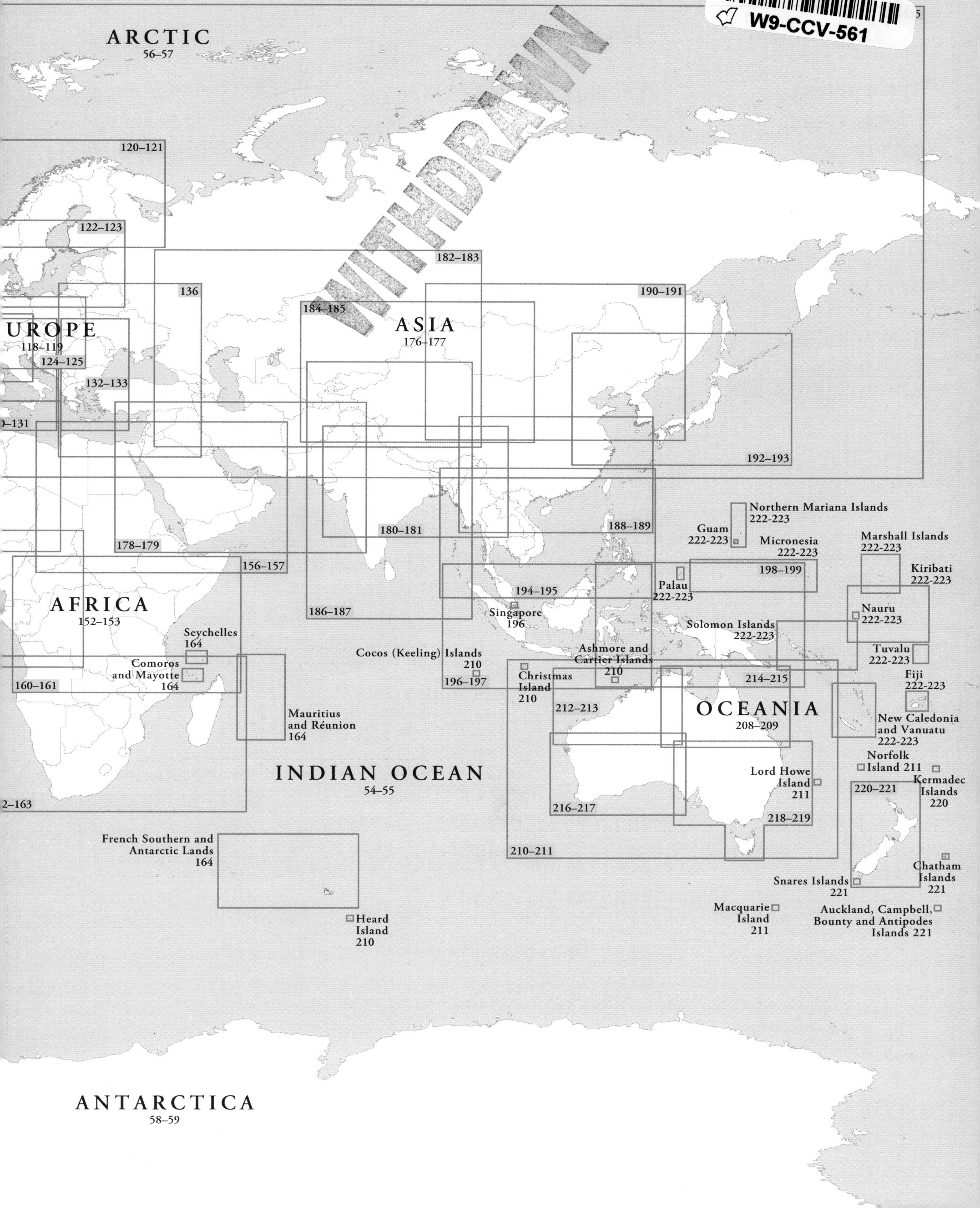
ARCTIC
56–57
120–121
122–123
UROPE
118–119
124–125
132–133
136
182–183
184–185
ASIA
176–177
190–191
192–193
180–181
188–189
178–179
156–157
186–187
AFRICA
152–153
Seychelles
164
Comoros
and Mayotte
164
160–161
Mauritius
and Réunion
164
2–163
INDIAN OCEAN
54–55
French Southern and
Antarctic Lands
164
Heard
Island
210
Cocos (Keeling) Islands
210
196–197
194–195
Singapore
196
Christmas
Island
210
Ashmore and
Cartier Islands
210
Northern Mariana Islands
222-223
Guam
222-223
Micronesia
222-223
Marshall Islands
222-223
198–199
Palau
222-223
Kiribati
222-223
Nauru
222-223
Solomon Islands
222-223
Tuvalu
222-223
214–215
Fiji
222-223
212–213
OCEANIA
208–209
New Caledonia
and Vanuatu
222-223
Norfolk
Island 211
Kermadec
Islands
220
Lord Howe
Island
211
220–221
216–217
218–219
210–211
Chatham
Islands
221
Snares Islands
221
Macquarie
Island
211
Auckland, Campbell,
Bounty and Antipodes
Islands 221
ANTARCTICA
58–59

EARTH

ESSENTIAL ATLAS

READER'S DIGEST
EXCLUSIVE CANADIAN EDITION

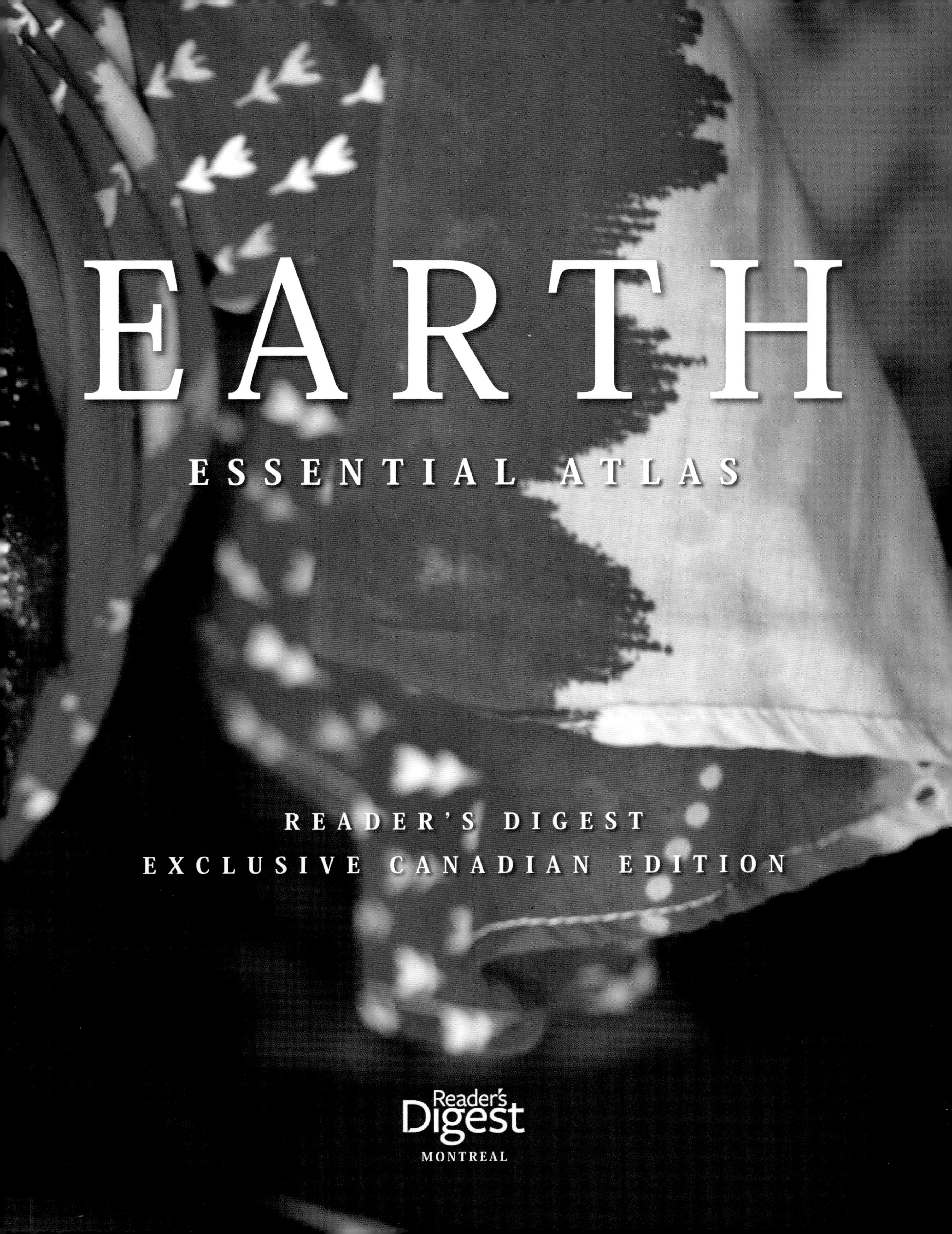

EARTH

ESSENTIAL ATLAS

READER'S DIGEST
EXCLUSIVE CANADIAN EDITION

Reader's Digest
MONTREAL

C o n t

SPOTLIGHT ON CANADA 6

GLOBAL PERSPECTIVE 12

Global Statistics 14

Plate Tectonics 16

Earth's Landforms 18

Temperature 20

Climate 22

Plants and Animals 24

World Energy 26

Population 28

Religions of the World 30

Human Migration 32

Human Impact on the Environment 34

Global Trade and Communication 36

THE WORLD 38

Introduction 40

MAPPING

World Political 42
1:75,000,000

World Physical 44
1:75,000,000

OCEANS AND POLES 46

Introduction 48

MAPPING

Atlantic Ocean 50
1:41,300,000

Pacific Ocean 52
1:50,600,000

Indian Ocean 54
1:37,500,000

Arctic 56
1:18,700,000

Antarctic 58
1:18,700,000

NORTH AMERICA 60

Northern America 62

Middle America 66

MAPPING

North America Political 70
1:25,300,000

Alaska, Northern Canada, and Greenland 72
1:15,950,000

Western Canada 74
1:5,630,000

Central Canada 76
1:5,630,000

Eastern Canada 78
1:5,630,000

Northwestern USA 80
1:5,630,000

Northeastern USA 82
1:5,630,000

Southwestern USA 84
1:5,630,000

Southeastern USA 86
1:5,630,000

Mexico 88
1:7,880,000

Central America and the Caribbean 90
1:7,880,000

SOUTH AMERICA 92

South America 94

MAPPING

South America Political 98
1:20,600,000

Northwestern South America 100
1:7,880,000

Eastern South America 102
1:7,880,000

Central South America 104
1:7,880,000

South Central South America 106
1:7,880,000

Southern South America 108
1:7,880,000

Islands Around South America 109

e n t s

EUROPE 110

Northern and Western Europe 112

Eastern Europe 114

Southern Europe 116

MAPPING

Europe Political 118
1:15,000,000

Northern Scandinavia and Iceland 120
1:3,750,000

Southern Scandinavia and the Baltic States 122
1:3,750,000

Central Europe 124
1:3,750,000

Western Europe 126
1:3,750,000

Spain and Portugal 128
1:3,750,000

Italy and Eastern Central Europe 130
1:3,750,000

Southeastern Europe 132
1:3,750,000

Russian Federation 134
1:19,710,000

Turkey and Eastern Europe 136
1:10,320,000

British Isles 137
1:4,700,000

Southern England and Wales 138
1:1,410,000

Northern England 140
1:1,410,000

Scotland 142
1:1,880,000

Ireland 143
1:1,880,000

AFRICA 144

Northern Africa 146

Central Africa 148

Southern Africa 150

MAPPING

Africa Political 152
1:29,000,000

Northwestern Africa 154
1:10,320,000

Northeastern Africa and the Middle East 156
1:10,320,000

Western Central Africa 158
1:10,320,000

Eastern Central Africa 160
1:10,320,000

Southern Africa and Madagascar 162
1:10,320,000

Islands Around Africa 164

ASIA 166

Southwest Asia 168

Asia 170

Southeast Asia 174

MAPPING

Asia Political 176
1:37,500,000

Middle East 178
1:10,320,000

Western Central Asia 180
1:7,880,000

Northwestern Asia 182
1:10,320,000

Central Asia 184
1:7,880,000

India 186
1:10,320,000

Eastern Central Asia 188
1:7,880,000

Northeastern China and Mongolia 190
1:7,880,000

Japan and Korea 192
1:7,880,000

Southeast Asia and the Philippines 194
1:9,390,000

Western Indonesia, Malaysia, and Singapore 196
1:9,390,000

Eastern Indonesia and Papua New Guinea 198
1:9,390,000

OCEANIA 200

Australia and New Zealand 202

Pacific Region 206

MAPPING

Oceania Political 208
1:31,900,000

Australia 210
1:14,080,000

Northwestern Australia 212
1:5,630,000

Northeastern Australia 214
1:5,630,000

Southwestern Australia 216
1:5,630,000

Southeastern Australia 218
1:5,630,000

New Zealand 220
1:3,750,000

Islands of the Pacific 222

Map Legend 224

Gazetteer 225

Credits and Acknowledgements 304

Spotlight on CANADA

ARCTIC OCEAN
Ellesmere Island
Beaufort Sea
Baffin Bay
UNITED STATES OF AMERICA
Victoria Island
Baffin Island
Gulf of Alaska
Whitehorse
Mt Logan
Iqaluit
Labrador Sea
Yellowknife
Queen Charlotte Islands
PACIFIC OCEAN
Vancouver Island
C A N A D A
Hudson Bay
Newfoundland
St John's
Edmonton
Vancouver
Victoria
Calgary
Saskatoon
Regina
Winnipeg
Thunder Bay
Chicoutimi
Charlottetown
Fredericton
Halifax
Québec
North Bay
Montréal
Sudbury
OTTAWA
ATLANTIC OCEAN
UNITED STATES OF AMERICA
Toronto
Oshawa
London
Hamilton

The second-largest country in the world, Canada covers a vast expanse of almost 10 million km^2 (4 million square miles). Stretching from the West Coast and the rugged Rocky Mountains, to the sweeping Prairies, the harsh Arctic region, and the verdant Atlantic Provinces, Canada boasts not only a diverse climate and landscape, but also a rich and varied culture, and some of the world's most dynamic cities.

Physical Geography

Canada's landscape reflects the two major divisions in its geology—a large core of massive, old, crystalline Precambrian rocks known as the Canadian Shield, and an outer rim of younger, mainly stratified rocks known collectively as the Borderlands. The Borderlands region is at its most extensive in the west, where it includes all of British Columbia, Alberta, and the Yukon Territory, and stretches through Saskatchewan into southern Manitoba. In the north, it forms parts of the Northwest Territories and Nunavut, reaching as far as the tip of Ellesmere Island. In the east, it includes all of New Brunswick, Nova Scotia, Newfoundland, and Prince Edward Island, and small sections of Quebec and Ontario along the St Lawrence River to the Great Lakes. Both the Canadian Shield and the Borderlands extend south into the USA.

Right Long-time inhabitants of Canada's hostile and unforgiving Arctic region, these days the majority of Canada's Inuit population can be found in Nunavut, a territory that officially came into being in 1999.

The ancient, heavily glaciated surface of the Canadian Shield has relatively low relief, and for the most part the interior of Canada is a region of gently rolling landscapes with thousands of lakes. The geologically younger Borderlands has undergone a considerable amount of tectonic reshaping, particularly in the west, where the Coast, Cascade, and Rocky mountain ranges offer high mountains and deep trenches before dropping to the Western Plains of Alberta. In the east, a series of high mountains have since eroded, leaving a rugged landscape of hills, valleys, and fjords.

In general, Canada's climate is warmer on the West Coast than the East Coast; the center has a true continental climate with extreme highs and lows. The north exhibits low precipitation and cold temperatures, and hence has large areas of permafrost and tundra. Vegetation ranges from coniferous boreal forests (taiga) in the north to extensive prairies in the western provinces of Alberta and Saskatchewan. Temperate rainforests are a feature of the Pacific coast, and mixed deciduous forests cover the Atlantic seaboard.

Royal Bill 参茸國藥行 Trading Inc.
成興海味
IANNO

Below Brimming with restaurants and stores that offer a wide range of Asian cuisine and commodities, Toronto's bustling Chinatown district is one of the largest of its kind in North America.

History

Humans first crossed into present-day Canada via the Bering Strait from Asia, perhaps as early as 35,000 years ago. The first recorded landing of a European was by Viking seafarer Leif Ericsson, at what he called Vinland, in northern Newfoundland, about 1000 CE. Italian explorer Giovanni Caboto (John Cabot) sailed west at the behest of King Henry VII of England in 1497, exploring the northeastern seaboard. His reports brought fishing fleets to the abundant fish stocks of the Grand Banks off Newfoundland and Nova Scotia. By 1524, French king Francis I was also sending explorers, including Jacques Cartier, who made several voyages from 1534 and a failed attempt to found a colony in Quebec in 1541. It was not until 1605 that a successful colony was established at Port Royal in Nova Scotia. Samuel de Champlain founded the colony that became Quebec City in 1608. The English captured his garrison in 1629, but after peace was restored he returned to New France as Governor in 1633.

Provinces and Territories

Province/Territory	Capital
British Columbia	Victoria
Alberta	Edmonton
Saskatchewan	Regina
Manitoba	Winnipeg
Ontario	Toronto
Quebec	Quebec City
New Brunswick	Fredericton
Prince Edward Island	Charlottetown
Nova Scotia	Halifax
Newfoundland and Labrador	St John's
Yukon	Whitehorse
Northwest Territories	Yellowknife
Nunavut	Iqaluit

Left Spanning the St John River, Hartland Covered Bridge in New Brunswick is the world's longest structure of this kind. The heritage-listed bridge stretches across the river for a distance of 390 meters (1,282 feet).

French trappers and missionaries advanced throughout much of what was to become the Canadian nation. The British founded colonies along the eastern coast to the south. They founded the Hudson's Bay Company in 1670 and began exploration and fur trading far to the north, establishing forts along the margin of the bay. In 1759, the English general James Wolfe led a fleet of 140 ships and 9,000 soldiers against Quebec. After a long siege, he made the tactical move of scaling the cliffs at night, and after the battle on the Plains of Abraham, seized the city. In 1763, the Treaty of Paris ended the so-called Seven Years' War among Europe's main powers and ceded eastern North America to the British.

In 1775, during the American Revolutionary War, the 13 American colonies sent two armies north to capture Canada. Forces made up of British regulars, Canadian militia, and Indians defeated them, forcing the Americans to retreat. Until the end of the American war for independence in 1783, 40,000 American colonists, wishing to remain loyal to the British crown, fled north to Canada. They became known as the United Empire Loyalists, and many of them settled in Nova Scotia.

In 1791, British Parliament passed the Constitutional Act, creating two provinces, Upper and Lower Canada (essentially Ontario and Quebec). The French colonists in Lower Canada were allowed to retain their language, and their systems of education and law. Exploration continued, and by the early nineteenth century formal settlement efforts were being made in the west. Two rival trading companies, the Hudson's Bay Company

Below One of the jewels of Banff National Park in Alberta, Moraine Lake is located in the Valley of Ten Peaks, which provides a spectacular backdrop to its sparkling turquoise waters. The unusual color is caused by silt particles that are carried down by glacial meltwater.

Canada's Biggest Lakes

Freshwater lakes cover more than 747,000 km^2 (288,418 square miles), or some 7.6 percent of Canada's total area.

Lake	Area
Lake Superior	82,100 km^2 (31, 700 square miles)
Lake Huron	59,600 km^2 (23,011 square miles)
Great Bear Lake	31,328 km^2 (12,095 square miles)
Great Slave Lake	28,568 km^2 (11,030 square miles)
Lake Erie	25,700 km^2 (9,922 square miles)
Lake Ontario	19,000 km^2 (7,336 square miles)

Canada's Waterfalls

Canada's largest falls by area are Virginia Falls, in the South Nahanni River, Northwest Territories. At a height of 96 meters (316 feet), Virginia Falls is twice as high as Niagara's Horseshoe Falls (which has the greatest waterfall by volume), but not nearly as high as Della Falls in British Columbia, the highest falls in the country at 440 meters (1,312 feet) high.

Below Though not the world's largest waterfalls, Niagara Falls are arguably the most recognizable. Collectively, the scenic Horseshoe Falls—most of which lies in the province of Ontario—and the two smaller falls on the US side, account for a massive volume of up to 168,000 m^3 (6 million cubic feet) of water passing over the crest line every minute. Its potential as a source of hydroelectric power has been harnessed by both nations.

(HBC) and the North West Company, had interests in the area, and occasional physical conflict broke out between them. In 1812, the first wave of Scottish and Irish settlers sent by Thomas Douglas, Earl of Selkirk, began to arrive in the Red River Valley, Manitoba, but the conflicts prevented successful settlement until 1817.

War broke out between Britain and the United States in 1812, and several attacks on Canada were carried out by American troops. The war was fought in three major theaters but ultimately, forces of British soldiers, Canadian militiamen, and Indians—including legendary Shawnee war chief, Tecumseh—were able to repulse the attacks.

The British Parliament passed the British North America Act in 1867, and on July 1, 1867, the new Dominion of Canada was born with four provinces: Ontario, Quebec, New Brunswick, and Nova Scotia. Its first prime minister was Sir John A. Macdonald who, apart from a five-year break, was to remain in power until his death in 1891. But the Dominion he was to govern was incomplete. Prince Edward Island and Newfoundland had refused to join, the vast prairie lands to the west and north belonged to HBC, and British Columbia seemed remote.

In 1870, the fledgling government of Canada purchased Rupert's Land (much of what is now Manitoba, Alberta, Saskatchewan, Nunavut and the Northwest Territories) from HBC, who retained only a small amount of territory for settlements and trading posts.

In Manitoba, the Métis people (of mixed aboriginal and European descent) of the Red River Valley, fearing loss of their property rights, resisted the new government. Louis Riel led an uprising (that eventually resulted in Riel's execution), but with the passage of the Manitoba Act in 1870, Métis rights were recognized.

When the American Civil War ended in 1865, US army veterans made their way north to the Alberta and Saskatchewan plains, or "Whoop Up" country, as it was then known. These veterans were equipped with a new invention, the repeating rifle, and were capable of slaughtering buffalo on a scale not previously possible. They called themselves "free traders" to distinguish themselves from any legitimate fur trading company

Left Athabasca Glacier is part of the Columbia Icefield, and a much-visited natural feature. This slow-moving glacier is a victim of global warming, having receded and shrunk over the last century.

representatives, such as HBC's. They set up shop in a series of garrisons called "whisky forts" that flew the American flag. Initially, these free traders traded repeating rifles with the Indians for buffalo hides, but whisky soon became the commodity most sought after by the Indians.

The presence of the whisky forts had serious consequences. The Indians, especially the Blackfoot tribe, over-hunted the buffalo, which were already threatened with extinction. The native way of life was changed forever. They became alcohol-dependent and traded anything they could lay their hands on for whisky—including their women. When the women returned to the tribes, they brought with them syphilis and smallpox and the Indians died by the thousands.

It became imperative for the newly formed government of Canada to take some action to impose peace, order, and good government in the west if they were ever to attract settlers to the territory. So in 1873, Sir John A. Macdonald created the North West Mounted Police (NWMP)—predecessor to the Royal Canadian Mounted Police (RCMP)—to put an end to lawlessness and to show the flag of the Dominion in the west. He chose to outfit them in red coats, the serge tunic worn by the British army, to reassure the Indians that they would not be dealing with a blue-coated force similar to the American cavalry who were generally hated. Over the next several years, the NWMP rid the Canadian west of the free traders and established garrisons across the Prairies.

Meanwhile, on July 20, 1871, British Columbia entered Confederation, followed by Prince Edward Island in 1873. The last spike of the Canadian Pacific Railway, completing the line across the Dominion, was driven home on November 7, 1885. Saskatchewan and Alberta both joined in 1905, and in 1949, Newfoundland completed the nation.

Canada grew steadily during the early years of the twentieth century, primarily through immigration. Canada supported Britain during the Boer War (1899–1902) and in World War I (1914–18), although with increasing independence each time. In 1931, the Statute of Westminster established the British Commonwealth of Nations, and essentially set Canada and other dominions up as autonomous entities. Canada entered World War II in support of Britain, but with its own army, navy, and air force. On February 15, 1965, Canada raised the red-and-white maple leaf flag, replacing the former Red Ensign, and reducing symbolically the role of Britain in Canadian affairs.

The final act of severing legal ties with Britain took place in 1982, when the British North America Act was replaced by the Canadian Constitution. Since that time, threats of separation by Quebec were averted by the failure of referendums in the province in 1980 and 1995; and the Northwest Territories (NWT) were split into two with the formal creation of Nunavut in 1999. Nunavut, the former eastern portion of the NWT, has 750,000 square miles (1.9 million km^2) of territory, and is classed as a self-governing homeland for the Inuit inhabitants. Iqaliut on Baffin Island was selected as the seat of the administrative capital of the new territory.

Above With some 200 species of mammals, more than 460 species of birds, and thousands of plant species, Canada boasts a variety of flora and fauna as diverse as the country itself.

Canadian Time Zones

Standard time was invented by the Canadian Pacific Railway's chief engineer, Sandford Fleming, and went into effect worldwide on January 1, 1885. Canada was divided into seven time zones—Newfoundland, Atlantic, Eastern, Central, Mountain, Pacific, and Yukon. There was a 5½-hour difference from east coast to west coast. Subsequently, the Yukon switched in 1973 to Pacific Time, reducing the zones to six and the time difference to 4½ hours.

Canada's Road System

THE WORLD'S LONGEST NATIONAL HIGHWAY

Canada's national highway system is over 25,000 km (15,535 mi.) in length, the longest stretch of which is the Trans-Canada Highway (National Highway 1), extending 7,821 km (4,860 mi.) from Victoria, British Columbia (Mile 0), to St John's, Newfoundland—the longest national highway in the world. Building commenced on April 25, 1950, at a cost of $1 billion, and was fully completed in June 1965.

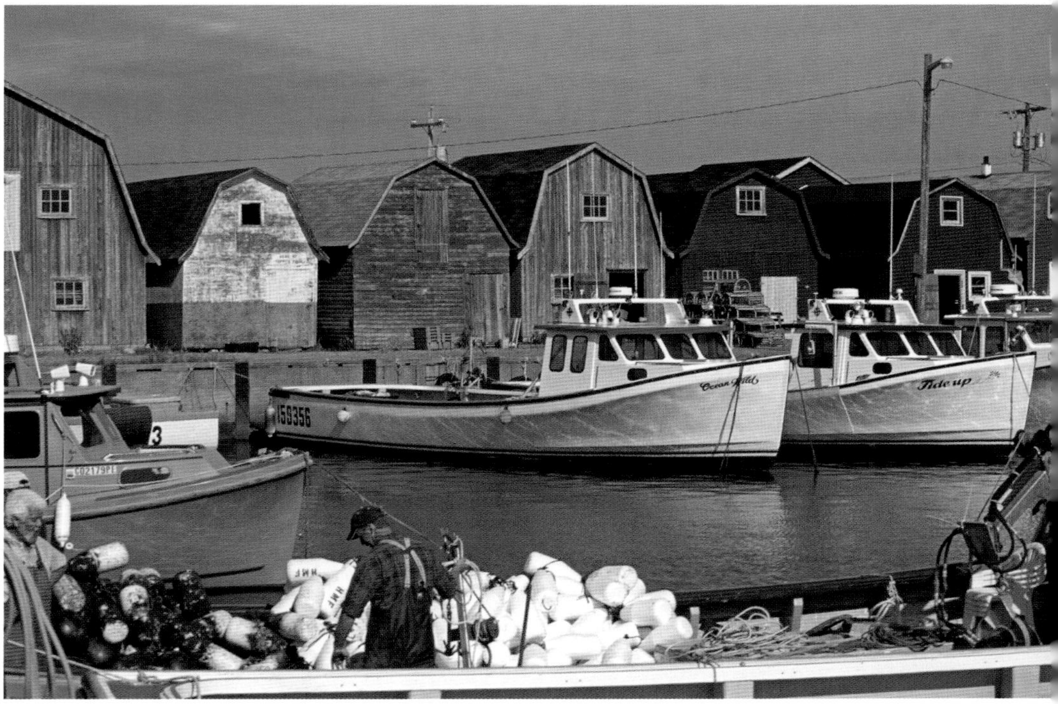

Below The picturesque town of Malpeque lies on Prince Edward Island's northern coastline. Farming and fishing are the principal industries, and Malpeque oysters are highly prized around the world.

Right Strategically located at the heart of four main city districts, the Palais de congrès is Montreal's convention center. A statement in architecture, the structure's external facade presents a "light show" of glass, while clever use of color remains a theme within.

Administration/Government

Canada is a federation comprising ten provinces and three territories. From east to west, the provinces are Newfoundland and Labrador, Nova Scotia, Prince Edward Island, New Brunswick, Quebec, Ontario, Manitoba, Saskatchewan, Alberta, and British Columbia. The three territories, all north of latitude 60 degrees, are Nunavut, Northwest Territories, and the Yukon.

The federal government has two houses: An elected House of Commons, and an appointed Senate that acts as a quasi House of Lords. Each province and territory also has an elected legislative assembly. The leader of the federal government bears the title of Prime Minister, while the leaders of the provincial governments are known as Premiers. Canada's head of state is Queen Elizabeth II, who is represented at the federal level by a Governor General appointed for a fixed term by the incumbent government. Each province and territory has similar representation in the form of a Lieutenant Governor. During federal elections, held for the most part at four-year intervals, unless the incumbent government loses a vote of confidence beforehand, voters are offered a choice of candidates, most of whom belong to one of a number of political parties. The two largest parties are the Liberal Party of Canada (which tends to the left) and the Conservative Party (which tends to the right). Other parties include the New Democratic Party, the Green Party and the Bloc Québécois.

Canada's written Constitution is a collection of 25 documents (14 Acts of the British Parliament, seven Acts of the Canadian Parliament, and four British Orders-in-Council). One of its principal documents is the British North America Act, of 1867, together with all its amendments up to 1975. All these elements, along with a Canadian Charter of Rights and Freedoms, were outlined in the Constitution Act of 1982.

Economy

Canada is one of the world's wealthiest nations; in 2006, the International Monetary Fund reported that Canada ranked eighth worldwide, with a Gross Domestic Product (GDP) of US$1,275,273 million. The service industry occupies some three-quarters of the labor force, while 15 percent are in manufacturing, 5 percent in construction, and 3 percent in agriculture. Much of Canada's wealth is in the form of natural resources, particularly oil, timber, and minerals. There is also a large manufacturing sector concentrated primarily in the Windsor–Quebec City corridor. In the Quebec portion, the emphasis is on aerospace and pharmaceuticals. The Canadarm, a mechanical arm used on the US Space Shuttle, was designed and built in Canada.

Newfoundland and Nova Scotia, both heavily reliant on fishing in the past, now have large revenues from offshore oil and gas deposits. British Columbia, New Brunswick, and Quebec also have large forestry industries, and Prince Edward Island is famous for potatoes. Alberta and Saskatchewan are well known for beef, wheat, and corn, but also produce oil and gas. The Alberta Tar Sands hold approximately 988 billion cubic feet (28 billion m^3) of recoverable crude bitumen, which

Below The annual Winter Carnival held in Quebec City has a long history. One of the events that has been held each time since the Carnival's inception in 1894 is the challenging canoe race along the icy waters of the St Lawrence River.

- **35,000 BCE** First inhabitants cross the Bering Strait from Asia into Canada
- **1000 CE** First European contact by Viking seafarer Leif Ericsson
- **1534** Jacques Cartier claims Gulf of St Lawrence for France
- **1605** France establishes settlement at Port Royal
- **1608** Quebec City founded
- **1642** Montreal founded
- **1763** Treaty of Paris cedes eastern North America to British
- **1774** Quebec Act defines boundaries and rights
- **1867** Passage of British North America Act forms Dominion of Canada uniting the provinces of Ontario, Quebec, New Brunswick, and Nova Scotia. John A. Macdonald becomes Canada's first prime minister.
- **1870** Manitoba joins Confederation
- **1871** Treaty of Washington recognizes Dominion of Canada; British Columbia joins Confederation
- **1873** Prince Edward Island joins Confederation
- **1885** Canadian Pacific Railway completed; Louis Riel is hanged for treason

Unique Canadian Cuisine

Immigration introduced Canadians to a wide variety of cuisines, including the ubiquitous Chinese (mostly Cantonese) food that followed the nineteenth-century railway workers from coast to coast. Although maple syrup is widely recognized as a Canadian symbol, it is also used commonly in other countries. There are a few specialties, however, that wear a truly Canadian stamp.

Poutine is an artery-clogging concoction of French-fried potatoes smothered with fresh cheese curds and gravy. It is the quintessential comfort food of Quebec.

Tourtière is a meat pie made from ground pork and veal, or beef. A Québécois product, it is often served as Christmas or holiday fare. Some family variations include potatoes.

Nanaimo Bars are dessert slices with a crumb base covered in vanilla butter icing and/or custard, then topped with chocolate. They are named after the city of Nanaimo, on Vancouver Island.

Fiddleheads are the young, unfurled fronds of certain varieties of fern.

Beaver Tails are made from deep-fried dough sprinkled with cinnamon, powdered sugar, or maple syrup. They are a particular favorite in Ottawa.

Arctic Char is a noted fish delicacy, native to glacial lakes in the far north. It is now being farmed commercially.

Cod Tongues are usually served breaded and fried. They are a popular specialty in Newfoundland.

amounts to three-quarters of North American petroleum reserves. Canada is the United States' largest trading partner, with yearly trade of well in excess of $620 billion Canadian dollars.

People and Culture

When Europeans arrived in what is now Canada, they found two aboriginal peoples—the Inuit (formerly known as Eskimos) in the Arctic, and the Indians in more southerly regions. In time, as European explorers worked their way westward, they intermarried with aboriginal people, creating a new population, the Métis. Métis come from many regions but are concentrated in the western provinces, particularly Manitoba. With the passing of the Constitution Act of 1982, all three groups are now classed legally as "Aboriginal Peoples of Canada." All Aboriginal Peoples of Canada, male and female, are guaranteed treaty rights under the Constitution, and in recent years many land claims made under such treaty rights have been settled across Canada; others are in the process of negotiation.

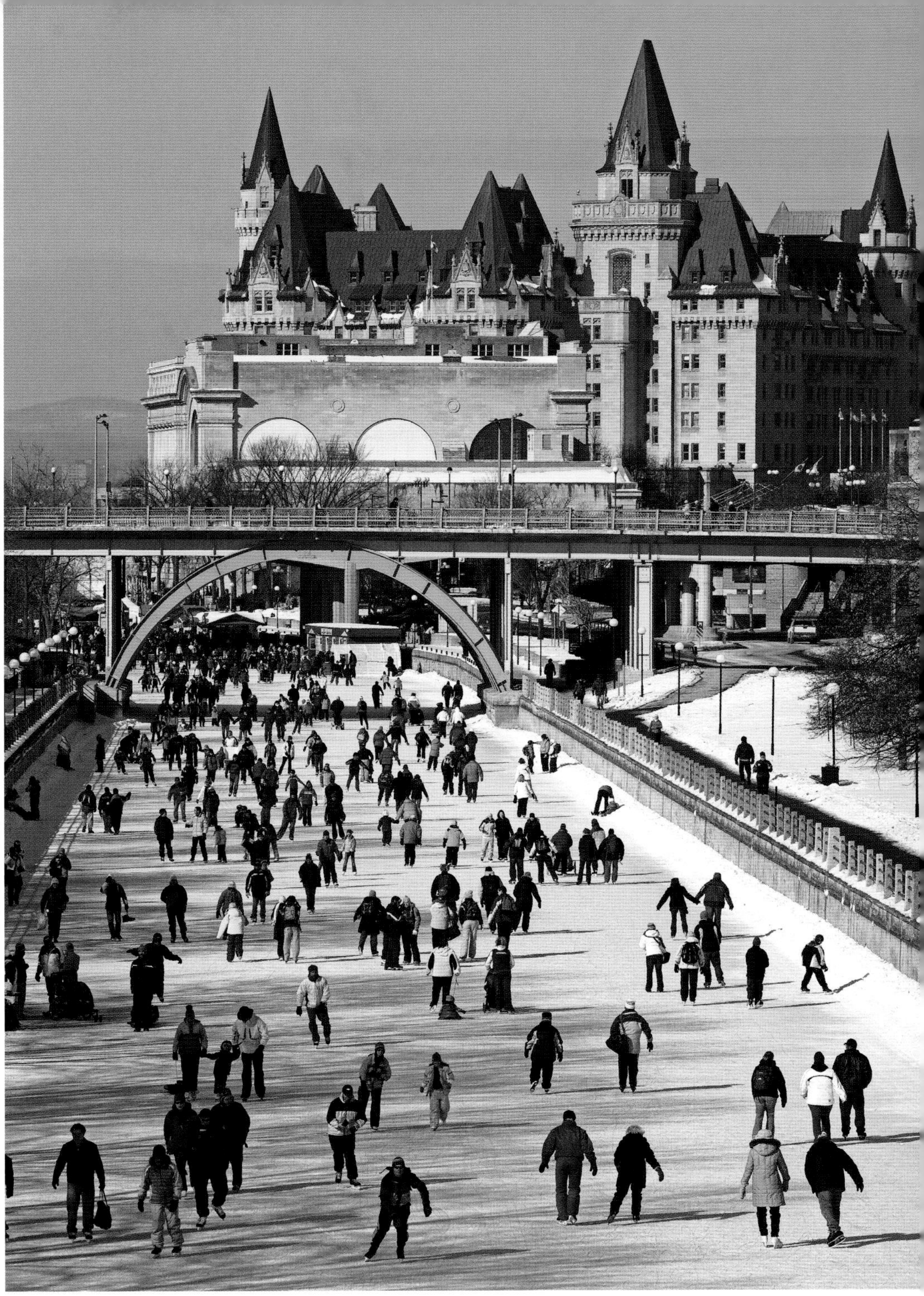

Above Ottawa's Winterlude festival is an opportunity for locals and visitors to celebrate the winter season. Chilly winter conditions see the waters of Rideau Canal freeze over to create the world's longest ice rink. Ice sculptures, concerts, and local fare are added attractions.

More recent cultural migrations were from English, Scottish, Irish, and French stock. Canada accepts about 200,000 immigrants per year from many ethnic groups—more than any other country. In 1985, the Canadian Multiculturalism Act was promulgated, which allows immigrants to practice (within reason) the traditional lifestyles of their countries of origin. A notable example has been allowing Sikh members of the Royal Canadian Mounted Police to wear their traditional turbans rather than the famous RCMP headgear.

- **1905** Alberta and Saskatchewan both join Confederation
- **1920** Royal Canadian Mounted Police formed when the forces of the North West Mounted Police and Dominion Police merge
- **1931** Statute of Westminster establishes British Commonwealth of Nations
- **1949** Newfoundland joins Confederation
- **1967** Montreal hosts World's Fair during Canada's Centennial year
- **1976** Montreal hosts the Summer Olympic Games
- **1980** Rejection of first referendum on Quebec separation
- **1982** Canadian Constitution replaces British North America Act
- **1988** Winter Olympics staged in Calgary
- **1995** Rejection of second referendum on Quebec separation
- **1999** Division of the Northwest Territories into Nunavut in the east, and Northwest Territories in the west
- **2005** Canada becomes the fourth nation in the world to legalize same-sex marriage
- **2010** Vancouver hosts the Winter Olympic Games

Western Hemisphere

Global Perspective

Eastern Hemisphere

GLOBAL STATISTICS

	NORTH AMERICA	SOUTH AMERICA	EUROPE
Number of Countries	23	12	45
Area	24,490,000 km^2/9,455,640 mi^2	17,840,000km^2/6,888,060 mi^2	10,180,000 km^2/3,930,520 mi^2
% of Global Population	8%	6%	11%
Population Density	*15/km^2, 39/mi^2	*28/km^2, 73/mi^2	32/km^2, 83/mi^2
Largest Country	Canada	Brazil	Russian Federation
Smallest Country	St Kitts and Nevis	Suriname	Vatican City
Largest Island	Greenland (2,166,086 km^2/836,330 mi^2)	Tierra del Fuego (47,990 km^2/18,530 mi^2)	Great Britain (230,465 km^2/88,985 mi^2)
Longest River	Mississippi–Missouri (6,019 km/3,740 miles)	Amazon (6,400 km/4,000 miles)	Yenisey (5,540 km/3,442 miles)
Largest Lake	Lake Superior, Canada/USA (12,100 km^3/2,900 mi^3)	Lake Titicaca, Bolivia/Peru (893 km^3/214 mi^3)	Lake Baikal, Russian Federation (23,600 km^3/5,700 mi^3)
Highest Mountain	Mt McKinley, Alaska, USA (6,198 m/20,330 ft)	Cerro Aconcagua, Argentina (6,962 m/22,841 ft)	Gora El'brus, Russian Federation (5,633 m/18,481 ft)
	* Indicates Canada and USA	* Indicates Latin America	

THE OCEANS

PACIFIC OCEAN
Area 155,557,000 km^2 (60,060,895 mi^2)
Deepest Point Challenger Deep, Mariana Trench

ATLANTIC OCEAN
Area 76,762,000 km^2 (29,637,975 mi^2)
Deepest Point Milwaukee Deep, Puerto Rico Trench

INDIAN OCEAN
Area 68,556,000 km^2 (26,469,620 mi^2)
Deepest Point Java Trench

SOUTHERN OCEAN
Area 20,327,000 km^2 (7,848,300 mi^2)
Deepest Point South Sandwich Trench

ARCTIC OCEAN
Area 14,056,000 km^2 (5,427,050 mi^2)
Deepest Point Fram Basin

Left The most physiographically varied archipelago in Micronesia, the islands of Palau are exposed peaks of undersea ridges that stretch for almost 200 kilometers (125 miles) between New Guinea and Japan. Mostly uninhabited, the 350 islands that make up the tiny island nation are of volcanic and coralline origin, and are home to Micronesia's greatest diversity of terrestrial flora and fauna.

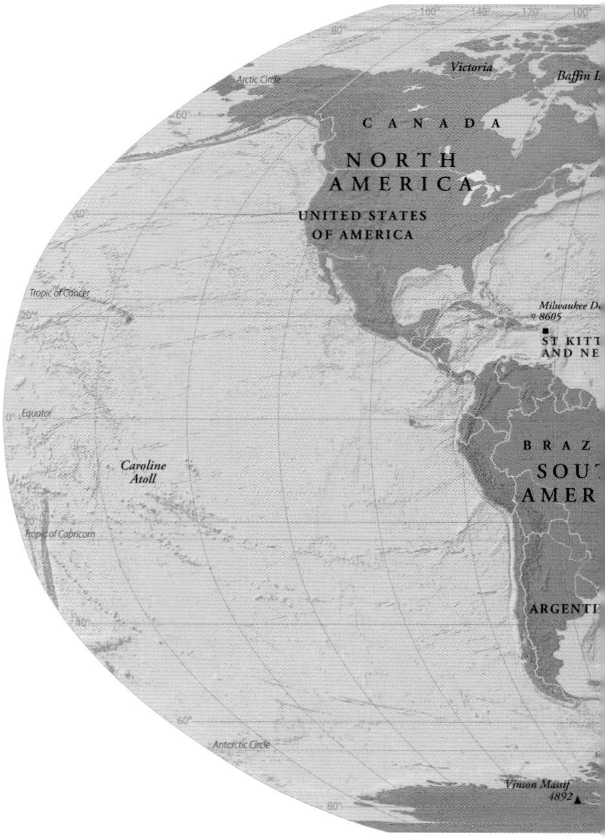
Victoria
CANADA
NORTH AMERICA
UNITED STATES OF AMERICA
Arctic Circle
Tropic of Cancer
Equator
Caroline Atoll
Tropic of Capricorn
Antarctic Circle
Vinson Massif 4892

Right The mighty Himalayas are the most vigorously growing mountains on Earth. The range includes 14 of the world's highest points, including the highest, Mt Everest, which soars to 8,844 meters (29,016 feet).

Right middle The Yukon and Klondike rivers merge at Dawson City. The Yukon River is navigable and—as the longest river in northwestern North America—it was a major transport system during the Klondike Gold Rush period.

Far right Most of Greenland—arguably the world's largest island—is covered by an extensive ice cap, with glaciers that carve out a rugged coastline as they reach the ocean.

AFRICA	ASIA	OCEANIA	ANTARCTICA
53	47	14	—
30,370,000 km^2/11,725,925 mi^2	43,810,000 km^2/6,915,135 mi^2	9,010,000 km^2/3,478,780 mi^2	13,720,000 km^2/5,297,320 mi^2
14%	61%	<1%	0.00002%
29/km^2, 80/mi^2	126/km^2, 326/mi^2	*2.7/km^2, 7.1/mi^2	0.00007/km^2
Sudan	China	Australia	—
Seychelles	Maldives	Nauru	—
Madagascar (581,540 km^2/224,534 mi^2)	Borneo (739,000 km/285,330 mi^2)	New Guinea (808,516 km^2/312,170 mi^2)	—
Nile (6,650 km/4,132 miles)	Yangtze (6,380 km/3,964 miles)	Murray River, Australia (2,375 km/1,476 miles)	—
Lake Tanganyika, Tanzania/DRC/Burundi/ Zambia (18,900 km^3/4,500 mi^3)	Lake Balkhash, Kazakhstan (106 km^3/25 mi^3)	Lake Taupo, New Zealand (60 km^3/14 mi^3)	—
Kilimanjaro, Tanzania (5,895 m/19,340 ft)	Mt Everest, Nepal/China (8,844 m/29,016 ft)	Mt Wilhelm, Papua New Guinea (4,509 m/14,793 ft)	Vinson Massif (4,897 m/16,066 ft)
		* Indicates Australia	

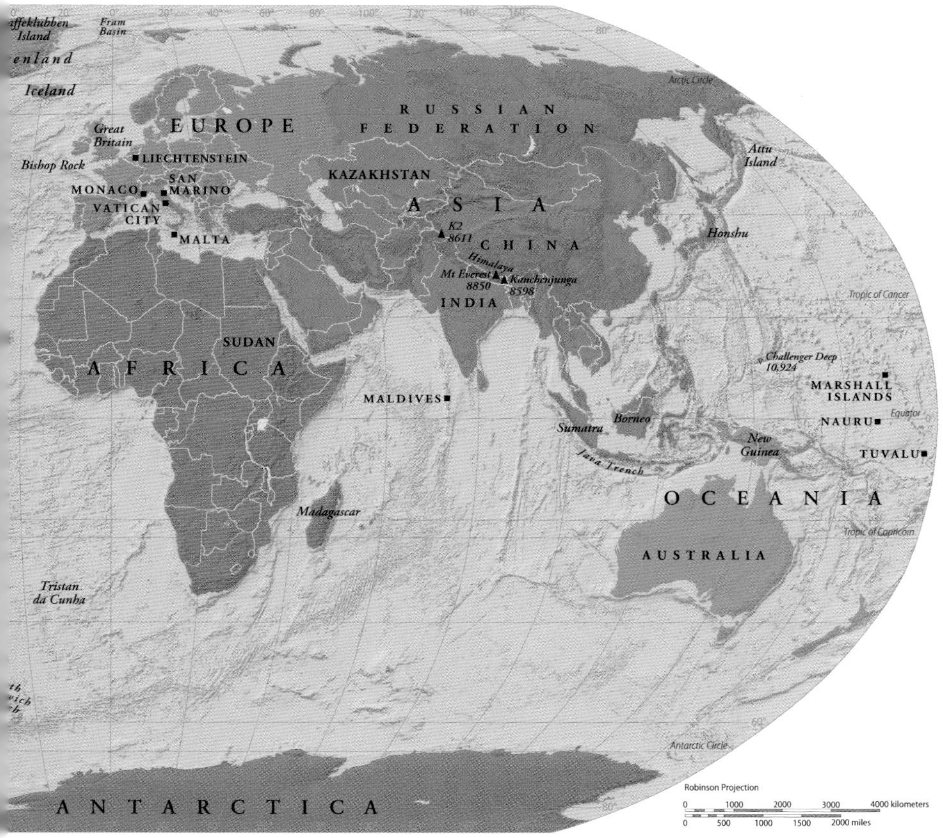
EUROPE
RUSSIAN FEDERATION
KAZAKHSTAN
ASIA
CHINA
INDIA
AFRICA
SUDAN
MALDIVES
OCEANIA
AUSTRALIA
ANTARCTICA
Iceland
Great Britain
Bishop Rock
LIECHTENSTEIN
SAN MARINO
MONACO
VATICAN CITY
MALTA
K2 8611
Himalaya
Mt Everest 8850
Kanchenjunga 8598
Honshu
Attu Island
Challenger Deep 10,924
MARSHALL ISLANDS
NAURU
TUVALU
Borneo
Sumatra
Java Trench
New Guinea
Madagascar
Tristan da Cunha
Arctic Circle
Tropic of Cancer
Equator
Tropic of Capricorn
Antarctic Circle
Robinson Projection

Above The Nile river is steeped in history, and a number of the world's great and ancient cities lie along its course, including Khartoum, Aswan, Luxor, and the Egyptian capital, Cairo.

Left Covering more than three-quarters of Russia, and often perceived as a frigid wasteland, Siberia encompasses a range of terrains, the world's widest coastal shelf, and the world's largest lake—Lake Baikal.

PLATE TECTONICS

In the beginning—4,600 million years ago—Earth formed by accretion in the flattened disk of debris that was spinning around the Sun. The protoplanet grew slowly, heating up and finally becoming a molten ball.

A lighter mantle formed around a heavier core as gravity pulled the denser elements, such as iron, toward its center, while less dense elements, such as silicon and aluminum, rose toward the surface. A thin, brittle crust formed, which acts as an insulating blanket around a boiling interior trying to shed its heat into outer space. This is the basis of Earth's internal heat engine or plate tectonic motor, which is responsible for all the features in Earth's landscape.

Earth's Plate Tectonic Motor

Earth's heat-driven motor is incredibly powerful yet, in human terms, is imperceptibly slow. However, evidence of its activity is everywhere. Boiling plumes of hot material push upward toward the crust, and eventually rip it apart. The lightest materials (aluminum- and silicon-rich rocks) accumulate like a thickened scum on the surface—this is how Earth's first permanent continents were formed, and the planet's surface has been in constant motion since that time.

In the 1950s and 1960s new ocean-floor bathymetric data led to the discovery of oceanic spreading ridges and deep trough-like subduction trenches. These oceanic spreading ridges are fiery cracks, tearing apart Earth's

Below The amazingly regular shapes of these rock divisions come from natural causes, not human action. Tectonic stress caused the initial fractures, with salt and water also working to produce this tessellated pavement.

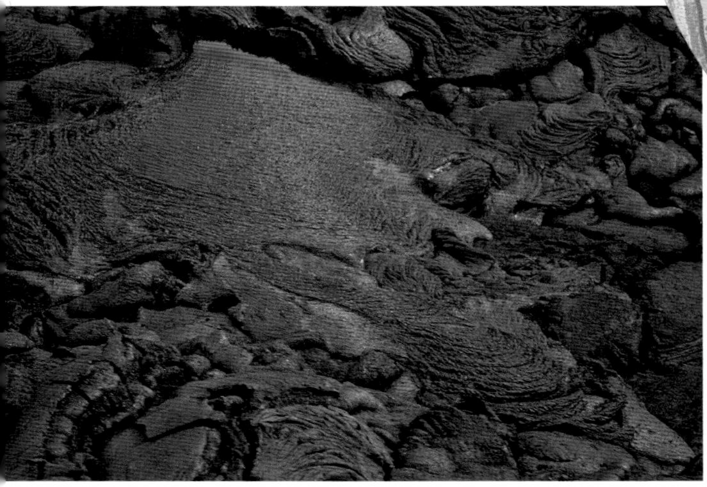

Left Red-hot lava comes from magma deep below the surface. As the molten rock cools, a hard crust forms first, and then the lava solidifies into igneous rock.

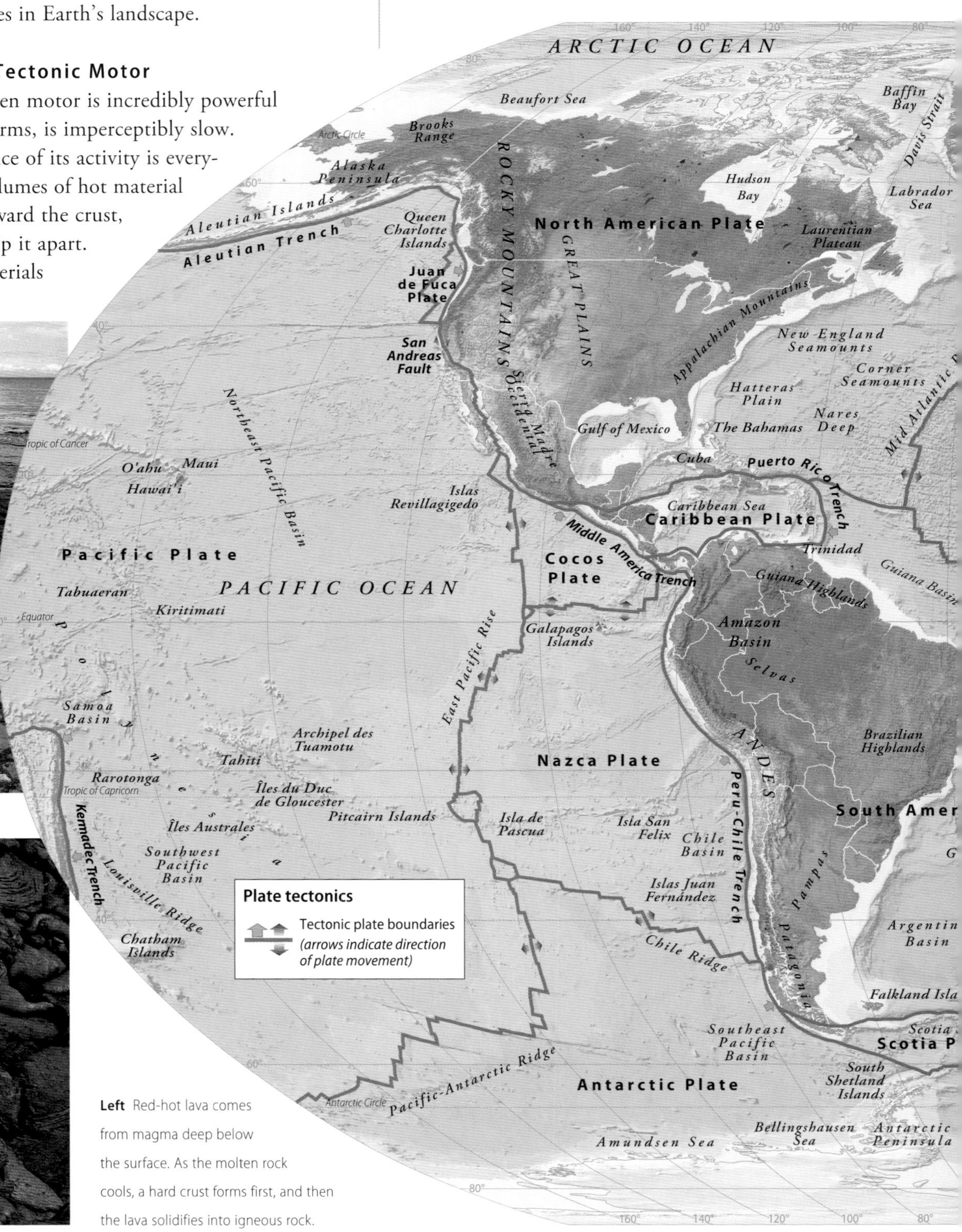
ARCTIC OCEAN
Beaufort Sea
Baffin Bay
Davis Strait
Brooks Range
Arctic Circle
Alaska Peninsula
Aleutian Islands
Aleutian Trench
Queen Charlotte Islands
ROCKY MOUNTAINS
GREAT PLAINS
Hudson Bay
Labrador Sea
North American Plate
Laurentian Plateau
Juan de Fuca Plate
San Andreas Fault
Appalachian Mountains
New England Seamounts
Corner Seamounts
Mid-Atlantic
Hatteras Plain
Nares Deep
The Bahamas
Sierra Madre Occidental
Gulf of Mexico
Cuba
Puerto Rico Trench
Northeast Pacific Basin
Tropic of Cancer
O'ahu
Maui
Hawai'i
Islas Revillagigedo
Caribbean Sea
Caribbean Plate
Middle America Trench
Trinidad
Guiana Basin
Pacific Plate
Cocos Plate
Guiana Highlands
PACIFIC OCEAN
Tabuaeran
Kiritimati
Equator
Galapagos Islands
Amazon Basin
Selvas
East Pacific Rise
Samoa Basin
Polynesia
Archipel des Tuamotu
Brazilian Highlands
Tahiti
Nazca Plate
ANDES
Rarotonga
Tropic of Capricorn
Îles du Duc de Gloucester
Pitcairn Islands
Îles Australes
Kermadec Trench
Isla de Pascua
Isla San Felix
Chile Basin
Peru-Chile Trench
South America
Southwest Pacific Basin
Louisville Ridge
Islas Juan Fernández
Pampas
Argentine Basin
Chatham Islands
Chile Ridge
Patagonia
Falkland Islands
Scotia
Scotia Plate
Southeast Pacific Basin
South Shetland Islands
Pacific-Antarctic Ridge
Antarctic Circle
Antarctic Plate
Amundsen Sea
Bellingshausen Sea
Antarctic Peninsula
Plate tectonics
Tectonic plate boundaries
(arrows indicate direction of plate movement)

tectonic plates. Magma rises to the surface along these cracks to fill the gap, and hardens to make new crust, which is, in turn, split apart. Topographically, these spreading ridges are long, broad, submerged mountain chains. Occasionally, these massive fracture zones are visible on land, as steep sheer-walled valleys, basalt volcanoes, intense thermal activity, and deep narrow lakes.

Growing new crust along the ridges means that older crust must be destroyed in equal amounts elsewhere. These lines of destruction, along which the tectonic plates are pushed together, are called subduction zones. One of the plates, usually the lighter one, slips on top of the other, which is pushed down into the mantle and melted. Subduction zones are marked by deep, narrow, submarine trenches and bordered by violently explosive, classically cone-shaped volcanoes fed by the molten products of the descending plate. Such activity is rife around the edge of the Pacific Ocean's "Ring of Fire," where the Pacific Plate is being steadily consumed on all sides by neighboring plates.

When the plates being pushed together are both buoyant, neither is able to easily slip beneath the other. The collision results in the land on both sides being crumpled and folded. The leading continental edges can be pushed miles skyward. The Himalaya mountain range is Earth's finest example of this process in action today, as the Indian subcontinent grinds steadily northward into the Asian mainland. Many of Earth's less significant ranges—such as the Appalachians of the USA and the Urals of Russia—were once Himalaya-sized ranges, but erosion has reduced their grandeur over time.

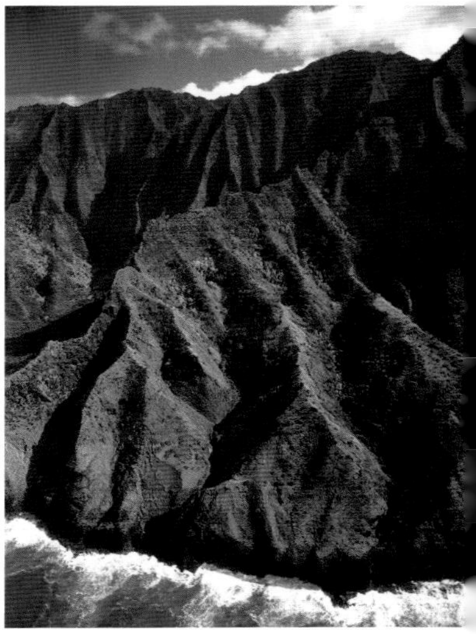

Above The rugged Na Pali coast of Hawaii's Kauai island shows spectacular sea cliffs created by the erosion of the shield volcano that first formed the island.

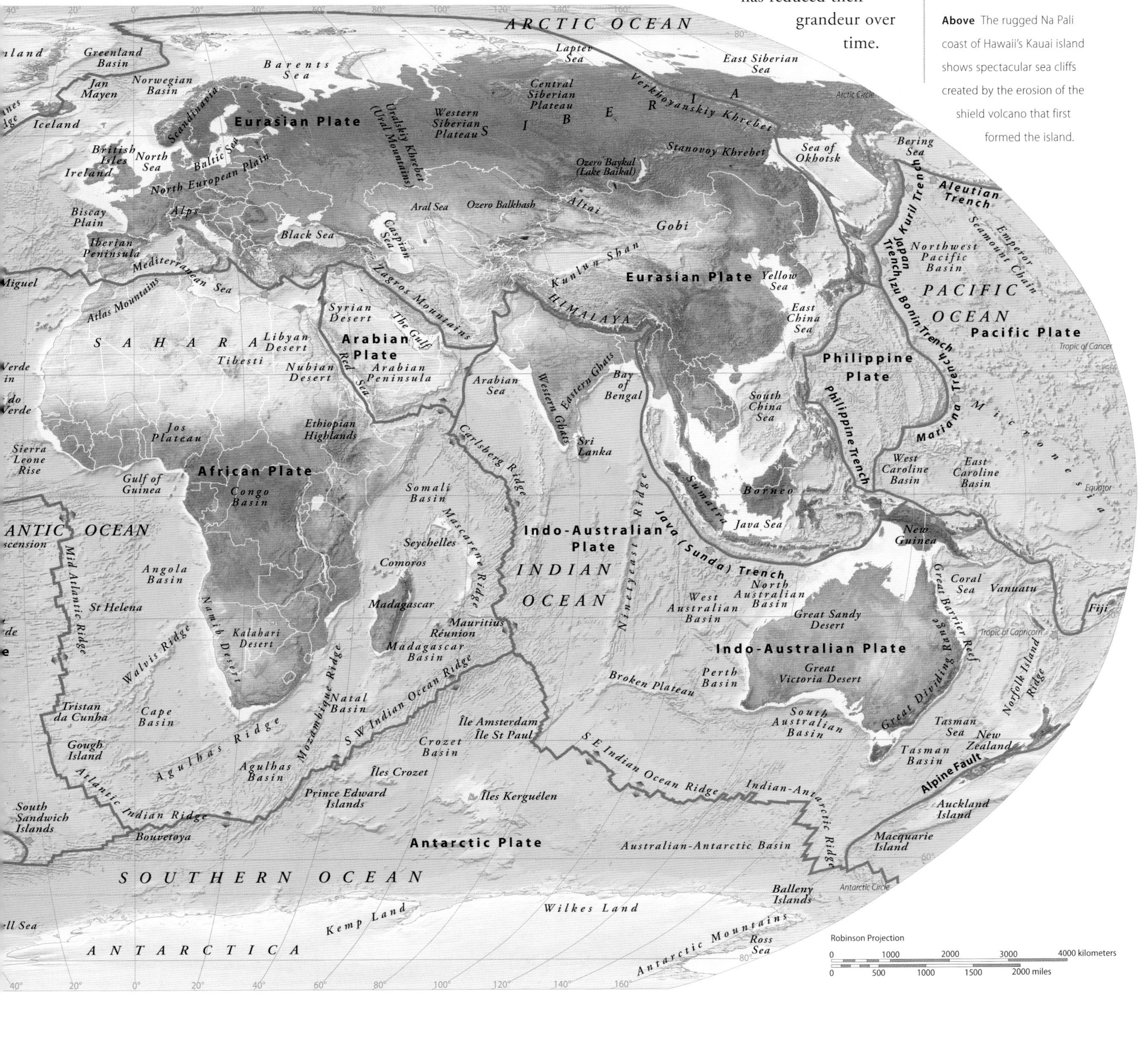
ARCTIC OCEAN
Greenland Basin
Jan Mayen
Norwegian Basin
Barents Sea
Iceland
Scandinavia
Eurasian Plate
British Isles
Ireland
North Sea
Baltic Sea
North European Plain
Uralskiy Khrebet (Ural Mountains)
Western Siberian Plateau
SIBERIA
Central Siberian Plateau
Laptev Sea
East Siberian Sea
Verkhoyanskiy Khrebet
Arctic Circle
Stanovoy Khrebet
Sea of Okhotsk
Bering Sea
Ozero Baykal (Lake Baikal)
Biscay Plain
Alps
Aral Sea
Ozero Balkhash
Altai
Gobi
Black Sea
Caspian Sea
Iberian Peninsula
Mediterranean Sea
Kunlun Shan
Eurasian Plate
Yellow Sea
Kuril Trench
Aleutian Trench
Emperor Seamount Chain
Northwest Pacific Basin
PACIFIC OCEAN
Japan Trench
Izu Bonin Trench
Pacific Plate
Tropic of Cancer
Atlas Mountains
Zagros Mountains
HIMALAYA
East China Sea
Syrian Desert
The Gulf
SAHARA
Libyan Desert
Arabian Plate
Tibesti
Nubian Desert
Red Sea
Arabian Peninsula
Philippine Plate
Philippine Trench
Mariana Trench
Arabian Sea
Western Ghats
Eastern Ghats
Bay of Bengal
South China Sea
Micronesia
Jos Plateau
Ethiopian Highlands
Carlsberg Ridge
Sri Lanka
Sierra Leone Rise
African Plate
Gulf of Guinea
Congo Basin
Somali Basin
Ninetyeast Ridge
Sumatra
Borneo
West Caroline Basin
East Caroline Basin
Equator
Java Sea
New Guinea
ATLANTIC OCEAN
Mascarene Ridge
Indo-Australian Plate
Java (Sunda) Trench
Seychelles
Comoros
INDIAN OCEAN
Angola Basin
Mid Atlantic Ridge
St Helena
Madagascar
North Australian Basin
West Australian Basin
Coral Sea
Vanuatu
Great Barrier Reef
Fiji
Great Sandy Desert
Namib Desert
Kalahari Desert
Mauritius
Réunion
Madagascar Basin
Indo-Australian Plate
Tropic of Capricorn
Walvis Ridge
Mozambique Ridge
SW Indian Ocean Ridge
Broken Plateau
Perth Basin
Great Victoria Desert
Great Dividing Range
Norfolk Island Ridge
Tristan da Cunha
Cape Basin
Natal Basin
Île Amsterdam
Île St Paul
South Australian Basin
Tasman Sea
New Zealand
Gough Island
Agulhas Ridge
Crozet Basin
SE Indian Ocean Ridge
Tasman Basin
Alpine Fault
Agulhas Basin
Îles Crozet
Atlantic Indian Ridge
Prince Edward Islands
Îles Kerguélen
Indian-Antarctic Ridge
Auckland Island
South Sandwich Islands
Bouvetøya
Antarctic Plate
Australian-Antarctic Basin
Macquarie Island
SOUTHERN OCEAN
Balleny Islands
Antarctic Circle
Kemp Land
Wilkes Land
Transantarctic Mountains
Ross Sea
ANTARCTICA
Robinson Projection
0 1000 2000 3000 4000 kilometers
0 500 1000 1500 2000 miles

EARTH'S LANDFORMS

Our planet's surface displays an amazing variety of breathtaking landforms, which are not just random features—each is a result of predictable geological circumstances and caused by Earth's powerful internal heat engine.

Above There are a variety of types of volcanic eruptions; this is a Vulcanian eruption in which thick clouds of ash-carrying gas are explosively discharged into the air.

Below Torres del Paine National Park in the Chilean Andes protects a spectacular landscape, including the jagged peaks of the Cuernos del Paine: Granite intrusions under a layer of glacially eroded shale.

An Earth whose surface was not being folded and pushed by heat from within—a cold-cored Earth—would be a swampy, flat landscape.

Mighty Mountains and Powerful Rivers

Mountain ranges occur along the edges of tectonic plates. Crumpled together, their edges push upward as in the Himalayas, or overlap to melt and form volcanic arcs such as those of Japan, the Philippines, and Indonesia. In these places, the forces of erosion—wind, water, and ice—carve the rising rocks and volcanic peaks into landforms such as V-shaped valleys and canyons. The spines of Earth's mightiest mountain ranges control the climate of entire continents. The North American Cordillera and the Andean Cordillera of South America together form Earth's longest subaerial mountain range. Earth's 14 tallest mountains, all higher than 8,000 meters (26,250 feet), are in the Himalayas, along the collision margin between the Indian and Asian subcontinents.

Earth's most powerful rivers are those that drain the biggest mountain ranges. Their sources of water are derived from the disruption of moisture-laden air. Mountain barriers force air to rise, and the cooling air drops its moisture as precipitation on the mountain slopes. The Amazon, by far the world's most powerful river, drains the forested eastern side of the northern Andean Cordillera, and travels the entire width of South America before discharging into the Atlantic Ocean. A river's power is determined by the volume of water discharged, not by its length. The Nile is the world's longest river; its water travels some 6,700 kilometers (4,160 miles)—longer than the Amazon's 6,516 kilometers (4,050 miles). But the Nile does not carry very much water. Its catchment is dry and it has been heavily dammed for agricultural use. In terms of volume of water discharged, the Nile is ranked twenty-fourth.

Earth's mightiest rivers carry millions of tons of sediment, which is deposited in huge fan-shaped deltas at their mouths. This load is so heavy that it depresses Earth's crust into enormous basins in these regions. Bangladesh lies almost entirely on the giant delta of the Brahmaputra and Ganges rivers. This fertile delta is ideal for multiple annual cultivations, but the ever-shifting and flooding channels of the delta make life challenging for the country's 120 million inhabitants.

Rift Valleys and Fault Lines

Some of the lowest points on Earth's land surface are found where it has been stretched to breaking point by rising mantle currents acting on the base of the crust—a process known as rifting. Long cracks appear in the surface, accompanied by enormous slices of crust slipping

downward to form deep steep-walled valleys. Some impressive examples include the East African Rift Valley and the Jordan Valley–Dead Sea Rift. The lowest subaerial point on Earth is found on the shore of the Dead Sea, on the Israel–Jordan border. This point is 394 meters (1,292 feet) below sea level, and is steadily lowering over time as the Dead Sea continues to slowly evaporate.

Ongoing irregular slippage along long fault planes is experienced in these regions in the form of abundant earthquakes. Some of the most dangerous and earthquake-prone areas are at the edges of major tectonic plates that slide sideways against one another. Large populations at risk include those living along California's San Andreas Fault and Turkey's North Anatolian Fault Zone.

Deserts Hot and Cold

About one-fifth of Earth's land surface is desert—a region that receives less than 250 millimeters (10 inches) of precipitation annually. (Cold dry regions are also considered deserts: Antarctica contains the world's largest ice desert, as what little snow that falls there tends not to melt.) The Sahara Desert is the world's largest hot desert, and extends across parts of Morocco, Algeria, Egypt, Libya, Chad, and Mauritania. Desert landscapes are mostly bare of vegetation, and may have a rocky or pebbly surface, or be covered with mobile sand dunes. Surface water is practically nonexistent, and flows only as a sudden deluge following rare instances of torrential rainfall. Extremely high evaporation rates and low rainfall combine to transport soluble salts to temporary salt lakes or playa lakes that form at the deserts' lowest points.

The major hot deserts—such as the Sahara, Kalahari, and the Great Australian deserts—occur in distinct bands around the globe, between the latitudes of about 20° to 35° north and south of the equator. In this zone, air masses are dry and warm, so there is very little chance of rain. Deserts lie toward the center and western side of large continents, far from the reach of the moisture-laden easterly trade winds—the strong winds driven by Earth's easterly rotation. Deserts also form on the downwind, or "rain-shadow," side of major mountain ranges.

Volcanoes Active and Extinct

All of the classic volcanic peaks—such as Mount Fuji in Japan or Mount Etna in Italy—are essentially active, although they may not have erupted in decades, or even millennia. There are about 1,500 such volcanoes on Earth. Geologically speaking, they could erupt any minute, as evidenced by the typical, clean-lined, conical peaks that are formed by periodic ash falls and lava flows, and have not yet been ravaged by the forces of erosion.

Extinct volcanoes are more difficult to recognize. Their cones have long been eroded, and often it is only the volcano's internal "plumbing system"—dykes and pipes that once brought lava to the surface—that remains. Some of Earth's most spectacular landforms are, in fact, volcanic remnants, such as Devils Tower in Wyoming, USA. In Europe, such volcanic remains have long been chosen as invincible sites on which to build fortresses or places of contemplation, such as monasteries. Sometimes, if the erosion of an ancient volcano has been absolute, all that may remain is the imprint of the radial drainage pattern on an essentially flat landscape.

Top This amazing desert landscape shows limestone "pinnacles," formed by plant roots breaking up a subterranean layer of limestone into pillars and then the erosion of the covering layer of soil and plant life it supported.

Above Lord Howe Island, off the eastern coast of Australia, is the topmost portion of an extinct underwater volcano that first erupted about seven million years ago.

TEMPERATURE

Air temperature affects many aspects of our daily lives. It is also one of the most important determining factors of the climate. Understanding what causes variations in air temperature leads to a better knowledge of our planet.

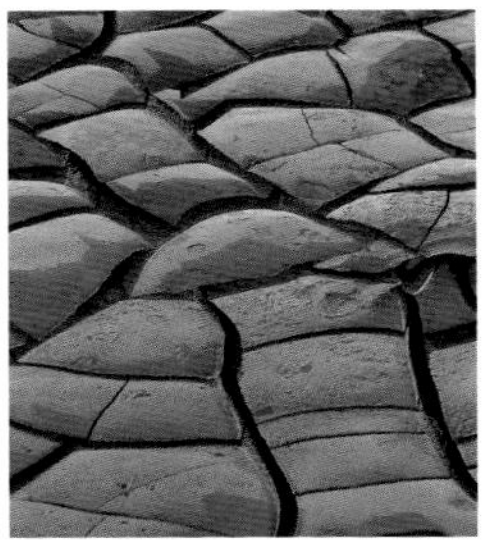

Above The combination of aridity and temperature extremes (38°C/100°F in summer, –9°C/16°F in winter) has dried the earth along the northwestern edge of China's Taklamakan Desert.

Below The Ross Ice Shelf is Antarctica's largest. These floating platforms of ice protect the continental glaciers that feed them, but may detach from the continent if air and water temperatures increase.

The temperature of Earth's atmosphere varies with altitude, but it is in the lowest layer of our atmosphere (the troposphere) that we experience the dynamic changes in temperature that occur on our planet.

Energy Balance

Temperature on Earth is determined by energy balance at the surface. This balance is maintained because heat is transferred via conduction, convection, and radiation, or a combination thereof. Conduction is the transfer of thermal energy through matter, from higher to lower, acting to equalize temperature differences. Convection transfers heat through the movement of currents within a fluid or gas; warm air is less dense than cool air, and air movement results as warmer air rises and cooler air sinks. Electromagnetic radiation is emitted from the surface of an object due to the object's temperature.

Another important heat transfer process is latent heat, energy that is taken up and stored when a substance changes state. Matter basically exist in three states—solid, liquid, or gas. Earth's temperature range allows water to exist in all three states (as ice, water, and steam) and to change from one state to another. Heat is released into the air by condensation (gas to liquid), melting (solid to liquid), and sublimation (solid to gas). Heat is absorbed from the air by evaporation (liquid to gas), freezing (liquid to solid), and deposition (gas to solid). Water can absorb energy in one location and transport it to another where it is released, redistributing energy.

Why Regions Differ in Temperature

Our Sun emits energy in the form of electromagnetic radiation, or insolation, which is absorbed, scattered, or reflected. Latitude determines the duration and intensity of insolation. The duration changes very little at the equator; the greatest change in duration of solar radiation occurs at the poles, 90° North and South latitude, when during the summer, the Sun stays above the horizon throughout the 24-hour day. Yet here the intensity of insolation is weak because solar rays strike the surface at a shallow angle.

In the tropics there is a net energy surplus; in middle and higher latitudes there is a net energy deficit. The atmospheric circulation transports energy toward the poles, reducing the equatorial and polar temperature contrast. Prevailing global wind systems also drive surface ocean currents, which transport warmer tropical water poleward and bring colder polar waters toward the tropics.

There are major differences in the rate of heating and cooling between a land surface and a body of water. First, solar radiation does not penetrate below the surface of rock and soil on land surfaces, but can penetrate several meters through water. Second, dry land heats and cools about four times faster than water. Third, warm water can mix with cooler water below, and redistribute the heat. Fourth, air over water surfaces can be cooled by evaporation, which is limited over land because there is not as much water in soil or vegetation.

Mountainous regions are cool to cold: Temperature decreases on average at about 6.5°C per 1,000 meter increase in elevation (3.5°F/1,000 feet). A sequence of temperatures in several thousand feet of elevation is similar to traveling several thousand miles toward the nearest pole. At very high elevations, low temperatures persist throughout the year and the ground may be covered in ice or snow, even in the tropics.

Above Hydrothermal activity can create warm micro-climates, as at Waimangu Thermal Valley, on New Zealand's North Island. The eruption of Mt Tarawera in 1886 was soon followed by the formation of hot springs and steaming fissures.

Left Areas with limited vegetation and soil moisture, like most of Australia's inland regions, experience intense heating during the day but at night will cool rapidly, thereby showing a large daily temperature range.

Global Temperature 1850–1880

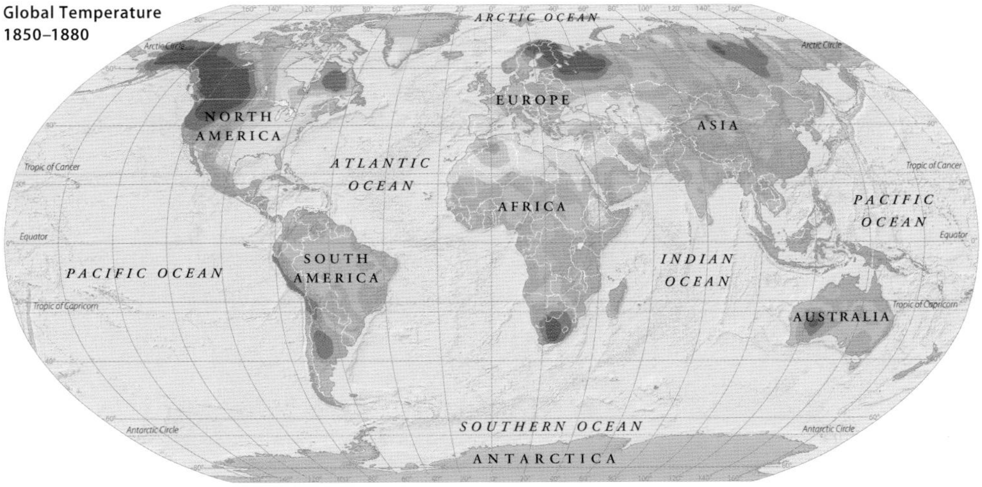
ARCTIC OCEAN
Arctic Circle
NORTH AMERICA
EUROPE
ASIA
ATLANTIC OCEAN
Tropic of Cancer
AFRICA
PACIFIC OCEAN
Equator
SOUTH AMERICA
INDIAN OCEAN
PACIFIC OCEAN
Tropic of Capricorn
AUSTRALIA
Antarctic Circle
SOUTHERN OCEAN
ANTARCTICA

Global Temperature 1880–1900

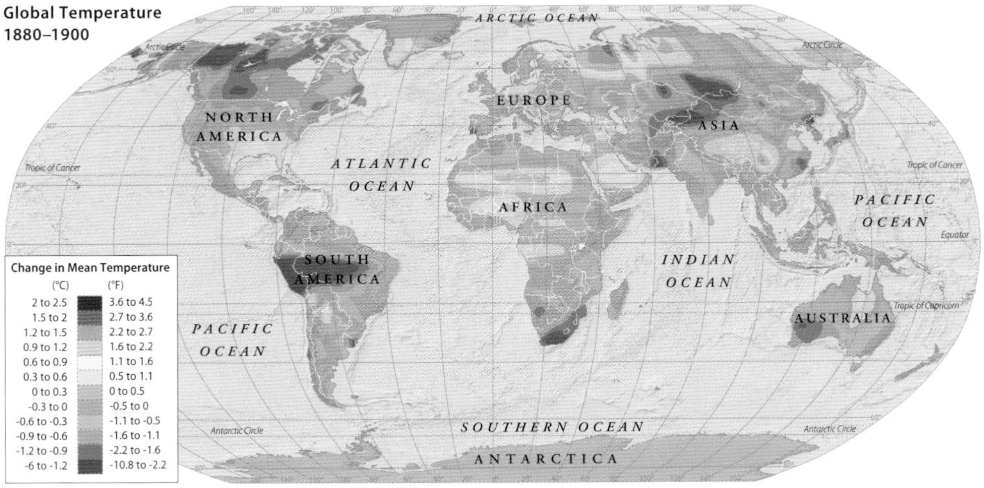
ARCTIC OCEAN
Arctic Circle
NORTH AMERICA
EUROPE
ASIA
ATLANTIC OCEAN
Tropic of Cancer
AFRICA
PACIFIC OCEAN
Equator
SOUTH AMERICA
INDIAN OCEAN
PACIFIC OCEAN
Tropic of Capricorn
AUSTRALIA
Antarctic Circle
SOUTHERN OCEAN
ANTARCTICA
Change in Mean Temperature
(°C) (°F)
2 to 2.5 3.6 to 4.5
1.5 to 2 2.7 to 3.6
1.2 to 1.5 2.2 to 2.7
0.9 to 1.2 1.6 to 2.2
0.6 to 0.9 1.1 to 1.6
0.3 to 0.6 0.5 to 1.1
0 to 0.3 0 to 0.5
-0.3 to 0 -0.5 to 0
-0.6 to -0.3 -1.1 to -0.5
-0.9 to -0.6 -1.6 to -1.1
-1.2 to -0.9 -2.2 to -1.6
-6 to -1.2 -10.8 to -2.2

Global Temperature 1900–1950

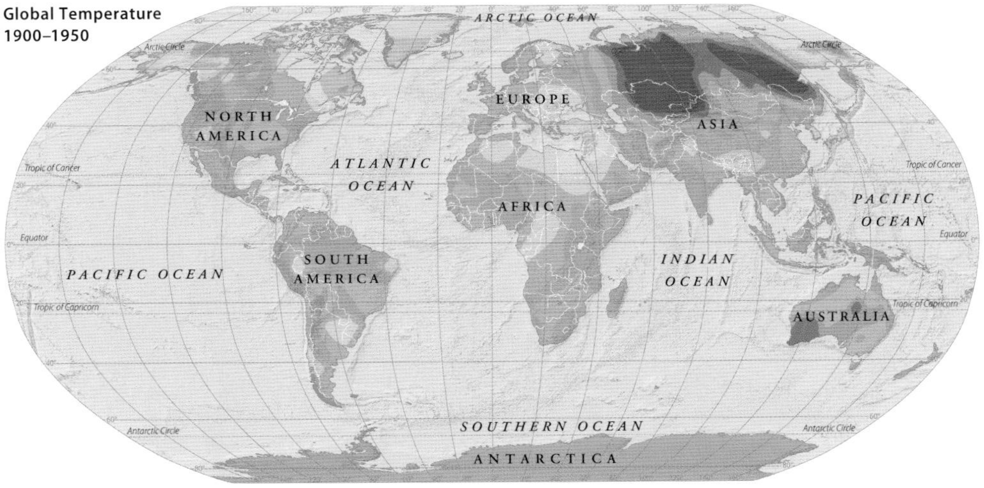
ARCTIC OCEAN
Arctic Circle
NORTH AMERICA
EUROPE
ASIA
ATLANTIC OCEAN
Tropic of Cancer
AFRICA
PACIFIC OCEAN
Equator
SOUTH AMERICA
INDIAN OCEAN
PACIFIC OCEAN
Tropic of Capricorn
AUSTRALIA
Antarctic Circle
SOUTHERN OCEAN
ANTARCTICA

Global Temperature 1950–2000

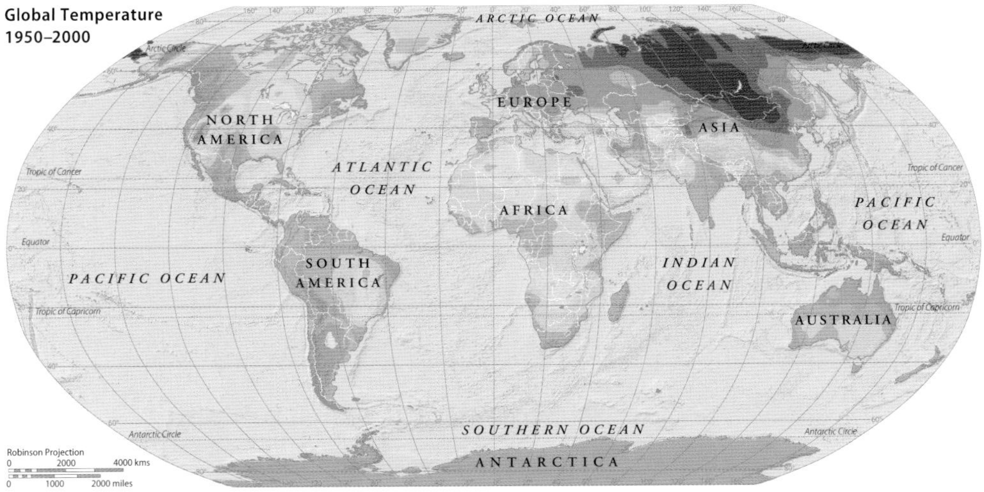
ARCTIC OCEAN
NORTH AMERICA
EUROPE
ASIA
ATLANTIC OCEAN
Tropic of Cancer
AFRICA
PACIFIC OCEAN
Equator
SOUTH AMERICA
INDIAN OCEAN
PACIFIC OCEAN
Tropic of Capricorn
AUSTRALIA
Antarctic Circle
SOUTHERN OCEAN
ANTARCTICA
Robinson Projection
0 2000 4000 kms
0 1000 2000 miles

CLIMATE

Climate is the average and variations of weather in a region over long periods of time. Weather, on the other hand, is the measurement of air temperature, precipitation, barometric pressure, and winds at a given moment.

Bottom About 12 percent of the world's land area experiences an arid climate, with the largest region being the Sahara–Saudi Arabia–Iran–Thar desert belt of North Africa and southern Asia.

Below New Zealand's Te Urewera National Park covers about 2,126 square kilometers (821 square miles), with enough variation in climate to provide habitats for a wide range of native plants and animals.

Climate, in its basic sense, is the statistical analysis of weather: It combines weather record parameters into averages, ranges, and extremes. Climate zones are arbitrarily defined regions that share similar long-term weather elements. Climate is one of the most important determining factors for the distribution of life on Earth, and is also an important factor in making informed economic and land use decisions.

Earth has a variety of climate types that range from tropical moist in equatorial regions to polar. Seven factors affect climate at a given location: Latitude, land/water distribution, ocean currents, wind patterns, high- and low-pressure circulations, mountain barriers, and elevation. In order to understand the general climate of a location, averages and ranges are used to group weather elements.

The most widely used classification system for world climates was devised by Wladimir Köppen in 1918 and applies a vegetation-based approach. The Köppen climate classification system uses five major types that are designated by the capital letters A, B, C, D, and E. A breakdown of the major climate regions follows. It should be noted that the Köppen climate classification system can distinguish many additional climate subtypes.

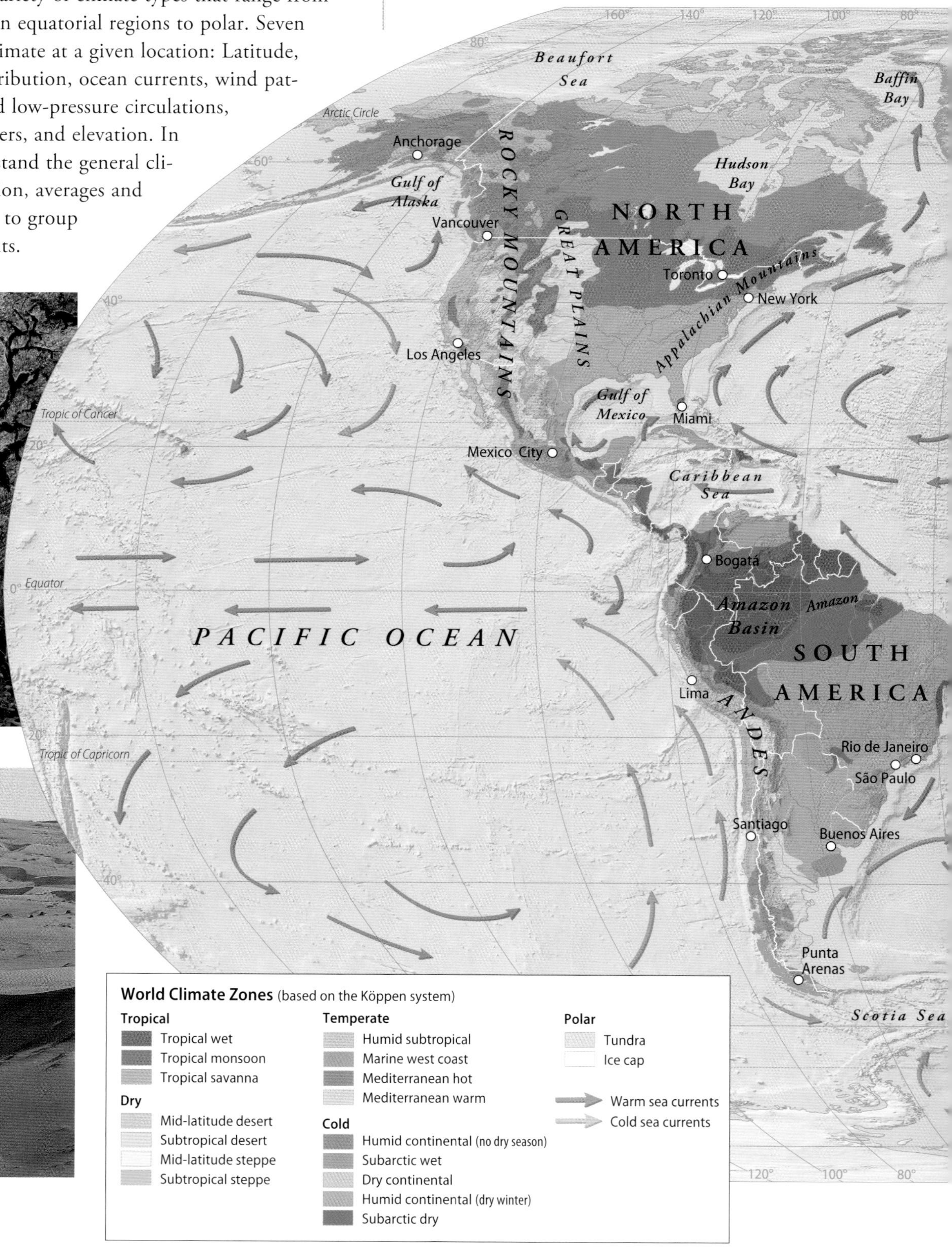
Beaufort Sea
Baffin Bay
Arctic Circle
Anchorage
Gulf of Alaska
Hudson Bay
ROCKY MOUNTAINS
GREAT PLAINS
NORTH AMERICA
Vancouver
Toronto
Appalachian Mountains
New York
Los Angeles
Tropic of Cancer
Gulf of Mexico
Miami
Mexico City
Caribbean Sea
Bogatá
Equator
Amazon Basin
Amazon
PACIFIC OCEAN
SOUTH AMERICA
Lima
ANDES
Tropic of Capricorn
Rio de Janeiro
São Paulo
Santiago
Buenos Aires
Punta Arenas
Scotia Sea
World Climate Zones (based on the Köppen system)
Tropical
Tropical wet
Tropical monsoon
Tropical savanna
Dry
Mid-latitude desert
Subtropical desert
Mid-latitude steppe
Subtropical steppe
Temperate
Humid subtropical
Marine west coast
Mediterranean hot
Mediterranean warm
Cold
Humid continental (no dry season)
Subarctic wet
Dry continental
Humid continental (dry winter)
Subarctic dry
Polar
Tundra
Ice cap
Warm sea currents
Cold sea currents

Tropical Moist (Group A)

Three major climate types are found in the low latitudes: Tropical wet climate (Af), tropical monsoon climate (Am), and wet–dry tropical climate (Aw).

Dry (Group B)

The two main types of B climates are based on degree of dryness—the arid (BW) and semiarid or steppe (BS).

Moist Subtropical Mid-latitude (Group C)

These regions are noted for hot humid summers, while winters tend to be mild, especially in the lower latitudes. Poleward regions are colder and harsher. Two other climate types, the marine west coast and Mediterranean, are included in group C.

Moist Continental and Boreal Forest (Group D)

The moist continental climate experiences a large temperature range due to its interior location in mid-latitude continents. The taiga or boreal forest region experiences cold winters and mild summers.

Polar (Group E)

Polar climates are the tundra and ice cap, both with very low temperatures. Although these regions are covered by snow and ice, they are extremely dry and snowfall is low.

Highland (Group H)

Highlands have many climate zones and the character of the climate is related to the surrounding lowlands. Temperature decreases with elevation, and temperature range and precipitation generally increase.

Above Hurricanes are associated with low-pressure systems over tropical or subtropical waters, thunderstorm activity, and low-level winds.

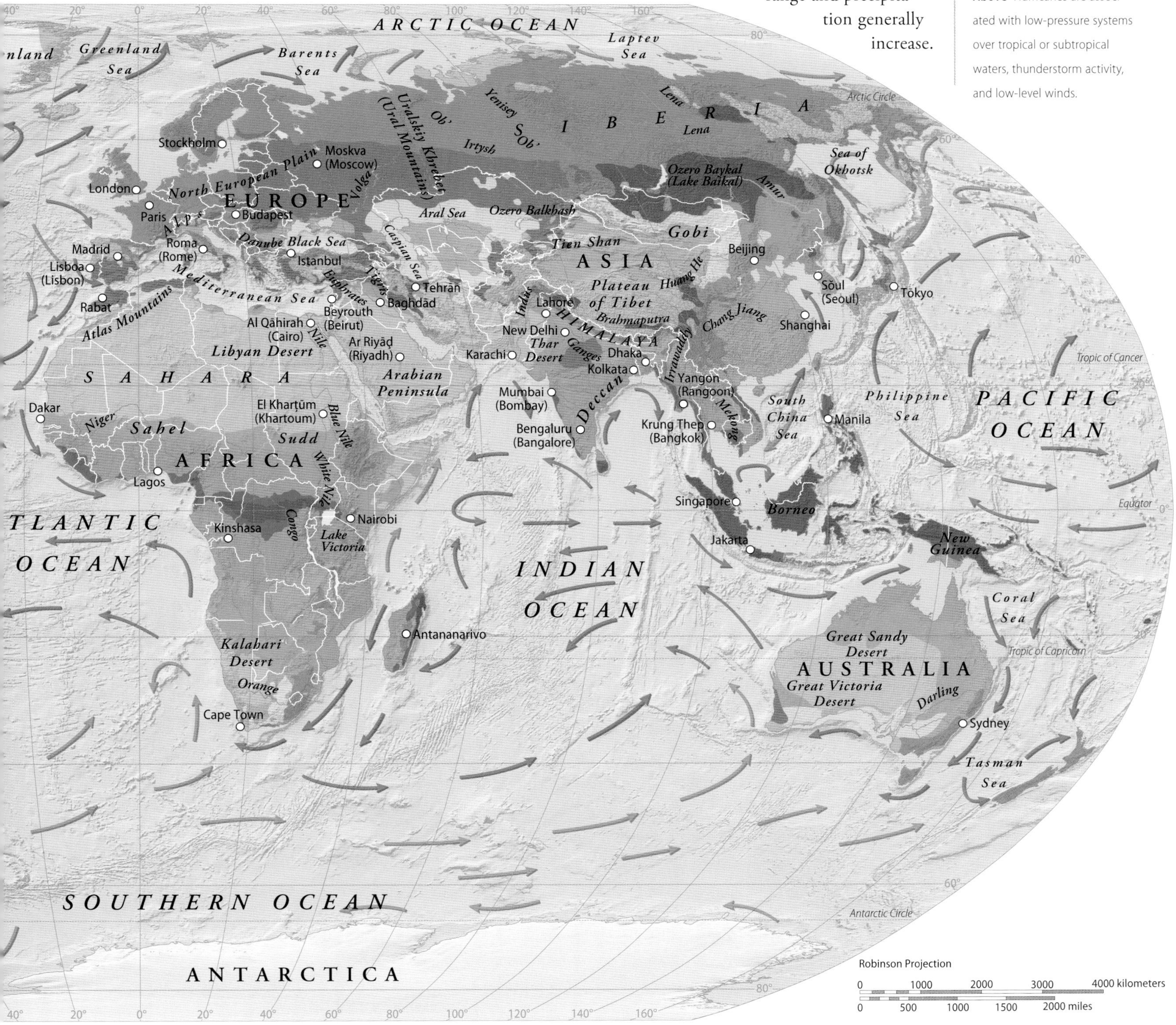
ARCTIC OCEAN
Greenland Sea
Barents Sea
Laptev Sea
SIBERIA
Arctic Circle
Sea of Okhotsk
Stockholm
Moskva (Moscow)
London
Paris
EUROPE
North European Plain
Budapest
Alps
Madrid
Roma (Rome)
Lisboa (Lisbon)
Istanbul
Black Sea
Mediterranean Sea
Rabat
Atlas Mountains
Al Qāhirah (Cairo)
Beyrouth (Beirut)
Baghdād
Tehrān
Ar Riyād (Riyadh)
Libyan Desert
SAHARA
Arabian Peninsula
Caspian Sea
Aral Sea
Ozero Balkhash
Tien Shan
ASIA
Gobi
Ozero Baykal (Lake Baikal)
Beijing
Sŏul (Seoul)
Tōkyo
Shanghai
Plateau of Tibet
HIMALAYA
Lahore
New Delhi
Thar Desert
Karachi
Dhaka
Kolkata
Mumbai (Bombay)
Bengaluru (Bangalore)
Deccan
Yangon (Rangoon)
Krung Thep (Bangkok)
South China Sea
Manila
Philippine Sea
PACIFIC OCEAN
Tropic of Cancer
Equator
Singapore
Borneo
Jakarta
New Guinea
Dakar
Sahel
El Kharṭūm (Khartoum)
Sudd
AFRICA
Lagos
Kinshasa
Nairobi
Lake Victoria
TLANTIC OCEAN
INDIAN OCEAN
Antananarivo
Kalahari Desert
Cape Town
Coral Sea
Tropic of Capricorn
Great Sandy Desert
AUSTRALIA
Great Victoria Desert
Sydney
Tasman Sea
SOUTHERN OCEAN
Antarctic Circle
ANTARCTICA
Robinson Projection
0 1000 2000 3000 4000 kilometers
0 500 1000 1500 2000 miles

PLANTS and ANIMALS

The complexity of life on Earth is truly staggering. Estimates of the total number of plant and animal species differ greatly, but about 1.75 million species have been formally classified, of which around half are insects.

Above Only about 400 Siberian tigers still live in the wild, due to hunting and habitat loss, and the species is now endangered.

Below The Arabian oryx was hunted almost to extinction, but the breeding of zoo animals has preserved the species.

With large areas of the planet remaining relatively unexplored, it is impossible to determine the exact number of species on Earth. Biodiversity is usually defined as "variability among living organisms." This variability is essential to the maintenance of a healthy environment. Plants and animals have evolved to fill almost every niche in nature, ensuring that living creatures are found in every environment from the extreme cold of Antarctica to the hottest deserts and the deepest oceans.

The Biophysical Environment

The biophysical environment is the collection of living (biotic) and non-living (abiotic) elements that make up Earth. There are four such elements: the biosphere—the collection of all living organisms, both plant and animal; the atmosphere—the layer of gases that surround Earth; the hydrosphere—water storages and the transfers between them; and the lithosphere—Earth's crust, including soils, landforms, and bedrock.The ways these four "spheres" interact create different environments and thus differences in biodiversity.

At the heart of all ecosystems is the Sun. Solar energy is absorbed by plants and, through photosynthesis, is converted into energy. Plants are then consumed by

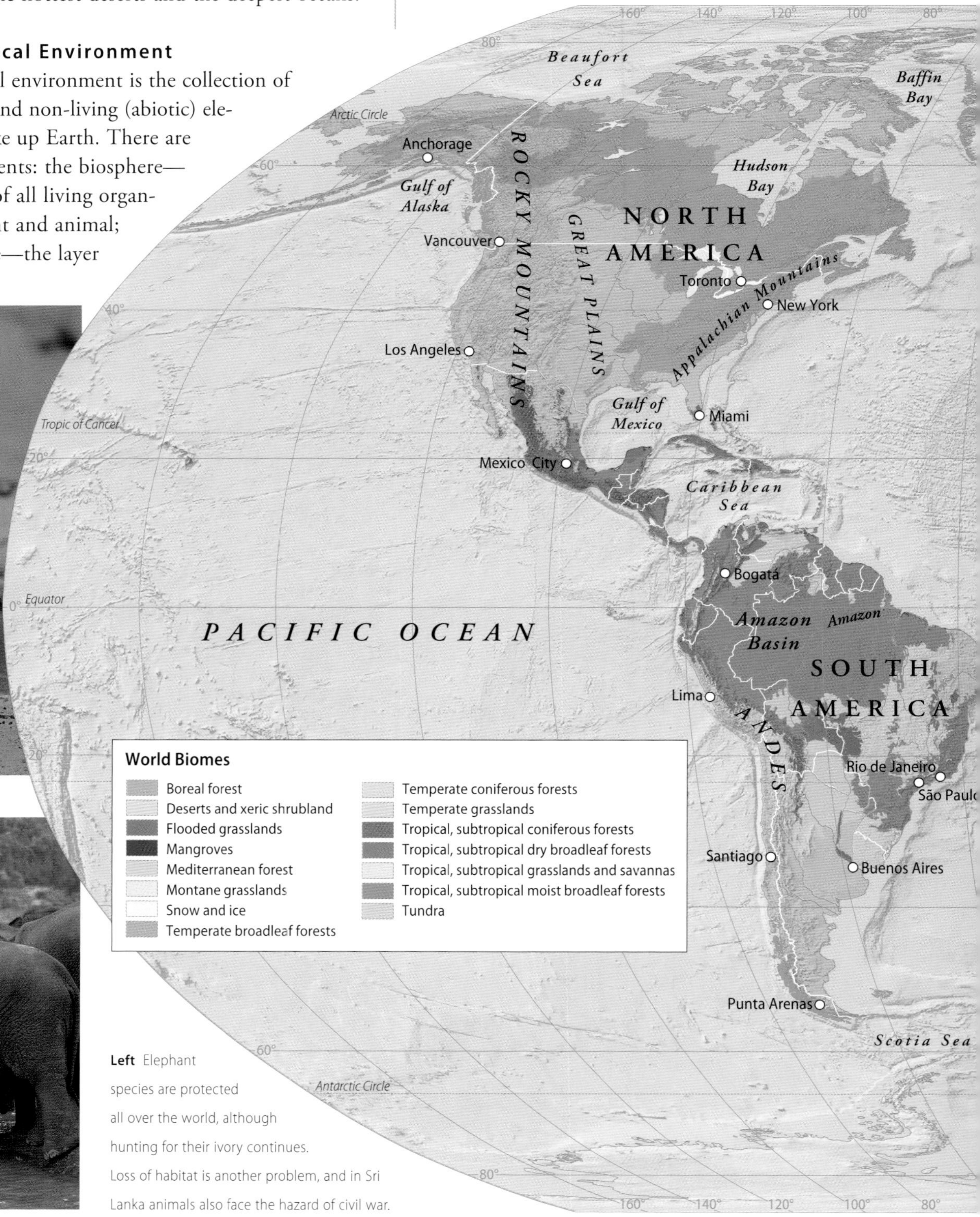
Beaufort Sea
Baffin Bay
Arctic Circle
Anchorage
Gulf of Alaska
Hudson Bay
ROCKY MOUNTAINS
GREAT PLAINS
NORTH AMERICA
Vancouver
Toronto
Appalachian Mountains
New York
Los Angeles
Gulf of Mexico
Miami
Tropic of Cancer
Mexico City
Caribbean Sea
Bogatá
Equator
PACIFIC OCEAN
Amazon Basin
Amazon
SOUTH AMERICA
Lima
ANDES
Rio de Janeiro
São Paulo
Santiago
Buenos Aires
Punta Arenas
Scotia Sea
Antarctic Circle
World Biomes
Boreal forest
Deserts and xeric shrubland
Flooded grasslands
Mangroves
Mediterranean forest
Montane grasslands
Snow and ice
Temperate broadleaf forests
Temperate coniferous forests
Temperate grasslands
Tropical, subtropical coniferous forests
Tropical, subtropical dry broadleaf forests
Tropical, subtropical grasslands and savannas
Tropical, subtropical moist broadleaf forests
Tundra

Left Elephant species are protected all over the world, although hunting for their ivory continues. Loss of habitat is another problem, and in Sri Lanka animals also face the hazard of civil war.

herbivores (plant-eating animals) which are, in turn, consumed by carnivores (meat-eating animals). Then plants and animals break down biological material and recycle it into the soil, spreading energy through the ecosystem.

Climate influences the plants and animals found in an area. The tropical zone is home to the most diverse ecosystems on earth, the rainforests. The polar regions receive such small amounts of solar energy that they are almost devoid of plant life on the land—highly adapted aquatic plants provide the basis of the polar food chains.

Forests are significant environments, covering huge areas of the continents. There are three main groups of forests, each determined by latitude. Around the equator are the tropical rainforests, where conditions encourage thousands of species to flourish in a tiny area. In the mid-latitudes temperate forests dominate. These forests tend to have a more open canopy and support grazing animals. In Canada, Northern Europe, and Siberia evergreen coniferous forests are prevalent, and many of the animal inhabitants typically hibernate to survive the harsh winters.

More than 40 percent of Earth's land surface is covered by grassland. Grasslands support a complex interrelationship between plants and animals: Grazing animals became the dominant fauna; in response, carnivores evolved.

Human activity has led to the destruction of vast areas of natural habitat. Recent research by the International Union for Conservation of Nature (IUCN) found that 22 percent of mammal species, 12 percent of birds, 30 percent of reptiles, 31 percent of amphibians, 39 percent of fish, and more than 50 percent of invertebrate species (mostly insects) are endangered now.

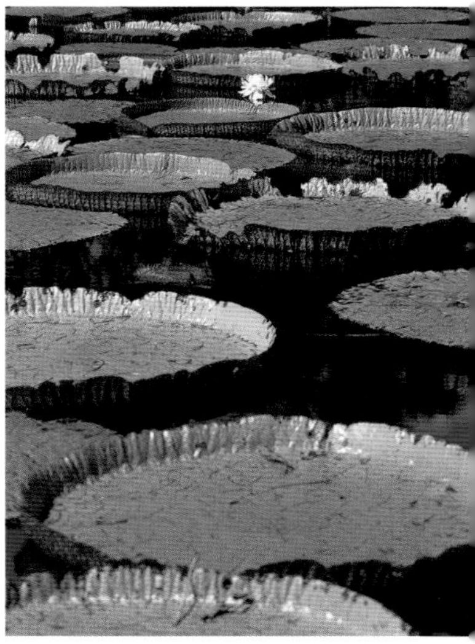

Above A native of the Amazon Basin of South America, the giant waterlily has leaves that reach more than 1.8 meters (6 ft) in diameter. Tropical habitats support a wide range of plant types.

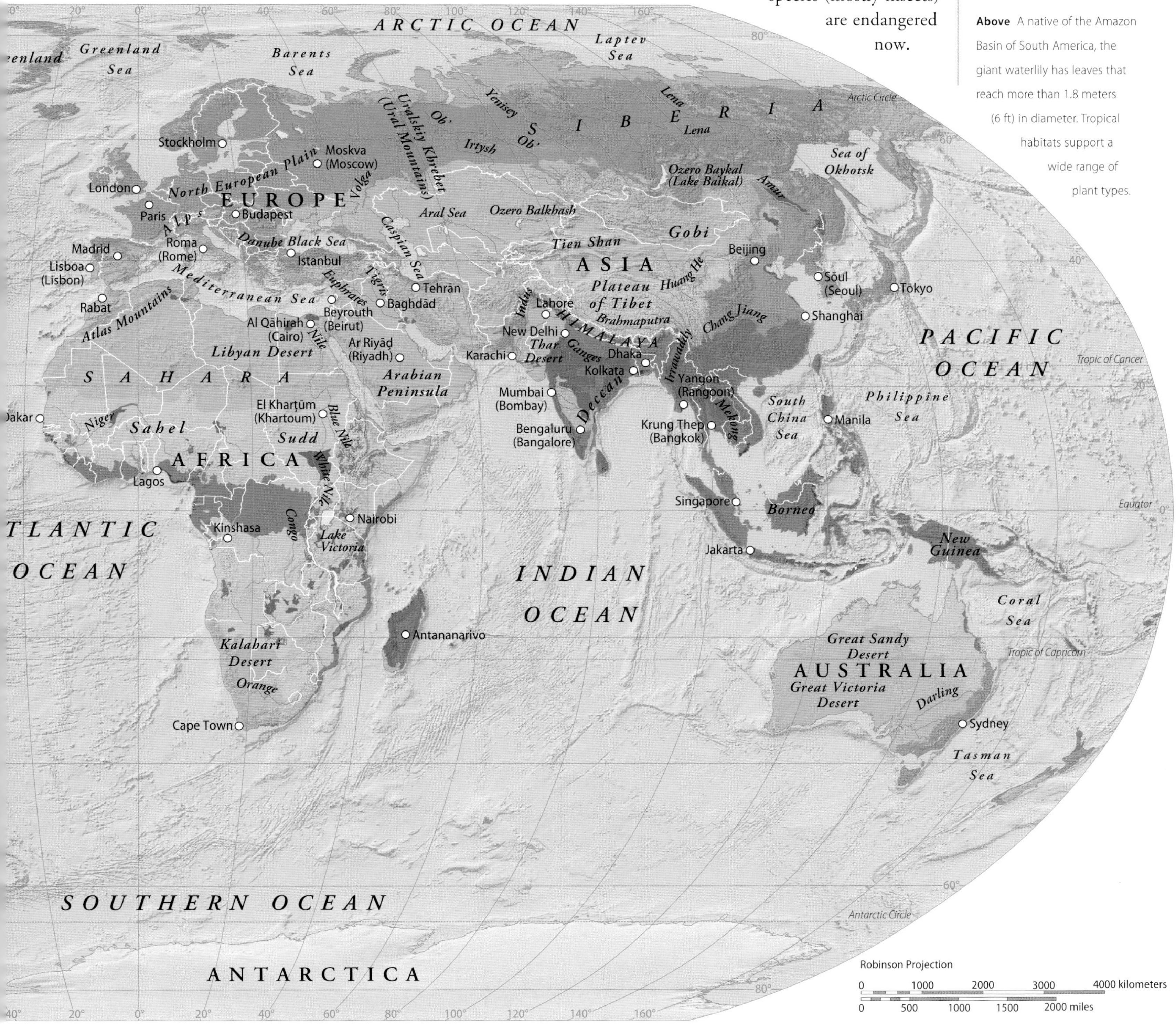
ARCTIC OCEAN
Greenland Sea
Barents Sea
Laptev Sea
Arctic Circle
SIBERIA
Uralskiy Khrebet (Ural Mountains)
Ob'
Yenisey
Lena
Irtysh
Stockholm
Moskva (Moscow)
North European Plain
London
EUROPE
Volga
Paris
Alps
Budapest
Madrid
Roma (Rome)
Danube
Black Sea
Lisboa (Lisbon)
Istanbul
Mediterranean Sea
Rabat
Atlas Mountains
Caspian Sea
Aral Sea
Ozero Balkhash
Sea of Okhotsk
Ozero Baykal (Lake Baikal)
Amur
Gobi
Tien Shan
Beijing
ASIA
Huang He
Sŏul (Seoul)
Tōkyo
Tehrān
Tigris
Euphrates
Baghdād
Beyrouth (Beirut)
Al Qāhirah (Cairo)
Nile
Ar Riyāḍ (Riyadh)
Libyan Desert
Plateau of Tibet
Indus
Lahore
HIMALAYA
Brahmaputra
Chang Jiang
Shanghai
PACIFIC OCEAN
Tropic of Cancer
New Delhi
Thar Desert
Ganges
Karachi
Dhaka
Kolkata
Irrawaddy
SAHARA
Arabian Peninsula
Mumbai (Bombay)
Deccan
Yangon (Rangoon)
South China Sea
Philippine Sea
Manila
El Kharṭūm (Khartoum)
Blue Nile
Dakar
Niger
Sahel
Sudd
Bengaluru (Bangalore)
Krung Thep (Bangkok)
Mekong
AFRICA
White Nile
Lagos
Singapore
Borneo
Equator
Congo
Nairobi
Kinshasa
Lake Victoria
ATLANTIC OCEAN
Jakarta
New Guinea
INDIAN OCEAN
Coral Sea
Antananarivo
Great Sandy Desert
Tropic of Capricorn
Kalahari Desert
AUSTRALIA
Great Victoria Desert
Darling
Orange
Cape Town
Sydney
Tasman Sea
SOUTHERN OCEAN
Antarctic Circle
ANTARCTICA
Robinson Projection
0 1000 2000 3000 4000 kilometers
0 500 1000 1500 2000 miles

WORLD ENERGY

Energy is essential to all life. In the natural world it is the Sun that provides the primary source of energy. In modern human society, where energy is consumed on a vast scale, most of our energy is derived from burning fossil fuels.

In recent years, the energy needs of developing nations have grown considerably. With oil, coal, and natural gas facing depletion by the end of this century—if current levels of consumption continue and no further reserves are found—the need to cultivate alternative sources of energy is vital. Until recently, decisions about energy have been based solely on economic factors such as cost and availability. The growing global debate on climate change, however, increasingly emphasizes non-economic environmental concerns.

Alternative Energy Sources

On the surface, nuclear energy appears to be a viable alternative to the three main fossil fuels—just 454 grams (1 pound) of uranium can release more energy than 1,500 tons of coal. Globally, nuclear power accounts for around 16 percent of all power production. A major energy source in Europe, nuclear power is considered a very clean technology in that there are no emissions from the actual site of generation. However, one of the main problems with nuclear power is secure storage of its highly toxic waste. Among other risks associated with it is the threat that nuclear technology may be diverted to nuclear weapons programs.

Below Solar power is well suited for use in isolated places not connected to the electricity grid. Research continues to improve the efficiency of collecting, storing and converting solar energy.

Left An aerial view of a coal strip-mining operation. One of the major fossil fuels, coal is a non-renewable resource that provides much of the world's energy supply.

Beaufort Sea
Baffin Bay
Arctic Circle
Anchorage
Hudson Bay
Gulf of Alaska
ROCKY MTS
Vancouver
NORTH AMERICA
Toronto
New York
Los Angeles
Tropic of Cancer
Gulf of Mexico
Miami
Mexico City
Caribbean Sea
Bogatá
Equator
PACIFIC OCEAN
SOUTH AMERICA
Lima
ANDES
Tropic of Capricorn
Rio de Jane
São Paulo
Santiago
Buenos Aires
Punta Arenas
Scotia Sea
Antarctic Circle
World Energy Resources
Oil
Coal
Gas
Uranium
Wind
Hydroelectric

Renewable resources—energy derived from the Sun, wind, the power of waves, and running water—represent alternative long-term solutions.

Solar energy is the most abundant alternative source. There are two main methods of solar-power generation. Photovoltaic cells are used for small- and medium-scale applications. Modern research is examining ways to produce flexible cells that can be used to cover roof surfaces, permitting individual homes to become power stations. Large-scale solar power stations are found in the dry, sun-drenched regions of countries like the USA, India, Spain, and Australia, with many more planned worldwide.

Wind power is again becoming attractive as an alternative energy source. At present around one percent of global electricity production is wind generated—modern wind turbines can produce up to 1 megawatt of power, and are capable of powering hundreds of homes.

Engineers have now developed the technology to use the energy of ocean waves to turn a turbine, and thus create electricity. A small wave plant installed in a harbor at Wollongong, Australia, produces around 450 kilowatts of energy per day, which is used to desalinate about 3,000,000 liters (792,516 gallons) of water a day.

Geothermal power is yet another alternative to fossil fuels. This technology uses the heat of Earth's interior to superheat water and create steam for turning electricity turbines. Bores are sunk deep into the earth to reach "hot rocks;" water is then pumped down through the bore and, heated by the rocks, is turned into steam. Geothermal plants have long been used in Iceland, which has five geothermal power plants.

Above Hydroelectricity provides almost 20 percent of the world's energy. The massive forces of flowing water are harnessed by turbines for power generation.

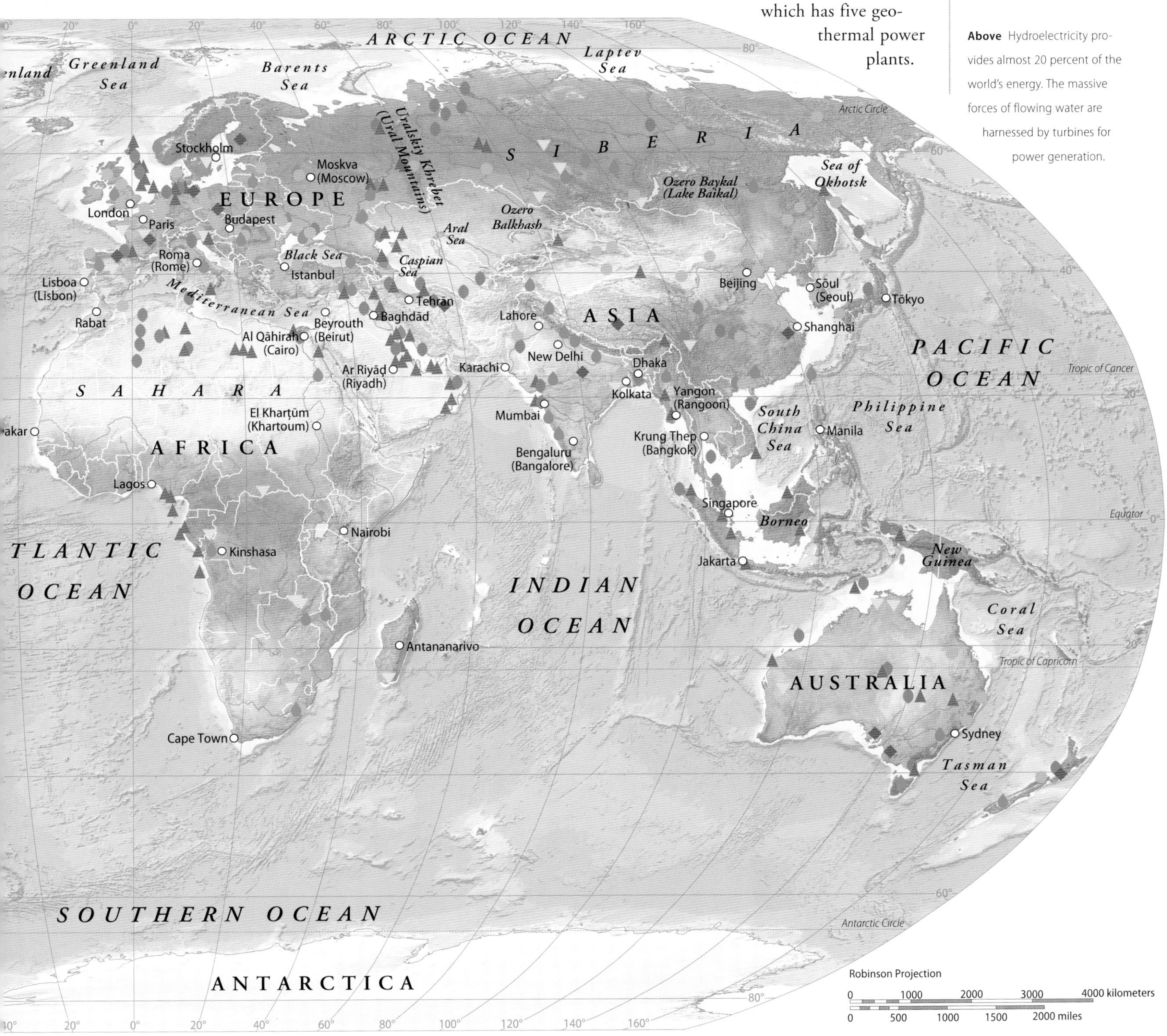
ARCTIC OCEAN
Greenland Sea
Barents Sea
Laptev Sea
Arctic Circle
SIBERIA
Uralskiy Khrebet (Ural Mountains)
Stockholm
Moskva (Moscow)
EUROPE
London
Paris
Budapest
Sea of Okhotsk
Ozero Baykal (Lake Baikal)
Ozero Balkhash
Aral Sea
Caspian Sea
Black Sea
Roma (Rome)
Istanbul
Lisboa (Lisbon)
Rabat
Mediterranean Sea
Beyrouth (Beirut)
Al Qāhirah (Cairo)
Tehrān
Baghdād
Ar Riyāḍ (Riyadh)
Beijing
Sŏul (Seoul)
Tōkyo
Shanghai
ASIA
Lahore
New Delhi
Karachi
Dhaka
Kolkata
PACIFIC OCEAN
Tropic of Cancer
SAHARA
El Kharṭūm (Khartoum)
Mumbai
Yangon (Rangoon)
South China Sea
Philippine Sea
Manila
Dakar
AFRICA
Bengaluru (Bangalore)
Krung Thep (Bangkok)
Lagos
Singapore
Borneo
Equator
Nairobi
ATLANTIC OCEAN
Kinshasa
Jakarta
New Guinea
INDIAN OCEAN
Coral Sea
Antananarivo
Tropic of Capricorn
AUSTRALIA
Cape Town
Sydney
Tasman Sea
SOUTHERN OCEAN
Antarctic Circle
ANTARCTICA
Robinson Projection
0 1000 2000 3000 4000 kilometers
0 500 1000 1500 2000 miles

POPULATION

Earth is home to nearly 7 billion human beings, a number that is projected to reach around 9.5 billion sometime during the middle of the century, then plateau and perhaps decline.

World population data figures disclose some interesting issues. For example, 61 percent of the world's population lives in Asia—home to six of the ten most populated countries. India—currently second in population—will soon overtake China to become the most populated country. Several top 10 countries experience a rate of natural increase (RNI) twice that of the world's 1.2 percent average. Europe, on the other hand, has become the first continent in modern history to achieve sustained zero population growth. RNI is a critical index of demographic, economic, and social conditions within a country. Typically, countries with a low RNI tend to have a longer life expectancy, be more urban, and have a higher gross national product (GNP) than do those with a high rate of growth.

Where people live is a reflection of many factors. The natural environment and its resources play a significant role, as does culture, including economic capability, available capital and technological resources, needs and aspirations, and perceptions of the natural environment and its potential. Today, about two-thirds of Earth's land surface is inhabited and in some way productive.

However, population density figures can be misleading. Europe has about 32 people per square kilometer

Below This satellite image shows the city lights of Tokyo, Japan. The world's largest urban agglomeration is the Tokyo–Yokohama metropolitan area, which is home to an estimated 34 million people.

Left Comprised of 53 countries, Africa is home to 14 percent of the global population—some 680 million people—a figure that is estimated will double within 30 years.

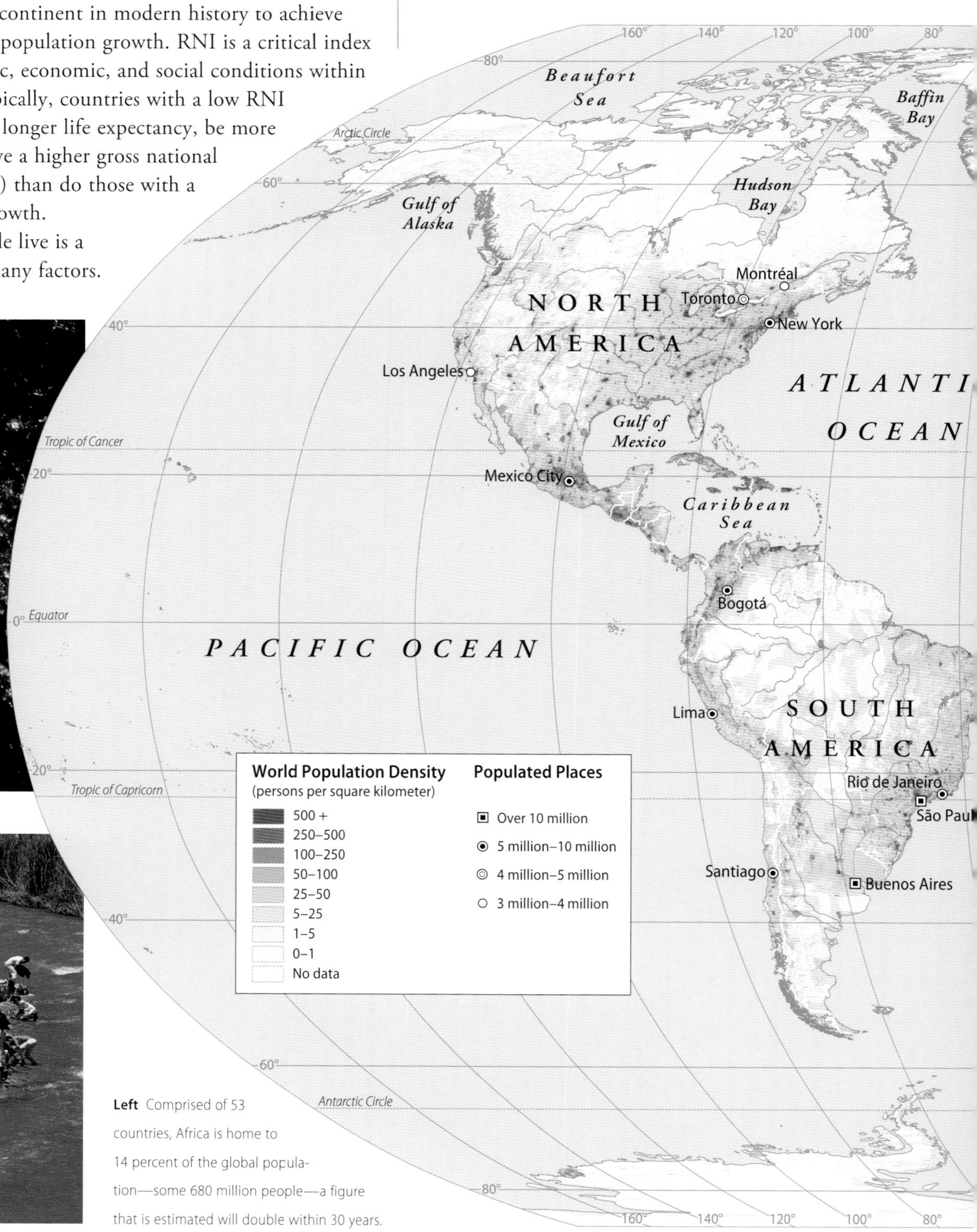

Beaufort Sea
Baffin Bay
Arctic Circle
Hudson Bay
Gulf of Alaska
Montréal
Toronto
New York
NORTH AMERICA
Los Angeles
ATLANTIC OCEAN
Gulf of Mexico
Tropic of Cancer
Mexico City
Caribbean Sea
Bogotá
Equator
PACIFIC OCEAN
Lima
SOUTH AMERICA
Rio de Janeiro
São Paulo
Santiago
Buenos Aires
Tropic of Capricorn
Antarctic Circle
World Population Density
(persons per square kilometer)
500 +
250–500
100–250
50–100
25–50
5–25
1–5
0–1
No data
Populated Places
Over 10 million
5 million–10 million
4 million–5 million
3 million–4 million

(83/square mile), but nearly the entire continent is settled. However in Asia—the most densely populated continent with 126 people per square kilometer (326/square mile)—about 75 percent of the territory is nearly inaccessible and largely unoccupied. Generally, many areas of low population density are places in which climatic conditions, terrain, or other physical features are too extreme to support economic development capable of sustaining extensive settlement.

Rural-to-urban migration has resulted in one of the most remarkable shifts in settlement patterns during recent centuries. Today, approximately 50 percent of the world's population is urban. About 400 cities have more than one million residents, including 26 "megacities" with more than eight million inhabitants.

Throughout most of history, population grew very slowly. However, a century ago, advances in hygiene, health care, and food production and distribution combined to create a population explosion. Since 1960, the population of the world has more than doubled—from 3.2 billion to 6.7 billion in 2009.

The so-called population dilemma—overpopulation and its consequences—is only remotely tied to numbers of people. Overpopulation is a condition reached when the human population of a defined geographic area exceeds the capacity of available land and resources to provide the essential elements of survival under existing conditions. Of greatest significance are a country's government and economy. With a stable democratic government and viable free-market economy, a society will prosper and thoughts of "overpopulation" will vanish.

Above The Greek island of Rhodes has a long history of habitation. The largest island in the Dodecanese, Rhodes also has the largest population of the group—approximately 117,000 people.

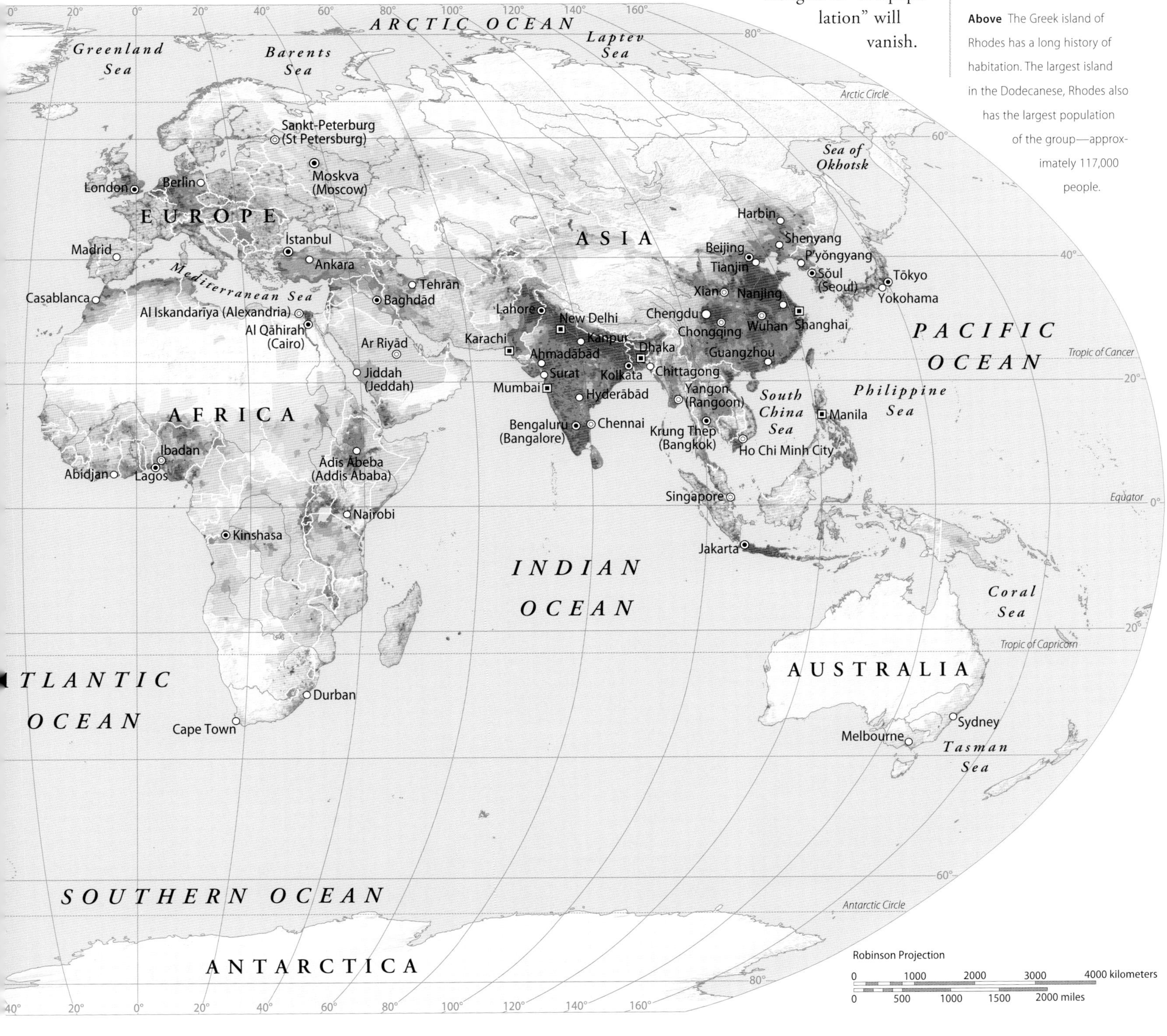
ARCTIC OCEAN
Greenland Sea
Barents Sea
Laptev Sea
Arctic Circle
Sankt-Peterburg (St Petersburg)
Moskva (Moscow)
London
Berlin
EUROPE
Madrid
Istanbul
Ankara
Mediterranean Sea
Casablanca
Tehrān
Baghdād
Al Iskandarīya (Alexandria)
Al Qāhirah (Cairo)
Ar Riyāḍ
Jiddah (Jeddah)
ASIA
Sea of Okhotsk
Harbin
Shenyang
Beijing
Tianjin
P'yŏngyang
Sŏul (Seoul)
Tōkyo
Yokohama
Xian
Nanjing
Lahore
New Delhi
Chengdu
Chongqing
Wuhan
Shanghai
Karachi
Kanpur
Ahmadābād
Dhaka
Guangzhou
Surat
Kolkata
Chittagong
Mumbai
Hyderābād
Yangon (Rangoon)
South China Sea
Manila
Philippine Sea
PACIFIC OCEAN
Tropic of Cancer
Bengaluru (Bangalore)
Chennai
Krung Thep (Bangkok)
Ho Chi Minh City
AFRICA
Ibadan
Abidjan
Lagos
Ādīs Ābeba (Addis Ababa)
Nairobi
Kinshasa
Singapore
Equator
Jakarta
INDIAN OCEAN
Coral Sea
Tropic of Capricorn
ATLANTIC OCEAN
AUSTRALIA
Durban
Cape Town
Sydney
Melbourne
Tasman Sea
SOUTHERN OCEAN
Antarctic Circle
ANTARCTICA
Robinson Projection
0 1000 2000 3000 4000 kilometers
0 500 1000 1500 2000 miles

RELIGIONS of the WORLD

For most societies, religions provide shared narratives, an integrated comprehensive view of the world, and an ethical code. In many cases, but not always, they are closely linked to cultural or ethnic identity.

There are some 450 million practitioners of Primal Religions. Each tribe has its own beliefs and sacred sites. The Adivasis of India find the sacred in the forest and its gifts. Mayan religion focuses on the calendar as determined by astronomical events.

There are more than a billion Hindus, 80 percent of whom live in India. The cornerstone of the Hindu belief is that reality is ultimately one, without division into individual persons or objects. Hindus also believe in reincarnation and karma—good actions bear good fruit for the doer, evil actions bad fruit.

The 400 million Buddhists, mainly living in the East, share with Hindus a belief in karma, reincarnation, and the illusory nature of the phenomenal world.

Of the world's 23 million Sikhs, 80 percent live in Punjab in northwest India. Sikhs are also a substantial minority in the United Kingdom and Canada. Sikhism, born in the fifteenth century CE, combines Islam's monotheism with the Hindu concepts of karma and reincarnation. However, its followers consider it a new divine revelation, not a synthesis.

The Jewish faith is embraced by 16.5 million people, less than one percent of the global population. The United States, with six million, has the world's largest

Below Christianity, Judaism and Islam regard Jerusalem as a holy city, with many sacred places. Al-Aqsa Mosque is part of the Islamic complex built on Temple Mount, one of Islam's most important sites. It was first built in the eighth century CE.

Bottom Incense is burned in many differnt types of religious rituals. Buddhists, the most prevalent religious group in Vietnam, offer incense as part of almost every ceremony, both to honor Buddha and as an aid for prayer and meditation.

160°
140°
120°
100°
80°
Beaufort Sea
Arctic Circle
Gulf of Alaska
Hudson Bay
NORTH AMERICA
Gulf of Mexico
Tropic of Cancer
MEXICO
Mexico City
Caribbean Sea
Equator
PACIFIC OCEAN
SOUTH AMERICA
PERU
Lago Titicaca
BOLIVIA
Tropic of Capricorn
Scotia Sea
World Religions
Protestant Christianity
Catholic Christianity
Orthodox Christianity
Judaism
Sunni Islam
Shia Islam
Hinduism
Sikhism
Mahayana Buddhism
Theravada Buddhism
Chinese religions
Shinto
Primal religions
Sparsely populated areas
Major Holy Sites
Christianity
Judaism
Islam
Hindu
Sikh
Buddhism
Chinese
Shinto
Primal

Jewish population. Judaism's God is both creator of the entire world and the God of Israel. As land, "Israel" refers to a part of the Middle East that, according to the Bible, God promised to Abraham's descendants. As people, "Israel" is the descendants of Abraham through Isaac.

The more than two billion Christians worldwide believe that Jesus Christ is the second person in a triune God (Father, Son and Holy Spirit), and that his death is the sacrifice through which anyone who believes in him is reconciled to God. Christianity's three main branches are Orthodox, Roman Catholic, and Protestant.

The Islamic religion began in the seventh century CE in what is now western Saudi Arabia. Most countries with Muslim majorities are in the Middle East or North Africa, but the largest Muslim populations are found in Indonesia and the Indian subcontinent. Of the world's 1.5 billion Muslim believers, 83 percent are Sunnis, and 16 percent are Shi'ite.

From ancient Chinese beliefs emerged two enduring traditions, Daoism and Confucianism. Both sought harmony, and both used the Dao (way) for the principle that established harmony—Daoism looked to nature while Confucians sought harmony in human relations. Buddhist monks reached China nearly 2,000 years ago, and many Chinese practice parts of these three traditions.

Shinto is the ancient indigenous religion of Japan. It is difficult to estimate the number of adherents—one is Shinto simply by virtue of being born Japanese. The Shinto way of life is encoded in its rituals; there is no written code of ethics. Shinto has a reverence for the land, culture, people, and nation of Japan.

Above In Malawi, Christianity and Islam flourish, but the tribal medicine men still use spiritual (and herbal) remedies to cure illness caused by evil spirits or witchcraft.

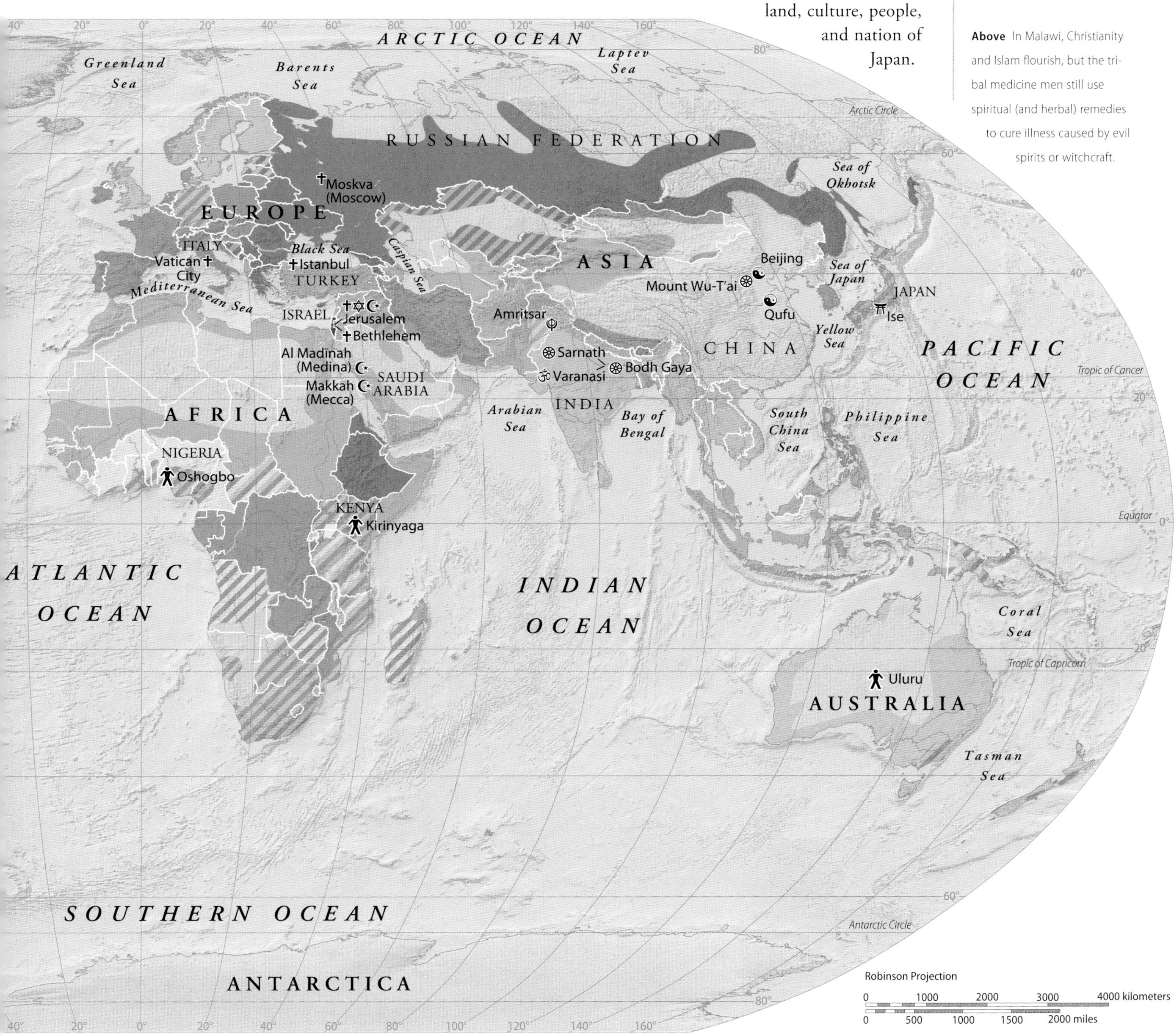
ARCTIC OCEAN
Greenland Sea
Barents Sea
Laptev Sea
RUSSIAN FEDERATION
Arctic Circle
Sea of Okhotsk
Moskva (Moscow)
EUROPE
ITALY
Vatican City
Black Sea
Istanbul
TURKEY
Caspian Sea
Mediterranean Sea
ASIA
Beijing
Sea of Japan
Mount Wu-T'ai
JAPAN
Qufu
Ise
ISRAEL
Jerusalem
Bethlehem
Amritsar
Yellow Sea
Al Madinah (Medina)
Makkah (Mecca)
SAUDI ARABIA
Sarnath
Varanasi
Bodh Gaya
CHINA
PACIFIC OCEAN
Tropic of Cancer
AFRICA
Arabian Sea
INDIA
Bay of Bengal
South China Sea
Philippine Sea
NIGERIA
Oshogbo
KENYA
Kirinyaga
Equator
ATLANTIC OCEAN
INDIAN OCEAN
Coral Sea
Tropic of Capricorn
Uluru
AUSTRALIA
Tasman Sea
SOUTHERN OCEAN
Antarctic Circle
ANTARCTICA
Robinson Projection
0 1000 2000 3000 4000 kilometers
0 500 1000 1500 2000 miles

HUMAN MIGRATION

In the animal kingdom, humans alone are not confined to a particular, biologically restricted habitat. Culture is humankind's adaptive mechanism. It has allowed our species to occupy any of Earth's diverse environments.

Currently, an estimated 200 million people—about 3 percent of the world's population—migrate across an international boundary each year.

Most migrants—about 120 million of them each year according to United Nations data—move from less developed to industrialized countries in search of a better life. Additionally, countless millions of people move without crossing a political boundary.

Migration is selective and generally voluntary. Throughout history, economic considerations have been the primary stimulus influencing migration. Other causes include physical conditions—natural disasters—and human-induced conditions, such as war and religious or political persecution.

History of Migration

Early humans migrated from place to place in search of a better food supply, but the movements were largely local. Seasonal migration in search of better pasture continues to this day. Open water was a much greater barrier to early migration than conditions on land. In fact, human settlement was limited to the "World Island" (the Afro-Eurasian landmass) throughout approximately 98 percent of human history. However, by the dawn of the Common Era, the two-thirds of Earth's land surface that

Below The similarities of the cultural relics that remain on Easter Island—including the iconic statues, known as moai—to those of Polynesian neighbors may indicate that the first travelers to the isolated island came from Polynesia.

Left Asia's massive Thar Desert is home to nomadic herders, who have adapted to the climatic conditions, and travel by camel across a landscape that has no oases.

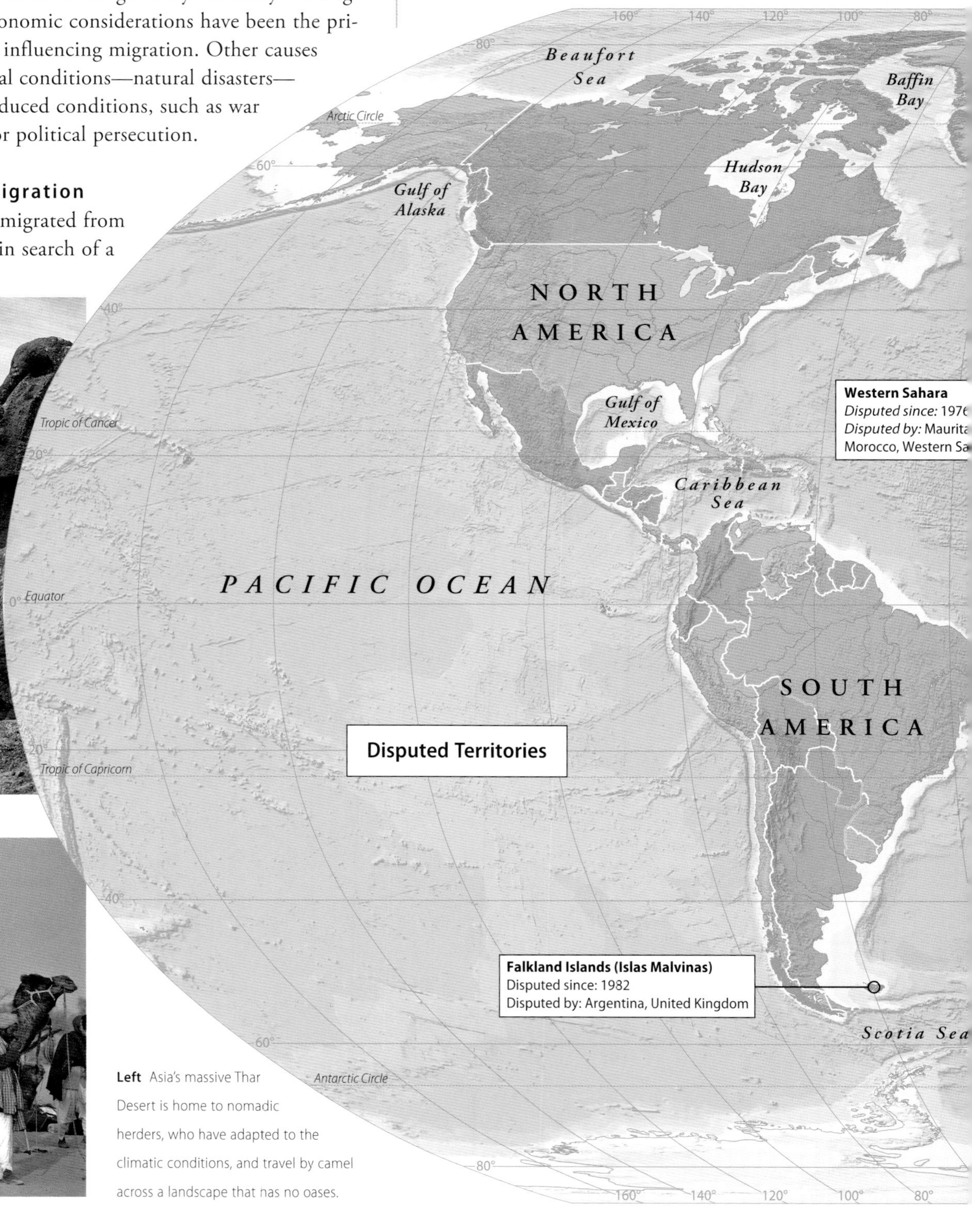
Beaufort Sea
Baffin Bay
Arctic Circle
Hudson Bay
Gulf of Alaska
NORTH AMERICA
Gulf of Mexico
Caribbean Sea
Tropic of Cancer
Equator
PACIFIC OCEAN
SOUTH AMERICA
Tropic of Capricorn
Disputed Territories
Western Sahara
Disputed since: 197
Disputed by: Maurit
Morocco, Western Sa
Falkland Islands (Islas Malvinas)
Disputed since: 1982
Disputed by: Argentina, United Kingdom
Scotia Sea
Antarctic Circle
160° 140° 120° 100° 80°
80° 60° 40° 20° 0° 20° 40° 60° 80°

are now inhabited were occupied. The Pacific Basin was the last settled frontier, yet most islands in that vast expanse of water were inhabited by Polynesian peoples long before Magellan's epic voyage.

Occasionally, there will be a mass migration such as the more than 60 million Europeans who, over a span of several centuries, moved to the Americas, Australia, New Zealand, South Africa, and elsewhere. Their reasons varied, although nearly all of them sought a better life.

Migration can also be compelled or involuntary. The enslavement of Africans and their transfer to the Americas, Europe, and Asia is a tragic example of this type of migration. So, too, are the millions of refugees worldwide who have been, and continue to be, displaced as a result of environmental, political, racial, ethnic, economic, social, and religious conflicts. There are many types of political conflicts. The most serious are international disputes.

Ethnic cleansing often has a political catalyst. Some groups become politically marginalized and their well-being is threatened when a power shift occurs within a country. Migration can result from such conflicts, giving rise to political refugees.

Future Migration

In regard to migration patterns, there are trends that appear likely. Migration from less-developed to developed countries will accelerate because of a shortage of workers in developed lands created by a rapidly aging population. Within developing nations, rural-to-urban migration will accelerate; whereas in developed nations, the trend will be from large to smaller cities or rural towns.

Above The Berlin Wall was long a symbol of a country divided. The fall of this edifice in 1989 signaled the beginning of a new era for the German people on both sides of the wall.

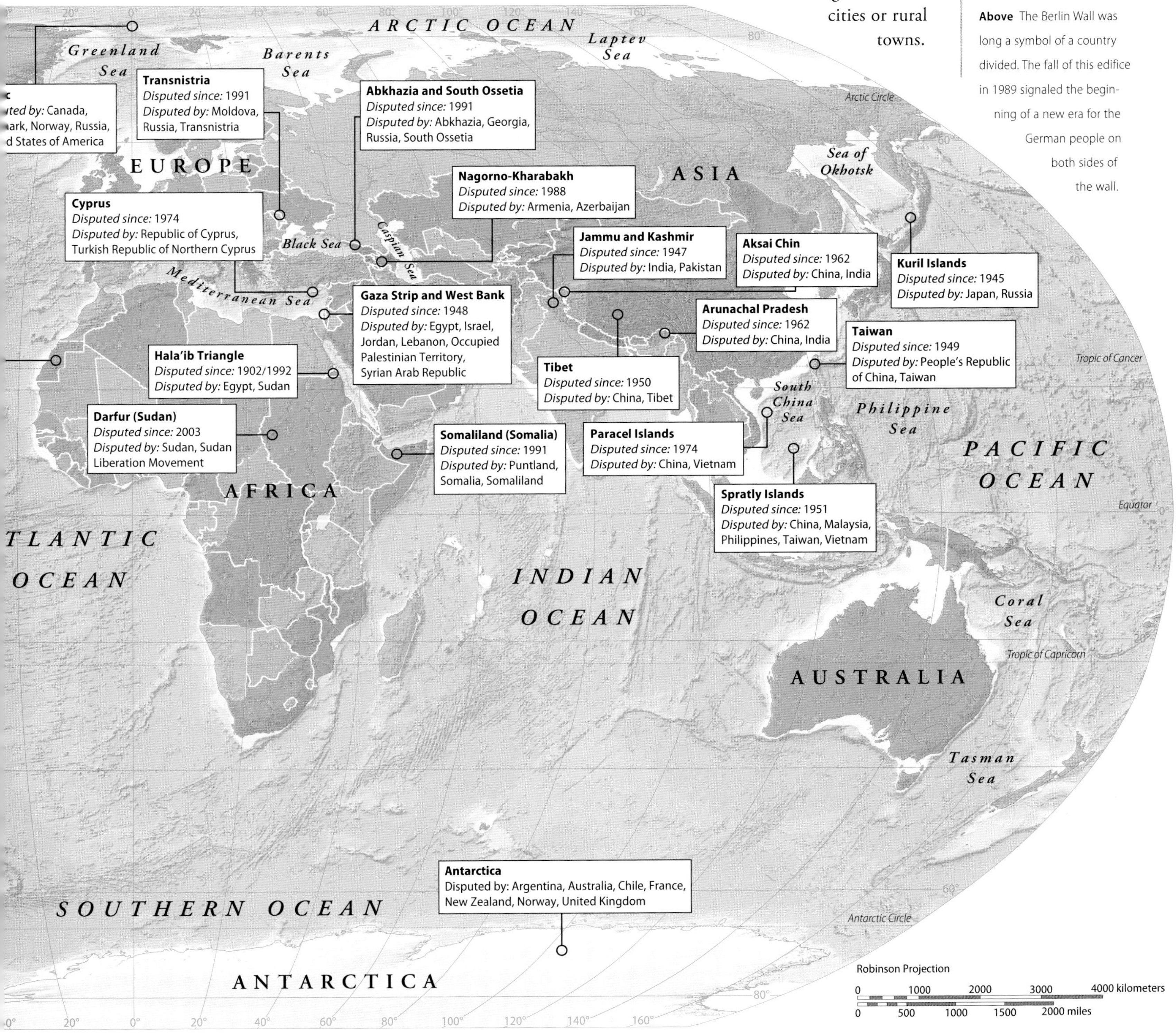
ARCTIC OCEAN
Greenland Sea
Barents Sea
Laptev Sea
Transnistria
Disputed since: 1991
Disputed by: Moldova, Russia, Transnistria
Abkhazia and South Ossetia
Disputed since: 1991
Disputed by: Abkhazia, Georgia, Russia, South Ossetia
Arctic Circle
EUROPE
ASIA
Sea of Okhotsk
Nagorno-Karabakh
Disputed since: 1988
Disputed by: Armenia, Azerbaijan
Cyprus
Disputed since: 1974
Disputed by: Republic of Cyprus, Turkish Republic of Northern Cyprus
Black Sea
Caspian Sea
Mediterranean Sea
Jammu and Kashmir
Disputed since: 1947
Disputed by: India, Pakistan
Aksai Chin
Disputed since: 1962
Disputed by: China, India
Kuril Islands
Disputed since: 1945
Disputed by: Japan, Russia
Gaza Strip and West Bank
Disputed since: 1948
Disputed by: Egypt, Israel, Jordan, Lebanon, Occupied Palestinian Territory, Syrian Arab Republic
Arunachal Pradesh
Disputed since: 1962
Disputed by: China, India
Taiwan
Disputed since: 1949
Disputed by: People's Republic of China, Taiwan
Tropic of Cancer
Hala'ib Triangle
Disputed since: 1902/1992
Disputed by: Egypt, Sudan
Tibet
Disputed since: 1950
Disputed by: China, Tibet
South China Sea
Philippine Sea
Darfur (Sudan)
Disputed since: 2003
Disputed by: Sudan, Sudan Liberation Movement
Somaliland (Somalia)
Disputed since: 1991
Disputed by: Puntland, Somalia, Somaliland
Paracel Islands
Disputed since: 1974
Disputed by: China, Vietnam
PACIFIC OCEAN
AFRICA
Spratly Islands
Disputed since: 1951
Disputed by: China, Malaysia, Philippines, Taiwan, Vietnam
Equator
TLANTIC OCEAN
INDIAN OCEAN
Coral Sea
Tropic of Capricorn
AUSTRALIA
Tasman Sea
Antarctica
Disputed by: Argentina, Australia, Chile, France, New Zealand, Norway, United Kingdom
SOUTHERN OCEAN
Antarctic Circle
ANTARCTICA
Robinson Projection
0 1000 2000 3000 4000 kilometers
0 500 1000 1500 2000 miles

HUMAN IMPACT on the ENVIRONMENT

Humans have altered the natural world in a far more dramatic way than any other species. The development of complex human societies has occurred through the taming and exploitation of Earth's environments and systems.

Below Although the larch is still the dominant tree of the eastern Siberian forests, climate change and loss of habitat due to development has caused its decline in other areas.

Humans are perhaps the first species with the potential to destroy Earth, although many other species can wreak havoc on the environment, particularly when their numbers reach unsustainable proportions. The difference with humans is the scale of the impact. Rubbish can be found throughout all the world's oceans, the global atmosphere has become a dump for the world's pollution, the rate of species extinction due to loss of habitat continues to increase, and environments all over the world are showing signs of significant stress.

Climate Change

Earth's climate is always changing. Evidence shows that Earth's temperature has gone through a number of warm (hothouse) and cold (icehouse) cycles—there is no evidence to suggest that it will not continue in the future. Factors responsible for past episodes of climate change include variations in incoming solar radiation, changes in atmospheric composition, and changes in Earth's surface.

Changes in atmospheric composition are a result of both natural processes and human activities, but it is human activities that are giving rise for concern about the environment and climate change. Over the last century, temperatures have again increased, but at a rate not seen before: The Intergovernmental Panel on Climate Change reported that from 1906 to 2005 global surface temperature increased by 0.74°C (1.33°F) and that the 12 years from 1995 to 2006 rank among the 12 warmest years since 1850.

The gases that affect surface temperatures are known as greenhouse gases: These gases trap radiation and prevent it from escaping back into space. The most important greenhouse gases are water vapor, carbon dioxide, methane, nitrous oxide, and fluorinated gases.

Water vapor is responsible for warming Earth by about 30°C (54°F). Human activity does not directly affect water vapor concentrations except at local levels; however, other greenhouse gases have had a quantifiable effect. Carbon dioxide occurs naturally in the atmosphere and is also emitted by processes such as the burning of fossil fuels. Atmospheric concentrations of carbon dioxide have increased by 36 percent from pre-industrial levels. Oil, for all its benefits, is a major contributor to this increase—being rich in carbon dioxide, it releases this gas into the atmosphere when burned. Methane is formed during the production and transport of coal, natural gas, and oil, as well as by livestock and agricultural activities. Concentrations of this gas increased during the twentieth century by 148 percent over pre-industrial levels. Nitrous oxide is emitted during agricultural and industrial activities, combustion of fossil fuels, and from solid waste. Atmospheric levels have increased from pre-industrial levels by 16 percent. Fluorinated gases—powerful synthetic gases emitted during a variety of industrial processes—are potent greenhouse gases.

Many scientists and researchers believe the role of human activity, which has clearly altered Earth's environment, is increasingly important in climate change. Although little can be done to affect natural changes, there are steps that humans could take to reduce our effects upon Earth's climate. However, it is also important to remember that change, rather than stability, is the natural order of Earth's climate.

Deforestation

One of humankind's more devastating impacts on the natural world is deforestation. Forests are cleared for timber and, most commonly, to create large areas of land for agriculture. Clearing is widespread in South America, particularly in the Amazon Basin, and in Southeast Asia, most notably in Indonesia, Malaysia, and Myanmar. Because forests are such complex ecosystems, deforestation has a dramatic effect on a large number of plant

Right Although Antarctica is relatively isolated, there is still a need to protect particular areas from human activity. The Port Foster and Deception Island area is actively volcanic, and the subject of much research, so some sections have restricted access.

and animal species.Not only are tree-dwelling species directly affected, but the impacts of deforestation are also seen in river systems where deforestation has increased soil erosion in surrounding areas.

Forests are also seen as one solution to the problem of global warming. As plants absorb carbon dioxide, the main greenhouse gas, forests can play a powerful role in mitigating the effects of the greenhouse effect.

The Oceans

The planet's oceans have long been both an important food source for millions of people and a dumping ground for waste. It is still common practice for many commercial ships and recreational boats to dispose of waste by simply throwing it overboard. Research conducted in 2007 found that a North Pacific "rubbish soup" that holds as much 2.5 percent of all the plastic manufactured worldwide since 1950 had enlarged to join up with another massive concentration of rubbish in the western Pacific near Japan; the total area affected is bigger than the land area of the continental United States. Scientists have labeled the area the Pacific Garbage Patch. At present, the patch lies well away from international shipping lanes and within international waters. Consequently there is little political will to clean it up, although this may change as the patch gets closer to land. The US National Oceanic and Atmospheric Administration (NOAA) is using unmanned aircraft to track the patch and collect further data.

The other major impact that humans have on the oceans is through commercial fishing. The average annual catch is estimated at around 80 million tonnes (90 million tons). Unsustainable fishing has seen many species of fish become virtually extinct. The North Atlantic cod fisheries of Canada are one such commercial fishing ground that has all but disappeared. As demand for seafood continues to grow, more pressure is being placed on marine environments. Many countries have adopted strict quotas for their fishing fleets, confining the amount that can be caught by each boat. Bycatch—the term used to describe unwanted species caught while fishing—can be as much as 3 kilograms (7 pounds) per 450 grams (1 pound) of commercial fish. This bycatch, deemed uneconomic, is discarded into the sea.

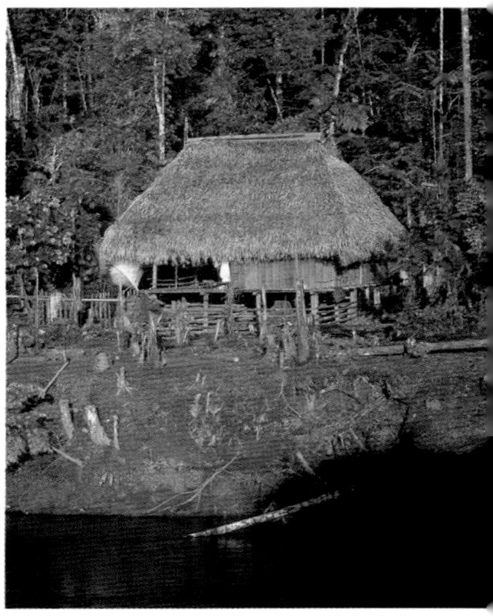

Above Even the simplest construction of a thatched hut along the Amazon River in South America has a slight environmental impact. Dense jungle vegetation is cleared down to the riverbank.

Left Natural forces also work to change the environment. Driftwood deposited on a barren Siberian beach becomes a source of organic matter that will eventually enrich the soil.

GLOBAL TRADE and COMMUNICATION

During the twentieth century the world became a much smaller place, in terms of the ability of humankind to communicate across the face of the planet, and to transport goods and services around it.

Yet there are still millions of people, particularly in Africa, who have never heard a telephone dial tone.

Until 1866, the fastest that a newly arrived Irish migrant in the United States could communicate with family back home was via a letter sent by ship, a journey of several days. Today, that same message can be instantaneously transmitted by telephone. There are now close to 1.5 billion mobile (cell) phone users worldwide, around a quarter of the world's population. The fastest growing regions for mobile phone use are China, India, and Russia—among the most populous countries on earth.

While telecommunication advances are staggering, there are still very large gaps with regard to access to this technology: around 5 percent of Africa's population had Internet access in 2007, compared to about 72 percent of North Americans.

Undersea Cables

The vast majority of the world's voice and Internet traffic is carried in fiber optic cables strung out across the ocean floors, with millions of separate data and voice transfers happening simultaneously.

The first cables carried telegraph traffic—in 1850 a cable was laid beneath the English Channel. In 1866, the SS *Great Eastern* laid the first transatlantic cable.

Below Linking the Atlantic and Pacific Oceans, the Panama Canal is a monumental engineering achievement that has greatly improved the efficiency of international trade since its completion in 1914.

PCC
63

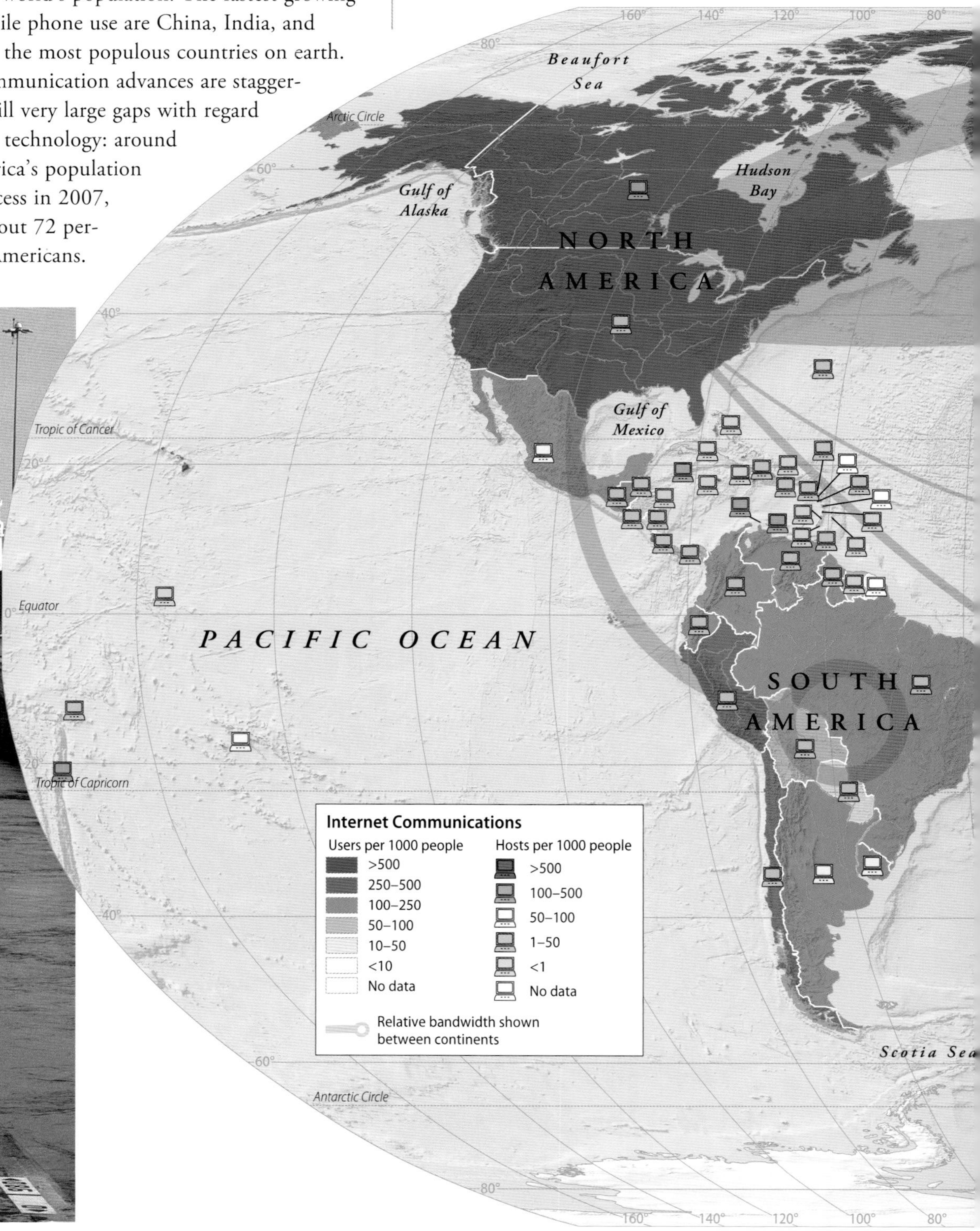
Beaufort Sea
Arctic Circle
Gulf of Alaska
Hudson Bay
NORTH AMERICA
Gulf of Mexico
Tropic of Cancer
Equator
PACIFIC OCEAN
SOUTH AMERICA
Tropic of Capricorn
Scotia Sea
Antarctic Circle
160°
140°
120°
100°
80°
60°
40°
20°
0°
Internet Communications
Users per 1000 people
>500
250–500
100–250
50–100
10–50
<10
No data
Hosts per 1000 people
>500
100–500
50–100
1–50
<1
No data
Relative bandwidth shown between continents

The World Wide Web

In 1990 Tim Berners-Lee created a communication tool for computers, a web browser called the World Wide Web. This has transformed the way that humans interact. By 1996, use of the Web had expanded at such a rapid rate that most large companies were beginning to use it for commercial reasons, leading to the development of e-commerce. Since this time the Web has continued to grow, with virtually all large companies offering their products for sale via websites.

The Web has also grown into an alternative recreational and news medium. The ability for individuals to create their own websites, using sites such as YouTube, has transformed the way that people receive and transmit information from a home desktop computer.

International Trade

Trade has always been an important link between nations. In the twentieth century a number of important trade organizations emerged, based on regional links. The European Union (EU) is one of the oldest trade organizations in the world. Formed after World War II as the European Economic Community (EEC), the EU has evolved into a vast political, economic, social, and legal institution. One of the most significant features of the EU is the concept of the single market: There are no import or export taxes between member nations and a single currency, the euro, is used by most of them.

Other trading partnerships include the North American Free Trade Agreement (NAFTA), which facilitates trade between the United States, Canada, and Mexico; and the Asia Pacific Economic Cooperation group.

Above A barge moves down the Grand Canal in China—the oldest and longest canal in the world. Some sections of this important trade and communications link are more than 2,000 years old.

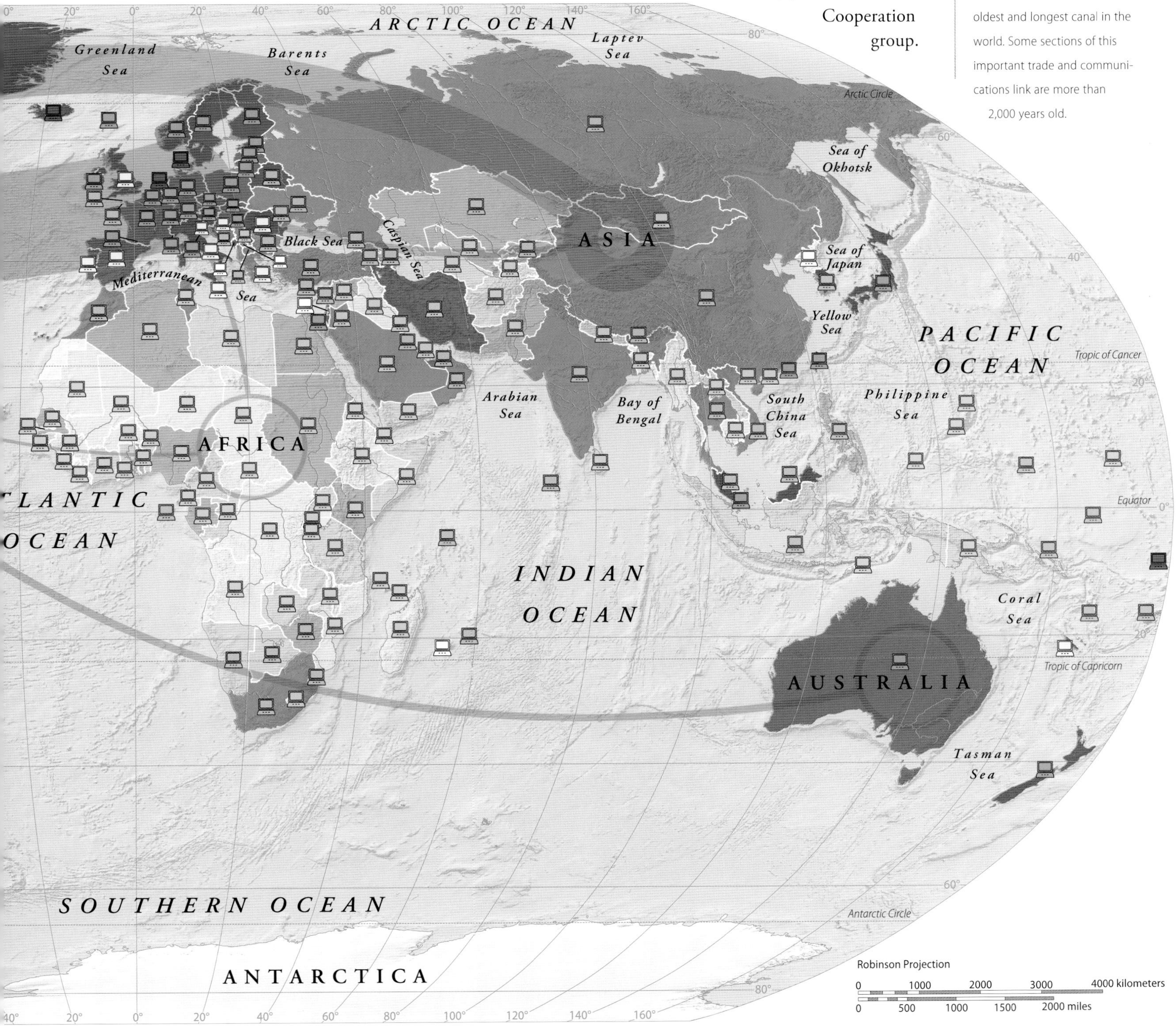
ARCTIC OCEAN
Greenland Sea
Barents Sea
Laptev Sea
Arctic Circle
Sea of Okhotsk
ASIA
Caspian Sea
Black Sea
Sea of Japan
Mediterranean Sea
Yellow Sea
PACIFIC OCEAN
Tropic of Cancer
Arabian Sea
Bay of Bengal
South China Sea
Philippine Sea
AFRICA
LANTIC OCEAN
Equator
INDIAN OCEAN
Coral Sea
Tropic of Capricorn
AUSTRALIA
Tasman Sea
SOUTHERN OCEAN
Antarctic Circle
ANTARCTICA
Robinson Projection
0 1000 2000 3000 4000 kilometers
0 500 1000 1500 2000 miles

The World

The WORLD

The world is an enormously complex place of flourishing diversity. Economic globalization and technological developments have ushered in a new age of prosperity for many people. The big picture suggests that, in general, humanity is better off today than ever before. It may not always appear that way at first glance, given the many negative side-effects of global progress—for example, increased pollution, widespread availability of drugs and weapons, and fast-spreading infectious diseases.

Right Dubai, the second-largest state of the United Arab Emirates, has developed rapidly over the last 40 or so years, and cars have replaced camels as the main mode of transport. However, camels are still valued as racing animals.

Below Thousands of years ago, in the Cappadocian region of modern Turkey, cones like these (the eroded remnants of a volcanic plateau) were hollowed out to provide housing. Nowadays they may be used for storage.

Anti-globalization proponents also criticize developed nations for exploiting local peoples and enlarging the income gap between wealthy and poor nations. Proponents of globalization argue that the path toward wealth is long and cannot be accomplished overnight. Overall, they say, the poor are in much better shape today than they were ever before.

Social and Economic Progress

Comparing a poor country from Africa or Latin America with a developed nation from, say, Europe leads nowhere. But if such countries are viewed in the context of their own historical experience, then the scale of positive development is evident. India, for example, has transformed itself from an undeveloped backwater into a food-exporting nation with a burgeoning economy. Social changes have also been remarkable. The rigid social fabric of India's caste hierarchy is being slowly eroded, while gender equality is becoming more than an impossible dream.

The affluence of nations depends on their socioeconomic and political imperatives which, when fulfilled, open space for the exercise of true personal liberties. Even though many totalitarian and autocratic regimes hold power worldwide, many more people now enjoy unprecedented freedom of choice. Most problems in today's world stem from internal disarray in countries whose governments refuse to share the responsibility of governing, and do not allow improvements for fear of losing their grip on power. The number of such countries, however, is declining.

Resources management is a growing global concern. The depletion of available resources such as timber and fossil fuels for the sake of economic growth is often noted as a cause of environmental problems, yet only an affluent society can afford the luxury of a clean and protected environment. In developing nations, a degraded environment is frequently regarded as a necessary byproduct of jobs, economic growth, and ultimately a better future for the next generation. Circumstances were no different for Europeans and Americans in the early stages of the Industrial Revolution. With the increase in quality of life and wealth, the notion of environmental protection will spread to the developing world.

That the world is getting better, rather than worse, is evident in the prices, availability, and variety of most foods compared to the past. Fewer people are malnourished. Demographic data also indicates progress—life expectancy is increasing, while infant mortality rates continue to fall. Many previously incurable diseases have been eradicated or contained.

With the world's human population projected to increase from its current 6.6 billion to perhaps 9.5 billion by mid-century, there is cause for optimism but also a need for action in the case of looming problems such as global warming. Natural resources must be conserved, alternative resources developed, and pollution reduced. Most important of all, human resources must be developed. This can only be achieved through good government, free markets, adequate health care and education, and respect for human rights.

Regions

To better understand the world, geographers systematize physical and cultural features into regional frameworks. The purpose of defining a region is to isolate the features of a particular area that make it different from others. The fact that regions do not exist in reality but are invented by geographers explains why there are so many of them. Each region has a core, a zone of highest distribution, and a periphery or transitional zone of overlap with surrounding regions. Natural regions can be based on landforms, climate, vegetation, soils, or other geographic criteria. Criteria for a cultural region may comprise single or multiple cultural traits.

Scholars frequently combine information from natural and cultural regions to expand their knowledge about people and places, cultural adaptation to natural environment, agriculture, and settlement, and to predict future patterns and distribution.

When measuring economic activity or transportation, the concept of a "functional region" is applied, that is, a region created on the basis of a specific function. Some examples of functional regions include areas covered by an airline carrier or the distribution of a newspaper.

Certain areas may be classed as regions because of an economic activity, or by virtue of their residents' own perceptions of homogeneity. Well-known examples of such perceptual regions include Canada's Maritime Provinces and Australia's Outback.

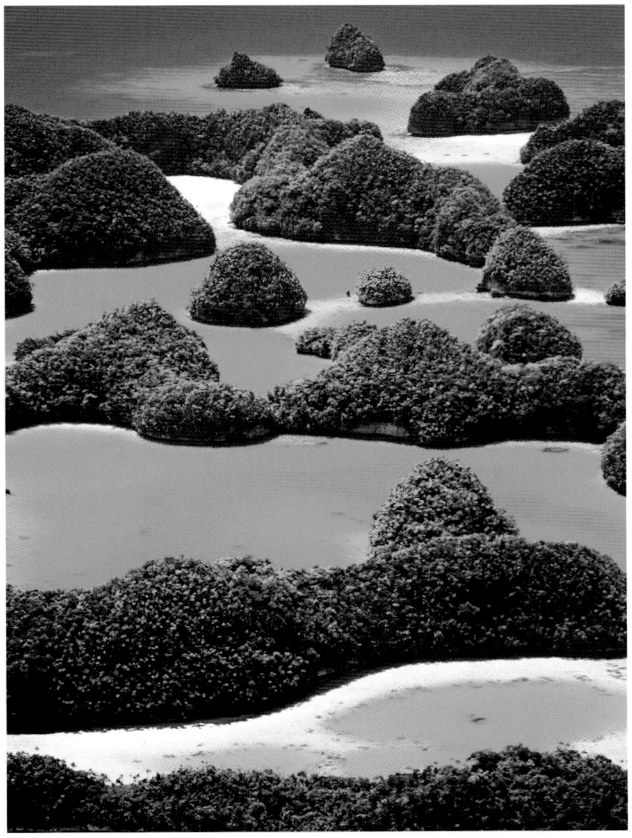

Left The world features an amazing variety of landscapes. The island nation of Palau includes the Rock Islands—more than 200 uninhabited, forest-covered, limestone islands that were formed by uplifted coral reefs.

Below The area around the historic city of Ljubljana was first settled around 2000 BCE. The city has been rebuilt a number of times and contains an interesting mix of architectural styles. Ljubljana is now the capital of Slovenia.

Greenland
(Kalaallit Nunaat)
(Denmark)
Queen Elizabeth Islands
Ellesmere Island
Parry Islands
Beaufort Sea
Baffin Bay
Davis Strait
Baffin I.
Victoria Island
Banks I.
McClure Str.
Amundsen G.
Devon I.
Bylot I.
Qaanaaq
Qeqertarsuaq
Nuuk
Nanortalik
Nunap Isua (Kap Farvel)
Denmark Strait
REYKJAVIK
ICELAND
Faroe Is
(Denmark)
Tórshavn
Orkney Is
Outer Hebrides
(UK)
DUBLIN
DEN HAAG/'S-GRAVENHAGE
IRELAND
BRUSSEL/BRUXELLES
Channel Islands
(UK)
Jan Mayen
Shannon Ø
RUS. FED.
Arctic Circle
ALASKA
(USA)
Barrow
Aklavik
Bering Str.
Seward Pen.
St Lawrence I.
St Matthew Island
Nunivak Island
Bering Sea
Pribilof Islands
Alaska Pen.
Perryville
Togiak
Stebbins
Fairbanks
Anchorage
Kodiak Island
Kenai Pen.
Gulf of Alaska
Yukon
Whitehorse
Juneau
Aleutian Islands
Queen Charlotte Is
Kugluktuk
Great Bear Lake
Yellowknife
Great Slave Lake
Wrigley
Fond-du-lac
Churchill
Hudson Bay
Belcher Islands
James Bay
Southampton I.
Coats I.
Hudson Strait
Ivujivik
Kimmirut
Taloyoak
Cape Chidley
Labrador Sea
Gillam
Cartwright
Lake Melville
Saint-Augustin
Wemindji
CANADA
ROCKY MTS
Edmonton
Saskatoon
Calgary
Regina
Winnipeg
L. Winnipeg
Kamloops
Kelowna
Vancouver
Victoria
Seattle
Tacoma
Portland
Eugene
Helena
Bismarck
International Falls
Sault Ste Marie
Chicoutimi
Quebec
Montreal
OTTAWA
Toronto
Augusta
Halifax
Newfoundland
St John's
Cape Race
St Pierre and Miquelon
(France)
Billings
Boise
Pierre
Minneapolis
St Paul
Chicago
Detroit
Pittsburgh
Boston
New York
Philadelphia
Baltimore
WASHINGTON DC
Columbus
Indianapolis
UNITED STATES OF AMERICA
Cape Mendocino
Reno
Sacramento
San Francisco
San Jose
Las Vegas
Denver
Los Angeles
San Diego
Tijuana
Mexicali
Phoenix
Albuquerque
Oklahoma City
Fort Worth
Dallas
Austin
San Antonio
Houston
New Orleans
Memphis
Nashville
Atlanta
Raleigh
Charlotte
Charleston
Savannah
Jacksonville
Orlando
Tampa
Miami
Bermuda
(UK)
Midway Islands
(USA)
Tropic of Cancer
Necker Island
Nihoa
Kaua'i
O'ahu
Honolulu
Maui
Wailuku
Hilo
Hawai'i
HAWAII
(USA)
Johnston Atoll
(USA)
Guadalupe
(Mexico)
Punta Eugenia
Ciudad Juárez
Chihuahua
Torreón
Monterrey
Saltillo
La Paz
Cabo Falso
G. of Mexico
MEXICO
Guadalajara
León
CIUDAD DE MÉXICO
Puebla
Veracruz
Bahía de Campeche
Acapulco
Islas Revillagigedo
(Mexico)
Cancún
LA HABANA
CUBA
NASSAU
BAHAMAS
Grand Bahama
Straits of Florida
Turks and Caicos Islands
(UK)
Cayman Is
(UK)
JAMAICA
KINGSTON
PORT-AU-PRINCE
DOM. REP.
SANTO DOMINGO
San Juan
Puerto Rico
(US)
British Virgin Islands
(UK)
US Virgin Islands
(US)
Anguilla (UK)
Sint Maarten (Netherlands)
St Martin (France)
St Barthélemy (France)
ST KITTS AND NEVIS
ANTIGUA AND BARBUDA
Montserrat (UK)
Guadeloupe (France)
Martinique (France)
ST LUCIA
DOMINICA
BARBADOS
ST VINCENT AND THE GRENADINES
GRENADA
TRINIDAD AND TOBAGO
Caribbean Sea
Aruba
(Neth.)
Neth. Antilles
(Neth.)
BELMOPAN
BELIZE
GUATEMALA
HONDURAS
TEGUCIGALPA
SAN SALVADOR
EL SALVADOR
NICARAGUA
MANAGUA
SAN JOSÉ
COSTA RICA
PANAMÁ
PANAMA
Barranquilla
Maracaibo
CARACAS
VENEZUELA
Cúcuta
Medellín
BOGOTÁ
Cali
COLOMBIA
GEORGETOWN
GUYANA
PARAMARIBO
SURINAME
Cayenne
French Guiana
(France)
Boa Vista
Isla del Coco
(Costa Rica)
Isla de Malpelo
(Colombia)
Isla Fernandina
Isla Isabela
Santa Cruz
Archipiélago de Colón
(Galapagos Islands)
(Ecuador)
QUITO
ECUADOR
Guayaquil
Iquitos
Mouths of the Amazon
Macapá
Belém
Santarém
Manaus
Parintins
Itaituba
Amazon Basin
São Luís
Fortaleza
Fernando de Noronha
(Brazil)
Caucaia
Marabá
Teresina
Mossoró
Natal
João Pessoa
Recife
Maceió
Aracaju
Jaboatão
BRAZIL
Chiclayo
Trujillo
Cajamarca
Huaraz
Callao
LIMA
PERU
Rio Branco
Ariquemes
Sinop
Vilhena
Palmas
Barreiras
Porangatu
Feira de Santana
Salvador
Cusco
BOLIVIA
Lago Titicaca
Arequipa
LA PAZ
Cochabamba
SUCRE
Santa Cruz
Cáceres
Cuiabá
BRASÍLIA
Goiânia
Porto Seguro
Belo Horizonte
Campo Grande
Ribeirão Preto
Campinas
Rio de Janeiro
São Paulo
Curitiba
Ilha da Trindade
(Brazil)
Ilhas Martin Vaz
(Brazil)
Iquique
Calama
Antofagasta
San Salvador de Jujuy
ASUNCIÓN
PARAGUAY
San Miguel de Tucumán
Copiapó
Isla San Felix
Isla San Ambrosio
(Chile)
Porto Alegre
Córdoba
Pelotas
Paysandú
URUGUAY
Mendoza
SANTIAGO
BUENOS AIRES
MONTEVIDEO
Río de la Plata
Archipiélago Juan Fernández
(Chile)
Concepción
Santa Rosa
Tandil
Mar del Plata
Bahía Blanca
Valdivia
Puerto Montt
Golfo San Matías
ANDES
CHILE
ARGENTINA
PATAGONIA
Comodoro Rivadavia
Falkland Islands
(UK)
Stanley
West Falkland
East Falkland
Bahía Grande
Punta Arenas
Estrecho de Magallanes
Isla Grande de Tierra del Fuego
Isla de los Estados
Cabo de Hornos (Cape Horn)
Drake Passage
Scotia Sea
South Georgia
South Georgia and South Sandwich Islands
(UK)
South Sandwich Islands
South Shetland Islands
South Orkney Islands
Antarctic Circle
Bellingshausen Sea
Amundsen Sea
Carney I.
Thurston Island
Alexander Island
Antarctic Peninsula
Ellsworth Land
Weddell Sea
Berkner Island
Marie Byrd Land
Roosevelt Island
Ross Sea
PACIFIC OCEAN
ATLANTIC OCEAN
Kingman Reef
(USA)
Palmyra Atoll
(USA)
Tabuaeran
Kiritimati
Howland I.
(USA)
Equator
Baker I.
(USA)
Phoenix Islands
KIRIBATI
Line Islands
Malden Island
Starbuck Island
Penrhyn Atoll
Manihiki Atoll
Nassau
Tokelau
(New Zealand)
Caroline Island
Flint Island
Îles Marquises
Wallis and Futuna
(France)
SAMOA
APIA
Pago Pago
American Samoa
(USA)
TONGA
FIJI
Niue
(New Zealand)
NUKU'ALOFA
Tropic of Capricorn
Cook Is
(New Zealand)
Avarua
Papeete
Archipel de la Société
Archipel des Tuamotu
French Polynesia
(France)
Archipel des Australes
Henderson Island
Pitcairn Islands
(UK)
Rapa Nui
(Chile)
Kermadec Islands
(New Zealand)
Chatham Islands
(New Zealand)
Cabo Fisterra
PORTUGAL
LISBOA
Pico
Terceira
São Miguel
Azores
(Portugal)
Str. of Gibraltar
Ceuta (Spain)
RABAT
Madeira
(Portugal)
Casablanca
Marrakech
Agadir
Islas Canarias
(Spain)
Santa Cruz de Tenerife
Las Palmas de Gran Canaria
Laâyoune
Western Sahara
(disputed)
Ad Dakhla
Zouérat
MAURITANIA
NOUAKCHOTT
Santo Antão
CAPE VERDE
PRAIA
Santiago
Saint Louis
DAKAR
SENEGAL
BANJUL
GAMBIA
BISSAU
GUINEA-BISSAU
BAMAKO
Arquipélago dos Bijagós
CONAKRY
GUINEA
FREETOWN
SIERRA LEONE
MONROVIA
LIBERIA
YAMOUSSOUKRO
Cape Palmas
Abidjan
OUAGADOUGOU
Ascension
(UK)
Saint Helena
(UK)
Tristan da Cunha Group
(UK)
Gough Island
(UK)
160°
140°
120°
100°
80°
60°
40°
20°
0°
1:75,000,000
Robinson Projection
0 1000 2000 3000 4000 kilometers
0 500 1000 1500 2000 miles

WORLD POLITICAL

RUSSIAN FEDERATION
KAZAKHSTAN
MONGOLIA
CHINA
INDIA
JAPAN
PACIFIC OCEAN
INDIAN OCEAN
AUSTRALIA
INDONESIA
PHILIPPINES
NEW ZEALAND
ANTARCTICA
LIBYA
SUDAN
CHAD
NIGER
NIGERIA
ETHIOPIA
KENYA
SOMALIA
TANZANIA
ANGOLA
ZAMBIA
NAMIBIA
BOTSWANA
SOUTH AFRICA
MADAGASCAR
SAUDI ARABIA
IRAN
IRAQ
TURKEY
EGYPT
YEMEN
OMAN
AFGHANISTAN
PAKISTAN
UZBEKISTAN
TURKMENISTAN
KYRGYZSTAN
TAJIKISTAN
MYANMAR
THAILAND
CAMBODIA
VIETNAM
LAOS
MALAYSIA
SRI LANKA
MALDIVES
PAPUA NEW GUINEA
SOLOMON ISLANDS
VANUATU
FIJI
TUVALU
KIRIBATI
MARSHALL ISLANDS
FEDERATED STATES OF MICRONESIA
PALAU
UKRAINE
POLAND
BELARUS
LATVIA
ESTONIA
FINLAND
SWEDEN
NORWAY
MOSKVA
Sankt-Peterburg
BEIJING
Shanghai
Hong Kong
TŌKYŌ
Ōsaka
SŎUL
P'YONGYANG
MANILA
JAKARTA
SINGAPORE
KUALA LUMPUR
BANGKOK
KRUNG THEP
YANGON
DHAKA
Kolkata
NEW DELHI
DELHI
MUMBAI
Chennai
BENGALURU
Karachi
ISLĀMĀBĀD
KĀBOL
TEHRĀN
BAGHDĀD
AR RIYĀD
ANKARA
İstanbul
AL QĀHIRAH
NAIROBI
ADDIS ABEBA
KINSHASA
LUANDA
Johannesburg
CAPE TOWN
Durban
ANTANANARIVO
CANBERRA
Sydney
Melbourne
Brisbane
Perth
Adelaide
Darwin
WELLINGTON
Auckland
Christchurch
Arabian Sea
Bay of Bengal
Coral Sea
Tasman Sea
Sea of Okhotsk
Barents Sea
Laptev Sea
Mediterranean Sea
Black Sea
Caspian Sea
SOUTHERN OCEAN
WILKES LAND
Queen Mary Land
Enderby Land
Davis Sea
Ross Sea
Îles Kerguelen
Îles Crozet
Heard Island
McDonald Islands
British Indian Ocean Territory (UK)
Cocos (Keeling) Islands (Australia)
Christmas Island (Australia)
Tropic of Cancer
Tropic of Capricorn
Arctic Circle
Antarctic Circle
Equator
20° 40° 60° 80° 100° 120° 140° 160°

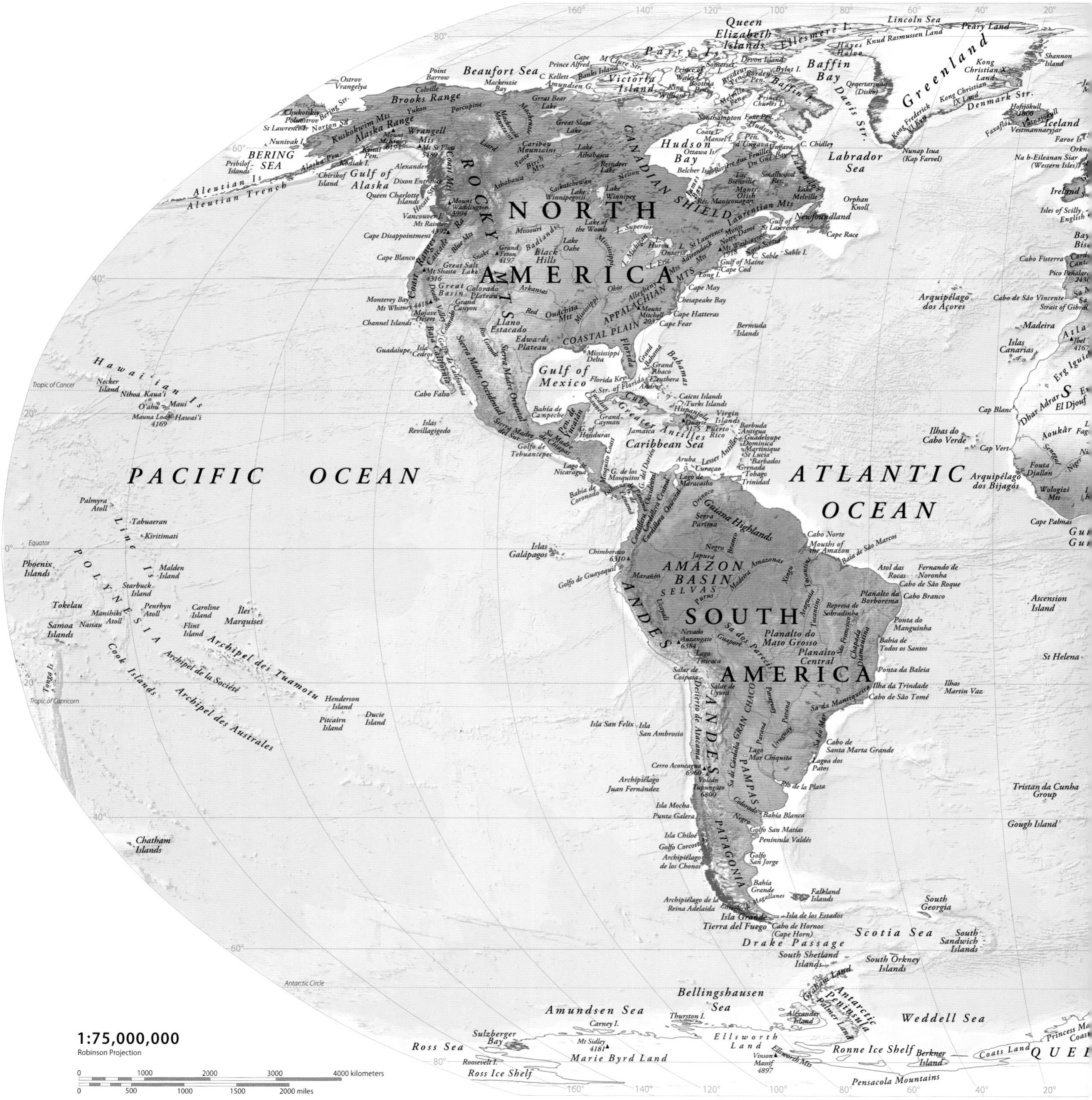
NORTH AMERICA
SOUTH AMERICA
PACIFIC OCEAN
ATLANTIC OCEAN
Beaufort Sea
Queen Elizabeth Islands
Parry Is.
Victoria Island
Baffin Bay
Greenland
Iceland
Hudson Bay
Labrador Sea
Gulf of Alaska
BERING SEA
Aleutian Is
Aleutian Trench
Brooks Range
Alaska Range
ROCKY MTS
CANADIAN SHIELD
APPALACHIAN MTS
COASTAL PLAIN
Great Basin
Colorado Plateau
Llano Estacado
Edwards Plateau
Gulf of Mexico
Caribbean Sea
Greater Antilles
Lesser Antilles
Newfoundland
Bermuda Islands
Arquipélago dos Açores
Madeira
Islas Canarias
Ilhas do Cabo Verde
Hawai'ian Is
Mauna Loa 4169
Line Is
POLYNESIA
Archipel des Tuamotu
Archipel de la Société
Archipel des Australes
Cook Islands
Îles Marquises
Islas Galápagos
Guiana Highlands
AMAZON BASIN
SELVAS
Planalto do Mato Grosso
ANDES
GRAN CHACO
PAMPAS
PATAGONIA
Falkland Islands
South Georgia
Tierra del Fuego
Cabo de Hornos (Cape Horn)
Drake Passage
Scotia Sea
South Sandwich Islands
South Shetland Islands
South Orkney Islands
Bellingshausen Sea
Amundsen Sea
Weddell Sea
Ross Sea
Ross Ice Shelf
Marie Byrd Land
Ellsworth Land
Ronne Ice Shelf
Antarctic Peninsula
Pensacola Mountains
Tristan da Cunha Group
Gough Island
Ascension Island
St Helena
Chatham Islands
Tropic of Cancer
Equator
Tropic of Capricorn
Antarctic Circle
1:75,000,000
Robinson Projection
0 1000 2000 3000 4000 kilometers
0 500 1000 1500 2000 miles

WORLD PHYSICAL

EUROPE
ASIA
AFRICA
AUSTRALIA
ANTARCTICA
PACIFIC OCEAN
INDIAN OCEAN
SOUTHERN OCEAN
Svalbard
Zemlya Frantsa-Iosifa
Barents Sea
Karskoye More
Severnaya Zemlya
Laptev Sea
Novosibirskiye Ostrova
Vostochno-Sibirskoye More
SIBIR' (SIBERIA)
SREDNE-SIBIRSKOYE PLOSKOGOR'YE
ZAPADNO-SIBIRSKAYA RAVNINA
URAL'SKIY KHREBET (URAL MOUNTAINS)
NORTHERN EUROPEAN PLAIN
Kol'skiy Poluostrov
Baltic Sea
Sea of Okhotsk
Sakhalin
Karaginskiy Zaliv
Komandorskiye Ostrova
Near Is
Rat Is
Kamchatka
Stanovoy Khrebet
Barabinskaya Steppe
Turgayskaya Stolovaya Strana
Kazakhskiy Melkosopochnik
Black Sea
Caspian Sea
Aral Sea
Sea of Azov
CAUCASUS
Mediterranean Sea
ALPS
Altai Mts
GOBI
TIEN SHAN
Taklimakan Shamo
KUNLUN SHAN
QINGZANG GAOYUAN
PAMIR
HINDU KUSH
KARAKORAM RA.
HIMALAYA
Mt Everest 8850
Peski Karakumy
Peski Kyzylkum
Hokkaidō
Honshū
Shikoku
Kyūshū
Sea of Japan (East Sea)
Yellow Sea
East China Sea
Okinawa
Taiwan
Ogasawara-shotō
ARABIAN PENINSULA
Ar Rub' al Khālī
Red Sea
G. of Aden
G. of Oman
The Gulf
Arabian Sea
Bay of Bengal
Andaman Sea
South China Sea
Philippine Sea
Luzon
Mindanao
Hainan
Sri Lanka
Deccan
Maldives
Lakshadweep
Andaman Islands
Nicobar Is
Borneo
Sumatera
Jawa
Sulawesi
Celebes Sea
Laut Jawa
Laut Banda
Laut Flores
Timor Sea
Arafura Sea
New Guinea
Halmahera
Mariana Is
Caroline Is
MELANESIA
Marshall Is
Solomon Sea
Coral Sea
New Caledonia
Fiji Islands
Tasman Sea
New Zealand
North Island
South Island
Tasmania
Bass Str.
Great Australian Bight
Nullarbor Plain
Great Victoria Desert
Great Sandy Desert
Tanami Desert
GREAT DIVIDING RA.
Great Barrier Reef
Gulf of Carpentaria
Kimberley
Macdonnell Ra.
Madagascar
Mozambique Channel
Seychelles
Mauritius
Réunion
Comoros
Kalahari Desert
Namib Desert
Congo Basin
Ethiopian Highlands
Somali Pen.
Sahara
Libyan Desert
Nubian Desert
Darfur
Tibesti
L. Victoria
Lake Tanganyika
Lake Nyasa
Kilimanjaro 5895
Drakensberg
Great Karoo
Cape of Good Hope
Cape Agulhas
Île Amsterdam
Île St-Paul
Îles Crozet
Île Kerguélen
McDonald Islands
Heard Island
Davis Sea
Amery Ice Shelf
Enderby Land
Queen Mary Land
WILKES LAND
Victoria Land
Ross Sea
Ross Ice Shelf
Mt Erebus 3794
Balleny Islands
Cape Adare
Tropic of Cancer
Tropic of Capricorn
Equator
Arctic Circle
Antarctic Circle

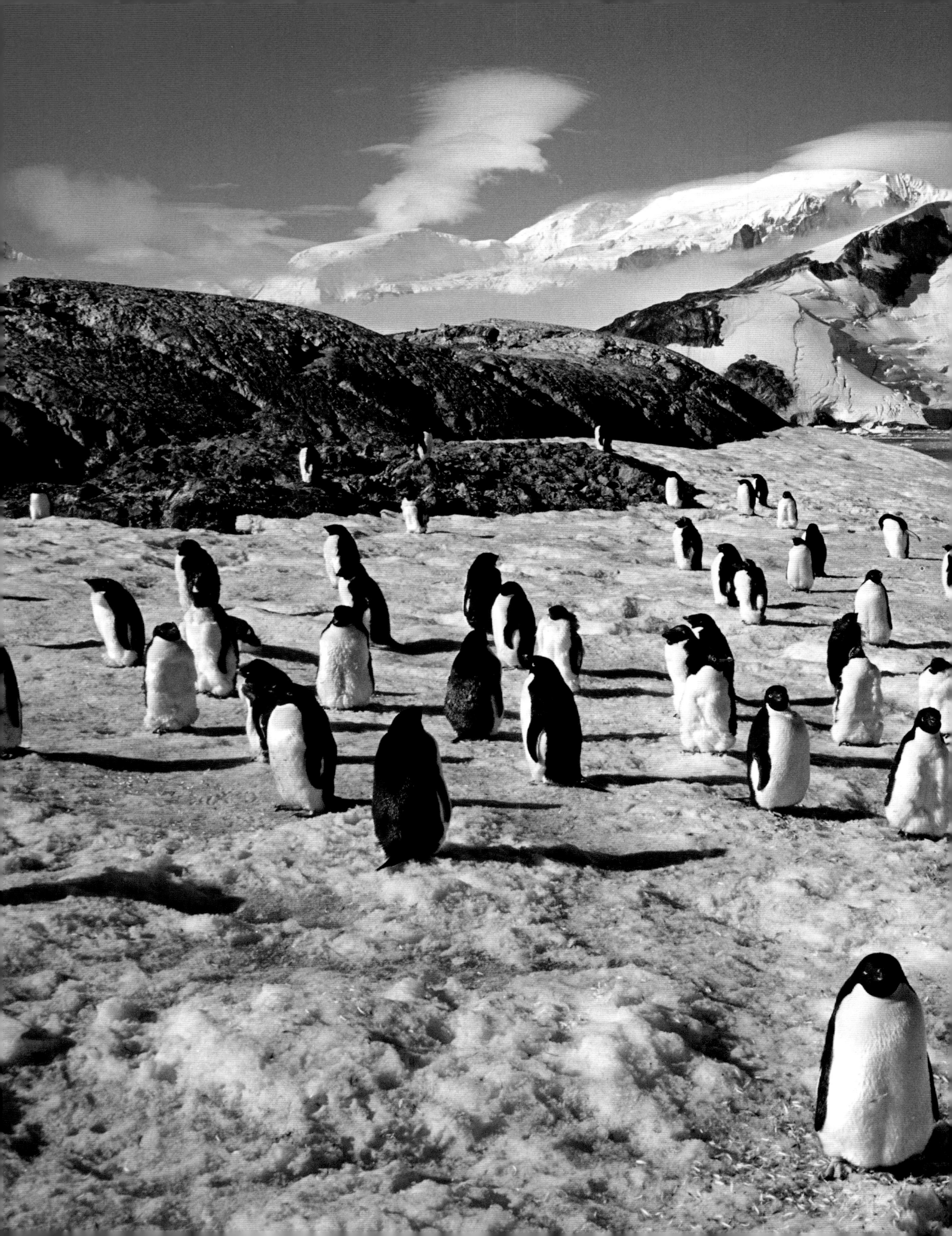

Oceans and Poles

OCEANS and POLES

Only 28 percent of our planet's surface is visible landmass, the other 72 percent is water. Oceanic currents gather all the world's oceans into a single connected system. The enormous global ocean contains the majority of life on Earth, much more than has ever been present on land. The vast, landless, ice-covered ocean that surrounds the North Pole was assumed by geographers to be matched around the South Pole until the discovery of the continent of Antarctica in the nineteenth century.

Below An amazing variety of underwater life can be found in the oceans. New species have been discovered in deep-sea hydrothermal vents in the Southwest Pacific, including an unusual tube worm.

Below A surprising number of the Arctic Ocean islands are inhabited, despite the extreme environment. Russian meteorologists on Novaya Zemlya conduct research into the climate there.

Previously, scientists assumed that oceans did not engage in major interactions; this is one of the reasons for their arbitrary division into five. The Atlantic, Pacific, and Indian oceans are the major oceans; the Arctic and Southern (or Antarctic) oceans are sometimes counted separately, at other times they are included in the main three.

Oceans show remarkable physical and biological diversity. With an average depth of more than 3,660 meters (12,000 feet), and with the deepest locations exceeding 10,670 meters (35,000 feet), the variation in their vertical range is simply too large to allow for uniformity. Modern technology has allowed us to map the physical geography of ocean floors and make accurate measurements of depth. Biological make-up, however, remains to be fully explored, especially in the deeps beyond the continental shelf zones.

The Pacific, Atlantic, and Indian Oceans

The Pacific Ocean, by far the largest in terms of area and volume, contains about half the world's water. The western Pacific holds the depth record as well. The Mariana Trench—where the Pacific Plate collides with the Philippine Plate and slides beneath it—has a current depth of 10,911.5 meters (35,799 feet), and is becoming deeper. In the middle of the Pacific, continental rifting causes spreading of the ocean's floor and expansion of the Pacific Plate. As a consequence, new islands are created near the rift by active vulcanism, while volcanic activity along the plate's peripheries provides evidence of an active tectonic cycle. These geological processes—where the collision of the Pacific Plate with the surrounding plates results in high levels of volcanic and seismic activity—have resulted in the "Pacific Ring of Fire." Earthquakes, for example, are not uncommon in countries such as Japan and the Philippines.

Until the sixteenth century most Pacific Ocean voyages were conducted between islands in the southern Pacific, for the purposes of trade and fishing. Once Europeans reached the New World, however, the Pacific became a transportation corridor, as it remains today.

Long before the discovery of the Americas, the North Atlantic and the Mediterranean Sea were busy waterways. Since then the Atlantic has been transformed into an avenue of commerce. Even today maritime transportation along the South American and African coasts is more effective than overland crossings of those continents. The Atlantic Ocean is generally less prone than the Pacific to destructive physical processes, and when they do occur they tend to be localized and isolated—for example, the volcanoes in Iceland.

The Atlantic Ocean exerts a great climatic influence on the surrounding continents. The warm Gulf Stream provides moisture to western Europe and prevents freezing of the northern Atlantic waters. Just off the West African coast, water and wind currents move westward. As they come closer to North America they form conditions that result in hurricanes during the summer and autumn months. The Atlantic south of the Equator displays less variety. Extreme storms are a rarity until one reaches the Antarctic region.

Although the smallest of the big three, the Indian Ocean is surrounded by the most culturally complex region; this ocean, unlike its larger counterparts, has been well traveled since antiquity. It acted as an excellent alternative to longer, more dangerous overland travel. The Indian Ocean's enclosed character plays a vital factor in the movement of air masses that cause torrential rains in South Asia during summer months. The summer monsoons originate near Mauritius and continue northward, resulting in flooding in lowland areas of the Indian sub-continent. Most of the Indian Ocean is relatively stable in terms of its seismic activity, except where it borders Southeast Asia, as illustrated by the devastating tsunami of 2004.

The Poles

The polar regions experience very limited daylight hours in the long winters and few hours of darkness in summer. Violent blizzards are frequent, but heavy snow is

DEPENDENCIES AND TERRITORIES	OFFICIAL NAME	AREA	POPULATION	CAPITAL	RELIGION	POPULATION DENSITY	HIGHEST POINT	CURRENCY
Bouvet Island (Norway)	Bouvetøya	49 km²/19 mi²	no permanent population	—	—	—	Olav Peak 935 m/3.068 ft	—
French Southern and Antarctic Lands (France)	Territoire des Terres Australes et Antarctiques Françaises	7,748 km²/2,992 mi²	no permanent population	—	—	—	Mont Ross 1,850 m/6,070 ft	—
Heard Island and McDonald Islands (Australia)	Territory of Heard Island and McDonald Islands	388 km²/150 mi²	no permanent population	—	—	—	Mawson Peak 2,745 m/9,006 ft	—

not; both the Arctic and Antarctic regions receive less than 250 millimeters (10 inches) of precipitation a year.

Despite the similarities of weather, ice, and snow, there are many pronounced differences between the two regions, mainly to do with physical geography. The southern hemisphere is predominantly ocean and the continental landmasses of South America and Australia are a great distance from Antarctica. In the high southern latitudes, rough seas and complex weather patterns create difficult conditions for navigation, with the result that shipping lanes have long bypassed this part of the globe in favour of less treacherous routes. Apart from scientific researchers at several experimental stations, Antarctica is uninhabited. In 1959 an international treaty banned all activities related to commercial and military use. By contrast, the Arctic region has been inhabited, and well traveled, for many millennia. Evidence in Siberia suggests human presence within the Arctic Circle dates back at least 30,000 years. Today, there are approximately 8 million people—of whom some 250,000 are members of indigenous groups—living within the Arctic Circle.

Antarctica, covered with thick glacial ice, and with temperatures that can fall below –73°C (–100°F), remains in a true sense the farthest corner of the world. Only 2 percent of the continent is not hidden by ice that, on average, is about 2.3 kilometers (1½ miles) thick. Beneath that ice, however, lie mountain ranges, ice-scoured valleys, low plateaus, and numerous islands. The landmass was first sighted from a Russian vessel in 1820, and by the mid-1800s, explorers who sailed along its coasts realized it was large enough to be considered a continent. Including its icecap, it is larger in area than Europe.

Left The Pacific Ocean is home to approximately 40 percent of the world's coral reefs, with the Great Barrier Reef off Australia's east coast the largest and best known. Coral reefs usually occur on moderately deep, stable continental margins.

Below Antarctica is the only continent with no indigenous population, but scientists and their support staff live there, and some 30,000 tourists visit each year. Wordie House is no longer used as a British research station, but has been designated as an historic site.

ASIA
EUROPE
AFRICA
NORTH AMERICA
ARCTIC OCEAN
ATLANTIC OCEAN
MID-ATLANTIC RIDGE
Greenland
Iceland
British Isles
BARENTS SEA
KARA SEA
NORWEGIAN SEA
NORTH SEA
BALTIC SEA
WHITE SEA
BLACK SEA
MEDITERRANEAN SEA
ADRIATIC SEA
AEGEAN SEA
TYRRHENIAN SEA
Ionian Sea
CELTIC SEA
LABRADOR SEA
HUDSON BAY
Baffin Bay
Davis Strait
Baffin Island
Hudson Strait
Queen Elizabeth Islands
Victoria Island
Beaufort Sea
BERING SEA
Gulf of Alaska
Aleutian Islands
Aleutian Trench
Tufts Plain
SARGASSO SEA
CARIBBEAN SEA
GULF OF MEXICO
Bahama Islands
Greater Antilles
Lesser Antilles
Puerto Rico Trench
Cayman Trench
Yucatan Channel
Middle America Trench
Guatemala Basin
GUIANA BASIN
Demerara Abyssal Plain
Demerara Plateau
Hatteras Abyssal Plain
Bermuda Rise
New England Seamounts
Newfoundland Basin
Grand Banks of Newfoundland
Charlie-Gibbs Fracture Zone
Reykjanes Ridge
Denmark Strait
Irminger Basin
Gloria Ridge
Eirik Ridge
Northwest Atlantic Mid-Ocean Canyon
Porcupine Abyssal Plain
Biscay Plain
Iberian Plain
Azores-Biscay Rise
Azores
Canary Basin
Madeira
CAPE VERDE ABYSSAL PLAIN
Gambia Plain
Doldrums Fracture Zone
Vema Fracture Zone
Cape Verde Fracture Zone
Kane Fracture Zone
Atlantis Fracture Zone
Oceanographer Fracture Zone
Nares Deep
Canada Basin
Makarov Basin
Lomonosov Ridge
Alpha Ridge
Mendeleyev Ridge
Gakkel Ridge
Nansen Basin
Fram Basin
Pole Abyssal Plain
Norwegian Basin
Iberian Peninsula
Anchorage
Vancouver
Houston
New Orleans
Miami
New York
Boston
Washington D.C.
Philadelphia
Halifax
Saint John's
Nuuk
Reykjavík
London
Amsterdam
Lisboa
Tunis
Istanbul
Casablanca
Dakar
Lagos
Accra
Abidjan
Caracas
Georgetown
Paramaribo
1:41,300,000
Lambert Azimuthal Equal Area Projection
0 750 1500 2250 3000 kilometers
0 500 1000 1500 2000 miles
Meters
Feet
0
LAND BELOW SEA LEVEL
100 328
200 656
1000 3281
2000 6562
4000 13123
6000 19685

ATLANTIC OCEAN

SOUTH AMERICA
ANTARCTICA
PACIFIC OCEAN
SOUTHERN OCEAN
MID-ATLANTIC RIDGE
ATLANTIC-INDIAN RIDGE
ANGOLA BASIN
BRAZIL BASIN
PERU-CHILE TRENCH
SCOTIA SEA
WEDDELL SEA
BELLINGSHAUSEN SEA
AMUNDSEN SEA
COSMONAUT SEA
Angola Abyssal Plain
Walvis Ridge
Namibia Abyssal Plain
Cape Abyssal Plain
Agulhas Ridge
Agulhas Basin
Agulhas Plateau
Orange Cone
Enderby Abyssal Plain
Kerguelen Plateau
Elan Bank
Ascension Fracture Zone
Chain Fracture Zone
Pernambuco Plain
Pernambuco Seamounts
Hotspur Fracture Zone
Rio Grande Rise
Argentine Basin
Argentine Abyssal Plain
Argentine Rise
Santos Plateau
Falkland Plateau
Falkland Escarpment
South Georgia Ridge
South Sandwich Trench
Islas Orcadas Rise
American-Antarctic Ridge
Atlantic-Indian Antarctic Basin
Shona Ridge
Maud Rise
Weddell Abyssal Plain
Belgrano Bank
Ronne Ice Shelf
Antarctic Peninsula
Drake Passage
Yaghan Basin
Chile Rise
Chile Basin
Nazca Ridge
Peru Basin
Galapagos Rise
Sala y Gómez Ridge
Roggeveen Basin
Southeast Pacific Basin
East Pacific Rise
Menard Fracture Zone
Eltanin Fracture Zone
Udintsev Fracture Zone
Pacific-Antarctic Ridge
Bellingshausen Abyssal Plain
Amundsen Ridges
South Pole
Meters
Feet
0
LAND BELOW SEA LEVEL
100
328
200
656
1000
3281
2000
6562
4000
13123
6000
19685

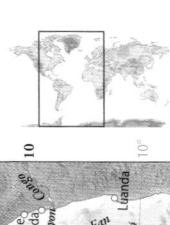

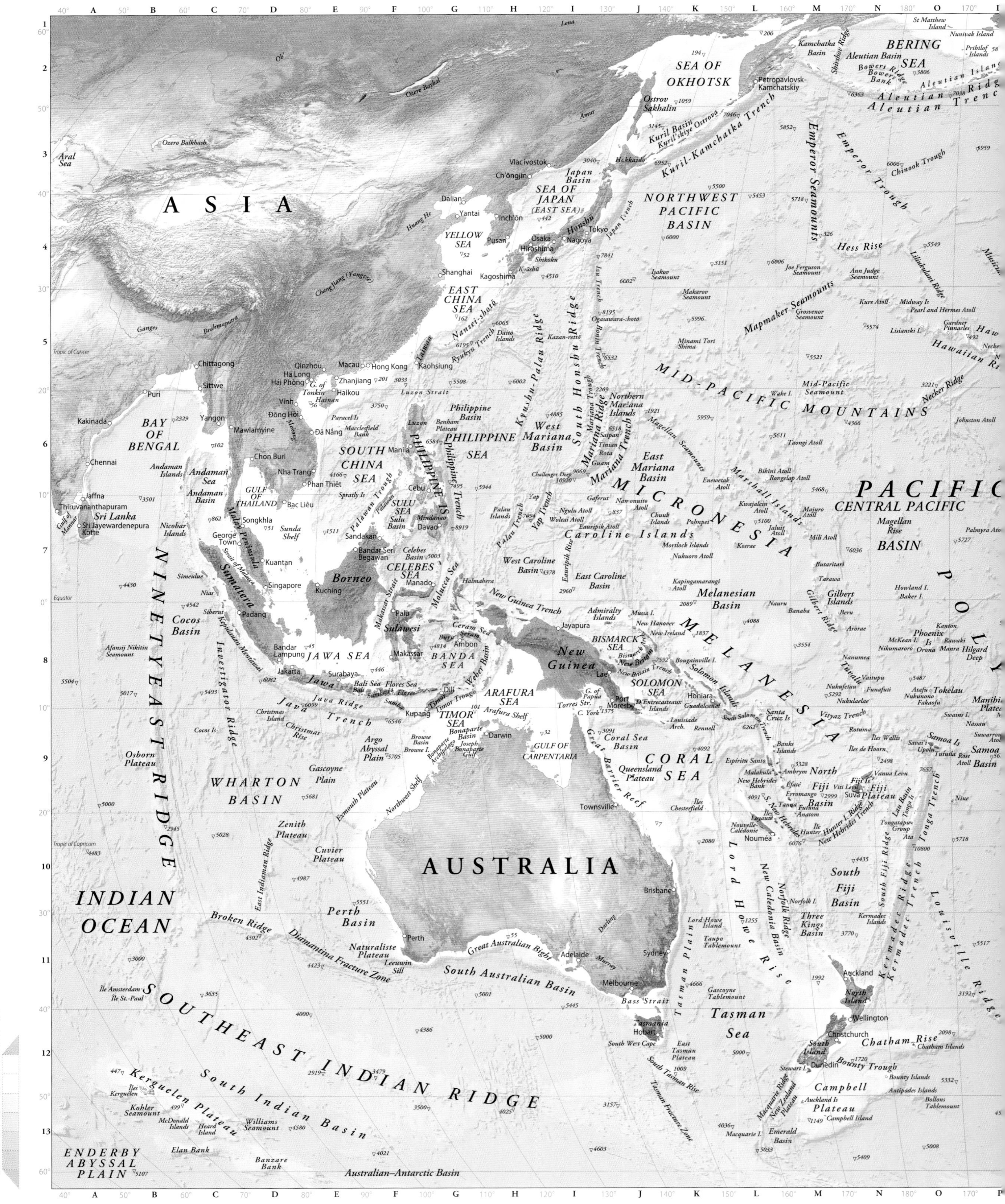
ASIA
AUSTRALIA
INDIAN OCEAN
PACIFIC
CENTRAL PACIFIC BASIN
SEA OF OKHOTSK
BERING SEA
Kamchatka Basin
Aleutian Basin
Bowers Ridge
Bowers Bank
Aleutian Islands
Aleutian Ridge
Aleutian Trench
Shirshov Ridge
Pribilof Islands
St Matthew Island
Nunivak Island
Petropavlovsk-Kamchatskiy
Ostrov Sakhalin
Kuril Basin
Kuril'skiye Ostrova
Kuril-Kamchatka Trench
Emperor Seamounts
Emperor Trough
Chinook Trough
Hess Rise
NORTHWEST PACIFIC BASIN
Japan Basin
SEA OF JAPAN (EAST SEA)
Vladivostok
Ch'ŏngjin
Hokkaidō
Honshū
Tōkyō
Nagoya
Ōsaka
Hiroshima
Shikoku
Kyūshū
Kagoshima
Pusan
Inch'ŏn
Dalian
Yantai
YELLOW SEA
Shanghai
EAST CHINA SEA
Nansei-shotō
Ryukyu Trench
Japan Trench
Izu Trench
Ogasawara-shotō
Bonin Trench
Daitō Islands
Kazan-rettō
Minami Tori Shima
Mapmaker Seamounts
MID-PACIFIC MOUNTAINS
Mid-Pacific Seamount
Necker Ridge
Hawaiian Ridge
Lili'uokalani Ridge
Kure Atoll
Midway Is
Pearl and Hermes Atoll
Lisianski I.
Gardner Pinnacles
Johnston Atoll
Wake I.
Marshall Islands
Bikini Atoll
Rongelap Atoll
Enewetak Atoll
Kwajalein Atoll
Majuro Atoll
Mili Atoll
Jaluit Atoll
Taongi Atoll
Magellan Rise
Magellan Seamounts
Isakov Seamount
Makarov Seamount
Joe Ferguson Seamount
Ann Judge Seamount
Grosvenor Seamount
Ozero Baykal
Ozero Balkhash
Aral Sea
Lena
Ob'
Amur
Huang He
Chang Jiang (Yangtze)
Brahmaputra
Ganges
Tropic of Cancer
Chittagong
Sittwe
Puri
Kakinada
Chennai
Jaffna
Thiruvananthapuram
Sri Lanka
Sri Jayewardenepura Kotte
Gulf of Mannar
BAY OF BENGAL
Yangon
Mawlamyine
Andaman Islands
Andaman Sea
Andaman Basin
Nicobar Islands
Chon Buri
GULF OF THAILAND
Bac Lieu
Songkhla
George Town
Malay Peninsula
Strait of Malacca
Kuantan
Singapore
Sumatera
Padang
Nias
Siberut
Simeulue
Qinzhou
Ha Long
Hai Phong
G. of Tonkin
Hainan
Zhanjiang
Haikou
Macau
Hong Kong
Taiwan
Kaohsiung
Luzon Strait
Vinh
Dong Hoi
Da Nang
Nha Trang
Phan Thiet
Paracel Is
Macclesfield Bank
SOUTH CHINA SEA
Spratly Is
Palawan Trough
Palawan
Sunda Shelf
Luzon
Manila
Benham Plateau
PHILIPPINE IS
Philippine Trench
PHILIPPINE SEA
Philippine Basin
Cebu
SULU SEA
Sulu Basin
Mindanao
Davao
Sandakan
Bandar Seri Begawan
Borneo
Kuching
CELEBES SEA
Celebes Basin
Manado
Halmahera
Molucca Sea
Makassar Strait
Palu
Sulawesi
Makassar
Ceram Sea
Seram
Buru
Ambon
BANDA SEA
Weber Basin
Bandar Lampung
JAWA SEA
Jakarta
Jawa
Surabaya
Bali
Bali Sea
Flores Sea
Flores
Sumba
Timor
Dili
Kupang
Timor Trough
TIMOR SEA
Java Ridge
Java Trench
Christmas Island
Christmas Rise
Kyushu-Palau Ridge
South Honshu Ridge
West Mariana Basin
Mariana Trough
Mariana Ridge
Mariana Trench
Northern Mariana Islands
Saipan
Tinian
Rota
Guam
Challenger Deep
East Mariana Basin
Magellan Seamounts
MICRONESIA
Caroline Islands
Palau Islands
Palau Trench
Yap
Yap Trench
Ngulu Atoll
Woleai Atoll
Eauripik Atoll
Eauripik Rise
Gaferut
Namonuito Atoll
Chuuk Islands
Pohnpei
Kosrae
Mortlock Islands
Nukuoro Atoll
West Caroline Basin
East Caroline Basin
Kapingamarangi Atoll
Melanesian Basin
Nauru
Banaba
Gilbert Islands
Gilbert Ridge
Butaritari
Tarawa
Beru
Arorae
Howland I.
Baker I.
Kanton
Phoenix Is
McKean I.
Nikumaroro
Orona
Rawaki
Manra
Hilgard Deep
Palmyra Atoll
POLYNESIA
New Guinea Trench
Admiralty Islands
Mussa I.
New Hanover
New Ireland
BISMARCK SEA
Bismarck Arch.
New Britain
New Britain Trench
Jayapura
New Guinea
Lae
Port Moresby
G. of Papua
Torres Str.
C. York
ARAFURA SEA
Arafura Shelf
Darwin
GULF OF CARPENTARIA
Bonaparte Basin
Joseph Bonaparte Gulf
Bonaparte Archipelago
Browse Basin
Browse I.
Argo Abyssal Plain
Gascoyne Plain
Exmouth Plateau
Northwest Shelf
SOLOMON SEA
D'Entrecasteaux Islands
Louisiade Arch.
Rennell
Honiara
Guadalcanal
Bougainville I.
Solomon Islands
MELANESIA
Santa Cruz Is
South Solomon Trench
Vityaz Trench
Tuvalu
Nanumea
Vaitupu
Nukufetau
Funafuti
Nukulaelae
Atafu
Nukunonu
Fakaofu
Tokelau
Swains I.
Nassau
Manihiki Plateau
Rotuma
Îles Wallis
Îles de Hoorn
Samoa Is
Savai'i
Upolu
Tutuila
Rose Atoll
Samoa Basin
Banks Islands
Espiritu Santo
Ambrym
Malakula
Efaté
Erromango
Tanna
Anatom
New Hebrides Bank
New Hebrides Trench
North Fiji Basin
Fiji
Fiji Is
Viti Levu
Vanua Levu
Suva
Fiji Plateau
Futuna
Île Hunter
Hunter I. Ridge
Lau Basin
Tonga Is
Tongatapu Group
Ata
Tonga Trench
Niue
Coral Sea Basin
CORAL SEA
Queensland Plateau
Great Barrier Reef
Îles Chesterfield
Townsville
Nouvelle-Calédonie
Loyauté
Nouméa
Brisbane
Darling
Murray
Sydney
Adelaide
Melbourne
Bass Strait
Tasmania
Hobart
South West Cape
Perth
Great Australian Bight
South Australian Basin
Naturaliste Plateau
Leeuwin Sill
Perth Basin
Cuvier Plateau
Zenith Plateau
East Indiaman Ridge
Broken Ridge
Diamantina Fracture Zone
Tropic of Capricorn
Equator
WHARTON BASIN
Investigator Ridge
Kepulauan Mentawai
Cocos Basin
Cocos Is
Osborn Plateau
NINETYEAST RIDGE
Afanasij Nikitin Seamount
SOUTHEAST INDIAN RIDGE
Île Amsterdam
Île St.-Paul
Kerguelen Plateau
Îles Kerguelen
Kohler Seamount
McDonald Islands
Heard Island
Williams Seamount
Elan Bank
Banzare Bank
South Indian Basin
ENDERBY ABYSSAL PLAIN
Australian–Antarctic Basin
South Tasman Rise
Tasman Fracture Zone
East Tasman Plateau
Tasman Plain
Tasman Sea
Lord Howe Island
Lord Howe Rise
Taupo Tablemount
Gascoyne Tablemount
New Caledonia Basin
Norfolk Ridge
Norfolk I.
Three Kings Basin
South Fiji Basin
South Fiji Ridge
Kermadec Islands
Kermadec Ridge
Kermadec Trench
Louisville Ridge
Auckland
North Island
Wellington
Christchurch
South Island
Dunedin
Chatham Rise
Chatham Islands
Bounty Trough
Bounty Islands
Antipodes Islands
Bollons Tablemount
Campbell Plateau
Campbell Island
Auckland Is
Stewart I.
Macquarie Ridge
New Zealand Plateau
Emerald Basin
Macquarie I.
Meters
Feet
0
LAND BELOW SEA LEVEL
100
328
200
656
1000
3281
2000
6562
4000
13123
6000
19685

1:50,600,000

Eckert IV Projection

0 750 1500 2250 3000 kilometers

0 500 1000 1500 2000 miles

PACIFIC OCEAN

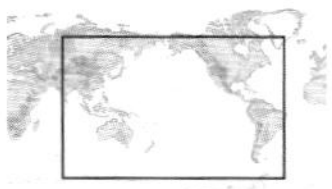

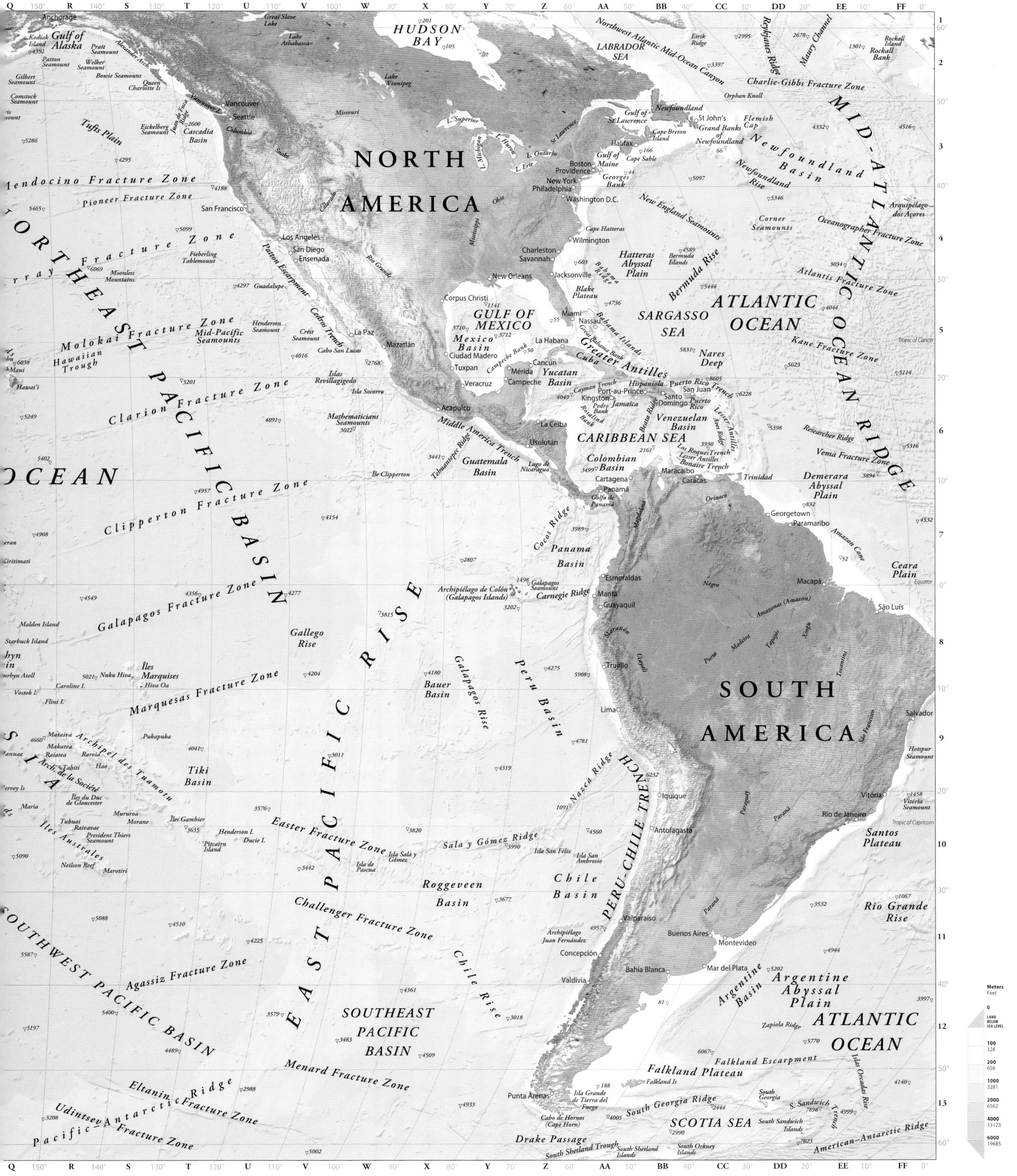
NORTH
AMERICA
SOUTH
AMERICA
HUDSON BAY
LABRADOR SEA
GULF OF MEXICO
CARIBBEAN SEA
SARGASSO SEA
ATLANTIC OCEAN
SCOTIA SEA
NORTHEAST PACIFIC BASIN
SOUTHEAST PACIFIC BASIN
SOUTHWEST PACIFIC BASIN
EAST PACIFIC RISE
OCEAN
Gulf of Alaska
Anchorage
Kodiak Island
Pratt Seamount
Welker Seamount
Patton Seamount
Gilbert Seamount
Bowie Seamount
Queen Charlotte Is
Comstock Seamount
Vancouver
Seattle
Columbia
Cascadia Basin
Eickelberg Seamount
Juan de Fuca Ridge
Tufts Plain
Mendocino Fracture Zone
Pioneer Fracture Zone
San Francisco
Los Angeles
San Diego
Ensenada
Fieberling Tablemount
Moonless Mountains
Guadalupe
Patton Escarpment
Murray Fracture Zone
Molokai Fracture Zone
Mid-Pacific Seamounts
Henderson Seamount
Crest Seamount
Cedros Trench
Cabo San Lucas
La Paz
Mazatlán
Hawaiian Trough
Maui
Hawai'i
Clarion Fracture Zone
Islas Revillagigedo
Isla Socorro
Mathematicians Seamounts
Acapulco
Middle America Trench
Tehuantepec Ridge
Guatemala Basin
Île Clipperton
Clipperton Fracture Zone
Kiritimati
Galapagos Fracture Zone
Gallego Rise
Malden Island
Starbuck Island
Nuku Hiva
Îles Marquises
Hiva Oa
Caroline I.
Vostok I.
Flint I.
Marquesas Fracture Zone
Pukapuka
Mataiva
Makatea
Raiatea
Tahiti
Raroia
Hao
Archipel des Tuamotu
Arch. de la Société
Tiki Basin
Îles du Duc de Gloucester
Tubuai
Raivavae
Mururoa
Morane
Îles Gambier
President Thiers Seamount
Îles Australes
Neilson Reef
Marotiri
Henderson I.
Ducie I.
Pitcairn Island
Easter Fracture Zone
Isla Sala y Gómez
Isla de Pascua
Sala y Gómez Ridge
Roggeveen Basin
Challenger Fracture Zone
Chile Rise
Agassiz Fracture Zone
Menard Fracture Zone
Eltanin Fracture Zone
Udintsev Fracture Zone
Pacific-Antarctic Ridge
Bauer Basin
Galapagos Rise
Peru Basin
Archipiélago de Colón (Galapagos Islands)
Galapagos Seamount
Carnegie Ridge
Cocos Ridge
Panama Basin
Nazca Ridge
PERU-CHILE TRENCH
Isla San Félix
Isla San Ambrosio
Chile Basin
Archipiélago Juan Fernández
Great Slave Lake
Lake Athabasca
Lake Winnipeg
Missouri
Snake
Colorado
Rio Grande
Mississippi
Ohio
L. Superior
L. Michigan
L. Huron
L. Erie
L. Ontario
St Lawrence
Gulf of St Lawrence
Newfoundland
St John's
Grand Banks of Newfoundland
Cape Breton Island
Halifax
Gulf of Maine
Cape Sable
Georges Bank
Boston
Providence
New York
Philadelphia
Washington D.C.
Cape Hatteras
Wilmington
Charleston
Savannah
Jacksonville
New Orleans
Corpus Christi
Blake Plateau
Bahama Ridge
Hatteras Abyssal Plain
Bermuda Islands
Bermuda Rise
New England Seamounts
Miami
Nassau
Bahama Islands
Great Bahama Bank
Mexico Basin
Ciudad Madero
Tuxpan
Veracruz
Campeche Bank
Mérida
Campeche
Cancún
La Habana
Cuba
Yucatan Basin
Cayman Trench
Greater Antilles
Hispaniola
Port-au-Prince
Kingston
Jamaica
Pedro Bank
Rosalind Bank
Beata Ridge
Santo Domingo
Puerto Rico
Puerto Rico Trench
San Juan
Lesser Antilles
Aves Ridge
Venezuelan Basin
La Ceiba
Usulután
Lago de Nicaragua
Colombian Basin
Los Roques Trench
Lesser Antilles
Bonaire Trench
Maracaibo
Caracas
Cartagena
Panamá
Golfo de Panamá
Trinidad
Orinoco
Magdalena
Georgetown
Paramaribo
Demerara Abyssal Plain
Amazon Cone
Ceara Plain
Esmeraldas
Manta
Guayaquil
Macapá
Negro
Amazonas (Amazon)
São Luís
Marañón
Ucayali
Purus
Madeira
Tapajós
Xingu
Tocantins
Trujillo
Lima
Salvador
São Francisco
Hotspur Seamount
Iquique
Antofagasta
Paraguay
Paraná
Vitória
Vitória Seamount
Rio de Janeiro
Santos Plateau
Rio Grande Rise
Valparaíso
Buenos Aires
Montevideo
Concepción
Valdivia
Bahía Blanca
Mar del Plata
Argentine Basin
Argentine Abyssal Plain
Zapiola Ridge
Falkland Escarpment
Falkland Plateau
Falkland Is
Punta Arenas
Isla Grande de Tierra del Fuego
Cabo de Hornos (Cape Horn)
Drake Passage
South Shetland Trough
South Shetland Islands
South Georgia Ridge
South Georgia
South Sandwich Islands
South Sandwich Trench
South Orkney Islands
Islas Orcadas Rise
American-Antarctic Ridge
Northwest Atlantic Mid-Ocean Canyon
Eirik Ridge
Reykjanes Ridge
Maury Channel
Rockall Island
Rockall Bank
Charlie-Gibbs Fracture Zone
Orphan Knoll
Flemish Cap
Newfoundland Basin
Newfoundland Rise
MID-ATLANTIC OCEAN RIDGE
Arquipélago dos Açores
Corner Seamounts
Oceanographer Fracture Zone
Atlantis Fracture Zone
Nares Deep
Kane Fracture Zone
Tropic of Cancer
Researcher Ridge
Vema Fracture Zone
Equator
Tropic of Capricorn
Meters
Feet
LAND BELOW SEA LEVEL

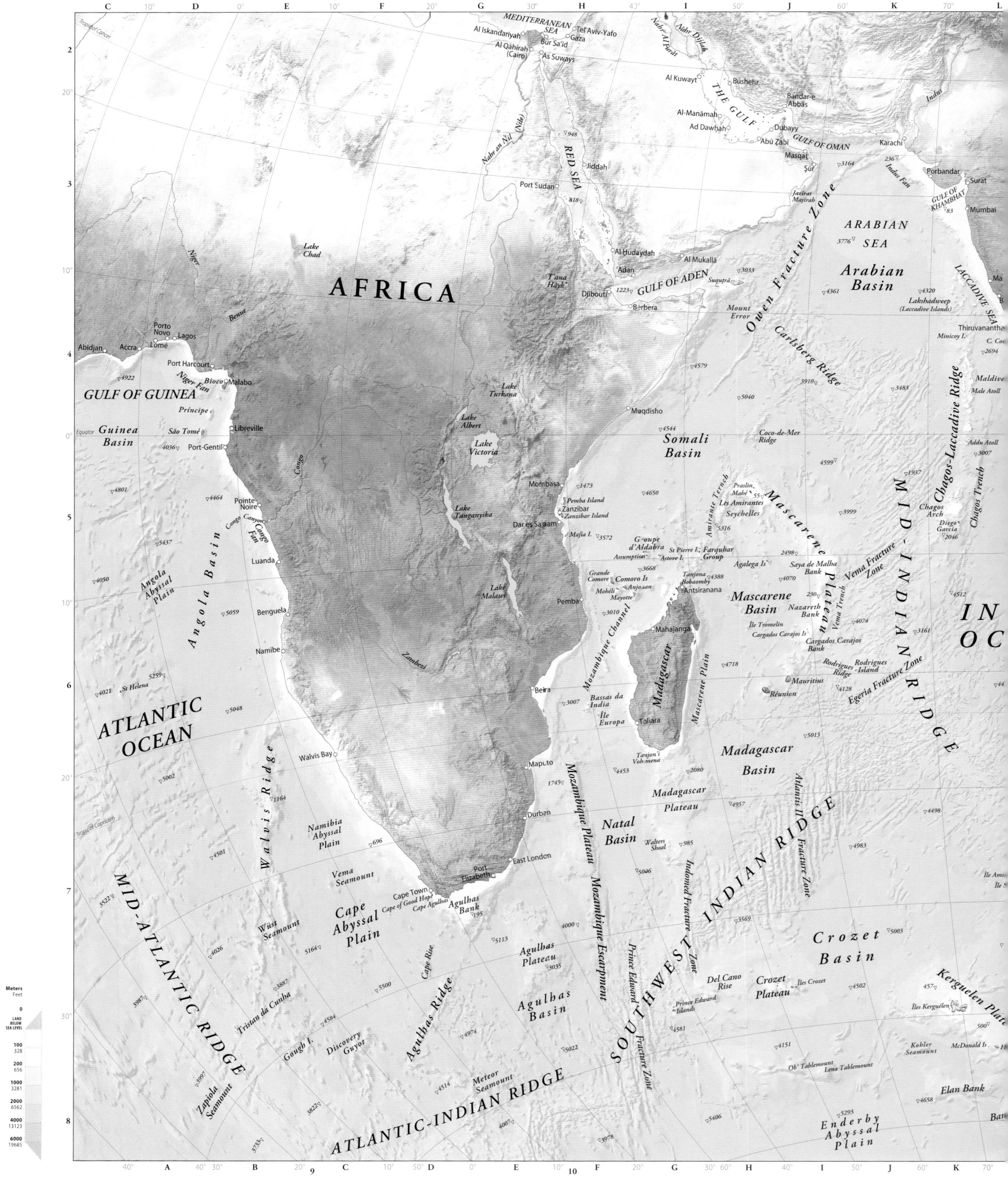

AFRICA
ATLANTIC OCEAN
GULF OF GUINEA
MEDITERRANEAN SEA
RED SEA
THE GULF
GULF OF OMAN
GULF OF ADEN
ARABIAN SEA
LACCADIVE SEA
GULF OF KHAMBHAT
IN
OC
Tropic of Cancer
Tropic of Capricorn
Equator
Al Iskandarīyah
Al Qāhirah (Cairo)
Tel Aviv-Yafo
Gaza
Būr Sa'īd
As Suways
Nahr an Nīl (Nile)
Nahr al Furāt
Nahr Dijlah
Al Kuwayt
Būshehr
Bandar-e Abbās
Al-Manāmah
Ad Dawhah
Dubayy
Abū Ẕabī
Karachi
Masqaṭ
Ṣūr
Indus
Indus Fan
Porbandar
Surat
Mumbai
Jiddah
Port Sudan
Jazīrat Maṣīrah
Al Ḥudaydah
Al Mukallā
Adan
Suquṭrā
Djibouti
Berbera
T'ana Hāyk'
Lake Chad
Niger
Benue
Porto Novo
Lagos
Abidjan
Accra
Lomé
Port Harcourt
Bioco
Malabo
Niger Fan
Príncipe
São Tomé
Libreville
Guinea Basin
Port-Gentil
Congo
Pointe-Noire
Congo Canyon
Congo Fan
Luanda
Angola Abyssal Plain
Angola Basin
Benguela
Namibe
St Helena
Walvis Ridge
Walvis Bay
Namibia Abyssal Plain
Vema Seamount
Cape Town
Cape of Good Hope
Cape Agulhas
Agulhas Bank
Port Elizabeth
East London
Durban
Maputo
Beira
Zambezi
Lake Malawi
Lake Tanganyika
Lake Victoria
Lake Albert
Lake Turkana
Mombasa
Pemba Island
Zanzibar
Zanzibar Island
Dar es Salaam
Mafia I.
Muqdisho
Somali Basin
Mount Error
Owen Fracture Zone
Carlsberg Ridge
Arabian Basin
Lakshadweep (Laccadive Islands)
Thiruvananthapuram
Minicoy I.
Maldives
Male Atoll
Addu Atoll
Chagos-Laccadive Ridge
Chagos Trench
Chagos Arch
Diego Garcia
Coco-de-Mer Ridge
Praslin
Mahé
Les Amirantes
Seychelles
Amirante Trench
Mascarene Plateau
Groupe d'Aldabra
Assumption
St Pierre I.
Astove I.
Farquhar Group
Agalega Is
Saya de Malha Bank
Nazareth Bank
Grande Comore
Comoro Is
Mohéli
Anjouan
Mayotte
Tanjona Bobaomby
Antsiranana
Mahajanga
Madagascar
Mozambique Channel
Bassas da India
Île Europa
Toliara
Tanjon'i Vohimena
Mascarene Plain
Mascarene Basin
Île Tromelin
Cargados Carajos Is
Cargados Carajos Bank
Vema Trench
Vema Fracture Zone
Rodrigues Ridge
Rodrigues Island
Mauritius
Réunion
Egeria Fracture Zone
MID-INDIAN RIDGE
Pemba
Madagascar Basin
Madagascar Plateau
Atlantis II Fracture Zone
Natal Basin
Walters Shoal
Mozambique Plateau
Mozambique Escarpment
Indomed Fracture Zone
SOUTHWEST INDIAN RIDGE
Prince Edward Fracture Zone
Prince Edward Islands
Del Cano Rise
Crozet Plateau
Îles Crozet
Crozet Basin
Kerguelen Plateau
Îles Kerguelen
Kohler Seamount
McDonald Is.
Ob' Tablemount
Lena Tablemount
Elan Bank
Enderby Abyssal Plain
Île Amsterdam
Agulhas Plateau
Agulhas Basin
Agulhas Ridge
Cape Rise
Cape Abyssal Plain
Wüst Seamount
Tristan da Cunha
Gough I.
Discovery Guyot
Meteor Seamount
MID-ATLANTIC RIDGE
Zapiola Seamount
ATLANTIC-INDIAN RIDGE
Meters
Feet
0
LAND BELOW SEA LEVEL
100 328
200 656
1000 3281
2000 6562
4000 13123
6000 19685

1:37,500,000
Lambert Azimuthal Equal Area

0 500 1000 1500 2000 kilometers
0 250 500 750 1000 miles

INDIAN OCEAN

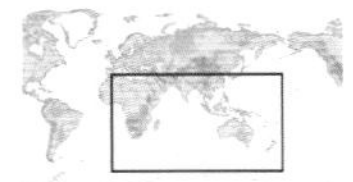

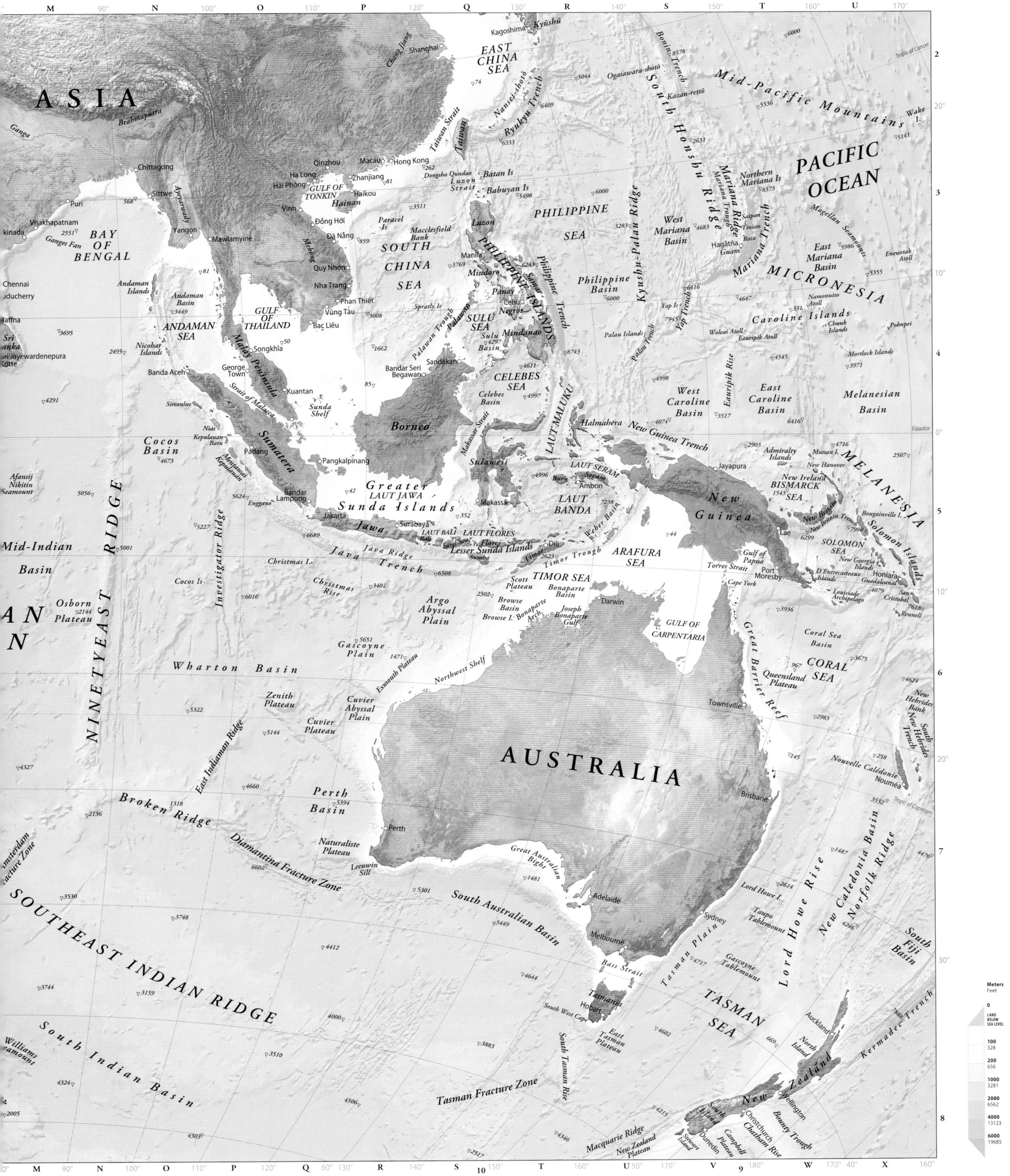
ASIA
PACIFIC OCEAN
AUSTRALIA
BAY OF BENGAL
ANDAMAN SEA
GULF OF THAILAND
GULF OF TONKIN
SOUTH CHINA SEA
EAST CHINA SEA
PHILIPPINE SEA
SULU SEA
CELEBES SEA
LAUT MALUKU
LAUT SERAM
LAUT BANDA
LAUT JAWA
LAUT BALI
LAUT FLORES
TIMOR SEA
ARAFURA SEA
GULF OF CARPENTARIA
BISMARCK SEA
SOLOMON SEA
CORAL SEA
TASMAN SEA
MICRONESIA
MELANESIA
Greater Sunda Islands
Lesser Sunda Islands
PHILIPPINE ISLANDS
Borneo
Sumatera
Jawa
Sulawesi
New Guinea
Luzon
Mindanao
Hainan
Taiwan
Kyūshū
Halmahera
Timor
Tasmania
New Zealand
North Island
South Island
Stewart Island
Kagoshima
Shanghai
Chang Jiang
Brahmaputra
Ganga
Chittagong
Puri
Visakhapatnam
Chennai
Puducherry
Jaffna
Sri Lanka
Sri Jayewardenepura Kotte
Sittwe
Yangon
Mawlamyine
Ayeyarwady
Mekong
Qinzhou
Macau
Hong Kong
Ha Long
Hai Phong
Zhanjiang
Haikou
Vinh
Đông Hới
Đà Nẵng
Quy Nhơn
Nha Trang
Phan Thiết
Vũng Tàu
Bạc Liêu
Songkhla
George Town
Kuantan
Banda Aceh
Malay Peninsula
Strait of Malacca
Padang
Pangkalpinang
Bandar Lampung
Jakarta
Surabaya
Bali
Sumbawa
Flores
Sumba
Dili
Makassar
Ambon
Seram
Buru
Jayapura
Lae
Port Moresby
Honiara
Manila
Mindoro
Panay
Cebu
Negros
Samar
Palawan
Sandakan
Bandar Seri Begawan
Darwin
Townsville
Brisbane
Sydney
Melbourne
Adelaide
Perth
Hobart
Auckland
Wellington
Christchurch
Dunedin
Nouméa
Hagåtña
Guam
Saipan
Tinian
Rota
Cape York
Torres Strait
Gulf of Papua
Bass Strait
South West Cape
Taiwan Strait
Luzon Strait
Batan Is
Babuyan Is
Dongsha Qundao
Paracel Is
Macclesfield Bank
Spratly Is
Andaman Islands
Nicobar Islands
Andaman Basin
Simeulue
Nias
Kepulauan Batu
Kepulauan Mentawai
Enggano
Christmas I.
Cocos Is
Ogasawara-shotō
Kazan-rettō
Nansei-shotō
Northern Mariana Is
Palau Islands
Yap Is
Woleai Atoll
Eauripik Atoll
Caroline Islands
Chuuk Islands
Pohnpei
Namonuito Atoll
Mortlock Islands
Enewetak Atoll
Wake I.
Admiralty Islands
Mussau I.
New Hanover
New Ireland
New Britain
Bougainville I.
Solomon Islands
New Georgia Island
Guadalcanal
San Cristobal
Rennell
D'Entrecasteaux Islands
Louisiade Archipelago
Nouvelle Calédonie
Lord Howe I.
Mid-Pacific Mountains
Magellan Seamounts
Bonin Trench
South Honshu Ridge
Ryukyu Trench
Mariana Trough
Mariana Ridge
Mariana Trench
Kyushu-Palau Ridge
Palau Trench
Yap Trench
Philippine Trench
Eauripik Rise
New Guinea Trench
New Britain Trench
Java Ridge
Java Trench
Timor Trough
Weber Basin
Makassar Strait
Palawan Trough
Sunda Shelf
Northwest Shelf
Exmouth Plateau
Great Barrier Reef
Great Australian Bight
Leeuwin Sill
Ninetyeast Ridge
Investigator Ridge
East Indiaman Ridge
Broken Ridge
Diamantina Fracture Zone
Southeast Indian Ridge
Amsterdam Fracture Zone
Tasman Fracture Zone
South Tasman Rise
East Tasman Plateau
Macquarie Ridge
New Zealand Plateau
Campbell Plateau
Chatham Rise
Bounty Trough
Kermadec Trench
Lord Howe Rise
New Caledonia Basin
Norfolk Ridge
South Fiji Basin
New Hebrides Bank
South New Hebrides Trench
Tasman Plain
Gascoyne Tablemount
Taupo Tablemount
Queensland Plateau
Coral Sea Basin
West Mariana Basin
East Mariana Basin
Philippine Basin
West Caroline Basin
East Caroline Basin
Melanesian Basin
Celebes Basin
Sulu Basin
Cocos Basin
Mid-Indian Basin
Wharton Basin
Osborn Plateau
Argo Abyssal Plain
Gascoyne Plain
Zenith Plateau
Cuvier Abyssal Plain
Cuvier Plateau
Perth Basin
Naturaliste Plateau
South Australian Basin
South Indian Basin
Scott Plateau
Browse Basin
Browse I.
Bonaparte Basin
Bonaparte Arch
Joseph Bonaparte Gulf
Christmas Rise
Afanasij Nikitin Seamount
Williams Seamount
Ganges Fan
Tropic of Cancer
Tropic of Capricorn
Equator
Meters
Feet
LAND BELOW SEA LEVEL
0
100 328
200 656
1000 3281
2000 6562
4000 13123
6000 19685

ASIA
NORTH AMERICA
ARCTIC OCEAN
PACIFIC OCEAN
SEA OF OKHOTSK
BERING SEA
CHUKCHI SEA
BEAUFORT SEA
VOSTOCHNO-SIBIRSKOYE MORE
(East Siberian Sea)
MORE LAPTEVYKH
(Laptev Sea)
POLUOSTROV KAMCHATKA
Ostrov Sakhalin
Kuril'skiye Ostrova
Kuril-Kamchatka Trench
Kronotskiy Zaliv
Kamchatskiy Zaliv
Zaliv Ozernoy
Kamchatka Basin
Karaginskiy Zaliv
Ostrov Karaginskiy
Olyutorskiy Zaliv
Komandorskiye Ostrova
Aleutian Trench
Aleutian Ridge
Aleutian Islands
Shirshov Ridge
Bowers Bank
Bowers Ridge
Bering Basin
Aleutian Basin
Zaliv Shelikhova
Magadan
Penzhinskaya Guba
Anadyr
Zaliv Kresta
Anadyrskiy Zaliv
Chukotskiy Poluostrov
Kolyuchinskaya Guba
Mys Dezhneva
Bering Strait
St Matthew Island
St Lawrence I.
Nunivak Island
Pribilof Islands
Norton Sound
Seward Peninsula
Kotzebue Sound
Point Barrow
Etolin Strait
Kuskokwim Bay
Bristol Bay
Unimak Island
Shumagin Islands
Alaska Peninsula
Shelikof Strait
Cook Inlet
Kodiak I.
Kenai Peninsula
Anchorage
Gulf of Alaska
Aleutian Trench
Kodiak Seamount
Patton Seamount
Gilbert Seamount
Pratt Seamount
Chichagof Island
Lena
Aldan
Indigirka
Kolyma
Yanskiy Zaliv
Proliv Dmitriya Lapteva
Lyakhovskiye Ostrova
Novosibirskiye Ostrova
Ostrov Kotel'nyy
Ostrov Faddeyevskiy
Ostrov Novaya Sibir
Chaunskaya Guba
O. Ayon
Proliv Longa
Ostrov Vrangelya
Kucherov Terrace
Wrangel Abyssal Plain
Pole Abyssal Plain
MAKAROV BASIN
Mendeleyev Ridge
Mendeleyev Abyssal Plain
Chukchi Abyssal Plain
Chukchi Plateau
Northwind Abyssal Plain
Northwind Ridge
Northwind Escarpment
Canada Abyssal Plain
CANADA BASIN
Alpha Ridge
North Magnetic Pole
Oleneskiy Zaliv
Ostrov Bol'shoy Begichev
Khatangskiy Zaliv
Mackenzie Bay
Mackenzie
Great Bear L.
Amundsen Gulf
Banks Island
Prince of Wales Str.
Prince Albert Peninsula
Victoria Island
Dolphin and Union Str.
Coronation G.
Dease Str.
Queen Maud Gulf
King William Island
M'Clure Strait
Melville I.
Viscount Melville Sd.
Prince Patrick Island
Prince Gustaf Adolf Sea
Parry Islands
M'Clintock Chan.
Prince of Wales Island
Victoria Str.
Hadley Bay
Larsen Sound
Franklin Str.
Wollaston Peninsula
Prince Albert Sd.
Borden Island
Mackenzie King Island
Hazen Strait
Lougheed I.
Byam Martin Chan.
Liddon G.
Ballantyne Strait
Crozier Chan.
Kellett Strait
Eglinton I.
Stefansson Island
P
O
N
M
Q
R
S
T
U
V
W
X
135°
120°
105°
150°
165°
180°
60°
75°
1
2
3
Meters
Feet
0
LAND BELOW SEA LEVEL
100
328
200
656
1000
3281
2000
6562
4000
13123
6000
19685

1:18,700,000

Lambert Conic Conformal Projection

0 200 400 600 800 kilometers

0 100 200 300 400 miles

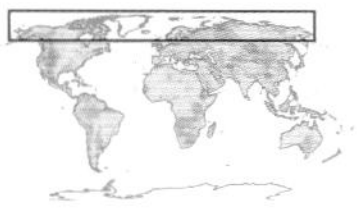

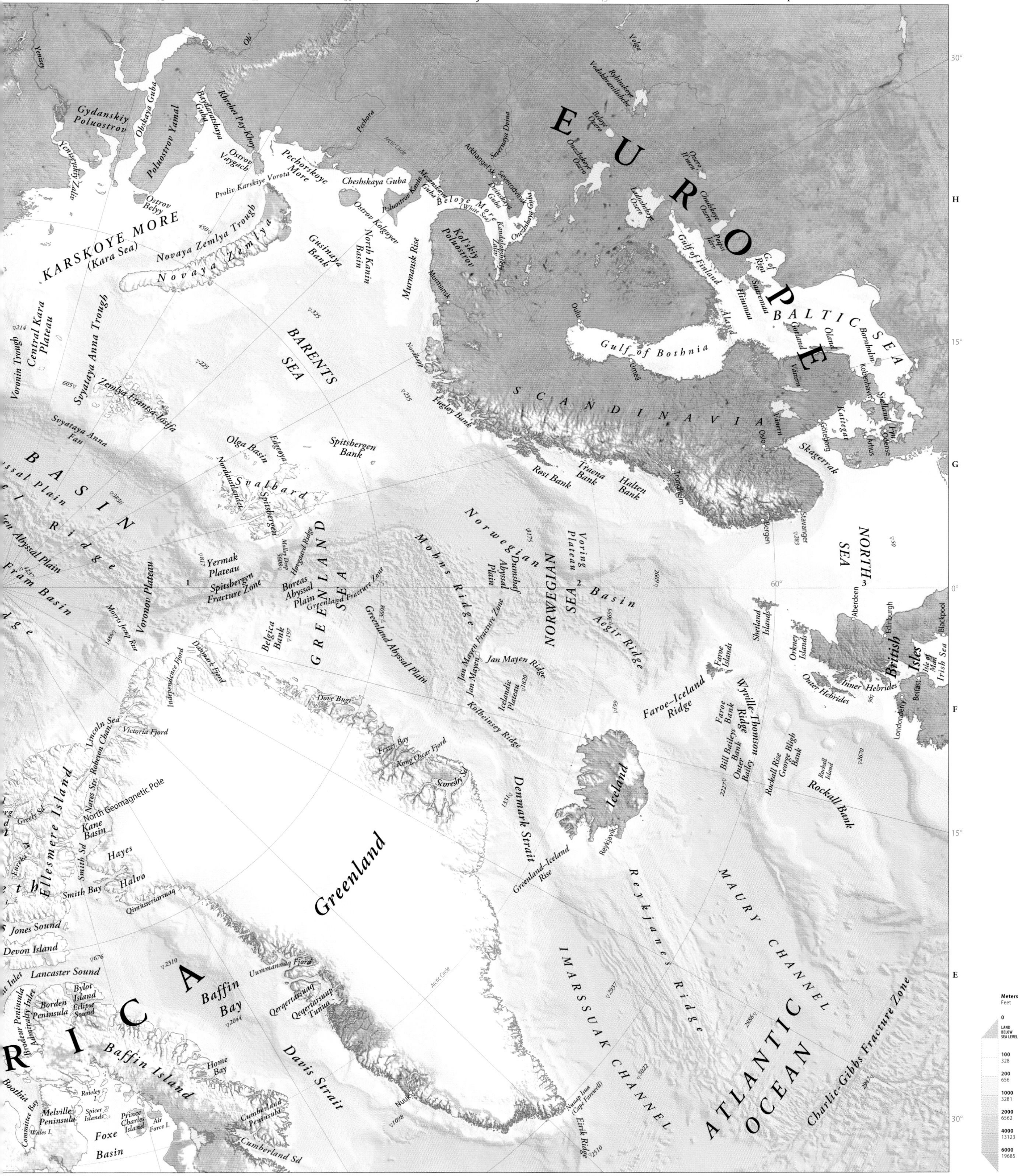
L
75°
K
60°
J
45°
I
A
B
C
D
H
G
F
E
30°
15°
0°
EUROPE
SCANDINAVIA
BALTIC SEA
Gulf of Bothnia
Gulf of Finland
G. of Riga
Saaremaa
Hiiumaa
Gotland
Öland
Åland
Bornholm
København
Sjælland
Fyn
Odense
Århus
Kattegat
Skagerrak
Göteborg
Oslo
Vänern
Vättern
Oulu
Umeå
Trondheim
Bergen
Stavanger
NORTH SEA
Aberdeen
Edinburgh
Blackpool
Belfast
Londonderry
Isle of Man
Irish Sea
British Isles
Inner Hebrides
Outer Hebrides
Orkney Islands
Shetland Islands
Faroe Islands
Faroe–Iceland Ridge
Faroe Bank
Wyville-Thomson Ridge
Bill Baileys Bank
Outer Bailey
Rockall Rise
George Bligh Bank
Rockall Island
Rockall Bank
Iceland
Reykjavík
Denmark Strait
Greenland–Iceland Rise
Reykjanes Ridge
MAURY CHANNEL
IMARSSUAK CHANNEL
ATLANTIC OCEAN
Charlie-Gibbs Fracture Zone
Eirik Ridge
Nunap Isua (Cape Farewell)
Nuuk
Davis Strait
Baffin Bay
Baffin Island
Greenland
Qimusseriarsuaq
Uummannaq Fjord
Qeqertarsuaq
Qeqertarsuup Tunua
Scoresby Sd
Kong Oscar Fjord
Fetter Bay
Dove Bugt
Danmark Fjord
Independence Fjord
Victoria Fjord
Lincoln Sea
Robeson Chan.
Nares Str.
North Geomagnetic Pole
Kane Basin
Hayes Halvø
Smith Sd
Smith Bay
Greely Sd
Ellesmere Island
Jones Sound
Devon Island
Lancaster Sound
Bylot Island
Eclipse Sound
Borden Peninsula
Admiralty Inlet
Brodeur Peninsula
Home Bay
Cumberland Peninsula
Cumberland Sd
Rowley I.
Spicer Islands
Prince Charles Island
Air Force I.
Melville Peninsula
Wales I.
Committee Bay
Boothia
Foxe Basin
RICA
Jan Mayen
Jan Mayen Ridge
Jan Mayen Fracture Zone
Icelandic Plateau
Kolbeinsey Ridge
Ægir Ridge
Norwegian Basin
NORWEGIAN SEA
Vøring Plateau
Dumshaf Abyssal Plain
Mohns Ridge
Greenland Abyssal Plain
Greenland Fracture Zone
GREENLAND SEA
Boreas Abyssal Plain
Belgica Bank
Hovgaard Ridge
Molloy Deep
Spitsbergen Fracture Zone
Yermak Plateau
Vøronoo Plateau
Morris Jesup Rise
Fram Basin
Svalbard
Spitsbergen
Nordaustlandet
Edgeøya
Olga Basin
Spitsbergen Bank
Røst Bank
Træna Bank
Halten Bank
Fugløy Bank
Nordkapp
BARENTS SEA
Murmansk
Murmansk Rise
North Kanin Basin
Gusinaya Bank
Kol'skiy Poluostrov
Kandalakshskiy Zaliv
Onezhskaya Guba
Beloye More (White Sea)
Dvinskaya Guba
Mezenskaya Guba
Poluostrov Kanin
Ostrov Kolguyev
Cheshskaya Guba
Pechorskoye More
Pechora
Arkhangel'sk
Severodvinsk
Severnaya Dvina
Onezhskoye Ozero
Ladozhskoye Ozero
Chudskoye Ozero
Peipsi Järv
Ozero Il'men
Beloye Ozero
Rybinskoye Vodokhranilishche
Volga
Arctic Circle
Proliv Karskiye Vorota
Ostrov Vaygach
Khrebet Pay-Khoy
Baydaratskaya Guba
Poluostrov Yamal
Obskaya Guba
Ob'
Gydanskiy Poluostrov
Yeniseyskiy Zaliv
Yenisey
Ostrov Belyy
KARSKOYE MORE (Kara Sea)
Novaya Zemlya
Novaya Zemlya Trough
Central Kara Plateau
Voronin Trough
Svyataya Anna Trough
Svyataya Anna Fan
Zemlya Frantsa-Iosifa
BASIN
Ridge
Abyssal Plain
Meters
Feet
0
LAND BELOW SEA LEVEL
100
328
200
656
1000
3281
2000
6562
4000
13123
6000
19685

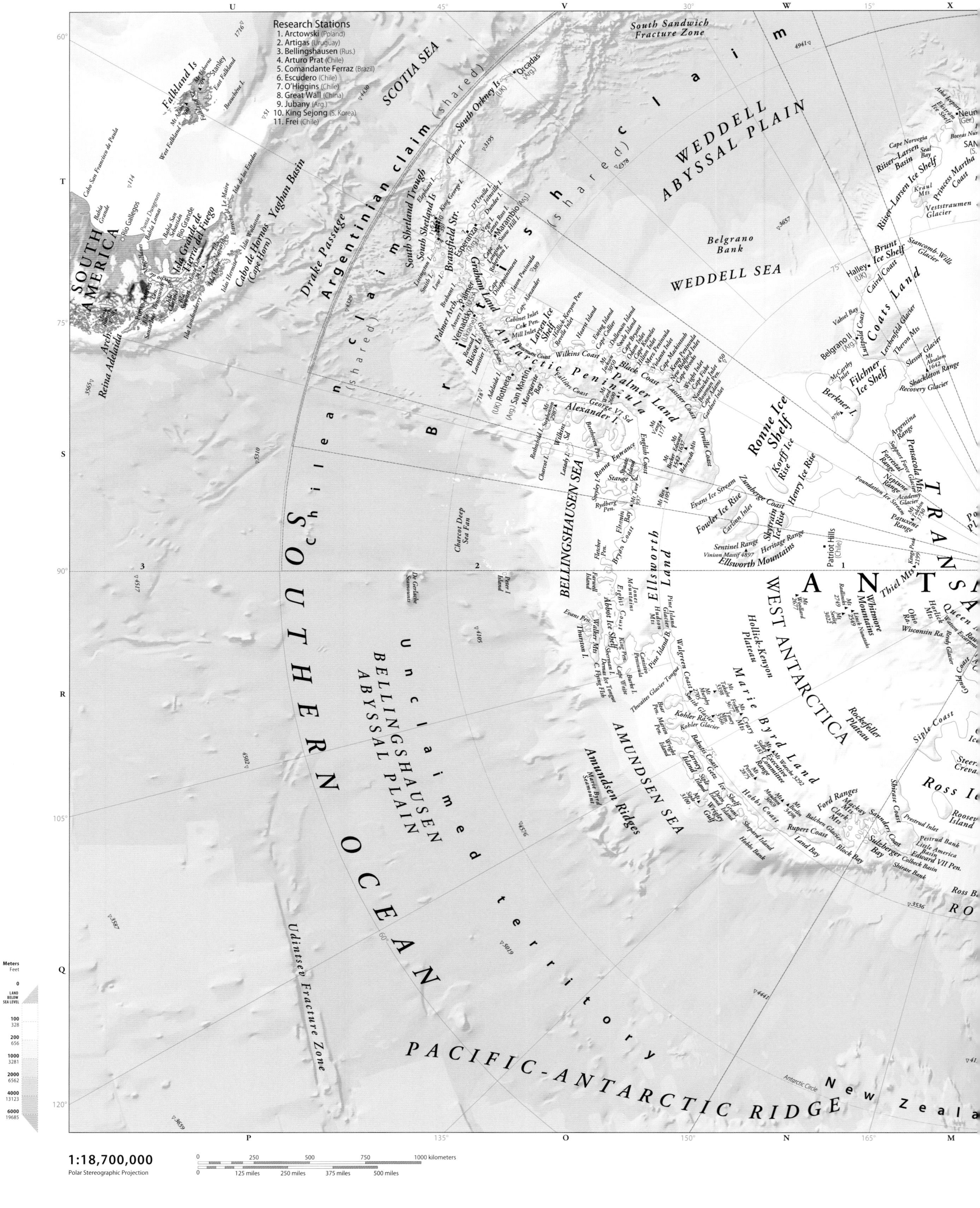

Research Stations
1. Arctowski (Poland)
2. Artigas (Uruguay)
3. Bellingshausen (Rus.)
4. Arturo Prat (Chile)
5. Comandante Ferraz (Brazil)
6. Escudero (Chile)
7. O'Higgins (Chile)
8. Great Wall (China)
9. Jubany (Arg.)
10. King Sejong (S. Korea)
11. Frei (Chile)
SCOTIA SEA
South Sandwich Fracture Zone
Falkland Is
Stanley
East Falkland
West Falkland
Beauchene I.
South Orkney Is (UK)
Orcadas (Arg.)
Argentinian claim (shared)
British claim (shared)
Chilean claim (shared)
WEDDELL ABYSSAL PLAIN
WEDDELL SEA
Belgrano Bank
Yaghan Basin
SOUTH AMERICA
Rio Gallegos
Rio Grande
Isla Grande de Tierra del Fuego
Cabo de Hornos (Cape Horn)
Drake Passage
South Shetland Trough
South Shetland Is
Bransfield Str.
Elephant I.
King George I.
Clarence I.
Esperanza
Marambio (Arg.)
Graham Land
Antarctic Peninsula
Palmer Land
Palmer Arch.
Palmer (USA)
Vernadsky (Ukraine)
Larsen Ice Shelf
Wilkins Coast
Black Coast
Lassiter Coast
Orville Coast
Rothera (UK)
San Martín (Arg.)
Marguerite Bay
Alexander I.
George VI Sd
Ronne Entrance
English Coast
BELLINGSHAUSEN SEA
Peter I Island
De Gerlache Seamounts
Charcot Deep Sea Fan
Ronne Ice Shelf
Korff Ice Rise
Henry Ice Rise
Berkner I.
Filchner Ice Shelf
Belgrano II (Arg.)
Coats Land
Caird Coast
Halley (UK)
Brunt Ice Shelf
Riiser-Larsen Ice Shelf
Princess Martha Coast
Stancomb-Wills Glacier
Shackleton Range
Recovery Glacier
Pensacola Mts
Foundation Ice Stream
Zumberge Coast
Fowler Ice Rise
Evans Ice Stream
Carlson Inlet
Skytrain Ice Rise
Sentinel Range
Vinson Massif 4897
Ellsworth Mountains
Heritage Range
Patriot Hills (Chile)
Ellsworth Land
Bryan Coast
Eights Coast
Abbot Ice Shelf
Thurston I.
Pine Island B.
Walgreen Coast
Thwaites Glacier Tongue
Hollick-Kenyon Plateau
WEST ANTARCTICA
ANTARCTICA
Whitmore Mountains
Thiel Mts
Marie Byrd Land
Executive Committee Range
Rockefeller Plateau
Siple Coast
Ross Ice Shelf
Roosevelt Island
Ruppert Coast
Hobbs Coast
Saunders Coast
Sulzberger Bay
Edward VII Pen.
Ford Ranges
Land Bay
Block Bay
AMUNDSEN SEA
Amundsen Ridges
unclaimed territory
BELLINGSHAUSEN ABYSSAL PLAIN
SOUTHERN OCEAN
Udintsev Fracture Zone
PACIFIC-ANTARCTIC RIDGE
Antarctic Circle
New Zealand
Meters
Feet
LAND BELOW SEA LEVEL
1:18,700,000
Polar Stereographic Projection
0 250 500 750 1000 kilometers
0 125 miles 250 miles 375 miles 500 miles

ANTARCTIC

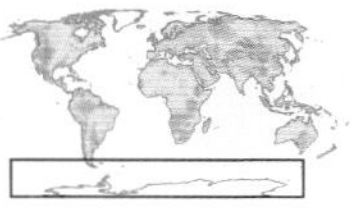

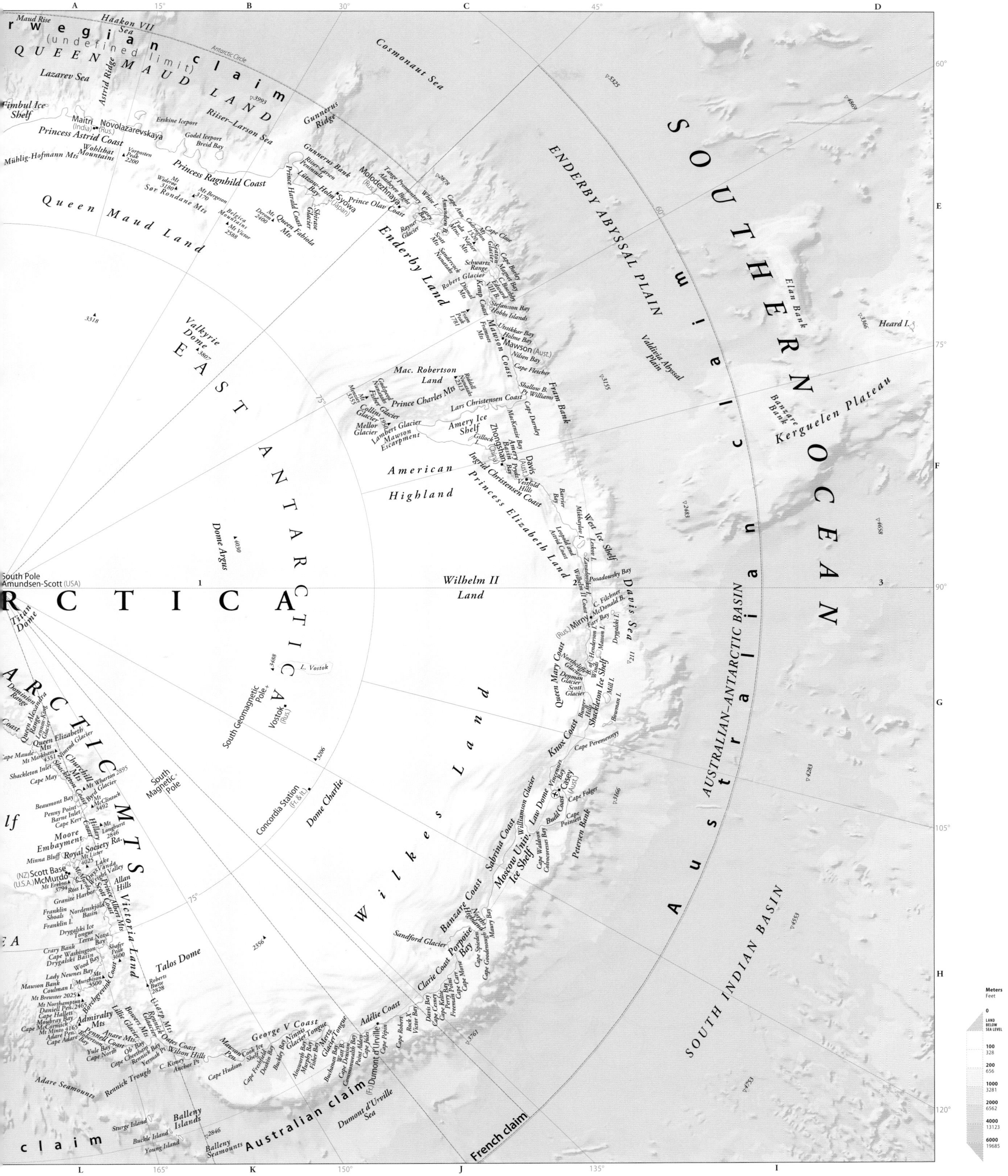

A
B
C
D
E
F
G
H
I
J
K
L
15°
30°
45°
60°
75°
90°
105°
120°
135°
150°
165°
1
2
3
Maud Rise
Haakon VII Sea
Norwegian claim (undefined limit)
QUEEN MAUD LAND
Antarctic Circle
Lazarev Sea
Astrid Ridge
Fimbul Ice Shelf
Maitri (India)
Novolazarevskaya (Rus.)
Princess Astrid Coast
Erskine Iceport
Riiser-Larsen Sea
Godel Iceport
Breid Bay
Mühlig-Hofmann Mts
Wohlthat Mountains
Vorposten Peak 2200
Princess Ragnhild Coast
Sør Rondane Mts
Mt Bergeson 3170
Queen Maud Land
Belgica Mountains
Mt Victor 2588
Queen Fabiola Mts
Prince Harald Coast
Lützow-Holm Bay
Shirase Glacier
Syowa (Japan)
Prince Olav Coast
Molodezhnaya (Rus.)
Gunnerus Ridge
Gunnerus Bank
Riiser-Larsen Peninsula
Cosmonaut Sea
Enderby Land
Amundsen Bay
Cape Ann
Scott Mts
Napier Mts
Rayner Glacier
Cape Close
Casey Bay
Schwartz Range
Robert Glacier
Kemp Coast
Stefansson Bay
Hobbs Islands
Framnes Mts
Mawson (Aust.)
Holme Bay
Nilsen Bay
Cape Fletcher
Mawson Coast
Shallow B.
Pt Williams
Lars Christensen Coast
Cape Darnley
Fram Bank
Mac. Robertson Land
Prince Charles Mts
Fisher Glacier
Collins Glacier
Mellor Glacier
Lambert Glacier
Mawson Escarpment
Amery Ice Shelf
Gillock I.
MacKenzie Bay
Zhongshan (China)
Davis (Aust.)
Vestfold Hills
Ingrid Christensen Coast
American Highland
Princess Elizabeth Land
Barrier Bay
West Ice Shelf
Leopold and Astrid Coast
Posadowsky Bay
Wilhelm II Coast
Wilhelm II Land
Davis Sea
C. Filchner
McDonald B.
Mirny (Rus.)
Drygalski I.
Queen Mary Coast
Denman Glacier
Scott Glacier
Shackleton Ice Shelf
Mill I.
Bowman I.
Knox Coast
Cape Peremennyy
Casey (Aust.)
Vincennes Bay
Cape Folger
Budd Coast
Law Dome
Cape Poinsett
Petersen Bank
Williamson Glacier
Sabrina Coast
Moscow Univ. Ice Shelf
Banzare Coast
Porpoise Bay
Sandford Glacier
Clarie Coast
Adélie Coast
Dumont d'Urville (Fr.)
Dumont d'Urville Sea
French claim
Australian claim
George V Coast
Ninnis Glacier Tongue
Mertz Glacier Tongue
Commonwealth Bay
Cape Hudson
Cook Ice Shelf
Oates Coast
Wilson Hills
Anchor Pt
Balleny Islands
Sturge Island
Buckle Island
Young Island
Balleny Seamounts
Adare Seamounts
Rennick Trough
Wilkes Land
Talos Dome
Dome Charlie
Concordia Station (Fr. & It.)
South Magnetic Pole
South Geomagnetic Pole
Vostok (Rus.)
L. Vostok
Dome Argus
Valkyrie Dome
EAST ANTARCTICA
South Pole
Amundsen-Scott (USA)
Titan Dome
TRANSANTARCTIC MTS
Queen Alexandra Range
Queen Elizabeth Mts
Churchill Mts
Shackleton Inlet
Cape May
Beaumont Bay
Hillary Coast
Moore Embayment
Royal Society Ra.
Minna Bluff
(NZ) Scott Base
(U.S.A.) McMurdo
Mt Erebus 3794
Ross I.
Granite Harbor
Allan Hills
Victoria Land
Franklin Shoals
Franklin I.
Drygalski Ice Tongue
Terra Nova Bay
Crary Bank
Cape Washington
Drygalski Basin
Wood Bay
Lady Newnes Bay
Mawson Bank
Coulman I.
Borchgrevink Coast
Admiralty Mts
Pennell Coast
Cape Adare
Robertson Bay
Usarp Mts
Roberts Butte 2828
Lillie Glacier
Anare Mts
Yule Bay
Cape North
SOUTHERN OCEAN
ENDERBY ABYSSAL PLAIN
Valdivia Abyssal Plain
Elan Bank
Banzare Bank
Kerguelen Plateau
Heard I.
AUSTRALIAN-ANTARCTIC BASIN
SOUTH INDIAN BASIN
Meters
Feet
0
LAND BELOW SEA LEVEL
100
328
200
656
1000
3281
2000
6562
4000
13123
6000
19685

North America

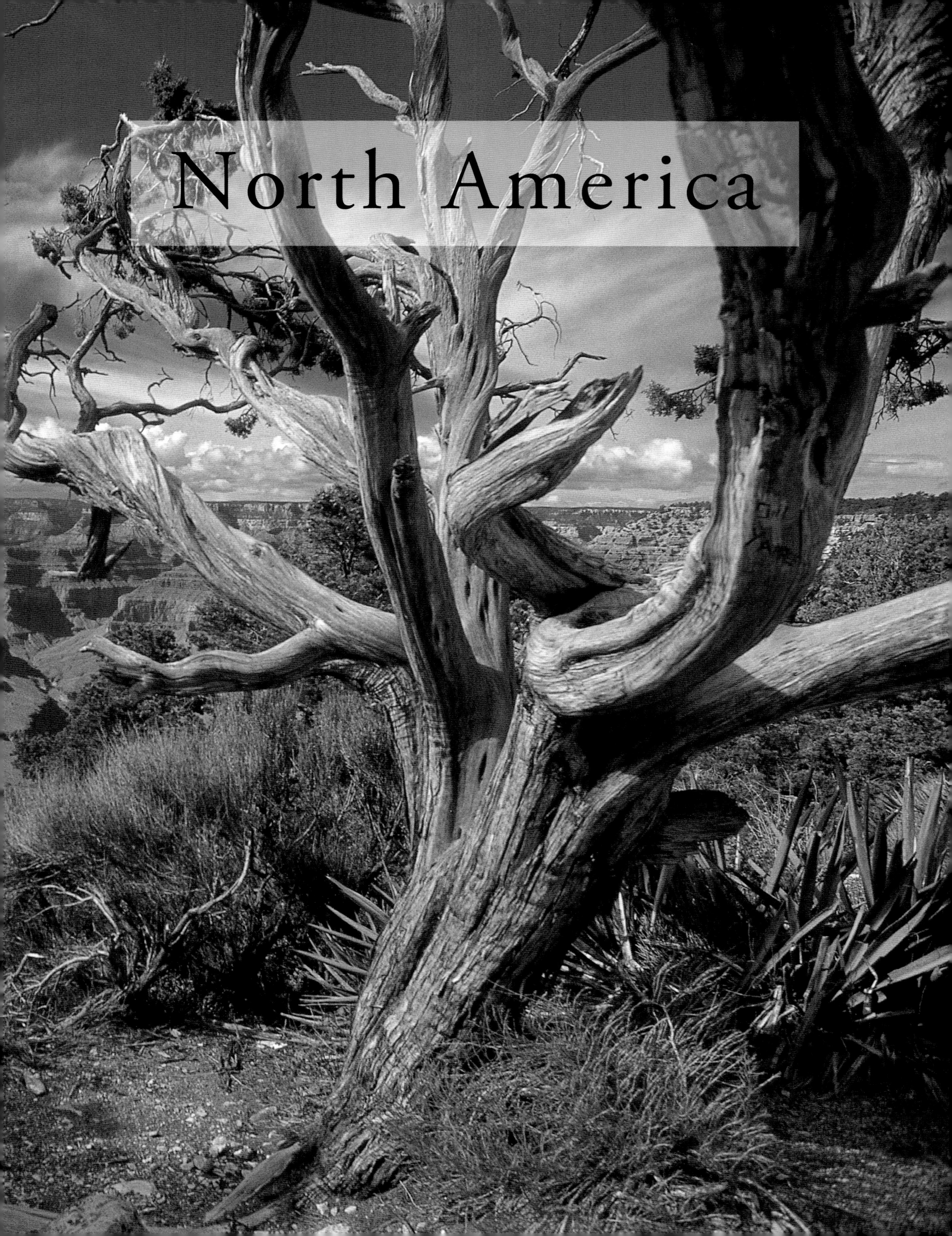

NORTHERN AMERICA

Northern America consists of the United States of America and Canada (Greenland, St Pierre and Miquelon, and Bermuda are also included in this region), and covers an area of 21,977,681 square kilometers (8,485,613 square miles). The continent contains the second- (Canada) and the third- (USA) largest countries in the world, as measured by size. Greenland, at 2,175,600 square kilometers (840,000 square miles), is the world's largest island, and is more than twice the area of the next-largest island, New Guinea.

Previous pages The plateaus and basins of the Colorado Plateau of southwestern USA have been deeply eroded by water over millions of years, forming many steep-walled canyons. The Grand Canyon is 1,828 meters (6,000 feet) deep at its deepest point.

Right Declared the national symbol of the USA in 1782, the bald eagle *(Haliaeetus leucocephalus)* is the only species of eagle endemic to North America. Its range extends across the breadth of Canada and the United States.

Below Boasting one of the most famous skylines in the world, New York City—known as "The Big Apple" and "the city that never sleeps"—attracts millions of domestic and international visitors every year.

The most northerly point is Kap Morris Jesup, 83°N, in Greenland, while Dry Tortuga Island, Florida, 24°N, is the furthest south. The most easterly inhabited location is Nord, Greenland, and the most westerly inhabited point is Attu Island, in the Aleutian Islands, off Alaska.

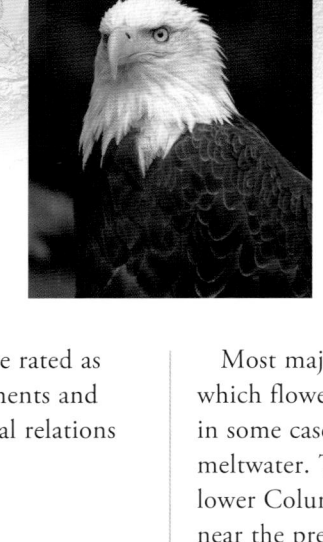

Political Geography

North America's political geographical components are the USA and Canada, while Greenland (Kalaallit Nunaat) is an integral, but self-governing, part of Denmark, Bermuda is a self-governing overseas territory of Great Britain, and St Pierre and Miquelon is a self-governing overseas collectivity of France. The USA and Canada are rated as strong democracies with very stable governments and have experienced generally good international relations for more than 150 years.

Physical Geography

The physical geography of North America is quite spectacular. Within US territory can be found both its highest point, Mt McKinley, in Denali National Park, Alaska, at 6,198 meters (20,335 feet), and its lowest elevation, Badwater, –86 meters (–282 feet), at Death Valley National Park, California. Both features were produced by tectonic forces, working positively and negatively, through which faulting generated upthrust areas for mountains and downthrown sections for very deep valleys. McKinley is a granitic intrusion, and Badwater is a graben (rift valley). Within 129 kilometers (80 miles) of Badwater is Mt Whitney, which at 4,418 meters (14,494 feet) is the highest elevation in the USA outside Alaska.

Canada's highest peak is Mt Logan, which at 5,951 meters (19,524 feet) is part of the St Elias Mountains located in the southwestern corner of the Yukon Territory.

Most major valleys were cut by the rivers which flowed through them, supplemented, in some cases, by massive volumes of glacial meltwater. This is what occurred with the lower Columbia River when a glacial dam near the present-day city of Missoula, Montana, burst some 15,000 years ago and produced what was probably the largest flood in prehistory. The Channeled Scablands topography of eastern Washington State is an example of the impact of that epic flash flood. Glacial meltwaters sculpted parts of the valleys of the upper Mississippi River system and the St Lawrence watershed as well.

Much of Greenland is covered by the world's second-largest ice sheet. The island's extensive glaciers provide a laboratory for the study of glacial processes, in particular how continental-size glaciers may have functioned. Greenland's ice sheet expanded considerably during the Pleistocene Epoch, engulfing the entire island as, worldwide, the sea level declined because of glacier development on land. Most of Canada and much of the northern USA were also glaciated during the Pleistocene Epoch, which concluded with lower elevation ice melting away between 10000 and 8000 BCE. As many as 18 advances and retreats of the continental glaciers occurred during the past one million years, transforming the areas over which the ice passed through erosion and deposits.

COUNTRIES	OFFICIAL NAME	AREA	POPULATION	CAPITAL	RELIGION	POPULATION DENSITY	HIGHEST POINT	CURRENCY
Canada	Canada	9,984,670 km²/3,855,103 mi²	33,487,000	Ottawa	✝76.6, ☪2%, ✡1.1%, ☸1%, ॐ1%, ☬0.9%, ○17.4%	3.4/km², 8.7/mi²	Mt Logan 5,959 m/19,551 ft	Dollar
United States of America	United States of America	9,826,630 km²/3,794,066 mi²	307,212,000	Washington DC	✝76%, ○24%	31/km², 81/mi²	Mt McKinley 6,198 m/20,335 ft	Dollar

DEPENDENCIES AND TERRITORIES	OFFICIAL NAME	AREA	POPULATION	CAPITAL	RELIGION	POPULATION DENSITY	HIGHEST POINT	CURRENCY
Greenland (Denmark)	Greenland (Kalaallit Nunaat)	2,166,086 km²/836,330 mi²	58,000	Nuuk (Godthåb)	✝97%, ○3%	0.027/km², 0.069/mi²	Gunnbjorn 3,700 m/12,139 ft	Krone
St Pierre and Miquelon (France)	Collectivité territoriale de Saint-Pierre-et-Miquelon	241 km²/93 mi²	7,000	Saint-Pierre	✝99%, ○1%	29/km²,75/mi²	Morne de la Grande Montagne 240 m/787 ft	Euro
Bermuda (UK)	Bermuda	54 km²/21 mi²	68,000	Hamilton	✝67%, ○33%	1,259/km², 3,238/mi²	Town Hill 76 m/249 ft	Dollar

Thousands of square kilometers across the region owe their appearance to the effects of this glacial visitation. Source areas for the main North American glaciations in Canada were located on the Ungava Plateau in northern Quebec and on the western side of Hudson Bay.

Bermuda is a chain of about 140 islands, the highest parts of an underwater volcano seamount. St Pierre and Miquelon is an archipelago of 8 small rocky islands.

Rivers and Lakes

Several of the world's longer or larger rivers in terms of discharge flow across the region; these are the Missouri–Mississippi system (the world's fourth-longest river, after the Nile, the Amazon, and the Yangtze), the Yukon, the Mackenzie, the Columbia, and the St Lawrence rivers. The Missouri–Mississippi River network is the largest in North America, draining all or parts of 32 American states and two Canadian provinces. Its total length is 6,019 kilometers (3,740 miles).

The world's largest surface resource of fresh water is found in the Great Lakes, shared between Canada and the USA with the exception of Lake Michigan, which is entirely within the USA. Total volume of the five lakes is 22,800 cubic kilometers (5,472 cubic miles), which is

Below Most of Canada was covered by ice 10,000–20,000 years ago. British Columbia's Green Lake is so named for the color of its water. Minerals contained in glacial meltwater encourage the growth of the algae that creates this attractive verdant hue.

about one-fifth, or 22 percent, of all of the world's accessible fresh water. Northwestern Canada is the location of additional huge freshwater bodies such as Lake Winnipeg, Great Slave Lake, and Great Bear Lake. Great Slave Lake in Northwest Territories is the deepest lake in North America at 614 meters (2,015 feet). It is followed by Crater Lake, Oregon, at 589 meters (1,932 feet), and Lake Chelan, Washington, at 489 meters (1,605 feet). A volcanic caldera eruption and subsequent collapse formed the basin of Crater Lake, whereas Chelan's basin was carved out by valley glacier action.

Mountains and Lowlands

The geological spine of the region is the Rocky Mountain system, which traverses western sectors of both Canada and the USA, with outliers of the Mackenzie and Yukon mountains in the far north of Canada, and the Brooks and Alaska ranges in Alaska. The highest elevation of the Rockies on the US side is Mt Elbert in Colorado at 4,399 meters (14,433 feet). On the Canadian side, Mt Robson in British Columbia is the highest point, at 3,954 meters (12,972 feet). Other major mountain ranges include the Cascades, running from northern California to southern British Columbia, and the Appalachians, which extend from southeastern USA into eastern Canada. Active volcanism occurs in the Cascades, with volcanoes situated in California, Oregon, Washington, and British Columbia. Volcanoes also occur in southern and southwestern Alaska on the mainland and in the Aleutian Island chain. The eruption of Mt St

Below right The iconic Golden Gate Bridge—one of the longest suspension bridges in the world—spans San Francisco Bay. Measuring 2.7 kilometers (1.7 miles) long, the bridge links San Francisco to Marin County.

Right Greenland is geographically part of Northern America, although politically the island is included in the Kingdom of Denmark. Most of the island's population lives in the ice-free coastal areas.

Below New York City, with more than 8 million residents, is the most highly populated city in the United States. This color-enhanced satellite image shows the island of Manhattan, Staten Island, and Long Island.

Helens, Washington, in 1980 was the most recent activity in the coterminous USA. Alaskan outbursts have been much more recent. Sited within Yellowstone National Park, Wyoming, is a huge caldera, the result of volcanic explosive activity several hundred thousand years ago. The area remains volcanically and seismically active.

The Canadian Shield—a significant lowland—forms the geologic and geographical core of North America. It covers an extensive area of eastern and central Canada with outliers in the adjacent USA. The Shield is a conglomeration of ancient, Precambrian, metamorphic, and igneous rocks that have been geologically quiescent for a considerable period of time. Many valuable minerals, ranging from iron ore and copper to diamonds, occur in Canadian Shield rocks. Superimposed over part of the Shield is Hudson Bay, which extends the world ocean deeply into the region. It ranks as the eleventh-largest of the world's seas, gulfs, and bays, occupying some 1,239,000 square kilometers (475,000 square miles). The Hudson Bay area is undergoing a process called isostatic rebound. The tremendous volume of ice that covered the area and depressed the Earth's crust is now melting. With this immense weight now dispersed, the land is readjusting itself, or rebounding, and large swathes of formerly submerged terrain are now above sea level.

Historical and Human Geography

Many pre-historians, anthropologists, and researchers hold that immigrants from two sources first populated North America: Asia and Europe. Some early people may have traversed Beringia, the Bering Strait land bridge, but it is believed that others arrived by coasting—traveling by sea, mostly within sight of land. Many native peoples assert, however, that their ancestors have always been here. These earliest or first peoples became paleo- or proto-Indians—later to be called Native Americans or First Nations—and occupied the land for thousands of years before the arrival of the first Europeans, the Norsemen, who landed at L'Anse aux Meadows, Newfoundland, about 1000 CE. Their tenure was brief. Several centuries later, fishermen from European countries crossed the Atlantic to seek more productive waters and established shore stations, making contact with the native inhabitants. Later, during the 1600s and 1700s, European explorers sponsored by governments or merchant associations came from Spain, England, France, Russia, and other countries. European colonizers aggressively claimed, settled, and developed North American landscapes.

The USA gained its independence from Britain in 1783, and the Dominion of Canada was founded in 1867 through less violent means—the passing of the British Parliament's Act of Union. During the nineteenth century, great multitudes of European immigrants settled in the USA and Canada. These groups were supplemented with lesser migrant streams from Asia, Latin America, and other regions.

Economic and Urban Geography

The USA, with an estimated population of 307 million people, represents the world's largest economy in terms of gross domestic product, while Canada, with one-tenth of the US's population, at 33 million people, is America's largest trading partner.

Great cities have been built across the continent in both Canada and the USA. Canada's urban places encompass Quebec City, Montreal, Toronto, Winnipeg, Edmonton, Calgary, and Vancouver, among others. In the USA, major cities include New York City, Boston, Philadelphia, Pittsburgh, Chicago, Atlanta, Miami, Houston, San Antonio, St Louis, Denver, Salt Lake City, San Francisco, Seattle, Los Angeles, and San Diego.

Above Consistently ranking highly among the "most liveable cities in the world," Vancouver is British Columbia's largest city, and host city of the 2010 Winter Olympics and Paralympics.

Left Bermuda is one of the Atlantic's most popular sailing centers, and the large number of private yachts reflect the thriving economy, based on financial services for international business, and tourism.

Above The wheat belt region of North America extends from the Prairie provinces of Canada through central USA. The two countries are among the top wheat producers in the world.

MIDDLE AMERICA

Middle America extends from the United States of Mexico in the north, through six other countries to Panama in the south, and also encompasses the islands of the Caribbean. Mainland Middle America occupies 2,496,335 square kilometers (963,839 square miles)—about 11 percent of the area of the USA and Canada combined. At 2,753,000 square kilometers (1,063,000 square miles), the Caribbean Sea stretches over an area about one-third the size of Canada.

MAINLAND MIDDLE AMERICA

Eight countries make up the region of mainland Middle America, with Mexico being the largest in area and population (110 million people). The smallest in area is El Salvador, while Belize has the lowest population at 308,000. Middle American countries have been independent since the 1820s, when Spanish colonial rule was overthrown. However, their political paths have not been straightforward because of problems generated both internally—resulting in coups and revolutions—and by outside forces, such as US interventions.

Above The keel-billed toucan *(Ramphastos sulfuratus)* is found throughout mainland Middle America, with a distribution range from southern Mexico to northern Colombia. This brightly colored toucan is the national bird of Belize.

Physical Geography

The mighty Rio Grande river marks much of the northern boundary of the region, while the Panama–Colombia border is its southern extremity. Mainland Middle America, besides being the connector between North and South America, has a fascinating physical geography that is marked by mountain ranges, deserts and rainforests, tropical lowlands and temperate highlands, all hemmed into a comparatively narrow area by the Atlantic and Pacific oceans. The region's highest elevations are volcanic peaks, and are located in central Mexico—Pico de Orizaba at 5,610 meters (18,406 feet); Volcán Popocatépetl at 5,465 meters (17,930 feet); and Iztaccíhuatl with a height of 5,230 meters (17,159 feet).

Because of Middle America's location in relation to the world-wide pattern of lithospheric or tectonic crustal plates, the region is subject to major earthquakes, volcanism, and seismic sea waves. Most of the region forms part of the North American Plate; the rest of the area is situated on the Caribbean Plate. In contact with both plates on their western margins is the Cocos Plate, consisting of oceanic crust that is being subducted beneath the other two plates. This tectonic plate movement results in seismic activity—the most destructive manifestation so far was the devastating Mexico City earthquake of 1985 measuring 8.1 on the Richter Scale—with a chain of volcanoes running from Mexico to Costa Rica, and an occasional tsunami striking the Pacific coasts of several of the countries.

Lake Nicaragua, the largest lake in Middle America, is found in Nicaragua, and measures 164 kilometers (102 miles) long, and 170 kilometers (230 feet) deep, with an area of 8,400 square kilometers (3,200 square miles). It feeds the San Juan River, which empties into the Caribbean Sea. Since the topography in the vicinity is relatively low, the river and lake corridor has recently been considered as a possible site for a second canal to link the Atlantic and Pacific oceans.

Middle American countries are also known for their tropical revolving storms—hurricanes—which develop over both the western Atlantic and eastern Pacific oceans. Atlantic storms track across the Caribbean Sea and often strike the eastern coast of Middle America; Pacific Ocean hurricanes begin southwest of Mexico and track north and east to devastate northwestern Mexican coastal regions.

Economic Geography—Panama Canal

Perhaps the most significant change to occur in the entire region's geography, since the arrival of Europeans, has been the construction of the Panama Canal. The Isthmus of Panama is the shortest distance between the world's two greatest oceans; in addition, the continental divide has the lowest elevation. The canal was completed in 1914 by the US government after a French company failed in its attempt to connect the oceans.

Panama was a province of Colombia, and a separatist movement declared Panama independent in November 1903. Colombia tried to retain Panama as a province but the USA, quickly followed by France and other European countries, recognized the country's independence,

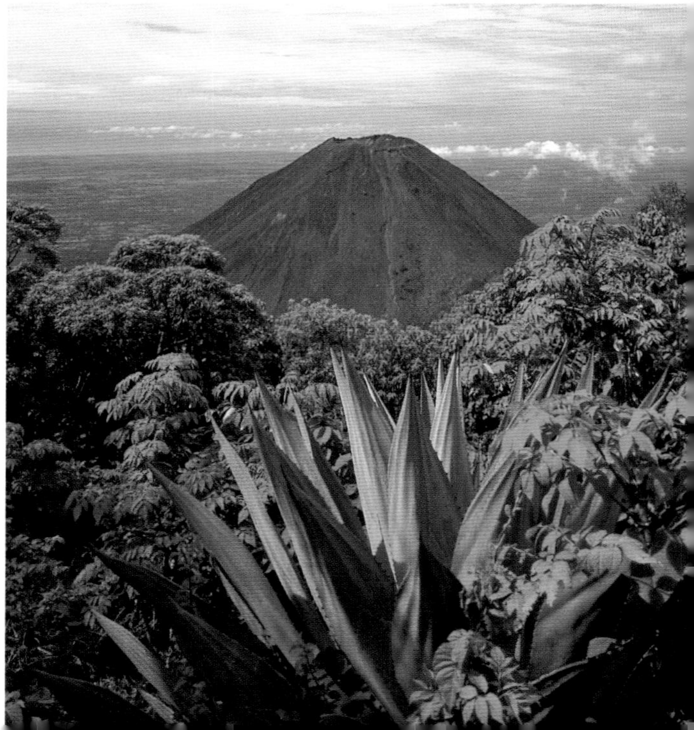

COUNTRIES	OFFICIAL NAME	AREA	POPULATION	CAPITAL	RELIGION	POPULATION DENSITY	HIGHEST POINT	CURRENCY
Antigua and Barbuda	Antigua and Barbuda	441 km^2/170 mi^2	86,000	St John's	✝92.2%, ○7.8%	195/km^2, 506/mi^2	Boggy Peak 402 m/1,319 ft	Dollar
Bahamas	Commonwealth of The Bahamas	10,070 km^2/3,888 mi^2	309,000	Nassau	✝96.3%, ○3.7%	31/km^2, 79/mi^2	Mt Alvernia 63 m/207 ft	Dollar
Barbados	Barbados	431 km^2/166 mi^2	284,000	Bridgetown	✝71%, ○29%	659/km^2, 1,711/mi^2	Mt Hillaby 336 m/1,102 ft	Dollar
Belize	Belize	22,966 km^2/8,867 mi^2	308,000	Belmopan	✝76.6%, ○23.4%	13/km^2, 35/mi^2	Doyle's Delight 1,160 m/3,806 ft	Dollar
Costa Rica	República de Costa Rica	50,660 km^2/19,560 mi^2	4,254,000	San José	✝90%, ○10%	84/km^2, 217/mi^2	Cerro Chirripó 3,810 m/12,500 ft	Colón
Cuba	República de Cuba	110,860 km^2/42,803 mi^2	11,452,000	Havana (La Habana)	✝85%, ○15%	103/km^2, 268/mi^2	Pico Turquino 2,005 m/6,578 ft	Peso
Dominica	Commonwealth of Dominica	754 km^2/291 mi^2	73,000	Roseau	✝92.3%, ○7.7%	97/km^2, 251/mi^2	Morne Diablotins 1,447 m/4,747 ft	Dollar
Dominican Republic	República Dominicana	48,380 km^2/18,680 mi^2	9,650,000	Santo Domingo	✝95%, ○5%	199/km^2, 517/mi^2	Pico Duarte 3,175 m/10,417 ft	Peso
El Salvador	República de El Salvador	21,040 km^2/8,124 mi^2	7,185,000	San Salvador	✝78%, ○22%	342/km^2, 884/mi^2	Cerro El Pital 2,730 m/8,957 ft	US dollar
Grenada	Grenada	344 km^2/133 mi^2	91,000	St George's	✝100%	264/km^2, 684/mi^2	Mt St Catherine 840 m/2,756 ft	Dollar
Guatemala	República de Guatemala	109,117 km^2/42,139 mi^2	13,276,000	Guatemala City	✝85%, 🚶15%	122/km^2, 315/mi^2	Volcán Tajamulco 4,211 m/13,816 ft	Quetzal
Haiti	République d'Haïti; Repiblik d'Ayiti	27,560 km^2/10,641 mi^2	9,035,000	Port-au-Prince	✝100%	328/km^2, 849/mi^2	Chaîne de la Selle 2,680 m/8,793 ft	Gourde
Honduras	República de Honduras	111,890 km^2/43,201mi^2	7,793,000	Tegucigalpa	✝100%	70/km^2, 180/mi^2	Cerro Las Minas 2,870 m/9,416 ft	Lempira
Jamaica	Jamaica	10,831 km^2/4,182 mi^2	2,826,000	Kingston	✝65.1%, ○34.9%	261/km^2, 676/mi^2	Blue Mountain Peak 2,256 m/7,402 ft	Dollar
Mexico	Estados Unidos Mexicanos	1,972,550 km^2/761,606 mi^2	111,212,000	Mexico City	✝84%, ○16%	56/km^2, 146/mi^2	Volcán Pico de Orizaba 5,610 m/18,406 ft	Peso
Nicaragua	República de Nicaragua	120,254 km^2/46,430 mi^2	5,891,000	Managua	✝100%	49/km^2, 127/mi^2	Pico Mogatón 2,438 m/7,999 ft	Córdoba
Panama	República de Panamá	75,990 km^2/29,340 mi^2	3,360,000	Panama City	✝100%	44/km^2, 115/mi^2	Volcán Barú 3,475 m/11,400 ft	Balboa/ US dollar
St Kitts and Nevis	Federation of Saint Kitts and Nevis	261 km^2/101 mi^2	40,000	Basseterre	✝100%	153/km^2, 397/mi^2	Mt Liamuiga 1,156 m/3,792 ft	Dollar
St Lucia	Saint Lucia	606 km^2/234 mi^2	160,000	Castries	✝90.8%, ○9.2%	264/km^2, 684/mi^2	Mt Gimie 950 m/3,117 ft	Dollar
St Vincent and the Grenadines	Saint Vincent and the Grenadines	389 km^2/150 mi^2	104,000	Kingstown	✝88%, ○12%	268/km^2, 693/mi^2	La Soufrière 1,234 m/4,049 ft	Dollar
Trinidad and Tobago	Republic of Trinidad and Tobago	5,128 km^2/1,980 mi^2	1,230,000	Port-of-Spain	✝57.6%, ॐ22.5%, ☪5.8%, ○14.1%	240/km^2, 621/mi^2	El Cerro del Aripo 940 m/3,084 ft	Dollar

DEPENDENCIES AND TERRITORIES	OFFICIAL NAME	AREA	POPULATION	CAPITAL	RELIGION	POPULATION DENSITY	HIGHEST POINT	CURRENCY
Anguilla (UK)	Anguilla	102 km^2/39 mi^2	14,000	The Valley	✝90.5%, ○9.5%	137/km^2, 359/mi^2	Crocus Hill 65 m/3,213 ft	Dollar
Aruba (Netherlands)	Aruba	193 km^2/75 mi^2	103,000	Oranjestad	✝90.1%, ✡0.2%, ○9.7%	534/km^2, 1,374/mi^2	Mt Jamanota 188 m/617 ft	Guilder/ florin
British Virgin Islands (UK)	British Virgin Islands	153 km^2/59 mi^2	24,000	Road Town	✝96%, ○4%	157/km^2, 407/mi^2	Mt Sage 521 m/1,709 ft	Dollar
Cayman Islands (UK)	Cayman Islands	262 km^2/100 mi^2	49,000	George Town	✝79.4%, ○20.6%	187/km^2, 490/mi^2	The Bluff 43 m/141 ft	Dollar
Guadeloupe (France)	Département de la Guadeloupe	1,629 km^2/629 mi^2	453,000	Basse-Terre	✝96%, ॐ4%	278/km^2, 720/mi^2	Soufrière 1,484 m/4,869 ft	Euro
Martinique (France)	Département de la Martinique	1,128 km^2/ 436 mi^2	398,000	Fort-de-France	✝95%, ॐ5%	353/km^2, 913/mi^2	Montagne Pelée 1,397 m/4,583 ft	Euro
Montserrat (UK)	Montserrat	102 km^2/39 mi^2	5,000	Brades	✝100%	49/km^2, 128/mi^2	English's Crater 930 m/3,051 ft	Dollar
Navassa Island (USA)	Navassa Island	5.4 km^2/2 mi^2	None	—	—	—	77 m/253 ft	—
Netherlands Antilles (Netherlands)	Nederlandse Antillen	960 km^2/371 mi^2	227,000	Willemstad	✝92.3%, ✡1.3%, ○6.4%	237/km^2, 612/mi^2	Mt Scenery 862 m/2828 ft	Guilder
Puerto Rico (USA)	Commonwealth of Puerto Rico	8,870 km^2/3,425 mi^2	3,971,000	San Juan	✝85%, ○15%	448/km^2, 1,159/mi^2	Cerro de Punta 1,339 m/4,393 ft	Dollar
St Barthélemy (France)	Collectivité d'Outre-Mer de Saint-Barthélemy	21 km^2/8 mi^2	7,000	Gustavia	✝100%	333/km^2, 875/mi^2	Morne du Vitet 286 m/938 ft	Euro
St Martin (France)	Collectivité d'Outre-Mer de Saint-Martin	54.4 km^2/21 mi^2	30,000	Marigot	✝95%, ॐ6%	551/km^2, 1,428/mi^2	Pic du Paradis 424 m/1,391 ft	Euro
Turks and Caicos Islands (UK)	Turks and Caicos Islands	430 km^2/267 mi^2	23,000	Grand Turk (Cockburn Town)	✝86%, ○14%	53/km^2, 86/mi^2	Blue Hills 49 m/161 ft	Dollar
US Virgin Islands (USA)	United States Virgin Islands	346 km^2/134 mi^2	110,000	Charlotte Amalie	✝93%, ○7%	317/km^2, 821/mi^2	Crown Mountain 475 m/1,558 ft	Dollar

Left Following its birth in 1770, El Salvador's Izalco volcano experienced regular eruptions for over 200 years. For this reason, it became known as the "Lighthouse of the Pacific," its glowing Strombolian eruptions acting as a beacon to seafarers up until the mid-1960s, when activity declined.

PEPSI

Right A roadside stall selling fresh produce in Tegucigalpa (meaning "silver mountain"). Founded by the Spanish in 1578, the city—a center for gold and silver mining—became the official capital of Honduras in 1880.

Below Barbados exhibits a mix of influences—from Spanish and English to buccaneer—blended with local culture. Built in 1743, the stately architecture of Codrington College in St John is a fine example of the English architectural style of the times.

and supported it against Colombia. In the same month Panama and the USA signed a treaty to begin work on the canal. The 82-kilometer- (51-mile-) long canal, with its three sets of navigation locks, was extremely well designed and has operated almost flawlessly since it opened. It reduces the sea route between the Atlantic and Pacific oceans by 13,500 kilometers (8,000 miles), compared with circumnavigating South America. The current decade has seen Panama's approval for construction of a second canal to handle ships that are too large for the original and to cope with increased global maritime traffic.

CARIBBEAN MIDDLE AMERICA

The Caribbean sub-region of Middle America consists of the islands in the Caribbean Sea, a western extension of the North Atlantic Ocean. The region may be divided into the larger islands, the Greater Antilles, from Puerto Rico westward to Cuba, and the island arc of the Lesser Antilles, to the east and south of Puerto Rico. The Bahamas, although located north of the Caribbean Sea, are usually linked to the region because of cultural ties.

Historical Perspective

Discovery by Europeans of the Caribbean region was made by Christopher Columbus in 1492. Spanish colonization started with his second voyage in 1493, on the island of Hispaniola, at Santo Domingo, and proceeded from island to island. Other European powers quickly became interested in the region, and colonial holdings were established. This has led to a variegated cultural mosaic comprised of the indigenous "Indios," the imported African slaves, and the European colonists.

Today, the Caribbean islands are a conglomeration of independent countries; various dependencies of European states; and Puerto Rico, which is an unincorporated, organized territory of the USA. Approximately 38.5 million people reside within the various jurisdictions of the Caribbean region.

Physical Geography

The Caribbean's physical geography is highly varied; the latitudinal extent ranges from 10°N. to 23°N. Volcanic peaks, tropical rainforests, white sandy beaches, extensive coral reefs, low-lying limestone islands, and many other features are found within the region. The highest elevation is Pico Duarte, at 3,187 meters (10,417 feet), in the Cordillera Central of the Dominican Republic. The next four highest of the Caribbean regional summits are also on the island of Hispaniola. The deepest point in the Caribbean Sea is the Cayman Trench, south of the Cayman Islands, at 7,686 meters (25,216 feet).

A large part of the Caribbean region, with the notable exception of the island of Cuba, is located on the Caribbean Plate. Much of its oceanic crust is being subducted, drawn down under the South American Plate, causing both earthquake and volcanic activity along the plate's eastern margin. A volcanic eruption of Mount Pelée on the island of Martinique in 1902 generated a special type of pyroclastic flow, a nuée ardente—a glowing gas cloud that engulfed the city of Saint-Pierre, killing more than 29,000 people in a few minutes.

In addition, the Caribbean is well known for its tropical revolving storms—hurricanes—which have tracked

across the area for millennia causing untold loss of human life, and damaging the economies of the islands over which they pass. Typically, the hurricane season begins around June and concludes in November. Many of the hurricanes that have caused great havoc on the Middle and North American mainlands first crossed over islands in the Caribbean.

Economic Geography

The modern economic infrastructure of the Caribbean region, in terms of crops produced for subsistence and exportable commodities, is almost exclusively the result of the developments that occurred during the European colonial period. There is widespread dependence on prices set outside of the region for its produce—sugar and tropical fruits among others.

Only two basic items in the modern period have changed in the equation—the independence of many of the island states, and the rise of tourism. The economies of many of the countries and dependencies are increasingly tied to foreign tourists, especially Americans and Canadians, with a good representation of Europeans. The image of a tropical isle with a white sandy beach as an escape from twenty-first century life is appealing to many. The result has been an explosive increase in tourism in the region with both positive and negative impacts.

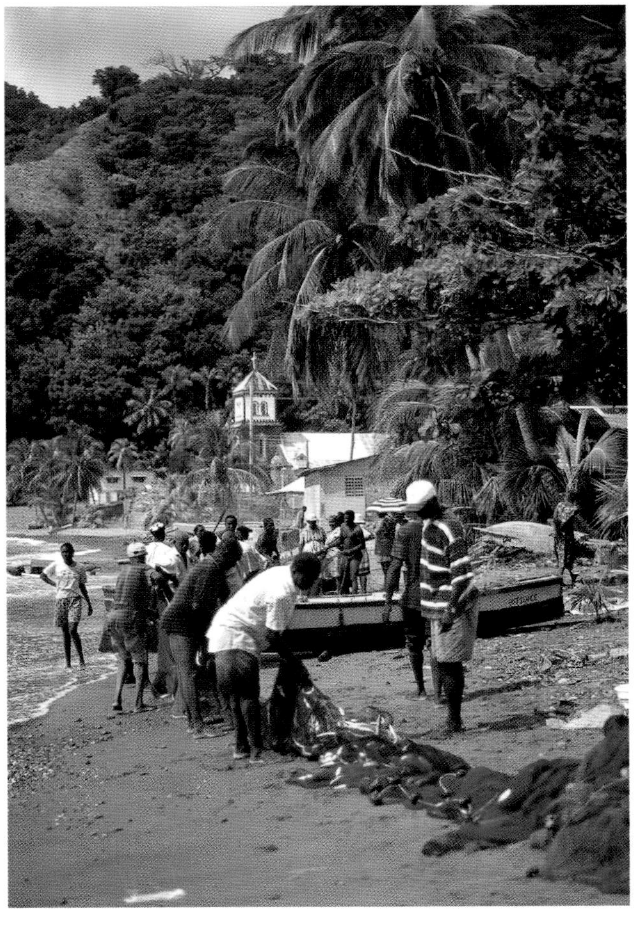

Above The principal islands of the US Virgin Islands are: St Thomas, St Croix, and St John. The capital—Charlotte Amalie, on St Thomas—is a popular Caribbean port-of-call for cruise ships.

Left Lying between Martinique and Guadeloupe, the volcanic island of Dominica offers a splendid venue for diving and fishing.

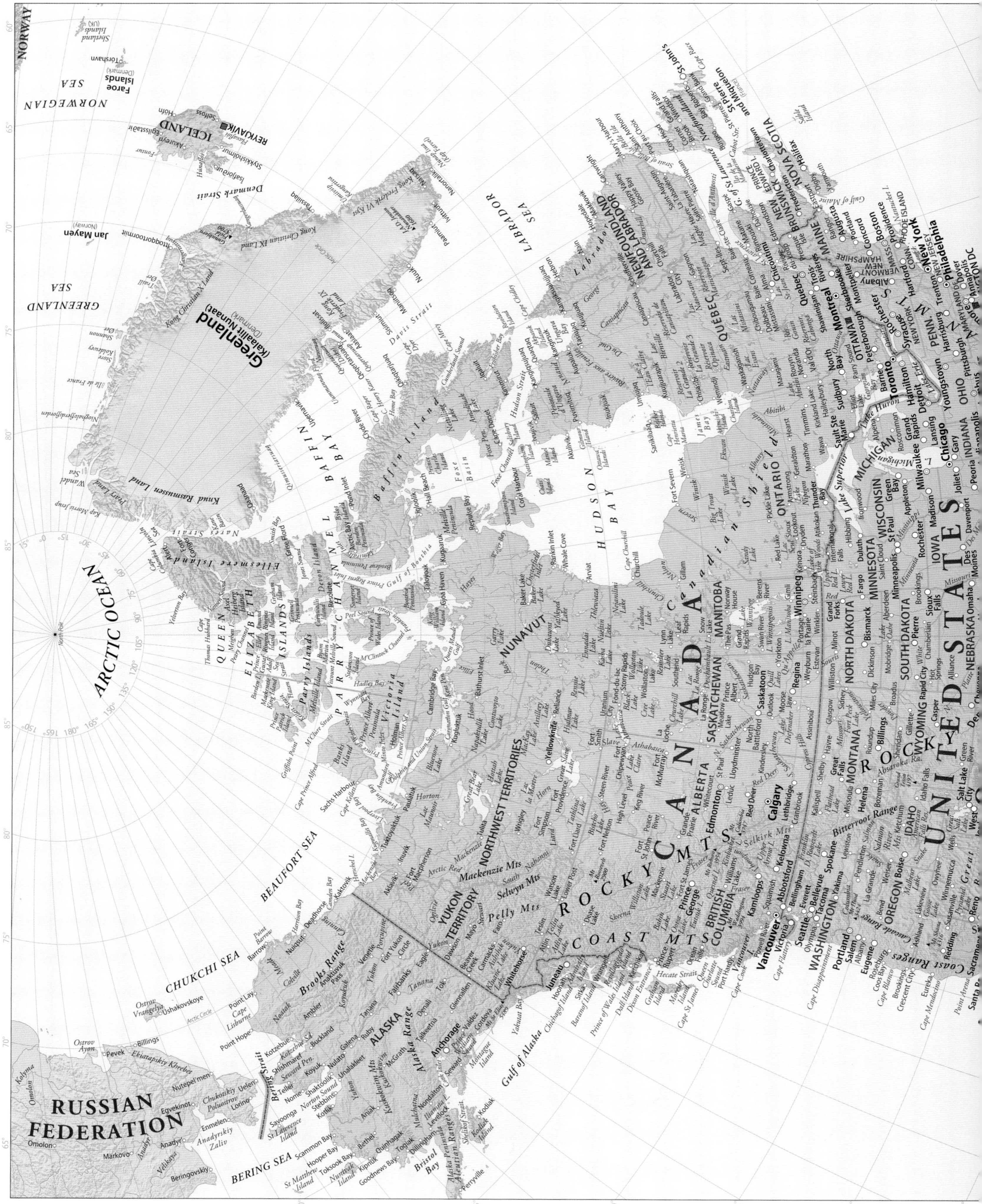
ARCTIC OCEAN
NORWEGIAN SEA
GREENLAND SEA
LABRADOR SEA
BAFFIN BAY
BEAUFORT SEA
CHUKCHI SEA
BERING SEA
HUDSON BAY
Gulf of Alaska
Greenland
(Kalaallit Nunaat)
(Denmark)
ICELAND
REYKJAVIK
Faroe Islands
(Denmark)
Jan Mayen
(Norway)
Shetland Islands
(UK)
NORWAY
RUSSIAN FEDERATION
CANADA
UNITED STATES
ALASKA
YUKON TERRITORY
NORTHWEST TERRITORIES
NUNAVUT
BRITISH COLUMBIA
ALBERTA
SASKATCHEWAN
MANITOBA
ONTARIO
QUEBEC
NEWFOUNDLAND AND LABRADOR
NEW BRUNSWICK
NOVA SCOTIA
PRINCE EDWARD I.
St Pierre and Miquelon
(France)
WASHINGTON
OREGON
IDAHO
MONTANA
WYOMING
NORTH DAKOTA
SOUTH DAKOTA
NEBRASKA
MINNESOTA
IOWA
WISCONSIN
MICHIGAN
INDIANA
OHIO
PENN.
NEW YORK
MAINE
ROCKY MTS
COAST MTS
Mackenzie Mts
Selwyn Mts
Pelly Mts
Brooks Range
Alaska Range
Baffin Island
Victoria Island
Ellesmere Island
Banks Island
QUEEN ELIZABETH ISLANDS
PARRY CHANNEL
Davis Strait
Denmark Strait
Bering Strait
Hudson Strait
Foxe Basin
Nares Strait
Canadian Shield
Lake Superior
Lake Huron
Lake Michigan
Great Bear Lake
Great Slave Lake
Anchorage
Fairbanks
Juneau
Whitehorse
Yellowknife
Vancouver
Victoria
Seattle
Portland
Edmonton
Calgary
Saskatoon
Regina
Winnipeg
Thunder Bay
Chicago
Detroit
Toronto
OTTAWA
Montreal
Quebec
Halifax
St John's
Boston
New York
Philadelphia
Churchill
Iqaluit
North Pole
Arctic Circle

1:25,300,000

Lambert Azimuthal Equal Area

0 250 500 750 1000 kilometers

0 125 250 375 500 miles

NORTH AMERICA POLITICAL

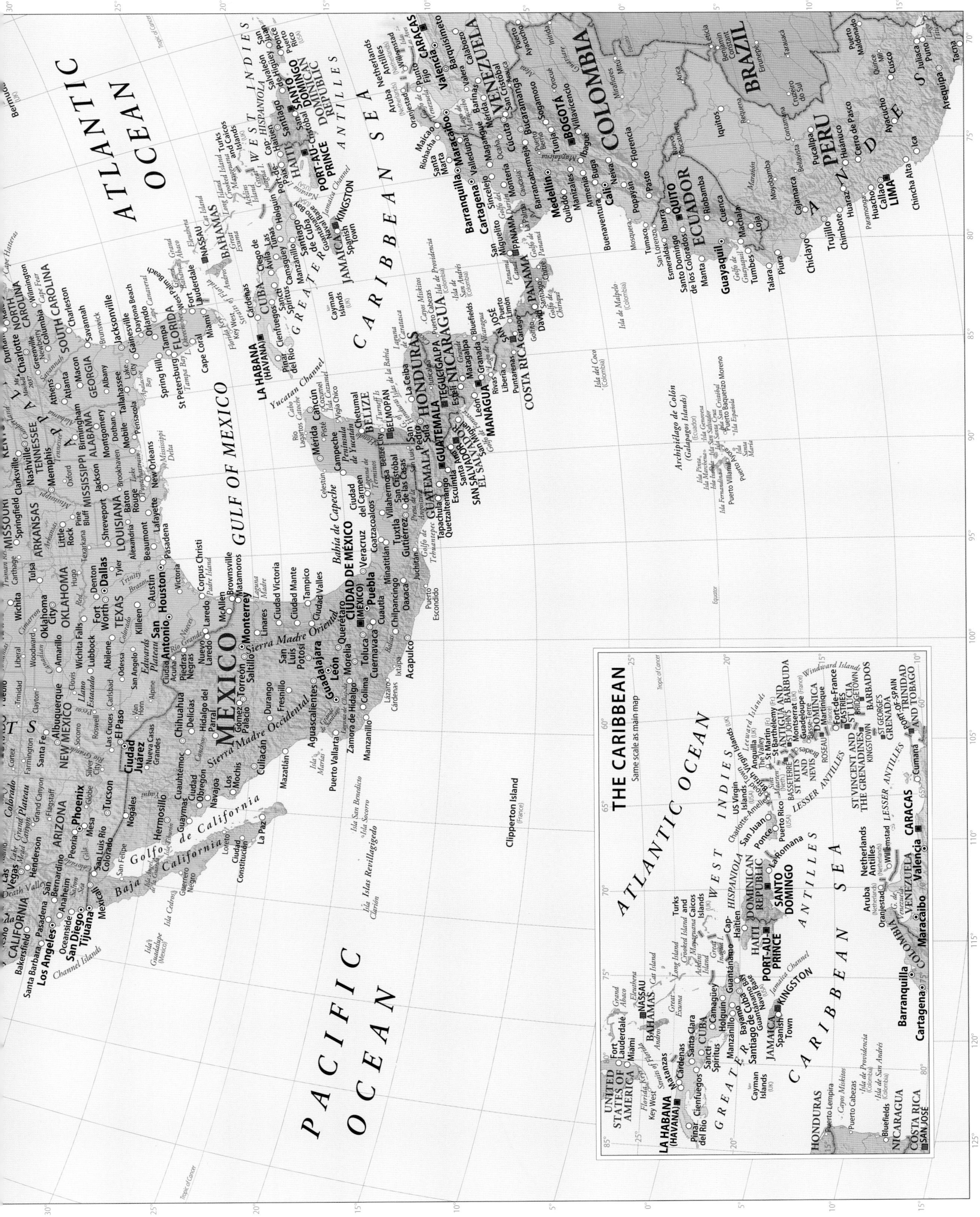

ATLANTIC OCEAN
PACIFIC OCEAN
GULF OF MEXICO
CARIBBEAN SEA
MEXICO
CIUDAD DE MÉXICO (MEXICO)
CUBA
LA HABANA (HAVANA)
BAHAMAS
NASSAU
JAMAICA
KINGSTON
HAITI
PORT-AU-PRINCE
DOMINICAN REPUBLIC
SANTO DOMINGO
BELIZE
BELMOPAN
GUATEMALA
HONDURAS
TEGUCIGALPA
EL SALVADOR
SAN SALVADOR
NICARAGUA
MANAGUA
COSTA RICA
SAN JOSÉ
PANAMA
COLOMBIA
BOGOTÁ
VENEZUELA
CARACAS
ECUADOR
QUITO
PERU
LIMA
BRAZIL
GREATER ANTILLES
WEST INDIES
THE CARIBBEAN
Same scale as main map
LESSER ANTILLES
Clipperton Island (France)
Archipiélago de Colón (Galapagos Islands) (Ecuador)

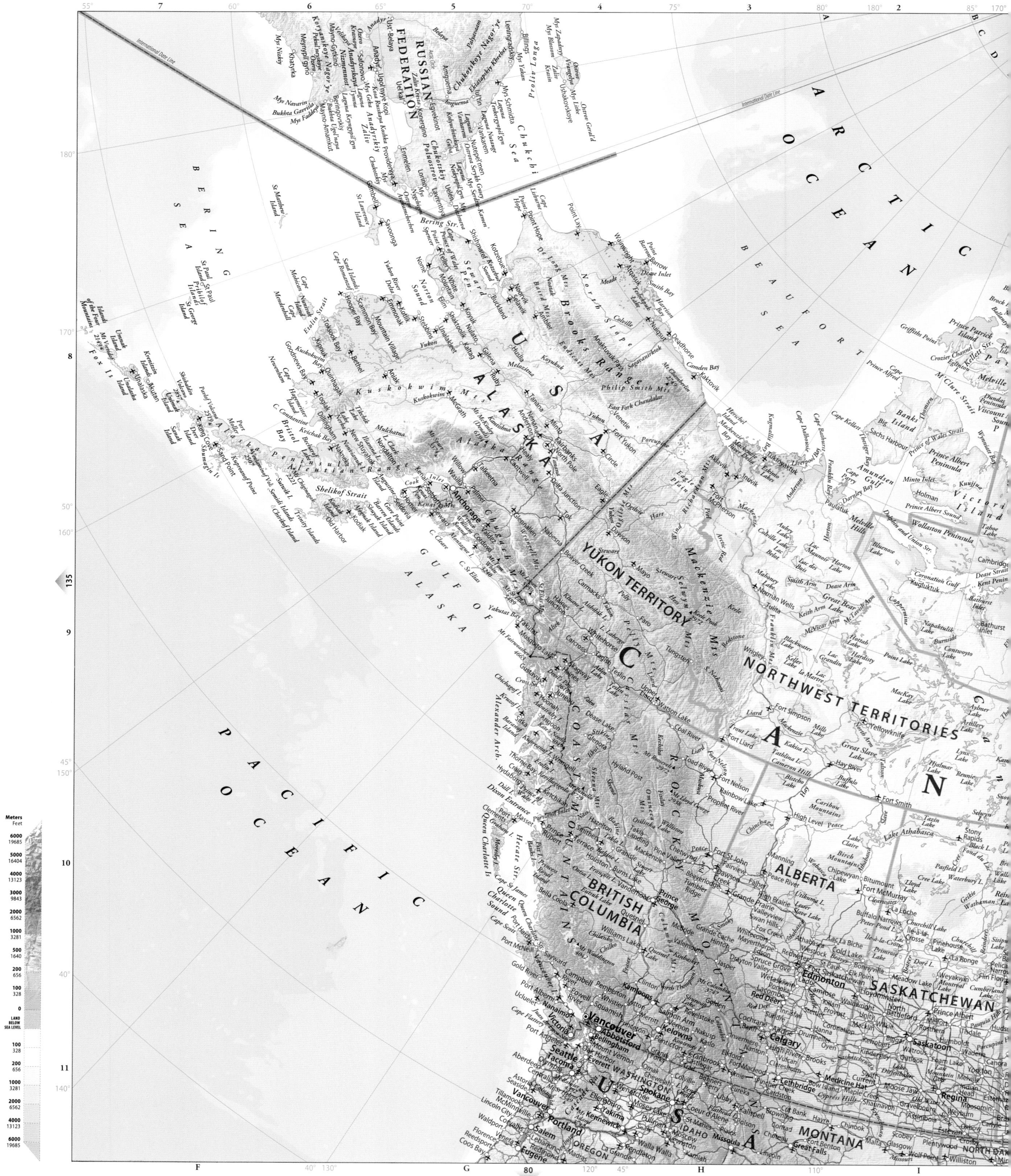
RUSSIAN FEDERATION
BERING SEA
ARCTIC OCEAN
BEAUFORT SEA
Chukchi Sea
U.S.A.
ALASKA
Brooks Range
Gulf of Alaska
PACIFIC OCEAN
YUKON TERRITORY
NORTHWEST TERRITORIES
CANADA
BRITISH COLUMBIA
ALBERTA
SASKATCHEWAN
WASHINGTON
OREGON
IDAHO
MONTANA
NORTH DAKOTA
Anchorage
Fairbanks
Whitehorse
Yellowknife
Edmonton
Calgary
Vancouver
Victoria
Seattle
Portland
Spokane
Saskatoon
Regina
Prince George
Kelowna
Kamloops
International Date Line
Meters
Feet
6000 19685
5000 16404
4000 13123
3000 9843
2000 6562
1000 3281
500 1640
200 656
100 328
0
LAND BELOW SEA LEVEL
100 328
200 656
1000 3281
2000 6562
4000 13123
6000 19685
135
80

1:15,950,000

Lambert Conic Conformal Projection

0 200 400 600 800 kilometers

0 100 200 300 400 miles

ALASKA, NORTHERN CANADA, and GREENLAND

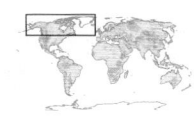

Greenland
(Kalaallit Nunaat)
(Denmark)
ICELAND
REYKJAVIK
GREENLAND SEA
NORWEGIAN SEA
Jan Mayen (Norway)
Faroe Islands (Denmark)
Tórshavn
Denmark Strait
BAFFIN BAY
Davis Strait
LABRADOR SEA
ATLANTIC OCEAN
HUDSON BAY
Hudson Strait
Foxe Basin
Foxe Channel
Baffin Island
Ellesmere Island
Devon Island
Bylot Island
Somerset Island
Prince of Wales Island
Southampton Island
Coats Island
Melville Peninsula
Boothia Peninsula
Gulf of Boothia
QUEEN ELIZABETH ISLANDS
Axel Heiberg Island
Lancaster Sd
Jones Sound
Lincoln Sea
Wandel Sea
Peary Land
Knud Rasmussen Land
Kong Christian X Land
Kong Christian IX Land
Kong Frederik VI Kyst
Kong Frederik VIII Land
Dronning Louise Land
Kong Wilhelm Land
Nuuk
Qaanaaq
Upernavik
Uummannaq
Sisimiut
Maniitsoq
Paamiut
Narsaq
Qaqortoq
Nanortalik
Tasiilaq
Ittoqqortoormiit
NUNAVUT
Iqaluit
Pond Inlet
Clyde River
Qikiqtarjuaq
Pangnirtung
Cape Dorset
Kimmirut
Igloolik
Hall Beach
Repulse Bay
Coral Harbour
Chesterfield Inlet
Rankin Inlet
Whale Cove
Arviat
Baker Lake
Gjoa Haven
Kugaaruk
Taloyoak
Resolute
Grise Fiord
Arctic Bay
NUNAVIK
Péninsule d'Ungava
Ungava Bay
Kuujjuaq
Kangiqsujuaq
Salluit
Ivujivik
Akulivik
Puvirnituq
Inukjuak
Umiujaq
Kuujjuarapik
Sanikiluaq
Belcher Islands
James Bay
QUÉBEC
ONTARIO
MANITOBA
NEWFOUNDLAND AND LABRADOR
LABRADOR
Nain
Hopedale
Happy Valley-Goose Bay
Labrador City
Churchill Falls
Schefferville
Fermont
Sept-Îles
Île d'Anticosti
Gulf of St Lawrence
NEWFOUNDLAND
St John's
Corner Brook
Gander
Grand Falls
Cape Race
St-Pierre and Miquelon (France)
Cabot Str.
Gulf of Maine
PRINCE EDWARD ISLAND
NEW BRUNSWICK
NOVA SCOTIA
Halifax
Saint John
Fredericton
Moncton
Sable Island
Québec
Chicoutimi
Trois-Rivières
Sherbrooke
USA
MAINE
Churchill
Winnipeg
Thompson
Thunder Bay
L. Superior
Kenora
Dryden
Timmins
Cochrane
Moosonee
Rouyn-Noranda
Val-d'Or
Chibougamau
MINNESOTA
International Falls
Fort Severn
Cape Churchill
83

YUKON TERRITORY
BRITISH COLUMBIA
CANADA
USA
ALASKA
NORTH
WASHINGTON
PACIFIC OCEAN
ROCKY MOUNTAINS
COAST MOUNTAINS
ALEXANDER ARCHIPELAGO
Queen Charlotte Islands
Queen Charlotte Sound
Hecate Strait
Dixon Entrance
Fraser Plateau
Vancouver
Richmond
Coquitlam
Surrey
Abbotsford
Chilliwack
Victoria
Saanich
Nanaimo
Kamloops
Kelowna
Prince George
Prince Rupert
Whitehorse
Juneau
Fort St John
Dawson Creek
Grande Prairie
Fort Nelson
Meters
Feet
6000 19685
5000 16404
4000 13123
3000 9843
2000 6562
1000 3281
500 1640
200 656
100 328
0
LAND BELOW SEA LEVEL
100 328
200 656
1000 3281
2000 6562
4000 13123
6000 19685

1:5,630,000
Lambert Conic Conformal Projection

WESTERN CANADA

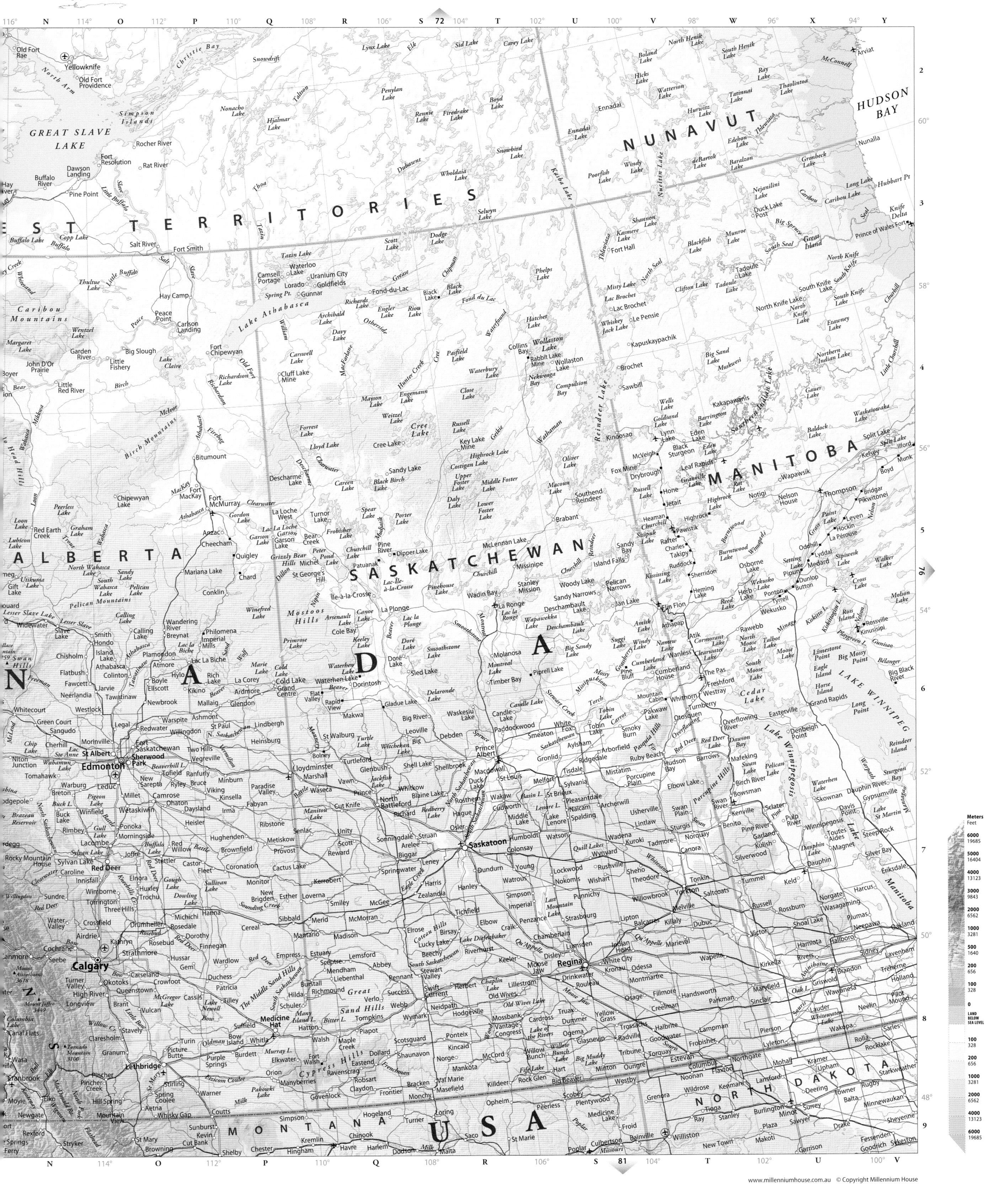

NORTHWEST TERRITORIES
NUNAVUT
ALBERTA
SASKATCHEWAN
MANITOBA
CANADA
USA
MONTANA
NORTH DAKOTA
HUDSON BAY
GREAT SLAVE LAKE
Lake Athabasca
Reindeer Lake
Wollaston Lake
Lake Winnipeg
Lake Winnipegosis
Lake Manitoba
Cedar Lake
Caribou Mountains
Birch Mountains
Pelican Mountains
Swan Hills
Mostoos Hills
Cypress Hills
Great Sand Hills
The Middle Sand Hills
Yellowknife
Fort Resolution
Hay River
Fort Smith
Fort Chipewyan
Fort McMurray
Uranium City
Arviat
Churchill
Thompson
The Pas
Flin Flon
Lynn Lake
Prince Albert
Lloydminster
North Battleford
Saskatoon
Regina
Moose Jaw
Swift Current
Yorkton
Brandon
Edmonton
St Albert
Sherwood Park
Red Deer
Calgary
Lethbridge
Medicine Hat
Minot
Williston
Meters
Feet
6000 19685
5000 16404
4000 13123
3000 9843
2000 6562
1000 3281
500 1640
200 656
100 328
0
LAND BELOW SEA LEVEL
100 328
200 656
1000 3281
2000 6562
4000 13123
6000 19685
72
76
81

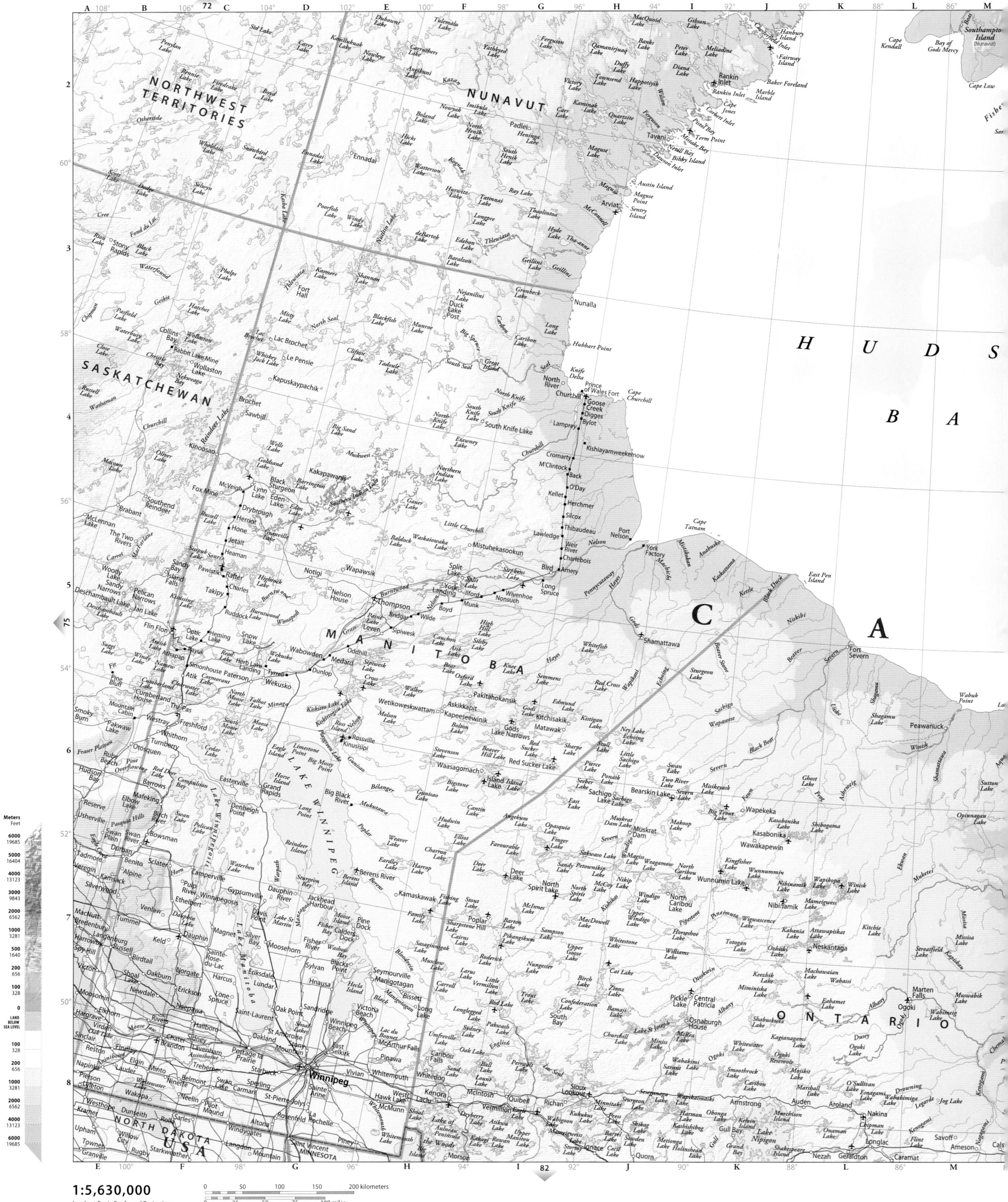
72
75
82
NORTHWEST TERRITORIES
NUNAVUT
SASKATCHEWAN
MANITOBA
ONTARIO
HUDSON BAY
CANADA
NORTH DAKOTA
USA
MINNESOTA
LAKE WINNIPEG
Lake Winnipegosis
Lake Manitoba
Southampton Island (Nunavut)
Cape Kendall
Bay of Gods Mercy
Cape Low
Hanbury Island
Chesterfield Inlet
Fairway Island
Rankin Inlet
Baker Foreland
Marble Island
Cape Jones
Tavani
Term Point
Bibby Island
Dawson Inlet
Austin Island
Arviat
Maguse Point
Sentry Island
Nunalla
Hubbart Point
Knife Delta
North River
Churchill
Prince of Wales Fort
Cape Churchill
Goose Creek
Digges
Bylot
Lamprey
Kishiayamweekemow
Cromarty
M'Clintock
Back
O'Day
Kellet
Herchmer
Silcox
Thibaudeau
Lawledge
Weir River
Charlebois
Amery
Bird
Long Spruce
Port Nelson
Cape Tatnam
York Factory
East Pen Island
Shamattawa
Fort Severn
Wabuk Point
Peawanuck
Ennadai
Nueltin Lake
Kasba Lake
Fort Hall
Lac Brochet
Le Pensie
Kapuskaypachik
Brochet
Sawbill
Kinoosao
Wollaston Lake
Rabbit Lake Mine
Collins Bay
Stony Rapids
Fond du Lac
Black Lake
Tadoule Lake
South Knife Lake
Kakapawanis
Southern Indian Lake
Lynn Lake
Fox Mine
McVeigh
Drybrough
Herriot
Hone
Jetait
Heaman
Pukatawagan
Pawistik
Rafter
Charles
Takipy
Ruddock
Flin Flon
Snow Lake
Sherridon
Southend
Reindeer Lake
Brabant
McLennan Lake
The Two Rivers
Sandy Bay
Island Falls
Pelican Narrows
Deschambault Lake
Jan Lake
Nelson House
Thompson
Split Lake
York Landing
Ilford
Wivenhoe
Munk
Nonsuch
Boyd
Wilde
Bridgar
Sipiwesk
Wabowden
Medard
Oddhill
Dunlop
Tyrrell
Wekusko
Herb Lake Landing
Paterson
Simonhouse
Cormorant
Atik
Cranberry Portage
Cumberland House
The Pas
Westray
Freshford
Whithorn
Turnberry
Otosquen
Mistuhekasookun
Wapawsik
Notigi
Gillam
Pakitahokansik
Askikkapit
Kapeeseewinik
Wetikoweskwattam
Rossville
Kinusisipi
Norway House
Gods Lake Narrows
Red Sucker Lake
Island Lake
Waasagomach
Big Black River
Berens River
Kamaskawak
Poplar River
Sachigo Lake
Bearskin Lake
Muskrat Dam
Wapekeka
Kasabonika
Wawakapewin
Kingfisher Lake
Wunnummin Lake
Nibinamik
North Caribou Lake
North Spirit Lake
Deer Lake
Sandy Lake
Neskantaga
Pickle Lake
Central Patricia
Osnaburgh House
Marten Falls
Ogoki
Webequie
Easterville
Grand Rapids
Denbeigh Point
Mafeking
Birch River
Bowsman
Swan River
Minitonas
Benito
Sclater
Camperville
Pulp River
Winnipegosis
Ethelbert
Gypsumville
Dauphin River
Davis Point
Jackhead Harbour
Pine Dock
Fisher River
Dauphin
Gilbert Plains
Grandview
Roblin
Russell
Langenburg
Yorkton
Kamsack
Canora
Tummel
Silver Bay
Moosehorn
Eriksdale
Lundar
Ste. Rose du Lac
Neepawa
Minnedosa
Hamiota
Oak Point
Saint-Laurent
St. Ambroise
Portage la Prairie
Oakland
Stonewall
Selkirk
Winnipeg Beach
Victoria Beach
Pinawa
Whitemouth
Lac du Bonnet
Manigotagan
Bissett
Seymourville
Hnausa
Winnipeg
Steinbach
Sainte Anne
Carman
Morden
Brandon
Virden
Moosomin
Reston
Souris
Melita
Boissevain
Killarney
Pilot Mound
Rosenfeld
Emerson
La Rochelle
Kenora
Hawk Lake
Keewatin
Vermilion Bay
Dryden
Sioux Lookout
Minnitaki
Ignace
Savant Lake
Armstrong
Nakina
Geraldton
Longlac
Caramat
Savoff
Ameson
Nipigon
Gull Bay
Nezah
Quorn
McIntosh
Richan
Quibell
Red Lake
Ear Falls
Umfreville
Caribou Falls
Whitedog
Minaki
Lake of the Woods
Lake Nipigon
Lake St. Joseph
Lac Seul
Albany
Attawapiskat
Winisk
Severn
Hayes
Nelson
Churchill
Seal
Thlewiaza
Kazan
1:5,630,000
Lambert Conic Conformal Projection
0 50 100 150 200 kilometers
0 25 50 75 100 miles
Meters Feet
6000 19685
5000 16404
4000 13123
3000 9843
2000 6562
1000 3281
500 1640
200 656
100 328
0
LAND BELOW SEA LEVEL
100 328
200 656
1000 3281
2000 6562
4000 13123
6000 19685

CENTRAL CANADA

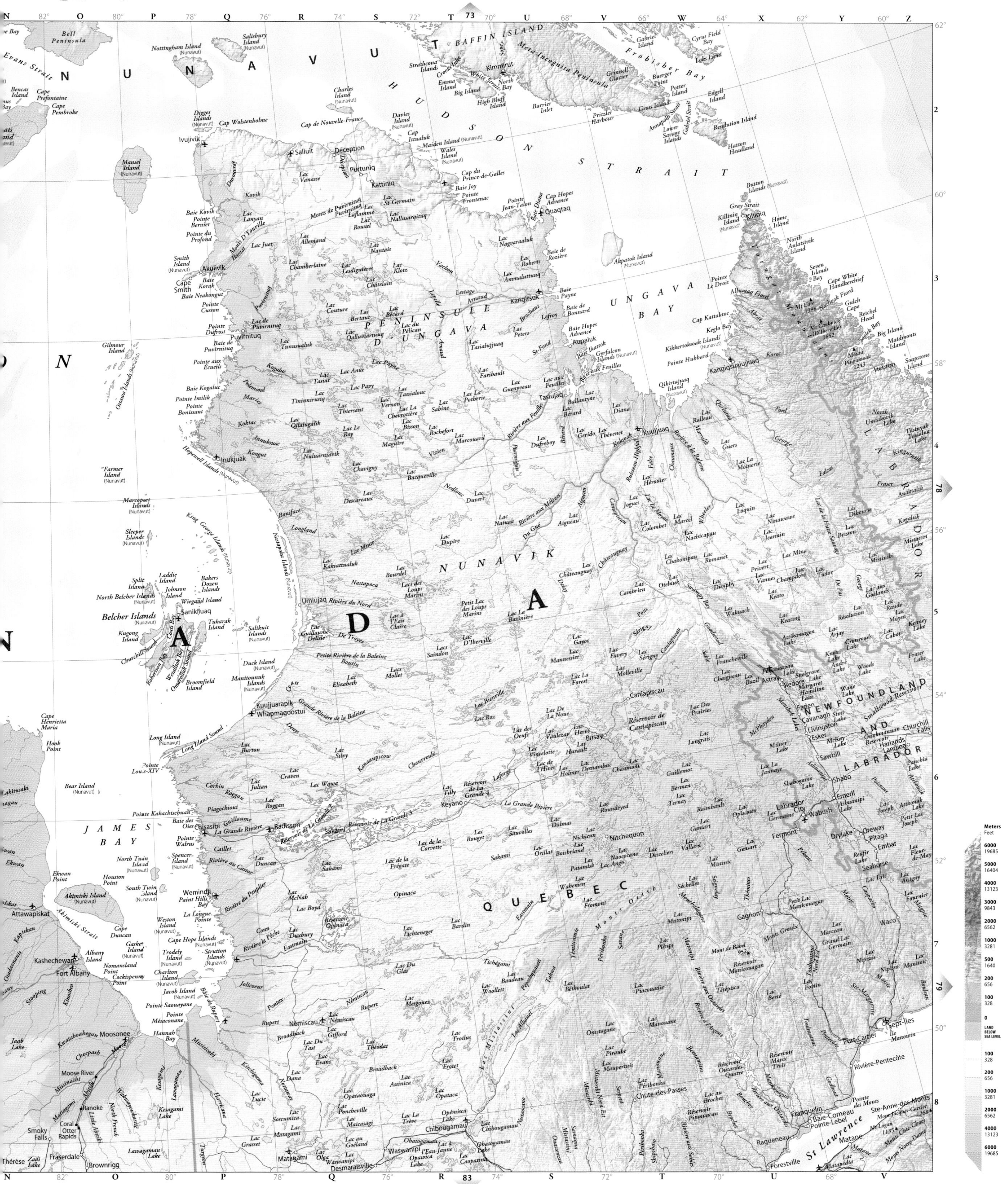

N U N A V U T
BAFFIN ISLAND
HUDSON STRAIT
UNGAVA BAY
PÉNINSULE D'UNGAVA
NUNAVIK
C A N A D A
JAMES BAY
QUEBEC
NEWFOUNDLAND AND LABRADOR
LABRADOR
Bell Peninsula
Evans Strait
Nottingham Island (Nunavut)
Salisbury Island (Nunavut)
Mansel Island (Nunavut)
Digges Islands (Nunavut)
Cap Wolstenholme
Ivujivik
Salluit
Déception
Purtuniq
Kattiniq
Charles Island (Nunavut)
Cap de Nouvelle-France
Davies Island (Nunavut)
Maiden Island (Nunavut)
Wales Island (Nunavut)
Cap du Prince-de-Galles
Kimmirut
Meta Incognita Peninsula
Frobisher Bay
Resolution Island
Button Islands (Nunavut)
Killiniq Island (Nunavut)
Killiniq
Akpatok Island (Nunavut)
Quaqtaq
Kangirsuk
Aupaluk
Tasiujaq
Kuujjuaq
Kangiqsualujjuaq
Hebron
Torngat Mountains
Akulivik
Puvirnituq
Inukjuak
Umiujaq
Kuujjuarapik
Whapmagoostui
Belcher Islands (Nunavut)
Sanikiluaq
North Belcher Islands (Nunavut)
Sleeper Islands (Nunavut)
King George Islands (Nunavut)
Nastapoka Islands (Nunavut)
Hopewell Islands (Nunavut)
Ottawa Islands (Nunavut)
Long Island (Nunavut)
Bear Island (Nunavut)
Chisasibi
Radisson
Sakami
Keyano
Réservoir de La Grande 3
Réservoir de La Grande 4
La Grande Rivière
Wemindji
Eastmain
Akimiski Island (Nunavut)
Attawapiskat
Kashechewan
Fort Albany
Moosonee
Moose River
Ranoke
Coral Rapids
Otter Rapids
Smoky Falls
Fraserdale
Brownrigg
Nemiscau
Matagami
Chibougamau
Waswanipi
Desmaraisville
Chute-des-Passes
Lac Mistassini
Nitchequon
Réservoir de Caniapiscau
Caniapiscau
Brisay
Schefferville
Astray
Redore
Faden
Cavanagh
Livingston
Esker
Sawbill
Shabo
Emeril
Labrador City
Wabush
Fermont
Gagnon
Réservoir Manicouagan
Mont de Babel 952
Churchill Falls
Smallwood Reservoir
Harlands Landing
Oreway
Pitaga
Drylake
Embar
Seahorse
Waco
Sept-Îles
Port-Cartier
Rivière-Pentecôte
Baie-Comeau
Pointe-Lebel
Franquelin
Ragueneau
Forestville
Matane
St Lawrence
Ste-Anne-des-Monts
Mont Jacques Cartier 1268
Mt Logan 1135
Monts Chic-Chocs
Monts Notre-Dame
Matapédia
Réservoir Outardes Quatre
Réservoir Manic Trois
Réservoir Pipmuacan
Monts Otish
Mt Caubvick 1652
Mt Eliot 1388
Mount Pingitkalik 1243
Meters / Feet
6000 19685
5000 16404
4000 13123
3000 9843
2000 6562
1000 3281
500 1640
200 656
100 328
0
LAND BELOW SEA LEVEL
100 328
200 656
1000 3281
2000 6562
4000 13123
6000 19685

LABRADOR SEA
DAVIS STRAIT
HUDSON STRAIT
UNGAVA BAY
NEWFOUNDLAND AND LABRADOR
CANADA
NUNAVUT
Baffin Island
Greenland (Kalaallit Nunaat) (Denmark)
PÉNINSULE D'UNGAVA
Qeqertarsuatsiaat
Kangigdlermiut
Paamiut
Qeqertarsuaq
Narsalik
Neria
Kangilinnguit
Ivittuut
Arsuk
Saqqamiut
Qassimiut
Saarloq
Cape Murchison
Lady Franklin Island
Monumental Island
Lemieux Islands
Cyrus Field Bay
Loks Land
Edgell Island
Resolution Island
Hatton Headland
Frobisher Bay
Meta Incognita Peninsula
Grinnell Glacier
Gross Island
Lower Savage Islands
Peters Point
Button Islands (Nunavut)
Gray Strait
Home Island
Killiniq Island (Nunavut)
Killiniq
Cape William-Smith
Eclipse Harbour
North Aulatsivik Island
Torngat Mountains
Mt. Caubvick (D'Iberville) 1652
Hebron
Hebron Fiord
Nain
Natuashish
Davis Inlet
Hopedale
Makkovik
Cape Harrison
Rigolet
Cartwright
Paradise River
Black Tickle
Port Hope Simpson
Lake Melville
Happy Valley-Goose Bay
North West River
Churchill Falls
Smallwood Reservoir
Labrador City
Wabush
Fermont
Schefferville
Kangiqsualujjuaq
Kuujjuaq
Tasiujaq
Aupaluk
Kangirsuk
Quaqtaq
Kangiqsujuaq
Salluit
Kattiniq
Kimmirut
Akpatok Island (Nunavut)
Charles Island (Nunavut)
Baie Déception
Déception
Purtuniq
Rivière à la Baleine
Rivière George
Caniapiscau
Réservoir de Caniapiscau
Lac Le Moyne
Lac Minto
Lac Bienville
Goodwood
Swampy Bay
Kawawachikamach
Menihek Lakes
Ashuanipi
Sawbill
Nitchequon

1:5,630,000

Lambert Conic Conformal Projection

0 50 100 150 200 kilometers

0 25 50 75 100 miles

Meters	Feet
6000	19685
5000	16404
4000	13123
3000	9843
2000	6562
1000	3281
500	1640
200	656
100	328
0 LAND BELOW SEA LEVEL	
100	328
200	656
1000	3281
2000	6562
4000	13123
6000	19685

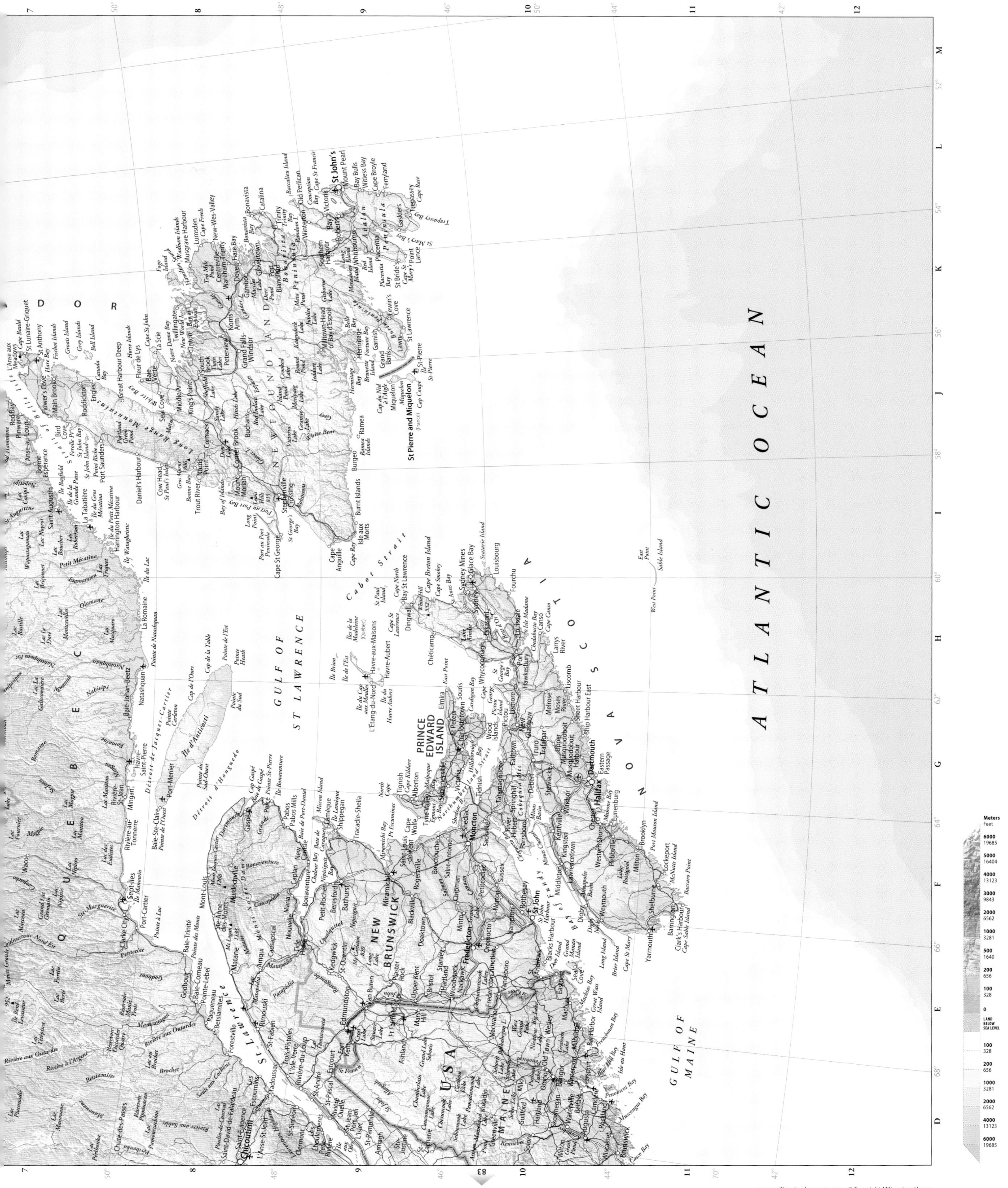
ATLANTIC OCEAN
GULF OF ST LAWRENCE
GULF OF MAINE
NEWFOUNDLAND
NOVA SCOTIA
NEW BRUNSWICK
PRINCE EDWARD ISLAND
QUEBEC
USA
MAINE
St Pierre and Miquelon
(France)
Cabot Strait
St John's
Halifax
Dartmouth
Charlottetown
Fredericton
Moncton
Saint John
Sydney
Corner Brook
Gander
Sept-Îles
Rimouski
Chicoutimi
Bangor
Augusta
Île d'Anticosti
Sable Island
Meters
Feet
6000
19685
5000
16404
4000
13123
3000
9843
2000
6562
1000
3281
500
1640
200
656
100
328
0
LAND BELOW SEA LEVEL
100
328
200
656
1000
3281
2000
6562
4000
13123
6000
19685

83

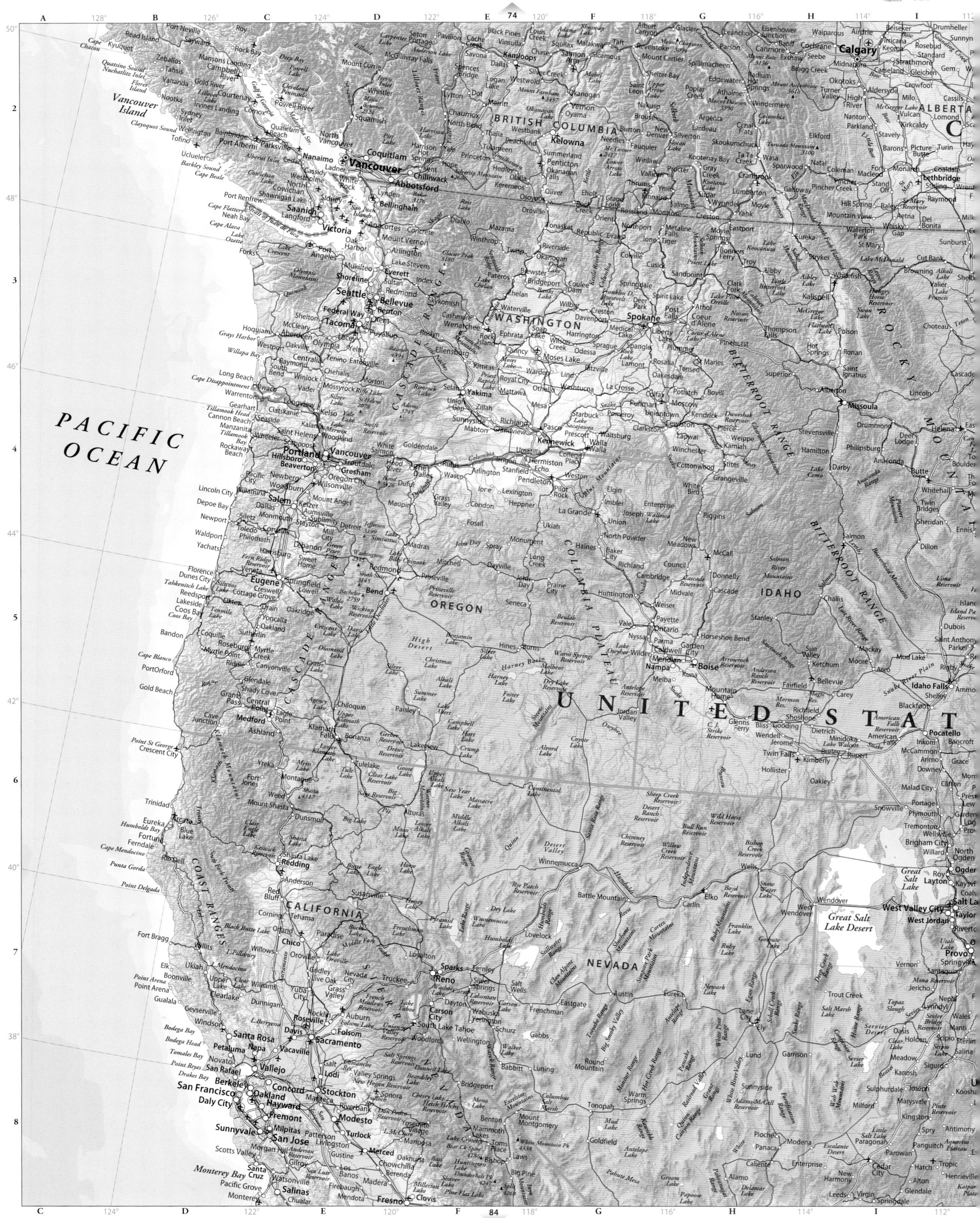
PACIFIC OCEAN
UNITED STATES
BRITISH COLUMBIA
ALBERTA
WASHINGTON
OREGON
IDAHO
CALIFORNIA
NEVADA
Vancouver Island
Vancouver
Victoria
Seattle
Tacoma
Spokane
Portland
Salem
Eugene
Boise
Calgary
Kelowna
Kamloops
Reno
Sacramento
San Francisco
Oakland
San Jose
Fresno
Stockton
Modesto
Great Salt Lake
Great Salt Lake Desert
Salt Lake City
Ogden
Provo
Missoula
Pocatello
Idaho Falls
Medford
Redding
Santa Rosa
Monterey Bay
CASCADE RANGE
COAST RANGES
COLUMBIA PLATEAU
BITTERROOT RANGE
ROCKY MOUNTAINS
SIERRA NEVADA

1:5,630,000

Lambert Conic Conformal Projection

0 50 100 150 200 kilometers

0 25 50 75 100 miles

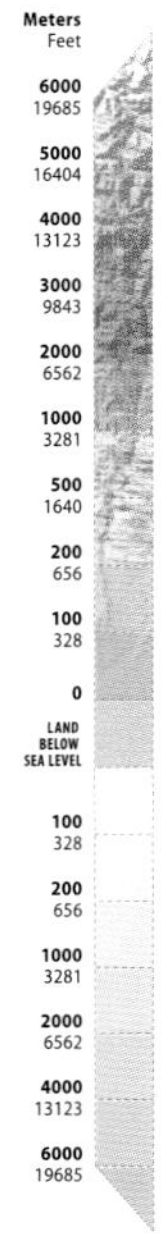
Meters
Feet
6000 19685
5000 16404
4000 13123
3000 9843
2000 6562
1000 3281
500 1640
200 656
100 328
0
LAND BELOW SEA LEVEL
100 328
200 656
1000 3281
2000 6562
4000 13123
6000 19685

NORTHWESTERN USA

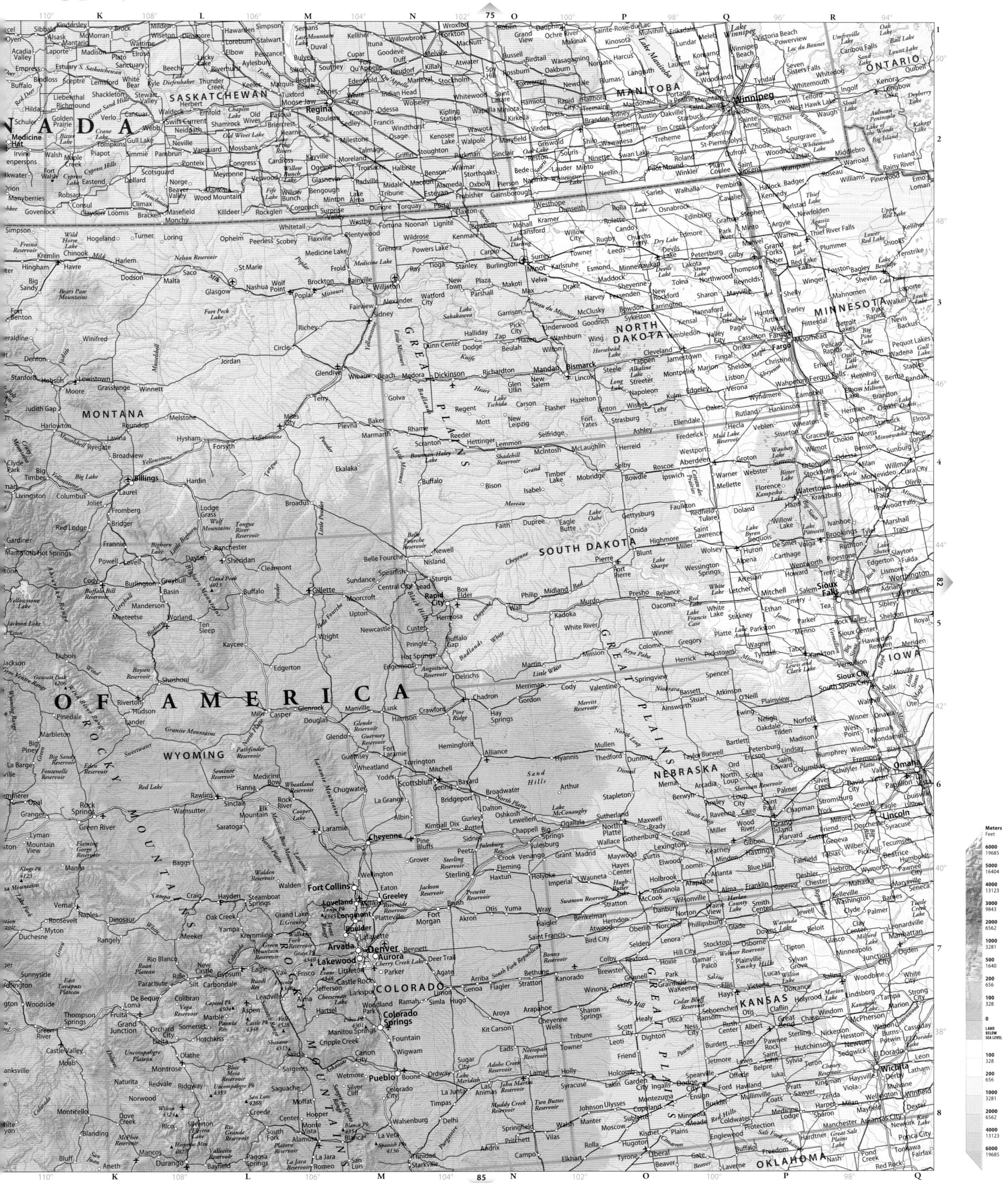

SASKATCHEWAN
MANITOBA
ONTARIO
NADA
MONTANA
NORTH DAKOTA
SOUTH DAKOTA
MINNESOTA
WYOMING
NEBRASKA
IOWA
COLORADO
KANSAS
OKLAHOMA
OF AMERICA
ROCKY MOUNTAINS
GREAT PLAINS
Regina
Winnipeg
Bismarck
Pierre
Cheyenne
Denver
Lincoln
Omaha
Sioux Falls
Rapid City
Billings
Fargo
Wichita
Colorado Springs
Pueblo
Fort Collins
75
82
85
Meters
Feet
6000
19685
5000
16404
4000
13123
3000
9843
2000
6562
1000
3281
500
1640
200
656
100
328
0
LAND BELOW SEA LEVEL

MANITOBA
ONTARIO
NORTH DAKOTA
SOUTH DAKOTA
NEBRASKA
KANSAS
OKLAHOMA
MINNESOTA
IOWA
MISSOURI
WISCONSIN
ILLINOIS
MICHIGAN
INDIANA
OHIO
KENTUCKY
UNITED STATES OF A
Lake Superior
Lake Michigan
Winnipeg
Thunder Bay
Duluth
Minneapolis
Saint Paul
Fargo
Sioux Falls
Omaha
Des Moines
Milwaukee
Chicago
Detroit
Indianapolis
Kansas City
Saint Louis
Springfield
Louisville
Cincinnati
Columbus
Tulsa
Meters
Feet
LAND BELOW SEA LEVEL
76
81
86

1:5,630,000

Lambert Conic Conformal Projection

0 50 100 150 200 kilometers

0 25 50 75 100 miles

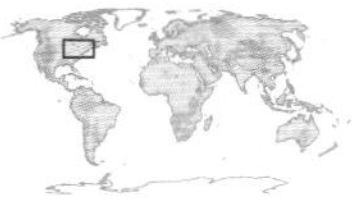

NORTHEASTERN USA

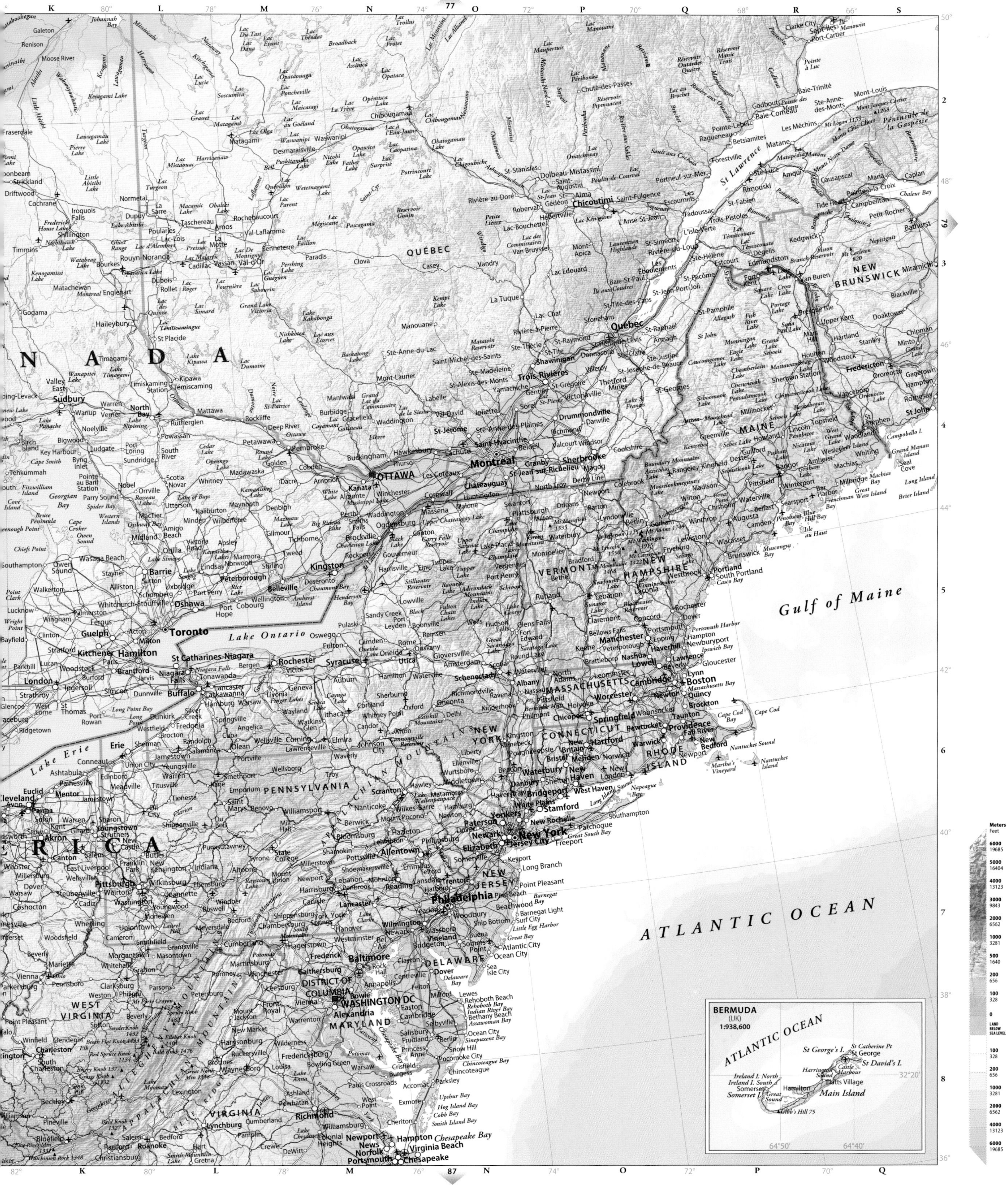

QUÉBEC
NEW BRUNSWICK
MAINE
VERMONT
NEW HAMPSHIRE
MASSACHUSETTS
CONNECTICUT
RHODE ISLAND
NEW YORK
PENNSYLVANIA
NEW JERSEY
DELAWARE
MARYLAND
DISTRICT OF COLUMBIA
WASHINGTON DC
WEST VIRGINIA
VIRGINIA
Gulf of Maine
ATLANTIC OCEAN
Lake Ontario
Lake Erie
OTTAWA
Montreal
Québec
Toronto
Boston
New York
Philadelphia
Baltimore
Pittsburgh
Buffalo
Rochester
Syracuse
Albany
Hartford
Providence
Portland
Richmond
Norfolk
Virginia Beach
BERMUDA
(UK)
1:938,600
ATLANTIC OCEAN
St George's I.
St George
St David's I.
Main Island
Hamilton
Somerset
Gibb's Hill 75
Meters
Feet
6000
19685
5000
16404
4000
13123
3000
9843
2000
6562
1000
3281
500
1640
200
656
100
328
0
LAND BELOW SEA LEVEL

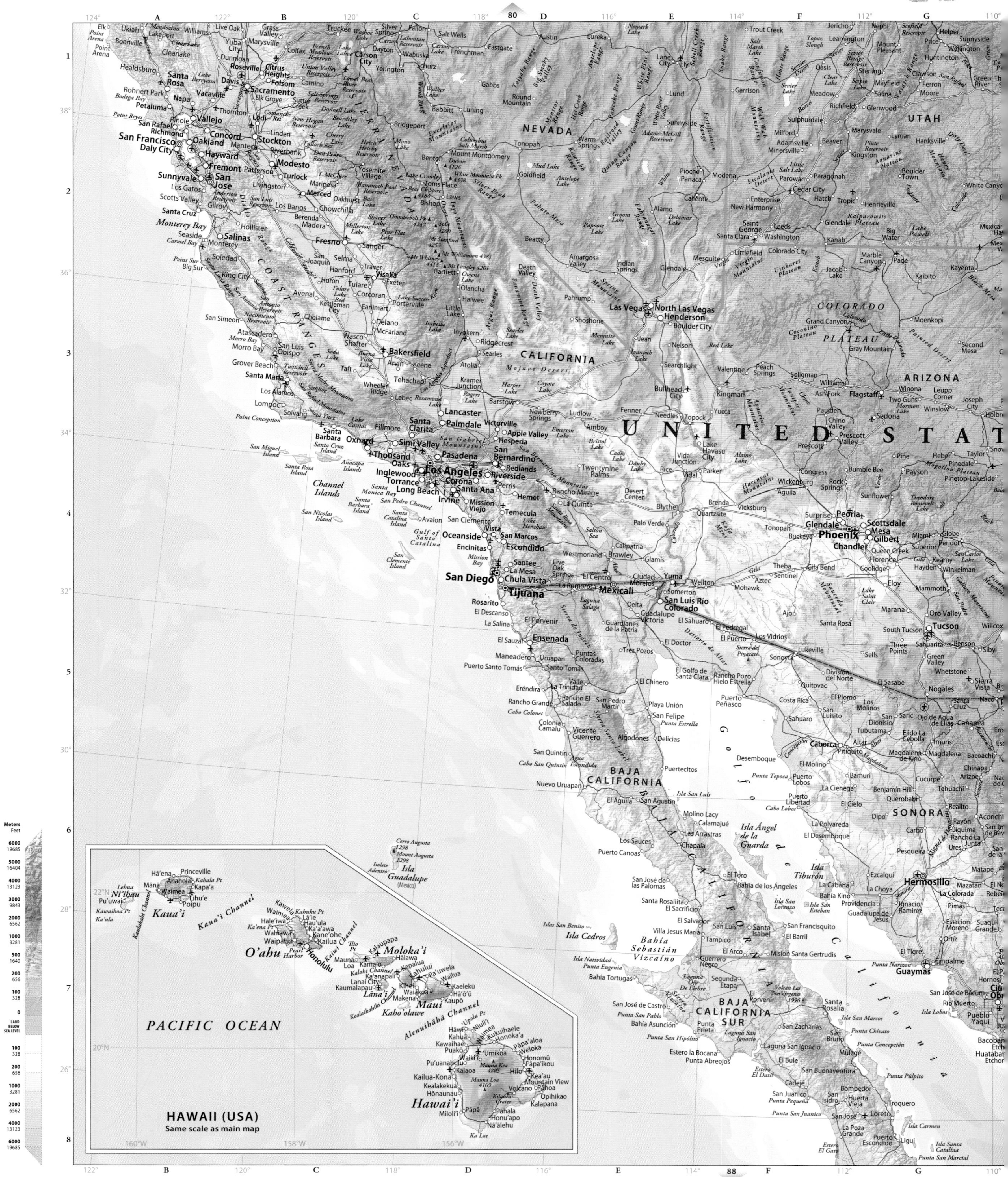
80
88
NEVADA
UTAH
CALIFORNIA
ARIZONA
UNITED STAT
SONORA
BAJA CALIFORNIA
BAJA CALIFORNIA SUR
COLORADO PLATEAU
COAST RANGES
SIERRA NEVADA
Mojave Desert
Golfo de California
Channel Islands
Monterey Bay
San Francisco
Oakland
Sacramento
San Jose
Stockton
Modesto
Fresno
Bakersfield
Las Vegas
North Las Vegas
Henderson
Los Angeles
Long Beach
Santa Ana
Riverside
San Bernardino
San Diego
Tijuana
Mexicali
Yuma
Phoenix
Tucson
Hermosillo
Guaymas
Ensenada
Isla Ángel de la Guarda
Isla Tiburón
Isla Cedros
Bahía Sebastián Vizcaíno
Isla Guadalupe (Mexico)
HAWAII (USA)
Same scale as main map
PACIFIC OCEAN
Ni'ihau
Kaua'i
O'ahu
Honolulu
Moloka'i
Lāna'i
Maui
Kaho'olawe
Hawai'i
Mauna Kea 4205
Mauna Loa 4169
Meters
Feet
LAND BELOW SEA LEVEL

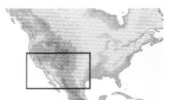

1:5,630,000

Lambert Conic Conformal Projection

0 50 100 150 200 kilometers

0 25 50 75 100 miles

SOUTHWESTERN USA

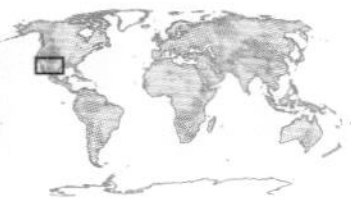

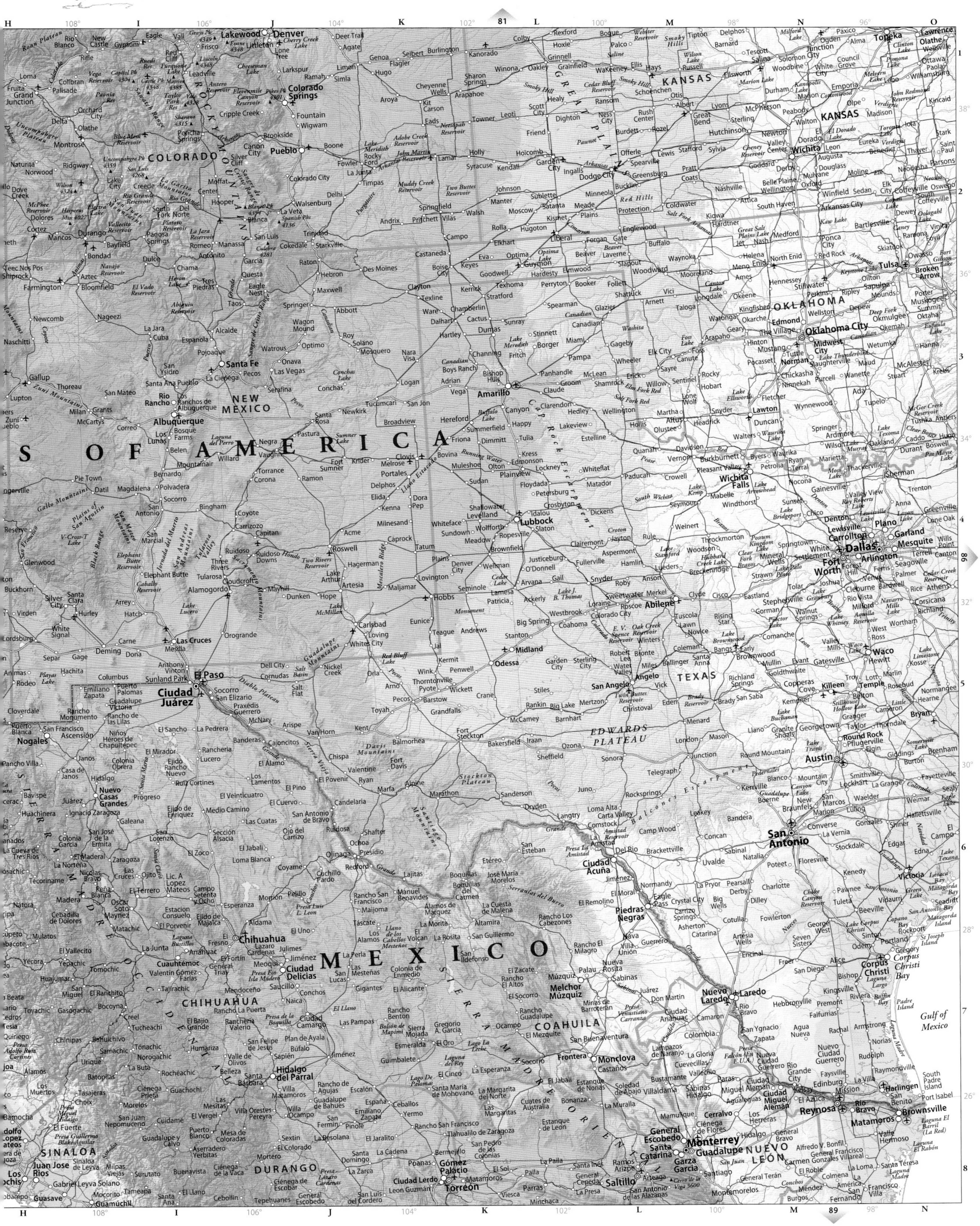
UNITED STATES OF AMERICA
MEXICO
COLORADO
KANSAS
OKLAHOMA
NEW MEXICO
TEXAS
CHIHUAHUA
COAHUILA
NUEVO LEÓN
DURANGO
SINALOA
ROCKY MOUNTAINS
GREAT PLAINS
EDWARDS PLATEAU
SIERRA MADRE OCCIDENTAL
SIERRA MADRE ORIENTAL
Gulf of Mexico
Denver
Colorado Springs
Pueblo
Santa Fe
Albuquerque
Wichita
Oklahoma City
Tulsa
Amarillo
Lubbock
Dallas
Fort Worth
Austin
San Antonio
El Paso
Ciudad Juárez
Chihuahua
Monterrey
Saltillo
Torreón
Laredo
Nuevo Laredo
Corpus Christi
Brownsville
Matamoros
Reynosa
H
I
J
K
L
M
N
O
108°
106°
104°
102°
100°
98°
96°
1
2
3
4
5
6
7
8
38°
36°
34°
32°
30°
28°
26°
81
86
89

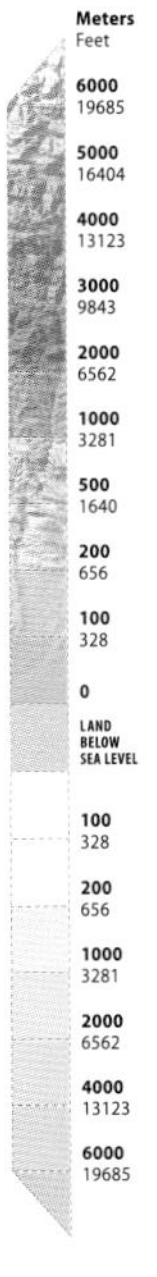
Meters
Feet
6000
19685
5000
16404
4000
13123
3000
9843
2000
6562
1000
3281
500
1640
200
656
100
328
0
LAND BELOW SEA LEVEL
100
328
200
656
1000
3281
2000
6562
4000
13123
6000
19685

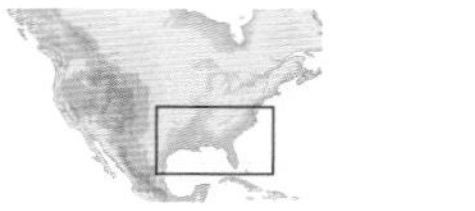

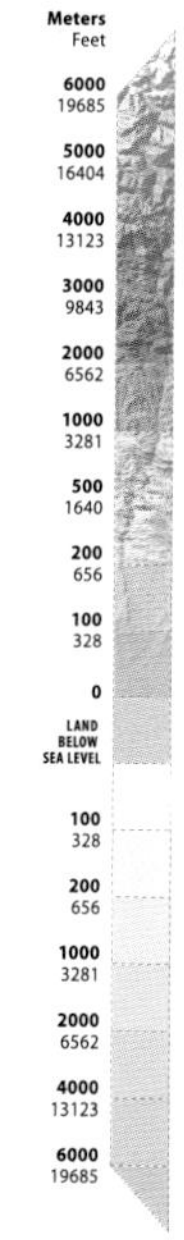

Meters
Feet
6000
19685
5000
16404
4000
13123
3000
9843
2000
6562
1000
3281
500
1640
200
656
100
328
0
LAND BELOW SEA LEVEL
100
328
200
656
1000
3281
2000
6562
4000
13123
6000
19685

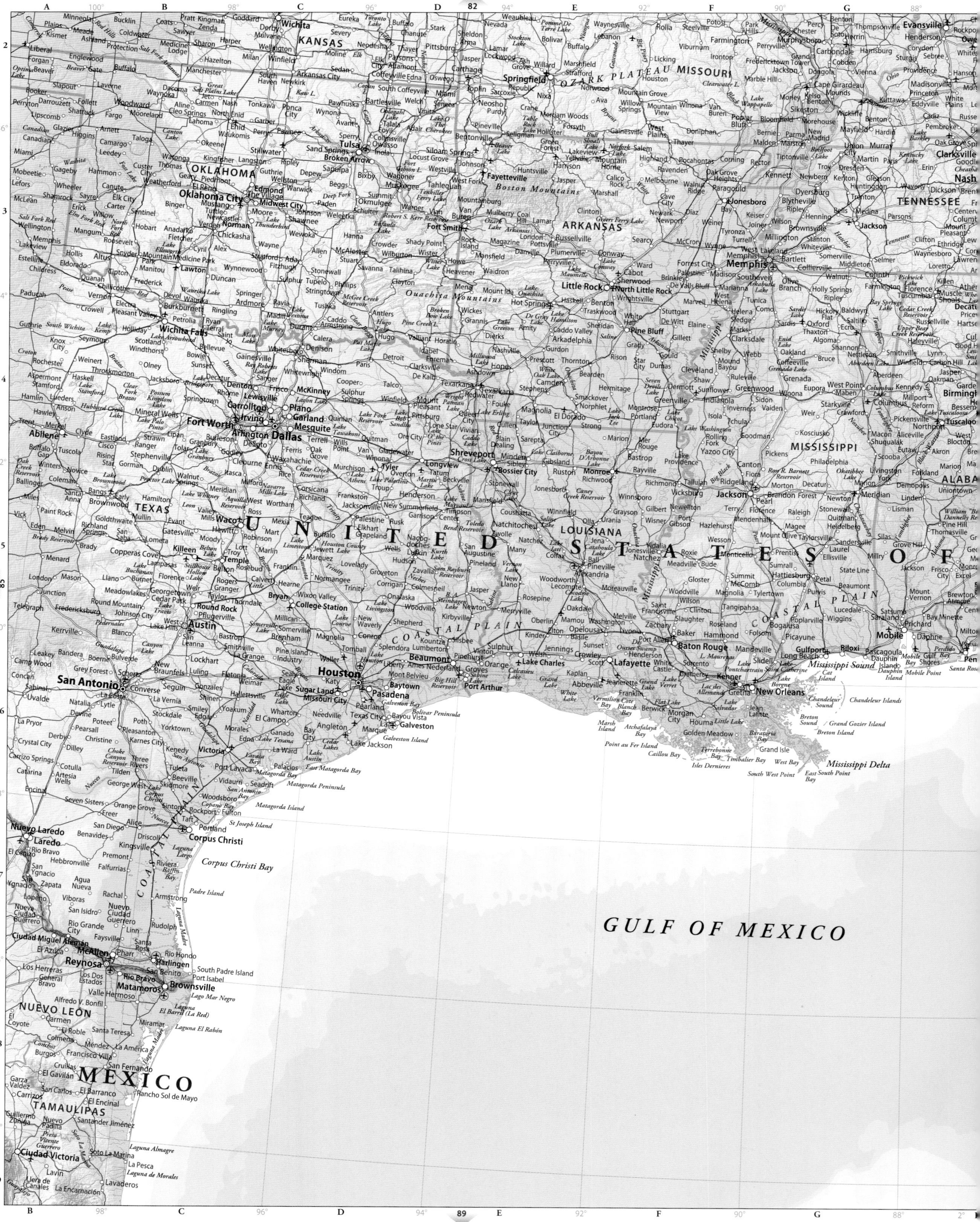

A
B
C
D
E
F
G
82
85
89
100°
98°
96°
94°
92°
90°
88°
36°
34°
32°
30°
28°
26°
24°
KANSAS
MISSOURI
OKLAHOMA
ARKANSAS
TENNESSEE
TEXAS
LOUISIANA
MISSISSIPPI
UNITED STATES OF
MEXICO
NUEVO LEÓN
TAMAULIPAS
GULF OF MEXICO
OZARK PLATEAU
Boston Mountains
Ouachita Mountains
COASTAL PLAIN
Wichita
Tulsa
Oklahoma City
Springfield
Fayetteville
Fort Smith
Little Rock
Memphis
Jackson
Dallas
Fort Worth
Arlington
Shreveport
Waco
Austin
San Antonio
Houston
Beaumont
Lake Charles
Lafayette
Baton Rouge
New Orleans
Mobile
Gulfport
Biloxi
Galveston
Corpus Christi
Laredo
Nuevo Laredo
McAllen
Reynosa
Matamoros
Brownsville
Ciudad Victoria
Evansville
Clarksville
Mississippi Sound
Mississippi Delta
Chandeleur Islands
Padre Island
Corpus Christi Bay
Matagorda Island

1:5,630,000

Lambert Conic Conformal Projection

0 50 100 150 200 kilometers

0 25 50 75 100 miles

SOUTHEASTERN USA

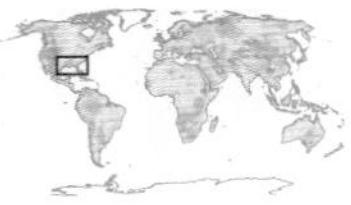

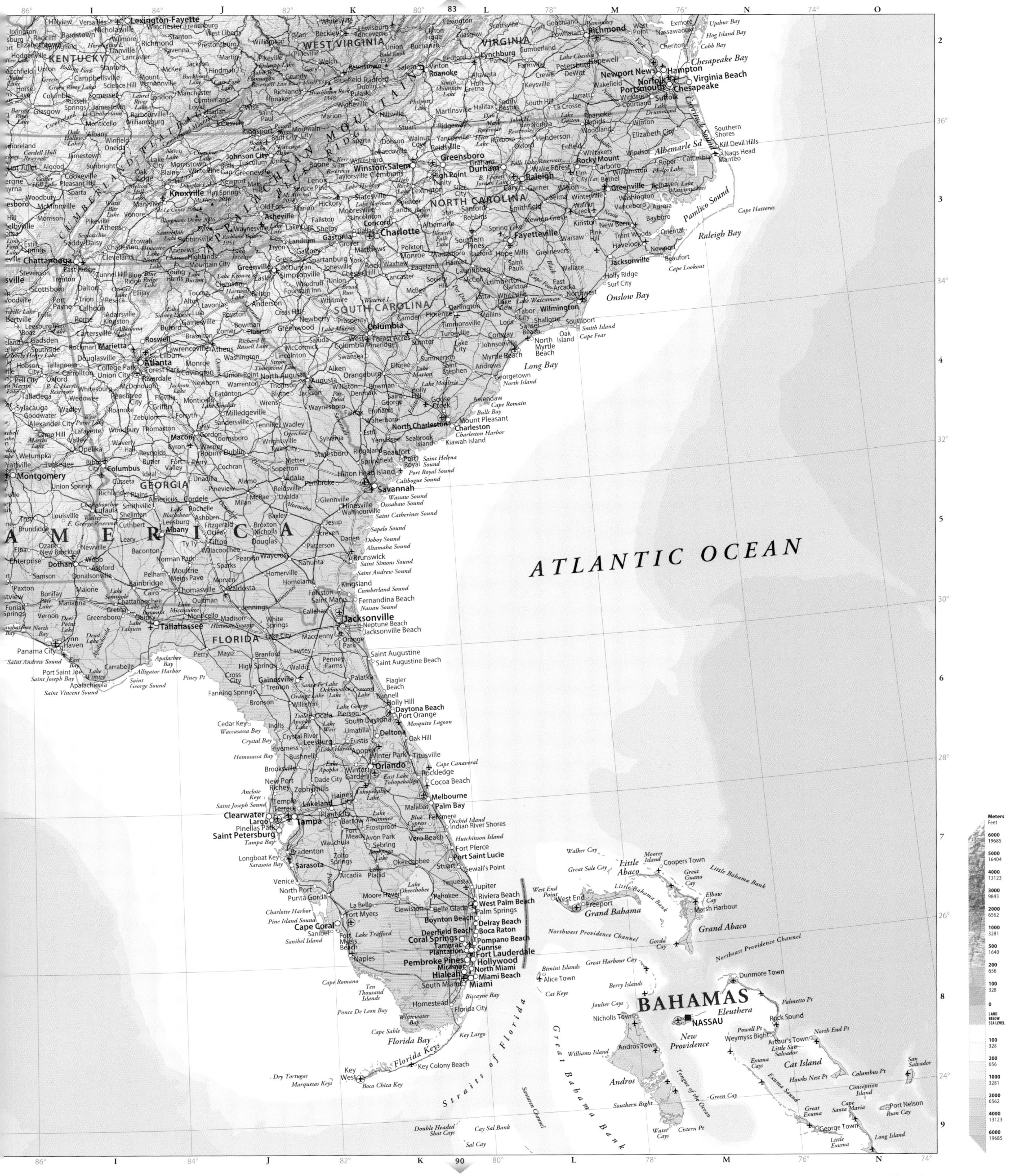

ATLANTIC OCEAN
AMERICA
KENTUCKY
WEST VIRGINIA
VIRGINIA
NORTH CAROLINA
SOUTH CAROLINA
GEORGIA
FLORIDA
BAHAMAS
NASSAU
CUMBERLAND PLATEAU
APPALACHIAN MOUNTAINS
BLUE RIDGE
Lexington-Fayette
Richmond
Newport News
Hampton
Norfolk
Virginia Beach
Portsmouth
Chesapeake
Chesapeake Bay
Roanoke
Lynchburg
Knoxville
Johnson City
Asheville
Greensboro
Winston-Salem
High Point
Durham
Raleigh
Charlotte
Fayetteville
Greenville
Wilmington
Jacksonville
Albemarle Sd
Pamlico Sound
Cape Hatteras
Raleigh Bay
Onslow Bay
Cape Lookout
Cape Fear
Long Bay
Chattanooga
Spartanburg
Columbia
Augusta
Charleston
North Charleston
Savannah
Atlanta
Marietta
Roswell
Macon
Columbus
Montgomery
Albany
Dothan
Tallahassee
Panama City
Gainesville
Daytona Beach
Orlando
Melbourne
Palm Bay
Tampa
Clearwater
Saint Petersburg
Sarasota
Cape Coral
Fort Myers
Naples
West Palm Beach
Boynton Beach
Delray Beach
Boca Raton
Coral Springs
Pompano Beach
Fort Lauderdale
Hollywood
Pembroke Pines
Miramar
Hialeah
North Miami
Miami Beach
Miami
Homestead
Key West
Florida Bay
Florida Keys
Straits of Florida
Lake Okeechobee
Cape Canaveral
Grand Bahama
Freeport
Little Abaco
Great Abaco
Marsh Harbour
Andros
New Providence
Eleuthera
Cat Island
Great Bahama Bank
Tongue of the Ocean
Northeast Providence Channel
Northwest Providence Channel
Little Bahama Bank
Meters
Feet
6000 19685
5000 16404
4000 13123
3000 9843
2000 6562
1000 3281
500 1640
200 656
100 328
0
LAND BELOW SEA LEVEL
100 328
200 656
1000 3281
2000 6562
4000 13123
6000 19685

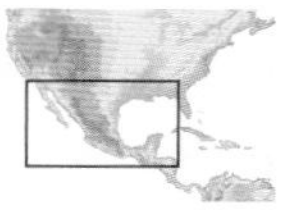

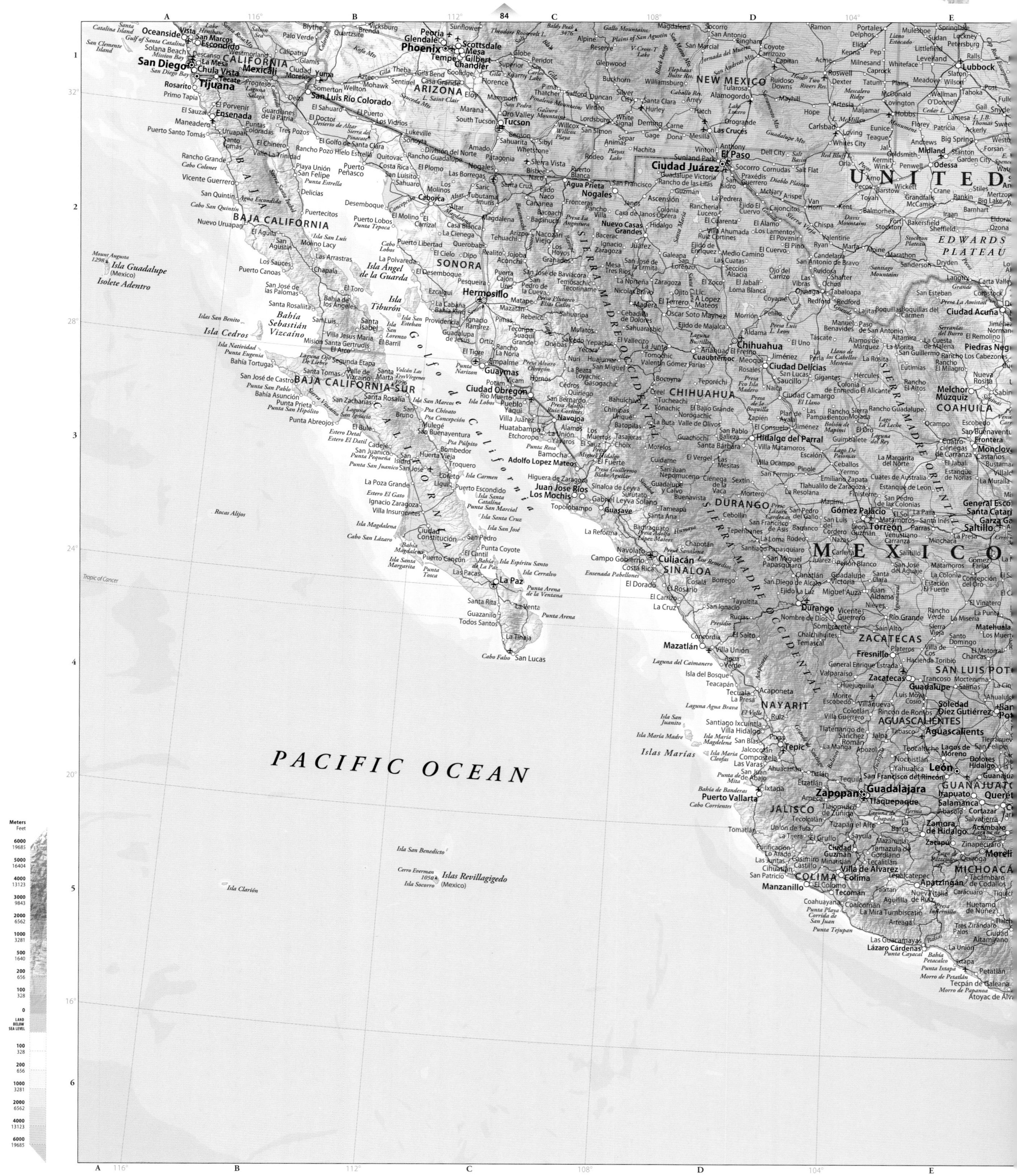
84
PACIFIC OCEAN
Golfo de California
UNITED
MEXICO
CALIFORNIA
ARIZONA
NEW MEXICO
BAJA CALIFORNIA
BAJA CALIFORNIA SUR
SONORA
CHIHUAHUA
COAHUILA
SINALOA
DURANGO
ZACATECAS
NAYARIT
AGUASCALIENTES
JALISCO
COLIMA
MICHOACÁN
GUANAJUATO
SAN LUIS POT
SIERRA MADRE OCCIDENTAL
SIERRA MADRE ORIENTAL
EDWARDS PLATEAU
San Diego
Tijuana
Mexicali
Phoenix
Tucson
El Paso
Ciudad Juárez
Chihuahua
Hermosillo
Guaymas
Ciudad Obregón
Los Mochis
Culiacán
Mazatlán
Durango
Torreón
Saltillo
La Paz
Cabo San Lucas
Tepic
Guadalajara
Zapopan
Puerto Vallarta
Manzanillo
Colima
Aguascalientes
León
Lubbock
Odessa
Midland
Isla Guadalupe (Mexico)
Isla Cedros
Isla Tiburón
Isla Ángel de la Guarda
Islas Marías
Islas Revillagigedo (Mexico)
Isla Socorro
Isla Clarión
Isla San Benedicto
Tropic of Cancer
A
B
C
D
E
1
2
3
4
5
6
116°
112°
108°
104°
32°
28°
24°
20°
16°
Meters
Feet
6000 19685
5000 16404
4000 13123
3000 9843
2000 6562
1000 3281
500 1640
200 656
100 328
0
LAND BELOW SEA LEVEL
100 328
200 656
1000 3281
2000 6562
4000 13123
6000 19685

1:7,880,000
Lambert Conic Conformal Projection

0 50 100 150 200 250 300 kilometers
0 25 50 75 100 125 150 miles

MEXICO

GULF OF MEXICO
UNITED STATES OF AMERICA
TEXAS
LOUISIANA
MISSISSIPPI
ALABAMA
GEORGIA
FLORIDA
COASTAL PLAIN
NUEVO LEON
TAMAULIPAS
HIDALGO
TLAXCALA
VERACRUZ
DISTRITO FEDERAL
MORELOS
PUEBLA
OAXACA
TABASCO
CHIAPAS
CAMPECHE
YUCATÁN
QUINTANA ROO
PENÍNSULA DE YUCATÁN
SIERRA MADRE DEL SUR
BELIZE
GUATEMALA
HONDURAS
NICARAGUA
CUBA
PINAR DEL RÍO
ISLA DE LA JUVENTUD
MOSQUITIA
Bahía de Campeche
Gulf of Honduras
Golfo de Tehuantepec
Yucatán Channel
Mississippi Delta
Mississippi Sound
Corpus Christi Bay
Dry Tortugas
Arrecife Alacrán
Tropic of Cancer
CIUDAD DE MÉXICO
GUATEMALA
TEGUCIGALPA
BELMOPAN
Houston
Dallas
San Antonio
New Orleans
Mérida
Cancún
Veracruz
Puebla
Tampico
Villahermosa
Campeche
Belize City
San Pedro Sula
Oaxaca
Tuxtla Gutiérrez
Tampa
Jacksonville
Birmingham
Montgomery
Shreveport
Austin
Corpus Christi
Laredo
Matamoros
F
G
H
I
J
96°
92°
88°
84°
32°
28°
24°
20°
16°
87
90
1
2
3
4
5
6
Meters
Feet
6000
19685
5000
16404
4000
13123
3000
9843
2000
6562
1000
3281
500
1640
200
656
100
328
0
LAND BELOW SEA LEVEL

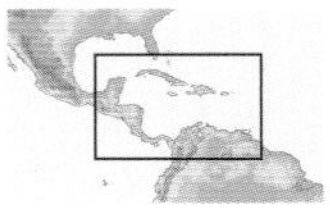

GULF OF MEXICO
Gulf of Honduras
PACIFIC OCEAN
UNITED STATES OF AMERICA
MEXICO
YUCATÁN
CAMPECHE
QUINTANA ROO
TABASCO
CHIAPAS
BELIZE
GUATEMALA
HONDURAS
EL SALVADOR
NICARAGUA
COSTA RICA
PANAMA
CUBA
JAMAICA
CHOCÓ
LA HABANA (HAVANA)
Cayman Islands (UK)
Mérida
Cancún
Campeche
Chetumal
BELMOPAN
Belize City
GUATEMALA
SAN SALVADOR
TEGUCIGALPA
MANAGUA
SAN JOSÉ
PANAMÁ
KINGSTON
NASSAU
Bahía de Campeche
Tropic of Cancer
Isla de Coco (Costa Rica)
A
B
C
D
E
1
2
3
4
5
6
92°
88°
84°
80°
24°
20°
16°
12°
8°
87
89

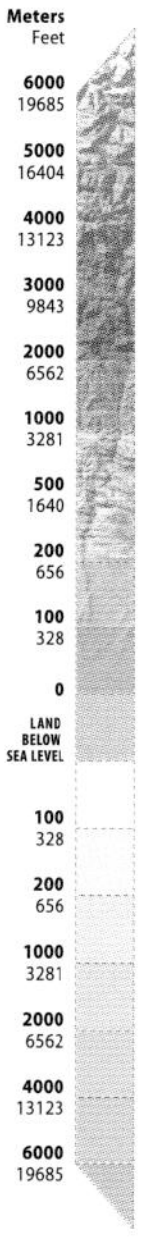

Meters
Feet
6000
19685
5000
16404
4000
13123
3000
9843
2000
6562
1000
3281
500
1640
200
656
100
328
0
LAND BELOW SEA LEVEL
100
328
200
656
1000
3281
2000
6562
4000
13123
6000
19685

1:7,880,000

Lambert Conic Conformal Projection

0 50 100 150 200 250 300 kilometers

0 25 50 75 100 125 150 miles

CENTRAL AMERICA and the CARIBBEAN

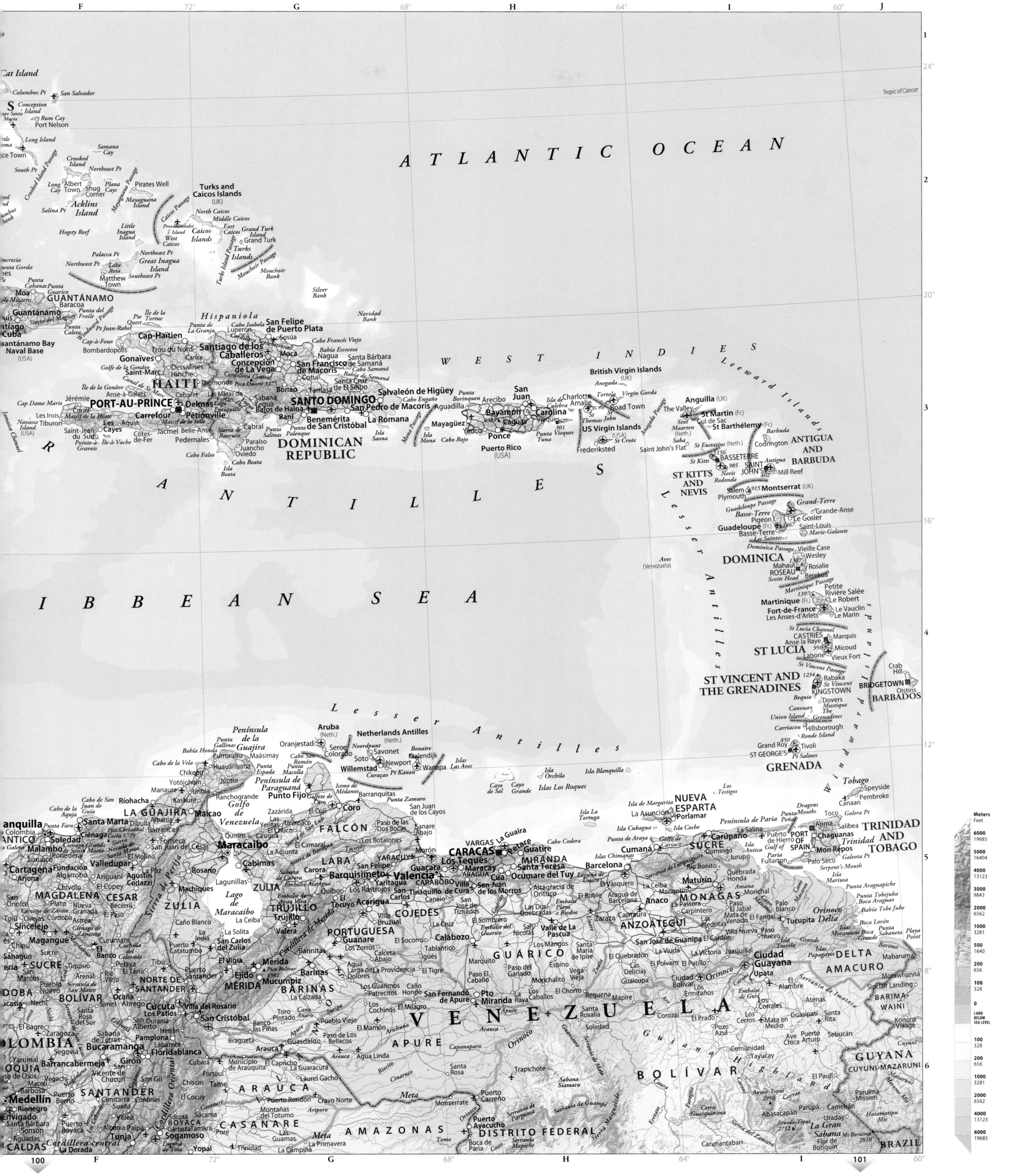

ATLANTIC OCEAN
CARIBBEAN SEA
WEST INDIES
ANTILLES
Lesser Antilles
Leeward Islands
Windward Islands
Tropic of Cancer
Turks and Caicos Islands
(UK)
Acklins Island
Great Inagua Island
Hispaniola
HAITI
PORT-AU-PRINCE
DOMINICAN REPUBLIC
SANTO DOMINGO
Santiago de los Caballeros
Puerto Rico
(USA)
San Juan
British Virgin Islands
US Virgin Islands
Anguilla (UK)
St Martin (Fr.)
St Barthélemy (Fr.)
ST KITTS AND NEVIS
BASSETERRE
ANTIGUA AND BARBUDA
SAINT JOHN'S
Montserrat (UK)
Guadeloupe (Fr.)
DOMINICA
ROSEAU
Martinique (Fr.)
Fort-de-France
ST LUCIA
CASTRIES
ST VINCENT AND THE GRENADINES
KINGSTOWN
BARBADOS
BRIDGETOWN
GRENADA
ST GEORGE'S
Tobago
TRINIDAD AND TOBAGO
PORT OF SPAIN
Aruba
(Neth.)
Netherlands Antilles
(Neth.)
Willemstad
Islas Los Roques
Isla Blanquilla
NUEVA ESPARTA
Golfo de Venezuela
Lago de Maracaibo
Maracaibo
CARACAS
Valencia
Barquisimeto
Maracay
Barcelona
Cumaná
Maturín
Ciudad Guayana
Ciudad Bolívar
VENEZUELA
ZULIA
FALCÓN
LARA
TRUJILLO
PORTUGUESA
COJEDES
GUÁRICO
ANZOÁTEGUI
MONAGAS
SUCRE
DELTA AMACURO
BARINAS
APURE
BOLÍVAR
AMAZONAS
DISTRITO FEDERAL
Orinoco
COLOMBIA
LA GUAJIRA
MAGDALENA
CESAR
NORTE DE SANTANDER
SANTANDER
ARAUCA
CASANARE
BOYACA
Cúcuta
Bucaramanga
Barranquilla
Santa Marta
Cartagena
Medellín
GUYANA
CUYUNI-MAZARUNI
BARIMA-WAINI
BRAZIL
Meters
Feet
LAND BELOW SEA LEVEL
F
G
H
I
J
72°
68°
64°
60°
24°
20°
16°
12°
8°
100
101

South America

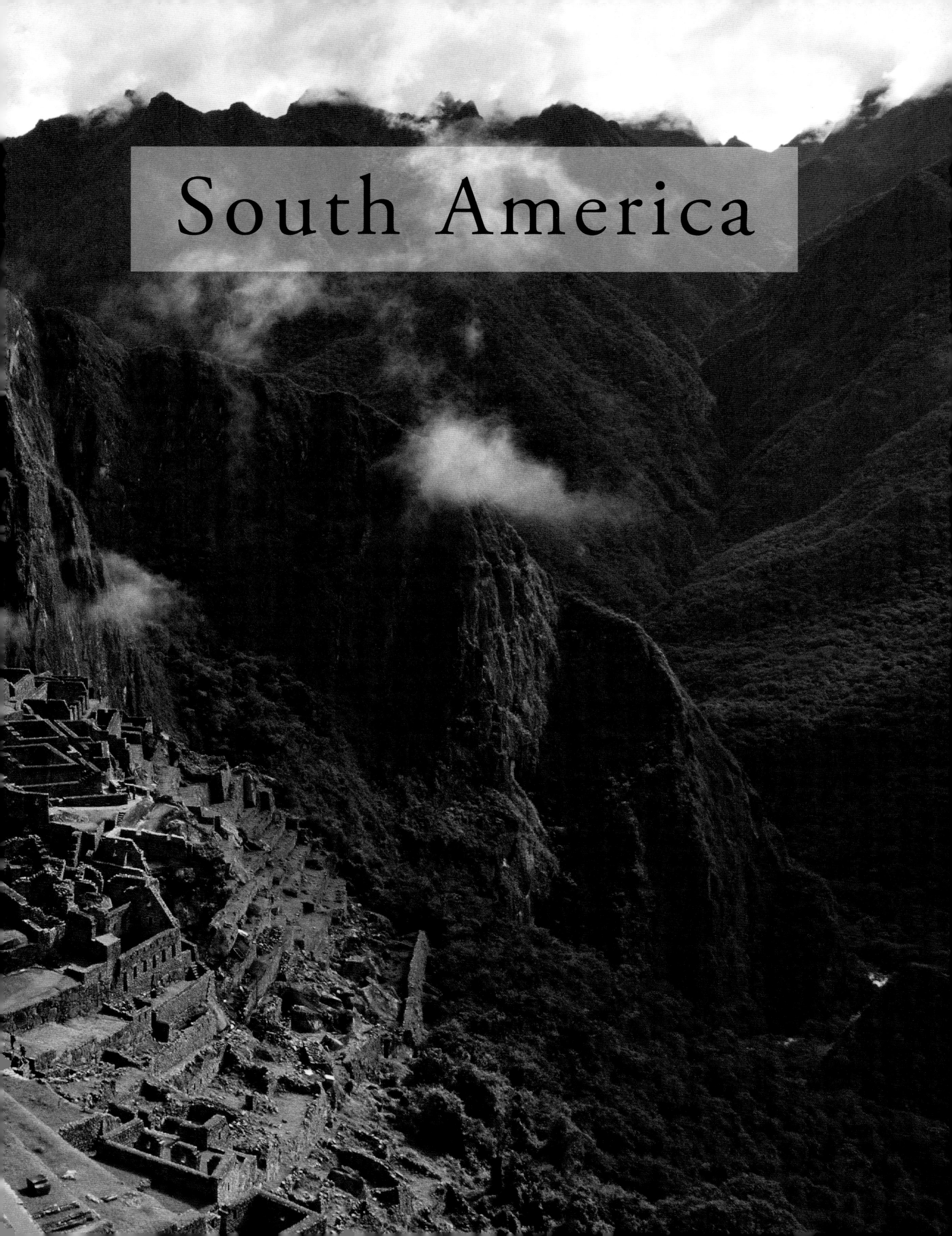

SOUTH AMERICA

Most of the continent is in the Southern Hemisphere, as the equator cuts across South America in its northern third, running through Ecuador, southern Colombia, and northern Brazil. History has divided the continent into 12 countries, the largest of which is Portuguese-speaking Brazil. Most of the rest of South America was colonized by Spain and the inhabitants speak Spanish, although Ecuador, Peru, and Bolivia especially have large native Indian populations who speak indigenous languages.

Previous pages The remains of Machu Picchu stand proudly among the mighty mountains of the Andes as a testament to the ingenuity and skill of Incan engineers and craftsmen.

Right Spanish and Portuguese influence is evident in the architectural styles seen in many South American towns and cities.

Below Cuzco in Peru was the capital of the Incan empire, and evidence of this once-powerful civilization remains today, with the ruins of well-built fortresses and buildings still standing.

Prior to the Spanish conquest, Peru was the center of a highly advanced Inca civilization, centered around the cities of Cuzco and Machu Picchu.

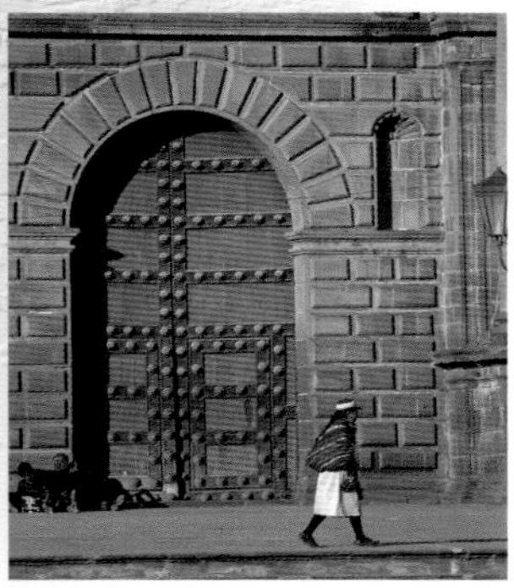

Three small territories in Caribbean South America—Guyana, Suriname, and French Guiana—were colonized by the English, Dutch, and French respectively. These three countries have diverse populations of East Asians, Amerindians, and descendants of African slaves. Like all the other countries of South America, Guyana and Suriname are independent, but French Guiana is an overseas department of France.

The Andes

There is a great diversity of landforms and climates in South America. Most prominent is a chain of high mountains called the Andes, which extends for more than 7,000 kilometers (4,400 miles) along the north–south length of the continent near the Pacific coast. It is the longest mountain chain in the world, and the highest outside Asia. The highest peak—at 6,962 meters (22,841 feet)—is Aconcagua, located in Argentina, close to its long border with Chile. The mountain chain was formed by tectonic subduction of the Pacific Basin's Nazca Plate beneath the continental South American plate, and is geologically unstable, with frequent earthquakes and volcanic eruptions. The many active volcanoes are arranged in four clusters along the length of the mountain chain. Llaima Volcano in south-central Chile and Pichincha Volcano near Ecuador's capital, Quito, are two of the many volcanic mountains in the Andes that have experienced spectacular eruptions in recent years.

The widest part of the Andes Mountains is in the south-center of the chain—in Bolivia and neighboring parts of Peru and Chile. Here, associated most especially with Bolivia, are the Altiplano—the world's second

COUNTRIES	OFFICIAL NAME	AREA	POPULATION	CAPITAL	RELIGION	POPULATION DENSITY	HIGHEST POINT	CURRENCY
Argentina	República Argentina	3,761,274 km^2/1,452,236 mi^2	40,914,000	Buenos Aires	✝94%, ✡2%, ○4%	11/km^2, 28/mi^2	Cerro Aconcagua 6,962 m/22,841 ft	Peso
Bolivia	República de Bolivia	1,084,390 km^2/418,685 mi^2	9,775,000	La Paz; Sucre	✝100%	9/km^2, 23/mi^2	Nevado Sajama 6,452 m/21,463 ft	Boliviano
Brazil	República Federativa do Brasil	8,514,877 km^2/3,300,000 mi^2	198,739,000	Brasília	✝90%, ○10%	23/km^2, 60/mi^2	Pico da Neblina 3,014 m/10,184 ft	Real
Chile	República de Chile	756,950 km^2/292,260 mi^2	16,602,000	Santiago	✝87.1%, ○12.9%	22/km^2, 57/mi^2	Nevado Ojos del Salado 6,880 m/22,572 ft	Peso
Colombia	República de Colombia	1,038,700 km^2/401,044 mi^2	45,644,000	Bogota	✝90%, ○10%	44/km^2, 114/mi^2	Pico Cristóbal Colón 5,775 m/18,945 ft	Peso
Ecuador	República del Ecuador	276,840 km^2/106,889 mi^2	14,573,000	Quito	✝95%, ○5%	53/km^2, 136/mi^2	Chimborazo 6,267 m/20,561 ft	US dollar
Guyana	Cooperative Republic of Guyana	196,850 km^2/76,004 mi^2	772,000	Georgetown	✝50%, ॐ35%, ☪10%, ○5%	4/km^2, 10/mi^2	Mt Roraima 2,835 m/9,301 ft	Dollar
Paraguay	República del Paraguay; Paraguay Retân	406,750 km^2/157,047 mi^2	6,996,000	Asunción	✝97%, ○3%	17/km^2, 45/mi^2	Cerro Pero 842 m/2,762 ft	Guarani
Peru	República del Perú	1,280,000 km^2/463,323 mi^2	29,547,000	Lima	✝83.1%, ○16.9%	23/km^2, 64/mi^2	Nevado Huascarán 6,768 m/22,205 ft	Nuevo sol
Suriname	Republiek Suriname	161,470 km^2/62,344 mi^2	481,000	Paramaribo	✝48%, ॐ27.4%, ☪19.6%, 🯅5%	3/km^2, 8/mi^2	Juliana Top 1,230 m/4,035 ft	Dollar
Uruguay	República Oriental del Uruguay	176,220 km^2/68,039 mi^2	3,494,000	Montevideo	✝68%, ✡1%, ○31%	20/km^2, 51/mi^2	Cerro Catedral 514 m/1,686 ft	Peso
Venezuela	República Bolivariana de Venezuela	882,050 km^2/340,561 mi^2	26,815,000	Caracas	✝98%, ○2%	30/km^2, 79/mi^2	Pico Bolivar 5,007 m/16,427 ft	Bolivar

DEPENDENCIES AND TERRITORIES		AREA	POPULATION	CAPITAL	RELIGION	POPULATION DENSITY	HIGHEST POINT	CURRENCY
Falkland Islands/ Islas Malvinas (UK)	Isla Malvinas	12,173 km^2/4,700 mi^2	3,100	Stanley	✝67%, ○33%	0.3/km^2, 0.6/mi^2	Mt Usborne 705 m/2,313 ft	Pound
French Guiana (France)	Department of Guiana	89,150 km^2/34,421 mi^2	221,500	Cayenne	✝100%	2/km^2, 6/mi^2	Bellevue de l'Inini 851 m/2,792 ft	Euro
South Georgia and South Sandwich Islands (UK)	South Georgia and the South Sandwich Islands	3,903 km^2/1,507 mi^2	no permanent population	—	—	—	Mt Paget 2,934 m/9,626 ft	—

largest high plain after Tibet—and Lake Titicaca, one of the world's highest large lakes, situated on the Peru–Bolivia boundary. In Ecuador, the Andes are split into two ranges—Cordillera Oriental and Cordillera Occidental—while to the north in Colombia they form three ranges, the easternmost of which extends into Venezuela. For most of their length, the Andes Mountains form a high wall that separates rainy climates on one side from dry climates on the other. In west-central South America, the mountains block moisture-bearing winds and rain from the distant Atlantic, creating the rain-shadow Atacama Desert along the Pacific Coast of northern Chile and neighboring Peru. It is the world's driest desert. In the southernmost part of the continent, where the prevailing winds are from west to east, the Pacific Ocean side of the mountains receives considerable rainfall and snow, making southern Chile a land of thick forests, high glaciers, and deep fjords. By contrast, the land to the east of the mountains is dry and barren. This is the Patagonia region of southern Argentina, a large plain of shingle rock, sparse vegetation, and few settlers.

Above Paramaribo, Suriname's capital, retains much of the architecture and cultural influences acquired when the country was a Dutch colony. Paramaribo's Old City was proclaimed a UNESCO World Heritage Site in 2002.

The Mighty Rivers of South America

About 40 percent of South America lies in the basin of the Amazon River—the largest and longest river basin in the world. The basin measures about 6,915,000 square kilometers (2,670,000 square miles). The largest part of the Amazonia (54 percent) is in Brazil, but the basin also extends to eastern Ecuador and Peru, southern Colombia and Venezuela, and northern Bolivia. The basin supports the world's largest tropical rainforest—the Amazon rainforest. It is home to a rich diversity of plant and animal species, as well as to scattered and isolated tribes of traditional hunters and gatherers. Increasing exploitation of the rainforest for timber, gold, petroleum, and other resources, along with the conversion of forests to farmland and ranches, threaten flora, fauna, and traditional human cultures with extinction. The Amazon River itself is by far the largest in the world when measured by volume of water, and the longest—or second-longest after the Nile River in Africa, depending on where one pinpoints the

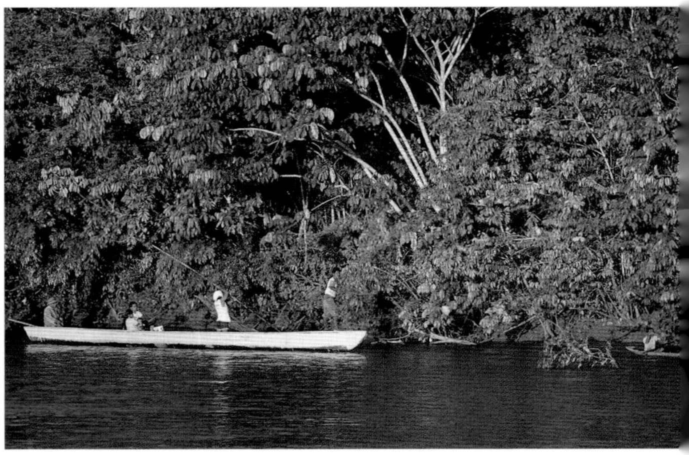

Above Founded in1567 by Diego de Losada, Caracas is the capital and largest city of Venezuela. This cosmopolitan city is flanked by Avila National Park and nearby hills, creating ideal conditions for pleasant year-round temperatures..

Above Right The mighty Amazon River, which flows from the Andes to the Atlantic, is one of the world's most navigable rivers, and locals have used the river as a transport route for centuries.

sources of each river. At its mouth, near the port city of Belém in northern Brazil, the Amazon is some 330 kilometers (210 miles) wide. The biggest tributaries of the Amazon are the Rio Negro, the Putumayo River, and the Madeira River. Because of sparse population and few roads in the Amazon region, there is not one bridge along the entire length of the river or its tributaries.

Other major rivers in South America are the Rio Paraná in Brazil, Paraguay, and Argentina—the continent's second-longest river; its main tributary, the Paraguay River; and the Uruguay River, which flows into the Paraná to form the Rio de la Plata, the wide estuary between Argentina and Uruguay on the South Atlantic coast. Itaipu Dam, the world's second largest source of hydroelectricity after the Three Gorges Dam in China, spans the Paraná on the border of Brazil and Paraguay, supplying both countries with much of their energy needs. Not far from the dam on the tributary Iguaçu River is Iguaçu Falls, one of the largest waterfalls in the world, and an acknowledged natural wonder. A second globally famous South American waterfall is Angel Falls—at 979 meters (3,212 feet), it is the highest waterfall in the world. Angel Falls is located in the Guyana Highlands of Venezuela, in a remote tropical rainforest, and plunges directly from the top of a tabletop mountain to a river far below.

The largest river in northern South America is the Orinoco. Originating in the tropical highlands—at the boundary of Brazil and Venezuela—the Orinoco forms part of the Venezuelan border with Colombia, and then flows through the middle of Venezuela to its delta on the Atlantic coast. The lower reaches of the river are navigable and support heavy industry in two large Venezuelan river towns, Ciudad Bolivar and Ciudad Guyana.

Natural Resources and Agriculture

A broad valley to the north of the Orinoco River holds the world's largest deposits of heavy crude oil. These deposits, and Venezuela's reserves of conventional crude oil in the vicinity of Lake Maracaibo near its Caribbean coast, make the country one of the world's major producers and exporters of oil. Colombia and Ecuador also export significant quantities of oil. Other major industrial resources in South America include about one-fifth of the world's iron reserves, most notably in southern Brazil and in the highlands of Venezuela; one-quarter of the world's copper ore, almost all of which is in Chile and Peru; major deposits of bauxite in Guyana and Suriname; and tin in Bolivia. Two open-pit copper mines in Chile—Chuquicamata and Escondida—rank among the largest mines in the world.

Gold and silver production has long been important in South America, especially during the time of European conquest and colonization in the sixteenth through late eighteenth centuries. The city of Potosí in Bolivia, arguably the world's highest elevation city at 4,090 meters (13,420 feet), has been a notable producer of silver since its founding in 1546 by Spanish conquistadors at the base of an ore-laden mountain they called Cerro Rico ("rich mountain").

Right Polylepis forests are native to the Andes region, and are mostly found in Bolivia's Western Cordillera. The effects of climate change and human impact have seen the once-flourishing forests reduced by a staggering 90 percent.

In addition, Pacific islands offshore from Peru have been exploited for centuries for their thick deposits of guano, a nitrate-rich fertilizer formed from the droppings of seabirds and cave bats.

The agricultural geography of South America reflects the climatic and physiographic diversity of the continent. Coffee and bananas are the major crops in Brazil, Colombia, and Ecuador, with the world's highest quality coffee said to come from the volcanic soils of Colombia's Cordillera Central region.

Brazil has an exceptionally diverse agricultural base and also grows sugar cane, corn, wheat, rice, and soybeans, as well as cocoa, cotton, latex, and various oil palms. The country's sugar production is rooted in its history of colonialism and slave labor transported from the African continent.

Along with Argentina and neighboring Uruguay, Brazil is a world leader in beef production. Argentina's La Pampa province—an expansive grassy plain in the very center of the country—is an agricultural heartland known for its many large cattle ranches called estancias. Further south, in Patagonia, sheep are raised. Alpacas are farmed for their wool in the Altiplano of Bolivia and Peru, while llamas are used more for transportation.

The foothills of the Andes in both Argentina and Chile are wine country, and wine is a lucrative export for both countries. Chile, Argentina, and Brazil also produce a variety of fruits, milk, cheese, and other dairy products, and fish—all of which are exported. The remote highlands of Colombia produce a less desirable export—illegal narcotics.

Below One of the most spectacular sections of Iguaçu Falls is the Garganta del Diablo Falls (Devil's Throat). At 150 meters (500 feet) wide, and running over a course of approximately 700 meters (2,300 feet), these falls mark the border between Argentina and Brazil.

ATLANTIC OCEAN
CARIBBEAN SEA
WEST INDIES
GREATER ANTILLES
LESSER ANTILLES
Leeward Islands
Windward Islands
BAHAMAS
CUBA
LA HABANA (HAVANA)
HAITI
PORT-AU-PRINCE
DOMINICAN REPUBLIC
SANTO DOMINGO
JAMAICA
KINGSTON
Cayman Islands (UK)
Turks and Caicos Islands (UK)
Puerto Rico (USA)
ANTIGUA AND BARBUDA
ST KITTS AND NEVIS
DOMINICA
ST LUCIA
BARBADOS
ST VINCENT AND THE GRENADINES
GRENADA
TRINIDAD AND TOBAGO
PORT-OF-SPAIN
Netherlands Antilles
Aruba (Netherlands)
HONDURAS
NICARAGUA
COSTA RICA
SAN JOSÉ
PANAMA
PANAMÁ
COLOMBIA
BOGOTÁ
VENEZUELA
CARACAS
GUYANA
GEORGETOWN
SURINAME
PARAMARIBO
French Guiana (France)
Cayenne
ECUADOR
QUITO
PERU
LIMA
BOLIVIA
LA PAZ
BRAZIL
BRASÍLIA
AMAZON BASIN
GUIANA HIGHLANDS
PLANALTO DO MATO GROSSO
PLANALTO CENTRAL
ANDES
SELVAS
Mouths of the Amazon
Manaus
Belém
Fortaleza
Recife
Salvador
Maceió
Natal
Medellín
Cali
Barranquilla
Cartagena
Maracaibo
Valencia
Guayaquil
Santa Cruz
Cochabamba
Goiânia

1:20,600,000

Lambert Azimuthal Equal Area Projection

0 250 500 750 1000 kilometers

0 125 250 375 500 miles

SOUTH AMERICA POLITICAL

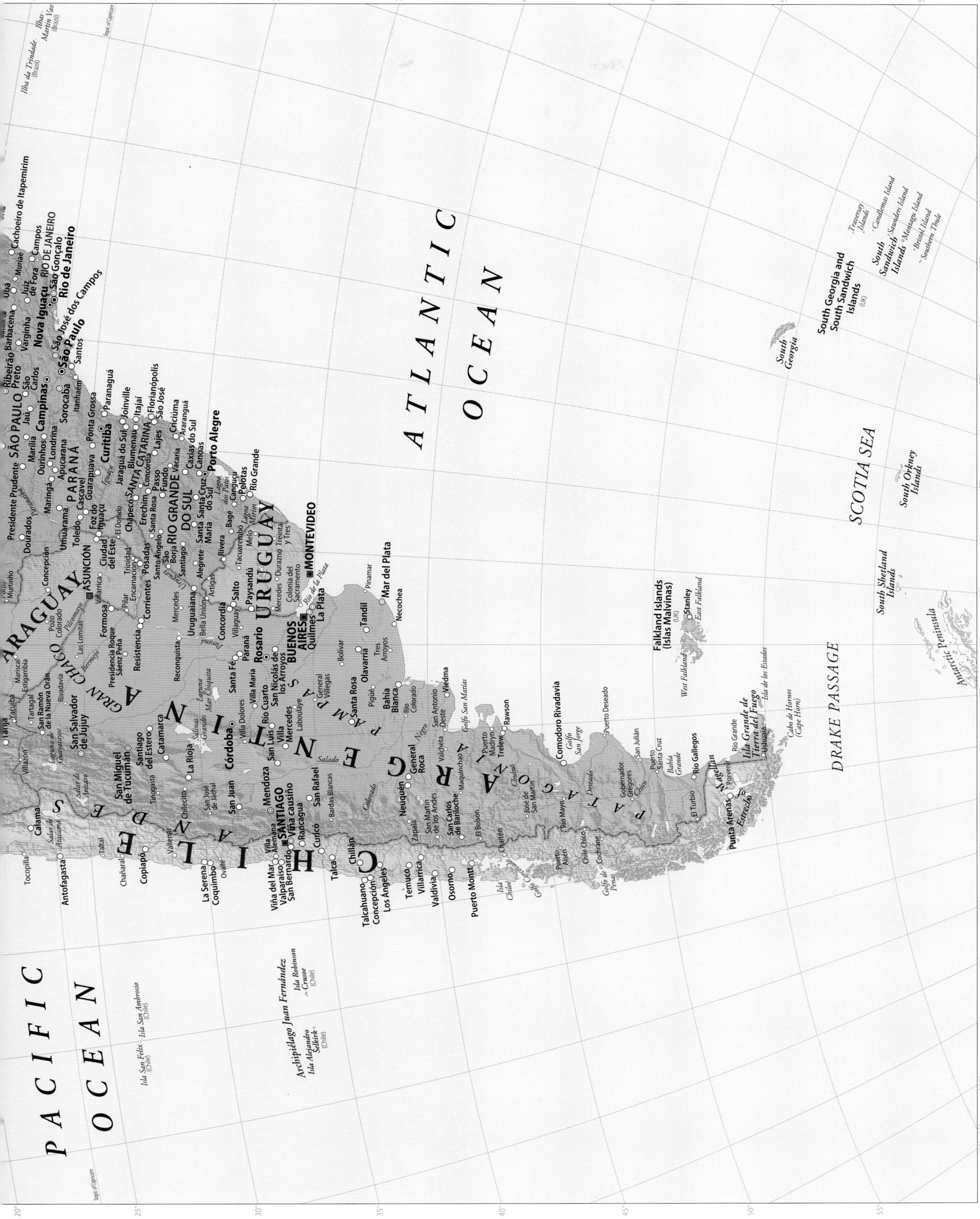

ATLANTIC OCEAN
PACIFIC OCEAN
SCOTIA SEA
DRAKE PASSAGE
ARGENTINA
CHILE
URUGUAY
PARAGUAY
GRAN CHACO
PAMPAS
PATAGONIA
SÃO PAULO
PARANÁ
SANTA CATARINA
RIO GRANDE DO SUL
RIO DE JANEIRO
Rio de Janeiro
São Paulo
Campinas
Curitiba
Porto Alegre
Nova Iguaçu
São Gonçalo
São José dos Campos
Santos
Ribeirão Preto
Sorocaba
Londrina
Maringá
Florianópolis
Joinville
Blumenau
Pelotas
Rio Grande
Caxias do Sul
Canoas
Foz do Iguaçu
Ciudad del Este
ASUNCIÓN
Concepción
Encarnación
MONTEVIDEO
Salto
Paysandú
Rivera
Tacuarembó
Melo
BUENOS AIRES
La Plata
Quilmes
Mar del Plata
Necochea
Tandil
Olavarría
Bahía Blanca
Santa Rosa
Rosario
Santa Fé
Paraná
Córdoba
Río Cuarto
Villa María
Corrientes
Resistencia
Posadas
Formosa
San Miguel de Tucumán
Santiago del Estero
San Salvador de Jujuy
Salta
Catamarca
La Rioja
San Juan
Mendoza
San Luis
San Rafael
Neuquén
General Roca
Viedma
Rawson
Trelew
Puerto Madryn
San Carlos de Bariloche
Comodoro Rivadavia
Puerto Deseado
San Julián
Río Gallegos
Río Grande
Ushuaia
Punta Arenas
Estrecho de Magallanes
Isla Grande de Tierra del Fuego
Isla de los Estados
Cabo de Hornos (Cape Horn)
SANTIAGO
Valparaíso
Viña del Mar
Rancagua
Curicó
Talca
Chillán
Concepción
Talcahuano
Los Angeles
Temuco
Villarrica
Valdivia
Osorno
Puerto Montt
Isla Chiloé
Coquimbo
La Serena
Copiapó
Antofagasta
Calama
Tocopilla
Falkland Islands (Islas Malvinas) (UK)
Stanley
West Falkland
East Falkland
South Georgia and South Sandwich Islands (UK)
South Georgia
South Sandwich Islands
South Orkney Islands
South Shetland Islands
Antarctic Peninsula
Archipiélago Juan Fernández
Isla Robinson Crusoe (Chile)
Isla Alejandro Selkirk (Chile)
Isla San Félix (Chile)
Isla San Ambrosio (Chile)
Ilha da Trindade (Brazil)
Ilhas Martin Vaz (Brazil)
Tropic of Capricorn

CARIBBEAN SEA
PACIFIC OCEAN
Lesser Antilles
PANAMA
COLOMBIA
ECUADOR
PERU
ANDES
LLANOS
SELVAS
BOGOTÁ
QUITO
CARACAS
Medellín
Cali
Barranquilla
Cartagena
Maracaibo
Guayaquil
Iquitos
Golfo de Panamá
Golfo de Venezuela
Lago de Maracaibo
Golfo de Guayaquil
Península de la Guajira
Península de Paraguaná
Isla de Malpelo
Aruba (Netherlands)
Netherlands Antilles (Netherlands)
Administrative regions in Ecuador numbered on the map:
1. SANTO DOMINGO DE LOS TSÁCHILAS
Administrative regions in Venezuela numbered on the map:
1. YARACUY
2. CARABOBO
3. ARAGUA
4. VARGAS
5. DISTRITO CAPITAL
Meters
Feet
6000 19685
5000 16404
4000 13123
3000 9843
2000 6562
1000 3281
500 1640
200 656
100 328
0
LAND BELOW SEA LEVEL
100 328
200 656
1000 3281
2000 6562
4000 13123
6000 19685
90
104
A
B
C
D
80°
76°
72°
68°

1:7,880,000

Lambert Conic Conformal Projection

0 50 100 150 200 250 300 kilometers

0 25 50 75 100 125 150 miles

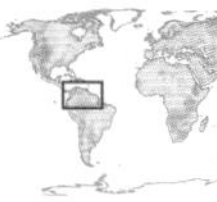

NORTHWESTERN SOUTH AMERICA

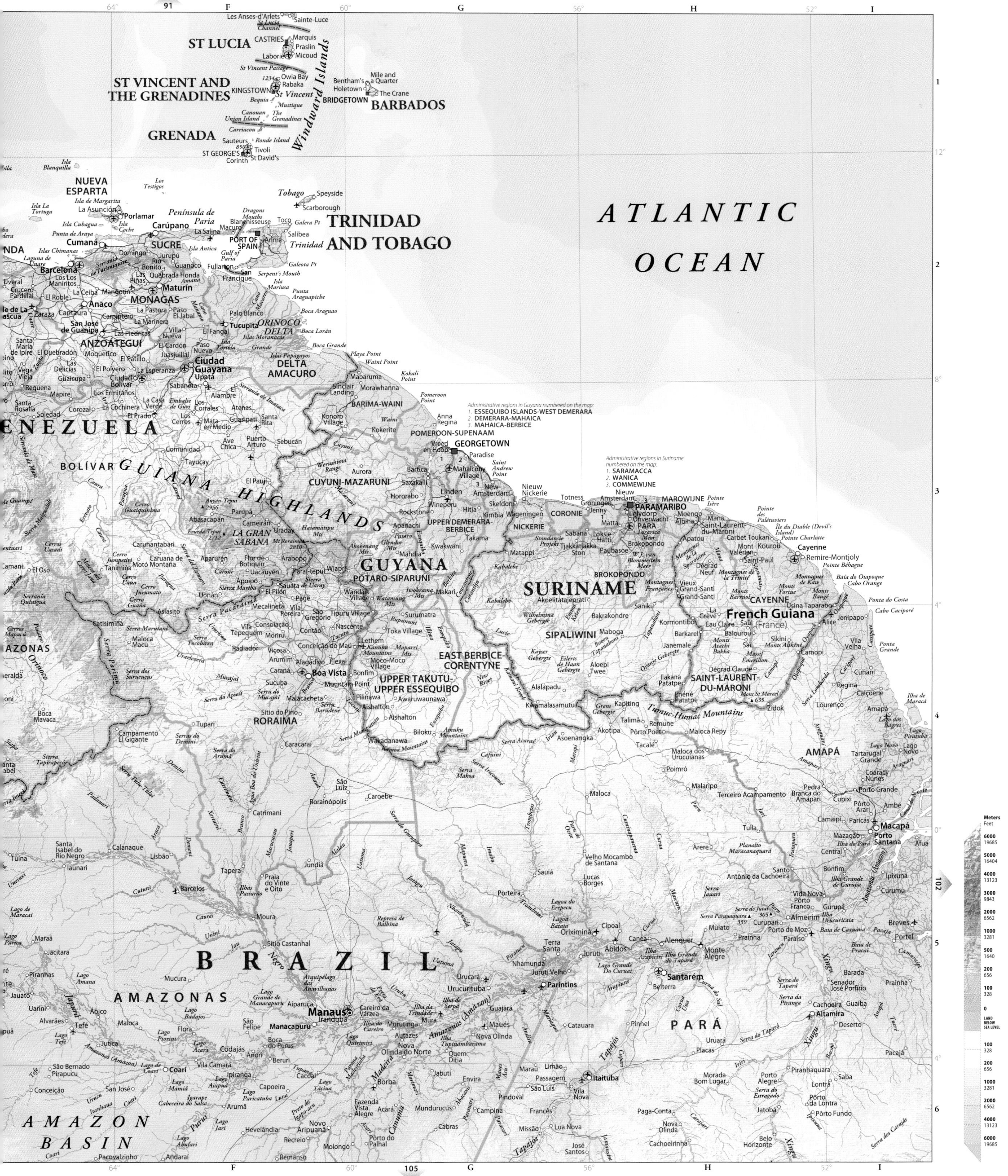
91
105
102
ATLANTIC OCEAN
ST LUCIA
ST VINCENT AND THE GRENADINES
GRENADA
BARBADOS
TRINIDAD AND TOBAGO
Windward Islands
CASTRIES
KINGSTOWN
BRIDGETOWN
ST GEORGE'S
PORT OF SPAIN
NUEVA ESPARTA
SUCRE
MONAGAS
ANZOÁTEGUI
DELTA AMACURO
BOLÍVAR
AMAZONAS
VENEZUELA
GUIANA HIGHLANDS
LA GRAN SABANA
GUYANA
GEORGETOWN
BARIMA-WAINI
POMEROON-SUPENAAM
CUYUNI-MAZARUNI
UPPER DEMERARA-BERBICE
POTARO-SIPARUNI
EAST BERBICE-CORENTYNE
UPPER TAKUTU-UPPER ESSEQUIBO
Administrative regions in Guyana numbered on the map:
1. ESSEQUIBO ISLANDS-WEST DEMERARA
2. DEMERARA-MAHAICA
3. MAHAICA-BERBICE
SURINAME
PARAMARIBO
Administrative regions in Suriname numbered on the map:
1. SARAMACCA
2. WANICA
3. COMMEWIJNE
MAROWIJNE
CORONIE
NICKERIE
PARA
BROKOPONDO
SIPALIWINI
French Guiana
(France)
CAYENNE
SAINT-LAURENT-DU-MARONI
Tumuc-Humac Mountains
RORAIMA
Boa Vista
AMAPÁ
Macapá
BRAZIL
AMAZONAS
PARÁ
Manaus
Santarém
AMAZON BASIN
Meters
Feet
6000 19685
5000 16404
4000 13123
3000 9843
2000 6562
1000 3281
500 1640
200 656
100 328
0
LAND BELOW SEA LEVEL
100 328
200 656
1000 3281
2000 6562
4000 13123
6000 19685

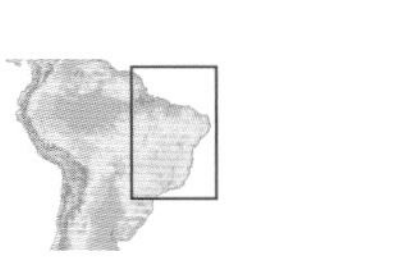

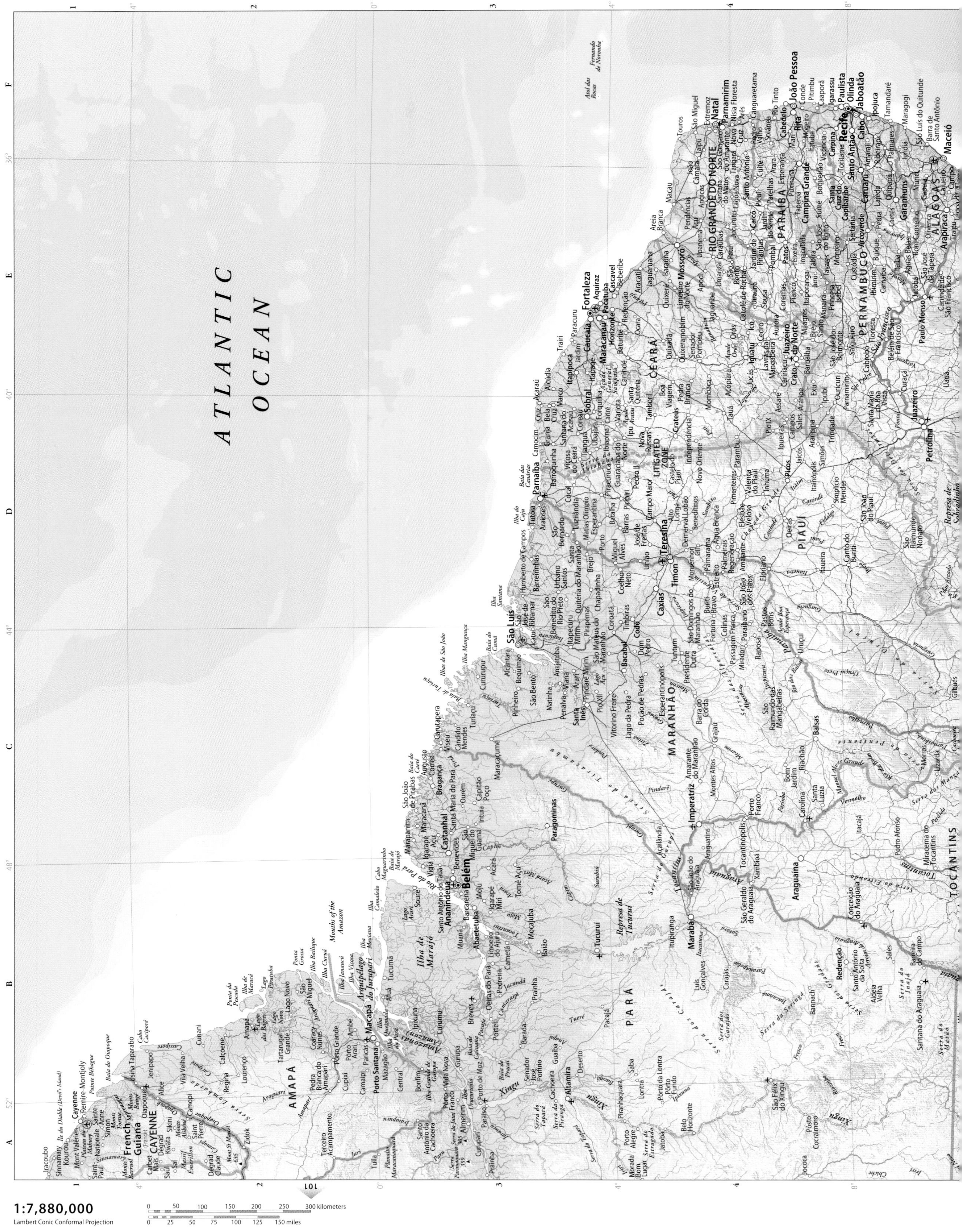
ATLANTIC
OCEAN
French Guiana
(France)
CAYENNE
Cayenne
AMAPÁ
Macapá
PARÁ
Belém
MARANHÃO
São Luís
Teresina
PIAUÍ
CEARÁ
Fortaleza
RIO GRANDE DO NORTE
Natal
PARAÍBA
João Pessoa
PERNAMBUCO
Recife
ALAGOAS
Maceió
TOCANTINS
Ilha de Marajó
Mouths of the Amazon
LITIGATED ZONE

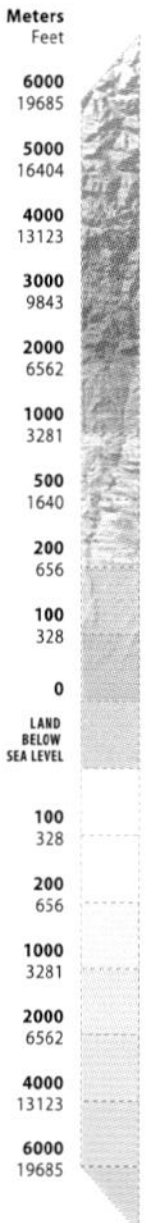
Meters
Feet
6000 19685
5000 16404
4000 13123
3000 9843
2000 6562
1000 3281
500 1640
200 656
100 328
0
LAND BELOW SEA LEVEL
100 328
200 656
1000 3281
2000 6562
4000 13123
6000 19685

1:7,880,000

Lambert Conic Conformal Projection

0 50 100 150 200 250 300 kilometers

0 25 50 75 100 125 150 miles

EASTERN SOUTH AMERICA

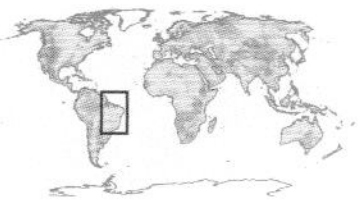

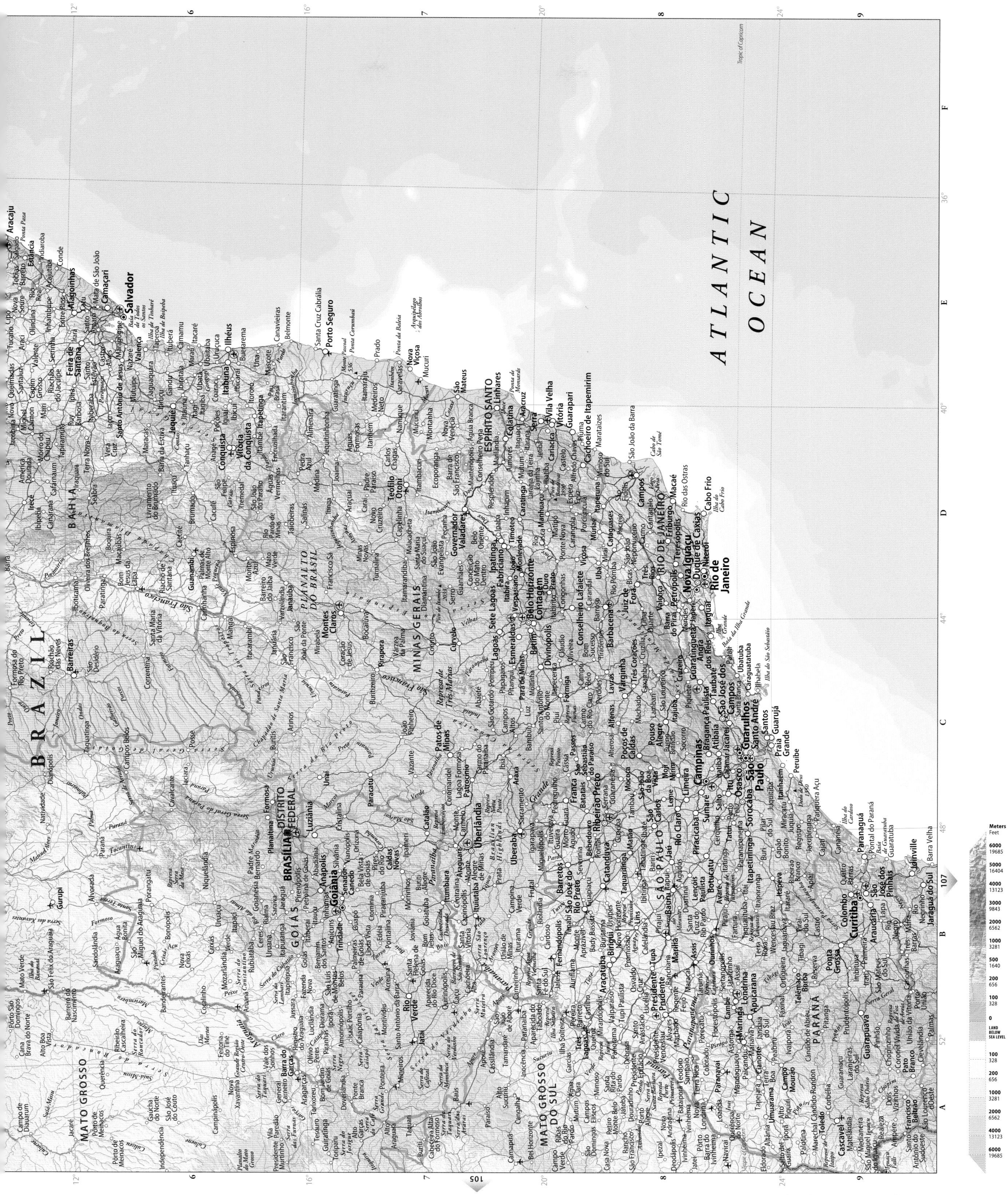
ATLANTIC OCEAN
BRAZIL
BAHIA
MINAS GERAIS
GOIÁS
SÃO PAULO
MATO GROSSO
MATO GROSSO DO SUL
PARANÁ
ESPÍRITO SANTO
RIO DE JANEIRO
DISTRITO FEDERAL
PLANALTO DO BRASIL
Salvador
Brasília
Belo Horizonte
Rio de Janeiro
São Paulo
Curitiba
107
105
Meters
Feet
6000
19685
5000
16404
4000
13123
3000
9843
2000
6562
1000
3281
500
1640
200
656
100
328
0
LAND BELOW SEA LEVEL
100
328
200
656
1000
3281
2000
6562
4000
13123
6000
19685

A
B
C
D
80°
76°
72°
68°
100
106
4°
8°
12°
16°
20°
1
2
3
4
5
6
ECUADOR
PERU
CHILE
PACIFIC OCEAN
AMAZON BASIN
Machala
Tumbes
Talara
Sullana
Piura
Chiclayo
Trujillo
Chimbote
Huacho
Callao
LIMA
Pisco
Ica
Nazca
Camaná
Arequipa
Moquegua
Ilo
Tacna
Arica
Iquique
Tocopilla
Calama
ANTOFAGASTA
Iquitos
Pucallpa
Tingo María
Huánuco
Cerro de Pasco
Huancayo
Ayacucho
Abancay
Cusco
Juliaca
Puno
Lago Titicaca
LA PAZ
Oruro
Rio Branco
Cruzeiro do Sul
Tabatinga
LORETO
AMAZONAS
CAJAMARCA
LAMBAYEQUE
PIURA
TUMBES
SAN MARTÍN
LA LIBERTAD
ANCASH
HUÁNUCO
PASCO
JUNÍN
UCAYALI
MADRE DE DIOS
HUANCAVELICA
ICA
AYACUCHO
APURÍMAC
CUSCO
PUNO
AREQUIPA
MOQUEGUA
TACNA
ARICA Y PARINACOTA
TARAPACÁ
ACRE
PANDO
ORURO
CORDILLERA CENTRAL
CORDILLERA OCCIDENTAL
CORDILLERA ORIENTAL
DESIERTO DE ATACAMA
Amazonas (Amazon)
Marañón
Ucayali
Huallaga

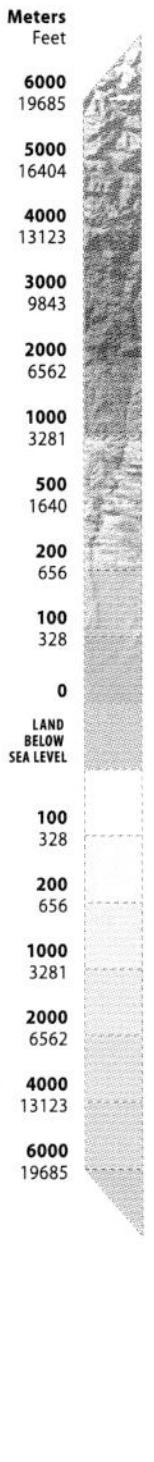
Meters
Feet
6000
19685
5000
16404
4000
13123
3000
9843
2000
6562
1000
3281
500
1640
200
656
100
328
0
LAND BELOW SEA LEVEL
100
328
200
656
1000
3281
2000
6562
4000
13123
6000
19685

1:7,880,000

Lambert Conic Conformal Projection

0 50 100 150 200 250 300 kilometers

0 25 50 75 100 125 150 miles

CENTRAL SOUTH AMERICA

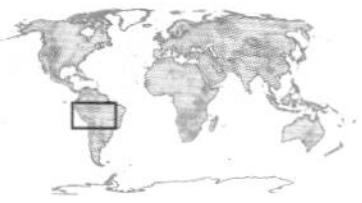

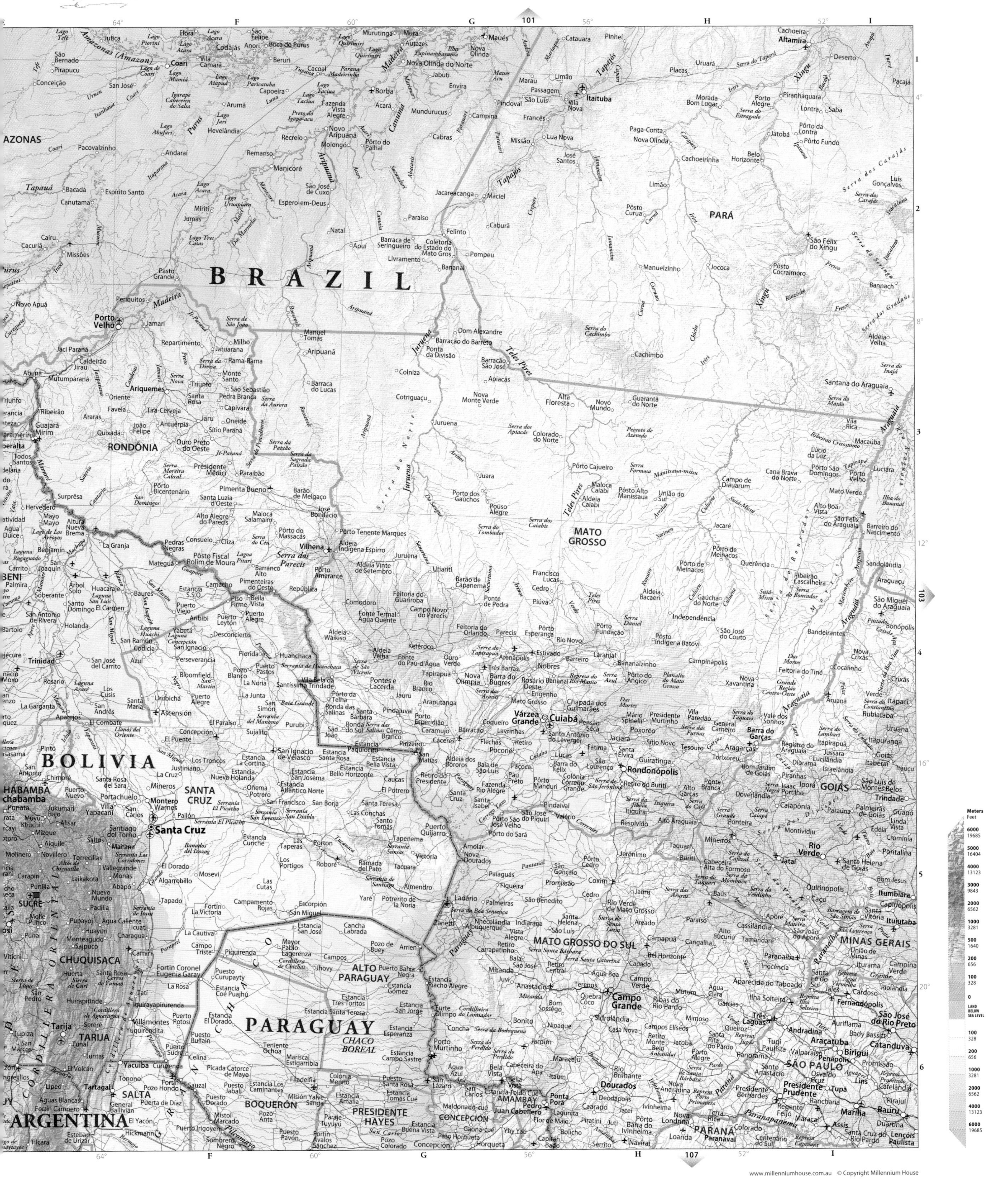
101
103
107
F
G
H
I
64°
60°
56°
52°
4°
8°
12°
16°
20°
1
2
3
4
5
6
BRAZIL
BOLIVIA
PARAGUAY
ARGENTINA
PARÁ
MATO GROSSO
MATO GROSSO DO SUL
RONDÔNIA
GOIÁS
MINAS GERAIS
SÃO PAULO
PARANÁ
SANTA CRUZ
CHUQUISACA
TARIJA
SALTA
BENI
ALTO PARAGUAY
PRESIDENTE HAYES
BOQUERÓN
CONCEPCIÓN
AMAMBAY
GRAN CHACO
CHACO BOREAL
CORDILLERA ORIENTAL
Amazonas (Amazon)
Madeira
Tapajós
Xingu
Araguaia
Juruena
Teles Pires
Paraguai
Paraná
Paranapanema
Pilcomayo
Mamoré
Guaporé
Serra dos Parecis
Serra do Cachimbo
Serra do Roncador
Serra dos Carajás
Porto Velho
Cuiabá
Várzea Grande
Campo Grande
Rondonópolis
Ariquemes
Vilhena
Itaituba
Altamira
Coari
Santa Cruz
Sucre
Trinidad
Tarija
Montero
Dourados
Corumbá
Rio Verde
Presidente Prudente
Marília
Bauru
Araçatuba
São José do Rio Preto
Catanduva
Ponta Porã
Pedro Juan Caballero
Concepción
Três Lagoas
Jataí
Barra do Garças
Meters
Feet
6000
19685
5000
16404
4000
13123
3000
9843
2000
6562
1000
3281
500
1640
200
656
100
328
0
LAND BELOW SEA LEVEL

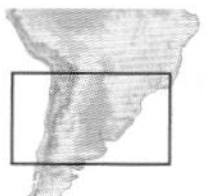

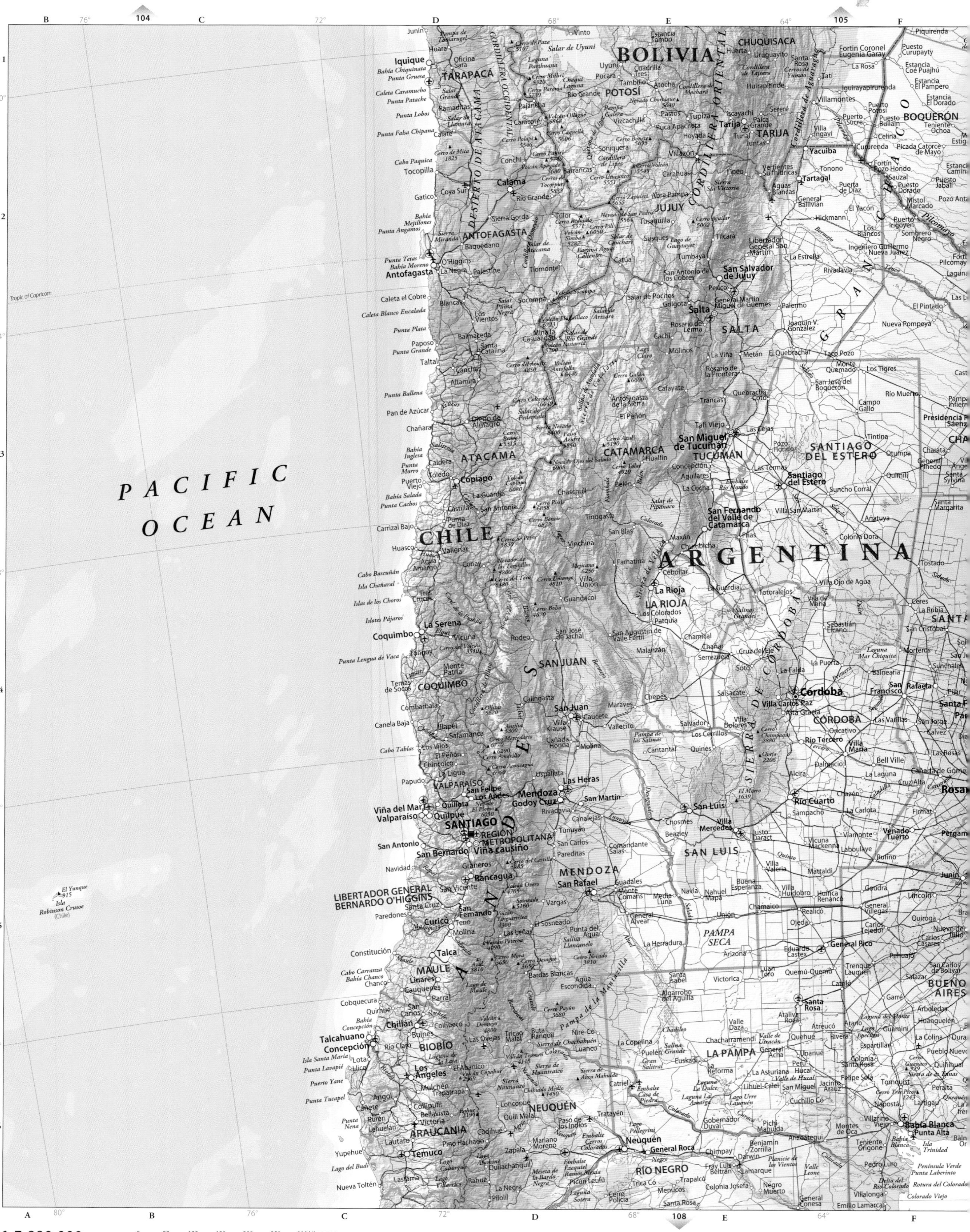

104
105
108
B
C
D
E
F
A
76°
72°
68°
64°
80°
20°
24°
28°
32°
36°
1
2
3
4
5
6
PACIFIC OCEAN
BOLIVIA
CHILE
ARGENTINA
ANDES
GRAN CHACO
Tropic of Capricorn
CHUQUISACA
POTOSÍ
TARIJA
BOQUERÓN
TARAPACÁ
ANTOFAGASTA
JUJUY
SALTA
ATACAMA
CATAMARCA
TUCUMÁN
SANTIAGO DEL ESTERO
LA RIOJA
COQUIMBO
SAN JUAN
CÓRDOBA
VALPARAÍSO
REGIÓN METROPOLITANA
MENDOZA
SAN LUIS
LIBERTADOR GENERAL BERNARDO O'HIGGINS
MAULE
BIOBÍO
ARAUCANÍA
NEUQUÉN
LA PAMPA
RÍO NEGRO
BUENOS AIRES
PAMPA SECA
DESIERTO DE ATACAMA
CORDILLERA OCCIDENTAL
CORDILLERA ORIENTAL
SIERRA DE CÓRDOBA
Salar de Uyuni
Salar de Atacama
Iquique
Calama
Antofagasta
Tocopilla
Tarija
Yacuiba
San Salvador de Jujuy
Salta
San Miguel de Tucumán
Santiago del Estero
San Fernando del Valle de Catamarca
Copiapó
La Rioja
La Serena
Coquimbo
San Juan
Córdoba
Mendoza
Viña del Mar
Valparaíso
SANTIAGO
San Antonio
Rancagua
San Rafael
Talca
Chillán
Talcahuano
Concepción
Los Ángeles
Temuco
Neuquén
General Roca
Bahía Blanca
San Luis
Río Cuarto
Villa María
Santa Rosa
El Yunque 915
Isla Robinson Crusoe (Chile)

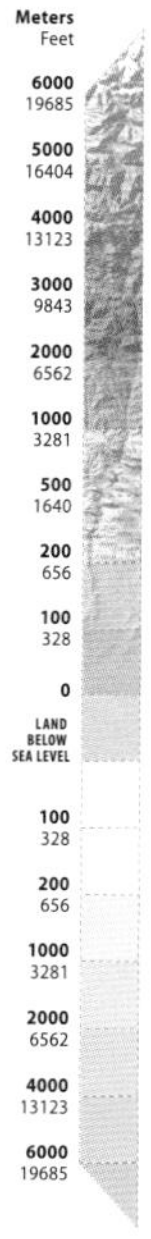

Meters
Feet
6000
19685
5000
16404
4000
13123
3000
9843
2000
6562
1000
3281
500
1640
200
656
100
328
0
LAND BELOW SEA LEVEL
100
328
200
656
1000
3281
2000
6562
4000
13123
6000
19685

1:7,880,000
Lambert Conic Conformal Projection

0 50 100 150 200 250 300 kilometers
0 25 50 75 100 125 150 miles

SOUTH CENTRAL SOUTH AMERICA

103
BRAZIL
PARAGUAY
URUGUAY
ATLANTIC OCEAN
MATO GROSSO DO SUL
SÃO PAULO
MINAS GERAIS
PARANÁ
SANTA CATARINA
RIO GRANDE DO SUL
São Paulo
Rio de Janeiro
Belo Horizonte
Campinas
Curitiba
Florianópolis
Porto Alegre
Campo Grande
Londrina
Joinville
Pelotas
Rio Grande
ASUNCIÓN
MONTEVIDEO
BUENOS AIRES
La Plata
Mar del Plata
Corrientes
Posadas
Encarnación
Foz do Iguaçu
Ciudad del Este
Santos
Niterói
Ribeirão Preto
Uberaba
Sorocaba
Ponta Grossa
Caxias do Sul
Santa Maria
Uruguaiana
Concordia
Paysandú
Salto
Tacuarembó
Rivera
Melo
Maldonado
Tandil
Necochea
Tropic of Capricorn
Rio de la Plata
Lagoa dos Patos
Lagoa Mirim
Meters
Feet
6000 19685
5000 16404
4000 13123
3000 9843
2000 6562
1000 3281
500 1640
200 656
100 328
0
LAND BELOW SEA LEVEL
100 328
200 656
1000 3281
2000 6562
4000 13123
6000 19685

SOUTHERN SOUTH AMERICA

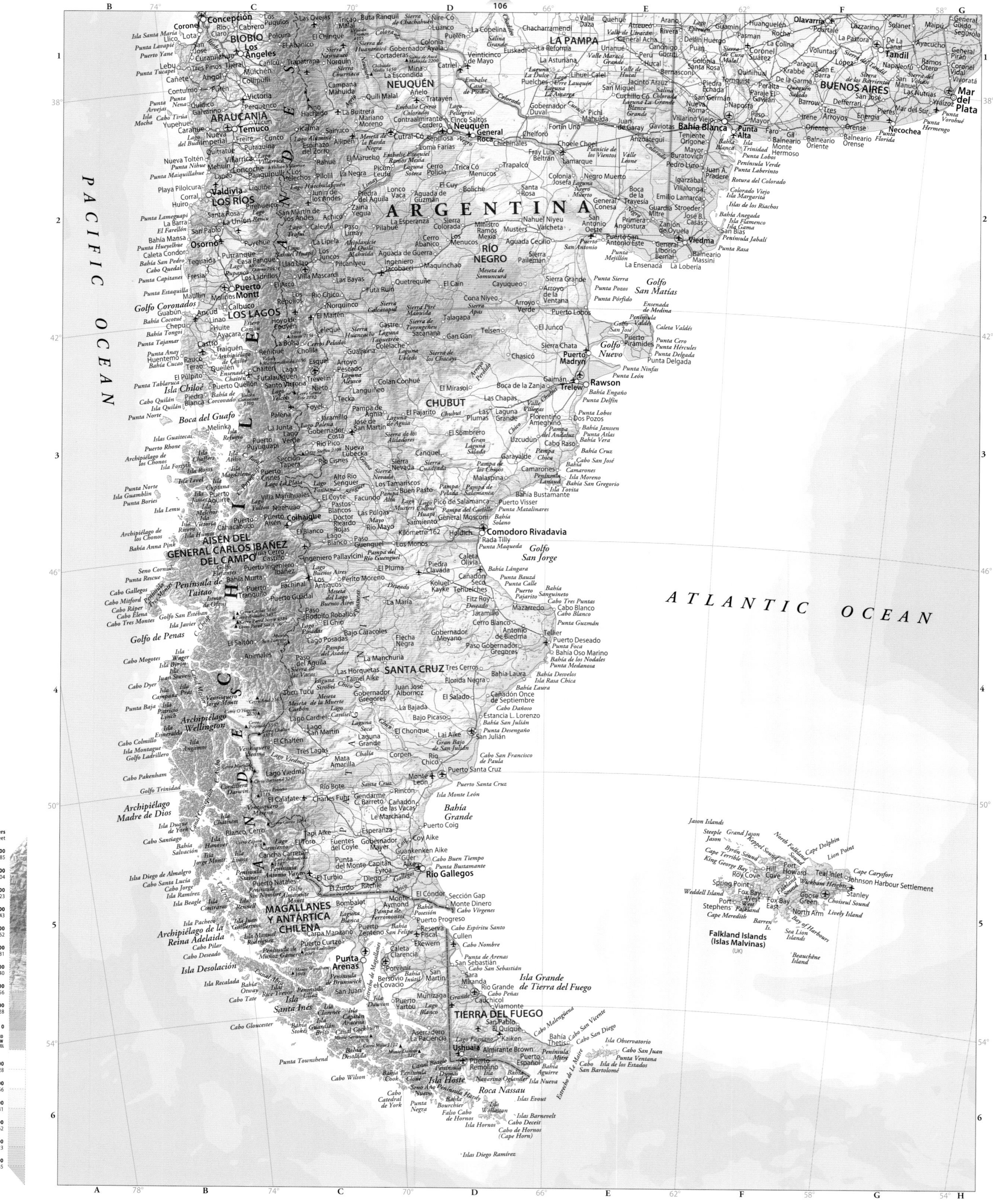
106
PACIFIC OCEAN
ATLANTIC OCEAN
ARGENTINA
CHILE
LA PAMPA
BUENOS AIRES
NEUQUÉN
RÍO NEGRO
CHUBUT
SANTA CRUZ
TIERRA DEL FUEGO
BIOBÍO
ARAUCANÍA
LOS RÍOS
LOS LAGOS
AISÉN DEL GENERAL CARLOS IBÁÑEZ DEL CAMPO
MAGALLANES Y ANTÁRTICA CHILENA
Concepción
Los Ángeles
Temuco
Valdivia
Osorno
Puerto Montt
Castro
Coihaique
Punta Arenas
Ushuaia
Río Gallegos
Comodoro Rivadavia
Rawson
Trelew
Puerto Madryn
Viedma
Bahía Blanca
Neuquén
Mar del Plata
Tandil
Necochea
Olavarría
Golfo San Matías
Golfo Nuevo
Golfo San Jorge
Golfo de Penas
Golfo Coronados
Boca del Guafo
Isla Chiloé
Isla Grande de Tierra del Fuego
Isla Desolación
Isla Hoste
Isla Navarino
Cabo de Hornos (Cape Horn)
Islas Diego Ramírez
Falkland Islands (Islas Malvinas) (UK)
Stanley
Meters
Feet
6000 19685
5000 16404
4000 13123
3000 9843
2000 6562
1000 3281
500 1640
200 656
100 328
0
LAND BELOW SEA LEVEL
100 328
200 656
1000 3281
2000 6562
4000 13123
6000 19685

1:7,880,000

Lambert Conic Conformal Projection

0 50 100 150 200 250 300 kilometers

0 25 50 75 100 125 150 miles

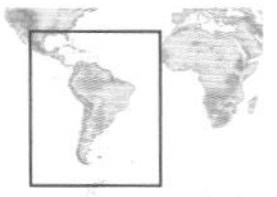

ISLANDS Around SOUTH AMERICA

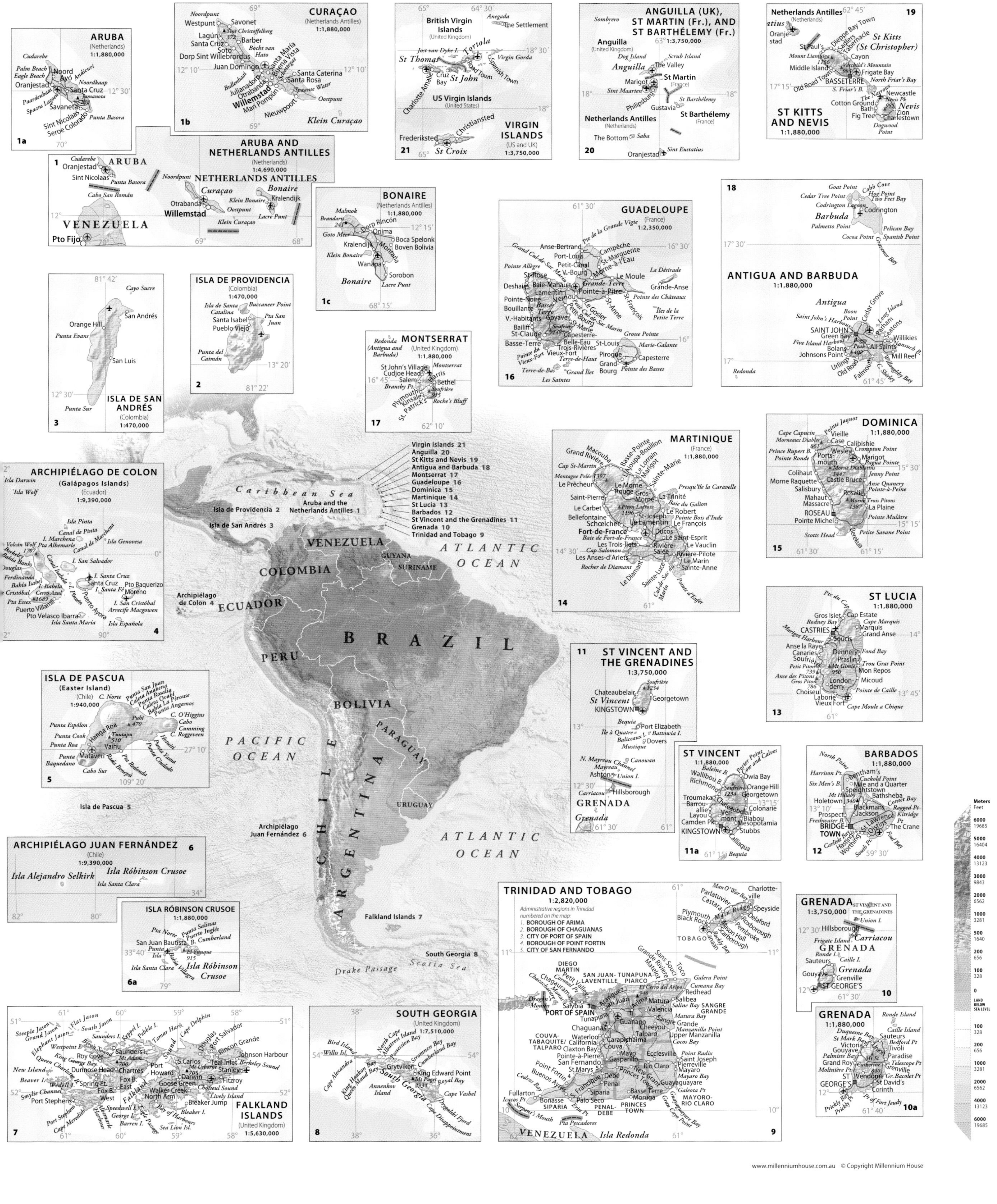
ARUBA
(Netherlands)
1:1,880,000
1a
CURAÇAO
(Netherlands Antilles)
1:1,880,000
1b
British Virgin Islands
(United Kingdom)
US Virgin Islands
(United States)
VIRGIN ISLANDS
(US and UK)
1:3,750,000
21
ANGUILLA (UK), ST MARTIN (Fr.), AND ST BARTHÉLEMY (Fr.)
1:3,750,000
20
Netherlands Antilles
ST KITTS AND NEVIS
1:1,880,000
19
ARUBA AND NETHERLANDS ANTILLES
(Netherlands)
1:4,690,000
1
VENEZUELA
BONAIRE
(Netherlands Antilles)
1:1,880,000
1c
GUADELOUPE
(France)
1:2,350,000
16
18
ANTIGUA AND BARBUDA
1:1,880,000
ISLA DE PROVIDENCIA
(Colombia)
1:470,000
2
ISLA DE SAN ANDRÉS
(Colombia)
1:470,000
3
MONTSERRAT
(United Kingdom)
1:1,880,000
17
MARTINIQUE
(France)
1:1,880,000
14
DOMINICA
1:1,880,000
15
Virgin Islands 21
Anguilla 20
St Kitts and Nevis 19
Antigua and Barbuda 18
Montserrat 17
Guadeloupe 16
Dominica 15
Martinique 14
St Lucia 13
Barbados 12
St Vincent and the Grenadines 11
Grenada 10
Trinidad and Tobago 9
Caribbean Sea
Isla de Providencia 2
Isla de San Andrés 3
Aruba and the Netherlands Antilles 1
ARCHIPIÉLAGO DE COLON
(Galápagos Islands)
(Ecuador)
1:9,390,000
4
Archipiélago de Colon 4
VENEZUELA
GUYANA
SURINAME
COLOMBIA
ECUADOR
ATLANTIC OCEAN
BRAZIL
PERU
BOLIVIA
PARAGUAY
CHILE
ARGENTINA
URUGUAY
PACIFIC OCEAN
ST LUCIA
1:1,880,000
13
ISLA DE PASCUA
(Easter Island)
(Chile)
1:940,000
5
Isla de Pascua 5
11 ST VINCENT AND THE GRENADINES
1:3,750,000
ST VINCENT
1:1,880,000
11a
BARBADOS
1:1,880,000
12
Archipiélago Juan Fernández 6
ARCHIPIÉLAGO JUAN FERNÁNDEZ
(Chile)
1:9,390,000
6
ISLA RÓBINSON CRUSOE
1:1,880,000
6a
Falkland Islands 7
South Georgia 8
Scotia Sea
Drake Passage
TRINIDAD AND TOBAGO
1:2,820,000
Administrative regions in Trinidad numbered on the map:
1. BOROUGH OF ARIMA
2. BOROUGH OF CHAGUANAS
3. CITY OF PORT OF SPAIN
4. BOROUGH OF POINT FORTIN
5. CITY OF SAN FERNANDO
9
GRENADA
1:3,750,000
10
GRENADA
1:1,880,000
10a
FALKLAND ISLANDS
(United Kingdom)
1:5,630,000
7
SOUTH GEORGIA
(United Kingdom)
1:7,510,000
8
Meters
Feet
6000 19685
5000 16404
4000 13123
3000 9843
2000 6562
1000 3281
500 1640
200 656
100 328
0
LAND BELOW SEA LEVEL
100 328
200 656
1000 3281
2000 6562
4000 13123
6000 19685

Europe

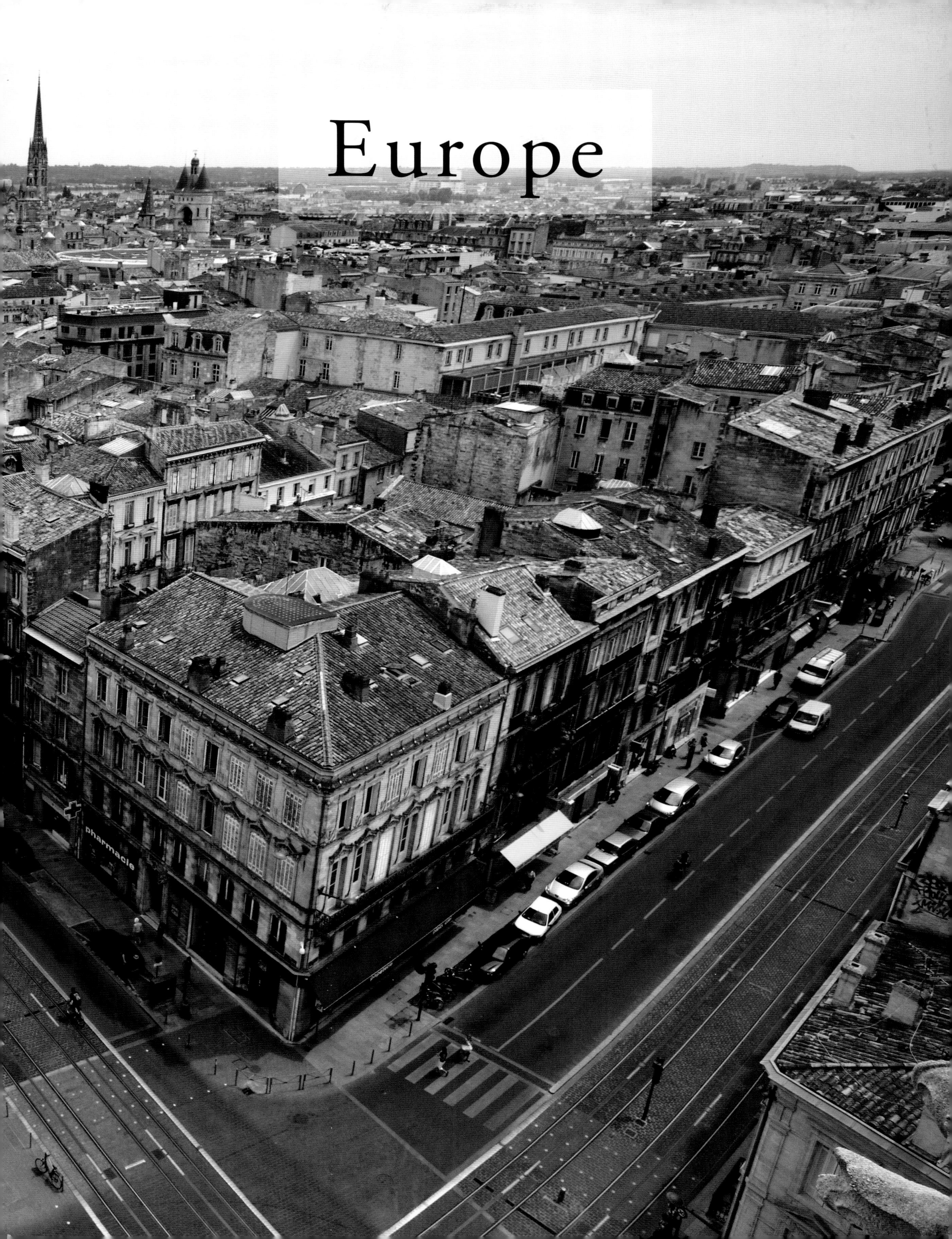
pharmacie

NORTHERN and WESTERN EUROPE

The combined regions of Western and Northern Europe include the countries of Scandinavia, the Baltic states, Iceland, the British Isles, and a swathe of mainland territory from France to the eastern boundaries of Germany and Austria. About one-third of all European territory is covered by the region. North Cape (Nordkapp) marks the northernmost point of the European mainland; the French island of Corsica is the southernmost point of the region. Iceland lies the farthest west and eastern Finland is the eastern boundary.

Right Best known for his fairy tales, Hans Christian Andersen is one of Denmark's most famous authors. Statues of him and especially of "the little mermaid" are popular features of the city of Copenhagen.

Previous pages Although Bordeaux is well known as a French wine-producing area, the city itself is an important regional commercial center. Its busy port, beautiful public gardens, and historic buildings (many built in the 1700s) bring many visitors.

Below The imposing grandeur of the Bernese Alps draws many climbers to this area. Schreckhorn, in Switzerland, is one of the most challenging peaks, with the first successful ascent made in 1861.

Nineteen countries make up Western and Northern Europe. These may be subdivided through the following classifications: Northern (Nordic) Europe—including the island nation of Iceland, Norway, Sweden, Finland, Estonia, Latvia, Lithuania, and Denmark; the British Isles—comprised of the United Kingdom and Ireland; and Western Europe—consisting of France, Liechtenstein, Monaco, Germany, Belgium, Netherlands, Luxembourg, Switzerland, and Austria.

Germany has the largest population at 82 million, followed by France at 64 million, and United Kingdom with 61 million. At the other end of the scale, the microstates of Monaco and Liechtenstein have 33,000 and 35,000 inhabitants respectively.

Climate and Vegetation

The mild climate of Western Europe is due to the effect of the Gulf Stream—a warm oceanic current that originates in the Gulf of Mexico, then flows north along the coast of North America, where it splits in two. Its northern arm flows across the Atlantic to the western coasts of Europe, helping to make temperatures in that region less cold than those experienced by the inland areas of the European landmass. The climate of northern Europe is dominated by the cold arctic winds that flow south from polar regions.

Much of Western and Northern Europe's natural flora and fauna has been lost to human development. In Scandinavia and Finland boreal forests still dominate much of the landscape, particularly in Sweden. These forests also dominate the Baltic states. Norway also has substantial areas of alpine ecosystems.

Within Western Europe much of the natural vegetation is confined to nature reserves and national parks. Within the mountain regions, extensive areas of alpine vegetation, particularly alpine heath, are found on the upper slopes, although centuries of summer grazing and more recently the ski industry have had an impact. Boreal evergreen forests are also found on the lower slopes, particularly in the Alps. In the valleys and the lowlands most of the original temperate deciduous forests have been cleared and now form the great agricultural lands of the region.

Physical Geography

The physical geography of the region is diverse, with a wide variety of geological features evident. Extensive lowlands extend across northern France into Belgium and the Netherlands, where large areas are below sea level. Extensive mountain ranges span the region—the Alps run east to west, stretching 1,200 kilometers (750 miles) from France through Switzerland, Liechtenstein, southern Germany, and Austria. At 4,807 meters (15,771 feet), France's Mont Blanc is the highest point. Separating Spain from France, the Pyrenees mark the southern boundary of the region.

Extensive mountain ranges run from north to south, hugging Norway's western coast. This coastline is dominated by extensive fjord systems that have been carved by the extensive glaciers found there. Further west, the large island of Iceland lies midway between Northern Europe and Canada. Dominated by an extensive iceshelf in the southwest corner of the island, Iceland is also the most volcanically active part of the region. To the north of Norway is Svalbard, lying well within the Arctic Circle. Lakes are also a key feature of Scandinavia, Lake Vänern in southern Sweden is the region's largest lake, and contains over 20,000 small islands and rocky outcrops.

The other major islands of the region are the British Isles. Britain is separated from Europe by the narrow and shallow English Channel, where a number of small islands, including Guernsey and Jersey, are found. Lying further west, the Irish Sea separates Britain from Ireland, which is often referred to as the Emerald Isle due to its green hue, created by vast rainfall.

COUNTRIES	OFFICIAL NAME	AREA	POPULATION	CAPITAL	RELIGION	POPULATION DENSITY	HIGHEST POINT	CURRENCY
Austria	Republik Österreich	82,444 km²/31,834 mi²	8,210,000	Vienna (Wien)	✝78.3%, ☪4.2%, ◯17.5%	100/km², 258/mi²	Großglockner 3,797 m/12,457 ft	Euro
Belgium	Royaume de Belgique; Koninkrijk België; Königreich Belgien	30,278 km²/11,691 mi²	10,414,000	Brussels (Bruxelles/Brussel)	✝75%, ◯25%	344/km², 891/mi²	Botrange 694 m/2,277 ft	Euro
Denmark	Kongeriget Danmark	42,394 km²/16,370 mi²	5,501,000	Copenhagen (København)	✝98%, ☪2%	130/km², 336/mi²	Yding Skovhøj 173 m/568 ft	Krone
Estonia	Eesti Vabariik	43,211 km²/16,685 mi²	1,299,000	Tallinn	✝27.8%, ◯72.2%	30/km², 78/mi²	Suur Munamägi 318 m/1,043 ft	Kroon
Finland	Suomen Tasavalta; Republiken Finland	304,473 km²/117,557 mi²	5,250,000	Helsinki	✝85.3%, ◯14.7%	17/km², 45/mi²	Haltiatunturi 1,324 m/4,343 ft	Euro
France	République Française	545,630 km²/210,668 mi²	64,058,000	Paris	✝83–90%, ☪5–10%, ✡1%, ◯4%	117/km², 304/mi²	Mont Blanc 4,807 m/15,771 ft	Euro
Germany	Bundesrepublik Deutschland	349,223 km²/134,845mi²	82,330,000	Berlin	✝68%, ☪3.7%, ◯28.3%	236/km², 611/mi²	Zugspitze 2,962 m/9,718 ft	Euro
Iceland	Lýðveldið Ísland	100,250 km²/38,706 mi²	307,000	Reykjavík	✝93.8%, ◯6.2%	3/km², 8/mi²	Hvannadalshnúkur 2,110 m/6,952 ft	Króna
Ireland	Éire; Ireland	70,282 km²/27,136 mi²	4,203,000	Dublin (Baile Átha Cliath)	✝93%, ◯7%	60/km², 155/mi²	Carrauntuohil 1,041 m/3,414 ft	Euro
Latvia	Latvijas Republika	63,589 km²/24,554 mi²	2,232,000	Riga	✝35.9%, ◯64.1%	35/km², 91/mi²	Gaizina Kalns 312 m/1,024 ft	Lat
Liechtenstein	Fürstentum Liechtenstein	160 km²/61.8 mi²	35,000	Vaduz	✝83.2%, ◯16.8%	218/km², 566/mi²	Vorder-Grauspitz 2,599 m/8,527 ft	Franc
Lithuania	Lietuvos Respublika	65,200 km²/25,176 mi²	3,555,000	Vilnius	✝85%, ◯15%	55/km², 141/mi²	Juozapinės Kalnas 293 m/963 ft	Litas
Luxembourg	Grand Duché de Luxembourg; Großherzogtum Luxemburg	2,586 km²/999 mi²	492,000	Luxembourg	✝87%, ◯13%	190/km², 492/mi²	Buurgplaatz 562 m/1,843 ft	Euro
Monaco	Principauté de Monaco	1.95 km²/¾ mi²	33,000	Monaco	✝90%, ◯10%	16,923/km², 44,000/mi²	Mont Agel 140 m/459 ft	Euro
Netherlands	Koninkrijk der Nederlanden	41,528 km²/16,034 mi²	16,716,000	Amsterdam, The Hague (Den Haag/'s-Gravenhage)	✝43.7%, ☪5.8%, ◯50.5%	403/km², 1,043/mi²	Vaalserberg 321 m/1,053 ft	Euro
Norway	Kongeriket Noreg; Kongeriket Norge	307,422 km²/118,703 mi²	4,661,000	Oslo	✝90.1%, ☪1.8%, ◯8.1%	15/km², 39/mi²	Galdhøpiggen 2,469 m/8,100 ft	Krone
Sweden	Konungariket Sverige	410,934 km²/158,662 mi²	9,060,000	Stockholm	✝87%, ◯13%	22/km², 57/mi²	Kebnekaise 2,111 m/6,926 ft	Krona
Switzerland	Schweizerische Eidgenossenschaft; Confédération Suisse; Confederazione Svizzera; Confederaziun Svizra	39,770 km²/15,355 mi²	7,604,000	Bern	✝79.3%, ☪4.3%, ◯16.4%	191/km², 495/mi²	Dufourspitze 4,634 m/15,200 ft	Franc
United Kingdom	United Kingdom of Great Britain and Northern Ireland	244,820 km²/94,526 mi²	61,113,000	London	✝72%, ☪2.7%, ॐ1%, ☬0.6%, ✡0.5%, ◯23.2%	250/km², 647/mi²	Ben Nevis 1,343 m/4,406 ft	Pound Sterling

DEPENDENCIES AND TERRITORIES	OFFICIAL NAME	AREA	POPULATION	CAPITAL	RELIGION	POPULATION DENSITY	HIGHEST POINT	CURRENCY
Aland (Finland)	Ahvenanmaan Lääni	1,481 km²/572 mi²	27,000	Mariehamn (Maarianhamina)	✝94.8%, ◯5.2%	18/km², 47/mi²	Orrdals Hill 129 m/423 ft	Euro
Faroe Islands (Denmark)	Færoerne; Føroyar	1,399 km²/540 mi²	49,000	Torshavn	✝83.8%, ◯16.2%	35/km², 90/mi²	Slaettaratindur 882 m/2,894 ft	Krone
Guernsey (UK)	Bailiwick of Guersey	78 km²/30 mi²	66,000	St Peter Port	✝99%, ◯1%	846/km², 2,200/mi²	Le Moulin 114 m/375 ft	Pound
Isle of Man (UK)	Isle of Man	572 km²/221 mi²	77,000	Douglas	✝99%, ◯1%	135/km², 348/mi²	Snaefell 621 m/2,037 ft	Pound
Jan Mayen (Norway)	Jan Mayen	377 km²/145 mi²	no permanent population	—	—	—	Beerenberg 2,277 m/7,469 ft	—
Jersey (UK)	Bailiwick of Jersey	116 km²/45 mi²	92,000	St Helier	✝95%, ☪0.5%, ◯4.5%	793/km², 2,044/mi²	Les Platons 143 m/469 ft	Pound
Svalbard (Norway)	Svalbard	61,020 km²/23,560 mi²	2,100	Longyearbyen	✝99%, ◯1%	0.03/km², 0.09/mi²	Newtontoppen 1,717 m/5,632 ft	Krone

Numerous rivers crisscross the region, fed by melting snow in upland areas. At 1,320 kilometers (820 miles) long, the Rhine is Western Europe's longest river. It rises in the Swiss Alps, and empties into the North Sea at Rotterdam, in the Netherlands.

The coastlines of the region are long and varied. Extensive coastal flats dominate the shorelines of northern France, and are also found along the Baltic Sea coastlines of Denmark, Germany and the Baltic states. Britain's east coast also contains mostly depositional features, such as dunes and beaches. Rocky coastlines are found along France's southern Mediterranean Sea and the west coast of Norway, where deep fjords formed by glacial action are found in abundance. Ireland's west coast adjacent to the Atlantic is also dominated by rocky landforms.

Left Chenonceau Castle, in France's Loire Valley, is one of the best known chateaus of the area. Built in the sixteenth century as a residence rather than a fortified castle, it has since been embellished with spectacular gardens, and extended and restored.

EASTERN EUROPE

Eastern Europe constitutes all of the territory stretching eastward from the German and Austrian borders to the Urals in Russian Federation, as well as the eastern Balkan states of Bulgaria, Romania, and Moldova. The land to the east of the Urals and south to the Caspian Sea is considered to be in Asia, and Russian Federation is therefore considered to be in both Europe and Asia. Eastern Europe's southernmost state is Bulgaria; Russian Federation is the northernmost state.

Geographically, ten nations, including Russian Federation, make up this region. Five countries of the region have landlocked status; these are Belarus, Czech Republic, Hungary, Moldova, and Slovakia. Countries with access to the world ocean are, from north to south: Russian Federation, Poland, Ukraine, Romania, and Bulgaria. Russian Federation is the largest country in the region and indeed the world, followed within Eastern Europe by Ukraine; Moldova has the smallest area.

Right Street performers add color and interest to many European cityscapes. Here an Austrian organ grinder prepares to ply his trade in Budapest.

Climate and Vegetation

Like the other regions of Europe, Eastern Europe has a diverse physical environment. The climate of the region is similarly highly variable. Typically the region experiences cold winters, with average temperatures often below freezing. Yet summers tend to be mild to warm, and significant parts of the region experience low rainfalls, particularly Romania. With much of the region being some distance from the coast, continental weather patterns tend to dominate over coastal systems, with Poland in the north, and European Russia being the exceptions.

The plateau between the Ural and Carpathian mountain ranges experiences lower rainfall than further western areas, and a vast system of grassland ecosystems, known as steppes, dominates the area. These highly fertile lands have largely been taken over by agricultural development.

The vegetation in other parts of the region is dominated by temperate deciduous forests, which once covered most of western Poland, Slovakia, Czech Republic, Moldova, Hungary, and western Romania. Evergreen boreal forests are found in the colder climates of Belarus, eastern Poland, and parts of Ukraine. These forests also dominate in northwestern Russia.

Below Prague's Old Town Square has been the Czech capital's central marketplace for more than 600 years. It is surrounded by historic buildings from a variety of styles. The Church of Our Lady before Tyn was built during the 1300s.

Physical Features

The environment of the western portion of Eastern Europe, centered around southern Poland, Czech Republic, and Slovakia, is heavily influenced by alpine environments. Here, the geology is less stable and the topography tends to be associated with mountain ranges and steep-sided river valleys carved out of the landscape by ancient glacial systems. The Carpathian Mountains stretch 1,450 kilometers (900 miles) in a sweeping arc from Poland in the north through Slovakia and into Romania. Although not excessively high, with a maximum of 2,655 meters (8,711 feet) at Mt Gerlachovka in Slovakia, the extent of the mountains has a significant impact on the region's environment. Sometimes referred to as the South Carpathians, the Transylvanian Alps run off the Carpathians running east to west for around 250 kilometers (150 miles) through Romania.

The far eastern boundary of Eastern Europe is formed by the Ural Mountains. These rugged mountains run north to south for 2,500 kilometers (1,550 miles) and have traditionally been seen as the boundary between European Russia in the west and the Asian portion of Russia that extends to the east. The mountains have three distinct parts with the central part containing the highest mountains, Mt Narodnaya, at 1,895 meters (6,217 feet), being the highest in the range. This region, along with the northern section, is alpine-like, with glaciers and large areas of permafrost. To the south, as the range stretches toward the Caspian Sea, the mountains are highly eroded and eventually give way to hills.

Stretching between the Urals and the Carpathians is the Central Russian Upland, which is a vast plateau that is the result of considerable geological stability. The

COUNTRIES	OFFICIAL NAME	AREA	POPULATION	CAPITAL	RELIGION	POPULATION DENSITY	HIGHEST POINT	CURRENCY
Belarus	Respublika Belarus; Respublika Byelarus'	207,600 km^2/80,161 mi^2	9,649,000	Minsk	✝80%, ○20%	46/km^2, 120/mi^2	Dzyarzhynskaya Hara 346 m/1,135 ft	Rouble
Bulgaria	Republika Bŭlgariya	110,550 km^2/42,687 mi^2	7,205,000	Sofia (Sofiya)	✝83.8%, ☪12.2%, ○4%	65/km^2, 169/mi^2	Musala 2,925 m/9,596 ft	Lev
Czech Republic	Česká Republika	77,276 km^2/29,839 mi^2	10,212,000	Prague (Praha)	✝28.9%, ○71.1%	132/km^2, 342/mi^2	Sněžka 1,602 m/5,259 ft	Koruna
Hungary	Magyar Köztársaság	92,340 km^2/35,655 mi^2	9,906,000	Budapest	✝74%, ○26%	107/km^2, 278/mi^2	Kékes 1,014 m/3,327 ft	Forint
Moldova	Republica Moldova	33,371 km^2/12,886 mi^2	4,321,000	Kishinev (Chişinău)	✝95.3%, ○4.7%	129/km^2, 335/mi^2	Dealul Bălăneşti 430 m/1,411 ft	Leu
Poland	Rzeczpospolita Polska	304,465 km^2/117,563 mi^2	38,483,000	Warsaw (Warszawa)	✝91.4%, ○8.6%	126/km^2, 327/mi^2	Rysy 2,499 m/8,199 ft	Zloty
Romania	România	230,340 km^2/88,941 mi^2	22,215,000	Bucharest (Bucureşti)	✝99%, ○1%	96/km^2, 250/mi^2	Moldoveanu 2,544 m/8,346 ft	Leu
Russian Federation	Rossiysjaya Federatsiya	16,995,800 km^2/6,562,591 mi^2	140,041,000	Moscow (Moskva)	✝22%, ☪15%, ○63%	8/km^2, 21/mi^2	Gora El'brus 5,633 m/18,481 ft	Ruble
Slovakia	Slovenská Republika	48,800 km^2/18,843 mi^2	5,463,000	Bratislava	✝84%, ○16%	112/km^2, 290/mi^2	Gerlachovský Štít 2,655 m/8,711 ft	Koruna
Ukraine	Ukrayina	603,700 km^2/233,107 mi^2	45,700,000	Kiev (Kyiv/Kyyiv)	✝51.7%, ○48.3%	76/km^2, 196/mi^2	Hora Hoverla 2,061 m/6,762 ft	Hryvnia

Great Hungarian Plain is another large lowland area, extending from southeastern Hungary to western Romania, and covering an area of around 100,000 square kilometers (38,000 square miles).

Europe's longest rivers (the Volga and the Danube) flow through Eastern Europe, and both are important transport links. Much of Eastern Europe is continental, and Czech Republic, Slovakia, Hungary, Moldova, and Belarus are all landlocked. Poland has a shoreline along the Baltic, where vast dune systems are found along the flat open coastline. European Russia has a short Baltic coastline and then a vast coastline along the Arctic, much of which is frozen for most of the year. Bulgaria, Ukraine, and Russia all have coastlines along the virtually enclosed Black Sea. The northern coastline—occupied by Ukraine and Romania—tends to be rocky with plunging cliff faces in parts. Much of the rest of the coast is generally indented with wide bays. Ukraine and Russia also border the Sea of Azov, a small bay-like sea branching off the northern Black Sea.

Below The Russian city of St Petersburg was founded in 1703 by Peter the Great on the Neva River. The new city's impressive buildings included palaces, cathedrals, and places of learning, most designed by European architects.

SOUTHERN EUROPE

Southern Europe is defined traditionally as a combination of the peninsular and island countries framing the northern shores of the Mediterranean Sea—it is known also as Mediterranean Europe. The Iberian and Italian peninsulas and the western half of the Balkan Peninsula, proceeding from west to east, make up this region. Southern or Mediterranean Europe forms about a quarter of the continent of Europe. Of the sixteen countries of this region, only six have no coastline, with four of these found on the Balkan Peninsula.

Below This hand was once part of a giant marble statue of Constantine, the first Christian Roman Emperor. It stands in a courtyard of the Capitoline Hill and Museum, Rome, Italy.

Below Venice and its southern islands, as seen from outer space. The island of Giudecca is shaped like a fishbone, and San Giorgio is opposite the mouth of the Grand Canal.

The region's most northerly point occurs along the Italian–Austrian boundary, while the southernmost location is the tiny island of Gavdos, Greece. The most westerly point is Cabo de Roca, Portugal; the most easterly is the Dodecanese island of Strongyli, Greece. Sixteen countries and one colony constitute Southern Europe. The countries are Portugal, Andorra, Spain, Italy, San Marino, Vatican City, Malta, Slovenia, Croatia, Bosnia and Herzegovina, Serbia, Montenegro, Kosovo, Albania, Macedonia, and Greece, while Gibraltar is a colony of the United Kingdom. Italy has the largest population at 58 million, while Vatican City (the Holy See) has fewer than 1,000 people.

Climate and Vegetation

Southern Europe is strongly influenced by its Mediterranean climate, which provides dry and hot summers with wet but reasonably mild winters. Winter temperatures tend to be lower further from the coast.

Agricultural development has replaced most of the endemic flora and fauna.Where natural environments do exist, the Mediterranean climate provides for ecosystems well adapted to long periods of low rainfall, with grasses and more open forests tending to dominate. Separated from Africa by the Strait of Gibraltar, which measures only 13 kilometers (8 miles) across at its most narrow point, the Iberian Peninsula shares many common features with North Africa. The native vegetation across the southern part of the peninsula, including all of Portugal and the southwest of Spain, is evergreen forest, typical of subtropical regions. These forests once also lined the west coast of the Italian Peninsula. The drier eastern part of the peninsula is dominated by low-growing scrub, known as chaparral; this is also found in small pockets along the southern coastlines of mainland Italy and Sicily. Within the areas of elevated altitude in northern Spain, central Italy, and the southwest Balkans, deciduous forests thrive. Boreal forests are found in the higher mountains of Greece and the Balkan region.

Physical Features

The geology of the region is characterized by considerable tectonic activity. Fault lines caused by the northward drift of the African Plate into the Eurasian Plate are the cause of this activity, and Europe's most active volcanoes are found in the region.

Mt Vesuvius, in southwestern Italy, most famously erupted in 79 CE, causing the destruction of the ancient city of Pompeii, and it remains highly active, with the most recent significant eruption in 1944. A number of other significant volcanoes are found in the islands of the Tyrrhenian Sea. Mt Etna, on the Italian island of Sicily, is the most active European volcano. Earthquakes are also common in much of Southern Europe. In April 2009, a significant earthquake struck the Italian city of L'Aquila, causing widespread damage and leading to the death of hundreds of people.

Significant mountain ranges are found throughout the region. Most notable are the Pyrenees, which run east to west, separating the Iberian Peninsula from Western Europe. It is within these mountains that the nation of Andorra is found. The Apennines run along much of the length of the Italian Peninsula, effectively splitting it into distinct halves. In the extreme north of Italy, in the Friuli-Venezia Giulia and Tyrol regions, the Dolomites rise up to join with the Alps of Western Europe. The Balkan Mountains are the principal range of the Balkan Peninsula; it runs generally southward but has numerous spurs running off the main range, crisscrossing the region.

COUNTRIES	OFFICIAL NAME	AREA	POPULATION	CAPITAL	RELIGION	POPULATION DENSITY	HIGHEST POINT	CURRENCY
Albania	Republika e Shqipërisë	27,398 km²/10,579 mi²	3,640,000	Tirana (Tiranë)	☪70%, ✝30%	133/km², 344/mi²	Maja e Korabit/Golem Korab 2,764 m/9,068 ft	Lek
Andorra	Principat d'Andorra	469 km²/181 mi²	84,000	Andorra la Vella	✝90%, ○10%	179/km², 464/mi²	Coma Pedrosa 2,496 m/9,665 ft	Euro
Bosnia and Herzegovina	Bosna i Hercegovina	51,129 km²/19,742 mi²	4,613,000	Sarajevo	✝46%, ☪40%, ○14%	90/km², 234/mi²	Maglić 2,386 m/7,828 ft	Mark
Croatia	Republica Hrvatska	56,414 km²/21,781 mi²	4,490,000	Zagreb	✝92.6%, ☪1.3%, ○6.1%	80/km², 206/mi²	Dinara 1,831 m/6,007 ft	Kuna
Greece	Ellinikí Dhimokratía	130,800 km²/50,505 mi²	10,737,000	Athens (Athina)	✝98%, ☪1.3%, ○0.7%	82/km², 213/mi²	Ólympos 2,917 m/9,570 ft	Euro
Italy	Repubblica Italiana	294,020 km²/113,530 mi²	58,126,000	Rome (Roma)	✝90%, ○10%	198/km², 512/mi²	Monte Bianco 4,748 m/15,577 ft	Euro
Kosovo	Republika e Kosovës; Republika Kosovo	10,887 km²/4,203 mi²	1,805,000	Priština	✝, ☪, ○	166/km², 429/mi²	Gjeravica/Đeravica 2,565 m/8,415 ft	Euro, Dinar
Macedonia	Republika Makedonija	24,586 km²/9,493 mi²	2,067,000	Skopje	✝64.7%, ☪33.3%, ○2%	84/km², 218/mi²	Golem Korab 2,764 m/9,068 ft	Denar
Malta	Republic of Malta; Repubblika ta' Malta	316 km²/122 mi²	405,000	Valletta	✝98%, ○2%	1,282/km², 3,320/mi²	Ta' Dmejrek 253 m/830 ft	Euro
Montenegro	Republika Crna Gora	13,812 km²/5,333 mi²	672,000	Podgorica	✝75%, ☪20%, ○5%	49/km², 126/mi²	Bobotov Kuk 2,522 m/8,274 ft	Euro
Portugal	República Portuguesa	91,951 km²/35,505 mi²	10,708,000	Lisbon (Lisboa)	✝86.7%, ○13.3%	116/km², 301/mi²	Ponta do Pico 2,351 m/7,713 ft	Euro
San Marino	Repubblica di San Marino	61.2 km²/23½ mi²	30,000	San Marino	✝100%	490/km², 1,296/mi²	Monte Titano 755 m/2,477 ft	Euro
Serbia	Republika Srbija	77,474 km²/29,915 mi²	7,379,000	Belgrade (Beograd)	✝91.6%, ☪3.2%, ○5.2%	95/km², 247/mi²	Midžor 2,169 m/7,116 ft	Dinar
Slovenia	Republika Slovenija	20,151 km²/7,781 mi²	2,006,000	Ljubljana	✝61%, ☪2.4%, ○36.6%	100/km², 258/mi²	Triglav 2,864 m/9,396 ft	Euro
Spain	Reino de España	499,542 km²/192,873 mi²	40,525,000	Madrid	✝94%, ○6%	81/km², 210/mi²	Pico de Tiede (Islas Canarias) 3,718 m/12,198 ft	Euro
Vatican City	Stato della Città del Vaticano	0.44 km²/⅙ mi²	824	Vatican City (Città del Vaticano)	✝100%	1,872/km², 4,944/mi²	75 m/246 ft	Euro

DEPENDENCIES AND TERRITORIES	OFFICIAL NAME	AREA	POPULATION	CAPITAL	RELIGION	POPULATION DENSITY	HIGHEST POINT	CURRENCY
Gibraltar (UK)	Gibraltar	6.5 km²/2½ mi²	28,034	Gibraltar	✝88.3%, ☪4%, ✡2.1%, ॐ1.8%, ○3.8%	4,312/km², 11,214/mi²	Rock of Gibraltar 426 m/1,398 ft	Pound

Far left The Parthenon, Athens, was built in the fifth century BCE in honor of the Greek goddess Athena. Since then the building has served as a treasury, a Christian church, and a mosque.

Left Wooden farm buildings in Gorenjska, Slovenia. Tourists flock to this most Alpine region of Slovenia for skiing and mountain climbing.

The region's seas are another key feature of Southern Europe. The Adriatic lies between the Balkan and Italian peninsulas and contains several large islands that hug the coastlines of Croatia. In the north of the sea, a huge delta and barrier system is found along the north and northeastern Italian coastlines. Within this system the famous canal city of Venice is found.

The large islands of Sardinia and Sicily (both part of Italy) are found within the Tyrrhenian Sea. South of Sicily, within the Mediterranean and midway to North Africa, the small island nation of Malta is found. Further west, the Balearic Islands are found off the east coast of Spain. The Ionian Sea, off the coast of Greece, also hosts hundreds of islands, most of which are rocky and arid.

ICELAND
REYKJAVÍK
Akureyri
Höfn
Ísafjörður
Hraunhafnartangi
Arctic Circle
NORWEGIAN SEA
NORTH SEA
ATLANTIC OCEAN
MEDITERRANEAN SEA
Faroe Islands (Denmark)
Tórshavn
Shetland Islands
Orkney Islands
Na h-Eileanan Siar (Western Isles)
Inner Hebrides
UNITED KINGDOM
SCOTLAND
ENGLAND
WALES
NORTHERN IRELAND
Aberdeen
Dundee
Glasgow
Edinburgh
Belfast
Newcastle upon Tyne
Sunderland
Middlesbrough
Isle of Man (UK)
Liverpool
Leeds
Manchester
Derby
Nottingham
Birmingham
Coventry
Norwich
Gloucester
Swansea
Cardiff
Bristol
Luton
LONDON
Southampton
Brighton
Plymouth
Exeter
Bournemouth
Portsmouth
Isles of Scilly
St George's Channel
English Channel
Channel Islands (UK)
IRELAND
DUBLIN (BAILE ATHA CLIATH)
Galway
Limerick
Cork
NORWAY
SWEDEN
OSLO
Bergen
Stavanger
Trondheim
Drammen
Skien
Skagerrak
Kattegat
STOCKHOLM
Uppsala
Västerås
Örebro
Göteborg
Jönköping
Linköping
Norrköping
Umeå
Gulf of Bothnia
Baltic Sea
Gotland
Öland
Lofoten
Vesterålen
DENMARK
KØBENHAVN (COPENHAGEN)
Odense
Århus
Aalborg
Malmö
Bornholm
NETHERLANDS
AMSTERDAM
DEN HAAG/'S-GRAVENHAGE (THE HAGUE)
Rotterdam
Haarlem
Groningen
Arnhem
BELGIUM
BRUSSEL/BRUXELLES (BRUSSELS)
Antwerpen
Liège
Namur
LUXEMBOURG
LUX.
GERMANY
BERLIN
Hamburg
Bremen
Bremerhaven
Kiel
Lübeck
Rostock
Hannover
Essen
Dortmund
Düsseldorf
Köln
Bonn
Siegen
Frankfurt am Main
Wiesbaden
Mannheim
Heidelberg
Karlsruhe
Stuttgart
Nürnberg
Würzburg
Regensburg
Ingolstadt
München (Munich)
Ulm
Leipzig
Dresden
Chemnitz
Erfurt
Jena
Gera
Potsdam
Trier
Heilbronn
FRANCE
PARIS
Le Havre
Caen
Rouen
Amiens
Reims
Metz
Nancy
Strasbourg
Mulhouse
Brest
Rennes
Le Mans
Orléans
Angers
Tours
Nantes
La Rochelle
Dijon
Limoges
Clermont-Ferrand
Lyon
St-Étienne
Grenoble
Bordeaux
Toulouse
Montpellier
Nîmes
Marseille
Aix-en-Provence
Toulon
Nice
Perpignan
Bay of Biscay
Golfe du Lion
MONACO
ANDORRA
ANDORRA LA VELLA
SWITZ.
BERN
Zürich
Basel
Lausanne
Genève
LIECH.
VADUZ
AUSTRIA
WIEN (VIENNA)
Salzburg
Innsbruck
Graz
Klagenfurt
CZECH REPUBLIC
PRAHA (PRAGUE)
Plzeň
Brno
Ostrava
Olomouc
SLOVAKIA
BRATISLAVA
Košice
HUNGARY
BUDAPEST
Győr
Pécs
Szeged
POLAND
WARSZAWA (WARSAW)
Gdańsk
Gdynia
Szczecin
Poznań
Łódź
Wrocław
Kraków
Katowice
Bydgoszcz
Toruń
Częstochowa
Opole
Zielona Góra
Legnica
Koszalin
Elbląg
Olsztyn
Kaliningrad
RUSS. FED.
SLOVENIA
LJUBLJANA
CROATIA
ZAGREB
Split
BOSNIA AND HERZEGOVINA
SARAJEVO
Mostar
SERBIA
MONTENEGRO
PODGORICA
ALBANIA
TIRANË (TIRANA)
Durrës
GREECE
ITALY
ROMA (ROME)
VATICAN CITY
SAN MARINO
Milano (Milan)
Torino (Turin)
Genova
Bergamo
Brescia
Verona
Trento
Venezia (Venice)
Trieste
Padova
Bologna
Parma
Modena
Firenze (Florence)
Perugia
Pescara
Napoli (Naples)
Salerno
Bari
Foggia
Taranto
Brindisi
Lecce
Reggio di Calabria
Messina
Palermo
Catania
Siracusa
Cagliari
Sassari
Sardegna (Sardinia)
Sicilia (Sicily)
Corse (Corsica)
Ajaccio
Adriatic Sea
Tyrrhenian Sea
Ionian Sea
Ligurian Sea
MALTA
VALLETTA
PORTUGAL
LISBOA (LISBON)
Porto
Braga
Coimbra
Setúbal
SPAIN
MADRID
Barcelona
Valencia
Sevilla
Málaga
Granada
Córdoba
Bilbao
Zaragoza
A Coruña
Vigo
Oviedo
Gijón
Santander
San Sebastián
Vitoria-Gasteiz
Pamplona
León
Burgos
Valladolid
Salamanca
Toledo
Guadalajara
Badajoz
Cáceres
Huelva
Cádiz
Jerez de la Frontera
Almería
Murcia
Cartagena
Alicante
Elche
Albacete
Tarragona
Lleida
Girona
Palma
Mallorca (Majorca)
Menorca (Minorca)
Eivissa (Ibiza)
Islas Baleares (Balearic Islands)
Pyrenees
Sierra Nevada
Strait of Gibraltar
Gibraltar (UK)
Ceuta (Spain)
Melilla (Spain)
MOROCCO
RABAT
Casablanca
Tangier
Fès
Meknès
Marrakech
Agadir
Oujda
Safi
Essaouira
El Jadida
Atlas Mts
ALGERIA
ALGER (ALGIERS)
Oran
Constantine
Annaba
Sétif
Batna
Biskra
Tlemcen
Béchar
TUNISIA
TUNIS
Sfax
Sousse
Kairouan
Gabès

1:15,000,000
Lambert Conformal Conic Projection

0 250 500 750 1000 kilometers
0 125 250 375 500 miles

EUROPE POLITICAL

RUSSIAN FEDERATION
KAZAKHSTAN
UZBEKISTAN
TURKMENISTAN
BELARUS
UKRAINE
MOLDOVA
ROMANIA
BULGARIA
TURKEY
GEORGIA
ARMENIA
AZERBAIJAN
AZ.
IRAN
IRAQ
SYRIA
CYPRUS
LEBANON
ISRAEL
JORDAN
SAUDI ARABIA
KUWAIT
Barents Sea
Beloye More
BLACK SEA
Sea of Azov
CASPIAN SEA
Aral Sea
Aegean Sea
The Gulf
Ural'skiy Khrebet (Ural Mountains)
Timanskiy Kryazh
Zapadno-Sibirskaya Ravnina
Obshchiy Syrt
Kazakhskiy Melkosopochnik
Turgayskaya Stolovaya Strana
Peski Priaral'skiye Karakumy
Peski Kyzyl Kum
Plato Ustyurt
Garagum
Kopet Dag
Caucasus
Anadolu Dağlari
Toros Dağlari
Küre Dağlari
Doğu Toroslar
Reshteh-ye Kūhhā-ye Alborz
Kūhhā-ye Zagros
Iranian Plateau
Dasht-e Kavīr
Dasht-e Lūt
Syrian Desert
Ladozhskoye Ozero
Onezhskoye Ozero
Poluostrov Kanin
Kol'skiy Poluostrov
Ostrov Kolguyev
MOSKVA (MOSCOW)
Sankt-Peterburg (St Petersburg)
MINSK
KYIV/KYYIV (KIEV)
CHIŞINĂU
BUCUREŞTI (BUCHAREST)
ANKARA
ASTANA
AŞGABAT (AŞHGABAT)
T'BILISI
YEREVAN
BAKI (BAKU)
TEHRĀN
BAGHDĀD
DIMASHQ (DAMASCUS)
BEYROUTH (BEIRUT)
LEFKOSIA (NICOSIA)
AL KUWAYT (KUWAIT)
Murmansk
Arkhangel'sk
Severodvinsk
Petrozavodsk
Vologda
Yaroslavl'
Nizhniy Novgorod
Kazan'
Perm'
Yekaterinburg
Chelyabinsk
Ufa
Samara
Saratov
Volgograd
Rostov-na-Donu
Krasnodar
Voronezh
Omsk
Novosibirsk
Tyumen'
Kharkiv
Odesa
Dnipropetrovs'k
Istanbul
Bursa
İzmir
Adana
Konya
Halab (Aleppo)
Al Mawşil (Mosul)
Tabrīz
Eşfahān
Shīrāz
Mashhad
Al Başrah

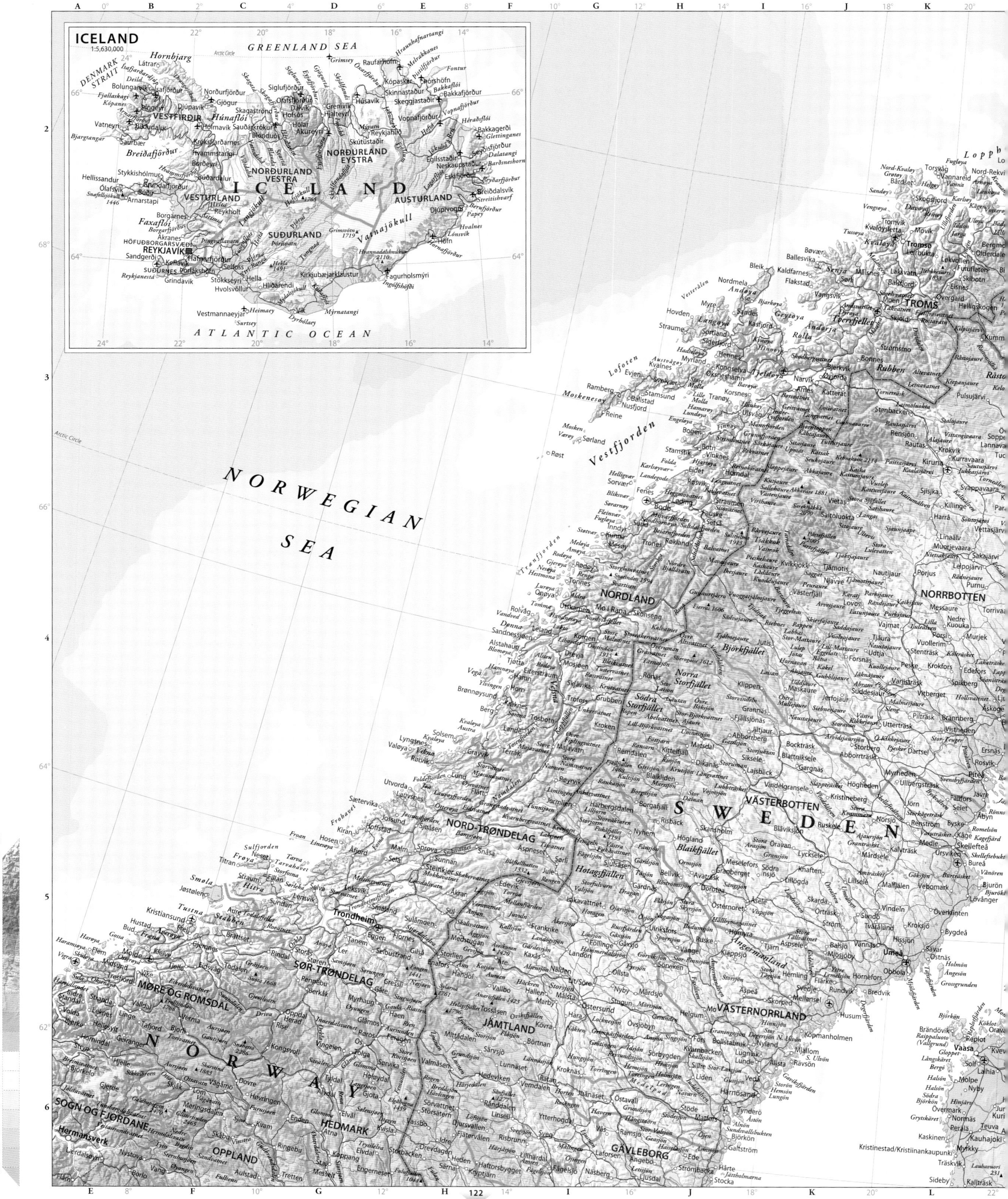
ICELAND
1:5,630,000
GREENLAND SEA
DENMARK STRAIT
ATLANTIC OCEAN
Arctic Circle
I C E L A N D
VESTFIRÐIR
NORÐURLAND VESTRA
NORÐURLAND EYSTRA
VESTURLAND
AUSTURLAND
SUÐURLAND
HÖFUÐBORGARSVÆÐI
SUÐURNES
REYKJAVÍK
Akureyri
Húsavík
Ísafjörður
Hornbjarg
Húnaflói
Breiðafjörður
Faxaflói
Vatnajökull
Langjökull
Hofsjökull
Mýrdalsjökull
Hafnarfjörður
Keflavík
Grindavík
Selfoss
Hveragerði
Vestmannaeyjar
Heimaey
Surtsey
Egilsstaðir
Seyðisfjörður
Höfn
Grímsey
Siglufjörður
Sauðárkrókur
Blönduós
Borgarnes
Akranes
Stykkishólmur
Kirkjubæjarklaustur
Vík
NORWEGIAN SEA
Vestfjorden
Lofoten
Arctic Circle
Tranfjorden
N O R W A Y
S W E D E N
NORDLAND
TROMS
NORRBOTTEN
VÄSTERBOTTEN
VÄSTERNORRLAND
JÄMTLAND
GÄVLEBORG
NORD-TRØNDELAG
SØR-TRØNDELAG
MØRE OG ROMSDAL
SOGN OG FJORDANE
OPPLAND
HEDMARK
Tromsø
Narvik
Kiruna
Bodø
Mo i Rana
Trondheim
Kristiansund
Molde
Ålesund
Östersund
Umeå
Skellefteå
Piteå
Luleå
Vaasa
Sundsvall
Härnösand
Örnsköldsvik
Hudiksvall
Lofoten
Vesterålen
Andøya
Hinnøya
Senja
Moskenesøy
Røst
Smøla
Hitra
Frøya
Kebnekaise 2114
Sulitjelma
Storsjön
Ångermanälven
Kristinestad/Kristiinankaupunki
Meters
Feet
LAND BELOW SEA LEVEL

122

NORTHERN SCANDINAVIA and ICELAND

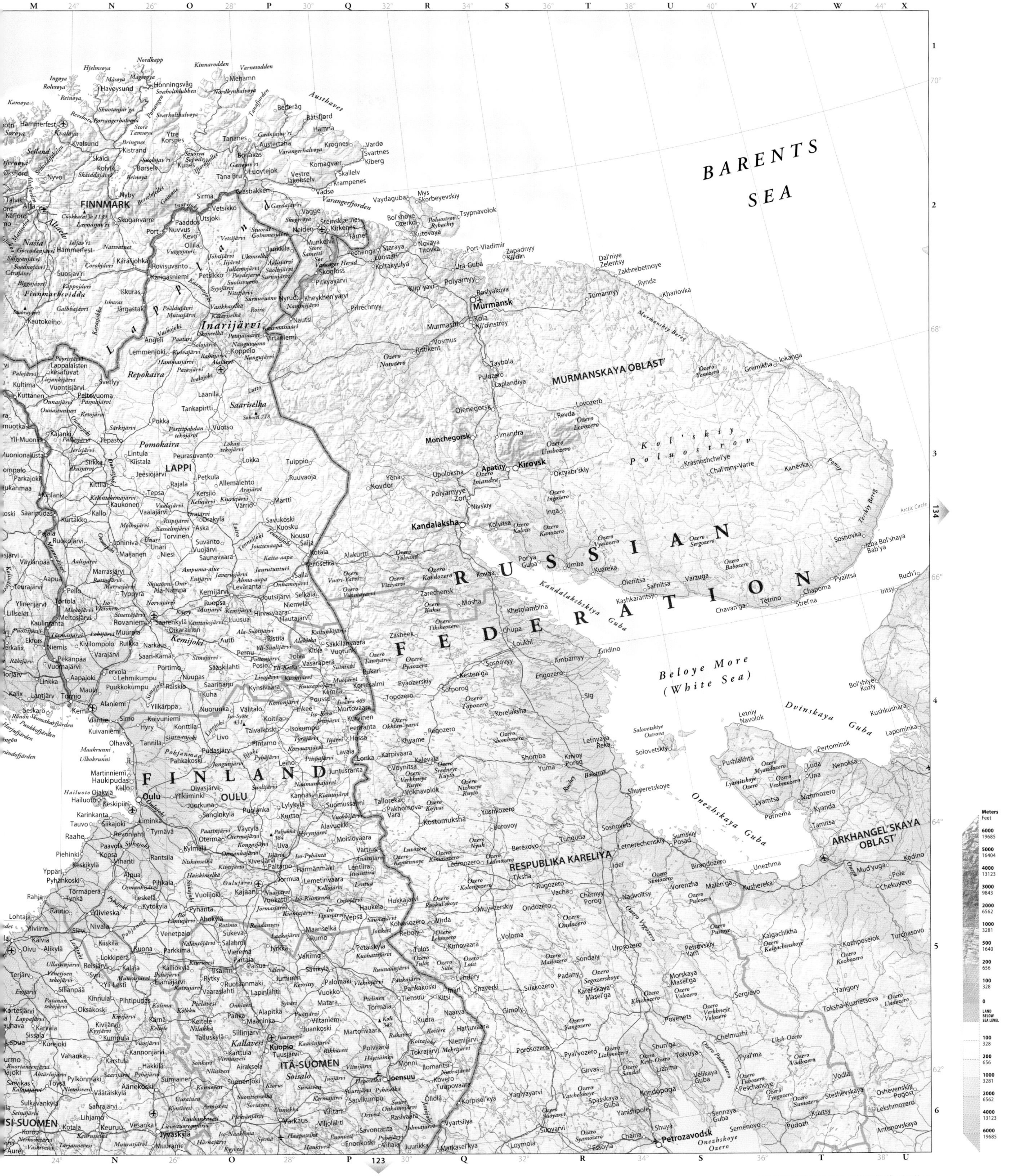
M N O P Q R S T U V W X
24° 26° 28° 30° 32° 34° 36° 38° 40° 42° 44°
1 2 3 4 5 6
70° 68° 66° 64° 62°
BARENTS SEA
Beloye More (White Sea)
RUSSIAN FEDERATION
FINLAND
MURMANSKAYA OBLAST'
RESPUBLIKA KARELIYA
ARKHANGEL'SKAYA OBLAST'
FINNMARK
LAPPI
OULU
ITÄ-SUOMEN
Lappland
Kol'skiy Poluostrov
Kandalakshskiya Guba
Onezhskaya Guba
Dvinskaya Guba
Varangerfjorden
Austhavet
Inarijärvi
Murmansk
Kirovsk
Apatity
Monchegorsk
Kandalaksha
Olenegorsk
Petrozavodsk
Oulu
Kuopio
Joensuu
Jyväskylä
Rovaniemi
Kemi
Tornio
Kajaani
Hammerfest
Honningsvåg
Kirkenes
Vardø
Vadsø
Nordkapp
Arctic Circle
134
123
Meters Feet
6000 19685
5000 16404
4000 13123
3000 9843
2000 6562
1000 3281
500 1640
200 656
100 328
0
LAND BELOW SEA LEVEL
100 328
200 656
1000 3281
2000 6562
4000 13123
6000 19685

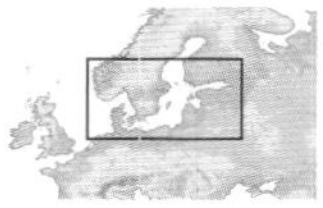

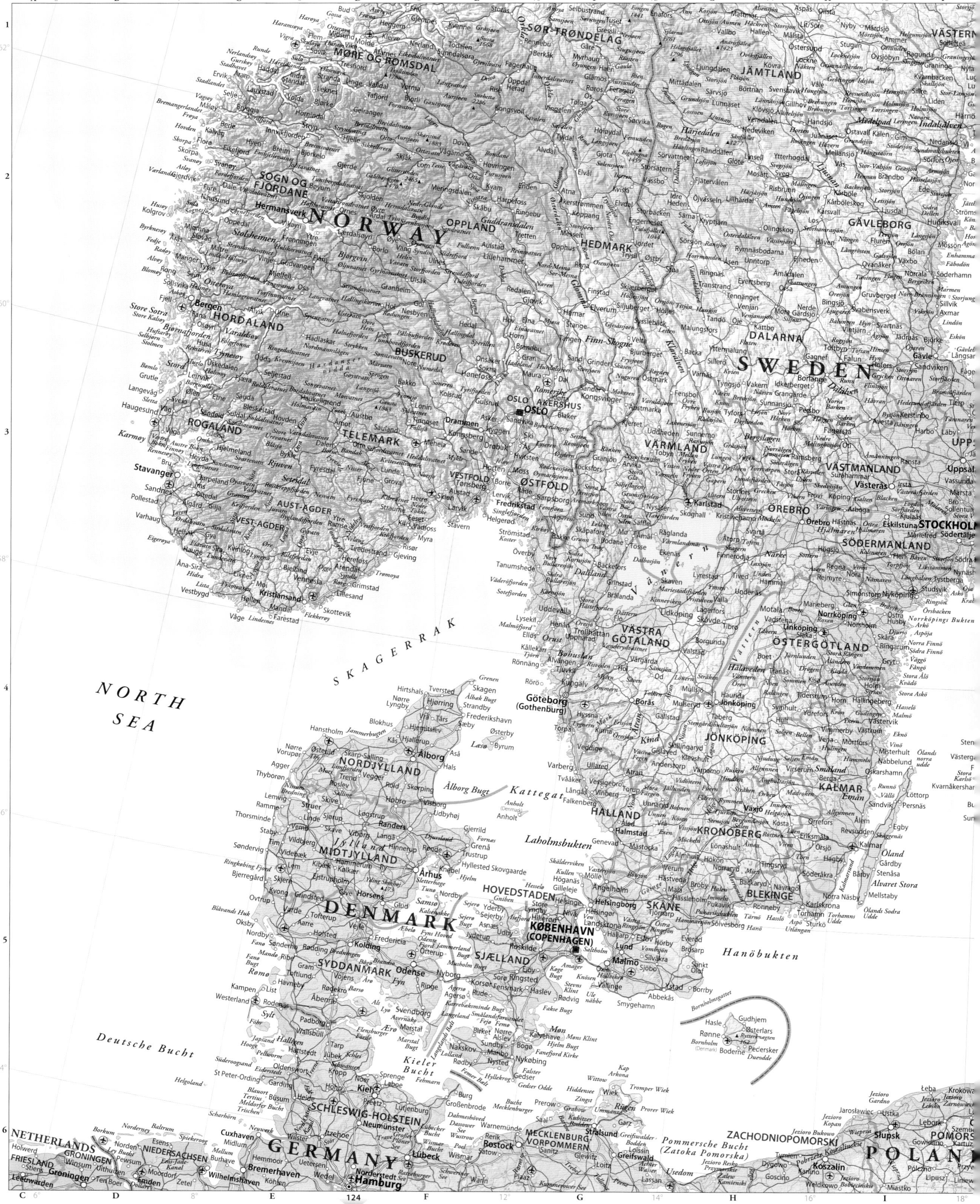

120
124
A B C D E F G H I
1 2 3 4 5 6
NORWAY
SWEDEN
DENMARK
GERMANY
POLAND
NETHERLANDS
NORTH SEA
SKAGERRAK
Kattegat
Ålborg Bugt
Laholmsbukten
Hanöbukten
Deutsche Bucht
Kieler Bucht
Pommersche Bucht (Zatoka Pomorska)
Vänern
Vättern
MØRE OG ROMSDAL
SØR-TRØNDELAG
SOGN OG FJORDANE
OPPLAND
HEDMARK
HORDALAND
BUSKERUD
OSLO
AKERSHUS
ROGALAND
TELEMARK
VESTFOLD
ØSTFOLD
AUST-AGDER
VEST-AGDER
JÄMTLAND
GÄVLEBORG
DALARNA
VÄRMLAND
VÄSTMANLAND
ÖREBRO
SÖDERMANLAND
ÖSTERGÖTLAND
VÄSTRA GÖTALAND
JÖNKÖPING
HALLAND
KRONOBERG
KALMAR
BLEKINGE
SKÅNE
NORDJYLLAND
MIDTJYLLAND
SYDDANMARK
HOVEDSTADEN
SJÆLLAND
SCHLESWIG-HOLSTEIN
NIEDERSACHSEN
MECKLENBURG-VORPOMMERN
ZACHODNIOPOMORSKIE
FRIESLAND
GRONINGEN
Oslo
Bergen
Stavanger
Kristiansand
Drammen
Hermansverk
Göteborg (Gothenburg)
Karlstad
Örebro
Västerås
Uppsala
Stockholm
Norrköping
Linköping
Jönköping
Växjö
Halmstad
Kalmar
Karlskrona
Malmö
Lund
Helsingborg
København (Copenhagen)
Ålborg
Århus
Odense
Kolding
Esbjerg
Kiel
Lübeck
Hamburg
Bremerhaven
Wilhelmshaven
Emden
Cuxhaven
Rostock
Stralsund
Greifswald
Koszalin
Słupsk
Groningen
Leeuwarden
Gävle
Falun
Östersund
Bornholm
Rønne
Öland
Gotland
Fyn
Sjælland
Læsø
Anholt
Rügen
Usedom
Helgoland
Sylt
Karmøy

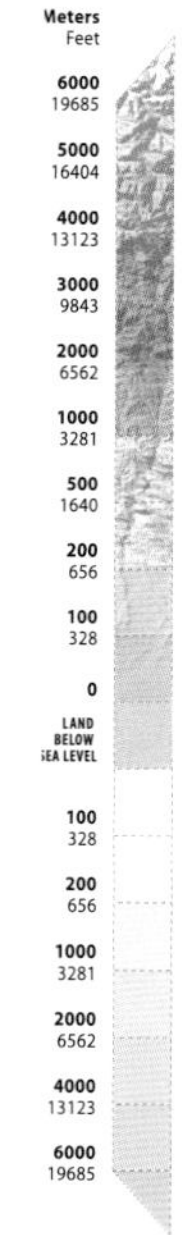

Meters
Feet
6000 19685
5000 16404
4000 13123
3000 9843
2000 6562
1000 3281
500 1640
200 656
100 328
0
LAND BELOW SEA LEVEL
100 328
200 656
1000 3281
2000 6562
4000 13123
6000 19685

1:3,750,000

Lambert Conic Conformal Projection

0 50 100 150 200 kilometers

0 25 50 75 100 miles

SOUTHERN SCANDINAVIA and the BALTIC STATES

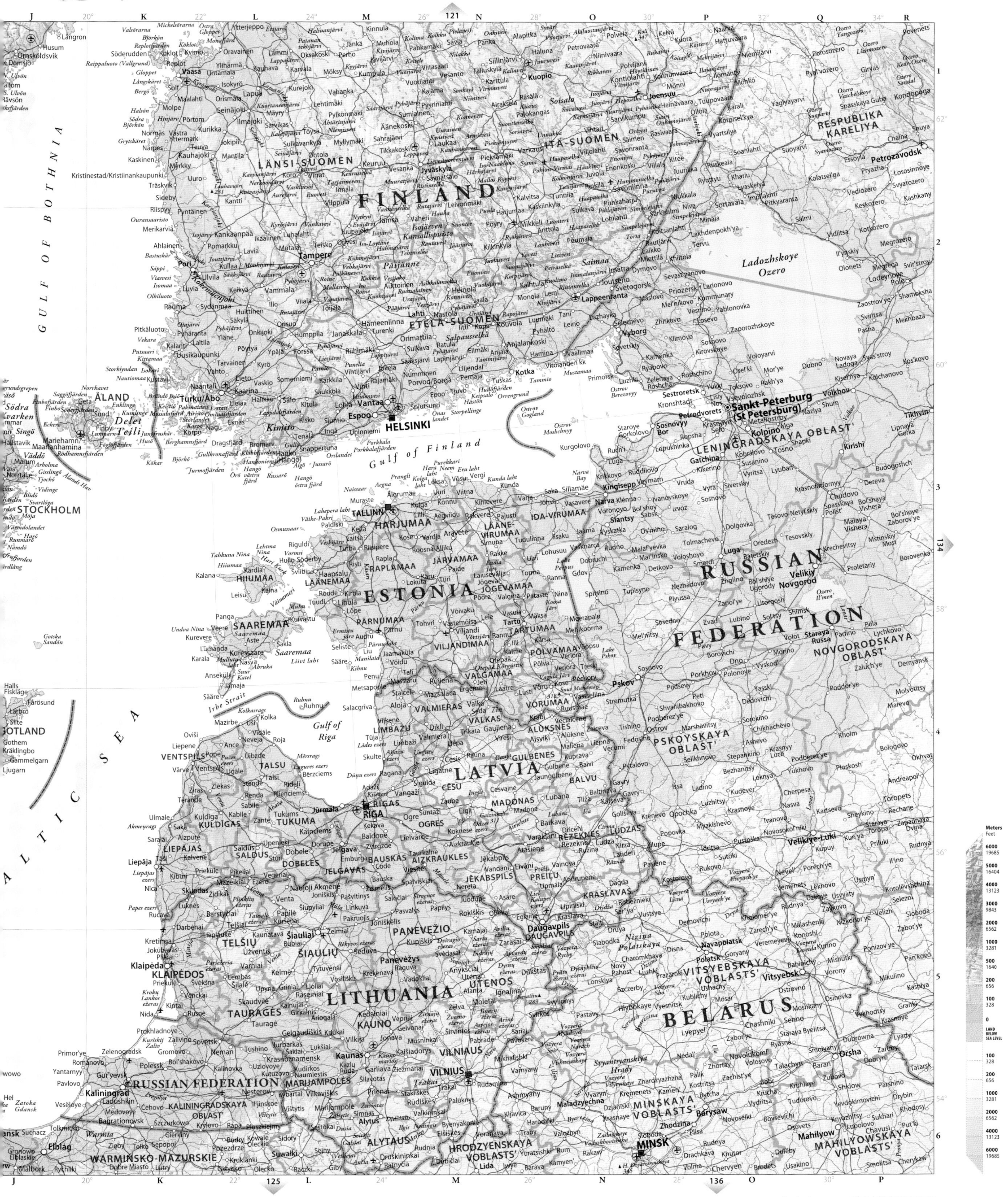
121
125
136
134
FINLAND
ESTONIA
LATVIA
LITHUANIA
BELARUS
RUSSIAN FEDERATION
RUSSIAN
FEDERATION
RESPUBLIKA KARELIYA
LÄNSI-SUOMEN
ITÄ-SUOMEN
ETELÄ-SUOMEN
ÅLAND
LENINGRADSKAYA OBLAST'
NOVGORODSKAYA OBLAST'
PSKOVSKAYA OBLAST'
KALININGRADSKAYA OBLAST'
WARMIŃSKO-MAZURSKIE
VITSYEBSKAYA VOBLASTS'
MINSKAYA VOBLASTS'
HRODZYENSKAYA VOBLASTS'
MAHILYOWSKAYA VOBLASTS'
HELSINKI
TALLINN
RIGA
VILNIUS
MINSK
STOCKHOLM
Sankt-Peterburg (St Petersburg)
GULF OF BOTHNIA
BALTIC SEA
Gulf of Finland
Gulf of Riga
Ladozhskoye Ozero
Irbe Strait
Meters
Feet
LAND BELOW SEA LEVEL

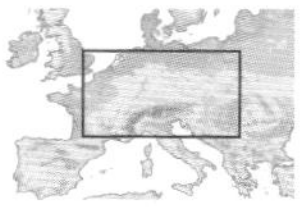

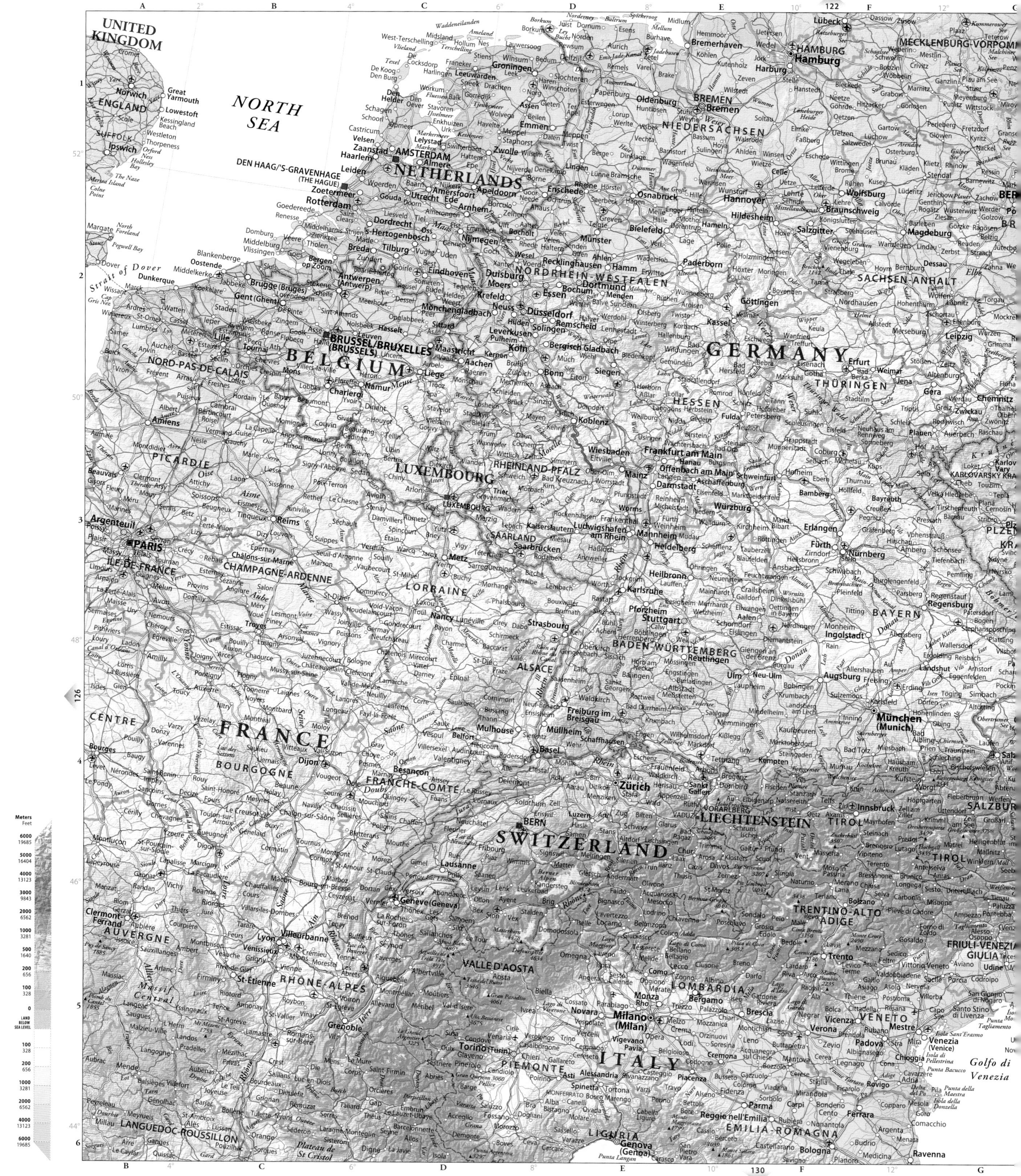
UNITED KINGDOM
NORTH SEA
NETHERLANDS
BELGIUM
LUXEMBOURG
GERMANY
FRANCE
SWITZERLAND
LIECHTENSTEIN
ITALY
ENGLAND
NIEDERSACHSEN
NORDRHEIN-WESTFALEN
SACHSEN-ANHALT
MECKLENBURG-VORPOMMERN
HESSEN
THÜRINGEN
RHEINLAND-PFALZ
SAARLAND
BADEN-WÜRTTEMBERG
BAYERN
NORD-PAS-DE-CALAIS
PICARDIE
ÎLE-DE-FRANCE
CHAMPAGNE-ARDENNE
LORRAINE
ALSACE
CENTRE
BOURGOGNE
FRANCHE-COMTÉ
AUVERGNE
RHÔNE-ALPES
LANGUEDOC-ROUSSILLON
VORARLBERG
TIROL
SALZBURG
TRENTINO-ALTO ADIGE
FRIULI-VENEZIA GIULIA
VALLE D'AOSTA
LOMBARDIA
PIEMONTE
VENETO
LIGURIA
EMILIA-ROMAGNA
Golfo di Venezia
Strait of Dover
Meters
Feet
LAND BELOW SEA LEVEL
122
126
130

1:3,750,000

Lambert Conic Conformal Projection

0 50 100 150 200 kilometers

0 25 50 75 100 miles

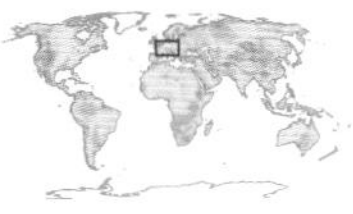

CENTRAL EUROPE

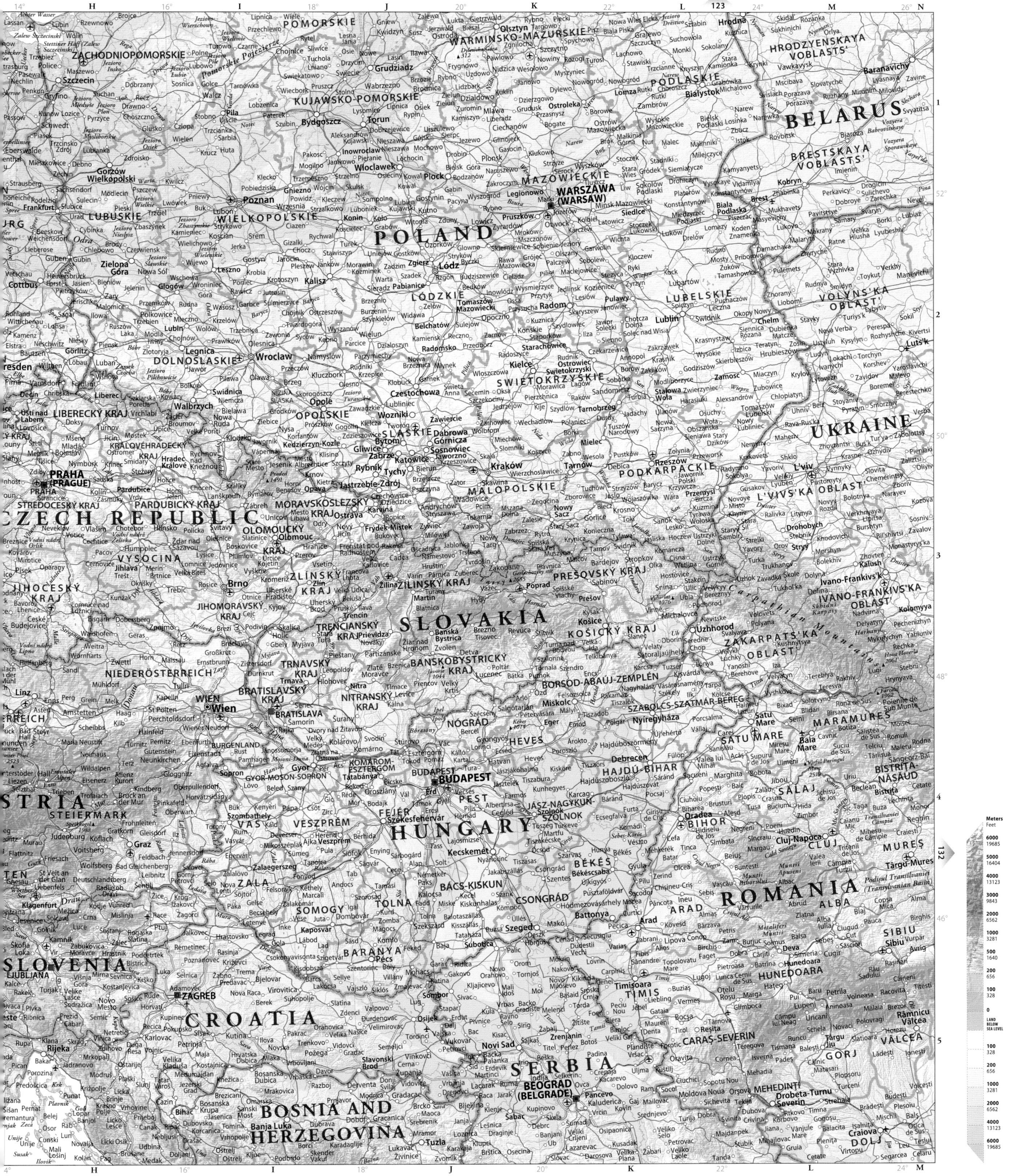

POLAND
CZECH REPUBLIC
SLOVAKIA
HUNGARY
AUSTRIA
SLOVENIA
CROATIA
BOSNIA AND HERZEGOVINA
SERBIA
ROMANIA
UKRAINE
BELARUS
POMORSKIE
ZACHODNIOPOMORSKIE
WARMINSKO-MAZURSKIE
KUJAWSKO-POMORSKIE
PODLASKIE
MAZOWIECKIE
WIELKOPOLSKIE
LUBUSKIE
LODZKIE
LUBELSKIE
DOLNOSLASKIE
OPOLSKIE
SLASKIE
SWIETOKRZYSKIE
MALOPOLSKIE
PODKARPACKIE
HRODZYENSKAYA VOBLASTS'
BRESTSKAYA VOBLASTS'
VOLYNS'KA OBLAST'
L'VIVS'KA OBLAST'
IVANO-FRANKIVS'KA OBLAST'
ZAKARPATS'KA OBLAST'
LIBERECKÝ KRAJ
KRÁLOVÉHRADECKÝ KRAJ
PARDUBICKÝ KRAJ
STREDOCESKÝ KRAJ
MORAVSKOSLEZSKÝ KRAJ
OLOMOUCKÝ KRAJ
VYSOCINA
JIHOCESKÝ KRAJ
JIHOMORAVSKÝ KRAJ
ZLÍNSKÝ KRAJ
ZILINSKÝ KRAJ
PRESOVSKÝ KRAJ
KOSICKÝ KRAJ
TRENCIANSKÝ KRAJ
BANSKOBYSTRICKÝ KRAJ
TRNAVSKÝ KRAJ
NITRANSKÝ KRAJ
BRATISLAVSKÝ KRAJ
NIEDERÖSTERREICH
STEIERMARK
BURGENLAND
BORSOD-ABAÚJ-ZEMPLÉN
SZABOLCS-SZATMÁR-BEREG
NÓGRÁD
HEVES
HAJDÚ-BIHAR
KOMÁROM-ESZTERGOM
GYOR-MOSON-SOPRON
PEST
JÁSZ-NAGYKUN-SZOLNOK
FEJÉR
VESZPRÉM
VAS
ZALA
SOMOGY
TOLNA
BÁCS-KISKUN
CSONGRÁD
BÉKÉS
BARANYA
SATU MARE
MARAMURES
BIHOR
SALAJ
CLUJ
BISTRITA-NASAUD
MURES
ARAD
ALBA
TIMIS
HUNEDOARA
SIBIU
CARAS-SEVERIN
GORJ
VÂLCEA
MEHEDINTI
DOLJ
WARSZAWA (WARSAW)
PRAHA (PRAGUE)
WIEN
BRATISLAVA
BUDAPEST
ZAGREB
LJUBLJANA
BEOGRAD (BELGRADE)
Gdansk
Szczecin
Bydgoszcz
Torun
Olsztyn
Bialystok
Poznan
Lódz
Wroclaw
Kraków
Katowice
Lublin
Rzeszów
Kielce
Radom
Opole
Czestochowa
Brest
Hrodna
L'viv
Lutsk
Kalush
Ivano-Frankivs'k
Uzhhorod
Brno
Olomouc
Ostrava
Liberec
Zilina
Poprad
Presov
Kosice
Miskolc
Debrecen
Nyíregyháza
Szeged
Pécs
Gyor
Szombathely
Székesfehérvár
Kecskemét
Szolnok
Oradea
Cluj-Napoca
Satu Mare
Baia Mare
Arad
Timisoara
Novi Sad
Osijek
Rijeka
Graz
Linz
Klagenfurt
Craiova
Drobeta-Turnu Severin
Carpathian Mountains
Meters
Feet
6000
19685
5000
16404
4000
13123
3000
9843
2000
6562
1000
3281
500
1640
200
656
100
328
0
LAND BELOW SEA LEVEL
100
328
200
656
1000
3281
2000
6562
4000
13123
6000
19685
123
132
H
I
J
K
L
M
N
14°
16°
18°
20°
22°
24°
26°
52°
50°
48°
46°
1
2
3
4
5

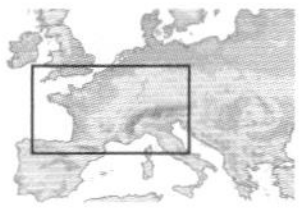

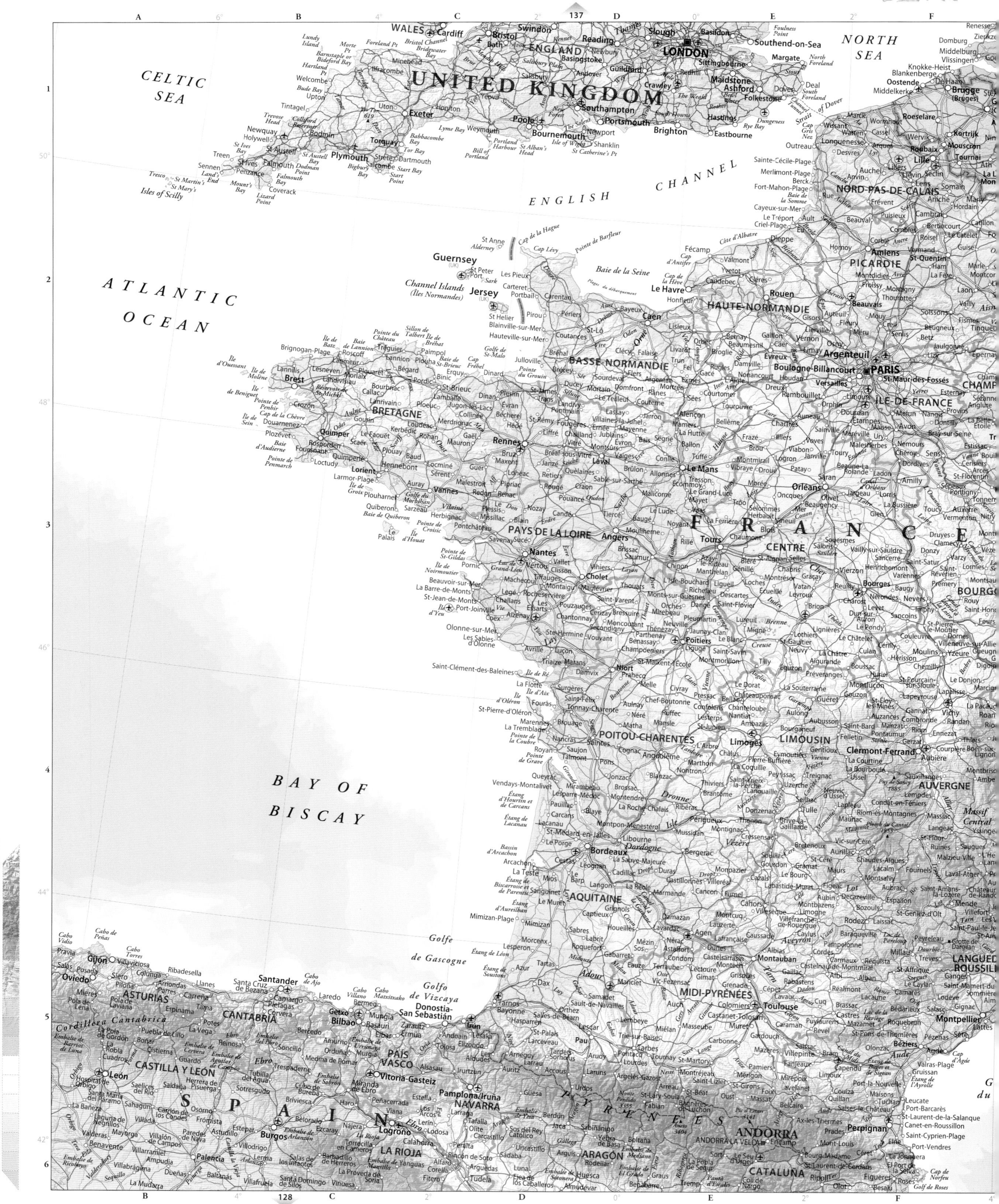

137
128
A B C D E F
1 2 3 4 5 6
CELTIC SEA
ATLANTIC OCEAN
BAY OF BISCAY
ENGLISH CHANNEL
NORTH SEA
UNITED KINGDOM
ENGLAND
WALES
LONDON
Channel Islands (Îles Normandes)
Guernsey (UK)
Jersey (UK)
Isles of Scilly
F R A N C E
PARIS
ÎLE-DE-FRANCE
NORD-PAS-DE-CALAIS
PICARDIE
HAUTE-NORMANDIE
BASSE-NORMANDIE
BRETAGNE
PAYS DE LA LOIRE
CENTRE
POITOU-CHARENTES
LIMOUSIN
AUVERGNE
AQUITAINE
MIDI-PYRÉNÉES
LANGUEDOC-ROUSSILLON
S P A I N
ASTURIAS
CANTABRIA
PAÍS VASCO
NAVARRA
LA RIOJA
CASTILLA Y LEÓN
ARAGÓN
CATALUÑA
ANDORRA
P Y R E N E E S
Golfe de Gascogne
Golfo de Vizcaya
Cordillera Cantábrica
Meters
Feet
6000 19685
5000 16404
4000 13123
3000 9843
2000 6562
1000 3281
500 1640
200 656
100 328
0
LAND BELOW SEA LEVEL
100 328
200 656
1000 3281
2000 6562
4000 13123
6000 19685

1:3,750,000

Lambert Conic Conformal Projection

0 50 100 150 200 kilometers

0 25 50 75 100 miles

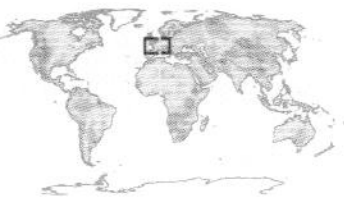

WESTERN EUROPE

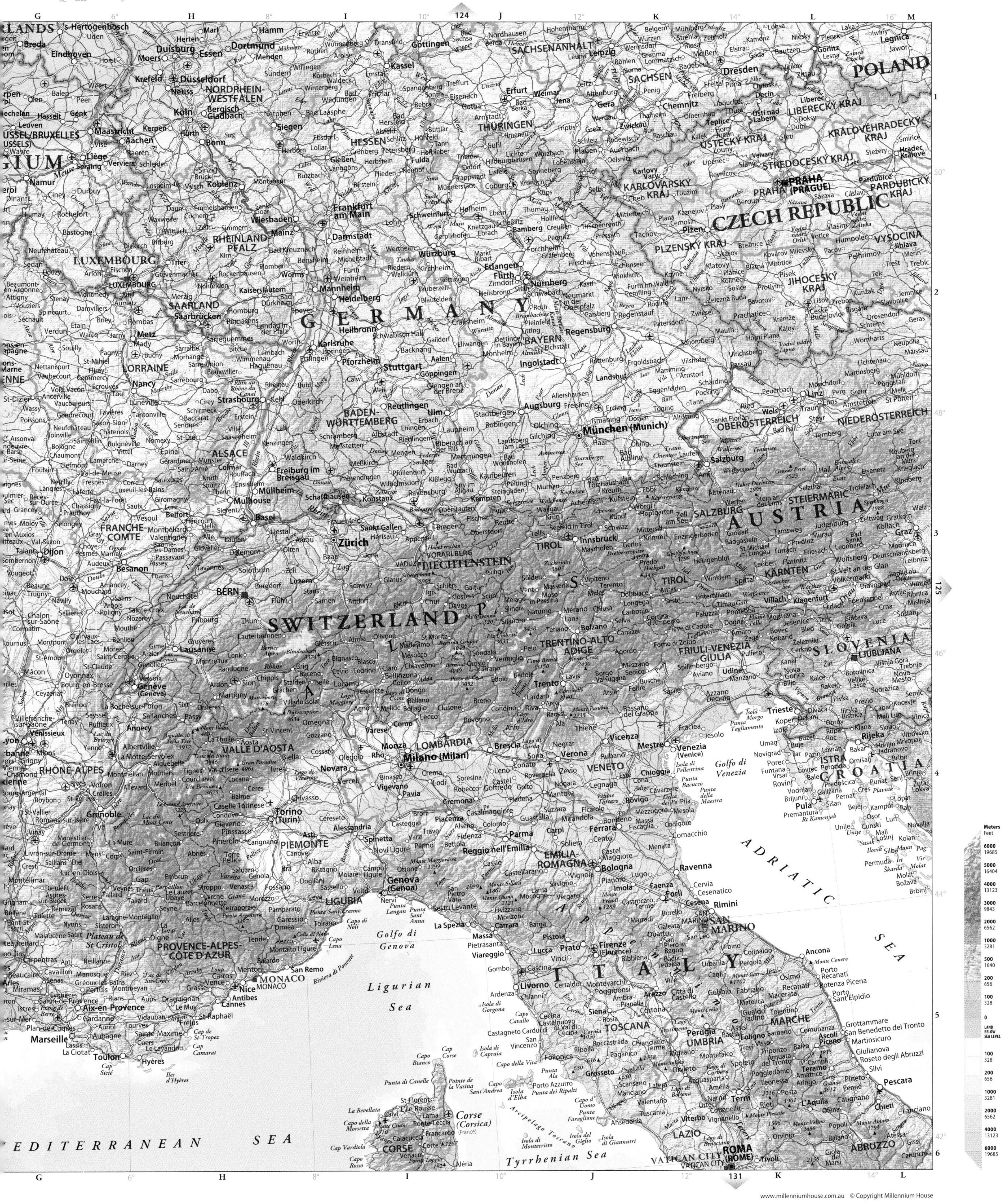
GERMANY
POLAND
CZECH REPUBLIC
AUSTRIA
SWITZERLAND
LIECHTENSTEIN
LUXEMBOURG
SLOVENIA
CROATIA
ITALY
MONACO
SAN MARINO
VATICAN CITY
ALPS
APENNINES
ADRIATIC SEA
Ligurian Sea
Tyrrhenian Sea
MEDITERRANEAN SEA
Golfo di Genova
Golfo di Venezia
Corse (Corsica) (France)
NORDRHEIN-WESTFALEN
HESSEN
THÜRINGEN
SACHSEN
SACHSENANHALT
RHEINLAND-PFALZ
SAARLAND
BADEN-WÜRTTEMBERG
BAYERN
LORRAINE
ALSACE
FRANCHE-COMTE
RHÔNE-ALPES
PROVENCE-ALPES-CÔTE D'AZUR
TIROL
SALZBURG
STEIERMARK
KÄRNTEN
OBERÖSTERREICH
NIEDERÖSTERREICH
LOMBARDIA
PIEMONTE
LIGURIA
VALLE D'AOSTA
TRENTINO-ALTO ADIGE
VENETO
FRIULI-VENEZIA GIULIA
EMILIA-ROMAGNA
TOSCANA
UMBRIA
MARCHE
LAZIO
ABRUZZO
ISTRA
PRAHA (PRAGUE)
München (Munich)
Milano (Milan)
Torino (Turin)
Genova (Genoa)
Firenze (Florence)
ROMA (ROME)
Venezia (Venice)
Genève (Geneva)
BERN
Zürich
LJUBLJANA
Frankfurt am Main
Stuttgart
Nürnberg
Köln
Düsseldorf
Dresden
Leipzig
Strasbourg
Marseille
Nice
Bologna
Verona
Trieste
Innsbruck
Salzburg
Linz
Graz
Meters
Feet
6000
19685
5000
16404
4000
13123
3000
9843
2000
6562
1000
3281
500
1640
200
656
100
328
0
LAND BELOW SEA LEVEL
100
328
200
656
1000
3281
2000
6562
4000
13123
6000
19685
124
125
131

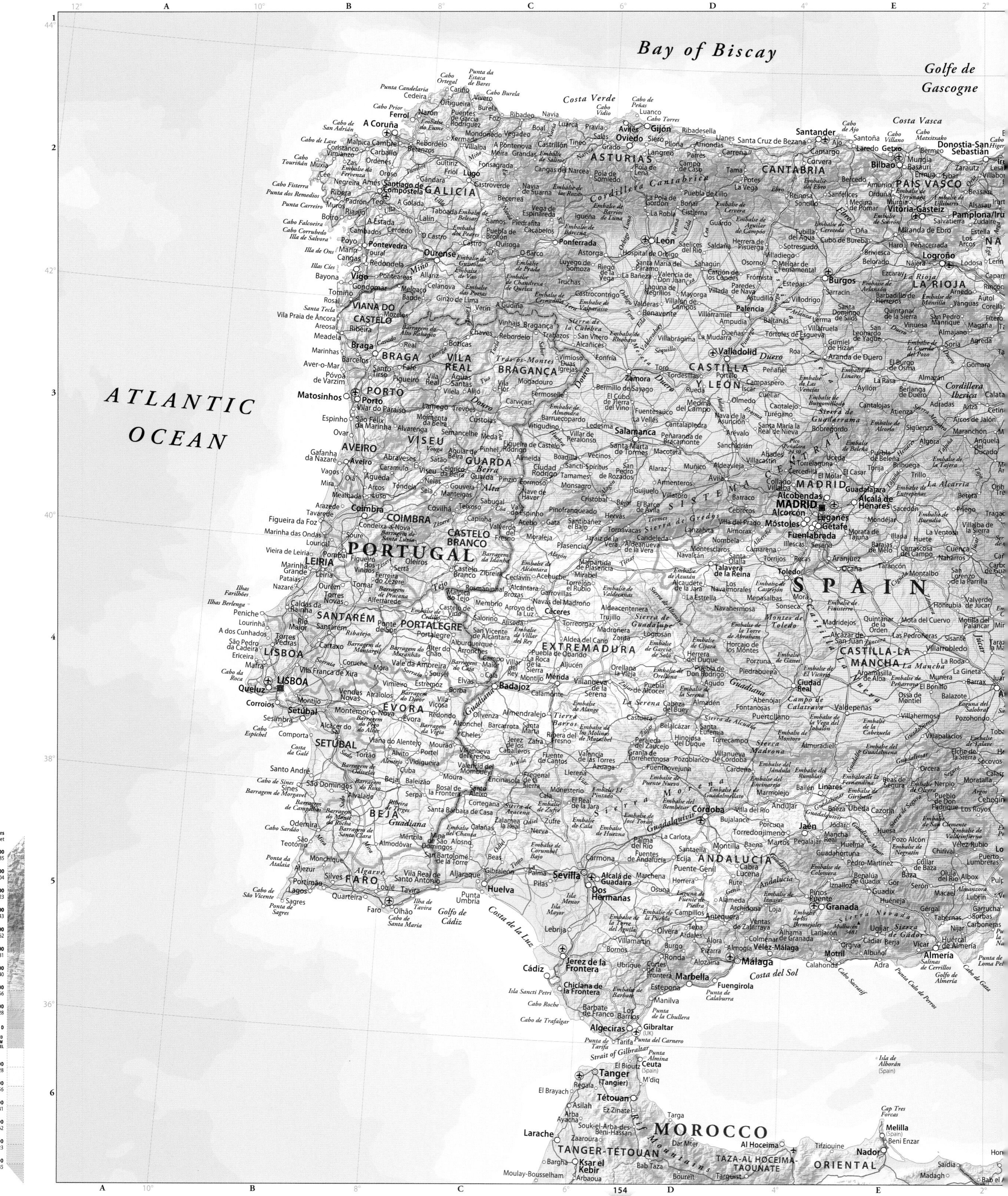
Bay of Biscay
Golfe de Gascogne
ATLANTIC OCEAN
PORTUGAL
SPAIN
MOROCCO
GALICIA
ASTURIAS
CANTABRIA
PAÍS VASCO
LA RIOJA
CASTILLA Y LEÓN
MADRID
CASTILLA-LA MANCHA
EXTREMADURA
ANDALUCÍA
VIANA DO CASTELO
BRAGA
VILA REAL
BRAGANÇA
PORTO
AVEIRO
VISEU
GUARDA
COIMBRA
CASTELO BRANCO
LEIRIA
SANTARÉM
PORTALEGRE
LISBOA
SETÚBAL
ÉVORA
BEJA
FARO
TANGER-TÉTOUAN
TAZA-AL HOCEIMA-TAOUNATE
ORIENTAL
Costa Verde
Costa Vasca
Cordillera Cantabrica
Sistema Central
Sierra de Gredos
Sierra Morena
Sierra Nevada
Costa del Sol
Costa de la Luz
Strait of Gibraltar
Golfo de Cádiz
Rif Mountains
A Coruña
Santiago de Compostela
Lugo
Ourense
Vigo
Pontevedra
Oviedo
Gijón
Santander
Bilbao
Donostia-San Sebastián
Vitoria-Gasteiz
Pamplona/Iruña
Logroño
León
Burgos
Palencia
Valladolid
Zamora
Salamanca
Ávila
Segovia
Madrid
Alcalá de Henares
Toledo
Cáceres
Badajoz
Mérida
Ciudad Real
Córdoba
Jaén
Granada
Sevilla
Huelva
Cádiz
Jerez de la Frontera
Málaga
Marbella
Almería
Algeciras
Gibraltar (UK)
Ceuta (Spain)
Melilla (Spain)
Tanger (Tangier)
Tétouan
Larache
Al Hoceima
Nador
Porto
Braga
Coimbra
Lisboa
Setúbal
Évora
Faro
Cabo de São Vicente
Cabo de Trafalgar
Cabo Fisterra
Miño
Duero
Douro
Tejo
Tajo
Guadiana
Guadalquivir
Ebro
Isla de Alborán (Spain)
Meters Feet
6000 19685
5000 16404
4000 13123
3000 9843
2000 6562
1000 3281
500 1640
200 656
100 328
0
LAND BELOW SEA LEVEL
100 328
200 655
1000 3281
2000 6562
4000 13123
6000 19685

154

1:3,750,000

0 50 100 150 200 kilometers
0 25 50 75 100 miles

Lambert Conic Conformal Projection

SPAIN and PORTUGAL

FRANCE
MIDI-PYRÉNÉES
LANGUEDOC-ROUSSILLON
PROVENCE-ALPES-CÔTE D'AZUR
AQUITAINE
ITALY
MONACO
Golfo di Genova
LIGURIAN SEA
Golfe du Lion
ANDORRA
ANDORRA LA VELLA
CATALUÑA
ARAGÓN
VALENCIANA
Toulouse
Montpellier
Marseille
Toulon
Nice
Cannes
Perpignan
Nîmes
Avignon
Aix-en-Provence
Béziers
Zaragoza
Lleida
Tarragona
Barcelona
Sabadell
Terrassa
Santa Coloma de Gramanet
Mataró
Manresa
Girona
Figueres
Reus
Castelló de la Plana
Sagunto
Valencia
Gandía
Alcoi
Benidorm
Alicante (Alacant)
Elche-Elx
Murcia
Cartagena
Costa Brava
Costa Dorada
Islas Baleares (Balearic Islands)
ISLAS BALEARES
Mallorca (Majorca)
Menorca (Minorca)
Eivissa (Ibiza)
Formentera
Cabrera
Palma
Mahón
MEDITERRANEAN SEA
CORSE
Ajaccio
Sassari
SARDEGNA (Italy)
ALGERIA
ALGER (ALGIERS)
ALGER
BOUMERDÈS
TIPAZA
BLIDA
TIZI OUZOU
BÉJAÏA
JIJEL
SKIKDA
ANNABA
EL TARF
CONSTANTINE
GUELMA
SOUK AHRAS
MILA
SÉTIF
BORDJ BOU ARRÉRIDJ
BOUIRA
MÉDÉA
AÏN DEFLA
CHLEF
MOSTAGANEM
ORAN
RELIZANE
TISSEMSILT
TIARET
MASCARA
AÏN TEMOUCHENT
SIDI BEL ABBÈS
SAÏDA
DJELFA
M'SILA
BATNA
BISKRA
OUM EL BOUAGHI
KHENCHELA
TÉBESSA
Tellien Atlas
Haut Plateaux
Meters
Feet
6000 19685
5000 16404
4000 13123
3000 9843
2000 6562
1000 3281
500 1640
200 656
100 328
0
LAND BELOW SEA LEVEL
100 328
200 656
1000 3281
2000 6562
4000 13123
6000 19685
126
131
155

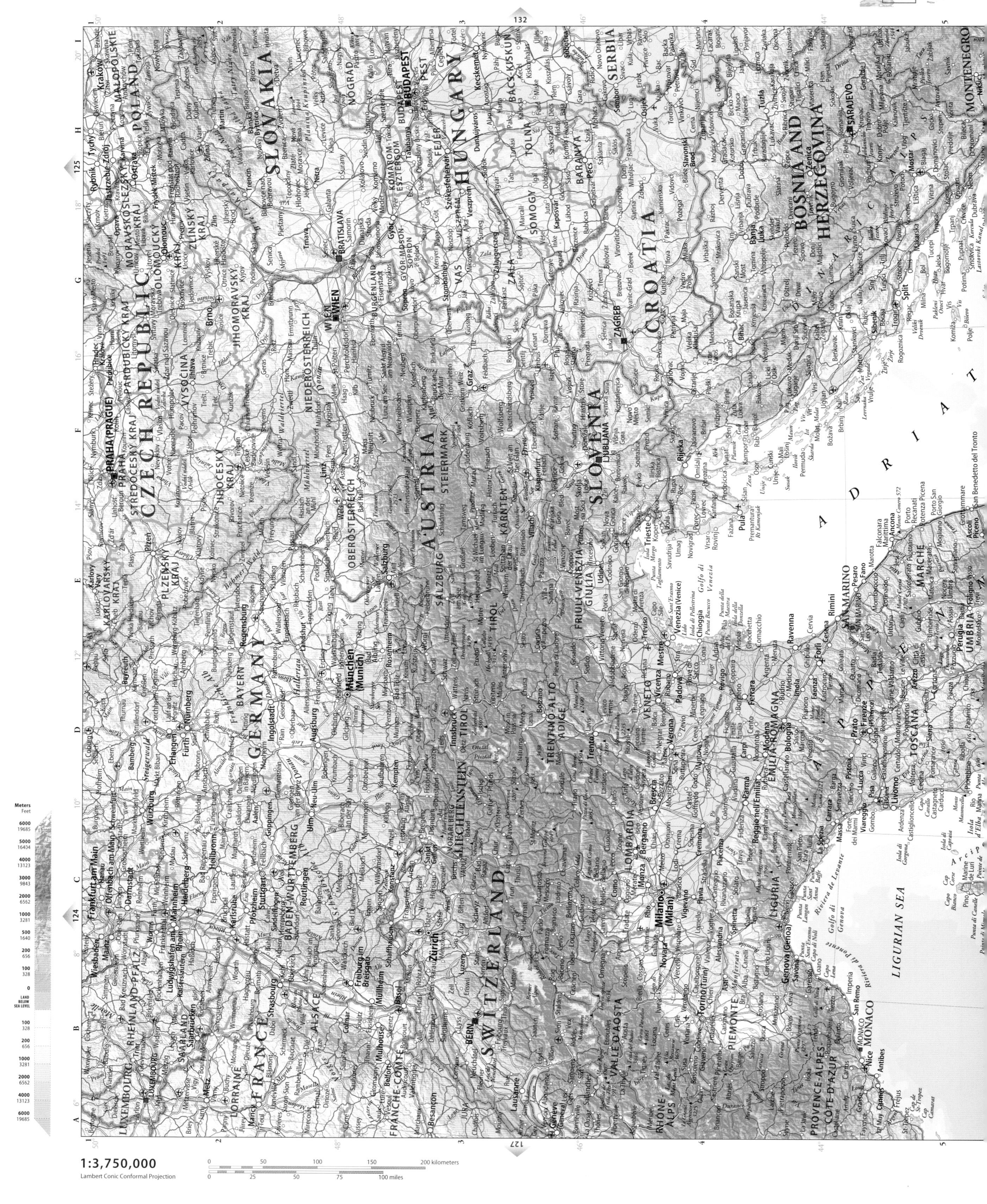
CZECH REPUBLIC
SLOVAKIA
POLAND
HUNGARY
AUSTRIA
GERMANY
SWITZERLAND
LIECHTENSTEIN
SLOVENIA
CROATIA
BOSNIA AND HERZEGOVINA
SERBIA
MONTENEGRO
FRANCE
MONACO
SAN MARINO
LIGURIAN SEA
ADRIATIC SEA
Meters
Feet
LAND BELOW SEA LEVEL

1:3,750,000

Lambert Conic Conformal Projection

0 50 100 150 200 kilometers

0 25 50 75 100 miles

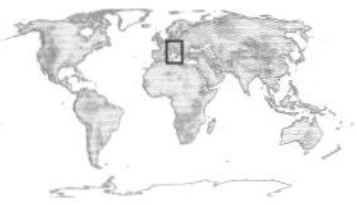

ITALY and EASTERN CENTRAL EUROPE

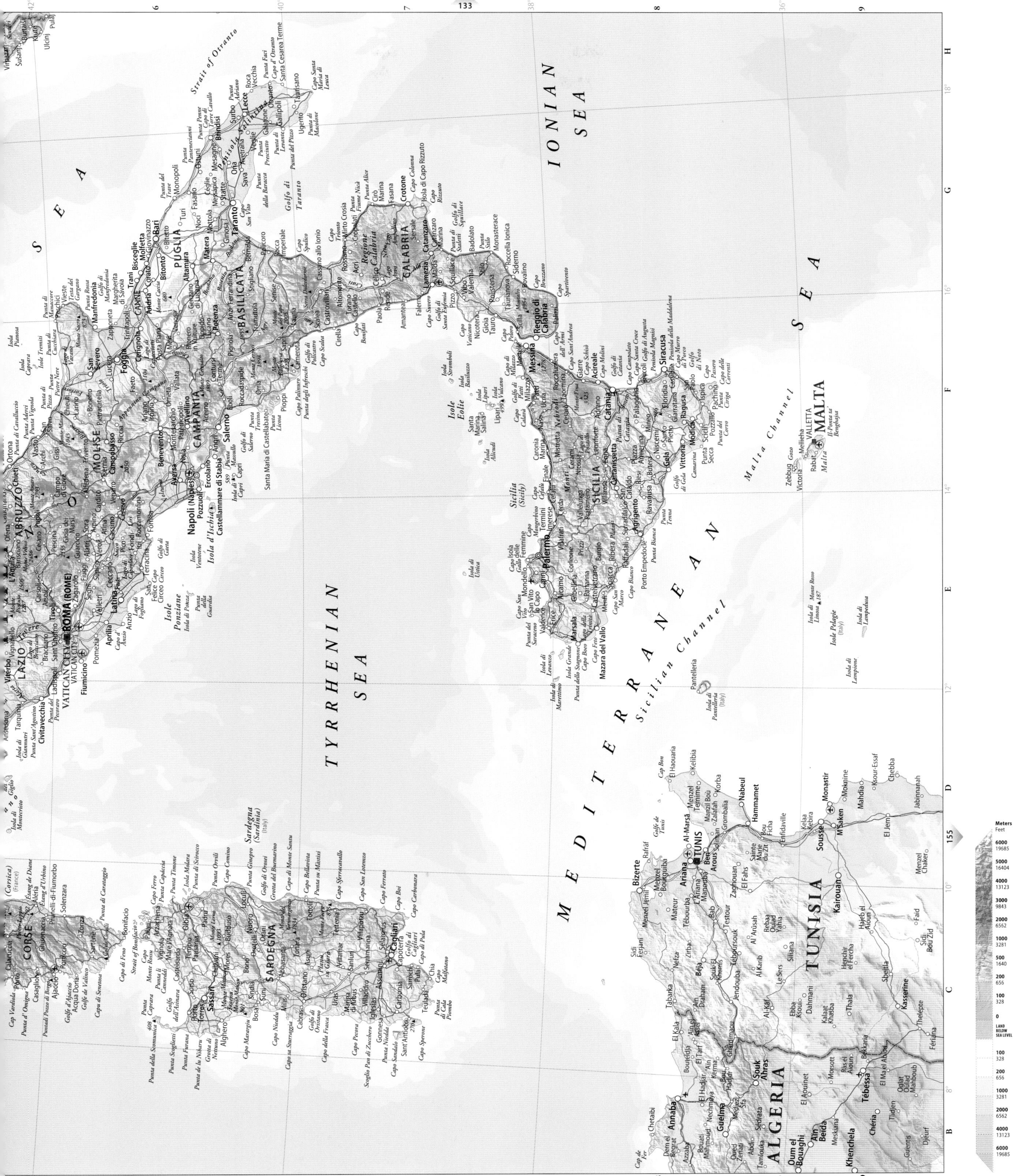

133
129
155
TYRRHENIAN SEA
IONIAN SEA
MEDITERRANEAN SEA
Strait of Otranto
Sicilian Channel
Malta Channel
Strait of Bonifacio
Golfo di Taranto
PUGLIA
BASILICATA
CALABRIA
CAMPANIA
MOLISE
ABRUZZO
LAZIO
SICILIA
SARDEGNA
CORSE
TUNISIA
ALGERIA
MALTA
VALLETTA
ROMA (ROME)
VATICAN CITY
Napoli (Naples)
Palermo
Messina
Reggio di Calabria
Catania
Siracusa
Bari
Taranto
Brindisi
Lecce
Foggia
Salerno
Cagliari
Sassari
TUNIS
Bizerte
Sousse
Annaba
Pantelleria
Isole Eolie
Isole Ponziane
Sicilia (Sicily)
Sardegna (Sardinia) (Italy)
Meters
Feet
6000 19685
5000 16404
4000 13123
3000 9843
2000 6562
1000 3281
500 1640
200 656
100 328
0
LAND BELOW SEA LEVEL

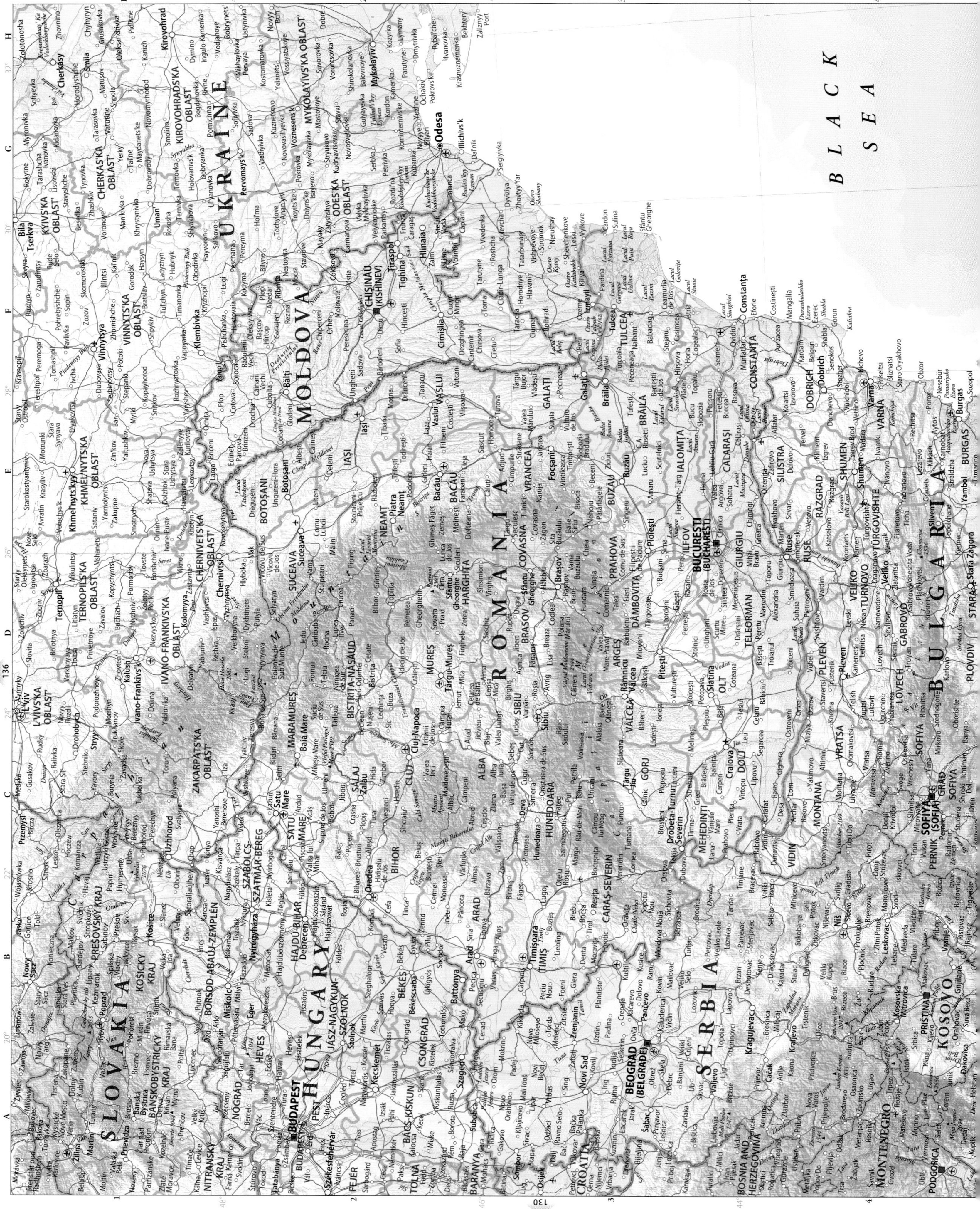
BLACK SEA
UKRAINE
MOLDOVA
ROMANIA
BULGARIA
SERBIA
HUNGARY
SLOVAKIA
KOSOVO
MONTENEGRO
BOSNIA AND HERZEGOVINA
CROATIA
Odesa
CHIŞINĂU (KISHINEV)
BUCUREŞTI (BUCHAREST)
BEOGRAD (BELGRADE)
BUDAPEST
SOFIYA (SOFIA)
PRISHTINA
PODGORICA
Constanţa
Varna
Burgas
136
130

Meters / Feet
6000 19685
5000 16404
4000 13123
3000 9843
2000 6562
1000 3281
500 1640
200 656
100 328
0
LAND BELOW SEA LEVEL
100 328
200 656
1000 3281
2000 6562
4000 13123
6000 19685

1:3,750,000

Lambert Conic Conformal Projection

0 50 100 150 200 kilometers

0 25 50 75 100 miles

SOUTHEASTERN EUROPE

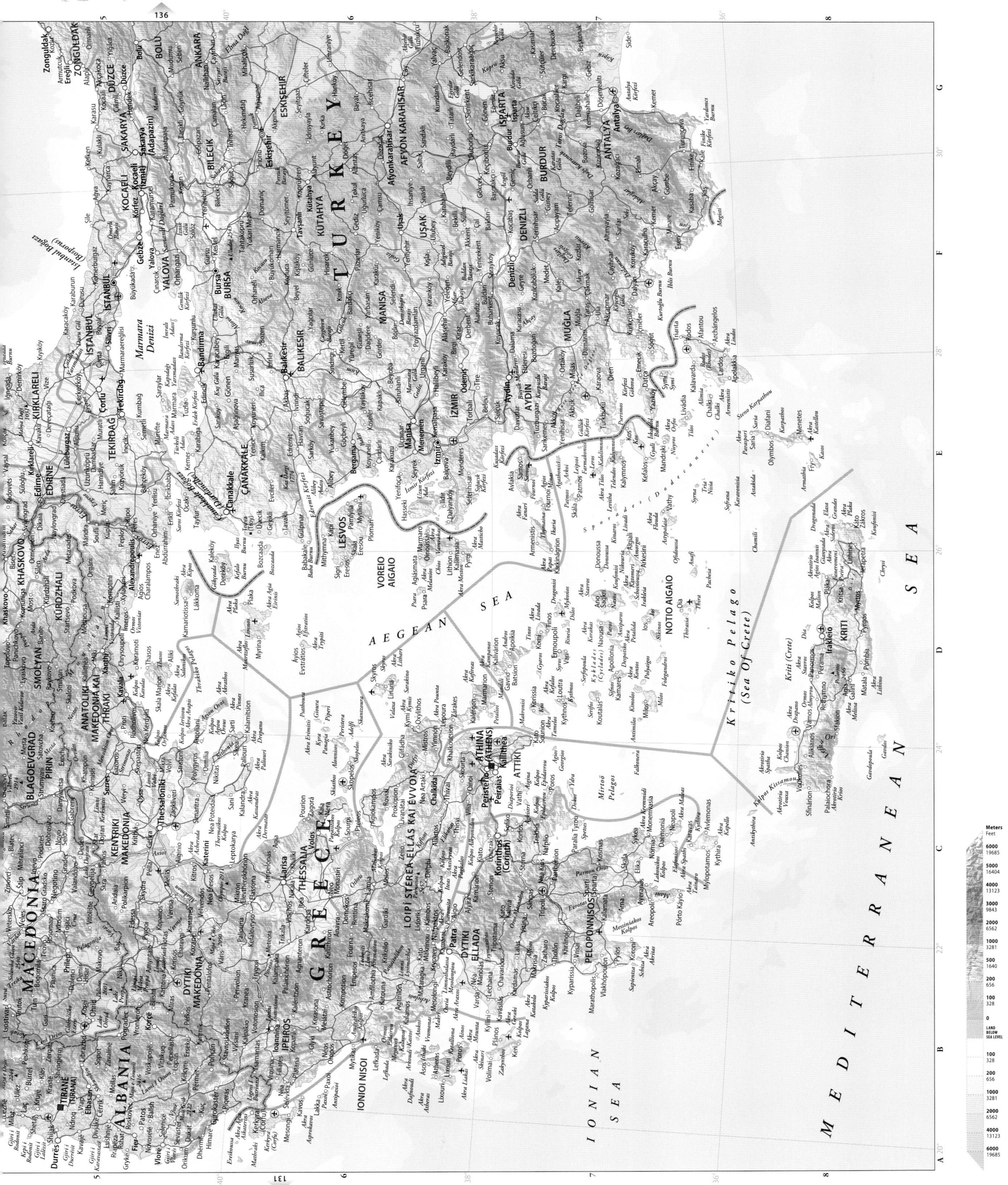
TURKEY
GREECE
ALBANIA
MACEDONIA
AEGEAN SEA
IONIAN SEA
MEDITERRANEAN SEA
Kritiko Pelago (Sea Of Crete)
Marmara Denizi
VOREIO AIGAIO
NOTIO AIGAIO
IONIOI NISOI
PELOPONNISOS
KRITI
ATTIKI
ATHINA (ATHENS)
İSTANBUL
İZMİR
ANKARA
TIRANË (TIRANA)
Meters
Feet
6000
19685
5000
16404
4000
13123
3000
9843
2000
6562
1000
3281
500
1640
200
656
100
328
0
LAND BELOW SEA LEVEL
100
328
200
656
1000
3281
2000
6562
4000
13123
6000
19685

Meters
Feet
6000 19685
5000 16404
4000 13123
3000 9843
2000 6562
1000 3281
500 1640
200 656
100 328
0
LAND BELOW SEA LEVEL
100 328
200 656
1000 3281
2000 6562
4000 13123
6000 19685
ARCTIC
Barents Sea
Norwegian Sea
North Sea
Baltic Sea
Gulf of Bothnia
Black Sea
Caspian Sea
Sea of Azov
Aral Sea
The Gulf
Karskoye More (Kara Sea)
Svalbard (Norway)
Zemlya Frantsa-Iosifa (Franz Josef Land)
Novaya Zemlya
UNITED KINGDOM
LONDON
DEN HAAG/ 's-GRAVENHAGE (THE HAGUE)
BRUSSEL/BRUXELLES
DENMARK
KØBENHAVN (COPENHAGEN)
NORWAY
OSLO
SWEDEN
STOCKHOLM
FINLAND
HELSINKI
ESTONIA
TALLINN
LATVIA
RIGA
LITHUANIA
VILNIUS
GERMANY
BERLIN
POLAND
WARSZAWA
CZECH REP.
PRAHA (PRAGUE)
SLOVAKIA
WIEN (VIENNA)
BRATISLAVA
HUNGARY
BUDAPEST
ROMANIA
MOLDOVA
CHIŞINĂU
BELARUS
MINSK
UKRAINE
KYIV (KIEV)
RUSSIA
MOSKVA (MOSCOW)
Sankt-Peterburg
TURKEY
GEORGIA
T'BILISI
ARMENIA
YEREVAN
AZERBAIJAN
BAKI (BAKU)
IRAQ
IRAN
TEHRĀN
KAZAKHSTAN
ASTANA
UZBEKISTAN
TOSHKENT (TASHKENT)
TURKMENISTAN
ASGABAT (ASHGABAT)
KYRGYZSTAN
BISHKEK
TAJIKISTAN
DUSHANBE
AFGHANISTAN
KĀBOL (KABUL)
HINDU KUSH
TIEN SHAN
PAMIR
ALTAY
Taklimakan Shamo
Tarim Pendi
Ürümqi
Almaty
Novosibirsk
Omsk
Yekaterinburg
Chelyabinsk
Samara
Volgograd
Rostov-na-Donu
Nizhniy Novgorod
Kazan'
Perm'
Ufa
Murmansk
Arkhangel'sk
YAMALO-NENETSKIY AVTONOMNYY OKRUG
KHANTY-MANSIYSKIY AVTONOMNYY OKRUG
RESPUBLIKA KOMI
ZAPADNO-SIBIRSKAYA RAVNINA
Kazakhskiy Melkosopochnik
Garagum
Kyzylkum
Betpak-Dala

1:19,700,000

Conic Equidistant Projection

0 100 200 300 400 500 600 700 kilometers

0 100 200 300 400 miles

RUSSIAN FEDERATION

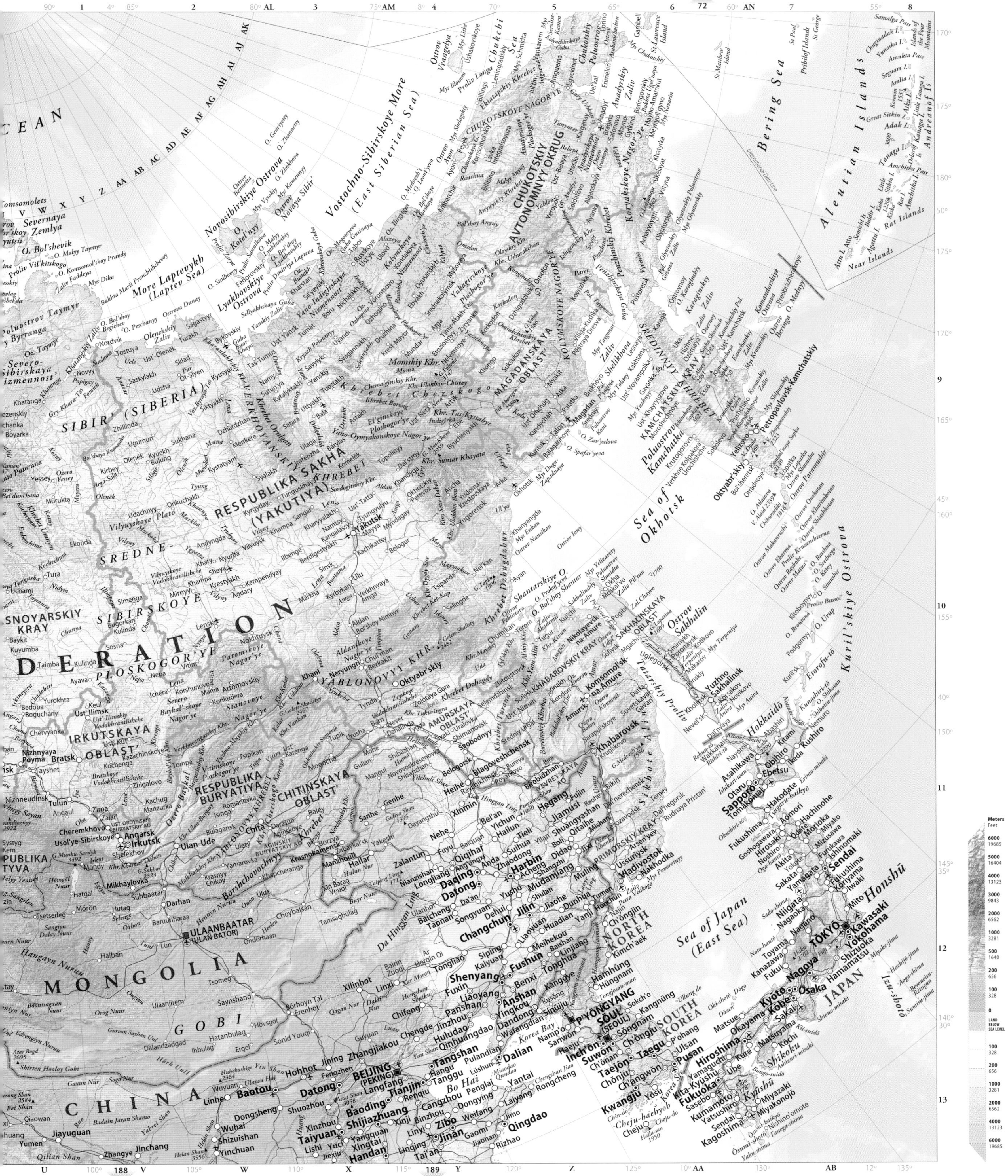

RUSSIAN FEDERATION
SIBIR' (SIBERIA)
RESPUBLIKA SAKHA (YAKUTIYA)
CHUKOTSKIY AVTONOMNYY OKRUG
MAGADANSKAYA OBLAST'
KAMCHATSKIY KRAY
KHABAROVSKIY KRAY
SAKHALINSKAYA OBLAST'
AMURSKAYA OBLAST'
CHITINSKAYA OBLAST'
RESPUBLIKA BURYATIYA
IRKUTSKAYA OBLAST'
KRASNOYARSKIY KRAY
PRIMORSKIY KRAY
SREDNE-SIBIRSKOYE PLOSKOGOR'YE
MONGOLIA
CHINA
NORTH KOREA
SOUTH KOREA
JAPAN
GOBI
More Laptevykh (Laptev Sea)
Vostochno-Sibirskoye More (East Siberian Sea)
Chukchi Sea
Bering Sea
Sea of Okhotsk
Sea of Japan (East Sea)
Aleutian Islands
Kuril'skiye Ostrova
Sakhalin
Hokkaidō
Honshū
Novosibirskiye Ostrova
Ostrov Vrangelya
Yakutsk
Magadan
Petropavlovsk-Kamchatskiy
Khabarovsk
Vladivostok
Irkutsk
Ulan-Ude
Chita
Blagoveshchensk
Komsomol'sk-na-Amure
Yuzhno-Sakhalinsk
ULAANBAATAR (ULAN BATOR)
BEIJING (PEKING)
P'YONGYANG
SŎUL (SEOUL)
TŌKYŌ
Harbin
Shenyang
Dalian
Tianjin
Sapporo
Sendai
Yokohama
Nagoya
Ōsaka
Kōbe
Hiroshima
Fukuoka
Pusan
Meters
Feet
6000 19685
5000 16404
4000 13123
3000 9843
2000 6562
1000 3281
500 1640
200 656
100 328
0
LAND BELOW SEA LEVEL
100 328
200 656
1000 3281
2000 6562
4000 13123
6000 19685

TURKEY and EASTERN EUROPE

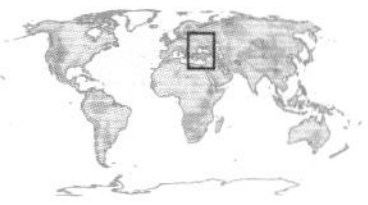

Baltic Sea
POLAND
WARSZAWA (WARSAW)
LITHUANIA
VILNIUS
BELARUS
MINSK
RUSSIAN FEDERATION
UKRAINE
KYIV/KYYIV (KIEV)
SLOVAKIA
HUNGARY
BUDAPEST
MOLDOVA
CHIŞINĂU (KISHINEV)
ROMANIA
BUCUREŞTI (BUCHAREST)
SERBIA
BEOGRAD (BELGRADE)
KOSOVO
PRISTINA
BULGARIA
SOFIYA (SOFIA)
MACEDONIA
SKOPJE
ALBANIA
TIRANË (TIRANA)
GREECE
ATHINA (ATHENS)
Aegean Sea
Black Sea
Sea of Azov
GEORGIA
T'BILISI
ARMENIA
YEREVAN
TURKEY
ANKARA
İSTANBUL
IRAN
IRAQ
BAGHDĀD
SYRIA
DIMASHQ (DAMASCUS)
LEBANON
BEYROUTH (BEIRUT)
CYPRUS
NICOSIA (LEFKOSIA)
ISRAEL
YERUSHALAYIM/AL QUDS (JERUSALEM)
JORDAN
'AMMAN
SAUDI ARABIA
EGYPT
AL QĀHIRAH (CAIRO)
LIBYA
MEDITERRANEAN SEA
Administrative regions in Turkey Numbered on the map:
1. İSTANBUL
2. YALOVA
3. KOCAELİ
4. SAKARYA
5. DÜZCE
Administrative regions in Russian Federation Numbered on the map:
1. KABARDINO BALKARSKAYA RESP.
2. RESPUBLIKA SEVERNAYA OSETIYA-ALANIYA
3. RESPUBLIKA INGUSHETIYA

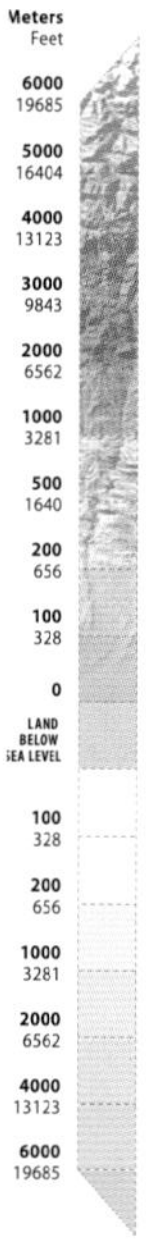
Meters Feet
6000 19685
5000 16404
4000 13123
3000 9843
2000 6562
1000 3281
500 1640
200 656
100 328
0
LAND BELOW SEA LEVEL
100 328
200 656
1000 3281
2000 6562
4000 13123
6000 19685

1:10,320,000

Conic Equidistant Projection

0 100 200 300 400 500 kilometers

0 50 100 150 200 250 300 miles

BRITISH ISLES

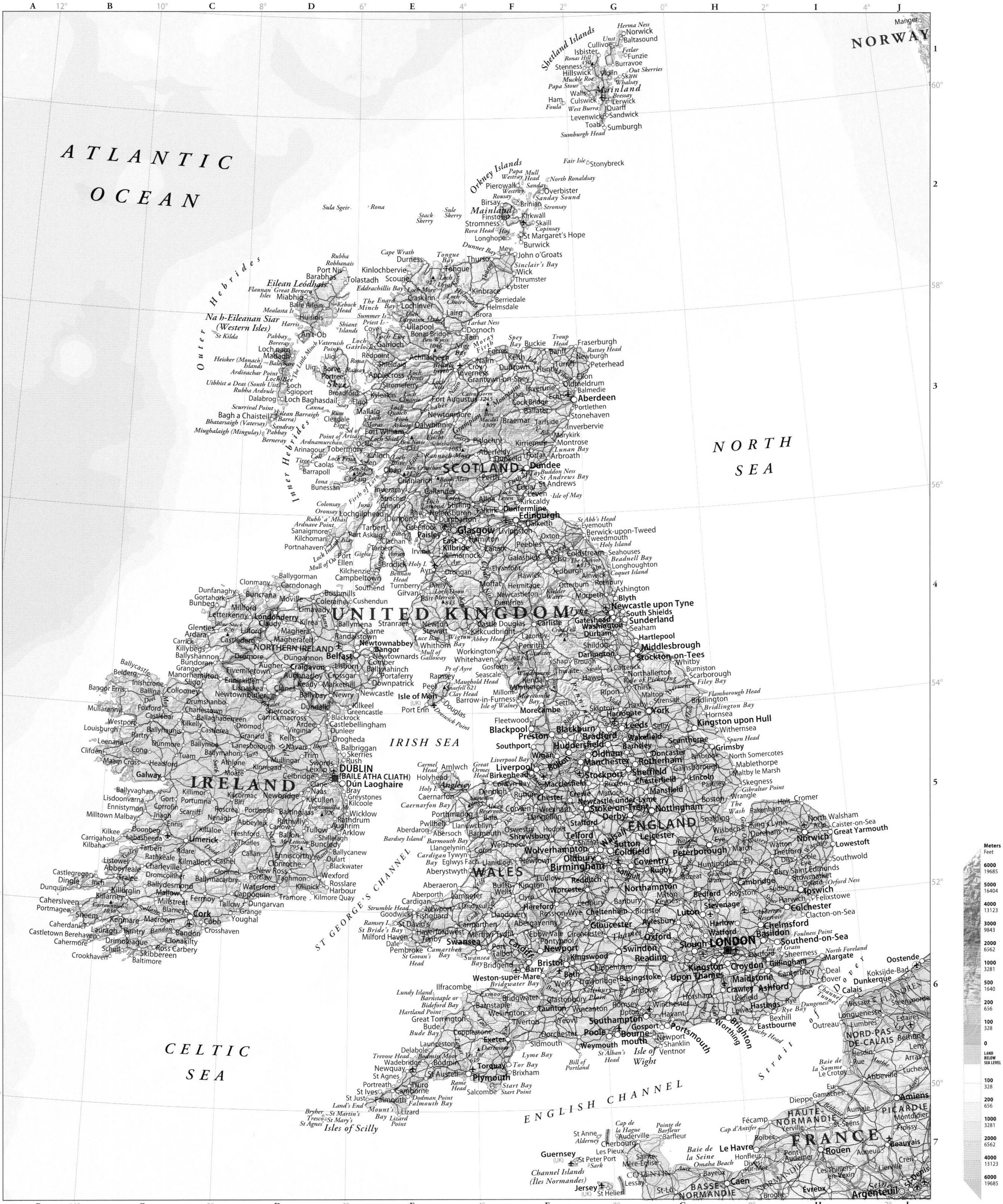

A
B
C
D
E
F
G
H
I
J
12°
10°
8°
6°
4°
2°
0°
60°
58°
56°
54°
52°
50°
ATLANTIC OCEAN
NORTH SEA
IRISH SEA
CELTIC SEA
ENGLISH CHANNEL
ST GEORGE'S CHANNEL
Strait of Dover
NORWAY
UNITED KINGDOM
SCOTLAND
NORTHERN IRELAND
ENGLAND
WALES
IRELAND
FRANCE
Shetland Islands
Orkney Islands
Outer Hebrides
Inner Hebrides
Na h-Eileanan Siar (Western Isles)
Isles of Scilly
Channel Islands (Îles Normandes)
Isle of Man (UK)
Isle of Wight
Lerwick
Sumburgh
Kirkwall
Stornoway
John o'Groats
Thurso
Wick
Ullapool
Inverness
Fort William
Fort Augustus
Aberdeen
Dundee
Perth
Stirling
Edinburgh
Glasgow
Paisley
Kilmarnock
Ayr
Dumfries
Berwick-upon-Tweed
Newcastle upon Tyne
Sunderland
Carlisle
Middlesbrough
Stockton-on-Tees
York
Leeds
Bradford
Blackpool
Preston
Liverpool
Manchester
Sheffield
Kingston upon Hull
Nottingham
Leicester
Birmingham
Coventry
Wolverhampton
Stoke-on-Trent
Derby
Lincoln
Norwich
Great Yarmouth
Ipswich
Cambridge
Peterborough
Northampton
Oxford
Reading
LONDON
Southend-on-Sea
Chelmsford
Colchester
Dover
Canterbury
Margate
Brighton
Eastbourne
Hastings
Southampton
Portsmouth
Bournemouth
Poole
Weymouth
Exeter
Plymouth
Torquay
Truro
Penzance
Falmouth
Bristol
Bath
Swansea
Cardiff
Newport
Gloucester
Cheltenham
Hereford
Worcester
Aberystwyth
Holyhead
Belfast
Londonderry
Armagh
Newry
DUBLIN (BAILE ÁTHA CLIATH)
Dún Laoghaire
Drogheda
Dundalk
Sligo
Galway
Limerick
Ennis
Tralee
Killarney
Cork
Cobh
Waterford
Wexford
Kilkenny
Athlone
Mullingar
Castlebar
Westport
Letterkenny
Douglas
St Helier
Guernsey (UK)
Jersey (UK)
St Peter Port
Cherbourg
Le Havre
Rouen
Caen
Dieppe
Calais
Dunkerque
Boulogne
Amiens
Oostende
NORD-PAS-DE-CALAIS
HAUTE-NORMANDIE
BASSE-NORMANDIE
PICARDIE
Meters Feet
6000 19685
5000 16404
4000 13123
3000 9843
2000 6562
1000 3281
500 1640
200 656
100 328
0
LAND BELOW SEA LEVEL
100 328
200 656
1000 3281
2000 6562
4000 13123
6000 19685

1:4,700,000

Lambert Conic Conformal Projection

0 50 100 150 200 250 kilometers

0 25 50 75 100 150 miles

140
143
A
B
C
D
E
7°
6°
5°
4°
3°
53°
52°
51°
50°
1
2
3
4
5
IRELAND
KILDARE
WICKLOW
CARLOW
WEXFORD
IRISH
SEA
St George's Channel
Cardigan
Bay
Caernarfon
Bay
CELTIC
SEA
Bristol Channel
Lyme Bay
WALES
CONWY
GWYNEDD
DENBIGHSHIRE
WREXHAM
CEREDIGION
POWYS
PEMBROKESHIRE
CARMARTHENSHIRE
SWANSEA
NEATH PORT TALBOT
BRIDGEND
VALE OF GLAMORGAN
CARDIFF
NEWPORT
SHROPSHIRE
HEREFORDSHIRE
TELFORD AND WREKIN
CHESHIRE
MONMOUTHSHIRE
NORTH SOMERSET
SOMERSET
DEVON
CORNWALL
TORBAY
Cambrian Mountains
Brecon Beacons
Black Mountains
Exmoor
Dartmoor
Bodmin Moor
Wicklow Mountains
Snowdon 1085
Lundy Island
Bardsey
Isles of Scilly
ISLES OF SCILLY
St Mary's
St Agnes
St Martin's
Tresco
Bryher
Land's End
Lizard Point
Start Point
Hartland Point
St David's Head
St Govan's Head
Worms Head
Carnsore Point
Hook Head
Saltee Islands
Skomer Island
Skokholm Island
Ramsey Island
Caldey Island
Wexford Harbour
Rosslare Harbour
Swansea
Cardiff
Newport
Bristol
Plymouth
Torquay
Exeter
Taunton
Hereford
Shrewsbury
Telford
Barnstaple
Bodmin
Truro
Penzance
Falmouth
Newquay
Aberystwyth
Carmarthen
Wexford
Arklow
Bray
Dinas
Weston-super-Mare
Bridgwater
Yeovil
Barry
Rhondda
Caerphilly
Pontypridd
Merthyr Tydfil
Neath
Port Talbot
Llanelli
Tenby
Pembroke
Milford Haven
Haverfordwest
Fishguard
Cardigan
Brecon
Abergavenny
Welshpool
Wrexham
Bangor
Caernarfon
Pwllheli
Dolgellau
Barmouth
Harlech
Bala

1:1,410,000

Lambert Conic Conformal Projection

0 50 100 kilometers

0 25 50 miles

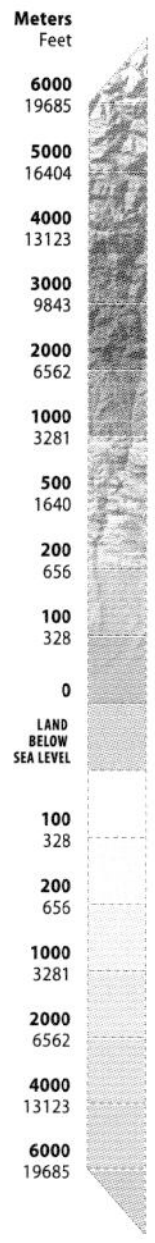
Meters
Feet
6000
19685
5000
16404
4000
13123
3000
9843
2000
6562
1000
3281
500
1640
200
656
100
328
0
LAND BELOW SEA LEVEL
100
328
200
656
1000
3281
2000
6562
4000
13123
6000
19685

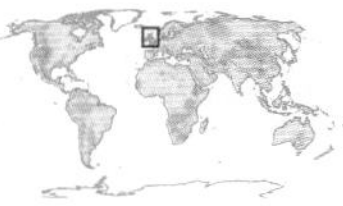

SOUTHERN ENGLAND and WALES

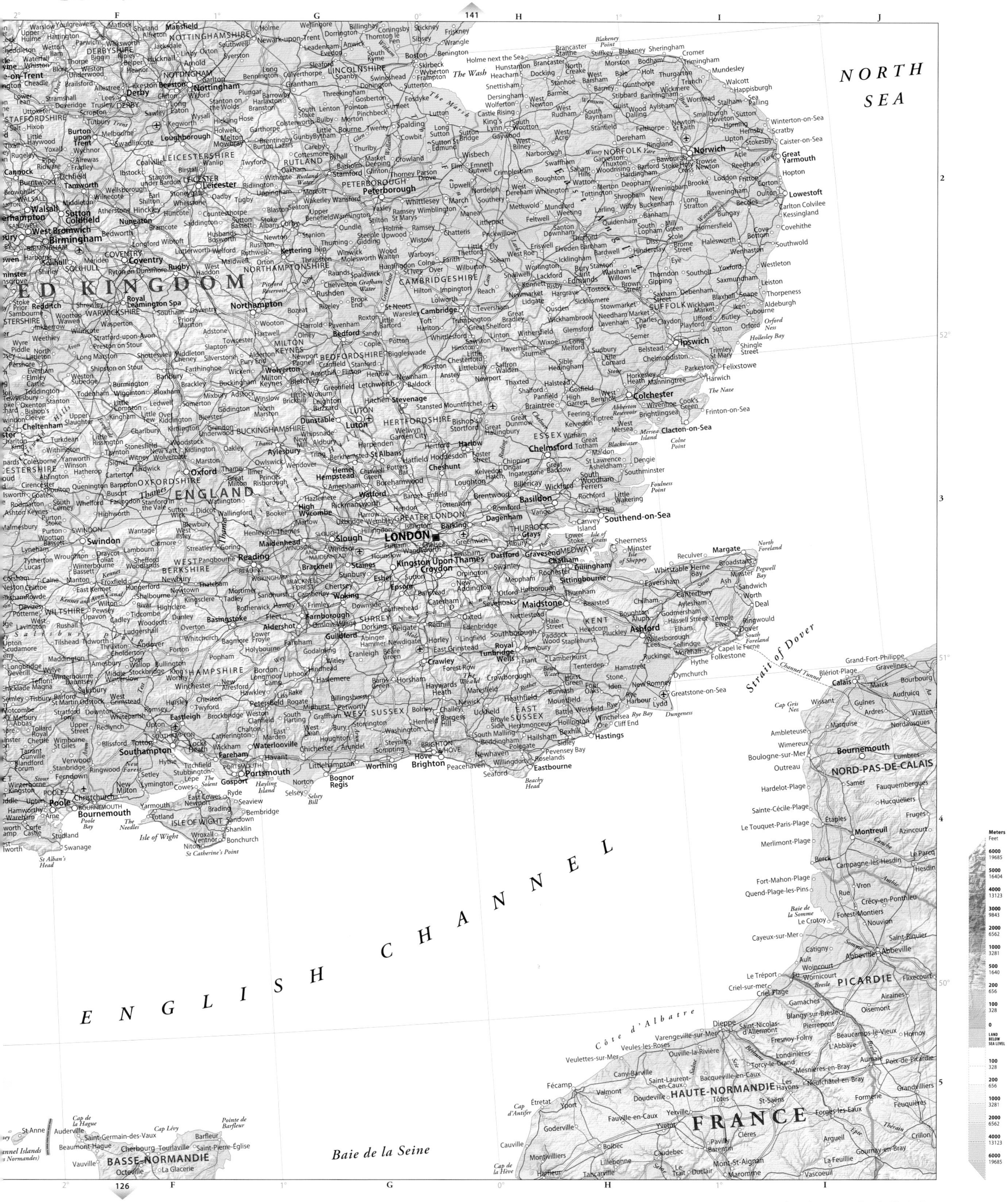
141
NORTH SEA
ENGLISH CHANNEL
UNITED KINGDOM
ENGLAND
FRANCE
LONDON
GREATER LONDON
Birmingham
Coventry
Leicester
Nottingham
Peterborough
Cambridge
Norwich
Great Yarmouth
Lowestoft
Ipswich
Colchester
Chelmsford
Southend-on-Sea
Oxford
Reading
Swindon
Southampton
Portsmouth
Bournemouth
Brighton
Hastings
Eastbourne
Dover
Folkestone
Margate
Ashford
Maidstone
Calais
Boulogne-sur-Mer
Abbeville
Dieppe
Fécamp
The Wash
Strait of Dover
Isle of Wight
Baie de la Seine
Côte d'Albatre
NORD-PAS-DE-CALAIS
PICARDIE
HAUTE-NORMANDIE
BASSE-NORMANDIE
126
Meters
Feet
6000
19685
5000
16404
4000
13123
3000
9843
2000
6562
1000
3281
500
1640
200
656
100
328
0
LAND BELOW SEA LEVEL

A
B
C
D
E
1
2
3
4
5
7°
6°
5°
4°
3°
55°
54°
53°
52°
142
143
138
UNITED KINGDOM
NORTHERN IRELAND
SCOTLAND
IRELAND
WALES
IRISH SEA
North Channel
St George's Channel
Cardigan Bay
Liverpool Bay
Solway Firth
Firth of Clyde
Isle of Man
(UK)
ISLE OF ANGLESEY
DUBLIN
(BAILE ÁTHA CLIATH)
Dún Laoghaire
Belfast
Londonderry
Craigavon
Bangor
Douglas
Carlisle
Dumfries
Ayr
Wexford
Wicklow
Drogheda
Dundalk
Newry
Holyhead
Aberystwyth
Blackpool
Morecambe
Southport
Liverpool
Wallasey
Malin Head
Rathlin Island
Mull of Kintyre
Mull of Galloway
Rinns of Galloway
Calf of Man
Bardsey
Saltee Islands
Lambay Island
DUMFRIES AND GALLOWAY
SOUTH AYRSHIRE
CUMBRIA
GWYNEDD
CONWY
DENBIGHSHIRE
FLINTSHIRE
CEREDIGION
POWYS
Snowdonia
Cambrian Mountains
Wicklow Mountains
LOUTH
MEATH
DUBLIN
KILDARE
WICKLOW
WEXFORD
CARLOW
KILKENNY
LAOIS
WESTMEATH
CAVAN
MONAGHAN
DONEGAL
INISHOWEN
LIMAVADY
COLERAINE
MOYLE
BALLYMONEY
BALLYMENA
LARNE
ANTRIM
NEWTOWNABBEY
CARRICKFERGUS
NORTH DOWN
ARDS
CASTLEREAGH
LISBURN
DOWN
BANBRIDGE
CRAIGAVON
ARMAGH
DUNGANNON
COOKSTOWN
MAGHERAFELT
OMAGH
STRABANE
LONDONDERRY
NEWRY AND MOURNE
Meters
Feet
6000
19685
5000
16404
4000
13123
3000
9843
2000
6562
1000
3281
500
1640
200
656
100
328
0
LAND BELOW SEA LEVEL

1:1,410,000

Lambert Conic Conformal Projection

0 50 100 kilometers

0 25 50 miles

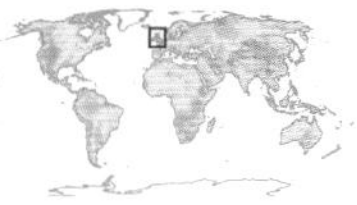

NORTHERN ENGLAND

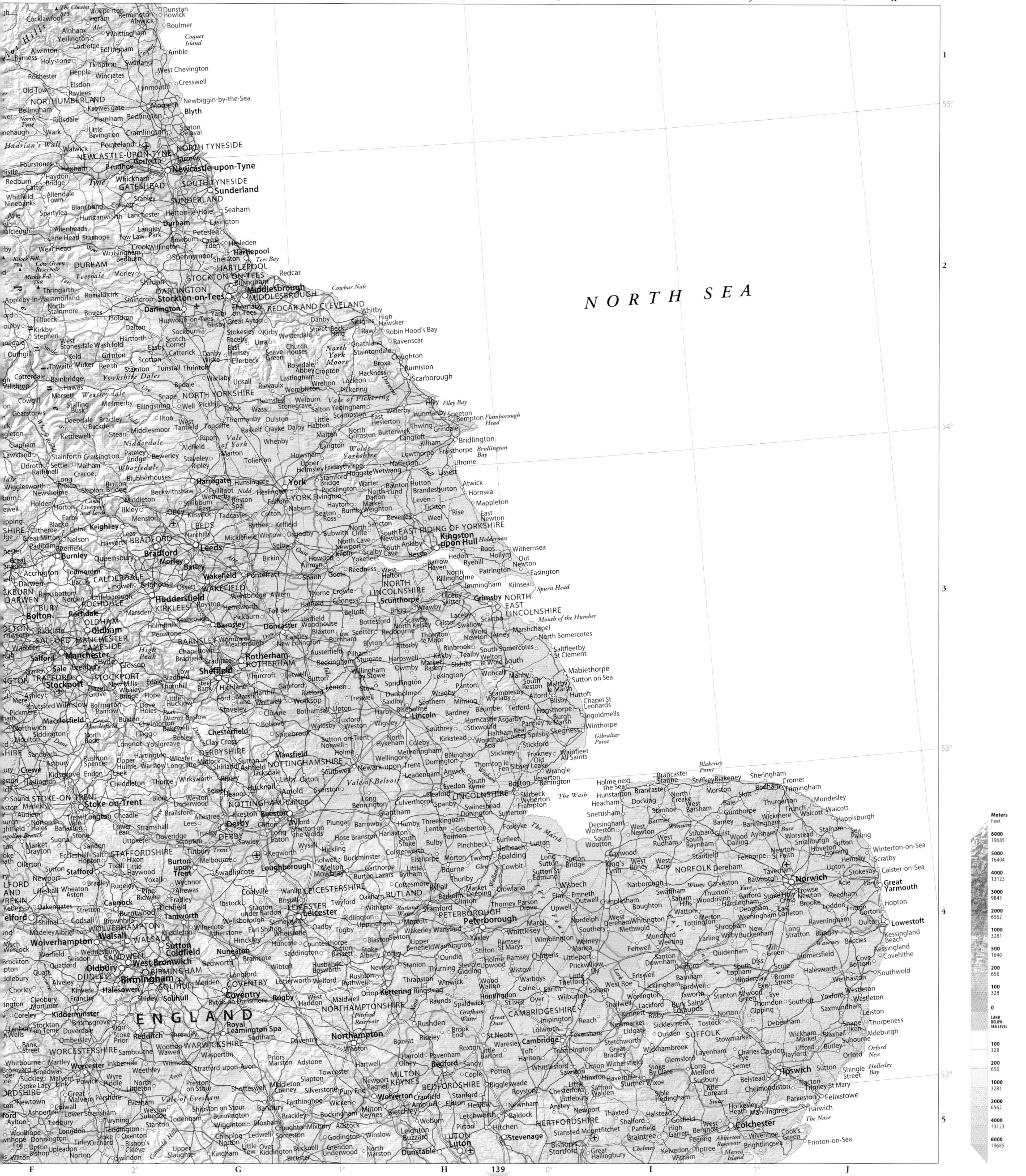

NORTH SEA
ENGLAND
NORTHUMBERLAND
NEWCASTLE-UPON-TYNE
Newcastle-upon-Tyne
NORTH TYNESIDE
SOUTH TYNESIDE
GATESHEAD
SUNDERLAND
Sunderland
Durham
DURHAM
HARTLEPOOL
Hartlepool
STOCKTON-ON-TEES
Stockton-on-Tees
DARLINGTON
Darlington
Middlesbrough
MIDDLESBROUGH
REDCAR AND CLEVELAND
NORTH YORKSHIRE
York
YORK
Harrogate
Scarborough
Bridlington
EAST RIDING OF YORKSHIRE
Kingston upon Hull
NORTH LINCOLNSHIRE
NORTH EAST LINCOLNSHIRE
Grimsby
Scunthorpe
Leeds
LEEDS
Bradford
BRADFORD
WAKEFIELD
Wakefield
CALDERDALE
KIRKLEES
Huddersfield
BARNSLEY
Barnsley
Doncaster
Sheffield
Rotherham
ROTHERHAM
Manchester
MANCHESTER
SALFORD
Salford
OLDHAM
Oldham
ROCHDALE
Rochdale
BURY
Bolton
TAMESIDE
TRAFFORD
STOCKPORT
Stockport
Burnley
Blackburn
DARWEN
Macclesfield
Chesterfield
DERBYSHIRE
Derby
DERBY
NOTTINGHAMSHIRE
Nottingham
NOTTINGHAM
Mansfield
Lincoln
LINCOLNSHIRE
Boston
The Wash
STOKE-ON-TRENT
Stoke-on-Trent
STAFFORDSHIRE
Stafford
LEICESTERSHIRE
Leicester
LEICESTER
RUTLAND
PETERBOROUGH
Peterborough
Norwich
NORFOLK
Great Yarmouth
Lowestoft
SUFFOLK
Ipswich
Colchester
CAMBRIDGESHIRE
Cambridge
HERTFORDSHIRE
Stevenage
LUTON
Luton
BEDFORDSHIRE
Bedford
MILTON KEYNES
Northampton
NORTHAMPTONSHIRE
Coventry
COVENTRY
WARWICKSHIRE
Birmingham
BIRMINGHAM
Wolverhampton
WOLVERHAMPTON
Walsall
WALSALL
SANDWELL
DUDLEY
SOLIHULL
WORCESTERSHIRE
Worcester
Kidderminster
Redditch
Telford
Yorkshire Dales
North York Moors
Vale of York
Vale of Pickering
Flamborough Head
Spurn Head
Mouth of the Humber
Gibraltar Point
Blakeney Point
Orford Ness
Hollesley Bay
The Naze
Hadrian's Wall
2° G 1° H 0° I 1° J 2° K
F 2° G 1° H 139 0° I 1° J
1 2 3 4 5
55° 54° 53° 52°
Meters
Feet
6000 19685
5000 16404
4000 13123
3000 9843
2000 6562
1000 3281
500 1640
200 656
100 328
0
LAND BELOW SEA LEVEL
100 328
200 656
1000 3281
2000 6562
4000 13123
6000 19685

SCOTLAND

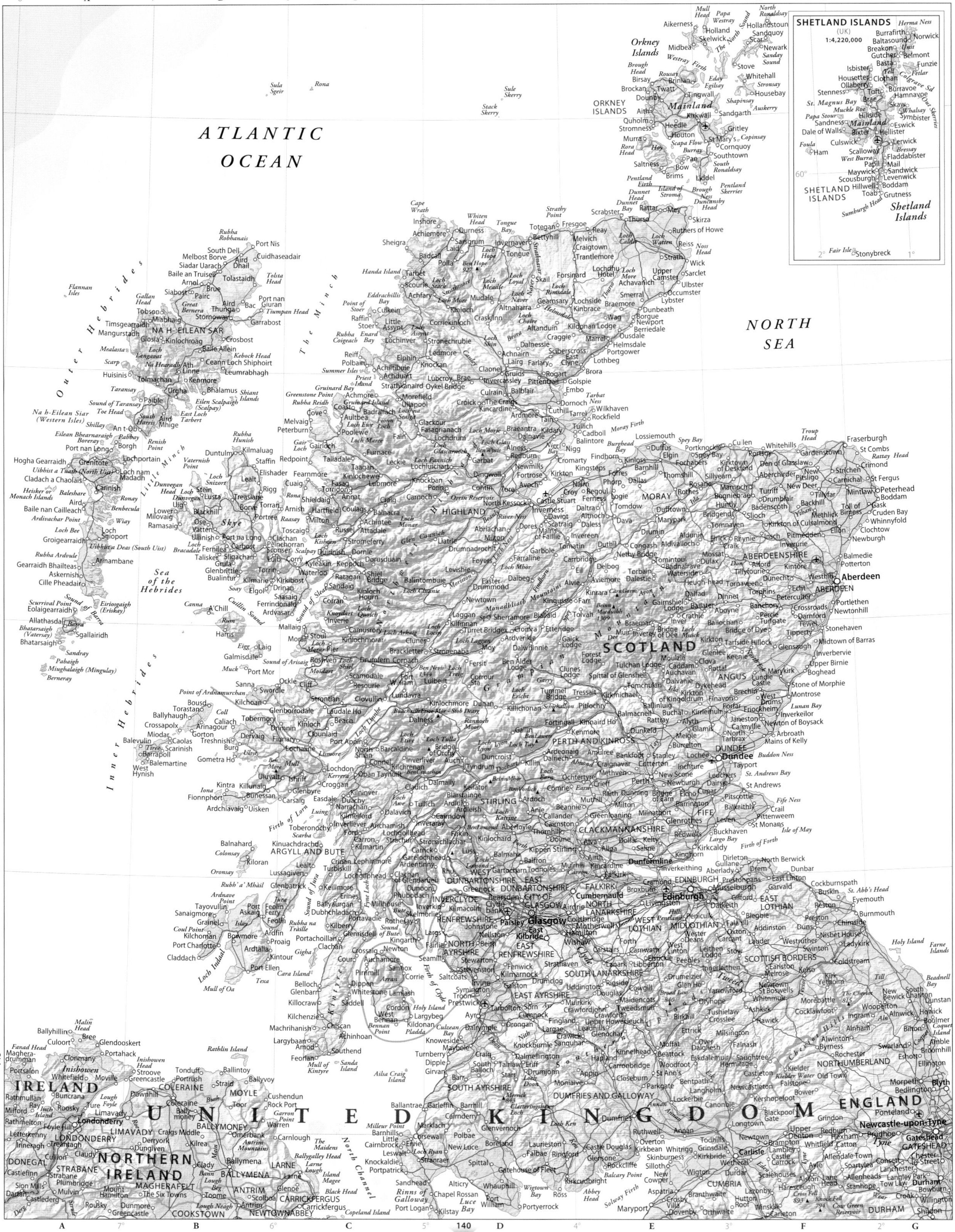
ATLANTIC OCEAN
NORTH SEA
SHETLAND ISLANDS (UK) 1:4,220,000
Shetland Islands
Orkney Islands
ORKNEY ISLANDS
Outer Hebrides
Inner Hebrides
NA H-EILEAN SAR
The Minch
Little Minch
Sea of the Hebrides
HIGHLAND
MORAY
ABERDEENSHIRE
Aberdeen
SCOTLAND
Grampian Mountains
ANGUS
PERTH AND KINROSS
DUNDEE
Dundee
FIFE
STIRLING
CLACKMANNANSHIRE
ARGYLL AND BUTE
Edinburgh
EDINBURGH
Glasgow
SCOTTISH BORDERS
SOUTH LANARKSHIRE
EAST AYRSHIRE
SOUTH AYRSHIRE
DUMFRIES AND GALLOWAY
NORTHUMBERLAND
ENGLAND
Newcastle-upon-Tyne
CUMBRIA
DURHAM
UNITED KINGDOM
IRELAND
NORTHERN IRELAND
North Channel
Solway Firth
Firth of Forth
Firth of Clyde
Firth of Lorn
Moray Firth
Meters
Feet
LAND BELOW SEA LEVEL
143
140

1:1,880,000

Lambert Conic Conformal Projection

0 50 100 kilometers

0 25 50 miles

IRELAND

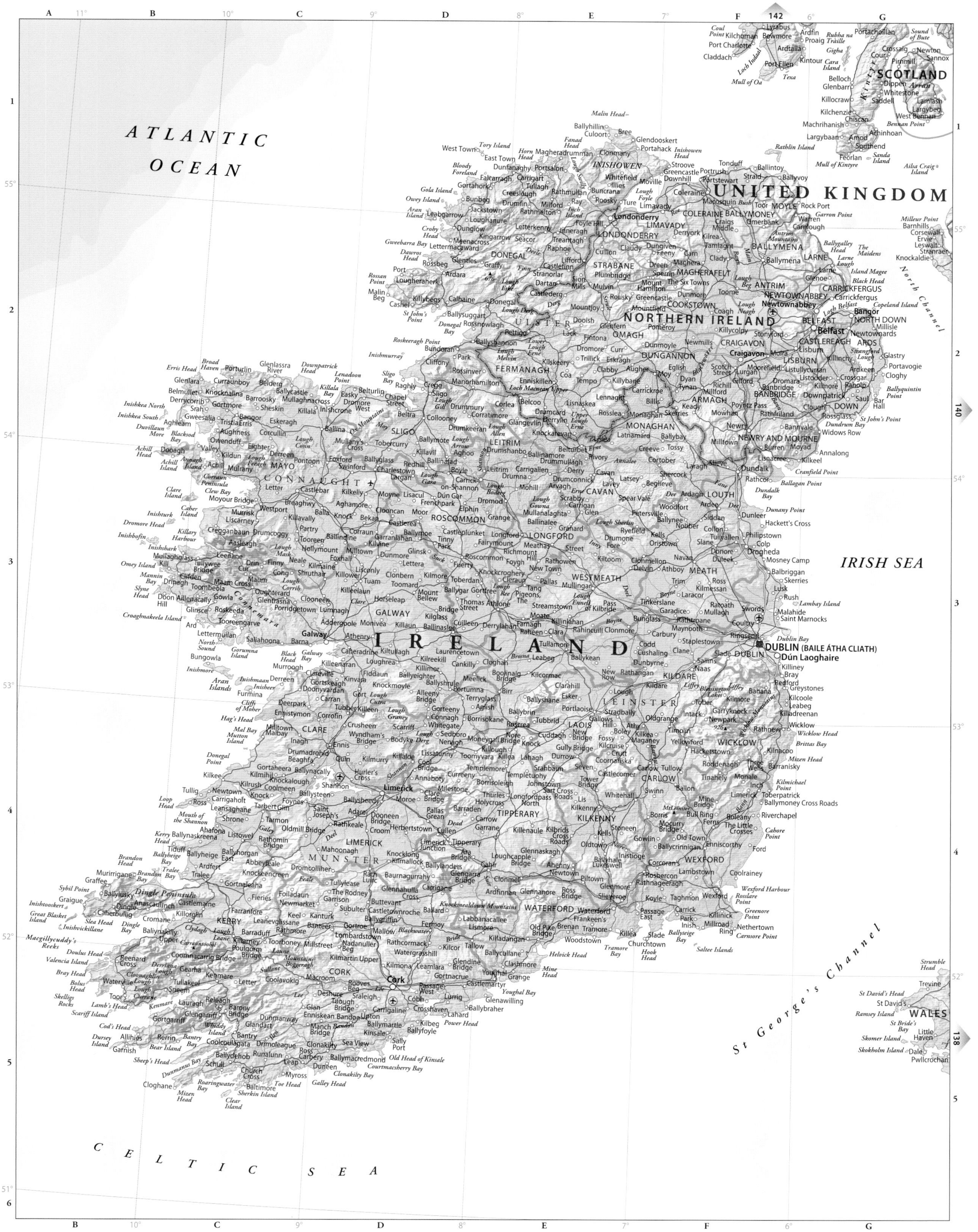

ATLANTIC OCEAN
CELTIC SEA
IRISH SEA
St George's Channel
North Channel
UNITED KINGDOM
NORTHERN IRELAND
SCOTLAND
WALES
IRELAND
ULSTER
CONNAUGHT
LEINSTER
MUNSTER
DUBLIN (BAILE ÁTHA CLIATH)
Dún Laoghaire
Belfast
Londonderry
Newtownabbey
Craigavon
Galway
Limerick
Cork
Waterford
Wexford
Kilkenny
Sligo
DONEGAL
SLIGO
LEITRIM
MAYO
ROSCOMMON
LONGFORD
WESTMEATH
MEATH
LOUTH
CAVAN
MONAGHAN
GALWAY
CLARE
LIMERICK
TIPPERARY
KERRY
CORK
WATERFORD
WEXFORD
WICKLOW
KILDARE
LAOIS
CARLOW
KILKENNY
FERMANAGH
OMAGH
STRABANE
LIMAVADY
COLERAINE
BALLYMONEY
MOYLE
BALLYMENA
LARNE
CARRICKFERGUS
ANTRIM
NEWTOWNABBEY
BELFAST
NORTH DOWN
ARDS
CASTLEREAGH
LISBURN
CRAIGAVON
BANBRIDGE
DOWN
NEWRY AND MOURNE
ARMAGH
DUNGANNON
COOKSTOWN
MAGHERAFELT
LONDONDERRY
INISHOWEN
142
140
138
A
B
C
D
E
F
G
1
2
3
4
5
6
11°
10°
9°
8°
7°
6°
55°
54°
53°
52°
51°

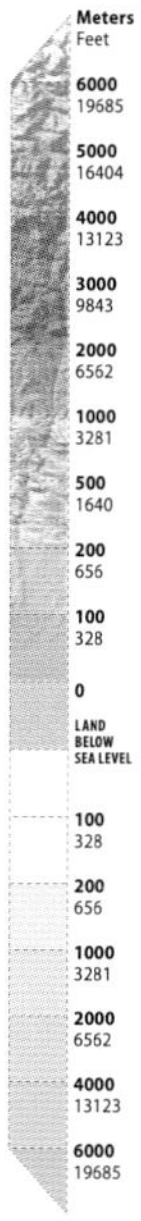

Meters
Feet
6000
19685
5000
16404
4000
13123
3000
9843
2000
6562
1000
3281
500
1640
200
656
100
328
0
LAND BELOW SEA LEVEL
100
328
200
656
1000
3281
2000
6562
4000
13123
6000
19685

1:1,880,000

Lambert Conic Conformal Projection

0 50 100 kilometers

0 25 50 miles

Africa

NORTHERN AFRICA

Africa is the second-largest continent (Asia is larger both in size and population), and northern Africa extends from the North Atlantic Ocean in the west to a narrow land bridge to western Asia—the Sinai Peninsula—and the Red Sea in the east. It covers the area from the southern shores of the Mediterranean Sea south to a transition zone—the Sahel. Northern Africa is defined by graduations from extremely dry climates in the north to progressively more humid zones as far south as latitude 10° North.

Above These women come from a small village in Eritrea, one of the hottest and driest countries in the world. Approximately two-thirds of Eritrea's population receives food aid, and a high percentage serve in the armed forces.

The region can also be defined by country borders—think of northern Africa as being eleven countries arranged in two west–east tiers between the Atlantic Ocean and the Red Sea. The northern tier has the Mediterranean countries of Morocco, Algeria, Tunisia, Libya, and Egypt, while the southern tier is comprised of Mauritania, Mali, Niger, Chad, Sudan, and Eritrea. The region also includes the disputed Western Sahara on the Atlantic coast, three small Spanish possessions (Canary Islands and the cities of Ceuta, and Melilla), and the Portuguese Madeira Islands.

The Vast Sahara

The major geographic characteristic of northern Africa is dry climate. Most of the region forms part of the Sahara Desert, which, with an area of 9,000,000 square kilometers (3,500,000 square miles) is the world's largest hot desert. It receives less than 7.6 centimeters (3 inches) of rain per year. The most arid section is the Libyan Desert toward the northeast, a landscape of sand dunes, windswept plains, ridges, and depressions. The descriptively named Great Sand Sea on the Libya–Egypt border is part of the Libyan Desert.

There are three notable mountain areas within the Sahara—the Hoggar Mountains in southern Algeria, the Tibesti Mountains in northern Chad, and the Aïr Mountains in northern Niger. All are volcanic in origin. The highest peak in the region—Emi Koussi at 3,415 meters (11,204 feet)—is located in the Tibesti group.

In the Sahara's western region, in Mauritania, is a barren sand dune zone called El Djouf, or "Empty Quarter." To the south, the Sahara grades into the Sahel, a belt of grasses and shrub land that receives more rainfall. The Sahel is the boundary between dry northern Africa and the more humid, central region.

The Atlas Mountains

To the northwest of the Sahara Desert are the Atlas Mountains. They are a geological offshoot of the European Alps and cover much of Morocco, northern Algeria, and northern Tunisia, separating the northern coastal region from the desert. There are six separate ranges: Middle Atlas, High Atlas, Anti-Atlas, Tell Atlas, and Saharan Atlas mountains, and the Aurès Mountains. The highest peak is Jebel Toubkal (4,165 meters; 13,665 feet) in the High Atlas range in central Morocco.

Right Marketplace in Luxor, Egypt. Luxor is world-famous for its dense concentration of ancient monuments, including the temple complex of Karnak and the tombs in the Valley of the Kings and the Valley of the Queens.

Previous pages A satellite image of sand dunes in Namib-Naukluft Park, Namibia. The world's tallest sand dunes are formed here by coastal winds, with some reaching 300 meters (980 ft) high. Desert covers most of the park, which is Africa's largest.

	COUNTRIES	OFFICIAL NAME	AREA	POPULATION	CAPITAL	RELIGION	POPULATION DENSITY	HIGHEST POINT	CURRENCY
	Algeria	Al Jumhūrīyah al Jazā'irīyah ad Dīmuqrāṭīyah ash Sha'bīyah	2,381,240 km²/919,595 mi²	34,178,000	Algiers (Alger)	☪99%, ○1%	14/km², 37/mi²	Tahat 3,003 m/9,852 ft	Dinar
	Chad	République du Tchad; Jumhūrīyat Tshād	1,259,200 km²/486,178 mi²	10,329,000	N'Djamena	☪53.1%, ✝34.3%, 🧍7.3%, ○5.3%	8/km², 21/mi²	Emi Koussi 3,415 m/11,204 ft	Franc
	Egypt	Jumhūrīyat Miṣr al 'Arabīyah	995,450 km²/384,344 mi²	83,083,000	Cairo (Al-Qāhirah)	☪90%, ✝10%	83/km², 216/mi²	Jabal Kātrīnā 2,629 m/8,623 ft	Pound
	Eritrea	Hagere Ērtra	121,320 km²/46,842 mi²	5,647,000	Asmara	☪45%, ✝45%, ○10%	47/km², 121/mi²	Soira 3,018 m/9,900 ft	Nafka
	Libya	Al Jamāhīrīyah al 'Arabīyah al Lībīyah ash Sha'bīyah al Ishtirākīyah	1,759,540 km²/679,359 mi²	6,310,000	Tripoli (Ṭarābulus)	☪97%, ○3%	4/km², 9/mi²	Bīkkū Bīttī 2,267 m/7,437 ft	Dinar
	Mali	République du Mali	1,230,244 km²/475,000 mi²	12,667,000	Bamako	☪90%, ✝1%, 🧍9%	10/km², 27/mi²	Hombori Tondo 1,155 m/3,789 ft	Franc
	Mauritania	Al Jumhūrīyah al Islāmīyah al Mūrītānīyah	1,030,700 km²/397,954 mi²	3,129,000	Nouakchott	☪100%	3/km², 8/mi²	Kediet ej Jill 915 m/3,002 ft	Ouguyia
	Morocco	Al Mamlakah al Maghribīyah	446,300 km²/172,317 mi²	34,859,000	Rabat	☪98.7%, ✝1.1%, ✡0.2%	78/km², 202/mi²	Jbel Toubkal 4,165 m/13,665 ft	Dirham
	Niger	République du Niger	1,266,700 km²/489,678 mi²	15,306,000	Niamey	☪80%, ○20%	12/km², 31/mi²	Bagzane 2,022 m/6,633 ft	Franc
	Sudan	Jumhūrīyat as Sūdan	2,505,810 km²/967,499 mi²	41,088,000	Khartoum (Al Kharṭūm)	☪70%, 🧍25%, ✝5%	16/km², 42/mi²	Kinyeti 3,187 m/10,456 ft	Dinar
	Tunisia	Al Jumhūrīyah at Tūnisīyah	163,610 km²/63,170 mi²	10,486,340	Tunis	☪98%, ✝1%, ○1%	64/km², 166/mi²	Jebel ech Chambi 1,544 m/5,064 ft	Dinar

	DEPENDENCIES AND TERRITORIES	OFFICIAL NAME	AREA	POPULATION	CAPITAL	RELIGION	POPULATION DENSITY	HIGHEST POINT	CURRENCY
	Canary Islands (Spain)	Comunidad Autónoma de Canarias	7,770 km²/3,000 mi²	1,996,000	Las Palmas; Santa Cruz	N/A	257/km², 665/mi²	Pico de Teide 3,718 m/12,198 ft	Euro
	Ceuta (Spain)	Ceuta (Plaza de Soberania)	20 km²/7¾ mi²	76,000	—	N/A	3,800/km², 9,806/mi²	Mt Anyera 345 m/1,132 ft	Euro
	Madeira (Portugal)	Região Autónoma da Madeira	828 km²/320 mi²	250,000	Funchal	N/A	302/km², 781/mi²	Pico Ruivo 1,862 m/6,109 ft	Euro
	Melilla (Spain)	Melilla (Plaza de Soberania)	12 km²/4½ mi²	67,000	—	☪45%, ✝45%, ॐ5% ✡5%	5,583/km², 14,889/mi²	N/A	Euro
	Western Sahara (disputed)	As-Sahra al-Garbiyah	266,000 km²/102,702 mi²	405,210	El Aaiún (Laâyoune)	N/A	2/km², 4/mi²	805 m/2,641 ft	Moroccan

The natural resources of the Atlas Mountains include iron ore, lead, copper, silver, marble, and natural gas. They are also the source of water, which supports oasis agriculture and larger urban settlements.

Northern Africa's Rivers

The Nile River is the main geographical feature in the eastern part of northern Africa. Its waters come from two main tributaries—the White Nile and the Blue Nile—that originate in different parts of east-central Africa and converge near Khartoum, the capital city of Sudan. The united river then flows north through the deserts of northern Sudan and Egypt to its delta in the Mediterranean Sea. The river—the longest in the world—is the lifeline of both Sudan and Egypt, and supports irrigated agriculture along its length, as well as populated areas. Two dams near the city of Aswan in southern Egypt regulate seasonal water flow and prevent flooding; they also generate electrical power. Lake Nasser is the reservoir that formed behind the newer dam, the Aswan High Dam, which was completed in 1970. The lake is about 550 kilometers (342 miles) long, with a maximum width of about 35 kilometers (22 miles).

The Nile Delta is one of the largest in the world. It starts nearly 160 kilometers (100 miles) south from the sea, and is some 240 kilometers (150 miles) wide along its curved Mediterranean coastline. The land in the delta is highly fertile and intensively farmed with two to three crops produced each year, although chemical fertilizers are now required to replenish soil fertility that was lost when the river's annual rich-sediment-bearing floods were brought under control by the dams at Aswan.

The only other river of note in northern Africa is the Niger, a crescent-shaped river with a middle course through the heart of Mali and neighboring Niger. The river has an unusual "inland delta" of braided streams and wetlands. This delta provides Mali with rich agricultural lands and fishing resources. Its seasonal wetlands are important to migratory birds, and have been included in UNESCO's Ramsar Convention on Wetlands.

Above Once the cultural, religious, and economic center of West Africa, Tombouctou (Timbuktu) in Mali is in danger of being smothered by the drifting sands of the Sahara. When not threatened by sandstorms, people use the flat roofs of their dwellings as outdoor living and working spaces.

CENTRAL AFRICA

The middle of Africa straddles the Equator and extends about 10° North and South. Its northern boundary spans the continent from its great bulge along the Atlantic Ocean in the west to the Horn of Africa in the east. Here the continent measures some 8,000 kilometers (5,000 miles) across, from the westernmost point at Cape Verde in Senegal to the tip of the horn in Somalia. Central Africa encompasses extremely diverse climates, landforms, and vegetation patterns, as well as human cultures and livelihoods.

Above The widespread greater flamingo, the largest flamingo species, is found in the shallow salt lakes and lagoons of eastern and central Africa, among many other locations.

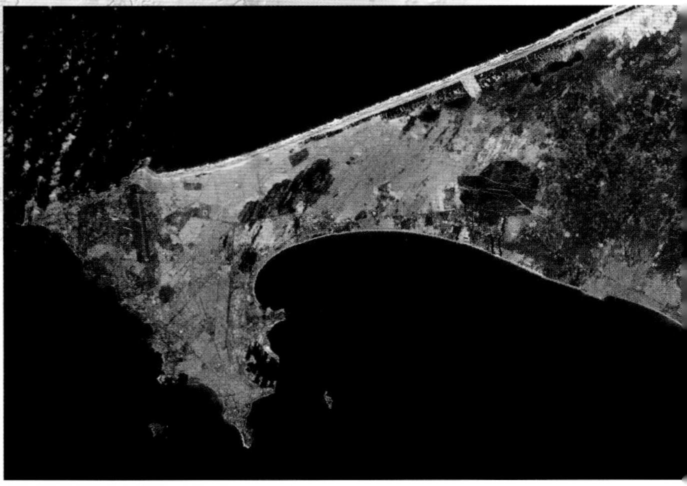

Above right Senegal's capital, Dakar, is located on the Cape Verde Peninsula, and its sheltered harbor is one of western Africa's most important ports.

The northern edge of central Africa is savanna, a grassland biome between deserts to the north and lush vegetation further south. The heart of the region is the equatorial jungle in the large basin of the Congo River in the Democratic Republic of the Congo, still mostly an area of low population density and expansive rainforest. Other rainforest areas are found in the western part of central Africa in the countries bordering the Atlantic Ocean. To the east are the Ethiopian Highlands, a plateau that rarely descends below 1,500 meters (5,000 feet) and has been called the "Roof of Africa." Between this area of high elevation and the Indian Ocean to the east lies the arid region of Ogaden.

Elsewhere, particularly in Kenya, Tanzania, and Uganda, central Africa is a world of rich farmlands, spectacular plains, and beautiful lakes. In Tanzania, near the border with Kenya, is the continent's highest mountain, the triple-peaked Mt Kilimanjaro (5,895 meters; 19,340 feet). Off the Indian Ocean coast is Zanzibar, famous as an ancient trading port, a spice island, and a tropical resort with spectacular beaches.

The Congo River

At 4,700 kilometers (2,922 miles) long, the Congo is the longest river in central Africa, and, after the Nile, it is the second-longest in Africa as a whole, and the eighth-longest in the world. Because of heavy rainfall in its catchment area it ranks second in the world, after the Amazon River, in volume of water. Its drainage basin, measuring 3,380,000 square kilometers (1,420,848 square miles), is also the world's second-largest. The area is rich in underground resources, particularly copper, cobalt, and industrial diamonds, as well as timber. In the decades just before and after 1900, forest lands along the Congo River were exploited by European colonialists for rubber, at great cost to the native population. The rich environment of the Congo is now in danger from over-logging, and loss of plant and animal habitat. There is special concern among conservationists about the endangered species of common chimpanzees, bonobos (pygmy chimpanzees), and gorillas in the Congo Basin.

The Great Rift Valley

The main geographical feature in the eastern part of central Africa is the Great Rift Valley, a long and narrow depression in Earth's surface created by active divergence of continental plates. There are numerous active volcanoes in the region, of which Kilimanjaro is but one, as well as a prominent chain of lakes that is often referred to as the Great Lakes of Africa. Among the largest of these are Lake Victoria, Africa's largest lake; Lake Tanganyika, the longest lake in the world at 673 kilometers (418 miles) long; and Lake Malawi (Lake Nyasa), between Malawi, Mozambique, and Tanzania.

Left The Ngorongoro Conservation Area, Tanzania, is a protected habitat for the Cape buffalo (pictured), as well as herds of rhinoceros, lion, leopard, elephant, zebra, gazelle, and wildebeest.

COUNTRIES	OFFICIAL NAME	AREA	POPULATION	CAPITAL	RELIGION	POPULATION DENSITY	HIGHEST POINT	CURRENCY
Benin	République du Bénin	110,620 km²/42,710 mi²	8,792,000	Porto-Novo	✝42.8%, ☪24.4%, 🧍17.3%, ○15.5%	79/km², 206/mi²	Mont Sokbaro 658 m/2,159 ft	Franc
Burkina Faso	Burkina Faso	273,800 km²/105,714 mi²	15,746,000	Ouagadougou	☪50%, 🧍40%, ✝10%	57/km², 149/mi²	Tena Kourou 749 m/2,457 ft	Franc
Burundi	République du Burundi; Republika y'u Burundi	25,650 km²/9,904 mi²	8,988,000	Bujumbura	✝67%, 🧍23%, ☪10%	350/km², 908/mi²	Mt Heha 2,670 m/8,760 ft	Franc
Cameroon	République du Cameroun; Republic of Cameroon	475,440 km²/183,568 mi²	18,879,000	Yaoundé	🧍40%, ✝40%, ☪20%	40/km², 103/mi²	Fako 4,095 m/13,425 ft	Franc
Cape Verde	República de Cabo Verde	4,030 km²/1,556 mi²	429,000	Praia	✝100%	106/km², 276/mi²	Mt Fogo 2,829 m/9,281 ft	Escudo
Central African Republic	Kodorosese ti Beafrika; République Centrafricaine	622,984 km²/240,534 mi²	4,511,000	Bangui	✝50%, 🧍35%, ☪15%	7/km², 19/mi²	Mont Ngaoui 1,420 m/4,658 ft	Franc
Congo	République du Congo	341,500 km²/131,854 mi²	4,013,000	Brazzaville	✝50%, 🧍48%, ☪2%	12/km², 30/mi²	Berongou 903 m/2,963 ft	Franc
Côte d'Ivoire	République de Côte d'Ivoire	318,000 km²/122,780 mi²	20,617,000	Yamoussoukro	🧍40%, ☪35%, ✝25%	65/km², 168/mi²	Mont Nimba 1,752 m/5,748 ft	Franc
Democratic Republic of Congo	République Démocratique du Congo	2,345,410 km²/905,568 mi²	68,693,000	Kinshasa	✝70%, ☪10%, 🧍10%, ○10%	29/km², 76/mi²	Pic Marguerite 5,110 m/16,761 ft	Franc
Djibouti	République de Djibouti; Jumhūriyat Jībūtī	23,201 km²/8,960 mi²	516,000	Djibouti	☪94%, ✝6%	22/km², 58/mi²	Moussa Ali 2,028 m/6,652 ft	Franc
Equatorial Guinea	República de Guinea Ecuatorial; République de Guinée Équatoriale	28,051 km²/10,830 mi²	633,000	Malabo	N/A	23/km², 58/mi²	Pico Basile 3,008 m/9,870 ft	Franc
Ethiopia	Ye'ītyop'īya Fēdēralawī Dēmokrasīyawī Rīpeblīk	1,127,127 km²/435,184 mi²	85,237,000	Addis Ababa (Ādīs Ābeba)	✝60.8%, ☪32.8%, 🧍4.6%, ○1.8%	76/km², 196/mi²	Ras Dejen 4,620 m/15,154 ft	Birr
Gabon	République Gabonais	267,667 km²/103,346 mi²	1,515,000	Libreville	✝65%, 🧍35%	6/km², 15/mi²	Iboundji 1,575 m/5,166 ft	Franc
Gambia	Republic of The Gambia	11,300 km²/4,363 mi²	1,783,000	Banjul	☪90%, ✝9%, 🧍1%	158/km², 409/mi²	53 m/173 ft	Dalasi
Ghana	Republic of Ghana	230,940 km²/89,166 mi²	23,832,000	Accra	✝68.8%, ☪15.9%, 🧍8.5%, ○6.8%	103/km², 267/mi²	Mt Afadjato 880 m/2,887 ft	Ced
Guinea	République de Guinée	245,857 km²/94,526 mi²	10,058,000	Conakry	☪85%, ✝8%, 🧍7%	41/km², 106/mi²	Mont Nimba 1,752 m/5,748 ft	Franc
Guinea-Bissau	República da Guiné-Bissau	28,000 km²/10,811 mi²	1,534,000	Bissau	🧍50%, ☪45%, ✝5%	55/km², 142/mi²	300 m/984 ft	Franc
Kenya	Jamhuri ya Kenya Republic of Kenya	569,250 km²/219,789 mi²	39,003,000	Nairobi	✝78%, ☪10%, 🧍10%, ○2%	68/km², 177/mi²	Mt Kenya 5,199 m/17,057 ft	Shilling
Liberia	Republic of Liberia	96,320 km²/37,189 mi²	3,442,000	Monrovia	✝40%, 🧍40%, ☪20%	36/km², 93/mi²	Wuteve 1,380 m/ 4,528 ft	Dollar
Nigeria	Federal Republic of Nigeria	923,768 km²/356,669 mi²	149,229,000	Abuja	☪50%, ✝40%, 🧍10%	162/km², 418/mi²	Chappal Waddi/Tchabal Ouadé 2,410 m/7,936 ft	Naira
Rwanda	Republika y'u Rwanda; Republic of Rwanda; République du Rwanda	24,948 km²/9,632 mi²	10,473,000	Kigali	✝93.6%, ☪4.6%, ○1.8%	420/km², 1,087/mi²	Volcan Karisimbi 4,510 m/14,826 ft	Franc
São Tomé and Príncipe	República Democrática de São Tomé e Príncipe	1,001 km²/386 mi²	213,000	São Tomé	✝77.5%, ○22.5%	212/km², 551/mi²	Pico de São Tomé 2,024 m/6,639 ft	Dobra
Senegal	République du Sénégal	196,190 km²/75,794 mi²	13,712,000	Dakar	☪94%, ✝5%, 🧍1%	70/km², 181/mi²	581 m/1,906 ft	Franc
Sierra Leone	Republic of Sierra Leone	71,620 km²/27,653 mi²	6,440,000	Freetown	☪60%, 🧍30%, ✝10%	90/km², 233/mi²	Loma Mansa 1,948 m/6,391 ft	Leone
Somalia	Jamhuuriyada Demuqraadiga Soomaaliyeed	637,657 km²/246,201 mi²	9,832,000	Mogadishu (Muqdisho)	☪100%	15/km², 40/mi²	Shimbiris 2,416 m/7,927 ft	Shilling
Tanzania	Jamhuri ya Muungano wa Tanzania; United Republic of Tanzania	886,037 km²/342,101 mi²	41,049,000	Dar es Salaam, Dodoma	✝30%, ☪35%, 🧍35%	46/km², 120/mi²	Kilimanjaro 5,895 m/19,340 ft	Shilling
Togo	République Togolaise	54,385 km²/20,998 mi²	6,020,000	Lomé	🧍51%, ✝29%, ☪20%	111/km², 287/mi²	Mont Agou 986 m/2,335 ft	Franc
Uganda	Republic of Uganda	199,710 km²/77,108 mi²	32,370,000	Kampala	✝83.9%, ☪12.1%, ○4%	162/km², 420/mi²	Margherita Peak 5,109 m/16,762 ft	Shilling

To the east of the Rift Valley are some of Africa's greatest plains, most notably the Serengeti Plain in Kenya and Tanzania, which is famous for its wildlife, especially the annual mass migration of wildebeest, gazelle, and zebra.

The Niger River Delta

In the western part of central Africa, along the coast of Nigeria, is the Niger River Delta, where the waters of the Niger River and its main tributary, the Benue, reach the Gulf of Guinea. It covers some 70,000 square kilometers (27,000 square miles) and is a rich and varied ecosystem. The area was once called Oil Rivers because it was a major producer of oil palm, but now the main products are petroleum and natural gas.

Left High-altitude hillsides in Rwanda are well suited to tea growing, and tea plantations are major contributors to the nation's economy, with most of the tea grown sold overseas.

SOUTHERN AFRICA

The southern part of the African continent is a diverse region of bone-dry deserts, tropical rainforests, expansive swamps, rolling grasslands teeming with wildlife, and fertile farmland. It is also rich in natural resources and biological diversity. The region extends from tropical jungles at latitude 10° South in Angola on the Atlantic Ocean coast to Africa's southernmost tip, Cape Agulhas (34.5°S) in the Republic of South Africa, where the climate is Mediterranean.

Right A man maneuvers his mekoro (dugout canoe) through the wetlands of the Okavango Delta in Botswana's otherwise arid north. The world's largest inland delta, it is famous for its wildlife, particularly the 400-plus bird species.

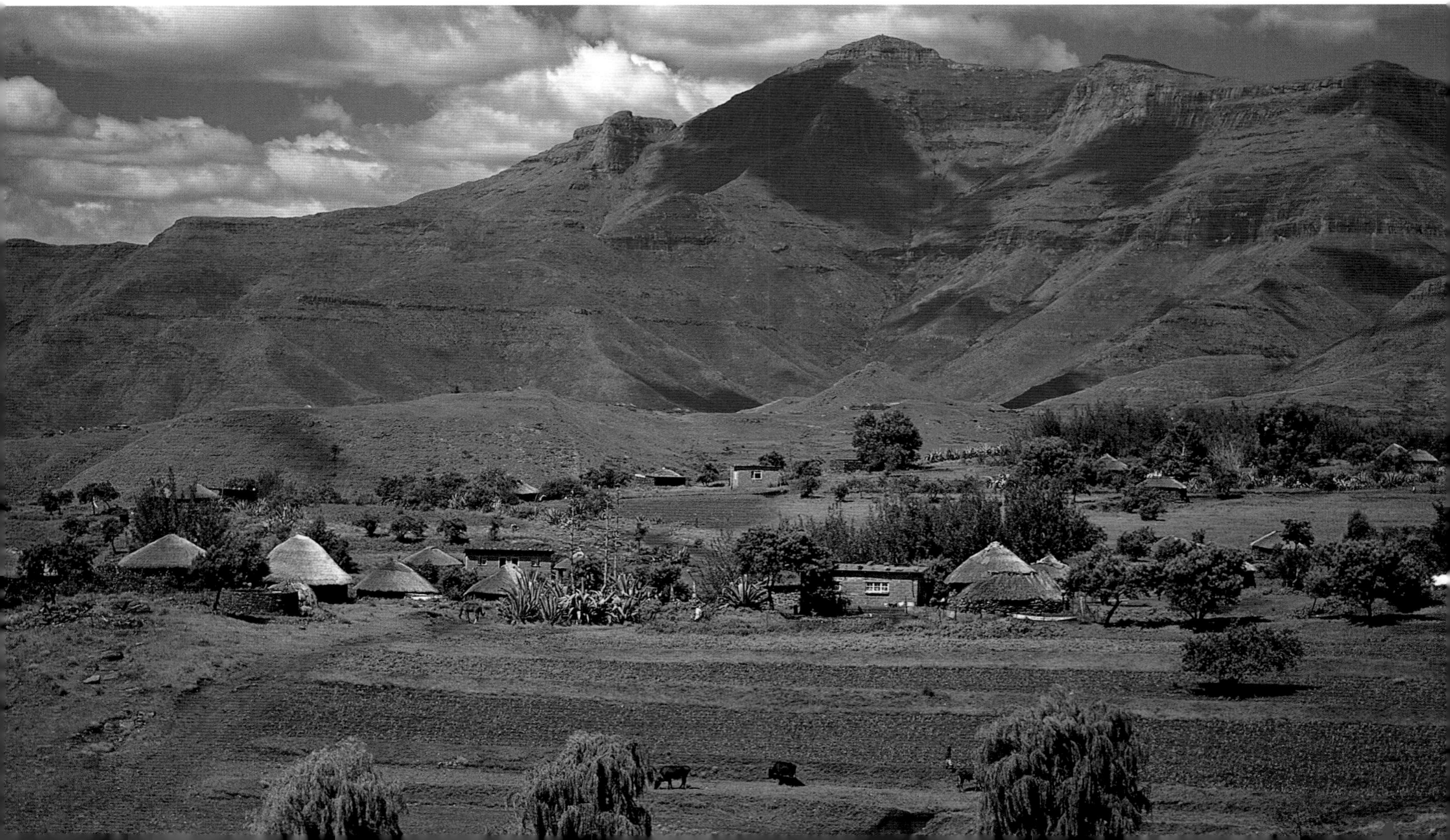

Below Village of traditional Basotho huts in western Lesotho. Nearly 90 percent of the population is involved in subsistence agriculture. Wheat, maize, and sorghum are the principal crops; however much food has to be imported in times of drought.

The northern limits of mainland southern Africa stretch east from Angola across the continent and include Zambia, Malawi, and Mozambique on the eastern seaboard. To the south lie the nations of Namibia, Botswana, Zimbabwe, Swaziland, Lesotho, and South Africa.

Southern Africa also includes the large island of Madagascar (587,041 square kilometers; 226,597 square miles), which lies across the Mozambique Channel in the Indian Ocean. Madagascar is the fourth-largest island in the world. The island nations of Comoros, Mauritius, and Seychelles, together with the dependencies of Réunion (Fr.), Mayotte (Fr.), and St Helena (UK), which also includes Ascension, complete the region.

The islands around southern Africa are mostly of volcanic or coralline origin, although some of the islands of the Seychelles are granitic—they are the peaks of the Indian Ocean ridge known as the Mascarene Plateau.

The Cape of Good Hope, near Africa's southern tip, is the place where, in 1488, voyagers from Europe first began to navigate east instead of south as they searched for a route around Africa to Asia.

Southern Africa's Rivers

Two of the largest rivers in southern Africa are the Zambezi and the Limpopo. Both flow through the east of the continent and drain into the Indian Ocean. The Zambezi is 2,574 kilometers (1,600 miles) long and has along its course the spectacular Victoria Falls between Zambia and Zimbabwe, and two major hydroelectric dams, Cahora Bassa and Kariba. The Limpopo is 1,750 kilometers (1,087 miles) long, and its sluggish, lower course runs through Mozambique where its banks are fertile, and the region is heavily populated.

The Orange River rises in Lesotho and flows 2,200 kilometers (1,360 miles) southwest to the Atlantic. It forms

COUNTRIES	OFFICIAL NAME	AREA	POPULATION	CAPITAL	RELIGION	POPULATION DENSITY	HIGHEST POINT	CURRENCY
Angola	República de Angola	1,246,700 km^2/481,354 mi^2	12,799,000	Luanda	✝53%, 🧍47%	10/km^2, 26/mi^2	Morro de Môco 2,620 m/8,596 ft	Kwanza
Botswana	Republic of Botswana	585,370 km^2/226,013 mi^2	1,991,000	Gaborone	✝71.6%, 🧍6%, ○22.4%	3/km^2, 9/mi^2	Tsodilo Hills 1,489 m/4,885 ft	Pula
Comoros	Union des Comores; Udzima wa Komori; Jumhūrīyat al Qamar al Muttahidah	2,170 km^2/838 mi^2	752,000	Moroni	☪98%, ✝2%	347/km^2, 897/mi^2	Le Kartala 2,360 m/7,743 ft	Franc
Lesotho	Kingdom of Lesotho	30,355 km^2/11,720 mi^2	2,131,000	Maseru	✝80%, 🧍20%	70/km^2, 182/mi^2	Thabana-Ntlenyana 3,482 m/11,424 ft	Loti
Madagascar	République de Madagascar; Repoblikan'i Madagasikara	581,540 km^2/224,534 mi^2	20,654,000	Antananarivo	🧍52%, ✝41%, ☪7%	36/km^2, 92/mi^2	Maromokotro 2,876 m/9,436 ft	Ariary
Malawi	Dziko la Malaŵi; Republic of Malawi	94,080 km^2/36,324 mi^2	14,269,000	Lilongwe	✝79.9%, ☪12.8%, ○7.3%	152/km^2, 393/mi^2	Sapitwa 3,002 m/9,849 ft	Kwacha
Mauritius	Republic of Mauritius	2,030 km^2/784 mi^2	1,284,000	Port Louis	ॐ48%, ✝32.2%, ☪16.6%, ○3.2%	633/km^2, 1,638/mi^2	Piton 828 m/2,717 ft	Rupee
Mozambique	República de Moçambique	784,090 km^2/302,739 mi^2	21,669,000	Maputo	✝41.3%, ☪17.8%, ○40.9%	28/km^2, 72/mi^2	Binga 2,436 m/7,992 ft	Metical
Namibia	Republic of Namibia	825,418 km^2/318,694 mi^2	2,109,000	Windhoek	✝85%, 🧍15%	2/km^2, 7/mi^2	Königstein 2,606 m/8,411 ft	Dollar
Seychelles	Republic of Seychelles; Repiblik Sesel; République des Seychelles	455 km^2/176 mi^2	87,000	Victoria	✝93.2%, ॐ2.1%, ☪1.1%, ○3.6%	191/km^2, 494/mi^2	Morne Seychellois 905 m/2,969 ft	Rupee
South Africa	Republic of South Africa; Republiek van Suid-Afrika	1,219,912 km^2/471,008 mi^2	49,052,000	Pretoria (Tshwane)	✝79.7%, ☪1.5%, ○18.8%	40/km^2, 104/mi^2	Njesuthi 3,408 m/11,181 ft	Rand
Swaziland	Umbuso weSwatini; Kingdom of Swaziland	17,203 km^2/6,642 mi^2	1,124,000	Mbabane, Lobamba	🧍40%, ✝20%, ☪10%, ○30%	65/km^2, 169/mi^2	Emiembe 1,862 m/6,109 ft	Lilangeni
Zambia	Republic of Zambia	720,724 km^2/285,994 mi^2	11,863,000	Lusaka	✝50–75%, ☪, ॐ 24–49%, 🧍1%	16/km^2, 41/mi^2	2,301 m/7,549 ft	Kwacha
Zimbabwe	Republic of Zimbabwe	386,670 km^2/149,294 mi^2	11,393,000	Harare	✝50%, 🧍49%, ☪1%	29/km^2, 76/mi^2	Inyangani 2,592 m/8,504 ft	Dollar

DEPENDENCIES AND TERRITORIES	OFFICIAL NAME	AREA	POPULATION	CAPITAL	RELIGION	POPULATION DENSITY	HIGHEST POINT	CURRENCY
Mayotte (France)	Collectivité Territoriale de Mayotte	374/ km^2, 145/mi^2	224,000	Mamoudzou	☪97%, ✝3%	598/km^2, 1,545/mi^2	Benara 660 m/2,165 ft	Euro
Réunion (France)	Département de la Réunion	2,512 km^2, 970 mi^2	782,000	St-Denis	✝86%, ○14%	311/km^2, 806/mi^2	Piton des Neiges 3,070 m/10,069 ft	Euro
St Helena (UK)	St Helena	413 km^2, 160 mi^2	8,000	Jamestown	N/A	19 km^2, 50/mi^2	2,062 m/6,765 ft	Pound

part of South Africa's northern border, and provides the country with hydroelectric power, and water for irrigation.

In Botswana, in the very heart of southern Africa, is the Okavango Delta, the world's largest inland river delta, and one of Africa's most bountiful wildlife habitats. It is where the Okavango River (length 1,600 kilometers; 1,000 miles) breaks up into a wide wetland before its waters disappear into the Kalahari Desert. The desert is the central geographical feature of southern Africa and the site of an ancient lake, Lake Makgadikgadi, which dried up thousands of years ago. Despite its aridity, the Kalahari is also rich in flora and fauna and becomes excellent grazing land after rain. Nearby are other remnants of the ancient lake, including several extensive salt pans, the most prominent of which is the Etosha Pan in northeastern Namibia.

Namib Desert

The main geographical feature on the Atlantic side of southern Africa is the Namib Desert. It stretches along the Atlantic coast for some 1,600 kilometers (1,000 miles) from southern Angola through the length of Namibia, but is only 50 to 160 kilometers (30 to 100 miles) wide. It is one of the driest places on Earth.

A feature of the Namib Desert is the Sossusvlei, a unique landscape with an extensive clay pan surrounded by red sand dunes, which are among the world's highest at nearly 300 meters (1,000 feet). The northern edge of the desert is known as the Skeleton Coast, because of the many shipwrecks, and skeletons of beached whales and seals, found there. The sea offshore is turbulent and foggy. The region's native Bushmen call this the "land that God made in anger." To the south of the Namib Desert along the coast of Namibia and South Africa is the Succulent Karoo, a distinctive eco-region known for its thousands of varieties of succulent plants.

Major Natural Resources

The desert and adjoining parts of Namibia are important sources of uranium, lead, zinc, tin, silver, tungsten, and most famously, gem-quality diamonds. Other major resources in southern Africa include huge deposits of copper in Zambia, historically the main sustenance of that country; chromium, platinum, and nickel in the Great Dyke geological formation of central Zimbabwe; and petroleum in Angola. An extraordinarily wide range of valuable minerals and precious stones can be found in South Africa, most famously the huge deposits of gold in the Witwatersrand Basin and diamonds near Kimberley in the center of the country.

The fynbos vegetation of South Africa's Western Cape and Eastern Cape provinces is remarkable for both its diversity and its rarity; about two-thirds of its species are found only there. The Mediterranean climate also supports numerous vineyards and a wine export industry in the area around Cape Town. South Africa's rich mineral resources coupled with excellent farmlands have made it the wealthiest nation on the African continent.

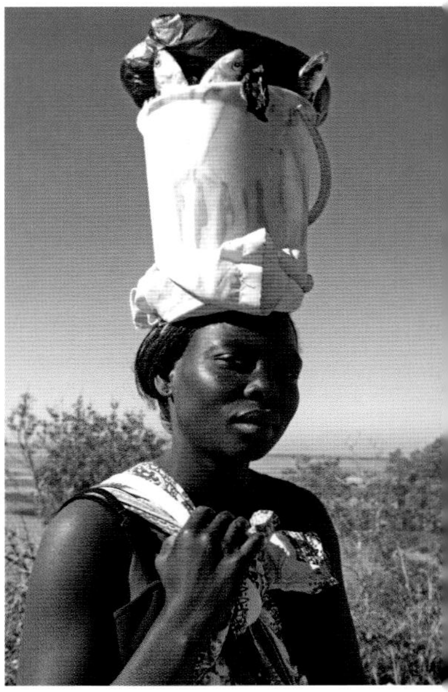

Above A woman from Maputo—the capital of Mozambique—balances a bucket of fish on her head. Seafood is an important part of Maputo's diverse cuisine, which shows Portuguese, Arab, Indian, and Chinese influences.

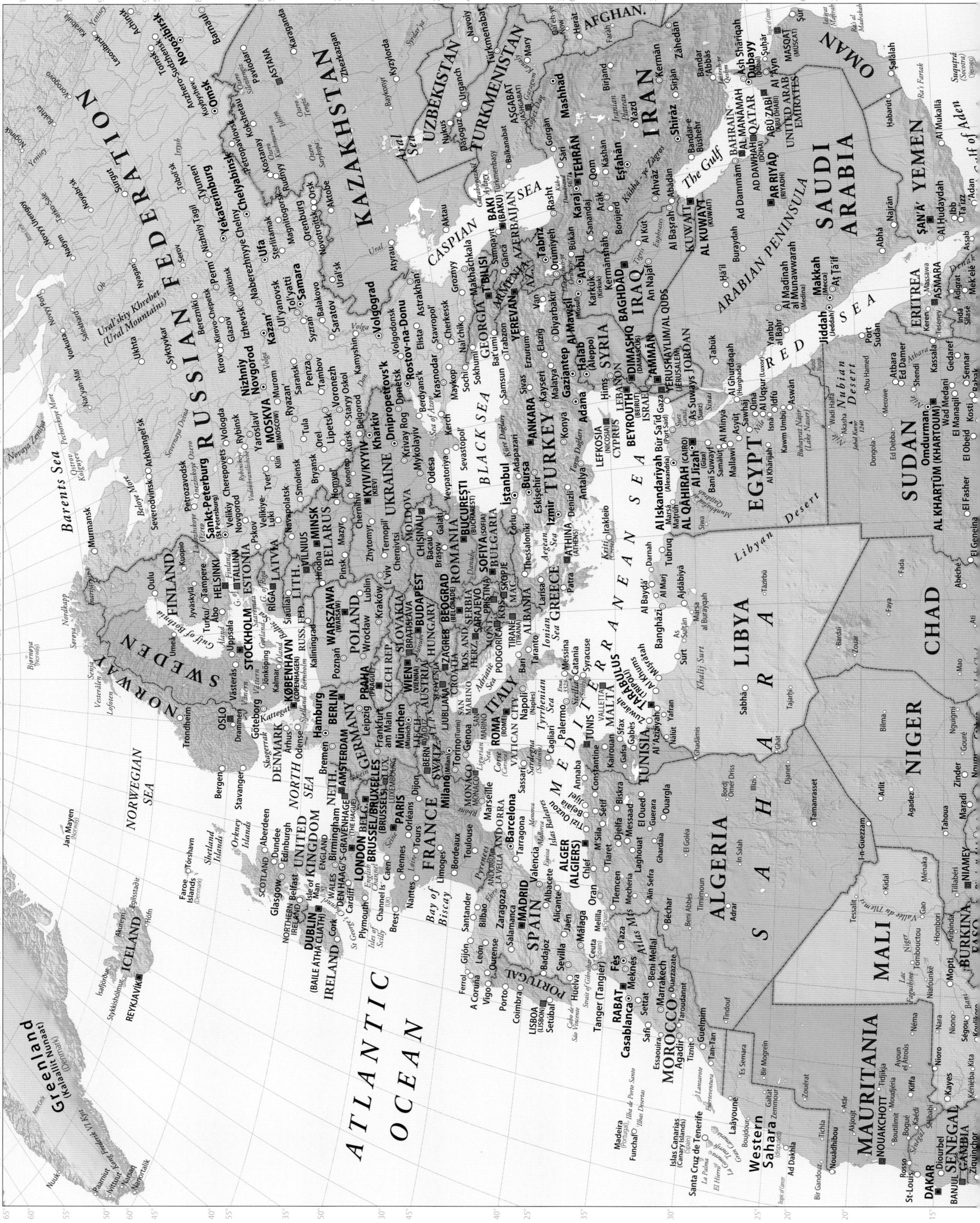
RUSSIAN FEDERATION
KAZAKHSTAN
UZBEKISTAN
TURKMENISTAN
AFGHAN.
IRAN
IRAQ
SYRIA
TURKEY
SAUDI ARABIA
YEMEN
OMAN
EGYPT
SUDAN
LIBYA
CHAD
NIGER
MALI
ALGERIA
MAURITANIA
MOROCCO
TUNISIA
SPAIN
PORTUGAL
FRANCE
ITALY
GERMANY
POLAND
UKRAINE
ROMANIA
BELARUS
FINLAND
SWEDEN
NORWAY
ICELAND
IRELAND
UNITED KINGDOM
GREECE
Greenland (Kalaallit Nunaat) (Denmark)
ATLANTIC OCEAN
NORWEGIAN SEA
NORTH SEA
Barents Sea
BLACK SEA
CASPIAN SEA
MEDITERRANEAN SEA
RED SEA
The Gulf
ARABIAN PENINSULA
SAHARA
Libyan Desert
Western Sahara (Disputed)

1:29,000,000

Lambert Azimuthal Equal Area Projection

0 250 500 750 1000 kilometers

0 125 250 375 500 miles

AFRICA POLITICAL

ATLANTIC OCEAN
INDIAN OCEAN
Gulf of Guinea
Mozambique Channel
SOMALIA
ETHIOPIA
KENYA
UGANDA
RWANDA
BURUNDI
TANZANIA
CENTRAL AFRICAN REPUBLIC
DEMOCRATIC REPUBLIC OF CONGO
CONGO
GABON
CAMEROON
EQUATORIAL GUINEA
SÃO TOMÉ AND PRÍNCIPE
ANGOLA
ZAMBIA
MALAWI
MOZAMBIQUE
ZIMBABWE
BOTSWANA
NAMIBIA
SOUTH AFRICA
LESOTHO
SWAZILAND
MADAGASCAR
COMOROS
SEYCHELLES
MAURITIUS
GHANA
TOGO
CÔTE D'IVOIRE
LIBERIA
SIERRA LEONE
MUQDISHO (MOGADISHU)
NAIROBI
KAMPALA
KIGALI
BUJUMBURA
DODOMA
DAR ES SALAAM
BANGUI
KINSHASA
BRAZZAVILLE
LIBREVILLE
YAOUNDÉ
MALABO
SÃO TOMÉ
LUANDA
LUSAKA
LILONGWE
HARARE
MAPUTO
GABORONE
WINDHOEK
PRETORIA
CAPE TOWN
BLOEMFONTEIN
MASERU
MBABANE
ANTANANARIVO
MORONI
VICTORIA
PORT LOUIS
ACCRA
LOMÉ
YAMOUSSOUKRO
MONROVIA
FREETOWN
ABUJA
Namib Desert
Kalahari Desert
Saint Helena (UK)
Ascension (UK)
Tristan da Cunha (St Helena)
Gough Island (St Helena)
Réunion (France)
Prince Edward Islands (South Africa)
Îles Crozet (French Southern and Antarctic Territories)

A
B
C
D
E
128
158
25°
20°
15°
10°
5°
35°
30°
1
2
3
4
5
6
Azores
(Portugal)
São Miguel
LISBOA
(LISBON)
Queluz
Setúbal
Cabo Espichel
SETÚBAL
Costa da Galé
Cabo de Sines
ÉVORA
Évora
Badajoz
EXTREMADURA
Mérida
Beja
BEJA
PORTUGAL
Sevilla
Córdoba
Huelva
FARO
Faro
Dos Hermanas
Cabo de São Vicente
Sagres
Cabo de Santa Maria
Golfo de Cádiz
Jerez de la Frontera
ANDALUCÍA
Cádiz
Marbella
Cabo de Trafalgar
Algeciras
Tanger
(Tangier)
Ceuta
M'diq
Tétouan
Asilah
Larache
Ksar el Kebir
Bargha
Moulay- Bousselham
Ouezzane
Kénitra
Sidi Slimane
Sidi Kacem
Taza
RABAT
Meknès
Fès
Mohammedia
Casablanca
Khemisset
Sefrou
Rommani
Berrechid
El Jadida
Settat
Oued Zem
Sidi Smaïl
Khouribga
Boujad
Khenifra
Khemis Zemamra
Safi
Fkih Ben Salah
El Kelaâ des Srarhna
Beni Mellal
Midelt
Er Rachidia
MOROCCO
Essaouira
Chichaoua
Marrakech
Boumaine Dadès
Tinerhir
Tamanar
Ouarzazate
Jbel Toubkal 4167
Cap Rhir
Agadir
Biougra
Tazzarine
Tiznit
Tafraoute
Zagora
Sidi Ifni
Tata
Hassi el Khebi
Guelmim
Cap Drâa
Tan-Tan
Assa
Tinfouchy
Hamada du Drâa
Hamada Tounassine
Tindouf
Sebkha de Tindouf
Hamada ed Douakel
Arquipélago de Madeira
Ilha de Porto Santo
Pico Ruivo 1862
Madeira
(Portugal)
Funchal
Ilhas Desertas
ATLANTIC OCEAN
Ilhas Selvagens
(Madeira)
Canary Islands
(Spain)
San Cristóbal de la Laguna
Santa Cruz de Tenerife
La Palma
Las Indias
Puerto de la Estaca
El Hierro
Frontera
Calera
La Gomera
Tenerife
Pico del Teide
Las Palmas de Gran Canaria
Agaete
Gran Canaria
Playa del Ingles
Islas Canarias
Lanzarote
Alegranza
Graciosa
Orzola
Arrecife
Playa Blanca
Tindaya
Puerto del Rosario
Fuerteventura
Tarfaya
Cap Juby
Laâyoune
Al Haggounia
Es Semara
Boukra
Al Mahbas
Idiriya
Cap Boujdour
Aoufist
Zemmour
Skaymat
Tropic of Cancer
Bîr Mogreïn
Galtat Zemmour
Western Sahara
(disputed)
RIO DE ORO
TIRIS ZEMMOUR
GHALLAMANE
Chegga
Ad Dakhla
Imlili
Awserd
Bir Gandouz
Tichla
Fdérik
Zouérat
El Hammâmi
Touajil
Agâraktem
Nouâdhibou
Ras Nouâdhibou
DAKHLET NOUÂDHIBOU
Ras Agâdir
Choûm
MAQTEÏR
Azefal
Atâr
Chinguetti
ADRAR
El Mreyyé
Iouîk
Châmi
INCHIRI
Akjoujt
Nouâmghâr
El Mhaijrat
Boû Rjeimât
MAURITANIA
TOMBOUCTOU
NOUAKCHOTT
Ouâd Nâga
TRARZA
Tidjikja
TAGANT
Tîchît
Lekhcheb
Moudjéria
Boutilimit
Magta Lahjar
Cangrâfa
Tiguent
Mederdra
Rkîz
Boumdeït
BRAKNA
Aleg
Bogué
Barkéwol el Abiod
Guérou
Tâmchekket
HODH ECH CHARGUI
Oualâta
Rosso
Dagana
Podor
St-Louis
Kiffa
ASSABA
HODH EL GHARBI
Ayoun el Atroûs
Kankossa
Tintâne
Timbedgha
Néma
Louga
Kébémèr
Linguère
Lagbar
Thilogne
Kaédi
Mbout
GORGOL
Tivaouane
Matam
Kobenni
Amourj
Bassikounou
DAKAR
Cap Vert
Thiès
Mbacké
Diourbel
Touba
Ranérou
Sélibabi
GUIDIMAKA
Djiguéni
Adel Bagrou
Mbour
Joal-Fadiout
Fatick
Kaolack
SENEGAL
Kayes
KAYES
Nioro
Nara
Nampala
MOPTI
Mopti
GAMBIA
Serekunda
BANJUL
Farafenni
Tambacounda
KOULIKORO
Ségou
SÉGOU
Kolda
Ziguinchor
Sédhiou
GUINEA-BISSAU
BISSAU
Bafatá
Gabú
GUINEA
Kédougou
BAMAKO
Bafoulabé
Kita
Koulikoro
Djenné
CAPE VERDE
Santo Antão
São Vicente
Mindelo
São Nicolau
Sal
Pedra Lume
Sal Rei
Boa Vista
Fundo das Figuerias
Curral Velho
Ilhas do Cabo Verde
Tarrafal
Fogo 2828
Fogo
Santiago
Maio
PRAIA
São Filipe

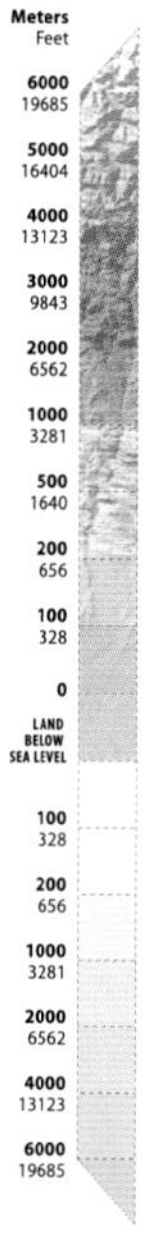
Meters
Feet
6000
19685
5000
16404
4000
13123
3000
9843
2000
6562
1000
3281
500
1640
200
656
100
328
0
LAND BELOW SEA LEVEL
100
328
200
656
1000
3281
2000
6562
4000
13123
6000
19685

1:10,320,000

Lambert Conic Conformal Projection

0 100 200 300 400 500 kilometers

0 50 100 150 200 250 300 miles

NORTHWESTERN AFRICA

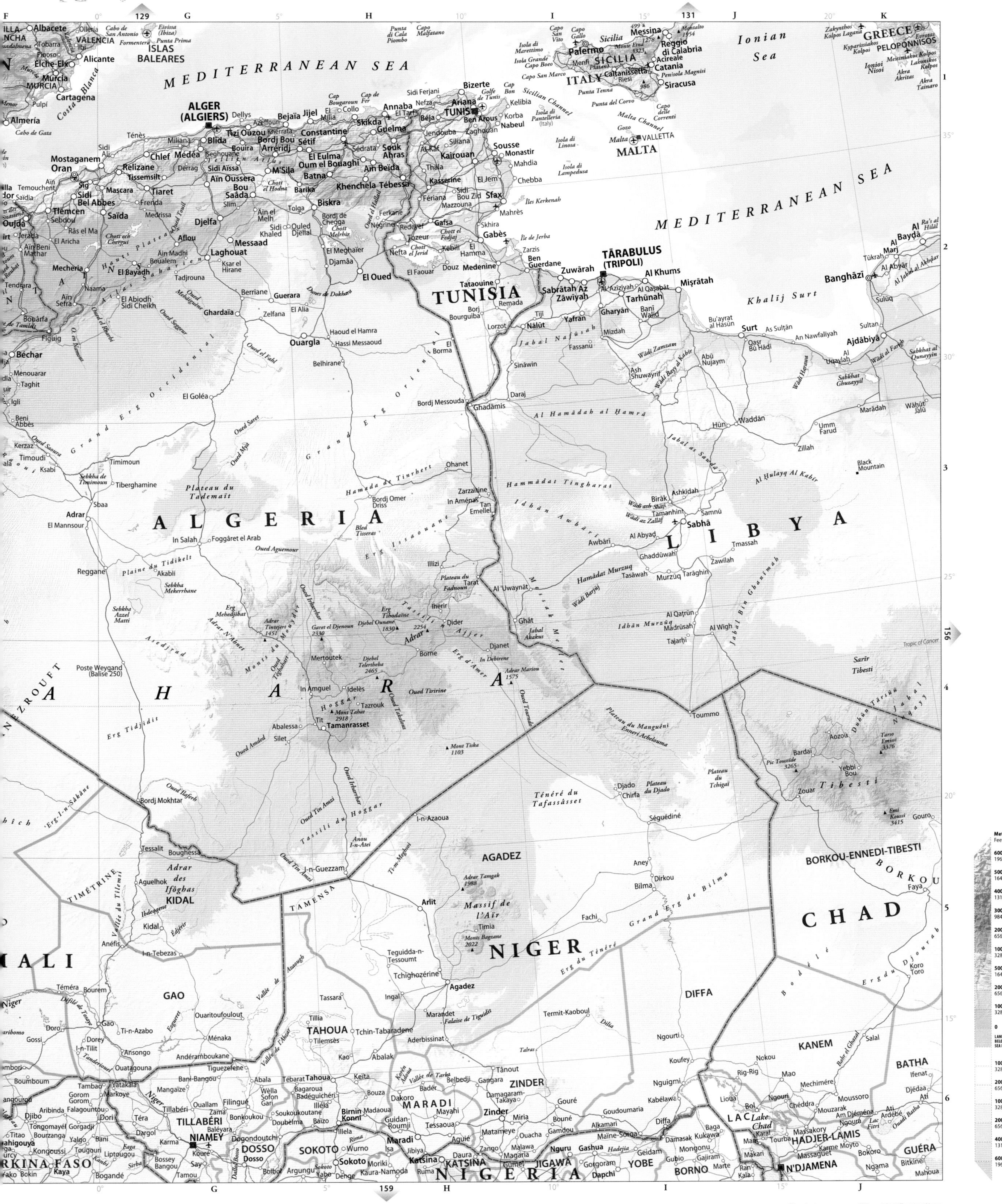
MEDITERRANEAN SEA
Ionian Sea
ALGER (ALGIERS)
TUNIS
TUNISIA
ALGERIA
LIBYA
NIGER
CHAD
MALI
NIGERIA
MALTA
VALLETTA
ITALY
SICILIA
GREECE
ISLAS BALEARES
VALENCIA
MURCIA
TĀRABULUS (TRIPOLI)
NIAMEY
N'DJAMENA
SAHARA
Grand Erg Occidental
Grand Erg Oriental
Tassili n' Ajjer
Hoggar
Tibesti
Massif de l'Aïr
Ténéré du Tafassâsset
Al Hamādah al Ḩamrā
Khalīj Surt
Tamanrasset
Ghardaïa
Ouargla
Béchar
Constantine
Oran
Banghāzī
Sabhā
Misrātah
Agadez
Arlit
Zinder
Maradi
Tahoua
Gao
Kidal
AGADEZ
TAHOUA
TILLABÉRI
DOSSO
MARADI
ZINDER
DIFFA
GAO
KIDAL
TIMÉTRINE
TAMENSA
BORKOU-ENNEDI-TIBESTI
BORKOU
KANEM
LAC
BATHA
HADJER-LAMIS
GUÉRA
SOKOTO
KATSINA
JIGAWA
YOBE
BORNO
Lake Chad
Tropic of Cancer
Meters
Feet
LAND BELOW SEA LEVEL
129
131
156
159

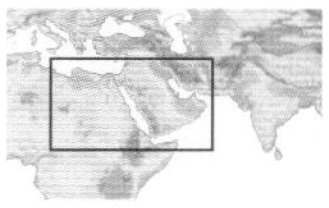

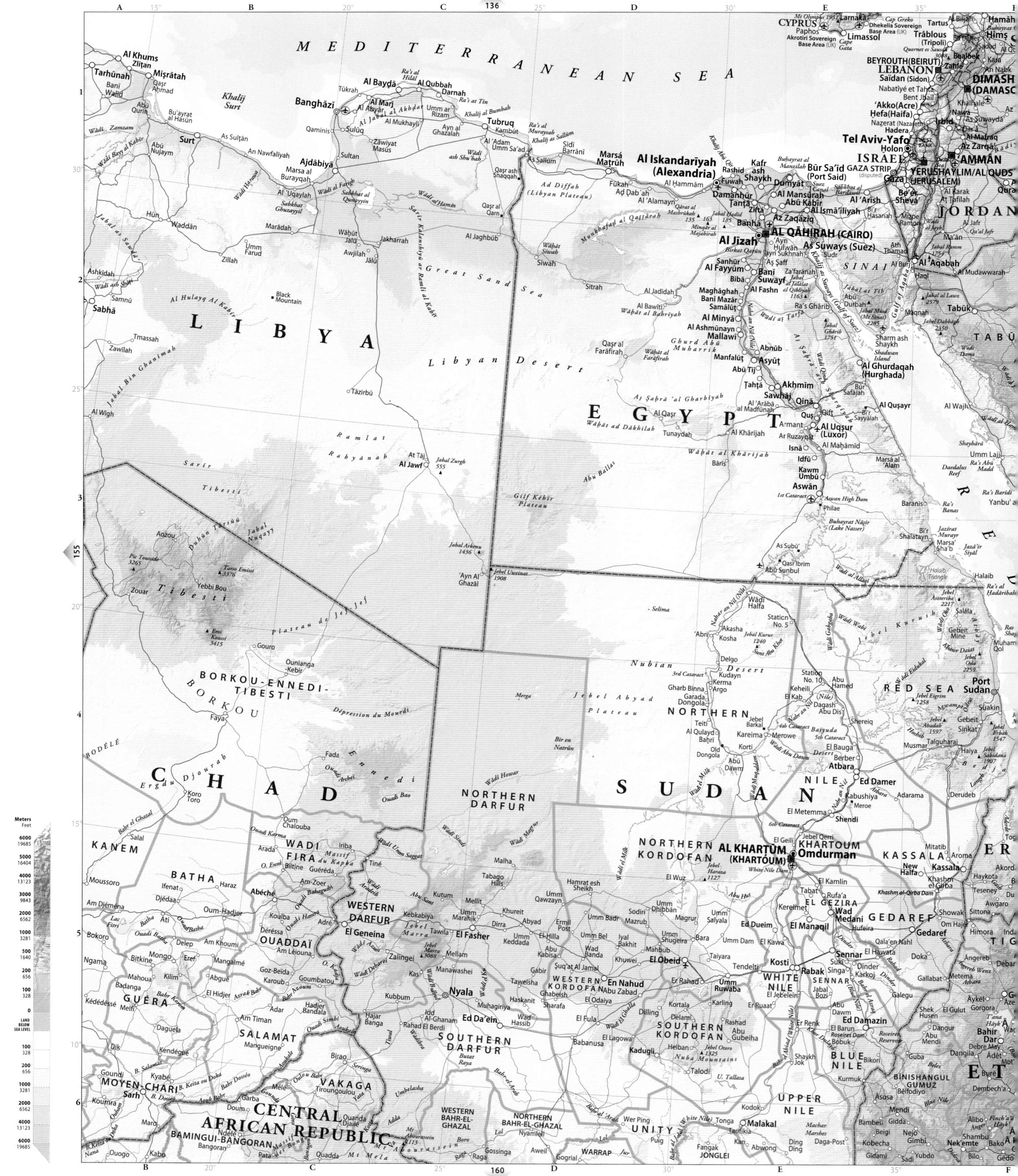

136
155
160
MEDITERRANEAN SEA
LIBYA
EGYPT
SUDAN
CHAD
CENTRAL AFRICAN REPUBLIC
ISRAEL
LEBANON
JORDAN
RED SEA
Libyan Desert
Great Sand Sea
Nubian Desert
Tibesti
BORKOU-ENNEDI-TIBESTI
BORKOU
Ennedi
Ad Diffah (Libyan Plateau)
Gilf Kebir Plateau
Jebel Abyad Plateau
Ramlat Rabyānah
Khalij Surt
Al Khums
Zlīţan
Mişrātah
Tarhūnah
Surt
Ajdābiyā
Banghāzī
Al Bayḑā
Darnah
Tubruq
Marsá Maţrūh
Al Iskandarīyah (Alexandria)
Būr Sa'īd (Port Said)
AL QĀHIRAH (CAIRO)
Al Jīzah
As Suways (Suez)
Al Fayyūm
Banī Suwayf
Al Minyā
Asyūţ
Sawhāj
Qinā
Al Uqşur (Luxor)
Aswān
Al Ghurdaqah (Hurghada)
Tel Aviv-Yafo
YERUSHALAYIM/AL QUDS (JERUSALEM)
'AMMĀN
BEYROUTH(BEIRUT)
DIMASHQ (DAMASCUS)
Al Jawf
Sabhā
Aozou
Faya
Wadi Halfa
Dongola
Atbara
Port Sudan
AL KHARTŪM (KHARTOUM)
Omdurman
Kassala
Wad Medani
Gedaref
Kosti
El Obeid
En Nahud
El Fasher
El Geneina
Nyala
Ed Da'ein
Kadugli
Malakal
Abéché
Sarh
NORTHERN
NILE
NORTHERN DARFUR
WESTERN DARFUR
SOUTHERN DARFUR
NORTHERN KORDOFAN
WESTERN KORDOFAN
SOUTHERN KORDOFAN
KHARTOUM
KASSALA
EL GEZIRA
GEDAREF
SENNAR
WHITE NILE
BLUE NILE
UPPER NILE
UNITY
WARRAP
JONGLEI
NORTHERN BAHR-EL-GHAZAL
WESTERN BAHR-EL-GHAZAL
KANEM
BATHA
WADI FIRA
OUADDAÏ
GUÉRA
SALAMAT
MOYEN-CHARI
VAKAGA
BAMINGUI-BANGORAN
Meters
Feet
LAND BELOW SEA LEVEL

1:10,320,000

Lambert Conic Conformal Projection

0 100 200 300 400 500 kilometers

0 50 100 150 200 250 300 miles

NORTHEASTERN AFRICA and the MIDDLE EAST

IRAQ
BAGHDAD
IRAN
KUWAIT
BAHRAIN
QATAR
AD DAWḤAH (DOHA)
ABŪ ẒABĪ (ABU DHABI)
UNITED ARAB EMIRATES
SAUDI ARABIA
AR RIYĀḌ (RIYADH)
ARABIAN PENINSULA
AR RUB' AL KHĀLĪ
OMAN
MASQAṬ (MUSCAT)
YEMEN
ṢAN'Ā' (SANAA)
DJIBOUTI
SOMALIA
AFGHANISTAN
The Gulf
Gulf of Oman
GULF OF ADEN
INDIAN OCEAN
Makkah (Mecca)
Al Madinah al Munawwarah (Medina)
Dubayy (Dubai)
Adan (Aden)
Meters
Feet

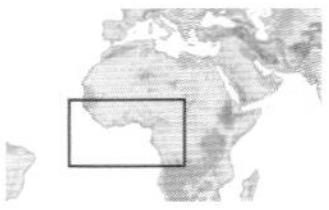

154
SENEGAL
GAMBIA
GUINEA-BISSAU
GUINEA
SIERRA LEONE
LIBERIA
MALI
CÔTE D'IVOIRE
BURKINA FASO
GHANA
TOGO
DAKAR
Thiès
Tivaouane
Mbour
Joal-Fadiout
Diourbel
Kaolack
Tambacounda
BANJUL
Serekunda
BISSAU
Ziguinchor
Kolda
Kayes
KAYES
KOULIKORO
BAMAKO
SIKASSO
Sikasso
SEGOU
Ségou
MOPTI
Mopti
Djenné
CONAKRY
Kindia
Labé
Mamou
Kankan
Siguiri
Guékédou
Nzérékoré
FREETOWN
Makeni
Bo
Kenema
MONROVIA
Buchanan
Harper
Abidjan
YAMOUSSOUKRO
Bouaké
Korhogo
Daloa
Man
San Pédro
Sassandra
Grand-Bassam
Abengourou
OUAGADOUGOU
Bobo Dioulasso
Koudougou
Kaya
Tamale
Kumasi
Sekondi
Takoradi
Cape Coast
ACCRA
Tema
LOMÉ
Cotonou
NIAM
TILLABÉRI
Bight of Ben
GULF OF GUINE
ATLANTIC OCEAN
Ascension (United Kingdom)
Georgetown
Two Boats Village
Meters
Feet
6000
19685
5000
16404
4000
13123
3000
9843
2000
6562
1000
3281
500
1640
200
656
100
328
0
LAND BELOW SEA LEVEL
100
328
200
656
1000
3281
2000
6562
4000
13123
6000
19685

1:10,320,000
Lambert Conic Conformal Projection

0 100 200 300 400 500 kilometers
0 50 100 150 200 250 300 miles

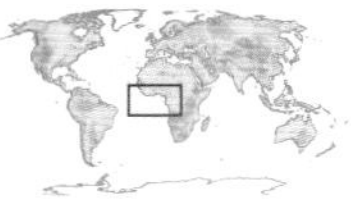

WESTERN CENTRAL AFRICA

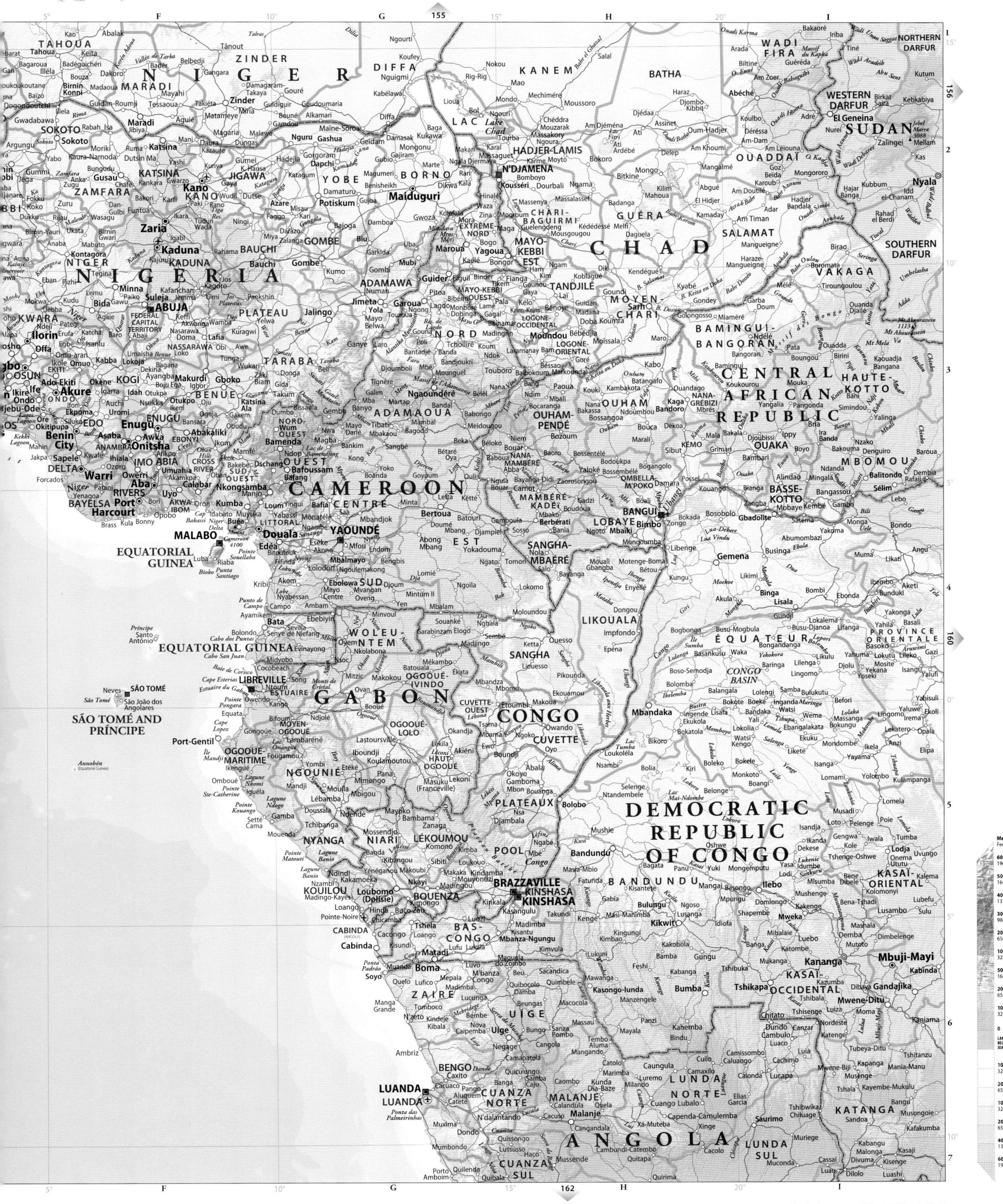

155
156
160
162
F
G
H
I
5°
10°
15°
20°
NIGER
NIGERIA
CHAD
CAMEROON
EQUATORIAL GUINEA
SÃO TOMÉ AND PRÍNCIPE
GABON
CONGO
CENTRAL AFRICAN REPUBLIC
DEMOCRATIC REPUBLIC OF CONGO
ANGOLA
SUDAN
TAHOUA
ZINDER
MARADI
DIFFA
KANEM
BATHA
WADI FIRA
NORTHERN DARFUR
WESTERN DARFUR
SOUTHERN DARFUR
LAC
HADJER-LAMIS
OUADDAÏ
SALAMAT
GUÉRA
CHARI-BAGUIRMI
MAYO-KEBBI EST
MAYO-KEBBI OUEST
TANDJILÉ
MOYEN-CHARI
LOGONE-OCCIDENTAL
LOGONE-ORIENTAL
SOKOTO
KATSINA
ZAMFARA
KANO
JIGAWA
YOBE
BORNO
KADUNA
BAUCHI
GOMBE
ADAMAWA
NIGER
KWARA
PLATEAU
NASSARAWA
TARABA
FEDERAL CAPITAL TERRITORY
OSUN
EKITI
ONDO
KOGI
BENUE
ENUGU
EDO
EBONYI
ANAMBRA
IMO
ABIA
CROSS RIVER
AKWA IBOM
DELTA
RIVERS
BAYELSA
EXTRÊME-NORD
NORD
ADAMAOUA
NORD-OUEST
SUD-OUEST
OUEST
LITTORAL
CENTRE
EST
SUD
BAMINGUI-BANGORAN
VAKAGA
HAUTE-KOTTO
OUHAM
OUHAM-PENDÉ
NANA-GRÉBIZI
KÉMO
OUAKA
MBOMOU
BASSE-KOTTO
NANA-MAMBÉRÉ
MAMBÉRÉ-KADÉÏ
OMBELLA-M'POKO
LOBAYE
SANGHA-MBAÉRÉ
WOLEU-NTEM
ESTUAIRE
MOYEN-OGOOUÉ
OGOOUÉ-IVINDO
OGOOUÉ-LOLO
OGOOUÉ-MARITIME
NGOUNIÉ
NYANGA
HAUT-OGOOUÉ
LIKOUALA
SANGHA
CUVETTE-OUEST
CUVETTE
PLATEAUX
LÉKOUMOU
NIARI
POOL
BOUENZA
KOUILOU
PROVINCE ORIENTALE
ÉQUATEUR
CONGO BASIN
BANDUNDU
BAS-CONGO
KASAÏ-ORIENTAL
KASAÏ-OCCIDENTAL
KATANGA
ZAIRE
UÍGE
BENGO
CUANZA NORTE
CUANZA SUL
MALANJE
LUNDA NORTE
LUNDA SUL
CABINDA
ABUJA
N'DJAMENA
YAOUNDÉ
MALABO
LIBREVILLE
SÃO TOMÉ
BANGUI
BRAZZAVILLE
KINSHASA
LUANDA
Lake Chad
Meters
Feet
6000
19685
5000
16404
4000
13123
3000
9843
2000
6562
1000
3281
500
1640
200
656
100
328
0
LAND BELOW SEA LEVEL

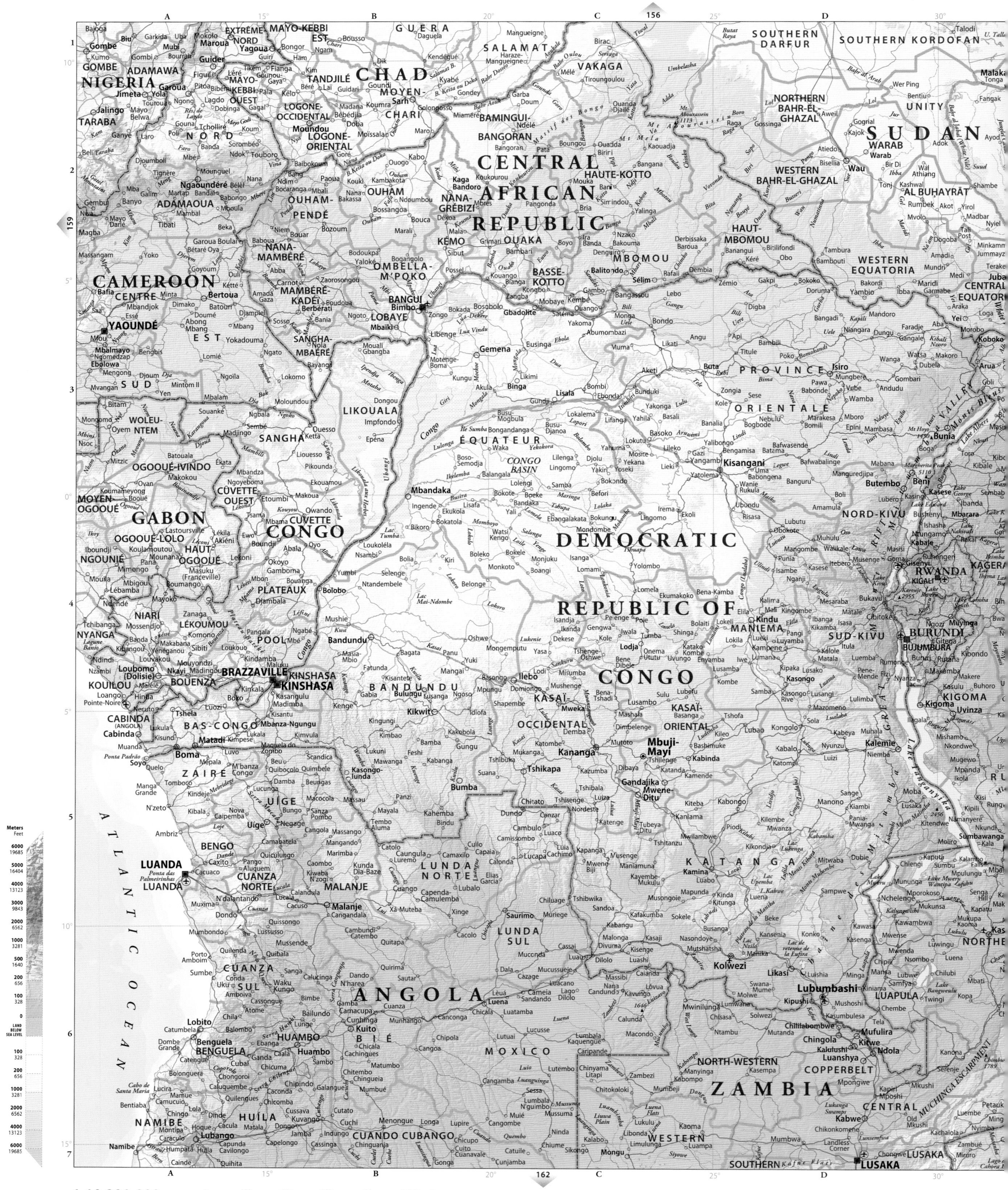

CHAD
NIGERIA
CAMEROON
CENTRAL AFRICAN REPUBLIC
SUDAN
GABON
CONGO
DEMOCRATIC REPUBLIC OF CONGO
RWANDA
BURUNDI
ANGOLA
ZAMBIA
ATLANTIC OCEAN
YAOUNDÉ
BANGUI
BRAZZAVILLE
KINSHASA
LUANDA
KIGALI
BUJUMBURA
LUSAKA
CONGO BASIN
Lac Mai-Ndombe
Lake Tanganyika
Lake Mweru
Lake Kivu
Lake Edward
Lake Albert
Muchinga Escarpment
Meters
Feet
6000
19685
5000
16404
4000
13123
3000
9843
2000
6562
1000
3281
500
1640
200
656
100
328
0
LAND BELOW SEA LEVEL
156
159
162

1:10,320,000

Lambert Conic Conformal Projection

0 100 200 300 400 500 kilometers

0 50 100 150 200 250 300 miles

EASTERN CENTRAL AFRICA

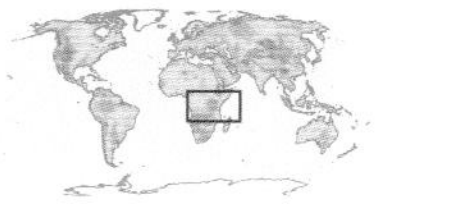

157
163
ETHIOPIA
SOMALIA
KENYA
TANZANIA
MOZAMBIQUE
MALAWI
MADAGASCAR
COMOROS
SEYCHELLES
INDIAN OCEAN
ĀDĪS ĀBEBA (ADDIS ABABA)
MUQDISHO (MOGADISHU)
NAIROBI
DODOMA
DAR ES SALAAM
LILONGWE
MORONI
Ethiopian Highlands
RIFT VALLEY
Mombasa
Kismaayo
Zanzibar
Hargeysa
Berbera
Nampula
Mozambique Channel
Meters
Feet
6000
19685
5000
16404
4000
13123
3000
9843
2000
6562
1000
3281
500
1640
200
656
100
328
0
LAND BELOW SEA LEVEL

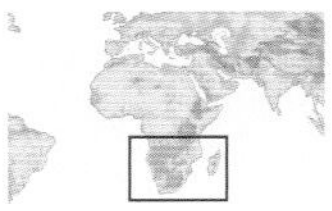

160
ATLANTIC OCEAN
ANGOLA
NAMIBIA
BOTSWANA
ZAMBIA
SOUTH AFRICA
ZIMBABWE
LESOTHO
LUANDA
WINDHOEK
GABORONE
LUSAKA
PRETORIA (TSHWANE)
MASERU
CAPE TOWN
BLOEMFONTEIN
Johannesburg
Soweto
Port Elizabeth
East London
Walvis Bay
Swakopmund
Lüderitz
Lubango
Huambo
Benguela
Lobito
Livingstone
Bulawayo
Kimberley
Upington
Maun
Francistown
Lubumbashi
Ndola
Kitwe
Tropic of Capricorn
Cape of Good Hope
Cape Agulhas
KALAHARI DESERT
NAMIB DESERT
Skeleton Coast
Etosha Pan
Okavango Delta
CAPRIVI STRIP

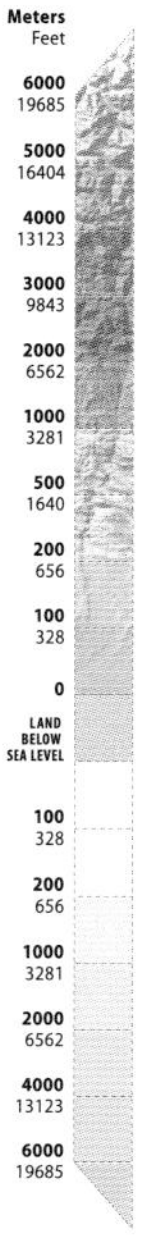
Meters
Feet
6000
19685
5000
16404
4000
13123
3000
9843
2000
6562
1000
3281
500
1640
200
656
100
328
0
LAND BELOW SEA LEVEL
100
328
200
656
1000
3281
2000
6562
4000
13123
6000
19685

1:10,320,000

Lambert Conic Conformal Projection

0 100 200 300 400 500 kilometers

0 50 100 150 200 250 300 miles

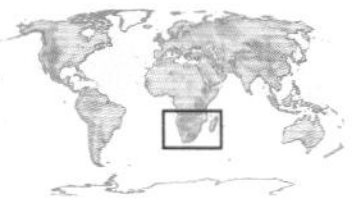

SOUTHERN AFRICA and MADAGASCAR

161
SEYCHELLES
Group d'Aldabra
(Seychelles)
Assumption
Cosmoledo Islands
Astove
St Pierre Island
Providence
Île au Cerf
Farquhar Group
COMOROS
Mitsamiouli
Mbéni
MORONI
Koimbani
Njazidja
(Grand Comore)
Karthala 2361
Pidjani
Mutsamudu
Anjouan (Nzwani)
Mwali (Mohéli)
Fomboni
Domoni
Mamoudzou
Sada
Mayotte (France)
Îles Glorieuses (France)
MOZAMBIQUE CHANNEL
Île Juan de Nova (France)
Bassas da India (France)
Île Europa (France)
MADAGASCAR
ANTANANARIVO
Antsiranana
ANTSIRANANA
Nosy Be
Ambilobe
Ambanja
Sambava
Antalaha
Andapa
Maroantsetra
Mahajanga
MAHAJANGA
Marovoay
Besalampy
Maintirano
Tambohorano
Morondava
TOAMASINA
Toamasina
Antsirabe
Fianarantsoa
FIANARANTSOA
Manakara
Farafangana
TOLIARA
Toliara
Ihosy
Ambovombe
Tôlanaro
Tropic of Capricorn
MALAWI
LILONGWE
CENTRAL
NORTHERN
SOUTHERN
Mzuzu
Blantyre
Zomba
Kasungu
MOZAMBIQUE
CABO DELGADO
NIASSA
NAMPULA
ZAMBÉZIA
TETE
MANICA
SOFALA
INHAMBANE
GAZA
MAPUTO
Pemba
Nacala
Nampula
Mocambique
Angoche
Quelimane
Beira
Chimoio
Tete
Lichinga
Cuamba
Mocuba
Inhambane
Maxixe
Xai-Xai
Chibuto
Vilankulos
Mocimboa da Praia
MTWARA
Mtwara
RUVUMA
Songea
SWAZILAND
Richards Bay
Durban
INDIAN OCEAN
F
G
H
I
J
K
35°
40°
45°
50°
55°
10°
15°
20°
25°
30°
1
2
3
4
5
6

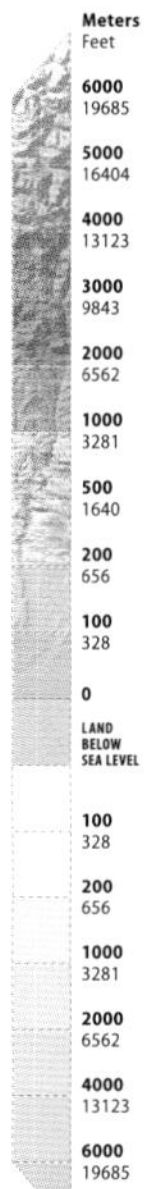

Meters
Feet
6000
19685
5000
16404
4000
13123
3000
9843
2000
6562
1000
3281
500
1640
200
656
100
328
0
LAND BELOW SEA LEVEL
100
328
200
656
1000
3281
2000
6562
4000
13123
6000
19685

ISLANDS Around AFRICA

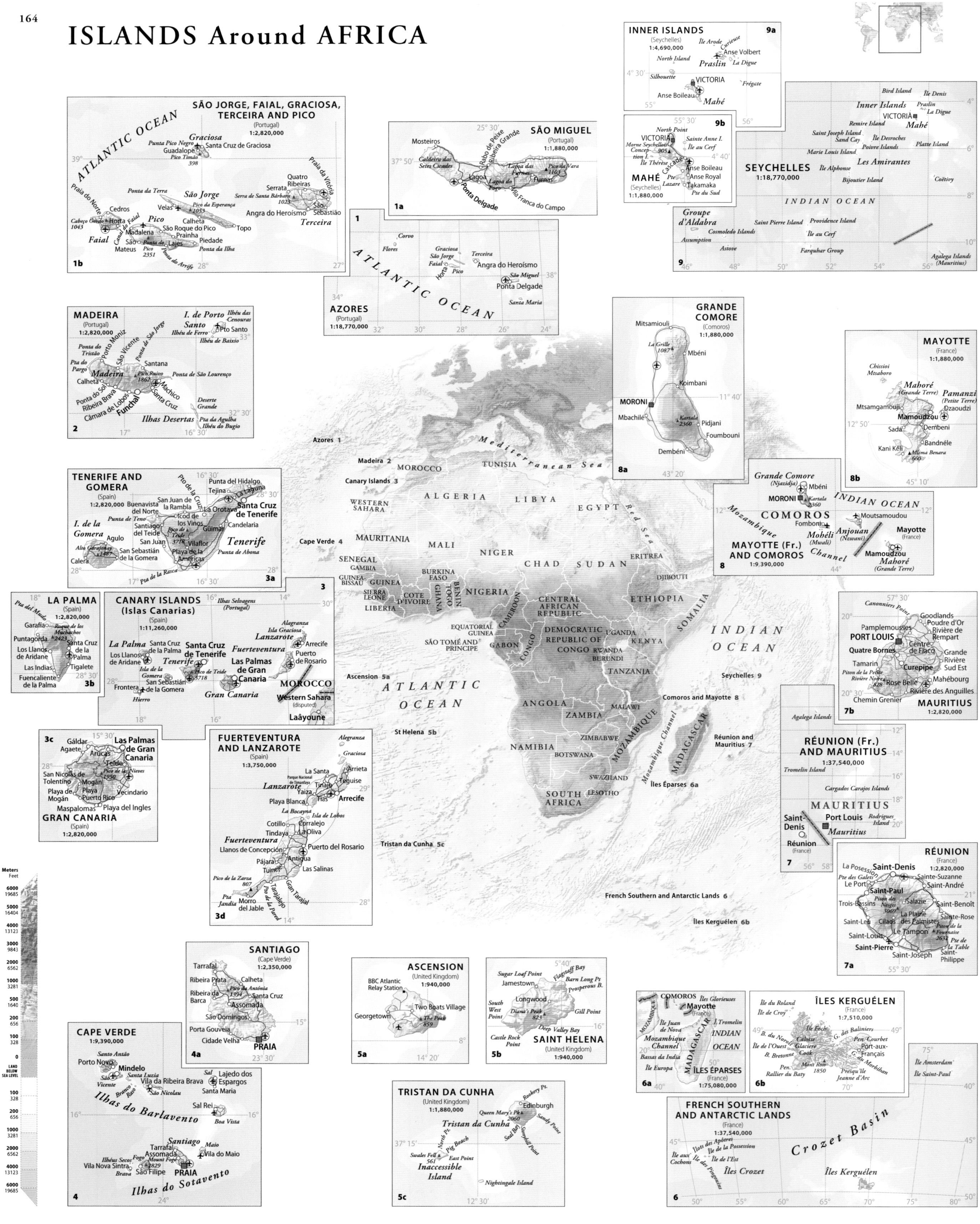
INNER ISLANDS 9a
(Seychelles)
1:4,690,000
Île Arode
Curieuse
Anse Volbert
North Island
Praslin
La Digue
Silhouette
VICTORIA
Frégate
Anse Boileau
Mahé
9b
North Point
VICTORIA
Sainte Anne I.
Île au Cerf
Morne Seychellois 905
Conception I.
Île Thérèse
Cascade
Anse Boileau
Anse Royal
Takamaka
Pte du Sud
MAHÉ
(Seychelles)
1:1,880,000
Bird Island
Île Denis
Inner Islands
Praslin
La Digue
VICTORIA
Mahé
Remire Island
Saint Joseph Island
Sand Cay
Île Desroches
Poivre Islands
Platte Island
Marie Louis Island
SEYCHELLES
1:18,770,000
Île Alphonse
Les Amirantes
Bijoutier Island
Coëtivy
INDIAN OCEAN
Groupe d'Aldabra
Saint Pierre Island
Providence Island
Cosmoledo Islands
Île au Cerf
Assumption
Astove
Farquhar Group
Agalega Islands (Mauritius)
9
SÃO JORGE, FAIAL, GRACIOSA, TERCEIRA AND PICO
(Portugal)
1:2,820,000
ATLANTIC OCEAN
Graciosa
Punta Pico Negro
Santa Cruz de Graciosa
Guadalope
Pico Timão 398
Praia da Vitória
Quatro Ribeiras
Serrata
Ponta da Terra
São Jorge
Serra de Santa Bárbara 1023
Praia do Norte
Cedros
Velas
Pico da Esperança 1053
São Sebastião
Angra do Heroísmo
Terceira
Cabeço Gordo 1043
Horta
Canal do Faial
Pico
Calheta
São Roque do Pico
Topo
Madalena
Prainha
Faial
São Mateus
Piedade
Pico 2351
Lajes
Ponta da Ilha
Ponta do Arrife
1b
SÃO MIGUEL
(Portugal)
1:1,880,000
Mosteiros
Caldeira das Sete Cidades
Rabo de Peixe
Ribeira Grande
Lagoa
Lagoa das Furnas
Pico da Vara 1103
Furnas
Lagoa do Fogo
Ponta Delgada
Vila Franca do Campo
1a
1
Corvo
Flores
Graciosa
São Jorge
Faial
Terceira
Angra do Heroísmo
Horta
Pico
São Miguel
Ponta Delgada
Santa Maria
ATLANTIC OCEAN
AZORES
(Portugal)
1:18,770,000
MADEIRA
(Portugal)
1:2,820,000
I. de Porto Santo
Ilhéu das Cenouras
Ilhéu de Ferro
Pto Santo
Ilhéu de Baixio
Ponta do Tristão
Porto Moniz
São Vicente
Ponta de São Jorge
Pta do Pargo
Santana
Madeira
Pico Ruivo 1862
Ponta de São Lourenço
Calheta
Machico
Ponta do Sol
Ribeira Brava
Santa Cruz
Câmara de Lobos
Funchal
Deserte Grande
Ilhas Desertas
Pta da Agulha
Ilhéu do Bugio
2
GRANDE COMORE
(Comoros)
1:1,880,000
Mitsamiouli
La Grille 1087
Mbéni
Koimbani
MORONI
Mbachilé
Kartala 2360
Pidjani
Foumbouni
Dembéni
8a
MAYOTTE
(France)
1:1,880,000
Chissioi Mtsaboro
Mahoré (Grande Terre)
Pamanzi (Petite Terre)
Mtsamgamouji
Dzaoudzi
Mamoudzou
Sada
Dembeni
Bandréle
Kani Kéli
Mlima Benara 660
8b
Grande Comore (Njazidja)
Mbéni
MORONI
Kartala 2360
INDIAN OCEAN
COMOROS
Moutsamoudou
Fomboni
Mohéli (Mwali)
Anjouan (Nzwani)
Mayotte (France)
Mozambique Channel
MAYOTTE (Fr.) AND COMOROS
1:9,390,000
Mamoudzou
Mahoré (Grande Terre)
8
TENERIFE AND GOMERA
(Spain)
1:2,820,000
Pto de la Cruz
Punta del Hidalgo
Tejina
La Laguna
San Juan de la Rambla
Buenavista del Norte
La Orotava
Santa Cruz de Tenerife
Punta de Teno
Icod de los Vinos
Candelaria
I. de la Gomera
Santiago del Teide
Güímar
Pico de Teide 3718
Tenerife
Agulo
San Juan
Vilaflor
Alto Garajonay 1487
San Sebastián de la Gomera
Playa de las Américas
Punta de Abona
Calera
Pta de la Rasca
3a
LA PALMA
(Spain)
1:2,820,000
Pta del Mudo
Garafía
Roque de los Muchachos 2423
Puntagorda
Santa Cruz de la Palma
Los Llanos de Aridane
Las Indias
Tigalete
Fuencaliente de la Palma
3b
CANARY ISLANDS (Islas Canarias)
(Spain)
1:11,260,000
Ilhas Selvagens (Portugal)
Alagranza
Isla Graciosa
Lanzarote
Arrecife
La Palma
Santa Cruz de la Palma
Santa Cruz de Tenerife
Fuerteventura
Los Llanos de Aridane
Tenerife
Las Palmas de Gran Canaria
Puerto de Rosario
Isla de la Gomera
Pico de Teide 3718
San Sebastián de la Gomera
Frontera
Hierro
Gran Canaria
MOROCCO
Western Sahara (disputed)
Laâyoune
3
Gáldar
Las Palmas de Gran Canaria
Agaete
Arucas
Telde
San Nicolás de Tolentino
Pico de las Nieves 1950
Mogán
Vecindario
Playa de Mogán
Playa
Puerto Rico
Maspalomas
Playa del Ingles
GRAN CANARIA
(Spain)
1:2,820,000
3c
FUERTEVENTURA AND LANZAROTE
(Spain)
1:3,750,000
Alegranza
Graciosa
Arrieta
La Santa
Parque Nacional de Timanfaya
Teguise
Lanzarote
Tinajo
Yaiza
Tías
Arrecife
Playa Blanca
La Bocayna
Isla de Lobos
Cotillo
Corralejo
Tindaya
Oliva
Fuerteventura
Llanos de Concepción
Puerto del Rosario
Antigua
Pájara
Tuineje
Las Salinas
Pico de la Zarza 807
Gran Tarajal
Pta Jandía
Morro del Jable
Tarajalejo
Pta de la Pared
3d
Azores 1
Madeira 2
Canary Islands 3
Cape Verde 4
Ascension 5a
St Helena 5b
Tristan da Cunha 5c
French Southern and Antarctic Lands 6
Îles Éparses 6a
Îles Kerguélen 6b
Réunion and Mauritius 7
Comoros and Mayotte 8
Seychelles 9
MOROCCO
TUNISIA
Mediterranean Sea
ALGERIA
LIBYA
EGYPT
Red Sea
WESTERN SAHARA
MAURITANIA
MALI
NIGER
CHAD
SUDAN
ERITREA
SENEGAL
GAMBIA
GUINEA-BISSAU
GUINEA
BURKINA FASO
BENIN
TOGO
GHANA
NIGERIA
DJIBOUTI
ETHIOPIA
SIERRA LEONE
COTE D'IVOIRE
LIBERIA
CENTRAL AFRICAN REPUBLIC
CAMEROON
SOMALIA
EQUATORIAL GUINEA
SÃO TOMÉ AND PRINCIPE
GABON
CONGO
DEMOCRATIC REPUBLIC OF CONGO
UGANDA
KENYA
RWANDA
BURUNDI
TANZANIA
INDIAN OCEAN
ATLANTIC OCEAN
ANGOLA
ZAMBIA
MALAWI
MOZAMBIQUE
ZIMBABWE
NAMIBIA
BOTSWANA
MADAGASCAR
Mozambique Channel
SWAZILAND
LESOTHO
SOUTH AFRICA
RÉUNION (Fr.) AND MAURITIUS
1:37,540,000
Agalega Islands
Tromelin Island
Cargados Carajos Islands
MAURITIUS
Saint-Denis
Port Louis
Rodrigues Island
Mauritius
Réunion (France)
7
MAURITIUS
1:2,820,000
Canonniers Point
Goodlands
Poudre d'Or
Pamplemousses
Rivière de Rempart
PORT LOUIS
Centre de Flacq
Quatre Bornes
Grande Rivière Sud Est
Tamarin
Curepipe
Piton de la Petite Rivière Noire 828
Rose Belle
Mahébourg
Chemin Grenier
Rivière des Anguilles
7b
RÉUNION
(France)
1:2,820,000
La Possession
Saint-Denis
Pte des Galets
Sainte-Suzanne
Le Port
Saint-André
Saint-Paul
Piton des Neiges 3069
Salazie
Saint-Benoît
Trois-Bassins
La Plaine des Palmistes
Sainte-Rose
Saint-Leu
Cilaos
Piton de la Fournaise 2632
Le Tampon
Saint-Louis
Pte de la Table
Saint-Pierre
Saint-Joseph
Saint-Philippe
7a
SANTIAGO
(Cape Verde)
1:2,350,000
Tarrafal
Ribeira Prata
Calheta
Pico da Antónia 1394
Ribeira da Barca
Santa Cruz
Assomada
São Domingos
Porta Gouveia
Cidade Velha
PRAIA
4a
ASCENSION
(United Kingdom)
1:940,000
BBC Atlantic Relay Station
Georgetown
Two Boats Village
The Peak 859
5a
Sugar Loaf Point
Flagstaff Bay
Jamestown
Barn Long Pt
Prosperous B.
South West Point
Longwood
Diana's Peak 823
Gill Point
Deep Valley Bay
Castle Rock Point
SAINT HELENA
(United Kingdom)
1:940,000
5b
CAPE VERDE
1:9,390,000
Santo Antão
Porto Novo
Mindelo
São Vicente
Santa Luzia
Sal
Lajedo dos Espargos
Vila da Ribeira Brava
Branco
Raso
São Nicolau
Santa Maria
Ilhas do Barlavento
Sal Rei
Boa Vista
Santiago
Maio
Tarrafal
Assomada
Vila do Maio
Ilhéus Secos
Fogo
Mount Fogo 2829
Vila Nova Sintra
Brava
São Filipe
PRAIA
Ilhas do Sotavento
4
TRISTAN DA CUNHA
(United Kingdom)
1:1,880,000
Rookery Pt.
Edinburgh
Queen Mary's Pk 2060
Sandy Point
Tristan da Cunha
Seal Bay
Stonyhill Point
North Pt.
Pig Beach
Swales Fell 561
East Point
Inaccessible Island
Nightingale Island
5c
COMOROS
Îles Glorieuses
Mayotte (France)
MOZAMBIQUE
Île Juan de Nova
I. Tromelin
Mozambique Channel
MADAGASCAR
INDIAN OCEAN
Bassas da India
Île Europa
ÎLES ÉPARSES
(France)
1:75,080,000
6a
ÎLES KERGUÉLEN
1:7,510,000
Île du Roland
Île de Croy
Île Foch
G. des Baliniers
B. du Nord
Île de l'Ouest
Calotte Glaciere Cook
Pen. Courbet
Port-aux-Français
B. Bretonne
G. du Morbihan
Pen. Rallier du Baty
Mont Ross 1850
Presqu'île Jeanne d'Arc
6b
Île Amsterdam
Île Saint-Paul
FRENCH SOUTHERN AND ANTARCTIC LANDS
(France)
1:37,540,000
Îlots des Apôtres
Île de la Possession
Île aux Cochons
Île de l'Est
Île des Pingouins
Crozet Basin
Îles Crozet
Îles Kerguélen
6
Meters
Feet
6000 19685
5000 16404
4000 13123
3000 9843
2000 6562
1000 3281
500 1640
200 656
100 328
0
LAND BELOW SEA LEVEL
100 328
200 656
1000 3281
2000 6562
4000 13123
6000 19685

Asia

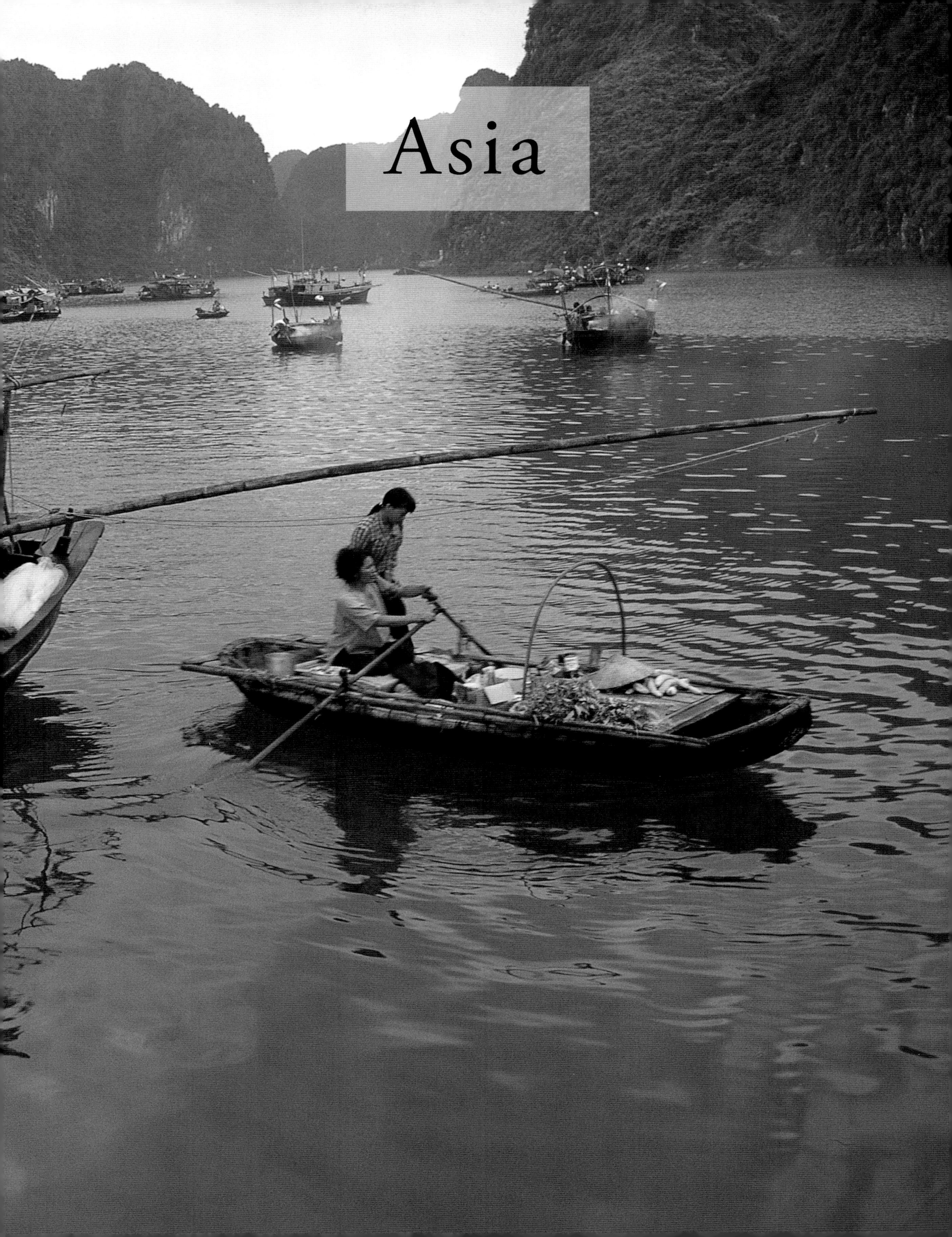

SOUTHWEST ASIA

Southwest Asia, the region sometimes referred to as the Middle East, is a vast and complexly shaped area separated from Africa and Europe by four seas—the Red Sea, the Mediterranean Sea, the Black Sea, and the Caspian Sea. Its natural boundaries with the other parts of Asia consist of rugged terrain, high mountains, and harsh deserts, while to the south lies the Arabian Sea, an extension of the Indian Ocean.

Above Like many Syrians, this young goatherd follows a traditional lifestyle, which has changed little over several thousand years. The country's economy is largely agricultural.

Previous pages Some 1,600 islands dot Vietnam's Ha Long Bay in the Gulf of Tonkin. With its spectacular limestone pillars and amazing diversity of marine life, this unique location was inscribed as a UNESCO World Heritage Site in 1994.

The eastern Mediterranean Sea, to the west of Southwest Asia, contains the island country of Cyprus and borders Turkey, Syria, Lebanon, and Israel. There is a land bridge across the Sinai Peninsula that connects Southwest Asia with Africa. The Red Sea and the Gulf of Aden separate the Arabian Peninsula portion of Southwest Asia from the African continent.

Borders with Europe include the Mediterranean Sea, the Black Sea, and the Caspian Sea, with the narrow Bosporus Channel in northwestern Turkey separating the Sea of Marmara from the Black Sea, and the high and rugged Caucasus mountain range separating Georgia and Azerbaijan from the Russian Federation. Boundaries between Southwest Asia and the remainder of Asia include the Hindu Kush and Karakoram mountain ranges in the east, an extension of the Himalayas.

The Thar Desert (also called the Great Indian Desert or the Great South Asian Desert) lies between Southwest Asia and Pakistan and India to the southeast; while various mountains, salt deserts, and other difficult terrain in Iran and Afghanistan, form a natural border to the north, separating the region from Turkmenistan and other central Asian countries. Reaching 1,070 meters (3,510 feet) in height, the historic Khyber Pass—located in mountains between Afghanistan and Pakistan—provides a difficult overland connection between different parts of the Asian world.

Right This NASA satellite image shows the hundreds of artificial islands off Dubai's Persian Gulf coastline, which were created to maximize potential for beachfront tourism. The islands, built from sand dredged from the sea floor, are shielded from erosion by rock breakwaters.

The Region's Deserts

Southwest Asia is part of the dry world. The largest desert in the region is the Arabian Desert, covering some 2,330,000 square kilometers (900,000 square miles), and occupying most of the Arabian Peninsula from Yemen and Oman in the south to Jordan and Iraq in the north. In its center is the Rub'al-Khali (known as the Empty Quarter), an expansive terrain of sandy plains and high dunes. Other desert areas are found in Israel, Syria, Iran, and Pakistan.

In Iran, the largest desert area is Dasht-e Kavir, also known as the Great Salt Desert. It lies in the center of the Plateau of Iran and measures some 77,600 square kilometers (30,000 square miles).

The Dead Sea—located at the boundary between Israel and the West Bank on the west and Jordan to the east—is a saline desert lake in a deep rift valley. Sitting at 422 meters (1,385 feet) below sea level, the shores of the Dead Sea are the lowest point on the surface of Earth.

Far right The ruins of Palmyra are set in an oasis in central Syria, 210 kilometers (130 miles) to the northeast of Damascus. The ancient city comprises temples, palaces, and porticos, and extends over a distance of several miles.

COUNTRIES	OFFICIAL NAME	AREA	POPULATION	CAPITAL	RELIGION	POPULATION DENSITY	HIGHEST POINT	CURRENCY
Afghanistan	Dê Afghānistān Islāmī Jumhūriyat; Jomhūrī-ye Eslāmī-ye Afghānestān	647,500 km^2/250,001 mi^2	33,610,000	Kabul (Kābol)	☪99%, ○1%	52/km^2, 134/mi^2	Nowshāk 7,486 m/24,557 ft	Afghani
Armenia	Hayastani Hanrapetut'yun	28,450 km^2/10,965 mi^2	2,967,000	Yerevan	✝98.7%, ○1.3%	104/km^2, 271/mi^2	Aragats Lerrnagagat' 4,090 m/13,419 ft	Dram
Azerbaijan	Azərbaycan Respublikası	86,100 km^2/33,243 mi^2	8,238,000	Baku (Bakı)	☪93.4%, ✝2.2%, ○4.4%	95/km^2, 247/mi^2	Bazardüzü Dağı 4,466 m/14,652 ft	Manat
Bahrain	Mamlakat al Baḩrayn	665 km^2/257 mi^2	727,700	Manama (Al Manāmah)	☪81.2%, ✝9%, ○9.8%	1,094/km^2, 2,831/mi^2	Jabal ad Dukhan 122 m/400 ft	Dinar
Cyprus	Kypriakí Dimokratía; Kıbrıs Cumhuriyeti	9,250 km^2/3,570 mi^2	796,700	Nicosia (Lefkosia)	✝78%, ☪18%, ○4%	86/km^2, 223/mi^2	Mt Olympus 1,950 m/6,400 ft	Pound, Euro
Georgia	Sak'art'velo	69,700 km^2/26,911 mi^2	4,615,000	T'bilisi	✝88.6%, ☪9.9%, ○1.5%	66/km^2, 171/mi^2	Schchara Berg 5,068 m/16,627 ft	Lari
Iran	Jomhūrī-ye Eslāmī-ye Īrān	1,636,000 km^2/631,663 mi^2	66,429,000	Tehran	☪98%, ○2%	40/km^2, 105/mi^2	Kūh-e Damāvand 5,671 m/18,606 ft	Rial
Iraq	Al Jumhūrīyah al'Irāqīyah	432,162 km^2/166,859 mi^2	28,945,000	Baghdād	☪97%, ○3%	67/km^2, 173/mi^2	11,847 m/3,611 ft	Dinar
Israel	Medinat Yisra'el; Dawlat Isrā'īl	20,330 km^2/7,849 mi^2	7,233,000	Jerusalem (Yerushalayim/Al Quds)	✡76.4%, ☪17.6%, ✝2.1%, ○3.9%	356/km^2, 921/mi^2	Har Meron 1,208 m/3,963 ft	Shekel
Jordan	Al Mamlakah al Urdunīyah al Hāshimīyah	92,300 km^2/35,627 mi^2	6,343,000	Amman ('Ammān)	☪92%, ✝6%, ○2%	69/km^2, 178/mi^2	Jabal Ram 1,734 m/5,689 ft	Dinar
Kuwait	Dawlat al Kuwayt	17,820 km^2/6,880 mi^2	2,691,000	Kuwait (Al Kuwayt)	☪85%, ✝6%, ॐ6%, ○3%	151/km^2, 391/mi^2	306 m/1,004 ft	Dinar
Lebanon	Al Jumhūrīyah al Lubnānīyah	10,230 km^2/3,950 mi^2	4,017,000	Beirut (Beyrouth)	☪59.7%, ✝39%, ○1.3%	393/km^2, 1,017/mi^2	Qurnat as Sawdā' 3,088 m/10,131 ft	Pound
Oman	Salṭanat 'Umān	212,460 km^2/82,031 mi^2	3,418,000	Muscat (Masqaṭ)	☪88%, ॐ7%, ✝4%, ○1%	16/km^2, 42/mi^2	Jabal Shams 2,980 m/9,777 ft	Rial
Pakistan	Islamic Republic of Pakistan; Jamhūryat Islāmī Pākistān	778,720 km^2/300,665 mi^2	176,243,000	Islamabad	☪97%, ○3%	226/km^2, 586/mi^2	K2/Qogir Feng 8,611 m/28,251 ft	Rupee
Qatar	Dawlat Qaṭar	11,437 km^2/4,416 mi^2	883,000	Doha (Ad Dawḩah)	☪77.5%, ✝8.5%, ○14%	77/km^2, 200/mi^2	Qurayn Abū al Bawl 103 m/338 ft	Riyal
Saudi Arabia	Al Mamlakah Al Arabiyyah Al Su'ūdiyyah	2,149,690 km^2/830,000 mi^2	28,686,000	Riyadh (Ar Riyāḑ)	☪100%	13/km^2, 34/mi^2	Jabal Sawdā' 3,133 m/10,279 ft	Riyal
Syria	Al Jumhūrīyah al 'Arabīyah as Sūrīyah	184,050 km^2/71,062 mi^2	20,178,000	Damascus (Dimashq)	☪89%, ✝10%, ○1%	110/km^2, 284/mi^2	Tall ash Shaykhah 2,814 m/9,232 ft	Pound
Turkey	Türkiye Cumhuriyeti	780,580 km^2/301,380 mi^2	76,805,000	Ankara	☪99.8%, ○0.2%	98/km^2, 255/mi^2	Ağrı Dağı 5,166 m/16,948 ft	Lira
United Arab Emirates	Al Imārāt al 'Arabīyah al Muttaḩidah	83,600 km^2/32,278 mi^2	4,798,000	Abu Dhabi (Abu Ẓabī)	☪95%, ✝2%, ॐ2%, ○1%	57/km^2, 149/mi^2	Jabal Yibir 1,527 m/5,010 ft	Dirham
Yemen	Al Jumhūrīyah al Yamanīyah	527,970 km^2/203,850 mi^2	23,822,000	Şan'ā'	☪99.9% ○0.1%	45/km^2, 117/mi^2	Jabal an Nabī Shu'ayb 3,760 m/12,336 ft	Rial

DEPENDENCIES AND TERRITORIES	OFFICIAL NAME	AREA	POPULATION	CAPITAL	RELIGION	POPULATION DENSITY	HIGHEST POINT	CURRENCY
Akrotiri Sovereign Base Area (UK)	Akrotiri Sovereign Base Area	123 km^2, 47 mi^2	6,300	Episkopi Cantonment	N/A	51/km^2, 134/mi^2	Nowshak 7,485 m/24,557 ft	Pound
Dhekelia Sovereign Base Area (UK)	Dhekelia Sovereign Base Area	130 km^2, 50 mi^2	7,200	Episkopi Cantonment	N/A	55/km^2, 144/mi^2	—	Pound
Gaza Strip (disputed)	Gaza Strip; Qiṭā Ghazzah	360 km^2, 139 mi^2	1,551,000	Gaza	☪99.3%, ✝0.7%	4,308 km^2, 11,158/mi^2	Abu 'Awdah (Joz Abu 'Auda) 105 m/344 ft	Shekel
West Bank (disputed)	Aḑ Ḑaffah al Gharbīyah; West Bank	5,640 km^2, 2,178 mi^2	2,461,200	Disputed	☪75%, ✡17%, ✝8%	436/km^2, 1,130/mi^2	Tall Asur 1,033 m/3,353 ft	Shekel, Dinar

Water Sources and Mountains

There are numerous aquifers throughout the desert region that determine human settlement patterns and potential for irrigated agriculture. The Tigris–Euphrates river system is located in the heart of Southwest Asia. Its two main rivers rise in the mountains of southeastern Turkey, flowing through Iraq, and join to form the Shatt al-Arab, the 200-kilometer- (120-mile-) long waterway that empties into the Gulf. These are the two main rivers of ancient Mesopotamia, an early center of civilization and part of the Fertile Crescent. This historically important zone includes southern Turkey and the Levant along the eastern Mediterranean. In northern Iran, on the southern shores of the Caspian Sea, is the Shomal, or Jungles of Iran, a lush rainforest environment that is a striking exception to the overall dryness of Southwest Asia.

The nearby Alborz Mountains capture considerable winter snow and have numerous outstanding ski resorts. Their highest peak is Mt Damavand, a symmetrical volcanic cone with a height of 5,671 meters (18,606 feet). The highest mountain in Turkey is Mt Ararat (Agri Dagi), located near the border with Armenia; it too is a dormant snow-capped volcano, standing 5,166 meters (16,948 feet) high.

Oil

The Gulf, the northern extension of the Indian Ocean via the Gulf of Oman and Strait of Hormuz, separates the Arabian Peninsula from Iran. It is the largest source of crude oil on Earth and the basis for a prosperous export economy for countries along its shores. Kuwait, Qatar, and the United Arab Emirates depend almost wholly on oil revenues, while the larger Saudi Arabia and Iran have additional resources and more diversified economies. Oil is also found in other countries in Southwest Asia, namely in northern Iraq, the interiors of Saudi Arabia and Iran, in Azerbaijan along the Caspian Sea, and in smaller amounts in Oman and Yemen.

Above The Margham Desert sand dunes lie to the south of Dubai, in the United Arab Emirates. Visitors can experience the wonder of these dunes on four-wheel-drive safari tours.

ASIA

Asia is the larger part of the enormous Eurasian continental land mass and is commonly considered to be a continent in its own right to differentiate it from the European world. It extends from the Arctic Circle into the southern hemisphere and is the world's largest continent. Apart from Southwest Asia and Southeast Asia, Asia's major subregions include South Asia, Central Asia, and East Asia. Geographically, part of Russian Federation is North or Siberian Asia.

Right Facade of a Hindu temple in Sri Lanka. Hinduism is the predominant religion of the Tamil people there, although most of the population practice Buddhism.

Below Thyangboche monastery, in Nepal's Everest region, suffered severe earthquake damage in 1934, and was almost completely destroyed by fire in 1989. Monks, sherpas, and local craftspeople rebuilt the monastery with the help of the Himalayan Trust.

SOUTH ASIA

South Asia is basically India and its neighbors, although Pakistan, which borders India on the northwest, can also be considered part of Southwest Asia, with which it shares a dry climate. Other than that ambiguity, South Asia is an unusually well-defined region that is sometimes referred to as a subcontinent.

The Himalayas—the highest mountain chain in the world—form a sharp boundary to the north with Central Asia, while the other limits are various bodies of the Indian Ocean—the Bay of Bengal to the east and the Arabian Sea to the west. The island nation of Sri Lanka in the Indian Ocean, lying just off the southern tip of India, and the Maldives island chain in the Laccadive Sea of the Indian Ocean, are also part of South Asia. Mt Everest, the highest peak in the world at 8,844 meters (29,016 feet), is in the Himalayas on the boundary between Nepal and China.

The border region between India and Pakistan is the Thar (Great Indian or Great South Asian) Desert. To the north is Kashmir, a boundary region between India, Pakistan, and China, with rugged mountains and fertile river valleys. Kashmir is the source of numerous major rivers, most notably the Indus River. The Ganges River originates in the Himalayan highlands. This is the holy river of Hindu India and flows through the heart of the fertile and extremely crowded Indo-Gangetic Plain before emptying via multiple channels into the Bay of Bengal. The Mouths of the Ganges is shared with the Brahmaputra River, which originates on the far side of the Himalayas in China and cuts a complicated path through the mountains into Bangladesh. The center of

	COUNTRIES	OFFICIAL NAME	AREA	POPULATION	CAPITAL	RELIGION	POPULATION DENSITY	HIGHEST POINT	CURRENCY
	Bangladesh	Gana Prajātantrī Bānlādesh	133,910 km^2/51,703 mi^2	156,051,000	Dhaka	☪83%, ॐ16%, ○1%	1,165/km^2, 3,018/mi^2	1,063 m/3,488 ft	Taka
	Bhutan	Druk Gyalkhap	47,000 km^2/18,147 mi^2	691,000	Thimphu	☸68%, ॐ30%, ○2%	15/km^2, 38/mi^2	Kula Kangri 7,553 m/24,780 ft	Ngultrum, Rupee
	China	Zhonghua Renmin Gongheguo	9,596,960 km^2/3,705,390 mi^2	1,338,613,000	Beijing	✝☸☯4%, ☪2%, ○94%	139/km^2, 361/mi^2	Qomolangma (Everest) 8,844 m/29,016 ft	Renminbi
	India	Bhāratīya Ganarājya; Republic of India	2,973,190 km^2/1,147,955 mi^2	1,166,079,000	New Delhi	ॐ80.5%, ☪13.4%, ✝2.3%, ☬1.9%, ○1.9%	392/km^2, 1,015/mi^2	Kānchenjunga 8,598 m/28,209 ft	Rupee
	Japan	Nippon-koku	377,835 km^2/145,882 mi^2	127,079,000	Tokyo	⛩☸84%, ○16%	336/km^2, 871/mi^2	Fuji 3,776 m/12,388 ft	Yen
	Kazakhstan	Qazaqstan Respūblīkasy; Respublica Kazakhstan	2,669,800 km^2/1,030,816 mi^2	15,399,000	Astana	☪47%, ✝46%, ○7%	6/km^2, 15/mi^2	Khan Tängiri Shyngy 6,995 m/22,949 ft	Tenga
	Kyrgyzstan	Kyrgyz Respublikasy; Kyrgyzskaya Respublika	191,300 km^2/73,861 mi^2	5,432,000	Bishkek (Frunze)	☪75%, ✝20%, ○5%	28/km^2, 73/mi^2	Jengish Chokusu 7,439 m/24,406 ft	Som
	Maldives	Dhivehi Raajjeyge Jumhooriyyaa	300 km^2/116 mi^2	396,000	Male	☪100%	1,321/km^2, 3,413/mi^2	2.4 m/8 ft	Rufiyaa
	Mongolia	Mongol Uls	1,564,116 km^2/603,906 mi^2	3,041,000	Ulan Bator (Ulaanbaatar)	🯅50%, ✝6%, ☪4%, ○40%	2/km^2, 5/mi^2	Nayramadlin Orgil 4,374 m/14,350 ft	Tugrik
	Nepal	Saṅghīya Loktāntrik Ganatantra Nepāl	147,181 km^2/56,827 mi^2	28,563,000	Kathmandu	ॐ86%, ☸8%, ☪3%, ○3%	194/km^2, 502/mi^2	Sagarmāthā (Everest) 8,844 m/29,016 ft	Rupee
	North Korea	Chosŏn-minjujuŭi-inmin-konghwaguk	120,410 km^2/46,490 mi^2	22,665,000	Pyongyang	✝, ☸, ☯, ○	188/km^2, 488/mi^2	Paektu-san 2,744 m/9,003 ft	Won
	South Korea	Taehan-min'guk	98,190 km^2/37,911 mi^2	48,509,000	Seoul (Sŏul)	☸26%, ✝26%, ☯1%, ○47%	494/km^2, 1,280/mi^2	Halla-san 1,950 m/6,398 ft	Won
	Sri Lanka	Shrī Lamkā Prajātāntrika Samājavādī Janarajaya; Ilankai Jananāyaka Choșalichak Kutiyarachu	64,740 km^2/24,996 mi^2	21,325,000	Sri Jayewardenepura Kotte; Colombo	☸69.1%, ☪7.6%, ॐ7.1%, ✝6.2%, ○10%	329/km^2, 853/mi^2	Pidurutalagala 2,524 m/8,281 ft	Rupee
	Tajikistan	Jumhurii Tojikiston	142,700 km^2/55,097 mi^2	7,349,000	Dushanbe	☪90%, ○10%	51/km^2, 133/mi^2	Imeni Ismail Samani 7,495 m/24,590 ft	Somoni
	Turkmenistan	Türkmenistan	488,100 km^2/188,456 mi^2	4,885,000	Ashgabat (Aşgabat)	☪89%, ✝9%, ○2%	10/km^2, 26/mi^2	Gora Ayribaba 3,139 m/10,299 ft	Manat
	Uzbekistan	O'zbekiston Respublikasi	425,400 km^2/164,248 mi^2	27,606,000	Tashkent (Toshkent)	☪88%, ✝9%, ○3%	65/km^2, 168/mi^2	Adelunga Toghi 4,301 m/14,111 ft	Soum

	DEPENDENCIES AND TERRITORIES	OFFICIAL NAME	AREA	POPULATION	CAPITAL	RELIGION	POPULATION DENSITY	HIGHEST POINT	CURRENCY
	British Indian Ocean Territory (UK)	British Indian Ocean Territory	60 km^2/23 mi^2	4,000 (military personnel)	Diego Garcia	N/A	67 km^2, 174/mi^2	15 m/49 ft	Pound Sterling

the Indian Peninsula is mostly a plateau region cut by locally important rivers. Along the coasts of the Bay of Bengal and Arabian Sea are low mountain chains called, respectively, the Eastern Ghats and the Western Ghats.

Sri Lanka's central southern interior is mountainous. The foothills support tea plantations, rice paddies, and other agriculture. The Maldives are low-lying coral atolls with an average elevation of less than 1.5 meters (5 feet)—the highest point is only 2.3 meters (7½ feet). The very existence of the Maldives is endangered by rising sea levels brought on by global warming.

Most of South Asia is subject to the seasonal winds of the monsoon. In winter months, it is the dry season, with the prevailing winds from the continent. By June the pattern reverses, with moist winds from the Indian Ocean bringing heavy rains.

The slopes of the Himalayas in northeast India are the wettest places on earth. Severe flooding often takes place downstream, especially in low-lying Bangladesh. Deforestation in the mountains of northern India and Nepal has added to the severity of flooding.

CENTRAL ASIA

Central Asia is a complex world of rugged mountains, hostile deserts, lush river valleys and desert oases, high plateaus and some of the world's most enormous grassy plains. The region is bounded by the Caspian Sea and the dry lands of Southwest Asia to the west, the Himalayas and South Asia to the south, and the more humid parts of China's interior to the east. To the north are the forests of Russian Siberia.

The major countries of Central Asia are the "stans"—Tajikistan, Turkmenistan, Kyrgyzstan, Uzbekistan, and Kazakhstan—and Mongolia. China's Tibetan Plateau and desert to the northwest can also be considered to be part of Central Asia. The region is often associated with

Above Landlocked Mongolia has a varied topography, encompassing mountains, deserts, and steppes. The most mountainous regions are found mainly in the western and southwestern parts of the country.

Above The traditional Tibetan hat is designed for all seasons with the flaps turned up or down according to the temperature. It is usually made of felt, and the flaps are sometimes lined with rabbit or fox fur.

Above right Postcards to the gods, Kyoto, Japan. Shinto votive plaques (called Ema) for sale on the street leading to a Kyoto temple display an array of wishes and prayers.

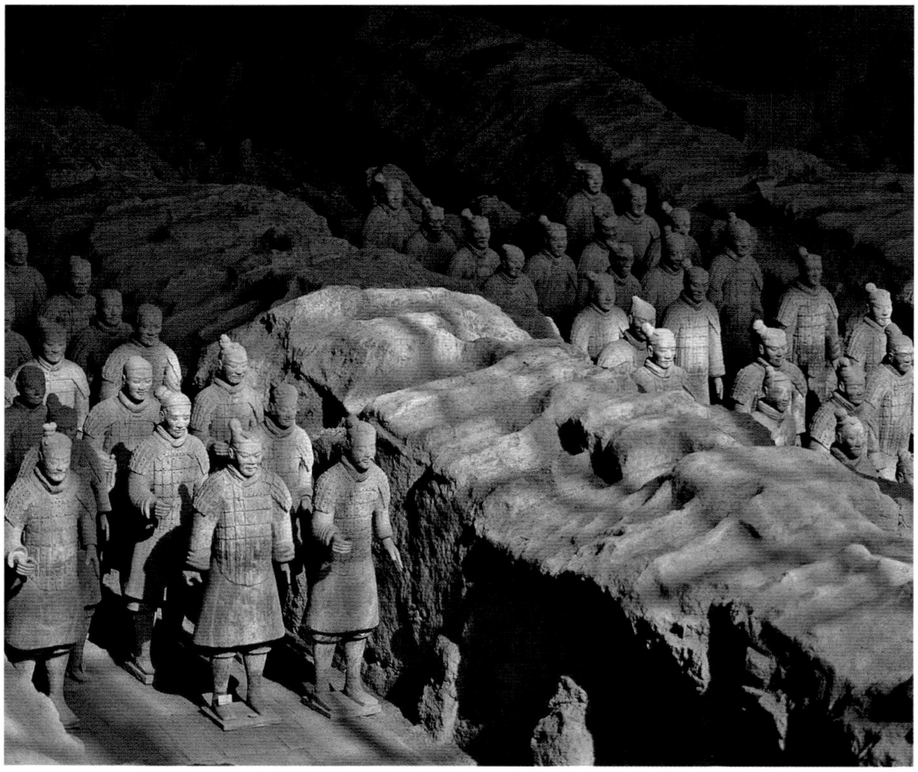

Below The "terracotta army" is a collection of about 6,000 life-size statues commissioned by Chinese Emperor Q'in Shih-huang-ti (256–206 BCE). The figures were discovered in the Shaanxi province in 1975.

the Silk Road, an ancient route of caravan trade between China, Mediterranean Europe, and the Middle East.

The Caspian Sea is the largest inland body of water in the world, having a surface area of 371,000 square kilometers (143,244 square miles). Its waters have a saline content about one-third that of the oceans. To the east, in a closed basin at the boundary between Kazakhstan and Uzbekistan, is what is left of the Aral Sea—once a prominent saline sea but now rapidly shrinking and becoming small remnant lakes because of diversion for irrigation of the river waters that feed it. Its rivers are the Amu Darya and the Syr Darya, both of which originate in the Tian Shan Mountains to the south. Major deserts in the area are the Kyzyl Kum in the doab (plain) between these two rivers; the Kara Kum to the west in Turkmenistan; and the Taklamakan across the high mountains in northwestern China. The Gobi Desert—in the border region of China and Mongolia—is the largest desert in Asia, with an area of about 1,295,000 square kilometers (500,000 square miles), while the Sistan Basin in southwestern Afghanistan and neighboring parts of Iran and Pakistan is one of the driest zones on earth. The highest point in the Tian Shan range is Jengish Chokusu, or Pobeda Peak, on the boundary between China and Kyrgyzstan. It rises to 7,439 meters (24,406 feet). Central Asia's landmark grassy steppes stretch across much of Kazakhstan, adjacent portions of Russia, and Mongolia, where the sparse population practices subsistence herding much as it has for centuries.

All of the countries of Central Asia are landlocked, but one, Uzbekistan, is one of only two doubly landlocked nations in the world, meaning that all countries that border it are also landlocked. (Liechtenstein is the other doubly landlocked country.) Uzbekistan's irrigated river valleys and desert oases—most notably the fertile Fergana Valley—produce many types of grains, cotton and are also home to vineyards. Turkmenistan also produces cotton. Turkmenistan and Kazakhstan have substantial oil and natural gas resources, and pipe their products to Russia and other parts of Europe. Central Asia is also rich in various mineral resources, including uranium and gold. Tajikistan is one of the world's main sources of aluminum.

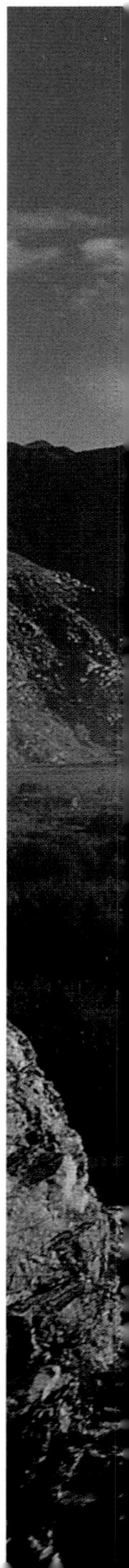

EAST ASIA

East Asia consists of China, North Korea, and South Korea on the mainland of the continent, the islands that comprise Japan, and the island of Taiwan in the western Pacific Ocean. Because China is so large and geographically diverse, its western lands such as the Tibetan Plateau and deserts in the northwest, as well as its Gobi Desert border with Mongolia, are often assigned to Central Asia. The Gulf of Tongking and the South China Sea border the region to the south, while the East China Sea lies to the east of the continent. The Sea of Japan, or East Sea, lies between Japan and the eastern side of the Korean Peninsula. There is considerable nationalistic dispute between the two Koreas and Japan about what that body of water should be named. The Yellow Sea separates the western side of the Korean Peninsula from China. The Taiwan Strait separates the island of Taiwan and the Asian continent.

The topography of East Asia is mostly mountainous and rugged, with its population concentrated in river valleys and delta lands, and along coastal plains. Except in the northern reaches, where climate is much less hospitable, all of the lower lands are exceptionally densely populated, with huge metropolitan areas: Tokyo in Japan, Seoul in South Korea, and Shanghai, Beijing, and Guangdong Province–Hong Kong in China. The longest river in East Asia (as well as in all of Asia, and the third longest in the world) is the Chang Jiang or Yangtze River (6,380 kilometers; 3,964 miles). It flows west to east through the heart of China, dividing the country into roughly equal-sized northern and southern halves, and empties into the East China Sea near Shanghai through one of the most densely settled deltas in the world. The world's biggest dam, the Three Gorges Dam, is on the Chang Jiang, and is scheduled to be the world's single largest source of electric power. The Huang He—the Yellow River—is China's second longest river at 5,464 kilometers (3,395 miles), and winds through loosely compacted loess (loamy) deposits in the north. It is muddy and prone to changes in course and flooding. Because of the flooding, it has been referred to as "China's Sorrow." Other major rivers include the Zhu Jiang or Pearl River in the south of China, the Liao and Songhua (Sungari) rivers in the heavily industrial northeast, and the Heilong Jiang, or Amur River, along China's border with Russia's Siberia. In the southwest of China, near the city of Guilin, is a spectacular landscape of karst (limestone) hills.

The four main islands of Japan—Hokkaido in the north, Honshu in the center, and Shikoku and Kyushu in the south—are all mountainous. At 3,776 meters (12,388 feet), Mt Fuji is the country's highest peak. This exceptionally symmetrical volcanic cone is located on the Pacific Ocean side of the island of Honshu, near Tokyo. Japan's major islands and much of the rest of East Asia are highly vulnerable to earthquakes.

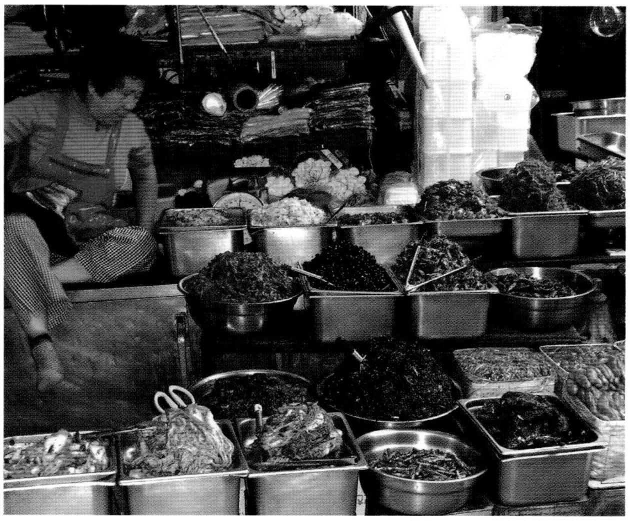

Left A vendor sells kimchi at a street market in Seoul, South Korea. Kimchi is a side dish made of seasoned pickled cabbage or other vegetables, and is a staple of the Korean diet.

Below Tibetan village in the Himalayas. Tibet is known as the "roof of the world" because most parts of the country are higher than 3,000 meters (9,843 feet). Many visitors experience altitude sickness due to lack of oxygen.

SOUTHEAST ASIA

Southeast Asia is comprised of eleven countries, including three that are quite small—Singapore, Brunei, and Timor-Leste (East Timor). The countries are situated on groups of islands and peninsulas at the southeastern edge of the Eurasian landmass. Southeast Asia lies between the Indian and Pacific oceans, and is bordered on the north by rugged terrain in southern China. Australia lies to the south across the Timor Sea and the Arafura Sea.

The countries of peninsular Southeast Asia consist of Myanmar, Thailand, Malaysia, Vietnam, Cambodia, and Laos. Malaysia is divided in two—the economic center of the country is situated in the southern region of the Malay Peninsula, while East Malaysia consists of two provinces on the north of the island of Borneo. Brunei is an enclave nation also in northern Borneo, while Singapore is an island nation off the tip of the Malay Peninsula. Other island countries in Southeast Asia are Philippines, in the northeastern part of the region lying between the Philippine Sea and the South China Sea, and Indonesia, a large archipelago of 17,508 islands that stretches some 4,820 kilometers (3,000 miles) west to east, from the northwestern tip of Sumatra to the center of New Guinea. East Timor, the eastern part of the island of Timor, is part of that archipelago. While the western part of New Guinea is a province of Indonesia, the eastern half of the island belongs to Papua New Guinea, a country more commonly associated with Oceania than with Southeast Asia. Laos is the only country of Southeast Asia that is landlocked.

Right Members of a Vietnamese hill tribe work in a rice paddy. More than 50 recognized ethnic minorities live in the mountainous regions of Vietnam.

Above Women carry offerings to the deities in this Balinese religious procession. The procession is an integral part of Balinese life, and often starts from a temple and ends at the sea or other sacred body of water.

Physical Geography

The geography of mainland Southeast Asia is one of alternating mountain terrain and other highlands with the fertile valleys of large rivers. The mountains are home to ethnic minorities and so-called hill tribes, while the valleys are the heartlands of nation-states and are dominated by national majority populations. The Burmese peoples of Myanmar (Burma) are concentrated in the large valley of the Ayeyarwady River and its enormous delta. The core of Thailand is the Chao Phraya River and its valley, and is home to the Thai people, while in Cambodia the majority Khmer population lives in lowlands associated with the Mekong River and a connected lake, Tonle Sap. In Vietnam, the population is concentrated in the Red River valley and delta in the north and in the delta region of the Mekong in the south near Ho Chi Minh City (Saigon).

The most rugged mountains of mainland Southeast Asia are in northwestern Myanmar near the boundaries with Bangladesh and India, and in the Golden Triangle region where northern Myanmar, Thailand, and Laos share boundaries. The Mekong is Southeast Asia's longest river. Its 4,350 kilometer- (2,703 mile-) course begins in China, where it is called the Lancang, and then flows through or along the borders of Myanmar, Thailand, Laos, and Cambodia before emptying into the South China Sea off Vietnam. Dam construction across the upper reaches of the river in China has altered water flow for downriver countries, bringing negative consequences for livelihoods and environmental quality. Habitats of large species such as the Mekong dolphins and manatees are also threatened.

The islands of Southeast Asia are mostly volcanic and are characterized by numerous spectacular volcanic cones; periodic eruptions; fertile, well-watered valleys; and dense populations. The Indonesian island of Java and the center of the large Philippine island of Luzon in particular share these features. Other parts of maritime Southeast Asia—including Indonesia's Sumatra, most

	COUNTRIES	OFFICIAL NAME	AREA	POPULATION	CAPITAL	RELIGION	POPULATION DENSITY	HIGHEST POINT	CURRENCY
	Brunei	Brunei Darussalam; Negara Brunei Darussalam	5,270 km^2/2,035 mi^2	388,000	Bandar Seri Begawan	☪67%, ☸13%, ✝10%, ○10%	74/km^2, 191/mi^2	Bukit Pagon 1,850 m/6,070 ft	Dollar
	Cambodia	Preăhréachéanachâkr Kâmpŭchéa	176,520 km^2/68,155 mi^2	14,494,000	Phnom Penh (Phnum Pénh)	☸95%, ○5%	82/km^2, 213/mi^2	Phnum Aôral 1,810 m/5,938 ft	Riel
	Indonesia	Republik Indonesia	1,826,440 km^2/705,192 mi^2	240,271,000	Jakarta	☪86.1%, ✝8.7%, ॐ1.8%, ☸3.4%	131/km^2, 341/mi^2	Puncak Jaya 5,030 m/16,503 ft	Rupiah
	Laos	Sathalanalat Paxathipatai Paxaxôn Lao	230,800 km^2/89,112 mi^2	6,835,000	Vientiane (Viangchan)	☸65%, 🚶32.9%, ✝1.3%, ○0.8%	30/km^2, 77/mi^2	Phou Bia 2,817 m/9,242 ft	Kip
	Malaysia	Malaysia	328,550 km^2/126,854 mi^2	25,716,000	Kuala Lumpur	☪60.4%, ☸19.2%, ✝9.1%, ॐ6.3%, ☯2.6%, ○2.4%	78/km^2, 203/mi^2	Kinabalu 4,100 m/13,451 ft	Ringgit
	Myanmar	Pyidaungzu Myanma Naingngandaw	657,740 km^2/253,955 mi^2	48,138,000	Rangoon (Yangon), Naypyidaw	☸89%, ✝4%, ☪4%, ○3%	73/km^2, 189/mi^2	Hkakabo Razi 5,881 m/19,295 ft	Kyat
	Philippines	Republika ng Pilipinas; Republic of the Philippines	298,170 km^2/115,124 mi^2	97,977,000	Manila	✝88.2%, ☪5%, ○6.8%	329/km^2, 851/mi^2	Apo Mountain 2,954 m/9,692 ft	Peso
	Singapore	Republic of Singapore; Republik Singapura	683 km^2/264 mi^2	4,657,000	Singapore	☸42.5%, ☪14.9%, ✝14.6%, ☯8.5%, ॐ4%, ○15.5%	6,819/km^2, 17,640/mi^2	Bukit Timah 166 m/545 ft	Dollar
	Thailand	Ratcha Anachak Thai	511,770 km^2/197,596 mi^2	65,905,000	Bangkok (Krung Thep)	☸94.6%, ☪4.6%, ✝0.8%	129/km^2, 334/mi^2	Doi Inthanon 2,576 m/8,451 ft	Baht
	Timor-Leste	Repúblika Demokrátika Timor Lorosa'e; República Democrática de Timor-Leste	15,007 km^2/5,794 mi^2	1,131,000	Dili	✝99%, ☪1%	75/km^2, 195/mi^2	Foho Tatamailau 2,963 m/9,721 ft	US dollar
	Vietnam	Công Hòa Xã Hội Chủ Nghĩa Việt Nam	325,360 km^2/125,622 mi^2	86,967,000	Hanoi (Hà Nội)	☸70%, ○30%	267/km^2, 692/mi^2	Fan Si Pan 3,144 m/10,315 ft	Dong

DEPENDENCIES AND TERRITORIES	OFFICIAL NAME	AREA	POPULATION	CAPITAL	RELIGION	POPULATION DENSITY	HIGHEST POINT	CURRENCY
Paracel Islands (disputed)	Paracel Islands	N/A	N/A	—	N/A	N/A	14 m/46 ft	—
Spratly Islands (disputed)	Spratly Islands	N/A	N/A	—	N/A	N/A	4 m/13 ft	—

Above Fishing boats, Vietnam. Fishing is a viable industry in Vietnam due to the country's extensive system of lakes and rivers, as well as its lengthy coastline.

of Borneo, Indonesia's province on New Guinea, and the island of Mindanao in southern Philippines—are rugged and lightly settled frontier zones.

Natural Resources

The region has dense stands of tropical rainforests, countless endemic species of flora and fauna, and many distinctive cultures and languages, all of which are under increasing threat from frontier expansion and resource exploitation. Timber, crude oil, and various minerals are important products of the Southeast Asian islands. Indonesia is especially rich in natural resources. The mountain slopes in northern and central Luzon in Philippines and on Indonesia's Bali are spectacularly terraced for paddy fields and other crops. Considerable land has been converted in Indonesia and other countries to plantation agriculture. The dry-season burning of jungle to enable expansion of farmlands has caused considerable air pollution over a wide area of Southeast Asia. The American-owned Grasberg Mine in the high mountains of eastern Indonesia in western New Guinea is the world's largest gold mine and third largest copper mine.

ATLANTIC OCEAN
NORWEGIAN SEA
NORTH SEA
Greenland
(Kalaallit Nunaat)
(Denmark)
ICELAND
REYKJAVIK
NORWAY
SWEDEN
FINLAND
RUSSIA
KAZAKHSTAN
UZBEKISTAN
TURKMENISTAN
KYRGYZSTAN
TAJIKISTAN
AFGHANISTAN
PAKISTAN
INDIA
IRAN
IRAQ
SYRIA
TURKEY
JORDAN
SAUDI ARABIA
ARABIAN PENINSULA
YEMEN
OMAN
UNITED ARAB EMIRATES
KUWAIT
QATAR
BAHRAIN
EGYPT
LIBYA
ALGERIA
MOROCCO
TUNISIA
MAURITANIA
MALI
NIGER
CHAD
SUDAN
S A H A R A
NIGERIA
CAMEROON
CENTRAL AFRICAN REPUBLIC
CONGO
DEMOCRATIC REPUBLIC OF CONGO
GABON
ANGOLA
NAMIBIA
BOTSWANA
ZAMBIA
ZIMBABWE
MOZAMBIQUE
MALAWI
TANZANIA
KENYA
UGANDA
RWANDA
BURUNDI
ETHIOPIA
ERITREA
DJIBOUTI
SOMALIA
SEYCHELLES
COMOROS
MALDIVES
MEDITERRANEAN SEA
BLACK SEA
CASPIAN SEA
RED SEA
ARABIAN SEA
Gulf of Aden
Gulf of Guinea
INDIAN
British Indian Ocean Territory
(UK)
Lakshadweep
(Laccadive Islands)
(India)
Barents Sea
Gulf of Bothnia
Bay of Biscay
MOSKVA
(MOSCOW)
Sankt-Peterburg
ANKARA
BAGHDAD
TEHRĀN
AR RIYĀḌ
(RIYADH)
AL QĀHIRAH
(CAIRO)
ṢAN'Ā'
MUQDISHO
(MOGADISHU)
NAIROBI
DAR ES SALAAM
ADIS ABEBA
(ADDIS ABABA)
AL KHARṬŪM
(KHARTOUM)
KINSHASA
LUANDA
LONDON
PARIS
MADRID
ROMA
BERLIN
KARACHI
MUMBAI
(BOMBAY)
DELHI
COLOMBO
MALE

1:37,500,000

Lambert Azimuthal Equal Area Projection

0 500 1000 1500 2000 kilometers

0 250 500 750 1000 miles

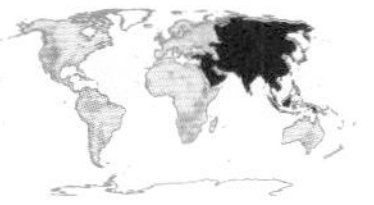

ASIA POLITICAL

OCEAN
FEDERATION
SIBIR' (SIBERIA)
Laptev Sea
Bering Strait
Chukchi Sea
Bering Sea
Aleutian Islands
ALASKA (USA)
HAWAII (USA)
Honolulu
Kauai
Oahu
Molokai
Maui
Hawai'i
SEA OF OKHOTSK
Sakhalin
Poluostrov Kamchatka
Petropavlovsk-Kamchatskiy
Magadan
Yakutsk
Tiksi
Saskylakh
Olenek
Zhigansk
Sangar
Nyurba
Lensk
Olekminsk
Aldan
Neryungri
Tynda
Bodaybo
Ust'-Ilimsk
Kirensk
Ust'-Kut
Severobaykal'sk
Taksimo
Skovorodino
Svobodnyy
Blagoveshchensk
Khabarovsk
Komsomol'sk-na-Amure
Nikolayevsk-na-Amure
Chumikan
Okha
Yuzhno-Sakhalinsk
Bratsk
Kansk
Achinsk
Krasnoyarsk
Lesosibirsk
Noginsk
Bakhta
Tura
Vorogovo
Nizhneudinsk
Tulun
Cheremkhovo
Angarsk
Irkutsk
Ulan-Ude
Chita
Sretensk
Mogocha
Krasnokamensk
Novokuznetsk
Abakan
Biysk
Kyzyl
Kyakhta
Darhan-Uul
ULAANBAATAR (ULAN BATOR)
Choybalsan
Manzhouli
Hulun Buir
Heihe
Qiqihar
Suihua
Harbin
Jixi
Jiamusi
Hegang
Shuangyashan
Birobidzhan
Mudanjiang
Jilin
Siping
Changchun
Baicheng
Shenyang
Fushun
Benxi
Anshan
Fuxin
Vladivostok
Ch'ongjin
NORTH KOREA
P'YONGYANG
Wonsan
SOUTH KOREA
SOUL (SEOUL)
Inch'on
Taegu
Pusan
Kwangju
SEA OF JAPAN (EAST SEA)
JAPAN
Sapporo
Hokkaido
Asahikawa
Kitami
Kushiro
Hakodate
Aomori
Hachinohe
Morioka
Akita
Sendai
Niigata
Honshu
Koriyama
Iwaki
Mito
TOKYO
Yokohama
Shizuoka
Nagoya
Nagano
Fukui
Kyoto
Osaka
Kobe
Okayama
Hiroshima
Shikoku
Fukuoka
Kumamoto
Miyazaki
Kagoshima
Nagasaki
Kyushu
Tanega-shima
MONGOLIA
Ulaangom
Ölgiy
Hovd
Uliastay
Altay
Bayanhongor
Saynshand
Dalandzadgad
Mörön
Bulgan
GOBI
CHINA
BEIJING (PEKING)
Zhangjiakou
Hohhot
Baotou
Datong
Baoding
Tianjin
Tangshan
Dalian
Yantai
Qingdao
Jinan
Shijiazhuang
Taiyuan
Handan
Anyang
Zhengzhou
Xuzhou
Yancheng
Yinchuan
Wuzhong
Lanzhou
Xi'ning
Linxia
Changzhi
Luoyang
Xi'an
Bengbu
Nanjing
Wuxi
SHANGHAI
Suzhou
Huainan
Hefei
Wuhan
Hangzhou
Ningbo
Wenzhou
Quzhou
Xinyang
Shiyan
Hanzhong
Guangyuan
Mianyang
Deyang
Chengdu
Nanchong
Chongqing
Yueyang
Nanchang
Changde
Changsha
Zhuzhou
Xiangtan
Hengyang
Fuzhou
T'aipei
T'aichung
Taiwan
T'aitung
Kaohsiung
Quanzhou
Zhangzhou
Shantou
Yongzhou
Zigong
Zunyi
Leshan
Guiyang
Guilin
Anshun
Lupanshui
Xingyi
Qujing
Kunming
Liuzhou
Shaoguan
Guangzhou
Shenzhen
Hong Kong
Jiangmen
Yulin
Nanning
Maoming
Zhanjiang
Haikou
Hainan
Beihai
Wulumuqi
Shihezi
Kelamayi
Turpan
Yumen
Jiayuguan
Jinchang
Ruoqiang
Altun Shan
Hob Xil Shan
Tanggula Shan
Nyainqêntanglha Shan
Nyima
Nagqu
Qamdo
Darlag
Nyingchi
Dêqên
Dali
Baoshan
Gejiu
Xigazê
THIMPHU
BHUTAN
NEPAL
KATHMANDU
Mt Everest 8850
Dibrugarh
Guwahati
Shiliguri
BANGLADESH
DHAKA (DACCA)
Khulna
Chittagong
Haora
Kolkata (Calcutta)
Mouths of the Ganges
Bhubaneshwar
Visakhapatnam
BAY OF BENGAL
MYANMAR
Mandalay
NAYPYIDAW
YANGON (RANGOON)
Bassein
Mawlamyine
Tavoy
Andaman Islands (India)
Port Blair
ANDAMAN SEA
Nicobar Islands (India)
HÀ NÔI
Hai Phong
Thanh Hoa
Vinh
G. of Tonkin
LAOS
VIANGCHAN (VIENTIANE)
Udon Thani
Chiang Mai
Phitsanulok
THAILAND
KRUNG THEP (BANGKOK)
Nakhon Ratchasima
Pakxé
Huê
Da Nang
Quang Ngai
VIETNAM
Quy Nhon
Nha Trang
CAMBODIA
PHNUM PÉNH
Kampong Cham
Biên Hòa
Hô Chí Minh
Cân Tho
Rach Gia
Chon Buri
Batdambang
Gulf of Thailand
Surat Thani
Nakhon Si Thammarat
Phuket
Songkhla
Hat Yai
Alor Setar
George Town
Kota Bahru
Kuala Terengganu
Taiping
Ipoh
MALAYSIA
Kuantan
KUALA LUMPUR
Klang
Johor Bahru
SINGAPORE
Medan
Banda Aceh
Binjai
Pematangsiantar
Simeulue
Nias
Pekanbaru
Padang
Siberut
Sumatera
Jambi
Palembang
Bengkulu
Bandar Lampung
JAKARTA
Bandung
Semarang
Yogyakarta
Surakarta
Surabaya
Malang
Jawa
LAUT JAWA
Bangka
Belitung
Banjarmasin
Pontianak
Borneo
Balikpapan
Samarinda
Martapura
Kuching
Sibu
Miri
BRUNEI
BANDAR SERI BEGAWAN
Kota Kinabalu
Sandakan
Tawau
Tarakan
Tanjungredeb
CELEBES SEA
Sulawesi
Palu
Gorontalo
Kendari
Parepare
Makassar
LAUT FLORES
Flores
Sumbawa
Bima
Sumba
Kupang
Timor
DILI
TIMOR-LESTE (EAST TIMOR)
LAUT BANDA
Ambon
Buru
Seram
Ternate
Halmahera
Sorong
Manokwari
Biak
Jayapura
New Guinea
INDONESIA
Kepulauan Aru
Kepulauan Tanimbar
Pulau Dolak
Merauke
PAPUA NEW GUINEA
Gulf of Papua
PORT MORESBY
Popondetta
Lae
New Britain
New Ireland
Bougainville
SOLOMON ISLANDS
HONIARA
SOLOMON SEA
CORAL SEA
Torres Strait
Cape York
Bamaga
Weipa
Aurukun
Coen
Lockhart River
Kowanyama
Cooktown
Cairns
Innisfail
Atherton
Ingham
Townsville
Mornington I.
Gulf of Carpentaria
Groote Eylandt
Nhulunbuy
Galiwinku
Maningrida
Minjilang
Melville Island
Darwin
Jabiru
Katherine
Adelaide River
Mataranka
Ngukurr
Joseph Bonaparte Gulf
AUSTRALIA
SOUTH CHINA SEA
Paracel Islands (disputed)
Spratly Islands (disputed)
Palawan
SULU SEA
PHILIPPINES
MANILA
Quezon City
Luzon
Baguio
Laoag
Tuguegarao
Babuyan Islands
Dagupan
Tarlac
Olongapo
Batangas
Lucena
Legazpi
Mindoro
Panay
Samar
Ormoc
Iloilo
Bacolod
Cebu
Negros
Surigao
Butuan
Iligan
Cagayan de Oro
Mindanao
Davao
Pagadian
Zamboanga
Mount Apo 2954
General Santos
PHILIPPINE SEA
EAST CHINA SEA
Okinawa
Naha
Yellow Sea
Cheju-do
PACIFIC OCEAN
Kazan Retto (Japan)
Northern Mariana Islands (USA)
Saipan
Tinian
Capitol Hill
Guam (USA)
Hagåtña
Wake Island (USA)
Caroline Islands
FEDERATED STATES OF MICRONESIA
PALIKIR
Pohnpei
Chuuk
Mortlock Islands
MARSHALL ISLANDS
MELEKEOK
PALAU
MELANESIA
Kuril'skiye Ostrova
Iturup
Rat Islands
Near Is
Komandorskiye Ostrova
International Date Line
Tropic of Cancer
Equator
Tropic of Capricorn
INDIAN OCEAN

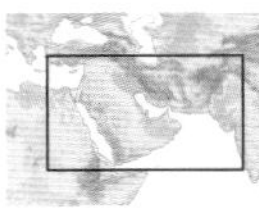

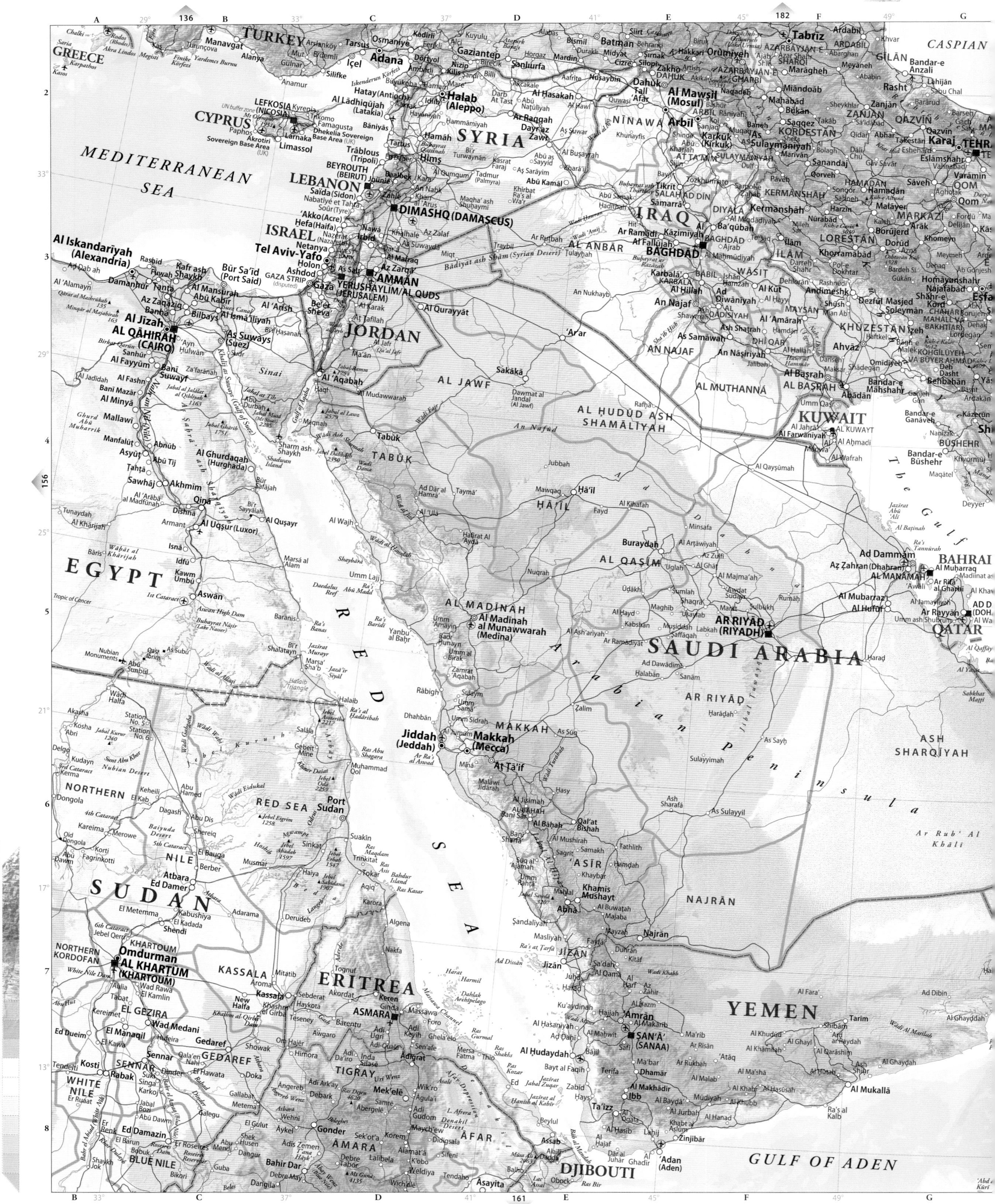

TURKEY
SYRIA
IRAQ
CYPRUS
LEBANON
ISRAEL
JORDAN
EGYPT
SUDAN
ERITREA
SAUDI ARABIA
KUWAIT
YEMEN
DJIBOUTI
QATAR
BAHRAIN
GREECE
MEDITERRANEAN SEA
RED SEA
GULF OF ADEN
CASPIAN
The Gulf
Arabian Peninsula
Ar Rub' Al Khālī
Bādiyat ash Shām (Syrian Desert)
An Nafūd
Sinai
Nubian Desert
LEFKOSIA (NICOSIA)
BEYROUTH (BEIRUT)
DIMASHQ (DAMASCUS)
'AMMAN
YERUSHALAYIM/AL QUDS (JERUSALEM)
Tel Aviv-Yafo
GAZA STRIP (disputed)
AL QĀHIRAH (CAIRO)
Al Iskandarīyah (Alexandria)
Būr Sa'īd (Port Said)
As Suways (Suez)
Al Jīzah
Aswān
Al Uqşur (Luxor)
BAGHDĀD
Al Mawşil (Mosul)
Arbīl
Karkūk (Kirkuk)
Al Başrah
Ḩalab (Aleppo)
Ḩimş
Ḩamāh
Adana
Gaziantep
Şanlıurfa
Tabrīz
Kermānshāh
Hamadān
Qom
Karaj
Ahvāz
AL KUWAYT
AR RIYĀḐ (RIYADH)
Jiddah (Jeddah)
Makkah (Mecca)
Al Madīnah al Munawwarah (Medina)
At Ṭā'if
Ad Dammām
AL MANĀMAH
AD DAWḨAH (DOHA)
SAN'Ā' (SANAA)
'Adan (Aden)
Al Ḩudaydah
Al Mukallā
Ta'izz
ASMARA
Massawa
Port Sudan
Kassala
Omdurman
AL KHARṬŪM (KHARTOUM)
Wad Medani
Gonder
Mek'ele
Bahir Dar
Asayita
Tropic of Cancer

1:10,320,000
Conic Equidistant Projection

0 100 200 300 400 500 kilometers
0 50 100 150 200 250 300 miles

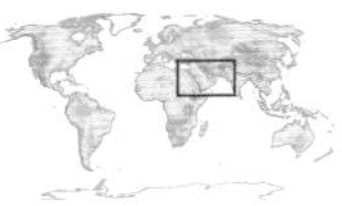

MIDDLE EAST

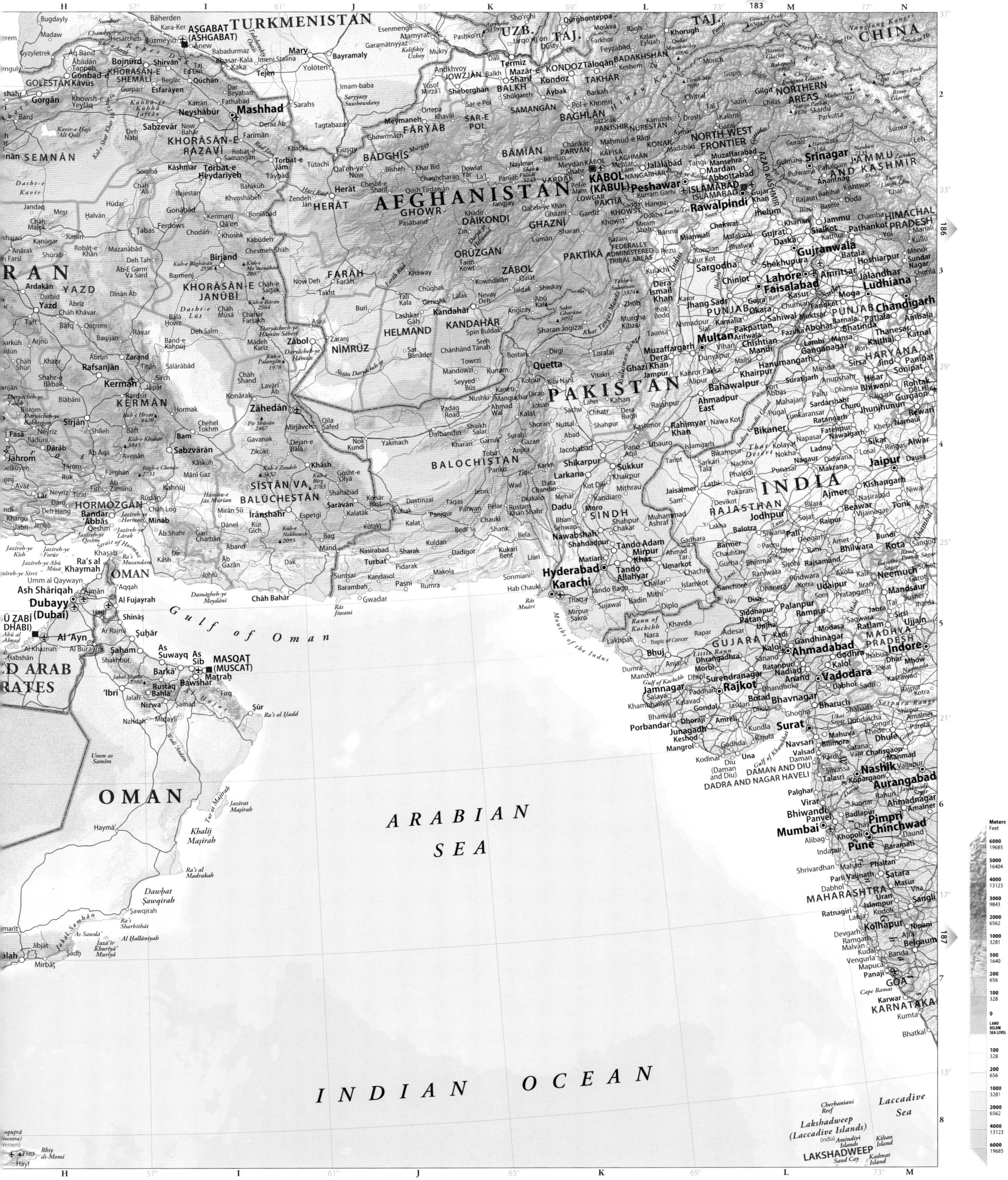

TURKMENISTAN
AFGHANISTAN
PAKISTAN
INDIA
OMAN
IRAN
CHINA
UZB.
TAJ.
ARABIAN SEA
INDIAN OCEAN
Gulf of Oman
ASGABAT (ASHGABAT)
KĀBOL (KABUL)
ISLAMABAD
MASQAT (MUSCAT)
Mashhad
Herāt
Kandahār
Quetta
Peshawar
Rawalpindi
Lahore
Faisalabad
Multan
Hyderabad
Karachi
Srinagar
Amritsar
Ludhiana
Chandigarh
Jaipur
Jodhpur
Ahmadabad
Vadodara
Surat
Rajkot
Mumbai
Pune
Nashik
Aurangabad
Indore
Dubayy (Dubai)
Zāhedān
Kermān
SINDH
PUNJAB
BALOCHISTAN
GUJARAT
RAJASTHAN
MAHARASHTRA
HARYANA
GOA
KARNATAKA
JAMMU AND KASHMIR
NORTH-WEST FRONTIER
HIMACHAL PRADESH
MADHYA PRADESH
DAMAN AND DIU
DADRA AND NAGAR HAVELI
LAKSHADWEEP
Lakshadweep (Laccadive Islands)
Laccadive Sea
Meters
Feet
6000
19685
5000
16404
4000
13123
3000
9843
2000
6562
1000
3281
500
1640
200
656
100
328
0
LAND BELOW SEA LEVEL
183
186
187

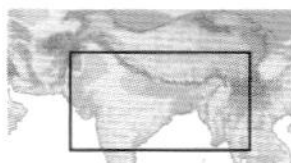

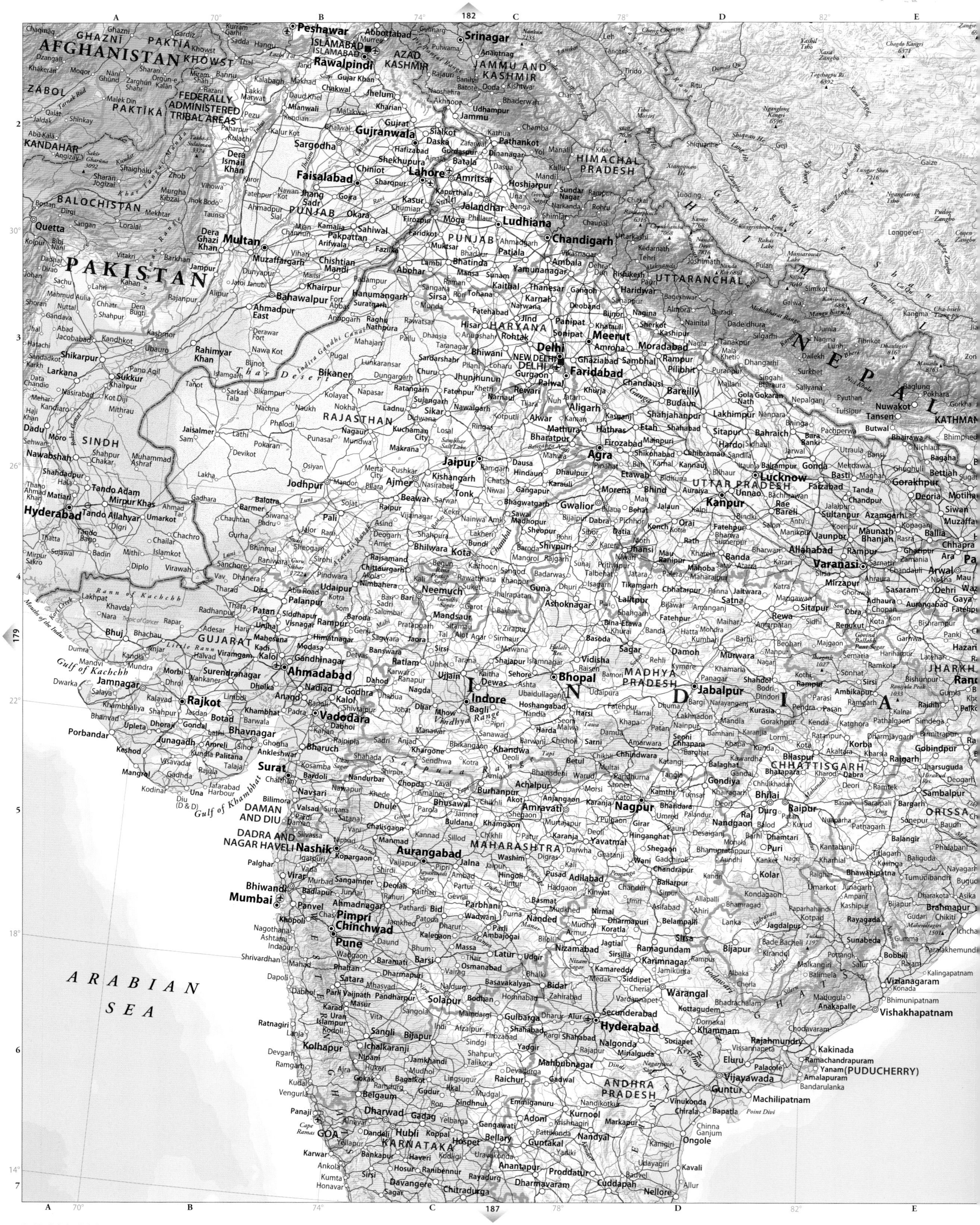

182
187
179
A
B
C
D
E
70°
74°
78°
82°
30°
26°
22°
18°
14°
AFGHANISTAN
PAKISTAN
INDIA
NEPAL
ARABIAN SEA
Gulf of Kachchh
Gulf of Khambhat
Rann of Kachchh
Thar Desert
Tropic of Cancer
Mouths of the Indus
ISLAMABAD
Rawalpindi
Peshawar
Srinagar
JAMMU AND KASHMIR
AZAD KASHMIR
FEDERALLY ADMINISTERED TRIBAL AREAS
KHOWST
PAKTIA
PAKTIKA
ZABOL
KANDAHAR
BALOCHISTAN
PUNJAB
SINDH
HIMACHAL PRADESH
UTTARANCHAL
HARYANA
RAJASTHAN
UTTAR PRADESH
GUJARAT
MADHYA PRADESH
MAHARASHTRA
CHHATTISGARH
ORISSA
ANDHRA PRADESH
KARNATAKA
GOA
DAMAN AND DIU
DADRA AND NAGAR HAVELI
JHARKHAND
Lahore
Faisalabad
Gujranwala
Multan
Quetta
Hyderabad
Delhi
NEW DELHI
Faridabad
Agra
Meerut
Jaipur
Lucknow
Kanpur
Varanasi
Allahabad
Ahmadabad
Surat
Vadodara
Rajkot
Indore
Bhopal
Jabalpur
Nagpur
Nashik
Mumbai
Pune
Pimpri Chinchwad
Aurangabad
Hyderabad
Vishakhapatnam
Vijayawada
Chandigarh
Ludhiana
Amritsar
Jalandhar
Kathmandu

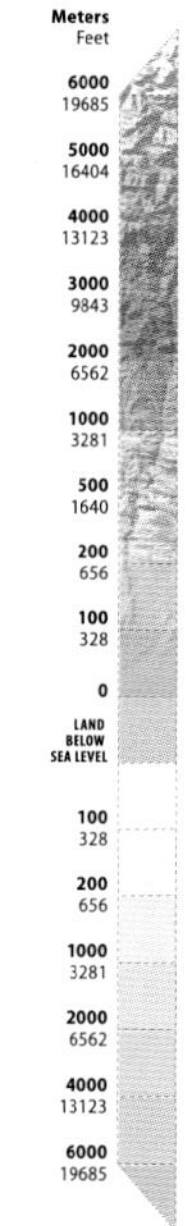

Meters
Feet
6000
19685
5000
16404
4000
13123
3000
9843
2000
6562
1000
3281
500
1640
200
656
100
328
0
LAND BELOW SEA LEVEL

1:7,880,000

Conic Equidistant Projection

0 50 100 150 200 250 300 kilometers

0 25 50 75 100 125 150 miles

WESTERN CENTRAL ASIA

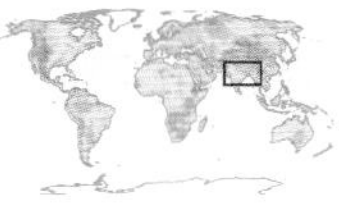

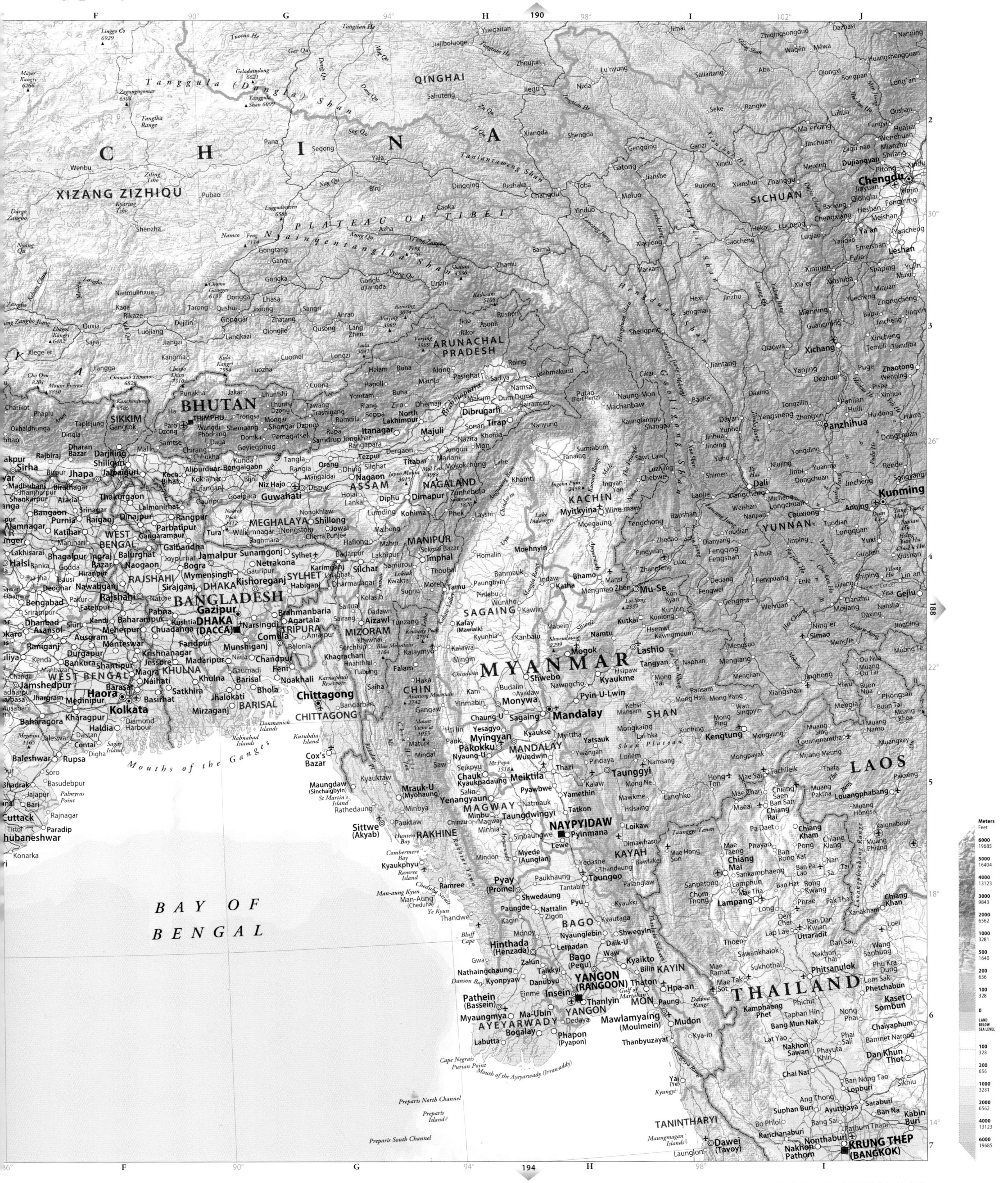
CHINA
XIZANG ZIZHIQU
QINGHAI
SICHUAN
YUNNAN
PLATEAU OF TIBET
Tanggula (Dangla) Shan
Nyainqentanglha Shan
Taniantaweng Shan
Hengduan Shan
Gaoligong Shan
Chengdu
Kunming
Lhasa
BHUTAN
THIMPHU
SIKKIM
ARUNACHAL PRADESH
ASSAM
NAGALAND
MEGHALAYA
MANIPUR
MIZORAM
TRIPURA
WEST BENGAL
BANGLADESH
DHAKA (DACCA)
Chittagong
Kolkata
Haora
Mouths of the Ganges
BAY OF BENGAL
MYANMAR
KACHIN
SAGAING
CHIN
MANDALAY
Mandalay
SHAN
Shan Plateau
MAGWAY
RAKHINE
NAYPYIDAW
KAYAH
BAGO
KAYIN
MON
YANGON
YANGON (RANGOON)
AYEYARWADY
TANINTHARYI
Mouth of the Ayeyarwady (Irrawaddy)
LAOS
THAILAND
KRUNG THEP (BANGKOK)
Meters
Feet
LAND BELOW SEA LEVEL

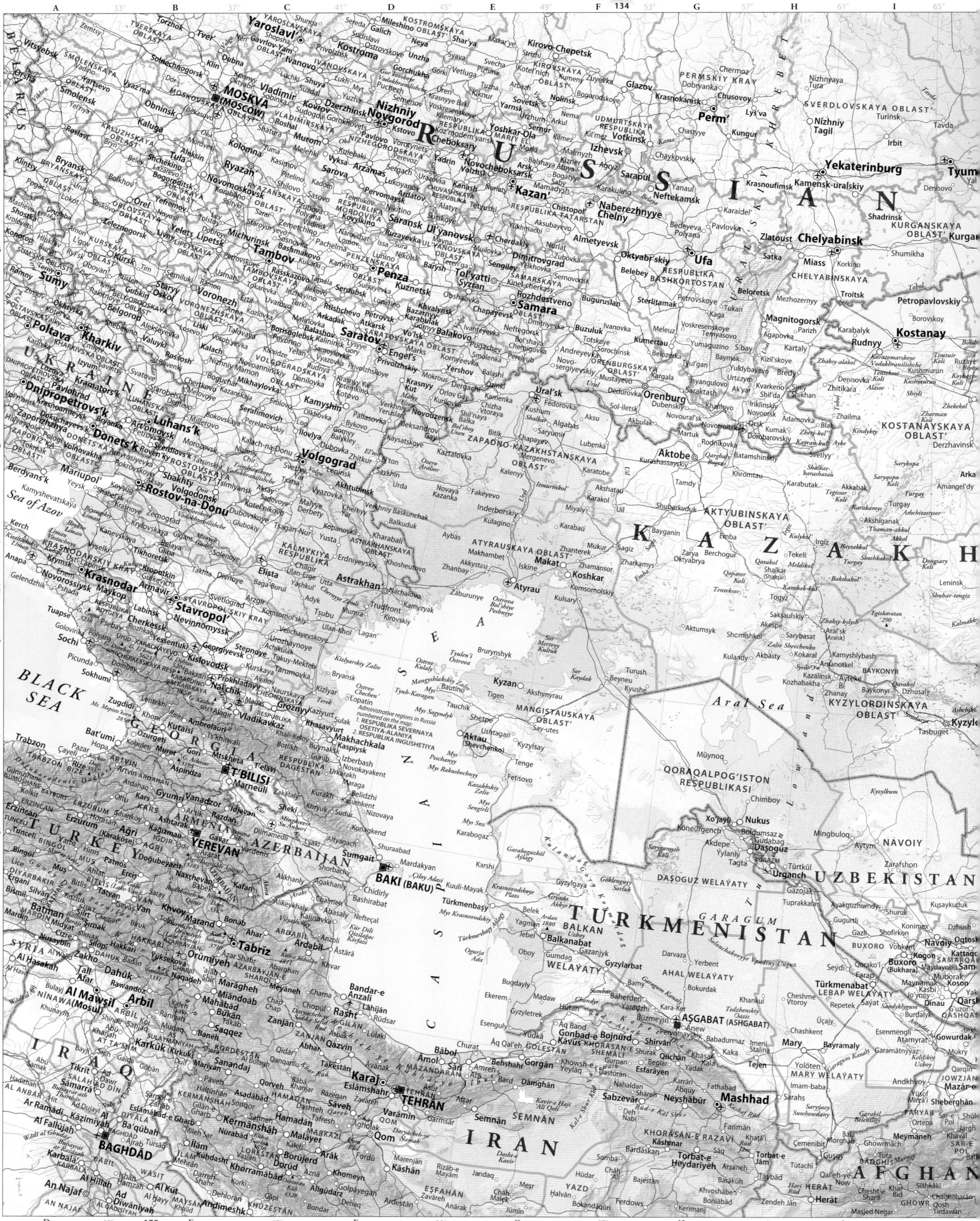
A
B
C
D
E
F
G
H
I
33°
37°
41°
45°
49°
53°
57°
61°
65°
134
136
178
2
3
4
5
6
7
8
RUSSIAN
KAZAKH
UKRAINE
BELARUS
GEORGIA
ARMENIA
AZERBAIJAN
TURKEY
IRAQ
IRAN
TURKMENISTAN
UZBEKISTAN
AFGHAN
BLACK SEA
Sea of Azov
CASPIAN SEA
Aral Sea
GARAGUM
MOSKVA (MOSCOW)
Yaroslavl'
Kostroma
Ivanovo
Vladimir
Tver'
Smolensk
Kaluga
Tula
Ryazan'
Nizhniy Novgorod
Cheboksary
Kazan'
Perm'
Yekaterinburg
Chelyabinsk
Ufa
Samara
Penza
Tambov
Lipetsk
Voronezh
Kursk
Belgorod
Kharkiv
Poltava
Sumy
Dnipropetrovs'k
Donets'k
Luhans'k
Mariupol'
Rostov-na-Donu
Volgograd
Saratov
Engel's
Orenburg
Ural'sk
Aktobe
Magnitogorsk
Kostanay
Kurgan
Astrakhan'
Atyrau
Elista
Krasnodar
Stavropol'
Sochi
Kutaisi
T'BILISI
YEREVAN
BAKI (BAKU)
Makhachkala
Groznyy
Vladikavkaz
Nal'chik
Aktau (Shevchenko)
Nukus
Dasoguz
Urganch
AŞGABAT (ASHGABAT)
Mashhad
Mary
Türkmenabat
Buxoro (Bukhara)
TEHRAN
Karaj
Qom
Tabriz
Orūmīyeh
Rasht
Kermānshāh
Hamadān
Arbīl
Al Mawṣil (Mosul)
Kirkūk
BAGHDĀD
Al Ḥillah
An Najaf
Herāt
Sumgait
Balkanabat
Türkmenbaşy
Karshi
Kyzylorda
Izhevsk
Naberezhnyye Chelny
Ul'yanovsk
Tol'yatti
Syzran'
Krasnodarskiy Kray
Stavropol'skiy Kray
ATYRAUSKAYA OBLAST'
AKTYUBINSKAYA OBLAST'
MANGISTAUSKAYA OBLAST'
KOSTANAYSKAYA OBLAST'
KYZYLORDINSKAYA OBLAST'
QORAQALPOG'ISTON RESPUBLIKASI
DAŞOGUZ WELAÝATY
AHAL WELAÝATY
BALKAN WELAÝATY
LEBAP WELAÝATY
MARY WELAÝATY
NAVOIY
KHORASAN-E RAZAVI
MĀZANDARĀN
SEMNĀN
ESFAHĀN
YAZD

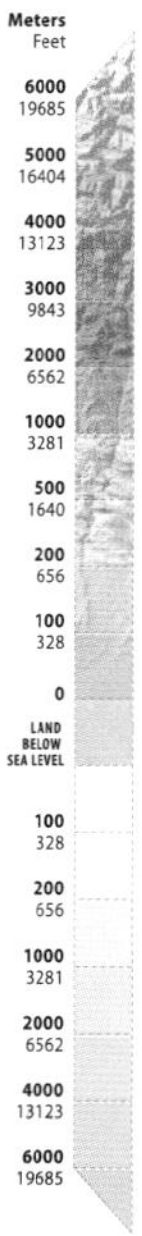
Meters
Feet
6000
19685
5000
16404
4000
13123
3000
9843
2000
6562
1000
3281
500
1640
200
656
100
328
0
LAND BELOW SEA LEVEL
100
328
200
656
1000
3281
2000
6562
4000
13123
6000
19685

1:10,320,000

Conic Equidistant Projection

0 100 200 300 400 500 kilometers

0 50 100 150 200 250 300 miles

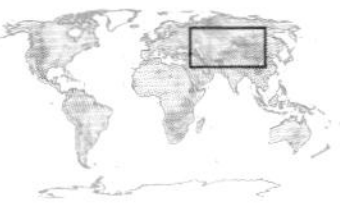

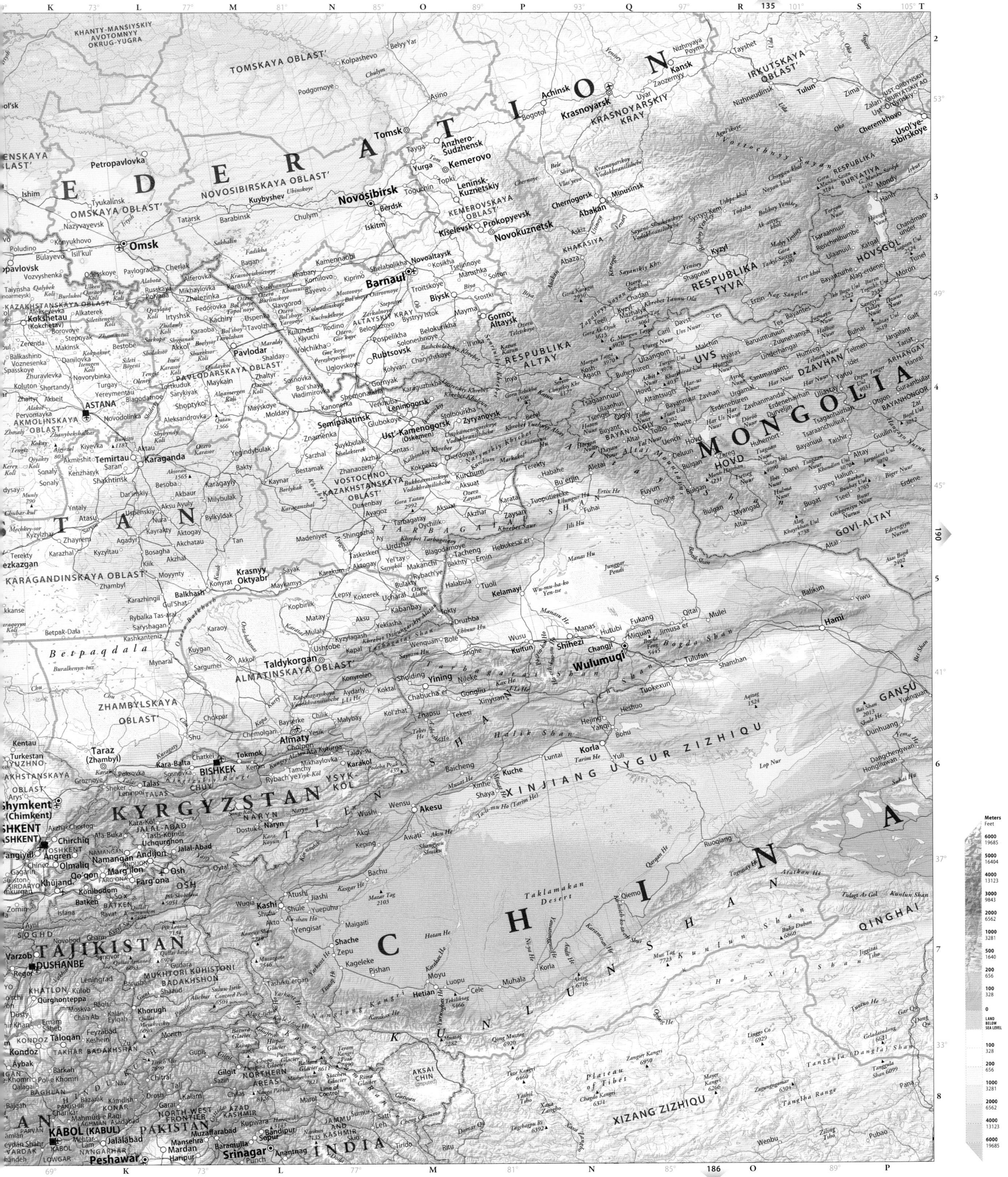
RUSSIAN FEDERATION
KAZAKHSTAN
KYRGYZSTAN
TAJIKISTAN
MONGOLIA
CHINA
PAKISTAN
INDIA
XINJIANG UYGUR ZIZHIQU
XIZANG ZIZHIQU
QINGHAI
GANSU
Tomsk
Novosibirsk
Omsk
Barnaul
Kemerovo
Novokuznetsk
Krasnoyarsk
Abakan
Kyzyl
Pavlodar
ASTANA
Karaganda
Semipalatinsk
Ust'-Kamenogorsk
Almaty
BISHKEK
DUSHANBE
KABOL (KABUL)
Peshawar
Srinagar
Wulumuqi
Kashi
Hetian
Hami
Taklamakan Desert
Plateau of Tibet
Meters
Feet
6000
19685
5000
16404
4000
13123
3000
9843
2000
6562
1000
3281
500
1640
200
656
100
328
0
LAND BELOW SEA LEVEL

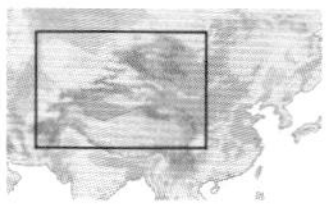

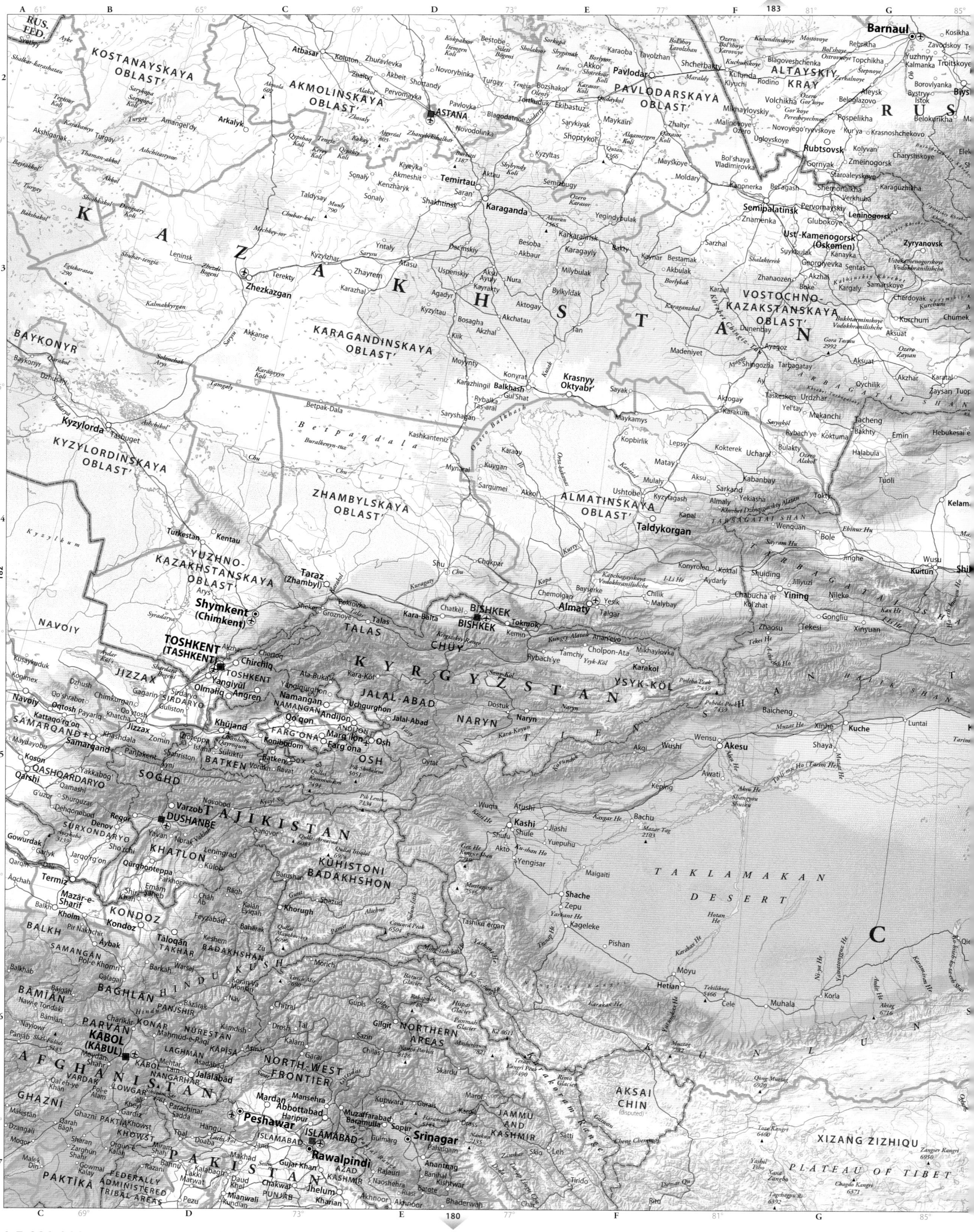

183
182
180
A B C D E F G
61° 65° 69° 73° 77° 81° 85°
49° 45° 41° 37° 33°
2 3 4 5 6 7
K A Z A K H S T A N
KOSTANAYSKAYA OBLAST'
AKMOLINSKAYA OBLAST'
PAVLODARSKAYA OBLAST'
ALTAYSKIY KRAY
KARAGANDINSKAYA OBLAST'
VOSTOCHNO-KAZAKSTANSKAYA OBLAST'
BAYKONYR
KYZYLORDINSKAYA OBLAST'
ZHAMBYLSKAYA OBLAST'
ALMATINSKAYA OBLAST'
YUZHNO-KAZAKHSTANSKAYA OBLAST'
NAVOIY
ASTANA
Barnaul
Pavlodar
Semipalatinsk
Ust'-Kamenogorsk (Öskemen)
Karaganda
Temirtau
Zhezkazgan
Arkalyk
Kyzylorda
Balkhash
Taldykorgan
Almaty
Taraz (Zhambyl)
Shymkent (Chimkent)
Turkestan
TOSHKENT (TASHKENT)
BISHKEK
Betpaqdala
K Y R G Y Z S T A N
TALAS
CHÜY
YSYK-KÖL
JALAL-ABAD
NARYN
OSH
BATKEN
Namangan
Andijon
Farg'ona
Osh
Khŭjand
Samarqand
Jizzax
Navoiy
Qarshi
Termiz
T A J I K I S T A N
DUSHANBE
SOGHD
KHATLON
KŬHISTONI BADAKHSHON
Khorugh
Yining
Akesu
Kashi
Shache
Hetian
TAKLAMAKAN DESERT
C
XIZANG ZIZHIQU
PLATEAU OF TIBET
AKSAI CHIN (disputed)
JAMMU AND KASHMIR
NORTHERN AREAS
NORTH-WEST FRONTIER
Srinagar
Peshawar
ISLĀMĀBĀD
Rawalpindi
Gilgit
K2 8611
P A K I S T A N
A F G H A N I S T A N
KĀBOL (KĀBUL)
Mazār-e-Sharif
Jalalabad
HINDU KUSH
K U N L U N
T I E N S H A N

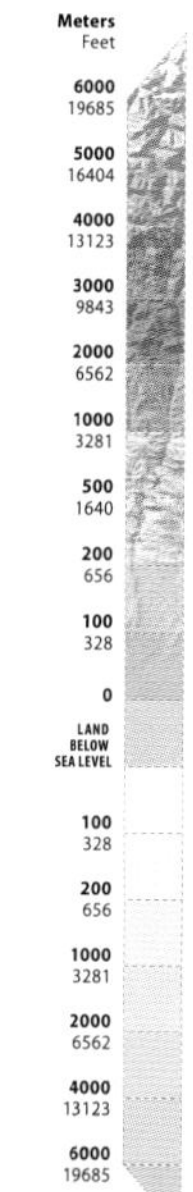

Meters
Feet
6000 19685
5000 16404
4000 13123
3000 9843
2000 6562
1000 3281
500 1640
200 656
100 328
0
LAND BELOW SEA LEVEL
100 328
200 656
1000 3281
2000 6562
4000 13123
6000 19685

1:7,880,000
Conic Equidistant Projection

0 50 100 150 200 250 300 kilometers
0 25 50 75 100 125 150 miles

CENTRAL ASIA

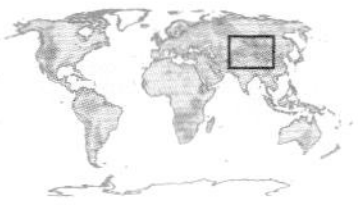

RESPUBLIKA KHAKASIYA
KEMEROVSKAYA OBLAST'
KRASNOYARSKIY KRAY
IRKUTSKAYA OBLAST'
RESPUBLIKA TYVA
RESPUBLIKA BURYATIYA
CHITINSKAYA OBLAST'
RESPUBLIKA ALTAY
Kyzyl
Irkutsk
Ulan-Ude
Ozero Baykal
UVS
BAYAN-ÖLGIY
HÖVSGÖL
SELENGE
DARHAN-UUL
BULGAN
ORHON
HENTIY
ULAANBAATAR (ULAN BATOR)
TÖV
ARHANGAY
DZAVHAN
HOVD
GOVĬSUMBER
BAYANHONGOR
ÖVÖRHANGAY
DUNDGOVI
DORNOGOVI
GOVĬ-ALTAY
ÖMNÖGOVĬ
M O N G O L I A
MONGOLIAN PLATEAU
Wulumuqi
BOGDA SHAN
Hami
XINJIANG UYGUR ZIZHIQU
NEI MONGOL ZIZHIQU
NINGXIA HUIZU ZIZHIQU
Yinchuan
Lanzhou
Xining
QILIAN SHAN
QINGHAI
GANSU
SICHUAN
KUNLUN SHAN
HOH XIL SHAN
C H I N A
Meters
Feet

191

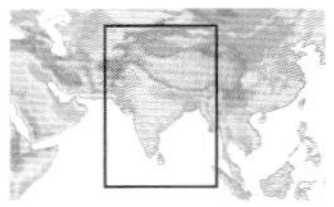

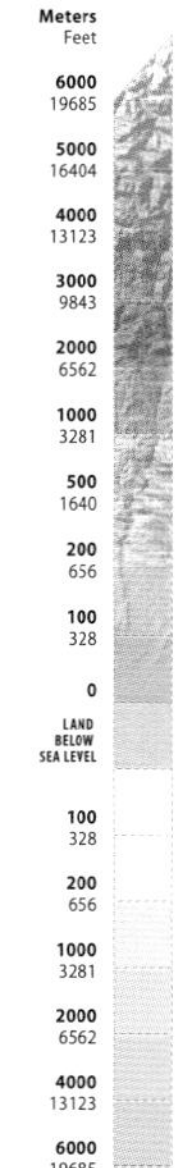

Meters
Feet
6000
19685
5000
16404
4000
13123
3000
9843
2000
6562
1000
3281
500
1640
200
656
100
328
0
LAND BELOW SEA LEVEL
100
328
200
656
1000
3281
2000
6562
4000
13123
6000
19685

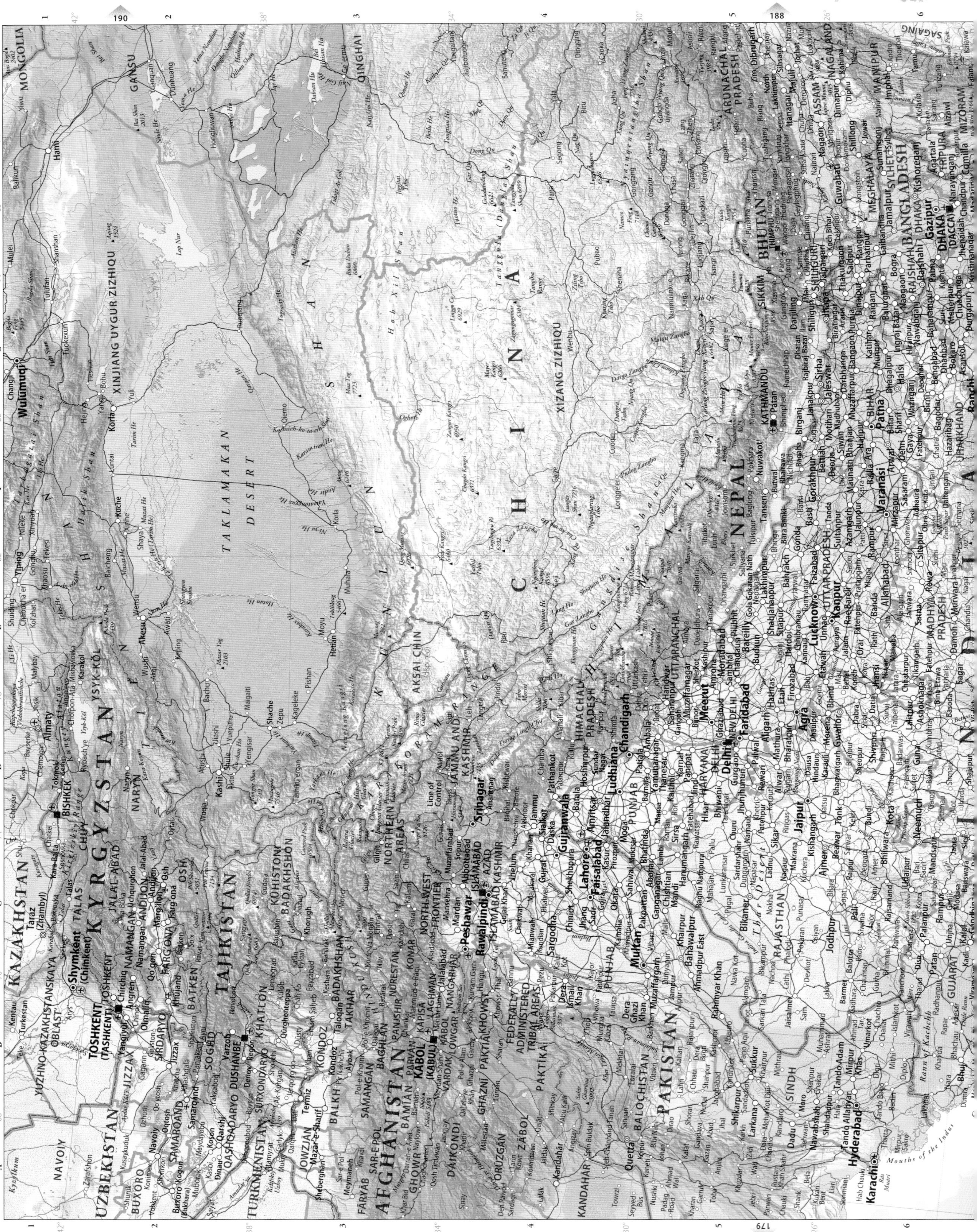

190
188
183
179
MONGOLIA
GANSU
QINGHAI
XINJIANG UYGUR ZIZHIQU
XIZANG ZIZHIQU
CHINA
TAKLAMAKAN DESERT
KUNLUN SHAN
KAZAKHSTAN
KYRGYZSTAN
TAJIKISTAN
UZBEKISTAN
TURKMENISTAN
AFGHANISTAN
PAKISTAN
NEPAL
BHUTAN
BANGLADESH
INDIA
KATHMANDU
THIMPHU
DHAKA (DACCA)
ISLAMABAD
KABUL
TOSHKENT (TASHKENT)
BISHKEK
DUSHANBE
NEW DELHI
Delhi
Lahore
Karachi
Hyderabad
Almaty
Wulumuqi
Kashi
Srinagar
AKSAI CHIN (disputed)
UTTAR PRADESH
RAJASTHAN
PUNJAB
SINDH
BALOCHISTAN
ARUNACHAL PRADESH

1:10,320,000

Conic Equidistant Projection

0 100 200 300 400 500 kilometers

0 50 100 150 200 250 300 miles

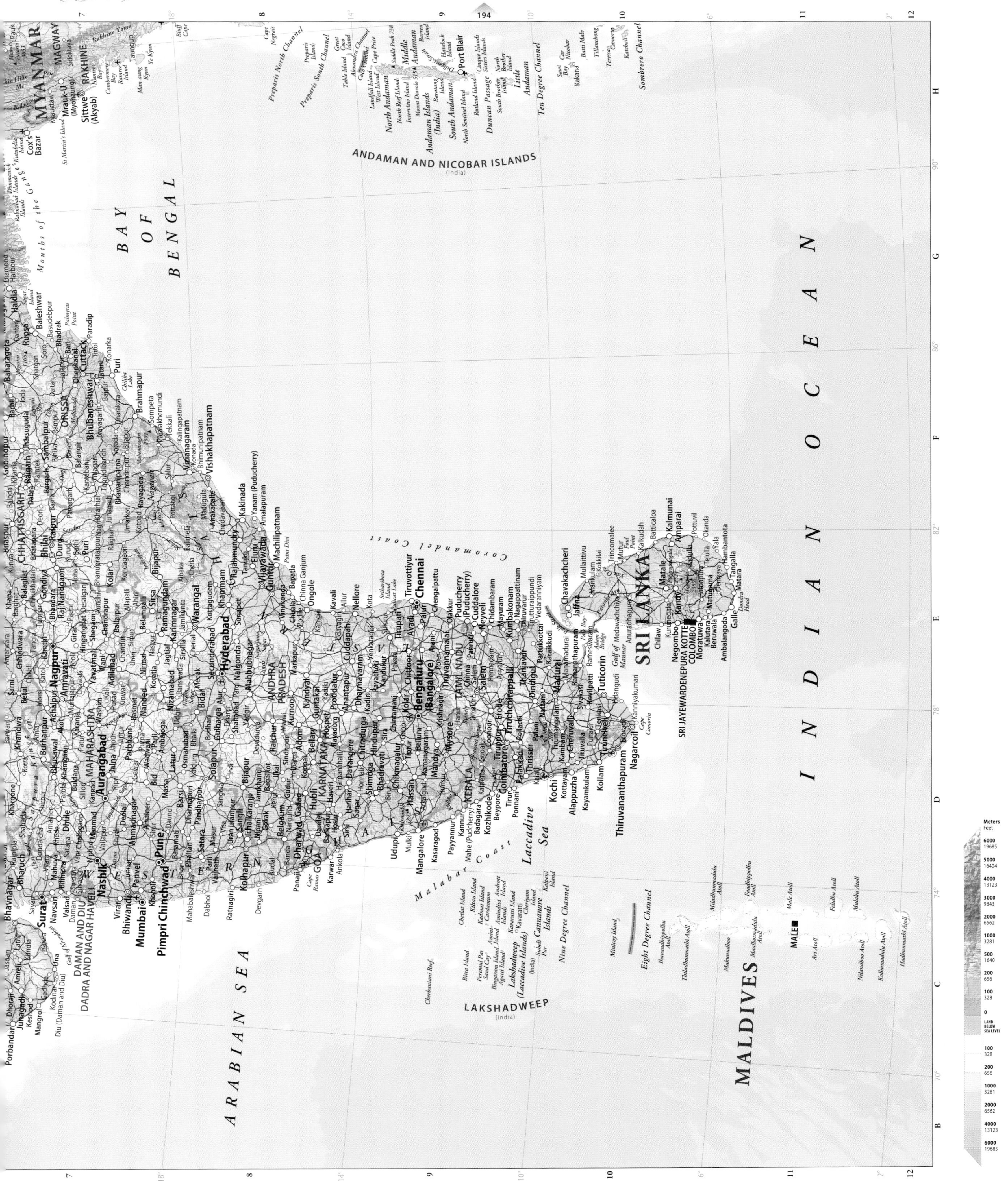
MYANMAR
BAY OF BENGAL
ANDAMAN AND NICOBAR ISLANDS
(India)
Port Blair
ARABIAN SEA
INDIAN OCEAN
SRI LANKA
SRI JAYEWARDENEPURA KOTTE
COLOMBO
MALDIVES
MALE
LAKSHADWEEP
(India)
Laccadive Sea
Mumbai
Pune
Hyderabad
Chennai
Bengaluru (Bangalore)
Nagpur
Surat
Aurangabad
Pimpri Chinchwad
Visakhapatnam
Madurai
Thiruvananthapuram
Meters
Feet
6000
19685
5000
16404
4000
13123
3000
9843
2000
6562
1000
3281
500
1640
200
656
100
328
0
LAND BELOW SEA LEVEL
100
328
200
656
1000
3281
2000
6562
4000
13123
6000
19685

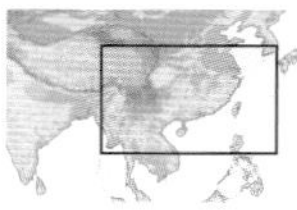

QINGHAI
XIZANG ZIZHIQU
PLATEAU OF TIBET
SICHUAN
GANSU
SHAANXI
CHONGQING
GUIZHOU
YUNNAN
GUANGXI ZHUANGZU ZIZHIQU
NINGXIA HUIZU ZIZHIQU
HAINAN
C H I N A
ARUNACHAL PRADESH
ASSAM
NAGALAND
MANIPUR
I N D I A
KACHIN
SAGAING
MANDALAY
SHAN
MAGWAY
KAYAH
KAYIN
BAGO
RAKHINE
AYEYARWADY
YANGON
MON
M Y A N M A R
L A O S
V I E T N A M
T H A I L A N D
Gulf of Tonkin
Gulf of Martaban
Khorat Plateau
Chengdu
Chongqing
Kunming
Guiyang
Nanning
Xi'an
Lanzhou
Mandalay
NAYPYIDAW
YANGON (RANGOON)
HÀ NỘI
VIANGCHAN (VIENTIANE)
Zhanjiang
Liuzhou
Panzhihua
Meters
Feet
6000 19685
5000 16404
4000 13123
3000 9843
2000 6562
1000 3281
500 1640
200 656
100 328
0
LAND BELOW SEA LEVEL
100 328
200 656
1000 3281
2000 6562
4000 13123
6000 19685
190
181
194

1:7,880,000

Conic Equidistant Projection

0 50 100 150 200 250 300 kilometers

0 25 50 75 100 125 150 miles

EASTERN CENTRAL ASIA

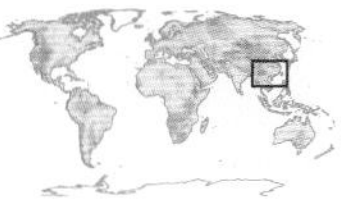

191
195
113°
117°
121°
125°
129°
G
H
I
J
K
1
2
3
4
5
6
33°
29°
25°
21°
17°
YELLOW SEA
(HUANG HAI)
EAST CHINA SEA
SOUTH CHINA SEA
PACIFIC OCEAN
PHILIPPINE SEA
SOUTH KOREA
JAPAN
TAIWAN
PHILIPPINES
SHANDONG
JIANGSU
ANHUI
HENAN
SHANXI
HUBEI
HUNAN
JIANGXI
ZHEJIANG
FUJIAN
GUANGDONG
SHANGHAI
HONG KONG (XIANGGANG) S.A.R.
Shanghai
Nanjing
Hangzhou
Wuhan
Nanchang
Fuzhou
Xiamen
Guangzhou
Shenzhen
Kowloon
Hong Kong (Xianggang)
Macau (Aomen)
Zhengzhou
Luoyang
Hefei
Changsha
Xuzhou
Linyi
Huainan
Wuxi
Changzhou
Suzhou
Ningbo
Wenzhou
Taizhou
Shantou
Dongguan
Zhongshan
Kaohsiung
T'aipei
T'aichung
T'ainan
Keelung
Hualien
Kwangju
Pusan (Busan)
Cheju
Fukuoka
Nagasaki
Okinawa
Naha
Korea Strait
Taiwan Strait
Bashi Channel
Luzon Strait
Balintang Channel
Babuyan Channel
Batan Islands
Babuyan Islands
Sakishima-shotō
Nansei-shotō (Ryukyu Islands)
Okinawa-shotō
Amami-shotō
Senkaku-shotō (disputed)
Pratas Island
PARACEL ISLANDS (disputed)
Laoag
Tuguegarao
Baguio
Dagupan
Luzon
Meters
Feet
6000
19685
5000
16404
4000
13123
3000
9843
2000
6562
1000
3281
500
1640
200
656
100
328
0
LAND BELOW SEA LEVEL

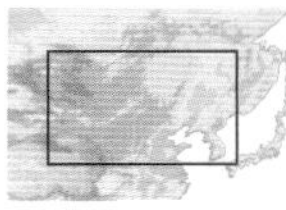

A
B
C
D
E
F
G
134
183
188
89°
93°
97°
101°
105°
109°
49°
45°
41°
37°
33°
2
3
4
5
6
7
RUSSIAN FEDERATION
RESPUBLIKA KHAKASIYA
KRASNOYARSKIY KRAY
RESPUBLIKA ALTAY
RESPUBLIKA TYVA
IRKUTSKAYA OBLAST'
UST'-ORDYNSKIY BURYATSKIY AO
RESPUBLIKA BURYATIYA
KAZAK.
MONGOLIA
CHINA
UVS
BAYAN-ÖLGIY
HOVD
DZAVHAN
HÖVSGÖL
BULGAN
ORHON
DARHAN-UUL
SELENGE
ARHANGAY
GOVĬ-ALTAY
BAYANHONGOR
ÖVÖRHANGAY
DUNDGOVĬ
ÖMNÖGOVĬ
DORNOGOVĬ
TÖV
HENTIY
GOVĬSUMBER
ULAANBAATAR (ULAN BATOR)
XINJIANG UYGUR ZIZHIQU
GANSU
QINGHAI
NEI MONGOL ZIZHIQU
NINGXIA HUIZU ZIZHIQU
SHAANXI
Mongolian Plateau
Gobi
Badain Jaran Shamo
Tengger Shamo
Altay
Hangayn Nuruu
Qilian Shan
Kunlun Shan
Bogda Shan
Bei Shan
Yin Shan
Loess Plateau
Ozero Baykal (Lake Baikal)
Uvs Nuur
Hövsgöl Nuur
Qinghai Hu
Abakan
Kyzyl
Irkutsk
Angarsk
Ulan-Ude
Darhan
Erdenet
Ulaangom
Hovd
Ölgiy
Uliastay
Altay
Bayanhongor
Mörön
Hami
Yumen
Jiayuguang
Jiuquan
Zhangye
Jinchang
Wuwei
Xining
Lanzhou
Baiyin
Yinchuan
Shizuishan
Wuhai
Baotou
Hohhot
Yan'an
Tianshui
Tongchuan
Dunhuang
Golmud
Delingha
1:7,880,000

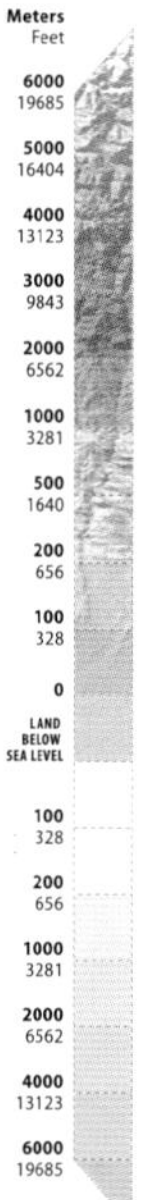
Meters
Feet
6000
19685
5000
16404
4000
13123
3000
9843
2000
6562
1000
3281
500
1640
200
656
100
328
0
LAND BELOW SEA LEVEL
100
328
200
656
1000
3281
2000
6562
4000
13123
6000
19685

1:7,880,000

Conic Equidistant Projection

0 50 100 150 200 250 300 kilometers

0 25 50 75 100 125 150 miles

NORTHEASTERN CHINA and MONGOLIA

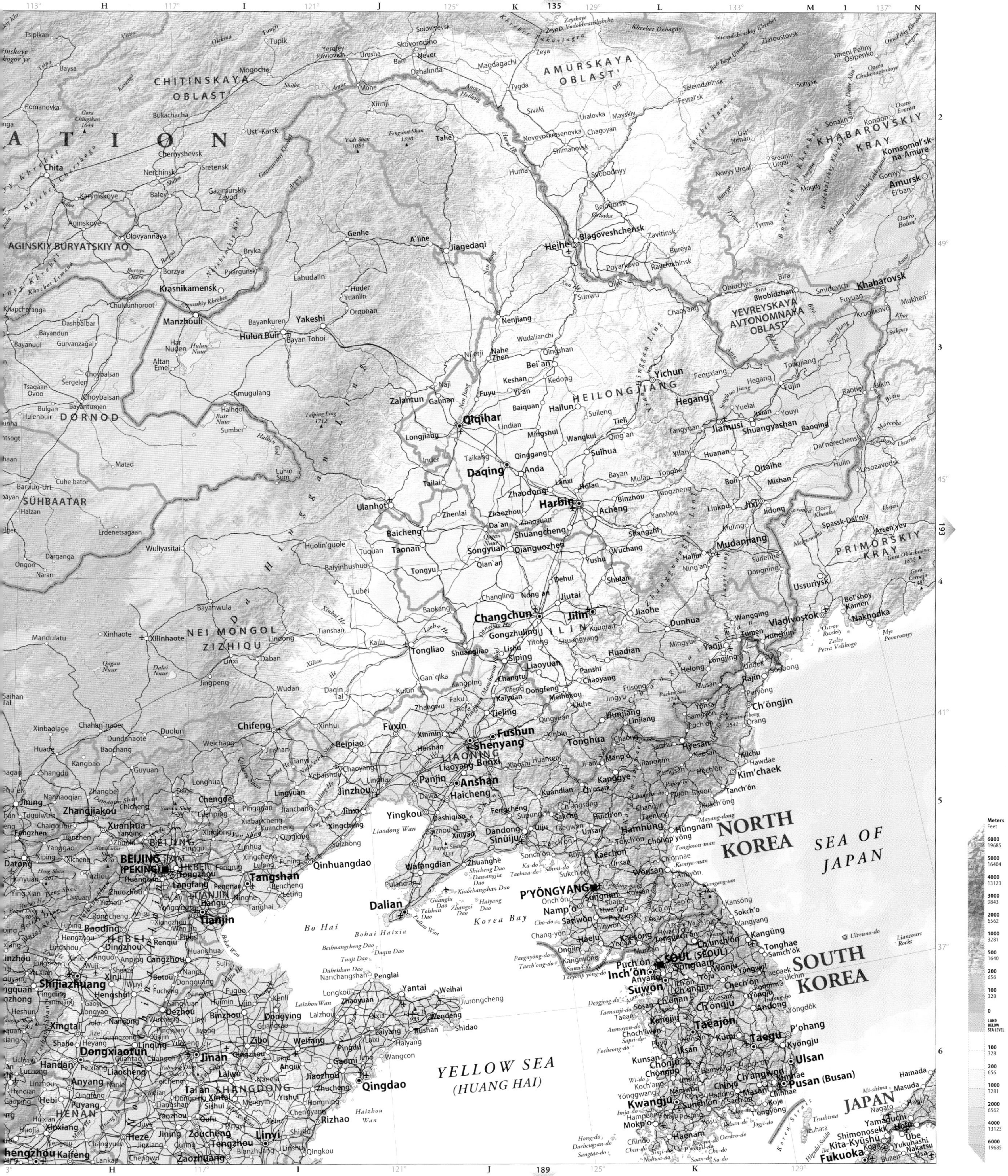

135
193
189
CHITINSKAYA OBLAST'
AMURSKAYA OBLAST'
KHABAROVSKIY KRAY
YEVREYSKAYA AVTONOMNAYA OBLAST'
PRIMORSKIY KRAY
AGINSKIY BURYATSKIY AO
DORNOD
SÜHBAATAR
HEILONGJIANG
JILIN
LIAONING
NEI MONGOL ZIZHIQU
HEBEI
BEIJING
TIANJIN
SHANDONG
HENAN
NORTH KOREA
SOUTH KOREA
JAPAN
SEA OF JAPAN
YELLOW SEA (HUANG HAI)
Bo Hai
Korea Bay
Liaodong Wan
Chita
Blagoveshchensk
Khabarovsk
Vladivostok
Harbin
Qiqihar
Daqing
Changchun
Jilin
Shenyang
Fushun
Anshan
Dalian
BEIJING (PEKING)
Tianjin
Tangshan
Shijiazhuang
Jinan
Qingdao
P'YŎNGYANG
SOUL (SEOUL)
Inch'ŏn
Taegu
Pusan (Busan)
Kwangju
Ulsan
Fukuoka
Meters
Feet
LAND BELOW SEA LEVEL

MONGOLIA
DORNOD
SÜHBAATAR
C H I N A
NEI MONGOL ZIZHIQU
Da Hinggan Ling
HEILONGJIANG
JILIN
LIAONING
HEBEI
SHANDONG
JIANGSU
ANHUI
ZHEJIANG
JIANGXI
SHANGHAI
TIANJIN
BEIJING (PEKING)
NORTH KOREA
SOUTH KOREA
P'YŎNGYANG
SŎUL (SEOUL)
YEVREYSKAYA AVTONOMNAYA OBLAST'
PRIMOR KRAY
Bo Hai
Korea Bay
YELLOW SEA (HUANG HAI)
EAST CHINA SEA
SE JA (EA
Korea Strait
Kyūshū
Shikoku
Ulreung-do
Liancourt Rocks
Oki-shotō
Ōsumi-shotō
Satsunan-shotō
Qiqihar
Daqing
Ha`erbin
Changchun
Jilin
Shenyang
Fushun
Anshan
Dalian
Dandong
Sinŭiju
Ch'ŏngjin
Hamhŭng
Kaesŏng
Inch'ŏn
Suwŏn
Taejŏn
Taegu
Kwangju
Ulsan
Pusan (Busan)
Cheju
Vladivostok
Nakhodka
Ussuriysk
Birobidzhan
Jiamusi
Mudanjiang
Hegang
Yichun
Tianjin
Tangshan
Qinhuangdao
Shijiazhuang
Baoding
Zhangjiakou
Chifeng
Jinzhou
Jinan
Qingdao
Yantai
Weihai
Linyi
Xuzhou
Lianyungang
Nanjing
Hefei
Wuxi
Changzhou
Suzhou
Shanghai
Hangzhou
Ningbo
Taizhou
Wenling
Fukuoka
Kita-Kyūshū
Hiroshima
Kumamoto
Kagoshima
Miyazaki
Nagasaki
Matsuyama
Okayama
1
2
3
4
5
6
A
B
C
D
E
F
G
112°
116°
120°
124°
128°
132°
46°
42°
38°
34°
30°
189
190
191

Meters / Feet
6000 19685
5000 16404
4000 13123
3000 9843
2000 6562
1000 3281
500 1640
200 656
100 328
0
LAND BELOW SEA LEVEL
100 328
200 656
1000 3281
2000 6562
4000 13123
6000 19685

1:7,880,000
Conic Equidistant Projection

0 50 100 150 200 250 300 kilometers
0 25 50 75 100 125 150 miles

JAPAN and KOREA

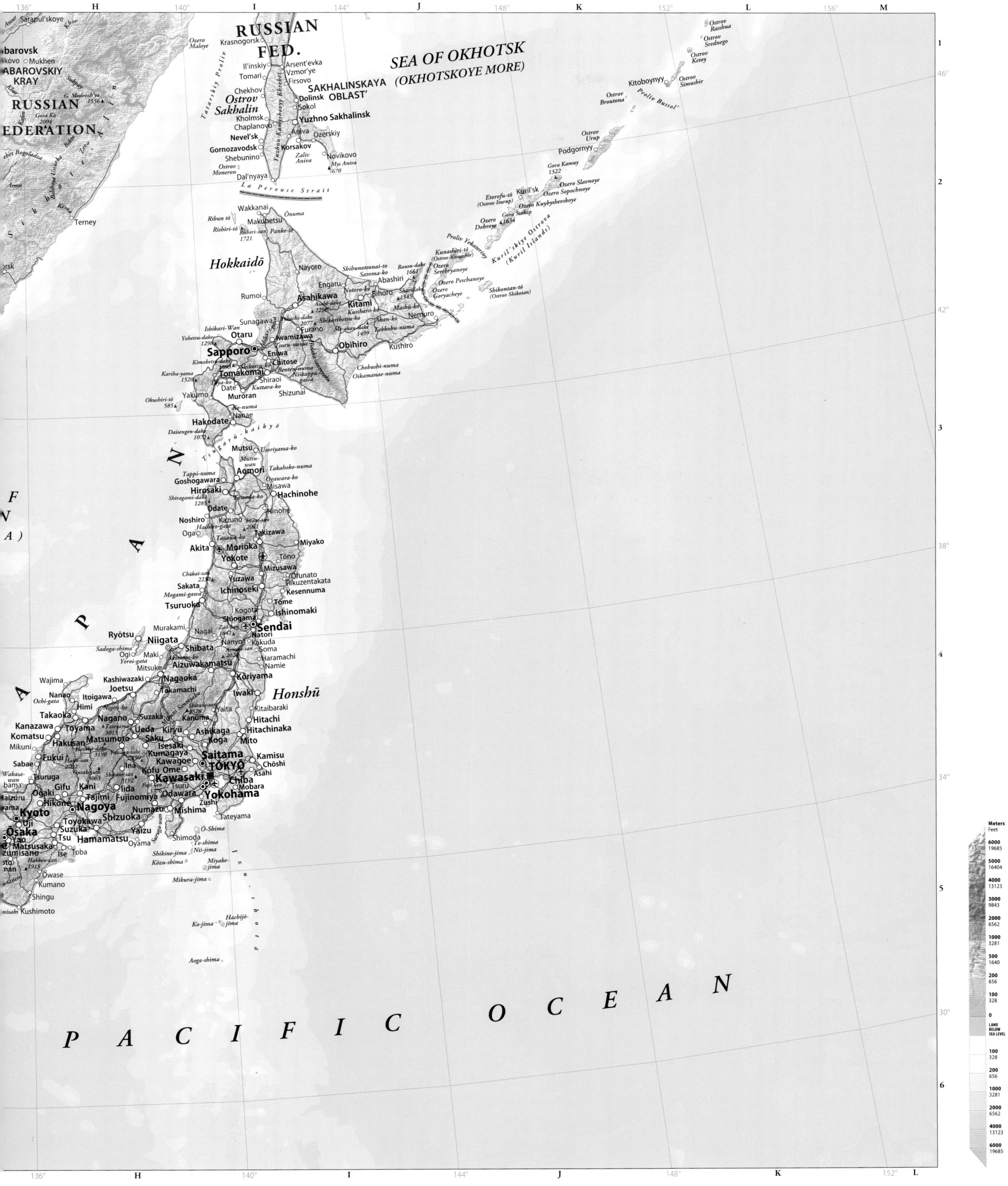

RUSSIAN FED.
SEA OF OKHOTSK (OKHOTSKOYE MORE)
SAKHALINSKAYA OBLAST'
Ostrov Sakhalin
RUSSIAN FEDERATION
KHABAROVSKIY KRAY
La Perouse Strait
Hokkaidō
Honshū
Kuril'skiye Ostrova (Kuril Islands)
Proliv Bussol'
Proliv Yekateriny
Tsugarū-kaikyō
PACIFIC OCEAN
Krasnogorsk
Il'inskiy
Tomari
Chekhov
Kholmsk
Chaplanovo
Nevel'sk
Gornozavodsk
Shebunino
Dal'nyaya
Arsent'evka
Vzmor'ye
Firsovo
Dolinsk
Sokol
Yuzhno Sakhalinsk
Aniva
Ozerskiy
Korsakov
Novikovo
Terney
Kitoboynyy
Podgornyy
Kuril'sk
Wakkanai
Makubetsu
Nayoro
Rumoi
Asahikawa
Engaru
Abashiri
Bihoro
Kitami
Nemuro
Kushiro
Obihiro
Furano
Sunagawa
Otaru
Sapporo
Iwamizawa
Eniwa
Chitose
Tomakomai
Shiraoi
Date
Muroran
Yakumo
Shizunai
Hakodate
Nanae
Mutsu
Aomori
Goshogawara
Hirosaki
Hachinohe
Odate
Noshiro
Kazuno
Oga
Takizawa
Akita
Morioka
Miyako
Yokote
Tōno
Mizusawa
Ōfunato
Rikuzentakata
Yuzawa
Sakata
Ichinoseki
Kesennuma
Tsuruoka
Tome
Ishinomaki
Kogota
Shiogama
Sendai
Murakami
Nagai
Natori
Ryōtsu
Niigata
Shibata
Kakuda
Soma
Haramachi
Namie
Aizuwakamatsu
Mitsuke
Kashiwazaki
Nagaoka
Kōriyama
Wajima
Joetsu
Tokamachi
Iwaki
Nanao
Itoigawa
Takaoka
Himi
Nagano
Suzaka
Kanuma
Kitaibaraki
Hitachi
Kanazawa
Toyama
Ueda
Kiryū
Ashikaga
Hitachinaka
Komatsu
Matsumoto
Saku
Mito
Mikuni
Hakusan
Isesaki
Koga
Kumagaya
Saitama
Kamisu
Sabae
Fukui
Kawagoe
TŌKYŌ
Chōshi
Ina
Kōfu
Ome
Asahi
Tsuruga
Kawasaki
Chiba
Gifu
Kani
Iida
Tsuru
Mobara
Ōgaki
Tajimi
Fujinomiya
Odawara
Yokohama
Hikone
Nagoya
Zushi
Kyoto
Numazu
Mishima
Uji
Toyokawa
Shizuoka
Tateyama
Ōsaka
Suzuka
Yaizu
Tsu
Hamamatsu
Shimoda
Matsusaka
Oyama
Ise
Toba
Owase
Kumano
Shingu
Kushimoto
Ō-Shima
To-shima
Nii-jima
Shikine-jima
Kōzu-shima
Miyake-jima
Mikura-jima
Ko-jima
Hachijō-jima
Aoga-shima
Meters
Feet
6000 19685
5000 16404
4000 13123
3000 9843
2000 6562
1000 3281
500 1640
200 656
100 328
0
LAND BELOW SEA LEVEL
100 328
200 656
1000 3281
2000 6562
4000 13123
6000 19685

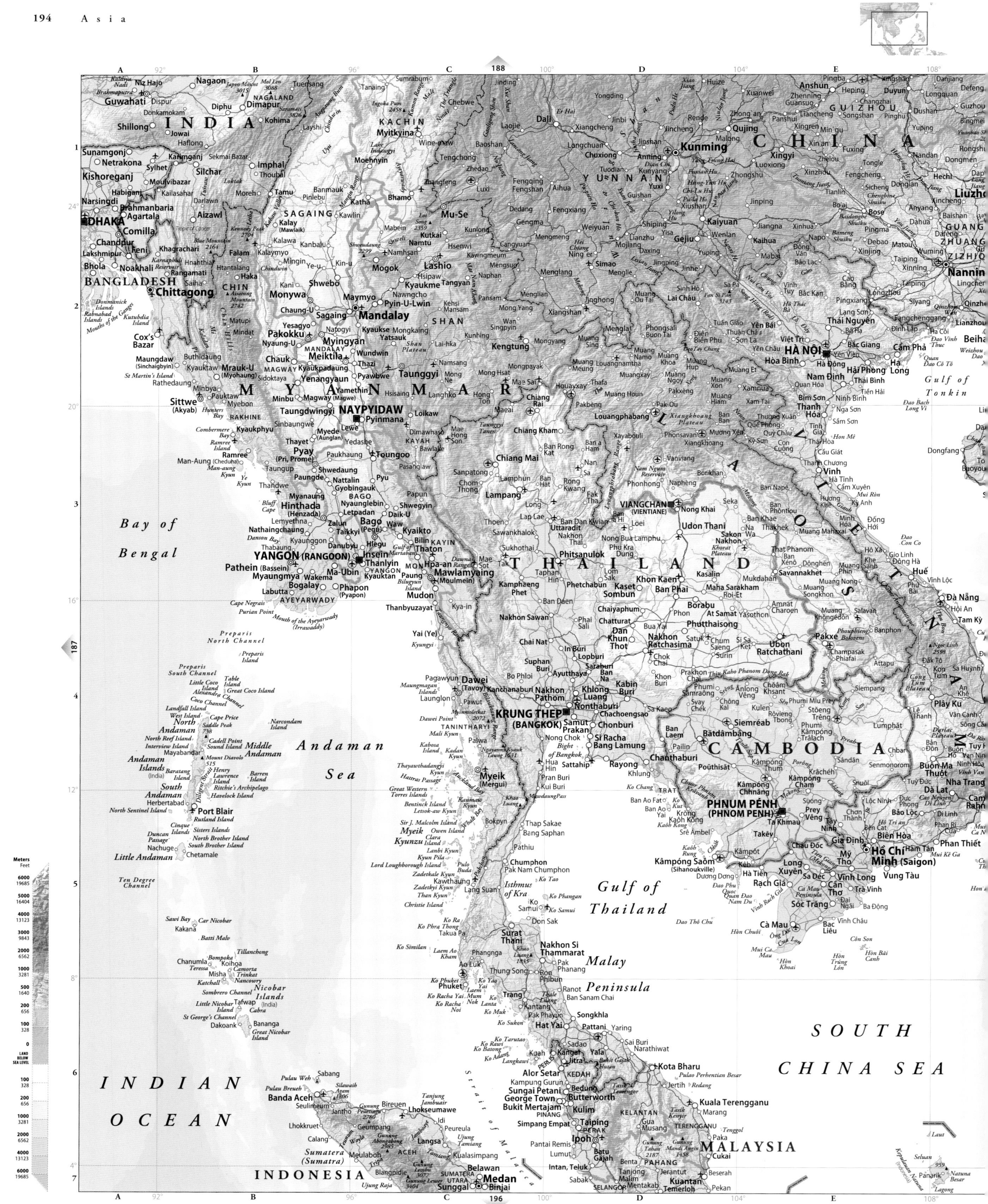
188
187
196
INDIA
BANGLADESH
DHAKA
Chittagong
MYANMAR
NAYPYIDAW
YANGON (RANGOON)
Mandalay
CHINA
YUNNAN
Kunming
LAOS
VIANGCHAN (VIENTIANE)
HÀ NỘI
VIETNAM
THAILAND
KRUNG THEP (BANGKOK)
CAMBODIA
PHNUM PÉNH (PHNOM PENH)
Hồ Chí Minh (Saigon)
MALAYSIA
INDONESIA
Medan
Bay of Bengal
Andaman Sea
Andaman Islands (India)
Nicobar Islands (India)
Gulf of Thailand
Gulf of Tonkin
Malay Peninsula
SOUTH CHINA SEA
INDIAN OCEAN
Strait of Malacca
Sumatera (Sumatra)

1:9,390,000
Mercator Projection
0 150 300 450 600 kilometers
0 100 200 300 400 miles

SOUTHEAST ASIA and the PHILIPPINES

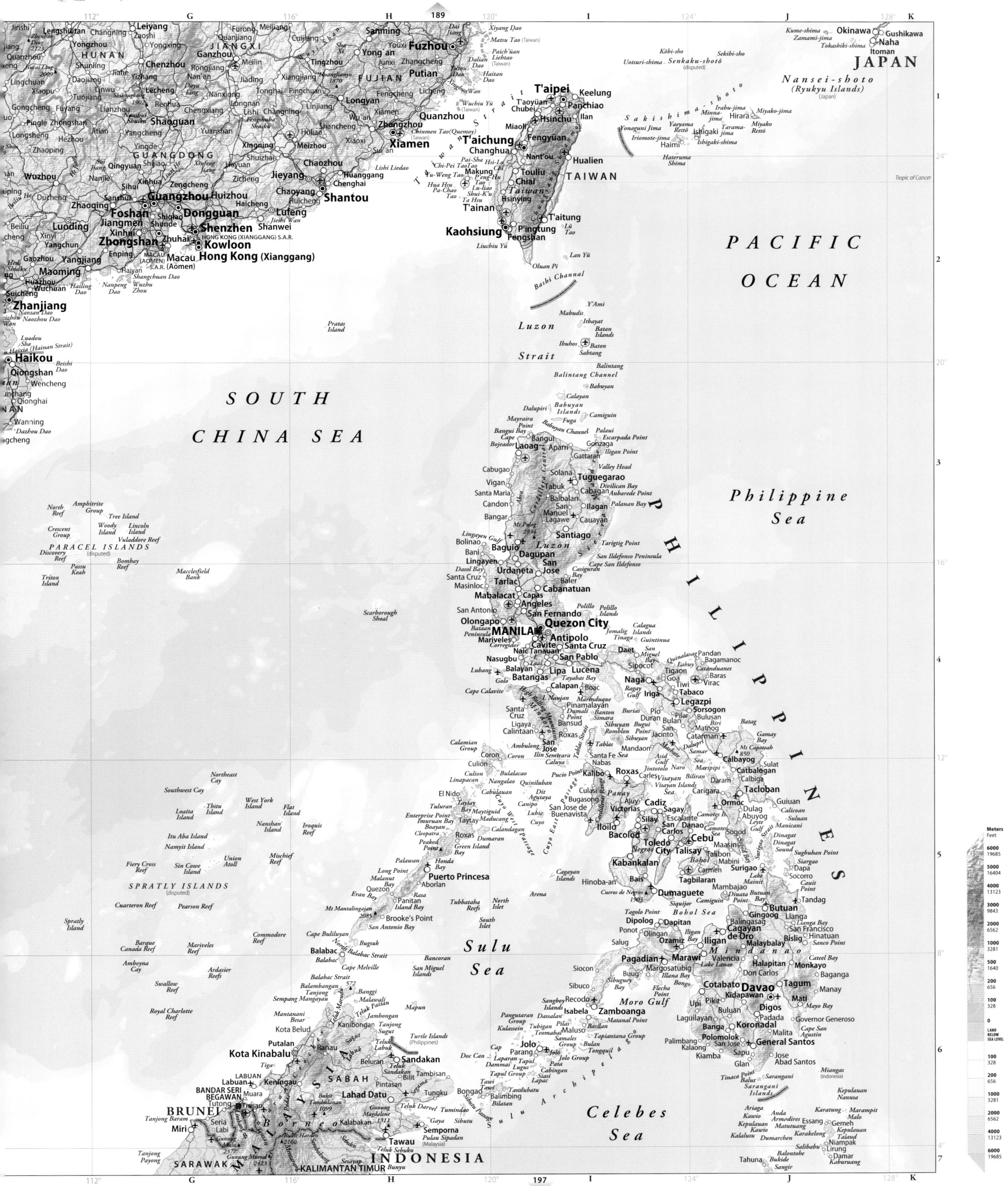
189
197
112°
116°
120°
124°
128°
G
H
I
J
K
1
2
3
4
5
6
7
24°
20°
16°
12°
8°
4°
Tropic of Cancer
PACIFIC OCEAN
SOUTH CHINA SEA
Philippine Sea
Sulu Sea
Celebes Sea
PHILIPPINES
TAIWAN
JAPAN
MALAYSIA
INDONESIA
BRUNEI
SABAH
SARAWAK
KALIMANTAN TIMUR
HUNAN
JIANGXI
FUJIAN
GUANGDONG
Luzon Strait
Bashi Channel
Balintang Channel
Babuyan Channel
Taiwan Strait
Moro Gulf
Bohol Sea
Sulu Archipelago
PARACEL ISLANDS (disputed)
SPRATLY ISLANDS (disputed)
Nansei-shoto (Ryukyu Islands) (Japan)
Sakishima-shoto
Senkaku-shotō (disputed)
Okinawa
Naha
Gushikawa
Itoman
T'aipei
Keelung
Panchiao
Hsinchu
T'aichung
Changhua
Hualien
T'ainan
Kaohsiung
P'ingtung
Fengshan
T'aitung
Lan Yü
Fuzhou
Putian
Xiamen
Quanzhou
Zhangzhou
Shantou
Chaozhou
Jieyang
Meizhou
Longyan
Sanming
Guangzhou
Foshan
Dongguan
Shenzhen
Kowloon
Hong Kong (Xianggang)
HONG KONG (XIANGGANG) S.A.R.
Macau (Aomen)
MACAU (AOMEN) S.A.R.
Zhuhai
Zhongshan
Jiangmen
Huizhou
Shaoguan
Zhaoqing
Maoming
Zhanjiang
Haikou
Qiongshan
Wenchang
Qionghai
Wanning
Chenzhou
Pratas Island
Scarborough Shoal
Macclesfield Bank
Woody Island
Lincoln Island
Tree Island
Amphitrite Group
Crescent Group
North Reef
Bombay Reef
Triton Island
Itu Aba Island
Namyit Island
Sin Cowe Island
Union Atoll
Mischief Reef
Fiery Cross Reef
Spratly Island
Laoag
Aparri
Vigan
Tuguegarao
Ilagan
Santiago
Baguio
Dagupan
San Jose
Cabanatuan
Tarlac
Angeles
San Fernando
Olongapo
Quezon City
MANILA
Antipolo
Cavite
Santa Cruz
San Pablo
Batangas
Lucena
Lipa
Naga
Legazpi
Sorsogon
Virac
Calapan
Puerto Princesa
Roxas
Kalibo
Iloilo
Bacolod
Cebu
Toledo City
Talisay
Tagbilaran
Dumaguete
Tacloban
Ormoc
Catbalogan
Calbayog
Surigao
Butuan
Cagayan de Oro
Iligan
Dipolog
Dapitan
Ozamiz
Pagadian
Marawi
Malaybalay
Zamboanga
Isabela
Jolo
Cotabato
Davao
Tagum
Digos
Koronadal
General Santos
Mindanao
Luzon
Mt Pulog 2934
Mt Apo
Kota Kinabalu
Sandakan
Lahad Datu
Tawau
Semporna
Labuan
BANDAR SERI BEGAWAN
Miri
Tahuna
Miangas (Indonesia)
Meters
Feet
LAND BELOW SEA LEVEL

194
A
B
C
D
E
92°
96°
100°
104°
108°
8°
4°
0°
1
2
3
4
5
6
7
Andaman Sea
ANDAMAN AND NICOBAR ISLANDS (India)
Nicobar Islands (India)
Car Nicobar
Kakana
Batti Malv
Tillanchong
Chanumla
Bompoka
Teressa
Koihoa
Camorta
Misha
Trinkat
Nancowry
Katchall
Little Nicobar Island
Tafwap
Cabra
Dakoank
Bananga
Great Nicobar Island
Ko Ra
Ko Phra Thong
Don Sak
Surat Thani
Nakhon Si Thammarat
Pak Phanang
Ko Similan
Laem Ao Kham
Khao Luang 1835
Phangnga
Thung Song
THAILAND
Krabi
Ko Yao Yai
Phuket
Laem Mum Nok
Ko Racha Yai
Ko Racha Noi
Ko Lanta
Ko Muk
Phatthalung
Trang
Kantang
Ranot
Ban Sanam Chai
Pak Phayun
Songkhla
Malay Peninsula
Ko Sukon
Hat Yai
Pattani
Yaring
Sai Buri
Ko Tarutao
Ko Rawi
Ko Adang
Satun
Sadao
Yala
Narathiwat
PERLIS
Kangar
Langkawi
Bukit Gajah Hutan
Kota Bharu
Pulao Perhentian Besar
Redang
Alor Setar
KEDAH
Kampung Gurun
Sungai Petani
George Town
Butterworth
PINANG
Bukit Mertajam
Kulim
Simpang Empat
Taiping
PERAK
Ipoh
Kuala Terengganu
Marang
KELANTAN
TERENGGANU
Gua Musang
Tenggol
Paka
Gunung Tahan 2187
Gunung Mandi Angin 1458
Pantai Remis
Lumut
Batu Gajah
Cukai
PAHANG
Intan, Teluk
Tanjong Malim
Jerantut
Beserah
Kuantan
Sabak
SELANGOR
Besar Hantu 1462
Pekan
KUALA LUMPUR
Shah Alam
Petaling Jaya
Klang
Semenyih
Seremban
NEGERI SEMBILAN
Port Dickson
MALAYSIA
Tioman
Aur
Mersing
Melaka
MELAKA
Muar
Keluang
JOHOR
Batu Pahat
Sekudai
Kota Tinggi
Johor Bahru
SINGAPORE
Tanjung Belungkor
Singapore Strait
Nongsapura
Kijang
Tanjungpinang
Batam
Sugi
Numbing
Mesanak
Sebangka
Kepulauan Lingga
Rangsang
Tanjungbatu
Teluknibung
Sungaiguntung
Temiang
Bakung
Tanjung Datuk
Baso
1154
Tanjung Basu
478
Singkep
Tanjung Buku
Tanjung Perkat
Tanjung Jabung
Selat Berhala
Teluk Kelabat
Strait of Malacca
Pulau Weh
Sabang
Banda Aceh
Seulimeum
Silawaih Agam 1806
Jantho
Gunung Peuetsagoe 2780
Bireuen
Tanjung Jambuair
Lhokseumawe
Idi
Peureula
Lhokkruet
Geumpang
Calang
ACEH
Langsa
Ujung Tamiang
Kualasimpang
Meulaboh
Gunung Abongabong 2985
Blangpidie
Gunung Lembu 3077
Gunung Leuser 3404
Ujung Raja
Belawan
Medan
Sunggal
Binjai
Tapaktuan
Kabanjahe
Labuhanruku
Kisaran
Pematangsiantar
Tanjung Dewa
Sibigo
Bakongan
Simeulue
Sinabang
Samosir
Prapat
Pangkalanlunang
Labuhanbilik
Porsea
Kepulauan Banyak
Reusam
Babi
Singkil
Tuangku
Bangkaru
SUMATERA UTARA
Rantauprapat
Perbaungan
Kotapinang
Dumai
Rupat
Sibolga
Langgapayung
Tanjung Dowi
Musala
Ladara
Batangtoru
Lahewa
Padangsidempuan
Rantaukampar
Balaipungut
Sungaiapit
Gunung Malea 2012
Nias
Sirombu
Lolowau
Hinako
Sorikmarapi 2145
Gunung Kulabu 2122
Minas
Buatan
Natal
Bangkinang
Pekanbaru
Telukdalam
Pini
2274
Airbangis
Talu
Bonjol
Payakumbuh
RIAU
Pulautelo
Simuk
Tanahmasa
Sasak
Tembilahan
Bukittinggi
2891
2262
270
Tanahbala
Pariaman
Sijunjung
Rengat
Pegunungan Tigapuluh
Selat Siberut
Muarasigep
384
Padang
Gunung Talang 2599
Selatpanjang
Kagologolo
Siberut
SUMATERA BARAT
Dusunmudo
Hari
Simpang
Muarasiberut
Sabulubek
Painan
Tebo
Muaratebo
Tanjung Melalo
Tanjung Samak
Belinyu
Tanjung Tiung
Taileleo
Kambang
Muaralabuh
Muarabungo
Jambi
Kampa
692
Sungailiat
JAMBI
Muarabulian
Alanggantang
Mentok
Pangkalpinang
Selat Bungalaut
Kepulauan Mentawai
Indrapura
Sungaipenuh
Bayunglincir
Tanjung Carat
Sipura
Katiet
Tanjung Indrapura
Bukit Masurai 2935
Sarolangun
Karanggadung
BANGKA-BELITUNG
Tanjung Berikat
Sungalpadang
Mailepp
Selat Siberut
Pagai Utara
Mukomuko
Surulangun
Penuguan
Bedinggong
Sikakap
368
Pagai Selatan
Pasarbantal
Rawas
Muaralakitan
Palembang
Batubetumbang
Mendanau
Liat
Tanjungpandan
Belitung
Burai
Taitaitanopo
Bukit Dueen 2467
Muarabeliti
SUMATERA SELATAN
Plaju
Kertapati
Tanjungraja
Toboali
Lepar
Tanjung Baginda
Selat Gaspar
Gantung
Teluk Balok
Sanding
Ketahun
Pendopo
Kayuagung
Tanjung Kait
Selat Lepar
Selat Gelasa
Lais
BENGKULU
Prabumulih
Bengkulu
Gunung Dempo 3159
Lahat
Baturaja
Wiralaga
Tanjung Lumut
Tanjung Kerbau
Gunung Patah 2817
Pasarseluma
Bukit Nanti 1619
Talangbatu
Dintiteladas
Manna
Sputih
Tanjung Kenam
Bintuhan
Terbanggi-besar
LAMPUNG
Metro
Tanjung Palausekopong
Enggano
281
Kayaapu
Krui
Pringsewu
Bandar Lampung
Ngaras
Bandaragung
Belimbing
Teluk Semangka
Tanjung Cina
Selat Sunda
Cilegon
1179
Serang
JAKARTA
Bekasi
Depok
Bogor
BANTEN
Rangkasbitung
Pamanukan
Indramay
Bojong Gede
Subang
Paseh
Cirebo
Bandung
Cianjur
Panaitan
Tanjung Guhakolak
Deli
Tinjil
Cicalengka
Garut
Ciamis
JAWA BARAT
Sindangbarang
Tasikmalaya
Purwok
Pameungpeuk
Cilaca
Jawa
Laut (J
INDIAN OCEAN
SOUTH CHIN
INDIA
Dao Thô Chu
Cà Mau
Bac Liêu
Hòn Chuôi
VIETNAM
Cua Lon
Mui Ca Mau
Hòn Khoai
Côn Son
Hòn Trùng Lón
Hòn Bài Canh
Laut
Seluan
959
Natuna Besar
Panarik
Lagong
Kepulauan Natuna
Kepulauan Anambas
Mubur
Matak
Siantan
Bajau
Jemaja
Letung
Raibu
Midai
Subi Besar
Serasan
Seraya
KEPULAUAN RIAU
Murih
Tanjung Mungguree
Mendarik
Uwi
Tambelan Besar
Pemangkat
Sekura
Kepulauan Tambelan
Benua
Singkawang
Lemukutan
Sungairaya
Kepulauan Badas
Temaju
Pengiki Datu
Pejantan
Pontiana
Tanjungsaleh
Laut
Penebangan
Kepulauan Karimata
Selat Karimata
Padang
Karima
Equator
Christmas Island (Australia)
North Keeling Island
West Island (Panjang)
South Island (Atas)
Cocos (Keeling) Islands (Australia)
Meters
Feet
6000 19685
5000 16404
4000 13123
3000 9843
2000 6562
1000 3281
500 1640
200 656
100 328
0
LAND BELOW SEA LEVEL
100 328
200 656
1000 3281
2000 6562
4000 13123
6000 19685
MALAYSIA
Masai
Johore Strait
Pasir Gudang
Sungai Johor
Johor Bahru
SEMBAWANG
Sungei Buloh Nature Park
Kranji Res.
WOODLANDS
YISHUN
Tanjung Belungkor
Lower Seletar Res.
Seletar Airport
Sarimbun Res.
Murai Res.
Singapore Zoological Gardens
Night Safari
Serangoon Harbour
Pulau Ubin
Pulau Tekong Kechil
Pulau Tekong
CHOA CHU KANG
PUNGGOL
SENGKANG
Pasir Ris Park
CHANGI VILLAGE
Changi Beach Park
Restricted Area
Poyan Res.
BUKIT PANJANG
Upper Seletar Res.
ANG MO KIO
HOUGANG
PASIR RIS
Changi
SINGAPORE
Singapore I.
Upper Peirce Res.
Kranji Expressway
Tampines Expressway (TPE)
BUKIT BATOK
Bukit Timah 162
MacRitchie Res.
BISHAN
SERANGOON
TAMPINES
Bedok Res. Park
Singapore Changi International Airport
Bukit Timah Nature Reserve
BUKIT TIMAH
TOA PAYOH
Bedok Res.
SIMEI
Ayer Rajah Expressway (AYE)
JURONG
BEDOK
TUAS
Pan Island Expressway (PIE)
Jurong Park
CLEMENTI
HOLLAND VILLAGE
Botanic Gardens
NOVENA
GEYLANG
KATONG
Jurong Bird Park
Pandan Reservoir
East Coast Parkway (ECP)
Tanah Merah
QUEENSTOWN
Raffles Hotel
Marina Bay
East Coast Park
Selat Jurong
West Coast Park
PASIR PANJANG
Mt Faber Park
TELOK BLANGAH
Fort Canning Park
CHINATOWN
Jurong Island
Selat Pandan
Singapore Cruise Centre
Pulau Brani
Singapore Strait
Pulau Bintan
Sentosa
Pulau Bukum
Pulau Busing
Pulau Bukum Kechil
Pulau Sakijang Bendera
Pulau Sakijang Pelepah
Pulau Sudong
Pulau Sebarok
SINGAPORE
1:469,250
Lambert Conic Conformal Projection
Pulau Semakau
Nongsapura
Pulau Pawai
Pulau Senang
Main Strait
INDONESIA
Batu Ampar
Pulau Batam
Sekupang
10 kilometers
5 miles
103°40'
103°45'
103°50'
103°55'
104°
104°05'
1°30'
1°25'
1°20'
1°15'
1°10'

1:9,390,000

Mercator Projection

0 150 300 450 600 kilometers

0 100 200 300 400 miles

WESTERN INDONESIA, MALAYSIA, and SINGAPORE

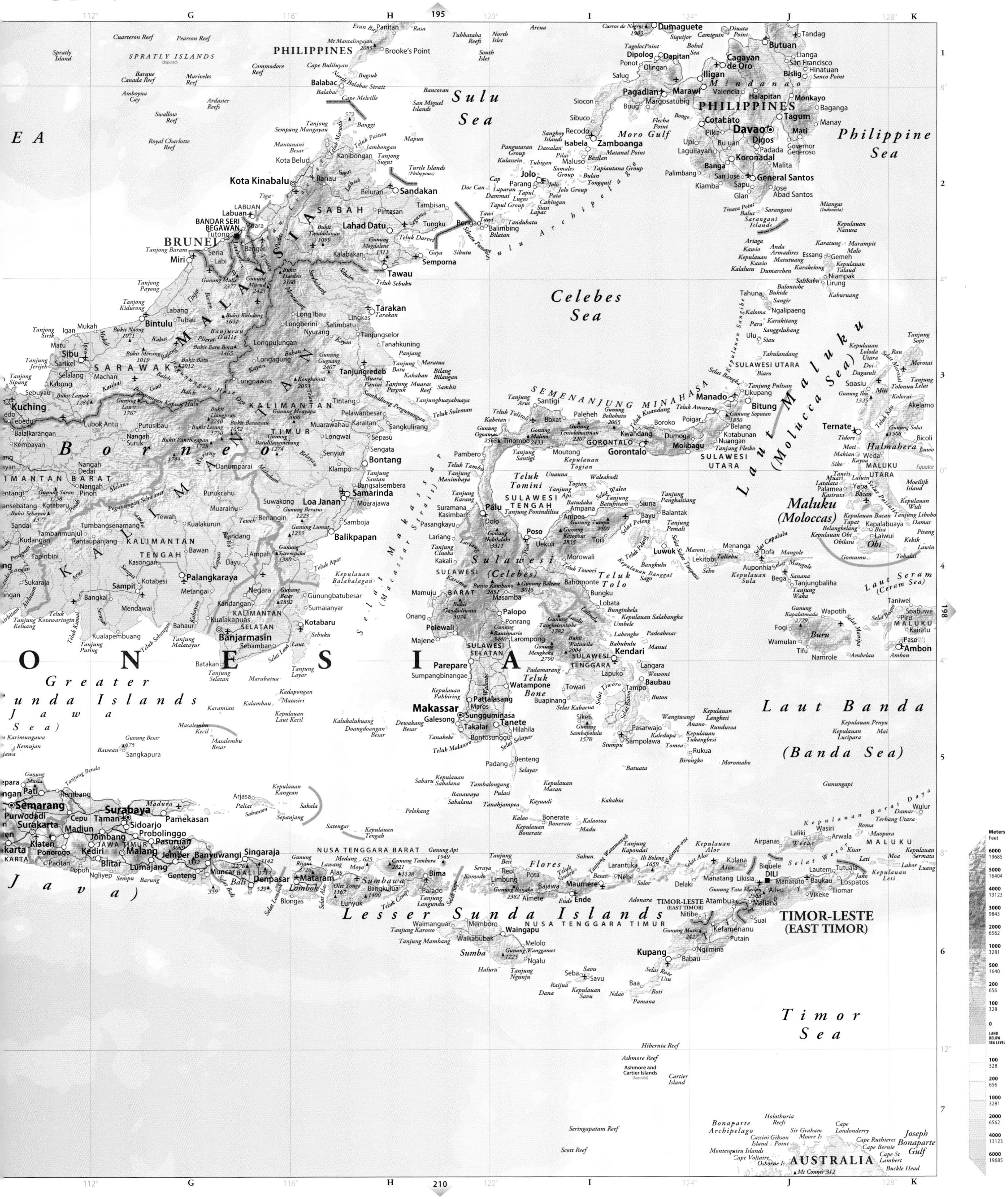

PHILIPPINES
SPRATLY ISLANDS
Sulu Sea
Celebes Sea
Philippine Sea
Mindanao
Davao
Zamboanga
General Santos
Cagayan de Oro
Iligan
Butuan
Cotabato
Kota Kinabalu
SABAH
Sandakan
Lahad Datu
Tawau
BRUNEI
BANDAR SERI BEGAWAN
Miri
Bintulu
Sibu
Kuching
SARAWAK
MALAYSIA
Borneo
KALIMANTAN
KALIMANTAN TIMUR
KALIMANTAN BARAT
KALIMANTAN TENGAH
KALIMANTAN SELATAN
Tarakan
Samarinda
Balikpapan
Palangkaraya
Banjarmasin
Tanjungredeb
Bontang
Selat Makassar (Macassar Strait)
Sulawesi (Celebes)
SULAWESI UTARA
SULAWESI TENGAH
SULAWESI SELATAN
SULAWESI TENGGARA
SULAWESI BARAT
GORONTALO
Manado
Bitung
Gorontalo
Palu
Poso
Kendari
Makassar
Parepare
Palopo
Baubau
Teluk Tomini
Teluk Tolo
Teluk Bone
Laut Maluku (Molucca Sea)
Maluku (Moloccas)
MALUKU
MALUKU UTARA
Halmahera
Ternate
Obi
Buru
Ambon
Laut Seram (Ceram Sea)
Laut Banda (Banda Sea)
INDONESIA
Greater Sunda Islands
Java Sea
Java
Semarang
Surabaya
Malang
Madura
Lesser Sunda Islands
NUSA TENGGARA BARAT
NUSA TENGGARA TIMUR
Bali
Denpasar
Lombok
Mataram
Sumbawa
Bima
Flores
Sumba
Waingapu
Ende
Maumere
Kupang
TIMOR-LESTE (EAST TIMOR)
DILI
Timor Sea
Ashmore and Cartier Islands (Australia)
AUSTRALIA
Joseph Bonaparte Gulf
Bonaparte Archipelago
Meters
Feet
6000
19685
5000
16404
4000
13123
3000
9843
2000
6562
1000
3281
500
1640
200
656
100
328
0
LAND BELOW SEA LEVEL

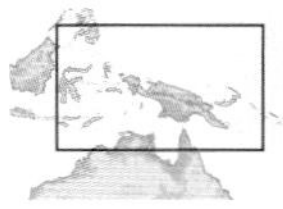

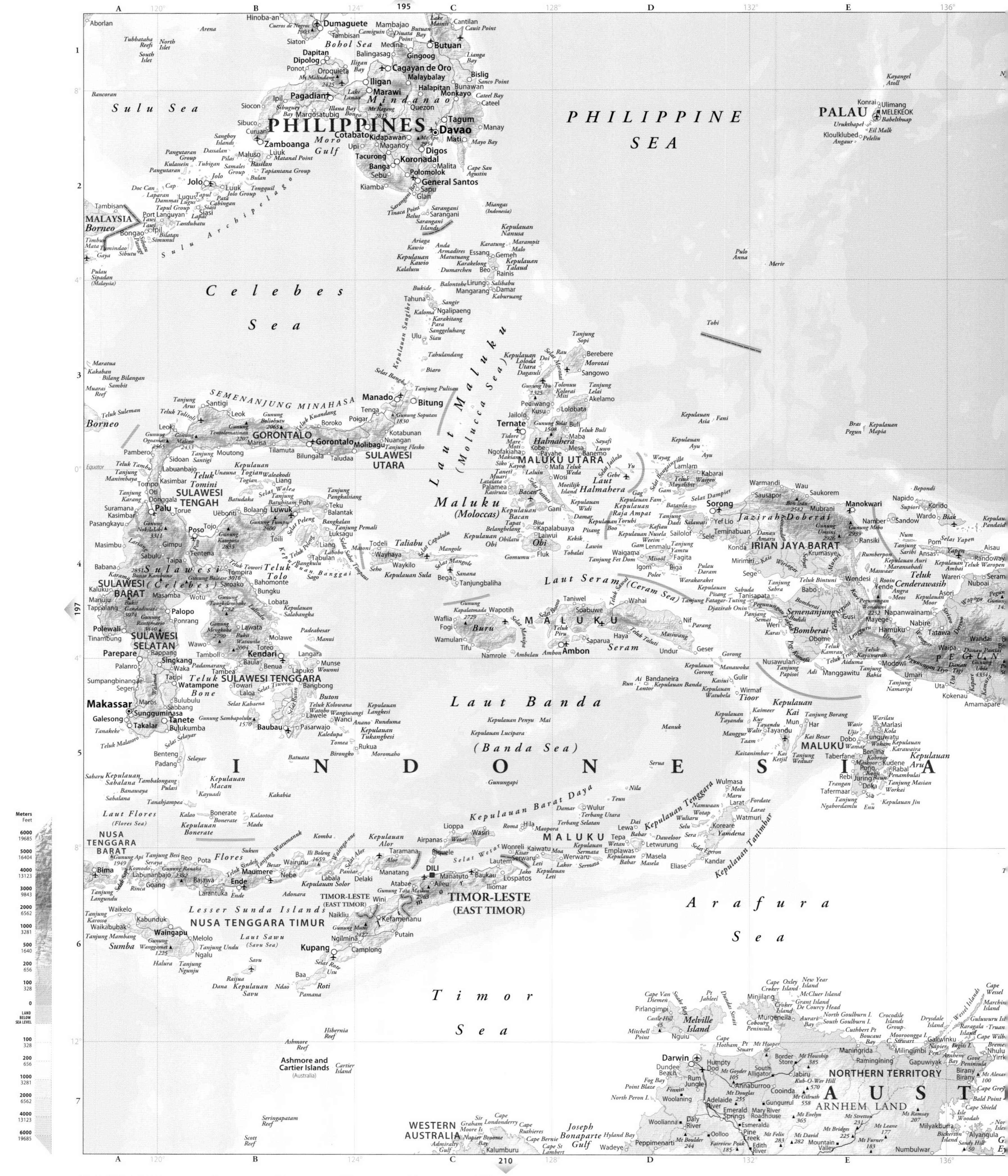

195
A
B
C
D
E
120°
124°
128°
132°
136°
1
2
3
4
5
6
7
8°
4°
0° Equator
4°
8°
12°
197
210
Sulu Sea
PHILIPPINE SEA
PHILIPPINES
Mindanao
Bohol Sea
Dumaguete
Butuan
Dapitan
Dipolog
Oroquieta
Gingoog
Cagayan de Oro
Malaybalay
Iligan
Marawi
Halapitan
Monkayo
Pagadian
Tagum
Davao
Mati
Cotabato
Kidapawan
Moro Gulf
Digos
Koronadal
Polomolok
General Santos
Zamboanga
Jolo
Sulu Archipelago
Tacurong
PALAU
Melekeok
Babelthuap
Koror
Ulimang
Konrai
MALAYSIA
Borneo
Celebes Sea
Laut Maluku (Molucca Sea)
Manado
Bitung
Gorontalo
GORONTALO
SULAWESI UTARA
Semenanjung Minahasa
Ternate
Halmahera
MALUKU UTARA
Laut Halmahera
Teluk Tomini
SULAWESI TENGAH
Palu
Poso
Luwuk
Sulawesi (Celebes)
SULAWESI BARAT
SULAWESI SELATAN
SULAWESI TENGGARA
Kendari
Palopo
Parepare
Makassar
Sungguminasa
Takalar
Baubau
Teluk Bone
Teluk Tolo
Kepulauan Sula
Taliabu
Kepulauan Banggai
Maluku (Moloccas)
Obi
Bacan
Sorong
Manokwari
IRIAN JAYA BARAT
Jazirah Doberai
Teluk Cenderawasih
Laut Seram (Ceram Sea)
Seram
Buru
Ambon
MALUKU
Laut Banda (Banda Sea)
INDONESIA
Kepulauan Kai
Kepulauan Aru
Kepulauan Tanimbar
Kepulauan Barat Daya
Laut Flores (Flores Sea)
Flores
NUSA TENGGARA BARAT
NUSA TENGGARA TIMUR
Lesser Sunda Islands
Bima
Maumere
Ende
Sumba
Waingapu
Laut Sawu (Savu Sea)
Kupang
Timor
DILI
TIMOR-LESTE (EAST TIMOR)
Timor Sea
Arafura Sea
Ashmore and Cartier Islands (Australia)
WESTERN AUSTRALIA
Joseph Bonaparte Gulf
Darwin
Melville Island
NORTHERN TERRITORY
ARNHEM LAND
AUSTRALIA
Meters
Feet
6000 19685
5000 16404
4000 13123
3000 9843
2000 6562
1000 3281
500 1640
200 656
100 328
0
LAND BELOW SEA LEVEL
100 328
200 656
1000 3281
2000 6562
4000 13123
6000 19685

1:9,390,000

Mercator Projection

0 150 300 450 600 kilometers

0 100 200 300 400 miles

EASTERN INDONESIA and PAPUA NEW GUINEA

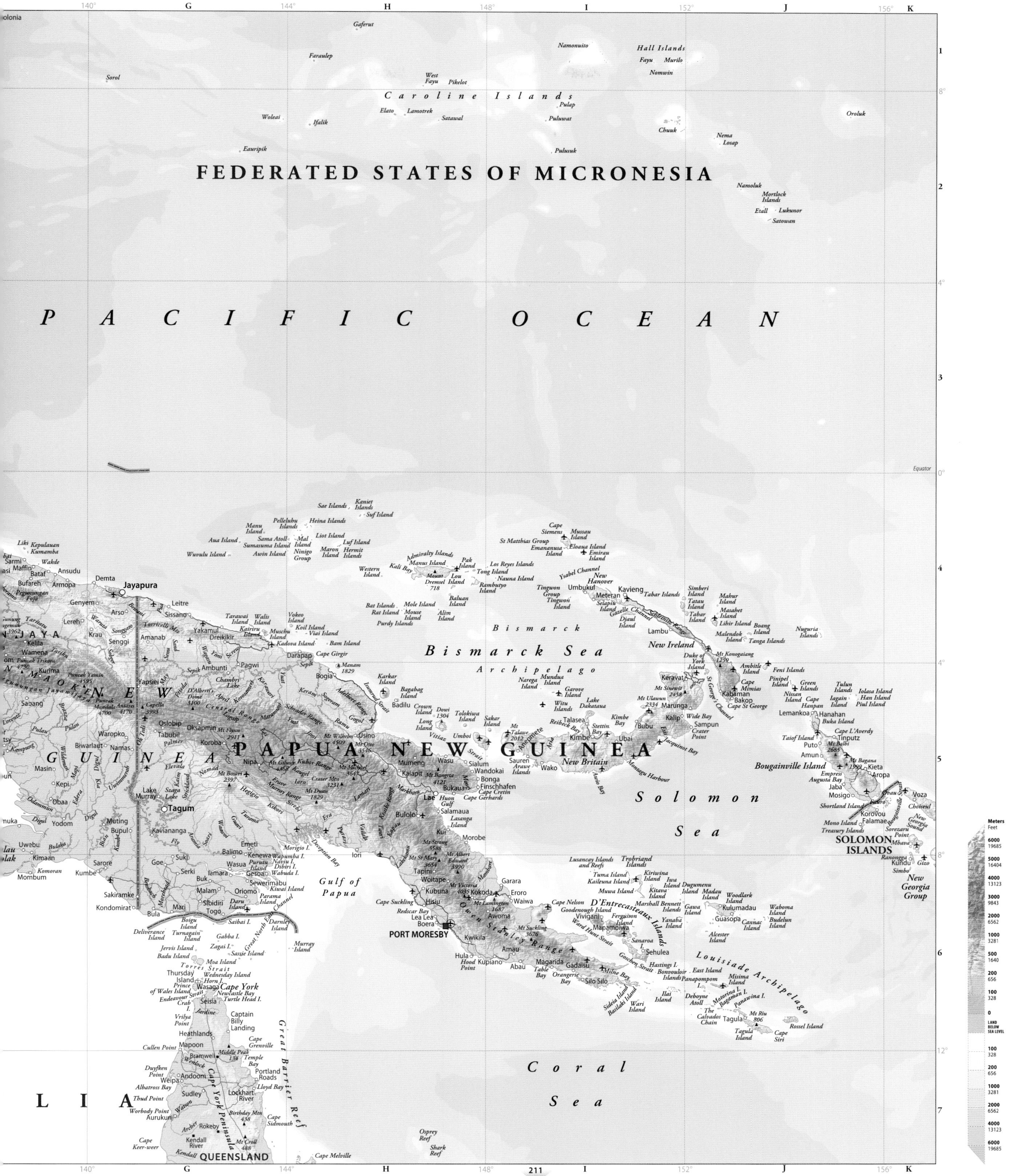

FEDERATED STATES OF MICRONESIA
PACIFIC OCEAN
Caroline Islands
Gaferut
Faraulep
Sorol
West Fayu
Pikelot
Namonuito
Hall Islands
Fayu
Murilo
Nomwin
Elato
Lamotrek
Satawal
Pulap
Puluwat
Woleai
Ifalik
Chuuk
Nema
Losap
Oroluk
Eauripik
Pulusuk
Namoluk
Mortlock Islands
Etall
Lukunor
Satowan
Equator
Jayapura
PAPUA NEW GUINEA
NEW GUINEA
Bismarck Sea
Bismarck Archipelago
New Ireland
New Britain
Kavieng
Admiralty Islands
Manus Island
Solomon Sea
Gulf of Papua
PORT MORESBY
Lae
Madang
Mt Wilhelm 4509
Owen Stanley Range
D'Entrecasteaux Islands
Louisiade Archipelago
Trobriand Islands
Bougainville Island
Buka Island
SOLOMON ISLANDS
New Georgia Group
Choiseul
Coral Sea
Torres Strait
Cape York
Cape York Peninsula
QUEENSLAND
Great Barrier Reef
Thursday Island
Tagum
Wewak
Mt Hagen
Rabaul
Kokoda
Kimbe
Alotau
Misima Island
Rossel Island
Tagula Island
Woodlark Island
Feni Islands
Green Islands
Nissan Island
Tanga Islands
Lihir Island
Tabar Islands
Mussau Island
Emirau Island
St Matthias Group
Ninigo Group
Hermit Islands
Wuvulu Island
Aua Island
Karkar Island
Manam
Fly
Sepik
Ramu
Markham
Central Range
Weipa
Kimaan
Merauke
Kiunga
Daru Island
Mt Victoria 4035
Mt Lamington 1687
Goodenough Island
Ferguson Island
Normanby Island
Sideia Island
Basilaki Island
Cape Melville
Osprey Reef
Shark Reef
Meters
Feet
6000
19685
5000
16404
4000
13123
3000
9843
2000
6562
1000
3281
500
1640
200
656
100
328
0
LAND BELOW SEA LEVEL
140°
144°
148°
152°
156°
G
H
I
J
K

Oceania

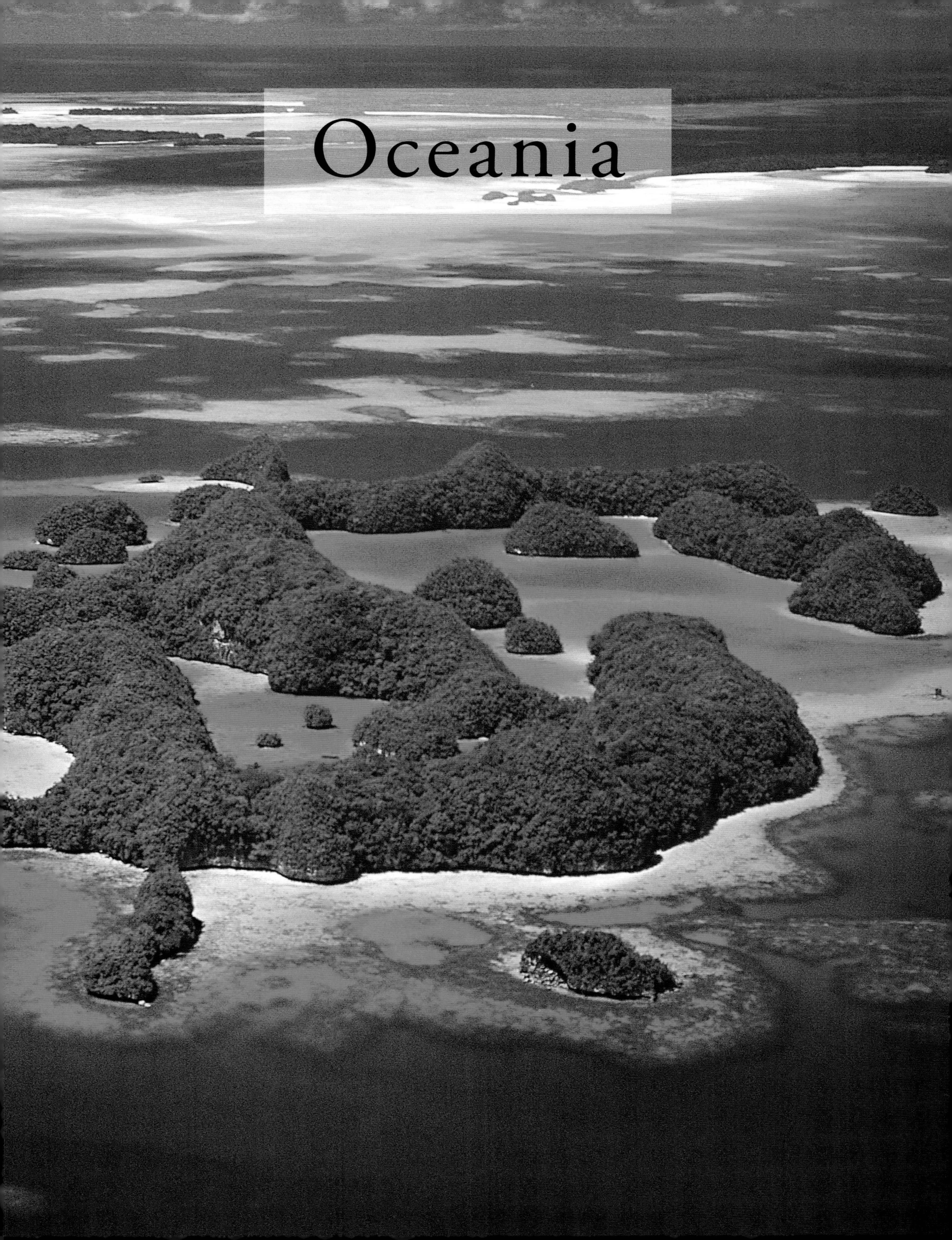

AUSTRALIA and NEW ZEALAND

While the continent of Oceania covers a large area spattered with numerous islands—most of which are quite small and located far apart—it is Australia and New Zealand that account for over 90 percent of the land and population. The Australian continent, because of its size, enjoys a variety of climates, including Mediterranean climatic regions in the south and southwest. Over 90 percent of Australians reside in urban areas, and a majority of New Zealanders prefer the northern island.

Previous pages Lapped by crystal clear waters, and including a number of islands known as the "Rock Islands"—Palau is a popular tourist destination and a magnet for diving enthusiasts.

AUSTRALIA

Australia is unique inasmuch as it is the world's sixth largest country occupying an entire continent. Surrounded by ocean with no land borders, it is sometimes called Earth's largest island. The country's coastline is bordered by the Timor and Arafura seas to the north, the South Pacific to the east, the wild Southern Ocean to the south, and the Indian Ocean to the west. Australia is an ancient land that time has eroded—it is also home to the oldest continuous culture in the world, that of the Australian Aborigines.

The Ranges

The Great Dividing Range runs along Australia's eastern seaboard, stretching from Queensland's Cape York Peninsula in the north to the island of Tasmania in the south. Mt Kosciuszko, the highest peak on the range, is 2,229 meters (7,313 feet) above sea level, and is part of the small alpine region near the New South Wales–Victoria border. West of the dividing range, the topography is predominately flat—a few low ranges are scattered around the continent, including the Grampians in Victoria, the Flinders in South Australia, the MacDonnells near Alice Springs, and the Hammersley Range in Western Australia. Two of the country's most well-known landforms rise up near the center of Australia. These are Uluru, known to European settlers as Ayers Rock, and Kata Tjuta, also referred to as the Olgas.

The heavily eroded country has an average elevation of just 330 meters (1,083 feet) above sea level—which makes it the lowest continent in the world. The lowest point is 15 meters (49 feet) below sea level at Lake Eyre. Located in South Australia, this is the largest salt pan in the world, and it covers about 1,170,000 square kilometers (450,000 square miles)—about one-sixth of the entire country.

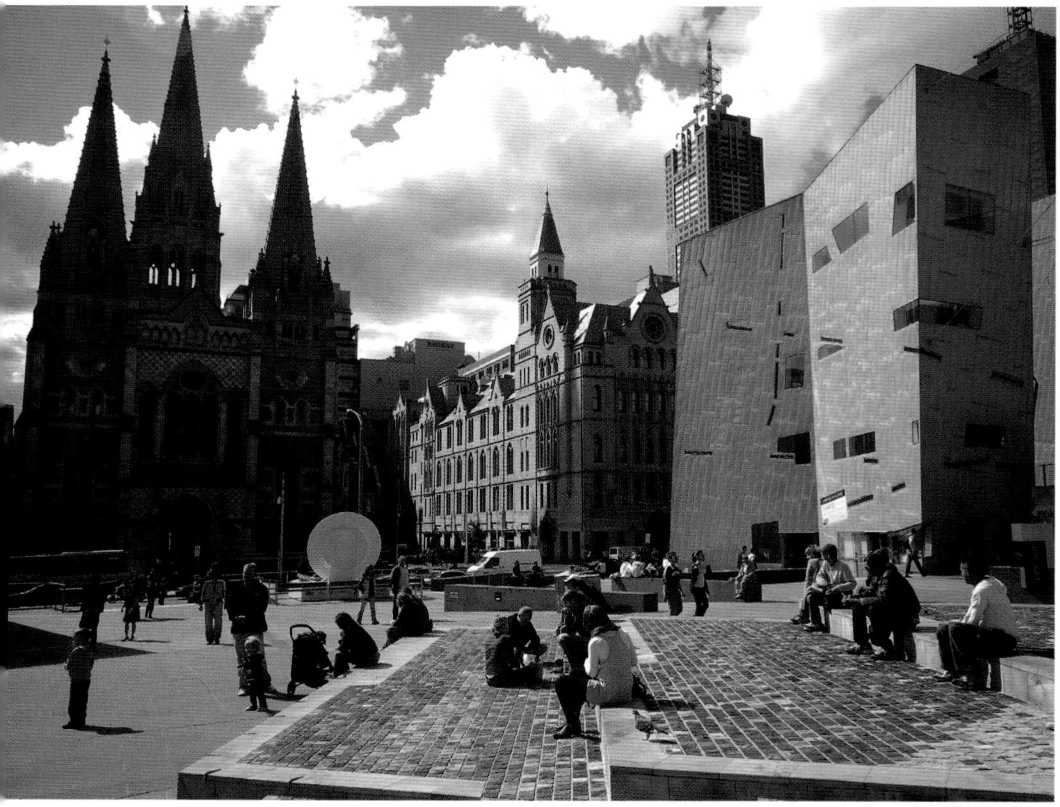

Below Melbourne is a bustling cosmopolitan city, where old and new stand side-by-side. Stately St Paul's Cathedral, on Flinders Street, overlooks the metallic facade of the modern buildings of Federation Square.

Australia's Spectacular Gorges

The Australian landmass is geologically stable, experiencing no significant earthquake or volcanic activity. Its ancient sandstone gorges are, in some cases, more than 100 million years old. The dried-up river beds at the base of the gorges feature red boulders and, occasionally, deep waterholes, while waterfalls flow down the gouged sides of the high sandstone walls. There are awe-inspiring gorges throughout Australia—in Far North Queensland spectacular examples include the gorges at Carnarvon, Mossman, and Lawn Hills, while Western Australia boasts the Geike and Windjana gorges. Kakadu and Katherine Gorge in the Northern Territory are situated in the wet tropics, and their flora reflects the benefit of extra rainfall. The deepest gorges are, however, found under the sea. The Murray Canyons reach a depth of 4,575 meters (15,000 feet), and extend for more than 150 kilometers (93 miles) off South Australia. Geologic evidence indicates that this region is similar to the geology of Antarctica, reinforcing the fact that the two landmasses were once one.

Desert Landscape

Australia is a semiarid to arid land—10 deserts comprise almost 20 percent of the landmass, and it is the driest continent on Earth. The desert areas are located mainly in the central lowlands and western plateau.

The Simpson Desert, which covers parts of South Australia, Queensland, and the Northern Territory, is a sand desert with dunes that stretch 160 kilometers (100 miles). These dunes can reach an amazing 40 meters (130 feet) in height, and are stationary, anchored by vegetation. The dips in between the dunes—which can be up to

COUNTRIES	OFFICIAL NAME	AREA	POPULATION	CAPITAL	RELIGION	POPULATION DENSITY	HIGHEST POINT	CURRENCY
Australia	Commonwealth of Australia	7,686,850 km^2/2,967,910 mi^2	21,262,000	Canberra	✝67.4%, ☸1.9%, ☪1.5%, ○29.2%	2.7/km^2, 7.1/mi^2	Mt Kosciuszko 2,229 m/7,313 ft	Dollar
New Zealand	New Zealand	268,021 km^2/103,483 mi^2	4,213,000	Wellington	✝53.5%, ○46.5%	16/km^2, 40/mi^2	Aoraki (Mt Cook) 3,754 m/12,316 ft	Dollar

DEPENDENCIES AND TERRITORIES	OFFICIAL NAME	AREA	POPULATION	CAPITAL	RELIGION	POPULATION DENSITY	HIGHEST POINT	CURRENCY
Ashmore and Cartier Islands (Australia)	Territory of Ashmore and Cartier Islands	5 km^2/2 mi^2	None	None	—	—	3 m/10 ft	—
Christmas Island (Australia)	Territory of Christmas Island	135 km^2/52 mi^2	1,400	The Settlement	☸36%, ✡25%, ✝18%, ○21%	10/km^2, 27/mi^2	Murray Hill 361 m/1,184 ft	Dollar
Cocos (Keeling) Islands (Australia)	Territory of Cocos (Keeling) Islands	14 km^2/5 mi^2	600	West Island	☪180%, ○20%	43/km^2, 120/mi^2	5 m/16 ft	Dollar
Coral Sea Islands (Australia)	Coral Sea Islands Territory	3 km^2/1 mi^2	None	None	—	—	6 m/20 ft	—
Norfolk Island (Australia)	Territory of Norfolk Island	35 km^2/13 mi^2	2,140	Kingston	✝62.7%, ○37.3%	61/km^2, 165/mi^2	Mt Bates 319 m/1,047 ft	Dollar

140 meters (450 feet) apart—feature eucalyptus and acacia trees, and sometimes large groups of bloodwood trees.

The main deserts of south-central Australia are stony deserts—the Tirari Desert and Sturt's Stony Desert. These consist of large areas of wind-eroded rock and gravel known as gibber plains. Their soils contain iron oxide which gives them their rich, characteristic, red color.

The Nullarbor Plain runs across southwestern Australia, to the north of the Great Australian Bight. At around 200,000 square kilometers (77,220 square miles), it is one of the largest areas of karst topography in the world. This vast expanse of limestone harbors huge caverns and dolines (sinkholes) that are not always immediately discernible on the surface. While this is an arid landscape—

Above The giant rock stacks known as the Twelve Apostles are the star attractions of Victoria's Great Ocean Road. Due to erosion, only eight formations are left standing above the water line.

Left Geike Gorge is a spectacular 30 meter (98 ft) gorge in the rugged, remote Kimberley region in the northwest of Western Australia.

Right Uluru (Ayers Rock) in Australia's Northern Territory, has been inscribed as a World Heritage Site. Because the local Aboriginal people revere the site as a sacred place, climbing the rock is discouraged.

Nullarbor being derived from the Latin for "no trees"—it does support hardy shrubs such as bluebush and saltbush.

The Driest Continent

The majority of Australia's rivers lie in the eastern part of the continent. River flows are erratic and salinity is a growing problem. The climate is affected by the irregular fluctuations of the El Niño and La Niña cycles of the Southern Oscillation that in some years result in droughts accompanied by bushfires, and in other years in heavy rains, flooding, and more frequent tropical cyclones in the north. Median annual rainfall ranges from 180 centimeters (71 inches) on the northeast Queensland coast to 20 centimeters (8 inches) in the arid center, but the overall average for the continent is less than 50 centimeters (20 inches) a year. Artesian (underground) water is often the only source of water for inland towns such as Alice Springs—central Australia is inhospitable and very sparsely populated. Temperatures across the continent vary—the average daytime winter temperature in Tasmania is 12°C (52°F), and over 30°C (86°F) during the wet season in the tropical north.

Above The carnivorous marsupial known as the Tasmanian devil *(Sarcophilus harrisii)* was declared an endangered species in 2008. Its survival is threatened by "devil facial tumor disease," a highly contagious transmissible cancer.

NEW ZEALAND

New Zealand is a remote group of islands located in the South Pacific Ocean. The nearest significant landmass is Australia, which is 1,198 nautical miles to the west, across the Tasman Sea. To the north and east of the country lies the Pacific Ocean, and to its south, the Southern Ocean.

Below The Groom River flows through the lush Blue Tier rainforest region of Tasmania's northeast highlands. It is the last pristine, intact tributary of the George River.

It is a land of snow-capped mountains, deep fjords, bubbling mud pools, and excellent wine-growing regions.

The Country's Topography

Mountains and uplands are defining features of New Zealand, with approximately three-quarters of its surface higher than 200 meters (656 feet). The small archipelago straddles two geophysical plates. Twenty million years ago the land was low-lying or submerged, and remained so until tectonic activity, which continues to this day, gave it shape. The mountain ranges are mostly soft metamorphic rocks and show the effects of crustal movement. The only active volcanoes are located on the North Island, but there is evidence of volcanic activity on the South Island, where Dunedin and Christchurch lie on or beside long-extinct volcanoes. There are few flat expanses in New Zealand—the largest flat region is the Canterbury Plains on South Island. This fertile area produces 80 percent of New Zealand's crops and grains.

New Zealand's coastline is deeply indented with fjords, sounds, and bays. The waters around North Island are warm and subtropical, while Stewart Island in the south is surrounded by sub-Antarctic waters. Northland, to the northwest of Auckland, is a region of coastal incisions, whereas the coastal areas further south are less indented—apart from Fiordland in the southwest, and the sounds of South Island's Marlborough region.

Climate

The Southern Alps and the mountain ranges of the North Island are not very high, but a combination of

length, height, and SSW–NNE orientation creates a lively interaction with prevailing westerly winds. Near the main divide, annual precipitation can exceed 500 centimeters (197 inches), but a few miles east, the total may be just 50 centimeters (20 inches). Most precipitation falls as rain, but snow does occur, and along the Southern Alps lie 360 glaciers that cover about 1,160 square kilometers (448 square miles). Tropical weather systems are fairly common in Northland, and sometimes penetrate into higher latitudes, causing floods and triggering landslides.

The tempering effect of the oceans is felt throughout the country. While seasonal differences in weather and climate primarily reflect the duration of daylight, in some years the principal driver is the Southern Oscillation, and in the north and east of the country the El Niño phase is associated with frequent southwesterlies and less than average rainfall, while the La Niña phase is characterized by frequent northeasterlies and higher than average rainfall. It is therefore wrong to speak of only one New Zealand environment, even though in the mid-1800s land companies and government officials promoted the image of a uniform Mediterranean environment where crops of olives, grapes, and wheat would thrive. Experience has shown that these plants can be successfully grown, but not everywhere. In the lowlands, conditions range from cool temperate in Southland to marginally subtropical in Northland, and from an almost continental temperature regime in the dry inland basins of Otago and Canterbury to persistently cool and wet weather in Stewart Island and the sub-Antarctic islands.

Geysers

North Island is situated on the Pacific "Ring of Fire," where the Pacific Plate is being subducted beneath the Indo-Australian Plate. This tectonic activity has given rise not only to the volcanoes of North Island, but also to its world-famous geysers. Here at a depth of only 5 kilometers (3 miles) below ground level the temperature of Earth's crust reaches 660°F (350°C). Groundwater is heated and rises to the surface as hot springs. When the heat is such that the groundwater becomes steam, it shoots out of the earth as a fountain known as a geyser.

There are only about 1,000 active geysers worldwide, and New Zealand has the fourth-largest concentration of these geothermal springs—with the majority located in the Waikato region.

Left There are around 100 geothermal pools in New Zealand, many of them concentrated in the Rotorua area of the North Island. Bathing in the mineral-rich pools may help to soften the skin, ease muscle pain, and improve circulation.

Below Queenstown on New Zealand's South Island offers visitors all manner of extreme sports. Many visitors also come to this district to follow in the steps of Frodo and Sam on a *Lord of the Rings* tour.

PACIFIC REGION

There are some 20,000–30,000 islands in the Pacific Ocean, most of which are grouped into one of three clusters: Melanesia, Micronesia, and Polynesia. Melanesia means "black islands" and originated in the nineteenth century as a racial classification by Europeans; it now has currency as a geopolitical designation. Micronesia means "small islands" and refers to a wide zone of islands north of Melanesia. Polynesia means "many islands" and is the largest of the three divisions.

Above A Huri dancer participates in a ritual. Many tribal people in Papua New Guinea have a strong belief in witchcraft, sorcery, and ancestral spirits. Those found guilty of sorcery are usually punished and sometimes even killed.

Right The tropical paradise of Bora Bora—230 kilometers (140 miles) from Papeete—is considered the most beautiful island in French Polynesia. During World War II, it served as a US military supply base.

Territorial Clusters

The islands that make up Pacific Oceania are generally small and very far apart. Melanesia refers to the islands and island nations between the western part of the South Pacific and the Arafura Sea north and northeast of Australia, and includes Papua New Guinea and the Bismarck Archipelago, New Caledonia, the Solomon Islands, Vanuatu, and Fiji. Micronesia takes in Guam, Kiribati, the Marianas, the Marshall Islands, Nauru, Palau, and the Federated States of Micronesia. Most of Micronesia is north of the equator.

Polynesia—sometimes referred to as the "Polynesian Triangle"—encompasses islands in the central Pacific both north and south of the equator within a triangular shape that has the Hawaiian Islands as a northern apex, New Zealand at the south-southwest, and Easter Island (Rapa Nui) at the east-southeastern extremity. Within this region lie French Polynesia, the Cook Islands, Tonga, Samoa, American Samoa, Tuvalu, and the Midway Islands, among others.

The definition of Pacific Oceania is as much a social construction as it is based on the geographic position of islands. The western part of Melanesia, for instance, is mostly a part of Indonesia and is, therefore, often more commonly associated with Southeast Asia than with the Pacific. The divide between Melanesia and Southeast Asia is envisioned as the meridian on New Guinea that separates Indonesian provinces from those of Papua New Guinea.

Other examples of islands in the Pacific where populations are identified more with the continent they are near than with the ocean include Japan, the Philippines, and the Galapagos Islands off Ecuador in South America in the east. Historically, the Hawaiian Islands had been part of the Pacific Ocean cultural realm, but their status as a state in the United States and the large majority non-Pacific Islander population links them today with that country rather than with the Islander cultures that they once epitomized.

Topography

There are generally two types of island in Pacific Oceania, high islands and low islands. High islands are typically volcanic, are larger, have fertile soils, more fresh water to support agriculture, and topography ranging from dramatic mountaintops to sea level beaches. The climate of the region is mainly tropical, but many of the high islands also have climatic variety, with the lee sides of mountains being dry in comparison to heavy downpours and lush greenery on windward sides.

Large islands that have prominent, beautiful, two-volcano centers include Tahiti, the principal island of French Polynesia; and Moorea, another island in the same chain that is especially popular as a tourist and honeymoon destination.

By contrast, the larger islands of Melanesia are made of multiple volcanic peaks and distinct mountain ranges separated by domesticated valleys. These large islands include: New Guinea, the largest island in Pacific Oceania; the larger islands of the Bismarck Archipelago; Bougainville in the Solomon Islands group (but politically in Papua New Guinea); Grand Terre, the main island of New Caledonia; and Guadalcanal, the main island of the Solomon Islands. Reaching a height of 4,509 meters (14,793 feet), Mount Wilhelm—located in the center of Papua New Guinea—is the tallest peak in Pacific Oceania.

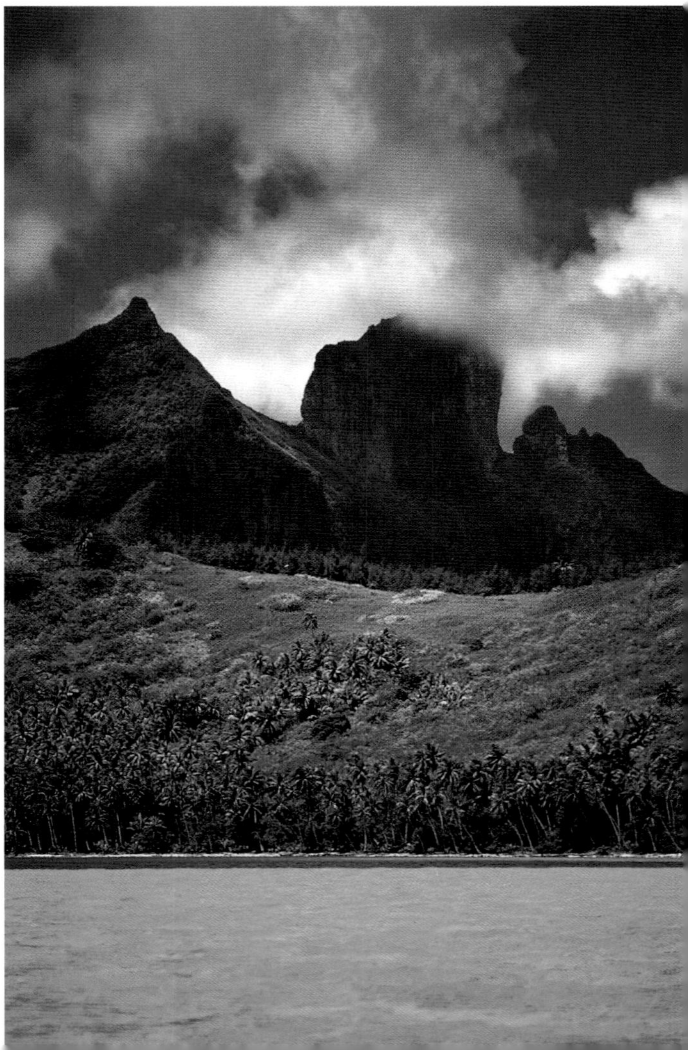

COUNTRIES	OFFICIAL NAME	AREA	POPULATION	CAPITAL	RELIGION	POPULATION DENSITY	HIGHEST POINT	CURRENCY
Fiji	Matanitu ko Viti; Republic of the Fiji Islands	18,270 km²/7,054 mi²	944,000	Suva	✝53%, ॐ34%, ☪7%, ○6%	52/km², 134/mi²	Tomanivi 1,324 m/4,344 ft	Dollar
Kiribati	Republic of Kiribati	811 km²/313 mi²	112,000	Tarawa	✝92%, ○8%	139/km², 361/mi²	81 m/266 ft	Australian dollar
Marshall Islands	Republic of the Marshall Islands	181.3 km²/70 mi²	64,500	Majuro	✝97.5%, ○2.5%	356/km², 922/mi²	10 m/33 ft	US dollar
Micronesia	Federated States of Micronesia	702 km²/271 mi²	107,000	Palikir	✝97%, ○3%	153/km², 396/mi²	Dolohmwar (Totolom) 791 m/2,595 ft	US dollar
Nauru	Republic of Nauru	21 km²/8 mi²	14,000	Yaren	✝79%, ○21%	667/km², 1,750/mi²	61 m/200 ft	Australian dollar
Palau	Beluu er a Belau; Republic of Palau	458 km²/177 mi²	20,700	Melekeok	✝71.7%, 🯅8.8%, ○19.5%	45/km², 117/mi²	Ngerchelchuus 242 m/794 ft	US dollar
Papua New Guinea	Independent State of Papua New Guinea	452,860 km²/174,850 mi²	6,057,000	Port Moresby	✝66%, 🯅34%	13/km², 34/mi²	Mt Wilhelm 4,509 m/14,793 ft	Kina
Samoa	Malo Sa'oloto Tuto'atasi o Samoa; Independent State of Samoa	2,934 km²/1,133 mi²	220,000	Apia	✝98%, ○2%	75/km², 194/mi²	Mauga Silisili 1,857 m/6,093 ft	Tala
Solomon Islands	Solomon Islands	27,450 km²/10,633 mi²	595,000	Honiara	✝97.1%, 2.9%	22/km², 56/mi²	Mt Makarakomburu 2,477 m/8,028 ft	Dollar
Tonga	Pule'anga Tonga; Kingdom of Tonga	718 km²/277 mi²	120,000	Nuku'alofa	-	168/km², 436/mi²	1,033 m/3,389 ft	Pa'anga
Tuvalu	Tuvalu	26 km²/10 mi²	12,000	Funafuti	✝98.4%, ○1.6%	473/km², 1,230/mi²	5 m/16 ft	Australian dollar Tuvaluan dollar
Vanuatu	Ripablik blong Vanuatu; Republic of Vanuatu; République de Vanuatu	12,200 km²/4,710 mi²	218,000	Port Vila	✝82.5%, 🯅5.6%, ○11.9%	18/km², 46/mi²	Tabwémasana 1,877 m/6,158 ft	Vatu

DEPENDENCIES AND TERRITORIES	OFFICIAL NAME	AREA	POPULATION	CAPITAL	RELIGION	POPULATION DENSITY	HIGHEST POINT	CURRENCY
American Samoa (USA)	Territory of American Samoa	199 km²/77 mi²	65,600	Pago Pago	✝100%	330/km², 852/mi²	Lata Mountain 964 m/3,163 ft	US dollar
Baker and Howland Islands (USA)	Baker and Howland Islands	4.7 km²/2 mi²	None	None	—	—	—	—
Cook Islands (New Zealand)	Cook Islands	237 km²/92 mi²	11,800	Avarua	✝90.2%, ○9.8%	50/km², 129/mi²	Te Manga 652 m/2,140 ft	NZ dollar
French Polynesia (France)	Pays d'Outre-mer de la Polynésie Française	541 km²/209 mi²	287,000	Papeete	✝84%, ○16%	530/km², 1,373/mi²	Mont Orohena 2,241 m/7,352 ft	Franc
Guam (USA)	Territory of Guam (Guåhån)	199 km²/77 mi²	178,400	Hågatña (Agana)	✝85%, ○15%	896/km², 2,264/mi²	Mt Lamlam 406 m/1,332 ft	US dollar
Jarvis Island (USA)	Jarvis Island	4.5 km²/2 mi²	None	None	—	—	7 m/23 ft	—
Johnston Atoll (USA)	Johnston Atoll	2.6 km²/1 mi²	None	None	—	—	10 m/33 ft	—
Kingman Reef (USA)	Kingman Reef	1 ha/2½ acres	None	None	—	—	2 m/7 ft	—
Midway Islands (USA)	Midway Islands	6.2 km²/2 mi²	40 (US FWS staff)	None	—	6/km², 20/mi²	13 m/43 ft	US dollar
New Caledonia (France)	Territoire des Nouvelle-Calédonie et Dépendances	18,575 km²/7,172 mi²	227,000	Nouméa	✝90%, ○10%	12/km², 32/mi²	Mont Panie 1,628 m/5,341 m	Franc
Niue (New Zealand)	Niue	260 km²/100 mi²	1,400	Alofi	✝81%, ○19%	5.4/km², 14/mi²	68 m/223 ft	NZ dollar
Northern Mariana Islands (USA)	Commonwealth of the Northern Mariana Islands	477 km²/184 mi²	88,600	Saipan	N/A	186/km², 482/mi²	965 m/3,166 ft	US dollar
Palmyra Atoll (USA)	Palmyra Atoll	4 km²/1½ mi²	None	None	—	—	3 m/10 ft	—
Pitcairn Islands (UK)	Pitcairn, Henderson, Ducie, and Oeno Islands	47 km²/18 mi²	48	Adamstown	✝100%	1/km², 2.7/mi²	Pawala Valley Ridge 347 m/1,138 ft	NZ dollar
Tokelau (New Zealand)	Tokelau	10 km²/4 mi²	1,400	None	✝98%, ○2%	142/km², 354/mi²	5 m/16 ft	NZ dollar
Wake Island (USA)	Wake Island	6.5 km²/2½ mi²	None	None	—	—	6 m/20 ft	—
Wallis and Futuna (France)	Territoire des Îles Wallis et Futuna; Territory of the Wallis and Futuna Islands	274 km²/106 mi²	15,200	Mata-Utu	✝99%, ○1%	56/km², 143/mi²	Mont Singavi 765 m/2,510 ft	Franc

There are 22 active volcanoes is Papua New Guinea: Rabaul volcano erupted in 1994, and most of the inhabitants of Manam Island have relocated to the mainland after increased activity from the island's volcano in 2004 to 2005.

The low islands are typically coral reef islands or phosphate rock islands and lack fresh water and agricultural land. Many of these are vulnerable to a potential rise in the level of the ocean due to global warming. The low islands include Nauru, Niue, the Marshall Islands, Kiribati, the northern Cook Islands, and the islands of Palau. These islands depend variously on tourism, phosphate mining, fishing, postage stamp sales, tax haven services, foreign aid, and remittances from abroad for income.

The US territory of Guam—the southernmost of the Marianas Islands—is a mix of coralline and volcanic origins, and while tourism is responsible for its largest source of income, it is also heavily dependent on US military spending. The island is host to the Andersen Air Force Base, which has the longest airstrip in the Pacific region.

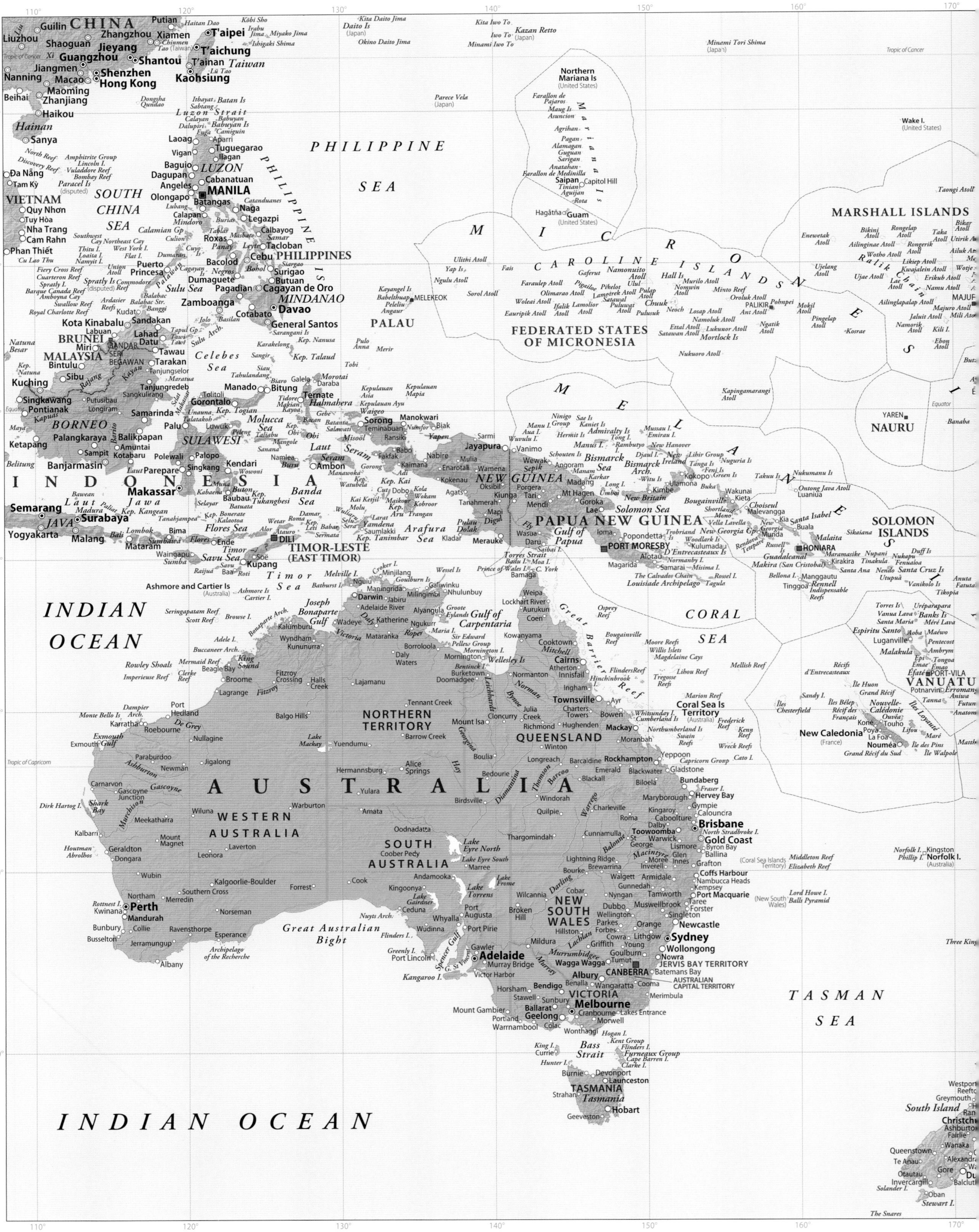
CHINA
T'aipei
T'aichung
Taiwan
Kaohsiung
Guangzhou
Shenzhen
Hong Kong
Macao
Hainan
Haikou
Sanya
VIETNAM
Đa Nẵng
PHILIPPINE SEA
SOUTH CHINA SEA
LUZON
MANILA
PHILIPPINES
MINDANAO
Davao
Zamboanga
Cebu
Northern Mariana Is (United States)
Saipan
Guam (United States)
Wake I. (United States)
MARSHALL ISLANDS
MICRONESIA
CAROLINE ISLANDS
FEDERATED STATES OF MICRONESIA
PALAU
MELEKEOK
PALIKIR
MAJURO
BRUNEI
BANDAR SERI BEGAWAN
MALAYSIA
Kota Kinabalu
Kuching
BORNEO
SULAWESI
Celebes Sea
Molucca Sea
Halmahera
INDONESIA
Java
Laut Jawa
JAVA
Surabaya
Semarang
Yogyakarta
Makassar
Banda Sea
Flores Sea
Savu Sea
Timor Sea
DILI
TIMOR-LESTE (EAST TIMOR)
Arafura Sea
Jayapura
NEW GUINEA
PAPUA NEW GUINEA
PORT MORESBY
Gulf of Papua
Bismarck Sea
Solomon Sea
SOLOMON ISLANDS
HONIARA
NAURU
YAREN
MELANESIA
CORAL SEA
Coral Sea Is Territory (Australia)
VANUATU
PORT-VILA
New Caledonia (France)
Nouméa
Norfolk I. (Australia)
INDIAN OCEAN
Gulf of Carpentaria
Great Barrier Reef
Darwin
NORTHERN TERRITORY
QUEENSLAND
WESTERN AUSTRALIA
SOUTH AUSTRALIA
AUSTRALIA
NEW SOUTH WALES
VICTORIA
TASMANIA
Tasmania
Great Australian Bight
Perth
Adelaide
Melbourne
Sydney
Brisbane
Gold Coast
Newcastle
Wollongong
CANBERRA
AUSTRALIAN CAPITAL TERRITORY
JERVIS BAY TERRITORY
Hobart
Bass Strait
TASMAN SEA
Townsville
Cairns
Alice Springs
Rockhampton
Kalgoorlie-Boulder
Geelong
Launceston
South Island
Tropic of Cancer
Tropic of Capricorn
Equator
110°
120°
130°
140°
150°
160°
170°
20°
10°
0°
30°
40°

1:31,900,000

Mercator Projection

0 500 1000 1500 2000 kilometers

0 250 500 750 1000 miles

OCEANIA POLITICAL

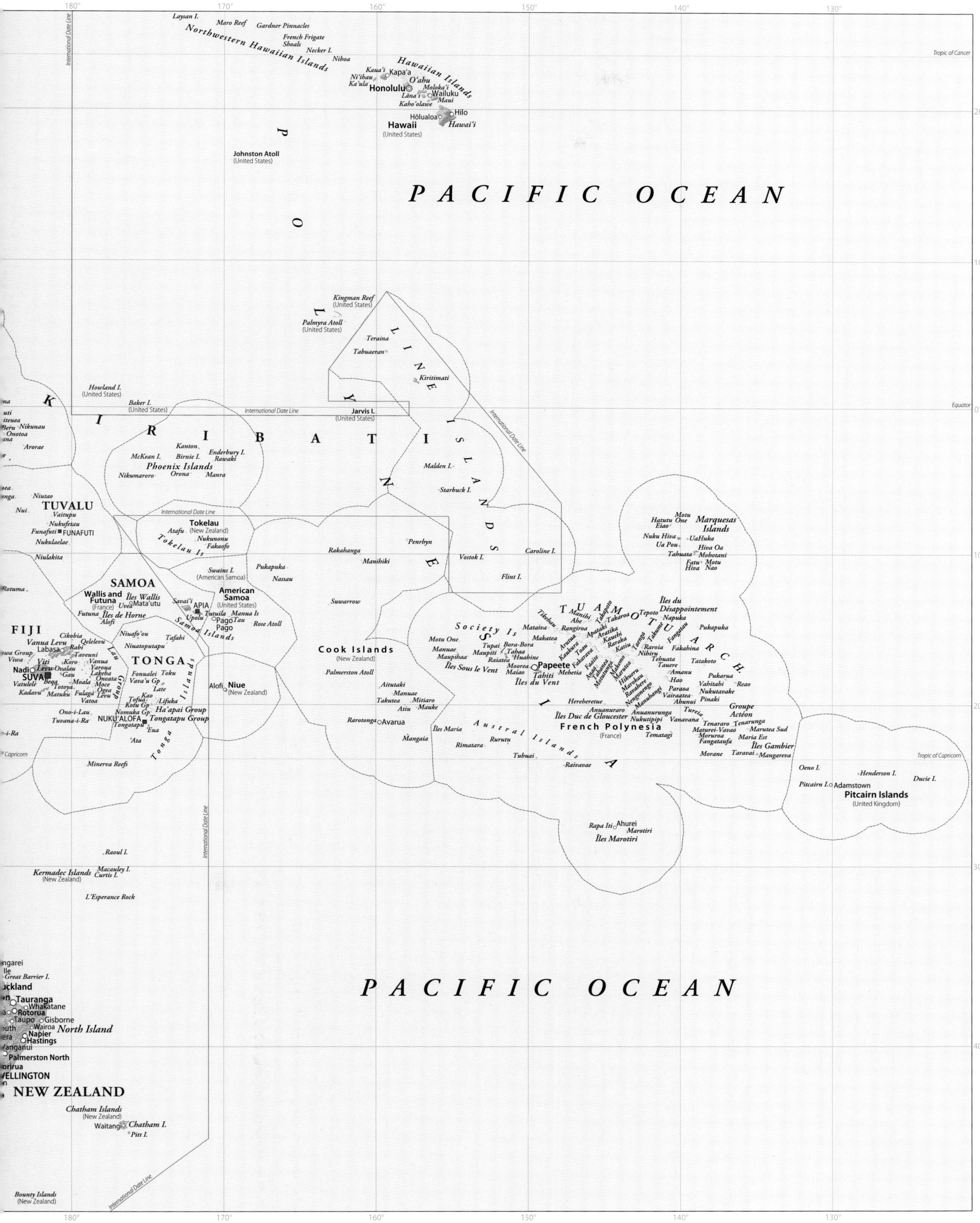

PACIFIC OCEAN
PACIFIC OCEAN
International Date Line
Tropic of Cancer
Equator
Tropic of Capricorn
Laysan I.
Maro Reef
Gardner Pinnacles
Northwestern Hawaiian Islands
French Frigate Shoals
Necker I.
Nihoa
Hawaiian Islands
Kaua'i
Kapa'a
Ni'ihau
Ka'ula
O'ahu
Honolulu
Moloka'i
Wailuku
Lāna'i
Maui
Kaho'olawe
Hilo
Hōlualoa
Hawaii
(United States)
Hawai'i
Johnston Atoll
(United States)
P O L Y N E S I A
Kingman Reef
(United States)
Palmyra Atoll
(United States)
Teraina
Tabuaeran
Kiritimati
LINE ISLANDS
Howland I.
(United States)
Baker I.
(United States)
Jarvis I.
(United States)
K I R I B A T I
Nikunau
Onotoa
Arorae
Kanton
Enderbury I.
McKean I.
Birnie I.
Rawaki
Phoenix Islands
Nikumaroro
Orona
Manra
Malden I.
Starbuck I.
Niutao
TUVALU
Nui
Vaitupu
Nukufetau
Funafuti
FUNAFUTI
Nukulaelae
Niulakita
Tokelau
(New Zealand)
Atafu
Nukunonu
Fakaofo
Tokelau Is
Swains I.
(American Samoa)
Pukapuka
Nassau
Rakahanga
Manihiki
Penrhyn
Vostok I.
Caroline I.
Flint I.
Hatutu
Motu One
Eiao
Marquesas Islands
Nuku Hiva
UaHuka
Ua Pou
Hiva Oa
Tahuata
Mohotani
Fatu Hiva
Motu Nao
Rotuma
SAMOA
Wallis and Futuna
(France)
Îles Wallis
Uvea
Mata'utu
Futuna
Îles de Horne
Alofi
Savai'i
APIA
Upolu
Tutuila
Pago Pago
Manua Is
Tau
American Samoa
(United States)
Rose Atoll
Samoa Islands
Suwarrow
FIJI
Cikobia
Qelelevu
Vanua Levu
Labasa
Rabi
Taveuni
Viti Levu
Nadi
SUVA
Koro
Ovalau
Gau
Vanua Balavu
Lakeba
Oneata
Moala
Moce
Beqa
Totoya
Ogea Levu
Vatulele
Kadavu
Matuku
Fulaga
Vatoa
Lau Group
Niuafo'ou
Niuatoputapu
Tafahi
TONGA
Fonualei
Toku
Vava'u Gp
Late
Kao
Tofua
Kotu Gp
Lifuka
Ha'apai Group
Nomuka Gp
NUKU'ALOFA
Tongatapu
Tongatapu Group
'Eua
'Ata
Tonga Islands
Ono-i-Lau
Tuvana-i-Ra
Minerva Reefs
Alofi
Niue
(New Zealand)
Cook Islands
(New Zealand)
Palmerston Atoll
Aitutaki
Manuae
Takutea
Mitiaro
Atiu
Mauke
Rarotonga
Avarua
Mangaia
Society Is
Motu One
Manuae
Maupihaa
Tupai
Bora-Bora
Maupiti
Tahaa
Raiatea
Huahine
Îles Sous le Vent
Moorea
Maiao
Papeete
Tahiti
Mehetia
Îles du Vent
Mataiva
Tikehau
Makatea
Rangiroa
Manihi
Ahe
Takapoto
Takaroa
Apataki
Arutua
Kaukura
Aratika
Toau
Kauehi
Fakarava
Raraka
Katiu
Faaite
Tepoto
Napuka
Îles du Désappointement
Pukapuka
Fangatau
Fakahina
Raroia
Nihiru
Tatakoto
Tehuata
Tauere
Amanu
Hao
Pukarua
Vahitahi
Reao
Nukutavake
Paraoa
Vairaatea
Ahunui
Pinaki
Hereheretue
Anuanuraro
Anuanurunga
Îles Duc de Gloucester
Nukutipipi
Tureia
Vanavana
Groupe Actéon
Tenararo
Tenarunga
Maturei-Vavao
Marutea Sud
Moruroa
Fangataufa
Maria Est
Îles Gambier
Morane
Taravai
Mangareva
Tematagi
French Polynesia
(France)
T U A M O T U A R C H.
Îles Maria
Austral Islands
Rimatara
Rurutu
Tubuai
Raivavae
Rapa Iti
Ahurei
Marotiri
Îles Marotiri
Oeno I.
Henderson I.
Ducie I.
Pitcairn I.
Adamstown
Pitcairn Islands
(United Kingdom)
Raoul I.
Kermadec Islands
(New Zealand)
Macauley I.
Curtis I.
L'Esperance Rock
Great Barrier I.
Tauranga
Whakatane
Rotorua
Taupo
Gisborne
Wairoa
North Island
Napier
Hastings
Palmerston North
NEW ZEALAND
Chatham Islands
(New Zealand)
Waitangi
Chatham I.
Pitt I.
Bounty Islands
(New Zealand)
180°
170°
160°
150°
140°
130°
20°
10°
0°
30°
40°

197
INDIAN OCEAN
INDONESIA
Jawa (Java)
JAWA BARAT
JAWA TENGAH
JAWA TIMUR
YOGYAKARTA
BALI
NUSA TENGGARA BARAT
NUSA TENGGARA TIMUR
TIMOR-LESTE (EAST TIMOR)
TIMOR SEA
LAUT SAWU (SAVU SEA)
Depok
Bogor
Bandung
Tasikmalaya
Yogyakarta
Surakarta
Malang
Denpasar
Mataram
Kupang
Christmas Island (Australia)
Ashmore and Cartier Islands (Australia)
Darwin
Broome
Port Hedland
Karratha
Carnarvon
Geraldton
Perth
Fremantle
Rockingham
Mandurah
Bunbury
Albany
Kalgoorlie-Boulder
Esperance
KIMBERLEY
PILBARA
GREAT SANDY DESERT
GIBSON DESERT
GREAT VICTORIA DESERT
Little Sandy Desert
TANAMI DESERT
Nullarbor Plain
WESTERN AUSTRALIA
Great Australian Bight
Tropic of Capricorn
Meters
Feet
CHRISTMAS ISLAND
1:1,400,000
1
INDIAN OCEAN
ASHMORE REEF AND CARTIER ISLAND
1:2,800,000
2
3
COCOS (KEELING) ISLANDS
1:1,400,000
South Keeling Islands
HEARD ISLAND
1:2,800,000
4
SOUTHERN OCEAN

1:14,000,000

Lambert Conic Conformal Projection

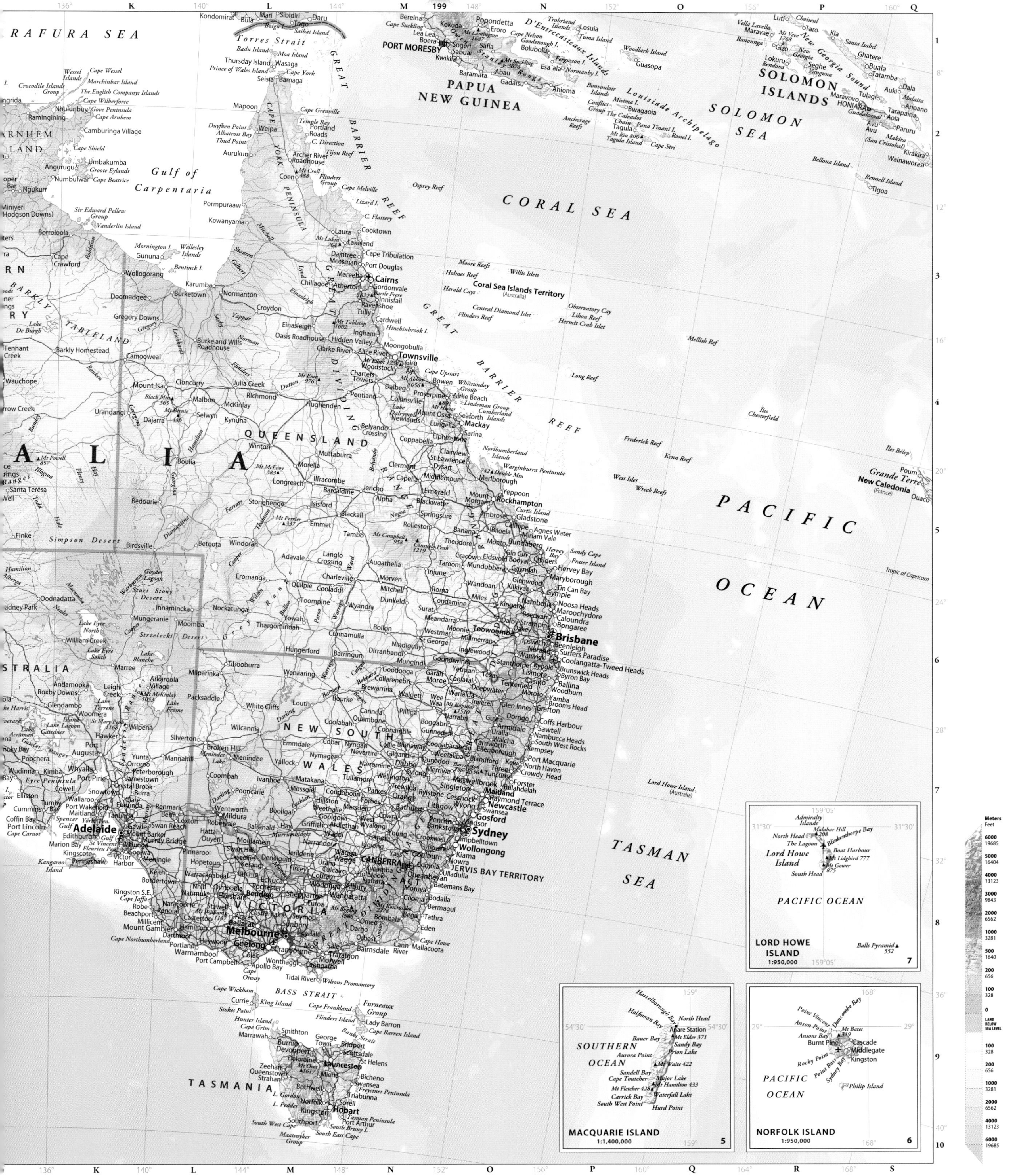
ARAFURA SEA
Torres Strait
PORT MORESBY
PAPUA NEW GUINEA
SOLOMON ISLANDS
SOLOMON SEA
HONIARA
Gulf of Carpentaria
CAPE YORK PENINSULA
GREAT BARRIER REEF
CORAL SEA
Coral Sea Islands Territory (Australia)
Cairns
Townsville
Mackay
Rockhampton
QUEENSLAND
GREAT DIVIDING RANGE
BARKLY TABLELAND
Simpson Desert
PACIFIC OCEAN
New Caledonia (France)
Tropic of Capricorn
Brisbane
Gold Coast
NEW SOUTH WALES
Newcastle
Sydney
Wollongong
CANBERRA
JERVIS BAY TERRITORY
TASMAN SEA
Lord Howe Island (Australia)
Adelaide
VICTORIA
Melbourne
Geelong
BASS STRAIT
TASMANIA
Launceston
Hobart
LORD HOWE ISLAND 1:950,000
PACIFIC OCEAN
Lord Howe Island
Balls Pyramid 552
7
MACQUARIE ISLAND 1:1,400,000
SOUTHERN OCEAN
5
NORFOLK ISLAND 1:950,000
PACIFIC OCEAN
Kingston
Philip Island
6
Meters Feet
6000 19685
5000 16404
4000 13123
3000 9843
2000 6562
1000 3281
500 1640
200 656
100 328
0
LAND BELOW SEA LEVEL

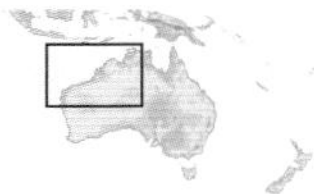

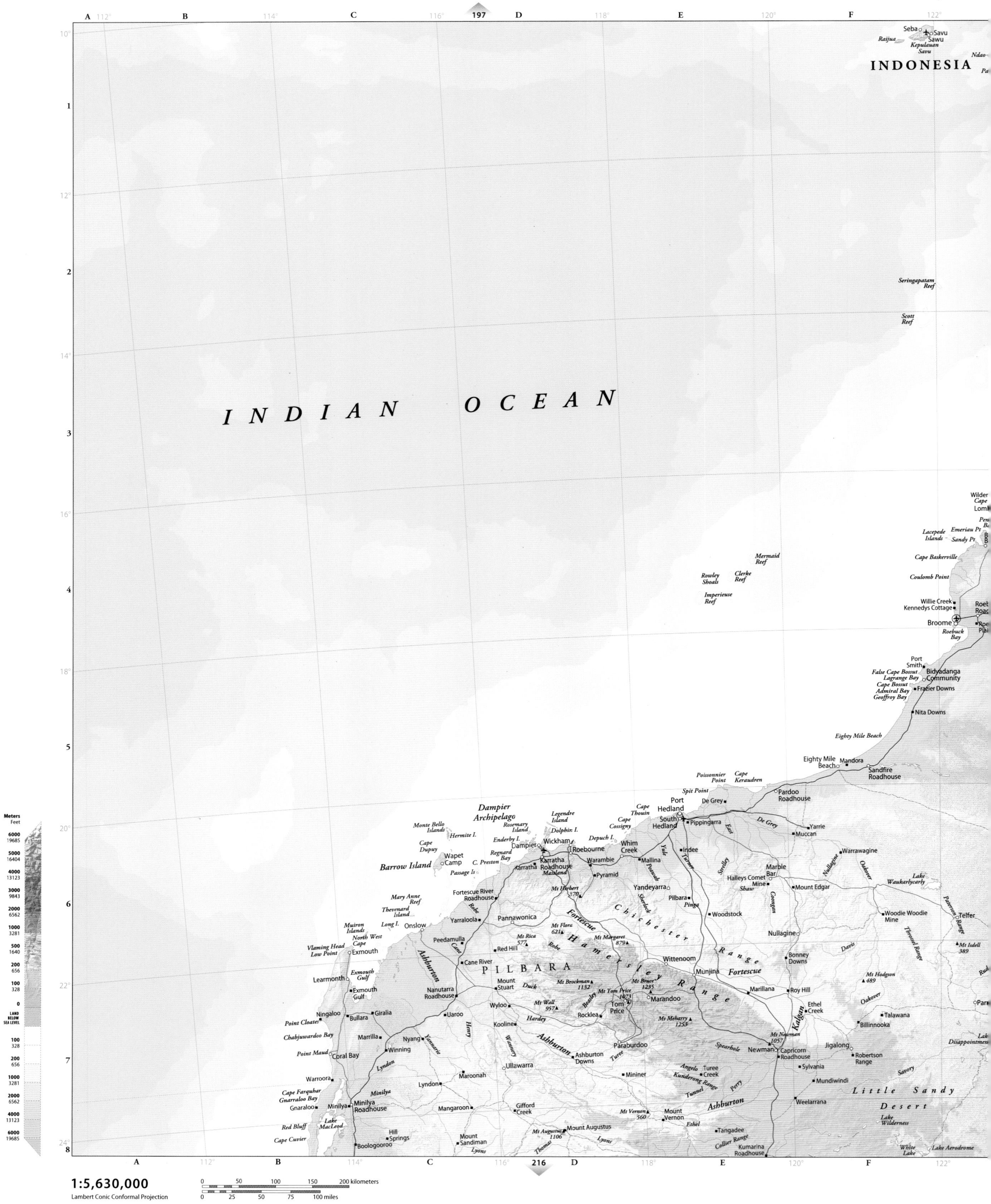

197
216
INDIAN OCEAN
INDONESIA
Seba
Savu
Sawu
Raijua
Kepulauan Savu
Ndao
Seringapatam Reef
Scott Reef
Mermaid Reef
Rowley Shoals
Clerke Reef
Imperieuse Reef
Lacepede Islands
Emeriau Pt
Sandy Pt
Cape Baskerville
Coulomb Point
Willie Creek
Kennedys Cottage
Broome
Roebuck Bay
Port Smith
False Cape Bossut
Lagrange Bay
Cape Bossut
Admiral Bay
Geoffroy Bay
Bidyadanga Community
Frazier Downs
Nita Downs
Eighty Mile Beach
Mandora
Sandfire Roadhouse
Poissonnier Point
Cape Keraudren
Pardoo Roadhouse
Spit Point
De Grey
Port Hedland
South Hedland
Pippingarra
Cape Thouin
Cape Cossigny
Dampier Archipelago
Legendre Island
Rosemary Island
Dolphin I.
Monte Bello Islands
Hermite I.
Enderby I.
Depuch I.
Dampier
Wickham
Roebourne
Whim Creek
Cape Dupuy
Wapet Camp
Barrow Island
C. Preston
Regnard Bay
Karratha
Karratha Roadhouse
Maitland
Warambie
Mallina
Indee
Yarrie
Muccan
Warrawagine
Pyramid
Yandeyarra
Marble Bar
Halleys Comet Mine
Mount Edgar
Lake Waukarlycarly
Mt Herbert 570
Fortescue River Roadhouse
Mary Anne Reef
Thevenard Island
Yarraloola
Pannawonica
Pilbara
Woodstock
Woodie Woodie Mine
Telfer
Muiron Islands
Long I.
Onslow
Mt Flora 621
Chichester
Nullagine
Vlaming Head
North West Cape
Low Point
Exmouth
Peedamulla
Mt Rica 577
Red Hill
Mt Margaret 879
Hamersley Range
Wittenoom
Bonney Downs
Mt Isdell 389
Exmouth Gulf
Learmonth
Cane River
PILBARA
Munjina
Fortescue
Mt Brockman 1132
Mt Bruce 1235
Mt Hodgson 489
Nanutarra Roadhouse
Mount Stuart
Mt Tom Price 1073
Tom Price
Marandoo
Marillana
Roy Hill
Ningaloo
Bullara
Giralia
Uaroo
Wyloo
Mt Wall 957
Rocklea
Ethel Creek
Talawana
Point Cloates
Koolinee
Mt Meharry 1253
Billinnooka
Chabjuwardoo Bay
Marrilla
Nyang
Paraburdoo
Mt Newman 1057
Newman
Capricorn Roadhouse
Jigalong
Robertson Range
Lake Disappointment
Point Maud
Coral Bay
Winning
Ashburton Downs
Ullawarra
Sylvania
Warroora
Maroonah
Mininer
Turee Creek
Mundiwindi
Cape Farquhar
Gnarraloo Bay
Lyndon
Weelarrana
Little Sandy Desert
Gnaraloo
Minilya Roadhouse
Mangaroon
Gifford Creek
Mt Vernon 560
Mount Vernon
Ashburton
Lake Wilderness
Red Bluff
Lake MacLeod
Hill Springs
Mt Augustus 1106
Mount Augustus
Tangadee
Cape Cuvier
Boologooroo
Mount Sandiman
Kumarina Roadhouse
White Lake
Lake Aerodrome
Meters Feet
LAND BELOW SEA LEVEL
1:5,630,000
Lambert Conic Conformal Projection
0 50 100 150 200 kilometers
0 25 50 75 100 miles

NORTHWESTERN AUSTRALIA

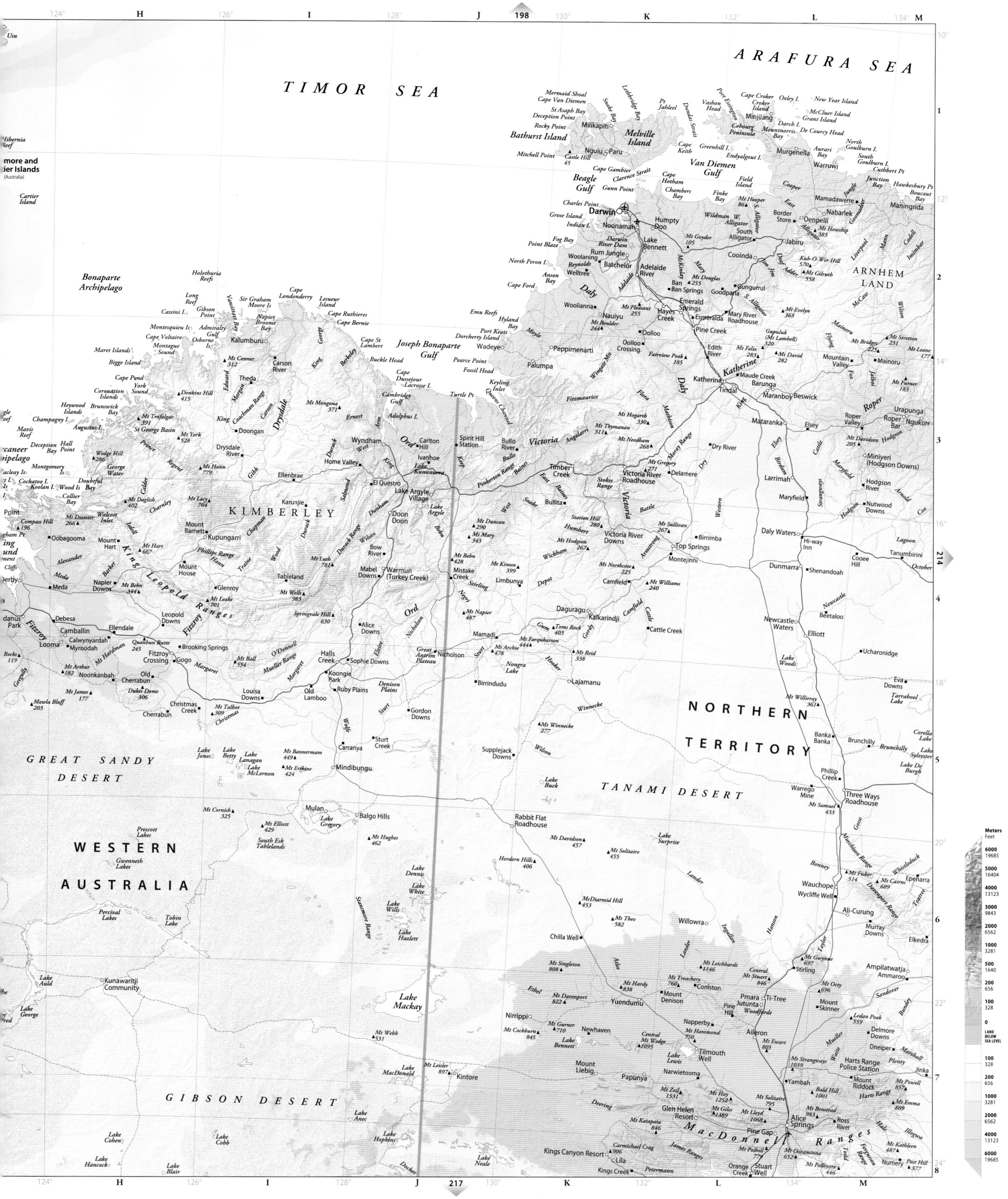

124° H 126° I 128° J 198 130° K 132° L 134° M
TIMOR SEA
ARAFURA SEA
Joseph Bonaparte Gulf
Bonaparte Archipelago
Van Diemen Gulf
Beagle Gulf
Bathurst Island
Melville Island
Darwin
Katherine
KIMBERLEY
King Leopold Ranges
ARNHEM LAND
NORTHERN TERRITORY
WESTERN AUSTRALIA
GREAT SANDY DESERT
TANAMI DESERT
GIBSON DESERT
MacDonnell Ranges
Alice Springs
Lake Mackay
Kununurra
Wyndham
Derby
Fitzroy Crossing
Halls Creek
Tennant Creek
Daly Waters
Mataranka
Jabiru
Hibernia Reef
Ashmore and Cartier Islands (Australia)
Cartier Island
Three Ways Roadhouse
Lajamanu
Yuendumu
Papunya
Hermannsburg
Kings Canyon Resort
Kintore
Kunawaritji Community
Balgo Hills
Rabbit Flat Roadhouse
Victoria River Downs
Timber Creek
Ali-Curung
Wauchope
Barrow Creek
Ti-Tree
Tilmouth Well
Glen Helen Resort
Lake Argyle
Meters Feet
6000 19685
5000 16404
4000 13123
3000 9843
2000 6562
1000 3281
500 1640
200 656
100 328
0
LAND BELOW SEA LEVEL
100 328
200 656
1000 3281
2000 6562
4000 13123
6000 19685
124° H 126° I 128° J 217 130° K 132° L 134° M
214

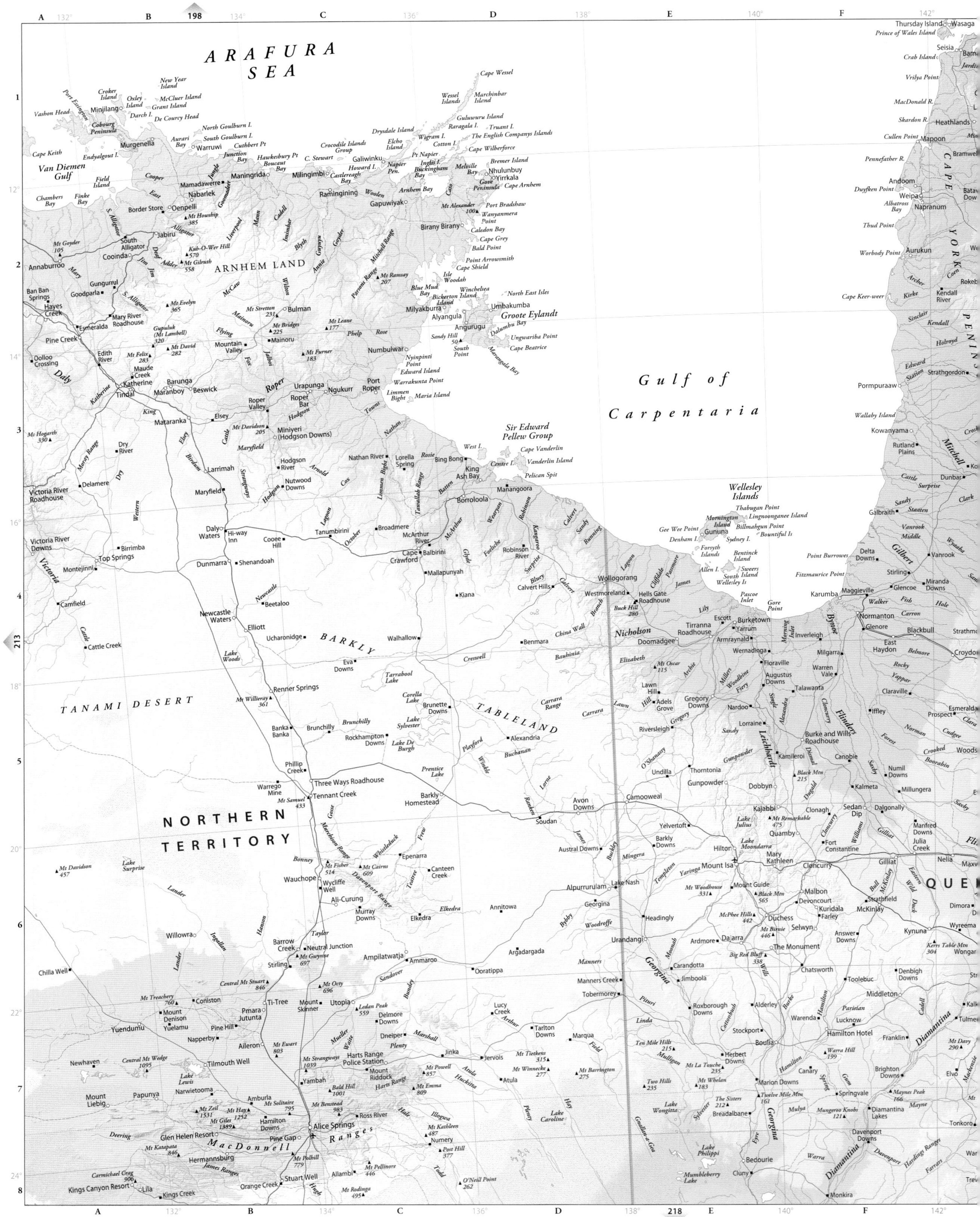

A
B
C
D
E
F
132°
134°
136°
138°
140°
142°
198
213
218
1
2
3
4
5
6
7
8
12°
14°
16°
18°
20°
22°
24°
ARAFURA SEA
Thursday Island
Wasaga
Prince of Wales Island
Seisia
Crab Island
Vrilya Point
MacDonald R.
Skardon R.
Heathlands
Cullen Point
Mapoon
Pennefather R.
Andoom
Duyfken Point
Weipa
Albatross Bay
Napranum
Thud Point
Worbody Point
Aurukun
Cape Keer-weer
Kendall River
CAPE YORK PENINSULA
Cape Wessel
Wessel Islands
Marchinbar Island
Guluwuru Island
Raragala I.
Truant I.
The English Companys Islands
Cape Wilberforce
New Year Island
McCluer Island
Croker Island
Oxley Island
Grant Island
Port Essington
Vashon Head
Minjilang
Darch I.
De Courcy Head
Cobourg Peninsula
North Goulburn I.
South Goulburn I.
Aurari Bay
Warruwi
Cuthbert Pt
Murgenella
Cape Keith
Endyalgout I.
Van Diemen Gulf
Field Island
Cooper
Mamadawerre
Nabarlek
Junction Bay
Hawkesbury Pt
Boucaut Bay
Maningrida
Milingimbi
C. Stewart
Crocodile Islands Group
Galiwinku
Drysdale Island
Elcho Island
Wigram I.
Cotton I.
Howard I.
Castlereagh Bay
Napier Pen.
Ramingining
Wooleen
Gapuwiyak
Pt Napier
Inglis I.
Buckingham Bay
Arnhem Bay
Melville Bay
Bremer Island
Nhulunbuy
Yirrkala
Gove Peninsula
Cape Arnhem
Chambers Bay
Finke Bay
Border Store
Oenpelli
Mt Howship 385
Mt Alexander 100
Port Bradshaw
Wanyanmera Point
Birany Birany
Caledon Bay
Cape Grey
Bald Point
Point Arrowsmith
Cape Shield
Jabiru
South Alligator
Mt Goyder 105
Kub-O-Wer Hill 570
Mt Gilruth 558
Cooinda
ARNHEM LAND
Annaburroo
Mt Ramsay 207
Isle Woodah
Winchelsea Island
North East Isles
Blue Mud Bay
Bickerton Island
Umbakumba
Groote Eylandt
Milyakburra
Alyangula
Angurugu
Dalumbu Bay
Ungwariba Point
Cape Beatrice
Sandy Hill 50
South Point
Gungurrul
Ban Ban Springs
Goodparla
Hayes Creek
Mt Evelyn 365
Mary River Roadhouse
Esmeralda
Mt Stretton 231
Bulman
Mt Bridges 225
Mainoru
Mt Leane 177
Phelp
Rose
Pine Creek
Gupuluk (Mt Lambell) 320
Mt David 282
Mountain Valley
Mt Furner 183
Numbulwar
Oolloo Crossing
Edith River
Mt Felix 283
Maude Creek
Katherine
Tindal
Barunga
Maranboy
Beswick
Roper
Urapunga
Ngukurr
Port Roper
Nyinpinti Point
Edward Island
Warrakunta Point
Limmen Bight
Maria Island
Gulf of Carpentaria
Roper Valley
Roper Bar
Mataranka
Elsey
Mt Davidson 205
Miniyeri (Hodgson Downs)
Mt Hogarth 330
Dry River
Sir Edward Pellew Group
West I.
Centre I.
Cape Vanderlin
Vanderlin Island
Pelican Spit
Nathan River
Lorella Spring
Bing Bong
King Ash Bay
Hodgson River
Larrimah
Nutwood Downs
Delamere
Victoria River Roadhouse
Maryfield
Manangoora
Borroloola
Wellesley Islands
Thabugan Point
Mornington Island
Lingnoonganee Island
Gununa
Billmabgun Point
Bountiful Is
Gee Wee Point
Denham I.
Sydney I.
Forsyth Islands
Bentinck Island
Allen I.
Sweers Island
South Wellesley Is
Pascoe Inlet
Gore Point
Point Burrowes
Fitzmaurice Point
Daly Waters
Hi-way Inn
Cooee Hill
Tanumbirini
Broadmere
McArthur River
Cape Crawford
Balbirini
Robinson River
Victoria River Downs
Birrimba
Top Springs
Montejinni
Dunmarra
Shenandoah
Mallapunyah
Calvert Hills
Wollogorang
Westmoreland
Hells Gate Roadhouse
Buck Hill 280
Kiana
Camfield
Beetaloo
Newcastle Waters
Elliott
Karumba
Maggieville
Glencoe
Miranda Downs
Normanton
Glenore
Blackbull
Burketown
Yarrum
Escott
Tirranna Roadhouse
Armraynald
Doomadgee
Nicholson
Inverleigh
Cattle Creek
Ucharonidge
BARKLY TABLELAND
Walhallow
Benmara
Eva Downs
Creswell
Elizabeth
Mt Oscar 115
Wernadinga
Floraville
Augustus Downs
Milgarra
Warren Vale
Talawanta
East Haydon
Tarrabool Lake
Renner Springs
Mt Willieray 361
Corella Lake
Brunette Downs
Lawn Hill
Adels Grove
Gregory Downs
Nardoo
Iffley
Claraville
TANAMI DESERT
Banka Banka
Brunchilly
Lake Sylvester
Rockhampton Downs
Lake De Burgh
Alexandria
Riversleigh
Lorraine
Burke and Wills Roadhouse
Kamileroi
Canobie
Leichhardt
Flinders
Phillip Creek
Prentice Lake
Undilla
Thorntonia
Gunpowder
Black Mtn 215
Numil Downs
Three Ways Roadhouse
Warrego Mine
Tennant Creek
Mt Samuel 433
Barkly Homestead
Dobbyn
Kalmeta
Millungera
NORTHERN TERRITORY
Avon Downs
Camooweal
Soudan
Kajabbi
Clonagh
Sedan Dip
Dalgonally
Lake Julius
Mt Remarkable 475
Yelvertoft
Barkly Downs
Quamby
Manfred Downs
Julia Creek
Fort Constantine
Austral Downs
Lake Moondarra
Hilton
Mount Isa
Mary Kathleen
Cloncurry
Gilliat
Nelia
QUEENSLAND
Mt Davidson 457
Lake Surprise
Mt Fisher 514
Mt Cairns 609
Epenarra
Canteen Creek
Wauchope
Wycliffe Well
Davenport Range
Ali-Curung
Murray Downs
Elkedra
Annitowa
Alpurrurulam
Lake Nash
Georgina
Mt Woodhouse 331
Mount Guide
Black Mtn 565
Malbon
Devoncourt
Stratfield
McKinlay
Kuridala
Duchess
Farley
Selwyn
McPhee Hills 442
Mt Birnie 446
Headingly
Dimora
Kynuna
Wyreema
Willowra
Barrow Creek
Neutral Junction
Mt Gwynne 697
Stirling
Ampilatwatja
Ammaroo
Argadargada
Urandangi
Ardmore
Dajarra
The Monument
Answer Downs
Kerrs Table Mtn 304
Wongar
Chilla Well
Ooratippa
Carandotta
Big Red Bluff 338
Chatsworth
Denbigh Downs
Central Mt Stuart 846
Mt Ooty 696
Manners Creek
Jimboola
Toolebuc
Mt Treachery 760
Coniston
Ti-Tree
Mount Skinner
Utopia
Tobermorey
Middleton
Mount Denison
Yuelamu
Pmara Jutunta
Ledan Peak 559
Delmore Downs
Lucy Creek
Roxborough Downs
Alderley
Warenda
Lucknow
Hamilton Hotel
Yuendumu
Pine Hill
Dneiper
Tarlton Downs
Marqua
Stockport
Boulia
Franklin
Mt Datty 290
Napperby
Aileron
Mt Ewart 803
Plenty
Jinka
Jervois
Mt Tietkens 315
Ten Mile Hills 215
Herbert Downs
Warra Hill 199
Newhaven
Central Mt Wedge 1095
Tilmouth Well
Mt Strangways 1039
Harts Range Police Station
Mount Riddock
Mt Powell 857
Mt Winnecke 277
Mt Barrington 275
Mt La Touche 235
Canary
Brighton Downs
Elvo
Lake Lewis
Narwietooma
Yambah
Bald Hill 1001
Mt Emma 809
Atula
Two Hills 235
Mt Whelan 183
Marion Downs
Mount Liebig
Papunya
Amburla
Mt Solitaire 795
Mt Benstead 983
Ross River
Lake Wongitta
The Sisters 212
Twelve Mile Mtn 161
Springvale
Maynes Peak 166
Mt Zeil 1531
Mt Hay 1252
Mt Giles 1389
Hamilton Downs
Alice Springs
Mt Kathleen 487
Lake Caroline
Breadalbane
Mungeroo Knobs 121
Diamantina Lakes
Tonkoro
Deering
Glen Helen Resort
Pine Gap
MacDonnell Ranges
Numery
Post Hill 377
Davenport Downs
Mt Katapata 846
Hermannsburg
James Ranges
Mt Polhill 779
Mt Pellinore 446
Lake Philippi
Bedourie
Carmichael Crag 906
Kings Canyon Resort
Lila
Kings Creek
Stuart Well
Orange Creek
Allambi
Mt Rodinga 495
O'Neill Point 262
Mumbleberry Lake
Cluny
Monkira
Diamantina
Georgina
Hugh
Todd

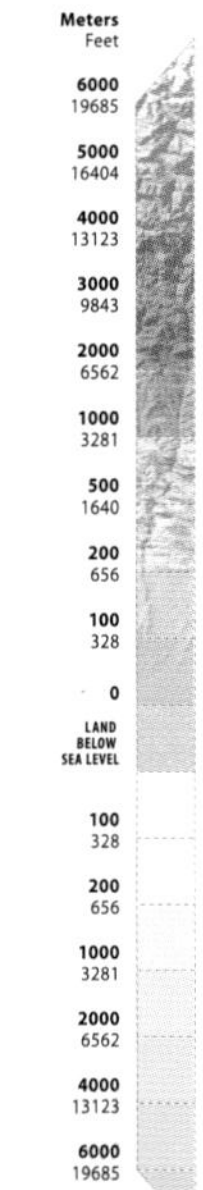

Meters
Feet
6000 19685
5000 16404
4000 13123
3000 9843
2000 6562
1000 3281
500 1640
200 656
100 328
0
LAND BELOW SEA LEVEL
100 328
200 656
1000 3281
2000 6562
4000 13123
6000 19685

1:5,630,000

Lambert Conic Conformal Projection

0 50 100 150 200 kilometers

0 25 50 75 100 miles

NORTHEASTERN AUSTRALIA

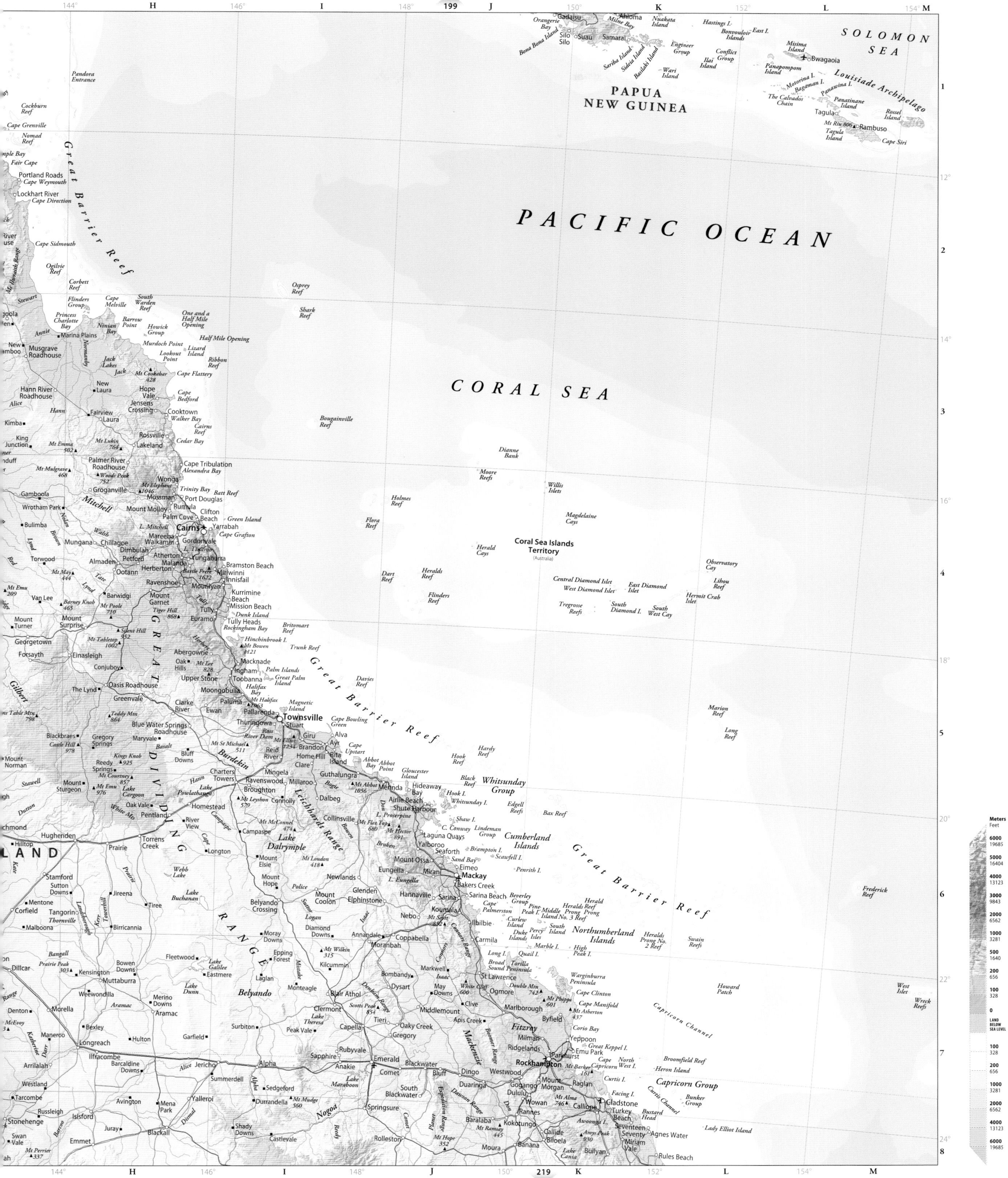

199
219
144°
146°
148°
150°
152°
154°
12°
14°
16°
18°
20°
22°
24°
H
I
J
K
L
M
1
2
3
4
5
6
7
8
PACIFIC OCEAN
CORAL SEA
SOLOMON SEA
PAPUA NEW GUINEA
Louisiade Archipelago
Great Barrier Reef
GREAT DIVIDING RANGE
Coral Sea Islands Territory
(Australia)
Capricorn Channel
Capricorn Group
Whitsunday Group
Cumberland Islands
Northumberland Islands
Bunker Group
Gadaisu
Ahioma
Milne Bay
Nuakata Island
Orangerie Bay
Bona Bona Island
Silo
Suau
Samarai
Sariba Island
Sideia Island
Basilaki Island
Engineer Group
Wari Island
Hastings I.
Bonvouloir Islands
East I.
Conflict Group
Ilai Island
Misima Island
Bwagaoia
Panapompom Island
Motorina I.
Bagaman I.
Panawina I.
The Calvados Chain
Panatinane Island
Rossel Island
Tagula
Mt Riu 806
Rambuso
Tagula Island
Cape Siri
Pandora Entrance
Cockburn Reef
Cape Grenville
Nomad Reef
Fair Cape
Portland Roads
Cape Weymouth
Lockhart River
Cape Direction
Cape Sidmouth
Ogilvie Reef
Corbett Reef
Stewart
Flinders Group
Cape Melville
South Warden Reef
Princess Charlotte Bay
Barrow Point
Ninian Bay
Howick Group
One and a Half Mile Opening
Half Mile Opening
Marina Plains
Annie
Musgrave Roadhouse
Normanby
Murdoch Point
Lookout Point
Lizard Island
Ribbon Reef
Jack Lakes
Jack
Mt Cook 428
Cape Flattery
Hann River Roadhouse
New Laura
Hope Vale
Cape Bedford
Jensens Crossing
Cooktown
Walker Bay
Fairview
Laura
Hann
Alice
Kimba
Cairns Reef
Cedar Bay
Rossville
Lakeland
King Junction
Mt Emma 502
Mt Lukin 764
Palmer River Roadhouse
Cape Tribulation
Alexandra Bay
Woods Peak 752
Mt Mulgrave 468
Wonga
Mt Elephant 1046
Trinity Bay
Batt Reef
Gamboola
Groganville
Mossman
Port Douglas
Wrotham Park
Mitchell
Mount Molloy
Rumula
Clifton Beach
Green Island
Bulimba
Palm Cove
Yarrabah
Cape Grafton
L. Mitchell
Cairns
Walsh
Mareeba
Gordonvale
Lynd
Mungana
Chillagee
Walkamin
Dimbulah
Tinaroo
Petford
Atherton
Yungaburra
Torwood
Almaden
Malanda
Bramston Beach
Ootann
Herberton
Bartle Frere 1622
Mirriwinni
Innisfail
Mt May 444
Tate
Ravenshoe
Mourilyan
Mt Emu 209
Barwidgi
Kurrimine Beach
Van Lee
Mount Garnet
Mission Beach
Barney Knob 465
Mt Poole 710
Tiger Hill 868
Tully
Dunk Island
Mount Turner
Mount Surprise
Euramo
Tully Heads
Rockingham Bay
Britomart Reef
Silent Hill 952
Mt Tabletop 1002
Herbert
Hinchinbrook I.
Georgetown
Mt Bowen 1121
Trunk Reef
Forsayth
Einasleigh
Abergowrie
Conjuboy
Oak Hills
Mt Lee 828
Macknade
Ingham
Palm Islands
Toobanna
Great Palm Island
Davies Reef
Upper Stone
Gilbert
The Lynd
Oasis Roadhouse
Moongobulla
Halifax Bay
Greenvale
Paluma
Mt Halifax 1063
Magnetic Island
Table Mtn 798
Teddy Mtn 864
Clarke River
Ewan
Pallarenda
Townsville
Stuart
Cape Bowling Green
Marion Reef
Thuringowa
Blue Water Springs Roadhouse
Ross River Dam
Giru
Alva
Long Reef
Blackbraes
Maryvale
Mt Elliot 1234
Ayr
Gregory Springs
Basalt
Mt St Michael 511
Reid River
Brandon
Cape Upstart
Castle Hill 978
Bluff Downs
Home Hill
Rita Island
Hardy Reef
Kings Knob 925
Burdekin
Clare
Abbot Bay
Abbot Point
Hook Reef
Mount Norman
Reedy Springs
Charters Towers
Guthalungra
Gloucester Island
Mt Courtney 857
Hann
Ravenswood
Millaroo
Bogie
Mt Abbot 1056
Black Reef
Stawell
Mount Sturgeon
Mt Emu 976
Lake Cargoon
Lake Powlathanga
Broughton
Merinda
Hideaway Bay
Whitsunday Group
Mt Leyshon 579
Connolly
Dalbeg
Airlie Beach
Hook I.
Whitsunday I.
Edgell Reefs
Oak Vale
Homestead
Pentland
Shute Harbour
White Mts
Leichhardt Range
L. Proserpine
Bax Reef
Dutton
River View
Collinsville
Bowen
Mt Flat Top 680
Shaw I.
Richmond
Campaspe
Mt McConnel 474
Mt Hector 891
C. Conway
Lindeman Group
Hughenden
Prairie
Torrens Creek
Laguna Quays
Lake Dalrymple
Yalboroo
Brampton I.
Hilltop
Cape
Longton
Mount Elsie
Mt Loudon 418
Broken
Seaforth
Scawfell I.
Sand Bay
Eimeo
Mount Ossa
Eungella
Mirani
Penrith I.
Kate
Webb Lake
Mount Hope
Newlands
L. Eungella
Mackay
Bakers Creek
Stamford
Sutton Downs
Prairie
Police
Glenden
Elphinstone
Hannaville
Sarina
Sarina Beach
Beverley Group
Herald Reef
Lake Buchanan
Jireena
Mount Coolon
Cape Palmerston
Pine Peak I.
Middle Island
Herald Prong
Herald Prong No. 3 Reef
Mentone
Corfield
Tangorin
Thornville
Tree
Belyando Crossing
Suttor
Logan
Isaac
Nebo
Mt Scott 892
Curlew Island
Frederick Reef
Malboona
Birricannia
Diamond Downs
Annandale
Coppabella
Illbilbie
Duke Islands
Percy Isles
South Island
Heralds Prong No. 2 Reef
Swain Reefs
Moray Downs
Moranbah
Carmila
Marble I.
High Peak I.
Bangall
Prairie Peak 303
Fleetwood
Epping Forest
Mistake
Mt Wilkin 315
Kilcummin
Connors
Long I.
Broad Sound
Tarilla Peninsula
Quail I.
Dillcar
Kensington
Bowen Downs
Lake Galilee
Eastmere
Laglan
Bombandy
Markwell
Isaac
Warginburra Peninsula
Muttaburra
Lake Dunn
Monteagle
Dysart
May Downs
St Lawrence
White Cliff 600
Double Mtn 742
Howard Patch
West Islet
Range
Weewondilla
Aramac
Merino Downs
Belyando
Denham Range
Blair Athol
Ogmore
Cape Clinton
Wreck Reefs
Denton
Morella
Aramac
Clermont
Scotts Peak 854
Clive
Mt Phipps 601
Cape Manifold
McEvoy
Bexley
Lake Theresa
Tieri
Middlemount
Apis Creek
Marlborough
Mt Atherton 437
Byfield
Katherine
Maneroo
Hulton
Surbiton
Peak Vale
Capella
Oaky Creek
Gregory
Mackenzie
Fitzroy
Corio Bay
Yeppoon
Longreach
Garfield
Milman
Ridgelands
Great Keppel I.
Emu Park
Parkhurst
Rubyvale
Sapphire
Anakie
Emerald
Blackwater
Rockhampton
Cape Capricorn
North West I.
Broomfield Reef
Heron Island
Arrilalah
Ilfracombe
Barcaldine Downs
Alice
Jericho
Alpha
Comet
Bluff
Dingo
Westwood
Mt Barker 181
Mount Morgan
Raglan
Curtis I.
Westland
Summerdell
Alpha
Sedgeford
Lake Maraboon
South Blackwater
Duaringa
Gogango
Dululu
Facing I.
Curtis Channel
Tarcombe
Avington
Mena Park
Yalleroi
Durrandella
Mt Mudge 560
Nogoa
Springsure
Dawson Range
Expedition Range
Wowan
Mt Alma 746
Calliope
Gladstone
Russleigh
Isisford
Dismal
Shady Downs
Comet
Planet
Baralaba
Kokotungo
Rannes
Turkey Beach
Bustard Head
Stonehenge
Juray
Blackall
Castlevale
Reedy
Rolleston
Mt Ramsay 445
Callide
Awoonga L.
Seventeen Seventy
Agnes Water
Lady Elliot Island
Swan Vale
Barcoo
Emmet
Mt Hope 352
Biloela
Amys Peak 930
Miriam Vale
Mt Perrier 337
Moura
Banana
Lake Cania
Bullyan
Rules Beach
Osprey Reef
Shark Reef
Bougainville Reef
Dianne Bank
Moore Reefs
Willis Islets
Holmes Reef
Flora Reef
Magdelaine Cays
Herald Cays
Observatory Cay
Dart Reef
Heralds Reef
Central Diamond Islet
East Diamond Islet
West Diamond Islet
Libou Reef
Flinders Reef
Hermit Crab Islet
Tregrosse Reefs
South Diamond I.
South West Cay
Meters
Feet
6000
19685
5000
16404
4000
13123
3000
9843
2000
6562
1000
3281
500
1640
200
656
100
328
0
LAND BELOW SEA LEVEL
100
328
200
656
1000
3281
2000
6562
4000
13123
6000
19685

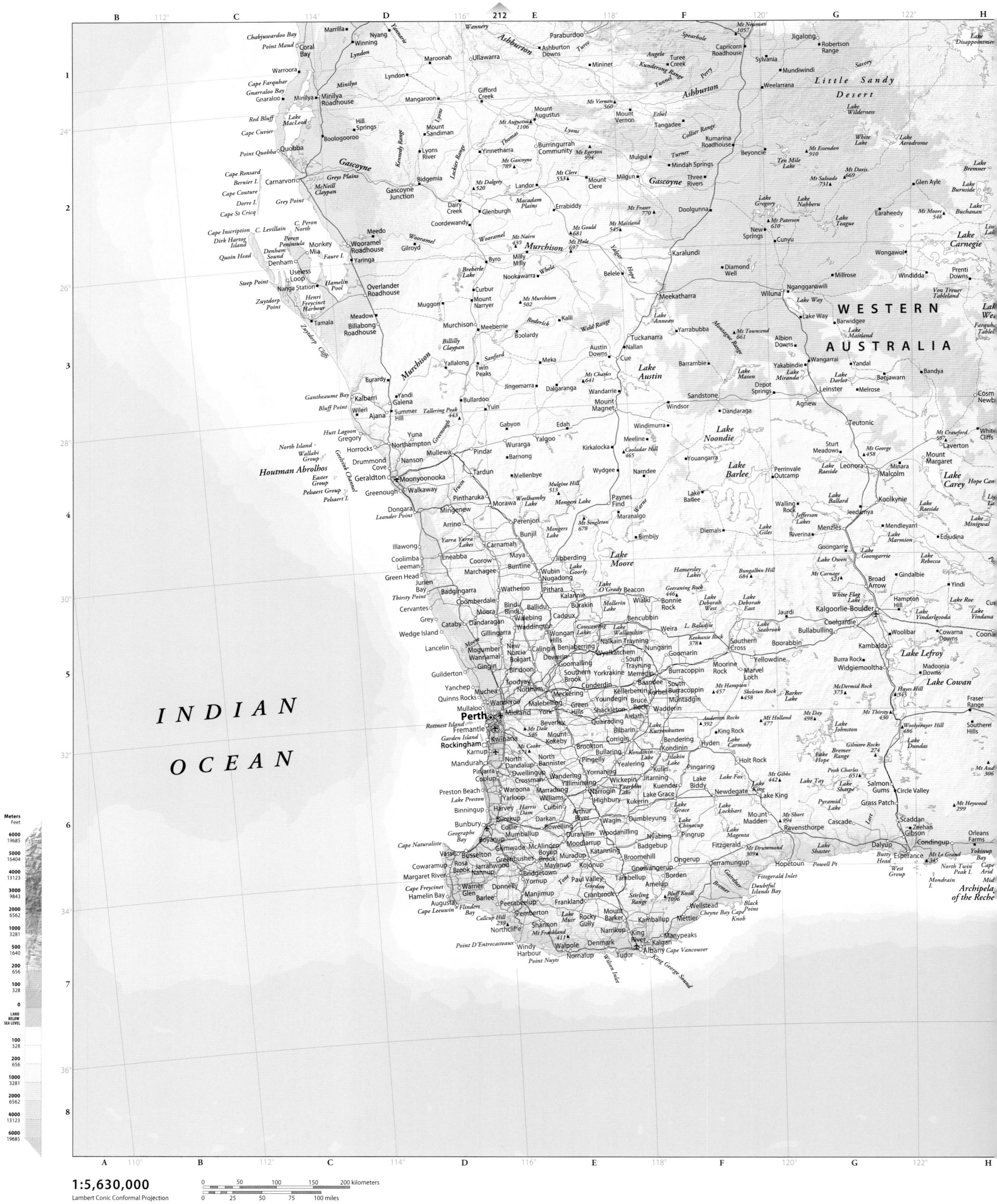

212
INDIAN
OCEAN
WESTERN
AUSTRALIA
Little Sandy
Desert
Perth
Fremantle
Rockingham
Kwinana
Mandurah
Pinjarra
Bunbury
Busselton
Margaret River
Augusta
Cape Leeuwin
Cape Naturaliste
Geographe Bay
Albany
King George Sound
Denmark
Walpole
Esperance
Ravensthorpe
Hopetoun
Kalgoorlie-Boulder
Coolgardie
Southern Cross
Merredin
Northam
York
Toodyay
Narrogin
Katanning
Wagin
Collie
Manjimup
Bridgetown
Geraldton
Houtman Abrolhos
Dongara
Northampton
Kalbarri
Carnarvon
Shark Bay
Denham
Dirk Hartog Island
Cape Inscription
Steep Point
Coral Bay
Point Maud
Exmouth Gulf
Lake MacLeod
Gascoyne
Murchison
Ashburton
Meekatharra
Cue
Mount Magnet
Sandstone
Wiluna
Leinster
Leonora
Laverton
Menzies
Norseman
Lake Lefroy
Lake Cowan
Lake Barlee
Lake Moore
Lake Austin
Lake Noondie
Lake Carnegie
Lake Way
Lake Raeside
Lake Carey
Mt Augustus 1106
Mt Egerton 994
Mt Newman 1057
Newman
Paraburdoo
Chabjuwardoo Bay
Warroora
Cape Farquhar
Gnaraloo Bay
Red Bluff
Cape Cuvier
Point Quobba
Cape Ronsard
Bernier I.
Dorre I.
Cape St Cricq
Peron Peninsula
Faure I.
Useless Loop
Hamelin Pool
Zuytdorp Point
Zuytdorp Cliffs
Gantheaume Bay
Bluff Point
Hutt Lagoon
North Island
Wallabi Group
Easter Group
Pelsaert Group
Leander Point
Jurien Bay
Thirsty Point
Cervantes
Lancelin
Guilderton
Yanchep
Rottnest Island
Garden Island
Preston Beach
Cape Freycinet
Hamelin Bay
Point D'Entrecasteaux
Point Nuyts
Wilson Inlet
Cape Vancouver
Stirling Range
Bluff Knoll 1096
Fitzgerald Inlet
Doubtful Islands Bay
Mondrain I.
Archipelago of the Recherche
1:5,630,000
Lambert Conic Conformal Projection
Meters
Feet
6000 19685
5000 16404
4000 13123
3000 9843
2000 6562
1000 3281
500 1640
200 656
100 328
0
LAND BELOW SEA LEVEL
100 328
200 656
1000 3281
2000 6562
4000 13123
6000 19685
0 50 100 150 200 kilometers
0 25 50 75 100 miles

SOUTHWESTERN AUSTRALIA

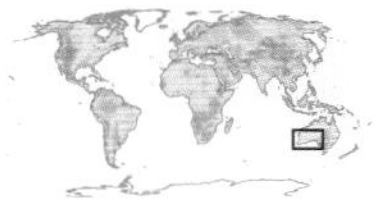

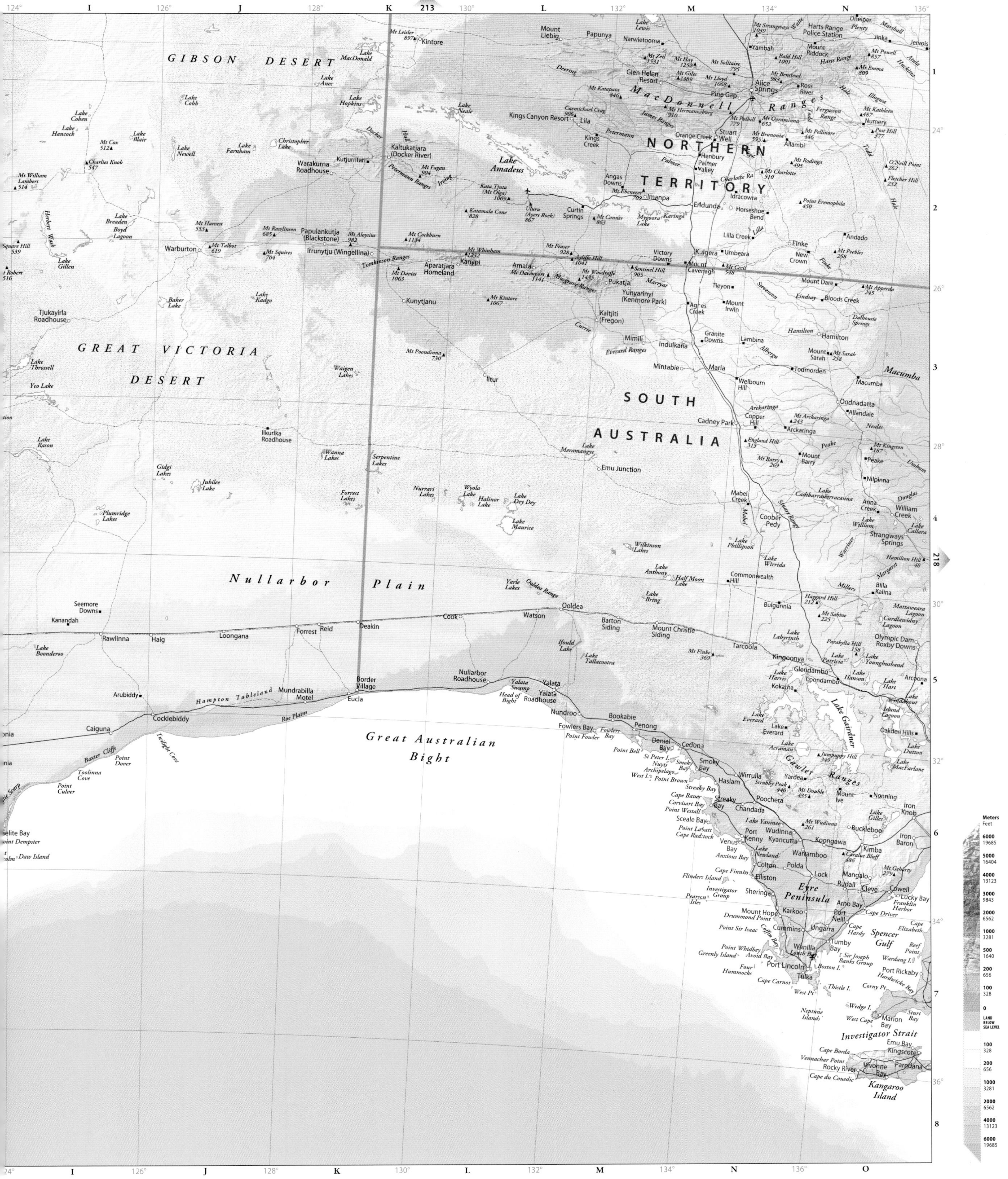

124°
I
126°
J
128°
K
213
130°
L
132°
M
134°
N
136°
O
GIBSON DESERT
Lake MacDonald
Mt Leisler 897
Kintore
Lake Anec
Lake Hopkins
Lake Neale
Lake Cobb
Lake Cohen
Lake Hancock
Lake Blair
Mt Cox 512
Lake Newell
Lake Farnham
Christopher Lake
Charlies Knob 547
Mt William Lambert 514
Kaltukatjara (Docker River)
Kutjuntari
Warakurna Roadhouse
Mt Fagan 904
Petermann Ranges
Lake Amadeus
Kata Tjuta (Mt Olga) 1069
Uluru (Ayers Rock) 867
Katamala Cone 828
Curtin Springs
Mt Conner 863
Lake Breaden
Boyd Lagoon
Mt Harvest 553
Mt Rawlinson 685
Papulankutja (Blackstone)
Mt Aloysius 982
Mt Cockburn 1134
Square Hill 539
Herbert Wash
Lake Gillen
Warburton
Mt Talbot 619
Mt Squires 704
Irrunytju (Wingellina)
Tomkinson Ranges
Mt Whinham 1232
Kanypi
Aparatjara Homeland
Mt Davies 1063
Amata
Mt Davenport 1141
Musgrave Ranges
Mt Fraser 928
Ayliffe Hill 1041
Mt Woodroffe 1435
Pukatja
Sentinel Hill 905
Marryat
Yunyarinyi (Kenmore Park)
Mt Robert 516
Baker Lake
Lake Kadgo
Kunytjanu
Mt Kintore 1067
Tjukayirla Roadhouse
Kaltjiti (Fregon)
Currie
Mimili
Everard Ranges
Indulkana
GREAT VICTORIA DESERT
Lake Throssell
Yeo Lake
Waigen Lakes
Mt Poondinna 730
Iltur
Mintabie
Lake Rason
Ilkurlka Roadhouse
Wanna Lakes
Serpentine Lakes
Lake Meramangye
Emu Junction
Gidgi Lakes
Jubilee Lake
Forrest Lakes
Nurrari Lakes
Wyola Lake
Halinor Lake
Lake Dey Dey
Lake Maurice
Plumridge Lakes
Wilkinson Lakes
Lake Anthony
Half Moon Lake
Nullarbor Plain
Yarle Lakes
Ooldea Range
Lake Bring
Commonwealth Hill
Seemore Downs
Kanandah
Cook
Watson
Ooldea
Barton Siding
Mount Christie Siding
Rawlinna
Haig
Loongana
Forrest
Reid
Deakin
Lake Boonderoo
Ifould Lake
Lake Tallacootra
Tarcoola
Mt Finke 369
Nullarbor Roadhouse
Yalata Swamp
Yalata
Head of Bight
Yalata Roadhouse
Border Village
Eucla
Arubiddy
Hampton Tableland
Mundrabilla Motel
Cocklebiddy
Roe Plains
Caiguna
Twilight Cove
Baxter Cliffs
Point Dover
Toolinna Cove
Point Culver
Great Australian Bight
Nundroo
Bookabie
Fowlers Bay
Point Fowler
Penong
Point Bell
Denial Bay
Ceduna
St Peter I.
Nuyts Archipelago
Smoky Bay
West I.
Point Brown
Streaky Bay
Cape Bauer
Corvisart Bay
Point Westall
Sceale Bay
Point Labatt
Cape Radstock
Venus Bay
Anxious Bay
Cape Finniss
Flinders Island
Investigator Group
Pearson Isles
Elliston
Sheringa
Mount Hope
Drummond Point
Point Sir Isaac
Coffin Bay
Point Whidbey
Avoid Bay
Greenly Island
Four Hummocks
Port Lincoln
Cape Carnot
West Pt
Neptune Islands
Daw Island
Point Dempster
NORTHERN TERRITORY
SOUTH AUSTRALIA
Mount Liebig
Papunya
Lake Lewis
Narwietooma
Mt Zeil 1531
Mt Hay 1252
Glen Helen Resort
Mt Giles 1389
Mt Lloyd 1068
Mt Solitaire 795
Alice Springs
Pine Gap
MacDonnell Ranges
Mt Katapata 846
Mt Hermannsburg 910
Carmichael Crag 906
Lila
Kings Canyon Resort
Kings Creek
James Ranges
Mt Pollrill 779
Mt Ooraminna 652
Orange Creek
Stuart Well
Henbury
Palmer Valley
Palmer
Angas Downs
Mt Ebenezer 702
Imanpa
Mygoora Lake
Karinga
Erldunda
Idracowra
Charlotte Ra
Mt Charlotte 510
Horseshoe Bend
Lilla Creek
Finke
Victory Downs
Kalgera
Umbeara
Mount Cavenagh
Mt Cecil 548
Tieyon
New Crown
Mount Dare
Agnes Creek
Mount Irwin
Granite Downs
Lambina
Alberga
Marla
Welbourn Hill
Todmorden
Mt Strangways 1039
Yambah
Harts Range Police Station
Mount Riddock
Harts Range
Bald Hill 1001
Mt Benstead 983
Ross River
Mt Brunonia 595
Mt Pellinore 446
Allambi
Mt Rodinga 495
Point Eremophila 450
Andado
Mt Peebles 258
Lindsay
Bloods Creek
Dalhousie Springs
Hamilton
Mount Sarah
Mt Sarah 258
Macumba
Dneiper
Plenty
Marshall
Jinka
Jervois
Mt Powell 857
Mt Emma 809
Illogwa
Mt Kathleen 487
Numery
Post Hill 377
O'Neill Point 262
Fletcher Hill 232
Fergusson Range
Oodnadatta
Allandale
Arckaringa
Copper Hill
Mt Arckaringa 243
Cadney Park
Neales
England Hill 315
Mt Barry 269
Mount Barry
Peake
Mt Kingston 187
Nilpinna
Mabel Creek
Coober Pedy
Stuart Range
Lake Cadibarrawirracanna
Anna Creek
William Creek
Lake William
Lake Phillipson
Lake Wirrida
Strangways Springs
Lake Callara
Hamilton Hill 40
Billa Kalina
Millers
Bulgunnia
Haggard Hill 212
Mt Sabine 225
Mattawearra Lagoon
Curdlawidny Lagoon
Lake Labyrinth
Parakylia Hill 158
Olympic Dam
Roxby Downs
Kingoonya
Glendambo
Lake Patricia
Lake Younghusband
Lake Harris
Coondambo
Lake Hanson
Lake Hart
Arcoona
Kokatha
Lake Gairdner
Island Lagoon
Lake Everard
Everard
Oakden Hills
Lake Acraman
Jumbuppy Hill 349
Lake Dutton
Lake MacFarlane
Gawler Ranges
Wirrulla
Haslam
Yardea
Scrubby Peak 440
Mt Double 435
Mount Ive
Nonning
Poochera
Chandada
Lake Yaninee
Port Kenny
Wudinna
Mt Wudinna 261
Kyancutta
Lake Gilles
Iron Knob
Buckleboo
Koongawa
Iron Baron
Lake Newland
Warramboo
Caralue Bluff 486
Kimba
Colton
Polda
Lock
Mangalo
Mt Gebbery 279
Rudall
Cleve
Cowell
Eyre Peninsula
Arno Bay
Lucky Bay
Franklin Harbor
Karkoo
Port Neill
Cape Driver
Cummins
Ungarra
Cape Hardy
Spencer Gulf
Cape Elizabeth
Wanilla
Louth Bay
Tumby Bay
Sir Joseph Banks Group
Reef Point
Wardang I.
Boston I.
Port Rickaby
Hardwicke Bay
Tulka
Thistle I.
Corny Pt
Wedge I.
West Cape
Marion Bay
Sturt Bay
Investigator Strait
Emu Bay
Kingscote
Cape Borda
Vennachar Point
Rocky River
Vivonne Bay
Parndana
Cape du Couedic
Kangaroo Island
218
24°
26°
28°
30°
32°
34°
36°
1
2
3
4
5
6
7
8
Meters
Feet
6000
19685
5000
16404
4000
13123
3000
9843
2000
6562
1000
3281
500
1640
200
656
100
328
0
LAND BELOW SEA LEVEL
100
328
200
656
1000
3281
2000
6562
4000
13123
6000
19685

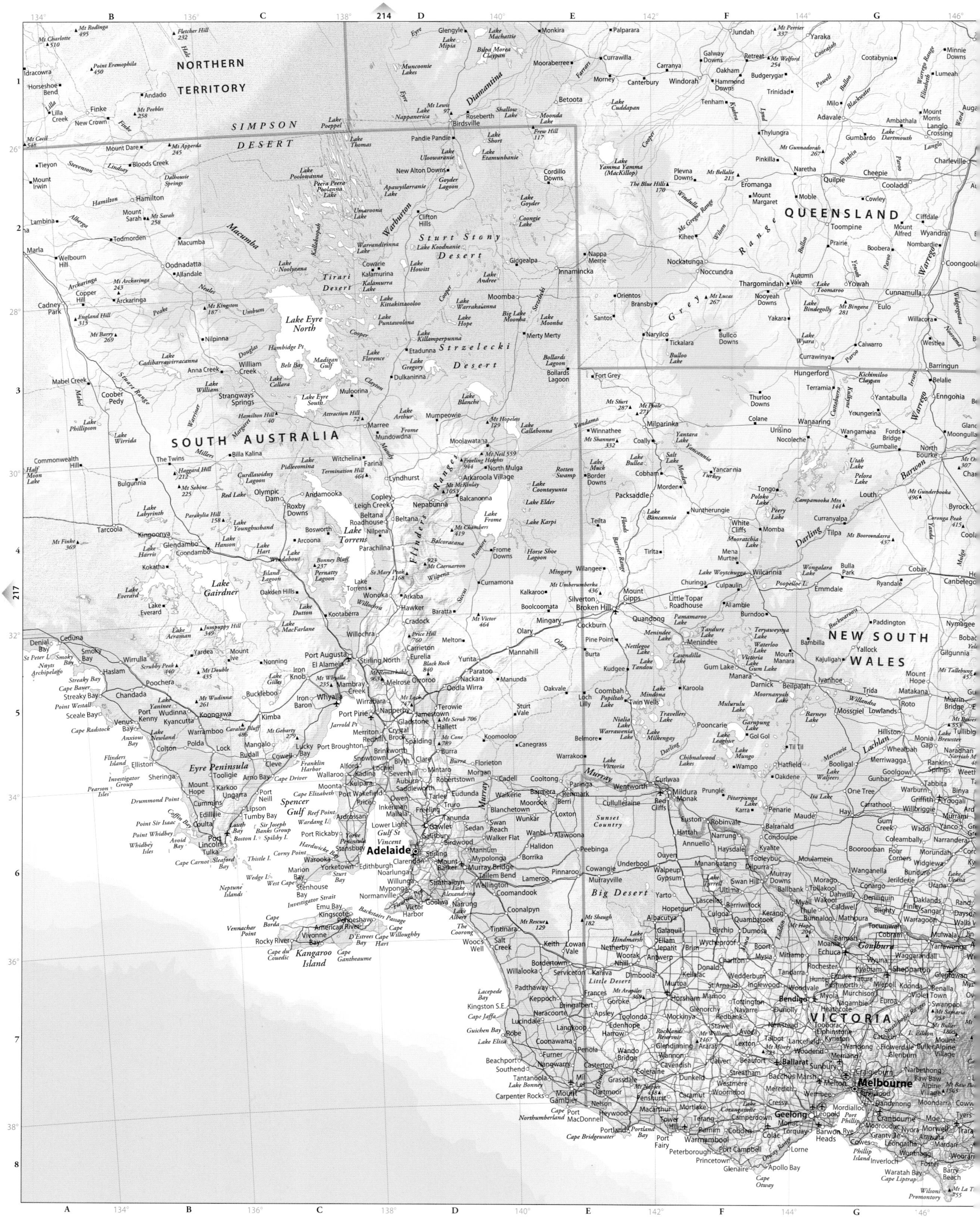

NORTHERN TERRITORY
SIMPSON DESERT
SOUTH AUSTRALIA
QUEENSLAND
NEW SOUTH WALES
VICTORIA
Lake Eyre North
Lake Eyre South
Lake Torrens
Lake Gairdner
Lake Frome
Sturt Stony Desert
Strzelecki Desert
Tirari Desert
Flinders Ranges
Grey Range
Eyre Peninsula
Spencer Gulf
Gulf St Vincent
Kangaroo Island
Adelaide
Melbourne
Geelong
Ballarat
Bendigo
Port Augusta
Whyalla
Port Pirie
Port Lincoln
Mount Gambier
Broken Hill
Mildura
Birdsville
Oodnadatta
Coober Pedy
Innamincka
Charleville
Cunnamulla
Bourke
Wilcannia
Murray
Darling
Big Desert
Little Desert
214
217
134°
136°
138°
140°
142°
144°
146°
26°
28°
30°
32°
34°
36°
38°
A
B
C
D
E
F
G
1
2
3
4
5
6
7
8

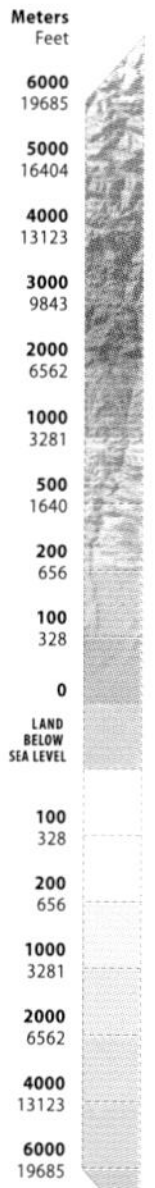

Meters
Feet
6000
19685
5000
16404
4000
13123
3000
9843
2000
6562
1000
3281
500
1640
200
656
100
328
0
LAND BELOW SEA LEVEL
100
328
200
656
1000
3281
2000
6562
4000
13123
6000
19685

1:5,630,000

Lambert Conic Conformal Projection

0 50 100 150 200 kilometers

0 25 50 75 100 miles

SOUTHEASTERN AUSTRALIA

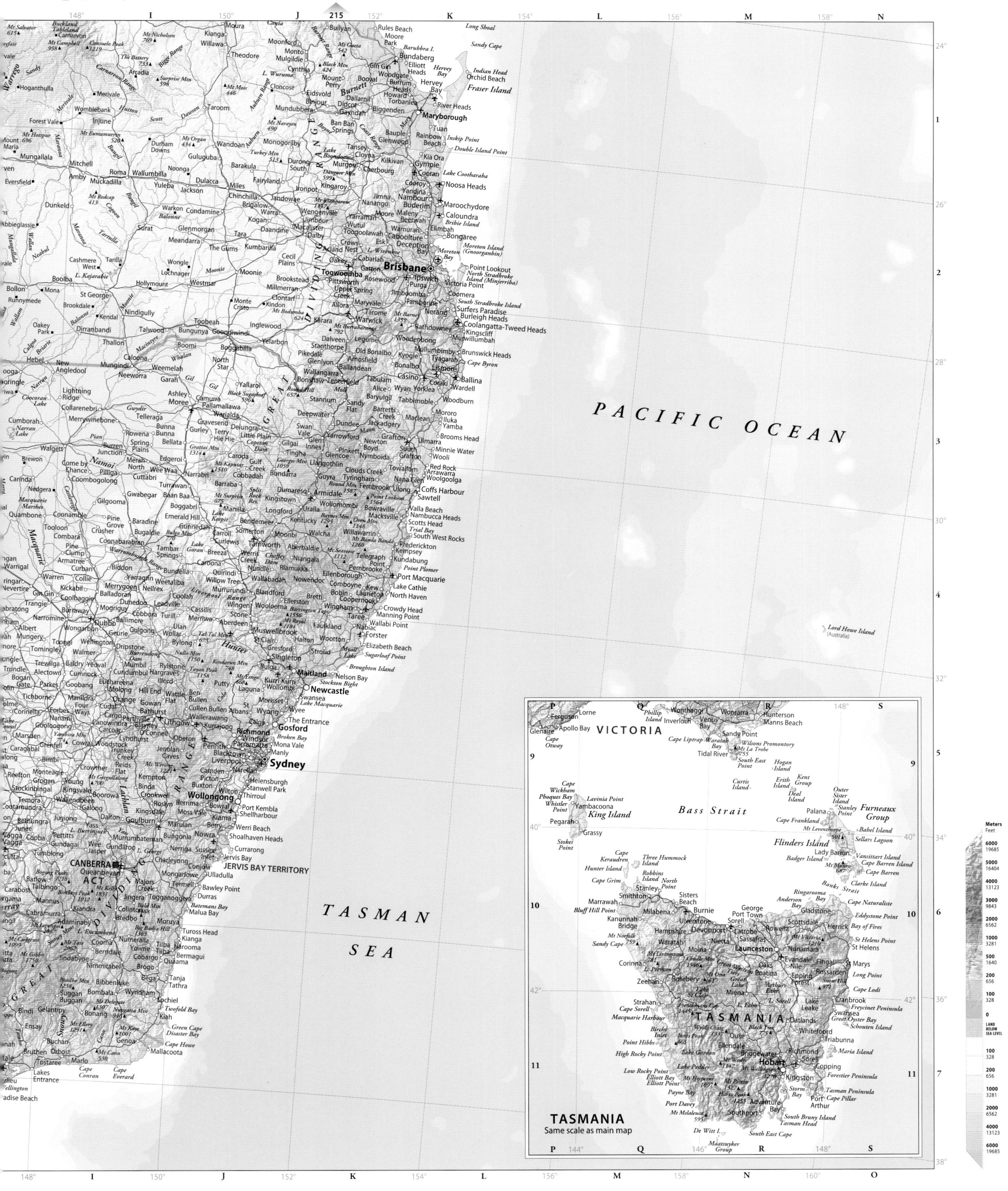

PACIFIC OCEAN
TASMAN SEA
Bass Strait
VICTORIA
TASMANIA
JERVIS BAY TERRITORY
ACT
CANBERRA
Brisbane
Sydney
Newcastle
Wollongong
Gosford
Toowoomba
Maryborough
Bundaberg
Hobart
Launceston
Devonport
Burnie
Fraser Island
Lord Howe Island (Australia)
King Island
Flinders Island
Furneaux Group
TASMANIA
Same scale as main map
Meters
Feet
LAND BELOW SEA LEVEL

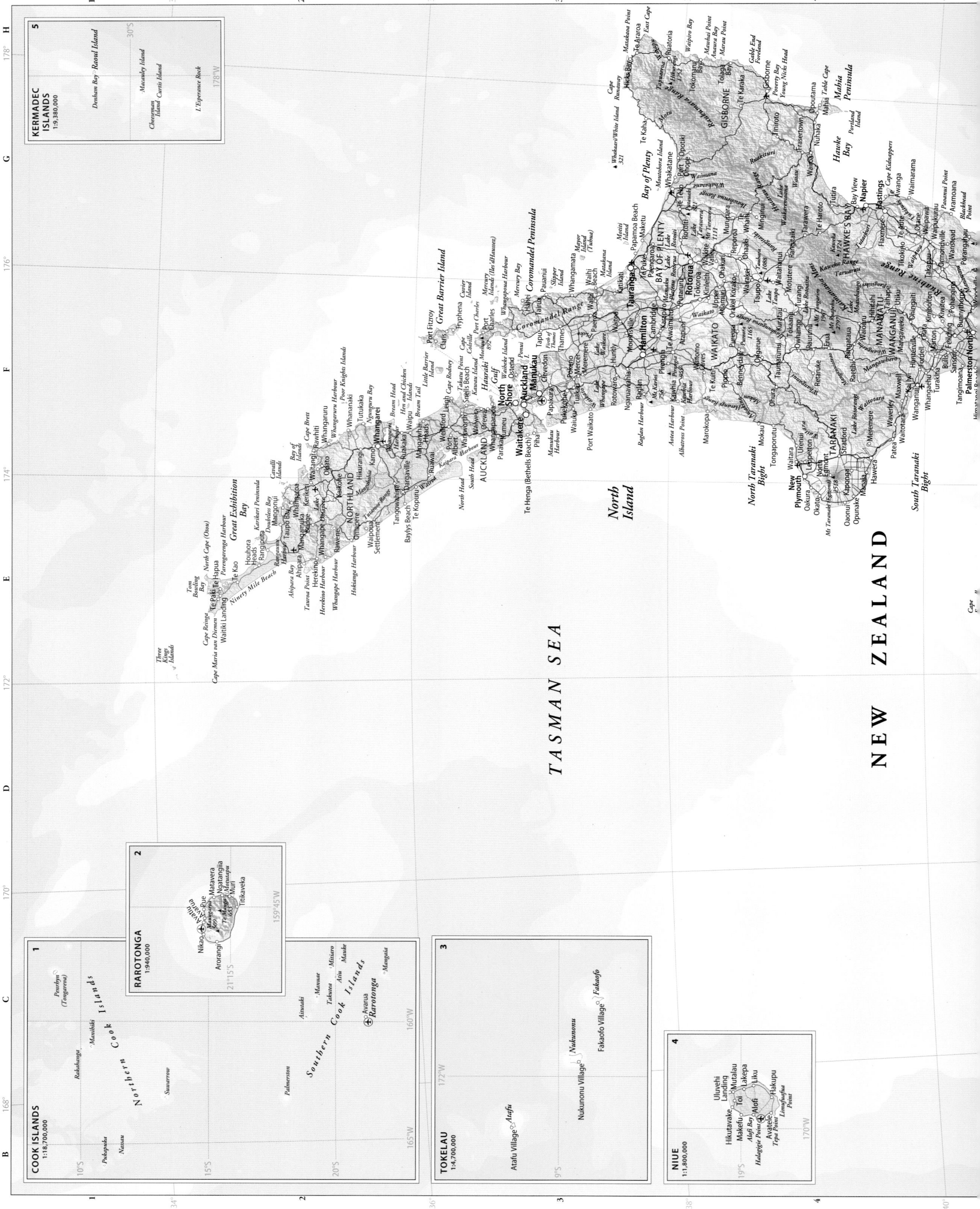
NEW ZEALAND
TASMAN SEA
North Island
NORTHLAND
AUCKLAND
WAIKATO
BAY OF PLENTY
GISBORNE
HAWKE'S BAY
TARANAKI
MANAWATU-WANGANUI
Auckland
Manukau
Waitakere
North Shore
Hamilton
Tauranga
Rotorua
Gisborne
Napier
Hastings
New Plymouth
Whangarei
Taupo
Palmerston North
Bay of Plenty
Hauraki Gulf
Great Barrier Island
Coromandel Peninsula
Hawke Bay
Mahia Peninsula
North Taranaki Bight
South Taranaki Bight
Great Exhibition Bay
Ninety Mile Beach
Cape Reinga
Cape Maria van Diemen
Three Kings Islands
East Cape
KERMADEC ISLANDS
1:9,380,000
Raoul Island
Denham Bay
Macauley Island
Curtis Island
Cheeseman Island
L'Esperance Rock
COOK ISLANDS
1:18,700,000
Northern Cook Islands
Southern Cook Islands
Penrhyn (Tongareva)
Manihiki
Rakahanga
Suwarrow
Pukapuka
Nassau
Palmerston
Aitutaki
Manuae
Takutea
Atiu
Mitiaro
Mauke
Mangaia
Rarotonga
Avarua
RAROTONGA
1:940,000
Avarua
Nikao
Arorangi
Matavera
Ngatangiia
Muri
Titikaveka
TOKELAU
1:4,700,000
Atafu
Atafu Village
Nukunonu
Nukunonu Village
Fakaofo
Fakaofo Village
NIUE
1:1,800,000
Alofi
Hikutavake
Makefu
Tuapa
Uluvehi Landing
Mutalau
Lakepa
Liku
Hakupu
Avatele
Alofi Bay
Halagigie Point
Tepa Point
Limufuafua Point

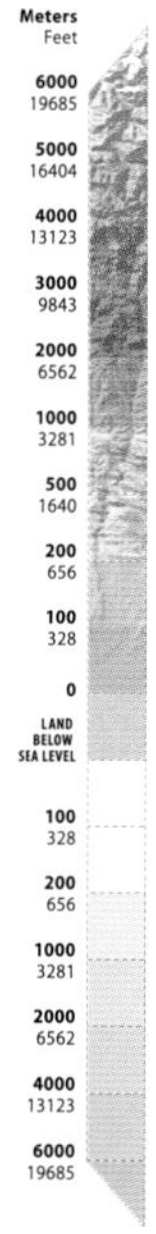
Meters
Feet
6000 19685
5000 16404
4000 13123
3000 9843
2000 6562
1000 3281
500 1640
200 656
100 328
0
LAND BELOW SEA LEVEL
100 328
200 656
1000 3281
2000 6562
4000 13123
6000 19685

1:3,750,000

Lambert Conic Conformal Projection

0 50 100 150 200 kilometers

0 25 50 75 100 miles

NEW ZEALAND

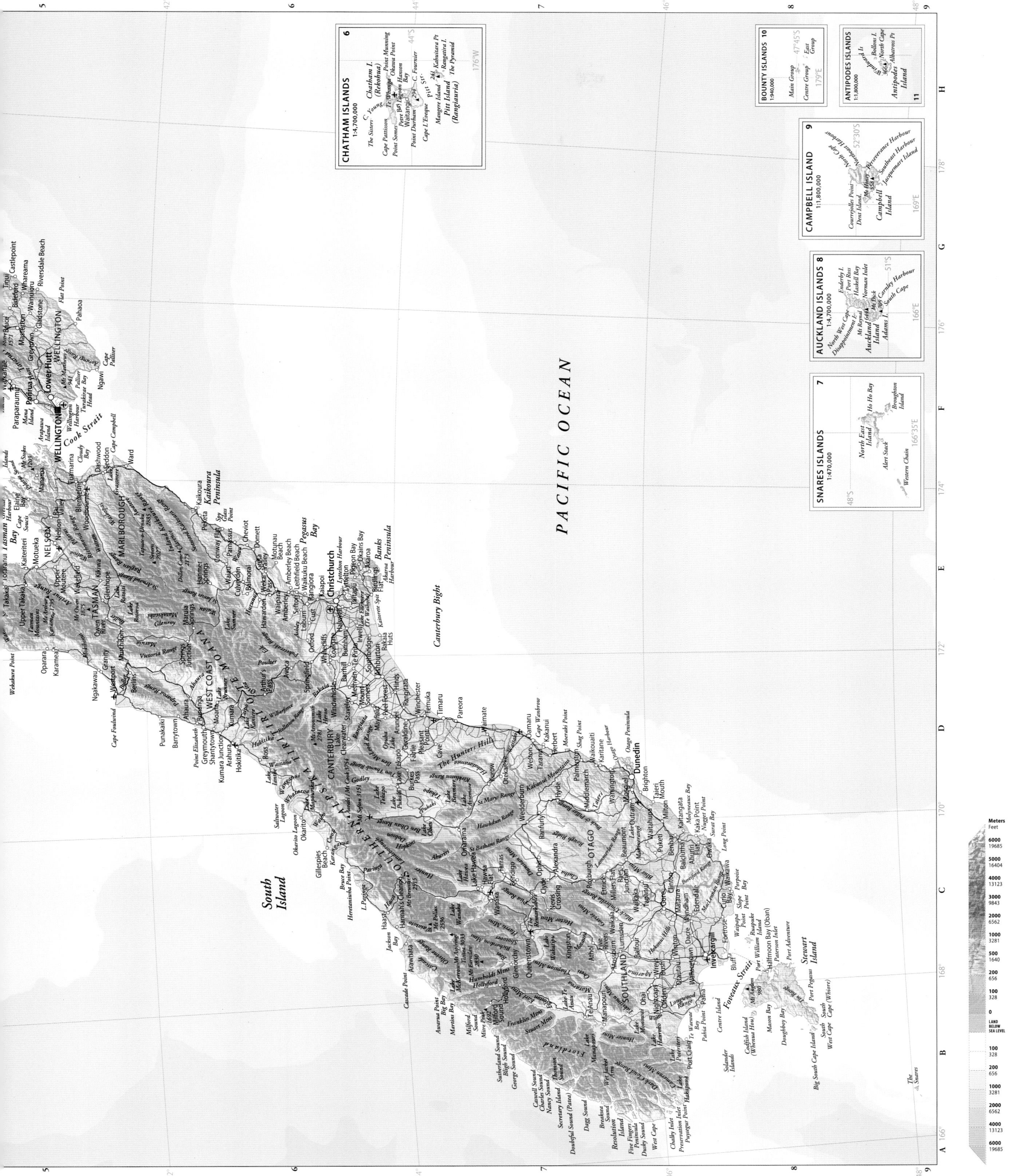
PACIFIC OCEAN
South Island
Canterbury Bight
Cook Strait
Foveaux Strait
Stewart Island
Pegasus Bay
Banks Peninsula
Kaikoura Peninsula
CHATHAM ISLANDS 1:4,700,000
BOUNTY ISLANDS 1:940,000
ANTIPODES ISLANDS 1:1,800,000
CAMPBELL ISLAND 1:1,800,000
AUCKLAND ISLANDS 1:4,700,000
SNARES ISLANDS 1:470,000
WELLINGTON
Christchurch
Dunedin
Invercargill
CANTERBURY
OTAGO
SOUTHLAND
MARLBOROUGH
TASMAN
NELSON
WEST COAST
SOUTHERN ALPS
Meters
Feet
LAND BELOW SEA LEVEL

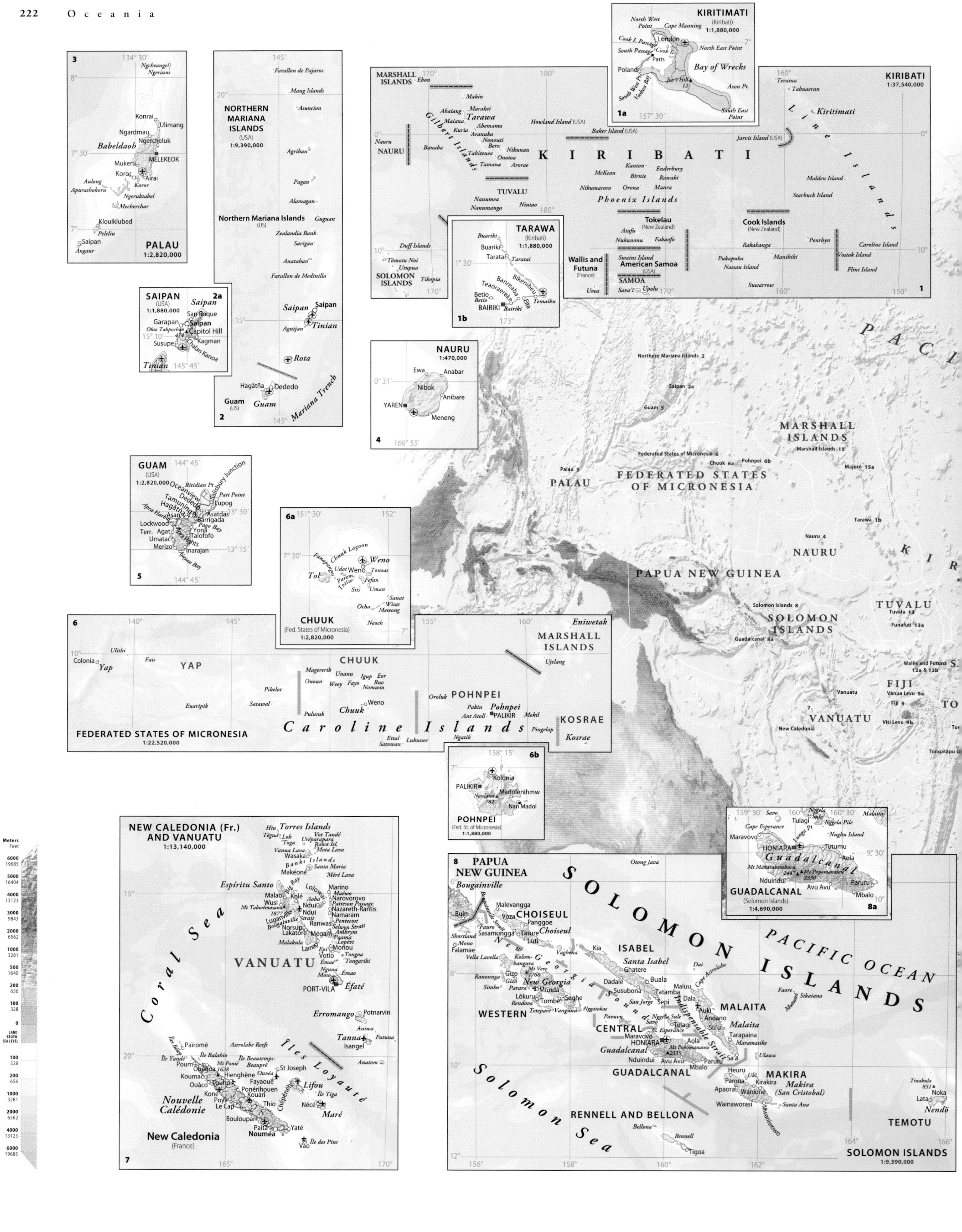
3
134° 30′
Ngcheangel
Ngeriuns
8°
Konrai
Ulimang
Ngardmau
Ngercheluk
Babeldaob
7° 30′
MELEKEOK
Mukeru
Koror
Airai
Aulong
Apurashokoru
Koror
Ngeruktabel
Mecherchar
Kloulklubed
7°
Peleliu
Saipan
Angaur
PALAU
1:2,820,000
145°
Farallon de Pajaros
Maug Islands
20°
NORTHERN MARIANA ISLANDS
(USA)
1:9,390,000
Asuncion
Agrihan
Pagan
Alamagan
Northern Mariana Islands
(US)
Guguan
Zealandia Bank
Sarigan
Anatahan
Farallon de Medinilla
Saipan
Saipan
Tinian
Aguijan
15°
Rota
Hagåtña
Dededo
Guam
(US)
Guam
Mariana Trench
2
145°
SAIPAN
(USA)
1:1,880,000
2a
Saipan
San Roque
Garapan
Saipan
Okso Takpochao
Capitol Hill
474
15° 10′
Kagman
Susupe
Chalan Kanoa
Tinian
145° 45′
MARSHALL ISLANDS
Ebon
170°
180°
Makin
Abaiang
Marakei
Tarawa
Maiana
Abemama
Kuria
Aranuka
Gilbert Islands
Nonouti
Beru
Nikunau
Tabiteuea
Onotoa
Tamana
Arorae
Howland Island (USA)
Baker Island (USA)
0°
Nauru
NAURU
Banaba
K I R I B A T I
TUVALU
Nanumea
Niutao
Nanumanga
180°
McKean
Kanton
Enderbury
Birnie
Rawaki
Nikumaroro
Orona
Manra
Phoenix Islands
Tokelau
(New Zealand)
Atafu
Nukunonu
Fakaofo
Duff Islands
10°
Tömotu Noi
Utupua
SOLOMON ISLANDS
Tikopia
170°
Wallis and Futuna
(France)
Uvea
Swains Island
American Samoa
(USA)
SAMOA
Sava'i
Upolu
170°
KIRITIMATI
(Kiribati)
1:1,880,000
North West Point
Cape Manning
Cook I. Passage
London
2°
South Passage
Cook I.
North East Point
Paris
Poland
Bay of Wrecks
South West Pt.
Vaskess Bay
Joe's Hill
12
Aeon Pt.
1a
157° 30′
South East Point
KIRIBATI
1:37,540,000
160°
Teraina
Tabuaeran
Kiritimati
Line Islands
Jarvis Island (USA)
0°
Malden Island
Starbuck Island
Cook Islands
(New Zealand)
Rarakanga
Penrhyn
Caroline Island
Vostok Island
Manihiki
10°
Pukapuka
Nassau Island
Flint Island
Suwarrow
160°
150°
1
TARAWA
(Kiribati)
1:1,880,000
Buariki
Buariki
Taratai
Taratai
1° 30′
Bikenibeu
Banreaba
Teaoraereke
Betio
Betio
Eita
Temaiku
BAIRIKI
Bairiki
1b
173°
NAURU
1:470,000
Ewa
Anabar
0° 31′
Nibok
Anibare
YAREN
Meneng
4
166° 55′
Northern Mariana Islands 2
Saipan 2a
Guam 5
MARSHALL ISLANDS
Marshall Islands 15
Federated States of Micronesia 6
Chuuk 6a
Pohnpei 6b
Majuro 15a
Palau 3
PALAU
FEDERATED STATES OF MICRONESIA
Tarawa 1b
Nauru 4
NAURU
PAPUA NEW GUINEA
Solomon Islands 8
SOLOMON ISLANDS
Guadalcanal 8a
TUVALU
Tuvalu 13
Funafuti 13a
Wallis and Futuna 12a & 12b
FIJI
Vanuatu
Vanua Levu 9a
Fiji 9
VANUATU
Viti Levu 9b
New Caledonia
Tongatapu
PACIFIC
GUAM
144° 45′
(USA)
1:2,820,000
Ritidian Pt
Salisbury Junction
Pati Point
Oceanview
Dededo
Tamuning
Lupog
Apra Harbor
Hagåtña
Asan
Asatdas
13° 30′
Barrigada
Pago Bay
Lockwood Terr.
Agat
Yona
Umatac
Talofofo
Merizo
Inarajan
13° 15′
Ajayan Bay
5
144° 45′
6a
151° 30′
152°
Chuuk Lagoon
7° 30′
Weno
Faichuk
Tol
Udot
Weno
Tonoas
Parem
Fefan
Totiw
Uman
Siis
Sanat
Ocha
Wisas
Meseong
CHUUK
(Fed. States of Micronesia)
1:2,820,000
Neoch
7°
6
140°
145°
155°
160°
Eniwetak
MARSHALL ISLANDS
10°
Ulithi
Colonia
Yap
Fais
YAP
CHUUK
Ujelang
Magererik
Unanu
Igup
Eor
Onoun
Weey
Fayo
Ruo
Nomwin
Pikelot
Weno
Oroluk
POHNPEI
Euaripik
Satawal
Pulusuk
Chuuk
Pakin
Pohnpei
Ant Atoll
PALIKIR
Mokil
KOSRAE
Caroline Islands
Pingelap
FEDERATED STATES OF MICRONESIA
1:22,520,000
Ettal
Satowan
Lukunor
Ngatik
Kosrae
158° 15′
6b
7°
Kolonia
PALIKIR
Madolenihmw
Nanlaud
782
Nan Madol
POHNPEI
(Fed. St. of Micronesia)
1:1,880,000
NEW CALEDONIA (Fr.) AND VANUATU
1:13,140,000
Hiu
Torres Islands
Tégua
Vot Tandé
Loh
Uréparapara
Toga
Rowa Isl.
Vanua Lava
Mota Lava
Wasaka
Banks Islands
Santa Maria
Makéone
Méré Lava
Espíritu Santo
Marino
Lolowai
Maéwo
Malao
Narovorovo
Aoba
Patteson Passage
Wusi
Big Bay
Nazareth-Rantis
Nduindui
Mt Tabwémasana 1877
Namaram
Luganville
Ndui
Pentecost
Bougainville Strait
Selwyn Strait
Norsup
Ranwas
Ambrym
Lakatoro
Mégam
Paama
Malakula
Lopévi
Lamap
Moriou
Epi
Tongoa
Votlo
Tongariki
Emaé
Nguna
Émao
Moso
PORT-VILA
Éfaté
15°
Coral Sea
VANUATU
Erromango
Potnarvin
Aniwa
Tanna
Futuna
Isangel
Anatom
Païromé
Astrolabe Reefs
Île Balabio
Île Beautemps-Beaupré
Îles Loyauté
Île Yandé
20°
Poum
Ouégoa
Mt Panié 1628
Ouvéa
St Joseph
Koumac
Touho
Hienghène
Fayaoué
Ouaco
Lifou
Ponérihouen
Île Tiga
Koné
Poya
Kouari
Chépénéhé
Nouvelle Calédonie
Le Cap
Thio
Nécé
Maré
Bouloupari
Païta
Yaté
Nouméa
New Caledonia
(France)
Vao
Île des Pins
7
165°
170°
Meters
Feet
6000
19685
5000
16404
4000
13123
3000
9843
2000
6562
1000
3281
500
1640
200
656
100
328
0
LAND BELOW SEA LEVEL
100
328
200
656
1000
3281
2000
6562
4000
13123
6000
19685
159° 30′
Savo
160°
Nggela Sule
160° 30′
Malaita
Tulagi
Nggela Pile
Cape Esperance
Maravovo
Lunga Pt
Nughu Island
HONIARA
Tutumu
9° 30′
Guadalcanal
Aola
Mt Makarakomburu 2447
Mt Popomanaseu 2330
Nduindui
Paruru
Avu Avu
GUADALCANAL
(Solomon Islands)
1:4,690,000
Mbalo
10°
8a
8
PAPUA NEW GUINEA
Bougainville
Otong Java
SOLOMON ISLANDS
PACIFIC OCEAN
Buin
Malevangga
Voza
CHOISEUL
Panggoe
Fauro
Bougainville Strait
Shortland
Sasamungga
Tasure
Choiseul
Mono
Luti
Falamae
New Georgia Sound
Kia
ISABEL
Vella Lavella
Vaghena
Kolombangara
Santa Isabel
Mt Veve 1768
Ghatere
Dai
8°
Ranongga
Gizo
Gizo
New Georgia
Buala
Cape Astrolabe
Simbo
Parara
Dadale
Maluu
Munda
Susubona
Tatamba
Faore
Sikaiana
Lokuru
Tombe
Seghe
San Jorge
Sepi
Dala
Manaoba
Rendova
Indispensable Strait
Tetepare
Vangunu
Nggatokae
MALAITA
WESTERN
Auki
Pavuvu
Nggela Sule
Anoano
Savo
Tulagi
Su'u
CENTRAL
C. Esperance
Malaita
Maravovo
Aola
Tarapaina
HONIARA
Maramasike
Mt Popomanaseu
Guadalcanal
2335
Ulawa
Nduindui
Avu Avu
Paruru
Sa'a
10°
Mbalo
GUADALCANAL
Heuru
MAKIRA
Pamua
Uki
Kirakira
Makira
(San Cristobal)
Tinakula 851
Apaora
Waniore
Noka
Lata
Wainaworasi
Santa Ana
Nendö
Solomon Sea
RENNELL AND BELLONA
Mwaniwowo
TEMOTU
Bellona
Rennell
164°
166°
Tigoa
12°
156°
158°
160°
162°
SOLOMON ISLANDS
1:9,390,000

ISLANDS of the PACIFIC

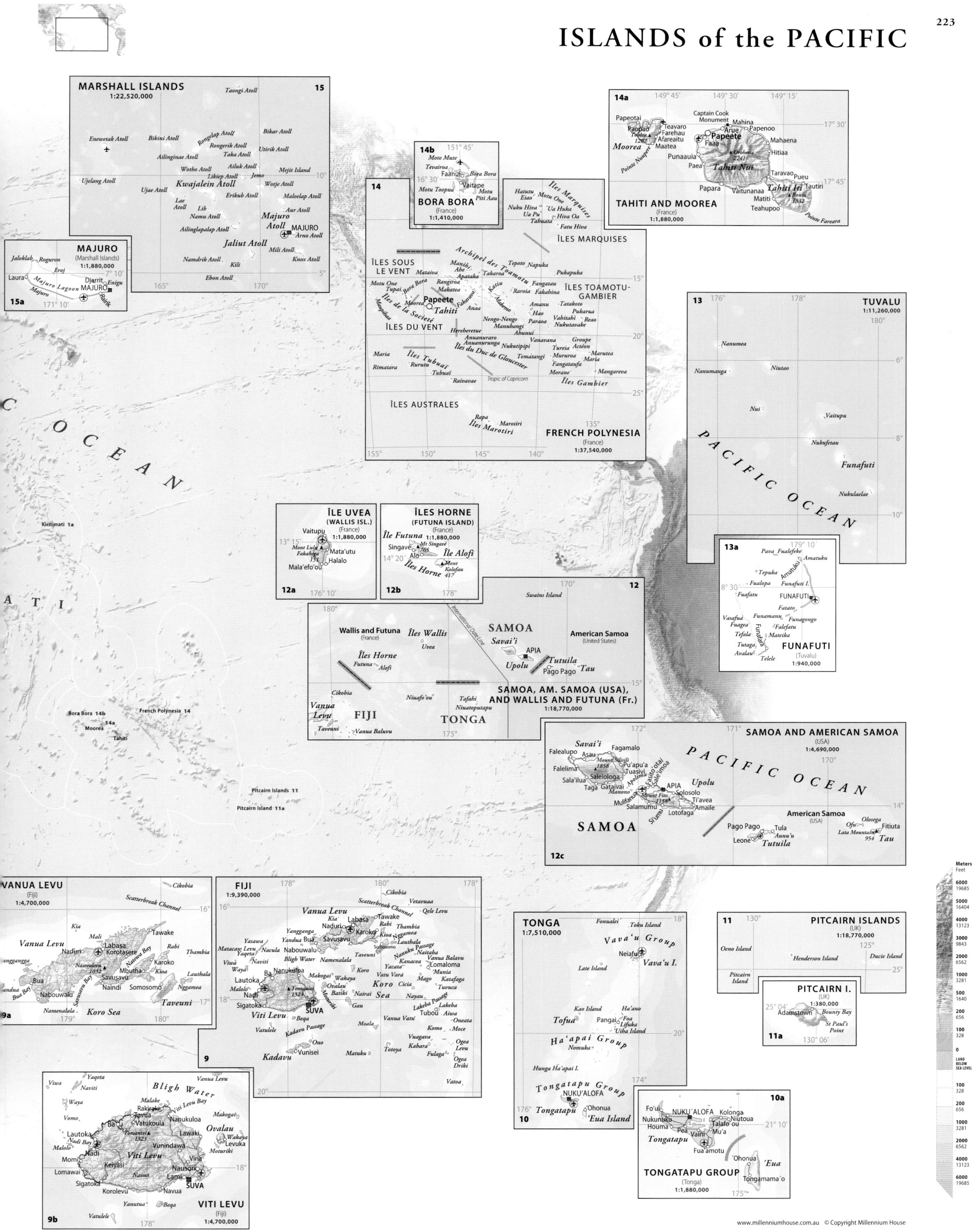

MARSHALL ISLANDS
1:22,520,000
15
Taongi Atoll
Enewetak Atoll
Bikini Atoll
Rongelap Atoll
Rongerik Atoll
Bikar Atoll
Utirik Atoll
Taka Atoll
Ailinginae Atoll
Wotho Atoll
Ailuk Atoll
Mejit Island
Likiep Atoll
Jemo
Ujelang Atoll
Kwajalein Atoll
Wotje Atoll
Ujae Atoll
Erikub Atoll
Maloelap Atoll
Lae Atoll
Lib
Aur Atoll
Namu Atoll
Majuro Atoll
Ailinglapalap Atoll
MAJURO
Arno Atoll
Jaliut Atoll
Mili Atoll
Namdrik Atoll
Kili
Knox Atoll
Ebon Atoll
MAJURO
(Marshall Islands)
1:1,880,000
15a
Jaloklab
Rongrong
Eroj
Laura
Majuro Lagoon
Djarrit
Enigu
Majuro
MAJURO
Rairik
14b
BORA BORA
(France)
1:1,410,000
Moto Mute
Tevairoa
Faanui
Bora Bora
Vaitape
Motu Toopua
Motu Piti Aau
14a
Papeotai
Captain Cook Monument
Mahina
Papenoo
Teavaro
Arue
Farehau
Papeete
Afareaitu
Faaa
Mahaena
Moorea
Maatea
Punaauia
Orohena 2241
Hitiaa
Paea
Tahiti Nui
Pointe Nuuparu
Taravao
Pueu
Papara
Vaitunanaa
Tahiti Iti
Tautiri
Matiti
Ronui 1332
Teahupoo
Pointe Fareara
TAHITI AND MOOREA
(France)
1:1,880,000
14
Îles Marquises
Hatutu
Eiao
Motu One
Nuku Hiva
Ua Huka
Ua Pu
Hiva Oa
Tahuata
Fatu Hiva
ÎLES MARQUISES
Archipel des Tuamotu
ÎLES SOUS LE VENT
Manihi
Ahe
Tepoto
Napuka
Mataiva
Apataki
Takaroa
Pukapuka
Motu One
Tupai
Bora Bora
Rangiroa
Makatea
Fangatau
Fakahina
Raroia
ÎLES TOAMOTU-GAMBIER
Papeete
Moorea
Tahiti
Îles de la Société
Anaa
Makemo
Katiu
Fakarava
Amanu
Hao
Tatakoto
Pukarua
Vahitahi
Reao
Nukutavake
Maupihaa
ÎLES DU VENT
Nengo-Nengo
Manuhangi
Paraoa
Ahunui
Hereheretue
Anuanuraro
Anuanurunga
Vanavana
Groupe Actéon
Îles du Duc de Gloucester
Nukutipipi
Tureia
Maria
Îles Tubuaï
Rurutu
Tubuaï
Rimatara
Tematangi
Mururoa
Marutea
Fangataufa
Morane
Mangareva
Îles Gambier
Raivavae
Tropic of Capricorn
ÎLES AUSTRALES
Rapa
Marotiri
Îles Marotiri
FRENCH POLYNESIA
(France)
1:37,540,000
13
TUVALU
1:11,260,000
Nanumea
Niutao
Nanumanga
Nui
Vaitupu
Nukufetau
Funafuti
Nukulaelae
PACIFIC OCEAN
13a
Pava
Fualefeke
Amatuku
Tepuka
Fualopa
Funafuti I.
Fuafatu
FUNAFUTI
Fatato
Funamanu
Funagongo
Vasafua
Fuagea
Falefatu
Tefala
Mateika
Tutaga
Avalau
Telele
FUNAFUTI
(Tuvalu)
1:940,000
ÎLE UVEA
(WALLIS ISL.)
(France)
1:1,880,000
Vaitupu
Mont Lulu Fakahega 151
Mata'utu
Halalo
Mala'efo'ou
12a
ÎLES HORNE
(FUTUNA ISLAND)
(France)
1:1,880,000
Île Futuna
Mt Singavé 765
Singavé
Alo
Île Alofi
Îles Horne
Mont Kolofau 417
12b
12
Swains Island
International Date Line
Wallis and Futuna
(France)
Îles Wallis
Uvea
SAMOA
Savai'i
American Samoa
(United States)
APIA
Îles Horne
Futuna
Alofi
Upolu
Tutuila
Pago Pago
Tau
Cikobia
Niuafo'ou
Tafahi
Niuatoputapu
SAMOA, AM. SAMOA (USA), AND WALLIS AND FUTUNA (Fr.)
1:18,770,000
Vanua Levu
FIJI
TONGA
Taveuni
Vanua Balavu
PACIFIC OCEAN
Kiritimati 1a
Bora Bora 14b
French Polynesia 14
14a
Moorea
Tahiti
Pitcairn Islands 11
Pitcairn Island 11a
SAMOA AND AMERICAN SAMOA
(USA)
1:4,690,000
Savai'i
Fagamalo
Falealupo
Asau
Mount Silisili 1858
Pu'apu'a
Tuasivi
Falelima
Salelologa
Sala'ilua
Taga
Gataivai
Manono
Apolima
APIA
Solosolo
Upolu
Mulifanua
Mount Fito 1158
Ti'avea
Salamumu
Amaile
Lotofaga
SAMOA
American Samoa
(USA)
Pago Pago
Tula
Ofu
Olosega
Fitiuta
Lata Mountain 954
Leone
Aunu'u
Tutuila
Tau
12c
VANUA LEVU
(Fiji)
1:4,700,000
Cikobia
Scatterbreak Channel
Kia
Mali
Tawake
Vanua Levu
Labasa
Naduri
Korotasere
Rabi
Thambia
Natewa Bay
Savusavu
Karoko
Nasorolevu 1032
Mbutha
Kioa
Lauthala
Bua
Bua Bay
Naindi
Somosomo
Nggamea
Nabouwalu
Taveuni
Namenalala
Koro Sea
9a
FIJI
1:9,390,000
Cikobia
Vetauuaa
Scatterbreak Channel
Qele Levu
Vanua Levu
Labasa
Rabi
Thambia
Yanggannga
Naduri
Karoko
Yandua
Bua
Savusavu
Kioa
Nggamea
Lauthala
Yasawa
Matacawa Levu
Nacula
Nabouwalu
Somosomo
Taveuni
Nanuku Passage
Naitaba
Yageta
Naviti
Bligh Water
Namenalala
Kanacea
Vanua Balavu
Lomaloma
Viwa
Waya
Nanukuloa
Koro
Yacata
Munia
Makogai
Vatu Vara
Lautoka
Wakaya
Mago
Katafaga
Malolo
Nadi
Ovalau
Cicia
Tuvuca
Tomanivi 1324
Batiki
Koro Sea
Sigatoka
Nairai
Nayau
Lakeba Passage
Lakeba
SUVA
Gau
Viti Levu
Beqa
Vanua Vatu
Tubou
Aiwa
Vatulele
Kadavu Passage
Moala
Oneata
Komo
Moce
Ono
Vuagava
Kabara
Ogea Levu
Totoya
Vunisei
Matuku
Fulaga
Ogea Driki
Kadavu
Vatoa
9
TONGA
1:7,510,000
Fonualei
Toku Island
Vava'u Group
Neiafu
Vava'u I.
Late Island
Kao Island
Ha'ano
Tofua
Pangai
Foa
Lifuka
'Uiha Island
Ha'apai Group
Nomuka
Hunga Ha'apai I.
Tongatapu Group
NUKU'ALOFA
Tongatapu
'Ohonua
'Eua Island
10
11
PITCAIRN ISLANDS
(UK)
1:18,770,000
Oeno Island
Henderson Island
Ducie Island
Pitcairn Island
PITCAIRN I.
(UK)
1:380,000
Adamstown
Bounty Bay
St Paul's Point
11a
10a
Fo'ui
NUKU'ALOFA
Kolonga
Nukuntuku
Niutoua
Talafo'ou
Houma
Mu'a
Pea
Vaini
Tongatapu
Fua'amotu
'Ohonua
'Eua
TONGATAPU GROUP
(Tonga)
1:1,880,000
Tongamama'o
Viwa
Yaqeta
Naviti
Bligh Water
Vanua Levu
Waya
Malake
Rakiraki
Viti Levu Bay
Vomo
Tavua
Nanukuloa
Makogai
Ba
Vatukoula
Lautoka
Nadi Bay
Tomanivi 1323
Lawaki
Ovalau
Wakaya
Levuka
Malolo
Nadi
Vunindawa
Moturiki
Momi
Viti Levu
Viria
Lomawai
Keiyasi
Nausori
Sigatoka
Navua
Lami
SUVA
Korolevu
Navua
Yanutua
Beqa
VITI LEVU
(Fiji)
1:4,700,000
Vatulele
9b
Meters
Feet
6000
19685
5000
16404
4000
13123
3000
9843
2000
6562
1000
3281
500
1640
200
656
100
328
0
LAND BELOW SEA LEVEL
100
328
200
656
1000
3281
2000
6562
4000
13123
6000
19685

GAZETTEER

FOREIGN TERMS

Açude Reservoir or lake *PORTUGUESE*
Ada, Adası Island *TURKISH*
Adaları Islands *TURKISH*
Adrar Hill or mountain *BERBER*
Akra, Akrotirio Cape or point *GREEK*
Älv, -älv, -älven River *SWEDISH*
Archipel Archipelago *FRENCH*
Archipiélago Archipelago *SPANISH*
Arquipélago Archipelago *PORTUGUESE*
Arrecife Reef *SPANISH*
Arroio River *PORTUGUESE, SPANISH*
Bahía Bay *SPANISH*
Baḩr Sea or large body of water *ARABIC*
Baía Bay *PORTUGUESE*
Baie Bay *FRENCH*
Banco Reef *SPANISH*
Banjaran Range *MALAY*
Barragem Dam or reservoir *PORTUGUESE*
Boca River mouth *PORTUGUESE, SPANISH*
Buchta Bay *UKRAINIAN*
Bugt Bay *DANISH*
Bukit Hill *INDONESIAN, MALAY*
Burnu Cape or point *TURKISH*
Cabo Cape *PORTUGUESE, SPANISH*
Cachoeira Waterfall *PORTUGUESE*
Caleta Bay or inlet *SPANISH*
Câmpia Plain *ROMANIAN*
Caño River *SPANISH*
Cap Cape *FRENCH*
Capo Cape *ITALIAN*
Cayo, Cayos Island, Islands *SPANISH*
Cerro Mountain *SPANISH*
Chaîne Mountain range *FRENCH*
Chott Lake or swamp *ARABIC*
Cienago Swamp *SPANISH*
Cima Mountain *ITALIAN*
Cordillera Mountain chain *SPANISH*
Colle Pass *ITALIAN*
Collina Hill or mountain *ITALIAN*
Cordillera Mountain chain *SPANISH*
Costa Coast *SPANISH*
Côte Coast *FRENCH*
Cuchillo Mountain range *SPANISH*
Dağ, Dağı Mountain or mountain range *TURKISH*
Dağlar, Dağları Mountains *TURKISH*
Dahr Escarpment *ARABIC*
Danau Lake *INDONESIAN*
Dao Island *CHINESE*
Đao Island *VIETNAMESE*
Dasht Desert *PERSIAN*
Denizi Sea *TURKISH*
Desierto Desert *SPANISH*
-do Island *KOREAN*
Eilean Island *GAELIC*
Embalse Dam or reservoir *SPANISH*
Ensenada Bay or cove *SPANISH*
Erg Large sand-covered desert area or sand dunes *ARABIC*
Estero Estuary or inlet *SPANISH*
Estrecho Strait *SPANISH*
Étang Lagoon or lake *FRENCH*
Ežeras Lake *LITHUANIAN*
Fiume River *ITALIAN*
-fjell Mountain *NORWEGIAN*
Falaise Cliff or escarpment *FRENCH*
Fleuve River *FRENCH*
Ghard Sand dune or sand dunes *ARABIC*
Gjiri Bay *ALBANIAN*
Gletscher Glacier *DANISH, GERMAN*
Gol, Golü Lake *TURKISH*
Golfe Gulf *FRENCH*
Golfo Gulf *ITALIAN, PORTUGUESE, SPANISH*
Gora Mountain *BULGARIAN, CROATIAN, RUSSIAN, SERBIAN, SLOVENIAN*
Gory Mountain range *RUSSIAN*
Guba Bay *RUSSIAN*
Gunung Mountain *INDONESIAN, MALAY*
Hamada, Hammadat Rocky desert plateau *ARABIC*
-hana Point *JAPANESE*
He River *CHINESE*
Hòn Island *VIETNAMESE*
Hora Mountain *CZECH, UKRAINIAN*
Île Island *FRENCH*
Îles Islands *FRENCH*
Ilha Island *PORTUGUESE*
Ilhas Islands *PORTUGUESE*
Isla Island *SPANISH*
Islas Islands *SPANISH*
Isola Island *ITALIAN*
Isole Islands *ITALIAN*
Istmo Isthmus *SPANISH*
Jabal, Jebel Mountain *ARABIC*
-jarv, -jarvi Lake or lagoon *ESTONIAN*
-jarvi Lake or lagoon *FINNISH*
Jazirat Island *ARABIC*
Jezero Lake *SLOVENIAN*
Jeziero Lake *POLISH*
Jiang River *CHINESE*
-jima Island *JAPANESE*
-jökull Glacier or ice cap *ICELANDIC*
Kap, Kapp Cape *DANISH, GERMAN, NORWEGIAN*
Kavir Salt desert *PERSIAN*
Kepulauan Archipelago or islands *INDONESIAN*
Khrebet Mountain range *RUSSIAN*
Khālij Bay or gulf *ARABIC*
Khao Mountain or peak *THAI*
Ko Island *THAI*
-ko Lake *JAPANESE*
Kolī Lake *KAZAKH*
Kólpos Gulf *GREEK*
Körfezi Gulf or bay *TURKISH*
Kuh, Kuh-e Mountains *PERSIAN*
Kŭli Lake *UZBEK*
Kyun Island *BURMESE*
Lac Lake *FRENCH*
Lacul Lake *ROMANIAN*
Laem Cape or point *THAI*
Lago, Laguna Lake *ITALIAN, PORTUGUESE, SPANISH*
Laut Sea *INDONESIAN, MALAY*
Liedao Islands *CHINESE*
Limnothalassa Bay or inlet *GREEK*
Llano Plain *SPANISH*
Ormos Bay *GREEK*
Loch, Lough Lake *GAELIC*
Maja Mountain *ALBANIAN*
Mar Sea *SPANISH*
Mare Sea *ITALIAN*
Massif Mountain *FRENCH*
Meer Lake *DUTCH, GERMAN*
Mesa, Meseta Plateau or tableland *SPANISH*
Melkosopochnik Sandy plateau with small hills *RUSSIAN*
-misaki Point *JAPANESE*
Mont, Montagne Mountain *FRENCH*
Monte Mountain *ITALIAN, PORTUGUESE, SPANISH*
Monti Mountain *ITALIAN*
Monts Mountain range *FRENCH*
More Sea *RUSSIAN*
Mui Cape or Point *VIETNAMESE*
Mys Cape or Point *RUSSIAN*
Nam River *BURMESE, LAOTIAN*
Nehri Stream *TURKISH*
Nevado Mountain range *SPANISH*
Nisoi Islands *GREEK*
Nizmennost' Lowlands, plain *RUSSIAN*
Novaya New *BELORUSSIAN, RUSSIAN*
Nuur Lake **Mongolian**
Ø, Øer Island *DANISH*
Oblast' Administrative division *RUSSIAN*
Okrug Administrative area *RUSSIAN*
Ormos Bay *GREEK*
Oros Mountain or mountains *GREEK*
Ostrov, Ostrova Island, islands *RUSSIAN*
Ouad, Oued River or wadi *ARABIC*
-øy, -øya Island, islands *NORWEGIAN*
Ozero Lake *RUSSIAN*
Pantà Reservoir or lake *CATALAN*
Passo Pass *ITALIAN*
Pegunungan Mountain range *INDONESIAN, MALAY*
Pendi Basin *CHINESE*
Péninsula Peninsula *SPANISH*
Péninsule Peninsula *FRENCH*
Peski Desert or sands *RUSSIAN*
Pic Peak *FRENCH*
Pico Peak *SPANISH*
Pik Peak *RUSSIAN*
Pivostriv Peninsula *UKRAINIAN*
Plaine Plain *FRENCH*
Planalto Plateau *PORTUGUESE*
Planina Mountain, Mountains *BULGARIAN*
Pointe Cape or point *FRENCH*
Poluostrov Peninsula *RUSSIAN*
Ponta Cape or point *PORTUGUESE*
Porto Port *ITALIAN, PORTUGUESE, SPANISH*
Pôrto Port *PORTUGUESE*
Potamos River *GREEK*
Presa Dam, reservoir, or lake *SPANISH*
Proliv Strait *RUSSIAN*
Promontório Promontory *SPANISH*
Puerto Port *SPANISH*
Pulau Island *INDONESIAN, MALAY*
Punta Cape or point *ITALIAN*
Puy Hill or peak *FRENCH*
Ra's, Raas Cape or point *ARABIC*
Ramlat Desert *ARABIC*
Represa Dam or reservoir *PORTUGUESE*
Ribeirão, Rio River *PORTUGUESE*
Río River *SPANISH*
Rivière River *FRENCH*
Rubha Cape *GAELIC*
Sabkhat Salt flat or salt marsh *ARABIC*
Sainte Saint *FRENCH*
Salina, Salinas Salt pan *SPANISH*
San, Santa, Santo Saint *ITALIAN, PORTUGUESE, SPANISH*
-san Mountain or volcano *JAPANESE*
São Saint *PORTUGUESE*
Selat Strait *INDONESIAN*
Semenanjung Peninsula *INDONESIAN*
Serra Mountain range *PORTUGUESE*
Serranía, Sierra Mountain range *SPANISH*
Shamo Desert *CHINESE*
Shan Mountain or mountains *CHINESE*
-shima Island *JAPANESE*
-shotō Islands *JAPANESE*
Slieve Mountain *GAELIC*
Sud South *FRENCH*
Sul South *PORTUGUESE*
Sund Sound *DANISH, GERMAN, NORWEGIAN, SWEDISH*
Sur South *SPANISH*
Tanjona Cape or point *MALAGASY*
Tanjong Cape or point *MALAY*
Tanjung Cape or point *INDONESIAN*
Tasik Lake *MALAY*
Tassili Plateau *BERBER*
Techniti Limni Reservoir *GREEK*
Tell Mountain *ARABIC*
Teluk Bay or gulf *INDONESIAN, MALAY*
Tierra Land *SPANISH*
Ujung Cape or point *INDONESIAN*
Vinh Bay or gulf *VIETNAMESE*
Vodokhranilishche Dam or reservoir *RUSSIAN*
Volcan Volcano *FRENCH*
Volcán Volcano *SPANISH*
Vozyera Lake *BELORUSSIAN*
Vozvyshennost' Region *RUSSIAN*
Vũng Bay *VIETNAMESE*
Wadi Watercourse *ARABIC*
Wāḩāt Oasis *ARABIC*
-wan Bay *JAPANESE*
-zaki Cape *JAPANESE*
Zaliv Bay or gulf *RUSSIAN*
Zemlya Land *RUSSIAN*

ABBREVIATIONS

AO Avtonomnyy Okrug
Arch./Archip. Archipelago
At. Atoll
B. Bay
Bgt Bight
Bn Basin
Br. Bridge
C. Cape
Can. Canyon
Cd Ciudad
Chan. Channel
DC District of Columbia
Dep. Depression
E East, Eastern, Easterly
Esc. Escarpment
Est. Estuary
For. Forest
Ft. Fort
Fj. Fjord
Fr. France
FYROM Former Yugoslav Republic of Macedonia
G. Gulf
Harb. Harbor, Harbour
Hd Headland
I. Island
Is Islands
It. Italy
Isth. Isthmus
L. Lake
Lag. Lagoon
Mt Mount, Mountain
Mts Mountains
N North, Northern, Northerly
Neth. Netherlands
Pass. Passage
Pen. Peninsula
Pln Plain
Plat. Plateau
Pk Park
Pt Point
R. River, Rivers
Res. Reserve
Resr Reservoir
S South, Southern, Southerly
Sea Chan. Sea Channel
St/Ste Saint
Str. Strait
Terr. Territory
UAE United Arab Emirates
UK United Kingdom
USA United States of America
Vol. Crater Volcanic Crater
Vol. Volcano
W West, Western, Westerly

Australian States
ACT Australian Capital Territory
NSW New South Wales
NT Northern Territory
Qld Queensland
SA South Australia
Tas. Tasmania
Vic. Victoria
WA Western Australia

MAP LEGEND

POPULATED PLACES

Population	National capital	Administrative capital	Other city or town
Over 5 million	■ **PARIS**	◉ **Hyderabad**	◉ **New York**
1 million–5 million	■ **BUDAPEST**	◉ **Zürich**	◉ **Vsevolozhsk**
500,000–1 million	■ **SKOPJE**	◎ **Kraków**	◎ **Argenteuil**
100,000–500,000	■ **PRIŠTINA**	○ **Ostrava**	○ **Korinthos**
50,000–100,000	■ **LUXEMBOURG**	○ **Zlín**	○ **Eastbourne**
10,000–50,000	■ MONACO	○ Neuchâtel	○ Exmouth
Less than 10,000	■ VADUZ	○ Sarnen	○ Campodolcino

Research station, homestead, point of interest, historic site, tourist feature ▪ Mawson
Built-up area

ADMINISTRATIVE FEATURES

Boundaries
International boundary – defined
International boundary – claimed, disputed, or undefined
Line of control, demarcation or ceasefire line
Internal administrative boundary – defined
Internal administrative boundary – claimed, disputed, or undefined
Other administrative boundary
Indication of extent of country or territory

Lettering Styles

ASIA	Continent name
KENYA	Country or independent nation
ALSACE	Main internal administrative area
DORSET	Other administrative area
New Caledonia (France)	Dependency (administering or parent country in parenthesis)
ARTOIS	Cultural region, historic area, or physical region or area

TRANSPORTATION

Motorway, freeway, expressway, or divided highway
Motorway, freeway, expressway, or divided highway (under construction)
Motorway, freeway, expressway, or divided highway (through a tunnel)
NOTE: Motorways are only shown at scales of 1:3 million or larger
Major road
Major road (under construction)
Major road (through a tunnel)
Secondary or minor road
Secondary or minor road (under construction)
Secondary or minor road (through a tunnel)
Track (shown in remote and sparsely populated areas only)
Primary or major railway
Primary or major railway (under contruction)
Primary or major railway (through a tunnel)
International airport
Major regional airport

OTHER FEATURES

Tropic of Cancer	Tropics and polar circles
International Date Line	International date line
50°	Graticule (lines of latitude and longitude) with value in degrees

PHYSICAL FEATURES

Lettering Styles

Holy Island	Small island or island group, peninsula, cape, reef, or other coastal feature
Shetland Islands	Major island or island group, peninsula, cape, reef, or other coastal feature
Mendip Hills	Small mountain range, plateau, valley, desert, or other landform
ANDES	Major or extensive mountain range, plateau, valley, desert, or other landform
Thames	Small hydrographic feature – river, lake, bay, gulf, glacier, channel
Loch Lomond	Large or extensive hydrographic feature – river, lake, bay, gulf, glacier, channel
Yellow Sea	Small sea name
North Sea	Large sea name
ARCTIC OCEAN	Ocean name
Chile Basin	Small ocean floor feature: ridge, trench, basin, or plateau (ocean maps only)
Perth Basin	Large ocean floor feature: ridge, trench, basin, or plateau (ocean maps only)

Hydrographic Features
Coastline or shoreline – definite
Coastline or shoreline – undefined, fluctuating, or indefinite
Major river
Minor or secondary river
Intermittent stream (main seasonal river)
Minor or secondary seasonal or intermittent river or wadi
Irrigation or drainage canal
Aqueduct
average extent of sea ice Extent of sea ice or drift ice in polar regions
Significant waterfall, rapids, dam or barrage (major rivers only)
Reef or coral atoll
Perennial lake, reservoir, or other water body
Seasonal, intermittent or impermanent lake
(salt) Perennial salt lake (significant)
(salt) Seasonal salt lake (significant)
Mainly dry lake, salt pan, salt flat, or claypan
Glacier, ice cap, ice sheet, ice shelf, permanent ice, or snow
Area of swamp, marsh, or land subject to inundation
Important spring, well, waterhole, or oasis

Topographic Features

Mt Bogong ▲ *1986*	Mountain peak (height in meters above sea level)
Glacier Peak ▲ *3180*	Volcano – active or inactive (height in meters above sea level)
2025 ▽	Ocean depth (meters below sea level) or land below sea level
	Significant mountain pass
	Significant escarpment or cliff
Great Wall	Significant wall or other linear man-made structure
	Desert or significant area of sand

Relief
All maps portray relief using elevation layer tints based on the intervals in the diagram at right, overlaid with specially prepared hill shading to give a three- dimensional effect for the topography of the area being mapped.

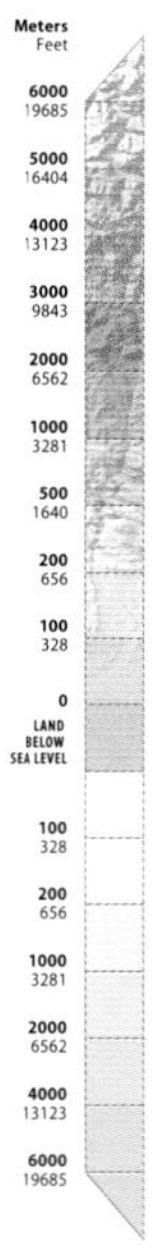
Meters
Feet
6000
19685
5000
16404
4000
13123
3000
9843
2000
6562
1000
3281
500
1640
200
656
100
328
0
LAND BELOW SEA LEVEL
100
328
200
656
1000
3281
2000
6562
4000
13123
6000
19685

Iceland place names may incorporate two letters not used in the English language (Þ, þ and Ð, ð). The letters Þ, þ represent "Th" and are indexed as such.

74 I5 **12 Mile** British Columbia Canada
74 F4 **40 Mile Flats** British Columbia Canada
74 K7 **70 Mile House** British Columbia Canada
74 K6 **150 Mile House** British Columbia Canada

A

120 H3 **Å** Norway
184 G4 **A-chi-chih Ho** *watercourse* Xinjiang Uygur Zizhiqu China
128 B2 **A Coruña** Spain
128 B4 **A dos Cunhados** Portugal
128 B2 **A Estada** Spain
128 B2 **A Golada** Spain
128 C2 **A Gudiña** Spain
128 C2 **A Pontenova** Spain
194 F4 **A Yun Pa** Vietnam
126 F1 **Aa** *watercourse* France
124 D2 **Aachen** Germany
136 G6 **Aafrîte** Syria
136 E6 **Aakrak** Syria
124 F3 **Aalen** Germany
121 P2 **Äälisjärvi** *lake* Finland
126 G1 **Aalst** Belgium
124 D2 **Aalten** Netherlands
121 N5 **Äänekoski** Finland
121 N3 **Aapajärvi** Finland
121 N3 **Aapajoki** Finland
121 M3 **Aapua** Sweden
127 I3 **Aarau** Switzerland
130 B3 **Aare** *watercourse* Switzerland
122 E5 **Aarre** Denmark
73 N5 **Aasiaat** Greenland
143 C3 **Aasleagh** Ireland
179 H3 **Āb Anbār-e Kān Sorkh** Iran
179 H4 **Āb Āqā** Iran
178 G3 **Āb-e Bāzoft** *watercourse* Iran
179 I3 **Āb-e Garm Va Sard** Iran
179 I4 **Āb Gazān** Iran
178 G3 **Āb Gonjeshk** Iran
179 H4 **Āb Kahūr** Iran
178 G3 **Āb Pardeh** Iran
179 H4 **Āb Sardū** Iran
179 I4 **Āb Shahr** Iran
179 H4 **Āb Zaminū** Iran
188 D2 **Aba** Sichuan China
160 E3 **Aba** Democratic Republic of Congo
159 F3 **Aba** Nigeria
182 E6 **Abābīn** Iran
105 G2 **Abacaxis** *watercourse* Brazil
120 J4 **Åbacka** Sweden
179 K4 **Abad** Pakistan
156 F4 **Abadab, Jebel** *mountain* Sudan
178 F3 **Ābādān** Iran
182 G6 **Ābādān Tappeh** Iran
178 G3 **Ābādeh** Iran
128 D3 **Abades** Spain
103 B7 **Abadiânia** Brazil
155 F2 **Abadla** Algeria
103 C7 **Abaeté** Brazil
102 B3 **Abaetetuba** Brazil
107 H3 **Abaí** Paraguay
222 1 **Abaiang** *island* Kiribati
159 F3 **Abaji** Nigeria
159 F3 **Abakaliki** Nigeria
183 P2 **Abakan** Russian Federation
183 O3 **Abakan** *watercourse* Russian Federation
159 H5 **Abala** Congo
155 G6 **Abala** Niger
155 H5 **Abalak** Niger
155 G4 **Abalessa** Algeria
135 U7 **Aban** Russian Federation
104 C4 **Abancay** Peru
179 I4 **Āband** Iran
100 B5 **Abanico** Ecuador
105 F5 **Abapó** Bolivia
182 E6 **Abarghan** Iran
179 H3 **Abarkūh** Iran
101 F3 **Abasacapán** Venezuela
182 E6 **Abasaly** Azerbaijan
193 J2 **Abashiri** Japan
88 E4 **Abasolo** Mexico
199 I6 **Abau** Papua New Guinea
123 L4 **Abava** *watercourse* Latvia
156 F5 **Abay Wenz (Blue Nile)** *watercourse* Ethiopia
183 P3 **Abaza** Russian Federation
159 H3 **Abba** Central African Republic
131 C6 **Abbasanta** Sardinia Italy
122 G5 **Abbekås** Sweden
139 H3 **Abberton Reservoir** England UK
139 I4 **Abbeville** France
86 E6 **Abbeville** Louisiana USA
75 Q7 **Abbey** Saskatchewan Canada
142 E6 **Abbey Head** *cape* Scotland UK
140 E2 **Abbey Town** Cumbria England UK
143 C4 **Abbeyfeale** Ireland
219 H2 **Abbieglassie** Qld Australia
120 J4 **Abborrberg** Sweden
120 K4 **Abborrträsk** Sweden
215 I6 **Abbot, Mount** Qld Australia
215 I5 **Abbot Bay** Qld Australia
59 R2 **Abbot Ice Shelf** Antarctica
215 J5 **Abbot Point** Qld Australia
138 E4 **Abbotsbury** Dorset England UK
74 J8 **Abbotsford** British Columbia Canada
85 J2 **Abbott** New Mexico USA
179 M2 **Abbottabad** Pakistan
157 I5 **Abd Al Kūrī** *island* Yemen
179 H3 **Ābdān Anjīr** Iran
178 F3 **Ābdānān** Iran
179 H4 **Ābdasht** Iran
161 G1 **Abdelcader** Somalia
157 G5 **Abdelcader** Somalia
131 B8 **Abdi** Algeria
133 E5 **Abdürrahim** Turkey
156 C5 **Abéché** Chad
120 G4 **Abelvær** Norway
120 I4 **Abelvattnet** *lake* Sweden
222 1 **Abemama** *island* Kiribati
162 C3 **Abenab** Namibia
158 D3 **Abengourou** Côte d'Ivoire
128 D4 **Abenójar** Spain
122 E5 **Åbenrå** Denmark
124 F3 **Abens** *watercourse* Germany
124 F3 **Abensberg** Germany
158 E3 **Abeokuta** Nigeria
138 C2 **Aber Arth** Ceredigion Wales UK
138 D2 **Aber Cowarch** Gwynedd Wales UK
138 C2 **Aberaeron** Ceredigion Wales UK
138 D2 **Aberangell** Gwynedd Wales UK
219 J4 **Aberbaldie** NSW Australia
142 F3 **Aberchirder** Aberdeenshire Scotland UK
138 D3 **Aberdare** Rhondda Cynon Taff Wales UK
138 C2 **Aberdaron** Gwynedd Wales UK
219 J5 **Aberdeen** NSW Australia
162 D6 **Aberdeen** South Africa
142 F3 **Aberdeen** Aberdeen Scotland UK
142 F3 **Aberdeen** *admin. area* Scotland UK
86 G4 **Aberdeen** Mississippi USA
81 P4 **Aberdeen** South Dakota USA
80 D3 **Aberdeen** Washington USA
73 J6 **Aberdeen Lake** Nunavut Canada
86 G4 **Aberdeen Lake** Mississippi USA
142 E3 **Aberdeenshire** *admin. area* Scotland UK
138 C2 **Aberdyfi** Gwynedd Wales UK
138 C1 **Aberffraw** Isle of Anglesey Wales UK
142 D4 **Aberfoyle** Stirling Scotland UK
157 F5 **Ābergelē** Ethiopia
215 H5 **Abergowrie** Qld Australia
138 D3 **Abergwynfi** Neath Port Talbot Wales UK
138 D2 **Abergynolwyn** Gwynedd Wales UK
142 F4 **Aberlady** East Lothian Scotland UK
138 D2 **Aberllefenni** Gwynedd Wales UK
85 L4 **Abernathy** Texas USA
138 C2 **Aberporth** Ceredigion Wales UK
126 B2 **Abers, Les** *region* France
138 C2 **Abersoch** Gwynedd Wales UK
80 E5 **Abert, Lake** Oregon USA
138 C2 **Aberystwyth** Ceredigion Wales UK
156 B5 **Abgué** Chad
178 E6 **Abhā** Saudi Arabia
182 F7 **Abhar** Iran
157 G5 **Abhe, Lac** *lake* Djibouti
159 F3 **Abia** *admin. area* Nigeria
156 E5 **Abiad, Bahr el (White Nile)** *watercourse* Sudan
101 E5 **Ábico** Brazil
158 D3 **Abidjan** Côte d'Ivoire
101 H5 **Ábidos** Brazil
86 B4 **Abilene** Texas USA
139 G3 **Abinger Hammer** Surrey England UK
142 E5 **Abington** South Lanarkshire Scotland UK
85 I2 **Abiquiu Reservoir** New Mexico USA
77 O7 **Abitibi** *watercourse* Ontario Canada
73 L9 **Abitibi, Lake** Ontario Canada
120 H4 **Åbjørvatnet** *lake* Norway
179 I2 **Ābkesht** Iran
139 F3 **Ablington** Gloucestershire England UK
156 E2 **Abnūb** Egypt
186 D4 **Abohar** Punjab India
158 D3 **Aboisso** Côte d'Ivoire
121 M2 **Abojárvi** *lake* Norway
158 E3 **Abomey** Benin
164 3a **Abona, Punta de** *cape* Canary Islands
124 D4 **Abondance** France
159 G4 **Abong Mbang** Cameroon
196 C2 **Abongabong, Gunung** *mountain* Indonesia
195 H5 **Aborlan** Philippines
136 F6 **Abou Hanâya** Syria
160 C2 **Abourassein, Mont** *mountain* Sudan
142 F3 **Aboyne** Aberdeenshire Scotland UK
182 H7 **Ābqūy** Iran
195 I3 **Abra** *watercourse* Philippines
108 B5 **Abra, Canal** *strait* Chile
106 E2 **Abra Pampa** Argentina
75 M6 **Abraham Lake** Alberta Canada
78 F3 **Abrat** *watercourse* Quebec Canada
120 K3 **Abraur** *lake* Sweden
128 C3 **Abraveses** Portugal
100 C2 **Ábrego** Colombia
156 E3 **'Abri** Sudan
142 D3 **Abriachan** Highland Scotland UK
130 B4 **Abriès** France
179 H3 **Ābrīz** Iran
51 O11 **Abrolhos Bank** *underwater feature* Atlantic Ocean
103 E7 **Abrolhos, Arquipélago dos** *islands* Brazil
178 G3 **Ābrū** Iran
132 C2 **Abrud** Romania
123 L3 **Abruka** *island* Estonia
179 H3 **Ābrūn** Iran
131 E5 **Abruzzo** *admin. area* Italy
178 E7 **'Abs** Yemen
59 W1 **Absalom, Mount** *mountain* Antarctica
81 K4 **Absaroka Range** Wyoming USA
127 K3 **Abtenau** Austria
179 H5 **Abū al Abyaḑ** *island* United Arab Emirates
178 G4 **Abū 'Alī, Jazīrat** *island* Saudi Arabia
136 F6 **Abū as Sayyid** Syria
156 D3 **Abū Ballāş** *range* Egypt
156 E4 **Abū Dawm** Sudan
156 E5 **Abū Dawm** Sudan
156 E4 **Abū Dawm, Wādī** *watercourse* Sudan
Abu Dhabi *see* **Abū Z̧abī** United Arab Emirates
156 E4 **Abu Dis** Sudan
156 E2 **Abū Durbah** Egypt
156 E5 **Abu Gubeiha** Sudan
156 E4 **Abu Hamed** Sudan
156 E5 **Abū Ḩūt** *watercourse* Sudan
156 E1 **Abū Kabīr** Egypt
156 D5 **Abū Kabisa** Sudan
179 K3 **Abū Kalā** Afghanistan
136 G6 **Abū Kamāl** Syria
178 E2 **Abū Kharjah** Iraq
178 D5 **Abū Madd, Ra's** *cape* Saudi Arabia
156 F5 **Abu Mendi** Ethiopia
179 H4 **Abū Mūsā, Jazīreh-ye** *island* Iran
136 F6 **Abū Naţūlīyah** Syria
155 J2 **Abū Nujaym** Libya
156 E1 **Abū Qīr, Khalīj** *bay* Egypt
155 J2 **Abū Qurīn** Libya
186 C6 **Abu Road** Rajasthan India
178 E2 **Abū Samak** Iraq
159 I2 **Abū Sanţ** *watercourse* Sudan
156 F3 **Abu Shagara, Ras** *cape* Sudan
156 E3 **Abū Sunbul** Egypt
156 E2 **Abū Tīj** Egypt
156 D5 **Abū Zabad** Sudan
179 H5 **Abū Z̧abī (Abu Dhabi)** United Arab Emirates
105 F2 **Abufari, Lago** *lake* Brazil
159 F3 **Abuja** Nigeria
195 I3 **Abulong** *watercourse* Philippines
160 C3 **Abumombazi** Democratic Republic of Congo
104 E3 **Abuna** *watercourse* Bolivia
105 E3 **Abunã** Brazil
100 E5 **Abunaí** Brazil
158 D3 **Aburi** Ghana
158 D3 **Abuso** Ghana
195 J5 **Abuyog** Philippines
160 E2 **Abwong** Sudan
156 D5 **Abyad** Sudan
120 L4 **Åbyn** Sweden
100 C4 **Acacías** Colombia
59 U1 **Academy Glacier** *ice* Antarctica
75 P7 **Acadia Valley** Alberta Canada
102 C4 **Açailândia** Brazil
103 E5 **Acajutiba** Brazil
89 G5 **Acala** Mexico
88 E4 **Acámbaro** Mexico
100 B2 **Acandí** Colombia
88 D4 **Acaponeta** Mexico
89 F5 **Acapulco** Mexico
105 G2 **Acará** Brazil
102 B3 **Acará** Brazil
102 B3 **Acará** *watercourse* Brazil
105 F2 **Acará, Lago** *lake* Brazil
102 B3 **Acará Miri** *watercourse* Brazil
102 D3 **Acaraú** Brazil
107 H3 **Acaray** *watercourse* Paraguay
105 G2 **Acari** *watercourse* Brazil
104 C4 **Acarí** Peru
104 C4 **Acari, Rio de** *watercourse* Peru
101 G4 **Acari, Serra** *mountains* Brazil
100 D4 **Acaricuará** Colombia
100 D2 **Acarigua** Venezuela
125 L4 **Acâş** Romania
130 B4 **Acceglio** France
83 N8 **Accomac** Virginia USA
126 D5 **Accous** France
158 D3 **Accra** Ghana
141 F3 **Accrington** Lancashire England UK
128 C3 **Acebo** Spain
85 K6 **Acebuches** Mexico
196 C2 **Aceh** *admin. area* Indonesia
128 C4 **Acehuche** Spain
131 F6 **Acerno** Italy
104 D5 **Achacachi** Bolivia
187 D7 **Achalpur** Maharashtra India
142 E2 **Achavanich** Highland Scotland UK
135 AJ6 **Achayvayam** Russian Federation
142 C3 **Achduart** Highland Scotland UK
133 B6 **Acheloös** *watercourse* Greece
191 K3 **Acheng** Heilongjiang China
124 F4 **Achenkirch** Austria
124 F4 **Achensee** *lake* Austria
133 C5 **Acherada, Akra** *cape* Greece
124 E3 **Achern** Germany
142 D2 **Achfary** Highland Scotland UK
108 B2 **Achicó** Argentina
142 D2 **Achiemore** Highland Scotland UK
182 D5 **Achikulak** Russian Federation
143 C3 **Achill** Ireland
142 B3 **A'Chill** Highland Scotland UK
143 B3 **Achill Head** *cape* Ireland
142 C2 **Achiltibuie** Highland Scotland UK
142 C5 **Achinhoan** Argyll and Bute Scotland UK
134 T7 **Achinsk** Russian Federation
142 C3 **Achintee** Highland Scotland UK
185 I2 **Achit Nuur** *lake* Mongolia
142 C3 **Achmore** Highland Scotland UK
142 D2 **Achnairn** Highland Scotland UK
122 G6 **Achter Wasser** *bay* Germany
161 E3 **Achwa** *watercourse* Uganda
136 E5 **Aciçay** *watercourse* Turkey
133 F7 **Acıgöl** *lake* Turkey
133 F7 **Acıpayam** Turkey
131 F8 **Acireale** Italy
182 D5 **Ackasar, Gora** *mountain* Georgia
85 L4 **Ackerly** Texas USA
91 F2 **Acklins Island** Bahamas
219 J2 **Acland** Qld Australia
139 I2 **Acle** Norfolk England UK
85 J4 **Acme** New Mexico USA
104 C3 **Acolla** Peru
106 D5 **Aconcagua, Cerro** *mountain* Argentina
84 G6 **Aconchi** Mexico
102 E4 **Acopiara** Brazil
104 C4 **Acoria** Peru
90 C5 **Acoyapa** Nicaragua
131 C6 **Acqua Doria** Corsica France
124 F5 **Acquanegra sul Chiese** Italy
124 E4 **Acquarossa** Switzerland
130 E5 **Acquasparta** Italy
217 N6 **Acraman, Lake** SA Australia
104 D3 **Acre** *admin. area* Brazil
105 I5 **Acreúna** Brazil
131 G7 **Acri** Italy
130 H3 **Ács** Hungary
223 14 **Actéon, Groupe** *islands* French Polynesia
83 K5 **Acton** Ontario Canada
143 F2 **Acton** Armagh Northern Ireland UK
84 C3 **Acton** California USA
89 F4 **Actopan** Mexico
102 E4 **Açu** Brazil
102 C3 **Açu, Lago** *lake* Brazil
156 D1 **Aḑ Ḑab'ah** Egypt
178 E7 **Aḑ Ḑaḩī** Yemen
178 F4 **Ad Dahnā'** Saudi Arabia
154 C4 **Ad Dakhla** Western Sahara
178 G4 **Ad Dammām** Saudi Arabia
178 D4 **Ad Dār al Ḩamrā'** Saudi Arabia
178 E5 **Ad Dawādimī** Saudi Arabia
178 G4 **Ad Dawḩah (Doha)** Qatar
178 E2 **Ad Dawr** Iraq
178 G7 **Ad Dibīn** Yemen
156 D1 **Aḑ Ḑiffah (Libyan Plateau)** *plateau* Egypt
178 E7 **Ad Dissān** *island* Saudi Arabia
178 E3 **Ad Dīwānīyah** Iraq
178 E2 **Ad Dujayl** Iraq
161 G2 **Ada** Ethiopia
81 Q3 **Ada** Minnesota USA
86 C3 **Ada** Oklahoma USA
190 F3 **Adaatsar** Mongolia
82 D8 **Adair** Oklahoma USA
87 I3 **Adairsville** Georgia USA
128 D3 **Adaja** *watercourse* Spain
135 AL8 **Adak Island** Alaska USA
109 7 **Adam, Mount** Falkland Islands
159 G3 **Adamaoua** *admin. area* Cameroon
159 G3 **Adamaoua, Massif de l'** *range* Cameroon
159 G3 **Adamawa** *admin. area* Nigeria
219 I7 **Adaminaby** NSW Australia
125 I5 **Adamovec** Croatia
182 H3 **Adamovka** Russian Federation
74 L7 **Adams** *watercourse* British Columbia Canada
80 F4 **Adams** Oregon USA
59 T1 **Adams, Cape** Antarctica
83 P4 **Adams, Mount** New Hampshire USA
187 E10 **Adam's Bridge** *island* Tamil Nadu India
221 8 **Adams Island** Auckland Islands New Zealand
74 L7 **Adams Lake** British Columbia Canada
84 E1 **Adams-McGill Reservoir** Nevada USA
223 11a **Adamstown** Pitcairn Islands
84 F1 **Adamsville** Utah USA
178 F8 **'Adan (Aden)** Yemen
136 E6 **Adana** Turkey
136 E6 **Adana** *admin. area* Turkey
194 C6 **Adang, Ko** *island* Thailand
197 H4 **Adang, Teluk** *bay* Indonesia
Adapazırı *see* **Sakarya** Turkey
156 C5 **Adar** Chad
156 E4 **Adarama** Sudan
143 D4 **Adare** Ireland
59 L2 **Adare, Cape** Antarctica
59 L2 **Adare Peninsula** Antarctica
59 L2 **Adare Seamounts** *underwater feature* Southern Ocean
218 G1 **Adavale** Qld Australia
123 M4 **Ādaži** Latvia
130 C3 **Adda** *watercourse* Italy
160 C2 **Adda** *watercourse* Sudan
143 C3 **Addergoole** Ireland
142 F5 **Addinston** Scottish Borders Scotland UK
86 F5 **Addis** Louisiana USA
Addis Ababa *see* **Ādīs Ābeba** Ethiopia
154 E5 **Adel Bagrou** Mauritania
213 K2 **Adelaide** *watercourse* NT Australia
218 D6 **Adelaide** SA Australia
59 T2 **Adelaide Island** Antarctica
73 J5 **Adelaide Peninsula** Nunavut Canada
213 K2 **Adelaide River** NT Australia
84 D3 **Adelanto** California USA
199 H5 **Adelbert Range** Papua New Guinea
213 G3 **Adele Island** WA Australia
133 D6 **Adelfi** *island* Greece
59 J2 **Adélie Coast** Antarctica
214 E5 **Adels Grove** Qld Australia
129 F3 **Ademuz** Spain
Aden *see* **'Adan** Yemen
178 F8 **Aden, Gulf of** Middle East
155 H5 **Aderbissinat** Niger
131 F5 **Aderci, Punta** *cape* Italy
156 F4 **Aderde** *watercourse* Eritrea
186 C6 **Adesar** Gujarat India
156 F5 **Ādēt** Ethiopia
186 F6 **Adhaura** Bihar India
198 E5 **Adi** *island* Indonesia
156 F5 **Ādī Ark'ay** Ethiopia
156 F5 **Ādī Da'iro** Ethiopia
157 F5 **Adi Gudom** Ethiopia
157 F5 **Adi Keyh** Eritrea
157 F5 **Ādī-Quala** Eritrea
157 F5 **Ādī Ugrī** Eritrea
158 D3 **Adiaso** Ghana
130 D4 **Adige** *watercourse* Italy
157 F5 **Ādīgrat** Ethiopia
133 F6 **Adıgüzel Barajı** *lake* Turkey
187 E7 **Adilabad** Andhra Pradesh India
161 F2 **Ādīs Ābeba (Addis Ababa)** Ethiopia
161 F2 **Ādīs Ābeba** *admin. area* Ethiopia
156 F5 **Ādīs Zemen** Ethiopia
136 F6 **Adıyaman** Turkey
136 F6 **Adiyaman** *admin. area* Turkey
132 E2 **Adjud** Romania
78 I5 **Adlavik Islands** Newfoundland and Labrador Canada
212 F5 **Admiral Bay** WA Australia
213 H3 **Admiralty Gulf** WA Australia
73 K4 **Admiralty Inlet** Nunavut Canada
73 I5 **Admiralty Island** Nunavut Canada
74 D4 **Admiralty Island** Alaska USA
211 inset **Admiralty Islands** Lord Howe Island Australia
199 H4 **Admiralty Islands** Papua New Guinea
59 L2 **Admiralty Mountains** Antarctica
85 N1 **Admire** Kansas USA
159 F3 **Ado-Ekiti** Nigeria
81 N7 **Adobe Creek Reservoir** Colorado USA
160 E2 **Adok** Sudan
85 H7 **Adolfo López Mateos** Mexico
88 D3 **Adolfo López Mateos, Presa** *lake* Mexico
88 C3 **Adolfo Ruíz Cortines** Mexico
120 J3 **Adolfsström** Sweden
213 J3 **Adolphus Island** WA Australia
198 B6 **Adonara** *island* Indonesia
187 D8 **Adoni** Andhra Pradesh India
124 G2 **Adorf** Germany
126 D5 **Adour** *watercourse* France
128 E5 **Adra** Spain
128 E3 **Adradas** Spain
131 F8 **Adrano** Italy
155 F3 **Adrar** Algeria
159 I2 **Adré** Chad
124 G5 **Adria** Italy
87 J4 **Adrian** Georgia USA
82 I6 **Adrian** Michigan USA
81 R5 **Adrian** Minnesota USA
85 K3 **Adrian** Texas USA
163 I4 **Adriandampy** Madagascar
131 H6 **Adriano, Punta** *cape* Italy
130 F5 **Adriatic Sea** Europe
139 G3 **Adstock** Buckinghamshire England UK
139 F2 **Adstone** Northamptonshire England UK
221 C8 **Adventure, Port** New Zealand
219 R11 **Adventure Bay** Tas. Australia
182 E4 **Adyk** Russian Federation
158 D3 **Adzopé** Côte d'Ivoire
134 N5 **Adz'va** *watercourse* Russian Federation
134 M5 **Adz'vavom** Russian Federation
122 F5 **Æbelø** *island* Denmark
133 D6 **Aegean Sea** Greece
50 R3 **Aegir Ridge** *underwater feature* Norwegian Sea
123 M3 **Aegna** *island* Estonia
123 M3 **Aegviidu** Estonia
222 1a **Aeon Point** Kiribati
122 F5 **Ærø** *island* Denmark
216 G2 **Aerodrome, Lake** WA Australia
75 O8 **Aetna** Alberta Canada
157 F4 **Afabet** Eritrea
157 G5 **Āfambo Hāyk'** *lake* Ethiopia
52 E8 **Afansij Nikitin Seamount** *underwater feature* Indian Ocean
133 F7 **Afantou** Greece
161 G2 **Āfar** *admin. area* Ethiopia
157 G5 **Afar Depression** *pan* Ethiopia
223 14a **Afareaitu** French Polynesia
120 E5 **Åfarnes** Norway
126 C3 **Aff** *watercourse* France
158 D3 **Afferi** Côte d'Ivoire
215 G8 **Affleck, Mount** Qld Australia
182 J7 **Afghanistan** *country* Asia
161 H3 **Afgooye** Somalia
161 F3 **Afgundud** *watercourse* Kenya
159 F3 **Afikpo** Nigeria
120 G5 **Åfjord** Norway
125 H4 **Aflenz Kurort** Austria
155 G2 **Aflou** Algeria
72 D7 **Afognak Island** Alaska USA
157 G5 **Afrera, Lac** *lake* Ethiopia
133 F6 **Afşar Barajı** *lake* Turkey
179 H2 **Aftar** Iran
85 I4 **Afton** New Mexico USA
83 N5 **Afton** New York USA
82 D8 **Afton** Oklahoma USA
81 J5 **Afton** Wyoming USA
102 B3 **Afuá** Brazil
136 D5 **Afyon Karahisar** *admin. area* Turkey
133 G6 **Afyonkarahisar** Turkey
187 D8 **Afzalpur** Karnataka India
155 H5 **Agadez** Niger
154 E2 **Agadir** Morocco
183 K4 **Agadyr** Kazakhstan
164 3b **Agaete** Canary Islands
159 F3 **Agaie** Nigeria
182 E6 **Agakhanly** Azerbaijan
164 7 **Agalega Islands** Mauritius
90 C4 **Agalta, Sierra de** *range* Honduras
134 Q6 **Agan** *watercourse* Russian Federation
134 S4 **Agapa** *watercourse* Russian Federation
133 G6 **Ağapınar** Turkey
134 S5 **Agapitovo** Russian Federation
182 H2 **Agapovka** Russian Federation
186 D6 **Agar** Madhya Pradesh India
161 F2 **Āgaro** Ethiopia
181 G4 **Agartala** Tripura India
53 S11 **Agassiz Fracture Zone** *underwater feature* Pacific Ocean
82 D2 **Agassiz Pool** *lake* Minnesota USA
222 5 **Agat** Guam
134 T5 **Agata, Ozero** *lake* Russian Federation
85 K1 **Agate** Colorado USA
133 E7 **Agathonisi** *island* Greece
187 C9 **Agatti Island** Lakshadweep India
135 AJ8 **Agattu Island** Alaska USA
82 I3 **Agawa Bay** Ontario Canada
158 D3 **Agboville** Côte d'Ivoire
135 Y6 **Agdary** Russian Federation
126 F5 **Agde** France
126 F5 **Agde, Cap d'** *cape* France
120 F5 **Agdenes** Norway
126 E4 **Agen** France
80 E5 **Agency Lake** Oregon USA
161 F2 **Āgere Maryam** Ethiopia
122 F5 **Agersø** *island* Denmark
125 I4 **Ágfalva** Hungary
162 C5 **Aggeneys** South Africa
122 E4 **Agger** Denmark
120 H5 **Äggsjön** *lake* Sweden
140 B2 **Aghalee** Armagh Northern Ireland UK
143 D3 **Aghamore** Ireland
140 B1 **Aghanloo** Limavady Northern Ireland UK
143 B2 **Aghleam** Ireland
140 B2 **Aghnagap** Ireland
178 G2 **Āgholak** Iran
143 D2 **Aghoo** Ireland
143 F4 **Aghow** Ireland
133 C6 **Agia** Greece
133 A6 **Agia Aikaterini, Akra** *cape* Greece
133 D6 **Agia Eirinis, Akra** *cape* Greece
133 D8 **Agia Galini** Greece
133 D6 **Agiásmata** Greece
191 H2 **Aginskiy Buryatskiy AO** *admin. area* Russian Federation
191 H2 **Aginskoye** Russian Federation
133 C6 **Agiokampos** Greece
133 D5 **Agion Oros** *range* Greece
133 D5 **Agios Charalampos** Greece
133 D6 **Agios Efstratios** *island* Greece
133 C7 **Agios Georgios** *island* Greece
133 D8 **Agios Ioannis, Akrotirio** *cape* Greece
133 E7 **Agios Minas** *island* Greece
133 D5 **Agiou Orous, Kolpos** *bay* Greece
133 C7 **Agkistri** *island* Greece
133 G7 **Ağlasun** Turkey
143 D3 **Aglish** Ireland
126 F5 **Agly** *watercourse* France
133 B6 **Agnanteron** Greece
217 M3 **Agnes Creek** SA Australia
82 F2 **Agnes Lake** Ontario Canada
215 K8 **Agnes Water** Qld Australia
216 G4 **Agnew** WA Australia
83 K3 **Agnew Lake** Ontario Canada
108 C3 **Agnia, Laguna de** *bay* Argentina
132 D3 **Agnita** Romania
127 I4 **Agno** Switzerland
122 I2 **Agön** *island* Sweden
158 D3 **Agona** Ghana
127 K3 **Agordo** Italy
104 D3 **Agostinho** Brazil
126 E5 **Agout** *watercourse* France
186 E5 **Agra** Uttar Pradesh India
128 F3 **Agreda** Spain
131 F6 **Agri** *watercourse* Italy
136 G5 **Ağri** *admin. area* Turkey
136 G5 **Ağri (Karaköse)** Turkey
136 H5 **Ağrı Dağı (Mount Ararat)** *mountain* Turkey
131 E8 **Agrigento** Italy
222 2 **Agrihan** *island* Northern Mariana Islands
133 B6 **Agrinion** Greece
108 B2 **Agrio** *watercourse* Argentina
182 F2 **Agryz** Russian Federation
122 I2 **Ågsjön** *lake* Sweden
106 D4 **Agua Amargo** Chile
107 G2 **Água Azul** Brazil
107 H2 **Água Boa** Brazil
101 F4 **Agua Boa do Univini** *watercourse* Brazil
103 B6 **Água Bonita** Brazil
102 D4 **Água Branca** Brazil
88 D4 **Agua Brava, Laguna** *lake* Mexico
105 E5 **Agua Caliente** Bolivia
104 E6 **Agua Castilla** Bolivia
103 A8 **Água Clara** Brazil
105 E4 **Agua Dulce** Bolivia
89 G5 **Agua Dulce** Mexico
106 D6 **Agua Escondida** Argentina
88 B2 **Agua Escondida** *watercourse* Mexico
100 D2 **Agua Larga de Dolores** Venezuela
100 D3 **Agua Linda** Venezuela
86 B7 **Agua Nueva** Texas USA
105 E3 **Água Preta** Brazil
88 C2 **Agua Prieta** Mexico
88 D4 **Agua Verde** Mexico
103 B8 **Agua Vermelha, Represa** *lake* Brazil
100 D2 **Agua Viva, Embalse de** *lake* Venezuela
100 A4 **Aguada, Punta** *cape* Ecuador
108 D2 **Aguada Cecilio** Argentina
108 C2 **Aguada de Guerra** Argentina
108 C2 **Aguada de Guzmán** Argentina
100 C3 **Aguadas** Colombia
91 H3 **Aguadilla** Puerto Rico
104 D4 **Aguajal** Peru
86 B7 **Agualeguas** Mexico
90 C4 **Aguan, Rio** *watercourse* Honduras
88 E3 **Aguanaval** *watercourse* Mexico
79 G7 **Aguanish** Quebec Canada
103 B8 **Aguapeí** *watercourse* Brazil
107 G4 **Aguapey** *watercourse* Argentina
106 F2 **Aguarague, Cordillera de** *range* Bolivia
100 B4 **Aguarico** *watercourse* Ecuador
102 E5 **Águas Belas** Brazil
105 E6 **Aguas Blancas** Argentina
106 E2 **Aguas Calientes, Laguna** *lake* Chile
103 D7 **Águas Formosas** Brazil
128 C3 **Águas Santas** Portugal
103 D6 **Águas Vermelhas** Brazil
88 E4 **Aguascalientes** Mexico
88 E4 **Aguascalientes** *admin. area* Mexico
129 F3 **Aguaviva** Spain
104 C3 **Aguaytia** *watercourse* Peru
100 C3 **Aguazul** Colombia
128 D4 **Agudo** Spain
103 B8 **Agudos** Brazil
128 B3 **Águeda** Portugal
155 G5 **Aguelhok** Mali
103 D7 **Águia Branca** Brazil
128 C3 **Aguiar de Beira** Portugal
155 H6 **Aguié** Niger
222 2 **Aguijan** *island* Northern Mariana Islands
84 F4 **Aguila** Arizona USA
105 E6 **Aguilar, Cerro** *mountain* Argentina
128 D2 **Aguilar de Campóo, Embalse de** *lake* Spain
106 E3 **Aguilares** Argentina
128 F5 **Águilas** Spain
88 E5 **Aguililla** Mexico
108 D6 **Aguirre, Bahía** *bay* Argentina
104 A2 **Aguja, Punta** *cape* Peru
157 F5 **Āgula'i** Ethiopia
164 2 **Agulha, Ponta da** *cape* Madeira
162 C6 **Agulhas, Cape** South Africa
54 G8 **Agulhas Bank** *underwater feature* Southern Ocean
103 C8 **Agulhas Negras** *mountain* Brazil
54 G9 **Agulhas Plateau** *underwater feature* Southern Ocean
54 F9 **Agulhas Ridge** *underwater feature* Southern Ocean
164 3a **Agulo** Canary Islands
183 Q2 **Agul'skoye** *lake* Russian Federation
189 J3 **Aguni-jima** *island* Japan
100 C2 **Agustín Codazzi** Colombia
195 I5 **Agutaya** *island* Philippines
133 F5 **Ağva** Turkey
156 F4 **Agwampt** *watercourse* Sudan
159 E2 **Agwara** Nigeria
161 E2 **Agwei** *watercourse* Sudan
143 C4 **Ahafona** Ireland
182 H6 **Ahal Welaýaty** *admin. area* Turkmenistan
182 E6 **Ahar** Iran
221 D6 **Ahaura** New Zealand
221 D6 **Ahaura** *watercourse* New Zealand
124 D1 **Ahaus** Germany
223 14 **Ahe** *island* French Polynesia
140 A4 **Ahenny** Ireland
215 K1 **Ahioma** Papua New Guinea
220 E2 **Ahipara** New Zealand
220 E2 **Ahipara Bay** New Zealand
187 E7 **Ahiri** Maharashtra India
123 K2 **Ahlainen** Finland
136 G5 **Ahlat** Turkey
124 E1 **Ahlden** Germany
124 D2 **Ahlen** Germany
121 O3 **Ahma-aapa** *island* Finland
179 L4 **Ahmad Tar** Pakistan
179 K3 **Ahmad Wal** Pakistan
186 C6 **Ahmadabad** Gujarat India
186 D4 **Ahmadgarh** Punjab India
187 D7 **Ahmadnagar** Maharashtra India
179 L3 **Ahmadpur East** Pakistan
179 L3 **Ahmadpur Sial** Pakistan
161 G2 **Ahmar** *range* Ethiopia
121 O4 **Ahmas** Finland
121 O5 **Ahokylä** Finland
121 P3 **Ahola** Finland
124 D2 **Ahr** *watercourse* Germany
186 F6 **Ahraura** Uttar Pradesh India
121 N5 **Ähtäri** Finland
123 M1 **Ähtärinjärvi** *lake* Finland
88 D4 **Ahuacatlán** Mexico
90 B4 **Ahuachapán** El Salvador
88 E4 **Ahualulco** Mexico
223 14 **Ahunui** *island* French Polynesia
221 C8 **Ahuriri Flat** New Zealand
221 C7 **Ahuriri** *watercourse* New Zealand
178 F3 **Ahvāz** Iran
121 O5 **Ahveninen** Finland
121 P3 **Ahvenselkä** Finland
198 D5 **Ai** *island* Indonesia
162 C5 **Ai-ais** Namibia
105 F2 **Aiapuá, Lago** *lake* Brazil
100 D4 **Aiari** *watercourse* Brazil
198 E5 **Aiduma** *island* Indonesia
133 D7 **Aigiali** Greece
133 C7 **Aigina** *island* Greece
133 C5 **Aiginio** Greece
133 C6 **Aigio** Greece
127 H3 **Aigle** Switzerland
78 C4 **Aigneau** *watercourse* Quebec Canada
78 C4 **Aigneau, Lac** *lake* Quebec Canada
123 M3 **Äigrumäe** Estonia
107 H5 **Aiguá** Uruguay
127 H4 **Aiguebelle** France
124 C5 **Aigues** *watercourse* France
126 G5 **Aigues-Mortes** France
126 E3 **Aigurande** France
188 C4 **Aihua** Yunnan China
123 M4 **Aijažu ezers** *lake* Latvia
87 K4 **Aiken** South Carolina USA
142 F1 **Aikerness** Orkney Islands Scotland UK
140 F2 **Aiketgate** Cumbria England UK
214 B7 **Aileron** NT Australia
198 C6 **Aileu** Timor-Leste (East Timor)
100 B2 **Ailigandí** Panama
223 15 **Ailinginae Atoll** Marshall Islands
223 15 **Ailinglapalap Atoll** Marshall Islands
143 C3 **Aillenacally** Ireland
78 I5 **Aillik** Newfoundland and Labrador Canada
140 C1 **Ailsa Craig** *island* Scotland UK
223 15 **Ailuk Atoll** Marshall Islands
126 G5 **Aimargues** France
198 B6 **Aimere** Indonesia
103 D7 **Aimorés** Brazil
127 G4 **Ain** *watercourse* France
155 H1 **Aïn Beïda** Algeria
154 E3 **'Aïn Ben Tili** Mauritania
155 F2 **Aïn Beni Mathar** Morocco
155 G1 **'Aïn Defla** Algeria
155 G2 **'Aïn Deheb** Algeria
131 C8 **Aïn Draham** Tunisia
131 C8 **'Aïn el Assel** Algeria
155 G1 **'Aïn el Hadjel** Algeria
155 G2 **'Aïn el Melh** Algeria
129 H6 **Aïn Feka** Algeria
129 J5 **Aïn Kechera** Algeria
131 C8 **'Aïn Kerma** Algeria
155 G2 **'Aïn Madhi** Algeria
155 H1 **Aïn-M'lila** Algeria
129 G6 **Aïn Nouissy** Algeria
155 H1 **Aïn Oulmene** Algeria
129 I6 **'Aïn Oum Chemel** Algeria
155 G1 **Aïn Oussera** Algeria
155 F2 **Aïn Sefra** Algeria
129 F6 **Aïn Temouchent** Algeria
133 B6 **Ainos** *cape* Greece
140 E3 **Ainsdale** Merseyside England UK
79 H9 **Ainslie, Lake** Nova Scotia Canada
81 P5 **Ainsworth** Nebraska USA
59 J2 **Ainsworth Bay** Antarctica
192 G4 **Aioi** Japan
190 G3 **Aipar** Mongolia
101 F5 **Aiparuça** Brazil
105 E5 **Aiquile** Bolivia
73 L5 **Air Force Island** Nunavut Canada
222 3 **Airai** Palau
139 I5 **Airaines** France
121 O5 **Airaksela** Finland
196 C3 **Airbangis** Indonesia
142 A3 **Aird** Na h-Eileanan Siar Scotland UK
142 B2 **Aird Dhail** Na h-Eileanan Siar Scotland UK
142 B3 **Aird Mhige** Na h-Eileanan Siar Scotland UK
142 B2 **Aird Thunga** Na h-Eileanan Siar Scotland UK
80 H1 **Airdrie** Alberta Canada
142 E5 **Airdrie** North Lanarkshire Scotland UK
127 G2 **Aire** *watercourse* France
141 G3 **Aire** *watercourse* England UK
126 D5 **Aire-sur-l'Adour** France
197 F4 **Airhitam** *watercourse* Indonesia
197 F4 **Airhitam, Teluk** *bay* Indonesia
123 L2 **Airisto** *bay* Finland
215 J6 **Airlie Beach** Qld Australia
141 H3 **Airmyn** East Riding of Yorkshire England UK
124 E4 **Airolo** Switzerland
197 J5 **Airpanas** Indonesia
142 E4 **Airth** Falkirk Scotland UK
181 G4 **Aisatung Mountain** Myanmar
198 F4 **Aisau** Indonesia
130 D2 **Aisch** *watercourse* Germany
108 B3 **Aisén del General Carlos Ibáñez del Campo** *admin. area* Chile
101 G4 **Aishalton** Guyana
72 F6 **Aishihik Lake** Yukon Territory Canada
120 J3 **Aisjaure** *bay* Sweden
108 C3 **Aisladores, Sierra de los** *range* Argentina
126 F2 **Aisne** *watercourse* France
124 D4 **Aissey** France
142 E1 **Aith** Orkney Islands Scotland UK
142 E3 **Aitnoch** Moray Scotland UK
121 O5 **Aittojärvi** Finland
220 1 **Aitutaki** *island* Cook Islands New Zealand
125 L4 **Aiud** Romania
123 N4 **Aiviekste** *watercourse* Latvia
223 9 **Aiwa** *island* Fiji
126 D3 **Aix, Île d'** *island* France
127 G5 **Aix-en-Provence** France
127 G4 **Aix-les-Bains** France
133 C6 **Aíyira** Greece
181 G4 **Aizawl** Mizoram India
126 D3 **Aizenay** France
123 M4 **Aizkraukle** Latvia
123 M4 **Aizkraukles Rajon** *admin. area* Latvia
123 K4 **Aizpute** Latvia
193 H4 **Aizuwakamatsu** Japan
182 E6 **'Ajab Shīr** Iran
131 C6 **Ajaccio** Corsica France
131 C6 **Ajaccio, Golfe d'** *bay* Corsica France
186 E6 **Ajaigarh** Madhya Pradesh India
89 F5 **Ajalpan** Mexico
216 D3 **Ajana** WA Australia
121 M3 **Ajankijärvi** *lake* Finland
120 I4 **Ajaure** *bay* Sweden
120 I4 **Ajaureforsen** Sweden
120 K4 **Ajaursjön** *lake* Sweden
222 5 **Ajayan Bay** Guam
156 C1 **Ajdābiyā** Libya
183 K3 **Ajgyrzal** *mountain* Kazakhstan
178 E2 **Ajīj, Wādī al** *watercourse* Iraq
130 G3 **Ajka** Hungary
179 H4 **'Ajmān** United Arab Emirates
186 D5 **Ajmer** Rajasthan India
186 D4 **Ajnala** Punjab India
128 E2 **Ajo** Spain
84 F4 **Ajo** Arizona USA
126 C5 **Ajo, Cabo de** *cape* Spain
104 C4 **Ajpi** Peru
187 D8 **Ajra** Maharashtra India
178 E2 **Ajrab** Iraq
158 D3 **Ajumaku** Ghana
195 I5 **Ajuy** Philippines
183 R3 **Ak-attyg-khol'** *lake* Russian Federation
182 J6 **Ak-Kurgan** Uzbekistan
183 P3 **Ak-Ojuk, Gora** *mountain* Russian Federation
155 G3 **Akabli** Algeria
135 AC8 **Akademii, Zaliv** *bay* Russian Federation
187 F7 **Akaltara** Chhattisgarh India
159 F3 **Akamkpa** Nigeria
193 J2 **Akan-ko** *lake* Japan
221 E6 **Akaroa** New Zealand
221 E6 **Akaroa Harbour** New Zealand
156 E3 **Akasha** Sudan
193 G4 **Akashi** Japan
121 N3 **Äkäsjärvi** *lake* Finland
121 N3 **Äkäslompolo** Finland
133 E6 **Akbaş** Turkey
182 H4 **Akbasty** Kazakhstan
183 L3 **Akbaur** Kazakhstan
183 K3 **Akbeit** Kazakhstan
155 G1 **Akbou** Algeria
133 E7 **Akbük** Turkey
183 M3 **Akbulak** Kazakhstan
182 G3 **Akbulak** Russian Federation
136 F6 **Akcakale** Turkey
133 G5 **Akçakoca** Turkey
133 F7 **Akçapınar** Turkey
133 F7 **Akçay** Turkey
136 D6 **Akçay** *watercourse* Turkey
154 D5 **Akchâr** *region* Mauritania
183 L4 **Akchatau** Kazakhstan
133 F7 **Akdağlar** *range* Turkey
182 H5 **Akdepe** Turkmenistan
136 G6 **Akdiken** Turkey
198 D3 **Akelamo** Indonesia
161 E2 **Akelo** Sudan
182 E6 **Akera** *watercourse* Azerbaijan
120 L4 **Åkerholmen** Sweden
122 F2 **Akershus** *admin. area* Norway
120 I5 **Åkersjön** *lake* Sweden
122 F2 **Åkerstrømmen** Norway
182 H4 **Akespe** Kazakhstan
184 F4 **Akesu** Xinjiang Uygur Zizhiqu China
160 C3 **Aketi** Democratic Republic of Congo
156 E2 **Akhmim** Egypt
186 D4 **Akhnoor** Jammu and Kashmir India/Pakistan
179 M3 **Akhnoor** Pakistan
133 E4 **Akhtopol** Bulgaria
182 E4 **Akhtubinsk** Russian Federation
192 G5 **Aki** Japan
78 O2 **Akia** *island* Greenland
159 G5 **Akiéni** Gabon
178 E1 **Akīka** Iraq
73 K8 **Akimiski Island** Nunavut Canada
77 N6 **Akimiski Strait** Nunavut/Ontario Canada
193 H4 **Akimoto-ko** *lake* Japan
193 I3 **Akita** Japan
221 G5 **Akitio** New Zealand
154 D5 **Akjoujt** Mauritania
182 I3 **Akkabak** Kazakhstan
120 J3 **Akkajaure** *lake* Sweden
183 J4 **Akkanse** Kazakhstan
120 J3 **Akkavare** *mountain* Sweden
133 F6 **Akkent** Turkey
178 C3 **'Akko (Acre)** Israel
Akkol *see* **Alekseyevka** Kazakhstan
183 L3 **Akkol'** Kazakhstan
183 L4 **Akkol'** Kazakhstan
182 I4 **Akkol** *lake* Kazakhstan
133 E7 **Akköy** Turkey
182 F4 **Akkystau** Kazakhstan
72 F5 **Aklavik** Northwest Territories Canada
123 K4 **Akmeņrags** *cape* Latvia
183 K3 **Akmeshit** Kazakhstan
Akmola *see* **Astana** Kazakhstan

182 J3 **Akmola** *mountain* Kazakhstan
183 K3 **Akmolinskaya Oblast'** *admin. area* Kazakhstan
154 F2 **Aknoul** Morocco
101 G3 **Akobenang Mountains** Guyana
101 H3 **Akoelitatajeprati** Suriname
186 D6 **Akola** Rajasthan India
159 G4 **Akom** Cameroon
159 G4 **Akono** Cameroon
156 F4 **Akordat** Eritrea
187 D7 **Akot** Maharashtra India
160 D2 **Akot** Sudan
101 H4 **Akotipa** Brazil
78 D2 **Akpatok Island** Nunavut Canada
133 G6 **Akpınar** Turkey
184 F5 **Akqi** Xinjiang Uygur Zizhiqu China
120 H5 **Åkran** Norway
120 inset **Akranes** Iceland
133 D5 **Akrathos, Akra** *cape* Greece
133 B7 **Akritas, Akra** *cape* Greece
86 H4 **Akron** Alabama USA
81 N6 **Akron** Colorado USA
83 K6 **Akron** Ohio USA
136 E6 **Akrotiri Sovereign Base Area** *British overseas territory* Cyprus
133 C8 **Akrotirio Spatha** *cape* Greece
186 E3 **Aksai Chin** *disputed territory* China/India
136 E5 **Aksaray** Turkey
136 E5 **Aksaray** *admin. area* Turkey
182 C4 **Aksay** Russian Federation
133 G6 **Akşehir Gölü** *lake* Turkey
182 G3 **Akshatau** Kazakhstan
182 I3 **Akshiganak** Kazakhstan
182 F5 **Akshynyrau** Kazakhstan
183 L3 **Aksoran** *mountain* Kazakhstan
182 G3 **Aksu** Kazakhstan
183 M4 **Aksu** Kazakhstan
133 G7 **Aksu** Turkey
133 G7 **Aksu** *watercourse* Turkey
183 L4 **Aksu Ayuly** Kazakhstan
184 F5 **Aksu He** *watercourse* Xinjiang Uygur Zizhiqu China
183 N4 **Aksuat** Kazakhstan
182 F2 **Aksubayevo** Russian Federation
157 F5 **Åksum** Ethiopia
136 E4 **Aksyuru-Konrat** Ukraine
184 G6 **Aktag** *mountain* Xinjiang Uygur Zizhiqu China
182 F5 **Aktau (Shevchenko)** Kazakhstan
183 L3 **Aktau** Kazakhstan
184 E5 **Akto** Xinjiang Uygur Zizhiqu China
182 H3 **Aktobe** Kazakhstan
183 L4 **Aktogay** Kazakhstan
183 M4 **Aktogay** Kazakhstan
182 H4 **Aktumsyk** Kazakhstan
Aktyubinsk *see* **Aktobe** Kazakhstan
182 H3 **Aktyubinskaya Oblast'** *admin. area* Kazakhstan
161 F2 **Akūbū** *watercourse* Sudan
160 C3 **Akula** Democratic Republic of Congo
77 P2 **Akulivik** Quebec Canada
120 L4 **Åkullsjön** Sweden
192 F5 **Akune** Japan
159 F3 **Akure** Nigeria
120 inset **Akureyri** Iceland
192 F6 **Akuseki-shima** *island* Japan
72 C8 **Akutan** Alaska USA
159 F4 **Akwa Ibom** *admin. area* Nigeria
159 F3 **Akwanga** Nigeria
Akyab *see* **Sittwe** Myanmar
183 N3 **Akzhal** Kazakhstan
183 L4 **Akzhal** Kazakhstan
183 N4 **Akzhar** Kazakhstan
183 K5 **Akzhar** Kazakhstan
155 I3 **Al Abyaḍ** Libya
156 C1 **Al Abyār** Libya
156 C1 **Al 'Adam** Libya
178 F3 **Al Aḥmadī** Kuwait
156 D1 **Al 'Alamayn** Egypt
178 F3 **Al 'Amārah** Iraq
178 C3 **Al 'Aqabah** Jordan
156 E2 **Al 'Arābā al Madfūnah** Egypt
156 E1 **Al 'Arīsh** Egypt
178 F4 **Al Arṭāwīyah** Saudi Arabia
131 C8 **Al 'Arûsah** Tunisia
178 E5 **Al Ash'arīyah** Saudi Arabia
156 E2 **Al Ashmūnayn** Egypt
179 H5 **Al 'Ayn** United Arab Emirates
155 I2 **Al 'Azīzīyah** Libya
178 E6 **Al Bāḥah** Saudi Arabia
156 E1 **Al Bardawīl, Sabkhat** *lake* Egypt
178 F3 **Al Başrah** Iraq
178 F3 **Al Başrah** *admin. area* Iraq
156 D2 **Al Bawītī** Egypt
156 C1 **Al Bayḍā** Libya
178 F7 **Al Bayḍā'** Yemen
136 F6 **Al Biljah** Syria
182 E7 **Al Bolagh** Iran
156 C1 **al Bumbah, Khalīj** *bay* Libya
179 H5 **Al Buraymī** Oman
178 C3 **Al Burj** Jordan
136 G6 **Al Buşayrah** Syria
178 E6 **Al Buwaţah** Saudi Arabia
178 E2 **Al Fallūjah** Iraq
178 F7 **Al Fara'** Yemen
178 F3 **Al Farwānīyah** Kuwait
156 E2 **Al Fashn** Egypt
156 E2 **Al Fayyûm** Egypt
179 H4 **Al Fujayrah** United Arab Emirates
178 E6 **Al Fukah** Saudi Arabia
178 E8 **Al Ghadīr** Yemen
178 E4 **Al Ghāţ** Saudi Arabia
178 G7 **Al Ghaydah** Yemen
178 G7 **Al Ghayḍdah** Yemen
178 F7 **Al Ghayl** Yemen
156 E2 **Al Ghurdaqah (Hurghada)** Egypt
178 E7 **Al Ḥadīd** Yemen
154 D3 **Al Haggounia** Western Sahara
178 F5 **Al Ḥā'ir** Saudi Arabia
178 E8 **Al Ḥajaf** Yemen
178 F3 **Al Ḥallah** Iraq
179 H6 **Al Ḥallānīyah** *island* Oman
156 D1 **Al Ḥammām** Egypt
178 F7 **Al Hanad** Yemen
178 E7 **Al Ḥarf** Yemen
136 G6 **Al Ḥasakah** Syria
178 E7 **Al Ḥasanīyah** Yemen
178 E7 **Al Ḥasīb** Yemen
178 F7 **Al Ḥasūsah** Yemen
136 G6 **Al Hawl** Syria
178 E5 **Al Ḥayd** Saudi Arabia
178 F3 **Al Ḥayy** Iraq
178 E7 **Al Ḥazm** Yemen
178 E3 **Al Ḥillah** Iraq
178 F5 **Al Ḥillah** Saudi Arabia
154 F1 **Al Hoceima** Morocco
178 E7 **Al Ḥudaydah** Yemen
178 E3 **Al Ḥudūd Ash Shamālīyah** *admin. area* Saudi Arabia
178 G4 **Al Hufūf** Saudi Arabia
155 J3 **Al Ḥulayq al Kabīr** *range* Libya
178 F7 **Al Ḥūtah** Yemen
156 D1 **Al Iskandarīyah (Alexandria)** Egypt
156 E1 **Al Ismā'īlīyah** Egypt
160 E2 **Al Jabal, Baḥr** *watercourse* Sudan
156 D2 **Al Jadīdah** Egypt
178 C3 **Al Jafr** Jordan
156 C2 **Al Jaghbūb** Libya
178 F3 **Al Jahrā'** Kuwait
178 G4 **Al Jamaylīyah** Qatar
156 C3 **Al Jawf** Libya
Al Jawf *see* **Dawmat al Jandal** Saudi Arabia
178 F5 **Al Jifārah** Saudi Arabia
178 E6 **Al Jisimah** Saudi Arabia
156 E2 **Al Jīzah** Egypt
178 D5 **Al Jumūm** Saudi Arabia
178 F7 **Al Jurbah** Yemen
131 C8 **Al-Kāf** Tunisia
179 I5 **Al Kāmil** Oman
178 C3 **Al Karak** Jordan
131 C8 **Al Karib** Tunisia
178 E2 **Al Kāẓimīyah** Iraq
178 F7 **Al Khabr** Yemen
179 I5 **Al Khābūrah** Oman
178 F7 **Al Khāmilah** Yemen
156 E2 **Al Khārijah** Egypt
178 F5 **Al Kharj** Saudi Arabia
156 E4 **Al Kharṭūm (Khartoum)** Sudan
178 G4 **Al Khawr** Qatar
179 H5 **Al Khaznah** United Arab Emirates
178 F7 **Al Khubb** Yemen
178 F7 **Al Khudūd** Yemen
155 I2 **Al Khums** Libya
178 E4 **Al Kihafah** Saudi Arabia
178 F3 **Al Kūt** Iraq
178 F3 **Al Kuwayt (Kuwait City)** Kuwait
136 E6 **Al Lādhiqīyah (Latakia)** Syria
178 F7 **Al Lazif** Yemen
178 D5 **Al Madīnah al Munawwarah (Medina)** Saudi Arabia
178 C3 **Al Mafraq** Jordan
156 E2 **Al Maḥāmīd** Egypt
154 E3 **Al Mahbas** Western Sahara
178 E2 **Al Maḥmūdīyah** Iraq
178 E7 **Al Maḥwit** Yemen
178 F4 **Al Majma'ah** Saudi Arabia
178 E7 **Al Makārib** Yemen
178 E7 **Al Makhādir** Yemen
178 F7 **Al Malab** Yemen
178 G4 **Al Manāmah** Bahrain
156 E1 **Al Manşūrah** Egypt
178 F3 **Al Maqwa'** Kuwait
178 E7 **Al Marāshī** Yemen
156 C1 **Al Marj** Libya
131 D8 **Al-Marsā** Tunisia
178 F7 **Al Ma'shā** Yemen
178 G7 **Al Masīlah, Wādī** *watercourse* Yemen
178 E7 **Al Maţāhif** Yemen
178 E2 **Al Mawşil (Mosul)** Iraq
156 E2 **Al Minyā** Egypt
178 E2 **Al Miqdādīyah** Iraq
178 G4 **Al Mubarraz** Saudi Arabia
178 C3 **Al Mudawwarah** Jordan
179 I5 **Al Muḍaybī** Oman
178 G4 **Al Muḥarraq** Bahrain
178 G7 **Al Mukallā** Yemen
156 C1 **Al Mukhaylī** Libya
178 F3 **Al Muşandaq** Iraq
178 E6 **Al Mushīrah** Saudi Arabia
178 E7 **Al Ogala** Yemen
136 F6 **Al Qadmus** Syria
156 E1 **Al Qāhirah (Cairo)** Egypt
178 E7 **Al Qamā** Yemen
178 F7 **Al Qarāshīm** Yemen
155 I2 **Al Qaşabāt** Libya
156 D2 **Al Qaşr** Egypt
155 I4 **Al Qaţrūn** Libya
178 F4 **Al Qayşūmah** Saudi Arabia
156 C1 **Al Qubbah** Libya
Al Quds *see* **Yerushalayim (Jerusalem)** Israel
156 E4 **Al Qulayd Baḥrī** Sudan
136 F6 **Al Qumqum** Syria
155 K2 **Al Qunayyin, Sabkhat** *lake* Libya
178 E6 **Al Qunfundah** Saudi Arabia
178 D3 **Al Qurayyāt** Saudi Arabia
156 E2 **Al Quşayr** Egypt
178 D4 **Al 'Ulá** Saudi Arabia
156 B1 **Al ´Uqaylah** Libya
156 E2 **Al Uqşur (Luxor)** Egypt
155 I3 **Al 'Uwaynāt** Libya
179 I5 **Al Wāfī** Oman
178 F4 **Al Wafrah** Kuwait
178 C4 **Al Wajh** Saudi Arabia
178 G4 **Al Wakrah** Qatar
136 G6 **Al Walīd** Syria
155 I4 **Al Wīgh** Libya
127 J4 **Ala** Italy
123 J4 **Ala** Sweden
130 D5 **Ala, Punta** *cape* Italy
183 K5 **Ala-Buka** Uzbekistan
121 O3 **Ala-Nampa** Finland
121 O3 **Ala-Suolijärvi** *lake* Finland
121 M4 **Ala-Viirre** Finland
71 **Alabama** *admin. area* USA
87 H4 **Alabama** *watercourse* Alabama USA
136 G6 **Alabas** Turkey
86 H4 **Alabaster** Alabama USA
183 L2 **Alabota** *lake* Russian Federation
136 E5 **Alaca** Turkey
Alacant *see* **Alicante** Spain
89 H4 **Alacrán, Arrecife** *reef* Mexico
190 D2 **Alag-erdene** Mongolia
185 J3 **Alag Khayrkhan Uul** *mountain* Mongolia
101 F4 **Alagadiço** Brazil
182 D5 **Alagir** Russian Federation
126 F4 **Alagnon** *watercourse* France
102 E5 **Alagoas** *admin. area* Brazil
103 E6 **Alagoinhas** Brazil
129 F3 **Alagón** Spain
128 D3 **Alagón** *watercourse* Spain
164 3 **Alagranza** *island* Canary Islands
135 AG8 **Alaid** *volcano* Kuril Islands
126 F5 **Alaigne** France
157 G5 **Alaïli Dadda'** Djibouti
129 I4 **Alaior** Spain
121 O2 **Alajärvi** *lake* Finland
120 L2 **Alajaure** *lake* Sweden
90 E5 **Alajuela, Lago** *lake* Panama
121 P3 **Alakitka** *lake* Finland
186 E4 **Alaknanda** *watercourse* Uttaranchal India
183 K3 **Alakol'** *lake* Kazakhstan
183 N4 **Alakol', Ozero** *lake* Kazakhstan
121 Q3 **Alakurtti** Russian Federation
121 N3 **Alakylä** Finland
101 G4 **Alalapadu** Suriname
101 F5 **Alalau** *watercourse* Brazil
121 O4 **Alalivo** Finland
121 P5 **Alaluostanjärvi** *lake* Finland
222 2 **Alamagan** *island* Northern Mariana Islands
157 F5 **Ālamat'ā** Ethiopia
81 N2 **Alameda** Saskatchewan Canada
128 D5 **Alameda** Spain
186 G6 **Alamnagar** Bihar India
89 F4 **Álamo** Mexico
84 E4 **Alamo** *watercourse* California USA
87 J4 **Alamo** Georgia USA
84 E2 **Alamo** Nevada USA
84 F3 **Alamo Lake** Arizona USA
85 J4 **Alamogordo** New Mexico USA
88 C3 **Álamos** Mexico
85 K6 **Álamos de Márquez** Mexico
81 M8 **Alamosa** Colorado USA
182 F2 **Alan-polyan** Russian Federation
121 P4 **Alanäljänkä** Finland
124 F1 **Aland** *watercourse* Germany
123 K2 **Åland** *Finnish autonomous state* Finland
122 H3 **Åländern** *lake* Sweden
133 F6 **Alandız** Turkey
123 J3 **Ålands Hav** *bay* Sweden
196 D3 **Alang Besar** *island* Indonesia
128 C4 **Alange, Embalse de** *lake* Spain
196 E4 **Alanggantang** *island* Indonesia
121 N4 **Alaniemi** Finland
123 M5 **Alanta** Lithuania
159 G3 **Alantika Mountains** *range* Cameroon
136 E6 **Alanya** Turkey
132 A2 **Alap** Hungary
159 E3 **Alapa** Nigeria
121 O5 **Alapitkä** Finland
133 G5 **Alaplı** Turkey
187 D10 **Alappuzha** Kerala India
128 D3 **Alaraz** Spain
197 H6 **Alas** Indonesia
197 H6 **Alas, Selat** *strait* Indonesia
133 F6 **Alaşehir** Turkey
59 D2 **Alasheyev Bight** *bay* Antarctica
74 C3 **Alaska** *admin. area* USA
72 D7 **Alaska, Gulf of** Alaska USA
72 C7 **Alaska Peninsula** Alaska USA
72 D6 **Alaska Range** Alaska USA
182 I3 **Alasor** *lake* Kazakhstan
131 E6 **Alatri** Italy
182 E2 **Alatyr** Russian Federation
80 C2 **Alava, Cape** Washington USA
121 P4 **Alavuokki** Finland
140 D3 **Alaw, Llyn** *lake* Wales UK
218 E6 **Alawoona** SA Australia
133 G6 **Alayunt** Turkey
135 AF4 **Alazeya** *watercourse* Russian Federation
135 AE5 **Alazeyskoye Ploskogor'ye** *region* Russian Federation
124 E4 **Alb** *watercourse* Germany
124 E5 **Alba** Italy
132 C2 **Alba** *admin. area* Romania
132 C2 **Alba Iulia** Romania
132 C2 **Albac** Romania
128 F4 **Albacete** Spain
218 F6 **Albacutya** Vic. Australia
122 F4 **Ålbæk Bugt** *bay* Denmark
187 E7 **Albaka** Andhra Pradesh India
129 G3 **Albalate de Cinca** Spain
126 F5 **Alban** France
77 S7 **Albanel, Lac** *lake* Quebec Canada
100 C4 **Albania** Colombia
100 C3 **Albania** Colombia
100 C2 **Albania** Colombia
133 B5 **Albania** *country* Europe
216 E7 **Albany** WA Australia
76 K7 **Albany** *watercourse* Ontario Canada
87 I5 **Albany** Georgia USA
87 I2 **Albany** Kentucky USA
82 D6 **Albany** Missouri USA
83 O5 **Albany** New York USA
77 O6 **Albany Island** Ontario Canada
129 I2 **Albaron** France
214 F2 **Albatross Bay** Qld Australia
109 8 **Albatross Island** South Georgia
221 11 **Albatross Point** Antipodes Islands New Zealand
131 D5 **Albegna** *watercourse* Italy
87 K3 **Albemarle** North Carolina USA
109 4 **Albemarle, Punta** *cape* Archipiélago de Colón (Galapagos Islands)
109 7 **Albemarle Harbour** Falkland Islands
87 M2 **Albemarle Sound** North Carolina USA
128 D3 **Alberche** *watercourse* Spain
120 G5 **Ålberg** Norway
217 N3 **Alberga** *watercourse* SA Australia
129 F4 **Alberique** Spain
80 C2 **Alberni Inlet** British Columbia Canada
219 H5 **Albert** NSW Australia
126 F1 **Albert** France
85 M1 **Albert** Kansas USA
218 D6 **Albert, Lake** SA Australia
160 E3 **Albert, Lake** Uganda
80 G1 **Albert Canyon** British Columbia Canada
199 H6 **Albert Edward, Mount** Papua New Guinea
82 E5 **Albert Lea** Minnesota USA
160 E3 **Albert Nile** *watercourse* Uganda
91 F2 **Albert Town** Bahamas
72 H7 **Alberta** *admin. area* Canada
162 D6 **Albertinia** South Africa
132 A2 **Albertirsa** Hungary
79 F9 **Alberton** Prince Edward Island Canada
80 H3 **Alberton** Montana USA
127 H4 **Albertville** France
87 H3 **Albertville** Alabama USA
132 E2 **Albeşti** Romania
126 F5 **Albi** France
126 E4 **Albias** France
124 F5 **Albignasego** Italy
81 M6 **Albin** Wyoming USA
101 H3 **Albina** Suriname
124 E5 **Albino** Italy
216 G3 **Albion Downs** WA Australia
129 G3 **Albocácer** Spain
155 F1 **Alborán, Isla de** *island* Spain
122 E4 **Ålborg** Denmark
122 F4 **Ålborg Bugt** *bay* Denmark
128 E5 **Albox** Spain
74 L6 **Albreda** British Columbia Canada
138 E2 **Albrighton** Shropshire England UK
124 E3 **Albstadt** Germany
128 E5 **Albuñol** Spain
105 G5 **Albuquerque** Brazil
85 I3 **Albuquerque** New Mexico USA
100 A1 **Albuquerque, Cayos de** *islands* Colombia
128 C4 **Alburquerque** Spain
218 H7 **Albury** NSW Australia
120 I5 **Alby** Sweden
128 B4 **Alcácer do Sal** Portugal
195 I3 **Alcala** Philippines
128 D5 **Alcalá de Guadaira** Spain
128 E3 **Alcalá de Henares** Spain
85 I2 **Alcalde** New Mexico USA
131 E8 **Alcamo** Italy
129 G3 **Alcanar** Spain
128 C3 **Alcañices** Spain
129 F3 **Alcañiz** Spain
102 C3 **Alcântara** Brazil
128 C4 **Alcántara** Spain
128 C4 **Alcántara, Embalse de** *lake* Spain
129 F5 **Alcantarilla** Spain
128 E3 **Alcarria, La** *region* Spain
128 D4 **Alcaudete de la Jara** Spain
128 E4 **Alcázar de San Juan** Spain
132 F2 **Alcedar** Moldova
199 J6 **Alcester Island** Papua New Guinea
136 F6 **Alçi** Turkey
106 F5 **Alcira** Argentina
128 E3 **Alcobendas** Spain
129 F4 **Alcoi** Spain
128 C4 **Alconchel** Spain
128 E3 **Alcorcón** Spain
129 F3 **Alcorisa** Spain
128 E3 **Alcorlo, Embalse de** *lake* Spain
129 G3 **Alcover** Spain
129 F3 **Alcubierre** Spain
129 H4 **Alcúdia** Spain
128 D4 **Alcudia, Sierra de** *range* Spain
164 9 **Aldabra, Groupe d'** *islands* Seychelles
89 F4 **Aldama** Mexico
85 J6 **Aldama** Mexico
135 AA7 **Aldan** Russian Federation
135 AB6 **Aldan** *watercourse* Russian Federation
135 Z7 **Aldanskoye Nagor'ye** *region* Russian Federation
185 J3 **Aldarhaan** Mongolia
139 G3 **Aldbury** Hertfordshire England UK
140 F2 **Aldcliffe** Lancashire England UK
128 C4 **Aldea del Cano** Spain
128 D4 **Aldeacentenera** Spain
128 D3 **Aldeanueva de la Vera** Spain
128 D3 **Aldeavieja** Spain
139 I2 **Aldeburgh** Suffolk England UK
105 H4 **Aldeia Bacaeri** Brazil
105 H3 **Aldeia Caiabi** Brazil
105 G5 **Aldeia dos Bororos** Brazil
105 G4 **Aldeia Indígena Espirro** Brazil
163 G2 **Aldeia Milepa** Mozambique
105 G4 **Aldeia Velha** Brazil
105 I3 **Aldeia Velha** Brazil
105 G4 **Aldeia Vinte de Setembro** Brazil
105 G4 **Aldeia Waikiso** Brazil
59 J2 **Alden, Point** Antarctica
214 E7 **Alderley** Qld Australia
126 C2 **Alderney** *island* Channel Islands UK
139 G3 **Aldershot** Hampshire England UK
75 O7 **Aldersyde** Alberta Canada
139 G2 **Alderton** Northamptonshire England UK
141 G2 **Aldfield** North Yorkshire England UK
142 E3 **Aldivalloch** Moray Scotland UK
120 H3 **Aldra** *island* Norway
142 E3 **Aldunie** Moray Scotland UK
219 I5 **Alectown** NSW Australia
122 G4 **Åled** Sweden
154 D5 **Aleg** Mauritania
164 3d **Alegranza** *island* Canary Islands
107 H4 **Alegrete** Brazil
158 E3 **Aléhéride** Togo
109 6 **Alejandro Selkirk, Isla** *island* Juan Fernández Archipiélago
182 E3 **Aleksandrov Gay** Russian Federation
183 L3 **Aleksandrovka** Kazakhstan
135 AD8 **Aleksandrovsk Sakhalinskiy** Russian Federation
125 J1 **Aleksandrów Kujawski** Poland
183 K2 **Alekseyevka** Kazakhstan
136 F2 **Alekseyevka** Russian Federation
136 F1 **Aleksin** Russian Federation
122 I4 **Ålem** Sweden
161 G2 **Alem Maya** Ethiopia
83 L2 **Alembert, Lac d'** *lake* Quebec Canada
120 G5 **Ålen** Norway
126 E2 **Alençon** France
101 H5 **Alenquer** Brazil
128 C4 **Alentejo** *region* Portugal
84 inset **Alenuihāhā Channel** Hawai'i USA
Aleppo *see* **Halab** Syria
131 C5 **Aléria** Corsica France
73 M2 **Alert** Nunavut Canada
221 7 **Alert Stack** *island* Snares Islands New Zealand
104 D3 **Alerta** Peru
126 G4 **Alès** France
125 L4 **Aleşd** Romania
124 E5 **Alessandria** Italy
130 E3 **Alesso** Italy
120 E5 **Ålesund** Norway
185 H3 **Aletai** Xinjiang Uygur Zizhiqu China
108 B3 **Aleusco, Laguna** *bay* Argentina
52 N2 **Aleutian Basin** *underwater feature* Pacific Ocean
135 AL8 **Aleutian Islands** Alaska USA
72 D7 **Aleutian Range** Alaska USA
52 O2 **Aleutian Ridge** *underwater feature* Pacific Ocean
52 N2 **Aleutian Trench** *underwater feature* Pacific Ocean
86 C3 **Alex** Oklahoma USA
213 H4 **Alexander** *watercourse* WA Australia
81 N3 **Alexander** North Dakota USA
59 T2 **Alexander, Cape** Antarctica
214 D2 **Alexander, Mount** NT Australia
74 C4 **Alexander Archipelago** Alaska USA
162 C5 **Alexander Bay** South Africa
87 I4 **Alexander City** Alabama USA
59 T2 **Alexander Island** Antarctica
214 F5 **Alexandra** *watercourse* Qld Australia
221 C7 **Alexandra** New Zealand
109 8 **Alexandra, Cape** South Georgia
194 B4 **Alexandra Channel** Andaman and Nicobar Islands India
214 D5 **Alexandria** NT Australia
74 J6 **Alexandria** British Columbia Canada
Alexandria *see* **Al Iskandarīyah** Egypt
90 E3 **Alexandria** Jamaica
162 E6 **Alexandria** South Africa
86 E5 **Alexandria** Louisiana USA
83 M7 **Alexandria** Virginia USA
100 E4 **Alexandrina** Brazil
218 D6 **Alexandrina, Lake** SA Australia
133 D5 **Alexandropoulis** Greece
78 J6 **Alexis** *watercourse* Newfoundland and Labrador Canada
74 J6 **Alexis Creek** British Columbia Canada
125 L2 **Alexsandrów** Poland
183 N3 **Aleysk** Russian Federation
128 F2 **Alfaro** Spain
132 E4 **Alfatar** Bulgaria
131 F6 **Alfedena** Italy
133 B7 **Alfeios** *watercourse* Greece
103 C8 **Alfenas** Brazil
183 L2 **Alferovka** Russian Federation
128 B4 **Alferrarede** Portugal
138 D4 **Alfington** Devon England UK
218 C5 **Alford** SA Australia
141 I3 **Alford** Lincolnshire England UK
142 F3 **Alford** Aberdeenshire Scotland UK
103 D8 **Alfredo Chaves** Brazil
89 F3 **Alfredo V. Bonfil** Mexico
221 F5 **Alfredton** New Zealand
139 F1 **Alfreton** Derbyshire England UK
182 F3 **Algabas** Kazakhstan
127 I5 **Algajola** Corsica France
135 AJ6 **Alganskaya** Russian Federation
122 C3 **Ålgård** Norway
105 F5 **Algarrobillo** Bolivia
100 C2 **Algarrobo** Colombia
106 E6 **Algarrobo del Aguilla** Argentina
128 B5 **Algarve** *region* Portugal
100 C4 **Algeciras** Colombia
128 D5 **Algeciras** Spain
157 F4 **Algena** Eritrea
155 G1 **Alger (Algiers)** Algeria
155 G3 **Algeria** *country* Africa
131 C6 **Alghero** Sardinia Italy
Algiers *see* **Alger** Algeria
123 L3 **Älgö** *island* Finland
84 E5 **Algodones** Mexico
84 G7 **Algodones, Estero Los** *bay* Mexico
86 G3 **Algoma** Mississippi USA
82 D5 **Algona** Iowa USA
87 I2 **Algood** Tennessee USA
128 E3 **Algora** Spain
128 E5 **Alhama de Granada** Spain
129 F5 **Alhama de Murcia** Spain
120 L4 **Alhamn** Sweden
138 E3 **Alhampton** Somerset England UK
178 F3 **'Alī Al Gharbī** Iraq
214 C6 **Ali-Curung** NT Australia
179 L2 **'Alī Kheyl** Afghanistan
157 G5 **Ali Sabieh** Djibouti
129 F3 **Aliaga** Spain
104 B2 **Alianza** Peru
133 C6 **Aliartos** Greece
187 C7 **Alibag** Maharashtra India
133 E6 **Alibey** Turkey
133 E6 **Alibey Adası** *island* Turkey
161 F2 **Ālībo** Ethiopia
158 E2 **Alibori** *watercourse* Benin
129 F4 **Alicante (Alacant)** Spain
219 K3 **Alice** NSW Australia
215 G3 **Alice** *watercourse* Qld Australia
101 I4 **Alice** Brazil
86 B7 **Alice** Texas USA
131 G7 **Alice, Punta** *cape* Italy
74 G5 **Alice Arm** British Columbia Canada
213 I4 **Alice Downs** WA Australia
214 B7 **Alice Springs** NT Australia
87 L8 **Alice Town** Bahamas
86 G4 **Aliceville** Alabama USA
183 L6 **Alichur** *watercourse* Tajikistan
195 I3 **Alicia** Philippines
215 G6 **Alick** *watercourse* Qld Australia
131 F7 **Alicudi, Isola** *island* Italy
133 G5 **Alifuatpaşa** Turkey
186 E5 **Aliganj** Uttar Pradesh India
186 E5 **Aligarh** Uttar Pradesh India
178 G2 **Alīgūdarz** Iran
191 J2 **A`lihe** Nei Mongol Zizhiqu China
128 C3 **Alijó** Portugal
101 H4 **Alikéné, Monts** *range* French Guiana
182 E6 **Alikeykhaly** Azerbaijan
182 E6 **Alikhanly** Azerbaijan
133 D5 **Alikí** Greece
133 C8 **Alikianos** Greece
121 M5 **Alikylä** Finland
199 H4 **Alim Island** Papua New Guinea
159 H5 **Alima** *watercourse* Congo
133 E7 **Alimia** *island* Greece
159 I3 **Alindao** Central African Republic
86 B2 **Aline** Oklahoma USA
132 B2 **Alioş** Romania
136 D5 **Aliova** *watercourse* Turkey
179 L3 **Alipur** Pakistan
181 F3 **Alipurduar** West Bengal India
105 E5 **Alisar** Bolivia
128 C4 **Aliseda** Spain
162 E6 **Aliwal North** South Africa
159 E2 **Aljanare** Nigeria
128 C5 **Aljaraque** Spain
128 B5 **Aljezur** Portugal
128 C4 **Aljucén** Spain
80 I2 **Alkali Lake** Montana USA
81 P3 **Alkaline Lake** North Dakota USA
155 I6 **Alkamari** Niger
183 K2 **Alkaterek** Kazakhstan
122 H3 **Alkvettern** *bay* Sweden
133 C6 **Alkyonidon, Kolpos** *bay* Greece
109 18 **All Saints** Antigua and Barbuda
158 E3 **Allada** Benin
83 Q3 **Allagash** *watercourse* Maine USA
186 E6 **Allahabad** Uttar Pradesh India
214 C8 **Allambi** NT Australia
218 F4 **Allambie** NSW Australia
59 K1 **Allan Hills** *mountain* Antarctica
76 J7 **Allan Water** Ontario Canada
218 B2 **Allandale** SA Australia
162 E5 **Allanridge** South Africa
187 E7 **Allapalli** Maharashtra India
156 E3 **Allāqi, Wādī Al** *watercourse* Egypt
128 C2 **Allariz** Spain
142 A4 **Allathasdal** Na h-Eileanan Siar Scotland UK
87 I3 **Allatoona Lake** Georgia USA
162 E4 **Alldays** South Africa
127 H3 **Alle** Switzerland
219 H6 **Alleena** NSW Australia
143 D3 **Alleeny Bridge** Ireland
83 L7 **Allegheny Mountains** USA
109 16 **Allègre, Pointe** *cape* Guadeloupe
121 O3 **Allemalehto** Finland
77 R2 **Allemand, Lac** *lake* Quebec Canada
86 F6 **Allemands, Lac des** *lake* Louisiana USA
86 C3 **Allen** Oklahoma USA
143 E2 **Allen, Lough** *lake* Ireland
214 E4 **Allen Island** Qld Australia
87 K4 **Allendale** South Carolina USA
141 F2 **Allendale Town** Northumberland England UK
141 F2 **Allenheads** Northumberland England UK
83 N6 **Allentown** Pennsylvania USA
124 F1 **Aller** *watercourse* Germany
138 E3 **Aller** Somerset England UK
130 D2 **Allershausen** Germany
139 F2 **Allestree** Derby England UK
127 H4 **Allevard** France
122 H4 **Allgunnen** *lake* Sweden
131 G7 **Alli** *watercourse* Italy
81 N5 **Alliance** Nebraska USA
126 F4 **Allier** *watercourse* France
213 L2 **Alligator** *watercourse* NT Australia
87 I6 **Alligator Harbor** Florida USA
143 B5 **Allihies** Ireland
108 C2 **Allipén** Chile
83 L4 **Alliston** Ontario Canada
142 E4 **Alloa** Clackmannanshire Scotland UK
126 E3 **Allonnes** France
219 J3 **Allora** Qld Australia
127 H4 **Allos** France
121 M3 **Allsån** Sweden
120 J5 **Ållsjön** Sweden
120 K5 **Allsta** Sweden
124 F2 **Allstedt** Germany
138 C3 **Alltwalis** Carmarthenshire Wales UK
187 E8 **Allur** Andhra Pradesh India
78 F3 **Alluviaq** *watercourse* Quebec Canada
78 F3 **Alluviaq Fiord** Quebec Canada
139 I2 **Allwood Green** Suffolk England UK
73 L9 **Alma** Quebec Canada
132 D2 **Alma** Romania
85 I1 **Alma** Colorado USA
87 J5 **Alma** Georgia USA
85 N1 **Alma** Kansas USA
81 P6 **Alma** Nebraska USA
215 K7 **Alma, Mount** Qld Australia
Alma-Ata *see* **Almaty** Kazakhstan
129 G3 **Almacellas** Spain
215 H4 **Almaden** Qld Australia
128 D4 **Almadén** Spain
89 F4 **Almagre, Laguna** *lake* Mexico
128 E3 **Almajano** Spain
183 M4 **Almaly** Kazakhstan
129 F4 **Almansa** Spain
128 E5 **Almanzora** *watercourse* Spain
132 C2 **Almaş** Romania
103 B6 **Almas, Rio das** *watercourse* Brazil
183 M4 **Almatinskaya Oblast'** *admin. area* Kazakhstan
183 M5 **Almaty** Kazakhstan
128 E3 **Almazán** Spain
128 C3 **Almeida** Portugal
102 A3 **Almeirim** Brazil
103 D7 **Almenara** Brazil
129 F4 **Almenara** Spain
128 C3 **Almendra, Embalse de** *lake* Spain
128 C4 **Almendralejo** Spain
105 G5 **Almendro** Bolivia
124 C1 **Almere** Netherlands
128 E5 **Almería** Spain
155 F1 **Almería, Golfe de** *bay* Spain
Al'met'yevsk *see* **Almetyevsk** Russian Federation
182 F2 **Almetyevsk** Russian Federation
122 H4 **Älmhult** Sweden
128 D6 **Almina, Punta** *cape* Morocco
108 C6 **Almirante Brown** Argentina
108 B5 **Almirante Montt, Golfo** *bay* Chile
128 B5 **Almodôvar** Portugal
128 D5 **Almogía** Spain
142 E4 **Almond** *watercourse* Scotland UK
85 I1 **Almont** Colorado USA
82 J5 **Almont** Michigan USA
83 M4 **Almonte** Ontario Canada
186 E5 **Almora** Uttaranchal India
128 D3 **Almorax** Spain
129 F4 **Almordi** Spain
120 J4 **Almsele** Sweden
129 F2 **Almudévar** Spain
128 E4 **Ålmuradiel** Spain
133 D8 **Almyrou, Ormos** *bay* Greece
141 G1 **Aln** *watercourse* England UK
187 D8 **Alnavar** Karnataka India
142 D3 **Alness** Highland Scotland UK
141 F1 **Alnham** Northumberland England UK
120 J5 **Alnö** Sweden
120 J5 **Alnön** *island* Sweden
141 G1 **Alnwick** Northumberland England UK
223 12a **Alo** Wallis and Futuna
101 H4 **Aloepi Twee** Suriname
220 4 **Alofi** Niue New Zealand
223 12a **Alofi, Île** *island* Wallis and Futuna
123 M4 **Aloja** Latvia
181 H3 **Along** Arunachal Pradesh India
133 C6 **Alonnisos** *island* Greece
198 C6 **Alor** *island* Indonesia
198 C5 **Alor, Kepulauan** *islands* Indonesia
197 J6 **Alor, Selat** *strait* Indonesia
196 D2 **Alor Setar** Malaysia
128 D5 **Álora** Spain
128 C5 **Alosno** Spain
186 D6 **Alot** Madhya Pradesh India
217 K2 **Aloysius, Mount** WA Australia
128 D5 **Alozaina** Spain
82 J4 **Alpena** Michigan USA
81 P4 **Alpena** South Dakota USA
102 C4 **Alpercatas** *watercourse* Brazil
215 I7 **Alpha** Qld Australia
215 I7 **Alpha** *watercourse* Qld Australia
50 I1 **Alpha Ridge** *underwater feature* Arctic Ocean
164 9 **Alphonse, Île** *island* Seychelles
75 U7 **Alpine** Manitoba Canada
85 H4 **Alpine** Arizona USA
85 K5 **Alpine** Texas USA
81 J5 **Alpine** Wyoming USA
89 F5 **Alpoyeca** Mexico
127 I3 **Alps** *range* Switzerland
121 N4 **Alpua** Finland
133 E5 **Alpullu** Turkey
214 D6 **Alpurrurulam** NT Australia
183 L3 **Alqamergen Koli** *lake* Kazakhstan
139 F2 **Alrewas** Staffordshire England UK
122 E5 **Als** *island* Denmark
127 H2 **Alsace** *region* France
128 E2 **Alsasau** Spain
81 K1 **Alsask** Saskatchewan Canada
74 C3 **Alsek** *watercourse* British Columbia Canada
72 F6 **Alsek** *watercourse* Yukon Territory Canada
120 H5 **Alsen** Sweden
124 E5 **Alseno** Italy
120 H5 **Alsensjön** *bay* Sweden
120 G5 **Alset** Norway
127 I1 **Alsfeld** Germany
120 J5 **Alsjö** Sweden
135 AC8 **Al'skiy Khrebet** *range* Russian Federation
120 I3 **Ålstad** Norway
120 H4 **Alstahaug** Norway
120 H4 **Alsten** *island* Norway
122 G3 **Alstern** *lake* Sweden
141 F2 **Alston** Cumbria England UK
123 N4 **Alsviķi** Latvia
138 D4 **Alswear** Devon England UK
121 M2 **Alta** Norway
128 C3 **Alta** *island* Portugal
122 J3 **Älta** Sweden
108 C3 **Alta, Pampa** *region* Argentina
105 H3 **Alta Floresta** Brazil
106 E4 **Alta Gracia** Argentina
121 M2 **Altaelv** *watercourse* Norway
121 M1 **Altafjorden** *bay* Norway
104 D3 **Altagracia** Bolivia
100 E2 **Altagracia de Orituco** Venezuela
185 J4 **Altai** Mongolia
185 I3 **Altai** Mongolia
185 I3 **Altai** Mongolia
185 I3 **Altai Mountains** Mongolia
89 J2 **Altamaha** *watercourse* Georgia USA
87 K5 **Altamaha Sound** Georgia USA
102 A3 **Altamira** Brazil
106 D3 **Altamira** Chile
88 E2 **Altamira** Mexico
128 D4 **Altamira, Sierra de** *range* Spain
82 D8 **Altamont** Kansas USA
131 G6 **Altamura** Italy
191 H3 **Altan Emel** Nei Mongol Zizhiqu China
190 G5 **Altan Shiret** Nei Mongol Zizhiqu China
190 F3 **Altanbulag** Mongolia
190 F2 **Altanbulag** Mongolia
142 D2 **Altanduin** Highland Scotland UK
103 A8 **Altânia** Brazil
190 G3 **Altanshiree** Mongolia
185 I3 **Altantsugts** Mongolia
88 C2 **Altar** Mexico
88 C2 **Altar** *watercourse* Mexico
84 F5 **Altar, Desierto de** *desert* Mexico
121 N4 **Altatornio** Finland
127 J4 **Altavilla Vicentina** Italy
83 L8 **Altavista** Virginia USA
185 J3 **Altay** Mongolia
183 O3 **Altay** *admin. area* Russian Federation
185 I3 **Altay Shan** *range* Xinjiang Uygur Zizhiqu China
183 M3 **Altayskiy Kray** *admin. area* Russian Federation
127 I3 **Altdorf** Switzerland
129 F4 **Altea** Spain
121 M1 **Alteidet** Norway
124 E2 **Altenau** *watercourse* Germany
127 K1 **Altenburg** Germany
128 C4 **Alter do Chão** Portugal
103 C8 **Alterosa** Brazil
120 K2 **Altevatnet** *lake* Norway
142 D6 **Alticry** Dumfries and Galloway Scotland UK
132 C4 **Altimir** Bulgaria
133 G6 **Altıntaş** Turkey
133 F7 **Altınyayla** Turkey
127 H3 **Altkirch** France
140 A2 **Altmover** Limavady Northern Ireland UK
130 D2 **Altmühl** *watercourse* Germany
142 D2 **Altnaharra** Highland Scotland UK
87 J3 **Alto** Georgia USA
86 D5 **Alto** Texas USA
105 F4 **Alto Alegre do Parecis** Brazil
103 A7 **Alto Araguaia** Brazil
100 D2 **Alto Barinas** Venezuela
105 I3 **Alto Boa Vista** Brazil
104 C3 **Alto Conazo** Peru
164 3a **Alto Garajonay** *volcano* Canary Islands
103 A7 **Alto Garças** Brazil
163 G3 **Alto Ligonha** Mozambique
102 D4 **Alto Longá** Brazil
104 D4 **Alto Madre de Dios** *watercourse* Peru
163 G3 **Alto Mólocuè** Mozambique
107 G2 **Alto Paraguay** *admin. area* Paraguay
107 H3 **Alto Paraná** *admin. area* Paraguay
107 H3 **Alto Piquiri** Brazil
104 D3 **Alto Purus** *watercourse* Peru
128 C3 **Alto Rabagão, Barragem do** *lake* Portugal
108 B3 **Alto Río Senguer** Argentina
100 C3 **Alto San Mateo** *mountain* Colombia
103 A7 **Alto Sucuriú** Brazil
131 G7 **Altomonte** Italy
81 R5 **Alton** Iowa USA
80 I8 **Alton** Utah USA
76 G8 **Altona** Manitoba Canada
82 F6 **Altona** Illinois USA
82 E6 **Altoona** Iowa USA
83 L6 **Altoona** Pennsylvania USA
124 G3 **Altötting** Germany
127 I3 **Altstätten** Switzerland
105 E4 **Altura Nueva Brema** Bolivia
80 E6 **Alturas** California USA
86 B3 **Altus** Oklahoma USA
182 E6 **Altyagach** Azerbaijan
163 G2 **Alua** Mozambique
136 F5 **Alucra** Turkey
123 N4 **Alūksne** Latvia
123 N4 **Alūksnes** *admin. area* Latvia
108 B2 **Aluminé, Lago** *lake* Argentina
136 E4 **Alupka** Ukraine
187 E8 **Alur** Andhra Pradesh India
136 E4 **Alushta** Ukraine
215 I5 **Alva** Qld Australia
142 E4 **Alva** Clackmannanshire Scotland UK
121 N5 **Alvajärvi** Finland
128 B5 **Alvalade** Portugal
178 F2 **Alvand, Kūh-e** *mountain* Iran
122 G4 **Älvängen** Sweden
89 G5 **Alvarado** Mexico
89 G5 **Alvarado, Laguna de** *lake* Mexico
101 E5 **Alvarães** Brazil
128 B3 **Alvarenga** Portugal
103 B8 **Álvares Machado** Brazil
88 C3 **Alvaro Obregón, Presa** *lake* Mexico
120 G5 **Alvdal** Norway
138 E2 **Alveley** Shropshire England UK
131 E5 **Alviano** Italy
142 E3 **Alvie** Highland Scotland UK
120 L4 **Alvik** Sweden
122 D2 **Ålvik** Norway
86 D6 **Alvin** Texas USA
128 C4 **Alvito** Portugal
103 B6 **Alvorada** Brazil
80 F5 **Alvord Lake** Oregon USA
122 C2 **Alvøy** *island* Norway
120 I5 **Älvros** Sweden
120 L4 **Älvsbyn** Sweden
186 D5 **Alwar** Rajasthan India
138 D1 **Alwen Reservoir** Wales UK
161 E2 **Alwero** *watercourse* Ethiopia
141 F1 **Alwinton** Northumberland England UK
214 D2 **Alyangula** NT Australia
123 M5 **Alytaus** *admin. area* Lithuania
142 E4 **Alyth** Perth and Kinross Scotland UK
123 M5 **Alytus** Lithuania
124 G3 **Alz** *watercourse* Germany
124 E3 **Alzey** Germany
126 F5 **Alzon** France
159 I2 **Am-Dam** Chad
155 J6 **Am Djéména** Chad
156 C5 **Am Doutilé** Chad
156 B5 **Am Khoumi** Chad
156 C5 **Am Léiouna** Chad
156 C5 **Am Timan** Chad
156 C5 **Am-Zoer** Chad
159 H4 **Amada Gaza** Central African Republic
122 H2 **Åmådalen** Sweden
217 L2 **Amadeus, Lake** NT Australia
160 E2 **Amadi** Sudan
73 L5 **Amadjuak Lake** Nunavut Canada
84 G5 **Amado** Arizona USA
84 B1 **Amador City** California USA
122 G5 **Amager** *island* Denmark
223 12c **Amaile** Samoa
89 F4 **Amajac** *watercourse* Mexico
192 F5 **Amakusa-shimoshima** *island* Japan
122 G3 **Åmål** Sweden
187 F8 **Amalapuram** Andhra Pradesh India
187 D7 **Amalner** Maharashtra India
198 F5 **Amamapare** Indonesia
107 H2 **Amambaí** *watercourse* Brazil
107 G2 **Amambay** *admin. area* Paraguay
189 J3 **Amami-o-shima** *island* Japan
189 J3 **Amami-shotō** *island* Japan
160 D4 **Amamula** Democratic Republic of Congo
101 F2 **Amana** *watercourse* Venezuela
101 E5 **Amana, Lago** *lake* Brazil
199 G4 **Amanab** Papua New Guinea
127 G2 **Amance, Lac** *lake* France
127 H3 **Amancey** France
186 E6 **Amanganj** Madhya Pradesh India
182 J3 **Amangel'dy** Kazakhstan
122 I3 **Åmänningen** *lake* Sweden
182 I4 **Amanotkel** Kazakhstan
131 G7 **Amantea** Italy
223 14 **Amanu** *island* French Polynesia
101 I4 **Amapá** Brazil
102 B2 **Amapá** *admin. area* Brazil
102 A2 **Amapari** *watercourse* Brazil
157 F5 **Āmara** *admin. area* Ethiopia
132 E3 **Amara, Lacul** *lake* Romania
102 F5 **Amaraji** Brazil
163 G2 **Amaramba, Lagon** *lake* Mozambique
102 D4 **Amarante** Brazil
102 C4 **Amarante do Maranhão** Brazil
108 C2 **Amarga, Laguna La** *lake* Argentina
84 D2 **Amargosa Valley** Nevada USA
85 L3 **Amarillo** Texas USA
106 D5 **Amarillo, Cerro** *mountain* Argentina
130 E3 **Amaro** Italy
127 L5 **Amaro, Monte** *mountain* Italy
186 E6 **Amarpatan** Madhya Pradesh India

181 G4 **Amarpur** Tripura India
132 E3 **Amaru** Romania
198 E4 **Amaru, Danau** *lake* Indonesia
187 E6 **Amarwara** Madhya Pradesh India
136 E5 **Amasya** Turkey
136 E5 **Amasya** *admin. area* Turkey
217 L3 **Amata** SA Australia
90 C3 **Amatique, Bahía de** *bay* Belize
130 E5 **Amatrice** Italy
223 13a **Amatuku** *island* Tuvalu
199 I6 **Amau** Papua New Guinea
161 F3 **Amaya** *watercourse* Kenya
102 B2 **Amazon, Mouths of the** Brazil
101 D2 **Amazon Basin** *depression* Brazil
53 BB7 **Amazon Cone** *underwater feature* Atlantic Ocean
101 I5 **Amazon River** *watercourse* Brazil
101 E5 **Amazonas** *admin. area* Brazil
102 B3 **Amazonas** *watercourse* Brazil
100 B6 **Amazonas** *admin. area* Peru
100 D5 **Amazonas** *watercourse* Peru
101 E4 **Amazonas** *admin. area* Venezuela
187 D7 **Ambad** Maharashtra India
198 F4 **Ambai, Kepulauan** *islands* Indonesia
187 D7 **Ambajogai** Maharashtra India
186 D4 **Ambala** Haryana India
187 E10 **Ambalangoda** Sri Lanka
197 H3 **Ambalat** Indonesia
159 G4 **Ambam** Cameroon
163 I2 **Ambanja** Madagascar
135 AH5 **Ambarchik** Russian Federation
136 F6 **Ambarli** Syria
121 R4 **Ambarnyy** Russian Federation
163 I4 **Ambatafinandrahama** Madagascar
218 G1 **Ambathala** Qld Australia
100 B5 **Ambato** Ecuador
163 I3 **Ambato Boeny** Madagascar
163 I3 **Ambatolampy** Madagascar
163 I3 **Ambatondrazaka** Madagascar
126 E4 **Ambazac** France
101 I4 **Ambé** Brazil
198 C4 **Ambelau** *island* Indonesia
124 F3 **Amberg** Germany
90 C3 **Ambergris Cay** *island* Belize
127 G4 **Ambérieu-en-Bugey** France
221 E6 **Amberley** New Zealand
221 E6 **Amberley Beach** New Zealand
126 F4 **Ambert** France
154 D6 **Ambidédi** Mali
186 F6 **Ambikapur** Chhattisgarh India
163 I2 **Ambilobe** Madagascar
163 I3 **Ambinaninony** Madagascar
199 J5 **Ambitle Island** Papua New Guinea
141 G1 **Amble** Northumberland England UK
72 D5 **Ambler** Alaska USA
140 F2 **Ambleside** Cumbria England UK
139 I4 **Ambleteuse** France
163 I3 **Ambodifotatra** Madagascar
163 I4 **Ambohimanga Atsimo** Madagascar
163 I4 **Ambohinihaonana** Madagascar
162 B2 **Amboiva** Angola
198 D4 **Ambon** Indonesia
198 D4 **Ambon** *island* Indonesia
161 F4 **Amboseli, Lake** Kenya
163 I4 **Ambositra** Madagascar
163 I5 **Ambovombe** Madagascar
84 E3 **Amboy** California USA
195 G6 **Amboyna Cay** *island* Spratly Islands
127 J5 **Ambra** Italy
160 A5 **Ambriz** Angola
182 D5 **Ambrolauri** Georgia
222 7 **Ambrym** *island* Vanuatu
195 I4 **Ambulong** *island* Philippines
197 G6 **Ambulu** Indonesia
197 G5 **Ambunten** Indonesia
199 G5 **Ambunti** Papua New Guinea
214 B7 **Amburla** NT Australia
219 I2 **Amby** Qld Australia
135 AK8 **Amchitka Island** Alaska USA
135 AL8 **Amchitka Pass** *strait* Alaska USA
88 D4 **Ameca** Mexico
127 H1 **Amel** Belgium
124 C1 **Ameland** *island* Netherlands
131 E5 **Amelia** Italy
216 F7 **Amelup** WA Australia
129 H4 **Amer, Punta de n'** *cape* Spain
103 D5 **América Dourada** Brazil
53 EE13 **American-Antarctic Ridge** *underwater feature* Southern Ocean
80 I5 **American Falls** Idaho USA
80 I5 **American Falls Reservoir** Idaho USA
59 F2 **American Highland** Antarctica
218 C6 **American River** SA Australia
223 12c **American Samoa** *unincorporated US territory* Pacific Ocean
103 C8 **Americana** Brazil
87 I4 **Americus** Georgia USA
124 C1 **Amerongen** Netherlands
124 C1 **Amersfoort** Netherlands
139 G3 **Amersham** Buckinghamshire England UK
76 H4 **Amery** Manitoba Canada
59 E2 **Amery Basin** *underwater feature* Southern Ocean
59 E2 **Amery Ice Shelf** Antarctica
128 B2 **Amés** Spain
82 E5 **Ames** Iowa USA
86 B2 **Ames** Oklahoma USA
86 D5 **Ames** Texas USA
139 F3 **Amesbury** Wiltshire England UK
76 M8 **Ameson** Ontario Canada
186 C6 **Amet** Rajasthan India
133 B6 **Amfilochia** Greece
135 AB6 **Amga** *watercourse* Russian Federation
135 AL5 **Amguema** Russian Federation
135 AL5 **Amguema** *watercourse* Russian Federation
135 AC8 **Amgun'** *watercourse* Russian Federation
181 H3 **Amguri** Assam India
83 Q4 **Amherst** Maine USA
85 K3 **Amherst** Texas USA
83 M4 **Amherst Island** Ontario Canada
126 F2 **Amiens** France
83 L4 **Amigo Beach** Ontario Canada
178 E2 **'Amij, Wādī** *watercourse* Iraq
126 F3 **Amilly** France
187 C9 **Amindivi Islands** Lakshadweep India
187 C9 **Amini Island** Lakshadweep India
161 G3 **Amino** Ethiopia
162 C4 **Aminuis** Namibia
54 J5 **Amirante Trench** *underwater feature* Indian Ocean
164 9 **Amirantes, Les** *islands* Seychelles
76 D5 **Amisk Lake** Saskatchewan Canada
88 E2 **Amistad, Presa La** *lake* Mexico
88 E2 **Amistad Reservoir** Texas USA
86 E3 **Amity** Arkansas USA
187 D7 **Amla** Madhya Pradesh India
186 D6 **Amli** Rajasthan India
135 AM8 **Amlia Island** Alaska USA
140 D3 **Amlwch** Isle of Anglesey Wales UK
78 C2 **Ammaluttuuq, Lac** *lake* Quebec Canada
178 C3 **'Ammān** Jordan
120 I3 **Ammarfjället** *island* Sweden
120 J4 **Ammarnäs** Sweden
214 C6 **Ammaroo** NT Australia
120 J5 **Ammer** Sweden
124 D1 **Ammerland** *region* Germany
124 F3 **Ammersee** *lake* Germany
80 J5 **Ammon** Idaho USA
194 E4 **Amnat Charoen** Thailand
142 C5 **Amod** Argyll and Bute Scotland UK
182 F7 **Āmol** Iran
105 G5 **Amolar** Brazil
133 C5 **Amolianí** Greece
136 E2 **Amon'** Russian Federation
107 G4 **Amores** *watercourse* Argentina
133 E7 **Amorgos** *island* Greece
105 I5 **Amorinópolis** Brazil
73 L9 **Amos** Quebec Canada
219 K3 **Amosfield** NSW Australia
122 D3 **Åmot** Norway
129 I5 **Amoucha** Algeria
154 E5 **Amourj** Mauritania
158 D3 **Amoya** Ghana
120 H3 **Amøya** *island* Norway
197 G4 **Ampah** Indonesia
198 B4 **Ampana** Indonesia
187 F7 **Ampani** Orissa India
163 H4 **Ampanihy** Madagascar
187 E10 **Amparai** Sri Lanka
163 I3 **Ampasimanolotra** Madagascar
133 C6 **Ampelonas** Greece
124 F3 **Amper** *watercourse* Germany
107 H3 **Ampére** Brazil
50 Q6 **Ampère Seamount** *underwater feature* Atlantic Ocean
124 G4 **Ampezzo** Italy
195 G3 **Amphitrite Group** *islands* Paracel Islands
214 C6 **Ampilatwatja** NT Australia
198 B4 **Ampoa** Indonesia
131 G7 **Ampollino, Lago** *lake* Italy
129 G3 **Amposta** Spain
139 G2 **Ampthill** Bedfordshire England UK
128 D3 **Ampudia** Spain
121 O3 **Ampuma-alue** *island* Finland
77 V8 **Amqui** Quebec Canada
178 E7 **'Amrān** Yemen
187 D7 **Amravati** Maharashtra India
182 G7 **Amreh** Iran
187 C7 **Amreli** Gujarat India
186 D4 **Amritsar** Punjab India
186 E5 **Amroha** Uttar Pradesh India
120 K4 **Åmsele** Sweden
122 H2 **Amsen** *lake* Sweden
124 C1 **Amsterdam** Netherlands
83 N5 **Amsterdam** New York USA
164 6 **Amsterdam, Île** *island* French Southern and Antarctic Lands
127 L2 **Amstetten** Austria
120 K4 **Åmträsket** *lake* Sweden
130 C3 **Amtzell** Germany
136 G6 **'Āmūdah** Syria
182 J6 **Amudar'ya** *watercourse* Turkmenistan
191 I3 **Amugulang** Nei Mongol Zizhiqu China
135 AM8 **Amukta Pass** *strait* Alaska USA
101 G4 **Amuku Mountains** Guyana
142 E4 **Amulree** Perth and Kinross Scotland UK
199 J5 **Amun** Papua New Guinea
73 J3 **Amund Ringnes Island** Nunavut Canada
56 M1 **Amundsen Abyssal Plain** *underwater feature* Arctic Ocean
59 D2 **Amundsen Bay** Antarctica
59 N1 **Amundsen Coast** Antarctica
72 G4 **Amundsen Gulf** Northwest Territories Canada
51 F16 **Amundsen Ridges** *underwater feature* Southern Ocean
59 G1 **Amundsen-Scott (USA)** *research station* Antarctica
59 P2 **Amundsen Sea** Antarctica
56 V2 **Amundsen Trough** *underwater feature* Beaufort Sea
122 H2 **Amungen** *lake* Sweden
197 G4 **Amuntai** Indonesia
135 AB9 **Amur** *watercourse* China
158 D3 **Amur** *watercourse* Ghana
135 AC8 **Amur** *watercourse* Russian Federation
198 C3 **Amurang, Teluk** *bay* Indonesia
128 E2 **Amurrio** Spain
191 M2 **Amursk** Russian Federation
135 AA8 **Amurskaya Oblast'** *admin. area* Russian Federation
133 B6 **Amvrakikos Kolpos** *bay* Greece
136 F3 **Amvrosiyevka** Ukraine
133 B5 **Amyntaio** Greece
215 K8 **Amys Peak** Qld Australia
132 F4 **Amzacea** Romania
194 F4 **An Khê** Vietnam
136 F7 **An Nabk** Syria
178 E3 **An Najaf** Iraq
178 E3 **An Najaf** *admin. area* Iraq
178 F3 **An Nāşirīyah** Iraq
155 J2 **An Nawfalīyah** Libya
178 E3 **An Nukhayb** Iraq
142 A3 **An t-Òb** Na h-Eileanan Siar Scotland UK
191 H5 **Ansu** Hebei China
90 E2 **Ana María, Golfo de** *bay* Cuba
122 D3 **Åna-Sira** Norway
223 14 **Anaa** *island* French Polynesia
159 E2 **Anaba** Nigeria
222 4 **Anabar** Nauru
135 X4 **Anabar** *watercourse* Russian Federation
76 J4 **Anabusko** *watercourse* Manitoba Canada
84 C4 **Anacapa Islands** California USA
101 E2 **Anaco** Venezuela
80 I3 **Anaconda** Montana USA
80 I4 **Anaconda Range** Montana USA
80 D2 **Anacortes** Washington USA
86 B3 **Anadarko** Oklahoma USA
135 AK6 **Anadyr'** Russian Federation
135 AI6 **Anadyr'** *watercourse* Russian Federation
135 AJ6 **Anadyrskaya Nizmennost'** *region* Russian Federation
135 AL6 **Anadyrskiy Zaliv** *bay* Russian Federation
135 AJ5 **Anadyrskoye Ploskogor'ye** *region* Russian Federation
133 D7 **Anafi** *island* Greece
91 I3 **Anagada Passage** *strait* Caribbean Sea/Atlantic Ocean
103 D6 **Anagé** Brazil
84 D4 **Anaheim** California USA
84 inset **Anahola** Hawai'i USA
88 D2 **Anáhuac** Mexico
187 D9 **Anai Mudi** *mountain* Kerala India
102 C3 **Anajatuba** Brazil
163 H4 **Anakao** Madagascar
187 F8 **Anakapalle** Andhra Pradesh India
109 5 **Anakena, Caleta** *bay* Isla de Pascua (Easter Island)
215 I7 **Anakie** Qld Australia
78 G4 **Anaktalik** *watercourse* Newfoundland and Labrador Canada
72 D5 **Anaktuvuk Pass** Alaska USA
104 D5 **Anallajchi, Cerro** *mountain* Bolivia
135 U5 **Anama, Ozero** *lake* Russian Federation
196 E3 **Anambas, Kepulauan** *islands* Indonesia
136 E6 **Anamur** Turkey
192 G5 **Anan** Japan
187 C6 **Anand** Gujarat India
187 G7 **Anandapur** Orissa India
183 M5 **Anan'evo** Kyrgyzstan
102 B3 **Ananindeua** Brazil
198 C5 **Anano** *island* Indonesia
187 D8 **Anantapur** Andhra Pradesh India
186 D4 **Anantnag** Jammu and Kashmir India/Pakistan
Ananyev *see* **Anan'yiv** Ukraine
132 F2 **Anan'yiv** Ukraine
182 C5 **Anapa** Russian Federation
103 B7 **Anápolis** Brazil
105 I1 **Anapú** *watercourse* Brazil
179 H2 **Anārak** Iran
59 L2 **Anare Mountains** Antarctica
211 inset **Anare Station** Macquarie Island Australia
120 H5 **Anarisfjälen** *mountain* Sweden
100 D2 **Anaro, Caño** *watercourse* Venezuela
143 B4 **Anascaul** Ireland
120 L4 **Ånäset** Sweden
107 H2 **Anastácio** Brazil
222 2 **Anatahan** *island* Northern Mariana Islands
133 D5 **Anatoliki Makedonia kai Thraki** *admin. area* Greece
222 7 **Anatom** *island* Vanuatu
121 P4 **Änättijärvi** *lake* Finland
106 F4 **Añatuya** Argentina
101 F4 **Anaua** *watercourse* Brazil
220 H4 **Anaura Bay** New Zealand
101 F5 **Anavilhanas, Arquipélago das** *islands* Brazil
133 C6 **Anavra** Greece
108 A3 **Anay, Punta** *cape* Chile
178 E3 **Anbār, Al** *admin. area* Iraq
192 E3 **Anbyŏn** North Korea
104 B3 **Ancash** *admin. area* Peru
123 L4 **Ance** Latvia
127 G2 **Ancerville** France
135 AC6 **Ancha** Russian Federation
104 C4 **Anchivay** Peru
108 A4 **Ancho, Canal** *strait* Chile
72 E6 **Anchorage** Alaska USA
123 L5 **Ančia** *lake* Lithuania
89 J2 **Anclote Keys** *islands* Florida USA
100 A5 **Ancón, Punta** *cape* Ecuador
100 B4 **Ancón de Sardinas, Bahía de** *bay* Ecuador
130 E5 **Ancona** Italy
126 F2 **Ancre** *watercourse* France
163 G2 **Ancuabe** Mozambique
108 B2 **Ancud** Chile
191 K3 **Anda** Heilongjiang China
198 C2 **Anda** *island* Indonesia
218 B1 **Andado** NT Australia
104 C4 **Andahuaylas** Peru
163 I3 **Andaingo Gara** Madagascar
163 I4 **Andalatanosy** Madagascar
120 E5 **Åndalsnes** Norway
154 F1 **Andalucía** *admin. area* Spain
128 D5 **Andalucía** *region* Spain
108 D3 **Andaluz, Pampa del** *region* Argentina
179 I5 **'Andām, Wādī** *watercourse* Oman
187 H9 **Andaman and Nicobar Islands** *admin. area* India
52 F6 **Andaman Basin** *underwater feature* Bay of Bengal
194 B4 **Andaman Islands** Andaman and Nicobar Islands India
194 B4 **Andaman Sea** Asia
218 C4 **Andamooka** SA Australia
163 I2 **Andapa** Madagascar
162 D3 **Andara** Namibia
105 F2 **Andaraí** Brazil
188 E4 **Ande** Guangxi Zhuangzu Zizhiqu China
120 J2 **Andenes** Norway
155 G5 **Andéramboukane** Niger
127 I3 **Andermatt** Switzerland
126 D4 **Andernos-les-Bains** France
222 5 **Andersen Air Force Base** Guam
72 G5 **Anderson** *watercourse* Northwest Territories Canada
72 E6 **Anderson** Alaska USA
80 D6 **Anderson** California USA
82 I6 **Anderson** Indiana USA
87 J3 **Anderson** South Carolina USA
219 R10 **Anderson Bay** Tas. Australia
80 H5 **Anderson Ranch Reservoir** Idaho USA
84 B2 **Anderson Reservoir** California USA
216 F6 **Anderson Rocks** *mountain* WA Australia
122 G4 **Anderstorp** Sweden
108 B2 **Andes** *range* Argentina
105 E6 **Andes** *range* Bolivia
108 B3 **Andes** *range* Chile
100 C3 **Andes** *range* Colombia
100 B4 **Andes** *range* Ecuador
104 C4 **Andes** *range* Peru
187 E8 **Andhra Pradesh** *admin. area* India
109 1a **Andicuri** *bay* Aruba
183 K6 **Andijon** Uzbekistan
183 K6 **Andijon** *admin. area* Uzbekistan
163 I3 **Andilamena** Madagascar
178 F3 **Andīmeshk** Iran
184 G5 **Andir He** *watercourse* Xinjiang Uygur Zizhiqu China
105 G1 **Andira** *watercourse* Brazil
Andizhan *see* **Andijon** Uzbekistan
182 J7 **Andkhvoy** Afghanistan
126 C5 **Andoain** Spain
163 I2 **Andoany** Madagascar
130 G3 **Andocs** Hungary
192 F4 **Andong** South Korea
192 F4 **Andong-ho** *lake* South Korea
214 F2 **Andoom** Qld Australia
120 J2 **Andørja** Norway
120 J2 **Andørja** *island* Norway
129 G2 **Andorra** *country* Europe
129 F3 **Andorra** Spain
129 G2 **Andorra La Vella** Andorra
139 F3 **Andover** Hampshire England UK
120 I2 **Andøya** *island* Norway
84 E4 **Andrade** California USA
103 B8 **Andradina** Brazil
163 H4 **Andranolava** Madagascar
163 I3 **Andranomavo** Madagascar
78 F5 **André Lake** Newfoundland and Labrador Canada
163 H3 **Andrea** Madagascar
135 AL8 **Andreanof Islands** Alaska USA
123 Q4 **Andreapol'** Russian Federation
218 D2 **Andree, Lake** SA Australia
216 H6 **Andrew, Mount** WA Australia
87 J3 **Andrews** North Carolina USA
87 L4 **Andrews** South Carolina USA
85 K4 **Andrews** Texas USA
182 F3 **Andreyevka** Russian Federation
131 G6 **Andria** Italy
85 K2 **Andrix** Colorado USA
181 H4 **Andro** Manipur India
163 H4 **Androka** Madagascar
163 I2 **Androranga** *watercourse* Madagascar
87 L8 **Andros** *island* Bahamas
133 D7 **Andros** *island* Greece
90 E1 **Andros Town** Bahamas
83 P4 **Androscoggin** *watercourse* Maine USA
187 C9 **Andrott Island** Lakshadweep India
123 N4 **Andrupene** Latvia
130 H2 **Andrychów** Poland
120 L1 **Andsnes** Norway
120 K2 **Andsvatnet** *lake* Norway
160 D3 **Andudu** Democratic Republic of Congo
128 D4 **Andújar** Spain
162 C2 **Andulo** Angola
135 Y6 **Andyngda** Russian Federation
213 J7 **Anec, Lake** WA Australia
155 G5 **Anéfis** Mali
109 21 **Anegada** *island* British Virgin Islands
108 E2 **Anegada, Bahía** *bay* Argentina
100 A3 **Anegada, Punta** *cape* Panama
106 D6 **Añelo** Argentina
199 I5 **Anepmete** Papua New Guinea
85 H2 **Aneth** Utah USA
129 G2 **Aneto** *mountain* Spain
182 H6 **Änew** Turkmenistan
108 B3 **Anexo, Cerro** *mountain* Argentina
155 I5 **Aney** Niger
124 F5 **Anfo** Italy
196 D3 **Ang Mo Kio** *admin. area* Singapore
194 D4 **Ang Thong** Thailand
163 I2 **Angadoka, Lohatunjona** *cape* Madagascar
213 K3 **Angalarri** *watercourse* NT Australia
108 A4 **Angamos, Isla** *island* Chile
109 5 **Angamos, Punta** *cape* Isla de Pascua (Easter Island)
190 E2 **Angara** *watercourse* Russian Federation
190 E2 **Angarsk** Russian Federation
217 M2 **Angas Downs** NT Australia
135 V8 **Angaul** Russian Federation
222 3 **Angaur** *island* Palau
120 I5 **Ånge** Sweden
120 J6 **Ängebo** Sweden
76 I6 **Angekum Lake** Ontario Canada
88 B2 **Ángel de la Guarda, Isla** *island* Mexico
85 J2 **Angel Fire** New Mexico USA
195 I4 **Angeles** Philippines
122 G4 **Ängelholm** Sweden
121 N2 **Angeli** Finland
83 L5 **Angelica** New York USA
212 E7 **Angelo** *watercourse* WA Australia
88 E2 **Angelo** Texas USA
199 F4 **Angemuk, Gunung** *mountain* Indonesia
161 F2 **Anger** *watercourse* Ethiopia
130 C4 **Angera** Italy
156 F5 **Ängereb** Ethiopia
156 F5 **Ängereb Wenz** *watercourse* Ethiopia
120 J5 **Ångermanälven** *watercourse* Sweden
120 J5 **Ångermanland** *region* Sweden
126 D3 **Angers** France
121 M3 **Ängesån** Sweden
120 L3 **Ängesån** *watercourse* Sweden
120 L5 **Ängesön** Sweden
120 L5 **Ängesön** *island* Sweden
197 H4 **Anggana** Indonesia
122 H4 **Änghultasjön** *lake* Sweden
102 E4 **Angicos** Brazil
76 F1 **Angikuni Lake** Nunavut Canada
179 K3 **Angizay** Afghanistan
138 B3 **Angle** Pembrokeshire Wales UK
221 B8 **Anglem, Mount** New Zealand
140 D3 **Anglesey, Isle of** *admin. area* England UK
86 D6 **Angleton** Texas USA
126 E3 **Anglin** *watercourse* France
124 B3 **Anglure** France
78 C6 **Ango, Lac** *lake* Quebec Canada
163 G3 **Angoche** Mozambique
179 I4 **Angohrān** Iran
106 C6 **Angol** Chile
162 C2 **Angola** *country* Africa
51 S11 **Angola Abyssal Plain** *underwater feature* Atlantic Ocean
51 S11 **Angola Basin** *underwater feature* Atlantic Ocean
74 D4 **Angoon** Alaska USA
88 C2 **Angostura, Presa La** *lake* Mexico
81 N5 **Angostura Reservoir** South Dakota USA
163 H2 **Angouan (Nzwani)** *island* Comoros
126 E4 **Angoulême** France
126 E4 **Angoumois** *region* France
181 H3 **Angpawng Bum** Myanmar
164 1b **Angra do Heroísmo** Azores
103 C8 **Angra dos Reis** Brazil
198 E4 **Angra Meos** *island* Indonesia
183 K5 **Angren** Uzbekistan
131 F6 **Angri** Italy
120 H5 **Ängsfjärden** *bay* Sweden
160 C3 **Angu** Democratic Republic of Congo
109 20 **Anguilla** *British overseas territory* Caribbean
90 E2 **Anguilla Cays** *islands* Bahamas
191 H5 **Anguo** Hebei China
214 D2 **Angurugu** NT Australia
142 F4 **Angus** *admin. area* Scotland UK
120 F5 **Angvik** Norway
162 E3 **Angwa** *watercourse* Zimbabwe
107 H2 **Anhanduí** *watercourse* Brazil
122 F4 **Anholt** Denmark
189 H2 **Anhui** *admin. area* China
72 D6 **Aniak** Alaska USA
222 4 **Anibare** Nauru
126 F1 **Aniche** France
103 B7 **Anicuns** Brazil
158 E3 **Anie** Togo
142 D4 **Anie** Stirling Scotland UK
124 G4 **Anif** Austria
108 B4 **Animales** Chile
85 H5 **Animas** New Mexico USA
85 I2 **Animas** *watercourse* New Mexico USA
132 C3 **Aninoasa** Romania
133 G6 **Anıtkaya** Turkey
193 I1 **Aniva** Russian Federation
135 AD9 **Aniva, Mys** *cape* Russian Federation
135 AD9 **Aniva, Zaliv** *bay* Russian Federation
222 7 **Aniwa** *island* Vanuatu
187 D6 **Anjad** Madhya Pradesh India
123 N2 **Anjala** Finland
123 N2 **Anjalankoski** Finland
120 H5 **Anjan** *lake* Sweden
187 D7 **Anjangaon** Maharashtra India
186 C6 **Anjar** Gujarat India
188 F3 **Anjiang** Hunan China
179 K4 **Anjira** Pakistan
164 8 **Anjouan (Nzwani)** *island* Comoros
163 I3 **Anjozorobe** Madagascar
192 E3 **Anju** North Korea
159 F2 **Anka** Nigeria
163 H4 **Ankaboa, Tanjona** *cape* Madagascar
188 F2 **Ankang** Shaanxi China
136 E5 **Ankara** Turkey
136 E5 **Ankara** *admin. area* Turkey
120 I4 **Ankarede Kapell** Sweden
120 I4 **Ankarvattnet** Sweden
120 I4 **Ankarvattnet** *lake* Sweden
163 I3 **Ankavandra** Madagascar
163 H4 **Ankazoabo** Madagascar
163 I3 **Ankazobe** Madagascar
82 E6 **Ankeny** Iowa USA
187 C7 **Ankleshwar** Gujarat India
187 D8 **Ankola** Karnataka India
141 H3 **Anlaby** East Riding of Yorkshire England UK
194 E4 **Ânlong Vêng** Cambodia
189 G2 **Anlu** Hubei China
192 E4 **Anmoyon-do** *island* South Korea
120 H5 **Ånn** *lake* Sweden
59 D2 **Ann, Cape** Antarctica
82 J5 **Ann Arbor** Michigan USA
52 N4 **Ann Judge Seamount** *underwater feature* Pacific Ocean
78 H6 **Ann Marie Lake** Newfoundland and Labrador Canada
182 C3 **Anna** Russian Federation
86 C4 **Anna** Texas USA
83 M7 **Anna, Lake** Virginia USA
218 C3 **Anna Creek** SA Australia
87 J7 **Anna Maria** Florida USA
108 A3 **Anna Pink, Bahía** *bay* Chile
101 C3 **Anna Regina** Guyana
155 H1 **Annaba** Algeria
143 D4 **Annaboty** Ireland
214 A2 **Annaburroo** NT Australia
140 C2 **Annacloy** Down Northern Ireland UK
143 C3 **Annagh Island** Ireland
140 B2 **Annahilt** Lisburn Northern Ireland UK
140 A2 **Annalee** *watercourse* Ireland
140 C2 **Annalong** Newry and Mourne Northern Ireland UK
142 E6 **Annan** Dumfries and Galloway Scotland UK
142 E5 **Annan** *watercourse* Scotland UK
215 J6 **Annandale** Qld Australia
83 M7 **Annapolis** Maryland USA
78 E2 **Annapolis Strait** Nunavut Canada
140 E2 **Annaside** Cumbria England UK
142 C3 **Annat** Highland Scotland UK
216 F3 **Annean, Lake** WA Australia
127 H4 **Annecy** France
109 8 **Annenkov Island** South Georgia
215 G3 **Annie** *watercourse* Qld Australia
188 D4 **Anning** Yunnan China
214 D6 **Annitowa** NT Australia
159 F5 **Annobón** *island* Equatorial Guinea
124 C5 **Annonay** France
125 K2 **Annopol** Poland
127 H5 **Annot** France
90 E3 **Annotto Bay** Jamaica
218 F6 **Annuello** Vic. Australia
82 J8 **Annville** Kentucky USA
127 H2 **Annweiler** Germany
108 C6 **Año Nuevo, Seno** *bay* Chile
133 D7 **Ano Sagkri** Greece
222 8 **Anoano** Solomon Islands
124 C2 **Anor** France
101 F5 **Anori** Brazil
161 H6 **Anorontany, Tanjona** *cape* Madagascar
122 F1 **Anoya** *lake* Norway
191 H5 **Anping** Hebei China
189 H2 **Anqing** Anhui China
191 I6 **Anqiu** Shandong China
128 E3 **Anquela del Ducado** Spain
181 G3 **Anrao** Xizang Zizhiqu China
127 K3 **Anras** Austria
189 G3 **Anren** Hunan China
198 E4 **Ansas** Indonesia
124 F3 **Ansbach** Germany
91 F3 **Anse-à-Galets** Haiti
109 16 **Anse-Bertrand** Guadeloupe
164 9a **Anse Boileau** Seychelles
109 13 **Anse la Raye** St Lucia
164 9b **Anse Royal** Seychelles
164 9a **Anse Volbert** Seychelles
131 D5 **Ansedónia** Italy
123 L3 **Anseküla** Estonia
191 J4 **Anshan** Liaoning China
188 E3 **Anshun** Guizhou China
106 D4 **Ansilta** *mountain* Argentina
122 H1 **Ansjön** *lake* Sweden
81 P6 **Ansley** Nebraska USA
86 B4 **Anson** Texas USA
213 K2 **Anson Bay** *watercourse* NT Australia
211 inset **Anson Point** Norfolk Island Australia
155 G5 **Ansongo** Mali
211 inset **Ansons Bay** Norfolk Island Australia
139 H3 **Anstey** Hertfordshire England UK
199 F4 **Ansudu** Indonesia
214 F6 **Answer Downs** Qld Australia
222 6 **Ant Atoll** *island* Federated States of Micronesia
104 C4 **Antabamba** Peru
163 J2 **Antalaha** Madagascar
136 D6 **Antalya** *admin. area* Turkey
133 G7 **Antalya Körfezi** *bay* Turkey
163 I3 **Antananarivo** Madagascar
163 I3 **Antananarivo** *admin. area* Madagascar
59 T2 **Antarctic Peninsula** Antarctica
59 G1 **Antarctica** *continent*
199 G5 **Antares** *mountain* Indonesia
107 I4 **Antas** *watercourse* Brazil
196 E5 **Antatai** Indonesia
84 D2 **Antelope Lake** Nevada USA
84 D1 **Antelope Range** Nevada USA
80 G5 **Antelope Reservoir** Oregon USA
128 D5 **Antequera** Spain
85 J1 **Antero Reservoir** Colorado USA
130 E3 **Anterselva** Italy
85 I5 **Anthony** Texas USA
217 M4 **Anthony, Lake** SA Australia
Anti-Taurus Mountains *see* **Güney Doğu Toroslar** Turkey
127 H5 **Antibes** France
101 F2 **Antica, Isla** *island* Venezuela
79 F8 **Anticosti, Île d'** *island* Quebec Canada
126 E2 **Antifer, Cap d'** *cape* France
82 G4 **Antigo** Wisconsin USA
109 18 **Antigua** *island* Antigua and Barbuda
164 3d **Antigua** Canary Islands
91 I3 **Antigua and Barbuda** *country* Caribbean
89 F4 **Antiguo Morelos** Mexico
133 C6 **Antikyras, Kolpos** *bay* Greece
133 D7 **Antimilos** *island* Greece
80 J7 **Antimony** Utah USA
121 M3 **Antinrova** Sweden
Antioch *see* **Hatay** Turkey
100 C3 **Antioquia** Colombia
100 C3 **Antioquia** *admin. area* Colombia
133 D7 **Antiparos** *island* Greece
133 B6 **Antipaxoi** *island* Greece
134 Q5 **Antipayuta** Russian Federation
221 11 **Antipodes Island** New Zealand
195 I4 **Antipolo** Philippines
100 B5 **Antisana** *volcano* Ecuador
86 D3 **Antlers** Oklahoma USA
106 D2 **Antofagasta** Chile
106 D2 **Antofagasta** *admin. area* Chile
106 E3 **Antofagasta de la Sierra** Argentina
106 E3 **Antofalla, Salina de** *lake* Argentina
106 D3 **Antofalla, Volcán** *volcano* Argentina
90 D5 **Antón** Panama
85 K4 **Anton** Texas USA
163 J3 **Antongila, Helodranon'** *bay* Madagascar
164 4a **Antónia, Pico da** *volcano* Cape Verde
163 I3 **Antonibe** Madagascar
108 C4 **Antonio de Biedma** Argentina
108 B5 **Antonio Varas, Península** *peninsula* Chile
85 J2 **Antonito** Colorado USA
121 U6 **Antonovskaya** Russian Federation
140 B2 **Antrim** Antrim Northern Ireland UK
140 B2 **Antrim** *admin. area* Northern Ireland UK
140 B2 **Antrim Mountains** Northern Ireland UK
163 I3 **Antsiafabositra** Madagascar
163 I3 **Antsirabe** Madagascar
163 I2 **Antsiranana** Madagascar
163 I2 **Antsiranana** *admin. area* Madagascar
163 H3 **Antsoha** Madagascar
163 I2 **Antsohihy** Madagascar
163 I2 **Antsohimbondrona** Madagascar
123 N2 **Anttola** Finland
186 E5 **Antu** Uttar Pradesh India
105 F3 **Antuérpia** Brazil
218 F7 **Antwerp** Vic. Australia
127 G1 **Antwerpen** Belgium
127 G1 **Antwerpen** *admin. area* Belgium
223 14 **Anuanuraro** *island* French Polynesia
223 14 **Anuanurunga** *island* French Polynesia
77 R3 **Anuc, Lac** *lake* Quebec Canada
186 C5 **Anupgarh** Rajasthan India
186 D5 **Anupshahr** Rajasthan India
187 E10 **Anuradhapura** Sri Lanka
59 T2 **Anvers Island** Antarctica
126 F1 **Anvin** France
189 H2 **Anwen** Zhejiang China
139 G1 **Anwick** Lincolnshire England UK
191 H5 **Anxin** Hebei China
218 B5 **Anxious Bay** SA Australia
158 D3 **Anyama** Côte d'Ivoire
188 E4 **Anyang** Guangxi Zhuangzu Zizhiqu China
191 H6 **Anyang** Henan China
192 E4 **Anyang** South Korea
188 C1 **A'nyemaoen Shan** *range* Jiangsu China
189 H1 **Anyi** Jiangsu China
158 D3 **Anyinam** Ghana
123 M5 **Anykščiai** Lithuania
135 AI5 **Anyuyskiy Khrebet** *range* Russian Federation
75 P4 **Anzac** Alberta Canada
74 J5 **Anzac** British Columbia Canada
210 inset **Anzac Peak** Heard Island Australia
183 O2 **Anzhero-Sudzhensk** Russian Federation
160 C4 **Anzi** Democratic Republic of Congo
131 F6 **Anzi** Italy
131 E6 **Anzio** Italy
131 E6 **Anzio, Capo d'** *cape* Italy
106 F6 **Anzoátegui** Argentina
101 E2 **Anzoátegui** *admin. area* Venezuela
182 E6 **Anzoli** Azerbaijan
194 C5 **Ao Luk** Thailand
222 7 **Aoba** *island* Vanuatu
193 H5 **Aoga-shima** *island* Japan
129 I5 **Aokas** Algeria
222 8a **Aola** Solomon Islands
Aomen *see* **Macau** China
193 I3 **Aomori** Japan
221 D6 **Aoraki (Mt Cook)** New Zealand
221 F5 **Aorangi Range** New Zealand
221 E5 **Aorere** *watercourse* New Zealand
124 D5 **Aosta** Italy
220 F4 **Aotea Harbour** New Zealand
154 D3 **Aoufist** Western Sahara
160 B2 **Aouk, Bahr** *watercourse* Central African Republic
159 I2 **Aoukale** *watercourse* Central African Republic
159 I2 **Aoukale** *watercourse* Chad
154 D5 **Aourou** Mali
154 E2 **Aoutime, Jbel** *mountain* Morocco
189 G3 **Aoxi** Jiangxi China
189 H3 **Aoyang** Fujian China
189 G3 **Aoyang** Jiangxi China
155 J4 **Aozou** Chad
107 G2 **Apa** *watercourse* Brazil
161 E3 **Apac** Uganda
84 G4 **Apache Junction** Arizona USA
106 E2 **Apagado, Volcán** *volcano* Chile
89 I2 **Apalachee Bay** Florida USA
87 I6 **Apalachicola** Florida USA
89 I2 **Apalachicola** *watercourse* Florida USA
158 D3 **Apam** Ghana
101 G3 **Apanachi** Guyana
222 8 **Apaora** Solomon Islands
100 D5 **Apaporis, Rio** *watercourse* Brazil
197 H4 **Apar, Teluk** *bay* Indonesia
217 K3 **Aparatjara Homeland** SA Australia
105 I5 **Aparecida do Rio Doce** Brazil
103 B8 **Aparecida do Taboado** Brazil
105 E4 **Aparejos** Bolivia
221 C7 **Aparima** *watercourse* New Zealand
195 I3 **Aparri** Philippines
100 B3 **Apartadó** Colombia
101 F3 **Aparurén** Venezuela
108 C3 **Apas, Sierra** *range* Argentina
223 14 **Apataka** *island* French Polynesia
121 R3 **Apatity** Russian Federation
101 H3 **Apatou** French Guiana
88 E5 **Apatzingán** Mexico
218 D2 **Apawyilarranie** *watercourse* SA Australia
124 C1 **Apeldoorn** Netherlands
105 E4 **Apere** *watercourse* Bolivia
160 D3 **Api** Democratic Republic of Congo
198 A6 **Api, Gunung** *volcano* Indonesia
198 B4 **Api, Tanjung** *cape* Indonesia
223 12c **Apia** Samoa
105 G3 **Apiacás** Brazil
105 G3 **Apiacás, Serra dos** *range* Brazil
103 B9 **Apiaí** Brazil
101 F4 **Apiaú, Serra do** *range* Brazil
215 J7 **Apis Creek** Qld Australia
195 J6 **Apo, Mount** *mountain* Philippines
88 E3 **Apodaca** Mexico
102 E4 **Apodi** Brazil
102 E4 **Apodi** *watercourse* Brazil
133 D7 **Apoikia** Greece
101 F3 **Apoipó** Venezuela
133 E7 **Apolakkia** Greece
223 12c **Apolima** *island* Samoa
218 F8 **Apollo Bay** Vic. Australia
133 D7 **Apollonia** Greece
90 B4 **Apopa** El Salvador
87 K6 **Apopka** Florida USA
87 K6 **Apopka, Lake** Florida USA
105 H5 **Apore** *watercourse* Brazil
105 I5 **Aporé** Brazil
104 D4 **Aporoma** Peru
132 A2 **Apostag** Hungary
73 O6 **Apostelen Tommelfinger** *mountain* Greenland
82 F3 **Apostle Islands** Wisconsin USA
107 H3 **Apóstoles** Argentina
164 6 **Apôtres, Îlots des** *islands* French Southern and Antarctic Lands
88 E4 **Apozol** Mexico
83 M6 **Appalachian Mountains** USA
127 K5 **Appennino** *range* Italy
127 I3 **Appenzell** Switzerland
218 B2 **Apperda, Mount** SA Australia
127 J3 **Appiano sulla Strada del Vino** Italy
142 E5 **Appin** Dumfries and Galloway Scotland UK
84 D3 **Apple Valley** California USA
141 F2 **Appleby-in-Westmorland** Cumbria England UK
138 C3 **Appledore** Devon England UK
82 G4 **Appleton** Wisconsin USA
102 A1 **Approuague** *watercourse* French Guiana
222 5 **Apra Harbor** Guam
222 5 **Apra Heights** Guam
199 G5 **April** *watercourse* Papua New Guinea
131 E6 **Aprilia** Italy
218 E7 **Apsley** Vic. Australia
83 L4 **Apsley** Ontario Canada
127 G5 **Apt** France
103 B8 **Apucarana** Brazil
105 G2 **Apuí** Brazil
222 3 **Apurashokoru** *island* Palau
100 D3 **Apure** *admin. area* Venezuela
100 D3 **Apure** *watercourse* Venezuela
104 C4 **Apurímac** *admin. area* Peru
123 N5 **Apvardų ežeras** *lake* Lithuania
182 G6 **Āq Band** Iran
182 E7 **Aq Gadok, Gardanehye** *pass* Iran
182 G6 **Āq Qal'eh** Iran
178 C4 **Aqaba, Gulf of** Red Sea
182 J7 **Āqchah** Afghanistan
156 F4 **Aqiq** Sudan
185 I4 **Aqitag** *mountain* Xinjiang Uygur Zizhiqu China
179 H4 **'Aqqah** United Arab Emirates
218 H2 **Aqua Downs** Qld Australia
84 F3 **Aquarius Mountains** Arkansas USA
84 G1 **Aquarius Plateau** Utah USA
76 M5 **Aquatuk** *watercourse* Ontario Canada
104 D2 **Aquidabã** Brazil
124 G5 **Aquileia** Italy
86 C5 **Aquilla Reservoir** Texas USA
91 F3 **Aquin** Haiti
102 E3 **Aquiraz** Brazil
126 D4 **Aquitaine** *admin. area* France
100 C2 **Aquja, Cabo de la** *cape* Colombia
179 H5 **Ar Rajmī** Oman
178 E2 **Ar Ramādī** Iraq
178 E5 **Ar Ramādīyāt** Saudi Arabia
136 F6 **Ar Raqqah** Syria
178 G4 **Ar Rayyān** Qatar
178 G4 **Ar Rifā' al Gharbī** Bahrain
178 F7 **Ar Rīsān** Yemen
178 F5 **Ar Riyāḍ (Riyadh)** Saudi Arabia
178 F7 **Ar Rukbah** Yemen
178 D2 **Ar Ruţbah** Iraq
178 G5 **Ar Ruways** United Arab Emirates
156 E2 **Ar Ruzayqāt** Egypt
186 F6 **Ara** Bihar India
161 G2 **Āra Ārba** Ethiopia
143 D4 **Ara Bridge** Ireland
87 H3 **Arab** Alabama USA
160 D1 **'Arab, Baḩr al** *watercourse* Sudan
54 K3 **Arabian Basin** *underwater feature* Arabian Sea
178 F5 **Arabian Peninsula** Saudi Arabia
179 J6 **Arabian Sea** Asia
101 F3 **Arabopó** Venezuela
101 F4 **Araca** *watercourse* Brazil
103 E5 **Aracaju** Brazil
102 E4 **Aracati** Brazil
104 C3 **Aracati** Brazil
103 B8 **Araçatuba** Brazil
100 E5 **Araçatuba, Ilhas de** *islands* Brazil
128 C5 **Aracena, Sierra de** *range* Spain
103 E5 **Araci** Brazil
103 D7 **Aracruz** Brazil
103 D7 **Araçuaí** Brazil
103 D7 **Araçuaí** *watercourse* Brazil
132 B2 **Arad** Romania
132 B2 **Arad** *admin. area* Romania
159 I2 **Arada** Chad
159 I2 **Aradeib, Wadi** *watercourse* Sudan
198 D6 **Arafura Sea** Australia
52 J9 **Arafura Shelf** *underwater feature* Arafura Sea
103 A6 **Aragarças** Brazil
129 F3 **Aragón** *admin. area* Spain
129 F2 **Aragón** *watercourse* Spain
100 E2 **Aragua** *admin. area* Venezuela
101 E2 **Aragua de Barcelona** Venezuela
103 B6 **Araguaçu** Brazil
103 B5 **Araguaia** *watercourse* Brazil
102 B5 **Araguaia, Arroios do** *watercourse* Brazil
102 B4 **Araguaína** Brazil
101 F2 **Araguao, Boca** *bay* Venezuela
101 F2 **Araguapiche, Punta** *cape* Venezuela
103 B7 **Araguari** Brazil
102 A2 **Araguari** *watercourse* Brazil
102 B4 **Araguatins** Brazil
221 D6 **Arahura** New Zealand
102 D3 **Araioses** Brazil
121 O3 **Arajärvi** *lake* Finland
178 G2 **Arāk** Iran
160 E3 **Araka** Sudan
135 AM5 **Arakamchechen, Ostrov** *island* Russian Federation
182 E6 **Araks** *watercourse* Azerbaijan
182 H4 **Aral Sea** *lake* Kazakhstan
182 I4 **Aral'sk (Aralsk)** Kazakhstan
Aral'skoye More *see* **Aral Sea**
182 E3 **Aralsor, Ozero** *lake* Kazakhstan
122 C1 **Åram** Norway
215 H7 **Aramac** Qld Australia
215 H7 **Aramac** *watercourse* Qld Australia
199 G5 **Aramia** *watercourse* Papua New Guinea
220 G5 **Aramoana** New Zealand
143 C3 **Aran Islands** Ireland
128 E3 **Aranda de Duero** Spain
109 9 **Aranguez** Trinidad and Tobago
187 E9 **Arani** Tamil Nadu India
128 E3 **Aranjuez** Spain
106 F6 **Arano** Argentina
162 C4 **Aranos** Namibia
103 B7 **Arantes** *watercourse* Brazil
222 1 **Aranuka** *island* Kiribati
154 F5 **Araouane** Mali
104 D4 **Arapa, Lago de** *lake* Peru
86 B3 **Arapaho** Oklahoma USA
85 K1 **Arapahoe** Colorado USA
81 P6 **Arapahoe** Nebraska USA
221 F5 **Arapawa Island** New Zealand
107 G4 **Arapey Grande** *watercourse* Uruguay
218 E7 **Arapiles, Mount** Vic. Australia
102 E5 **Arapiraca** Brazil
101 H5 **Arapiriri, Ilha** *island* Brazil
133 D5 **Arapis, Akra** *cape* Greece
101 H5 **Arapiuns** *watercourse* Brazil
220 F4 **Arapuni** New Zealand
105 G4 **Araputanga** Brazil

178 E3 **'Ar'ar** Saudi Arabia
102 F4 **Arara** Brazil
100 C5 **Araracuara, Mesa** *region* Colombia
107 I4 **Araranguá** Brazil
105 E3 **Araras** Brazil
103 A7 **Araras, Serra das** *range* Brazil
100 C5 **Araras de Coemas** Colombia
182 D6 **Ararat** Armenia
182 E6 **Ararat** *pass* Armenia
218 F7 **Ararat** Vic. Australia
Ararat, Mount *see* **Ağrı Dağı** Turkey
105 E4 **Araré, Laguna** *lake* Bolivia
102 C3 **Arari** Brazil
102 B3 **Arari, Lago** *lake* Brazil
186 G5 **Araria** Bihar India
102 D4 **Araripe** Brazil
102 D4 **Araripina** Brazil
122 C2 **Årås** Norway
129 F4 **Aras de Alpuente** Spain
102 D4 **Aratas, Açude** *lake* Brazil
100 D3 **Arauca** *admin. area* Colombia
100 D3 **Arauca** Venezuela
91 G6 **Arauca** *watercourse* Venezuela
108 B2 **Araucania** *admin. area* Chile
103 B9 **Araucária** Brazil
186 C6 **Aravali Range** Rajasthan India
123 M3 **Aravete** Estonia
218 G8 **Arawata** Vic. Australia
199 I5 **Arawe Islands** Papua New Guinea
221 C7 **Arawhata** New Zealand
103 C7 **Araxá** Brazil
133 B6 **Araxos, Akra** *cape* Greece
101 E2 **Araya, Punta de** *cape* Venezuela
128 B3 **Arazede** Portugal
128 D6 **Arba Ayacha** Morocco
161 F2 **Ārba Minch** Ethiopia
128 D6 **Arbaoua** Morocco
129 I5 **Arbaoun** Algeria
182 E1 **Arbazh** Russian Federation
178 E2 **Arbīl** Iraq
178 E2 **Arbīl** *admin. area* Iraq
122 H3 **Arboga** Sweden
127 G3 **Arbois** France
105 E4 **Árbol Solo** Bolivia
106 F6 **Arboledas** Argentina
100 B2 **Arboletes** Colombia
127 I3 **Arbon** Switzerland
75 T6 **Arborfield** Saskatchewan Canada
142 F4 **Arbroath** Angus Scotland UK
129 H3 **Arbúcies** Spain
84 A1 **Arbuckle** California USA
185 K2 **Arbulag** Mongolia
127 H4 **Arc** *watercourse* France
126 D4 **Arcachon** France
219 I1 **Arcadia** Qld Australia
87 K7 **Arcadia** Florida USA
81 P6 **Arcadia** Nebraska USA
80 C6 **Arcata** California USA
88 E5 **Arcelia** Mexico
126 F2 **Arces** France
133 F7 **Archángelos** Greece
132 C4 **Archar** Bulgaria
156 C4 **Archeï, Ouadi** *watercourse* Chad
129 F4 **Archena** Spain
214 F2 **Archer** *watercourse* Qld Australia
59 K2 **Archer Point** *cape* Antarctica
215 G2 **Archer River Roadhouse** Qld Australia
75 T6 **Archerwill** Saskatchewan Canada
131 F5 **Archi** Italy
75 Q3 **Archibald Lake** Saskatchewan Canada
128 D5 **Archidona** Spain
214 E5 **Archie** *watercourse* Qld Australia
213 J5 **Archie, Mount** NT Australia
218 B2 **Arckaringa** SA Australia
217 N3 **Arckaringa** *watercourse* SA Australia
218 B2 **Arckaringa, Mount** SA Australia
124 F5 **Arco** Italy
80 I5 **Arco** Idaho USA
124 C4 **Arconce** *watercourse* France
218 C4 **Arcoona** SA Australia
103 C8 **Arcos** Brazil
128 B3 **Arcos** Portugal
128 E3 **Arcos de Jalón** Spain
102 E5 **Arcoverde** Brazil
73 K4 **Arctic Bay** Nunavut Canada
72 B3 **Arctic Ocean**
72 F5 **Arctic Red** *watercourse* Northwest Territories Canada
59 U2 **Arctowski (Poland)** *research station* Antarctica
130 C5 **Arcu, Punta di** *cape* Corsica France
143 C3 **Ard** Ireland
178 F7 **Arḑ ar Raydah** Yemen
133 D5 **Arda** *watercourse* Bulgaria
127 I4 **Arda** *watercourse* Italy
182 E6 **Ardabīl** Iran
182 E6 **Ardabīl** *admin. area* Iran
140 B3 **Ardagh** Ireland
140 B2 **Ardaghy** Ireland
136 G5 **Ardahan** Turkey
136 G5 **Ardahan** *admin. area* Turkey
178 G3 **Ardakān** Iran
179 H3 **Ardakān** Iran
128 D5 **Ardales** Spain
120 E6 **Årdalstangen** Norway
182 G6 **Ardan** *mountain* Turkmenistan
143 D2 **Ardara** Ireland
195 G6 **Ardasier Reefs** Spratly Islands
216 F6 **Ardath** WA Australia
182 E2 **Ardatov** Russian Federation
140 B2 **Ardboe** Cookstown Northern Ireland UK
142 B4 **Ardchiavaig** Highland Scotland UK
127 G4 **Ardèche** *watercourse* France
143 F3 **Ardee** Ireland
142 D4 **Ardentinny** Argyll and Bute Scotland UK
130 D5 **Ardenza** Italy
142 D4 **Ardeonaig** Perth and Kinross Scotland UK
178 G2 **Ardestān** Iran
143 C4 **Ardfert** Ireland
142 B5 **Ardfin** Argyll and Bute Scotland UK
143 E4 **Ardfinnan** Ireland
154 E1 **Ardila** *watercourse* Spain
142 A3 **Ardivachar Point** Scotland UK
140 C2 **Ardkeen** Ards Northern Ireland UK
140 A4 **Ardlea** Ireland
142 D4 **Ardleish** Argyll and Bute Scotland UK
218 H6 **Ardlethan** NSW Australia
142 D4 **Ardlui** Argyll and Bute Scotland UK
214 E6 **Ardmore** Qld Australia
75 P5 **Ardmore** Alberta Canada
142 D3 **Ardmore** Highland Scotland UK
86 H3 **Ardmore** Alabama USA
86 C3 **Ardmore** Oklahoma USA
142 B4 **Ardnamurchan, Point of** Scotland UK
142 B5 **Ardnave Point** Scotland UK
142 D4 **Ardoch** Stirling Scotland UK
127 H3 **Ardon** Switzerland
124 A2 **Ardres** France
218 C6 **Ardrossan** SA Australia
140 C2 **Ards** *admin. area* Northern Ireland UK
142 B5 **Ardtalla** Argyll and Bute Scotland UK
132 C2 **Ardud** Romania
142 C3 **Ardvasar** Highland Scotland UK
142 D4 **Ardverikie** Highland Scotland UK
142 A3 **Ardvule, Rubha** *cape* Scotland UK
140 D2 **Ardwell** Dumfries and Galloway Scotland UK
120 H5 **Åre** Sweden
105 H5 **Areado** Brazil
103 D8 **Areal** Brazil
91 H3 **Arecibo** Puerto Rico
107 G3 **Aregua** Paraguay
102 E4 **Areia Branca** Brazil
157 F5 **Arekwa** *watercourse* Ethiopia
75 R6 **Arelee** Saskatchewan Canada
122 F3 **Aremarksjøen** *lake* Norway
195 I5 **Arena** *island* Philippines
80 C7 **Arena, Point** California USA
88 C4 **Arena, Punta** *cape* Mexico
88 C3 **Arena de la Ventana, Punta** *cape* Mexico
100 C2 **Arenal** Colombia
90 C5 **Arenal, Laguna de** *lake* Costa Rica
108 B4 **Arenales, Cerro** *mountain* Chile
105 G4 **Arenápolis** Brazil
106 D2 **Arenas, Punta** *cape* Chile
100 B4 **Arenas, Punta** *cape* Ecuador
108 C5 **Arenas, Punta de** *cape* Argentina
122 E3 **Arendal** Norway
124 F1 **Arendsee** *lake* Germany
129 F3 **Arenos, Embalse de** *lake* Spain
133 C7 **Areopoli** Greece
128 B3 **Areosa** Portugal
104 D5 **Arequipa** Peru
104 C4 **Arequipa** *admin. area* Peru
101 H5 **Arere** Brazil
161 F3 **Ārēro** Ethiopia
102 F4 **Arês** Brazil
120 H5 **Åreskutan** *mountain* Sweden
126 D5 **Arette** France
128 D3 **Arévalo** Spain
130 D5 **Arezzo** Italy
135 AE5 **Arga** Russian Federation
126 D5 **Arga** *watercourse* Spain
135 W5 **Arga-Sala** *watercourse* Russian Federation
214 D6 **Argadargada** NT Australia
190 F3 **Argalant** Mongolia
128 E4 **Argamasilla de Alba** Spain
120 G4 **Årgård** Norway
126 D5 **Argelès-Gazost** France
126 F5 **Argelès-sur-Mer** France
127 H5 **Argens** *watercourse* France
83 Q1 **Argent, Rivière à l'** *watercourse* Quebec Canada
74 M7 **Argenta** British Columbia Canada
130 D4 **Argenta** Italy
126 D2 **Argentan** France
126 E4 **Argentat** France
130 B4 **Argentera, Cima dell'** *mountain* Italy
124 D5 **Argentera, Punta** *mountain* Italy
126 F2 **Argenteuil** France
105 E6 **Argentina** *country* South America
59 V1 **Argentina Range** Antarctica
53 BB12 **Argentine Abyssal Plain** *underwater feature* Atlantic Ocean
53 AA12 **Argentine Basin** *underwater feature* Atlantic Ocean
51 N13 **Argentine Rise** *underwater feature* Atlantic Ocean
132 D3 **Argeş** *admin. area* Romania
156 E4 **Argo** Sudan
52 H9 **Argo Abyssal Plain** *underwater feature* Indian Ocean
128 E4 **Argos** *watercourse* Spain
128 F2 **Arguedas** Spain
139 I5 **Argueil** France
129 F2 **Arguís** Spain
191 I2 **Argun** *watercourse* Russian Federation
159 E2 **Argungu** Nigeria
198 E4 **Arguni, Teluk** *bay* Indonesia
191 I2 **Argunskiy Khrebet** *range* Russian Federation
59 F1 **Argus, Dome** *mountain* Antarctica
84 D2 **Argus Range** California USA
81 Q2 **Argyle** Minnesota USA
213 J4 **Argyle, Lake** WA Australia
140 C1 **Argyll and Bute** *admin. area* Scotland UK
190 E3 **Arhangay** *admin. area* Mongolia
123 J3 **Arholma** *island* Sweden
122 F4 **Århus** Denmark
190 F3 **Arhust** Mongolia
187 C11 **Ari Atoll** Maldives
199 I5 **Aria** *watercourse* Papua New Guinea
198 C2 **Ariaga** *island* Indonesia
219 H6 **Ariah Park** NSW Australia
162 C5 **Ariamsvlei** Namibia
131 D8 **Ariana** Tunisia
131 F6 **Ariano Irpino** Italy
100 C4 **Ariari** *watercourse* Colombia
105 F4 **Aribibi** Bolivia
158 D2 **Aribinda** Burkina Faso
104 D5 **Arica** Chile
100 D5 **Arica** Colombia
104 D5 **Arica, Bahía de** *lake* Peru
104 D5 **Arica-Parinacota** *admin. area* Chile
142 C4 **Arichamish** Argyll and Bute Scotland UK
100 D3 **Arichuna** *watercourse* Venezuela
216 H7 **Arid, Cape** WA Australia
216 H6 **Arid, Mount** WA Australia
193 G4 **Arida** Japan
133 C5 **Aridaia** Greece
126 E5 **Ariège** *watercourse* France
179 M3 **Arifwala** Pakistan
100 C2 **Ariguaní** Colombia
132 B4 **Arilje** Serbia
109 9 **Arima** Trinidad and Tobago
109 9 **Arima** *admin. area* Trinidad and Tobago
90 C4 **Arimís** Honduras
80 I5 **Arimo** Idaho USA
142 B4 **Arinagour** Highland Scotland UK
142 A3 **Arinambane** Na h-Eileanan Siar Scotland UK
131 E5 **Aringo** Italy
123 M5 **Arino ežeras** *lake* Lithuania
103 C6 **Arinos** Brazil
105 G3 **Arinos** *watercourse* Brazil
123 L5 **Ariogala** Lithuania
109 9 **Aripo, El Cerro del** *mountain* Trinidad and Tobago
100 D3 **Ariporo** *watercourse* Colombia
105 F3 **Aripuanã** Brazil
101 F6 **Aripuana** *watercourse* Brazil
105 F3 **Ariquemes** Brazil
142 C4 **Arisaig, Sound of** *bay* Scotland UK
85 J5 **Arispe** Texas USA
74 G6 **Aristazabal Island** British Columbia Canada
87 I5 **Ariton** Alabama USA
187 E9 **Ariyalur** Tamil Nadu India
128 E3 **Ariza** Spain
106 E3 **Arizaro, Salar de** *lake* Argentina
126 E5 **Arize** *watercourse* France
106 E5 **Arizona** Argentina
89 I6 **Arizona** Honduras
71 **Arizona** *admin. area* USA
84 G5 **Arizpe** Mexico
197 G5 **Arjasa** Indonesia
196 F5 **Arjawinangun** Indonesia
78 F5 **Arjay, Lac** *lake* Quebec Canada
120 J3 **Arjeplog** Sweden
179 H3 **Arjnū** Iran
161 F2 **Ārjo** Ethiopia
100 C2 **Arjona** Colombia
135 AD6 **Arka** Russian Federation
218 D4 **Arkaba** SA Australia
86 F3 **Arkabutla Lake** Mississippi USA
182 D3 **Arkadak** Russian Federation
86 E3 **Arkadelphia** Arkansas USA
142 C4 **Arkaig, Loch** *lake* Scotland UK
187 D9 **Arkalgud** Karnataka India
182 J3 **Arkalyk** Kazakhstan
179 H3 **Arkān** Iran
71 **Arkansas** *admin. area* USA
86 E3 **Arkansas** *watercourse* Arkansas USA
85 I1 **Arkansas** *watercourse* Colorado USA
85 L2 **Arkansas** *watercourse* Kansas USA
81 Q8 **Arkansas City** Kansas USA
218 D4 **Arkaroola Village** SA Australia
156 C3 **Arkenu, Jabal** *mountain* Libya
133 D7 **Arkesini** Greece
134 J6 **Arkhangel'sk** Russian Federation
134 J6 **Arkhangel'skaya Oblast'** *admin. area* Russian Federation
143 F4 **Arklow** Ireland
122 I3 **Arkö** *island* Sweden
133 E7 **Arkoi** *island* Greece
122 G5 **Arkona Kap** *cape* Germany
133 B6 **Arkoudi** *island* Greece
134 Q3 **Arkticheskogo Instituta, Ostrova** *islands* Russian Federation
182 F1 **Arkul** Russian Federation
126 F4 **Arlanc** France
126 C5 **Arlanza** *watercourse* Spain
126 C5 **Arlanzón, Embalse de** *lake* Spain
127 G5 **Arles** France
126 F5 **Arles-sur-Tech** France
158 E2 **Arli** Burkina Faso
85 K1 **Arlington** Colorado USA
85 M2 **Arlington** Kansas USA
80 E4 **Arlington** Oregon USA
86 C4 **Arlington** Texas USA
80 D2 **Arlington** Washington USA
155 H5 **Arlit** Niger
125 K3 **Arló** Hungary
127 G2 **Arlon** Belgium
82 D8 **Arma** Kansas USA
192 C2 **Armadires** *island* Indonesia
79 C9 **Armagh** Quebec Canada
140 B2 **Armagh** Armagh Northern Ireland UK
140 B2 **Armagh** *admin. area* Northern Ireland UK
179 H4 **Armak** Iran
124 C4 **Armançon** *watercourse* France
156 E2 **Armant** Egypt
133 E8 **Armathia** *island* Greece
219 I4 **Armatree** NSW Australia
182 D6 **Armavir** *pass* Armenia
182 D5 **Armavir** Russian Federation
182 D6 **Armenia** *country* Asia
100 C3 **Armenia** Colombia
100 B5 **Armenia** Ecuador
133 E7 **Armenistis** Greece
133 E7 **Armenistis, Akra** *cape* Greece
128 D3 **Armenteros** Spain
126 F1 **Armentières** France
131 F8 **Armi, Capo dell'** *cape* Italy
219 J4 **Armidale** NSW Australia
123 N1 **Armisvesi** *lake* Finland
199 F4 **Armopa** Indonesia
140 B1 **Armoy** Moyle Northern Ireland UK
214 E4 **Armraynald** Qld Australia
120 J5 **Armsjön** *lake* Sweden
217 L2 **Armstrong** *watercourse* NT Australia
76 K7 **Armstrong** Ontario Canada
82 D5 **Armstrong** Iowa USA
86 C3 **Armstrong** Oklahoma USA
86 C7 **Armstrong** Texas USA
193 G1 **Armu** *watercourse* Russian Federation
187 E7 **Armur** Andhra Pradesh India
133 G5 **Armutcuk** Turkey
133 C7 **Arna** Greece
126 E4 **Arnac-Pompadour** France
120 inset **Arnarfjörður** *bay* Iceland
120 inset **Arnarstapi** Iceland
78 C2 **Arnaud** *watercourse* Quebec Canada
183 K6 **Arnavad, Qullai** *mountain* Tajikistan
139 E4 **Arne** Dorset England UK
128 E2 **Arnedo** Spain
126 D5 **Arnéguy** France
120 J2 **Arnes** Norway
129 G3 **Arnes** Spain
120 F5 **Årnes** Norway
86 B2 **Arnett** Oklahoma USA
124 C2 **Arnhem** Netherlands
214 D2 **Arnhem, Cape** NT Australia
214 D2 **Arnhem Bay** NT Australia
214 C2 **Arnhem Land** *region* NT Australia
142 B3 **Arnish** Highland Scotland UK
85 K5 **Arno** Texas USA
223 15 **Arno Atoll** Marshall Islands
218 C5 **Arno Bay** SA Australia
142 B2 **Arnol** Na h-Eileanan Siar Scotland UK
214 C3 **Arnold** *watercourse* NT Australia
139 F1 **Arnold** Nottinghamshire England UK
84 B1 **Arnold** California USA
82 F7 **Arnold** Missouri USA
126 F3 **Arnon** *watercourse* France
120 L1 **Arnøya** *island* Norway
83 M4 **Arnprior** Ontario Canada
140 F2 **Arnside** Cumbria England UK
127 J1 **Arnstadt** Germany
124 G3 **Arnstorf** Germany
122 E5 **Ārø** *island* Denmark
101 E3 **Aro** *watercourse* Venezuela
162 C5 **Aroab** Namibia
164 9a **Arode, Île** *island* Seychelles
125 K4 **Ároktő** Hungary
76 L7 **Aroland** Ontario Canada
124 E2 **Arolsen** Germany
156 F4 **Aroma** Sudan
120 M5 **Aronkylä** Finland
199 J5 **Aropa** Papua New Guinea
222 1 **Arorae** *island* Kiribati
220 2 **Arorangi** Cook Islands New Zealand
130 C3 **Arosa** Switzerland
120 K3 **Årosjåkk** Sweden
85 K1 **Aroya** Colorado USA
124 B3 **Arpajon** France
131 E6 **Arpino** Italy
127 K5 **Arquata del Tronto** Italy
126 F1 **Arques** France
129 F3 **Arquillo de San Blás, Embalse del** *lake* Spain
105 H3 **Arraias** *watercourse* Brazil
90 E5 **Arraiján** Panama
128 C4 **Arraiolos** Portugal
140 C1 **Arran** *island* Scotland UK
74 K5 **Arras** British Columbia Canada
124 B2 **Arras** France
126 E5 **Arrats** *watercourse* France
219 K4 **Arrawarra** NSW Australia
126 F5 **Arre** France
126 E5 **Arreau** France
164 3d **Arrecife** Canary Islands
109 4 **Arrecife Macgowen** *reef* Archipiélago de Colón (Galapagos Islands)
106 F5 **Arrecifes** Argentina
85 I4 **Arrey** New Mexico USA
89 G5 **Arriaga** Mexico
81 N7 **Arriba** Colorado USA
105 G5 **Arrien** Paraguay
164 3d **Arrieta** Canary Islands
215 G7 **Arrilalah** Qld Australia
216 D4 **Arrino** WA Australia
128 D2 **Arriondas** Spain
107 H5 **Arroio Grande** Brazil
128 C4 **Arronches** Portugal
126 G3 **Arroux** *watercourse* France
143 D2 **Arrow, Lough** *lake* Ireland
82 F2 **Arrow Lake** Ontario Canada
86 B4 **Arrowhead, Lake** Texas USA
80 H5 **Arrowrock Reservoir** Idaho USA
221 D6 **Arrowsmith, Mount** New Zealand
214 D2 **Arrowsmith Point** NT Australia
105 E4 **Arroyo Agustin** *watercourse* Bolivia
128 C4 **Arroyo de la Luz** Spain
108 C2 **Arroyo de la Ventana** Argentina
84 B3 **Arroyo Grande** California USA
108 C3 **Arroyo Perdido** *watercourse* Argentina
108 B3 **Arroyo Pescado** Argentina
108 C2 **Arroyo Verde** Argentina
105 E4 **Arroyos, Lago de los** *lake* Bolivia
120 H4 **Årsand** Norway
179 H3 **Arsanjān** Iran
75 Q5 **Arsenault Lake** Saskatchewan Canada
193 I1 **Arsent'evka** Russian Federation
192 G2 **Arsen'yev** Russian Federation
124 F5 **Arsiè** Italy
182 F2 **Arsk** Russian Federation
136 E6 **Arslanköy** Turkey
199 G4 **Arso** Indonesia
131 E5 **Arsoli** Italy
127 G2 **Arsonval** France
120 J2 **Årstein** Norway
78 N2 **Arsuk** Greenland
78 N2 **Arsuutaa** *island* Greenland
124 B3 **Arsy** France
88 E5 **Arteaga** Mexico
85 L8 **Arteaga** Mexico
129 G3 **Artesa de Segre** Spain
85 J4 **Artesia** New Mexico USA
86 B6 **Artesia Wells** Texas USA
81 Q5 **Artesian** South Dakota USA
124 E4 **Arth** Switzerland
138 C2 **Arthog** Gwynedd Wales UK
214 D7 **Arthur** *watercourse* NT Australia
81 O6 **Arthur** Nebraska USA
81 Q3 **Arthur** North Dakota USA
218 G4 **Arthur, Lake** NSW Australia
213 H5 **Arthur, Mount** WA Australia
221 E5 **Arthur, Mount** New Zealand
221 E5 **Arthur Range** New Zealand
216 E6 **Arthur River** WA Australia
219 R10 **Arthurs Lake** Tas. Australia
221 D6 **Arthur's Pass** New Zealand
91 F1 **Arthur's Town** Bahamas
107 G4 **Artigas** Uruguay
107 G4 **Artigas** *admin. area* Uruguay
59 U2 **Artigas (Uruguay)** *research station* Antarctica
182 D6 **Ar'tik** Armenia
72 I6 **Artillery Lake** Northwest Territories Canada
178 E1 **Artish** Iraq
136 F3 **Art'omovsk** Ukraine
135 X7 **Artomovskiy** Russian Federation
129 H4 **Artrutx, Cap d'** *cape* Spain
190 E4 **Arts Bogd Uul** Mongolia
127 H5 **Artuby** *watercourse* France
59 U2 **Arturo Prat (Chile)** *research station* Antarctica
136 G5 **Artvin** Turkey
136 G5 **Artvin** *admin. area* Turkey
135 AE6 **Artyk** Russian Federation
100 E4 **Aru** Brazil
198 E5 **Aru, Kepulauan** *islands* Indonesia
160 E3 **Arua** Uganda
103 B6 **Aruanã** Brazil
100 D1 **Aruba** *admin. area* Caribbean Netherlands Antilles
217 I5 **Arubiddy** WA Australia
164 3b **Arucas** Canary Islands
126 D5 **Arudy** France
223 14a **Arue** French Polynesia
105 F2 **Arumã** Brazil
101 F4 **Arumã, Serra do** *range* Brazil
101 F4 **Arumim** Brazil
186 G5 **Arun** *watercourse* Nepal
139 G4 **Arun** *watercourse* England UK
181 H3 **Arunachal Pradesh** *admin. area* India
139 G4 **Arundel** West Sussex England UK
198 B3 **Arus, Tanjung** *cape* Indonesia
161 F4 **Arusha** Tanzania
161 F4 **Arusha** *admin. area* Tanzania
197 F4 **Arut** *watercourse* Indonesia
160 C3 **Aruwimi** *watercourse* Democratic Republic of Congo
81 M7 **Arvada** Colorado USA
143 E3 **Arvagh** Ireland
85 L4 **Arvana** Texas USA
190 E3 **Arvayheer** Mongolia
108 A2 **Arvejas, Punta** *cape* Chile
120 K3 **Arvesjaure** *lake* Sweden
75 X2 **Arviat** Nunavut Canada
120 K4 **Arvidsjaur** Sweden
120 K4 **Arvidsjaursjön** *lake* Sweden
122 G3 **Arvika** Sweden
120 L1 **Årviksand** Norway
84 C3 **Arvin** California USA
131 G7 **Arvo, Lago** *lake* Italy
186 F6 **Arwal** Bihar India
198 C5 **Arwala** Indonesia
183 J5 **Arys'** Kazakhstan
131 C6 **Arzachena** Italy
126 D5 **Arzacq-Arraziquet** France
182 D2 **Arzamas** Russian Federation
178 G5 **Arzanah** *island* United Arab Emirates
179 I2 **Arzaneh** Iran
155 F1 **Arzew** Algeria
182 D4 **Arzgir** Russian Federation
127 H3 **Arzier** Switzerland
124 C2 **As** Belgium
124 G2 **Aš** Czech Republic
122 F3 **Ås** Norway
156 E2 **Aş Şaff** Egypt
156 D2 **Aş Şaḩrā' al Gharbīyah** *desert* Egypt
178 B4 **Aş Şaḩrā' Ash Sharqīyah** Egypt
156 D1 **As Sallūm** Egypt
178 C3 **As Salţ** Jordan
178 F3 **As Samāwah** Iraq
136 F6 **Aş Sarāyim** Syria
178 F5 **As Sayḩ** Saudi Arabia
179 I5 **As Sib** Oman
178 B5 **As Subū'** Egypt
178 F2 **As Sulaymānīyah** Iraq
178 F6 **As Sulayyil** Saudi Arabia
155 J2 **As Sulţān** Libya
178 E5 **As Sūq** Saudi Arabia
136 G6 **Aş Şuwar** Syria
136 F7 **As Suwaydā'** Syria
179 I5 **As Suwayq** Oman
156 E2 **As Suways (Suez)** Egypt
160 D3 **Asa** *watercourse* Democratic Republic of Congo
122 F4 **Aså** Denmark
159 F3 **Asaba** Nigeria
179 L2 **Asadābād** Afghanistan
178 F2 **Asadābād** Iran
108 B4 **Asador, Pampa del** *region* Argentina
133 E5 **Aşağıinova** Turkey
136 H6 **Asagikiran** Turkey
196 C3 **Asahan** *watercourse* Indonesia
193 I4 **Asahi** Japan
193 I2 **Asahi-dake** *volcano* Japan
193 I2 **Asahikawa** Japan
179 J3 **Asaji** Iran
157 G5 **Āsalē** *lake* Ethiopia
222 5 **Asan** Guam
192 E4 **Asan** South Korea
192 E4 **Asan-man** *bay* South Korea
186 G6 **Asansol** West Bengal India
123 M4 **Asare** Latvia
120 I5 **Åsarna** Sweden
222 5 **Asatdas** Guam
223 12c **Asau** Samoa
157 G5 **Āsayita** Ethiopia
124 D2 **Asbach** Germany
182 F7 **Asbak** Iran
105 F4 **Ascensión** Bolivia
88 D2 **Ascensión** Mexico
90 C3 **Ascensión, Bahía de la** *bay* Mexico
51 R10 **Ascension Fracture Zone** *underwater feature* Atlantic Ocean
124 E3 **Aschaffenburg** Germany
129 G3 **Ascó** Spain
130 E5 **Ascoli Piceno** Italy
127 I3 **Ascona** Switzerland
104 B2 **Ascope** Peru
120 I2 **Åse** Norway
161 F2 **Āsela** Ethiopia
120 J4 **Åsele** Sweden
121 N4 **Asemankylä** Finland
161 E4 **Asembo** Kenya
122 G2 **Åsen** Sweden
108 C6 **Aserradero La Paciencia** Chile
85 I7 **Aserradero Yerbitas** Mexico
90 D5 **Aserrío de Gariché** Panama
182 H6 **Aşgabat (Ashgabat)** Turkmenistan
141 H3 **Asgarby** Lincolnshire England UK
185 J2 **Asgat** Mongolia
139 I3 **Ash** Kent England UK
84 F3 **Ash Fork** Arizona USA
82 E8 **Ash Grove** Missouri USA
178 E6 **Ash Sharafá** Saudi Arabia
179 H4 **Ash Shāriqah** United Arab Emirates
178 C4 **Ash Sharmah, Wādī** *watercourse* Saudi Arabia
178 G5 **Ash Sharqīyah** *admin. area* Saudi Arabia
178 F3 **Ash Shaţrah** Iraq
178 E3 **Ash Shawmalī** Iraq
178 G7 **Ash Shiḩr** Yemen
155 I2 **Ash Shuwayrif** Libya
87 J5 **Ashburn** Georgia USA
212 C7 **Ashburton** *watercourse* WA Australia
221 D6 **Ashburton** New Zealand
216 E1 **Ashburton Downs** WA Australia
182 J5 **Ashchikol'** *lake* Kazakhstan
182 I3 **Ashchitastysor** *lake* Kazakhstan
74 K7 **Ashcroft** British Columbia Canada
178 C3 **Ashdod** Israel
86 D4 **Ashdown** Arkansas USA
139 H3 **Asheldham** Essex England UK
86 B6 **Asherton** Texas USA
87 J3 **Asheville** North Carolina USA
123 O4 **Ashevo** Russian Federation
76 L5 **Asheweig** *watercourse* Ontario Canada
139 H3 **Ashford** Kent England UK
87 I5 **Ashford** Alabama USA
Ashgabat *see* **Aşgabat** Turkmenistan
193 H4 **Ashikaga** Japan
192 F5 **Ashikita** Japan
155 I3 **Ashkīdah** Libya
142 F5 **Ashkirk** Scottish Borders Scotland UK
81 P8 **Ashland** Kansas USA
82 J7 **Ashland** Kentucky USA
83 Q3 **Ashland** Maine USA
83 J6 **Ashland** Ohio USA
80 D5 **Ashland** Oregon USA
83 M8 **Ashland** Virginia USA
82 F3 **Ashland** Wisconsin USA
219 I3 **Ashley** NSW Australia
221 E6 **Ashley** *watercourse* New Zealand
141 F3 **Ashley** Cheshire England UK
82 G7 **Ashley** Illinois USA
81 P3 **Ashley** North Dakota USA
80 H2 **Ashley Lake** Montana USA
75 P5 **Ashmont** Alberta Canada
139 E4 **Ashmore** Dorset England UK
213 G2 **Ashmore and Cartier Islands** *Australian territory* Indian Ocean
210 inset **Ashmore Reef** Ashmore Reef and Cartier Island Australia
123 M5 **Ashmyany** Belarus
186 D6 **Ashoknagar** Madhya Pradesh India
138 E2 **Ashperton** Herefordshire England UK
138 D4 **Ashprington** Devon England UK
186 D6 **Ashta** Madhya Pradesh India
83 K6 **Ashtabula** Ohio USA
82 C3 **Ashtabula, Lake** North Dakota USA
187 C7 **Ashtami** Maharashtra India
182 D6 **Ashtarak** Armenia
109 11 **Ashton** St Vincent and the Grenadines
80 J4 **Ashton** Idaho USA
139 F3 **Ashton Keynes** Wiltshire England UK
77 V6 **Ashuanipi** Newfoundland and Labrador Canada
78 E6 **Ashuanipi** *watercourse* Newfoundland and Labrador Canada
78 E6 **Ashuanipi Lake** Newfoundland and Labrador Canada
83 O2 **Ashuapmuchuan** *watercourse* Quebec Canada
87 H4 **Ashville** Alabama USA
108 B5 **Asia, Estero** *bay* Chile
104 B4 **Asia, Isla** *island* Peru
198 D3 **Asia, Kepulauan** *islands* Indonesia
130 D4 **Asiago** Italy
101 F4 **Asiasito** Venezuela
195 I4 **Asid Gulf** Philippines
187 E7 **Asifabad** Andhra Pradesh India
187 F7 **Asika** Orissa India
123 M2 **Asikkalanselkä** *bay* Finland
154 E1 **Asilah** Morocco
104 D4 **Asillo** Peru
131 C6 **Asinara, Golfo dell'** *bay* Italy
186 D6 **Asind** Rajasthan India
183 O2 **Asino** Russian Federation
136 D2 **Asipovichy** Belarus
178 E6 **'Asīr** *admin. area* Saudi Arabia
156 F4 **Asis, Ras** *cape* Sudan
121 O3 **Aska** Finland
136 G5 **Aşkale** Turkey
122 F3 **Asker** Norway
141 G3 **Askern** South Yorkshire England UK
142 A3 **Askernish** Na h-Eileanan Siar Scotland UK
76 H5 **Askikkapit** Manitoba Canada
183 P2 **Askiz** Russian Federation
122 I3 **Askö** *island* Sweden
120 L4 **Åskogen** Sweden
122 C2 **Askøy** *island* Norway
179 L2 **Asmār** Afghanistan
157 F4 **Asmara** Eritrea
122 F5 **Asnæs** Denmark
122 H4 **Åsnen** *bay* Sweden
192 F5 **Aso** Japan
193 G4 **Aso-kai** *lake* Japan
192 F5 **Aso-san** *volcano* Japan
101 G4 **Asoenangka** Brazil
124 F5 **Asolo** Italy
181 H3 **Asonli** Arunachal Pradesh India
198 F4 **Asori** Indonesia
133 B6 **Ásos** Greece
156 E5 **Āsosa** Ethiopia
156 F3 **Asoteriba, Jebel** *mountain* Sudan
178 G3 **Āspās** Iran
120 I5 **Aspås** Sweden
140 E2 **Aspatria** Cumbria England UK
120 J5 **Aspeå** Sweden
81 L7 **Aspen** Colorado USA
74 K8 **Aspen Grove** British Columbia Canada
122 F3 **Asperen** *lake* Norway
86 A4 **Aspermont** Texas USA
182 D5 **Aspindza** Georgia
221 C7 **Aspiring, Mt (Tititea)** New Zealand
120 H4 **Aspneset** Norway
122 H4 **Aspö** *island* Sweden
122 I3 **Aspöja** *island* Sweden
127 G4 **Aspres-sur-Buëch** France
133 A6 **Asprokavos, Akra** *cape* Greece
120 K5 **Aspsele** Sweden
190 F3 **Asralt Hairhan** *mountain* Mongolia
154 E3 **Assa** Morocco
157 G5 **Assab** Eritrea
104 D1 **Assacaio** Brazil
103 B8 **Assaí** Brazil
157 G5 **Assal, Lac** *lake* Djibouti
181 G3 **Assam** *admin. area* India
102 E4 **Assaré** Brazil
124 C2 **Asse** Belgium
130 B4 **Asse** *watercourse* France
131 C7 **Assemini** Italy
124 D1 **Assen** Netherlands
126 F1 **Assenede** Belgium
79 F7 **Assigny, Lac** *lake* Newfoundland and Labrador Canada
159 H2 **Assinet** Chad
82 A2 **Assiniboine** *watercourse* Manitoba Canada
80 H1 **Assiniboine, Mount** British Columbia Canada
83 N1 **Assinica, Lac** *lake* Quebec Canada
103 B8 **Assis** Brazil
130 E5 **Assisi** Italy
124 E2 **Aßlar** Germany
164 4a **Assomada** Cape Verde
164 9 **Assumption** *island* Seychelles
142 C2 **Assynt, Loch** *lake* Scotland UK
126 E4 **Astaffort** France
135 AC5 **Astakh** Russian Federation
178 A2 **Astakida** *island* Greece
183 K3 **Astana** Kazakhstan
120 J3 **Ästansjö** Sweden
182 E6 **Āstārā** Iran
138 E1 **Astbury** Cheshire England UK
123 L3 **Aste** Estonia
125 H3 **Asten** Austria
124 E5 **Asti** Italy
120 J5 **Åstön** *island* Sweden
138 E1 **Aston** Cheshire England UK
107 I2 **Astorga** Brazil
128 C2 **Astorga** Spain
164 9 **Astove** *island* Seychelles
182 E4 **Astrakhan'** Russian Federation
182 E4 **Astrakhanskaya Oblast'** *admin. area* Russian Federation
120 K4 **Åsträsk** Sweden
77 V5 **Astray** Newfoundland and Labrador Canada
100 C2 **Astrea** Colombia
59 A2 **Astrid Ridge** *underwater feature* Southern Ocean
133 B6 **Astrochórion** Greece
222 8 **Astrolabe, Cape** Solomon Islands
222 7 **Astrolabe Reefs** Vanuatu
128 D2 **Astudillo** Spain
128 C2 **Asturias** *admin. area* Spain
133 E7 **Astypalaia** *island* Greece
222 2 **Asuncion** *island* Northern Mariana Islands
107 G3 **Asunción** Paraguay
90 B4 **Asunción Mita** Guatemala
89 F5 **Asunción Nochixtlán** Mexico
122 H4 **Åsunden** *lake* Sweden
131 C7 **Asuni** Italy
178 G2 **Āsūr** Iran
120 H3 **Åsvaer** *island* Norway
123 M5 **Asvejos ežeras** *lake* Lithuania
178 D5 **Aswad, Ar Ra's al** *cape* Saudi Arabia
156 E3 **Aswān** Egypt
156 E2 **Asyūţ** Egypt
194 D4 **At Samat** Thailand
178 C3 **Aţ Ţafīlah** Jordan
178 D5 **Aţ Ţā'if** Saudi Arabia
156 C3 **At Tāj** Libya
178 D5 **Aţ Ţuwāl** Saudi Arabia
198 C6 **Atabae** Timor-Leste (East Timor)
106 D3 **Atacama** *admin. area* Chile
106 D3 **Atacama, Desierto de** *desert* Chile
106 D2 **Atacama, Salar de** *lake* Chile
101 H4 **Atachi Bakka, Monts** *range* French Guiana
100 C4 **Ataco** Colombia
220 3 **Atafu** *island* Tokelau New Zealand
220 3 **Atafu Village** Tokelau New Zealand
158 E2 **Atakora, Châine de l'** *range* Benin
158 E3 **Atakpamé** Togo
128 B5 **Atalaia, Ponta da** *cape* Portugal
106 E6 **Ataliva Roca** Argentina
198 C6 **Atambua** Indonesia
182 J6 **Atamyrat** Turkmenistan
197 H2 **Atap** Indonesia
104 D4 **Atapata** Peru
178 F7 **'Atāq** Yemen
132 E4 **Ataqnasovsko Ezero** *lake* Bulgaria
154 D4 **Atâr** Mauritania
100 D2 **Atarigua, Embalse** *lake* Venezuela
186 E6 **Atarra** Uttar Pradesh India
Atas *see* **South Island** Australia
185 J4 **Atas Bogd** *mountain* Mongolia
84 B3 **Atascadero** California USA
123 N4 **Atašiene** Latvia
183 K4 **Atasu** Kazakhstan
185 I5 **Atatkan He** *watercourse* Xinjiang Uygur Zizhiqu China
136 F6 **Atatürk Barajı** *lake* Turkey
156 F5 **Atbara** *watercourse* Ethiopia
156 E4 **Atbara** Sudan
156 E4 **Atbara** *watercourse* Sudan
183 J3 **Atbasar** Kazakhstan
156 F3 **Atbāy** *range* Sudan
86 F6 **Atchafalaya Bay** Louisiana USA
82 D7 **Atchison** Kansas USA
101 F3 **Atenas** Venezuela
131 F5 **Atessa** Italy
124 B2 **Ath** Belgium
142 B2 **Ath Linne** Na h-Eileanan Siar Scotland UK
156 E2 **Ath Thamad** Egypt
75 O5 **Athabasca** Alberta Canada
75 P3 **Athabasca, Lake** Alberta/Saskatchewan Canada
80 G1 **Athalmer** British Columbia Canada
75 U5 **Athapap** Manitoba Canada
143 F3 **Athboy** Ireland
143 D3 **Athenry** Ireland
Athens *see* **Athina** Greece
86 H3 **Athens** Alabama USA
87 J4 **Athens** Georgia USA
83 J7 **Athens** Ohio USA
87 I3 **Athens** Tennessee USA
86 D4 **Athens** Texas USA
86 D4 **Athens, Lake** Texas USA
133 B6 **Atheras** Greece
133 B6 **Atheras, Akra** *cape* Greece
139 F2 **Atherstone** Warwickshire England UK
215 H4 **Atherton** Qld Australia
215 K7 **Atherton, Mount** Qld Australia
161 F4 **Athi** *watercourse* Kenya
133 C7 **Athina (Athens)** Greece
143 E3 **Athlone** Ireland
74 E6 **Athlow Bay** British Columbia Canada
221 C7 **Athol** New Zealand
80 G3 **Athol** Idaho USA
143 F4 **Athy** Ireland
156 B5 **Ati** Chad
155 J6 **Ati Ardébé** Chad
160 E3 **Atiak** Uganda
103 C8 **Atibaia** Brazil
79 I7 **Aticonipi, Lac** *lake* Quebec Canada
160 D2 **Atiedo** Sudan
128 E3 **Atienza** Spain
75 U5 **Atik** Manitoba Canada
76 H5 **Atik Lake** Manitoba Canada
75 N5 **Atikameg** Alberta Canada
77 N7 **Atikameg** *watercourse* Ontario Canada
78 F6 **Atikonak** *watercourse* Newfoundland and Labrador Canada
78 F6 **Atikonak Lake** Newfoundland and Labrador Canada
82 E2 **Atikwa Lake** Ontario Canada
108 B3 **Atilio, Isla** *island* Chile
131 E6 **Atina** Italy
220 1 **Atiu** *island* Cook Islands New Zealand
135 AF6 **Atka** Russian Federation
59 X2 **Atka Iceport** Antarctica
135 AL8 **Atka Island** Alaska USA
182 D3 **Atkarsk** Russian Federation
81 P5 **Atkinson** Nebraska USA
87 I4 **Atlanta** Georgia USA
82 I4 **Atlanta** Michigan USA
81 P6 **Atlanta** Nebraska USA
83 N7 **Atlantic City** New Jersey USA
51 S16 **Atlantic–Indian Antarctic Basin** *underwater feature* Southern Ocean
51 T15 **Atlantic–Indian Ridge** *underwater feature* Southern Ocean
50 **Atlantic Ocean**
100 C2 **Atlantico** *admin. area* Colombia
162 C6 **Atlantis** South Africa
50 N6 **Atlantis Fracture Zone** *underwater feature* Atlantic Ocean
54 J8 **Atlantis II Fracture Zone** *underwater feature* Indian Ocean
108 D3 **Atlas, Punta** *cape* Argentina
135 AG8 **Atlasova, Ostrov** *island* Kuril Islands
214 A6 **Atlee** *watercourse* NT Australia
81 J1 **Atlee** Alberta Canada
74 E3 **Atlin** British Columbia Canada
74 E3 **Atlin Lake** British Columbia Canada
122 C2 **Atløy** *island* Norway
75 O5 **Atmore** Alberta Canada
86 H5 **Atmore** Alabama USA
120 G6 **Atna** Norway
74 I6 **Atnarko** British Columbia Canada
120 G6 **Atnfoss** Norway
105 E6 **Atocha** Bolivia
133 B6 **Atokos** *island* Greece
84 D3 **Atolia** California USA
162 B2 **Atome** Angola
122 H3 **Åtorp** Sweden
89 F5 **Atoyac** *watercourse* Mexico
88 E5 **Atoyac de Álvarez** Mexico
72 D4 **Atqasuk** Alaska USA
122 G4 **Ätran** Sweden
122 G4 **Ätran** *watercourse* Sweden
100 B3 **Atrato** *watercourse* Colombia
106 F6 **Atreucó** Argentina
199 F5 **Atsy** Indonesia
142 C3 **Attadale** Highland Scotland UK
140 A4 **Attanagh** Ireland
194 E4 **Attapu** Laos
77 N6 **Attawapiskat** Ontario Canada
76 L6 **Attawapiskat Lake** Ontario Canada
83 P4 **Attean Pond** Maine USA
141 H3 **Atterby** Lincolnshire England UK
124 C3 **Attert** *watercourse* Luxembourg
81 P8 **Attica** Kansas USA
124 B3 **Attichy** France
127 G2 **Attigny** France
78 E5 **Attikamagen Lake** Newfoundland and Labrador Canada
133 C7 **Attiki** *admin. area* Greece
218 D3 **Attraction Hill** SA Australia
135 AJ8 **Attu** Alaska USA
135 AJ8 **Attu Island** Alaska USA
182 G7 **Atū** Iran
106 D5 **Atuel** *watercourse* Argentina
214 D7 **Atula** NT Australia
214 C7 **Atula** *watercourse* NT Australia
161 E3 **Atura** Uganda
184 E5 **Atushi** Xinjiang Uygur Zizhiqu China
75 T7 **Atwater** Saskatchewan Canada
81 R4 **Atwater** Minnesota USA
141 H3 **Atwick** East Riding of Yorkshire England UK
81 O7 **Atwood** Kansas USA
182 F4 **Atyrau** Kazakhstan
182 F4 **Atyrauskaya Oblast'** *admin. area* Kazakhstan
130 C3 **Au** Austria
124 F3 **Au** Germany
82 J4 **Au Sable** *watercourse* Michigan USA
199 G4 **Aua Island** Papua New Guinea
90 C4 **Auas** Honduras
127 G5 **Aubagne** France
195 I3 **Aubarede Point** Philippines
126 G2 **Aube** *watercourse* France
124 C2 **Aubel** Belgium
124 C5 **Aubenas** France
126 F4 **Aubière** France
126 F4 **Aubin** France
126 F4 **Aubrac** France
126 F4 **Aubrac** *region* France
72 G5 **Aubry Lake** Northwest Territories Canada
219 J2 **Auburn** *watercourse* Qld Australia
218 D6 **Auburn** SA Australia
87 I4 **Auburn** Alabama USA
80 E7 **Auburn** California USA
82 I6 **Auburn** Indiana USA
83 M5 **Auburn** New York USA
219 J1 **Auburn Range** Qld Australia
126 F4 **Aubusson** France

106 D6 **Aucá Mahuida, Sierra de** *mountain* Argentina
126 E5 **Auch** France
142 D4 **Auch** Argyll and Bute Scotland UK
142 C5 **Auchamore** North Ayrshire Scotland UK
142 E4 **Auchavan** Angus Scotland UK
126 F1 **Auchel** France
142 E6 **Auchencairn** Dumfries and Galloway Scotland UK
159 F3 **Auchi** Nigeria
220 F3 **Auckland** New Zealand
220 F3 **Auckland** *admin. area* New Zealand
194 C4 **Auckland Bay** Myanmar
221 8 **Auckland Island** New Zealand
126 D5 **Aucun** France
126 F5 **Aude** *watercourse* France
76 L7 **Auden** Ontario Canada
139 F5 **Auderville** France
127 G3 **Audeux** France
126 B2 **Audierne** France
126 B3 **Audierne, Baie d'** *bay* France
130 B3 **Audincourt** France
138 E2 **Audlem** Cheshire England UK
161 G2 **Audo Range** Ethiopia
123 M3 **Audru** Estonia
139 J4 **Audruicq** France
127 K1 **Aue** Germany
127 K1 **Auerbach** Germany
218 H1 **Augathella** Qld Australia
140 A2 **Augher** Dungannon Northern Ireland UK
140 B2 **Aughnacloy** Dungannon Northern Ireland UK
143 C2 **Aughness** Ireland
143 F4 **Aughrim** Ireland
124 F3 **Augsburg** Germany
216 D7 **Augusta** WA Australia
87 K4 **Augusta** Georgia USA
81 Q8 **Augusta** Kansas USA
83 Q4 **Augusta** Maine USA
131 F8 **Augusta, Golfo di** *bay* Italy
72 D7 **Augustine Island** Alaska USA
102 C3 **Augusto Corrêa** Brazil
216 E2 **Augustus, Mount** WA Australia
214 E5 **Augustus Downs** Qld Australia
213 H3 **Augustus Island** WA Australia
90 D4 **Auka** Honduras
120 F5 **Aukan** Norway
121 M3 **Aukea** Sweden
222 8 **Auki** Solomon Islands
120 E5 **Aukra** Norway
213 G7 **Auld, Lake** WA Australia
156 E4 **Aulia** Sudan
130 C4 **Aulla** Italy
126 D3 **Aulnay** France
126 C2 **Aulne** *watercourse* France
82 D2 **Aulneau Peninsula** Ontario Canada
126 E3 **Aulong** France
222 3 **Aulong** *island* Palau
120 G6 **Aulstad** Norway
126 E1 **Ault** France
142 C3 **Aultbea** Highland Scotland UK
139 I5 **Aumale** France
120 H5 **Aumen** *bay* Sweden
124 C3 **Aumetz** France
80 D4 **Aumsville** Oregon USA
159 E2 **Auna** Nigeria
187 E7 **Aundhi** Maharashtra India
126 E2 **Auneau** France
Aunglan *see* **Myede** Myanmar
126 D3 **Aunis** *region* France
223 12c **Aunu'u** *island* American Samoa
77 U3 **Aupaluk** Quebec Canada
198 C4 **Auponhia** Indonesia
127 H5 **Aups** France
196 E3 **Aur** *island* Malaysia
223 15 **Aur Atoll** Marshall Islands
186 E5 **Auraiya** Uttar Pradesh India
186 F6 **Aurangabad** Bihar India
187 D7 **Aurangabad** Maharashtra India
214 B1 **Aurari Bay** NT Australia
126 C3 **Auray** France
126 D2 **Aure** *watercourse* France
120 F5 **Aure** Norway
126 D4 **Aureilhan, Étang d'** *lake* France
121 M5 **Aurejärvi** *lake* Finland
198 E4 **Auri, Kepulauan** *islands* Indonesia
124 D1 **Aurich** Germany
103 B8 **Auriflama** Brazil
126 E5 **Aurignac** France
126 F4 **Aurillac** France
129 I2 **Auriol** France
129 F2 **Auritz** Spain
126 F3 **Auron** *watercourse* France
102 E4 **Aurora** Brazil
101 G3 **Aurora** Guyana
81 M7 **Aurora** Colorado USA
82 G6 **Aurora** Illinois USA
82 I7 **Aurora** Indiana USA
87 M3 **Aurora** North Carolina USA
105 F3 **Aurora, Serra da** *range* Brazil
211 inset **Aurora Point** *cape* Macquarie Island Australia
120 K2 **Aursfjordgård** Norway
122 E2 **Aursjøen** *lake* Norway
122 F1 **Aursunden** *lake* Norway
214 F2 **Aurukun** Qld Australia
162 C5 **Aus** Namibia
186 G6 **Ausgram** West Bengal India
142 F1 **Auskerry** *island* Scotland UK
122 D3 **Aust-Agder** *admin. area* Norway
122 E3 **Austad** Norway
120 G4 **Austafjord** Norway
122 E3 **Austbø** Norway
120 H4 **Austborg** Norway
141 G3 **Austerfield** South Yorkshire England UK
121 P1 **Austertana** Norway
121 Q1 **Austhavet** *bay* Norway
81 P2 **Austin** Manitoba Canada
82 E5 **Austin** Minnesota USA
84 D1 **Austin** Nevada USA
86 C5 **Austin** Texas USA
216 F3 **Austin, Lake** WA Australia
86 D6 **Austin, Lake** Texas USA
216 E3 **Austin Downs** WA Australia
76 I2 **Austin Island** Nunavut Canada
122 G2 **Austmarka** Norway
120 H4 **Austnes** Norway
120 G4 **Austra** *island* Norway
214 D6 **Austral Downs** NT Australia
223 14 **Australes, Îles** *admin. area* French Polynesia
198 E7 **Australia** *country* Oceania
52 F13 **Australian-Antarctic Basin** *underwater feature* Southern Ocean
211 N8 **Australian Capital Territory** *admin. area* Australia
122 C3 **Austre Bokn** *island* Norway
130 E3 **Austria** *country* Europe
120 inset **Austurland** *admin. area* Iceland
120 I2 **Austvågøy** *island* Norway
105 G1 **Autazes** Brazil
126 E5 **Auterive** France
126 F2 **Auteuil** France
126 E1 **Authie** *watercourse* France
126 E3 **Authion** *watercourse* France
218 H2 **Authoringa** Qld Australia
128 E2 **Autol** Spain
136 E4 **Autonomous Republic of Krym** *admin. area* Ukraine
121 O3 **Autti** Finland
123 M2 **Auttoinen** Finland
218 F2 **Autumn Vale** Qld Australia
126 F4 **Auvergne** *admin. area* France
126 F4 **Auvergne** *region* France
126 E4 **Auvézère** *watercourse* France
126 F3 **Auxerre** France
126 F2 **Auxon** France
101 F3 **Auyan-Tepui** *mountain* Venezuela
126 F3 **Auzances** France
82 E8 **Ava** Missouri USA
187 E9 **Avadi** Tamil Nadu India
120 M3 **Avafors** Sweden
223 13a **Avalau** *island* Tuvalu
126 F3 **Avallon** France
84 C4 **Avalon** California USA
79 L9 **Avalon Peninsula** Newfoundland and Labrador Canada
182 D5 **Avalov** Russian Federation
120 L4 **Avan** Sweden
182 F7 **Āvānak** Iran
178 G3 **Avanjān** Iran
86 C2 **Avant** Oklahoma USA
103 B8 **Avaré** Brazil
220 1 **Avarua** Cook Islands New Zealand
220 4 **Avatele** Niue New Zealand
220 2 **Avatiu** Cook Islands New Zealand
120 J4 **Avaträsk** Sweden
120 K4 **Avaviken** Sweden
179 H4 **Avaz** Iran
133 D5 **Avdira** Greece
101 F3 **Ave Chica** Venezuela
128 B3 **Aveiro** Portugal
128 B3 **Aveiro** *admin. area* Portugal
124 B2 **Avelgem** Belgium
131 F6 **Avellino** Italy
84 B3 **Avenal** California USA
179 H4 **Avenān** Iran
128 B3 **Aver-o-Mar** Portugal
122 H3 **Avern** *lake* Sweden
122 F5 **Avernakø** *island* Denmark
122 D1 **Averøya** *island* Norway
131 F6 **Aversa** Italy
91 I4 **Aves** *island* Venezuela
50 L8 **Aves Ridge** *underwater feature* Caribbean Sea
122 I2 **Avesta** Sweden
131 G6 **Avetrana** Italy
126 E4 **Aveyron** *watercourse* France
130 E3 **Aviano** Italy
142 E3 **Aviemore** Highland Scotland UK
221 D7 **Aviemore, Lake** New Zealand
127 G5 **Avignon** France
128 D3 **Ávila** Spain
128 D2 **Avilés** Spain
123 M5 **Avilių ežeras** *lake* Lithuania
100 D3 **Avimi** Colombia
215 H8 **Avington** Qld Australia
124 C3 **Avioth** France
133 E7 **Avlakia** Greece
133 C7 **Avlemonas** Greece
218 F7 **Avoca** Vic. Australia
218 F7 **Avoca** *watercourse* Vic. Australia
143 F4 **Avoca** Ireland
221 D6 **Avoca** New Zealand
142 D3 **Avoch** Highland Scotland UK
217 N7 **Avoid Bay** SA Australia
74 L7 **Avola** British Columbia Canada
124 B3 **Avon** France
139 E3 **Avon** *watercourse* England UK
142 E3 **Avon** *watercourse* Scotland UK
83 J6 **Avon** Ohio USA
214 D6 **Avon Downs** NT Australia
87 K7 **Avon Park** Florida USA
138 E3 **Avonmouth** Bristol England UK
132 E1 **Avratin** Ukraine
126 E2 **Avre** *watercourse* France
132 D3 **Avrig** Romania
126 D3 **Avrillé** France
130 H5 **Avtovac** Bosnia and Herzegovina
222 8 **Avu Avu** Solomon Islands
220 F4 **Awakino** *watercourse* New Zealand
178 G4 **'Awālī** Bahrain
197 H6 **Awang** Indonesia
197 G5 **Awarawar, Tanjung** *cape* Indonesia
161 G2 **Āwarē** Ethiopia
221 C7 **Awarua Point** *cape* New Zealand
101 G4 **Awaruwaunawa** Guyana
161 F2 **Āwasa** Ethiopia
161 F2 **Awasa, Lake** Ethiopia
161 G2 **Āwash** Ethiopia
157 G5 **Āwash Wenz** *watercourse* Ethiopia
161 F2 **Awata** *watercourse* Ethiopia
221 E5 **Awatere** *watercourse* New Zealand
184 F5 **Awati** Xinjiang Uygur Zizhiqu China
157 I3 **Awbārī** Libya
155 G5 **Awdal** *admin. area* Somalia
178 F4 **'Awdat Sudayr** Saudi Arabia
159 F3 **Awe** Nigeria
142 C4 **Awe, Loch** *lake* Scotland UK
160 D2 **Aweil** Sudan
87 L4 **Awendaw** South Carolina USA
156 F5 **Awgaro** Eritrea
199 H4 **Awin Island** Papua New Guinea
199 I5 **Awio Bay** Papua New Guinea
156 C2 **Awjilah** Libya
159 F3 **Awka** Nigeria
199 H6 **Awoma** Papua New Guinea
215 K8 **Awoonga Lake** Qld Australia
154 D4 **Awserd** Western Sahara
159 E3 **Awun** *watercourse* Nigeria
126 E5 **Ax-les-Thermes** France
124 F4 **Axams** Austria
73 J3 **Axel Heiberg Island** Nunavut Canada
158 D4 **Axim** Ghana
133 C5 **Axios** *watercourse* Greece
122 I2 **Axmar** Sweden
138 E4 **Axminster** Devon England UK
89 F5 **Axochiapan** Mexico
183 M4 **Ay** Kazakhstan
104 B2 **Ayabaca** Peru
108 B3 **Ayacara** Chile
154 F2 **Ayachi, Jbel** *mountain* Morocco
107 G6 **Ayacucho** Argentina
104 C4 **Ayacucho** Peru
104 C4 **Ayacucho** *admin. area* Peru
181 H4 **Ayadaw** Myanmar
183 M4 **Ayagoz** Kazakhstan
183 M4 **Ayagoz** *watercourse* Kazakhstan
182 I6 **Ayakguzhumdy** Uzbekistan
135 U4 **Ayakli** *watercourse* Russian Federation
158 D3 **Ayamé** Côte d'Ivoire
158 D3 **Ayamé, Lac d'** *lake* Côte d'Ivoire
159 G4 **Ayamikem** Equatorial Guinea
100 A5 **Ayampe, Punta** *cape* Ecuador
135 AC7 **Ayan** Russian Federation
135 T5 **Ayan** *watercourse* Russian Federation
136 E5 **Ayancık** Turkey
158 D3 **Ayanfuri** Ghana
159 F3 **Ayangba** Nigeria
135 AI6 **Ayanka** Russian Federation
104 D4 **Ayapata** Peru
100 C2 **Ayapel** Colombia
100 B5 **Ayasa** Ecuador
135 V7 **Ayava** Russian Federation
183 J7 **Āybak** Afghanistan
182 F4 **Aybas** Kazakhstan
183 J3 **Aydabul** Kazakhstan
136 F2 **Aydar** Russian Federation
136 F3 **Aydar** *watercourse* Ukraine
182 J6 **Aydar Kŭl'i** *lake* Uzbekistan
183 M5 **Aydarly** Kazakhstan
136 D6 **Aydın** *admin. area* Turkey
124 D4 **Ayent** Switzerland
133 C7 **Ayeranós** Greece
Ayers Rock *see* **Uluru** Australia
194 B4 **Ayeyarwady** *admin. area* Myanmar
181 H4 **Ayeyarwady** *watercourse* Myanmar
133 D6 **Áyios Evstrátios** Greece
182 I3 **Ayke** *lake* Kazakhstan
156 F5 **Āykel** Ethiopia
141 F2 **Ayle** Cumbria England UK
81 M1 **Aylesbury** Saskatchewan Canada
139 G3 **Aylesbury** Buckinghamshire England UK
139 I3 **Aylesham** Kent England UK
217 L3 **Ayliffe Hill** SA Australia
128 E3 **Ayllón** Spain
72 I6 **Aylmer Lake** Northwest Territories Canada
75 T6 **Aylsham** Saskatchewan Canada
139 I2 **Aylsham** Norfolk England UK
138 E2 **Aylton** Herefordshire England UK
156 C3 **'Ayn Al Ghazāl** Libya
156 C1 **Ayn al Ghazalah** Libya
156 E2 **'Ayn Ḩulwān** Egypt
156 E2 **'Ayn Şukhnah** Egypt
104 C4 **Ayna** Peru
183 J6 **Ayní** Tajikistan
109 1a **Ayó** Aruba
160 E2 **Ayod** Sudan
107 G3 **Ayolas** Paraguay
135 AI5 **Ayon** Russian Federation
135 AI4 **Ayon, Ostrov** *island* Russian Federation
129 F4 **Ayora** Spain
155 G6 **Ayorou** Niger
154 E5 **Ayoun el Atroûs** Mauritania
215 I5 **Ayr** Qld Australia
140 D1 **Ayr** North Ayrshire Scotland UK
140 D1 **Ayr** *watercourse* Scotland UK
140 E3 **Ayr, Point of** *cape* England UK
185 J3 **Ayrag Nuur** *lake* Mongolia
140 D2 **Ayre, Point of** *cape* Isle of Man UK
126 F5 **Ayrolle, Étang de l'** *lake* France
182 J6 **Ayrybaba** *mountain* Uzbekistan
157 G5 **Aysha** Ethiopia
182 I4 **Ayteke Bi** Kazakhstan
132 E4 **Aytos** Bulgaria
182 I5 **Aytym** Uzbekistan
198 D3 **Ayu** *island* Indonesia
198 D3 **Ayu, Kepulauan** *islands* Indonesia
194 D4 **Ayutthaya** Thailand
136 F6 **Ayvacik** Turkey
127 G1 **Aywaille** Belgium
178 E7 **Az Zāhir** Yemen
178 G4 **Aẓ Ẓahran (Dhahran)** Saudi Arabia
136 F7 **Az Zalaf** Syria
156 E1 **Az Zaqāzīq** Egypt
178 C3 **Az Zarqā'** Jordan
155 I2 **Az Zāwiyah** Libya
178 E4 **Az Zulfī** Saudi Arabia
179 M2 **Azad Kashmir** *admin. area* Pakistan
129 F3 **Azaila** Spain
186 F5 **Azamgarh** Uttar Pradesh India
104 D4 **Azángaro** Peru
182 E6 **Āzar Shahr** Iran
182 E6 **Āzarbāyjān-e Gharbī** *admin. area* Iran
182 E6 **Āzarbāyjān-e Sharqī** *admin. area* Iran
159 G2 **Azare** Nigeria
126 E3 **Azay-le-Rideau** France
129 I5 **Azeffoun** Algeria
182 E6 **Azerbaijan** *country* Asia
105 H3 **Azevedo, Peixoto de** *watercourse* Brazil
156 F5 **Āzezo** Ethiopia
181 G2 **Azha** Xizang Zizhiqu China
139 J4 **Azincourt** France
83 P4 **Aziscohos Lake** Maine USA
178 G2 **Aznā** Iran
100 B5 **Azogues** Ecuador
210 inset **Azorella Peninsula** Heard Island Australia
50 Q5 **Azores-Biscay Rise** *underwater feature* Atlantic Ocean
50 P5 **Azores Plain** *underwater feature* Atlantic Ocean
104 E3 **Azotes** Bolivia
159 I2 **Azoum, Bahr** *watercourse* Chad
136 F3 **Azov, Sea of** Asia
159 I2 **Azrak, Bahr** *watercourse* Chad
156 E5 **Azraq, Bahr el** *watercourse* Sudan
84 F4 **Aztec** Arizona USA
85 I2 **Aztec** New Mexico USA
128 D4 **Azuaga** Spain
129 F3 **Azuara** Spain
100 B5 **Azuay** *admin. area* Ecuador
106 D3 **Azúcar** *watercourse* Chile
100 B3 **Azuero, Península de** *peninsula* Panama
106 D3 **Azufre, Cerro del** *mountain* Chile
107 G6 **Azul** Argentina
105 F4 **Azul** Bolivia
106 D5 **Azul** *volcano* Chile
109 4 **Azul, Cerro** *volcano* Archipiélago de Colon (Galapagos Islands)
106 E3 **Azul, Cerro** *mountain* Argentina
108 B4 **Azul, Cerro** *mountain* Chile
104 C3 **Azul, Cordillera d'** *range* Peru
105 H4 **Azul, Serra** *range* Brazil
159 I2 **Azum, Wadi** *watercourse* Sudan
193 I4 **Azuma-san** *volcano* Japan
126 D5 **Azur** France
74 L6 **Azure Lake** British Columbia Canada
128 D4 **Azután, Embalse de** *lake* Spain
131 B8 **Azzaba** Algeria
130 E4 **Azzano Decimo** Italy

B

86 D5 **B. A. Steinhagen Lake** Texas USA
87 L3 **B. Everett Jordan Lake** North Carolina USA
223 9 **Ba** Fiji
194 E5 **Ba Đông** Vietnam
198 B6 **Baa** Indonesia
178 C2 **Baalbek** Lebanon
219 I4 **Baan Baa** NSW Australia
216 E5 **Baandee** WA Australia
127 I3 **Baar** Switzerland
161 G3 **Baardheere** Somalia
124 C2 **Baarle-Hertog** Netherlands
124 C1 **Baarn** Netherlands
190 D3 **Baatsagaan** Mongolia
131 C8 **Bab** Tunisia
128 E6 **Bab el Assa** Algeria
157 G5 **Bab el Mandeb** *strait* Djibouti
128 D6 **Bab Taza** Morocco
136 C5 **Baba Burnu** *cape* Turkey
178 F2 **Bābā Khanjar** Iran
154 D5 **Bababé** Mauritania
132 F3 **Babadag** Romania
196 E5 **Babadan** Indonesia
182 H6 **Babadurmaz** Turkmenistan
100 B5 **Babahoyo** Ecuador
100 B5 **Babahoyo** *watercourse* Ecuador
133 E6 **Babakale** Turkey
198 A4 **Babana** Indonesia
156 D5 **Babanusa** Sudan
129 J6 **Babar** Algeria
198 D6 **Babar, Kepulauan** *islands* Indonesia
197 G5 **Babat** Indonesia
161 F4 **Babati** Tanzania
198 B6 **Babau** Indonesia
138 D4 **Babbacombe Bay** England UK
84 C1 **Babbitt** Nevada USA
182 E6 **Babek** Azerbaijan
79 D7 **Babel, Mont de** *mountain* Quebec Canada
219 S9 **Babel Island** Tas. Australia
222 3 **Babeldaob** *island* Palau
198 E2 **Babelthuap** *island* Palau
132 D3 **Băbeni** Romania
196 C3 **Babi** *island* Indonesia
132 D3 **Băbiciu** Romania
178 E3 **Bābil** *admin. area* Iraq
161 G2 **Babile** Ethiopia
72 G7 **Babine** *watercourse* British Columbia Canada
123 P5 **Babinichy** Belarus
198 E4 **Babo** Indonesia
130 G3 **Babócsa** Hungary
182 F7 **Bābol** Iran
160 D3 **Babonde** Democratic Republic of Congo
160 D3 **Babongena** Democratic Republic of Congo
159 G3 **Babongo** Cameroon
159 G3 **Baboua** Central African Republic
121 T3 **Babozero, Ozero** *lake* Russian Federation
125 M1 **Babrovitskaye, Vozyera** *lake* Belarus
136 D2 **Babruysk** Belarus
190 F2 **Babushkin** Russian Federation
195 I3 **Babuyan** *island* Philippines
195 I3 **Babuyan Channel** Philippines
195 I3 **Babuyan Islands** Philippines
142 B2 **Bac** Na h-Eileanan Siar Scotland UK
133 B5 **Bač** Macedonia
132 A3 **Bač** Serbia
194 E2 **Bắc Giang** Vietnam
194 E2 **Bắc Kạn** Vietnam
194 E5 **Bac Liêu** Vietnam
161 H2 **Bacaadweyn** Somalia
104 E2 **Bacaba** Brazil
102 C4 **Bacabal** Brazil
105 E2 **Bacada** Brazil
102 B3 **Bacajá** *watercourse* Brazil
89 H5 **Bacalar** Mexico
90 B3 **Bacalar, Laguna** *lake* Mexico
88 C2 **Bacamuchi** *watercourse* Mexico
198 C4 **Bacan** *island* Indonesia
198 C4 **Bacan, Kepulauan** *islands* Indonesia
84 G5 **Bacanuchi** Mexico
132 E2 **Bacău** Romania
132 E2 **Bacău** *admin. area* Romania
79 L8 **Baccalieu Island** Newfoundland and Labrador Canada
127 H2 **Baccarat** France
79 F11 **Baccaro Point** *cape* Nova Scotia Canada
218 G7 **Bacchus Marsh** Vic. Australia
124 E4 **Baceno** Italy
85 H5 **Bacerac** Mexico
194 E2 **Bach Long Vi, Đao** *island* Vietnam
80 E5 **Bachelor, Mount** *volcano* Oregon USA
186 E5 **Bachhrawan** Uttar Pradesh India
184 F5 **Bachu** Xinjiang Uygur Zizhiqu China
188 E2 **Bachuan** Chongqing China
214 G4 **Back** *watercourse* Qld Australia
76 H4 **Back** Manitoba Canada
73 J5 **Back** *watercourse* Nunavut Canada
122 G2 **Backa** Sweden
130 H4 **Bačka Palanka** Serbia
120 I6 **Bäckan** Sweden
122 H4 **Backaryd** Sweden
120 J5 **Backe** Sweden
122 G3 **Bäckefors** Sweden
122 H2 **Backesjön** *lake* Sweden
142 F3 **Backhill** Aberdeenshire Scotland UK
124 E3 **Backnang** Germany
132 B3 **Bačko Gradište** Serbia
218 D6 **Backstairs Passage** SA Australia
81 R3 **Backus** Minnesota USA
84 H5 **Bacoachi** Mexico
84 H7 **Bacobampo** Mexico
195 I5 **Bacolod** Philippines
87 I5 **Baconton** Georgia USA
78 B3 **Bacqueville, Lac** *lake* Quebec Canada
139 H5 **Bacqueville-en-Caux** France
132 A2 **Bács-Kiskun** *admin. area* Hungary
130 E4 **Bacucco, Punta** *cape* Italy
141 F3 **Bacup** Lancashire England UK
104 D2 **Bacuri** Brazil
81 O4 **Bad** *watercourse* South Dakota USA
124 G4 **Bad Aibling** Germany
127 J1 **Bad Berka** Germany
127 I2 **Bad Dürkheim** Germany
124 E3 **Bad Dürrheim** Germany
125 H4 **Bad Gleichenberg** Austria
127 L2 **Bad Hall** Austria
127 I1 **Bad Hersfeld** Germany
125 G4 **Bad Ischl** Austria
124 D3 **Bad Kreuznach** Germany
127 I1 **Bad Laasphe** Germany
124 E2 **Bad Orb** Germany
130 C3 **Bad Ragaz** Switzerland
124 E3 **Bad Rappenau** Germany
127 J1 **Bad Sachsa** Germany
127 L3 **Bad Sankt Leonhard** Austria
124 F4 **Bad Tölz** Germany
124 E2 **Bad Wildungen** Germany
127 J2 **Bad Wörishofen** Germany
124 E4 **Bad Wurzach** Germany
188 E4 **Bada** Guangxi Zhuangzu Zizhiqu China
187 D9 **Badagara** Kerala India
190 E5 **Badain Jaran Shamo** Nei Mongol Zizhiqu China
121 M2 **Badajokka** *watercourse* Norway
101 F5 **Badajos, Lago** *lake* Brazil
128 C4 **Badajoz** Spain
183 K7 **BadakhshÂn** *admin. area* Afghanistan
178 E1 **Badān** Iraq
159 H2 **Badanga** Chad
181 G4 **Badarpur** Assam India
186 D6 **Badarwas** Madhya Pradesh India
197 G2 **Badas** Brunei
196 E3 **Badas, Kepulauan** *islands* Indonesia
142 C2 **Badcall** Highland Scotland UK
120 L2 **Badderfjorden** *bay* Norway
187 E7 **Bade Bacheli** Chhattisgarh India
155 H6 **Badéguichéri** Niger
127 I3 **Baden** Switzerland
124 E3 **Baden-Württemberg** *admin. area* Germany
129 F3 **Badenas** Spain
142 F3 **Badenscoth** Aberdeenshire Scotland UK
155 H6 **Badér** Niger
124 G4 **Badgastein** Austria
216 E6 **Badgebup** WA Australia
81 Q2 **Badger** Minnesota USA
219 R10 **Badger Island** Tas. Australia
179 J2 **Bādghīs** *admin. area* Afghanistan
216 D5 **Badgingarra** WA Australia
158 B2 **Badi** *watercourse* Guinea
127 K5 **Badia Tedalda** Italy
199 H5 **Badilu** Papua New Guinea
179 K5 **Badin** Pakistan
87 K3 **Badin Lake** North Carolina USA
88 D3 **Badiraguato** Mexico
178 D3 **Bādiyat ash Shām (Syrian Desert)** Jordan
81 N3 **Badlands** *range* North Dakota USA
81 N5 **Badlands** *range* South Dakota USA
187 C7 **Badlapur** Maharashtra India
142 E3 **Badnafrave** Moray Scotland UK
131 G7 **Badolato** Italy
158 E3 **Badou** Togo
178 D5 **Badr Ḩunayn** Saudi Arabia
142 C3 **Badrallach** Highland Scotland UK
199 G6 **Badu Island** Australia
187 E10 **Badulla** Sri Lanka
179 H4 **Bādūnī** Iran
187 E8 **Badvel** Andhra Pradesh India
103 B8 **Bady Bassitt** Brazil
135 AC8 **Badzhal'skiy Khrebet** *range* Russian Federation
129 G2 **Baells, Pantà de la** *lake* Spain
128 D5 **Baena** Spain
128 E5 **Baeza** Spain
74 I6 **Baezaeko** *watercourse* British Columbia Canada
159 G3 **Bafang** Cameroon
158 B2 **Bafatá** Guinea-Bissau
130 C4 **Baffe, Punta** *cape* Italy
73 L4 **Baffin Bay** Canada/Greenland
86 C7 **Baffin Bay** Texas USA
78 C1 **Baffin Island** Nunavut Canada
159 G4 **Bafia** Cameroon
158 B2 **Bafing** *watercourse* Guinea
158 B2 **Bafing-Makana** Mali
154 D6 **Bafoulabé** Mali
159 G3 **Bafoussam** Cameroon
179 H3 **Bāfq** Iran
179 H3 **Bāft** Iran
160 D3 **Bafwabalinge** Democratic Republic of Congo
160 D3 **Bafwasende** Democratic Republic of Congo
179 J4 **Bag** Iran
159 G2 **Baga** Nigeria
182 D4 **Baga-Burul** Russian Federation
199 H5 **Bagabag Island** Papua New Guinea
100 B3 **Bagadó** Colombia
186 F5 **Bagaha** Bihar India
187 D8 **Bagalkot** Karnataka India
199 J6 **Bagaman Island** Papua New Guinea
195 J4 **Bagamanoc** Philippines
183 M2 **Bagan** Russian Federation
196 D3 **Bagan Datuk** Malaysia
159 F3 **Bagana** Nigeria
199 J5 **Bagana, Mount** *volcano* Papua New Guinea
195 J6 **Baganga** Philippines
162 D3 **Bagani** Namibia
196 D3 **Bagansiapiapi** Indonesia
190 F3 **Baganuur** Mongolia
155 G6 **Bagaroua** Niger
160 B4 **Bagata** Democratic Republic of Congo
158 B3 **Bagbe** *watercourse* Sierra Leone
107 H4 **Bagé** Brazil
126 F5 **Bages et de Sigean, Étang de** *lake* France
186 E5 **Bageshwar** Uttaranchal India
120 L4 **Baggen** *island* Sweden
140 E2 **Baggrow** Cumbria England UK
81 L6 **Baggs** Wyoming USA
138 C3 **Baggy Point** *cape* England UK
179 H4 **Bāgh-e Chenār** *mountain* Iran
178 G3 **Bāgh-e Malek** Iran
179 I3 **Bāghārān, Kūh-e** *mountain* Iran
178 E2 **Baghdād** Iraq
178 E2 **Baghdād** *admin. area* Iraq
183 J7 **Baghlān** *admin. area* Afghanistan
181 G4 **Baghmara** Meghalaya India
140 E3 **Bagillt** Flintshire Wales UK
196 E4 **Baginda, Tanjung** *cape* Indonesia
133 G6 **Bağkonak** Turkey
81 R3 **Bagley** Minnesota USA
187 D6 **Bagli** Madhya Pradesh India
186 F5 **Baglung** Nepal
139 F3 **Bagmore** Hampshire England UK
126 E5 **Bagnères-de-Bigorre** France
126 E5 **Bagnères-de-Luchon** France
124 F5 **Bagnolo Mella** Italy
127 G4 **Bagnols-sur-Cèze** France
122 E5 **Bågø** *island* Denmark
194 C3 **Bago** *admin. area* Myanmar
194 C3 **Bago (Pegu)** Myanmar
186 F6 **Bagodar** Jharkhand India
159 G3 **Bagodo** Cameroon
158 C2 **Bagoé** *watercourse* Mali
188 E3 **Bagong** Guizhou China
123 K5 **Bagrationovsk** Russian Federation
Bagrax *see* **Bohu** China
101 I4 **Bagres, Lago dos** *lake* Brazil
104 B2 **Bagua Grande** Peru
195 I3 **Baguio** Philippines
155 H5 **Bagzane, Monts** *mountain* Niger
186 E5 **Bah** Uttar Pradesh India
178 E6 **Bāḩah, Al** *admin. area* Saudi Arabia
50 K6 **Bahama Ridge** *underwater feature* Atlantic Ocean
91 F2 **Bahamas** *country* Caribbean
143 F3 **Bahana** Ireland
187 G6 **Baharagora** Jharkhand India
183 K7 **Bahārak** Afghanistan
186 G6 **Baharampur** West Bengal India
197 G3 **Bahau** *watercourse* Indonesia
197 G4 **Bahaur** Indonesia
179 L3 **Bahawalpur** Pakistan
133 E5 **Bahçeköy** Turkey
157 F4 **Bahdur Island** *island* Sudan
182 H6 **Bäherden** Turkmenistan
161 F5 **Bahi** Tanzania
103 D6 **Bahia** *admin. area* Brazil
90 C3 **Bahía, Islas de la** *island* Honduras
198 E5 **Bahia, Tanjung** *cape* Indonesia
88 B3 **Bahía Asunción** Mexico
106 F6 **Bahía Blanca** Argentina
108 C3 **Bahía Bustamante** Argentina
100 A5 **Bahía de Caráquez** Ecuador
84 F6 **Bahía de los Ángeles** Mexico
90 D2 **Bahía Honda** Cuba
88 C2 **Bahía Kino** Mexico
108 C4 **Bahía Laura** Argentina
108 B2 **Bahía Mansa** Chile
108 B4 **Bahía Murta** Chile
108 D4 **Bahía Oso Marino** Argentina
108 D6 **Bahía Thetis** Argentina
88 B3 **Bahía Tortugas** Mexico
156 F5 **Bahir Dar** Ethiopia
179 I5 **Bahlā'** Oman
158 C3 **Bahn** Liberia
198 B4 **Bahomonte** Indonesia
155 J6 **Bahr el Ghazal** *watercourse* Chad
186 E5 **Bahraich** Uttar Pradesh India
178 G4 **Bahrain** *country* Middle East
156 D2 **Bahriyah, Wāḩāt Al** *spring* Egypt
198 B4 **Bahubulu** *island* Indonesia
85 H7 **Bahuichivo** Mexico
185 J5 **Bai Shan** *mountain* Gansu China
105 G5 **Baía** Brazil
105 G5 **Baía de São Luís** Brazil
101 I5 **Baía do Pracaí** *lake* Brazil
162 B3 **Baía dos Tigres** Angola
132 C2 **Baia Mare** Romania
102 B3 **Baião** Brazil
127 H5 **Baiardo** Italy
159 H3 **Baibokoum** Chad
189 G1 **Baicheng** Henan China
191 J3 **Baicheng** Jilin China
184 G4 **Baicheng** Xinjiang Uygur Zizhiqu China
188 E4 **Baidonghe Shuiku** *lake* Guangxi Zhuangzu Zizhiqu China
77 U8 **Baie-Comeau** Quebec Canada
79 G7 **Baie-Johan-Beetz** Quebec Canada
109 16 **Baie-Mahault** Guadeloupe
79 C9 **Baie-St-Paul** Quebec Canada
79 F8 **Baie-Ste-Claire** Quebec Canada
77 V8 **Baie-Trinité** Quebec Canada
79 J8 **Baie Verte** Newfoundland and Labrador Canada
188 F2 **Baihe** Shaanxi China
Baikal, Lake *see* **Baykal, Ozero** Russian Federation
142 B2 **Baile Ailein** Na h-Eileanan Siar Scotland UK
142 B2 **Baile an Truiseil** Na h-Eileanan Siar Scotland UK
Baile Átha Cliath *see* **Dublin** Ireland
142 A3 **Baile nan Cailleach** Na h-Eileanan Siar Scotland UK
132 D3 **Băile Olăneşti** Romania
132 E3 **Băile Siriu** Romania
128 E4 **Bailén** Spain
109 16 **Bailiff** Guadeloupe
190 G4 **Bailingmiao** Nei Mongol Zizhiqu China
102 B2 **Bailique, Ilha** *island* Brazil
188 D1 **Bailong Jiang** *watercourse* Jiangsu China
162 C2 **Bailundo** Angola
181 H2 **Baima** Xizang Zizhiqu China
80 C2 **Bainbridge** British Columbia Canada
141 F2 **Bainbridge** North Yorkshire England UK
87 I5 **Bainbridge** Georgia USA
188 E3 **Baini** Guizhou China
141 H3 **Bainton** East Riding of Yorkshire England UK
81 M2 **Bainville** Montana USA
191 K3 **Baiquan** Heilongjiang China
72 C5 **Baird Mountains** Alaska USA
222 1b **Bairiki** *island* Kiribati
219 H7 **Bairnsdale** Vic. Australia
126 D2 **Bais** France
195 I5 **Bais** Philippines
126 E5 **Baïse** *watercourse* France
188 E2 **Baisha** Sichuan China
188 E4 **Baishan** Guangxi Zhuangzu Zizhiqu China
189 H3 **Baishanzu** *mountain* Zhejiang China
188 F1 **Baishui** Shaanxi China
186 E5 **Baitadi** Nepal
164 2 **Baixio, Ilhéu de** *island* Madeira
162 C3 **Baixo Longa** Angola
190 F5 **Baiya Shan** *range* Shaanxi China
190 F6 **Baiyang** Ningxia Huizu Zizhiqu China
190 E6 **Baiyin** Gansu China
191 H4 **Baiyinchagan** Nei Mongol Zizhiqu China
191 J3 **Baiyinhushuo** Nei Mongol Zizhiqu China
156 E4 **Baiyuda Desert** Sudan
155 G6 **Baïzo** Niger
125 J4 **Baja** Hungary
108 A4 **Baja, Punta** *cape* Chile
84 E6 **Baja, Punta** *cape* Mexico
88 B2 **Baja California** *admin. area* Mexico
88 B2 **Baja California** *peninsula* Mexico
88 B3 **Baja California Sur** *admin. area* Mexico
196 E3 **Bajau** *island* Indonesia
198 B6 **Bajawa** Indonesia
179 I2 **Bajestān** Iran
179 K2 **Bājgāh** Afghanistan
178 E7 **Bājil** Yemen
108 B4 **Bajo Caracoles** Argentina
108 C4 **Bajo Picaso** Argentina
159 G2 **Bajoga** Nigeria
91 G3 **Bajos de Haina** Dominican Republic
187 F7 **Bajpur** Orissa India
197 G4 **Baka, Bukit** *mountain* Indonesia
159 I3 **Bakala** Central African Republic
186 D6 **Bakani** Rajasthan India
159 I1 **Bakaoré** Chad
130 F4 **Bakar** Croatia
159 F4 **Bakassi, Cap** *cape* Cameroon
197 H4 **Bakaucengal** Indonesia
159 F3 **Bakebe** Cameroon
154 D6 **Bakel** Senegal
86 F5 **Baker** Louisiana USA
81 M3 **Baker** Montana USA
222 1 **Baker and Howland Islands** *unincorporated US territory* Pacific Ocean
80 G4 **Baker City** Oregon USA
76 J1 **Baker Foreland** Nunavut Canada
222 1 **Baker Island** Pacific Ocean
217 J3 **Baker Lake** WA Australia
73 J6 **Baker Lake** Nunavut Canada
215 J6 **Bakers Creek** Qld Australia
77 P4 **Bakers Dozen Islands** Nunavut Canada
84 C3 **Bakersfield** California USA
85 K5 **Bakersfield** Texas USA
141 G3 **Bakewell** Derbyshire England UK
136 D2 **Bakhan'** Belarus
136 E2 **Bakhmach** Ukraine
134 S6 **Bakhta** Russian Federation
134 S6 **Bakhta** *watercourse* Russian Federation
179 H3 **Bakhtegan, Daryācheh-ye** *lake* Iran
184 G3 **Bakhty** Xinjiang Uygur Zizhiqu China
157 G5 **Baki** Somalia
182 F6 **Bakı (Baku)** Azerbaijan
133 E6 **Bakır** *watercourse* Turkey
120 inset **Bakkafjörður** Iceland
120 inset **Bakkaflói** *bay* Iceland
120 inset **Bakkagerði** Iceland
122 F3 **Bakke** Norway
120 L2 **Bakkeby** Norway
122 E3 **Bakko** Norway
133 F7 **Baklan** Turkey
158 C3 **Bako** Côte d'Ivoire
161 F2 **Bako** Ethiopia
196 C3 **Bakongan** Indonesia
161 G3 **Bakool** *admin. area* Somalia
199 J5 **Bakop** Papua New Guinea
160 D3 **Bakordi** Sudan
159 F2 **Bakori** Nigeria
159 I3 **Bakouma** Central African Republic
130 F4 **Bakovac** Croatia
101 H4 **Bakrakondre** Suriname
182 D5 **Baksan** Russian Federation
182 I4 **Bakshakol'** *lake* Kazakhstan
183 L3 **Bakty** Kazakhstan
Baku *see* **Bakı** Azerbaijan
196 E3 **Bakung** *island* Indonesia
59 P2 **Bakutis Coast** Antarctica
123 J4 **Bäl** Sweden
135 AB5 **Bala** Russian Federation
154 D6 **Bala** Senegal
138 D2 **Bala** Gwynedd Wales UK
179 I3 **Bālā Ḩowz** Iran
179 J2 **Bālā Morghāb** Afghanistan
195 H5 **Balabac** Philippines
197 H2 **Balabac** *island* Philippines
195 H6 **Balabac Strait** Malaysia
197 H1 **Balabac Strait North** Philippines
197 H4 **Balabalagan, Kepulauan** *islands* Indonesia
222 7 **Balabio, Île** *island* New Caledonia
132 C3 **Bălăciţa** Romania
216 F5 **Baladjie, Lake** WA Australia
135 AE7 **Balagannoye** Russian Federation
187 E7 **Balaghat** Madhya Pradesh India
129 G3 **Balaguer** Spain
197 F4 **Balaiberkuak** Indonesia
197 F3 **Balaikarangan** Indonesia
196 D3 **Balaipungut** Indonesia
197 F4 **Balairiam** Indonesia
163 F3 **Balaka** Malawi
182 E3 **Balakovo** Russian Federation
163 G2 **Balama** Mozambique
197 H2 **Balambangan** *island* Malaysia
89 H5 **Balancán de Domínguez** Mexico
160 B3 **Balangala** Democratic Republic of Congo
161 F4 **Balangida, Lake** *lake* Tanzania
187 F7 **Balangir** Orissa India
198 B4 **Balantak** Indonesia
100 B5 **Baláo** Ecuador
182 F3 **Balashi** Russian Federation
182 D3 **Balashov** Russian Federation
132 B2 **Balástya** Hungary
130 G3 **Balaton** *lake* Hungary
195 I4 **Balayan** Philippines
128 E4 **Balazote** Spain
195 I3 **Balbalan** Philippines
199 J5 **Balbi, Mount** *volcano* Papua New Guinea
100 D5 **Balbina** Brazil
214 C4 **Balbirini** NT Australia
142 D3 **Balblair** Highland Scotland UK
143 F3 **Balbriggan** Ireland
125 L4 **Balc** Romania
218 D4 **Balcanonna** SA Australia
81 N1 **Balcarres** Saskatchewan Canada
140 E2 **Balcary Point** *cape* Scotland UK
132 D3 **Bălceşti** Romania
59 O1 **Balchen Glacier** *ice* Antarctica
221 C8 **Balclutha** New Zealand
86 B6 **Balcones Escarpment** Texas USA
218 D4 **Balcoracana** *watercourse* SA Australia
133 E6 **Balçova** Turkey
214 C7 **Bald Hill** NT Australia
83 K8 **Bald Knob** *mountain* Virginia USA
219 I6 **Bald Mountain** NSW Australia
214 D2 **Bald Point** NT Australia
138 B4 **Baldhu** Cornwall England UK
139 G3 **Baldock** Hertfordshire England UK
76 G4 **Baldock Lake** Manitoba Canada
123 M4 **Baldone** Latvia
219 I5 **Baldry** NSW Australia
87 K5 **Baldwin** Florida USA
82 I5 **Baldwin** Michigan USA
82 E4 **Baldwin** Wisconsin USA
86 G3 **Baldwyn** Mississippi USA
74 L7 **Baldy Mount** British Columbia Canada
84 H4 **Baldy Peak** Arkansas USA
130 E4 **Bale** Croatia
158 B2 **Bale** *watercourse* Guinea
196 D4 **Bale** Indonesia
139 H2 **Bale** Norfolk England UK
129 H4 **Balearic Islands** *island* Spain
198 B4 **Balease, Gunung** *mountain* Indonesia
197 G3 **Baleh** *watercourse* Malaysia
103 E7 **Baleia, Ponta da** *cape* Brazil
77 Q5 **Baleine, Petite Rivière de la** *watercourse* Quebec Canada
78 E4 **Baleine, Rivière à la** *watercourse* Quebec Canada
109 11a **Baleine Bay** St Vincent and the Grenadines
126 D3 **Baleines, Pointe des** *cape* France
128 C4 **Baleizão** Portugal
142 B4 **Balemartine** Highland Scotland UK
127 G1 **Balen** Belgium
142 B4 **Balephuil** Highland Scotland UK
195 I4 **Baler** Philippines
195 I4 **Baler Bay** Philippines
142 A3 **Baleshare** *island* Scotland UK
187 G7 **Baleshwar** Orissa India
132 C3 **Băleşti** Romania
142 B4 **Balevulin** Highland Scotland UK
191 H2 **Baley** Russian Federation
155 G6 **Baléyara** Niger
221 C7 **Balfour** New Zealand
142 D4 **Balfron** Stirling Scotland UK
213 I6 **Balgo Hills** WA Australia
101 G5 **Balhina, Represa de** *lake* Brazil
157 G5 **Balho** Djibouti
197 G6 **Bali** *admin. area* Indonesia
197 G6 **Bali** *island* Indonesia
197 G5 **Bali, Laut (Bali Sea)** Indonesia
197 G6 **Bali, Selat** *strait* Indonesia
Bali Sea *see* **Bali, Laut** Indonesia
109 11 **Baliceaux Island** St Vincent and the Grenadines
187 F7 **Baliguda** Orissa India
136 D5 **Balıkesir** *admin. area* Turkey
197 H4 **Balikpapan** Indonesia
197 H4 **Balikpapan, Teluk** *bay* Indonesia
185 J4 **Balikun** Xinjiang Uygur Zizhiqu China
195 H6 **Balimbing** Philippines
187 F7 **Balimela** Orissa India
199 G6 **Balimo** Papua New Guinea
195 J5 **Balingasag** Philippines
124 E3 **Balingen** Germany
197 G3 **Balingian** Malaysia
164 6b **Baliniers, Golfe des** *bay* French Southern and Antarctic Lands
195 I3 **Balintang** *island* Philippines
195 I3 **Balintang Channel** Philippines
142 D3 **Balintombuie** Highland Scotland UK
142 E3 **Balintore** Highland Scotland UK
159 I3 **Balitondo** Central African Republic
143 C4 **Baliynakilly Upper** Ireland
124 C1 **Balk** Netherlands
142 F4 **Balkaithly** Fife Scotland UK
182 G6 **Balkan Welaýaty** *admin. area* Turkmenistan
182 G6 **Balkanabat** Turkmenistan
183 J3 **Balkashino** Kazakhstan
182 J7 **Balkh** Afghanistan

179 K2 **Balkh** *admin. area* Afghanistan
179 K2 **Balkhāb** Afghanistan
183 L4 **Balkhash** Kazakhstan
183 L4 **Balkhash, Ozero** *lake* Kazakhstan
182 E4 **Balkuduk** Kazakhstan
86 E5 **Ball** Louisiana USA
213 I5 **Ball, Mount** WA Australia
82 D1 **Ball Lake** Ontario Canada
143 C3 **Balla** Ireland
217 H6 **Balladonia** WA Australia
219 I4 **Balladoran** NSW Australia
140 B3 **Ballagan Point** *cape* Ireland
219 J3 **Ballandean** Qld Australia
120 J2 **Ballangen** Norway
142 C5 **Ballantrae** South Ayrshire Scotland UK
78 D3 **Ballantyne, Lac** *lake* Quebec Canada
72 H3 **Ballantyne Strait** Northwest Territories Canada
218 F7 **Ballarat** Vic. Australia
143 D4 **Ballard** Ireland
216 G4 **Ballard, Lake** WA Australia
187 E7 **Ballarpur** Maharashtra India
142 E3 **Ballater** Aberdeenshire Scotland UK
218 F6 **Ballbank** NSW Australia
154 E5 **Ballé** Mali
106 D3 **Ballena, Punta** *cape* Chile
59 K2 **Balleny Islands** Antarctica
59 K2 **Balleny Seamounts** *underwater feature* Southern Ocean
120 J2 **Ballesvika** Norway
186 F6 **Ballia** Uttar Pradesh India
216 E5 **Ballidu** WA Australia
219 I5 **Ballimore** NSW Australia
219 K3 **Ballina** NSW Australia
143 C2 **Ballina** Ireland
140 A3 **Ballinabrackey** Ireland
143 D2 **Ballinafad** Ireland
143 E3 **Ballinalack** Ireland
143 E3 **Ballinalee** Ireland
143 E2 **Ballinamore** Ireland
143 D3 **Ballinasloe** Ireland
143 D3 **Ballindine** Ireland
86 B5 **Ballinger** Texas USA
142 E4 **Ballinluig** Perth and Kinross Scotland UK
138 A1 **Ballintober** Ireland
140 B1 **Ballintoy** Moyle Northern Ireland UK
140 B3 **Ballivor** Ireland
142 F3 **Ballochan** Aberdeenshire Scotland UK
126 E2 **Ballon** France
143 F4 **Ballon** Ireland
127 J5 **Ballone Poggio** *mountain* Italy
211 inset **Balls Pyramid** Lord Howe Island Australia
133 A5 **Ballsh** Albania
120 H2 **Ballstad** Norway
82 F7 **Ballwin** Missouri USA
142 C5 **Ballyaurgan** Argyll and Bute Scotland UK
143 F2 **Ballybay** Ireland
140 A2 **Ballybegly** Ireland
143 D5 **Ballybraher** Ireland
143 E3 **Ballybrin** Ireland
143 C2 **Ballycastle** Ireland
140 B1 **Ballycastle** Moyle Northern Ireland UK
140 A3 **Ballycollin** Ireland
143 F4 **Ballycrinnigan** Ireland
143 E4 **Ballycullane** Ireland
143 C5 **Ballydehob** Ireland
143 D3 **Ballyeighter** Ireland
138 A2 **Ballyell** Ireland
140 B4 **Ballyellis** Ireland
143 E3 **Ballyfore** Ireland
143 D5 **Ballyfoyle** Ireland
140 C2 **Ballygalley Head** *cape* Northern Ireland UK
143 D3 **Ballygar** Ireland
143 D3 **Ballyglass** Ireland
140 C2 **Ballygowan** Ards Northern Ireland UK
143 D4 **Ballygriffin** Ireland
143 E4 **Ballyhale** Ireland
142 B4 **Ballyhaugh** Highland Scotland UK
143 C4 **Ballyheige** Ireland
143 C4 **Ballyheige Bay** Ireland
143 E1 **Ballyhillin** Ireland
140 B4 **Ballyhitt** Ireland
143 C4 **Ballyhorgan East** Ireland
143 E3 **Ballyjamesduff** Ireland
143 E3 **Ballykean** Ireland
143 D4 **Ballylanders** Ireland
143 B4 **Ballylusky** Ireland
143 E4 **Ballylynan** Ireland
143 D5 **Ballymacredmond** Ireland
140 A4 **Ballymartin** Ireland
143 D5 **Ballymartle** Ireland
140 B2 **Ballymena** Ballymena Northern Ireland UK
140 B2 **Ballymena** *admin. area* Northern Ireland UK
143 D3 **Ballymoe** Ireland
140 B1 **Ballymoney** Ballymoney Northern Ireland UK
140 B1 **Ballymoney** *admin. area* Northern Ireland UK
140 B4 **Ballymoney Cross Roads** Ireland
143 D2 **Ballymote** Ireland
143 C4 **Ballynacally** Ireland
140 C2 **Ballynahinch** Down Northern Ireland UK
143 C4 **Ballynaskreena** Ireland
140 B3 **Ballynee** Ireland
140 B4 **Ballyoliver** Ireland
140 C2 **Ballyquintin Point** *cape* Northern Ireland UK
143 E4 **Ballyragget** Ireland
143 E3 **Ballyshane** Ireland
143 D2 **Ballyshannon** Ireland
143 D4 **Ballysheedy** Ireland
143 D3 **Ballyshrule** Ireland
143 D4 **Ballysteen** Ireland
143 D2 **Ballysuggart** Ireland
140 B4 **Ballyteige Bay** Ireland
143 F4 **Ballyvaldon** Ireland
143 F4 **Ballyvallooo** Ireland
140 B1 **Ballyvoy** Moyle Northern Ireland UK
140 C2 **Ballywalter** Ards Northern Ireland UK
140 B2 **Ballyward** Banbridge Northern Ireland UK
106 D3 **Balmaceda** Chile
108 B5 **Balmaceda, Cerro** *mountain* Chile
142 E4 **Balmacneil** Perth and Kinross Scotland UK
142 D4 **Balmaha** Stirling Scotland UK
130 B4 **Balme** Italy
142 F3 **Balmedie** Aberdeenshire Scotland UK
221 E6 **Balmoral** New Zealand
85 K5 **Balmorhea** Texas USA
140 A3 **Balnacart** Ireland
142 C3 **Balnacra** Highland Scotland UK
142 B4 **Balnahard** Argyll and Bute Scotland UK
106 F4 **Balnearia** Argentina
108 D2 **Balneario Massini** Argentina
106 F6 **Balneario Monte Hermoso** Argentina
107 G6 **Balneario Orense** Argentina
106 F6 **Balneario Oriente** Argentina
179 J4 **Balochistan** *admin. area* Pakistan
187 E7 **Balod** Chhattisgarh India
187 F6 **Baloda** Chhattisgarh India
196 E4 **Balok, Teluk** *bay* Indonesia
162 B2 **Balombo** Angola
219 I2 **Balonne** *watercourse* Qld Australia
198 C3 **Balontohe** *island* Indonesia
130 H3 **Balotaszállás** Hungary
186 C6 **Balotra** Rajasthan India
101 H4 **Balourou** French Guiana
132 G2 **Balovnoye** Ukraine
186 E5 **Balrampur** Uttar Pradesh India
218 F6 **Balranald** NSW Australia
140 B3 **Balrath** Ireland
132 D3 **Balş** Romania
125 L4 **Balşa** Romania
102 C4 **Balsas** Brazil
88 E5 **Balsas** *watercourse* Mexico
102 C4 **Balsas, Rio das** *watercourse* Brazil
120 K2 **Balsfjord** Norway
126 F4 **Balsièges** France
120 K5 **Balsjö** Sweden
122 I2 **Bålsön** *island* Sweden
127 H3 **Balsthal** Switzerland
75 U8 **Balta** North Dakota USA
132 E3 **Balta Amara** *lake* Romania
132 F3 **Balta Jijilei** *lake* Romania
132 E3 **Balta Jirlăul** *lake* Romania
128 D3 **Baltanás** Spain
107 G4 **Baltasar Brum** Uruguay
142 inset **Baltasound** Shetland Scotland UK
132 E2 **Bălţi** Moldova
123 J4 **Baltic Sea**
143 C5 **Baltimore** Ireland
83 M7 **Baltimore** Maryland USA
123 N4 **Baltinava** Latvia
143 F4 **Baltinglass** Ireland
179 M2 **Baltoro Glacier** Pakistan
109 4 **Baltra, Isla** *island* Archipiélago de Colon (Galapagos Islands)
124 D1 **Baltrum** *island* Germany
199 H4 **Baluan Island** Papua New Guinea
197 G3 **Balui** *watercourse* Malaysia
196 C3 **Balumundam** Indonesia
122 H2 **Balungen** *lake* Sweden
186 G6 **Balurghat** West Bengal India
195 J6 **Balut** *island* Philippines
120 I3 **Balvatnet** *lake* Norway
124 D2 **Balve** Germany
123 N4 **Balvi** Latvia
123 N4 **Balvu** *admin. area* Latvia
100 B5 **Balzar** Ecuador
130 E5 **Balzo** Italy
159 H3 **Bam** Chad
179 I3 **Bam** Iran
191 J1 **Bam** Russian Federation
199 H4 **Bam Island** Papua New Guinea
214 G1 **Bamaga** Qld Australia
76 J7 **Bamaji Lake** Ontario Canada
154 E6 **Bamako** Mali
159 I3 **Bamba** *watercourse* Central African Republic
160 B5 **Bamba** Democratic Republic of Congo
159 G5 **Bambama** Congo
104 B2 **Bambamarca** Peru
90 C4 **Bambana, Rio** *watercourse* Nicaragua
159 I3 **Bambari** Central African Republic
196 C3 **Bambel** Indonesia
130 D2 **Bamberg** Germany
156 E6 **Bambesi** Ethiopia
160 D3 **Bambili** Democratic Republic of Congo
218 G5 **Bambilla** NSW Australia
158 D3 **Bamboi** Ghana
160 D2 **Bambouti** Sudan
103 C8 **Bambuí** Brazil
197 G4 **Bambulung** Indonesia
159 G3 **Bamenda** Cameroon
159 G3 **Bamendjing, Lac de** *lake* Cameroon
188 E4 **Bameng Shuiku** *lake* Guangxi Zhuangzu Zizhiqu China
80 C2 **Bamfield** British Columbia Canada
187 E6 **Bamhani** Madhya Pradesh India
179 K2 **Bāmiān** Afghanistan
179 K2 **Bāmiān** *admin. area* Afghanistan
159 I3 **Bamingui** Central African Republic
159 I3 **Bamingui-Bangoran** *admin. area* Central African Republic
194 D4 **Bamnet Narong** Thailand
85 H7 **Bamocha** Mexico
186 E6 **Bamori** Madhya Pradesh India
138 D4 **Bampton** Devon England UK
139 F3 **Bampton** Oxfordshire England UK
179 I2 **Bamrūd** Iran
84 F5 **Bamuri** Mexico
182 G6 **Bamy** Turkmenistan
158 D2 **Ban** Burkina Faso
194 D3 **Ban a Ham** Thailand
194 D3 **Ban a Hi** Thailand
194 D5 **Ban Ao Fat** Thailand
194 D5 **Ban Ao Yai** Thailand
194 D3 **Ban Ban** Laos
214 A2 **Ban Ban Springs** NT Australia
219 J1 **Ban Ban Springs** Qld Australia
194 C4 **Ban Daen** Thailand
194 D3 **Ban Dan Kwian** Thailand
194 F4 **Ban Đao Hon Gom** *island* Vietnam
194 E4 **Bản Đôn** Vietnam
194 D3 **Ban Dung** Thailand
194 C3 **Ban Hat** Thailand
194 E3 **Ban Khae** Thailand
194 D4 **Ban Laem** Thailand
194 D4 **Ban Na** Thailand
194 E3 **Ban Nakang** Laos
194 E3 **Ban Napè** Laos
194 D4 **Ban Nong Tao** Thailand
194 D3 **Ban Pa Lao** Thailand
194 D3 **Ban Phai** Thailand
194 E3 **Ban Phôntiou** Laos
194 D3 **Ban Phu** Thailand
194 C3 **Ban Rong Kat** Thailand
194 C3 **Ban San** Thailand
194 D6 **Ban Sanam Chai** Thailand
194 E3 **Ban Xénô** Laos
178 F7 **Banā, Wādī** *watercourse* Yemen
161 H3 **Banaadir** *admin. area* Somalia
222 1 **Banaba** *island* Kiribati
102 E4 **Banabuiu** *watercourse* Brazil
160 D3 **Banalia** Democratic Republic of Congo
163 F4 **Banamana, Lago** *lake* Mozambique
154 E6 **Banamba** Mali
84 G5 **Banámichi** Mexico
215 K8 **Banana** Qld Australia
158 B3 **Banana Islands** Sierra Leone
105 H4 **Bananal** Brazil
105 G2 **Bananal** Brazil
103 B5 **Bananal, Ilha do** *island* Brazil
105 H4 **Bananalzinho** Brazil
194 B6 **Bananga** Andaman and Nicobar Islands India
160 D2 **Banangui** Central African Republic
109 16 **Bananier** Guadeloupe
158 C3 **Banankoro** Guinea
186 D6 **Banas** *watercourse* Rajasthan India
156 F3 **Banās, Ra's** *cape* Egypt
198 A5 **Banawaya** *island* Indonesia
140 B2 **Banbridge** Banbridge Northern Ireland UK
140 B2 **Banbridge** *admin. area* Northern Ireland UK
139 F2 **Banbury** Oxfordshire England UK
138 C3 **Banc-y-felin** Carmarthenshire Wales UK
197 H1 **Bancalan** *island* Philippines
218 E4 **Bancannia, Lake** NSW Australia
142 F3 **Banchory** Aberdeenshire Scotland UK
100 D3 **Banco las Piñas** Venezuela
197 H2 **Bancoran** *island* Philippines
80 J5 **Bancroft** Idaho USA
179 I3 **Band-e Kahnūj** Iran
159 G3 **Banda** Cameroon
159 G5 **Banda** Congo
186 E6 **Banda** Madhya Pradesh India
187 C8 **Banda** Maharashtra India
186 E6 **Banda** Uttar Pradesh India
198 D5 **Banda, Kepulauan** *islands* Indonesia
198 C5 **Banda, Laut (Banda Sea)** Indonesia
196 B2 **Banda Aceh** Indonesia
219 K4 **Banda Banda, Mount** NSW Australia
Banda Sea *see* **Banda, Laut** Indonesia
196 C3 **Bandahara, Gunung** *mountain* Indonesia
122 E3 **Bandak** *lake* Norway
160 C4 **Bandaka** Democratic Republic of Congo
160 A2 **Bandal** Cameroon
158 D3 **Bandama, Vallée du** *admin. area* Côte d'Ivoire
158 C3 **Bandama Blanc** *watercourse* Côte d'Ivoire
158 C3 **Bandama Rouge** *watercourse* Côte d'Ivoire
198 D5 **Bandaneira** Indonesia
196 C3 **Bandar** Indonesia
179 H4 **Bandar 'Abbās** Iran
182 F6 **Bandar-e Anzali** Iran
178 G4 **Bandar-e Būshehr** Iran
178 G3 **Bandar-e Ganāveh** Iran
179 H4 **Bandar-e Lengeh** Iran
178 G3 **Bandar-e Māhshahr** Iran
196 E5 **Bandar Lampung** Indonesia
197 G2 **Bandar Seri Begawan** Brunei
197 F3 **Bandar Sri Aman** Malaysia
196 E5 **Bandaragung** Indonesia
181 G4 **Bandarban** Bangladesh
186 E4 **Bandarpunch** *mountain* Uttaranchal India
187 F8 **Bandarulanka** Andhra Pradesh India
128 C2 **Bande** Spain
103 B6 **Bandeirantes** Brazil
103 D8 **Bandeiras, Pico de** *mountain* Brazil
86 B6 **Bandera** Texas USA
85 J5 **Banderas** Mexico
88 D4 **Banderas, Bahía de** *bay* Mexico
154 F6 **Bandiagara** Mali
158 D2 **Bandiagara, Falaise de** *range* Mali
186 D3 **Bandipur** Jammu and Kashmir India/Pakistan
133 E5 **Bandırma** Turkey
133 F5 **Bandırma Körfezi** *bay* Turkey
159 G3 **Bandjoukri** Cameroon
164 8b **Bandnéle** Mayotte
143 D5 **Bandon** Ireland
143 D5 **Bandon** *watercourse* Ireland
80 C5 **Bandon** Oregon USA
160 B4 **Bandundu** Democratic Republic of Congo
160 B4 **Bandundu** *admin. area* Democratic Republic of Congo
196 E5 **Bandung** Indonesia
216 H3 **Bandya** WA Australia
182 E7 **Banēh** Iran
198 D3 **Banemo** Indonesia
91 F2 **Banes** Cuba
158 B2 **Banfélé** Guinea
80 H1 **Banff** Alberta Canada
158 D2 **Banfora** Burkina Faso
159 H3 **Bang** Central African Republic
194 D4 **Bang Lamung** Thailand
194 D3 **Bang Mun Nak** Thailand
194 D4 **Bang Sai** Thailand
194 C5 **Bang Saphan** Thailand
160 B5 **Banga** Angola
159 I3 **Banga** *watercourse* Central African Republic
160 C5 **Banga** Democratic Republic of Congo
186 D4 **Banga** Punjab India
195 J6 **Banga** Philippines
160 D3 **Bangadi** Democratic Republic of Congo
215 H7 **Bangall** *watercourse* Qld Australia
Bangalore *see* **Bengaluru** India
159 I3 **Bangana** Central African Republic
186 D5 **Banganga Nadi** *watercourse* Rajasthan India
186 G6 **Bangaon** Bihar India
197 G2 **Bangar** Brunei
195 I3 **Bangar** Philippines
159 I4 **Bangassou** Central African Republic
198 B5 **Bangbong** Indonesia
199 H5 **Bangeta, Mount** Papua New Guinea
198 B4 **Banggai, Kepulauan** *islands* Indonesia
197 H2 **Banggi** *island* Malaysia
156 C1 **Banghāzī** Libya
194 E3 **Banghiang** *watercourse* Laos
198 C3 **Bangka** *island* Indonesia
198 C3 **Bangka, Selat** *strait* Indonesia
196 E4 **Bangka-Belitung** *admin. area* Indonesia
197 G4 **Bangkal** Indonesia
197 G5 **Bangkalan** Indonesia
196 C3 **Bangkaru** *island* Indonesia
196 D3 **Bangkinang** Indonesia
196 D4 **Bangko** Indonesia
Bangkok *see* **Krung Thep** Thailand
197 G4 **Bangkuang** Indonesia
198 B4 **Bangkulu** *island* Indonesia
197 H6 **Bangkulua** Indonesia
181 G4 **Bangladesh** *country* Asia
162 C2 **Bango, Serra do** *range* Angola
138 C2 **Bangor** Ceredigion Wales UK
140 C2 **Bangor** North Down Northern Ireland UK
83 Q4 **Bangor** Maine USA
143 C2 **Bangor Erris** Ireland
159 I3 **Bangoran** Central African Republic
86 B5 **Bangs** Texas USA
197 H4 **Bangsalsembera** Indonesia
120 G4 **Bangsjøen** *lake* Norway
120 G4 **Bangsund** Norway
160 C5 **Bangu** Democratic Republic of Congo
195 I3 **Bangued** Philippines
159 H4 **Bangui** Central African Republic
195 I3 **Bangui** Philippines
195 I3 **Bangui Bay** Philippines
160 D3 **Banguru** Democratic Republic of Congo
162 F2 **Bangweulu, Lake** *lake* Zambia
156 E1 **Banhā** Egypt
139 I2 **Banham** Norfolk England UK
158 D2 **Bani** Burkina Faso
159 I3 **Bani** Central African Republic
91 G3 **Baní** Dominican Republic
154 E6 **Bani** *watercourse* Mali
195 H3 **Bani** Philippines
155 G5 **Bani-Bangou** Niger
156 E2 **Banī Mazār** Egypt
178 E6 **Banī Sār** Saudi Arabia
178 E6 **Banī Sharfā'** Saudi Arabia
156 E2 **Banī Suwayf** Egypt
155 I2 **Banī Walīd** Libya
159 H4 **Bania** Central African Republic
129 J6 **Baniane** Algeria
158 B2 **Banie** *watercourse* Guinea
158 C2 **Banifing** *watercourse* Mali
186 D4 **Banihal** Jammu and Kashmir India/Pakistan
158 E2 **Banikoara** Benin
159 G5 **Banio, Lagune** *lake* Gabon
129 I6 **Baniou** Algeria
132 D4 **Baniski Lom** *watercourse* Bulgaria
133 D5 **Banite** Bulgaria
136 E6 **Bāniyās** Syria
130 G4 **Banja Luka** Bosnia and Herzegovina
132 A3 **Banjani** Serbia
196 E5 **Banjaran** Indonesia
197 G4 **Banjarmasin** Indonesia
216 G3 **Banjawarn** WA Australia
125 H5 **Banjol** Croatia
158 A2 **Banjul** Gambia
138 E2 **Bank Street** Worcestershire England UK
186 G6 **Banka** Bihar India
214 B5 **Banka Banka** NT Australia
187 D8 **Bankapur** Karnataka India
154 F6 **Bankass** Mali
142 E4 **Bankfoot** Perth and Kinross Scotland UK
155 G6 **Bankilare** Niger
159 G3 **Bankim** Cameroon
158 B2 **Banko, Massif du** *mountain* Guinea
197 H5 **Bankobankoang** *island* Indonesia
158 C2 **Bankon** Guinea
140 F3 **Banks** Lancashire England UK
109 4 **Banks, Bahía** *bay* Archipiélago de Colón (Galapagos Islands)
74 F6 **Banks Island** British Columbia Canada
222 7 **Banks Islands** Vanuatu
76 H1 **Banks Lake** Nunavut Canada
80 F3 **Banks Lake** Washington USA
221 E6 **Banks Peninsula** New Zealand
219 S10 **Banks Strait** Tas. Australia
186 G6 **Bankura** West Bengal India
132 B3 **Banloc** Romania
181 H4 **Banmauk** Myanmar
140 B2 **Bann** *watercourse* Northern Ireland UK
105 I2 **Bannach** Brazil
213 I5 **Bannermam, Mount** WA Australia
84 D4 **Banning** California USA
139 I2 **Banningham** Norfolk England UK
179 L3 **Bannu** Pakistan
140 B2 **Bannvale** Newry and Mourne Northern Ireland UK
130 H2 **Bánovce nad Bebravou** Slovakia
194 E4 **Banphon** Laos
222 1b **Banreaba** Kiribati
159 F3 **Bansara** Nigeria
186 F5 **Bansi** Uttar Pradesh India
125 J3 **Banská Bystrica** Slovakia
125 J3 **Banská Štiavnica** Slovakia
125 J3 **Banskobystrický** *admin. area* Slovakia
139 G3 **Banstead** Surrey England UK
195 I4 **Bansud** Philippines
187 D7 **Banswada** Andhra Pradesh India
186 D6 **Banswara** Rajasthan India
159 G3 **Bantadjé** Cameroon
196 C7 **Bantam** Cocos (Keeling) Islands Australia
158 E3 **Banté** Benin
143 D4 **Banteer** Ireland
196 E5 **Banten** *admin. area* Indonesia
195 I4 **Banton** *island* Philippines
143 C5 **Bantry** Ireland
143 C5 **Bantry Bay** Ireland
132 D4 **Banya** Bulgaria
196 C3 **Banyak, Kepulauan** *islands* Indonesia
159 G3 **Banyo** Cameroon
129 H2 **Banyoles** Spain
196 E4 **Banyuasin** *watercourse* Indonesia
197 G6 **Banyuwangi** Indonesia
52 D13 **Banzare Bank** *underwater feature* Southern Ocean
59 I2 **Banzare Coast** Antarctica
156 C4 **Bao, Ouadi** *watercourse* Chad
194 E2 **Bảo Lạc** Vietnam
194 E5 **Bảo Lộc** Vietnam
190 F6 **Bao'an** Shaanxi China
191 H4 **Baochang** Nei Mongol Zizhiqu China
191 I5 **Baodi** Tianjin China
191 H5 **Baoding** Hebei China
188 C3 **Baohe** Yunnan China
188 E1 **Baoji** Shaanxi China
189 F2 **Baokang** Hubei China
191 J4 **Baokang** Nei Mongol Zizhiqu China
191 L3 **Baoqing** Heilongjiang China
159 H3 **Baoro** Central African Republic
91 G3 **Baoruco, Sierra de** *range* Dominican Republic
188 C3 **Baoshan** Yunnan China
188 F5 **Baoting** Hainan China
190 G5 **Baotou** Nei Mongol Zizhiqu China
158 C2 **Baoulé** *watercourse* Mali
188 D2 **Baoxing** Sichuan China
188 F5 **Baoyou** Hainan China
187 E8 **Bapatla** Andhra Pradesh India
132 A3 **Bapska** Croatia
188 D3 **Bapu** Sichuan China
179 H3 **Baqījān** Iran
189 G3 **Baqiu** Jiangxi China
178 E2 **Ba'qūbah** Iraq
106 D2 **Baquedano** Chile
109 5 **Baquedano, Punta** *cape* Chile
131 H5 **Bar** Montenegro
132 E1 **Bar** Ukraine
140 C2 **Bar Hall** Ards Northern Ireland UK
79 D10 **Bar Harbor** Maine USA
138 E2 **Bar Hill** Staffordshire England UK
127 G2 **Bar-sur-Seine** France
156 E5 **Bara** Sudan
186 F5 **Bara Banki** Uttar Pradesh India
161 G3 **Baraawe** Somalia
197 G4 **Barabai** Indonesia
183 M2 **Barabinsk** Russian Federation
82 G5 **Baraboo** Wisconsin USA
131 G6 **Baracca, Punta della** *cape* Italy
91 F2 **Baracoa** Cuba
101 I5 **Barada** Brazil
219 I4 **Baradine** NSW Australia
82 G3 **Baraga** Michigan USA
100 D2 **Baragua, Sierra de** *range* Venezuela
128 E3 **Barajas de Melo** Spain
179 I2 **Barākūh** Iran
219 J2 **Barakula** Qld Australia
215 J8 **Baralaba** Qld Australia
76 G2 **Baralzon Lake** Nunavut Canada
197 G3 **Baram** *watercourse* Malaysia
197 G2 **Baram, Tanjong** *cape* Malaysia
187 D7 **Baramati** Maharashtra India
179 J4 **Barambah** Pakistan
186 D3 **Baramulla** Jammu and Kashmir India/Pakistan
123 P5 **Baran'** Belarus
179 I3 **Bārān, Kūh-e** *mountain* Iran
140 A2 **Baranailt** Limavady Northern Ireland UK
136 C2 **Baranavichy** Belarus
132 B2 **Báránd** Hungary
158 D2 **Barani** Burkina Faso
156 F3 **Baranīs** Egypt
74 D4 **Baranof Island** Alaska USA
132 A2 **Baranya** *admin. area* Hungary
105 G4 **Barão de Capanema** Brazil
105 F3 **Barão de Melgaço** Brazil
154 E6 **Baraouéli** Mali
126 F4 **Baraqueville** France
182 F7 **Barārūd** Iran
195 J4 **Baras** Philippines
187 G6 **Barasat** West Bengal India
198 C5 **Barat Daya, Kepulauan** *islands* Indonesia
194 B4 **Baratang Island** Andaman and Nicobar Islands India
86 G6 **Barataria Bay** Louisiana USA
218 D4 **Baratta** SA Australia
102 E4 **Baraúna** Brazil
123 M6 **Barava** Belarus
100 C2 **Barbacáos, Bahía de** *bay* Colombia
103 D8 **Barbacena** Brazil
128 E2 **Barbadillo de Herreros** Spain
101 G1 **Barbados** *country* Caribbean
50 M8 **Barbados Ridge** *underwater feature* Atlantic Ocean
102 E4 **Barbalha** Brazil
100 C5 **Bárbara** Colombia
82 H2 **Barbara Lake** Ontario Canada
129 G2 **Barbastro** Spain
128 D5 **Barbate, Embalse de** *lake* Spain
128 D5 **Barbate de Franco** Spain
126 D4 **Barbezieux-St-Hilaire** France
187 F6 **Barbil** Orissa India
132 F2 **Bărboieni** Moldova
141 F2 **Barbon** Cumbria England UK
100 C3 **Barbosa** Colombia
87 J2 **Barbourville** Kentucky USA
109 18 **Barbuda** *island* Antigua and Barbuda
132 D3 **Bărbuleţu** Romania
122 I4 **Bårby** Sweden
127 I5 **Barcaggio** France
142 C4 **Barcaldine** Argyll and Bute Scotland UK
215 H7 **Barcaldine Downs** Qld Australia
102 B3 **Barcarena** Brazil
128 C4 **Barcarrota** Spain
104 D3 **Barcelona** Peru
129 H3 **Barcelona** Spain
101 E2 **Barcelona** Venezuela
127 H4 **Barcelonnette** France
101 F5 **Barcelos** Brazil
128 B3 **Barcelos** Portugal
128 C2 **Bárcena, Embalse de** *lake* Spain
215 H8 **Barcoo** *watercourse* Qld Australia
100 B4 **Barcos** Colombia
130 G4 **Barcs** Hungary
182 G7 **Bard** Iran
108 C2 **Barda Negra, Meseta de la** *plateau* Argentina
161 H2 **Bardaale** Somalia
155 J4 **Bardaï** Chad
133 F6 **Bardakçı** Turkey
106 D5 **Bardas Blancas** Argentina
179 I2 **Bardāskan** Iran
186 G6 **Barddhaman** West Bengal India
178 G2 **Bardeh Sī** Iran
125 K3 **Bardejov** Slovakia
77 R6 **Bardin, Lac** *lake* Quebec Canada
141 H3 **Bardney** Lincolnshire England UK
187 C7 **Bardoli** Gujarat India
140 D2 **Bardrochwood** Dumfries and Galloway Scotland UK
120 K1 **Bårdset** Norway
138 C2 **Bardsey** *island* Wales UK
179 H3 **Bardsīr** Iran
120 inset **Barðsneshorn** *cape* Iceland
82 I8 **Bardstown** Kentucky USA
120 K2 **Bardujord** Norway
139 H2 **Bardwell** Suffolk England UK
86 C4 **Bardwell** Texas USA
161 G3 **Barē** Ethiopia
132 B3 **Bare** Serbia
140 F2 **Bare** Lancashire England UK
186 E5 **Bareilly** Uttar Pradesh India
139 H5 **Barentin** France
57 L1 **Barents Abyssal Plain** *underwater feature* Arctic Ocean
56 I2 **Barents Sea**
134 F3 **Barentsøya** *island* Norway
156 F4 **Barentu** Eritrea
197 G3 **Bareo** Malaysia
139 F5 **Barfleur** France
126 D2 **Barfleur, Pointe de** *cape* France
139 I2 **Barford** Norfolk England UK
139 F3 **Barford St Martin** Wiltshire England UK
130 D4 **Barga** Italy
187 F7 **Bargarh** Orissa India
124 D5 **Barge** Italy
128 C6 **Bargha** Morocco
187 E6 **Barghat** Madhya Pradesh India
186 E6 **Bargi** Madhya Pradesh India
190 G1 **Barguzin** Russian Federation
135 X7 **Barguzinskiy Khrebet** *range* Russian Federation
187 E7 **Barhi** Chhattisgarh India
186 E6 **Barhi** Madhya Pradesh India
139 G2 **Barholm** Lincolnshire England UK
187 G7 **Bari** Orissa India
186 D6 **Bari** Rajasthan India
131 G6 **Bari** Italy
161 I1 **Bari** *admin. area* Somalia
186 D6 **Bari Sadri** Rajasthan India
178 D5 **Barīdī, Ra's** *cape* Saudi Arabia
155 H1 **Barika** Algeria
101 F2 **Barima** *watercourse* Venezuela
101 G3 **Barima-Waini** *admin. area* Guyana
100 D2 **Barinas** Venezuela
100 D2 **Barinas** *admin. area* Venezuela
159 I4 **Baringa** Democratic Republic of Congo
161 F3 **Baringo, Lake** *lake* Kenya
100 D2 **Barinitas** Venezuela
103 B8 **Bariri** Brazil
156 E3 **Bārīs** Egypt
181 G4 **Barisal** Bangladesh
181 G4 **Barisal** *admin. area* Bangladesh
196 D5 **Barisan, Pegunungan** *range* Indonesia
131 E5 **Barisciano** Italy
197 G4 **Barito** *watercourse* Indonesia
127 G4 **Barjac** France
127 H5 **Barjols** France
179 I5 **Barkā'** Oman
183 K7 **Barkah** Afghanistan
156 E4 **Barkal, Jebel** *mountain* Sudan
101 H4 **Barkarel** French Guiana
123 N4 **Barkava** Latvia
213 H4 **Barker** *watercourse* WA Australia
215 K7 **Barker, Mount** Qld Australia
216 G5 **Barker Lake** WA Australia
154 D5 **Barkéwol el Abiod** Mauritania
179 L3 **Barkhan** Pakistan
139 H3 **Barking** Greater London England UK
86 H2 **Barkley, Lake** Kentucky USA
80 C2 **Barkley Sound** British Columbia Canada
214 E6 **Barkly Downs** Qld Australia
214 C5 **Barkly Homestead** NT Australia
214 C5 **Barkly Tableland** NT Australia
162 D5 **Barkly West** South Africa
85 L6 **Barksdale** Texas USA
142 D6 **Barlae** Dumfries and Galloway Scotland UK
139 E2 **Barlaston** Staffordshire England UK
164 4 **Barlavento, Ilhas do** *islands* Cape Verde
124 F1 **Barleben** Germany
216 D7 **Barlee** WA Australia
216 F4 **Barlee, Lake** WA Australia
158 B3 **Barlo Point** *cape* Sierra Leone
218 G7 **Barmah** Vic. Australia
179 I3 **Barmenj** Iran
186 C6 **Barmer** Rajasthan India
139 H2 **Barmer** Norfolk England UK
218 E6 **Barmera** SA Australia
138 C2 **Barmouth Bay** Wales UK
164 5b **Barn Long Point** *cape* St Helena
143 C3 **Barna** Ireland
140 A4 **Barnadown** Ireland
186 D4 **Barnala** Punjab India
143 E3 **Barnan** Ireland
85 M1 **Barnard** Kansas USA
130 E2 **Bärnau** Germany
183 N2 **Barnaul** Russian Federation
59 K1 **Barne Inlet** *bay* Antarctica
83 O7 **Barnegat Bay** New Jersey USA
83 N7 **Barnegat Light** New Jersey USA
81 Q7 **Barnes** Kansas USA
73 L4 **Barnes Ice Cap** Nunavut Canada
139 G3 **Barnet** Greater London England UK
108 C6 **Barnevelt, Islas** *islands* Chile
124 G1 **Barnewitz** Germany
139 H2 **Barney** Norfolk England UK
219 K3 **Barney, Mount** Qld Australia
215 G4 **Barney Knob** *mountain* Qld Australia
218 G5 **Barneys Lake** NSW Australia
139 H2 **Barnham** Suffolk England UK
85 L5 **Barnhart** Texas USA
142 E3 **Barnhill** Moray Scotland UK
142 C5 **Barnhills** Dumfries and Galloway Scotland UK
216 E4 **Barnong** WA Australia
139 G3 **Barns Green** West Sussex England UK
141 G3 **Barnsley** South Yorkshire England UK
138 C3 **Barnstaple** Devon England UK
138 C3 **Barnstaple or Bideford Bay** England UK
124 E1 **Barnstorf** Germany
82 E3 **Barnum** Minnesota USA
87 K4 **Barnwell** South Carolina USA
159 F3 **Baro** Nigeria
186 D6 **Baroda** Madhya Pradesh India
186 D6 **Baroda** Rajasthan India
179 M2 **Baroghil Pass** Pakistan
80 I2 **Barons** Alberta Canada
143 C5 **Barony Bridge** Ireland
160 C2 **Baroua** Central African Republic
120 I2 **Barøya** *island* Norway
195 G5 **Barque Canada Reef** Spratly Islands
100 D2 **Barquisimeto** Venezuela
142 D5 **Barr** South Ayrshire Scotland UK
103 D5 **Barra** Brazil
163 G4 **Barra, Ponta da** *cape* Mozambique
142 A3 **Barra, Sound of** *bay* Scotland UK
103 D6 **Barra da Estiva** Brazil
102 F5 **Barra de Santo Antônio** Brazil
103 D7 **Barra de São Francisco** Brazil
105 G4 **Barra do Bugres** Brazil
102 C4 **Barra do Corda** Brazil
105 H5 **Barra do Félix** Brazil
103 A6 **Barra do Garças** Brazil
103 D8 **Barra do Piraí** Brazil
163 G4 **Barra Falsa, Ponta da** *cape* Mozambique
90 C4 **Barra Patuca** Honduras
103 B9 **Barra Velha** Brazil
219 J4 **Barraba** NSW Australia
105 G2 **Barraca de Seringueiro** Brazil
105 F3 **Barraca do Lucas** Brazil
105 G4 **Barracão** Brazil
105 G3 **Barracão do Barreto** Brazil
105 G3 **Barracão São José** Brazil
129 F3 **Barrachina** Spain
128 D3 **Barraco** Spain
143 D4 **Barraden** Ireland
143 C4 **Barraduff** Ireland
216 F3 **Barrambie** WA Australia
104 B2 **Barranca** Peru
100 C3 **Barranca de Upía** Colombia
100 C3 **Barrancabermeja** Colombia
106 D6 **Barrancas** *watercourse* Argentina
104 E6 **Barrancas** Bolivia
100 C2 **Barrancas** Colombia
88 D3 **Barranco** Mexico
105 F4 **Barranco Alto** Brazil
140 B4 **Barranisky** Ireland
100 C2 **Barranquilla** Colombia
100 D2 **Barranquitas** Venezuela
142 B4 **Barrapoll** Highland Scotland UK
102 D4 **Barras** Brazil
128 E4 **Barrax** Spain
126 F4 **Barre-des-Cévennes** France
105 I3 **Barreira do Campo** Brazil
103 C6 **Barreiras** Brazil
102 D3 **Barreirinhas** Brazil
105 H4 **Barreiro** Brazil
103 D6 **Barreiro do Jaíba** Brazil
105 I3 **Barreiro do Nascimento** Brazil
82 F2 **Barrel Lake** Ontario Canada
219 S10 **Barren, Cape** Tas. Australia
109 7 **Barren Island** Falkland Islands
194 B4 **Barren Island** Andaman and Nicobar Islands India
72 D7 **Barren Islands** Alaska USA
87 H2 **Barren River Lake** Kentucky USA
103 B8 **Barretos** Brazil
219 K3 **Barretts Creek** NSW Australia
221 D6 **Barrhill** New Zealand
142 D5 **Barrhill** South Ayrshire Scotland UK
83 L4 **Barrie** Ontario Canada
108 E1 **Barrientos, Sierra de los** *range* Argentina
59 F2 **Barrier Bay** Antarctica
78 D1 **Barrier Inlet** Nunavut Canada
218 E4 **Barrier Range** NSW Australia
222 5 **Barrigada** Guam
89 F3 **Barril, Laguna El** *lake* Mexico
79 F11 **Barrington** Nova Scotia Canada
142 E4 **Barrington** Fife Scotland UK
214 D7 **Barrington, Mount** NT Australia
76 E4 **Barrington Lake** Manitoba Canada
219 J5 **Barrington Tops** NSW Australia
218 G3 **Barringun** Qld Australia
126 B5 **Barrios de Luna, Embalse de** *lake* Spain
143 C2 **Barroosky** Ireland
102 D3 **Barroquinha** Brazil
103 D8 **Barroso** Brazil
104 D5 **Barroso, Nevado** *mountain* Peru
109 11a **Barrouallie** St Vincent and the Grenadines
106 F6 **Barrow** Argentina
140 B4 **Barrow** *watercourse* Ireland
72 D4 **Barrow** Alaska USA
72 D4 **Barrow, Point** Alaska USA
214 B6 **Barrow Creek** NT Australia
141 H3 **Barrow Haven** North Lincolnshire England UK
212 C6 **Barrow Island** WA Australia
215 H3 **Barrow Point** Qld Australia
73 J4 **Barrow Strait** Nunavut Canada
139 G2 **Barrowby** Lincolnshire England UK
75 U6 **Barrows** Manitoba Canada
128 C3 **Barruecopardo** Spain
101 H3 **Barruol, Monts** *range* French Guiana
138 D3 **Barry** Vale of Glamorgan Wales UK
218 B3 **Barry, Mount** SA Australia
218 H8 **Barry Beach** Vic. Australia
221 D6 **Barrytown** New Zealand
158 D2 **Barsalogo** Burkina Faso
125 M4 **Bârsana** Romania
182 F7 **Barseh** Iran
187 D7 **Barsi** Maharashtra India
122 E5 **Barsø** *island* Denmark
84 D3 **Barstow** California USA
85 K5 **Barstow** Texas USA
123 K4 **Barstyčiai** Lithuania
120 J3 **Bartaurte** *range* Sweden
122 G5 **Barthe** *watercourse* Germany
101 G3 **Bartica** Guyana
136 E5 **Bartin** Turkey
136 E5 **Bartin** *admin. area* Turkey
215 H4 **Bartle Frere** *mountain* Qld Australia
82 D8 **Bartlesville** Oklahoma USA
84 C2 **Bartlett** California USA
81 P6 **Bartlett** Nebraska USA
86 G3 **Bartlett** Tennessee USA
83 O4 **Barton** Vermont USA
76 I6 **Barton Lake** Ontario Canada
217 M5 **Barton Siding** SA Australia
87 K7 **Bartow** Florida USA
125 L5 **Baru** Romania
100 C2 **Baru, Isla de** *island* Colombia
100 C2 **Baru, Punta** *cape* Colombia
219 K1 **Barubbra Island** Qld Australia
101 F4 **Barudene, Serra** *range* Brazil
103 C8 **Barueri** Brazil
196 C3 **Barumun** *watercourse* Indonesia
190 G2 **Barun-Sabartuj, Gora** *mountain* Russian Federation
197 G6 **Barung** *island* Indonesia
214 B3 **Barunga** NT Australia
123 N5 **Baruny** Belarus
196 C3 **Barus** Indonesia
183 K6 **Barushan** Tajikistan
125 G1 **Baruth** Germany
191 H3 **Baruun-Urt** Mongolia
190 E3 **Baruunbayan-ylaan** Mongolia
190 E2 **Baruunburen** Mongolia
185 J2 **Baruunturuun** Mongolia
187 C6 **Barwala** Gujarat India
187 D6 **Barwani** Madhya Pradesh India
216 G3 **Barwidgee** WA Australia
215 H4 **Barwidgi** Qld Australia
218 G4 **Barwon** *watercourse* NSW Australia
218 G8 **Barwon Heads** Vic. Australia
125 L3 **Barycz** Poland
125 I2 **Barycz** *watercourse* Poland
135 AB5 **Barylas** Russian Federation
136 D1 **Barysaw** Belarus
182 E2 **Barysh** Russian Federation
219 K3 **Baryulgil** NSW Australia
132 B2 **Bârzava** Romania
160 A5 **Bas-Congo** *admin. area* Democratic Republic of Congo
132 B3 **Bašaid** Serbia
160 C3 **Basali** Democratic Republic of Congo
215 H5 **Basalt** *watercourse* Qld Australia
160 C5 **Basanga** Democratic Republic of Congo
160 B3 **Basankusu** Democratic Republic of Congo
128 E2 **Basauri** Spain
187 D8 **Basavakalyan** Karnataka India
195 I2 **Basco** Philippines
106 D4 **Bascuñán, Cabo** *cape* Chile
127 H3 **Basel** Switzerland
131 G6 **Basento** *watercourse* Italy
132 D3 **Băseşti** Romania
183 N3 **Bashchelakskiy Khrebet** *range* Russian Federation
189 I4 **Bashi Channal** *sea* Taiwan China
160 C5 **Bashimuke** Democratic Republic of Congo
182 F6 **Bashirabat** Azerbaijan
182 D2 **Bashmakovo** Russian Federation
178 G3 **Bāsht** Iran
132 H2 **Bashtanka** Ukraine
178 E2 **Bāshūr** Iraq
199 I6 **Basilaki Island** Papua New Guinea
195 I6 **Basilan** *island* Philippines
139 H3 **Basildon** Essex England UK
86 E5 **Basile** Louisiana USA
131 F6 **Basilicata** *admin. area* Italy
131 F7 **Basiluzzo, Isola** *island* Italy
81 K4 **Basin** Wyoming USA
75 S6 **Basin Lake** Saskatchewan Canada
122 I2 **Båsingen** *lake* Sweden
139 F3 **Basingstoke** Hampshire England UK
187 G6 **Basirhat** West Bengal India
83 R4 **Baskahegan Lake** Maine USA
136 H5 **Başkale** Turkey
73 L9 **Baskatong, Réservoir** Quebec Canada
83 N3 **Baskatong Lake** Quebec Canada
212 G4 **Baskerville, Cape** WA Australia
120 J4 **Bäsksjö** Sweden
141 G3 **Baslow** Derbyshire England UK
133 G7 **Başmakçı** Turkey
187 D7 **Basmat** Maharashtra India
187 F7 **Basna** Chhattisgarh India
196 D4 **Baso** *island* Indonesia
186 D6 **Basoda** Madhya Pradesh India
160 C3 **Basoko** Democratic Republic of Congo
160 C4 **Basongo** Democratic Republic of Congo
109 1a **Basora, Punta** *cape* Aruba
84 C2 **Bass Lake** California USA
130 D4 **Bassano del Grappa** Italy
164 6a **Bassas da India** Îles Éparses
159 I3 **Basse-Kotto** *admin. area* Central African Republic
126 D2 **Basse-Normandie** *admin. area* France
109 14 **Basse-Pointe** Martinique
158 B2 **Basse Santa Su** Gambia
109 16 **Basse-Terre** Guadeloupe
109 16 **Basse-Terre** *island* Guadeloupe
109 9 **Basse Terre** Trinidad and Tobago
Bassein *see* **Pathein** Myanmar
140 E2 **Bassenthwaite Lake** England UK
109 16 **Basses, Pointe des** *cape* Guadeloupe
109 19 **Basseterre** St Kitts and Nevis
81 P5 **Bassett** Nebraska USA
154 E5 **Bassikounou** Mauritania
126 D4 **Bassin d'Arcachon** *bay* France
124 E1 **Bassum** Germany

82 F2 **Basswood Lake** Ontario Canada
142 inset **Basta** Shetland Scotland UK
186 F5 **Basti** Uttar Pradesh India
127 I5 **Bastia** France
130 E5 **Bastia** Italy
79 H7 **Bastille, Lac** *lake* Quebec Canada
127 G1 **Bastogne** Belgium
103 B8 **Bastos** Brazil
86 F4 **Bastrop** Louisiana USA
86 C5 **Bastrop** Texas USA
123 K2 **Bastuskär** *island* Finland
120 L4 **Bastuträsk** Sweden
196 D4 **Basu, Tanjung** *cape* Indonesia
187 G7 **Basudebpur** Orissa India
199 H4 **Bat Islands** Papua New Guinea
190 E3 **Bat ulzai** Mongolia
159 F4 **Bata** Equatorial Guinea
195 I4 **Bataan Peninsula** *cape* Philippines
90 D2 **Batabanó, Golfo de** *bay* Cuba
195 I3 **Batac** Philippines
199 F4 **Bataf** Indonesia
195 J4 **Batag** *island* Philippines
135 AB5 **Batagay-Alyta** Russian Federation
103 A8 **Bataiporã** Brazil
133 D5 **Batak** Bulgaria
197 G5 **Batakan** Indonesia
186 D4 **Batala** Punjab India
102 D4 **Batalha** Brazil
196 E3 **Batam** *island* Indonesia
160 D3 **Batama** Democratic Republic of Congo
182 H3 **Batamshinskiy** Kazakhstan
195 I2 **Batan Islands** Philippines
196 F5 **Batang** Indonesia
197 F3 **Batang Tarang** Indonesia
159 H3 **Batangafo** Central African Republic
195 I4 **Batangas** Philippines
196 C3 **Batangtoru** Indonesia
198 D4 **Batanta** *island* Indonesia
132 B2 **Batăr** Romania
132 A2 **Bátaszék** Hungary
101 G5 **Batata, Lagoa** *lake* Brazil
103 C8 **Batatais** Brazil
214 G2 **Batavia Downs** Qld Australia
213 K2 **Batchelor** NT Australia
82 I3 **Batchewine Bay** Michigan USA
194 D4 **Bătdâmbâng** Cambodia
160 A4 **Batéké, Plateaux** *plain* Congo
219 J6 **Batemans Bay** NSW Australia
82 I7 **Batesville** Indiana USA
123 P3 **Batetskiy** Russian Federation
109 19 **Bath** St Kitts and Nevis
128 E3 **Bath** Bath and North East Somerset England UK
138 E3 **Bath and North East Somerset** *admin. area* England UK
159 H2 **Batha** *admin. area* Chad
159 H2 **Batha, Ouadi** *watercourse* Chad
138 C4 **Bathpool** Cornwall England UK
109 12 **Bathsheba** Barbados
219 I5 **Bathurst** NSW Australia
79 F9 **Bathurst** New Brunswick Canada
72 G4 **Bathurst, Cape** Northwest Territories Canada
72 I5 **Bathurst Inlet** Nunavut Canada
213 G4 **Bathurst Island** WA Australia
73 J3 **Bathurst Island** Nunavut Canada
157 F5 **Batī** Ethiopia
133 E7 **Batı Menteşe Dağları** *range* Turkey
158 E2 **Batia** Benin
158 D3 **Batié** Burkina Faso
223 9 **Batiki** *island* Fiji
130 H4 **Batina** Croatia
178 G4 **Baţinah, Al** *island* Saudi Arabia
125 K3 **Bátka** Slovakia
183 K6 **Batken** Kyrgyzstan
183 K6 **Batken** *admin. area* Kyrgyzstan
179 H3 **Bāţlāq-e Gāvkhūnī** *lake* Iran
141 G3 **Batley** West Yorkshire England UK
219 I6 **Batlow** NSW Australia
136 G6 **Batman** Turkey
136 G6 **Batman** *admin. area* Turkey
136 G6 **Batman Barajı** *lake* Turkey
155 H1 **Batna** Algeria
190 G3 **Batnarov** Mongolia
195 I2 **Baton** *island* Philippines
86 F5 **Baton Rouge** Louisiana USA
194 C6 **Batong, Ko** *island* Thailand
85 I7 **Batopilas** Mexico
186 D4 **Batote** Jammu and Kashmir India/Pakistan
159 G4 **Batouala** Gabon
159 G4 **Batouri** Cameroon
132 C3 **Bătrîna** Romania
120 K3 **Båtsa** *lake* Sweden
121 P1 **Båtsfjord** Norway
190 G3 **Batshireet** Mongolia
133 D7 **Batsíon** Greece
120 J3 **Båtsjaur** Sweden
190 F3 **Batsumber** Mongolia
215 H4 **Batt Reef** Qld Australia
78 K6 **Batteau** Newfoundland and Labrador Canada
214 D4 **Batten** *watercourse* NT Australia
196 B1 **Batti Malv** *island* Andaman and Nicobar Islands India
194 B5 **Batti Malv** *island* Nicobar Islands India
187 E10 **Batticaloa** Sri Lanka
214 A4 **Battle** *watercourse* NT Australia
75 Q6 **Battle** *watercourse* Alberta/Saskatchewan Canada
139 H4 **Battle** East Sussex England UK
138 D3 **Battle** Powys Wales UK
82 I5 **Battle Creek** Michigan USA
80 G6 **Battle Mountain** Nevada USA
132 B2 **Battonya** Hungary
190 E3 **Battsengel** Mongolia
161 F2 **Batu** *mountain* Ethiopia
197 G3 **Batu, Bukit** *mountain* Malaysia
196 C4 **Batu, Kepulauan** *islands* Indonesia
197 H3 **Batu, Tanjung** *cape* Indonesia
196 E6 **Batu Ampar** Indonesia
196 D3 **Batu Besar** Indonesia
197 G3 **Batu Bora, Bukit** *mountain* Malaysia
196 D2 **Batu Gajah** Malaysia
196 D3 **Batu Pahat** Malaysia
196 D2 **Batu Puteh, Gunung** *mountain* Malaysia
198 B5 **Batuata** *island* Indonesia
197 G3 **Batuayau, Bukit** *mountain* Indonesia
196 E4 **Batubetumbang** Indonesia
198 B4 **Batudaka** *island* Indonesia
198 B4 **Batuhitam, Tanjung** *cape* Indonesia
197 H4 **Batulicin** Indonesia
197 G3 **Batulilangmebang, Gunung** *mountain* Indonesia
182 D5 **Bat'umi** Georgia
196 D4 **Batumonga** Indonesia
179 M2 **Batura Glacier** Pakistan
196 E5 **Baturaja** Indonesia
102 E4 **Baturité** Brazil
126 B2 **Batz, Île de** *island* France
197 F3 **Bau** Malaysia
198 B5 **Baubau** Indonesia
159 F2 **Bauchi** Nigeria
159 F2 **Bauchi** *admin. area* Nigeria
126 C3 **Baud** France
77 S7 **Baudeau, Lac** *lake* Quebec Canada
187 F7 **Baudh** Orissa India
100 B3 **Baudó, Bahía de** *bay* Colombia
100 B3 **Baudó, Serranía de** *range* Colombia
218 B5 **Bauer, Cape** SA Australia
53 V8 **Bauer Basin** *underwater feature* Pacific Ocean
211 inset **Bauer Bay** Macquarie Island Australia
126 D3 **Baugé** France
101 H3 **Baugé, Monts** *range* French Guiana
126 F3 **Baugy** France
214 D5 **Bauhinia** *watercourse* NT Australia
198 C6 **Baukau** Timor-Leste (East Timor)
198 B5 **Baula** Indonesia
79 K7 **Bauld, Cape** Newfoundland and Labrador Canada
73 K3 **Baumann Fiord** Nunavut Canada
141 H3 **Baumber** Lincolnshire England UK
127 H3 **Baume-les-Dames** France
198 E5 **Baun** *island* Indonesia
219 K1 **Bauple** Qld Australia
105 F4 **Baures** Bolivia
143 D4 **Baurnagurrahy** Ireland
103 B8 **Bauru** Brazil
103 A7 **Baús** Brazil
186 G6 **Bausi** Bihar India
123 M4 **Bauska** Latvia
123 M4 **Bauskas** *admin. area* Latvia
182 F5 **Bautino** Kazakhstan
125 H2 **Bautzen** Germany
108 C4 **Bauzá, Punta** *cape* Argentina
124 B2 **Bavay** France
122 I3 **Båven** *lake* Sweden
88 C2 **Bavispe** Mexico
88 C2 **Bavispe** *watercourse* Mexico
130 F2 **Bavorov** Czech Republic
218 H7 **Baw Baw, Mount** Vic. Australia
218 H7 **Baw Baw Alpine Village** Vic. Australia
197 F4 **Bawal** *island* Indonesia
197 G4 **Bawan** Indonesia
197 F4 **Bawang, Tanjung** *cape* Indonesia
139 I2 **Bawburgh** Norfolk England UK
197 G5 **Bawean** *island* Indonesia
158 D2 **Bawku** Ghana
181 H5 **Bawlake** Myanmar
219 J6 **Bawley Point** NSW Australia
158 C3 **Bawo** Liberia
179 I5 **Bawshar** Oman
215 K6 **Bax Reef** Qld Australia
87 J5 **Baxley** Georgia USA
217 I6 **Baxter Cliffs** WA Australia
161 G3 **Bay** *admin. area* Somalia
86 F3 **Bay** Arkansas USA
79 L9 **Bay Bulls** Newfoundland and Labrador Canada
82 J5 **Bay City** Michigan USA
86 D6 **Bay City** Texas USA
86 H5 **Bay Minette** Alabama USA
220 G3 **Bay of Plenty** *admin. area* New Zealand
79 L9 **Bay Roberts** Newfoundland and Labrador Canada
79 H9 **Bay St Lawrence** Nova Scotia Canada
86 G3 **Bay Springs Lake** Mississippi USA
220 G4 **Bay View** New Zealand
196 E5 **Bayah** Indonesia
90 E2 **Bayamo** Cuba
91 H3 **Bayamón** Puerto Rico
191 K3 **Bayan** Heilongjiang China
190 E6 **Bayan** Qinghai China
190 D5 **Bayan** Qinghai China
197 H6 **Bayan** Indonesia
190 E2 **Bayan** Mongolia
190 F3 **Bayan** Mongolia
190 G3 **Bayan-adarga** Mongolia
190 F5 **Bayan Hot** Nei Mongol Zizhiqu China
185 I2 **Bayan-Ölgiy** *admin. area* Mongolia
190 F4 **Bayan-ovoo** Mongolia
191 I2 **Bayan Tohoi** Nei Mongol Zizhiqu China
190 F3 **Bayan-unjuul** Mongolia
190 E4 **Bayandalai** Mongolia
191 G3 **Bayandelger** Mongolia
191 H2 **Bayandun** Mongolia
190 E3 **Bayandun** Mongolia
160 B3 **Bayanga** Central African Republic
159 H3 **Bayanga-Didi** Central African Republic
190 F5 **Bayangaole** Nei Mongol Zizhiqu China
190 E3 **Bayangol** Mongolia
190 F3 **Bayangol** Mongolia
190 D4 **Bayangov** Mongolia
185 J2 **Bayanhairhan** Mongolia
190 F3 **Bayanhangai** Mongolia
190 D3 **Bayanhongor** Mongolia
190 D3 **Bayanhongor** *admin. area* Mongolia
190 G3 **Bayanhutag** Mongolia
190 F3 **Bayanjargalan** Mongolia
191 I2 **Bayankuren** Nei Mongol Zizhiqu China
190 D4 **Bayanlig** Mongolia
191 G3 **Bayanmunha** Mongolia
190 E3 **Bayannuur** Mongolia
185 I3 **Bayannuur** Mongolia
100 B2 **Bayano, Lago** *lake* Panama
190 G3 **Bayanovoo** Mongolia
190 F3 **Bayantal** Mongolia
190 E3 **Bayanteeg** Mongolia
185 J2 **Bayantes** Mongolia
190 D3 **Bayantsagaan** Mongolia
190 F3 **Bayantsagaan** Mongolia
190 F3 **Bayantsogt** Mongolia
191 H3 **Bayantumen** Mongolia
190 E3 **Bayanunder** Mongolia
191 G2 **Bayanuul** Mongolia
191 I4 **Bayanwula** Nei Mongol Zizhiqu China
185 K2 **Bayanzurhe** Mongolia
81 N6 **Bayard** Nebraska USA
85 H4 **Bayard** New Mexico USA
133 G6 **Bayat** Turkey
87 M3 **Bayboro** North Carolina USA
140 E2 **Baycliff** Cumbria England UK
134 O5 **Baydaratskaya Guba** *bay* Russian Federation
161 G3 **Baydhabo** Somalia
159 F4 **Bayelsa** *admin. area* Nigeria
130 D2 **Bayern** *admin. area* Germany
126 D2 **Bayeux** France
183 M2 **Bayevo** Russian Federation
83 K5 **Bayfield** Ontario Canada
85 I2 **Bayfield** Colorado USA
82 F3 **Bayfield** Wisconsin USA
79 I7 **Bayfield, Île** *island* Quebec Canada
182 G4 **Bayganin** Kazakhstan
178 E2 **Bayjī** Iraq
190 F1 **Baykal (Lake Baikal), Ozero** *lake* Russian Federation
135 W7 **Baykal'skiy Khrebet** *range* Russian Federation
135 U6 **Baykit** Russian Federation
182 I4 **Baykonyr** Kazakhstan
220 E2 **Baylys Beach** New Zealand
182 H3 **Baymak** Russian Federation
219 J4 **Baynes Mountain** NSW Australia
127 H2 **Bayon** France
128 B2 **Bayona** Spain
126 D5 **Bayonne** France
86 E4 **Bayou D'Arbonne Lake** Louisiana USA
86 D6 **Bayou Vista** Texas USA
104 A2 **Bayovar** Peru
182 I4 **Bayqonyr** *admin. area* Kazakhstan
182 I6 **Bayramaly** Turkmenistan
124 F3 **Bayreuth** Germany
83 L4 **Bays, Lake of** Ontario Canada
191 H1 **Baysa** Russian Federation
183 M5 **Bayserke** Kazakhstan
178 E7 **Bayt al Faqīh** Yemen
182 I4 **Baytakkol'** *lake* Kazakhstan
185 I3 **Baytik Shan** *range* Xinjiang Uygur Zizhiqu China
86 D6 **Baytown** Texas USA
198 B4 **Bayu** Indonesia
196 D4 **Bayunglincir** Indonesia
128 E5 **Baza** Spain
179 L2 **Bāzārak** Afghanistan
182 E3 **Bazarnyy-Karabulak** Russian Federation
163 G4 **Bazaruto, Ilha do** *island* Mozambique
126 D4 **Bazas** France
188 E2 **Bazhong** Sichuan China
191 H5 **Bazhou** Hebei China
179 I4 **Bāzīgar** Iran
78 E5 **Bazil, Lac** *lake* Quebec Canada
164 5a **BBC Atlantic Relay Station** Ascension
194 E5 **Be** *watercourse* Vietnam
163 I2 **Bé, Nosy** *island* Madagascar
142 C4 **Beach** Highland Scotland UK
81 N3 **Beach** North Dakota USA
218 D7 **Beachport** SA Australia
83 N7 **Beachwood** New Jersey USA
139 H4 **Beachy Head** *cape* England UK
216 E5 **Beacon** WA Australia
83 O6 **Beacon** New York USA
138 C4 **Beaford** Devon England UK
143 C4 **Beaghfa** Ireland
108 C6 **Beagle, Canal** *strait* Chile
108 A5 **Beagle, Isla** *island* Chile
212 G4 **Beagle Bay** WA Australia
213 K2 **Beagle Gulf** NT Australia
213 G3 **Beagle Reef** WA Australia
163 I2 **Bealanana** Madagascar
80 C2 **Beale, Cape** British Columbia Canada
142 E4 **Beannie** Perth and Kinross Scotland UK
75 N3 **Bear** *watercourse* Alberta Canada
80 J5 **Bear** *watercourse* Idaho USA
74 C3 **Bear Camp** British Columbia Canada
76 M1 **Bear Cove** Nunavut Canada
75 Q4 **Bear Creek** Saskatchewan Canada
80 F8 **Bear Creek Spire** *mountain* California USA
77 O5 **Bear Island** Nunavut Canada
143 C5 **Bear Island** Ireland
74 J5 **Bear Lake** British Columbia Canada
76 H5 **Bear Lake** Manitoba Canada
80 J6 **Bear Lake** Utah USA
59 Q2 **Bear Peninsula** Antarctica
86 E4 **Bearden** Arkansas USA
82 H2 **Beardmore** Ontario Canada
84 B1 **Beardsley Lake** California USA
139 G3 **Beare Green** Surrey England UK
126 D5 **Béarn** *region* France
140 A2 **Bearney** Strabane Northern Ireland UK
81 K2 **Bears Paw Mountains** Montana USA
142 D5 **Bearsden** East Dunbartonshire Scotland UK
76 J6 **Bearskin Lake** Ontario Canada
139 H3 **Bearsted** Kent England UK
128 C5 **Beas** Spain
128 E4 **Beas de Segura** Spain
128 E2 **Beasain** Spain
212 D7 **Beasley** *watercourse* WA Australia
91 G3 **Beata, Cabo** *cape* Dominican Republic
91 G3 **Beata, Isla** *island* Dominican Republic
50 K8 **Beata Ridge** *underwater feature* Caribbean Sea
81 Q6 **Beatrice** Nebraska USA
214 D3 **Beatrice, Cape** NT Australia
81 Q7 **Beattie** Kansas USA
142 E5 **Beattock** Dumfries and Galloway Scotland UK
74 K4 **Beatton** *watercourse* British Columbia Canada
84 D2 **Beatty** Nevada USA
127 G5 **Beaucaire** France
139 I5 **Beaucamps-le-Vieux** France
126 E2 **Beauce** *region* France
108 E5 **Beauchêne Island** Falkland Islands
218 F7 **Beaufort** Vic. Australia
127 H4 **Beaufort** France
197 G2 **Beaufort** Malaysia
87 M3 **Beaufort** North Carolina USA
87 K4 **Beaufort** South Carolina USA
72 D4 **Beaufort Sea** Canada/USA
162 D6 **Beaufort West** South Africa
126 E3 **Beaugency** France
142 D3 **Beauly** *watercourse* Scotland UK
140 D3 **Beaumaris** Isle of Anglesey Wales UK
126 E2 **Beaumesnil** France
127 G1 **Beaumont** Belgium
143 F3 **Beaumont** Ireland
221 C7 **Beaumont** New Zealand
86 G5 **Beaumont** Mississippi USA
86 D5 **Beaumont** Texas USA
59 K1 **Beaumont Bay** Antarctica
126 E4 **Beaumont-du-Périgord** France
127 G2 **Beaumont-en-Argonne** France
139 F5 **Beaumont-Hague** France
127 G3 **Beaune** France
126 F2 **Beaune-La Rolande** France
127 G1 **Beauraing** Belgium
222 7 **Beautemps-Beaupré, Île** *island* New Caledonia
126 F2 **Beauvais** France
126 F1 **Beauval** France
126 C3 **Beauvoir-sur-Mer** France
72 H/I8 **Beaver** *watercourse* Alberta/Saskatchewan Canada
78 H6 **Beaver** *watercourse* Newfoundland and Labrador Canada
76 K5 **Beaver** *watercourse* Ontario Canada
81 O8 **Beaver** Oklahoma USA
86 A2 **Beaver** *watercourse* Oklahoma USA
80 I7 **Beaver** Utah USA
80 I7 **Beaver** *watercourse* Utah USA
72 E6 **Beaver Creek** Yukon Territory Canada
82 G5 **Beaver Dam** Wisconsin USA
76 H5 **Beaver Hill Lake** Manitoba Canada
109 7 **Beaver Island** Falkland Islands
82 I4 **Beaver Island** Michigan USA
74 M2 **Beaver Lake** Northwest Territories Canada
86 E2 **Beaver Lake** Arkansas USA
76 J5 **Beaver Stone** *watercourse* Ontario Canada
75 R8 **Beaver Valley** Saskatchewan Canada
80 I4 **Beaverhead Mountains** Montana USA
75 O6 **Beaverhill Lake** Alberta Canada
74 L5 **Beaverlodge** Alberta Canada
80 D4 **Beaverton** Oregon USA
186 D5 **Beawar** Rajasthan India
106 E5 **Beazley** Argentina
159 H3 **Bébédjia** Chad
103 B8 **Bebedouro** Brazil
102 E4 **Beberibe** Brazil
140 E3 **Bebington** Merseyside England UK
127 I1 **Bebra** Germany
129 H4 **Beca, Punta** *cape* Spain
89 H4 **Becal** Mexico
78 B2 **Bécard, Lac** *lake* Quebec Canada
139 I2 **Beccles** Suffolk England UK
132 E3 **Beceni** Romania
128 C2 **Becerreá** Spain
100 C2 **Becerril** Colombia
155 F2 **Béchar** Algeria
72 D7 **Becharof Lake** Alaska USA
126 D2 **Bécherel** France
141 H2 **Beck Hole** North Yorkshire England UK
59 T1 **Becker, Mount** *mountain* Antarctica
141 H3 **Beckingham** Nottinghamshire England UK
83 K8 **Beckley** West Virginia USA
86 D4 **Beckville** Texas USA
141 G3 **Beckwithshaw** North Yorkshire England UK
132 D2 **Beclean** Romania
125 I4 **Becsehely** Hungary
140 B3 **Bective** Ireland
141 G2 **Bedale** North Yorkshire England UK
126 F5 **Bédarieux** France
141 G2 **Bedburn** Durham England UK
139 H4 **Beddingham** East Sussex England UK
75 U8 **Bede** Manitoba Canada
161 F2 **Bedelē** Ethiopia
182 G2 **Bedeyeva Polyana** Russian Federation
139 G2 **Bedford** Bedfordshire England UK
82 H7 **Bedford** Indiana USA
83 L6 **Bedford** Pennsylvania USA
83 L8 **Bedford** Virginia USA
215 H3 **Bedford, Cape** Qld Australia
213 G4 **Bedford Island** WA Australia
109 10a **Bedford Point** Grenada
139 G2 **Bedfordshire** *admin. area* England UK
179 K4 **Bedi** Pakistan
196 E4 **Bedinggong** Indonesia
156 F4 **Bedja** *range* Sudan
125 J2 **Będków** Poland
141 G1 **Bedlington** Northumberland England UK
135 U7 **Bedoba** Russian Federation
196 E4 **Bedok** *admin. area* Singapore
196 E3 **Bedok Reservoir** Singapore
124 F4 **Bedole** Italy
214 E8 **Bedourie** Qld Australia
124 D1 **Bedum** Netherlands
196 D2 **Bedung** Malaysia
139 F2 **Bedworth** Warwickshire England UK
142 A3 **Bee, Loch** *bay* Scotland UK
83 L7 **Beech Flat Knob** *mountain* West Virginia USA
81 L1 **Beechy** Saskatchewan Canada
141 G3 **Beeley** Derbyshire England UK
178 C3 **Be'ér Sheva'** Israel
219 K2 **Beerwah** Qld Australia
125 H1 **Beeskow** Germany
139 F2 **Beeston** Nottinghamshire England UK
214 B4 **Beetaloo** NT Australia
59 T2 **Beethoven Peninsula** Antarctica
86 C6 **Beeville** Texas USA
163 I3 **Befandriana** Madagascar
160 C3 **Befori** Democratic Republic of Congo
163 I4 **Befotaka** Madagascar
140 B2 **Beg, Lough** *lake* Northern Ireland UK
219 I7 **Bega** NSW Australia
198 C4 **Bega** Indonesia
126 C2 **Bégard** France
86 C3 **Beggs** Oklahoma USA
182 H6 **Beglar** Iran
140 A3 **Beglieve** Ireland
122 E2 **Begna** *watercourse* Norway
78 C2 **Bégon, Pointe** *cape* Quebec Canada
186 D6 **Begun** Rajasthan India
129 H3 **Begur, Cap de** *cape* Spain
102 B1 **Béhague, Pointe** *cape* French Guiana
186 E5 **Behat** Madhya Pradesh India
186 D4 **Behat** Uttar Pradesh India
178 G3 **Behbahān** Iran
74 F5 **Behm Canal** Alaska USA
213 J4 **Behn** *watercourse* WA Australia
213 H4 **Behn, Mount** WA Australia
136 G6 **Behranci** Turkey
59 T1 **Behrendt Mountains** Antarctica
182 G7 **Behshahr** Iran
185 J6 **Bei Huisan Hu** *lake* Qinghai China
189 F4 **Bei Jiang** *watercourse* Guangdong China
185 J4 **Bei Shan** *range* Gansu China
191 K3 **Bei`an** Heilongjiang China
120 I3 **Beiarnfjorden** *lake* Norway
190 D5 **Beida Shan** *range* Nei Mongol Zizhiqu China
161 E2 **Beigi** Ethiopia
189 H3 **Beiguan Dao** *island* Fujian China
188 F4 **Beihai** Guangxi Zhuangzu Zizhiqu China
191 I5 **Beihuangcheng Dao** *island* Shandong China
191 H5 **Beijing (Peking)** Beijing China
191 H5 **Beijing** *admin. area* China
124 D1 **Beilen** Netherlands
188 F4 **Beiliu** Guangxi Zhuangzu Zizhiqu China
188 F4 **Beiliu He** *watercourse* Guangxi Zhuangzu Zizhiqu China
189 I3 **Beilong Shan** *range* Zhejiang China
218 F5 **Beilpajah** NSW Australia
185 J6 **Beilu He** *lake* Qinghai China
159 H3 **Béinamar** Chad
142 E3 **Beinn Macduibh** *mountain* Scotland UK
142 D4 **Beinn Mhòr** *mountain* Scotland UK
191 I4 **Beipiao** Liaoning China
163 F3 **Beira** Mozambique
128 C3 **Beira** *island* Portugal
Beirut *see* **Beyrouth** Lebanon
80 I1 **Beiseker** Alberta Canada
120 J2 **Beisfjord** Norway
189 F5 **Beishi Dao** *island* Hainan China
191 H5 **Beitai Ding** Shanxi China
191 H5 **Beitai Ding** *mountain* Shanxi China
162 E4 **Beitbridge** Zimbabwe
142 D5 **Beith** North Ayrshire Scotland UK
125 L4 **Beiuş** Romania
128 C4 **Beja** Portugal
128 C5 **Beja** *admin. area* Portugal
131 C8 **Béja** Tunisia
155 H1 **Bejaïa** Algeria
128 D3 **Béjar** Spain
159 G3 **Beka** Cameroon
143 D3 **Bekan** Ireland
196 E5 **Bekasi** Indonesia
160 D5 **Beke** Democratic Republic of Congo
132 B2 **Békés** Hungary
132 B2 **Békés** *admin. area* Hungary
132 B2 **Békéscsaba** Hungary
132 H2 **Bekhtery** Ukraine
133 F6 **Bekilli** Turkey
163 I4 **Bekily** Madagascar
163 I3 **Bekipay** Madagascar
163 I4 **Bekitro** Madagascar
131 C9 **Bekkaria** Algeria
163 H4 **Bekoropoka-Antongo** Madagascar
182 D3 **Bekovo** Russian Federation
83 M7 **Bel Air** Maryland USA
89 H5 **Bel-Ha** Mexico
105 H5 **Bel Horizonte** Brazil
179 K4 **Bela** Pakistan
162 E4 **Bela-Bela** South Africa
102 D3 **Bela Cruz** Brazil
107 G2 **Bela Vista** Brazil
103 B7 **Bela Vista de Goiás** Brazil
197 G3 **Belaga** Malaysia
183 M3 **Bel'agash** Kazakhstan
128 D4 **Belalcázar** Spain
218 G3 **Belalie** NSW Australia
187 E7 **Belampalli** Andhra Pradesh India
198 C3 **Belang** Indonesia
198 C4 **Belangbelang** *island* Indonesia
76 G6 **Bélanger** *watercourse* Manitoba Canada
129 F6 **Belarbi** Algeria
219 H4 **Belaringar** NSW Australia
136 C2 **Belarus** *country* Europe
196 C3 **Belawan** Indonesia
72 A5 **Belaya** *watercourse* Russian Federation
182 C4 **Belaya Glina** Russian Federation
136 D3 **Belaya Tserkov** Ukraine
197 H3 **Belayan** *watercourse* Indonesia
155 H6 **Belbedji** Niger
126 E5 **Belcaire** France
125 J2 **Bełchatów** Poland
73 L7 **Belcher Islands** Nunavut Canada
129 F3 **Belchite** Spain
143 E2 **Belcoo** Fermanagh Northern Ireland UK
143 C2 **Belderg** Ireland
135 U5 **Bel'dunchana, Ozero** *lake* Russian Federation
183 P2 **Bele** *lake* Russian Federation
182 G2 **Belebey** Russian Federation
125 I4 **Beled** Hungary
161 H3 **Beledweyne** Somalia
157 F5 **Beleghes** *watercourse* Ethiopia
130 F4 **Belej** Croatia
182 G6 **Belek** Turkmenistan
158 C2 **Beleko** Mali
159 G3 **Bélèl** Cameroon
216 F3 **Belele** WA Australia
102 B3 **Belém** Brazil
102 E5 **Belém de São Francisco** Brazil
106 E3 **Belén** Argentina
106 E3 **Belén** *watercourse* Argentina
90 C5 **Belén** Costa Rica
107 G2 **Belén** Paraguay
107 G4 **Belén** Uruguay
104 D5 **Belén, Cerro** *mountain* Chile
100 C3 **Belén de Umbria** Colombia
85 I3 **Belen** New Mexico USA
128 E3 **Beleña, Embalse de** *lake* Spain
222 7 **Bélep, Îles** *islands* New Caledonia
156 F5 **Beles** *watercourse* Ethiopia
128 C2 **Belesar, Embalse de** *lake* Spain
132 F3 **Beleţ, Lacul** *lake* Moldova
133 E6 **Belevi** Turkey
140 C2 **Belfast** Belfast Northern Ireland UK
140 C2 **Belfast** *admin. area* Northern Ireland UK
83 Q4 **Belfast** Maine USA
143 G2 **Belfast Lough** *bay* Northern Ireland UK
156 F5 **Bēlfodiyo** Ethiopia
127 H3 **Belfort** France
187 D8 **Belgaum** Karnataka India
127 K1 **Belgern** Germany
57 F1 **Belgica Bank** *underwater feature* Greenland Sea
59 C2 **Belgica Mountains** Antarctica
124 E5 **Belgioioso** Italy
124 C2 **Belgium** *country* Europe
136 F2 **Belgorod** Russian Federation
136 F2 **Belgorodskaya Oblast'** *admin. area* Russian Federation
Belgrade *see* **Beograd** Serbia
51 N17 **Belgrano Bank** *underwater feature* Southern Ocean
59 V1 **Belgrano II (Argentina)** *research station* Antarctica
132 F4 **Belgun** Bulgaria
142 D5 **Belhamie** South Ayrshire Scotland UK
87 M3 **Belhaven** North Carolina USA
155 H2 **Belhirane** Algeria
159 G3 **Beli** Nigeria
132 B4 **Beli Drim** *watercourse* Kosovo
132 E4 **Beli Lom** Bulgaria
132 E4 **Beli Lom, Yazovir** *reservoir* Bulgaria
132 C4 **Beli Potok** Serbia
132 C4 **Beli Timok** *watercourse* Serbia
182 E5 **Belidzhi** Russian Federation
196 E5 **Belimbing** Indonesia
182 D3 **Belinskiy** Russian Federation
196 E4 **Belinyu** Indonesia
196 E4 **Belitung** *island* Indonesia
90 B3 **Belize** *watercourse* Belize
90 B3 **Belize** *country* Central America
90 B3 **Belize City** Belize
83 M2 **Bell** *watercourse* Quebec Canada
217 M6 **Bell, Point** SA Australia
74 G4 **Bell II** British Columbia Canada
79 K7 **Bell Island** Newfoundland and Labrador Canada
77 O1 **Bell Peninsula** Nunavut Canada
106 F5 **Bell Ville** Argentina
74 G6 **Bella Bella** British Columbia Canada
74 H6 **Bella Coola** British Columbia Canada
107 G4 **Bella Unión** Uruguay
107 G4 **Bella Vista** Argentina
105 F4 **Bella Vista** Bolivia
107 G2 **Bella Vista** Paraguay
126 E3 **Bellac** France
124 E5 **Bellagio** Italy
218 F2 **Bellalie, Mount** Qld Australia
130 C3 **Bellano** Italy
187 D8 **Bellary** Karnataka India
219 I3 **Bellata** NSW Australia
108 B2 **Bellavista** Chile
100 B3 **Bellavista** Colombia
104 B2 **Bellavista** Peru
131 C7 **Bellavista, Capo** *cape* Sardinia Italy
91 F3 **Belle-Anse** Haiti
79 K9 **Belle Bay** Newfoundland and Labrador Canada
81 N4 **Belle Fourche** South Dakota USA
81 M5 **Belle Fourche** *watercourse* Wyoming USA
81 N4 **Belle Fourche Reservoir** South Dakota USA
87 K7 **Belle Glade** Florida USA
126 C3 **Belle-Île** *island* France
79 K7 **Belle Isle** Newfoundland and Labrador Canada
79 J7 **Belle Isle, Strait of** Newfoundland and Labrador Canada
86 C2 **Belle Plaine** Kansas USA
140 B2 **Belleek** Newry and Mourne Northern Ireland UK
109 14 **Bellefontaine** Martinique
82 J6 **Bellefontaine** Ohio USA
126 E2 **Bellême** France
122 H4 **Bellen** *lake* Sweden
83 M4 **Belleville** Ontario Canada
127 G3 **Belleville** France
81 Q7 **Belleville** Kansas USA
83 J6 **Belleville** Ohio USA
80 H5 **Bellevue** Idaho USA
86 B4 **Bellevue** Texas USA
80 D3 **Bellevue** Washington USA
127 G4 **Belley** France
88 D3 **Belleza** Mexico
141 F1 **Bellingham** Northumberland England UK
59 U2 **Bellingshausen (Russia)** *research station* Antarctica
51 H16 **Bellingshausen Abyssal Plain** *underwater feature* Southern Ocean
59 S2 **Bellingshausen Sea** Antarctica
127 I3 **Bellinzona** Switzerland
100 C3 **Bello** Colombia
142 C5 **Belloch** Argyll and Bute Scotland UK
222 8 **Bellona** *island* Solomon Islands
83 O5 **Bellows Falls** Vermont USA
86 G3 **Bells** Tennessee USA
187 D9 **Belluru** Karnataka India
120 J4 **Bellvik** Sweden
86 C6 **Bellville** Texas USA
81 P2 **Belmont** Manitoba Canada
142 inset **Belmont** Shetland Scotland UK
103 E6 **Belmonte** Brazil
90 B3 **Belmopan** Belize
218 E5 **Belmore** NSW Australia
214 F5 **Belmore** *watercourse* Qld Australia
143 C2 **Belmullet** Ireland
163 H4 **Belo** Madagascar
102 A4 **Belo Horizonte** Brazil
103 D7 **Belo Oriente** Brazil
163 H3 **Belo-Tsiribihina** Madagascar
83 O4 **Beloeil** Quebec Canada
183 N3 **Beloglazovo** Russian Federation
191 K2 **Belogorsk** Russian Federation
136 E4 **Belogorsk** Ukraine
163 I5 **Beloha** Madagascar
81 P7 **Beloit** Kansas USA
159 G3 **Béloko** Central African Republic
183 N3 **Belokurikha** Russian Federation
134 H6 **Belomorsk** Russian Federation
160 B4 **Belonge** Democratic Republic of Congo
181 G4 **Belonia** Tripura India
128 E2 **Belorado** Spain
182 H2 **Beloretsk** Russian Federation
72 G5 **Belot, Lac** *lake* Northwest Territories Canada
74 C2 **Beloud Post** Yukon Territory Canada
134 I5 **Beloye More (White Sea)** *sea* Russian Federation
182 G3 **Belozerka** Russian Federation
126 E5 **Belpech** France
139 F1 **Belper** Derbyshire England UK
81 P8 **Belpre** Kansas USA
139 I2 **Belstead** Suffolk England UK
81 J3 **Belt** Montana USA
218 C3 **Belt Bay** SA Australia
218 D4 **Beltana** SA Australia
218 D4 **Beltana Roadhouse** SA Australia
101 H5 **Belterra** Brazil
140 B3 **Beltichburne** Ireland
141 H3 **Beltoft** North Lincolnshire England UK
82 D7 **Belton** Missouri USA
87 J3 **Belton** South Carolina USA
86 C5 **Belton** Texas USA
86 C5 **Belton Lake** Texas USA
143 D2 **Beltra** Ireland
143 E2 **Belturbet** Ireland
143 D2 **Belturlin** Ireland
183 O3 **Belukha, Gora** *mountain* Kazakhstan
196 F2 **Belungkor, Tanjung** *cape* Malaysia
197 H2 **Beluran** Malaysia
125 J3 **Beluša** Slovakia
134 L4 **Belush'ya Guba** Russian Federation
139 G1 **Belvoir, Vale of** *valley* England UK
215 I7 **Belyando** *watercourse* Qld Australia
215 I6 **Belyando Crossing** Qld Australia
134 P4 **Belyy, Ostrov** *island* Russian Federation
183 O1 **Belyy Yar** Russian Federation
125 M2 **Belz** Ukraine
124 G1 **Belzig** Germany
163 H3 **Bemaraha** *range* Madagascar
163 I3 **Bemarivo** *watercourse* Madagascar
160 A5 **Bembe** Angola
128 D5 **Bembézar, Embalse del** *lake* Spain
139 F4 **Bembridge** Isle of Wight England UK
81 R3 **Bemidji** Minnesota USA
82 D3 **Bemidji, Lake** Minnesota USA
141 H2 **Bempton** East Riding of Yorkshire England UK
142 D4 **Ben Alder Lodge** Highland Scotland UK
131 D8 **Ben Arous** Tunisia
129 F6 **Ben Badis** Algeria
219 J5 **Ben Bullen** NSW Australia
194 E5 **Bên Cat** Vietnam
142 C4 **Ben Cruachan** *mountain* Scotland UK
155 I2 **Ben Guerdane** Tunisia
142 D2 **Ben Hope** *mountain* Scotland UK
142 D4 **Ben Lawers** *mountain* Scotland UK
142 D4 **Ben Lomond** *mountain* Scotland UK
221 D6 **Ben McLeod Range** New Zealand
142 B4 **Ben More** *mountain* Scotland UK
221 C7 **Ben Ohau Range** New Zealand
158 C3 **Ben Town** Liberia
142 D4 **Ben Vorlich** *mountain* Scotland UK
142 D3 **Ben Wyvis** *mountain* Scotland UK
219 H5 **Bena** NSW Australia
81 R3 **Bena** Minnesota USA
160 D4 **Bena-Kamba** Democratic Republic of Congo
160 C4 **Bena-Tshadi** Democratic Republic of Congo
129 G2 **Benabarre** Spain
129 F4 **Benaguacil** Spain
218 H7 **Benalla** Vic. Australia
128 E5 **Benalúa de Guadix** Spain
197 G4 **Benanga** Indonesia
197 G4 **Benangin** Indonesia
126 E3 **Benassay** France
128 D2 **Benavente** Spain
104 E4 **Benavides** Bolivia
86 B7 **Benavides** Texas USA
77 N1 **Bencas Island** Nunavut Canada
191 I5 **Bencheng** Hebei China
216 E5 **Bencubbin** WA Australia
80 E4 **Bend** Oregon USA
197 F5 **Benda, Tanjung** *cape* Indonesia
162 E6 **Bendearg** *mountain* South Africa
219 J4 **Bendemeer** NSW Australia
161 I2 **Bender Beyla** Somalia
216 F6 **Bendering** WA Australia
218 G7 **Bendigo** Vic. Australia
221 C7 **Bendigo** New Zealand
163 F3 **Bene** Mozambique
160 C4 **Bene Dibele** Democratic Republic of Congo
86 D2 **Benedict** Kansas USA
78 I5 **Benedict, Mount** Newfoundland and Labrador Canada
102 D4 **Beneditinos** Brazil
91 G3 **Benemérita de San Cristóbal** Dominican Republic
89 H5 **Benemérito de las Américas** Mexico
154 F6 **Bénéna** Mali
163 I4 **Benenitra** Madagascar
131 F6 **Benevento** Italy
102 B3 **Benevides** Brazil
127 H2 **Benfeld** France
194 D2 **Bèng** *watercourse* Laos
186 G6 **Bengabad** Jharkhand India
194 A3 **Bengal, Bay of**
187 D9 **Bengaluru (Bangalore)** Karnataka India
160 D3 **Bengamisa** Democratic Republic of Congo
159 G4 **Bengbis** Cameroon
189 H2 **Bengbu** Anhui China
131 F9 **Benghajsa, Il-Ponta ta'** *cape* Malta
Benghazi *see* **Banghāzī** Libya
196 D3 **Bengkalis** Indonesia
196 D3 **Bengkalis** *island* Indonesia
196 F3 **Bengkayang** Indonesia
196 D4 **Bengkulu** Indonesia
196 D4 **Bengkulu** *admin. area* Indonesia
197 H4 **Bengkung** Indonesia
160 A5 **Bengo** *admin. area* Angola
81 M2 **Bengough** Saskatchewan Canada
162 B2 **Benguela** Angola
162 B2 **Benguela** *admin. area* Angola
163 G4 **Benguérua, Ilha** *island* Mozambique
Benha *see* **Banhā** Egypt
52 I6 **Benham Plateau** *underwater feature* Philippine Sea
221 C8 **Benhar** New Zealand
105 E4 **Beni** *admin. area* Bolivia
104 E4 **Beni** *watercourse* Bolivia
160 D3 **Beni** Democratic Republic of Congo
155 F2 **Beni Abbès** Algeria
128 E6 **Beni Enzar** Morocco
154 E2 **Beni Mellal** Morocco
129 I5 **Beni Ouaggag** Algeria
155 F1 **Beni Saf** Algeria
Beni Suef *see* **Bani Suwayf** Egypt
129 G3 **Benicarló** Spain
129 G3 **Benicasim** Spain
105 E3 **Benicito** *watercourse* Bolivia
129 F4 **Benidorm** Spain
126 B2 **Beniguet, Île de** *island* France
158 E3 **Benin** *country* Africa
159 F3 **Benin** *watercourse* Nigeria
158 E4 **Benin, Bight of** *bay*
159 F3 **Benin City** Nigeria
139 H2 **Benington** Lincolnshire England UK
159 G2 **Benisheikh** Nigeria
75 U7 **Benito** Manitoba Canada
89 F4 **Benito Juárez** Mexico
216 E5 **Benjaberring** WA Australia
105 E4 **Benjamín** Bolivia
107 G3 **Benjamín Aceval** Paraguay
104 D2 **Benjamin Constant** Brazil
105 I5 **Benjamin dos Santos** Brazil
88 C2 **Benjamín Hill** Mexico
80 E5 **Benjamin Lake** Oregon USA
106 E6 **Benjamín Zorrilla** Argentina
198 E5 **Benjina** Indonesia
81 O6 **Benkelman** Nebraska USA
130 F4 **Benkovac** Croatia
214 D4 **Benmara** NT Australia
221 D7 **Benmore, Lake** New Zealand
138 C4 **Bennacott** Cornwall England UK
142 C5 **Bennan Point** Scotland UK
74 D3 **Bennett** British Columbia Canada
81 M7 **Bennett** Colorado USA
214 A7 **Bennett, Lake** NT Australia
74 D2 **Bennett Lake** Yukon Territory Canada
135 AE3 **Bennetta, Ostrov** *island* Russian Federation
143 E4 **Bennettsbridge** Ireland
220 F4 **Benneydale** New Zealand
162 E5 **Benoni** South Africa
159 H3 **Bénoye** Chad
90 B3 **Benque Viejo del Carmen** Belize
199 G6 **Bensbach** *watercourse* Papua New Guinea
127 I2 **Bensheim** Germany
75 T8 **Benson** Saskatchewan Canada
84 G5 **Benson** Arizona USA
81 R4 **Benson** Minnesota USA
214 C7 **Benstead, Mount** NT Australia
178 C2 **Bent Jbail** Lebanon
196 D2 **Benta** Malaysia
193 I2 **Benten-numa** *lake* Japan
198 B5 **Benteng** Indonesia
109 12 **Bentham's** Barbados
158 B3 **Benti** Guinea
162 B2 **Bentiaba** Angola
194 C5 **Bentinck Island** Myanmar
107 I4 **Bento Gonçalves** Brazil
86 E3 **Benton** Arkansas USA
84 C2 **Benton** California USA
82 G8 **Benton** Illinois USA
86 G2 **Benton** Kentucky USA
82 G8 **Benton** Missouri USA
82 H5 **Benton Harbor** Michigan USA
80 J3 **Benton Lake** Montana USA
196 D3 **Bentong** Malaysia
86 D2 **Bentonville** Arkansas USA
140 E1 **Bentpath** Dumfries and Galloway Scotland UK
198 B5 **Benua** Indonesia
196 E3 **Benua** *island* Indonesia
197 G3 **Benua Martinus** Indonesia
159 F3 **Benue** *admin. area* Nigeria
159 F3 **Benue** *watercourse* Nigeria
196 D3 **Benum, Gunung** *mountain* Malaysia
191 J4 **Benxi** Liaoning China
198 C2 **Beo** Indonesia
198 F4 **Beoga** Indonesia
132 B3 **Beograd (Belgrade)** Serbia
186 E6 **Beohari** Madhya Pradesh India
158 C3 **Béoumi** Côte d'Ivoire
198 E4 **Bepondi** *island* Indonesia
192 F5 **Beppu** Japan
223 9 **Beqa** *island* Fiji
109 11 **Bequia** *island* St Vincent and the Grenadines
102 C3 **Bequimão** Brazil
140 A2 **Beragh** Omagh Northern Ireland UK
163 I4 **Beraketa** Madagascar
197 H4 **Berangas** Indonesia
78 C3 **Bérard** *watercourse* Quebec Canada
78 C3 **Bérard, Lac** *lake* Quebec Canada
196 C3 **Berastagi** Indonesia
197 H4 **Beratus, Gunung** *mountain* Indonesia
197 H3 **Berau** *watercourse* Indonesia
163 I3 **Beravina** Madagascar
129 F3 **Berbegal** Spain
156 E4 **Berber** Sudan
157 G5 **Berbera** Somalia
159 H4 **Berbérati** Central African Republic
101 G3 **Berbice** *watercourse* Guyana
128 E2 **Bercedo** Spain
130 H3 **Bercel** Hungary
124 E5 **Berceto** Italy
182 H4 **Berchogur** Kazakhstan

139 I4 **Berck** France
135 AA6 **Berdigestyakh** Russian Federation
183 N2 **Berdsk** Russian Federation
129 F2 **Berdún** Spain
136 F3 **Berdyans'k** Ukraine
136 D3 **Berdychiv** Ukraine
159 H3 **Béré** Chad
138 C4 **Bere Alston** Devon England UK
198 D3 **Berebere** Indonesia
157 I5 **Bereeda** Somalia
132 C1 **Berehove** Ukraine
125 I5 **Berek** Croatia
109 15 **Berekua** Dominica
183 O3 **Berel** Kazakhstan
84 B2 **Berenda** California USA
76 G6 **Berens** *watercourse* Manitoba Canada
76 G6 **Berens Island** Manitoba Canada
76 G6 **Berens River** Manitoba Canada
79 F9 **Beresford** New Brunswick Canada
74 E5 **Beresford Bay** Alaska USA
221 C8 **Beresford Range** New Zealand
125 M2 **Berestechko** Ukraine
136 D2 **Berezan** Ukraine
134 M7 **Berezniki** Russian Federation
121 R4 **Berëzovo** Russian Federation
123 O2 **Berezovyy, Ostrov** *island* Russian Federation
120 H4 **Berg** Norway
127 J1 **Berga** Germany
129 G2 **Berga** Spain
122 I4 **Berga** Sweden
133 E6 **Bergama** Turkey
124 E5 **Bergamo** Italy
124 D1 **Berge** Germany
120 I5 **Berge** Sweden
122 C2 **Bergen** Norway
83 M5 **Bergen** New York USA
124 C2 **Bergen op Zoom** Netherlands
126 E4 **Bergerac** France
59 B2 **Bergeson, Mount** Antarctica
123 K2 **Berghamnsfjärd** *bay* Finland
124 D2 **Bergisch Gladbach** Germany
120 L2 **Bergmo** Norway
120 M4 **Bergnäset** Sweden
120 K4 **Bergnäsudden/Bergnäs** Sweden
120 L5 **Bergö** Finland
121 M4 **Bergön** *island* Sweden
121 L1 **Bergsfjord** Norway
122 H3 **Bergslagen** *region* Sweden
122 H4 **Bergundasjön** *lake* Sweden
120 K3 **Bergviken** Sweden
122 I2 **Bergviken** *lake* Sweden
190 G3 **Berh** Mongolia
196 D4 **Berhala, Selat** *strait* Indonesia
130 H3 **Berhida** Hungary
196 E4 **Berikat, Tanjung** *cape* Indonesia
72 A7 **Bering Sea** Russian Federation/USA
72 C6 **Bering Strait** Russian Federation/USA
135 AI8 **Beringa, Ostrov** *island* Russian Federation
127 G1 **Beringen** Belgium
135 AK6 **Beringovskiy** Russian Federation
128 E5 **Berja** Spain
120 G5 **Berkåk** Norway
135 Z7 **Berkakit** Russian Federation
124 D2 **Berkel** *watercourse* Netherlands/Germany
213 I3 **Berkeley** *watercourse* WA Australia
80 D8 **Berkeley** California USA
82 F7 **Berkeley** Missouri USA
109 4 **Berkeley, Cabo** *cape* Archipiélago de Colon (Galapagos Islands)
109 7 **Berkeley Sound** *bay* Falkland Islands
139 G3 **Berkhamsted** Hertfordshire England UK
139 E3 **Berkley** Somerset England UK
59 U1 **Berkner Island** Antarctica
83 O5 **Berkshire Hills** Massachusetts USA
74 M6 **Berland** *watercourse* Alberta Canada
128 E3 **Berlanga de Duero** Spain
122 C2 **Berle** Norway
128 B4 **Berlenga, Ilhas** *islands* Portugal
121 P1 **Berlevåg** Norway
124 G1 **Berlin** Germany
124 G1 **Berlin** *admin. area* Germany
89 H6 **Berlín** Honduras
83 N7 **Berlin** Maryland USA
83 P4 **Berlin** New Hampshire USA
59 O1 **Berlin, Mount** Antarctica
73 K4 **Berlinguet Inlet** Nunavut Canada
221 D5 **Berlins** New Zealand
219 J7 **Bermagui** NSW Australia
128 E5 **Bermejales, Embalse de los** *lake* Spain
88 E3 **Bermejillo** Mexico
106 E4 **Bermejo** *watercourse* Argentina
106 E2 **Bermejo** *watercourse* Bolivia
100 B5 **Bermejos** Ecuador
78 D6 **Bermen, Lac** *lake* Quebec Canada
128 E2 **Bermeo** Spain
128 C3 **Bermillo de Sayago** Spain
83 inset **Bermuda** *UK overseas territory* Atlantic Ocean
50 L6 **Bermuda Rise** *underwater feature* Atlantic Ocean
127 H3 **Bern** Switzerland
131 G6 **Bernalda** Italy
85 I3 **Bernalillo** New Mexico USA
85 I3 **Bernardo** New Mexico USA
106 F6 **Bernasconi** Argentina
125 G1 **Bernau** Germany
126 E2 **Bernay** France
124 F2 **Bernburg** Germany
124 D4 **Berner Alpen** *range* Switzerland
142 A4 **Berneray** *island* Scotland UK
86 G2 **Bernie** Missouri USA
213 I2 **Bernie, Cape** WA Australia
77 Q2 **Bernier, Pointe** *cape* Quebec Canada
73 K4 **Bernier Bay** Nunavut Canada
216 C2 **Bernier Island** WA Australia
83 P3 **Bernierville** Quebec Canada
127 I3 **Bernina, Piz** *mountain* Switzerland
127 I3 **Bernina Gruppe** *mountain* Switzerland
162 B3 **Bero** *watercourse* Angola
163 I4 **Beroroha** Madagascar
130 F2 **Beroun** Czech Republic
125 G3 **Berounka** *watercourse* Czech Republic
127 G5 **Berre, Étang de** *lake* France
154 E2 **Berrechid** Morocco
218 E6 **Berri** SA Australia
155 G2 **Berriane** Algeria
219 I7 **Berridale** NSW Australia
142 E2 **Berriedale** Highland Scotland UK
219 J6 **Berrima** NSW Australia
89 G5 **Berriozábal** Mexico
218 F6 **Berriwillock** Vic. Australia
155 G1 **Berrouaghia** Algeria
138 D3 **Berrow** Somerset England UK
219 J6 **Berry** NSW Australia
126 F3 **Berry** *region* France
90 E1 **Berry Islands** Bahamas
80 D7 **Berryessa, Lake** California USA
162 C5 **Berseba** Namibia
108 B5 **Bersovio el Covacio** Chile
196 D2 **Bertam** Malaysia
78 A3 **Bertaut, Lac** *lake* Quebec Canada
79 D7 **Berté, Lac** *lake* Quebec Canada
132 E3 **Berteştii de Jos** Romania
81 R3 **Bertha** Minnesota USA
124 B2 **Bertincourt** France
130 A1 **Bertogne** Belgium
159 G4 **Bertoua** Cameroon
108 B4 **Bertrand, Cerro** *mountain* Argentina
124 C3 **Bertrix** Belgium
222 1 **Beru** *island* Kiribati
120 inset **Berufjörður** *bay* Iceland
105 F1 **Beruri** Brazil
187 E10 **Beruwala** Sri Lanka
86 F6 **Berwick** Louisiana USA
83 M6 **Berwick** Pennsylvania USA
81 P6 **Berwyn** Nebraska USA
132 B3 **Berzasca** Romania
123 L4 **Bērzciems** Latvia
130 G3 **Berzence** Hungary
126 F4 **Bès** *watercourse* France
74 J4 **Besa** *watercourse* British Columbia Canada
197 H3 **Besah** Indonesia
163 H3 **Besalampy** Madagascar
129 H2 **Besalú** Spain
127 H3 **Besançon** France
198 B6 **Besar** *island* Indonesia
196 D3 **Besar** *mountain* Malaysia
196 D2 **Besar, Gunung** *mountain* Malaysia
196 D3 **Besar Hantu** *mountain* Malaysia
126 F3 **Besbre** *watercourse* France
132 G1 **Besedka** Ukraine
196 D3 **Beserah** Malaysia
157 F5 **Beshio** *spring* Ethiopia
198 B6 **Besi, Tanjung** *cape* Indonesia
124 E3 **Besigheim** Germany
196 C2 **Besitang** Indonesia
125 K5 **Beška** Serbia
133 G7 **Beşkonak** Turkey
136 F6 **Besni** Turkey
183 L3 **Besoba** Kazakhstan
159 H3 **Béssao** Chad
86 H4 **Bessemer** Alabama USA
124 C2 **Best** Netherlands
183 M3 **Bestamak** Kazakhstan
183 L3 **Bestobe** Kazakhstan
134 J6 **Bestuzhevo** Russian Federation
214 B3 **Beswick** NT Australia
163 I3 **Betafo** Madagascar
163 H3 **Betanatanana** Madagascar
163 I5 **Betanty** Madagascar
128 B2 **Betanzos** Spain
159 G3 **Bétaré Oya** Cameroon
158 E3 **Bétérou** Benin
128 E3 **Beteta** Spain
162 C5 **Bethanie** Namibia
82 D6 **Bethany** Missouri USA
126 D5 **Bétharram, Grottes de** *point of interest* France
109 17 **Bethel** Montserrat
138 C1 **Bethel** Isle of Anglesey Wales UK
72 C6 **Bethel** Alaska USA
87 M3 **Bethel** North Carolina USA
83 O5 **Bethel** Vermont USA
Bethells Beach *see* **Te Henga** New Zealand
138 C1 **Bethesda** Gwynedd Wales UK
162 E5 **Bethlehem** South Africa
77 S7 **Béthoulat, Lac** *lake* Quebec Canada
85 K1 **Bethune** Colorado USA
126 E2 **Béthune** *watercourse* France
219 H6 **Bethungra** NSW Australia
103 C7 **Betim** Brazil
222 1b **Betio** *island* Kiribati
163 H4 **Betioky** Madagascar
218 E1 **Betoota** Qld Australia
159 H4 **Bétou** Congo
183 K4 **Betpak-Dala** Kazakhstan
183 K4 **Betpaqdala** Kazakhstan
163 I4 **Betroka** Madagascar
77 U8 **Betsiamites** Quebec Canada
79 C7 **Betsiamites** *watercourse* Quebec Canada
163 I3 **Betsiboka** *watercourse* Madagascar
186 F5 **Bettiah** Bihar India
138 E2 **Bettisfield** Wrexham Wales UK
124 E5 **Bettola** Italy
138 D3 **Bettws** Newport Wales UK
138 D2 **Bettws y Crwyn** Shropshire England UK
213 I5 **Betty, Lake** WA Australia
142 D2 **Bettyhill** Highland Scotland UK
143 F3 **Bettystown** Ireland
187 D7 **Betul** Madhya Pradesh India
186 D6 **Betwa** *watercourse* Madhya Pradesh India
126 F2 **Betz** France
160 B5 **Beu** Angola
104 E4 **Beu, Serranía del** *range* Bolivia
126 F2 **Beugneux** France
138 D2 **Beulah** Powys Wales UK
81 O3 **Beulah** North Dakota USA
80 F5 **Beulah Reservoir** Oregon USA
160 B5 **Beungas** Angola
126 E3 **Beuvron** *watercourse* France
216 E6 **Beverley** WA Australia
141 H3 **Beverley** East Riding of Yorkshire England UK
215 J6 **Beverley Group** *islands* Qld Australia
85 N1 **Beverly** Kansas USA
83 P5 **Beverly** Massachusetts USA
83 K7 **Beverly** Ohio USA
83 L7 **Beverly** West Virginia USA
199 G4 **Bewani** Papua New Guinea
199 G4 **Bewani** *watercourse* Papua New Guinea
141 G2 **Bewerley** North Yorkshire England UK
139 H3 **Bewl Water** *lake* England UK
127 H3 **Bex** Switzerland
139 H4 **Bexhill** East Sussex England UK
215 H7 **Bexley** Qld Australia
133 G7 **Bey Dağları** *range* Turkey
133 F6 **Beydilli** Turkey
133 F6 **Beyel** Turkey
158 C3 **Beyla** Guinea
157 G5 **Beylul** Eritrea
182 G4 **Beyneu** Kazakhstan
133 E6 **Beyoba** Turkey
216 G2 **Beyondie** WA Australia
136 D5 **Beypazari** Turkey
187 D9 **Beypore** Kerala India
161 H2 **Beyra** Somalia
178 C2 **Beyrouth (Beirut)** Lebanon
133 G7 **Beyşehir Gölü** *lake* Turkey
182 C4 **Beysugskiy Liman** *lake* Russian Federation
163 H4 **Bezaha** Madagascar
123 O4 **Bezhanitsy** Russian Federation
126 F5 **Béziers** France
186 C6 **Bhachau** Gujarat India
186 D4 **Bhadaur** Punjab India
186 D4 **Bhaderwah** Jammu and Kashmir India/Pakistan
187 E8 **Bhadrachalam** Andhra Pradesh India
187 G7 **Bhadrak** Orissa India
187 D9 **Bhadravati** Karnataka India
186 G6 **Bhagalpur** Bihar India
186 D5 **Bhagwatgarh** Rajasthan India
187 D7 **Bhainsdehi** Madhya Pradesh India
186 F5 **Bhairawa** Uttar Pradesh India
142 B3 **Bhalamus** Na h-Eileanan Siar Scotland UK
187 D7 **Bhalki** Karnataka India
179 L3 **Bhalwal** Pakistan
181 H4 **Bhamo** Myanmar
187 E7 **Bhamragad** Maharashtra India
179 K4 **Bhan** Pakistan
187 E7 **Bhandara** Maharashtra India
187 E7 **Bhanupratappur** Chhattisgarh India
187 B7 **Bhanvad** Gujarat India
186 D5 **Bharatpur** Rajasthan India
186 F6 **Bharno** Jharkhand India
187 C7 **Bharuch** Gujarat India
186 E6 **Bharwa Sumerpur** Uttar Pradesh India
186 E6 **Bharwari** Uttar Pradesh India
187 E7 **Bhatapara** Chhattisgarh India
142 A4 **Bhatarsaigh** Na h-Eileanan Siar Scotland UK
186 D4 **Bhatinda** Punjab India
187 D9 **Bhatkal** Karnataka India
187 D9 **Bhavani Sagar** *lake* Tamil Nadu India
187 C7 **Bhavnagar** Gujarat India
187 F7 **Bhawanipatna** Orissa India
142 A3 **Bhearnaraigh, Eilean** *island* Scotland UK
186 F5 **Bheri** *watercourse* Nepal
187 D7 **Bhikangaon** Madhya Pradesh India
187 E7 **Bhilai** Chhattisgarh India
186 D6 **Bhilwara** Rajasthan India
186 F5 **Bhimphedi** Nepal
187 F8 **Bhimunipatnam** Andhra Pradesh India
186 E5 **Bhind** Madhya Pradesh India
186 E5 **Bhinga** Uttar Pradesh India
186 C6 **Bhinmal** Rajasthan India
162 E6 **Bhisho** South Africa
187 C7 **Bhiwandi** Maharashtra India
186 D5 **Bhiwani** Haryana India
181 G4 **Bhola** Bangladesh
186 D6 **Bhopal** Madhya Pradesh India
187 C7 **Bhor** Maharashtra India
187 F7 **Bhubaneshwar** Orissa India
186 B6 **Bhuj** Gujarat India
187 D7 **Bhum** Maharashtra India
187 D7 **Bhusawal** Maharashtra India
181 G3 **Bhutan** *country* Asia
104 E2 **Bia** *watercourse* Brazil
179 H3 **Biābānī** Iran
109 11a **Biabou** St Vincent and the Grenadines
198 E4 **Biak** *island* Indonesia
125 L1 **Biała Piska** Poland
125 L1 **Biała Podlaska** Poland
142 D3 **Biallaid** Highland Scotland UK
125 L1 **Białystok** Poland
199 G5 **Bian** *watercourse* Indonesia
127 I5 **Bianco, Capo** *cape* Corsica France
131 E8 **Bianco, Capo** *cape* Italy
189 H1 **Biandangang Kou** *sea* Jiangsu China
159 I4 **Bianga** Central African Republic
189 H1 **Bianzhuang** Shandong China
198 C3 **Biaro** *island* Indonesia
126 D5 **Biarritz** France
127 I3 **Biasca** Switzerland
156 E2 **Bibā** Egypt
162 B2 **Bibala** Angola
87 I4 **Bibb City** Georgia USA
219 I7 **Bibbenluke** NSW Australia
130 D5 **Bibbiena** Italy
76 I2 **Bibby Island** Nunavut Canada
159 G3 **Bibémi** Cameroon
124 E3 **Biberach an der Riß** Germany
179 K3 **Bibi Nani** Pakistan
158 D3 **Bibiani** Ghana
133 B5 **Bicaj** Albania
103 D8 **Bicas** Brazil
139 F3 **Bicester** Oxfordshire England UK
72 H7 **Biche, Lac la** *lake* Alberta Canada
214 D2 **Bickerton Island** NT Australia
198 D3 **Bicoli** Indonesia
130 H3 **Bicske** Hungary
138 E2 **Bicton** Shropshire England UK
187 D7 **Bid** Maharashtra India
179 I3 **Bīd** Iran
159 F3 **Bida** Nigeria
197 H2 **Bidadari, Tanjong** *cape* Malaysia
178 E6 **Bīdah, Wādī** *watercourse* Saudi Arabia
187 D8 **Bidar** Karnataka India
219 I4 **Biddon** NSW Australia
221 F5 **Bideford** New Zealand
138 C3 **Bideford** Devon England UK
216 D2 **Bidgemia** WA Australia
186 E5 **Bidhuna** Uttar Pradesh India
121 M2 **Bidjovagge** Norway
212 F5 **Bidyadanga Community** WA Australia
191 L3 **Bidzhar** *watercourse* Russian Federation
162 C2 **Bié** *admin. area* Angola
125 K3 **Biecz** Poland
124 E2 **Biedenkopf** Germany
127 H3 **Biel** Switzerland
136 A2 **Bielawa** Poland
131 G2 **Biele Karpaty** *range* Slovakia
124 E1 **Bielefeld** Germany
124 E5 **Biella** Italy
125 J1 **Bielsk** Poland
125 L1 **Bielsk Podlaski** Poland
194 E5 **Biên Hòa** Vietnam
125 H2 **Bieniów** Poland
78 B5 **Bienville, Lac** *lake* Quebec Canada
129 F2 **Bierge** Spain
125 J2 **Bieruń** Poland
125 K1 **Biesal** Poland
125 G1 **Biesenthal** Germany
127 G2 **Bièvre** Belgium
131 F6 **Biferno** *watercourse* Italy
159 G5 **Bifoum** Gabon
72 G4 **Big** *watercourse* Northwest Territories Canada
75 R6 **Big** *watercourse* Saskatchewan Canada
219 I7 **Big Badja Hill** NSW Australia
78 H5 **Big Bay** Newfoundland and Labrador Canada
221 C7 **Big Bay** New Zealand
222 7 **Big Bay** Vanuatu
82 H4 **Big Bay De Noc** Michigan USA
84 D3 **Big Bear Lake** California USA
75 S8 **Big Beaver** Saskatchewan Canada
81 J3 **Big Bell Mountains** Montana USA
86 F4 **Big Black** *watercourse* Mississippi USA
75 W6 **Big Black River** Manitoba Canada
82 C6 **Big Blue** *watercourse* Nebraska USA
86 G5 **Big Creek Lake** Alabama USA
218 E6 **Big Desert** Vic. Australia
81 S2 **Big Falls** Minnesota USA
82 E2 **Big Fork** *watercourse* Minnesota USA
86 D6 **Big Hill Reservoir** Texas USA
78 G3 **Big Island** Newfoundland and Labrador Canada
76 H8 **Big Island** Ontario Canada
83 R4 **Big Lake** Maine USA
81 K4 **Big Lake** Montana USA
85 L5 **Big Lake** Texas USA
218 E3 **Big Lake Moonba** SA Australia
76 G6 **Big Mossy Point** Manitoba Canada
75 S8 **Big Muddy Lake** Saskatchewan Canada
84 C2 **Big Pine** California USA
82 D3 **Big Pine Lake** Minnesota USA
86 E2 **Big Piney** *watercourse* Missouri USA
81 J5 **Big Piney** Wyoming USA
82 I5 **Big Rapids** Michigan USA
214 E6 **Big Red Bluff** *mountain* Qld Australia
83 M4 **Big Rideau Lake** Ontario Canada
75 R6 **Big River** Saskatchewan Canada
80 E6 **Big Sage Reservoir** California USA
74 E2 **Big Salmon Range** Yukon Territory Canada
76 F4 **Big Sand Lake** Manitoba Canada
81 J2 **Big Sandy** Montana USA
75 S5 **Big Sandy Lake** Saskatchewan Canada
82 E3 **Big Sandy Lake** Minnesota USA
81 K5 **Big Sandy Reservoir** Wyoming USA
82 C4 **Big Sioux** *watercourse* South Dakota USA
75 O3 **Big Slough** Alberta Canada
84 D1 **Big Smoky Valley** Nevada USA
221 B8 **Big South Cape Island** New Zealand
85 L4 **Big Spring** Texas USA
81 N6 **Big Springs** Nebraska USA
76 G3 **Big Spruce** *watercourse* Manitoba Canada
75 P7 **Big Stone** Alberta Canada
84 B2 **Big Sur** California USA
81 K4 **Big Timber** Montana USA
76 K6 **Big Trout Lake** Ontario Canada
84 G2 **Big Water** Utah USA
86 B6 **Big Wells** Texas USA
198 D4 **Biga** Indonesia
138 D4 **Bigbury Bay** England UK
154 C6 **Bigene** Senegal
185 J3 **Biger Nuur** *lake* Mongolia
121 M2 **Biggajávri** *lake* Norway
75 Q6 **Biggar** Saskatchewan Canada
213 H3 **Bigge Island** WA Australia
219 I1 **Bigge Range** Qld Australia
219 K1 **Biggenden** Qld Australia
139 F1 **Biggin** Derbyshire England UK
139 G2 **Biggleswade** Bedfordshire England UK
81 K5 **Bighorn** *watercourse* Wyoming USA
81 K4 **Bighorn Lake** Wyoming USA
81 L4 **Bighorn Mountains** Wyoming USA
194 D4 **Bight of Bangkok** *bay* Thailand
127 I3 **Bignasco** Switzerland
154 C6 **Bignona** Senegal
132 A4 **Bigor** Montenegro
138 A2 **Bigstone** Ireland
76 H6 **Bigstone Lake** Manitoba Canada
107 I3 **Biguaçu** Brazil
83 K3 **Bigwood** Ontario Canada
130 F4 **Bihać** Bosnia and Herzegovina
186 F6 **Bihar** *admin. area* India
186 F6 **Bihar Sharif** Bihar India
160 E4 **Biharamulo** Tanzania
132 B2 **Biharea** Romania
132 C2 **Bihor** *admin. area* Romania
193 J2 **Bihoro** Japan
132 C2 **Bihorului, Munţii** *range* Romania
104 D4 **Bihua** Bolivia
158 A2 **Bijagós, Arquipélago dos** *islands* Guinea-Bissau
186 D5 **Bijaipur** Madhya Pradesh India
187 E7 **Bijapur** Chhattisgarh India
187 D8 **Bijapur** Karnataka India
187 F7 **Bijapur** Orissa India
186 E6 **Bijawar** Madhya Pradesh India
130 H4 **Bijeljina** Bosnia and Herzegovina
188 E3 **Bijie** Guizhou China
181 G3 **Bijni** Assam India
186 E5 **Bijnor** Uttar Pradesh India
179 L4 **Bijnot** Pakistan
164 9 **Bijoutier Island** Seychelles
186 C5 **Bikampur** Rajasthan India
186 C5 **Bikaner** Rajasthan India
223 15 **Bikar Atoll** Marshall Islands
222 1b **Bikenibeu** Kiribati
192 G1 **Bikin** Russian Federation
192 G1 **Bikin** *watercourse* Russian Federation
223 15 **Bikini Atoll** Marshall Islands
163 F4 **Bikita** Zimbabwe
156 E5 **Bikori** Sudan
160 B4 **Bikoro** Democratic Republic of Congo
132 G1 **Bila Tserkva** Ukraine
198 A3 **Bilang Bilangan** *island* Indonesia
186 C5 **Bilara** Rajasthan India
187 F6 **Bilaspur** Chhattisgarh India
195 I6 **Bilatan** *island* Philippines
186 E5 **Bilaua** Madhya Pradesh India
194 C4 **Bilauktaung Range** Thailand
128 E2 **Bilbao** Spain
216 E6 **Bilbarin** WA Australia
156 E1 **Bilbays** Egypt
143 E4 **Bilboa** Ireland
132 D2 **Bilbor** Romania
120 inset **Bíldudalur** Iceland
130 H5 **Bileća** Bosnia and Herzegovina
136 D5 **Bilecik** *admin. area* Turkey
125 K5 **Biled** Romania
186 E5 **Bilhaur** Uttar Pradesh India
160 C3 **Bili** *watercourse* Democratic Republic of Congo
135 AI5 **Bilibino** Russian Federation
163 H2 **Bilibiza** Mozambique
130 G4 **Bilice** Croatia
187 C7 **Bilimora** Gujarat India
194 C3 **Bilin** Myanmar
125 G2 **Bílina** Czech Republic
195 J5 **Biliran** *island* Philippines
161 G3 **Bilis Qooqaani** Somalia
133 B5 **Bilisht** Albania
197 H2 **Bilit** Malaysia
127 K4 **Bilje** Slovenia
50 Q3 **Bill Baileys Bank** *underwater feature* Atlantic Ocean
138 E4 **Bill of Portland** *cape* England UK
218 C3 **Billa Kalina** SA Australia
216 D3 **Billabong Roadhouse** WA Australia
139 H3 **Billericay** Essex England UK
136 F6 **Billi** Syria
216 D3 **Billilly Claypan** WA Australia
120 E5 **Billingen** Norway
141 G2 **Billingham** Stockton-on-Tees England UK
139 G1 **Billinghay** Lincolnshire England UK
135 AK5 **Billings** Russian Federation
81 K4 **Billings** Montana USA
139 G3 **Billingshurst** West Sussex England UK
212 F7 **Billinnooka** WA Australia
140 B2 **Billis** Ireland
214 E4 **Billmahgun Point** Qld Australia
123 J1 **Billsta** Sweden
80 E4 **Billy Chinook, Lake** Oregon USA
155 I5 **Bilma** Niger
161 F2 **Bilo** Ethiopia
215 K8 **Biloela** Qld Australia
101 G4 **Biloku** Guyana
187 D7 **Biloli** Maharashtra India
130 H2 **Bílovec** Czech Republic
86 G5 **Biloxi** Mississippi USA
218 D1 **Bilpea Morea Claypan** *pan* Qld Australia
141 I3 **Bilsby** Lincolnshire England UK
132 D1 **Bil'shivtsi** Ukraine
125 M2 **Bil's'ka Volya** Ukraine
124 E4 **Bilten** Switzerland
156 C5 **Biltine** Chad
120 L2 **Bilto** Norway
141 G1 **Bilton** Northumberland England UK
194 C3 **Bilugyun Island** Myanmar
198 B3 **Bilungala** Indonesia
132 G2 **Bilyayivka** Ukraine
132 F2 **Bilyne** Ukraine
194 E2 **Bim Sơn** Vietnam
160 D3 **Bima** *watercourse* Democratic Republic of Congo
198 A6 **Bima** Indonesia
162 C2 **Bimbe** Angola
219 I6 **Bimberi Peak** NSW Australia
219 H6 **Bimbi** NSW Australia
216 F4 **Bimbijy** WA Australia
158 E3 **Bimbila** Ghana
159 H4 **Bimbo** Central African Republic
87 L8 **Bimini Islands** Bahamas
179 H5 **Bin Aḥmad** United Arab Emirates
188 E1 **Bin Xian** Shaanxi China
186 E6 **Bina-Etawa** Madhya Pradesh India
140 A1 **Binalt** Ireland
127 I4 **Binasco** Italy
141 H3 **Binbrook** Lincolnshire England UK
126 G1 **Binche** Belgium
219 I6 **Binda** NSW Australia
218 G3 **Bindegolly, Lake** Qld Australia
159 G3 **Binder** Chad
190 G3 **Binder** Mongolia
219 H7 **Bindi** Vic. Australia
216 E5 **Bindi Bindi** WA Australia
186 E5 **Bindki** Uttar Pradesh India
81 J1 **Bindloss** Alberta Canada
216 E5 **Bindoon** WA Australia
160 B5 **Bindu** Democratic Republic of Congo
163 F3 **Bindura** Zimbabwe
158 D3 **Bineda** *watercourse* Côte d'Ivoire
129 G3 **Binefar** Spain
214 D3 **Bing Bong** NT Australia
160 C3 **Binga** Democratic Republic of Congo
162 E3 **Binga** Zimbabwe
163 F3 **Binga, Monte** *mountain* Mozambique
218 G3 **Bingara, Mount** Qld Australia
187 C9 **Bingaram Island** Lakshadweep India
86 B3 **Binger** Oklahoma USA
85 I4 **Bingham** New Mexico USA
188 E3 **Bingmei** Guizhou China
136 G5 **Bingöl** Turkey
136 G5 **Bingöl** *admin. area* Turkey
122 H2 **Bingsjö** Sweden
189 H3 **Bingxi** Jiangxi China
194 E2 **Bình Gia** Vietnam
194 E2 **Bình Mỹ** Vietnam
126 C2 **Binic** France
187 F7 **Binika** Orissa India
129 H4 **Binisalem** Spain
196 C3 **Binjai** Indonesia
219 J1 **Binjour** Qld Australia
158 B3 **Binkolo** Sierra Leone
157 I5 **Binne, Raas** *island* Somalia
216 D6 **Binningup** WA Australia
161 F1 **Binshangul Gumuz** *admin. area* Ethiopia
196 E3 **Bintan** *island* Indonesia
196 D2 **Bintang, Banjaran** *range* Malaysia
196 D5 **Bintuhan** Indonesia
197 G3 **Bintulu** Malaysia
198 E4 **Bintuni, Teluk** *bay* Indonesia
218 H6 **Binya** NSW Australia
188 E4 **Binzhou** Guangxi Zhuangzu Zizhiqu China
191 K3 **Binzhou** Heilongjiang China
191 I5 **Binzhou** Shandong China
106 D6 **Biobío** *admin. area* Chile
106 C6 **Biobío** *watercourse* Chile
159 F4 **Bioko** *island* Equatorial Guinea
154 E2 **Biougra** Morocco
198 C6 **Biquele** Timor-Leste (East Timor)
157 G5 **Bir, Ras** *cape* Djibouti
129 J6 **Bir Chouhada** Algeria
160 D2 **Bir Di** Sudan
156 D4 **Bir en Natrûn** *spring* Sudan
154 C4 **Bir Gandouz** Western Sahara
129 I6 **Bir Ghellalia** Algeria
156 E1 **Bi'r Ḩasanah** Egypt
154 D3 **Bîr Mogreïn** Mauritania
156 E2 **Bi'r Sayyālah** *place of interest* Egypt
156 F3 **Bi'r Shalatayn** Egypt
136 F6 **Bi'r Turwaynān** Syria
191 L2 **Bira** Russian Federation
191 M3 **Bira** *watercourse* Russian Federation
155 I3 **Birāk** Libya
121 T4 **Birandozero** Russian Federation
214 D2 **Birany Birany** NT Australia
156 C5 **Birao** Central African Republic
186 G5 **Biratnagar** Nepal
75 O3 **Birch** *watercourse* Alberta Canada
83 K3 **Birch Island** Ontario Canada
75 M1 **Birch Lake** Northwest Territories Canada
76 I7 **Birch Lake** Ontario Canada
72 H7 **Birch Mountains** Alberta Canada
75 U6 **Birch River** Manitoba Canada
82 F8 **Birch Tree** Missouri USA
218 F6 **Birchip** Vic. Australia
132 C3 **Birchiş** Romania
219 Q11 **Birchs Inlet** Tas. Australia
161 G2 **Bircot** Ethiopia
125 L3 **Bircza** Poland
76 H4 **Bird** Manitoba Canada
81 O7 **Bird City** Kansas USA
79 J7 **Bird Cove** Newfoundland and Labrador Canada
164 9 **Bird Island** Seychelles
109 8 **Bird Island** South Georgia
221 E6 **Birdlings Flat** New Zealand
218 D1 **Birdsville** Qld Australia
75 U7 **Birdtail** Manitoba Canada
214 B3 **Birdum** *watercourse* NT Australia
218 D6 **Birdwood** SA Australia
136 F6 **Birecik** Turkey
194 C6 **Bireun** Indonesia
179 J4 **Bīrg, Kūh-e** *mountain* Iran
186 F5 **Birganj** Nepal
132 D3 **Bîrghiş** Romania
133 F6 **Birgi** Turkey
195 J4 **Biri** *island* Philippines
160 D2 **Biri** *watercourse* Sudan
103 B8 **Birigui** Brazil
159 I3 **Birini** Central African Republic
179 I3 **Bīrjand** Iran
156 E2 **Birkat Qarūn** *lake* Egypt
159 I2 **Birkat Saira** Sudan
130 B2 **Birkenfeld** Germany
122 F5 **Birket** Denmark
140 E1 **Birkhill** Scottish Borders Scotland UK
141 G3 **Birkin** North Yorkshire England UK
139 F2 **Birmingham** West Midlands England UK
86 H4 **Birmingham** Alabama USA
187 F6 **Birmitrapur** Orissa India
186 F6 **Birni** Jharkhand India
222 1 **Birnie** *island* Kiribati
214 E6 **Birnie, Mount** Qld Australia
159 F2 **Birnin Gwari** Nigeria
159 E2 **Birnin Kebbi** Nigeria
155 H6 **Birnin Konni** Niger
159 E2 **Birnin-Yauri** Nigeria
191 L3 **Birobidzhan** Russian Federation
198 B5 **Birongko** *island* Indonesia
186 G5 **Birpur** Bihar India
143 E3 **Birr** Ireland
124 E4 **Birr** Switzerland
215 H6 **Birricannia** Qld Australia
214 B4 **Birrimba** NT Australia
213 J5 **Birrindudu** NT Australia
132 D2 **Bîrsana** Romania
81 L1 **Birsay** Saskatchewan Canada
142 E1 **Birsay** Orkney Islands Scotland UK
139 F2 **Birstall** Leicester England UK
124 E2 **Birstein** Germany
199 G7 **Birthday Mountain** Australia
181 G2 **Biru** Xizang Zizhiqu China
199 F5 **Birufu** Indonesia
136 G6 **Biruk** Turkey
187 D9 **Birur** Karnataka India
135 U7 **Biryusa** *watercourse* Russian Federation
198 C4 **Bisa** *island* Indonesia
84 H5 **Bisbee** Arizona USA
126 D4 **Biscarrosse** France
126 D4 **Biscarrosse et de Parentis, Étang de** *lake* France
126 D4 **Biscarrosse-Plage** France
126 C4 **Biscay, Bay of** Atlantic Ocean
50 R5 **Biscay Plain** *underwater feature* Atlantic Ocean
87 K8 **Biscayne Bay** Florida USA
131 G6 **Bisceglie** Italy
124 G4 **Bischofswiesen** Germany
127 H2 **Bischwiller** France
59 T2 **Biscoe Islands** Antarctica
83 J3 **Biscotasing** Ontario Canada
160 D2 **Bisellia** Sudan
133 D5 **Biser** Bulgaria
134 L7 **Biserovo** Russian Federation
130 G5 **Biševo** *island* Croatia
196 D3 **Bishan** *admin. area* Singapore
179 J2 **Bīsheh** Afghanistan
183 L5 **Bishkek** Kyrgyzstan
80 F8 **Bishop** California USA
86 C7 **Bishop** Texas USA
80 H6 **Bishop Creek Reservoir** Nevada USA
85 L3 **Bishop Hills** Texas USA
139 E3 **Bishop's Cleeve** Gloucestershire England UK
139 H3 **Bishop's Stortford** Hertfordshire England UK
138 C3 **Bishops Tawton** Devon England UK
186 F6 **Bishrampur** Jharkhand India
189 G2 **Bishui** Henan China
186 F6 **Bishunpur** Jharkhand India
161 E3 **Bisina, Lake** Uganda
100 D3 **Bisinaca** Colombia
90 D5 **Bisira** Panama
83 J3 **Biskotasi Lake** Ontario Canada
155 H2 **Biskra** Algeria
195 J5 **Bislig** Philippines
81 O3 **Bismarck** North Dakota USA
199 I5 **Bismarck Archipelago** *islands* Papua New Guinea
199 I4 **Bismarck Sea** Papua New Guinea
136 G6 **Bismil** Turkey
120 F6 **Bismoen** Norway
132 E3 **Bisoca** Romania
81 N4 **Bison** South Dakota USA
75 M4 **Bison Lake** Alberta Canada
179 H3 **Bisrom** Iran
158 A2 **Bissau** Guinea-Bissau
159 G3 **Bissaula** Nigeria
76 H7 **Bissett** Manitoba Canada
158 B2 **Bissikrima** Guinea
78 B3 **Bisson, Lac** *lake* Quebec Canada
127 I4 **Bistagno** Italy
74 L3 **Bistcho Lake** Alberta Canada
86 E4 **Bistineau, Lake** Louisiana USA
132 B4 **Bistra** *mountain* Macedonia/Kosovo
132 D2 **Bistraţa-Năsăud** *admin. area* Romania
130 F3 **Bistrica** Slovenia
132 D2 **Bistriţa** Romania
132 D2 **Bistriţa** *watercourse* Romania
160 C2 **Bita** *watercourse* Central African Republic
159 G4 **Bitam** Gabon
124 D3 **Bitburg** Germany
124 D3 **Bitche** France
131 G6 **Bitetto** Italy
182 F3 **Bitik** Kazakhstan
160 D2 **Bitilifondi** Central African Republic
155 J6 **Bitkine** Chad
136 G5 **Bitlis** Turkey
136 G5 **Bitlis** *admin. area* Turkey
131 G6 **Bitonto** Italy
159 G4 **Bitoutouk** Cameroon
187 C9 **Bitra Island** Lakshadweep India
75 Q7 **Bitter Lake** Saskatchewan Canada
81 Q4 **Bitter Lake** South Dakota USA
162 C6 **Bitterfontein** South Africa
80 G3 **Bitterroot Range** Idaho USA
75 P4 **Bitumount** Alberta Canada
198 C3 **Bitung** Indonesia
159 G2 **Biu** Nigeria
199 F5 **Biwarlaut** Indonesia
132 C2 **Bixad** Romania
86 D3 **Bixby** Oklahoma USA
142 inset **Bixter** Shetland Scotland UK
183 O3 **Biya** *watercourse* Russian Federation
189 H2 **Biyang** Anhui China
182 J3 **Biyesoygan** *lake* Kazakhstan
183 O3 **Biysk** Russian Federation
155 H1 **Bizerte** Tunisia
120 inset **Bjargtangar** *cape* Iceland
120 J2 **Bjarkøya** *island* Norway
125 M1 **Bjaroza** Belarus
120 K5 **Bjästa** Sweden
122 D3 **Bjelland** Norway
130 G4 **Bjelovar** Croatia
120 H3 **Bjerka** Norway
120 J2 **Bjerkvik** Norway
122 E5 **Bjerregård** Denmark
122 D2 **Bjørgvin** *region* Norway
120 J5 **Björkå** Sweden
120 E5 **Bjørke** Norway
122 I2 **Björke** Sweden
122 F3 **Bjørkelangen** *lake* Norway
122 D2 **Björkelo** Norway
120 J3 **Björkfjället** *island* Sweden
121 M4 **Björkfors** Sweden
120 J5 **Björkhöjden** Sweden
120 G5 **Bjørklia** Norway
120 K2 **Björkliden** Sweden
123 K3 **Björkö** *island* Finland
120 L5 **Björköby** Finland
120 L5 **Björkön** *island* Finland
120 J5 **Björkön** Sweden
121 M4 **Björkön** *island* Sweden
120 K4 **Björksele** Sweden
120 F5 **Bjorli** Norway
120 K5 **Björna** Sweden
121 P2 **Bjørnevatn** Norway
120 I5 **Björnön** Sweden
134 E4 **Bjørnøya** *island* Norway
120 H4 **Bjørnstad** Norway
120 J2 **Bjørntoppen** *lake* Norway
122 G2 **Bjurberget** Sweden
120 L4 **Bjurfors** Sweden
120 L4 **Bjuröklubb** *cape* Sweden
120 L4 **Bjurön** Sweden
120 K4 **Bjurträsk** Sweden
122 G4 **Bjuv** Sweden
154 E6 **Bla** Mali
132 B4 **Blace** Serbia
76 G7 **Black** *watercourse* Manitoba Canada
84 G4 **Black** *watercourse* Arkansas USA
86 F2 **Black** *watercourse* Missouri USA
83 N5 **Black** *watercourse* New York USA
87 L3 **Black** *watercourse* North Carolina USA
82 G2 **Black Bay** Ontario Canada
76 K5 **Black Bear** *watercourse* Ontario Canada
75 R4 **Black Birch Lake** Saskatchewan Canada
80 D7 **Black Butte Lake** California USA
59 T2 **Black Coast** Antarctica
74 K6 **Black Creek** British Columbia Canada
76 K4 **Black Duck** *watercourse* Ontario Canada
82 E2 **Black Hawk** Ontario Canada
143 G2 **Black Head** *cape* Northern Ireland UK
81 N5 **Black Hills** South Dakota USA
78 J5 **Black Island** Newfoundland and Labrador Canada
75 S3 **Black Lake** Saskatchewan Canada
82 I4 **Black Lake** Michigan USA
83 N4 **Black Lake** New York USA
84 G2 **Black Mesa** Arkansas USA
219 J1 **Black Mountain** Qld Australia
155 J3 **Black Mountain** Libya
138 D3 **Black Mountains** Wales UK
80 E1 **Black Pines** British Columbia Canada
216 D7 **Black Point** WA Australia
88 D1 **Black Range** New Mexico USA
215 J5 **Black Reef** Qld Australia
82 F4 **Black River Falls** Wisconsin USA
218 D5 **Black Rock** *mountain* SA Australia
109 9 **Black Rock** Trinidad and Tobago
182 C5 **Black Sea**
136 D4 **Black Sea** Asia/Europe
75 U4 **Black Sturgeon** Manitoba Canada
82 G2 **Black Sturgeon Lake** Ontario Canada
219 J3 **Black Sugarloaf** *mountain* NSW Australia
78 K6 **Black Tickle** Newfoundland and Labrador Canada
219 R11 **Black Tier** *mountain* Tas. Australia
221 C7 **Black Umbrella Range** New Zealand
Black Volta *see* **Mouhoun** Ghana
86 H4 **Black Warrior** *watercourse* Alabama USA
215 H8 **Blackall** Qld Australia
215 H5 **Blackbraes** Qld Australia
214 F4 **Blackbull** Qld Australia
141 F3 **Blackburn with Darwen** *admin. area* England UK
122 I3 **Blacken** *bay* Sweden
76 F3 **Blackfish Lake** Manitoba Canada
80 I5 **Blackfoot** Idaho USA
80 J5 **Blackfoot Reservoir** Idaho USA
140 B1 **Blackheath** Coleraine Northern Ireland UK
142 B3 **Blackhill** Highland Scotland UK
109 12 **Blackmans** Barbados
141 F3 **Blacko** Lancashire England UK
140 E3 **Blackpool** Blackpool England UK
140 E3 **Blackpool** *admin. area* England UK
140 F1 **Blackpool Gate** Cumbria England UK
79 E10 **Blacks Harbour** New Brunswick Canada
76 G7 **Blacks Point** Manitoba Canada
89 J2 **Blackshear, Lake** Georgia USA
143 B2 **Blacksod Bay** Ireland
Blackstone *see* **Papulankutja** Australia
219 J5 **Blacktown** NSW Australia
79 F9 **Blackville** New Brunswick Canada
215 J7 **Blackwater** Qld Australia
218 G1 **Blackwater** *watercourse* Qld Australia
74 J6 **Blackwater** British Columbia Canada
143 F4 **Blackwater** Ireland
143 D4 **Blackwater** *watercourse* Ireland
139 H3 **Blackwater** *watercourse* England UK
72 G6 **Blackwater Lake** Northwest Territories Canada
83 P5 **Blackwater Reservoir** New Hampshire USA
142 C5 **Blackwaterfoot** North Ayrshire Scotland UK
142 E5 **Blackwood** Dumfries and Galloway Scotland UK
138 D2 **Blaenau Ffestiniog** Gwynedd Wales UK
138 D3 **Blaenau Gwent** *admin. area* Wales UK
138 D3 **Blaenavon** Torfaen Wales UK
138 C3 **Blaenwaun** Carmarthenshire Wales UK
120 H4 **Blåfiellhatten** *mountain* Norway
130 G5 **Blagaj** Bosnia and Herzegovina
138 E3 **Blagdon** North Somerset England UK
183 N4 **Blagodarnoye** Kazakhstan
182 D4 **Blagodarnoyy** Russian Federation
183 K3 **Blagodatnoe** Kazakhstan
Blagodatnoye *see* **Blagodatnoe** Kazakhstan
133 C4 **Blagoevgrad** Bulgaria
133 C5 **Blagoevgrad** *admin. area* Bulgaria
191 K2 **Blagoveshchensk** Russian Federation
120 J4 **Blaikfjället** *island* Sweden
120 I4 **Blaikliden** Sweden
126 D3 **Blain** France
87 J2 **Blaine** Tennessee USA
75 R6 **Blaine Lake** Saskatchewan Canada
126 D2 **Blainville-sur-Mer** France
81 Q6 **Blair** Nebraska USA
82 F4 **Blair** Wisconsin USA
213 H8 **Blair, Lake** WA Australia
215 I7 **Blair Athol** Qld Australia
140 D1 **Blairquhan** South Ayrshire Scotland UK
132 C2 **Blaj** Romania
182 I3 **Blak** Russian Federation
50 K7 **Blake Plateau** *underwater feature* Atlantic Ocean
87 I5 **Blakely** Georgia USA
138 E3 **Blakeney** Gloucestershire England UK
139 I2 **Blakeney** Norfolk England UK
139 H2 **Blakeney Point** England UK
122 F3 **Blaker** Norway
196 E5 **Blambangan** Indonesia
197 G6 **Blambangan, Semenanjung** *peninsula* Indonesia
130 B2 **Blâmont** France
129 H4 **Blanc, Cap** *cape* Spain
124 D5 **Blanc, Mont** *mountain* France/Italy
81 M8 **Blanca** Colorado USA
108 D2 **Blanca, Bahía** *bay* Argentina
104 b3 **Blanca, Cordillera** *range* Peru
129 F4 **Blanca, Costa** *region* Spain
108 B5 **Blanca, Laguna** *bay* Chile
108 D2 **Blanca Grande, Laguna La** *lake* Argentina
81 M8 **Blanca Peak** Colorado USA
106 D3 **Blancas** Chile
218 D3 **Blanche, Lake** SA Australia

213 G7 **Blanche, Lake** WA Australia
218 D6 **Blanchetown** SA Australia
141 F2 **Blanchland** Durham England UK
106 D4 **Blanco** *watercourse* Argentina
105 F4 **Blanco** *watercourse* Bolivia
104 C2 **Blanco** *watercourse* Peru
86 B5 **Blanco** Texas USA
108 D4 **Blanco, Cabo** *cape* Argentina
90 C5 **Blanco, Cabo** *cape* Costa Rica
80 C5 **Blanco, Cape** California USA
108 B5 **Blanco, Cerro** *mountain* Chile
108 C6 **Blanco, Lago** *lake* Chile
106 D3 **Blanco Encalada, Caleta** *bay* Chile
120 inset **Blanda** *watercourse* Iceland
219 J4 **Blandford** NSW Australia
139 E4 **Blandford Forum** Dorset England UK
81 K8 **Blanding** Utah USA
129 H3 **Blanes** Spain
196 C2 **Blangkejeren** Indonesia
196 C3 **Blangpidie** Indonesia
139 I5 **Blangy-sur-Bresle** France
126 F1 **Blankenberge** Belgium
101 E2 **Blanquilla, Isla** *island* Venezuela
163 F3 **Blantyre** Malawi
126 E4 **Blanzac** France
142 D4 **Blarstainge** Argyll and Bute Scotland UK
122 D3 **Blåsjø** *lake* Norway
139 G2 **Blaston** Leicester England UK
133 C5 **Blatec** Macedonia
125 G3 **Blatná** Czech Republic
132 A1 **Blatnica** Slovakia
120 J4 **Blattniksele** Sweden
124 E3 **Blaufelden** Germany
122 E5 **Blauort** *island* Germany
122 D5 **Blåvands Huk** *cape* Denmark
120 K4 **Blåviken** *bay* Sweden
120 K4 **Blåviksjön** Sweden
139 I2 **Blaxhall** Suffolk England UK
141 H3 **Blaxton** South Yorkshire England UK
126 D4 **Blaye** France
219 I5 **Blayney** NSW Australia
213 K2 **Blaze, Point** NT Australia
109 7 **Bleaker Island** Falkland Islands
109 7 **Bleaker Jump** Falkland Islands
124 F1 **Bleckede** Germany
125 H4 **Bled** Slovenia
142 F5 **Blegbie** East Lothian Scotland UK
124 D2 **Bleialf** Germany
120 I2 **Bleik** Norway
120 H4 **Bleikvasslia** Norway
120 I4 **Bleikvatnet** *lake* Norway
122 H4 **Blekinge** *admin. area* Sweden
158 C2 **Blendio** Mali
221 E5 **Blenheim** New Zealand
127 H4 **Bléone** *watercourse* France
126 E3 **Bléré** France
139 I4 **Blériot-Plage** France
122 D3 **Bleskestad** Norway
126 F4 **Blesle** France
140 B3 **Blessington Lakes** *watercourse* Ireland
139 G2 **Bletchley** Milton Keynes England UK
124 C4 **Bletterans** France
160 E3 **Bleus, Monts** *range* Democratic Republic of Congo
139 F3 **Blewbury** Oxfordshire England UK
87 L3 **Blewett Falls Lake** North Carolina USA
132 A1 **Blhovce** Slovakia
155 G1 **Blida** Algeria
132 C2 **Blidari** Romania
130 G5 **Blidinje Jezero** *lake* Bosnia and Herzegovina
123 J3 **Blidö** *island* Sweden
130 B2 **Blies** *watercourse* Germany
221 B7 **Bligh Sound** New Zealand
223 9a **Bligh Water** *strait* Fiji
218 G6 **Blighty** NSW Australia
120 H3 **Bliksvær** *island* Norway
82 J3 **Blind River** Ontario Canada
124 E4 **Blindenhorn** *mountain* Switzerland
133 A5 **Blinisht** Albania
211 inset **Blinkenthorpe Bay** Lord Howe Island Australia
80 H5 **Bliss** Idaho USA
139 F4 **Blissford** Hampshire England UK
197 G6 **Blitar** Indonesia
132 E4 **Bliznatsi** Bulgaria
Bliznyuki *see* **Blyznyuky** Ukraine
59 O1 **Block Bay** Antarctica
162 E5 **Bloemfontein** South Africa
162 E5 **Bloemhof** South Africa
126 E3 **Blois** France
122 E4 **Blokhus** Denmark
122 C2 **Blomøy** *island* Norway
120 inset **Blönduós** Iceland
197 H6 **Blongas** Indonesia
218 B2 **Bloods Creek** SA Australia
76 G7 **Bloodvein** *watercourse* Manitoba Canada
140 C2 **Bloody Bridge** Newry and Mourne Northern Ireland UK
143 D1 **Bloody Foreland** *cape* Ireland
82 F4 **Bloomer** Wisconsin USA
105 F4 **Bloomfield** Bolivia
82 H7 **Bloomfield** Indiana USA
82 I8 **Bloomfield** Kentucky USA
82 G8 **Bloomfield** Missouri USA
85 I2 **Bloomfield** New Mexico USA
82 G6 **Bloomington** Illinois USA
82 H7 **Bloomington** Indiana USA
82 E4 **Bloomington** Minnesota USA
83 M6 **Bloomsburg** Pennsylvania USA
197 F5 **Blora** Indonesia
139 F1 **Blore** Staffordshire England UK
73 Q5 **Blosseville Kyst** *coast* Greenland
135 AK4 **Blossom, Mys** *cape* Russian Federation
139 F2 **Bloxham** Oxfordshire England UK
141 G3 **Blubberhouses** North Yorkshire England UK
87 K7 **Blue Cypress Lake** Florida USA
81 P6 **Blue Hill** Nebraska USA
83 Q4 **Blue Hill Bay** Maine USA
80 D6 **Blue Lake** California USA
81 L7 **Blue Mesa Reservoir** Colorado USA
181 G4 **Blue Mountain** Mizoram India
221 C7 **Blue Mountains** New Zealand
80 F4 **Blue Mountains** Oregon USA
214 C2 **Blue Mud Bay** NT Australia
Blue Nile *see* **Abay Wenz** *and* **Azraq, Bahr el** Africa
161 F1 **Blue Nile** *watercourse* Ethiopia
81 Q7 **Blue Rapids** Kansas USA
87 I3 **Blue Ridge** Georgia USA
87 K2 **Blue Ridge** North Carolina USA
83 L8 **Blue Ridge** *range* Virginia USA
87 I3 **Blue Ridge Lake** Georgia USA
215 H5 **Blue Water Springs Roadhouse** Qld Australia
74 K4 **Blueberry** *watercourse* British Columbia Canada
83 K8 **Bluefield** West Virginia USA
90 E3 **Bluefields** Jamaica
90 D4 **Bluefields** Nicaragua
72 H5 **Bluenose Lake** Nunavut Canada
214 D4 **Bluey** *watercourse* NT Australia
215 J7 **Bluff** Qld Australia
221 C8 **Bluff** New Zealand
84 H2 **Bluff** Utah USA
194 B3 **Bluff Cape** Myanmar
87 J2 **Bluff City** Tennessee USA
215 H5 **Bluff Downs** Qld Australia
219 Q10 **Bluff Hill Point** Tas. Australia
216 F7 **Bluff Knoll** *mountain* WA Australia
216 D3 **Bluff Point** WA Australia
107 I3 **Blumenau** Brazil
81 P4 **Blunt** South Dakota USA
214 C2 **Blyth** *watercourse* NT Australia
218 D5 **Blyth** SA Australia
141 G1 **Blyth** Northumberland England UK
84 E4 **Blythe** California USA
87 J4 **Blythe** Georgia USA
86 G3 **Blytheville** Arkansas USA
141 H3 **Blyton** Lincolnshire England UK
158 B3 **Bo** Sierra Leone
194 E2 **Bố Hạ** Vietnam
191 I5 **Bo Hai** *bay* China
194 C4 **Bo Phloi** Thailand
103 C8 **Boa Esperança** Brazil
102 D4 **Boa Esperança, Açude** *lake* Brazil
105 G5 **Boa Sentença, Serra da** *range* Brazil
102 E4 **Boa Viagem** Brazil
104 C2 **Boa Vista** Brazil
164 4 **Boa Vista** *island* Cape Verde
100 D5 **Boa Vista, Ilhas** *islands* Brazil
103 B6 **Boa Vista, Serra da** *range* Brazil
195 I4 **Boac** Philippines
90 C4 **Boaco** Nicaragua
128 C3 **Boadilla** Spain
188 E4 **Bo'ai** Yunnan China
128 C2 **Boal** Spain
159 H4 **Boali** Central African Republic
159 G3 **Boanda** Cameroon
199 J4 **Boang Island** Papua New Guinea
160 C4 **Boangi** Democratic Republic of Congo
198 D4 **Boano, Selat** *strait* Indonesia
73 K6 **Boas** *watercourse* Nunavut Canada
211 inset **Boast Harbour** Lord Howe Island Australia
90 D3 **Boatswain Point** Cayman Islands
195 H5 **Boayan** *island* Philippines
87 H3 **Boaz** Alabama USA
74 F4 **Bob Quinn Lake** British Columbia Canada
86 D4 **Bob Sandlin, Lake** Texas USA
218 H5 **Bobadah** NSW Australia
188 F4 **Bobai** Guangxi Zhuangzu Zizhiqu China
161 H6 **Bobaomby, Tanjona** *cape* Madagascar
187 F7 **Bobbili** Andhra Pradesh India
122 I6 **Bobięcińskie Wielkie, Jezioro** *lake* Poland
219 K4 **Bobin** NSW Australia
130 D2 **Bobingen** Germany
124 E3 **Böblingen** Germany
158 D2 **Bobo Dioulasso** Burkina Faso
162 E4 **Bobonong** Botswana
132 C2 **Bobota** Romania
123 O5 **Bobr** Belarus
125 H2 **Bóbr** *watercourse* Poland
132 H1 **Bobrynets'** Ukraine
156 E5 **Bobuk** Sudan
124 F1 **Bobzin** Germany
90 D1 **Boca Chica Key** *island* Florida USA
108 D2 **Boca de la Travesía** Argentina
108 D3 **Boca de la Zanja** Argentina
100 E3 **Boca de Paria** Venezuela
89 F5 **Boca del Río** Mexico
104 E3 **Boca do Acre** Brazil
104 D2 **Bôca do Mutum** Brazil
105 F1 **Boca do Purus** Brazil
101 E4 **Boca Mavaca** Venezuela
87 K7 **Boca Raton** Florida USA
109 1c **Boca Spelonk** Netherlands Antilles
100 B5 **Boca Suno** Ecuador
104 C3 **Boca Tibeni** Peru
103 D7 **Bocaiúva** Brazil
158 D3 **Bocanda** Côte d'Ivoire
159 H3 **Bocaranga** Central African Republic
100 D3 **Bocas del Guaturia** Colombia
90 D5 **Bocas del Toro** Panama
90 D5 **Bocas del Toro, Archipiélago de** *islands* Panama
89 G5 **Bochil** Mexico
124 D2 **Bocholt** Germany
124 D2 **Bochum** Germany
162 E4 **Bochum** South Africa
120 K4 **Bockträsk** Sweden
162 B2 **Bocoio** Angola
85 I7 **Bocoyna** Mexico
132 B3 **Bocşa** Romania
132 C3 **Bocuşniţa** Romania
125 J4 **Bodajk** Hungary
122 G3 **Bodane** Sweden
142 G3 **Boddam** Aberdeenshire Scotland UK
142 inset **Boddam** Shetland Scotland UK
124 F2 **Bode** *watercourse* Germany
80 D7 **Bodega Bay** California USA
80 D7 **Bodega Head** *point* California USA
120 L4 **Boden** Sweden
124 E4 **Bodensee** *lake* Germany
143 D3 **Boderg, Lough** *lake* Ireland
122 H5 **Boderne** Denmark
139 I2 **Bodham** Norfolk England UK
187 D8 **Bodhan** Karnataka India
158 E3 **Bodi** Benin
138 C4 **Bodmin** Cornwall England UK
138 C4 **Bodmin Moor** Cornwall England UK
120 I3 **Bodø** Norway
107 G2 **Bodoquena, Serra da** *range* Brazil
159 H3 **Bodoukpa** Central African Republic
186 E6 **Bodri** Madhya Pradesh India
219 J3 **Bodumba, Mount** Qld Australia
120 J5 **Bodumsjön** *lake* Sweden
179 H3 **Bodūr Bahman** Iran
143 D4 **Bodyke** Ireland
125 K1 **Bodzanów** Poland
160 C3 **Boeke** Democratic Republic of Congo
126 F4 **Boën-sur-Lignon** France
131 E8 **Boeo, Capo** *cape* Italy
199 H6 **Boera** Papua New Guinea
86 B6 **Boerne** Texas USA
122 H3 **Boet** Sweden
160 D3 **Boga** Democratic Republic of Congo
194 B3 **Bogalay** Myanmar
86 G5 **Bogalusa** Louisiana USA
219 H5 **Bogan** *watercourse* NSW Australia
219 H5 **Bogan Gate** NSW Australia
158 D2 **Bogandé** Burkina Faso
159 H3 **Bogangolo** Central African Republic
219 H1 **Bogarella** Qld Australia
86 D4 **Bogata** Texas USA
125 K1 **Bogate** Poland
125 J5 **Bogatić** Serbia
182 F2 **Bogatyye Saby** Russian Federation
160 D3 **Bogbode** Democratic Republic of Congo
160 B3 **Bogbonga** Democratic Republic of Congo
190 D3 **Bogd** Mongolia
190 E4 **Bogd** Mongolia
185 K3 **Bogd Uul** *mountain* Mongolia
185 H4 **Bogda Feng** *mountain* Xinjiang Uygur Zizhiqu China
185 I4 **Bogda Shan** *range* Xinjiang Uygur Zizhiqu China
132 G1 **Bogdanovka** Ukraine
124 G3 **Bogen** Germany
120 I3 **Bogen** Norway
219 J3 **Boggabilla** NSW Australia
219 J4 **Boggabri** NSW Australia
143 C4 **Boggeragh Mountains** Ireland
109 18 **Boggy Peak** *volcano* Antigua and Barbuda
142 F4 **Boghead** Aberdeenshire Scotland UK
199 H5 **Bogia** Papua New Guinea
215 I6 **Bogie** *watercourse* Qld Australia
192 E4 **Bogil-do** *island* South Korea
142 F3 **Bogniebrae** Aberdeenshire Scotland UK
139 G4 **Bognor Regis** West Sussex England UK
159 G2 **Bogo** Cameroon
122 G5 **Bogø** Denmark
193 G1 **Bogoladza, Khrebet** *range* Russian Federation
133 B5 **Bogomila** Macedonia
130 G5 **Bogomolje** Croatia
219 H7 **Bogong, Mount** Vic. Australia
219 I6 **Bogong Peaks** NSW Australia
196 E5 **Bogor** Indonesia
182 F1 **Bogorodskoye** Russian Federation
100 C3 **Bogotá** Colombia
134 S7 **Bogotol** Russian Federation
183 P2 **Bogotol** Russian Federation
181 F4 **Bogra** Bangladesh
135 U7 **Boguchany** Russian Federation
182 C3 **Boguchar** Russian Federation
140 D1 **Bogue** Dumfries and Galloway Scotland UK
81 P7 **Bogue** Kansas USA
154 D5 **Bogué** Mauritania
127 M1 **Boguszów-Gorce** Poland
191 I5 **Bohai Haixia** *bay* China
191 I5 **Bohai Wan** *bay* Hebei China
140 B3 **Bohermeen** Ireland
158 E3 **Bohicon** Benin
127 K1 **Böhlen** Germany
130 E2 **Böhmer Wald** *region* Germany
195 J5 **Bohol** *island* Philippines
195 J5 **Bohol Sea** Philippines
138 C4 **Bohortha** Cornwall England UK
185 H4 **Bohu** Xinjiang Uygur Zizhiqu China
122 F3 **Bohuslan** *region* Sweden
131 C7 **Boi, Capo** *cape* Italy
199 G6 **Boigu Island** Australia
103 E6 **Boipeba, Ilha de** *island* Brazil
128 B2 **Boiro** Spain
103 B7 **Bois** *watercourse* Brazil
72 G5 **Bois, Lac des** *lake* Northwest Territories Canada
82 I4 **Bois Blanc Island** Michigan USA
82 C3 **Bois de Sioux** *watercourse* North Dakota USA
109 14 **Bois d'Inde, Pointe** *cape* Martinique
78 C6 **Boisbriand, Lac** *lake* Quebec Canada
80 G5 **Boise** Idaho USA
81 N8 **Boise City** Oklahoma USA
195 I3 **Bojeador, Cape** Philippines
182 H6 **Bojnūrd** Iran
197 F5 **Bojonegoro** Indonesia
196 E5 **Bojong** Indonesia
196 E5 **Bojong Gede** Indonesia
120 I4 **Bojtiken** Sweden
159 F3 **Boju Ega** Nigeria
159 G4 **Bok** *watercourse* Cameroon
160 B3 **Bokada** Democratic Republic of Congo
179 H2 **Bokandāqūn** Iran
186 G6 **Bokaro** Jharkhand India
198 B3 **Bokat** Indonesia
160 B4 **Bokatola** Democratic Republic of Congo
183 N3 **Boke** Kazakhstan
158 B2 **Boké** Guinea
160 C4 **Bokele** Democratic Republic of Congo
194 D2 **Bokeo** *admin. area* Laos
219 H3 **Bokhara** *watercourse* NSW Australia
158 D2 **Bokin** Burkina Faso
159 G5 **Boko** Congo
Boko *see* **Boke** Kazakhstan
125 J4 **Bokod** Hungary
160 D3 **Bokoko** Democratic Republic of Congo
161 G3 **Bokol Mayo** Ethiopia
160 C3 **Bokondo** Democratic Republic of Congo
155 J6 **Bokoro** Chad
160 C4 **Bokote** Democratic Republic of Congo
182 D3 **Bokovskaya** Russian Federation
194 C5 **Bokpyn** Myanmar
162 D5 **Bokspits** South Africa
160 C4 **Bokungu** Democratic Republic of Congo
182 H6 **Bokurdak** Turkmenistan
155 I6 **Bol** Chad
130 G5 **Bol** Croatia
Bol Shoy Kavkaz *see* **Caucasus** Asia
198 B4 **Bolaang** Indonesia
160 C4 **Bolaiti** Democratic Republic of Congo
122 I2 **Bölan** Sweden
76 F2 **Boland Lake** Nunavut Canada
88 E4 **Bolaños** *watercourse* Mexico
109 18 **Bolans** Antigua and Barbuda
102 C5 **Bolas, Rio das** *watercourse* Brazil
139 H5 **Bolbec** France
155 G6 **Bolbol** Niger
124 F5 **Bolca** Italy
141 G2 **Boldron** Durham England UK
182 H5 **Boldumsaz** Turkmenistan
184 G4 **Bole** Xinjiang Uygur Zizhiqu China
158 D3 **Bole** Ghana
120 L4 **Böle** Sweden
138 A2 **Boleany** Ireland
132 C1 **Bolekhiv** Ukraine
160 B4 **Boleko** Democratic Republic of Congo
198 B6 **Boleng, Ili** *volcano* Indonesia
140 A4 **Boley** Ireland
120 H3 **Bolga** Norway
216 E5 **Bolgart** WA Australia
158 D2 **Bolgatanga** Ghana
132 F3 **Bolhrad** Ukraine
191 L3 **Boli** Heilongjiang China
160 D4 **Boli** Democratic Republic of Congo
160 B4 **Bolia** Democratic Republic of Congo
108 C2 **Boliche** Argentina
107 H2 **Bolicho** Brazil
120 L4 **Boliden** Sweden
195 H3 **Bolinao** Philippines
143 F4 **Bolinaspick** Ireland
82 G6 **Bolingbrook** Illinois USA
198 B3 **Boliohutu, Gunung** *mountain* Indonesia
104 E4 **Bolívar** Bolivia
100 C2 **Bolívar** *admin. area* Colombia
82 E8 **Bolivar** Missouri USA
101 F3 **Bolívar** *admin. area* Venezuela
91 G5 **Bolivar, Pico** *mountain* Venezuela
86 D6 **Bolivar Peninsula** Texas USA
106 E2 **Bolivia** *country* South America
130 H5 **Boljanići** Montenegro
125 I2 **Bolków** Poland
218 E3 **Bollards Lagoon** SA Australia
129 I1 **Bollène** France
141 F3 **Bollington** Cheshire England UK
219 H3 **Bollon** Qld Australia
221 11 **Bollons Island** Antipodes Island New Zealand
52 O13 **Bollons Tablemount** *underwater feature* Southern Ocean
120 J5 **Bollstabruk** Sweden
122 G4 **Bolmen** *lake* Sweden
75 Q6 **Bolney** Saskatchewan Canada
139 G4 **Bolney** West Sussex England UK
160 B4 **Bolobo** Democratic Republic of Congo
124 F5 **Bologna** Italy
127 G2 **Bologne** France
123 P4 **Bologovo** Russian Federation
135 AB6 **Bologur** Russian Federation
160 B3 **Bolomba** Democratic Republic of Congo
160 C3 **Bolombo** *watercourse* Democratic Republic of Congo
135 AC9 **Bolon', Ozero** *lake* Russian Federation
89 H5 **Bolonchencahuich** Mexico
159 F4 **Bolondo** Equatorial Guinea
162 B2 **Bolonguera** Angola
132 D1 **Bolotnya** Ukraine
106 D4 **Bolsa, Cerro** *mountain* Argentina
131 D5 **Bolsena, Lago di** *lake* Italy
123 K5 **Bol'shakovo** Russian Federation
182 F2 **Bolshaya Atnya** Russian Federation
182 F3 **Bol'shaya Chernigovka** Russian Federation
135 W5 **Bol'shaya Kuonamka** *watercourse* Russian Federation
191 L1 **Bols'haya Ussurka** *watercourse* Russian Federation
192 G2 **Bol'shaya Ussurka** *watercourse* Russian Federation
123 Q3 **Bol'shaya Vishera** Russian Federation
183 M3 **Bol'shaya Vladimirovka** Kazakhstan
135 AG8 **Bol'sheretsk** Russian Federation
135 W3 **Bol'shevik, Ostrov** *island* Russian Federation
134 M5 **Bol'shezemel'skaya Tundra** *region* Russian Federation
121 U4 **Bol'shiye Kozly** Russian Federation
182 F4 **Bol'shiye Peshnyye, Ostrova** *islands* Kazakhstan
123 P3 **Bol'shiye Ugorody** Russian Federation
135 AH5 **Bol'shoy Anyuy** *watercourse* Russian Federation
135 X4 **Bol'shoy Begichev, Ostrov** *island* Russian Federation
192 G2 **Bol'shoy Kamen'** Russian Federation
135 AD4 **Bol'shoy Lyakhovskiy, Ostrov** *island* Russian Federation
135 AA7 **Bol'shoy Nimnyr** Russian Federation
123 O3 **Bol'shoy Sabsk** Russian Federation
135 AC8 **Bol'shoy Shantar, Ostrov** *island* Russian Federation
183 M3 **Bol'shoy Tavolzhan** *lake* Kazakhstan
182 F3 **Bol'shoy Uzen** *watercourse* Kazakhstan
183 Q3 **Bolshoy Yenisey** *watercourse* Russian Federation
135 X8 **Bol'shoy Yeravnoye, Ozero** *lake* Russian Federation
193 H1 **Bolshoya Ussurka** *watercourse* Russian Federation
135 AH4 **Bol'shoye Morskoye, Ozero** *lake* Russian Federation
183 N3 **Bol'shoye Ostrovnoye** *lake* Russian Federation
121 R2 **Bol'shoye Ozerko** Russian Federation
183 M2 **Bol'shoye Topol'noye, Ozero** *lake* Russian Federation
183 M3 **Bol'shoye Yarovoye, Ozero** *lake* Russian Federation
123 Q3 **Bol'shoye Zaborov'ye** Russian Federation
88 D3 **Bolsón de Mapimi** *region* Mexico
141 G3 **Bolsover** Derbyshire England UK
122 C2 **Bolstadfjorden** *lake* Norway
129 G2 **Boltaña** Spain
141 F3 **Bolton** Greater Manchester England UK
141 G3 **Bolton Bridge** North Yorkshire England UK
76 H5 **Bolton Lake** Manitoba Canada
140 F2 **Bolton le Sands** Lancashire England UK
136 D5 **Bolu** *admin. area* Turkey
120 inset **Bolungarvík** Iceland
143 B5 **Bolus Head** *cape* Ireland
138 C4 **Bolventor** Cornwall England UK
125 J5 **Bóly** Hungary
133 E4 **Bolyarovo** Bulgaria
130 D3 **Bolzano** Italy
102 E5 **Bom Conselho** Brazil
103 C7 **Bom Despacho** Brazil
102 C4 **Bom Jardim** Brazil
105 H5 **Bom Jardim de Goiás** Brazil
103 B7 **Bom Jesus** Brazil
103 D6 **Bom Jesus da Lapa** Brazil
107 H2 **Bom Sossêgo** Brazil
103 C8 **Bom Sucesso** Brazil
160 A5 **Boma** Democratic Republic of Congo
219 I7 **Bombala** NSW Australia
108 B5 **Bombalot** Chile
215 J7 **Bombandy** Qld Australia
91 F3 **Bombardopolis** Haiti
Bombay *see* **Mumbai** India
195 G3 **Bombay Reef** Paracel Islands
88 C3 **Bombedor** Mexico
198 E4 **Bomberai** *watercourse* Indonesia
198 E4 **Bomberai, Semenanjung** *peninsula* Indonesia
160 C3 **Bombi** Democratic Republic of Congo
155 J6 **Bomboyo** Chad
181 G3 **Bomdila** Arunachal Pradesh India
160 D3 **Bomili** Democratic Republic of Congo
122 C3 **Bømlo** *island* Norway
160 D3 **Bomokandi** *watercourse* Democratic Republic of Congo
196 B1 **Bompoka** *island* India
194 B5 **Bompoka** *island* Andaman and Nicobar Islands India
120 I5 **Bomsund** Sweden
155 I1 **Bon, Cap** *cape* Tunisia
199 I6 **Bona Bona Island** Papua New Guinea
182 E6 **Bonāb** Iran
109 1 **Bonaire** *island* Netherlands Antilles
50 L8 **Bonaire Trench** *underwater feature* Caribbean Sea
121 P1 **Bonakas** Norway
219 K3 **Bonalbo** NSW Australia
219 I7 **Bonang** Vic. Australia
88 E3 **Bonanza** Mexico
90 C4 **Bonanza** Nicaragua
80 E5 **Bonanza** Oregon USA
91 G3 **Bonao** Dominican Republic
213 H3 **Bonaparte Archipelago** *islands* WA Australia
52 I9 **Bonaparte Basin** *underwater feature* Timor Sea
128 D2 **Boñar** Spain
109 9 **Bonasse** Trinidad and Tobago
79 F8 **Bonaventure** Quebec Canada
79 F8 **Bonaventure** *watercourse* Quebec Canada
79 F8 **Bonaventure, Île** *island* Quebec Canada
79 L8 **Bonavista** Newfoundland and Labrador Canada
79 L8 **Bonavista Bay** Newfoundland and Labrador Canada
79 L8 **Bonavista Peninsula** Newfoundland and Labrador Canada
139 F4 **Bonchurch** Isle of Wight England UK
130 B3 **Boncourt** Switzerland
85 I2 **Bondad** Colorado USA
178 G3 **Bondar** Iran
130 D4 **Bondeno** Italy
121 M4 **Bondersbyn** Sweden
160 C3 **Bondo** Democratic Republic of Congo
158 D3 **Bondoukou** Côte d'Ivoire
158 D2 **Bondoukui** Burkina Faso
197 G5 **Bondowoso** Indonesia
82 G4 **Bonduel** Wisconsin USA
198 B5 **Bone, Teluk** *bay* Indonesia
218 H3 **Boneda** NSW Australia
131 F6 **Bonefro** Italy
198 B5 **Bonerate** Indonesia
198 B5 **Bonerate** *island* Indonesia
198 B5 **Bonerate, Kepulauan** *islands* Indonesia
129 F4 **Bonete** Spain
106 D4 **Bonete, Cerro** *mountain* Argentina
101 I5 **Bonfim** Brazil
101 G4 **Bonfim** Guyana
161 F2 **Bonga** Ethiopia
199 H5 **Bonga** Papua New Guinea
181 G3 **Bongaigaon** Assam India
160 C3 **Bongandanga** Democratic Republic of Congo
195 H6 **Bongao** Philippines
219 K2 **Bongaree** Qld Australia
195 J6 **Bongo** *island* Philippines
159 I3 **Bongo, Massif des** *range* Central African Republic
163 I3 **Bongolava** *range* Madagascar
159 H2 **Bongor** Chad
155 F5 **Boni** Mali
179 I2 **Boniābād** Iran
158 D3 **Boniérédougou** Côte d'Ivoire
77 Q4 **Boniface** *watercourse* Quebec Canada
131 C6 **Bonifacio** Corsica France
131 C6 **Bonifacio, Strait of** Corsica France
131 F7 **Bonifati, Capo** *cape* Italy
87 I5 **Bonifay** Florida USA
52 K5 **Bonin Trench** *underwater feature* Pacific Ocean
77 P3 **Bonissant, Pointe** *cape* Quebec Canada
107 G2 **Bonito** Brazil
196 D4 **Bonjol** Indonesia
155 G6 **Bonkoukou** Niger
127 G3 **Bonlieu** France
127 H1 **Bonn** Germany
78 D3 **Bonnard, Baie de** *bay* Quebec Canada
79 I8 **Bonne Bay** Newfoundland and Labrador Canada
79 J7 **Bonne-Espérance** Quebec Canada
80 G2 **Bonners Ferry** Idaho USA
120 K2 **Bonnes** Norway
127 H3 **Bonneville** France
214 B6 **Bonney** *watercourse* NT Australia
218 E7 **Bonney, Lake** SA Australia
218 C4 **Bonney Bluff** *mountain* SA Australia
212 E7 **Bonney Downs** WA Australia
216 F5 **Bonnie Rock** WA Australia
159 F4 **Bonny** Nigeria
85 K1 **Bonny Reservoir** Colorado USA
131 C6 **Bono** Sardinia Italy
199 F4 **Bonoi** Indonesia
105 I4 **Bonópolis** Brazil
219 J3 **Bonshaw** NSW Australia
197 H3 **Bontang** Indonesia
138 D2 **Bontddu** Gwynedd Wales UK
158 B3 **Bonthe** Sierra Leone
198 A5 **Bontosunggu** Indonesia
120 L3 **Bönträsket** *lake* Sweden
199 I6 **Bonvouloir Islands** Papua New Guinea
158 C3 **Bonzo** Côte d'Ivoire
198 D4 **Boo, Kepulauan** *islands* Indonesia
218 G2 **Boobera** Qld Australia
217 M5 **Bookabie** SA Australia
139 G3 **Booker** Buckinghamshire England UK
86 A2 **Booker** Texas USA
158 C3 **Boola** Guinea
216 E3 **Boolardy** WA Australia
219 I2 **Boolba** Qld Australia
218 E4 **Boolcoomata** SA Australia
218 G5 **Booligal** NSW Australia
143 E3 **Boolinaig Bridge** Ireland
216 D2 **Boologooroo** WA Australia
215 J7 **Boomer Range** Qld Australia
219 I3 **Boomi** NSW Australia
109 18 **Boon Point** Antigua and Barbuda
217 I5 **Boonderoo, Lake** WA Australia
219 J2 **Boondooma, Lake** Qld Australia
81 M7 **Boone** Colorado USA
87 K2 **Boone** North Carolina USA
87 J2 **Boone Lake** Tennessee USA
190 D3 **Bööntsagaan Nuur** *lake* Mongolia
84 A1 **Boonville** California USA
83 N5 **Boonville** New York USA
216 G5 **Boorabbin** WA Australia
214 F5 **Boorabin** *watercourse* Qld Australia
161 G2 **Boorama** Somalia
218 G4 **Booroondarra, Mount** NSW Australia
218 G6 **Booroorban** NSW Australia
219 I6 **Boorowa** NSW Australia
218 F7 **Boort** Vic. Australia
157 H5 **Boosaaso** Somalia
140 E2 **Boot** Cumbria England UK
59 D2 **Boothby, Cape** Antarctica
73 J4 **Boothia, Gulf of** Nunavut Canada
73 J4 **Boothia Peninsula** Nunavut Canada
140 E2 **Bootle** Cumbria England UK
159 G5 **Booué** Gabon
219 K1 **Booyal** Qld Australia
102 E4 **Boqueirão** Brazil
103 C6 **Boqueirão, Serra do** *range* Brazil
105 F6 **Boquerón** *admin. area* Paraguay
88 D3 **Boquilla, Presa de la** *lake* Mexico
88 E3 **Boquillas** Mexico
88 E2 **Boquillas** Texas USA
88 E2 **Boquillas del Carmen** Mexico
103 D6 **Boquira** Brazil
160 E2 **Bor** Sudan
185 K4 **Bor Ul Shan** *range* Nei Mongol Zizhiqu China
223 14 **Bora Bora** *island* French Polynesia
194 D3 **Borabu** Thailand
163 I3 **Boraha, Nosy** *island* Madagascar
130 G5 **Boraja** Croatia
198 E5 **Borang, Tanjung** *cape* Indonesia
122 G4 **Borås** Sweden
178 G3 **Borāzjān** Iran
105 G2 **Borba** Brazil
128 C4 **Borba** Portugal
132 E3 **Borcea** Romania
59 L2 **Borchgrevink Coast** Antarctica
130 G4 **Borci** Bosnia and Herzegovina
124 D1 **Borculo** Netherlands
217 O7 **Borda, Cape** SA Australia
122 D3 **Bordalsvatnet** *lake* Norway
126 D4 **Bordeaux** France
216 F7 **Borden** WA Australia
72 H3 **Borden Island** Northwest Territories/ Nunavut Canada
73 K4 **Borden Peninsula** Nunavut Canada
218 E4 **Border Downs** NSW Australia
214 B2 **Border Store** NT Australia
217 K5 **Border Village** SA Australia
218 E7 **Bordertown** SA Australia
120 inset **Borðeyri** Iceland
155 G1 **Bordj Bou Arréridj** Algeria
155 G1 **Bordj Bounaama** Algeria
155 H2 **Bordj de Chegga** Algeria
129 H5 **Bordj Emir Khaled** Algeria
155 H2 **Bordj Messouda** Algeria
155 G4 **Bordj Mokhtar** Algeria
129 H5 **Bordj Okhriss** Algeria
155 H3 **Bordj Omer Driss** Algeria
139 G3 **Bordon** Hampshire England UK
73 S6 **Borðoy** *island* Faroe Islands
130 C4 **Bore** Italy
154 F5 **Boré** Mali
57 F1 **Boreas Abyssal Plain** *underwater feature* Greenland Sea
59 X2 **Boreas Nunatak** *mountain* Antarctica
139 G3 **Borehamwood** Hertfordshire England UK
142 D6 **Boreland** Dumfries and Galloway Scotland UK
127 K4 **Borello** Italy
125 M2 **Boremel'** Ukraine
122 H3 **Boren** *lake* Sweden
142 A3 **Boreray** *island* Scotland UK
120 I4 **Borgafjäll** Sweden
120 inset **Borgarfjörður** *bay* Iceland
120 inset **Borgarnes** Iceland
120 I4 **Borgasjön** *lake* Sweden
85 L3 **Borger** Texas USA
142 A3 **Borgh** Na h-Eileanan Siar Scotland UK
86 G5 **Borgne, Lake** Louisiana USA
130 D3 **Borgo Valsugana** Italy
142 E2 **Borgue** Highland Scotland UK
122 G3 **Borgunda** Sweden
122 C3 **Borgundøy** *island* Norway
120 I5 **Borgvattnet** Sweden
159 F4 **Bori** Nigeria
108 A3 **Bories, Punta** *cape* Chile
194 D3 **Borikhan** Laos
91 H3 **Borinquen, Punta** *cape* Puerto Rico
182 D3 **Borisoglebsk** Russian Federation
163 I3 **Boriziny** Madagascar
155 H2 **Borj Bourguiba** Tunisia
179 H3 **Borj-e Dargāh** Iran
125 K2 **Borki** Poland
125 M2 **Borki** Ukraine
155 J5 **Borkou** *region* Chad
156 B4 **Borkou-Ennedi-Tibesti** *admin. area* Chad
124 D1 **Borkum** Germany
124 D1 **Borkum** *island* Germany
122 H2 **Borlänge** Sweden
59 D2 **Borley, Cape** Antarctica
120 E6 **Borlo** Norway
133 F6 **Borlu** Turkey
183 M4 **Borlykak** *lake* Kazakhstan
183 L3 **Borlysor** *lake* Kazakhstan
130 C4 **Bormida** *watercourse* Italy
127 K1 **Borna** Germany
155 H4 **Borne** Algeria
124 D1 **Borne** Netherlands
198 A3 **Borneo** *island* Indonesia
142 D6 **Borness** Dumfries and Galloway Scotland UK
122 H5 **Bornholm** *island* Denmark
122 H5 **Bornholmsgattet** *bay* Sweden
160 A1 **Borno** *admin. area* Nigeria
128 D5 **Bornos** Spain
190 F3 **Bornuur** Mongolia
160 D2 **Boro** *watercourse* Sudan
198 B3 **Boroko** Indonesia
159 I2 **Boromata** Central African Republic
158 D2 **Boromo** Burkina Faso
158 C3 **Boron** Côte d'Ivoire
135 AD5 **Borong, Khrebet** *range* Russian Federation
132 A2 **Borota** Hungary
123 Q3 **Borovenka** Russian Federation
123 O4 **Borovichi** Russian Federation
183 N3 **Borovlyanka** Russian Federation
130 F4 **Borovnica** Slovenia
121 R4 **Borovoy** Russian Federation
183 K2 **Borovoye** Kazakhstan
182 I2 **Borovskoy** Kazakhstan
125 K2 **Borów** Poland
125 K1 **Borowe** Poland
100 A5 **Borrachos, Punta** *cape* Ecuador
122 H5 **Borrby** Sweden
122 F3 **Borre** Norway
88 D3 **Borrego** Mexico
218 E6 **Borrika** SA Australia
143 F4 **Borris** Ireland
143 D4 **Borrisokane** Ireland
143 E4 **Borrisoleigh** Ireland
214 D4 **Borroloola** NT Australia
187 C6 **Borsad** Gujarat India
122 D3 **Borsæ** *lake* Norway
121 N1 **Børselv** Norway
121 N1 **Borselvjellet** *region* Norway
132 E1 **Borshchiv** Ukraine
191 G2 **Borshchovochnyy Khrebet** *range* Russian Federation
132 B1 **Borsod-Abaúj-Zemplén** *admin. area* Hungary
120 J2 **Børsvatnet** *lake* Norway
126 F4 **Bort-les-Orgues** France
Bortala *see* **Bole** China
120 H5 **Börtnan** Sweden
135 AD4 **Boru** Russian Federation
178 G3 **Borūjen** Iran
178 F2 **Borūjerd** Iran
142 B3 **Borve** Highland Scotland UK
140 F2 **Borwick** Lancashire England UK
132 C1 **Borynia** Ukraine
191 H2 **Borzya** Russian Federation
191 H2 **Borzya** *watercourse* Russian Federation
191 H2 **Borzya Ozero** *lake* Russian Federation
131 C6 **Bosa** Sardinia Italy
183 K4 **Bosagha** Kazakhstan
130 G4 **Bosanska Dubica** Bosnia and Herzegovina
125 I5 **Bosanska Krupa** Bosnia and Herzegovina
199 G5 **Bosavi, Mount** Papua New Guinea
124 E5 **Bosco Marengo** Italy
188 E4 **Bose** Guangxi Zhuangzu Zizhiqu China
162 E5 **Boshof** South Africa
179 I2 **Boshrūyeh** Iran
125 I3 **Boskovice** Czech Republic
130 H4 **Bosna** *watercourse* Bosnia and Herzegovina
130 G4 **Bosnia and Herzegovina** *country* Europe
160 B3 **Boso-Semodja** Democratic Republic of Congo
160 B3 **Bosobolo** Democratic Republic of Congo
85 I3 **Bosque Farms** New Mexico USA
159 H3 **Bossangoa** Central African Republic
160 B2 **Bossembélé** Central African Republic
159 H3 **Bossentélé** Central African Republic
155 G6 **Bossey Bangou** Niger
86 E4 **Bossier City** Louisiana USA
162 C4 **Bossiesvlei** Namibia
212 F5 **Bossut, Cape** WA Australia
179 K3 **Bostan** Pakistan
139 G2 **Boston** Lincolnshire England UK
83 P5 **Boston** Massachusetts USA
74 K8 **Boston Bar** British Columbia Canada
217 N7 **Boston Island** SA Australia
86 D3 **Boston Mountains** Arkansas USA
141 G3 **Boston Spa** West Yorkshire England UK
86 D3 **Boswell** Oklahoma USA
83 L6 **Boswell** Pennsylvania USA
218 C4 **Bosworth** SA Australia
187 C6 **Botad** Gujarat India
104 D3 **Botafogo** Brazil
196 C4 **Botanic Gardens** *point of interest* Singapore
162 D4 **Boteti** *watercourse* Botswana
141 H3 **Bothamsall** Nottinghamshire England UK
123 J2 **Bothnia, Gulf of** Finland
128 C3 **Boticas** Portugal
132 D2 **Botiza** Romania
182 E5 **Botlikh** Russian Federation
120 I3 **Botn** Norway
120 F5 **Botngard** Norway
120 J2 **Botnhamn** Norway
132 B3 **Botoš** Serbia
132 E2 **Botoşani** Romania
132 E2 **Botoşani** Romania
132 E2 **Botoşani** *admin. area* Romania
191 H5 **Botou** Hebei China
158 C3 **Botro** Côte d'Ivoire
162 E5 **Botshabelo** South Africa
120 L4 **Botsmark** Sweden
162 D4 **Botswana** *country* Africa
141 H3 **Bottesford** North Lincolnshire England UK
103 B8 **Botucatu** Brazil
158 C3 **Bou** *watercourse* Côte d'Ivoire
131 D8 **Bou Ficha** Tunisia
131 C8 **Bou Hadjdr** Algeria
129 H5 **Bou Medfaa** Algeria
129 I6 **Bou Mellal** Algeria
154 F2 **Bou Naceur, Jbel** *mountain* Morocco
129 G6 **Bou Noual** Algeria
154 C5 **Boû Rjeïmât** Mauritania
155 G1 **Bou Saâda** Algeria
158 C3 **Bouaflé** Côte d'Ivoire
158 C3 **Bouaké** Côte d'Ivoire
155 G2 **Boualem** Algeria
155 F2 **Bouânane** Morocco
159 H5 **Bouanga** Congo
159 H3 **Bouar** Central African Republic
155 F2 **Bouârfa** Morocco
131 B8 **Bouati Mahmoud** Algeria
127 G5 **Bouc-Bel-Air** France
159 H3 **Bouca** Central African Republic
214 C1 **Boucaut Bay** NT Australia
79 D8 **Boucher** *watercourse* Quebec Canada
79 I7 **Boucher, Lac** *lake* Quebec Canada
79 F9 **Bouctouche** New Brunswick Canada
154 F2 **Boudenib** Morocco
159 H4 **Boudoua** Central African Republic
159 G5 **Bouenza** *admin. area* Congo
159 G5 **Bouenza** *watercourse* Congo
155 H1 **Bougaa** Algeria
222 8 **Bougainville** *island* Papua New Guinea
198 D4 **Bougainville, Selat** *strait* Indonesia
215 I3 **Bougainville Reef** Coral Sea Islands Territory Australia
222 8 **Bougainville Strait** Solomon Islands
222 7 **Bougainville Strait** Vanuatu
155 H1 **Bougaroûn, Cap** *cape* Algeria
155 G4 **Boughessa** Mali
139 H2 **Boughton** Norfolk England UK
139 H3 **Boughton Aluph** Kent England UK
158 C2 **Bougouni** Mali
155 G1 **Bougzoul** Algeria
129 J6 **Bouhamama** Algeria
109 16 **Bouillante** Guadeloupe
127 G2 **Bouillon** Belgium
124 C3 **Bouilly** France
159 G4 **Bouinandjé** *watercourse* Gabon
155 G1 **Bouira** Algeria
154 E2 **Boujad** Morocco
154 D3 **Boukra** Western Sahara
130 B2 **Boulay-Moselle** France
81 M7 **Boulder** Colorado USA
80 I3 **Boulder** Montana USA
213 K2 **Boulder, Mount** NT Australia
74 G3 **Boulder City** British Columbia Canada
84 E3 **Boulder City** Nevada USA
84 G2 **Boulder Town** Utah USA
79 F7 **Bouleau** *watercourse* Quebec Canada
129 J6 **Boulehilet** Algeria
154 F2 **Boulemane** Morocco
158 E2 **Boulgou** Burkina Faso
214 E7 **Boulia** Qld Australia
141 G1 **Boulmer** Northumberland England UK
126 F2 **Boulogne-Billancourt** France
126 E5 **Boulogne-sur-Gesse** France
139 I4 **Boulogne-sur-Mer** France
159 I3 **Boulou** *watercourse* Central African Republic
222 7 **Bouloupari** New Caledonia
158 D2 **Boulsa** Burkina Faso
154 E2 **Boumaine Dadès** Morocco
159 G5 **Boumango** Gabon
159 G4 **Boumba** *watercourse* Cameroon
159 H4 **Boumbé** *watercourse* Central African Republic
155 F5 **Boumboum** Mali
154 D5 **Boumdeït** Mauritania
155 G1 **Boumerdes** Algeria
158 D3 **Bouna** Côte d'Ivoire
83 P4 **Boundary Mountains** Maine USA
158 C3 **Boundiali** Côte d'Ivoire
159 H5 **Boundji** Congo
140 B4 **Bounds Bridge** Ireland
155 I6 **Bouné** Niger
159 I3 **Boungou** Central African Republic
159 I3 **Boungou** *watercourse* Central African Republic
154 C6 **Bounkiling** Senegal
214 E4 **Bountiful Islands** Qld Australia
223 11a **Bounty Bay** Pitcairn Islands
221 10 **Bounty Islands** New Zealand
52 N12 **Bounty Trough** *underwater feature* Pacific Ocean
158 D2 **Boura** Burkina Faso
126 F3 **Bourbonnais** *region* France
82 H6 **Bourbonnais** Illinois USA
127 G3 **Bourbonne-les-Bains** France
139 J4 **Bourbourg** France

126 C2 **Bourbriac** France
108 C6 **Bourchier, Bahía** *bay* Chile
127 G4 **Bourdeaux** France
77 R4 **Bourdel, Lac** *lake* Quebec Canada
128 D6 **Boureït** Morocco
155 F5 **Bourem** Mali
127 G4 **Bourg-Argental** France
127 G3 **Bourg-en-Bresse** France
127 G4 **Bourg-lès-Valence** France
126 E5 **Bourg-Madame** Spain
127 H4 **Bourg-St-Maurice** France
126 E4 **Bourganeuf** France
126 F3 **Bourges** France
127 G4 **Bourget, Lac du** *lake* France
126 F3 **Bourgogne** *admin. area* France
127 G4 **Bourgoin-Jallieu** France
83 K2 **Bourkes** Ontario Canada
139 G2 **Bourne** Lincolnshire England UK
139 F4 **Bournemouth** Bournemouth England UK
139 F4 **Bournemouth** *admin. area* England UK
159 G2 **Bourrah** Cameroon
126 E4 **Bourran** France
158 D2 **Bourzanga** Burkina Faso
142 B4 **Bousd** Highland Scotland UK
129 H5 **Bouskene** Algeria
126 F3 **Boussac** France
159 H2 **Bousso** Chad
131 C8 **Bouteldja** Algeria
154 D5 **Boutilimit** Mauritania
77 R5 **Boutin** *watercourse* Quebec Canada
126 D3 **Boutonne** *watercourse* France
51 I5 **Boutougou Fara** Senegal
Bouvet Island *see* **Bouvetøya** Antarctica
51 S15 **Bouvetøya** *Norwegian dependency* Antarctica
127 H2 **Bouxwiller** France
160 D2 **Bouyé** *watercourse* Central African Republic
155 H6 **Bouza** Niger
129 G5 **Bouzghaïa** Algeria
120 J2 **Bøvær** Norway
131 G7 **Bovalino** Italy
130 E3 **Bovec** Slovenia
127 J4 **Bovegno** Italy
109 1c **Boven Bolivia** Netherlands Antilles
101 H4 **Boven Tapanahoni** *watercourse* Suriname
124 E2 **Bovenden** Germany
120 F5 **Bøverfjorden** Norway
124 D5 **Boves** Italy
80 G3 **Bovill** Idaho USA
85 K3 **Bovina** Texas USA
123 O5 **Bovsevichi** Belarus
142 E2 **Bow** Orkney Islands Scotland UK
75 P8 **Bow Island** Alberta Canada
213 J4 **Bow River** WA Australia
138 C2 **Bow Street** Ceredigion Wales UK
188 E1 **Bowang** Shaanxi China
81 N2 **Bowbells** North Dakota USA
141 G2 **Bowburn** Durham England UK
81 P4 **Bowdle** South Dakota USA
81 P3 **Bowdon** North Dakota USA
216 E6 **Bowelling** WA Australia
215 I6 **Bowen** *watercourse* Qld Australia
218 H5 **Bowen, Mount** NSW Australia
215 I5 **Bowen, Mount** Qld Australia
215 H7 **Bowen Downs** Qld Australia
141 F1 **Bower** Northumberland England UK
52 N2 **Bowers Bank** *underwater feature* Bering Sea
59 K2 **Bowers Mountains** Antarctica
52 N2 **Bowers Ridge** *underwater feature* Bering Sea
141 F2 **Bowes** Durham England UK
83 M7 **Bowie** Maryland USA
86 C4 **Bowie** Texas USA
53 S2 **Bowie Seamount** *underwater feature* Pacific Ocean
82 H8 **Bowling Green** Kentucky USA
82 J6 **Bowling Green** Ohio USA
83 M7 **Bowling Green** Virginia USA
215 I5 **Bowling Green, Cape** Qld Australia
87 J3 **Bowman** Georgia USA
87 K4 **Bowman** South Carolina USA
74 K7 **Bowman, Mount** British Columbia Canada
59 T2 **Bowman Coast** Antarctica
81 N4 **Bowman-Haley Lake** North Dakota USA
59 G2 **Bowman Island** Antarctica
59 U2 **Bowman Peninsula** Antarctica
142 B5 **Bowmore** Argyll and Bute Scotland UK
219 J6 **Bowral** NSW Australia
219 K4 **Bowraville** NSW Australia
74 K6 **Bowron** *watercourse* British Columbia Canada
74 G4 **Bowser Lake** British Columbia Canada
75 U6 **Bowsman** Manitoba Canada
82 E3 **Bowstring Lake** Minnesota USA
139 E3 **Box** Wiltshire England UK
81 N4 **Box Elder** South Dakota USA
191 I5 **Boxing** Shandong China
100 C3 **Boyaca** *admin. area* Colombia
133 F5 **Boyalı** Turkey
216 D6 **Boyanup** WA Australia
135 U4 **Boyarka** Russian Federation
75 W5 **Boyd** Manitoba Canada
77 Q6 **Boyd, Lac** *lake* Quebec Canada
217 I2 **Boyd Lagoon** WA Australia
76 D2 **Boyd Lake** Northwest Territories Canada
80 H6 **Boyd Reservoir** Nevada USA
75 M3 **Boyer** Alberta Canada
82 D5 **Boyer** *watercourse* Iowa USA
182 C4 **Boykov Liman** *lake* Russian Federation
75 O5 **Boyle** Alberta Canada
143 D3 **Boyle** Ireland
219 J1 **Boyne** *watercourse* Qld Australia
140 A3 **Boyne** *watercourse* Ireland
87 K7 **Boynton Beach** Florida USA
159 I3 **Boyo** Central African Republic
197 F5 **Boyolali** Indonesia
85 K3 **Boys Ranch** Texas USA
81 K5 **Boysen Reservoir** Wyoming USA
183 J6 **Boysun** Uzbekistan
120 E6 **Bøyum** Norway
216 E6 **Boyup Brook** WA Australia
130 F4 **Božava** Croatia
133 E6 **Bozcaada** Turkey
133 D6 **Bozcaada** *island* Turkey
133 F7 **Bozdoğan** Turkey
139 G2 **Bozeat** Northamptonshire England UK
81 J4 **Bozeman** Montana USA
133 F6 **Bozen** Turkey
189 G1 **Bozhou** Anhui China
134 L6 **Bozhyudor** Russian Federation
132 C4 **Božica** Serbia
126 F4 **Bozouls** France
159 H3 **Bozoum** Central African Republic
133 G7 **Bozova** Turkey
183 L3 **Bozshakol'** Kazakhstan
182 J2 **Bozshakol** *lake* Kazakhstan
124 F5 **Bozzolo** Italy
124 D5 **Bra** Italy
101 H3 **Braams Punt** *cape* Suriname
127 G1 **Brabant** *admin. area* Belgium
75 T4 **Brabant** Saskatchewan Canada
59 T2 **Brabant Island** Antarctica
142 B3 **Bracadale, Loch** *bay* Scotland UK
131 E5 **Bracciano** Italy
131 E5 **Bracciano, Lago di** *lake* Italy
132 C3 **Braćevac** Serbia
120 I5 **Bräcke** Sweden
75 Q8 **Bracken** Saskatchewan Canada
85 L6 **Brackettville** Texas USA
142 D4 **Brackletter** Highland Scotland UK
139 F2 **Brackley** Northamptonshire England UK
139 G3 **Bracknell** Bracknell Forest England UK
139 G3 **Bracknell Forest** *admin. area* England UK
131 G6 **Bradano** *watercourse* Italy
87 J7 **Bradenton** Florida USA
132 C3 **Brădești** Romania
141 G3 **Bradfield** South Yorkshire England UK
141 G3 **Bradford** West Yorkshire England UK
82 G6 **Bradford** Illinois USA
83 O5 **Bradford** Vermont USA
138 E4 **Bradford Abbas** Dorset England UK
141 G3 **Bradgate** South Yorkshire England UK
139 F4 **Brading** Isle of Wight England UK
141 G2 **Bradley** North Yorkshire England UK
139 E2 **Bradley** Staffordshire England UK
84 B3 **Bradley** California USA
214 D2 **Bradshaw, Port** NT Australia
81 O6 **Brady** Nebraska USA
86 B5 **Brady** Texas USA
86 B5 **Brady Reservoir** Texas USA
142 D3 **Brae** Highland Scotland UK
142 inset **Brae** Shetland Scotland UK
142 D3 **Braeantra** Highland Scotland UK
142 E3 **Braemar** Aberdeenshire Scotland UK
142 E2 **Braemore** Highland Scotland UK
128 B3 **Braga** Portugal
128 B3 **Braga** *admin. area* Portugal
106 F5 **Bragado** Argentina
102 C3 **Bragança** Brazil
128 C3 **Bragança** Portugal
128 C3 **Bragança** *admin. area* Portugal
103 C8 **Bragança Paulista** Brazil
75 N7 **Bragg Creek** Alberta Canada
135 AK6 **Bragina** Russian Federation
100 D3 **Bragueta** Venezuela
82 E4 **Braham** Minnesota USA
181 H3 **Brahmakund** Arunachal Pradesh India
181 G4 **Brahmanbaria** Bangladesh
187 F7 **Brahmapur** Orissa India
181 H3 **Brahmaputra** *watercourse* Assam India
132 E3 **Brăila** Romania
132 E3 **Brăila** *admin. area* Romania
139 F2 **Brailsford** Derbyshire England UK
82 D3 **Brainerd** Minnesota USA
139 H3 **Braintree** Essex England UK
162 E4 **Brak** *watercourse* South Africa
124 E1 **Brake** Germany
122 G3 **Brålanda** Sweden
126 F5 **Bram** France
139 F2 **Bramcote** Warwickshire England UK
120 J5 **Brämön** *island* Sweden
140 F2 **Brampton** Cumbria England UK
215 J6 **Brampton Island** Qld Australia
124 D1 **Bramsche** Germany
122 I2 **Bramsöfjärden** *bay* Sweden
215 I4 **Bramston Beach** Qld Australia
214 G2 **Bramwell** Qld Australia
132 D3 **Bran** Romania
120 J4 **Brånaberg** Sweden
139 H2 **Brancaster** Norfolk England UK
139 H2 **Brancaster Staithe** Norfolk England UK
214 D4 **Branch** *watercourse* NT Australia
101 F4 **Branco** *watercourse* Brazil
164 4 **Branco** *island* Cape Verde
130 C3 **Brand** Austria
109 1c **Brandaris** *mountain* Netherlands Antilles
120 J5 **Brändbo** Sweden
122 F2 **Brandbu** Norway
124 G1 **Brandenburg** *admin. area* Germany
141 H3 **Brandesburton** East Riding of Yorkshire England UK
123 K2 **Brändö** *island* Finland
215 I5 **Brandon** Qld Australia
81 P2 **Brandon** Manitoba Canada
81 R4 **Brandon** Minnesota USA
86 G4 **Brandon** Mississippi USA
120 M4 **Brändön** Sweden
143 B4 **Brandon Bay** Ireland
143 B4 **Brandon Head** *cape* Ireland
120 L5 **Brändövik** Finland
122 E5 **Brandsø** *island* Denmark
162 D6 **Brandvlei** South Africa
87 J6 **Branford** Florida USA
196 D4 **Brani, Pulau** *island* Singapore
130 F4 **Branica** *watercourse* Slovenia
120 L4 **Brännberg** Sweden
120 L5 **Brännland** Sweden
218 F3 **Bransby** Qld Australia
109 17 **Bransby Point** *cape* Montserrat
59 U2 **Bransfield Strait** Antarctica
82 E8 **Branson** Missouri USA
139 G2 **Branston** Leicester England UK
75 O7 **Brant** Alberta Canada
77 N5 **Brant** *watercourse* Ontario Canada
83 K5 **Brantford** Ontario Canada
140 E2 **Branthwaite** Cumbria England UK
126 E4 **Brantôme** France
198 E3 **Bras** *island* Indonesia
79 H10 **Bras d'Or Lake** Nova Scotia Canada
87 J3 **Braselton** Georgia USA
103 D7 **Brasil, Planalto do** *region* Brazil
104 D3 **Brasiléia** Brazil
103 C6 **Brasília** Brazil
132 D3 **Brașov** Romania
132 D3 **Brasóv** *admin. area* Romania
159 F4 **Brass** Nigeria
126 F5 **Brassac** France
127 G1 **Brasschaat** Belgium
197 H2 **Brassey, Banjaran** *range* Malaysia
125 I3 **Bratislava** Slovakia
125 I3 **Bratislavský** *admin. area* Slovakia
133 D4 **Bratsigovo** Bulgaria
135 V7 **Bratsk** Russian Federation
132 F1 **Bratslav** Ukraine
120 I4 **Brattbäcken** Sweden
120 K4 **Bratten** Sweden
83 O5 **Brattleboro** Vermont USA
138 D3 **Bratton** Somerset England UK
120 F5 **Brattset** Norway
120 E5 **Brattvåg** Norway
124 F1 **Braunschweig** Germany
138 C3 **Braunton** Devon England UK
164 4 **Brava** *island* Cape Verde
129 H3 **Brava, Costa** *region* Spain
100 A5 **Brava, Punta** *cape* Ecuador
122 I3 **Bråviken** *bay* Sweden
106 D3 **Bravo, Cerro** *mountain* Chile
84 E4 **Brawley** California USA
143 F3 **Bray** Ireland
143 B5 **Bray Head** *cape* Ireland
73 L5 **Bray Island** Nunavut Canada
126 F2 **Bray-sur-Seine** France
126 E3 **Braye** *watercourse* France
138 D3 **Brayford** Devon England UK
75 M6 **Brazeau** *watercourse* Alberta Canada
74 M6 **Brazeau, Mount** Alberta Canada
75 N6 **Brazeau Reservoir** Alberta Canada
158 B3 **Brazier Point** *cape* Liberia
103 C5 **Brazil** *country* South America
51 P11 **Brazil Basin** *underwater feature* Atlantic Ocean
86 B4 **Brazos** *watercourse* Texas USA
199 F5 **Brazza** *watercourse* Indonesia
159 H5 **Brazzaville** Congo
130 F4 **Brbinj** Croatia
132 A3 **Brčko** Bosnia and Herzegovina
125 G3 **Brdy** *range* Czech Republic
214 E7 **Breadalbane** Qld Australia
217 I2 **Breaden, Lake** WA Australia
143 C3 **Breaghwy** Ireland
142 inset **Breakon** Shetland Scotland UK
221 B7 **Breaksea Sound** New Zealand
126 D2 **Bréal-sous-Vitré** France
220 F2 **Bream Head** *cape* New Zealand
220 F3 **Bream Tail** *cape* New Zealand
138 D3 **Brean** Somerset England UK
132 D3 **Breaza** Romania
216 E3 **Breberle Lake** WA Australia
196 F5 **Brebes** Indonesia
196 F5 **Brebes, Tanjung** *cape* Indonesia
132 B3 **Brebu** Romania
126 D2 **Brécey** France
138 C3 **Brechfa** Carmarthenshire Wales UK
142 F4 **Brechin** Angus Scotland UK
86 B4 **Breckenridge** Texas USA
125 I3 **Břeclav** Czech Republic
138 D3 **Brecon** Powys Wales UK
138 D3 **Brecon Beacons** *range* Wales UK
124 C2 **Breda** Netherlands
162 D6 **Bredasdorp** South Africa
122 G1 **Bredåsjön** *lake* Sweden
219 I6 **Bredbo** NSW Australia
141 F3 **Bredbury** Greater Manchester England UK
120 I5 **Bredbyn** Sweden
78 P2 **Bredefjord** *bay* Greenland
81 N1 **Bredenbury** Saskatchewan Canada
122 E5 **Bredningen** *bay* Denmark
122 H2 **Bredsjön** *lake* Sweden
123 J1 **Bredvik** Sweden
182 H3 **Bredy** Russian Federation
127 G1 **Bree** Belgium
143 E1 **Bree** Ireland
219 J4 **Breeza** NSW Australia
133 C5 **Bregalnica** *watercourse* Macedonia
124 E4 **Bregenz** Austria
126 D2 **Bréhal** France
126 C2 **Bréhat, Île de** *island* France
122 H1 **Brehungen** *lake* Sweden
59 B2 **Breid Bay** Antarctica
120 inset **Breiðafjörður** *bay* Iceland
122 D1 **Breidalsvatn** *lake* Norway
120 inset **Breiðdalsvík** Iceland
127 H5 **Breil-sur-Roya** France
122 D2 **Breim** Norway
122 D2 **Breimsvatnet** *lake* Norway
121 M1 **Breivikbotn** Norway
120 K2 **Breivikeidet** Norway
102 D3 **Brejo** Brazil
102 D5 **Brejo** *watercourse* Brazil
102 E4 **Brejo Santo** Brazil
120 G5 **Brekken** Norway
122 C2 **Bremangerlandet** *island* Norway
130 C4 **Brembo** *watercourse* Italy
124 E1 **Bremen** Germany
124 E1 **Bremen** *admin. area* Germany
216 F7 **Bremer** *watercourse* WA Australia
214 D2 **Bremer Island** NT Australia
216 G6 **Bremer Range** WA Australia
124 E1 **Bremerhaven** Germany
216 H2 **Bremner, Lake** WA Australia
140 A4 **Brenan** Ireland
84 F4 **Brenda** Arizona USA
130 D4 **Brendola** Italy
86 C5 **Brenham** Texas USA
158 E3 **Breniase** Ghana
138 D1 **Brenig, Llyn** *lake* Wales UK
126 E3 **Brenne** *region* France
124 F4 **Brennero** Italy
124 F5 **Breno** Italy
124 C4 **Brénod** France
86 H4 **Brent** Alabama USA
124 F4 **Brenta, Cima** *mountain* Italy
139 G2 **Brentingby** Leicester England UK
139 H3 **Brentwood** Essex England UK
86 H2 **Brentwood** Tennessee USA
124 F5 **Brescia** Italy
126 E1 **Bresle** *watercourse* France
132 B4 **Bresnica** Serbia
124 F4 **Bressanone** Italy
127 G3 **Bresse** *region* France
126 D3 **Bressuire** France
136 B2 **Brest** Belarus
126 B2 **Brest** France
132 B4 **Brestovac** Serbia
136 C2 **Brestskaya Voblasts'** *admin. area* Belarus
126 C2 **Bretagne** *admin. area* France
126 C3 **Bretagne** *region* France
126 E4 **Bretenoux** France
75 N6 **Breton** Alberta Canada
89 H2 **Breton Island** *island* Louisiana USA
89 H2 **Breton Sound** Louisiana USA
164 6b **Bretonne, Baie** *bay* French Southern and Antarctic Lands
220 F2 **Brett, Cape** New Zealand
219 J4 **Bretti** NSW Australia
138 E1 **Bretton** Flintshire Wales UK
196 B2 **Breueh, Pulau** *island* Indonesia
102 B3 **Breves** Brazil
82 I3 **Brevort** Michigan USA
158 B3 **Brewerville** Liberia
219 H4 **Brewon** NSW Australia
85 L1 **Brewster** Kansas USA
80 F2 **Brewster** Washington USA
Brewster, Kap *see* **Kangikajik** Greenland
218 H5 **Brewster, Lake** NSW Australia
59 L2 **Brewster, Mount** Antarctica
221 C7 **Brewster, Mount** New Zealand
86 H5 **Brewton** Alabama USA
75 O5 **Breynat** Alberta Canada
132 B3 **Brežđe** Serbia
125 I3 **Březí** Czech Republic
125 I5 **Brezičani** Bosnia and Herzegovina
125 G3 **Březnice** Czech Republic
125 J3 **Brezno** Slovakia
132 D3 **Brezoi** Romania
130 G4 **Brezovac** Croatia
159 I3 **Bria** Central African Republic
84 F2 **Brian Head** Utah USA
127 H4 **Briançon** France
138 D2 **Brianne, Llyn** *lake* Wales UK
219 H3 **Briarie** *watercourse* Qld Australia
219 K2 **Bribie Island** Qld Australia
130 F4 **Bribir** Croatia
132 E1 **Briceni** Moldova
79 H7 **Briçonnet, Lac** *lake* Quebec Canada
143 D4 **Bride** *watercourse* Ireland
138 C4 **Bridestowe** Devon England UK
138 D4 **Bridfordmills** Devon England UK
75 W5 **Bridgar** Manitoba Canada
142 E3 **Bridge of Dee** Aberdeenshire Scotland UK
142 F4 **Bridge of Dye** Aberdeenshire Scotland UK
142 E4 **Bridge of Earn** Perth and Kinross Scotland UK
142 D4 **Bridge of Orchy** Argyll and Bute Scotland UK
142 F3 **Bridgend** Aberdeenshire Scotland UK
138 D3 **Bridgend** Bridgend Wales UK
138 D3 **Bridgend** *admin. area* Wales UK
84 C1 **Bridgeport** California USA
83 O6 **Bridgeport** Connecticut USA
81 N6 **Bridgeport** Nebraska USA
80 F3 **Bridgeport** Washington USA
86 C4 **Bridgeport, Lake** Texas USA
84 C1 **Bridgeport Reservoir** California USA
81 K4 **Bridger** Montana USA
214 C2 **Bridges, Mount** NT Australia
83 N7 **Bridgeton** New Jersey USA
216 E6 **Bridgetown** WA Australia
91 J4 **Bridgetown** Barbados
138 D3 **Bridgetown** Somerset England UK
219 R11 **Bridgewater** Tas. Australia
218 E8 **Bridgewater, Cape** Vic. Australia
138 D3 **Bridgwater** Somerset England UK
138 D3 **Bridgwater Bay** England UK
141 H2 **Bridlington** East Riding of Yorkshire England UK
141 H2 **Bridlington Bay** England UK
138 E4 **Bridport** Dorset England UK
126 B2 **Briec** France
79 E10 **Brier Island** Nova Scotia Canada
81 M1 **Briercrest** Saskatchewan Canada
141 F3 **Brierfield** Lancashire England UK
83 K7 **Briery Knob** *mountain* West Virginia USA
124 C3 **Briey** France
127 H3 **Brig** Switzerland
219 J2 **Brigalow** Qld Australia
141 H3 **Brigg** North Lincolnshire England UK
80 I6 **Brigham City** Utah USA
141 G3 **Brighouse** West Yorkshire England UK
139 I3 **Brightlingsea** Essex England UK
221 D7 **Brighton** New Zealand
139 G4 **Brighton** Brighton and Hove England UK
139 G4 **Brighton and Hove** *admin. area* England UK
214 F7 **Brighton Downs** Qld Australia
126 B2 **Brignogan-Plage** France
127 H5 **Brignoles** France
128 E3 **Brihuega** Spain
130 E4 **Brijuni** Croatia
107 H2 **Brilhante** *watercourse* Brazil
100 D5 **Brilla Nueva** Peru
218 F7 **Brim** Vic. Australia
142 E2 **Brims** Orkney Islands Scotland UK
85 I7 **Brincadero** Mexico
131 G6 **Brindisi** Italy
217 M5 **Bring, Lake** SA Australia
218 E7 **Bringalbert** Vic. Australia
121 N1 **Bringnes** *island* Norway
142 E1 **Brinian** Orkney Islands Scotland UK
127 L4 **Brinje** Croatia
86 F3 **Brinkley** Arkansas USA
218 D5 **Brinkworth** SA Australia
132 E1 **Brînzeni** Moldova
126 E3 **Brion** France
79 H9 **Brion, Île** *island* Quebec Canada
126 F4 **Brioude** France
77 T5 **Brisay** Quebec Canada
219 K2 **Brisbane** Qld Australia
75 M7 **Brisco** British Columbia Canada
126 D3 **Brissac** France
127 I3 **Brissago** Switzerland
78 F4 **Brisson, Lac** *lake* Quebec Canada
79 E9 **Bristol** New Brunswick Canada
138 E3 **Bristol** Bristol England UK
138 E3 **Bristol** *admin. area* England UK
83 O6 **Bristol** Connecticut USA
72 D7 **Bristol Bay** Alaska USA
138 D3 **Bristol Channel** England UK
84 E3 **Bristol Lake** California USA
74 J8 **Britannia Beach** British Columbia Canada
73 K2 **British Empire Range** Nunavut Canada
137 **British Isles** Europe
176 **British Indian Ocean Territory** *UK overseas territory* Indian Ocean
91 H3 **British Virgin Islands** *UK overseas territory* Caribbean
215 I5 **Britomart Reef** Qld Australia
162 E5 **Brits** South Africa
162 D6 **Britstown** South Africa
82 E5 **Britt** Iowa USA
138 B2 **Brittas Bay** Ireland
81 Q4 **Britton** South Dakota USA
126 E4 **Brive-la-Gaillarde** France
128 E2 **Briviesca** Spain
138 D4 **Brixham** Torbay England UK
125 I3 **Brno** Czech Republic
122 I3 **Bro** Sweden
90 D2 **Broa, Ensenada de la** *bay* Cuba
216 G5 **Broad Arrow** WA Australia
143 C2 **Broad Haven** *bay* Ireland
142 E5 **Broad Law** *mountain* Scotland UK
87 K3 **Broad Run** *watercourse* South Carolina USA
215 J7 **Broad Sound** Qld Australia
83 L1 **Broadback** *watercourse* Quebec Canada
214 C4 **Broadmere** NT Australia
124 A2 **Broadstairs** Kent UK
81 M4 **Broadus** Montana USA
81 K3 **Broadview** Montana USA
85 K3 **Broadview** New Mexico USA
138 E2 **Broadwas** Worcestershire England UK
81 N6 **Broadwater** Nebraska USA
138 C3 **Broadway** Carmarthenshire Wales UK
138 E4 **Broadwey** Dorset England UK
122 H4 **Broby** Sweden
78 C3 **Brochant** *watercourse* Quebec Canada
75 U4 **Brochet** Manitoba Canada
79 D8 **Brochet** *watercourse* Quebec Canada
76 E3 **Brochet, Lac** *lake* Manitoba Canada
73 M9 **Brochet, Lac au** *lake* Quebec Canada
75 Q7 **Brock** Saskatchewan Canada
72 H3 **Brock Island** Northwest Territories Canada
142 E1 **Brockan** Orkney Islands Scotland UK
139 F4 **Brockbridge** Hampshire England UK
124 F2 **Brocken** *mountain* Germany
212 D7 **Brockman, Mount** WA Australia
138 E2 **Brockton** Shropshire England UK
83 P5 **Brockton** Massachusetts USA
81 M2 **Brockton** Montana USA
83 N4 **Brockville** Ontario Canada
83 L5 **Brocton** New York USA
132 A4 **Brodarevo** Serbia
123 O6 **Brodets** Belarus
73 K4 **Brodeur Peninsula** Nunavut Canada
125 K5 **Brodica** Serbia
125 J1 **Brodnica** Poland
125 H1 **Brody** Poland
126 E2 **Broglie** France
219 I7 **Brogo** NSW Australia
125 H1 **Brojce** Poland
125 K1 **Brok** Poland
215 J6 **Broken** *watercourse* Qld Australia
86 D2 **Broken Arrow** Oklahoma USA
219 J5 **Broken Bay** NSW Australia
86 D3 **Broken Bow Lake** Oklahoma USA
218 E4 **Broken Hill** NSW Australia
52 F11 **Broken Ridge** *underwater feature* Indian Ocean
135 AF7 **Brokhovo** Russian Federation
101 H3 **Brokopondo** Suriname
101 H3 **Brokopondo** *admin. area* Suriname
123 L3 **Bromarv** Finland
130 D2 **Brombachsee** *lake* Germany
124 F1 **Brome** Germany
139 I2 **Brome Street** Suffolk England UK
138 D3 **Brompton Regis** Somerset England UK
139 E2 **Bromsgrove** Worcestershire England UK
138 E2 **Bromyard** Herefordshire England UK
124 E5 **Broni** Italy
138 D2 **Bronllys** Powys Wales UK
134 O7 **Bronnikovo** Russian Federation
120 H4 **Brønnøysund** Norway
87 J6 **Bronson** Florida USA
86 A5 **Bronte** Texas USA
139 G2 **Brook End** Bedfordshire England UK
219 I3 **Brookdale** Qld Australia
139 I2 **Brooke** Norfolk England UK
195 H5 **Brooke's Point** Philippines
82 E7 **Brookfield** Missouri USA
213 H5 **Brooking Springs** WA Australia
81 Q4 **Brookings** South Dakota USA
79 F10 **Brooklyn** Nova Scotia Canada
82 E4 **Brooklyn Park** Minnesota USA
59 U2 **Brooks, Cape** Antarctica
74 H7 **Brooks Bay** British Columbia Canada
74 E2 **Brooks Brook** Yukon Territory Canada
72 D5 **Brooks Range** Alaska USA
85 J1 **Brookside** Colorado USA
219 J2 **Brookstead** Qld Australia
87 J6 **Brooksville** Florida USA
216 E6 **Brookton** WA Australia
82 I7 **Brookville Lake** Indiana USA
212 G4 **Broome** WA Australia
216 E6 **Broomehill** WA Australia
77 P5 **Broomfield Island** Nunavut Canada
215 K7 **Broomfield Reef** Qld Australia
141 G1 **Broomhill** Northumberland England UK
219 K3 **Brooms Head** NSW Australia
142 E2 **Brora** Highland Scotland UK
142 D2 **Brora** *watercourse* Scotland UK
122 H5 **Brösarp** Sweden
140 A3 **Brosna** *watercourse* Ireland
126 D4 **Brossac** France
132 C3 **Broșteni** Romania
126 E2 **Brou** France
126 D4 **Brouage** France
142 E1 **Brough Head** *cape* Scotland UK
142 F2 **Brough Ness** *cape* Scotland UK
215 I6 **Broughton** Qld Australia
138 E1 **Broughton** Flintshire Wales UK
140 F3 **Broughton** Lancashire England UK
219 K5 **Broughton Island** NSW Australia
221 7 **Broughton Island** Snares Islands New Zealand
125 I2 **Broumov** Czech Republic
74 M7 **Brouse** British Columbia Canada
135 AF9 **Broutona, Ostrov** *island* Kuril Islands
215 G4 **Brown** *watercourse* Qld Australia
217 M6 **Brown, Point** SA Australia
139 I2 **Brown Street** Suffolk England UK
75 P6 **Brownfield** Alberta Canada
85 K4 **Brownfield** Texas USA
139 F2 **Brownhills** West Midlands England UK
80 I2 **Browning** Montana USA
74 L2 **Brownings Landing** Northwest Territories Canada
83 K2 **Brownrigg** Ontario Canada
82 H7 **Brownstown** Indiana USA
86 G3 **Brownsville** Tennessee USA
86 C8 **Brownsville** Texas USA
86 B5 **Brownwood** Texas USA
86 B5 **Brownwood, Lake** Texas USA
52 I9 **Browse Basin** *underwater feature* Indian Ocean
141 H2 **Broxa** North Yorkshire England UK
142 E5 **Broxburn** West Lothian Scotland UK
87 J5 **Broxton** Georgia USA
139 H4 **Broyle Side** East Sussex England UK
128 C4 **Brozas** Spain
132 A3 **Brštica** Serbia
130 F2 **Brtnice** Czech Republic
122 C3 **Bru** Norway
126 F1 **Bruay-la-Bussière** France
75 O6 **Bruce** Alberta Canada
86 G4 **Bruce** Mississippi USA
82 F4 **Bruce** Wisconsin USA
212 E7 **Bruce, Mount** WA Australia
221 C6 **Bruce Bay** New Zealand
82 G3 **Bruce Crossing** Michigan USA
83 K4 **Bruce Peninsula** Ontario Canada
216 F5 **Bruce Rock** WA Australia
127 H2 **Bruche** *watercourse* France
124 E3 **Bruchsal** Germany
124 D2 **Brück** Germany
130 F3 **Bruck an der Mur** Austria
131 F8 **Brucoli** Italy
138 E3 **Brue** *watercourse* England UK
142 B2 **Brue** Na h-Eileanan Siar Scotland UK
126 F1 **Brugge** Belgium
124 D2 **Brühl** Germany
120 H5 **Bruksvallarna** Sweden
82 F3 **Brule** Wisconsin USA
74 M6 **Brûlé** Alberta Canada
78 G6 **Brûlé, Lac** *lake* Quebec Canada
126 D3 **Brûlon** France
103 D6 **Brumado** Brazil
127 H2 **Brumath** France
124 F1 **Brunau** Germany
214 C5 **Brunchilly** NT Australia
214 C5 **Brunchilly** *watercourse* NT Australia
87 I5 **Brundidge** Alabama USA
80 H5 **Bruneau** *watercourse* Idaho USA
197 G2 **Brunei** *country* Asia
197 G2 **Brunei Bay** Brunei/Malaysia
214 C5 **Brunette Downs** NT Australia
79 K9 **Brunette Island** Newfoundland and Labrador Canada
124 F4 **Brunico** Italy
221 D6 **Brunner, Lake** New Zealand
214 C8 **Brunonia, Mount** NT Australia
87 K5 **Brunswick** Georgia USA
79 D11 **Brunswick** Maine USA
108 B5 **Brunswick, Península de** *peninsula* Chile
213 H3 **Brunswick Bay** WA Australia
219 K3 **Brunswick Heads** NSW Australia
82 J2 **Brunswick Lake** Ontario Canada
59 W1 **Brunt Ice Shelf** Antarctica
130 G2 **Bruntál** Czech Republic
182 F4 **Brurynshyk** Kazakhstan
132 B4 **Brus** Serbia
125 H5 **Brušane** Croatia
81 N6 **Brush** Colorado USA
125 J3 **Brusno** Slovakia
107 I3 **Brusque** Brazil
Brussel *see* **Bruxelles** Belgium
Brussels *see* **Bruxelles** Belgium
132 C2 **Brusturi** Romania
219 H7 **Bruthen** Vic. Australia
138 E3 **Bruton** Somerset England UK
124 C2 **Bruxelles (Brussels)** Belgium
126 D2 **Bruz** France
131 G7 **Bruzzano, Capo** *cape* Italy
82 I6 **Bryan** Ohio USA
86 C5 **Bryan** Texas USA
59 S2 **Bryan Coast** Antarctica
136 F3 **Bryanka** Ukraine
136 E2 **Bryansk** Russian Federation
182 E5 **Bryansk** Russian Federation
136 E2 **Bryanskaya Oblast'** *admin. area* Russian Federation
Bryanskoye *see* **Bryansk** Russian Federation
86 E2 **Bryant** *watercourse* Missouri USA
59 U2 **Bryant, Cape** Antarctica
122 C2 **Bryggja** Norway
138 A5 **Bryher** *island* England UK
191 I2 **Bryka** Russian Federation
138 C2 **Bryn-crug** Gwynedd Wales UK
138 D3 **Brynamman** Carmarthenshire Wales UK
138 C2 **Brynkir** Gwynedd Wales UK
138 D3 **Brynna** Rhondda Cynon Taff Wales UK
138 D3 **Brynsadler** Rhondda Cynon Taff Wales UK
140 D3 **Brynteg** Isle of Anglesey Wales UK
132 B3 **Brzan** Serbia
132 B4 **Brzeće** Serbia
125 I2 **Brzeg** Poland
130 H2 **Brzeszcze** Poland
125 K3 **Brzezie** Poland
125 J2 **Brzeżnio** Poland
125 J1 **Brzozie** Poland
179 I4 **Bū Rang** Iran
185 H3 **Bu`erjin** Xinjiang Uygur Zizhiqu China
223 9 **Bua** Fiji
194 D4 **Bua Yai** Thailand
161 G3 **Bu'aale** Somalia
142 D4 **Buachaille Etive Mòr-Stob Dearg** *mountain* Scotland UK
158 D3 **Buaka** Ghana
222 8 **Buala** Solomon Islands
142 B3 **Bualintur** Highland Scotland UK
198 B5 **Buapinang** Indonesia
222 1b **Buariki** *island* Kiribati
196 D3 **Buatan** Indonesia
155 J2 **Bu'ayrat al Hasūn** Libya
158 B2 **Buba** Guinea-Bissau
158 A2 **Bubaque** Guinea-Bissau
162 F4 **Bubi** *watercourse* Zimbabwe
123 L5 **Bubiai** Lithuania
178 F3 **Būbiyān, Jazīrat** *island* Kuwait
199 I5 **Bubu** Papua New Guinea
161 F5 **Bubu** *watercourse* Tanzania
141 H3 **Bubwith** East Riding of Yorkshire England UK
133 G7 **Bucak** Turkey
100 C3 **Bucaramanga** Colombia
213 G3 **Buccaneer Archipelago** WA Australia
109 2 **Buccaneer Point** Isla de Providencia
132 D1 **Buchach** Ukraine
142 E4 **Buchal** Perth and Kinross Scotland UK
219 I7 **Buchan** Vic. Australia
73 L4 **Buchan Gulf** Nunavut Canada
214 D5 **Buchanan** *watercourse* NT Australia
83 L8 **Buchanan** Virginia USA
215 H6 **Buchanan, Lake** Qld Australia
216 H2 **Buchanan, Lake** WA Australia
86 B5 **Buchanan, Lake** Texas USA
59 J2 **Buchanan Bay** Antarctica
79 J8 **Buchans** Newfoundland and Labrador Canada
Bucharest *see* **București** Romania
130 C3 **Buchs** Switzerland
130 B2 **Buchy** France
130 D5 **Bucine** Italy
133 C5 **Bučište** Macedonia
132 C2 **Buciumi** Romania
213 K5 **Buck, Lake** NT Australia
214 E4 **Buck Hill** Qld Australia
75 N6 **Buck Lake** Alberta Canada
141 F2 **Buckden** North Yorkshire England UK
84 F4 **Buckeye** Arizona USA
138 D4 **Buckfastleigh** Devon England UK
142 E4 **Buckhaven** Fife Scotland UK
85 H4 **Buckhorn** New Mexico USA
87 J2 **Buckhorn Lake** Kentucky USA
83 N4 **Buckingham** Quebec Canada
139 G3 **Buckingham** Buckinghamshire England UK
214 C2 **Buckingham Bay** NT Australia
139 G3 **Buckinghamshire** *admin. area* England UK
72 C5 **Buckland** Alaska USA
219 H1 **Buckland Tableland** Qld Australia
213 I3 **Buckle Head** WA Australia
59 K2 **Buckle Island** Antarctica
218 C5 **Buckleboo** SA Australia
214 D6 **Buckley** *watercourse* NT Australia
138 D1 **Buckley** Flintshire Wales UK
82 I4 **Buckley** Michigan USA
59 J2 **Buckley Bay** Antarctica
81 P8 **Bucklin** Kansas USA
139 G2 **Buckminster** Leicester England UK
139 F3 **Bucknell** Oxfordshire England UK
80 E7 **Bucks Lake** California USA
218 G5 **Buckwaroon** *watercourse* NSW Australia
160 A4 **Buco Zau** Angola
132 D3 **Bucșani** Romania
132 E3 **Bucu** Romania
132 E3 **București (Bucharest)** Romania
82 J6 **Bucyrus** Ohio USA
120 E5 **Bud** Norway
181 H4 **Budalin** Myanmar
132 D1 **Budaniv** Ukraine
130 H3 **Budaörs** Hungary
132 A2 **Budapest** Hungary
130 H3 **Budapest** *admin. area* Hungary
120 inset **Búðardalur** Iceland
132 G2 **Budats'kyy Lyman** *lake* Ukraine
186 E5 **Budaun** Uttar Pradesh India
59 H2 **Budd Coast** Antarctica
161 G2 **Buddi** Ethiopia
142 F4 **Buddon Ness** *cape* Scotland UK
131 C6 **Buddusò** Sardinia Italy
138 C4 **Bude** Cornwall England UK
86 F5 **Bude** Mississippi USA
138 C4 **Bude Bay** England UK
124 C2 **Budel** Netherlands
199 J6 **Budelun Island** Papua New Guinea
219 K2 **Buderim** Qld Australia
132 C3 **Budești** Romania
218 F1 **Budgerygar** Qld Australia
108 B2 **Budi, Lago del** *lake* Chile
198 E4 **Budidi** *watercourse* Indonesia
120 inset **Búðir** Iceland
138 D4 **Budleigh Salterton** Devon England UK
123 Q3 **Budogoshch'** Russian Federation
130 D4 **Budrio** Italy
123 K5 **Budry** Poland
131 H5 **Budva** Montenegro
Budweis *see* **České Budějovice** Czech Republic
125 J2 **Budziszewice** Poland
159 F4 **Buéa** Cameroon
127 G4 **Buëch** *watercourse* France
84 B3 **Buellton** California USA
131 C6 **Buemarino, Grotta del** Sardinia Italy
108 C3 **Buen Pasto** Argentina
108 C5 **Buen Tiempo, Cabo** *cape* Argentina
83 N7 **Buena** New Jersey USA
106 E5 **Buena Esperanza** Argentina
104 E4 **Buena Hora** Bolivia
109 1b **Buena Vista** Netherlands Antilles
104 C2 **Buena Vista** Peru
90 E2 **Buena Vista, Bahía de** *bay* Cuba
84 C3 **Buena Vista Lake Bed** California USA
106 D2 **Buenaventura** Chile
100 B4 **Buenaventura** Colombia
88 D3 **Buenavista** Mexico
164 3a **Buenavista del Norte** Canary Islands
128 E3 **Buendia, Embalse de** *lake* Spain
107 J2 **Bueno Brandão** Brazil
107 G5 **Buenos Aires** Argentina
108 E1 **Buenos Aires** *admin. area* Argentina
90 D5 **Buenos Aires** Costa Rica
104 B2 **Buenos Aires** Peru
108 B4 **Buenos Aires, Lago** *lake* Argentina
109 9 **Buenos Ayres** Trinidad and Tobago
103 E6 **Buerarema** Brazil
78 E1 **Buerger Point** Nunavut Canada
88 D3 **Búfalo** Mexico
199 F4 **Bufareh** Indonesia
75 P7 **Buffalo** Alberta Canada
75 N2 **Buffalo** *watercourse* Northwest Territories Canada
86 D2 **Buffalo** Kansas USA
82 E8 **Buffalo** Missouri USA
83 L5 **Buffalo** New York USA
81 P8 **Buffalo** Oklahoma USA
81 N4 **Buffalo** South Dakota USA
86 C5 **Buffalo** Texas USA
83 K7 **Buffalo** West Virginia USA
81 L4 **Buffalo** Wyoming USA
81 K4 **Buffalo Bill Reservoir** Wyoming USA
81 N5 **Buffalo Gap** South Dakota USA
86 B4 **Buffalo Gap** Texas USA
75 M4 **Buffalo Head Hills** Alberta Canada
75 O6 **Buffalo Lake** Alberta Canada
72 H6 **Buffalo Lake** Northwest Territories Canada
85 K3 **Buffalo Lake** Texas USA
75 N2 **Buffalo River** Northwest Territories Canada
87 J3 **Buford** Georgia USA
125 K1 **Bug** *watercourse* Poland
100 B4 **Buga** Colombia
132 A2 **Bugac** Hungary
161 E4 **Bugala Island** Uganda
219 I4 **Bugaldie** NSW Australia
195 I5 **Bugasong** Philippines
185 J3 **Bugat** Mongolia
190 E2 **Bugat** Mongolia
182 G6 **Bugdayly** Turkmenistan
132 E3 **Bugeac, Lacul** *lake* Romania
164 2 **Bugio, Ilhéu do** *island* Madeira
130 G4 **Bugojno** Bosnia and Herzegovina
135 W6 **Bugorkan** Russian Federation
134 K5 **Bugrino** Russian Federation
197 H1 **Bugsuk** *island* Philippines
198 F4 **Buguba** Indonesia
187 F7 **Buguda** Orissa India
195 I4 **Bugui Point** Philippines
182 F2 **Buguruslan** Russian Federation
185 K5 **Buh He** *watercourse* Qinghai China
181 G3 **Buha** Arunachal Pradesh India
181 G3 **Buha** Arunachal Pradesh India
133 F7 **Buharkent** Turkey
178 E3 **Buḩayrat ar Razāzah** *lake* Iraq
178 E2 **Buḩayrat ath Tharthār** *lake* Iraq
136 F6 **Buhayrat Qattinah** *lake* Syria
185 I2 **Buhemuren** Mongolia
163 F3 **Buhera** Zimbabwe
124 E3 **Bühl** Germany
160 E4 **Buhoro** Tanzania
138 D2 **Builth Road** Powys Wales UK
219 J1 **Builyan** Qld Australia
102 E5 **Buíque** Brazil
191 I3 **Buir Nuur** *lake* Mongolia
162 C4 **Buitepos** Namibia
128 D5 **Bujalance** Spain
129 F3 **Bujaraloz** Spain
125 G5 **Buje** Croatia
160 D4 **Bujumbura** Burundi
199 G6 **Buk** Papua New Guinea
125 I1 **Buk** Poland
130 G3 **Bük** Hungary
185 I6 **Buka Duban** *mountain* Xinjiang Uygur Zizhiqu China
199 J5 **Buka Island** Papua New Guinea
191 H1 **Bukachacha** Russian Federation
162 D3 **Bukalo** Namibia
182 E7 **Būkān** Iran
199 H5 **Bukaua** Papua New Guinea
160 D4 **Bukavu** Democratic Republic of Congo
Bukhara *see* **Buxoro** Uzbekistan
183 N4 **Bukhtarminskoye Vodokhranilishche** *lake* Kazakhstan
198 C3 **Bukide** *island* Indonesia
196 B3 **Bukit Batok** *admin. area* Singapore
194 D6 **Bukit Gajah Hutan** *mountain* Thailand
196 D2 **Bukit Mertajam** Malaysia
196 C3 **Bukit Panjang** *admin. area* Singapore
196 C3 **Bukit Timah** *admin. area* Singapore
196 C3 **Bukit Timah** *mountain* Singapore
196 D4 **Bukittinggi** Indonesia
160 E4 **Bukoba** Tanzania
125 J3 **Bukovec** Czech Republic
122 I5 **Bukowo, Jezioro** *bay* Poland
196 E4 **Buku, Tanjung** *cape* Indonesia
196 C5 **Bukum, Pulau** *island* Singapore
196 C5 **Bukum Kechil, Pulau** *island* Singapore
199 G6 **Bula** Papua New Guinea
127 I3 **Bülach** Switzerland
135 X8 **Bulagansk** Russian Federation
190 G2 **Bulagansk** Russian Federation
199 F5 **Bulaka** *watercourse* Indonesia
183 N4 **Bulakty** Kazakhstan
195 I5 **Bulalacao** *island* Philippines
195 I4 **Bulan** Philippines
195 I6 **Bulan** *island* Philippines
162 E4 **Bulawayo** Zimbabwe
162 E4 **Bulawayo** *admin. area* Zimbabwe
183 K2 **Bulayevo** Kazakhstan
178 E2 **Bulayj** Iraq
159 I2 **Bulbul, Wadi** *watercourse* Sudan
139 G2 **Bulby** Lincolnshire England UK

133 F6 Buldan Turkey
133 F6 Buldan Barajı lake Turkey
187 D7 Buldana Maharashtra India
135 AK8 Buldir Island Alaska USA
158 D3 Bulenga Ghana
219 J5 Bulga NSW Australia
219 I4 Bulga Mountain NSW Australia
185 I3 Bulgan Mongolia
185 I3 Bulgan Mongolia
185 I3 Bulgan Mongolia
190 E3 Bulgan Mongolia
191 H3 Bulgan Mongolia
190 E4 Bulgan Mongolia
190 E2 Bulgan admin. area Mongolia
132 D4 Bulgaria country Europe
131 F6 Bulgheria, Monte mountain Italy
127 G2 Bulgnéville France
218 B4 Bulgunnia SA Australia
198 D3 Buli Indonesia
198 D3 Buli, Teluk bay Indonesia
197 H1 Buliluyan, Cape Philippines
215 G4 Bulimba Qld Australia
74 H5 Bulkley House British Columbia Canada
74 G5 Bulkley Ranges British Columbia Canada
214 F6 Bull watercourse Qld Australia
75 N8 Bull watercourse British Columbia Canada
140 B4 Bull Ring Ireland
80 G6 Bull Run Reservoir Nevada USA
86 E2 Bull Shoals Lake Arkansas USA
218 G4 Bulla Park NSW Australia
216 G5 Bullabulling WA Australia
212 C7 Bullara WA Australia
216 D3 Bullardoo WA Australia
216 E6 Bullaring WA Australia
161 G1 Bullaxaar Somalia
218 E4 Bullea, Lake NSW Australia
109 1b Bullenbaai bay Netherlands Antilles
221 D5 Buller watercourse New Zealand
218 H7 Buller, Mount Vic. Australia
84 E3 Bullhead City Arizona USA
139 F3 Bullington Hampshire England UK
213 K4 Bullita NT Australia
120 L4 Bullmark Sweden
213 J3 Bullo watercourse NT Australia
213 J3 Bullo River NT Australia
218 G1 Bulloo watercourse Qld Australia
218 F3 Bulloo Downs Qld Australia
218 F3 Bulloo Lake Qld Australia
220 F5 Bulls New Zealand
87 L4 Bulls Bay South Carolina USA
87 J2 Bulls Gap Tennessee USA
162 C4 Büllsport Namibia
214 C2 Bulman NT Australia
74 K1 Bulmer Lake Northwest Territories Canada
185 K3 Bulnai Mongolia
185 K2 Bulnay Uul mountain Mongolia
106 C6 Bulnes Chile
199 H5 Bulolo Papua New Guinea
195 J6 Buluan Philippines
198 B5 Bulubulu Indonesia
198 B5 Bulukumba Indonesia
160 C3 Bulukutu Democratic Republic of Congo
160 B4 Bulungu Democratic Republic of Congo
195 J4 Bulusan Philippines
86 B6 Bulverde Texas USA
81 M1 Bulyea Saskatchewan Canada
160 B5 Bumba Democratic Republic of Congo
190 D3 Bumbeger Mongolia
160 E4 Bumbire Island Tanzania
84 F3 Bumble Bee Arizona USA
196 F5 Bumiayu Indonesia
161 F3 Buna Kenya
142 C4 Bunavullin Highland Scotland UK
195 J5 Bunawan Philippines
143 D1 Bunbeg Ireland
216 D6 Bunbury WA Australia
138 E1 Bunbury Cheshire England UK
100 A4 Bunche Ecuador
143 F4 Bunclody Ireland
143 E1 Buncrana Ireland
161 E4 Bunda Tanzania
219 K1 Bundaberg Qld Australia
218 H3 Bundaleer Qld Australia
219 J4 Bundarra NSW Australia
219 I4 Bundella NSW Australia
214 C7 Bundey watercourse NT Australia
186 D6 Bundi Rajasthan India
143 D2 Bundoran Ireland
186 F6 Bundu Jharkhand India
160 C3 Bunduki Democratic Republic of Congo
218 G6 Bundure NSW Australia
142 B4 Bunessan Highland Scotland UK
159 F2 Bunga watercourse Nigeria
196 C4 Bungalaut, Selat strait Indonesia
216 F5 Bungalbin Hill WA Australia
139 I2 Bungay Suffolk England UK
59 G2 Bunger Hills mountain Antarctica
219 I2 Bungil watercourse Qld Australia
219 H7 Bungil Vic. Australia
198 B4 Bunginkela island Indonesia
198 B4 Bungku Indonesia
140 B3 Bunglass Ireland
160 B5 Bungo Angola
192 G5 Bungo-suidō strait Japan
161 E3 Bungoma Kenya
219 I6 Bungonia NSW Australia
143 C3 Bungowla Ireland
159 F2 Bungudu Nigeria
219 I3 Bungunya Qld Australia
160 E3 Bunia Democratic Republic of Congo
216 E4 Bunjil WA Australia
215 L7 Bunker Group Qld Australia
85 M1 Bunker Hill Kansas USA
160 D6 Bunkeya Democratic Republic of Congo
143 E4 Bunlacken Ireland
219 I3 Bunna Bunna NSW Australia
218 G6 Bunnaloo NSW Australia
87 K6 Bunnell Florida USA
220 F5 Bunnythorpe New Zealand
129 F4 Buñol Spain
132 C2 Buntești Romania
216 E4 Buntine WA Australia
197 G4 Buntok Indonesia
197 G4 Buntokecil Indonesia
197 H3 Bunyu island Indonesia
121 N2 Buollannjar'ga Norway
194 F4 Buôn Hồ Vietnam
194 F4 Buôn Ma Thuột Vietnam
194 D2 Buon Nua Laos
194 D2 Buon Tai Laos
135 AB4 Buor-Khaya, Guba bay Russian Federation
135 AB4 Buor-Khaya, Mys cape Russian Federation
135 AA6 Buotama watercourse Russian Federation
199 G5 Bupul Indonesia
156 E2 Būr Safājah Egypt
156 E1 Būr Sa'īd (Port Said) Egypt
Bur Sudan see Port Sudan Sudan
161 F4 Bura Kenya
216 E5 Burakin WA Australia
183 K4 Buralkenyn-tuz lake Kazakhstan
178 E4 Buraydah Saudi Arabia
83 M3 Burbidge Quebec Canada
182 I6 Burdalyk Turkmenistan
215 I5 Burdekin watercourse Qld Australia
75 P8 Burdett Alberta Canada
81 P7 Burdett Kansas USA
136 D6 Burdur admin. area Turkey
136 D6 Burdur Gölü lake Turkey
120 J4 Bure Sweden
139 I2 Bure watercourse England UK
161 F1 Burē Ethiopia
120 L4 Bureå Sweden
135 AB8 Bureinskiy Khrebet range Russian Federation
216 D6 Burekup WA Australia
128 C2 Burela Spain
128 C2 Burela, Cabo cape Spain
190 D2 Buren Togtokh Uul mountain Mongolia
190 G3 Burenhaan Mongolia
190 E3 Burenhangai Mongolia
191 L2 Bureya Russian Federation
191 L2 Bureya watercourse Russian Federation
121 M2 Burfjord Norway
83 K5 Burford Ontario Canada
122 F5 Burg Germany
142 B4 Burg Highland Scotland UK
132 E4 Burgas Bulgaria
132 E4 Burgas admin. area Bulgaria
124 F3 Burgau Germany
127 H3 Burgdorf Switzerland
130 G3 Burgenland admin. area Austria
79 J9 Burgeo Newfoundland and Labrador Canada
162 E6 Burgersdorp South Africa
83 M8 Burgess Virginia USA
139 G4 Burgess Hill West Sussex England UK
141 I3 Burgh le Marsh Lincolnshire England UK
142 E3 Burghead Bay Scotland UK
131 E8 Burgio Italy
124 G3 Burglengenfeld Germany
128 D5 Burgo Spain
128 E3 Burgomillodo, Embalse de lake Spain
86 B8 Burgos Mexico
128 E2 Burgos Spain
124 E2 Burgsinn Germany
122 J4 Burgsvik Sweden
185 J3 Burhan Buubay Uul mountain Mongolia
187 D7 Burhanpur Madhya Pradesh India
124 E1 Burhave Germany
103 B8 Buri Brazil
179 J3 Burī Afghanistan
196 D4 Buriai Indonesia
195 I4 Burias island Philippines
90 D6 Burica, Punta cape Panama
160 E4 Burigi, Lake Tanzania
79 K9 Burin Peninsula Newfoundland and Labrador Canada
103 B8 Buritama Brazil
105 H5 Buriti Brazil
102 C5 Buriti, Cachoeira do watercourse Brazil
103 B7 Buriti Alegre Brazil
102 D4 Buriti Bravo Brazil
103 C6 Buritis Brazil
103 C7 Buritizeiro Brazil
129 F4 Burjassot Spain
132 C3 Burjuc Romania
86 B3 Burkburnett Texas USA
214 F7 Burke watercourse Qld Australia
214 F5 Burke and Wills Roadhouse Qld Australia
59 Q2 Burke Island Antarctica
221 D7 Burkes Pass New Zealand
214 E4 Burketown Qld Australia
155 F6 Burkina Faso country Africa
183 K3 Burkitti mountain Kazakhstan
126 D5 Burlada Spain
130 C2 Burladingen Germany
215 G6 Burleigh Qld Australia
219 K3 Burleigh Heads Qld Australia
86 C4 Burleson Texas USA
80 I5 Burley Idaho USA
81 N7 Burlington Colorado USA
82 F6 Burlington Iowa USA
81 O2 Burlington North Dakota USA
81 K4 Burlington Wyoming USA
183 M2 Burlinskoye, Ozero lake Russian Federation
183 K2 Burlukol' lake Kazakhstan
Burma see Myanmar
134 N6 Burmantovo Russian Federation
139 F2 Burmington Warwickshire England UK
141 H3 Burnby East Riding of Yorkshire England UK
218 F5 Burndoo NSW Australia
140 F2 Burneside Cumbria England UK
86 B5 Burnet Texas USA
219 J1 Burnett watercourse Qld Australia
219 J1 Burnett Range Qld Australia
221 E6 Burnham New Zealand
138 E3 Burnham-on-Sea Somerset England UK
219 Q10 Burnie Tas. Australia
141 H2 Burniston North Yorkshire England UK
141 F3 Burnley Lancashire England UK
142 F5 Burnmouth Scottish Borders Scotland UK
81 Q7 Burns Kansas USA
80 F5 Burns Oregon USA
74 I5 Burns Lake British Columbia Canada
72 H5 Burnside watercourse Nunavut Canada
216 H2 Burnside, Lake WA Australia
82 E4 Burnsville Minnesota USA
79 I9 Burnt Islands Newfoundland and Labrador Canada
211 inset Burnt Pine Norfolk Island Australia
76 E5 Burntwood watercourse Manitoba Canada
139 F2 Burntwood Staffordshire England UK
76 E5 Burntwood Lake Manitoba Canada
120 K1 Burøysund Norway
218 D5 Burra SA Australia
218 D5 Burra watercourse SA Australia
216 G5 Burra Rock WA Australia
219 J3 Burrabaranga, Mount Qld Australia
216 F5 Burracoppin WA Australia
142 inset Burrafirth Shetland Scotland UK
219 J6 Burragorang, Lake NSW Australia
142 inset Burravoe Shetland Scotland UK
219 I5 Burraway NSW Australia
142 F2 Burray island Scotland UK
133 B5 Burrel Albania
142 E4 Burrelton Perth and Kinross Scotland UK
143 F2 Burren Newry and Mourne Northern Ireland UK
219 I4 Burren Junction NSW Australia
219 I5 Burrendong Dam NSW Australia
129 F4 Burriana Spain
138 D4 Burrington Devon England UK
216 E2 Burringurrah Community WA Australia
219 I6 Burrinjuck, Lake NSW Australia
88 E2 Burro, Serranías del range Mexico
140 D2 Burrow Head cape Scotland UK
214 F4 Burrowes Point Qld Australia
219 K1 Burrum Heads Qld Australia
138 C3 Burry Port Carmarthenshire Wales UK
136 D5 Bursa admin. area Turkey
140 F3 Burscough Bridge Lancashire England UK
132 D1 Burshtyn Ukraine
81 K1 Burstall Saskatchewan Canada
82 I4 Burt Lake Michigan USA
218 E5 Burta NSW Australia
131 H5 Burtaiši Montenegro
74 M8 Burton British Columbia Canada
82 J5 Burton Michigan USA
86 C5 Burton Texas USA
73 L8 Burton, Lac lake Quebec Canada
87 J3 Burton, Lake Georgia USA
138 E4 Burton Bradstock Dorset England UK
139 G2 Burton Lazars Leicester England UK
139 F2 Burton upon Trent Staffordshire England UK
120 L4 Burträsk Sweden
120 L4 Burträsket lake Sweden
198 C4 Buru island Indonesia
160 D4 Burundi country Africa
160 D4 Bururi Burundi
139 H4 Burwash East Sussex England UK
81 P6 Burwell Nebraska USA
139 G4 Bury West Sussex England UK
139 H2 Bury St Edmunds Suffolk England UK
136 E2 Buryn Ukraine
125 J2 Burzenin Poland
178 D5 Busai Saudi Arabia
Busan see Pusan South Korea
160 D6 Busanga Democratic Republic of Congo
124 D5 Busca Italy
124 F4 Busche Italy
139 F3 Buscot Oxfordshire England UK
140 B1 Bush watercourse Northern Ireland UK
178 G3 Būshehr admin. area Iran
160 E4 Bushenyi Uganda
87 J6 Bushnell Florida USA
196 B5 Busing, Pulau island Singapore
160 C3 Businga Democratic Republic of Congo
160 B4 Busira watercourse Democratic Republic of Congo
122 G2 Busjön lake Sweden
125 M3 Bus'k Ukraine
122 E2 Buskerud admin. area Norway
142 F5 Buskin Scottish Borders Scotland UK
130 F5 Buško Jezero lake Bosnia and Herzegovina
124 D4 Bussang France
216 D6 Busselton WA Australia
160 D2 Busseri watercourse Sudan
124 F5 Busseto Italy
135 AF9 Bussol', Proliv strait Kuril Islands
193 K1 Bussol', Proliv lake Russian Federation
130 B4 Bussoleno Italy
135 AD4 Bustakh, Ozero lake Russian Federation
88 E3 Bustamante Mexico
215 K8 Bustard Head Qld Australia
88 D2 Bustillos, Laguna lake Mexico
160 C3 Busu-Djanoa Democratic Republic of Congo
160 C3 Busu-Mogbula Democratic Republic of Congo
122 E5 Büsum Germany
160 C3 Buta Democratic Republic of Congo
106 D6 Buta Ranquil Argentina
160 D1 Butat Raya lake Sudan
142 C5 Bute island Scotland UK
142 C5 Bute, Sound of bay Scotland UK
161 F3 Bute Giarti Ethiopia
74 G6 Butedale British Columbia Canada
160 D3 Butembo Democratic Republic of Congo
131 F8 Butera Italy
181 G5 Buthidaung Myanmar
107 I4 Butiá Brazil
160 E3 Butiaba Uganda
86 G4 Butler Alabama USA
87 I4 Butler Georgia USA
83 L6 Butler Pennsylvania USA
143 E2 Butlers Bridge Ireland
139 I2 Butley Suffolk England UK
198 B5 Buton island Indonesia
198 B5 Buton, Selat strait Indonesia
130 D4 Buttapietra Italy
80 I4 Butte Montana USA
80 E6 Butte Lake California USA
140 E2 Buttermere Cumbria England UK
141 H2 Butterwick North Yorkshire England UK
196 D2 Butterworth Malaysia
162 E6 Butterworth South Africa
143 D4 Buttevant Ireland
138 D2 Buttington Powys Wales UK
127 I1 Buttlar Germany
75 V5 Button Manitoba Canada
78 F2 Button Islands Nunavut Canada
216 G6 Butty Head WA Australia
195 J5 Butuan Philippines
195 J5 Butuan Bay Philippines
182 C3 Buturlinovka Russian Federation
186 F5 Butwal Nepal
127 I1 Butzbach Germany
195 I6 Buug Philippines
161 H2 Buuhoodle Somalia
161 H3 Buulobarde Somalia
185 J3 Buur Nuur lake Mongolia
161 G3 Buurhabaka Somalia
185 K3 Buutsagaan Mongolia
120 I2 Buvåg Norway
120 G5 Buvika Norway
182 I6 Buxoro admin. area Uzbekistan
182 I6 Buxoro (Bukhara) Uzbekistan
219 J6 Buxton NSW Australia
141 G3 Buxton Derbyshire England UK
185 I3 Buyant Mongolia
185 I3 Buyant Mongolia
190 G4 Buyant-Uhaa Mongolia
182 E5 Buynaksk Russian Federation
158 C3 Buyo Côte d'Ivoire
158 C3 Buyo, Lac de lake Côte d'Ivoire
133 E7 Büyük Menderes Nehri watercourse Turkey
133 F5 Büyükada Turkey
136 E6 Büyükoba Turkey
133 F6 Büyükorhan Turkey
191 J5 Buyun Shan mountain Liaoning China
132 D2 Buza Romania
132 E3 Buzău Romania
132 E3 Buzău admin. area Romania
132 E3 Buzău watercourse Romania
192 F5 Buzen Japan
130 E4 Buzet Croatia
163 F3 Buzi Mozambique
132 B3 Buziaş Romania
182 H6 Büzmeýin Turkmenistan
182 F3 Buzuluk Russian Federation
199 J6 Bwagaoia Papua New Guinea
160 E4 Bwanga Tanzania
158 A2 Bwiam Gambia
138 C3 Bwlchygroes Pembrokeshire Wales UK
219 I7 Byadbo Mountain NSW Australia
73 I3 Byam Martin Island Nunavut Canada
136 D2 Byarezina watercourse Belarus
214 D6 Bybby watercourse NT Australia
125 K2 Byczki Poland
120 H5 Bydalen Sweden
125 J1 Bydgoszcz Poland
123 M5 Byenyakoni Belarus
86 B3 Byers Texas USA
215 K7 Byfield Qld Australia
120 L4 Bygdeå Sweden
120 L4 Bygdeträsket lake Sweden
122 E2 Bygdin lake Norway
120 L4 Bygdsiljum Sweden
122 D3 Byglandsfjorden lake Norway
136 D2 Bykhaw Belarus
122 D3 Bykle Norway
182 E3 Bykovo Russian Federation
135 AA4 Bykovskiy Russian Federation
183 L4 Bylkyldak Kazakhstan
219 J5 Bylong NSW Australia
76 H3 Bylot Manitoba Canada
73 L4 Bylot Island Nunavut Canada
83 K4 Byng Inlet Ontario Canada
214 F4 Bynoe watercourse Qld Australia
135 Z4 Byraya-Tas, Vozvyshennost' range Russian Federation
59 K1 Byrd Glacier ice Antarctica
122 C2 Byrknesøy island Norway
141 F1 Byrness Northumberland England UK
216 E3 Byro WA Australia
218 H4 Byrock NSW Australia
87 J4 Byron Georgia USA
219 K3 Byron, Cape NSW Australia
108 A4 Byron, Isla island Chile
81 P4 Byron, Lake South Dakota USA
109 7 Byron Sound Falkland Islands
135 U4 Byrranga, Gory range Russian Federation
122 F4 Byrum Denmark
122 I2 Bysjön bay Sweden
120 L4 Byske Sweden
120 L4 Byskeälven watercourse Sweden
183 N3 Bystryy Istok Russian Federation
135 AB5 Bytantay watercourse Russian Federation
123 O5 Bytcha Belarus
125 J2 Bytom Poland
135 AD6 Byuchenyakh Russian Federation
125 J3 Bzenica Slovakia

C

132 E3 C. A. Rosetti Romania
80 H5 C. J. Strike Reservoir Idaho USA
194 E3 Ca watercourse Vietnam
194 E5 Cà Mau Vietnam
196 E1 Cà Mau, Mũi cape Vietnam
194 E5 Ca Mau Peninsula cape Vietnam
180 E2 Ca Qu watercourse Xizang Zizhiqu China
107 G3 Caacupe Paraguay
107 H3 Caaguazú admin. area Paraguay
162 C2 Caala Angola
74 G6 Caamaño Sound British Columbia Canada
102 F4 Caaporã Brazil
107 G3 Caapucú Paraguay
107 H2 Caarapó Brazil
107 G3 Caazapà Paraguay
107 G3 Caazapá admin. area Paraguay
161 H2 Cabaad, Raas cape Somalia
195 I3 Cabagan Philippines
104 C4 Caballas, Bahía de bay Peru
88 D1 Caballo Reservoir New Mexico USA
100 B4 Caballos Colombia
138 D2 Caban Coch Reservoir Wales UK
91 F2 Cabañas, Punta cape Cuba
195 I4 Cabanatuan Philippines
130 F4 Čabar Croatia
91 F3 Cabaret Haiti
219 J2 Cabarlah Qld Australia
105 H5 Cabeceira Alta do Formoso Brazil
107 H2 Cabeceira do Apa Brazil
101 F6 Cabeceira do Salsa, Igarapé watercourse Brazil
164 1b Cabeço Gordo volcano Azores
102 F4 Cabedelo Brazil
130 C4 Cabella Ligure Italy
88 D2 Cabellos Mesteños, Llano de los plain Mexico
126 F5 Cabestany France
128 D4 Cabeza del Buey Spain
128 E4 Cabezuela, Embalse de la lake Spain
100 D2 Cabimas Venezuela
160 A5 Cabinda Angola
160 A4 Cabinda admin. area Angola
59 T2 Cabinet Inlet bay Antarctica
80 G2 Cabinet Mountains Idaho USA
195 I6 Cabingan island Philippines
102 F5 Cabo Brazil
108 D4 Cabo Blanco Argentina
106 H5 Cabo Castillo Uruguay
163 G2 Cabo Delgado admin. area Mozambique
103 D8 Cabo Frio Brazil
103 D8 Cabo Frio, Ilha do island Brazil
108 D3 Cabo Raso Argentina
73 L9 Cabonga, Réservoir Quebec Canada
219 K2 Caboolture Qld Australia
88 B2 Caborca Mexico
86 E3 Cabot Arkansas USA
78 F5 Cabot, Lac lake Quebec Canada
78 G4 Cabot Lake Newfoundland and Labrador Canada
196 B2 Cabra island India
194 B6 Cabra island Andaman and Nicobar Islands India
128 D5 Cabra Spain
91 G3 Cabral Dominican Republic
219 I6 Cabramurra NSW Australia
105 G2 Cabras Brazil
131 C7 Cabras Sardinia Italy
129 H4 Cabrera island Spain
106 C6 Cabrero Chile
129 F4 Cabriel watercourse Spain
102 E5 Cabrobó Brazil
158 B2 Cabuco Guinea-Bissau
195 I3 Cabugao Philippines
195 I5 Cabulauan island Philippines
105 G2 Caburã Brazil
108 B2 Caburgua, Lago lake Chile
128 C2 Cacabelos Spain
107 I3 Caçador Brazil
132 B4 Čačak Serbia
100 D3 Cacao Colombia
107 H4 Caçapava do Sul Brazil
131 G6 Caccia, Monte mountain Italy
107 H4 Cacequi Brazil
105 G5 Cáceres Brazil
100 C3 Cáceres Colombia
128 C4 Cáceres Spain
104 B2 Cachachi Peru
74 K7 Cache Creek British Columbia Canada
158 A2 Cacheau watercourse Guinea-Bissau
108 B4 Cachet, Cerro mountain Chile
158 A2 Cacheu Guinea-Bissau
106 E3 Cachi Argentina
106 E3 Cachi watercourse Argentina
105 H3 Cachimbo Brazil
105 H3 Cachimbo, Serra do range Brazil
160 C5 Cachimo Angola
162 C2 Cachingues Angola
105 H1 Cachoeira Brazil
105 I5 Cachoeira Alta Brazil
107 H4 Cachoeira do Sul Brazil
105 H2 Cachoeirinha Brazil
103 D8 Cachoeiro de Itapemirim Brazil
106 D3 Cachos, Punta cape Chile
158 A2 Cacine Guinea-Bissau
102 B2 Caciporé watercourse Brazil
102 B2 Caciporé, Cabo cape Brazil
105 F2 Cacoal Brazil
162 C2 Cacolo Angola
162 C2 Caconda Angola
160 A5 Cacongo Angola
100 C3 Cácota Colombia
85 L2 Cactus Texas USA
75 Q6 Cactus Lake Saskatchewan Canada
103 B7 Caçu Brazil
160 A5 Cacuaco Angola
162 C2 Cacuchi watercourse Angola
162 B2 Cacula Angola
103 D6 Caculé Brazil
105 E2 Cacuriã Brazil
162 C1 Cacuso Angola
161 G2 Cadaadley Somalia
161 H3 Cadale Somalia
142 E3 Cadboll Highland Scotland UK
130 H2 Čadca Slovakia
142 E4 Caddam Angus Scotland UK
86 C3 Caddo Oklahoma USA
86 D4 Caddo Lake Texas USA
86 E3 Caddo Valley Arkansas USA
88 B3 Cadejé Mexico
214 F7 Cadell watercourse Qld Australia
218 D6 Cadell SA Australia
194 B4 Cadell Point Andaman and Nicobar Islands India
127 G5 Cadenet France
85 M8 Cadereyta Jiménez Mexico
126 E5 Cadí, Serra del range Spain
128 E5 Cádiar Spain
217 N4 Cadibarrawirracanna, Lake SA Australia
83 L2 Cadillac Quebec Canada
126 D4 Cadillac France
82 I4 Cadillac Michigan USA
195 I5 Cadiz Philippines
128 C5 Cádiz Spain
86 H2 Cadiz Kentucky USA
83 K6 Cadiz Ohio USA
84 E3 Cadiz Lake California USA
139 F3 Cadley Wiltshire England UK
218 B2 Cadney Park SA Australia
74 M6 Cadomin Alberta Canada
74 M4 Cadotte watercourse Alberta Canada
75 M4 Cadotte Lake Alberta Canada
216 E5 Cadoux WA Australia
126 D2 Caen France
126 E2 Caër France
138 E3 Caerleon Newport Wales UK
138 C1 Caernarfon Gwynedd Wales UK
138 C1 Caernarfon Bay Wales UK
218 D4 Caernarvon, Mount SA Australia
138 D3 Caerphilly admin. area Wales UK
138 D2 Caersws Powys Wales UK
138 C2 Caerwedros Ceredigion Wales UK
104 D3 Caete watercourse Brazil
102 C3 Caeté, Baía do bay Brazil
102 e5 Caetés Brazil
103 D6 Caetité Brazil
103 D5 Cafarnaum Brazil
106 E3 Cafayate Argentina
105 H5 Café, Serra do range Brazil
103 B8 Cafelândia Brazil
105 H5 Cafèzal, Serra do range Brazil
101 G4 Cafuini watercourse Brazil
195 I3 Cagayan watercourse Philippines
195 J5 Cagayan de Oro Philippines
195 I5 Cagayan Islands Philippines
130 E5 Cagli Italy
131 C7 Cagliari Italy
131 C7 Cagliari, Golfo di bay Sardinia Italy
127 H5 Cagnes-sur-Mer France
100 C4 Caguan watercourse Colombia
91 H3 Caguas Puerto Rico
162 B3 Cahama Angola
143 B3 Caher Island Ireland
143 D3 Caheradrine Ireland
143 B4 Caherbullig Ireland
143 E4 Cahir Ireland
163 F3 Cahora Bassa, Lago de lake Mozambique
163 F3 Cahora Bassa Dam Mozambique
138 A2 Cahore Point Ireland
126 E4 Cahors France
90 D5 Cahuita Costa Rica
90 D5 Cahuita, Punta cape Costa Rica
194 E2 Cái Bâu, Đao island Vietnam
194 E2 Cái Chiên, Đao island Vietnam
128 C4 Caia Portugal
128 C4 Caia, Barragem do lake Portugal
105 G3 Caiabis, Serra dos range Brazil
162 D2 Caianda Angola
132 C2 Căianu Mic Romania
103 B7 Caiapó watercourse Brazil
105 H5 Caiapó, Serra range Brazil
103 B7 Caiapônia Brazil
102 E4 Caicó Brazil
91 G2 Caicos Islands Turks and Caicos Islands
91 F2 Caicos Passage channel Caribbean
217 I6 Caiguna WA Australia
120 K2 Caihnavarre island Norway
109 13 Caille, Pointe de cape St Lucia
77 P6 Caillet watercourse Quebec Canada
86 F6 Caillou Bay Louisiana USA
109 2 Caimán, Punta del cape Isla de Providencia
88 D4 Caimanero, Laguna del lake Mexico
132 F1 Căinarii Vechi Moldova
162 B3 Cainde Angola
132 D3 Câineni Romania
84 G1 Caineville Utah USA
138 D2 Caio Carmarthenshire Wales UK
59 W1 Caird Coast Antarctica
142 D5 Cairnderry Dumfries and Galloway Scotland UK
142 D4 Cairndow Argyll and Bute Scotland UK
142 C6 Cairnryan Dumfries and Galloway Scotland UK
215 H4 Cairns Qld Australia
214 C6 Cairns, Mount NT Australia
76 H7 Cairns Lake Ontario Canada
215 H3 Cairns Reef Qld Australia
142 E4 Cairnston Stirling Scotland UK
Cairo see Al Qāhirah Egypt
87 I5 Cairo Georgia USA
81 P6 Cairo Nebraska USA
82 I6 Cairo Ohio USA
105 E2 Cairu Brazil
139 I2 Caister-on-Sea Norfolk England UK
141 H3 Caistor Lincolnshire England UK
162 B2 Caitou Angola
162 C3 Caiundo Angola
132 E2 Căiuți Romania
218 G3 Caiwarro Qld Australia
189 I2 Caiyuan Zhejiang China
104 B2 Cajabamba Peru
103 C8 Cajamar Brazil
104 B2 Cajamarca Peru
104 B2 Cajamarca admin. area Peru
103 B9 Cajati Brazil
100 C5 Cajón Colombia
84 D3 Cajon Junction California USA
85 J5 Cajoncitos Mexico
89 F5 Cajonos watercourse Mexico
102 D3 Caju, Ilha do island Brazil
102 E5 Cajueiro Brazil
85 H6 Cajurichic Mexico
103 C8 Cajuru Brazil
133 F7 Çakmak Turkey
133 F6 Çal Turkey
128 C5 Cala Spain
128 C5 Cala, Embalse de lake Spain
129 H4 Cala Figuera, Cap de cape Spain
131 C7 Cala Piombo, Punta di cape Sardinia Italy
159 F4 Calabar Nigeria
100 E2 Calabozo Venezuela
131 F7 Calabria admin. area Italy
128 D5 Calaburra, Punta de cape Spain
129 G3 Calaceite Spain
104 C4 Calachane Peru
104 D5 Calacoto Bolivia
127 I5 Calacuccia Corsica France
132 C4 Calafat Romania
195 I4 Calagua Islands Philippines
128 E5 Calahonda Spain
128 F2 Calahorra Spain
162 C3 Calai Angola
139 I4 Calais France
106 E3 Calalaste, Sierra de range Argentina
106 D2 Calama Chile
84 E6 Calamajué Mexico
100 C4 Calamar Colombia
100 C3 Calambre, Cerros de mountains Colombia
195 H4 Calamian Group islands Philippines
129 F3 Calamocha Spain
128 C4 Calamonte Spain
104 D5 Calana Peru
101 E5 Calanaque Brazil
128 C5 Calañas Spain
129 F3 Calanda Spain
195 I5 Calandagan island Philippines
160 B5 Calandula Angola
196 B2 Calang Indonesia
77 N1 Calanus Bay Nunavut Canada
195 I4 Calapan Philippines
132 E3 Călărași Romania
132 E3 Călărași admin. area Romania
128 F4 Calasparra Spain
128 F3 Calatayud Spain
106 D2 Calate Chile
129 F3 Calatorao Spain
128 E4 Calatrava, Campo de region Spain
131 F7 Calavà, Capo cape Italy
195 I4 Calavite, Cape Philippines
195 I3 Calayan island Philippines
195 J4 Calbayog Philippines
195 J5 Calbiga Philippines
108 B2 Calbuco Chile
104 D4 Calca Peru
86 E6 Calcasieu Lake Louisiana USA
108 C3 Calcatapul, Sierra range Argentina
100 A5 Calceta Ecuador
100 D2 Calceta Abajo Venezuela
106 F4 Calchaqui Argentina
101 I4 Calçoene Brazil
Calcutta see Kolkata India
100 C3 Caldas admin. area Colombia
128 B4 Caldas da Rainha Portugal
103 B7 Caldas Novas Brazil
105 E3 Caldeirão Brazil
213 H4 Calder watercourse WA Australia
142 E2 Calder, Loch lake Scotland UK
106 D3 Caldera Chile
141 G3 Calderdale admin. area England UK
89 H5 Calderitas Mexico
76 G7 Calders Dock Manitoba Canada
219 H1 Caldervale Qld Australia
138 C3 Caldey Island Wales UK
138 E3 Caldicot Monmouthshire Wales UK
136 G5 Çaldıran Turkey
218 G6 Caldwell NSW Australia
80 G5 Caldwell Idaho USA
140 B2 Caledon Dungannon Northern Ireland UK
214 D2 Caledon Bay NT Australia
164 3a Calera Canary Islands
86 H4 Calera Alabama USA
86 C4 Calera Oklahoma USA
91 F2 Caleta, Punta cape Cuba
108 B5 Caleta Clarencia Chile
108 B2 Caleta Condor Chile
106 D3 Caleta el Cobre Chile
108 C4 Caleta Olivia Argentina
108 B2 Caleufú Argentina
84 E4 Calexico California USA
140 D2 Calf of Man island Isle of Man UK
219 J5 Calga NSW Australia
80 H1 Calgary Alberta Canada
143 D2 Calhaine Ireland
164 1b Calheta Azores
164 4a Calheta Cape Verde
164 2 Calheta Madeira
87 I3 Calhoun Georgia USA
86 G4 Calhoun City Mississippi USA
100 B4 Cali Colombia
142 B4 Caliach Highland Scotland UK
109 15 Calibishie Dominica
87 K4 Calibogue Sound South Carolina USA
195 J5 Calicoan island Philippines
80 H8 Caliente Nevada USA
109 9 California Trinidad and Tobago
71 California admin. area USA
88 B2 California, Golfo de bay Mexico
84 C3 California Aqueduct California USA
84 D3 California City California USA
129 G3 Cálig Spain
132 E2 Călinești Moldova
106 D4 Calingasta Argentina
216 E5 Calingiri WA Australia
195 I4 Calintaan Philippines
84 E4 Calipatria California USA
218 E3 Callabonna, Lake SA Australia
126 C2 Callac France
87 K5 Callahan Florida USA
143 E4 Callan Ireland
142 D4 Callander Stirling Scotland UK
104 B4 Callao Peru
217 O4 Callara, Lake SA Australia
216 D7 Callcup Hill WA Australia
108 C4 Calle, Punta cape Argentina
219 H5 Calleen NSW Australia
90 B4 Callejones Honduras
109 11a Calliaqua St Vincent and the Grenadines
215 K8 Callide Qld Australia
75 O5 Calling Lake Alberta Canada
138 C4 Callington Cornwall England UK
215 K8 Calliope Qld Australia
74 F3 Callison Ranch British Columbia Canada
139 E3 Calne Wiltshire England UK
132 C3 Câlnic Romania
160 C5 Calonda Angola
129 H3 Calonge Spain
219 I3 Caloona NSW Australia
100 B4 Caloto Colombia
219 K2 Caloundra Qld Australia
76 M8 Calstock Ontario Canada
131 F8 Caltanissetta Italy
160 B5 Caluango Angola
162 C2 Calucinga Angola
162 D2 Calunda Angola
162 B2 Caluquembe Angola
157 I5 Caluula Somalia
195 I5 Caluya island Philippines
199 J6 Calvados Chain, The islands Papua New Guinea
214 D4 Calvert watercourse NT Australia
218 F7 Calvert Vic. Australia
86 C5 Calvert Texas USA
214 D4 Calvert Hills NT Australia
74 G7 Calvert Island British Columbia Canada
106 F5 Calvez Argentina
127 I5 Calvi Corsica France
129 H4 Calvià Spain
162 C6 Calvinia South Africa
124 F1 Calvörde Germany
124 E3 Calw Germany
213 H4 Calwynyardah WA Australia
139 H2 Cam watercourse England UK
194 E3 Cam Lộ Vietnam
194 E2 Cẩm Phả Vietnam
194 F5 Cam Rahn Vietnam
194 F5 Cam Rahn, Vinh bay Vietnam
194 E3 Cẩm Xuyên Vietnam
160 B5 Camabatela Angola
103 E6 Camaçari Brazil
105 F4 Camacho Bolivia
107 I4 Camacho, Lagoa do lake Brazil
162 C2 Camacupa Angola
90 E2 Camagüey Cuba
90 E2 Camagüey admin. area Cuba
90 E2 Camagüey, Archipiélago de islands Cuba
196 D2 Camah, Gunung mountain Malaysia
101 I4 Camaipi Brazil
105 G2 Camaiu watercourse Brazil
133 G5 Çamalan Turkey
102 B3 Camaleão, Ilha island Brazil
103 E6 Camamu Brazil
104 C5 Camaná Peru
103 A7 Camapuã Brazil
107 I4 Camaquã Brazil
164 2 Câmara de Lobos Madeira
102 B3 Camaraipi watercourse Brazil
127 H5 Camarat, Cap cape France
128 D3 Camarena Spain
126 F5 Camarès France
126 B2 Camaret-sur-Mer France
128 E2 Camargo Spain
86 B2 Camargo Oklahoma USA
84 C3 Camarillo California USA
131 F8 Camarina bay Italy
85 L7 Camaron Mexico
90 C3 Camarón, Cabo cape Honduras
108 D3 Camarones Argentina
108 D3 Camarones, Bahía bay Argentina
138 C3 Camarthen Bay Wales UK
104 D4 Camata Bolivia
160 B5 Camaxilo Angola
128 B2 Cambados Spain
213 H4 Camballin WA Australia
103 B8 Cambé Brazil
139 G3 Camberley Surrey England UK
126 D5 Cambo-les-Bains France
194 E4 Cambodia country Asia
138 B4 Camborne Cornwall England UK
126 F1 Cambrai France
128 B2 Cambre Spain
84 B3 Cambria California USA
74 G5 Cambria Icefield British Columbia Canada
138 D2 Cambrian Mountains Wales UK
220 F3 Cambridge New Zealand
139 H2 Cambridge Cambridgeshire England UK
80 G4 Cambridge Idaho USA
83 M7 Cambridge Maryland USA
83 P5 Cambridge Massachusetts USA
82 E4 Cambridge Minnesota USA
72 I5 Cambridge Bay Nunavut Canada
213 J3 Cambridge Gulf WA Australia
139 H2 Cambridgeshire admin. area England UK
78 D4 Cambrien, Lac lake Quebec Canada
160 C5 Cambulo Angola
162 C2 Cambundi-Catembo Angola
219 J6 Camden NSW Australia
86 E4 Camden Arkansas USA
79 D10 Camden Maine USA
83 N7 Camden New Jersey USA
83 N5 Camden New York USA
87 K3 Camden South Carolina USA
72 E4 Camden Bay Alaska USA
109 11a Camden Park St Vincent and the Grenadines
72 I9 Camduff Saskatchewan Canada
162 D2 Cameia Angola
101 F3 Cameirán Venezuela
138 C4 Camelford Cornwall England UK
84 G3 Cameron Arizona USA
86 C5 Cameron Texas USA
83 K7 Cameron West Virginia USA
82 G2 Cameron Falls Ontario Canada
72 H6 Cameron Hills Northwest Territories Canada
73 I3 Cameron Island Nunavut Canada
82 I2 Cameron Lake Ontario Canada
221 B8 Cameron Mountains New Zealand
159 G3 Cameroon country Africa
159 F4 Cameroon, Mount Cameroon
131 F6 Camerota Italy
102 B3 Cametá Brazil
214 A4 Camfield NT Australia
214 A4 Camfield watercourse NT Australia
104 D5 Camiara Peru
195 I3 Camiguin island Philippines
87 I5 Camilla Georgia USA
84 B1 Camino California USA
105 F6 Camiri Bolivia
104 C3 Camisea watercourse Peru
160 C5 Camissombo Angola
90 C4 Camoapa Nicaragua

102 D3 **Camocim** Brazil
214 E5 **Camooweal** Qld Australia
101 H4 **Camopi** French Guiana
102 A2 **Camopi** *watercourse* French Guiana
194 B5 **Camorta** *island* Andaman and Nicobar Islands India
195 J5 **Camotes Islands** Philippines
195 J5 **Camotes Sea** Philippines
87 I4 **Camp Hill** Alabama USA
84 G3 **Camp Verde** Arizona USA
86 A6 **Camp Wood** Texas USA
139 I4 **Campagne-lès-Hesdin** France
101 F4 **Campamento El Gigante** Brazil
105 F5 **Campamento Rojas** Bolivia
218 G4 **Campamooka Mountain** NSW Australia
107 G5 **Campana** Argentina
108 A4 **Campana, Isla** *island* Chile
106 D6 **Campana Mahuida** Argentina
107 H2 **Campanha** Brazil
131 F6 **Campania** *admin. area* Italy
131 F6 **Campano, Appennino** *range* Italy
104 B1 **Campanquiz, Cerro** *mountain* Peru
215 I6 **Campaspe** Qld Australia
215 I6 **Campaspe** *watercourse* Qld Australia
128 D3 **Campaspero** Spain
81 Q3 **Campbell** Minnesota USA
221 F5 **Campbell, Cape** New Zealand
219 H1 **Campbell, Mount** Qld Australia
221 9 **Campbell Island** New Zealand
80 F5 **Campbell Lake** Oregon USA
52 N12 **Campbell Plateau** *underwater feature* Pacific Ocean
80 C2 **Campbell River** British Columbia Canada
82 I8 **Campbellsville** Kentucky USA
79 E9 **Campbellton** New Brunswick Canada
89 H5 **Campeche** Mexico
90 B3 **Campeche** *admin. area* Mexico
109 I6 **Campêche** Guadeloupe
90 A2 **Campeche, Bahía de** *bay* Mexico
50 I7 **Campeche Bank** *underwater feature* Gulf of Mexico
90 C2 **Campechén, Laguna** *bay* Mexico
90 E2 **Campechuela** Cuba
132 C2 **Câmpeni** Romania
218 F8 **Camperdown** Vic. Australia
75 U7 **Camperville** Manitoba Canada
132 C2 **Câmpia Turzii** Romania
128 B5 **Campilhas, Barragem de** *lake* Portugal
128 D5 **Campillos** Spain
101 G6 **Campina** Brazil
102 F4 **Campina Grande** Brazil
103 B7 **Campina Verde** Brazil
105 H4 **Campinápolis** Brazil
103 C8 **Campinas** Brazil
130 E5 **Campli** Italy
198 B6 **Camplong** Indonesia
159 F4 **Campo** Cameroon
129 G2 **Campo** Spain
81 N8 **Campo** Colorado USA
159 F4 **Campo, Punto de** *cape* Equatorial Guinea
102 E5 **Campo Alegre** Brazil
100 D3 **Campo Alegre** Colombia
103 C8 **Campo Belo** Brazil
128 D2 **Campo de Caso** Spain
103 A5 **Campo de Diauarum** Brazil
106 F3 **Campo Gallo** Argentina
88 D3 **Campo Gobierno** Mexico
127 I4 **Campo Ligure** Italy
102 D4 **Campo Maior** Brazil
128 C4 **Campo Maior** Portugal
103 A9 **Campo Mourão** Brazil
105 G4 **Campo Novo do Parecis** Brazil
100 C5 **Campo Serio** Peru
88 D2 **Campo Setenta y Ocho** Mexico
105 F6 **Campo Triste** Bolivia
103 A8 **Campo Verde** Brazil
100 C4 **Campoalegre** Colombia
131 F6 **Campobasso** Italy
79 E10 **Campobello Island** New Brunswick Canada
131 F8 **Campolato, Capo** *cape* Italy
103 D8 **Campos** Brazil
107 G2 **Campos** Paraguay
126 B5 **Campos, Tierra de** *region* Spain
103 C7 **Campos Altos** Brazil
103 C6 **Campos Belos** Brazil
107 H2 **Campos Elíseos** Brazil
102 D4 **Campos Sales** Brazil
104 C3 **Campoverde** Peru
132 C3 **Câmpu lui Neag** Romania
75 O6 **Camrose** Alberta Canada
75 Q3 **Camsell Portage** Saskatchewan Canada
133 F6 **Çamsu** Turkey
162 B2 **Camucuio** Angola
219 I3 **Camurra** NSW Australia
142 C3 **Camusrory** Highland Scotland UK
194 E5 **Cần Thơ** Vietnam
105 I3 **Cana Brava do Norte** Brazil
79 F10 **Canaan** *watercourse* New Brunswick Canada
109 9 **Canaan** Trinidad and Tobago
197 H1 **Canabungan** *island* Philippines
76 C5 **Canada** *country* North America
56 U1 **Canada Abyssal Plain** *underwater feature* Arctic Ocean
50 D2 **Canada Basin** *underwater feature* Arctic Ocean
79 J7 **Canada Bay** Newfoundland and Labrador Canada
106 F5 **Cañada de Gómez** Argentina
106 D4 **Cañada Honda** Argentina
85 J2 **Canadian** *watercourse* New Mexico USA
86 C3 **Canadian** *watercourse* Oklahoma USA
86 A3 **Canadian** Texas USA
72 I5 **Canadian Shield** *region* Canada
108 C5 **Cañadón de las Vacas** Argentina
108 C4 **Cañadón Once de Septiembre** Argentina
108 C4 **Cañadón Seco** Argentina
130 F4 **Čanak** Croatia
136 C5 **Çanakkale** *admin. area* Turkey
133 E5 **Çanakkale Boğazı (Dardanelles)** *watercourse* Turkey
75 N7 **Canal Flats** British Columbia Canada
106 D5 **Canalejas** Argentina
100 B2 **Canalete** Colombia
129 F4 **Canals** Spain
104 C2 **Canamã** Brazil
88 C2 **Cananea** Mexico
103 C9 **Cananéia** Brazil
100 B5 **Cañar** *admin. area* Ecuador
103 D5 **Canarana** Brazil
102 D3 **Canárias, Baía das** *inlet* Brazil
109 13 **Canaries** St Lucia
90 D2 **Canarreos, Archipiélago de los** *islands* Cuba
214 F7 **Canary** Qld Australia
154 C3 **Canary Islands** *Spanish autonomous community* Atlantic Ocean
50 Q6 **Canary Basin** *underwater feature* Atlantic Ocean
90 C5 **Cañas** Costa Rica
83 N5 **Canastota** New York USA
107 J1 **Canastra, Serra da** *range* Brazil
88 D3 **Canatlán** Mexico
87 K6 **Canaveral, Cape** Florida USA
103 E6 **Canavieiras** Brazil
90 D5 **Cañazas** Panama
127 J3 **Canazei** Italy
218 H4 **Canbelego** NSW Australia
219 I6 **Canberra** ACT Australia
108 B5 **Cancha Carrera** Argentina
105 G5 **Cancha Labrada** Paraguay
106 D3 **Canchas** Chile
126 E1 **Canche** *watercourse* France
126 E4 **Cancon** France
162 C2 **Canconga** Angola
89 I4 **Cancún** Mexico
133 E6 **Çandarlı** Turkey
126 D3 **Candé** France
105 F3 **Candeias** *watercourse* Brazil
88 E3 **Candela** *watercourse* Mexico
105 E3 **Candelaria** Bolivia
107 H4 **Candelária** Brazil
164 3a **Candelaria** Canary Islands
85 J5 **Candelaria** Texas USA
128 B2 **Candelaria, Punta** *cape* Spain
128 D3 **Candeleda** Spain
103 B9 **Cândido de Abreu** Brazil
102 C3 **Cândido Mendes** Brazil
124 D5 **Candiolo** Italy
75 S6 **Candle Lake** Saskatchewan Canada
81 P2 **Cando** North Dakota USA
195 I3 **Candon** Philippines
83 M5 **Candor** New York USA
212 C6 **Cane** *watercourse* WA Australia
212 C7 **Cane River** WA Australia
101 H5 **Canea** Brazil
218 E5 **Canegrass** SA Australia
100 E2 **Caneio** Venezuela
106 D4 **Canela Baja** Chile
130 C5 **Canelle, Punta di** *cape* Corsica France
130 C4 **Canelli** Italy
107 G5 **Canelones** Uruguay
107 H5 **Canelones** *admin. area* Uruguay
100 B5 **Canelos** Ecuador
129 H2 **Canet-en-Roussillon** France
104 C4 **Canete** *watercourse* Peru
106 C6 **Cañete** Chile
128 F3 **Cañete** Spain
86 C3 **Caney** Oklahoma USA
82 D8 **Caney** *watercourse* Oklahoma USA
86 E4 **Caney Creek Reservoir** Louisiana USA
103 A7 **Cangalha** Brazil
162 C2 **Cangamba** Angola
162 C1 **Cangandala** Angola
128 B2 **Cangas** Spain
128 C2 **Cangas del Narcea** Spain
162 C2 **Cangoa** Angola
160 B5 **Cangola** Angola
162 C2 **Cangombe** Angola
154 D5 **Cangrâfa** Mauritania
106 E2 **Cangrejillos** Argentina
102 F4 **Canguaretama** Brazil
107 H4 **Canguçu** Brazil
162 C2 **Canguenjo, Serra** *range* Angola
188 C4 **Cangyuan** Yunnan China
191 H5 **Cangzhou** Hebei China
215 K8 **Cania, Lake** Qld Australia
77 U5 **Caniapiscau** Quebec Canada
78 D4 **Caniapiscau** *watercourse* Quebec Canada
78 D5 **Caniapiscau, Réservoir de** Quebec Canada
106 D6 **Cañicú** Chile
74 K7 **Canim Lake** British Columbia Canada
102 E4 **Canindé** Brazil
102 D4 **Canindé** *watercourse* Brazil
102 E5 **Canindé de São Francisco** Brazil
107 H3 **Canindeyú** *admin. area* Paraguay
195 I5 **Canipo** *island* Philippines
59 R2 **Canisteo Peninsula** Antarctica
143 D3 **Cankilly** Ireland
136 E5 **Çankiri** Turkey
136 E5 **Çankiri** *admin. area* Turkey
80 H1 **Canmore** Alberta Canada
219 I7 **Cann** *watercourse* Vic. Australia
219 I7 **Cann, Mount** Vic. Australia
142 B3 **Canna** *island* Scotland UK
199 J6 **Cannac Island** Papua New Guinea
187 C9 **Cannanore Islands** Lakshadweep India
131 G6 **Canne** *ruin* Italy
131 C6 **Canneddi, Punta li** *cape* Sardinia Italy
127 H5 **Cannes** France
139 E2 **Cannock** Staffordshire England UK
80 D4 **Cannon Beach** Oregon USA
83 N5 **Cannonsville Reservoir** New York USA
100 C2 **Caño Blanco** Venezuela
100 D2 **Caño Hondo** Venezuela
100 C2 **Canoas, Punta** *cape* Colombia
107 I3 **Canõas, Rio das** *watercourse* Brazil
214 F5 **Canobie** Qld Australia
103 B9 **Canoinhas** Brazil
81 M7 **Canon City** Colorado USA
142 F5 **Canonbie** Dumfries and Galloway Scotland UK
106 F6 **Canónigo Gorriti** Argentina
164 7b **Canonniers Point** *cape* Mauritius
75 T7 **Canora** Saskatchewan Canada
101 F1 **Canouan** *island* St Vincent and the Grenadines
130 C4 **Canove** Italy
109 11 **Canowan** St Vincent and the Grenadines
219 I5 **Canowindra** NSW Australia
108 C3 **Canquel** Argentina
104 D6 **Canquella** Bolivia
90 D5 **Canquintú** Panama
79 H10 **Canso** Nova Scotia Canada
79 H10 **Canso, Cape** Nova Scotia Canada
133 F5 **Çanta** Turkey
128 D2 **Cantabria** *admin. area* Spain
128 D2 **Cantabrica, Cordillera** *range* Spain
103 D8 **Cantagalo** Brazil
126 F4 **Cantal** *region* France
128 D3 **Cantalapiedra** Spain
128 E3 **Cantalejo** Spain
128 E3 **Cantalojas** Spain
106 E5 **Cantantal** Argentina
101 E2 **Cantaura** Venezuela
214 C6 **Canteen Creek** NT Australia
132 F2 **Cantemir** Moldova
218 E1 **Canterbury** Qld Australia
139 I3 **Canterbury** Kent England UK
221 E7 **Canterbury Bight** New Zealand
195 J5 **Cantilan** Philippines
76 H6 **Cantin Lake** Manitoba Canada
141 G3 **Cantley** South Yorkshire England UK
102 D5 **Canto do Buriti** Brazil
86 F4 **Canton** Mississippi USA
83 N4 **Canton** New York USA
83 K6 **Canton** Ohio USA
86 D4 **Canton** Texas USA
86 B2 **Canton Lake** Oklahoma USA
75 Q7 **Cantuar** Saskatchewan Canada
72 E6 **Cantwell** Alaska USA
107 G5 **Cañuelas** Argentina
101 G6 **Canuma** *watercourse* Brazil
105 E2 **Canutama** Brazil
86 B3 **Canute** Oklahoma USA
85 J7 **Canutillo** Mexico
139 H3 **Canvey Island** Essex England UK
163 F3 **Canxixe** Mozambique
139 H5 **Cany-Barville** France
74 C2 **Canyon** Yukon Territory Canada
85 L3 **Canyon** Texas USA
80 J3 **Canyon Ferry Lake** Montana USA
86 B6 **Canyon Lake** Texas USA
80 D5 **Canyonville** Oregon USA
160 C5 **Canzar** Angola
194 E2 **Cao Bằng** Vietnam
194 F5 **Cao Nguyen Di Linh** Vietnam
188 D3 **Caohai** Guizhou China
189 G2 **Caohe** Hubei China
181 H2 **Caoka** Xizang Zizhiqu China
142 B4 **Caolas** Highland Scotland UK
160 B5 **Caombo** Angola
79 E7 **Caopacho** *watercourse* Quebec Canada
83 N2 **Caopatina, Lac** *lake* Quebec Canada
130 C4 **Caorso** Italy
195 I6 **Cap** *island* Philippines
109 13 **Cap, Pointe du** *cape* St Lucia
79 H9 **Cap aux Meules, Île du** *island* Quebec Canada
109 13 **Cap Estate** St Lucia
91 F3 **Cap-Haïtien** Haiti
88 E1 **Cap Rock Escarpment** Texas USA
131 C6 **Capáccia, Punta** *cape* Sardinia Italy
131 F6 **Capacciotti, Lago di** *lake* Italy
107 H1 **Capado** Brazil
160 C5 **Capaia** Angola
198 C4 **Capalulu, Selat** *strait* Indonesia
100 D5 **Capana** Brazil
100 E3 **Capanaparo** *watercourse* Venezuela
103 B9 **Capâo Bonito** Brazil
107 I4 **Capão da Canoa** Brazil
128 F2 **Caparroso** Spain
195 I4 **Capas** Philippines
104 E3 **Capatará** Brazil
126 D5 **Capbreton** France
215 H6 **Cape** *watercourse* Qld Australia
54 E8 **Cape Abyssal Plain** *underwater feature* Atlantic Ocean
79 I9 **Cape Anguille** Newfoundland and Labrador Canada
219 S10 **Cape Barren Island** Tas. Australia
79 H9 **Cape Breton Island** Nova Scotia Canada
79 L9 **Cape Broyle** Newfoundland and Labrador Canada
158 D3 **Cape Coast** Ghana
87 K7 **Cape Coral** Florida USA
214 C4 **Cape Crawford** NT Australia
73 L6 **Cape Dorset** Nunavut Canada
74 E4 **Cape Fanshaw** Alaska USA
87 L3 **Cape Fear** *watercourse* North Carolina USA
82 G8 **Cape Girardeau** Missouri USA
109 7 **Cape Meredith** Falkland Islands
54 F8 **Cape Rise** *underwater feature* Atlantic Ocean
79 I8 **Cape St George** Newfoundland and Labrador Canada
77 P2 **Cape Smith** Nunavut Canada
162 C6 **Cape Town** South Africa
215 H4 **Cape Tribulation** Qld Australia
154 B5 **Cape Verde** *country* Africa
50 P7 **Cape Verde Abyssal Plain** *underwater feature* Atlantic Ocean
50 O8 **Cape Verde Fracture Zone** *underwater feature* Atlantic Ocean
50 P8 **Cape Verde Seamount** *underwater feature* Atlantic Ocean
79 F9 **Cape Wolfe** Prince Edward Island Canada
214 G2 **Cape York Peninsula** Qld Australia
138 D2 **Capel Bangor** Ceredigion Wales UK
138 D1 **Capel-Curig** Conwy Wales UK
138 C3 **Capel Hendre** Carmarthenshire Wales UK
138 C3 **Capel Isaac** Carmarthenshire Wales UK
139 I3 **Capel le Ferne** Kent England UK
102 E5 **Capela** Brazil
103 D7 **Capelinha** Brazil
215 J7 **Capella** Qld Australia
199 G5 **Capella** *mountain* Papua New Guinea
162 C2 **Capelongo** Angola
160 B5 **Capenda-Camulemba** Angola
126 F5 **Capendu** France
109 16 **Capesterre** Guadeloupe
109 16 **Capesterre-Belle-Eau** Guadeloupe
107 G3 **Capiatá** Paraguay
162 C3 **Capico** Angola
129 G3 **Capicorp, Punta de** *cape* Spain
104 E3 **Capihuara** Bolivia
102 B3 **Capim** *watercourse* Brazil
103 D5 **Capim Grosso** Brazil
128 C3 **Capinha** Portugal
103 B7 **Capinópolis** Brazil
90 E5 **Capira** Panama
85 J4 **Capitan** New Mexico USA
108 B6 **Capitán Aracena, Isla** *island* Chile
108 B5 **Capitán Eyroa** Argentina
108 A2 **Capitanes, Punta** *cape* Chile
102 C3 **Capitão Poço** Brazil
222 2 **Capitol Hill** Northern Mariana Islands
81 L7 **Capitol Peak** Colorado USA
105 F3 **Capivara** Brazil
107 I2 **Capivara, Reservatório** *lake* Brazil
79 F8 **Caplan** Quebec Canada
132 F2 **Căplani** Moldova
124 G5 **Capo Sile** Italy
163 F2 **Capoche** *watercourse* Mozambique
105 F2 **Capoeira** Brazil
131 C7 **Capoterra** Sardinia Italy
195 J4 **Capotoah, Mount** *mountain* Philippines
140 E1 **Capplegill** Dumfries and Galloway Scotland UK
140 B3 **Cappoge** Ireland
130 C5 **Capraia, Isola di** *island* Italy
131 F5 **Caprara, Isola** *island* Italy
131 C6 **Caprara, Punta** *cape* Italy
131 F6 **Capri** Italy
131 F6 **Capri, Isola di** *island* Italy
215 K7 **Capricorn, Cape** Qld Australia
215 K7 **Capricorn Channel** Qld Australia
215 L7 **Capricorn Group** *islands* Qld Australia
216 F1 **Capricorn Roadhouse** WA Australia
162 D3 **Caprivi** *admin. area* Namibia
162 D3 **Caprivi Strip** *region* Botswana
85 K4 **Caprock** New Mexico USA
131 E6 **Caprolace, Lago di** *lake* Italy
214 G1 **Captain Billy Landing** Qld Australia
223 14a **Captain Cook Monument** *landmark* French Polynesia
126 D4 **Captieux** France
109 15 **Capucin, Cape** Dominica
162 B2 **Capunda Cavilongo** Angola
104 E6 **Caquella, Cerro** *mountain* Bolivia
100 C4 **Caqueta** *admin. area* Colombia
100 C4 **Caqueta** *watercourse* Colombia
194 B5 **Car Nicobar** *island* Andaman and Nicobar Islands India
142 C5 **Cara Island** Scotland UK
100 D2 **Carabobo** *admin. area* Venezuela
219 H6 **Carabost** NSW Australia
101 F4 **Caracaraí** Brazil
100 E2 **Caracas** Venezuela
100 B3 **Caracoles, Punta** *cape* Panama
100 C3 **Caracolí** Colombia
106 D2 **Caracote** Chile
88 E5 **Carácuaro** Mexico
162 B2 **Caraculo** Angola
219 H5 **Caragabal** NSW Australia
132 F2 **Caragaş** Moldova
127 H4 **Caraglio** Italy
107 H5 **Caraguatá** *watercourse* Uruguay
103 C8 **Caraguatatuba** Brazil
106 E2 **Carahuasi** Argentina
106 C6 **Carahue** Chile
103 D7 **Caraí** Brazil
105 H2 **Carajari** *watercourse* Brazil
102 B4 **Carajás** Brazil
102 B4 **Carajás, Serra dos** *range* Brazil
121 M2 **Cárajávri** *lake* Norway
218 C5 **Caralue Bluff** *mountain* SA Australia
129 G2 **Caraman** France
82 H2 **Caramat** Ontario Canada
106 D2 **Caramucho, Caleta** *bay* Chile
105 G4 **Caramujo** Brazil
128 B3 **Caramulo** Portugal
218 F7 **Caramut** Vic. Australia
101 F4 **Caraná** Brazil
103 D8 **Carandaí** Brazil
214 E6 **Carandotta** Qld Australia
103 D8 **Carangola** Brazil
109 9 **Carapichaima** Trinidad and Tobago
105 E5 **Carapiri** Bolivia
79 F9 **Caraquet, Baie de** *bay* New Brunswick Canada
104 B3 **Carás** Peru
132 C3 **Caraş-Severin** *admin. area* Romania
124 E5 **Carasco** Italy
104 E5 **Carasilla** Bolivia
196 E4 **Carat, Tanjung** *island* Indonesia
131 C6 **Carataggio, Punta di** *cape* Corsica France
90 D4 **Caratasca, Laguna de** *bay* Honduras
103 D7 **Caratinga** Brazil
104 E2 **Carauari** Brazil
102 E4 **Caraúbas** Brazil
103 E7 **Caravelas** Brazil
107 H4 **Carazinho** Brazil
128 B2 **Carballo** Spain
81 P2 **Carberry** Manitoba Canada
101 H4 **Carbet Maïs** French Guiana
101 H3 **Carbet Toukan** French Guiana
138 B4 **Carbis Bay** Cornwall England UK
84 G6 **Carbó** Mexico
86 B4 **Carbon** Texas USA
108 B4 **Carbón, Meseta** *plateau* Argentina
86 H4 **Carbon Hill** Alabama USA
131 C7 **Carbonara, Capo** *cape* Sardinia Italy
81 L7 **Carbondale** Colorado USA
82 G8 **Carbondale** Illinois USA
85 O1 **Carbondale** Kansas USA
128 F5 **Carboneras** Spain
128 F4 **Carboneras de Guadazaón** Spain
131 C7 **Carbonia** Sardinia Italy
130 E3 **Carbonin** Italy
126 E5 **Carbonne** France
142 B3 **Carbost** Highland Scotland UK
143 F3 **Carbury** Ireland
129 F4 **Carcaixent** Spain
126 D4 **Carcans** France
142 E5 **Carcant** Scottish Borders Scotland UK
106 F5 **Carcaraña** *watercourse* Argentina
124 E5 **Carcare** Italy
100 C3 **Carcasí** Colombia
126 F5 **Carcassonne** France
129 F2 **Carcastillo** Spain
219 I5 **Carcoar** NSW Australia
74 D2 **Carcross Cutoff** Yukon Territory Canada
107 G5 **Cardal** Uruguay
187 C9 **Cardamum** *island* Lakshadweep India
128 D4 **Cardeña** Spain
90 D2 **Cárdenas** Cuba
89 F4 **Cárdenas** Mexico
90 C5 **Cárdenas** Nicaragua
108 B4 **Cardiel, Lago** *lake* Argentina
138 D3 **Cardiff** Wales UK
138 D3 **Cardiff** *admin. area* Wales UK
138 C2 **Cardigan** Ceredigion Wales UK
79 G9 **Cardigan Bay** Prince Edward Island Canada
138 C2 **Cardigan Bay** Wales UK
74 M4 **Cardinal Lake** Alberta Canada
131 E6 **Cardito** Italy
100 A5 **Cardo Grande, Punta** *cape* Peru
132 F3 **Cardon** Romania
129 G3 **Cardona** Spain
103 B8 **Cardoso** Brazil
81 M2 **Cardross** Saskatchewan Canada
140 E2 **Cardurnock** Cumbria England UK
139 G2 **Careby** Lincolnshire England UK
75 Q4 **Careen Lake** Saskatchewan Canada
84 G4 **Carefree** Arizona USA
132 C2 **Carei** Romania
101 G5 **Careiro, Ilha do** *island* Brazil
101 G5 **Careiro da Várzea** Brazil
126 D2 **Carentan** France
100 B3 **Carepa** Colombia
80 I5 **Carey** Idaho USA
216 H4 **Carey, Lake** WA Australia
76 D1 **Carey Lake** Northwest Territories Canada
54 K6 **Cargados Carajos Bank** *underwater feature* Indian Ocean
164 7 **Cargados Carajos Islands** Mauritius
143 F2 **Cargan** Ballymena Northern Ireland UK
127 I5 **Cargèse** France
219 I5 **Cargo** NSW Australia
215 H6 **Cargoon, Lake** Qld Australia
140 A1 **Carha** Ireland
104 B3 **Carhuamayo** Peru
104 C4 **Carhuanca** Peru
103 D8 **Cariacica** Brazil
101 E2 **Cariaco, Golfo de** *bay* Venezuela
100 B6 **Cariamanga** Ecuador
100 B2 **Caribana, Punta** *cape* Colombia
91 F4 **Caribbean Sea**
89 H5 **Caribe** *watercourse* Mexico
74 K6 **Cariboo Mountains** British Columbia Canada
76 G3 **Caribou** *watercourse* Manitoba Canada
76 H7 **Caribou Falls** Ontario Canada
82 I3 **Caribou Island** Ontario Canada
76 G3 **Caribou Lake** Manitoba Canada
82 G1 **Caribou Lake** Ontario Canada
83 Q4 **Caribou Lake** Maine USA
72 H7 **Caribou Mountains** Alberta Canada
91 G3 **Carice** Haiti
195 J5 **Carigara** Philippines
124 D5 **Carignano** Italy
185 I2 **Caril** Mongolia
219 H4 **Carinda** NSW Australia
129 F3 **Cariñena** Spain
103 D6 **Carinhanha** Brazil
103 C6 **Carinhanha** *watercourse* Brazil
131 E7 **Carini** Italy
142 A3 **Carinish** Na h-Eileanan Siar Scotland UK
128 C2 **Cariño** Spain
160 C6 **Caripande** Angola
104 D5 **Cariquima** Chile
103 E5 **Carira** Brazil
102 D3 **Cariré** Brazil
102 E4 **Caririaçu** Brazil
125 L5 **Cârjiti** Romania
143 F3 **Carlanstown** Ireland
88 E3 **Carleña** Mexico
195 I5 **Carles** Philippines
140 F2 **Carleton** Cumbria England UK
79 E9 **Carleton, Mount** New Brunswick Canada
79 G8 **Carleton, Pointe** *cape* Quebec Canada
132 D2 **Cârlibaba** Romania
80 G6 **Carlin** Nevada USA
140 F2 **Carlisle** Cumbria England UK
83 M6 **Carlisle** Pennsylvania USA
109 12 **Carlisle Bay** Barbados
89 G5 **Carlos A. Carrillo** Mexico
106 F5 **Carlos Casares** Argentina
103 D7 **Carlos Chagas** Brazil
107 G5 **Carlos Reyles** Uruguay
106 F5 **Carlos Tejedor** Argentina
143 F4 **Carlow** Ireland
138 A2 **Carlow** *admin. area* Ireland
84 D4 **Carlsbad** California USA
85 J4 **Carlsbad** New Mexico USA
54 K4 **Carlsberg Ridge** *underwater feature* Indian Ocean
74 J5 **Carlson** British Columbia Canada
59 S1 **Carlson Inlet** *bay* Antarctica
75 P3 **Carlson Landing** Alberta Canada
139 F2 **Carlton** Nottinghamshire England UK
139 I2 **Carlton Colvilee** Suffolk England UK
213 J3 **Carlton Hill** WA Australia
82 G7 **Carlyle** Illinois USA
82 G7 **Carlyle Lake** Illinois USA
72 F6 **Carmacks** Yukon Territory Canada
76 G8 **Carman** Manitoba Canada
132 F2 **Carmanova** Moldova
138 C3 **Carmarthen** Carmarthenshire Wales UK
138 C3 **Carmarthenshire** *admin. area* Wales UK
126 F4 **Carmaux** France
82 H7 **Carmel** Indiana USA
84 A2 **Carmel Bay** California USA
140 D3 **Carmel Head** *cape* England UK
90 B3 **Carmelita** Guatemala
107 G5 **Carmelo** Uruguay
104 E3 **Carmen** Bolivia
86 B8 **Carmen** Mexico
195 J5 **Carmen** Philippines
81 P8 **Carmen** Oklahoma USA
90 B3 **Carmen, Isla del** *island* Mexico
89 G5 **Carmen, Laguna del** *lake* Mexico
104 D4 **Carmen de Toromonas** Bolivia
80 F2 **Carmi** British Columbia Canada
214 A8 **Carmichael Crag** *mountain* NT Australia
215 J6 **Carmila** Qld Australia
103 D8 **Carmo** Brazil
103 C8 **Carmo do Cajuru** Brazil
103 C7 **Carmo do Paranaíba** Brazil
107 J2 **Carmo do Rio Claro** Brazil
216 F6 **Carmody, Lake** WA Australia
128 D5 **Carmona** Spain
142 F4 **Carmyllie** Angus Scotland UK
143 F2 **Carn** Limavady Northern Ireland UK
142 E3 **Càrn Gorm** *mountain* Scotland UK
216 G5 **Carnage, Mount** WA Australia
140 B2 **Carnagh** Armagh Northern Ireland UK
102 E5 **Carnaíba** Brazil
216 D4 **Carnamah** WA Australia
140 B3 **Carnaross** Ireland
219 H1 **Carnarvon** Qld Australia
216 C2 **Carnarvon** WA Australia
162 D6 **Carnarvon** South Africa
219 I1 **Carnarvon Range** Qld Australia
143 E1 **Carndonagh** Ireland
138 C4 **Carne** Cornwall England UK
85 I4 **Carne** New Mexico USA
138 C1 **Carnedd Llewelyn** *mountain* Wales UK
216 H3 **Carnegie, Lake** WA Australia
51 J10 **Carnegie Ridge** *underwater feature* Pacific Ocean
103 B7 **Carneirinho** Brazil
128 D5 **Carnero, Punta del** *cape* Spain
140 B4 **Carnew** Ireland
59 P2 **Carney Island** Antarctica
140 F2 **Carnforth** Lancashire England UK
142 F3 **Carnichal** Aberdeenshire Scotland UK
221 8 **Carnley Harbour** Auckland Islands New Zealand
140 C2 **Carnlough** Larne Northern Ireland UK
138 D2 **Carno** Powys Wales UK
142 D3 **Carnoch** Highland Scotland UK
159 H4 **Carnot** Central African Republic
217 N7 **Carnot, Cape** SA Australia
138 A2 **Carnsore Point** Ireland
140 B2 **Carnteel** Dungannon Northern Ireland UK
142 E5 **Carnwath** South Lanarkshire Scotland UK
219 J4 **Caroda** NSW Australia
101 G4 **Caroebe** Brazil
102 C4 **Carolina** Brazil
104 D2 **Carolina** Peru
91 H3 **Carolina** Puerto Rico
75 N6 **Caroline** Alberta Canada
214 D7 **Caroline, Lake** NT Australia
222 1 **Caroline Island** Kiribati
199 H2 **Caroline Islands** Federated States of Micronesia
101 F3 **Caroní, Río** *watercourse* Venezuela
131 F7 **Caronia Marina** Italy
219 J4 **Caroona** NSW Australia
100 D2 **Carora** Venezuela
100 D2 **Carora, Sabana de** *region* Venezuela
127 H3 **Carouge** France
74 J5 **Carp Lake** British Columbia Canada
108 B5 **Carpa Manzano** Chile
125 L3 **Carpathian Mountains** *range* Slovakia
132 D3 **Carpaţii Meridionali** *range* Romania
132 C3 **Carpen** Romania
199 F7 **Carpentaria, Gulf of** *bay* Australia
80 D1 **Carpenter Lake** British Columbia Canada
218 E7 **Carpenter Rocks** SA Australia
127 G4 **Carpentras** France
124 F5 **Carpi** Italy
102 F4 **Carpina** Brazil
132 B3 **Cărpiniş** Romania
84 C3 **Carpinteria** California USA
101 F2 **Carpintero** Venezuela
81 O2 **Carpio** North Dakota USA
104 B3 **Carpo Bajo, Cerro** *mountain* Peru
59 I2 **Carr, Cape** Antarctica
87 J2 **Carr Fork Lake** Kentucky USA
76 H1 **Carr Lake** Nunavut Canada
87 I6 **Carrabelle** Florida USA
143 C3 **Carran** Ireland
218 F1 **Carranya** Qld Australia
213 I5 **Carranya** WA Australia
106 C5 **Carranza, Cabo** *cape* Chile
100 F4 **Carrao** *watercourse* Venezuela
214 D5 **Carrara** *watercourse* NT Australia
130 D4 **Carrara** Italy
214 D5 **Carrara Range** NT Australia
128 E3 **Carrascosa del Campo** Spain
143 E2 **Carraskea** Ireland
218 G6 **Carrathool** NSW Australia
143 C4 **Carrauntoohil** *mountain* Ireland
142 E3 **Carrbridge** Highland Scotland UK
91 F3 **Carrefour** Haiti
128 B2 **Carreiro, Punta** *cape* Spain
128 D2 **Carreña** Spain
104 B4 **Carretas, Punta** *cape* Peru
109 10 **Carriacou** *island* Grenada
140 B4 **Carrick** Ireland
142 D4 **Carrick** Argyll and Bute Scotland UK
211 inset **Carrick Bay** Macquarie Island Australia
143 D3 **Carrick-on-Shannon** Ireland
140 C2 **Carrickfergus** Carrickfergus Northern Ireland UK
140 C2 **Carrickfergus** *admin. area* Northern Ireland UK
140 A2 **Carrickmore** Omagh Northern Ireland UK
140 A2 **Carrickroe** Ireland
218 D5 **Carrieton** SA Australia
143 C4 **Carrigaholt** Ireland
83 P4 **Carrigain, Mount** New Hampshire USA
143 D5 **Carrigaline** Ireland
143 E3 **Carrigallen** Ireland
140 A3 **Carrigan** Ireland
143 D4 **Carrigane** Ireland
140 B2 **Carrigans** Ireland
143 E1 **Carrigart** Ireland
140 A4 **Carrigeen** Ireland
81 P3 **Carrington** North Dakota USA
128 D2 **Carrión de los Condes** Spain
105 E4 **Carrito** Bolivia
90 C4 **Carrizal** Honduras
106 D4 **Carrizal Bajo** Chile
85 M6 **Carrizo Springs** Texas USA
86 B8 **Carrizos** Mexico
85 J4 **Carrizozo** New Mexico USA
219 J4 **Carroll** NSW Australia
82 D5 **Carroll** Iowa USA
76 H7 **Carroll Lake** Ontario Canada
87 I4 **Carrollton** Georgia USA
82 E7 **Carrollton** Missouri USA
86 C4 **Carrollton** Texas USA
214 F4 **Carron** *watercourse* Qld Australia
142 C4 **Carron** Argyll and Bute Scotland UK
142 E4 **Carron** *watercourse* Scotland UK
142 E5 **Carronbridge** Dumfries and Galloway Scotland UK
129 J2 **Carros** France
75 T6 **Carrot** *watercourse* Saskatchewan Canada
143 D4 **Carrow** Ireland
76 E1 **Carruthers Lake** Nunavut Canada
83 N4 **Carry Falls Reservoir** New York USA
142 C4 **Carsaig** Highland Scotland UK
80 I1 **Carseland** Alberta Canada
142 D6 **Carseriggan** Dumfries and Galloway Scotland UK
142 D5 **Carskeoch** East Ayrshire Scotland UK
131 E5 **Carsoli** Italy
213 I3 **Carson** *watercourse* WA Australia
84 C1 **Carson** *watercourse* Nevada USA
81 O3 **Carson** North Dakota USA
80 F7 **Carson City** Nevada USA
213 I3 **Carson River** WA Australia
142 E5 **Carstairs** South Lanarkshire Scotland UK
75 Q3 **Carswell Lake** Saskatchewan Canada
85 L6 **Carta Valley** Texas USA
100 C2 **Cartagena** Colombia
100 C5 **Cartagena** Peru
129 F5 **Cartagena** Spain
100 C4 **Cartagena del Chairá** Colombia
128 B4 **Cartaxo** Portugal
86 B3 **Carter** Oklahoma USA
126 D2 **Carteret** France
87 I3 **Carters Lake** Georgia USA
87 I3 **Cartersville** Georgia USA
139 F3 **Carterton** Oxfordshire England UK
82 D8 **Carthage** Missouri USA
81 Q4 **Carthage** South Dakota USA
210 inset **Cartier Island** Ashmore Reef and Cartier Island Australia
140 B3 **Carton** Ireland
78 J6 **Cartwright** Newfoundland and Labrador Canada
210 inset **Cartwright, Cape** Heard Island Australia
101 F3 **Caruana de Montaña** Venezuela
102 F5 **Caruaru** Brazil
101 F3 **Carunantabari** Venezuela
131 F6 **Carunchio** Italy
101 F2 **Carúpano** Venezuela
100 D4 **Carurú** Colombia
102 C3 **Carutapera** Brazil
128 C3 **Carviçais** Portugal
138 C3 **Carway** Carmarthenshire Wales UK
87 L3 **Cary** North Carolina USA
108 F5 **Carysfort, Cape** Falkland Islands
100 C4 **Casa Agapito** Colombia
84 G5 **Casa Blanca** Mexico
85 H5 **Casa de Janos** Mexico
104 E4 **Casa de Lienzo** Bolivia
108 D2 **Casa de Piedra, Embalse** *lake* Argentina
84 G4 **Casa Grande** Arizona USA
103 A8 **Casa Nova** Brazil
108 B2 **Casa Pangue** Chile
106 E2 **Casabindo, Cerro de** *mountain* Argentina
154 E2 **Casablanca** Morocco
131 C5 **Casaglione** Corsica France
124 D5 **Casalborgone** Italy
107 G6 **Casalins** Argentina
127 J4 **Casalmaggiore** Italy
154 C6 **Casamance** *watercourse* Senegal
127 I5 **Casamozza** Corsica France
100 D3 **Casanare** *watercourse* Colombia
128 F4 **Casas de Juan Núñez** Spain
129 F4 **Casas-Ibáñez** Spain
216 G6 **Cascade** WA Australia
221 C7 **Cascade** *watercourse* New Zealand
211 inset **Cascade** Norfolk Island Australia
164 9b **Cascade** Seychelles
80 G4 **Cascade** Idaho USA
82 F5 **Cascade** Iowa USA
80 J3 **Cascade** Montana USA
221 C7 **Cascade Point** New Zealand
80 D5 **Cascade Range** Oregon/Washington USA
80 G4 **Cascade Reservoir** Idaho USA
101 H3 **Cascades, Plateau des** *region* Suriname
53 T3 **Cascadia Basin** *underwater feature* Pacific Ocean
104 A2 **Cascajal** *watercourse* Peru
79 E8 **Cascapédia** *watercourse* Quebec Canada
104 B2 **Cascas** Peru
103 A9 **Cascavel** Brazil
102 E4 **Cascavel** Brazil
130 D5 **Cascina** Italy
83 Q5 **Casco Bay** Maine USA
127 H4 **Caselle Torinese** Italy
100 D3 **Caserío El Banco** Colombia
83 N3 **Casey** Quebec Canada
59 H2 **Casey (Australia)** *research station* Antarctica
59 D2 **Casey Bay** Antarctica
143 D2 **Cashel** Ireland
80 E3 **Cashmere** Washington USA
219 I2 **Cashmere West** Qld Australia
100 D2 **Casigua** Venezuela
195 I4 **Casiguran Bay** Philippines
132 F3 **Casimcea** Romania
88 D5 **Casimiro Castillo** Mexico
219 K3 **Casino** NSW Australia
84 C3 **Casitas, Lake** California USA
125 H3 **Čáslav** Czech Republic
104 B3 **Casma** Peru
129 F3 **Caspe** Spain
81 L5 **Casper** Wyoming USA
182 F5 **Caspian Sea**
82 D3 **Cass Lake** Minnesota USA
163 F2 **Cassacatiza** Mozambique
162 D2 **Cassai** Angola
162 D2 **Cassamba** Angola
131 G7 **Cassano allo Ionio** Italy
126 F1 **Cassel** France
81 Q3 **Casselton** North Dakota USA
103 C8 **Cássia** Brazil
74 F2 **Cassiar Mountains** British Columbia/ Yukon Territory Canada
131 F8 **Cassibile** Italy
80 D2 **Cassidy** British Columbia Canada
103 B7 **Cassilândia** Brazil
219 I5 **Cassilis** NSW Australia
215 G6 **Cassilis** Qld Australia
80 I1 **Cassils** Alberta Canada
162 C3 **Cassinga** Angola
213 H2 **Cassini Island** WA Australia
131 E6 **Cassino** Italy
124 F5 **Cassio** Italy
101 I4 **Cassipore** *watercourse* Brazil
127 G5 **Cassis** France
142 D2 **Cassley** *watercourse* Scotland UK
81 Q7 **Cassoday** Kansas USA
162 C2 **Cassongue** Angola
82 H6 **Cassopolis** Michigan USA
130 D5 **Castagneto Carducci** Italy
85 K2 **Castaneda** Oklahoma USA
126 E5 **Castanet-Tolosan** France
102 C3 **Castanhal** Brazil
104 D3 **Castanheira** Brazil
88 E3 **Castaños** Mexico
109 9 **Castara** Trinidad and Tobago
130 C4 **Casteggio** Italy
127 J4 **Castel Goffredo** Italy
127 J4 **Castel Maggiore** Italy
130 D5 **Castelfiorentino** Italy
126 E4 **Casteljaloux** France
131 F6 **Castellammare di Stabia** Italy
127 H5 **Castellane** France
127 J4 **Castellarano** Italy
106 F3 **Castelli** Argentina
129 F4 **Castelló de la Plana** Spain
126 D4 **Castelnau-de-Médoc** France
129 G2 **Castelnau-de-Montmiral** France
126 F5 **Castelnau-le-Lez** France
126 E5 **Castelnau-Magnoac** France
126 E5 **Castelnaudary** France
130 D5 **Castelnuovo di Val di Cecina** Italy
103 D8 **Castelo** Brazil
128 C4 **Castelo Branco** Portugal
128 C3 **Castelo Branco** *admin. area* Portugal
128 C4 **Castelo de Vide** Portugal
102 D4 **Castelo do Piauí** Brazil
131 C6 **Castelsardo** Sardinia Italy
126 E4 **Castelsarrasin** France
131 E8 **Castelvetrano** Italy
218 E7 **Casterton** Vic. Australia
129 F2 **Castets** France
130 D5 **Castiglioncello** Italy
103 B8 **Castilho** Brazil
106 D3 **Castilla** Chile
128 E4 **Castilla–La Mancha** *admin. area* Spain
128 D4 **Castilla la Nueva** *region* Spain
128 D3 **Castilla la Vieja** *region* Spain
128 D3 **Castilla y Léon** *admin. area* Spain
101 E3 **Castillero** Venezuela
106 D5 **Castillo, Cerro del** *mountain* Chile
108 C3 **Castillo, Pampa del** *region* Argentina
126 E4 **Castillonnès** France
107 H5 **Castillos** Uruguay
104 D5 **Castilluma** Chile
138 D2 **Castle Caereinion** Powys Wales UK
140 F2 **Castle Carrock** Cumbria England UK
138 E3 **Castle Cary** Somerset England UK
81 J7 **Castle Dale** Utah USA
82 F3 **Castle Danger** Minnesota USA
142 E6 **Castle Douglas** Dumfries and Galloway Scotland UK
141 G2 **Castle Eden** Durham England UK
83 inset **Castle Harbour** Bermuda
213 K1 **Castle Hill** NT Australia
215 H5 **Castle Hill** Qld Australia
218 H7 **Castle Hill** Vic. Australia
81 L7 **Castle Peak** Colorado USA
139 H2 **Castle Rising** Norfolk England UK
81 M7 **Castle Rock** Colorado USA
82 G5 **Castle Rock Lake** Wisconsin USA
164 5b **Castle Rock Point** *cape* St Helena
142 D3 **Castle Stuart** Highland Scotland UK
85 H1 **Castle Valley** Utah USA
143 C3 **Castlebar** Ireland
143 F3 **Castlebellingham** Ireland
143 F2 **Castleblayney** Ireland
138 C3 **Castlebythe** Pembrokeshire Wales UK
143 E4 **Castlecomer** Ireland
140 A2 **Castlederg** Strabane Northern Ireland UK
143 E2 **Castlefinn** Ireland
143 C4 **Castlemaine** Ireland
143 D5 **Castlemartyr** Ireland
143 D3 **Castleplunket** Ireland
221 G5 **Castlepoint** New Zealand
143 D3 **Castlerea** Ireland
140 C2 **Castlereagh** *admin. area* Northern Ireland UK
214 C2 **Castlereagh Bay** NT Australia
140 A3 **Castlereban North** Ireland
219 I4 **Castlereigh** *watercourse* NSW Australia
143 F1 **Castlerock** Coleraine Northern Ireland UK
142 F5 **Castleton** Scottish Borders Scotland UK
140 D2 **Castletown** Isle of Man UK
143 D4 **Castletownroche** Ireland
215 I8 **Castlevale** Qld Australia
140 C2 **Castlewellan** Banbridge Northern Ireland UK
75 P6 **Castor** Alberta Canada
77 P6 **Castor, Rivière au** *watercourse* Quebec Canada
128 D4 **Castrejón, Embalse de** *lake* Spain

126 F5 **Castres** France
124 C1 **Castricum** Netherlands
109 13 **Castries** St Lucia
128 C2 **Castrillón** Spain
103 B9 **Castro** Brazil
108 B3 **Castro** Chile
128 C2 **Castro** Spain
103 E6 **Castro Alves** Brazil
127 J4 **Castrocaro Terme** Italy
128 C2 **Castrocontrigo** Spain
128 C2 **Castroverde** Spain
131 G7 **Castrovillari** Italy
128 D4 **Castuera** Spain
107 H5 **Casupá** Uruguay
221 B7 **Caswell Sound** New Zealand
Cat *see* **Çat** Turkey
194 E2 **Cát Bà, Đao** *island* Vietnam
91 F1 **Cat Island** Bahamas
89 H2 **Cat Island** Mississippi USA
87 L8 **Cat Keys** Bahamas
76 J7 **Cat Lake** Ontario Canada
216 D5 **Cataby** WA Australia
104 A2 **Catacaos** Peru
100 B6 **Catacocha** Ecuador
103 D8 **Cataguases** Brazil
86 E5 **Catahoula Lake** Louisiana USA
136 G6 **Çataksuyu** *watercourse* Turkey
103 C7 **Catalão** Brazil
133 F5 **Çatalca Yarımadası** *region* Turkey
79 L8 **Catalina** Newfoundland and Labrador Canada
129 G3 **Cataluña** *region* Spain
129 G3 **Catalunya** *admin. area* Spain
106 E3 **Catamarca** *admin. area* Argentina
100 B5 **Catamayo** Ecuador
163 F3 **Catandica** Mozambique
195 J4 **Catanduanes** *island* Philippines
103 B8 **Catanduva** Brazil
131 F8 **Catania** Italy
131 F8 **Catania, Golfo di** *bay* Italy
131 F8 **Catania, Piana di** *island* Italy
131 G7 **Catanzaro** Italy
131 G7 **Catanzaro Marina** Italy
86 B6 **Catarina** Texas USA
195 J4 **Catarman** Philippines
129 F4 **Catarroja** Spain
101 G5 **Catauara** Brazil
163 F3 **Cataxa** Mozambique
195 J5 **Catbalogan** Philippines
108 B6 **Catedral de York, Cabo** *cape* Chile
195 J6 **Cateel** Philippines
195 J6 **Cateel Bay** Philippines
89 G5 **Catemaco** Mexico
162 B2 **Catengue** Angola
139 G3 **Caterham** Surrey England UK
162 B1 **Catete** Angola
84 D4 **Cathedral City** California USA
139 F4 **Catherington** Hampshire England UK
84 B2 **Catheys Valley** California USA
218 G7 **Cathkin** Vic. Australia
100 E2 **Catia La Mar** Venezuela
131 E5 **Catignano** Italy
139 I4 **Catigny** France
126 F1 **Catillon** France
158 A2 **Catió** Guinea-Bissau
101 F4 **Catisimiña** Brazil
139 F3 **Catmore** West Berkshire England UK
214 D2 **Cato** *watercourse* NT Australia
90 C2 **Catoche, Cabo** *cape* Mexico
102 E4 **Catolé do Rocha** Brazil
160 B5 **Catolo** Angola
130 E5 **Catria, Monte** *mountain* Italy
106 E6 **Catriel** Argentina
106 F6 **Catriló** Argentina
101 F4 **Catrimani** Brazil
101 F4 **Catrimani** *watercourse* Brazil
100 B3 **Catripe, Ensenada** *bay* Colombia
83 N5 **Catskill Mountains** New York USA
141 G2 **Catterick** North Yorkshire England UK
140 F2 **Catterlen** Cumbria England UK
214 F4 **Cattle** *watercourse* Qld Australia
214 A4 **Cattle Creek** NT Australia
141 F2 **Catton** Northumberland England UK
103 E6 **Catu** Brazil
106 E2 **Catúa** Argentina
162 D3 **Catuile** Angola
162 B2 **Catumbela** Angola
163 G2 **Catur** Mozambique
194 E3 **Cầu Giát** Vietnam
101 E4 **Cauaburi** *watercourse* Brazil
195 I3 **Cauayan** Philippines
78 G3 **Caubvick, Mount (D'Iberville)** Newfoundland and Labrador/Quebec Canada
100 C2 **Cauca** *watercourse* Colombia
102 E3 **Caucaia** Brazil
105 G5 **Caucas** Bolivia
100 C3 **Caucasia** Colombia
134 J10 **Caucasus** *range* Asia
106 D4 **Caucete** Argentina
106 E2 **Cauchari, Salar de** *lake* Argentina
108 C5 **Cauchicol** Argentina
76 G5 **Cauchon Lake** Manitoba Canada
79 D9 **Caucomgomoc Lake** Maine USA
139 H5 **Caudebec** France
195 J5 **Cauit Point** Philippines
160 B5 **Caungula** Angola
162 C3 **Cauno** Angola
106 C5 **Cauquenes** Chile
101 E3 **Caura** *watercourse* Venezuela
101 F5 **Caures** *watercourse* Brazil
79 E8 **Causapscal** Quebec Canada
126 E4 **Caussade** France
105 E3 **Cautario** *watercourse* Brazil
126 D5 **Cauterets** France
139 H5 **Cauville** France
128 B3 **Cavado** *watercourse* Portugal
127 I4 **Cavaglià** Italy
129 I2 **Cavaillon** France
127 H5 **Cavalaire-sur-Mer** France
103 C6 **Cavalcante** Brazil
81 Q2 **Cavalier** North Dakota USA
129 I3 **Cavalleria, Cap de** *cape* Spain
220 E2 **Cavalli Islands** New Zealand
130 D5 **Cavallo, Capo** *cape* Italy
131 F5 **Cavalluccio, Punta di** *cape* Italy
158 C3/4 **Cavally** *watercourse* Côte d'Ivoire/Liberia
143 E3 **Cavan** Ireland
143 E3 **Cavan** *admin. area* Ireland
77 V5 **Cavanagh** Newfoundland and Labrador Canada
124 G5 **Cavarzere** Italy
221 D7 **Cave** New Zealand
86 F3 **Cave City** Arkansas USA
84 G4 **Cave Creek** Arizona USA
80 D5 **Cave Junction** Oregon USA
82 J7 **Cave Run Lake** Kentucky USA
104 E4 **Cavedor** Bolivia
218 F7 **Cavendish** Vic. Australia
82 H2 **Cavers** Ontario Canada
195 I4 **Cavite** Philippines
132 C2 **Cavnic** Romania
127 H4 **Cavour** Italy
82 G4 **Cavour** Wisconsin USA
130 H5 **Cavtat** Croatia
218 F5 **Cawndilla Lake** NSW Australia
103 C8 **Caxambu** Brazil
102 D4 **Caxias** Brazil
107 I4 **Caxias do Sul** Brazil
160 A5 **Caxito** Angola
101 I5 **Caxuana, Baia de** *bay* Brazil
133 G6 **Çay** Turkey
90 D2 **Cay Sal Bank** Bahamas
88 E5 **Cayacal, Punta** *cape* Mexico
100 B4 **Cayagama** Ecuador
83 M3 **Cayamant, Lac** *lake* Quebec Canada
100 B4 **Cayambe** Ecuador
136 G5 **Çayeli** Turkey
101 H3 **Cayenne** French Guiana
101 H4 **Cayenne** *admin. area* French Guiana
139 I4 **Cayeux-sur-Mer** France
133 F6 **Çaygören Barajı** *lake* Turkey
133 F7 **Çayhisar** Turkey
133 G5 **Çayırhan** Turkey
126 E4 **Caylus** France
90 E3 **Cayman Brac** *island* Cayman Islands
90 D3 **Cayman Islands** *British overseas territory* Caribbean
50 K8 **Cayman Trench** *underwater feature* Caribbean
161 H2 **Caynabo** Somalia
100 A5 **Cayo, Ensenada de** *bay* Ecuador
109 19 **Cayon** St Kitts and Nevis
83 M5 **Cayuga Lake** New York USA
108 C2 **Cayuqueo** Argentina
107 G4 **Caza Pava** Argentina
162 D2 **Cazage** Angola
126 E4 **Cazals** France
130 F4 **Cazin** Bosnia and Herzegovina
130 C3 **Cazis** Switzerland
162 D2 **Cazombo** Angola
128 E5 **Cazorla** Spain
163 F3 **Cazula** Mozambique
104 D4 **Ccolo** Peru
128 D2 **Cea** *watercourse* Spain
132 F3 **Ceamurlia de Jos** Romania
142 B2 **Ceann Loch Shiphoirt** Na h-Eileanan Siar Scotland UK
102 E4 **Ceará** *admin. area* Brazil
50 N9 **Ceara Plain** *underwater feature* Atlantic Ocean
90 D6 **Cebaco, Isla de** *island* Panama
85 H6 **Cebadilla de Dolores** Mexico
85 J7 **Ceballos** Mexico
106 E4 **Cebollar** Argentina
85 I8 **Cebollin** Mexico
128 D3 **Cebreros** Spain
195 I5 **Cebu** Philippines
131 E6 **Ceccano** Italy
132 A2 **Cece** Hungary
125 H3 **Čechtice** Czech Republic
217 M2 **Cecil, Mount** NT Australia
82 F2 **Cecil Lake** Ontario Canada
219 J2 **Cecil Plains** Qld Australia
130 D5 **Cecina** Italy
130 D5 **Cecina** *watercourse* Italy
128 C4 **Ceclavín** Spain
74 J8 **Cedar** British Columbia Canada
82 F5 **Cedar** *watercourse* Iowa USA
215 H3 **Cedar Bay** Qld Australia
85 L1 **Cedar Bluff Reservoir** Kansas USA
80 I8 **Cedar City** Utah USA
86 H3 **Cedar Creek Reservoir** Alabama USA
86 C4 **Cedar Creek Reservoir** Texas USA
90 B3 **Cedar Crossing** Belize
82 E5 **Cedar Falls** Iowa USA
109 18 **Cedar Grove** Antigua and Barbuda
87 J6 **Cedar Key** Florida USA
76 E6 **Cedar Lake** Manitoba Canada
88 E1 **Cedar Lake** Texas USA
86 D6 **Cedar Lakes** Texas USA
86 C5 **Cedar Park** Texas USA
82 F5 **Cedar Rapids** Iowa USA
109 18 **Cedar Tree Point** *cape* Antigua and Barbuda
128 B2 **Cedeira** Spain
128 C4 **Cedillo, Embalse de** *lake* Portugal
105 H5 **Cedro** Brazil
105 G4 **Cedro** Brazil
102 E4 **Cedro** Brazil
164 1b **Cedros** Azores
90 C4 **Cedros** Honduras
85 H7 **Cedros** Mexico
84 E6 **Cedros, Isla** *island* Mexico
109 9 **Cedros Bay** Trinidad and Tobago
53 U5 **Cedros Trench** *underwater feature* Pacific Ocean
218 A5 **Ceduna** SA Australia
128 B2 **Cée** Spain
161 H2 **Ceel Dhaab** Somalia
161 H3 **Ceel Dheere** Somalia
161 H3 **Ceel Huur** Somalia
161 H3 **Ceelbuur** Somalia
157 H5 **Ceerigaabo** Somalia
132 B2 **Cefa** Romania
131 F7 **Cefalù** Italy
131 F7 **Cefalù, Capo** *cape* Italy
132 A2 **Cegléd** Hungary
131 G6 **Céglie Messápica** Italy
128 F4 **Cehegín** Spain
123 K5 **Čehovo** Russian Federation
107 G5 **Ceibas** Argentina
125 I3 **Čejč** Czech Republic
131 E5 **Celano** Italy
128 C2 **Celanova** Spain
132 D3 **Celaru** Romania
88 E4 **Celaya** Mexico
143 F3 **Celbridge** Ireland
184 F6 **Cele** Xinjiang Uygur Zizhiqu China
126 E4 **Célé** *watercourse* France
Celebes *see* **Sulawesi** Indonesia
55 Q4 **Celebes Basin** *underwater feature* Celebes Sea
198 B3 **Celebes Sea** Indonesia/Philippines
104 B2 **Celendín** Peru
90 B2 **Celestún, Estero** *bay* Mexico
100 B6 **Celica** Ecuador
131 G7 **Celico** Italy
106 F2 **Celina** Paraguay
82 I6 **Celina** Ohio USA
129 F3 **Cella** Spain
138 C2 **Cellan** Ceredigion Wales UK
124 F1 **Celle** Germany
128 C3 **Celorico da Beira** Portugal
107 I3 **Celso Ramos** Brazil
143 C5 **Celtic Sea** Europe
133 G7 **Çeltikçi** Turkey
138 D2 **Celyn, Llyn** *lake* Wales UK
182 I7 **Çemenibit** Turkmenistan
138 D2 **Cemmaes Road** Powys Wales UK
197 H6 **Cempi, Teluk** *bay* Indonesia
132 B2 **Cenad** Romania
138 C2 **Cenarth** Carmarthenshire Wales UK
198 E4 **Cenderawasih, Teluk** *bay* Indonesia
125 K5 **Cenei** Romania
126 D4 **Cenon** France
89 H4 **Cenotillo** Mexico
164 2 **Cenouras, Ilhéu das** *island* Madeira
132 B3 **Čenta** Serbia
129 H3 **Centellas** Spain
103 B8 **Centenário do Sul** Brazil
163 F3 **Centenary** Zimbabwe
81 L8 **Center** Colorado USA
86 D5 **Center** Texas USA
87 I3 **Center Hill Lake** Tennessee USA
86 H3 **Centerville** Tennessee USA
130 D4 **Cento** Italy
162 E4 **Central** *admin. area* Botswana
101 I5 **Central** Brazil
161 F4 **Central** *admin. area* Kenya
163 F2 **Central** *admin. area* Malawi
107 G3 **Central** *admin. area* Paraguay
222 8 **Central** *admin. area* Solomon Islands
162 E2 **Central** *admin. area* Zambia
100 C3 **Central, Cordillera** *range* Colombia
91 G3 **Central, Cordillera** *range* Dominican Republic
104 B3 **Central, Cordillera** *range* Peru
195 I3 **Central, Cordillera** *range* Philippines
159 I3 **Central African Republic** *country* Africa
81 N4 **Central City** South Dakota USA
215 K4 **Central Diamond Islet** Coral Sea Islands Territory Australia
160 E3 **Central Equatoria** *admin. area* Sudan
57 L1 **Central Kara Plateau** *underwater feature* Arctic Ocean
214 B6 **Central Mt Stuart** *mountain* NT Australia
214 A7 **Central Mt Wedge** *mountain* NT Australia
52 O7 **Central Pacific Basin** *underwater feature* Pacific Ocean
76 J7 **Central Patricia** Ontario Canada
80 D5 **Central Point** Oregon USA
199 G5 **Central Range** Papua New Guinea
82 G7 **Centralia** Illinois USA
80 D3 **Centralia** Washington USA
103 B7 **Centralina** Brazil
159 G3 **Centre** *admin. area* Cameroon
124 B4 **Centre** *admin. area* France
127 G3 **Centre, Canal du** *watercourse* France
164 7b **Centre de Flacq** Mauritius
221 10 **Centre Group** *islands* Bounty Islands New Zealand
214 D3 **Centre Island** NT Australia
221 B8 **Centre Island** New Zealand
83 M7 **Centreville** Maryland USA
79 L8 **Centreville-Wareham-Trinity** Newfoundland and Labrador Canada
104 D4 **Centro Firmeza** Bolivia
127 I5 **Centuri** Corsica France
86 H5 **Century** Florida USA
188 F4 **Cenxi** Guangxi Zhuangzu Zizhiqu China
189 H3 **Cenyang** Jiangxi China
126 E5 **Cépet** France
197 F5 **Cepu** Indonesia
Ceram Sea *see* **Seram, Laut** Indonesia
131 F8 **Cerami** Italy
128 D3 **Cercedilla** Spain
131 E8 **Cerda** Italy
126 E5 **Cerdanya** *region* Spain
128 B2 **Cerdedo** Spain
126 E4 **Cère** *watercourse* France
124 F5 **Cerea** Italy
75 P7 **Cereal** Alberta Canada
128 E2 **Cereceda, Embalse de** *lake* Spain
138 D2 **Ceredigion** *admin. area* Wales UK
132 A4 **Cerem** Albania
106 F4 **Ceres** Argentina
103 B6 **Ceres** Brazil
124 D5 **Ceres** Italy
124 F5 **Cerese** Italy
127 I4 **Cereseto** Italy
126 F5 **Céret** France
100 C2 **Cereté** Colombia
164 9 **Cerf, Île au** *island* Seychelles
124 E5 **Cergnago** Italy
131 F6 **Cerignola** Italy
124 B4 **Cérilly** France
100 C3 **Cerinza** Colombia
126 F2 **Cerisiers** France
126 D3 **Cerizay** France
133 F5 **Çerkezköy** Turkey
125 G4 **Cerkno** Slovenia
132 B2 **Cermei** Romania
125 J5 **Cerna** Croatia
128 C2 **Cernadilla, Embalse de** *lake* Spain
192 G2 **Cernaja, Gora** *mountain* Russian Federation
132 E3 **Cernica** Romania
127 K2 **Černošín** Czech Republic
125 H3 **Černovice** Czech Republic
108 D3 **Cero, Punta** *cape* Argentina
103 C8 **Cerquilho** Brazil
85 M7 **Cerralvo** Mexico
88 C3 **Cerralvo, Isla** *island* Mexico
133 A5 **Cërrik** Albania
128 E5 **Cerrillos, Salinas de** *lake* Spain
107 G3 **Cerrito** Paraguay
88 E4 **Cerritos** Mexico
108 C2 **Cerro Abanico** Argentina
89 F4 **Cerro Azul** Mexico
108 C4 **Cerro Blanco** Argentina
105 G4 **Cêrro Branco** Brazil
107 H5 **Cerro Colorado** Uruguay
104 B3 **Cerro de Pasco** Peru
101 E3 **Cerro Jaua, Meseta del** *mountain* Venezuela
107 H5 **Cerro Largo** *admin. area* Uruguay
106 D6 **Cerro Policía** Argentina
90 D5 **Cerro Punta** Panama
108 C2 **Cerros Colorados, Embalse** *lake* Argentina
130 D5 **Certaldo** Italy
216 D5 **Cervantes** WA Australia
131 E6 **Cervaro** Italy
131 F6 **Cervati, Monte** *mountain* Italy
128 D2 **Cervera, Embalse de** *lake* Spain
130 E4 **Cervia** Italy
131 F6 **Cervialto, Monte** *mountain* Italy
100 C2 **Cesar** *admin. area* Colombia
131 F8 **Cesarò** Italy
130 E4 **Cesena** Italy
130 E4 **Cesenatico** Italy
123 M4 **Cēsis** Latvia
125 H3 **České Budějovice (Budweis)** Czech Republic
125 J3 **Český Těšín** Czech Republic
59 I2 **Cesney, Cape** Antarctica
126 D4 **Cestas** France
158 C3 **Cestos** *watercourse* Liberia
158 C3 **Cestos Point** *cape* Liberia
123 M4 **Cēsu** *admin. area* Latvia
123 N4 **Cesvaine** Latvia
132 D2 **Cetatea de Baltă** Romania
128 F3 **Cetina** Spain
105 F4 **Céu, Serra do** *range* Brazil
104 E2 **Céu Aberto** Brazil
128 D6 **Ceuta** *Spanish autonomous city* North Africa
124 E5 **Ceva** Italy
126 B6 **Cevico de la Torre** Spain
127 I3 **Cevio** Switzerland
124 C4 **Ceyzériat** France
180 E3 **Cha-hsieh Tsang-pu** *watercourse* Xizang Zizhiqu China
180 E2 **Cha-ko-mo Ho** *watercourse* Xizang Zizhiqu China
196 D3 **Chaah** Malaysia
126 F2 **Chaalis, Abbaye de** *point of interest* France
216 C1 **Chabjuwardoo Bay** WA Australia
126 E3 **Chabris** France
184 G4 **Chabucha`er** Xinjiang Uygur Zizhiqu China
109 9 **Chacachacare** *island* Trinidad and Tobago
90 C5 **Chacarita** Costa Rica
108 C3 **Chacays, Sierra de los** *range* Argentina
108 C1 **Chachahuén, Sierra de** *range* Argentina
104 B2 **Chachapoyas** Peru
106 E6 **Chacharramendi** Argentina
194 D4 **Chachoengsao** Thailand
179 L4 **Chachro** Pakistan
106 F3 **Chaco** *admin. area* Argentina
106 F2 **Chaco Boreal** *region* Paraguay
74 E5 **Chacon, Cape** Alaska USA
100 B4 **Chacón, Punta** *cape* Colombia
160 B2 **Chad** *country* Africa
159 G2 **Chad, Lake** Chad
183 P3 **Chadan** Russian Federation
106 E6 **Chadileo** *watercourse* Argentina
163 F2 **Chadiza** Zambia
135 U7 **Chadobets** *watercourse* Russian Federation
81 N5 **Chadron** Nebraska USA
159 F2 **Chafe** Nigeria
108 B3 **Chaffers, Isla** *island* Chile
219 J4 **Chaffey Dam** NSW Australia
124 D4 **Chaffois** France
109 9 **Chagaunas** *admin. area* Trinidad and Tobago
109 9 **Chagauramas** Trinidad and Tobago
184 G6 **Chagdo Kangri** *mountain* Xizang Zizhiqu China
179 K2 **Chaghcharān** Afghanistan
54 L4 **Chagos-Laccadive Ridge** *underwater feature* Indian Ocean
54 L5 **Chagos Trench** *underwater feature* Indian Ocean
191 K2 **Chagoyan** Russian Federation
109 9 **Chaguanas** Trinidad and Tobago
183 K6 **Chāh Āb** Afghanistan
179 I2 **Chāh 'Alī** Iran
179 I4 **Chāh Bahār** Iran
179 H3 **Chāh-e Dozdān** Iran
179 I3 **Chāh-e Sagak** Iran
179 H2 **Chāh Farsī** Iran
179 H4 **Chāh Gūni** Iran
179 H3 **Chāh Khāvar** Iran
179 I4 **Chāh Log** Iran
179 H2 **Chāh Malek** Iran
179 I3 **Chāh Mūsá** Iran
179 I3 **Chāh Shand** Iran
179 H3 **Chāh Shūr** Iran
90 B4 **Chahal** Guatemala
191 H4 **Chahan`naoer** Nei Mongol Zizhiqu China
185 K6 **Chahanwusu** Qinghai China
179 I3 **Chahār Farsakh** Iran
178 G3 **Chahār Maḩāll Va Bakhtīārī** *admin. area* Iran
155 G1 **Chahbounia** Algeria
163 H2 **Chai** Mozambique
194 D4 **Chai Nat** Thailand
187 F6 **Chaibasa** Jharkhand India
78 E5 **Chaigneau, Lac** *lake* Quebec Canada
191 H5 **Chaigoubu** Hebei China
179 L5 **Chailar** Pakistan
139 G4 **Chailey** East Sussex England UK
126 D2 **Chailland** France
82 I3 **Chaillon, Cape** Ontario Canada
51 P10 **Chain Fracture Zone** *underwater feature* Atlantic Ocean
194 C4 **Chainat** *admin. area* Thailand
194 E4 **Chaîne Annamitique** *mountain* Vietnam
108 B3 **Chaitén** Chile
108 B3 **Chaitén, Ensenada** *bay* Chile
194 D4 **Chaiyaphum** Thailand
107 G4 **Chajarí** Argentina
90 B4 **Chajul** Guatemala
161 F5 **Chake Chake** Tanzania
78 D4 **Chakonipau, Lac** *lake* Quebec Canada
187 F6 **Chakradharpur** Jharkhand India
179 L3 **Chakwal** Pakistan
222 2a **Chalan Kanoa** Northern Mariana Islands
90 B4 **Chalatenango** El Salvador
161 F3 **Chalbi Desert** Kenya
88 E4 **Chalchihuites** Mexico
79 F9 **Chaleur Bay** New Brunswick/Quebec Canada
108 B4 **Chalía** *watercourse* Argentina
187 D7 **Chalisgaon** Maharashtra India
187 D9 **Chaliyar** *watercourse* Kerala India
133 E7 **Chalki** Greece
133 E7 **Chalki** *island* Greece
133 C6 **Chalkida** Greece
221 B8 **Chalky Inlet** New Zealand
126 D3 **Challans** France
104 E5 **Challapata** Bolivia
52 K6 **Challenger Deep** *underwater feature* Pacific Ocean
53 V11 **Challenger Fracture Zone** *underwater feature* Pacific Ocean
80 H4 **Challis** Idaho USA
182 E6 **Chalmeh** Iran
121 T3 **Chal'mny-Varre** Russian Federation
123 R2 **Chalna** Russian Federation
124 C4 **Chalon-sur-Saône** France
127 G2 **Châlons-en-Champagne** France
127 G2 **Châlons-sur-Marne** France
108 B4 **Chaltén, Cerro** *mountain* Argentina
187 C7 **Chalthan** Gujarat India
139 G4 **Chalton** Hampshire England UK
126 E4 **Châlus** France
127 I3 **Cham** Switzerland
81 L8 **Chama** New Mexico USA
163 F2 **Chama** Zambia
106 E5 **Chamaico** Argentina
124 G3 **Chamb** *watercourse* Germany
186 D4 **Chamba** Himachal Pradesh India
161 F6 **Chamba** Tanzania
186 E5 **Chambal** *watercourse* Madhya Pradesh India
186 D6 **Chambal** *watercourse* Rajasthan India
75 S7 **Chamberlain** Saskatchewan Canada
79 D9 **Chamberlain Lake** Maine USA
77 R2 **Chamberlaine, Lac** *lake* Quebec Canada
85 K2 **Chamberlin** Texas USA
72 E5 **Chamberlin, Mount** Alaska USA
85 H3 **Chambers** Arizona USA
218 D4 **Chambers, Mount** SA Australia
214 A2 **Chambers Bay** NT Australia
83 M7 **Chambersburg** Pennsylvania USA
127 G4 **Chambéry** France
163 F2 **Chambeshi** *watercourse* Zambia
100 B5 **Chambira** Peru
104 C2 **Chambira** *watercourse* Peru
199 G5 **Chambri Lake** Papua New Guinea
100 B2 **Chame, Punta** *cape* Panama
154 C5 **Châmi** Mauritania
106 E4 **Chamical** Argentina
133 E8 **Chamili** *island* Greece
74 C2 **Champagne** Yukon Territory Canada
124 C3 **Champagne-Ardenne** *admin. area* France
126 E4 **Champagne-Mouton** France
127 G3 **Champagnole** France
213 H3 **Champagny Island** WA Australia
82 G6 **Champaign** Illinois USA
106 E5 **Champaqui, Cerro** *mountain* Argentina
194 E4 **Champasak** Laos
126 F2 **Champaubert** France
126 D3 **Champdeniers** France
78 F5 **Champdoré, Lac** *lake* Quebec Canada
126 F4 **Champeix** France
194 E3 **Champhon** *watercourse* Laos
83 O4 **Champlain, Lake** Vermont USA
89 H5 **Champotón** Mexico
106 E4 **Chañar** Argentina
106 D3 **Chañaral** Chile
106 D4 **Chañaral** *watercourse* Chile
106 D4 **Chañaral, Isla** *island* Chile
104 B3 **Chancay** Peru
104 C3 **Chanchavocaia** Brazil
106 C5 **Chanco** Chile
106 C5 **Chanco, Bahía** *bay* Chile
218 B5 **Chandada** SA Australia
161 F5 **Chandama** Tanzania
186 F6 **Chandauli** Uttar Pradesh India
186 E5 **Chandausi** Uttar Pradesh India
89 H2 **Chandeleur Islands** Louisiana USA
89 H2 **Chandeleur Sound** Louisiana USA
186 E6 **Chandia** Madhya Pradesh India
186 D4 **Chandigarh** Haryana India
186 G6 **Chandil** Jharkhand India
84 G4 **Chandler** Arizona USA
104 D3 **Chandless** *watercourse* Brazil
185 K3 **Chandman** Mongolia
185 I3 **Chandman** Mongolia
190 D2 **Chandman-under** Mongolia
181 G4 **Chandpur** Bangladesh
187 F7 **Chandpur** Orissa India
186 F5 **Chandpur** Uttar Pradesh India
187 E7 **Chandrapur** Maharashtra India
187 F7 **Chandrapur** Orissa India
128 C2 **Chandrexa de Queixa, Embalse de** *lake* Spain
187 E7 **Chandur** Maharashtra India
182 G6 **Chandyr** *watercourse* Turkmenistan
189 F2 **Chang Hu** *lake* Hubei China
189 H2 **Chang Jiang (Yangtze)** *watercourse* Anhui China
192 E3 **Chang-yŏn** North Korea
188 F3 **Chang`an** Guangxi Zhuangzu Zizhiqu China
163 F4 **Changane** *watercourse* Mozambique
191 K4 **Changbai Shan** *range* Jilin China
191 K4 **Changchun** Jilin China
189 F2 **Changde** Hunan China
181 H2 **Changdu** Xizang Zizhiqu China
189 G1 **Changge** Henan China
188 E5 **Changhua** *watercourse* Hainan China
189 H4 **Changhua** Taiwan China
196 F3 **Changi Beach Park** Singapore
196 E3 **Changi Village** *admin. area* Singapore
185 H4 **Changji** Xinjiang Uygur Zizhiqu China
192 E3 **Changjin** North Korea
192 E3 **Changjin-ho** *lake* North Korea
181 H3 **Changland** Arunachal Pradesh India
191 I5 **Changli** Hebei China
191 J4 **Changling** Jilin China
196 D2 **Changlun** Malaysia
189 F3 **Changning** Hunan China
189 G4 **Changning** Jiangxi China
188 D3 **Changning** Sichuan China
188 F3 **Changpu** Hunan China
191 H6 **Changqing** Shandong China
189 F3 **Changsha** Hunan China
189 H2 **Changshu** Jiangsu China
192 E3 **Ch'angsŏng** North Korea
191 J4 **Changtu** Liaoning China
192 F4 **Ch'angwon** South Korea
189 I2 **Changxing Dao** *island* Shanghai China
188 E2 **Changyuan** Chongqing China
189 G1 **Changyuan** Henan China
188 E3 **Changzhai** Guizhou China
191 H6 **Changzhi** Shanxi China
189 H2 **Changzhou** Jiangsu China
133 C8 **Chanion, Kolpos** *bay* Greece
84 C4 **Channel Islands** California USA
126 C2 **Channel Islands (Îles Normandes)** UK
139 I3 **Channel Tunnel** France/UK
85 K3 **Channing** Texas USA
126 E3 **Chanteloube** France
194 D4 **Chanthaburi** Thailand
126 D3 **Chantonnay** France
73 J5 **Chantrey Inlet** Nunavut Canada
196 B1 **Chanumla** India
194 B5 **Chanumla** Andaman and Nicobar Islands India
82 D8 **Chanute** Kansas USA
128 C5 **Chanza, Embalse del** *lake* Spain
189 H2 **Chao Hu** *lake* Anhui China
189 H2 **Chaohu** Anhui China
192 E3 **Chaŏng** North Korea
124 C3 **Chaource** France
189 G4 **Chaoyang** Guangdong China
191 L3 **Chaoyang** Heilongjiang China
191 K4 **Chaoyang** Jilin China
191 I4 **Chaoyang** Liaoning China
189 G4 **Chaozhou** Guangdong China
182 E6 **Chap Chap** Iran
105 H4 **Chapada dos Guimarães** Brazil
102 D4 **Chapada Grande** *region* Brazil
102 D3 **Chapadinha** Brazil
84 E6 **Chapala** Mexico
88 E4 **Chapala, Laguna de** *lake* Mexico
100 C4 **Chaparral** Colombia
182 F3 **Chapayev** Kazakhstan
182 F3 **Chapayevsk** Russian Federation
107 H3 **Chapecó** Brazil
107 H3 **Chapecó** *watercourse* Brazil
87 H3 **Chapel Hill** Tennessee USA
140 D2 **Chapel Rossan** Dumfries and Galloway Scotland UK
141 I3 **Chapel St Leonards** Lincolnshire England UK
143 D2 **Chapel Street** Ireland
140 C2 **Chapeltown** Down Northern Ireland UK
141 G3 **Chapeltown** South Yorkshire England UK
193 I1 **Chaplanovo** Russian Federation
82 J3 **Chapleau** Ontario Canada
81 L1 **Chaplin, Lake** Saskatchewan Canada
Chaplinka *see* **Chaplynka** Ukraine
136 E3 **Chaplynka** Ukraine
213 I4 **Chapman** *watercourse* WA Australia
81 P6 **Chapman** Nebraska USA
74 L7 **Chapman, Mount** British Columbia Canada
121 U3 **Chapoma** Russian Federation
88 D3 **Chapotán** Mexico
81 N6 **Chappell** Nebraska USA
179 K2 **Chaqmāq** Afghanistan
104 D5 **Chaqui** Chile
106 E2 **Chaqui Laguna** *lake* Bolivia
186 D4 **Char** Jammu and Kashmir India/Pakistan
135 Y7 **Chara** *watercourse* Russian Federation
107 G3 **Charadai** Argentina
105 F5 **Charagua** Bolivia
100 B3 **Charambirá, Punta** *point* Colombia
100 A5 **Charapotó, Punta** *cape* Ecuador
106 F3 **Charata** Argentina
133 B5 **Charavgi** Greece
88 E4 **Charcas** Mexico
100 C4 **Charco Caimán** Colombia
59 S2 **Charcot Deep Sea Fan** *underwater feature* Southern Ocean
59 S2 **Charcot Island** Antarctica
75 P5 **Chard** Alberta Canada
138 E3 **Charfield** South Gloucestershire England UK
159 H2 **Chari** *watercourse* Chad
159 H2 **Chari-Baguirmi** *admin. area* Chad
179 L2 **Chārīkār** Afghanistan
186 G5 **Charikot** Nepal
82 E6 **Chariton** Iowa USA
82 E6 **Chariton** *watercourse* Missouri USA
134 L5 **Charkayuvom** Russian Federation
139 F3 **Charlbury** Oxfordshire England UK
76 H4 **Charlebois** Manitoba Canada
127 G1 **Charleroi** Belgium
75 U5 **Charles** Manitoba Canada
78 K6 **Charles, Cape** Newfoundland and Labrador Canada
216 E3 **Charles, Mount** WA Australia
220 F3 **Charles, Port** New Zealand
108 B5 **Charles Fuhr** Argentina
78 A1 **Charles Island** Nunavut Canada
213 K2 **Charles Point** NT Australia
221 B7 **Charles Sound** New Zealand
139 H2 **Charles Tye** Suffolk England UK
87 L4 **Charleston** South Carolina USA
87 I3 **Charleston** Tennessee USA
83 K7 **Charleston** West Virginia USA
87 L4 **Charleston Harbor** South Carolina USA
83 M4 **Charleston Lake** Ontario Canada
143 D3 **Charlestown** Ireland
109 19 **Charlestown** St Kitts and Nevis
218 H2 **Charleville** Qld Australia
219 I6 **Charleyong** NSW Australia
59 I2 **Charlie, Dome** *mountain* Antarctica
50 O4 **Charlie-Gibbs Fracture Zone** *underwater feature* Atlantic Ocean
74 K4 **Charlie Lake** British Columbia Canada
217 I2 **Charlies Knob** *mountain* WA Australia
87 K3 **Charlotte** North Carolina USA
86 B6 **Charlotte** Texas USA
218 B1 **Charlotte, Mount** NT Australia
101 H3 **Charlotte, Pointe** *cape* French Guiana
109 21 **Charlotte Amalie** US Virgin Islands
89 J3 **Charlotte Harbor** Florida USA
74 I6 **Charlotte Lake** British Columbia Canada
217 M2 **Charlotte Range** NT Australia
79 G9 **Charlottetown** Prince Edward Island Canada
109 9 **Charlotteville** Trinidad and Tobago
218 H4 **Charlton** NSW Australia
218 F7 **Charlton** Vic. Australia
138 E3 **Charlton Horethorne** Somerset England UK
73 L8 **Charlton Island** Nunavut Canada
139 E3 **Charlton Kings** Gloucestershire England UK
124 D3 **Charmes** France
138 E4 **Charmouth** Dorset England UK
182 E6 **Charna** Iran
213 H4 **Charnley** *watercourse* WA Australia
127 G3 **Charollais** *region* France
123 N5 **Charomkhava** Belarus
126 F3 **Chârost** France
76 H6 **Charron Lake** Manitoba Canada
215 I6 **Charters Towers** Qld Australia
109 7 **Chartres** Falkland Islands
126 E2 **Chartres** France
183 N3 **Charyshskoye** Russian Federation
107 G5 **Chas** Argentina
186 G6 **Chas** Jharkhand India
187 C7 **Chas** Maharashtra India
106 D3 **Chaschuil** Argentina
107 G5 **Chascomús** Argentina
74 L7 **Chase** British Columbia Canada
81 P7 **Chase** Kansas USA
182 I6 **Chashkent** Turkmenistan
179 H3 **Chashmēh Mārī** Iran
123 O5 **Chashniki** Belarus
158 D3 **Chasia** Ghana
108 C3 **Chasicó** Argentina
126 E4 **Chasseneuil-sur-Bonnieure** France
127 G3 **Chassigny** France
126 D3 **Chassiron, Pointe de** *cape* France
127 G1 **Chastre** Belgium
182 G1 **Chastyye** Russian Federation
126 C2 **Château, Pointe du** *cape* France
127 H2 **Château-Salins** France
83 O4 **Châteauguay** Quebec Canada
78 D4 **Châteauguay** *watercourse* Quebec Canada
78 C4 **Châteauguay, Lac** *lake* Quebec Canada
126 F4 **Châteauneuf-de-Randon** France
126 E3 **Châteauponsac** France
127 G5 **Châteaurenard** France
124 C3 **Châteauvillain** France
109 16 **Châteaux, Pointe des** *cape* Guadeloupe
127 H3 **Châtel-St-Denis** Switzerland
126 D3 **Châtelaillon-Plage** France
78 A2 **Châtelain, Lac** *lake* Quebec Canada
127 G1 **Châtelet** Belgium
124 C3 **Châtenois** France
81 P2 **Chater** Manitoba Canada
139 H3 **Chatham** Medway England UK
74 D4 **Chatham** Alaska USA
86 E4 **Chatham** Louisiana USA
108 A5 **Chatham, Isla** *island* Chile
221 6 **Chatham Island (Rekohua)** New Zealand
52 O12 **Chatham Rise** *underwater feature* Pacific Ocean
74 F5 **Chatham Sound** British Columbia/Alaska Canada/USA
74 D4 **Chatham Strait** Alaska USA
183 L5 **Chatkël** Kyrgyzstan
186 F6 **Chatra** Jharkhand India
186 D5 **Chatsu** Rajasthan India
214 F6 **Chatsworth** Qld Australia
87 I5 **Chattahoochee** Florida USA
89 I1 **Chattahoochee** *watercourse* Georgia USA
87 I3 **Chattanooga** Tennessee USA
139 H2 **Chatteris** Cambridgeshire England UK
194 D4 **Chatturat** Thailand
87 J3 **Chatuge Lake** North Carolina USA
194 E5 **Châu Đốc** Vietnam
126 F4 **Chaudes-Aigues** France
127 G3 **Chauffailles** France
186 C6 **Chauhtan** Rajasthan India
181 H5 **Chauk** Myanmar
186 E4 **Chaukhamba** *mountain* Uttaranchal India
179 K4 **Chauki** Pakistan
78 E4 **Chaumaux** *watercourse* Quebec Canada
126 E3 **Chaumont** France
78 D6 **Chaumont, Lac** *lake* Quebec Canada
74 K8 **Chaumox** British Columbia Canada
181 H5 **Chaung-U** Myanmar
135 AI5 **Chaunskaya Guba** *bay* Russian Federation
186 D4 **Chaupal** Himachal Pradesh India
124 C4 **Chaussin** France
82 F6 **Chautauqua, Lake** Illinois USA
77 R5 **Chauvreulx** *watercourse* Quebec Canada
187 E10 **Chavakachcheri** Sri Lanka
121 T3 **Chavan'ga** Russian Federation
133 B7 **Chavarion** Greece
128 C3 **Chaves** Portugal
77 R3 **Chavigny, Lac** *lake* Quebec Canada
162 D2 **Chavuma** Zambia
123 P6 **Chavusi** Belarus
187 D7 **Chawala** Maharashtra India
135 AC8 **Chayatyn, Khrebet** *range* Russian Federation
182 G2 **Chaykovskiy** Russian Federation
135 AD8 **Chayvo, Zaliv** *bay* Russian Federation
106 F5 **Chazón** Argentina
104 B2 **Chazuta** Peru
194 E4 **Chbar** Cambodia
188 D4 **Che-kan Ho** *watercourse* Yunnan China
139 F2 **Cheadle** Staffordshire England UK
108 A4 **Cheap, Canal** *strait* Chile
86 H2 **Cheatham Lake** Tennessee USA
124 G2 **Cheb** Czech Republic
155 I1 **Chebba** Tunisia
182 E2 **Cheboksary** Russian Federation
82 I4 **Cheboygan** Michigan USA
181 I4 **Chebwe** Myanmar
182 E5 **Chechen', Ostrov** *island* Russian Federation
182 E5 **Chechenskaya Respublika** *admin. area* Russian Federation
192 F4 **Chech'ŏn** South Korea
79 H10 **Chedabucto Bay** Nova Scotia Canada
138 E3 **Cheddar** Somerset England UK
139 E1 **Cheddleton** Staffordshire England UK
155 J6 **Chéddra** Chad
181 G5 **Cheduba Strait** Myanmar
Cheduha *see* **Man-Aung** Myanmar
75 P4 **Cheecham** Alberta Canada
83 K1 **Cheepash** *watercourse* Ontario Canada
82 J1 **Cheepay** *watercourse* Ontario Canada
218 G2 **Cheepie** Qld Australia
220 5 **Cheeseman Island** Kermadec Islands New Zealand
85 J1 **Cheeseman Lake** Colorado USA
59 K2 **Cheetham, Cape** Antarctica
109 9 **Cheeyou** Trinidad and Tobago
126 D3 **Chef-Boutonne** France
154 E3 **Chegga** Mauritania
80 D3 **Chehalis** Washington USA
129 G6 **Chehama** Algeria
179 I3 **Chehel Tokhm** Iran
132 D3 **Cheia** Romania
132 B3 **Cheile Nerei** *range* Romania
192 E5 **Cheju** South Korea
192 E5 **Cheju-do** *island* South Korea
192 E5 **Cheju-Haehyŏp** *strait* South Korea
136 F1 **Chekhov** Russian Federation
121 U5 **Chekuyevo** Russian Federation
162 B3 **Chela, Serra da** *range* Angola
80 E3 **Chelan** Washington USA
80 E2 **Chelan, Lake** Washington USA
128 C4 **Cheles** Spain
106 E6 **Chelforó** Argentina
155 H1 **Chelghoum el Aïd** Algeria
163 G4 **Cheline** Mozambique
125 L2 **Chełm** Poland
139 H3 **Chelmer** *watercourse* England UK
139 I3 **Chelmondiston** Suffolk England UK
141 G3 **Chelmorton** Derbyshire England UK
139 H3 **Chelmsford** Essex England UK
121 S5 **Chelmuzhi** Russian Federation
139 G3 **Chelsea** Greater London England UK
82 I5 **Chelsea** Michigan USA
139 E3 **Cheltenham** Gloucestershire England UK
139 G2 **Chelveston** Northamptonshire England UK
182 I2 **Chelyabinsk** Russian Federation
182 H2 **Chelyabinskaya** *admin. area* Russian Federation
82 I1 **Chemahagan** *watercourse* Ontario Canada
154 E2 **Chemaïa** Morocco
135 AD5 **Chemalginskiy Khrebet** *range* Russian Federation
89 I4 **Chemax** Mexico
162 E2 **Chembe** Zambia
125 M3 **Chemerintsy** Ukraine
126 F3 **Chemilly** France
164 7b **Chemin Grenier** Mauritius
129 J6 **Chemmora** Algeria
127 K1 **Chemnitz** Germany
183 L5 **Chemolgan** Kazakhstan
188 E3 **Chen Shui** *watercourse* Guizhou China
179 M3 **Chenab** *watercourse* Pakistan
85 M2 **Cheney Reservoir** Kansas USA
186 E3 **Cheng Chemmo** *watercourse* Jammu and Kashmir India/Pakistan
187 E9 **Chengalpattu** Tamil Nadu India
188 E4 **Chengbine Shuiku** *lake* Guangxi Zhuangzu Zizhiqu China
191 I5 **Chengde** Hebei China
189 G2 **Chengdong Hu** *lake* Anhui China
188 D2 **Chengdu** Sichuan China
189 G4 **Chenghai** Guangdong China
189 G3 **Chengjiang** Jiangxi China
189 I2 **Chengqiao** Shanghai China
189 G1 **Chengwu** Shandong China
189 G4 **Chengxiang** Jiangxi China
188 D2 **Chengxiang** Sichuan China
191 I6 **Chengyang** Shandong China
188 E4 **Chengzhong** Guangxi Zhuangzu Zizhiqu China
187 E9 **Chennai** Tamil Nadu India
188 F3 **Chenyang** Hunan China
189 H3 **Chenying** Jiangxi China
189 G3 **Chenzhou** Hunan China
104 B2 **Chepén** Peru
222 7 **Chépénéhé** New Caledonia
106 E4 **Chepes** Argentina
161 F3 **Chephotet** *mountain* Kenya
104 E4 **Chepite, Serranía** *range* Bolivia
138 E3 **Chepstow** Monmouthshire Wales UK
108 B3 **Chepu** Chile
82 F3 **Chequamegon Bay** Wisconsin USA
82 F4 **Chequamegon Waters** *lake* Wisconsin USA
126 E3 **Cher** *watercourse* France
187 C9 **Cherbaniani Reef** Lakshadweep I ndia
219 J2 **Cherbourg** Qld Australia
139 F5 **Cherbourg** France
155 G1 **Cherchell** Algeria
182 E2 **Cherdakly** Russian Federation
183 N4 **Cherdoyak** Kazakhstan
135 V8 **Cheremkhovo** Russian Federation
75 N6 **Cherhill** Alberta Canada
155 H1 **Chéria** Algeria

187 E8 **Cherial** Andhra Pradesh India
139 F3 **Cheriton** Hampshire England UK
138 C3 **Cheriton** Swansea Wales UK
83 N8 **Cheriton** Virginia USA
187 C9 **Cheriyam Island** Lakshadweep India
136 D3 **Cherkas'ka Oblast'** *admin. area* Ukraine
132 H1 **Cherkasy** Ukraine
182 D5 **Cherkessk** Russian Federation
187 E7 **Cherla** Andhra Pradesh India
183 L2 **Cherlak** Russian Federation
182 G1 **Chermoz** Russian Federation
136 D2 **Chernihiv** Ukraine
136 D2 **Chernihivs'ka Oblast'** *admin. area* Ukraine
136 C3 **Chernivets'ka Oblast'** *admin. area* Ukraine
132 D1 **Chernivtsi** Ukraine
Chernobyl *see* **Chornobyl'** Ukraine
183 P2 **Chernogorsk** Russian Federation
183 O2 **Chernoye** *lake* Russian Federation
136 F2 **Chernyanka** Russian Federation
191 I2 **Chernyshevsk** Russian Federation
134 T6 **Chërnyy Ostrov** Russian Federation
121 R5 **Chërnyy Porog** Russian Federation
182 E4 **Chernyy Yar** Russian Federation
182 E4 **Chernyye Zemli** Russian Federation
86 D4 **Cherokee, Lake** Texas USA
87 J2 **Cherokee Lake** Tennessee USA
126 F2 **Chéroy** France
123 P4 **Cherpesa** Russian Federation
181 G4 **Cherra Punjee** Meghalaya India
213 H5 **Cherrabun** WA Australia
85 J1 **Cherry Creek La ke** Colorado USA
84 C1 **Cherry Lake** California USA
135 X8 **Cherskogo, Khrebet** *range* Russian Federation
136 G3 **Chertkovo** Ukraine
139 G3 **Chertsey** Surrey England UK
187 D10 **Cheruvalli** Kerala India
135 U7 **Chervyanka** Russian Federation
123 O6 **Chervyen'** Belarus
123 P6 **Cherykaw** Belarus
83 M8 **Chesapeake** Virginia USA
83 M7 **Chesapeake Bay** Maryland USA
87 N2 **Chesapeake Bay** Virginia USA
87 M2 **Chesdin, Lake** Virginia USA
141 F3 **Cheshire** *admin. area* England UK
182 I6 **Cheshme Vtoroy** Turkmenistan
134 K5 **Cheshskaya Guba** *bay* Russian Federation
179 J2 **Chesht-e Sharif** Afghanistan
139 G3 **Cheshunt** Hertfordshire England UK
138 E4 **Chesil Beach** Dorset England UK
179 I2 **Chesmeh Shāh** Iran
79 F10 **Chester** Nova Scotia Canada
140 F3 **Chester** Cheshire England UK
82 G8 **Chester** Illinois USA
81 J2 **Chester** Montana USA
81 Q7 **Chester** Nebraska USA
87 K3 **Chester** South Carolina USA
141 G2 **Chester-le-Street** Durham England UK
141 G3 **Chesterfield** Derbyshire England UK
76 J1 **Chesterfield Inlet** Nunavut Canada
79 D9 **Chesuncook Lake** Maine USA
129 J5 **Chetaibi** Algeria
194 B5 **Chetamale** Andaman and Nicobar Islands India
82 F4 **Chetek** Wisconsin USA
79 H9 **Chéticamp** Nova Scotia Canada
187 C9 **Chetlat Island** Lakshadweep India
139 E4 **Chettle** Dorset England UK
89 H5 **Chetumal** Mexico
221 F5 **Chetwode Islands** New Zealand
74 K5 **Chetwynd** British Columbia Canada
124 B4 **Chevagnes** France
105 E4 **Chevejécure** Bolivia
221 E6 **Cheviot** New Zealand
141 F1 **Cheviot, The** *mountain* England UK
142 F5 **Cheviot Hills** *range* England UK
126 B2 **Chèvre, Cap de la** *cape* France
138 E3 **Chew Magna** Bath and North East Somerset England UK
138 E3 **Chew Valley Lake** England UK
81 N5 **Cheyenne** *watercourse* South Dakota USA
81 M6 **Cheyenne** Wyoming USA
81 N7 **Cheyenne Wells** Colorado USA
216 F7 **Cheyne Bay** WA Australia
194 D5 **Chhâk** *island* Cambodia
186 F6 **Chhapra** Bihar India
186 E6 **Chhatarpur** Madhya Pradesh India
179 K4 **Chhatr** Pakistan
187 F7 **Chhattisgarh** *admin. area* India
186 E5 **Chhibramau** Uttar Pradesh India
187 E6 **Chhindwara** Madhya Pradesh India
194 E4 **Chhlong** *watercourse* Cambodia
187 E7 **Chhuikhadan** Chhattisgarh India
181 F3 **Chhukha** Bhutan
189 H2 **Chi He** *watercourse* Anhui China
188 D4 **Chi-Lu Hu** *lake* Yunnan China
180 E3 **Chi-lung Ho** *watercourse* Xizang Zizhiqu China
189 H4 **Chi-Pei Tao** *island* Taiwan China
100 C3 **Chía** Colombia
131 C7 **Chia** Sardinia Italy
189 H4 **Chiai** Taiwan China
185 H3 **Chianassu Hu** *lake* Xinjiang Uygur Zizhiqu China
127 J5 **Chianciano Terme** Italy
194 D3 **Chiang Kham** Thailand
194 D3 **Chiang Khan** Thailand
194 D3 **Chiang Klang** Thailand
194 C3 **Chiang Mai** Thailand
194 C3 **Chiang Mai** *admin. area* Thailand
194 C3 **Chiang Rai** Thailand
194 D2 **Chiang Saen** Thailand
162 B3 **Chiange** Angola
130 D5 **Chianni** Italy
89 G5 **Chiapa de Corzo** Mexico
89 G5 **Chiapas** *admin. area* Mexico
90 A4 **Chiapas, Sierra Madre de** *range* Mexico
130 C4 **Chiari** Italy
89 F5 **Chiautla de Tapia** Mexico
124 E4 **Chiavenna** Italy
193 I4 **Chiba** Japan
189 G2 **Chibi** Hubei China
218 F5 **Chibnalwood Lakes** NSW Australia
77 R8 **Chibougamau** Quebec Canada
77 R8 **Chibougamau, Lac** *lake* Quebec Canada
192 G4 **Chiburi-jima** *island* Japan
163 F4 **Chibuto** Mozambique
79 E8 **Chic-Chocs, Monts** *range* Quebec Canada
106 D2 **Chica** Chile
108 C3 **Chica, Pampa** *region* Argentina
82 H6 **Chicago** Illinois USA
162 C2 **Chicala** Angola
162 C2 **Chicala** Angola
104 B2 **Chicama** Peru
159 G5 **Chicamba** Congo
163 F3 **Chicamba** Mozambique
162 C2 **Chicapa** *watercourse* Angola
100 B3 **Chicha Bay** Colombia
104 D4 **Chichacori** Peru
74 C4 **Chichagof** Alaska USA
74 C3 **Chichagof Island** Alaska USA
154 E2 **Chichaoua** Morocco
106 E/F2 **Chichas, Cordillera de** *range* Bolivia/Paraguay
105 H3 **Chiche** *watercourse* Brazil
191 H5 **Chicheng** Hebei China
188 E2 **Chicheng** Sichuan China
139 G4 **Chichester** West Sussex England UK
212 E6 **Chichester Range** WA Australia
90 D5 **Chichica** Panama
90 B4 **Chichicastenango** Guatemala
89 F5 **Chichihualco** Mexico
106 E6 **Chichinales** Argentina
100 B5 **Chichirota** Ecuador
187 D6 **Chicholi** Madhya Pradesh India
86 G5 **Chickasawhay** *watercourse* Mississippi USA
86 C3 **Chickasha** Oklahoma USA
139 E3 **Chicklade** Wiltshire England UK
128 C5 **Chiclana de la Frontera** Spain
104 B2 **Chiclayo** Peru
108 B4 **Chico** *watercourse* Argentina
80 E7 **Chico** California USA
86 C4 **Chico** Texas USA
107 G5 **Chico, Lago** *lake* Argentina
104 C3 **Chico Mana** Brazil
163 F3 **Chicoa** Mozambique
162 B2 **Chicomba** Angola
163 G2 **Chiconono** Mozambique
83 O5 **Chicopee** Massachusetts USA
86 F4 **Chicot, Lake** Mississippi USA
79 C8 **Chicoutimi** Quebec Canada
162 B2 **Chicuma** Angola
160 B6 **Chicupo** Angola
187 E9 **Chidambaram** Tamil Nadu India
138 E4 **Chideock** Dorset England UK
182 F6 **Chidirly** Azerbaijan
73 M6 **Chidley, Cape** Nunavut Canada
162 C3 **Chiede** Angola
83 K4 **Chiefs Point** Ontario Canada
130 E3 **Chiemsee** *lake* Germany
160 D5 **Chiengi** Zambia
130 B4 **Chieri** Italy
127 G2 **Chiers** *watercourse* France
130 D3 **Chiese Fiume** *watercourse* Italy
131 F5 **Chieti** Italy
131 F6 **Chieuti** Italy
124 B2 **Chièvres** Belgium
191 I4 **Chifeng** Nei Mongol Zizhiqu China
163 F2 **Chifunde** Mozambique
72 D7 **Chiginagak, Mount** Alaska USA
79 F10 **Chignecto Bay** New Brunswick/Nova Scotia Canada
100 B3 **Chigorodó** Colombia
83 O2 **Chigoubiche, Lac** *lake* Quebec Canada
105 E5 **Chiguailla, Altos de** *range* Bolivia
163 F4 **Chigubo** Mozambique
88 D2 **Chihuahua** Mexico
88 D3 **Chihuahua** *admin. area* Mexico
100 C2 **Chikepu** Colombia
123 O4 **Chikhachëvo** Russian Federation
187 E7 **Chikhli** Madhya Pradesh India
187 D7 **Chikhli** Maharashtra India
187 F7 **Chikiti** Orissa India
187 D9 **Chikmagalur** Karnataka India
162 E2 **Chikonkomene** Zambia
190 F2 **Chikoy** *watercourse* Russian Federation
135 AG8 **Chikurachki** *volcano* Kuril Islands
163 F2 **Chikwa** Zambia
162 B2 **Chila** Angola
104 C4 **Chila** Peru
104 C4 **Chila Pillune, Cerro** *mountain* Peru
74 J6 **Chilako** *watercourse* British Columbia Canada
72 G8 **Chilanko** *watercourse* British Columbia Canada
179 M2 **Chilas** Pakistan
187 E10 **Chilaw** Sri Lanka
104 B4 **Chilca** Peru
74 J7 **Chilcotin** *watercourse* British Columbia Canada
74 J7 **Chilcotin Ranges** British Columbia Canada
85 L3 **Childress** Texas USA
104 D6 **Chile** *country* South America
53 Y11 **Chile Basin** *underwater feature* Pacific Ocean
53 X12 **Chile Rise** *underwater feature* Pacific Ocean
104 E6 **Chilena** Bolivia
160 B6 **Chilengue, Serra do** *range* Angola
104 B2 **Chilete** *watercourse* Peru
182 E4 **Chilgir** Russian Federation
139 H3 **Chilham** Kent England UK
183 M5 **Chilik** Kazakhstan
187 F7 **Chilika Lake** Orissa India
162 E2 **Chililabombwe** Zambia
131 C6 **Chilivani** Sardinia Italy
74 D3 **Chilkat Inlet** Alaska USA
72 G8 **Chilko** *watercourse* British Columbia Canada
74 I7 **Chilko Lake** British Columbia Canada
214 A6 **Chilla Well** NT Australia
215 H4 **Chillagoe** Qld Australia
106 C6 **Chillán** Chile
82 E7 **Chillicothe** Missouri USA
82 J7 **Chillicothe** Ohio USA
86 B3 **Chillicothe** Texas USA
138 D4 **Chillington** Devon England UK
138 E4 **Chillington** Somerset England UK
74 K8 **Chilliwack** British Columbia Canada
108 B3 **Chiloé, Archipiélago de** *islands* Chile
108 B3 **Chiloé, Isla** *island* Chile
163 F2 **Chilonga** Zambia
80 E5 **Chiloquin** Oregon USA
89 F5 **Chilpancingo** Mexico
139 G3 **Chiltern Hills** *range* England UK
138 D3 **Chilton Trinity** Somerset England UK
160 C5 **Chiluage** Angola
162 E2 **Chilubi** Zambia
163 F2 **Chilumba** Malawi
163 G3 **Chilwa, Lake** Malawi
90 B4 **Chimaltenango** Guatemala
90 E5 **Chimán** Panama
101 E2 **Chimanas, Islas** *islands* Venezuela
127 G1 **Chimay** Belgium
104 B3 **Chimbote** Peru
104 B3 **Chimbote, Bahía** *bay* Peru
182 H5 **Chimboy** Uzbekistan
163 F2 **Chimbwingombe** *mountain* Zambia
Chimkent *see* **Shymkent** Kazakhstan
159 I3 **Chimko** *watercourse* Central African Republic
183 J6 **Chimkurgan** Uzbekistan
80 G6 **Chimney Reservoir** Nevada USA
163 F3 **Chimoio** Mozambique
105 E5 **Chimoré** Bolivia
106 E6 **Chimpay** Argentina
181 G4 **Chin** *admin. area* Myanmar
192 E4 **Chin-do** *island* South Korea
181 G5 **Chin Hills** Myanmar
181 F2 **China** *country* Asia
89 H5 **Chiná** Mexico
214 D4 **China Wall** *range* NT Australia
90 C4 **Chinandega** Nicaragua
88 C2 **Chinapa** Mexico
196 D4 **Chinatown** *admin. area* Singapore
90 B4 **Chinautla** Guatemala
104 B4 **Chincha Alta** Peru
72 H7 **Chinchaga** *watercourse* Alberta Canada
219 J2 **Chinchilla** Qld Australia
90 C3 **Chinchorro, Banco** *reef* Mexico
106 D5 **Chincolco** Chile
83 N8 **Chincoteague** Virginia USA
83 N8 **Chincoteague Bay** Virginia USA
163 G3 **Chinde** Mozambique
192 E4 **Chindo** South Korea
181 H4 **Chindwin** *watercourse* Myanmar
191 H2 **Chingikan, Gora** *mountain* Russian Federation
183 M4 **Chingiz-Tau, Khrebet** *range* Kazakhstan
162 B2 **Chingo** Angola
162 E2 **Chingola** Zambia
162 C3 **Chinguanja** Angola
162 C2 **Chinguar** Angola
162 C2 **Chingueia** Angola
105 H6 **Chingüelo** Paraguay
154 D4 **Chinguetti** Mauritania
192 F4 **Chinhae** South Korea
163 F3 **Chinhanda** Mozambique
162 F3 **Chinhoyi** Zimbabwe
179 L3 **Chiniot** Pakistan
85 H7 **Chinipas** Mexico
104 E4 **Chiñiri** Bolivia
192 F4 **Chinju** South Korea
159 I3 **Chinko** *watercourse* Central African Republic
84 H2 **Chinle** Arizona USA
84 H2 **Chinle** *watercourse* Arkansas USA
189 H4 **Chinmen Tao (Quemoy)** *island* Taiwan China
187 E8 **Chinna Ganjum** Andhra Pradesh India
187 E9 **Chinna Salem** Tamil Nadu India
84 F3 **Chino** *watercourse* Arkansas USA
84 F3 **Chino Valley** Arizona USA
216 F6 **Chinocup, Lake** WA Australia
126 E3 **Chinon** France
81 K2 **Chinook** Montana USA
52 O3 **Chinook Trough** *underwater feature* Pacific Ocean
104 B3 **Chinos, Bahía Los** *bay* Peru
183 J6 **Chinoz** Uzbekistan
163 F2 **Chinsali** Zambia
187 E9 **Chintamani** Karnataka India
100 C2 **Chinú** Colombia
124 C3 **Chiny** Belgium
162 D2 **Chinyama Litapi** Zambia
181 H5 **Chinzu** Myanmar
124 G5 **Chioggia** Italy
133 D6 **Chios** *island* Greece
75 N6 **Chip Lake** Alberta Canada
163 F2 **Chipata** Zambia
132 F2 **Chiperceni** Moldova
163 G3 **Chiperone, Mount** Mozambique
75 O4 **Chipewyan Lake** Alberta Canada
162 E2 **Chipili** Zambia
162 C2 **Chipindo** Angola
163 F4 **Chipinge** Zimbabwe
79 F9 **Chipman** New Brunswick Canada
75 S3 **Chipman** *watercourse* Saskatchewan Canada
82 H2 **Chipman Lake** Ontario Canada
162 C2 **Chipoia** Angola
163 F2 **Chipoka** Malawi
160 B6 **Chipola** Angola
82 F4 **Chippewa** *watercourse* Wisconsin USA
82 F4 **Chippewa Falls** Wisconsin USA
141 F3 **Chipping** Lancashire England UK
139 F3 **Chipping Norton** Oxfordshire England UK
139 H3 **Chipping Ongar** Essex England UK
127 H3 **Chippis** Switzerland
79 E10 **Chiputneticook Lakes** New Brunswick Canada
90 B4 **Chiquimula** Guatemala
106 D2 **Chiquinata, Bahía** *bay* Chile
187 E8 **Chirala** Andhra Pradesh India
181 G3 **Chirang** Bhutan
138 D2 **Chirbury** Shropshire England UK
183 K5 **Chirchiq** Uzbekistan
163 G3 **Chire** Mozambique
155 I4 **Chirfa** Niger
100 C2 **Chiriguaná** Colombia
72 D7 **Chirikof Island** Alaska USA
100 A3 **Chiriquí, Golfo de** *bay* Panama
100 A2 **Chiriquí, Laguna de** *bay* Panama
100 A2 **Chiriquí, Punta** *cape* Panama
100 A2 **Chiriquí, Volcán de** *volcano* Panama
90 D5 **Chiriquí Grande** Panama
128 E5 **Chirival** Spain
138 D2 **Chirk** Wrexham Wales UK
132 E3 **Chirnogi** Romania
142 F5 **Chirnside** Scottish Borders Scotland UK
90 D5 **Chirripó, Cerro** *mountain* Costa Rica
90 D5 **Chirripó, Rio** *watercourse* Costa Rica
132 F2 **Chirsova** Moldova
104 D4 **Chiru Choricha, Serranía** *range* Bolivia
162 E3 **Chirundu** Zimbabwe
162 E2 **Chisasa** Zambia
77 P6 **Chisasibi** Quebec Canada
142 C5 **Chiscan** Argyll and Bute Scotland UK
100 C3 **Chiscas** Colombia
90 B4 **Chisec** Guatemala
163 F1 **Chisenga** Malawi
75 N5 **Chisholm** Alberta Canada
79 C10 **Chisholm** Maine USA
179 L3 **Chishtian Mandi** Pakistan
188 E3 **Chishui** Guizhou China
188 E3 **Chishui He** *watercourse* Sichuan China
132 F2 **Chişinău (Kishinev)** Moldova
125 K4 **Chişineu-Criş** Romania
85 J5 **Chispa** Texas USA
163 F4 **Chissibuca** Mozambique
163 F4 **Chissinguane** Mozambique
164 8b **Chissio Mtsaboro** *island* Mayotte
182 F2 **Chistopol'** Russian Federation
139 G3 **Chiswell Green** Hertfordshire England UK
191 H2 **Chita** Russian Federation
161 F5 **Chita** Tanzania
162 B3 **Chitado** Angola
160 C5 **Chitato** Angola
162 C2 **Chitembo** Angola
135 Y8 **Chitinskaya Oblast'** *admin. area* Russian Federation
161 E5 **Chitipa** Malawi
186 E4 **Chitkal** Himachal Pradesh India
163 F4 **Chitobe** Mozambique
162 D2 **Chitokoloki** Zambia
162 E3 **Chitongo** Zambia
193 I2 **Chitose** Japan
187 D8 **Chitradurga** Karnataka India
179 L2 **Chitral** Pakistan
90 D6 **Chitré** Panama
181 G4 **Chittagong** Bangladesh
181 G4 **Chittagong** *admin. area* Bangladesh
186 D6 **Chittaurgarh** Rajasthan India
139 E3 **Chittoe** Wiltshire England UK
187 E9 **Chittoor** Andhra Pradesh India
163 F3 **Chitungwiza** Zimbabwe
163 G2 **Chiulezi** *watercourse* Mozambique
162 D3 **Chiume** Angola
163 G2 **Chiúre** Mozambique
124 F4 **Chiusa** Italy
130 D5 **Chiusi** Italy
163 G2 **Chiuta, Lake** Mozambique
124 D5 **Chivasso** Italy
88 C3 **Chívato, Punta** *cape* Mexico
163 F3 **Chivhu** Zimbabwe
107 F5 **Chivilcoy** Argentina
100 C2 **Chivolo** Colombia
108 C3 **Chivos, Pampa de los** *region* Argentina
89 H6 **Chixoy** *watercourse* Guatemala
162 E3 **Chizarira Hills** *range* Zimbabwe
182 F3 **Chizha Vtoraya** Kazakhstan
189 H2 **Chizhou** Anhui China
125 H1 **Chlebowo** Poland
155 G1 **Chlef** Algeria
125 L2 **Chłopiatyn** Poland
130 F2 **Chlum u Třeboně** Czech Republic
194 E2 **Chợ Chu** Vietnam
192 E3 **Cho-do** *island* North Korea
192 E4 **Cho-do** *island* South Korea
181 F3 **Cho Oyu** *mountain* Xizang Zizhiqu China
196 B3 **Choa Chu Kang** *admin. area* Singapore
194 E4 **Chŏâm Khsant** Cambodia
106 D4 **Choapa** *watercourse* Chile
193 I2 **Chobushi-numa** *lake* Japan
125 I2 **Choceň** Czech Republic
192 E4 **Choch'iwon** South Korea
100 B3 **Chocó** *admin. area* Colombia
100 B4 **Chocó, Bahía** *bay* Colombia
87 H5 **Choctawhatchee Bay** Florida USA
125 I2 **Chocz** Poland
179 I2 **Chodān** Iran
187 E8 **Chodavaram** Andhra Pradesh India
106 E6 **Choele Choel** Argentina
163 F2 **Chofombo** Mozambique
179 M2 **Chogo Lungma Glacier** Pakistan
190 F4 **Chogtovoo** Mongolia
190 F4 **Chogttsetsii** Mongolia
142 D2 **Choire, Loch** *lake* Scotland UK
222 8 **Choiseul** *admin. area* Solomon Islands
222 8 **Choiseul** *island* Solomon Islands
109 7 **Choiseul Sound** *bay* Falkland Islands
88 C3 **Choix** Mexico
125 I1 **Chojnice** Poland
125 I2 **Chojnik** Poland
125 H2 **Chojnów** Poland
194 D4 **Chok Chai** Thailand
193 I3 **Chōkai-zan** *volcano* Japan
86 B6 **Choke Canyon Reservoir** Texas USA
81 Q4 **Chokio** Minnesota USA
183 L5 **Chokpar** Kazakhstan
163 F4 **Chokwé** Mozambique
84 B3 **Cholame** California USA
139 F3 **Cholderton** Wiltshire England UK
126 D3 **Cholet** France
108 B3 **Cholila** Argentina
100 D3 **Chololobo** Colombia
90 C4 **Choloma** Honduras
183 M5 **Cholpon-Ata** Kyrgyzstan
89 F5 **Cholula** Mexico
192 E3 **Ch'ŏlwon** South Korea
194 C3 **Chom Thong** Thailand
162 E3 **Choma** Zambia
132 D4 **Chomakovtsi** Bulgaria
181 F3 **Chommo Yummo** *mountain* Xizang Zizhiqu China
181 G3 **Chomo Ganggar** *mountain* Xizang Zizhiqu China
181 F3 **Chomo Lhari** *mountain* Bhutan
194 E5 **Chơn Thành** Vietnam
135 W6 **Chona** *watercourse* Russian Federation
192 E4 **Ch'ŏnan** South Korea
194 D4 **Chonburi** Thailand
100 A5 **Chone** Ecuador
194 D4 **Chông Kal** Cambodia
192 F3 **Ch'ŏngjin** North Korea
192 E4 **Ch'ŏngju** South Korea
188 D2 **Chonglong** Sichuan China
189 I2 **Chongming Dao** *island* Shanghai China
162 B2 **Chongoroi** Angola
104 B2 **Chongoyape** Peru
192 E3 **Chŏngp'yŏng** North Korea
188 E2 **Chongqing** Chongqing China
188 E2 **Chongqing** *admin. area* China
192 E4 **Chŏngup** South Korea
162 E3 **Chongwe** Zambia
192 E4 **Chŏnju** South Korea
192 E3 **Ch'onnae** North Korea
108 A3 **Chonos, Archipiélago de los** *islands* Chile
100 B5 **Chontal** Ecuador
89 G5 **Chontalpa** Mexico
132 C1 **Chop** Ukraine
186 F6 **Chopan** Uttar Pradesh India
187 D7 **Chopda** Maharashtra India
103 A9 **Chopim** *watercourse* Brazil
103 A9 **Chopinzinho** Brazil
182 F6 **Chopūl** Iran
190 F3 **Chor** Mongolia
138 E2 **Chorley** Shropshire England UK
136 D2 **Chornobyl'** Ukraine
136 E4 **Chornomors'ke** Ukraine
105 E6 **Chorolque, Nevado** *mountain* Bolivia
106 D4 **Choros, Islas de los** *islands* Chile
125 L1 **Choroszcz** Poland
183 K5 **Chortoq** Uzbekistan
192 E3 **Ch'osan** North Korea
193 I4 **Chōshi** Japan
106 E5 **Chosmes** Argentina
125 H1 **Choszczno** Poland
104 B2 **Chota** Peru
125 K2 **Chotcza Dolna** Poland
80 I3 **Choteau** Montana USA
130 F2 **Chotěboř** Czech Republic
154 D4 **Choûm** Mauritania
80 E8 **Chowchilla** California USA
191 H3 **Choybalsan** Mongolia
191 H3 **Choybalsan** Mongolia
127 G3 **Choye** France
183 R3 **Choygan-khol'** *lake* Russian Federation
129 H5 **Chrea** Algeria
125 H2 **Chřibská** Czech Republic
82 H7 **Chrisney** Indiana USA
221 E6 **Christchurch** New Zealand
139 F4 **Christchurch** Dorset England UK
74 D4 **Christian Sound** Alaska USA
83 K8 **Christiansburg** Virginia USA
109 21 **Christiansted** US Virgin Islands
75 P1 **Christie Bay** Northwest Territories Canada
194 C5 **Christie Island** Myanmar
81 Q3 **Christine** North Dakota USA
86 B6 **Christine** Texas USA
213 I5 **Christmas** *watercourse* WA Australia
213 H5 **Christmas Creek** WA Australia
210 inset **Christmas Island** *Australian territory* Indian Ocean
80 E5 **Christmas Lake** Oregon USA
55 O6 **Christmas Rise** *underwater feature* Indian Ocean
217 J2 **Christopher Lake** WA Australia
85 L5 **Christoval** Texas USA
133 D8 **Chrysi** *island* Greece
133 D5 **Chrysoupoli** Greece
183 L5 **Chu** *watercourse* Kazakhstan
90 B4 **Chuacús, Sierra de** *range* Guatemala
181 F4 **Chuadanga** Bangladesh
84 B2 **Chualar** California USA
163 F4 **Chuáli, Lagoa** *lake* Mozambique
183 J4 **Chubar-kul'** *lake* Kazakhstan
189 I4 **Chubei** Taiwan China
108 C3 **Chubut** *admin. area* Argentina
108 C3 **Chubut** *watercourse* Argentina
104 C4 **Chuchaujasa, Cerro** *mountain* Peru
104 B2 **Chuchuhuasi** Peru
100 B2 **Chucunaque** *watercourse* Panama
123 P3 **Chudovo** Russian Federation
72 E6 **Chugach Mountains** Alaska USA
135 AM8 **Chuginadak Island** Alaska USA
81 M6 **Chugwater** Wyoming USA
190 E6 **Chuimatan** Gansu China
192 E5 **Chuja-gundo** *island* South Korea
189 F2 **Chujiang** Hunan China
135 AC8 **Chukchagirskoye, Ozero** *lake* Russian Federation
56 S1 **Chukchi Abyssal Plain** *underwater feature* Arctic Ocean
56 S1 **Chukchi Plateau** *underwater feature* Arctic Ocean
72 B5 **Chukchi Sea** Russian Federation/USA
135 AG5 **Chukoch'ye** *watercourse* Russian Federation
135 AM6 **Chukotskiy, Mys** *cape* Russian Federation
135 AJ5 **Chukotskiy Avtonomnyy Okrug** *admin. area* Russian Federation
135 AM5 **Chukotskiy Poluostrov** *peninsula* Russian Federation
135 AK5 **Chukotskoye Nagor'ye** *range* Russian Federation
84 D4 **Chula Vista** California USA
104 C4 **Chulca** Peru
128 D5 **Chullera, Punta de la** *cape* Spain
135 Z7 **Chul'man** Russian Federation
138 D4 **Chulmleigh** Devon England UK
104 A2 **Chulucanas** Peru
104 E5 **Chulumani** Bolivia
191 H2 **Chuluunhoroot** Mongolia
190 D3 **Chuluut** Mongolia
190 D3 **Chuluut Gol** *watercourse* Mongolia
183 M2 **Chulym** Russian Federation
183 N1 **Chulym** *watercourse* Russian Federation
134 N5 **Chum** Russian Federation
194 D3 **Chum Phae** Thailand
194 D4 **Chum Saeng** Thailand
106 E4 **Chumbicha** Argentina
183 O4 **Chumek** Kazakhstan
132 D4 **Chumerna** *mountain* Bulgaria
179 M3 **Chumian** Pakistan
135 AC8 **Chumikan** Russian Federation
194 C5 **Chumphon** Thailand
135 U7 **Chuna** *watercourse* Russian Federation
89 H5 **Chunchintoc** Mexico
192 E4 **Ch'unch'ŏn** South Korea
104 D5 **Chuncoroco** Peru
194 E2 **Chung** *watercourse* Vietnam
192 E4 **Ch'ungju** South Korea
189 I4 **Chungyang Shanmo** *range* Taiwan China
188 E1 **Chunhua** Shaanxi China
189 H2 **Chunxi** Jiangsu China
135 V6 **Chunya** *watercourse* Russian Federation
89 I4 **Chunyaxche, Laguna** *lake* Mexico
194 E5 **Chuôi, Hòn** *island* Vietnam
194 D5 **Chuor Phnum Krâvanh** Cambodia
121 R3 **Chupa** Russian Federation
179 J3 **Chūqhak** Afghanistan
104 B3 **Chuquicara** *watercourse* Peru
105 E6 **Chuquisaca** *admin. area* Bolivia
104 D5 **Chuquitira** Peru
127 I3 **Chur** Switzerland
182 G7 **Churat** Iran
143 C5 **Church Cross** Ireland
141 H2 **Church Houses** North Yorkshire England UK
75 X3 **Churchill** Manitoba Canada
76 E5 **Churchill** *watercourse* Manitoba Canada
78 G6 **Churchill** *watercourse* Newfoundland and Labrador Canada
76 D5 **Churchill** *watercourse* Saskatchewan Canada
76 I3 **Churchill, Cape** Manitoba Canada
78 F6 **Churchill Falls** Newfoundland and Labrador Canada
82 F1 **Churchill Lake** Ontario Canada
75 Q4 **Churchill Lake** Saskatchewan Canada
59 K1 **Churchill Mountains** Antarctica
77 O4 **Churchill Sound** Nunavut Canada
75 V8 **Churchs Ferry** North Dakota USA
140 B4 **Churchtown** Ireland
183 P3 **Chureg Tag** *mountain* Russian Federation
218 F4 **Churinga** NSW Australia
108 B1 **Churriaca, Sierra** *range* Argentina
186 D5 **Churu** Rajasthan India
85 H2 **Chuska Mountains** New Mexico USA
182 H1 **Chusovoy** Russian Federation
77 T8 **Chute-des-Passes** Quebec Canada
181 G3 **Chutia** Assam India
74 E4 **Chutine** *watercourse* British Columbia Canada
222 6 **Chuuk** *admin. area* Federated States of Micronesia
222 6 **Chuuk** *island* Federated States of Micronesia
222 6a **Chuuk Lagoon** Federated States of Micronesia
135 AI6 **Chuvanskiye Gory** *range* Russian Federation
182 E2 **Chuvashskaya Respublika** *admin. area* Russian Federation
188 D3 **Chuxiong** Yunnan China
183 L5 **Chüy** *admin. area* Kyrgyzstan
189 H2 **Chuzhou** Anhui China
136 E3 **Chyhyryn** Ukraine
132 F2 **Ciadîr-Lunga** Moldova
196 F5 **Ciamis** Indonesia
196 E5 **Cianjur** Indonesia
103 A8 **Cianorte** Brazil
125 I1 **Ciążeń** Poland
196 E5 **Cibadak** Indonesia
160 D4 **Cibitoke** Burundi
126 D5 **Ciboure** France
196 E5 **Cicalengka** Indonesia
223 9 **Cicia** *island* Fiji
164 4a **Cidade Velha** Cape Verde
107 I4 **Cidreira** Brazil
125 K1 **Ciechanów** Poland
90 E2 **Ciego de Ávila** Cuba
90 E2 **Ciego de Ávila** *admin. area* Cuba
125 K2 **Cielądz** Poland
196 E5 **Ciemas** Indonesia
100 C2 **Ciénaga** Colombia
85 J8 **Ciénega de Escobar** Mexico
88 E3 **Ciénega de Flores** Mexico
85 I8 **Ciénega de la Vaca** Mexico
85 I7 **Ciénega Prieta** Mexico
90 D2 **Cienfuegos** Cuba
90 D2 **Cienfuegos** *admin. area* Cuba
128 B2 **Cíes, Ilhas** *islands* Spain
129 F4 **Cieza** Spain
133 G6 **Çifteler** Turkey
128 E4 **Cigüela** *watercourse* Spain
88 D5 **Cihuatlán** Mexico
132 F2 **Ciietu** Moldova
128 D4 **Cijara, Embalse de** *lake* Spain
196 F5 **Cijulang** Indonesia
188 C3 **Cikai** Yunnan China
196 F5 **Cikalong** Indonesia
196 E5 **Cikampek** Indonesia
223 9 **Cikobia** *island* Fiji
196 F5 **Cilacap** Indonesia
164 7a **Cilaos** Réunion
196 E5 **Cilegon** Indonesia
133 G5 **Çilimli** Turkey
143 F4 **Cill Mhucraise** Ireland
142 A3 **Cille Pheadair** Na h-Eileanan Siar Scotland UK
182 F6 **Çiloy Adasi** *island* Azerbaijan
196 E5 **Cimahi** Indonesia
86 A2 **Cimarron** *watercourse* Kansas USA
85 J2 **Cimarron** New Mexico USA
132 F2 **Cimişlia** Moldova
100 C3 **Cimitarra** Colombia
132 E2 **Cîmpia Moldovei de Nord** *range* Moldova
132 F2 **Cîmpia Moldovei de Sud** *range* Moldova
132 E2 **Cîmpurile** Romania
196 E5 **Cina, Tanjung** *cape* Indonesia
133 F5 **Çınarcık** Turkey
100 D3 **Cinaruco** *watercourse* Venezuela
129 G3 **Cinca** *watercourse* Spain
82 I7 **Cincinnati** Ohio USA
106 D6 **Cinco Saltos** Argentina
138 E3 **Cinderford** Gloucestershire England UK
74 J6 **Cinema** British Columbia Canada
127 G1 **Ciney** Belgium
198 A4 **Cinoka, Tanjung** *cape* Indonesia
194 B5 **Cinque Islands** Andaman and Nicobar Islands India
89 G5 **Cintalapa de Figueroa** Mexico
126 E5 **Cintegabelle** France
126 D5 **Cintruénigo** Spain
196 F5 **Cipatujah** Indonesia
103 E5 **Cipó** Brazil
101 H5 **Cipoal** Brazil
196 E5 **Ciputat** Indonesia
131 E6 **Circeo, Capo** *cape* Italy
72 E5 **Circle** Alaska USA
81 M3 **Circle** Montana USA
216 G6 **Circle Valley** WA Australia
82 J7 **Circleville** Ohio USA
196 F5 **Cirebon** Indonesia
131 F7 **Cirella** Italy
139 F3 **Cirencester** Gloucestershire England UK
124 D3 **Cirey** France
104 C4 **Cirialo** Peru
124 D5 **Ciriè** Italy
131 F8 **Ciriga, Punta** *cape* Italy
123 N4 **Cirma** *lake* Latvia
131 G7 **Cirò Marina** Italy
126 D4 **Ciron** *watercourse* France
132 D2 **Cîrța** Romania
196 E5 **Cisarua** Indonesia
86 B4 **Cisco** Texas USA
125 L3 **Cisna** Poland
90 E2 **Cistern Point** Bahamas
128 D2 **Cistierna** Spain
80 E7 **Citrus Heights** California USA
162 C6 **Citrusdal** South Africa
130 E5 **Città di Castello** Italy
Città del Vaticano *see* **Vatican City**
124 F5 **Cittadella** Italy
142 E5 **City of Edinburgh** *admin. area* Scotland UK
142 D5 **City of Glasgow** *admin. area* Scotland UK
132 B3 **Ciuchici** Romania
132 F2 **Ciucur-Mingir** Moldova
88 E2 **Ciudad Acuña** Mexico
86 B7 **Ciudad Alemán** Mexico
88 E5 **Ciudad Altamirano** Mexico
88 E3 **Ciudad Anáhuac** Mexico
90 B4 **Ciudad Arce** El Salvador
100 B3 **Ciudad Bolívar** Colombia
101 F2 **Ciudad Bolívar** Venezuela
88 D3 **Ciudad Camargo** Mexico
90 C4 **Ciudad Choluteca** Honduras
88 C3 **Ciudad Constitución** Mexico
90 C4 **Ciudad Darío** Nicaragua
90 D2 **Ciudad de La Habana** *admin. area* Cuba
89 F5 **Ciudad de México (México City)** Mexico
89 H5 **Ciudad del Carmen** Mexico
106 H3 **Ciudad del Este** Paraguay
89 F4 **Ciudad del Maíz** Mexico
88 D2 **Ciudad Delicias** Mexico
101 F2 **Ciudad Guayana** Venezuela
85 I6 **Ciudad Guerrero** Mexico
88 E5 **Ciudad Guzmán** Mexico
88 D2 **Ciudad Juárez** Mexico
88 E3 **Ciudad Lerdo** Mexico
89 F5 **Ciudad López Mateos** Mexico
89 F4 **Ciudad Madero** Mexico
89 F4 **Ciudad Mante** Mexico
90 B3 **Ciudad Melchor de Mencos** Guatemala
89 F3 **Ciudad Miguel Alemán** Mexico
84 E4 **Ciudad Morelos** Mexico
88 C3 **Ciudad Obregón** Mexico
89 G5 **Ciudad Pemex** Mexico
128 E4 **Ciudad Real** Spain
128 C3 **Ciudad Rodrigo** Spain
90 C4 **Ciudad Sandino** Nicaragua
89 F4 **Ciudad Valles** Mexico
89 F4 **Ciudad Victoria** Mexico
109 5 **Ciudado, Punta** *cape* Isla de Pascua (Easter Island)
125 L4 **Ciugud** Romania
132 C2 **Ciuhoiu** Romania
132 F3 **Ciumai** Moldova
127 I5 **Ciuttone, Punta di** *cape* Corsica France
127 K3 **Cividale del Friuli** Italy
131 D5 **Civitavecchia** Italy
126 E3 **Civray** France
189 I2 **Cixi** Zhejiang China
136 G6 **Cizre** Turkey
140 A2 **Clabby** Fermanagh Northern Ireland UK
142 C5 **Clachan** Argyll and Bute Scotland UK
142 B3 **Clachan** Highland Scotland UK
142 C4 **Clachan of Glendaruel** Argyll and Bute Scotland UK
142 E4 **Clackmannanshire** *admin. area* Scotland UK
139 I3 **Clacton-on-Sea** Essex England UK
142 A3 **Cladach a' Chaolais** Na h-Eileanan Siar Scotland UK
142 B5 **Claddach** Argyll and Bute Scotland UK
142 C4 **Cladich** Argyll and Bute Scotland UK
140 B2 **Clady** Magherafelt Northern Ireland UK
138 D2 **Claerwen Reservoir** Wales UK
81 P7 **Claflin** Kansas USA
140 A1 **Claggan** Ireland
86 E4 **Claiborne, Lake** Louisiana USA
126 E3 **Clain** *watercourse* France
80 D6 **Clair Engle Lake** California USA
72 H7 **Claire, Lake** Alberta Canada
85 L4 **Clairemont** Texas USA
127 G3 **Clairvaux-les-Lacs** France
126 F3 **Clamecy** France
80 G7 **Clan Alpine Mountains** Nevada USA
143 F3 **Clane** Ireland
139 F4 **Clanfield** Hampshire England UK
87 H4 **Clanton** Alabama USA
162 C6 **Clanwilliam** South Africa
142 D2 **Claonel** Highland Scotland UK
141 F2 **Clapham** North Yorkshire England UK
214 G5 **Clara** *watercourse* Qld Australia
143 E3 **Clara** Ireland
81 R4 **Clara City** Minnesota USA
194 C5 **Clara Island** Myanmar
143 E3 **Clarahill** Ireland
214 F5 **Claraville** Qld Australia
215 I5 **Clare** Qld Australia
218 D5 **Clare** SA Australia
143 C4 **Clare** *admin. area* Ireland
143 D3 **Clare** *watercourse* Ireland
82 I5 **Clare** Michigan USA
143 D4 **Clare Bridge** Ireland
143 B3 **Clare Island** Ireland
83 O5 **Claremont** New Hampshire USA
221 E6 **Clarence** *watercourse* New Zealand
108 B6 **Clarence, Isla** *island* Chile
59 U2 **Clarence Island** Antarctica
213 K2 **Clarence Strait** NT Australia
74 E4 **Clarence Strait** Alaska USA
91 F2 **Clarence Town** Bahamas
218 D6 **Clarendon** SA Australia
85 L3 **Clarendon** Texas USA
75 O7 **Claresholm** Alberta Canada
143 C3 **Clareville** Ireland
59 I2 **Clarie Coast** Antarctica
82 E5 **Clarion** Iowa USA
83 L6 **Clarion** *watercourse* Pennsylvania USA
88 B5 **Clarión, Isla** *island* Mexico
53 S6 **Clarion Fracture Zone** *underwater feature* Pacific Ocean
220 F3 **Claris** New Zealand
214 G4 **Clark** *watercourse* Qld Australia
72 D6 **Clark, Lake** Alaska USA
83 K4 **Clark, Point** Ontario Canada
80 G2 **Clark Fork** Idaho USA
59 O1 **Clark Mountains** Antarctica
84 F3 **Clarkdale** Arizona USA
77 V7 **Clarke City** Quebec Canada
219 S10 **Clarke Island** Tas. Australia
215 H5 **Clarke River** Qld Australia
79 F11 **Clark's Harbour** Nova Scotia Canada
83 K7 **Clarksburg** West Virginia USA
86 F3 **Clarksdale** Mississippi USA
82 H8 **Clarkson** Kentucky USA
80 G3 **Clarkston** Washington USA
86 H2 **Clarksville** Tennessee USA
86 D4 **Clarksville** Texas USA
87 L3 **Clarkton** North Carolina USA
103 B6 **Claro** *watercourse* Brazil
127 I3 **Claro** Switzerland
106 E3 **Claro, Lago** *lake* Argentina
140 A4 **Clasheen Bridge** Ireland
143 E4 **Clashmore** Ireland
80 D3 **Clatskanie** Oregon USA
140 D1 **Clatteringshaws Loch** *lake* Scotland UK
85 L3 **Claude** Texas USA
103 C8 **Cláudio** Brazil
140 A2 **Claudy** Londonderry Northern Ireland UK
73 Q4 **Clavering Øer** *island* Greenland
84 G1 **Clawson** Utah USA
109 9 **Claxton Bay** Trinidad and Tobago
81 Q7 **Clay Center** Kansas USA
141 G3 **Clay Cross** Derbyshire England UK
140 D2 **Clay Head** *cape* Isle of Man UK
75 Q8 **Claydon** Saskatchewan Canada
139 I2 **Claydon** Suffolk England UK
74 K4 **Clayhurst** British Columbia Canada
80 B2 **Clayoquot Sound** British Columbia Canada
218 D3 **Clayton** *watercourse* SA Australia
83 N7 **Clayton** Delaware USA
85 K2 **Clayton** New Mexico USA
86 D3 **Clayton** Oklahoma USA
86 D3 **Clear Boggy** *watercourse* Oklahoma USA
86 B4 **Clear Fork Brazos** *watercourse* Texas USA
219 R11 **Clear Hill** Tas. Australia
74 L4 **Clear Hills** Alberta Canada
143 C5 **Clear Island** Ireland
84 A1 **Clear Lake** California USA
86 E4 **Clear Lake** Louisiana USA
84 F1 **Clear Lake** Utah USA
80 E6 **Clear Lake Reservoir** California USA
74 L4 **Clear Prairie** Alberta Canada
74 L4 **Cleardale** Alberta Canada
72 E7 **Cleare, Cape** Alaska USA
80 D7 **Clearlake** California USA
81 L4 **Clearmont** Wyoming USA
72 H7 **Clearwater** *watercourse* Alberta Canada
74 K7 **Clearwater** British Columbia Canada
75 Q4 **Clearwater** *watercourse* Saskatchewan Canada
87 J7 **Clearwater** Florida USA
80 G3 **Clearwater** *watercourse* Idaho USA
74 K6 **Clearwater Lake** British Columbia Canada
86 F2 **Clearwater Lake** Missouri USA
80 H4 **Clearwater Mountains** Idaho USA
140 E2 **Cleator Moor** Cumbria England UK
86 C4 **Cleburne** Texas USA
126 D2 **Clécy** France
124 C3 **Clefmont** France
132 E2 **Cleja** Romania
196 C4 **Clementi** *admin. area* Singapore
87 K2 **Clemmons** North Carolina USA
87 J3 **Clemson** South Carolina USA
83 K7 **Clendenin** West Virginia USA
86 B2 **Cleo Springs** Oklahoma USA
138 E2 **Cleobury Mortimer** Shropshire England UK
195 H5 **Cleopatra Needle** *mountain* Philippines
143 E3 **Cleraun** Ireland
216 E2 **Clere, Mount** WA Australia
139 I5 **Cléres** France
212 E4 **Clerke Reef** WA Australia
215 I7 **Clermont** Qld Australia
79 C9 **Clermont** Quebec Canada
124 B3 **Clermont** France
126 F4 **Clermont-Ferrand** France
126 F5 **Clermont-l'Hérault** France
127 H1 **Clervaux** Luxembourg

218 C5 **Cleve** SA Australia
220 F3 **Clevedon** New Zealand
138 E3 **Clevedon** North Somerset England UK
87 H4 **Cleveland** Alabama USA
86 F4 **Cleveland** Mississippi USA
81 P3 **Cleveland** North Dakota USA
83 K6 **Cleveland** Ohio USA
87 I3 **Cleveland** Tennessee USA
82 H5 **Cleveland** Wisconsin USA
74 E5 **Cleveland Peninsula** Alaska USA
103 A9 **Clevelândia** Brazil
143 C3 **Clew Bay** Ireland
87 K7 **Clewiston** Florida USA
143 B3 **Clifden** Ireland
221 B8 **Clifden** New Zealand
142 C4 **Cliff** Highland Scotland UK
139 H4 **Cliff End** East Sussex England UK
218 G2 **Cliffdale** Qld Australia
214 E4 **Cliffdale** *watercourse* Qld Australia
143 D2 **Cliffony** Ireland
143 C4 **Cliffs of Moher** *point of interest* Ireland
140 F2 **Clifton** Cumbria England UK
139 F2 **Clifton** Nottingham England UK
85 H4 **Clifton** Arizona USA
80 I5 **Clifton** Idaho USA
86 H3 **Clifton** Tennessee USA
86 C5 **Clifton** Texas USA
215 H4 **Clifton Beach** Qld Australia
83 L8 **Clifton Forge** Virginia USA
218 D2 **Clifton Hills** SA Australia
76 F3 **Clifton Lake** Manitoba Canada
75 Q8 **Climax** Saskatchewan Canada
74 M6 **Cline River** Alberta Canada
85 J3 **Clines Corners** New Mexico USA
87 J3 **Clingmans Dome** *mountain* North Carolina USA
85 I5 **Clint** Texas USA
74 K7 **Clinton** British Columbia Canada
83 K5 **Clinton** Ontario Canada
221 C8 **Clinton** New Zealand
86 E3 **Clinton** Arkansas USA
82 F6 **Clinton** Iowa USA
86 F5 **Clinton** Louisiana USA
82 G5 **Clinton** Wisconsin USA
215 K7 **Clinton, Cape** Qld Australia
82 D7 **Clinton Lake** Kansas USA
214 G6 **Clio** Qld Australia
82 J5 **Clio** Michigan USA
53 S7 **Clipperton Fracture Zone** *underwater feature* Pacific Ocean
53 V6 **Clipperton Island** *French possession* Pacific Ocean
126 D3 **Clisson** France
132 C2 **Clit** Romania
141 F3 **Clitheroe** Lancashire England UK
215 J7 **Clive** Qld Australia
105 F4 **Cliza** Brazil
80 C2 **Clo-oose** British Columbia Canada
212 B7 **Cloates, Point** WA Australia
142 G3 **Clochtow** Aberdeenshire Scotland UK
140 B2 **Clogh** Ballymena Northern Ireland UK
140 B2 **Clogh Mills** Ballymena Northern Ireland UK
143 E3 **Cloghan** Ireland
143 C5 **Cloghane** Ireland
140 A2 **Clogher** Dungannon Northern Ireland UK
140 B2 **Cloghoge** Newry and Mourne Northern Ireland UK
140 C2 **Cloghy** Ards Northern Ireland UK
214 F6 **Clonagh** Qld Australia
143 D5 **Clonakilty** Ireland
143 D5 **Clonakilty Bay** Ireland
140 B3 **Clonalvy** Ireland
140 A3 **Clonarrow** Ireland
143 D3 **Clonbern** Ireland
140 A3 **Cloncanon** Ireland
219 J1 **Cloncose** Qld Australia
214 F6 **Cloncurry** Qld Australia
214 F5 **Cloncurry** *watercourse* Qld Australia
143 E2 **Clones** Ireland
140 B2 **Clonfeacle** Dungannon Northern Ireland UK
140 A2 **Clonleigh** Ireland
143 E1 **Clonmany** Ireland
143 E4 **Clonmel** Ireland
140 A3 **Clonmellon** Ireland
140 A3 **Clonmore** Ireland
143 F4 **Clonroche** Ireland
219 J2 **Clontarf** Qld Australia
140 B3 **Cloon** Ireland
143 B5 **Cloonaghlin Lough** *lake* Ireland
143 D3 **Clooncan** Ireland
143 C3 **Clooneen** Ireland
82 E3 **Cloquet** Minnesota USA
59 D2 **Close, Cape** Antarctica
75 S4 **Close Lake** Saskatchewan Canada
142 E5 **Closeburn** Dumfries and Galloway Scotland UK
142 inset **Clothan** Shetland Scotland UK
81 L4 **Cloud Peak** Wyoming USA
85 J4 **Cloudcroft** New Mexico USA
219 K4 **Clouds Creek** NSW Australia
221 F5 **Cloudy Bay** New Zealand
108 C6 **Cloué, Península** Chile
140 C2 **Clough** Down Northern Ireland UK
141 H2 **Cloughton** North Yorkshire England UK
142 C4 **Clounlaid** Highland Scotland UK
83 N2 **Clova** Quebec Canada
142 E4 **Clova** Angus Scotland UK
138 C4 **Clovelly** Devon England UK
85 H5 **Cloverdale** New Mexico USA
82 H8 **Cloverport** Kentucky USA
80 F8 **Clovis** California USA
85 K3 **Clovis** New Mexico USA
142 C4 **Clovullin** Highland Scotland UK
141 G3 **Clowne** Derbyshire England UK
138 E2 **Clows Top** Worcestershire England UK
219 J2 **Cloyna** Qld Australia
142 C3 **Cluanie, Loch** *lake* Scotland UK
75 Q3 **Cluff Lake Mine** Saskatchewan Canada
132 C2 **Cluj** *admin. area* Romania
132 C2 **Cluj-Napoca** Romania
138 D2 **Clun** Shropshire England UK
142 D4 **Clunes** Highland Scotland UK
142 E4 **Clunes Lodge** Perth and Kinross Scotland UK
214 E8 **Cluny** Qld Australia
127 H3 **Cluses** France
124 E5 **Clusone** Italy
86 D6 **Clute** Texas USA
221 C7 **Clutha** *watercourse* New Zealand
143 C4 **Clydagh** *watercourse* Ireland
221 C7 **Clyde** New Zealand
140 E1 **Clyde** *watercourse* Scotland UK
81 Q7 **Clyde** Kansas USA
86 B4 **Clyde** Texas USA
142 D5 **Clyde, Firth of** *bay* Scotland UK
81 J4 **Clyde Park** Montana USA
73 M4 **Clyde River** Nunavut Canada
142 D5 **Clydebank** West Dunbartonshire Scotland UK
138 D2 **Clyro** Powys Wales UK
140 A2 **Coa** Fermanagh Northern Ireland UK
128 C3 **Côa** *watercourse* Portugal
84 D4 **Coachella** California USA
213 I3 **Coachman Range** WA Australia
140 B2 **Coagh** Cookstown Northern Ireland UK
85 L4 **Coahoma** Texas USA
88 E5 **Coahuayana** Mexico
88 E3 **Coahuila** *admin. area* Mexico
74 H2 **Coal** *watercourse* Yukon Territory Canada
74 H7 **Coal Harbour** British Columbia Canada
86 E3 **Coal Hill** Arkansas USA
72 G7 **Coal River** British Columbia Canada
141 F2 **Coalcleugh** Northumberland England UK
88 E5 **Coalcomán** Mexico
75 O8 **Coaldale** Alberta Canada
221 D6 **Coalgate** New Zealand
84 B2 **Coalinga** California USA
218 F3 **Coally** NSW Australia
139 F2 **Coalville** Leicester England UK
80 J6 **Coalville** Utah USA
100 B5 **Coangos** Ecuador
103 E6 **Coaraci** Brazil
101 I4 **Coaracy Nunes** Brazil
105 F2 **Coari** Brazil
101 E6 **Coari** *watercourse* Brazil
101 F6 **Coari, Lago de** *lake* Brazil
161 F4 **Coast** *admin. area* Kenya
142 C3 **Coast** Highland Scotland UK
72 F7 **Coast Mountains** British Columbia Canada
219 K1 **Coast Range** Qld Australia
84 B2 **Coast Ranges** California USA
86 G5 **Coastal Plain** Louisiana USA
86 C7 **Coastal Plain** Texas USA
142 D5 **Coatbridge** North Lanarkshire Scotland UK
139 E3 **Coates** Gloucestershire England UK
77 Q5 **Coats** *watercourse* Quebec Canada
81 P8 **Coats** Kansas USA
77 P4 **Coats Bay** Nunavut Canada
73 K6 **Coats Island** Nunavut Canada
59 W1 **Coats Land** *plain* Antarctica
89 G5 **Coatzacoalcos** Mexico
90 B4 **Cobán** Guatemala
132 E2 **Cobani** Moldova
218 G4 **Cobar** NSW Australia
100 C3 **Cobardes, Serranía Los** *range* Colombia
219 I7 **Cobargo** NSW Australia
213 I8 **Cobb, Lake** WA Australia
87 N2 **Cobb Bay** Virginia USA
109 18 **Cobb Cove** *bay* Antigua and Barbuda
219 J4 **Cobbadah** NSW Australia
219 H7 **Cobbannah** Vic. Australia
219 I5 **Cobbora** NSW Australia
218 F8 **Cobden** Vic. Australia
83 M4 **Cobden** Ontario Canada
82 G8 **Cobden** Illinois USA
79 F10 **Cobequid Mountains** Nova Scotia Canada
143 D5 **Cóbh** Cork Ireland
218 F4 **Cobham** NSW Australia
104 D3 **Cobija** Brazil
83 L5 **Cobourg** Ontario Canada
214 B1 **Cobourg Peninsula** NT Australia
106 C6 **Cobquecura** Chile
218 G6 **Cobram** Vic. Australia
163 F2 **Cobué** Mozambique
130 D1 **Coburg** Germany
73 L3 **Coburg Island** Nunavut Canada
100 B5 **Coca** *watercourse* Ecuador
124 E4 **Coca, Pizzo di** *mountain* Italy
104 D5 **Cocachacra** Peru
102 D3 **Cocal** Brazil
103 B6 **Cocalinho** Brazil
105 E5 **Cochabamba** Bolivia
105 E5 **Cochabamba** *admin. area* Bolivia
101 F2 **Coche, Isla** *island* Venezuela
130 B1 **Cochem** Germany
90 D2 **Cochinos, Bahía de** *bay* Cuba
164 6 **Cochons, Île aux** *island* French Southern and Antarctic Lands
83 Q2 **Cochons, Sault aux** *watercourse* Quebec Canada
87 J4 **Cochran** Georgia USA
75 N7 **Cochrane** Alberta Canada
73 K9 **Cochrane** Ontario Canada
213 G4 **Cockatoo Island** WA Australia
215 G4 **Cockburn** *watercourse* Qld Australia
218 E5 **Cockburn** SA Australia
108 B6 **Cockburn, Canal** *strait* Chile
214 A7 **Cockburn, Mount** NT Australia
82 J4 **Cockburn Island** Ontario Canada
215 G1 **Cockburn Reef** Qld Australia
91 F1 **Cockburn Town** Bahamas
142 F5 **Cockburnspath** Scottish Borders Scotland UK
140 F3 **Cockerham** Lancashire England UK
77 O7 **Cockispenny Point** Ontario Canada
142 F5 **Cocklawfoot** Scottish Borders Scotland UK
217 J6 **Cocklebiddy** WA Australia
90 D5 **Coclé** Panama
90 E2 **Coco, Cayo** *island* Cuba
90 C6 **Coco, Isla de** *island* Costa Rica
100 B4 **Coco, Punta** *cape* Colombia
90 D4 **Coco, Rio** *watercourse* Nicaragua
194 B4 **Coco Channel** Andaman and Nicobar Islands India
54 J4 **Coco-de-Mer Ridge** *underwater feature* Indian Ocean
87 K6 **Cocoa Beach** Florida USA
109 18 **Cocoa Point** *cape* Antigua and Barbuda
159 F4 **Cocobeach** Gabon
86 E5 **Cocodrie Lake** Louisiana USA
84 F3 **Coconino Plateau** Arkansas USA
210 inset **Cocos (Keeling) Islands** *Australian territory* Pacific Ocean
55 N5 **Cocos Basin** *underwater feature* Indian Ocean
109 9 **Cocos Bay** *bay* Trinidad and Tobago
53 X7 **Cocos Ridge** *underwater feature* Pacific Ocean
108 A2 **Cocotué, Bahía** *bay* Chile
83 Q6 **Cod, Cape** Massachusetts USA
83 P6 **Cod Bay, Cape** Massachusetts USA
78 H4 **Cod Island** Newfoundland and Labrador Canada
105 F1 **Codajás** Brazil
143 E3 **Codd** Ireland
123 M4 **Code** Latvia
101 E2 **Codera, Cabo** *cape* Venezuela
221 B8 **Codfish Island (Whenua Hou)** New Zealand
105 F4 **Codicia** Bolivia
124 G5 **Codigoro** Italy
106 D6 **Codihué** Argentina
132 D3 **Codlea** Romania
102 D4 **Codó** Brazil
124 E5 **Codogno** Italy
91 I3 **Codrington** Antigua and Barbuda
59 D2 **Codrington, Mount** Antarctica
109 18 **Codrington Lagoon** *lake* Antigua and Barbuda
130 E4 **Codroipo** Italy
143 B5 **Cod's Head** *cape* Ireland
139 E2 **Codsall** Staffordshire England UK
81 O5 **Cody** Nebraska USA
81 K4 **Cody** Wyoming USA
138 C2 **Coed Ystumgwern** Gwynedd Wales UK
138 D3 **Coelbren** Powys Wales UK
102 D4 **Coelho Neto** Brazil
215 G2 **Coen** Qld Australia
214 G2 **Coen** *watercourse* Qld Australia
164 9 **Coëtivy** *island* Seychelles
80 G3 **Coeur d'Alene** Idaho USA
80 G3 **Coeur d'Alene Lake** Idaho USA
126 D3 **Coëx** France
86 G4 **Coffeeville** Mississippi USA
82 D8 **Coffeyville** Kansas USA
218 B6 **Coffin Bay** SA Australia
219 K4 **Coffs Harbour** NSW Australia
90 B4 **Cofradía** Honduras
132 F3 **Cogealac** Romania
126 D4 **Cognac** France
127 H5 **Cogolin** France
219 I2 **Cogoon** *watercourse* Qld Australia
213 H8 **Cohen, Lake** WA Australia
160 E4 **Cohoha South, Lake** Burundi
100 A3 **Coiba, Isla de** *island* Panama
108 C5 **Coig** *watercourse* Argentina
142 C2 **Coigeach, Rubha** *cape* Scotland UK
108 B3 **Coihaique** Chile
106 D6 **Coihueco** Chile
187 D9 **Coimbatore** Tamil Nadu India
128 B3 **Coimbra** Portugal
128 B3 **Coimbra** *admin. area* Portugal
104 D5 **Coipasa, Lago de** *lake* Bolivia
104 D5 **Coipasa, Salar de** *pan* Bolivia
100 D2 **Cojedes** *admin. area* Venezuela
100 A4 **Cojimíes, Punta** *cape* Ecuador
104 B3 **Cojup, Nevado** *mountain* Peru
81 M8 **Cokedale** Colorado USA
81 J5 **Cokeville** Wyoming USA
218 F8 **Colac** Vic. Australia
100 B5 **Colai, Cerro** *mountain* Ecuador
108 C3 **Colan Conhué** Argentina
218 F3 **Colane** NSW Australia
103 D7 **Colatina** Brazil
59 N1 **Colbeck Basin** *underwater feature* Southern Ocean
81 O7 **Colby** Kansas USA
104 C4 **Colca** Peru
104 E5 **Colcha** Bolivia
139 H3 **Colchester** Essex England UK
75 P5 **Cold Lake** Alberta Canada
142 F5 **Coldstream** Scottish Borders Scotland UK
81 P8 **Coldwater** Kansas USA
82 I6 **Coldwater** Michigan USA
138 E3 **Cole** Somerset England UK
75 Q5 **Cole Bay** Saskatchewan Canada
59 T2 **Cole Peninsula** Antarctica
218 G6 **Coleambally** NSW Australia
138 D2 **Colebatch** Shropshire England UK
83 P4 **Colebrook** New Hampshire USA
141 H3 **Coleby** Lincolnshire England UK
108 C3 **Colelache** Argentina
75 N8 **Coleman** Alberta Canada
86 B5 **Coleman** Texas USA
82 G4 **Coleman** Wisconsin USA
218 E7 **Coleraine** Vic. Australia
140 B1 **Coleraine** Coleraine Northern Ireland UK
143 F1 **Coleraine** *admin. area* Northern Ireland UK
162 E6 **Colesberg** South Africa
139 E3 **Colesborne** Gloucestershire England UK
105 G2 **Coletoria do Estado do Mato Gros** Brazil
80 E7 **Colfax** California USA
86 E5 **Colfax** Louisiana USA
80 G3 **Colfax** Washington USA
108 C3 **Colhué Huapí, Lago** *lake* Argentina
124 E4 **Colico** Italy
162 E5 **Coligny** South Africa
88 E5 **Colima** Mexico
88 D5 **Colima** *admin. area* Mexico
102 C4 **Colinas** Brazil
126 C5 **Colindres** Spain
219 I6 **Colinton** NSW Australia
75 O5 **Colinton** Alberta Canada
142 B4 **Coll** *island* Scotland UK
129 G2 **Coll de Nargó** Spain
128 E3 **Collado Villalba** Spain
130 E3 **Collalto** *mountain* Italy
219 I3 **Collarenebri** NSW Australia
81 L7 **Collbran** Colorado USA
87 I4 **College Park** Georgia USA
80 F3 **College Place** Washington USA
86 C5 **College Station** Texas USA
219 I4 **Collie** NSW Australia
216 E6 **Collie** WA Australia
59 T2 **Collier, Cape** Antarctica
213 H4 **Collier Bay** WA Australia
212 E8 **Collier Range** WA Australia
86 G3 **Collierville** Tennessee USA
138 C4 **Colliford Reservoir** England UK
126 C2 **Collinée** France
82 E6 **Collins** Iowa USA
86 G5 **Collins** Mississippi USA
75 T3 **Collins Bay** Saskatchewan Canada
59 E2 **Collins Glacier** *ice* Antarctica
73 I4 **Collinson Peninsula** Nunavut Canada
215 I6 **Collinsville** Qld Australia
86 D2 **Collinsville** Oklahoma USA
106 C6 **Collipulli** Chile
155 H1 **Collo** Algeria
143 F3 **Collon** Ireland
143 D2 **Collooney** Ireland
85 L1 **Collyer** Kansas USA
127 H2 **Colmar** France
86 B8 **Colmena** Mexico
128 D5 **Colmenar** Spain
86 D5 **Colmesneil** Texas USA
108 A4 **Colmillo, Cabo** *cape* Chile
142 D5 **Colmonell** South Ayrshire Scotland UK
139 H2 **Colne** Cambridgeshire England UK
141 F3 **Colne** Lancashire England UK
139 I3 **Colne Point** England UK
105 G3 **Colniza** Brazil
219 J5 **Colo** *watercourse* NSW Australia
104 E3 **Colocação Vertente** Brazil
82 D4 **Cologne** Minnesota USA
90 B4 **Cololaca** Honduras
78 D4 **Colombet, Lac** *lake* Quebec Canada
86 B7 **Colombia** Mexico
100 D4 **Colombia** *country* South America
50 K8 **Colombian Basin** *underwater feature* Caribbean
103 B9 **Colombo** Brazil
187 E10 **Colombo** Sri Lanka
81 P5 **Colome** South Dakota USA
128 E5 **Colomera, Embalse de** *lake* Spain
126 E5 **Colomiers** France
100 B4 **Colón** Colombia
90 D2 **Colón** Cuba
90 E5 **Colón** Panama
109 4 **Colón, Archipiélago de (Galapagos Islands)** *islands* Ecuador Pacific Ocean
90 C4 **Colón, Montañas de** *range* Honduras
109 11a **Colonarie** St Vincent and the Grenadines
109 11a **Colonarie** *watercourse* St Vincent and the Grenadines
88 A2 **Colonet, Cabo** *cape* Mexico
222 6 **Colonia** Federated States of Micronesia
107 G5 **Colonia** *admin. area* Uruguay
104 C2 **Colonia Angamos** Peru
88 C2 **Colonia Aribabi** Mexico
84 D5 **Colonia Camalu** Mexico
105 H5 **Colônia Córrego Grande** Brazil
88 E2 **Colonia de Enmedio** Mexico
107 G5 **Colonia de Sacramento** Uruguay
106 F4 **Colonia Dora** Argentina
85 H6 **Colonia Garcia** Mexico
106 D6 **Colonia Gobernador Ayala** Argentina
106 E6 **Colonia Josefa** Argentina
107 G2 **Colonia Menno** Paraguay
106 F2 **Colonia Neuland** Paraguay
88 D2 **Colonia Obrera** Mexico
106 F6 **Colonia Santa Rosa** Argentina
83 M8 **Colonial Heights** Virginia USA
131 G6 **Colonna, Capo** *cape* Italy
75 S7 **Colonsay** Saskatchewan Canada
142 B4 **Colonsay** *island* Scotland UK
85 O1 **Colony** Kansas USA
106 F6 **Colorada Grande, Salina** *pan* Argentina
108 C2 **Colorado** *watercourse* Argentina
103 B8 **Colorado** Brazil
106 D5 **Colorado** *watercourse* Chile
88 B2 **Colorado** *lake* Mexico
71 **Colorado** *admin. area* USA
84 E4 **Colorado** *watercourse* Arkansas USA
85 H1 **Colorado** *watercourse* Colorado USA
86 C6 **Colorado** *watercourse* Texas USA
84 G2 **Colorado** *watercourse* Utah USA
100 C2 **Colorado, Cuchilla del** *range* Colombia
84 F2 **Colorado City** Arizona USA
85 J2 **Colorado City** Colorado USA
85 L4 **Colorado City** Texas USA
105 G3 **Colorado do Norte** Brazil
84 F2 **Colorado Plateau** Arkansas USA
81 M7 **Colorado Springs** Colorado USA
106 F6 **Colorado Viejo** *watercourse* Argentina
106 D3 **Colorados, Cerro** *mountain* Argentina
130 D4 **Colorno** Italy
132 F2 **Colosova** Moldova
219 H4 **Colossal** NSW Australia
88 E4 **Colotlán** Mexico
143 F3 **Colp** Ireland
125 G1 **Cölpin** Germany
104 E5 **Colquiri** Bolivia
87 I5 **Colquitt** Georgia USA
139 G2 **Colsterworth** Lincolnshire England UK
218 B5 **Colton** SA Australia
141 G3 **Colton** North Yorkshire England UK
84 D3 **Colton** California USA
72 H8 **Columbia** *watercourse* British Columbia Canada
82 I8 **Columbia** Kentucky USA
86 G5 **Columbia** Mississippi USA
82 E7 **Columbia** Missouri USA
87 M3 **Columbia** North Carolina USA
72 G9 **Columbia** *watercourse* Oregon USA
87 k4 **Columbia** South Carolina USA
86 H3 **Columbia** Tennessee USA
80 E3 **Columbia** *watercourse* Washington USA
73 M2 **Columbia, Cape** Nunavut Canada
72 H8 **Columbia, Mount** Alberta/British Columbia Canada
74 L6 **Columbia Icefield** British Columbia Canada
80 H1 **Columbia Lake** British Columbia Canada
72 G8 **Columbia Mountains** British Columbia Canada
80 F4 **Columbia Plateau** Oregon USA
51 O12 **Columbia Seamount** *underwater feature* Pacific Ocean
162 C6 **Columbine, Cape** South Africa
87 I4 **Columbus** Georgia USA
82 I7 **Columbus** Indiana USA
86 G4 **Columbus** Mississippi USA
81 K4 **Columbus** Montana USA
81 Q6 **Columbus** Nebraska USA
85 I5 **Columbus** New Mexico USA
81 N2 **Columbus** North Dakota USA
82 J7 **Columbus** Ohio USA
91 F2 **Columbus Bank** Bahamas
86 G4 **Columbus Lake** Mississippi USA
91 F1 **Columbus Point** Bahamas
84 C1 **Columbus Salt Marsh** Nevada USA
128 D2 **Colunga** Spain
106 D2 **Colupo, Cerro** *mountain* Chile
72 D5 **Colville** *watercourse* Alaska USA
80 G2 **Colville** Washington USA
220 F3 **Colville, Cape** New Zealand
72 G5 **Colville Lake** Northwest Territories Canada
59 H2 **Colvocoresses Bay** Antarctica
138 E2 **Colwall** Herefordshire England UK
140 E3 **Colwyn Bay** Conwy Wales UK
124 G5 **Comacchio** Italy
89 G5 **Comalcalco** Mexico
104 D5 **Comanche** Bolivia
86 B5 **Comanche** Texas USA
84 B1 **Comanche Reservoir** California USA
59 U2 **Comandante Ferraz (Brazil)** *research station* Antarctica
106 F3 **Comandante Fontana** Argentina
106 D5 **Comandante Salas** Argentina
132 D3 **Comarnic** Romania
108 B3 **Comau, Estero** *bay* Chile
90 C4 **Comayagua** Honduras
219 I4 **Combara** NSW Australia
106 D4 **Combarbala** Chile
138 C3 **Combe Martin** Devon England UK
127 G3 **Combeaufontaine** France
140 C2 **Comber** Ards Northern Ireland UK
181 G5 **Combermere Bay** Myanmar
126 F1 **Combles** France
163 F4 **Combomune** Mozambique
219 K4 **Comboyne** NSW Australia
126 F4 **Combronde** France
219 I4 **Come by Chance** NSW Australia
87 J3 **Comer** Georgia USA
215 J7 **Comet** Qld Australia
215 J8 **Comet** *watercourse* Qld Australia
181 G4 **Comilla** Bangladesh
131 C6 **Comino, Capo** *cape* Sardinia Italy
89 G5 **Comitán de Domínguez** Mexico
126 F3 **Commentry** France
86 D4 **Commerce** Texas USA
124 C3 **Commercy** France
83 O2 **Commissaires, Lac des** *lake* Quebec Canada
73 K5 **Committee Bay** Nunavut Canada
195 G5 **Commodore Reef** Spratly Islands
59 J2 **Commonwealth Bay** Antarctica
218 B3 **Commonwealth Hill** SA Australia
124 E5 **Como** Italy
86 G3 **Como** Mississippi USA
130 C3 **Como, Lago di** *lake* Italy
82 J3 **Como, Lake** Ontario Canada
80 H3 **Como, Lake** Montana USA
105 G4 **Comodoro** Brazil
108 C3 **Comodoro Rivadavia** Argentina
187 D10 **Comorin, Cape** Tamil Nadu India
164 6a **Comoros** *country* Africa
80 C2 **Comox** British Columbia Canada
213 G4 **Compass Hill** WA Australia
128 B4 **Comporta** Portugal
88 D4 **Compostela** Mexico
103 C9 **Comprida, Ilha** *island* Brazil
127 H5 **Comps-sur-Artuby** France
126 B5 **Compuerto, Embalse de** *lake* Spain
76 D4 **Compulsion Bay** Saskatchewan Canada
142 E4 **Comrie** Perth and Kinross Scotland UK
85 L6 **Comstock** Texas USA
53 Q2 **Comstock Seamount** *underwater feature* Pacific Ocean
127 K5 **Comunanza** Italy
101 F3 **Comunidad** Venezuela
194 E3 **Con Co, Đao** *island* Vietnam
194 E3 **Con Cuông** Vietnam
196 E1 **Côn Son** *island* Vietnam
124 G5 **Cona** Italy
108 C2 **Cona Niyeo** Argentina
104 C4 **Conaica** Peru
158 B3 **Conakry** Guinea
218 G6 **Conargo** NSW Australia
106 D4 **Conay** Chile
104 D4 **Concacj** Peru
86 B6 **Concan** Texas USA
105 E2 **Conceição** Brazil
103 B7 **Conceição das Alagoas** Brazil
102 B5 **Conceição do Araguaia** Brazil
103 D7 **Conceição do Mato Dentro** Brazil
101 G4 **Conceição do Maú** Brazil
106 E3 **Concepción** Argentina
105 F5 **Concepción** Bolivia
106 C6 **Concepción** Chile
88 B2 **Concepción** *watercourse* Mexico
107 G2 **Concepción** Paraguay
107 G2 **Concepción** *admin. area* Paraguay
104 C3 **Concepción** Peru
106 C6 **Concepción, Bahía** *bay* Chile
108 A5 **Concepción, Canal** *strait* Chile
105 F4 **Concepción, Laguna** *lake* Bolivia
88 C3 **Concepción, Punta** *cape* Mexico
91 G3 **Concepción de La Vega** Dominican Republic
88 E3 **Concepción del Oro** Mexico
84 B3 **Conception, Point** California USA
79 L9 **Conception Bay** Newfoundland and Labrador Canada
162 B4 **Conception Bay** Namibia
91 F2 **Conception Island** Bahamas
164 9b **Conception Island** Seychelles
105 G6 **Concha** Brazil
103 B8 **Conchas** Brazil
85 J3 **Conchas** New Mexico USA
85 J3 **Conchas Lake** New Mexico USA
106 D2 **Conchi** Chile
84 H3 **Concho** Arizona USA
85 J7 **Conchos** Mexico
86 B8 **Conchos** *watercourse* Mexico
80 F2 **Conconully** Washington USA
80 D8 **Concord** California USA
83 P5 **Concord** New Hampshire USA
87 K3 **Concord** North Carolina USA
183 L6 **Concord Peak** *mountain* Tajikistan
107 H3 **Concórdia** Brazil
90 C4 **Concordia** Honduras
88 D4 **Concordia** Mexico
162 C5 **Concordia** South Africa
107 G4 **Concordia** Uruguay
59 I1 **Concordia Station (France and Italy)** *research station* Antarctica
74 K8 **Concrete** Washington USA
162 B2 **Conda** Angola
90 E2 **Condado** Cuba
219 J2 **Condamine** Qld Australia
126 F4 **Condat-en-Féniers** France
103 E5 **Conde** Brazil
128 B3 **Condeixa-a-Nova** Portugal
216 H6 **Condingup** WA Australia
127 J4 **Condino** Italy
219 H5 **Condobolin** NSW Australia
126 E5 **Condom** France
80 E4 **Condon** Oregon USA
104 B2 **Condor, Cordillera del** *range* Peru
218 F6 **Condoulpe** NSW Australia
130 B4 **Condove** Italy
218 D5 **Cone, Mount** SA Australia
130 E5 **Conero, Monte** *mountain* Italy
76 I7 **Confederation Lake** Ontario Canada
100 C3 **Confines** Colombia
215 K1 **Conflict Group** *islands* Papua New Guinea
126 E3 **Confolens** France
84 F1 **Confusion Range** Utah USA
107 G3 **Confuso** *watercourse* Paraguay
143 C3 **Cong** Ireland
194 E4 **Cong Tum Plateau** Vietnam
142 E3 **Congash** Highland Scotland UK
159 H5 **Congo** *country* Africa
159 G6 **Congo** *watercourse* Angola
159 H5 **Congo** *watercourse* Congo
160 C4 **Congo, Democratic Republic of** *country* Africa
160 D5 **Congo (Lualaba)** *watercourse* Democratic Republic of Congo
160 C3 **Congo Basin** Democratic Republic of Congo
54 F5 **Congo Canyon** *underwater feature* Atlantic Ocean
54 F5 **Congo Fan** *underwater feature* Atlantic Ocean
103 D8 **Congonhas** Brazil
75 R8 **Congress** Saskatchewan Canada
84 F3 **Congress** Arizona USA
89 H5 **Conhuas** Mexico
139 G1 **Coningsby** Lincolnshire England UK
214 B7 **Coniston** NT Australia
140 E2 **Coniston** Cumbria England UK
140 E2 **Coniston Water** *lake* England UK
219 J6 **Conjola** NSW Australia
215 H5 **Conjuboy** Qld Australia
75 P5 **Conklin** Alberta Canada
126 D2 **Conlie** France
140 C2 **Conlig** Ards Northern Ireland UK
77 Q6 **Conn** *watercourse* Quebec Canada
143 C2 **Conn, Lough** *lake* Ireland
143 D4 **Connagh** Ireland
83 K6 **Conneaut** Ohio USA
70 **Connecticut** *admin. area* USA
142 C4 **Connel** Argyll and Bute Scotland UK
143 C3 **Connemara** *region* Ireland
217 L2 **Conner, Mount** NT Australia
213 I3 **Conner, Mount** WA Australia
215 I6 **Connolly** Qld Australia
140 B2 **Connor** Ballymena Northern Ireland UK
215 J7 **Connors** *watercourse* Qld Australia
215 J6 **Connors Range** Qld Australia
132 B2 **Conop** Romania
100 E4 **Conorochite** *watercourse* Venezuela
103 D6 **Conquista** Brazil
80 J2 **Conrad** Montana USA
219 I7 **Conran, Cape** Vic. Australia
86 D5 **Conroe** Texas USA
86 D5 **Conroe, Lake** Texas USA
103 D8 **Conselheiro Lafaiete** Brazil
103 D7 **Conselheiro Pena** Brazil
109 12 **Conset Bay** Barbados
141 G2 **Consett** Durham England UK
101 F4 **Consolação** Brazil
90 D2 **Consolación del Sur** Cuba
132 F3 **Constanța** Romania
132 F3 **Constanța** *admin. area* Romania
155 H1 **Constantine** Algeria
72 D7 **Constantine, Cape** Alaska USA
103 B6 **Constantino, Serra do** *range* Brazil
106 C5 **Constitución** Chile
107 G4 **Constitución** Uruguay
105 F4 **Consuelo** Brazil
219 I1 **Consuelo Peak** Qld Australia
75 Q8 **Consul** Saskatchewan Canada
103 C7 **Contagem** Brazil
187 G7 **Contai** West Bengal India
104 C2 **Contamana** Peru
101 F4 **Contão** Brazil
103 D6 **Contas, Rio de** *watercourse* Brazil
131 H6 **Contessa, Punta della** *cape* Italy
142 D3 **Contin** Highland Scotland UK
80 F6 **Continental Lake** Nevada USA
85 I2 **Continental Reservoir** Colorado USA
89 I4 **Contoy, Isla** *island* Mexico
106 D6 **Contraalmirante Cordero** Argentina
108 A5 **Contraras, Isla** *island* Chile
128 F4 **Contreras, Embalse de** *lake* Spain
100 A3 **Contreras, Islas** *islands* Panama
106 C6 **Contulmo** Chile
104 B2 **Contumazá** Peru
131 F6 **Contursi Terme** Italy
72 H5 **Contwoyto Lake** Nunavut Canada
100 D4 **Conuco de Ciucar** Colombia
86 B6 **Converse** Texas USA
221 E6 **Conway Flat** New Zealand
86 E3 **Conway** Arkansas USA
87 L4 **Conway** South Carolina USA
215 J6 **Conway, Cape** Qld Australia
86 E3 **Conway, Lake** Arkansas USA
140 E3 **Conwy** Conwy Wales UK
138 D1 **Conwy** *admin. area* Wales UK
138 D1 **Conwy** *watercourse* Wales UK
219 H6 **Cooba** NSW Australia
218 B3 **Coober Pedy** SA Australia
219 H3 **Coocoran Lake** NSW Australia
214 C4 **Cooee Hill** NT Australia
214 B2 **Cooinda** NT Australia
214 G6 **Cooinda** Qld Australia
217 L5 **Cook** SA Australia
221 C6 **Cook** *watercourse* New Zealand
108 B6 **Cook, Bahía** *bay* Chile
164 6b **Cook, Calotte Glaciaire** *glacier* French Southern and Antarctic Lands
Cook, Mount *see* **Aoraki** New Zealand
109 5 **Cook, Punta** *cape* Isla de Pascua (Easter Island)
59 K2 **Cook Ice Shelf** Antarctica
72 D7 **Cook Inlet** Alaska USA
222 1a **Cook Island** Kiribati
222 1a **Cook Island Passage** *strait* Kiribati
220 1 **Cook Islands** *NZ territory* Pacific Ocean
221 F5 **Cook Strait** New Zealand
215 H3 **Cookabar, Mount** Qld Australia
216 E6 **Cooke, Mount** WA Australia
87 I2 **Cookeville** Tennessee USA
139 I3 **Cook's Green** Essex England UK
83 P4 **Cookshire** Quebec Canada
143 F2 **Cookstown** Cookstown Northern Ireland UK
143 F2 **Cookstown** *admin. area* Northern Ireland UK
215 H3 **Cooktown** Qld Australia
143 D4 **Cool Bridge** Ireland
218 H4 **Coolabah** NSW Australia
216 E4 **Cooladar Hill** WA Australia
218 G2 **Cooladdi** Qld Australia
219 I4 **Coolah** NSW Australia
219 H6 **Coolamon** NSW Australia
219 K3 **Coolangatta-Tweed Heads** NSW Australia
143 C5 **Coolavokig** Ireland
140 A3 **Coolayna Haggard** Ireland
219 I5 **Coolbaggie** NSW Australia
143 C5 **Coolcoulagata** Ireland
140 A3 **Coole** Ireland
216 G5 **Coolgardie** WA Australia
84 G4 **Coolidge** Arizona USA
216 D4 **Coolimba** WA Australia
143 C4 **Coolmeen** Ireland
143 F4 **Coolnacon** Ireland
140 B4 **Coolnahorna** Ireland
140 B4 **Coolrainey** Ireland
143 F4 **Coolroe** Ireland
218 E6 **Cooltong** SA Australia
216 D6 **Coolup** WA Australia
219 I7 **Cooma** NSW Australia
218 D6 **Coomandook** SA Australia
218 E5 **Coombah** NSW Australia
216 E5 **Coomberdale** WA Australia
219 I4 **Coombogolong** NSW Australia
219 K2 **Coomera** Qld Australia
143 C5 **Coomnacarrig Bridge** Ireland
82 E4 **Coon Rapids** Minnesota USA
219 I4 **Coonabarabran** NSW Australia
218 D6 **Coonalpyn** SA Australia
219 I4 **Coonamble** NSW Australia
216 H5 **Coonana** WA Australia
218 E7 **Coonawarra** SA Australia
218 B4 **Coondambo** SA Australia
140 A2 **Cooneen** Fermanagh Northern Ireland UK
212 E6 **Coongan** *watercourse* WA Australia
218 E2 **Coongie Lake** SA Australia
218 G2 **Coongoola** Qld Australia
187 D9 **Coonoor** Tamil Nadu India
218 E4 **Coontayunta, Lake** SA Australia
214 B1 **Cooper** *watercourse* NT Australia
218 D2 **Cooper** *watercourse* SA Australia
86 D4 **Cooper** Texas USA
217 H7 **Cooper Island** WA Australia
81 M6 **Cooper Lake** Wyoming USA
219 K4 **Coopernook** NSW Australia
87 M7 **Coopers Town** Bahamas
218 G1 **Coorajah** *watercourse* Qld Australia
219 K2 **Cooran** Qld Australia
216 D2 **Coordewandy** WA Australia
143 E4 **Coorlaghan** Ireland
140 A4 **Coornariska** Ireland
218 D6 **Coorong, The** *watercourse* SA Australia
216 E4 **Coorow** WA Australia
219 K2 **Cooroy** Qld Australia
80 C5 **Coos Bay** Oregon USA
80 C5 **Coos Bay** Oregon USA
218 G1 **Cootabynia** Qld Australia
219 I6 **Cootamundra** NSW Australia
219 K2 **Cootharaba, Lake** Qld Australia
104 B3 **Copa, Nevado** *mountain* Peru
106 D6 **Copahue, Volcán** *volcano* Chile
89 F5 **Copala** Mexico
105 E3 **Copallora** Bolivia
86 D2 **Copan Lake** Oklahoma USA
86 C6 **Copano Bay** Texas USA
129 F5 **Cope, Cabo** *cape* Spain
81 O8 **Copeland** Kansas USA
140 C2 **Copeland Island** *island* Down Northern Ireland UK
90 C4 **Copén** Honduras
Copenhagen *see* **København** Denmark
219 J3 **Copeton Dam** NSW Australia
106 D3 **Copiapó** Chile
106 D3 **Copiapó** *watercourse* Chile
106 D3 **Copiapo, Volcán** *volcano* Chile
142 F2 **Copinsay** *island* Scotland UK
139 G2 **Cople** Bedfordshire England UK
218 D4 **Copley** SA Australia
162 B2 **Coporolo** *watercourse* Angola
75 N2 **Copp Lake** Northwest Territories Canada
215 J6 **Coppabella** Qld Australia
140 A2 **Coppanagh Mills** Ireland
124 F5 **Copparo** Italy
138 C4 **Coppathorne** Cornwall England UK
82 J2 **Coppell** Ontario Canada
82 H3 **Copper Harbor** Michigan USA
218 B2 **Copper Hill** SA Australia
80 E2 **Copper Mountain** British Columbia Canada
86 C5 **Copperas Cove** Texas USA
162 E2 **Copperbelt** *admin. area* Zambia
72 H5 **Coppermine** *watercourse* Nunavut Canada
162 D5 **Copperton** South Africa
219 R11 **Copping** Tas. Australia
138 D4 **Copplestone** Devon England UK
132 D2 **Copşa Mică** Romania
180 E2 **Coqen Zangbo** *watercourse* Xizang Zizhiqu China
105 G4 **Coqueiro** Brazil
141 G1 **Coquet** *watercourse* England UK
141 G1 **Coquet Island** England UK
80 C5 **Coquille** Oregon USA
106 D4 **Coquimbo** Chile
106 D4 **Coquimbo** *admin. area* Chile
74 J8 **Coquitlam** British Columbia Canada
103 C7 **Coração de Jesus** Brazil
91 F3 **Corail** Haiti
219 K3 **Coraki** NSW Australia
77 O7 **Coral** Ontario Canada
216 C1 **Coral Bay** WA Australia
197 H1 **Coral Bay** Philippines
73 K6 **Coral Harbour** Nunavut Canada
52 **Coral Sea** Oceania
52 K9 **Coral Sea Basin** *underwater feature* Coral Sea
215 J4 **Coral Sea Islands** *Australian territory* Pacific Ocean
87 K7 **Coral Springs** Florida USA
131 C6 **Coralli, Col de** *pass* Corsica France
82 F6 **Coralville** Iowa USA
218 F8 **Corangamite, Lake** Vic. Australia
101 G3 **Corantijn** *watercourse* Suriname
131 G6 **Corato** Italy
130 E5 **Corbara, Lago di** *lake* Italy
103 A9 **Corbélia** Brazil
76 I1 **Corbett Inlet** Nunavut Canada
215 H2 **Corbett Reef** Qld Australia
126 F2 **Corbie** France
77 P5 **Corbin** *watercourse* Quebec Canada
139 G2 **Corby** Northamptonshire England UK
84 C2 **Corcoran** California USA
140 B4 **Corcoran's** Ireland
108 B3 **Corcovado, Bahía de** *bay* Chile
143 C2 **Corcullin** Ireland
87 J5 **Cordele** Georgia USA
87 I2 **Cordell Hull Reservoir** Tennessee USA
126 E4 **Cordes** France
195 I5 **Cordilleras Range** Philippines
218 E2 **Cordillo Downs** SA Australia
106 E4 **Córdoba** Argentina
106 F4 **Córdoba** *admin. area* Argentina
100 C2 **Córdoba** Colombia
100 C2 **Córdoba** *admin. area* Colombia
89 F5 **Córdoba** Mexico
128 D5 **Córdoba** Spain
106 E4 **Córdoba, Sierra de** *mountain* Argentina
142 C5 **Cordon** North Ayrshire Scotland UK
72 E6 **Cordova** Alaska USA
85 J3 **Cordova** New Mexico USA
102 D3 **Coreaú** Brazil
138 E2 **Coreley** Shropshire England UK
128 F2 **Corella** Spain
214 C5 **Corella Lake** NT Australia
102 E4 **Coremas** Brazil
138 D4 **Corfe** Somerset England UK
139 E4 **Corfe Castle** Dorset England UK
215 G6 **Corfield** Qld Australia
Corfu *see* **Kerkyra** Greece
130 E5 **Corinaldo** Italy
219 H5 **Corinella** NSW Australia
219 Q10 **Corinna** Tas. Australia
Corinth *see* **Korinthos** Greece
109 10a **Corinth** Grenada
86 G3 **Corinth** Mississippi USA
86 C4 **Corinth** Texas USA
210 inset **Corinthian Bay** Heard Island Australia
103 C7 **Corinto** Brazil
100 C4 **Corinto** Colombia
90 C4 **Corinto** El Salvador
90 B4 **Corinto** Honduras
215 K7 **Corio Bay** Qld Australia
104 E5 **Coripata** Bolivia
159 F4 **Corisco, Baie de** *bay* Gabon
128 B2 **Coristanco** Spain
143 D5 **Cork** Ireland
143 D5 **Cork** *admin. area* Ireland
143 E2 **Corlea** Ireland
131 E8 **Corleone** Italy
133 E5 **Çorlu** Turkey
79 J8 **Cormack** Newfoundland and Labrador Canada
74 K2 **Cormack Lake** Northwest Territories Canada
124 C4 **Cormatin** France
127 K4 **Cormòns** Italy
76 E5 **Cormorant Lake** Manitoba Canada
124 C4 **Cormoz** France
85 M3 **Corn** Oklahoma USA
124 D4 **Cornaux** Switzerland
132 C3 **Cornea** Romania
82 G6 **Cornell** Illinois USA
82 F4 **Cornell** Wisconsin USA
129 H3 **Cornellà** Spain
79 J8 **Corner Brook** Newfoundland and Labrador Canada
50 N6 **Corner Seamounts** *underwater feature* Atlantic Ocean
86 H3 **Cornersville** Tennessee USA
130 D5 **Cornia** *watercourse* Italy
127 J4 **Cornicello** *mountain* Italy
124 D4 **Cornimont** France
86 F2 **Corning** Arkansas USA
80 D7 **Corning** California USA
83 M5 **Corning** New York USA

213 I6 **Cornish, Mount** WA Australia
108 A4 **Cornish, Seno** *bay* Chile
127 I5 **Corno di Becco, Punta** *cape* Corsica France
142 F2 **Cornquoy** Orkney Islands Scotland UK
132 D3 **Cornu de Sus** Romania
132 E2 **Cornu Luncii** Romania
85 J5 **Cornudas** Texas USA
126 F5 **Cornus** France
83 N4 **Cornwall** Ontario Canada
138 C4 **Cornwall** *admin. area* England UK
73 J3 **Cornwall Island** Nunavut Canada
73 J3 **Cornwallis Island** Nunavut Canada
218 C6 **Corny Point** SA Australia
100 D2 **Coro** Venezuela
100 D2 **Coro, Golfete de** *bay* Venezuela
102 C4 **Coroatá** Brazil
218 H6 **Corobimilla** NSW Australia
104 E5 **Coroico** Bolivia
121 N2 **Corokjávri** *lake* Norway
103 C7 **Coromandel** Brazil
187 E9 **Coromandel Coast** Tamil Nadu India
220 F3 **Coromandel Peninsula** New Zealand
220 F3 **Coromandel Range** New Zealand
195 I5 **Coron** Philippines
195 I4 **Coron** *island* Philippines
84 D4 **Corona** California USA
85 J3 **Corona** New Mexico USA
75 S8 **Coronach** Saskatchewan Canada
84 D4 **Coronado** California USA
90 D5 **Coronado, Bahía de** *bay* Costa Rica
108 A2 **Coronados, Golfo** *bay* Chile
75 P6 **Coronation** Alberta Canada
72 H5 **Coronation Gulf** Nunavut Canada
213 H3 **Coronation Islands** WA Australia
106 C6 **Coronel** Chile
107 G3 **Coronel Oviedo** Paraguay
106 F6 **Coronel Suárez** Argentina
107 G6 **Coronel Vidal** Argentina
103 A9 **Coronel Vivida** Brazil
218 H4 **Coronga Peak** NSW Australia
101 G3 **Coronie** *admin. area* Suriname
104 C4 **Coropuna, Nevado** *mountain* Peru
90 B3 **Corozal** Belize
101 E3 **Corozal** Venezuela
109 9 **Corozal Point** *cape* Trinidad and Tobago
142 C4 **Corpach** Highland Scotland UK
108 C4 **Corpen** Argentina
127 G4 **Corps** France
126 D3 **Corps-Nuds** France
86 C7 **Corpus Christi** Texas USA
86 C6 **Corpus Christi, Lake** Texas USA
86 C7 **Corpus Christi Bay** Texas USA
108 B2 **Corral** Chile
164 3d **Corralejo** Canary Islands
89 F5 **Corralero, Laguna** *lake* Mexico
85 I3 **Corrales** New Mexico USA
90 D2 **Corralillo** Cuba
105 F5 **Corralones, Serranía Los** *range* Bolivia
142 C3 **Corran** Highland Scotland UK
143 D2 **Corratimore** Ireland
143 D3 **Corraun** Ireland
143 C3 **Corraun Peninsula** Ireland
127 H3 **Corre** France
90 D5 **Corredor** Costa Rica
195 I4 **Corregidor** *island* Philippines
105 G5 **Corrego Taxo** *watercourse* Brazil
103 A7 **Correntes** *watercourse* Brazil
105 E3 **Correnteza** Bolivia
131 F8 **Correnti, Capo delle** *cape* Italy
103 C6 **Correntina** Brazil
85 I3 **Correo** New Mexico USA
126 E4 **Corrèze** *watercourse* France
143 C3 **Corrib, Lough** *lake* Ireland
142 C5 **Corrie** North Ayrshire Scotland UK
142 C5 **Corriecravie** North Ayrshire Scotland UK
142 D2 **Corriekinloch** Highland Scotland UK
107 G3 **Corrientes** Argentina
107 G4 **Corrientes** *admin. area* Argentina
107 G4 **Corrientes** *watercourse* Argentina
104 C1 **Corrientes** *watercourse* Peru
100 B3 **Corrientes, Cabo** *cape* Colombia
90 C2 **Corrientes, Cabo** *cape* Cuba
88 D4 **Corrientes, Cabo** *cape* Mexico
86 D5 **Corrigan** Texas USA
216 E6 **Corrigin** WA Australia
138 D2 **Corris** Gwynedd Wales UK
143 C4 **Corrofin** Ireland
128 B4 **Corroios** Portugal
142 D4 **Corrour Sta** Highland Scotland UK
128 B2 **Corrubedo, Cabo** *cape* Spain
142 C3 **Corry** Highland Scotland UK
129 K2 **Corse** *admin. area* Corsica France
130 C5 **Corse, Cap** *cape* France
140 C2 **Corsewall** Dumfries and Galloway Scotland UK
139 E3 **Corsham** Wiltshire England UK
Corsica *see* **Corse**
86 C4 **Corsicana** Texas USA
106 D6 **Cortaderas** Argentina
88 E4 **Cortazar** Mexico
127 I5 **Corte** Corsica France
128 C5 **Cortegana** Spain
128 D5 **Cortes de la Frontera** Spain
81 K8 **Cortez** Colorado USA
80 G6 **Cortez Mountains** Nevada USA
130 E3 **Cortina d'Ampezzo** Italy
83 M5 **Cortland** New York USA
140 B2 **Cortober** Ireland
139 I2 **Corton** Suffolk England UK
130 D5 **Cortona** Italy
140 B3 **Cortown** Ireland
128 B4 **Coruche** Portugal
136 E5 **Çorum** Turkey
136 E5 **Çorum** *admin. area* Turkey
103 B7 **Corumbá** *watercourse* Brazil
103 E7 **Corumbaú, Ponta** *cape* Brazil
128 C5 **Corumbel Bajo, Embalse de** *lake* Spain
102 E5 **Coruripe** Brazil
80 D4 **Corvallis** Oregon USA
128 E2 **Corvera** Spain
77 R6 **Corvette, Lac de la** *lake* Quebec Canada
218 B5 **Corvisart Bay** SA Australia
164 1 **Corvo** *island* Azores
131 F8 **Corvo, Punta del** *cape* Italy
138 D2 **Corwen** Denbighshire Wales UK
82 E6 **Corydon** Iowa USA
82 H8 **Corydon** Kentucky USA
88 D3 **Cosalá** Mexico
104 C2 **Cosca** Peru
83 K6 **Coshocton** Ohio USA
104 E4 **Cosincho** Bolivia
88 E4 **Cosío** Mexico
216 H3 **Cosmo Newbery** WA Australia
164 9 **Cosmoledo Islands** Seychelles
59 C2 **Cosmonaut Sea** Southern Ocean
124 E5 **Cossato** Italy
212 D6 **Cossigny, Cape** WA Australia
126 E3 **Cosson** *watercourse* France
100 E2 **Costa, Cordillera de la** *range* Venezuela
101 I3 **Costa, Ponta do** *cape* Brazil
128 D5 **Costa del Sol,** *region* Spain
129 H3 **Costa Dorada** *region* Spain
84 D4 **Costa Mesa** California USA
107 H2 **Costa Rica** Brazil
90 D5 **Costa Rica** *country* Central America
88 D3 **Costa Rica** Mexico
88 B2 **Costa Rica** Mexico
132 E2 **Costeşti** Romania
75 S4 **Costigan Lake** Saskatchewan Canada
132 F4 **Costineşti** Romania
195 J6 **Cotabato** Philippines
100 B4 **Cotacachi** Ecuador
104 E5 **Cotacajes** *watercourse* Bolivia
103 D7 **Cotaxé** *watercourse* Brazil
86 F6 **Cote Blanch Bay** Louisiana USA
126 E1 **Côte d'Albâtre** *region* France
126 C2 **Côte du Granit Rose** *region* France
132 D3 **Coteana** Romania
81 P4 **Coteau des Prairies** *valley* South Dakota USA
81 O3 **Coteau du Missouri** *valley* North Dakota USA
75 R7 **Coteau Hills** Saskatchewan Canada
91 F3 **Côtes-de-Fer** Haiti
138 C3 **Cothi** *watercourse* Wales UK
164 3d **Cotillo** Canary Islands
132 F2 **Cotiujeni** Moldova
158 E3 **Cotonou** Benin
100 B5 **Cotopaxi** *volcano* Ecuador
132 E1 **Cotova** Moldova
105 G3 **Cotriguaçu** Brazil
139 F3 **Cotswold Hills** England UK
80 D5 **Cottage Grove** Oregon USA
131 E5 **Cottanello** Italy
125 H2 **Cottbus** Germany
141 F2 **Cotterdale** North Yorkshire England UK
142 E4 **Cotterton** Perth and Kinross Scotland UK
139 G2 **Cottesmore** Rutland England UK
109 19 **Cotton Ground** St Kitts and Nevis
214 D1 **Cotton Island** NT Australia
214 E7 **Cottonbush** *watercourse* Qld Australia
80 G3 **Cottonwood** Idaho USA
82 C7 **Cottonwood** *watercourse* Kansas USA
85 N1 **Cottonwood Falls** Kansas USA
91 G3 **Cotuí** Dominican Republic
86 B6 **Cotulla** Texas USA
126 D4 **Coubre, Pointe de la** *cape* France
83 P3 **Coudres, Île aux** *island* Quebec Canada
126 F5 **Couiza** France
142 B5 **Coul Point** Scotland UK
142 C3 **Coulags** Highland Scotland UK
80 F3 **Coulee Dam** Washington USA
126 F3 **Couleuvre** France
59 L2 **Coulman Island** Antarctica
127 G3 **Coulmier-le-Sec** France
212 G4 **Coulomb Point** WA Australia
127 G5 **Coulon** *watercourse* France
83 M3 **Coulonge** *watercourse* Quebec Canada
218 B6 **Coulta** SA Australia
140 B3 **Coultry** Ireland
80 G4 **Council** Idaho USA
81 R6 **Council Bluffs** Iowa USA
81 Q7 **Council Grove** Kansas USA
138 E2 **Cound** Shropshire England UK
139 F2 **Countesthorpe** Leicester England UK
79 J9 **Coupé, Cap** *cape* St Pierre and Miquelon
142 C5 **Cour** Argyll and Bute Scotland UK
101 G3 **Courantyne** *watercourse* Guyana
164 6b **Courbet, Péninsule** *peninsula* French Southern and Antarctic Lands
124 D5 **Courchevel** France
126 F4 **Courpière** France
221 9 **Courrejolles Point** Campbell Island New Zealand
124 C4 **Cours** France
127 G4 **Courthézon** France
140 B4 **Courthoyle** Ireland
87 M2 **Courtland** Virginia USA
143 D5 **Courtmacsherry Bay** Ireland
215 H6 **Courtney, Mount** Qld Australia
126 E2 **Courtomer** France
143 F4 **Courtown** Ireland
86 E4 **Coushatta** Louisiana USA
126 D2 **Coutances** France
126 D2 **Couterne** France
75 P8 **Coutts** Alberta Canada
216 C2 **Couture, Cape** WA Australia
77 R2 **Couture, Lac** *lake* Quebec Canada
109 9 **Couva** Trinidad and Tobago
109 9 **Couva-Tabaquite/Talparo** Trinidad and Tobago
124 C2 **Couvin** Belgium
132 E3 **Covasna** Romania
132 D3 **Covasna** *admin. area* Romania
142 C3 **Cove** Highland Scotland UK
139 I2 **Cove Bottom** Suffolk England UK
139 I2 **Covehithe** Suffolk England UK
139 F2 **Coventry** West Midlands England UK
138 B4 **Coverack** Cornwall England UK
128 C3 **Covilhã** Portugal
87 J4 **Covington** Georgia USA
109 11a **Cow and Calves** *cape* St Vincent and the Grenadines
141 F2 **Cow Green Reservoir** England UK
79 J8 **Cow Head** Newfoundland and Labrador Canada
219 H5 **Cowal, Lake** NSW Australia
216 H5 **Cowan, Lake** WA Australia
218 E6 **Cowangie** Vic. Australia
216 D6 **Cowaramup** WA Australia
218 D2 **Cowarie** SA Australia
216 H5 **Cowarna Downs** WA Australia
141 H2 **Cowbar Nab** *cape* England UK
139 G2 **Cowbit** Lincolnshire England UK
138 D3 **Cowbridge** Vale of Glamorgan Wales UK
216 E5 **Cowcowing Lake** WA Australia
82 G7 **Cowden** Illinois USA
218 C5 **Cowell** SA Australia
218 G8 **Cowes** Vic. Australia
139 F4 **Cowes** Isle of Wight England UK
141 F2 **Cowgill** Cumbria England UK
142 E5 **Cowgill** South Lanarkshire Scotland UK
80 C2 **Cowichan Lake** British Columbia Canada
218 G2 **Cowley** Qld Australia
219 I5 **Cowra** NSW Australia
218 H8 **Cowwarr** Vic. Australia
214 C3 **Cox** *watercourse* NT Australia
126 E5 **Cox** France
217 I2 **Cox, Mount** WA Australia
107 H4 **Coxilha Grande** *region* Brazil
105 H5 **Coxim** Brazil
79 I7 **Coxipi** *watercourse* Quebec Canada
79 I7 **Coxipi, Lac** *lake* Quebec Canada
181 G5 **Cox's Bazar** Bangladesh
108 C5 **Coy Aike** Argentina
106 D2 **Coya Sur** Chile
158 B3 **Coyah** Guinea
88 D2 **Coyame** Mexico
80 E1 **Coyle** British Columbia Canada
142 D5 **Coylton** Ayrshire Scotland UK
85 J4 **Coyote** New Mexico USA
85 H2 **Coyote** *watercourse* New Mexico USA
84 D3 **Coyote Lake** California USA
80 F5 **Coyote Lake** Oregon USA
84 E4 **Coyote Wells** California USA
88 E5 **Coyuca de Benítez** Mexico
81 P6 **Cozad** Nebraska USA
126 D4 **Cozes** France
89 I4 **Cozumel** Mexico
90 C2 **Cozumel, Isla** *island* Mexico
91 J4 **Crab Hill** Barbados
214 G1 **Crab Island** Qld Australia
138 C4 **Crackington Haven** Cornwall England UK
141 F2 **Cracoe** North Yorkshire England UK
219 Q10 **Cradle Mountain** Tas. Australia
218 D5 **Cradock** SA Australia
162 E6 **Cradock** South Africa
142 E2 **Craggie** Highland Scotland UK
132 D2 **Crăieşti** Romania
142 C3 **Craig** Highland Scotland UK
140 D1 **Craig** South Ayrshire Scotland UK
74 E5 **Craig** Alaska USA
81 L6 **Craig** Colorado USA
138 D2 **Craig Goch Reservoir** Wales UK
140 B2 **Craigavole** Coleraine Northern Ireland UK
140 B2 **Craigavon** Armagh Northern Ireland UK
143 F2 **Craigavon** *admin. area* Northern Ireland UK
140 D1 **Craigdarroch** East Ayrshire Scotland UK
218 G7 **Craigieburn** Vic. Australia
142 E4 **Craignavar** Perth and Kinross Scotland UK
140 B2 **Craigs Middle** Ballymoney Northern Ireland UK
142 E2 **Craigtown** Highland Scotland UK
75 S7 **Craik** Saskatchewan Canada
142 F3 **Craik** Aberdeenshire Scotland UK
142 F4 **Crail** Fife Scotland UK
124 F3 **Crailsheim** Germany
132 C3 **Craiova** Romania
141 G1 **Cramlington** Northumberland England UK
142 E5 **Cramond** City of Edinburgh Scotland UK
143 E2 **Cranagh** Strabane Northern Ireland UK
74 G5 **Cranberry Junction** British Columbia Canada
218 G8 **Cranbourne** Vic. Australia
219 S11 **Cranbrook** Tas. Australia
216 E7 **Cranbrook** WA Australia
75 N8 **Cranbrook** British Columbia Canada
82 G4 **Crandon** Wisconsin USA
82 E8 **Crane** Missouri USA
85 K5 **Crane** Texas USA
81 K1 **Crane Lake** Saskatchewan Canada
82 E2 **Crane Lake** Minnesota USA
139 G2 **Cranfield** Bedfordshire England UK
143 G2 **Cranfield Point** Northern Ireland UK
139 G3 **Cranleigh** Surrey England UK
126 D3 **Craon** France
132 F3 **Crapina, Lacul** *lake* Ukraine
59 L2 **Crary Bank** *underwater feature* Ross Sea
59 M1 **Crary Ice Rise** Antarctica
59 P1 **Crary Mountains** Antarctica
142 D2 **Crask Inn** Highland Scotland UK
132 C2 **Crasna** Romania
80 D5 **Crater Lake** Oregon USA
199 H5 **Crater Mountain** Papua New Guinea
199 J5 **Crater Point** Papua New Guinea
102 D4 **Crateús** Brazil
142 E3 **Crathie** Aberdeenshire Scotland UK
131 G7 **Crati** *watercourse* Italy
102 E4 **Crato** Brazil
77 Q5 **Craven, Lac** *lake* Quebec Canada
100 D3 **Cravo Norte** Colombia
100 D3 **Cravo Sur** *watercourse* Colombia
142 E5 **Crawford** South Lanarkshire Scotland UK
86 G4 **Crawford** Mississippi USA
81 N5 **Crawford** Nebraska USA
216 H4 **Crawford, Mount** WA Australia
142 E5 **Crawfordjohn** South Lanarkshire Scotland UK
82 H6 **Crawfordsville** Indiana USA
142 E5 **Crawick** Dumfries and Galloway Scotland UK
139 G3 **Crawley** West Sussex England UK
138 D3 **Cray** Powys Wales UK
141 G2 **Crayke** North Yorkshire England UK
81 J3 **Crazy Mountains** Montana USA
138 D4 **Creacombe** Devon England UK
124 B3 **Crécy** France
139 I4 **Crécy-en-Ponthieu** France
138 E2 **Credenhill** Herefordshire England UK
138 D4 **Crediton** Devon England UK
72 I7 **Cree** *watercourse* Saskatchewan Canada
75 R4 **Cree Lake** Saskatchewan Canada
75 R4 **Cree Lake** Saskatchewan Canada
81 L8 **Creede** Colorado USA
88 D3 **Creel** Mexico
75 T8 **Creelman** Saskatchewan Canada
143 E1 **Creeslough** Ireland
142 D6 **Creetown** Dumfries and Galloway Scotland UK
140 B2 **Creeve** Ireland
140 A2 **Creevelea** Ireland
143 D2 **Cregg** Ireland
140 A1 **Creggan** Londonderry Northern Ireland UK
143 C3 **Cregganbaun** Ireland
126 F2 **Creil** France
130 C4 **Crema** Italy
127 G4 **Crémieu** France
130 D4 **Cremona** Italy
86 G5 **Creola** Alabama USA
127 K3 **Crep Nudo** *mountain* Italy
132 B3 **Crepaja** Serbia
105 G2 **Crepori** *watercourse* Brazil
125 H5 **Cres** Croatia
80 D2 **Crescent, Lake** Washington USA
80 C6 **Crescent City** California USA
195 F3 **Crescent Group** *islands* Paracel Islands
87 K6 **Crescent Lake** Florida USA
80 E5 **Crescent Lake** Oregon USA
124 B2 **Crespin** France
106 F5 **Crespo** Argentina
126 E4 **Cressensac** France
141 G1 **Cresswell** Northumberland England UK
218 F8 **Cressy** Vic. Australia
127 G4 **Crest** France
53 U5 **Crest Seamount** *underwater feature* Pacific Ocean
74 M8 **Creston** British Columbia Canada
80 F3 **Creston** Washington USA
87 H5 **Crestview** Florida USA
214 D5 **Creswell** *watercourse* NT Australia
80 D5 **Creswell** Oregon USA
Crete *see* **Kriti** Greece
Crete, Sea of *see* **Kritiko Pelago** Europe
199 I5 **Cretin, Cape** Papua New Guinea
126 F5 **Creus, Cap de** *cape* Spain
126 E3 **Creuse** *watercourse* France
124 F3 **Creußen** Germany
138 E1 **Crewe** Cheshire England UK
83 L8 **Crewe** Virginia USA
138 E4 **Crewkerne** Somerset England UK
138 C2 **Criccieth** Gwynedd Wales UK
107 I4 **Criciúma** Brazil
138 D2 **Crickadarn** Powys Wales UK
138 D3 **Crickhowell** Powys Wales UK
142 E4 **Crieff** Perth and Kinross Scotland UK
126 E1 **Criel-Plage** France
139 I4 **Criel-sur-mer** France
139 I5 **Crillon** France
82 E2 **Crilly** Ontario Canada
142 G3 **Crimond** Aberdeenshire Scotland UK
139 H2 **Crimplesham** Norfolk England UK
142 C4 **Crinan** Argyll and Bute Scotland UK
140 B1 **Crindle** Limavady Northern Ireland UK
81 M7 **Cripple Creek** Colorado USA
132 C2 **Crişcior** Romania
83 N8 **Crisfield** Maryland USA
159 G4 **Cristal, Monts de** *range* Gabon
103 C7 **Cristalina** Brazil
100 A3 **Cristo, Punta** *cape* Panama
128 D3 **Cristóbal** Spain
109 4 **Cristóbal, Punta** *cape* Archipiélago de Colón (Galapagos Islands)
100 C2 **Cristóbal Colón, Pico** *mountain* Colombia
132 C2 **Crişul Alb** *watercourse* Romania
132 C2 **Crişul Negru** *watercourse* Romania
132 C3 **Crivina** Romania
124 F1 **Crivitz** Germany
103 B6 **Crixás** Brazil
103 B6 **Crixás Açu** *watercourse* Brazil
130. G5 **Crkvice** Croatia
133 B5 **Crna** *watercourse* Macedonia
127 L3 **Črna** Slovenia
132 B4 **Crna Gora** *region* Serbia
132 A3 **Crnča** Serbia
133 B5 **Crni Drim** *watercourse* Macedonia
143 B3 **Croaghnakeela Island** Ireland
130 **Croatia** *country* Europe
124 F4 **Croce, Monte** *mountain* Italy
197 G2 **Crocker, Banjaran** *range* Malaysia
214 C1 **Crocodile Islands Group** NT Australia
82 H8 **Crofton** Kentucky USA
142 C4 **Croggan** Highland Scotland UK
143 D2 **Crohy Head** *cape* Ireland
142 D3 **Croick** Highland Scotland UK
126 C3 **Croisic, Pointe de** *cape* France
214 B1 **Croker, Cape** NT Australia
83 K4 **Croker, Cape** Ontario Canada
214 B1 **Croker Island** NT Australia
215 G2 **Croll, Mount** Qld Australia
124 C5 **Crolles** France
143 C4 **Cromane** Ireland
76 H4 **Cromarty** Manitoba Canada
142 D3 **Cromarty** Highland Scotland UK
139 I2 **Cromer** Norfolk England UK
105 I5 **Cromínia** Brazil
109 15 **Crompton Point** *cape* Dominica
142 D4 **Cromra** Highland Scotland UK
140 B3 **Crone** Ireland
141 G2 **Crook** Durham England UK
81 N6 **Crook** Colorado USA
214 G5 **Crooked** *watercourse* Qld Australia
91 F2 **Crooked Island Passage** Bahamas
79 J8 **Crooked Lake** Newfoundland and Labrador Canada
140 A3 **Crookedwood** Ireland
78 C1 **Crooks Inlet** Nunavut Canada
219 I6 **Crookwell** NSW Australia
143 D4 **Croom** Ireland
131 G7 **Cropalati** Italy
141 H2 **Cropton** North Yorkshire England UK
214 G3 **Crosbie** *watercourse* Qld Australia
142 B2 **Crosbost** Na h-Eileanan Siar Scotland UK
140 E2 **Crosby** Cumbria England UK
140 E3 **Crosby** Merseyside England UK
140 E2 **Crosby Villa** Cumbria England UK
85 L4 **Crosbyton** Texas USA
159 F3 **Cross** *watercourse* Nigeria
87 J6 **Cross City** Florida USA
141 F2 **Cross Fell** *mountain* England UK
87 K3 **Cross Hill** South Carolina USA
76 G5 **Cross Lake** Manitoba Canada
86 D4 **Cross Lake** Louisiana USA
83 Q3 **Cross Lake** Maine USA
138 B4 **Cross Lanes** Cornwall England UK
159 F3 **Cross River** *admin. area* Nigeria
74 C3 **Cross Sound** Alaska USA
142 C5 **Crossaig** Argyll and Bute Scotland UK
142 B4 **Crossapolx** Highland Scotland UK
75 N7 **Crossfield** Alberta Canada
140 C2 **Crossgar** Down Northern Ireland UK
143 D5 **Crosshaven** Ireland
140 B4 **Crosslaghroe** Ireland
140 E1 **Crosslee** Scottish Borders Scotland UK
216 E6 **Crossman** WA Australia
142 F3 **Crossroads** Aberdeenshire Scotland UK
78 F5 **Crossroads Lake** Newfoundland and Labrador Canada
86 A4 **Croton** *watercourse* Texas USA
131 G7 **Crotone** Italy
139 F3 **Croughton** Northamptonshire England UK
139 H3 **Crowborough** East Sussex England UK
86 D3 **Crowder** Oklahoma USA
219 K4 **Crowdy Head** NSW Australia
86 B4 **Crowell** Texas USA
80 I1 **Crowfoot** Alberta Canada
139 G2 **Crowland** Lincolnshire England UK
141 H3 **Crowle** North Lincolnshire England UK
86 E5 **Crowley** Louisiana USA
84 C2 **Crowley, Lake** California USA
199 H5 **Crown Island** Papua New Guinea
219 K2 **Crows Nest** Qld Australia
219 I6 **Crowther** NSW Australia
142 D3 **Croy** Highland Scotland UK
164 6b **Croy, Île de** *island* French Southern and Antarctic Lands
214 G5 **Croydon** Qld Australia
139 G3 **Croydon** Greater London England UK
164 6 **Crozet, Îles** *islands* French Southern and Antarctic Lands
54 J9 **Crozet Basin** *underwater feature* Southern Ocean
54 J9 **Crozet Plateau** *underwater feature* Southern Ocean
72 G3 **Crozier Channel** Northwest Territories Canada
126 B2 **Crozon** France
132 D2 **Crucea** Romania
101 E2 **Crucero Pardillal** Venezuela
100 B3 **Cruces, Punta** *cape* Colombia
142 G3 **Cruden Bay** Aberdeenshire Scotland UK
142 D6 **Cruggleton** Dumfries and Galloway Scotland UK
89 F3 **Cruillas** Mexico
50 P6 **Cruiser Seamount** *underwater feature* Atlantic Ocean
140 B3 **Cruisetown** Ireland
80 F5 **Crump Lake** Oregon USA
138 C3 **Crundale** Pembrokeshire Wales UK
143 D4 **Crusheen** Ireland
219 I4 **Crusher** NSW Australia
143 E4 **Crutt** Ireland
102 D3 **Cruz** Brazil
108 D3 **Cruz, Bahía** *bay* Argentina
104 A2 **Cruz, Bahía La** *bay* Peru
90 E3 **Cruz, Cabo** *cape* Cuba
106 F5 **Cruz Alta** Argentina
107 H4 **Cruz Alta** Brazil
109 21 **Cruz Bay** US Virgin Islands
106 E4 **Cruz del Eje** Argentina
104 D4 **Cruz Pampa** Peru
103 C8 **Cruzeiro** Brazil
104 C2 **Cruzeiro do Sul** Brazil
103 C8 **Cruzília** Brazil
74 G3 **Cry Lake** British Columbia Canada
74 K5 **Crysdale, Mount** British Columbia Canada
87 J6 **Crystal Bay** Florida USA
218 D5 **Crystal Brook** SA Australia
86 B6 **Crystal City** Texas USA
82 G3 **Crystal Falls** Michigan USA
82 H4 **Crystal Lake** Michigan USA
87 J6 **Crystal River** Florida USA
130 H3 **Csávoly** Hungary
125 K3 **Cserehát** *region* Hungary
125 I4 **Csokonyavisonta** Hungary
125 K4 **Csongrád** Hungary
125 K4 **Csongrád** *admin. area* Hungary
125 I4 **Csót** Hungary
194 F4 **Cu Lao Re** *island* Vietnam
194 F5 **Cu Lao Thu** *island* Vietnam
100 E2 **Cúa** Venezuela
196 E1 **Cua Lon** *watercourse* Vietnam
108 C3 **Cuadrada, Sierra** *range* Argentina
104 E6 **Cuadrilla Tres** Bolivia
128 D2 **Cuadros** Spain
142 C3 **Cuaig** Highland Scotland UK
163 G2 **Cuamba** Mozambique
162 D3 **Cuando** *watercourse* Angola
162 C3 **Cuando Cubango** *admin. area* Angola
162 C3 **Cuangar** Angola
160 B5 **Cuango** Angola
160 B5 **Cuango** *watercourse* Angola
160 B5 **Cuango** *watercourse* Democratic Republic of Congo
162 C2 **Cuanza** Angola
162 B1 **Cuanza** *watercourse* Angola
162 B1 **Cuanza Norte** *admin. area* Angola
162 C2 **Cuanza Sul** *admin. area* Angola
100 E3 **Cuao, Macizo del** *range* Venezuela
101 E3 **Cuao, Río** *watercourse* Venezuela
100 E3 **Cuao, Serranía de** *range* Venezuela
107 G4 **Cuaro** *watercourse* Uruguay
195 G5 **Cuarteron Reef** Spratly Islands
85 K7 **Cuates de Australia** Mexico
162 C3 **Cuatir** *watercourse* Angola
85 K7 **Cuatrociénegas de Carranza** Mexico
88 D2 **Cuauhtémoc** Mexico
89 F5 **Cuautitlán** Mexico
89 F5 **Cuautla** Mexico
90 E2 **Cuba** *country* Caribbean
128 C4 **Cuba** Portugal
82 F7 **Cuba** Missouri USA
85 I2 **Cuba** New Mexico USA
83 L5 **Cuba** New York USA
101 E2 **Cubagua, Isla** *island* Venezuela
162 B2 **Cubal** Angola
162 B3 **Cubal** *watercourse* Angola
160 B6 **Cubango** *watercourse* Angola
100 C3 **Cubará** Colombia
103 C8 **Cubatão** Brazil
103 B6 **Cubatão, Serra do** *range* Brazil
128 E2 **Cubo de Bureba** Spain
132 F2 **Cubolta** Moldova
108 A3 **Cucao, Bahía** *bay* Chile
131 F6 **Cucchiara, Punta di** *cape* Italy
162 C2 **Cuchi** Angola
162 C3 **Cuchi** *watercourse* Angola
106 E6 **Cuchillo Có** Argentina
85 J6 **Cuchillo Pardo** Mexico
90 B4 **Cuchumatanes, Sierra los** *range* Guatemala
109 12 **Cuckold Point** *cape* Barbados
100 E4 **Cucui** Venezuela
88 C2 **Cucurpé** Mexico
100 B3 **Cucurrupí** Colombia
100 C3 **Cúcuta** Colombia
219 I5 **Cudal** NSW Australia
109 1a **Cudarebe** *cape* Aruba
140 A4 **Cuddagh** Ireland
187 E9 **Cuddalore** Tamil Nadu India
187 E8 **Cuddapah** Andhra Pradesh India
218 E1 **Cuddapan, Lake** Qld Australia
214 G5 **Cudgee** *watercourse* Qld Australia
219 H7 **Cudgewa, Mount** Vic. Australia
126 A5 **Cudillero** Spain
109 17 **Cudjoe Head** Montserrat
75 S6 **Cudworth** Saskatchewan Canada
216 E3 **Cue** WA Australia
162 C3 **Cuebe** *watercourse* Angola
162 C3 **Cueio** *watercourse* Angola
162 C2 **Cuelei** *watercourse* Angola
128 D3 **Cuéllar** Spain
162 C2 **Cuemba** Angola
100 B5 **Cuenca** Ecuador
128 E3 **Cuenca** Spain
128 F3 **Cuenca, Serrania de** *range* Spain
128 E3 **Cuerda del Pozo, Embalse de la** *lake* Spain
89 F5 **Cuernavaca** Mexico
195 I5 **Cueros de Negros** *mountain* Philippines
129 J2 **Cuers** France
85 J6 **Cuerva, Laguna El** *lake* Mexico
91 F2 **Cueto** Cuba
89 F3 **Cuevecillas** Mexico
100 B3 **Cuevita, Bahía** *bay* Colombia
132 C3 **Cugir** Romania
182 C5 **Cugus, Gora** *mountain* Russian Federation
191 H3 **Cuhe bator** Mongolia
105 G4 **Cuiabá** Brazil
105 G5 **Cuiabá** *watercourse* Brazil
88 D3 **Cuidame** Mexico
142 B2 **Cuidhaseadair** Na h-Eileanan Siar Scotland UK
188 D3 **Cuihua** Yunnan China
189 G3 **Cuijiang** Fujian China
90 B4 **Cuilapa** Guatemala
143 D3 **Cuilleen** Ireland
142 B3 **Cuillin Sound** Scotland UK
160 B5 **Cuilo** Angola
102 E4 **Cuité** Brazil
162 C3 **Cuito** *watercourse* Angola
162 C3 **Cuito Cuanavale** Angola
88 E5 **Cuitzeo, Laguna de** *lake* Mexico
101 F5 **Cuiuni** *watercourse* Brazil
82 F7 **Cuivre** *watercourse* Missouri USA
196 D2 **Cukai** Malaysia
109 14 **Cul-de-Sac du Marin** *bay* Martinique
126 F3 **Culan** France
195 I5 **Culasi** Philippines
81 M2 **Culbertson** Montana USA
216 E6 **Culbin** WA Australia
138 D3 **Culbone** Somerset England UK
218 H6 **Culcairn** NSW Australia
91 H3 **Culebra, Isla de** *island* Puerto Rico
85 J2 **Culebra, Mount** Colorado USA
128 C3 **Culebra, Sierra de la** *range* Spain
218 H3 **Culgoa** *watercourse* NSW Australia
218 F6 **Culgoa** Vic. Australia
88 D3 **Culiacán** Mexico
195 I5 **Culion** Philippines
195 H5 **Culion** *island* Philippines
105 H4 **Culiseu** *watercourse* Brazil
142 C2 **Culkein** Highland Scotland UK
129 F3 **Culla** Spain
128 E5 **Cúllar de Baza** Spain
108 C5 **Cullen** Argentina
143 D4 **Cullen** Ireland
142 F3 **Cullen** Moray Scotland UK
86 E4 **Cullen** Louisiana USA
219 J5 **Cullen Bullen** NSW Australia
214 F1 **Cullen Point** Qld Australia
129 F4 **Cullera** Spain
140 A2 **Cullion** Strabane Northern Ireland UK
86 H3 **Cullman** Alabama USA
138 D4 **Cullompton** Devon England UK
218 E6 **Cullulleraine** Vic. Australia
140 D2 **Culmalzie** Dumfries and Galloway Scotland UK
128 E5 **Culo de Perros, Punta** *cape* Spain
140 A1 **Culoort** Ireland
218 F4 **Culpaulin** NSW Australia
142 D3 **Culrain** Highland Scotland UK
140 D2 **Culshabbin** Dumfries and Galloway Scotland UK
142 inset **Culswick** Shetland Scotland UK
103 A6 **Culuene** *watercourse* Brazil
217 I6 **Culver, Point** WA Australia
221 E6 **Culverden** New Zealand
139 G2 **Culverthorpe** Lincolnshire England UK
142 D5 **Culzean Bay** Scotland UK
102 C3 **Cumã, Baía do** *bay* Brazil
101 E2 **Cumaná** Venezuela
109 9 **Cumana Bay** *bay* Trinidad and Tobago
100 C3 **Cumaral** Colombia
100 D3 **Cumaribo** Colombia
87 J2 **Cumberland** Kentucky USA
87 I2 **Cumberland** *watercourse* Kentucky USA
83 L7 **Cumberland** Maryland USA
83 L8 **Cumberland** Virginia USA
109 6a **Cumberland, Bahía** *bay* Isla Róbinson Crusoe
87 I2 **Cumberland, Lake** Kentucky USA
109 8 **Cumberland Bay** South Georgia
75 T6 **Cumberland House** Saskatchewan Canada
215 J6 **Cumberland Islands** Qld Australia
76 D5 **Cumberland Lake** Saskatchewan Canada
87 J2 **Cumberland Mountains** Kentucky USA
73 M5 **Cumberland Peninsula** Nunavut Canada
87 I3 **Cumberland Plateau** Tennessee USA
73 M5 **Cumberland Sound** Nunavut Canada
87 K5 **Cumberland Sound** Georgia USA
142 E5 **Cumbernauld** North Lanarkshire Scotland UK
100 B4 **Cumbitara** Colombia
219 H3 **Cumborah** NSW Australia
140 E2 **Cumbria** *admin. area* England UK
101 H5 **Cuminapanema** *watercourse* Brazil
109 5 **Cumming, Cabo** *cape* Isla de Pascua (Easter Island)
218 B6 **Cummins** SA Australia
219 I5 **Cumnock** NSW Australia
142 D5 **Cumnock** East Ayrshire Scotland UK
101 I4 **Cunani** Brazil
106 C6 **Cunco** Chile
216 H5 **Cundeelee** WA Australia
216 E5 **Cunderdin** WA Australia
219 I5 **Cundumbul** NSW Australia
162 C3 **Cunene** *admin. area* Angola
162 B3 **Cunene** *watercourse* Angola
162 C2 **Cunhinga** Angola
104 D3 **Cunhupuca** Brazil
129 G3 **Cunit** Spain
162 D3 **Cunjamba** Angola
218 G3 **Cunnamulla** Qld Australia
213 G4 **Cunningham Point** WA Australia
104 C2 **Cunshamayo** Peru
130 F4 **Ćunski** Croatia
216 G2 **Cunyu** WA Australia
121 N2 **Čuokkaraš'ša** *mountain* Norway
181 G3 **Cuomei** Xizang Zizhiqu China
181 G3 **Cuona** Xizang Zizhiqu China
180 E2 **Cuoqin** Xizang Zizhiqu China
75 S7 **Cupar** Saskatchewan Canada
142 E4 **Cupar** Fife Scotland UK
105 H1 **Cupari** *watercourse* Brazil
100 B3 **Cupica, Golfo de** *bay* Colombia
101 I4 **Cupixi** Brazil
108 B3 **Cuptana, Isla** *island* Chile
126 F5 **Cuq** France
143 C3 **Cur** Ireland
90 D2 **Cura, Laguna del** *lake* Cuba
108 D1 **Cura Malal, Sierra de** *range* Argentina
102 E5 **Curaçá** Brazil
100 D2 **Curaçao** *island* Netherlands Antilles
108 E2 **Curacó** *watercourse* Argentina
101 E4 **Curamoni** Venezuela
106 C6 **Curanilahue** Chile
100 B5 **Curaray** *watercourse* Ecuador
100 C5 **Curaray** *watercourse* Peru
107 G4 **Curaya** *watercourse* Argentina
219 I4 **Curban** NSW Australia
216 D3 **Curbur** WA Australia
217 O5 **Curdlawidny Lagoon** SA Australia
126 F3 **Cure** *watercourse* France
85 H6 **Curea** Mexico
164 7b **Curepipe** Mauritius
105 E3 **Curequete** *watercourse* Brazil
105 E6 **Curi, Sierra de** *range* Bolivia
104 D3 **Curichón** Bolivia
106 D5 **Curicó** Chile
100 E5 **Curicuriari** *watercourse* Brazil
164 9a **Curieuse** *island* Seychelles
100 C4 **Curillo** Colombia
100 D5 **Curinga** Peru
221 C8 **Curio Bay** New Zealand
103 B9 **Curitiba** Brazil
107 I3 **Curitibanos** Brazil
215 J6 **Curlew Island** Qld Australia
219 J4 **Curlewis** NSW Australia
218 E6 **Curlwaa** NSW Australia
218 D4 **Curnamona** SA Australia
162 B3 **Curoca** *watercourse* Angola
140 A2 **Curr** Omagh Northern Ireland UK
143 F3 **Curragha** Ireland
143 E4 **Currahill** Ireland
101 G5 **Curral Velho** Brazil
154 B5 **Curral Velho** Cape Verde
105 H6 **Curralinho** Brazil
143 B5 **Currane, Lough** *lake* Ireland
218 G4 **Curranyalpa** NSW Australia
219 J6 **Currarong** NSW Australia
143 C2 **Curraunboy** Ireland
218 E1 **Currawilla** Qld Australia
218 G3 **Currawinya** Qld Australia
143 D4 **Curreeny** Ireland
217 L3 **Currie** *watercourse* SA Australia
87 N2 **Currituck Sound** North Carolina USA
132 B2 **Curtici** Romania
217 L2 **Curtin Springs** NT Australia
81 O6 **Curtis** Nebraska USA
215 K7 **Curtis Channel** Qld Australia
215 K7 **Curtis Island** Qld Australia
219 R9 **Curtis Island** Tas. Australia
220 5 **Curtis Island** Kermadec Islands New Zealand
105 H2 **Curuá** *watercourse* Brazil
102 B2 **Curuá, Ilha** *island* Brazil
101 H5 **Curua do Sul** *watercourse* Brazil
105 H1 **Curua Una** *watercourse* Brazil
105 H2 **Curuaes** *watercourse* Brazil
101 H5 **Curuai, Lago Grande do** *lake* Brazil
195 I6 **Curuan** Philippines
104 C2 **Curuçá** *watercourse* Brazil
162 B3 **Curue** *watercourse* Angola
100 C2 **Curumaní** Colombia
101 I5 **Curumu** Brazil
196 D4 **Curup** Indonesia
101 H5 **Curupari** Brazil
105 F6 **Cururenda** Bolivia
102 C3 **Cururupu** Brazil
107 G4 **Curuzú Cuatiá** Argentina
103 C7 **Curvelo** Brazil
90 D5 **Cusapín** Panama
104 D4 **Cusco** Peru
104 C4 **Cusco** *admin. area* Peru
104 C2 **Cushabatay** *watercourse* Peru
140 A3 **Cushaling** Ireland
140 B1 **Cushendun** Moyle Northern Ireland UK
100 C3 **Cusiana** *watercourse* Colombia
80 G2 **Cusick** Washington USA
130 D4 **Cusna, Monte** *mountain* Italy
162 C2 **Cussava** Angola
126 F3 **Cusset** France
87 I4 **Cusseta** Georgia USA
77 Q2 **Cusson, Pointe** *cape* Quebec Canada
221 E6 **Cust** New Zealand
81 N5 **Custer** South Dakota USA
86 B3 **Custer City** Oklahoma USA
127 H2 **Custines** France
102 E5 **Custódia** Brazil
128 C3 **Custoias** Portugal
132 C3 **Cut** Romania
80 I2 **Cut Bank** Montana USA
75 Q6 **Cut Knife** Saskatchewan Canada
162 C2 **Cutato** Angola
74 L5 **Cutbank** *watercourse* Alberta Canada
140 D2 **Cutcloy** Dumfries and Galloway Scotland UK
162 C2 **Cutenda** Angola
87 I5 **Cuthbert** Georgia USA
214 B1 **Cuthbert Point** NT Australia
142 D3 **Cuthill** Highland Scotland UK
143 D3 **Cutra, Lough** *lake* Ireland
106 D6 **Cutral-Có** Argentina
219 I4 **Cuttabri** NSW Australia
218 G3 **Cuttaburra** *watercourse* NSW Australia
187 F7 **Cuttack** Orissa India
100 B5 **Cutucú, Cordillera de** *range* Ecuador
159 H5 **Cuvette** *admin. area* Congo
159 G4 **Cuvette-Ouest** *admin. area* Congo
212 B8 **Cuvier, Cape** WA Australia
55 P7 **Cuvier Abyssal Plain** *underwater feature* Indian Ocean
220 F3 **Cuvier Island** New Zealand
55 O7 **Cuvier Plateau** *underwater feature* Indian Ocean
124 E1 **Cuxhaven** Germany
195 I5 **Cuyo** *island* Philippines
195 I5 **Cuyo East Passage** *strait* Philippines
195 I5 **Cuyo West Passage** *strait* Philippines
101 F3 **Cuyuni** *watercourse* Guyana
140 E3 **Cwm** Denbighshire Wales UK
138 C3 **Cwm Duad** Carmarthenshire Wales UK
138 C2 **Cwmann** Carmarthenshire Wales UK
138 D3 **Cwmbran** Torfaen Wales UK
138 D3 **Cwmdu** Powys Wales UK
138 C3 **Cwmfelin Mynach** Carmarthenshire Wales UK
125 H1 **Cybinka** Poland
Cyclades *see* **Kyklades** Greece
82 J6 **Cygnet** Ohio USA
218 C6 **Cygnet River** SA Australia
219 J1 **Cynthia** Qld Australia
81 K2 **Cypress Hills** Saskatchewan Canada
81 K2 **Cypress Lake** Saskatchewan Canada
136 E6 **Cyprus** *country* Asia
86 B3 **Cyril** Oklahoma USA
78 F1 **Cyrus Field Bay** Nunavut Canada
125 I1 **Czarne** Poland
125 H3 **Czech Republic** *country* Europe
125 J3 **Czechowice-Dziedzice** Poland
125 K2 **Czekarzewice** Poland
125 H1 **Czerwieńsk** Poland
125 J2 **Częstochowa** Poland
125 I1 **Człopa** Poland

D

191 I3 **Da Hinggan Ling** *range* Nei Mongol Zizhiqu China
194 F5 **Dà Lat** Vietnam
194 F3 **Đà Nẵng** Vietnam
194 F4 **Đa Râng** *watercourse* Vietnam
189 H1 **Da Yunhe (Grand Canal)** *watercourse* Jiangsu China
191 J3 **Da`an** Jilin China
190 G6 **Da`ning** Shanxi China
219 J2 **Daandine** Qld Australia
120 I6 **Dåasen** *lake* Sweden
188 E2 **Daba Shan** *range* Chongqing China
158 D3 **Dabakala** Côte d'Ivoire
191 I4 **Daban** Nei Mongol Zizhiqu China
178 C4 **Dabbāgh, Jabel** *mountain* Saudi Arabia
100 B3 **Dabeiba** Colombia
187 C6 **Dabhoi** Gujarat India
187 C8 **Dabhol** Maharashtra India
189 G2 **Dabie Shan** *range* Anhui China
124 D3 **Dabo** France
154 D6 **Dabo** Senegal
158 D3 **Dabou** Côte d'Ivoire
158 D3 **Daboya** Ghana
190 F5 **Dabqig** Nei Mongol Zizhiqu China
187 F7 **Dabra** Chhattisgarh India
186 E6 **Dabra** Madhya Pradesh India
125 J2 **Dąbrowa Górnicza** Poland
185 J5 **Dabsan Hu** *lake* Qinghai China
Dacca *see* **Dhaka** Bangladesh
189 I2 **Dachangtu Shan** *range* Zhejiang China
189 I2 **Dachu Shan** *range* Zhejiang China
86 B2 **Dacoma** Oklahoma USA
83 M4 **Dacre** Ontario Canada

221 C8 **Dacre** New Zealand
190 G2 **Dadal** Mongolia
222 8 **Dadale** Solomon Islands
87 J6 **Dade City** Florida USA
186 E5 **Dadeldhura** Nepal
179 K3 **Dadhar** Pakistan
198 D4 **Dadi, Tanjung** *cape* Indonesia
179 J4 **Dadigor** Pakistan
126 F5 **Dadou** *watercourse* France
187 C7 **Dadra and Nagar Haveli** *admin. area* India
179 K4 **Dadu** Pakistan
188 D2 **Dadu He** *watercourse* Sichuan China
178 C5 **Daedalus Reef** Saudi Arabia
Daegu *see* **Taegu** South Korea
192 E4 **Daeheugsan-do** *island* South Korea
133 C7 **Daemoniá** Greece
195 I4 **Daet** Philippines
188 E3 **Dafang** Guizhou China
188 E4 **Dafeng** Guangxi Zhuangzu Zizhiqu China
189 H1 **Dafeng** Jiangsu China
133 B6 **Dafnoudi, Akra** *cape* Greece
181 F3 **Daga** Bhutan
161 E2 **Daga-Post** Sudan
162 E3 **Dagamela** Zimbabwe
154 C5 **Dagana** Senegal
156 E4 **Dagash** Sudan
198 C3 **Dagasuli** *island* Indonesia
133 G7 **Dağbeli** Turkey
123 N4 **Dagda** Latvia
133 F6 **Dağdere** Turkey
191 H4 **Dage** Hebei China
139 H3 **Dagenham** Greater London England UK
221 B7 **Dagg Sound** New Zealand
213 H4 **Daglish, Mount** WA Australia
122 H3 **Daglösen** *lake* Sweden
159 H2 **Daguela** Chad
195 I3 **Dagupan** Philippines
213 K4 **Daguragu** NT Australia
191 I5 **Daheishan Dao** *island* Shandong China
157 G4 **Dahlak Archipelago** *islands* Eritrea
178 E2 **Dahluj** Iraq
155 H1 **Dahmani** Tunisia
125 G2 **Dahme** *watercourse* Germany
122 F5 **Dahmeshöved** *cape* Germany
186 D6 **Dahod** Gujarat India
189 F2 **Dahong Shan** *mountain* Hubei China
161 H1 **Dahot** *watercourse* Somalia
188 E4 **Dahua** Guangxi Zhuangzu Zizhiqu China
178 E2 **Dahūk** Iraq
178 E2 **Dahūk** *admin. area* Iraq
218 G6 **Dahwilly** NSW Australia
198 D5 **Dai** *island* Indonesia
222 8 **Dai** *island* Solomon Islands
189 H3 **Dai Jiang** *watercourse* Fujian China
194 E5 **Đại Ngãi** Vietnam
192 G4 **Dai-sen** *volcano* Japan
191 G5 **Dai Xian** Shanxi China
196 E4 **Daik** Indonesia
194 C3 **Daik-U** Myanmar
120 J4 **Daikanvik** Sweden
179 K2 **Dāikondi** *admin. area* Afghanistan
186 E5 **Dailekh** Nepal
142 D5 **Dailly** South Ayrshire Scotland UK
142 F4 **Dairsie** Fife Scotland UK
216 D2 **Dairy Creek** WA Australia
82 E3 **Dairyland** Wisconsin USA
193 I3 **Daisengen-dake** *volcano* Japan
189 I2 **Daishan Dao** *island* Zhejiang China
187 F7 **Daitari** Orissa India
214 E6 **Dajarra** Qld Australia
188 D4 **Dajie** Yunnan China
188 D2 **Dajin Chuan** *watercourse* Sichuan China
189 F4 **Dajin Dao** *island* Guangdong China
179 I4 **Dak** Iran
194 E4 **Đắk Tô** Vietnam
154 C6 **Dakar** Senegal
154 C6 **Dakar** *admin. area* Senegal
161 G2 **Dakata** *watercourse* Ethiopia
199 I5 **Dakataua, Lake** Papua New Guinea
156 D2 **Dākhilah, Wāḥāt Ad** *spring* Egypt
196 B2 **Dakoank** Andaman and Nicobar Islands India
155 H6 **Dakoro** Niger
132 B4 **Đakovica** Kosovo
122 F2 **Dal** Norway
162 D2 **Dala** Angola
222 8 **Dala** Solomon Islands
158 B2 **Dalaba** Guinea
154 D6 **Dalaba** Senegal
191 H4 **Dalai Nuur** *lake* Nei Mongol Zizhiqu China
185 J5 **Dalai Shan** *mountain* Gansu China
190 E4 **Dalain Hob** Nei Mongol Zizhiqu China
122 H2 **Dalälven** *watercourse* Sweden
133 F7 **Dalama** Turkey
133 F7 **Dalaman** *watercourse* Turkey
190 E4 **Dalandzadgad** Mongolia
190 G3 **Dalanjargalan** Mongolia
122 H2 **Dalarna** *admin. area* Sweden
197 F3 **Dalat** Malaysia
120 inset **Dalatangi** *cape* Iceland
142 C4 **Dalavich** Argyll and Bute Scotland UK
179 J4 **Dalbandin** Pakistan
142 E6 **Dalbeattie** Dumfries and Galloway Scotland UK
215 I6 **Dalbeg** Qld Australia
142 D3 **Dalbeg** Highland Scotland UK
199 G5 **D'Albertis Dome** *mountain* Papua New Guinea
122 G3 **Dalbosjön** *bay* Sweden
219 J2 **Dalby** Qld Australia
141 G2 **Dalby** North Yorkshire England UK
122 C2 **Dale** Norway
138 B3 **Dale** Pembrokeshire Wales UK
216 E6 **Dale, Mount** WA Australia
87 I2 **Dale Hollow Lake** Tennessee USA
142 inset **Dale of Walls** Shetland Scotland UK
124 D1 **Dalen** Netherlands
122 E3 **Dalen** Norway
142 E3 **Daless** Highland Scotland UK
142 E3 **Dalestie** Moray Scotland UK
142 E3 **Dalfad** Aberdeenshire Scotland UK
179 I4 **Dalgān** Iran
216 E3 **Dalgaranga** WA Australia
216 E2 **Dalgety, Mount** WA Australia
214 F6 **Dalgonally** Qld Australia
85 K2 **Dalhart** Texas USA
120 F5 **Dalholen** Norway
72 G4 **Dalhousie, Cape** Northwest Territories Canada
217 N3 **Dalhousie Springs** SA Australia
188 F1 **Dali** Shaanxi China
188 C3 **Dali** Yunnan China
182 J6 **Dālī** Afghanistan
178 F2 **Dālī Chū** Iran
191 J5 **Dalian** Liaoning China
189 H3 **Dalian Dao** *island* Fujian China
191 J5 **Dalian Wan** *bay* Liaoning China
191 I4 **Daling He** *watercourse* Liaoning China
130 H4 **Dalj** Croatia
142 E5 **Dalkeith** Midlothian Scotland UK
74 E5 **Dall Island** Alaska USA
219 K1 **Dallarnil** Qld Australia
80 E1 **Dallas** British Columbia Canada
142 E3 **Dallas** Moray Scotland UK
87 K3 **Dallas** North Carolina USA
80 D4 **Dallas** Oregon USA
86 C4 **Dallas** Texas USA
155 G6 **Dallol Bosso** *watercourse* Niger
178 G5 **Dalmā** *island* United Arab Emirates
106 F5 **Dalmacio** Argentina
142 D4 **Dalmally** Argyll and Bute Scotland UK
78 C6 **Dalmas, Lac** *lake* Quebec Canada
142 D5 **Dalmellington** East Ayrshire Scotland UK
142 D3 **Dalnavie** Highland Scotland UK
193 G2 **Daln'egorsk** Russian Federation
192 G1 **Dal'nerechensk** Russian Federation
142 D4 **Dalness** Highland Scotland UK
142 D2 **Dalnessie** Highland Scotland UK
132 G2 **Dal'nik** Ukraine
121 T2 **Dal'niye Zelentsy** Russian Federation
135 AD9 **Dal'nyaya** Russian Federation
158 C3 **Daloa** Côte d'Ivoire
142 E4 **Dalriech** Perth and Kinross Scotland UK
142 D5 **Dalrymple** East Ayrshire Scotland UK
215 I6 **Dalrymple, Lake** Qld Australia
122 F3 **Dalsland** *region* Sweden
135 AC6 **Dal'stroy** Russian Federation
186 F6 **Daltenganj** Jharkhand India
219 I6 **Dalton** NSW Australia
141 G2 **Dalton** North Yorkshire England UK
87 I3 **Dalton** Georgia USA
81 N6 **Dalton** Nebraska USA
140 E2 **Dalton-in-Furness** Cumbria England UK
142 E3 **Daltra** Highland Scotland UK
196 D3 **Daludalu** Indonesia
214 D3 **Dalumbu Bay** NT Australia
195 I3 **Dalupiri** *island* Philippines
195 J4 **Dalupri** *island* Philippines
142 E4 **Dalvanie** Angus Scotland UK
219 J3 **Dalveen** Qld Australia
120 inset **Dalvík** Iceland
142 D4 **Dalwhinnie** Highland Scotland UK
214 A3 **Daly** *watercourse* NT Australia
80 D8 **Daly City** California USA
75 S4 **Daly Lake** Saskatchewan Canada
213 K2 **Daly River** NT Australia
214 B4 **Daly Waters** NT Australia
133 F7 **Dalyan** Turkey
133 E6 **Dalyanköy** Turkey
216 G6 **Dalyup** WA Australia
194 E2 **Đầm Hà** Vietnam
181 G2 **Dam Qu** *watercourse* Qinghai China
178 C4 **Damā, Wādī** *watercourse* Saudi Arabia
125 L2 **Damachava** Belarus
155 H6 **Damagaram-Takaya** Niger
179 I4 **Damāgheh-ye Meydānī** *cape* Iran
187 C7 **Daman** Daman and Diu India
187 C7 **Daman and Diu** *admin. area* India
156 E1 **Damanhūr** Egypt
191 H4 **Damaqun Shan** *range* Hebei China
198 C3 **Damar** Indonesia
198 D4 **Damar** *island* Indonesia
85 M1 **Damar** Kansas USA
159 H4 **Damara** Central African Republic
133 F7 **Damarası** Turkey
159 G2 **Damasak** Nigeria
Damascus *see* **Dimashq** Syria
159 G2 **Damaturu** Nigeria
129 G1 **Damazan** France
160 B5 **Damba** Angola
158 E3 **Dambai** Ghana
133 E5 **Dambaslar** Turkey
159 G2 **Damboa** Nigeria
132 D3 **Dâmbovita** *admin. area* Romania
91 F3 **Dame Marie, Cap** *cape* Haiti
189 I3 **Damen Dao** *island* Zhejiang China
182 G7 **Dāmghān** Iran
191 H6 **Daming** Hebei China
195 I6 **Dammai** *island* Philippines
186 E6 **Damoh** Madhya Pradesh India
212 D6 **Dampier** WA Australia
198 D4 **Dampier, Selat** *strait* Indonesia
212 D6 **Dampier Archipelago** WA Australia
213 G5 **Dampier Downs** WA Australia
197 G6 **Dampit** Indonesia
187 E6 **Damua** Madhya Pradesh India
126 E2 **Damville** France
124 C3 **Damvillers** France
126 D3 **Damvix** France
133 C5 **Damyanitsa** Bulgaria
87 L2 **Dan** *watercourse* Virginia USA
159 F2 **Dan-Gulbi** Nigeria
188 F1 **Dan Jiang** *watercourse* Shaanxi China
194 D4 **Dan Khun Thot** Thailand
194 D3 **Dan Sai** Thailand
198 B6 **Dana** *island* Indonesia
83 M1 **Dana, Lac** *lake* Quebec Canada
84 D4 **Dana Point** California USA
158 C3 **Danané** Côte d'Ivoire
195 J5 **Danao** Philippines
83 O6 **Danbury** Connecticut USA
81 O6 **Danbury** Nebraska USA
141 H2 **Danby** North Yorkshire England UK
84 E3 **Danby Lake** California USA
141 G2 **Danby Wiske** North Yorkshire England UK
189 G1 **Dancheng** Henan China
189 I2 **Dancheng** Zhejiang China
216 F4 **Dandaraga** WA Australia
216 D5 **Dandaragan** WA Australia
160 A5 **Dande** *watercourse* Angola
161 F3 **Dande** Ethiopia
187 D8 **Dandeli** Karnataka India
218 G7 **Dandenong** Vic. Australia
162 C2 **Dando** Angola
191 J5 **Dandong** Liaoning China
141 F3 **Dane** *watercourse* England UK
179 I4 **Dānel** Iran
188 D4 **Danfeng** Yunnan China
198 B6 **Danga** Indonesia
143 E4 **Dangan Bridge** Ireland
189 G4 **Dangan Dao** *island* Guangdong China
188 D1 **Dangchang** Gansu China
185 J5 **Dangchengwan** Gansu China
126 E3 **Dangé** France
162 C6 **Danger Point** *cape* South Africa
185 J5 **Danghe Nanshan** *range* Gansu China
156 F5 **Dangila** Ethiopia
Dangla Shan *see* **Tanggula Shan** China
219 J2 **Dangore Mountain** Qld Australia
181 E2 **Dangra Tssho** *lake* Xizang Zizhiqu China
90 B3 **Dangriga** Belize
189 G1 **Dangshan** Anhui China
156 F5 **Dangur** Ethiopia
105 H4 **Daniel, Serra** *range* Brazil
90 D5 **Daniel Flores** Costa Rica
59 L2 **Daniell Peninsula** Antarctica
79 J7 **Daniel's Harbour** Newfoundland and Labrador Canada
162 D5 **Daniëlskuil** South Africa
183 K3 **Danilovka** Kazakhstan
182 D3 **Danilovka** Russian Federation
188 E3 **Danjiang** Guizhou China
189 F2 **Danjiangkou** Hubei China
189 F2 **Danjiangkou Shuiku** *lake* Hubei China
90 C4 **Danlí** Honduras
73 Q2 **Danmark Fjord** Greenland
158 D2 **Dano** Burkina Faso
108 C4 **Dañoso, Cabo** *cape* Argentina
74 I6 **Danskin** British Columbia Canada
194 B3 **Danson Bay** Myanmar
187 G7 **Dantan** West Bengal India
Danube *see* **Donau** Europe
194 B3 **Danubyu** Myanmar
197 G3 **Danumparai** Indonesia
83 O4 **Danville** Quebec Canada
86 E3 **Danville** Arkansas USA
82 H6 **Danville** Illinois USA
82 I8 **Danville** Kentucky USA
189 H2 **Danyang** Jiangsu China
188 F5 **Danzhou** Hainan China
190 G6 **Danzhou** Shaanxi China
189 F3 **Daojiang** Hunan China
195 J5 **Dapa** Philippines
158 E2 **Dapaong** Togo
159 G2 **Dapchi** Nigeria
86 H5 **Daphne** Alabama USA
195 I5 **Dapitan** Philippines
187 C8 **Dapoli** Maharashtra India
188 F4 **Dapu** Guangxi Zhuangzu Zizhiqu China
191 J5 **Daqin Dao** *island* Shandong China
191 I4 **Daqin Tal** Nei Mongol Zizhiqu China
191 J3 **Daqing** Heilongjiang China
190 G5 **Daqing Shan** *range* Nei Mongol Zizhiqu China
178 E8 **Dār al Juhār** Yemen
182 H7 **Dar Beyaban** Iran
161 F5 **Dar es Salaam** Tanzania
161 F5 **Dar es Salaam** *admin. area* Tanzania
179 I4 **Dar Gol** Iran
128 D6 **Dar Mter** Morocco
154 C5 **Dara** Senegal
136 F7 **Dar'ā** Syria
179 H4 **Dārāb** Iran
155 I2 **Daraj** Libya
195 J5 **Daram** Philippines
198 D4 **Daram, Pulau** *island* Indonesia
199 H4 **Darapap** Papua New Guinea
159 G2 **Darazo** Nigeria
136 F6 **Darb At Tast** Syria
123 K4 **Darbėnai** Lithuania
186 F5 **Darbhanga** Bihar India
179 H3 **Darbīd** Iran
80 H3 **Darby** Montana USA
214 B1 **Darch Island** NT Australia
74 J7 **D'Arcy** British Columbia Canada
Dardanelles *see* **Çanakkale Boğazı** Turkey
161 F4 **Dareda** Tanzania
130 D4 **Darfo** Italy
127 J4 **Darfo Boario Terme** Italy
191 H3 **Darganga** Mongolia
220 E2 **Dargaville** New Zealand
126 F4 **Dargilan, Grotte de** *point of interest* France
158 D2 **Dargo** Burkina Faso
181 F2 **Dargo Zangbo** *watercourse* Xizang Zizhiqu China
155 G6 **Dargol** Niger
190 F2 **Darhan** Mongolia
190 G3 **Darhan** Mongolia
190 F2 **Darhan-Uul** *admin. area* Mongolia
87 K5 **Darien** Georgia USA
82 G5 **Darien** Wisconsin USA
100 B2 **Darién, Golfo del** *bay* Colombia/Panama
90 E5 **Darién, Serranía del** *range* Colombia/Panama
90 C4 **Dariense, Cordillera** *range* Nicaragua
183 K3 **Dar'inskiy** Kazakhstan
100 D5 **Dário** Brazil
178 F3 **Dariseh** Iran
186 G5 **Darjiling** West Bengal India
221 B7 **Dark Cloud Range** New Zealand
216 E6 **Darkan** WA Australia
140 B2 **Darkley** Armagh Northern Ireland UK
194 F4 **Darlac Plateau** Vietnam
181 G4 **Darlawn** Mizoram India
218 F5 **Darling** *watercourse* NSW Australia
81 O2 **Darling, Lake** North Dakota USA
73 L3 **Darling Peninsula** Nunavut Canada
141 G2 **Darlington** Darlington England UK
141 G2 **Darlington** *admin. area* England UK
87 L3 **Darlington** South Carolina USA
138 E2 **Darliston** Shropshire England UK
216 G3 **Darlot, Lake** WA Australia
130 C2 **Darmstadt** Germany
187 C7 **Darna** *watercourse* Maharashtra India
156 C1 **Darnah** Libya
127 H2 **Darney** France
142 F3 **Darnford** Aberdeenshire Scotland UK
218 F5 **Darnick** NSW Australia
59 E2 **Darnley, Cape** Antarctica
72 G5 **Darnley Bay** Northwest Territories Canada
199 G6 **Darnley Island** Qld Australia
129 F3 **Daroca** Spain
132 B3 **Darosova** Serbia
154 E6 **Darouma** *watercourse* Mali
215 G7 **Darr** *watercourse* Qld Australia
179 K2 **Darrah-e Awd** Afghanistan
178 F2 **Darreh Shahr** Iran
161 G2 **Darro** *watercourse* Ethiopia
86 A2 **Darrouzett** Texas USA
157 I5 **Darsah** *island* Yemen
138 D4 **Dart** *watercourse* England UK
215 J4 **Dart Reef** Coral Sea Islands Territory Australia
143 E2 **Dartan** Ireland
139 H3 **Dartford** Kent England UK
138 D4 **Dartmeet** Devon England UK
218 E7 **Dartmoor** Vic. Australia
79 G10 **Dartmouth** Nova Scotia Canada
79 F8 **Dartmouth** *watercourse* Quebec Canada
138 D4 **Dartmouth** Devon England UK
218 G2 **Dartmouth, Lake** Qld Australia
120 L4 **Dartsel** Sweden
179 H4 **Darū** Iran
199 G6 **Daru Island** Papua New Guinea
158 B3 **Darul** Sierra Leone
182 H6 **Darvaza** Turkmenistan
195 H6 **Darvel, Teluk** *bay* Malaysia
185 J3 **Darvi** Mongolia
185 J3 **Darvi** Mongolia
161 G3 **Darwa** *watercourse* Ethiopia
141 F3 **Darwen** Blackburn with Darwen England UK
162 F3 **Darwendale** Zimbabwe
187 D7 **Darwha** Maharashtra India
106 E6 **Darwin** Argentina
213 K2 **Darwin** NT Australia
109 7 **Darwin** Falkland Islands
108 B5 **Darwin, Cordillera** *range* Chile
109 4 **Darwin, Isla** *island* Archipiélago de Colon (Galapagos Islands)
108 C6 **Darwin, Monte** *mountain* Chile
213 K2 **Darwin River Dam** NT Australia
191 H2 **Dashbalbar** Mongolia
190 E3 **Dashintsilen** Mongolia
191 J5 **Dashiqiao** Liaoning China
178 G2 **Dashteh** Iran
221 F5 **Dashwood** New Zealand
179 M3 **Daska** Pakistan
182 H5 **Daşoguz** Turkmenistan
182 H5 **Daşoguz Welaýaty** *admin. area* Turkmenistan
195 H4 **Dasol Bay** Philippines
195 I6 **Dassalan** *island* Philippines
124 F1 **Dassow** Germany
122 F5 **Dassower See** *bay* Germany
182 G7 **Dastūrān** Iran
186 D4 **Dasua** Punjab India
179 K4 **Data Chandio** Pakistan
197 G3 **Datadian** Indonesia
133 E7 **Datça** Turkey
193 I2 **Date** Japan
186 E6 **Datia** Madhya Pradesh India
189 F4 **Datian Ding** *mountain* Guangdong China
85 I3 **Datil** New Mexico USA
191 H5 **Datong** Shanxi China
135 AD9 **Datta** Russian Federation
122 G3 **Dättern** *bay* Sweden
196 F3 **Datu** *island* Indonesia
196 F3 **Datu, Tanjung** *cape* Indonesia
196 D4 **Datuk, Tanjung** *cape* Indonesia
125 G1 **Datze** *watercourse* Germany
179 H4 **Dāu** *island* United Arab Emirates
179 L3 **Daud Khel** Pakistan
123 N5 **Daugavpils** Latvia
123 N5 **Daugavpils** *admin. area* Latvia
127 H1 **Daun** Germany
187 D7 **Daund** Maharashtra India
75 U7 **Dauphin** Manitoba Canada
86 G5 **Dauphin Island** Alabama USA
76 F7 **Dauphin Lake** Manitoba Canada
75 V7 **Dauphin River** Manitoba Canada
159 F2 **Daura** Nigeria
190 G2 **Daurskiy Khrebet** *range* Russian Federation
186 D5 **Dausa** Rajasthan India
142 E3 **Dava** Moray Scotland UK
187 D8 **Davangere** Karnataka India
195 J6 **Davao** Philippines
197 J2 **Davao Gulf** *bay* Philippines
162 E5 **Davel** South Africa
214 F8 **Davenport** *watercourse* Qld Australia
84 A2 **Davenport** California USA
82 F6 **Davenport** Iowa USA
80 F3 **Davenport** Washington USA
217 L3 **Davenport, Mount** SA Australia
214 F8 **Davenport Downs** Qld Australia
214 C6 **Davenport Range** NT Australia
139 F2 **Daventry** Northamptonshire England UK
219 Q11 **Davey, Port** Tas. Australia
90 D5 **David** Panama
214 B3 **David, Mount** NT Australia
81 Q6 **David City** Nebraska USA
86 B3 **Davidson** Oklahoma USA
214 A6 **Davidson, Mount** NT Australia
217 K3 **Davies, Mount** SA Australia
78 B1 **Davies Island** Nunavut Canada
215 I5 **Davies Reef** Qld Australia
142 D3 **Daviot** Highland Scotland UK
212 F7 **Davis** *watercourse* WA Australia
80 E7 **Davis** California USA
81 Q5 **Davis** South Dakota USA
216 G2 **Davis, Mount** WA Australia
59 F2 **Davis (Australia)** *research station* Antarctica
59 J2 **Davis Bay** Antarctica
78 H5 **Davis Inlet** Newfoundland and Labrador Canada
80 E5 **Davis Lake** Oregon USA
88 D2 **Davis Mountains** Texas USA
76 F7 **Davis Point** Manitoba Canada
59 G2 **Davis Sea** Antarctica
78 G1 **Davis Strait** Canada/Greenland
158 C3 **Davo** *watercourse* Côte d'Ivoire
130 G4 **Davor** Croatia
127 I3 **Davos** Switzerland
120 K1 **Davøya** *island* Norway
185 I2 **Davst** Mongolia
133 E7 **Davutlar** Turkey
214 G7 **Davy, Mount** Qld Australia
75 Q3 **Davy Lake** Saskatchewan Canada
217 I6 **Daw Island** WA Australia
191 J5 **Dawa** Liaoning China
191 J5 **Dawangjia Dao** *island* Liaoning China
194 C4 **Dawei (Tavoy)** Myanmar
194 C4 **Dawei Point** Myanmar
198 D5 **Daweloor** *island* Indonesia
179 I6 **Dawḥat Şawqirah** *sea* Oman
138 D4 **Dawlish** Devon England UK
138 D4 **Dawlish Warren** Devon England UK
178 D3 **Dawmat al Jandal (Al Jawf)** Saudi Arabia
194 C3 **Dawna Range** Myanmar
143 D2 **Dawros Head** *cape* Ireland
219 I1 **Dawson** *watercourse* Qld Australia
72 F6 **Dawson** Yukon Territory Canada
108 B6 **Dawson, Isla** *island* Chile
80 G1 **Dawson, Mount** British Columbia Canada
74 K5 **Dawson Creek** British Columbia Canada
76 I2 **Dawson Inlet** Nunavut Canada
75 N2 **Dawson Landing** Northwest Territories Canada
215 J7 **Dawson Range** Qld Australia
74 H7 **Dawsons Landing** British Columbia Canada
189 G2 **Dawu** Hubei China
188 C1 **Dawu** Qinghai China
179 I6 **Dawwah** Oman
126 D5 **Dax** France
188 E2 **Daxian** Sichuan China
189 I2 **Daxie Dao** *island* Zhejiang China
188 C3 **Daxing** Yunnan China
188 D4 **Daxing** Yunnan China
194 E2 **Đáy** *watercourse* Vietnam
216 G6 **Day, Mount** WA Australia
188 C3 **Dayan** Yunnan China
185 H3 **Dayan Nuur** *lake* Mongolia
189 G2 **Daye Hu** *lake* Hubei China
107 G4 **Daymán** *watercourse* Uruguay
82 I2 **Dayohessarah Lake** Ontario Canada
136 G6 **Dayr az Zawr** Syria
218 H6 **Daysdale** NSW Australia
75 O6 **Daysland** Alberta Canada
84 C1 **Dayton** Nevada USA
82 I7 **Dayton** Ohio USA
81 L4 **Dayton** Wyoming USA
87 K6 **Daytona Beach** Florida USA
197 G4 **Dayu** Indonesia
189 G3 **Dayu Ling** *range* Guangdong China
189 H3 **Dayu Shan** *range* Fujian China
80 F4 **Dayville** Oregon USA
191 I6 **Daze Shan** *range* Shandong China
188 D1 **Dazhasi** Sichuan China
188 F5 **Dazhou Dao** *island* Hainan China
162 D6 **De Aar** South Africa
88 D4 **De Acaponeta, Rio** *watercourse* Mexico
81 K7 **De Beque** Colorado USA
214 C5 **De Burgh, Lake** NT Australia
124 C1 **De Cocksdorp** Netherlands
214 B1 **De Courcy Head** NT Australia
87 H5 **De Funiak Springs** Florida USA
59 R2 **De Gerlache Seamounts** *underwater feature* Southern Ocean
81 R4 **De Graff** Minnesota USA
86 E3 **De Gray Lake** Arkansas USA
212 E6 **De Grey** WA Australia
212 E6 **De Grey** *watercourse* WA Australia
126 F1 **De Haan** Belgium
86 D4 **De Kalb** Texas USA
124 C1 **De Koog** Netherlands
107 G6 **De La Canal** Argentina
106 F6 **De la Garma** Argentina
72 C5 **De Long Mountains** Alaska USA
78 F5 **De Pas** *watercourse* Quebec Canada
82 G4 **De Pere** Wisconsin USA
124 B2 **De Pinte** Belgium
81 Q4 **De Smet** South Dakota USA
82 G8 **De Soto** Illinois USA
77 R4 **De Troyes** *watercourse* Quebec Canada
86 F3 **De Valls Bluff** Arkansas USA
74 L6 **De Veber, Mount** Alberta Canada
74 D2 **De Wette** Yukon Territory Canada
86 F3 **De Witt** Arkansas USA
219 R11 **De Witt Island** Tas. Australia
78 G3 **Deacon Head** Newfoundland and Labrador Canada
143 D4 **Dead** *watercourse* Ireland
78 K6 **Dead Islands** Newfoundland and Labrador Canada
87 I5 **Dead Lake** Florida USA
178 C3 **Dead Sea** Israel/Jordan
72 E4 **Deadhorse** Alaska USA
74 M4 **Deadwood** Alberta Canada
214 B2 **Deaf Adder** *watercourse* NT Australia
217 K5 **Deakin** WA Australia
59 K2 **Deakin Bay** Antarctica
139 I3 **Deal** Kent England UK
219 R9 **Deal Island** Tas. Australia
74 I6 **Dean** *watercourse* British Columbia Canada
59 P2 **Dean Island** Antarctica
74 G3 **Dease** *watercourse* British Columbia Canada
72 H5 **Dease Arm** Northwest Territories Canada
72 D4 **Dease Inlet** Alaska USA
74 F3 **Dease Lake** British Columbia Canada
74 F3 **Dease Lake** British Columbia Canada
72 I5 **Dease Strait** Nunavut Canada
84 D2 **Death Valley** California USA
197 F3 **Debak** Malaysia
188 E4 **Debao** Guangxi Zhuangzu Zizhiqu China
159 I2 **Debarei, Wadi** *watercourse* Sudan
156 F5 **Debark** Ethiopia
76 F2 **Debartok Lake** Nunavut Canada
75 R6 **Debden** Saskatchewan Canada
155 F2 **Debdou** Morocco
109 9 **Débé** Trinidad and Tobago
139 I2 **Debenham** Suffolk England UK
79 G10 **Debert** Nova Scotia Canada
213 H4 **Debesa** WA Australia
125 K2 **Dębica** Poland
125 H1 **Dębno** Poland
154 F5 **Débo, Lac** *lake* Mali
216 F5 **Deborah East, Lake** WA Australia
216 F5 **Deborah West, Lake** WA Australia
199 J6 **Deboyne Atoll** *reef* Papua New Guinea
105 H6 **Debrasa** Brazil
132 A3 **Debrc** Serbia
161 F2 **Debre Birhan** Ethiopia
161 H2 **Debre Birhan** Somalia
161 F1 **Debre Markos** Ethiopia
156 F5 **Debre May** Ethiopia
156 F5 **Debre Tabor** Ethiopia
161 F2 **Debre Zeyit** Ethiopia
132 B2 **Debrecen** Hungary
86 H3 **Decatur** Alabama USA
82 G7 **Decatur** Illinois USA
86 G4 **Decatur** Mississippi USA
86 C4 **Decatur** Texas USA
126 F4 **Decazeville** France
108 C6 **Deceit, Cabo** *cape* Chile
77 R1 **Déception** Quebec Canada
78 A1 **Déception** *watercourse* Quebec Canada
78 A1 **Déception, Baie** *bay* Quebec Canada
219 K2 **Deception Bay** Qld Australia
213 H3 **Deception Bay** WA Australia
199 H5 **Deception Bay** Papua New Guinea
162 D4 **Deception Pans** *pan* Botswana
213 K1 **Deception Point** NT Australia
189 F4 **Decheng** Guangdong China
125 H2 **Děčín** Czech Republic
124 B4 **Decize** France
82 F5 **Decorah** Iowa USA
132 A2 **Decs** Hungary
132 A4 **Dedaj** Albania
188 C4 **Dedang** Yunnan China
194 B3 **Dedaya** Myanmar
222 5 **Dededo** Guam
133 C5 **Dedeli** Macedonia
161 G2 **Deder** Ethiopia
103 C9 **Dedo de Deus** *mountain* Brazil
158 D2 **Dédougou** Burkina Faso
123 O4 **Dedovichi** Russian Federation
182 G3 **Dedurovka** Russian Federation
161 E6 **Dedza** Malawi
140 B3 **Dee** *watercourse* Ireland
142 E4 **Dee** *watercourse* Scotland UK
138 D2 **Dee** *watercourse* Wales UK
140 A3 **Deel** *watercourse* Ireland
85 N3 **Deep** *watercourse* Oklahoma USA
75 M2 **Deep Bay** Northwest Territories Canada
80 I7 **Deep Creek Range** Utah USA
86 C3 **Deep Fork** *watercourse* Oklahoma USA
78 H5 **Deep Inlet** Newfoundland and Labrador Canada
83 M3 **Deep River** Ontario Canada
164 5b **Deep Valley Bay** St Helena
141 F2 **Deepdale** North Yorkshire England UK
219 J3 **Deepwater** NSW Australia
82 E7 **Deepwater** Missouri USA
79 E10 **Deer Island** New Brunswick Canada
72 C8 **Deer Island** Alaska USA
79 J8 **Deer Lake** Newfoundland and Labrador Canada
76 H6 **Deer Lake** Ontario Canada
76 H6 **Deer Lake** Ontario Canada
80 I3 **Deer Lodge** Montana USA
80 G3 **Deer Park** Washington USA
87 I5 **Deer Point Lake** Florida USA
79 K8 **Deer Pond** Newfoundland and Labrador Canada
81 M7 **Deer Trail** Colorado USA
87 K7 **Deerfield Beach** Florida USA
214 A7 **Deering** *watercourse* NT Australia
81 O2 **Deering** North Dakota USA
143 C3 **Deerpark** Ireland
82 E3 **Deerwood** Minnesota USA
188 F3 **Defeng** Guizhou China
107 G6 **Defferrari** Argentina
82 I6 **Defiance** Ohio USA
85 H3 **Defiance Plateau** Arkansas USA
74 F3 **Defot** British Columbia Canada
161 G2 **Dega Medo** Ethiopia
161 G2 **Degeh Bur** Ethiopia
79 D9 **Dégelis** Quebec Canada
120 K5 **Degerfjärden** *bay* Sweden
120 L3 **Degerselet** *lake* Sweden
120 L3 **Degervattnet** *lake* Sweden
122 H2 **Deglunden** *lake* Sweden
101 H4 **Dégrad Claude** French Guiana
101 H4 **Dégrad Kwata** French Guiana
101 H3 **Dégrad Neuf** French Guiana
182 C3 **Degtevo** Russian Federation
178 G3 **Deh Dasht** Iran
179 I4 **Deh Dāti** Iran
179 H4 **Deh Hang** Iran
179 I2 **Deh Nabī** Iran
179 K3 **Deh Rāwod** Afghanistan
179 I3 **Deh Salm** Iran
179 I2 **Deh Tah** Iran
178 G3 **Dehak** Iran
178 G2 **Dehaq** Iran
178 F3 **Dehlorān** Iran
182 J6 **Dehqonobod** Uzbekistan
186 E4 **Dehra Dun** Uttaranchal India
186 F6 **Dehri** Bihar India
191 K4 **Dehui** Jilin China
120 inset **Deild** *cape* Iceland
126 F1 **Deinze** Belgium
179 I4 **Dejan-e Bālā** Iran
161 F1 **Dejen** Ethiopia
156 F5 **Dejen, Ras** *mountain* Ethiopia
133 B5 **Dejës, Maja e** *mountain* Albania
181 F3 **Dejilin** Xizang Zizhiqu China
130 E4 **Dekani** Slovenia
160 C4 **Dekese** Democratic Republic of Congo
159 F3 **Dekina** Nigeria
159 H3 **Dékoa** Central African Republic
75 O8 **Del Bonita** Alberta Canada
54 I9 **Del Cano Rise** *underwater feature* Southern Ocean
84 D4 **Del Mar** California USA
81 L8 **Del Norte** Colorado USA
85 L6 **Del Rio** Texas USA
138 C4 **Delabole** Cornwall England UK
109 9 **Delaford** Trinidad and Tobago
198 C6 **Delaki** Indonesia
84 E2 **Delamar Lake** Nevada USA
214 A3 **Delamere** NT Australia
156 E5 **Delami** Sudan
84 C3 **Delano** California USA
135 AL8 **Delarof Islands** Alaska USA
75 R5 **Delaronde Lake** Saskatchewan Canada
70 **Delaware** *admin. area* USA
82 J6 **Delaware** Ohio USA
83 N6 **Delaware** *watercourse* Pennsylvania USA
83 N7 **Delaware Bay** Delaware USA
78 C4 **Delay** *watercourse* Quebec Canada
142 E3 **Delbog** Highland Scotland UK
219 I7 **Delegate, Mount** Vic. Australia
127 H3 **Delémont** Switzerland
132 E2 **Deleni** Romania
155 J6 **Delep** Chad
156 B5 **Delep** Chad
123 K2 **Delet Teili** *bay* Finland
108 D3 **Delfín, Punta** *cape* Argentina
106 F6 **Delfín Huergo** Argentina
124 D1 **Delfzijl** Netherlands
80 C6 **Delgada, Point** California USA
108 D3 **Delgada, Punta** *cape* Argentina
163 H2 **Delgado, Cabo** *cape* Mozambique
185 K3 **Delger** Mongolia
190 G3 **Delgereh** Mongolia
190 E3 **Delgerhaan** Mongolia
190 G3 **Delgerhaan** Mongolia
190 E3 **Delgerhangai** Mongolia
190 G3 **Delgerkhaan Uul** *mountain* Mongolia
190 F3 **Delgertsogt** Mongolia
156 E3 **Delgo** Sudan
186 D5 **Delhi** Delhi India
186 D5 **Delhi** *admin. area* India
85 J2 **Delhi** Colorado USA
83 N5 **Delhi** New York USA
196 E5 **Deli** *island* Indonesia
88 B2 **Delicias** Mexico
132 B4 **Deligrad** Serbia
178 G2 **Delījān** Iran
185 K5 **Delingha** Qinghai China
196 C3 **Delitua** Indonesia
199 G6 **Deliverance Island** Qld Australia
85 J5 **Dell City** Texas USA
81 Q5 **Dell Rapids** South Dakota USA
130 B3 **Delle** Switzerland
155 G1 **Dellys** Algeria
91 F3 **Delmas** Haiti
214 C7 **Delmore Downs** NT Australia
133 C6 **Delphi** Greece
82 H6 **Delphi** Indiana USA
81 Q7 **Delphos** Kansas USA
85 K3 **Delphos** New Mexico USA
87 K7 **Delray Beach** Florida USA
120 J6 **Delsbo** Sweden
88 B1 **Delta** Mexico
159 F3 **Delta** *admin. area* Nigeria
81 K7 **Delta** Colorado USA
101 F2 **Delta Amacuro** *admin. area* Venezuela
214 F4 **Delta Downs** Qld Australia
72 E6 **Delta Junction** Alaska USA
87 K6 **Deltona** Florida USA
219 J3 **Delungra** NSW Australia
185 I3 **Deluun** Mongolia
143 E3 **Delvin** Ireland
132 D1 **Delyatyn** Ukraine
129 J5 **Dem el Begrat** Algeria
59 R2 **Demas Ice Tongue** Antarctica
160 C5 **Demba** Democratic Republic of Congo
156 F5 **Dembech'a** Ethiopia
164 8b **Dembeni** Mayotte
164 8a **Dembéni** Comoros
161 E2 **Dembī Dolo** Ethiopia
159 I3 **Dembia** Central African Republic
101 F5 **Demeni** *watercourse* Brazil
50 M8 **Demerara Abyssal Plain** *underwater feature* Atlantic Ocean
50 M9 **Demerara Plateau** *underwater feature* Atlantic Ocean
102 D4 **Demerval Lobão** Brazil
85 I4 **Deming** New Mexico USA
101 F4 **Demini** *watercourse* Brazil
101 F4 **Demini, Serras do** *range* Brazil
133 B5 **Demir Hisar** Macedonia
133 F6 **Demirköprü Barajı** *lake* Turkey
133 E5 **Demirköy** Turkey
130 B4 **Demonte** Italy
86 H4 **Demopolis** Alabama USA
196 D5 **Dempo, Gunung** *volcano* Indonesia
217 H6 **Dempster, Point** WA Australia
199 G4 **Demta** Indonesia
134 P7 **Dem'yanka** *watercourse* Russian Federation
123 Q4 **Demyansk** Russian Federation
134 O7 **Dem'yanskoye** Russian Federation
124 C1 **Den Burg** Netherlands
194 D3 **Den Chai** Thailand
124 C1 **Den Haag/'s-Gravenhage (The Hague)** Netherlands
124 C1 **Den Helder** Netherlands
124 C1 **Den Oever** Netherlands
142 F3 **Den of Glasslaw** Aberdeenshire Scotland UK
157 G5 **Denakil** *range* Ethiopia
157 G5 **Denakil Desert** Ethiopia
Denali *see* **McKinley, Mt** USA
161 G2 **Denan** Ethiopia
75 V6 **Denbeigh Point** Manitoba Canada
83 M4 **Denbigh** Ontario Canada
138 D1 **Denbigh** Denbighshire Wales UK
214 F7 **Denbigh Downs** Qld Australia
138 D1 **Denbighshire** *admin. area* Wales UK
196 E4 **Dendang** Indonesia
124 D1 **Denekamp** Netherlands
159 F2 **Denge** Nigeria
139 H3 **Dengie** Essex England UK
191 J4 **Dengta** Liaoning China
159 I3 **Denguiro** Central African Republic
216 C2 **Denham** WA Australia
220 5 **Denham Bay** Kermadec Islands New Zealand
214 E4 **Denham Island** Qld Australia
215 J7 **Denham Range** Qld Australia
216 C2 **Denham Sound** WA Australia
142 F5 **Denholm** Scottish Borders Scotland UK
129 G4 **Denia** Spain
218 A5 **Denial Bay** SA Australia
218 G6 **Deniliquin** NSW Australia
164 9 **Denis, Île** *island* Seychelles
86 C4 **Denison** Texas USA
59 J2 **Denison, Cape** Antarctica
213 J5 **Denison Plains** WA Australia
182 I3 **Denisovka** Kazakhstan
182 J2 **Denisovo** Russian Federation
187 E10 **Deniyaya** Sri Lanka
136 D6 **Denizli** *admin. area* Turkey
59 G2 **Denman Glacier** *ice* Antarctica
216 E7 **Denmark** WA Australia
122 F5 **Denmark** *country* Europe
87 K4 **Denmark** South Carolina USA
73 P5 **Denmark Strait** Greenland/Iceland
109 13 **Dennery** St Lucia
213 J6 **Dennis, Lake** WA Australia
183 J6 **Denov** Uzbekistan
197 G6 **Denpasar** Indonesia
221 9 **Dent Island** Campbell Island New Zealand
132 B3 **Denta** Romania
215 G7 **Denton** Qld Australia
81 K3 **Denton** Montana USA
86 C4 **Denton** Texas USA
89 F1 **Denton** *watercourse* Texas USA
199 I6 **D'Entrecasteaux Islands** Papua New Guinea
81 M7 **Denver** Colorado USA
85 K4 **Denver City** Texas USA
77 Q5 **Denys** *watercourse* Quebec Canada
186 D5 **Deoband** Uttar Pradesh India
103 A8 **Deodápolis** Brazil
186 F6 **Deogarh** *mountain* Chhattisgarh India
187 F7 **Deogarh** Orissa India
186 C6 **Deogarh** Rajasthan India
186 G6 **Deoghar** Jharkhand India
192 E4 **Deogjeog-do** *island* South Korea
194 E3 **DeoKeo Nua** *mountain* Laos
187 D7 **Deolali** Maharashtra India
187 D7 **Deoli** Madhya Pradesh India
187 E7 **Deoli** Maharashtra India
194 E3 **DeoMu Gia** *mountain* Laos
139 I2 **Deopham** Norfolk England UK
187 F7 **Deori** Chhattisgarh India
187 E7 **Deori** Maharashtra India
186 F5 **Deoria** Uttar Pradesh India
194 D2 **DeoTay Chang** *mountain* Laos
159 F3 **Dep** *watercourse* Nigeria
191 L2 **Dep** *watercourse* Russian Federation
86 C3 **Depew** Oklahoma USA
80 C4 **Depoe Bay** Oregon USA
196 E5 **Depok** Indonesia
213 K4 **Depot** *watercourse* NT Australia
216 G3 **Depot Springs** WA Australia
212 D6 **Depuch Island** WA Australia
179 L3 **Dera Bugti** Pakistan
179 L3 **Dera Ghazi Khan** Pakistan
179 L3 **Dera Ismail Khan** Pakistan
132 B4 **Đeravica** *mountain* Kosovo
179 L4 **Derawar Fort** Pakistan
182 H7 **Derāz Āb** Iran
135 AC5 **Derbeke** *watercourse* Russian Federation
133 F6 **Derbent** Turkey
160 C2 **Derbissaka** Central African Republic
213 G4 **Derby** WA Australia
139 F2 **Derby** Derby England UK
139 F2 **Derby** *admin. area* England UK
81 Q8 **Derby** Kansas USA
86 B6 **Derby** Texas USA
83 O4 **Derby Line** Vermont USA
141 G3 **Derbyshire** *admin. area* England UK
133 G7 **Derebucak** Turkey
139 H2 **Dereham** Norfolk England UK
133 D5 **Dereköy** Turkey
190 F3 **Deren** Mongolia
156 C5 **Déréssa** Chad
123 Q3 **Dereva** Russian Federation
198 F4 **Derewo** *watercourse* Indonesia
140 A2 **Derg** *watercourse* Northern Ireland UK
143 D4 **Derg, Lough** *lake* Ireland
182 E3 **Dergachi** Russian Federation
181 G3 **Dergaon** Assam India
162 C4 **Derm** Namibia
133 C6 **Dermatas, Akra** *cape* Greece
140 B3 **Dermotstown** Ireland
86 F4 **Dermott** Arkansas USA
89 H2 **Dernieres, Isles** *islands* Louisiana USA
123 O5 **Dernovichi** Belarus
59 C2 **Derom, Mount** Antarctica
129 H6 **Derrag** Algeria
163 G3 **Derre** Mozambique
143 C3 **Derreen** Ireland
161 H3 **Derri** Somalia
143 C5 **Derriana Lough** *lake* Ireland
140 A3 **Derry** Ireland
143 E2 **Derry** *admin. area* Northern Ireland UK
143 C2 **Derrycorrib** Ireland
140 A3 **Derrygolan** Ireland
143 D3 **Derrylahan** Ireland
140 A2 **Derrylin** Fermanagh Northern Ireland UK
140 B3 **Derrymullen** Ireland
140 B2 **Derryork** Limavady Northern Ireland UK
140 A3 **Derryrobinson** Ireland
139 H2 **Dersingham** Norfolk England UK
156 F4 **Derudeb** Sudan
142 B4 **Dervaig** Highland Scotland UK
130 G4 **Derventa** Bosnia and Herzegovina
140 B1 **Dervock** Ballymoney Northern Ireland UK
138 D1 **Derwen** Denbighshire Wales UK
141 H2 **Derwent** *watercourse* England UK
134 R4 **Deryabino** Russian Federation
182 J3 **Derzhavinsk** Kazakhstan
82 E6 **Des Moines** Iowa USA
82 D5 **Des Moines** *watercourse* Minnesota USA

85 K2 **Des Moines** New Mexico USA
86 F5 **Des Ourses Swamp** Louisiana USA
78 D5 **Des Prairies, Lac** *lake* Quebec Canada
132 C4 **Desa** Romania
106 E5 **Desaguadero** *watercourse* Argentina
104 D5 **Desaguadero** *watercourse* Bolivia
104 D5 **Desaguadero** Peru
106 D5 **Desague, Cerro** *mountain* Argentina
187 E7 **Desaiganj** Maharashtra India
84 D4 **Descanso** California USA
77 R4 **Descareaux, Lac** *lake* Quebec Canada
126 E3 **Descartes** France
78 C6 **Desceliers, Lac** *lake* Quebec Canada
75 T5 **Deschambault Lake** Saskatchewan Canada
75 Q4 **Descharme** *watercourse* Saskatchewan Canada
75 Q4 **Descharme Lake** Saskatchewan Canada
80 E4 **Deschutes** *watercourse* Oregon USA
105 F4 **Desconcierto** Bolivia
108 C4 **Deseado** *watercourse* Argentina
108 A5 **Deseado, Cabo** *cape* Chile
84 F5 **Desemboque** Mexico
108 C4 **Desengaño, Punta** *cape* Argentina
83 M4 **Deseronto** Ontario Canada
84 E4 **Desert Center** California USA
84 D4 **Desert Hot Springs** California USA
80 G6 **Desert Ranch Reservoir** Nevada USA
80 F6 **Desert Valley** Nevada USA
164 2 **Desertas, Ilhas** *islands* Madeira
164 2 **Deserte Grande** *island* Madeira
105 I1 **Deserto** Brazil
109 16 **Deshaies** Guadeloupe
81 Q6 **Deshler** Nebraska USA
143 D5 **Deshure** Ireland
77 Q8 **Desmaraisville** Quebec Canada
136 D2 **Desna** *watercourse* Ukraine
78 C5 **Desnambuc, Lac** *lake* Quebec Canada
108 A5 **Desolación, Isla** *island* Chile
108 B6 **Desolada, Bahía** *bay* Chile
86 C4 **DeSoto** Texas USA
133 D7 **Despotiko** *island* Greece
132 B3 **Despotovac** Serbia
164 9 **Desroches, Île** *island* Seychelles
91 F3 **Dessalines** Haiti
124 G2 **Dessau** Germany
124 C2 **Dessel** Belgium
87 H5 **Destin** Florida USA
108 D4 **Desvelos, Bahía** *bay* Argentina
126 E1 **Desvres** France
132 B2 **Deszk** Hungary
162 E3 **Dete** Zimbabwe
132 A4 **Đetinja** *watercourse* Serbia
123 O3 **Detkovo** Russian Federation
82 H4 **Detour, Point** Michigan USA
82 J5 **Detroit** Michigan USA
80 D4 **Detroit** Oregon USA
86 D4 **Detroit** Texas USA
81 R3 **Detroit Lakes** Minnesota USA
130 H2 **Detva** Slovakia
186 C6 **Detvas** Rajasthan India
122 D5 **Deutsche Bucht** *bay* Germany
125 H4 **Deutschlandsberg** Austria
132 C3 **Deva** Romania
187 D8 **Devadurga** Karnataka India
133 E5 **Deveçatağı** Turkey
130 G3 **Devecser** Hungary
136 E5 **Develi** Turkey
187 C8 **Devgarh** Maharashtra India
186 C5 **Devikot** Rajasthan India
138 D2 **Devil's Bridge** Ceredigion Wales UK
Devil's Island *see* **Diable, Île du** French Guiana
81 P2 **Devils Lake** North Dakota USA
74 E3 **Devil's Paw** *mountain* British Columbia/Alaska Canada/USA
86 B6 **Devine** Texas USA
139 F3 **Devizes** Wiltshire England UK
86 B3 **Devol** Oklahoma USA
138 D4 **Devon** *admin. area* England UK
73 K3 **Devon Island** Nunavut Canada
214 F6 **Devoncourt** Qld Australia
219 R10 **Devonport** Tas. Australia
163 F3 **Devure** *watercourse* Zimbabwe
196 B3 **Dewa, Tanjung** *cape* Indonesia
197 H5 **Dewakang Besar** *island* Indonesia
186 D6 **Dewas** Madhya Pradesh India
84 F3 **Dewey** Arizona USA
82 D8 **Dewey** Oklahoma USA
83 M8 **DeWitt** Virginia USA
139 E4 **Dewlish** Dorset England UK
189 H3 **Dexing** Jiangxi China
86 C2 **Dexter** Kansas USA
79 D10 **Dexter** Maine USA
85 J4 **Dexter** New Mexico USA
217 L4 **Dey Dey, Lake** SA Australia
188 D2 **Deyang** Sichuan China
178 G4 **Deyyer** Iran
178 F3 **Dezfūl** Iran
132 F2 **Dezghingea** Moldova
72 C5 **Dezhneva, Mys** *cape* Russian Federation
191 H5 **Dezhou** Shandong China
188 D3 **Dezhou** Sichuan China
178 D5 **Dhahbān** Saudi Arabia
Dhahran *see* **Az Zahran** Saudi Arabia
181 G4 **Dhaka** Bangladesh
181 G4 **Dhaka** *admin. area* Bangladesh
186 F5 **Dhaka** Bihar India
129 J6 **Dhalaa** Algeria
178 E7 **Dhamār** Yemen
187 E7 **Dhamtari** Chhattisgarh India
186 G6 **Dhanbad** Jharkhand India
187 C6 **Dhandhuka** Gujarat India
186 C6 **Dhanera** Gujarat India
186 E5 **Dhangarhi** Nepal
186 D5 **Dhansia** Rajasthan India
186 F6 **Dhanwar** Jharkhand India
187 D6 **Dhar** Madhya Pradesh India
187 F7 **Dharakota** Orissa India
186 G5 **Dharan Bazar** Nepal
181 G4 **Dharmanagar** Tripura India
187 E7 **Dharmapuri** Andhra Pradesh India
187 D8 **Dharmapuri** Maharashtra India
187 D8 **Dharmavaram** Andhra Pradesh India
187 F6 **Dharmjaygarh** Chhattisgarh India
187 D8 **Dharur** Andhra Pradesh India
187 D7 **Dharur** Maharashtra India
187 D8 **Dharwad** Karnataka India
186 F5 **Dhaulagiri** *mountain* Nepal
186 D5 **Dhaulpur** Rajasthan India
136 E6 **Dhekelia Sovereign Base Area** *UK overseas territory* Cyprus
181 H3 **Dhemaji** Assam India
187 F7 **Dhenkanal** Orissa India
133 A5 **Dhërmi** Albania
178 F3 **Dhī Qār** *admin. area* Iraq
181 G3 **Dhing** Assam India
187 C7 **Dhola** Gujarat India
186 C6 **Dholka** Gujarat India
161 G3 **Dhoomadeere** Somalia
187 C7 **Dhoraji** Gujarat India
186 C6 **Dhrangadhra** Gujarat India
186 C6 **Dhrol** Gujarat India
187 D7 **Dhule** Maharashtra India
187 E6 **Dhuma** Madhya Pradesh India
186 F5 **Dhunche** Nepal
186 D6 **Dhuri** Madhya Pradesh India
161 I2 **Dhuudo** Somalia
161 H2 **Dhuusa Marreeb** Somalia
194 F5 **Di Linh** Vietnam
133 D8 **Dia** *island* Greece
101 H3 **Diable, Île du (Devil's Island)** *island* French Guiana
109 15 **Diables, Morne aux** *volcano* Dominica
74 K8 **Diablo** Washington USA
88 D2 **Diablo Plateau** Texas USA
84 B2 **Diablo Range** California USA
109 15 **Diablotins, Morne** *volcano* Dominica
133 E8 **Diafani** Greece
154 E6 **Diafarabé** Mali
154 F6 **Diaka** *watercourse* Mali
154 D6 **Diakon** Mali
154 D6 **Dialafara** Mali
154 D6 **Dialakoto** Senegal
109 14 **Diamant, Rocher de** *cape* Martinique
106 F5 **Diamante** Argentina
104 C3 **Diamante Auúl** Peru
104 C1 **Diamante Azul** Peru
218 D1 **Diamantina** *watercourse* Qld Australia
103 D7 **Diamantina** Brazil
103 D6 **Diamantina, Chapada** *region* Brazil
55 O8 **Diamantina Fracture Zone** *underwater feature* Indian Ocean
214 F7 **Diamantina Lakes** Qld Australia
215 I6 **Diamond Downs** Qld Australia
187 G6 **Diamond Harbour** West Bengal India
80 D5 **Diamond Lake** Oregon USA
216 F3 **Diamond Well** WA Australia
154 D6 **Diamou** Mali
188 D4 **Dian Chi** *lake* Yunnan China
78 D2 **Diana, Baie** *bay* Quebec Canada
78 D3 **Diana, Lac** *lake* Quebec Canada
76 I1 **Diana Lake** Nunavut Canada
164 5b **Diana's Peak** *volcano* St Helena
189 H2 **Dianbu** Anhui China
127 I5 **Diane, Étang de** *lagoon* Corsica France
188 D1 **Dianga** Gansu China
154 E6 **Diangounte Kamara** Mali
215 J3 **Dianne Bank** Coral Sea Islands Territory Australia
103 C5 **Dianópolis** Brazil
158 C3 **Dianra** Côte d'Ivoire
188 C4 **Dianyang** Yunnan China
188 E4 **Diao Jiang** *watercourse* Guangxi Zhuangzu Zizhiqu China
158 E2 **Diapaga** Burkina Faso
133 C7 **Diaporioi** *island* Greece
194 B4 **Diavolo, Mount** Andaman and Nicobar Islands India
86 F3 **Diaz** Arkansas USA
100 B5 **Díaz de Pineda** Ecuador
162 C5 **Diaz Point** *cape* Namibia
160 C5 **Dibaya** Democratic Republic of Congo
162 D5 **Dibeng** South Africa
D'Iberville *see* **Caubvick, Mount** Canada
78 B5 **D'Iberville, Lac** *lake* Quebec Canada
199 G6 **Dibiri Island** Papua New Guinea
181 H3 **Dibrugarh** Assam India
100 C2 **Dibulla** Colombia
221 8 **Dick, Mount** Auckland Islands New Zealand
85 L4 **Dickens** Texas USA
81 N3 **Dickinson** North Dakota USA
86 H2 **Dickson** Tennessee USA
130 D5 **Dicomano** Italy
219 J1 **Didcot** Qld Australia
139 F3 **Didcot** Oxfordshire England UK
138 E2 **Diddlebury** Shropshire England UK
155 H3 **Dider** Algeria
161 F2 **Didesa** *watercourse* Ethiopia
154 E6 **Didiéni** Mali
157 F5 **Didigsala** Ethiopia
158 D2 **Didir** Burkina Faso
186 D5 **Didwana** Rajasthan India
123 M5 **Didžiulis** *lake* Lithuania
127 G4 **Die** France
188 D1 **Die Shan** *range* Jiangsu China
158 D2 **Diébougou** Burkina Faso
130 D5 **Diecimo** Italy
107 H5 **Dieciocho de Julio** Uruguay
72 I8 **Diefenbaker, Lake** Saskatchewan Canada
106 D3 **Diego de Almagro** Chile
108 A5 **Diego de Almagro, Isla** *island* Chile
54 L5 **Diego Garcìa** *island* British Indian Ocean Territory
109 9 **Diego Martin** *admin. area* Trinidad and Tobago
108 C6 **Diego Ramírez, Islas** *islands* Chile
108 B5 **Diego Ritchie** Argentina
127 H2 **Diekirch** Luxembourg
154 E6 **Diéma** Mali
216 F4 **Diemals** WA Australia
124 F3 **Diemantstein** Germany
124 E2 **Diemel** *watercourse* Germany
124 E2 **Diemelsee** *lake* Germany
194 D2 **Điện Biên Phu** Vietnam
194 E3 **Diễn Châu** Vietnam
126 E2 **Dieppe** France
109 19 **Dieppe Bay Town** St Kitts and Nevis
86 D3 **Dierks** Arkansas USA
80 H5 **Dietrich** Idaho USA
127 G4 **Dieulefit** France
127 H2 **Dieuze** France
104 B2 **Diez de Agosto** Peru
159 G2 **Diffa** Niger
160 D3 **Digba** Democratic Republic of Congo
79 F10 **Digby** Nova Scotia Canada
79 E10 **Digby Neck** *peninsula* Nova Scotia Canada
76 H3 **Digges** Manitoba Canada
77 Q1 **Digges Islands** Nunavut Canada
187 G7 **Digha** West Bengal India
81 O7 **Dighton** Kansas USA
127 H4 **Digne** France
124 B4 **Digoin** France
195 J6 **Digos** Philippines
187 D7 **Digras** Maharashtra India
179 L4 **Digri** Pakistan
199 G5 **Digul** *watercourse* Indonesia
78 F4 **Dihourse, Lac** *lake* Quebec Canada
161 G3 **Diinsoor** Somalia
178 F3 **Dijlah, Nahr** *watercourse* Iraq
127 G3 **Dijon** France
159 H3 **Dik** Chad
135 X3 **Dika, Mys** *cape* Russian Federation
133 E5 **Dikaia** Greece
120 J4 **Dikanäs** Sweden
157 G5 **Dikhil** Djibouti
123 M4 **Dikļi** Latvia
158 C3 **Dikodougou** Côte d'Ivoire
134 R4 **Dikson** Russian Federation
133 D8 **Dikti** *range* Greece
159 G2 **Dikwa** Nigeria
161 F2 **Dila** Ethiopia
198 C6 **Dili** Timor-Leste (East Timor)
155 I5 **Dilia** *watercourse* Niger
194 B4 **Diligent Strait** Andaman and Nicobar Islands India
182 D6 **Dilizhan** Armenia
215 G7 **Dillcar** Qld Australia
86 B6 **Dilley** Texas USA
154 E6 **Dilli** Mali
156 D5 **Dilling** Sudan
72 D7 **Dillingham** Alaska USA
75 Q5 **Dillon** *watercourse* Saskatchewan Canada
80 I4 **Dillon** Montana USA
221 E6 **Dillon Cone** *mountain* New Zealand
82 I7 **Dillsboro** Indiana USA
182 E6 **Dilmamedli** Azerbaijan
160 C6 **Dilolo** Democratic Republic of Congo
133 D7 **Dilos** *island* Greece
218 F6 **Dilpurra** NSW Australia
159 G4 **Dimako** Cameroon
181 G4 **Dimapur** Nagaland India
136 F7 **Dimashq (Damascus)** Syria
181 H5 **Dimawhaso** Myanmar
160 C5 **Dimbelenge** Democratic Republic of Congo
158 D3 **Dimbokro** Côte d'Ivoire
218 F7 **Dimboola** Vic. Australia
215 H4 **Dimbulah** Qld Australia
182 F2 **Dimitrovgrad** Russian Federation
85 K3 **Dimmitt** Texas USA
214 G6 **Dimora** Qld Australia
195 J5 **Dinagat** *island* Philippines
195 J5 **Dinagat Sound** Philippines
181 F4 **Dinajpur** Bangladesh
126 C2 **Dinan** France
179 H3 **Dīnān Āb** Iran
186 D4 **Dinanagar** Punjab India
155 F6 **Dinangourou** Mali
127 G1 **Dinant** Belgium
178 G3 **Dīnār, Kūh-e** *mountain* Iran
126 C2 **Dinard** France
138 C1 **Dinas** Gwynedd Wales UK
138 C2 **Dinas** Pembrokeshire Wales UK
182 J6 **Dinau** Uzbekistan
161 F2 **Dinchiya** *watercourse* Ethiopia
162 B2 **Dinde** Angola
156 E5 **Dinder** Sudan
156 E5 **Dinder** *watercourse* Sudan
187 E8 **Dindi** *watercourse* Andhra Pradesh India
187 D9 **Dindigul** Tamil Nadu India
163 F4 **Dindiza** Mozambique
186 E6 **Dindori** Madhya Pradesh India
161 E2 **Ding Ding** Sudan
190 F5 **Dingbian** Shaanxi China
189 H2 **Dingcheng** Anhui China
188 F5 **Dingcheng** Hainan China
186 G5 **Dingla** Nepal
143 B4 **Dingle** Ireland
143 B4 **Dingle Bay** Ireland
143 B4 **Dingle Peninsula** Ireland
215 J7 **Dingo** Qld Australia
181 H2 **Dingqing** Xizang Zizhiqu China
189 G1 **Dingtao** Shandong China
158 B2 **Dinguiraye** Guinea
79 H9 **Dingwall** Nova Scotia Canada
142 D3 **Dingwall** Highland Scotland UK
190 E6 **Dingxi** Gansu China
191 G5 **Dingxiang** Shanxi China
191 H5 **Dingzhou** Hebei China
194 E2 **Đình Lập** Vietnam
124 F3 **Dinkelsbühl** Germany
124 E1 **Dinklage** Germany
142 F3 **Dinnet** Aberdeenshire Scotland UK
138 C1 **Dinorwic** Gwynedd Wales UK
81 K6 **Dinosaur** Colorado USA
130 B2 **Dinozé** France
75 R7 **Dinsmore** Saskatchewan Canada
196 E5 **Dintiteladas** Indonesia
84 C2 **Dinuba** California USA
105 I5 **Diorama** Brazil
158 C3 **Dioulatie-Dougou** Côte d'Ivoire
154 C6 **Diouloulou** Senegal
154 E6 **Dioura** Mali
154 C6 **Diourbel** Senegal
181 G4 **Diphu** Assam India
90 C4 **Dipilto** Nicaragua
179 L5 **Diplo** Pakistan
84 G6 **Dipo** Mexico
195 I5 **Dipolog** Philippines
142 C5 **Dippen** Argyll and Bute Scotland UK
75 R5 **Dipper Lake** Saskatchewan Canada
142 D5 **Dipple** South Ayrshire Scotland UK
189 H2 **Dipu** Zhejiang China
100 B3 **Dipurdú** Colombia
179 I4 **Dīr** Iran
179 K3 **Dirao** Pakistan
154 F5 **Diré** Mali
161 G2 **Dirē Dawa** Ethiopia
161 G2 **Dirē Dawa** *admin. area* Ethiopia
215 G2 **Direction, Cape** Qld Australia
210 inset **Direction Island (Tikus)** Cocos (Keeling) Islands Australia
133 C6 **Dirfys** *range* Greece
179 K3 **Dirgi** Pakistan
162 D3 **Dirico** Angola
216 C2 **Dirk Hartog Island** WA Australia
155 I5 **Dirkou** Niger
142 F4 **Dirleton** East Lothian Scotland UK
156 D5 **Dirra** Sudan
219 I3 **Dirranbandi** Qld Australia
84 G1 **Dirty Devil** *watercourse* Utah USA
186 C6 **Disa** Gujarat India
59 T2 **Disappointment, Cape** Antarctica
109 8 **Disappointment, Cape** South Georgia
80 C3 **Disappointment, Cape** Washington USA
212 G7 **Disappointment, Lake** WA Australia
221 8 **Disappointment Island** Auckland Islands New Zealand
213 H4 **Disaster, Mount** WA Australia
219 J7 **Disaster Bay** *watercourse* NSW Australia
54 D9 **Discovery Guyot** *underwater feature* Southern Ocean
195 F3 **Discovery Reef** Paracel Islands
127 I3 **Disentis** Switzerland
127 I3 **Disentis Muster** Switzerland
156 E2 **Dishnā** Egypt
Disko *see* **Qeqertarsuaq** Greenland
75 S7 **Disley** Saskatchewan Canada
214 F5 **Dismal** *watercourse* Qld Australia
81 O6 **Dismal** *watercourse* Nebraska USA
59 D2 **Dismal Mountains** Antarctica
123 O5 **Disna** Belarus
181 G3 **Dispur** Assam India
139 I2 **Diss** Norfolk England UK
140 E2 **Distington** Cumbria England UK
107 G5 **Distrito Federal** *admin. area* Argentina
103 C6 **Distrito Federal** *admin. area* Brazil
89 F5 **Distrito Federal** *admin. area* Mexico
195 I5 **Dit** *island* Philippines
158 B2 **Ditinn** Guinea
187 C7 **Diu** Daman and Diu India
197 J1 **Diuata Mountains** *range* Philippines
195 J5 **Diuata Point** Philippines
126 D5 **Diusse** France
125 G5 **Divača** Slovenia
132 B3 **Divci** Serbia
126 D3 **Dive** *watercourse* France
182 D2 **Diveyevo** Russian Federation
187 E8 **Divi, Point** Andhra Pradesh India
130 G4 **Divičani** Bosnia and Herzegovina
120 K2 **Dividalen** *valley* Norway
195 I3 **Divilican Bay** Philippines
130 H2 **Divín** Slovakia
103 C8 **Divinópolis** Brazil
105 F3 **Divisa, Serra da** *range* Brazil
88 B2 **División del Norte** Mexico
103 B7 **Divisões, Serra das** *range* Brazil
133 A5 **Divjakë** Albania
182 D4 **Divnoye** Russian Federation
158 C3 **Divo** Côte d'Ivoire
128 C4 **Divor, Barragem do** *lake* Portugal
160 C6 **Divuma** Democratic Republic of Congo
81 N6 **Dix** Nebraska USA
82 G6 **Dixon** Illinois USA
74 E5 **Dixon Entrance** British Columbia/Alaska Canada/USA
74 M4 **Dixonville** Alberta Canada
178 F2 **Diyālá** *admin. area* Iraq
136 G6 **Diyarbakır** Turkey
136 G6 **Diyarbakir** *admin. area* Turkey
126 F2 **Dizy** France
160 A3 **Dja** *watercourse* Cameroon
155 I4 **Djado** Niger
120 L4 **Djäkneboda** Sweden
155 H2 **Djamâa** Algeria
159 G5 **Djambala** Congo
159 G4 **Djampiel** Cameroon
155 H4 **Djanet** Algeria
223 15a **Djarrit** Marshall Islands
199 I4 **Djaul Island** Papua New Guinea
156 B5 **Djédaa** Chad
155 G2 **Djelfa** Algeria
154 F6 **Djenné** Mali
132 C3 **Djerdap** *region* Serbia
159 G3 **Djerem** *watercourse* Cameroon
155 J6 **Djermaya** Chad
129 J6 **Djeurf** Algeria
158 D2 **Djibo** Burkina Faso
157 G5 **Djibouti** *country* Africa
157 G5 **Djibouti** Djibouti
154 E5 **Djiguéni** Mauritania
129 G6 **Djilali Ben Amar** Algeria
158 C2 **Djinko** *watercourse* Guinea
160 C3 **Djolu** Democratic Republic of Congo
156 B5 **Djombo Kibbit** Chad
158 C3 **Djon** *watercourse* Guinea
159 G4 **Djoua** *watercourse* Congo
159 I3 **Djoubissi** Central African Republic
158 E3 **Djougou** Benin
159 G4 **Djoum** Cameroon
159 G3 **Djoumboli** Cameroon
155 J5 **Djourab, Erg du** *desert* Chad
120 inset **Djúpavík** Iceland
120 inset **Djúpivogur** Iceland
120 K5 **Djupsjö** Sweden
121 M3 **Djupträsket** *lake* Sweden
120 L2 **Djupvik** Norway
122 F4 **Djursland** *region* Denmark
122 I3 **Djursö** *island* Sweden
120 H5 **Djursvallen** Sweden
135 AD4 **Dmitriya Lapteva, Proliv** *strait* Russian Federation
182 F3 **Dmitriyevka** Russian Federation
132 G2 **Dmytrivka** Ukraine
214 C7 **Dneiper** NT Australia
182 A2 **Dnepr** *watercourse* Russian Federation
Dneprodzerzhinsk *see* **Dniprodzerzhyns'k** Ukraine
136 C2 **Dnieper** *watercourse* Belarus
Dniepro *see* **Dnipro** Ukraine
136 D2 **Dnipro (Dniepro)** *watercourse* Ukraine
136 E3 **Dnipropetrovs'k** Ukraine
136 E3 **Dnipropetrovs'ka Oblast'** *admin. area* Ukraine
136 C3 **Dnister** *watercourse* Ukraine
123 O4 **Dno** Russian Federation
194 E3 **Đô Lương** Vietnam
163 F3 **Doa** Mozambique
179 L2 **Doaba** Pakistan
79 E9 **Doaktown** New Brunswick Canada
197 H5 **Doangdoangan Besar** *island* Indonesia
197 H5 **Doangdoangan Kecil** *island* Indonesia
159 H3 **Doba** Chad
130 E3 **Dobbiaco** Italy
214 E5 **Dobbyn** Qld Australia
123 L4 **Dobele** Latvia
123 L4 **Dobeles** *admin. area* Latvia
198 E4 **Doberai, Jazirah** *peninsula* Indonesia
125 H3 **Dobersberg** Austria
159 G3 **Dobinga** Cameroon
198 E5 **Dobo** Indonesia
130 H4 **Doboj** Bosnia and Herzegovina
87 K5 **Doboy Sound** Georgia USA
132 C3 **Dobra** Romania
132 B3 **Dobra** Serbia
132 H2 **Dobre** Ukraine
123 K6 **Dobre Miasto** Poland
132 E4 **Dobrich** Bulgaria
132 E4 **Dobrich** *admin. area* Bulgaria
130 H4 **Dobrinje** Bosnia and Herzegovina
182 C3 **Dobrinka** Russian Federation
130 H5 **Dobro Polje** Bosnia and Herzegovina
125 J4 **Döbrököz** Hungary
130 H5 **Dobromani** Bosnia and Herzegovina
133 C5 **Dobrošinci** Macedonia
132 G1 **Dobrovody** Ukraine
125 M1 **Dobroye** Belarus
182 C3 **Dobroye** Russian Federation
193 J2 **Dobroye, Ozero** *lake* Russian Federation
123 N3 **Dobruchi** Russian Federation
132 F3 **Dobruja** *region* Romania
182 G1 **Dobryanka** Russian Federation
132 G1 **Dobryanka** Ukraine
123 P5 **Dobryn'** Belarus
125 H1 **Dobrzany** Poland
125 J1 **Dobrzejewice** Poland
221 C6 **Dobson** *watercourse* New Zealand
87 K2 **Dobson** North Carolina USA
195 H6 **Doc Can** *island* Philippines
100 B3 **Docampó, Ensenada de** *bay* Colombia
103 D7 **Doce** *watercourse* Brazil
142 D4 **Dochart** *watercourse* Scotland UK
217 K2 **Docker** *watercourse* WA Australia
Docker River *see* **Kaltukatjara** Australia
139 H2 **Docking** Norfolk England UK
120 I5 **Dockmyr** Sweden
120 K5 **Docksta** Sweden
88 E4 **Doctor Arroyo** Mexico
108 B3 **Doctor Ricardo Rojas** Argentina
186 D4 **Doda** Jammu and Kashmir India/Pakistan
186 D4 **Doda** *watercourse* Jammu and Kashmir India/Pakistan
Dodecanese *see* **Sporades** Greece
81 N3 **Dodge** North Dakota USA
81 O8 **Dodge City** Kansas USA
76 C3 **Dodge Lake** Saskatchewan Canada
138 C4 **Dodman Point** England UK
158 C3 **Dodo** *watercourse* Côte d'Ivoire
161 F5 **Dodoma** Tanzania
161 F5 **Dodoma** *admin. area* Tanzania
81 K2 **Dodson** Montana USA
198 C4 **Dofa** Indonesia
132 E2 **Dofteana** Romania
74 J7 **Dog Creek** British Columbia Canada
109 20 **Dog Island** Anguilla
78 H4 **Dog Island** Newfoundland and Labrador Canada
82 G2 **Dog Lake** Ontario Canada
133 G6 **Döğer** Turkey
130 B4 **Dogliani** Italy
127 K3 **Dogna** Italy
192 G4 **Dōgo** *island* Japan
192 G4 **Dōgo** *mountain* Japan
160 D2 **Dogoba** Sudan
158 D2 **Dogon Plateau** *plain* Burkina Faso
155 G6 **Dogondoutchi** Niger
136 H5 **Doğubeyazit** Turkey
136 G5 **Doğukaradeniz Dağları** Turkey
109 18 **Dogwood Point** St Kitts and Nevis
181 E3 **Dogxung Zangbo** *watercourse* Xizang Zizhiqu China
Doha *see* **Ad Dawḩah** Qatar
198 C3 **Doi** *island* Indonesia
74 K4 **Doig** *watercourse* British Columbia Canada
102 D5 **Dois Irmãos, Serra dos** *range* Brazil
103 A9 **Dois Vizinhos** Brazil
127 G1 **Doische** Belgium
133 C5 **Dojran, Lake** Greece
198 E5 **Doka** Indonesia
156 F5 **Doka** Sudan
122 F2 **Dokka** *watercourse* Norway
158 C2 **Doko** Guinea
133 C7 **Dokos** *island* Greece
127 L1 **Doksy** Czech Republic
136 F3 **Dokuchayevs'k** Ukraine
199 F5 **Dolak, Pulau** *island* Indonesia
81 P4 **Doland** South Dakota USA
138 D2 **Dolau** Powys Wales UK
73 L9 **Dolbeau-Mistassini** Quebec Canada
138 C2 **Dolbenmaen** Gwynedd Wales UK
131 G7 **Dolcedorme, Serra** *mountain* Italy
50 O9 **Doldrums Fracture Zone** *underwater feature* Atlantic Ocean
127 G3 **Dole** France
133 B5 **Dolenci** Macedonia
134 M5 **Dolgiy, Ostrov** *island* Russian Federation
123 O3 **Dolgovka** Russian Federation
132 D1 **Dolina** Ukraine
193 I1 **Dolinsk** Russian Federation
160 A4 **Dolisie (Loubomo)** Congo
132 C3 **Dolj** *admin. area* Romania
130 G4 **Doljani** Croatia
142 E4 **Dollar** Clackmannanshire Scotland UK
75 Q8 **Dollard** Saskatchewan Canada
124 D1 **Dollart** *bay* Netherlands
59 U2 **Dolleman Island** Antarctica
140 B3 **Dollys Grove** Ireland
125 I2 **Dolnośląskie** *admin. area* Poland
125 J3 **Dolný Kubín** Slovakia
198 A4 **Dolo** Indonesia
161 G3 **Dolo Odo** Ethiopia
107 G6 **Dolores** Argentina
90 B3 **Dolores** Guatemala
107 G5 **Dolores** Uruguay
81 K8 **Dolores** Colorado USA
85 H1 **Dolores** *watercourse* Colorado USA
88 E4 **Dolores Hidalgo** Mexico
125 K5 **Dolovo** Serbia
109 7 **Dolphin, Cape** Falkland Islands
72 H5 **Dolphin and Union Strait** Nunavut Canada
162 B5 **Dolphin Head** *cape* Namibia
212 D6 **Dolphin Island** WA Australia
138 D1 **Dolwyddelan** Conwy Wales UK
132 D1 **Dolyna** Ukraine
132 F2 **Dolyns'ke** Ukraine
132 E1 **Dolzhok** Ukraine
198 F4 **Dom, Gunung** *mountain* Indonesia
105 G3 **Dom Alexandre** Brazil
107 H4 **Dom Pedrito** Brazil
102 C4 **Dom Pedro** Brazil
159 F3 **Doma** Nigeria
79 F7 **Domagaya Lake** Newfoundland and Labrador Canada
133 F6 **Domaniç** Turkey
130 G5 **Domanovići** Bosnia and Herzegovina
180 D2 **Domar Qu** *watercourse* Xizang Zizhiqu China
182 C5 **Dombaj, Gora** *mountain* Russian Federation
182 H3 **Dombarovskiy** Russian Federation
120 F5 **Dombås** Norway
182 D5 **Dombay** Russian Federation
163 F3 **Dombe** Mozambique
162 B2 **Dombe Grande** Angola
127 G3 **Dombes** *region* France
125 J4 **Dombóvár** Hungary
132 B1 **Dombrád** Hungary
124 B2 **Domburg** Netherlands
74 K6 **Dome Creek** British Columbia Canada
106 D2 **Domeyko, Cordillera** *range* Chile
126 D2 **Domfront** France
101 F2 **Domingo** Venezuela
91 I4 **Dominica** *country* Caribbean
91 I4 **Dominica Passage** Guadeloupe
91 G3 **Dominican Republic** *country* Caribbean
73 L5 **Dominion, Cape** Nunavut Canada
78 H6 **Dominion Lake** Newfoundland and Labrador Canada
59 L1 **Dominion Range** Antarctica
160 C4 **Domiongo** Democratic Republic of Congo
181 G3 **Domka** Bhutan
161 H2 **Domo** Ethiopia
124 E4 **Domodossola** Italy
133 C6 **Domokos** Greece
163 H2 **Domoni** Comoros
127 H2 **Dompaire** France
197 H6 **Dompu** Indonesia
120 K5 **Domsjö** Sweden
106 D6 **Domuyo, Volcán** *volcano* Argentina
125 H4 **Domžale** Slovenia
215 J6 **Don** *watercourse* Qld Australia
126 D3 **Don** *watercourse* France
182 D4 **Don** *watercourse* Russian Federation
141 G3 **Don** *watercourse* England UK
142 F3 **Don** *watercourse* Scotland UK
195 J6 **Don Carlos** Philippines
85 L7 **Don Martin** Mexico
84 B2 **Don Pedro Reservoir** California USA
194 C5 **Don Sak** Thailand
85 I4 **Dona** New Mexico USA
140 B3 **Donabate** Ireland
140 A2 **Donagh** Fermanagh Northern Ireland UK
140 C2 **Donaghadee** Ards Northern Ireland UK
140 B2 **Donaghmore** Dungannon Northern Ireland UK
218 F7 **Donald** Vic. Australia
74 M7 **Donald** British Columbia Canada
87 I5 **Donalsonville** Georgia USA
130 F2 **Donau (Danube)** *watercourse* Austria
130 C2 **Donau (Danube)** *watercourse* Germany
141 G3 **Doncaster** South Yorkshire England UK
132 E4 **Donchevo** Bulgaria
187 D7 **Dondaicha** Maharashtra India
162 B1 **Dondo** Angola
163 F3 **Dondo** Mozambique
187 E11 **Dondra Head** *cape* Sri Lanka
143 D2 **Donegal** Ireland
143 E1 **Donegal** *admin. area* Ireland
143 D2 **Donegal Bay** Ireland
143 C4 **Donegal Point** Ireland
136 F3 **Donets'k** Ukraine
136 F3 **Donets'ka Oblast'** *admin. area* Ukraine
194 E3 **Đông Hà** Vietnam
188 E2 **Dong He** *watercourse* Sichuan China
194 E3 **Đồng Hới** Vietnam
189 G4 **Dong Jiang** *watercourse* Guangdong China
194 E2 **Đồng Mỏ** Vietnam
181 G2 **Dong Qu** *watercourse* Qinghai China
194 E2 **Đồng Văn** Vietnam
159 G3 **Donga** Nigeria
159 G3 **Donga** *watercourse* Nigeria
163 G4 **Dongane, Lagoa** *lake* Mozambique
216 D4 **Dongara** WA Australia
191 J4 **Dongbei Pingyuan (Manchurian Plain)** China
188 D3 **Dongchuan** Yunnan China
188 D3 **Dongchuan** Yunnan China
190 G5 **Dongcun** Shanxi China
188 E5 **Dongfang** Hainan China
191 K4 **Dongfeng** Jilin China
181 G3 **Dongga** Xizang Zizhiqu China
198 A4 **Donggala** Indonesia
185 K6 **Donggi Conag** *lake* Qinghai China
189 G4 **Dongguan** Guangdong China
190 G5 **Dongguan** Shanxi China
191 H5 **Dongguang** Hebei China
188 E2 **Donghe** Sichuan China
194 E3 **Dônghén** Laos
188 E1 **Donghua** Gansu China
188 E3 **Donghuang** Guizhou China
189 H1 **Dongkan** Jiangsu China
188 F3 **Dongkou** Hunan China
188 E4 **Donglan** Guangxi Zhuangzu Zizhiqu China
191 J4 **Dongliao He** *watercourse* Jilin China
188 E4 **Dongmen** Guangxi Zhuangzu Zizhiqu China
191 L4 **Dongning** Heilongjiang China
162 C2 **Dongo** Angola
124 E4 **Dongo** Italy
156 E4 **Dongola** Sudan
82 G8 **Dongola** Illinois USA
160 B3 **Dongou** Congo
189 F3 **Dongping** Hunan China
191 H6 **Dongping** Shandong China
182 I4 **Dongsary Koli** *lake* Kazakhstan
189 H4 **Dongshan Dao** *island* Fujian China
190 G5 **Dongsheng** Nei Mongol Zizhiqu China
189 H2 **Dongtai** Jiangsu China
189 F2 **Dongting Hu** *lake* Hunan China
189 I3 **Dongtou Dao** *island* Zhejiang China
162 D2 **Dongwe** *watercourse* Zambia
188 E2 **Dongxiang** Sichuan China
191 H6 **Dongxiaotun** Hebei China
189 H2 **Dongyang** Zhejiang China
191 I5 **Dongying** Shandong China
139 G2 **Donington** Lincolnshire England UK
86 F2 **Doniphan** Missouri USA
132 C4 **Donji Krivodol** Serbia
130 H4 **Donji Miholjac** Croatia
130 G4 **Donji Mujdžići** Bosnia and Herzegovina
130 G4 **Donji Srb** Croatia
132 C4 **Donji Striževac** Serbia
130 H4 **Donji Svilaj** Bosnia and Herzegovina
181 G4 **Donkamokam** Assam India
213 H3 **Donkins Hill** WA Australia
181 G5 **Donmanick Islands** Bangladesh
120 H3 **Dønna** *island* Norway
83 P3 **Donnacona** Quebec Canada
84 C1 **Donnell Lake** California USA
216 D7 **Donnelly** WA Australia
80 G4 **Donnelly** Idaho USA
81 R4 **Donnelly** Minnesota USA
138 E2 **Donnington** Herefordshire England UK
140 B3 **Donore** Ireland
128 F2 **Donostia-San Sebastián** Spain
133 D7 **Donoussa** Greece
133 D7 **Donoussa** *island* Greece
124 B3 **Dontilly** France
130 E4 **Donzella, Isola della** *island* Italy
126 E4 **Donzenac** France
124 B4 **Donzy** France
143 B3 **Dooagh** Ireland
140 A2 **Dooish** Omagh Northern Ireland UK
216 F2 **Doolgunna** WA Australia
214 E4 **Doomadgee** Qld Australia
140 D1 **Doon** *watercourse* Scotland UK
140 D1 **Doon, Loch** *lake* Scotland UK
213 J4 **Doon Doon** WA Australia
143 B3 **Doon Hill** Ireland
143 D4 **Dooneen Bridge** Ireland
213 I3 **Doongan** WA Australia
143 C3 **Doonyvardan** Ireland
82 H4 **Door Peninsula** Wisconsin USA
124 C1 **Doorn** Netherlands
85 K4 **Dora** New Mexico USA
212 G7 **Dora, Lake** WA Australia
130 B4 **Dora Baltea** *watercourse* Italy
213 J3 **Dorcherty Island** NT Australia
138 E4 **Dorchester** Dorset England UK
81 Q6 **Dorchester** Nebraska USA
73 L5 **Dorchester, Cape** Nunavut Canada
162 C4 **Dordabis** Namibia
126 F2 **Dordives** France
126 E4 **Dordogne** *watercourse* France
124 C2 **Dordrecht** Netherlands
162 E6 **Dordrecht** South Africa
126 F4 **Dore** *watercourse* France
75 R5 **Doré Lake** Saskatchewan Canada
75 R5 **Doré Lake** Saskatchewan Canada
124 E1 **Dörentrup** Germany
142 D3 **Dores** Highland Scotland UK
103 C7 **Dores do Indaiá** Brazil
155 F5 **Dorey** Mali
124 G3 **Dorfen** Germany
158 D2 **Dori** Burkina Faso
75 Q5 **Dorintosh** Saskatchewan Canada
139 G3 **Dorking** Surrey England UK
187 E8 **Dornakal** Andhra Pradesh India
130 F3 **Dornava** Slovenia
124 E4 **Dornbirn** Austria
124 D2 **Dorndorf** Germany
126 F3 **Dornes** France
142 C3 **Dornie** Highland Scotland UK
142 D3 **Dornoch** Highland Scotland UK
191 H3 **Dornod** *admin. area* Mongolia
190 G4 **Dornogovi** *admin. area* Mongolia
124 D1 **Dornum** Germany
155 F5 **Doro** Mali
185 J3 **Döröö Nuur** *lake* Mongolia
120 J4 **Dorotea** Sweden
75 O7 **Dorothy** Alberta Canada
134 K7 **Dorovitsa** Russian Federation
109 1c **Dorp Rincón** Netherlands Antilles
109 1b **Dorp Sint Willebrordus** Netherlands Antilles
85 M1 **Dorrance** Kansas USA
216 C2 **Dorre Island** WA Australia
139 G1 **Dorrington** Lincolnshire England UK
139 E4 **Dorset** *admin. area* England UK
127 G3 **Dortan** France
127 H1 **Dortmund** Germany
136 F6 **Dörtyol** Turkey
178 G2 **Dorūd** Iran
160 D3 **Doruma** Democratic Republic of Congo
123 L4 **Dorupe** Latvia
142 C3 **Dorusduain** Highland Scotland UK
128 D5 **Dos Hermanas** Spain
105 F2 **Dos Marmelos** *watercourse* Brazil
108 D3 **Dos Pozos** Argentina
133 G7 **Döşemealtı** Turkey
124 G1 **Dosse** *watercourse* Germany
159 I3 **Dosséo, Bahr** *watercourse* Chad
155 G6 **Dosso** Niger
155 G6 **Dosso** *admin. area* Niger
179 J4 **Dostinzai** Pakistan
183 L5 **Dostuk** Kyrgyzstan
80 E1 **Dot** British Columbia Canada
87 I5 **Dothan** Alabama USA
158 B3 **Douako** Guinea
159 F4 **Douala** Cameroon
126 B2 **Douarnenez** France
155 G6 **Doubèlma** Niger
218 B5 **Double, Mount** SA Australia
90 D2 **Double Headed Shot Cays** *islands* Bahamas
78 I5 **Double Island** Newfoundland and Labrador Canada
219 K1 **Double Island Point** Qld Australia
78 I5 **Double Mer** *lake* Newfoundland and Labrador Canada
215 K7 **Double Mountain** Qld Australia
127 G3 **Doubs** *watercourse* France
213 H4 **Doubtful Bay** WA Australia
216 F7 **Doubtful Islands Bay** WA Australia
221 B7 **Doubtful Sound (Patea)** New Zealand
220 E2 **Doubtless Bay** New Zealand
139 H5 **Doudeville** France
154 F6 **Douentza** Mali
221 B8 **Doughboy Bay** New Zealand
218 C3 **Douglas** *watercourse* SA Australia
109 7 **Douglas** Falkland Islands
140 D2 **Douglas** Isle of Man UK
162 D5 **Douglas** South Africa
142 E5 **Douglas** South Lanarkshire Scotland UK
84 H5 **Douglas** Arizona USA
87 J5 **Douglas** Georgia USA
81 M5 **Douglas** Wyoming USA
214 A2 **Douglas, Mount** NT Australia
74 G6 **Douglas Channel** British Columbia Canada
87 J3 **Douglas Lake** Tennessee USA
81 Q8 **Douglass** Kansas USA
87 I4 **Douglasville** Georgia USA
158 B2 **Dougountouni** Guinea
189 F2 **Douhudi** Hubei China
143 B5 **Doulus Head** *cape* Ireland
159 I3 **Doum** Central African Republic
159 G4 **Doumé** Cameroon
142 E1 **Dounby** Orkney Islands Scotland UK
142 D4 **Doune** Stirling Scotland UK
103 B7 **Dourada, Cachoeirada** *watercourse* Brazil
105 H6 **Douradinho** Brazil
105 H6 **Dourados** Brazil
107 H2 **Dourados** *watercourse* Brazil
159 H2 **Dourbali** Chad
126 F4 **Dourbie** *watercourse* France
126 F2 **Dourdan** France
126 F5 **Dourgne** France
128 C3 **Douro** *watercourse* Portugal
189 G3 **Doushui Shuiku** *lake* Jiangxi China
159 G5 **Doussala** Gabon
126 D2 **Douve** *watercourse* France
155 H2 **Douz** Tunisia
126 E5 **Douze** *watercourse* France
127 G2 **Douzy** France
139 F2 **Dove** *watercourse* England UK
73 R3 **Dove Bugt** *bay* Greenland
81 K8 **Dove Creek** Colorado USA
141 G3 **Dove Holes** Derbyshire England UK
140 E2 **Dovenby** Cumbria England UK
79 L8 **Dover** Newfoundland and Labrador Canada
139 I3 **Dover** Kent England UK
83 N7 **Dover** Delaware USA
83 P5 **Dover** New Hampshire USA
83 N6 **Dover** New Jersey USA
83 K6 **Dover** Ohio USA
217 I6 **Dover, Point** WA Australia
139 I3 **Dover, Strait of** France/UK
139 E2 **Doverdale** Worcestershire England UK
139 F2 **Doveridge** Derbyshire England UK
105 H5 **Doverlândia** Brazil
109 11 **Dovers** St Vincent and the Grenadines
120 F6 **Dovre** Norway
216 E5 **Dowerin** WA Australia
199 H5 **Dowi** *volcano* Papua New Guinea
196 C3 **Dowi, Tanjung** *cape* Indonesia
179 K2 **Dowlat Yār** Afghanistan
75 O7 **Dowling Lake** Alberta Canada
143 G2 **Down** *admin. area* Northern Ireland UK
80 I5 **Downey** Idaho USA
140 B1 **Downhill** Coleraine Northern Ireland UK
140 C2 **Downpatrick** Down Northern Ireland UK
143 C2 **Downpatrick Head** *cape* Ireland
81 P7 **Downs** Kansas USA
139 G3 **Downside** Surrey England UK
139 F4 **Downton** Wiltshire England UK
74 I6 **Downton, Mount** British Columbia Canada
73 L9 **Dozois, Réservoir** Quebec Canada
127 H4 **Drac** *watercourse* France
129 H4 **Drac, Coves del** Spain
123 O6 **Drachkava** Belarus
124 D1 **Drachten** Netherlands
132 D3 **Drăcşani** Romania
120 J2 **Drag** Norway
120 I4 **Dragan** *bay* Sweden
132 D4 **Draganovo** Bulgaria
132 B4 **Dragaš** Kosovo
132 A3 **Draginje** Serbia
133 E8 **Dragonada** *island* Greece
133 D7 **Dragonisi** *island* Greece
101 F2 **Dragons Mouths** *strait* Trinidad and Tobago/Venezuela
132 B4 **Dragoševac** Serbia
123 L2 **Dragsfjärd** Finland
127 H5 **Draguignan** France
132 E1 **Drăguşeni** Romania
80 D5 **Drain** Oregon USA
179 K4 **Drakalo** Pakistan
81 O3 **Drake** North Dakota USA
59 T3 **Drake Passage** *strait* Antarctica
84 A2 **Drakes Bay** California USA
122 F3 **Drammen** Norway
132 F2 **Drânceni** Romania
120 inset **Drangajökull** *mountain* Iceland
127 I1 **Dransfeld** Germany

133 D8 **Drapano, Akra** *cape* Greece
140 B2 **Draperstown** Magherafelt Northern Ireland UK
186 D3 **Drass** Jammu and Kashmir India/ Pakistan
130 E3 **Drau** *watercourse* Austria
130 G3 **Drava** *watercourse* Croatia
125 H4 **Dravograd** Slovenia
125 H1 **Drawa** *watercourse* Poland
125 H1 **Drawno** Poland
139 F3 **Draycot Foliat** Swindon England UK
140 A2 **Dreen** Londonderry Northern Ireland UK
138 C3 **Drefach** Carmarthenshire Wales UK
127 K3 **Dreiherrnspitze** *mountain* Austria
199 G4 **Dreikikir** Papua New Guinea
124 D3 **Dreisam** *watercourse* Germany
125 L2 **Drelów** Poland
142 F4 **Drem** East Lothian Scotland UK
199 H4 **Dremsel, Mount** Papua New Guinea
132 C4 **Dren** Bulgaria
130 H4 **Drenovci** Croatia
133 C6 **Drepano, Akra** *cape* Greece
125 G2 **Dresden** Germany
86 G2 **Dresden** Tennessee USA
140 D2 **Dreswick Point** Isle of Man UK
126 E2 **Dreux** France
120 H6 **Drevdagen** Sweden
120 H4 **Drevja** Norway
120 H6 **Drevsjø** Norway
80 E5 **Drews Reservoir** Oregon USA
123 N4 **Dricēni** Latvia
123 N5 **Dridža** *lake* Latvia
83 K2 **Driftwood** Ontario Canada
140 E2 **Drigg** Cumbria England UK
142 C4 **Drimnin** Highland Scotland UK
143 C5 **Drimoleague** Ireland
138 E4 **Drimpton** Dorset England UK
132 A4 **Drin** *watercourse* Albania
143 C3 **Drin** Ireland
143 B3 **Drinagh** Ireland
142 B3 **Drinan** Highland Scotland UK
75 S7 **Drinkwater** Saskatchewan Canada
219 I5 **Dripstone** NSW Australia
86 C7 **Driscoll** Texas USA
122 E1 **Driva** *watercourse* Norway
218 C5 **Driver, Cape** SA Australia
122 F3 **Drøbak** Norway
132 C3 **Drobeta-Turnu Severin** Romania
126 G4 **Drobie** *watercourse* France
125 J1 **Drobin** Poland
132 E1 **Drochia** Moldova
122 H3 **Drögen** *lake* Sweden
143 F3 **Drogheda** Ireland
125 L1 **Drogičin** Belarus
Drogobych *see* **Drohobych** Ukraine
125 L1 **Drohiczyn** Poland
132 C1 **Drohobych** Ukraine
140 B2 **Dromara** Banbridge Northern Ireland UK
143 D4 **Dromcolliher** Ireland
126 D2 **Drôme** *watercourse* France
143 E3 **Dromod** Ireland
140 A2 **Dromore** Omagh Northern Ireland UK
143 B3 **Dromore Head** *cape* Ireland
143 D2 **Dromore West** Ireland
127 H4 **Dronero** Italy
142 D5 **Drongan** East Ayrshire Scotland UK
126 E4 **Dronne** *watercourse* France
73 O5 **Dronning Ingrid Land** Greenland
73 Q3 **Dronning Louise Land** Greenland
126 E4 **Dropt** *watercourse* France
127 L2 **Drosendorf** Austria
179 L2 **Drosh** Pakistan
126 E2 **Droué** France
82 I1 **Drowning** *watercourse* Ontario Canada
143 C4 **Drumadrohid** Ireland
140 A2 **Drumbeg** Ireland
142 F3 **Drumblair** Aberdeenshire Scotland UK
143 E2 **Drumcard** Fermanagh Northern Ireland UK
142 D5 **Drumclog** South Lanarkshire Scotland UK
143 C3 **Drumcoggy** Ireland
140 A2 **Drumcondra** Ireland
143 E3 **Drumconnick** Ireland
143 E3 **Drumcree** Ireland
138 A2 **Drumdangan** Ireland
215 G4 **Drumduff** Qld Australia
142 E5 **Drumelzier** Scottish Borders Scotland UK
142 C4 **Drumfern** Highland Scotland UK
143 E1 **Drumfin** Ireland
140 A2 **Drumgoon** Ireland
75 O7 **Drumheller** Alberta Canada
142 E3 **Drumin** Moray Scotland UK
142 D5 **Drumjohn** Dumfries and Galloway Scotland UK
143 D2 **Drumkeeran** Ireland
80 I3 **Drummond** Montana USA
87 M2 **Drummond, Lake** Virginia USA
216 F6 **Drummond, Mount** WA Australia
216 D4 **Drummond Cove** WA Australia
82 I4 **Drummond Island** Michigan USA
218 B6 **Drummond Point** SA Australia
215 I7 **Drummond Range** Qld Australia
73 L9 **Drummondville** Quebec Canada
140 A2 **Drummullagh** Ireland
143 D2 **Drummury** Ireland
143 E3 **Drumna** Ireland
142 D3 **Drumnadrochit** Highland Scotland UK
140 B2 **Drumnasoo** Armagh Northern Ireland UK
143 E3 **Drumone** Ireland
140 A2 **Drumquin** Omagh Northern Ireland UK
140 A3 **Drumroe** Ireland
143 D2 **Drumshanbo** Ireland
140 B2 **Drumshanbo** Cookstown Northern Ireland UK
140 B3 **Drumsru** Ireland
123 L5 **Druskininkai** Lithuania
123 N5 **Druya** Belarus
126 F3 **Druyes** France
183 N4 **Druzhba** Kazakhstan
136 E2 **Druzhba** Ukraine
135 AE5 **Druzhina** Russian Federation
130 G4 **Drvar** Bosnia and Herzegovina
125 J1 **Drwęca** *watercourse* Poland
214 B3 **Dry** *watercourse* NT Australia
74 B3 **Dry Bay** Alaska USA
80 F6 **Dry Lake** Nevada USA
80 F5 **Dry Lake Reservoir** Oregon USA
214 B3 **Dry River** NT Australia
90 D1 **Dry Tortugas** *island* Florida USA
82 E2 **Dryberry Lake** Ontario Canada
123 P5 **Drybin** Belarus
75 U4 **Drybrough** Manitoba Canada
76 I8 **Dryden** Ontario Canada
85 K5 **Dryden** Texas USA
59 L2 **Drygalski Basin** *underwater feature* Ross Sea
109 8 **Drygalski Fjord** South Georgia
59 L1 **Drygalski Ice Tongue** Antarctica
59 G2 **Drygalski Island** Antarctica
140 E1 **Dryhope** Scottish Borders Scotland UK
77 W6 **Drylake** Newfoundland and Labrador Canada
120 E5 **Dryna** Norway
123 O5 **Drysa** *watercourse* Belarus
213 I3 **Drysdale** *watercourse* WA Australia
214 C1 **Drysdale Island** NT Australia
213 I3 **Drysdale River** WA Australia
125 J1 **Drzycim** Poland
159 G3 **Dschang** Cameroon
83 L6 **Du Bois** Pennsylvania USA
218 C7 **du Couedic, Cape** SA Australia
77 R7 **Du Glas, Lac** *lake* Quebec Canada
78 C4 **Du Gué** *watercourse* Quebec Canada
160 C3 **Dua** *watercourse* Democratic Republic of Congo
142 C4 **Duachy** Argyll and Bute Scotland UK
215 J7 **Duaringa** Qld Australia
103 B8 **Duartina** Brazil
128 C3 **Duas Igrejas** Portugal
199 H5 **Duau, Mount** Papua New Guinea
127 L1 **Dubá** Czech Republic
Dubai *see* **Dubayy** United Arab Emirates
76 E1 **Dubawnt Lake** Nunavut Canada
82 G4 **Dubay, Lake** Wisconsin USA
179 H4 **Dubayy (Dubai)** United Arab Emirates
219 I5 **Dubbo** NSW Australia
158 C3 **Dube** *watercourse* Liberia
160 D3 **Dubela** Democratic Republic of Congo
182 G3 **Dubenskiy** Russian Federation
142 C5 **Dubhchladach** Argyll and Bute Scotland UK
127 K1 **Dubí** Czech Republic
123 M5 **Dubičiai** Lithuania
160 D5 **Dubie** Democratic Republic of Congo
125 L2 **Dubienka** Poland
143 F3 **Dublin (Baile Átha Cliath)** Ireland
143 F3 **Dublin** *admin. area* Ireland
87 J4 **Dublin** Georgia USA
86 B4 **Dublin** Texas USA
83 K8 **Dublin** Virginia USA
143 F3 **Dublin Bay** Ireland
123 P2 **Dubno** Russian Federation
83 L2 **Dubois** Quebec Canada
80 I4 **Dubois** Idaho USA
81 K5 **Dubois** Wyoming USA
80 F8 **Dubois, Mount** California USA
132 C3 **Dubova** Romania
132 E1 **Dubovaya** Ukraine
182 D3 **Dubovka** Russian Federation
125 I5 **Dubovsko** Bosnia and Herzegovina
182 D4 **Dubovskoye** Russian Federation
130 G4 **Dubrava** Bosnia and Herzegovina
130 G5 **Dubrava** Croatia
130 H5 **Dubrovnik** Croatia
134 O7 **Dubrovnoye** Russian Federation
123 P5 **Dubrowna** Belarus
75 T7 **Dubuc** Saskatchewan Canada
82 F5 **Dubuque** Iowa USA
223 14 **Duc de Gloucester, Îles du** *islands* French Polynesia
194 F4 **Đức Phổ** Vietnam
194 E5 **Đức Phong** Vietnam
126 D2 **Ducey** France
189 F4 **Ducheng** Guangdong China
81 J6 **Duchesne** Utah USA
214 E6 **Duchess** Qld Australia
75 P7 **Duchess** Alberta Canada
214 G2 **Ducie** *watercourse* Qld Australia
223 11 **Ducie Island** Pitcairn Islands
214 F6 **Duck** *watercourse* Qld Australia
212 D7 **Duck** *watercourse* WA Australia
77 Q5 **Duck Island** Nunavut Canada
75 R6 **Duck Lake** Saskatchewan Canada
75 W3 **Duck Lake Post** Manitoba Canada
139 H5 **Duclair** France
109 14 **Ducos** Martinique
138 E1 **Duddon** Cheshire England UK
127 H2 **Dudelange** Luxembourg
132 B2 **Dudeştii Vechi** Romania
134 S5 **Dudinka** Russian Federation
187 D7 **Dudna** *watercourse* Maharashtra India
134 T4 **Dudypta** *watercourse* Russian Federation
158 C3 **Duékoué** Côte d'Ivoire
196 D4 **Duen, Bukit** *volcano* Indonesia
128 D3 **Dueñas** Spain
122 H5 **Dueodde** *cape* Denmark
128 D3 **Duero** *watercourse* Spain
59 L1 **Dufek Coast** Antarctica
75 T7 **Duff** Saskatchewan Canada
222 1 **Duff Islands** Solomon Islands
142 E3 **Dufftown** Moray Scotland UK
142 E3 **Duffus** Moray Scotland UK
76 H1 **Duffy Lake** Nunavut Canada
127 H4 **Dufourspitze** *mountain* Switzerland
78 C3 **Dufreboy, Lac** *lake* Quebec Canada
81 Q2 **Dufrost** Manitoba Canada
77 Q2 **Dufrost, Pointe** *cape* Quebec Canada
80 E4 **Dufur** Oregon USA
130 F4 **Duga Resa** Croatia
135 AE7 **Duga-Zapadnaya, Mys** *cape* Russian Federation
214 F5 **Dugald** *watercourse* Qld Australia
199 J6 **Dugumenu Island** Papua New Guinea
178 E6 **Duhrān** Yemen
155 J4 **Duhūn Tārsū** *range* Chad
127 K4 **Duino** Italy
142 C3 **Duirinish** Highland Scotland UK
124 D2 **Duisburg** Germany
100 C3 **Duitama** Colombia
162 F4 **Duiwelskloof** South Africa
189 G1 **Duji-Xiangsha** Anhui China
188 D2 **Dujiangyan** Sichuan China
161 G3 **Düjuuma** Somalia
160 E2 **Duk Faiwil** Sudan
156 F5 **Dukambio** Eritrea
133 A5 **Dukat** Albania
74 F5 **Duke Island** Alaska USA
215 K6 **Duke Islands** Qld Australia
199 J5 **Duke of York Island** Papua New Guinea
213 H5 **Dukes Dome** *mountain* WA Australia
159 E2 **Dukku** Nigeria
123 N5 **Dūkštas** Lithuania
162 E4 **Dukwe** Botswana
190 F2 **Dulaanhan** Mongolia
219 I2 **Dulacca** Qld Australia
195 J5 **Dulag** Philippines
142 E3 **Dulax** Aberdeenshire Scotland UK
106 F4 **Dulce** *watercourse* Argentina
85 I2 **Dulce** New Mexico USA
90 D5 **Dulce, Golfo** *bay* Costa Rica
123 O6 **Dulëby** Belarus
143 F3 **Duleek** Ireland
178 F2 **Dulf** Iraq
135 AB5 **Dulgalakh** *watercourse* Russian Federation
190 E3 **Dulgeen** Mongolia
197 G3 **Dulit, Banjuran** *range* Malaysia
218 D3 **Dulkaninna** SA Australia
162 F5 **Dullstroom** South Africa
132 E4 **Dulovo** Bulgaria
215 K7 **Dululu** Qld Australia
82 E3 **Duluth** Minnesota USA
138 D3 **Dulverton** Somerset England UK
181 H3 **Dum Duma** Assam India
195 I5 **Dumaguete** Philippines
196 D3 **Dumai** Indonesia
195 I4 **Dumali Point** Philippines
195 I5 **Dumaran** *island* Philippines
198 C2 **Dumarchen** *island* Indonesia
219 J4 **Dumaresq** NSW Australia
86 F4 **Dumas** Arkansas USA
85 L3 **Dumas** Texas USA
108 C6 **Dumas, Península** Chile
216 E6 **Dumbleyung** WA Australia
159 G3 **Dumbo** Cameroon
142 E5 **Dumfries** Dumfries and Galloway Scotland UK
142 D5 **Dumfries and Galloway** *admin. area* Scotland UK
75 S8 **Dummer** Saskatchewan Canada
124 E1 **Dümmer** *lake* Germany
198 C3 **Dumoga** Indonesia
83 M3 **Dumoine, Lac** *lake* Quebec Canada
59 J2 **Dumont d'Urville (France)** *research station* Antarctica
59 J2 **Dumont d'Urville Sea** Antarctica
218 F6 **Dumosa** Vic. Australia
186 B6 **Dumra** Gujarat India
57 G2 **Dumshaf Abyssal Plain** *underwater feature* Norwegian Sea
156 E1 **Dumyāt** Egypt
143 D3 **Dún Gar** Ireland
143 F3 **Dún Laoghaire** Ireland
126 E3 **Dun-le-Palestel** France
126 F3 **Dun-sur-Auron** France
132 B1 **Dunajec** *watercourse* Poland
125 I4 **Dunajská Streda** Slovakia
142 D4 **Dunan** Perth and Kinross Scotland UK
143 F3 **Dunany** Ireland
140 B3 **Dunany Point** Ireland
125 J4 **Dunaújváros** Hungary
132 C4 **Dunavtsi** Bulgaria
135 Z4 **Dunay, Ostrova** *islands* Russian Federation
214 G4 **Dunbar** Qld Australia
142 F4 **Dunbar** East Lothian Scotland UK
142 E2 **Dunbeath** Highland Scotland UK
143 F3 **Dunboyne** Ireland
143 F4 **Dunbur** Ireland
140 B3 **Dunbyrne** Ireland
74 J8 **Duncan** British Columbia Canada
85 H4 **Duncan** Arizona USA
86 C3 **Duncan** Oklahoma USA
87 J3 **Duncan** South Carolina USA
77 O6 **Duncan, Cape** Nunavut Canada
77 Q6 **Duncan, Lac** *lake* Quebec Canada
213 J4 **Duncan, Mount** NT Australia
194 B5 **Duncan Passage** *strait* Andaman and Nicobar Islands India
91 F2 **Duncan Town** Bahamas
142 F2 **Duncansby Head** *cape* Scotland UK
211 inset **Duncombe Bay** Norfolk Island Australia
143 F4 **Duncormick** Ireland
142 D4 **Duncroist** Stirling Scotland UK
191 H4 **Dundahaote** Nei Mongol Zizhiqu China
143 F2 **Dundalk** Ireland
140 B3 **Dundalk Bay** Ireland
216 G6 **Dundas, Lake** WA Australia
74 F5 **Dundas Island** British Columbia Canada
72 H4 **Dundas Peninsula** Northwest Territories Canada
214 A1 **Dundas Strait** NT Australia
219 J3 **Dundee** NSW Australia
214 G6 **Dundee** Qld Australia
162 F5 **Dundee** South Africa
142 F4 **Dundee** Dundee Scotland UK
142 F4 **Dundee** *admin. area* Scotland UK
82 J6 **Dundee** Michigan USA
213 K2 **Dundee Beach** NT Australia
59 U2 **Dundee Island** Antarctica
190 F3 **Dundgovi** *admin. area* Mongolia
160 C5 **Dundo** Angola
142 E6 **Dundrennan** Dumfries and Galloway Scotland UK
140 B2 **Dundrod** Antrim Northern Ireland UK
140 C2 **Dundrum** Down Northern Ireland UK
140 C2 **Dundrum Bay** Northern Ireland UK
75 R7 **Dundurn** Saskatchewan Canada
142 F3 **Dunecht** Aberdeenshire Scotland UK
221 D7 **Dunedin** New Zealand
219 I5 **Dunedoo** NSW Australia
143 D5 **Duneen** Ireland
183 M4 **Dunenbay** Kazakhstan
126 E4 **Dunes** France
80 C5 **Dunes City** Oregon USA
143 E1 **Dunfanaghy** Ireland
142 E4 **Dunfermline** Fife Scotland UK
140 B2 **Dungannon** Dungannon Northern Ireland UK
143 E2 **Dungannon** *admin. area* Northern Ireland UK
186 D5 **Dungargarh** Rajasthan India
155 H6 **Dungas** Niger
139 H4 **Dungeness** *cape* England UK
140 B2 **Dungiven** Londonderry Northern Ireland UK
143 D2 **Dunglow** Ireland
140 B2 **Dungooly** Ireland
160 D3 **Dungu** Democratic Republic of Congo
196 D2 **Dungun** Malaysia
213 J4 **Dunham** *watercourse* WA Australia
141 H3 **Dunholme** Lincolnshire England UK
189 G3 **Dunhou** Jiangxi China
191 K4 **Dunhua** Jilin China
185 J5 **Dunhuang** Gansu China
215 I4 **Dunk Island** Qld Australia
219 I2 **Dunkeld** Qld Australia
218 F7 **Dunkeld** Vic. Australia
142 E4 **Dunkeld** Perth and Kinross Scotland UK
85 J4 **Dunken** New Mexico USA
124 B2 **Dunkerque** France
83 L5 **Dunkirk** New York USA
82 J6 **Dunkirk** Ohio USA
81 R6 **Dunlap** Iowa USA
143 F3 **Dunlavin** Ireland
143 F3 **Dunleer** Ireland
139 F3 **Dunley** Hampshire England UK
75 V5 **Dunlop** Manitoba Canada
143 C5 **Dunmanus Bay** Ireland
143 C5 **Dunmanway** Ireland
214 B4 **Dunmarra** NT Australia
143 D3 **Dunmore** Ireland
140 B2 **Dunmore** Cookstown Northern Ireland UK
140 C2 **Dunmore** Down Northern Ireland UK
143 F4 **Dunmore East** Ireland
90 E1 **Dunmore Town** Bahamas
140 A2 **Dunmoyle** Omagh Northern Ireland UK
140 B2 **Dunmurry** Lisburn Northern Ireland UK
215 H7 **Dunn, Lake** Qld Australia
81 N3 **Dunn Center** North Dakota USA
142 E2 **Dunnet Bay** Scotland UK
142 E2 **Dunnet Head** *cape* Scotland UK
84 B1 **Dunnigan** California USA
142 E4 **Dunning** Perth and Kinross Scotland UK
81 O6 **Dunning** Nebraska USA
109 7 **Dunnose Head** Falkland Islands
83 L5 **Dunnville** Ontario Canada
218 F7 **Dunolly** Vic. Australia
142 D5 **Dunoon** Argyll and Bute Scotland UK
78 E4 **Dunphy, Lac** *lake* Quebec Canada
142 D6 **Dunragit** Dumfries and Galloway Scotland UK
142 F5 **Duns** Scottish Borders Scotland UK
81 O2 **Dunseith** North Dakota USA
74 I8 **Dunsmuir** British Columbia Canada
80 D6 **Dunsmuir** California USA
139 G3 **Dunstable** Bedfordshire England UK
141 G1 **Dunstan** Northumberland England UK
221 C7 **Dunstan Mountains** New Zealand
138 D3 **Dunster** Somerset England UK
142 B3 **Duntulm** Highland Scotland UK
123 M4 **Dūņu ezers** *lake* Latvia
142 B3 **Dunvegan, Loch** *bay* Scotland UK
142 B3 **Dunvegan Head** *cape* Scotland UK
140 A2 **Dunwish** Omagh Northern Ireland UK
179 L3 **Dunyapur** Pakistan
191 H4 **Duolun** Nei Mongol Zizhiqu China
194 E2 **Duong** *watercourse* Vietnam
194 D5 **Dương Đông** Vietnam
78 B4 **Dupire, Lac** *lake* Quebec Canada
132 C4 **Dupnitsa** Bulgaria
81 O4 **Dupree** South Dakota USA
83 L2 **Dupuy** Quebec Canada
212 C6 **Dupuy, Cape** WA Australia
103 D8 **Duque de Caxias** Brazil
109 10a **Duquesne Bay** Grenada
213 I3 **Durack** *watercourse* WA Australia
213 I4 **Durack Range** WA Australia
136 G6 **Duraklı** Turkey
127 G5 **Durance** *watercourse* France
88 D3 **Durango** Mexico
84 E4 **Durango** Mexico
88 D3 **Durango** *admin. area* Mexico
126 C5 **Durango** Spain
81 L8 **Durango** Colorado USA
100 C3 **Durania** Colombia
216 E6 **Duranillin** WA Australia
132 F4 **Durankulashko Ezero** *lake* Bulgaria
106 F6 **Durañona** Argentina
86 C4 **Durant** Oklahoma USA
126 E4 **Duras** France
107 G5 **Durazno** Uruguay
107 H5 **Durazno** *admin. area* Uruguay
75 U7 **Durban** Manitoba Canada
163 F5 **Durban** South Africa
127 G1 **Durbuy** Belgium
140 F2 **Durdar** Cumbria England UK
130 H4 **Đurđenovac** Croatia
161 I2 **Durdura, Raas** *cape* Somalia
125 K2 **Durdy** Poland
187 E7 **Durg** Chhattisgarh India
186 G6 **Durgapur** West Bengal India
141 G2 **Durham** Durham England UK
141 G2 **Durham** *admin. area* England UK
85 N1 **Durham** Kansas USA
87 L3 **Durham** North Carolina USA
221 6 **Durham, Point** Chatham Islands New Zealand
219 I2 **Durham Downs** Qld Australia
196 D3 **Duri** Indonesia
197 F4 **Duriansebatang** Indonesia
142 E5 **Durisdeer** Dumfries and Galloway Scotland UK
142 D2 **Durness** Highland Scotland UK
125 I3 **Dürnkrut** Austria
219 J2 **Durong South** Qld Australia
77 Q2 **Durouvray** *watercourse* Quebec Canada
215 I8 **Durrandella** Qld Australia
219 J6 **Durras** NSW Australia
133 A5 **Durrës** Albania
133 A5 **Durrësit, Gjiri i** *bay* Albania
143 E4 **Durrow** Ireland
143 B5 **Dursey Island** Ireland
138 E3 **Dursley** Gloucestershire England UK
188 E3 **Duru** Guizhou China
133 F5 **Duru Göl** *lake* Turkey
161 H2 **Durukhsi** Somalia
133 F5 **Durusu** Turkey
185 J3 **Durveljin** Mongolia
198 F4 **d'Urville, Tanjung** *cape* Indonesia
59 U2 **D'Urville Island** Antarctica
221 E5 **D'Urville Island** New Zealand
82 H1 **Dusey** *watercourse* Ontario Canada
188 E3 **Dushan** Guizhou China
183 J6 **Dushanbe** Tajikistan
123 L5 **Dusia** *lake* Lithuania
221 B7 **Dusky Sound** New Zealand
191 M2 **Dusse-Alin', Khrebet** *range* Russian Federation
213 J3 **Dussejour, Cape** WA Australia
127 H1 **Düsseldorf** Germany
74 B2 **Dusty** *watercourse* Yukon Territory Canada
183 J6 **Dŭsty** Tajikistan
196 D4 **Dusunmudo** Indonesia
142 E3 **Duthil** Highland Scotland UK
159 F2 **Dutse** Nigeria
159 F2 **Dutsin Ma** Nigeria
215 G6 **Dutton** *watercourse* Qld Australia
80 J3 **Dutton** Montana USA
218 C4 **Dutton, Lake** SA Australia
185 I3 **Duut** Mongolia
75 S7 **Duval** Saskatchewan Canada
78 B4 **Duvert, Lac** *lake* Quebec Canada
143 B2 **Duvillaun More** *island* Ireland
77 Q6 **Duxbury, Lac** *lake* Quebec Canada
214 F2 **Duyfken Point** Qld Australia
188 E3 **Duyun** Guizhou China
133 G6 **Düzağaç** Turkey
136 D5 **Düzce** *admin. area* Turkey
121 U4 **Dvinskaya Guba** *bay* Russian Federation
123 M5 **Dviragio ežeras** *lake* Lithuania
130 H3 **Dvory nad Žitavou** Slovakia
161 G3 **Dwaa** *watercourse* Ethiopia
163 F2 **Dwangwa** Malawi
187 B6 **Dwarka** Gujarat India
162 E4 **Dwarsberg** South Africa
216 E6 **Dwellingup** WA Australia
82 G6 **Dwight** Illinois USA
85 N1 **Dwight** Kansas USA
80 G3 **Dworshak Reservoir** Idaho USA
132 E1 **D'yakovtsy** Ukraine
158 E3 **Dyan** *watercourse* Nigeria
140 B2 **Dyan** Dungannon Northern Ireland UK
108 A4 **Dyer, Cabo** *cape* Chile
73 M5 **Dyer, Cape** Nunavut Canada
83 K4 **Dyer Bay** Ontario Canada
86 G2 **Dyersburg** Tennessee USA
138 C2 **Dyffryn** Gwynedd Wales UK
138 D2 **Dyffryn-Castell** Ceredigion Wales UK
138 D2 **Dyfi** *watercourse* Wales UK
135 AB7 **Dygdy-Sise, Khrebet** *range* Russian Federation
122 H5 **Dygowo** Poland
182 D5 **Dyhtau, Gora** *mountain* Russian Federation
125 I3 **Dyje** *watercourse* Czech Republic
142 E4 **Dykehead** Angus Scotland UK
125 M3 **Dykhtinets** Ukraine
125 K1 **Dylewo** Poland
125 J1 **Dylewska Góra** *mountain* Poland
138 D2 **Dylife** Powys Wales UK
139 H3 **Dymchurch** Kent England UK
82 E2 **Dyment** Ontario Canada
132 G1 **Dymino** Ukraine
123 O2 **Dymovo** Russian Federation
120 inset **Dyrhólaey** *cape* Iceland
120 E5 **Dyrnes** Norway
120 J2 **Dyrøya** *island* Norway
120 J2 **Dyrøyhamn** Norway
215 J7 **Dysart** Qld Australia
143 E3 **Dysart** Ireland
123 N5 **Dysna** *watercourse* Belarus
123 N5 **Dysnų ežeras** *lake* Lithuania
123 N5 **Dysnykščio ežeras** *lake* Belarus
133 B6 **Dytiki Ellada** *admin. area* Greece
133 B5 **Dytiki Makedonia** *admin. area* Greece
135 U5 **Dyupkun, Ozero** *lake* Russian Federation
132 F3 **Dyviziya** Ukraine
190 G4 **Dzamïn Üüd** Mongolia
179 K3 **Dzangalī** Afghanistan
164 8b **Dzaoudzi** Mayotte
185 J3 **Dzavhan** *admin. area* Mongolia
182 D2 **Dzerzhinsk** Russian Federation
135 AB8 **Dzhagdy, Khrebet** *range* Russian Federation
191 M2 **Dzhaki-Unakhta Yakbyyana, Khrebet** *range* Russian Federation
135 Z8 **Dzhalinda** Russian Federation
135 Z5 **Dzhardzhan** Russian Federation
190 E2 **Dzhida** *watercourse* Russian Federation
135 AG6 **Dzhigudzhak** Russian Federation
Dzhizak *see* **Jizzax** Uzbekistan
135 AC7 **Dzhugdzhur, Khrebet** *range* Russian Federation
183 M4 **Dzhungarskiy Alatau, Khrebet** *range* Kazakhstan
182 I4 **Dzhusaly** Kazakhstan
182 J6 **Dzhush** Uzbekistan
125 K1 **Działdowo** Poland
125 J2 **Działoszyn** Poland
125 K1 **Dzierzgowo** Poland
89 H4 **Dzilam de Bravo** Mexico
89 H4 **Dzilam González** Mexico
123 N5 **Dzisna** *watercourse* Belarus
89 H4 **Dzitás** Mexico
89 H4 **Dzitbalché** Mexico
123 N5 **Dzjanīski** Belarus
89 H5 **Dzuiché** Mexico
184 G3 **Dzungarian Gate** *pass* Xinjiang Uygur Zizhiqu China
190 D2 **Dzuun Nuur** *lake* Mongolia

E

88 E2 **E. V. Spence Reservoir** Texas USA
76 L7 **Eabamet Lake** Ontario Canada
81 N7 **Eads** Colorado USA
82 E4 **Eagan** Minnesota USA
85 H3 **Eagar** Arizona USA
78 J6 **Eagle** *watercourse* Newfoundland and Labrador Canada
81 L7 **Eagle** Colorado USA
81 Q6 **Eagle** Nebraska USA
109 1a **Eagle Beach** *bay* Aruba
81 O4 **Eagle Butte** South Dakota USA
75 R7 **Eagle Creek** Saskatchewan Canada
76 F6 **Eagle Island** Manitoba Canada
82 E2 **Eagle Lake** Ontario Canada
80 E6 **Eagle Lake** California USA
86 C6 **Eagle Lake** Texas USA
85 J2 **Eagle Nest** New Mexico USA
85 J2 **Eagle Nest Reservoir** New Mexico USA
85 L6 **Eagle Pass** Texas USA
109 7 **Eagle Passage** *strait* Falkland Islands
72 F5 **Eagle Plain** Yukon Territory Canada
80 D5 **Eagle Point** Oregon USA
82 G3 **Eagle River** Michigan USA
82 G4 **Eagle River** Wisconsin USA
216 G2 **Earaheedy** WA Australia
141 F3 **Earby** Lancashire England UK
76 G6 **Eardley Lake** Manitoba Canada
139 H2 **Earith** Cambridgeshire England UK
221 B7 **Earl Mountains** New Zealand
139 F2 **Earl Shilton** Leicester England UK
84 C3 **Earlimart** California USA
142 F5 **Earlston** Scottish Borders Scotland UK
79 G10 **Earltown** Nova Scotia Canada
86 B5 **Early** Texas USA
142 E4 **Earn** *watercourse* Scotland UK
142 D4 **Earn, Loch** *lake* Scotland UK
221 C7 **Earnslaw, Mount** New Zealand
85 K3 **Earth** Texas USA
141 G2 **Easby** North Yorkshire England UK
142 C4 **Easdale** Argyll and Bute Scotland UK
141 G2 **Easington** Durham England UK
141 I3 **Easington** East Riding of Yorkshire England UK
143 D2 **Easky** Ireland
87 J3 **Easley** South Carolina USA
212 E6 **East** *watercourse* WA Australia
59 D1 **East Antarctica** *region* Antarctica
87 L3 **East Arcadia** North Carolina USA
142 D5 **East Ayrshire** *admin. area* Scotland UK
213 K3 **East Baines** *watercourse* NT Australia
87 I5 **East Bay** Florida USA
86 G6 **East Bay** Louisiana USA
101 G4 **East Berbice-Corentyne** *admin. area* Guyana
82 E4 **East Bethel** Minnesota USA
86 H5 **East Brewton** Alabama USA
91 G2 **East Caicos** *island* Turks and Caicos Islands
220 H3 **East Cape** New Zealand
139 I2 **East Carleton** Norfolk England UK
52 K7 **East Caroline Basin** *underwater feature* Pacific Ocean
189 J2 **East China Sea** Asia
142 E2 **East Clyne** Highland Scotland UK
139 F4 **East Cowes** Isle of Wight England UK
215 K4 **East Diamond Islet** Coral Sea Islands Territory Australia
142 D5 **East Dunbartonshire** *admin. area* Scotland UK
161 E2 **East Equatoria** *admin. area* Sudan
72 E5 **East Fork Chandalar** *watercourse* Alaska USA
139 G3 **East Grinstead** West Sussex England UK
221 10 **East Group** *islands* Bounty Islands New Zealand
141 G2 **East Harlsey** North Yorkshire England UK
214 F4 **East Haydon** Qld Australia
80 J3 **East Helena** Montana USA
141 H2 **East Heslerton** North Yorkshire England UK
138 E3 **East Huntspill** Somerset England UK
138 D3 **East Ilkerton** Devon England UK
55 N7 **East Indiaman Ridge** *underwater feature* Indian Ocean
199 J6 **East Island** Papua New Guinea
210 inset **East Islet** Ashmore Reef and Cartier Island Australia
139 F3 **East Kennet** Wiltshire England UK
141 G3 **East Keswick** West Yorkshire England UK
142 D5 **East Kilbride** South Lanarkshire Scotland UK
76 I6 **East Lake** Ontario Canada
87 K6 **East Lake Tohopekaliga** Florida USA
82 I5 **East Lansing** Michigan USA
142 F5 **East Linton** East Lothian Scotland UK
83 K6 **East Liverpool** West Virginia USA
142 B3 **East Loch Tarbert** *bay* Scotland UK
162 E6 **East London** South Africa
138 C4 **East Looe** Cornwall England UK
142 F5 **East Lothian** *admin. area* Scotland UK
139 G4 **East Marden** West Sussex England UK
52 L6 **East Mariana Basin** *underwater feature* Pacific Ocean
86 D6 **East Matagorda Bay** Texas USA
82 F6 **East Moline** Illinois USA
141 H3 **East Newton** East Riding of Yorkshire England UK
53 U10 **East Pacific Rise** *underwater feature* Pacific Ocean
76 K4 **East Pen Island** Nunavut Canada
79 I10 **East Point** Nova Scotia Canada
79 H9 **East Point** Prince Edward Island Canada
164 5c **East Point** *cape* St Helena
142 D5 **East Renfrewshire** *admin. area* Scotland UK
87 I3 **East Ridge** Tennessee USA
141 H3 **East Riding of Yorkshire** *admin. area* England UK
83 K8 **East River Mountain** Virginia USA
East Sea *see* **Japan, Sea of**
76 G7 **East Selkirk** Manitoba Canada
135 AI4 **East Siberian Sea** Russian Federation
139 H4 **East Sussex** *admin. area* England UK
55 T9 **East Tasman Plateau** *underwater feature* Tasman Sea
84 H1 **East Tavaputs Plateau** Utah USA
East Timor *see* **Timor-Leste**
143 D1 **East Town** Ireland
139 H4 **Eastbourne** East Sussex England UK
75 Q8 **Eastend** Saskatchewan Canada
142 D3 **Easter Drummond** Highland Scotland UK
53 U10 **Easter Fracture Zone** *underwater feature* Pacific Ocean
216 C4 **Easter Group** *islands* WA Australia
Easter Island *see* **Isla de Pascua**
214 F6 **Eastern** *watercourse* Qld Australia
161 F3 **Eastern** *admin. area* Kenya
162 E6 **Eastern Cape** *admin. area* South Africa
Eastern Desert *see* **Aş Şaḩrā' Ash Sharqīyah** Egypt
79 G10 **Eastern Passage** Nova Scotia Canada
75 V6 **Easterville** Manitoba Canada
84 D1 **Eastgate** Nevada USA
86 B4 **Eastland** Texas USA
139 F4 **Eastleigh** Hampshire England UK
73 L8 **Eastmain** *watercourse* Quebec Canada
215 H7 **Eastmere** Qld Australia
138 E4 **Easton** Dorset England UK
83 M7 **Easton** Maryland USA
75 M8 **Eastport** Idaho USA
83 R4 **Eastport** Maine USA
142 E6 **Eastriggs** Dumfries and Galloway Scotland UK
81 M6 **Eaton** Colorado USA
138 E2 **Eaton upon Tern** Shropshire England UK
87 J4 **Eatonton** Georgia USA
80 D3 **Eatonville** Washington USA
101 H4 **Eau Claire** French Guiana
82 F4 **Eau Claire** Wisconsin USA
73 L7 **Eau Claire, Lac à l'** *lake* Quebec Canada
83 N2 **Eau-Jaune, Lac à l'** *lake* Quebec Canada
199 G2 **Eauripik** *island* Federated States of Micronesia
55 S4 **Eauripik Atoll** *reef* Caroline Islands
55 S4 **Eauripik Rise** *underwater feature* Pacific Ocean
126 E5 **Eauze** France
199 G7 **Ebagoola** Qld Australia
159 E3 **Eban** Nigeria
162 B2 **Ebanga** Angola
160 C4 **Ebangalakata** Democratic Republic of Congo
131 C9 **Ebba Ksoui** Tunisia
124 G4 **Ebbs** Austria
74 J1 **Ebbutt Hills** Northwest Territories Canada
138 D3 **Ebbw Vale** Blaenau Gwent Wales UK
135 AD6 **Ebe** Russian Federation
159 G4 **Ebebiyin** Equatorial Guinea
125 G4 **Ebene Reichenau** Austria
217 M2 **Ebenezer, Mount** NT Australia
125 I4 **Ebenfurth** Austria
83 L6 **Ebensburg** Pennsylvania USA
127 J1 **Ebern** Germany
130 F3 **Eberndorf** Austria
125 G1 **Eberswalde** Germany
127 I3 **Ebikon** Switzerland
184 G4 **Ebinur Hu** *lake* Xinjiang Uygur Zizhiqu China
160 C3 **Ebola** *watercourse* Democratic Republic of Congo
131 F6 **Eboli** Italy
159 G4 **Ebolowa** Cameroon
223 15 **Ebon Atoll** Marshall Islands
160 C3 **Ebonda** Democratic Republic of Congo
159 F3 **Ebonyi** *admin. area* Nigeria
127 J2 **Ebrach** Germany
129 F3 **Ebro** *watercourse* Spain
128 E2 **Ebro, Embalse del** *lake* Spain
127 I1 **Ebsdorf** Germany
135 AF5 **Ebyakh** Russian Federation
142 E5 **Ecclefechan** Dumfries and Galloway Scotland UK
138 E2 **Eccleshall** Staffordshire England UK
109 9 **Ecclesville** Trinidad and Tobago
80 F4 **Echo** Oregon USA
219 R11 **Echo, Lake** Tas. Australia
76 J5 **Echoing** *watercourse* Manitoba Canada
76 I5 **Echoing Lake** Ontario Canada
142 F3 **Echt** Aberdeenshire Scotland UK
218 G7 **Echuca** Vic. Australia
128 D5 **Écija** Spain
123 J2 **Eckerö** *island* Finland
78 F3 **Eclipse Harbour** Newfoundland and Labrador Canada
73 L4 **Eclipse Sound** Nunavut Canada
126 E3 **Écommoy** France
103 D7 **Ecoporanga** Brazil
83 M3 **Écorces, Lac aux** *lake* Quebec Canada
127 G2 **Écrouves** France
86 G3 **Ecru** Mississippi USA
125 I4 **Écs** Hungary
132 A2 **Ecséd** Hungary
132 B2 **Ecsegfalva** Hungary
100 B5 **Ecuador** *country* South America
126 E3 **Écueillé** France
77 Q3 **Écueils, Pointe aux** *cape* Quebec Canada
157 G5 **Ed** Eritrea
156 D5 **Ed Da'ein** Sudan
178 C2 **Ed Daher** Lebanon
156 E5 **Ed Damazin** Sudan
156 E4 **Ed Damer** Sudan
156 E5 **Ed Dueim** Sudan
216 E4 **Edah** WA Australia
141 G3 **Edale** Derbyshire England UK
142 F1 **Eday** *island* Scotland UK
142 C2 **Eddrachillis Bay** Scotland UK
74 K6 **Eddy** British Columbia Canada
219 S10 **Eddystone Point** Tas. Australia
82 G8 **Eddyville** Kentucky USA
124 C1 **Ede** Netherlands
120 J5 **Ede** Sweden
159 G4 **Edéa** Cameroon
123 J2 **Edebo** Sweden
120 L3 **Edefors** Sweden
76 G2 **Edehon Lake** Nunavut Canada
103 B7 **Edéia** Brazil
107 H3 **Edelira** Paraguay
140 F2 **Eden** *watercourse* England UK
86 B5 **Eden** Texas USA
75 U4 **Eden Lake** Manitoba Canada
82 E4 **Eden Prairie** Minnesota USA
81 K5 **Eden Reservoir** Wyoming USA
139 H3 **Edenbridge** Kent England UK
221 C8 **Edendale** New Zealand
143 E3 **Edenderry** Ireland
218 E7 **Edenhope** Vic. Australia
75 S7 **Edenwold** Saskatchewan Canada
124 E2 **Eder** *watercourse* Germany
199 F5 **Edera** *watercourse* Indonesia
133 C5 **Edessa** Greece
120 H5 **Edevik** Sweden
86 C6 **Edgar** Texas USA
81 P3 **Edgeley** North Dakota USA
78 F2 **Edgell Island** Nunavut Canada
215 J6 **Edgell Reefs** Qld Australia
81 N5 **Edgemont** South Dakota USA
134 F3 **Edgeøya** *island* Norway
219 I4 **Edgeroi** NSW Australia
85 O1 **Edgerton** Kansas USA
81 Q5 **Edgerton** Minnesota USA
81 L5 **Edgerton** Wyoming USA
75 M7 **Edgewater** British Columbia Canada
82 G7 **Edgewood** Illinois USA
218 B6 **Edillilie** SA Australia
83 K6 **Edinboro** Pennsylvania USA
81 Q2 **Edinburg** North Dakota USA
86 B7 **Edinburg** Texas USA
164 5c **Edinburgh** St Helena
142 E5 **Edinburgh** City of Edinburgh Scotland UK
133 E5 **Edincik** Turkey
132 E1 **Edineţ** Moldova
163 F2 **Edingeni** Malawi
136 C5 **Edirne** *admin. area* Turkey
84 C3 **Edison** California USA
87 K4 **Edisto** *watercourse* South Carolina USA
214 B3 **Edith River** NT Australia
218 C6 **Edithburgh** SA Australia
216 H4 **Edjudina** WA Australia
141 G1 **Edlingham** Northumberland England UK
86 C3 **Edmond** Oklahoma USA
85 L3 **Edmonson** Texas USA
75 O6 **Edmonton** Alberta Canada
81 P2 **Edmore** North Dakota USA
76 I5 **Edmund Lake** Manitoba Canada
79 D9 **Edmundston** New Brunswick Canada
86 D2 **Edna** Kansas USA
86 C6 **Edna** Texas USA
159 F3 **Edo** *admin. area* Nigeria
124 F4 **Edolo** Italy
133 E6 **Edremit** Turkey
133 E6 **Edremit Körfezi** *bay* Turkey
185 J4 **Edrengiyn Nuruu** Mongolia
75 M6 **Edson** Alberta Canada
106 E5 **Eduardo Castex** Argentina
214 F3 **Edward** *watercourse* Qld Australia
160 D4 **Edward, Lake** Democratic Republic of Congo
59 T1 **Edward, Mount** Antarctica
214 C3 **Edward Island** NT Australia
59 N1 **Edward VII Peninsula** Antarctica
59 D2 **Edward VIII Bay** Antarctica
88 E2 **Edwards Plateau** Texas USA
140 A2 **Edymore** Strabane Northern Ireland UK
80 D7 **Eel** *watercourse* California USA
162 C3 **Eenhana** Namibia
222 7 **Éfaté** *island* Vanuatu
82 G7 **Effingham** Illinois USA
82 D7 **Effingham** Kansas USA
132 F3 **Eforie** Romania
128 F2 **Ega** *watercourse* Spain
84 E1 **Egan Range** Nevada USA
159 F3 **Egbe** Nigeria
122 I4 **Egby** Sweden
124 G2 **Eger** *watercourse* Germany
132 B2 **Eger** Hungary
54 K7 **Egeria Fracture Zone** *underwater feature* Indian Ocean
210 inset **Egeria Point** Christmas Island Australia
198 D6 **Egeron, Selat** *strait* Indonesia
216 E2 **Egerton, Mount** WA Australia
125 I4 **Egervár** Hungary
120 L2 **Egga** Norway
120 K3 **Eggelats** *lake* Sweden
120 G5 **Eggen** Norway
127 K2 **Eggenfelden** Germany
138 D4 **Eggesford** Devon England UK
142 F1 **Egilsay** *island* Scotland UK
120 inset **Egilsstaðir** Iceland
133 G7 **Eğirdir** Turkey
133 G6 **Eğirdir Gölü** *lake* Turkey
190 E2 **Egiyn Gol** *watercourse* Mongolia
182 I4 **Egizkaratau** *mountain* Kazakhstan
123 N5 **Eglaine** Latvia
126 F4 **Égletons** France
221 B7 **Eglinton** *watercourse* New Zealand
72 H3 **Eglinton Island** Northwest Territories Canada
140 B2 **Eglish** Dungannon Northern Ireland UK
138 D2 **Eglwys Fach** Ceredigion Wales UK
Egmont, Mount *see* **Taranaki, Mount** New Zealand
79 F9 **Egmont Bay** Prince Edward Island Canada
140 E2 **Egremont** Cumbria England UK
124 B3 **Égreville** France
126 E3 **Éguzon** France
135 AL5 **Egvekinot** Russian Federation
156 D2 **Egypt** *country* Africa

124 E3 **Ehingen** Germany
80 F2 **Eholt** British Columbia Canada
87 K4 **Ehrhardt** South Carolina USA
223 I4 **Eiao** *island* French Polynesia
122 D3 **Eiavatn** *lake* Norway
126 C5 **Eibar** Spain
124 F2 **Eichsfeld** *region* Germany
124 F3 **Eichstätt** Germany
53 S3 **Eickelberg Seamount** *underwater feature* Pacific Ocean
120 E5 **Eide** Norway
122 E5 **Eider** *watercourse* Germany
122 E5 **Eiderstedt** *peninsula* Germany
120 F5 **Eidet** Norway
120 I3 **Eidet** Norway
120 E5 **Eidsdal** Norway
120 I2 **Eidsfjord** Norway
122 E1 **Eidsvåg** Norway
120 G4 **Eidsvatnet** *lake* Norway
219 J1 **Eidsvold** Qld Australia
156 E4 **Eidukal, Wādī** *watercourse* Sudan
122 C3 **Eigerøya** *island* Norway
142 B4 **Eigg** *island* Scotland UK
187 C10 **Eight Degree Channel** Maldives
143 C2 **Eighter** Ireland
59 R2 **Eights Coast** Antarctica
212 F5 **Eighty Mile Beach** WA Australia
156 F4 **Eigrim, Jebel** *mountain* Sudan
122 C2 **Eikefjord** Norway
122 E1 **Eikesdalsvatnet** *lake* Norway
142 E3 **Eil** Highland Scotland UK
198 E2 **Eil Malk** *island* Palau
218 G7 **Eildon, Lake** Vic. Australia
124 G2 **Eilenburg** Germany
101 G4 **Eilerts de Haan Gebergte** *range* Suriname
215 J6 **Eimeo** Qld Australia
124 F1 **Eimke** Germany
122 F2 **Eina** Norway
215 H5 **Einasleigh** Qld Australia
122 F2 **Einavatnet** *lake* Norway
124 C2 **Eindhoven** Netherlands
194 B3 **Einme** Myanmar
57 D3 **Eirik Ridge** *underwater feature* Atlantic Ocean
104 D2 **Eirunepé** Brazil
127 G2 **Eischen** Luxembourg
162 D3 **Eiseb** *watercourse* Botswana
162 C4 **Eiseb** *watercourse* Namibia
127 J1 **Eisenach** Germany
125 H4 **Eisenerz** Austria
80 H1 **Eisenhower Junction** Alberta Canada
127 L3 **Eisenkappel** Austria
125 I4 **Eisenstadt** Austria
124 F2 **Eisfeld** Germany
127 L2 **Eisgarn** Austria
123 M5 **Eišiškės** Lithuania
127 J1 **Eisleben** Germany
124 E3 **Eislingen** Germany
222 1b **Eita** Kiribati
120 H4 **Eiterstraum** Norway
124 D2 **Eitorf** Germany
129 G4 **Eivissa (Ibiza)** *island* Spain
122 G5 **Ejby** Denmark
129 F2 **Ejea de los Caballeros** Spain
163 H4 **Ejeda** Madagascar
122 H2 **Ejheden** Sweden
100 D2 **Ejido** Venezuela
85 I5 **Ejido de Enriquez** Mexico
88 D2 **Ejido de Majalca** Mexico
88 D2 **Ejido El Cuervo** Mexico
84 G5 **Ejido La Cebolla** Mexico
88 D3 **Ejido La Luz** Mexico
84 H5 **Ejido Naco** Mexico
85 I5 **Ejido Rancho Nuevo** Mexico
122 E5 **Ejstrupholm** Denmark
158 D3 **Ejura** Ghana
89 F5 **Ejutla** Mexico
81 M4 **Ekalaka** Montana USA
135 AF9 **Ekarma, Ostrov** *island* Russian Federation
159 G4 **Ékata** Gabon
122 G3 **Ekenäs** Sweden
190 E5 **E'kenhuduge** Nei Mongol Zizhiqu China
182 G6 **Ekerem** Turkmenistan
221 F5 **Eketahuna** New Zealand
108 C5 **Ekewern** Chile
121 M3 **Ekfors** Sweden
135 AK5 **Ekiatapskiy Khrebet** *range* Russian Federation
183 L3 **Ekibastuz** Kazakhstan
159 F3 **Ekiti** *admin. area* Nigeria
123 L2 **Eknäs** Finland
122 I4 **Eknö** *island* Sweden
159 F3 **Ekok** Cameroon
160 C4 **Ekoli** Democratic Republic of Congo
135 W5 **Ekonda** Russian Federation
159 H4 **Ekouamou** Congo
159 F3 **Ekpoma** Nigeria
162 C5 **Eksteenfontein** South Africa
59 X2 **Ekström Ice Shelf** Antarctica
120 K4 **Ekträsk** Sweden
159 E3 **Eku** *watercourse* Nigeria
160 B4 **Ekukola** Democratic Republic of Congo
160 C4 **Ekuku** Democratic Republic of Congo
160 C4 **Ekumakoko** Democratic Republic of Congo
73 K8 **Ekwan** *watercourse* Ontario Canada
77 N6 **Ekwan Point** Ontario Canada
106 D6 **El Abanico** Chile
155 G2 **El Abiodh Sidi Cheikh** Algeria
88 B2 **El Águila** Mexico
101 F3 **El Alambre** Venezuela
218 C5 **El Alamein** SA Australia
88 D2 **El Álamo** Mexico
155 H2 **El Alia** Algeria
88 E3 **El Alicante** Mexico
104 A2 **El Alto** Peru
100 B4 **El Ángel** Ecuador
129 I5 **El Aouana** Algeria
155 H1 **El Aouinet** Algeria
108 B2 **El Arco** Chile
88 B2 **El Arco** Mexico
155 F2 **El Aricha** Algeria
155 H1 **El Arrouch** Algeria
100 B4 **El Aticito** Colombia
90 C4 **El Ayote** Nicaragua
86 B7 **El Azúca** Mexico
100 C3 **El Bagre** Colombia
88 D3 **El Bajío Grande** Mexico
100 C2 **El Banco** Colombia
128 D3 **El Barco de Ávila** Spain
86 B8 **El Barranco** Mexico
84 F6 **El Barril** Mexico
156 E5 **El Barun** Sudan
156 E4 **El Bauga** Sudan
155 G2 **El Bayadh** Algeria
100 C4 **El Billar** Colombia
128 D6 **El Bioutz** Morocco
108 B3 **El Blanco** Chile
128 E4 **El Bonillo** Spain
129 G6 **El Bordj** Algeria
100 B4 **El Bordo** Colombia
155 H2 **El Borma** Algeria
128 D6 **El Brayach** Morocco
88 B3 **El Bule** Mexico
128 E3 **El Burgo de Osma** Spain
108 C2 **El Caín** Argentina
84 D4 **El Cajon** California USA
108 B5 **El Calafate** Argentina
100 D2 **El Camaral** Venezuela
86 C6 **El Campo** Texas USA
88 E3 **El Canelo** Mexico
88 C3 **El Cantil** Mexico
100 D3 **El Capricho** Colombia
101 F2 **El Cardón** Venezuela
105 F4 **El Carmen** Bolivia
84 F5 **El Carrizal** Mexico
88 D3 **El Carrizo** Mexico
128 E3 **El Casar** Spain
100 B5 **El Castañán** *range* Ecuador
90 C5 **El Castillo de La Concepción** Nicaragua
104 A1 **El Caucho** Peru
100 C4 **El Cayman** Colombia
86 B7 **El Cenizo** Texas USA
84 E4 **El Centro** California USA
108 B4 **El Chaltén** Argentina
88 B2 **El Chinero** Mexico
106 D6 **El Chinque** Argentina
108 C4 **El Chonque** Argentina
101 E2 **El Chorro** Venezuela
100 D2 **El Chuco** Venezuela
88 B2 **El Cielo** Mexico
88 E3 **El Cinco** Mexico
100 C3 **El Cocuy** Colombia
88 D5 **El Colomo** Mexico
88 D3 **El Colorado** Mexico
105 E4 **El Combate** Bolivia
108 C5 **El Cóndor** Argentina
88 D3 **El Consuelo** Mexico
90 D5 **El Copé** Panama
100 C2 **El Copey** Colombia
100 E2 **El Corozo** Venezuela
90 D5 **El Cortezo** Panama
86 B8 **El Coyote** Mexico
108 B3 **El Coyte** Argentina
85 I5 **El Cuarenta** Mexico
128 D3 **El Cubo de Tierra del Vino** Spain
85 J6 **El Cuerva, Laguna** *bay* Mexico
88 D2 **El Cuervo** Mexico
100 D2 **El Cují** Venezuela
108 C2 **El Cuy** Argentina
88 B3 **El Datil, Estero** *lake* Mexico
84 D4 **El Descanso** Mexico
88 B2 **El Desemboque** Mexico
100 D2 **El Diario de Yaracuy** Venezuela
88 B2 **El Doctor** Mexico
100 C4 **El Doncello** Colombia
105 F5 **El Dorado** Bolivia
88 D3 **El Dorado** Mexico
86 E4 **El Dorado** Arkansas USA
81 Q8 **El Dorado** Kansas USA
82 C8 **El Dorado Lake** Kansas USA
86 B8 **El Encinal** Mexico
90 C4 **El Escaño de Tepale** Honduras
90 B4 **El Estor** Guatemala
129 I5 **El Eulima** Algeria
155 H1 **El Fahs** Tunisia
101 F2 **El Fangal** Venezuela
155 H2 **El Faouar** Tunisia
108 A2 **El Farellón** *island* Chile
156 D5 **El Fasher** Sudan
88 D2 **El Fortín** Mexico
85 I6 **El Fresno** Mexico
161 G2 **El Fud** Ethiopia
88 C3 **El Fuerte** Mexico
156 D5 **El Fula** Sudan
88 B3 **El Gato, Estero** *lake* Mexico
86 B8 **El Gavilán** Mexico
156 E4 **El Geili** Sudan
156 C5 **El Geneina** Sudan
156 E5 **El Gezira** *admin. area* Sudan
108 B4 **El Ghio** Argentina
155 G2 **El Goléa** Algeria
84 E5 **El Golfo de Santa Clara** Mexico
129 G2 **El Grado, Embalse de** *lake* Spain
88 D5 **El Grullo** Mexico
100 C4 **El Guamo** Colombia
129 J5 **El Guerrah** Algeria
156 F5 **El Gulut** Ethiopia
155 H1 **El Hadjar** Algeria
154 E2 **El Hajeb** Morocco
155 H2 **El Hallail, Oued** *watercourse* Algeria
129 I6 **El Hamel** Algeria
155 H2 **El Hamma** Tunisia
131 D8 **El Haouaria** Tunisia
156 E5 **El Hawata** Sudan
156 B5 **El Hidjer** Chad
89 F4 **El Higo** Mexico
156 D5 **El-Hilla** Sudan
85 K7 **El Jabali** Mexico
85 J6 **El Jabali** Mexico
154 E2 **El Jadida** Morocco
88 D3 **El Jaralito** Mexico
156 E5 **El Jebelein** Sudan
155 I1 **El Jem** Tunisia
108 C3 **El Junco** Argentina
156 E4 **El Kab** Sudan
156 E4 **El Kadada** Sudan
155 H1 **El Kala** Algeria
156 E4 **El Kamlin** Sudan
129 I6 **El Kantara** Algeria
156 E5 **El Kawa** Sudan
154 E2 **El Kelaâ Srarhna** Morocco
161 G2 **El Kerē** Ethiopia
156 D5 **El Lagowa** Sudan
161 F3 **El Lēh** Ethiopia
89 I6 **El Llano** Honduras
89 F4 **El Llano** Mexico
88 D3 **El Llano** Mexico
131 C9 **El Ma el Abiod** Algeria
85 H6 **El Maderal** Mexico
129 J6 **El Mahder** Algeria
108 B3 **El Maitén** Argentina
100 D3 **El Mamón** Venezuela
156 E5 **El Manaqil** Sudan
155 F3 **El Mannsour** Algeria
106 D6 **El Marucho** Argentina
88 E4 **El Matorral** Mexico
100 E4 **El Médano** Colombia
161 G2 **El Medo** Ethiopia
155 H2 **El Meghaïer** Algeria
156 E4 **El Metemma** Sudan
85 K7 **El Mezquite** Mexico
154 C5 **El Mhaijrat** Mauritania
100 D3 **El Milagro** Venezuela
155 H1 **El Milia** Algeria
100 D4 **El Mirador** Colombia
85 I5 **El Mirador** Mexico
108 C3 **El Mirasol** Argentina
128 E3 **El Molar** Spain
100 C2 **El Molino** Colombia
88 B2 **El Molino** Mexico
84 C3 **El Monte** California USA
85 L6 **El Moral** Mexico
106 E5 **El Morro** *mountain* Argentina
84 H6 **El Novillo** Mexico
156 E5 **El Obeid** Sudan
156 D5 **El Odaiya** Sudan
106 E6 **El Odre** Argentina
86 B9 **El Ojital** Mexico
100 D4 **El Olvido** Colombia
104 B1 **El Oro** *admin. area* Ecuador
88 E3 **El Oro** Mexico
101 E3 **El Oso** Venezuela
155 H2 **El Oued** Algeria
129 I6 **El Outaya** Algeria
108 C3 **El Pajarito** Argentina
88 C3 **El Palmarito** Mexico
105 F4 **El Paraíso** Bolivia
90 C4 **El Paraíso** Honduras
100 C2 **El Paso** Colombia
85 I5 **El Paso** Texas USA
101 F2 **El Patillo** Venezuela
100 C4 **El Pato** Colombia
101 F3 **El Paují** Venezuela
100 C4 **El Paujil** Colombia
84 F4 **El Pedregal** Mexico
100 E4 **El Peligro** Venezuela
106 E3 **El Peñón** Argentina
106 D5 **El Peñón** *mountain* Chile
100 D3 **El Percal** Colombia
129 G3 **El Perelló** Spain
101 F3 **El Pilón** Brazil
85 J5 **El Pino** Mexico
106 F3 **El Pintado** Argentina
128 D4 **El Pintado, Embalse** *lake* Spain
104 A1 **El Plátano** Peru
88 B2 **El Plomo** Mexico
106 D5 **El Plomo, Nevado** *mountain* Chile
108 B4 **El Pluma** Argentina
101 E2 **El Polvero** Venezuela
126 F5 **El Port de la Selva** Spain
100 D3 **El Porvenir** Colombia
88 B3 **El Porvenir** Mexico
88 D2 **El Porvenir** Mexico
85 J5 **El Porvenir** Mexico
84 D4 **El Porvenir** Mexico
90 E5 **El Porvenir** Panama
105 G5 **El Potrero** Bolivia
88 D2 **El Povenir** Mexico
101 F3 **El Prado** Venezuela
90 C4 **El Progreso** Honduras
105 F5 **El Puente** Bolivia
88 B1 **El Puerto** Mexico
108 B3 **El Púlpito** Chile
106 F3 **El Quebrachal** Argentina
101 E2 **El Quebradón** Venezuela
213 I3 **El Questro** WA Australia
108 C6 **El Quique** Argentina
85 N8 **El Rabón, Laguna** *lake* Mexico
88 D3 **El Ranchito** Mexico
89 I6 **El Rancho** Honduras
128 C5 **El Real de la Jara** Spain
90 E5 **El Real de Santa María** Panama
100 C5 **El Refugio** Colombia
85 L6 **El Remolino** Mexico
86 C3 **El Reno** Oklahoma USA
100 C4 **El Retorno** Colombia
88 E4 **El Retorno** Mexico
89 H5 **El Roble** Mexico
89 F3 **El Roble** Mexico
101 E2 **El Roble** Venezuela
90 C4 **El Rodeo** Honduras
100 A5 **El Rosario** Ecuador
88 D3 **El Rosario** Mexico
88 B2 **El Sacrificio** Mexico
88 B1 **El Sahuaro** Mexico
100 D2 **El Saladillo** Venezuela
108 C4 **El Salado** Argentina
88 D4 **El Salto** Mexico
108 B4 **El Saltón** Chile
90 B4 **El Salvador** *country* Central America
88 E3 **El Salvador** Mexico
88 B2 **El Salvador** Mexico
85 I5 **El Sancho** Mexico
84 G5 **El Sasabe** Mexico
90 C4 **El Sauce** Nicaragua
85 H7 **El Sauz** Mexico
86 B7 **El Sauz** Texas USA
88 A2 **El Sauzal** Mexico
85 K7 **El Socorro** Mexico
100 D2 **El Socorro** Venezuela
88 E3 **El Sol** Mexico
108 C3 **El Sombrero** Argentina
100 E2 **El Sombrero** Venezuela
106 D5 **El Sosneado** Argentina
88 C2 **El Tabacote** Mexico
100 B4 **El Tambo** Colombia
155 H1 **El Tarf** Algeria
100 C2 **El Tarra** Colombia
129 H3 **El Ter** *watercourse* Spain
85 I6 **El Terrero** Mexico
88 C2 **El Tigre** Mexico
100 D2 **El Tigre** Venezuela
100 D2 **El Tocuyo** Venezuela
108 B5 **El Toro** Chile
84 F6 **El Toro** Mexico
108 B5 **El Turbio** Argentina
88 D2 **El Uno** Mexico
85 I2 **El Vado Reservoir** New Mexico USA
88 D4 **El Valle** *lake* Mexico
85 H6 **El Vallecito** Mexico
101 E2 **El Vasquero** Venezuela
85 J5 **El Veinticuatro** Mexico
129 G3 **El Vendrell** Spain
85 I7 **El Vergel** Mexico
128 E4 **El Vicario, Embalse de** *lake* Spain
90 C4 **El Viejo** Nicaragua
100 D2 **El Vigía** Venezuela
88 E3 **El Vinatero** Mexico
105 E6 **El Volcán** Bolivia
85 K6 **El Volcan** Mexico
161 G3 **El Wak** Kenya
156 E5 **El Wuz** Sudan
106 F2 **El Yacón** Argentina
109 6a **El Yunque** *volcano* Isla Róbinson Crusoe
88 E3 **El Zacate** Mexico
88 D2 **El Zoco** Mexico
100 C3 **El Zulia** Colombia
108 B5 **El Zurdo** Argentina
133 C7 **Elafonisos** *island* Greece
86 F3 **Elaine** Arkansas USA
221 E5 **Elaine Bay** New Zealand
121 N5 **Elämäjärvi** Finland
121 N5 **Elämäjärvi** *lake* Finland
59 E3 **Elan Bank** *underwater feature* Southern Ocean
133 E8 **Elasa** *island* Greece
133 C6 **Elassona** Greece
199 H2 **Elato** *island* Federated States of Micronesia
136 F5 **Elaziğ** Turkey
136 F5 **Elazığ** *admin. area* Turkey
87 H5 **Elba** Alabama USA
130 D5 **Elba, Isola d'** *island* Italy
191 M2 **El'ban** Russian Federation
133 B5 **Elbasan** Albania
125 H2 **Elbe** *watercourse* Czech Republic
124 G2 **Elbe** *watercourse* Germany
82 H7 **Elberfeld** Indiana USA
87 J3 **Elberton** Georgia USA
124 F4 **Elbigenalp** Austria
85 N1 **Elbing** Kansas USA
123 J5 **Elbląg** Poland
75 R7 **Elbow** Saskatchewan Canada
87 M7 **Elbow Cay** Bahamas
75 U6 **Elbow Lake** Saskatchewan Canada
81 R4 **Elbow Lake** Minnesota USA
182 D5 **El'brus, Gora** *mountain* Russian Federation
128 E4 **Elche de la Sierra** Spain
129 F4 **Elche-Elx** Spain
142 E4 **Elcho** Perth and Kinross Scotland UK
214 C1 **Elcho Island** NT Australia
129 F4 **Elda** Spain
161 F3 **Eldama Ravine** Kenya
218 E4 **Elder, Lake** SA Australia
211 inset **Elder, Mount** Macquarie Island Australia
133 F7 **Elderesi** Turkey
103 A8 **Eldorado** Brazil
86 B3 **Eldorado** Oklahoma USA
85 L5 **Eldorado** Texas USA
161 F3 **Eldoret** Kenya
141 F2 **Eldroth** North Yorkshire England UK
86 B3 **Electra** Texas USA
85 I2 **Electra Lake** Colorado USA
108 B4 **Elefantes, Golfo** *bay* Chile
132 B2 **Elek** Hungary
183 O3 **Elekmonar** Russian Federation
161 F4 **Elementeita, Lake** Kenya
108 A4 **Elena, Cabo** *cape* Chile
215 H4 **Elephant, Mount** Qld Australia
85 I4 **Elephant Butte** New Mexico USA
88 D1 **Elephant Butte Reservoir** New Mexico USA
59 U2 **Elephant Island** Antarctica
109 7 **Elephant Jason** *island* Falkland Islands
138 D2 **Elerch** Ceredigion Wales UK
102 D4 **Elesbão Veloso** Brazil
90 E1 **Eleuthera** *island* Bahamas
82 F4 **Eleva** Wisconsin USA
199 G5 **Elevala** *watercourse* Papua New Guinea
85 J1 **Elevenmile Canyon Reservoir** Colorado USA
74 C3 **Elfin Cove** Alaska USA
84 H5 **Elfrida** Arizona USA
120 H5 **Elgåhogna** *mountain* Norway
81 O2 **Elgin** Manitoba Canada
142 E3 **Elgin** Moray Scotland UK
82 G5 **Elgin** Illinois USA
80 G4 **Elgin** Oregon USA
86 C5 **Elgin** Texas USA
135 AC5 **El'ginskoye Ploskogor'ye** *region* Russian Federation
142 B3 **Elgol** Highland Scotland UK
161 E3 **Elgon, Mount** Uganda
135 AJ5 **El'gygytgyn, Ozero** *lake* Russian Federation
139 I3 **Elham** Kent England UK
160 C5 **Elias Garcia** Angola
198 D6 **Eliase** Indonesia
85 K4 **Elida** New Mexico USA
157 G5 **Ēlīda'ār** Ethiopia
133 C7 **Elika** Greece
133 C6 **Elikonas** *range* Greece
160 D4 **Elila** Democratic Republic of Congo
160 D4 **Elila** *watercourse* Democratic Republic of Congo
72 C6 **Elim** Alaska USA
123 N2 **Elimäki** Finland
219 K2 **Elimbah** Qld Australia
188 E3 **Eling** Guizhou China
78 G3 **Eliot, Mount** Newfoundland and Labrador Canada
160 C4 **Elipa** Democratic Republic of Congo
142 B3 **Elishader** Highland Scotland UK
182 D4 **Elista** Russian Federation
218 D7 **Eliza, Lake** SA Australia
214 E5 **Elizabeth** *watercourse* Qld Australia
83 N6 **Elizabeth** New Jersey USA
218 C6 **Elizabeth, Cape** SA Australia
77 R5 **Elizabeth, Lac** *lake* Quebec Canada
221 D6 **Elizabeth, Point** New Zealand
219 K5 **Elizabeth Beach** NSW Australia
87 M2 **Elizabeth City** North Carolina USA
82 I8 **Elizabethtown** Kentucky USA
128 F2 **Elizondo** Spain
80 H2 **Elk** *watercourse* British Columbia Canada
75 S1 **Elk** *watercourse* Northwest Territories Canada
86 H3 **Elk** *watercourse* Alabama USA
84 A1 **Elk** California USA
82 C8 **Elk** *watercourse* Kansas USA
83 K7 **Elk** *watercourse* West Virginia USA
86 D2 **Elk City** Kansas USA
86 B3 **Elk City** Oklahoma USA
84 B1 **Elk Grove** California USA
82 D6 **Elk Horn** Iowa USA
82 I4 **Elk Lake** Michigan USA
81 L6 **Elk Mountain** Wyoming USA
82 I4 **Elk Rapids** Michigan USA
82 E4 **Elk River** Minnesota USA
214 C6 **Elkedra** NT Australia
214 C6 **Elkedra** *watercourse* NT Australia
75 N7 **Elkford** British Columbia Canada
82 I6 **Elkhart** Indiana USA
81 O8 **Elkhart** Kansas USA
86 D5 **Elkhart** Texas USA
75 U8 **Elkhorn** Manitoba Canada
75 N8 **Elko** British Columbia Canada
80 H6 **Elko** Nevada USA
86 H2 **Elkton** Kentucky USA
80 D5 **Elkton** Oregon USA
75 P8 **Elkwater** Alberta Canada
218 F7 **Ellam** Vic. Australia
126 C3 **Ellé** *watercourse* France
83 L7 **Elleber Knob** *mountain* West Virginia USA
73 I3 **Ellef Ringnes Island** Nunavut Canada
219 K4 **Ellenborough** NSW Australia
213 I3 **Ellenbrae** WA Australia
219 R11 **Ellendale** Tas. Australia
213 H4 **Ellendale** WA Australia
143 F4 **Ellendale** Ireland
81 P4 **Ellendale** North Dakota USA
80 E3 **Ellensburg** Washington USA
83 N6 **Ellenville** New York USA
141 G2 **Ellerbeck** North Yorkshire England UK
219 J4 **Ellerston** NSW Australia
219 I7 **Ellery, Mount** Vic. Australia
138 E2 **Ellesmere** Shropshire England UK
221 E6 **Ellesmere (Te Waihora), Lake** New Zealand
73 K3 **Ellesmere Island** Nunavut Canada
140 F3 **Ellesmere Port** Cheshire England UK
72 I5 **Ellice** *watercourse* Nunavut Canada
87 I3 **Ellijay** Georgia USA
141 G2 **Ellingstring** North Yorkshire England UK
141 G1 **Ellington** Northumberland England UK
82 F8 **Ellington** Missouri USA
215 I5 **Elliot, Mount** Qld Australia
76 H6 **Elliot Lake** Manitoba Canada
82 J3 **Elliot Lake** Ontario Canada
214 B4 **Elliott** NT Australia
213 I6 **Elliott, Mount** WA Australia
219 Q11 **Elliott Bay** Tas. Australia
219 K1 **Elliott Heads** Qld Australia
219 Q11 **Elliott Point** Tas. Australia
81 P7 **Ellis** Kansas USA
74 L8 **Ellison** British Columbia Canada
Ellisras *see* **Lephalale** South Africa
218 B5 **Elliston** SA Australia
86 G5 **Ellisville** Mississippi USA
142 F3 **Ellon** Aberdeenshire Scotland UK
87 K4 **Elloree** South Carolina USA
122 F3 **Ellös** Sweden
75 O5 **Ellscott** Alberta Canada
82 E5 **Ellsworth** Iowa USA
81 P7 **Ellsworth** Kansas USA
86 B3 **Ellsworth, Lake** Oklahoma USA
59 S2 **Ellsworth Land** *plain* Antarctica
59 S1 **Ellsworth Mountains** Antarctica
124 F3 **Ellwangen** Germany
139 H2 **Elm** Cambridgeshire England UK
87 M3 **Elm City** North Carolina USA
76 F8 **Elm Creek** Manitoba Canada
86 B3 **Elm Fork Red** *watercourse* Oklahoma USA
136 E5 **Elma Dağı** Turkey
133 F7 **Elmalı** Turkey
79 G9 **Elmira** Prince Edward Island Canada
83 M5 **Elmira** New York USA
139 E2 **Elmley Castle** Worcestershire England UK
81 J7 **Elmo** Utah USA
218 G7 **Elmore** Vic. Australia
86 A2 **Elmwood** Oklahoma USA
126 F5 **Elne** France
120 E5 **Elnesvågen** Norway
75 O7 **Elnora** Alberta Canada
199 I4 **Eloaua Island** Papua New Guinea
159 G4 **Elogo** Congo
84 G4 **Eloy** Arizona USA
143 D3 **Elphin** Ireland
142 C2 **Elphin** Highland Scotland UK
215 J6 **Elphinstone** Qld Australia
218 G7 **Elphinstone** Vic. Australia
106 D4 **Elqui** *watercourse* Chile
142 F3 **Elrick** Aberdeenshire Scotland UK
81 R4 **Elrosa** Minnesota USA
75 Q7 **Elrose** Saskatchewan Canada
130 D5 **Elsa** *watercourse* Italy
141 F1 **Elsdon** Northumberland England UK
124 E3 **Elsenfeld** Germany
130 C2 **Elsenz** *watercourse* Germany
214 B3 **Elsey** NT Australia
214 B3 **Elsey** *watercourse* NT Australia
120 L2 **Elsnes** Norway
142 E5 **Elsrickle** South Lanarkshire Scotland UK
124 C2 **Elst** Netherlands
139 G2 **Elsthorpe** Lincolnshire England UK
125 H2 **Elstra** Germany
59 S2 **Eltanin Bay** Antarctica
51 F15 **Eltanin Fracture Zone** *underwater feature* Southern Ocean
182 E3 **El'ton** Russian Federation
182 E3 **El'ton** *lake* Russian Federation
140 F3 **Elton** Cheshire England UK
86 E5 **Elton** Louisiana USA
124 E2 **Eltville** Germany
187 E8 **Eluru** Andhra Pradesh India
120 G6 **Elvål** Norway
142 E5 **Elvanfoot** South Lanarkshire Scotland UK
128 C4 **Elvas** Portugal
120 G6 **Elvdal** Norway
139 H2 **Elveden** Suffolk England UK
218 H2 **Elverston** Qld Australia
122 E2 **Elverum** Norway
141 H3 **Elvington** York England UK
213 J5 **Elvire** *watercourse* WA Australia
214 G7 **Elvo** Qld Australia
81 P6 **Elwood** Nebraska USA
155 F1 **Elx** Spain
139 H2 **Ely** Cambridgeshire England UK
138 D3 **Ely** Cardiff Wales UK
82 F3 **Ely** Minnesota USA
80 H7 **Ely** Nevada USA
83 J6 **Elyria** Ohio USA
124 E3 **Elz** *watercourse* Germany
124 D2 **Elzbach** *watercourse* Germany
222 7 **Émaé** *island* Vanuatu
121 P4 **Emäjoki** *watercourse* Finland
183 J6 **Emām Şāḩeb** Afghanistan
122 I4 **Emån** *watercourse* Sweden
199 I4 **Emananusa Island** Papua New Guinea
222 7 **Émao** *island* Vanuatu
182 H4 **Emba** Kazakhstan
182 G4 **Emba** *watercourse* Kazakhstan
162 E5 **Embalenhle** South Africa
77 W6 **Embar** Newfoundland and Labrador Canada
135 U5 **Embenchime** *watercourse* Russian Federation
104 D3 **Embira** *watercourse* Brazil
142 E3 **Embo** Highland Scotland UK
103 C7 **Emborcaçao, Represa** *lake* Brazil
127 H4 **Embrun** France
161 F4 **Embu** Kenya
107 J2 **Embu Guaçu** Brazil
162 C3 **Embundo** Angola
123 L4 **Emburga** Latvia
122 D6 **Emden** Germany
133 E7 **Emecik** Turkey
188 D2 **Emeishan** Sichuan China
215 J7 **Emerald** Qld Australia
52 M13 **Emerald Basin** *underwater feature* Southern Ocean
219 J4 **Emerald Hill** NSW Australia
72 H3 **Emerald Isle** Northwest Territories Canada
214 A2 **Emerald Springs** NT Australia
212 G4 **Emeriau Point** WA Australia
77 V6 **Emeril** Newfoundland and Labrador Canada
101 H4 **Émerillon, Massif** *range* French Guiana
84 D3 **Emerson Lake** California USA
81 Q5 **Emery** South Dakota USA
80 J7 **Emery** Utah USA
199 G5 **Emeti** Papua New Guinea
122 C2 **Emhjellevatnet** *lake* Norway
155 J5 **Emi Koussi** *mountain* Chad
84 B1 **Emigrant Gap** California USA
130 C4 **Emilia-Romagna** *admin. area* Italy
89 H5 **Emiliano Zapata** Mexico
85 J7 **Emiliano Zapata** Mexico
85 H5 **Emiliano Zapata** Mexico
106 F7 **Emilio Lamarca** Argentina
184 G3 **Emin** Xinjiang Uygur Zizhiqu China
199 I4 **Emirau Island** Papua New Guinea
163 F5 **Emjindini** South Africa
214 C7 **Emma, Mount** NT Australia
78 C1 **Emma Island** Nunavut Canada
101 G4 **Emma Keten** *range* Suriname
83 N6 **Emmaus** Pennsylvania USA
218 G4 **Emmdale** NSW Australia
127 H1 **Emmelshausen** Germany
124 D1 **Emmen** Netherlands
124 D2 **Emmerich** Germany
215 H8 **Emmet** Qld Australia
187 D8 **Emmiganuru** Andhra Pradesh India
72 C6 **Emmonak** Alaska USA
139 H2 **Emneth** Norfolk England UK
81 S2 **Emo** Manitoba Canada
132 B2 **Emőd** Hungary
88 C3 **Empalme** Mexico
107 G3 **Empedrado** Argentina
52 M3 **Emperor Seamount** *underwater feature* Pacific Ocean
52 N3 **Emperor Trough** *underwater feature* Pacific Ocean
133 B6 **Empesos** Greece
198 D6 **Emplawas** Indonesia
82 C7 **Emporia** Kansas USA
83 L6 **Emporium** Pennsylvania USA
75 P7 **Empress** Alberta Canada
199 J5 **Empress Augusta Bay** Papua New Guinea
124 D1 **Ems** *watercourse* Germany
124 D1 **Ems-Jade-Kanal** *watercourse* Germany
127 I1 **Emstal** Germany
215 G4 **Emu, Mount** Qld Australia
218 C6 **Emu Bay** SA Australia
217 M4 **Emu Junction** SA Australia
215 K7 **Emu Park** Qld Australia
213 J2 **Emu Reefs** NT Australia
156 D5 **En Nahud** Sudan
120 H5 **Enafors** Sweden
142 C2 **Enard Bay** Scotland UK
89 G5 **Encajonado** *watercourse* Mexico
129 G2 **Encamp** Andorra
107 H4 **Encantadas, Serra das** *range* Brazil
107 H3 **Encarnación** Paraguay
86 B6 **Encinal** Texas USA
128 D4 **Encinarejo, Embalse del** *lake* Spain
128 C4 **Encinasola** Spain
84 D4 **Encinitas** California USA
103 D6 **Encruzilhada** Brazil
107 H4 **Encruzilhada do Sul** Brazil
132 B1 **Encs** Hungary
196 D3 **Endau** *watercourse* Malaysia
198 B6 **Ende** Indonesia
198 B6 **Ende** *island* Indonesia
219 Q11 **Endeavour Bay** Tas. Australia
214 G1 **Endeavour Strait** Qld Australia
120 G6 **Enden** Norway
222 1 **Enderbury** *island* Kiribati
74 L7 **Enderby** British Columbia Canada
59 D2 **Enderby Abyssal Plain** *underwater feature* Southern Ocean
221 8 **Enderby Island** Auckland Islands New Zealand
212 D6 **Enderby Island** WA Australia
59 D2 **Enderby Land** *plain* Antarctica
72 D5 **Endicott Mountains** Alaska USA
104 E3 **Endimari** *watercourse* Brazil
123 N3 **Endla järv** *lake* Estonia
159 G4 **Endom** Cameroon
139 E1 **Endon** Staffordshire England UK
214 B1 **Endyalgout Island** NT Australia
104 C3 **Ene** *watercourse* Peru
216 D4 **Eneabba** WA Australia
182 C5 **Enem** Russian Federation
101 H4 **Enéné Patatpe** Suriname
107 G6 **Energía** Argentina
223 15 **Enewetak Atoll** *reef* Marshall Islands
133 E5 **Enez** Turkey
109 14 **Enfer, Pointe d'** *cape* Martinique
162 B3 **Enfião, Ponta do** *cape* Angola
131 D8 **Enfidaville** Tunisia
139 G3 **Enfield** Greater London England UK
87 M2 **Enfield** North Carolina USA
82 I3 **Engadine** Michigan USA
120 F5 **Engan** Norway
108 D3 **Engaño, Bahía** *bay* Argentina
91 G3 **Engaño, Cabo** *cape* Dominican Republic
193 I2 **Engaru** Japan
120 F5 **Engdal** Norway
120 I3 **Engeløya** *island* Norway
182 E3 **Engel's** Russian Federation
75 R4 **Engemann Lake** Saskatchewan Canada
124 E4 **Engen** Germany
105 G4 **Engenho** Brazil
124 E1 **Enger** Germany
120 H6 **Engerneset** Norway
196 D5 **Enggano** *island* Indonesia
199 I6 **Engineer Group** *islands* Papua New Guinea
196 F3 **Engkilili** Malaysia
137 G5 **England** *admin. area* UK
218 B3 **England Hill** SA Australia
79 J7 **Englee** Newfoundland and Labrador Canada
73 L9 **Englehart** Ontario Canada
75 R3 **Engler Lake** Saskatchewan Canada
81 P8 **Englewood** Kansas USA
82 E1 **English** *watercourse* Ontario Canada
139 G4 **English Channel (La Manche)** *strait* UK/France
59 T2 **English Coast** Antarctica
214 D1 **English Companys Islands, The** NT Australia
121 R4 **Engozero** Russian Federation
124 E3 **Engstingen** Germany
123 L4 **Engures ezers** *lake* Latvia
122 I2 **Enhammarsfjärden** *bay* Sweden
86 C2 **Enid** Oklahoma USA
86 G3 **Enid Lake** Mississippi USA
223 15a **Enigu** *island* Marshall Islands
121 O3 **Enijärvi** *lake* Finland
193 I2 **Eniwa** Japan
222 6 **Eniwetak** *island* Marshall Islands
189 G3 **Enjiang** Jiangxi China
135 AD7 **Enkan, Mys** *cape* Russian Federation
124 C1 **Enkhuizen** Netherlands
123 K2 **Enklinge** *island* Finland
188 C4 **Enle** Yunnan China
135 AL5 **Enmelen** Russian Federation
131 F8 **Enna** Italy
75 U2 **Ennadai** Nunavut Canada
76 E2 **Ennadai Lake** Nunavut Canada
159 I2 **Enné, Ouadi** *watercourse* Chad
156 C4 **Ennedi** *range* Chad
140 A3 **Ennell, Lough** *lake* Ireland
126 F4 **Ennezat** France
218 G3 **Enngonia** NSW Australia
143 D4 **Ennis** Ireland
80 J4 **Ennis** Montana USA
86 C4 **Ennis** Texas USA
80 J4 **Ennis Lake** Montana USA
143 F4 **Enniscorthy** Ireland
143 D5 **Enniskean** Ireland
143 F3 **Enniskerry** Ireland
143 E2 **Enniskillen** Fermanagh Northern Ireland UK
143 C4 **Ennistymon** Ireland
127 L2 **Enns** Austria
130 E3 **Enns** *watercourse* Austria
130 F3 **Ennstaler Alpen** *range* Austria
121 Q5 **Eno** Finland
196 D4 **Enok** Indonesia
121 P5 **Enonkoski** Finland
121 O4 **Enonkylä** Finland
121 M2 **Enontekiö** Finland
123 O1 **Enonvesi** *bay* Finland
123 O1 **Enonvesi** *lake* Finland
189 F4 **Enping** Guangdong China
91 G3 **Enriquillo, Lago** *lake* Dominican Republic
219 H7 **Ensay** Vic. Australia
124 D1 **Enschede** Netherlands
88 A2 **Ensenada** Mexico
188 F2 **Enshi** Hubei China
81 O8 **Ensign** Kansas USA
127 H3 **Ensisheim** France
161 E3 **Entebbe** Uganda
142 E5 **Enterkinfoot** Dumfries and Galloway Scotland UK
87 I5 **Enterprise** Alabama USA
80 G4 **Enterprise** Oregon USA
80 I8 **Enterprise** Utah USA
195 H5 **Enterprise Point** Philippines
100 A3 **Entrada, Punta** *cape* Panama
74 M6 **Entrance** Alberta Canada
126 F4 **Entraygues** France
107 G4 **Entre Ríos** *admin. area* Argentina
103 E5 **Entre Rios** Brazil
128 E3 **Entrepeñas, Embalse de** *lake* Spain
198 E5 **Enu** *island* Indonesia
159 F3 **Enugu** Nigeria
159 F3 **Enugu** *admin. area* Nigeria
100 C3 **Envigado** Colombia
104 D2 **Envira** Brazil
105 G2 **Envira** Brazil
160 C4 **Enyamba** Democratic Republic of Congo
159 H4 **Enyéllé** Congo
130 H3 **Enying** Hungary
130 C2 **Enz** *watercourse* Germany
130 D4 **Enza** *watercourse* Italy
124 G4 **Enzingerboden** Austria
128 C2 **Eo** *watercourse* Spain
192 E4 **Eocheong-do** *island* South Korea
142 A3 **Eolaigearraidh** Na h-Eileanan Siar Scotland UK
131 F7 **Eolie, Isole** *island* Italy
222 6 **Eor** *island* Federated States of Micronesia
124 C1 **Epe** Netherlands
108 D1 **Epecuén, Lago** *lake* Argentina
159 H4 **Epéna** Congo
214 C6 **Epenarra** NT Australia
126 F2 **Épernay** France
80 F3 **Ephrata** Washington USA
222 7 **Epi** *island* Vanuatu
133 C7 **Epidavrou, Kolpos** *bay* Greece
129 F3 **Épila** Spain
127 G3 **Épinac** France
127 H2 **Épinal** France
160 D3 **Epini** Democratic Republic of Congo
123 M2 **Epoo** Finland
83 P5 **Epping** New Hampshire USA
215 I7 **Epping Forest** Qld Australia
219 R10 **Epping Forest** Tas. Australia
130 C2 **Eppingen** Germany
139 G3 **Epsom** Surrey England UK
126 E2 **Epte** *watercourse* France
162 C4 **Epukiro** Namibia
160 D3 **Epulu** *watercourse* Democratic Republic of Congo
178 G3 **Eqlīd** Iran
159 F5 **Equata** Gabon
160 C3 **Équateur** *admin. area* Democratic Republic of Congo
159 F4 **Equatorial Guinea** *country* Africa
188 C3 **Er Hai** *lake* Yunnan China
154 F2 **Er Rachidia** Morocco
156 E5 **Er Rahad** Sudan
156 E5 **Er Renk** Sudan
156 E5 **Er Roseires** Sudan
156 E5 **Er Ruaat** Sudan
130 D5 **Era** *watercourse* Italy
199 H5 **Era** *watercourse* Papua New Guinea
124 G5 **Eraclea** Italy
197 H1 **Eran Bay** Philippines
90 B4 **Erandique** Honduras
199 G5 **Erave** *watercourse* Papua New Guinea
156 F4 **Erbab, Jebel** *mountain* Sudan
136 G5 **Erciş** Turkey
131 F6 **Ercolano** Italy
130 H3 **Ercsi** Hungary
130 H3 **Érd** Hungary
133 E5 **Erdek Körfezi** *bay* Turkey
136 E6 **Erdemli** Turkey
185 K3 **Erdene** Mongolia
190 G4 **Erdene** Mongolia
185 I3 **Erdeneburen** Mongolia
190 E3 **Erdenedalai** Mongolia
185 J3 **Erdenehairhan** Mongolia
190 E3 **Erdenesant** Mongolia
190 E2 **Erdenet** Mongolia
191 H3 **Erdenetsagaan** Mongolia
190 D3 **Erdenetsogt** Mongolia
132 A3 **Erdevik** Serbia
124 F3 **Erding** Germany
182 E4 **Erdniyevskiy** Russian Federation
126 D3 **Erdre** *watercourse* France
125 J5 **Erdut** Croatia
59 L1 **Erebus, Mount** *volcano* Antarctica
107 H3 **Erechim** Brazil
190 F2 **Eree** Mongolia
191 G2 **Ereen** Mongolia
156 B5 **Eref** Chad
136 D5 **Ereğli** Turkey
136 E6 **Ereğli** Turkey
133 A6 **Ereikoussa** *island* Greece
84 D5 **Eréndira** Mexico
190 G4 **Erenhot** Nei Mongol Zizhiqu China
101 G5 **Erepecu, Lagoa do** *lake* Brazil
161 G2 **Erer** *watercourse* Ethiopia
128 D3 **Eresma** *watercourse* Spain
133 D6 **Eresos** Greece
101 E3 **Erevato** *watercourse* Venezuela
154 F2 **Erfoud** Morocco
124 F2 **Erfurt** Germany
136 F5 **Ergani** Turkey
123 M4 **Ērģeme** Latvia
136 C5 **Ergene** *watercourse* Turkey
133 F5 **Ergili** Turkey
123 M4 **Ērgļi** Latvia
124 G3 **Ergolding** Germany
127 K2 **Ergoldsbach** Germany
81 Q3 **Erhard** Minnesota USA
79 F7 **Éric, Lac** *lake* Quebec Canada
131 E7 **Erice** Italy
128 B4 **Ericeira** Portugal
142 D4 **Ericht, Loch** *lake* Scotland UK
86 B3 **Erick** Oklahoma USA
75 V7 **Erickson** Manitoba Canada
81 P6 **Ericson** Nebraska USA
83 K5 **Erie** Pennsylvania USA
83 K5 **Erie, Lake** Canada/USA
142 D5 **Eriff** East Ayrshire Scotland UK
133 E5 **Erikli** Turkey
75 V7 **Eriksdale** Manitoba Canada
122 H4 **Eriksmåla** Sweden
223 15 **Erikub Atoll** *reef* Marshall Islands
133 D6 **Erimitis, Akra** *cape* Greece
86 H2 **Erin** Tennessee USA
109 9 **Erin Point** Trinidad and Tobago
142 C5 **Erines** Argyll and Bute Scotland UK
139 H2 **Eriswell** Suffolk England UK
130 B3 **Eriswil** Switzerland
219 R9 **Erith Island** Tas. Australia
156 F4 **Eritrea** *country* Africa
123 J3 **Erken** *lake* Sweden
190 E3 **Erkhet Uul** *mountain* Mongolia
127 J2 **Erlangen** Germany
217 M2 **Erldunda** NT Australia
86 E4 **Erling, Lake** Arkansas USA

191 H2 **Ermana, Khrebet** *range* Russian Federation
162 E5 **Ermelo** South Africa
156 D5 **Ermil Post** Sudan
123 M3 **Ermistu järv** *lake* Estonia
133 D7 **Ermoupoli** Greece
128 E2 **Ermúa** Spain
140 A3 **Erne** *watercourse* Ireland
126 D2 **Ernée** France
213 I3 **Ernest** *watercourse* WA Australia
81 L1 **Ernfold** Saskatchewan Canada
130 G2 **Ernstbrunn** Austria
187 D9 **Erode** Tamil Nadu India
223 15a **Eroj** *island* Marshall Islands
218 F2 **Eromanga** Qld Australia
162 C4 **Erongo** *admin. area* Namibia
199 I6 **Eroro** Papua New Guinea
135 AE5 **Erozionnyy** Russian Federation
188 E1 **Erqu** Shaanxi China
126 C2 **Erquy** France
216 E2 **Errabiddy** WA Australia
143 B2 **Erris Head** *cape* Ireland
222 7 **Erromango** *island* Vanuatu
127 I2 **Ersbach** Germany
133 B5 **Ersekë** Albania
120 J2 **Ersfjord** Norway
179 M2 **Ershād Owin, Kowtal-e** *pass* Pakistan
213 I5 **Erskine, Mount** WA Australia
59 B2 **Erskine Iceport** Antarctica
120 L5 **Ersmark/Ume-Ersmark** Sweden
120 L4 **Ersnäs** Sweden
120 I3 **Erstein** France
127 H2 **Erstein** France
182 C3 **Ertil** Russian Federation
185 H3 **Ertix He** *watercourse* Xinjiang Uygur Zizhiqu China
120 M3 **Ertsjärv** Sweden
120 F5 **Ertvågøya** *island* Norway
123 M3 **Eru laht** *bay* Estonia
220 F4 **Erua** New Zealand
101 F3 **Erueda-Tepui** *mountain* Venezuela
159 F3 **Erufa** Nigeria
187 D10 **Eruvadi** Tamil Nadu India
126 D2 **Erve** *watercourse* France
142 C6 **Ervie** Dumfries and Galloway Scotland UK
122 C1 **Ervik** Norway
124 E2 **Erwitte** Germany
138 D2 **Erwood** Powys Wales UK
133 B7 **Erymanthos** *range* Greece
183 Q3 **Erzin** Russian Federation
136 F5 **Erzincan** Turkey
136 F5 **Erzincan** *admin. area* Turkey
136 G5 **Erzurum** Turkey
136 G5 **Erzurum** *admin. area* Turkey
154 D3 **Es Semara** Western Sahara
104 C5 **Esbilla** Peru
195 I5 **Escalante** Philippines
80 J8 **Escalante** Utah USA
84 G2 **Escalante** *watercourse* Utah USA
84 F2 **Escalante Desert** Utah USA
126 E5 **Escales, Pantà d'** *lake* Spain
129 G4 **Escaleta, Punta de la** *cape* Spain
88 D3 **Escalón** Mexico
82 H4 **Escanaba** Michigan USA
89 H5 **Escárcega** Mexico
195 I3 **Escarpada Point** Philippines
127 G2 **Esch-sur-Alzette** Luxembourg
124 F4 **Eschede** Germany
124 E4 **Eschenz** Switzerland
127 H3 **Escholzmatt** Switzerland
124 F2 **Eschwege** Germany
88 E3 **Escobedo** Mexico
91 G3 **Escocesa, Bahía** *bay* Dominican Republic
84 D4 **Escondido** California USA
90 D4 **Escondido, Rio** *watercourse* Nicaragua
105 F5 **Escorpión** Bolivia
129 G2 **Escosse** France
214 E4 **Escott** Qld Australia
59 U2 **Escudero (Chile)** *research station* Antarctica
90 B4 **Escuintla** Guatemala
79 F9 **Escuminac, Point** New Brunswick Canada
159 G4 **Eséke** Cameroon
178 C2 **Eşen** Turkey
133 F7 **Eşen** *watercourse* Turkey
182 G6 **Esenguly** Turkmenistan
182 I6 **Esenmengli** Turkmenistan
122 D6 **Esens** Germany
129 G2 **Esera** *watercourse* Spain
178 G3 **Eşfahān** Iran
178 G3 **Eşfahān** *admin. area* Iran
182 H6 **Esfarāyen** Iran
138 C3 **Esgair** Carmarthenshire Wales UK
178 G2 **Eshehārd** Iran
139 G3 **Esher** Surrey England UK
139 G1 **Eshott** Northumberland England UK
163 F5 **Esikhawini** South Africa
130 E5 **Esino** *watercourse* Italy
163 I4 **Esira** Madagascar
199 I5 **Esis** *watercourse* Papua New Guinea
219 K2 **Esk** Qld Australia
221 E6 **Esk** *watercourse* New Zealand
140 E1 **Esk** *watercourse* Scotland UK
79 H10 **Eskasoni** Nova Scotia Canada
142 E5 **Eskdalemuir** Dumfries and Galloway Scotland UK
142 E2 **Eske, Lough** *lake* Ireland
77 V6 **Esker** Newfoundland and Labrador Canada
140 A3 **Esker** Ireland
143 C2 **Eskeragh** Ireland
120 inset **Eskifjörður** Iceland
122 I3 **Eskilstuna** Sweden
72 F5 **Eskimo Lakes** Northwest Territories Canada
136 D5 **Eskişehir** *admin. area* Turkey
121 N5 **Eskola** Finland
122 I2 **Eskön** *island* Sweden
143 E2 **Eskragh** Omagh Northern Ireland UK
126 B5 **Esla** *watercourse* Spain
104 D4 **Eslabón, Serranía de** *range* Bolivia
178 F2 **Eslāmābād-e Gharb** Iran
178 G2 **Eslāmshahr** Iran
122 G5 **Eslöv** Sweden
214 A2 **Esmeralda** NT Australia
214 G5 **Esmeralda** Qld Australia
88 E3 **Esmeralda** Mexico
104 A4 **Esmeralda, Isla** *island* Chile
103 C7 **Esmeraldas** Brazil
100 B4 **Esmeraldas** Ecuador
81 P2 **Esmond** North Dakota USA
82 H1 **Esnagami Lake** Ontario Canada
82 I2 **Esnagi Lake** Ontario Canada
100 D1 **Espada, Punta** *cape* Venezuela
126 F4 **Espalion** France
129 G4 **Espalmador, Isla** *island* Spain
88 D3 **España** Mexico
85 I3 **Espanola** New Mexico USA
109 4 **Española, Isla** *island* Archipiélago de Colón (Galapagos Islands)
106 F5 **Espartillar** Argentina
100 C4 **Espejo, Lago** *lake* Colombia
103 D8 **Espera Feliz** Brazil
102 F4 **Esperança** Brazil
164 1b **Esperança, Pico da** *volcano* Azores
216 G6 **Esperance** WA Australia
222 8 **Esperance, Cape** Solomon Islands
102 D3 **Esperantina** Brazil
102 C4 **Esperantinópolis** Brazil
108 B5 **Esperanza** Argentina
85 I6 **Esperanza** Mexico
90 C4 **Esperanza, Sierra la** *range* Honduras
59 U2 **Esperanza (Argentina)** *research station* Antarctica
105 F2 **Espero-em-Deus** Brazil
179 I4 **Espetgi** Iran
128 B4 **Espichel, Cabo** *cape* Portugal
107 I3 **Espigão, Serra do** *range* Brazil
126 F5 **Espiguette, Pointe de l'** *cape* France
100 C3 **Espinal** Colombia
104 C3 **Espinal** Peru
128 D2 **Espinama** Spain
106 D6 **Espinazo del Zorro** Argentina
103 D7 **Espinhaço, Serra do** *range* Brazil
128 B3 **Espinho** Portugal
107 H4 **Espinilho, Serra do** *range* Brazil
101 E2 **Espino** Venezuela
103 D6 **Espinosa** Brazil
105 E2 **Espírito Santo** Brazil
103 D7 **Espírito Santo** *admin. area* Brazil
Espiritu *see* **Banna** Philippines
222 7 **Espiritu Santo** *island* Vanuatu
90 C3 **Espíritu Santo, Bahía del** *bay* Mexico
108 C5 **Espíritu Santo, Cabo** *cape* Argentina
88 C3 **Espíritu Santo, Isla** *island* Mexico
89 H4 **Espita** Mexico
109 5 **Espólon, Punta** *cape* Isla de Pascua (Easter Island)
123 M2 **Espoo** Finland
179 I4 **Espor** Iran
107 H4 **Espumoso** Brazil
88 C2 **Esqueda** Mexico
108 B3 **Esquel** Argentina
107 G4 **Esquina** Argentina
120 L3 **Esrange** Sweden
198 C2 **Essang** Indonesia
154 E2 **Essaouira** Morocco
158 A2 **Essau** Gambia
159 G4 **Essé** Cameroon
127 G1 **Essen** Belgium
124 D2 **Essen** Germany
126 E2 **Essendon, Mount** WA Australia
101 G4 **Essequibo** *watercourse* Guyana
101 G3 **Essequibo Islands-West Demerara** *admin. area* Guyana
139 H3 **Essex** *admin. area* England UK
109 4 **Essex, Punta** *cape* Archipiélago de Colón (Galapagos Islands)
214 B1 **Essington, Port** NT Australia
135 AG7 **Esso** Russian Federation
126 E3 **Essonne** France
121 R6 **Essoyla** Russian Federation
159 G4 **Est** *admin. area* Cameroon
79 H9 **Est, Île de l'** *island* Quebec Canada
164 6 **Est, Île de l'** *island* French Southern and Antarctic Lands
79 H8 **Est, Pointe de l'** Quebec Canada
128 C2 **Estaca de Bares, Punta da** *cape* Spain
85 I6 **Estacion Consuelo** Mexico
88 E3 **Estación El Fuerte** Mexico
85 I7 **Estacion Golandrinas** Mexico
84 G6 **Estacion Moreno** Mexico
108 D6 **Estados, Isla de los** *island* Argentina
126 F5 **Estagel** France
126 F3 **Estaimpuis** Belgium
124 B2 **Estaires** France
85 I3 **Estancia** New Mexico USA
103 E5 **Estância** Brazil
107 G2 **Estancia Amalia** Paraguay
104 D5 **Estancia Añutani** Bolivia
105 F5 **Estancia Atlántico Norte** Bolivia
105 G5 **Estancia Bella Vista** Bolivia
105 G5 **Estancia Bello Horizonte** Bolivia
107 G2 **Estancia Buena Vista** Paraguay
104 E6 **Estancia Cala Horno** Bolivia
107 G2 **Estancia Campo Sastre** Paraguay
104 E5 **Estancia Catchi Vinto** Bolivia
107 G2 **Estancia Coé Puajhú** Paraguay
105 F5 **Estancia Curiche** Bolivia
106 F2 **Estancia El Dorado** Paraguay
106 F2 **Estancia El Pampero** Paraguay
107 G2 **Estancia Esperanza** Paraguay
107 G2 **Estancia Gómez** Paraguay
105 E5 **Estancia Kayorani** Bolivia
108 C4 **Estancia L. Lorenzo** Argentina
105 F5 **Estancia La Cortina** Bolivia
107 F2 **Estancia Los Caminantes** Paraguay
105 F6 **Estancia Nueva Holanda** Bolivia
105 G5 **Estancia Paquiocito** Bolivia
105 G6 **Estancia Riacho Alegre** Paraguay
105 F4 **Estancia S.S.O.** Bolivia
107 G2 **Estancia San Jorge** Paraguay
105 F5 **Estancia San José** Paraguay
105 F5 **Estancia San Josema** Bolivia
105 G5 **Estancia Santa Rosa** Bolivia
107 G2 **Estancia Santa Teresa** Paraguay
104 D6 **Estancia Sinalaco** Bolivia
104 E6 **Estancia Tambo** Bolivia
107 G2 **Estancia Toldo Cué** Paraguay
107 G2 **Estancia Tomas Cué** Paraguay
107 G2 **Estancia Tres Toritos** Paraguay
104 D5 **Estancia Vinto** Bolivia
85 K7 **Estanque de Leon** Mexico
84 G6 **Estanque de Norias** Mexico
108 A2 **Estaquilla, Punta** *cape* Chile
129 G2 **Estats, Pic d'** *mountain* Spain
79 D9 **Estcourt** Quebec Canada
162 E5 **Estcourt** South Africa
124 F5 **Este** Italy
106 E2 **Esteban de Urizar** Argentina
90 C4 **Estelí** Nicaragua
122 E4 **Estella** Spain
86 A3 **Estelline** Texas USA
128 E4 **Estepar** Spain
128 D5 **Estepona** Spain
159 F4 **Esterias, Cape** Gabon
124 B3 **Esternay** France
84 B3 **Estero Bay** California USA
84 G7 **Estero la Bocana** Mexico
84 B5 **Esteros** Paraguay
106 F2 **Esteros** Paraguay
124 D1 **Esterwegen** Germany
75 T8 **Estevan** Saskatchewan Canada
75 P7 **Esther** Alberta Canada
87 H4 **Estill** South Carolina USA
87 H3 **Estill Springs** Tennessee USA
163 F3 **Estima** Mozambique
126 F2 **Estissac** France
105 G4 **Estivado** Brazil
123 **Estonia** *country* Europe
127 H5 **Estoublon** France
102 A4 **Estragado, Serra do** *range* Brazil
102 D4 **Estreito** Brazil
107 I4 **Estrela** Brazil
84 E5 **Estrella, Punta** *cape* Mexico
126 C4 **Estremoz** Portugal
102 B5 **Estrondo, Serra do** *range* Brazil
159 G4 **Estuaire** *admin. area* Gabon
75 Q7 **Estuary** Saskatchewan Canada
142 inset **Eswick** Shetland Scotland UK
130 H3 **Esztergom** Hungary
216 E3 **Etadunna** SA Australia
78 I6 **Etagaulet Bay** Newfoundland and Labrador Canada
186 E5 **Etah** Uttar Pradesh India
127 G2 **Étain** France
199 J2 **Etal** *island* Federated States of Micronesia
79 H7 **Etamamiou** *watercourse* Quebec Canada
126 F2 **Étampes** France
218 D2 **Etamunbanie, Lake** SA Australia
139 I4 **Étaples** France
186 E5 **Etawah** Uttar Pradesh India
76 G4 **Etawney Lake** Manitoba Canada
88 C3 **Etchojoa** Mexico
88 C3 **Etchoropo** Mexico
123 M2 **Etelä-Suomen** *admin. area* Finland
123 N2 **Eteläjoki** *watercourse* Finland
104 B2 **Eten** Peru
88 E2 **Etéreo** Mexico
81 Q4 **Ethan** South Dakota USA
216 F2 **Ethel** *watercourse* WA Australia
212 F7 **Ethel Creek** WA Australia
75 U7 **Ethelbert** Manitoba Canada
215 G3 **Etheldale** Qld Australia
215 G4 **Etheridge** *watercourse* Qld Australia
153 G4 **Ethiopia** *country* Africa
161 F1 **Ethiopian Highlands** *range* Ethiopia
86 H3 **Ethridge** Tennessee USA
104 D4 **Etive** *watercourse* Scotland UK
142 C4 **Etive, Loch** *lake* Scotland UK
131 I8 **Etna, Monte** *volcano* Italy
122 C3 **Etne** Norway
72 C7 **Etolin Strait** Alaska USA
193 J2 **Etorofu-tō (Ostrov Iturup)** *island* Russian Federation
162 C3 **Etosha Pan** Namibia
159 G4 **Etoumbi** Congo
87 I3 **Etowah** Tennessee USA
139 H5 **Étretat** France
126 E4 **Etroubles** Italy
162 D3 **Etsha** Botswana
222 6 **Ettal** *island* Federated States of Micronesia
127 H2 **Ettelbruck** Luxembourg
142 D3 **Etteridge** Highland Scotland UK
127 I2 **Ettlingen** Germany
221 E7 **Ettrick** New Zealand
142 E5 **Ettrick** Scottish Borders Scotland UK
88 D4 **Etzatlán** Mexico
75 O8 **Etzicom Coulee** *watercourse* Alberta Canada
75 P8 **Etzikom** Alberta Canada
139 I4 **Eu** France
223 10 **'Eua Island** Tonga
218 H5 **Euabalong** NSW Australia
222 6 **Euaripik** *island* Federated States of Micronesia
219 I5 **Euchareena** NSW Australia
217 K5 **Eucla** WA Australia
83 K6 **Euclid** Ohio USA
219 I7 **Eucumbene, Lake** NSW Australia
79 F7 **Eudistes, Lac des** *lake* Quebec Canada
86 F4 **Eudora** Arkansas USA
218 D6 **Eudunda** SA Australia
87 I5 **Eufaula** Alabama USA
86 D3 **Eufaula Lake** Oklahoma USA
80 D4 **Eugene** Oregon USA
84 E7 **Eugenia, Punta** *cape* Mexico
89 H5 **Eugenio Echeverría Castellot** Mexico
218 G3 **Eulo** Qld Australia
219 I2 **Eumamurrin, Mount** Qld Australia
128 B2 **Eume, Embalse do** *lake* Spain
215 J6 **Eungella** Qld Australia
215 J6 **Eungella, Lake** Qld Australia
85 K4 **Eunice** New Mexico USA
127 H1 **Eupen** Belgium
Euphrates *see* **Furāt, Nahr al** Middle East
86 G4 **Eupora** Mississippi USA
215 H5 **Euramo** Qld Australia
216 D5 **Eurardy** WA Australia
126 E2 **Eure** *watercourse* France
82 C8 **Eureka** Kansas USA
80 H2 **Eureka** Montana USA
84 E1 **Eureka** Nevada USA
74 L4 **Eureka River** Alberta Canada
73 K3 **Eureka Sound** Nunavut Canada
218 D5 **Eurelia** SA Australia
218 G7 **Euroa** Vic. Australia
164 6a **Europa, Île** *island* Îles Éparses
106 E6 **Euskadi** Argentina
87 K6 **Eustis** Florida USA
218 F6 **Euston** NSW Australia
86 H4 **Eutaw** Alabama USA
85 K6 **Eutimias** Mexico
74 G8 **Eutsuk Lake** British Columbia Canada
159 I8 **Euwo** *watercourse* Central African Republic
85 L2 **Eva** Oklahoma USA
214 C5 **Eva Downs** NT Australia
104 E4 **Eva Eva, Serranía** *range* Bolivia
123 M2 **Eväjärvi** *lake* Finland
162 C3 **Evale** Angola
219 R10 **Evandale** Tas. Australia
104 E3 **Evangelista** Bolivia
74 L8 **Evans** Washington USA
108 A5 **Evans, Isla** *island* Chile
83 M1 **Evans, Lac** *lake* Quebec Canada
109 3 **Evans, Punta** *cape* Isla de San Andrés
59 S1 **Evans Ice Stream** Antarctica
59 R2 **Evans Peninsula** Antarctica
73 K6 **Evans Strait** Nunavut Canada
81 J6 **Evanston** Wyoming USA
82 H8 **Evansville** Indiana USA
86 B5 **Evant** Texas USA
82 I5 **Evart** Michigan USA
133 E6 **Evciler** Turkey
139 G2 **Evedon** Lincolnshire England UK
214 B2 **Evelyn, Mount** NT Australia
139 F3 **Evenlode** *watercourse* England UK
120 J2 **Evenskjær** Norway
219 J7 **Everard, Cape** Vic. Australia
218 B4 **Everard, Lake** SA Australia
217 M3 **Everard Ranges** SA Australia
181 F3 **Everest, Mount** Himalaya Asia
80 D3 **Everett** Washington USA
126 F1 **Evergem** Belgium
88 C5 **Evermann, Cerro** *volcano* Mexico
122 H5 **Everöd** Sweden
218 H2 **Eversfield** Qld Australia
129 H2 **Evertsberg** Sweden
139 F2 **Evesham** Worcestershire England UK
139 F2 **Evesham, Vale of** *valley* England UK
121 M5 **Evijärvi** Finland
159 G4 **Evinayong** Equatorial Guinea
122 D3 **Evje** Norway
120 H3 **Evjen** Norway
127 H3 **Evolène** Switzerland
128 C4 **Évora** Portugal
128 C4 **Évora** *admin. area* Portugal
135 AC8 **Evoron, Ozero** *lake* Russian Federation
108 C6 **Evout, Islas** *islands* Chile
126 D2 **Évran** France
126 E2 **Èvre** *watercourse* France
126 E2 **Évreux** France
126 D2 **Évron** France
133 E5 **Evros** *watercourse* Turkey
133 C7 **Evrotas** *watercourse* Greece
133 C6 **Evvoia** *island* Greece
222 4 **Ewa** Nauru
215 H5 **Ewan** Qld Australia
214 B7 **Ewart, Mount** NT Australia
90 E3 **Ewarton** Jamaica
161 E3 **Ewaso Ngiro** *watercourse* Kenya
142 C3 **Ewe, Loch** *bay* Scotland UK
81 P5 **Ewing** Nebraska USA
59 U2 **Ewing Island** Antarctica
159 G5 **Ewo** Congo
104 E4 **Exaltación** Bolivia
138 D4 **Exbourne** Devon England UK
81 J1 **Excel** Alberta Canada
86 H5 **Excel** Alabama USA
81 E5 **Excelsior** South Africa
84 D1 **Excelsior Mountains** Nevada USA
127 J1 **Exdorf** Germany
138 D4 **Exe** *watercourse* England UK
59 P1 **Executive Committee Range** Antarctica
122 G4 **Exen** *lake* Sweden
84 C2 **Exeter** California USA
138 D3 **Exford** Somerset England UK
126 E2 **Exmes** France
138 D3 **Exminster** Devon England UK
138 D4 **Exmoor** England UK
83 N8 **Exmore** Virginia USA
212 C6 **Exmouth** WA Australia
138 D4 **Exmouth** Devon England UK
212 C7 **Exmouth Gulf** WA Australia
55 P6 **Exmouth Plateau** *underwater feature* Indian Ocean
142 inset **Exnaboe** Shetland Scotland UK
133 C5 **Exochi** Greece
215 J7 **Expedition Range** Qld Australia
79 J8 **Exploits** *watercourse* Newfoundland and Labrador Canada
79 K8 **Exploits, Bay of** Newfoundland and Labrador Canada
75 N7 **Exshaw** Alberta Canada
128 C4 **Extremadura** *admin. area* Spain
159 G2 **Extrême-Nord** *admin. area* Cameroon
102 F4 **Extremoz** Brazil
102 E4 **Exu** Brazil
90 E1 **Exuma Cays** *islands* Bahamas
90 E1 **Exuma Sound** *bay* Bahamas
161 F4 **Eyasi, Lake** Tanzania
139 I2 **Eye** Suffolk England UK
142 F5 **Eyemouth** Scottish Borders Scotland UK
129 I2 **Eyguières** France
120 inset **Eyjafjarðará** *watercourse* Iceland
120 inset **Eyjafjörður** *bay* Iceland
161 I2 **Eyl** Somalia
161 H2 **Eyl** *watercourse* Somalia
126 E4 **Eymoutiers** France
82 E5 **Eyota** Minnesota USA
218 E2 **Eyre** *watercourse* Qld Australia
218 D1 **Eyre** *watercourse* Qld Australia
217 M6 **Eyre Island** SA Australia
218 D3 **Eyre North, Lake** SA Australia
218 B5 **Eyre Peninsula** SA Australia
218 C3 **Eyre South, Lake** SA Australia
127 G4 **Eyrieux** *watercourse* France
73 S6 **Eysturoy** *island* Faroe Islands
138 E2 **Eyton** Herefordshire England UK
128 D6 **Ez Zinate** Morocco
162 F5 **Ezakheni** South Africa
88 C2 **Ezcalqui** Mexico
128 E2 **Ezcaray** Spain
108 C2 **Ezequiel Ramos Mexía, Embalse** *lake* Argentina
123 L4 **Ezere** Latvia
132 F4 **Ezerec** Bulgaria
189 G2 **Ezhou** Hubei China

F

223 14a **Faaa** French Polynesia
187 D11 **Faadhippolhu Atoll** Maldives
161 G3 **Faafxadhuun** Somalia
223 14b **Faanui** French Polynesia
129 G2 **Fabian** France
120 J4 **Fåbodliden** Sweden
122 I2 **Fäbodön** *cape* Sweden
130 E5 **Fabriano** Italy
103 D7 **Fabriciano** Brazil
75 P6 **Fabyan** Alberta Canada
141 G2 **Faceby** North Yorkshire England UK
155 I5 **Fachi** Niger
108 B4 **Fachinal** Chile
131 H6 **Faci, Punta** *cape* Italy
215 K7 **Facing Island** Qld Australia
108 C3 **Facundo** Argentina
156 C4 **Fada** Chad
158 E2 **Fada N'gourma** Burkina Faso
132 A2 **Fadd** Hungary
72 A6 **Faddeya, Mys** *cape* Russian Federation
135 W3 **Faddeya, Zaliv** *bay* Russian Federation
135 AD3 **Faddeyevskiy, Ostrov** *island* Russian Federation
77 V5 **Faden** Newfoundland and Labrador Canada
183 M2 **Fadikha** *lake* Russian Federation
130 D4 **Faenza** Italy
131 F6 **Faeto** Italy
159 H3 **Fafa** *watercourse* Central African Republic
128 B3 **Fafe** Portugal
161 G2 **Fafen** *watercourse* Ethiopia
158 E2 **Faga** *watercourse* Burkina Faso
223 12c **Fagamalo** Samoa
217 K2 **Fagan, Mount** NT Australia
132 D3 **Făgăraș** Romania
120 I6 **Fågelsjö** Sweden
120 I4 **Fågelsjön** *bay* Sweden
122 H2 **Fågelsjön** *lake* Sweden
122 I2 **Fågelsundet** Sweden
122 E1 **Fagerhaug** Norway
120 L4 **Fagerheden** Sweden
120 J3 **Fagerli** Norway
122 H3 **Fagersta** Sweden
132 C3 **Făget** Romania
159 F2 **Faggo** Nigeria
198 D4 **Fagita** Indonesia
108 C6 **Fagnano, Lago** *lake* Argentina
156 E4 **Fagrinkotti** Sudan
120 inset **Fagurholsmýri** Iceland
164 1b **Faial** *island* Azores
164 1b **Faial, Canal do** *strait* Azores
131 C9 **Faid** Tunisia
127 I3 **Faido** Switzerland
83 M2 **Faillon, Lac** *lake* Quebec Canada
142 C3 **Fain** Highland Scotland UK
215 G2 **Fair Cape** Qld Australia
72 E5 **Fairbanks** Alaska USA
81 Q6 **Fairbury** Nebraska USA
76 D6 **Fairfax** Missouri USA
81 Q8 **Fairfax** Oklahoma USA
87 K4 **Fairfax** South Carolina USA
80 H5 **Fairfield** Idaho USA
81 P6 **Fairfield** Nebraska USA
86 C5 **Fairfield** Texas USA
219 H5 **Fairholme** NSW Australia
86 D2 **Fairland** Oklahoma USA
221 D7 **Fairlie** New Zealand
142 D5 **Fairlie** North Ayrshire Scotland UK
82 D5 **Fairmont** Minnesota USA
215 H3 **Fairview** Qld Australia
74 L4 **Fairview** Alberta Canada
82 H4 **Fairview** Michigan USA
81 M3 **Fairview** Montana USA
80 J7 **Fairview** Utah USA
214 A3 **Fairview Peak** NT Australia
76 J1 **Fairway Island** Nunavut Canada
74 C3 **Fairweather, Mount** British Columbia/Alaska Canada/USA
140 A4 **Fairybush** Ireland
219 J2 **Fairyland** Qld Australia
143 D3 **Fairymount** Ireland
222 6 **Fais** *island* Federated States of Micronesia
179 M3 **Faisalabad** Pakistan
81 N4 **Faith** South Dakota USA
131 E6 **Faiti** Italy
186 F5 **Faizabad** Uttar Pradesh India
178 D3 **Fajr, Wādī** *watercourse* Saudi Arabia
193 D3 **Fak Tha** Thailand
223 14 **Fakahina** *island* French Polynesia
220 3 **Fakaofo Village** Tokelau New Zealand
223 14 **Fakarava** *island* French Polynesia
182 F4 **Fakeyevo** Kazakhstan
198 E4 **Fakfak, Pegunungan** *range* Indonesia
132 E4 **Fakija** Bulgaria
130 H4 **Fakovići** Bosnia and Herzegovina
122 G5 **Fakse Bugt** *bay* Denmark
189 J4 **Faku** Liaoning China
158 B3 **Falaba** Sierra Leone
158 E2 **Falagountou** Burkina Faso
142 F5 **Falahill** Scottish Borders Scotland UK
126 D2 **Falaise** France
75 M2 **Falaise Lake** Northwest Territories Canada
181 G4 **Falam** Myanmar
222 8 **Falamae** Solomon Islands
142 D6 **Falbae** Dumfries and Galloway Scotland UK
143 D1 **Falcarragh** Ireland
128 B2 **Falceira, Cabo** *cape* Spain
101 E2 **Falcón** *admin. area* Venezuela
89 F3 **Falcón, Presa** *lake* Mexico
130 E5 **Falconara Marittima** Italy
78 F4 **Falcoz** *watercourse* Quebec Canada
158 B2 **Falea** Mali
223 12c **Falealupo** Samoa
223 13a **Falefatu** *island* Tuvalu
223 12c **Falelima** Samoa
154 D6 **Falémé** *watercourse* Mali
131 G7 **Falerna** Italy
88 B7 **Falfurrias** Texas USA
74 M5 **Falher** Alberta Canada
122 G4 **Falkenberg** Sweden
142 E4 **Falkirk** Falkirk Scotland UK
142 E5 **Falkirk** *admin. area* Scotland UK
51 N14 **Falkland Escarpment** *underwater feature* Atlantic Ocean
108 F5 **Falkland Islands (Islas Malvinas)** *UK territory* Atlantic Ocean
51 M15 **Falkland Plateau** *underwater feature* Atlantic Ocean
109 7 **Falkland Sound** *strait* Falkland Islands
133 D7 **Falkonera** *island* Greece
83 P6 **Fall River** Massachusetts USA
140 A1 **Fallask** Ireland
142 E5 **Fallford** Dumfries and Galloway Scotland UK
120 L4 **Fällfors** Sweden
59 T2 **Fallières Coast** Antarctica
80 F7 **Fallon** Nevada USA
86 B6 **Falls City** Texas USA
87 L3 **Falls Lake Reservoir** North Carolina USA
87 K3 **Fallston** North Carolina USA
109 8 **Falmouth** Antigua and Barbuda
138 B4 **Falmouth** Cornwall England UK
83 J7 **Falmouth** Kentucky USA
138 B4 **Falmouth Bay** England UK
142 F5 **Falnash** Scottish Borders Scotland UK
154 E6 **Falo** Mali
158 D2 **Falou** Mali
106 D2 **Falsa Chipana, Punta** *cape* Chile
78 D4 **False** *watercourse* Quebec Canada
78 I5 **False Cape** Newfoundland and Labrador Canada
212 F5 **False Cape Bossut** WA Australia
129 G3 **Falset** Spain
91 G3 **Falso, Cabo** *cape* Dominican Republic
90 D4 **Falso, Cabo** *cape* Honduras
88 C4 **Falso, Cabo** *cape* Mexico
106 B3 **Falso Azufre** *mountain* Chile
122 G5 **Falster** *island* Denmark
141 F1 **Falstone** Northumberland England UK
122 H2 **Falun** Sweden
198 D4 **Fam, Kepulauan** *islands* Indonesia
136 E6 **Famagusta** Cyprus
106 E4 **Famatina** Argentina
106 E4 **Famatina, Sierra de** *range* Argentina
75 Q4 **Family Lake** Manitoba Canada
194 D2 **Fan Si Pan** *mountain* Vietnam
154 E6 **Fana** Mali
122 C2 **Fana** Norway
143 E1 **Fanad Head** *cape* Ireland
74 6a **Fananani, Mochun** *strait* Federated States of Micronesia
222 6a **Fanapanges** *island* Federated States of Micronesia
133 E7 **Fanari, Akra** *cape* Greece
158 B2 **Fandana** Mali
143 F3 **Fane** *watercourse* Ireland
122 G5 **Fanefjord Kirke** *bay* Denmark
133 D8 **Faneromeni, Akra** *cape* Greece
222 6a **Fanew, Mochun** *strait* Federated States of Micronesia
188 F2 **Fang Xian** Hubei China
160 E2 **Fangak** Sudan
223 14 **Fangatau** *island* French Polynesia
223 14 **Fangataufa** *island* French Polynesia
188 E4 **Fangchenggang** Guangxi Zhuangzu Zizhiqu China
188 E2 **Fangdou Shan** *range* Chongqing China
131 C5 **Fango** *watercourse* Corsica France
122 I3 **Fångö** *island* Sweden
191 K3 **Fangzheng** Heilongjiang China
198 D3 **Fani** *island* Indonesia
126 F5 **Fanjeaux** France
142 D3 **Fannich, Loch** *lake* Scotland UK
87 J6 **Fanning Springs** Florida USA
122 E5 **Fanø** *island* Denmark
130 E5 **Fano** Italy
122 E5 **Fanø Bugt** *bay* Denmark
133 C5 **Fanós** Greece
122 I4 **Fansgölen** *lake* Sweden
222 8 **Faore** *island* Solomon Islands
154 D6 **Faraba** Mali
160 D3 **Faradje** Democratic Republic of Congo
163 I4 **Farafangana** Madagascar
154 C6 **Farafenni** Gambia
156 D2 **Farāfirah, Wāḥāt Al** *spring* Egypt
131 D5 **Faraglione, Punta** *cape* Italy
179 J3 **Farāh** Afghanistan
179 J3 **Farāh** *admin. area* Afghanistan
179 J3 **Farāh Rūd** *watercourse* Afghanistan
222 2 **Farallon de Medinilla** *island* Northern Mariana Islands
222 2 **Farallon de Pajaros** *island* Northern Mariana Islands
132 E2 **Faraoani** Romania
182 I6 **Farap** Turkmenistan
199 H1 **Faraulep** *island* Federated States of Micronesia
132 D2 **Farcău** *mountain* Romania
223 14a **Fareara, Pointe** *cape* French Polynesia
139 F4 **Fareham** Hampshire England UK
223 14a **Farehau** French Polynesia
122 D4 **Farestad** Norway
220 F5 **Farewell, Cape** New Zealand
179 H7 **Farghāna** Iran
81 Q3 **Fargo** North Dakota USA
86 B2 **Fargo** Oklahoma USA
183 K6 **Farg'ona** Uzbekistan
183 K6 **Farg'ona** *admin. area* Uzbekistan
82 E4 **Faribault** Minnesota USA
78 C3 **Faribault, Lac** *lake* Quebec Canada
186 D5 **Faridabad** Haryana India
186 D4 **Faridkot** Punjab India
181 F4 **Faridpur** Bangladesh
155 K2 **Farigh, Wādī al** *watercourse* Libya
120 I6 **Färila** Sweden
128 B4 **Farilhões, Ilhas** *islands* Portugal
158 A2 **Farim** Guinea-Bissau
179 I2 **Farīmān** Iran
218 D4 **Farina** SA Australia
139 F3 **Faringdon** Oxfordshire England UK
102 C4 **Farinha** *watercourse* Brazil
183 K6 **Farkhor** Tajikistan
134 S5 **Farkovo** Russian Federation
142 D2 **Farlary** Highland Scotland UK
214 F6 **Farley** Qld Australia
126 E7 **Farmakonisi** *island* Greece
77 O3 **Farmer Island** Nunavut Canada
84 C2 **Farmersville** California USA
82 F6 **Farmington** Iowa USA
82 E4 **Farmington** Minnesota USA
86 G3 **Farmington** Mississippi USA
82 F8 **Farmington** Missouri USA
85 H2 **Farmington** New Mexico USA
82 J5 **Farmington Hills** Michigan USA
132 A2 **Farmos** Hungary
83 L8 **Farmville** Virginia USA
130 H3 **Farná** Slovakia
143 E3 **Farnagh** Ireland
139 F3 **Farnborough** Hampshire England UK
138 E1 **Farndon** Cheshire England UK
139 G3 **Farnham** Surrey England UK
217 J2 **Farnham, Lake** WA Australia
74 M7 **Farnham, Mount** British Columbia Canada
141 F3 **Farnworth** Greater Manchester England UK
106 F6 **Faro** Argentina
159 G3 **Faro** *watercourse* Cameroon
72 F6 **Faro** Yukon Territory Canada
128 C5 **Faro** *admin. area* Portugal
128 B5 **Faro** Portugal
91 F5 **Faro, Punta** *cape* Colombia
57 F2 **Faroe Bank** *underwater feature* Atlantic Ocean
57 F2 **Faroe–Iceland Ridge** *underwater feature* Atlantic Ocean
73 S6 **Faroe Islands** *Danish admin. area* North Atlantic Ocean
123 J4 **Fårösund** Sweden
212 B7 **Farquhar, Cape** WA Australia
164 9 **Farquhar Group** *islands* Seychelles
213 K4 **Farquharson, Mount** NT Australia
216 H3 **Farquharson Tableland** WA Australia
142 E3 **Farr** Highland Scotland UK
59 G2 **Farr Bay** Antarctica
142 D3 **Farraline** Highland Scotland UK
143 C4 **Farranfore** Ireland
218 E1 **Farrars** *watercourse* Qld Australia
74 K4 **Farrell Creek** British Columbia Canada
178 G3 **Fārs** *admin. area* Iran
178 F7 **Farsakh, Ra's** *cape* Yemen
139 F2 **Farthinghoe** Northamptonshire England UK
103 B8 **Fartura** Brazil
Farvel, Kap *see* **Nunap Isua** Greenland
85 K3 **Farwell** Texas USA
59 R2 **Farwell Island** Antarctica
182 I7 **Fāryāb** *admin. area* Afghanistan
179 H3 **Fasā** Iran
179 H4 **Fasā** Iran
142 C3 **Fasag** Highland Scotland UK
142 C3 **Fasagrianach** Highland Scotland UK
131 G7 **Fasana** Italy
131 G6 **Fasano** Italy
223 12c **Fasito'otai** Samoa
122 H3 **Fåsjön** *lake* Sweden
155 I2 **Fassanu** Libya
124 F1 **Faßberg** Germany
198 D4 **Fatagar-Tuting, Tanjung** *cape* Indonesia
158 B2 **Fatala** *watercourse* Guinea
223 13a **Fatato** *island* Tuvalu
186 D5 **Fatehabad** Haryana India
186 D6 **Fatehgarh** Madhya Pradesh India
186 F5 **Fatehpur** Bihar India
186 E6 **Fatehpur** Madhya Pradesh India
186 D5 **Fatehpur** Rajasthan India
186 E5 **Fatehpur** Uttar Pradesh India
186 G6 **Fatehpur** West Bengal India
179 L3 **Fatehpur** Pakistan
182 H7 **Fatehabad** Iran
160 E2 **Fathai** Sudan
83 N2 **Father Lake** Quebec Canada
154 C6 **Fatick** Senegal
105 H5 **Fátima** Brazil
120 I4 **Fatmomakke** Sweden
154 D6 **Fatoto** Gambia
136 F5 **Fatsa** Turkey
120 I4 **Fättjarn** *lake* Sweden
223 14 **Fatu Hiva** *island* French Polynesia
160 B4 **Fatunda** Democratic Republic of Congo
179 H4 **Fatūyeh** Iran
120 I3 **Faulevatnet** *lake* Norway
219 J5 **Faulkland** NSW Australia
81 P4 **Faulkton** South Dakota USA
139 J4 **Fauquembergues** France
74 L8 **Fauquier** British Columbia Canada
216 C2 **Faure Island** WA Australia
222 8 **Fauro** *island* Solomon Islands
120 I3 **Fauske** Norway
139 H5 **Fauville-en-Caux** France
105 F3 **Favela** Brazil
127 H4 **Faverges** France
139 H3 **Faversham** Kent England UK
78 C5 **Favery, Lac** *lake* Quebec Canada
127 G2 **Favières** France
76 I6 **Favourable Lake** Ontario Canada
75 N5 **Fawcett** Alberta Canada
76 K6 **Fawn** *watercourse* Ontario Canada
140 A2 **Fawney** Strabane Northern Ireland UK
120 inset **Faxaflói** *bay* Iceland
120 J5 **Faxälven** *watercourse* Sweden
103 B9 **Faxinal** Brazil
156 B4 **Faya** Chad
158 C2 **Faya** *watercourse* Mali
222 7 **Fayaoué** New Caledonia
178 E4 **Fayd** Saudi Arabia
127 H5 **Fayence** France
84 G1 **Fayette** Utah USA
86 D2 **Fayetteville** Arkansas USA
87 L3 **Fayetteville** North Carolina USA
87 H3 **Fayetteville** Tennessee USA
86 C6 **Fayetteville** Texas USA
178 E6 **Fayfā'** Saudi Arabia
127 G3 **Fayl-la-Forêt** France
178 F3 **Faylakā, Jazīrat** *island* Kuwait
222 6 **Fayo** *island* Federated States of Micronesia
86 B7 **Faysville** Texas USA
199 I1 **Fayu** *island* Federated States of Micronesia
130 E4 **Fažana** Croatia
158 E3 **Fazao, Monts** *range* Togo
105 I5 **Fazenda Nova** Brazil
105 G5 **Fazenda Rio Alegre** Brazil
105 E5 **Fazenda São José** Brazil
101 F6 **Fazenda Vista Alegre** Brazil
186 D4 **Fazilka** Punjab India
154 D5 **Fdérik** Mauritania
143 C4 **Feale** *watercourse* Ireland
87 M4 **Fear, Cape** North Carolina USA
142 C3 **Fearnmore** Highland Scotland UK
139 H5 **Fécamp** France
159 F3 **Federal Capital Territory** *admin. area* Nigeria
80 D3 **Federal Way** Washington USA
179 L3 **Federally Administered Tribal Areas** *admin. area* Pakistan
199 I2 **Federated States of Micronesia** *country* Oceania
124 E3 **Federsee** *lake* Germany
122 C2 **Fedje** *island* Norway
183 L2 **Fedorovka** Kazakhstan
182 F3 **Fëdorovka** Kazakhstan
135 AD4 **Fëdorovskiy** Russian Federation
123 O4 **Fedosino** Russian Federation
143 C3 **Feeagh, Lough** *lake* Ireland
143 E2 **Feeny** Limavady Northern Ireland UK
139 H3 **Feering** Essex England UK
222 6a **Fefan** *island* Federated States of Micronesia
122 F5 **Fehmarn** *island* Germany
103 D8 **Feia, Lago** *lake* Brazil
191 H6 **Feicheng** Shandong China
104 D3 **Feijó** Brazil
220 F5 **Feilding** New Zealand
103 E6 **Feira de Santana** Brazil
125 H4 **Feistritz** *watercourse* Austria
105 G4 **Feitoria do Guariroba** Brazil
105 G4 **Feitoria do Orlando** Brazil
105 I4 **Feitoria do Tiné** Brazil
191 H6 **Feixiang** Hebei China
130 H3 **Fejér** *admin. area* Hungary
122 F5 **Fejø** *island* Denmark
130 H3 **Feked** Hungary
135 AC7 **Feklistova, Ostrov** *island* Russian Federation
126 E2 **Fel** France
129 H4 **Felanitx** Spain
125 H4 **Feldbach** Austria
124 F3 **Feldberg** Germany
107 G4 **Feliciano** *watercourse* Argentina
187 C11 **Felidhu Atoll** Maldives
138 D2 **Felindre** Powys Wales UK
105 G2 **Felinto** Brazil
89 H5 **Felipe Carrillo Puerto** Mexico
106 F6 **Felipe Solá** Argentina
214 B3 **Felix, Mount** NT Australia
139 I3 **Felixstowe** Suffolk England UK
130 C2 **Fellbach** Germany
126 F4 **Felletin** France
87 K7 **Fellsmere** Florida USA
130 G3 **Felsőrajk** Hungary
125 K3 **Felsőszolca** Hungary
138 D4 **Feltham** Somerset England UK
139 I2 **Felthorpe** Norfolk England UK
83 N7 **Felton** Delaware USA
124 F4 **Feltre** Italy
139 H2 **Feltwell** Norfolk England UK
122 F5 **Femer Bælt** *bay* Denmark
122 F5 **Femø** *island* Denmark
122 F3 **Femsjøen** *lake* Norway
122 G5 **Femsjön** Sweden
120 G6 **Femundsundet** Norway
190 G6 **Fen He** *watercourse* Shanxi China
85 H3 **Fence Lake** New Mexico USA
120 I3 **Fenes** Norway
127 H2 **Fénétrange** France
124 D5 **Fenêtre, Col de** *pass* France/Switzerland
181 H2 **Feng** *mountain* Xizang Zizhiqu China
181 G2 **Feng** *mountain* Xizang Zizhiqu China
189 G3 **Fengcheng** Fujian China
189 G4 **Fengcheng** Fujian China
189 G6 **Fengcheng** Guangdong China
188 E4 **Fengcheng** Guangxi Zhuangzu Zizhiqu China
189 G1 **Fengcheng** Jiangsu China
189 G3 **Fengcheng** Jiangxi China
191 J5 **Fengcheng** Liaoning China
189 I2 **Fenghua** Zhejiang China
191 H5 **Fenghuang** Hebei China
188 E3 **Fengle** Sichuan China
188 D2 **Fengming** Sichuan China
191 I5 **Fengnan** Hebei China
190 G6 **Fengqi** Shaanxi China
188 C4 **Fengqing Fengshan** Yunnan China
189 G1 **Fengqiu** Henan China
191 I5 **Fengrun** Hebei China
189 H3 **Fengshan** Fujian China
189 H4 **Fengshan** Taiwan China
189 G4 **Fengshuba Shuiku** *lake* Guangdong China
191 J2 **Fengshui Shan** *mountain* Heilongjiang China
189 G2 **Fengtai** Anhui China
188 C4 **Fengwei** Yunnan China
191 L3 **Fengxiang** Heilongjiang China
188 E1 **Fengxiang** Shaanxi China
188 C4 **Fengxiang** Yunnan China
188 E3 **Fengyi** Guizhou China
188 D2 **Fengyi** Sichuan China
189 H4 **Fengyüan** Taiwan China
191 H5 **Fengzhen** Nei Mongol Zizhiqu China
191 H5 **Fengzhou** Hebei China
181 G4 **Feni** Bangladesh
199 J5 **Feni Islands** Papua New Guinea
84 E3 **Fenner** California USA
131 C6 **Feno, Capo di** *cape* Corsica France
163 I3 **Fenoarivo Atsinanana** Madagascar
139 H2 **Fens, The** *region* England UK
122 G2 **Fensbol** Sweden
189 H2 **Fenshui Jiang** *watercourse* Zhejiang China
122 F5 **Fensmark** Denmark
141 H3 **Fenton** Nottinghamshire England UK
82 J5 **Fenton** Michigan USA
142 D5 **Fenwick** East Ayrshire Scotland UK

190 G5 **Fenyang** Shanxi China
142 C5 **Feochaig** Argyll and Bute Scotland UK
136 E4 **Feodosiya** Ukraine
142 C5 **Feolin** Argyll and Bute Scotland UK
142 B5 **Feolin Ferry** Argyll and Bute Scotland UK
142 C5 **Feorlan** Argyll and Bute Scotland UK
129 J5 **Fer, Cap de** *cape* Algeria
120 G5 **Feragen** Norway
120 G5 **Feragen** *lake* Norway
109 4 **Ferdinanda, Isla** *island* Archipiélago de Colón (Galapagos Islands)
179 I2 **Ferdows** Iran
133 E5 **Feres** Greece
83 K5 **Fergus** Ontario Canada
81 Q3 **Fergus Falls** Minnesota USA
218 F8 **Ferguson** Vic. Australia
76 I1 **Ferguson** *watercourse* Nunavut Canada
76 G1 **Ferguson Lake** Nunavut Canada
199 I6 **Fergusson Island** Papua New Guinea
214 C7 **Fergusson Range** NT Australia
155 H2 **Fériana** Tunisia
136 F6 **Ferikli** Turkey
129 J6 **Ferkane** Algeria
158 C3 **Ferkessedougou** Côte d'Ivoire
130 F3 **Ferlach** Austria
143 E2 **Fermanagh** *admin. area* Northern Ireland UK
77 V6 **Fermont** Quebec Canada
128 C3 **Fermoselle** Spain
143 D4 **Fermoy** Ireland
80 D4 **Fern Ridge Reservoir** Oregon USA
128 E4 **Fernandina, Embalse de la** *lake* Spain
87 K5 **Fernandina Beach** Florida USA
51 **Fernando de Noronha** *island* Brazil
105 I6 **Fernandópolis** Brazil
163 H2 **Fernão Veloso** Mozambique
163 H2 **Fernão Veloso, Baía de** *bay* Mozambique
219 K4 **Fernbrook** NSW Australia
80 C6 **Ferndale** California USA
139 F4 **Ferndown** Dorset England UK
142 E3 **Ferness** Highland Scotland UK
142 B3 **Fernilea** Highland Scotland UK
80 F7 **Fernley** Nevada USA
143 F4 **Ferns** Ireland
79 J7 **Ferolle Point** Newfoundland and Labrador Canada
131 G6 **Ferrandina** Italy
124 F5 **Ferrara** Italy
131 C7 **Ferrato, Capo** *cape* Sardinia Italy
128 B4 **Ferreira do Zêzere** Portugal
142 C3 **Ferrindonald** Highland Scotland UK
86 C4 **Ferris** Texas USA
131 C6 **Ferro, Capo** *cape* Sardinia Italy
164 2 **Ferro, Ilhéu de** *island* Madeira
100 D5 **Ferro Velho** Brazil
128 B2 **Ferrol** Spain
80 J7 **Ferron** Utah USA
131 C7 **Ferru, Monte** *mountain* Sardinia Italy
131 F5 **Ferruccio, Punta di** *cape* Italy
129 H4 **Ferrutx, Cap** *cape* Spain
140 B4 **Ferrybank** Ireland
79 L9 **Ferryland** Newfoundland and Labrador Canada
142 D4 **Fersit** Highland Scotland UK
142 D5 **Ferter** South Ayrshire Scotland UK
81 Q3 **Fertile** Minnesota USA
130 G3 **Fertőrákos** Hungary
128 B2 **Fervenza, Embalse da** *lake* Spain
154 E2 **Fès** Morocco
122 E3 **Feset** Norway
160 B5 **Feshi** Democratic Republic of Congo
81 P3 **Fessenden** North Dakota USA
120 I3 **Festvåg** Norway
198 D4 **Fet Dom, Tanjung** *cape* Indonesia
154 D6 **Fété Bowé** Senegal
132 E3 **Feteşti** Romania
140 B4 **Fethard** Ireland
182 F5 **Fetisovo** Kazakhstan
131 E8 **Feto, Capo** *cape* Italy
124 F3 **Feuchtwangen** Germany
78 D3 **Feuilles, Baie aux** *bay* Quebec Canada
78 D3 **Feuilles, Lac aux** *lake* Quebec Canada
78 C3 **Feuilles, Rivière aux** *watercourse* Quebec Canada
139 I5 **Feuquières** France
126 G4 **Feurs** France
120 F5 **Fevåg** Norway
191 L2 **Fevral'sk** Russian Federation
183 K6 **Feyẕābād** Afghanistan
138 D1 **Ffrith** Wrexham Wales UK
106 E3 **Fiambala** *watercourse* Argentina
158 D2 **Fian** Ghana
163 I4 **Fianarantsoa** Madagascar
163 I4 **Fianarantsoa** *admin. area* Madagascar
159 H3 **Fianga** Chad
132 B3 **Fibis** Romania
124 F5 **Ficarolo** Italy
161 F2 **Fichē** Ethiopia
124 G3 **Fichtelnaab** *watercourse* Germany
102 D4 **Fidalgo** *watercourse* Brazil
143 D3 **Fiddaun** Ireland
130 D4 **Fidenza** Italy
124 G4 **Fieberbrunn** Austria
53 T4 **Fieberling Tablemount** *underwater feature* Pacific Ocean
214 D7 **Field** *watercourse* NT Australia
214 B2 **Field Island** NT Australia
132 D3 **Fieni** Romania
133 A5 **Fier** Albania
127 G4 **Fier** *watercourse* France
132 E3 **Fierbinţi-Târg** Romania
143 C4 **Fieries** Ireland
120 I3 **Fierras** *mountain* Sweden
214 E5 **Fiery** *watercourse* Qld Australia
195 G5 **Fiery Cross Reef** Spratly Islands
127 I3 **Fiesch** Switzerland
158 C2 **Fifa** Guinea
142 E4 **Fife** *admin. area* Scotland UK
75 S8 **Fife Lake** Saskatchewan Canada
142 F4 **Fife Ness** *cape* Scotland UK
159 G4 **Fifinda** Cameroon
109 19 **Fifth Cabin** British Columbia Canada
126 F4 **Figeac** France
130 D5 **Figline Valdarno** Italy
105 G5 **Figueira** Brazil
128 B3 **Figueira da Foz** Portugal
128 C3 **Figueira de Castelo Rodrigo** Portugal
128 B3 **Figueiró** Portugal
128 B4 **Figueiró dos Vinhos** Portugal
129 H2 **Figueres** Spain
155 F2 **Figuig** Morocco
159 G3 **Figuil** Cameroon
223 9 **Fiji** *country* Oceania
52 O9 **Fiji Plateau** *underwater feature* Pacific Ocean
161 G2 **Fik'** Ethiopia
104 D3 **Filadelfia** Bolivia
107 F2 **Filadelfia** Paraguay
158 C2 **Filamana** Mali
132 E4 **Filaretovo** Bulgaria
59 G2 **Filchner, Cape** Antarctica
59 V1 **Filchner Ice Shelf** Antarctica
141 H2 **Filey** North Yorkshire England UK
141 H2 **Filey Bay** England UK
133 B6 **Filiates** Greece
155 G6 **Filingué** Niger
132 E2 **Filipeni** Romania
132 D3 **Filipeştii de Pădure** Romania
120 F5 **Fillan** Norway
138 D3 **Filleigh** Devon England UK
75 T8 **Fillmore** Saskatchewan Canada
84 C3 **Fillmore** California USA
133 B5 **Filotas** Greece
130 E5 **Filottrano** Italy
161 G2 **Fīltu** Ethiopia
59 A2 **Fimbul Ice Shelf** Antarctica
179 H4 **Fin** Iran
131 F7 **Finale** Italy
130 D4 **Finale Emilia** Italy
142 F4 **Finavon** Angus Scotland UK
123 J2 **Finbo** *island* Finland
123 J2 **Finbofjärden** *bay* Finland
123 K2 **Finby** Finland
161 F2 **Finch'a'ā Hāyk'** *lake* Ethiopia
140 A2 **Findermore** Dungannon Northern Ireland UK
142 E3 **Findhorn** Moray Scotland UK
142 D3 **Findhorn** *watercourse* Scotland UK
75 U8 **Findlay** Manitoba Canada
82 J6 **Findlay** Ohio USA
83 N4 **Fine** New York USA
219 R10 **Fingal** Tas. Australia
81 Q3 **Fingal** North Dakota USA
78 G4 **Finger Hill Island** Newfoundland and Labrador Canada
76 I6 **Finger Lake** Ontario Canada
83 M5 **Finger Lakes** New York USA
142 E5 **Fingland** Dumfries and Galloway Scotland UK
163 F3 **Fingoé** Mozambique
133 G7 **Finike** Turkey
133 G7 **Finike Körfezi** *bay* Turkey
85 K8 **Finisterre** Mexico
128 E4 **Finisterre, Embalse de** *lake* Spain
218 B1 **Finke** NT Australia
218 B4 **Finke, Mount** SA Australia
214 B2 **Finke Bay** NT Australia
82 E2 **Finland** Ontario Canada
121 O3 **Finland** *country* Europe
123 M3 **Finland, Gulf of** Europe
74 I4 **Finlay** *watercourse* British Columbia Canada
218 G6 **Finley** NSW Australia
143 E2 **Finn** *watercourse* Ireland
122 G2 **Finn-Skogne** *island* Norway
140 A3 **Finnea** Ireland
75 O7 **Finnegan** Alberta Canada
122 H3 **Finnerödja** Sweden
213 K2 **Finniss** *watercourse* NT Australia
218 B5 **Finniss, Cape** SA Australia
120 K2 **Finnkroken** Norway
121 N2 **Finnmark** *admin. area* Norway
121 N2 **Finnmarksvidda** *region* Norway
122 C3 **Finnøy** *island* Norway
120 J2 **Finnsnes** Norway
143 C3 **Finny** Ireland
199 H5 **Finschhafen** Papua New Guinea
122 F2 **Finstad** Norway
132 D2 **Fînţinele** Romania
143 E2 **Fintona** Omagh Northern Ireland UK
142 C3 **Fionn Loch** *lake* Scotland UK
142 B4 **Fionnphort** Highland Scotland UK
221 B7 **Fiordland** *region* New Zealand
75 T6 **Fir** *watercourse* Saskatchewan Canada
75 P4 **Firebag** *watercourse* Alberta Canada
80 E8 **Firebaugh** California USA
76 C2 **Firedrake Lake** Northwest Territories Canada
130 D5 **Firenze (Florence)** Italy
219 S10 **Fires, Bay of** Tas. Australia
74 H3 **Fireside** British Columbia Canada
74 H4 **Firesteel** *watercourse* British Columbia Canada
158 B3 **Firestone Plantation** *place of interest* Liberia
142 D4 **Firkin** Argyll and Bute Scotland UK
106 F5 **Firmat** Argentina
124 C5 **Firminy** France
187 D8 **Firozabad** Karnataka India
186 E5 **Firozabad** Uttar Pradesh India
186 D4 **Firozpur** Punjab India
179 I5 **Firq** Oman
193 I1 **Firsovo** Russian Federation
142 inset **Firth** Shetland Scotland UK
179 G2 **Fīrūz Kūh** Iran
124 F4 **Fischen** Germany
79 K7 **Fischot Islands** Newfoundland and Labrador Canada
162 C5 **Fish** *watercourse* Namibia
214 F4 **Fish Hole** *watercourse* Qld Australia
82 E3 **Fish Lake Reservoir** Minnesota USA
83 Q3 **Fish River Lake** Maine USA
81 Q3 **Fisher** Minnesota USA
214 C6 **Fisher, Mount** NT Australia
59 J2 **Fisher Bay** Antarctica
76 G7 **Fisher Bay** Manitoba Canada
59 E2 **Fisher Glacier** *ice* Antarctica
76 G7 **Fisher River** Manitoba Canada
73 K6 **Fisher Strait** Nunavut Canada
163 H4 **Fisherenana** *watercourse* Madagascar
76 H6 **Fishing Lake** Manitoba Canada
87 J2 **Fishtrap Lake** Kentucky USA
120 I4 **Fiskåfjället** *mountain* Sweden
59 U2 **Fiske, Cape** Antarctica
126 F2 **Fismes** France
128 B2 **Fisterra, Cabo** *cape* Spain
83 P5 **Fitchburg** Massachusetts USA
128 F2 **Fitero** Spain
223 12c **Fitiuta** American Samoa
223 12c **Fito, Mount** *volcano* Samoa
155 J6 **Fitri, Lac** *lake* Chad
138 E2 **Fitz** Shropshire England UK
74 H7 **Fitz Hugh Sound** British Columbia Canada
108 C4 **Fitz Roy** Argentina
216 F6 **Fitzgerald** WA Australia
87 J5 **Fitzgerald** Georgia USA
216 F7 **Fitzgerald Inlet** WA Australia
86 C3 **Fitzhugh** Oklahoma USA
213 K3 **Fitzmaurice** *watercourse* NT Australia
214 F4 **Fitzmaurice Point** Qld Australia
215 K7 **Fitzroy** *watercourse* Qld Australia
213 G5 **Fitzroy** *watercourse* WA Australia
213 H5 **Fitzroy Crossing** WA Australia
109 7 **Fitzroy Settlement** Falkland Islands
83 K4 **Fitzwilliam Island** Ontario Canada
131 E6 **Fiuggi** Italy
131 G7 **Fiume Nicà, Punta** *cape* Italy
131 E6 **Fiumicino** Italy
142 C4 **Fiunary** Highland Scotland UK
221 B7 **Five Fingers Peninsula** New Zealand
109 18 **Five Island Harbour** *bay* Antigua and Barbuda
221 C7 **Five Rivers** New Zealand
219 H5 **Five Ways** NSW Australia
130 D4 **Fivizzano** Italy
160 D4 **Fizi** Democratic Republic of Congo
120 I3 **Fjær** Norway
122 D3 **Fjæra** Norway
120 inset **Fjallaskagi** *cape* Iceland
120 I4 **Fjällfjällen** *mountain* Sweden
120 J4 **Fjällsjönäs** Sweden
120 H6 **Fjätervålen** Sweden
120 J2 **Fjelbu** Norway
122 C2 **Fjell** Norway
120 J2 **Fjelldal** Norway
120 K2 **Fjellfrøsvatnet** *lake* Norway
122 E3 **Fjone** Norway
121 M4 **Fjuskön** *island* Sweden
154 E2 **Fkih Ben Salah** Morocco
142 inset **Fladdabister** Shetland Scotland UK
141 G3 **Flagg** Derbyshire England UK
81 N7 **Flagler** Colorado USA
87 K6 **Flagler Beach** Florida USA
84 G3 **Flagstaff** Arizona USA
164 5b **Flagstaff Bay** St Helena
120 J2 **Flakstad** Norway
120 E6 **Flåm** Norway
141 I2 **Flamborough Head** *cape* England UK
108 E2 **Flamenco, Isla** *island* Argentina
81 K6 **Flaming Gorge Reservoir** Wyoming USA
82 E2 **Flanders** Ontario Canada
142 A2 **Flannan Isles** Scotland UK
122 H4 **Flåren** *lake* Sweden
120 K5 **Flärke** Sweden
120 L4 **Flarken** Sweden
81 O3 **Flasher** North Dakota USA
120 H5 **Flåsjön** *lake* Sweden
138 D3 **Flat Holm** *island* England UK
195 G5 **Flat Island** Spratly Islands
109 7 **Flat Jason** *island* Falkland Islands
86 F6 **Flat Lake** Louisiana USA
221 F5 **Flat Point** New Zealand
215 J6 **Flat Top, Mount** Qld Australia
75 Q5 **Flat Valley** Saskatchewan Canada
75 N5 **Flatbush** Alberta Canada
122 H2 **Flaten** *lake* Sweden
75 N8 **Flathead** *watercourse* Montana USA
80 H3 **Flathead Lake** Montana USA
120 I5 **Flatnor** Sweden
86 C6 **Flatonia** Texas USA
120 H4 **Flått** Norway
215 H3 **Flattery, Cape** Qld Australia
80 C2 **Flattery, Cape** Washington USA
125 H4 **Flattnitz** Austria
83 inset **Flatts Village** Bermuda
220 G4 **Flaxmere** New Zealand
75 T8 **Flaxton** North Dakota USA
75 S8 **Flaxville** Montana USA
108 C4 **Flecha Negra** Argentina
195 I6 **Flecha Point** *island* Philippines
105 G5 **Flechas** Brazil
75 P6 **Fleet** Alberta Canada
139 G3 **Fleet** Hampshire England UK
215 H7 **Fleetwood** Qld Australia
140 E3 **Fleetwood** Lancashire England UK
120 H3 **Fleinvær** *island* Norway
122 E3 **Flekkerøy** *island* Norway
122 D1 **Flem** Norway
81 N6 **Fleming** Colorado USA
50 N5 **Flemish Cap** *underwater feature* Atlantic Ocean
122 I3 **Flen** Sweden
122 F5 **Flensburger Förde** *bay* Denmark
126 D2 **Flers** France
198 C3 **Flesko, Tanjung** *cape* Indonesia
86 B3 **Fletcher** Oklahoma USA
59 E2 **Fletcher, Cape** Antarctica
211 inset **Fletcher, Mount** Macquarie Island Australia
218 B1 **Fletcher Hill** NT Australia
59 S2 **Fletcher Peninsula** Antarctica
79 J7 **Fleur de Lys** Newfoundland and Labrador Canada
79 F7 **Fleur-de-May, Lac** *lake* Newfoundland and Labrador Canada
126 E5 **Fleurance** France
130 B3 **Fleurier** Switzerland
218 D6 **Fleurieu Peninsula** SA Australia
126 F5 **Fleury** France
126 E2 **Fleury** France
101 F4 **Flexal** Brazil
127 I1 **Flieden** Germany
127 I3 **Flims** Switzerland
75 U5 **Flin Flon** Manitoba Canada
214 F4 **Flinders** *watercourse* Qld Australia
216 D7 **Flinders Bay** WA Australia
215 G3 **Flinders Group** *islands* Australia
218 B5 **Flinders Island** SA Australia
219 R10 **Flinders Island** Tas. Australia
218 D4 **Flinders Ranges** SA Australia
215 J4 **Flinders Reef** Coral Sea Islands Territory Australia
122 I2 **Flinssjön** *lake* Sweden
140 E3 **Flint** Flintshire Wales UK
87 H3 **Flint** *watercourse* Alabama USA
87 I4 **Flint** *watercourse* Georgia USA
82 J5 **Flint** Michigan USA
222 1 **Flint Island** Kiribati
76 M8 **Flint Lake** Ontario Canada
140 E3 **Flintshire** *admin. area* Wales UK
127 G2 **Flirey** France
139 G2 **Flitton** Bedfordshire England UK
139 J4 **Flixecourt** France
122 G3 **Flo** Sweden
124 B2 **Flobecq** Belgium
126 F3 **Flogny** France
124 G2 **Flöha** Germany
124 G2 **Flöha** *watercourse* Germany
86 H5 **Flomaton** Alabama USA
127 I2 **Flomborn** Germany
218 E4 **Floods** *watercourse* NSW Australia
140 F2 **Flookburgh** Cumbria England UK
100 C5 **Flor de Agosto** Peru
101 F3 **Flor de Botiquín** Venezuela
105 H6 **Flor de Maio** Brazil
213 K3 **Flora** *watercourse* NT Australia
101 F5 **Flora** Brazil
86 F4 **Flora** Mississippi USA
212 D6 **Flora, Mount** WA Australia
215 I4 **Flora Reef** Coral Sea Islands Territory Australia
126 F4 **Florac** France
214 E5 **Floraville** Qld Australia
124 C2 **Floreffe** Belgium
Florence *see* **Firenze** Italy
86 H3 **Florence** Alabama USA
84 G4 **Florence** Arizona USA
86 F4 **Florence** Mississippi USA
80 C5 **Florence** Oregon USA
87 L3 **Florence** South Carolina USA
81 Q4 **Florence** South Dakota USA
86 C5 **Florence** Texas USA
82 G4 **Florence** Wisconsin USA
218 D3 **Florence, Lake** SA Australia
107 G4 **Florencia** Argentina
100 C4 **Florencia** Colombia
126 F5 **Florensac** France
108 D3 **Florentino Ameghino** Argentina
127 G2 **Florenville** Belgium
107 G5 **Flores** *watercourse* Argentina
164 1 **Flores** *island* Azores
90 B3 **Flores** Guatemala
198 B6 **Flores** *island* Indonesia
107 G5 **Flores** *admin. area* Uruguay
197 H5 **Flores, Laut (Flores Sea)** Indonesia
74 H8 **Flores Island** British Columbia Canada
Flores Sea *see* **Flores, Laut** Indonesia
101 E5 **Floresta** Brazil
102 E5 **Floresta** Brazil
103 B8 **Florestópolis** Brazil
86 B6 **Floresville** Texas USA
85 K4 **Florey** Texas USA
102 D4 **Floriano** Brazil
107 I3 **Florianópolis** Brazil
105 F4 **Florida** Bolivia
90 E2 **Florida** Cuba
107 G5 **Florida** Uruguay
107 H5 **Florida** *admin. area* Uruguay
71 **Florida** *admin. area* USA
108 E2 **Florida, Punta** *cape* Argentina
90 D1 **Florida, Straits of** North America
87 K8 **Florida Bay** USA
87 K8 **Florida City** Florida USA
87 K8 **Florida Keys** *islands* USA
108 C4 **Florida Negra** Argentina
100 C3 **Floridablanca** Colombia
131 F8 **Floridia** Italy
218 D5 **Florieton** SA Australia
82 F7 **Florissant** Missouri USA
120 G5 **Flornes** Norway
122 C2 **Florø** Norway
120 H6 **Flötningen** Sweden
133 E7 **Flouda, Akra** *cape* Greece
87 J4 **Flovilla** Georgia USA
218 G7 **Flowerdale** Vic. Australia
79 J7 **Flower's Cove** Newfoundland and Labrador Canada
82 C5 **Floyd** *watercourse* Iowa USA
85 L4 **Floydada** Texas USA
124 C1 **Fluessen** *lake* Netherlands
122 I2 **Flugen** *lake* Sweden
127 H3 **Flühli** Switzerland
198 C4 **Fluk** Indonesia
122 I2 **Fluren** Sweden
138 B4 **Flushing** Cornwall England UK
129 H2 **Fluvià** *watercourse* Spain
199 G5 **Fly** *watercourse* Papua New Guinea
213 L2 **Flying** *watercourse* NT Australia
59 R2 **Flying Fish, Cape** Antarctica
210 inset **Flying Fish Cove** Christmas Island Australia
120 inset **Fnjóská** *watercourse* Iceland
223 10 **Foa** *island* Tonga
108 D4 **Foca, Punta** *cape* Argentina
100 A6 **Foca, Punta** *cape* Peru
142 E3 **Fochabers** Moray Scotland UK
132 E3 **Focşani** Romania
138 D2 **Foel** Powys Wales UK
214 D4 **Foelsche** *watercourse* NT Australia
132 B3 **Foeni** Romania
198 D7 **Fog Bay** Australia
122 I3 **Fogdön** *island* Sweden
155 G3 **Foggâret el Arab** Algeria
131 F6 **Foggia** Italy
198 C4 **Fogi** Indonesia
130 E5 **Foglia** *watercourse* Italy
131 E6 **Fogliano, Lago di** *lake* Italy
123 K2 **Föglöfjärden** *bay* Finland
164 4 **Fogo** *island* Cape Verde
164 1a **Fogo, Lagoa do** *lake* Azores
164 4 **Fogo, Mount** *volcano* Cape Verde
79 K8 **Fogo Island** Newfoundland and Labrador Canada
122 E5 **Föhr** *island* Germany
143 C4 **Foiladaun** Ireland
126 E5 **Foix** France
199 F4 **Foja, Pegunungan** *range* Indonesia
159 E2 **Fokku** Nigeria
120 G4 **Folda** *bay* Norway
120 G4 **Foldefjorden** *bay* Norway
132 B2 **Földes** Hungary
86 H5 **Foley** Alabama USA
73 L5 **Foley Island** Nunavut Canada
83 J2 **Foleyet** Ontario Canada
122 D2 **Folgefonna** *lake* Norway
59 H2 **Folger, Cape** Antarctica
130 E5 **Foligno** Italy
120 E5 **Folkestad** Norway
139 I3 **Folkestone** Kent England UK
87 K5 **Folkston** Georgia USA
120 G5 **Follafoss** Norway
120 G5 **Folldal** Norway
86 A2 **Follett** Texas USA
141 G3 **Follifoot** North Yorkshire England UK
120 I5 **Föllinge** Sweden
130 D5 **Follonica** Italy
122 E3 **Follsjå** *lake* Norway
80 E7 **Folsom** California USA
86 F5 **Folsom** Louisiana USA
80 E7 **Folsom Lake** California USA
163 H2 **Fomboni** Comoros
135 W4 **Fomich** *watercourse* Russian Federation
158 C3 **Fon Going** *range* Guinea
109 13 **Fond Bay** St Lucia
75 R3 **Fond-du-Lac** Saskatchewan Canada
82 G5 **Fond du Lac** Wisconsin USA
131 E6 **Fondi** Italy
128 C3 **Fonfría** Spain
120 G5 **Fongen** *mountain* Norway
128 C2 **Fonsagrada** Spain
100 C2 **Fonseca** Colombia
90 C4 **Fonseca, Golfo de** *bay* Honduras
127 G4 **Fontaine** France
108 B3 **Fontana, Lago** *lake* Argentina
128 D4 **Fontanosas** Spain
74 K3 **Fontas** British Columbia Canada
74 K3 **Fontas** *watercourse* British Columbia Canada
101 E5 **Fonte Boa** Brazil
105 G4 **Fonte do Pau-d'Água** Brazil
105 G4 **Fonte Termal Água Quente** Brazil
79 H7 **Fonteneau, Lac** *lake* Quebec Canada
81 J5 **Fontenelle Reservoir** Wyoming USA
120 inset **Fontur** *cape* Iceland
223 10 **Fonualei** *island* Tonga
130 G3 **Fonyód** Hungary
129 G2 **Fonz** Spain
74 M6 **Foothills** Alberta Canada
74 M3 **Footner Lake** Alberta Canada
219 I5 **Forbes** NSW Australia
74 M7 **Forbes, Mount** Alberta/British Columbia Canada
159 F3 **Forcados** Nigeria
130 D2 **Forchheim** Germany
78 F4 **Ford** *watercourse* Quebec Canada
143 F4 **Ford** Ireland
141 G3 **Ford** Derbyshire England UK
138 E2 **Ford** Shropshire England UK
142 C4 **Ford** Argyll and Bute Scotland UK
81 P8 **Ford** Kansas USA
213 J2 **Ford, Cape** Australia
59 O1 **Ford Ranges** Antarctica
198 D5 **Fordate** *island* Indonesia
134 B6 **Førdefjorden** *strait* Norway
220 F4 **Fordell** New Zealand
138 D2 **Forden** Powys Wales UK
218 G3 **Fords Bridge** NSW Australia
82 H8 **Fordsville** Kentucky USA
178 G2 **Fordū** Iran
81 Q2 **Fordville** North Dakota USA
140 A3 **Fore** Ireland
158 B3 **Forécariah** Guinea
73 P5 **Forel, Mont** *mountain* Greenland
138 D3 **Foreland Point** England UK
86 D4 **Foreman** Arkansas USA
75 P8 **Foremost** Alberta Canada
214 F5 **Forest** *watercourse* Qld Australia
86 G4 **Forest** Mississippi USA
87 K3 **Forest Acres** South Carolina USA
82 E5 **Forest City** Iowa USA
86 C4 **Forest Hill** Texas USA
142 E4 **Forest Lodge** Perth and Kinross Scotland UK
139 I4 **Forest-Montiers** France
87 I4 **Forest Park** Georgia USA
139 H3 **Forest Row** East Sussex England UK
219 H1 **Forest Vale** Qld Australia
219 S11 **Forestier Peninsula** Tas. Australia
77 U8 **Forestville** Quebec Canada
126 D4 **Forêt des Landes** *region* France
142 F4 **Forfar** Angus Scotland UK
81 O8 **Forgan** Oklahoma USA
139 I5 **Forges-les-Eaux** France
130 D3 **Forggensee** *lake* Germany
140 B2 **Forkill** Newry and Mourne Northern Ireland UK
86 H4 **Forkland** Alabama USA
80 C3 **Forks** Washington USA
130 E4 **Forlì** Italy
81 Q3 **Forman** North Dakota USA
130 C3 **Formazza** Italy
140 E3 **Formby** Merseyside England UK
129 G4 **Formentera** *island* Spain
129 H4 **Formentor, Cap de** *cape* Spain
139 I5 **Formerie** France
131 E6 **Formia** Italy
107 J2 **Formiga** Brazil
107 G3 **Formosa** Argentina
107 G3 **Formosa** *admin. area* Argentina
103 C6 **Formosa** Brazil
105 H3 **Formosa, Serra** *range* Brazil
103 C5 **Formosa do Rio Preto** Brazil
103 B6 **Formoso** *watercourse* Brazil
128 C3 **Formoso** Portugal
122 F4 **Fornæs** *cape* Denmark
129 I3 **Fornells** Spain
120 J2 **Forneset** Norway
127 K3 **Forno di Zoldo** Italy
163 F4 **Fornos** Mozambique
157 F4 **Foro** Eritrea
132 B3 **Forotic** Romania
102 D3 **Forquilha** Brazil
107 I4 **Forquilhinha** Brazil
142 E3 **Forres** Moray Scotland UK
217 K5 **Forrest** WA Australia
82 G6 **Forrest** Illinois USA
86 F3 **Forrest City** Arkansas USA
75 Q4 **Forrest Lake** Saskatchewan Canada
217 K4 **Forrest Lakes** WA Australia
59 U1 **Forrestal Range** Antarctica
74 E5 **Forrester Island** Alaska USA
120 J5 **Fors** Sweden
120 J2 **Forsa** Norway
85 L4 **Forsan** Texas USA
215 G5 **Forsayth** Qld Australia
120 J2 **Forsbakken** Norway
142 E2 **Forsinard** Highland Scotland UK
120 H3 **Forsland** Norway
120 K3 **Forsnäs** Sweden
120 F5 **Forsnes** Norway
123 L2 **Forssa** Finland
125 H2 **Forst** Germany
219 K5 **Forster** NSW Australia
87 J4 **Forsyth** Georgia USA
82 E8 **Forsyth** Missouri USA
81 L3 **Forsyth** Montana USA
108 A3 **Forsyth, Isla** *island* Chile
214 E4 **Forsyth Islands** Qld Australia
215 G7 **Forsyth Range** Qld Australia
179 L3 **Fort Abbas** Pakistan
77 O6 **Fort Albany** Ontario Canada
162 E6 **Fort Beaufort** South Africa
72 I9 **Fort Belknap** Montana USA
81 J3 **Fort Benton** Montana USA
80 D7 **Fort Bragg** California USA
75 P3 **Fort Chipewyan** Alberta Canada
81 M6 **Fort Collins** Colorado USA
73 M2 **Fort Conger** Nunavut Canada
214 F6 **Fort Constantine** Qld Australia
85 K5 **Fort Davis** Texas USA
91 I4 **Fort-de-France** Martinique
109 14 **Fort-de-France, Baie de** *bay* Martinique
87 H5 **Fort Deposit** Alabama USA
82 D5 **Fort Dodge** Iowa USA
83 O5 **Fort Edward** New York USA
79 E9 **Fort Fairfield** Maine USA
74 I5 **Fort Fraser** British Columbia Canada
86 D2 **Fort Gibson Lake** Oklahoma USA
218 E3 **Fort Grey** NSW Australia
75 U3 **Fort Hall** Manitoba Canada
85 J5 **Fort Hancock** Texas USA
Fort Hertz *see* **Putao** Myanmar
109 10a **Fort Jeudy, Point of** Grenada
80 D6 **Fort Jones** California USA
83 Q3 **Fort Kent** Maine USA
81 M5 **Fort Laramie** Wyoming USA
87 K7 **Fort Lauderdale** Florida USA
74 J2 **Fort Liard** Northwest Territories Canada
75 P4 **Fort MacKay** Alberta Canada
75 O8 **Fort Macleod** Alberta Canada
75 P4 **Fort McMurray** Alberta Canada
72 F5 **Fort McPherson** Northwest Territories Canada
82 F6 **Fort Madison** Iowa USA
139 I4 **Fort-Mahon-Plage** France
87 K7 **Fort Meade** Florida USA
81 N6 **Fort Morgan** Colorado USA
87 K7 **Fort Myers** Florida USA
87 K7 **Fort Myers Beach** Florida USA
74 J3 **Fort Nelson** British Columbia Canada
74 J3 **Fort Nelson** *watercourse* British Columbia Canada
87 I3 **Fort Payne** Alabama USA
81 L3 **Fort Peck Lake** Montana USA
87 K7 **Fort Pierce** Florida USA
81 O4 **Fort Pierre** South Dakota USA
74 M2 **Fort Providence** Northwest Territories Canada
75 T7 **Fort Qu'Appelle** Saskatchewan Canada
75 O2 **Fort Resolution** Northwest Territories Canada
74 I5 **Fort St James** British Columbia Canada
74 K4 **Fort St John** British Columbia Canada
75 O6 **Fort Saskatchewan** Alberta Canada
76 L5 **Fort Severn** Ontario Canada
74 K2 **Fort Simpson** Northwest Territories Canada
75 P2 **Fort Smith** Northwest Territories Canada
86 D3 **Fort Smith** Arkansas USA
85 K5 **Fort Stockton** Texas USA
85 J3 **Fort Sumner** New Mexico USA
87 J4 **Fort Valley** Georgia USA
75 M3 **Fort Vermilion** Alberta Canada
75 Q8 **Fort Walsh** Saskatchewan Canada
87 H5 **Fort Walton Beach** Florida USA
82 I6 **Fort Wayne** Indiana USA
142 C4 **Fort William** Highland Scotland UK
86 C4 **Fort Worth** Texas USA
81 O3 **Fort Yates** North Dakota USA
72 E5 **Fort Yukon** Alaska USA
104 E4 **Fortaleza** Bolivia
104 E3 **Fortaleza** Brazil
129 F3 **Fortanete** Spain
130 D5 **Forte dei Marmi** Italy
212 D6 **Fortescue** *watercourse* WA Australia
212 D6 **Fortescue River Roadhouse** WA Australia
142 D4 **Forth** *watercourse* Scotland UK
142 E5 **Forth** South Lanarkshire Scotland UK
142 F4 **Forth, Firth of** *bay* Scotland UK
80 H7 **Fortification Range** Nevada USA
79 E7 **Fortin, Lac** *lake* Quebec Canada
106 F2 **Fortín Ávalos Sánchez** Paraguay
106 E2 **Fortín Campero** Argentina
106 F2 **Fortín Coronel Eugenia Garay** Paraguay
105 F5 **Fortín La Victoria** Bolivia
106 F3 **Fortín Lavalle** Argentina
106 F2 **Fortín Pilcomayo** Argentina
106 F2 **Fortín Pozo Hondo** Paraguay
107 G3 **Fortín Sargento Primero Leyes** Argentina
106 E6 **Fortín Uno** Argentina
142 D4 **Fortingall** Perth and Kinross Scotland UK
139 F3 **Forton** Hampshire England UK
140 F3 **Forton** Lancashire England UK
131 F6 **Fortore** *watercourse* Italy
100 D3 **Fortoul** Colombia
221 C8 **Fortrose** New Zealand
142 D3 **Fortrose** Highland Scotland UK
102 C4 **Fortuna** Brazil
80 C6 **Fortuna** California USA
75 T8 **Fortuna** North Dakota USA
132 F3 **Fortuna, Lacul** *lake* Romania
79 K9 **Fortune Bay** Newfoundland and Labrador Canada
179 H4 **Forūr, Jazīreh-ye** *island* Iran
127 G5 **Fos-sur-Mer** France
139 G2 **Fosdyke** Lincolnshire England UK
189 G4 **Foshan** Guangdong China
73 K2 **Fosheim Peninsula** Nunavut Canada
120 G4 **Fosna** *region* Norway
158 D3 **Foso** Ghana
86 B3 **Foss** Oklahoma USA
124 D5 **Fossano** Italy
80 E4 **Fossil** Oregon USA
213 J3 **Fossil Head** NT Australia
81 R3 **Fosston** Minnesota USA
140 A4 **Fossy** Ireland
218 H8 **Foster** Vic. Australia
73 Q4 **Foster Bugt** *bay* Greenland
80 F5 **Foster Lake** Oregon USA
139 H3 **Foster Street** Essex England UK
82 J6 **Fostoria** Ohio USA
126 C3 **Fouesnant** France
159 G5 **Fougamou** Gabon
126 D2 **Fougères** France
223 10a **Fo'ui** Tonga
86 E4 **Fouke** Arkansas USA
109 12 **Foul Bay** Barbados
187 E10 **Foul Point** Sri Lanka
158 C2 **Foulabala** Mali
127 G2 **Foulain** France
158 B2 **Foulamôri** Guinea
139 H3 **Foulness Point** England UK
221 D5 **Foulwind, Cape** New Zealand
154 E2 **Foum Zguid** Morocco
164 8a **Foumbouni** Comoros
59 T1 **Foundation Ice Stream** Antarctica
158 E2 **Founouyo** Benin
81 M7 **Fountain** Colorado USA
84 G4 **Fountain Hills** Arizona USA
87 J3 **Fountain Inn** South Carolina USA
218 G6 **Four Corners** NSW Australia
218 B6 **Four Hummocks** *island* SA Australia
72 C8 **Four Mountains, Islands of the** Alaska USA
139 H4 **Four Oaks** East Sussex England UK
219 I5 **Four Ways** NSW Australia
126 D4 **Fouras** France
79 H10 **Fourchu** Nova Scotia Canada
79 H6 **Fourmont, Lac** *lake* Newfoundland and Labrador Canada
133 B6 **Fourna** Greece
164 7a **Fournaise, Piton de la** *volcano* Réunion
126 F4 **Fournels** France
221 6 **Fournier, Cape** Chatham Islands New Zealand
79 F7 **Fournier, Lac** *lake* Quebec Canada
133 E7 **Fournoi** Greece
133 E7 **Fournoi** *island* Greece
126 F3 **Fours** France
141 F1 **Fourstones** Northumberland England UK
74 H4 **Fourth Cabin** British Columbia Canada
158 B2 **Fouta Djallon** *range* Guinea
91 F3 **Foux, Cap-à-** *cape* Haiti
221 B8 **Foveaux Strait** New Zealand
138 C4 **Fowey** *watercourse* England UK
74 F4 **Fowler** British Columbia Canada
81 M7 **Fowler** Colorado USA
217 M6 **Fowler, Point** SA Australia
59 S1 **Fowler Ice Rise** Antarctica
217 M5 **Fowlers Bay** SA Australia
217 M6 **Fowlers Bay** SA Australia
86 B6 **Fowlerton** Texas USA
138 E2 **Fownhope** Herefordshire England UK
213 L3 **Fox** *watercourse* NT Australia
74 I4 **Fox** *watercourse* British Columbia Canada
216 F6 **Fox, Lake** WA Australia
109 7 **Fox Bay East** Falkland Islands
109 7 **Fox Bay West** Falkland Islands
74 M5 **Fox Creek** Alberta Canada
72 C8 **Fox Islands** Alaska USA
75 U4 **Fox Mine** Manitoba Canada
73 L5 **Foxe Basin** Nunavut Canada
73 K5 **Foxe Channel** Nunavut Canada
73 L6 **Foxe Peninsula** Nunavut Canada
143 C3 **Foxford** Ireland
143 C3 **Foxhall** Ireland
220 F5 **Foxton Beach** New Zealand
75 U7 **Foxwarren** Manitoba Canada
138 E3 **Foy** Herefordshire England UK
108 B3 **Foyel** Argentina
142 D3 **Foyers** Highland Scotland UK
143 E3 **Foygh** Ireland
86 D2 **Foyil** Oklahoma USA
143 E1 **Foyle, Lough** *bay* Northern Ireland UK
143 E2 **Foyle Hill** Londonderry Northern Ireland UK
143 C4 **Foynes** Ireland
128 C2 **Foz** Spain
107 I3 **Foz de Areia, Represa do** *reservoir* Brazil
162 B3 **Foz do Cunene** Angola
107 H3 **Foz do Iguaçu** Brazil
139 F2 **Fradley** Staffordshire England UK
120 E5 **Fræna** *island* Norway
129 G3 **Fraga** Spain
91 F2 **Fraile, Punta del** *cape* Cuba
141 H2 **Fraisthorpe** East Riding of Yorkshire England UK
59 Q1 **Frakes, Mount** Antarctica
59 E2 **Fram Bank** *underwater feature* Antarctica
57 F1 **Fram Basin** *underwater feature* Arctic
59 D2 **Fram Peak** *mountain* Antarctica
59 E2 **Framnes Mountains** Antarctica
139 G2 **Frampton** Lincolnshire England UK
122 D3 **Framvaren** *bay* Norway
107 J2 **Franca** Brazil
101 H3 **Françaises, Montagnes** *range* Suriname
126 **France** *country* Europe
73 R3 **France, Île de** *island* Greenland
218 E7 **Frances** SA Australia
74 G2 **Frances** *watercourse* Yukon Territory Canada
101 G6 **Francês** Brazil
90 D2 **Francés, Punta** *cape* Cuba
74 G2 **Frances Lake** Yukon Territory Canada
Franceville *see* **Masuku** Gabon
138 E2 **Franche** Worcestershire England UK
127 G3 **Franche-Comté** *admin. area* France
78 E5 **Francheville, Lac** *lake* Quebec Canada
90 C4 **Francia** Honduras
75 T7 **Francis** Saskatchewan Canada
80 I2 **Francis, Lake** Montana USA
81 P5 **Francis Case, Lake** South Dakota USA
107 H3 **Francisco Beltrão** Brazil
85 K8 **Francisco I. Madero** Mexico
105 H4 **Francisco Lucas** Brazil
103 D7 **Francisco Sá** Brazil
86 B8 **Francisco Villa** Mexico
162 E4 **Francistown** Botswana
74 H5 **François Lake** British Columbia Canada
130 H2 **Francova Lhota** Czech Republic
124 C1 **Franeker** Netherlands
140 A4 **Frankeen's** Ireland
130 C2 **Frankenthal** Germany
82 H6 **Frankfort** Indiana USA
82 I7 **Frankfort** Kentucky USA
125 H1 **Frankfurt** Germany
127 I1 **Frankfurt am Main** Germany
124 F3 **Fränkische Alb** *region* Germany
216 E7 **Frankland** WA Australia
219 R9 **Frankland, Cape** Tas. Australia
216 E7 **Frankland, Mount** WA Australia
214 F7 **Franklin** Qld Australia
86 F6 **Franklin** Louisiana USA
81 P6 **Franklin** Nebraska USA
83 L6 **Franklin** Pennsylvania USA
86 H3 **Franklin** Tennessee USA
86 C5 **Franklin** Texas USA
83 L7 **Franklin** West Virginia USA
72 G5 **Franklin Bay** Northwest Territories Canada
80 F2 **Franklin D. Roosevelt Lake** Washington USA
218 C5 **Franklin Harbor** SA Australia
59 L1 **Franklin Island** Antarctica
80 H6 **Franklin Lake** Nevada USA
72 G6 **Franklin Mountains** Northwest Territories Canada
221 B7 **Franklin Mountains** New Zealand
83 K6 **Franklin Park** Pennsylvania USA
50 P4 **Franklin Seamount** *underwater feature* Atlantic Ocean
59 L1 **Franklin Shoals** *underwater feature* Ross Sea
73 J4 **Franklin Strait** Nunavut Canada
86 F5 **Franklinton** Louisiana USA
120 H5 **Frankrike** Sweden
86 D4 **Frankston** Texas USA
81 K4 **Frannie** Wyoming USA
77 V8 **Franquelin** Quebec Canada
162 B4 **Fransfontein** Namibia
73 R3 **Franske Øer** *island* Greenland
120 J5 **Fränsta** Sweden
139 H3 **Frant** East Sussex England UK
134 M3 **Frantsa Iosifa, Zemlya (Franz Josef Land)** *island* Russian Federation
Franz Josef Land *see* **Frantsa Iosifa, Zemlya** Russian Federation
122 G5 **Franzburg** Germany
131 C7 **Frasca, Capo della** *cape* Sardinia Italy
74 D3 **Fraser** British Columbia Canada
74 J6 **Fraser** *watercourse* British Columbia Canada
78 G4 **Fraser** *watercourse* Newfoundland and Labrador Canada
217 L2 **Fraser, Mount** NT Australia
216 F2 **Fraser, Mount** WA Australia
219 K1 **Fraser Island** Qld Australia
74 I5 **Fraser Lake** British Columbia Canada
78 G5 **Fraser Lake** Newfoundland and Labrador Canada
74 J6 **Fraser Plateau** British Columbia Canada
216 H6 **Fraser Range** WA Australia
162 D6 **Fraserburg** South Africa
142 F3 **Fraserburgh** Aberdeenshire Scotland UK
77 O8 **Fraserdale** Ontario Canada
220 G4 **Frasertown** New Zealand
82 I3 **Frater** Ontario Canada
127 I3 **Frauenfeld** Switzerland
107 G5 **Fray Bentos** Uruguay
106 E6 **Fray Luis Beltrán** Argentina
127 H2 **Fraze** France
126 E2 **Frazé** France
212 F5 **Frazier Downs** WA Australia
140 F3 **Freckleton** Lancashire England UK
130 D4 **Freddi, Monte** *mountain* Italy
82 E4 **Frederic** Wisconsin USA
122 E5 **Fredericia** Denmark
83 M7 **Frederick** Maryland USA
86 B3 **Frederick** Oklahoma USA
81 P4 **Frederick** South Dakota USA
73 P2 **Frederick E. Hyde Fjord** Greenland
83 K2 **Frederick House Lake** Ontario Canada
215 M6 **Frederick Reef** Coral Sea Islands Territory Australia
86 B5 **Fredericksburg** Texas USA
83 M7 **Fredericksburg** Virginia USA
219 K4 **Frederickton** NSW Australia
82 F8 **Fredericktown** Missouri USA
79 E10 **Fredericton** New Brunswick Canada
79 E10 **Fredericton Junction** New Brunswick Canada
78 M1 **Frederikhåb Isblink** *ice* Greenland
122 F4 **Frederikshavn** Denmark
109 21 **Frederiksted** US Virgin Islands
84 F2 **Fredonia** Arizona USA
83 L5 **Fredonia** New York USA
120 K4 **Fredrika** Sweden
122 F3 **Fredrikstad** Norway
162 E5 **Free State** *admin. area* South Africa
86 B2 **Freedom** Oklahoma USA
218 D6 **Freeling** SA Australia
218 D4 **Freeling Heights** *mountain* SA Australia
79 L8 **Freels, Cape** Newfoundland and Labrador Canada
75 N5 **Freeman** *watercourse* Alberta Canada
59 I2 **Freeman Point** Antarctica

87 L7 **Freeport** Bahamas
82 G5 **Freeport** Illinois USA
83 O6 **Freeport** New York USA
86 D6 **Freeport** Texas USA
86 B7 **Freer** Texas USA
158 B3 **Freetown** Sierra Leone
164 9a **Frégate** *island* Seychelles
77 R6 **Frégate, Lac de la** *lake* Quebec Canada
128 C4 **Fregenal de la Sierra** Spain
Fregon *see* **Kaltjiti** Australia
126 C2 **Fréhel, Cap** *cape* France
120 E5 **Frei** Norway
59 U2 **Frei (Chile)** *research station* Antarctica
127 K1 **Freiberg** Germany
124 G2 **Freiberger Mulde** *watercourse* Germany
124 D4 **Freiburg im Breisgau** Germany
106 C6 **Freire** Chile
124 F3 **Freising** Germany
125 G2 **Freital** Germany
127 H5 **Fréjus** France
216 D6 **Fremantle** WA Australia
138 C3 **Fremington** Devon England UK
80 E8 **Fremont** California USA
81 Q6 **Fremont** Nebraska USA
82 J6 **Fremont** Ohio USA
82 G4 **Fremont** Wisconsin USA
101 H4 **French Guiana** *French overseas department* South America
90 C3 **French Harbor** Honduras
82 H7 **French Lick** Indiana USA
80 E7 **French Meadows Reservoir** California USA
223 I4 **French Polynesia** *French overseas land* Pacific Ocean
82 F3 **French River** Minnesota USA
164 6 **French Southern and Antarctic Lands** *French overseas territory* Indian Ocean/Southern Ocean
82 J8 **Frenchburg** Kentucky USA
72 I9 **Frenchman** *watercourse* Saskatchewan Canada
84 C1 **Frenchman** Nevada USA
83 Q4 **Frenchman Bay** Maine USA
80 E7 **Frenchman Lake** California USA
219 Q11 **Frenchmans Cap** *mountain* Tas. Australia
143 D3 **Frenchpark** Ireland
155 G1 **Frenda** Algeria
130 H2 **Frenštát pod Radhoštěm** Czech Republic
102 B4 **Fresco** *watercourse* Brazil
142 E2 **Fresgoe** Highland Scotland UK
59 K2 **Freshfield, Cape** Antarctica
75 U6 **Freshford** Manitoba Canada
143 E4 **Freshford** Ireland
109 12 **Freshwater Bay** Barbados
108 B2 **Fresia** Chile
127 G3 **Fresnes** France
124 B2 **Fresnes** France
88 E4 **Fresnillo** Mexico
80 F8 **Fresno** California USA
81 J2 **Fresno Reservoir** Montana USA
139 I5 **Fresnoy-Folny** France
124 G1 **Fretzdorf** Germany
129 H4 **Freu, Cap des** *cape* Spain
126 F1 **Frévent** France
214 C6 **Frew** *watercourse* NT Australia
218 E2 **Frew Hill** SA Australia
216 D7 **Freycinet, Cape** WA Australia
219 S11 **Freycinet Peninsula** Tas. Australia
130 E2 **Freyung** Germany
158 B2 **Fria** Guinea
162 B3 **Fria, Cape** Namibia
106 E4 **Frias** Argentina
127 H3 **Fribourg** Switzerland
103 D8 **Friburgo** Brazil
141 H2 **Fridaythorpe** East Riding of Yorkshire England UK
199 G5 **Frieda** *watercourse* Papua New Guinea
85 L1 **Friend** Kansas USA
81 Q6 **Friend** Nebraska USA
125 H4 **Friesach** Austria
109 19 **Frigate Bay** St Kitts and Nevis
139 G3 **Frimley** Surrey England UK
139 I3 **Frinton-on-Sea** Essex England UK
142 F4 **Friockheim** Angus Scotland UK
128 C2 **Friol** Spain
85 K3 **Friona** Texas USA
81 L7 **Frisco** Colorado USA
86 C4 **Frisco** Texas USA
86 H5 **Frisco City** Alabama USA
122 G4 **Frisjön** *lake* Sweden
139 H1 **Friskney** Lincolnshire England UK
85 L3 **Fritch** Texas USA
139 I2 **Fritton** Norfolk England UK
127 I1 **Fritzlar** Germany
130 E3 **Friuli-Venezia Giulia** *admin. area* Italy
140 E2 **Frizington** Cumbria England UK
120 F4 **Froan** *island* Norway
75 T8 **Frobisher** Saskatchewan Canada
73 M6 **Frobisher Bay** Nunavut Canada
75 Q4 **Frobisher Lake** Saskatchewan Canada
140 F3 **Frodsham** Cheshire England UK
76 K5 **Frog** *watercourse* Ontario Canada
120 F4 **Frohavet** *bay* Norway
125 H4 **Frohnleiten** Austria
81 M2 **Froid** Montana USA
126 F2 **Froissy** France
122 J4 **Fröjel** Sweden
182 D3 **Frolovo** Russian Federation
81 K4 **Fromberg** Montana USA
218 D3 **Frome** *watercourse* SA Australia
90 E3 **Frome** Jamaica
139 E3 **Frome** Somerset England UK
218 D4 **Frome, Lake** SA Australia
218 D4 **Frome Downs** SA Australia
213 G5 **Frome Rocks** *mountain* WA Australia
138 E4 **Frome St Quinton** Dorset England UK
128 D2 **Frómista** Spain
78 C6 **Fromont, Lac** *lake* Quebec Canada
81 M6 **Front Range** Colorado USA
83 L7 **Front Royal** Virginia USA
78 C2 **Frontenac, Pointe** *cape* Quebec Canada
164 3 **Frontera** Canary Islands
89 G5 **Frontera** Mexico
88 E3 **Frontera** Mexico
89 G5 **Frontera, Punta** *cape* Mexico
89 G6 **Frontera Comalapa** Mexico
84 H5 **Fronteras** Mexico
75 Q8 **Frontier** Saskatchewan Canada
126 F5 **Frontignan** France
126 E5 **Fronton** France
120 I2 **Frøskeland** Norway
120 J4 **Frostberget** Sweden
87 K7 **Frostproof** Florida USA
77 R7 **Frotet, Lac** *lake* Quebec Canada
122 H3 **Frövi** Sweden
139 F3 **Froxfield** Wiltshire England UK
120 F5 **Frøya** *island* Norway
139 J4 **Fruges** France
81 K7 **Fruita** Colorado USA
83 N7 **Fruitland** Maryland USA
74 M8 **Fruitvale** British Columbia Canada
132 F2 **Frunza** Moldova
Frunze *see* **Bishkek** Kyrgyzstan
107 I2 **Frutal** Brazil
133 E8 **Fry** Greece
125 J3 **Frýdek-Místek** Czech Republic
125 H2 **Frýdlant** Czech Republic
83 P4 **Fryeburg** Maine USA
125 K1 **Frygnowo** Poland
122 G2 **Frysjøen** *lake* Norway
188 E2 **Fu Jiang** *watercourse* Chongqing China
188 D2 **Fu Jiang** *watercourse* Sichuan China
189 H3 **Fu`an** Fujian China
223 10a **Fua'amotu** Tonga
223 13a **Fuafatu** *island* Tuvalu
223 13a **Fuagea** *island* Tuvalu
223 13a **Fualefeke** *island* Tuvalu
223 13a **Fualopa** *island* Tuvalu
124 D4 **Fuans** France
190 E6 **Fucheng** Gansu China
191 H5 **Fucheng** Hebei China
189 H1 **Fucheng** Jiangsu China
190 G6 **Fucheng** Shaanxi China
189 H2 **Fuchun Jiang** *watercourse* Zhejiang China
164 3b **Fuencaliente de la Palma** Canary Islands
128 D5 **Fuengirola** Spain
128 E3 **Fuenlabrada** Spain
128 C4 **Fuente de Cantos** Spain
100 C4 **Fuente de Oro** Colombia
128 D5 **Fuente de Piedra, Laguna de** *lake* Spain
128 D4 **Fuenteovejuna** Spain
128 D5 **Fuentes de Andalucía** Spain
108 B5 **Fuentes del Coyle** Argentina
128 D3 **Fuentesaúco** Spain
90 E5 **Fuerte, Isla** *island* Colombia
164 3d **Fuerteventura** *island* Canary Islands
143 D3 **Fuerty** Ireland
195 I3 **Fuga** *island* Philippines
120 J2 **Fugleberg** Norway
57 H2 **Fugløy Bank** *underwater feature* Barents Sea
120 H3 **Fugløya** *island* Norway
189 G1 **Fugou** Henan China
191 I5 **Fuguo** Shandong China
185 H3 **Fuhai** Xinjiang Uygur Zizhiqu China
124 G2 **Fuhne** *watercourse* Germany
193 H4 **Fuji-san** *volcano* Japan
189 H3 **Fujian** *admin. area* China
191 L3 **Fujin** Heilongjiang China
193 H4 **Fujinomiya** Japan
156 D1 **Fūkah** Egypt
185 H4 **Fukang** Xinjiang Uygur Zizhiqu China
193 G4 **Fukuchiyama** Japan
192 F5 **Fukue-jima** *island* Japan
189 I3 **Fukuei Chiao** *island* Taiwan China
193 H4 **Fukui** Japan
192 F5 **Fukuoka** Japan
192 G4 **Fukuyama** Japan
223 9 **Fulaga** *island* Fiji
122 G2 **Fulan** *watercourse* Sweden
124 E2 **Fulda** Germany
124 E2 **Fulda** *watercourse* Germany
81 R5 **Fulda** Minnesota USA
141 G3 **Fulford** York England UK
139 G3 **Fulham** Greater London England UK
189 H2 **Fuliang** Jiangxi China
188 D2 **Fulin** Sichuan China
188 E2 **Fuling** Chongqing China
109 9 **Fullarton** Trinidad and Tobago
85 L4 **Fullerville** Texas USA
120 F6 **Fullsenn** *lake* Norway
132 C2 **Fülöp** Hungary
82 F7 **Fulton** Missouri USA
83 M5 **Fulton** New York USA
86 C6 **Fulton** Texas USA
83 N5 **Fulton Chain Lakes** New York USA
126 E4 **Fumel** France
223 13a **Funafuti** Tuvalu
223 13a **Funafuti Island** Tuvalu
223 13a **Funagongo** *island* Tuvalu
223 13a **Funamanu** *island* Tuvalu
189 G2 **Funan** Anhui China
164 2 **Funchal** Madeira
100 C2 **Fundación** Colombia
132 D3 **Fundata** Romania
154 B5 **Fundo das Figuerias** Cape Verde
79 E10 **Fundy, Bay of** New Brunswick/Nova Scotia Canada
191 I5 **Funing** Hebei China
124 G5 **Funtana** Croatia
159 F2 **Funtua** Nigeria
100 C3 **Funza** Colombia
142 inset **Funzie** Shetland Scotland UK
191 H5 **Fuping** Hebei China
131 C6 **Furana, Punta** *cape* Sardinia Italy
163 F2 **Furancungo** Mozambique
193 I2 **Furano** Japan
157 G1 **Furāt, Nahr al** *watercourse* Middle East
122 C2 **Fure** Norway
122 H4 **Furen** *lake* Sweden
143 C3 **Furmina** Ireland
142 C3 **Furnace** Highland Scotland UK
164 1a **Furnas** Azores
164 1a **Furnas, Lagoa das** *lake* Azores
107 J2 **Furnas, Represa** *reservoir* Brazil
105 H4 **Furnas, Serra das** *range* Brazil
219 S9 **Furneaux Group** *islands* Tas. Australia
218 E7 **Furner** SA Australia
214 C3 **Furner, Mount** NT Australia
189 G3 **Furong** Jiangxi China
132 B2 **Furta** Hungary
105 G6 **Furte Olimpo** Paraguay
124 F3 **Fürth** Germany
124 E3 **Fürth** Germany
124 G3 **Furth im Wald** Germany
120 L2 **Furuflaten** Norway
120 L4 **Furuögrund** Sweden
120 F6 **Furusjøen** *lake* Norway
73 K5 **Fury and Hecla Strait** Nunavut Canada
100 C3 **Fusagasuga** Colombia
190 G6 **Fushan** Shanxi China
191 J4 **Fushun** Liaoning China
191 K4 **Fusong** Jilin China
108 B2 **Futa Ruín** Argentina
189 H3 **Futun Xi** *watercourse* Fujian China
222 7 **Futuna** *island* Vanuatu
223 12a **Futuna, Île** *island* Wallis and Futuna
104 D4 **Futuro** Bolivia
156 E1 **Fuwah** Egypt
188 D4 **Fuxian Hu** *lake* Yunnan China
191 J4 **Fuxin** Liaoning China
188 E3 **Fuxing** Guizhou China
189 G2 **Fuyang** Anhui China
189 F4 **Fuyang** Guangxi Zhuangzu Zizhiqu China
189 H2 **Fuyang** Zhejiang China
189 H3 **Fuying Dao** *island* Fujian China
191 J3 **Fuyu** Heilongjiang China
191 M3 **Fuyuan** Heilongjiang China
185 I3 **Fuyun** Xinjiang Uygur Zizhiqu China
189 H3 **Fuzhou** Fujian China
87 I3 **Fyffe** Alabama USA
122 F5 **Fyn** *island* Denmark
142 C5 **Fyne, Loch** *bay* Scotland UK
122 F5 **Fyns Hoved** *cape* Denmark
122 E3 **Fyresdal** Norway
122 E3 **Fyreselv** *watercourse* Norway
122 E3 **Fyresvatn** *lake* Norway
120 I5 **Fyrsjön** *lake* Sweden

G

161 H2 **Gaalkacyo** Somalia
197 G3 **Gaat** *watercourse* Malaysia
126 E5 **Gabarret** France
126 D5 **Gabas** *watercourse* France
190 D6 **Gabasongduo** Qinghai China
199 G6 **Gabba Island** Australia
84 D1 **Gabbs** Nevada USA
162 B2 **Gabela** Angola
155 I2 **Gabès** Tunisia
156 E3 **Gabgaba, Wādī** *watercourse* Sudan
160 B4 **Gabia** Democratic Republic of Congo
125 J1 **Gąbin** Poland
156 D5 **Gabir** Sudan
220 H4 **Gable End Foreland** *cape* New Zealand
159 G5 **Gabon** *country* Africa
159 F4 **Gabon, Estuaire du** *bay* Gabon
162 E4 **Gaborone** Botswana
133 C5 **Gabrene** Bulgaria
134 T4 **Gabrey, Vozvyshennost'** *range* Russian Federation
78 E1 **Gabriel Island** Nunavut Canada
88 C3 **Gabriel Leyva Solano** Mexico
78 F2 **Gabriel Strait** Nunavut Canada
132 D4 **Gabrovo** *admin. area* Bulgaria
158 B2 **Gabú** Guinea-Bissau
216 E4 **Gabyon** WA Australia
126 E2 **Gacé** France
182 F7 **Gach Sar** Iran
100 C3 **Gachalá** Colombia
100 C3 **Gachetá** Colombia
130 H5 **Gacko** Bosnia and Herzegovina
120 I5 **Gåda** Sweden
187 D8 **Gadag** Karnataka India
199 I6 **Gadaisu** Papua New Guinea
187 E7 **Gadchiroli** Maharashtra India
120 I4 **Gäddede** Sweden
186 C6 **Gadhara** Rajasthan India
187 C7 **Gadhda** Gujarat India
128 E5 **Gádor, Sierra de** *range* Spain
87 I3 **Gadsden** Alabama USA
187 D8 **Gadwal** Andhra Pradesh India
159 H4 **Gadzi** Central African Republic
121 P1 **Gædnjajav'ri** *lake* Norway
126 C2 **Gaël** France
73 Q4 **Gael Hamke Bugt** *bay* Greenland
138 D3 **Gaer** Powys Wales UK
138 E3 **Gaer-fawr** Monmouthshire Wales UK
121 O1 **Gæssejav'ri** *lake* Norway
132 D3 **Găești** Romania
131 E6 **Gaeta, Golfo di** *bay* Italy
219 J1 **Gaeta, Mount** Qld Australia
128 B3 **Gafanha da Nazaré** Portugal
199 H1 **Gaferut** *island* Federated States of Micronesia
87 K3 **Gaffney** South Carolina USA
155 H2 **Gafsa** Tunisia
198 D4 **Gag** *island* Indonesia
159 H3 **Gagal** Chad
183 J6 **Gagarin** Uzbekistan
85 H4 **Gage** New Mexico USA
86 A3 **Gageby** Texas USA
79 E10 **Gagetown** New Brunswick Canada
122 H2 **Gagnef** Sweden
158 C3 **Gagnoa** Côte d'Ivoire
77 U7 **Gagnon** Quebec Canada
181 F4 **Gaibandha** Bangladesh
142 D4 **Gaick Lodge** Highland Scotland UK
178 E2 **Gaida** Iraq
130 E3 **Gail** *watercourse* Austria
85 L4 **Gail** Texas USA
124 E3 **Gaildorf** Germany
126 E5 **Gaillac** France
126 E2 **Gaillon** France
108 D3 **Gaimán** Argentina
87 J6 **Gainesville** Florida USA
87 J3 **Gainesville** Georgia USA
82 E8 **Gainesville** Missouri USA
86 C4 **Gainesville** Texas USA
81 O2 **Gainsborough** Saskatchewan Canada
142 C3 **Gair Loch** *bay* Scotland UK
216 F7 **Gairdner** *watercourse* WA Australia
218 B4 **Gairdner, Lake** SA Australia
142 C3 **Gairloch** Highland Scotland UK
142 E3 **Gairnshiel Lodge** Aberdeenshire Scotland UK
161 F5 **Gairo** Tanzania
121 O1 **Gaissane** *region* Norway
83 M7 **Gaithersburg** Maryland USA
180 E2 **Gaize** Xizang Zizhiqu China
191 J5 **Gaizhou** Liaoning China
123 M4 **Gaiziņkalns** *mountain* Latvia
125 K5 **Gaj** Serbia
192 F6 **Gaja-shima** *island* Japan
159 G2 **Gajiram** Nigeria
162 D5 **Gakarosa** *mountain* South Africa
159 F3 **Gakem** Nigeria
56 N1 **Gakkel Ridge** *underwater feature* Arctic Ocean
125 J5 **Gakovo** Serbia
160 D3 **Gakpi** Democratic Republic of Congo
106 E3 **Galán, Cerro** *mountain* Argentina
161 F4 **Galana** *watercourse* Kenya
196 E3 **Galang Besar** *island* Indonesia
162 C2 **Galangue** Angola
125 I3 **Galanta** Slovakia
53 S8 **Galapagos Fracture Zone** *underwater feature* Pacific Ocean
Galapagos Islands *see* **Colon, Archipiélago de** Ecuador
53 W9 **Galapagos Rise** *underwater feature* Pacific Ocean
53 X8 **Galapagos Seamount** *underwater feature* Pacific Ocean
218 F6 **Galaquil** Vic. Australia
132 F3 **Galați** Romania
132 E3 **Galați** *admin. area* Romania
131 H6 **Galatone** Italy
121 N2 **Galbbajávri** *lake* Norway
214 F4 **Galbraith** Qld Australia
164 3b **Gáldar** Canary Islands
120 F6 **Galdhøpiggen** *mountain* Norway
154 E6 **Galé** Mali
128 B4 **Galé, Costa da** *region* Portugal
85 I5 **Galeana** Mexico
130 D4 **Galeata** Italy
156 E5 **Galegu** Sudan
197 J3 **Galela** Indonesia
216 D3 **Galena** WA Australia
72 D6 **Galena** Alaska USA
125 G1 **Galenbecker See** *lake* Germany
109 9 **Galeota Point** Trinidad and Tobago
104 E6 **Galera, Pampa** *region* Bolivia
100 A4 **Galera, Punta** *cape* Ecuador
89 F6 **Galera, Punta** *cape* Mexico
100 C2 **Galera, Punta de la** *cape* Colombia
109 9 **Galera Point** Trinidad and Tobago
100 B5 **Galeras, Cordillera de** *range* Ecuador
82 F6 **Galesburg** Illinois USA
198 A5 **Galesong** Indonesia
82 F4 **Galesville** Wisconsin USA
161 G2 **Galeti** *watercourse* Ethiopia
77 O7 **Galeton** Ontario Canada
164 7a **Galets, Pointe des** *cape* Réunion
143 C4 **Galey** *watercourse* Ireland
140 F3 **Galgate** Lancashire England UK
161 H3 **Galguduud** *admin. area* Somalia
103 C6 **Galheirão** *watercourse* Brazil
182 D5 **Gali** Georgia
182 D1 **Galich** Russian Federation
134 J6 **Galichskaya Vozvyshennost'** *range* Russian Federation
128 C2 **Galicia** *admin. area* Spain
215 H7 **Galilee, Lake** Qld Australia
159 G3 **Galim** Cameroon
158 A2 **Galinhas, Ilha das** *island* Guinea-Bissau
82 J6 **Galion** Ohio USA
109 14 **Galion, Baie du** *bay* Martinique
84 G4 **Galiuro Mountains** Arkansas USA
214 C1 **Galiwinku** NT Australia
125 G5 **Galižana** Croatia
156 F5 **Gallabat** Sudan
142 A2 **Gallan Head** *cape* Scotland UK
124 E5 **Gallareto** Italy
81 J4 **Gallatin** *watercourse* Montana USA
187 E11 **Galle** Sri Lanka
126 D5 **Gállego** *watercourse* Spain
53 U8 **Gallego Rise** *underwater feature* Pacific Ocean
108 B5 **Gallegos** *watercourse* Argentina
108 A4 **Gallegos, Cabo** *cape* Chile
130 D5 **Galleno** Italy
124 E5 **Gallereto** Italy
143 D5 **Galley Head** *cape* Ireland
130 C4 **Galliate** Italy
142 D4 **Gallin** Perth and Kinross Scotland UK
100 D1 **Gallinas, Punta** *cape* Colombia
124 F5 **Gallio** Italy
131 G6 **Gallipoli** Italy
Gallipoli *see* **Gelibolu** Turkey
120 L3 **Gällivare** Sweden
131 E7 **Gallo, Capo** *cape* Italy
85 H3 **Gallo Mountains** New Mexico USA
90 B3 **Gallon Jug** Belize
75 N8 **Galloway** British Columbia Canada
140 D2 **Galloway, Mull of** *cape* Scotland UK
140 A4 **Gallows Hill** Ireland
122 G4 **Gällstad** Sweden
85 H3 **Gallup** New Mexico USA
129 F3 **Gallur** Spain
142 B4 **Galmisdale** Highland Scotland UK
104 E4 **Galo** Bolivia
219 I6 **Galong** NSW Australia
190 G3 **Galshar** Mongolia
123 L5 **Galstas** *lake* Lithuania
142 D5 **Galston** East Ayrshire Scotland UK
190 D3 **Galt** Mongolia
80 E7 **Galt** California USA
154 D3 **Galtat Zemmour** Western Sahara
122 I3 **Galten** *bay* Sweden
120 J5 **Galtström** Sweden
124 F4 **Galtür** Austria
82 F6 **Galva** Illinois USA
106 C6 **Galvarino** Chile
86 D6 **Galveston** Texas USA
86 D6 **Galveston Bay** Texas USA
86 D6 **Galveston Island** Texas USA
122 I2 **Galvsjön** *lake* Sweden
186 E5 **Galwa** Nepal
143 C3 **Galway** Ireland
143 D3 **Galway** *admin. area* Ireland
143 C3 **Galway Bay** Ireland
218 F1 **Galway Downs** Qld Australia
198 D4 **Gam** *island* Indonesia
194 E2 **Gâm** *watercourse* Vietnam
108 E2 **Gama, Isla** *island* Argentina
139 I5 **Gamaches** France
159 F3 **Gamana** *watercourse* Nigeria
78 D6 **Gamart, Lac** *lake* Quebec Canada
195 J4 **Gamay Bay** Philippines
162 C2 **Gamba** Angola
159 F5 **Gamba** Gabon
161 E2 **Gambēla** Ethiopia
161 E2 **Gambēla Hizboch** *admin. area* Ethiopia
72 B6 **Gambell** Alaska USA
158 A2 **Gambia** *country* Africa
158 B2 **Gambia** *watercourse* Gambia
50 P9 **Gambia Plain** *underwater feature* Atlantic Ocean
158 B2 **Gambie** *watercourse* Guinea
198 D6 **Gambier, Cape** Australia
223 14 **Gambier, Îles** *islands* French Polynesia
79 K8 **Gambo** Newfoundland and Labrador Canada
159 I4 **Gambo** Central African Republic
159 H5 **Gamboma** Congo
215 G4 **Gamboola** Qld Australia
159 H4 **Gamboula** Central African Republic
155 H6 **Gamdou** Niger
100 C3 **Gámeza** Colombia
121 M4 **Gammelgården** Sweden
123 J4 **Gammelgarn** Sweden
120 M4 **Gammelstaden** Sweden
162 C4 **Gamsberg** *mountain* Namibia
108 C3 **Gan Gan** Argentina
84 H3 **Ganado** Arizona USA
86 C6 **Ganado** Texas USA
162 B2 **Ganda** Angola
198 A4 **Gandadiwata, Bukit** *mountain* Indonesia
187 E7 **Gandai** Chhattisgarh India
160 C5 **Gandajika** Democratic Republic of Congo
128 B2 **Gándara** Spain
179 K4 **Gandava** Pakistan
79 K8 **Gander** *watercourse* Newfoundland and Labrador Canada
79 K8 **Gander Lake** Newfoundland and Labrador Canada
129 G3 **Gandesa** Spain
186 D6 **Gandhi Sagar** *lake* Madhya Pradesh India
186 C6 **Gandhinagar** Gujarat India
129 F4 **Gandía** Spain
103 E6 **Gandu** Brazil
121 P1 **Gandvik** Norway
186 E5 **Ganga (Ganges)** *watercourse* Uttar Pradesh India
160 D3 **Gangale** Democratic Republic of Congo
186 C5 **Ganganagar** Rajasthan India
186 D5 **Gangapur** Rajasthan India
155 H6 **Gangara** Niger
186 G6 **Gangarampur** West Bengal India
181 H4 **Gangaw** Myanmar
187 D8 **Gangawati** Karnataka India
180 E2 **Gangdise Shan** *range* Xizang Zizhiqu China
126 F5 **Ganges** France
Ganges *see* **Ganga** India
187 H7 **Ganges, Mouths of the** *delta* Bangladesh
55 M3 **Ganges Fan** *underwater feature* Indian Ocean
186 D5 **Gangoh** Uttar Pradesh India
186 G5 **Gangtok** Sikkim India
188 E1 **Gangu** Gansu China
160 C3 **Gangu** *watercourse* Democratic Republic of Congo
198 D4 **Gani** Indonesia
178 G3 **Ganjeh Gūn** Iran
191 J3 **Gannan** Heilongjiang China
126 F3 **Gannat** France
81 K5 **Gannett Peak** Wyoming USA
191 J4 **Gan'qika** Nei Mongol Zizhiqu China
181 G2 **Ganqu** Xizang Zizhiqu China
190 G6 **Ganquan** Shaanxi China
162 C6 **Gansbaai** South Africa
188 D1 **Gansu** *admin. area* China
158 C3 **Ganta** Liberia
161 G3 **Gantama** Somalia
218 C7 **Gantheaume, Cape** SA Australia
216 D3 **Gantheaume Bay** WA Australia
87 H5 **Gantt Lake** Alabama USA
196 F4 **Gantung** Indonesia
159 G3 **Ganye** Nigeria
158 D3 **Ganze** Côte d'Ivoire
189 G3 **Ganzhou** Jiangxi China
188 C2 **Ganzi** Sichuan China
124 G1 **Ganzlin** Germany
155 F5 **Gao** Mali
188 C2 **Gaocheng** Sichuan China
188 F3 **Gaocun** Hunan China
190 E6 **Gaolan** Gansu China
189 G4 **Gaolan Liedao** *islands* Guangdong China
188 F2 **Gaoleshan** Hubei China
188 C3 **Gaoligong Shan** *range* Yunnan China
191 I6 **Gaomi** Shandong China
107 G2 **Gaona-cué** Paraguay
191 G6 **Gaoping** Shanxi China
190 D5 **Gaotai** Gansu China
158 D2 **Gaoua** Burkina Faso
158 B2 **Gaoual** Guinea
191 H5 **Gaoyang** Hebei China
191 H5 **Gaoyi** Hebei China
189 H2 **Gaoyou** Jiangsu China
189 H2 **Gaoyou Hu** *lake* Jiangsu China
188 F4 **Gaozhou** Guangdong China
127 H4 **Gap** France
122 G3 **Gapern** *lake* Sweden
120 J2 **Gapøya** *island* Norway
214 C2 **Gapuwiyak** NT Australia
185 I6 **Gar Qu** *lake* Qinghai China
180 D2 **Gar Zangbo** *watercourse* Xizang Zizhiqu China
132 A2 **Gara** Hungary
143 D3 **Gara, Lough** *lake* Ireland
182 I7 **Garabil Belentligi** *lake* Turkmenistan
159 G4 **Garabinzam** Congo
182 G5 **Garabogazköl Aýlagy** *lake* Turkmenistan
90 E5 **Garachiné** Panama
90 E5 **Garachiné, Punta** *cape* Panama
156 E4 **Garada** Sudan
140 B3 **Garadice** Ireland
164 3b **Garafía** Canary Islands
100 C3 **Garagoa** Colombia
182 H6 **Garagum** Turkmenistan
182 I6 **Garagum Kanaly** *watercourse* Turkmenistan
219 I3 **Garah** NSW Australia
179 L2 **Garai** Pakistan
182 I6 **Garamätnyýaz** Turkmenistan
158 D2 **Garango** Burkina Faso
102 E5 **Garanhuns** Brazil
222 2a **Garapan** Northern Mariana Islands
199 I6 **Garara** Papua New Guinea
108 C3 **Garayalde** Argentina
159 I3 **Garba** Central African Republic
161 F3 **Garba Tula** Kenya
161 G3 **Garbahaarrey** Somalia
142 D3 **Garbat** Highland Scotland UK
125 I2 **Garbce** Poland
86 C2 **Garber** Oklahoma USA
142 D3 **Garbole** Highland Scotland UK
103 A6 **Garças, Rio das** *watercourse* Brazil
129 G3 **Garcia** Spain
85 J2 **Garcia** Colorado USA
128 D4 **Garcia de Sola, Embalse de** *lake* Spain
100 B3 **García Gómez** Colombia
107 H2 **Garcias** Brazil
126 F4 **Gard** *watercourse* France
130 D4 **Garda, Lago di** *lake* Italy
121 P2 **Gardajav'ri** *lake* Norway
129 I2 **Gardanne** France
122 I4 **Gårdby** Sweden
80 G5 **Garden City** Idaho USA
81 O8 **Garden City** Kansas USA
85 L5 **Garden City** Texas USA
80 J6 **Garden City** Utah USA
216 D6 **Garden Island** WA Australia
82 G2 **Garden Lake** Ontario Canada
75 O3 **Garden River** Alberta Canada
86 H4 **Gardendale** Alabama USA
142 F3 **Gardenstown** Aberdeenshire Scotland UK
120 H5 **Gärdessjön** *lake* Sweden
133 B6 **Gardiki** Greece
81 J4 **Gardiner** Montana USA
122 E5 **Garding** Germany
179 L2 **Gardīz** Afghanistan
120 I4 **Gärdnäs** Sweden
59 T1 **Gardner Inlet** *bay* Antarctica
122 I5 **Gardno, Jezioro** *lake* Poland
130 D4 **Gardone Riviera** Italy
126 E5 **Gardouch** France
120 I4 **Gärdsjön** *lake* Sweden
120 G5 **Gåre** Norway
142 D4 **Garelochhead** Argyll and Bute Scotland UK
124 E5 **Garessio** Italy
155 H4 **Garet el Djenoun** *mountain* Algeria
215 H7 **Garfield** Qld Australia
131 G6 **Gargano, Testa del** *cape* Italy
82 I3 **Gargantua, Cape** Ontario Canada
182 E6 **Gargar** Iran
120 J4 **Gargnäs** Sweden
186 F6 **Garhwa** Jharkhand India
133 B5 **Gari** Macedonia
179 I4 **Garī Charbān** Iran
74 J8 **Garibaldi, Mount** British Columbia Canada
162 C6 **Garies** South Africa
178 F2 **Garīn, Kūh-e** *mountain* Iran
161 F4 **Garissa** Kenya
104 A2 **Garita Garcia** Peru
159 G2 **Garkida** Nigeria
75 U7 **Garland** Manitoba Canada
86 C4 **Garland** Texas USA
142 D5 **Garleffin** South Ayrshire Scotland UK
123 L5 **Garliava** Lithuania
142 D6 **Garlieston** Dumfries and Galloway Scotland UK
182 J6 **Garlyk** Turkmenistan
160 D3 **Garmabe** Sudan
178 G2 **Garmsār** Iran
125 J2 **Garnek** Poland
82 E5 **Garner** Iowa USA
87 L3 **Garner** North Carolina USA
79 K9 **Garnish** Newfoundland and Labrador Canada
143 B5 **Garnish** Ireland
218 F5 **Garnpung Lake** NSW Australia
126 E5 **Garonne** *watercourse* France
129 G1 **Garonne, Canal latéral à la** *watercourse* France
161 H2 **Garoowe** Somalia
186 D6 **Garot** Madhya Pradesh India
159 G3 **Garoua** Cameroon
159 G3 **Garoua Boulai** Cameroon
199 I5 **Garove Island** Papua New Guinea
142 B2 **Garrabost** Na h-Eileanan Siar Scotland UK
143 E4 **Garrane** Ireland
143 D3 **Garranlahan** Ireland
106 F6 **Garré** Argentina
143 D4 **Garrison** Ireland
81 O3 **Garrison** North Dakota USA
86 D5 **Garrison** Texas USA
84 E1 **Garrison** Utah USA
140 D1 **Garroch** Dumfries and Galloway Scotland UK
140 C1 **Garron Point** Northern Ireland UK
128 C4 **Garrovillas** Spain
128 F5 **Garrucha** Spain
179 K4 **Garruk** Pakistan
142 D4 **Garry** *watercourse* Scotland UK
73 I5 **Garry Lake** Nunavut Canada
143 F1 **Garryduff** Ballymoney Northern Ireland UK
138 A1 **Garryknock** Ireland
75 Q4 **Garson** *watercourse* Saskatchewan Canada
75 P4 **Garson Lake** Alberta Canada
75 Q4 **Garson Lake** Saskatchewan Canada
140 F3 **Garstang** Lancashire England UK
126 E3 **Gartempe** *watercourse* France
120 F5 **Garten** Norway
138 D2 **Garth** Powys Wales UK
138 D2 **Garthmyl** Powys Wales UK
139 G2 **Garthorpe** Leicester England UK
142 D4 **Gartocharn** West Dunbartonshire Scotland UK
124 F1 **Gartow** Germany
196 E5 **Garut** Indonesia
143 F2 **Garvagh** Coleraine Northern Ireland UK
140 A2 **Garvaghy** Omagh Northern Ireland UK
142 F5 **Garvald** East Lothian Scotland UK
139 H2 **Garveston** Norfolk England UK
221 C7 **Garvie Mountains** New Zealand
125 K2 **Garwolin** Poland
82 H6 **Gary** Indiana USA
83 K8 **Gary** West Virginia USA
122 G5 **Garz** Germany
85 L8 **Garza Garcia** Mexico
86 B8 **Garza Valdez** Mexico
100 C4 **Garzón** Colombia
120 F5 **Gåsbue** Norway
126 E5 **Gascogne** *region* France
126 C5 **Gascogne, Golfe de** *bay* France
86 E2 **Gasconade** *watercourse* Missouri USA
216 E2 **Gascoyne** *watercourse* WA Australia
216 E2 **Gascoyne, Mount** WA Australia
216 D2 **Gascoyne Junction** WA Australia
52 G9 **Gascoyne Plain** *underwater feature* Pacific Ocean
52 L11 **Gascoyne Tablemount** *underwater feature* Pacific Ocean
156 F4 **Gash** *watercourse* Eritrea
159 G2 **Gashua** Nigeria
142 G3 **Gask** Aberdeenshire Scotland UK
77 O6 **Gasket Island** Nunavut Canada
79 L9 **Gaskiers** Newfoundland and Labrador Canada
125 K1 **Gąsocin** Poland
85 H7 **Gasogachic** Mexico
196 E4 **Gaspar, Selat** *strait* Indonesia
109 9 **Gasparillo** Trinidad and Tobago
79 F8 **Gaspé** Quebec Canada
79 F8 **Gaspé, Baie de** *bay* Quebec Canada
79 F8 **Gaspé, Cap** *cape* Quebec Canada
79 E8 **Gaspésie, Péninsule de la** *peninsula* Quebec Canada
158 D2 **Gassan** Burkina Faso
154 C6 **Gassane** Senegal
83 K7 **Gassaway** West Virginia USA
128 D4 **Gasset, Embalse de** *lake* Spain
120 J5 **Gässjö** Sweden
87 M2 **Gaston, Lake** North Carolina USA
87 K3 **Gastonia** North Carolina USA
108 C3 **Gastre** Argentina
128 C3 **Gata** Spain
128 E5 **Gata, Cabo de** *cape* Spain
136 E6 **Gata, Cape** Cyprus
74 H3 **Gataga** *watercourse* British Columbia Canada
132 B3 **Gătaia** Romania
223 12c **Gataivai** Samoa
123 P3 **Gatchina** Russian Federation
81 O8 **Gate** Oklahoma USA
141 G3 **Gateford** Nottinghamshire England UK
142 D6 **Gatehouse of Fleet** Dumfries and Galloway Scotland UK
140 E2 **Gatesgarth** Cumbria England UK
141 G2 **Gateshead** Tyne and Wear England UK
141 G2 **Gateshead** *admin. area* England UK
73 I4 **Gateshead Island** Nunavut Canada
86 C5 **Gatesville** Texas USA
106 D2 **Gatico** Chile
73 L9 **Gatineau** *watercourse* Quebec Canada
188 C2 **Gatong** Xizang Zizhiqu China
195 I3 **Gattaran** Philippines
219 K2 **Gatton** Qld Australia
127 I4 **Gattorna** Italy
90 E5 **Gatún, Lago** *lake* Panama
186 E3 **Gatwan** *watercourse* Jammu and Kashmir India/Pakistan
223 9 **Gau** *island* Fiji
105 H4 **Gaúcha do Norte** Brazil
124 B3 **Gauchy** France
100 D5 **Gaudencio** Colombia
76 G4 **Gauer Lake** Manitoba Canada
123 M4 **Gauja** *watercourse* Latvia
123 N4 **Gaujiena** Latvia
120 G5 **Gaula** *watercourse* Norway
120 E6 **Gaupne** Norway
181 G4 **Gauripur** Bangladesh
181 F3 **Gauripur** Assam India
181 G4 **Gaurnadi** Bangladesh
122 E3 **Gausta** *mountain* Norway
120 J2 **Gausvik** Norway
120 I4 **Gäutan** *bay* Sweden
162 E5 **Gauteng** *admin. area* South Africa
120 F5 **Gautsjøen** *bay* Norway
178 F2 **Gāv Savār** Iran
179 I4 **Gavanak** Iran
135 AG7 **Gavanka** Russian Federation
182 E6 **Gavar** Armenia
126 D5 **Gavarnie** France
179 H4 **Gāvbandī** Iran
133 C8 **Gavdopoula** *island* Greece
133 D8 **Gavdos** *island* Greece
126 D5 **Gave** *watercourse* France
103 D6 **Gavião** *watercourse* Brazil
120 K5 **Gaviksfjärden** *bay* Sweden
84 B3 **Gaviota** California USA
106 F6 **Gaviotas** Argentina
122 I2 **Gävle** Sweden
120 I6 **Gävleborgs** *admin. area* Sweden
122 I2 **Gävlebukten** *bay* Sweden
72 A6 **Gavriila, Bukhta** *bay* Russian Federation
133 D7 **Gavrio** Greece
182 C1 **Gavrlov-Yam** Russian Federation
123 O4 **Gavry** Russian Federation
123 N4 **Gavry** Russian Federation
199 J6 **Gawa Island** Papua New Guinea
186 F6 **Gawan** Jharkhand India
218 D6 **Gawler** SA Australia
159 F3 **Gawu** Nigeria
120 I5 **Gåxsjö** Sweden
120 I5 **Gåxsjön** *lake* Sweden
186 F6 **Gaya** Bihar India
197 G2 **Gaya** *island* Malaysia
159 E2 **Gaya** Niger
159 F2 **Gaya** Nigeria
82 I4 **Gaylord** Michigan USA
219 J1 **Gayndah** Qld Australia
134 L6 **Gayny** Russian Federation
78 C5 **Gayot, Lac** *lake* Quebec Canada
139 H2 **Gaywood** Norfolk England UK
178 C3 **Gaza** Gaza Strip Middle East
163 F4 **Gaza** *admin. area* Mozambique
178 C4 **Gaza Strip** *disputed territory* Middle East
179 K4 **Gazan** Pakistan
182 G6 **Gazanjyk** Turkmenistan
199 I4 **Gazelle Channel** *strait* Papua New Guinea
210 inset **Gazert, Cape** Heard Island Australia
160 C3 **Gazi** Democratic Republic of Congo
136 F6 **Gaziantep** Turkey
136 F6 **Gaziantep** *admin. area* Turkey
191 I2 **Gazimurskiy Khrebet** *range* Russian Federation
191 I2 **Gazimurskiy Zavod** Russian Federation
181 G4 **Gazipur** Bangladesh
182 I6 **Gazli** Uzbekistan
182 I5 **Gazojak** Turkmenistan
133 C5 **Gazoros** Greece
130 D4 **Gazzuolo** Italy
160 C3 **Gbadolite** Democratic Republic of Congo
158 C3 **Gbarnga** Liberia
158 E2 **Gbassa** Benin
125 I3 **Gbely** Slovakia
159 F3 **Gboko** Nigeria
123 J5 **Gdańsk** Poland
123 J5 **Gdańsk, Zatoka** *bay* Poland
123 N3 **Gdov** Russian Federation
123 J5 **Gdynia** Poland
143 C5 **Gearha** Ireland
80 D3 **Gearhart** Oregon USA
142 D2 **Gearnsary** Highland Scotland UK
142 A3 **Gearraidh Bhailteas** Na h-Eileanan Siar Scotland UK
141 F2 **Gearstones** North Yorkshire England UK
86 B3 **Geary** Oklahoma USA
120 J5 **Geasjön** *lake* Sweden
158 B2 **Geba** *watercourse* Guinea-Bissau
198 D4 **Gebe** *island* Indonesia
156 F4 **Gebeit** Sudan
156 F3 **Gebeit Mine** Sudan
133 G7 **Gebiz** Turkey
133 F5 **Gebze** Turkey
188 E2 **Gecheng** Chongqing China
196 D4 **Gedang, Gunung** *mountain* Indonesia
156 F5 **Gedaref** Sudan
156 E5 **Gedaref** *admin. area* Sudan
124 E2 **Gedern** Germany
127 G2 **Gedinne** Belgium
133 F6 **Gediz** Turkey
133 E6 **Gediz** *watercourse* Turkey
161 G2 **Gedlegubē** Ethiopia
161 G3 **Gedo** *admin. area* Somalia
161 F2 **Gēdo** Ethiopia
190 G5 **Gedong** Shanxi China
197 F3 **Gedong** Malaysia
126 E5 **Gèdre** France
122 F5 **Gedser** Denmark
122 G5 **Gedser Odde** *cape* Denmark
214 E4 **Gee Wee Point** Qld Australia
219 I6 **Geegullalong, Mount** NSW Australia
213 G5 **Geegully** *watercourse* WA Australia
127 G1 **Geel** Belgium
218 G8 **Geelong** Vic. Australia
216 C4 **Geelvink Channel** WA Australia
216 F5 **Geeraning Rock** *mountain* WA Australia
185 J6 **Ge'ermu** Qinghai China
133 C5 **Gefira** Greece
218 C5 **Geharty, Mount** SA Australia
159 G2 **Geidam** Nigeria
75 S4 **Geikie** *watercourse* Saskatchewan Canada
76 H2 **Geillini** *watercourse* Nunavut Canada
76 H2 **Geillini Lake** Nunavut Canada
120 E5 **Geiranger** Norway
130 D2 **Geisenfeld** Germany
130 B2 **Geisenheim** Germany
160 E4 **Geita** Tanzania
120 J2 **Geitvatnet** *lake* Norway
180 D2 **Geji** Xizang Zizhiqu China
188 D4 **Gejiu** Yunnan China
72 A6 **Geka, Mys** *cape* Russian Federation
160 D2 **Gel** *watercourse* Sudan
131 F8 **Gela** Italy
131 F8 **Gela, Golfo di** *bay* Italy
181 G2 **Geladaindong** *mountain* Qinghai China
161 H2 **Geladī** Ethiopia
197 F4 **Gelam** *island* Indonesia
196 D2 **Gelang, Tanjong** *cape* Malaysia
219 I7 **Gelantipy** Vic. Australia
133 E6 **Gelembe** Turkey
161 G2 **Gelemso** Ethiopia
133 G6 **Gelendost** Turkey
182 C5 **Gelendzhik** Russian Federation
123 L5 **Gelgaudiškis** Lithuania
161 H2 **Gelinsoor** Somalia
179 H4 **Gelkūyeh** Iran
130 G3 **Gelse** Hungary
196 E4 **Gelumbang** Indonesia
123 M5 **Gelvonai** Lithuania
75 O7 **Gem** Alberta Canada
127 G1 **Gembloux** Belgium
159 G3 **Gembu** Nigeria
198 C2 **Gemeh** Indonesia
160 B3 **Gemena** Democratic Republic of Congo
157 G5 **Gemerī Hāyk'** *lake* Ethiopia
133 F7 **Gemiç** Turkey
133 F5 **Gemlik Körfezi** *bay* Turkey
127 K3 **Gemona del Friuli** Italy
126 D4 **Gémozac** France

124 E2 **Gemünden** Germany
161 G2 **Genale** *watercourse* Ethiopia
108 B5 **Gendarme C. Barreto** Argentina
126 G3 **Génelard** France
106 E6 **General Acha** Argentina
107 F6 **General Alvear** Argentina
106 E5 **General Alvear** Argentina
106 F2 **General Ballivián** Argentina
107 G5 **General Belgrano** Argentina
89 F3 **General Bravo** Mexico
105 H4 **General Carneiro** Brazil
88 E3 **General Cepeda** Mexico
106 E7 **General Conesa** Argentina
88 E4 **General Enrique Estrada** Mexico
88 E3 **General Escobedo** Mexico
85 N8 **General Francisco Gonzales Villareal** Mexico
107 G6 **General Guido** Argentina
107 G6 **General Juan Madariaga** Argentina
108 D2 **General Liborio Bernal** Argentina
106 E3 **General Martín Miguel de Güemes** Argentina
108 C3 **General Mosconi** Argentina
107 G3 **General Paz** Argentina
106 F5 **General Pico** Argentina
106 F3 **General Pinedo** Argentina
107 G6 **General Pirán** Argentina
106 E6 **General Roca** Argentina
195 J6 **General Santos** Philippines
89 F3 **General Terán** Mexico
85 I6 **General Trias** Mexico
106 F5 **General Villegas** Argentina
129 F4 **Generalísimo, Embalse del** *lake* Spain
83 M5 **Genesee** *watercourse* New York USA
85 M1 **Geneseo** Kansas USA
Geneva *see* **Genève** Switzerland
81 Q6 **Geneva** Nebraska USA
83 M5 **Geneva** New York USA
122 G4 **Genevad** Sweden
130 B3 **Genève (Geneva)** Switzerland
124 E3 **Gengenbach** Germany
188 C4 **Gengma** Yunnan China
188 C2 **Gengqing** Sichuan China
160 C4 **Gengwa** Democratic Republic of Congo
191 J2 **Genhe** Nei Mongol Zizhiqu China
128 D5 **Genil** *watercourse* Spain
126 E3 **Génillé** France
186 C6 **Genji** Rajasthan India
127 G1 **Genk** Belgium
131 C6 **Gennargentu, Monte del** *mountain* Sardinia Italy
124 C2 **Gennep** Netherlands
108 B3 **Genoa** *watercourse* Argentina
219 I7 **Genoa** Vic. Australia
Genoa *see* **Genova** Italy
81 N7 **Genoa** Colorado USA
124 D5 **Genola** Italy
129 H1 **Génolhac** France
127 H3 **Genolier** Switzerland
130 C5 **Genova, Golfo di** *bay* Italy
130 C4 **Genova (Genoa)** Italy
109 4 **Genovesa, Isla** *island* Archipiélago de Colon (Galapagos Islands)
135 AG3 **Genriyetty, Ostrov** *island* Russian Federation
78 E6 **Gensart, Lac** *lake* Quebec Canada
126 F1 **Gent** Belgium
196 E5 **Genteng** Indonesia
197 G6 **Genteng** Indonesia
197 G5 **Genteng** *island* Indonesia
124 G1 **Genthin** Germany
83 O3 **Gentilly** Quebec Canada
126 E4 **Gentioux** France
199 G4 **Genyem** Indonesia
131 G6 **Genzano di Lucania** Italy
212 F5 **Geoffroy Bay** WA Australia
216 D6 **Geographe Bay** WA Australia
73 Q4 **Geographical Society Øer** *island* Greenland
78 F4 **George** *watercourse* Quebec Canada
162 D6 **George** South Africa
79 H10 **George, Cape** Nova Scotia Canada
213 G7 **George, Lake** WA Australia
160 E3 **George, Lake** Uganda
87 K6 **George, Lake** Florida USA
82 I3 **George, Lake** Michigan USA
83 O5 **George, Lake** New York USA
216 G4 **George, Mount** WA Australia
50 Q4 **George Bligh Bank** *underwater feature* Atlantic Ocean
109 7 **George Island** Falkland Islands
221 B7 **George Sound** New Zealand
219 R10 **George Town** Tas. Australia
91 F2 **George Town** Bahamas
90 D3 **George Town** Cayman Islands
196 D2 **George Town** Malaysia
59 J2 **George V Coast** Antarctica
59 T2 **George VI Sound** *strait* Antarctica
213 H3 **George Water** *bay* WA Australia
86 B6 **George West** Texas USA
50 L5 **Georges Bank** *underwater feature* Atlantic Ocean
219 J4 **Georges Mountain** NSW Australia
164 5a **Georgetown** Ascension
215 G5 **Georgetown** Qld Australia
101 G3 **Georgetown** Guyana
109 11a **Georgetown** St Vincent and the Grenadines
82 I7 **Georgetown** Kentucky USA
87 L4 **Georgetown** South Carolina USA
86 C5 **Georgetown** Texas USA
182 D5 **Georgia** *country* Asia
71 **Georgia** *admin. area* USA
80 C2 **Georgia, Gulf of** British Columbia Canada
74 I7 **Georgia, Strait of** British Columbia Canada
83 K4 **Georgian Bay** Ontario Canada
86 H5 **Georgiana** Alabama USA
214 D6 **Georgina** NT Australia
214 E6 **Georgina** *watercourse* Qld Australia
183 N3 **Georgiyevka** Kazakhstan
182 D5 **Georgiyevsk** Russian Federation
127 K1 **Gera** Germany
133 B7 **Geraki, Akra** *cape* Greece
103 D6 **Geral, Serra** *range* Brazil
72 B4 **Geral'd, Ostrov** *island* Russian Federation
221 D7 **Geraldine** New Zealand
81 J3 **Geraldine** Montana USA
216 D4 **Geraldton** WA Australia
76 L8 **Geraldton** Ontario Canada
127 H2 **Gérardmer** France
130 F2 **Geras** Austria
80 E5 **Gerber Reservoir** Oregon USA
179 H3 **Gerdeh Kūh** Iran
136 E5 **Gerede** Turkey
179 J3 **Gereshk** Afghanistan
128 E5 **Gérgal** Spain
199 H5 **Gerhards, Cape** Papua New Guinea
78 D3 **Gerido, Lac** *lake* Quebec Canada
196 D2 **Gerik** Malaysia
81 N6 **Gering** Nebraska USA
125 K3 **Gerlachovský štít** *mountain* Slovakia
124 F4 **Gerlos** Austria
78 E6 **Germaine, Lac** *lake* Quebec Canada
73 R3 **Germania Land** *peninsula* Greenland
124 **Germany** *country* Europe
124 C3 **Germay** France
127 I2 **Germersheim** Germany
127 J2 **Gerolzhofen** Germany
138 C4 **Gerrans** Cornwall England UK
129 G2 **Gers** *watercourse* France
126 F4 **Gerzat** France
198 D4 **Geser** Indonesia
199 G6 **Gesoa** Papua New Guinea
120 J5 **Gesunden** *bay* Sweden
123 J2 **Geta** Finland
128 E3 **Getafe** Spain
81 P4 **Gettysburg** South Dakota USA
128 E2 **Getxo** Spain
59 P2 **Getz Ice Shelf** Antarctica
196 C2 **Geumpang** Indonesia
219 I5 **Geurie** NSW Australia
136 G5 **Gevaş** Turkey
133 C5 **Gevgelija** Macedonia
187 D7 **Gevrai** Maharashtra India
120 H5 **Gevsjön** *lake* Sweden
127 H3 **Gex** France
133 E6 **Geyikli** Turkey
196 D4 **Geylang** *admin. area* Singapore
181 G3 **Geylegphug** Bhutan
133 F7 **Geyre** Turkey
84 A1 **Geyserville** California USA
184 E5 **Gez He** *watercourse* Xinjiang Uygur Zizhiqu China
162 D5 **Ghaap Plateau** *plain* South Africa
156 D5 **Ghabeish** Sudan
155 H2 **Ghadāmis** Libya
155 I3 **Ghaddūwah** Libya
186 F5 **Ghaghara** *watercourse* Uttar Pradesh India
156 D5 **Ghalla, Wādī El** *watercourse* Sudan
154 E4 **Ghallamane** *region* Mauritania
158 D3 **Ghana** *country* Africa
162 D4 **Ghanzi** Botswana
162 D4 **Ghanzi** *admin. area* Botswana
156 E4 **Gharb Binna** Sudan
155 G2 **Ghardaïa** Algeria
131 C8 **Ghardimaou** Tunisia
156 E2 **Ghārib, Jabal** *mountain* Egypt
183 K6 **Gharm** Tajikistan
155 I2 **Gharyān** Libya
155 I3 **Ghāt** Libya
187 E7 **Ghatanji** Maharashtra India
222 8 **Ghatere** Solomon Islands
187 F7 **Ghatgan** Orissa India
187 E8 **Ghats, Eastern** *range* Andhra Pradesh India
187 D8 **Ghats, Western** *range* Maharashtra India
155 F1 **Ghazaouet** Algeria
186 D5 **Ghaziabad** Uttar Pradesh India
186 F6 **Ghazipur** Uttar Pradesh India
179 K2 **Ghaznī** Afghanistan
179 K2 **Ghaznī** *admin. area* Afghanistan
157 G4 **Ghela'elo** Eritrea
130 C4 **Ghemme** Italy
132 D2 **Gheorgheni** Romania
130 E4 **Ghibullo** Italy
132 F2 **Ghidighici, Lacul** *lake* Moldova
132 E2 **Ghimeş-Făget** Romania
131 C5 **Ghisonaccia** Corsica France
187 C7 **Ghogha** Gujarat India
186 F6 **Ghorawal** Uttar Pradesh India
75 N7 **Ghost Lake** Alberta Canada
78 H5 **Ghost Lake** Newfoundland and Labrador Canada
76 K5 **Ghost Lake** Ontario Canada
83 L2 **Ghost Range** Ontario Canada
179 J2 **Ghowr** *admin. area* Afghanistan
179 J2 **Ghowrmāch** Afghanistan
178 E3 **Ghudāf, Wādī al** *watercourse* Iraq
186 F5 **Ghughuli** Uttar Pradesh India
179 M2 **Ghujerab** *watercourse* Pakistan
156 D2 **Ghurd Abū Muharrik** *range* Egypt
155 J3 **Ghuzayyil, Sabkhat** *lake* Libya
194 E5 **Gia Định** Vietnam
194 E3 **Gianh** *watercourse* Vietnam
131 D5 **Giannutri, Isola di** *island* Italy
133 E8 **Gianysada** *island* Greece
131 F8 **Giarratana** Italy
131 F8 **Giarre** Italy
127 H4 **Giaveno** Italy
213 I3 **Gibb** *watercourse* WA Australia
219 H7 **Gibbo, Mount** Vic. Australia
81 P6 **Gibbon** Nebraska USA
216 G6 **Gibbs, Mount** WA Australia
83 inset **Gibb's Hill** Bermuda
161 F2 **Gibe** *watercourse* Ethiopia
131 E8 **Gibellina** Italy
162 C5 **Gibeon** Namibia
128 C5 **Gibraleón** Spain
128 D5 **Gibraltar** *UK overseas territory* Europe
128 D5 **Gibraltar** Gibraltar
154 E1 **Gibraltar, Strait of** Mediterranean Sea/Atlantic Ocean
141 I3 **Gibraltar Point** England UK
86 E4 **Gibsland** Louisiana USA
216 G6 **Gibson** WA Australia
213 I7 **Gibson Desert** WA Australia
76 I1 **Gibson Lake** Nunavut Canada
213 H2 **Gibson Point** WA Australia
123 L5 **Giby** Poland
130 G3 **Gic** Hungary
185 J3 **Gichgeniyn Nuruu** Mongolia
159 G3 **Gida** Nigeria
161 E2 **Gīdamī** Ethiopia
120 K5 **Gidböle** Sweden
161 F2 **Gidda** Ethiopia
86 C5 **Giddings** Texas USA
120 K5 **Gideå** Sweden
120 K5 **Gideälven** *watercourse* Sweden
218 E2 **Gidgealpa** SA Australia
217 J4 **Gidgi Lakes** WA Australia
161 F2 **Gīdolē** Ethiopia
126 F3 **Gien** France
127 J2 **Giengen an der Brenz** Germany
132 B3 **Giera** Romania
123 K5 **Gierkiny** Poland
120 J4 **Giertsjaure** *lake* Sweden
Giesecke Isfjord *see* **Kangerlussuaq** Greenland
127 I1 **Gießen** Germany
124 D1 **Gieten** Netherlands
125 K1 **Gietrzwałd** Poland
142 F5 **Gifford** East Lothian Scotland UK
77 Q7 **Gifford, Lac** *lake* Quebec Canada
212 D8 **Gifford Creek** WA Australia
75 N5 **Gift Lake** Alberta Canada
193 H4 **Gifu** Japan
182 D4 **Gigant** Russian Federation
88 D3 **Gigantes** Mexico
142 C5 **Gigha** *island* Scotland UK
132 C4 **Ghighera** Romania
131 D5 **Giglio, Isola del** *island* Italy
131 C6 **Giglio, Punta del** *cape* Sardinia Italy
129 H2 **Gignac** France
179 I3 **Gījī** Iran
128 D2 **Gijón** Spain
106 F6 **Gil** Argentina
219 I3 **Gil Gil** *watercourse* NSW Australia
84 F4 **Gila** *watercourse* Arkansas USA
84 F4 **Gila Bend** Arizona USA
182 F7 **Gīlān** *admin. area* Iran
178 F2 **Gīlān-e Gharb** Iran
214 F4 **Gilbert** *watercourse* Qld Australia
78 J6 **Gilbert** *watercourse* Newfoundland and Labrador Canada
84 G4 **Gilbert** Arizona USA
86 F4 **Gilbert** Louisiana USA
222 1 **Gilbert Islands** Kiribati
52 N8 **Gilbert Ridge** *underwater feature* Pacific Ocean
214 G5 **Gilbert River** Qld Australia
53 Q2 **Gilbert Seamount** *underwater feature* Pacific Ocean
102 C5 **Gilbués** Brazil
81 Q2 **Gilby** North Dakota USA
130 D2 **Gilching** Germany
163 G3 **Gilé** Mozambique
216 F4 **Giles, Lake** WA Australia
214 B7 **Giles, Mount** NT Australia
156 D3 **Gilf Kébir Plateau** *plain* Egypt
143 F2 **Gilford** Banbridge Northern Ireland UK
219 J3 **Gilgai** NSW Australia
179 M2 **Gilgit** Pakistan
179 M2 **Gilgit** *watercourse* Pakistan
219 I4 **Gilgooma** NSW Australia
218 H5 **Gilgunnia** NSW Australia
197 G6 **Gilimanuk** Indonesia
122 D3 **Gilja** Norway
143 D2 **Gill, Lough** *lake* Ireland
164 5b **Gill Point** *cape* St Helena
122 G4 **Gilleleje** Denmark
217 I3 **Gillen, Lake** WA Australia
218 C5 **Gilles, Lake** SA Australia
221 C6 **Gillespies Beach** New Zealand
86 F3 **Gillett** Arkansas USA
82 G4 **Gillett** Wisconsin USA
81 M4 **Gillette** Wyoming USA
120 I5 **Gillhov** Sweden
214 F6 **Gilliat** Qld Australia
214 F6 **Gilliat** *watercourse* Qld Australia
77 V5 **Gilling** Newfoundland and Labrador Canada
216 E5 **Gillingarra** WA Australia
139 E3 **Gillingham** Dorset England UK
139 H3 **Gillingham** Medway England UK
59 E2 **Gillock Island** Antarctica
216 G6 **Gilmore Rocks** *mountain* WA Australia
83 M4 **Gilmour** Ontario Canada
73 L7 **Gilmour Island** Nunavut Canada
161 E2 **Gilo** *watercourse* Ethiopia
80 E8 **Gilroy** California USA
216 D2 **Gilroyd** WA Australia
214 B2 **Gilruth, Mount** NT Australia
120 G5 **Gilså** Norway
199 G5 **Giluwe, Mount** Papua New Guinea
138 D3 **Gilwern** Monmouthshire Wales UK
120 J5 **Gim** Sweden
126 E5 **Gimat** France
161 F2 **Gimbī** Ethiopia
130 B3 **Gimel** Switzerland
159 F3 **Gimi** Nigeria
109 13 **Gimie, Mount** *volcano* St Lucia
121 R5 **Gimoly** Russian Federation
126 E5 **Gimone** *watercourse* France
126 E5 **Gimont** France
198 A4 **Gimpu** Indonesia
219 I4 **Gin Gin** NSW Australia
219 J1 **Gin Gin** Qld Australia
161 F2 **Ginchi** Ethiopia
157 F4 **Ginda** Eritrea
216 G5 **Gindalbie** WA Australia
131 C6 **Ginepro, Punta** *cape* Sardinia Italy
216 D5 **Gingin** WA Australia
195 J5 **Gingoog** Philippines
161 G2 **Ginir** Ethiopia
131 G6 **Ginosa** Italy
128 C2 **Ginzo de Lima** Spain
194 E3 **Gio Linh** Vietnam
131 E6 **Gioia dei Marsi** Italy
131 F7 **Gioia Tauro** Italy
142 B2 **Giosla** Na h-Eileanan Siar Scotland UK
133 D6 **Gioura** *island* Greece
131 G6 **Giovinazzo** Italy
139 I2 **Gipping** Suffolk England UK
212 C7 **Giralia** WA Australia
187 E7 **Girar** Maharashtra India
83 K6 **Girard** Ohio USA
162 B3 **Giraúl** *watercourse* Angola
136 F5 **Giresun** Turkey
136 F5 **Giresun** *admin. area* Turkey
199 H4 **Girgir, Cape** Papua New Guinea
160 B3 **Giri** *watercourse* Democratic Republic of Congo
128 E4 **Giribaile, Embalse de** *lake* Spain
120 I4 **Girisjön** *lake* Sweden
132 B2 **Girişu de Criş** Romania
123 L5 **Girkalnis** Lithuania
132 E2 **Girleni** Romania
187 D7 **Girna** *watercourse* Maharashtra India
127 H3 **Giromagny** France
100 C3 **Girón** Colombia
129 H3 **Girona** Spain
126 D4 **Gironde** *watercourse* France
126 E5 **Girou** *watercourse* France
218 H5 **Girral** NSW Australia
141 G2 **Girsby** Darlington England UK
215 I5 **Giru** Qld Australia
107 H4 **Giruá** Brazil
142 D5 **Girvan** South Ayrshire Scotland UK
121 R5 **Girvas** Russian Federation
220 H4 **Gisborne** New Zealand
220 G4 **Gisborne** *admin. area* New Zealand
79 K9 **Gisborne Lake** Newfoundland and Labrador Canada
160 D4 **Gisenyi** Rwanda
122 G4 **Gislaved** Sweden
126 E2 **Gisors** France
131 F5 **Gissi** Italy
123 J3 **Gisslingö** *island* Sweden
160 D4 **Gitega** Burundi
179 M2 **Gittidas** *watercourse* Pakistan
130 C3 **Giubiasco** Switzerland
130 E5 **Giulianova** Italy
132 E3 **Giurgiu** *admin. area* Romania
122 E5 **Give** Denmark
124 C2 **Givet** France
127 G4 **Givors** France
162 F4 **Giyani** South Africa
161 F2 **Giyon** Ethiopia
125 I1 **Giżałki** Poland
222 8 **Gizo** *island* Solomon Islands
123 K5 **Giżycko** Poland
120 E5 **Gjemnes** Norway
120 F6 **Gjendebu** Norway
120 E6 **Gjerde** Norway
122 C2 **Gjerdvik** Norway
120 H3 **Gjerøya** *island* Norway
122 F4 **Gjerrild** Denmark
122 G2 **Gjesåssjøen** *lake* Norway
120 F5 **Gjevilvatn** *lake* Norway
122 E3 **Gjeving** Norway
120 H4 **Gjevsjøen** *lake* Sweden
133 B5 **Gjirokastër** Albania
73 J5 **Gjoa Haven** Nunavut Canada
120 inset **Gjögur** Iceland
120 inset **Gjögurtá** *cape* Iceland
120 F5 **Gjølme** Norway
120 F5 **Gjøra** Norway
120 G5 **Gjota** Norway
122 F2 **Gjøvik** Norway
133 B5 **Gjugjë** Albania
79 I9 **Glace Bay** Nova Scotia Canada
80 G1 **Glacier** British Columbia Canada
74 C3 **Glacier Bay** Alaska USA
80 E2 **Glacier Peak** *volcano* Washington USA
142 C3 **Glackour** Highland Scotland UK
81 P7 **Glade** Kansas USA
86 D4 **Gladewater** Texas USA
120 G4 **Gladstad** Norway
215 K7 **Gladstone** Qld Australia
218 D5 **Gladstone** SA Australia
219 R10 **Gladstone** Tas. Australia
221 F5 **Gladstone** New Zealand
82 H4 **Gladstone** Michigan USA
75 R5 **Gladue Lake** Saskatchewan Canada
82 I5 **Gladwin** Michigan USA
138 D3 **Glais** Swansea Wales UK
120 G5 **Glåma** *watercourse* Norway
142 E4 **Glamis** Angus Scotland UK
84 E4 **Glamis** California USA
130 G4 **Glamoč** Bosnia and Herzegovina
120 G5 **Glåmos** Norway
124 D3 **Glan** *watercourse* Germany
143 C5 **Glan** Ireland
195 J6 **Glan** Philippines
122 H3 **Glan** *lake* Sweden
143 C5 **Glandart** Ireland
218 H3 **Glandore** NSW Australia
143 E2 **Glangevlin** Ireland
127 I3 **Glarus** Switzerland
138 D2 **Glasbury** Powys Wales UK
142 D3 **Glascarnoch, Loch** *lake* Scotland UK
81 Q7 **Glasco** Kansas USA
143 G2 **Glasdrumman** Newry and Mourne Northern Ireland UK
72 I9 **Glasglow** Montana USA
142 D5 **Glasgow** City of Glasgow Scotland UK
82 I8 **Glasgow** Kentucky USA
82 E7 **Glasgow** Missouri USA
81 L2 **Glasgow** Montana USA
83 L8 **Glasgow** Virginia USA
75 S8 **Glasnevin** Saskatchewan Canada
142 D3 **Glass, Loch** *lake* Scotland UK
83 N7 **Glassboro** New Jersey USA
140 D2 **Glasserton** Dumfries and Galloway Scotland UK
140 F3 **Glasson** Lancashire England UK
138 E3 **Glastonbury** Somerset England UK
143 G2 **Glastry** Ards Northern Ireland UK
86 A2 **Glazier** Texas USA
134 L7 **Glazov** Russian Federation
86 G2 **Gleason** Tennessee USA
154 E5 **Gleïbat Boukenni** Mauritania
75 O7 **Gleichen** Alberta Canada
125 H4 **Gleisdorf** Austria
139 H2 **Glemsford** Suffolk England UK
140 A3 **Glen** Ireland
139 G2 **Glen** *watercourse* England UK
216 H2 **Glen Ayle** WA Australia
142 D3 **Glen Cannich** *valley* Scotland UK
214 B7 **Glen Helen Resort** NT Australia
142 E5 **Glen Ho** Scottish Borders Scotland UK
219 J3 **Glen Innes** NSW Australia
81 O3 **Glen Ullin** North Dakota USA
218 F8 **Glenaire** Vic. Australia
143 G2 **Glenarm** Larne Northern Ireland UK
143 F2 **Glenavy** Lisburn Northern Ireland UK
143 E5 **Glenawilling** Ireland
140 A4 **Glenballyvally** Ireland
142 C5 **Glenbarr** Argyll and Bute Scotland UK
142 C5 **Glenbatrick** Argyll and Bute Scotland UK
75 V8 **Glenboro** Manitoba Canada
142 C4 **Glenborrodale** Highland Scotland UK
140 B4 **Glenbrien** Ireland
142 B3 **Glenbrittle** Highland Scotland UK
216 E2 **Glenburgh** WA Australia
218 G7 **Glenburn** Vic. Australia
75 R6 **Glenbush** Saskatchewan Canada
142 C4 **Glenbyre** Highland Scotland UK
219 J3 **Glencoe** NSW Australia
214 F4 **Glencoe** Qld Australia
83 K5 **Glencoe** Ontario Canada
84 F4 **Glendale** Arizona USA
84 C3 **Glendale** California USA
84 E2 **Glendale** Nevada USA
80 D5 **Glendale** Oregon USA
80 I8 **Glendale** Utah USA
82 H5 **Glendale** Wisconsin USA
218 B4 **Glendambo** SA Australia
215 J6 **Glenden** Qld Australia
143 D4 **Glendine Bridge** Ireland
218 E7 **Glendinning** Vic. Australia
81 M3 **Glendive** Montana USA
81 M5 **Glendo** Wyoming USA
81 M5 **Glendo Reservoir** Wyoming USA
75 P5 **Glendon** Alberta Canada
140 A1 **Glendooskert** Ireland
101 G3 **Glendor Mountains** Guyana
140 D1 **Glendoune** South Ayrshire Scotland UK
143 E1 **Gleneely** Ireland
218 E7 **Glenelg** *watercourse* Vic. Australia
140 A2 **Glenfern** Omagh Northern Ireland UK
81 P3 **Glenfield** North Dakota USA
143 D4 **Glengarra Bridge** Ireland
143 C5 **Glengarriff** Ireland
218 D1 **Glengyle** Qld Australia
221 E5 **Glenhope** New Zealand
143 C2 **Glenlara** Ireland
143 C2 **Glenlassra River** Ireland
142 F4 **Glenlee** Angus Scotland UK
142 D6 **Glenluce** Dumfries and Galloway Scotland UK
219 J3 **Glenlyon** Qld Australia
143 E4 **Glenmore** Ireland
219 I2 **Glenmorgan** Qld Australia
143 D4 **Glennahulla Cross** Ireland
72 E6 **Glennallen** Alaska USA
143 E4 **Glennanore** Ireland
143 E4 **Glennaskagh** Ireland
80 H5 **Glenns Ferry** Idaho USA
87 K5 **Glennville** Georgia USA
142 E5 **Glenochar** South Lanarkshire Scotland UK
143 G2 **Glenoe** Larne Northern Ireland UK
74 F4 **Glenora** British Columbia Canada
218 F7 **Glenorchy** Vic. Australia
221 C7 **Glenorchy** New Zealand
214 F4 **Glenore** Qld Australia
140 F2 **Glenridding** Cumbria England UK
142 C5 **Glenrisdell** Argyll and Bute Scotland UK
143 E2 **Glenroan** Strabane Northern Ireland UK
81 M5 **Glenrock** Wyoming USA
142 E4 **Glenrothes** Fife Scotland UK
218 H7 **Glenrowan** Vic. Australia
213 I4 **Glenroy** WA Australia
221 E6 **Glenroy** *watercourse* New Zealand
83 O5 **Glens Falls** New York USA
142 F4 **Glensaugh** Aberdeenshire Scotland UK
142 E6 **Glensone** Dumfries and Galloway Scotland UK
143 D2 **Glenties** Ireland
143 C3 **Glentrasna** Ireland
142 D5 **Glenvernoch** Dumfries and Galloway Scotland UK
219 K1 **Glenwood** Qld Australia
85 H4 **Glenwood** New Mexico USA
84 G1 **Glenwood** Utah USA
127 I3 **Gletsch** Switzerland
120 inset **Glettinganes** *cape* Iceland
122 G5 **Glewitz** Germany
133 C6 **Glifádha** Greece
132 C3 **Glimboca** Romania
143 C4 **Glin** Ireland
125 K1 **Glinojeck** Poland
143 C3 **Glinsce** Ireland
143 D3 **Glinsk** Ireland
139 G2 **Glinton** Peterborough England UK
120 I5 **Glissjöberg** Sweden
120 F6 **Glittertinden** *mountain* Norway
125 J2 **Gliwice** Poland
84 G4 **Globe** Arizona USA
133 B5 **Globočičko Ezero** *lake* Macedonia
132 E2 **Glodeni** Moldova
125 H4 **Gloggnitz** Austria
125 I2 **Głogów** Poland
120 H3 **Glomfjord** Norway
122 F2 **Glomma** *watercourse* Norway
120 K4 **Glommersträsk** Sweden
122 E2 **Glonde** *lake* Norway
124 F3 **Glonn** *watercourse* Germany
120 L5 **Gloppet** *bay* Finland
50 N4 **Gloria Ridge** *underwater feature* Atlantic Ocean
164 6a **Glorieuses, Îles** *islands* Îles Éparses
141 G3 **Glossop** Derbyshire England UK
86 F5 **Gloster** Mississippi USA
120 H5 **Glöte** Sweden
139 E3 **Gloucester** Gloucestershire England UK
83 P5 **Gloucester** Massachusetts USA
108 B6 **Gloucester, Cabo** *cape* Chile
215 J5 **Gloucester Island** Qld Australia
139 F3 **Gloucestershire** *admin. area* England UK
127 H3 **Glovelier** Switzerland
79 J8 **Glover Island** Newfoundland and Labrador Canada
83 N5 **Gloversville** New York USA
79 K8 **Glovertown** Newfoundland and Labrador Canada
124 G1 **Glöwen** Germany
125 J2 **Głowno** Poland
182 D4 **Glubokiy** Russian Federation
183 N3 **Glubokoye** Kazakhstan
122 E5 **Glud** Denmark
136 D2 **Glusha** Belarus
125 H1 **Głusko** Poland
214 D4 **Glyde** *watercourse* NT Australia
133 B6 **Glykí** Greece
138 D3 **Glyncorwg** Neath Port Talbot Wales UK
130 E3 **Gmunden** Austria
214 E7 **Gnallan-a-Gea** *watercourse* Qld Australia
216 C1 **Gnaraloo** WA Australia
120 J5 **Gnarp** Sweden
212 B7 **Gnarraloo Bay** WA Australia
125 G4 **Gnesau** Austria
122 F4 **Gniben** *cape* Denmark
125 J1 **Gniew** Poland
125 I1 **Gniezno** Poland
132 B4 **Gnjilane** Kosovo
124 G5 **Gnocchetta** Italy
Gnoorganbin *see* **Moreton Island** Australia
216 F6 **Gnowangerup** WA Australia
187 D8 **Goa** *admin. area* India
195 I4 **Goa** Philippines
181 G3 **Goalpara** Assam India
197 H6 **Goang** Indonesia
158 D3 **Goaso** Ghana
109 18 **Goat Point** Antigua and Barbuda
141 H2 **Goathland** North Yorkshire England UK
161 F2 **Goba** Ethiopia
162 C4 **Gobabis** Namibia
178 F2 **Gōbān** Iraq
161 G2 **Gobele** *watercourse* Ethiopia
100 A6 **Gobernador, Punta** *cape* Peru
108 B3 **Gobernador Costa** Argentina
106 F4 **Gobernador Crespo** Argentina
106 E6 **Gobernador Duval** Argentina
108 B4 **Gobernador Gregores** Argentina
108 B5 **Gobernador Mayer** Argentina
108 C4 **Gobernador Moyano** Argentina
107 G4 **Gobernador Virasoro** Argentina
190 E4 **Gobi** *desert* Mongolia
187 F6 **Gobindpur** Orissa India
133 E6 **Göçbeyli** Turkey
121 M2 **Goccadanjávri** *lake* Norway
124 D2 **Goch** Germany
162 C4 **Gochas** Namibia
127 L1 **Göda** Germany
139 G3 **Godalming** Surrey England UK
187 E7 **Godawari** *watercourse* Andhra Pradesh India
77 V8 **Godbout** Quebec Canada
79 E8 **Godbout** *watercourse* Quebec Canada
186 G6 **Godda** Jharkhand India
81 Q8 **Goddard** Kansas USA
161 G2 **Godē** Ethiopia
161 F5 **Godegode** Tanzania
120 H4 **Godejorda** Norway
59 B2 **Godel Iceport** Antarctica
139 H5 **Goderville** France
82 F7 **Godfrey** Illinois USA
186 C6 **Godhra** Gujarat India
139 F3 **Godington** Oxfordshire England UK
161 H2 **Godinlabe** Somalia
221 D6 **Godley** *watercourse* New Zealand
86 C4 **Godley** Texas USA
139 H3 **Godmersham** Kent England UK
106 D5 **Godoy Cruz** Argentina
130 G3 **Gödre** Hungary
76 I4 **Gods** *watercourse* Manitoba Canada
76 H5 **Gods Lake** Manitoba Canada
76 H5 **Gods Lake Narrows** Manitoba Canada
76 L1 **Gods Mercy, Bay of** Nunavut Canada
59 E2 **Godspeed Nunataks** *range* Antarctica
125 L2 **Godziszów** Poland
199 G6 **Goe** Papua New Guinea
124 B2 **Goedereede** Netherlands
73 L8 **Goéland, Lac au** *lake* Quebec Canada
73 M7 **Goélands, Lac aux** *lake* Quebec Canada
124 B2 **Goes** Netherlands
83 K3 **Gogama** Ontario Canada
215 K7 **Gogango** Qld Australia
82 G3 **Gogebic, Lake** Michigan USA
82 G3 **Gogebic Range** *range* Michigan USA
123 N2 **Gogland, Ostrov** *island* Russian Federation
213 H5 **Gogo** WA Australia
163 F4 **Gogói** Mozambique
199 H5 **Gogol** *watercourse* Papua New Guinea
125 J2 **Gogolin** Poland
132 C3 **Gogoşu** Romania
158 E2 **Gogounou** Benin
160 D2 **Gogrial** Sudan
124 F1 **Göhrde** Germany
104 D2 **Goiabal** Brazil
103 B6 **Goianésia** Brazil
103 B7 **Goiânia** Brazil
103 B6 **Goiás** Brazil
103 B7 **Goiás** *admin. area* Brazil
103 C6 **Goiás, Serra Geral de** *range* Brazil
103 B7 **Goiatuba** Brazil
122 G4 **Göinge** *region* Sweden
124 C2 **Goirle** Netherlands
124 F5 **Goito** Italy
161 F2 **Gojeb** *watercourse* Ethiopia
179 L3 **Gojra** Pakistan
125 J1 **Gójsk** Poland
187 D8 **Gokak** Karnataka India
133 D5 **Gökçeada** *island* Turkey
133 F6 **Gökçek** Turkey
182 G6 **Gökleńguýy Şorluk** *lake* Turkmenistan
133 E7 **Gökova Körfezi** *bay* Turkey
120 L4 **Göksjön** *lake* Sweden
136 F5 **Göksu Nehri** *watercourse* Turkey
122 E2 **Gol** Norway
218 F5 **Gol Gol** NSW Australia
130 G3 **Gola** Croatia
186 E5 **Gola Gokaran Nath** Uttar Pradesh India
143 D1 **Gola Island** Ireland
181 G3 **Golaghat** Assam India
125 I1 **Golce** Poland
133 F6 **Gölcük** *watercourse* Turkey
80 C5 **Gold Beach** Oregon USA
74 J7 **Gold Bridge** British Columbia Canada
158 D4 **Gold Coast** West Africa
74 H8 **Gold River** British Columbia Canada
74 M7 **Golden** British Columbia Canada
83 M4 **Golden** Ontario Canada
220 E5 **Golden Bay** New Zealand
86 F6 **Golden Meadow** Louisiana USA
75 Q7 **Golden Prairie** Saskatchewan Canada
80 E4 **Goldendale** Washington USA
84 D2 **Goldfield** Nevada USA
75 Q3 **Goldfields** Saskatchewan Canada
82 J2 **Goldie Lake** Ontario Canada
76 E4 **Goldsand Lake** Manitoba Canada
85 K5 **Goldsmith** Texas USA
86 B5 **Goldthwaite** Texas USA
161 F2 **Golecha** Ethiopia
182 G6 **Golestān** *admin. area* Iran
84 C3 **Goleta** California USA
90 D5 **Golfito** Costa Rica
133 F7 **Gölgeli, Dağları** *range* Turkey
106 E3 **Golgota** Argentina
133 F7 **Gölhisar** Turkey
130 F4 **Goli** *island* Croatia
160 E3 **Goli** Uganda
123 N4 **Goliševa** Latvia
127 L3 **Golnik** Slovenia
195 I4 **Golo** *island* Philippines
188 D1 **Golog Shan** *range* Jiangsu China
159 H3 **Golongosso** Central African Republic
182 C5 **Golovinka** Russian Federation
132 F3 **Goloviţa, Lacul** *lake* Romania
178 G2 **Golpāyegān** Iran
133 G5 **Gölpazarı** Turkey
142 E3 **Golspie** Highland Scotland UK
130 G4 **Golubić** Croatia
81 N3 **Golva** North Dakota USA
136 G5 **Gölyurt Geçidi** *pass* Turkey
124 G1 **Golzow** Germany
160 E4 **Goma** Uganda
128 E3 **Gómara** Spain
186 E5 **Gomati** *watercourse* Uttar Pradesh India
163 G2 **Gomba** Mozambique
160 D3 **Gombari** Democratic Republic of Congo
159 G2 **Gombe** Nigeria
159 G3 **Gombe** *admin. area* Nigeria
160 E4 **Gombe** *watercourse* Tanzania
133 F7 **Gömbe** Turkey
159 G2 **Gombi** Nigeria
130 D5 **Gombo** Italy
142 B4 **Gometra House** Highland Scotland UK
88 E3 **Gómez Farías** Mexico
88 E3 **Gómez Palacio** Mexico
198 C4 **Gomumu** *island* Indonesia
179 I2 **Gonābād** Iran
91 F3 **Gonaïves** Haiti
135 AA7 **Gonam** *watercourse* Russian Federation
91 F3 **Gonâve, Île de la** *island* Haiti
182 G6 **Gonbad-e Kāvūs** Iran
132 B1 **Gönc** Hungary
186 E5 **Gonda** Uttar Pradesh India
187 C7 **Gondal** Gujarat India
156 F5 **Gonder** Ethiopia
136 G5 **Gonderme Gecidi** *pass* Turkey
159 H3 **Gondey** Chad
187 E7 **Gondiya** Maharashtra India
158 B3 **Gondolahun** Liberia
128 B2 **Gondomar** Spain
127 G2 **Gondrecourt** France
133 G7 **Gönen** Turkey
133 E5 **Gönen** Turkey
162 C3 **Gonga** Angola
181 G3 **Gongb ujiangda** Xizang Zizhiqu China
188 F4 **Gongcheng** Guangxi Zhuangzu Zizhiqu China
181 G3 **Gonggar** Xizang Zizhiqu China
189 G3 **Gongjiang** Jiangxi China
181 G3 **Gongka** Xizang Zizhiqu China
184 G4 **Gongliu** Xinjiang Uygur Zizhiqu China
103 E6 **Gongogi** *watercourse* Brazil
159 G2 **Gongola** *watercourse* Nigeria
159 F5 **Gongoúe** Gabon
181 G2 **Gongtang** Xizang Zizhiqu China
191 J4 **Gongzhuling** Jilin China
131 C7 **Gonnesa** Sardinia Italy
162 E6 **Gonubie** South Africa
81 R3 **Gonvick** Minnesota USA
195 I3 **Gonzaga** Philippines
84 B2 **Gonzales** California USA
86 C6 **Gonzales** Texas USA
219 I5 **Goobang** NSW Australia
83 M8 **Goochland** Virginia USA
86 H3 **Good Hope** Alabama USA
162 C6 **Good Hope, Cape of** South Africa
74 G3 **Good Hope Lake** British Columbia Canada
59 I2 **Goodenough, Cape** Antarctica
199 I6 **Goodenough Island** Papua New Guinea
75 T7 **Goodeve** Saskatchewan Canada
80 H5 **Gooding** Idaho USA
164 7b **Goodlands** Mauritius
86 H2 **Goodlettsville** Tennessee USA
86 G4 **Goodman** Mississippi USA
72 C7 **Goodnews Bay** Alaska USA
219 H3 **Goodooga** NSW Australia
214 B2 **Goodparla** NT Australia
81 O3 **Goodrich** North Dakota USA
75 T8 **Goodwater** Saskatchewan Canada
87 H4 **Goodwater** Alabama USA
85 L2 **Goodwell** Oklahoma USA
138 C2 **Goodwick** Pembrokeshire Wales UK
78 E5 **Goodwood** *watercourse* Quebec Canada
124 C2 **Gooik** Belgium
141 H3 **Goole** East Riding of Yorkshire England UK
218 G5 **Goolgowi** NSW Australia
219 I5 **Goolma** NSW Australia
219 I5 **Gooloogong** NSW Australia
218 D6 **Goolwa** SA Australia
214 B2 **Goomadeer** *watercourse* NT Australia
216 E5 **Goomalling** WA Australia
216 F5 **Goomarin** WA Australia
219 J3 **Goondiwindi** Qld Australia
216 G4 **Goongarrie** WA Australia
216 G4 **Goongarrie, Lake** WA Australia
138 B4 **Goonhavern** Cornwall England UK
124 D1 **Goor** Netherlands
216 E5 **Goorly, Lake** WA Australia
78 H6 **Goose** *watercourse* Newfoundland and Labrador Canada
78 H6 **Goose Bay** Newfoundland and Labrador Canada
76 H3 **Goose Creek** Manitoba Canada
87 K4 **Goose Creek** South Carolina USA
109 7 **Goose Green** Falkland Islands
80 E6 **Goose Lake** California USA
138 C4 **Gooseham** Cornwall England UK
127 I2 **Göppingen** Germany
128 E5 **Gor** Spain
125 I2 **Góra** Poland
125 K1 **Góra** Poland
187 E6 **Gorakhpur** Madhya Pradesh India
186 F5 **Gorakhpur** Uttar Pradesh India
219 J4 **Goran, Lake** NSW Australia
130 H5 **Goražde** Bosnia and Herzegovina
182 D1 **Gorchukha** Russian Federation
90 D2 **Gorda, Punta** *cape* Cuba
90 D4 **Gorda, Punta** *cape* Nicaragua
80 C6 **Gorda, Punta** *cape* California USA
87 M7 **Gorda Cay** *island* Bahamas
133 F6 **Gördes** Turkey
216 E7 **Gordon** *watercourse* WA Australia
87 J4 **Gordon** Georgia USA
81 N5 **Gordon** Nebraska USA
219 R11 **Gordon, Lake** Tas. Australia
213 J5 **Gordon Downs** WA Australia
75 P4 **Gordon Lake** Alberta Canada
74 L5 **Gordondale** Alberta Canada
215 H4 **Gordonvale** Qld Australia
214 A4 **Gordy** *watercourse* NT Australia
159 H3 **Goré** Chad
161 F2 **Gore** Ethiopia
221 C8 **Gore** New Zealand
214 E4 **Gore Point** Qld Australia
72 D7 **Gore Point** Alaska USA
86 B4 **Goree** Texas USA
82 G8 **Goreville** Illinois USA
143 F4 **Gorey** Wexford Ireland
179 I3 **Gorg** Iran
158 D2 **Gorgadji** Burkina Faso
182 G7 **Gorgān** Iran
126 F5 **Gorges** France
100 B4 **Gorgona, Isla** *island* Colombia
130 C5 **Gorgona, Isola di** *island* Italy
156 F5 **Gorgora** Ethiopia
159 G2 **Gorgoram** Nigeria
132 F3 **Gorgova, Lacul** *lake* Romania
85 M1 **Gorham** Kansas USA
83 P4 **Gorham** New Hampshire USA
182 D5 **Gori** Georgia
139 F3 **Goring** Oxfordshire England UK
124 G5 **Gorizia** Italy
132 C3 **Gorj** *admin. area* Romania
186 F5 **Gorkha** Nepal
134 O5 **Gorki** Russian Federation
182 E1 **Gorki** Russian Federation
134 J7 **Gor'kovskoye Vodokhranilishche** *lake* Russian Federation
183 M3 **Gor'koye, Ozero** *lake* Russian Federation
183 M3 **Gor'koye Peresheyechnoye** *lake* Russian Federation
125 K3 **Gorlice** Poland
127 L1 **Görlitz** Germany
124 F1 **Gorlosen** Germany
86 B4 **Gorman** Texas USA
186 E5 **Gormi** Madhya Pradesh India
127 L4 **Gornje Jelenje** Croatia
125 I4 **Gornji Petrovci** Slovenia
183 O3 **Gorno-Altaysk** Russian Federation
193 I1 **Gornozavodsk** Russian Federation
183 N3 **Gornyak** Russian Federation
191 M2 **Gornyy** Russian Federation
182 E3 **Gornyy** Russian Federation
182 E3 **Gornyy Balykley** Russian Federation
159 I3 **Goro** *watercourse* Central African Republic
124 G5 **Goro** Italy
132 F1 **Gorodok** Ukraine
218 E7 **Goroke** Vic. Australia
182 D2 **Gorokhovets** Russian Federation
158 D2 **Gorom Gorom** Burkina Faso
198 D5 **Gorong** *island* Indonesia
198 D5 **Gorong, Kepulauan** *islands* Indonesia
163 F3 **Gorongosa** Mozambique
163 F3 **Gorongoza, Monte** *mountain* Mozambique
198 B3 **Gorontalo** Indonesia
198 B3 **Gorontalo** *admin. area* Indonesia
108 B5 **Gorra, Cerro** *mountain* Chile
124 D1 **Gorredijk** Netherlands
140 E3 **Gorsedd** Flintshire Wales UK
138 C3 **Gorseinon** Swansea Wales UK
143 D3 **Gort** Ireland
143 C4 **Gortaheera** Ireland
143 D1 **Gortahork** Ireland
138 A2 **Gorteens** Ireland
143 D3 **Gorteeny** Ireland
143 D3 **Gortfree** Ireland
143 C5 **Gortgarriff** Ireland
143 C2 **Gortmore** Ireland
143 D5 **Gortnacrue** Ireland
140 A4 **Gortnagan** Ireland
143 C4 **Gortnaleaha** Ireland
142 B4 **Gorton** Highland Scotland UK
143 D4 **Gortroe** Ireland
143 D3 **Gortskeagh** Ireland
143 C3 **Gorumna Island** Ireland
132 F4 **Gorun** Bulgaria
120 I5 **Görviksjön** *lake* Sweden
193 J2 **Goryacheye, Ozero** *lake* Russian Federation
190 F2 **Goryachinsk (Gremyachinsk)** Russian Federation
123 O5 **Goryany** Belarus
124 G1 **Görzke** Germany
125 H1 **Gorzów Wielkopolski** Poland
130 D3 **Gosaldo** Italy
139 G2 **Gosberton** Lincolnshire England UK
199 I6 **Goschen Strait** Papua New Guinea
122 H5 **Gościno** Poland
139 H3 **Gosfield** Essex England UK
219 J5 **Gosford** NSW Australia
140 E2 **Gosforth** Cumbria England UK
141 G1 **Gosforth** Tyne and Wear England UK
82 I6 **Goshen** Indiana USA

193 I3 **Goshogawara** Japan
179 J4 **Gosht-e 'Olyā** Iran
80 H6 **Goshute Lake** Nevada USA
139 F4 **Gosport** Hampshire England UK
120 E5 **Gossa** *island* Norway
154 C6 **Gossas** Senegal
214 C5 **Gosse** *watercourse* NT Australia
155 F5 **Gossi** Mali
160 D2 **Gossinga** Sudan
133 B5 **Gostivar** Macedonia
125 J2 **Gostków** Poland
125 I2 **Gostyń** Poland
125 J1 **Gostynin** Poland
122 F4 **Göteborg (Gothenburg)** Sweden
159 G3 **Gotel Mountains** *range* Nigeria
127 J1 **Gotha** Germany
123 J4 **Gothem** Sweden
Gothenburg *see* **Göteborg** Sweden
81 O6 **Gothenburg** Nebraska USA
155 G6 **Gothèye** Niger
123 J4 **Gotland** *island* Sweden
109 1c **Goto Meer** *lake* Netherlands Antilles
127 L3 **Gotovlje** Slovenia
123 J3 **Gotska Sandön** *island* Sweden
192 G4 **Gōtsu** Japan
127 I1 **Göttingen** Germany
120 K5 **Gottne** Sweden
158 C3 **Gouan** *watercourse* Côte d'Ivoire
124 C1 **Gouda** Netherlands
154 D6 **Goudiry** Senegal
155 I6 **Goudoumaria** Niger
106 F5 **Goudra** Argentina
158 C3 **Gouéké** Guinea
75 O6 **Gough Lake** Alberta Canada
73 L9 **Gouin, Réservoir** Quebec Canada
158 E3 **Gouka** Benin
219 I6 **Goulburn** NSW Australia
218 G7 **Goulburn** *watercourse* Vic. Australia
86 F4 **Gould** Arkansas USA
216 E2 **Gould, Mount** WA Australia
59 O1 **Gould Coast** Antarctica
158 C2 **Goulia** Côte d'Ivoire
159 I2 **Goumbatou** Chad
154 E6 **Goumbou** Mali
159 G3 **Gouna** Cameroon
159 I3 **Gounda** *watercourse* Central African Republic
154 F5 **Goundam** Mali
159 H3 **Goundi** Chad
159 H3 **Gounou-Gaya** Chad
189 I2 **Gouqi Dao** *island* Zhejiang China
155 G1 **Gouraya** Algeria
154 D6 **Gouraye** Mauritania
158 D2 **Gourcy** Burkina Faso
126 E4 **Gourdon** France
155 I6 **Gouré** Niger
126 C2 **Gourin** France
82 I2 **Gourlay Lake** Ontario Canada
139 I5 **Gournay-en-Bray** France
155 J5 **Gouro** Chad
156 B4 **Gouro** Chad
128 C3 **Gouveia** Portugal
83 N4 **Gouverneur** New York USA
127 G1 **Gouvy** Belgium
109 10a **Gouyave** Grenada
126 F3 **Gouzon** France
190 F3 **Gov-ugtaal** Mongolia
214 D2 **Gove Peninsula** NT Australia
135 Al7 **Govena, Poluostrov** *peninsula* Russian Federation
75 Q8 **Govenlock** Saskatchewan Canada
103 D7 **Governador Valadares** Brazil
185 J4 **Govi-Altay** *admin. area* Mongolia
190 E4 **Govi Altayn Nuruu** Mongolia
186 F6 **Govind Ballabh Pant Sagar** *lake* Uttar Pradesh India
186 D4 **Govind Sagar** *lake* Himachal Pradesh India
190 F3 **Govisumber** *admin. area* Mongolia
219 I5 **Gowan** NSW Australia
82 E3 **Gowan** Minnesota USA
82 D7 **Gower** Missouri USA
211 inset **Gower, Mount** Lord Howe Island Australia
74 F6 **Gowgaia Bay** British Columbia Canada
122 I5 **Gowidlino** Poland
143 C3 **Gowla** Ireland
140 B4 **Gowlin** Ireland
179 K3 **Gowmal Kalay** Afghanistan
143 E3 **Gowna, Lough** *lake* Ireland
182 J6 **Gowurdak** Turkmenistan
107 G4 **Goya** Argentina
109 16 **Goyave** Guadeloupe
214 C2 **Goyder** NT Australia
218 E2 **Goyder, Lake** SA Australia
214 A2 **Goyder, Mount** NT Australia
218 D2 **Goyder Lagoon** SA Australia
133 G5 **Göynük** Turkey
159 G3 **Goyoum** Cameroon
122 E3 **Gøystvatn** *lake* Norway
159 I2 **Goz Beïda** Chad
156 C5 **Goz-Beïda** Chad
131 F8 **Gozo** *island* Malta
127 I4 **Gozzano** Italy
162 D6 **Graaff-reinet** South Africa
158 C4 **Grabo** Côte d'Ivoire
124 F1 **Grabow** Germany
122 G5 **Grabow** *bay* Germany
125 J1 **Grabów** Poland
125 L1 **Grabówka** Poland
125 J5 **Gračanica** Bosnia and Herzegovina
126 E3 **Graçay** France
80 J5 **Grace** Idaho USA
216 F6 **Grace, Lake** WA Australia
82 G3 **Grace Harbor** Michigan USA
140 B3 **Gracedieu** Ireland
83 M3 **Gracefield** Quebec Canada
140 B2 **Gracehill** Ballymena Northern Ireland UK
81 Q4 **Graceville** Minnesota USA
130 B3 **Grächen** Switzerland
90 B4 **Gracias** Honduras
90 D4 **Gracias a Dios, Cabo** *cape* Nicaragua
164 1b **Graciosa** *island* Azores
164 3d **Graciosa** *island* Canary Islands
125 I5 **Gradac** Croatia
130 H4 **Gradačac** Bosnia and Herzegovina
102 B4 **Gradaús, Serra dos** *range* Brazil
133 C5 **Gradec** Macedonia
132 E4 **Gradets** Bulgaria
133 C5 **Gradevo** Bulgaria
132 C4 **Gradište** Serbia
128 C2 **Grado** Spain
86 F3 **Grady** Arkansas USA
127 J2 **Gräfenberg** Germany
143 B4 **Graffee** Ireland
139 G4 **Graffham** West Sussex England UK
143 D2 **Graffy** Ireland
139 G2 **Grafham Water** *lake* England UK
120 H5 **Gräftåvallen** Sweden
219 K3 **Grafton** NSW Australia
81 Q2 **Grafton** North Dakota USA
83 K7 **Grafton** West Virginia USA
215 H4 **Grafton, Cape** Qld Australia
74 J4 **Graham** *watercourse* British Columbia Canada
82 F2 **Graham** Ontario Canada
87 L2 **Graham** North Carolina USA
74 E6 **Graham Island** British Columbia Canada
73 J3 **Graham Island** Nunavut Canada
75 N4 **Graham Lake** Alberta Canada
83 Q4 **Graham Lake** Maine USA
59 T2 **Graham Land** *plain* Antarctica
73 L4 **Graham Moore, Cape** Nunavut Canada
162 E6 **Grahamstown** South Africa
143 B4 **Graigue** Ireland
139 H3 **Grain, Isle of** England UK
142 B5 **Grainel** Argyll and Bute Scotland UK
81 O7 **Grainfield** Kansas USA
102 C4 **Grajaú** Brazil
102 C4 **Grajaú** *watercourse* Brazil
125 L1 **Grajewo** Poland
122 E5 **Gram** Denmark
126 E4 **Gramat** France
50 M8 **Gramberg Seamount** *underwater feature* Atlantic Ocean
86 F5 **Gramercy** Louisiana USA
185 K4 **Grampian Mountains** *range* Scotland UK
122 F2 **Gran** Norway
164 3 **Gran Canaria** *island* Canary Islands
109 9 **Gran Cayo Point** Trinidad and Tobago
100 B4 **Gran Macizo Colombiano** *range* Colombia
104 C3 **Gran Pajonal** *region* Peru
124 D5 **Gran Paradiso** *mountain* Italy
130 B4 **Gran Queyron** *mountain* France/Italy
106 E6 **Gran Salitral** *lake* Argentina
164 3d **Gran Tarajal** Canary Islands
130 B4 **Grana** *watercourse* Italy
90 C5 **Granada** Nicaragua
128 E5 **Granada** Spain
85 H6 **Granados** Mexico
143 E3 **Gránard** Ireland
120 H6 **Granåsen** Norway
120 J4 **Granåsen** Sweden
120 J4 **Granberget** Sweden
120 I5 **Granboda** Sweden
86 C4 **Granbury** Texas USA
86 C4 **Granbury, Lake** Texas USA
83 O4 **Granby** Quebec Canada
81 M6 **Granby, Lake** Colorado USA
127 G3 **Grancey** France
82 I5 **Grand** *watercourse* Michigan USA
82 D6 **Grand** *watercourse* Missouri USA
81 O4 **Grand** *watercourse* South Dakota USA
87 M7 **Grand Abaco** *island* Bahamas
109 13 **Grand Anse** St Lucia
130 B4 **Grand Argentier, Le** *mountain* France
87 L7 **Grand Bahama** *island* Bahamas
79 K9 **Grand Bank** Newfoundland and Labrador Canada
50 M5 **Grand Banks of Newfoundland** *underwater feature* Atlantic Ocean
158 D3 **Grand-Bassam** Côte d'Ivoire
82 G2 **Grand Bay** Ontario Canada
158 C4 **Grand Bérébi** Côte d'Ivoire
109 16 **Grand-Bourg** Guadeloupe
84 F2 **Grand Canyon** Arizona USA
90 D3 **Grand Cayman** *island* Cayman Islands
75 P5 **Grand Centre** Alberta Canada
105 F6 **Grand Chaco** *range* Paraguay
109 16 **Grand Cul-de-Sac Marin** *bay* Guadeloupe
79 K8 **Grand Falls-Windsor** Newfoundland and Labrador Canada
74 L8 **Grand Forks** British Columbia Canada
81 Q3 **Grand Forks** North Dakota USA
139 J4 **Grand-Fort-Philippe** France
86 G6 **Grand Gozier Island** Louisiana USA
82 H5 **Grand Haven** Michigan USA
109 16 **Grand Îlet** *island* Guadeloupe
82 H3 **Grand Island** Michigan USA
81 P6 **Grand Island** Nebraska USA
86 G6 **Grand Isle** Louisiana USA
109 7 **Grand Jason** *island* Falkland Islands
81 K7 **Grand Junction** Colorado USA
83 N3 **Grand Lac du Commissaire** *lake* Quebec Canada
79 E7 **Grand Lac Germain** *lake* Quebec Canada
158 D3 **Grand-lahou** Côte d'Ivoire
79 E10 **Grand Lake** New Brunswick Canada
78 H6 **Grand Lake** Newfoundland and Labrador Canada
81 M6 **Grand Lake** Colorado USA
86 E6 **Grand Lake** Louisiana USA
83 Q3 **Grand Lake Seboeis** Maine USA
83 M3 **Grand Lake Victoria** Quebec Canada
126 D3 **Grand-Lieu, Lac de** *lake* France
79 E10 **Grand Manan Island** New Brunswick Canada
82 I3 **Grand Marais** Michigan USA
82 F3 **Grand Marais** Minnesota USA
82 G3 **Grand Portage** Minnesota USA
86 C4 **Grand Prairie** Texas USA
74 I5 **Grand Rapids** British Columbia Canada
75 V6 **Grand Rapids** Manitoba Canada
82 I5 **Grand Rapids** Michigan USA
82 E3 **Grand Rapids** Minnesota USA
109 14 **Grand Rivière** Martinique
109 10a **Grand Roy** Grenada
101 H3 **Grand-Santi** French Guiana
91 I3 **Grand-Terre** *island* Montserrat
81 J5 **Grand Teton** *mountain* Wyoming USA
82 G8 **Grand Tower** Illinois USA
82 I4 **Grand Traverse Bay** Michigan USA
91 G2 **Grand Turk** Turks and Caicos Islands
91 G2 **Grand Turk Island** Turks and Caicos Islands
81 O1 **Grand View** Manitoba Canada
128 C2 **Grandas** Spain
108 C5 **Grande** *watercourse* Argentina
105 F5 **Grande** *watercourse* Bolivia
107 H2 **Grande** Brazil
103 C5 **Grande** *watercourse* Brazil
79 F8 **Grande** *watercourse* Quebec Canada
85 J5 **Grande** *watercourse* New Mexico USA
88 D2 **Grande** *watercourse* Texas USA
108 C5 **Grande, Bahía** *bay* Argentina
105 F4 **Grande, Baía** *bay* Brazil
101 F2 **Grande, Boca** *bay* Venezuela
100 E2 **Grande, Cayo** *island* Venezuela
107 H5 **Grande, Cuchilla** *range* Uruguay
103 C8 **Grande, Ilha** *island* Brazil
131 E8 **Grande, Isola** *island* Italy
101 I4 **Grande, Ponta** *cape* Brazil
106 D3 **Grande, Punta** *cape* Chile
106 D2 **Grande, Salar** *pan* Chile
106 E6 **Grande, Salina** *pan* Argentina
105 H5 **Grande, Serra** *range* Brazil
109 16 **Grande-Anse** Guadeloupe
74 L6 **Grande Cache** Alberta Canada
Grand Canal *see* **Da Yunhe** China
164 8 **Grande Comore (Njazidja)** *island* Comoros
102 B3 **Grande de Gurupa, Ilha** *island* Brazil
106 E2 **Grande de Jujuy, Rio** *watercourse* Argentina
107 H5 **Grande del Durazno, Cuchilla** *range* Uruguay
107 G5 **Grande Inferior, Cuchilla** *range* Uruguay
74 L5 **Grande Prairie** Alberta Canada
103 A6 **Grande Região Centro-Oeste** *region* Brazil
109 9 **Grande Riviere** Trinidad and Tobago
73 L7 **Grande Riviére de la Baleine** *watercourse* Quebec Canada
164 7b **Grande Rivière Sud Est** Mauritius
109 16 **Grande-Terre** *island* Guadeloupe
Grande Terre *see* **Mahorê** Mayotte
133 E8 **Grandes** *island* Greece
85 K5 **Grandfalls** Texas USA
59 T2 **Grandidier Channel** *strait* Antarctica
72 H6 **Grandin, Lac** *lake* Northwest Territories Canada
74 F4 **Granduc** British Columbia Canada
80 F3 **Grandview** Washington USA
139 I5 **Grandvilliers** France
129 F3 **Grañén** Spain
106 D5 **Graneros** Chile
143 D4 **Graney, Lough** *lake* Ireland
122 H2 **Grangärde** Sweden
143 E5 **Grange** Ireland
138 A2 **Grange** Ireland
143 D3 **Grange** Ireland
86 C5 **Granger** Texas USA
81 K6 **Granger** Wyoming USA
80 G4 **Grangeville** Idaho USA
120 J5 **Grängsjö** Sweden
122 E2 **Granheim** Norway
120 L3 **Granhult** Sweden
120 J5 **Graninge** Sweden
120 J5 **Graningesjön** *lake* Sweden
74 H5 **Granisle** British Columbia Canada
217 M3 **Granite Downs** SA Australia
59 L1 **Granite Harbor** *bay* Antarctica
79 J8 **Granite Lake** Newfoundland and Labrador Canada
81 L5 **Granite Mountains** Wyoming USA
80 F6 **Granite Range** Nevada USA
86 B5 **Granite Shoals** Texas USA
82 I2 **Granitehill Lake** Ontario Canada
221 D5 **Granity** New Zealand
102 D3 **Granja** Brazil
128 D4 **Granja de Torrehermosa** Spain
122 G3 **Gränjön** Sweden
123 P5 **Granki** Russian Federation
90 E2 **Granma** *admin. area* Cuba
122 G3 **Grann** *lake* Sweden
120 J4 **Grannäs** Sweden
86 D3 **Grannis** Arkansas USA
120 K4 **Granö** Sweden
104 B4 **Grano de Oro, Punta** *cape* Peru
106 D6 **Granole** *watercourse* Argentina
124 G1 **Gransee** Germany
140 C2 **Gransha** Larne Northern Ireland UK
120 L3 **Gransjö** Sweden
120 J4 **Gransjön** *lake* Sweden
81 O6 **Grant** Nebraska USA
59 P2 **Grant Island** Antarctica
198 E6 **Grant Island** NT Australia
84 E1 **Grant Range** Nevada USA
139 G2 **Grantham** Lincolnshire England UK
142 E5 **Granton House** Dumfries and Galloway Scotland UK
120 K4 **Granträsket** *lake* Sweden
85 I3 **Grants** New Mexico USA
80 D5 **Grants Pass** Oregon USA
83 L7 **Grantsville** Maryland USA
218 G8 **Grantville** Vic. Australia
120 K3 **Granudden** Sweden
75 O8 **Granum** Alberta Canada
140 B2 **Granville** Dungannon Northern Ireland UK
85 H4 **Granville** Arizona USA
81 O2 **Granville** North Dakota USA
73 I7 **Granville Lake** Manitoba Canada
86 D5 **Grapeland** Texas USA
129 J5 **Grarem** Algeria
121 P1 **Grasbakken** Norway
120 F5 **Gråsjøen** *lake* Norway
140 E2 **Grasmere** Cumbria England UK
123 J2 **Gräsö** *island* Sweden
76 F5 **Grass** *watercourse* Manitoba Canada
216 G6 **Grass Patch** WA Australia
80 E7 **Grass Valley** California USA
80 E4 **Grass Valley** Oregon USA
75 T5 **Grassberry** *watercourse* Saskatchewan Canada
218 E7 **Grassdale** Vic. Australia
127 H5 **Grasse** France
83 L2 **Grasset, Lac** *lake* Quebec Canada
141 G2 **Grassington** North Yorkshire England UK
120 I5 **Gråssjön** Sweden
122 G3 **Gråssjön** *lake* Sweden
221 F5 **Grassmere, Lake** New Zealand
81 K3 **Grassrange** Montana USA
219 Q10 **Grassy** Tas. Australia
83 K7 **Grassy Knob** *mountain* West Virginia USA
120 I3 **Grasvatnet** *lake* Norway
120 J2 **Gratangen** Norway
125 H4 **Gratkorn** Austria
120 K5 **Grätnäs** Sweden
219 J4 **Grattai Mountain** NSW Australia
124 E4 **Graubünden** *admin. area* Switzerland
126 E5 **Graulhet** France
129 G2 **Graus** Spain
107 I4 **Gravataí** Brazil
122 D3 **Gravatn** *lake* Norway
126 D4 **Grave, Pointe de** *cape* France
139 J4 **Gravelines** France
109 18 **Gravenor Bay** Antigua and Barbuda
219 J3 **Gravesend** NSW Australia
139 H3 **Gravesend** Kent England UK
78 H4 **Graveyard Island** Newfoundland and Labrador Canada
91 F3 **Gravois, Pointe-à-** *cape* Haiti
120 G4 **Gravvik** Norway
124 C4 **Gray** France
87 J4 **Gray** Georgia USA
80 G2 **Gray Creek** British Columbia Canada
84 G3 **Gray Mountain** Arizona USA
78 F2 **Gray Strait** Nunavut Canada
139 H3 **Grays** Thurrock England UK
80 C3 **Grays Harbor** Washington USA
80 J5 **Grays Lake** Idaho USA
81 M7 **Grays Peak** Colorado USA
86 E4 **Grayson** Louisiana USA
125 H4 **Graz** Austria
132 E3 **Greaca** Romania
75 R3 **Grease** *watercourse* Saskatchewan Canada
213 J5 **Great Antrim Plateau** WA Australia
217 L6 **Great Australian Bight** SA Australia
141 G2 **Great Ayton** North Yorkshire England UK
109 10a **Great Bacolet Point** *cape* Grenada
139 H3 **Great Baddow** Essex England UK
53 Y5 **Great Bahama Bank** *underwater feature* Atlantic Ocean
220 F3 **Great Barrier Island** New Zealand
215 G2 **Great Barrier Reef** Qld Australia
84 E1 **Great Basin** Nevada USA
83 N7 **Great Bay** New Jersey USA
72 G5 **Great Bear Lake** Northwest Territories Canada
81 P7 **Great Bend** Kansas USA
81 Q3 **Great Bend** North Dakota USA
142 B2 **Great Bernera** *island* Scotland UK
143 B4 **Great Blasket Island** Ireland
139 H2 **Great Bradley** Suffolk England UK
140 E2 **Great Broughton** Cumbria England UK
74 I8 **Great Central Lake** British Columbia Canada
194 B4 **Great Coco Island** Andaman and Nicobar Islands India
219 J3 **Great Dividing Range** NSW Australia
215 H6 **Great Dividing Range** Qld Australia
219 H7 **Great Dividing Range** Vic. Australia
82 J4 **Great Duck Island** Ontario Canada
139 H3 **Great Dunmow** Essex England UK
220 E2 **Great Exhibition Bay** New Zealand
91 F2 **Great Exuma** *island* Bahamas
80 J3 **Great Falls** Montana USA
87 M7 **Great Guana Cay** *island* Bahamas
139 H3 **Great Hallingbury** Essex England UK
87 M8 **Great Harbour Cay** *island* Bahamas
79 J7 **Great Harbour Deep** Newfoundland and Labrador Canada
141 F3 **Great Harwood** Lancashire England UK
91 F2 **Great Inagua Island** Bahamas
76 G3 **Great Island** Manitoba Canada
162 D6 **Great Karoo** *plain* South Africa
215 K7 **Great Keppel Island** Qld Australia
219 R10 **Great Lake** Tas. Australia
138 E2 **Great Malvern** Worcestershire England UK
140 E3 **Great Marton** Blackpool England UK
50 P7 **Great Meteor Bank** *underwater feature* Atlantic Ocean
139 F3 **Great Milton** Oxfordshire England UK
141 F3 **Great Mitton** Lancashire England UK
162 C5 **Great Namaqualand** *region* Namibia
194 B6 **Great Nicobar Island** Andaman and Nicobar Islands India
199 G6 **Great North East Channel** *strait* Papua New Guinea
83 L7 **Great North Mountain** Virginia USA
140 E3 **Great Ormes Head** *cape* England UK
139 G2 **Great Ouse** *watercourse* England UK
219 S11 **Great Oyster Bay** Tas. Australia
215 I5 **Great Palm Island** Qld Australia
90 E3 **Great Pedro Bluff** *cape* Jamaica
81 N4 **Great Plains** South Dakota USA
83 Q4 **Great Pond** Maine USA
160 D5 **Great Rift Valley** Democratic Republic of Congo
161 F5 **Great Ruaha** *watercourse* Tanzania
83 N5 **Great Sacandaga Lake** New York USA
87 L7 **Great Sale Cay** *island* Bahamas
80 I6 **Great Salt Lake** Utah USA
80 I6 **Great Salt Lake Desert** Utah USA
86 B2 **Great Salt Plains Lake** Oklahoma USA
75 Q7 **Great Sand Hills** Saskatchewan Canada
156 C2 **Great Sand Sea** *desert* Libya
213 H5 **Great Sandy Desert** WA Australia
139 H2 **Great Shelford** Cambridgeshire England UK
135 AL8 **Great Sitkin Island** Alaska USA
75 N2 **Great Slave Lake** Northwest Territories Canada
83 inset **Great Sound** *bay* Bermuda
83 O6 **Great South Bay** New York USA
139 H3 **Great Totham** Essex England UK
217 I4 **Great Victoria Desert** WA Australia
59 U2 **Great Wall (China)** *research station* Antarctica
83 R4 **Great Wass Island** Maine USA
219 R10 **Great Western Tiers** *range* Tas. Australia
194 C5 **Great Western Torres Islands** Myanmar
139 I2 **Great Yarmouth** Norfolk England UK
91 F3 **Greater Antilles** *islands* Caribbean Sea
90 E2 **Greater Bahama Bank** *underwater feature* Atlantic Ocean
139 G3 **Greater London** *admin. area* England UK
197 F5 **Greater Sunda Islands** *islands* Indonesia
139 H4 **Greatstone-on-Sea** Kent England UK
132 C3 **Greci** Romania
122 H3 **Grecken** *bay* Sweden
108 B3 **Greda Este, Cerro** *mountain* Argentina
133 C6 **Greece** *country* Europe
81 M6 **Greeley** Colorado USA
85 O1 **Greeley** Kansas USA
73 K2 **Greeley Fiord** Nunavut Canada
87 I2 **Green** *watercourse* Kentucky USA
84 G1 **Green** *watercourse* Utah USA
81 J5 **Green** *watercourse* Wyoming USA
109 18 **Green Bay** Antigua and Barbuda
82 H4 **Green Bay** Wisconsin USA
82 G4 **Green Bay** Wisconsin USA
219 J7 **Green Cape** NSW Australia
90 E2 **Green Cay** *island* Bahamas
75 N5 **Green Court** Alberta Canada
86 E2 **Green Forest** Arkansas USA
216 D5 **Green Head** WA Australia
216 E5 **Green Hills** WA Australia
215 I4 **Green Island** Qld Australia
195 H5 **Green Island Bay** Philippines
199 J5 **Green Islands** Papua New Guinea
86 C6 **Green Lake** Texas USA
81 L7 **Green Mountain Reservoir** Colorado USA
83 O5 **Green Mountains** Vermont USA
138 E3 **Green Ore** Somerset England UK
80 D4 **Green Peter Lake** Oregon USA
81 J7 **Green River** Utah USA
81 K6 **Green River** Wyoming USA
82 I8 **Green River Lake** Kentucky USA
84 G5 **Green Valley** Arizona USA
143 F3 **Greenanstown** Ireland
87 K2 **Greenbrier** *watercourse* West Virginia USA
81 Q2 **Greenbush** Minnesota USA
216 E6 **Greenbushes** WA Australia
140 B1 **Greencastle** Ireland
143 F2 **Greencastle** Newry and Mourne Northern Ireland UK
143 E2 **Greencastle** Omagh Northern Ireland UK
82 H7 **Greencastle** Indiana USA
87 J2 **Greeneville** Tennessee USA
139 G2 **Greenfield** Bedfordshire England UK
84 B2 **Greenfield** California USA
82 D6 **Greenfield** Iowa USA
214 B1 **Greenhill Island** NT Australia
82 G3 **Greenland** Michigan USA
73 N4 **Greenland (Kalaallit Nunaat)** *Danish dependency* Atlantic Ocean
50 R2 **Greenland Abyssal Plain** *underwater feature* Atlantic Ocean
50 S2 **Greenland Fracture Zone** *underwater feature* Atlantic Ocean
57 E2 **Greenland-Iceland Rise** *underwater feature* Atlantic Ocean
73 R4 **Greenland Sea** Greenland
142 E4 **Greenloaning** Perth and Kinross Scotland UK
218 B6 **Greenly Island** SA Australia
142 D5 **Greenock** Inverclyde Scotland UK
143 F2 **Greenore** Ireland
143 F4 **Greenore Point** Ireland
216 D4 **Greenough** WA Australia
216 D4 **Greenough** *watercourse* WA Australia
83 K4 **Greenough Point** Ontario Canada
87 I5 **Greensboro** Florida USA
87 L2 **Greensboro** North Carolina USA
82 I7 **Greensburg** Indiana USA
81 P8 **Greensburg** Kansas USA
142 C3 **Greenstone Point** Scotland UK
215 H5 **Greenvale** Qld Australia
158 C3 **Greenville** Liberia
87 H5 **Greenville** Alabama USA
82 G7 **Greenville** Illinois USA
79 D10 **Greenville** Maine USA
86 F4 **Greenville** Mississippi USA
87 M3 **Greenville** North Carolina USA
82 I6 **Greenville** Ohio USA
87 J3 **Greenville** South Carolina USA
86 C4 **Greenville** Texas USA
82 F2 **Greenwater Lake** Ontario Canada
139 G3 **Greenwich** Greater London England UK
86 F4 **Greenwood** Mississippi USA
87 J3 **Greenwood** South Carolina USA
82 F4 **Greenwood** Wisconsin USA
87 J3 **Greer** South Carolina USA
86 E3 **Greers Ferry Lake** Arkansas USA
86 E3 **Greeson, Lake** Arkansas USA
138 E2 **Greete** Shropshire England UK
104 D3 **Gregorio** *watercourse* Brazil
85 K7 **Gregorio A. Garcia** Mexico
215 J7 **Gregory** Qld Australia
214 E5 **Gregory** *watercourse* Qld Australia
216 D4 **Gregory** WA Australia
81 P5 **Gregory** South Dakota USA
86 C7 **Gregory** Texas USA
218 D3 **Gregory, Lake** SA Australia
216 F2 **Gregory, Lake** WA Australia
214 A3 **Gregory, Mount** NT Australia
214 E5 **Gregory Downs** Qld Australia
214 G5 **Gregory Range** Qld Australia
215 H5 **Gregory Springs** Qld Australia
122 G5 **Greifswald** Germany
122 G5 **Greifswalder Bodden** *bay* Germany
125 H3 **Grein** Austria
124 G2 **Greiz** Germany
136 E6 **Greko, Cap** *cape* Cyprus
121 U2 **Gremikha** Russian Federation
Gremyachinsk *see* **Goryachinsk** Russian Federation
122 F4 **Grenå** Denmark
109 10 **Grenada** *country* Caribbean
86 G4 **Grenada** Mississippi USA
86 G4 **Grenada Lake** Mississippi USA
129 G2 **Grenade** France
126 D5 **Grenade-sur-l'Adour** France
91 I4 **Grenadines, The** *islands* St Vincent and the Grenadines
127 H3 **Grenchen** Switzerland
139 F3 **Grendon Underwood** Buckinghamshire England UK
122 F4 **Grenen** *cape* Denmark
219 I5 **Grenfell** NSW Australia
142 A3 **Grenitote** Na h-Eileanan Siar Scotland UK
120 inset **Grenivík** Iceland
127 G4 **Grenoble** France
81 N2 **Grenora** North Dakota USA
101 H4 **Grens Gebergte** *range* Brazil
121 Q2 **Grense-Jakobselv** Norway
215 G1 **Grenville, Cape** Qld Australia
127 G5 **Gréoux-les-Bains** France
219 J5 **Gresford** NSW Australia
80 D4 **Gresham** Oregon USA
197 G5 **Gresik** Indonesia
196 D4 **Gresik** Indonesia
120 G5 **Gressli** Norway
221 E6 **Greta Valley** New Zealand
142 E6 **Gretna** Dumfries and Galloway Scotland UK
87 I5 **Gretna** Florida USA
86 F6 **Gretna** Louisiana USA
83 L8 **Gretna** Virginia USA
124 D1 **Greven** Germany
127 H2 **Grevenmacher** Luxembourg
127 H2 **Grevenmacher** *admin. area* Luxembourg
221 E5 **Greville Harbour** New Zealand
216 D5 **Grey** WA Australia
79 J9 **Grey** *watercourse* Newfoundland and Labrador Canada
214 D2 **Grey, Cape** NT Australia
86 B6 **Grey Forest** Texas USA
73 N8 **Grey Islands** Newfoundland and Labrador Canada
216 C2 **Grey Point** WA Australia
218 F2 **Grey Range** Qld Australia
81 K4 **Greybull** Wyoming USA
81 K4 **Greybull** *watercourse* Wyoming USA
221 D6 **Greymouth** New Zealand
221 F5 **Greytown** New Zealand
216 D2 **Greys Plains** WA Australia
143 F3 **Greystones** Ireland
133 A5 **Grib, Mali** *mountain* Albania
121 S4 **Gridino** Russian Federation
80 E7 **Gridley** California USA
85 O1 **Gridley** Kansas USA
75 T8 **Griffin** Saskatchewan Canada
87 I4 **Griffin** Georgia USA
218 H6 **Griffith** NSW Australia
72 G3 **Griffiths Point** Northwest Territories Canada
127 G4 **Grignan** France
126 D4 **Grignols** France
127 G4 **Grigny** France
132 A4 **Grilë** Albania
219 Q10 **Grim, Cape** Tas. Australia
159 I3 **Grimari** Central African Republic
124 G2 **Grimma** Germany
78 H4 **Grimmington Island** Newfoundland and Labrador Canada
120 I5 **Grimnäsfjärden** *bay* Sweden
138 E2 **Grimpo** Shropshire England UK
120 inset **Grimsá** *watercourse* Iceland
141 H3 **Grimsby** North East Lincolnshire England UK
120 inset **Grimsey** *island* Iceland
74 M4 **Grimshaw** Alberta Canada
122 E3 **Grimstad** Norway
120 inset **Grimsvötn** *mountain* Iceland
216 E6 **Grimwade** WA Australia
120 F5 **Grindal** Norway
141 H2 **Grindale** East Riding of Yorkshire England UK
120 inset **Grindavik** Iceland
122 G2 **Grinder** Norway
141 F1 **Grindon** Northumberland England UK
122 E5 **Grindsted** Denmark
90 D5 **Grindstone Bay Chiquita, Punta** *cape* Nicaragua
123 L5 **Griniai** Lithuania
85 L1 **Grinnell** Kansas USA
78 E1 **Grinnell Glacier** Nunavut Canada
73 J3 **Grinnell Peninsula** Nunavut Canada
140 F2 **Grinsdale** Cumbria England UK
122 G3 **Grinstad** Sweden
132 D2 **Grinties** Romania
141 G2 **Grinton** North Yorkshire England UK
162 D5 **Griquatown** South Africa
139 I4 **Gris Nez, Cap** *cape* France
73 K3 **Grise Fiord** Nunavut Canada
129 G2 **Grisolles** France
81 O2 **Griswold** Manitoba Canada
142 F2 **Gritley** Orkney Islands Scotland UK
140 E2 **Grizedale** Cumbria England UK
75 Q4 **Grizzly Bear Hills** Saskatchewan Canada
79 K7 **Groais Island** Newfoundland and Labrador Canada
162 D5 **Groblershoop** South Africa
125 L1 **Gródek** Poland
125 I2 **Grodków** Poland
162 C6 **Groen** *watercourse* South Africa
138 D3 **Groesffordd** Powys Wales UK
219 H6 **Grogan** NSW Australia
215 H4 **Groganville** Qld Australia
142 A3 **Groigearraidh** Na h-Eileanan Siar Scotland UK
126 C3 **Groix, Île de** *island* France
125 K2 **Grójec** Poland
131 D8 **Grombalia** Tunisia
130 H5 **Gromiljak** Bosnia and Herzegovina
123 K5 **Gromovo** Russian Federation
76 G3 **Gronbeck Lake** Manitoba Canada
120 L4 **Grönbo** Sweden
120 H4 **Grong** Norway
218 H6 **Grong Grong** NSW Australia
120 H4 **Grongstadvatnet** *lake* Norway
124 D1 **Groningen** Netherlands
122 D6 **Groningen** *admin. area* Netherlands
101 H3 **Groningen** Suriname
75 S6 **Gronlid** Saskatchewan Canada
120 E5 **Grønnes** Norway
123 J5 **Gronowo Elbląskie** Poland
85 L3 **Groom** Texas USA
84 E2 **Groom Lake** Nevada USA
162 D6 **Groot** *watercourse* South Africa
162 C5 **Groot Karas Berg** *range* Namibia
162 D5 **Grootdrink** South Africa
214 D2 **Groote Eylandt** *island* NT Australia
162 C3 **Grootfontein** Namibia
109 13 **Gros Islet** St Lucia
79 I7 **Gros Mécatina, Île du** *island* Quebec Canada
79 J8 **Gros Morne** *mountain* Newfoundland and Labrador Canada
109 14 **Gros-Morne** Martinique
109 13 **Gros Piton** *volcano* St Lucia
81 J5 **Gros Ventre Range** Wyoming USA
213 K2 **Grose Island** NT Australia
124 F4 **Grosio** Italy
138 E3 **Grosmont** Monmouthshire Wales UK
127 G3 **Grosne** *watercourse* France
78 F1 **Gross Island** Nunavut Canada
162 C4 **Gross Ums** Namibia
102 B2 **Grossa, Ponta** *cape* Brazil
129 G4 **Grossa, Punta** *cape* Spain
127 K3 **Großarl** Austria
109 16 **Grosse Pointe** *cape* Guadeloupe
124 G3 **Große Vils** *watercourse* Germany
122 F5 **Großenbrode** Germany
124 F1 **Großer Graben** *watercourse* Germany
122 F5 **Großer Plöner See** *lake* Germany
125 H4 **Grosser Priel** *mountain* Austria
125 G1 **Großer Selchower See** *lake* Germany
130 D5 **Grosseto** Italy
124 G4 **Großglockner** *mountain* Austria
120 L5 **Grossgrunden** *island* Sweden
125 I3 **Großkrut** Austria
130 C2 **Großostheim** Germany
127 H2 **Grostenquin** France
127 L4 **Grosuplje** Slovenia
52 N5 **Grosvenor Seamount** *underwater feature* Pacific Ocean
78 J5 **Groswater Bay** Newfoundland and Labrador Canada
120 J2 **Grøtavær** Norway
120 I5 **Grötingen** *lake* Sweden
81 P4 **Groton** South Dakota USA
120 K1 **Grøtøy** *island* Norway
130 E5 **Grottammare** Italy
83 L7 **Grottoes** Virginia USA
75 M5 **Grouard** Alberta Canada
126 D2 **Grouin, Pointe du** *cape* France
79 D7 **Groulx, Monts** *range* Quebec Canada
74 K5 **Groundbirch** British Columbia Canada
122 E3 **Grova** Norway
82 J7 **Grove City** Ohio USA
86 H5 **Grove Hill** Alabama USA
81 M6 **Grover** Colorado USA
87 K3 **Grover** North Carolina USA
84 B3 **Grover Beach** California USA
86 E6 **Groves** Texas USA
86 D5 **Groveton** Texas USA
183 K5 **Groznoye** Kyrgyzstan
182 E5 **Groznyy** Russian Federation
120 I4 **Grubben** Norway
121 M3 **Grubbnäsudden** Sweden
125 K1 **Grudusk** Poland
125 J1 **Grudziądz** Poland
106 D2 **Gruesa, Punta** *cape* Chile
132 C3 **Gruia** Romania
142 D2 **Gruids** Highland Scotland UK
142 C3 **Gruinard Bay** Scotland UK
142 C3 **Gruinard Island** Scotland UK
126 F5 **Gruissan** France
142 B3 **Grula** Highland Scotland UK
122 G3 **Grumsfjorden** *bay* Sweden
127 I1 **Grünberg** Germany
120 inset **Grundarfjörður** Iceland
120 H5 **Grundsjön** *lake* Sweden
83 J8 **Grundy** Virginia USA
120 J3 **Grunnfjorden** *bay* Norway
132 H1 **Grushkovka** Ukraine
122 C3 **Grutle** Norway
142 inset **Grutness** Shetland Scotland UK
122 I2 **Gruvberget** Sweden
85 L2 **Gruver** Texas USA
127 H3 **Gruyères** Switzerland
182 G6 **Gryada Akkyr** Turkmenistan
122 I2 **Grycken** *lake* Sweden
125 H1 **Gryfino** Poland
81 R2 **Grygla** Minnesota USA
133 A5 **Grykë** Albania
122 I3 **Gryt** Sweden
120 J2 **Grytøya** *island* Norway
120 L5 **Grytskäret** *island* Finland
109 8 **Grytviken** South Georgia
190 G6 **Gu Xian** Shanxi China
196 D2 **Gua Musang** Malaysia
108 A2 **Guabún** Chile
100 D3 **Guacamayas** Colombia
90 E2 **Guacanayabo, Golfo de** *bay* Cuba
100 E2 **Guacara** Venezuela
85 I7 **Guachochi** Mexico
128 E5 **Guadahortuna** Spain
128 D5 **Guadajoz** *watercourse* Spain
88 E4 **Guadalajara** Mexico
128 E3 **Guadalajara** Spain
222 8 **Guadalcanal** *admin. area* Solomon Islands
222 8 **Guadalcanal** *island* Solomon Islands
128 E4 **Guadalén** *watercourse* Spain
106 E5 **Guadales** Argentina
128 E4 **Guadalimar** *watercourse* Spain
128 D4 **Guadalmellato, Embalse de** *lake* Spain
128 E4 **Guadalmena** *watercourse* Spain
128 E4 **Guadalmena, Embalse del** *lake* Spain
164 1b **Guadalope** Azores
129 F3 **Guadalope** *watercourse* Spain
128 D5 **Guadalquivir** *watercourse* Spain
88 C2 **Guadalupa de Jesús** Mexico
100 C4 **Guadalupe** Colombia
88 E4 **Guadalupe** Mexico
88 E3 **Guadalupe** Mexico
84 C6 **Guadalupe** *volcano* Mexico
104 B2 **Guadalupe** Peru
84 B3 **Guadalupe** California USA
86 C6 **Guadalupe** *watercourse* Texas USA
84 C6 **Guadalupe, Isla** *island* Mexico
128 D4 **Guadalupe, Sierra de** *range* Spain
85 J7 **Guadalupe de Bahues** Mexico
85 J4 **Guadalupe Mountains** New Mexico USA
88 D3 **Guadalupe Victoria** Mexico
88 D2 **Guadalupe Victoria** Mexico
88 B1 **Guadalupe Victoria** Mexico
88 D3 **Guadalupe y Calvo** Mexico
128 E3 **Guadarrama, Sierra de** *range* Spain
91 I3 **Guadeloupe** *French overseas territory* Caribbean
109 I6 **Guadeloupe** *island* Caribbean
91 I3 **Guadeloupe Passage** Caribbean
128 C4 **Guadiana** *watercourse* Portugal
128 D4 **Guadiana** *watercourse* Spain
90 C2 **Guadiana, Bahía** *bay* Cuba
128 E5 **Guadiana Menor** *watercourse* Spain
128 E5 **Guadix** Spain
108 B3 **Guafo, Boca del** *bay* Chile
101 I5 **Guaíba** Brazil
101 E2 **Guaicupa** Venezuela
104 D5 **Guaiguasi, Cerro** *mountain* Chile
100 D4 **Guainia** *admin. area* Colombia
100 D4 **Guainia** *watercourse* Colombia
101 F3 **Guaiquinima, Cerro** *mountain* Venezuela
103 B8 **Guaíra** Brazil
107 G3 **Guairá** *admin. area* Paraguay
108 B3 **Guaitecas, Islas** *islands* Chile
90 E2 **Guajaba, Cayo** *island* Cuba
101 G5 **Guajará** Brazil
105 E3 **Guajará Mirim** Brazil
100 B5 **Gualaceo** Ecuador
90 C4 **Gualaco** Honduras
84 A1 **Gualala** California USA
90 B4 **Gualán** Guatemala
100 B5 **Gualaquiza** Ecuador
130 E5 **Gualdo Tadino** Italy
107 G5 **Gualeguay** Argentina
107 G4 **Gualeguay** *watercourse* Argentina
108 B3 **Gualjaina** Argentina
222 2 **Guam** *island* Pacific Ocean
222 2 **Guam** *unincorporated US territory* Pacific Ocean
100 C4 **Guamal** Colombia
100 C5 **Guamareyes** Colombia
108 A3 **Guamblin, Isla** *island* Chile
107 H2 **Guami Taperé** Paraguay
106 F6 **Guaminí** Argentina
100 C3 **Guamo** Colombia
101 E3 **Guampí, Serranía de** *range* Venezuela
88 C3 **Guamúchil** Mexico
191 H5 **Gu'an** Hebei China
101 F3 **Guaña, Cerro** *mountain* Venezuela
104 D3 **Guanabara** Brazil
90 C5 **Guanacaste, Cordillera de** *range* Costa Rica
106 F6 **Guanaco, Cerro** *mountain* Argentina
108 B2 **Guanaco, Cerro del** *mountain* Argentina
90 C2 **Guanahacabibes, Península** Cuba
90 C3 **Guanaja** Honduras
90 C3 **Guanaja, Isla de** *island* Honduras
90 D2 **Guanajay** Cuba
88 E4 **Guanajuato** Mexico
88 E4 **Guanajuato** *admin. area* Mexico
103 D6 **Guanambi** Brazil
104 B3 **Guañape, Punta** *cape* Peru
109 9 **Guanapo** Trinidad and Tobago
100 D2 **Guanare** Venezuela
104 E4 **Guanay** Bolivia
191 H6 **Guancheng** Shandong China
106 D4 **Guandacol** Argentina
90 C2 **Guane** Cuba
188 E2 **Guang'an** Sichuan China
189 G4 **Guangdong** *admin. area* China
188 D2 **Guanghan** Sichuan China
190 E6 **Guanghe** Gansu China
191 J5 **Guanglu Dao** *island* Liaoning China
188 D3 **Guangming** Sichuan China
191 I5 **Guangrao** Shandong China
189 G2 **Guangshui** Hubei China
188 E4 **Guangxi Zhuangzu Zizhiqu** *admin. area* China
188 E2 **Guangyuan** Sichuan China
189 G4 **Guangzhou** Guangdong China
191 H5 **Guangzong** Hebei China
103 D7 **Guanhães** Brazil
101 E3 **Guaniamo, Rio** *watercourse* Venezuela
90 D6 **Guánico, Punta** *cape* Panama
90 D2 **Guaniguanico, Cordillera de** *range* Cuba
108 C5 **Guankenken Aike** Argentina
188 F2 **Guanmian Shan** *range* Chongqing China
100 B5 **Guano** Ecuador
101 F2 **Guanoco** Venezuela
188 E3 **Guansuo** Guizhou China
91 F2 **Guantánamo** Cuba
91 F2 **Guantánamo** *admin. area* Cuba
91 F3 **Guantánamo Bay Naval Base** *US military base* Cuba
191 H6 **Guantao** Hebei China
100 B4 **Guapi** Colombia
100 B4 **Guapí, Bahía de** *bay* Colombia
103 B8 **Guapiaçu** Brazil
103 B7 **Guapó** Brazil
105 F4 **Guapore** *watercourse* Bolivia
107 J2 **Guará** Brazil
102 D4 **Guaraciaba do Norte** Brazil
107 I3 **Guaramirim** Brazil
100 B5 **Guaranda** Ecuador
107 J2 **Guaranésia** Brazil
107 H3 **Guaraniaçu** Brazil
105 H3 **Guarantã do Norte** Brazil
103 D8 **Guarapari** Brazil
107 I3 **Guarapuava** Brazil
103 E7 **Guaratinga** Brazil
107 J2 **Guaratinguetá** Brazil
107 I3 **Guaratuba** Brazil
107 I3 **Guaratuba, Baía de** *bay* Brazil
104 D4 **Guarayos** Bolivia
104 D4 **Guarayos, Altiplanicie de los** *region* Bolivia
131 E6 **Guarcino** Italy
128 C3 **Guarda** Portugal
128 C3 **Guarda** *admin. area* Portugal
131 E6 **Guardia, Punta della** *cape* Italy

108 D2 **Guardia Mitre** Argentina
108 B6 **Guardián Brito, Isla** *island* Chile
84 E4 **Guardianes de la Patria** Mexico
128 D2 **Guardo** Spain
100 E2 **Guarenas** Venezuela
107 I2 **Guariba** Brazil
100 E2 **Guarico** *admin. area* Venezuela
100 E2 **Guárico** *watercourse* Venezuela
100 E2 **Guarico, Embalse del** *lake* Venezuela
91 F2 **Guarico, Punta** *cape* Cuba
103 C8 **Guarujá** Brazil
103 C8 **Guarulhos** Brazil
88 C3 **Guasave** Mexico
100 B4 **Guascama, Punta** *cape* Colombia
100 D3 **Guasdalito** Venezuela
101 F3 **Guasipati** Venezuela
199 J6 **Guasopa** Papua New Guinea
124 F5 **Guastalla** Italy
90 B4 **Guastatoya** Guatemala
90 B4 **Guatemala** *country* Central America
90 B4 **Guatemala** Guatemala
53 W6 **Guatemala Basin** *underwater feature* Pacific Ocean
100 E2 **Guatire** Venezuela
199 G5 **Guavi** *watercourse* Papua New Guinea
100 C4 **Guaviare** *admin. area* Colombia
100 D4 **Guaviare** *watercourse* Colombia
107 G4 **Guaviraví** Argentina
107 J2 **Guaxupé** Brazil
100 C4 **Guayabero** *watercourse* Colombia
109 9 **Guayaguayare** Trinidad and Tobago
109 9 **Guayaguayare Bay** Trinidad and Tobago
89 F4 **Guayalejo** *watercourse* Mexico
100 E3 **Guayapo, Serranía** *range* Venezuela
100 B5 **Guayaquil** Ecuador
100 A5 **Guayaquil, Golfo de** *bay* Ecuador
105 E3 **Guayaramerín** Bolivia
107 G3 **Guayaybi** Paraguay
107 G3 **Guaycuru** *watercourse* Argentina
88 C3 **Guaymas** Mexico
107 G4 **Guayquiraró** *watercourse* Argentina
106 E2 **Guaytayoc, Lago de** *lake* Argentina
88 C4 **Guazanilo** Mexico
90 B4 **Guazapa** El Salvador
156 F5 **Guba** Ethiopia
187 D9 **Gubbi** Karnataka India
130 E5 **Gubbio** Italy
120 K3 **Gubblijaure** *lake* Sweden
125 H2 **Guben** Germany
125 H2 **Gubin** Poland
159 G2 **Gubio** Nigeria
136 F2 **Gubkin** Russian Federation
189 F2 **Gucheng** Hubei China
189 H2 **Gucheng Hu** *lake* Jiangsu China
190 E3 **Guchin-us** Mongolia
182 H5 **Gudabag** Turkmenistan
187 D9 **Gudalur** Tamil Nadu India
183 K6 **Gudara** Tajikistan
187 F7 **Gudari** Orissa India
122 F2 **Gudbrandsdalen** *valley* Norway
122 H5 **Gudhjem** Denmark
122 I4 **Gudingen** *bay* Sweden
187 D8 **Gudur** Karnataka India
120 E6 **Gudvangen** Norway
127 H3 **Guebwiller** France
83 M2 **Guéguen, Lac** *lake* Quebec Canada
158 B3 **Guékédou** Guinea
154 D4 **Guelb er Rîchât** *mountain* Mauritania
159 H2 **Guelengdeng** Chad
155 H1 **Guelma** Algeria
154 D3 **Guelmim** Morocco
83 K5 **Guelph** Ontario Canada
126 C2 **Guémené-sur-Scorff** France
131 B9 **Guentis** Algeria
78 C3 **Guenyveau, Lac** *lake* Quebec Canada
126 C3 **Guer** France
108 C5 **Güer Aike** Argentina
159 H2 **Guera** *admin. area* Chad
155 G2 **Guerara** Algeria
159 I2 **Guéréda** Chad
126 E3 **Guéret** France
126 C2 **Guernsey** *British crown dependency* English Channel
81 M5 **Guernsey** Wyoming USA
81 M5 **Guernsey Reservoir** Wyoming USA
154 D5 **Guérou** Mauritania
85 L6 **Guerrero** Mexico
89 F5 **Guerrero** *admin. area* Mexico
84 E7 **Guerrero Negro** Mexico
78 E4 **Guers, Lac** *lake* Quebec Canada
129 F2 **Güesa** Spain
124 C4 **Gueugnon** France
158 C3 **Gueyo** Côte d'Ivoire
189 H3 **Gufeng** Fujian China
188 F2 **Gufu** Hubei China
222 2 **Guguan** *island* Northern Mariana Islands
197 H3 **Guguang, Gunung** *mountain* Indonesia
182 I6 **Gugurtli** Uzbekistan
196 E5 **Guhakolak, Tanjung** *cape* Indonesia
107 G2 **Guia Lopes da Laguna** Brazil
50 N9 **Guiana Basin** *underwater feature* Atlantic Ocean
101 F3 **Guiana Highlands** *range* Guyana/Venezuela
158 C3 **Guibéroua** Côte d'Ivoire
218 D7 **Guichen Bay** SA Australia
188 F4 **Guicheng** Guangxi Zhuangzu Zizhiqu China
155 H6 **Guidan-Roumji** Niger
159 H3 **Guidari** Chad
159 G3 **Guider** Cameroon
155 H6 **Guidiguir** Niger
154 D5 **Guidimaka** *admin. area* Mauritania
188 E3 **Guiding** Guizhou China
189 G3 **Guidong** Hunan China
158 C3 **Guiglo** Côte d'Ivoire
124 B3 **Guignes** France
100 E2 **Güigüe** Venezuela
120 I3 **Guijaurtjårro** *lake* Sweden
189 H2 **Guiji Shan** *range* Zhejiang China
128 D3 **Guijuelo** Spain
216 D5 **Guilderton** WA Australia
139 G3 **Guildford** Surrey England UK
83 Q4 **Guilford** Maine USA
188 F3 **Guilin** Guangxi Zhuangzu Zizhiqu China
77 P6 **Guillaume** *watercourse* Quebec Canada
73 L7 **Guillaume Delisle, Lac** *lake* Quebec Canada
127 H4 **Guillaumes** France
78 D6 **Guillemot, Lac** *lake* Quebec Canada
88 C3 **Guillermo Blake Aguilar, Presa** *lake* Mexico
89 F3 **Guillermo Zúñiga** Mexico
127 H4 **Guillestre** France
164 3a **Güimar** Canary Islands
88 E3 **Guimbalete** Mexico
158 B2 **Guinea** *country* Africa
158 E4 **Guinea, Gulf of** Africa
50 R9 **Guinea Basin** *underwater feature* Atlantic Ocean
158 B2 **Guinea-Bissau** *country* Africa
139 I4 **Guînes** France
90 D2 **Güines** Cuba
79 H6 **Guines, Lac** *lake* Newfoundland and Labrador Canada
126 C2 **Guingamp** France
195 I4 **Guintinua** *island* Philippines
90 C5 **Guiones, Punta** *cape* Costa Rica
188 F4 **Guiping** Guangxi Zhuangzu Zizhiqu China
105 H5 **Guiratinga** Brazil
159 H2 **Guiri** Cameroon
90 E2 **Guisa** Cuba
126 F2 **Guise** France
188 D4 **Guishan** Yunnan China
139 H2 **Guist** Norfolk England UK
128 C2 **Guistolas, Embalse de** *lake* Spain
128 C2 **Guitiriz** Spain
195 J5 **Guiuan** Philippines
188 E3 **Guiyang** Guizhou China
189 F3 **Guiyang** Hunan China
188 E3 **Guizhou** *admin. area* China
126 D4 **Gujan-Mestras** France
179 M2 **Gujar Khan** Pakistan
186 C6 **Gujarat** *admin. area* India
159 G2 **Gujba** Nigeria
190 G5 **Gujiao** Shanxi China
179 M3 **Gujranwala** Pakistan
179 M3 **Gujrat** Pakistan
178 G3 **Gūkān** Iran
190 E5 **Gulang** Gansu China
187 D8 **Gulbarga** Karnataka India
123 N4 **Gulbene** Latvia
123 N4 **Gulbenes** *admin. area* Latvia
78 G3 **Gulch Cape** Newfoundland and Labrador Canada
178 G4 **Gulf, The** Middle East
219 J4 **Gulf Creek** NSW Australia
86 H5 **Gulf Shores** Alabama USA
87 J7 **Gulfport** Florida USA
86 G5 **Gulfport** Mississippi USA
219 I5 **Gulgong** NSW Australia
135 Z8 **Gulian** Heilongjiang China
188 E3 **Gulin** Sichuan China
198 D5 **Gulir** Indonesia
183 J6 **Guliston** Uzbekistan
182 C4 **Gulkevichi** Russian Federation
76 K8 **Gull** *watercourse* Ontario Canada
76 K8 **Gull Bay** Ontario Canada
75 O6 **Gull Lake** Alberta Canada
78 H6 **Gull Lake** Newfoundland and Labrador Canada
75 Q7 **Gull Lake** Saskatchewan Canada
82 D3 **Gull Lake** Minnesota USA
142 F4 **Gullane** East Lothian Scotland UK
123 L3 **Gullkronafjärd** *bay* Finland
123 L3 **Gullö** *island* Finland
133 E7 **Güllük Körfezi** *bay* Turkey
140 A4 **Gully Bridge** Ireland
186 D3 **Gulmarg** Jammu and Kashmir India/Pakistan
136 E6 **Gülnar** Turkey
124 G1 **Gülper See** *lake* Germany
133 E6 **Gülpınar** Turkey
183 L4 **Gul'Shat** Kazakhstan
122 F2 **Gulsrud** Norway
161 E3 **Gulu** Uganda
219 J2 **Guluguba** Qld Australia
189 G2 **Guluu** Henan China
214 D1 **Guluwuru Island** NT Australia
132 G2 **Gulyayevka** Ukraine
213 K4 **Gum** *watercourse* NT Australia
214 F7 **Gum** *watercourse* Qld Australia
218 G6 **Gum Creek** NSW Australia
218 F5 **Gum Lake** NSW Australia
218 F5 **Gum Lake** NSW Australia
162 D3 **Gumare** Botswana
218 G3 **Gumbalie** NSW Australia
218 G2 **Gumbardo** Qld Australia
182 G6 **Gumdag** Turkmenistan
159 F2 **Gumel** Nigeria
128 E3 **Gumiel de Hizán** Spain
186 F6 **Gumla** Jharkhand India
187 F7 **Gumma** Orissa India
159 F2 **Gummi** Nigeria
136 F5 **Gümüşhane** Turkey
136 G5 **Gümüşhane** *admin. area* Turkey
85 N4 **Gun Barrel City** Texas USA
186 D6 **Guna** Madhya Pradesh India
157 F5 **Guna, Mount** *mountain* Ethiopia
188 E2 **Gu'nan** Chongqing China
218 G6 **Gunbar** NSW Australia
139 G2 **Gunby** Lincolnshire England UK
219 I6 **Gundagai** NSW Australia
219 I6 **Gundaroo** NSW Australia
218 G4 **Gunderbooka, Mount** NSW Australia
160 C3 **Gundji** Democratic Republic of Congo
218 H5 **Gunebang** NSW Australia
133 F6 **Güneşli** Turkey
133 F7 **Güney** Turkey
136 G5 **Güney Doğu Toroslar** Turkey
160 B5 **Gungu** Democratic Republic of Congo
162 C2 **Gungue** Angola
214 B2 **Gungurrul** NT Australia
182 E5 **Gunib** Russian Federation
76 G6 **Gunisao** *watercourse* Manitoba Canada
76 G6 **Gunisao Lake** Manitoba Canada
130 H4 **Gunja** Croatia
133 F6 **Günlüce** Turkey
213 K2 **Gunn Point** NT Australia
218 G2 **Gunnadorah, Mount** Qld Australia
75 Q3 **Gunnar** Saskatchewan Canada
120 J4 **Gunnarn** Sweden
121 M4 **Gunnarsfjärden** *bay* Sweden
73 Q5 **Gunnbjørn Fjeld** *mountain* Greenland
219 J4 **Gunnedah** NSW Australia
59 C2 **Gunnerus Bank** *underwater feature* Southern Ocean
59 C2 **Gunnerus Ridge** *underwater feature* Southern Ocean
141 H3 **Gunness** North Lincolnshire England UK
138 C4 **Gunnislake** Cornwall England UK
120 L5 **Gunnismark** Sweden
214 E5 **Gunpowder** Qld Australia
214 E5 **Gunpowder** *watercourse* Qld Australia
183 K6 **Gunt** *watercourse* Tajikistan
187 D8 **Guntakal** Andhra Pradesh India
87 H3 **Guntersville Lake** Alabama USA
139 H2 **Gunthorpe** Norfolk England UK
187 E8 **Guntur** Andhra Pradesh India
214 E4 **Gununa** Qld Australia
197 F3 **Gunung Ayer** Malaysia
198 C5 **Gunungapi** *island* Indonesia
197 H4 **Gunungbatubesar** Indonesia
196 C3 **Gunungsitoli** Indonesia
196 E5 **Gunungsugih** Indonesia
196 C3 **Gunungtua** Indonesia
130 D2 **Günz** *watercourse* Germany
189 G1 **Guo He** *watercourse* Anhui China
189 G1 **Guoyang** Anhui China
188 E1 **Guozhen** Shaanxi China
179 M2 **Gupis** Pakistan
214 B3 **Gupuluk (Mount Lambell)** *mountain* NT Australia
185 K3 **Guraanbular** Mongolia
186 D3 **Gurais** Jammu and Kashmir India/Pakistan
160 D3 **Gurba** *watercourse* Democratic Republic of Congo
186 D4 **Gurdaspur** Punjab India
86 E4 **Gurdon** Arkansas USA
186 D5 **Gurgaon** Haryana India
102 D4 **Gurgueia** *watercourse* Brazil
186 C6 **Gurha** Rajasthan India
101 F3 **Guri, Embalse de** *lake* Venezuela
125 H4 **Gurk** *watercourse* Austria
219 I3 **Gurley** NSW Australia
81 N6 **Gurley** Nebraska USA
157 G5 **Gurmal, Ras** *cape* Eritrea
214 A7 **Gurner, Mount** NT Australia
163 F3 **Guro** Mozambique
182 H7 **Gurpan** Iran
122 C1 **Gurskøy** *island* Norway
133 F5 **Gürsu** Turkey
186 C6 **Guru Sikhar** *mountain* Rajasthan India
163 G3 **Gurué** Mozambique
102 B3 **Gurupá** Brazil
103 B5 **Gurupi** Brazil
102 C3 **Gurupi** *watercourse* Brazil
102 B4 **Gurupi, Serra do** *range* Brazil
101 G4 **Gurupira, Serra do** *range* Brazil
162 F3 **Guruve** Zimbabwe
190 E4 **Gurvan Sayhan Uul** Mongolia
190 G3 **Gurvanbayan** Mongolia
190 E3 **Gurvanbular** Mongolia
190 F3 **Gurvansaihan** Mongolia
190 E4 **Gurvantes** Mongolia
191 H2 **Gurvanzagal** Mongolia
Gur'yev *see* **Atyrau** Kazakhstan
123 K5 **Gur'yevsk** Russian Federation
125 L3 **Gusakov** Ukraine
159 F2 **Gusau** Nigeria
182 I7 **Guşgy** Turkmenistan
189 G2 **Gushi** Henan China
189 J3 **Gushikawa** Japan
198 E4 **Gusi** Indonesia
135 AF4 **Gusinaya, Guba** *bay* Russian Federation
57 J2 **Gusinaya Bank** *underwater feature* Barents Sea
190 F2 **Gusinoozërsk** Russian Federation
135 AH4 **Gusmp, Ostrov** *island* Russian Federation
125 I4 **Güssing** Austria
120 J5 **Gussjön** *lake* Sweden
109 I9 **Gustavia** St Barthélemy
74 D3 **Gustavus** Alaska USA
80 E8 **Gustine** California USA
142 inset **Gutcher** Shetland Scotland UK
125 H4 **Gutenstein** Austria
215 I5 **Guthalungra** Qld Australia
86 C3 **Guthrie** Oklahoma USA
86 A4 **Guthrie** Texas USA
189 H3 **Gutian Shuiku** *lake* Fujian China
89 F4 **Gutiérrez Zamora** Mexico
189 G1 **Guting** Shandong China
82 F5 **Guttenberg** Iowa USA
163 F3 **Gutu** Zimbabwe
185 K3 **Guulin** Mongolia
181 G3 **Guwahati** Assam India
101 G3 **Guyana** *country* South America
188 F3 **Guyang** Hunan China
126 D4 **Guyenne** *region* France
188 F3 **Guyi** Guangxi Zhuangzu Zizhiqu China
85 L2 **Guymon** Oklahoma USA
189 H3 **Guyong** Fujian China
87 J3 **Guyot, Mount** North Carolina USA
219 J4 **Guyra** NSW Australia
87 K4 **Guyton** Georgia USA
191 H4 **Guyuan** Hebei China
190 F6 **Guyuan** Ningxia Huizu Zizhiqu China
214 C2 **Guyuyu** *watercourse* NT Australia
189 H1 **Guzhen** Anhui China
188 E3 **Guzhou** Guizhou China
85 I5 **Guzmán** Mexico
85 I5 **Guzmán, Laguna de** *bay* Mexico
108 D4 **Guzmán, Punta** *cape* Argentina
182 J6 **G'uzor** Uzbekistan
130 H5 **Gvozd** Montenegro
194 B3 **Gwa** Myanmar
219 I4 **Gwabegar** NSW Australia
159 F2 **Gwadabawa** Nigeria
179 J4 **Gwadar** Pakistan
186 E5 **Gwalior** Madhya Pradesh India
159 E2 **Gwambara** Nigeria
162 E4 **Gwanda** Zimbabwe
157 I5 **Gwardafuy, Gees** *cape* Somalia
159 F2 **Gwarzo** Nigeria
162 E3 **Gwayi** Zimbabwe
125 I1 **Gwda** *watercourse* Poland
143 D2 **Gweebarra Bay** Ireland
138 B4 **Gweek** Cornwall England UK
143 C2 **Gweesalia** Ireland
162 E3 **Gwembe** Zambia
213 H6 **Gwenneth Lakes** WA Australia
138 C3 **Gwernogle** Carmarthenshire Wales UK
162 E3 **Gweru** Zimbabwe
162 E3 **Gweru** *watercourse* Zimbabwe
162 E4 **Gweta** Botswana
81 Q3 **Gwinner** North Dakota USA
159 G2 **Gwoza** Nigeria
138 D1 **Gwyddelwern** Denbighshire Wales UK
219 I3 **Gwydir** *watercourse* NSW Australia
138 D2 **Gwynedd** *admin. area* Wales UK
214 B6 **Gwynne, Mount** NT Australia
138 D2 **Gwystre** Powys Wales UK
127 G3 **Gy** France
122 D3 **Gya** Norway
132 A2 **Gyál** Hungary
133 E7 **Gyali** *island* Greece
185 K6 **Gyaring Hu** *lake* Qinghai China
133 D7 **Gyaros** *island* Greece
134 Q4 **Gyda** Russian Federation
134 Q4 **Gydanskaya Guba** *bay* Russian Federation
134 Q4 **Gydanskiy Poluostrov** *peninsula* Russian Federation
138 D1 **Gyfelia** Wrexham Wales UK
219 K2 **Gympie** Qld Australia
194 B3 **Gyobingauk** Myanmar
125 J4 **Gyöngyös** Hungary
130 G3 **Győr** Hungary
130 G3 **Győr-Moson-Sopron** *admin. area* Hungary
218 F6 **Gypsum** Vic. Australia
81 L7 **Gypsum** Colorado USA
85 N1 **Gypsum** Kansas USA
75 V7 **Gypsumville** Manitoba Canada
78 D3 **Gyrfalcon Islands** Nunavut Canada
122 E2 **Gyrinosvatnet** *lake* Norway
138 C1 **Gyrn-gôch** Gwynedd Wales UK
132 B2 **Gyula** Hungary
182 D6 **Gyumri** Armenia
122 D3 **Gyvatn** *lake* Norway
182 G6 **Gyzylarbat** Turkmenistan
182 G6 **Gyzyletrek** Turkmenistan
182 G6 **Gyzylgaya** Turkmenistan

H

123 N6 **H. Dzyarzhynskaya** *mountain* Belarus
87 H4 **H. Neely Henry Lake** Alabama USA
181 F3 **Ha** Bhutan
194 E2 **Ha Côi** Vietnam
194 E2 **Hà Đông** Vietnam
184 H4 **Ha-erh-kuo-ssu Ho** *watercourse* Xinjiang Uygur Zizhiqu China
194 E2 **Hạ Long** Vietnam
194 E2 **Hà Nội (Hanoi)** Vietnam
194 E5 **Hà Tiên** Vietnam
194 E3 **Hà Tĩnh** Vietnam
130 F2 **Haag** Austria
59 A2 **Haakon VII Sea** Antarctica
223 10 **Ha'ano** *island* Tonga
223 10 **Ha'apai Group** *islands* Tonga
121 N5 **Haapajärvi** Finland
121 O5 **Haapajärvi** *lake* Finland
121 O5 **Haapakoski** Finland
121 N5 **Haapamäki** Finland
123 O1 **Haapaselkä** *lake* Finland
121 N4 **Haapavesi** Finland
123 L3 **Haapsalu** Estonia
130 D2 **Haar** Germany
121 O5 **Haarajoki** Finland
124 C1 **Haarlem** Netherlands
221 C6 **Haast** New Zealand
221 C6 **Haast** *watercourse* New Zealand
161 G3 **Haaway** Somalia
179 K4 **Hab Chauki** Pakistan
185 H3 **Habahe** Xinjiang Uygur Zizhiqu China
178 G6 **Ḩabarūt** Yemen
161 F3 **Habaswein** Kenya
127 G2 **Habay la Neuve** Belgium
181 G4 **Habiganj** Bangladesh
127 L2 **Habry** Czech Republic
179 H5 **Ḩabshān** United Arab Emirates
193 I5 **Hachijō-jima** *island* Japan
193 I3 **Hachinohe** Japan
193 H3 **Hachiro-gata** *lake* Japan
85 H5 **Hachita** New Mexico USA
88 E4 **Hacienda Toribio** Mexico
120 I5 **Hackås** Sweden
143 F4 **Hacketstown** Ireland
143 F3 **Hackett's Cross** Ireland
141 H2 **Hackness** North Yorkshire England UK
120 H5 **Håckren** *bay* Sweden
162 C2 **Haco** Angola
163 F4 **Hacufera** Mozambique
156 F3 **Ḩadāribah, Ra's al** *cape* Sudan
179 I5 **Ḩadd, Ra's al** *cape* Oman
122 C1 **Haddal** Norway
159 G2 **Hadejia** Nigeria
159 G2 **Hadejia** *watercourse* Nigeria
122 F2 **Hadeland** *region* Norway
178 C3 **Hadera** Israel
179 H5 **Ḩadf** United Arab Emirates
187 D7 **Hadgaon** Maharashtra India
187 C12 **Hadhunmathi Atoll** Maldives
156 E1 **Ḩadīd, Jabal** *mountain* Egypt
178 E2 **Ḩadīthah** Iraq
156 C5 **Hadjer Bandala** Chad
159 H2 **Hadjer-Lamis** *admin. area* Chad
122 D2 **Hadlaskar** Norway
72 I4 **Hadley Bay** Nunavut Canada
192 E4 **Hadong** South Korea
141 F1 **Hadrian's Wall** *physical feature* England UK
120 I2 **Hadseløya** *island* Norway
192 E3 **Haeju** North Korea
192 E4 **Haeju-man** *bay* North Korea
121 M1 **Haen** Norway
84 inset **Hā'ena** Hawai'i USA
192 E4 **Haenam** South Korea
191 K3 **Ha'erbin** Heilongjiang China
178 D4 **Ḩafirat Al 'Aydā** Saudi Arabia
179 M3 **Hafizabad** Pakistan
181 G4 **Haflong** Assam India
120 inset **Hafnarfjörður** Iceland
122 D2 **Hafslovatnet** *lake* Norway
178 G3 **Haftkel** Iran
120 H6 **Haftorsbygget** Sweden
222 2 **Hagåtña** Guam
122 I4 **Hagby** Sweden
72 C7 **Hagemeister Island** Alaska USA
124 D1 **Hagen** Germany
85 J4 **Hagerman** New Mexico USA
83 M7 **Hagerstown** Maryland USA
126 D5 **Hagetmau** France
218 B4 **Haggard Hill** SA Australia
120 J5 **Häggdånger** Sweden
122 H2 **Haggen** *lake* Sweden
192 F4 **Hagi** Japan
143 C4 **Hag's Head** *cape* Ireland
75 R6 **Hague** Saskatchewan Canada
139 F5 **Hague, Cap de la** *cape* France
124 D3 **Haguenau** France
220 F3 **Hahei** New Zealand
123 M2 **Hahmajärvi** *lake* Finland
194 E2 **Hải Phòng (Haiphong)** Vietnam
194 F5 **Hai, Hon** *island* Vietnam
101 F3 **Haiamatipu Mountains** Guyana
189 H2 **Hai'an** Jiangsu China
162 C5 **Haib** *watercourse* Namibia
189 G4 **Haicheng** Guangdong China
191 J5 **Haicheng** Liaoning China
190 F6 **Haicheng** Ningxia Huizu Zizhiqu China
Haifa *see* **Hefa** Israel
217 J5 **Haig** WA Australia
81 O7 **Haigler** Nebraska USA
188 F5 **Haikou** Hainan China
178 E4 **Ḩā'il** Saudi Arabia
178 E4 **Ḩā'īl** *admin. area* Saudi Arabia
73 L9 **Haileybury** Ontario Canada
191 L4 **Hailin** Heilongjiang China
189 F4 **Hailing Dao** *island* Guangdong China
190 F4 **Hailiutu** Nei Mongol Zizhiqu China
139 H4 **Hailsham** East Sussex England UK
191 K3 **Hailun** Heilongjiang China
121 N4 **Hailuoto** Finland
121 N4 **Hailuoto** *island* Finland
189 I2 **Haimen** Jiangsu China
189 I4 **Haimi** Japan
188 F5 **Hainan** *admin. area* China
188 F5 **Hainan** *island* Hainan China
Hainan Strait *see* **Qiongzhou Haixia** China
158 B3 **Haindi** Liberia
80 G4 **Haines** Oregon USA
87 K6 **Haines City** Florida USA
74 C2 **Haines Junction** Yukon Territory Canada
125 H3 **Hainfeld** Austria
Haiphong *see* **Hải Phòng** Vietnam
190 E3 **Hairhan** Mongolia
190 E3 **Hairhandulaan** Mongolia
121 O4 **Haiskinselkä** *bay* Finland
189 H3 **Haitan Dao** *island* Fujian China
91 F3 **Haiti** *country* Caribbean
84 D2 **Haiwee** California USA
156 F4 **Haiya** Sudan
189 F4 **Haiyan** Guangdong China
189 H2 **Haiyang** Anhui China
191 J6 **Haiyang** Shandong China
191 J5 **Haiyang Dao** *island* Liaoning China
189 I2 **Haiyou** Zhejiang China
191 I6 **Haizhou Wan** *bay* Shandong China
120 J2 **Håja** *island* Norway
179 I5 **Ḩajar, Al** *range* Oman
156 C5 **Ḩajar Banga** Sudan
132 B2 **Hajdú-Bihar** *admin. area* Hungary
125 K4 **Hajdúböszörmény** Hungary
132 B2 **Hajdúszoboszló** Hungary
132 B2 **Hajdúszovát** Hungary
131 C9 **Hajeb el Aioun** Tunisia
179 K4 **Haji Khan** Pakistan
186 F6 **Hajipur** Bihar India
178 E7 **Ḩajjah** Yemen
178 F7 **Ḩajr, Wādī** *watercourse* Yemen
190 G3 **Hajuuuln** Mongolia
181 G4 **Haka** Myanmar
221 B8 **Hakapoua, Lake** New Zealand
221 D7 **Hakataramea** *watercourse* New Zealand
136 G6 **Hakkari** Turkey
136 H6 **Hakkāri** *admin. area* Turkey
193 G4 **Hakken-zan** *mountain* Japan
121 N5 **Häkkilä** Finland
193 I3 **Hakodate** Japan
121 M1 **Hakstabben** Norway
193 H4 **Haku-san** *volcano* Japan
220 4 **Hakupu** Niue New Zealand
193 H4 **Hakusan** Japan
120 J2 **Håkvik** Norway
179 K4 **Hala** Pakistan
136 F6 **Halab (Aleppo)** Syria
178 E5 **Ḩalabān** Saudi Arabia
184 G3 **Halabula** Xinjiang Uygur Zizhiqu China
89 H4 **Halachó** Mexico
220 4 **Halagigie Point** Niue New Zealand
156 F3 **Halaib** Halaib Triangle
156 F3 **Halaib Triangle** *disputed territory* Egypt/Sudan
186 D6 **Halali Reservoir** Madhya Pradesh India
223 12b **Halalo** Wallis and Futuna
195 J6 **Halapitan** Philippines
122 H3 **Hålaveden** *region* Sweden
84 inset **Hālawa** Hawai'i USA
75 T8 **Halbrite** Saskatchewan Canada
132 D3 **Hălchiu** Romania
187 G6 **Haldia** West Bengal India
214 C7 **Hale** *watercourse* NT Australia
216 E3 **Hale, Mount** WA Australia
85 L3 **Hale Center** Texas USA
139 H3 **Hale Street** Kent England UK
84 inset **Hale'iwa** Hawai'i USA
127 G1 **Halen** Belgium
122 H4 **Halen** *lake* Sweden
139 E2 **Halesowen** West Midlands England UK
139 I2 **Halesworth** Suffolk England UK
86 H3 **Haleyville** Alabama USA
158 D3 **Half Assini** Ghana
215 H3 **Half Mile Opening** *reef* Qld Australia
218 A3 **Half Moon Lake** SA Australia
211 inset **Halfmoon Bay** Macquarie Island Australia
221 C8 **Halfmoon Bay (Oban)** New Zealand
74 J4 **Halfway** *watercourse* British Columbia Canada
190 E2 **Halganat** Mongolia
191 I3 **Halhgol** Mongolia
191 I3 **Halhin Gol** *watercourse* Mongolia
83 L4 **Haliburton** Ontario Canada
218 E6 **Halidon** SA Australia
79 G10 **Halifax** Nova Scotia Canada
87 L2 **Halifax** Virginia USA
215 I5 **Halifax, Mount** Qld Australia
215 I5 **Halifax Bay** Qld Australia
184 G4 **Halik Shan** *range* Xinjiang Uygur Zizhiqu China
123 L2 **Halikko** Finland
133 E6 **Halilbeyli** Turkey
217 L4 **Halinor Lake** SA Australia
185 J3 **Haliun** Mongolia
122 G5 **Häljarp** Sweden
121 O5 **Halkokumpu** Finland
125 H4 **Hall** Austria
123 J4 **Hall** Sweden
73 K5 **Hall Beach** Nunavut Canada
199 I1 **Hall Islands** Federated States of Micronesia
73 M6 **Hall Peninsula** Nunavut Canada
213 H3 **Hall Point** WA Australia
120 J5 **Hälla** Sweden
192 E5 **Halla-san** *mountain* South Korea
122 G4 **Halland** *admin. area* Sweden
179 H6 **Ḩallāniyah, Al** *island* Oman
121 P4 **Hallavaara** Finland
81 P1 **Hallboro** Manitoba Canada
120 J5 **Hällbymagasinet** *lake* Sweden
127 G1 **Halle** Belgium
124 E1 **Halle** Germany
120 I5 **Hallen** Sweden
124 E2 **Hallenburg** Germany
130 D2 **Hallertau** *region* Germany
218 D5 **Hallett** SA Australia
86 C2 **Hallett** Oklahoma USA
59 L2 **Hallett, Cape** Antarctica
86 C6 **Hallettsville** Texas USA
59 W1 **Halley (UK)** *research station* Antarctica
212 E6 **Halleys Comet Mine** WA Australia
59 X2 **Hallgreen, Mount** Antarctica
81 N3 **Halliday** North Dakota USA
122 E5 **Halligen** *island* Germany
122 E2 **Hallingdal** *valley* Norway
122 E2 **Hallingdalselva** *watercourse* Norway
122 I4 **Hallingeberg** Sweden
122 D2 **Hallingskarvet** *region* Norway
81 Q2 **Hallock** Minnesota USA
213 I5 **Halls Creek** WA Australia
123 J4 **Halls Fiskläge** Sweden
123 J2 **Hallstavik** Sweden
120 I5 **Hallviken** Sweden
138 C4 **Hallworthy** Cornwall England UK
198 D3 **Halmahera** *island* Indonesia
198 D4 **Halmahera, Laut** *sea* Indonesia
125 L4 **Halmeu** Romania
120 G4 **Halmøya** *island* Norway
122 G4 **Halmstad** Sweden
122 D2 **Halnefjorden** *lake* Norway
122 F4 **Hals** Denmark
120 F5 **Hals** Norway
120 H3 **Halsa** Norway
140 F3 **Halsall** Lancashire England UK
138 B4 **Halsetown** Cornwall England UK
186 G6 **Halsi** Bihar India
122 C3 **Halsnøy** *island* Norway
120 L5 **Halsön** *island* Finland
139 H3 **Halstead** Essex England UK
121 N5 **Halsua** Finland
121 M5 **Halsuanjärvi** *lake* Finland
221 E6 **Halswell** New Zealand
185 J5 **Haltang He** *watercourse* Qinghai China
120 G5 **Haltdalen** Norway
50 S3 **Halten Bank** *underwater feature* Norwegian Sea
124 D2 **Haltern** Germany
141 H3 **Haltham** Lincolnshire England UK
134 F5 **Haltia** *mountain* Finland
219 J5 **Halton** NSW Australia
140 F3 **Halton** *admin. area* England UK
178 F2 **Haltūshān** Iran
141 F2 **Haltwhistle** Northumberland England UK
178 G4 **Ḩālūl** *island* Qatar
121 P5 **Haluna** Finland
198 B6 **Halura** *island* Indonesia
186 C6 **Halvad** Gujarat India
179 H2 **Ḩalvān** Iran
124 D2 **Halver** Germany
191 G3 **Halzan** Mongolia
159 H2 **Ham** Chad
126 F2 **Ham** France
142 inset **Ham** Shetland Scotland UK
194 E5 **Hàm Tân** Vietnam
192 G4 **Hamada** Japan
178 F2 **Hamadān** Iran
182 E7 **Hamadān** *admin. area* Iran
155 F2 **Hamaguir** Algeria
136 F6 **Ḩamāh (Hamath)** Syria
136 F6 **Hamam** Turkey
193 H4 **Hamamatsu** Japan
178 G4 **Hamandeh** Iran
122 F2 **Hamar** Norway
120 I2 **Hamarøy** Norway
120 I2 **Hamarøy** *island* Norway
161 G2 **Hamarro Hadad** Ethiopia
Hamath *see* **Ḩamāh** Syria
187 E10 **Hambantota** Sri Lanka
218 C3 **Hambidge Point** SA Australia
124 E1 **Hamburg** Germany
124 F1 **Hamburg** *admin. area* Germany
83 N6 **Hamburg** New Jersey USA
83 L5 **Hamburg** New York USA
178 E6 **Ḩamḑah** Saudi Arabia
178 D4 **Ḩamḑah, Wādī al** *watercourse* Saudi Arabia
178 F3 **Ḩamdān** Iraq
123 M2 **Hämeenlinna** Finland
216 D7 **Hamelin Bay** WA Australia
216 D3 **Hamelin Pool** WA Australia
124 E1 **Hameln** Germany
216 F5 **Hamersley Lakes** WA Australia
192 F3 **Hamgyŏng-Sanmaek** North Korea
192 E3 **Hamhŭng** North Korea
185 J4 **Hami** Xinjiang Uygur Zizhiqu China
133 E5 **Hamidiye** Turkey
214 G6 **Hamilton** *watercourse* Qld Australia
218 B2 **Hamilton** SA Australia
218 B2 **Hamilton** *watercourse* SA Australia
83 inset **Hamilton** Bermuda
83 L5 **Hamilton** Ontario Canada
220 F3 **Hamilton** New Zealand
142 D5 **Hamilton** South Lanarkshire Scotland UK
85 N2 **Hamilton** Kansas USA
82 E7 **Hamilton** Missouri USA
80 H3 **Hamilton** Montana USA
83 N5 **Hamilton** New York USA
82 I7 **Hamilton** Ohio USA
86 B5 **Hamilton** Texas USA
86 E3 **Hamilton, Lake** Arkansas USA
211 inset **Hamilton, Mount** Macquarie Island Australia
214 B7 **Hamilton Downs** NT Australia
218 C3 **Hamilton Hill** SA Australia
214 F7 **Hamilton Hotel** Qld Australia
78 I6 **Hamilton Inlet** Newfoundland and Labrador Canada
79 K8 **Hamilton Sound** Newfoundland and Labrador Canada
156 C1 **Hamīn, Wādī Al** *watercourse* Libya
123 N2 **Hamina** Finland
121 O5 **Haminalahti** Finland
75 U7 **Hamiota** Manitoba Canada
122 D2 **Hamlagrovatnet** *lake* Norway
87 L3 **Hamlet** North Carolina USA
86 A4 **Hamlin** Texas USA
124 D2 **Hamm** Germany
155 I1 **Hammamet** Tunisia
136 F6 **Ḩammāmīyah** Syria
122 H3 **Hammar** Sweden
120 I5 **Hammarnäset** Sweden
122 H5 **Hammarsjön** *lake* Sweden
121 O2 **Hammasjärvi** *lake* Finland
121 P5 **Hammaslahti** Finland
124 E1 **Hamme** *watercourse* Germany
120 I5 **Hammerdal** Sweden
120 I5 **Hammerdalssjön** *lake* Sweden
121 M2 **Hammerfest** Norway
121 D1 **Hammerfest** Norway
122 E4 **Hammerum** Denmark
86 B3 **Hammon** Oklahoma USA
82 H6 **Hammond** Indiana USA
86 F5 **Hammond** Louisiana USA
214 B7 **Hammond, Mount** NT Australia
218 F1 **Hammond Downs** Qld Australia
79 J7 **Hammone, Lac** *lake* Quebec Canada
120 H4 **Hamn** Norway
121 Q1 **Hamna** Norway
142 inset **Hamnavoe** Shetland Scotland UK
120 L2 **Hamneidet** Norway
120 L2 **Hamnes** Norway
120 H4 **Hamnøya** *island* Norway
192 E4 **Hampeong** South Korea
219 Q10 **Hampshire** Tas. Australia
139 F3 **Hampshire** *admin. area* England UK
79 F10 **Hampton** New Brunswick Canada
83 P5 **Hampton** New Hampshire USA
83 M8 **Hampton** Virginia USA
216 F5 **Hampton, Mount** WA Australia
216 G5 **Hampton Hill** WA Australia
217 J6 **Hampton Tableland** WA Australia
159 I2 **Hamra, Ouadi** *watercourse* Chad
156 D5 **Hamrat esh Sheikh** Sudan
139 H3 **Hamstreet** Kent England UK
198 E4 **Hamuku** Indonesia
179 J3 **Hāmūn, Daryācheh-ye** *lake* Iran
179 I4 **Hāmūn-e Jāz Mūrīan** *lake* Iran
179 J3 **Hāmūn Şāberī, Daryāchech-ye** *lake* Iran
139 E4 **Hamworthy** Poole England UK
192 E4 **Hamyang** South Korea
199 J5 **Han Island** Papua New Guinea
189 G4 **Han Jiang** *watercourse* Guangdong China
130 H4 **Han Pijesak** Bosnia and Herzegovina
188 E2 **Han Shui** *watercourse* Shaanxi China
190 E2 **Han-Ula, Gora** *mountain* Russian Federation
199 J5 **Hanahan** Papua New Guinea
124 E2 **Hanau** Germany
190 F4 **Hanbogd** Mongolia
76 J1 **Hanbury Island** Nunavut Canada
74 J7 **Hanceville** British Columbia Canada
189 G3 **Hanchang** Hunan China
190 G6 **Hancheng** Shaanxi China
189 G2 **Hanchuan** Hubei China
81 R4 **Hancock** Minnesota USA
217 I2 **Hancock, Lake** WA Australia
142 C2 **Handa Island** Scotland UK
191 H6 **Handan** Hebei China
161 F5 **Handeni** Tanzania
187 D6 **Handia** Madhya Pradesh India
191 H6 **Handian** Shanxi China
120 H3 **Handnesøya** *island* Norway
120 H5 **Handöl** Sweden
120 I5 **Handsjö** Sweden
75 T8 **Handsworth** Saskatchewan Canada
120 G6 **Hanestad** Norway
188 E2 **Hanfeng** Chongqing China
84 C2 **Hanford** California USA
109 5 **Hanga Roa** Isla de Pascua (Easter Island)
190 E2 **Hangal** Mongolia
185 K3 **Hangayn Nuruu** *range* Mongolia
189 H3 **Hangchuan** Fujian China
Hangö *see* **Hanko** Finland
123 L3 **Hangö östra fjärd** *bay* Finland
123 L3 **Hangö västra fjärd** *bay* Finland
122 I1 **Hångstaörn** *lake* Sweden
191 I5 **Hangu** Tianjin China
179 L2 **Hangu** Pakistan
189 H2 **Hangzhou** Zhejiang China
189 I2 **Hangzhou Wan** *bay* Zhejiang China
190 D2 **Hanh** Mongolia
138 E3 **Hanham** South Gloucestershire England UK
190 E4 **Hanhongor** Mongolia
178 E7 **Ḩanīsh al Kabīr, Jazīrat al** *island* Yemen
210 inset **Hanitch Hill** Christmas Island Australia
197 G4 **Hanjalipan** Indonesia
190 E6 **Hanji** Gansu China
188 E2 **Hanjia** Chongqing China
179 J4 **Hanjīrak** Iran
121 P5 **Hankamäki** Finland
121 O5 **Hankasalem asema** Finland
121 O5 **Hankasalmi** Finland
81 Q3 **Hankinson** North Dakota USA
123 L3 **Hanko (Hangö)** Finland
123 L3 **Hankoniemi** *cape* Finland
133 G6 **Hanköy** Turkey
84 G1 **Hanksville** Utah USA
75 R7 **Hanley** Saskatchewan Canada
81 R4 **Hanley Falls** Minnesota USA
221 E6 **Hanmer Springs** New Zealand
215 G3 **Hann** *watercourse* Qld Australia
213 I4 **Hann** *watercourse* WA Australia
213 H3 **Hann, Mount** WA Australia
215 G3 **Hann River Roadhouse** Qld Australia
75 P7 **Hanna** Alberta Canada
86 D3 **Hanna** Oklahoma USA
81 L6 **Hanna** Wyoming USA
81 P3 **Hannaford** North Dakota USA
77 P7 **Hannah Bay** Ontario Canada
221 C6 **Hannah's Clearing** New Zealand
215 J6 **Hannaville** Qld Australia
82 F7 **Hannibal** Missouri USA
124 E1 **Hannover** Germany
215 G5 **Hanns Table Mountain** Qld Australia
127 G1 **Hannut** Belgium
122 H5 **Hanö** *island* Sweden
122 H5 **Hanöbukten** *bay* Sweden
Hanoi *see* **Ha Nội** Vietnam
162 D6 **Hanover** South Africa
83 M7 **Hanover** Pennsylvania USA
108 A5 **Hanover, Isla** *island* Chile
199 J5 **Hanpan, Cape** Papua New Guinea
190 D3 **Hanrai** Mongolia
130 G3 **Hanság** *range* Hungary
189 F3 **Hanshou** Hunan China
214 B6 **Hanson** *watercourse* NT Australia
82 H8 **Hanson** Kentucky USA
218 C4 **Hanson, Lake** SA Australia
221 6 **Hanson Bay** Chatham Islands New Zealand
124 F1 **Hanstedt** Germany
122 E4 **Hanstholm** Denmark
186 D5 **Hanumangarh** Rajasthan India
187 D9 **Hanur** Karnataka India
190 E3 **Hanuy Gol** *watercourse* Mongolia
188 E2 **Hanyin** Shaanxi China
188 E1 **Hanzhong** Shaanxi China
223 14 **Hao** *reef* French Polynesia
190 E5 **Haomen** Qinghai China
187 G6 **Haora** West Bengal India
84 inset **Hā'ō'ū** Hawai'i USA
155 H2 **Haoud el Hamra** Algeria
121 N4 **Haparanda** Sweden
192 F4 **Hapch'on** South Korea
142 E5 **Hapland** Dumfries and Galloway Scotland UK
181 G3 **Hapoli** Arunachal Pradesh India
139 I2 **Happisburgh** Norfolk England UK
76 H1 **Happotiyik Lake** Nunavut Canada
85 L3 **Happy** Texas USA
178 C3 **Ḩaql** Saudi Arabia
198 E5 **Har** Indonesia
185 K5 **Har Hu** *lake* Qinghai China
191 H3 **Har Nuden** Nei Mongol Zizhiqu China
185 J3 **Har Nuur** *lake* Mongolia
185 I2 **Har-us Nuur** *lake* Mongolia
185 I3 **Har Us Nuur** *lake* Mongolia
120 I5 **Hara** Sweden
123 M3 **Hara laht** *bay* Estonia
178 G5 **Ḩaraḑ** Saudi Arabia
178 E7 **Ḩaraḑ** Yemen
178 F5 **Ḩarāḑah** Saudi Arabia
120 L3 **Harads** Sweden
120 E5 **Haram** *island* Norway
193 I4 **Haramachi** Japan
120 E5 **Haramsøya** *island* Norway
186 D3 **Haramukh** *mountain* Jammu and Kashmir India/Pakistan
163 F3 **Harare** Zimbabwe
163 F3 **Harare** *admin. area* Zimbabwe
161 G2 **Hārarī Hizb** *admin. area* Ethiopia
125 L2 **Harasiuki** Poland
155 J2 **Harāwah, Wādī** *watercourse* Libya
159 H2 **Haraz** Chad
156 E4 **Haraza, Jebel** *mountain* Sudan
159 I3 **Haraze-Mangueigne** Chad
120 I4 **Härbergsdalen** Sweden
122 I2 **Harbo** Sweden
82 J5 **Harbor Beach** Michigan USA
139 F2 **Harborne** West Midlands England UK
109 7 **Harbours, Bay of** Falkland Islands
124 E1 **Harburg** Germany
141 H3 **Harby** Nottinghamshire England UK
81 P1 **Harcus** Manitoba Canada
84 F3 **Harcuvar Mountains** Arkansas USA
187 D6 **Harda** Madhya Pradesh India
122 D2 **Hardanger vidda** *region* Norway
162 C4 **Hardap** *admin. area* Namibia
139 I4 **Hardelot-Plage** France
197 G2 **Harden, Bukit** *mountain* Indonesia
86 A2 **Hardesty** Oklahoma USA
212 D7 **Hardey** *watercourse* WA Australia
86 G2 **Hardin** Kentucky USA
81 L4 **Hardin** Montana USA
139 I2 **Hardingham** Norfolk England UK
214 F8 **Hardings Ranges** Qld Australia
82 H8 **Hardinsburg** Kentucky USA
72 H6 **Hardisty Lake** Northwest Territories Canada
186 E5 **Hardoi** Uttar Pradesh India
86 B2 **Hardtner** Kansas USA
139 F3 **Hardwick** Oxfordshire England UK
218 C6 **Hardwicke Bay** SA Australia
218 C6 **Hardy, Cape** SA Australia
214 A7 **Hardy, Mount** NT Australia
108 C6 **Hardy, Península** Chile
82 I5 **Hardy Dam Pond** Michigan USA
215 J5 **Hardy Reef** Qld Australia

79 K8 **Hare Bay** Newfoundland and Labrador Canada
79 K7 **Hare Bay** Newfoundland and Labrador Canada
122 G3 **Harefjorden** *lake* Sweden
141 G3 **Harehills** West Yorkshire England UK
122 C1 **Hareidlandet** *island* Norway
124 D1 **Haren** Netherlands
161 G2 **Härer** Ethiopia
141 F2 **Haresceugh** Cumbria England UK
139 H5 **Harfleur** France
138 D4 **Harford** Devon England UK
161 G2 **Hargele** Ethiopia
161 G2 **Hargeysa** Somalia
132 D2 **Harghita** *admin. area* Romania
81 O2 **Hargrave** Manitoba Canada
139 H2 **Hargrave** Suffolk England UK
219 I5 **Hargraves** NSW Australia
190 F5 **Harhatan** Nei Mongol Zizhiqu China
185 I2 **Harhiraa** Mongolia
190 E3 **Harhorin** Mongolia
196 D4 **Hari** *watercourse* Indonesia
123 L3 **Hari Kurk** *bay* Estonia
179 J2 **Harī Rūd** *watercourse* Afghanistan
186 E5 **Haridwar** Uttaranchal India
187 D8 **Harihar** Karnataka India
186 F6 **Hariharpur** Chhattisgarh India
186 C6 **Harij** Gujarat India
179 L2 **Haripur** Pakistan
122 H2 **Härjåsjön** *lake* Sweden
122 G1 **Härjedalen** *valley* Sweden
121 M4 **Harjufjärden** *bay* Sweden
123 M3 **Harjumaa** *admin. area* Estonia
123 N2 **Harjumaa** Finland
121 O5 **Härkajärvi** *lake* Finland
82 D6 **Harlan** Iowa USA
87 J2 **Harlan** Kentucky USA
81 P6 **Harlan County Lake** Nebraska USA
78 F6 **Harlands Landing** Newfoundland and Labrador Canada
139 G2 **Harlaxton** Lincolnshire England UK
138 C2 **Harlech** Gwynedd Wales UK
81 K2 **Harlem** Montana USA
124 C1 **Harlingen** Netherlands
86 C7 **Harlingen** Texas USA
139 H3 **Harlow** Essex England UK
81 K3 **Harlowton** Montana USA
139 H2 **Harlton** Cambridgeshire England UK
133 F6 **Harmancık** Turkey
120 J6 **Harmånger** Sweden
121 P4 **Härmänmäki** Finland
157 G4 **Harmil** *island* Eritrea
82 F2 **Harmon Lake** Ontario Canada
84 B3 **Harmony** California USA
81 F5 **Harney Basin** *pan* Oregon USA
80 F5 **Harney Lake** Oregon USA
141 G1 **Harnham** Northumberland England UK
120 K5 **Härnön** *island* Sweden
120 J5 **Härnösand** Sweden
128 E2 **Haro** Spain
123 J3 **Harö** *island* Sweden
123 N5 **Harodz'ki** Belarus
120 E5 **Harøya** *island* Norway
78 G5 **Harp Lake** Newfoundland and Labrador Canada
187 D8 **Harpanahalli** Karnataka India
120 F6 **Harpefoss** Norway
139 G3 **Harpenden** Hertfordshire England UK
158 C4 **Harper** Liberia
81 P8 **Harper** Kansas USA
84 D3 **Harper Lake** California USA
141 H3 **Harpswell** Lincolnshire England UK
120 L3 **Harrå** Sweden
187 E6 **Harrai** Madhya Pradesh India
120 L3 **Harrejaur** Sweden
83 L2 **Harricanaw** *watercourse* Quebec Canada
140 E2 **Harrington** Cumbria England UK
80 F3 **Harrington** Washington USA
73 N8 **Harrington Harbour** Quebec Canada
83 inset **Harrington Sound** Bermuda
75 R7 **Harris** Saskatchewan Canada
109 17 **Harris** Montserrat
142 B4 **Harris** Highland Scotland UK
218 B4 **Harris, Lake** SA Australia
87 K6 **Harris, Lake** Florida USA
216 E6 **Harris Dam** WA Australia
217 H5 **Harris Lake** WA Australia
221 C7 **Harris Mountains** New Zealand
53 Q3 **Harris Seamount** *underwater feature* Pacific Ocean
82 G8 **Harrisburg** Illinois USA
80 D4 **Harrisburg** Oregon USA
83 M6 **Harrisburg** Pennsylvania USA
162 E5 **Harrismith** South Africa
86 E2 **Harrison** Arkansas USA
82 I4 **Harrison** Michigan USA
81 N5 **Harrison** Nebraska USA
78 J5 **Harrison, Cape** Newfoundland and Labrador Canada
72 D4 **Harrison Bay** Alaska USA
74 K8 **Harrison Hot Springs** British Columbia Canada
74 K8 **Harrison Lake** British Columbia Canada
109 12 **Harrison Point** *cape* Barbados
83 L7 **Harrisonburg** Virginia USA
82 J4 **Harrisville** Michigan USA
83 N4 **Harrisville** New York USA
141 G3 **Harrogate** North Yorkshire England UK
139 G2 **Harrold** Bedfordshire England UK
76 H6 **Harrop Lake** Manitoba Canada
218 E7 **Harrow** Vic. Australia
139 G3 **Harrow** Greater London England UK
81 O1 **Harrowby** Manitoba Canada
120 I4 **Harrsjön** Sweden
120 J4 **Harrvik** Sweden
82 E7 **Harry S. Truman Reservoir** Missouri USA
120 J2 **Harstad** Norway
81 M2 **Hart** Saskatchewan Canada
72 F5 **Hart** *watercourse* Yukon Territory Canada
82 H5 **Hart** Michigan USA
85 K3 **Hart** Texas USA
218 D6 **Hart, Cape** SA Australia
218 C4 **Hart, Lake** SA Australia
213 H4 **Hart, Mount** WA Australia
80 F5 **Hart Lake** Oregon USA
74 J5 **Hart Range** British Columbia Canada
132 A2 **Harta** Hungary
162 D5 **Hartbees** *watercourse* South Africa
120 J6 **Hårte** Sweden
142 C3 **Hartfield** Highland Scotland UK
83 O6 **Hartford** Connecticut USA
82 H8 **Hartford** Kentucky USA
81 Q5 **Hartford** South Dakota USA
141 G2 **Hartforth** North Yorkshire England UK
138 E1 **Harthill** Cheshire England UK
141 G3 **Harthill** South Yorkshire England UK
139 F1 **Hartington** Derbyshire England UK
79 E9 **Hartland** New Brunswick Canada
79 D10 **Hartland** Maine USA
138 C3 **Hartland Point** England UK
141 G2 **Hartlepool** Hartlepool England UK
141 G2 **Hartlepool** *admin. area* England UK
85 K3 **Hartley** Texas USA
74 G6 **Hartley Bay** British Columbia Canada
214 C7 **Harts Range** NT Australia
214 C7 **Harts Range Police Station** NT Australia
85 J1 **Hartsel** Colorado USA
86 H3 **Hartselle** Alabama USA
162 D5 **Hartswater** South Africa
139 G2 **Hartwell** Northamptonshire England UK
87 J3 **Hartwell Lake** South Carolina USA
219 R11 **Hartz Peak** Tas. Australia
81 P6 **Harvard** Nebraska USA
217 J2 **Harvest, Mount** WA Australia
216 D6 **Harvey** WA Australia
81 P3 **Harvey** North Dakota USA
85 O1 **Harveyville** Kansas USA
139 I3 **Harwich** Essex England UK
186 D5 **Haryana** *admin. area* India
178 F2 **Harzin** Iran
124 D1 **Hase** *watercourse* Germany
107 G4 **Hasenkamp** Argentina
190 E3 **Hashaat** Mongolia
193 G4 **Hashimoto** Japan
156 D5 **Haskanit** Sudan
86 E3 **Haskell** Arkansas USA
86 B4 **Haskell** Texas USA
221 8 **Haskell Bay** Auckland Islands New Zealand
125 H3 **Haslach an der Mühl** Austria
124 E3 **Haslach im Kinzigtal** Germany
218 B5 **Haslam** SA Australia
122 H5 **Hasle** Denmark
124 E4 **Hasle** Switzerland
139 G3 **Haslemere** Surrey England UK
122 F5 **Haslev** Denmark
138 E1 **Haslington** Cheshire England UK
126 D5 **Hasparren** France
187 D9 **Hassan** Karnataka India
133 E6 **Hasseki** Turkey
73 J3 **Hassel Sound** Nunavut Canada
120 J5 **Hassela** Sweden
120 J5 **Hasselasjön** *lake* Sweden
211 inset **Hasselborough Bay** Macquarie Island Australia
139 H3 **Hassell Street** Kent England UK
122 I4 **Hasselö** *island* Sweden
127 G1 **Hasselt** Belgium
154 F3 **Hassi el Khebi** Algeria
155 H2 **Hassi Messaoud** Algeria
120 J5 **Hässjö** Sweden
122 G2 **Hassjön** *lake* Sweden
122 G4 **Hässleholm** Sweden
122 H4 **Hasslö** *island* Sweden
130 C2 **Haßloch** Germany
82 E3 **Hassman** Minnesota USA
109 12 **Hastings** Barbados
220 G4 **Hastings** New Zealand
139 H4 **Hastings** East Sussex England UK
82 I5 **Hastings** Michigan USA
82 E4 **Hastings** Minnesota USA
81 P6 **Hastings** Nebraska USA
199 I6 **Hastings Island** Papua New Guinea
122 H3 **Hästnäs** Sweden
123 N2 **Hästön** *island* Finland
122 G4 **Hästveda** Sweden
178 E6 **Ḩasy** Saudi Arabia
194 D6 **Hat Yai** Thailand
179 K4 **Hatachi** Pakistan
190 G4 **Hatanbular** Mongolia
136 F6 **Hatay (Antioch)** Turkey
136 F6 **Hatay** *admin. area* Turkey
83 N6 **Hatboro** Pennsylvania USA
85 I4 **Hatch** New Mexico USA
80 I8 **Hatch** Utah USA
76 D3 **Hatchet Lake** Saskatchewan Canada
86 G3 **Hatchie** *watercourse* Tennessee USA
132 C3 **Haţeg** Romania
189 I4 **Hateruma Shima** *island* Japan
218 F5 **Hatfield** NSW Australia
139 G3 **Hatfield** Hertfordshire England UK
141 G3 **Hatfield** South Yorkshire England UK
141 H3 **Hatfield Woodhouse** South Yorkshire England UK
139 F3 **Hatherop** Gloucestershire England UK
186 E5 **Hathras** Uttar Pradesh India
109 1b **Hato, Bocht van** *bay* Netherlands Antilles
186 E6 **Hatta** Madhya Pradesh India
218 F6 **Hattah** Vic. Australia
124 D1 **Hattem** Netherlands
87 N3 **Hatteras, Cape** North Carolina USA
50 K6 **Hatteras Abyssal Plain** *underwater feature* Atlantic Ocean
86 G5 **Hattiesburg** Mississippi USA
81 K1 **Hatton** Saskatchewan Canada
78 F2 **Hatton Headland** Nunavut Canada
194 C4 **Hattras Passage** *strait* Myanmar
122 E5 **Hattstedt** Germany
121 Q5 **Hattuvaara** Finland
121 O4 **Hatulanmäki** Finland
223 14 **Hatutu** *island* French Polynesia
130 H3 **Hatvan** Hungary
161 G2 **Haud** *plain* Ethiopia
122 D3 **Hauge** Norway
122 C3 **Haugesund** Norway
142 E6 **Haugh of Urr** Dumfries and Galloway Scotland UK
120 H3 **Haugland** Norway
120 L1 **Haugnes** Norway
123 M2 **Hauha** *lake* Finland
220 F4 **Hauhungaroa Range** New Zealand
121 Q4 **Haukela** Finland
122 D3 **Haukeligrend** Norway
121 N4 **Haukipudas** Finland
121 P5 **Haukivesi** *bay* Finland
120 J2 **Haukøy** *island* Norway
106 F3 **Haumonia** Argentina
220 F3 **Hauraki Gulf** New Zealand
122 H4 **Haurida** Sweden
221 B8 **Hauroko, Lake** New Zealand
127 J3 **Hausham** Germany
Haussez, Iles d' *see* **Mercury Islands** New Zealand
83 Q5 **Haut, Isle au** *island* Maine USA
160 D2 **Haut-Mbomou** *admin. area* Central African Republic
159 G5 **Haut-Ogooué** *admin. area* Gabon
121 P3 **Hautajärvi** Finland
159 I3 **Haute-Kotto** *admin. area* Central African Republic
126 E2 **Haute-Normandie** *admin. area* France
126 D2 **Hauteville-sur-Mer** France
155 G2 **Hauts Plateaux** *range* Algeria
84 inset **Hau'ula** Hawai'i USA
125 G3 **Hauzenberg** Germany
125 K3 **Havaj** Slovakia
Havana *see* **La Habana** Cuba
82 F6 **Havana** Illinois USA
139 G4 **Havant** Hampshire England UK
124 G1 **Havel** *watercourse* Germany
87 M3 **Havelock** North Carolina USA
194 B5 **Havelock Island** Andaman and Nicobar Islands India
124 D1 **Havelte** Netherlands
122 H2 **Håven** Sweden
138 C3 **Haverfordwest** Pembrokeshire Wales UK
139 H2 **Haverhill** Suffolk England UK
83 P5 **Haverhill** Massachusetts USA
187 D8 **Haveri** Karnataka India
120 I5 **Havern** *bay* Sweden
83 O6 **Haverstraw** New York USA
81 P8 **Haviland** Kansas USA
120 H5 **Hävlingen** *lake* Sweden
122 E5 **Havneby** Denmark
121 N1 **Havøya** *island* Norway
121 N1 **Havøysund** Norway
122 I2 **Håvran** *lake* Sweden
133 E6 **Havran** Turkey
81 K2 **Havre** Montana USA
79 H9 **Havre-Aubert** Quebec Canada
79 G9 **Havre Aubert, Île du** *island* Quebec Canada
79 H9 **Havre-aux-Maisons** Quebec Canada
79 G7 **Havre-Saint-Pierre** Quebec Canada
132 E1 **Havrylivtsi** Ukraine
120 I4 **Havsnäs** Sweden
84 inset **Hawai'i** *admin. area* USA
52 P5 **Hawaiian Ridge** *underwater feature* Pacific Ocean
53 R5 **Hawaiian Trough** *underwater feature* Pacific Ocean
178 G4 **Ḩawār, Jazīrat** *island* Bahrain
75 R7 **Hawarden** Saskatchewan Canada
221 E6 **Hawarden** New Zealand
138 D1 **Hawarden** Flintshire Wales UK
81 Q5 **Hawarden** Iowa USA
192 F3 **Hawdae** North Korea
221 C7 **Hawea Flat** New Zealand
221 C7 **Hawea, Lake** New Zealand
220 F4 **Hawera** New Zealand
141 F2 **Hawes** North Yorkshire England UK
140 F2 **Haweswater Reservoir** England UK
142 F5 **Hawick** Scottish Borders Scotland UK
74 M4 **Hawk Hills** Alberta Canada
221 D7 **Hawkdun Range** New Zealand
78 J6 **Hawke** *watercourse* Newfoundland and Labrador Canada
220 G4 **Hawke Bay** New Zealand
218 D4 **Hawker** SA Australia
83 N4 **Hawkesbury** Ontario Canada
214 C1 **Hawkesbury Point** NT Australia
86 D4 **Hawkins** Texas USA
139 G3 **Hawkley** Hampshire England UK
91 F1 **Hawks Nest Point** Bahamas
140 F2 **Hawkshead** Cumbria England UK
139 G3 **Hawley** Hampshire England UK
83 N6 **Hawley** Pennsylvania USA
86 B4 **Hawley** Texas USA
141 G3 **Haworth** West Yorkshire England UK
178 F3 **Hawr al Ḩammār** *lake* Iraq
178 E2 **Ḩawrān, Wādī** *watercourse* Iraq
84 C4 **Hawthorne** California USA
157 F5 **Hawzēn** Ethiopia
81 N6 **Haxtun** Colorado USA
218 G6 **Hay** NSW Australia
214 D7 **Hay** *watercourse* NT Australia
75 M2 **Hay** *watercourse* Northwest Territories Canada
138 C4 **Hay** Cornwall England UK
214 B7 **Hay, Mount** NT Australia
75 P3 **Hay Camp** Alberta Canada
74 L3 **Hay Lake** Alberta Canada
138 D2 **Hay-on-Wye** Powys Wales UK
75 N2 **Hay River** Northwest Territories Canada
81 N5 **Hay Springs** Nebraska USA
198 D4 **Haya** Indonesia
136 F6 **Ḩayānīyah** Syria
179 H5 **Ḩaybī** Oman
136 F3 **Haychur** *watercourse* Ukraine
133 G6 **Haydarlı** Turkey
84 G4 **Hayden** Arizona USA
81 L6 **Hayden** Colorado USA
141 F2 **Haydon Bridge** Northumberland England UK
76 I5 **Hayes** *watercourse* Manitoba Canada
73 J5 **Hayes** *watercourse* Nunavut Canada
81 O6 **Hayes Center** Nebraska USA
214 A2 **Hayes Creek** NT Australia
73 M3 **Hayes Halvø** *plain* Greenland
216 G5 **Hayes Hill** WA Australia
157 I5 **Hayf** Yemen
82 E5 **Hayfield** Minnesota USA
157 F5 **Hāyk'** Ethiopia
157 F5 **Hayk Hayk** *lake* Ethiopia
156 F4 **Haykota** Eritrea
138 B4 **Hayle** Cornwall England UK
139 F4 **Hayling Island** England UK
179 H6 **Haymā'** Oman
87 H4 **Hayneville** Alabama USA
75 P7 **Hays** Alberta Canada
81 P7 **Hays** Kansas USA
178 E7 **Ḩays** Yemen
59 N1 **Hays Mountains** Antarctica
218 F6 **Haysdale** Vic. Australia
81 Q8 **Haysville** Kansas USA
132 F1 **Haysyn** Ukraine
141 H3 **Hayton** East Riding of Yorkshire England UK
132 F1 **Hayvoron** Ukraine
80 D8 **Hayward** California USA
82 F3 **Hayward** Wisconsin USA
139 G4 **Haywards Heath** West Sussex England UK
186 F6 **Hazaribag** Jharkhand India
81 Q4 **Hazel** South Dakota USA
141 F3 **Hazel Grove** Greater Manchester England UK
74 H5 **Hazelton** British Columbia Canada
81 P8 **Hazelton** Kansas USA
81 O3 **Hazelton** North Dakota USA
81 O3 **Hazen** North Dakota USA
73 M2 **Hazen, Lake** Nunavut Canada
73 I3 **Hazen Strait** Northwest Territories/ Nunavut Canada
86 F5 **Hazlehurst** Mississippi USA
139 G3 **Hazlemere** Buckinghamshire England UK
83 N6 **Hazleton** Pennsylvania USA
213 J6 **Hazlett, Lake** WA Australia
191 I4 **He** *lake* Nei Mongol Zizhiqu China
189 F4 **He Jiang** *watercourse* Guangxi Zhuangzu Zizhiqu China
139 H2 **Heacham** Norfolk England UK
217 L5 **Head of Bight** *bay* SA Australia
139 H3 **Headcorn** Kent England UK
214 E6 **Headingly** Qld Australia
86 B3 **Headrick** Oklahoma USA
140 C2 **Headwood** Larne Northern Ireland UK
80 D7 **Healdsburg** California USA
86 C3 **Healdton** Oklahoma USA
72 E6 **Healy** Alaska USA
85 L1 **Healy** Kansas USA
75 U5 **Heaman** Manitoba Canada
139 F1 **Heanor** Derbyshire England UK
210 inset **Heard Island** Indian Ocean
210 inset **Heard Island and McDonald Island** *Australian territory* Indian Ocean
75 S7 **Hearne** Saskatchewan Canada
86 C5 **Hearne** Texas USA
76 N8 **Hearst** Ontario Canada
59 T2 **Hearst Island** Antarctica
81 N3 **Heart** *watercourse* North Dakota USA
79 H8 **Heath, Pointe** *cape* Quebec Canada
218 G7 **Heathcote** Vic. Australia
139 H4 **Heathfield** East Sussex England UK
214 G1 **Heathlands** Qld Australia
86 D3 **Heavener** Oklahoma USA
86 B7 **Hebbronville** Texas USA
79 F10 **Hebbville** Nova Scotia Canada
191 H5 **Hebei** *admin. area* China
219 H3 **Hebel** Qld Australia
84 G3 **Heber** Arizona USA
83 P2 **Hébertville** Quebec Canada
81 J4 **Hebgen Lake** Montana USA
191 H6 **Hebi** Henan China
142 B3 **Hebrides, Sea of the** Scotland UK
77 X3 **Hebron** Newfoundland and Labrador Canada
82 H6 **Hebron** Indiana USA
81 Q6 **Hebron** Nebraska USA
85 J2 **Hebron** New Mexico USA
184 H3 **Hebukesai`er** Xinjiang Uygur Zizhiqu China
74 F6 **Hecate Strait** British Columbia Canada
189 H3 **Hecheng** Jiangxi China
189 H3 **Hecheng** Zhejiang China
188 E4 **Hechi** Guangxi Zhuangzu Zizhiqu China
188 E2 **Hechuan** Chongqing China
189 G3 **Hechuan** Jiangxi China
81 P4 **Hecla** South Dakota USA
76 G7 **Hecla Island** Manitoba Canada
215 J6 **Hector, Mount** Qld Australia
221 C7 **Hector Mountains** New Zealand
122 E2 **Hedal** Norway
122 E3 **Heddalsvatnet** *lake* Norway
126 D2 **Hédé** France
120 H5 **Hede** Sweden
120 H6 **Heden** Sweden
121 M3 **Hedenäset** Sweden
122 I2 **Hedesundafjärden** *bay* Sweden
120 H5 **Hedeviken** Sweden
188 F4 **Hedi Shuiku** *lake* Guangdong China
80 E2 **Hedley** British Columbia Canada
86 A3 **Hedley** Texas USA
122 F2 **Hedmark** *admin. area* Norway
141 H3 **Hedon** East Riding of Yorkshire England UK
142 E2 **Heedle** Orkney Islands Scotland UK
178 C3 **Hefa (Haifa)** Israel
189 H2 **Hefei** Anhui China
191 L3 **Hegang** Heilongjiang China
191 L3 **Hegang** Heilongjiang China
120 E5 **Heggem** Norway
120 F6 **Heggenes** Norway
120 H6 **Heggeriset** Norway
120 I3 **Heggmovatnet** *lake* Norway
199 G5 **Hegigio** *watercourse* Papua New Guinea
142 inset **Heglibister** Shetland Scotland UK
120 G5 **Hegra** Norway
188 C4 **Hei Chiang** *watercourse* Yunnan China
190 D5 **Hei He** *watercourse* Gansu China
188 D2 **Hei-shui Ho** *watercourse* Sichuan China
156 E5 **Heiban** Sudan
122 E5 **Heide** Germany
124 E3 **Heidelberg** Germany
162 D6 **Heidelberg** South Africa
162 E5 **Heidelberg** South Africa
86 G5 **Heidelberg** Mississippi USA
191 K2 **Heihe** Heilongjiang China
124 E3 **Heilbronn** Germany
124 G4 **Heiligenblut** Austria
191 K1 **Heilong** *watercourse* Heilongjiang China
191 K3 **Heilongjiang** *admin. area* China
124 F3 **Heilsbronn** Germany
120 inset **Heimaey** *island* Iceland
190 D6 **Heimahe** Qinghai China
199 H4 **Heina Islands** Papua New Guinea
121 O5 **Heinämäki** Finland
121 Q5 **Heinävaara** Finland
121 P5 **Heinävesi** Finland
125 H2 **Heinersbrück** Germany
123 N2 **Heinola** Finland
75 P6 **Heinsburg** Alberta Canada
191 J4 **Heishan** Liaoning China
188 D3 **Heishui He** *watercourse* Sichuan China
Heisker Islands *see* **Monach Islands** UK
75 O6 **Heisler** Alberta Canada
123 J4 **Hejde** Sweden
191 H5 **Hejian** Hebei China
188 E3 **Hejiang** Sichuan China
190 G6 **Hejin** Shanxi China
185 H4 **Hejing** Xinjiang Uygur Zizhiqu China
133 G6 **Hekimdağ** Turkey
120 inset **Hekla** *mountain* Iceland
189 H3 **Hekou** Jiangxi China
188 D2 **Hekou** Sichuan China
123 J5 **Hel** Poland
120 H5 **Helagsfjället** *mountain* Sweden
181 G3 **Helam** Arunachal Pradesh India
190 F5 **Helan Shan** *range* Ningxia Huizu Zizhiqu China
124 C2 **Helden** Netherlands
138 D4 **Hele** Devon England UK
82 G2 **Helen Lake** Ontario Canada
86 F3 **Helena** Arkansas USA
80 I3 **Helena** Montana USA
86 B2 **Helena** Oklahoma USA
219 J6 **Helensburgh** NSW Australia
125 H3 **Helfenberg** Austria
122 H4 **Helgasjön** *lake* Sweden
122 G4 **Helge** *watercourse* Sweden
122 F3 **Helgerød** Norway
122 D5 **Helgoland** *island* Germany
120 K1 **Helgøy** Norway
120 K1 **Helgøy** *island* Norway
120 J5 **Helgum** Sweden
120 J5 **Helgumsjön** *lake* Sweden
122 E2 **Helin** *lake* Norway
190 G5 **Helin`ge`er** Nei Mongol Zizhiqu China
189 H2 **Helixi** Anhui China
120 inset **Hella** Iceland
120 F5 **Helland** Norway
122 D1 **Hellesylt** Norway
120 L2 **Helligskogen** Norway
120 H3 **Helligvær** *island* Norway
128 F4 **Hellín** Spain
120 inset **Hellissandur** Iceland
142 inset **Hellister** Shetland Scotland UK
120 L1 **Hellnes** Norway
214 E4 **Hells Gate Roadhouse** Qld Australia
122 C3 **Hellvik** Norway
84 B2 **Helm** California USA
179 J3 **Helmand** *admin. area* Afghanistan
179 K2 **Helmand, Daryā-ye** *watercourse* Afghanistan
124 F2 **Helme** *watercourse* Germany
162 C5 **Helmeringhausen** Namibia
142 E2 **Helmsdale** Highland Scotland UK
142 E2 **Helmsdale** *watercourse* Scotland UK
141 G2 **Helmsley** North Yorkshire England UK
191 L4 **Helong** Jilin China
81 J7 **Helper** Utah USA
132 B4 **Helshan** Albania
122 G4 **Helsingborg** Sweden
122 G4 **Helsinge** Denmark
122 G4 **Helsingør** Denmark
123 M2 **Helsinki** Finland
123 J5 **Helska** *bay* Poland
138 B4 **Helston** Cornwall England UK
143 E4 **Helvick Head** *cape* Ireland
127 J2 **Hemau** Germany
139 G3 **Hemel Hempstead** Hertfordshire England UK
138 C4 **Hemerdon** Devon England UK
84 D4 **Hemet** California USA
75 U5 **Heming Lake** Manitoba Canada
81 N5 **Hemingford** Nebraska USA
138 E3 **Hemington** Somerset England UK
120 K5 **Hemling** Sweden
122 E6 **Hemmoor** Germany
120 H3 **Hemnesberget** Norway
139 I2 **Hemsby** Norfolk England UK
123 J4 **Hemse** Sweden
120 I5 **Hemsjön** *lake* Sweden
120 K5 **Hemsö** Sweden
120 K5 **Hemsön** *island* Sweden
141 G3 **Hemsworth** West Yorkshire England UK
220 F2 **Hen and Chicken Islands** New Zealand
189 F1 **Henan** *admin. area* China
122 F3 **Henån** Sweden
128 E3 **Henares** *watercourse* Spain
214 B8 **Henbury** NT Australia
131 C9 **Henchir el Fercha** Tunisia
133 G5 **Hendek** Turkey
82 H8 **Henderson** Kentucky USA
86 F5 **Henderson** Louisiana USA
84 E2 **Henderson** Nevada USA
87 L2 **Henderson** North Carolina USA
86 D4 **Henderson** Texas USA
83 M5 **Henderson Bay** New York USA
59 G2 **Henderson Island** Antarctica
223 11 **Henderson Island** Pitcairn Islands
53 T5 **Henderson Seamount** *underwater feature* Pacific Ocean
139 G3 **Hendon** Greater London England UK
179 H4 **Hendorābī, Jazīreh-ye** *island* Iran
139 G4 **Henfield** West Sussex England UK
191 H5 **Heng Shan** *mountain* Shanxi China
191 H5 **Heng Shan** *range* Shanxi China
189 F3 **Hengdong** Hunan China
181 I3 **Hengduan Shan** *range* Xizang Zizhiqu China
189 I2 **Hengsha Dao** *island* Shanghai China
191 H5 **Hengshui** Hebei China
189 G3 **Hengshui** Jiangxi China
189 F3 **Hengyang** Hunan China
188 F4 **Hengzhou** Guangxi Zhuangzu Zizhiqu China
191 H5 **Hengzhou** Hebei China
76 G2 **Heninga Lake** Nunavut Canada
79 K7 **Henley Harbour** Newfoundland and Labrador Canada
139 G3 **Henley-on-Thames** Oxfordshire England UK
139 G2 **Henlow** Bedfordshire England UK
120 I5 **Hennan** Sweden
120 I5 **Hennan** *lake* Sweden
126 C3 **Hennebont** France
82 G6 **Hennepin** Illinois USA
120 I2 **Hennes** Norway
86 C2 **Hennessey** Oklahoma USA
81 R3 **Henning** Minnesota USA
86 G3 **Henning** Tennessee USA
216 C3 **Henri Freycinet Harbour** WA Australia
126 F3 **Henrichemont** France
77 N5 **Henrietta Maria, Cape** Ontario Canada
84 G2 **Henrieville** Utah USA
212 C7 **Henry** *watercourse* WA Australia
59 T1 **Henry Ice Rise** Antarctica
73 M5 **Henry Kater, Cape** Nunavut Canada
194 B4 **Henry Lawrence Island** Andaman and Nicobar Islands India
84 G1 **Henry Mountains** Utah USA
80 J4 **Henrys Lake** Idaho USA
84 D4 **Henshaw, Lake** California USA
162 B4 **Henties Bay** Namibia
190 G3 **Hentiy** *admin. area* Mongolia
218 H6 **Henty** NSW Australia
Henzada *see* **Hinthada** Myanmar
188 E3 **Heping** Guizhou China
188 E3 **Heping** Guizhou China
189 G4 **Hepo** Guangdong China
121 P5 **Heposelkä** *bay* Finland
141 F1 **Hepple** Northumberland England UK
80 F4 **Heppner** Oregon USA
190 G5 **Hequ** Shanxi China
120 inset **Héraðsflói** *bay* Iceland
120 inset **Héraðsvötn** *watercourse* Iceland
215 J4 **Herald Cays** *islands* Coral Sea Islands Territory Australia
215 K6 **Herald Reef Prong** Qld Australia
215 K6 **Heralds Prong No. 2 Reef** Qld Australia
215 K6 **Heralds Prong No. 3 Reef** Qld Australia
215 J4 **Heralds Reef** Coral Sea Islands Territory Australia
220 F4 **Herangi Range** New Zealand
179 J2 **Herāt** Afghanistan
179 J2 **Herāt** *admin. area* Afghanistan
126 F5 **Hérault** *watercourse* France
75 V5 **Herb Lake** Manitoba Canada
75 V5 **Herb Lake Landing** Manitoba Canada
126 E3 **Herbault** France
215 H5 **Herbert** *watercourse* Qld Australia
217 I2 **Herbert** *watercourse* WA Australia
75 R7 **Herbert** Saskatchewan Canada
221 D7 **Herbert** New Zealand
212 D6 **Herbert, Mount** WA Australia
214 E7 **Herbert Downs** Qld Australia
194 B5 **Herbertabad** Andaman and Nicobar Islands India
215 H4 **Herberton** Qld Australia
143 D4 **Herbertstown** Ireland
126 C3 **Herbignac** France
124 E2 **Herborn** Germany
127 I1 **Herbstein** Germany
76 H4 **Herchmer** Manitoba Canada
85 K6 **Hércules** Mexico
108 D3 **Hércules, Punta** *cape* Argentina
59 P1 **Hercules Dome** *mountain* Antarctica
51 S14 **Herdman Seamount** *underwater feature* Pacific Ocean
138 E2 **Hereford** Herefordshire England UK
85 K3 **Hereford** Texas USA
138 E2 **Herefordshire** *admin. area* England UK
122 E3 **Herefoss** Norway
223 14 **Hereheretue** *island* French Polynesia
220 E2 **Herekino** New Zealand
220 E2 **Herekino Harbour** New Zealand
130 G3 **Herend** Hungary
221 C6 **Heretaniwha Point** New Zealand
127 H3 **Héricourt** France
127 I3 **Herisau** Switzerland
126 F3 **Hérisson** France
59 S1 **Heritage Range** Antarctica
190 G3 **Herlen** Mongolia
190 G3 **Herlen** Mongolia
81 Q4 **Herman** Minnesota USA
214 B7 **Hermannsburg** NT Australia
214 B8 **Hermannsburg, Mount** NT Australia
120 J5 **Hermansjö** Sweden
122 D2 **Hermansverk** Norway
108 F2 **Hermengo, Punta** *cape* Argentina
218 H4 **Hermidale** NSW Australia
80 F4 **Hermiston** Oregon USA
215 K4 **Hermit Crab Islet** *island* Coral Sea Islands Territory Australia
199 H4 **Hermit Islands** Papua New Guinea
79 K9 **Hermitage** Newfoundland and Labrador Canada
142 F5 **Hermitage** Scottish Borders Scotland UK
86 E4 **Hermitage** Arkansas USA
79 J9 **Hermitage Bay** Newfoundland and Labrador Canada
212 C6 **Hermite Island** WA Australia
81 N5 **Hermosa** South Dakota USA
88 C2 **Hermosillo** Mexico
125 J4 **Hernád** Hungary
125 K3 **Hernád** *watercourse* Hungary
81 O7 **Herndon** Kansas USA
139 I3 **Herne Bay** Kent England UK
78 D4 **Hérodier, Lac** *lake* Quebec Canada
124 C2 **Héron** Belgium
221 D6 **Heron, Lake** New Zealand
215 K7 **Heron Island** Qld Australia
100 C3 **Herrán** Colombia
122 E3 **Herre** Norway
81 O4 **Herreid** South Dakota USA
124 E3 **Herrenberg** Germany
128 D5 **Herrera** Spain
128 D2 **Herrera de Pisuerga** Spain
128 D4 **Herrera del Duque** Spain
90 C3 **Herrero, Punta** *cape* Mexico
219 R10 **Herrick** Tas. Australia
81 P5 **Herrick** South Dakota USA
82 G8 **Herrin** Illinois USA
87 I2 **Herrington Lake** Kentucky USA
75 U4 **Herriot** Manitoba Canada
126 E5 **Hers** *watercourse* France
72 F5 **Herschel Island** Yukon Territory Canada
127 G1 **Herstal** Belgium
139 H4 **Herstmonceux** East Sussex England UK
127 H1 **Herten** Germany
139 G3 **Hertford** Hertfordshire England UK
139 G3 **Hertfordshire** *admin. area* England UK
107 H5 **Herval** Brazil
128 D3 **Hervás** Spain
78 C5 **Hervé, Lac** *lake* Quebec Canada
105 E4 **Hervedero** Bolivia
219 K1 **Hervey Bay** Qld Australia
219 K1 **Hervey Bay** Qld Australia
130 C2 **Herxheim** Germany
182 G6 **Hesarcheh** Iran
139 J4 **Hesdin** France
189 F4 **Heshan** Guangdong China
189 F3 **Heshan** Hunan China
188 D2 **Heshan** Sichuan China
191 H5 **Heshun** Shanxi China
185 H4 **Heshuo** Xinjiang Uygur Zizhiqu China
141 G2 **Hesleden** Durham England UK
141 G3 **Heslington** York England UK
84 D3 **Hesperia** California USA
219 R11 **Hesperus, Mount** Tas. Australia
81 K8 **Hesperus Mountain** Colorado USA
74 H8 **Hesquiat** British Columbia Canada
72 F6 **Hess** *watercourse* Yukon Territory Canada
52 N4 **Hess Rise** *underwater feature* Pacific Ocean
122 F4 **Hesselø** *island* Denmark
124 E2 **Hessen** *admin. area* Germany
121 P2 **Hesseng** Norway
141 H3 **Hessle** East Riding of Yorkshire England UK
81 Q7 **Hesston** Kansas USA
120 H3 **Hestmona** *island* Norway
140 E3 **Heswall** Merseyside England UK
80 F8 **Hetch Hetchy Reservoir** California USA
184 F5 **Hetian** Xinjiang Uygur Zizhiqu China
120 I4 **Hetögeln** *bay* Sweden
81 N4 **Hettinger** North Dakota USA
141 G2 **Hetton-le-Hole** Tyne and Wear England UK
142 E3 **Heugh-head** Aberdeenshire Scotland UK
222 8 **Heuru** Solomon Islands
139 G5 **Hève, Cap de la** *cape* France
105 F2 **Hevelândia** Brazil
125 K4 **Heves** Hungary
125 K4 **Heves** *admin. area* Hungary
86 C5 **Hewitt** Texas USA
141 F2 **Hexham** Northumberland England UK
188 C3 **Hexi** Sichuan China
189 H3 **Hexi** Zhejiang China
191 H6 **Heyang** Hebei China
188 F1 **Heyang** Shaanxi China
190 E6 **Heyin** Qinghai China
140 F2 **Heysham** Lancashire England UK
189 G4 **Heyuan** Guangdong China
218 E8 **Heywood** Vic. Australia
216 H6 **Heywood, Mount** WA Australia
213 H3 **Heywood Islands** WA Australia
179 I3 **Hezār, Kūh-e** *mountain* Iran
189 G1 **Heze** Shandong China
188 D3 **Hezhang** Guizhou China
189 F4 **Hezhou** Guangxi Zhuangzu Zizhiqu China
214 B4 **Hi-way Inn** NT Australia
87 K8 **Hialeah** Florida USA
82 D7 **Hiawatha** Kansas USA
82 E3 **Hibbing** Minnesota USA
210 inset **Hibernia Reef** Ashmore Reef and Cartier Island Australia
104 D5 **Hichocollo** Peru
139 G2 **Hickling** Nottinghamshire England UK
106 F2 **Hickmann** Argentina
87 K3 **Hickory** North Carolina USA
87 K3 **Hickory, Lake** North Carolina USA
86 G3 **Hickory Flat** Mississippi USA
220 H3 **Hicks Bay** New Zealand
75 V2 **Hicks Lake** Nunavut Canada
132 C2 **Hida** Romania
193 I2 **Hidaka-sanmyaku** Japan
89 F3 **Hidalgo** Mexico
89 F4 **Hidalgo** *admin. area* Mexico
88 D3 **Hidalgo del Parral** Mexico
125 J4 **Hidas** Hungary
213 G4 **Hidden Island** WA Australia
122 G5 **Hiddensee** *island* Germany
215 J6 **Hideaway Bay** Qld Australia
132 C2 **Hidişelu de Jos** Romania
122 D3 **Hidra** *island* Norway
222 7 **Hienghène** New Caledonia
164 3 **Hierro** *island* Canary Islands
121 M3 **Hietanen** Sweden
121 P4 **Hietaperä** Finland
192 F5 **Higashi-Suidō** *strait* Japan
128 F2 **Higer, Cabo** *cape* France
86 A2 **Higgins** Texas USA
82 I4 **Higgins Lake** Michigan USA
77 T1 **High Bluff Island** Nunavut Canada
138 D3 **High Bray** Devon England UK
80 E5 **High Desert** Oregon USA
139 H3 **High Garrett** Essex England UK
141 H2 **High Hawsker** North Yorkshire England UK
76 H5 **High Hill Lake** Manitoba Canada
74 M3 **High Level** Alberta Canada
141 G3 **High Peak** *region* England UK
215 K6 **High Peak Island** Qld Australia
87 L3 **High Point** North Carolina USA
75 O7 **High River** Alberta Canada
87 K3 **High Rock Lake** North Carolina USA
219 Q11 **High Rocky Point** Tas. Australia
195 I4 **High Rolling Mountains** Philippines
87 J6 **High Springs** Florida USA
139 G3 **High Wycombe** Buckinghamshire England UK
216 E6 **Highbury** WA Australia
139 F3 **Highclere** Hampshire England UK
138 D2 **Highgate** Powys Wales UK
142 D3 **Highland** *admin. area* Scotland UK
86 F2 **Highland** Arkansas USA
82 D7 **Highland** Kansas USA
87 J3 **Highlands** North Carolina USA
141 G3 **Highlane** Derbyshire England UK
81 P4 **Highmore** South Dakota USA
138 E3 **Highnam** Gloucestershire England UK
75 U5 **Highrock** Manitoba Canada
75 U5 **Highrock Lake** Manitoba Canada
75 S4 **Highrock Lake** Saskatchewan Canada
139 F3 **Highworth** Swindon England UK
88 C3 **Higuera de Zaragoza** Mexico
220 F4 **Hihitahi** New Zealand
123 M2 **Hiidenvesi** *lake* Finland
161 H3 **Hiiraan** *admin. area* Somalia
123 L3 **Hiiumaa** *admin. area* Estonia
123 L3 **Hiiumaa** *island* Estonia
193 H4 **Hikone** Japan
220 F2 **Hikurangi** New Zealand
220 H3 **Hikurangi** *mountain* New Zealand
220 4 **Hikutavake** Niue New Zealand
198 C5 **Hila** Indonesia
198 B5 **Hilahila** Indonesia
75 P7 **Hilda** Alberta Canada
84 F2 **Hildale** Utah USA
127 J1 **Hildburghausen** Germany
124 D2 **Hilden** Germany
124 E1 **Hildesheim** Germany
52 P8 **Hilgard Deep** *underwater feature* Pacific Ocean
196 C3 **Hilialawa** Indonesia
81 P7 **Hill City** Kansas USA
108 E5 **Hill Cove** Falkland Islands
219 I5 **Hill End** NSW Australia
75 O8 **Hill Spring** Alberta Canada
216 D2 **Hill Springs** WA Australia
109 12 **Hillaby, Mount** Barbados
59 K1 **Hillary Coast** Antarctica
124 E1 **Hille** Germany
122 G5 **Hillerød** Denmark
138 E3 **Hillesley** Gloucestershire England UK
143 F2 **Hillhead** Banbridge Northern Ireland UK
87 K5 **Hilliard** Florida USA
139 G3 **Hillingdon** Greater London England UK
82 J4 **Hillman** Michigan USA
142 F4 **Hillock** Angus Scotland UK
120 I4 **Hillsand** Sweden
80 D4 **Hillsboro** Oregon USA
91 I4 **Hillsborough** Grenada
79 G9 **Hillsborough Bay** Prince Edward Island Canada
142 inset **Hillside** Shetland Scotland UK
218 G5 **Hillston** NSW Australia
87 K2 **Hillsville** Virginia USA
215 G6 **Hilltop** Qld Australia
143 F4 **Hilltown** Ireland
82 I7 **Hillview** Kentucky USA
142 inset **Hillwell** Shetland Scotland UK
84 inset **Hilo** Hawai'i USA
214 E6 **Hilton** Qld Australia
139 G2 **Hilton** Cambridgeshire England UK
139 E4 **Hilton** Dorset England UK
87 K4 **Hilton Head Island** South Carolina USA
59 U2 **Hilton Inlet** *bay* Antarctica
186 D4 **Himachal Pradesh** *admin. area* India
180 E2 **Himalaya** *range* Asia
121 M4 **Himanka** Finland
133 A5 **Himarë** Albania
220 F5 **Himatangi Beach** New Zealand
186 C6 **Himatnagar** Gujarat India
192 F5 **Hime-shima** *island* Japan
193 H4 **Himi** Japan
156 F5 **Himora** Ethiopia
136 F6 **Ḩimş** Syria
196 C3 **Hinako** *island* Indonesia
159 G2 **Hinalé** Cameroon
195 J5 **Hinatuan** Philippines
132 F2 **Hînceşti** Moldova
91 F3 **Hinche** Haiti
215 I5 **Hinchinbrook Island** Qld Australia
139 F2 **Hinckley** Leicester England UK
82 E3 **Hinckley** Minnesota USA
159 G5 **Hinda** Congo
186 D5 **Hindaun** Rajasthan India
139 H2 **Hinderclay** Suffolk England UK
139 G3 **Hindhead** Surrey England UK
82 J8 **Hindman** Kentucky USA
218 E7 **Hindmarsh, Lake** Vic. Australia
221 D7 **Hinds** New Zealand
79 J8 **Hinds Lake** Newfoundland and Labrador Canada
122 H4 **Hindsen** *lake* Sweden
183 K7 **Hindu Kush** *range* Afghanistan
187 D9 **Hindupur** Andhra Pradesh India
80 F5 **Hines** Oregon USA
74 L4 **Hines Creek** Alberta Canada
87 K5 **Hinesville** Georgia USA
187 E7 **Hinganghat** Maharashtra India
81 J2 **Hingham** Montana USA
187 D7 **Hingoli** Maharashtra India
136 G5 **Hinis** Turkey
123 K1 **Hinjärv** *lake* Finland
120 L5 **Hinjärvträsket** *lake* Finland
122 F4 **Hinnerup** Denmark
120 J2 **Hinnøya** *island* Norway
120 K5 **Hinnsjön** *lake* Sweden
195 I5 **Hinoba-an** Philippines
128 D4 **Hinojosa del Duque** Spain
122 I2 **Hinsen** *lake* Sweden
130 F3 **Hinterstoder** Austria
194 B3 **Hinthada (Henzada)** Myanmar
74 M6 **Hinton** Alberta Canada
86 B3 **Hinton** Oklahoma USA
139 H2 **Hinxton** Cambridgeshire England UK
192 F5 **Hirado-shima** *island* Japan
138 C3 **Hiraeth** Carmarthenshire Wales UK
187 F7 **Hirakud Reservoir** Orissa India
161 F4 **Hiraman** *watercourse* Kenya
186 G6 **Hiranpur** Jharkhand India
189 J4 **Hirara** Japan
161 G2 **Hīrna** Ethiopia
138 D2 **Hirnant** Powys Wales UK
193 I3 **Hirosaki** Japan
192 G4 **Hiroshima** Japan
130 D2 **Hirschau** Germany

124 C3 **Hirson** France
132 E3 **Hîrșova** Romania
132 F2 **Hîrtop** Moldova
122 E4 **Hirtshals** Denmark
121 P3 **Hirvasvaara** Finland
186 D5 **Hisar** Haryana India
133 F6 **Hisarcık** Turkey
190 E3 **Hishigunder** Mongolia
199 H6 **Hisiu** Papua New Guinea
91 G2 **Hispaniola** *island* Caribbean
179 M2 **Hispar Glacier** Pakistan
120 L5 **Hissjön** Sweden
178 E2 **Hit** Iraq
192 F5 **Hita** Japan
193 I4 **Hitachi** Japan
193 I4 **Hitachinaka** Japan
139 G3 **Hitchen** Hertfordshire England UK
101 G3 **Hitia** Guyana
223 14a **Hitiaa** French Polynesia
120 F5 **Hitra** *island* Norway
81 Q3 **Hitterdal** Minnesota USA
124 F1 **Hitzacker** Germany
222 7 **Hiu** *island* Vanuatu
223 14 **Hiva Oa** *island* French Polynesia
77 S5 **Hiver, Lac de l'** *lake* Quebec Canada
87 I3 **Hiwassee Lake** Virginia USA
74 J6 **Hixon** British Columbia Canada
139 F2 **Hixon** Staffordshire England UK
87 J5 **Hixtown Swamp** Florida USA
120 L4 **Hjåggböleliden** Sweden
122 F4 **Hjallerup** Denmark
75 Q2 **Hjalmar Lake** Northwest Territories Canada
122 H3 **Hjälmaren** *bay* Sweden
120 inset **Hjalteyri** Iceland
120 I3 **Hjartøya** *island* Norway
120 E6 **Hjelle** Norway
122 F4 **Hjelm** *island* Denmark
122 G5 **Hjelm Bugt** *bay* Denmark
122 D3 **Hjelmeland** Norway
121 N1 **Hjelmsøya** *island* Norway
122 E4 **Hjemitslev** Denmark
120 F5 **Hjerkinn** Norway
122 F4 **Hjørring** Denmark
120 E5 **Hjørungavåg** Norway
194 C3 **Hlaingbwe** Myanmar
132 F3 **Hlavani** Ukraine
194 C3 **Hlegu** Myanmar
132 F2 **Hlinaia** Moldova
125 H3 **Hlinsko** Czech Republic
120 inset **Hlíðarendi** Iceland
125 I3 **Hlohovec** Slovakia
162 E5 **Hlotse** Lesotho
136 E2 **Hlukhiv** Ukraine
132 D1 **Hlyboka** Ukraine
123 N5 **Hlybokaye** Belarus
181 G4 **Hnahthial** Mizoram India
76 G7 **Hnausa** Manitoba Canada
125 J3 **Hnúšťa** Slovakia
158 E3 **Ho** Ghana
194 E5 **Hồ Chí Minh (Saigon)** Vietnam
221 7 **Ho Ho Bay** Snares Islands New Zealand
194 E2 **Hồ Thác Bà** *lake* Vietnam
194 E5 **Hồ Tri an** *watercourse* Vietnam
194 E3 **Hồ Xá** Vietnam
194 E2 **Hòa Bình** Vietnam
162 C4 **Hoachanas** Namibia
162 B3 **Hoanib** *watercourse* Namibia
219 R11 **Hobart** Tas. Australia
86 B3 **Hobart** Oklahoma USA
85 K4 **Hobbs** New Mexico USA
59 O2 **Hobbs Bank** *underwater feature* Amundsen Sea
59 P1 **Hobbs Coast** Antarctica
59 E2 **Hobbs Islands** Antarctica
100 C4 **Hobo** Colombia
122 E4 **Hobro** Denmark
81 K3 **Hobson** Montana USA
87 I4 **Hobson City** Alabama USA
74 K6 **Hobson Lake** British Columbia Canada
161 H2 **Hobyo** Somalia
89 H4 **Hocabá** Mexico
130 C2 **Hochdorf** Germany
162 C4 **Hochfeld** Namibia
124 G4 **Hochgall** *mountain* Italy
192 F3 **Hŏch'ŏn** North Korea
75 W5 **Hockin** Manitoba Canada
132 C1 **Hoczew** Poland
139 G3 **Hoddesdon** Hertfordshire England UK
82 I8 **Hodgenville** Kentucky USA
75 R7 **Hodgeville** Saskatchewan Canada
214 B3 **Hodgson** *watercourse* NT Australia
213 K4 **Hodgson, Mount** NT Australia
212 F7 **Hodgson, Mount** WA Australia
Hodgson Downs *see* **Miniyeri** Australia
214 C3 **Hodgson River** NT Australia
125 K4 **Hódmezővásárhely** Hungary
161 H1 **Hodmo** *watercourse* Somalia
192 E3 **Hoeyang** North Korea
127 J1 **Hof** Germany
127 I1 **Hofbieber** Germany
120 G4 **Hoffstad** Norway
124 F2 **Hofheim** Germany
120 G4 **Hofles** Norway
162 E6 **Hofmeyr** South Africa
120 inset **Höfn** Iceland
122 I2 **Hofors** Sweden
120 inset **Hofsá** *watercourse* Iceland
120 inset **Hofsjökull** *mountain* Iceland
120 inset **Hofsós** Iceland
192 F4 **Hofu** Japan
120 inset **Höfuðborgarsvæði** *admin. area* Iceland
83 N8 **Hog Island Bay** Virginia USA
109 I8 **Hog Point** Antigua and Barbuda
219 R9 **Hogan Island** Tas. Australia
122 G4 **Höganäs** Sweden
219 H1 **Hoganthulla** Qld Australia
214 A3 **Hogarth, Mount** NT Australia
75 Q8 **Hogeland** Montana USA
142 A3 **Hogha Gearraidh** Na h-Eileanan Siar Scotland UK
120 K4 **Högheden** Sweden
120 I4 **Högland** Sweden
122 H3 **Högsjö** Sweden
141 I3 **Hogsthorpe** Lincolnshire England UK
91 F2 **Hogsty Reef** Bahamas
120 H5 **Högvålen** Sweden
185 K3 **Hoh Nuur** *lake* Mongolia
185 I6 **Hoh Xil Shan** *range* Xizang Zizhiqu China
185 K6 **Hoh Yanhu** *lake* Qinghai China
124 E4 **Hohe Freschen** *mountain* Austria
124 F3 **Hohenlinden** Germany
127 K1 **Hohenthurm** Germany
124 G4 **Hoher Dachstein** *mountain* Austria
190 G5 **Hohhot** Nei Mongol Zizhiqu China
122 E5 **Hohn** Germany
158 E3 **Hohoe** Ghana
194 F4 **Hội An** Vietnam
181 G3 **Hojai** Assam India
220 E2 **Hokianga Harbour** New Zealand
221 F5 **Hokio Beach** New Zealand
221 D6 **Hokitika** New Zealand
221 D6 **Hokitika** *watercourse* New Zealand
193 I2 **Hokkaidō** *island* Japan
122 H4 **Hökön** Sweden
221 C8 **Hokonui Hills** New Zealand
122 E2 **Hol** Norway
120 J2 **Hol** Norway
122 G4 **Hol** Sweden
104 D3 **Holanda** Bolivia
105 E4 **Holanda** Bolivia
120 inset **Hólar** Iceland
139 H2 **Holbeach** Lincolnshire England UK
74 G7 **Holberg** British Columbia Canada
185 K2 **Holboo Nuur** *lake* Mongolia
139 H3 **Holborough** Kent England UK
84 G3 **Holbrook** Arizona USA
81 P6 **Holbrook** Nebraska USA
81 O8 **Holcomb** Kansas USA
120 G4 **Holden** *lake* Norway
141 F3 **Holden** Lancashire England UK
80 I7 **Holden** Utah USA
120 H4 **Holdern** *lake* Sweden
141 H3 **Holderness** *cape* England UK
108 C3 **Holdich** Argentina
91 J4 **Holetown** Barbados
90 E2 **Holguín** Cuba
90 E2 **Holguin** *admin. area* Cuba
125 I3 **Holíč** Slovakia
125 H2 **Holice** Czech Republic
82 G2 **Holinshead Lake** Ontario Canada
122 G2 **Höljes** Sweden
122 G2 **Höljessjön** *lake* Sweden
138 C4 **Hollacombe** Devon England UK
75 V8 **Holland** Manitoba Canada
142 F1 **Holland** Orkney Islands Scotland UK
82 H5 **Holland** Michigan USA
216 F6 **Holland, Mount** WA Australia
196 D4 **Holland Village** *admin. area* Singapore
142 F1 **Hollandstoun** Orkney Islands Scotland UK
124 F1 **Holle** Germany
122 D3 **Høllen** Norway
139 I2 **Hollesley Bay** England UK
127 J2 **Hollfeld** Germany
59 T2 **Hollick-Kenyon Peninsula** Antarctica
59 Q1 **Hollick-Kenyon Plateau** Antarctica
86 B4 **Holliday** Texas USA
139 H4 **Hollington** East Sussex England UK
86 B3 **Hollis** Oklahoma USA
80 E8 **Hollister** California USA
80 H5 **Hollister** Idaho USA
82 E8 **Hollister** Missouri USA
120 L4 **Hollsvattnet** *lake* Sweden
124 C1 **Hollum** Netherlands
122 G5 **Höllviken** *bay* Sweden
81 N7 **Holly** Colorado USA
87 K6 **Holly Hill** Florida USA
87 K4 **Holly Hill** South Carolina USA
87 M3 **Holly Ridge** North Carolina USA
86 G3 **Holly Springs** Mississippi USA
142 D5 **Hollybush** East Ayrshire Scotland UK
221 C7 **Hollyford** New Zealand
221 C7 **Hollyford** *watercourse* New Zealand
141 I3 **Hollym** East Riding of Yorkshire England UK
219 I2 **Hollymount** Qld Australia
143 C3 **Hollymount** Ireland
87 K7 **Hollywood** Florida USA
121 M5 **Holm** Finland
120 H4 **Holm** Norway
122 I4 **Holm** Sweden
120 J5 **Holm** Sweden
132 F2 **Hol'ma** Ukraine
72 H4 **Holman** Northwest Territories Canada
122 D3 **Holmavatn** *lake* Norway
120 inset **Hólmavík** Iceland
139 G2 **Holme** Cambridgeshire England UK
139 G1 **Holme** Nottinghamshire England UK
59 E2 **Holme Bay** Antarctica
138 E2 **Holme Lacy** Herefordshire England UK
139 H2 **Holme next the Sea** Norfolk England UK
77 T5 **Holmer, Lac** *lake* Quebec Canada
215 J4 **Holmes Reef** Coral Sea Islands Territory Australia
138 A2 **Holmestown** Ireland
141 G3 **Holmfirth** West Yorkshire England UK
120 K4 **Holmfors** Sweden
120 L5 **Holmön** Sweden
120 L5 **Holmön** *island* Sweden
120 J5 **Holmsjön** *bay* Sweden
120 I5 **Holmsjön** *lake* Sweden
120 L5 **Holmsund** Sweden
120 L4 **Holmträsk** Sweden
138 D4 **Holne** Devon England UK
178 C3 **Holon** Israel
162 C5 **Holoog** Namibia
213 I2 **Holothuria Reefs** WA Australia
132 G1 **Holovanivs'k** Ukraine
120 G5 **Holøydal** Norway
214 F3 **Holroyd** *watercourse* Qld Australia
124 C2 **Holsbeek** Belgium
122 D2 **Holskarvatnet** *lake* Norway
122 C2 **Holsnøy** *island* Norway
122 E5 **Holsted** Denmark
87 J2 **Holston** *watercourse* Tennessee USA
138 C4 **Holsworthy** Devon England UK
120 K2 **Holt** Norway
138 E1 **Holt** Cheshire England UK
139 I2 **Holt** Norfolk England UK
216 F6 **Holt Rock** WA Australia
78 J5 **Holton** Newfoundland and Labrador Canada
120 G5 **Holtsjøen** *lake* Norway
84 E4 **Holtville** California USA
139 G2 **Holwell** Leicester England UK
124 C1 **Holwerd** Netherlands
140 D3 **Holy Island** England UK
142 D5 **Holy Island** Scotland UK
139 G3 **Holybourne** Hampshire England UK
143 E4 **Holycross** Ireland
140 D3 **Holyhead** Isle of Anglesey Wales UK
140 D3 **Holyhead Bay** Wales UK
81 N6 **Holyoke** Colorado USA
83 O5 **Holyoke** Massachusetts USA
85 M1 **Holyrood** Kansas USA
141 F1 **Holystone** Northumberland England UK
138 B4 **Holywell** Cornwall England UK
140 E3 **Holywell** Flintshire Wales UK
124 E2 **Holzminden** Germany
161 E4 **Homa Bay** Kenya
181 H4 **Homalin** Myanmar
74 I7 **Homathko** *watercourse* British Columbia Canada
74 I7 **Homathko Icefield** British Columbia Canada
178 G3 **Homāyunshahr** Iran
155 F5 **Hombori** Mali
127 H2 **Homburg** Germany
73 M5 **Home Bay** Nunavut Canada
215 I5 **Home Hill** Qld Australia
77 W2 **Home Island** Newfoundland and Labrador Canada
210 inset **Home Island** Cocos (Keeling) Islands Australia
213 I3 **Home Valley** WA Australia
87 J5 **Homeland** Georgia USA
72 D7 **Homer** Alaska USA
86 E4 **Homer** Louisiana USA
82 I5 **Homer** Michigan USA
139 I2 **Homersfield** Norfolk England UK
87 J5 **Homerville** Georgia USA
215 H6 **Homestead** Qld Australia
87 K8 **Homestead** Florida USA
120 H4 **Hommelstø** Norway
120 G5 **Hommelvik** Norway
187 D8 **Homnabad** Karnataka India
132 E2 **Homocea** Romania
89 J2 **Homosassa Bay** Florida USA
126 F5 **Homps** France
136 D2 **Homyel'** Belarus
136 D2 **Homyel'skaya Voblasts'** *admin. area* Belarus
120 J5 **Hömyra** Sweden
194 E5 **Hòn Bãi Canh** *island* Vietnam
128 F6 **Honaïne** Algeria
83 K8 **Honaker** Virginia USA
84 inset **Hōnaunau** Hawai'i USA
187 D8 **Honavar** Karnataka India
100 C3 **Honda** Colombia
100 C1 **Honda, Bahía** *bay* Colombia
195 H5 **Honda Bay** Philippines
162 C6 **Hondeklipbaai** South Africa
75 N5 **Hondo** Alberta Canada
192 F5 **Hondo** Japan
85 J4 **Hondo** *watercourse* New Mexico USA
86 B6 **Hondo** Texas USA
90 C4 **Honduras** *country* Central America
90 C3 **Honduras, Gulf of** Honduras
75 U4 **Hone** Manitoba Canada
122 F2 **Hønefoss** Norway
221 9 **Honey, Mount** Campbell Island New Zealand
80 E6 **Honey Lake** California USA
126 E2 **Honfleur** France
192 E4 **Hong-do** *island* South Korea
189 G1 **Hong He** *watercourse* Henan China
189 G4 **Hong Kong (Xianggang)** Hong Kong (Zianggiang) S.A.R. China
189 G4 **Hong Kong (Xianggang) S.A.R.** *admin. area* China
181 I5 **Hong Ton** Myanmar
189 G2 **Hong'an** Hubei China
189 G2 **Honghu** Hubei China
188 F3 **Hongjiang** Hunan China
185 J5 **Hongliuwan** Gansu China
189 G3 **Hongmen Shuiku** *lake* Jiangxi China
191 I6 **Hongning** Shandong China
188 F4 **Hongshui He** *watercourse* Guangxi Zhuangzu Zizhiqu China
190 G6 **Hongtong** Shanxi China
79 F8 **Honguedo, Détroit d'** *strait* Quebec Canada
192 E3 **Hongwŏn** North Korea
189 H1 **Hongze Hu** *lake* Jiangsu China
222 8a **Honiara** Solomon Islands
138 D4 **Honiton** Devon England UK
187 D8 **Honnali** Karnataka India
121 O1 **Honningsvåg** Norway
84 inset **Honoka'a** Hawai'i USA
84 inset **Honolulu** Hawai'i USA
84 inset **Honomū** Hawai'i USA
128 E4 **Honrubia** Spain
193 I4 **Honshū** *island* Japan
84 inset **Honu'apo** Hawai'i USA
80 E4 **Hood, Mount** *volcano* Oregon USA
199 H6 **Hood Point** Papua New Guinea
122 E5 **Hooge** *island* Germany
75 M3 **Hoohey Creek** Alberta Canada
143 F4 **Hook Head** *cape* Ireland
215 J6 **Hook Island** Qld Australia
77 N5 **Hook Point** Ontario Canada
215 J5 **Hook Reef** Qld Australia
213 K5 **Hooker** *watercourse* NT Australia
86 D4 **Hooks** Texas USA
72 F7 **Hoonah** Alaska USA
81 M8 **Hooper** Colorado USA
214 B2 **Hooper, Mount** NT Australia
72 C6 **Hooper Bay** Alaska USA
81 Q2 **Hoople** North Dakota USA
162 E5 **Hoopstad** South Africa
86 H4 **Hoover** Alabama USA
136 G5 **Hopa** Turkey
216 F3 **Hope** *watercourse* WA Australia
74 K8 **Hope** British Columbia Canada
141 G3 **Hope** Derbyshire England UK
138 D4 **Hope** Devon England UK
86 E4 **Hope** Arkansas USA
85 N1 **Hope** Kansas USA
85 J4 **Hope** New Mexico USA
218 D3 **Hope, Lake** SA Australia
216 G6 **Hope, Lake** WA Australia
142 D2 **Hope, Loch** *lake* Scotland UK
72 C5 **Hope, Point** Alaska USA
216 H4 **Hope Campbell Lake** WA Australia
87 L3 **Hope Mills** North Carolina USA
138 E2 **Hope under Dinmore** Herefordshire England UK
215 H3 **Hope Vale** Qld Australia
78 H5 **Hopedale** Newfoundland and Labrador Canada
89 H5 **Hopelchén** Mexico
218 D3 **Hopeless, Mount** SA Australia
134 G3 **Hopen** *island* Norway
77 U3 **Hopes Advance, Baie** *bay* Quebec Canada
218 F6 **Hopetoun** Vic. Australia
216 G6 **Hopetoun** WA Australia
162 D5 **Hopetown** South Africa
83 M8 **Hopewell** Virginia USA
77 P3 **Hopewell Islands** Nunavut Canada
124 G4 **Hopfgarten** Austria
221 C7 **Hopkins** *watercourse* New Zealand
217 K2 **Hopkins, Lake** WA Australia
139 I2 **Hopton** Norfolk England UK
139 E2 **Hopton** Staffordshire England UK
162 B2 **Hoque** Angola
80 D3 **Hoquiam** Washington USA
136 G5 **Horasan** Turkey
86 D4 **Horatio** Arkansas USA
124 E3 **Horb am Neckar** Germany
122 G5 **Hörby** Sweden
128 D4 **Horcajo de los Montes** Spain
126 F1 **Hordain** France
122 D2 **Hordaland** *admin. area* Norway
213 K6 **Hordern Hills** NT Australia
138 C2 **Horeb** Ceredigion Wales UK
132 C3 **Horezu** Romania
136 F6 **Horgaz** Turkey
185 H3 **Horgon Nuur** *lake* Mongolia
132 A2 **Horgoš** Serbia
132 D1 **Horhany** *range* Ukraine
132 F3 **Horia** Romania
102 E4 **Horizonte** Brazil
104 D3 **Horizonte** Brazil
139 H3 **Horkesley Heath** Essex England UK
139 G3 **Horley** Surrey England UK
59 Q1 **Horlick Mountains** Antarctica
179 I3 **Hormak** Iran
104 B3 **Hormigas de Afuera, Islas** *islands* Peru
179 H4 **Hormoz, Jazīreh-ye** *island* Iran
179 H4 **Hormozgān** *admin. area* Iran
179 H4 **Hormuz, Strait of** Middle East
125 H3 **Horn** Austria
74 M2 **Horn** *watercourse* Northwest Territories Canada
120 inset **Horn** *cape* Iceland
122 F2 **Horn** Norway
120 H4 **Horn** Norway
122 H4 **Horn** Sweden
Horn, Cape *see* **Hornos, Cabo de** Chile
218 H7 **Horn, The** *mountain* Vic. Australia
143 E1 **Horn Head** *cape* Ireland
214 G1 **Horn Island** Qld Australia
74 L1 **Horn Plateau** Northwest Territories Canada
125 K3 **Hornád** *watercourse* Slovakia
120 inset **Hornafjörður** *bay* Iceland
120 J3 **Hornavan** *bay* Sweden
141 H3 **Horncastle** Lincolnshire England UK
120 I3 **Horndal** Norway
138 C4 **Horndon** Devon England UK
223 12 **Horne, Îles** *islands* Wallis and Futuna
120 K5 **Hörnefors** Sweden
74 L1 **Hornell Lake** Northwest Territories Canada
82 I2 **Hornepayne** Ontario Canada
125 I3 **Horní Benešov** Czech Republic
124 G3 **Horní Bříza** Czech Republic
125 I2 **Horní Jelení** Czech Republic
127 K1 **Horní Jiřetín** Czech Republic
125 H3 **Horní Planá** Czech Republic
120 E6 **Hornindal** Norway
139 I2 **Horning** Norfolk England UK
104 D5 **Horno Chico** Peru
120 J5 **Hornön** Sweden
88 C3 **Hornos** Mexico
108 C6 **Hornos, Cabo de (Cape Horn)** *cape* Chile
108 C6 **Hornos, Falso Cabo de** *cape* Chile
108 C6 **Hornos, Isla** *island* Chile
126 E2 **Hornoy** France
141 H3 **Hornsea** East Riding of Yorkshire England UK
120 J4 **Hornsjö** Sweden
120 K5 **Hörnsjö** Sweden
122 I2 **Hornslandet** *cape* Sweden
132 F3 **Horodnye** Ukraine
132 G1 **Horodyshche** Ukraine
101 G3 **Hororabo** Guyana
191 G3 **Horovlin** Mongolia
107 G2 **Horqueta** Paraguay
138 C4 **Horrabridge** Devon England UK
122 G2 **Horrmunden** *lake* Sweden
216 D4 **Horrocks** WA Australia
210 inset **Horsburgh Island (Luar)** Cocos (Keeling) Islands Australia
82 I8 **Horse Cave** Kentucky USA
75 V6 **Horse Island** Manitoba Canada
79 K7 **Horse Islands** Newfoundland and Labrador Canada
80 E6 **Horse Lake** California USA
218 E4 **Horse Shoe Lagoon** SA Australia
138 C4 **Horsebridge** Devon England UK
74 K6 **Horsefly Lake** British Columbia Canada
143 D3 **Horseleap** Ireland
122 E5 **Horsens** Denmark
218 B1 **Horseshoe Bend** NT Australia
80 G5 **Horseshoe Bend** Idaho USA
76 J6 **Horseshoe Lake** Ontario Canada
50 Q6 **Horseshoe Seamounts** *underwater feature* Atlantic Ocean
218 F7 **Horsham** Vic. Australia
139 G3 **Horsham** West Sussex England UK
124 D2 **Horst** Netherlands
124 D1 **Hörstel** Germany
164 1 **Horta** Azores
122 F3 **Horten** Norway
122 H1 **Horten** *lake* Sweden
72 G5 **Horton** *watercourse* Northwest Territories Canada
141 F3 **Horton** Lancashire England UK
82 D7 **Horton** Kansas USA
72 G5 **Horton Lake** Northwest Territories Canada
125 H5 **Horvati** Croatia
125 I4 **Horvátzsidány** Hungary
83 J2 **Horwood Lake** Ontario Canada
136 C2 **Horyn** *watercourse* Ukraine
161 F2 **Hosai'na K'olito** Ethiopia
139 G2 **Hose** Leicester England UK
197 G3 **Hose, Pegunungan** *range* Malaysia
120 F4 **Hosen** Norway
179 I3 **Ḩoseynābād** Iran
187 D6 **Hoshangabad** Madhya Pradesh India
186 D4 **Hoshiarpur** Punjab India
156 F4 **Hoshib** *watercourse* Sudan
187 D8 **Hospet** Karnataka India
128 D2 **Hospital de Orbigo** Spain
121 P4 **Hossa** Finland
120 K5 **Hössjö** Sweden
108 C6 **Hoste, Isla** *island* Chile
125 L3 **Hostovice** Slovakia
120 H6 **Höstsätern** Sweden
187 D8 **Hosur** Karnataka India
80 G7 **Hot Creek Range** Nevada USA
86 E3 **Hot Springs** Arkansas USA
80 H3 **Hot Springs** Montana USA
87 J3 **Hot Springs** North Carolina USA
81 N5 **Hot Springs** South Dakota USA
120 I5 **Hotagen** *lake* Sweden
120 I4 **Hotagsfjällen** *island* Sweden
193 H4 **Hotaka-dake** *volcano* Japan
184 F5 **Hotan He** *lake* Xinjiang Uygur Zizhiqu China
162 D5 **Hotazel** South Africa
74 M4 **Hotchkiss** Alberta Canada
81 L7 **Hotchkiss** Colorado USA
213 K2 **Hotham, Cape** NT Australia
120 J4 **Hoting** Sweden
185 H3 **Hoton Nuur** *lake* Mongolia
190 E3 **Hotont** Mongolia
219 H2 **Hotspur, Mount** Qld Australia
51 Q11 **Hotspur Fracture Zone** *underwater feature* Atlantic Ocean
51 O11 **Hotspur Seamount** *underwater feature* Atlantic Ocean
72 H5 **Hottah Lake** Northwest Territories Canada
91 F3 **Hotte, Massif de la** *range* Haiti
162 B5 **Hottentot Bay** *bay* Namibia
109 5 **Hotuiti** *cape* Isla de Pascua (Easter Island)
126 C3 **Houat, Île d'** *island* France
194 D2 **Houayxay** Laos
142 inset **Houbie** Shetland Scotland UK
126 E2 **Houdan** France
124 C3 **Houdelaincourt** France
142 D5 **Houdston** South Ayrshire Scotland UK
126 E4 **Houeillès** France
196 D3 **Hougang** *admin. area* Singapore
139 G4 **Houghton** West Sussex England UK
82 G3 **Houghton** Michigan USA
82 I4 **Houghton Lake** Michigan USA
220 E2 **Houhora Heads** New Zealand
83 R3 **Houlton** Maine USA
190 G6 **Houma** Shanxi China
223 10a **Houma** Tonga
86 F6 **Houma** Louisiana USA
139 G3 **Hounslow** Greater London England UK
126 D4 **Hourtin et de Carcans, Étang d'** *lake* France
80 I7 **House Range** Utah USA
142 F1 **Housebay** Orkney Islands Scotland UK
142 inset **Housetter** Shetland Scotland UK
74 H5 **Houston** British Columbia Canada
82 F8 **Houston** Missouri USA
86 D6 **Houston** Texas USA
86 D6 **Houston, Lake** Texas USA
86 D5 **Houston County Lake** Texas USA
77 O6 **Houston Point** Nunavut Canada
216 C4 **Houtman Abrolhos** *reef* WA Australia
142 E2 **Houton** Orkney Islands Scotland UK
124 C2 **Houyet** Belgium
122 F2 **Hov** Norway
120 H3 **Hov** Norway
132 D1 **Hova Hoverla** *mountain* Ukraine
185 I3 **Hovd** Mongolia
185 J3 **Hovd** Mongolia
185 I2 **Hovd** Mongolia
185 I3 **Hovd** *admin. area* Mongolia
122 D3 **Hovda** Norway
122 D3 **Hovden** Norway
120 I2 **Hovden** Norway
122 C2 **Hovden** *island* Norway
139 G4 **Hove** Brighton and Hove England UK
122 F4 **Hovedstaden** *admin. area* Denmark
139 I2 **Hoveton** Norfolk England UK
57 G1 **Hovgaard Ridge** *underwater feature* Greenland Sea
121 M3 **Hovlössjön** *lake* Sweden
120 F6 **Høvringen** Norway
190 G4 **Hövsgöl** Mongolia
185 K2 **Hövsgöl** *admin. area* Mongolia
190 D2 **Hövsgöl Nuur** *lake* Mongolia
190 E4 **Hövüün** Mongolia
156 D4 **Howar, Wādī** *watercourse* Sudan
219 K1 **Howard** Qld Australia
81 Q5 **Howard** South Dakota USA
82 G4 **Howard** Wisconsin USA
214 C2 **Howard Island** NT Australia
215 L7 **Howard Patch** *reef* Qld Australia
85 L3 **Howardwick** Texas USA
141 H3 **Howden** East Riding of Yorkshire England UK
86 D3 **Howe** Oklahoma USA
219 I7 **Howe, Cape** NSW Australia
164 6b **Howe, Île** *island* French Southern and Antarctic Lands
59 O1 **Howe, Mount** *mountain* Antarctica
138 D2 **Howey** Powys Wales UK
162 F5 **Howick** South Africa
141 G1 **Howick** Northumberland England UK
215 H3 **Howick Group** *islands* Qld Australia
218 D2 **Howitt, Lake** SA Australia
218 H7 **Howitt, Mount** Vic. Australia
83 Q4 **Howland** Maine USA
222 1 **Howland Island** *USA territory* Pacific Ocean
141 H2 **Howsham** North Yorkshire England UK
214 B2 **Howship, Mount** NT Australia
143 F3 **Howth** Ireland
81 O7 **Hoxie** Kansas USA
124 E2 **Höxter** Germany
142 E2 **Hoy** *island* Scotland UK
124 E1 **Hoya** Germany
105 E6 **Hoyada** Bolivia
124 F2 **Hoym** Germany
160 D3 **Hoyo, Mount** *mountain* Democratic Republic of Congo
108 B3 **Hoyo de Epuyén** Argentina
121 P5 **Höytiäinen** *lake* Finland
194 C3 **Hpa-an** Myanmar
125 H2 **Hradec Králové** Czech Republic
130 G2 **Hranice** Czech Republic
130 F3 **Hrastnik** Slovenia
125 I4 **Hrastovsko** Croatia
120 inset **Hraunhafnartangi** *cape* Iceland
125 H5 **Hreljin** Croatia
132 F1 **Hristovaia** Moldova
136 B2 **Hrodna** Belarus
136 C2 **Hrodzyenskaya Voblasts'** *admin. area* Belarus
125 J3 **Hron** *watercourse* Slovakia
125 L2 **Hrubieszów** Poland
132 A1 **Hruštín** Slovakia
125 I5 **Hrvatska Dubica** Croatia
132 D2 **Hrynyava** Ukraine
181 H4 **Hsenwi** Myanmar
189 H4 **Hsi-Lo Chi** *lake* Taiwan China
189 H4 **Hsinchu** Taiwan China
188 D4 **Hsing-Yun Hu** *lake* Yunnan China
189 H4 **Hsinying** Taiwan China
181 H4 **Hsipaw** Myanmar
181 H5 **Hsisaing** Myanmar
189 I4 **Hsüen Shan** *mountain* Taiwan China
181 G4 **Htantalang** Myanmar
181 H5 **Hti lin** Myanmar
194 C4 **Hua Hin** Thailand
189 H4 **Hua Hsu** *island* Taiwan China
162 B4 **Huab** *watercourse* Namibia
100 A5 **Huaca, Punta La** *cape* Ecuador
105 F4 **Huacaraje** Bolivia
104 D5 **Huachacalla** Bolivia
105 F4 **Huachi, Laguna** *lake* Bolivia
104 C3 **Huachicña** Peru
85 H5 **Huachinera** Mexico
104 B3 **Huacho** Peru
84 G5 **Huachuca City** Arizona USA
104 B3 **Huacrachuco** Peru
191 H4 **Huade** Nei Mongol Zizhiqu China
191 K4 **Huadian** Jilin China
189 H4 **Huafeng** Fujian China
188 D2 **Huahai** Sichuan China
189 H2 **Huai He** *watercourse* Anhui China
189 G2 **Huai He** *watercourse* Jiangsu China
189 H1 **Huai`an** Jiangsu China
189 G2 **Huaibin** Henan China
188 F3 **Huaihua** Hunan China
189 H2 **Huainan** Anhui China
191 H5 **Huaiyang** Hebei China
189 H1 **Huaiyin** Jiangsu China
189 H2 **Huaiyuan** Anhui China
89 F5 **Huajuapan de León** Mexico
85 H6 **Huajumar** Mexico
198 C5 **Huaki** Indonesia
104 D4 **Hualca Hualca, Nevado** *mountain* Peru
104 C3 **Hualcará, Cerro** *mountain* Peru
106 E3 **Hualfín** Argentina
189 I4 **Hualien** Taiwan China
104 B3 **Huallaga** *watercourse* Peru
104 B2 **Huamachuco** Peru
162 C2 **Huambo** Angola
162 C2 **Huambo** *admin. area* Angola
191 L3 **Huanan** Heilongjiang China
104 B2 **Huancabamba** Peru
108 B3 **Huancache, Sierra** *range* Argentina
104 C4 **Huancaray** Peru
104 C4 **Huancavelica** Peru
104 C4 **Huancayo** Peru
105 F4 **Huanchaca** Bolivia
105 F4 **Huanchaca, Serranía de** *range* Bolivia
190 F6 **Huancheng** Gansu China
189 H2 **Huanfeng** Anhui China
Huang Hai *see* **Yellow Sea** China/North Korea/South Korea
189 G1 **Huang He** *watercourse* Henan China
189 F1 **Huang He** *watercourse* Jiangsu China
190 F5 **Huang He** *watercourse* Nei Mongol Zizhiqu China
190 F5 **Huang He** *watercourse* Ningxia Huizu Zizhiqu China
185 K6 **Huang He** *watercourse* Qinghai China
191 I5 **Huang He** *watercourse* Shandong China
188 D1 **Huang He** *watercourse* Sichuan China
189 H2 **Huang Shan** *range* Anhui China
189 G2 **Huangchuan** Henan China
191 H5 **Huangcun** Beijing China
189 H4 **Huanggang** Guangdong China
189 H3 **Huanggang Shan** *mountain* Jiangxi China
191 I5 **Huanghua** Hebei China
188 F4 **Huanghua He** *watercourse* Guangxi Zhuangzu Zizhiqu China
189 G3 **Huanglianyu** *mountain* Fujian China
188 D3 **Huangni He** *watercourse* Yunnan China
189 H2 **Huangshan** Anhui China
188 D2 **Huangshengguan** Sichuan China
189 G2 **Huangshi** Hubei China
106 F6 **Huanguelén** Argentina
190 E6 **Huangyuan** Qinghai China
191 G5 **Huangzhai** Shanxi China
104 C4 **Huanipaca** Peru
191 K4 **Huanren** Liaoning China
104 C4 **Huanta** Peru
106 D6 **Huantraicó, Sierra de** *range* Argentina
104 B3 **Huánuco** Peru
104 B3 **Huánuco** *admin. area* Peru
104 E5 **Huanuni** Bolivia
106 D1 **Huara** Chile
104 B3 **Huaraz** Peru
104 B3 **Huarmey** Peru
104 B3 **Huarmey, Bahía** *bay* Peru
104 B4 **Huarochirí** Peru
104 B1 **Huasaga** Peru
100 B5 **Huasaga** *watercourse* Peru
104 C2 **Huáscar** Peru
106 D4 **Huasco** Chile
106 D4 **Huasco** *watercourse* Chile
88 C3 **Huatabampo** Mexico
104 C4 **Huataca** Peru
89 F6 **Huatulco** Mexico
105 E4 **Huatunas, Laguna** *lake* Bolivia
100 D1 **Huauáriuaha** Colombia
104 B3 **Huaura** Peru
104 B3 **Huaura, Grupo de** *islands* Peru
104 B3 **Huayán** Peru
189 H2 **Huayang** Anhui China
188 F1 **Huayin** Shaanxi China
104 C4 **Huayllampi** Peru
104 C4 **Huaytane, Cerro** *mountain* Peru
189 G2 **Huayuan** Hubei China
188 F3 **Huayuan** Hunan China
105 E5 **Huayurí** Bolivia
190 E6 **Huazang** Gansu China
188 F4 **Huazhou** Guangdong China
82 E5 **Hubbard** Iowa USA
74 B2 **Hubbard, Mount** Yukon Territory Canada
77 V3 **Hubbard, Pointe** Quebec Canada
86 B4 **Hubbard Creek Lake** Texas USA
75 X3 **Hubbart Point** Manitoba Canada
189 F2 **Hubei** *admin. area* China
187 D8 **Hubli** Karnataka India
132 F1 **Hubnyk** Ukraine
106 E6 **Hucal** Argentina
106 E6 **Hucal, Valle de** *valley* Argentina
214 C7 **Huckitta** *watercourse* NT Australia
139 F1 **Hucknall** Nottinghamshire England UK
139 I4 **Hucqueliers** France
179 H2 **Hūdar** Iran
141 G3 **Huddersfield** West Yorkshire England UK
191 J2 **Huder** Nei Mongol Zizhiqu China
190 F2 **Huder** Mongolia
122 I2 **Hudiksvall** Sweden
123 N2 **Hudöfjärden** *bay* Finland
85 M1 **Hudson** Kansas USA
86 D5 **Hudson** Texas USA
81 K5 **Hudson** Wyoming USA
59 K2 **Hudson, Cape** Antarctica
82 D8 **Hudson, Lake** Oklahoma USA
75 Y2 **Hudson Bay** Canada
75 T6 **Hudson Bay** Saskatchewan Canada
83 O5 **Hudson Falls** New York USA
73 Q4 **Hudson Land** *plain* Greenland
59 R2 **Hudson Mountains** Antarctica
77 S1 **Hudson Strait** Nunavut/Quebec Canada
74 J5 **Hudson's Hope** British Columbia Canada
76 H6 **Hudwin Lake** Manitoba Canada
194 E3 **Huế** Vietnam
128 C3 **Huebra** *watercourse* Spain
108 B2 **Huechulafquén, Lago** *lake* Argentina
132 C2 **Huedin** Romania
90 B4 **Huehuetenango** Guatemala
88 E4 **Huejuquilla** Mexico
128 E5 **Huelma** Spain
128 C5 **Huelva** Spain
128 E5 **Huéneja** Spain
108 A3 **Huentemó** Chile
128 E5 **Huércal de Almería** Spain
105 E6 **Huerta** Bolivia
88 C3 **Huerta Vieja** Mexico
129 F4 **Huertas, Cabo de las** *cape* Spain
129 F3 **Huerva** *watercourse* Spain
128 E5 **Huesa** Spain
129 F2 **Huesca** Spain
109 6a **Huesco Ballena, Punta** *cape* Isla Róbinson Crusoe
88 E5 **Huetamo de Núñez** Mexico
128 E3 **Huete** Spain
108 A2 **Hueyelhue, Punta** *cape* Chile
128 D5 **Huezna, Embalse de** *lake* Spain
156 E5 **Hufeira** Sudan
122 C2 **Huftarøy** *island* Norway
141 H3 **Huggate** East Riding of Yorkshire England UK
214 B8 **Hugh** *watercourse* NT Australia
215 H6 **Hughenden** Qld Australia
75 P6 **Hughenden** Alberta Canada
213 J6 **Hughes, Mount** WA Australia
122 C3 **Huglo** *island* Norway
81 N7 **Hugo** Colorado USA
86 D3 **Hugo** Oklahoma USA
86 D3 **Hugo Lake** Oklahoma USA
81 O8 **Hugoton** Kansas USA
191 H6 **Huguan** Shanxi China
185 J3 **Huhemort** Mongolia
89 H4 **Huhí** Mexico
121 Q5 **Huhtilampi** Finland
121 Q5 **Huhus** Finland
188 E1 **Hui Xian** Gansu China
220 G4 **Huiarau Range** New Zealand
189 H2 **Huicheng** Anhui China
189 G4 **Huicheng** Guangdong China
192 E3 **Huich'on** North Korea
104 B2 **Huicungo** Peru
188 D3 **Huidong** Sichuan China
100 B5 **Huijin** Peru
162 B3 **Huila** Angola
162 B2 **Huíla** *admin. area* Angola
100 C4 **Huila** *admin. area* Colombia
162 B3 **Huíla, Planalto da** *plain* Angola
188 D3 **Huili** Sichuan China
191 I5 **Huimin** Shandong China
189 I2 **Huinan** Shanghai China
104 D5 **Huiñaymarca, Lago** *lake* Bolivia
106 F5 **Huinca Renancó** Argentina
190 E6 **Huining** Gansu China
105 F6 **Huirapitinde** Bolivia
108 B2 **Huiro** Chile
138 C4 **Huish** Devon England UK
142 A3 **Huisinis** Na h-Eileanan Siar Scotland UK
126 E2 **Huisne** *watercourse* France
108 B3 **Huite** Chile
100 B5 **Huito** Ecuador
123 L2 **Huittinen** Finland
89 F5 **Huitzuco de los Figueroa** Mexico
191 H6 **Huixian** Henan China
89 F5 **Huixquilucan** Mexico
89 G6 **Huixtla** Mexico
188 D3 **Huize** Yunnan China
189 G4 **Huizhou** Guangdong China
121 M3 **Hukanmaa** Sweden
187 D8 **Hukeri** Karnataka India
121 Q4 **Hukkajärvi** Finland
199 H6 **Hula** Papua New Guinea
191 K3 **Hulan** Heilongjiang China
190 F3 **Huld** Mongolia
191 G3 **Hulenbuir** Mongolia
189 G4 **Huliao** Guangdong China
191 L3 **Hulin** Heilongjiang China
122 H4 **Hulingen** *lake* Sweden
217 K2 **Hull** *watercourse* NT Australia
141 H3 **Hull** *watercourse* England UK
123 L3 **Hullo** Estonia
185 J3 **Hulma Nuur** *lake* Mongolia
122 H4 **Hult** Sweden
215 H7 **Hulton** Qld Australia
191 I2 **Hulun Buir** Nei Mongol Zizhiqu China
191 I3 **Hulun Nuur** *lake* Nei Mongol Zizhiqu China
136 F3 **Hulyaypole** Ukraine
191 K2 **Huma** Heilongjiang China
191 K2 **Huma He** *watercourse* Heilongjiang China
104 C3 **Humaitá** Brazil
85 I7 **Humariza** Mexico
88 D3 **Humaya** *watercourse* Mexico
162 B3 **Humbe** Angola
141 I3 **Humber, Mouth of the** *bay* England UK
213 K4 **Humbert** *watercourse* NT Australia
102 D3 **Humberto de Campos** Brazil
162 C2 **Humbi, Serra** *range* Angola
86 D6 **Humble** Texas USA
75 S6 **Humboldt** Saskatchewan Canada
82 D6 **Humboldt** Nebraska USA
80 G6 **Humboldt** *watercourse* Nevada USA
80 C6 **Humboldt Bay** California USA
Humboldt Gletscher *see* **Sermersuaq** Greenland
80 F7 **Humboldt Lake** Nevada USA
221 C7 **Humboldt Mountains** New Zealand
80 F6 **Humboldt Range** Nevada USA
139 G2 **Humby** Lincolnshire England UK
219 H7 **Hume, Lake** Vic. Australia
125 K3 **Humenné** Slovakia
82 E6 **Humeston** Iowa USA
122 I4 **Hummeln** *lake* Sweden
123 O2 **Hummonselkä** *bay* Finland
108 B3 **Humos, Isla** *island* Chile
162 B3 **Humpata** Angola
81 Q6 **Humphrey** Nebraska USA
130 F2 **Humpolec** Czech Republic
121 N5 **Humppi** Finland
123 L2 **Humppila** Finland
213 K2 **Humpty Doo** NT Australia
185 J3 **Humreg** Mongolia
155 J3 **Hūn** Libya
120 inset **Húnaflói** *bay* Iceland
189 F3 **Hunan** *admin. area* China
191 L4 **Hunchun** Jilin China
139 F2 **Huncote** Leicester England UK
120 I6 **Hundsjön** *lake* Sweden
132 C3 **Hunedoara** Romania
132 C3 **Hunedoara** *admin. area* Romania
127 I1 **Hünfeld** Germany
223 10 **Hunga Ha'apai Island** Tonga
125 J4 **Hungary** *country* Europe
218 G3 **Hungerford** Qld Australia
139 F3 **Hungerford** West Berkshire England UK
192 E3 **Hŭngnam** North Korea
80 I2 **Hungry Horse Reservoir** Montana USA
120 I5 **Hungsjön** *lake* Sweden
162 C2 **Hungulo** Angola
142 B3 **Hunish, Rubha** *cape* Scotland UK
191 K4 **Hunjiang** Jilin China
191 K4 **Hunjiang** *watercourse* Liaoning China
141 H2 **Hunmanby** North Yorkshire England UK
141 G3 **Hunsingore** North Yorkshire England UK
139 H2 **Hunstanton** Norfolk England UK
141 F2 **Hunstanworth** Durham England UK
187 D9 **Hunsur** Karnataka India
78 H5 **Hunt** *watercourse* Newfoundland and Labrador Canada
124 E1 **Hunte** *watercourse* Germany
219 J5 **Hunter** *watercourse* NSW Australia
218 G7 **Hunter** Vic. Australia
221 C7 **Hunter** *watercourse* New Zealand
81 Q3 **Hunter** North Dakota USA
75 R3 **Hunter Creek** Saskatchewan Canada
219 Q10 **Hunter Island** Tas. Australia
52 N10 **Hunter Island Ridge** *underwater feature* Pacific Ocean
221 B7 **Hunter Mountains** New Zealand
181 G5 **Hunters Bay** Myanmar
221 D7 **Hunters Hills, The** *range* New Zealand
218 H8 **Hunterson** Vic. Australia
220 F4 **Hunterville** New Zealand
83 N4 **Huntingdon** Quebec Canada
139 G2 **Huntingdon** Cambridgeshire England UK
86 G3 **Huntingdon** Tennessee USA
138 D2 **Huntington** Herefordshire England UK
80 G4 **Huntington** Oregon USA
81 J7 **Huntington** Utah USA
83 J7 **Huntington** West Virginia USA
84 D4 **Huntington Beach** California USA
80 F8 **Huntington Lake** California USA
124 E1 **Huntlosen** Germany
220 F3 **Huntly** New Zealand
142 F3 **Huntly** Aberdeenshire Scotland UK
138 E3 **Huntspill** Somerset England UK
87 H3 **Huntsville** Alabama USA
86 E2 **Huntsville** Arkansas USA
86 D5 **Huntsville** Texas USA
89 H4 **Hunucmá** Mexico
125 K4 **Hunya** Hungary
191 H5 **Hunyuan** Shanxi China

189 G1 **Huojia** Henan China
191 I3 **Huolin'guole** Nei Mongol Zizhiqu China
199 H5 **Huon Gulf** *bay* Papua New Guinea
194 E3 **Hương Khê** Vietnam
121 N5 **Huopana** Finland
189 G2 **Huoqiu** Anhui China
189 G2 **Huoshan** Anhui China
190 G6 **Huozhou** Shanxi China
77 T5 **Hurault, Lac** *lake* Quebec Canada
83 K4 **Hurd, Cape** Ontario Canada
211 inset **Hurd Point** Macquarie Island Australia
122 F2 **Hurdalssjøen** *lake* Norway
161 I1 **Hurdiyo** Somalia
Hurghada *see* **Al Ghurdaqah** Egypt
124 B4 **Huriel** France
185 J5 **Hurleg Hu** *lake* Qinghai China
143 D4 **Hurler's Cross** Ireland
85 H4 **Hurley** New Mexico USA
190 E4 **Hurmen** Mongolia
84 B2 **Huron** California USA
81 P4 **Huron** South Dakota USA
82 J4 **Huron, Lake** Canada/USA
139 F3 **Hursley** Hampshire England UK
139 H3 **Hurst Green** East Sussex England UK
83 L8 **Hurt** Virginia USA
127 H1 **Hürth** Germany
221 E6 **Hurunui** *watercourse* New Zealand
75 V2 **Hurwitz Lake** Nunavut Canada
141 G2 **Hurworth-on-Tees** Darlington England UK
122 C2 **Husa** Norway
120 inset **Húsavík** Iceland
139 F2 **Husbands Bosworth** Leicester England UK
120 K4 **Husbondliden** Sweden
190 F2 **Hushaat** Mongolia
72 D5 **Huslia** Alaska USA
123 K2 **Husö** *island* Finland
122 C2 **Husøy** *island* Norway
75 O7 **Hussar** Alberta Canada
120 E5 **Hustad** Norway
120 K5 **Husum** Sweden
120 H4 **Husvika** Norway
125 I1 **Huta** Poland
182 G6 **Hūtan** Iran
190 E2 **Hutar-under** Mongolia
74 M3 **Hutch Lake** Alberta Canada
162 D6 **Hutchinson** South Africa
81 Q7 **Hutchinson** Kansas USA
82 D4 **Hutchinson** Minnesota USA
87 K7 **Hutchinson Island** Florida USA
83 K8 **Hutchinson Rock** *mountain* Virginia USA
190 F2 **Hutel** Mongolia
178 E7 **Ḩūth** Yemen
221 F5 **Hutt** *watercourse* New Zealand
216 D4 **Hutt Lagoon** WA Australia
77 W4 **Hutte Sauvage, Lac de la** *lake* Quebec Canada
141 I3 **Huttoft** Lincolnshire England UK
219 I1 **Hutton** *watercourse* Qld Australia
141 H3 **Hutton** East Riding of Yorkshire England UK
140 F2 **Hutton Roof** Cumbria England UK
185 H4 **Hutubi** Xinjiang Uygur Zizhiqu China
191 H5 **Hutuo He** *watercourse* Shanxi China
121 M3 **Huuki** Sweden
75 O7 **Huxley** Alberta Canada
127 G1 **Huy** Belgium
189 H2 **Huzhou** Zhejiang China
120 inset **Hvalnes** *cape* Iceland
120 inset **Hvammsfjörður** *bay* Iceland
120 inset **Hvammstangi** Iceland
120 inset **Hvannadalshnúkur** *mountain* Iceland
130 G5 **Hvar** Croatia
120 inset **Hvítá** *watercourse* Iceland
122 F3 **Hvitsten** Norway
120 inset **Hvolsvöllur** Iceland
192 E3 **Hwach'on** South Korea
162 E3 **Hwange** Zimbabwe
192 E3 **Hwangju** North Korea
192 E4 **Hwasun** South Korea
163 F3 **Hwedza** Zimbabwe
81 O6 **Hyannis** Nebraska USA
185 J2 **Hyaras** Mongolia
185 J2 **Hyargas Nuur** *lake* Mongolia
125 J3 **Hyby** Slovakia
140 E2 **Hycemoor** Cumbria England UK
87 L2 **Hyco Lake** North Carolina USA
74 E5 **Hydaburg** Alaska USA
221 D7 **Hyde** New Zealand
141 F3 **Hyde** Greater Manchester England UK
76 H2 **Hyde Lake** Nunavut Canada
140 B2 **Hyde Park** Antrim Northern Ireland UK
216 F6 **Hyden** WA Australia
187 E8 **Hyderabad** Andhra Pradesh India
179 K4 **Hyderabad** Pakistan
122 C2 **Hyen** Norway
127 H5 **Hyères** France
127 H5 **Hyères, Iles d'** *islands* France
192 F3 **Hyesan** North Korea
122 F3 **Hyggen** Norway
74 G2 **Hyland** *watercourse* Yukon Territory Canada
213 J2 **Hyland Bay** NT Australia
74 G4 **Hyland Post** British Columbia Canada
122 F5 **Hyllekrog** *cape* Denmark
122 F4 **Hyllested Skovgaarde** Denmark
75 O5 **Hylo** Alberta Canada
122 I2 **Hyn** *lake* Sweden
192 G4 **Hyono-sen** *volcano* Japan
121 N4 **Hyry** Finland
121 P4 **Hyrynjärvi** *lake* Finland
121 P4 **Hyrynsalmi** Finland
81 L3 **Hysham** Montana USA
122 G4 **Hyssna** Sweden
74 L5 **Hythe** Alberta Canada
139 F4 **Hythe** Hampshire England UK
139 I3 **Hythe** Kent England UK
121 O5 **Hytölä** Finland
192 F5 **Hyuga** Japan

I

184 G4 **I-Li He** *watercourse* Xinjiang Uygur Zizhiqu China
183 M5 **I-Li He** *lake* Kazakhstan
155 H4 **I-n-Azaoua** Niger
155 H5 **I-n-Guezzam** Algeria
155 G5 **I-n-Tebezas** Mali
155 F5 **I-n-Tilit** Mali
103 C6 **Iaciara** Brazil
104 D3 **Iaco** *watercourse* Brazil
103 D6 **Iaçu** Brazil
199 J5 **Iagain Island** Papua New Guinea
132 E3 **Ialomita** *admin. area* Romania
199 G6 **Iamara** Papua New Guinea
87 I5 **Iamonia, Lake** Florida USA
221 D6 **Ianthe, Lake** New Zealand
199 H5 **Iaro** *watercourse* Papua New Guinea
132 E2 **Iaşi** Romania
132 E2 **Iaşi** *admin. area* Romania
86 E5 **Iatt, Lake** Louisiana USA
101 E5 **Iaunari** Brazil
159 E3 **Ibadan** Nigeria
100 C3 **Ibagué** Colombia
103 B8 **Ibaiti** Brazil
160 E4 **Ibanda** Uganda
160 D4 **Ibanga** Democratic Republic of Congo
132 B4 **Ibar** *watercourse* Kosovo
100 B4 **Ibarra** Ecuador
103 C8 **Ibaté** Brazil
103 D8 **Ibatiba** Brazil
178 E7 **Ibb** Yemen
160 D3 **Ibba** Sudan
160 D2 **Ibba** *watercourse* Sudan
160 C3 **Ibembo** Democratic Republic of Congo
159 H4 **Ibenga** *watercourse* Congo
107 G4 **Iberá, Esteros del** *bay* Argentina
104 D3 **Iberia** Peru
50 Q5 **Iberian Plain** *underwater feature* Atlantic Ocean
129 F3 **Iberica, Cordillera** *range* Spain
120 J2 **Ibestad** Norway
74 D2 **Ibex Valley** Yukon Territory Canada
129 F4 **Ibi** Spain
103 C7 **Ibiá** Brazil
102 D3 **Ibiapina** Brazil
103 E6 **Ibicaraí** Brazil
103 E6 **Ibicuí** Brazil
107 G4 **Ibicuí** Brazil
107 G4 **Ibicuí** *watercourse* Brazil
102 E5 **Ibimirim** Brazil
103 D5 **Ibipeba** Brazil
103 E6 **Ibirataia** Brazil
103 C8 **Ibirité** Brazil
133 E6 **İbirler** Turkey
107 H4 **Ibirubá** Brazil
103 B8 **Ibitinga** Brazil
129 G4 **Ibiza** Spain
Ibiza *see* **Eivissa** Spain
102 D4 **Ibjapaba, Serra da** *range* Brazil
133 F7 **İblis Burnu** *cape* Turkey
163 H2 **Ibo** Mozambique
103 D6 **Ibotirama** Brazil
159 G5 **Iboundji** Gabon
179 H5 **'Ibrī** Oman
133 E5 **İbrikbaba** Turkey
139 F2 **Ibstock** Leicester England UK
198 C3 **Ibu, Gunung** *mountain* Indonesia
195 I2 **Ibuhos** *island* Philippines
192 F5 **Ibusuki** Japan
104 C4 **Ica** Peru
104 C4 **Ica** *admin. area* Peru
100 D5 **Içá** *watercourse* Brazil
109 9 **Icacos Point** Trinidad and Tobago
106 D6 **Icalma** Chile
100 E4 **Icana** *watercourse* Brazil
90 E5 **Icantí** Panama
107 I4 **Içara** Brazil
102 C3 **Icatu** Brazil
136 E6 **Içel** Turkey
136 E6 **Içel** *admin. area* Turkey
120 inset **Iceland** *country* Europe
57 F2 **Icelandic Plateau** *underwater feature* Norwegian Sea
187 D8 **Ichalkaranji** Maharashtra India
187 F7 **Ichchapuram** Orissa India
135 W7 **Ichëra** Russian Federation
135 AI6 **Ichigemskiy Khrebet** *range* Russian Federation
105 E5 **Ichilo** *watercourse* Bolivia
193 I3 **Ichinoseki** Japan
192 E3 **Ich'on** North Korea
192 E4 **Ich'ŏn** South Korea
139 H2 **Icklingham** Suffolk England UK
133 F7 **İçmeler** Turkey
102 E4 **Icó** Brazil
164 3a **Icod de los Vinos** Canary Islands
105 F5 **Icuati** Bolivia
74 D3 **Icy Strait** Alaska USA
81 R5 **Ida Grove** Iowa USA
123 N3 **Ida-Virumaa** *admin. area* Estonia
159 F4 **Idabato** Cameroon
86 D4 **Idabel** Oklahoma USA
159 F3 **Idah** Nigeria
70 **Idaho** *admin. area* USA
80 I5 **Idaho Falls** Idaho USA
85 L4 **Idalou** Texas USA
128 C4 **Idanha, Barragem da** *lake* Portugal
159 I2 **Idd Al-Ghanam** Sudan
156 C5 **Idd el-Chanam** Sudan
161 H2 **Iddan** Somalia
75 P7 **Iddesleigh** Alberta Canada
120 L2 **Iddon** *island* Norway
87 I4 **Ideal** Georgia USA
132 D2 **Ideciu de Jos** Romania
121 S4 **Idel'** Russian Federation
155 H4 **Idelès** Algeria
139 H4 **Iden** East Sussex England UK
185 K3 **Ider** Mongolia
156 E3 **Idfū** Egypt
157 F5 **Idga Hamus** Ethiopia
196 C2 **Idi** Indonesia
160 B4 **Idiofa** Democratic Republic of Congo
121 M2 **Idivuoma** Sweden
182 E6 **Idjevan** Armenia
122 H2 **Idkerberget** Sweden
141 H3 **Idle** *watercourse* England UK
136 F6 **Idlib** Syria
161 F5 **Idodi** Tanzania
218 A1 **Idracowra** NT Australia
120 H6 **Idre** Sweden
133 G6 **İdrisyayla** Turkey
123 O4 **Idritsa** Russian Federation
130 D4 **Idro, Lago d'** *lake* Italy
120 I5 **Idsjön** *lake* Sweden
130 C1 **Idstein** Germany
161 F5 **Idugalo** Tanzania
160 C4 **Idumbe** Democratic Republic of Congo
135 AB7 **Idyum** *watercourse* Russian Federation
189 J3 **Ie-shima** *island* Japan
132 D2 **Iedu** Romania
126 F1 **Ieper** Belgium
133 D8 **Ierapetra** Greece
133 D5 **Ierissou, Kolpos** *bay* Greece
125 M4 **Iernut** Romania
121 N2 **Iešjav'ri** *lake* Norway
161 F5 **Ifakara** Tanzania
199 H2 **Ifalik** *island* Federated States of Micronesia
163 I4 **Ifanadiana** Madagascar
159 E3 **Ife** Nigeria
156 B5 **Ifenat** Chad
214 F5 **Iffley** Qld Australia
121 O1 **Ifjordfjellet** *region* Norway
159 F3 **Ifon** Nigeria
217 M5 **Ifould Lake** SA Australia
138 E2 **Ifton Heath** Shropshire England UK
162 D3 **Ifuluta Plain** *plain* Zambia
125 H5 **Ig** Slovenia
159 F2 **Igabi** Nigeria
125 I4 **Igal** Hungary
197 F3 **Igan** Malaysia
197 F3 **Igan** *watercourse* Malaysia
161 E3 **Iganga** Uganda
103 C8 **Igarapava** Brazil
102 C3 **Igarapé Açu** Brazil
102 B3 **Igarapé Miri** Brazil
102 F4 **Igarassu** Brazil
134 S5 **Igarka** Russian Federation
159 F3 **Igarra** Nigeria
106 F6 **Igarzábal** Argentina
187 C7 **Igatpuri** Maharashtra India
159 E3 **Igboho** Nigeria
159 F3 **Igbor** Nigeria
136 G5 **Iğdir** Turkey
136 G5 **Iğdir** *admin. area* Turkey
138 E2 **Ightfield** Shropshire England UK
127 I3 **Igis** Switzerland
108 F2 **Iglesia, Punta** *cape* Argentina
131 C7 **Iglesias** Sardinia Italy
155 F2 **Igli** Algeria
73 K5 **Igloolik** Nunavut Canada
78 H4 **Iglosiatik Island** Newfoundland and Labrador Canada
78 H4 **Iglusuaktalialuk Island** Newfoundland and Labrador Canada
76 J8 **Ignace** Ontario Canada
85 I2 **Ignacio** Colorado USA
84 G6 **Ignacio Ramirez** Mexico
88 C3 **Ignacio Zaragoza** Mexico
88 D2 **Ignacio Zaragoza** Mexico
123 N5 **Ignalina** Lithuania
133 E5 **İğneada** Turkey
136 D5 **İğneada Burnu** *cape* Turkey
198 D4 **Igom** Indonesia
161 E5 **Igoma** Tanzania
161 E4 **Igombe** *watercourse* Tanzania
132 D1 **Igrovitsa** Ukraine
103 B9 **Iguaçu** *watercourse* Brazil
107 H3 **Iguaçu Falls** *waterfall* Argentina/Brazil
103 D6 **Iguaí** Brazil
100 C4 **Iguaje, Mesas de** *region* Colombia
89 F5 **Iguala** Mexico
129 G3 **Igualada** Spain
90 E6 **Iguana, Isla** *island* Panama
103 C9 **Iguape** Brazil
107 H2 **Iguatemi** Brazil
102 E4 **Iguatu** Brazil
159 F5 **Iguéla** Gabon
128 C2 **Igueña** Spain
100 D2 **Igüés** Venezuela
105 F6 **Iguirayapirurenda** Bolivia
161 E4 **Igunga** Tanzania
222 6 **Igup** *island* Federated States of Micronesia
190 D3 **Ih Bogd Uul** Mongolia
190 E2 **Ih-uul** Mongolia
187 C10 **Ihavandhippolhu Atoll** Maldives
160 E4 **Ihema, Lac** *lake* Tanzania
155 H3 **Iherir** Algeria
185 J3 **Ihes Nuur** *lake* Mongolia
189 J3 **Iheya-shima** *island* Japan
190 G3 **Ihhet** Mongolia
159 F3 **Ihiala** Nigeria
126 D5 **Iholdy** France
163 I4 **Ihosy** Madagascar
163 I4 **Ihosy** *watercourse* Madagascar
133 F6 **İhsaniye** Turkey
190 E3 **Ihtamir** Mongolia
221 F5 **Ihuraua** New Zealand
121 N4 **Ii** Finland
193 H4 **Iida** Japan
121 O4 **Iijärvi** *lake* Finland
121 N4 **Iijoki** *watercourse* Finland
123 N3 **Iisaku** Estonia
121 O5 **Iisalmi** Finland
123 N2 **Iitti** Finland
121 P4 **Iivaara** *mountain* Finland
121 P4 **Iivantiira** *lake* Finland
159 E3 **Ijebu-Ode** Nigeria
124 D2 **IJssel, Oude** *watercourse* Netherlands
124 C1 **IJsselmeer** *bay* Netherlands
107 H4 **Ijuí** Brazil
107 H4 **Ijuí** *watercourse* Brazil
123 L2 **Ikaalinen** Finland
163 I4 **Ikalamavony** Madagascar
160 C4 **Ikanda** Democratic Republic of Congo
159 F2 **Ikara** Nigeria
133 E7 **Ikaria** *island* Greece
77 U3 **Ikattok, Baie** *bay* Quebec Canada
220 G4 **Ikawhenua Range** New Zealand
159 E3 **Ikeja** Nigeria
160 C4 **Ikela** Democratic Republic of Congo
160 B3 **Ikelemba** *watercourse* Democratic Republic of Congo
139 I2 **Iken** Suffolk England UK
159 F5 **Ikengué** Gabon
159 F3 **Ikeni** Nigeria
120 J3 **Ikesjaure** *lake* Sweden
185 K2 **Ikh Bogo Uul** *mountain* Mongolia
132 C4 **Ikhtiman** Bulgaria
192 F5 **Iki** *island* Japan
Iki-Burul *see* **Baga-Burul** Russian Federation
160 E4 **Ikimba, Lake** *lake* Tanzania
159 E3 **Ikire** Nigeria
192 F5 **Ikitsuki-shima** *island* Japan
160 E5 **Ikola** Tanzania
159 F3 **Ikole** Nigeria
159 F3 **Ikom** Nigeria
163 I4 **Ikongo** Madagascar
161 E3 **Ikoto** Sudan
159 G5 **Ikoy** *watercourse* Gabon
192 E4 **Iksan** South Korea
77 Q2 **Iktotat** *watercourse* Quebec Canada
161 F5 **Ikwiriri** Tanzania
104 D5 **Ilabaya** Peru
160 D5 **Ilagala** Tanzania
195 I3 **Ilagan** Philippines
199 I6 **Ilai Island** Papua New Guinea
121 Q5 **Ilajanjärvi** *lake* Finland
101 H4 **Ilakana Patatpe** French Guiana
186 G5 **Ilam** Nepal
139 F1 **Ilam** Staffordshire England UK
178 F2 **Īlām** Iran
178 F2 **Īlām** *admin. area* Iran
90 B4 **Ilama** Honduras
189 I4 **Ilan** Taiwan China
127 I3 **Ilanz** Switzerland
158 E3 **Ilaro** Nigeria
125 J3 **Ilava** Slovakia
104 D5 **Ilave** Peru
125 J1 **Iława** Poland
135 Z6 **Ilbenge** Russian Federation
215 J6 **Ilbilbie** Qld Australia
138 E3 **Ilchester** Somerset England UK
133 E6 **Ildır** Turkey
75 R5 **Île-à-la-Crosse** Saskatchewan Canada
72 I7 **Île-à-la-Crosse, Lac** *lake* Saskatchewan Canada
126 F2 **Île-de-France** *admin. area* France
132 E3 **Ileana** Romania
160 C4 **Ilebo** Democratic Republic of Congo
136 E6 **Ilemin** Turkey
143 C5 **Ilen** *watercourse* Ireland
161 F3 **Ileret** Kenya
223 14 **Îles du Vent** *admin. area* French Polynesia
223 14 **Îles Marquises** *admin. area* French Polynesia
223 14 **Îles Sous-le-Vent** *admin. area* French Polynesia
223 14 **Îles Tuamotu-Gambier** *admin. area* French Polynesia
219 I5 **Ilford** NSW Australia
76 H4 **Ilford** Manitoba Canada
215 H7 **Ilfracombe** Qld Australia
138 C3 **Ilfracombe** Devon England UK
123 M5 **Ilgis** *lake* Lithuania
103 B8 **Ilha Solteira** Brazil
105 I6 **Ilha Solteira, Represa** *lake* Brazil
107 J2 **Ilhabela** Brazil
103 E6 **Ilhéus** Brazil
183 L4 **Ili** *watercourse* Kazakhstan
72 D7 **Iliamna Lake** Alaska USA
133 E6 **Ilıca** Turkey
161 H2 **Ilig, Raas** *cape* Somalia
195 J5 **Iligan** Philippines
195 J5 **Iligan Bay** Philippines
195 I3 **Iligan Point** Philippines
73 Q4 **Ilimananngip Nunaa** *island* Greenland
135 W6 **Ilimpeya** *watercourse* Russian Federation
195 I4 **Ilin** *island* Philippines
183 O3 **Il'inka** Russian Federation
123 P5 **Il'ino** Russian Federation
135 AD9 **Il'inskiy** Russian Federation
193 I1 **Il'inskiy** Russian Federation
84 inset **'Ilio Point** Hawai'i USA
198 C6 **Iliomar** Timor-Leste (East Timor)
135 AG4 **Ilirgytgyn, Ozero** *lake* Russian Federation
127 L4 **Ilirska Bistrica** Slovenia
123 L5 **Il'jinskoe** Russian Federation
132 C1 **Ilk** Hungary
187 D8 **Ilkal** Karnataka India
139 F2 **Ilkeston** Derbyshire England UK
141 G3 **Ilkley** West Yorkshire England UK
217 J4 **Ilkurlka Roadhouse** WA Australia
127 H2 **Ill** *watercourse* France
104 D3 **Illampu** Bolivia
128 E3 **Illana** Spain
195 I6 **Illana Bay** Philippines
106 D4 **Illapel** Chile
216 D4 **Illawong** WA Australia
159 F2 **Illela** Nigeria
155 H6 **Illéla** Niger
124 F4 **Iller** *watercourse* Germany
128 E3 **Illescas** Spain
123 N3 **Illi** Estonia
132 G2 **Illichivs'k** Ukraine
126 E2 **Illiers** France
143 E1 **Illies** Ireland
104 E5 **Illimani** *mountain* Bolivia
82 G6 **Illinois** *watercourse* Illinois USA
132 F1 **Illintsi** Ukraine
101 G4 **Illiwa** *watercourse* Guyana
155 H3 **Illizi** Algeria
123 L2 **Illo** Finland
214 C7 **Illogwa** *watercourse* NT Australia
128 F3 **Illueca** Spain
124 F2 **Ilm** *watercourse* Germany
120 M5 **Ilmajoki** Finland
123 P3 **Il'men', Ozero** *lake* Russian Federation
127 J1 **Ilmenau** Germany
139 G3 **Ilmer** Buckinghamshire England UK
104 D5 **Ilo** Peru
195 I5 **Iloilo** Philippines
130 H4 **Ilok** Croatia
121 Q5 **Ilomantsi** Finland
159 E3 **Ilorin** Nigeria
130 G4 **Ilova** Croatia
130 F4 **Ilovik** *island* Croatia
182 D3 **Ilovlya** Russian Federation
125 H2 **Iłowa** Poland
138 C3 **Ilston** Swansea Wales UK
141 G2 **Ilton** North Yorkshire England UK
217 L3 **Iltur** SA Australia
219 K3 **Iluka** NSW Australia
73 N5 **Ilulissat** Greenland
73 O5 **Ilulissat Gletscher** *ice* Greenland
161 E5 **Ilunde** Tanzania
161 E5 **Ilungu** Tanzania
121 N4 **Ilveskylä** Finland
80 C3 **Ilwaco** Washington USA
133 E5 **Ilyas Burnu** *cape* Turkey
134 M6 **Ilych** *watercourse* Russian Federation
123 Q2 **Il'ynskiy** Russian Federation
130 F3 **Ilz** Austria
125 K2 **Iłża** Poland
192 G4 **Imabari** Japan
101 G5 **Imabu** *watercourse* Brazil
102 E4 **Imaculada** Brazil
182 I7 **Imam-baba** Turkmenistan
121 R3 **Imandra** Russian Federation
121 R3 **Imandra, Ozero** *lake* Russian Federation
217 M2 **Imanpa** NT Australia
183 J3 **Imantau Koli** *lake* Kazakhstan
57 D2 **Imarssuak Channel** *underwater feature* Atlantic Ocean
101 F3 **Imataca, Serranía de** *range* Venezuela
123 O2 **Imatra** Finland
100 B4 **Imbabura** *admin. area* Ecuador
107 I4 **Imbituba** Brazil
103 B9 **Imbituva** Brazil
80 G4 **Imbler** Oregon USA
135 AC8 **Imeni Peliny Osipenko** Russian Federation
191 M2 **Imeni Peliny Osipenko** Russian Federation
182 H6 **Imeni Stalina** Turkmenistan
101 E4 **Imeri, Serra** *range* Brazil
133 D5 **Ímeros** Greece
161 G2 **Īmī** Ethiopia
125 M1 **Imienin** Belarus
76 G2 **Imikula Lake** Nunavut Canada
77 P3 **Imilik, Pointe** Quebec Canada
214 C2 **Imimbar** *watercourse* NT Australia
192 E4 **Imja-do** *island* South Korea
192 E3 **Imjin-gang** *watercourse* North Korea
154 C4 **Imlili** Western Sahara
123 O2 **Immalanjärvi** *lake* Finland
122 H4 **Immeln** *lake* Sweden
127 I3 **Immendingen** Germany
141 H3 **Immingham** North East Lincolnshire England UK
159 F3 **Imo** *admin. area* Nigeria
159 F3 **Imo** *watercourse* Nigeria
130 D4 **Imola** Italy
104 E2 **Imperatriz** Brazil
102 C4 **Imperatriz** Brazil
130 C5 **Imperia** Italy
75 S7 **Imperial** Saskatchewan Canada
84 E4 **Imperial** California USA
81 O6 **Imperial** Nebraska USA
75 P5 **Imperial Mills** Alberta Canada
212 E4 **Imperieuse Reef** WA Australia
159 H4 **Impfondo** Congo
181 G4 **Imphal** Manipur India
126 F3 **Imphy** France
123 P2 **Impilakhti** Russian Federation
139 H2 **Impington** Cambridgeshire England UK
133 F5 **İmralı Adası** *island* Turkey
122 C3 **Ims** Norway
192 E4 **Imsil** South Korea
124 F4 **Imst** Austria
135 AA5 **Imtenzha** Russian Federation
88 C2 **Imuris** Mexico
195 H5 **Imuruan Bay** Philippines
155 H3 **In Aménas** Algeria
155 H4 **In Amguel** Algeria
194 D4 **In Buri** Thailand
155 G3 **In Salah** Algeria
193 H4 **Ina** Japan
125 H1 **Ina** *watercourse* Poland
164 5c **Inaccessible Island** *island* St Helena
143 C4 **Inagh** Ireland
104 D3 **Inaiuini** *watercourse* Brazil
105 I3 **Inajá, Serra do** *range* Brazil
214 D3 **Inamalamandja Point** NT Australia
104 D4 **Inambari** Peru
104 D4 **Iñapari** Peru
222 5 **Inarajan** Guam
132 A2 **Inárcs** Hungary
121 Q5 **Inari** Finland
121 O2 **Inari** Finland
121 O2 **Inarijärvi** *bay* Finland
121 O2 **Inarijoki** *watercourse* Finland
121 N2 **Inarijoki** *watercourse* Norway
129 H4 **Inca** Spain
140 E3 **Ince Blundell** Merseyside England UK
136 E4 **Ince Burun** *cape* Turkey
143 C4 **Inch** Ireland
143 F4 **Inch** Ireland
143 E1 **Inch Island** Ireland
192 E4 **Inch'ŏn** South Korea
142 E4 **Inchture** Perth and Kinross Scotland UK
163 F5 **Incomati** *watercourse* Mozambique
156 F5 **Inda Silasē** Ethiopia
142 B5 **Indaal, Loch** *bay* Scotland UK
103 C7 **Indaiá** *watercourse* Brazil
103 C8 **Indaiatuba** Brazil
120 J5 **Indalsälven** *watercourse* Sweden
187 C7 **Indapur** Maharashtra India
181 H4 **Indaw** Myanmar
181 H4 **Indawgyi, Lake** Myanmar
212 E6 **Indee** WA Australia
84 C2 **Independence** California USA
82 F5 **Independence** Iowa USA
82 D8 **Independence** Kansas USA
82 I7 **Independence** Kentucky USA
82 D7 **Independence** Missouri USA
73 P2 **Independence Fjord** Greenland
80 G6 **Independence Mountains** Nevada USA
102 D4 **Independência** Brazil
105 H4 **Independência** Brazil
104 B4 **Independencia, Isla** *island* Peru
191 J3 **Inder** Nei Mongol Zizhiqu China
182 F4 **Inderborskiy** Kazakhstan
80 E3 **Index** Washington USA
187 D8 **Indi** Karnataka India
180 D4 **India** *country* Asia
219 K1 **Indian Head** Qld Australia
75 T7 **Indian Head** Saskatchewan Canada
213 K2 **Indian Island** NT Australia
82 H3 **Indian Lake** Michigan USA
83 N5 **Indian Lake** New York USA
55 **Indian Ocean**
87 K7 **Indian River Shores** Florida USA
75 V8 **Indian Springs** Manitoba Canada
84 E2 **Indian Springs** Nevada USA
70 **Indiana** *admin. area* USA
83 L6 **Indiana** Pennsylvania USA
82 H7 **Indianapolis** Indiana USA
82 E6 **Indianola** Iowa USA
86 F4 **Indianola** Mississippi USA
81 O6 **Indianola** Nebraska USA
105 G5 **Indiarana** Brazil
103 E5 **Indiaroba** Brazil
161 F2 **Indibir** Ethiopia
134 K5 **Indiga** Russian Federation
135 AD6 **Indigirka** *watercourse* Russian Federation
132 B3 **Inđija** Serbia
84 D4 **Indio** California USA
186 C5 **Indira Gandhi Canal** Rajasthan India
222 8 **Indispensable Strait** Solomon Islands
54 I9 **Indomed Fracture Zone** *underwater feature* Southern Ocean
198 E5 **Indonesia** *country* Asia
187 D6 **Indore** Madhya Pradesh India
196 D4 **Indragiri** *watercourse* Indonesia
123 M5 **Indrajų ežeras** *lake* Lithuania
196 F5 **Indramayu** Indonesia
196 F5 **Indramayu, Tanjung** *cape* Indonesia
196 D4 **Indrapura** Indonesia
196 D4 **Indrapura, Tanjung** *cape* Indonesia
187 E7 **Indravati** *watercourse* Chhattisgarh India
126 E3 **Indre** *watercourse* France
121 Q1 **Indre Kiberg** Norway
120 E5 **Indre Standal** Norway
120 J2 **Indre-Tysfjorden** *bay* Norway
120 G4 **Indre Vikna** *island* Norway
217 M3 **Indulkana** SA Australia
162 C2 **Indungo** Angola
179 L3 **Indus** *watercourse* Pakistan
54 K2 **Indus Fan** *underwater feature* Arabian Sea
82 F6 **Industry** Illinois USA
86 C6 **Industry** Texas USA
133 E5 **İnecik** Turkey
123 M4 **Inesis** *lake* Latvia
132 B2 **Ineu** Romania
133 C5 **Inevo** Macedonia
88 E5 **Infiernillo, Presa** *lake* Mexico
131 F7 **Infreschi, Punta degli** *cape* Italy
121 S3 **Inga** Russian Federation
123 M2 **Ingå** Finland
155 H5 **Ingal** Niger
213 L6 **Ingallan** *watercourse* NT Australia
85 L2 **Ingalls** Kansas USA
160 C4 **Inganda** Democratic Republic of Congo
123 J3 **Ingarö** *island* Sweden
139 H3 **Ingatestone** Essex England UK
127 I2 **Ingelheim** Germany
160 B4 **Ingende** Democratic Republic of Congo
106 F2 **Ingeniero Guillermo Nueva Juárez** Argentina
108 C2 **Ingeniero Jacobacci** Argentina
108 B4 **Ingeniero Pallavicini** Chile
74 I4 **Ingenika Mine** British Columbia Canada
83 K5 **Ingersoll** Ontario Canada
215 I5 **Ingham** Qld Australia
73 M3 **Inglefield Land** *plain* Greenland
106 D3 **Inglesa, Bahía** *bay* Chile
141 F2 **Ingleton** North Yorkshire England UK
219 J3 **Inglewood** Qld Australia
218 F7 **Inglewood** Vic. Australia
84 C4 **Inglewood** California USA
87 J6 **Inglis** Florida USA
214 D2 **Inglis Island** NT Australia
191 G2 **Ingoda** *watercourse* Russian Federation
181 H4 **Ingoka Pum** *mountain* Myanmar
141 I3 **Ingoldmells** Lincolnshire England UK
81 R2 **Ingolf** Ontario Canada
73 R2 **Ingolf Fjord** Greenland
124 F3 **Ingolstadt** Germany
121 M1 **Ingøya** *island* Norway
121 S3 **Ingozero, Ozero** *lake* Russian Federation
74 E6 **Ingraham Bay** British Columbia Canada
186 G6 **Ingraj Bazar** West Bengal India
141 G1 **Ingram** Northumberland England UK
86 B5 **Ingram** Texas USA
59 F2 **Ingrid Christensen Coast** Antarctica
136 E3 **Ingulets** *watercourse* Ukraine
132 H1 **Ingulo-Kamenka** Ukraine
182 D5 **Ingushetiya Respublika** *admin. area* Russian Federation
163 F5 **Ingwavuma** South Africa
162 E2 **Ingwe** Zambia
127 H2 **Ingwiller** France
181 H4 **Ingyan Yan** Myanmar
163 F5 **Inhaca** Mozambique
163 F4 **Inhafenga** Mozambique
163 G4 **Inhambane** Mozambique
163 F4 **Inhambane** *admin. area* Mozambique
103 E5 **Inhambupe** Brazil
163 F3 **Inhaminga** Mozambique
103 D7 **Inhapim** Brazil
163 I2 **Inharana** Madagascar
133 G5 **İnhisar** Turkey
102 D4 **Inhuma** Brazil
103 B7 **Inhumas** Brazil
123 K2 **Iniö** *island* Finland
100 E4 **Inírida** Colombia
100 D4 **Inírida** *watercourse* Colombia
143 F4 **Inish** Ireland
143 B3 **Inishbofin** *island* Ireland
143 C2 **Inishcrone** Ireland
143 C3 **Inisheer** *island* Ireland
143 B2 **Inishkea North** *island* Ireland
143 B2 **Inishkea South** *island* Ireland
143 C3 **Inishmaan** *island* Ireland
143 C3 **Inishmore** *island* Ireland
143 D2 **Inishmurray** *island* Ireland
143 E1 **Inishowen** *peninsula* Ireland
143 F1 **Inishowen Head** *cape* Ireland
143 B3 **Inishshark** *island* Ireland
143 B4 **Inishtooskert** *island* Ireland
143 B3 **Inishturk** *island* Ireland
143 B4 **Inishvickillane** *island* Ireland
140 A4 **Inistioge** Ireland
192 F3 **Inje** South Korea
219 I1 **Injune** Qld Australia
139 F2 **Inkberrow** Worcestershire England UK
125 I4 **Inke** Hungary
121 P4 **Inkee** Finland
218 D6 **Inkerman** SA Australia
74 E3 **Inklin** *watercourse* British Columbia Canada
80 I5 **Inkom** Idaho USA
221 E6 **Inland Kaikoura Range** New Zealand
124 G4 **Inn** *watercourse* Germany
121 N5 **Innala** Finland
218 E2 **Innamincka** SA Australia
122 H4 **Innaren** *lake* Sweden
120 I3 **Inndyr** Norway
142 B4 **Inner Hebrides** *islands* Scotland UK
164 9 **Inner Islands** Seychelles
120 G5 **Innerdalsvatnet** *lake* Norway
142 E5 **Innerleithen** Scottish Borders Scotland UK
124 F1 **Innerste** *watercourse* Germany
120 L5 **Innertavle** Sweden
219 Q11 **Innes Peak** Tas. Australia
124 F3 **Inning** Germany
215 I4 **Innisfail** Qld Australia
75 O6 **Innisfail** Alberta Canada
192 G4 **Innoshima** Japan
124 F4 **Innsbruck** Austria
120 K2 **Innset** Norway
77 Q3 **Innuksuac** *watercourse* Quebec Canada
120 E6 **Innvikfjorden** Norway
143 E3 **Inny** *watercourse* Ireland
103 B7 **Inocência** Brazil
86 D2 **Inola** Oklahoma USA
133 G6 **İnönü** Turkey
125 K2 **Inowłódz** Poland
125 J1 **Inowrocław** Poland
142 F3 **Insch** Aberdeenshire Scotland UK
216 C2 **Inscription, Cape** WA Australia
194 C3 **Insein** Myanmar
142 D2 **Inshore** Highland Scotland UK
219 K1 **Inskip Point** Qld Australia
125 H1 **Ińsko, Jezioro** *lake* Poland
134 N5 **Inta** Russian Federation
140 B3 **Intack** Ireland
196 D2 **Intan, Teluk** Malaysia
127 H3 **Interlaken** Switzerland
82 E2 **International Falls** Minnesota USA
194 B4 **Interview Island** Andaman and Nicobar Islands India
90 B4 **Intibucá** Honduras
107 F4 **Intiyaco** Argentina
121 V4 **Intsy** Russian Federation
100 C5 **Intuto** Peru
77 P3 **Inukjuak** Quebec Canada
108 C5 **Inútil, Bahía** *bay* Chile
72 F5 **Inuvik** Northwest Territories Canada
142 E3 **Inver** Aberdeenshire Scotland UK
142 C4 **Inveraray** Argyll and Bute Scotland UK
142 F4 **Inverbervie** Aberdeenshire Scotland UK
221 C8 **Invercargill** New Zealand
142 D3 **Invercassley** Highland Scotland UK
142 D5 **Inverclyde** *admin. area* Scotland UK
142 E3 **Invereen** Highland Scotland UK
142 E4 **Inverey** Aberdeenshire Scotland UK
142 C3 **Inverie** Highland Scotland UK
142 F4 **Inverkeilor** Angus Scotland UK
142 E4 **Inverkeithing** Fife Scotland UK
142 D5 **Inverkip** Inverclyde Scotland UK
214 F4 **Inverleigh** Qld Australia
142 C4 **Inverliever** Argyll and Bute Scotland UK
142 C4 **Inverliver** Argyll and Bute Scotland UK
218 G8 **Inverloch** Vic. Australia
142 D2 **Invernaver** Highland Scotland UK
142 D3 **Inverness** Highland Scotland UK
87 J6 **Inverness** Florida USA
86 F4 **Inverness** Mississippi USA
142 F3 **Inverurie** Aberdeenshire Scotland UK
218 B5 **Investigator Group** *islands* SA Australia
55 N5 **Investigator Ridge** *underwater feature* Indian Ocean
218 C6 **Investigator Strait** SA Australia
183 O3 **Inya** Russian Federation
135 AE6 **Inya** *watercourse* Russian Federation
163 F3 **Inyangani** *mountain* Zimbabwe
80 F8 **Inyo Mountains** California USA
84 D3 **Inyokern** California USA
100 B4 **Inzá** Colombia
130 E3 **Inzell** Germany
182 D3 **Inzhavino** Russian Federation
192 F5 **Iô-jima** *island* Japan
133 B6 **Ioannina** Greece
133 B6 **Ioanninon, Limni** *lake* Greece
121 U2 **Iokanga** Russian Federation
82 D8 **Iola** Kansas USA
199 J5 **Iolasa Island** Papua New Guinea
142 B4 **Iona** *island* Scotland UK
80 F4 **Ione** Oregon USA
80 G2 **Ione** Washington USA
132 D3 **Ioneşti** Romania
82 I5 **Ionia** Michigan USA
133 A6 **Ionian Islands** Greece
133 B7 **Ionian Sea** Greece
133 A6 **Ionioi Nisia** *island* Greece
133 B6 **Ionioi Nisoi** *admin. area* Greece
135 AD7 **Iony, Ostrov** *island* Russian Federation
199 H5 **Iori** Papua New Guinea
133 D7 **Ios** Greece
133 D7 **Ios** *island* Greece
74 M5 **Iosegun Lake** Alberta Canada
134 L6 **Iosser** Russian Federation
86 E5 **Iota** Louisiana USA
154 C5 **Iouîk** Mauritania
70 **Iowa** *admin. area* USA
82 F6 **Iowa** *watercourse* Iowa USA
82 F6 **Iowa City** Iowa USA
82 E5 **Iowa Falls** Iowa USA
85 M4 **Iowa Park** Texas USA
103 D7 **Ipaba** Brazil
103 B7 **Ipameri** Brazil
102 E5 **Ipanema** *watercourse* Brazil
103 D7 **Ipatinga** Brazil
103 B8 **Ipauçu** Brazil
133 B6 **Ipeiros** *admin. area* Greece
136 G5 **Ipek Geçidi** *pass* Turkey
125 J3 **Ipel'** *watercourse* Slovakia
162 E5 **Ipelegeng** South Africa
159 H4 **Ipendja** *watercourse* Congo
159 E3 **Iperu** Nigeria
90 E5 **Ipetí** Panama
105 H6 **Ipezal** Brazil
100 B4 **Ipiales** Colombia
197 I2 **Ipil** Philippines
195 I6 **Ipil** Philippines
103 E6 **Ipirá** Brazil
105 F2 **Ipiranga** Brazil
101 I5 **Ipixuna** Brazil
102 A4 **Ipixuna** *watercourse* Brazil
196 D2 **Ipoh** Malaysia
102 F5 **Ipojuca** Brazil
125 J3 **Ipoly** *watercourse* Hungary
103 A9 **Iporã** Brazil
103 B7 **Iporá** Brazil
159 I3 **Ippy** Central African Republic
219 K2 **Ipswich** Qld Australia
139 I2 **Ipswich** Suffolk England UK
81 P4 **Ipswich** South Dakota USA
83 P5 **Ipswich Bay** Massachusetts USA
102 D4 **Ipu** Brazil
103 B8 **Ipuã** Brazil
102 D4 **Ipubi** Brazil
102 D4 **Ipueiras** Brazil
196 D4 **Ipuh** Indonesia
104 D4 **Ipuni** Bolivia
73 M6 **Iqaluit** Nunavut Canada
185 J5 **Iqe He** *watercourse* Qinghai China
106 D2 **Iquique** Chile
104 C1 **Iquitos** Peru
159 I3 **Ira Banda** Central African Republic
85 L5 **Iraan** Texas USA
189 I4 **Irabu-jima** *island* Japan
104 D3 **Iracema** Brazil
101 H3 **Iracoubo** French Guiana
157 F4 **Irafayle** Eritrea
133 D7 **Irakleia** *island* Greece
133 D8 **Irakleio** Greece
90 D4 **Iralaya** Honduras
182 G7 **Iran** *country* Asia
101 F5 **Iranduba** Brazil
179 I4 **Īrānshahr** Iran
88 E4 **Irapuato** Mexico
178 D3 **Iraq** *country* Asia
182 D8 **Iraq** *country* Middle East
103 D6 **Iraquara** Brazil
103 E6 **Irará** Brazil
102 A3 **Iratapuru** *watercourse* Brazil
103 B9 **Irati** Brazil
198 E4 **Irau, Bon** *mountain* Indonesia
90 D5 **Irazú, Volcán** *volcano* Costa Rica
123 L4 **Irbe Strait** Estonia
178 C3 **Irbid** Jordan
182 I1 **Irbit** Russian Federation
103 D5 **Irecê** Brazil
143 E3 **Ireland** *country* Europe
83 inset **Ireland Islands** Bermuda
160 C4 **Irema** Democratic Republic of Congo
106 F6 **Irene** Argentina
81 Q5 **Irene** South Dakota USA
182 I4 **Irgiz** Kazakhstan
182 H4 **Irgiz** *watercourse* Kazakhstan
154 E2 **Irherm** Morocco
154 E2 **Irhil m'Goun** *mountain* Morocco
198 F4 **Irian Jaya** *admin. area* Indonesia
198 E4 **Irian Jaya Barat** *admin. area* Indonesia
101 G4 **Iriau** *watercourse* Brazil
159 I1 **Iriba** Chad
156 C4 **Iriba** Chad
101 G4 **Iricoumé, Serra** *range* Brazil
132 A3 **Irig** Serbia
195 I4 **Iriga** Philippines
182 H3 **Iriklinskiy** Russian Federation
143 E2 **Irineragh** Ireland
161 F5 **Iringa** Tanzania
161 F5 **Iringa** *admin. area* Tanzania
189 I4 **Iriomote-jima** *island* Japan
102 A4 **Iriri** *watercourse* Brazil
102 A5 **Iriri Novo** *watercourse* Brazil
143 G3 **Irish Sea** Ireland/UK
143 E2 **Irish Town** Omagh Northern Ireland UK
140 B3 **Irishford** Ireland
102 C3 **Irituia** Brazil
135 U7 **Irkineyeva** *watercourse* Russian Federation
190 E2 **Irkut** *watercourse* Russian Federation
135 V8 **Irkutsk** Russian Federation
135 V7 **Irkutskaya Oblast'** *admin. area* Russian Federation
75 P6 **Irma** Alberta Canada
121 P4 **Irnijärvi** *lake* Finland
121 P4 **Irninniemi** Finland
163 I2 **Irodo** *watercourse* Madagascar
218 C5 **Iron Baron** SA Australia
218 C5 **Iron Knob** SA Australia
82 G4 **Iron Mountain** Michigan USA
82 G3 **Iron River** Michigan USA
78 I5 **Ironbound Islands** Newfoundland and Labrador Canada
219 J2 **Ironpot** Qld Australia
82 E3 **Ironton** Minnesota USA
82 F8 **Ironton** Missouri USA
82 J7 **Ironton** Ohio USA
82 F3 **Ironwood** Michigan USA
195 H5 **Iroquis Reef** Spratly Islands
81 Q4 **Iroquois** South Dakota USA
218 G3 **Irrara** *watercourse* NSW Australia

Irrawaddy *see* **Ayeyarwady** Myanmar
75 O7 **Irricana** Alberta Canada
80 F4 **Irrigon** Oregon USA
217 K3 **Irrunytju (Wingellina)** WA Australia
123 M4 **Irši** Latvia
122 I3 **Irsta** Sweden
134 O7 **Irtysh** *watercourse* Russian Federation
183 L2 **Irtyshsk** Kazakhstan
128 F2 **Irún** Spain
128 F2 **Irurtzun** Spain
75 P8 **Irvine** Alberta Canada
142 D5 **Irvine** North Ayrshire Scotland UK
84 D4 **Irvine** California USA
80 C2 **Irvines Landing** British Columbia Canada
217 K2 **Irving** *watercourse* NT Australia
86 C4 **Irving** Texas USA
82 H8 **Irvington** Kentucky USA
221 E6 **Irwell** New Zealand
216 D4 **Irwin** *watercourse* WA Australia
80 J5 **Irwin** Idaho USA
87 J4 **Irwinton** Georgia USA
159 F2 **Isa** Nigeria
215 I6 **Isaac** *watercourse* Qld Australia
105 I5 **Isaac Portilho** Brazil
222 8 **Isabel** *admin. area* Solomon Islands
81 O4 **Isabel** South Dakota USA
195 I6 **Isabela** Philippines
91 G3 **Isabela, Cabo** *cape* Dominican Republic
109 4 **Isabela, Canal** *strait* Archipiélago de Colon (Galapagos Islands)
109 4 **Isabela, Isla** *island* Archipiélago de Colon (Galapagos Islands)
90 C4 **Isabelia, Cordillera** *range* Nicaragua
82 F3 **Isabella** Minnesota USA
84 C3 **Isabella Lake** California USA
134 S3 **Isachenko, Ostrov** *island* Russian Federation
73 I3 **Isachsen, Cape** Nunavut Canada
120 inset **Ísafjarðardjúp** *bay* Iceland
120 inset **Ísafjörður** Iceland
186 D6 **Isagarh** Madhya Pradesh India
192 F5 **Isahaya** Japan
52 L4 **Isakov Seamount** *underwater feature* Pacific Ocean
125 L5 **Işalniţa** Romania
163 I4 **Isalo, Massif d'** *range* Madagascar
160 D4 **Isambe** Democratic Republic of Congo
160 C4 **Isandja** Democratic Republic of Congo
160 C4 **Isanga** Democratic Republic of Congo
222 7 **Isangel** Vanuatu
160 C3 **Isangi** Democratic Republic of Congo
159 F3 **Isanlu** Nigeria
160 D4 **Isasa** Democratic Republic of Congo
132 G2 **Isayevo** Ukraine
142 inset **Isbister** Shetland Scotland UK
128 D3 **Íscar** Spain
105 E6 **Iscayachi** Bolivia
133 G6 **İscehisar** Turkey
124 F4 **Ischgl** Austria
131 E6 **Ischia, Isola d'** *island* Italy
100 B4 **Iscuande** *watercourse* Colombia
100 B4 **Iscuandé** Colombia
213 H4 **Isdell** *watercourse* WA Australia
212 G7 **Isdell, Mount** WA Australia
124 B4 **Isdes** France
193 H4 **Ise** Japan
122 F5 **Isefjord** *bay* Denmark
161 E5 **Iseke** Tanzania
124 G4 **Isel** *watercourse* Austria
59 M2 **Iselin Bank** *underwater feature* Southern Ocean
124 E4 **Iselle** Italy
124 G3 **Isen** *watercourse* Germany
130 D4 **Iseo** Italy
127 G4 **Isère** *watercourse* France
101 H3 **Isère, Pointe** *cape* French Guiana
131 F6 **Isernia** Italy
193 H4 **Isesaki** Japan
183 K6 **Isfana** Kyrgyzstan
134 D3 **Isfjorden** *strait* Norway
178 E3 **Ishān Ḩamzah** Iraq
160 D4 **Ishasha** Uganda
134 M6 **Isherim, Gora** *mountain* Russian Federation
101 G4 **Isherton** Guyana
189 I4 **Ishigaki** Japan
189 I4 **Ishigaki-shima** *island* Japan
193 I2 **Ishikari-gawa** *watercourse* Japan
193 I2 **Ishikari-Wan** *bay* Japan
183 K2 **Ishim** Russian Federation
193 I3 **Ishinomaki** Japan
192 G5 **Ishizuchi-san** *volcano* Japan
82 H3 **Ishpeming** Michigan USA
142 C4 **Ishriff** Highland Scotland UK
107 H4 **Isidoro Noblía** Uruguay
183 K2 **Isil'kul'** Russian Federation
160 E5 **Isimbira** Tanzania
135 X8 **Isinga** Russian Federation
191 G2 **Isinga** Russian Federation
161 F3 **Isiolo** Kenya
160 D3 **Isiro** Democratic Republic of Congo
215 H8 **Isisford** Qld Australia
133 E7 **İskandil Burnu** *cape* Turkey
136 E6 **İskenderun Körfezi** *sea* Turkey
136 E5 **İskilip** Turkey
182 F4 **Iskine** Kazakhstan
183 N2 **Iskitm** Russian Federation
132 C4 **Iskrovci** Serbia
132 C4 **Iskur** *watercourse* Bulgaria
121 N2 **Iškuras** Norway
121 N2 **Iskuras** *mountain* Norway
161 I1 **Iskushuban** Somalia
74 F4 **Iskut** *watercourse* British Columbia Canada
142 E4 **Isla** *watercourse* Scotland UK
109 6a **Isla, Punta** *cape* Isla Róbinson Crusoe
89 H5 **Isla de Aguada** Mexico
109 5 **Isla de Pascua (Easter Island)** *island* Chile
88 D4 **Isla del Bosque** Mexico
100 C5 **Isla Inayuga** Peru
88 D2 **Isla Madero, Presa Fco.** *lake* Mexico
89 I4 **Isla Mujeres** Mexico
90 E5 **Isla Tigre** Panama
104 D1 **Isla Tigre** Peru
107 G3 **Isla Umbú** Paraguay
179 L2 **Islamabad** *admin. area* Pakistan
179 M2 **Islāmābād** Pakistan
179 L4 **Islamgarh** Pakistan
179 L5 **Islamkot** Pakistan
186 D6 **Islamnagar** Madhya Pradesh India
195 H5 **Island Bay** Philippines
75 T5 **Island Falls** Saskatchewan Canada
218 C4 **Island Lagoon** SA Australia
75 O5 **Island Lake** Alberta Canada
76 H6 **Island Lake** Manitoba Canada
82 E3 **Island Lake Reservoir** Minnesota USA
143 G2 **Island Magee** Northern Ireland UK
80 J4 **Island Park** Idaho USA
80 J4 **Island Park Reservoir** Idaho USA
79 J8 **Island Pond** Newfoundland and Labrador Canada
78 I5 **Islands, Bay of** Newfoundland and Labrador Canada
220 F2 **Islands, Bay of** New Zealand
Islas Malvinas *see* **Falkland Islands** Atlantic Ocean
51 P15 **Islas Orcadas Rise** *underwater feature* Atlantic Ocean
142 B5 **Islay** *island* Scotland UK
126 E4 **Isle** *watercourse* France
79 I9 **Isle aux Morts** Newfoundland and Labrador Canada
140 D2 **Isle of Man** *British crown dependency* UK
142 D6 **Isle of Whithorn** Dumfries and Galloway Scotland UK
139 F4 **Isle of Wight** *admin. area* England UK
214 D2 **Isle Woodah** NT Australia
155 G1 **Isles Baleares** *admin. area* Spain
138 A5 **Isles of Scilly** England UK
138 A5 **Isles of Scilly** *admin. area* England UK
142 inset **Islesburgh** Shetland Scotland UK
139 G3 **Islington** Greater London England UK
139 G2 **Islip** Northamptonshire England UK
127 J2 **Ismaning** Germany
156 E2 **Isnā** Egypt
123 M5 **Išnarų ežeras** *lake* Lithuania
124 F4 **Isny** Germany
127 J3 **Isny im Allgäu** Germany
121 P4 **Iso-Kero** *lake* Finland
121 P4 **Iso-Kiimanen** *lake* Finland
121 O5 **Iso Lamujärvi** *lake* Finland
123 M2 **Iso-Loytäne** *lake* Finland
121 O5 **Iso-Naaklima** *lake* Finland
121 P4 **Iso-Pyhäntä** *lake* Finland
123 M2 **Iso Roine** *lake* Finland
121 O4 **Iso-Syöte** *mountain* Finland
121 P5 **Iso Tipasjärvi** *lake* Finland
121 N3 **Iso Vietonen** *lake* Finland
123 M2 **Isojärvi** *lake* Finland
120 L5 **Isojoki** Finland
163 F2 **Isoka** Zambia
123 K2 **Isokari** *island* Finland
121 P4 **Isokumpu** Finland
120 M5 **Isokyrö** Finland
127 H4 **Isola** France
86 F4 **Isola** Mississippi USA
131 E7 **Isola delle Femmine** Italy
131 G7 **Isola di Capo Rizzuto** Italy
123 K2 **Isomaa** *island* Finland
160 E5 **Isopa** Tanzania
136 D6 **Isparta** *admin. area* Turkey
132 D1 **Ispas** Ukraine
131 F8 **Ispica** Italy
124 E5 **Ispra** Italy
182 D5 **Ispravnaya** Russian Federation
124 E3 **Ispringen** Germany
178 C3 **Israel** *country* Middle East
103 B7 **Israelândia** Brazil
217 H6 **Israelite Bay** WA Australia
123 O4 **Issa** Russian Federation
182 D2 **Issa** Russian Federation
183 L3 **Issen** *lake* Kazakhstan
158 C3 **Issia** Côte d'Ivoire
126 F4 **Issoire** France
130 F4 **Ist** *island* Croatia
136 D5 **İstanbul** *admin. area* Turkey
133 F5 **İstanbul Boğazı (Bosporus)** *watercourse* Turkey
120 G6 **Isteren** *lake* Norway
194 C5 **Isthmus of Kra** *sea* Thailand
100 B2 **Isthmus of Panama** *land feature*
183 K6 **Istiqlol, Qullai** *mountain* Tajikistan
100 B3 **Istmina** Colombia
132 B4 **Istok** Kosovo
125 L1 **Istok** Poland
87 K7 **Istokpoga Lake** Florida USA
127 G5 **Istres** France
132 F3 **Istria** Romania
121 O5 **Istunmäki** Finland
199 H5 **Isumrud Strait** Papua New Guinea
132 C3 **Isverna** Romania
182 G3 **Isyangulovo** Russian Federation
123 L1 **Itä-Aure** Finland
218 G6 **Ita Lake** NSW Australia
123 O1 **Itä-Suomen** *admin. area* Finland
104 E2 **Itabaiana** Brazil
103 E5 **Itabaiana** Brazil
103 B8 **Itaberá** Brazil
103 D6 **Itaberaba** Brazil
103 B7 **Itaberaí** Brazil
103 D7 **Itabira** Brazil
103 E6 **Itabuna** Brazil
102 B4 **Itacaiuna** *watercourse* Brazil
102 C5 **Itacajá** Brazil
103 C6 **Itacarambi** Brazil
103 E6 **Itacaré** Brazil
100 D6 **Itacuai** *watercourse* Brazil
107 G3 **Itacurubí del Rosario** Paraguay
103 D6 **Itagi** Brazil
103 E6 **Itagibá** Brazil
103 D7 **Itaguaçu** Brazil
103 D8 **Itaguaí** Brazil
100 C3 **Itagüí** Colombia
103 B8 **Itaí** Brazil
102 E5 **Itaíba** Brazil
102 D4 **Itaim** *watercourse* Brazil
107 H3 **Itaimbey** *watercourse* Paraguay
102 D4 **Itainópolis** Brazil
103 A9 **Itaipu, Represa de** *lake* Brazil
105 H2 **Itaituba** Brazil
107 I3 **Itajaí** Brazil
107 I3 **Itajaí** *watercourse* Brazil
103 B8 **Itajobi** Brazil
103 C8 **Itajubá** Brazil
131 **Italy** *country* Europe
103 E7 **Itamaraju** Brazil
103 D7 **Itamarandiba** Brazil
104 D2 **Itamarati** Brazil
103 D7 **Itambacuri** Brazil
103 D7 **Itambacuri** *watercourse* Brazil
103 D6 **Itambé** Brazil
103 D7 **Itambé, Pico de** *mountain* Brazil
163 H4 **Itampolo** Madagascar
181 G3 **Itanagar** Arunachal Pradesh India
107 H2 **Itanara** Paraguay
103 C9 **Itanhaém** Brazil
105 E2 **Itanhaua** *watercourse* Brazil
103 D7 **Itanhém** Brazil
103 E7 **Itanhém** *watercourse* Brazil
105 F5 **Itani, Serranía de** *range* Bolivia
103 B6 **Itapaci** Brazil
102 E3 **Itapagé** Brazil
105 F2 **Itaparana** *watercourse* Brazil
103 C8 **Itapecerica** Brazil
102 C3 **Itapecuru Mirim** Brazil
103 D8 **Itaperuna** Brazil
103 D6 **Itapetinga** Brazil
103 B8 **Itapetininga** Brazil
103 B8 **Itapeva** Brazil
107 I4 **Itapeva, Lagoa** *lake* Brazil
102 C4 **Itapicuru** *watercourse* Brazil
102 E3 **Itapipoca** Brazil
103 B6 **Itapirapuã** Brazil
103 B8 **Itápolis** Brazil
102 E4 **Itaporanga** Brazil
103 B8 **Itaporanga** Brazil
101 E5 **Itapuã** Brazil
107 I2 **Itapuí** Brazil
103 B6 **Itapuranga** Brazil
107 G4 **Itaqui** Brazil
103 D7 **Itarana** Brazil
103 D6 **Itarantim** Brazil
103 B9 **Itararé** Brazil
187 D6 **Itarsi** Madhya Pradesh India
86 C4 **Itasca** Texas USA
103 C8 **Itatiba** Brazil
103 B8 **Itatinga** Brazil
102 F4 **Itatuba** Brazil
105 I5 **Itauçu** Brazil
102 D4 **Itaueira** Brazil
102 D4 **Itaueira** *watercourse* Brazil
105 H6 **Itaum** Brazil
186 E5 **Itaunja** Uttar Pradesh India
195 I2 **Itbayat** *island* Philippines
133 C6 **Itéa** Greece
133 C6 **Iteas, Kolpos** *bay* Greece
160 D4 **Itebero** Democratic Republic of Congo
183 K3 **Itemgen Koli** *lake* Kazakhstan
161 E5 **Itende** Tanzania
78 N1 **Iterlak** *island* Greenland
83 M5 **Ithaca** New York USA
133 B6 **Ithaki** *island* Greece
160 C3 **Itimbiri** *watercourse* Democratic Republic of Congo
103 D7 **Itinga** Brazil
105 H5 **Itiquira** Brazil
105 H5 **Itiquira** *watercourse* Brazil
103 C8 **Itirapina** Brazil
103 D6 **Itiruçu** Brazil
104 D5 **Itiza** Chile
182 F3 **Itmurinkol'** *lake* Kazakhstan
193 H4 **Itoigawa** Japan
163 I4 **Itomampy** *watercourse* Madagascar
189 J3 **Itoman** Japan
126 E2 **Iton** *watercourse* France
103 D6 **Itororó** Brazil
131 E6 **Itri** Italy
86 F4 **Itta Bena** Mississippi USA
73 Q4 **Ittoqqortoormiit** Greenland
77 S1 **Ittualuk, Cap** *cape* Quebec Canada
103 C8 **Itu** Brazil
195 G5 **Itu Aba Island** Spratly Islands
103 D6 **Ituaçu** Brazil
100 C3 **Ituango** Colombia
103 E6 **Ituberá** Brazil
104 D2 **Itucumã** Brazil
104 D2 **Itui** *watercourse* Brazil
103 B7 **Ituiutaba** Brazil
160 D4 **Itula** Democratic Republic of Congo
161 E5 **Itumba** Tanzania
103 B7 **Itumbiara** Brazil
75 T7 **Ituna** Saskatchewan Canada
102 B4 **Itupiranga** Brazil
103 B7 **Iturama** Brazil
89 H5 **Iturbide** Mexico
160 D3 **Ituri** *watercourse* Democratic Republic of Congo
Iturup, Ostrov *see* **Etorofo-tō** Kuril Islands
103 C8 **Ituverava** Brazil
105 E3 **Ituxi** *watercourse* Brazil
107 G3 **Ituzaingo** Argentina
124 F2 **Itz** *watercourse* Germany
122 E6 **Itzehoe** Germany
81 P8 **Iuka** Kansas USA
135 AL5 **Iul'tin** Russian Federation
122 G3 **Iväg** *lake* Sweden
103 B9 **Ivaí** *watercourse* Brazil
107 I3 **Ivaiporã** Brazil
121 O2 **Ivalo** Finland
121 O2 **Ivalojoki** *watercourse* Finland
125 J4 **Iváncsa** Hungary
132 E1 **Ivane-Puste** Ukraine
218 G5 **Ivanhoe** NSW Australia
213 J3 **Ivanhoe** WA Australia
83 J2 **Ivanhoe** *watercourse* Ontario Canada
81 Q4 **Ivanhoe** Minnesota USA
82 J2 **Ivanhoe Lake** Ontario Canada
130 G4 **Ivanić-Grad** Croatia
132 D1 **Ivano-Frankivs'k** Ukraine
136 C3 **Ivano-Frankivs'ka Oblast'** *admin. area* Ukraine
182 G3 **Ivanovka** Russian Federation
132 H2 **Ivanovka** Ukraine
132 G1 **Ivanovka** Ukraine
132 E4 **Ivanovo** Bulgaria
123 P4 **Ivanovo** Russian Federation
134 J7 **Ivanovo** Russian Federation
182 C1 **Ivanovo** Russian Federation
182 C2 **Ivanovskaya** *admin. area* Russian Federation
134 J7 **Ivanovskaya Oblast'** *admin. area* Russian Federation
183 N3 **Ivanovskiy Khrebet** *range* Kazakhstan
123 O3 **Ivanovskoye** Russian Federation
84 E3 **Ivanpah Lake** California USA
132 E4 **Ivanski** Bulgaria
182 F3 **Ivanteyevka** Russian Federation
125 M2 **Ivanychi** Ukraine
120 H4 **Ivarrud** Norway
133 E5 **Ivaylovgrad** Bulgaria
132 F1 **Ivcha** Ukraine
134 N6 **Ivdel'** Russian Federation
87 J4 **Ivey** Georgia USA
105 H6 **Ivinheima** Brazil
78 N2 **Ivittuut** Greenland
136 F2 **Ivnya** Russian Federation
163 I4 **Ivohibe** Madagascar
136 E2 **Ivotka** *watercourse* Ukraine
124 D5 **Ivrea** Italy
133 E6 **İvrindi** Turkey
182 D5 **Ivris Ugheltekhili** *pass* Georgia
77 Q1 **Ivujivik** Quebec Canada
161 E5 **Ivuna** Tanzania
138 D4 **Ivybridge** Devon England UK
199 I6 **Iwa Island** Papua New Guinea
193 I4 **Iwaki** Japan
192 G4 **Iwakuni** Japan
160 C4 **Iwala** Democratic Republic of Congo
193 I2 **Iwamizawa** Japan
193 I3 **Iwate-san** *volcano* Japan
160 D4 **Iwe** Democratic Republic of Congo
161 F5 **Iwimbi** Tanzania
127 L1 **Iwiny** Poland
159 E3 **Iwo** Nigeria
101 G3 **Iwokrama Mountains** Guyana
123 M6 **Iwye** Belarus
104 D4 **Ixiamas** Bolivia
89 H4 **Ixil** Mexico
88 D4 **Ixtapa** Mexico
88 E5 **Ixtapa** Mexico
88 E5 **Ixtapa, Punta** *cape* Mexico
88 D4 **Ixtlán** Mexico
139 H2 **Ixworth** Suffolk England UK
135 V8 **Iya** *watercourse* Russian Federation
156 D5 **Iyal Bakhit** Sudan
161 E5 **Iyayi** Tanzania
192 G5 **Iyo-nada** *bay* Japan
125 L3 **Iza** Ukraine
90 B4 **Izabal, Lago de** *lake* Guatemala
125 I4 **Ižakovci** Slovenia
89 H4 **Izamal** Mexico
121 V3 **Izba Bol'shaya Bab'ya** Russian Federation
182 E5 **Izberbash** Russian Federation
125 L2 **Izbica** Poland
132 D4 **Izbiceni** Romania
178 G3 **Izeh** Iran
189 J3 **Izena-shima** *island* Japan
132 E4 **Izgrev** Bulgaria
182 G2 **Izhevsk** Russian Federation
134 L5 **Izhma** *watercourse* Russian Federation
132 F3 **Izmayil** Ukraine
136 C5 **İzmir** *admin. area* Turkey
133 E6 **İzmir Körfezi** *bay* Turkey
Izmit *see* **Kocaeli** Turkey
128 D5 **Iznajar, Embalse de** *lake* Spain
128 E5 **Iznalloz** Spain
133 F5 **İznik Gölü** *lake* Turkey
130 E4 **Izola** Slovenia
105 F5 **Izozog, Banados del** *watercourse* Bolivia
132 A2 **Izsák** Hungary
193 I5 **Izu-shotō** *island* Japan
52 K4 **Izu Trench** *underwater feature* Pacific Ocean
192 F4 **Izuhara** Japan
193 G4 **Izumisano** Japan
192 G4 **Izumo** Japan
134 R3 **Izvestiy Ts.I.K., Ostrova** *islands* Russian Federation
132 C4 **Izvor** Serbia
132 E4 **Izvorovo** Bulgaria
132 E2 **Izvorul Muntelui, Lacul** *lake* Romania
123 O3 **Izvoz** Russian Federation
136 F3 **Izyum** Ukraine

J

73 O6 **J. A. D. Jensen Nunatakker** *mountain* Greenland
85 L4 **J. B. Thomas, Lake** Texas USA
87 J4 **J. Strom Thurmond Lake** Georgia USA
77 N7 **Jaab Lake** Ontario Canada
123 N2 **Jaala** Finland
121 O4 **Jaalanka** Finland
123 N3 **Jaama** Estonia
123 M3 **Jaamaküla** Estonia
123 N2 **Jääsjärvi** *lake* Finland
199 J5 **Jaba** Papua New Guinea
178 E6 **Jabal Al Ḩijāz** *range* Saudi Arabia
156 E5 **Jabal Bozi** Sudan
179 H6 **Jabal Samhān** *range* Oman
178 E7 **Jabal Zuqar, Jazīrat** *island* Yemen
108 E2 **Jabalí, Península** Argentina
186 E6 **Jabalpur** Madhya Pradesh India
124 B2 **Jabbeke** Belgium
131 D9 **Jabinnanah** Tunisia
214 B2 **Jabiru** NT Australia
136 E6 **Jablah** Syria
127 L4 **Jablanac** Croatia
130 H5 **Jablaničko Jezero** *lake* Bosnia and Herzegovina
132 A1 **Jabłonka** Poland
102 F5 **Jaboatão** Brazil
179 H4 **Jabrī** Iran
132 A4 **Jabuka** Serbia
196 E4 **Jabung, Tanjung** *cape* Indonesia
104 C3 **Jaburu** Brazil
105 G2 **Jabuti** Brazil
129 F2 **Jaca** Spain
108 B3 **Jacaf, Canal** *strait* Chile
101 E5 **Jacaré** Brazil
103 A6 **Jacaré** Brazil
103 D5 **Jacaré** *watercourse* Brazil
105 G2 **Jacareacanga** Brazil
103 C8 **Jacareí** Brazil
104 D5 **Jacha Jipiña** Bolivia
106 D4 **Jáchal** *watercourse* Argentina
105 E3 **Jaci Paraná** Brazil
105 H4 **Jaciara** Brazil
106 F6 **Jacinto Arauz** Argentina
105 E3 **Jaciparana** *watercourse* Brazil
101 E5 **Jacitara** Brazil
215 H3 **Jack** *watercourse* Qld Australia
215 H3 **Jack Lakes** Qld Australia
86 E4 **Jack Lee, Lake** Arkansas USA
219 K3 **Jackadgery** NSW Australia
75 Q6 **Jackfish Lake** Saskatchewan Canada
76 G7 **Jackhead Harbour** Manitoba Canada
77 V1 **Jackman Sound** Nunavut Canada
86 B4 **Jacksboro** Texas USA
139 F1 **Jacksdale** Nottinghamshire England UK
219 I2 **Jackson** Qld Australia
109 12 **Jackson** Barbados
86 H5 **Jackson** Alabama USA
82 J8 **Jackson** Kentucky USA
82 I5 **Jackson** Michigan USA
89 H1 **Jackson** Mississippi USA
82 G8 **Jackson** Missouri USA
87 K4 **Jackson** South Carolina USA
86 G3 **Jackson** Tennessee USA
81 J5 **Jackson** Wyoming USA
59 T2 **Jackson, Mount** *mountain* Antarctica
221 C6 **Jackson Bay** New Zealand
221 C6 **Jackson Bay** New Zealand
87 J4 **Jackson Lake** Georgia USA
81 J5 **Jackson Lake** Wyoming USA
81 M6 **Jackson Reservoir** Colorado USA
74 F4 **Jacksons** British Columbia Canada
87 K5 **Jacksonville** Florida USA
87 M3 **Jacksonville** North Carolina USA
86 D5 **Jacksonville** Texas USA
87 K5 **Jacksonville Beach** Florida USA
143 D1 **Jackstown** Ireland
91 F3 **Jacmel** Haiti
77 P7 **Jacob Island** Nunavut Canada
84 F2 **Jacob Lake** Arizona USA
179 K4 **Jacobabad** Pakistan
103 D5 **Jacobina** Brazil
138 C4 **Jacobstowe** Devon England UK
221 9 **Jacquemart Island** Campbell Island New Zealand
79 G8 **Jacques-Cartier, Détroit de** *strait* Quebec Canada
79 F8 **Jacques-Cartier, Mont** *mountain* Quebec Canada
199 I5 **Jacquinot Bay** Papua New Guinea
84 D4 **Jacumba** California USA
102 B3 **Jacundá** *watercourse* Brazil
103 B9 **Jacupiranga** Brazil
100 D5 **Jacurapa, Parana de** *watercourse* Brazil
125 K2 **Jadachy** Poland
130 H4 **Jadar** Bosnia and Herzegovina
74 G3 **Jade City** British Columbia Canada
124 E1 **Jadebusen** *bay* Germany
122 I2 **Jädraås** Sweden
130 F4 **Jadranovo** Croatia
120 H3 **Jægtvik** Norway
104 B2 **Jaén** Peru
128 E5 **Jaén** Spain
122 C3 **Jæren** *region* Norway
187 C7 **Jafarabad Harbour** Gujarat India
Jaffa *see* **Tel Aviv-Yafo** Israel
218 D7 **Jaffa, Cape** SA Australia
187 E10 **Jaffna** Sri Lanka
187 F7 **Jagdalpur** Chhattisgarh India
124 E3 **Jagst** *watercourse* Germany
187 E7 **Jagtial** Andhra Pradesh India
103 E6 **Jaguaquara** Brazil
107 H5 **Jaguarão** Brazil
107 H5 **Jaguarão** *watercourse* Brazil
103 D5 **Jaguarari** Brazil
107 H4 **Jaguari** *watercourse* Brazil
103 B9 **Jaguariaíva** Brazil
102 E4 **Jaguaribe** Brazil
102 E4 **Jaguaribe** *watercourse* Brazil
102 E4 **Jaguaruana** Brazil
104 B4 **Jaguay** Peru
106 D4 **Jague** *watercourse* Argentina
219 I7 **Jagungal, Mount** NSW Australia
121 M5 **Jähdyspohja** Finland
213 K1 **Jahleel, Point** NT Australia
178 E7 **Jahnīyah** Yemen
130 H5 **Jahorina** *mountain* Bosnia and Herzegovina
179 H4 **Jahrom** Iran
104 B3 **Jahuí, Cerro** *mountain* Peru
102 D4 **Jaicós** Brazil
198 C3 **Jailolo** Indonesia
198 D4 **Jailolo, Selat** *strait* Indonesia
187 D7 **Jaipur** Maharashtra India
186 D5 **Jaipur** Rajasthan India
181 H3 **Jairampur** Assam India
186 C5 **Jaisalmer** Rajasthan India
186 E6 **Jaitwara** Madhya Pradesh India
187 G7 **Jajapur** Orissa India
125 I4 **Ják** Hungary
132 A2 **Jakabszállás** Hungary
121 O4 **Jäkäläväara** Finland
181 G3 **Jakar** Bhutan
196 E5 **Jakarta** Indonesia
196 E5 **Jakarta** *admin. area* Indonesia
156 C2 **Jakharrah** Libya
125 K3 **Jaklovce** Slovakia
120 K3 **Jäknajaure** *lake* Sweden
198 C6 **Jako** *island* Timor-Leste (East Timor)
120 K2 **Jakobnjargga** *peninsula* Norway
120 J3 **Jakobsbakken** Norway
121 M5 **Jakobstad/Pietarsaari** Finland
159 F3 **Jakpa** Nigeria
85 K4 **Jal** New Mexico USA
179 H5 **Jalah** Oman
183 L6 **Jalal-Abad** Kyrgyzstan
183 K5 **Jalal-Abad** *admin. area* Kyrgyzstan
179 L2 **Jalālābād** Afghanistan
156 E2 **Jalālat al Qibliyah, Jabal al** *mountain* Egypt
186 F5 **Jalalpur** Uttar Pradesh India
186 D4 **Jalandhar** Punjab India
90 C4 **Jalapa** Nicaragua
89 F5 **Jalapa Enríquez** Mexico
121 M5 **Jalasjärvi** Finland
186 E5 **Jalaun** Uttar Pradesh India
214 C3 **Jalboi** *watercourse* NT Australia
88 D4 **Jalcocotán** Mexico
179 K3 **Jaldak** Afghanistan
103 B8 **Jales** Brazil
187 G7 **Jaleswar** Orissa India
186 F5 **Jaleswar** Nepal
178 F3 **Jalībah** Iraq
159 G3 **Jalingo** Nigeria
88 D4 **Jalisco** *admin. area* Mexico
125 I4 **Jalkovec** Croatia
122 I3 **Jälla** Sweden
122 G4 **Jällunden** *lake* Sweden
187 D7 **Jalna** Maharashtra India
223 15a **Jaloklab** *island* Marshall Islands
128 F3 **Jalón** *watercourse* Spain
186 C6 **Jalor** Rajasthan India
88 E4 **Jalpa** Mexico
181 F3 **Jalpaiguri** West Bengal India
89 F4 **Jalpan** Mexico
89 G5 **Jaltepec** *watercourse* Mexico
156 C2 **Jālū** Libya
223 15 **Jaluit Atoll** *reef* Marshall Islands
161 G3 **Jamaame** Somalia
90 E3 **Jamaica** *country* Caribbean
91 F3 **Jamaica Channel** Caribbean
123 L3 **Jämaja** Estonia
179 I4 **Jamāl Pā'īn** Iran
181 F4 **Jamalpur** Bangladesh
109 1a **Jamanota** *mountain* Aruba
105 H2 **Jamanxim** *watercourse* Brazil
89 F5 **Jamapa** *watercourse* Mexico
105 F3 **Jamari** Brazil
105 F3 **Jamari** *watercourse* Brazil
162 C2 **Jamba** Angola
104 A1 **Jambelí, Punta** *cape* Ecuador
196 D4 **Jambi** Indonesia
196 D4 **Jambi** *admin. area* Indonesia
196 C2 **Jamboaye** *watercourse* Indonesia
197 H2 **Jambongan** *island* Malaysia
197 H4 **Jambu** Indonesia
196 C2 **Jambuair, Tanjung** *cape* Indonesia
214 E4 **James** *watercourse* Qld Australia
81 Q5 **James** *watercourse* South Dakota USA
83 M8 **James** *watercourse* Virginia USA
108 B3 **James, Isla** *island* Chile
213 H5 **James, Mount** WA Australia
77 O6 **James Bay** Ontario/Quebec Canada
214 B8 **James Ranges** NT Australia
59 U2 **James Ross Island** Antarctica
73 J5 **James Ross Strait** Nunavut Canada
73 Q4 **Jameson Land** *region* Greenland
218 D5 **Jamestown** SA Australia
164 5b **Jamestown** St Helena
87 I2 **Jamestown** Kentucky USA
83 L5 **Jamestown** New York USA
81 P3 **Jamestown** North Dakota USA
83 K6 **Jamestown** Pennsylvania USA
87 I2 **Jamestown** Tennessee USA
Jamieson *see* **Mantamaru** Australia
187 E7 **Jamikunta** Andhra Pradesh India
187 D8 **Jamkhandi** Karnataka India
187 D7 **Jamkhed** Maharashtra India
122 E4 **Jammerbugten** *bay* Denmark
122 F5 **Jammerland Bugt** *bay* Denmark
186 D4 **Jammu** Jammu and Kashmir India/Pakistan
186 D3 **Jammu and Kashmir** *admin. area* India
186 C6 **Jamnagar** Gujarat India
187 D7 **Jamner** Maharashtra India
196 E5 **Jampang Kulon** Indonesia
179 L3 **Jampur** Pakistan
123 M2 **Jämsä** Finland
121 N5 **Jämsä** Finland
186 G6 **Jamshedpur** Jharkhand India
122 G1 **Jämtland** *admin. area* Sweden
100 B4 **Jamundí** Colombia
75 T5 **Jan Lake** Saskatchewan Canada
73 S4 **Jan Mayen** *dependency* Norway
57 F2 **Jan Mayen Fracture Zone** *underwater feature* Norwegian Sea
57 F2 **Jan Mayen Ridge** *underwater feature* Norwegian Sea
123 M2 **Janakkala** Finland
186 E6 **Janakpur** Chhattisgarh India
186 F5 **Janakpur** Nepal
103 D6 **Janaúba** Brazil
102 B2 **Janaucú, Ilha** *island* Brazil
104 B2 **Jancala** Peru
179 L2 **Jand** Pakistan
103 B8 **Jandaia do Sul** Brazil
179 H2 **Jandaq** Iran
164 3d **Jandia, Punta** *cape* Canary Islands
104 D2 **Jandiatuba** *watercourse* Brazil
219 J2 **Jandowae** Qld Australia
128 D4 **Jándula, Embalse del** *lake* Spain
103 C5 **Janeiro** *watercourse* Brazil
101 H4 **Janemale** French Guiana
142 F4 **Janeston** Angus Scotland UK
82 G5 **Janesville** Wisconsin USA
163 G4 **Jangamo** Mozambique
179 K2 **Jangjay** Afghanistan
125 J1 **Janikowo** Poland
121 Q5 **Janisjoki** *watercourse* Finland
132 A3 **Janja** Bosnia and Herzegovina
121 N5 **Jänkä** Finland
121 M3 **Jänkisjärvi** Sweden
121 P2 **Jankkila** Finland
132 B4 **Jankov Kamen** *mountain* Serbia
125 I2 **Janków** Poland
85 H5 **Janos** Mexico
125 I4 **Jánossomorja** Hungary
125 K2 **Janowiec** Poland
125 K1 **Janowo** Poland
162 D6 **Jansenville** South Africa
120 H5 **Jänsmässholmen** Sweden
108 D3 **Janssen, Bahía** *bay* Argentina
196 B2 **Jantho** Indonesia
103 C6 **Januária** Brazil
126 E2 **Janville** France
126 D3 **Janzé** France
186 D6 **Jaora** Madhya Pradesh India
193 H3 **Japan** *country* Asia
192 G3 **Japan, Sea of (East Sea)** Japan
52 J3 **Japan Basin** *underwater feature* Sea of Japan (East Sea)
52 K4 **Japan Trench** *underwater feature* Pacific Ocean
103 D8 **Japeri** Brazil
121 O5 **Jäppilä** Finland
122 E5 **Japsand** *island* Germany
101 E5 **Japura** *watercourse* Brazil
196 D4 **Japura** Indonesia
181 G3 **Japvo Mount** Assam India
90 E6 **Jaqué** Panama
90 E6 **Jaque, Punta** *cape* Panama
109 15 **Jaquot, Pointe** *cape* Dominica
103 B6 **Jaraguá** Brazil
103 B9 **Jaraguá do Sul** Brazil
128 D3 **Jaraiz de la Vera** Spain
132 A3 **Jarak** Serbia
108 B3 **Jaramillo** Argentina
108 C4 **Jaramillo** Argentina
101 H5 **Jaraucu** *watercourse* Brazil
102 E3 **Jardim** Brazil
105 G6 **Jardim** Brazil
102 E4 **Jardim de Piranhas** Brazil
102 E4 **Jardim do Seridó** Brazil
214 G1 **Jardine** *watercourse* Qld Australia
90 E2 **Jardines de la Reina, Archipiélago de los** *islands* Cuba
120 L2 **Jarga** *island* Norway
185 J3 **Jargalan** Mongolia
190 D3 **Jargalant** Mongolia
190 D3 **Jargalant** Mongolia
190 D3 **Jargalant** Mongolia
190 E2 **Jargalant** Mongolia
190 F3 **Jargalant** Mongolia
185 K3 **Jargalant Uul** *mountain* Mongolia
190 G3 **Jargalthaan** Mongolia
121 N2 **Jårgastak** Norway
126 F3 **Jargeau** France
179 K2 **Jarghān** Afghanistan
121 M3 **Jarhois** Sweden
102 A3 **Jari** *watercourse* Brazil
105 F2 **Jari, Lago** *lake* Brazil
132 E3 **Jariştea** Romania
122 H3 **Järnlunden** *lake* Sweden
122 G3 **Järnsjön** *lake* Sweden
127 G2 **Jarny** France
125 I2 **Jarocin** Poland
122 I5 **Jarosławiec** Poland
120 H5 **Järpen** Sweden
183 J6 **Jarqo'rg'on** Uzbekistan
216 D6 **Jarrahwood** WA Australia
87 M2 **Jarratt** Virginia USA
218 C5 **Jarrold Point** SA Australia
126 D2 **Jarron** France
141 G2 **Jarrow** Tyne and Wear England UK
190 F5 **Jartai Yanchi** *lake* Nei Mongol Zizhiqu China
105 F3 **Jaru** Brazil
123 M3 **Järvamaa** *admin. area* Estonia
75 O5 **Jarvie** Alberta Canada
121 O4 **Järvikylä** Finland
83 L5 **Jarvis** Ontario Canada
222 1 **Jarvis Island** *unincorporated US territory* Pacific Ocean
120 I4 **Järvsand** Sweden
186 E5 **Jarwal** Uttar Pradesh India
187 C6 **Jasdan** Gujarat India
125 I5 **Jasenica** Bosnia and Herzegovina
125 H2 **Jasień** Poland
158 E3 **Jasikan** Ghana
125 K3 **Jasiołka** *watercourse* Poland
179 I4 **Jāsk** Iran
125 K3 **Jaśliska** Poland
125 K3 **Jasło** Poland
59 U2 **Jason Peninsula** Antarctica
74 L6 **Jasper** Alberta Canada
86 H4 **Jasper** Alabama USA
86 E3 **Jasper** Arkansas USA
87 J5 **Jasper** Florida USA
82 H7 **Jasper** Indiana USA
82 D8 **Jasper** Missouri USA
86 E5 **Jasper** Texas USA
125 J3 **Jastrzębie-Zdrój** Poland
125 K4 **Jasz-Nagykun-Szolnok** *admin. area* Hungary
130 H3 **Jászberény** Hungary
130 H3 **Jászjákóhalma** Hungary
132 B2 **Jásztelek** Hungary
103 B7 **Jataí** Brazil
107 I2 **Jataizinho** Brazil
187 F7 **Jatani** Orissa India
101 G5 **Jatapu** *watercourse* Brazil
186 E6 **Jatara** Madhya Pradesh India
186 D5 **Jatari** Uttar Pradesh India
105 H6 **Jateí** Brazil
197 F5 **Jatiroto** Indonesia
102 A4 **Jatobá** Brazil
102 E5 **Jatobá** Brazil
103 A8 **Jatobá** Brazil
179 L3 **Jatoi Janubi** Pakistan
120 J6 **Jättholmarna** *island* Sweden
105 F3 **Jatuarana** Brazil
105 E6 **Jatun** Bolivia
104 B3 **Jatun Patay** Peru
104 D4 **Jatunari, Serranía** *range* Bolivia
103 B8 **Jaú** Brazil
101 F5 **Jaú** *watercourse* Brazil
101 F5 **Jauaperi** *watercourse* Brazil
101 H5 **Jauari, Serra** *range* Brazil
101 E5 **Jauató** Brazil
126 F2 **Jaulgonne** France
89 F4 **Jaumave** Mexico
126 E3 **Jaunay-Clan** France
123 N4 **Jaungulbene** Latvia
186 F6 **Jaunpur** Uttar Pradesh India
121 O4 **Jaurakkajärvi** Finland
216 G5 **Jaurdi** WA Australia
105 G4 **Jauru** Brazil
105 H5 **Jauru** Brazil
121 P3 **Jaurutunturi** *island* Finland
Java *see* **Jawa** Indonesia
55 P5 **Java Ridge** *underwater feature* Indian Ocean
Java Sea *see* **Jawa, Laut** Indonesia
55 P6 **Java Trench** *underwater feature* Indian Ocean
104 C2 **Javari** *watercourse* Peru
104 C2 **Javari Mirim** *watercourse* Peru
121 O3 **Javarus** Finland
121 O3 **Javarusjärvi** *lake* Finland
190 F2 **Javhlant** Mongolia
108 A4 **Javier, Isla** *island* Chile
132 B4 **Javor** *range* Serbia
125 J3 **Javorie** *mountain* Slovakia
125 I2 **Javorník** Czech Republic
120 L4 **Jävre** Sweden
120 L4 **Jävrefjärden** *bay* Sweden
197 F5 **Jawa, Laut (Java Sea)** Indonesia
196 F6 **Jawa (Java)** *island* Indonesia
196 E5 **Jawa Barat** *admin. area* Indonesia
197 F5 **Jawa Tengah** *admin. area* Indonesia
197 G5 **Jawa Timur** *admin. area* Indonesia
186 C6 **Jawai** *lake* Rajasthan India
178 D3 **Jawf, Al** *admin. area* Saudi Arabia
161 H3 **Jawhar** Somalia
127 M1 **Jawor** Poland
125 K2 **Jawor Solecki** Poland
125 L3 **Jawornik Polski** Poland
125 J2 **Jaworzno** Poland
198 F5 **Jaya, Puncak** *mountain* Indonesia
187 D7 **Jayakwadi Sagar** *lake* Maharashtra India
199 G4 **Jayapura** Indonesia
199 F5 **Jayawijaya, Pegunungan** *range* Indonesia
178 C3 **Jayb, Wādī al** *watercourse* Jordan
86 A4 **Jayton** Texas USA
179 I4 **Jāz Mūrīan** Iran
154 D3 **Jdiriya** Western Sahara
84 E3 **Jean** Nevada USA
86 F6 **Jean Lafitte** Louisiana USA
91 F3 **Jean-Rabel, Pointe** Haiti
77 T2 **Jean-Talon, Pointe** Quebec Canada
86 F6 **Jeanerette** Louisiana USA
164 6b **Jeanne d'Arc, Presqu'île** *peninsula* French Southern and Antarctic Lands
83 L6 **Jeannette** Pennsylvania USA
77 V4 **Jeannin, Lac** *lake* Quebec Canada
159 E3 **Jebba** Nigeria
132 B3 **Jebel** Romania
182 G6 **Jebel** Turkmenistan
156 D4 **Jebel Abyad Plateau** *desert* Sudan
156 E4 **Jebel Qerri** Sudan
179 K4 **Jebri** Pakistan
196 E4 **Jebus** Indonesia
142 F5 **Jedburgh** Scottish Borders Scotland UK
Jeddah *see* **Jiddah** Saudi Arabia
79 J8 **Jeddore Lake** Newfoundland and Labrador Canada
125 K2 **Jedlińsk** Poland
130 G2 **Jedovnice** Czech Republic
125 K2 **Jędrzejów** Poland
216 G4 **Jeedamya** WA Australia
121 O3 **Jeesiö** Finland
121 N3 **Jeesiöjärvi** Finland
124 F1 **Jeetze** *watercourse* Germany
156 C3 **Jef-Jef, Plateau de** *plain* Chad
81 R4 **Jeffers** Minnesota USA
85 J1 **Jefferson** Colorado USA
80 D4 **Jefferson** Oregon USA
83 P4 **Jefferson, Mount** New Hampshire USA
82 E7 **Jefferson City** Missouri USA
216 G4 **Jefferson Lakes** WA Australia
159 E2 **Jega** Nigeria
Jeju *see* **Cheju** South Korea
123 M4 **Jēkabpils** Latvia
123 M4 **Jēkabspils** *admin. area* Latvia
59 X2 **Jelbart Ice Shelf** Antarctica
125 J3 **Jelenec** Slovakia
125 H2 **Jelenin** Poland
123 L4 **Jelgava** Latvia
123 L4 **Jelgavas** *admin. area* Latvia
122 F3 **Jeløy** *island* Norway
130 G5 **Jelsa** Croatia
122 D3 **Jelsa** Norway
154 E2 **Jemaa de Mrirt** Morocco
196 E3 **Jemaja** *island* Indonesia
197 G6 **Jember** Indonesia
85 I3 **Jemez Springs** New Mexico USA
159 F3 **Jemma** Nigeria
125 H3 **Jemnice** Czech Republic
223 15 **Jemo** *island* Marshall Islands
197 G4 **Jempang, Danau** *lake* Indonesia
124 F2 **Jena** Germany
86 E5 **Jena** Louisiana USA
179 H4 **Jenāḩ** Iran
163 F2 **Jenda** Malawi
155 H1 **Jendouba** Tunisia
101 I4 **Jenipapo** Brazil
75 P7 **Jenner** Alberta Canada
125 I4 **Jennersdorf** Austria
87 J5 **Jennings** Florida USA
86 E5 **Jennings** Louisiana USA
101 H3 **Jenny** Suriname
109 15 **Jenny Point** *cape* Dominica
219 J5 **Jenolan Caves** NSW Australia
215 H3 **Jensens Crossing** Qld Australia
197 F5 **Jepara** Indonesia
218 E7 **Jeparit** Vic. Australia
121 M5 **Jeppo** Finland
103 D6 **Jequié** Brazil
103 D7 **Jequitinhonha** Brazil
103 D7 **Jequitinhonha** *watercourse* Brazil
155 F2 **Jerada** Morocco
196 D3 **Jerantut** Malaysia
91 F3 **Jérémie** Haiti
102 E5 **Jeremoabo** Brazil
161 G2 **Jerer** *watercourse* Ethiopia
197 H6 **Jereweh** Indonesia
128 C5 **Jerez de la Frontera** Spain
128 C4 **Jerez de los Caballeros** Spain
120 K4 **Jerfojaur** Sweden
121 N2 **Jerggul** Norway
215 I7 **Jericho** Qld Australia
84 F1 **Jericho** Utah USA
124 G1 **Jerichow** Germany
197 F3 **Jerijeh, Tanjung** *cape* Malaysia
218 G6 **Jerilderie** NSW Australia
125 H2 **Jerischke** Germany
121 N3 **Jerisjärvi** *lake* Finland
125 I2 **Jerka** Poland
84 F3 **Jerome** Arizona USA
80 H5 **Jerome** Idaho USA
105 H5 **Jerônimo** Brazil
216 F6 **Jerramungup** WA Australia
143 F2 **Jerrettspass** Newry and Mourne Northern Ireland UK
126 C2 **Jersey** *British crown dependency* UK
83 N6 **Jersey City** New Jersey USA
196 D2 **Jertih** Malaysia
Jerusalem *see* **Yerushalayim (Al Quds)** Israel

219 J6 **Jervis Bay** NSW Australia
219 J6 **Jervis Bay Territory** *admin. area* Australia
74 J8 **Jervis Inlet** British Columbia Canada
199 G6 **Jervis Island** Australia
214 D7 **Jervois** NT Australia
125 J1 **Jerzwald** Poland
130 F3 **Jesenice** Slovenia
130 G1 **Jeseník** Czech Republic
130 E5 **Jesi** Italy
124 G5 **Jesolo** Italy
181 F4 **Jessore** Bangladesh
87 K5 **Jesup** Georgia USA
89 G5 **Jesús Carranza** Mexico
86 B2 **Jet** Oklahoma USA
158 A2 **Jeta, Ilha de** *island* Guinea-Bissau
75 U4 **Jetait** Manitoba Canada
123 M4 **Jeti** Estonia
103 D8 **Jetibá** Brazil
81 P7 **Jetmore** Kansas USA
125 I3 **Jevišovka** *watercourse* Czech Republic
81 P7 **Jewell** Kansas USA
86 C5 **Jewett** Texas USA
132 A4 **Jezercë, Maja** *mountain* Albania
130 G4 **Jezero** Bosnia and Herzegovina
125 I5 **Jezerski Grad** Bosnia and Herzegovina
125 J1 **Jeżewo** Poland
136 B2 **Jezioro Drestwo** *lake* Poland
186 G6 **Jha jha** Bihar India
186 D6 **Jhabua** Madhya Pradesh India
179 K4 **Jhal** Pakistan
181 G4 **Jhalokati** Bangladesh
186 D6 **Jhalrapatan** Rajasthan India
179 L3 **Jhang Sadr** Pakistan
186 G5 **Jhanjharpur** Bihar India
186 E6 **Jhansi** Uttar Pradesh India
186 G5 **Jhapa** Bihar India
186 D6 **Jharda** Madhya Pradesh India
187 G6 **Jhargram** West Bengal India
186 F6 **Jharkhand** *admin. area* India
187 F7 **Jharsuguda** Orissa India
179 M3 **Jhelum** Pakistan
179 L3 **Jhelum** *watercourse* Pakistan
181 F4 **Jhenaidah** Bangladesh
187 F6 **Jhinkpani** Jharkhand India
179 L3 **Jhok Bodo** Pakistan
106 F2 **Jhovy** Paraguay
186 D5 **Jhunjhunun** Rajasthan India
105 F3 **Ji-Paraná, Rio** *watercourse* Brazil
181 H2 **Ji Qu** *watercourse* Qinghai China
189 G3 **Ji`an** Jiangxi China
191 K4 **Ji`an** Jilin China
189 G1 **Jia Xian** Henan China
189 G3 **Jiading** Jiangxi China
191 J2 **Jiagedaqi** Heilongjiang China
189 F3 **Jiahe** Hunan China
180 E3 **Jiajia** Xizang Zizhiqu China
185 J6 **Jiajiboluoge** Qinghai China
188 E1 **Jialing Jiang** *watercourse* Jiangsu China
190 G5 **Jialu** Shaanxi China
191 L3 **Jiamusi** Heilongjiang China
189 F4 **Jian Jiang** *watercourse* Guangdong China
125 L5 **Jiana** Romania
191 I5 **Jianchang** Liaoning China
189 H2 **Jiande** Zhejiang China
189 H2 **Jiangdu** Jiangsu China
181 F3 **Jiangga** Xizang Zizhiqu China
188 E2 **Jiangkou** Sichuan China
189 G3 **Jiangkou Shuiku** *lake* Jiangxi China
189 G4 **Jiangmen** Guangdong China
188 D4 **Jiangna** Yunnan China
189 H1 **Jiangsu** *admin. area* China
189 G3 **Jiangxi** *admin. area* China
190 G6 **Jiangxian** Shanxi China
189 H2 **Jiangyan** Jiangsu China
189 H2 **Jiangyin** Jiangsu China
188 D2 **Jiangyou** Sichuan China
181 F3 **Jiangzi** Xizang Zizhiqu China
188 E1 **Jianjun** Shaanxi China
189 H3 **Jian'ou** Fujian China
188 C2 **Jianshe** Sichuan China
188 C3 **Jiantang** Yunnan China
189 H3 **Jianyang** Fujian China
188 D2 **Jianyang** Sichuan China
189 G4 **Jiaocheng** Guangdong China
191 K4 **Jiaohe** Jilin China
188 D3 **Jiaokui** Yunnan China
191 I6 **Jiaonan** Shandong China
191 I6 **Jiaozhou** Shandong China
189 G1 **Jiaozue** Henan China
189 G4 **Jiapeng Liedao** *islands* Guangdong China
184 E5 **Jiashi** Xinjiang Uygur Zizhiqu China
189 H2 **Jiaxing** Zhejiang China
185 K5 **Jiayuguang** Gansu China
178 F5 **Jibal Ţuwayq** *range* Saudi Arabia
216 E4 **Jibberding** WA Australia
132 D3 **Jibert** Romania
155 H6 **Jibiya** Niger
179 H6 **Jibjāt** Oman
105 H5 **Jibóia, Serra da** *range* Brazil
132 C2 **Jibou** Romania
125 L4 **Jichişu de Jos** Romania
125 H2 **Jičín** Czech Republic
178 D5 **Jiddah (Jeddah)** Saudi Arabia
100 C5 **Jidina** Colombia
181 H3 **Jido** Arunachal Pradesh India
191 L3 **Jidong** Heilongjiang China
132 D2 **Jidvieu** Romania
181 H2 **Jiegu** Qinghai China
120 K2 **Jiehkkevarri** *mountain* Norway
191 I6 **Jiehu** Shandong China
134 F5 **Jiek'kevarri** *mountain* Norway
189 G4 **Jieshi Wan** *bay* Guangdong China
189 G1 **Jieshou** Anhui China
190 G5 **Jiexiu** Shanxi China
189 G4 **Jieyang** Guangdong China
216 G1 **Jigalong** WA Australia
159 F2 **Jigawa** *admin. area* Nigeria
185 I6 **Jiggitai Tsho** *lake* Qinghai China
189 H4 **Jih-Yueh T'an** *lake* Taiwan China
125 H3 **Jihlava** Czech Republic
125 H3 **Jihlava** *watercourse* Czech Republic
125 H3 **Jihočeský Kraj** *admin. area* Czech Republic
125 I3 **Jihomoravský Kraj** *admin. area* Czech Republic
155 H1 **Jijel** Algeria
188 E2 **Jijiang** Chongqing China
161 G2 **Jijiga** Ethiopia
216 F6 **Jilakin Lake** WA Australia
185 H3 **Jili Hu** *lake* Xinjiang Uygur Zizhiqu China
161 G3 **Jilib** Somalia
191 K4 **Jilin** *admin. area* China
191 K4 **Jilin** Jilin China
184 G4 **Jiliyuzi** Xinjiang Uygur Zizhiqu China
120 J4 **Jiltjaur** Sweden
214 B2 **Jim Jim** *watercourse* NT Australia
161 F2 **Jīma** Ethiopia
90 E2 **Jimaguayu, Embalse de** *lake* Cuba
188 C1 **Jimai** Qinghai China
160 C6 **Jimbe** *watercourse* Zambia
161 F5 **Jimbo** Tanzania
214 E7 **Jimboola** Qld Australia
219 K2 **Jimboomba** Qld Australia
219 J2 **Jimbour** Qld Australia
85 J7 **Jiménez** Mexico
88 D2 **Jiménez** Mexico
88 E2 **Jiménez** Mexico
159 G3 **Jimeta** Nigeria
199 H5 **Jimi** *watercourse* Papua New Guinea
219 K2 **Jimna** Qld Australia
191 I6 **Jimo** Shandong China
185 I4 **Jimusa'er** Xinjiang Uygur Zizhiqu China
198 E5 **Jin, Kepulauan** *islands* Indonesia
189 G3 **Jin Jiang** *watercourse* Jiangxi China
189 H3 **Jin Xi** *watercourse* Fujian China
191 H6 **Jinan** Shandong China
188 D3 **Jinbi** Yunnan China
190 E5 **Jinchang** Gansu China
191 G6 **Jincheng** Shanxi China
188 E2 **Jincheng** Sichuan China
188 D3 **Jincheng** Sichuan China
188 D3 **Jincheng** Yunnan China
188 D2 **Jinchuan** Sichuan China
186 D5 **Jind** Haryana India
219 I7 **Jindabyne** NSW Australia
218 H6 **Jindera** NSW Australia
188 C3 **Jinding** Yunnan China
188 E2 **Jin'e** Sichuan China
188 E2 **Jinfo Shan** *mountain* Chongqing China
190 F6 **Jing He** *watercourse* Gansu China
188 E1 **Jing He** *watercourse* Shaanxi China
189 H2 **Jing Xian** Anhui China
190 F6 **Jingchuan** Gansu China
189 H2 **Jingdezhen** Jiangxi China
216 E3 **Jingemarra** WA Australia
219 I6 **Jingera** NSW Australia
189 G3 **Jinggangshan** Jiangxi China
184 G4 **Jinghe** Xinjiang Uygur Zizhiqu China
188 C4 **Jinghong** Yunnan China
190 G5 **Jingle** Shanxi China
189 F2 **Jingmen** Hubei China
190 F6 **Jingning** Gansu China
191 I4 **Jingpeng** Nei Mongol Zizhiqu China
188 D4 **Jingping** Yunnan China
188 D3 **Jingxin** Yunnan China
189 H2 **Jingyang** Anhui China
188 E2 **Jingyang** Shaanxi China
191 K4 **Jingyu** Jilin China
188 E1 **Jingyu Nao** *mountain* Shaanxi China
190 E6 **Jingyuan** Gansu China
189 F2 **Jingzhou** Hubei China
189 F2 **Jingzhou** Hubei China
188 D4 **Jinhe** Yunnan China
188 C3 **Jinhua** Yunnan China
189 H2 **Jinhua** Zhejiang China
191 H4 **Jining** Nei Mongol Zizhiqu China
189 G1 **Jining** Shandong China
191 H6 **Jining** Shandong China
189 H4 **Jinjiang** Fujian China
189 H2 **Jinjiazhuang** Anhui China
214 C7 **Jinka** NT Australia
161 F2 **Jinka** Ethiopia
189 G2 **Jinniu** *mountain* Hubei China
90 C4 **Jinotega** Nicaragua
90 C5 **Jinotepe** Nicaragua
190 F6 **Jinping** Gansu China
188 D4 **Jinping** Yunnan China
188 C4 **Jinping** Yunnan China
188 E3 **Jinsha** Guizhou China
188 C2 **Jinsha Jiang** *watercourse* Xizang Zizhiqu China
188 D3 **Jinsha Jiang** *watercourse* Yunnan China
191 I4 **Jinshan** Nei Mongol Zizhiqu China
190 G4 **Jinshan** Nei Mongol Zizhiqu China
188 D3 **Jinshan** Yunnan China
189 F2 **Jinshi** Hunan China
188 F3 **Jinshi** Hunan China
190 D3 **Jinst** Mongolia
185 K5 **Jinta** Gansu China
189 H2 **Jintan** Jiangsu China
189 I2 **Jintang Shan** *range* Zhejiang China
195 I5 **Jintotolo** *island* Philippines
187 D7 **Jintur** Maharashtra India
191 I5 **Jinxi** Liaoning China
189 G3 **Jinxi Hu** *lake* Jiangxi China
189 G1 **Jinxiang** Shandong China
188 F4 **Jinxiu** Guangxi Zhuangzu Zizhiqu China
188 D2 **Jinyuan** Sichuan China
191 G5 **Jinzhong** Shanxi China
191 J4 **Jinzhou** Liaoning China
188 C2 **Jinzhu** Sichuan China
100 A5 **Jipijapa** Ecuador
88 C2 **Jiquima** Mexico
186 D6 **Jiran** Madhya Pradesh India
105 E3 **Jirau** Brazil
215 H6 **Jireena** Qld Australia
127 L1 **Jiříkov** Czech Republic
161 H2 **Jirriban** Somalia
190 G6 **Jishan** Shanxi China
190 E6 **Jishi** Qinghai China
188 F3 **Jishou** Hunan China
216 E6 **Jitarning** WA Australia
103 E6 **Jitaúna** Brazil
189 F4 **Jitian** Guangdong China
196 D2 **Jitra** Malaysia
132 C3 **Jiu** *watercourse* Romania
189 F3 **Jiucai Ling** *mountain* Guangxi Zhuangzu Zizhiqu China
189 G2 **Jiujiang** Jiangxi China
189 G2 **Jiuling Shan** *range* Jiangxi China
188 E2 **Jiulong** Sichuan China
189 H3 **Jiulong Shan** *mountain* Zhejiang China
185 K5 **Jiuquan** Gansu China
191 J5 **Jiurongcheng** Shandong China
191 K4 **Jiutai** Jilin China
89 F5 **Jiutepec** Mexico
179 J5 **Jiwani, Rās** *cape* Pakistan
191 L3 **Jixi** Heilongjiang China
191 L3 **Jixian** Heilongjiang China
190 G6 **Jixian** Shanxi China
181 G3 **Jixiong** Xizang Zizhiqu China
191 I6 **Jiyang** Shandong China
189 F1 **Jiyuan** Henan China
178 G7 **Jiz', Wādī al** *watercourse* Yemen
178 E7 **Jīzan** *admin. area* Saudi Arabia
178 E7 **Jīzān** Saudi Arabia
191 H6 **Jize** Hebei China
178 D4 **Jizl, Wādī al** *watercourse* Saudi Arabia
183 J6 **Jizzax** Uzbekistan
183 J6 **Jizzax** *admin. area* Uzbekistan
120 G4 **Jøa** *island* Norway
107 I3 **Joaçaba** Brazil
103 D7 **Joaíma** Brazil
154 C6 **Joal-Fadiout** Senegal
102 F4 **João Câmara** Brazil
105 F3 **João Felipe** Brazil
107 H5 **João Maria, Albardão do** *watercourse* Brazil
103 D7 **João Monlevade** Brazil
102 F4 **João Pessoa** Brazil
103 C7 **João Pinheiro** Brazil
106 E3 **Joaquin V. González** Argentina
90 E2 **Jobabo** Cuba
187 D6 **Jobat** Madhya Pradesh India
132 A2 **Jobbágyi** Hungary
87 J3 **Jocassee, Lake** South Carolina USA
121 M3 **Jockfall/Jokk** Sweden
124 E3 **Jockgrim** Germany
105 H2 **Jococa** Brazil
90 C4 **Jocón** Honduras
187 F7 **Joda** Orissa India
128 E5 **Jódar** Spain
186 C5 **Jodhpur** Rajasthan India
52 N4 **Joe Ferguson Seamount** *underwater feature* Pacific Ocean
121 P5 **Joensuu** Finland
222 1a **Joe's Hill** Kiribati
120 I4 **Joesjö** Sweden
193 H4 **Joetsu** Japan
75 O6 **Joffre** Alberta Canada
75 N7 **Joffre, Mount** Alberta/British Columbia Canada
76 M7 **Jog Lake** Ontario Canada
123 N3 **Jõgeva** Estonia
123 N3 **Jõgevamaa** *admin. area* Estonia
192 F4 **Jogji-do** *island* South Korea
77 U4 **Jogues, Lac** *lake* Quebec Canada
179 K3 **Johan** Pakistan
73 L3 **Johan Peninsula** Nunavut Canada
162 E5 **Johannesburg** South Africa
179 I4 **Johlū** Iran
80 F4 **John Day** Oregon USA
80 E4 **John Day** *watercourse* Oregon USA
75 N3 **John D'Or Prairie** Alberta Canada
87 L2 **John H. Kerr Reservoir** Virginia USA
81 N7 **John Martin Reservoir** Colorado USA
82 D7 **John Redmond Reservoir** Kansas USA
83 J8 **John W. Flannagan Reservoir** Virginia USA
86 D2 **Johnson** Arkansas USA
85 L2 **Johnson** Kansas USA
86 C3 **Johnson** Oklahoma USA
210 inset **Johnson Bank** Ashmore Reef and Cartier Island Australia
83 N5 **Johnson City** New York USA
87 J2 **Johnson City** Tennessee USA
86 B5 **Johnson City** Texas USA
109 7 **Johnson Harbour Settlement** Falkland Islands
77 P4 **Johnson Island** Nunavut Canada
74 E2 **Johnsons Crossing** Yukon Territory Canada
109 18 **Johnsons Point** Antigua and Barbuda
87 L4 **Johnsonville** South Carolina USA
138 C3 **Johnston** Pembrokeshire Wales UK
216 G6 **Johnston, Lake** WA Australia
52 P6 **Johnston Atoll** *reef* Pacific Ocean
52 P6 **Johnston Atoll** *unincorporated US territory* Pacific Ocean
142 D5 **Johnstone** Renfrewshire Scotland UK
143 E4 **Johnstown** Ireland
196 D3 **Johor** *admin. area* Malaysia
196 D3 **Johor Bahru** Malaysia
196 D2 **Johore Strait** Singapore
121 O2 **Johtijärvi** *lake* Finland
123 N3 **Jõhvi** Estonia
124 B4 **Joigny** France
86 F3 **Joiner** Arkansas USA
103 B9 **Joinville** Brazil
124 C3 **Joinville** France
59 U2 **Joinville Island** Antarctica
88 C2 **Jojoba** Mexico
123 M2 **Jokela** Finland
73 Q3 **Jøkelbugten** *bay* Greenland
121 O5 **Jokijärvi** Finland
121 P4 **Jokijärvi** Finland
121 O4 **Jokikokko** Finland
121 N5 **Jokikylä** Finland
121 P4 **Jokikylä** Finland
121 M5 **Jokipii** Finland
120 K3 **Jokkmokk** Sweden
123 K5 **Jokūbavas** Lithuania
120 inset **Jökulsá á Brú** *watercourse* Iceland
120 inset **Jökulsá á Fjöllum** *watercourse* Iceland
121 N3 **Jolanki** Finland
77 P7 **Jolicoeur** *watercourse* Quebec Canada
82 G6 **Joliet** Illinois USA
81 K4 **Joliet** Montana USA
73 L9 **Joliette** Quebec Canada
86 B4 **Jolly** Texas USA
195 I6 **Jolo** Philippines
195 I6 **Jolo** *island* Philippines
195 I6 **Jolo Group** *island* Philippines
120 E6 **Jolstavatnet** *lake* Norway
195 I4 **Jomalig** *island* Philippines
197 G5 **Jombang** Indonesia
186 F5 **Jomsom** Nepal
127 I3 **Jona** Switzerland
123 M5 **Jonava** Lithuania
100 B5 **Jondachi** Ecuador
76 J1 **Jones, Cape** Nunavut Canada
213 I5 **Jones, Lake** WA Australia
59 R2 **Jones Mountains** Antarctica
210 inset **Jones Point** Christmas Island Australia
73 K3 **Jones Sound** Nunavut Canada
86 F3 **Jonesboro** Arkansas USA
86 E4 **Jonesboro** Louisiana USA
86 F5 **Jonesville** Louisiana USA
87 K3 **Jonesville** South Carolina USA
87 J2 **Jonesville** Virginia USA
121 O4 **Jongunjärvi** *lake* Finland
123 M4 **Joniškėlis** Lithuania
123 L4 **Joniškis** Lithuania
121 P5 **Jonkeri** *lake* Finland
122 H4 **Jönköping** Sweden
122 H4 **Jönköping** *admin. area* Sweden
120 G5 **Jonsvatn** *lake* Norway
89 G5 **Jonuta** Mexico
126 D4 **Jonzac** France
82 D8 **Joplin** Missouri USA
85 H7 **Jopopaco** Mexico
178 C3 **Jordan** *country* Middle East
81 L3 **Jordan** Montana USA
87 H4 **Jordan Lake** Alabama USA
80 G5 **Jordan Valley** Oregon USA
122 G2 **Jordet** Norway
108 A5 **Jorge, Cabo** *cape* Chile
108 A5 **Jorge Montt, Isla** *island* Chile
108 B4 **Jorge Montt, Ventisquero** *glacier* Chile
181 H3 **Jorhat** Assam India
105 H5 **Jorigue, Serra do** *range* Brazil
124 E1 **Jork** Germany
121 O4 **Jormasjärvi** *lake* Finland
120 H4 **Jormlien** Sweden
121 P4 **Jormua** Finland
120 L4 **Jörn** Sweden
85 I4 **Jornada del Muerto** New Mexico USA
121 O5 **Joroinen** Finland
122 D3 **Jørpeland** Norway
159 F3 **Jos** Nigeria
159 F3 **Jos Plateaux** *plain* Nigeria
195 J6 **Jose Abad Santos** Philippines
108 D2 **José B. Casás** Argentina
105 F4 **José Bonifácio** Brazil
102 D4 **José de Freitas** Brazil
108 B3 **José de San Martín** Argentina
85 K6 **José María Morelos** Mexico
105 G2 **José Santos** Brazil
128 D5 **José Torán, Embalse de** *lake* Spain
80 G4 **Joseph** Oregon USA
80 I7 **Joseph** Utah USA
77 W6 **Joseph, Lac** *lake* Newfoundland and Labrador Canada
213 J3 **Joseph Bonaparte Gulf** WA Australia
84 G3 **Joseph City** Arizona USA
50 Q6 **Josephine Bank** *underwater feature* Atlantic Ocean
186 E4 **Joshimath** Uttaranchal India
86 C4 **Joshua** Texas USA
120 G4 **Jøssund** Norway
120 G4 **Jøssundjorden** *bay* Norway
109 21 **Jost van Dyke Island** British Virgin Islands
120 E5 **Jøstølen** Norway
121 P4 **Joukokylä** Finland
90 E1 **Joulter Cays** *islands* Bahamas
178 C2 **Joünié** Lebanon
75 N5 **Joussard** Alberta Canada
121 P3 **Joutsenaapa** *island* Finland
123 O2 **Joutseno** Finland
121 O3 **Joutsijärvi** Finland
123 L2 **Joutsjärvi** *lake* Finland
103 B7 **Joviânia** Brazil
181 G4 **Jowai** Meghalaya India
182 J6 **JowzjĀn** *admin. area* Afghanistan
77 T2 **Joy, Baie** *bay* Quebec Canada
89 G6 **Joya, Laguna de la** *lake* Mexico
126 G4 **Joyeuse** France
182 J6 **Jo'ynoy** Uzbekistan
181 F4 **Joypurhat** Bangladesh
125 K1 **Józefów** Poland
106 F6 **Juan A. Pradere** Argentina
88 E3 **Juan Aldama** Mexico
53 T3 **Juan de Fuca Ridge** *underwater feature* Pacific Ocean
106 E6 **Juan de Garay** Argentina
164 6a **Juan de Nova, Île** *island* Îles Éparses
109 1b **Juan Domingo** Netherlands Antilles
106 F6 **Juan E. Barra** Argentina
108 A5 **Juan Guillermos, Isla** *island* Chile
108 C4 **Juan José Albornoz** Argentina
85 H8 **Juan Jose Rios** Mexico
74 F6 **Juan Perez Sound** British Columbia Canada
89 G5 **Juan Rodríguez Clara** Mexico
108 A4 **Juan Stuven, Isla** *island* Chile
120 I5 **Juånäset** Sweden
107 G6 **Juancho** Argentina
91 G3 **Juancho** Dominican Republic
161 F5 **Juani** *island* Tanzania
104 B2 **Juanjuí** Peru
121 P5 **Juankoski** Finland
189 G2 **Juanshui** Hubei China
158 E3 **Juapon** Ghana
105 G3 **Juara** Brazil
88 D3 **Juárez** Mexico
85 H5 **Juárez** Mexico
85 L7 **Juárez** Mexico
88 A1 **Juárez, Sierra de** *range* Mexico
101 F2 **Juasjuillal** Venezuela
104 D2 **Juati** *watercourse* Brazil
103 D5 **Juàzeiro** Brazil
102 E4 **Juazeiro do Norte** Brazil
158 C3 **Juazohn** Liberia
160 E3 **Juba** Sudan
59 U2 **Jubany (Argentina)** *research station* Antarctica
161 G3 **Jubba, Webi** *watercourse* Somalia
161 G3 **Jubbada Dhexe** *admin. area* Somalia
161 G3 **Jubbada Hoose** *admin. area* Somalia
178 D4 **Jubbah** Saudi Arabia
122 E5 **Jübek** Germany
217 J4 **Jubilee Lake** WA Australia
79 K8 **Jubilee Lake** Newfoundland and Labrador Canada
126 D2 **Jublains** France
128 E4 **Júcar** *watercourse* Spain
102 E4 **Jucás** Brazil
88 E4 **Juchipila** *watercourse* Mexico
103 E7 **Jucuruçu** *watercourse* Brazil
102 E4 **Jucurutu** Brazil
127 L3 **Judenburg** Austria
81 K3 **Judith** *watercourse* Montana USA
81 K3 **Judith Gap** Montana USA
189 I2 **Juegang** Jiangsu China
189 I2 **Juegang** Jiangsu China
77 Q2 **Juet, Lac** *lake* Quebec Canada
120 L3 **Juggijaur** Sweden
219 I6 **Jugiong** NSW Australia
185 K2 **Jugnayn Nuur** *lake* Mongolia
126 C2 **Jugon-les-Lacs** France
178 E7 **Juḥā** Saudi Arabia
179 I4 **Jūhānī** Iran
90 C4 **Juigalpa** Nicaragua
124 D1 **Juist** Germany
103 D8 **Juiz de Fora** Brazil
196 D4 **Jujuhan** *watercourse* Indonesia
106 E2 **Jujuy** *admin. area* Argentina
120 L3 **Jukkasjärvi** *bay* Sweden
105 E5 **Jukumari Bajo** Bolivia
120 H4 **Jule** Norway
59 J2 **Jules, Cape** Antarctica
81 N6 **Julesburg** Colorado USA
81 N6 **Julesburg Reservoir** Colorado USA
104 D5 **Juli** Peru
214 F6 **Julia Creek** Qld Australia
104 D4 **Juliaca** Peru
84 D4 **Julian** California USA
77 Q5 **Julian, Lac** *lake* Quebec Canada
109 1b **Julianadorp** Netherlands Antilles
85 J6 **Julimes** Mexico
107 H4 **Júlio de Castilhos** Brazil
214 E6 **Julius, Lake** Qld Australia
121 O2 **Jullamojärvi** *lake* Finland
126 D2 **Julloville** France
189 F2 **Julong Shan** *mountain* Hubei China
191 H5 **Julu** Hebei China
121 P4 **Jumalisjärvi** *lake* Finland
105 F2 **Jumas** Brazil
129 F4 **Jumilla** Spain
179 H2 **Jūmīn** Iran
121 O5 **Juminen** Finland
186 E5 **Jumla** Nepal
160 E2 **Jummayzah** Sudan
160 D2 **Jummayzah** Sudan
101 F3 **Jumpetiri, Cerro** *mountain* Venezuela
218 B5 **Jumpuppy Hill** SA Australia
187 C7 **Junagadh** Gujarat India
187 F7 **Junagarh** Orissa India
129 G3 **Juncosa** Spain
86 B5 **Junction** Texas USA
214 B1 **Junction Bay** *watercourse* NT Australia
81 Q7 **Junction City** Kansas USA
86 E4 **Junction City** Louisiana USA
218 F1 **Jundah** Qld Australia
101 F5 **Jundiá** Brazil
102 F5 **Jundiá** Brazil
191 H5 **Jundu Shan** *range* Beijing China
74 D3 **Juneau** Alaska USA
74 D3 **Juneau Icefield** Alaska USA
219 H6 **Junee** NSW Australia
123 J3 **Jungfrufjorden** *bay* Sweden
123 K2 **Jungfruskär** *island* Finland
185 H3 **Junggar Pendi** Xinjiang Uygur Zizhiqu China
214 B2 **Jungle** *watercourse* NT Australia
160 E2 **Junglel Canal** *watercourse* Sudan
160 E2 **Jungoli** *admin. area* Sudan
132 B4 **Junik** Kosovo
106 F5 **Junín** Argentina
106 D1 **Junín** Chile
100 B4 **Junín** Colombia
100 A5 **Junín** Ecuador
104 C3 **Junín** Peru
104 C3 **Junín** *admin. area* Peru
104 B3 **Junín, Lago** *lake* Peru
108 B2 **Junín de los Andes** Argentina
84 F3 **Juniper Mountains** Arkansas USA
124 C3 **Juniville** France
121 M4 **Junkön** *island* Sweden
188 D3 **Junlian** Sichuan China
187 C7 **Junnar** Maharashtra India
85 L5 **Juno** Texas USA
121 M3 **Junosuando** Sweden
120 J5 **Junsele** Sweden
189 G3 **Junshan Hu** *lake* Jiangxi China
105 E6 **Juntas** Bolivia
90 C5 **Juntas** Costa Rica
121 P4 **Juntusranta** Finland
189 H3 **Junxi** Fujian China
123 M4 **Juodupė** Lithuania
121 P5 **Juojärvi** *lake* Finland
121 M3 **Juoksengi** Sweden
121 M3 **Juoksenki** Finland
123 N2 **Juolasvesi** *bay* Finland
121 O4 **Juorkuna** Finland
179 I3 **Jūpār** Iran
103 B8 **Jupía, Represa** *lake* Brazil
87 K7 **Jupiter** Florida USA
100 D2 **Júptui** Colombia
103 C9 **Juquiá** Brazil
107 J2 **Juquitiba** Brazil
160 D2 **Jur** *watercourse* Sudan
142 B5 **Jura** *island* Scotland UK
142 C5 **Jura, Sound of** *bay* Scotland UK
100 B3 **Juradó** Colombia
215 H8 **Juray** Qld Australia
123 L5 **Jurbarkas** Lithuania
126 F4 **Juré** France
216 D5 **Jurien Bay** WA Australia
198 E5 **Juring** Indonesia
123 L4 **Jūrmala** Latvia
123 K3 **Jurmofjärden** *bay* Finland
121 O4 **Jurmu** Finland
189 H2 **Jurong** Jiangsu China
196 B3 **Jurong** *admin. area* Singapore
196 B4 **Jurong, Selat** *strait* Singapore
196 B4 **Jurong Island** *island* Singapore
196 B4 **Jurong Park** Singapore
102 E4 **Juru** Brazil
104 C3 **Juruá** *watercourse* Brazil
105 G3 **Juruena** Brazil
105 G4 **Juruena** Brazil
105 G3 **Juruena** *watercourse* Brazil
101 F3 **Jurumato, Cerro** *mountain* Venezuela
107 I2 **Jurumirim, Represa de** *lake* Brazil
101 I4 **Jurupari, Arquipélago do** *islands* Brazil
101 F2 **Jurupú** Venezuela
101 G5 **Juruti** Brazil
101 G5 **Juruti Velho** Brazil
120 L5 **Jurva** Finland
121 N5 **Jurvansalo** Finland
105 I4 **Jussara** Brazil
123 L3 **Jussarö** *island* Finland
127 G3 **Jussey** France
85 L4 **Justiceburg** Texas USA
105 F5 **Justiniano** Bolivia
106 E5 **Justo Daract** Argentina
125 I4 **Juta** Hungary
100 E5 **Jutaí** Brazil
104 D2 **Jutaí** Brazil
104 E1 **Jutaí** *watercourse* Brazil
102 A3 **Jutaí, Serra do** *mountain* Brazil
104 E5 **Jutalla** Bolivia
124 G1 **Jüterbog** Germany
105 H6 **Juti** Brazil
90 B4 **Jutiapa** Guatemala
90 C4 **Jutiapa** Honduras
105 E1 **Jutica** Brazil
90 C4 **Juticalpa** Honduras
89 I6 **Jutiquile** Honduras
120 J3 **Jutis** Sweden
125 I2 **Jutrosin** Poland
121 P5 **Juuka** Finland
123 M2 **Juupajoki** Finland
121 Q6 **Juurikka** Finland
121 P5 **Juuruvesi** *bay* Finland
122 D3 **Juvatn** *lake* Norway
89 J4 **Juventud, Isla de la** *island* Cuba
105 G6 **Juvi** Brazil
121 P5 **Juvola** Finland
120 H5 **Juvuln** *bay* Sweden
197 F5 **Juwana** Indonesia
191 H6 **Juye** Shandong China
124 C3 **Juzennecourt** France
162 D4 **Jwaneng** Botswana
122 F5 **Jyderup** Denmark
122 E4 **Jylland** *island* Denmark
120 M5 **Jyllinkoski** Finland
121 O5 **Jyrkkä** Finland
121 N5 **Jyväskylä** Finland

K

159 F2 **K. Hausa** Nigeria
184 E6 **K2** *mountain* (disputed)
179 M2 **K2** *mountain* Pakistan
159 E2 **Ka** *watercourse* Nigeria
192 E3 **Ka-do** *island* North Korea
84 inset **Ka Lae** *cape* Hawai'i USA
Ka Tiritiri O Te Moana *see* **Southern Alps** New Zealand
84 inset **Ka'a'awa** Hawai'i USA
161 E3 **Kaabong** Uganda
101 H3 **Kaaimans Hoofd** *cape* Suriname
120 L3 **Kaalasjärvi** Sweden
120 K3 **Kaalasjärvi** *lake* Sweden
121 O2 **Kaamanen** Finland
121 O2 **Kaamasjoki** *watercourse* Finland
84 inset **Ka'anapali** Hawai'i USA
121 M2 **Kaaresuvanto** Finland
123 L2 **Kaarina** Finland
121 P2 **Kaarmassaari** *bay* Finland
120 L3 **Kaartijärvi** Sweden
121 P5 **Kaavi** Finland
121 P5 **Kaavinjärvi** *lake* Finland
197 I5 **Kabaena** *island* Indonesia
198 B5 **Kabaena, Selat** *strait* Indonesia
158 B3 **Kabala** Sierra Leone
160 D4 **Kabale** Uganda
101 G3 **Kabalebe** *watercourse* Suriname
160 D5 **Kabalo** Democratic Republic of Congo
199 J5 **Kabaman** Papua New Guinea
160 D5 **Kabamba, Lac** *lake* Democratic Republic of Congo
183 M4 **Kabanbay** Kazakhstan
160 B5 **Kabanga** Democratic Republic of Congo
160 C6 **Kabangu** Democratic Republic of Congo
76 K6 **Kabania Lake** Ontario Canada
196 C3 **Kabanjahe** Indonesia
195 I5 **Kabankalan** Philippines
223 9 **Kabara** *island* Fiji
198 D4 **Kabarai** Indonesia
182 D5 **Kabardino Balkarskaya Resp.** *admin. area* Russian Federation
181 H4 **Kabaw Valley** Myanmar
159 F3 **Kabba** Nigeria
155 I6 **Kabélawa** Niger
82 I2 **Kabenung Lake** Ontario Canada
197 I3 **Kabetan** *island* Indonesia
82 E2 **Kabetogama Lake** Minnesota USA
160 D5 **Kabeya** Democratic Republic of Congo
123 L4 **Kabile** Latvia
194 D4 **Kabin Buri** Thailand
73 K9 **Kabinakagami Lake** Ontario Canada
160 C5 **Kabinda** Democratic Republic of Congo
159 H3 **Kabo** Central African Republic
179 L2 **Kābol** *admin. area* Afghanistan
179 L2 **Kābol (Kābul)** Afghanistan
162 D2 **Kabompo** Zambia
162 D2 **Kabompo** *watercourse* Zambia
197 F3 **Kabong** Malaysia
160 D5 **Kabongo** Democratic Republic of Congo
194 C4 **Kabosa Island** Myanmar
154 C6 **Kabrousse** Senegal
178 E5 **Kabshān** Saudi Arabia
120 J2 **Kåbtajaure** *lake* Sweden
179 I2 **Kabūdeh** Iran
163 F2 **Kabudira** *watercourse* Malawi
Kabul *see* **Kābol** Afghanistan
179 L2 **Kābul, Daryā-ye** *watercourse* Pakistan
198 A6 **Kabunduk** Indonesia
197 J3 **Kaburuang** *island* Indonesia
156 E4 **Kabushiya** Sudan
162 E2 **Kabwe** Zambia
160 D5 **Kabwe, Lac** *lake* Democratic Republic of Congo
132 B3 **Kačarevo** Serbia
162 F2 **Kachalola** Zambia
186 B6 **Kachchh, Gulf of** Gujarat India
135 AA6 **Kachikattsy** Russian Federation
181 H4 **Kachin** *admin. area* Myanmar
160 E4 **Kachira, Lake** *lake* Uganda
183 L2 **Kachiry** Kazakhstan
161 F2 **Kachīsī** Ethiopia
135 W8 **Kachug** Russian Federation
179 I3 **Kachūli** Iran
163 G3 **Kachulu** Malawi
161 E3 **Kachung** Uganda
136 G5 **Kaçkar Dağı** *mountain* Turkey
127 K1 **Kadaň** Czech Republic
194 C4 **Kadan Kyun** Myanmar
197 G5 **Kadapongan** *island* Indonesia
197 I5 **Kadatuang** *island* Indonesia
223 9 **Kadavu** *island* Fiji
223 9 **Kadavu Passage** *strait* Fiji
158 D3 **Kade** Ghana
160 B3 **Kadéi** *watercourse* Central African Republic
217 J3 **Kadgo, Lake** WA Australia
186 C6 **Kadi** Gujarat India
218 C5 **Kadina** SA Australia
158 B2 **Kadiondola, Mount** *mountain* Guinea
187 E8 **Kadiri** Andhra Pradesh India
136 F6 **Kadirli** Turkey
159 I2 **Kadja, Ouadi** *watercourse* Chad
187 C9 **Kadmat Island** Lakshadweep India
81 O5 **Kadoka** South Dakota USA
182 D2 **Kadom** Russian Federation
162 E3 **Kadoma** Zimbabwe
199 H4 **Kadova Island** Papua New Guinea
156 D5 **Kadugli** Sudan
159 F2 **Kaduna** Nigeria
159 F2 **Kaduna** *admin. area* Nigeria
159 F2 **Kaduna** *watercourse* Nigeria
219 H5 **Kadungle** NSW Australia
181 H3 **Kadusam** *mountain* Arunachal Pradesh India
192 E3 **Kaechon** North Korea
154 D5 **Kaédi** Mauritania
79 K8 **Kaegudeck Lake** Newfoundland and Labrador Canada
159 G2 **Kaélé** Cameroon
84 inset **Kaelekū** Hawai'i USA
84 inset **Ka'ena Point** Hawai'i USA
121 Q5 **Käenkoski** Finland
192 E4 **Kaesông** North Korea
160 C5 **Kafakumba** Democratic Republic of Congo
182 E6 **Kafan** Armenia
159 F3 **Kafanchan** Nigeria
193 G1 **Kafen** *watercourse* Russian Federation
136 F6 **Kafer ez Zaïta** Syria
198 D4 **Kafiau** *island* Indonesia
133 D6 **Kafireas, Akra** *cape* Greece
121 M2 **Kåfjord** Norway
120 L2 **Kåfjorddalen** Norway
162 E3 **Kafne Flats** Zambia
158 D3 **Kafolo** Côte d'Ivoire
156 E1 **Kafr ash Shaykh** Egypt
160 E3 **Kafu** *watercourse* Uganda
162 E3 **Kafue** *watercourse* Zambia
162 E3 **Kafue Gorge** Zambia
181 F3 **Kaga** Xizang Zizhiqu China
182 G2 **Kaga** Russian Federation
159 H3 **Kaga Bandoro** Central African Republic
83 J4 **Kagawong** Ontario Canada
120 L4 **Kåge** Sweden
120 L4 **Kagefjärd** *bay* Sweden
184 F5 **Kageleke** Xinjiang Uygur Zizhiqu China
120 L1 **Kågen** *island* Norway
160 E4 **Kagera** *admin. area* Tanzania
160 E4 **Kagera** *watercourse* Tanzania
76 K7 **Kagianagami Lake** Ontario Canada
194 B3 **Kagin** Myanmar
136 G5 **Kağızman** Turkey
222 2a **Kagman** Northern Mariana Islands
196 C4 **Kagologolo** Indonesia
159 F3 **Kagoro** Nigeria
192 F5 **Kagoshima** Japan
84 inset **Kahala Point** Hawai'i USA
179 K3 **Kahan** Pakistan
197 J3 **Kahatola** *island* Indonesia
197 G4 **Kahayan** *watercourse* Indonesia
160 B5 **Kahemba** Democratic Republic of Congo
179 I4 **Kahnūj** Iran
158 C3 **Kahnwia** Liberia
84 inset **Kaho'olawe** Hawai'i USA
136 F5 **Kahraman-Maraş** *admin. area* Turkey
136 F6 **Kahramanmaraş** Turkey
179 L3 **Kahror Pakka** Pakistan
84 inset **Kahuā** Hawai'i USA
221 6 **Kahuitara Point** Chatham Islands New Zealand
84 inset **Kahuku Point** Hawai'i USA
84 inset **Kahului** Hawai'i USA
221 E5 **Kahurangi Point** New Zealand
198 E5 **Kai, Kepulauan** *islands* Indonesia
198 E5 **Kai Besar** *island* Indonesia
220 F4 **Kai Iwi** New Zealand
198 E5 **Kai Ketjil** *island* Indonesia
159 E3 **Kaiama** Nigeria
199 H5 **Kaiapit** Papua New Guinea
221 E6 **Kaiapoi** New Zealand
84 G2 **Kaibito** Arizona USA
189 G1 **Kaifeng** Henan China
123 N2 **Kaihtula** Finland
188 D4 **Kaihua** Yunnan China
189 H2 **Kaihua** Zhejiang China
108 C6 **Kaiken** Argentina
220 E2 **Kaikohe** New Zealand
221 E6 **Kaikoura** New Zealand
221 E6 **Kaikoura Peninsula** New Zealand
181 G4 **Kailasahar** Tripura India
199 I6 **Kaileuna Island** Papua New Guinea
188 E3 **Kaili** Guizhou China
191 J4 **Kailu** Nei Mongol Zizhiqu China
84 inset **Kailua** Hawai'i USA
84 inset **Kailua-Kona** Hawai'i USA
199 G5 **Kaim** *watercourse* Papua New Guinea
220 F4 **Kaimanawa Mountains** New Zealand
198 E5 **Kaimeer** *island* Indonesia
123 L3 **Käina** Estonia
193 G4 **Kainan** Japan
159 E2 **Kainji Reservoir** *lake* Nigeria
121 M3 **Kainulasjärvi** Sweden
220 F3 **Kaipara Harbour** New Zealand
84 G2 **Kaiparowits Plateau** Utah USA
78 I5 **Kaipokok Bay** Newfoundland and Labrador Canada
198 D4 **Kairatu** Indonesia
199 G4 **Kairiru Island** Papua New Guinea
129 J6 **Kaïs** Algeria
198 E4 **Kais** *watercourse* Indonesia
127 K3 **Kaisergebirge** *range* Austria
124 D3 **Kaiserslautern** Germany
123 M5 **Kaišiadorys** Lithuania
74 E6 **Kaisun** British Columbia Canada
196 E4 **Kait, Tanjung** *cape* Indonesia
121 P3 **Kaita-aapa** *island* Finland
198 E5 **Kaitanimbar** *island* Indonesia
221 C8 **Kaitangata** New Zealand
221 E5 **Kaiteriteri** New Zealand
186 D6 **Kaitha** Madhya Pradesh India
186 D5 **Kaithal** Haryana India
186 D6 **Kaithoon** Rajasthan India
221 E6 **Kaitorete Spit** New Zealand
120 K3 **Kaitumälven** *watercourse* Sweden
121 O4 **Kaivanto** Finland
198 C6 **Kaiwatu** Indonesia
84 inset **Kaiwi Channel** Hawai'i USA
188 E3 **Kaiyang** Guizhou China
191 J4 **Kaiyuan** Liaoning China
188 D4 **Kaiyuan** Yunnan China
189 F3 **Kaiyun** Hunan China
121 O4 **Kajaani** Finland
214 F6 **Kajabbi** Qld Australia
121 N5 **Kajama** Finland
121 M2 **Kajanki** Finland
219 I2 **Kajarabie, Lake** Qld Australia
161 F4 **Kajiado** Kenya
160 D2 **Kajok** Sudan
130 F2 **Kájov** Czech Republic
218 G5 **Kajuligah** NSW Australia
159 F2 **Kajuru** Nigeria
104 E4 **Kaka** *watercourse* Bolivia
182 H6 **Kaka** Turkmenistan
221 C8 **Kaka Point** New Zealand
197 H3 **Kakaban** *island* Indonesia
197 I5 **Kakabia** *island* Indonesia
83 M3 **Kakabonga, Lake** Quebec Canada
77 P5 **Kakachischuan, Pointe** Quebec Canada
82 E2 **Kakagi Lake** Ontario Canada
198 A4 **Kakali** Indonesia
162 D5 **Kakamas** South Africa
161 E3 **Kakamega** Kenya
159 G5 **Kakamoéka** Congo
194 B5 **Kakana** Andaman and Nicobar Islands India
221 D7 **Kakanui** New Zealand
221 D7 **Kakanui Mountains** New Zealand
75 V4 **Kakapawanis** Manitoba Canada
80 C2 **Kakawis** British Columbia Canada
74 E4 **Kake** Alaska USA
120 K3 **Kakel** *bay* Sweden
160 C4 **Kakenge** Democratic Republic of Congo
189 J3 **Kakeroma-jima** *island* Japan
135 AG7 **Kakhtana** Russian Federation
77 R4 **Kakiattualuk, Lac** *lake* Quebec Canada
187 F8 **Kakinada** Andhra Pradesh India
74 M2 **Kakisa Lake** Northwest Territories Canada
160 B5 **Kakobola** Democratic Republic of Congo
158 B2 **Kakou** *mountain* Guinea
158 B2 **Kakrima** *watercourse* Guinea
121 O2 **Kakslauttanen** Finland
72 E4 **Kaktovik** Alaska USA
120 I5 **Kakuåsen** Sweden
193 I4 **Kakuda** Japan
161 E3 **Kakuma** Kenya
121 Q5 **Kakunkyulya** Russian Federation
197 G3 **Kakus** *watercourse* Malaysia
74 L5 **Kakwa** *watercourse* Alberta Canada
182 G7 **Kal-e Shur Khar Va Towain** *watercourse* Iran
155 I6 **Kala** Nigeria
160 E5 **Kala** Tanzania
133 C6 **Kala Nera** Greece
Kalaallit Nunaat *see* **Greenland**
131 C9 **Kalaat Khasba** Tunisia
179 L3 **Kalabagh** Pakistan
197 H2 **Kalabakan** Malaysia
161 F3 **Kalabata** *watercourse* Kenya
162 D2 **Kalabo** Zambia
182 D3 **Kalach** Russian Federation
182 D4 **Kalach-na-Donu** Russian Federation
181 G5 **Kaladan** *watercourse* Myanmar
187 D9 **Kaladi** Kerala India
162 D4 **Kalahari Desert** *desert* Botswana
121 N5 **Kalaja** Finland
123 L1 **Kalajäjärvi** *lake* Finland
121 M4 **Kalajoki** Finland
159 E2 **Kalalé** Benin
197 J2 **Kalalusu** *island* Indonesia
179 L2 **Kalam** Pakistan
80 D4 **Kalama** Washington USA
133 C7 **Kalamata** Greece
82 I5 **Kalamazoo** Michigan USA
197 G5 **Kalambau** *island* Indonesia
160 E5 **Kalambo Falls** Tanzania
133 C6 **Kalamítsion** Greece
133 B6 **Kalamos** Greece
133 B6 **Kalamos** *island* Greece
133 B6 **Kalampaka** Greece
197 H3 **Kalampising** Indonesia
218 D2 **Kalamurina** SA Australia
218 D2 **Kalamurra Lake** SA Australia
183 K6 **Kalān Eylqah** Afghanistan
123 L3 **Kalana** Estonia
136 E3 **Kalanchak** Ukraine
133 C6 **Kalandra** Greece
161 E5 **Kalangali** Tanzania

216 E5 **Kalannie** WA Australia
123 K2 **Kalanti** Finland
197 I5 **Kalao** *island* Indonesia
84 inset **Kalaoa** Hawai'i USA
195 J6 **Kalaong** Philippines
198 B5 **Kalaotoa** *island* Indonesia
196 E4 **Kalapa** Indonesia
84 inset **Kalapana** Hawai'i USA
135 Y7 **Kalar** *watercourse* Russian Federation
178 G3 **Kalār, Kūh-e** *mountain* Iran
179 K3 **Kalat** Pakistan
179 J4 **Kalat** Pakistan
179 J4 **Kalatāk** Iran
84 inset **Kalaupapa** Hawai'i USA
187 C6 **Kalavad** Gujarat India
133 E7 **Kalavarda** Greece
181 H5 **Kalaw** Myanmar
181 H4 **Kalawa** Myanmar
181 H4 **Kalay (Mawlaik)** Myanmar
181 H4 **Kalaymyo** Myanmar
179 I6 **Kalbān** Oman
216 D3 **Kalbarri** WA Australia
183 N3 **Kalbinskiy Khrebet** *range* Kazakhstan
125 H5 **Kalce** Slovenia
125 I4 **Káld** Hungary
120 J2 **Kaldfarnes** Norway
181 G3 **Kaldiya Nadi** *watercourse* Assam India
120 I2 **Kaldvåg** Norway
133 F7 **Kale** Turkey
74 L8 **Kaleden** British Columbia Canada
197 I5 **Kaledupa** *island* Indonesia
187 D7 **Kalegaon** Maharashtra India
178 G2 **Kaleh** Iran
182 E7 **Kaleh Gavi** Iran
127 K1 **Kalek** Czech Republic
161 F3 **Kalekol** Kenya
133 D5 **Kaleköy** Turkey
160 C4 **Kalema** Democratic Republic of Congo
160 D5 **Kalemie** Democratic Republic of Congo
120 J5 **Kälen** Sweden
133 B6 **Kaléntzion** Greece
182 F3 **Kalenyy** Kazakhstan
133 D6 **Kalérgon** Greece
121 Q4 **Kalevala** Russian Federation
121 T5 **Kalgachikha** Russian Federation
121 T5 **Kalgachinskoye, Ozero** *lake* Russian Federation
216 F7 **Kalgan** WA Australia
212 F7 **Kalgan** *watercourse* WA Australia
216 G5 **Kalgoorlie-Boulder** WA Australia
130 F4 **Kali** Croatia
187 D7 **Kali** Maharashtra India
186 D6 **Kali** Rajasthan India
186 E4 **Kali** *watercourse* Uttaranchal India
199 H4 **Kali Bay** Papua New Guinea
132 F4 **Kaliakra** *cape* Bulgaria
197 G5 **Kalianget** Indonesia
195 I5 **Kalibo** Philippines
160 D4 **Kalima** Democratic Republic of Congo
197 G4 **Kalimantan** *region* Indonesia
197 F4 **Kalimantan Barat** *admin. area* Indonesia
197 G4 **Kalimantan Selatan** *admin. area* Indonesia
197 G4 **Kalimantan Tengah** *admin. area* Indonesia
197 H3 **Kalimantan Timur** *admin. area* Indonesia
132 B4 **Kalimash** Albania
163 F2 **Kalinda** Zambia
187 F7 **Kalingapatnam** Andhra Pradesh India
123 K5 **Kaliningrad** Russian Federation
123 K5 **Kaliningradskaya Oblast'** *admin. area* Russian Federation
182 D3 **Kalininsk** Russian Federation
130 H5 **Kalinovik** Bosnia and Herzegovina
182 E6 **Kalinovka** Azerbaijan
123 K5 **Kalinovka** Russian Federation
199 I5 **Kalip** Papua New Guinea
80 H2 **Kalispell** Montana USA
125 J2 **Kalisz** Poland
160 E5 **Kaliua** Tanzania
133 D7 **Kalivárion** Greece
121 M4 **Kalix** Sweden
121 M3 **Kalixälven** *watercourse* Sweden
120 L3 **Kalixfors** Sweden
214 G7 **Kalkadoon** Qld Australia
214 A4 **Kalkarindji** NT Australia
218 E4 **Kalkaroo** SA Australia
82 I4 **Kalkaska** Michigan USA
162 C4 **Kalkfeld** Namibia
133 E6 **Kalkım** Turkey
162 C4 **Kalkrand** Namibia
187 E10 **Kalkudah** Sri Lanka
218 C2 **Kallakoopah** *watercourse* SA Australia
121 O5 **Kallavesi** *bay* Finland
120 M4 **Kallax** Sweden
122 F3 **Kållekärr** Sweden
121 M4 **Kallfjärden** *bay* Sweden
216 E3 **Kalli** WA Australia
133 E6 **Kallimasia** Greece
121 O5 **Kalliokylä** Finland
133 D5 **Kallísti** Greece
133 C7 **Kallithea** Greece
133 D5 **Kallithéa** Greece
133 B6 **Kallithiron** Greece
121 N3 **Kallo** Finland
125 J4 **Kálló** Hungary
120 K4 **Kallön** Sweden
120 H5 **Kallsjön** *bay* Sweden
120 I5 **Kallsta/Ringsta** Sweden
120 L5 **Kallträsk** Finland
121 P3 **Kallunki** Finland
121 P3 **Kallunkijärvi** *lake* Finland
183 J3 **Kalmakkol** *lake* Kazakhstan
182 J4 **Kalmakkyrgan** *watercourse* Kazakhstan
183 N3 **Kalmanka** Russian Federation
122 I4 **Kalmar** Sweden
122 I4 **Kalmar** *admin. area* Sweden
122 I4 **Kalmarsund** *bay* Sweden
123 N3 **Kalme** Estonia
214 F5 **Kalmeta** Qld Australia
127 G1 **Kalmthout** Belgium
187 E10 **Kalmunai** Sri Lanka
182 E4 **Kalmykiya Respublika** *admin. area* Russian Federation
132 A1 **Kálna** Slovakia
187 F6 **Kalnai** Chhattisgarh India
123 L4 **Kalnciems** Latvia
132 F1 **Kal'nik** Ukraine
123 L5 **Kalnujai** Lithuania
158 C3 **Kaloa** Côte d'Ivoire
125 J4 **Kalocsa** Hungary
84 inset **Kalohi Channel** Hawai'i USA
186 C6 **Kalol** Gujarat India
160 D4 **Kalole** Democratic Republic of Congo
133 E7 **Kalolimnos** *island* Greece
197 J3 **Kaloma** *island* Indonesia
162 E3 **Kalomo** Zambia
133 B6 **Kalpakio** Greece
187 C10 **Kalpeni Island** Lakshadweep India
187 D9 **Kalpetta** Kerala India
186 E5 **Kalpi** Uttar Pradesh India
122 F5 **Kalsenakke** *island* Denmark
72 D6 **Kaltag** Alaska USA
217 M3 **Kaltjiti (Fregon)** SA Australia
217 K2 **Kaltukatjara (Docker River)** NT Australia
132 B3 **Kaluđerica** Serbia
136 F1 **Kaluga** Russian Federation
197 H5 **Kalukalukuang** *island* Indonesia
197 H4 **Kaluku** Indonesia
197 G3 **Kalulong, Bukit** *mountain* Malaysia
162 E2 **Kalulushi** Zambia
213 I3 **Kalumburu** WA Australia
160 D5 **Kalungwishi** *watercourse* Zambia
179 L3 **Kalur Kot** Pakistan
132 D1 **Kalush** Ukraine
187 E10 **Kalutara** Sri Lanka
134 H8 **Kaluzhskaya Oblast'** *admin. area* Russian Federation
122 C2 **Kalvåg** Norway
120 I3 **Kalvatnet** *lake* Norway
122 G5 **Kalvehave** Denmark
123 K4 **Kalvene** Latvia
85 L1 **Kalvesta** Kansas USA
121 M5 **Kälviä** Finland
123 N2 **Kalvitsa** Finland
120 K4 **Kalvträsk** Sweden
133 E7 **Kalymnos** Greece
133 E7 **Kalymnos** *island* Greece
159 G3 **Kam** *watercourse* Nigeria
182 G2 **Kama** *lake* Russian Federation
159 I2 **Kamaday** Chad
123 M5 **Kamajai** Lithuania
197 G5 **Kamal** Indonesia
179 L3 **Kamalia** Pakistan
84 inset **Kamalō** Hawai'i USA
186 D5 **Kaman** Rajasthan India
198 E4 **Kamandan** *watercourse* Indonesia
101 G4 **Kamani Kreek** *watercourse* Guyana
83 M4 **Kamaniskeg Lake** Ontario Canada
162 B3 **Kamanjab** Namibia
179 J2 **Kamar Zard** Afghanistan
218 H6 **Kamarah** NSW Australia
133 B6 **Kamárai** Greece
187 E7 **Kamareddy** Andhra Pradesh India
133 D7 **Kamares** Greece
133 C6 **Kamárion** Greece
133 D5 **Kamariotissa** Greece
158 B3 **Kamaron** Sierra Leone
76 G6 **Kamaskawak** Manitoba Canada
162 E3 **Kamativi** Zimbabwe
159 E2 **Kamba** Nigeria
182 H4 **Kambak-kul'** *lake* Kazakhstan
159 H3 **Kambakota** Central African Republic
216 G5 **Kambalda** WA Australia
216 E7 **Kamballup** WA Australia
187 D10 **Kambam** Tamil Nadu India
196 D4 **Kambang** Indonesia
196 F5 **Kambangan, Nusa** *island* Indonesia
158 B3 **Kambia** Sierra Leone
158 E3 **Kambole** Togo
133 B6 **Kámbos** Greece
160 D6 **Kambove** Democratic Republic of Congo
198 B4 **Kambuno, Bunto** *mountain* Indonesia
156 C1 **Kambūt** Libya
135 AF7 **Kamchatka, Poluostrov** *peninsula* Russian Federation
56 R3 **Kamchatka Basin** *underwater feature* Bering Sea
135 AG7 **Kamchatskiy Kray** *admin. area* Russian Federation
135 AH7 **Kamchatskiy Zaliv** *bay* Russian Federation
132 E4 **Kamchiya** *watercourse* Bulgaria
179 L2 **Kāmdīsh** Afghanistan
123 O5 **Kamen'** Belarus
132 D4 **Kamen** Bulgaria
160 C5 **Kamende** Democratic Republic of Congo
132 D4 **Kamenets** Bulgaria
130 E4 **Kamenjak, Rt** *cape* Croatia
182 F3 **Kamenka** Kazakhstan
123 O3 **Kamenka** Russian Federation
123 O2 **Kamenka** Russian Federation
182 D2 **Kamenka** Russian Federation
132 G2 **Kamenka** Ukraine
Kamen'naobi *see* **Kamennaobi** Russian Federation
183 N2 **Kamennaobi** Russian Federation
121 Q4 **Kamennoye, Ozero** *lake* Russian Federation
135 AF3 **Kamennyy, Mys** *cape* Russian Federation
182 I2 **Kamensk-uralskiy** Russian Federation
125 I5 **Kamensko** Croatia
127 L1 **Kamenz** Germany
186 E4 **Kamet** *mountain* Uttaranchal India
192 F5 **Kami Koshiki-jima** *island* Japan
80 G3 **Kamiah** Idaho USA
125 I1 **Kamieniec** Poland
125 J2 **Kamieńsk** Poland
162 C6 **Kamieskroon** South Africa
214 F5 **Kamileroi** Qld Australia
76 E1 **Kamilukuak Lake** Nunavut Canada
160 C5 **Kamina** Democratic Republic of Congo
76 H1 **Kaminak Lake** Nunavut Canada
189 J3 **Kaminone-Sho** *island* Japan
193 I4 **Kamisu** Japan
74 K7 **Kamloops** British Columbia Canada
133 B5 **Kamnik** Albania
125 H4 **Kamnik** Slovenia
220 F2 **Kamo** New Zealand
101 G4 **Kamoa Mountains** Guyana
121 M1 **Kamøya** *island* Norway
130 F2 **Kamp** *watercourse* Austria
196 E4 **Kampa** Indonesia
161 E3 **Kampala** Uganda
133 D6 **Kampanos, Akra** *cape* Greece
196 D3 **Kampar** *watercourse* Indonesia
196 D2 **Kampar** Malaysia
196 D3 **Kamparkiri** *watercourse* Indonesia
122 E5 **Kampen** Germany
160 D4 **Kampene** Democratic Republic of Congo
81 Q4 **Kampeska, Lake** South Dakota USA
194 C3 **Kamphaeng Phet** *admin. area* Cambodia
194 C3 **Kamphaeng Phet** Thailand
161 E5 **Kampi Katoto** Tanzania
194 E5 **Kâmpóng Cham** Cambodia
194 E4 **Kâmpóng Chhnăng** Cambodia
196 D2 **Kampong Koh** Malaysia
194 D5 **Kâmpóng Saôm (Sihanoukville)** Cambodia
194 E4 **Kâmpóng Thum** Cambodia
130 F4 **Kampor** Croatia
194 E5 **Kâmpôt** Cambodia
158 D2 **Kampti** Burkina Faso
163 F2 **Kampumbu** Zambia
199 F5 **Kampung** *watercourse* Indonesia
196 D2 **Kampung Gurun** Malaysia
198 E4 **Kamrau, Teluk** *bay* Indonesia
75 U7 **Kamsack** Saskatchewan Canada
158 B2 **Kamsar** Guinea
179 I4 **Kamshahr** Iran
187 E7 **Kamthi** Maharashtra India
82 H2 **Kamuck** *watercourse* Ontario Canada
198 F5 **Kamura** *watercourse* Indonesia
193 K2 **Kamuy, Gora** *volcano* Russian Federation
125 L1 **Kamyanyets** Belarus
123 N6 **Kamyen'** Belarus
182 C4 **Kamyshevatskaya** Russian Federation
182 E3 **Kamyshin** Russian Federation
182 I4 **Kamyshlybash** Kazakhstan
182 E4 **Kamyzyak** Russian Federation
135 U7 **Kan** *watercourse* Russian Federation
160 E2 **Kan** Sudan
77 R5 **Kanaaupscow** *watercourse* Quebec Canada
84 F2 **Kanab** *watercourse* Arkansas USA
84 F2 **Kanab** Utah USA
223 9 **Kanacea** *island* Fiji
135 AL8 **Kanaga Island** Alaska USA
78 H5 **Kanairiktok Bay** Newfoundland and Labrador Canada
127 K3 **Kanal** Slovenia
121 N5 **Kanala** Finland
120 I4 **Kanan** Sweden
217 I5 **Kanandah** WA Australia
160 C5 **Kananga** Democratic Republic of Congo
182 E2 **Kanash** Russian Federation
89 H4 **Kanasín** Mexico
83 N4 **Kanata** Ontario Canada
183 N3 **Kanayka** Kazakhstan
193 H4 **Kanazawa** Japan
181 H4 **Kanbalu** Myanmar
158 D2 **Kanbi** *watercourse* Burkina Faso
89 I5 **Kancab-Ché** Mexico
194 C4 **Kanchanaburi** Thailand
194 C4 **Kanchanaburi** *admin. area* Thailand
186 G5 **Kanchenjunga** *mountain* Nepal
179 K3 **Kandahār** Afghanistan
179 K3 **Kandahār** *admin. area* Afghanistan
121 R3 **Kandalaksha** Russian Federation
134 I5 **Kandalakshskiy Zaliv** *bay* Russian Federation
121 S3 **Kandalakshskiya Guba** *bay* Russian Federation
196 C3 **Kandang** Indonesia
197 G4 **Kandangan** Indonesia
198 D6 **Kandar** Indonesia
179 J4 **Kandasol** Pakistan
127 H3 **Kandersteg** Switzerland
179 L4 **Kandhkot** Pakistan
158 E2 **Kandi** Benin
186 G6 **Kandi** West Bengal India
197 I3 **Kandi, Tanjung** *cape* Indonesia
179 K4 **Kandiaro** Pakistan
186 C6 **Kandla** Gujarat India
163 I3 **Kandreho** Madagascar
187 E7 **Kandri** Maharashtra India
187 E9 **Kandukur** Andhra Pradesh India
187 E10 **Kandy** Sri Lanka
135 AF6 **Kandychan** Russian Federation
83 L6 **Kane** Pennsylvania USA
73 M3 **Kane Basin** Greenland
50 N7 **Kane Fracture Zone** *underwater feature* Atlantic Ocean
154 D5 **Kanel** Senegal
155 J6 **Kanem** *admin. area* Chad
84 inset **Kane'ohe** Hawai'i USA
179 K3 **Kaneti** Pakistan
121 U3 **Kanëvka** Russian Federation
182 C4 **Kanevskaya** Russian Federation
130 E4 **Kanfanar** Croatia
162 D4 **Kang** Botswana
188 E1 **Kang Xian** Gansu China
78 N1 **Kangaarsuup Tasersua** *lake* Greenland
73 N5 **Kangaatsiaq** Greenland
158 C2 **Kangaba** Mali
136 F5 **Kangal** Turkey
135 AA6 **Kangalassy** Russian Federation
196 D2 **Kangar** Malaysia
158 C2 **Kangaré** Mali
214 D4 **Kangaroo** *watercourse* NT Australia
218 C7 **Kangaroo Island** SA Australia
121 M5 **Kangas** Finland
121 N4 **Kangas** Finland
121 N5 **Kangasaho** Finland
123 N1 **Kangasjärvi** *lake* Finland
121 O4 **Kangaskylä** Finland
121 P5 **Kangaslahti** Finland
121 P5 **Kangaslampi** Finland
191 H4 **Kangbao** Hebei China
192 E3 **Kangdong** North Korea
197 G5 **Kangean, Kepulauan** *islands* Indonesia
73 M5 **Kangeeak Point** Nunavut Canada
161 E2 **Kangen** *watercourse* Sudan
73 O6 **Kangeq** *cape* Greenland
78 O2 **Kangeq** *island* Greenland
73 N5 **Kangerlussuaq** Greenland
73 P5 **Kangerlussuaq** *bay* Greenland
73 N4 **Kangerlussuaq (Giesecke Isfjord)** *island* Greenland
73 N5 **Kangerlussuaq (Søndre Strømfjord)** *bay* Greenland
73 O6 **Kangerlussuatsiaq (Lindenow Fjord)** *bay* Greenland
73 Q4 **Kangertittivaq** *bay* Greenland
73 P5 **Kangertittivatsiaq** *bay* Greenland
192 E3 **Kanggye** North Korea
78 M1 **Kangigdlermiut** Greenland
73 Q4 **Kangikajik (Kap Brewster)** *cape* Greenland
78 N2 **Kangilinnguit** Greenland
77 W3 **Kangiqsualujjuaq** Quebec Canada
77 T2 **Kangiqsujuaq** Quebec Canada
77 T2 **Kangirsuk** Quebec Canada
189 G3 **Kangle** Jiangxi China
180 E3 **Kangma** Xizang Zizhiqu China
181 F3 **Kangma** Xizang Zizhiqu China
192 E4 **Kangnyŏng** North Korea
159 G4 **Kango** Gabon
121 M3 **Kangos/Kangosfors** Sweden
121 M3 **Kangosjärvi** Finland
191 J4 **Kangping** Liaoning China
180 D2 **Kangrinboqe Feng** *mountain* Xizang Zizhiqu China
192 F4 **Kangŭng** South Korea
158 C3 **Kani** Côte d'Ivoire
193 H4 **Kani** Japan
181 H4 **Kani** Myanmar
164 8b **Kani Kéli** Mayotte
160 C5 **Kaniama** Democratic Republic of Congo
197 H2 **Kanibongan** Malaysia
221 D6 **Kaniere, Lake** New Zealand
199 H4 **Kaniet Islands** Papua New Guinea
187 E8 **Kanigiri** Andhra Pradesh India
134 K5 **Kanin, Poluostrov** *peninsula* Russian Federation
134 J5 **Kanin Nos** Russian Federation
121 W2 **Kanin Nos, Mys** *cape* Russian Federation
134 J5 **Kaninskiy Bereg** *range* Russian Federation
218 E7 **Kaniva** Vic. Australia
132 G1 **Kanizh** Ukraine
186 F5 **Kanjiroba** *mountain* Nepal
123 L2 **Kankaanpää** Finland
82 H6 **Kankakee** Illinois USA
158 C2 **Kankan** Guinea
159 F2 **Kankara** Nigeria
158 C2 **Kankelaba** *watercourse* Mali
187 E7 **Kanker** Chhattisgarh India
154 D5 **Kankossa** Mauritania
195 I5 **Kanlaon, Mount** *volcano* Philippines
194 C5 **Kanmaw Kyun** Myanmar
187 D7 **Kannad** Maharashtra India
121 P4 **Kannas** Finland
186 E5 **Kannauj** Uttar Pradesh India
187 D10 **Kanniyakumari** Tamil Nadu India
123 M1 **Kannonjärvi** Finland
121 N5 **Kannonkoski** Finland
187 D9 **Kannur** Kerala India
121 M5 **Kannus** Finland
197 J4 **Kano** *island* Indonesia
159 F2 **Kano** Nigeria
159 F2 **Kano** *admin. area* Nigeria
91 G5 **Kanon, Point** Netherlands Antilles
162 F2 **Kanona** Zambia
183 M3 **Kanonerka** Kazakhstan
85 N1 **Kanopolis Lake** Kansas USA
81 N7 **Kanorado** Kansas USA
80 I7 **Kanosh** Utah USA
197 G3 **Kanowit** Malaysia
192 F5 **Kanoya** Japan
121 S3 **Kanozero, Ozero** *lake* Russian Federation
186 E5 **Kanpur** Uttar Pradesh India
162 E2 **Kansanshi** Zambia
71 **Kansas** *admin. area* USA
82 D7 **Kansas City** Missouri USA
160 D6 **Kansenia** Democratic Republic of Congo
135 U7 **Kansk** Russian Federation
183 Q2 **Kansk** Russian Federation
192 F3 **Kansŏng** South Korea
187 F7 **Kantabanji** Orissa India
194 C6 **Kantang** Thailand
158 E2 **Kantchari** Burkina Faso
72 D6 **Kantishna** *watercourse* Alaska USA
222 1 **Kanton** *island* Kiribati
52 O8 **Kanton** *reef* Phoenix Islands
120 M5 **Kantti** Finland
89 H4 **Kantunil** Mexico
89 I4 **Kantunilkin** Mexico
143 D4 **Kanturk** Ireland
179 H2 **Kanūgar** Iran
101 G4 **Kanuku Mountains** Guyana
193 H4 **Kanuma** Japan
219 Q10 **Kanunnah Bridge** Tas. Australia
162 C5 **Kanus** Namibia
160 D4 **Kanyaru** *watercourse* Burundi
162 E4 **Kanye** Botswana
217 L3 **Kanypi** SA Australia
155 H5 **Kao** Niger
223 10 **Kao Island** Tonga
194 D5 **Kaôh Kong** *island* Cambodia
194 D5 **Kaôh Rung** *island* Cambodia
189 H4 **Kaohsiung** Taiwan China
162 B3 **Kaokoveld** *range* Namibia
154 C6 **Kaolack** Senegal
162 D2 **Kaoma** Zambia
132 B4 **Kaona** Serbia
159 I3 **Kaouadja** Central African Republic
84 inset **Kapa'a** Hawai'i USA
133 E6 **Kapaklı** Turkey
183 M4 **Kapal** Kazakhstan
198 C4 **Kapalabuaya** Indonesia
198 C4 **Kapalatmada, Gunung** *mountain* Indonesia
84 inset **Kapalua** Hawai'i USA
158 D3 **Kapandae** Ghana
160 C5 **Kapanga** Democratic Republic of Congo
198 F5 **Kapare** *watercourse* Indonesia
160 E5 **Kapatu** Zambia
199 H5 **Kapau** *watercourse* Papua New Guinea
183 M5 **Kapchagayskoya Vodokhranilishche** *lake* Kazakhstan
161 E3 **Kapchorwa** Uganda
76 H5 **Kapeeseewinik** Manitoba Canada
125 H3 **Kapelln** Austria
133 C7 **Kapello, Akra** *cape* Greece
125 H4 **Kapfenberg** Austria
133 E6 **Kápi** Greece
133 F5 **Kapıdağı Yarımadası** *island* Turkey
160 D3 **Kapili** *watercourse* Democratic Republic of Congo
52 L7 **Kapingamarangi Atoll** *reef* Micronesia
162 E2 **Kapiri Mposhi** Zambia
179 L2 **Kāpīsā** *admin. area* Afghanistan
76 M6 **Kapiskau** *watercourse* Ontario Canada
197 G3 **Kapit** Malaysia
221 F5 **Kapiti Island** New Zealand
101 H4 **Kapiting** Brazil
220 F4 **Kaponga** New Zealand
159 I2 **Kapka, Massif du** *range* Chad
86 E6 **Kaplan** Louisiana USA
198 B6 **Kapondai, Tanjung** *cape* Indonesia
125 I4 **Kaposvár** Hungary
120 H4 **Kappfjällen** *mountain* Norway
192 F3 **Kapsan** North Korea
197 G4 **Kapuas** *watercourse* Indonesia
197 G3 **Kapuas Hulu, Pegunungan** *range* Malaysia
186 D4 **Kapurthala** Punjab India
73 K9 **Kapuskasing** Ontario Canada
75 U3 **Kapuskaypachik** Manitoba Canada
160 D5 **Kaputa** Zambia
219 J4 **Kaputar, Mount** NSW Australia
161 F3 **Kaputir** Kenya
158 E3 **Kara** *watercourse* Benin
134 N5 **Kara** *watercourse* Russian Federation
136 F6 **Kara** Syria
158 E3 **Kara** Togo
183 L5 **Kara-Balta** Kyrgyzstan
182 H6 **Kara-Ker** Turkmenistan
183 K5 **Kara-Köl** Kyrgyzstan
183 L5 **Kara-Koyun** *watercourse* Kyrgyzstan
134 Q3 **Kara Sea** Russian Federation
182 I2 **Karabalyk** Kazakhstan
182 F4 **Karabau** Kazakhstan
133 E5 **Karabiga** Turkey
182 F5 **Karabogaz** Turkmenistan
136 E5 **Karabük** Turkey
133 F5 **Karaburun** Turkey
136 F6 **Karaburun** Turkey
182 H3 **Karabutak** Kazakhstan
133 F5 **Karacabey** Turkey
133 F5 **Karacaköy** Turkey
133 F7 **Karacasu** Turkey
182 D5 **Karachayevo-Cherkesskaya Resp.** *admin. area* Russian Federation
179 K5 **Karachi** Pakistan
133 F7 **Karaçulha** Turkey
187 D8 **Karad** Maharashtra India
125 J5 **Karadaglije** Bosnia and Herzegovina
158 D3 **Karaga** Ghana
135 AH7 **Karaga** Russian Federation
183 L3 **Karaganda** Kazakhstan
183 K4 **Karagandinskaya oblast'** *admin. area* Kazakhstan
183 M4 **Karaganzhal** *lake* Kazakhstan
183 L3 **Karagayly** Kazakhstan
135 AI7 **Karaginskiy, Ostrov** *island* Russian Federation
135 AI7 **Karaginskiy Zaliv** *bay* Russian Federation
183 P3 **Karagos, Gora** *mountain* Russian Federation
183 N3 **Karaguzhikha** Kazakhstan
133 F6 **Karahallı** Turkey
182 G2 **Karaidel'** Russian Federation
187 E9 **Karaikkudi** Tamil Nadu India
197 H3 **Karaitan** Indonesia
182 F7 **Karaj** Iran
178 G2 **Karaj** Iran
125 J5 **Karakaja** Bosnia and Herzegovina
182 I3 **Karakamys** *lake* Kazakhstan
184 F5 **Karakax He** *watercourse* Xinjiang Uygur Zizhiqu China
197 J2 **Karakelong** *island* Indonesia
197 J3 **Karakitang** *island* Indonesia
182 G3 **Karakol** Kazakhstan
183 K5 **Karakol** *watercourse* Kazakhstan
183 M5 **Karakol** Kyrgyzstan
184 F6 **Karakoram Pass** Xinjiang Uygur Zizhiqu China
186 D3 **Karakoram Pass** Jammu and Kashmir India/Pakistan
179 N2 **Karakoram Pass** Pakistan
184 F6 **Karakoram Range** Xinjiang Uygur Zizhiqu China
186 D3 **Karakoram Range** Jammu and Kashmir India/Pakistan
Karaköse *see* **Ağri** Turkey
133 E6 **Karaköy** Turkey
182 G2 **Karakulino** Russian Federation
183 M4 **Karakum** Kazakhstan
133 F6 **Karakür** Turkey
162 C3 **Karakuwisa** Namibia
133 E6 **Karakuzu** Turkey
155 I6 **Karal** Chad
123 K3 **Karala** Estonia
121 Q5 **Karali** Russian Federation
216 F3 **Karalundi** WA Australia
197 H4 **Karama** *watercourse* Indonesia
136 E6 **Karaman** Turkey
136 E6 **Karaman** *admin. area* Turkey
179 M2 **Karambar Pass** Pakistan
197 H4 **Karambu** Indonesia
221 E5 **Karamea** New Zealand
221 E5 **Karamea** *watercourse* New Zealand
197 G5 **Karamian** *island* Indonesia
184 G5 **Karamiran He** *watercourse* Xinjiang Uygur Zizhiqu China
185 H6 **Karamiran Shankou** *pass* Xinjiang Uygur Zizhiqu China
133 F5 **Karamürsel** Turkey
154 C6 **Karang** Senegal
198 A4 **Karang, Tanjung** *cape* Indonesia
196 E4 **Karangagung** Indonesia
221 C6 **Karangarua** *watercourse* New Zealand
197 G6 **Karangasem** Indonesia
159 G4 **Karangoua** *watercourse* Congo
187 D7 **Karanja** Maharashtra India
187 E7 **Karanja** Maharashtra India
187 E6 **Karanjia** Madhya Pradesh India
121 N5 **Karankajärvi** *lake* Finland
183 L3 **Karaoba** Kazakhstan
133 E7 **Karaova** Turkey
183 L4 **Karaoy** Kazakhstan
136 E6 **Karapinar** Turkey
220 F3 **Karapiro** New Zealand
183 J4 **Karaqoyyn Koli** *lake* Kazakhstan
219 J3 **Karara** Qld Australia
186 E6 **Karari** Uttar Pradesh India
198 E4 **Karas** *island* Indonesia
162 C5 **Karas** *admin. area* Namibia
121 N2 **Kárášjohka** Norway
121 N2 **Karasjokka** *watercourse* Norway
183 L3 **Karasor, Ozero** *lake* Kazakhstan
183 L3 **Karasor Koli** *lake* Kazakhstan
133 G5 **Karasu** Turkey
183 M2 **Karasuk** Russian Federation
183 O4 **Karatal** Kazakhstan
183 M4 **Karatal** *watercourse* Kazakhstan
133 G7 **Karatas Gölü** *lake* Turkey
120 K3 **Karatj** *lake* Sweden
182 G3 **Karatobe** Kazakhstan
182 I3 **Karatomarskoye Vodokhranilishche** *lake* Kazakhstan
192 F5 **Karatsu** Japan
197 J2 **Karatung** *island* Indonesia
183 M4 **Karaul** Kazakhstan
134 R4 **Karaul** Russian Federation
186 D5 **Karauli** Rajasthan India
133 C7 **Karavas** Greece
133 A5 **Karavastasë, Gjiri i** *bay* Albania
133 E7 **Karavonisia** *island* Greece
198 E5 **Karawaira, Kepulauan** *island* Indonesia
196 E5 **Karawang, Tanjung** *cape* Indonesia
199 G5 **Karawari** *watercourse* Papua New Guinea
183 K4 **Karazhal** Kazakhstan
183 L4 **Karazhingil** Kazakhstan
178 E3 **Karbalā'** Iraq
178 E3 **Karbalā'** *admin. area* Iraq
120 I6 **Kårböle** Sweden
122 H2 **Kårböleskog** Sweden
125 K4 **Karcag** Hungary
125 K3 **Karcsa** Hungary
125 K1 **Karczew** Poland
132 F4 **Kardam** Bulgaria
133 B7 **Kardamás** Greece
133 B6 **Karditsa** Greece
123 L3 **Kärdla** Estonia
125 I4 **Kardos-ér** *watercourse* Hungary
162 D6 **Kareeberge** *range* South Africa
156 E4 **Kareima** Sudan
121 R5 **Karel'skaya Masel'ga** Russian Federation
135 Y8 **Karenga** *watercourse* Russian Federation
186 E6 **Karera** Madhya Pradesh India
159 F2 **Karfi** Nigeria
182 G3 **Kargala** Russian Federation
183 N3 **Kargaly** Kazakhstan
135 AK5 **Karganay** Russian Federation
133 G7 **Kargı** Turkey
186 D3 **Kargil** Jammu and Kashmir India/Pakistan
186 E5 **Karhal** Uttar Pradesh India
121 N4 **Karhukangas** Finland
159 G2 **Kari** Nigeria
162 E3 **Kariba** Zimbabwe
162 E3 **Kariba, Lake** *lake* Zimbabwe
193 H2 **Kariba-yama** *volcano* Japan
162 C4 **Karibib** Namibia
162 D6 **Kariega** *watercourse* South Africa
121 N2 **Karigasniemi** Finland
220 E2 **Karikari Peninsula** New Zealand
158 E2 **Karimama** Benin
196 F4 **Karimata** *island* Indonesia
196 F4 **Karimata, Kepulauan** *islands* Indonesia
196 F4 **Karimata, Selat** *strait* Indonesia
181 G4 **Karimganj** Assam India
187 E7 **Karimnagar** Andhra Pradesh India
196 D3 **Karimun** *island* Indonesia
197 F5 **Karimungawa, Kepulauan** *islands* Indonesia
197 F5 **Karimunjawa** *island* Indonesia
157 H5 **Karin** Somalia
217 M2 **Karinga** *watercourse* NT Australia
121 N4 **Karinkanta** Finland
220 F3 **Karioi, Mount** *volcano* New Zealand
221 D7 **Karitane** New Zealand
187 C6 **Karjan** Gujarat India
199 H5 **Karkar Island** Papua New Guinea
183 L3 **Karkaralinsk** Kazakhstan
179 K4 **Karkh** Pakistan
133 E7 **Karkinágrion** Greece
136 E4 **Karkinits'ka Zatoka** *sea* Ukraine
123 M2 **Karkkila** Finland
156 E5 **Karkoj** Sudan
218 B6 **Karkoo** SA Australia
178 E2 **Karkūk (Kirkuk)** Iraq
121 P1 **Karlebotn** Norway
124 D2 **Kärlich** Germany
156 E5 **Karling** Sudan
122 H5 **Karlino** Poland
136 E3 **Karlivka** Ukraine
130 F4 **Karlovac** Croatia
124 G2 **Karlovarský Kraj** *admin. area* Czech Republic
132 D4 **Karlovo** Bulgaria
124 G2 **Karlovy Vary** Czech Republic
121 M4 **Karlsborg** Sweden
124 F3 **Karlsfeld** Germany
122 H4 **Karlskrona** Sweden
120 L1 **Karlsøy** *island* Norway
120 I3 **Karlsøyvær** *island* Norway
124 E3 **Karlsruhe** Germany
81 O2 **Karlsruhe** North Dakota USA
122 G3 **Karlstad** Sweden
81 Q2 **Karlstad** Minnesota USA
130 C2 **Karlstadt** Germany
155 G6 **Karma** Niger
159 I1 **Karma, Ouadi** *watercourse* Chad
155 J6 **Karme** Chad
122 C3 **Karmøy** *island* Norway
121 N5 **Kärnä** Finland
186 D5 **Karnal** Haryana India
186 E5 **Karnali** *watercourse* Nepal
181 G4 **Karnaphuli Reservoir** Bangladesh
187 D8 **Karnataka** *admin. area* India
86 C6 **Karnes City** Texas USA
125 J1 **Karniszyn** Poland
132 E4 **Karnobat** Bulgaria
122 F3 **Kärnsjön** *lake* Sweden
124 G4 **Kärnten** *admin. area* Austria
216 D6 **Karnup** WA Australia
162 E3 **Karoi** Zimbabwe
223 9 **Karoko** Fiji
163 F1 **Karonga** Malawi
160 D4 **Karonje** *mountain* Rwanda
120 K4 **Karonsbo** Sweden
218 F5 **Karoola** NSW Australia
179 L3 **Karor** Pakistan
157 F4 **Karora** Eritrea
223 9a **Karorko** Fiji
198 A6 **Karosso, Tanjung** *cape* Indonesia
156 C5 **Karoub** Chad
121 P4 **Kärpänkylä** Finland
133 E8 **Karpathos** *island* Greece
218 E4 **Karpi, Lake** SA Australia
121 Q4 **Karpivaara** Russian Federation
133 E7 **Karpuzlu Barajı** *lake* Turkey
218 F6 **Karra** NSW Australia
182 H7 **Karrān** Iran
212 D6 **Karratha** WA Australia
212 D6 **Karratha Roadhouse** WA Australia
122 F5 **Karrebæksminde Bugt** *bay* Denmark
136 G5 **Kars** Turkey
136 G5 **Kars** *admin. area* Turkey
123 N3 **Kärsa** Estonia
121 N4 **Kärsämä** Finland
121 N5 **Kärsämäki** Finland
123 N4 **Kārsava** Latvia
182 F6 **Karshi** Turkmenistan
134 M4 **Karskiye Vorota, Proliv** *strait* Russian Federation
134 Q3 **Karskoye More** *sea* Russian Federation
121 N5 **Karstula** Finland
120 I6 **Karsvall** Sweden
132 A2 **Kartal** Hungary
164 8a **Kartala** *volcano* Comoros
182 H2 **Kartaly** Russian Federation
123 P4 **Kartsevo** Russian Federation
121 O5 **Karttula** Finland
122 J5 **Kartuzy** Poland
123 M3 **Käru** Estonia
214 F4 **Karumba** Qld Australia
121 M3 **Karungi** Sweden
161 E4 **Karungu** Kenya
213 I4 **Karunjie** WA Australia
120 E5 **Kårvåg** Norway
121 M5 **Karvala** Finland
120 M5 **Karvia** Finland
123 L1 **Karvianjärvi** *lake* Finland
123 L2 **Karvianjoki** *watercourse* Finland
125 J3 **Karviná** Czech Republic
121 N5 **Karvoskylä** Finland
187 D8 **Karwar** Karnataka India
186 D6 **Karwar** Madhya Pradesh India
191 H2 **Karymskoye** Russian Federation
134 S7 **Kas** *watercourse* Russian Federation
159 I2 **Kas** Sudan
156 C5 **Kas** Sudan
133 F7 **Kaş** Turkey
122 E4 **Kås** Denmark
133 F7 **Kasaba** Turkey
76 K6 **Kasabonika** Ontario Canada
76 K6 **Kasabonika Lake** Ontario Canada
160 C5 **Kasai** *watercourse* Democratic Republic of Congo
192 G4 **Kasai** Japan
160 C5 **Kasaï-Occidental** *admin. area* Democratic Republic of Congo
160 C4 **Kasaï-Oriental** *admin. area* Democratic Republic of Congo
160 C6 **Kasaji** Democratic Republic of Congo
194 D3 **Kasalin** Thailand
163 F2 **Kasama** Zambia
162 E3 **Kasane** Botswana
160 B4 **Kasangulu** Democratic Republic of Congo
157 F4 **Kasar, Ras** *cape* Eritrea/Sudan
187 D9 **Kasaragod** Kerala India
123 M3 **Kasari** *watercourse* Estonia
121 O2 **Kasariselkä** *bay* Finland
158 B3 **Kasasi** Sierra Leone
76 D2 **Kasba Lake** Northwest Territories/Nunavut Canada
182 J6 **Kasbi** Uzbekistan
162 E2 **Kasempa** Zambia
160 D6 **Kasenga** Democratic Republic of Congo
160 D4 **Kasese** Democratic Republic of Congo
160 E3 **Kasese** Uganda
194 D3 **Kaset Sombun** Thailand
120 J2 **Kasfjord** Norway
186 E5 **Kasganj** Uttar Pradesh India
179 I4 **Kash** Iran
179 I2 **Kashaf Rūd** *watercourse* Iran
178 G2 **Kāshān** Iran
77 O6 **Kashechewan** Ontario Canada
184 E5 **Kashi** Xinjiang Uygur Zizhiqu China
187 F7 **Kashipur** Orissa India
186 E5 **Kashipur** Uttaranchal India
76 K8 **Kashishibog Lake** Ontario Canada
193 H4 **Kashiwazaki** Japan
183 L4 **Kashkanteniz** Kazakhstan
123 Q2 **Kashkany** Russian Federation
121 T3 **Kashkarantsy** Russian Federation
179 I2 **Kāshmar** Iran
179 L4 **Kashmor** Pakistan
100 C2 **Kashure** Colombia
160 D2 **Kashwal** Sudan
198 A4 **Kasimbar** Indonesia
133 G7 **Kasımlar** Turkey
182 D2 **Kasimov** Russian Federation
160 D3 **Kasingi** Democratic Republic of Congo
197 J4 **Kasiruta** *island* Indonesia
198 D5 **Kasiui** *island* Indonesia
120 K3 **Kaska Kaitumjaure** *lake* Sweden
82 G7 **Kaskaskia** *watercourse* Illinois USA
76 J4 **Kaskattama** *watercourse* Manitoba Canada
120 J3 **Kaskaure** *lake* Sweden
123 O2 **Kaskiinkylä** Finland
120 L5 **Kaskinen** Finland
179 I4 **Kāskūh** Iran
74 M8 **Kaslo** British Columbia Canada
75 U3 **Kasmere Lake** Manitoba Canada
197 G4 **Kasongan** Indonesia
160 D4 **Kasongo** Democratic Republic of Congo
159 H6 **Kasongo-lunda** Democratic Republic of Congo
160 D4 **Kasongo Rive** Democratic Republic of Congo
133 E8 **Kasos** *island* Greece
182 E5 **Kaspiysk** Russian Federation
123 P5 **Kasplya** Russian Federation
136 F6 **KasratFaraj** Syria
187 D6 **Kasrawad** Madhya Pradesh India
156 F4 **Kassala** Sudan
156 F4 **Kassala** *admin. area* Sudan
133 C6 **Kassandras, Akra** *cape* Greece
127 I1 **Kassel** Germany
155 H1 **Kasserine** Tunisia
136 E5 **Kastamonu** Turkey
133 C5 **Kastanea** Greece
130 F4 **Kaštel Žegarski** Croatia
133 E8 **Kastellou, Akra** *cape* Greece
124 F3 **Kastl** Germany
133 B5 **Kastoria** Greece
133 B5 **Kastorias, Limni** *lake* Greece
133 B6 **Kastos** *island* Greece
136 E2 **Kastsyukovichy** Belarus
160 E4 **Kasulu** Tanzania
160 D6 **Kasumbulesa** Democratic Republic of Congo
182 E5 **Kasumkent** Russian Federation
78 H5 **Kasungatak Island** Newfoundland and Labrador Canada
163 F2 **Kasungu** Malawi
179 M3 **Kasur** Pakistan
217 L2 **Kata Tjuta (Mount Olga)** *mountain* NT Australia
223 9 **Katafaga** *island* Fiji
159 G2 **Katagum** Nigeria
159 F2 **Katagum** *watercourse* Nigeria
160 C4 **Katako-Kombe** Democratic Republic of Congo
133 B7 **Katakolo, Akra** *cape* Greece
161 E3 **Katakwi** Uganda
217 L2 **Katamala Cone** *mountain* NT Australia
160 C5 **Katanda** Democratic Republic of Congo
160 D5 **Katanga** *admin. area* Democratic Republic of Congo
135 V7 **Katanga** *watercourse* Russian Federation
187 E7 **Katangi** Madhya Pradesh India
216 E6 **Katanning** WA Australia
214 B7 **Katapata, Mount** NT Australia
159 F3 **Katcha** Nigeria
194 B6 **Katchall** *island* Andaman and Nicobar Islands India
215 G6 **Kate** *watercourse* Qld Australia
160 C5 **Katenge** Democratic Republic of Congo
133 C5 **Katerini** Greece
74 E4 **Kates Needle** *mountain* British Columbia/Alaska Canada/USA
140 B2 **Katesbridge** Banbridge Northern Ireland UK
161 F4 **Katesh** Tanzania
163 F2 **Katete** Zambia
187 F6 **Katghora** Chhattisgarh India
181 H4 **Katha** Myanmar
214 B3 **Katherine** NT Australia
214 B2 **Katherine** *watercourse* NT Australia
215 G7 **Katherine** *watercourse* Qld Australia
214 C7 **Kathleen, Mount** NT Australia
186 F5 **Kathmandu** Nepal
75 O7 **Kathryn** Alberta Canada
162 D5 **Kathu** South Africa
186 D4 **Kathua** Jammu and Kashmir India/Pakistan
154 E6 **Kati** Mali
197 G3 **Katibas** *watercourse* Malaysia
196 C4 **Katiet** Indonesia
186 G6 **Katihar** Bihar India
220 F3 **Katikati** New Zealand
162 D3 **Katima Mulilo** Namibia
158 C3 **Katiola** Côte d'Ivoire
223 14 **Katiu** *island* French Polynesia
121 M2 **Kätkäsuvanto** Finland
121 M2 **Kätkesuando** Sweden
132 F3 **Katlabukh, Ozero** *lake* Ukraine
133 C7 **Kato Kalívia** Greece
133 B6 **Kato Makrinou** Greece
133 D7 **Kato Sounion** Greece
133 E8 **Káto Zákros** Greece
187 E7 **Katol** Maharashtra India
121 M5 **Kåtölandet** *island* Finland
160 C5 **Katombe** Democratic Republic of Congo
133 D7 **Katomeri, Akra** *cape* Greece
160 D5 **Katompi** Democratic Republic of Congo
196 E4 **Katong** *admin. area* Singapore
198 B4 **Katoposa, Gunung** *mountain* Indonesia
133 B6 **Katouna** Greece
125 J2 **Katowice** Poland
186 E6 **Katra** Madhya Pradesh India
133 G7 **Katrancık Dağı** *range* Turkey
142 D4 **Katrine, Loch** *lake* Scotland UK
120 J3 **Kätsak** *lake* Sweden
132 E4 **Katselovo** Bulgaria
159 F2 **Katsina** Nigeria
159 F2 **Katsina** *admin. area* Nigeria
159 F3 **Katsina Ala** Nigeria
77 W3 **Kattaktoc, Cap** *cape* Quebec Canada
182 J6 **Kattaqo'rg'on** Uzbekistan
122 H2 **Kättbo** Sweden
122 F4 **Kattegat** *bay* Denmark
120 J2 **Katterat** Norway
77 S2 **Kattiniq** Quebec Canada
161 G3 **Katulo** *watercourse* Kenya
183 O3 **Katun** *watercourse* Russian Federation
86 D6 **Katy** Texas USA
134 Q7 **Katyl'ga** Russian Federation
197 J3 **Kau, Teluk** *bay* Indonesia
84 inset **Kaua'i** *island* Hawai'i USA
84 inset **Kaua'i Channel** Hawai'i USA
124 F4 **Kaufbeuren** Germany

199 H5 **Kaugel** *watercourse* Papua New Guinea
120 M5 **Kauhajoki** Finland
120 M5 **Kauhajoki** *watercourse* Finland
121 M5 **Kauhava** Finland
121 N3 **Kaukonen** Finland
84 inset **Ka'ula** *island* Hawai'i USA
84 inset **Kaulakahi Channel** Hawai'i USA
121 M3 **Kaulinranta** Finland
162 D3 **Kaulu Plain** *plain* Zambia
84 inset **Kaumalapau** Hawai'i USA
123 L5 **Kaunas** Lithuania
123 L5 **Kaunatava** Lithuania
181 I3 **Kaunglanhpu** Myanmar
123 L5 **Kauno** *admin. area* Lithuania
123 M5 **Kauno marios** *lake* Lithuania
120 E6 **Kaupanger** Norway
84 inset **Kaupō** Hawai'i USA
159 F2 **Kaura-Namoda** Nigeria
121 M5 **Kaustinen** Finland
121 M2 **Kautokeino** Norway
132 B4 **Kavadar** Serbia
133 A5 **Kavajë** Albania
133 E5 **Kavaklı** Turkey
133 D5 **Kavala** Greece
133 D5 **Kavalas, Kolpos** *bay* Greece
187 E8 **Kavali** Andhra Pradesh India
187 C9 **Kavaratti** Lakshadweep India
187 C9 **Kavaratti Island** Lakshadweep India
133 B7 **Kavásilas** Greece
199 G5 **Kavianange** Papua New Guinea
199 I4 **Kavieng** Papua New Guinea
162 D3 **Kavimba** Botswana
182 G7 **Kavīr-e Ḥājī 'Alī Qolī** *lake* Iran
179 H2 **Kavīr, Dasht-e** *desert* Iran
133 B6 **Kavos** Greece
162 D2 **Kavungo** Angola
101 H3 **Kaw, Montagnes de** *range* French Guiana
86 C2 **Kaw Lake** Oklahoma USA
193 H4 **Kawagoe** Japan
84 inset **Kawaihae** Hawai'i USA
84 inset **Kawaihoa Point** Hawai'i USA
160 D5 **Kawambwa** Zambia
162 E2 **Kawana** Zambia
187 E7 **Kawardha** Chhattisgarh India
83 L4 **Kawartha Lakes** Ontario Canada
160 D5 **Kawasa** Democratic Republic of Congo
193 H4 **Kawasaki** Japan
220 F3 **Kawau Island** New Zealand
77 V5 **Kawawachikamach** Quebec Canada
220 G4 **Kaweka** *mountain* New Zealand
220 G4 **Kaweka Range** New Zealand
84 inset **Kawela** Hawai'i USA
220 F4 **Kawhia** New Zealand
220 F4 **Kawhia Harbour** New Zealand
80 G8 **Kawich Range** Nevada USA
197 H6 **Kawinda** Indonesia
197 J2 **Kawio** *island* Indonesia
198 C2 **Kawio, Kepulauan** *islands* Indonesia
181 H4 **Kawlin** Myanmar
156 E3 **Kawm Umbū** Egypt
181 I4 **Kawngmeum** Myanmar
194 C5 **Kawthaung** Myanmar
184 G4 **Kax He** *watercourse* Xinjiang Uygur Zizhiqu China
120 H5 **Kaxås** Sweden
184 F5 **Kaxgar He** *watercourse* Xinjiang Uygur Zizhiqu China
158 D2 **Kaya** Burkina Faso
196 D5 **Kayaapu** Indonesia
136 F6 **Kayabasi** Turkey
181 H5 **Kayah** *admin. area* Myanmar
160 E5 **Kayambi** Zambia
187 D10 **Kayamkulam** Kerala India
197 H3 **Kayan** *watercourse* Indonesia
198 E1 **Kayangel Atoll** *reef* Palau
81 L5 **Kaycee** Wyoming USA
219 I7 **Kaye, Mount** Vic. Australia
160 C5 **Kayembe-Mukulu** Democratic Republic of Congo
84 G2 **Kayenta** Arizona USA
154 D6 **Kayes** Mali
154 D6 **Kayes** *admin. area* Mali
194 C3 **Kayin** *admin. area* Myanmar
124 D3 **Kayl** Luxembourg
121 P3 **Käylä** Finland
183 M3 **Kaynar** Kazakhstan
133 G5 **Kaynarca** Turkey
197 J3 **Kayoa** *island* Indonesia
183 L4 **Kayrakty** Kazakhstan
182 H3 **Kayran-kul** *lake* Russian Federation
182 E3 **Kaysatskoye** Russian Federation
101 G4 **Kayser Gebergte** *range* Suriname
136 E5 **Kayseri** Turkey
136 E5 **Kayseri** *admin. area* Turkey
80 J6 **Kaysville** Utah USA
197 I5 **Kayuadi** *island* Indonesia
196 E4 **Kayuagung** Indonesia
198 E4 **Kayumerah, Teluk** *bay* Indonesia
75 S8 **Kayville** Saskatchewan Canada
133 E6 **Kaz Dargi** *mountain* Turkey
135 W7 **Kazachinskoye** Russian Federation
182 F5 **Kazakhskiy Zaliv** *bay* Kazakhstan
182 I4 **Kazakhstan** *country* Asia
182 I4 **Kazalinsk** Kazakhstan
75 U2 **Kazan** *watercourse* Nunavut Canada
182 F2 **Kazan'** Russian Federation
182 D3 **Kazanskaja** Russian Federation
50 O7 **Kazanskiy Seamount** *underwater feature* Atlantic Ocean
159 F2 **Kazaure** Nigeria
182 D5 **Kazbek, Gora** *mountain* Russian Federation
178 G3 **Kāzerūn** Iran
182 E5 **Kaziyurt** Russian Federation
123 L5 **Kazlų Rūda** Lithuania
127 K2 **Kaznějov** Czech Republic
182 E3 **Kaztalovka** Kazakhstan
160 C5 **Kazumba** Democratic Republic of Congo
193 I3 **Kazuno** Japan
134 O6 **Kazymskiy Mys** Russian Federation
130 E2 **Kdyně** Czech Republic
133 D7 **Kea** *island* Greece
84 inset **Kea'au** Hawai'i USA
143 F2 **Keady** Armagh Northern Ireland UK
104 D5 **Keakeani, Cordillera** *range* Bolivia
141 I3 **Keal Coates** Lincolnshire England UK
84 inset **Kealaikahiki Channel** Hawai'i USA
84 inset **Kealakekua** Hawai'i USA
140 B3 **Kealstown** Ireland
143 G2 **Kearney** Ards Northern Ireland UK
81 P6 **Kearney** Nebraska USA
84 G4 **Kearny** Arizona USA
78 E5 **Keating, Lac** *lake* Quebec Canada
78 E5 **Keato, Lac** *lake* Quebec Canada
213 J3 **Keats, Port** NT Australia
194 E5 **Kêb** Cambodia
136 F5 **Keban Barajı.** *lake* Turkey
159 E2 **Kebbi** *admin. area* Nigeria
154 C5 **Kébémèr** Senegal
155 H2 **Kebili** Tunisia
159 I2 **Kebkabiya** Sudan
120 K3 **Kebnekaise** *mountain* Sweden
142 B2 **Kebock Head** *cape* Scotland UK
161 G2 **K'ebri Dehar** Ethiopia
191 G4 **Kebu'er** Nei Mongol Zizhiqu China
196 F5 **Kebumen** Indonesia
196 D4 **Kebur** Indonesia
132 A2 **Kecel** Hungary
72 G7 **Kechika** *watercourse* British Columbia Canada
133 G7 **Keçiborlu** Turkey
132 A2 **Kecskemét** Hungary
196 D2 **Kedah** *admin. area* Malaysia
123 L5 **Kėdainiai** Lithuania
186 E4 **Kedarnath** Uttaranchal India
159 H2 **Kédédéssé** Chad
159 G3 **Kedei** *watercourse* Cameroon
79 E9 **Kedgwick** New Brunswick Canada
197 G5 **Kediri** Indonesia
191 K3 **Kedong** Heilongjiang China
154 D6 **Kédougou** Senegal
123 R1 **Kedr-Ozero, Ozero** *lake* Russian Federation
196 F3 **Kedukul** Indonesia
196 F5 **Kedungwuni** Indonesia
134 L6 **Kedvavom** Russian Federation
125 J2 **Kędzierzyn-Koźle** Poland
143 C4 **Keel** Ireland
72 G6 **Keele** *watercourse* Northwest Territories Canada
72 F6 **Keele Peak** Yukon Territory Canada
81 M1 **Keeler** Saskatchewan Canada
75 Q5 **Keeley Lake** Saskatchewan Canada
Keeling Islands *see* **Cocos Islands**
189 I3 **Keelung** Taiwan China
84 C3 **Keene** California USA
83 O5 **Keene** New Hampshire USA
142 F4 **Keenie** Angus Scotland UK
213 J3 **Keep** *watercourse* NT Australia
219 J4 **Keepit, Lake** NSW Australia
214 F2 **Keer-weer, Cape** Qld Australia
140 A2 **Keeran** Fermanagh Northern Ireland UK
162 C5 **Keetmanshoop** Namibia
76 K7 **Keezhik Lake** Ontario Canada
133 D5 **Kefalas, Akra** *cape* Greece
133 D5 **Kefalo Burnu** *cape* Turkey
133 E7 **Kefalos** Greece
133 D7 **Kefalos, Akra** *cape* Greece
133 C6 **Kefalovryso** Greece
198 C6 **Kefamenanu** Indonesia
159 F3 **Keffi** Nigeria
133 G5 **Kefken** Turkey
74 M4 **Keg River** Alberta Canada
77 W3 **Keglo Bay** Quebec Canada
139 F2 **Kegworth** Leicester England UK
156 E4 **Keheili** Sudan
124 D3 **Kehl** Germany
124 D2 **Kehrig** Germany
181 H5 **Kehsi Mansam** Myanmar
141 G3 **Keighley** West Yorkshire England UK
123 L2 **Keikyä** Finland
123 M3 **Keila** Estonia
142 D4 **Keilator** Stirling Scotland UK
142 C5 **Keillmore** Argyll and Bute Scotland UK
123 N2 **Keipsalo** *island* Finland
86 F3 **Keiser** Arkansas USA
123 K2 **Keistiö** *island* Finland
155 H6 **Keïta** Niger
159 H3 **Keita ou Doka, Bahr** *watercourse* Central African Republic
121 O5 **Keitele** Finland
121 N5 **Keitele** *lake* Finland
121 N5 **Keitelepohja** Finland
218 E7 **Keith** SA Australia
214 A1 **Keith, Cape** NT Australia
72 G5 **Keith Arm** Northwest Territories Canada
74 K6 **Keithley Creek** British Columbia Canada
223 9a **Keiyasi** Fiji
80 D4 **Keizer** Oregon USA
178 G3 **Kejān** Iran
123 M4 **Ķekava** Latvia
125 K4 **Kékes** *mountain* Hungary
190 G4 **Kekeyiligeng** Nei Mongol Zizhiqu China
197 K4 **Kekik** *island* Indonesia
159 E3 **Kekki Lagoon** *bay* Nigeria
186 D6 **Kekri** Rajasthan India
131 D9 **Kelaa Kebira** Tunisia
161 G2 **K'elafo** Ethiopia
184 G3 **Kelamayi** Xinjiang Uygur Zizhiqu China
190 G5 **Kelan** Shanxi China
197 J4 **Kelang** *island* Indonesia
196 D2 **Kelantan** *admin. area* Malaysia
196 D2 **Kelantan** *watercourse* Malaysia
133 B5 **Këlcyrë** Albania
75 U7 **Keld** Manitoba Canada
141 F2 **Keld** North Yorkshire England UK
141 G3 **Kelfield** North Yorkshire England UK
155 I1 **Kelibia** Tunisia
182 I6 **Kelifskiy Uzboy** *lake* Turkmenistan
199 F4 **Kelila** Indonesia
136 F5 **Kelkit** Turkey
218 F7 **Kellalac** Vic. Australia
72 G6 **Keller Lake** Northwest Territories Canada
216 E5 **Kellerberrin** WA Australia
76 H4 **Kellet** Manitoba Canada
72 G4 **Kellett, Cape** Northwest Territories Canada
72 H3 **Kellett Strait** Northwest Territories Canada
75 T7 **Kelliher** Saskatchewan Canada
81 R3 **Kelliher** Minnesota USA
121 N4 **Kello** Finland
134 S6 **Kellog** Russian Federation
121 P4 **Kellojärvi** *lake* Finland
121 O3 **Kelloniemi** Finland
121 P3 **Kelloselkä** Finland
143 E4 **Kells** Ireland
143 F3 **Kells** Ireland
143 F2 **Kells** Ballymena Northern Ireland UK
219 I6 **Kelly, Mount** NSW Australia
123 L5 **Kelmė** Lithuania
159 H3 **Kélo** Chad
121 N3 **Kelontekemä** Finland
121 N3 **Kelontekemäjärvi** *lake* Finland
120 L2 **Kelottijärvi** *lake* Sweden
74 L8 **Kelowna** British Columbia Canada
86 B7 **Kelsay** Texas USA
75 W4 **Kelsey** Manitoba Canada
80 C1 **Kelsey Bay** British Columbia Canada
142 F5 **Kelso** Scottish Borders Scotland UK
82 G8 **Kelso** Missouri USA
80 D3 **Kelso** Washington USA
59 I2 **Keltie, Cape** Antarctica
142 E4 **Kelty** Fife Scotland UK
196 D3 **Keluang** Malaysia
197 F4 **Keluang, Tanjung** *cape* Indonesia
121 O3 **Kelujärvi** *lake* Finland
121 Q5 **Kelvä** Finland
139 H3 **Kelvedon** Essex England UK
139 H3 **Kelvedon Hatch** Essex England UK
76 K8 **Kelvin Island** Ontario Canada
193 H2 **Kema** *watercourse* Russian Federation
197 G2 **Kemabung** Malaysia
133 E6 **Kemalpaşa** Turkey
196 D2 **Kemasik** Malaysia
197 F3 **Kembayan** Indonesia
159 I4 **Kembé** Central African Republic
132 A1 **Kemence** Hungary
133 G7 **Kemer** Turkey
133 F7 **Kemer** Turkey
133 E5 **Kemer** Turkey
133 F5 **Kemerburgaz** Turkey
183 O2 **Kemerovo** Russian Federation
134 S7 **Kemerovskaya Oblast'** *admin. area* Russian Federation
183 O2 **Kemerovskayaoblast'** *admin. area* Russian Federation
121 N4 **Kemi** Finland
121 O3 **Kemijärvi** Finland
121 O3 **Kemijärvi** *lake* Finland
121 O3 **Kemijoki** *watercourse* Finland
121 P4 **Kemilä** Finland
183 L5 **Kemin** Kyrgyzstan
81 J6 **Kemmerer** Wyoming USA
130 D2 **Kemnath** Germany
159 H3 **Kémo** *admin. area* Central African Republic
85 M4 **Kemp, Lake** Texas USA
59 D2 **Kemp Coast** Antarctica
59 U2 **Kemp Peninsula** Antarctica
74 M4 **Kemp River** Alberta Canada
121 N4 **Kempele** Finland
135 Y6 **Kempendyay** Russian Federation
86 C5 **Kempner** Texas USA
219 K4 **Kempsey** NSW Australia
139 E2 **Kempsey** Worcestershire England UK
73 L9 **Kempt, Lac** *lake* Quebec Canada
124 F4 **Kempten** Germany
219 I6 **Kempton** NSW Australia
138 E2 **Kempton** Shropshire England UK
197 F5 **Kemujan** *island* Indonesia
142 E6 **Ken** *watercourse* Scotland UK
140 D1 **Ken, Loch** *lake* Scotland UK
155 F2 **Kenadsa** Algeria
72 D6 **Kenai** Alaska USA
72 D7 **Kenai Mountains** Alaska USA
72 D6 **Kenai Peninsula** Alaska USA
196 E5 **Kenam, Tanjung** *cape* Indonesia
78 H6 **Kenamu** *watercourse* Newfoundland and Labrador Canada
197 G6 **Kencong** Indonesia
187 F6 **Kenda** Chhattisgarh India
186 G6 **Kenda** West Bengal India
219 I3 **Kendal** Qld Australia
140 F2 **Kendal** Cumbria England UK
214 F3 **Kendall** *watercourse* Qld Australia
85 L2 **Kendall** Kansas USA
76 L1 **Kendall, Cape** Nunavut Canada
214 G2 **Kendall River** Qld Australia
198 B4 **Kendari** Indonesia
197 F4 **Kendawangan** Indonesia
197 F4 **Kendawangan** *watercourse* Indonesia
159 H2 **Kendégué** Chad
124 D2 **Kendel** *watercourse* Netherlands
80 G3 **Kendrick** Idaho USA
86 C6 **Kenedy** Texas USA
86 D5 **Kenefick** Texas USA
158 B3 **Kenema** Sierra Leone
78 I6 **Kenemich** *watercourse* Newfoundland and Labrador Canada
199 G5 **Kenewa** Papua New Guinea
160 B4 **Kenge** Democratic Republic of Congo
181 I5 **Kengtung** Myanmar
162 D5 **Kenhardt** South Africa
154 D6 **Kéniéba** Mali
197 H2 **Keningau** Malaysia
154 E2 **Kénitra** Morocco
138 E2 **Kenley** Shropshire England UK
191 I5 **Kenli** Shandong China
143 C5 **Kenmare** Ireland
143 C5 **Kenmare** *bay* Ireland
81 N2 **Kenmare** North Dakota USA
142 B3 **Kenmore** Na h-Eileanan Siar Scotland UK
142 D4 **Kenmore** Perth and Kinross Scotland UK
138 E3 **Kenn** North Somerset England UK
85 K4 **Kenna** New Mexico USA
83 Q4 **Kennebec** *watercourse* Maine USA
86 H4 **Kennedy** Alabama USA
81 Q2 **Kennedy** Minnesota USA
74 I7 **Kennedy, Mount** British Columbia Canada
181 G4 **Kennedy Peak** *mountain* Myanmar
216 D2 **Kennedy Range** WA Australia
212 G4 **Kennedys Cottage** WA Australia
86 F6 **Kenner** Louisiana USA
139 F3 **Kennet** *watercourse* England UK
139 F3 **Kennet and Avon Canal** England UK
139 H2 **Kennett** Cambridgeshire England UK
86 F2 **Kennett** Missouri USA
80 F3 **Kennewick** Washington USA
77 X5 **Kenney Lake** Newfoundland and Labrador Canada
82 I1 **Kenogami** *watercourse* Ontario Canada
83 P2 **Kénogami, Lac** *lake* Quebec Canada
83 K2 **Kenogamissi Lake** Ontario Canada
76 H8 **Kenora** Ontario Canada
75 T8 **Kenosee Lake** Saskatchewan Canada
82 H5 **Kenosha** Wisconsin USA
121 U5 **Kenozero, Ozero** *lake* Russian Federation
121 Q5 **Kenraalinkylä** Finland
81 P3 **Kensal** North Dakota USA
215 H7 **Kensington** Qld Australia
81 R4 **Kensington** Minnesota USA
74 K8 **Kent** British Columbia Canada
139 H3 **Kent** *admin. area* England UK
83 K6 **Kent** Ohio USA
85 J5 **Kent** Texas USA
80 D3 **Kent** Washington USA
82 I5 **Kent City** Michigan USA
219 R9 **Kent Group** *islands* Tas. Australia
72 I5 **Kent Peninsula** Nunavut Canada
183 J5 **Kentau** Kazakhstan
183 P3 **Kentegir** *watercourse* Russian Federation
138 D4 **Kentisbeare** Devon England UK
86 G2 **Kenton** Tennessee USA
133 C5 **Kentriki Makedonia** *admin. area* Greece
219 J4 **Kentucky** NSW Australia
71 **Kentucky** *admin. area* USA
82 I7 **Kentucky** *watercourse* Kentucky USA
86 G2 **Kentucky Lake** Tennessee USA
79 F10 **Kentville** Nova Scotia Canada
75 U6 **Kenville** Manitoba Canada
161 F3 **Kenya** *country* Africa
161 F3 **Kenya, Mount** *mountain* Kenya
125 I4 **Kenyeri** Hungary
196 D2 **Kenyir, Tasik** *watercourse* Malaysia
183 K3 **Kenzharyk** Kazakhstan
124 D3 **Kenzingen** Germany
216 F5 **Keokanie Rock** *mountain* WA Australia
82 F6 **Keokuk** Iowa USA
80 I1 **Keoma** Alberta Canada
87 J3 **Keowee, Lake** South Carolina USA
194 E2 **Kép** Vietnam
196 D4 **Kepahiang** Indonesia
197 G6 **Kepanjen** Indonesia
199 F5 **Kepi** Indonesia
133 A5 **Kepi i Rodonit** *cape* Albania
77 W6 **Kepimits Lake** Newfoundland and Labrador Canada
184 F5 **Keping** Xinjiang Uygur Zizhiqu China
125 I2 **Kępno** Poland
109 7 **Keppel Island** Falkland Islands
108 E5 **Keppel Sound** Falkland Islands
218 E7 **Keppoch** SA Australia
142 C3 **Keppoch** Highland Scotland UK
196 E3 **Kepulauan Riau** *admin. area* Indonesia
188 C1 **Kequ** Qinghai China
187 D9 **Kerala** *admin. area* India
199 H5 **Keram** *watercourse* Papua New Guinea
133 D5 **Keramoti** Greece
218 F6 **Kerang** Vic. Australia
133 B6 **Kerasona** Greece
212 E5 **Keraudren, Cape** WA Australia
199 I5 **Keravat** Papua New Guinea
196 D4 **Kerbau, Tanjung** *cape* Indonesia
126 C2 **Kerbédic** France
136 F4 **Kerch** Ukraine
160 D2 **Kéré** Central African Republic
156 E5 **Kereimet** Sudan
218 H5 **Kerein Hills** NSW Australia
74 L8 **Keremeos** British Columbia Canada
157 F4 **Keren** Eritrea
89 F1 **Kerens** Texas USA
183 J3 **Kerey Koli** *lake* Kazakhstan
164 6 **Kerguélen, Îles** *islands* French Southern and Antarctic Lands
59 F3 **Kerguelen Plateau** *underwater feature* Southern Ocean
133 B7 **Keri** Greece
161 F4 **Kericho** Kenya
220 E2 **Kerikeri** New Zealand
179 I2 **Kerimanj** Iran
196 D4 **Kerinci, Danau** *lake* Indonesia
196 D4 **Kerinci, Gunung** *volcano* Indonesia
161 F3 **Kerio** *watercourse* Kenya
133 C5 **Kerkinitis, Limni** *lake* Greece
133 A6 **Kerkyra** Greece
133 A6 **Kerkyra (Corfu)** *island* Greece
156 E4 **Kerma** Sudan
220 5 **Kermadec Islands** New Zealand
52 O11 **Kermadec Ridge** *underwater feature* Pacific Ocean
52 O11 **Kermadec Trench** *underwater feature* Pacific Ocean
121 P5 **Kermajärvi** *lake* Finland
179 I3 **Kermān** Iran
179 I3 **Kermān** *admin. area* Iran
178 F2 **Kermānshāh** Iran
178 F2 **Kermānshāh** *admin. area* Iran
132 E4 **Kermen** Bulgaria
85 K5 **Kermit** Texas USA
84 C3 **Kern** *watercourse* California USA
158 E2 **Kérou** Benin
158 C3 **Kérouané** Guinea
127 H1 **Kerpen** Germany
215 H6 **Kerr** *watercourse* Qld Australia
59 K1 **Kerr, Cape** Antarctica
142 C4 **Kerrera** *island* Scotland UK
85 K2 **Kerrick** Texas USA
219 H5 **Kerriwah** NSW Australia
75 Q7 **Kerrobert** Saskatchewan Canada
214 F6 **Kerrs Table Mountain** *mountain* Qld Australia
86 B5 **Kerrville** Texas USA
143 C4 **Kerry** *admin. area* Ireland
138 D2 **Kerry** Powys Wales UK
143 B4 **Kerry Head** *cape* Ireland
161 F2 **Kersa Dek** Ethiopia
140 F1 **Kershopefoot** Cumbria England UK
121 O3 **Kersilö** Finland
74 J6 **Kersley** British Columbia Canada
122 I2 **Kerstinbo** Sweden
196 E4 **Kertapati** Indonesia
196 D2 **Kerteh** Malaysia
133 F6 **Kertil** Turkey
187 D8 **Kerur** Karnataka India
155 F3 **Kerzaz** Algeria
77 O7 **Kesagami** *watercourse* Ontario Canada
77 O7 **Kesagami Lake** Ontario Canada
193 I3 **Kesennuma** Japan
191 K3 **Keshan** Heilongjiang China
183 K7 **Keshem** Afghanistan
187 C7 **Keshod** Gujarat India
187 F7 **Kesinga** Orissa India
121 N4 **Keskikylä** Finland
136 E5 **Keskin** Turkey
121 N4 **Keskipiiri** Finland
123 Q2 **Keskozero** Russian Federation
139 I2 **Kessingland** Suffolk England UK
139 I2 **Kessingland Beach** Suffolk England UK
133 F5 **Kestel** Turkey
121 Q4 **Kesten'ga** Russian Federation
121 O4 **Kestilä** Finland
140 E2 **Keswick** Cumbria England UK
80 D6 **Keswick Reservoir** California USA
134 R7 **Ket'** *watercourse* Russian Federation
135 AB7 **Ket-Kap, Khrebet** *range* Russian Federation
134 T5 **Keta, Ozero** *lake* Russian Federation
158 E3 **Keta Lagoon** *bay* Ghana
196 D4 **Ketahun** Indonesia
133 B6 **Ketalliona** *island* Greece
196 D3 **Ketamputih** Indonesia
196 F4 **Ketapang** Indonesia
74 H3 **Ketchika** *watercourse* British Columbia Canada
74 F5 **Ketchikan** Alaska USA
80 H5 **Ketchum** Idaho USA
124 C1 **Ketelmeer** *bay* Netherlands
105 G4 **Ketéroco** Brazil
130 G3 **Kéthely** Hungary
138 E2 **Ketley** Telford and Wrekin England UK
121 N2 **Ketojärvi** *lake* Finland
121 N2 **Ketomella** Finland
135 AF9 **Ketoy, Ostrov** *island* Kuril Islands
193 L1 **Ketoy, Ostrov** *lake* Russian Federation
159 H4 **Ketta** Congo
159 G4 **Kétté** Cameroon
139 G2 **Kettering** Northamptonshire England UK
82 I7 **Kettering** Ohio USA
74 L8 **Kettle** *watercourse* British Columbia Canada
76 K4 **Kettle** *watercourse* Manitoba Canada
80 F2 **Kettle Falls** Washington USA
83 J5 **Kettle Point** Ontario Canada
80 F2 **Kettle River Range** Washington USA
84 C2 **Kettleman City** California USA
141 F2 **Kettlewell** North Yorkshire England UK
197 F3 **Ketungau** *watercourse* Indonesia
196 B2 **Keude Teunom** Indonesia
135 V7 **Keul'** Russian Federation
124 F2 **Keula** Germany
121 N5 **Keurusselkä** *lake* Finland
121 N5 **Keuruu** Finland
158 E3 **Keve** Togo
80 J2 **Kevin** Montana USA
121 O2 **Kevo** Finland
121 P5 **Kevritty** *lake* Finland
219 K4 **Kew** NSW Australia
82 G6 **Kewanee** Illinois USA
82 H4 **Kewaunee** Wisconsin USA
82 G3 **Keweenaw Bay** Michigan USA
82 G3 **Keweenaw Peninsula** Michigan USA
82 H3 **Keweenaw Point** Michigan USA
141 G3 **Kexbrough** South Yorkshire England UK
87 K8 **Key Colony Beach** Florida USA
83 K4 **Key Harbour** Ontario Canada
75 S4 **Key Lake Mine** Saskatchewan Canada
87 K8 **Key Largo** *island* Florida USA
87 K8 **Key West** Florida USA
81 O5 **Keya Paha** *watercourse* South Dakota USA
77 S6 **Keyano** Quebec Canada
85 K2 **Keyes** Oklahoma USA
72 A6 **Keyngypil'gyn, Laguna** Russian Federation
138 E3 **Keynsham** Bath and North East Somerset England UK
83 N6 **Keyport** New Jersey USA
74 C3 **Keysall** *watercourse* British Columbia Canada
83 L7 **Keyser** West Virginia USA
82 C8 **Keystone Lake** Oklahoma USA
83 L8 **Keysville** Virginia USA
125 K3 **Kežmarok** Slovakia
162 D4 **Kgalagadi** *admin. area* Botswana
162 E4 **Kgatleng** *admin. area* Botswana
179 H4 **Khabar, Kūh-e** *mountain* Iran
191 M3 **Khabarovsk** Russian Federation
135 AC8 **Khabarovskiy Kray** *admin. area* Russian Federation
183 M2 **Khabary** Russian Federation
178 E7 **Khabb, Wādī** *watercourse* Yemen
179 H3 **Khabr** Iran
178 F7 **Khabt al Aslūm** Yemen
179 K2 **Khadīr** Afghanistan
182 C5 **Khadyzhensk** Russian Federation
132 G2 **Khadzhybeys'kyy Lyman** *lake* Ukraine
186 E6 **Khaga** Uttar Pradesh India
181 G4 **Khagrachari** Bangladesh
187 E7 **Khairagarh** Chhattisgarh India
179 L3 **Khairpur** Pakistan
179 K4 **Khairpur** Pakistan
190 E2 **Khaizan Burged Uul** *mountain* Mongolia
183 P2 **Khakasiya** *admin. area* Russian Federation
179 K3 **Khākerān** Afghanistan
162 D4 **Khakhea** Botswana
136 F7 **Khalhale** Syria
182 E5 **Khali-Keloy** Russian Federation
178 F3 **Khalid** Iraq
179 I6 **Khalīj Maşīrah** *sea* Oman
182 H3 **Khalilovo** Russian Federation
133 C6 **Khálki** Greece
133 C6 **Khalkoútsion** Greece
190 E2 **Khamar-Daban, Khrebet** *range* Russian Federation
186 E6 **Khamaria** Madhya Pradesh India
187 B6 **Khambhaliya** Gujarat India
187 C6 **Khambhat** Gujarat India
187 C7 **Khambhat, Gulf of** Gujarat India
187 D7 **Khamgaon** Maharashtra India
178 E6 **Khamīs Mushayt** Saudi Arabia
187 E8 **Khammam** Andhra Pradesh India
135 Y6 **Khampa** Russian Federation
135 Z6 **Khampa** Russian Federation
181 H3 **Khamti** Myanmar
136 F7 **Khan al 'Arus** Syria
187 D7 **Khandwa** Madhya Pradesh India
135 AC6 **Khandyga** Russian Federation
129 J6 **Khangat Sidi Nadji** Algeria
135 Z7 **Khani** Russian Federation
192 G2 **Khanka, Ozero** *lake* Russian Federation
182 H6 **Khankui** Turkmenistan
135 Y5 **Khannya** *watercourse* Russian Federation
186 D6 **Khanpur** Rajasthan India
190 E2 **Khantayn Nuruu Uul** *mountain* Mongolia
134 T5 **Khantayskoye, Ozero** *lake* Russian Federation
134 T5 **Khantayskoye Vodokhranilishche** *lake* Russian Federation
134 O6 **Khanty-Mansiysk** Russian Federation
134 O6 **Khanty-Mansiyskiy Avotomnyy Okrug-Yugra** *admin. area* Russian Federation
135 AD7 **Khanyangda** Russian Federation
194 C5 **Khao Luang** *mountain* Myanmar
194 C5 **Khao Luang** *mountain* Thailand
187 E6 **Khapa** Madhya Pradesh India
191 G2 **Khapcheranga** Russian Federation
179 J2 **Khar Bīd** Afghanistan
178 G2 **Khar Rūd** *watercourse* Iran
179 L3 **Khar Tangai Manda** *watercourse* Pakistan
135 W4 **Khara-Tas, Gory** *range* Russian Federation
182 E4 **Kharabali** Russian Federation
187 G6 **Kharagpur** West Bengal India
136 G6 **Kharā'ij** Syria
179 K4 **Kharan** Pakistan
135 AA4 **Kharaulakhskiy Khrebet** *range* Russian Federation
186 E6 **Kharela** Uttar Pradesh India
187 D7 **Khargone** Madhya Pradesh India
179 H4 **Khargū** Iran
187 F7 **Kharhial** Orissa India
179 M3 **Kharian** Pakistan
156 E3 **Khārijah, Wāḥāt Al** *spring* Egypt
135 AG9 **Kharimkotan, Ostrov** *island* Kuril Islands
185 I2 **Kharkhiraa Uul** *mountain* Mongolia
136 F2 **Kharkiv** Ukraine
136 F3 **Kharkivs'ka Oblast'** *admin. area* Ukraine
121 T2 **Kharlovka** Russian Federation
123 P2 **Kharlu** Russian Federation
133 D5 **Kharmanli** Bulgaria
187 F7 **Kharod** Chhattisgarh India
133 C5 **Kharopón** Greece
187 F7 **Kharsia** Chhattisgarh India
135 AD4 **Kharstan** Russian Federation
Khartoum *see* **Al Kharṭūm** Sudan
156 E4 **Khartoum** *admin. area* Sudan
135 AA6 **Kharyyalakh** Russian Federation
179 H4 **Khaşab** Oman
182 H6 **Khasar-Kala** Turkmenistan
182 E5 **Khasavyurt** Russian Federation
179 J4 **Khāsh** Iran
182 J6 **Khashdala** Uzbekistan
156 F5 **Khashm el Girba** Sudan
133 D5 **Khaskovo** Bulgaria
133 D4 **Khaskovo** *admin. area* Bulgaria
179 J2 **Khaţā'ī** Iran
135 V4 **Khatanga** Russian Federation
135 V4 **Khatanga** *watercourse* Russian Federation
135 W4 **Khatangskiy Zaliv** *bay* Russian Federation
186 D5 **Khatauli** Uttar Pradesh India
182 J6 **Khatcha** Uzbekistan
183 K6 **Khatlon** *admin. area* Tajikistan
135 Y6 **Khaty** Russian Federation
135 AK6 **Khatyrka** Russian Federation
179 L2 **Khāvāk, Kowtal-e** *pass* Afghanistan
179 K2 **Khavāl** Afghanistan
186 B6 **Khavda** Gujarat India
179 J3 **Khāway** Afghanistan
181 G4 **Khawhai** Mizoram India
156 F3 **Khawr Daiat** *spring* Sudan
178 E6 **Khaybar** Saudi Arabia
162 C6 **Khayelitsha** South Africa
194 E3 **Khe Sanh** Vietnam
187 D7 **Khede** Maharashtra India
155 G1 **Khemis Miliana** Algeria
154 E2 **Khemis Zemamra** Morocco
154 E2 **Khemisset** Morocco
155 H1 **Khenchela** Algeria
154 E2 **Khenifra** Morocco
155 H1 **Kherrata** Algeria
136 E3 **Kherson** Ukraine
136 E3 **Khersons'ka Oblast'** *admin. area* Ukraine
135 U4 **Kheta** *watercourse* Russian Federation
121 R3 **Khetolambina** Russian Federation
186 D5 **Khetri** Rajasthan India
121 P2 **Kheykhen'yarvi** Russian Federation
123 O2 **Khiitola** Russian Federation
190 G2 **Khilok** Russian Federation
190 G2 **Khilok** *watercourse* Russian Federation
136 F7 **Khirbat Ra's al Wa'r** Syria
121 S5 **Khizhozero, Ozero** *lake* Russian Federation
194 D4 **Khlong Luang** Thailand
194 D4 **Khlung** Thailand
136 C3 **Khmel'nyts'ka Oblast'** *admin. area* Ukraine
132 E1 **Khmel'nyts'kyy** Ukraine
194 E5 **Khoai, Hòn** *island* Vietnam
123 P6 **Khodosy** Belarus
132 C1 **Khodovichi** Ukraine
183 J7 **Kholm** Afghanistan
123 P4 **Kholm** Russian Federation
135 AD9 **Kholmsk** Russian Federation
193 I1 **Kholmsk** Russian Federation
123 O5 **Kholomer'ye** Belarus
183 N3 **Kholzun, Khrebet** *range* Russian Federation
162 C4 **Khomas** *admin. area* Namibia
178 G2 **Khomeyn** Iran
183 M2 **Khomutino** *lake* Russian Federation
194 D4 **Khon Buri** Thailand
194 D3 **Khon Kaen** Thailand
185 J3 **Khondlon Uul** *mountain* Mongolia
135 AF6 **Khongo** Russian Federation
182 D5 **Khoni** Georgia
179 H4 **Khonj** Iran
181 H3 **Khonsa** Arunachal Pradesh India
187 C7 **Khopoli** Maharashtra India
193 G1 **Khor** Russian Federation
193 H1 **Khor** *watercourse* Russian Federation
156 E3 **Khor Abu Sunt** *watercourse* Sudan
156 E5 **Khor Dulayb** *watercourse* Sudan
179 I3 **Khorāsān-e Janūbī** *admin. area* Iran
179 I2 **Khorāsān-e Razavī** *admin. area* Iran
182 G6 **Khorāsān-e Shemālī** *admin. area* Iran
194 D3 **Khorat Plateau** Thailand
190 G2 **Khorinsk** Russian Federation
162 B4 **Khorixas** Namibia
136 E2 **Khorol** *watercourse* Ukraine
178 F2 **Khorramābād** Iran
178 F3 **Khorramshahr** Iran
183 K6 **Khorugh** Tajikistan
182 E4 **Khosheutovo** Russian Federation
179 I2 **Khoshk** Iran
136 E2 **Khot'kovo** Russian Federation
132 E1 **Khotyn** Ukraine
179 H4 **Khour Fakkān** United Arab Emirates
154 E2 **Khouribga** Morocco
182 G7 **Khowsh-e Yeylāq** Iran
179 L2 **Khowst** Afghanistan
179 L2 **Khowst** *admin. area* Afghanistan
136 D2 **Khoyniki** Belarus
133 C7 **Khránoi** Greece
135 AE4 **Khromskaya Guba** *bay* Russian Federation
182 H3 **Khromtau** Kazakhstan
132 F1 **Khrystynivka** Ukraine
182 E5 **Khryuk** Russian Federation
162 D4 **Khudumalapye** Botswana
162 D5 **Khuis** Botswana
183 K6 **Khŭjand.** Tajikistan
134 N6 **Khulga** *watercourse* Russian Federation
181 F4 **Khulna** Bangladesh
181 F4 **Khulna** *admin. area* Bangladesh
190 F3 **Khulstayn Uul** *mountain* Mongolia
135 AC8 **Khummi, Ozero** *lake* Russian Federation
178 E2 **Khunayfis** Iraq
184 E6 **Khunjerab Pass** Xinjiang Uygur Zizhiqu China
186 F6 **Khunti** Jharkhand India
186 E6 **Khurai** Madhya Pradesh India
156 D5 **Khureit** Sudan
179 H6 **Khurīyā' Murīyā, Jazā'ir** *island* Oman
186 D5 **Khurja** Uttar Pradesh India
123 O6 **Khutor** Belarus
156 D5 **Khuwei** Sudan
179 K4 **Khuzdar** Pakistan
178 F3 **Khūzestān** *admin. area* Iran
182 E3 **Khvalynsk** Russian Federation
182 E6 **Khvar** Iran
178 G4 **Khvormūj** Iran
179 I2 **Khvoshābeh** Iran
182 D6 **Khvoy** Iran
121 Q4 **Khyame** Russian Federation
179 L2 **Khyber Pass** Pakistan
132 C1 **Khyriv** Ukraine
223 9 **Kia** *island* Fiji
199 G5 **Kia** *watercourse* Indonesia
222 8 **Kia** Solomon Islands
219 K2 **Kia Ora** Qld Australia
219 I7 **Kiah** NSW Australia
219 J6 **Kiama** NSW Australia
195 J6 **Kiamba** Philippines
160 D5 **Kiambi** Democratic Republic of Congo
214 D4 **Kiana** NT Australia
219 I6 **Kiandra** NSW Australia
219 J7 **Kianga** NSW Australia
219 J1 **Kianga** Qld Australia
219 J2 **Kiangarow, Mount** Qld Australia
121 P4 **Kiantajärvi** *bay* Finland
121 P4 **Kiantajärvi** *lake* Finland
73 N4 **Kiatassuaq** *island* Greenland
133 C6 **Kiato** Greece
90 C4 **Kiauban** Honduras
87 K4 **Kiawah Island** South Carolina USA
122 E4 **Kibæk** Denmark
161 F5 **Kibaha** Tanzania
160 A5 **Kibala** Angola
160 E3 **Kibale** Uganda
160 D3 **Kibali** *watercourse* Democratic Republic of Congo
159 G5 **Kibangou** Congo
186 D4 **Kibar** Himachal Pradesh India
160 D5 **Kibara, Monts** *range* Democratic Republic of Congo
161 F5 **Kibau** Tanzania
161 F5 **Kibaya** Tanzania
121 Q1 **Kiberg** Norway
160 E3 **Kiboga** Uganda
161 F4 **Kiboko** *watercourse* Kenya
160 E4 **Kibondo** Tanzania
161 F2 **Kibre Mengist** Ethiopia
123 K4 **Kiburi** Latvia
121 P1 **Kiby** Norway
132 E4 **Kichevo** Bulgaria
218 G3 **Kichimiloo Claypan** NSW Australia
219 I4 **Kickabil** NSW Australia
155 G5 **Kidal** Mali
132 G1 **Kidanovka** Ukraine
195 J6 **Kidapawan** Philippines
139 E2 **Kidderminster** Worcestershire England UK
161 E2 **Kidepo** *watercourse* Sudan
154 D6 **Kidira** Senegal
139 F3 **Kidlington** Oxfordshire England UK
220 G4 **Kidnappers, Cape** New Zealand
138 E1 **Kidsgrove** Staffordshire England UK
197 G3 **Kidurong, Tanjong** *cape* Malaysia
122 F5 **Kiel** Germany
82 G5 **Kiel** Wisconsin USA
125 K2 **Kielce** Poland
125 J2 **Kielcza** Poland
141 F1 **Kielder** Northumberland England UK
141 F1 **Kielder Water** *lake* England UK
122 F5 **Kieler Bucht** *bay* Germany
194 E2 **Kiến An** Vietnam
120 L2 **Kiepanjaure** *lake* Sweden
199 J5 **Kieta** Papua New Guinea
125 J2 **Kietrz** Poland
Kiev *see* **Kyyiv** Ukraine
161 F5 **Kifanyo** Tanzania
154 D5 **Kiffa** Mauritania
133 C6 **Kifisos** *watercourse* Greece
160 D4 **Kigali** Rwanda
78 H4 **Kiglapait, Cape** Newfoundland and Labrador Canada
158 C2 **Kignan** Mali
160 D4 **Kigoma** Tanzania
160 E4 **Kigoma** *admin. area* Tanzania
161 F5 **Kigwe** Tanzania
197 G4 **Kihambatang** Indonesia
197 H3 **Kihammawon** Indonesia
218 F2 **Kihee** Qld Australia
84 inset **Kīhei** Hawai'i USA
121 M3 **Kihlanki** Finland
123 N3 **Kihlevere** Estonia
121 M5 **Kihniö** Finland
123 M3 **Kihnu** *island* Estonia
193 G5 **Kii-sanchi** Japan
121 Q5 **Kiihtelysvaara** Finland
183 K4 **Kiik** Kazakhstan
121 N4 **Kiiminki** Finland
121 N5 **Kiiskilä** Finland
121 N3 **Kiistala** Finland
160 E4 **Kijanebalola, Lake** *lake* Uganda
196 E3 **Kijang** Indonesia
125 K2 **Kije** Poland
132 B4 **Kijevo** Kosovo
161 F5 **Kijunga** *spring* Tanzania
160 D4 **Kikamba** Democratic Republic of Congo
123 O3 **Kikerino** Russian Federation
78 H4 **Kikiktaksoak Island** Newfoundland and Labrador Canada
132 B3 **Kikinda** Serbia
75 O5 **Kikino** Alberta Canada
221 E5 **Kikiwa** New Zealand
78 H4 **Kikkertavak Island** Newfoundland and Labrador Canada
77 V3 **Kikkertoksoak Islands** Nunavut Canada
134 R6 **Kikkiakki** Russian Federation
133 D7 **Kikladhes** *island* Greece
182 E1 **Kiknur** Russian Federation
218 H5 **Kikoira** NSW Australia
160 D5 **Kikondja** Democratic Republic of Congo
199 G5 **Kikori** *watercourse* Papua New Guinea
182 D3 **Kikvidze** Russian Federation
160 B5 **Kikwit** Democratic Republic of Congo
122 E3 **Kil** Norway
84 inset **Kilauea Crater** *volcano* Hawai'i USA
130 F2 **Kilb** Austria
143 D5 **Kilbeg** Ireland
143 F3 **Kilberry** Ireland
142 C5 **Kilberry** Argyll and Bute Scotland UK
120 H3 **Kilboghamn** Norway
120 J2 **Kilbotn** Norway
140 B3 **Kilbride Cross Roads** Ireland
140 A4 **Kilbrids Cross Roads** Ireland
143 F4 **Kilcarney** Ireland
142 C5 **Kilchenzie** Argyll and Bute Scotland UK
142 B4 **Kilchoan** Highland Scotland UK
142 B5 **Kilchoman** Argyll and Bute Scotland UK
142 C4 **Kilchrenan** Argyll and Bute Scotland UK
142 C5 **Kilchrist** Argyll and Bute Scotland UK
192 F3 **Kilchu** North Korea
140 C2 **Kilclief** Down Northern Ireland UK
140 B2 **Kilcoo** Down Northern Ireland UK
143 F3 **Kilcoole** Ireland
143 D4 **Kilcor** Ireland
143 E3 **Kilcormac** Ireland
140 A4 **Kilcruise** Ireland
143 F3 **Kilcullen** Ireland
215 I7 **Kilcummin** Qld Australia
140 B2 **Kilcurly** Ireland
140 B3 **Kildalkey** Ireland
143 F3 **Kildare** Ireland
143 F3 **Kildare** *admin. area* Ireland
79 G9 **Kildare, Cape** Prince Edward Island Canada
142 D3 **Kildary** Highland Scotland UK
138 A2 **Kildavin** Ireland
143 F3 **Kilday** Ireland
134 I5 **Kil'din, Ostrov** *island* Russian Federation
121 R2 **Kil'dinstroy** Russian Federation
140 B2 **Kildoagh** Ireland
80 C2 **Kildonan** British Columbia Canada
142 C5 **Kildonan** North Ayrshire Scotland UK
142 E2 **Kildonan Lodge** Highland Scotland UK
143 C3 **Kildun** Ireland
122 D3 **Kilefjordan** *lake* Norway
182 E2 **Kilemary** Russian Federation
160 D5 **Kilembe** Democratic Republic of Congo
160 D5 **Kileo** Democratic Republic of Congo
122 E3 **Kilevatnet** *lake* Norway
142 D3 **Kilfinnan** Highland Scotland UK
143 D3 **Kilglass** Ireland
141 H2 **Kilham** East Riding of Yorkshire England UK
223 15 **Kili** *island* Marshall Islands
158 E3 **Kilibo** Benin
159 H2 **Kilim** Chad
156 B5 **Kilim** Chad
161 F4 **Kilimanjaro** *admin. area* Tanzania
161 F4 **Kilimanjaro** *volcano* Tanzania
136 F6 **Kilis** Turkey
136 F6 **Kilis** *admin. area* Turkey
132 F3 **Kiliya** Ukraine
143 F4 **Kilkea** Ireland
143 C4 **Kilkee** Ireland

143 F2 **Kilkeel** Newry and Mourne Northern Ireland UK
143 D3 **Kilkelly** Ireland
143 E4 **Kilkenny** Ireland
143 E4 **Kilkenny** *admin. area* Ireland
123 N2 **Kilkinkylä** Finland
219 K2 **Kilkivan** Qld Australia
143 B3 **Kill** Ireland
87 N2 **Kill Devil Hills** North Carolina USA
143 E4 **Killadangan** Ireland
143 F3 **Killadreenan** Ireland
143 C2 **Killala** Ireland
143 C2 **Killala Bay** Ireland
82 H2 **Killala Lake** Ontario Canada
143 D4 **Killaloe** Ireland
75 T7 **Killaly** Saskatchewan Canada
218 D3 **Killamperpunna, Lake** SA Australia
143 C4 **Killarney** Ireland
143 C3 **Killary Harbour** Ireland
140 A3 **Killasona** Ireland
143 D3 **Killaun** Ireland
143 C3 **Killavally** Ireland
143 D2 **Killavil** Ireland
75 R8 **Killdeer** Saskatchewan Canada
143 E4 **Killea** Ireland
143 D3 **Killeelaun** Ireland
143 D4 **Killeen** Ireland
86 C5 **Killeen** Texas USA
143 D3 **Killeenaran** Ireland
140 C1 **Killellan** Argyll and Bute Scotland UK
86 H3 **Killen** Alabama USA
143 E4 **Killenaule** Ireland
86 F5 **Killian** Louisiana USA
142 D4 **Killichonan** Perth and Kinross Scotland UK
143 D3 **Killimor** Ireland
142 D4 **Killin** Stirling Scotland UK
143 G2 **Killinchy** Ards Northern Ireland UK
140 B3 **Killiney** Ireland
120 L3 **Killinge** Sweden
143 F4 **Killinick** Ireland
77 W2 **Killiniq** Nunavut Canada
77 W2 **Killiniq Island** Nunavut Canada
121 M5 **Killinkoski** Finland
143 E3 **Killinlahan** Ireland
142 C5 **Killocraw** Argyll and Bute Scotland UK
143 C4 **Killorglin** Ireland
140 B3 **Killosseny** Ireland
143 E4 **Killough** Ireland
143 G2 **Killough** Down Northern Ireland UK
143 D3 **Killower** Ireland
142 B4 **Killunaig** Highland Scotland UK
140 A2 **Killybane** Dungannon Northern Ireland UK
143 D2 **Killybegs** Ireland
140 B2 **Killycolpy** Cookstown Northern Ireland UK
140 B3 **Killyon** Ireland
142 D5 **Kilmacolm** Inverclyde Scotland UK
143 E4 **Kilmacthomas** Ireland
143 C3 **Kilmaine** Ireland
143 D4 **Kilmallock** Ireland
142 B3 **Kilmaluag** Highland Scotland UK
142 B3 **Kilmarie** Highland Scotland UK
142 D5 **Kilmarnock** East Ayrshire Scotland UK
142 C4 **Kilmartin** Argyll and Bute Scotland UK
143 D5 **Kilmartin Upper** Ireland
142 C4 **Kilmelford** Argyll and Bute Scotland UK
140 B3 **Kilmessan** Ireland
182 F2 **Kilmez** Russian Federation
182 F2 **Kil'mez** Russian Federation
143 F4 **Kilmichael Point** Ireland
143 C4 **Kilmihil** Ireland
143 D5 **Kilmona** Ireland
143 F3 **Kilmore** Ireland
143 D3 **Kilmore** Ireland
143 G2 **Kilmore** Down Northern Ireland UK
143 F4 **Kilmore Quay** Ireland
140 B4 **Kilmurry** Ireland
143 D4 **Kilmurry** Ireland
143 F4 **Kilnacoo** Ireland
142 C4 **Kilninver** Argyll and Bute Scotland UK
141 I3 **Kilnsea** East Riding of Yorkshire England UK
108 D3 **Kilómetro 164** Argentina
142 B4 **Kiloran** Argyll and Bute Scotland UK
161 F5 **Kilosa** Tanzania
138 E3 **Kilpeck** Herefordshire England UK
140 B3 **Kilpedder** Ireland
143 F4 **Kilpierce** Ireland
141 H3 **Kilpin** East Riding of Yorkshire England UK
120 L2 **Kilpisjärvi** *lake* Sweden
121 R2 **Kilp"yavr** Russian Federation
140 B1 **Kilraghts** Ballymoney Northern Ireland UK
140 B2 **Kilrea** Coleraine Northern Ireland UK
143 D3 **Kilreekill** Ireland
143 C4 **Kilrush** Ireland
122 E3 **Kilsfjorden** *bay* Norway
143 E2 **Kilskeery** Omagh Northern Ireland UK
142 D6 **Kilstay** Dumfries and Galloway Scotland UK
187 C9 **Kiltan Island** Lakshadweep India
140 B3 **Kiltiernan** Ireland
140 A3 **Kiltoom** Ireland
121 O5 **Kiltuanjärvi** *lake* Finland
143 D3 **Kiltullagh** Ireland
160 D5 **Kilubi** *watercourse* Democratic Republic of Congo
143 D3 **Kilvine** Ireland
120 L3 **Kilvo** Sweden
161 F5 **Kilwa Kivinje** Tanzania
159 G3 **Kim** *watercourse* Cameroon
159 H3 **Kim** Chad
199 F5 **Kimaan** Indonesia
197 G2 **Kimanis, Teluk** *bay* Malaysia
121 Q4 **Kimasozero, Ozero** *lake* Russian Federation
215 G3 **Kimba** Qld Australia
218 C5 **Kimba** SA Australia
159 G5 **Kimba** Congo
82 D4 **Kimball** Minnesota USA
81 N6 **Kimball** Nebraska USA
160 B5 **Kimbao** Democratic Republic of Congo
199 I5 **Kimbe** Papua New Guinea
199 I5 **Kimbe Bay** Papua New Guinea
213 H4 **Kimberley** *region* NT Australia
162 D5 **Kimberley** South Africa
215 H4 **Kimberley, Cape** Qld Australia
80 H5 **Kimberly** Idaho USA
101 G3 **Kimbia** Guyana
220 F5 **Kimbolton** New Zealand
192 F3 **Kim'chaek** North Korea
192 F4 **Kimhae** South Korea
123 L2 **Kimito** *island* Finland
74 M5 **Kimiwan Lake** Alberta Canada
192 E4 **Kimje** South Korea
77 U1 **Kimmirut** Nunavut Canada
193 I2 **Kimobetsu-dake** *volcano* Japan
133 D7 **Kimolos** *island* Greece
213 J4 **Kimon, Mount** NT Australia
159 G5 **Kimongo** Congo
121 Q5 **Kimovaara** Russian Federation
154 F6 **Kimparana** Mali
160 A5 **Kimpese** Democratic Republic of Congo
74 H6 **Kimsquit** British Columbia Canada
160 B5 **Kimvula** Democratic Republic of Congo
181 H4 **Kin-u** Myanmar
197 H2 **Kinabalu, Gunung** *mountain* Malaysia
197 H2 **Kinabatangan** *watercourse* Malaysia
133 E7 **Kinaros** *island* Greece
197 H2 **Kinarut** Malaysia
74 F4 **Kinaskan Lake** British Columbia Canada
72 H8 **Kinbasket Lake** Alberta Canada
74 L6 **Kinbasket Lake** British Columbia Canada
142 E2 **Kinbrace** Highland Scotland UK
75 R8 **Kincaid** Saskatchewan Canada
85 O1 **Kincaid** Kansas USA
142 E4 **Kincardine** Fife Scotland UK
142 D3 **Kincardine** Highland Scotland UK
122 G4 **Kind** *region* Sweden
160 D5 **Kinda** Democratic Republic of Congo
122 H3 **Kinda** *region* Sweden
159 G5 **Kindamba** Congo
219 J5 **Kindarun Mountain** NSW Australia
125 H4 **Kindberg** Austria
160 A5 **Kindeje** Angola
86 E5 **Kinder** Louisiana USA
83 O5 **Kinderhook** New York USA
75 Q7 **Kindersley** Saskatchewan Canada
158 B2 **Kindia** Guinea
219 J3 **Kindon** Qld Australia
160 D4 **Kindu** Democratic Republic of Congo
182 I3 **Kindykty** *lake* Kazakhstan
182 F2 **Kinel-cherkasy** Russian Federation
214 B3 **King** *watercourse* NT Australia
213 J3 **King** *watercourse* WA Australia
216 F6 **King, Lake** WA Australia
214 D3 **King Ash Bay** NT Australia
73 I3 **King Christian Island** Nunavut Canada
84 B2 **King City** California USA
82 D6 **King City** Missouri USA
72 C7 **King Cove** Alaska USA
109 8 **King Edward Point** South Georgia
213 I3 **King George** *watercourse* WA Australia
109 7 **King George Bay** *bay* Falkland Islands
59 U2 **King George Island** Antarctica
77 P4 **King George Islands** Nunavut Canada
216 E7 **King George Sound** WA Australia
109 8 **King Haakon Bay** South Georgia
219 Q9 **King Island** Tas. Australia
215 G3 **King Junction** Qld Australia
213 H4 **King Leopold Ranges** WA Australia
59 S1 **King Peak** *mountain* Antarctica
59 R2 **King Peninsula** Antarctica
216 E7 **King River** WA Australia
216 F6 **King Rock** WA Australia
59 U2 **King Sejong (South Korea)** *research station* Antarctica
213 G4 **King Sound** WA Australia
73 J5 **King William Island** Nunavut Canada
219 J2 **Kingaroy** Qld Australia
143 D2 **Kingarrow** Ireland
142 C5 **Kingarth** Argyll and Bute Scotland UK
74 H7 **Kingcome** *watercourse* British Columbia Canada
83 P4 **Kingfield** Maine USA
86 C3 **Kingfisher** Oklahoma USA
76 K6 **Kingfisher Lake** *lake* Ontario Canada
139 F3 **Kingham** Oxfordshire England UK
142 E4 **Kinghorn** Fife Scotland UK
123 O3 **Kingisepp** Russian Federation
84 E3 **Kingman** Arizona USA
81 P8 **Kingman** Kansas USA
209 **Kingman Reef** *unincorporated US territory* Pacific Ocean
160 D4 **Kingombe** Democratic Republic of Congo
218 B4 **Kingoonya** SA Australia
214 A8 **Kings Canyon Resort** NT Australia
214 A8 **Kings Creek** NT Australia
215 H5 **Kings Knob** *mountain* Qld Australia
139 H2 **King's Lynn** Norfolk England UK
81 J6 **Kings Peak** Utah USA
79 J8 **King's Point** Newfoundland and Labrador Canada
139 F3 **King's Worthy** Hampshire England UK
138 D4 **Kingsbridge** Devon England UK
84 C2 **Kingsburg** California USA
139 F3 **Kingsclere** Hampshire England UK
219 K3 **Kingscliff** NSW Australia
139 E3 **Kingscote** Gloucestershire England UK
219 I6 **Kingsdale** NSW Australia
87 K5 **Kingsland** Georgia USA
141 F3 **Kingsley** Cheshire England UK
87 J2 **Kingsport** Tennessee USA
142 E3 **Kingsteps** Highland Scotland UK
138 E3 **Kingsthorne** Herefordshire England UK
211 inset **Kingston** Norfolk Island Australia
219 R11 **Kingston** Tas. Australia
79 F10 **Kingston** Nova Scotia Canada
83 M4 **Kingston** Ontario Canada
90 E3 **Kingston** Jamaica
221 C7 **Kingston** New Zealand
87 I3 **Kingston** Georgia USA
85 I4 **Kingston** New Mexico USA
83 O6 **Kingston** New York USA
84 F1 **Kingston** Utah USA
218 B3 **Kingston, Mount** SA Australia
139 E3 **Kingston Deverill** Wiltshire England UK
218 D7 **Kingston S.E.** SA Australia
141 H3 **Kingston upon Hull** East Riding of Yorkshire England UK
139 G3 **Kingston upon Thames** Greater London England UK
219 J4 **Kingstown** NSW Australia
109 11a **Kingstown** St Vincent and the Grenadines
219 I6 **Kingsvale** NSW Australia
86 C7 **Kingsville** Texas USA
138 E3 **Kingswood** South Gloucestershire England UK
138 D2 **Kington** Herefordshire England UK
160 B5 **Kingungi** Democratic Republic of Congo
77 X4 **Kingurutik** *watercourse* Newfoundland and Labrador Canada
142 D3 **Kingussie** Highland Scotland UK
160 D6 **Kiniama** Democratic Republic of Congo
133 F6 **Kınık** Turkey
159 G5 **Kinkala** Congo
158 D3 **Kinkane** *watercourse* Côte d'Ivoire
220 F4 **Kinleith** New Zealand
142 C4 **Kinloch** Highland Scotland UK
142 D2 **Kinloch** Highland Scotland UK
142 C3 **Kinloch Hourn** Highland Scotland UK
142 D4 **Kinlochard** Stirling Scotland UK
142 C3 **Kinlochewe** Highland Scotland UK
142 C4 **Kinlochmorar** Highland Scotland UK
142 D4 **Kinlochmore** Highland Scotland UK
142 B2 **Kinlochroag** Na h-Eileanan Siar Scotland UK
142 E3 **Kinloss** Moray Scotland UK
122 G4 **Kinna** Sweden
80 G2 **Kinnaird** British Columbia Canada
142 E4 **Kinnaird Ho** Perth and Kinross Scotland UK
121 O1 **Kinnarodden** *cape* Norway
143 E3 **Kinnegad** Ireland
140 E1 **Kinnelhead** Dumfries and Galloway Scotland UK
122 G3 **Kinneviken** *bay* Sweden
121 N5 **Kinnula** Finland
121 O5 **Kinnulanlahti** Finland
76 D4 **Kinoosao** Saskatchewan Canada
77 O7 **Kinosheo** *watercourse* Ontario Canada
75 V7 **Kinosota** Manitoba Canada
142 E3 **Kinrara** Highland Scotland UK
143 D5 **Kinsale** Ireland
109 17 **Kinsale** Montserrat
75 P6 **Kinsella** Alberta Canada
59 K2 **Kinsey, Cape** Antarctica
160 B4 **Kinshasa** Democratic Republic of Congo
160 B4 **Kinshasa** *admin. area* Democratic Republic of Congo
87 M3 **Kinston** North Carolina USA
123 K5 **Kintai** Lithuania
158 C2 **Kintinian** Guinea
217 K1 **Kintore** NT Australia
142 F3 **Kintore** Aberdeenshire Scotland UK
217 L3 **Kintore, Mount** SA Australia
142 B5 **Kintour** Argyll and Bute Scotland UK
142 B4 **Kintra** Highland Scotland UK
142 C5 **Kintyre, Mull of** *cape* Scotland UK
142 C4 **Kinuachdrachd** Argyll and Bute Scotland UK
77 N5 **Kinushseo** *watercourse* Ontario Canada
75 W6 **Kinusisipi** Manitoba Canada
143 D3 **Kinvara** Ireland
139 E2 **Kinvere** Staffordshire England UK
187 E7 **Kinwat** Maharashtra India
124 E2 **Kinzig** *watercourse* Germany
223 9a **Kioa** *island* Fiji
161 E4 **Kiomboi** Tanzania
121 O5 **Kiorus** *bay* Finland
81 P8 **Kiowa** Kansas USA
160 D4 **Kipaka** Democratic Republic of Congo
83 L3 **Kipawa** Quebec Canada
73 L9 **Kipawa, Lac** *lake* Quebec Canada
161 E5 **Kipembawe** Tanzania
161 E5 **Kipengere Range** *range* Tanzania
160 E5 **Kipili** Tanzania
121 O4 **Kipinä** Finland
81 N1 **Kipling Station** Saskatchewan Canada
72 C7 **Kipnuk** Alaska USA
133 E5 **Kípoi** Greece
133 D5 **Kipos, Akra** *cape* Greece
142 D4 **Kippen** Stirling Scotland UK
183 N2 **Kiprino** Russian Federation
160 D6 **Kipushi** Democratic Republic of Congo
222 8 **Kirakira** Solomon Islands
120 G4 **Kiran** Norway
187 E7 **Kirandul** Chhattisgarh India
154 D5 **Kirané** Mali
133 F6 **Kıranköy** Turkey
133 F6 **Kiraz** Turkey
135 X5 **Kirbey** Russian Federation
123 L3 **Kirbla** Estonia
141 G2 **Kirby** North Yorkshire England UK
86 E5 **Kirbyville** Texas USA
124 E3 **Kirchheim** Germany
136 G5 **Kireçli Geçidi** *pass* Turkey
135 W7 **Kirenga** *watercourse* Russian Federation
133 F7 **Kirenis** *watercourse* Turkey
183 L5 **Kirgizskiy Range** *range* Kyrgyzstan
160 B4 **Kiri** Democratic Republic of Congo
222 1 **Kiribati** *country* Oceania
161 H2 **Kiridh** Somalia
136 E5 **Kırıkkafe** *admin. area* Turkey
136 E5 **Kırıkkale** Turkey
123 P3 **Kirishi** Russian Federation
222 1 **Kiritimati** *island* Kiribati
199 I6 **Kiriwina Island** Papua New Guinea
140 D2 **Kirk Michael** Isle of Man UK
142 F5 **Kirk Yetholm** Scottish Borders Scotland UK
133 G6 **Kırka** Turkey
216 E4 **Kirkalocka** WA Australia
142 E6 **Kirkbean** Dumfries and Galloway Scotland UK
140 E2 **Kirkbride** Cumbria England UK
140 D1 **Kirkbride** South Ayrshire Scotland UK
141 H3 **Kirkby** Lincolnshire England UK
141 F2 **Kirkby Stephen** Cumbria England UK
75 O7 **Kirkcaldy** Alberta Canada
142 E4 **Kirkcaldy** Fife Scotland UK
142 D5 **Kirkconnel** Dumfries and Galloway Scotland UK
142 D6 **Kirkcowan** Dumfries and Galloway Scotland UK
142 D6 **Kirkcudbright** Dumfries and Galloway Scotland UK
214 F2 **Kirke** *watercourse* Qld Australia
81 O2 **Kirkella** Manitoba Canada
121 Q2 **Kirkenes** Norway
140 F3 **Kirkham** Lancashire England UK
142 B3 **Kirkibost** Highland Scotland UK
120 inset **Kirkjubæjarklaustur** Iceland
141 F2 **Kirkland** Cumbria England UK
142 D5 **Kirkland** Dumfries and Galloway Scotland UK
73 K9 **Kirkland Lake** Ontario Canada
136 C5 **Kırklareli** *admin. area* Turkey
141 G3 **Kirklees** *admin. area* England UK
82 H6 **Kirklin** Indiana USA
221 D7 **Kirkliston Range** New Zealand
140 D2 **Kirkmaiden** Dumfries and Galloway Scotland UK
142 E4 **Kirkmichael** Perth and Kinross Scotland UK
122 F3 **Kirkøy** *island* Norway
142 E5 **Kirkpatrick** Dumfries and Galloway Scotland UK
141 H3 **Kirkstead** Lincolnshire England UK
82 E6 **Kirksville** Missouri USA
142 F4 **Kirkton** Angus Scotland UK
142 D3 **Kirkton** Highland Scotland UK
142 F3 **Kirkton of Culsalmond** Aberdeenshire Scotland UK
142 E4 **Kirkton of Kingoldrum** Angus Scotland UK
142 F3 **Kirktown of Deskford** Moray Scotland UK
Kirkūk *see* **Karkūk** Iraq
142 F2 **Kirkwall** Orkney Islands Scotland UK
124 D3 **Kirn** Germany
134 L7 **Kirovo-Chepetsk** Russian Federation
182 F1 **Kirovo-Chepetsk** Russian Federation
132 H1 **Kirovohrad** Ukraine
136 D3 **Kirovohrads'ka Oblast'** *admin. area* Ukraine
121 R3 **Kirovsk** Russian Federation
134 K7 **Kirovskaya Oblast'** *admin. area* Russian Federation
182 E4 **Kirovskiy** Russian Federation
123 O2 **Kirovskoye** Russian Federation
142 E4 **Kirriemuir** Angus Scotland UK
131 D9 **Kirrouan** Tunisia
134 L7 **Kirs** Russian Federation
136 E5 **Kirşehir** Turkey
136 E5 **Kirşehir** *admin. area* Turkey
139 F3 **Kirtlington** Oxfordshire England UK
120 L3 **Kiruna** Sweden
59 X2 **Kirwan Escarpment** *range* Antarctica
193 H4 **Kiryū** Japan
122 H4 **Kisa** Sweden
125 J5 **Kisač** Serbia
161 F5 **Kisaki** Tanzania
160 D3 **Kisangani** Democratic Republic of Congo
160 B4 **Kisantete** Democratic Republic of Congo
160 B5 **Kisantu** Democratic Republic of Congo
197 J5 **Kisar** *island* Indonesia
196 C3 **Kisaran** Indonesia
125 I4 **Kisdobsza** Hungary
183 O2 **Kiselevsk** Russian Federation
123 Q2 **Kisel'nya** Russian Federation
160 C6 **Kisenge** Democratic Republic of Congo
123 M4 **Kišezers** *lake* Latvia
179 H4 **Kīsh, Jazireh-ye** *island* Iran
186 D5 **Kishangarh** Rajasthan India
159 E3 **Kishi** Nigeria
76 I3 **Kishiayamweekemow** Manitoba Canada
192 F5 **Kishiga-zaki** *island* Japan
76 I6 **Kishikas** *watercourse* Ontario Canada
Kishinev *see* **Chişinău** Moldova
181 G4 **Kishoreganj** Bangladesh
142 C3 **Kishorn, Loch** *bay* Scotland UK
186 D4 **Kishtwar** Jammu and Kashmir India/Pakistan
160 E5 **Kisi** Tanzania
161 E5 **Kisigo** *watercourse* Tanzania
161 E4 **Kisii** Kenya
135 AK8 **Kiska** *island* Alaska USA
74 K5 **Kiskatinaw** *watercourse* British Columbia Canada
75 V5 **Kiskitto Lake** Manitoba Canada
75 V5 **Kiskittogisu Lake** Manitoba Canada
123 L2 **Kisko** Finland
132 B2 **Kisköre** Hungary
132 A2 **Kiskunhalas** Hungary
133 F6 **Kışla** Turkey
133 F6 **Kışlaköy** Turkey
132 C2 **Kisléta** Hungary
182 D5 **Kislovodsk** Russian Federation
161 G4 **Kismaayo** Somalia
81 O8 **Kismet** Kansas USA
74 G5 **Kispiox** *watercourse* British Columbia Canada
133 C8 **Kissamou, Kolpos** *bay* Greece
158 B3 **Kissidougou** Guinea
87 K7 **Kissimmee, Lake** Florida USA
75 U5 **Kississing Lake** Manitoba Canada
130 C3 **Kißlegg** Germany
132 A2 **Kisszállás** Hungary
132 A2 **Kistelek** Hungary
76 I5 **Kistigan Lake** Manitoba Canada
121 N1 **Kistrand** Norway
161 E4 **Kisumu** Kenya
160 A5 **Kisundi** Democratic Republic of Congo
132 C1 **Kisvárda** Hungary
81 N7 **Kit Carson** Colorado USA
154 E6 **Kita** Mali
192 F5 **Kita-Kyūshū** Japan
178 E6 **Kitāf** Yemen
193 I4 **Kitaibaraki** Japan
161 E3 **Kitale** Kenya
193 I2 **Kitami** Japan
161 E4 **Kitangiri, Lake** *lake* Tanzania
199 I6 **Kitava Island** Papua New Guinea
161 G6 **Kitaya** Tanzania
83 K5 **Kitchener** Ontario Canada
76 L6 **Kitchie Lake** Ontario Canada
77 P7 **Kitchigama** *watercourse* Quebec Canada
76 I5 **Kitchisakik** Manitoba Canada
160 C5 **Kiteba** Democratic Republic of Congo
121 Q5 **Kitee** Finland
121 P5 **Kiteenjärvi** *lake* Finland
132 E4 **Kiten** Bulgaria
160 D5 **Kitendwe** Democratic Republic of Congo
161 E3 **Kitgum** Uganda
74 G5 **Kitimat** British Columbia Canada
74 G5 **Kitimat Ranges** British Columbia Canada
121 P3 **Kitka** Finland
121 M3 **Kitkiöjärvi** Sweden
121 M3 **Kitkiöjoki** Sweden
135 AF9 **Kitoboynyy** Kuril Islands
193 K1 **Kitoboynyy** Russian Federation
109 12 **Kitridge Point** *cape* Barbados
133 C5 **Kítros** Greece
121 Q5 **Kitsi** Finland
120 K3 **Kittajaur** Sweden
218 D3 **Kittakittaooloo, Lake** SA Australia
123 K2 **Kittamaa** *island* Finland
120 I4 **Kittelfjäll** Sweden
121 N3 **Kittilä** Finland
138 D4 **Kittisford** Somerset England UK
80 E3 **Kittitas** Washington USA
123 L2 **Kitula** Finland
161 F4 **Kitumbeine** *volcano* Tanzania
161 F5 **Kitumbini** Tanzania
161 E5 **Kitunda** Tanzania
160 C5 **Kitunga** Democratic Republic of Congo
162 E2 **Kitwe** Zambia
121 O3 **Kiurujärvi** *lake* Finland
121 O5 **Kiuruvesi** Finland
121 O5 **Kiuruvesi** *lake* Finland
74 E5 **Kiusta** British Columbia Canada
121 N3 **Kivalo** *island* Finland
125 M2 **Kivertsi** Ukraine
121 O4 **Kivesjärvi** Finland
121 O4 **Kivesjärvi** *lake* Finland
121 N5 **Kivijärvi** Finland
121 N5 **Kivijärvi** *lake* Finland
121 Q5 **Kivilahti** Finland
121 N3 **Kivilompolo** Finland
160 D4 **Kivu, Lake** *lake* Democratic Republic of Congo
135 AC8 **Kivun, Khrebet** *range* Russian Federation
160 B5 **Kiwaba N'zogi** Angola
199 G6 **Kiwai Island** Papua New Guinea
161 F5 **Kiwawa** Tanzania
220 F5 **Kiwitea** New Zealand
182 E6 **Kiyamaki Dagh** *mountain* Azerbaijan
183 K3 **Kiyevka** Kazakhstan
133 F5 **Kıyıköy** Turkey
184 E5 **Kizil He** *watercourse* Xinjiang Uygur Zizhiqu China
133 F7 **Kızılcabölük** Turkey
133 F7 **Kızılcadağ** Turkey
136 E5 **Kızılırmah** *watercourse* Turkey
182 H3 **Kizil'skoye** Russian Federation
182 C4 **Kiziltashskiy Liman** *lake* Russian Federation
182 E5 **Kizlyar** Russian Federation
182 E5 **Kizlyarskiy Zaliv** *bay* Russian Federation
182 F2 **Kizner** Russian Federation
120 J2 **Kjeldebotn** Norway
120 K2 **Kjerkesjora** Norway
120 J2 **Kjerr** Norway
122 G3 **Kjerret** Norway
120 I3 **Kjerringøy** Norway
120 F5 **Kjerringvåg** Norway
120 J2 **Kjerstad** Norway
121 O1 **Kjøllefjord** Norway
120 J2 **Kjøpsvik** Norway
122 I3 **Kjulaås** Sweden
196 E4 **Klabat, Teluk** *bay* Indonesia
199 F6 **Kladar** Indonesia
124 F1 **Kläden** Germany
197 H2 **Klagan** Malaysia
125 H4 **Klagenfurt** Austria
123 K5 **Klaipėda** Lithuania
123 K4 **Klaipėdos** *admin. area* Lithuania
80 D6 **Klamath** *watercourse* California USA
80 E5 **Klamath Falls** Oregon USA
80 D6 **Klamath Mountains** California USA
197 H3 **Klampo** Indonesia
130 F4 **Klana** Croatia
196 D3 **Klang** Malaysia
210 inset **Klapa Tuju** Cocos (Keeling) Islands Australia
120 K4 **Kläppen** Sweden
120 J5 **Kläppsjö** Sweden
122 G3 **Klarälven** *watercourse* Sweden
197 F5 **Klaten** Indonesia
124 G3 **Klatovy** Czech Republic
120 L2 **Klauvnes** Norway
162 C6 **Klawer** South Africa
74 E5 **Klawock** Alaska USA
158 B3 **Kle** Liberia
125 I1 **Kłecko** Poland
125 J1 **Kleczew** Poland
74 I7 **Kleena Kleene** British Columbia Canada
109 1c **Klein Bonaire** *island* Netherlands Antilles
109 1b **Klein Curaçao** *island* Netherlands Antilles
162 C5 **Klein Karas** Namibia
124 G3 **Kleine Laaber** *watercourse* Germany
120 E5 **Kleive** Norway
158 C2 **Kléla** Mali
132 F1 **Klembivka** Ukraine
130 H4 **Klenje** Serbia
123 O3 **Klenna** Russian Federation
162 E5 **Klerksdorp** South Africa
182 D3 **Kletskaya** Russian Federation
122 H4 **Klevshult** Sweden
124 G1 **Klietz** Germany
132 E4 **Klikach** Bulgaria
136 D2 **Klimavichy** Belarus
132 E4 **Kliment** Bulgaria
123 O2 **Klimovo** Russian Federation
136 E2 **Klimovo** Russian Federation
136 F1 **Klimovsk** Russian Federation
132 B4 **Klina** Kosovo
74 I7 **Klinaklini** *watercourse* British Columbia Canada
136 E2 **Klintsy** Russian Federation
120 J4 **Klippen** Sweden
162 D6 **Klipplaat** South Africa
125 I2 **Klisino** Poland
132 A3 **Kljajićevo** Serbia
123 M5 **Kljavica** Belarus
130 G4 **Ključ** Bosnia and Herzegovina
123 L3 **Klobbfjärden** *bay* Finland
125 J2 **Kłobuck** Poland
125 K2 **Kłoczew** Poland
125 I2 **Kłodzko** Poland
122 F2 **Kløfta** Norway
133 B5 **Klos** Albania
127 I3 **Klosters** Switzerland
78 B2 **Klotz, Lac** *lake* Quebec Canada
222 3 **Kloulklubed** Palau
120 I5 **Klövsjö** Sweden
72 F6 **Kluane Lake** Yukon Territory Canada
120 L4 **Klubbfors** Sweden
125 J2 **Kluczbork** Poland
182 D5 **Klukhoris Ugheltekhili** *pass* Georgia
125 K1 **Klukowo** Poland
74 C2 **Klukshu** Yukon Territory Canada
74 D3 **Klukwan** Alaska USA
197 H4 **Klumpang, Teluk** *bay* Indonesia
197 G6 **Klungkung** Indonesia
132 A3 **Klupci** Serbia
183 M3 **Klyuchi** Russian Federation
120 K4 **Knaften** Sweden
122 F4 **Knebel** Denmark
76 H5 **Knee Lake** Manitoba Canada
75 R5 **Knee Lake** Saskatchewan Canada
75 O6 **Kneehills Creek** Alberta Canada
127 J2 **Knetzgau** Germany
132 D4 **Knezha** Bulgaria
125 I5 **Knežica** Bosnia and Herzegovina
81 N3 **Knife** *watercourse* North Dakota USA
75 X3 **Knife Delta** Manitoba Canada
74 H7 **Knight Inlet** British Columbia Canada
138 D2 **Knighton** Powys Wales UK
130 G4 **Knin** Croatia
216 F7 **Knob, Cape** WA Australia
143 C4 **Knock** Ireland
143 E4 **Knock** Ireland
143 D3 **Knock** Ireland
141 F2 **Knock** Cumbria England UK
141 F2 **Knock Fell** *mountain* England UK
142 C6 **Knockaldie** Dumfries and Galloway Scotland UK
143 C4 **Knockalough** Ireland
142 C2 **Knockan** Highland Scotland UK
140 B3 **Knockaphrumpa** Ireland
140 A2 **Knockarevan** Fermanagh Northern Ireland UK
142 D3 **Knockban** Highland Scotland UK
140 B4 **Knockbane** Ireland
143 F3 **Knockbride** Ireland
142 D5 **Knockburnie** East Ayrshire Scotland UK
143 D3 **Knockcroghery** Ireland
143 C4 **Knockeencreen** Ireland
142 C5 **Knockenkelly** North Ayrshire Scotland UK
143 D4 **Knocklong** Ireland
143 D4 **Knockmealdown Mountains** Ireland
140 B2 **Knockmore** Lisburn Northern Ireland UK
143 D3 **Knockmoyle** Ireland
143 F1 **Knocknacarry** Moyle Northern Ireland UK
143 C2 **Knocknalina** Ireland
142 D5 **Knocknalling** Dumfries and Galloway Scotland UK
140 A3 **Knocks** Ireland
126 F1 **Knokke-Heist** Belgium
122 G2 **Knon** *lake* Sweden
122 G5 **Knösen** *cape* Sweden
140 D1 **Knowe** Dumfries and Galloway Scotland UK
141 F1 **Knowesgate** Northumberland England UK
142 D5 **Knoweside** South Ayrshire Scotland UK
59 U2 **Knowles, Cape** Antarctica
140 F3 **Knowsley** *admin. area* England UK
223 I5 **Knox Atoll** *reef* Marshall Islands
86 B4 **Knox City** Texas USA
59 H2 **Knox Coast** Antarctica
77 W5 **Knox Lake** Newfoundland and Labrador Canada
82 E6 **Knoxville** Iowa USA
87 J3 **Knoxville** Tennessee USA
142 C3 **Knoydart** *cape* Scotland UK
138 D2 **Knucklas** Powys Wales UK
73 M3 **Knud Rasmussen Land** *plain* Greenland
141 F3 **Knutsford** Cheshire England UK
123 P6 **Knyazhitsy** Belarus
162 D6 **Knysna** South Africa
125 L1 **Knyszyn** Poland
193 H1 **Ko, Gora** *mountain* Russian Federation
194 C6 **Ko Adang** *island* Thailand
194 D5 **Ko Chang** Thailand
184 H5 **Ko-hsieh-ko-ta-erh Shui** *watercourse* Xinjiang Uygur Zizhiqu China
193 H5 **Ko-jima** *island* Japan
194 D5 **Ko Kut** Thailand
184 E6 **Ko-le-ching Ho** *watercourse* Xinjiang Uygur Zizhiqu China
186 F5 **Ko-li Ho** *watercourse* Nepal
193 I3 **Ko-numa** *lake* Japan
194 D5 **Ko Phangan** Thailand
194 D5 **Ko Samui** Thailand
194 C5 **Ko Samui** Thailand
189 J2 **Ko-Takara-jima** *island* Japan
192 F6 **Ko-takara-shima** *island* Japan
194 C5 **Ko Tao** Thailand
158 D2 **Koalla** Burkina Faso
161 F5 **Koani** Tanzania
196 E4 **Koba** Indonesia
124 G4 **Kobarid** Slovenia
192 F5 **Kobayashi** Japan
73 O6 **Kobberminebugt** *bay* Greenland
198 C3 **Kobe** Indonesia
193 G4 **Kobe** Japan
161 E2 **Kobecha** Ethiopia
122 G5 **København (Copenhagen)** Denmark
154 E5 **Kobenni** Mauritania
74 K4 **Kobes** British Columbia Canada
189 I3 **Kōbi-sho** *island* Japan
159 H3 **Koblagué** Chad
127 H1 **Koblenz** Germany
157 F5 **K'obo** Ethiopia
160 E3 **Koboko** Uganda
159 I3 **Kobou** *watercourse* Central African Republic
123 P3 **Kobralovo** Russian Federation
198 E5 **Kobroor** *island* Indonesia
125 M1 **Kobryn** Belarus
182 D5 **Kobuleti** Georgia
133 G5 **Kocaali** Turkey
133 G7 **Kocaaliler** Turkey
133 F7 **Kocabaş** Turkey
136 D5 **Kocaeli** *admin. area* Turkey
133 F5 **Kocaeli (İzmit)** Turkey
136 D5 **Kocasu** *watercourse* Turkey
133 E4 **Kocayazı** Turkey
130 G5 **Kočerin** Bosnia and Herzegovina
125 H5 **Kočevje** Slovenia
181 F3 **Koch Bihar** West Bengal India
133 D5 **Kochan** Bulgaria
192 E4 **Koch'ang** South Korea
135 V6 **Kochechum** *watercourse* Russian Federation
124 F4 **Kochelsee** *lake* Germany
135 V7 **Kochenga** Russian Federation
124 E3 **Kocher** *watercourse* Germany
187 D10 **Kochi** Kerala India
192 G5 **Kochi** Japan
182 E2 **Kochkurovo** Russian Federation
125 L2 **Kock** Poland
132 A2 **Kocsér** Hungary
135 Y7 **Kodar, Khrebet** *range* Russian Federation
125 L2 **Kodeń** Poland
72 D7 **Kodiak** Alaska USA
72 D7 **Kodiak Island** Alaska USA
56 U3 **Kodiak Seamount** *underwater feature* Pacific Ocean
134 J6 **Kodima** Russian Federation
187 C7 **Kodinar** Gujarat India
121 U5 **Kodino** Russian Federation
158 E2 **Kodjar** Burkina Faso
159 H3 **Kodo** *watercourse* Central African Republic
160 E2 **Kodok** Sudan
156 E6 **Kodok** Sudan
187 D8 **Kodoli** Maharashtra India
132 F1 **Kodyma** Ukraine
124 B2 **Koekelare** Belgium
186 F5 **Koeripur** Uttar Pradesh India
162 C5 **Koës** Namibia
192 E4 **Koesan** South Korea
84 F4 **Kofa Mountains** Arkansas USA
133 E5 **Kofçaz** Turkey
162 D5 **Koffiefontein** South Africa
125 H4 **Köflach** Austria
158 D3 **Koforidua** Ghana
193 H4 **Kōfu** Japan
193 H4 **Koga** Japan
192 F5 **Koga** Japan
77 Q3 **Kogaluc** *watercourse* Quebec Canada
77 Q3 **Kogaluc, Baie** *bay* Quebec Canada
77 X4 **Kogaluk** *watercourse* Newfoundland and Labrador Canada
219 J2 **Kogan** Qld Australia
122 G5 **Køge Bugt** *bay* Denmark
159 F3 **Kogi** *admin. area* Nigeria
75 V2 **Kognak** *watercourse* Nunavut Canada
158 B2 **Kogon** *watercourse* Guinea
182 I6 **Kogon** Uzbekistan
193 I3 **Kogota** Japan
192 E4 **Kogum-do** *island* South Korea
178 G3 **Kohgīlūyeh Va Būyer Ahmad** *admin. area* Iran
181 H4 **Kohima** Nagaland India
122 E6 **Köhlen** Germany
59 Q1 **Kohler Glacier** Antarctica
59 Q1 **Kohler Range** Antarctica
54 K10 **Kohler Seamount** *underwater feature* Southern Ocean
198 E5 **Kohn** *island* Indonesia
178 E2 **Koi Sanjaq** Iraq
158 B3 **Koidu-Sefadu** Sierra Leone
194 B5 **Koihoa** Andaman and Nicobar Islands India
196 B1 **Koihoa** Tripura India
185 J6 **Koikyim Qu** *watercourse* Qinghai China
199 H4 **Koil Island** Papua New Guinea
164 8a **Koimbani** Comoros
133 C5 **Koímisis** Greece
158 B3 **Koindu** Sierra Leone
121 Q5 **Koitajoki** *watercourse* Finland
121 Q5 **Koitere** *lake* Finland
121 P4 **Koitila** Finland
123 O2 **Koitsanlahti** Finland
121 N3 **Koivu** Finland
121 O5 **Koivujärvi** *lake* Finland
121 P5 **Koivumäki** Finland
121 N4 **Koivuniemi** Finland
121 Q5 **Koivuvaara** Finland
192 F4 **Koje** South Korea
125 I3 **Kojetín** Czech Republic
216 E6 **Kojonup** WA Australia
161 F2 **Koka, Lake** *lake* Ethiopia
83 Q4 **Kokadjo** Maine USA
101 G2 **Kokali Point** *cape* Guyana
123 K3 **Kökar** *island* Finland
182 H4 **Kokaral** Kazakhstan
218 B4 **Kokatha** SA Australia
183 K3 **Kokay** *lake* Kazakhstan
Kokchetav *see* **Kokshetau** Kazakhstan
123 L2 **Kokemäenjoki** *watercourse* Finland
198 F5 **Kokenau** Indonesia
162 C5 **Kokerboom** Namibia
101 G3 **Kokerite** Guyana
187 E10 **Kokkilai** Sri Lanka
121 M5 **Kokkola** Finland
120 L5 **Köklot** Finland
120 L5 **Köklot** *island* Finland
123 M4 **Koknese** Latvia
159 E2 **Koko** Nigeria
199 H6 **Kokoda** Papua New Guinea
82 H6 **Kokomo** Indiana USA
162 D4 **Kokong** Botswana
162 E5 **Kokosi** South Africa
215 J8 **Kokotungo** Qld Australia
158 B2 **Kokoulo** *watercourse* Guinea
183 K3 **Kokpaksor** *lake* Kazakhstan
183 N4 **Kokpekty** Kazakhstan
181 G3 **Kokrajhar** Assam India
192 E3 **Koksan** North Korea
183 K2 **Kokshetau (Kokchetav)** Kazakhstan
126 F1 **Koksijde** Belgium
77 U4 **Koksoak** *watercourse* Quebec Canada
162 E6 **Kokstad** South Africa
77 Q3 **Koktac** *watercourse* Quebec Canada
183 M5 **Koktal** Kazakhstan
183 M4 **Kokterek** Kazakhstan
183 N4 **Koktuma** Kazakhstan
197 I5 **Koku, Tanjung** *cape* Indonesia
192 F5 **Kokubu** Japan
198 E5 **Kola** *island* Indonesia
121 R2 **Kola** Russian Federation
134 H5 **Kola** *watercourse* Russian Federation
127 L4 **Kolan** Croatia
198 C6 **Kolana** Indonesia
187 E7 **Kolar** Chhattisgarh India
187 E9 **Kolar** Karnataka India
121 M3 **Kolari** Finland
125 J4 **Kolárovo** Slovakia
132 E4 **Kolartsi** Bulgaria
120 H5 **Kolåsen** Sweden
181 G4 **Kolasib** Mizoram India
123 Q2 **Kolatsel'ga** Russian Federation
186 C5 **Kolayat** Rajasthan India
57 E2 **Kolbeinsey Ridge** *underwater feature* Norwegian Sea
125 K1 **Kołbiel** Poland
123 Q2 **Kolchanovo** Russian Federation
132 C1 **Kölcse** Hungary
154 D6 **Kolda** Senegal
122 E5 **Kolding** Denmark
160 C4 **Kole** Democratic Republic of Congo
160 D3 **Kole** Democratic Republic of Congo
222 7 **Kolé** Vanuatu
158 B3 **Kolenté** *watercourse* Guinea
120 L4 **Koler** Sweden
123 M3 **Kolga** Estonia
123 M3 **Kolga Laht** *bay* Estonia
122 C2 **Kolgrov** Norway
134 L5 **Kolguyev, Ostrov** *island* Russian Federation
187 D8 **Kolhapur** Maharashtra India
187 C11 **Kolhumadulu Atoll** Maldives
121 P5 **Koli** *mountain* Finland
158 B2 **Koliba** *watercourse* Guinea-Bissau
121 N5 **Kolima** *lake* Finland
125 H2 **Kolín** Czech Republic
127 K2 **Kolinec** Czech Republic
123 L4 **Kolka** Latvia
122 E4 **Kølkær** Denmark
123 L4 **Kolkasrags** *cape* Latvia
187 G6 **Kolkata** West Bengal India
121 O5 **Kolkku** *lake* Finland
123 N1 **Kolkonjärvi** *lake* Finland
121 O4 **Kollaja** Finland
187 D10 **Kollam** Kerala India
121 M3 **Kölmjärv** Sweden
127 H1 **Köln (Cologne)** Germany
125 J1 **Koło** Poland
161 F4 **Kolo** Tanzania
159 G2 **Kolofata** Cameroon
223 12a **Kolofau, Mont** *mountain* Wallis and Futuna
154 E6 **Kolokani** Mali
222 8 **Kolombangara** *island* Solomon Islands
136 F1 **Kolomna** Russian Federation
160 C4 **Kolomonyi** Democratic Republic of Congo
132 D1 **Kolomyya** Ukraine
158 C2 **Kolondieba** Mali
223 10a **Kolonga** Tonga
121 Q4 **Kolongozero, Ozero** *lake* Russian Federation
222 6b **Kolonia** Federated States of Micronesia
197 K3 **Kolorai** *island* Indonesia
197 I5 **Kolowana Watobo, Teluk** *bay* Indonesia
134 R7 **Kolpashevo** Russian Federation
183 N1 **Kolpashevo** Russian Federation
123 P3 **Kolpino** Russian Federation
124 G1 **Kölpinsee** *lake* Germany
133 C7 **Kolpos Epidavrou** *island* Greece
179 K3 **Kolpur** Pakistan
134 I5 **Kol'skiy Poluostrov** *peninsula* Russian Federation
122 I3 **Kolsnaren** *lake* Sweden
122 E3 **Kolsrud** Norway
121 Q2 **Koltakyulya** Russian Federation
120 L3 **Költräsket** *lake* Sweden
108 C4 **Koluel Kayke** Argentina
183 K3 **Koluton** Kazakhstan
121 Q5 **Kolvasozero** Russian Federation
120 G4 **Kolvereid** Norway
121 N1 **Kolvik** Norway
121 R3 **Kolvits, Ozero** *lake* Russian Federation
121 R3 **Kolvitsa** Russian Federation
160 D6 **Kolwezi** Democratic Republic of Congo
135 AG5 **Kolyma** *watercourse* Russian Federation
135 AF4 **Kolymskaya Nizmennost'** *region* Russian Federation
135 AG6 **Kolymskoye Nagor'ye** *mountain* Russian Federation
135 AM5 **Kolyuchinskaya Guba** *cape* Russian Federation
183 N3 **Kolyvan'** Russian Federation
183 M5 **Kol'zhat** Kazakhstan
190 F2 **Koma** *watercourse* Russian Federation
125 K4 **Komádi** Hungary
159 G2 **Komadugu-Gana** *watercourse* Nigeria

121 Q1 **Komagvær** Norway
125 L3 **Komańcza** Poland
135 AI7 **Komandorskiye Ostrova** *island* Russian Federation
76 G7 **Komarno** Manitoba Canada
125 J4 **Komárno** Slovakia
125 J4 **Komárom-Esztergom** *admin. area* Hungary
193 H4 **Komatsu** Japan
197 I5 **Komba** *island* Indonesia
162 C3 **Kombat** Namibia
160 D4 **Kombe** Democratic Republic of Congo
158 D2 **Kombissiri** Burkina Faso
135 AB6 **Komelëk** Russian Federation
196 E4 **Komering** *watercourse* Indonesia
133 D7 **Komi** Greece
130 G5 **Komin** Croatia
132 G2 **Kominternivs'ke** Ukraine
192 F2 **Komissorovka** *watercourse* Russian Federation
130 G5 **Komiža** Croatia
125 J4 **Komló** Hungary
123 P2 **Kommunary** Russian Federation
183 K6 **Kommunizm, Qullai** *mountain* Kyrgyzstan
223 9 **Komo** *island* Fiji
159 G4 **Komo** *watercourse* Gabon
197 H6 **Komodo** *island* Indonesia
158 D3 **Komoé** *watercourse* Côte d'Ivoire
159 G5 **Komono** Congo
199 F6 **Komoran** *island* Indonesia
133 D5 **Komotini** Greece
121 M3 **Kompelusvaara** Sweden
132 A2 **Kömpöc** Hungary
133 B6 **Kompotion** Greece
135 V2 **Komsomolets, Ostrov** *island* Russian Federation
135 AC8 **Komsomol'sk-na-Amure** Russian Federation
191 N2 **Komsomol'sk-na-Amure** Russian Federation
182 G4 **Komsomolskiy** Kazakhstan
182 E4 **Komsomol'skiy** Russian Federation
135 X3 **Komsomol'skoy Pravdy, Ostrova** *island* Russian Federation
133 D5 **Komuniga** Bulgaria
186 F6 **Kon** Uttar Pradesh India
181 I4 **Kon Kyan** Myanmar
194 F4 **Kon Tum** Vietnam
187 F7 **Konada** Andhra Pradesh India
182 E5 **Konagkend** Azerbaijan
183 K7 **Konar** *admin. area* Afghanistan
179 J4 **Konār Bast** Iran
179 I3 **Konārak** Iran
187 G7 **Konarka** Orissa India
133 C4 **Konarsko** Bulgaria
186 E6 **Konch** Uttar Pradesh India
198 D4 **Konda** Indonesia
134 N6 **Konda** *watercourse* Russian Federation
187 E7 **Kondagaon** Chhattisgarh India
135 AF5 **Kondakova** Russian Federation
216 F6 **Kondinin** WA Australia
216 F6 **Kondinin Lake** WA Australia
161 F4 **Kondoa** Tanzania
199 G6 **Kondomirat** Indonesia
135 AC8 **Kondon** Russian Federation
191 M2 **Kondon** Russian Federation
123 R1 **Kondopoga** Russian Federation
183 J7 **Kondoz** Afghanistan
183 J7 **Kondoz** *admin. area* Afghanistan
222 7 **Koné** New Caledonia
134 M6 **Konetsbor** Russian Federation
182 H5 **Köneürgench** Turkmenistan
194 E4 **Kong** *watercourse* Cambodia
159 G3 **Kong** Cameroon
158 D3 **Kong** Côte d'Ivoire
73 P5 **Kong Christian IX Land** *region* Greenland
73 Q4 **Kong Christian X Land** *region* Greenland
73 O5 **Kong Frederik IX Land** *region* Greenland
73 O6 **Kong Frederik VI Kyst** *coast* Greenland
73 Q3 **Kong Frederik VIII Land** *region* Greenland
73 Q4 **Kong Oscars Fjord** Greenland
73 Q3 **Kong Wilhelm Land** *region* Greenland
121 N3 **Köngäs** Finland
121 O4 **Kongasjärvi** *lake* Finland
159 I4 **Kongbo** Central African Republic
121 N5 **Konginkangas** Finland
135 AG6 **Konginskiye Gory** *range* Russian Federation
192 E4 **Kongjiu** South Korea
197 H3 **Kongkemul** *mountain* Indonesia
162 D3 **Kongola** Namibia
160 D5 **Kongolo** Democratic Republic of Congo
158 D2 **Kongoussi** Burkina Faso
122 E3 **Kongsberg** Norway
120 I2 **Kongselva** Norway
120 H4 **Kongsmoen** Norway
134 G3 **Kongsøya** *island* Norway
120 J2 **Kongsvik** Norway
122 G2 **Kongsvinger** Norway
120 F5 **Kongsvoll** Norway
184 E5 **Kongur Shan** *mountain* Xinjiang Uygur Zizhiqu China
77 Q3 **Kongut** *watercourse* Quebec Canada
135 AF7 **Koni, Poluostrov** *peninsula* Russian Federation
183 K6 **Konibodom** Tajikistan
125 K3 **Konieczna** Poland
124 F1 **Königslutter** Germany
124 G4 **Königssee** *lake* Germany
182 J6 **Konimex** Uzbekistan
125 J1 **Konin** Poland
127 H3 **Köniz** Switzerland
130 G5 **Konjic** Bosnia and Herzegovina
162 C5 **Konkiep** *watercourse* Namibia
160 D6 **Konko** Democratic Republic of Congo
158 B2 **Konkoure** *watercourse* Guinea
135 X7 **Konkudera** Russian Federation
154 F6 **Konna** Mali
121 O5 **Konnevesi** Finland
121 O5 **Konnevesi** *bay* Finland
123 M3 **Kõnnu** Estonia
123 P1 **Konnunvaara** Finland
199 J5 **Konogaiang, Mount** Papua New Guinea
101 F3 **Konoro Village** Guyana
123 P5 **Konoshi** Belarus
136 E2 **Konotop** Ukraine
222 3 **Konrai** Palau
158 B2 **Konrokota** Mali
122 I2 **Könsberg** *cape* Sweden
125 K2 **Końskie** Poland
161 F2 **Konso** Ethiopia
125 L1 **Konstantynów** Poland
127 I3 **Konstanz** Germany
159 F2 **Kontagora** Nigeria
159 E2 **Kontagora** *watercourse* Nigeria
123 O1 **Kontiolahti** Finland
121 P5 **Kontkala** Finland
133 D7 **Kontos, Akra** *cape* Greece
121 N3 **Konttajärvi** Finland
121 O4 **Konttila** Finland
136 E6 **Konya** Turkey
136 E5 **Konya** *admin. area* Turkey
132 C4 **Konyavo** Bulgaria
183 L4 **Konyrat** Kazakhstan
183 M5 **Konyrolen** Kazakhstan
183 K2 **Konyukhovo** Kazakhstan
80 H2 **Koocanusa, Lake** Montana USA
218 D2 **Koodnanie, Lake** SA Australia
213 G4 **Koolan Island** WA Australia
214 G3 **Koolatah** Qld Australia
212 D7 **Kooline** WA Australia
216 G4 **Koolkynie** WA Australia
218 D5 **Koomooloo** SA Australia
218 G7 **Koonda** Vic. Australia
218 B5 **Koongawa** SA Australia
213 I5 **Koongie Park** WA Australia
123 N3 **Koosa Järv** *lake* Estonia
80 J7 **Koosharem** Utah USA
218 C4 **Kootaberra** SA Australia
80 G2 **Kootanie Lake** British Columbia Canada
75 N8 **Kootenay** *watercourse* British Columbia Canada
74 M8 **Kootenay Bay** British Columbia Canada
74 M8 **Kootenay Lake** British Columbia Canada
183 L5 **Kopa** *watercourse* Kazakhstan
163 F2 **Kopa** Zambia
186 F5 **Kopaganj** Uttar Pradesh India
122 I5 **Kopań, Jezioro** *lake* Poland
120 inset **Kópanes** *cape* Iceland
133 B6 **Kopani** Greece
133 C5 **Kopanós** Greece
182 E4 **Kopanovka** Russian Federation
132 B4 **Kopaonik** *range* Kosovo
187 D7 **Kopargaon** Maharashtra India
120 inset **Kópasker** Iceland
132 E1 **Kopayhorod** Ukraine
183 M4 **Kopbirlik** Kazakhstan
130 E4 **Koper** Slovenia
182 H6 **Kopet Dag** *range* Iran
122 H3 **Köping** Sweden
132 A4 **Koplik** Albania
120 K5 **Köpmanholmen** Sweden
187 D8 **Koppal** Karnataka India
120 G6 **Koppang** Norway
120 L2 **Koppangen** Norway
121 O2 **Koppelo** Finland
120 G5 **Kopperå** Norway
132 D4 **Koprivets** Bulgaria
133 F6 **Köprüören** Turkey
121 N4 **Kopsa** Finland
132 D1 **Kopychyntsi** Ukraine
133 B5 **Korab** *mountain* Macedonia
182 C2 **Korablino** Russian Federation
77 Q2 **Korak, Baie** *bay* Quebec Canada
133 D7 **Korakas, Akra** *cape* Greece
183 K7 **Korān Va Monjān** Afghanistan
154 F5 **Korarou, Lac** *lake* Mali
187 E7 **Koratla** Andhra Pradesh India
187 F6 **Korba** Chhattisgarh India
155 I1 **Korba** Tunisia
124 E2 **Korbach** Germany
216 F5 **Korbel** WA Australia
132 C3 **Korbovo** Serbia
130 G4 **Korčanica** Bosnia and Herzegovina
133 B5 **Korçë** Albania
130 G5 **Korčula** *island* Croatia
182 E7 **KordestĀn** *admin. area* Iran
132 G2 **Kordon** Ukraine
192 D3 **Korea Bay** North Korea
192 F4 **Korea Strait** Japan
198 D5 **Koreare** Indonesia
121 R4 **Korelaksha** Russian Federation
157 F5 **Korem** Ethiopia
155 H6 **Korén Adoua** *watercourse* Niger
121 O4 **Korentokylä** Finland
134 M6 **Korepino** Russian Federation
125 I2 **Korfantów** Poland
133 F5 **Körfez** Turkey
59 T1 **Korff Ice Rise** Antarctica
133 C7 **Korfos** Greece
120 H3 **Korgen** Norway
158 C3 **Korhogo** Côte d'Ivoire
186 B6 **Kori Creek** Gujarat India
123 N2 **Koria** Finland
198 E4 **Korido** Indonesia
154 F5 **Korientzé** Mali
154 F5 **Korienzé, Lac** *lake* Mali
101 G3 **Korikori, Kaap** *cape* Suriname
133 C7 **Korinthos (Corinth)** Greece
133 B5 **Korisós** Greece
133 D7 **Korissia** Greece
130 H5 **Korita** Bosnia and Herzegovina
193 I4 **Kōriyama** Japan
121 Q5 **Korkeakangas** Finland
178 F2 **Korkī** Iran
182 I2 **Korkino** Russian Federation
135 AF6 **Korkodon** Russian Federation
135 AG5 **Korkodon** *watercourse* Russian Federation
184 H4 **Korla** Xinjiang Uygur Zizhiqu China
184 G5 **Korla** Xinjiang Uygur Zizhiqu China
101 H4 **Kormontibo** French Guiana
183 N2 **Kornilovo** Russian Federation
182 E3 **Kornyeevka** Russian Federation
158 C3 **Koro** Côte d'Ivoire
223 9 **Koro** *island* Fiji
121 M5 **Koro** Finland
154 F6 **Koro** Mali
223 9a **Koro Sea** Fiji
155 J5 **Koro Toro** Chad
156 B4 **Koro Toro** Chad
199 G5 **Koroba** Papua New Guinea
77 W3 **Koroc** *watercourse* Quebec Canada
123 P5 **Korolëvshchina** Russian Federation
223 9a **Korolevu** Fiji
159 H2 **Korom, Bahr** *watercourse* Chad
195 J6 **Koronadal** Philippines
133 B7 **Koroni** Greece
222 3 **Koror** Palau
222 3 **Koror** *island* Palau
125 K4 **Körös** *watercourse* Hungary
199 G5 **Korosameri** *watercourse* Papua New Guinea
136 D2 **Korosten'** Ukraine
223 9a **Korotasere** Fiji
199 J5 **Korovou** Solomon Islands
121 N5 **Korpi** Finland
123 N2 **Korpijärvi** *lake* Finland
121 M3 **Korpilombolo** Sweden
121 Q5 **Korpisel'kya** Russian Federation
121 P5 **Korpivaara** Finland
123 K2 **Korpo** Finland
123 K2 **Korpo** *island* Finland
121 N5 **Korppinen** Finland
135 AD9 **Korsakov** Russian Federation
193 I1 **Korsakov** Russian Federation
125 M2 **Korshev** Ukraine
135 X7 **Korshunovo** Russian Federation
120 J2 **Korsnes** Norway
122 F5 **Korsør** Denmark
120 L4 **Korsträsk** Sweden
120 H5 **Korsvattnet** *lake* Sweden
120 G5 **Korsvegen** Norway
156 E5 **Kortala** Sudan
121 P4 **Kortesalmi** Finland
121 M5 **Kortesjärvi** Finland
156 E4 **Korti** Sudan
126 F1 **Kortrijk** Belgium
121 P5 **Kortteinen** Finland
133 F7 **Koruköy** Turkey
121 P4 **Korvua** Finland
121 P4 **Korvuanjärvi** *lake* Finland
135 AJ6 **Koryakskoye Nagor'ye** *range* Russian Federation
134 K6 **Koryazhma** Russian Federation
133 E7 **Kos** Greece
133 E7 **Kos** *island* Greece
135 AL6 **Kosa Russkaya Koshka** *cape* Russian Federation
187 C7 **Kosamba** Gujarat India
192 E3 **Kosan** North Korea
125 I1 **Kościan** Poland
125 J1 **Kościelec** Poland
86 G4 **Kosciusko** Mississippi USA
123 N4 **Kose** Estonia
123 M3 **Kose** Estonia
133 B5 **Kosel** Macedonia
133 E6 **Köseler** Turkey
122 G4 **Kösen** *lake* Sweden
183 O3 **Kosh-Agach** Russian Federation
156 E3 **Kosha** Sudan
182 G4 **Koshkar** Kazakhstan
82 G5 **Koshkonong, Lake** Wisconsin USA
125 K3 **Košice** Slovakia
125 K3 **Košický** *admin. area* Slovakia
183 N2 **Kosikha** Russian Federation
120 H5 **Kosjön** *lake* Sweden
120 M5 **Koskenkorva** Finland
121 N4 **Koskenkylä** Finland
121 P4 **Koskenmäki** Finland
121 O2 **Koskenniska** Finland
121 N5 **Koskenpää** Finland
123 Q2 **Kos'kovo** Russian Federation
121 M5 **Koskue** Finland
134 K6 **Koslan** Russian Federation
133 C7 **Kosmas** Greece
182 J6 **Koson** Uzbekistan
132 B4 **Kosovo** *country* Europe
132 B4 **Kosovo Polje** *region* Kosovo
132 B4 **Kosovska Mitrovica** Kosovo
222 6 **Kosrae** *admin. area* Federated States of Micronesia
222 6 **Kosrae** *island* Federated States of Micronesia
86 C5 **Kosse** Texas USA
158 C3 **Kossou, Lac de** *lake* Côte d'Ivoire
122 H4 **Kosta** Sweden
125 I5 **Kostajnica** Bosnia and Herzegovina
182 I2 **Kostanay** Kazakhstan
182 I3 **Kostanayskaya Oblast'** *admin. area* Kazakhstan
125 H5 **Kostanjevica** Slovenia
122 F3 **Koster** *island* Sweden
156 E5 **Kosti** Sudan
134 S5 **Kostino** Russian Federation
132 H2 **Kostomarovka** Ukraine
121 Q4 **Kostomuksha** Russian Federation
121 P4 **Kostonjärvi** *lake* Finland
136 C2 **Kostopil'** Ukraine
123 O4 **Kostorovo** Russian Federation
123 O5 **Kostritsa** Belarus
134 J7 **Kostroma** Russian Federation
182 D1 **Kostroma** Russian Federation
182 E1 **Kostromskaya Oblast'** *admin. area* Russian Federation
158 E3 **Kosubosu** Nigeria
121 P5 **Kosula** Finland
122 I5 **Koszalin** Poland
125 K2 **Koszyce** Poland
179 K4 **Kot Diji** Pakistan
187 E8 **Kota** Andhra Pradesh India
187 F6 **Kota** Chhattisgarh India
186 D6 **Kota** Rajasthan India
186 F6 **Kota** Uttar Pradesh India
197 H2 **Kota Belud** Malaysia
196 D2 **Kota Bharu** Malaysia
197 H2 **Kota Kinabalu** Malaysia
197 F3 **Kota Samarahan** Malaysia
196 D3 **Kota Tinggi** Malaysia
196 E5 **Kotaagung** Indonesia
197 F4 **Kotabaru** Indonesia
197 H4 **Kotabaru** Indonesia
196 C3 **Kotabaru** Indonesia
197 G4 **Kotabesi** Indonesia
196 E5 **Kotabumi** Indonesia
198 C3 **Kotabunan** Indonesia
121 N5 **Kotala** Finland
121 P3 **Kotala** Finland
196 C3 **Kotanopan** Indonesia
196 D3 **Kotapinang** Indonesia
196 D3 **Kotatengah** Indonesia
197 F4 **Kotawaringin** Indonesia
197 F4 **Kotawaringin, Teluk** *bay* Indonesia
74 K3 **Kotcho Lake** British Columbia Canada
182 E1 **Kotel'nich** Russian Federation
182 D4 **Kotel'nikovo** Russian Federation
135 AC3 **Kotel'nyy, Ostrov** *island* Russian Federation
136 E2 **Kotel'va** Ukraine
186 F6 **Kothi** Madhya Pradesh India
161 E3 **Kotido** Uganda
135 AD9 **Kotikovo** Russian Federation
121 O4 **Kotila** Finland
121 P4 **Kotiranta** Finland
123 N2 **Kotka** Finland
123 Q2 **Kotkozero** Russian Federation
134 K6 **Kotlas** Russian Federation
72 C6 **Kotlik** Alaska USA
127 L3 **Kotlje** Slovenia
161 F3 **Kotome** *watercourse* Kenya
130 H4 **Kotorsko** Bosnia and Herzegovina
158 D3 **Kotouba** Côte d'Ivoire
182 D3 **Kotovo** Russian Federation
182 D3 **Kotovsk** Russian Federation
187 F7 **Kotpad** Chhattisgarh India
186 D5 **Kotputli** Rajasthan India
186 C6 **Kotra** Gujarat India
187 D7 **Kotra** Madhya Pradesh India
186 E6 **Kotra** Uttar Pradesh India
187 E8 **Kottagudem** Andhra Pradesh India
187 D10 **Kottayam** Kerala India
159 I3 **Kotto** *watercourse* Central African Republic
72 C5 **Kotzebue** Alaska USA
72 C5 **Kotzebue Sound** Alaska USA
159 H3 **Kouango** Central African Republic
158 F5 **Kouango, Pointe** Gabon
222 7 **Kouari** New Caledonia
158 B2 **Koubia** Guinea
158 D2 **Koudougou** Burkina Faso
158 D2 **Kouéré** Burkina Faso
155 I6 **Koufey** Niger
133 D7 **Koufonisi** *island* Greece
159 G5 **Kouilou** *admin. area* Congo
159 H3 **Kouki** Central African Republic
159 H3 **Koukourou** Central African Republic
159 I3 **Koukourou** *watercourse* Central African Republic
159 G5 **Koulamoutou** Gabon
159 I2 **Koulba** Chad
156 C5 **Koulbo** Chad
154 E6 **Koulikoro** Mali
154 E6 **Koulikoro** *admin. area* Mali
158 B2 **Kouloun** *watercourse* Guinea
159 G3 **Koum** Cameroon
159 H3 **Kouma** *watercourse* Central African Republic
222 7 **Koumac** New Caledonia
215 J6 **Koumala** Qld Australia
159 G4 **Koumameyong** Gabon
101 I3 **Koumarouman, Pointe** *cape* French Guiana
158 B2 **Koumbia** Guinea
159 I3 **Koumou** *watercourse* Central African Republic
159 H3 **Koumra** Chad
154 D6 **Koundian** Mali
158 D2 **Koundougou** Burkina Faso
154 D6 **Koungheul** Senegal
154 D6 **Kounkané** Senegal
86 D5 **Kountze** Texas USA
191 K4 **Kouqian** Jilin China
158 B2 **Kouragué** Mali
158 C3 **Kourai** *watercourse* Guinea
155 G6 **Kouré** Niger
189 J3 **Kouri-shima** *island* Japan
130 F1 **Kouřim** Czech Republic
101 H3 **Kourou** French Guiana
154 D5 **Koûroudjél** Mauritania
158 D2 **Kourouma** Burkina Faso
158 D2 **Koury** Mali
154 D6 **Koussanar** Senegal
154 D6 **Koussane** Senegal
155 J6 **Kousséri** Chad
133 D7 **Koutalás** Greece
158 C2 **Koutiala** Mali
121 O4 **Kouva** Finland
123 N2 **Kouvola** Finland
158 C2 **Kouya** *watercourse* Guinea
159 H5 **Kouyou** *watercourse* Congo
130 G5 **Kovači** Bosnia and Herzegovina
133 G7 **Kovada Gölü** *lake* Turkey
127 L2 **Kovářov** Czech Republic
121 R3 **Kovda** Russian Federation
121 Q3 **Kovdor** Russian Federation
121 Q3 **Kovdozero, Ozero** *lake* Russian Federation
123 P1 **Kovero** Finland
125 K4 **Kövesd** Romania
77 Q2 **Kovik** *watercourse* Quebec Canada
77 Q2 **Kovik, Baie** *bay* Quebec Canada
132 B3 **Kovilj** Serbia
187 D10 **Kovilpatti** Tamil Nadu India
132 B3 **Kovin** Serbia
121 M5 **Kovjoki** Finland
122 H1 **Kövra** Sweden
135 AH6 **Kovrizhka** Russian Federation
182 D2 **Kovrov** Russian Federation
182 D2 **Kovylkino** Russian Federation
125 J1 **Kowal** Poland
123 L5 **Kowale Oleckie** Poland
214 F3 **Kowanyama** Qld Australia
125 H2 **Kowary** Poland
189 G4 **Kowloon** Hong Kong China
179 K3 **Kowndalān** Afghanistan
179 M2 **Kowtal-e Ershād Owīn** *pass* Pakistan
179 L2 **Kowtal-e Khāvāk** *pass* Afghanistan
179 L2 **Kowtal-e Morgh** *pass* Afghanistan
179 K2 **Kowtal-e Shībar** *pass* Afghanistan
179 K2 **Kowtal-e Wonay** *pass* Afghanistan
182 J3 **Koybaghar Koli** *lake* Kazakhstan
133 F7 **Köyceğiz Gölü** *lake* Turkey
134 J5 **Koyda** Russian Federation
121 M5 **Köyhäjoki** Finland
140 B4 **Koyle** Ireland
182 G6 **Koymatdag, Gory** *range* Turkmenistan
121 O3 **Köyry** *lake* Finland
182 C4 **Koysug** Russian Federation
72 C6 **Koyuk** Alaska USA
72 D5 **Koyukuk** *watercourse* Alaska USA
133 E6 **Koyuneli** Turkey
133 E6 **Koyuneri** Turkey
121 Q4 **Koyvas, Ozero** *lake* Russian Federation
133 F7 **Kozağacı** Turkey
133 G5 **Kozan** Turkey
136 E6 **Kozan** Turkey
133 B5 **Kozani** Greece
157 G5 **Kozar, Ras** *cape* Eritrea
130 H2 **Kozelník** Slovakia
182 I4 **Kozhabakha** Kazakhstan
187 D9 **Kozhikode** Kerala India
121 U5 **Kozhozero, Ozero** *lake* Russian Federation
121 U5 **Kozhposëlok** Russian Federation
125 K2 **Kozienice** Poland
133 F7 **Kozlar** Turkey
182 D3 **Kozlovka** Russian Federation
133 G5 **Kozlu** Turkey
133 F6 **Kozluca** Turkey
136 G5 **Kozluk** Turkey
125 J2 **Koźminek** Poland
182 E2 **Koz'modem'yansk** Russian Federation
132 C4 **Koznitsa** *mountain* Bulgaria
132 D1 **Kozova** Ukraine
193 H4 **Kōzu-shima** *island* Japan
130 H2 **Kozy** Poland
133 E5 **Kozyörük** Turkey
132 G2 **Kozyrka** Ukraine
158 E2 **Kpako** *watercourse* Benin
158 E3 **Kpalimé** Togo
194 C5 **Kra Buri** Thailand
106 F6 **Krabbé** Argentina
122 I3 **Krabbfjärden** *bay* Sweden
123 N4 **Krabi** Estonia
194 C5 **Krabi** *admin. area* Thailand
194 E4 **Krâchéh** Cambodia
120 J4 **Kraddsele** Sweden
132 B3 **Kragujevac** Serbia
196 E5 **Krakatau** *volcano* Indonesia
120 K5 **Kråken** Sweden
123 J4 **Kräklingbo** Sweden
120 I3 **Kråkmo** Norway
120 H4 **Kråknes** Norway
125 L3 **Krakovets'** Ukraine
125 J2 **Kraków** Poland
197 G5 **Kraksaan** Indonesia
130 G1 **Králíky** Czech Republic
132 B4 **Kraljevo** Serbia
125 H2 **Královéhradecký Kraj** *admin. area* Czech Republic
136 F3 **Kramators'k** Ukraine
76 E8 **Kramer** North Dakota USA
84 D3 **Kramer Junction** California USA
120 J5 **Kramfors** Sweden
121 Q1 **Krampenes** Norway
133 B6 **Kranea** Greece
196 B2 **Kranji Reservoir** Singapore
125 G4 **Kranjska Gora** Slovenia
81 Q4 **Kranzburg** South Dakota USA
72 B4 **Krasin, Zaliv** *bay* Russian Federation
123 N5 **Krāslava** Latvia
123 N4 **Krāslavas** *admin. area* Latvia
123 N5 **Krasnaye** Belarus
125 M3 **Krasne** Ukraine
125 L2 **Kraśnik** Poland
191 I2 **Krasnikamensk** Russian Federation
130 F4 **Krasno Polje** Croatia
136 F3 **Krasnoarmeysk** Ukraine
182 C4 **Krasnodar** Russian Federation
182 C4 **Krasnodarskiy Kray** *admin. area* Russian Federation
123 P3 **Krasnofarfornyy** Russian Federation
193 I1 **Krasnogorsk** Russian Federation
134 M7 **Krasnokamsk** Russian Federation
182 G1 **Krasnokamsk** Russian Federation
132 F1 **Krasnopil'** Ukraine
134 R5 **Krasnosel'kup** Russian Federation
183 N3 **Krasnoshchekovo** Russian Federation
121 T3 **Krasnoshchel'ye** Russian Federation
134 N7 **Krasnotur'insk** Russian Federation
182 H2 **Krasnoufimsk** Russian Federation
134 N7 **Krasnoural'sk** Russian Federation
134 M6 **Krasnovishersk** Russian Federation
183 M2 **Krasnovishnevoye** *lake* Russian Federation
182 G6 **Krasnovodskiy, Mys** *cape* Turkmenistan
182 G6 **Krasnovodskoye Plato** Turkmenistan
134 T7 **Krasnoyarsk** Russian Federation
183 Q2 **Krasnoyarsk** Russian Federation
135 U6 **Krasnoyarskiy Kray** *admin. area* Russian Federation
183 P2 **Krasnoyarskoy Vodokhranilishche** *lake* Russian Federation
123 P5 **Krasnoye** Russian Federation
123 O4 **Krasnoye** Russian Federation
182 C4 **Krasnoye** Russian Federation
135 AJ6 **Krasnoye, Ozero** *lake* Russian Federation
123 P3 **Krasnoye Selo** Russian Federation
132 H2 **Krasnoznamenka** Ukraine
123 L5 **Krasnoznamensk** Russian Federation
125 L2 **Krasnystaw** Poland
190 F2 **Krasnyy Chikoy** Russian Federation
182 E3 **Krasnyy Kut** Russian Federation
123 P4 **Krasnyy Luch** Russian Federation
136 F3 **Krasnyy Luch** Ukraine
183 L4 **Krasnyy Oktyabr'** Kazakhstan
182 D3 **Krasnyy Yar** Russian Federation
182 E1 **Krasnyye Baki** Russian Federation
133 B5 **Krastë** Albania
132 E1 **Krasyliv** Ukraine
199 H5 **Kratke Range** Papua New Guinea
199 G4 **Krau** Indonesia
59 X2 **Kraul Mountains** Antarctica
130 H2 **Kravaře** Czech Republic
86 D3 **Krebs** Oklahoma USA
123 P3 **Krechevitsy** Russian Federation
127 H1 **Krefeld** Germany
123 M5 **Krekenava** Lithuania
136 E3 **Kremenchuk** Ukraine
136 E3 **Kremenchuts' Ka Vodoskhovyshche** *lake* Ukraine
123 N5 **Kremenets** Belarus
136 F3 **Kremennaya** Ukraine
75 P8 **Kremlin** Montana USA
133 C7 **Kremmidi, Akra** *cape* Greece
81 L6 **Kremmling** Colorado USA
132 A4 **Kremna** Serbia
130 F2 **Křemže** Czech Republic
123 O4 **Krenëvo** Russian Federation
72 C8 **Krenitzin Islands** Alaska USA
85 L3 **Kress** Texas USA
135 AD5 **Krest-Mayor** Russian Federation
72 B5 **Kresta, Zaliv** Russian Federation
134 L5 **Krestovka** Russian Federation
135 Y6 **Krestyakh** Russian Federation
123 K5 **Kretinga** Lithuania
124 F4 **Kreuth** Germany
159 F4 **Kribi** Cameroon
85 K3 **Krider** New Mexico USA
127 L3 **Krieglach** Austria
133 B6 **Krikello** Greece
123 O3 **Krikkovo** Russian Federation
159 H3 **Krim-Krim** Chad
124 G4 **Krimml** Austria
125 H2 **Křinec** Czech Republic
133 C8 **Krios, Akrotirio** *cape* Greece
187 E8 **Krishna** *watercourse* Andhra Pradesh India
187 D8 **Krishnagiri** Andhra Pradesh India
187 E9 **Krishnagiri** Tamil Nadu India
186 G6 **Krishnanagar** West Bengal India
122 D3 **Kristiansand** Norway
120 E5 **Kristiansund** Norway
120 K4 **Kristineberg** Sweden
122 H3 **Kristinehamn** Sweden
120 L5 **Kristinestad/Kristiinankaupunki** Finland
133 C5 **Krithiá** Greece
133 D8 **Kriti (Crete)** *admin. area* Greece
133 D7 **Kritiko Pelago (Sea of Crete)** *sea* Europe
133 D8 **Kritsa** Greece
123 L5 **Kriūkai** Lithuania
132 C4 **Kriva Reka** *watercourse* Macedonia
130 H2 **Kriváň** Slovakia
121 R4 **Krivoy Porog** Russian Federation
121 T6 **Krivtsy** Russian Federation
130 G2 **Křižanov** Czech Republic
130 G3 **Križevci** Croatia
130 F4 **Križpolje** Croatia
130 F4 **Krk** *island* Croatia
130 G4 **Krnjeuša** Bosnia and Herzegovina
125 I2 **Krnov** Czech Republic
125 I2 **Krobia** Poland
122 E2 **Krøderen** *lake* Norway
125 I4 **Krog** Slovenia
121 Q1 **Krognes** Norway
158 C4 **Krohnwodoke** Liberia
120 I4 **Kroken** Norway
120 J5 **Krokfors** Sweden
120 L3 **Krokfors** Sweden
120 I5 **Kroknäs** Sweden
120 I5 **Krokom** Sweden
197 F3 **Krokong** Malaysia
122 J5 **Krokowa** Poland
120 inset **Króksfjarðarnes** Iceland
120 L4 **Kroksjö** Sweden
120 J4 **Kroksjö** Sweden
123 K5 **Krokų Lankos ežeras** *lake* Lithuania
120 L3 **Krokvik** Sweden
136 E2 **Krolevets** Ukraine
130 G2 **Kroměříž** Czech Republic
122 H4 **Krön** *lake* Sweden
127 J1 **Kronach** Germany
75 S7 **Kronau** Saskatchewan Canada
194 D5 **Krŏng Kaôh Kŏng** Cambodia
122 H4 **Kronoberg** *admin. area* Sweden
121 M5 **Kronoby** Finland
135 AH8 **Kronotskiy, Mys** *cape* Russian Federation
135 AH8 **Kronotskiy Poluostrov** *peninsula* Russian Federation
135 AH8 **Kronotskiy Zaliv** *bay* Russian Federation
135 AH8 **Kronotskoye Ozero** *lake* Russian Federation
73 R2 **Kronprins Christian Land** *plain* Greenland
73 P5 **Kronprins Frederik Bjerge** *mountains* Greenland
123 O2 **Kronshtadt** Russian Federation
162 E5 **Kroonstad (Maokeng)** South Africa
182 C4 **Kropotkin** Russian Federation
122 E5 **Kropp** Germany
125 K3 **Krosno** Poland
120 F6 **Krossbu** Norway
125 I2 **Krotoszyn** Poland
125 H5 **Krško** Slovenia
123 O5 **Krucha** Belarus
125 I1 **Krucz** Poland
135 AC9 **Kruglikovo** Russian Federation
193 G1 **Kruglikovo** Russian Federation
123 O5 **Kruhlaye** Belarus
196 D5 **Krui** Indonesia
162 D6 **Kruisfontein** South Africa
133 A5 **Krujë** Albania
123 K5 **Kruklanki** Poland
198 E4 **Krumasye** Indonesia
124 E4 **Krumbach** Germany
124 F3 **Krumbach** Germany
124 F4 **Krün** Germany
194 D4 **Krung Thep (Bangkok)** Thailand
130 H5 **Krupac** Bosnia and Herzegovina
125 J3 **Krupinská planina** *region* Slovakia
132 E4 **Krushevets** Bulgaria
124 G2 **Krušné Hory** *range* Czech Republic
132 D4 **Krŭstets** Bulgaria
131 H5 **Krute** Montenegro
130 B3 **Kruth** France
135 AG7 **Krutogorovo** Russian Federation
120 I4 **Krutsjön** *lake* Sweden
120 I4 **Krutvatnet** *lake* Norway
135 AF9 **Kruzenshterna, Proliv** *strait* Russian Federation
74 D4 **Kruzof Island** Alaska USA
125 M2 **Krylov** Ukraine
50 O8 **Krylov Seamount** *underwater feature* Atlantic Ocean
123 K5 **Krylovo** Russian Federation
182 C4 **Krylovskaya** Russian Federation
136 E4 **Krym, Autonomous Republic of** *admin. area* Ukraine
182 C5 **Krymsk** Russian Federation
132 B1 **Krynica** Poland
125 L1 **Krynki** Poland
133 B6 **Kryoneri** Greece
122 G2 **Kryptjärn** Sweden
136 E3 **Kryvyy Rih** Ukraine
132 F1 **Kryzhopil'** Ukraine
125 I2 **Krzelów** Poland
125 J2 **Krzepice** Poland
125 J2 **Krzeszowice** Poland
125 L3 **Krzywcza** Poland
155 F3 **Ksabi** Algeria
154 F2 **Ksabi** Morocco
155 G1 **Ksar el Boukhari** Algeria
155 G2 **Ksar el Hirane** Algeria
154 E2 **Ksar el Kebir** Morocco
181 F3 **Ksham Chuu** *watercourse* Xizang Zizhiqu China
131 D9 **Ksour-Essaf** Tunisia
182 D2 **Kstovo** Russian Federation
156 D5 **Ku, Wādī El** *watercourse* Sudan
184 E5 **Ku-shan Ho** *watercourse* Xinjiang Uygur Zizhiqu China
196 C2 **Kuah** Malaysia
197 G2 **Kuala Belait** Brunei
196 D2 **Kuala Krai** Malaysia
196 D2 **Kuala Lipis** Malaysia
196 D3 **Kuala Lumpur** Malaysia
196 D3 **Kuala Lumpur** *admin. area* Malaysia
197 G2 **Kuala Penyu** Malaysia
196 D3 **Kuala Rompin** Malaysia
196 D2 **Kuala Terengganu** Malaysia
197 G4 **Kualakapuas** Indonesia
197 G4 **Kualakuayan** Indonesia
197 G4 **Kualakurun** Indonesia
196 C2 **Kualalangsa** Indonesia
197 G4 **Kualapembuang** Indonesia
197 G4 **Kualasampit** Indonesia
196 C2 **Kualasimpang** Indonesia
196 D4 **Kualatungkal** Indonesia
197 H2 **Kuamut** Malaysia
191 I5 **Kuancheng** Hebei China
198 B3 **Kuandang, Teluk** *bay* Indonesia
191 J5 **Kuandian** Liaoning China
196 D3 **Kuantan** Malaysia
178 E7 **Ku'aydinah** Yemen
214 B2 **Kub-O-Wer Hill** NT Australia
182 C4 **Kuban** *watercourse* Russian Federation
132 G2 **Kubanka** Ukraine
120 K5 **Kubbe** Sweden
159 I2 **Kubbum** Sudan
156 C5 **Kubbum** Sudan
122 G5 **Kubitzer Bodden** *bay* Germany
123 O5 **Kublichy** Belarus
199 H5 **Kubor Range** Papua New Guinea
197 G6 **Kubu** Indonesia
196 F4 **Kubu** Indonesia
197 G3 **Kubuang** Indonesia
197 G3 **Kubumesaai** Indonesia
199 H6 **Kubuna** Papua New Guinea
133 A5 **Kuç** Albania
186 D5 **Kuchaman City** Rajasthan India
184 G4 **Kuche** Xinjiang Uygur Zizhiqu China
134 J5 **Kuchema** Russian Federation
186 C5 **Kuchera** Rajasthan India
56 R1 **Kucherov Terrace** *underwater feature* Arctic Ocean
194 E3 **Kuchinarai** Thailand
196 F3 **Kuching** Malaysia
192 F5 **Kuchino-shima** *island* Japan
192 F5 **Kuchinoerabu-jima** *island* Japan
124 G4 **Kuchl** Austria
183 M3 **Kuchukskoye** *lake* Russian Federation
132 G2 **Kuchurhans'ke Vodoskhovyshche** *lake* Ukraine
120 inset **Kúðafljót** *watercourse* Iceland
187 C8 **Kudal** Maharashtra India
196 F4 **Kudangan** Indonesia
196 D3 **Kudap** Indonesia
197 H2 **Kudat** Malaysia
156 E4 **Kudayn** Sudan
198 E5 **Kudene** Indonesia
123 O4 **Kudever'** Russian Federation
218 E5 **Kudgee** NSW Australia
123 L5 **Kudirkos Naumiestis** Lithuania
187 D8 **Kudligi** Karnataka India
187 D9 **Kudremukh** *mountain* Karnataka India
132 G2 **Kudryavtsevka** Ukraine
159 F3 **Kudu** Nigeria
197 F5 **Kudus** Indonesia
189 I4 **Kueishan Tao** *island* Taiwan China
216 F6 **Kuender** WA Australia
130 E3 **Kufstein** Austria
73 K5 **Kugaaruk** Nunavut Canada
72 H5 **Kugluktuk** Nunavut Canada
72 F5 **Kugmallit Bay** Northwest Territories Canada
77 O4 **Kugong Island** Nunavut Canada
121 O4 **Kuha** Finland
179 J4 **Kūhak** Iran
178 F2 **Kūhdasht** Iran
179 H4 **Kūhej** Iran
182 H7 **Kūhhā-ye Kūhhā Jaftāy** *range* Iran
178 G3 **Kūhhā-Ye Zāgros** Iran
183 K6 **Kūhistoni Badakhshon** *admin. area* Tajikistan
123 M2 **Kuhmajärvi** *lake* Finland
121 P4 **Kuhmo** Finland
199 H5 **Kui** Papua New Guinea
194 C4 **Kui Buri** Thailand
121 N5 **Kuikka** Finland
90 C4 **Kuikuina** Nicaragua
162 C4 **Kuiseb** *watercourse* Namibia
162 C2 **Kuito** Angola
184 G4 **Kuitun** Xinjiang Uygur Zizhiqu China
74 D4 **Kuiu Island** Alaska USA
121 O2 **Kuivajärvi** *lake* Finland
121 M3 **Kuivakangas** Sweden
121 N4 **Kuivaniemi** Finland
121 M5 **Kuivasjärvi** *lake* Finland
121 N5 **Kuivasmäki** Finland
123 L3 **Kuivastu** Estonia
125 J1 **Kujawsko-Pomorskie** *admin. area* Poland
179 K4 **Kukari Bent** Pakistan
182 D3 **Kukarki** Russian Federation
121 Q3 **Kukas, Ozero** *lake* Russian Federation
159 G2 **Kukawa** Nigeria
216 F6 **Kukerin** WA Australia
132 B4 **Kukës** Albania
123 M2 **Kukkia** *lake* Finland
121 N5 **Kukko** Finland
125 K1 **Kuklin** Poland
84 inset **Kukuihaele** Hawai'i USA
76 J8 **Kukukus Lake** Ontario Canada
158 B3 **Kukuna** Sierra Leone
159 F4 **Kula** Nigeria
130 H4 **Kula** Serbia
181 G3 **Kula Kangri** *mountain* Bhutan
196 C3 **Kulabu, Gunung** *mountain* Indonesia
179 L3 **Kulachi** Pakistan
182 F4 **Kulagino** Kazakhstan
196 D3 **Kulai** Malaysia
179 J4 **Kūlakī** Iran
133 G5 **Kulaklı** Turkey
161 F3 **Kulal, Mount** *mountain* Kenya
182 F5 **Kulaly, Ostrov** *island* Kazakhstan
160 C4 **Kulampanga** Democratic Republic of Congo
182 G5 **Kulandag** *range* Turkmenistan
182 H4 **Kulandy** Kazakhstan
195 I6 **Kulassein** *island* Philippines
135 AC8 **Kul'chi** Russian Federation
179 J4 **Kuldan** Pakistan
123 K4 **Kuldīga** Latvia
123 K4 **Kuldīgas** *admin. area* Latvia
74 H5 **Kuldo** British Columbia Canada
162 D4 **Kule** Botswana
182 D2 **Kulebaki** Russian Federation
194 E4 **Kulen** Cambodia
132 F2 **Kulevcha** Ukraine
217 M2 **Kulgera** NT Australia
196 D2 **Kulim** Malaysia
216 F6 **Kulin** WA Australia
135 V6 **Kulinda** Russian Federation
75 U7 **Kulish** Manitoba Canada
218 G3 **Kulkyne** *watercourse* NSW Australia
123 L2 **Kullaa** Finland
122 G4 **Kullen** *cape* Sweden
186 D4 **Kullu** Himachal Pradesh India
81 P3 **Kulm** North Dakota USA
183 K6 **Kŭlob** Tajikistan
123 L2 **Kulovesi** *bay* Finland
218 D6 **Kulpara** SA Australia
158 D2 **Kulpawn** *watercourse* Ghana
182 G4 **Kulsary** Kazakhstan
121 M2 **Kultima** Finland
120 I4 **Kultsjön** *lake* Sweden
190 E2 **Kultuk** Russian Federation
135 AE6 **Kulu** *watercourse* Russian Federation
199 J6 **Kulumadau** Papua New Guinea
191 J4 **Kulun** Nei Mongol Zizhiqu China
183 M3 **Kulunda** Russian Federation
183 M2 **Kulundinskoye** *lake* Russian Federation
121 O5 **Kulvemäki** Finland
182 I4 **Kulykol'** *lake* Kazakhstan
133 E6 **Kum** *watercourse* Turkey
192 E4 **Kŭm-Gang** *watercourse* South Korea
182 D5 **Kuma** *watercourse* Russian Federation
198 E4 **Kumafa, Pegunungan** *range* Indonesia
193 H4 **Kumagaya** Japan
196 F4 **Kumai** Indonesia
197 F4 **Kumai, Teluk** *bay* Indonesia
182 H3 **Kumak** Russian Federation
199 F4 **Kumamba, Kepulauan** *islands* Indonesia
192 F5 **Kumamoto** Japan
193 H5 **Kumano** Japan
221 D6 **Kumara** New Zealand
221 D6 **Kumara Junction** New Zealand
216 F2 **Kumarina Roadhouse** WA Australia
158 D3 **Kumasi** Ghana
159 F4 **Kumba** Cameroon
133 E5 **Kumbağ** Turkey
187 E9 **Kumbakonam** Tamil Nadu India
219 J2 **Kumbarilla** Qld Australia
199 G6 **Kumbe** Indonesia
199 G5 **Kumbe** *watercourse* Indonesia
186 D6 **Kumbhraj** Madhya Pradesh India
192 E3 **Kumch'on** North Korea
133 G6 **Kumdanlı** Turkey
189 J3 **Kume-shima** *island* Japan
182 F1 **Kumeny** Russian Federation
182 G3 **Kumertau** Russian Federation
220 F3 **Kumeu** New Zealand
192 F3 **Kumgang-san** *mountain* North Korea
186 E6 **Kumhari** Madhya Pradesh India
192 F4 **Kumi** South Korea
123 K2 **Kumlinge** *island* Finland
120 L2 **Kummavuopio** Sweden
124 G1 **Kummerower See** *lake* Germany
159 G2 **Kumo** Nigeria
181 H3 **Kumon Range** Myanmar
121 N5 **Kumpula** Finland
187 D8 **Kumta** Karnataka India
192 E3 **Kumya-man** *bay* North Korea
80 G5 **Kuna** Idaho USA
Kunashir, Ostrov *see* **Kunashiri-tō** Kuril Islands
213 H7 **Kunawaritji Community** WA Australia
123 N3 **Kunda** Estonia
181 G3 **Kunda** Assam India
187 E6 **Kunda** Chhattisgarh India
159 H6 **Kunda Dīa-Baze** Angola
123 N3 **Kunda Laht** *bay* Estonia
219 K4 **Kundabung** NSW Australia
179 K3 **Kundar** *watercourse* Pakistan
212 E7 **Kunderong Range** WA Australia
187 E8 **Kunderu** *watercourse* Andhra Pradesh India
179 L3 **Kundian** Pakistan
130 D3 **Kundl** Austria
187 C7 **Kundla** Gujarat India
199 K6 **Kundu** Solomon Islands
196 D3 **Kundur** *island* Indonesia
162 B3 **Kunene** *admin. area* Namibia
162 B3 **Kunene** *watercourse* Namibia
121 O1 **Kunes** Norway
74 E5 **Kung** British Columbia Canada
122 F4 **Kungälv** Sweden
135 W4 **Kungasalakh, Ozero** *lake* Russian Federation
183 L5 **Kungey-Alatau** Kyrgyzstan
74 F6 **Kunghit Island** British Columbia Canada
160 B3 **Kungu** Democratic Republic of Congo
182 G1 **Kungur** Russian Federation
194 B3 **Kungyangon** Myanmar

125 K4 **Kunhegyes** Hungary
181 I5 **Kunhing** Myanmar
196 F5 **Kuningan** Indonesia
181 I4 **Kunlon** Myanmar
181 I4 **Kunlong** Myanmar
185 J6 **Kunlun Shan** *range* Qinghai China
185 H6 **Kunlun Shan** *range* Xinjiang Uygur Zizhiqu China
188 D3 **Kunming** Yunnan China
120 H3 **Kunna** Norway
125 H1 **Kunow** Germany
192 E4 **Kunsan** South Korea
135 AE7 **Kuntuk** Russian Federation
213 J3 **Kununurra, Lake** WA Australia
159 F2 **Kunya** Nigeria
123 P4 **Kun'ya** Russian Federation
188 D4 **Kunyang** Yunnan China
217 K3 **Kunytjanu** SA Australia
127 L2 **Kunžak** Czech Republic
189 H3 **Kuocang Shan** *mountain* Zhejiang China
189 H3 **Kuocang Shan** *range* Zhejiang China
120 J3 **Kuoddujaure** *lake* Sweden
121 P5 **Kuohattijärvi** *lake* Finland
123 M2 **Kuohijärvi** *lake* Finland
120 L3 **Kuoksu** Sweden
121 P3 **Kuolayarvi** Russian Federation
123 N2 **Kuolimo** *lake* Finland
120 K3 **Kuollejaur** Sweden
120 K3 **Kuollejaure** *lake* Sweden
121 N5 **Kuona** Finland
121 O5 **Kuopio** Finland
121 Q5 **Kuora** Finland
121 M5 **Kuortane** Finland
123 L1 **Kuortaneenjärvi** *lake* Finland
121 P3 **Kuosku** Finland
198 B6 **Kupang** Indonesia
197 I6 **Kupang, Teluk** *bay* Indonesia
199 I6 **Kupiano** Papua New Guinea
125 H5 **Kupinec** Croatia
132 B3 **Kupinovo** Serbia
123 M5 **Kupiškis** Lithuania
133 E5 **Küplü** Turkey
187 D9 **Kuppam** *watercourse* Kerala India
123 N4 **Kuprava** Latvia
72 F7 **Kupreanof Island** Alaska USA
72 D7 **Kupreanof Point** Alaska USA
127 J1 **Küps** Germany
213 H4 **Kupungarri** WA Australia
123 P4 **Kupuy** Russian Federation
186 D3 **Kupwara** Jammu and Kashmir India/Pakistan
182 E5 **Kur** *watercourse* Azerbaijan
198 E5 **Kur** *island* Indonesia
178 G4 **Kūr Deh** Iran
182 F6 **Kür Dili Qizilağac Körfazi** *island* Azerbaijan
179 I4 **Kūr Gich** Iran
183 K5 **Kuragaty** *watercourse* Kazakhstan
159 F3 **Kuragwi** Nigeria
182 E5 **Kurakh** Russian Federation
182 G3 **Kurashassayskiy** Kazakhstan
187 E6 **Kurasia** Madhya Pradesh India
220 F4 **Kuratau** New Zealand
192 G4 **Kurayoshi** Japan
183 N4 **Kurchum** Kazakhstan
183 N4 **Kurchum** *watercourse* Kazakhstan
125 J4 **Kurd** Hungary
182 D6 **Kurdistan** *region* Iran
133 D5 **Kŭrdzhali** Bulgaria
133 D5 **Kŭrdzhali** *admin. area* Bulgaria
192 G4 **Kure** Japan
52 O5 **Kure Atoll** *reef US dependency* Pacific Ocean
121 M5 **Kurejoki** Finland
123 L3 **Kuressaare** Estonia
123 K3 **Kurevere** Estonia
182 J2 **Kurgan** Russian Federation
182 I2 **Kurganskaya Oblast'** *admin. area* Russian Federation
123 O3 **Kurgolovo** Russian Federation
198 E4 **Kuri** *watercourse* Indonesia
222 1 **Kuria** *island* Kiribati
214 F6 **Kuridala** Qld Australia
120 M5 **Kurikka** Finland
52 K3 **Kuril Basin** *underwater feature* Pacific Ocean
52 L3 **Kuril-Kamchatka Trench** *underwater feature* Pacific Ocean
193 J2 **Kuril'skiye Ostrova (Kuril Islands)** Russian Federation
182 E3 **Kurilovka** Russian Federation
193 J2 **Kuril'sk** Russian Federation
199 F5 **Kurima** Indonesia
123 P5 **Kurino** Belarus
133 F7 **Kürkçüler** Turkey
121 P4 **Kurkijärvi** *lake* Finland
161 E1 **Kurmuk** Sudan
156 E5 **Kurmuk** Sudan
187 E8 **Kurnool** Andhra Pradesh India
192 F5 **Kuro-shima** *island* Japan
75 T7 **Kuroki** Saskatchewan Canada
221 D7 **Kurow** New Zealand
219 J5 **Kurrajong** NSW Australia
179 K3 **Kurram** Pakistan
179 L2 **Kurram Garhi** Pakistan
120 L3 **Kurravaara** Sweden
216 F6 **Kurrenkutten, Lake** WA Australia
219 J5 **Kurri Kurri** NSW Australia
215 I4 **Kurrimine Beach** Qld Australia
123 L4 **Kuršenaj** Lithuania
136 F2 **Kursk** Russian Federation
182 D5 **Kurskaya** Russian Federation
136 E2 **Kurskaya Oblast'** *admin. area* Russian Federation
121 P3 **Kursu** Finland
133 F5 **Kurşunlu** Turkey
121 N3 **Kurtakko** Finland
86 D5 **Kurth Lake** Texas USA
133 F7 **Kurtoğlu Burnu** *cape* Turkey
121 P4 **Kurtto** Finland
183 L5 **Kurty** *watercourse* Kazakhstan
160 D2 **Kuru** *watercourse* Sudan
187 E7 **Kurud** Chhattisgarh India
162 D5 **Kuruman** South Africa
162 D5 **Kuruman** *watercourse* South Africa
192 F5 **Kurume** Japan
190 G1 **Kurumkan** Russian Federation
184 E5 **Kurunduk** *watercourse* Xinjiang Uygur Zizhiqu China
187 E10 **Kurunegala** Sri Lanka
156 E3 **Kurush, Jebel** *range* Sudan
121 P4 **Kurvinen** Finland
134 S4 **Kur'ya** Russian Federation
183 N3 **Kur'ya** Russian Federation
192 E4 **Kurye** South Korea
133 E5 **Kuş Gölü** *lake* Turkey
132 B3 **Kusadak** Serbia
133 E7 **Kuşadası Körfezi** *bay* Greece
183 L4 **Kusak** *watercourse* Kazakhstan
74 C2 **Kusawa Lake** Yukon Territory Canada
182 J6 **Kusaykuduk** Uzbekistan
124 F1 **Kusey** Germany
121 T5 **Kushereka** Russian Federation
192 F5 **Kushikino** Japan
192 F5 **Kushima** Japan
193 G5 **Kushimoto** Japan
193 J2 **Kushiro** Japan
121 V4 **Kushkushara** Russian Federation
182 I3 **Kushmurun** Kazakhstan
182 J3 **Kushmurun** *lake* Kazakhstan
132 C1 **Kushnytsya** Ukraine
181 F4 **Kushtia** Bangladesh
182 F3 **Kushum** Kazakhstan
132 B3 **Kusiće** Serbia
72 D6 **Kuskokwim** *watercourse* Alaska USA
72 C7 **Kuskokwim Bay** Alaska USA
72 D6 **Kuskokwim Mountains** Alaska USA
120 L4 **Kusmark** Sweden
193 J2 **Kussharo-ko** *lake* Japan
123 K2 **Kustavi** Finland
132 B3 **Kuštilj** Serbia
198 C3 **Kusu** Indonesia
197 G6 **Kuta** Indonesia
196 C2 **Kutabagok** Indonesia
196 C3 **Kutacane** Indonesia
136 D5 **Kütahya** *admin. area* Turkey
182 D5 **Kutaisi** Georgia
124 E1 **Kutenholz** Germany
130 G4 **Kutina** Croatia
120 J3 **Kutjaure** *lake* Sweden
217 K2 **Kutjurntari** WA Australia
181 H4 **Kutkai** Myanmar
125 J1 **Kutno** Poland
121 Q2 **Kutovaya** Russian Federation
121 M2 **Kuttanen** Finland
193 I2 **Kuttara-ko** *lake* Japan
86 G2 **Kuttawa** Kentucky USA
181 G5 **Kutubdia Island** Bangladesh
159 I2 **Kutum** Sudan
156 C5 **Kutum** Sudan
183 M5 **Kuturga** Kyrgyzstan
123 L5 **Kutuzovo** Russian Federation
121 O5 **Kuuhankavesi** *lake* Finland
72 H4 **Kuujjua** *watercourse* Northwest Territories Canada
77 U3 **Kuujjuaq** Quebec Canada
77 Q5 **Kuujjuarapik** Quebec Canada
182 F6 **Kuuli-Mayak** Turkmenistan
121 N5 **Kuusa** Finland
121 N5 **Kuusaa** Finland
121 P4 **Kuusamo** Finland
121 P4 **Kuusamojärvi** *lake* Finland
121 O4 **Kuusiranta** Finland
162 C2 **Kuvango** Angola
178 F3 **Kuwait** *country* Middle East
Kuwait City *see* **Al Kuwayt** Kuwait
134 J5 **Kuya** Russian Federation
183 M2 **Kuybyshev** Russian Federation
193 J2 **Kuybyshevskoye, Ozero** *lake* Russian Federation
183 L4 **Kuygan** Kazakhstan
133 F7 **Kuyucak** Turkey
136 F6 **Kuyulu** Turkey
135 U6 **Kuyumba** Russian Federation
132 A3 **Kuzmin** Serbia
132 C1 **Kuźmina** Poland
134 T6 **Kuz'movka** Russian Federation
182 E2 **Kuznetsk** Russian Federation
132 G2 **Kuznetsovo** Ukraine
125 K2 **Kuźnica** Poland
125 L1 **Kuźnica** Poland
134 I5 **Kuzomen'** Russian Federation
136 F2 **Kuzovka** Russian Federation
121 S3 **Kuzreka** Russian Federation
122 I3 **Kvädö** *island* Sweden
120 L1 **Kvænangen** *bay* Norway
120 J2 **Kvæøya** *island* Norway
120 G5 **Kvål** Norway
120 H2 **Kvalnes** Norway
120 G4 **Kvaløya** *island* Norway
120 G4 **Kvaløysætra** Norway
120 K2 **Kvaloysletta** Norway
121 M1 **Kvalsund** Norway
120 F6 **Kvam** Norway
120 F5 **Kvanne** Norway
182 E5 **Kvareli** Georgia
182 H3 **Kvarkeno** Russian Federation
122 J4 **Kvarnåkershamn** Sweden
120 J5 **Kvarnbacken** Sweden
120 H4 **Kvarnbergsvattnet** *lake* Sweden
132 D1 **Kvasy** Ukraine
122 D2 **Kvennsjøen** *lake* Norway
120 H4 **Kvesjøen** *lake* Norway
120 L5 **Kvevlax** Finland
72 D7 **Kvichak Bay** Alaska USA
122 G2 **Kvien** *lake* Sweden
122 D3 **Kvifjorden** *lake* Norway
120 J3 **Kvikkjokk** Sweden
120 M5 **Kvimo** Finland
122 D3 **Kvina** *watercourse* Norway
122 D3 **Kvinlog** Norway
120 H6 **Kvisla** Norway
120 E5 **Kvisvik** Norway
122 E3 **Kviteseidvatnet** *lake* Norway
120 L1 **Kvitnes** Norway
134 H2 **Kvitøya** *island* Norway
122 E5 **Kvong** Denmark
160 B4 **Kwa** *watercourse* Democratic Republic of Congo
158 D3 **Kwadwokurom** Ghana
223 I5 **Kwajalein Atoll** *reef* Marshall Islands
181 G4 **Kwakta** Manipur India
101 G3 **Kwakwani** Guyana
161 F4 **Kwale** Kenya
159 F3 **Kwale** Nigeria
101 G4 **Kwamalasamutu** Suriname
163 F5 **Kwamashu** South Africa
198 B3 **Kwandang** Indonesia
162 D3 **Kwando** *watercourse* Botswana
192 E4 **Kwangju** South Korea
160 B4 **Kwango** *watercourse* Democratic Republic of Congo
192 F3 **Kwanmo-bong** *mountain* North Korea
162 E6 **Kwanobuhle** South Africa
159 E3 **Kwara** *admin. area* Nigeria
77 O7 **Kwataboahegan** *watercourse* Ontario Canada
163 F5 **Kwazulu Natal** *admin. area* South Africa
162 E3 **Kwekwe** Zimbabwe
162 D4 **Kweneng** *admin. area* Botswana
160 B5 **Kwenge** *watercourse* Democratic Republic of Congo
125 J1 **Kwidzyn** Poland
157 F5 **Kwīhzā** Ethiopia
199 H6 **Kwikila** Papua New Guinea
125 I1 **Kwilcz** Poland
160 B5 **Kwilu** *watercourse* Democratic Republic of Congo
216 D6 **Kwinana** WA Australia
194 E3 **Kỳ Anh** Vietnam
194 E3 **Kỳ Sơn** Vietnam
194 C4 **Kya-in** Myanmar
159 H3 **Kyabé** Chad
218 F1 **Kyabra** *watercourse* Qld Australia
218 G7 **Kyabram** Vic. Australia
194 B3 **Kyaiklat** Myanmar
194 C3 **Kyaikto** Myanmar
218 F6 **Kyalite** NSW Australia
218 B5 **Kyancutta** SA Australia
121 U4 **Kyanda** Russian Federation
181 F2 **Kyaring Tsho** *lake* Xizang Zizhiqu China
194 C3 **Kyaukki** Myanmar
181 H4 **Kyaukme** Myanmar
181 H5 **Kyaukpadaung** Myanmar
181 G5 **Kyaukphyu** Myanmar
181 H5 **Kyaukse** Myanmar
194 C3 **Kyauktan** Myanmar
181 G5 **Kyauktaw** Myanmar
194 B3 **Kyaunggon** Myanmar
194 C3 **Kyautaga** Myanmar
123 L5 **Kybartai** Lithuania
120 I4 **Kycklingvattnet** Sweden
219 H6 **Kyeamba** NSW Australia
161 E5 **Kyela** Tanzania
136 D2 **Kyiv/Kyyiv (Kiev)** Ukraine
136 D2 **Kyivs'ka Oblast** *admin. area* Ukraine
125 I3 **Kyjov** Czech Republic
133 D7 **Kyklades (Cyclades)** *islands* Greece
121 P5 **Kylänlahti** Finland
75 Q7 **Kyle** Saskatchewan Canada
142 C3 **Kyleakin** Highland Scotland UK
124 D2 **Kyll** *watercourse* Germany
133 B7 **Kyllini** Greece
121 O4 **Kylmälä** Finland
133 D6 **Kymi** Greece
133 D6 **Kymis, Akra** *cape* Greece
186 E6 **Kymore** Madhya Pradesh India
218 G7 **Kyneton** Vic. Australia
74 D2 **Kynocks** Yukon Territory Canada
121 P4 **Kynsivaara** Finland
121 O5 **Kynsivesi** *lake* Finland
214 F6 **Kynuna** Qld Australia
161 E3 **Kyoga, Lake** *lake* Uganda
219 K3 **Kyogle** NSW Australia
192 F4 **Kyŏngju** South Korea
192 F3 **Kyŏngsŏng** North Korea
194 B3 **Kyonpyaw** Myanmar
193 G4 **Kyoto** Japan
133 B7 **Kyparissia** Greece
133 B7 **Kyparissiakos Kolpos** *bay* Greece
133 C6 **Kyra Panagia** *island* Greece
135 AA6 **Kyrbykan** Russian Federation
136 E6 **Kyrenia** Cyprus
135 Z6 **Kyrgyday** Russian Federation
183 L5 **Kyrgyzstan** *country* Asia
124 G1 **Kyritz** Germany
123 L2 **Kyrö** Finland
121 N2 **Kyrö** Finland
120 L5 **Kyrönjoki** *watercourse* Finland
123 L2 **Kyrösjärvi** *lake* Finland
134 M6 **Kyrta** Russian Federation
125 K3 **Kysak** Slovakia
135 Z5 **Kystatyam** Russian Federation
130 H2 **Kysucké Nové Mesto** Slovakia
125 M2 **Kysylyn** Ukraine
135 AB5 **Kytalyktakh** Russian Federation
132 F3 **Kytay, Ozero** *lake* Ukraine
133 C7 **Kythira** Greece
133 C7 **Kythira** *island* Greece
133 D7 **Kythnos** Greece
133 D7 **Kythnos** *island* Greece
121 N4 **Kytökylä** Finland
121 P4 **Kytömäki** Finland
135 X5 **Kyuekh-Bulung** Russian Federation
194 C5 **Kyun Pila** Myanmar
194 C4 **Kyungyi** Myanmar
181 H4 **Kyunhla** Myanmar
74 H7 **Kyuquot** British Columbia Canada
182 G4 **Kyushe** Kazakhstan
192 F5 **Kyūshū** *island* Japan
55 R3 **Kyushu-Palau Ridge** *underwater feature* Pacific Ocean
132 C4 **Kyustendil** *admin. area* Bulgaria
135 AA4 **Kyusyur** Russian Federation
218 H6 **Kywong** NSW Australia
136 D2 **Kyyïvs'ka Misto** *admin. area* Ukraine
121 N5 **Kyyjärvi** Finland
121 N5 **Kyyjärvi** *lake* Finland
123 N1 **Kyyvesi** *lake* Finland
182 F5 **Kyzan** Kazakhstan
183 Q3 **Kyzyl** Russian Federation
183 P3 **Kyzyl-Mazhalyk** Russian Federation
183 K6 **Kyzyl-Su** *watercourse* Tajikistan
183 M4 **Kyzylagash** Kazakhstan
182 I5 **Kyzylkum** Uzbekistan
182 J5 **Kyzylorda** Kazakhstan
182 I4 **Kyzylordinskaya Oblast'** *admin. area* Kazakhstan
182 F5 **Kyzylsay** Kazakhstan
183 L3 **Kyzyltas** Kazakhstan
183 K4 **Kyzyltau** Kazakhstan
183 K4 **Kyzylzhar** Kazakhstan

L

100 D2 **La Adjunta** Venezuela
129 F3 **La Almunia de Doña Godina** Spain
89 F3 **La América** Mexico
85 L6 **La Amistad** Mexico
85 H5 **La Angostura, Presa** *lake* Mexico
106 E6 **La Asturiana** Argentina
101 F2 **La Asunción** Venezuela
106 F6 **La Aurora** Argentina
108 C4 **La Bajada** Argentina
128 D2 **La Bañeza** Spain
88 E4 **La Barca** Mexico
81 J5 **La Barge** Wyoming USA
108 B2 **La Barra** Chile
126 C3 **La Barre-de-Monts** France
124 B2 **La Bassée** France
78 C4 **La Bazinière, Lac** *lake* Quebec Canada
88 C3 **La Beata** Mexico
87 K7 **La Belle** Florida USA
126 F2 **La Belle Étoile** France
75 O5 **La Biche, Lac** *lake* Alberta Canada
164 3d **La Bocayna** *strait* Canary Islands
108 B3 **La Bolsa** Argentina
85 J7 **La Boquilla de Conchos** Mexico
126 F4 **La Bourboule** France
104 A2 **La Breita** Peru
127 G5 **La Brillanne** France
106 D6 **La Buitrera** Argentina
124 B4 **La Bussière** France
85 I7 **La Buta** Mexico
88 C2 **La Cabaña** Mexico
85 J8 **La Cadena** Mexico
100 D3 **La Calzada** Venezuela
100 D3 **La Campiña** Colombia
84 C3 **La Canada Flintridge** California USA
82 H3 **La Canadienne Point** Ontario Canada
126 F4 **La Canourgue** France
126 F2 **La Capelle** France
106 F5 **La Carlota** Argentina
128 D5 **La Carlota** Spain
101 F3 **La Casa Verde** Venezuela
85 I6 **La Casita** Mexico
105 F5 **La Cautiva** Bolivia
100 E4 **La Ceiba** Colombia
90 C4 **La Ceiba** Honduras
89 F4 **La Ceiba** Mexico
100 D2 **La Ceiba** Venezuela
101 E2 **La Ceiba** Venezuela
100 C3 **La Ceja** Colombia
127 G3 **La Chapelle-de-Guinchay** France
126 E3 **La Châtre** France
127 H3 **La Chaux-de-Fonds** Switzerland
78 B3 **La Chevrotière, Lac** *lake* Quebec Canada
90 E5 **La Chorrera** Panama
88 C2 **La Choya** Mexico
84 G5 **La Cienega** Mexico
85 I3 **La Cienega** New Mexico USA
88 E4 **La Cinta** Mexico
127 G5 **La Ciotat** France
124 D5 **La Clusaz** France
106 E3 **La Cocha** Argentina
101 F3 **La Cochinera** Venezuela
106 F6 **La Colina** Argentina
88 E3 **La Colonia** Mexico
88 C2 **La Colorada** Mexico
106 E6 **La Copelina** Argentina
126 E4 **La Coquille** France
75 P5 **La Corey** Alberta Canada
86 B6 **La Coste** Texas USA
126 F4 **La Courtine** France
87 L2 **La Crosse** Virginia USA
80 G3 **La Crosse** Washington USA
82 F5 **La Crosse** Wisconsin USA
107 G4 **La Cruz** Argentina
104 E3 **La Cruz** Bolivia
105 F5 **La Cruz** Bolivia
90 C5 **La Cruz** Costa Rica
88 D4 **La Cruz** Mexico
100 D2 **La Cruz** Venezuela
104 D6 **La Cruz de Pica** Chile
85 K6 **La Cuesta de Malena** Mexico
85 J3 **La Cueva** New Mexico USA
88 C2 **La Cueva de Tres Ríos** Mexico
109 I6 **La Désirade** *island* Guadeloupe
164 9a **La Digue** *island* Seychelles
100 C3 **La Dorada** Colombia
108 C2 **La Dulce, Laguna** *lake* Argentina
104 D4 **La Encañada** Peru
89 F4 **La Encarnación** Mexico
108 D2 **La Ensenada** Argentina
101 E4 **La Esmeralda** Venezuela
108 C2 **La Esperanza** Argentina
100 C4 **La Esperanza** Colombia
90 B4 **La Esperanza** Honduras
88 E3 **La Esperanza** Mexico
101 F2 **La Esperanza** Venezuela
104 E4 **La Estación** Bolivia
106 E2 **La Estrella** Argentina
128 D4 **La Estrella** Spain
106 E4 **La Falda** Argentina
126 F2 **La Fère** France
126 E3 **La Ferrière** France
124 B3 **La Ferté-Alais** France
124 B3 **La Ferté-Milon** France
139 I5 **La Feuillie** France
126 D3 **La Flotte** France
78 C5 **La Forest, Lac** *lake* Quebec Canada
100 C2 **La Fría** Venezuela
79 G7 **La Galissonnière, Lac** *lake* Quebec Canada
105 E4 **La Garganta** Bolivia
85 I2 **La Garita Mountains** Colorado USA
128 E4 **La Gineta** Spain
74 L5 **La Glace** Alberta Canada
139 F5 **La Glacerie** France
89 F3 **La Gloria** Mexico
164 3a **La Gomera, Isla de** *island* Canary Islands
101 F3 **La Gran Sabana** *region* Venezuela
80 F4 **La Grande** Oregon USA
77 Q6 **La Grande 2, Réservoir de** Quebec Canada
77 R6 **La Grande 3, Réservoir de** Quebec Canada
77 S5 **La Grande 4, Réservoir de** Quebec Canada
126 G4 **La Grande-Combe** France
126 G5 **La Grande-Motte** France
79 I7 **La Grande Passe, Île de** *island* Quebec Canada
77 P6 **La Grande Rivière** *watercourse* Quebec Canada
109 I6 **La Grande Vigie, Pointe de** *cape* Guadeloupe
87 I4 **La Grange** Georgia USA
86 C6 **La Grange** Texas USA
81 M6 **La Grange** Wyoming USA
105 E4 **La Granja** Bolivia
91 G3 **La Granja, Punta de** *cape* Dominican Republic
101 H4 **La Grève** French Guiana
164 8a **La Grille** *volcano* Comoros
91 F5 **La Guajira** *admin. area* Colombia
91 G4 **La Guajira, Península de** *peninsula* Colombia
100 D3 **La Guaracura** Colombia
106 E4 **La Guardia** Argentina
106 D3 **La Guardia** Chile
90 D2 **La Habana** *admin. area* Cuba
90 D2 **La Habana (Havana)** Cuba
106 E5 **La Herradura** Argentina
126 E2 **La Hutte** France
100 C2 **La India** Venezuela
89 F5 **La Isla** Mexico
100 C2 **La Jagua de Ibirico** Colombia
78 E6 **La Jannaye, Lac** *lake* Quebec Canada
85 J2 **La Jara** Colorado USA
85 I2 **La Jara** New Mexico USA
85 I2 **La Jara Reservoir** Colorado USA
127 H4 **La Javie** France
90 C4 **La Jicaral** Nicaragua
129 H2 **La Jonquera** Spain
104 E5 **La Joya** Bolivia
85 I6 **La Joya** Mexico
100 C4 **La Julia** Colombia
105 F4 **La Junta** Bolivia
108 B3 **La Junta** Chile
85 I6 **La Junta** Mexico
81 N8 **La Junta** Colorado USA
88 D5 **La Juntas** Mexico
106 F5 **La Laguna** Argentina
164 3a **La Laguna** Canary Islands
85 K7 **La Leche, Lago** *lake* Mexico
100 C4 **La Libertad** Colombia
100 A5 **La Libertad** Ecuador
104 B3 **La Libertad** *admin. area* Peru
106 D5 **La Ligua** Chile
108 B2 **La Lipela** Argentina
100 B4 **La Llanada** Colombia
108 D2 **La Lobería** Argentina
75 Q4 **La Loche, Lac** *lake* Saskatchewan Canada
75 Q4 **La Loche West** Saskatchewan Canada
88 D3 **La Loma** Mexico
89 F3 **La Loma** Mexico
77 P6 **La Longue Pointe** *cape* Quebec Canada
126 G1 **La Louvière** Belgium
100 C4 **La Macarena** Colombia
100 C4 **La Macarena, Serranía de** *range* Colombia
100 B5 **La Maná** Ecuador
128 E4 **La Mancha** *region* Spain
La Manche *see* **English Channel** UK/France
108 C4 **La Manchuria** Argentina
88 D4 **La Manga** Mexico
85 K7 **La Margarita del Norte** Mexico
108 C4 **La María** Argentina
100 B4 **La María** Colombia
101 F2 **La Marinera** Venezuela
88 E3 **La Maroma** Mexico
86 D6 **La Marque** Texas USA
90 D5 **La Mesa** Panama
84 D4 **La Mesa** California USA
88 E5 **La Mira Tumbiscatio** Mexico
88 E4 **La Miseria** Mexico
84 D4 **La Misíon** Mexico
104 C4 **La Misión** Peru
82 F6 **La Moine** *watercourse* Illinois USA
78 E4 **La Moinerie, Lac** *lake* Quebec Canada
100 C4 **La Montañita** Colombia
88 E2 **La Morita** Mexico
83 L2 **La Motte** Quebec Canada
127 G4 **La Motte-Servolex** France
128 D3 **La Mudarra** Spain
88 E3 **La Muralla** Mexico
127 G4 **La Mure** France
85 N8 **La Nacha, Laguna** *lake* Mexico
85 J7 **La Navecilla** Mexico
106 D6 **La Negra** Argentina
106 D2 **La Negra** Chile
105 F4 **La Noria** Bolivia
85 H6 **La Norteña** Mexico
164 3d **La Oliva** Canary Islands
164 3a **La Orotava** Canary Islands
104 C3 **La Oroya** Peru
126 F3 **La Pacaudière** France
88 E3 **La Paila** Mexico
164 3 **La Palma** *island* Canary Islands
90 E5 **La Palma** Panama
128 C5 **La Palma** Spain
90 D5 **La Palmas** Panama
126 D4 **La Palmyre** France
106 E6 **La Pampa** *admin. area* Argentina
107 G6 **La Pastora** Argentina
101 F2 **La Pastora** Venezuela
104 D5 **La Paz** Bolivia
104 D4 **La Paz** *admin. area* Bolivia
100 C2 **La Paz** Colombia
90 C4 **La Paz** Honduras
88 C3 **La Paz** Mexico
107 H3 **La Paz** Paraguay
90 C4 **La Paz Centro** Nicaragua
104 B2 **La Peca** Peru
100 D5 **La Pedrera** Colombia
88 D2 **La Pedrera** Mexico
85 J6 **La Perla** Mexico
76 G5 **La Pérouse** Manitoba Canada
109 5 **La Pérouse, Bahía** *bay* Isla de Pascua (Easter Island)
86 C9 **La Pesca** Mexico
90 C4 **La Pimienta** Honduras
109 15 **La Plaine** Dominica
164 7a **La Plaine des Palmistes** Réunion
89 H6 **La Planes** Honduras
107 G5 **La Plata** Argentina
100 C4 **La Plata** Colombia
82 E6 **La Plata** Missouri USA
104 B2 **La Playa** Peru
75 R5 **La Plonge** Saskatchewan Canada
75 R5 **La Plonge, Lac** *lake* Saskatchewan Canada
129 G2 **La Pobla de Lillet** Spain
129 G2 **La Pobla de Segur** Spain
128 D2 **La Pola de Gordón** Spain
88 B2 **La Polvareda** Mexico
164 7a **La Posession** Réunion
78 B3 **La Potherie, Lac** *lake* Quebec Canada
89 F4 **La Poza** Mexico
84 F8 **La Poza Grande** Mexico
82 E3 **La Prairie** Minnesota USA
88 D4 **La Presa** Mexico
85 L8 **La Presa** Mexico
100 D3 **La Primavera** Colombia
128 E2 **La Proveda de Soria** Spain
100 D2 **La Providencia** Venezuela
86 B6 **La Pryor** Texas USA
106 F4 **La Puerta** Argentina
88 E4 **La Punta** Mexico
84 D4 **La Quinta** California USA
128 E3 **La Rasa** Spain
100 E2 **La Raya** Venezuela
106 E6 **La Reforma** Argentina
100 D4 **La Reforma** Colombia
89 F3 **La Reforma** Mexico
88 C3 **La Reforma** Mexico
126 D4 **La Réole** France
88 D3 **La Resolana** Mexico
129 K2 **La Revellata** *cape* Corsica France
106 E4 **La Rioja** Argentina
106 E4 **La Rioja** *admin. area* Argentina
128 E2 **La Rioja** *admin. area* Spain
126 C5 **La Rioja** *region* Spain
128 D2 **La Robla** Spain
128 C4 **La Roca de la Sierra** Spain
126 E4 **La Roche-Chalais** France
127 G1 **La Roche-en-Ardenne** Belgium
127 H3 **La Roche-sur-Foron** France
126 E4 **La Rochefoucauld** France
76 G8 **La Rochelle** Manitoba Canada
126 D3 **La Rochelle** France
128 E4 **La Roda** Spain
79 H7 **La Romaine** Quebec Canada
91 G3 **La Romana** Dominican Republic
75 S5 **La Ronge** Saskatchewan Canada
72 I8 **La Ronge, Lac** *lake* Saskatchewan Canada
105 F6 **La Rosa** Bolivia
85 K6 **La Rosita** Mexico
106 F4 **La Rubia** Argentina
84 D4 **La Rumorosa** Mexico
107 G3 **La Sabana** Argentina
88 A1 **La Salina** Mexico
101 F2 **La Salina** Venezuela
164 3d **La Santa** Canary Islands
73 L9 **La Sarre** Quebec Canada
126 D4 **La Sauve-Majeure** France
79 K8 **La Scie** Newfoundland and Labrador Canada
129 G3 **La Sènia** Spain
106 D4 **La Serena** Chile
100 D2 **La Solita** Venezuela
126 E3 **La Souterraine** France
127 I4 **La Spezia** Italy
79 I7 **La Tabatière** Quebec Canada
88 E4 **La Tapona** Mexico
126 D4 **La Teste** France
130 B4 **La Thuile** Italy
88 D5 **La Tijera** Mexico
88 C4 **La Tinaja** Mexico
100 B4 **La Tola** Colombia
214 E7 **La Touche, Mount** Qld Australia
127 G4 **La Tour-du-Pin** France
126 D4 **La Tremblade** France
109 14 **La Trinité** Martinique
218 H8 **La Trobe, Mount** Vic. Australia
100 B5 **La Troncal** Ecuador
73 L9 **La Tuque** Quebec Canada
108 B2 **La Unión** Chile
100 B4 **La Unión** Colombia
90 C4 **La Unión** Honduras
88 E5 **La Unión** Mexico
88 C3 **La Unión** Mexico
104 A2 **La Unión** Peru
104 B3 **La Unión** Peru
129 F5 **La Unión** Spain
129 F4 **La Vall d'Uxó** Spain
128 D2 **La Vega** Spain
128 D3 **La Vellés** Spain
88 C4 **La Venta** Mexico
128 E3 **La Ventosa** Spain
87 H2 **La Vergne** Tennessee USA
86 B6 **La Vernia** Texas USA
81 M8 **La Veta** Colorado USA
101 F2 **La Victoria** Venezuela
86 C7 **La Villa** Texas USA
106 E3 **La Viña** Argentina
81 Q6 **La Vista** Nebraska USA
101 F2 **La Viuda** Venezuela
127 G4 **La Voulte-sur-Rhône** France
86 C6 **La Ward** Texas USA
88 D3 **La Zarca** Mexico
121 P5 **Laakajärvi** *lake* Finland
123 N3 **Lääne-Virumaa** *admin. area* Estonia
123 L3 **Läänemaa** *admin. area* Estonia
121 O2 **Laanila** Finland
161 H1 **Laas Dawaco** Somalia
161 H2 **Laascaanood** Somalia
123 N4 **Laatre** Estonia
124 E4 **Laax** Switzerland
154 D3 **Laâyoune** Western Sahara
198 B6 **Labala** Indonesia
197 G3 **Labang** Malaysia
223 9a **Labasa** Fiji
126 E4 **Labastide-Murat** France
126 F5 **Labastide-Rouairoux** France
126 E5 **Labastide-Saint-Pierre** France
100 C3 **Labateca** Colombia
218 B5 **Labatt, Point** SA Australia
143 D4 **Labbanacallee** Ireland
120 J3 **Labbas** *lake* Sweden
139 I5 **L'Abbaye** France
125 H2 **Labe** *watercourse* Czech Republic
158 B2 **Labé** Guinea
83 N3 **Labelle** Quebec Canada
198 B4 **Labengke** *island* Indonesia
74 D2 **Laberge, Lake** Yukon Territory Canada
106 F6 **Laberinto, Punta** *cape* Argentina
197 G2 **Labi** Brunei
182 C5 **Labinsk** Russian Federation
196 D3 **Labis** Malaysia
178 F5 **Labkah** Saudi Arabia
197 I4 **Labobo** *island* Indonesia
125 I4 **Lábod** Hungary
122 F5 **Laboe** Germany
109 13 **Laborie** St Lucia
126 D4 **Labouheyre** France
106 F5 **Laboulaye** Argentina
78 G4 **Labrador** *region* Newfoundland and Labrador Canada
77 V6 **Labrador City** Newfoundland and Labrador Canada
73 N7 **Labrador Sea** Canada/Greenland
126 D4 **Labrit** France
196 E4 **Labu** Indonesia
197 G2 **Labuan** Malaysia
197 G2 **Labuan** *admin. area* Malaysia
210 inset **Labuan, Cape** Heard Island Australia
197 I4 **Labuanbajo** Indonesia
191 I2 **Labudalin** Nei Mongol Zizhiqu China
196 D3 **Labuhanbilik** Indonesia
196 C3 **Labuhanhaji** Indonesia
196 C3 **Labuhanruku** Indonesia
195 H6 **Labuk** *watercourse* Malaysia
195 H6 **Labuk, Teluk** *bay* Malaysia
190 E6 **Labuleng** Gansu China
198 A6 **Labunanbajo** Indonesia
194 B3 **Labutta** Myanmar
122 I2 **Läby** Sweden
218 B4 **Labyrinth, Lake** SA Australia
133 A5 **Laç** Albania
155 I6 **Lac** *admin. area* Chad
79 H7 **Lac, Île du** *island* Quebec Canada
83 O2 **Lac-Bouchette** Quebec Canada
75 U3 **Lac Brochet** Manitoba Canada
83 O3 **Lac-Chat** Quebec Canada
76 G7 **Lac du Bonnet** Manitoba Canada
83 O3 **Lac Edouard** Quebec Canada
75 P5 **Lac La Biche** Alberta Canada
74 K7 **Lac la Hache** British Columbia Canada
83 L2 **Lac-Lois** Quebec Canada
81 R4 **Lac qui Parle** *lake* Minnesota USA
76 N8 **Lac-Ste-Thérèse** Ontario Canada
104 E5 **Laca Jahuira** *watercourse* Bolivia
126 F4 **Lacalm** France
126 D4 **Lacanau** France
126 D4 **Lacanau, Étang de** *lake* France
126 D4 **Lacanau-Océan** France
89 H5 **Lacandón, Laguna** *lake* Mexico
89 H5 **Lacantún** *lake* Mexico
132 A3 **Laćarak** Serbia
129 H2 **Lacaune** France
187 D9 **Laccadive Sea** India
141 H3 **Laceby** North East Lincolnshire England UK
218 D7 **Lacepede Bay** SA Australia
212 G4 **Lacepede Islands** WA Australia
80 D3 **Lacey** Washington USA
179 L2 **Lachi Toi** *watercourse* Pakistan
218 G5 **Lachlan** *watercourse* NSW Australia
125 L1 **Lachowo** Poland
83 N4 **Lachute** Quebec Canada
133 G5 **Lâçin** Turkey
140 A2 **Lack** Omagh Northern Ireland UK
83 L5 **Lackawanna** New York USA
139 H2 **Lackford** Suffolk England UK
76 H8 **Laclu** Ontario Canada
75 O6 **Lacombe** Alberta Canada
83 P5 **Laconia** New Hampshire USA
109 1c **Lacre Punt** *cape* Netherlands Antilles
109 14 **Lacroix, Piton** *volcano* Martinique
213 J3 **Lacrosse Island** WA Australia
213 H4 **Lacy, Mount** WA Australia
125 I4 **Lad** Hungary
196 C3 **Ladara** Indonesia
105 G5 **Ladário** Brazil
120 J3 **Låddaure** *lake* Sweden
77 P4 **Laddie Island** Nunavut Canada
123 M4 **Lādes ezers** *lake* Latvia
132 D3 **Lădești** Romania
123 O4 **Ladino** Russian Federation
131 E6 **Ladispoli** Italy
80 D2 **Ladner** British Columbia Canada
186 D5 **Ladnu** Rajasthan India
126 F2 **Ladon** France
123 P2 **Ladozhskoye Ozero** *lake* Russian Federation
108 C6 **Ladrillero, Cabo** *cape* Argentina
108 B5 **Ladrillero, Cerro** *mountain* Chile
108 A4 **Ladrillero, Golfo** *bay* Chile
181 G3 **Ladu** *mountain* Xizang Zizhiqu China
123 K5 **Ladushkin** Russian Federation
73 K3 **Lady Ann Strait** Nunavut Canada
219 S10 **Lady Barron** Tas. Australia
215 L8 **Lady Elliot Island** Qld Australia
78 G1 **Lady Franklin Island** Nunavut Canada
162 E6 **Lady Frere** South Africa
162 E6 **Lady Grey** South Africa
87 K6 **Lady Lake** Florida USA
59 L2 **Lady Newnes Bay** Antarctica
142 F5 **Ladykirk** Scottish Borders Scotland UK
74 J8 **Ladysmith** British Columbia Canada
162 E5 **Ladysmith** South Africa
82 F4 **Ladysmith** Wisconsin USA
132 F1 **Ladyzhyn** Ukraine
199 H5 **Lae** Papua New Guinea
223 I5 **Lae Atoll** *reef* Marshall Islands
194 C5 **Laem Ao Kham** *island* Thailand
194 C6 **Laem Mum Nok** *island* Thailand
122 H4 **Läen** *lake* Sweden
122 D2 **Lærdalsøyri** Norway
122 F4 **Læsø** *island* Denmark
121 N2 **Lævnasjav'ri** *lake* Norway
121 O2 **Lævvajåk** Norway
87 I4 **Lafayette** Alabama USA
81 M7 **Lafayette** Colorado USA
82 H6 **Lafayette** Indiana USA
86 E5 **Lafayette** Louisiana USA
124 C4 **Laferté** France
159 F3 **Lafia** Nigeria
83 M2 **Laflamme** *watercourse* Quebec Canada
78 B2 **Laflamme, Lac** *lake* Quebec Canada
125 I4 **Lafnitz** *watercourse* Austria
77 S5 **Laforge** *watercourse* Quebec Canada
120 I6 **Laforsen** Sweden
126 E4 **Lafrançaise** France
196 B2 **Laful** Andaman and Nicobar Islands India
143 E1 **Lagacurry** Ireland
199 G5 **Lagaip** *watercourse* Papua New Guinea
182 E4 **Lagan'** Russian Federation
122 H4 **Lagan** *watercourse* Sweden
133 B7 **Lagana, Kolpos** *bay* Greece
120 inset **Lagarfljót** *watercourse* Iceland
103 E5 **Lagarto** Brazil
195 I3 **Lagawe** Philippines
154 D5 **Lagbar** Senegal
159 G3 **Lagdo** Cameroon
160 A2 **Lagdo, Résevoir de** *lake* Cameroon
124 E2 **Lage** Germany
122 E2 **Lågen** *watercourse* Norway
124 E1 **Lägerdorf** Germany
122 H3 **Lagerfors** Sweden
107 I3 **Lages** Brazil
142 D3 **Laggan** Highland Scotland UK
142 D4 **Laggan, Loch** *lake* Scotland UK
120 M5 **Laggars** Finland
161 F3 **Lagh Bogal** *watercourse* Kenya
161 G3 **Lagh Bor** *watercourse* Kenya
179 L2 **Laghmān** *admin. area* Afghanistan
155 G2 **Laghouat** Algeria
215 I7 **Laglan** Qld Australia
108 B3 **Lago Blanco** Argentina
108 B4 **Lago Buenos Aires, Meseta del** *plateau* Argentina
108 B4 **Lago Cardiel** Argentina
102 C4 **Lago da Pedra** Brazil
162 D2 **Lago Dilolo** Angola
108 B3 **Lago Futalaufquen** Argentina
101 I4 **Lago Novo** Brazil
108 B4 **Lago Posadas** Argentina
108 B4 **Lago San Martín** Argentina
108 B3 **Lago Verde** Chile
108 B4 **Lago Viedma** Argentina
164 1a **Lagoa** Azores
102 E5 **Lagoa da Canoa** Brazil
103 C8 **Lagoa da Prata** Brazil
103 C7 **Lagoa Formosa** Brazil
102 E4 **Lagoa Nova** Brazil
107 I4 **Lagoa Vermelha** Brazil
103 C7 **Lagoas** Brazil
194 F7 **Lagong** *island* Indonesia
214 C4 **Lagoon** *watercourse* NT Australia
214 E4 **Lagoon** *watercourse* Qld Australia
211 inset **Lagoon, The** *lake* Lord Howe Island Australia
159 E3 **Lagos** Nigeria
159 E3 **Lagos** *admin. area* Nigeria
128 B5 **Lagos** Portugal
88 E4 **Lagos de Moreno** Mexico
159 E3 **Lagos Lagoon** *bay* Nigeria
125 K2 **Łagów** Poland
212 F5 **Lagrange Bay** WA Australia
120 H5 **Lågsjön** *lake* Sweden
195 J6 **Laguilayan** Philippines
219 J5 **Laguna** NSW Australia
84 D4 **Laguna Beach** California USA
128 D2 **Laguna de Negrillos** Spain
90 D4 **Laguna de Perlas** Nicaragua
108 B4 **Laguna Grande** Argentina
108 C3 **Laguna Grande** Argentina
84 D4 **Laguna Niguel** California USA
215 J6 **Laguna Quays** Qld Australia
84 F7 **Laguna San Ignacio** Mexico
135 AL5 **Laguna Tenkergynpil'gyn** *bay* Russian Federation
106 F3 **Laguna Yema** Argentina
104 C2 **Lagunas** Peru
85 J6 **Lagunetas** Mexico
100 D2 **Lagunillas** Venezuela
105 H6 **Lagunita** Brazil
197 H2 **Lahad Datu** Malaysia
143 E4 **Lahagh** Tipperary Ireland
143 D5 **Lahard** Cork Ireland
196 D4 **Lahat** Indonesia
181 H3 **Lahe** Myanmar
123 L3 **Lahepera Laht** *bay* Estonia
196 C3 **Lahewa** Indonesia
178 E7 **Laḥij** Yemen
182 F6 **Lāhījān** Iran
124 E2 **Lahn** *watercourse* Germany
121 M3 **Lahnajärvi** Sweden
121 M3 **Lahnasuando** Sweden
122 G4 **Laholmsbukten** *bay* Sweden
86 B2 **Lahoma** Oklahoma USA
80 F7 **Lahontan Reservoir** Nevada USA
179 M3 **Lahore** Pakistan
121 P5 **Lahovaara** Finland
124 D3 **Lahr** Germany
179 K3 **Lahri** Pakistan
123 M2 **Lahti** Finland
195 I4 **Lahuy** *island* Philippines
159 H3 **Laï** Chad
199 G5 **Lai** *watercourse* Papua New Guinea
108 C4 **Lai Aike** Argentina
194 D2 **Lai Châu** Vietnam
181 H5 **Lai-hka** Myanmar
188 F4 **Laibin** Guangxi Zhuangzu Zizhiqu China
142 D2 **Laid** Highland Scotland UK
84 inset **Lā'ie** Hawai'i USA
142 B4 **Laig** Highland Scotland UK
126 E2 **L'Aigle** France
124 C4 **Laignes** France
120 M5 **Laihia** Finland
105 E5 **Laikakota** Bolivia
123 O2 **Laikko** Finland
120 K2 **Laimoluokta** *bay* Sweden
121 M3 **Lainio** Sweden
142 D2 **Lairg** Highland Scotland UK
196 D4 **Lais** Indonesia
161 F3 **Laisamis** Kenya
120 J3 **Laisan** *lake* Sweden
126 F4 **Laissac** France
120 J3 **Laisvall** Sweden
123 K2 **Laitila** Finland
123 M3 **Laitse** Estonia
123 N3 **Laiusevälja** Estonia
191 I6 **Laiwu** Shandong China
198 C4 **Laiwui** Indonesia
191 I6 **Laixi** Shandong China
191 I6 **Laiyang** Shandong China
191 H5 **Laiyuan** Hebei China

191 I5 **Laizhou** Shandong China
191 I5 **LaizhouWan** *bay* Shandong China
106 D6 **Laja, Laguna de la** *lake* Chile
100 E4 **Laja Suiza** Venezuela
213 K5 **Lajamanu** NT Australia
102 D5 **Laje** Brazil
102 E5 **Lajedo** Brazil
164 4 **Lajedo dos Espargos** Cape Verde
164 1b **Lajes** Azores
103 D8 **Lajinha** Brazil
85 K6 **Lajitas** Texas USA
132 A2 **Lajosmizse** Hungary
109 14 **L'Ajoupa-Bouillon** Martinique
120 J4 **Lajsbäck** Sweden
125 I4 **Lajta** *watercourse* Hungary
125 H2 **Łąka** Poland
121 M5 **Lakaluoma** Finland
154 E6 **Lakamané** Mali
222 7 **Lakatoro** Vanuatu
120 L3 **Lakaträsk** Sweden
120 L3 **Lakaträsket** *lake* Sweden
120 I5 **Lakavattnet** Sweden
75 S8 **Lake Alma** Saskatchewan Canada
81 P5 **Lake Andes** South Dakota USA
213 J4 **Lake Argyle Village** WA Australia
85 J4 **Lake Arthur** New Mexico USA
216 F4 **Lake Barlee** WA Australia
213 K2 **Lake Bennett** NT Australia
216 F6 **Lake Biddy** WA Australia
87 J5 **Lake Butler** Florida USA
219 K4 **Lake Cathie** NSW Australia
86 E5 **Lake Charles** Louisiana USA
81 L7 **Lake City** Colorado USA
87 J5 **Lake City** Florida USA
82 I4 **Lake City** Michigan USA
87 L4 **Lake City** South Carolina USA
87 I2 **Lake City** Tennessee USA
221 D6 **Lake Clearwater** New Zealand
84 D4 **Lake Elsinore** California USA
218 B4 **Lake Everard** SA Australia
81 J6 **Lake Fork** *watercourse* Utah USA
86 D4 **Lake Fork Reservoir** Texas USA
216 F6 **Lake Grace** WA Australia
84 E3 **Lake Havasu City** Arizona USA
221 C7 **Lake Hawea** New Zealand
86 D6 **Lake Jackson** Texas USA
216 F6 **Lake King** WA Australia
219 R11 **Lake Leake** Tas. Australia
75 S6 **Lake Lenore** Saskatchewan Canada
82 G3 **Lake Linden** Michigan USA
75 M7 **Lake Louise** Alberta Canada
87 J3 **Lake Lure** North Carolina USA
82 E5 **Lake Mills** Iowa USA
84 G3 **Lake Montezuma** Arizona USA
199 G5 **Lake Murray** Papua New Guinea
214 D6 **Lake Nash** NT Australia
87 J5 **Lake Park** Georgia USA
81 R5 **Lake Park** Iowa USA
87 K7 **Lake Placid** Florida USA
83 O4 **Lake Placid** New York USA
86 F4 **Lake Providence** Louisiana USA
80 F6 **Lake Range** Nevada USA
80 D3 **Lake Stevens** Washington USA
85 L3 **Lake Tanglewood** Texas USA
221 D7 **Lake Tekapo** New Zealand
218 D4 **Lake Torrens** SA Australia
87 L3 **Lake View** South Carolina USA
216 G3 **Lake Way** WA Australia
76 F6 **Lake Winnipeg** Manitoba Canada
223 9 **Lakeba** *island* Fiji
223 9 **Lakeba Passage** *strait* Fiji
199 H6 **Lakekamu** *watercourse* Papua New Guinea
215 H3 **Lakeland** Qld Australia
87 K6 **Lakeland** Florida USA
86 G3 **Lakeland** Tennessee USA
74 G5 **Lakelse Lake** British Columbia Canada
122 G3 **Lakenesjön** *lake* Sweden
220 4 **Lakepa** Niue New Zealand
80 D7 **Lakeport** California USA
160 E2 **Lakes** *admin. area* Sudan
219 H7 **Lakes Entrance** Vic. Australia
80 C5 **Lakeside** Oregon USA
86 E2 **Lakeview** Arkansas USA
80 E5 **Lakeview** Oregon USA
86 A3 **Lakeview** Texas USA
82 E4 **Lakeville** Minnesota USA
81 M7 **Lakewood** Colorado USA
186 C5 **Lakha** Rajasthan India
123 P2 **Lakhdenpokh'ya** Russian Federation
186 D6 **Lakheri** Rajasthan India
186 E5 **Lakhimpur** Uttar Pradesh India
181 G3 **Lakhipur** Assam India
186 G6 **Lakhisarai** Bihar India
187 E6 **Lakhnadon** Madhya Pradesh India
186 B6 **Lakhpat** Gujarat India
81 O8 **Lakin** Kansas USA
77 N5 **Lakitusaki** *watercourse* Ontario Canada
133 B6 **Lakka** Greece
179 L3 **Lakki Marwat** Pakistan
133 D5 **Lákkoma** Greece
125 I5 **Lakócsa** Hungary
133 C7 **Lakonikos Kolpos** *bay* Greece
198 D6 **Lakor** *island* Indonesia
158 C3 **Lakota** Côte d'Ivoire
81 P2 **Lakota** North Dakota USA
121 N1 **Lakselv/Leavdnja** Norway
187 C9 **Lakshadweep** *admin. area* India
187 C9 **Lakshadweep (Laccadive Islands)** Lakshadweep India
181 G4 **Lakshmipur** Bangladesh
120 H4 **Laksjøen** *lake* Norway
120 K2 **Laksvatn** Norway
179 K2 **La'l** Afghanistan
181 G4 **Lalaghat** Assam India
179 K3 **Lālak** Afghanistan
89 G5 **Lalana** *watercourse* Mexico
133 B7 **Lalas** Greece
163 G2 **Lalaua** Mozambique
133 A5 **Lalëzit, Gjiri i** *bay* Albania
157 F5 **Lalībela** Ethiopia
198 C5 **Laliki** Indonesia
128 B2 **Lalín** Spain
198 B4 **Lalindu** *watercourse* Indonesia
186 E6 **Lalitpur** Uttar Pradesh India
120 F6 **Lalm** Norway
181 F4 **Lalmonirhat** Bangladesh
197 I5 **Laloa** Indonesia
198 C4 **Laluin** *island* Indonesia
124 G3 **Lam** Germany
127 I5 **Lama** Corsica France
134 T5 **Lama, Ozero** *lake* Russian Federation
127 J4 **Lama Mocogno** Italy
197 H2 **Lamag** Malaysia
222 7 **Lamap** Vanuatu
86 E3 **Lamar** Arkansas USA
81 N7 **Lamar** Colorado USA
82 D8 **Lamar** Missouri USA
124 C3 **Lamarche** France
199 H5 **Lamari** *watercourse* Papua New Guinea
106 E6 **Lamarque** Argentina
127 G4 **Lamastre** France
126 C2 **Lamballe** France
107 G3 **Lambaré** Paraguay
159 G5 **Lambaréné** Gabon
103 C8 **Lambari** Brazil
105 I4 **Lambari, Serra do** *range* Brazil
143 G3 **Lambay Island** Ireland
104 B2 **Lambayeque** *admin. area* Peru
Lambell, Mount *see* **Gupuluk** Australia
197 G4 **Lambeng** Indonesia
139 H3 **Lamberhurst** Kent England UK
59 E2 **Lambert Glacier** Antarctica
162 C6 **Lambert's Bay** South Africa
210 inset **Lambeth Bluff** *cape* Heard Island Australia
186 D4 **Lambi** Punjab India
218 B2 **Lambina** SA Australia
141 F2 **Lambley** Northumberland England UK
139 F3 **Lambourn** West Berkshire England UK
143 B5 **Lamb's Head** *cape* Ireland
140 B4 **Lambstown** Wexford Ireland
199 I4 **Lambu** Papua New Guinea
196 C3 **Lame** Indonesia
159 G3 **Lamé** Chad
128 C3 **Lamego** Portugal
108 A2 **Lameguapi, Punta** *cape* Chile
109 16 **Lamentin** Guadeloupe
79 F9 **Lamèque** New Brunswick Canada
79 F9 **Lamèque, Île** *island* New Brunswick Canada
218 E6 **Lameroo** SA Australia
85 L4 **Lamesa** Texas USA
129 G3 **L'Ametlla de Mar** Spain
131 G7 **Lamezia** Italy
223 9a **Lami** Fiji
133 C6 **Lamia** Greece
199 I6 **Lamington, Mount** *volcano* Papua New Guinea
198 D4 **Lamlam** Indonesia
142 C5 **Lamlash** North Ayrshire Scotland UK
221 C7 **Lammerlaw Range** New Zealand
121 M5 **Lammi** Finland
74 K6 **Lamming Mills** British Columbia Canada
140 A4 **Lamoge** Ireland
82 E6 **Lamoni** Iowa USA
80 G3 **Lamont** Washington USA
138 C4 **Lamorran** Cornwall England UK
199 H2 **Lamotrek** *island* Federated States of Micronesia
104 D4 **Lampa** Peru
194 C3 **Lampang** Thailand
194 C3 **Lampang** *admin. area* Thailand
86 B5 **Lampasas** Texas USA
126 B2 **Lampaul-Plouarzel** France
88 E3 **Lampazos de Naranjo** Mexico
131 E9 **Lampedusa, Isola di** *island* Italy
121 O5 **Lamperila** Finland
138 C2 **Lampeter** Ceredigion Wales UK
194 C3 **Lamphun** Thailand
131 E9 **Lampione, Isola di** *island* Italy
75 T8 **Lampman** Saskatchewan Canada
76 H3 **Lamprey** Manitoba Canada
196 E5 **Lampung** *admin. area* Indonesia
196 E5 **Lampung, Teluk** *bay* Indonesia
181 G4 **Lamsang** Manipur India
121 O4 **Lamu** Finland
161 G4 **Lamu** Kenya
161 G4 **Lamu Bay** Kenya
161 G4 **Lamu Island** *island* Kenya
189 I4 **Lan Yü** *island* Taiwan China
124 F4 **Lana** Italy
213 I5 **Lanagan, Lake** WA Australia
84 inset **Lāna'i** *island* Hawai'i USA
197 J2 **Lanao, Lake** Philippines
142 E5 **Lanark** South Lanarkshire Scotland UK
197 H2 **Lanas** Malaysia
108 D3 **Lanaud, Península** Argentina
194 C5 **Lanbi Kyun** Myanmar
181 H2 **Lancang Jiang** *watercourse* Xizang Zizhiqu China
188 C3 **Lancang Jiang (Mekong)** *watercourse* Yunnan China
141 F3 **Lancashire** *admin. area* England UK
84 C3 **Lancaster** California USA
82 I8 **Lancaster** Kentucky USA
82 E6 **Lancaster** Missouri USA
83 L5 **Lancaster** New York USA
82 J7 **Lancaster** Ohio USA
83 M6 **Lancaster** Pennsylvania USA
87 K3 **Lancaster** South Carolina USA
140 F3 **Lancaster Canal** England UK
73 K4 **Lancaster Sound** Nunavut Canada
218 G7 **Lancefield** Vic. Australia
216 D5 **Lancelin** WA Australia
141 G2 **Lanchester** Durham England UK
131 F5 **Lanciano** Italy
106 C6 **Lanco** Chile
59 O1 **Land Bay** Antarctica
197 F3 **Landak** *watercourse* Indonesia
124 E3 **Landau in der Pfalz** Germany
100 C3 **Landázuri** Colombia
120 H4 **Lande** Norway
120 I3 **Landegode** *island* Norway
214 B6 **Lander** *watercourse* NT Australia
81 K5 **Lander** Wyoming USA
126 B2 **Landerneau** France
129 F4 **Landete** Spain
126 C3 **Landévant** France
138 B5 **Landewednack** Cornwall England UK
194 B4 **Landfall Island** Andaman and Nicobar Islands India
196 D4 **Landik, Gunung** *mountain* Indonesia
87 K3 **Landis** North Carolina USA
126 B2 **Landivisiau** France
126 D2 **Landivy** France
162 E2 **Landless Corner** Zambia
120 H5 **Landögssjön** *lake* Sweden
120 I5 **Landön** Sweden
216 E2 **Landor** WA Australia
126 F4 **Landos** France
127 I3 **Landquart** Switzerland
87 J3 **Landrum** South Carolina USA
138 B4 **Land's End** *cape* England UK
127 J2 **Landsberg am Lech** Germany
215 H6 **Landsborough** *watercourse* Qld Australia
221 C6 **Landsborough** *watercourse* New Zealand
124 G3 **Landshut** Germany
122 G5 **Landskrona** Sweden
126 B2 **Landudec** France
138 C4 **Landulph** Cornwall England UK
84 E1 **Lane** Nevada USA
141 F2 **Lane Head** Durham England UK
126 C3 **Lanester** France
194 E2 **Lang Chánh** Vietnam
180 D2 **Lang Ho** *watercourse* Xizang Zizhiqu China
190 F4 **Lang Shan** *range* Nei Mongol Zizhiqu China
194 E2 **Lạng Sơn** Vietnam
194 C5 **Lang Suan** Thailand
181 G3 **Lang Zhen** Xizang Zizhiqu China
122 E4 **Langå** Denmark
130 C4 **Langan, Punta** *cape* Italy
161 F2 **Langano, Lake** *lake* Ethiopia
188 E2 **Langao** Shaanxi China
198 B5 **Langara** Indonesia
108 C4 **Lángara, Bahía** *bay* Argentina
120 K3 **Langas** *bay* Sweden
122 G4 **Långås** Sweden
142 B2 **Langavat, Loch** *lake* Scotland UK
140 F1 **Langburnshiels** Scottish Borders Scotland UK
188 E2 **Langchi** Sichuan China
81 P2 **Langdon** North Dakota USA
214 D2 **Langdon, Port** NT Australia
126 F4 **Langeac** France
156 F4 **Langeb** *watercourse* Sudan
122 F5 **Langeland** *island* Denmark
122 F5 **Langelands Bælt** *bay* Denmark
124 E2 **Langen** Germany
75 U7 **Langenburg** Saskatchewan Canada
124 E3 **Langenburg** Germany
120 I2 **Langenes** Norway
127 H3 **Langenthal** Switzerland
134 Q6 **Langepas** Russian Federation
122 E3 **Langesjå** *lake* Norway
122 C3 **Langevåg** Norway
191 H5 **Langfang** Hebei China
121 M1 **Langfjordjøkulen** *bay* Norway
74 J8 **Langford** British Columbia Canada
196 D3 **Langgam** Indonesia
196 C3 **Langgapayung** Indonesia
124 E2 **Langgöns** Germany
122 I3 **Långhalsen** *bay* Sweden
121 M3 **Långheden** Sweden
130 D4 **Langhirano** Italy
181 I5 **Langhko** Myanmar
142 E5 **Langholm** Dumfries and Galloway Scotland UK
189 I3 **Langji Shan** *range* Zhejiang China
120 inset **Langjökull** *ice* Iceland
196 C2 **Langka** Indonesia
194 C6 **Langkawi** *island* Thailand
181 G3 **Langkazi** Xizang Zizhiqu China
197 J5 **Langkesi, Kepulauan** *islands* Indonesia
197 H2 **Langkon** Malaysia
218 E7 **Langkoop** Vic. Australia
84 C2 **Langley, Mount** California USA
141 G2 **Langley Park** Durham England UK
218 G2 **Langlo** *watercourse* Qld Australia
218 G2 **Langlo Crossing** Qld Australia
126 F4 **Langogne** France
126 D4 **Langon** France
121 M4 **Långön** *island* Sweden
120 I2 **Langøya** *island* Norway
138 E3 **Langport** Somerset England UK
128 D2 **Langreo** Spain
124 C4 **Langres** France
120 K5 **Långron** Sweden
122 H2 **Långrösten** *lake* Sweden
75 V7 **Langruth** Manitoba Canada
196 C2 **Langsa** Indonesia
122 I2 **Långsand** Sweden
120 M3 **Långsel** Sweden
120 G5 **Langsjøen** *lake* Norway
122 I2 **Långsjön** *lake* Sweden
120 L5 **Långskäret** *island* Finland
120 L2 **Langslett** Norway
85 N3 **Langston** Oklahoma USA
141 H2 **Langtoft** East Riding of Yorkshire England UK
141 H2 **Langton** North Yorkshire England UK
120 L4 **Långträsk** Sweden
138 C4 **Langtree** Devon England UK
85 L6 **Langtry** Texas USA
188 F1 **Languan** Shaanxi China
124 C5 **Languedoc-Roussillon** *admin. area* France
108 B3 **Languiñeo** Argentina
197 H6 **Langundu, Tanjung** *cape* Indonesia
120 F5 **Langvatnet** *lake* Norway
120 J5 **Långvattnet** Sweden
120 H5 **Långvattnet** *lake* Sweden
120 K5 **Långviksmon** Sweden
189 H2 **Langxi** Anhui China
188 E2 **Langzhong** Sichuan China
187 C8 **Lanja** Maharashtra India
197 G3 **Lanjak, Bukit** *mountain* Malaysia
128 E5 **Lanjarón** Spain
181 G4 **Lanka** Assam India
187 E7 **Lanka** Chhattisgarh India
189 G1 **Lankao** Henan China
126 C2 **Lanmeur** France
120 I5 **Lännässjön** *lake* Sweden
120 L2 **Lannavaara** Sweden
126 E5 **Lannemezan** France
126 B2 **Lannilis** France
126 C2 **Lannion** France
126 C2 **Lannion, Baie de** *bay* France
126 E4 **Lanouaille** France
89 H6 **Lanquín** Guatemala
126 C2 **Lanrivain** France
83 N6 **Lansdale** Pennsylvania USA
82 G3 **L'Anse** Michigan USA
79 J7 **L'Anse-au-Loup** Newfoundland and Labrador Canada
79 K7 **L'Anse aux Meadows** Newfoundland and Labrador Canada
83 P2 **L'Anse-St-Jean** Quebec Canada
81 O2 **Lansford** North Dakota USA
123 L1 **Länsi-Suomen** *admin. area* Finland
82 I5 **Lansing** Michigan USA
120 M3 **Lansjärv** Sweden
125 I3 **Lanškroun** Czech Republic
127 H4 **Lanslebourg-Mont-Cenis** France
194 C6 **Lanta, Ko** *island* Thailand
121 M4 **Lantjärv** Sweden
191 K3 **Lanxi** Heilongjiang China
189 H2 **Lanxi** Zhejiang China
77 Q2 **Lanyan, Lac** *lake* Quebec Canada
128 D3 **Lanzahita** Spain
164 3d **Lanzarote** *island* Canary Islands
190 E6 **Lanzhou** Gansu China
131 F7 **Lao** *watercourse* Italy
194 D2 **Lào Cai** Vietnam
195 I3 **Laoag** Philippines
189 G3 **Laodao He** *watercourse* Hunan China
191 J4 **Laoha He** *watercourse* Nei Mongol Zizhiqu China
189 F2 **Laohekou** Hubei China
143 E3 **Laois** *admin. area* Ireland
188 C3 **Laojie** Yunnan China
126 F2 **Laon** France
194 E3 **Laos** *country* Southeast Asia
191 L4 **Laoye Ling** *range* Heilongjiang China
194 D3 **Lap Lae** Thailand
103 B9 **Lapa** Brazil
195 I6 **Lapac** *island* Philippines
107 G3 **Lapachito** Argentina
126 F3 **Lapalisse** France
90 D4 **Lapan** Nicaragua
195 I6 **Laparan** *island* Philippines
126 F3 **Lapeyrouse** France
123 N2 **Lapinjärvi** Finland
121 O5 **Lapinlahti** Finland
121 O5 **Lapinsalo** Finland
121 R2 **Laplandiya** Russian Federation
126 F4 **Lapleau** France
121 V4 **Lapominka** Russian Federation
75 Q7 **Laporte** Saskatchewan Canada
81 R3 **Laporte** Minnesota USA
132 B3 **Lapovo** Serbia
121 M5 **Lappajärvi** Finland
121 M5 **Lappajärvi** *lake* Finland
121 M2 **Lappalaisten kesätuvat** Finland
123 L2 **Lappdalsfjärden** *bay* Finland
123 O2 **Lappeenranta** Finland
120 L5 **Lappfjärd** Finland
121 M5 **Lappfors** Finland
121 O3 **Lappi** *admin. area* Finland
121 O2 **Lappland** *region* Finland
121 M2 **Lappojávri** *lake* Norway
120 L3 **Lappträsket** *lake* Sweden
Laptev Sea *see* **Laptevykh, More** Russian Federation
135 AA3 **Laptevykh, More (Laptev Sea)** *sea* Russian Federation
121 M5 **Lapua** Finland
121 M5 **Lapuanjoki** *watercourse* Finland
198 B5 **Lapuko** Indonesia
80 G3 **Lapwai** Idaho USA
131 E5 **L'Aquila** Italy
186 F5 **Lar** Uttar Pradesh India
179 H4 **Lār** Iran
100 D2 **Lara** *admin. area* Venezuela
158 D3 **Larabanga** Ghana
154 E1 **Larache** Morocco
140 B3 **Laracor** Ireland
140 B2 **Laragh** Ireland
127 G4 **Laragne-Montéglin** France
179 H4 **Lārak, Jazīreh-ye** *island* Iran
159 H3 **Laramanay** Chad
81 M6 **Laramie** Wyoming USA
81 M6 **Laramie** *watercourse* Wyoming USA
81 M6 **Laramie Mountains** Colorado USA
103 D7 **Laranja da Terra** Brazil
105 H4 **Laranjal** Brazil
103 A9 **Laranjeiras do Sul** Brazil
198 B6 **Larantuka** Indonesia
197 I6 **Larantuka** Indonesia
198 D5 **Larat** Indonesia
198 E5 **Larat** *island* Indonesia
155 G1 **Larba** Algeria
142 C6 **Larbrax** Dumfries and Galloway Scotland UK
126 E4 **L'Arbre** France
123 J4 **Lärbro** Sweden
126 D5 **Larceveau** France
127 H4 **Larche** France
127 J4 **Lardaro** Italy
74 M7 **Lardeau** British Columbia Canada
80 G1 **Lardo** British Columbia Canada
133 F7 **Lardos** Greece
104 B3 **Laredo** Peru
128 E2 **Laredo** Spain
86 B7 **Laredo** Texas USA
132 E1 **Larga** Moldova
142 D5 **Largae** Dumfries and Galloway Scotland UK
143 D3 **Largan** Ireland
87 J7 **Largo** Florida USA
90 D2 **Largo, Cayo** *island* Cuba
86 C7 **Largo, Laguna** *lake* Texas USA
142 F4 **Largo Bay** Scotland UK
142 D5 **Largs** North Ayrshire Scotland UK
142 C5 **Largybaan** Argyll and Bute Scotland UK
140 C1 **Largybeg** North Ayrshire Scotland UK
131 D8 **L'Ariana** Tunisia
198 A4 **Lariang** Indonesia
198 A4 **Lariang** *watercourse* Indonesia
81 Q3 **Larimore** North Dakota USA
131 F6 **Larino** Italy
123 P2 **Larionovo** Russian Federation
133 C6 **Larisa** Greece
139 H2 **Lark** *watercourse* England UK
179 K4 **Larkana** Pakistan
85 J1 **Larkspur** Colorado USA
139 H2 **Larling** Norfolk England UK
126 C3 **Larmor-Plage** France
136 E6 **Larnaka** Cyprus
143 G2 **Larne** Larne Northern Ireland UK
143 G2 **Larne** *admin. area* Northern Ireland UK
143 G2 **Larne Lough** *bay* Northern Ireland UK
159 G3 **Laro** Cameroon
198 B4 **Larompong** Indonesia
129 G1 **Laroque-Timbaut** France
126 F4 **Laroquebrou** France
128 F2 **Larraga** Spain
126 D5 **Larrau** France
214 B3 **Larrimah** NT Australia
79 H10 **Larrys River** Nova Scotia Canada
59 E2 **Lars Christensen Coast** Antarctica
59 T2 **Larsen Ice Shelf** Antarctica
82 F2 **Larson** Ontario Canada
106 F6 **Lartigau** Argentina
126 D5 **Laruns** France
76 H7 **Larus Lake** Ontario Canada
122 F3 **Larvik** Norway
81 N7 **Las Animas** Colorado USA
107 G6 **Las Armas** Argentina
88 B2 **Las Arrastras** Mexico
108 B2 **Las Bayas** Argentina
85 H7 **Las Bocas** Mexico
88 C2 **Las Borregas** Mexico
100 E3 **Las Carmelitas** Venezuela
106 E3 **Las Cejas** Argentina
108 C3 **Las Chapas** Argentina
89 G5 **Las Choapas** Mexico
129 F2 **Las Cinco Villas** *region* Spain
105 G5 **Las Conchas** Bolivia
85 I6 **Las Cruces** Mexico
85 I4 **Las Cruces** New Mexico USA
85 J5 **Las Cuatas** Mexico
90 E5 **Las Cumbres** Panama
105 F5 **Las Cutas** Bolivia
101 E2 **Las Delicias** Venezuela
101 E2 **Las Dos Quebradas** Venezuela
85 L7 **Las Esperanzas** Mexico
107 G6 **Las Flores** Argentina
88 E5 **Las Guacamayas** Mexico
100 D3 **Las Guamas** Colombia
106 D5 **Las Heras** Argentina
108 B4 **Las Horquetas** Argentina
164 3b **Las Indias** Canary Islands
106 D5 **Las Leñas** Argentina
90 D5 **Las Lomas** Panama
104 A2 **Las Lomas** Peru
106 F3 **Las Lomitas** Argentina
89 H5 **Las Margaritas** Mexico
88 E3 **Las Margaritas** Mexico
91 G3 **Las Matas de Farfán** Dominican Republic
88 D3 **Las Mesitas** Mexico
88 D2 **Las Mesteñas** Mexico
107 G6 **Las Nutrias** Argentina
106 D6 **Las Ovejas** Argentina
88 C3 **Las Pacas** Mexico
164 3b **Las Palmas de Gran Canaria** Canary Islands
85 J7 **Las Pampas** Mexico
128 E4 **Las Pedroñeras** Spain
101 F2 **Las Piedritas** Venezuela
101 F2 **Las Piñas** Venezuela
108 C3 **Las Plumas** Argentina
108 C3 **Las Pulgas** Argentina
157 H5 **Las Qoray** Somalia
106 F5 **Las Rosas** Argentina
164 3d **Las Salinas** Canary Islands
90 D6 **Las Tablas** Panama
105 F5 **Las Taperas** Bolivia
106 E3 **Las Termas** Argentina
88 B3 **Las Tres Vírgenes, Volcán** *volcano* Mexico
90 C4 **Las Trojes** Honduras
90 E2 **Las Tunas** Cuba
90 E2 **Las Tunas** *admin. area* Cuba
88 D4 **Las Varas** Mexico
106 F4 **Las Varillas** Argentina
84 E2 **Las Vegas** Nevada USA
85 J3 **Las Vegas** New Mexico USA
85 J6 **Las Vibras** Mexico
100 D2 **Las Yeritas** Venezuela
197 G3 **Lasan** Indonesia
199 H5 **Lasanga Island** Papua New Guinea
107 H5 **Lascano** Uruguay
218 F6 **Lascelles** Vic. Australia
197 F5 **Lasem** Indonesia
181 H4 **Lashio** Myanmar
179 J3 **Lashkar Gāh** Afghanistan
125 J1 **Łasin** Poland
198 B4 **Lasolo** *watercourse* Indonesia
125 G1 **Lassan** Germany
126 D2 **Lassay** France
59 T2 **Lassiter Coast** Antarctica
75 S7 **Last Mountain Lake** Saskatchewan Canada
106 C6 **Lastarria** Chile
106 D3 **Lastarria, Volcán** *volcano* Chile/Argentina
141 H2 **Lastingham** North Yorkshire England UK
159 G5 **Lastoursville** Gabon
130 G5 **Lastovo** *island* Croatia
130 G5 **Lastovski Kanal** *watercourse* Croatia
194 C4 **Lat Yao** Thailand
222 8 **Lata** Solomon Islands
223 12c **Lata Mountain** American Samoa
100 B5 **Latacunga** Ecuador
59 S2 **Latady Island** Antarctica
Latakia *see* **Al Lādhiqīyah** Syria
198 C4 **Latalata** *island* Indonesia
104 D5 **Latarana** Chile
223 10 **Late Island** Tonga
186 F6 **Latehar** Jharkhand India
127 J5 **Latera** Italy
186 D6 **Lateri** Madhya Pradesh India
86 C2 **Latham** Kansas USA
187 C7 **Lathi** Gujarat India
186 C5 **Lathi** Rajasthan India
120 J4 **Latikberg** Sweden
82 E5 **Latimer** Iowa USA
131 E6 **Latina** Italy
140 A2 **Latnamard** Ireland
125 K1 **Latowicz** Poland
120 inset **Látrar** Iceland
219 R10 **Latrobe** Tas. Australia
140 A3 **Latsey** Ireland
87 L3 **Latta** South Carolina USA
126 F5 **Lattes** France
120 K3 **Latunjaure** *lake* Sweden
187 D7 **Latur** Maharashtra India
123 M4 **Latvia** *country* Europe
52 O9 **Lau Basin** *underwater feature* Pacific Ocean
142 C4 **Laudale Ho** Highland Scotland UK
81 O2 **Lauder** Manitoba Canada
142 F5 **Lauder** Scottish Borders Scotland UK
123 O4 **Lauderi** Latvia
130 D2 **Lauf an der Pegnitz** Germany
124 G4 **Laufen** Germany
127 H3 **Laufen** Switzerland
124 E3 **Lauffen** Germany
73 M3 **Lauge Koch Kyst** *region* Greenland
120 M5 **Lauhavuori** *mountain* Finland
123 M1 **Laukaa** Finland
121 P5 **Laukansalo** Finland
120 K4 **Lauker** Sweden
120 L1 **Laukøya** *island* Norway
121 M1 **Laukvik** Norway
219 R10 **Launceston** Tas. Australia
138 C4 **Launceston** Cornwall England UK
143 C4 **Laune** *watercourse* Ireland
194 C4 **Launglon** Myanmar
124 E3 **Laupheim** Germany
215 H3 **Laura** Qld Australia
223 15a **Laura** Marshall Islands
108 C4 **Laura, Bahía** *bay* Argentina
143 C5 **Lauragh** Ireland
86 G5 **Laurel** Mississippi USA
81 K4 **Laurel** Montana USA
81 Q5 **Laurel** Nebraska USA
100 D3 **Laurel Gacho** Colombia
83 L6 **Laurel Hill** *range* Pennsylvania USA
87 I2 **Laurel River Lake** Kentucky USA
143 D3 **Laurencetown** Ireland
210 inset **Laurens Peninsula** Heard Island Australia
83 P3 **Laurentian Highlands** Quebec Canada
131 F6 **Lauria** Italy
142 D6 **Laurieston** Dumfries and Galloway Scotland UK
219 K4 **Laurieton** NSW Australia
87 L3 **Laurinburg** North Carolina USA
82 G3 **Laurium** Michigan USA
107 I4 **Lauro Muller** Brazil
127 H3 **Lausanne** Switzerland
196 F4 **Laut** *island* Indonesia
197 G4 **Laut, Selat** *strait* Indonesia
197 G5 **Laut Kecil, Kepulauan** *islands* Indonesia
121 M3 **Lautakoski** Sweden
106 C6 **Lautaro** Chile
198 C6 **Lautem** Timor-Leste (East Timor)
127 H3 **Lauterbrunnen** Switzerland
223 9 **Lauthala** *island* Fiji
223 9a **Lautoka** Fiji
120 G4 **Lauvøyfjorden** *bay* Norway
120 G4 **Lauvsnes** Norway
122 C1 **Lauvstad** Norway
124 D1 **Lauwersoog** Netherlands
126 E4 **Lauzerte** France
163 I2 **Lava, Nosy** *island* Madagascar
85 N6 **Lavaca Bay** Texas USA
86 B9 **Lavaderos** Mexico
126 D2 **Laval** France
126 F4 **Laval-Atger** France
121 P4 **Lavala** Finland
179 H4 **Lāvān, Jazīreh-ye** *island* Iran
106 C6 **Lavapié, Punta** *cape* Chile
129 G1 **Lavardac** France
179 I3 **Lavārī Āb** Iran
126 E5 **Lavaur** France
126 E5 **Lavelanet** France
76 F8 **Lavenham** Manitoba Canada
139 H2 **Lavenham** Suffolk England UK
124 E5 **Laveno** Italy
199 J5 **L'Averdy, Cape** Papua New Guinea
81 P8 **Laverne** Oklahoma USA
124 E4 **Lavertezzo** Switzerland
216 H4 **Laverton** WA Australia
140 A3 **Lavey** Ireland
127 I5 **Lavezzo, Col de** *pass* Corsica France
123 L2 **Lavia** Finland
86 B9 **Lavin** Mexico
81 K3 **Lavina** Montana USA
219 Q9 **Lavinia Point** Tas. Australia
130 D3 **Lavis** Italy
135 AI5 **Lavka Integralsoyuza** Russian Federation
59 T2 **Lavoisier Island** Antarctica
86 C4 **Lavon Lake** Texas USA
120 H3 **Låvong** Norway
87 J3 **Lavonia** Georgia USA
103 C8 **Lavras** Brazil
102 E4 **Lavras da Mangabeira** Brazil
72 B5 **Lavrentiya** Russian Federation
105 G4 **Lavrinhas** Brazil
59 H2 **Law Dome** *plain* Antarctica
77 P7 **Lawagamau** *watercourse* Ontario Canada
83 L2 **Lawagamau Lake** Ontario Canada
223 9a **Lawaki** Fiji
197 H6 **Lawang** *island* Indonesia
197 G2 **Lawas** Malaysia
77 N6 **Lawashi** *watercourse* Ontario Canada
198 B4 **Lawata** Indonesia
198 B5 **Lawele** Indonesia
197 K4 **Lawin** *island* Indonesia
197 G3 **Lawit, Gunung** *mountain* Indonesia
196 D2 **Lawit, Gunung** *mountain* Malaysia
141 F2 **Lawkland** North Yorkshire England UK
76 H4 **Lawledge** Manitoba Canada
79 K9 **Lawn** Newfoundland and Labrador Canada
86 B4 **Lawn** Texas USA
214 E5 **Lawn Hill** Qld Australia
214 E5 **Lawn Hill** *watercourse* Qld Australia
158 D2 **Lawra** Ghana
82 H7 **Lawrence** Indiana USA
82 D7 **Lawrence** Kansas USA
83 P5 **Lawrence** Massachusetts USA
86 H3 **Lawrenceburg** Tennessee USA
79 F10 **Lawrencetown** Nova Scotia Canada
140 B2 **Lawrencetown** Banbridge Northern Ireland UK
87 J4 **Lawrenceville** Georgia USA
83 M6 **Lawrenceville** Pennsylvania USA
84 C2 **Laws** California USA
87 J5 **Lawtey** Florida USA
86 B3 **Lawton** Oklahoma USA
178 C4 **Lawz, Jabal al** *mountain* Saudi Arabia
74 F5 **Lax Kw'alaams** British Columbia Canada
128 B2 **Laxe, Cabo de** *cape* Spain
140 D2 **Laxey** Isle of Man UK
142 inset **Laxo** Shetland Scotland UK
124 D3 **Laxou** France
120 I5 **Laxsjö** Sweden
122 H3 **Laxsjön** *lake* Sweden
158 D2 **Lay** Burkina Faso
126 D3 **Lay** *watercourse* France
87 H4 **Lay Lake** Alabama USA
197 G5 **Layar, Tanjung** *cape* Indonesia
134 K5 **Laydënnyy, Mys** *cape* Russian Federation
76 F8 **Layland** Manitoba Canada
104 D4 **Layo** Peru
126 D3 **Layon** *watercourse* France
109 11a **Layou** St Vincent and the Grenadines
181 H4 **Layshi** Myanmar
80 J6 **Layton** Utah USA
132 E2 **Laza** Romania
164 9b **Lazare, Pointe** *cape* Seychelles
59 A2 **Lazarev Sea** Southern Ocean
132 B3 **Lazarevac** Serbia
88 E5 **Lázaro Cárdenas** Mexico
85 J6 **Lázaro Cárdenas** Mexico
88 D3 **Lázaro Cárdenas, Presa** *lake* Mexico
131 E5 **Lazio** *admin. area* Italy
124 F5 **Lazise** Italy
132 B3 **Laznica** Serbia
140 F2 **Lazonby** Cumbria England UK
125 L4 **Lazuri** Romania
107 G6 **Lazzarino** Argentina
126 D4 **Le Barp** France
126 E3 **Le Blanc** France
126 E4 **Le Bourg** France
127 H4 **Le Bourg-d'Oisans** France
222 7 **Le Cap** New Caledonia
126 F5 **Le Cap d'Agde** France
109 14 **Le Carbet** Martinique
126 F1 **Le Catelet** France
126 F5 **Le Caylar** France
126 F3 **Le Châtelet** France
124 C3 **Le Chesne** France
124 C5 **Le Cheylard** France
126 B2 **Le Conquet** France
87 J3 **Le Conte, Mount** Tennessee USA
127 G3 **Le Creusot** France
139 I4 **Le Crotoy** France
109 14 **Le Diamant** Martinique
126 F3 **Le Donjon** France
126 E3 **Le Dorat** France
79 H7 **Le Doré, Lac** *lake* Quebec Canada
78 F3 **Le Droit, Pointe** *cape* Quebec Canada
126 C2 **Le Faouët** France
109 14 **Le François** Martinique
109 16 **Le Gosier** Guadeloupe
82 E5 **Le Grand** Iowa USA
216 H6 **Le Grand, Mount** WA Australia
126 E3 **Le Grand-Lucé** France
126 E2 **Le Grand-Quevilly** France
126 E2 **Le Havre** France
109 14 **Le Lamentin** Martinique
124 D5 **Le Lauzet-Ubaye** France
127 H5 **Le Lavandou** France
127 H3 **Le Locle** Switzerland
109 14 **Le Lorrain** Martinique
126 E3 **Le Lude** France
108 D6 **Le Maire, Estrecho de** *strait* Argentina
126 E2 **Le Mans** France
108 C5 **Le Marchand** Argentina
109 14 **Le Marin** Martinique
126 F4 **Le Monastier-sur-Gazeille** France
127 H4 **Le Monêtier-les-Bains** France
109 14 **Le Morne Rouge** Martinique
109 16 **Le Moule** Guadeloupe
78 D4 **Le Moyne, Lac** *lake* Quebec Canada
129 F1 **Le Muret** France
127 H5 **Le Muy** France
126 C3 **Le Palais** France
139 J4 **Le Parcq** France
126 E2 **Le Péage** France
127 G4 **Le Péage-de-Roussillon** France
75 U3 **Le Pensie** Manitoba Canada
126 D3 **Le Plessis** France
124 B4 **Le Pondy** France
127 G5 **Le Pontet** France
126 D4 **Le Porge** France
164 7a **Le Port** Réunion
109 14 **Le Prêcheur** Martinique
124 B2 **Le Quesnoy** France
109 14 **Le Robert** Martinique
82 G6 **Le Roy** Illinois USA
77 R3 **Le Roy, Lac** *lake* Quebec Canada
124 D4 **Le Russey** France
109 14 **Le Saint-Esprit** Martinique
131 C8 **Le Sers** Tunisia
129 G2 **Le Seu d'Urgell** Spain
164 7a **Le Tampon** Réunion
124 C5 **Le Teil** France
126 D2 **Le Teilleul** France
194 E4 **Lệ Thanh** Vietnam
139 I4 **Le Touquet-Paris-Plage** France
124 D4 **Le Tour** France
139 H5 **Le Trait** France
139 I4 **Le Tréport** France
109 14 **Le Vauclin** Martinique
130 E5 **Le Ville** Italy
199 H6 **Lea Lea** Papua New Guinea
138 A1 **Leabeg** Ireland
143 E3 **Leabeg** Ireland
143 D2 **Leabgarrow** Ireland
77 V1 **Leach Bay** Nunavut Canada
81 N4 **Lead** South Dakota USA
139 G1 **Leadenham** Lincolnshire England UK
142 E5 **Leadhills** South Lanarkshire Scotland UK
219 I5 **Leadville** NSW Australia
81 L7 **Leadville** Colorado USA
82 F8 **Leadwood** Missouri USA
75 V4 **Leaf Rapids** Manitoba Canada
218 F5 **Leaghur, Lake** NSW Australia
213 H4 **Leake, Mount** WA Australia
86 B6 **Leakey** Texas USA
142 C4 **Lealt** Argyll and Bute Scotland UK
142 B3 **Lealt** Highland Scotland UK
82 J5 **Leamington** Ontario Canada
80 I7 **Leamington** Utah USA
143 D5 **Leamlara** Ireland
80 G1 **Leanchoil** British Columbia Canada
216 D4 **Leander Point** WA Australia
143 C4 **Leane, Lough** *lake* Ireland
214 C2 **Leane, Mount** NT Australia
143 C4 **Leanevglissane** Ireland
163 I3 **Leanja** Madagascar
143 C4 **Leansaghane** Ireland
143 C5 **Leap** Ireland
212 C7 **Learmonth** WA Australia
87 I5 **Leary** Georgia USA
139 G3 **Leatherhead** Surrey England UK
82 D7 **Leavenworth** Kansas USA
122 I5 **Łeba** Poland
124 D3 **Lebach** Germany
159 G5 **Lébamba** Gabon
132 B4 **Lebane** Serbia
178 C2 **Lebanon** *country* Middle East
82 I8 **Lebanon** Kentucky USA
82 E8 **Lebanon** Missouri USA
83 O5 **Lebanon** New Hampshire USA
80 D4 **Lebanon** Oregon USA
83 M6 **Lebanon** Pennsylvania USA
182 I6 **Lebap Welaýaty** *admin. area* Turkmenistan
84 C3 **Lebec** California USA
158 B2 **Lébékéré** Guinea
73 L9 **Lebel-sur-Quévillon** Quebec Canada
160 C3 **Lebo** Democratic Republic of Congo
82 D7 **Lebo** Kansas USA
122 I5 **Lębork** Poland
162 E4 **Lebowakgomo** South Africa
128 C5 **Lebrija** Spain
122 I5 **Łebsko, Jezioro** *lake* Poland
106 C6 **Lebu** Chile
100 C3 **Lebvrija** *watercourse* Colombia
131 H6 **Lecce** Italy
124 E5 **Lecco** Italy
129 F3 **Lécera** Spain
133 B7 **Lechaina** Greece
88 E3 **Leche, Lago La** *lake* Mexico
90 E2 **Leche, Laguna de** *lake* Cuba
189 G3 **Lecheng** Guangdong China
132 D2 **Lechința** Romania
141 F2 **Leck** Lancashire England UK
142 C3 **Leckie** Highland Scotland UK
86 E5 **Lecompte** Louisiana USA
160 A4 **Léconi** Gabon
159 G5 **Léconi** *watercourse* Gabon
126 E5 **Lectoure** France
125 L2 **Łęczna** Poland
214 C7 **Ledan Peak** *mountain* NT Australia
196 D3 **Ledang, Gunung** *mountain* Malaysia
125 I4 **Ledava** *watercourse* Slovenia
138 E2 **Ledbury** Herefordshire England UK
128 D3 **Ledesma** Spain
142 D2 **Ledmore** Highland Scotland UK
121 Q4 **Ledmozero** Russian Federation
121 R4 **Ledmozero, Ozero** *lake* Russian Federation
196 F3 **Ledo** Indonesia
75 O6 **Leduc** Alberta Canada
139 F3 **Ledwell** Oxfordshire England UK
143 C5 **Lee** *watercourse* Ireland
138 C3 **Lee** Devon England UK
215 H5 **Lee, Mount** Qld Australia
140 E2 **Leece** Cumbria England UK
82 D3 **Leech Lake** Minnesota USA
86 B3 **Leedey** Oklahoma USA
141 G3 **Leeds** West Yorkshire England UK
87 H4 **Leeds** Alabama USA
81 P2 **Leeds** North Dakota USA
84 F2 **Leeds** Utah USA
141 F3 **Leeds and Liverpool Canal** England UK
124 D1 **Leek** Netherlands
139 E1 **Leek** Staffordshire England UK
216 D4 **Leeman** WA Australia
143 C3 **Leenane** Ireland
139 F2 **Lees** Derbyshire England UK
141 G3 **Lees** West Yorkshire England UK
82 D7 **Lees Summit** Missouri USA
87 I3 **Leesburg** Alabama USA
87 K6 **Leesburg** Florida USA
87 I5 **Leesburg** Georgia USA
82 I6 **Leesburg** Indiana USA
82 J7 **Leesburg** Ohio USA
83 M7 **Leesburg** Virginia USA
124 C1 **Leeuwarden** Netherlands
216 D7 **Leeuwin, Cape** WA Australia
55 P8 **Leeuwin Sill** *underwater feature* Indian Ocean
91 I3 **Leeward Islands** Caribbean
159 H5 **Léfini** *watercourse* Congo
133 D8 **Lefka Ori** *range* Greece
133 B6 **Lefkada** Greece
133 B6 **Lefkada** *island* Greece
Lefkosia *see* **Nicosia** Cyprus
86 A3 **Lefors** Texas USA
77 T3 **Lefroy** *watercourse* Quebec Canada
216 G5 **Lefroy, Lake** WA Australia
75 O6 **Legal** Alberta Canada
128 E3 **Leganés** Spain
76 M7 **Legarde** *watercourse* Ontario Canada
195 I4 **Legazpi** Philippines
126 D3 **Legé** France
212 D6 **Legendre Island** WA Australia
138 E2 **Legion Cross** Herefordshire England UK
125 K1 **Legionowo** Poland
124 F5 **Legnago** Italy
125 I2 **Legnica** Poland
196 F5 **Legokjawa** Indonesia
130 G3 **Legrad** Croatia
126 C2 **Léguer** *watercourse* France
219 K3 **Legume** NSW Australia
160 D3 **Legwe** *watercourse* Democratic Republic of Congo
186 D3 **Leh** Jammu and Kashmir India/Pakistan
83 N6 **Lehighton** Pennsylvania USA
132 E3 **Lehliu-Gară** Romania
120 M5 **Lehmäjoki** Finland
121 N3 **Lehmikumpu** Finland
121 P5 **Lehmo** Finland
81 P3 **Lehr** North Dakota USA
124 F1 **Lehre** Germany
124 E1 **Lehrte** Germany

121 M5 **Lehtimäki** Finland
123 L3 **Lehtma Nina** *cape* Estonia
121 O4 **Lehtovaara** Finland
106 C6 **Lehuelán** Chile
162 D4 **Lehututu** Botswana
125 H4 **Leibnitz** Austria
141 G4 **Leicester** *admin. area* England UK
139 F2 **Leicester** Leicester England UK
139 F2 **Leicestershire** *admin. area* England UK
214 E5 **Leichhardt** *watercourse* Qld Australia
214 B6 **Leichhardt, Mount** NT Australia
215 I6 **Leichhardt Range** Qld Australia
124 C1 **Leiden** Netherlands
123 N3 **Leie** Estonia
124 F1 **Leiferde** Germany
220 F3 **Leigh** New Zealand
139 E3 **Leigh** Gloucestershire England UK
141 F3 **Leigh** Greater Manchester England UK
81 Q6 **Leigh** Nebraska USA
218 D4 **Leigh Creek** SA Australia
139 G3 **Leighton Buzzard** Bedfordshire England UK
120 K2 **Leinavatnet** *lake* Norway
124 E1 **Leine** *watercourse* Germany
121 P4 **Leino** Finland
216 G3 **Leinster** WA Australia
143 F4 **Leinster, Mount** *mountain* Ireland
138 E2 **Leintwardine** Herefordshire England UK
120 L3 **Leipojärvi** Sweden
133 E7 **Leipsoi** *island* Greece
124 G2 **Leipzig** Germany
120 F5 **Leira** Norway
120 K2 **Leirbukta** Norway
128 B4 **Leiria** Portugal
128 B4 **Leiria** *admin. area* Portugal
122 C3 **Leirvik** Norway
217 K1 **Leisler, Mount** NT Australia
139 I2 **Leiston** Suffolk England UK
123 L3 **Leisu** Estonia
82 H8 **Leitchfield** Kentucky USA
142 E5 **Leithen Lodge** Scottish Borders Scotland UK
221 E6 **Leithfield Beach** New Zealand
199 G4 **Leitre** Papua New Guinea
143 D3 **Leitrim** Ireland
143 E2 **Leitrim** *admin. area* Ireland
100 B4 **Leiva** Colombia
123 N2 **Leivonmäki** Finland
121 P5 **Leivonmäki** Finland
189 F3 **Leiyang** Hunan China
188 F5 **Leizhou** Guangdong China
188 F5 **Leizhou Wan** *bay* Guangdong China
100 C4 **Lejanías** Colombia
120 G4 **Leka** *island* Norway
160 C4 **Lekatero** Democratic Republic of Congo
159 G5 **Lékéti** *watercourse* Congo
154 D5 **Lekhcheb** Mauritania
123 P5 **Lëkhovo** Russian Federation
159 G5 **Lékila** Gabon
198 C4 **Lekitobi** Indonesia
120 E5 **Leknes** Norway
159 G5 **Lékona** *watercourse* Congo
159 G5 **Lékoumou** *admin. area* Congo
120 G5 **Leksdalsvatn** *lake* Norway
121 U6 **Lekshmozero** Russian Federation
121 Q5 **Leksozero, Ozero** *lake* Russian Federation
120 G5 **Leksvik** Norway
197 K3 **Lelai, Tanjung** *cape* Indonesia
120 H3 **Leland** Norway
122 G3 **Lelång** *lake* Sweden
108 B3 **Leleque** Argentina
162 C6 **Leliefontein** South Africa
101 H3 **Lelydorp** Suriname
124 C1 **Lelystad** Netherlands
122 E4 **Lem** Denmark
161 G3 **Lema Shilindi** Ethiopia
127 H3 **Léman, Lac (Lake Geneva)** *lake* Switzerland/France
199 J5 **Lemankoa** Papua New Guinea
127 H2 **Lembach** France
197 H6 **Lembar** Indonesia
123 K5 **Lembas** Lithuania
126 D5 **Lembeye** France
197 H3 **Lembu** Indonesia
196 C2 **Lembu, Gunung** *mountain* Indonesia
103 C8 **Leme** Brazil
121 P4 **Lemetinvaara** Finland
80 I4 **Lemhi** *watercourse* Idaho USA
123 N2 **Lemi** Finland
73 M6 **Lemieux Islands** Nunavut Canada
121 O2 **Lemmenjoki** Finland
81 N4 **Lemmon** South Dakota USA
84 C2 **Lemoore** California USA
74 J5 **Lemoray** British Columbia Canada
124 B5 **Lempdes** France
75 Q7 **Lemsford** Saskatchewan Canada
159 F3 **Lemu** Nigeria
108 A3 **Lemu, Isla** *island* Chile
196 F3 **Lemukutan** *island* Indonesia
122 E4 **Lemvig** Denmark
194 B3 **Lemyethna** Myanmar
135 X7 **Lena** *watercourse* Russian Federation
127 I4 **Lena, Capo** *cape* Italy
54 J10 **Lena Tablemount** *underwater feature* Southern Ocean
143 C2 **Lenadoon Point** Ireland
143 E1 **Lenan** Ireland
197 H6 **Lenangguar** Indonesia
130 F3 **Lenart** Slovenia
103 B8 **Lençóis Paulista** Brazil
160 D3 **Lenda** *watercourse* Democratic Republic of Congo
142 D5 **Lendalfoot** South Ayrshire Scotland UK
121 Q5 **Lendery** Russian Federation
75 R6 **Leney** Saskatchewan Canada
198 E4 **Lengguru** *watercourse* Indonesia
120 H4 **Lenglingen** *lake* Norway
190 E5 **Lenglong Ling** *mountain* Gansu China
190 E5 **Lenglong Ling** *range* Gansu China
189 F3 **Lengshuijiang** Hunan China
189 F3 **Lengshuitan** Hunan China
106 C4 **Lengua de Vaca, Punta** *cape* Chile
183 K6 **Lenina, Pik** *mountain* Tajikistan
183 K6 **Leningrad** Tajikistan
123 P3 **Leningradskaya Oblast'** *admin. area* Russian Federation
135 AK5 **Leningradskiy** Russian Federation
183 N3 **Leninogorsk** Kazakhstan
183 K5 **Leninpol'** Kyrgyzstan
182 J4 **Leninsk** Kazakhstan
182 E4 **Leninsk** Russian Federation
183 O2 **Leninsk-Kuznetskiy** Russian Federation
124 D4 **Lenk** Switzerland
132 E1 **Lenkovtsy** Ukraine
198 D4 **Lenmalu** Indonesia
140 A2 **Lennaght** Ireland
124 E2 **Lenne** *watercourse* Germany
124 E2 **Lennestadt** Germany
59 K1 **Lennox-King Glacier** Antarctica
130 D4 **Leno** Italy
87 K3 **Lenoir** North Carolina USA
81 P7 **Lenora** Kansas USA
75 S6 **Lenore Lake** Saskatchewan Canada
126 F1 **Lens** France
135 X6 **Lensk** Russian Federation
120 F5 **Lensvik** Norway
182 D5 **Lentekhi** Georgia
125 I4 **Lenti** Hungary
121 P4 **Lentiira** Finland
139 G2 **Lenton** Lincolnshire England UK
121 P4 **Lentua** *lake* Finland
158 D2 **Léo** Burkina Faso
74 I5 **Leo Creek** British Columbia Canada
130 E3 **Leoben** Austria
126 D4 **Léognan** France
198 B3 **Leok** Indonesia
197 I3 **Leok** Indonesia
86 E3 **Leola** Arkansas USA
138 E2 **Leominster** Herefordshire England UK
83 P5 **Leominster** Massachusetts USA
126 D5 **Léon** France
88 E4 **León** Mexico
90 C4 **León** Nicaragua
128 D2 **León** Spain
86 C2 **Leon** Kansas USA
85 N5 **Leon** *watercourse* Texas USA
126 D5 **Léon, Étang de** *lake* France
88 D2 **Leon, Presa Luis L.** *lake* Mexico
108 D3 **León, Punta** *cape* Argentina
85 K8 **Leon Guzmán** Mexico
89 I4 **Leona Vicario** Mexico
86 C4 **Leonard** Texas USA
162 C4 **Leonardville** Namibia
81 Q7 **Leonardville** Kansas USA
223 12c **Leone** American Samoa
108 D2 **Leone, Valle** *valley* Argentina
131 E5 **Leonessa** Italy
131 F8 **Leonforte** Italy
218 G8 **Leongatha** Vic. Australia
216 G4 **Leonora** WA Australia
135 AH4 **Leont'yeva, Ostrov** *island* Russian Federation
140 B3 **Leopardstown** Ireland
218 G8 **Leopold** Vic. Australia
58 F2 **Leopold and Astrid Coast** Antarctica
213 H4 **Leopold Downs** WA Australia
130 G2 **Leopoldov** Slovakia
132 D3 **Leordeni** Romania
81 O7 **Leoti** Kansas USA
75 R6 **Leoville** Saskatchewan Canada
196 E4 **Lepar** *island* Indonesia
139 F4 **Lepe** Hampshire England UK
78 B2 **Lepellé** *watercourse* Quebec Canada
162 E4 **Lephalala** *watercourse* South Africa
162 E4 **Lephalale (Ellisras)** South Africa
162 E4 **Lephepe** Botswana
142 C4 **Lephinmore** Argyll and Bute Scotland UK
189 H3 **Leping** Jiangxi China
133 D6 **Lepoura** Greece
121 M2 **Leppäjärvi** Finland
121 N5 **Leppävesi** *lake* Finland
121 O5 **Leppävirta** Finland
220 F4 **Lepperton** New Zealand
183 M4 **Lepsy** Kazakhstan
133 C5 **Leptokarya** Greece
154 D5 **Leqceïba** Mauritania
189 H3 **Leqing** Zhejiang China
120 G5 **Ler** Norway
158 D3 **Léraba** *watercourse* Burkina Faso
162 E4 **Lerala** Botswana
58 W1 **Lerchenfeld Glacier** Antarctica
89 G5 **Lerdo de Tejada** Mexico
159 G3 **Léré** Chad
154 F5 **Léré** Mali
199 F4 **Lereh** Indonesia
128 F2 **Lerín** Spain
120 J5 **Leringen** *bay* Sweden
88 E4 **Lerma** *watercourse* Mexico
128 E2 **Lerma** Spain
131 C6 **Lerno, Monte** *mountain* Sardinia Italy
133 E7 **Leros** *island* Greece
122 F3 **Lervik** Norway
142 inset **Lerwick** Shetland Scotland UK
127 G4 **Les Abrets** France
109 16 **Les Abymes** Guadeloupe
126 D5 **Les Aldudes** France
164 9 **Les Amirantes** *island* Seychelles
109 14 **Les Anses-d'Arlets** Martinique
129 G3 **Les Borges Blanques** Spain
91 F3 **Les Cayes** Haiti
79 C9 **Les Éboulements** Quebec Canada
127 G4 **Les Échelles** France
79 D8 **Les Escoumins** Quebec Canada
126 D3 **Les Essarts** France
130 B3 **Les Gets** France
139 I5 **Les Hayons** France
91 F3 **Les Irois** Haiti
127 G3 **Les Laumes** France
77 V8 **Les Méchins** Quebec Canada
127 G4 **Les Mées** France
126 D2 **Les Pieux** France
126 D3 **Les Sables-d'Olonne** France
109 16 **Les Saintes** *island* Guadeloupe
109 14 **Les Trois-Îlets** Martinique
126 G4 **Les Vans** France
132 B4 **Lešak** Kosovo
128 F2 **Lesaka** Spain
129 H2 **L'Escala** Spain
126 D5 **Lescar** France
78 A2 **Lesdiguières, Lac** *lake* Quebec Canada
188 D2 **Leshan** Sichuan China
134 K6 **Leshukonskoye** Russian Federation
125 K2 **Lesiów** Poland
120 F5 **Lesja** Norway
121 N4 **Leskelä** Finland
132 F3 **Leski** Ukraine
125 L3 **Lesko** Poland
58 F2 **Leskov Island** Antarctica
132 B4 **Leskovac** Serbia
124 C3 **Lesmont** France
127 L1 **Leśna** Poland
125 J1 **Leśna Jania** Poland
135 AH7 **Lesnaya** Russian Federation
126 B2 **Lesneven** France
132 A3 **Lešnica** Serbia
134 T7 **Lesosibirsk** Russian Federation
162 E5 **Lesotho** *country* Africa
192 G2 **Lesozavodsk** Russian Federation
126 D4 **Lesparre-Médoc** France
220 5 **L'Esperance Rock** *island* Kermadec Islands New Zealand
129 F2 **Lesperon** France
129 G3 **L'Espluga de Francolí** Spain
91 H4 **Lesser Antilles** *islands* Caribbean
75 N5 **Lesser Slave** *watercourse* Alberta Canada
72 H7 **Lesser Slave Lake** Alberta Canada
198 B6 **Lesser Sunda Islands** Indonesia
77 T2 **Lestage** *watercourse* Quebec Canada
126 E3 **Lesterps** France
121 N5 **Lestijärvi** *lake* Finland
121 N5 **Lestijoki** *watercourse* Finland
213 I2 **Lesueur Island** WA Australia
197 G3 **Lesung, Bukit** *mountain* Indonesia
133 E6 **Lesvos** *island* Greece
142 C6 **Leswalt** Dumfries and Galloway Scotland UK
125 I2 **Leszno** Poland
79 H9 **L'Étang-du-Nord** Quebec Canada
81 P5 **Letcher** South Dakota USA
139 G3 **Letchworth** Hertfordshire England UK
130 G3 **Letenye** Hungary
181 G4 **Letha** Myanmar
75 O8 **Lethbridge** Alberta Canada
213 K1 **Lethbridge Bay** NT Australia
101 G4 **Lethem** Guyana
198 C6 **Leti** *island* Indonesia
198 C6 **Leti, Kepulauan** *islands* Indonesia
162 D4 **Letiahau** *watercourse* Botswana
104 D2 **Leticia** Colombia
191 I5 **Leting** Hebei China
162 E4 **Letlhakane** Botswana
162 E4 **Letlhakeng** Botswana
121 S4 **Letnerechenskiy** Russian Federation
132 D4 **Letnitsa** Bulgaria
121 T4 **Letniy Navolok** Russian Federation
121 S4 **Letnyaya Reka** Russian Federation
194 B3 **Letpadan** Myanmar
194 C5 **Letsok-aw Kyun** Myanmar
122 H2 **Letssjön** *lake* Sweden
159 G4 **Letta** Cameroon
122 G2 **Letten** *lake* Sweden
143 C5 **Letter** Ireland
143 C3 **Letter** Ireland
143 D3 **Lettera** Ireland
143 E2 **Letterkenny** Ireland
143 D2 **Lettermacaward** Ireland
143 C3 **Lettermullan** Ireland
81 R1 **Lettonia** Manitoba Canada
196 E3 **Letung** Indonesia
141 G3 **Letwell** South Yorkshire England UK
198 D5 **Letwurung** Indonesia
132 C3 **Leu** Romania
162 D2 **Lèuá** Angola
131 H7 **Leuca, Capo Santa Maria di** *cape* Italy
126 F5 **Leucate** France
142 F4 **Leuchers** Fife Scotland UK
124 D4 **Leukerbad** Switzerland
142 B2 **Leumrabhagh** Na h-Eileanan Siar Scotland UK
127 K1 **Leuna** Germany
84 G3 **Leupp Corner** Arizona USA
196 C3 **Leuser, Gunung** *mountain* Indonesia
127 G1 **Leuven** Belgium
196 E5 **Leuwiliang** Indonesia
182 C2 **Lev Tolstoy** Russian Federation
120 G5 **Levanger** Norway
130 C4 **Levante, Riviera de** *region* Italy
131 E7 **Levanzo, Isola di** *island* Italy
121 O3 **Leväranta** Finland
108 A3 **Level, Isla** *island* Chile
85 K4 **Levelland** Texas USA
75 W5 **Leven** Manitoba Canada
141 H3 **Leven** East Riding of Yorkshire England UK
142 E4 **Leven** Fife Scotland UK
140 F2 **Levens** Cumbria England UK
219 S10 **Leventhorpe, Mount** Tas. Australia
142 inset **Levenwick** Shetland Scotland UK
212 G4 **Leveque, Cape** WA Australia
221 6 **L'Eveque, Cape** Chatham Islands New Zealand
124 D2 **Leverkusen** Germany
139 H1 **Leverton** Lincolnshire England UK
126 F3 **Levet** France
125 J3 **Levice** Slovakia
124 F4 **Levico Terme** Italy
127 H3 **Levier** France
216 C2 **Levillain, Cape** WA Australia
221 F5 **Levin** New Zealand
142 D3 **Levishie** Highland Scotland UK
133 E7 **Levitha** *island* Greece
121 O4 **Levo-oja** Finland
130 F5 **Levrnaka** *island* Croatia
126 E3 **Levroux** France
132 D4 **Levski** Bulgaria
223 9a **Levuka** Fiji
126 D2 **Lévy, Cap** *cape* France
198 A6 **Lewa** Indonesia
181 H5 **Lewe** Myanmar
81 N6 **Lewellen** Nebraska USA
83 N7 **Lewes** Delaware USA
79 K9 **Lewin's Cove** Newfoundland and Labrador Canada
81 Q2 **Lewis** Manitoba Canada
85 M2 **Lewis** Kansas USA
214 B7 **Lewis, Lake** NT Australia
218 D1 **Lewis, Mount** Qld Australia
82 C5 **Lewis and Clark Lake** Nebraska USA
79 I8 **Lewis Hills** Newfoundland and Labrador Canada
80 I2 **Lewis Range** Montana USA
86 H3 **Lewis Smith Lake** Alabama USA
82 H8 **Lewisburg** Kentucky USA
86 H3 **Lewisburg** Tennessee USA
83 K8 **Lewisburg** West Virginia USA
139 G3 **Lewisham** Greater London England UK
80 G3 **Lewiston** Idaho USA
83 P4 **Lewiston** Maine USA
80 J6 **Lewiston** Utah USA
82 F6 **Lewistown** Illinois USA
81 K3 **Lewistown** Montana USA
86 C4 **Lewisville** Texas USA
87 C4 **Lewisville Lake** Texas USA
86 F4 **Lexington** Mississippi USA
81 P6 **Lexington** Nebraska USA
87 K3 **Lexington** North Carolina USA
80 F4 **Lexington** Oregon USA
83 L8 **Lexington** Virginia USA
82 I7 **Lexington-Fayette** Kentucky USA
218 F7 **Lexton** Vic. Australia
138 C4 **Ley** Cornwall England UK
164 6b **Leygues, Îles** *islands* French Southern and Antarctic Lands
140 F3 **Leyland** Lancashire England UK
126 D4 **Leyre** *watercourse* France
215 I6 **Leyshon, Mount** Qld Australia
127 H3 **Leysin** Switzerland
195 J5 **Leyte Gulf** Philippines
138 C4 **Lezant** Cornwall England UK
133 A5 **Lezhë** Albania
136 E2 **L'gov** Russian Federation
181 F3 **Lhagoi Kangri** *mountain* Xizang Zizhiqu China
181 G3 **Lhasa** Xizang Zizhiqu China
125 H3 **Lhenice** Czech Republic
126 F4 **L'Herm** France
196 B2 **Lhokkruet** Indonesia
196 C2 **Lhokseumawe** Indonesia
196 C2 **Lhoksukon** Indonesia
181 G3 **Lhuntshi** Bhutan
181 G3 **Lhuntsi Dzong** Bhutan
Li Jiang *see* **Dayan** China
188 F2 **Li Shui** *watercourse* Hunan China
133 B6 **Liakas, Akra** *cape* Greece
104 C4 **Liamayoc, Cerro** *mountain* Peru
162 D3 **Liambezi, Lake** *lake* Botswana
109 19 **Liamuiga, Mount** *volcano* St Kitts and Nevis
189 G4 **Lian Jiang** *lake* Guangdong China
188 E3 **Liancheng** Guizhou China
188 E4 **Liancheng** Yunnan China
192 G4 **Liancourt Rocks** *island*
189 G3 **Lianfeng** Fujian China
197 I4 **Liang** Indonesia
198 B4 **Liang** Indonesia
196 D3 **Liang Timur, Gunung** *mountain* Malaysia
195 J5 **Lianga** Philippines
195 J5 **Lianga Bay** Philippines
191 G5 **Liangcheng** Nei Mongol Zizhiqu China
188 E1 **Liangdan** Gansu China
188 D1 **Lianghekou** Gansu China
197 G3 **Liangpran, Bukit** *mountain* Indonesia
188 E2 **Liangshan** Chongqing China
191 H6 **Liangshan** Shandong China
188 F4 **Lianjiang** Guangdong China
189 G3 **Lianjiang** Jiangxi China
189 H1 **Lianyungang** Jiangsu China
189 F4 **Lianzhou** Guangdong China
188 F4 **Lianzhou** Guangxi Zhuangzu Zizhiqu China
188 D4 **Lianzhu** Yunnan China
191 H6 **Liaocheng** Shandong China
191 J5 **Liaodong Wan** *bay* Liaoning China
191 J4 **Liaoning** *admin. area* China
191 J4 **Liaoyang** Liaoning China
191 K4 **Liaoyuan** Jilin China
72 G7 **Liard** *watercourse* British Columbia Canada
74 J2 **Liard** *watercourse* Northwest Territories Canada
74 F2 **Liard** *watercourse* Yukon Territory Canada
74 I2 **Liard Range** Northwest Territories Canada
74 H3 **Liard River** British Columbia Canada
179 K4 **Liari** Pakistan
196 E4 **Liat** *island* Indonesia
142 D3 **Liatrie** Highland Scotland UK
223 15 **Lib** *island* Marshall Islands
100 C3 **Líbano** Colombia
142 E5 **Libberton** South Lanarkshire Scotland UK
80 H2 **Libby** Montana USA
127 J5 **Libeccio, Punta** *cape* Italy
160 B3 **Libenge** Democratic Republic of Congo
125 K1 **Liberadz** Poland
81 O8 **Liberal** Kansas USA
125 H2 **Liberec** Czech Republic
125 H2 **Liberecký Kraj** *admin. area* Czech Republic
158 C3 **Liberia** *country* Africa
90 C5 **Liberia** Costa Rica
106 D5 **Libertador General Bernardo O'Higgins** *admin. area* Chile
106 E2 **Libertador General San Martín** Argentina
82 D7 **Liberty** Missouri USA
83 N6 **Liberty** New York USA
86 D5 **Liberty** Texas USA
80 G3 **Liberty Lake** Washington USA
127 G2 **Libin** Belgium
197 K4 **Libobo, Tanjung** *cape* Indonesia
162 E6 **Libode** South Africa
161 G3 **Liboi** Kenya
162 D2 **Libonda** Zambia
125 H2 **Libouchec** Czech Republic
126 D4 **Libourne** France
133 B5 **Librazhd** Albania
159 F4 **Libreville** Gabon
155 J3 **Libya** *country* Africa
156 C2 **Libyan Desert** Libya
Libyan Plateau *see* **Aḍ Ḍiffah** Egypt
85 I6 **Lic. A Lopez Mateos** Mexico
136 G5 **Lice** Turkey
189 H3 **Licheng** Fujian China
189 H1 **Licheng** Jiangsu China
191 H6 **Licheng** Shanxi China
139 F2 **Lichfield** Staffordshire England UK
163 G2 **Lichinga** Mozambique
127 J1 **Lichte** Germany
125 H3 **Lichtenau** Austria
162 E5 **Lichtenburg** South Africa
77 R6 **Lichteneger, Lac** *lake* Quebec Canada
188 E2 **Lichuan** Hubei China
125 H5 **Lička Jesenica** Croatia
130 F4 **Lički Osik** Croatia
82 I7 **Licking** *watercourse* Kentucky USA
82 F8 **Licking** Missouri USA
125 H5 **Licko Lešće** Croatia
218 H7 **Licola** Vic. Australia
123 M6 **Lida** Belarus
142 F2 **Liddel** Orkney Islands Scotland UK
120 J5 **Liden** Sweden
162 C4 **Lidfontein** Namibia
139 H2 **Lidgate** Suffolk England UK
211 inset **Lidgbird, Mount** Lord Howe Island Australia
122 G3 **Lidköping** Sweden
130 E4 **Lido** *island* Italy
133 C6 **Lidoriki** Greece
120 I4 **Lidsjöberg** Sweden
120 K4 **Lidträsket** *lake* Sweden
125 J1 **Lidzbark** Poland
125 H4 **Liebenfels** Austria
75 Q7 **Liebenthal** Saskatchewan Canada
85 M1 **Liebenthal** Kansas USA
125 H2 **Lieberose** Germany
132 B3 **Liebling** Romania
124 **Liechtenstein** *country* Europe
127 G1 **Liège** Belgium
121 M2 **Liejankijärvi** *lake* Finland
160 C3 **Lieki** Democratic Republic of Congo
121 O4 **Liekola** Finland
121 Q5 **Lieksa** Finland
123 N4 **Liel Kalupes ezers** *lake* Latvia
123 L2 **Lielax** Finland
123 L4 **Lielupe** *watercourse* Latvia
123 M4 **Lielvārde** Latvia
123 M4 **Liepa** Latvia
123 K4 **Liepāja** Latvia
123 K4 **Liepājas** *admin. area* Latvia
123 K4 **Liepājas ezers** *lake* Latvia
123 K4 **Liepene** Latvia
123 L5 **Lieplaukė** Lithuania
123 N4 **Liepna** Latvia
127 G1 **Lier** Belgium
124 C4 **Liernais** France
126 E2 **Lierville** France
121 N5 **Liesjärvi** Finland
123 L2 **Liesjärvi** *lake* Finland
126 F2 **Liesse** France
127 H3 **Liestal** Switzerland
124 C2 **Liesveld** Netherlands
123 L2 **Lieto** Finland
123 N/O2 **Lietvesi** *lake* Finland
126 E2 **Lieurey** France
121 O5 **Lievestuore** Finland
123 M1 **Lievestuoreenjärvi** *lake* Finland
126 F1 **Liévin** France
83 N4 **Lièvre** *watercourse* Quebec Canada
125 H4 **Liezen** Austria
160 C3 **Lifanga** Democratic Republic of Congo
143 F3 **Liffey** *watercourse* Ireland
143 E2 **Lifford** Ireland
126 D2 **Liffré** France
222 7 **Lifou** *island* New Caledonia
223 10 **Lifuka** *island* Tonga
123 M4 **Līgatne** Latvia
195 I4 **Ligaya** Philippines
133 B6 **Ligeni I Butrintit** *lake* Albania
216 H4 **Lightfoot Lake** WA Australia
219 I3 **Lightning Ridge** NSW Australia
126 F3 **Lignières** France
81 N2 **Lignite** North Dakota USA
163 G3 **Ligonha** *watercourse* Mozambique
126 E3 **Ligueil** France
126 E3 **Ligugé** France
88 C3 **Ligui** Mexico
130 C4 **Liguria** *admin. area* Italy
127 I5 **Ligurian Sea** Europe
199 J4 **Lihir Island** Papua New Guinea
121 N5 **Lihjamo** Finland
215 K4 **Lihou Reef** Coral Sea Islands Territory Australia
120 H3 **Lihovdet** *island* Norway
84 inset **Līhu'e** Hawai'i USA
106 E6 **Lihuel-Calel** Argentina
123 L3 **Lihula** Estonia
123 L3 **Liivi laht** *bay* Estonia
188 D4 **Lijiang** Yunnan China
191 I5 **Lijin** Shandong China
160 D6 **Likasi** Democratic Republic of Congo
160 C3 **Likati** Democratic Republic of Congo
74 K6 **Likely** British Columbia Canada
160 C4 **Likete** Democratic Republic of Congo
199 F4 **Liki** *island* Indonesia
223 15 **Likiep Atoll** Marshall Islands
160 C3 **Likimi** Democratic Republic of Congo
198 C6 **Likisia** Timor-Leste (East Timor)
122 D3 **Liknes** Norway
159 H4 **Likouala** *admin. area* Congo
159 H5 **Likouala** *watercourse* Congo
159 H4 **Likouala aux Herbes** *watercourse* Congo
122 I3 **Likstammen** *lake* Sweden
196 F3 **Liku** Indonesia
197 G2 **Liku** Malaysia
220 4 **Liku** Niue New Zealand
160 C3 **Likulu** Democratic Republic of Congo
198 C3 **Likupang** Indonesia
214 A8 **Lila** NT Australia
87 I4 **Lilburn** Georgia USA
127 I5 **L'Île-Rousse** Corsica France
160 C3 **Lileko** Democratic Republic of Congo
160 C3 **Lilenga** Democratic Republic of Congo
52 O4 **Liliukulani Ridge** *underwater feature* Pacific Ocean
123 N2 **Liljendal** Finland
120 I4 **Lill-Björkvattnet** *bay* Sweden
120 K3 **Lill-Mattaure** *lake* Sweden
218 B1 **Lilla** *watercourse* NT Australia
218 B1 **Lilla Creek** NT Australia
120 L3 **Lilla Luleälven** *lake* Sweden
120 K5 **Lillarmsjö** Sweden
126 F1 **Lille** France
120 I2 **Lille Molla** *island* Norway
139 H5 **Lillebonne** France
122 F2 **Lillehammer** Norway
126 F1 **Lillers** France
122 E3 **Lillesand** Norway
138 E2 **Lilleshall** Telford and Wrekin England UK
120 L2 **Lillestraumen** *bay* Norway
75 S7 **Lillestrom** Saskatchewan Canada
120 I6 **Lillhärdal** Sweden
120 I5 **Lillholmsjö** Sweden
123 M3 **Lilli** Estonia
58 K2 **Lillie Glacier** Antarctica
120 I4 **Lilljorm** *bay* Sweden
120 L4 **Lillkågeträsk** Sweden
120 J4 **Lillögda** Sweden
74 K7 **Lillooet** British Columbia Canada
74 J7 **Lillooet** *watercourse* British Columbia Canada
74 J7 **Lillooet Lake** British Columbia Canada
74 J7 **Lillooet Range** British Columbia Canada
120 K4 **Lillsele** Sweden
121 M3 **Lillselet** Sweden
120 I5 **Lillsjöhögen** Sweden
163 F2 **Lilongwe** Malawi
163 F2 **Lilongwe** *watercourse* Malawi
214 E4 **Lily** *watercourse* Qld Australia
74 I6 **Lily Lake** British Columbia Canada
132 C4 **Lilyache** Bulgaria
159 H3 **Lim** *watercourse* Cameroon
132 A4 **Lim** *watercourse* Montenegro
104 B4 **Lima** Peru
104 B3 **Lima** *admin. area* Peru
82 I6 **Lima** Ohio USA
103 D8 **Lima Duarte** Brazil
80 I4 **Lima Reservoir** Montana USA
182 C4 **Liman Vostochnyy** *lake* Russian Federation
125 K3 **Limanowa** Poland
105 G2 **Limão** Brazil
105 H2 **Limão** Brazil
106 D4 **Limarí** *watercourse* Chile
196 E3 **Limas** Indonesia
136 E6 **Limassol** Cyprus
143 F1 **Limavady** Limavady Northern Ireland UK
143 F2 **Limavady** *admin. area* Northern Ireland UK
108 C2 **Limay** *watercourse* Argentina
126 E2 **Limay** France
90 C4 **Limbaica** Nicaragua
197 G2 **Limbang** Malaysia
195 G6 **Limbang** *watercourse* Malaysia
123 M4 **Limbaži** Latvia
123 M4 **Limbažu** *admin. area* Latvia
187 C6 **Limbdi** Gujarat India
198 B6 **Limbung** Indonesia
197 G4 **Limbungan** Indonesia
213 J4 **Limbunya** NT Australia
127 G1 **Limburg** *admin. area* Belgium
124 C2 **Limburg** *admin. area* Netherlands
130 F3 **Limbuš** Slovenia
103 C8 **Limeira** Brazil
143 D4 **Limerick** Ireland
143 D4 **Limerick** *admin. area* Ireland
143 D4 **Limerick Junction** Ireland
89 F2 **Limestone, Lake** Texas USA
75 V6 **Limestone Point** Manitoba Canada
90 C4 **Limeta** Honduras
122 E4 **Limfjorden** *lake* Denmark
120 H4 **Limingen** *lake* Norway
121 M3 **Limingojärvi** Sweden
121 N4 **Liminka** Finland
214 C3 **Limmen Bight** *bay* NT Australia
133 D6 **Limnos** *island* Greece
102 B3 **Limoeiro do Ajuru** Brazil
102 E4 **Limoeiro do Norte** Brazil
126 E4 **Limoges** France
126 E4 **Limogne** France
81 N7 **Limon** Colorado USA
89 H5 **Limones** Mexico
124 B3 **Limours** France
126 E4 **Limousin** *admin. area* France
126 F5 **Limoux** France
163 F4 **Limpopo** *watercourse* Mozambique
162 E4 **Limpopo** *admin. area* South Africa
162 E4 **Limpopo** *watercourse* South Africa
220 4 **Limufuafua Point** Niue New Zealand
188 D4 **Lin'an** Yunnan China
120 L3 **Linaälv** Sweden
120 L3 **Linaälven** *watercourse* Sweden
121 Q2 **Linakhamari** Russian Federation
108 B2 **Linao** Chile
195 H5 **Linapacan** *island* Philippines
106 D5 **Linares** Chile
89 F3 **Linares** Mexico
128 E4 **Linares** Spain
128 E3 **Linares, Embalse de** *lake* Spain
133 D6 **Linaria** Greece
127 J5 **Linaro, Capo** *cape* Italy
197 G3 **Linau Balui** *plain* Malaysia
139 F1 **Linby** Nottinghamshire England UK
124 C2 **Lincent** Belgium
188 F5 **Lincheng** Hainan China
188 F3 **Lincheng** Hunan China
189 G3 **Linchuan** Jiangxi China
58 R1 **Linck Nunataks** *mountain* Antarctica
106 F5 **Lincoln** Argentina
141 H3 **Lincoln** Lincolnshire England UK
87 H4 **Lincoln** Alabama USA
82 G6 **Lincoln** Illinois USA
83 Q4 **Lincoln** Maine USA
72 H9 **Lincoln** Montana USA
81 Q6 **Lincoln** Nebraska USA
81 O3 **Lincoln** North Dakota USA
83 P4 **Lincoln, Mount** New Hampshire USA
72 G10 **Lincoln City** Oregon USA
195 G3 **Lincoln Island** Paracel Islands
73 N2 **Lincoln Sea** Canada/Greenland
141 H3 **Lincolnshire** *admin. area* England UK
87 J4 **Lincolnton** Georgia USA
87 K3 **Lincolnton** North Carolina USA
80 F3 **Lind** Washington USA
214 E7 **Linda** *watercourse* Qld Australia
105 I5 **Linda Vista** Brazil
122 C2 **Lindås-Halvøya** *island* Norway
124 G1 **Lindau** Germany
75 P6 **Lindbergh** Alberta Canada
105 E5 **Linde** Bolivia
122 E4 **Linde** Denmark
215 J6 **Lindeman Group** *islands* Qld Australia
101 G3 **Linden** Guyana
86 H4 **Linden** Alabama USA
84 B1 **Linden** California USA
Lindenow Fjord *see* **Kangerlussuatsiaq** Greenland
122 D4 **Lindesnes** *bay* Norway
160 D3 **Lindi** *watercourse* Democratic Republic of Congo
161 F5 **Lindi** Tanzania
161 F5 **Lindi** *admin. area* Tanzania
191 J3 **Lindian** Heilongjiang China
107 G2 **Lindo, Monte** *watercourse* Paraguay
122 I2 **Lindön** *island* Sweden
191 I4 **Lindong** Nei Mongol Zizhiqu China
133 F7 **Lindos, Akra** *cape* Greece
217 N3 **Lindsay** *watercourse* SA Australia
83 L4 **Lindsay** Ontario Canada
84 C2 **Lindsay** California USA
81 Q6 **Lindsay** Nebraska USA
81 Q7 **Lindsborg** Kansas USA
141 G3 **Lindwell** West Yorkshire England UK
222 1 **Line Islands** Kiribati
179 M2 **Line of Control** Pakistan
120 F5 **Linesøya** *island* Norway
190 G6 **Linfen** Shanxi China
195 I3 **Lingayen** Philippines
195 H3 **Lingayen Gulf** Philippines
188 F1 **Lingbao** Henan China
189 H1 **Lingcheng** Anhui China
188 F4 **Lingcheng** Guangxi Zhuangzu Zizhiqu China
188 F5 **Lingcheng** Hainan China
188 F3 **Lingchuan** Guangxi Zhuangzu Zizhiqu China
191 H6 **Lingchuan** Shanxi China
120 E5 **Linge** Norway
124 D1 **Lingen** Germany
139 G3 **Lingfield** Surrey England UK
196 E4 **Lingga** *island* Indonesia
197 F3 **Lingga** Malaysia
196 E3 **Lingga, Kepulauan** *islands* Indonesia
185 H6 **Linggo Co** *mountain* Xizang Zizhiqu China
191 J4 **Linghai** Liaoning China
188 E2 **Lingjiang** Sichuan China
197 H2 **Lingkabau** Malaysia
197 H3 **Lingkas** Indonesia
214 E4 **Lingnoonganee Island** Qld Australia
160 C4 **Lingomo** Democratic Republic of Congo
160 C3 **Lingomo** Democratic Republic of Congo
190 G6 **Lingshi** Shanxi China
191 H5 **Lingshou** Hebei China
187 D8 **Lingsugur** Karnataka India
154 C5 **Linguère** Senegal
188 F3 **Lingui** Guangxi Zhuangzu Zizhiqu China
190 F5 **Lingwu** Ningxia Huizu Zizhiqu China
188 F2 **Lingxi** Hunan China
189 H3 **Lingxi** Zhejiang China
189 F2 **Lingyang** Hunan China
191 I4 **Lingyuan** Liaoning China
189 H1 **Linhai** Jiangsu China
189 I3 **Linhai** Zhejiang China
103 D7 **Linhares** Brazil
190 F5 **Linhe** Nei Mongol Zizhiqu China
122 J5 **Liniewo** Poland
189 G3 **Linjiang** Fujian China
191 K4 **Linjiang** Jilin China
216 H2 **Linke Lakes** WA Australia
121 M3 **Linkka** Sweden
122 H3 **Linköping** Sweden
191 L3 **Linkou** Heilongjiang China
123 L4 **Linkuva** Lithuania
86 B7 **Linn** Texas USA
121 N5 **Linnankylä** Finland
142 C4 **Linnhe, Loch** *bay* Scotland UK
82 E4 **Lino Lakes** Minnesota USA
131 E9 **Linosa, Isola di** *island* Italy
191 H6 **Linqing** Hebei China
191 I6 **Linqu** Shandong China
189 G1 **Linquan** Anhui China
104 D4 **Linquipata** Peru
103 B8 **Lins** Brazil
120 H5 **Linsell** Sweden
189 H1 **Linshu** Shandong China
163 H4 **Linta** *watercourse* Madagascar
188 D1 **Lintan** Gansu China
75 T6 **Lintlaw** Saskatchewan Canada
139 H2 **Linton** Cambridgeshire England UK
81 O3 **Linton** North Dakota USA
121 N3 **Lintula** Finland
189 F3 **Linwu** Hunan China
191 I4 **Linxi** Nei Mongol Zizhiqu China
190 E6 **Linxia** Gansu China
190 G5 **Linxian** Shanxi China
189 F3 **Linxiang** Hunan China
189 G2 **Linxiang** Hunan China
162 D3 **Linyati Swamp** *swamp* Namibia
189 H1 **Linyi** Shandong China
191 H5 **Linyi** Shandong China
188 F1 **Linyi** Shanxi China
189 G1 **Linying** Henan China
125 H3 **Linz** Austria
190 D5 **Linze** Gansu China
181 H3 **Linzhi** Xizang Zizhiqu China
191 H6 **Linzhou** Henan China
197 G3 **Lio Matoh** Malaysia
125 M2 **Lioboml'** Ukraine
123 L5 **Lioliai** Lithuania
163 G3 **Lioma** Mozambique
126 F5 **Lion, Golfe du** *bay* France
108 E5 **Lion Point** Falkland Islands
74 J8 **Lions Bay** British Columbia Canada
198 C5 **Lioppa** Indonesia
199 H4 **Liot Island** Papua New Guinea
155 I6 **Lioua** Chad
159 H4 **Liouesso** Congo
195 I4 **Lipa** Philippines
86 B4 **Lipan** Texas USA
125 K3 **Lipany** Slovakia
132 A3 **Lipar** Serbia
131 F7 **Lipari** Italy
131 F7 **Lipari, Isola** *island* Italy
196 D3 **Lipatkain** Indonesia
127 K1 **Lipenec** Czech Republic
106 E2 **Lipeo** Argentina
121 P5 **Liperi** Finland
182 C3 **Lipetsk** Russian Federation
182 C3 **Lipetskaya Oblast'** *admin. area* Russian Federation
104 E6 **Lipez, Cordillera de** *range* Bolivia
139 G3 **Liphook** Hampshire England UK
123 N5 **Lipiniški** Latvia
132 B4 **Lipkovo** Macedonia
123 Q3 **Lipnaya Gorka** Russian Federation
125 I1 **Lipnica** Poland
125 J1 **Lipnica** Poland
122 I6 **Lipnica** Poland
125 H3 **Lipno, Vodní nádrž** *lake* Czech Republic
132 A3 **Lipolist** Serbia
132 B2 **Lipova** Romania
132 C3 **Lipovu** Romania
86 A2 **Lipscomb** Texas USA
218 C6 **Lipson** SA Australia
75 T7 **Lipton** Saskatchewan Canada
158 E2 **Liptougou** Burkina Faso
218 G8 **Liptrap, Cape** Vic. Australia
122 I5 **Lipusz** Poland
105 E6 **Lique, Sierra de** *range* Bolivia
108 B2 **Liquiñe** Chile
161 E3 **Lira** Uganda
131 E6 **Liri** *watercourse* Italy
129 F4 **Liria** Spain
198 C3 **Lirung** Indonesia
143 E4 **Lis** Ireland
132 D3 **Lisa** Romania
143 D3 **Lisacul** Ireland
160 B4 **Lisafa** Democratic Republic of Congo
160 C3 **Lisala** Democratic Republic of Congo
101 F5 **Lisbão** Brazil
143 E2 **Lisbellaw** Fermanagh Northern Ireland UK
104 D3 **Lisboa** Bolivia
128 B4 **Lisboa** *admin. area* Portugal
128 B4 **Lisboa (Lisbon)** Portugal
Lisbon *see* **Lisboa** Portugal
81 Q3 **Lisbon** North Dakota USA
143 F2 **Lisburn** Lisburn Northern Ireland UK
143 F2 **Lisburn** *admin. area* Northern Ireland UK
72 C5 **Lisburne, Cape** Alaska USA
143 C3 **Liscarney** Ireland
79 G10 **Liscomb** Nova Scotia Canada
143 D3 **Lisconly** Ireland
189 G4 **Lishi** Jiangxi China
190 G5 **Lishi** Shanxi China
189 H4 **Lishi Liedao** *island* Fujian China
191 J4 **Lishu** Jilin China
189 H3 **Lishui** Zhejiang China
126 E2 **Lisieux** France
123 P2 **Lisiy Nos** Russian Federation
122 H2 **Lisjön** *lake* Sweden
138 C4 **Liskeard** Cornwall England UK
136 F2 **Liski** Russian Federation
143 E2 **Lislap** Omagh Northern Ireland UK
126 E3 **L'Isle-Bouchard** France
126 E5 **L'Isle-en-Dodon** France
127 G5 **L'Isle-sur-la-Sorgue** France
79 D8 **L'Isle-Verte** Quebec Canada
140 A2 **Lislea** Ireland
79 C9 **L'Islet** Quebec Canada
86 G4 **Lisman** Alabama USA
219 K3 **Lismore** NSW Australia
79 G10 **Lismore** Nova Scotia Canada
143 E4 **Lismore** Ireland
142 C4 **Lismore** *island* Scotland UK
81 R5 **Lismore** Minnesota USA
123 O4 **Lisna, Vozyera** *lake* Belarus
140 B2 **Lisnacree** Newry and Mourne Northern Ireland UK
140 B1 **Lisnagunogue** Moyle Northern Ireland UK
143 E2 **Lisnaskea** Fermanagh Northern Ireland UK
132 F2 **Lisne** Ukraine
130 G4 **Lišnja** Bosnia and Herzegovina
125 H3 **Lišov** Czech Republic
132 G1 **Lisovichi** Ukraine
140 A3 **Lisreagh** Ireland
143 E3 **Lisryan** Ireland
139 G3 **Liss** Hampshire England UK
143 D4 **Lissatunny** Ireland
141 H2 **Lissett** East Riding of Yorkshire England UK
141 H3 **Lissington** Lincolnshire England UK
122 E5 **List** Germany
122 D3 **Lista** *island* Norway
58 K1 **Lister, Mount** *mountain* Antarctica
130 G5 **Lištica** Bosnia and Herzegovina
140 C2 **Listooder** Down Northern Ireland UK
143 C4 **Listowel** Ireland
140 B2 **Listullycurran** Lisburn Northern Ireland UK
120 I5 **Lit/Söre** Sweden
188 C3 **Litang Qu** *watercourse* Sichuan China
82 G7 **Litchfield** Illinois USA
132 E2 **Liteni** Romania
133 D6 **Lithari, Akra** *cape* Greece
219 J5 **Lithgow** NSW Australia
133 E8 **Lithines** Greece
133 D8 **Lithino, Akra** *cape* Greece
133 D6 **Líthion** Greece
123 M5 **Lithuania** *country* Europe
125 M3 **Litiatyn** Ukraine
102 D4 **Litigated Zone** Brazil
135 AL4 **Litke, Mys** *cape* Russian Federation
130 G2 **Litomyšl** Czech Republic
125 I3 **Litovel** Czech Republic
85 N5 **Little** *watercourse* Texas USA
87 M7 **Little Abaco** *island* Bahamas
77 O7 **Little Abitibi** *watercourse* Ontario Canada
83 K2 **Little Abitibi Lake** Ontario Canada
58 N1 **Little America Basin** *bay* Antarctica
194 B5 **Little Andaman** *island* Andaman and Nicobar Islands India
142 C2 **Little Assynt** Highland Scotland UK
87 M7 **Little Bahama Bank** *reef* Bahamas
139 G2 **Little Barford** Bedfordshire England UK
220 F3 **Little Barrier Island** New Zealand
141 F1 **Little Bavington** Northumberland England UK
81 J3 **Little Bell Mountains** Montana USA

81 L4 **Little Bighorn** *watercourse* Montana USA
80 H2 **Little Bitterroot Lake** Montana USA
75 O7 **Little Bow** *watercourse* Alberta Canada
139 G3 **Little Brickhill** Milton Keynes England UK
75 O2/3 **Little Buffalo** *watercourse* Alberta/ Northwest Territories Canada
139 G2 **Little Bytham** Lincolnshire England UK
142 C6 **Little Cairnbrock** Dumfries and Galloway Scotland UK
90 D3 **Little Cayman** *island* Cayman Islands
139 H2 **Little Chesterford** Essex England UK
76 H4 **Little Churchill** *watercourse* Manitoba Canada
82 G4 **Little Chute** Wisconsin USA
194 B4 **Little Coco Island** Andaman and Nicobar Islands India
84 G3 **Little Colorado** *watercourse* Arkansas USA
139 F3 **Little Compton** Warwickshire England UK
139 H2 **Little Cornard** Suffolk England UK
76 M7 **Little Current** *watercourse* Ontario Canada
80 E5 **Little Deschutes** *watercourse* Oregon USA
218 E7 **Little Desert** Vic. Australia
83 O7 **Little Egg Harbor** New Jersey USA
91 F2 **Little Exuma** *island* Bahamas
75 O3 **Little Fishery** Alberta Canada
74 K7 **Little Fort** British Columbia Canada
141 H2 **Little Habton** North Yorkshire England UK
138 B3 **Little Haven** Pembrokeshire Wales UK
139 F2 **Little Haywood** Staffordshire England UK
141 G3 **Little Hucklow** Derbyshire England UK
91 F2 **Little Inagua Island** Bahamas
84 D3 **Little Lake** California USA
86 F6 **Little Lake** Louisiana USA
82 F3 **Little Marais** Minnesota USA
79 H6 **Little Mecatina** *watercourse* Newfoundland and Labrador Canada
142 B3 **Little Minch** *bay* Scotland UK
81 N3/4 **Little Missouri** *watercourse* North Dakota/South Dakota USA
80 E3 **Little Naches** *watercourse* Washington USA
194 B6 **Little Nicobar Island** Andaman and Nicobar Islands India
219 J3 **Little Plain** NSW Australia
81 M4 **Little Powder** *watercourse* Montana USA
186 C6 **Little Rann** Gujarat India
75 N3 **Little Red River** Alberta Canada
139 F3 **Little Rissington** Gloucestershire England UK
86 E3 **Little Rock** Arkansas USA
76 I5 **Little Sachigo Lake** Ontario Canada
80 I8 **Little Salt Lake** Utah USA
91 F1 **Little San Salvador** *island* Bahamas
216 G2 **Little Sandy Desert** WA Australia
82 D5 **Little Sioux** *watercourse* Iowa USA
135 AK8 **Little Sitkin Island** *island* Alaska USA
74 M5 **Little Smoky** Alberta Canada
74 M5 **Little Smoky** *watercourse* Alberta Canada
135 AL8 **Little Tanaga Island** Alaska USA
139 F3 **Little Tew** Oxfordshire England UK
139 H2 **Little Thetford** Cambridgeshire England UK
218 F4 **Little Topar Roadhouse** NSW Australia
82 I4 **Little Traverse Bay** Michigan USA
76 I7 **Little Vermilion Lake** Ontario Canada
139 H3 **Little Wakering** Essex England UK
81 O5 **Little White** *watercourse* South Dakota USA
141 F3 **Littleborough** Greater Manchester England UK
139 H2 **Littlebury** Essex England UK
84 F2 **Littlefield** Arizona USA
85 K4 **Littlefield** Texas USA
138 C4 **Littleham** Devon England UK
139 G4 **Littlehampton** West Sussex England UK
139 H2 **Littleport** Cambridgeshire England UK
81 M7 **Littleton** Colorado USA
159 G4 **Littoral** *admin. area* Cameroon
163 G2 **Litunde** Mozambique
74 C3 **Lituya Bay** Alaska USA
127 K1 **Litvínov** Czech Republic
132 C1 **Litynya** Ukraine
123 M3 **Liu** Estonia
189 H2 **Liucheng** Jiangsu China
189 H4 **Liuchiu Yü** *island* Taiwan China
188 E3 **Liuchuan** Guizhou China
191 K4 **Liuhe** Jilin China
189 I2 **Liuheng Dao** *island* Zhejiang China
190 E6 **Liujiaxia** Gansu China
161 E6 **Liuli** Tanzania
188 D1 **Liulin** Gansu China
190 F6 **Liupan Shan** *range* Ningxia Huizu Zizhiqu China
163 G3 **Liúpo** Mozambique
162 D2 **Liuwa Plain** *plain* Zambia
189 G4 **Liuxi He** *watercourse* Guangdong China
189 G3 **Liuyang** Hunan China
189 G3 **Liuyang He** *watercourse* Hunan China
188 F4 **Liuzhou** Guangxi Zhuangzu Zizhiqu China
133 D7 **Livada, Akra** *cape* Greece
133 C5 **Livadi** Greece
133 E7 **Livadi** *island* Greece
133 E7 **Livádia** Greece
133 C6 **Livanátai** Greece
123 N4 **Līvāni** Latvia
131 H5 **Livari** Montenegro
126 E2 **Livarot** France
80 E7 **Live Oak** California USA
87 J5 **Live Oak** Florida USA
84 D4 **Live Oak Springs** California USA
109 7 **Lively Island** Falkland Islands
219 J5 **Liverpool** NSW Australia
214 B2 **Liverpool** *watercourse* NT Australia
140 F3 **Liverpool** *admin. area* England UK
140 F3 **Liverpool** Merseyside England UK
73 L4 **Liverpool, Cape** Nunavut Canada
72 F5 **Liverpool Bay** Northwest Territories Canada
140 E3 **Liverpool Bay** England UK
219 J4 **Liverpool Range** NSW Australia
160 D5 **Lividjo** *watercourse* Democratic Republic of Congo
77 V6 **Livingston** Newfoundland and Labrador Canada
90 B4 **Lívingston** Guatemala
142 E5 **Livingston** West Lothian Scotland UK
86 G4 **Livingston** Alabama USA
80 E8 **Livingston** California USA
82 G7 **Livingston** Illinois USA
81 J4 **Livingston** Montana USA
86 D5 **Livingston, Lake** Texas USA
59 T2 **Livingston Island** Antarctica
162 E3 **Livingstone** Zambia
219 Q10 **Livingstone, Mount** Tas. Australia
130 G5 **Livno** Bosnia and Herzegovina
136 F2 **Livny** Russian Federation
121 O4 **Livo** Finland
121 O4 **Livojärvi** *lake* Finland
121 O4 **Livojoki** *watercourse* Finland
86 F5 **Livonia** Louisiana USA
82 J5 **Livonia** Michigan USA
83 M5 **Livonia** New York USA
130 D5 **Livorno** Italy
105 G2 **Livramento** Brazil
103 D6 **Livramento do Brumado** Brazil
127 G4 **Livron-sur-Drôme** France
125 K1 **Liw** Poland
163 F2 **Liwala** *watercourse* Malawi
161 F5 **Liwale** Tanzania
161 F5 **Liwale Juu** Tanzania
191 H5 **Liwu** Hebei China
188 E1 **Lixian** Gansu China
188 D4 **Lixian Jiang** *watercourse* Yunnan China
189 G1 **Lixin** Anhui China
133 B6 **Lixouri** Greece
189 H2 **Liyang** Anhui China
189 H2 **Liyang** Jiangsu China
188 F2 **Liyuan** Hunan China
138 B5 **Lizard** Cornwall England UK
215 H3 **Lizard Island** Qld Australia
138 B5 **Lizard Point** England UK
102 C5 **Lizarda** Brazil
121 S5 **Lizhma** Russian Federation
121 R5 **Lizhmozero, Ozero** *lake* Russian Federation
124 B3 **Lizy** France
132 B3 **Ljig** Serbia
125 H4 **Ljubljana** Slovenia
132 A3 **Ljubovija** Serbia
122 H2 **Ljugaren** *lake* Sweden
123 J4 **Ljugarn** Sweden
120 H5 **Ljungan** *watercourse* Sweden
120 H5 **Ljungdalen** Sweden
120 L4 **Ljuså** Sweden
120 J6 **Ljusdal** Sweden
120 I6 **Ljusnan** *watercourse* Sweden
122 H3 **Ljusnaren** *lake* Sweden
120 H5 **Ljusnedal** Sweden
104 C4 **Llaico** Peru
104 E5 **Llallagua** Bolivia
104 D6 **Llamara, Salar de** *pan* Chile
138 C2 **Llanaber** Gwynedd Wales UK
138 C2 **Llanaelhaiarn** Gwynedd Wales UK
138 D2 **Llanafan-fawr** Powys Wales UK
138 D2 **Llanarmon Dyffryn** Wrexham Wales UK
138 C2 **Llanbadarn-Fawr** Ceredigion Wales UK
140 D3 **Llanbadrig** Isle of Anglesey Wales UK
138 C2 **Llanbedr** Gwynedd Wales UK
138 C2 **Llanbedrog** Gwynedd Wales UK
138 C1 **Llanberis** Gwynedd Wales UK
138 C2 **Llancynfelyn** Ceredigion Wales UK
138 C2 **Llanddeiniol** Ceredigion Wales UK
138 D1 **Llanddoget** Conwy Wales UK
138 D2 **Llandegley** Powys Wales UK
138 D3 **Llandeilo** Carmarthenshire Wales UK
138 C3 **Llandissilio** Pembrokeshire Wales UK
138 D3 **Llandovery** Carmarthenshire Wales UK
138 D2 **Llandrillo** Denbighshire Wales UK
140 E3 **Llandudno** Conwy Wales UK
138 D2 **Llandulas** Powys Wales UK
138 C2 **Llandyssul** Carmarthenshire Wales UK
138 D3 **Llanedeyrn** Cardiff Wales UK
138 C3 **Llanedy** Carmarthenshire Wales UK
138 C3 **Llanegwad** Carmarthenshire Wales UK
138 C3 **Llanelli** Carmarthenshire Wales UK
138 D2 **Llanelwedd** Powys Wales UK
138 C2 **Llanengan** Gwynedd Wales UK
138 D2 **Llanerfyl** Powys Wales UK
128 D2 **Llanes** Spain
138 D2 **Llanfachreth** Gwynedd Wales UK
140 D3 **Llanfaethlu** Isle of Anglesey Wales UK
138 C2 **Llanfair** Gwynedd Wales UK
138 C2 **Llanfair Clydogau** Ceredigion Wales UK
140 E3 **Llanfair Talhaiarn** Conwy Wales UK
138 D2 **Llanfair Waterdine** Shropshire England UK
140 E3 **Llanfairfechan** Conwy Wales UK
138 C2 **Llanfihangel-y-pennant** Gwynedd Wales UK
138 D2 **Llanfyllin** Powys Wales UK
138 D2 **Llangadfan** Powys Wales UK
138 D2 **Llangadwaladr** Powys Wales UK
138 E3 **Llangattock nigh Usk** Monmouthshire Wales UK
140 D3 **Llangefni** Isle of Anglesey Wales UK
138 C2 **Llangeler** Carmarthenshire Wales UK
138 C2 **Llangelynin** Gwynedd Wales UK
138 D1 **Llangernyw** Conwy Wales UK
140 D3 **Llangoed** Isle of Anglesey Wales UK
138 D2 **Llangollen** Denbighshire Wales UK
138 E2 **Llangollen Branch** *watercourse* England UK
219 J4 **Llangothlin** NSW Australia
138 D2 **Llangower** Gwynedd Wales UK
138 C2 **Llangranog** Ceredigion Wales UK
138 D2 **Llangunllo** Powys Wales UK
138 D2 **Llangurig** Powys Wales UK
138 D2 **Llangwm** Conwy Wales UK
138 C2 **Llangwnadl** Gwynedd Wales UK
138 D3 **Llangynidr** Powys Wales UK
138 D2 **Llangynog** Powys Wales UK
138 D3 **Llanhamlach** Powys Wales UK
138 C2 **Llanilar** Ceredigion Wales UK
138 C2 **Llanina** Ceredigion Wales UK
138 C1 **Llanllechid** Gwynedd Wales UK
138 C1 **Llanllyfni** Gwynedd Wales UK
138 C3 **Llanmiloe** Carmarthenshire Wales UK
86 B5 **Llano** Texas USA
88 D3 **Llano, El** *plain* Mexico
85 J6 **Llano de los Cabellos Mesteños** Mexico
90 D6 **Llano de Piedra** Panama
88 E1 **Llano Estacado** *region* New Mexico USA
138 C2 **Llanon** Ceredigion Wales UK
100 D3 **Llanos** *region*
164 3d **Llanos de Concepción** Canary Islands
138 C3 **Llanrhidian** Swansea Wales UK
140 D3 **Llanrhyddlad** Isle of Anglesey Wales UK
138 B3 **Llanrian** Pembrokeshire Wales UK
138 D1 **Llanrwst** Conwy Wales UK
138 D2 **Llansaintffread in Elvel** Powys Wales UK
138 D1 **Llansannan** Conwy Wales UK
138 C2 **Llansantffraid** Ceredigion Wales UK
138 C2 **Llansawel** Carmarthenshire Wales UK
138 D2 **Llansilin** Powys Wales UK
138 E3 **Llansoy** Monmouthshire Wales UK
140 D3 **Llantrisaint** Isle of Anglesey Wales UK
138 D2 **Llantysilio** Denbighshire Wales UK
138 D2 **Llanuwchllyn** Gwynedd Wales UK
138 D2 **Llanwddyn** Powys Wales UK
138 C1 **Llanwnda** Gwynedd Wales UK
138 D2 **Llanwnog** Powys Wales UK
138 D3 **Llanwrda** Carmarthenshire Wales UK
138 D2 **Llanwrin** Powys Wales UK
138 D2 **Llanwrtyd Wells** Powys Wales UK
138 D2 **Llanyblodwel** Shropshire England UK
138 C2 **Llanychaiarn** Ceredigion Wales UK
138 D2 **Llanycil** Gwynedd Wales UK
138 D2 **Llanycrwys** Carmarthenshire Wales UK
138 D2 **Llanymawddwy** Gwynedd Wales UK
108 B2 **Llao Llao** Argentina
104 B3 **Llata** Peru
129 G2 **Llavorsí** Spain
138 E1 **Llay** Wrexham Wales UK
138 D2 **Lledrod** Ceredigion Wales UK
129 G3 **Lleida** Spain
89 F4 **Llera de Canales** Mexico
128 C4 **Llerena** Spain
106 C6 **Llico** Chile
129 H3 **Lloret de Mar** Spain
100 B3 **Lloró** Colombia
138 D2 **Llowes** Powys Wales UK
214 B7 **Lloyd, Mount** NT Australia
215 G2 **Lloyd Bay** Qld Australia
74 I4 **Lloyd George, Mount** British Columbia Canada
72 I7 **Lloyd Lake** Saskatchewan Canada
75 P6 **Lloydminster** Saskatchewan Canada
138 D2 **Lloyney** Shropshire England UK
129 H4 **Llucmajor** Spain
106 D3 **Llullaillaco, Volcán** *volcano* Chile
104 C5 **Lluta** Peru
138 C2 **Llwyngwril** Gwynedd Wales UK
138 D2 **Llynclys** Shropshire England UK
138 C3 **Llys-y fran** Pembrokeshire Wales UK
140 E3 **Llysfaen** Conwy Wales UK
125 J1 **Lniano** Poland
194 E2 **Lô** *watercourse* Vietnam
88 D5 **Lo Arado** Mexico
197 H4 **Loa Janan** Indonesia
195 G5 **Loaita Island** Spratly Islands
197 H4 **Loakulu** Indonesia
103 A8 **Loanda** Brazil
160 C5 **Loange** *watercourse* Democratic Republic of Congo
159 G5 **Loango** Congo
160 A5 **Loango** Democratic Republic of Congo
130 C4 **Loano** Italy
198 B4 **Lobata** Indonesia
162 E5 **Lobatse** Botswana
125 H2 **Löbau** Germany
159 H4 **Lobaye** *admin. area* Central African Republic
159 H3 **Lobaye** *watercourse* Central African Republic
124 C2 **Lobbes** Belgium
159 G4 **Lobe** *watercourse* Cameroon
127 J1 **Lobenstein** Germany
161 E3 **Lobira** Sudan
162 B2 **Lobito** Angola
124 2 **Löbnitz** Germany
89 F4 **Lobo, Isla de** *island* Mexico
107 G5 **Lobos** Argentina
88 B2 **Lobos, Cabo** *cape* Mexico
88 C3 **Lobos, Isla** *island* Mexico
164 3d **Lobos, Isla de** *island* Canary Islands
108 D3 **Lobos, Punta** *cape* Argentina
104 A2 **Lobos de Afuera, Islas** *islands* Peru
104 A2 **Lobos de Tierra, Isla** *island* Peru
221 E6 **Loburn** New Zealand
134 N7 **Lobva** Russian Federation
125 I1 **Łobżenica** Poland
194 E5 **Lôc Ninh** Vietnam
127 H4 **Locana** Italy
127 I3 **Locarno** Switzerland
218 E5 **Loch Lilly** NSW Australia
142 A3 **Loch nam Madadh** Na h-Eileanan Siar Scotland UK
142 A3 **Loch Sgioport** Na h-Eileanan Siar Scotland UK
142 C4 **Lochaline** Highland Scotland UK
140 C2 **Lochans** Dumfries and Galloway Scotland UK
142 E5 **Locharbriggs** Dumfries and Galloway Scotland UK
142 E2 **Lochdhu Hotel** Highland Scotland UK
142 C4 **Lochdon** Highland Scotland UK
142 D3 **Lochdrum** Highland Scotland UK
142 E4 **Lochee** Dundee Scotland UK
126 E3 **Loches** France
142 C4 **Lochgilphead** Argyll and Bute Scotland UK
219 I7 **Lochiel** NSW Australia
218 D5 **Lochiel** SA Australia
142 C2 **Lochinver** Highland Scotland UK
142 D3 **Lochluichart** Highland Scotland UK
142 E5 **Lochmaben** Dumfries and Galloway Scotland UK
219 I2 **Lochnager** Qld Australia
125 J1 **Łochocin** Poland
142 A3 **Lochportain** Na h-Eileanan Siar Scotland UK
142 E2 **Lochside** Highland Scotland UK
142 D3 **Lochy, Loch** *lake* Scotland UK
218 B5 **Lock** SA Australia
218 D5 **Lock, Mount** SA Australia
79 F11 **Lockeport** Nova Scotia Canada
142 E5 **Lockerbie** Dumfries and Galloway Scotland UK
218 H6 **Lockhart** NSW Australia
215 G2 **Lockhart** *watercourse* Qld Australia
89 I2 **Lockhart** Florida USA
86 C6 **Lockhart** Texas USA
216 F6 **Lockhart, Lake** WA Australia
216 D2 **Lockier Range** WA Australia
120 I5 **Lockne** Sweden
120 I5 **Locknesjön** *lake* Sweden
85 L3 **Lockney** Texas USA
139 F4 **Locks Heath** Hampshire England UK
141 H2 **Lockton** North Yorkshire England UK
75 S7 **Lockwood** Saskatchewan Canada
82 E8 **Lockwood** Missouri USA
222 5 **Lockwood Terrace** Guam
126 C3 **Locminé** France
126 B2 **Locronan** France
126 B3 **Loctudy** France
131 C6 **Loculi** Sardinia Italy
86 D2 **Locust Grove** Oklahoma USA
218 F6 **Loddon** *watercourse* Vic. Australia
139 I2 **Loddon** Norfolk England UK
161 E2 **Lodein** Sudan
126 F5 **Lodève** France
123 Q2 **Lodeynoye Pole** Russian Federation
81 L4 **Lodge Grass** Montana USA
75 N6 **Lodgepole** Alberta Canada
160 C4 **Lodi** Democratic Republic of Congo
124 E5 **Lodi** Italy
80 E7 **Lodi** California USA
219 S10 **Lodi, Cape** Tas. Australia
120 I3 **Løding** Norway
120 I2 **Lødingen** Norway
160 C4 **Lodja** Democratic Republic of Congo
128 E2 **Lodosa** Spain
127 I3 **Lodrino** Switzerland
161 F3 **Lodwar** Kenya
125 J2 **Łódź** Poland
125 J2 **Łódzkie** *admin. area* Poland
194 D3 **Loei** Thailand
194 D3 **Loei** *admin. area* Thailand
162 C6 **Loeriesfontein** South Africa
190 G5 **Loess Plateau** Nei Mongol Zizhiqu China
158 B3 **Lofa** *watercourse* Liberia
124 B2 **Loffre** France
120 H2 **Lofoten** *island* Norway
120 H5 **Lofssjön** *lake* Sweden
182 D3 **Log** Russian Federation
155 G6 **Loga** Niger
160 E3 **Loga** Sudan
215 I6 **Logan** *watercourse* Qld Australia
85 K3 **Logan** New Mexico USA
80 J6 **Logan** Utah USA
79 E8 **Logan, Mount** Quebec Canada
74 A2 **Logan, Mount** Yukon Territory Canada
74 K7 **Logan Lake** British Columbia Canada
87 H4 **Logan Martin Lake** Alabama USA
74 H2 **Logan Mountains** Yukon Territory Canada
82 H6 **Logansport** Indiana USA
120 K4 **Lögdasjön** *lake* Sweden
120 K4 **Lögdeälven** *watercourse* Sweden
142 E3 **Logie** Moray Scotland UK
161 F3 **Logipi, Lake** Kenya
122 D3 **Logna** *watercourse* Norway
159 H2 **Logne** *watercourse* Chad
159 H3 **Logone-Occidental** *admin. area* Chad
159 H3 **Logone-Oriental** *admin. area* Chad
126 E2 **Logron** France
128 E2 **Logroño** Spain
128 D4 **Logrosán** Spain
122 E4 **Løgstrup** Denmark
222 7 **Loh** *island* Vanuatu
186 D5 **Loharu** Haryana India
126 D3 **Lohéac** France
121 N3 **Lohijärvi** *lake* Finland
123 O2 **Lohilahti** Finland
121 N3 **Lohiniva** Finland
123 M2 **Lohja** Finland
127 I1 **Lohr** Germany
127 L1 **Lohsa** Germany
121 M4 **Lohtaja** Finland
123 N3 **Lohusuu** Estonia
181 H4 **Loi Song** *mountain* Myanmar
181 H5 **Loikaw** Myanmar
160 C4 **Loile** *watercourse* Democratic Republic of Congo
181 H5 **Loilem** Myanmar
123 L2 **Loimijoki** *watercourse* Finland
121 Q6 **Loimola** Russian Federation
126 F3 **Loing** *watercourse* France
126 F3 **Loir** *watercourse* France
126 F3 **Loire** *watercourse* France
126 F3 **Loire, Canal latéral à la** *watercourse* France
122 G5 **Loissin** Germany
122 G6 **Loitz** Germany
100 B5 **Loja** Ecuador
100 B6 **Loja** *admin. area* Ecuador
128 D5 **Loja** Spain
159 G6 **Loje** *watercourse* Angola
125 M2 **Lokachi** Ukraine
160 C3 **Lokalema** Democratic Republic of Congo
121 O3 **Lokan tekojärvi** *lake* Finland
160 D4 **Lokeli** Democratic Republic of Congo
130 E1 **Loket** Czech Republic
181 H3 **Lokhuni** Nagaland India
162 D4 **Lokhwabe** Botswana
161 F3 **Lokichar** Kenya
161 E3 **Lokichokio** Kenya
160 D4 **Lokila** Democratic Republic of Congo
161 F3 **Lokitaung** Kenya
121 O3 **Lokka** Finland
120 F5 **Løkken** Norway
121 N5 **Lokkiperä** Finland
123 P4 **Loknya** Russian Federation
159 F3 **Loko** Nigeria
159 F3 **Lokoja** Nigeria
160 C4 **Lokolia** Democratic Republic of Congo
160 B4 **Lokolo** *watercourse* Democratic Republic of Congo
160 B3 **Lokomo** Cameroon
160 C4 **Lokoro** *watercourse* Democratic Republic of Congo
158 E3 **Lokossa** Benin
136 E2 **Lokot** Russian Federation
73 M6 **Loks Land** *island* Nunavut Canada
123 M3 **Loksa** Estonia
101 H3 **Loksie Hatti** Suriname
120 H3 **Løkta** *island* Norway
181 G4 **Loktak** *lake* Manipur India
159 G4 **Lokundje** *watercourse* Cameroon
222 8 **Lokuru** Solomon Islands
123 M3 **Lokuta** Estonia
160 C3 **Lokutu** Democratic Republic of Congo
120 L2 **Løkvollen** Norway
160 D2 **Lol** *watercourse* Sudan
162 B2 **Lola** Angola
158 C3 **Lola** Guinea
160 C4 **Lolaka** *watercourse* Democratic Republic of Congo
160 C3 **Lolengi** Democratic Republic of Congo
122 F5 **Lolland** *island* Denmark
124 E2 **Lollar** Germany
198 D3 **Lolobata** Indonesia
198 C3 **Loloda Utara, Kepulauan** *islands* Indonesia
159 G4 **Lolodorf** Cameroon
222 7 **Lolowaï** Vanuatu
196 C3 **Lolowau** Indonesia
139 H2 **Lolworth** Cambridgeshire England UK
132 C4 **Lom** Bulgaria
159 G3 **Lom** *watercourse* Cameroon
120 F6 **Lom** Norway
194 D3 **Lom Sak** Thailand
85 H1 **Loma** Colorado USA
85 L6 **Loma Alta** Texas USA
88 D2 **Loma Blanca** Mexico
106 D6 **Loma Farías** Argentina
128 F5 **Loma Pelada, Punta de** *cape* Spain
223 9 **Lomaloma** Fiji
160 C4 **Lomami** Democratic Republic of Congo
160 D4 **Lomami** *watercourse* Democratic Republic of Congo
82 E2 **Loman** Minnesota USA
107 G3 **Lomas de Vallejos** Argentina
223 9a **Lomawai** Fiji
125 L2 **Łomazy** Poland
162 D3 **Lomba** *watercourse* Angola
212 G4 **Lombadina** WA Australia
102 B2 **Lombarda, Serra** *range* Brazil
130 C4 **Lombardia (Lombardy)** *admin. area* Italy
143 D4 **Lombardstown** Ireland
Lombardy *see* **Lombardia** Italy
126 E5 **Lombez** France
197 I6 **Lomblen** *island* Indonesia
197 H6 **Lombok** *island* Indonesia
197 G6 **Lombok, Selat** *strait* Indonesia
158 E3 **Lomé** Togo
160 C4 **Lomela** Democratic Republic of Congo
160 C4 **Lomela** *watercourse* Democratic Republic of Congo
130 C4 **Lomello** Italy
86 B5 **Lometa** Texas USA
159 G4 **Lomié** Cameroon
84 C4 **Lomita** California USA
100 C4 **Lomitas** Colombia
127 K1 **Lommatzsch** Germany
127 G1 **Lommel** Belgium
125 I3 **Lomnice** Czech Republic
125 H3 **Lomnice nad Lužnicí** Czech Republic
75 O7 **Lomond** Alberta Canada
142 D4 **Lomond, Loch** *lake* Scotland UK
56 P1 **Lomonosov Ridge** *underwater feature* Arctic Ocean
182 D2 **Lomov** Russian Federation
84 B3 **Lompoc** California USA
120 J4 **Lomselenäs** Sweden
120 J4 **Lomsjökullen** Sweden
125 L1 **Łomża** Poland
122 H4 **Lönashult** Sweden
130 D4 **Lonato** Italy
108 C2 **Lonco Vaca** Argentina
106 C6 **Loncoche** Chile
106 D6 **Loncopué** Argentina
139 I5 **Londinières** France
83 K5 **London** Ontario Canada
222 1a **London** Kiribati
139 G3 **London** Greater London England UK
86 E3 **London** Arkansas USA
82 I8 **London** Kentucky USA
86 B5 **London** Texas USA
109 13 **Londonderry** St Lucia
143 E1 **Londonderry** Londonderry Northern Ireland UK
213 I2 **Londonderry, Cape** WA Australia
103 B8 **Londrina** Brazil
74 K7 **Lone Butte** British Columbia Canada
86 D4 **Lone Oak** Texas USA
84 C2 **Lone Pine** California USA
75 V7 **Lone Spruce** Manitoba Canada
86 D4 **Lone Star** Texas USA
81 M7 **Lone Tree** Colorado USA
86 B3 **Lone Wolf** Oklahoma USA
122 G4 **Lönern** *lake* Sweden
194 C3 **Long** Thailand
138 E3 **Long Ashton** North Somerset England UK
87 L4 **Long Bay** South Carolina USA
84 C4 **Long Beach** California USA
86 G5 **Long Beach** Mississippi USA
80 C3 **Long Beach** Washington USA
139 G2 **Long Bennington** Lincolnshire England UK
83 O6 **Long Branch** New Jersey USA
91 F2 **Long Cay** *island* Bahamas
80 F4 **Long Creek** Oregon USA
139 F2 **Long Eaton** Derbyshire England UK
82 F6 **Long Grove** Iowa USA
197 H3 **Long Ibau** Indonesia
109 18 **Long Island** Antigua and Barbuda
215 J7 **Long Island** Qld Australia
212 C6 **Long Island** WA Australia
91 F2 **Long Island** Bahamas
83 R4 **Long Island** New Brunswick Canada
79 E10 **Long Island** Nova Scotia Canada
77 P5 **Long Island** Nunavut Canada
199 H5 **Long Island** Papua New Guinea
77 P5 **Long Island Sound** Nunavut/Quebec Canada
83 O6 **Long Island Sound** *bay* USA
188 F4 **Long Jiang** *watercourse* Guangxi Zhuangzu Zizhiqu China
76 H7 **Long Lake** Manitoba Canada
76 H3 **Long Lake** Manitoba Canada
79 E9 **Long Lake** New Brunswick Canada
73 K9 **Long Lake** Ontario Canada
83 Q3 **Long Lake** Maine USA
81 O3 **Long Lake** North Dakota USA
197 G3 **Long Lama** Malaysia
139 F2 **Long Marston** Warwickshire England UK
139 H2 **Long Melford** Suffolk England UK
197 G3 **Long Murum** Malaysia
219 S10 **Long Point** Tas. Australia
76 F6 **Long Point** Manitoba Canada
79 I8 **Long Point** Newfoundland and Labrador Canada
83 L5 **Long Point** Ontario Canada
221 C8 **Long Point** New Zealand
195 H5 **Long Point** Philippines
83 L5 **Long Point Bay** Ontario Canada
81 R4 **Long Prairie** Minnesota USA
141 F2 **Long Preston** North Yorkshire England UK
79 I9 **Long Range Mountains** Newfoundland and Labrador Canada
213 H2 **Long Reef** WA Australia
215 L8 **Long Shoal** *reef* Qld Australia
76 H4 **Long Spruce** Manitoba Canada
139 I2 **Long Stratton** Norfolk England UK
139 H2 **Long Sutton** Lincolnshire England UK
197 G3 **Long Teru** Malaysia
188 E1 **Long Xian** Shaanxi China
194 E5 **Long Xuyên** Vietnam
188 E4 **Long'an** Guangxi Zhuangzu Zizhiqu China
188 D2 **Long'an** Sichuan China
162 C2 **Longa** Angola
162 C3 **Longa** *watercourse* Angola
135 AK4 **Longa, Proliv** *strait* Russian Federation
197 G3 **Longagung** Indonesia
197 G3 **Longbawan** Indonesia
197 G3 **Longberini** Indonesia
197 H3 **Longbia** Indonesia
87 J7 **Longboat Key** Florida USA
197 G3 **Longboh** Indonesia
76 H8 **Longbow Lake** Ontario Canada
139 E3 **Longbridge Deverill** Wiltshire England UK
189 G1 **Longcheng** Anhui China
189 G4 **Longcheng** Guangdong China
189 G2 **Longcheng** Jiangxi China
188 D3 **Longchuan** Yunnan China
139 F1 **Longcliffe** Derbyshire England UK
86 B2 **Longdale** Oklahoma USA
190 F6 **Longde** Ningxia Huizu Zizhiqu China
139 E2 **Longdon** Worcestershire England UK
124 C4 **Longeau** France
130 D3 **Longega** Italy
127 H4 **Longet, Col de** *pass* France
219 J4 **Longford** NSW Australia
143 E3 **Longford** Ireland
143 E3 **Longford** *admin. area* Ireland
139 F2 **Longford** West Midlands England UK
143 E4 **Longfordpass North** Ireland
189 G2 **Longgan Hu** *lake* Anhui China
188 E2 **Longgang** Chongqing China
180 E2 **Longge'er** Xizang Zizhiqu China
191 I4 **Longhua** Hebei China
58 K1 **Longhurst, Mount** Antarctica
197 H4 **Longikis** Indonesia
58 U2 **Longing, Cape** Antarctica
197 G4 **Longiram** Indonesia
191 J3 **Longjiang** Heilongjiang China
189 G3 **Longjin** Jiangxi China
191 L4 **Longjing** Jilin China
188 F1 **Longjuzhai** Shaanxi China
197 H3 **Longkabinu** Indonesia
191 I5 **Longkou** Shandong China
76 L8 **Longlac** Ontario Canada
77 Q4 **Longland** *watercourse* Quebec Canada
76 H7 **Longlegged Lake** Ontario Canada
81 M6 **Longmont** Colorado USA
139 G3 **Longmoor Camp** Hampshire England UK
189 G4 **Longnan** Jiangxi China
197 G3 **Longnawan** Indonesia
141 G3 **Longnor** Staffordshire England UK
162 C2 **Longonjo** Angola
197 G3 **Longpahangai** Indonesia
76 G2 **Longpre Lake** Nunavut Canada
197 G3 **Longpujungan** Indonesia
188 E3 **Longquan** Guizhou China
189 F3 **Longquan** Hunan China
188 D4 **Longquan** Yunnan China
189 H3 **Longquan** Zhejiang China
78 D5 **Longrais, Lac** *lake* Quebec Canada
215 H7 **Longreach** Qld Australia
141 F3 **Longridge** Lancashire England UK
81 M6 **Longs Peak** Colorado USA
188 E3 **Longshan** Guizhou China
188 F4 **Longsheng** Guangxi Zhuangzu Zizhiqu China
188 F3 **Longsheng** Guangxi Zhuangzu Zizhiqu China
190 E5 **Longshou Shan** *range* Nei Mongol Zizhiqu China
215 H6 **Longton** Qld Australia
140 F3 **Longton** Lancashire England UK
139 E2 **Longton** Stoke-on-Trent England UK
140 F1 **Longtown** Cumbria England UK
126 F1 **Longuenesse** France
75 N7 **Longview** Alberta Canada
86 D4 **Longview** Texas USA
80 D3 **Longview** Washington USA
197 H3 **Longwai** Indonesia
140 B3 **Longwood** Ireland
164 5b **Longwood** St Helena
221 B8 **Longwood Range** New Zealand
74 K6 **Longworth** British Columbia Canada
190 E6 **Longwu** Qinghai China
188 D1 **Longxi** Gansu China
189 G4 **Longxian** Guangdong China
189 H3 **Longxun** Fujian China
189 H3 **Longyan** Fujian China
191 H5 **Longyao** Hebei China
134 3C **Longyearbyen** Svalbard
188 E4 **Longzhou** Guangxi Zhuangzu Zizhiqu China
181 G3 **Longzi** Xizang Zizhiqu China
122 E3 **Lonin** Norway
120 G4 **Lonin** Norway
121 P4 **Lonka** Russian Federation
160 C4 **Lonkonia** *watercourse* Democratic Republic of Congo
124 C3 **Lonny** France
123 N5 **Lonskiya** Belarus
120 inset **Lónsvík** *cape* Iceland
198 D5 **Lontor** *island* Indonesia
105 I2 **Lontra** Brazil
132 C1 **Lónya** Hungary
82 I5 **Looking Glass** *watercourse* Michigan USA
76 N5 **Lookout, Cape** Ontario Canada
87 M3 **Lookout, Cape** North Carolina USA
215 H3 **Lookout Point** Qld Australia
213 H5 **Looma** WA Australia
81 K2 **Loomis** Saskatchewan Canada
81 P6 **Loomis** Nebraska USA
75 N4 **Loon** *watercourse* Alberta Canada
75 N4 **Loon Lake** Alberta Canada
217 J5 **Loongana** WA Australia
143 B4 **Loop Head** *cape* Ireland
185 I5 **Lop Nur** *lake* Xinjiang Uygur Zizhiqu China
133 B5 **Lopan** Albania
130 F4 **Lopar** Croatia
182 E5 **Lopatin** Russian Federation
135 AD8 **Lopatina, Gora** *mountain* Russian Federation
182 E3 **Lopatino** Russian Federation
135 AG8 **Lopatka** Russian Federation
135 AG8 **Lopatka, Mys** *cape* Russian Federation
161 E2 **Lopaye** Sudan
194 D4 **Lopburi** Thailand
123 L3 **Lõpe** Estonia
138 E4 **Lopen** Somerset England UK
86 B7 **Lopeno** Texas USA
222 7 **Lopévi** *island* Vanuatu
107 G6 **López** Argentina
159 F5 **Lopez, Cape** *cape* Gabon
161 E3 **Lopodi** Sudan
160 C3 **Lopori** *watercourse* Democratic Republic of Congo
120 L1 **Loppa** Norway
120 L1 **Lopphavet** *bay* Norway
123 M2 **Loppijärvi** *lake* Finland
127 I5 **Loppio, Pointe** *mountain* Corsica France
120 I3 **Løpsmarka** Norway
123 O3 **Lopukhinka** Russian Federation
77 V4 **Loquin, Lac** *lake* Quebec Canada
75 Q3 **Lorado** Saskatchewan Canada
83 J6 **Lorain** Ohio USA
85 L4 **Loraine** Texas USA
179 K3 **Loralai** Pakistan
101 F2 **Lorán, Boca** *bay* Venezuela
141 G1 **Lorbottle** Northumberland England UK
128 F5 **Lorca** Spain
211 inset **Lord Howe Island** Australia
52 M11 **Lord Howe Rise** *underwater feature* Tasman Sea
194 C5 **Lord Loughborough Island** Myanmar
178 G3 **Lordegān** Iran
85 H4 **Lordsburg** New Mexico USA
75 R7 **Loreburn** Saskatchewan Canada
214 C3 **Lorella Spring** NT Australia
100 C3 **Lorena** Colombia
199 F5 **Lorentz** *watercourse* Indonesia
85 L4 **Lorenzo** Texas USA
178 F2 **Lorestān** *admin. area* Iran
100 B5 **Loreto** Ecuador
88 C3 **Loreto** Mexico
104 C2 **Loreto** *admin. area* Peru
86 H3 **Loretto** Tennessee USA
100 C2 **Lorica** Colombia
126 C3 **Lorient** France
73 J5 **Lorillard** *watercourse* Nunavut Canada
125 J4 **Lőrinci** Hungary
75 R8 **Loring** Montana USA
135 AM5 **Lorino** Russian Federation
104 D5 **Loripongo** Peru
87 L3 **Loris** South Carolina USA
126 F3 **Lormes** France
187 E6 **Lormi** Chhattisgarh India
142 C4 **Lorn, Firth of** *bay* Scotland UK
214 D5 **Lorne** *watercourse* NT Australia
218 F8 **Lorne** Vic. Australia
100 D4 **Loro** Colombia
158 D2 **Loropeni** Burkina Faso
214 E5 **Lorraine** Qld Australia
127 H2 **Lorraine** *admin. area* France
127 H2 **Lorraine** *region* France
85 M1 **Lorraine** Kansas USA
124 B4 **Lorris** France
216 G6 **Lort** *watercourse* WA Australia
124 D1 **Lorup** Germany
155 I2 **Lorzot** Tunisia
120 I6 **Los** Sweden
158 B3 **Los, Îles de** *islands* Guinea
85 J6 **Los Alamos** Mexico
84 B3 **Los Alamos** California USA
84 G7 **Los Algdones, Estero** Mexico
89 F4 **Los Altos** Mexico
106 D5 **Los Andes** Chile
106 C6 **Los Ángeles** Chile
84 C3 **Los Angeles** California USA
84 C3 **Los Angeles Aqueduct** *watercourse* California USA
108 B4 **Los Antiguos** Argentina
128 E2 **Los Arcos** Spain
80 E8 **Los Banos** California USA
104 D5 **Los Baños** Peru
128 D5 **Los Barrios** Spain
106 F2 **Los Blancos** Argentina
100 D2 **Los Botalones** Venezuela
100 E2 **Los Caballos** Venezuela
106 E4 **Los Cerrillos** Argentina
101 F3 **Los Cerros** Venezuela
100 D3 **Los Cochinos** Venezuela
106 E4 **Los Colorados** Argentina
101 F3 **Los Corrales** Venezuela
105 E4 **Los Cusis** Bolivia
89 H5 **Los Divorciados** Mexico
89 F3 **Los Dos Estados** Mexico
101 F3 **Los Ermitaños** Venezuela
104 E5 **Los Frailes, Cordillera de** *range* Bolivia
80 E8 **Los Gatos** California USA
100 D2 **Los Guarimos** Venezuela
106 D6 **Los Helechos** Argentina
85 M8 **Los Herreras** Mexico
88 C2 **Los Hoyos** Mexico
104 C4 **Los Incas** Peru
86 C7 **Los Indios** Texas USA
85 N8 **Los Indios El Control** Mexico
108 B2 **Los Juncos** Argentina
108 B2 **Los Ladrillos** Chile
106 C6 **Los Lagos** *admin. area* Chile
85 J5 **Los Lamentos** Mexico
164 3b **Los Llanos de Aridane** Canary Islands
85 I3 **Los Lunas** New Mexico USA
100 E2 **Los Mangos** Venezuela
101 E2 **Los Maniritos** Venezuela
90 C4 **los Marrabios, Cordillera** *range* Nicaragua
108 C2 **Los Menucos** Argentina
88 C3 **Los Mochis** Mexico
88 C2 **Los Molinos** Mexico
108 C4 **Los Monos** Argentina
88 E4 **Los Muertos** Mexico
88 C3 **Los Muertos** Mexico
128 D4 **Los Navalmorales** Spain
100 C2 **Los Palmitos** Colombia
100 C3 **Los Patios** Colombia
100 D5 **Los Patricio** Colombia
105 F5 **Los Portigos** Bolivia
106 D6 **Los Puquios** Chile
85 I3 **Los Ranchos de Albuquerque** New Mexico USA
100 D2 **Los Rastrojos** Venezuela
108 B2 **Los Repollos** Argentina
199 I4 **Los Reyes Islands** Papua New Guinea
108 B2 **Los Ríos** *admin. area* Chile
101 E2 **Los Roques, Islas** *islands* Venezuela
50 L8 **Los Roques Trench** *underwater feature* Caribbean Sea
128 E5 **Los Royos** Spain
88 B2 **Los Sauces** Mexico
108 B3 **Los Tamariscos** Argentina
101 F2 **Los Testigos** *islands* Venezuela
106 F3 **Los Tigres** Argentina
105 F5 **Los Troncos** Bolivia
84 F4 **Los Vidrios** Mexico
106 D3 **Los Vientos** Chile
106 D4 **Los Vilos** Chile
100 D2 **Los Zorros** Venezuela
129 F4 **Losa del Obispo** Spain
186 D5 **Losal** Rajasthan India
199 J2 **Losap** *island* Federated States of Micronesia
123 P2 **Losevo** Russian Federation
182 C3 **Losevo** Russian Federation
124 D2 **Losheim** Belgium
127 H1 **Losheim** Germany
125 L1 **Łosinka** Poland
120 J2 **Losivatnet** *lake* Norway
121 P5 **Losonmäki** Finland
123 R2 **Lososinnoye** Russian Federation
198 C6 **Lospatos** Timor-Leste (East Timor)
142 E3 **Lossiemouth** Moray Scotland UK
120 H5 **Lossnen** *lake* Sweden
80 I4 **Lost River Range** Idaho USA
138 C4 **Lostwithiel** Cornwall England UK
123 P5 **Losvida, Vozyera** *lake* Belarus
124 B5 **Lot** *watercourse* France
106 C6 **Lota** Chile
142 E2 **Lothbeg** Highland Scotland UK
126 E3 **Lothiers** France
160 C4 **Loto** Democratic Republic of Congo
160 C4 **Loto** *watercourse* Democratic Republic of Congo
223 12c **Lotofaga** Samoa
162 E4 **Lotsane** *watercourse* Botswana
86 C5 **Lott** Texas USA
122 I4 **Löttorp** Sweden
199 H4 **Lou Island** Papua New Guinea
194 D2 **Louangnamtha** Laos
194 D2 **Louangnamtha** *admin. area* Laos
194 D3 **Louangphabang** Laos
194 D3 **Louangphrabang** *range* Laos
Loubomo *see* **Dolisie** Congo
126 C2 **Loudéac** France
189 F3 **Loudi** Hunan China
215 I6 **Loudon, Mount** Qld Australia
127 H3 **Loue** *watercourse* France
159 G5 **Louéssé** *watercourse* Congo
190 G5 **Loufan** Shanxi China
154 C5 **Louga** Senegal
126 E5 **Louge** *watercourse* France
140 A3 **Lough** Ireland
143 E1 **Lough Swilly** *bay* Ireland
143 D2 **Loughanure** Ireland
139 F2 **Loughborough** Leicester England UK
143 E4 **Loughcapple Bridge** Ireland
73 I3 **Lougheed Island** Nunavut Canada
143 D2 **Lougheraherk** Ireland
143 D3 **Loughrea** Ireland
139 H3 **Loughton** Essex England UK
123 N2 **Louhivesi** *lake* Finland
74 K7 **Louis Creek** British Columbia Canada
162 E4 **Louis Trichardt** South Africa
77 P5 **Louis-XIV, Pointe** *cape* Quebec Canada
82 J7 **Louisa** Kentucky USA

83 L7 **Louisa** Virginia USA
213 I5 **Louisa Downs** WA Australia
79 I10 **Louisbourg** Nova Scotia Canada
82 D7 **Louisburg** Kansas USA
79 H10 **Louisdale** Nova Scotia Canada
74 F6 **Louise Island** British Columbia Canada
199 J6 **Louisiade Archipelago** *islands* Papua New Guinea
71 **Louisiana** *admin. area* USA
82 F7 **Louisiana** Missouri USA
87 I5 **Louisville** Alabama USA
82 I7 **Louisville** Kentucky USA
81 Q6 **Louisville** Nebraska USA
52 P11 **Louisville Ridge** *underwater feature* Pacific Ocean
121 R3 **Loukhi** Russian Federation
160 B4 **Loukoléla** Democratic Republic of Congo
159 G5 **Loukouo** Congo
128 B5 **Loulé** Portugal
158 C2 **Loulouni** Mali
159 F4 **Loum** Cameroon
76 H7 **Lount Lake** Ontario Canada
127 K1 **Louny** Czech Republic
127 H5 **Loup** *watercourse* France
81 P6 **Loup City** Nebraska USA
77 S4 **Loups Marins, Lacs des** Quebec Canada
129 F2 **Lourdes** France
101 I4 **Lourenço** Brazil
128 B3 **Louriçal** Portugal
128 B4 **Lourinhã** Portugal
124 B3 **Loury** France
121 Q5 **Lout, Ozero** *lake* Russian Federation
218 G4 **Louth** NSW Australia
143 F3 **Louth** *admin. area* Ireland
141 H3 **Louth** Lincolnshire England UK
218 B6 **Louth Bay** SA Australia
133 D7 **Loutra** Greece
133 C7 **Loutraki** Greece
159 G5 **Louvakou** Congo
124 C3 **Louvois** France
160 D5 **Lovai** *watercourse* Democratic Republic of Congo
120 L4 **Lövånger** Sweden
123 P4 **Lovat'** *watercourse* Russian Federation
120 E6 **Lovatnet** *lake* Norway
120 I4 **Lövberg** Sweden
120 I5 **Lövberga** Sweden
132 D4 **Lovech** Bulgaria
132 D4 **Lovech** *admin. area* Bulgaria
86 D5 **Lovelady** Texas USA
81 M6 **Loveland** Colorado USA
81 K4 **Lovell** Wyoming USA
80 F6 **Lovelock** Nevada USA
124 B2 **Lovendegem** Belgium
75 Q7 **Loverna** Saskatchewan Canada
120 I2 **Lovik** Norway
121 M3 **Lovikka** Sweden
85 J4 **Loving** New Mexico USA
85 K4 **Lovington** New Mexico USA
125 I4 **Lövő** Hungary
120 K3 **Lovos** Sweden
125 H2 **Lovosice** Czech Republic
121 S2 **Lovozero** Russian Federation
121 S3 **Lovozero, Ozero** *lake* Russian Federation
130 F4 **Lovran** Croatia
125 G5 **Lovreč** Croatia
132 B3 **Lovrin** Romania
120 I5 **Lövsjön** *lake* Sweden
120 I4 **Lövstrand** Sweden
162 D2 **Lôvua** Angola
76 M1 **Low, Cape** Nunavut Canada
141 G3 **Low Bradfield** South Yorkshire England UK
141 H3 **Low Burnham** North Lincolnshire England UK
58 T2 **Low Island** Antarctica
212 B6 **Low Point** WA Australia
210 inset **Low Point** Christmas Island Australia
219 Q11 **Low Rocky Point** Tas. Australia
160 D4 **Lowa** *watercourse* Democratic Republic of Congo
218 E7 **Lowan Vale** SA Australia
179 L2 **Lowarai Pass** Pakistan
83 P5 **Lowell** Massachusetts USA
80 D5 **Lowell** Oregon USA
74 L8 **Lower Arrow Lake** British Columbia Canada
84 B1 **Lower Bear River Reservoir** California USA
138 D2 **Lower Chapel** Powys Wales UK
75 S4 **Lower Foster Lake** Saskatchewan Canada
139 G3 **Lower Froyle** Hampshire England UK
138 D2 **Lower Hergest** Herefordshire England UK
221 F5 **Lower Hutt** New Zealand
80 E6 **Lower Klamath Lake** California USA
218 D6 **Lower Light** SA Australia
142 B3 **Lower Milovaig** Highland Scotland UK
74 G3 **Lower Post** British Columbia Canada
82 D3 **Lower Red Lake** Minnesota USA
78 F2 **Lower Savage Islands** Nunavut Canada
196 D2 **Lower Seletar Reservoir** Singapore
139 H3 **Lower Stoke** Medway England UK
139 E2 **Lower Strensham** Worcestershire England UK
139 F2 **Lower Tean** Staffordshire England UK
139 I2 **Lowestoft** Suffolk England UK
140 E2 **Loweswater** Cumbria England UK
179 L2 **Lowgar** *admin. area* Afghanistan
141 F2 **Lowgill** Lancashire England UK
125 J1 **Łowicz** Poland
218 G5 **Lowlands** NSW Australia
73 J4 **Lowther Island** Nunavut Canada
141 H2 **Lowthorpe** East Riding of Yorkshire England UK
83 N5 **Lowville** New York USA
218 E6 **Loxton** SA Australia
162 D6 **Loxton** South Africa
142 D2 **Loyal, Loch** *lake* Scotland UK
87 J2 **Loyall** Kentucky USA
80 E7 **Loyalton** California USA
222 7 **Loyauté, Îles** *islands* New Caledonia
121 Q6 **Loymola** Russian Federation
132 E4 **Lozarevo** Bulgaria
125 H1 **Łozice** Poland
132 A3 **Loznica** Serbia
136 F3 **Lozova** Ukraine
132 B3 **Lozovik** Serbia
134 N6 **Loz'va** *watercourse* Russian Federation
189 G2 **Lu Hu** *lake* Hubei China
189 H4 **Lu-liao Shui-K'u** *lake* Taiwan China
191 I6 **Lu Shan** *range* Shandong China
189 I4 **Lü Tao** *island* Taiwan China
160 B3 **Lua-Dekere** *watercourse* Democratic Republic of Congo
105 G2 **Lua Nova** Brazil
160 B3 **Lua Vindu** *watercourse* Democratic Republic of Congo
160 D5 **Luabo** Democratic Republic of Congo
163 G3 **Luabo** Mozambique
162 D2 **Luacano** Angola
160 C5 **Luaco** Angola
Lualaba *see* **Congo** Democratic Republic of Congo
160 D4 **Luama** *watercourse* Democratic Republic of Congo
162 D2 **Luambimba** *watercourse* Zambia
162 D3 **Luampa** Zambia
189 G2 **Lu'an** Anhui China
106 E6 **Luan Toro** Argentina
189 F1 **Luanchuan** Henan China
106 D6 **Luanco** Argentina
128 D2 **Luanco** Spain
160 A5 **Luanda** Angola
162 B1 **Luanda** *admin. area* Angola
162 C2 **Luando** Angola
197 K6 **Luang** *island* Indonesia
162 D2 **Luanginga** *watercourse* Zambia
160 B5 **Luangue** *watercourse* Angola
162 D2 **Luanguinga** *watercourse* Angola
160 E5 **Luangwa** *watercourse* Zambia
191 I5 **Luanping** Hebei China
162 E2 **Luanshya** Zambia
160 D6 **Luapula** *watercourse* Democratic Republic of Congo
162 E2 **Luapula** *admin. area* Zambia
Luar *see* **Horsburgh Island** Australia
128 C2 **Luarca** Spain
160 C6 **Luashi** Democratic Republic of Congo
162 C3 **Luassingua** *watercourse* Angola
162 D2 **Luatamba** Angola
163 G2 **Luatize** *watercourse* Mozambique
162 D2 **Luau** Angola
159 F4 **Luba** Equatorial Guinea
160 B5 **Lubalo** Angola
125 H2 **Lubań** Poland
123 N4 **Lubāna** Latvia
195 I4 **Lubang** *island* Philippines
162 B2 **Lubango** Angola
123 N4 **Lubāns** *lake* Latvia
160 D5 **Lubao** Democratic Republic of Congo
125 L2 **Lubartów** Poland
85 L4 **Lubbock** Texas USA
120 J4 **Lubbträsket** *lake* Sweden
142 D3 **Lubcroy** Highland Scotland UK
122 F6 **Lübeck** Germany
122 F5 **Lübecker Bucht** *bay* Germany
160 C4 **Lubefu** Democratic Republic of Congo
191 I4 **Lubei** Nei Mongol Zizhiqu China
125 L2 **Lubelskie** *admin. area* Poland
182 G3 **Lubenka** Kazakhstan
160 D4 **Lubero** Democratic Republic of Congo
126 E4 **Lubersac** France
125 H1 **Łubianka** Poland
125 M2 **Lubiaż** Ukraine
195 I5 **Lubic** *island* Philippines
75 N4 **Lubicon Lake** Alberta Canada
125 I1 **Lubie, Jezioro** *lake* Poland
125 J1 **Lubień Kujawski** Poland
125 I2 **Lubin** Poland
125 H1 **Lubin** Poland
123 P3 **Lubino** Russian Federation
125 L2 **Lublin** Poland
125 J2 **Lubliniec** Poland
142 C3 **Lubmore** Highland Scotland UK
197 F3 **Lubok Antu** Malaysia
125 I1 **Luboń** Poland
125 J1 **Luboniek** Poland
125 I1 **Łubowo** Poland
128 E5 **Lubrín** Spain
160 D5 **Lubudi** Democratic Republic of Congo
160 C5 **Lubudi** *watercourse* Democratic Republic of Congo
196 D4 **Lubuk Linggau** Indonesia
196 D3 **Lubuksikaping** Indonesia
160 D6 **Lubumbashi** Democratic Republic of Congo
125 H1 **Lubuskie** *admin. area* Poland
160 D4 **Lubutu** Democratic Republic of Congo
160 D4 **Lubutu** *watercourse* Democratic Republic of Congo
162 E2 **Lubwe** Zambia
83 R2 **Luc, Pointe à** *cape* Quebec Canada
127 G4 **Luc-en-Diois** France
162 C1 **Lucala** Angola
160 B5 **Lucala** *watercourse* Angola
83 K5 **Lucan** Ontario Canada
143 F3 **Lucan** Ireland
160 C5 **Lucapa** Angola
105 H5 **Lucas** Brazil
85 M1 **Lucas** Kansas USA
218 F3 **Lucas, Mount** Qld Australia
101 G5 **Lucas Borges** Brazil
130 D5 **Lucca** Italy
127 L3 **Luče** Slovenia
142 D6 **Luce Bay** Scotland UK
86 G5 **Lucedale** Mississippi USA
103 B8 **Lucélia** Brazil
195 I4 **Lucena** Philippines
128 D5 **Lucena** Spain
129 F3 **Lucena del Cid** Spain
125 J3 **Lučenec** Slovakia
131 F6 **Lucera** Italy
104 D4 **Lucerna** Peru
Lucerne *see* **Luzern** Switzerland
88 D2 **Lucero** Mexico
85 I4 **Lucero, Lake** New Mexico USA
100 B4 **Lucero, Punta** *cape* Ecuador
188 F4 **Lucheng** Guangxi Zhuangzu Zizhiqu China
191 H6 **Lucheng** Shanxi China
188 D2 **Lucheng** Sichuan China
163 G2 **Luchering** *watercourse* Mozambique
124 F1 **Lüchow** Germany
124 E4 **Luchsingen** Switzerland
105 I3 **Luciára** Brazil
101 G4 **Lucie** *watercourse* Suriname
77 P7 **Lucie, Lac** *lake* Quebec Canada
105 I5 **Lucilândia** Brazil
218 E7 **Lucindale** SA Australia
105 I3 **Lúcio da Luz** Brazil
197 J5 **Lucipara, Kepulauan** *islands* Indonesia
162 B2 **Lucira** Angola
132 E3 **Luciu** Romania
125 G2 **Luckau** Germany
214 F7 **Lucknow** Qld Australia
83 K5 **Lucknow** Ontario Canada
186 E5 **Lucknow** Uttar Pradesh India
218 C5 **Lucky Bay** SA Australia
75 R7 **Lucky Lake** Saskatchewan Canada
126 D3 **Luçon** France
91 F2 **Lucrecia, Cayo** *island* Cuba
160 A5 **Lucunga** Angola
162 D2 **Lucusse** Angola
214 D7 **Lucy Creek** NT Australia
121 U4 **Luda** Russian Federation
124 F1 **Lüderitz** Germany
162 C5 **Lüderitz** Namibia
83 K4 **Ludgate** Ontario Canada
139 F3 **Ludgershall** Wiltshire England UK
138 B4 **Ludgvan** Cornwall England UK
186 D4 **Ludhiana** Punjab India
160 C5 **Ludimba** *watercourse* Democratic Republic of Congo
82 H5 **Ludington** Michigan USA
138 E2 **Ludlow** Shropshire England UK
84 D3 **Ludlow** California USA
132 C3 **Ludoş** Romania
132 A2 **Ludoško Jezero** *lake* Serbia
124 E3 **Ludwigshafen am Rhein** Germany
125 M2 **Ludyn** Ukraine
123 N4 **Ludza** Latvia
123 N4 **Ludzas** *admin. area* Latvia
160 C5 **Luebo** Democratic Republic of Congo
86 B4 **Lueders** Texas USA
160 D4 **Lueki** Democratic Republic of Congo
160 D4 **Luemba** Democratic Republic of Congo
162 F2 **Luembe** Zambia
162 C2 **Luena** Angola
162 D2 **Luena** *watercourse* Angola
160 D5 **Luena** Democratic Republic of Congo
162 F2 **Luena** Zambia
162 D2 **Luena** *watercourse* Zambia
162 D2 **Luena Flats** *pan* Zambia
162 D3 **Luengué** Angola
188 E1 **Lueyang** Shaanxi China
199 H4 **Luf Island** Papua New Guinea
189 G4 **Lufeng** Guangdong China
188 F3 **Lufeng** Hunan China
160 A5 **Lufico** Angola
160 D5 **Lufila** *watercourse* Democratic Republic of Congo
162 E2 **Lufira, Lac de Retenue de la** *lake* Democratic Republic of Congo
86 D5 **Lufkin** Texas USA
160 A5 **Lufu** Democratic Republic of Congo
162 E1 **Lufubu** Zambia
160 E5 **Lufubu** *watercourse* Zambia
125 J5 **Lug** Croatia
123 O3 **Luga** Russian Federation
127 I3 **Lugano** Switzerland
222 7 **Luganville** Vanuatu
163 G3 **Lugela** *watercourse* Mozambique
163 G2 **Lugenda** *watercourse* Mozambique
138 E2 **Lugg** *watercourse* England UK
181 G2 **Luggudontsen** *mountain* Xizang Zizhiqu China
132 D1 **Lugi** Ukraine
132 F1 **Lugi** Ukraine
120 J5 **Lugnvik** Sweden
130 D4 **Lugo** Italy
128 C2 **Lugo** Spain
132 B3 **Lugoj** Romania
160 D4 **Lugulu** *watercourse* Democratic Republic of Congo
195 I6 **Lugus** Philippines
195 I6 **Lugus** *island* Philippines
123 L2 **Luhalahti** Finland
136 F3 **Luhans'k** Ukraine
136 F3 **Luhans'ka Oblast'** *admin. area* Ukraine
191 I3 **Luhin Sum** Nei Mongol Zizhiqu China
160 D4 **Luhoho** *watercourse* Democratic Republic of Congo
161 F5 **Luhombero** Tanzania
161 F5 **Luhombero** *mountain* Tanzania
188 D2 **Luhua** Sichuan China
160 B5 **Lui** *watercourse* Angola
160 C5 **Luia** Angola
163 F3 **Luia** *watercourse* Mozambique
162 D3 **Luiana** Angola
162 D3 **Luiana** *watercourse* Angola
142 B3 **Luib** Highland Scotland UK
142 D4 **Luibeilt** Highland Scotland UK
163 F4 **Luido** Mozambique
121 P5 **Luikonlahti** Finland
142 C4 **Luing** *island* Scotland UK
162 D2 **Luio** *watercourse* Angola
121 O3 **Luiro** Finland
121 O3 **Luiro** *watercourse* Finland
105 I2 **Luís Gonçalves** Brazil
88 E4 **Luis Moya** Mexico
160 D6 **Luishia** Democratic Republic of Congo
104 C4 **Luisiana** Peru
58 V1 **Luitpold Coast** Antarctica
160 C5 **Luiza** Democratic Republic of Congo
162 D2 **Luizavo** *watercourse* Angola
160 D5 **Luizi** Democratic Republic of Congo
189 H2 **Lujiang** Anhui China
130 F4 **Luka** Croatia
160 A5 **Lukala** Democratic Republic of Congo
162 E2 **Lukanga Swamps** *swamp* Zambia
130 H4 **Lukavac** Bosnia and Herzegovina
160 D5 **Lukenga, Lac** *lake* Democratic Republic of Congo
160 C4 **Lukenie** *watercourse* Democratic Republic of Congo
143 E4 **Lukeswell** Ireland
84 F5 **Lukeville** Mexico
88 B2 **Lukeville** Arizona USA
182 D1 **Lukh** Russian Federation
215 H3 **Lukin, Mount** Qld Australia
123 K4 **Luknės** Lithuania
189 G3 **Lukou** Hunan China
132 D4 **Lukovit** Bulgaria
125 M2 **Lukovo** Belarus
130 F4 **Lukovo Šugarje** Croatia
125 L2 **Łuków** Poland
182 D2 **Lukoyanov** Russian Federation
198 B4 **Luksagu** Indonesia
123 L5 **Lukšiai** Lithuania
125 K1 **Łukta** Poland
160 D5 **Lukuga** *watercourse* Democratic Republic of Congo
160 A5 **Lukula** Democratic Republic of Congo
162 D2 **Lukulu** Zambia
162 F2 **Lukulu** *watercourse* Zambia
160 D5 **Lukumbi** *watercourse* Democratic Republic of Congo
161 F5 **Lukumburu** Tanzania
160 B5 **Lukuni** Democratic Republic of Congo
222 6 **Lukunor** *island* Federated States of Micronesia
87 J3 **Lula** Georgia USA
182 F7 **Lūlaki** Iran
120 M4 **Luleå** Sweden
133 E5 **Lüleburgaz** Turkey
163 F4 **Lulekani** South Africa
120 J3 **Lulep Jutas** *lake* Sweden
190 G5 **Luliang Shan** *range* Shanxi China
160 D4 **Lulimba** Democratic Republic of Congo
86 C6 **Luling** Texas USA
191 I5 **Lulong** Hebei China
160 B3 **Lulonga** *watercourse* Democratic Republic of Congo
160 C3 **Lulu** *watercourse* Democratic Republic of Congo
223 12b **Lulu Fakahega, Mont** *mountain* Wallis and Futuna
160 C5 **Lulua** *watercourse* Democratic Republic of Congo
139 E4 **Lulworth Camp** Dorset England UK
159 E2 **Luma** Nigeria
162 C2 **Luma Cassai** Angola
197 G6 **Lumajang** Indonesia
179 K2 **Lūmān** Afghanistan
160 D4 **Lumana** Democratic Republic of Congo
123 L3 **Lümanda** Estonia
162 D2 **Lumbala Kaquengue** Angola
162 D2 **Lumbala N'guimbo** Angola
162 D3 **Lumbe** *watercourse* Zambia
75 N8 **Lumberton** British Columbia Canada
87 L3 **Lumberton** North Carolina USA
86 D5 **Lumberton** Texas USA
197 H2 **Lumbis** Indonesia
134 J5 **Lumbovka** Russian Federation
139 J4 **Lumbres** France
74 L7 **Lumby** British Columbia Canada
181 G4 **Lumding** Assam India
218 G1 **Lumeah** Qld Australia
133 B5 **Lumi I Osum** *watercourse* Albania
107 G2 **Lumiador, Cordilheira do** *range* Brazil
121 N4 **Lumijoki** Finland
127 G1 **Lummen** Belgium
143 C3 **Lumnagh** Ireland
123 K2 **Lumparn** *bay* Finland
194 E4 **Lumphăt** Cambodia
87 I4 **Lumpkin** Georgia USA
79 L8 **Lumsden** Newfoundland and Labrador Canada
75 S7 **Lumsden** Saskatchewan Canada
221 C7 **Lumsden** New Zealand
160 C7 **Lumulunga** Zambia
162 D3 **Lumuna** *watercourse* Angola
196 D2 **Lumut** Malaysia
197 H4 **Lumut, Gunung** *mountain* Indonesia
196 E4 **Lumut, Tanjung** *cape* Indonesia
162 E2 **Lumwana** Zambia
127 L4 **Lun** Croatia
190 F3 **Lün** Mongolia
105 F2 **Luna** *watercourse* Brazil
129 F2 **Luna** Spain
128 D2 **Luna** *watercourse* Spain
142 F4 **Lunan Bay** Scotland UK
125 L5 **Lunca Cernii de Sus** Romania
132 E2 **Lunca de Jos** Romania
132 D2 **Lunca Ilvei** Romania
74 I8 **Lund** British Columbia Canada
120 G4 **Lund** Norway
122 G5 **Lund** Sweden
141 H3 **Lund** East Riding of Yorkshire England UK
84 E1 **Lund** Nevada USA
162 C1 **Lunda Norte** *admin. area* Angola
162 D2 **Lunda Sul** *admin. area* Angola
76 F7 **Lundar** Manitoba Canada
142 C4 **Lundavra** Highland Scotland UK
163 F2 **Lundazi** Zambia
122 E3 **Lunde** Norway
120 J5 **Lunde** Sweden
120 H3 **Lundeura** *island* Norway
122 D3 **Lundevatn** *lake* Norway
142 F4 **Lundie Castle** Angus Scotland UK
120 I2 **Lundøya** *island* Norway
122 H3 **Lundsfjärden** *bay* Sweden
120 I5 **Lundsjön** Sweden
197 F3 **Lundu** Malaysia
138 C3 **Lundy Island** England UK
141 F2 **Lune** *watercourse* England UK
124 F1 **Lüneburger Heide** *region* Germany
129 I2 **Lunel** France
79 F10 **Lunenburg** Nova Scotia Canada
127 H2 **Lunéville** France
163 H3 **Lunga** Mozambique
222 8a **Lunga Point** Solomon Islands
180 E2 **Lungar Shan** *mountain* Xizang Zizhiqu China
162 C2 **Lunge** Angola
122 G3 **Lungen** *lake* Sweden
158 B3 **Lungi** Sierra Leone
120 K5 **Lungön** *island* Sweden
120 J5 **Lungsjön** Sweden
186 F5 **Lunh** Nepal
186 C6 **Luni** *watercourse* Rajasthan India
84 C1 **Luning** Nevada USA
182 E2 **Lunino** Russian Federation
186 C5 **Lunkaransar** Rajasthan India
142 inset **Lunna** Shetland Scotland UK
120 H5 **Lunnäset** Sweden
124 D1 **Lünne** Germany
162 E2 **Lunsemfwa** *watercourse* Zambia
184 G4 **Luntai** Xinjiang Uygur Zizhiqu China
197 H6 **Lunyuk** Indonesia
188 C1 **Lu'nyung** Sichuan China
125 H4 **Lunz am See** Austria
189 F1 **Luo He** *watercourse* Jiangsu China
189 F4 **Luoding** Guangdong China
188 F5 **Luodou Sha** *island* Guangdong China
189 G1 **Luohe** Henan China
181 F3 **Luojiang** Xizang Zizhiqu China
189 H1 **Luoma Hu** *lake* Jiangsu China
188 F1 **Luonan** Shaanxi China
123 N2 **Luonteri** *bay* Finland
184 F5 **Luopu** Xinjiang Uygur Zizhiqu China
189 G2 **Luoshan** Henan China
121 Q2 **Luostari** Russian Federation
121 M5 **Luoto** Finland
121 P1 **Luovtejok** Norway
189 G3 **Luoxiao Shan** *range* Hunan China
188 D4 **Luoxiong** Yunnan China
189 F1 **Luoyang** Henan China
181 G3 **Luozha** Xizang Zizhiqu China
160 A4 **Luozi** Democratic Republic of Congo
162 E3 **Lupane** Zimbabwe
188 D3 **Lupanshui** Guizhou China
197 F3 **Lupar** *watercourse* Malaysia
125 L5 **Lupeni** Romania
91 G3 **Luperón** Dominican Republic
163 G2 **Lupilichi** Mozambique
162 C2 **Lupire** Angola
161 F5 **Lupiro** Tanzania
222 5 **Lupog** Guam
123 P6 **Lupolovo** Belarus
195 J6 **Lupon** Philippines
138 D4 **Luppitt** Devon England UK
85 H3 **Lupton** Arizona USA
188 D2 **Luqiao** Sichuan China
188 D1 **Luqu** Gansu China
127 H3 **Lure** France
87 J3 **Lure, Lake** North Carolina USA
163 G2 **Lureco** *watercourse* Mozambique
160 B5 **Luremo** Angola
126 E3 **Lureuil** France
143 F3 **Lurgan** Ireland
143 F2 **Lurgan** Armagh Northern Ireland UK
104 E5 **Luribay** Bolivia
163 H2 **Lúrio** Mozambique
163 G2 **Lúrio** *watercourse* Mozambique
120 H3 **Lurøya** *island* Norway
143 D5 **Lurrig** Ireland
100 C2 **Luruaco** Colombia
160 D5 **Lusaka** Democratic Republic of Congo
162 E3 **Lusaka** Zambia
162 E3 **Lusaka** *admin. area* Zambia
160 D4 **Lusako** Democratic Republic of Congo
160 D4 **Lusamba** Democratic Republic of Congo
160 C4 **Lusambo** Democratic Republic of Congo
199 I6 **Lusancay Islands and Reefs** Papua New Guinea
160 B4 **Lusanga** Democratic Republic of Congo
160 D4 **Lusangi** Democratic Republic of Congo
74 M6 **Luscar** Alberta Canada
161 F6 **Lusewa** Tanzania
213 I4 **Lush, Mount** WA Australia
190 E6 **Lushaer** Qinghai China
188 F1 **Lushi** Henan China
133 A5 **Lushnjë** Albania
161 F4 **Lushoto** Tanzania
124 C3 **Lusigny** France
143 F3 **Lusk** Ireland
81 M5 **Lusk** Wyoming USA
130 G5 **Lusnić** Bosnia and Herzegovina
128 B3 **Luso** Portugal
142 D4 **Luss** Argyll and Bute Scotland UK
142 C4 **Lussagiven** Argyll and Bute Scotland UK
127 G4 **Lussan** France
162 B2 **Lussusso** Angola
142 B3 **Lusta** Highland Scotland UK
120 E6 **Luster** Norway
123 N4 **Lusti** Estonia
179 I3 **Lūt, Dasht-e** *desert* Iran
130 D3 **Lutago** Italy
86 F5 **Lutcher** Louisiana USA
162 D2 **Lutembo** Angola
222 8 **Luti** Solomon Islands
122 F5 **Lütjenburg** Germany
139 G3 **Luton** *admin. area* England UK
139 G3 **Luton** Luton England UK
197 G2 **Lutong** Malaysia
74 M3 **Lutose** Alberta Canada
123 K5 **Lutry** Poland
125 M2 **Luts'k** Ukraine
139 F2 **Lutterworth** Leicester England UK
121 P2 **Lutto** *watercourse* Finland
139 H2 **Lutton** Lincolnshire England UK
140 B3 **Luttrellstown** Ireland
162 D2 **Lutuai** Angola
58 C2 **Lützow-Holm Bay** Antarctica
190 F3 **Luuc** Mongolia
198 B2 **Luuk** Philippines
195 I6 **Luuk** Philippines
123 N2 **Luumäki** Finland
161 G3 **Luuq** Somalia
121 O3 **Luusua** Finland
160 C6 **Luveira** *watercourse* Democratic Republic of Congo
87 H5 **Luverne** Alabama USA
81 Q5 **Luverne** Minnesota USA
123 K2 **Luvia** Finland
160 A5 **Luvo** Angola
121 Q4 **Luvozero** *lake* Russian Federation
162 D2 **Luvuei** Angola
163 F2 **Luwawa** Malawi
161 F5 **Luwegu** *watercourse* Tanzania
161 E3 **Luwero** Uganda
162 E2 **Luwingu** Zambia
198 D3 **Luwo** *island* Indonesia
197 F4 **Luwuhuyu** Indonesia
198 B4 **Luwuk** Indonesia
127 **Luxembourg** *country* Europe
127 H2 **Luxembourg** Luxembourg
127 H3 **Luxeuil-les-Bains** France
126 D4 **Luxey** France
188 C4 **Luxi** Yunnan China
189 I3 **Luxi Dao** *island* Zhejiang China
Luxor *see* **Al Uqşur** Egypt
126 D5 **Luy** *watercourse* France
190 G5 **Luya Shan** *range* Shanxi China
160 D4 **Luyamba** Democratic Republic of Congo
128 C2 **Luyego de Somoza** Spain
189 G1 **Luyi** Henan China
103 C7 **Luz** Brazil
128 C5 **Luz, Costa de la** *region* Spain
134 K6 **Luza** Russian Federation
127 I3 **Luzern (Lucerne)** Switzerland
188 F4 **Luzhai** Guangxi Zhuangzu Zizhiqu China
188 C3 **Luzhang** Yunnan China
123 O2 **Luzhayka** Russian Federation
123 O4 **Luzhitsy** Russian Federation
123 N5 **Luzhki** Belarus
123 O2 **Luzhki** Russian Federation
188 E3 **Luzhou** Sichuan China
103 C7 **Luziânia** Brazil
125 H2 **Lužicka** *watercourse* Czech Republic
102 D3 **Luzilândia** Brazil
122 J5 **Luzino** Poland
125 H3 **Lužnice** *watercourse* Czech Republic
195 I3 **Luzon** *island* Philippines
195 I2 **Luzon Strait** Philippines
126 F3 **Luzy** France
132 D1 **L'viv** Ukraine
136 C2 **L'vivs'ka Oblast'** *admin. area* Ukraine
125 I1 **Lwówek** Poland
123 P5 **Lyady** Belarus
135 AC4 **Lyakhovskiye Ostrova** *island* Russian Federation
182 E6 **Lyaki** Azerbaijan
121 T4 **Lyamitskoye Ozero** *lake* Russian Federation
121 T4 **Lyamtsa** Russian Federation
123 P2 **Lyaskelya** Russian Federation
133 D5 **Lyaskovo** Bulgaria
125 M1 **Lyasnaya** Belarus
142 E2 **Lybster** Highland Scotland UK
125 M2 **Lybytiv** Ukraine
85 K2 **Lycan** Colorado USA
123 Q4 **Lychkovo** Russian Federation
120 K4 **Lycksele** Sweden
139 H4 **Lydd** Kent England UK
75 V5 **Lyddal** Manitoba Canada
138 C4 **Lydford** Devon England UK
138 E3 **Lydney** Gloucestershire England UK
74 F6 **Lyell Island** British Columbia Canada
123 O5 **Lyepyel'** Belarus
86 C7 **Lyford** Texas USA
122 D3 **Lygna** *watercourse* Norway
122 G4 **Lygnern** *lake* Sweden
81 O2 **Lyleton** Manitoba Canada
121 P4 **Lylykylä** Finland
84 G1 **Lyman** Utah USA
81 J6 **Lyman** Wyoming USA
132 G2 **Lymany** Ukraine
138 E4 **Lyme Bay** England UK
139 F4 **Lymington** Hampshire England UK
138 D4 **Lympstone** Devon England UK
83 L8 **Lynchburg** Virginia USA
215 G4 **Lynd** *watercourse* Qld Australia
80 D2 **Lynden** Washington USA
219 I5 **Lyndhurst** NSW Australia
218 D4 **Lyndhurst** SA Australia
216 D1 **Lyndon** WA Australia
212 C7 **Lyndon** *watercourse* WA Australia
82 G6 **Lyndon** Illinois USA
83 O4 **Lyndonville** Vermont USA
139 F3 **Lyneham** Wiltshire England UK
120 L2 **Lyngen** *bay* Norway
122 D3 **Lyngna** *lake* Norway
120 L2 **Lyngseidet** Norway
120 G4 **Lyngsnes** Norway
122 D3 **Lyngsvatnet** *lake* Norway
138 D3 **Lynmouth** Devon England UK
141 G1 **Lynmouth** Northumberland England UK
86 H3 **Lynn** Alabama USA
82 I6 **Lynn** Indiana USA
83 P5 **Lynn** Massachusetts USA
74 D3 **Lynn Canal** Alaska USA
87 I5 **Lynn Haven** Florida USA
75 U4 **Lynn Lake** Manitoba Canada
80 I7 **Lynndyl** Utah USA
138 D3 **Lynton** Devon England UK
75 R1 **Lynx Lake** Northwest Territories Canada
122 F5 **Lyø** *island* Denmark
127 G4 **Lyon** France
142 D4 **Lyon** *watercourse* Scotland UK
142 D4 **Lyon, Loch** *lake* Scotland UK
216 D2 **Lyons** *watercourse* WA Australia
81 P7 **Lyons** Kansas USA
82 I6 **Lyons** Ohio USA
216 D2 **Lyons River** WA Australia
142 B5 **Lyrabus** Argyll and Bute Scotland UK
122 H3 **Lyrestad** Sweden
126 F1 **Lys** *watercourse* France
122 F3 **Lysekil** Sweden
122 F3 **Lyseren** *lake* Norway
125 I3 **Lysice** Czech Republic
133 B6 **Lysimachia, Limni** *lake* Greece
125 J1 **Łysomice** Poland
120 F5 **Lysøysund** Norway
127 H3 **Lyss** Switzerland
134 M7 **Lys'va** Russian Federation
182 H1 **Lys'va** Russian Federation
132 G1 **Lysyanka** Ukraine
136 F3 **Lysychans'k** Ukraine
182 D3 **Lysyye Gory** Russian Federation
140 F3 **Lytham** Lancashire England UK
140 E3 **Lytham St Anne's** Lancashire England UK
86 B6 **Lytle** Texas USA
125 M2 **Lytovezh** Ukraine
221 E6 **Lyttelton** New Zealand
221 E6 **Lyttelton Harbour** New Zealand
74 K7 **Lytton** British Columbia Canada
123 P3 **Lyuban'** Russian Federation
125 M2 **Lyubeshiv** Ukraine
136 E2 **Lyudinovo** Russian Federation

M

194 E2 **Ma Song** *watercourse* Vietnam
194 B3 **Ma-Ubin** Myanmar
188 D2 **Ma'erkang** Sichuan China
121 N4 **Maakrunni** *island* Finland
120 L5 **Maalahti** Finland
187 C11 **Maalhosmadulu Atoll** Maldives
143 C3 **Maam Cross** Ireland
178 C3 **Ma'ān** Jordan
121 O5 **Maaninka** Finland
121 P5 **Maanselkä** Finland
Maarianhamina *see* **Mariehamn/ Maarianhamina** Aland Islands
124 C2 **Maas** *watercourse* Belgium/ Netherlands
127 G1 **Maaseik** Belgium
121 P4 **Maaselkä** Finland
100 D1 **Maásimay** Colombia
195 J5 **Maasin** Philippines
124 C2 **Maastricht** Netherlands
223 14a **Maatea** French Polynesia
219 R11 **Maatsuyker Group** *islands* Tas. Australia
121 N5 **Määttälä** Finland
189 G4 **Maba** Guangdong China
198 D3 **Maba** Indonesia
188 D4 **Mabai** Yunnan China
195 I4 **Mabalacat** Philippines
163 F4 **Mabalane** Mozambique
160 D3 **Mabana** Democratic Republic of Congo
178 E7 **Ma'bar** Yemen
101 G2 **Mabaruma** Guyana
162 D3 **Mabebe Depression** *pan* Botswana
181 H4 **Mabein** Myanmar
218 B3 **Mabel** *watercourse* SA Australia
82 F5 **Mabel** Minnesota USA
218 B3 **Mabel Creek** SA Australia
213 J4 **Mabel Downs** WA Australia
80 F1 **Mabel Lake** British Columbia Canada
86 B4 **Mabelle** Texas USA
86 G4 **Maben** Mississippi USA
195 J5 **Mabini** Philippines
141 I3 **Mablethorpe** Lincolnshire England UK
101 H4 **Maboga** Suriname
158 B3 **Mabole** *watercourse* Sierra Leone
80 F3 **Mabton** Washington USA
195 I2 **Mabudis** *island* Philippines
159 F2 **Mabuto** Nigeria
162 D4 **Mabutsane** Botswana
104 B2 **Macabí, Isla** *island* Peru
216 E2 **Macadam Plains** WA Australia
103 D8 **Macaé** Brazil
128 E5 **Macael** Spain
136 G5 **Macahel Gecidi** *pass* Turkey
86 D3 **McAlester** Oklahoma USA
216 E6 **McAlinden** WA Australia
219 J2 **Macalister** Qld Australia
74 J6 **Macalister** British Columbia Canada
86 B7 **McAllen** Texas USA
73 I5 **MacAlpine Lake** Nunavut Canada
83 L2 **Macamic Lake** Quebec Canada
197 I5 **Macan, Kepulauan** *islands* Indonesia
100 E4 **Macanacape, Laguna** *lake* Venezuela
163 F4 **Macandze** Mozambique
104 E3 **Macapá** Brazil
101 I4 **Macapá** Brazil
100 B6 **Macará** Ecuador
90 D6 **Macaracas** Panama
100 C4 **Macaranaima** Colombia
101 F2 **Macareo, Caño** *watercourse* Venezuela
214 D4 **McArthur** *watercourse* NT Australia
218 E8 **Macarthur** Vic. Australia
76 H7 **McArthur Falls** Manitoba Canada
214 C4 **McArthur River** NT Australia
100 B5 **Macas** Ecuador
Macassar Strait *see* **Makassar, Selat** Indonesia
102 E4 **Macau** Brazil
189 G4 **Macau (Aomen)** Macau (Aomen) S.A.R. China
189 G4 **Macau (Aomen) S.A.R.** *admin. area* China
105 I3 **Macaúba** Brazil
103 D6 **Macaúbas** Brazil
220 5 **Macauley Island** Kermadec Islands New Zealand
100 C4 **Macaya-tunia** *watercourse* Colombia
82 I4 **McBain** Michigan USA
161 I2 **Macbar, Raas** *cape* Somalia
87 K3 **McBee** South Carolina USA
74 K6 **McBride** British Columbia Canada
80 G4 **McCall** Idaho USA
85 K5 **McCamey** Texas USA
80 I5 **McCammon** Idaho USA
58 V1 **McCarthy Inlet** *bay* Antarctica
85 I3 **McCartys** New Mexico USA
214 B2 **McCaw** *watercourse* NT Australia
80 D3 **McCleary** Washington USA
87 J5 **Macclenny** Florida USA
79 K8 **Maccles Lake** Newfoundland and Labrador Canada
141 F3 **Macclesfield** Cheshire England UK
55 P3 **Macclesfield Bank** *underwater feature* South China Sea
141 F3 **Macclesfield Canal** England UK
58 K1 **McClintock, Mount** *mountain* Antarctica
214 B1 **McCluer Island** NT Australia
83 M6 **McClure** Pennsylvania USA
80 E8 **McClure, Lake** California USA
81 O3 **McClusky** North Dakota USA
87 L3 **McColl** South Carolina USA
86 F5 **McComb** Mississippi USA
81 O6 **McConaughy, Lake** Nebraska USA
215 I6 **McConnel, Mount** Qld Australia
76 H2 **McConnell** *watercourse* Nunavut Canada
81 O6 **McCook** Nebraska USA
75 R8 **McCord** Saskatchewan Canada
87 J4 **McCormick** South Carolina USA
58 L2 **McCormick, Cape** Antarctica
76 I6 **McCoy Lake** Ontario Canada
86 F3 **McCrory** Arkansas USA
216 G6 **McDermid Rock** *mountain* WA Australia
214 A6 **McDiarmid Hill** NT Australia
214 G1 **MacDonald** *watercourse* Qld Australia
75 V7 **Macdonald** Manitoba Canada
85 K4 **McDonald** New Mexico USA
213 J7 **MacDonald, Lake** WA Australia
80 I2 **McDonald, Lake** Montana USA
58 G2 **McDonald Bay** Antarctica
210 inset **McDonald Island** Heard Island Australia
80 H2 **MacDonald Range** British Columbia Canada
214 B7 **MacDonnell Ranges** NT Australia
87 I4 **McDonough** Georgia USA
163 F4 **McDougal, Lake** *lake* Zimbabwe
75 R6 **Macdowall** Saskatchewan Canada
73 J8 **MacDowell Lake** Ontario Canada
132 B2 **Macea** Romania
133 B5 **Macedonia** *country* Europe
102 F5 **Maceió** Brazil
100 C3 **Maceo** Colombia
130 E5 **Macerata** Italy
215 G7 **McEvoy, Mount** Qld Australia
84 C3 **McFarland** California USA
75 Q3 **MacFarlane** *watercourse* Saskatchewan Canada
218 C5 **MacFarlane, Lake** SA Australia
140 B1 **Macfinn Lower** Coleraine Northern Ireland UK
81 K1 **McGee** Saskatchewan Canada
86 D3 **McGee Creek Reservoir** Oklahoma USA
80 D1 **McGillivray Falls** British Columbia Canada
143 C5 **Macgillycuddy's Reeks** *range* Ireland
72 D6 **McGrath** Alaska USA
74 K5 **McGregor** British Columbia Canada
74 K5 **McGregor** *watercourse* British Columbia Canada
75 O7 **McGregor Lake** Alberta Canada
80 H3 **McGregor Lake** Montana USA
218 F2 **McGregor Range** Qld Australia
100 B5 **Machachi** Ecuador
103 C8 **Machado** Brazil
163 F4 **Machaila** Mozambique
100 B5 **Machala** Ecuador
185 K6 **Machali** Qinghai China
197 G3 **Machan** Malaysia
181 H3 **Machanbaw** Myanmar
161 E2 **Machar Marshes** *swamp* Sudan
214 E8 **Machattie, Lake** Qld Australia
76 K7 **Machawaian Lake** Ontario Canada
126 D3 **Machecoul** France
189 G2 **Macheng** Hubei China
79 E10 **Machias** Maine USA
83 R4 **Machias Bay** Maine USA
76 J4 **Machichi** *watercourse* Manitoba Canada
164 2 **Machico** Madeira
162 E3 **Machile** *watercourse* Zambia
187 E8 **Machilipatnam** Andhra Pradesh India
100 C2 **Machiques** Venezuela
142 C5 **Machrihanish** Argyll and Bute Scotland UK
105 E4 **Machupo** *watercourse* Bolivia
138 D2 **Machynlleth** Powys Wales UK
163 F4 **Macia** Mozambique
125 K2 **Maciejowice** Poland
105 G2 **Maciel** Brazil
107 G3 **Maciel** Paraguay
215 G2 **McIlwraith Range** Qld Australia
127 I5 **Macinaggio** Corsica France
76 I6 **McInnes Lake** Ontario Canada
82 E2 **McIntosh** Ontario Canada
81 O4 **McIntosh** South Dakota USA
219 I3 **Macintyre** *watercourse* Qld Australia
74 E5 **McIntyre Bay** British Columbia Canada
82 G2 **McIntyre Bay** Ontario Canada
215 J6 **Mackay** Qld Australia
75 O4 **MacKay** *watercourse* Alberta Canada
80 I5 **Mackay** Idaho USA
213 J7 **Mackay, Lake** WA Australia
78 F6 **McKay Lake** Newfoundland and Labrador Canada
72 H6 **MacKay Lake** Northwest Territories Canada
82 H2 **McKay Lake** Ontario Canada
58 O1 **Mackay Mountains** Antarctica
222 1 **McKean** *island* Kiribati
82 J8 **McKee** Kentucky USA
214 G7 **Mackenzie** *watercourse* Qld Australia
74 J5 **Mackenzie** British Columbia Canada
74 J1 **MacKenzie** *watercourse* Northwest Territories Canada
87 H5 **McKenzie** Alabama USA
58 E2 **MacKenzie Bay** Antarctica
72 F5 **Mackenzie Bay** Northwest Territories/Yukon Territory Canada
72 H3 **Mackenzie King Island** Northwest Territories/Nunavut Canada
72 F5 **Mackenzie Mountains** Northwest Territories Canada
72 F5 **Mackenzie River Delta** Northwest Territories Canada
221 C7 **McKerrow, Lake** New Zealand
MacKillop Lake *see* **Yamma Yamma Lake** Australia
82 I4 **Mackinaw City** Michigan USA
214 A2 **McKinlay** *watercourse* NT Australia
214 F6 **McKinlay** Qld Australia
214 F6 **McKinlay** *watercourse* Qld Australia
218 D4 **McKinlay, Mount** SA Australia
72 D6 **McKinley, Mount (Denali)** Alaska USA
86 C4 **McKinney** Texas USA
58 U2 **Mackintosh, Cape** Antarctica
215 I5 **Macknade** Qld Australia
219 K4 **Macksville** NSW Australia
86 G5 **McLain** Mississippi USA
81 O4 **McLaughlin** South Dakota USA
219 K3 **Maclean** NSW Australia
86 A3 **McLean** Texas USA
213 G3 **Macleay Island** WA Australia

75 S5 **McLennan Lake** Saskatchewan Canada
221 C8 **MacLennan Range** New Zealand
75 N6 **McLeod** *watercourse* Alberta Canada
216 C2 **MacLeod, Lake** WA Australia
75 P1 **McLeod Bay** Northwest Territories Canada
74 J5 **McLeod Lake** British Columbia Canada
213 I5 **McLernon, Lake** WA Australia
85 J6 **Maclovio Herrera** Mexico
88 D1 **McMillan, Lake** New Mexico USA
87 I3 **McMinnville** Tennessee USA
81 K1 **McMorran** Saskatchewan Canada
76 H8 **McMunn** Manitoba Canada
74 M7 **McMurdo** British Columbia Canada
58 L1 **McMurdo (USA)** *research station* Antarctica
58 K1 **McMurdo Sound** *strait* Antarctica
77 Q6 **McNab, Lac** *lake* Quebec Canada
85 J5 **McNary** Texas USA
143 E2 **Macnean, Upper Loch** *lake* Northern Ireland UK
216 C2 **McNeill Claypan** WA Australia
75 U7 **MacNutt** Saskatchewan Canada
79 F11 **McNutts Island** Nova Scotia Canada
104 E4 **Maco** Bolivia
163 F4 **Maçobere** Mozambique
160 B5 **Macocola** Angola
91 G4 **Macolla, Punta** *cape* Venezuela
131 G7 **Macolone, Punta di** *cape* Italy
82 F6 **Macomb** Illinois USA
87 J4 **Macon** Georgia USA
86 G4 **Macon** Mississippi USA
127 G3 **Mâcon** France
127 G3 **Mâconais** *region* France
162 D2 **Macondo** Angola
143 F1 **Macosquin** Coleraine Northern Ireland UK
128 D3 **Macotera** Spain
109 14 **Macouba** Martinique
81 N2 **Macoun** Saskatchewan Canada
76 D4 **Macoun Lake** Saskatchewan Canada
163 G4 **Macovane** Mozambique
78 E5 **McPhayden** *watercourse* Newfoundland and Labrador Canada
214 E6 **McPhee Hills** Qld Australia
85 H2 **McPhee Reservoir** Colorado USA
81 Q7 **McPherson** Kansas USA
58 E2 **Macpherson Robertson Land** *plain* Antarctica
219 H4 **Macquarie** *watercourse* NSW Australia
219 J5 **Macquarie, Lake** NSW Australia
219 Q11 **Macquarie Harbour** Tas. Australia
211 inset **Macquarie Island** Australia
219 H4 **Macquarie Marshes** *swamp* NSW Australia
55 U9 **Macquarie Ridge** *underwater feature* Southern Ocean
76 H1 **MacQuoid Lake** Nunavut Canada
87 J4 **McRae** Georgia USA
76 J7 **McRea Lake** Ontario Canada
196 C3 **MacRitchie Reservoir** Singapore
143 D5 **Macroom** Ireland
72 H5 **McTavish Arm** Northwest Territories Canada
83 L4 **MacTier** Ontario Canada
100 D4 **Macu** Brazil
101 F5 **Macucuau** *watercourse* Brazil
100 C4 **Macuje** Colombia
100 B5 **Macuma** Ecuador
218 B2 **Macumba** SA Australia
218 C2 **Macumba** *watercourse* SA Australia
100 E4 **Macuruco** Venezuela
104 D4 **Macusani** Peru
75 U4 **McVeigh** Manitoba Canada
72 G6 **McVictor Arm** Northwest Territories Canada
81 P3 **McVille** North Dakota USA
83 Q4 **Macwahoc** Maine USA
163 I4 **Madagascar** *country* Africa
54 J7 **Madagascar Basin** *underwater feature* Indian Ocean
54 I7 **Madagascar Plateau** *underwater feature* Indian Ocean
128 E6 **Madagh** Morocco
161 G3 **Madagoi** *watercourse* Somalia
164 1b **Madalena** Azores
79 H10 **Madame, Isle** *island* Nova Scotia Canada
159 H3 **Madana** Chad
155 H6 **Madaoua** Niger
132 E4 **Madara** Bulgaria
181 G4 **Madaripur** Bangladesh
199 J6 **Madau Island** Papua New Guinea
182 G6 **Madaw** Turkmenistan
83 L4 **Madawaska** Ontario Canada
161 G3 **Madax Gooy** *watercourse* Somalia
181 H4 **Madaya** Myanmar
160 E2 **Madbar** Sudan
127 J4 **Maddalena, Monte** *mountain* Italy
131 F8 **Maddalena, Penisola della** *cape* Italy
195 I3 **Maddela** Philippines
139 F3 **Maddington** Wiltshire England UK
81 P3 **Maddock** North Dakota USA
124 C2 **Made** Netherlands
179 I3 **Mādeh Karīz** Iran
101 G5 **Madeira** *watercourse* Brazil
164 2 **Madeira** *Portuguese autonomous region* Atlantic Ocean
164 2 **Madeira, Ilha de** *island* Atlantic Ocean
79 H9 **Madeleine, Îles de la** *islands* Quebec Canada
138 E2 **Madeley** Staffordshire England UK
138 E2 **Madeley** Telford and Wrekin England UK
82 D4 **Madelia** Minnesota USA
183 M4 **Madeniyet** Kazakhstan
88 C2 **Madera** Mexico
80 E8 **Madera** California USA
124 E4 **Madesimo** Italy
186 G5 **Madhubani** Bihar India
186 E6 **Madhya Pradesh** *admin. area* India
161 E5 **Madibira** Tanzania
104 D4 **Madidi** *watercourse* Bolivia
218 C3 **Madigan Gulf** SA Australia
178 G4 **Madīinat ash Shamāl** Qatar
86 C3 **Madill** Oklahoma USA
160 A5 **Madimba** Angola
160 B4 **Madimba** Democratic Republic of Congo
178 D4 **Madīnah, Al** *admin. area* Saudi Arabia
179 H5 **Madīnat Zāyid** United Arab Emirates
159 G5 **Madingo-Kayes** Congo
159 G5 **Madingou** Congo
159 G3 **Madingrin** Cameroon
163 I3 **Madirovalo** Madagascar
161 G2 **Madiso Shet** *watercourse* Ethiopia
81 K1 **Madison** Saskatchewan Canada
86 H3 **Madison** Alabama USA
86 F3 **Madison** Arkansas USA
87 J5 **Madison** Florida USA
82 I7 **Madison** Indiana USA
82 C7 **Madison** Kansas USA
79 D10 **Madison** Maine USA
81 Q4 **Madison** Minnesota USA
80 J4 **Madison** *watercourse* Montana USA
81 Q6 **Madison** Nebraska USA
82 G5 **Madison** Wisconsin USA
82 H8 **Madisonville** Kentucky USA
197 F5 **Madiun** Indonesia
159 G4 **Madjingo** Gabon
125 G4 **Madling** Austria
222 6b **Madolenihmw** Federated States of Micronesia
124 D3 **Madon** *watercourse* France
123 N4 **Madona** Latvia
123 N4 **Madonas** *admin. area* Latvia
216 H5 **Madoonia Downs** WA Australia
179 I6 **Madrakah, Ra's al** *cape* Oman
Madras *see* **Chennai** India
80 E4 **Madras** Oregon USA
89 F3 **Madre, Laguna** *lake* Mexico
86 C7 **Madre, Laguna** *lake* Texas USA
195 I3 **Madre, Sierra** *range* Philippines
104 D4 **Madre de Dios** *watercourse* Bolivia
104 D3 **Madre de Dios** *admin. area* Peru
108 A5 **Madre de Dios, Archipiélago** *islands* Chile
89 F5 **Madre Del Sur, Sierra** *range* Mexico
88 D4 **Madre Occidental, Sierra** *range* Mexico
85 K7 **Madre Oriental, Sierra** *range* Mexico
128 E3 **Madrid** Spain
128 E3 **Madrid** *admin. area* Spain
81 O6 **Madrid** Nebraska USA
128 E4 **Madridejos** Spain
122 H4 **Madroken** *lake* Sweden
128 D4 **Madrona, Sierra** *range* Spain
128 D4 **Madroñera** Spain
155 I4 **Madrūsah** Libya
197 I5 **Madu** *island* Indonesia
195 I5 **Maducang** *island* Philippines
187 F8 **Madugula** Andhra Pradesh India
197 G5 **Madura** *island* Indonesia
197 G5 **Madura, Selat** *strait* Indonesia
187 E10 **Madurai** Tamil Nadu India
161 E5 **Madyo** Tanzania
162 E3 **Madziwadzido** Zimbabwe
194 C2 **Mae Chan** Thailand
194 C3 **Mae Hong Son** Thailand
181 I4 **Mae Nam Khong** *watercourse* Myanmar
194 C3 **Mae Ramat** Thailand
181 I5 **Mae Sai** Myanmar
194 C3 **Mae Sot** Thailand
194 C3 **Mae Taeng** Thailand
194 C3 **Mae Tha** Thailand
194 C2 **Maeai** Thailand
129 G3 **Maella** Spain
138 D2 **Maesbrook** Shropshire England UK
138 D2 **Maesbury Marsh** Shropshire England UK
138 D3 **Maesteg** Bridgend Wales UK
130 E4 **Maestra, Punta della** *cape* Italy
90 E2 **Maestra, Sierra** *range* Cuba
222 7 **Maéwo** *island* Vanuatu
198 C3 **Mafa** Indonesia
178 E2 **Mafa** Iraq
163 G3 **Mafamede, Ilha de** Mozambique
75 U6 **Mafeking** Manitoba Canada
162 E5 **Mafeteng** Lesotho
199 F4 **Maffin** Indonesia
218 H7 **Maffra** Vic. Australia
161 F5 **Mafia Channel** *strait* Tanzania
161 F5 **Mafia** *island* Tanzania
162 E5 **Mafikeng** South Africa
158 B2 **Mafou** *watercourse* Guinea
103 B9 **Mafra** Brazil
128 B4 **Mafra** Portugal
159 G2 **Maga** Cameroon
135 AF7 **Magadan** Russian Federation
135 AF6 **Magadanskaya Oblast'** *admin. area* Russian Federation
161 F4 **Magadi, Lake** Kenya
163 F4 **Magaiza** Mozambique
108 B5 **Magallanes, Estrecho de (Magellan Strait)** *strait* Chile
108 B5 **Magallanes y de la Antártica Chilena** *admin. area* Chile
129 F3 **Magallón** Spain
128 E3 **Magaña** Spain
140 B4 **Maganey** Ireland
100 C2 **Magangué** Colombia
195 J6 **Maganoy** Philippines
155 H6 **Magaria** Niger
199 I6 **Magarida** Papua New Guinea
182 D5 **Magas** Russian Federation
86 E3 **Magazine** Arkansas USA
159 G3 **Magba** Cameroon
191 K1 **Magdagachi** Russian Federation
100 C2 **Magdalena** *admin. area* Colombia
100 C2 **Magdalena** *watercourse* Colombia
88 C2 **Magdalena** Mexico
84 G5 **Magdalena** *watercourse* Mexico
85 I3 **Magdalena** New Mexico USA
88 B3 **Magdalena, Bahía** *bay* Mexico
108 B3 **Magdalena, Isla** *island* Chile
88 B3 **Magdalena, Isla** *island* Mexico
84 G5 **Magdalena de Kino** Mexico
197 H2 **Magdalene, Gunung** *mountain* Malaysia
124 F1 **Magdeburg** Germany
215 K4 **Magdelaine Cays** *islands* Coral Sea Islands Territory Australia
192 F5 **Mage-shima** *island* Japan
86 G5 **Magee** Mississippi USA
197 F5 **Magelang** Indonesia
52 O7 **Magellan Rise** *underwater feature* Pacific Ocean
52 L6 **Magellan Seamounts** *underwater feature* Pacific Ocean
Magellan Strait *see* **Magallanes, Estrecho de** Chile
216 F6 **Magenta, Lake** WA Australia
222 6 **Magererik** *island* Federated States of Micronesia
121 N1 **Magerøya** *island* Norway
197 F5 **Magetan** Indonesia
214 F4 **Maggieville** Qld Australia
124 E5 **Maggiorasca, Monte** *mountain* Italy
130 C3 **Maggiore, Lago** *lake* Italy
156 E2 **Maghāghah** Egypt
154 D5 **Maghama** Mauritania
186 F5 **Maghar** Uttar Pradesh India
140 B2 **Maghera** Magherafelt Northern Ireland UK
143 E1 **Magheradrumman** Ireland
140 B2 **Magherafelt** Magherafelt Northern Ireland UK
143 F2 **Magherafelt** *admin. area* Northern Ireland UK
140 C2 **Magheramorne** Larne Northern Ireland UK
140 B2 **Maghereagh Cross** Ireland
178 E5 **Maghīb** Saudi Arabia
80 H5 **Magic Reservoir** Idaho USA
161 F5 **Magingo** Tanzania
76 J6 **Magiss Lake** Ontario Canada
75 V7 **Magnet** Manitoba Canada
58 D2 **Magnet Bay** Antarctica
215 I5 **Magnetic Island** Qld Australia
182 H2 **Magnitogorsk** Russian Federation
86 E4 **Magnolia** Arkansas USA
86 F5 **Magnolia** Mississippi USA
89 G2 **Magnolia** Texas USA
74 I3 **Magnum Mine** British Columbia Canada
223 9 **Mago** *island* Fiji
125 J4 **Mágocs** Hungary
163 F3 **Màgoé** Mozambique
83 O4 **Magog** Quebec Canada
79 F7 **Magpie** *watercourse* Quebec Canada
73 M8 **Magpie, Lac** *lake* Quebec Canada
186 G6 **Magra** West Bengal India
156 E5 **Magrur** Sudan
156 D4 **Magrur, Wādī** *watercourse* Sudan
154 D5 **Magta Lakjar** Mauritania
102 B3 **Maguarinho, Cabo** *cape* Brazil
91 F2 **Magüey, Sierra del** *range* Cuba
154 D6 **Magui, Mare de** *lake* Mali
77 S3 **Maguire, Lac** *lake* Quebec Canada
159 G2 **Magumeri** Nigeria
162 E3 **Magunue** Zimbabwe
76 H2 **Maguse** *watercourse* Nunavut Canada
76 H2 **Maguse Lake** Nunavut Canada
76 I2 **Maguse Point** Nunavut Canada
75 X2 **Maguse River** Nunavut Canada
181 H5 **Magway** *admin. area* Myanmar
181 H5 **Magway (Magwe)** Myanmar
Magwe *see* **Magway** Myanmar
194 D3 **Maha Sarakham** Thailand
182 E7 **Mahābād** Iran
187 C8 **Mahabaleshwar** Maharashtra India
163 I3 **Mahabe** Madagascar
186 E5 **Mahabharat Range** Nepal
187 C7 **Mahad** Maharashtra India
223 14a **Mahaena** French Polynesia
101 G3 **Mahaica-Berbice** *admin. area* Guyana
101 G3 **Mahaicony Village** Guyana
186 C5 **Mahajan** Rajasthan India
163 I3 **Mahajanga** Madagascar
163 I3 **Mahajanga** *admin. area* Madagascar
163 I3 **Mahajilo** *watercourse* Madagascar
197 G3 **Mahakam** *watercourse* Indonesia
162 E4 **Mahalapye** Botswana
187 F7 **Mahanadi** *watercourse* Chhattisgarh India
187 F7 **Mahanadi** *watercourse* Orissa India
163 I3 **Mahanoro** Madagascar
186 E6 **Maharajpur** Madhya Pradesh India
187 D7 **Maharashtra** *admin. area* India
178 G3 **Mahārlū, Daryācheh-ye** *lake* Iran
81 Q7 **Mahaska** Kansas USA
163 I3 **Mahasolo** Madagascar
163 I4 **Mahatalaky** Madagascar
163 I3 **Mahatsinjo** Madagascar
109 I5 **Mahaut** Dominica
163 I3 **Mahazoma** Madagascar
156 D5 **Mahbub** Sudan
187 E8 **Mahbubnagar** Andhra Pradesh India
155 G1 **Mahdia** Algeria
101 G3 **Mahdia** Guyana
155 I1 **Mahdia** Tunisia
164 9 **Mahé** *island* Seychelles
164 7b **Mahébourg** Mauritius
187 F7 **Mahendragiri** *mountain* Andhra Pradesh India
125 L2 **Maheriv** Ukraine
186 C6 **Mahesana** Gujarat India
186 D6 **Mahi** *watercourse* Rajasthan India
220 G4 **Mahia** New Zealand
220 G4 **Mahia Peninsula** New Zealand
123 P6 **Mahilyow** Belarus
136 D2 **Mahilyowskaya Voblasts'** *admin. area* Belarus
159 E3 **Mahin** Nigeria
223 14a **Mahina** French Polynesia
154 D6 **Mahina** Mali
221 C7 **Mahinerangi, Lake** New Zealand
178 E6 **Mahlal** Saudi Arabia
179 K4 **Mahmud Aulia** Pakistan
179 L2 **Mahmūd-e-Rāqī** Afghanistan
81 R3 **Mahnomen** Minnesota USA
186 E6 **Mahoba** Uttar Pradesh India
129 I4 **Mahón** Spain
79 F10 **Mahone Bay** Nova Scotia Canada
72 G5 **Mahoney Lake** Northwest Territories Canada
143 C4 **Mahoonagh** Ireland
128 F4 **Mahora** Spain
164 8 **Mahoré (Grande Terre)** *island* Mayotte
159 H2 **Mahoua** Chad
155 I2 **Mahrès** Tunisia
181 G4 **Mahur** Assam India
199 J4 **Mahur Island** Papua New Guinea
101 H3 **Mahury, Plateau du** *region* French Guiana
161 F6 **Mahuta** Tanzania
187 C7 **Mahuva** Gujarat India
186 D5 **Mahwa** Rajasthan India
133 E5 **Mahya Dağı** *mountain* Turkey
197 J5 **Mai** *island* Indonesia
160 B4 **Mai-Ndombe, Lac** *lake* Democratic Republic of Congo
222 1 **Maiana** *island* Kiribati
181 G4 **Maibong** Assam India
100 C2 **Maicao** Colombia
83 M1 **Maicasagi, Lac** *lake* Quebec Canada
127 H3 **Maîche** France
105 F2 **Maici** *watercourse* Brazil
85 H6 **Maicova** Mexico
101 H5 **Maicuru** *watercourse* Brazil
131 G7 **Maida** Italy
77 S1 **Maiden Island** Nunavut Canada
138 E4 **Maiden Newton** Dorset England UK
142 E5 **Maidencots** South Lanarkshire Scotland UK
139 G3 **Maidenhead** Windsor and Maidenhead England UK
143 G2 **Maidens, The** *islands* Northern Ireland UK
77 X3 **Maidmonts Island** Newfoundland and Labrador Canada
139 H3 **Maidstone** Kent England UK
159 G2 **Maiduguri** Nigeria
139 G2 **Maidwell** Northamptonshire England UK
125 M4 **Maieru** Romania
184 F5 **Maigaiti** Xinjiang Uygur Zizhiqu China
101 E3 **Maigualide, Sierra** *range* Venezuela
186 E6 **Maihar** Madhya Pradesh India
121 N3 **Maijanen** Finland
88 D2 **Maijoma** Mexico
160 D4 **Maiko** *watercourse* Democratic Republic of Congo
198 E5 **Maikoor** *island* Indonesia
142 inset **Mail** Shetland Scotland UK
186 E5 **Mailani** Uttar Pradesh India
196 C4 **Maileppe** Indonesia
125 K5 **Mailovac** Serbia
179 L3 **Mailsi** Pakistan
79 J8 **Main** *watercourse* Newfoundland and Labrador Canada
124 F3 **Main** *watercourse* Germany
143 F2 **Main** *watercourse* Northern Ireland UK
79 J7 **Main Brook** Newfoundland and Labrador Canada
124 F3 **Main-Donau-Kanal** *watercourse* Germany
221 10 **Main Group** *islands* Bounty Islands New Zealand
109 9 **Main Ridge** *range* Trinidad and Tobago
196 C5 **Main Strait** Singapore
133 C7 **Mainalon, Oros** *range* Greece
187 D8 **Maindargi** Maharashtra India
70 **Maine** *admin. area* USA
79 D11 **Maine, Gulf of** Canada/USA
155 I6 **Maïne-Soroa** Niger
124 E3 **Mainhardt** Germany
195 J5 **Mainit, Lake** Philippines
142 inset **Mainland** *island* Scotland UK
214 C3 **Mainoru** NT Australia
214 B2 **Mainoru** *watercourse* NT Australia
186 E5 **Mainpuri** Uttar Pradesh India
142 D3 **Mains of Faillie** Highland Scotland UK
142 F4 **Mains of Kelly** Angus Scotland UK
121 O4 **Mainua** Finland
124 E2 **Mainz** Germany
164 4 **Maio** *island* Cape Verde
107 G6 **Maipú** Argentina
104 C2 **Maipuco** Peru
100 E3 **Maipures** Colombia
181 F3 **Maiqu Zangbo** *watercourse* Xizang Zizhiqu China
108 B2 **Maiquillahue, Punta** *cape* Chile
105 F5 **Mairana** Bolivia
103 D5 **Mairi** Brazil
126 F5 **Maisons** France
127 L2 **Maissau** Austria
124 B3 **Maisse** France
162 E4 **Maitengwe** Botswana
219 J5 **Maitland** NSW Australia
218 C6 **Maitland** SA Australia
212 D6 **Maitland** *watercourse* WA Australia
216 G3 **Maitland, Lake** WA Australia
216 F2 **Maitland, Mount** WA Australia
58 A2 **Maitri (India)** *research station* Antarctica
90 D4 **Maíz, Islas del** *islands* Nicaragua
90 D4 **Maíz Grande, Isla del** *island* Nicaragua
193 G4 **Maizuru** Japan
130 G4 **Maja** Croatia
178 E6 **Majaba** Saudi Arabia
100 C2 **Majagual** Colombia
120 H4 **Majavatn** Norway
132 B3 **Majdanpek** Serbia
198 A4 **Majene** Indonesia
104 C5 **Majes** *watercourse* Peru
186 F6 **Majgaon** Madhya Pradesh India
189 G1 **Majia He** *watercourse* Henan China
191 I5 **Majia He** *watercourse* Shandong China
190 F5 **Majiawan** Ningxia Huizu Zizhiqu China
178 G3 **Majnavā** Iran
211 inset **Major Lake** Macquarie Island Australia
Majorca *see* **Mallorca** Spain
219 I6 **Majors Creek** NSW Australia
181 H3 **Majuli** Assam India
223 15a **Majuro** Marshall Islands
223 15 **Majuro Atoll** Marshall Islands
223 15a **Majuro Lagoon** Marshall Islands
162 E5 **Majwemasweu** South Africa
132 D1 **Mak** Ukraine
154 D6 **Maka** Senegal
159 G5 **Makabana** Congo
84 inset **Mākaha** Hawai'i USA
159 G5 **Makaka** Congo
160 D4 **Makamba** Burundi
161 E5 **Makambako** Tanzania
183 N4 **Makanchi** Kazakhstan
163 F2 **Makanjila** Malawi
135 AF9 **Makanrushi, Ostrov** *island* Russian Federation
100 D2 **Makaraipaho** Colombia
222 8a **Makarakomburu, Mount** Solomon Islands
159 G2 **Makari** Cameroon
101 G3 **Makari** Guyana
135 AD9 **Makarov** Russian Federation
56 R1 **Makarov Basin** *underwater feature* Arctic Ocean
52 L5 **Makarov Seamount** *underwater feature* Pacific Ocean
130 G5 **Makarska** Croatia
182 E1 **Makar'ye** Russian Federation
160 E5 **Makasa** Zambia
198 A5 **Makassar** Indonesia
197 H4 **Makassar, Selat (Macassar Strait)** Indonesia
182 G4 **Makat** Kazakhstan
161 F5 **Makatapora** Tanzania
223 14 **Makatea** *island* French Polynesia
53 R9 **Makatea** *reef* French Polynesia
163 F5 **Makatini Flats** *plain* South Africa
220 4 **Makefu** Niue New Zealand
223 14 **Makemo** *island* French Polynesia
84 inset **Makena** Hawai'i USA
158 B3 **Makeni** Sierra Leone
222 7 **Makéoné** Vanuatu
160 E4 **Makere** Tanzania
190 E6 **Maketang** Qinghai China
220 G3 **Maketu** New Zealand
162 E4 **Makgadikgadi** *pan* Botswana
182 E5 **Makhachkala** Russian Federation
179 L2 **Makhad** Pakistan
182 F4 **Makhambet** Kazakhstan
193 H4 **Maki** Japan
197 J3 **Makian** *island* Indonesia
222 1 **Makin** *island* Kiribati
75 V7 **Makinak** Manitoba Canada
183 K3 **Makinsk** Kazakhstan
222 8 **Makira** *admin. area* Solomon Islands
178 E5 **Makkah** *admin. area* Saudi Arabia
178 D5 **Makkah (Mecca)** Saudi Arabia
78 I5 **Makkovik** Newfoundland and Labrador Canada
78 I5 **Makkovik, Cape** Newfoundland and Labrador Canada
154 D6 **Mako** Senegal
132 B2 **Makó** Hungary
101 G4 **Makoa, Serra** *range* Brazil
223 9 **Makogai** *island* Fiji
159 G4 **Makokou** Gabon
179 J4 **Makola** Pakistan
161 E5 **Makongolosi** Tanzania
76 J6 **Makoop Lake** Ontario Canada
160 D3 **Makoro** Democratic Republic of Congo
81 O3 **Makoti** North Dakota USA
159 H5 **Makoua** Congo
159 G5 **Makoubi** Congo
132 B4 **Makovac** Kosovo
133 B5 **Makovo** Macedonia
134 S5 **Makovskoye, Ozero** *lake* Russian Federation
133 B6 **Makrakomi** Greece
186 D5 **Makrana** Rajasthan India
125 M2 **Makrany** Belarus
133 B6 **Makri** *island* Greece
133 B7 **Makrisia** Greece
133 D7 **Makronisi** *island* Greece
123 N3 **Mäksa** Estonia
178 F3 **Maksar** Iran
134 S7 **Maksimkin Yar** Russian Federation
193 I2 **Makubetsu** Japan
181 H3 **Makum** Assam India
162 D4 **Makunda** Botswana
189 H4 **Makung** Taiwan China
161 F5 **Makunguwiro** Tanzania
187 C11 **Makunudhoo** *island* Maldives
192 F5 **Makurazaki** Japan
159 F3 **Makurdi** Nigeria
75 Q6 **Makwa** Saskatchewan Canada
181 F3 **Mal** West Bengal India
143 C4 **Mal Bay** Ireland
199 H4 **Mal Island** Papua New Guinea
159 H3 **Mala** Central African Republic
104 B4 **Mala** Peru
122 G4 **Mala** Sweden
120 K4 **Malå** Sweden
90 E6 **Mala, Punta** *cape* Panama
125 J3 **Malá Fatra** *range* Slovakia
186 E5 **Mala Kheti** Nepal
87 K7 **Malabar** Florida USA
187 D9 **Malabar Coast** Kerala India
211 inset **Malabar Hill** Lord Howe Island Australia
159 F4 **Malabo** Equatorial Guinea
101 F4 **Malacacheta** Brazil
103 D7 **Malacacheta** Brazil
194 C6 **Malacca, Strait of**
196 D3 **Malacca, Strait of** Indonesia/Malaysia
80 I5 **Malad City** Idaho USA
123 N5 **Maladzyechna** Belarus
223 12b **Mala'efo'ou** Wallis and Futuna
123 O3 **Malaf'yevka** Russian Federation
100 C3 **Málaga** Colombia
128 D5 **Málaga** Spain
100 B4 **Málaga, Bahía de** *bay* Colombia
160 E5 **Malagarasi** *watercourse* Tanzania
90 E2 **Malagueta, Punta** *cape* Cuba
143 F3 **Malahide** Ireland
132 D3 **Malaia** Romania
163 I4 **Malaimbandy** Madagascar
222 8 **Malaita** *admin. area* Solomon Islands
222 8 **Malaita** *island* Solomon Islands
160 E2 **Malakal** Sudan
223 9a **Malake** *island* Fiji
86 D4 **Malakoff** Texas USA
222 7 **Malakula** *island* Vanuatu
80 F1 **Malakwa** British Columbia Canada
179 M3 **Malakwal** Pakistan
199 G6 **Malam** Papua New Guinea
197 I4 **Malamala** Indonesia
100 C2 **Malambo** Colombia
215 H4 **Malanda** Qld Australia
197 G5 **Malang** Indonesia
163 G2 **Malanga** Mozambique
161 E5 **Malangali** Tanzania
120 K2 **Malangen** Norway
120 K2 **Malangen** *bay* Norway
162 C1 **Malanje** Angola
162 C1 **Malanje** *admin. area* Angola
195 H5 **Malanut Bay** Philippines
106 E4 **Malanzán** Argentina
222 7 **Malao** Vanuatu
122 I3 **Mälaren** *bay* Sweden
101 H4 **Malaripo** Brazil
83 L2 **Malartic, Lac** *lake* Quebec Canada
125 M2 **Malaryta** Belarus
123 P5 **Malashenki** Belarus
197 H5 **Malasoro, Teluk** *bay* Indonesia
108 C3 **Malaspina** Argentina
74 I8 **Malaspina Strait** British Columbia Canada
197 G4 **Malatayur, Tanjung** *cape* Indonesia
136 F5 **Malatya** Turkey
136 F5 **Malatya** *admin. area* Turkey
124 C5 **Malaucène** France
155 H6 **Malawa** Niger
197 H2 **Malawali** *island* Malaysia
163 F2 **Malawi** *country* Africa
163 F2 **Malawi, Lake (Lake Nyasa)** *lake* Malawi/Mozambique
178 D6 **Malāwī Jidārah** Saudi Arabia
120 L5 **Malax** Finland
194 D5 **Malay Peninsula** *cape* Thailand
123 Q3 **Malaya Vishera** Russian Federation
195 J5 **Malaybalay** Philippines
178 F2 **Malāyer** Iran
196 E3 **Malaysia** *country* Asia
214 F6 **Malbon** Qld Australia
215 G6 **Malboona** Qld Australia
123 J5 **Malbork** Poland
185 J2 **Malchin** Mongolia
124 G1 **Malchiner See** *lake* Germany
216 G4 **Malcolm** WA Australia
217 H6 **Malcolm, Point** WA Australia
125 K3 **Malcov** Slovakia
86 G2 **Malden** Missouri USA
222 1 **Malden Island** Kiribati
187 C11 **Maldives** *country* Asia
139 H3 **Maldon** Essex England UK
107 H5 **Maldonado** Uruguay
107 H5 **Maldonado** *admin. area* Uruguay
89 F5 **Maldonado, Punta** *cape* Mexico
107 G2 **Maldonado-cué** Paraguay
130 D3 **Malè** Italy
187 C11 **Male** Maldives
187 C11 **Male Atoll** Maldives
158 C2 **Maléa** Guinea
196 C3 **Malea, Gunung** *mountain* Indonesia
133 C7 **Maleas, Akra** *cape* Greece
216 E5 **Malebelling** WA Australia
125 L1 **Malec** Poland
163 G3 **Malei** Mozambique
160 E2 **Malek** Sudan
179 K3 **Malek Din** Afghanistan
159 G5 **Malélé** Congo
163 G2 **Malema** Mozambique
159 F2 **Malendo** *watercourse* Nigeria
199 J4 **Malendok Island** Papua New Guinea
121 T5 **Malen'ga** Russian Federation
108 D6 **Malengüena, Cabo** *cape* Argentina
219 K2 **Maleny** Qld Australia
126 F2 **Malesherbes** France
179 K2 **Mālestān** Afghanistan
126 C3 **Malestroit** France
222 8 **Malevangga** Solomon Islands
125 M2 **Malevo** Ukraine
131 C7 **Malfatano, Capo** *cape* Sardinia Italy
120 K4 **Malfjälen** Sweden
156 D4 **Malha** Sudan
141 F2 **Malham** North Yorkshire England UK
80 F5 **Malheur Lake** Oregon USA
155 F5 **Mali** *country* Africa
188 D4 **Mali** Yunnan China
160 D4 **Mali** Democratic Republic of Congo
223 9a **Mali** *island* Fiji
181 H3 **Mali** *watercourse* Myanmar
132 A3 **Mali Iđoš** Serbia
194 C4 **Mali Kyun** Myanmar
130 F4 **Mali Lošinj** Croatia
130 F4 **Mali Lug** Croatia
133 C6 **Maliakos Kolpos** *bay* Greece
197 J6 **Maliana** Timor-Leste (East Timor)
84 C4 **Malibu** California USA
126 D3 **Malicorne** France
123 N4 **Maliena** Latvia
160 D5 **Malimba, Monts** *range* Democratic Republic of Congo
196 E5 **Malimping** Indonesia
140 A1 **Malin** Ireland
143 D2 **Malin Beg** Ireland
143 E1 **Malin Head** *cape* Ireland
195 I5 **Malindang, Mount** *mountain* Philippines
161 G4 **Malindi** Kenya
120 I6 **Målingen** *lake* Sweden
132 E2 **Mălini** Romania
125 L1 **Malinniki** Poland
198 B3 **Malino, Gunung** *mountain* Indonesia
182 D3 **Malinovka** Russian Federation
183 M3 **Malinovoye Ozero** Russian Federation
161 F5 **Malinyi** Tanzania
133 D8 **Malion, Kolpos** *bay* Greece
195 J6 **Malita** Philippines
85 K4 **Maljamar** New Mexico USA
161 G3 **Malka Mari** Kenya
187 E7 **Malkangiri** Orissa India
190 F2 **Malkhanskiy Khrebet** *range* Russian Federation
125 L1 **Małkinia Górna** Poland
219 I7 **Mallacoota** Vic. Australia
75 P5 **Mallaig** Alberta Canada
142 C3 **Mallaig** Highland Scotland UK
218 D6 **Mallala** SA Australia
100 B4 **Mallama** Colombia
214 C4 **Mallapunyah** NT Australia
123 M2 **Mallasvesi** *bay* Finland
156 E2 **Mallawī** Egypt
73 J6 **Mallery Lake** Nunavut Canada
212 E6 **Mallina** WA Australia
124 G4 **Mallnitz** Austria
129 H4 **Mallorca (Majorca)** *island* Spain
123 N1 **Mallos** *lake* Finland
143 D4 **Mallow** Ireland
138 D2 **Mallwyd** Gwynedd Wales UK
120 G4 **Malm** Norway
120 L3 **Malmberget** Sweden
127 H1 **Malmédy** Belgium
162 C6 **Malmesbury** South Africa
139 E3 **Malmesbury** Wiltshire England UK
120 K4 **Malmesjaure** *lake* Sweden
122 G5 **Malmö** Sweden
122 I4 **Malmö** *island* Sweden
122 F3 **Malmöfjord** *bay* Sweden
109 1c **Malmok** *cape* Netherlands Antilles
120 I5 **Malmsjön** *lake* Sweden
182 F2 **Malmyzh** Russian Federation
197 J2 **Malo** *island* Indonesia
130 G4 **Malo Tičevo** Bosnia and Herzegovina
101 H4 **Maloca** Brazil
101 F5 **Maloca** Brazil
104 D3 **Maloca** Brazil
105 H3 **Maloca Caiabi** Brazil
100 D4 **Maloca Capi Ponta** Brazil
100 D4 **Maloca do Chico** Brazil
101 H4 **Maloca dos Urucuianas** Brazil
100 D4 **Maloca Jutica** Brazil
101 F4 **Maloca Macu** Brazil
100 D4 **Maloca Pacu** Brazil
101 H4 **Maloca Repy** Brazil
105 F4 **Maloca Salamaim** Brazil
100 D4 **Maloca Uacari** Brazil
223 15 **Maloelap Atoll** Marshall Islands
223 9a **Malolo** *island* Fiji
163 G2 **Malombe, Lake** *lake* Malawi
125 H2 **Małomice** Poland
87 I5 **Malone** Florida USA
83 N4 **Malone** New York USA
188 D3 **Malong** Yunnan China
160 C6 **Malonga** Democratic Republic of Congo
160 E5 **Malonje** *mountain* Tanzania
125 J3 **Małopolskie** *admin. area* Poland
122 C2 **Måløy** Norway
136 F1 **Maloyaroslavets** Russian Federation
193 I1 **Maloye, Ozero** *lake* Russian Federation
134 L5 **Malozemel'skaya Tundra** *region* Russian Federation
128 C4 **Malpartida de Plasencia** Spain
100 A4 **Malpelo, Isla de** *island* Colombia
79 G9 **Malpeque Bay** Prince Edward Island Canada
128 B2 **Malpica** Spain
128 C4 **Malpica do Tejo** Portugal
125 H3 **Malše** *watercourse* Czech Republic
120 K2 **Målsnes** Norway
120 I5 **Målsta** Sweden
131 F9 **Malta** *country* Europe
81 L2 **Malta** Montana USA
155 J1 **Malta Channel** *strait* Malta
162 C4 **Maltahöhe** Namibia
141 I3 **Maltby le Marsh** Lincolnshire England UK
141 H2 **Malton** North Yorkshire England UK
89 F5 **Maltrata** Mexico
219 J6 **Malua Bay** NSW Australia
160 B4 **Maluku** Democratic Republic of Congo
197 K4 **Maluku** *admin. area* Indonesia
197 J3 **Maluku, Laut (Molucca Sea)** Indonesia
197 J4 **Maluku (Moluccas)** *islands* Indonesia
197 J3 **Maluku Utara** *admin. area* Indonesia
122 G2 **Malungsfors** Sweden
195 I6 **Maluso** Philippines
162 E5 **Maluti Mountains** *range* Lesotho
222 8 **Maluu** Solomon Islands
187 C8 **Malvan** Maharashtra India
138 E2 **Malvern Link** Worcestershire England UK
120 G5 **Malvik** Norway
Malvinas, Islas *see* **Falkland Islands** Atlantic Ocean
183 M5 **Malybay** Kazakhstan
125 K3 **Mályi** Hungary
135 AH5 **Malyy Anyuy** *watercourse* Russian Federation
135 AD4 **Malyy Lyakhovskiy, Ostrov** *island* Russian Federation
135 X3 **Malyy Taymyr, Ostrov** *island* Russian Federation
182 E3 **Malyy Uzen** *watercourse* Kazakhstan
183 Q3 **Malyy Yenisey** *watercourse* Russian Federation
182 D4 **Malyye Derbety** Russian Federation
126 F4 **Malzieu-Ville** France
135 X7 **Mama** Russian Federation
214 B2 **Mamadawerre** NT Australia
213 J4 **Mamadi** NT Australia
182 F2 **Mamadysh** Russian Federation
162 E5 **Mamafubedu** South Africa
82 I3 **Mamainse Point** Ontario Canada
220 G3 **Mamaku Plateau** New Zealand
154 D5 **Mamari** Senegal
101 H5 **Mamaru, Ilha Grande do** *island* Brazil
195 J5 **Mambajao** Philippines
159 G3 **Mambal** Cameroon
161 E4 **Mambali** Tanzania
197 H6 **Mambang, Tanjung** *cape* Indonesia
199 H6 **Mambare** *watercourse* Papua New Guinea
160 D3 **Mambasa** Democratic Republic of Congo
159 H4 **Mambére** *watercourse* Central African Republic
159 H4 **Mambéré-Kadéï** *admin. area* Central African Republic
159 G4 **Mambili** *watercourse* Congo
162 B3 **Mambonde** *watercourse* Angola
100 A5 **Mambra, Punta** *cape* Ecuador
218 C5 **Mambray Creek** SA Australia
76 J8 **Mameigweiss Lake** Ontario Canada
126 E2 **Mamers** France
159 F3 **Mamfé** Cameroon
101 F6 **Mamiá, Lago** *lake* Brazil
182 D5 **Mamison Pass** Russian Federation
124 G3 **Mamming** Germany
84 G4 **Mammoth** Arizona USA
81 J4 **Mammoth Hot Springs** Wyoming USA
80 F8 **Mammoth Lakes** California USA
80 F8 **Mammoth Pool Reservoir** California USA
105 E3/4 **Mamoré, Rio** *watercourse* Brazil/Bolivia
100 E5 **Mamori, Ilhas** *islands* Brazil
158 B2 **Mamou** Guinea
86 E5 **Mamou** Louisiana USA
164 8b **Mamoudzou** Mayotte
163 I3 **Mampikony** Madagascar
158 D3 **Mampong** Ghana
162 B2 **Mamue** Angola
198 A4 **Mamuju** Indonesia
88 E3 **Mamulique** Mexico
158 C3 **Man** Côte d'Ivoire
83 K8 **Man** West Virginia USA
181 G5 **Man-Aung (Cheduha)** Myanmar
181 G5 **Man-aung Kyun** Myanmar
181 E3 **Man Ho** *watercourse* Xizang Zizhiqu China
109 9 **Man O'War Bay** Trinidad and Tobago
78 H4 **Man O'War Peak** Newfoundland and Labrador Canada
101 H3 **Mana** French Guiana
101 H3 **Mana** *watercourse* French Guiana
134 T7 **Mana** *watercourse* Russian Federation
84 inset **Mānā** Hawai'i USA
221 F5 **Mana Island** New Zealand
100 A5 **Manabí** *admin. area* Ecuador
100 C3 **Manacacias** *watercourse* Colombia
101 F5 **Manacapuru** Brazil
101 F5 **Manacapuru, Lago Grande de** *lake* Brazil
131 G6 **Manaccore, Punta di** *cape* Italy
129 H4 **Manacor** Spain
198 C3 **Manado** Indonesia
90 C4 **Managua** Nicaragua
90 C4 **Managua, Lago de** *lake* Nicaragua
220 F4 **Manaia** New Zealand
102 E4 **Manaíra** Brazil
163 I4 **Manakara** Madagascar
186 D4 **Manali** Himachal Pradesh India
199 H5 **Manam** *volcano* Papua New Guinea
Manama *see* **Al Manāmah** Bahrain
187 E10 **Manamadurai** Tamil Nadu India
163 I4 **Manambondro** Madagascar
101 F2 **Manamo, Caño** *watercourse* Venezuela
163 I3 **Mananara** Madagascar
218 F6 **Manangatang** Vic. Australia
214 D3 **Manangoora** NT Australia
163 I4 **Mananjary** Madagascar
158 C2 **Manankoro** Mali
154 D6 **Manantali, Lac de** *lake* Mali
163 I4 **Manantenina** Madagascar
221 B7 **Manapouri** New Zealand
221 B7 **Manapouri, Lake** New Zealand
187 D7 **Manar** *watercourse* Maharashtra India
218 F5 **Manara** NSW Australia
221 F5 **Manaroa** New Zealand
184 H4 **Manas** Xinjiang Uygur Zizhiqu China
185 H3 **Manas Hu** *lake* Xinjiang Uygur Zizhiqu China
186 F5 **Manaslu** *mountain* Nepal
81 M8 **Manassa** Colorado USA
184 H4 **Manasu He** *watercourse* Xinjiang Uygur Zizhiqu China
198 C6 **Manatang** Indonesia
90 E2 **Manatí** Cuba
198 C6 **Manatuto** Timor-Leste (East Timor)
100 C2 **Manaure** Colombia
101 F5 **Manaus** Brazil
136 D6 **Manavgat** Turkey
187 D6 **Manawar** Madhya Pradesh India
156 C5 **Manawashei** Sudan
220 F5 **Manawatu** *watercourse* New Zealand
198 D5 **Manawoka** *island* Indonesia
195 J6 **Manay** Philippines
186 G6 **Manbazar** West Bengal India
141 I3 **Manby** Lincolnshire England UK
143 C5 **Manch Bridge** Cork Ireland
128 E5 **Mancha Real** Spain
100 B5 **Manchari** *watercourse* Peru
Manche, La *see* **English Channel** UK/France
141 F3 **Manchester** *admin. area* England UK
141 F3 **Manchester** Greater Manchester England UK
85 N1 **Manchester** Kansas USA
82 J8 **Manchester** Kentucky USA
83 P5 **Manchester** New Hampshire USA
81 P8 **Manchester** Oklahoma USA
141 F3 **Manchester Ship Canal** England UK
Manchurian Plain *see* **Dongbei Pingyuan** China
131 D5 **Manciano** Italy
126 E5 **Manciet** France
104 C2 **Mâncio Lima** Brazil
104 A2 **Máncora** Peru
81 K8 **Mancos** Colorado USA
179 J4 **Mand** Pakistan
161 E5 **Manda** Tanzania
161 E6 **Manda** Tanzania
103 A8 **Mandaguaçu** Brazil
196 D4 **Mandah** Indonesia
190 F4 **Mandah** Mongolia
196 D4 **Mandahara** Indonesia
190 F3 **Mandal** Mongolia
122 D3 **Mandal** Norway
199 G5 **Mandala, Puncak** *mountain* Indonesia
195 I5 **Mandalagan, Mount** *volcano* Philippines
181 H5 **Mandalay** Myanmar
181 H5 **Mandalay** *admin. area* Myanmar
190 F3 **Mandalgovī** Mongolia
190 E4 **Mandalovoo** Mongolia
158 C2 **Mandan** *watercourse* Guinea
81 O3 **Mandan** North Dakota USA
195 I4 **Mandaon** Philippines
197 H4 **Mandar, Teluk** *bay* Indonesia
159 G2 **Mandara Mountains** *range* Cameroon
90 C4 **Mandasta** Honduras
81 L4 **Manderson** Wyoming USA
86 F5 **Mandeville** Louisiana USA
186 D4 **Mandi** Himachal Pradesh India
196 D2 **Mandi Angin, Gunung** *mountain* Malaysia
154 F6 **Mandiakui** Mali
158 C2 **Mandiana** Guinea
163 F3 **Mandié** Mozambique
133 D7 **Mandili** *island* Greece
163 G2 **Mandimba** Mozambique
158 C2 **Mandingues, Mountains** *range* Mali
163 F5 **Mandini** South Africa
197 J4 **Mandioli** *island* Indonesia
159 G5 **Mandji** Gabon
159 F5 **Mandji, Île** *island* Gabon
187 E6 **Mandla** Madhya Pradesh India

122 E5 **Mandø** *island* Denmark
186 C5 **Mandor** Rajasthan India
196 F3 **Mandor** Indonesia
212 F5 **Mandora** WA Australia
160 D3 **Mandoro** Democratic Republic of Congo
163 I3 **Mandoto** Madagascar
179 K3 **Mandowzi** Afghanistan
133 E5 **Mándra** Greece
133 E7 **Mandraki** Greece
163 I4 **Mandrare** *watercourse* Madagascar
163 I3 **Mandritsara** Madagascar
163 I4 **Mandrosonor** Madagascar
186 D6 **Mandsaur** Madhya Pradesh India
197 H3 **Mandul** *island* Indonesia
191 H4 **Mandulatu** Nei Mongol Zizhiqu China
216 D6 **Mandurah** WA Australia
186 B6 **Mandvi** Gujarat India
187 D9 **Mandya** Karnataka India
139 H2 **Manea** Cambridgeshire England UK
88 A2 **Maneadero** Mexico
215 G7 **Maneroo** Qld Australia
136 C2 **Manevichi** Ukraine
156 E2 **Manfalût** Egypt
214 F6 **Manfred Downs** Qld Australia
131 F6 **Manfredonia** Italy
131 G6 **Manfredonia, Golfo di** *bay* Italy
103 D6 **Manga** Brazil
160 A5 **Manga Grande** Angola
102 C5 **Mangabeiras, Serra das** *range* Brazil
160 B4 **Mangai** Democratic Republic of Congo
220 1 **Mangaia** *island* Cook Islands New Zealand
155 G6 **Mangaïze** Niger
220 E2 **Mangakahia** *watercourse* New Zealand
181 G3 **Mangaldai** Assam India
132 F4 **Mangalia** Romania
159 H2 **Mangalmé** Chad
218 C5 **Mangalo** SA Australia
187 D9 **Mangalore** Karnataka India
220 E2 **Mangamuka Bridge** New Zealand
160 B5 **Mangando** Angola
220 F4 **Manganuioteao** *watercourse* New Zealand
198 C3 **Mangarang** Indonesia
223 I4 **Mangareva** *island* French Polynesia
216 D1 **Mangaroon** WA Australia
220 F5 **Mangatainoka** New Zealand
186 E6 **Mangawan** Madhya Pradesh India
220 F4 **Mangaweka** New Zealand
220 F3 **Mangawhai Heads** New Zealand
220 F4 **Mangawhero** *watercourse* New Zealand
122 C2 **Manger** Norway
221 6 **Mangere Island** Chatham Islands New Zealand
196 F4 **Manggar** Indonesia
199 F4 **Manggasi** Indonesia
198 E5 **Manggawitu** Indonesia
198 D5 **Manggur** *island* Indonesia
191 F4 **Mangin** Louisiana USA
181 H4 **Mangin Range** Myanmar
182 G5 **Mangistauskaya Oblast'** *admin. area* Kazakhstan
197 H3 **Mangkalihat, Tanjung** *cape* Indonesia
190 D6 **Manglaqiongtuo** Qinghai China
100 B4 **Manglares, Cabo** *cape* Colombia
158 E2 **Mango** Togo
158 D3 **Mangodara** Burkina Faso
163 H4 **Mangoky** *watercourse* Madagascar
197 J4 **Mangole** *island* Indonesia
197 J4 **Mangole, Selat** *strait* Indonesia
160 D4 **Mangombe** Democratic Republic of Congo
220 E2 **Mangonui** New Zealand
101 F2 **Mangotín** Venezuela
138 E3 **Mangotsfield** South Gloucestershire England UK
187 C7 **Mangrol** Gujarat India
186 D6 **Mangrol** Rajasthan India
186 E5 **Mangu Karnali** *watercourse* Nepal
179 K3 **Manguchar** Pakistan
159 I2 **Mangueigne** Chad
107 H5 **Mangueira, Lagoa** *lake* Brazil
90 C4 **Mangulile** Honduras
86 B3 **Mangum** Oklahoma USA
102 C3 **Mangunça, Ilha** *island* Brazil
160 D3 **Manguredjipa** Democratic Republic of Congo
142 A2 **Mangurstadh** Na h-Eileanan Siar Scotland UK
182 F5 **Mangyshlakskiy Zaliv** *bay* Kazakhstan
185 I3 **Manhan** Mongolia
81 Q7 **Manhattan** Kansas USA
80 J4 **Manhattan** Montana USA
103 D8 **Manhuaçu** Brazil
155 I6 **Mani** Chad
100 C3 **Maní** Colombia
133 C7 **Mani** *peninsula* Greece
159 F2 **Mani** Nigeria
179 I4 **Mānī Gaz** Iran
163 J4 **Mania** *watercourse* Madagascar
160 C5 **Mania-Manu** Democratic Republic of Congo
127 K3 **Maniago** Italy
161 F2 **Maniamba** Mozambique
159 I6 **Maniamuna** Democratic Republic of Congo
77 U7 **Manic Trois, Réservoir** Quebec Canada
163 F3 **Manica** Mozambique
163 F3 **Manica** *admin. area* Mozambique
163 F3 **Manicaland** *admin. area* Zimbabwe
195 J5 **Manicani** *island* Philippines
105 F2 **Manicoré** Brazil
105 F2 **Manicoré** *watercourse* Brazil
77 U8 **Manicouagan** *watercourse* Quebec Canada
160 D4 **Maniema** *admin. area* Democratic Republic of Congo
215 K7 **Manifold, Cape** Qld Australia
76 G7 **Manigotagan** Manitoba Canada
76 G7 **Manigotagan** *watercourse* Manitoba Canada
186 G6 **Manihari** Bihar India
223 I4 **Manihi** *island* French Polynesia
222 1 **Manihiki** *island* Cook Islands New Zealand
52 P9 **Manihiki Atoll** *reef* Cook Islands New Zealand
52 P8 **Manihiki Plateau** *underwater feature* Pacific Ocean
73 N5 **Maniitsoq** Greenland
160 D6 **Manika** Democratic Republic of Congo
160 D5 **Manika, Plateau de la** *plain* Democratic Republic of Congo
186 E6 **Manikpur** Uttar Pradesh India
195 I4 **Manila** Philippines
81 K6 **Manila** Utah USA
123 M3 **Manilaid** *island* Estonia
219 I5 **Manildra** NSW Australia
219 J4 **Manilla** NSW Australia
128 D5 **Manilva** Spain
197 H4 **Manimbaya, Tanjung** *cape* Indonesia
214 C2 **Maningrida** NT Australia
196 C4 **Maninjau, Danau** *lake* Indonesia
197 J4 **Manipa** *island* Indonesia
197 J4 **Manipa, Selat** *strait* Indonesia
181 H4 **Manipur** *admin. area* India
136 D5 **Manisa** *admin. area* Turkey
82 H4 **Manistee** Michigan USA
82 H4 **Manistee** *watercourse* Michigan USA
82 H4 **Manistique** Michigan USA
82 I3 **Manistique Lake** Michigan USA
76 E5 **Manitoba** *admin. area* Canada
75 V7 **Manitoba, Lake** Manitoba Canada
86 B3 **Manitou** Oklahoma USA
79 F7 **Manitou, Lac** *lake* Quebec Canada
82 H4 **Manitou Islands** Michigan USA
75 Q6 **Manitou Lake** Saskatchewan Canada
81 M7 **Manitou Springs** Colorado USA
83 J4 **Manitoulin Island** Ontario Canada
77 Q5 **Manitounuk Islands** Nunavut Canada
83 K4 **Manitowaning Bay** Ontario Canada
82 F3 **Manitowish** Wisconsin USA
82 H4 **Manitowoc** Wisconsin USA
105 H3 **Manitsaua-missu** *watercourse* Brazil
83 N3 **Maniwaki** Quebec Canada
100 C3 **Manizales** Colombia
163 H4 **Manja** Madagascar
192 E4 **Manjae-do** *island* South Korea
163 F4 **Manjalaze** Mozambique
216 E7 **Manjimup** WA Australia
159 F4 **Manjo** Cameroon
187 D7 **Manjra** *watercourse* Maharashtra India
82 E4 **Mankato** Minnesota USA
195 I3 **Mankayan** Philippines
132 G1 **Man'kivka** Ukraine
158 C3 **Mankono** Côte d'Ivoire
75 R8 **Mankota** Saskatchewan Canada
187 E10 **Mankulam** Sri Lanka
190 F4 **Manlai** Mongolia
129 H3 **Manlleu** Spain
219 J5 **Manly** NSW Australia
187 D7 **Manmad** Maharashtra India
219 K3 **Mann** *watercourse* NSW Australia
213 M2 **Mann** *watercourse* NT Australia
196 D5 **Manna** Indonesia
218 D5 **Mannahill** SA Australia
187 E10 **Mannar** Sri Lanka
214 D6 **Manners** *watercourse* NT Australia
214 D7 **Manners Creek** NT Australia
77 T5 **Mannessier, Lac** *lake* Quebec Canada
120 J2 **Mannfjorden** *bay* Norway
130 C2 **Mannheim** Germany
121 M3 **Männikkö** Sweden
143 B3 **Mannin Bay** Ireland
74 M4 **Manning** Alberta Canada
222 1a **Manning, Cape** Kiribati
219 K4 **Manning Point** NSW Australia
139 I3 **Manningtree** Essex England UK
120 M4 **Mannön** *island* Sweden
218 H8 **Manns Beach** Vic. Australia
131 C6 **Mannu** *watercourse* Sardinia Italy
131 C6 **Mannu, Capo** *cape* Sardinia Italy
131 C6 **Mannu, Monte** *mountain* Sardinia Italy
218 D6 **Mannum** SA Australia
219 H6 **Mannus** NSW Australia
104 E3 **Mano** Bolivia
158 B3 **Mano** Sierra Leone
163 H3 **Manoba** *watercourse* Madagascar
104 D3 **Manoel Urbano** Brazil
132 C4 **Manojlovce** Serbia
198 E4 **Manokwari** Indonesia
163 H4 **Manombo** Madagascar
105 F4 **Manomo, Serranía del** *range* Bolivia
160 D5 **Manono** Democratic Republic of Congo
223 12c **Manono** *island* Samoa
138 C3 **Manorbier** Pembrokeshire Wales UK
143 D2 **Manorhamilton** Ireland
138 B3 **Manorowen** Pembrokeshire Wales UK
127 G5 **Manosque** France
83 N3 **Manouane** Quebec Canada
77 T7 **Manouane** *watercourse* Quebec Canada
77 T7 **Manouane, Lac** *lake* Quebec Canada
131 D8 **Manouba** Tunisia
77 V7 **Manowin, Île** *island* Quebec Canada
192 E3 **Manp'o** North Korea
186 E6 **Manpur** Madhya Pradesh India
222 1 **Manra** *island* Kiribati
129 G3 **Manresa** Spain
186 D5 **Mansa** Punjab India
162 E2 **Mansa** Zambia
158 A2 **Mansa Konko** Gambia
158 A2 **Mansabá** Guinea-Bissau
180 D2 **Mansarowar Lake** Xizang Zizhiqu China
179 M2 **Mansehra** Pakistan
77 P1 **Mansel Island** Nunavut Canada
139 F1 **Mansfield** Nottinghamshire England UK
86 D3 **Mansfield** Arkansas USA
86 E4 **Mansfield** Louisiana USA
83 O4 **Mansfield, Mount** Vermont USA
181 H4 **Mansi** Myanmar
128 E2 **Mansilla, Embalse de** *lake* Spain
126 E4 **Mansle** France
158 A2 **Mansôa** Guinea-Bissau
74 I5 **Manson Creek** British Columbia Canada
74 I7 **Mansons Landing** British Columbia Canada
100 C3 **Manta** Colombia
100 A5 **Manta** Ecuador
76 G7 **Mantagao** *watercourse* Manitoba Canada
195 H5 **Mantalingajan, Mount** *mountain* Philippines
197 H2 **Mantanani Besar** *island* Malaysia
75 Q7 **Mantario** Saskatchewan Canada
104 C4 **Mantaro** *watercourse* Peru
80 E8 **Manteca** California USA
128 C3 **Manteigas** Portugal
103 D7 **Mantenópolis** Brazil
87 N3 **Manteo** North Carolina USA
81 O8 **Manter** Kansas USA
186 G6 **Manteswar** West Bengal India
126 F3 **Manthelan** France
80 J7 **Manti** Utah USA
121 M5 **Mantila** Finland
103 C8 **Mantiqueira, Serra da** *range* Brazil
139 F3 **Manton** Wiltshire England UK
130 D4 **Mantova** Italy
90 C2 **Mantua** Cuba
121 O4 **Mäntyjärvi** Finland
100 B5 **Manú** Ecuador
104 D4 **Manú** Peru
104 D3 **Manú** *watercourse* Peru
220 1 **Manuae** *island* Cook Islands New Zealand
53 Q9 **Manuae** *reef* French Polynesia
89 F4 **Manuel** Mexico
103 B5 **Manuel Alves** *watercourse* Brazil
102 C4 **Manuel Alves Grande** *watercourse* Brazil
88 E2 **Manuel Benavides** Mexico
108 B5 **Manuel Rodríguez, Isla** *island* Chile
105 F3 **Manuel Tomás** Brazil
106 D2 **Manuelzinho** Brazil
223 14 **Manuhangi** *island* French Polynesia
197 I4 **Manui** *island* Indonesia
195 I6 **Manuk Manka** *island* Philippines
220 F3 **Manukau** New Zealand
220 F3 **Manukau Harbour** New Zealand
218 D5 **Manunda** SA Australia
199 H4 **Manus Island** Papua New Guinea
81 Q2 **Manvel** North Dakota USA
86 D6 **Manvel** Texas USA
186 D8 **Manvi** Karnataka India
81 M5 **Manville** Wyoming USA
86 E5 **Many** Louisiana USA
84 H2 **Many Farms Lake** Arizona USA
75 P7 **Many Island Lake** Alberta Canada
162 F3 **Manyame, Lake** *lake* Zimbabwe
161 F4 **Manyara** *admin. area* Tanzania
161 F4 **Manyara, Lake** *lake* Tanzania
133 E5 **Manyas** Turkey
75 P8 **Manyberries** Alberta Canada
182 D4 **Manych Gudilo** *lake* Russian Federation
162 D4 **Manyinga** Zambia
216 F7 **Manypeaks** WA Australia
128 E3 **Manzanera** Spain
129 F3 **Manzanilla Point** Trinidad and Tobago
90 E2 **Manzanillo** Cuba
88 D5 **Manzanillo** Mexico
90 E5 **Manzanillo, Punta** *cape* Panama
80 D4 **Manzanita** Oregon USA
130 E4 **Manzano** Italy
126 F4 **Manzat** France
160 B5 **Manzengele** Democratic Republic of Congo
191 I2 **Manzhouli** Nei Mongol Zizhiqu China
131 D8 **Manzil Bou Zalafah** Tunisia
156 E1 **Manzilah, Buḩayrat al** *lake* Egypt
163 F5 **Manzini** Swaziland
135 W8 **Manzurka** Russian Federation
155 J6 **Mao** Chad
130 H4 **Maoča** Bosnia and Herzegovina
198 F4 **Maoke, Pegunungan** *range* Indonesia
Maokeng *see* **Kroonstad** South Africa
188 F4 **Maoming** Guangdong China
188 F2 **Maoping** Hubei China
197 J5 **Maopora** *island* Indonesia
101 E4 **Mapacú, Cerros** *range* Venezuela
163 F4 **Mapai** Mozambique
199 I6 **Mapamoiwa** Papua New Guinea
101 G4 **Maparri Mountains** Guyana
89 G6 **Mapastepec** Mexico
199 F5 **Mapi** *watercourse* Indonesia
104 E3 **Mapiá** Brazil
198 E3 **Mapia, Kepulauan** *island* Indonesia
100 E3 **Mapiche, Serranía** *range* Venezuela
89 E3 **Mapimí** Mexico
101 E3 **Mapire** Venezuela
104 D4 **Mapiri** Bolivia
100 C4 **Mapiripán** Colombia
100 C4 **Mapiriare** Colombia
82 D5 **Maple** *watercourse* Iowa USA
82 I5 **Maple** *watercourse* Michigan USA
82 C3 **Maple** *watercourse* North Dakota USA
75 Q8 **Maple Creek** Saskatchewan Canada
82 E4 **Maple Grove** Minnesota USA
86 H4 **Maplesville** Alabama USA
52 M5 **Mapmaker Seamounts** *underwater feature* Pacific Ocean
214 F1 **Mapoon** Qld Australia
196 E3 **Mapor** *island* Indonesia
221 D6 **Mapourika, Lake** New Zealand
141 H3 **Mappleton** East Riding of Yorkshire England UK
187 C8 **Mapuca** Goa India
101 G5 **Mapuera** *watercourse* Brazil
163 F5 **Mapulanguene** Mozambique
197 H2 **Mapun** *island* Philippines
160 C5 **Mapunda** Democratic Republic of Congo
163 F5 **Maputo** Mozambique
163 F5 **Maputo** *admin. area* Mozambique
178 G4 **Maqdam, Ras** *cape* Sudan
156 F4 **Maqha' ash Shuḩaymī** Syria
178 C4 **Maqnah** Saudi Arabia
154 D4 **Maqṭeïr** *region* Mauritania
180 E2 **Maquan He** *watercourse* Xizang Zizhiqu China
104 C2 **Maquea** Peru
108 C4 **Maqueda, Punta** *cape* Argentina
160 B5 **Maquela do Zombo** Angola
108 C2 **Maquinchao** Argentina
106 F4 **Mar Chiquita, Laguna** *lake* Argentina
107 G6 **Mar de Cobo** Argentina
107 G6 **Mar de Plata** Argentina
107 G6 **Mar del Sur** Argentina
89 F3 **Mar Negro, Lago** *lake* Mexico
161 F4 **Mara** *admin. area* Tanzania
101 E5 **Maraã** Brazil
102 B4 **Marabá** Brazil
197 G4 **Marabahan** Indonesia
197 H5 **Marabatua** *island* Indonesia
82 F2 **Marabœuf Lake** Ontario Canada
215 J7 **Maraboon, Lake** Qld Australia
158 C3 **Marabodé** *watercourse* Côte d'Ivoire
102 B2 **Maracá, Ilha de** *island* Brazil
102 C3 **Maracaçumé** Brazil
103 B8 **Maracaí** Brazil
101 E5 **Maracaí, Lago de** *lake* Brazil
100 D2 **Maracaibo** Venezuela
100 D2 **Maracaibo, Lago de** *lake* Venezuela
105 H6 **Maracaju** Brazil
105 H6 **Maracaju, Sierra de** *range* Brazil
102 C3 **Maracanã** Brazil
102 E3 **Maracanaú** Brazil
103 D6 **Maracás** Brazil
100 E2 **Maracay** Venezuela
106 E2 **Maracó Grande, Valle** *valley* Argentina
155 J3 **Marādah** Libya
158 F3 **Maradi** Niger
155 H6 **Maradi** *admin. area* Niger
182 E5 **Maraga** Russian Federation
182 E6 **Marāgheh** Iran
102 F5 **Maragogi** Brazil
103 E6 **Maragogipe** Brazil
100 E3 **Marairona, Cerros** *range* Venezuela
102 B3 **Marajó, Baía de** *bay* Brazil
102 B3 **Marajó, Ilha de** *island* Brazil
222 1 **Marakei** *island* Kiribati
160 D3 **Marakesa** Democratic Republic of Congo
161 F3 **Maralal** Kenya
183 M3 **Maraldy** *lake* Kazakhstan
160 C2 **Marali** Central African Republic
222 8 **Maramasike** *island* Solomon Islands
58 U2 **Marambio (Argentina)** *research station* Antarctica
197 J2 **Marampit** *island* Indonesia
199 G5 **Maramuni** *watercourse* Papua New Guinea
132 C2 **Maramureş** *admin. area* Romania
196 D3 **Maran** Malaysia
84 G4 **Marana** Arizona USA
216 E4 **Maranalgo** WA Australia
214 B3 **Maranboy** NT Australia
128 B3 **Maranchón** Spain
182 E6 **Marand** Iran
155 H5 **Marandet** Niger
212 E7 **Marandoo** WA Australia
196 D2 **Marang** Malaysia
214 F4 **Maranoa** NT Australia
102 C4 **Maranhão** *admin. area* Brazil
103 B6 **Maranhão** *watercourse* Brazil
128 C4 **Maranhão, Barragem do** *lake* Portugal
219 H2 **Maranoa** *watercourse* Qld Australia
104 B2 **Marañon** *watercourse* Peru
126 D3 **Marans** France
198 E4 **Maransabadi** *island* Indonesia
163 F4 **Marão** Mozambique
102 C3 **Marapanim** Brazil
101 G4 **Marapi** *watercourse* Brazil
196 D4 **Marapi, Gunung** *volcano* Indonesia
131 C6 **Marargiu, Capo** *cape* Sardinia Italy
221 C7 **Mararoa** *watercourse* New Zealand
197 H5 **Marasende** *island* Indonesia
178 F5 **Marāt** Saudi Arabia
103 D8 **Marataizes** Brazil
73 K9 **Marathon** Ontario Canada
85 K5 **Marathon** Texas USA
133 B7 **Marathopolis** Greece
197 H3 **Maratua** *island* Indonesia
105 G2 **Marau** Brazil
197 F4 **Marau** Indonesia
103 E6 **Maraú** Brazil
220 H4 **Marau Point** New Zealand
88 E5 **Maravatío** Mexico
105 E6 **Maraves** Argentina
222 8a **Maravovo** Solomon Islands
195 I5 **Marawi** Philippines
179 H5 **Marawwah, Jazīrat** *island* United Arab Emirates
104 C4 **Marayniocc** Peru
138 B4 **Marazion** Cornwall England UK
128 D5 **Marbella** Spain
80 G6 **Marble** Colorado USA
84 F2 **Marble Bar** WA Australia
84 G2 **Marble Canyon** Arizona USA
82 G8 **Marble Hill** Missouri USA
215 K6 **Marble Island** Qld Australia
76 J1 **Marble Island** Nunavut Canada
81 J5 **Marbleton** Wyoming USA
124 C4 **Marboz** France
138 E1 **Marbury** Cheshire England UK
122 H1 **Marby** Sweden
162 B3 **Marca, Ponta da** *cape* Angola
125 I4 **Marcali** Hungary
104 C4 **Marcapata** *watercourse* Peru
105 E4 **Marcavi** Bolivia
77 S6 **Marceau, Lac** *lake* Quebec Canada
77 U4 **Marcel, Lac** *lake* Quebec Canada
82 E3 **Marcell** Minnesota USA
104 C3 **Marcelo** Peru
139 H2 **March** Cambridgeshire England UK
216 E5 **Marchagee** WA Australia
81 Q2 **Marchand** Manitoba Canada
127 H3 **Marchaux** France
126 E3 **Marche** *region* France
130 E5 **Marche** *admin. area* Italy
127 G1 **Marche-en-Famenne** Belgium
128 D5 **Marchena** Spain
109 4 **Marchena, Canal de** *strait* Archipiélago de Colón (Galapagos Islands)
109 4 **Marchena, Isla** *island* Archipiélago de Colón (Galapagos Islands)
214 D1 **Marchinbar Island** NT Australia
126 G3 **Marcigny** France
139 I4 **Marck** France
103 D2 **Marco** Brazil
77 P4 **Marcopeet Islands** Nunavut Canada
104 C4 **Marcos** *watercourse* Brazil
77 S3 **Marcouard, Lac** *lake* Quebec Canada
81 R5 **Marcus** Iowa USA
182 F6 **Mardakyan** Azerbaijan
218 H8 **Mardan** Vic. Australia
179 L2 **Mardan** Pakistan
136 G6 **Mardin** Turkey
136 G6 **Mardin** *admin. area* Turkey
120 L3 **Mårdsel** Sweden
120 K4 **Mårdsele** Sweden
120 I5 **Mårdsjö** Sweden
197 J3 **Mare** *island* Indonesia
222 F8 **Maré** *island* New Caledonia
136 F6 **Mare'** Syria
130 E5 **Marecchia** *watercourse* Italy
103 A9 **Marechal Cândido Rondon** Brazil
104 C3 **Marechal Thaumaturgo** Brazil
142 C3 **Maree, Loch** *lake* Scotland UK
215 H4 **Mareeba** Qld Australia
131 D5 **Maremma** *region* Italy
154 D6 **Maréna** Mali
82 G5 **Marengo** Illinois USA
178 G2 **Marenjān** Iran
126 D4 **Marennes** France
163 H4 **Marerano** Madagascar
139 H4 **Maresfield** East Sussex England UK
213 H3 **Maret Islands** WA Australia
131 E8 **Marettimo, Isola di** *island* Italy
193 G1 **Marevka** *watercourse* Russian Federation
123 Q4 **Marevo** Russian Federation
85 J5 **Marfa** Texas USA
132 C3 **Marga** Romania
138 D3 **Margam** Neath Port Talbot Wales UK
213 H5 **Margaret** *watercourse* WA Australia
212 D6 **Margaret, Mount** WA Australia
74 H7 **Margaret Bay** British Columbia Canada
77 V5 **Margaret Hamilton Lake** Newfoundland and Labrador Canada
75 N3 **Margaret Lake** Alberta Canada
216 D6 **Margaret River** WA Australia
106 F6 **Margarita, Isla** *island* Argentina
101 E2 **Margarita, Isla de** *island* Venezuela
139 I3 **Margate** Kent England UK
132 C2 **Mărgău** Romania
131 G6 **Margherita di Savoia** Italy
160 D3 **Margherita Peak** *mountain* Uganda
132 C2 **Marghita** Romania
183 K6 **Marg'ilon** Uzbekistan
195 I6 **Margosatubig** Philippines
58 T2 **Marguerite Bay** Antarctica
136 E3 **Marhanets'** Ukraine
102 F4 **Mari** Brazil
199 G6 **Mari** Papua New Guinea
109 1b **Mari Pompoin** Netherlands Antilles
79 F8 **Maria** Quebec Canada
223 I4 **Maria** *reef* French Polynesia
88 D4 **María Cleofas, Isla** *island* Mexico
214 C3 **Maria Island** NT Australia
219 S11 **Maria Island** Tas. Australia
100 C2 **María la Baja** Colombia
88 D4 **María Madre, Isla** *island* Mexico
88 D4 **María Magdelena, Isla** *island* Mexico
130 F3 **Maria Neustift** Austria
220 E2 **Maria van Diemen, Cape** New Zealand
107 I2 **Marialva** Brazil
103 D8 **Mariana** Brazil
75 O5 **Mariana Lake** Alberta Canada
52 K6 **Mariana Ridge** *underwater feature* Pacific Ocean
52 K6 **Mariana Trench** *underwater feature* Pacific Ocean
52 K6 **Mariana Trough** *underwater feature* Pacific Ocean
181 H3 **Mariani** Assam India
86 F3 **Marianna** Arkansas USA
87 I5 **Marianna** Florida USA
107 G4 **Mariano Loza** Argentina
106 D6 **Mariano Moreno** Argentina
100 B4 **Mariapiri, Mesa de** *region* Colombia
101 G5 **Mariaqua** *watercourse* Brazil
100 E2 **Mariara** Venezuela
88 D4 **Marías, Islas** *islands* Mexico
100 E3 **Mariata** Venezuela
90 D6 **Mariato, Punta** *cape* Panama
178 F7 **Ma'rib** Yemen
101 F3 **Mariba, Sierra** *range* Venezuela
122 F5 **Maribo** Denmark
84 C3 **Maricopa** California USA
160 D3 **Maridi** Sudan
160 D2 **Maridi** *watercourse* Sudan
100 E5 **Marié** *watercourse* Brazil
58 P1 **Marie Byrd Land** *plain* Antarctica
58 Q2 **Marie Byrd Seamount** *underwater feature* Amundsen Sea
109 I6 **Marie-Galante** *island* Guadeloupe
75 P5 **Marie Lake** Alberta Canada
164 9 **Marie Louis Island** Seychelles
122 H3 **Mariebery** Sweden
120 I5 **Mariedal** Sweden
122 I3 **Mariefred** Sweden
123 J2 **Mariehamn/Maarianhamina** Aland Islands
90 D2 **Mariel** Cuba
103 B6 **Mariembero** *watercourse* Brazil
162 C4 **Mariental** Namibia
122 G3 **Mariestadsfjärden** *bay* Sweden
77 Q3 **Mariet** *watercourse* Quebec Canada
87 I4 **Marietta** Georgia USA
83 K7 **Marietta** Ohio USA
86 C4 **Marietta** Oklahoma USA
50 P4 **Marietta Seamount** *underwater feature* Atlantic Ocean
75 T7 **Marieval** Saskatchewan Canada
181 G3 **Marigaon** Assam India
127 G5 **Marignane** France
109 I5 **Marigot** Dominica
109 I4 **Marigot** Martinique
109 20 **Marigot** St Martin
109 I3 **Marigot Harbour** *bay* St Lucia
135 Y3 **Mariĭ Pronchishchevoy, Bukhta** *bay* Russian Federation
123 L5 **Marijampolė** Lithuania
123 L5 **Marijampolės** *admin. area* Lithuania
103 D7 **Marilândia** Brazil
103 B8 **Marília** Brazil
212 F7 **Marillana** WA Australia
101 G6 **Marimari** *watercourse* Brazil
160 B5 **Marimba** Angola
128 B2 **Marín** Spain
196 D4 **Marina Bay** Singapore
131 C7 **Marina di Arbus** Sardinia Italy
219 G3 **Marina Plains** Qld Australia
195 I4 **Marinduque** *island* Philippines
127 I5 **Marine de Luri** Corsica France
127 I5 **Marine de Sisco** Corsica France
124 A3 **Marines** France
82 H4 **Marinette** Wisconsin USA
103 B8 **Maringá** Brazil
160 C4 **Maringa** *watercourse* Democratic Republic of Congo
128 B3 **Marinha das Ondas** Portugal
128 B4 **Marinha Grande** Portugal
128 B3 **Marinhas** Portugal
222 7 **Marino** Vanuatu
123 O3 **Mar'insko** Russian Federation
104 H3 **Mário Spinelli** Brazil
86 H4 **Marion** Alabama USA
82 I6 **Marion** Indiana USA
82 F5 **Marion** Iowa USA
81 Q7 **Marion** Kansas USA
86 E4 **Marion** Louisiana USA
86 G4 **Marion** Mississippi USA
87 K3 **Marion** North Carolina USA
81 P3 **Marion** North Dakota USA
82 J6 **Marion** Ohio USA
86 B6 **Marion** Texas USA
87 K2 **Marion** Virginia USA
87 L4 **Marion, Lake** South Carolina USA
218 C6 **Marion Bay** SA Australia
214 E7 **Marion Downs** Qld Australia
81 Q7 **Marion Lake** Kansas USA
215 L5 **Marion Reef** Coral Sea Islands Territory Australia
155 H4 **Mariou, Adrar** *mountain* Algeria
100 C3 **Maripí** Colombia
195 J5 **Maripipi** *island* Philippines
84 C2 **Mariposa** California USA
100 E3 **Mariposa** Venezuela
193 B3 **Marisa** Indonesia
105 F6 **Mariscal Estigarribia** Paraguay
107 H5 **Mariscala** Uruguay
133 D4 **Maritsa** *watercourse* Bulgaria
136 F3 **Mariupol'** Ukraine
101 F2 **Mariusa, Isla** *island* Venezuela
182 E7 **Marivān** Iran
195 I4 **Mariveles** Philippines
195 G5 **Mariveles Reef** Spratly Islands
121 Q5 **Marjovaara** Finland
159 G2 **Mark** *region* Sweden
82 F7 **Mark Twain Lake** Missouri USA
161 G3 **Marka** Somalia
183 O4 **Markakol'** *lake* Kazakhstan
188 C2 **Markam** Xizang Zizhiqu China
187 E8 **Markapur** Andhra Pradesh India
178 G2 **Markazi** *admin. area* Iran
124 E4 **Markdorf** Germany
124 G1 **Markee** Germany
124 C1 **Marken** *island* Netherlands
162 E4 **Marken** South Africa
124 C1 **Markermeer** *bay* Netherlands
139 G2 **Market Deeping** Lincolnshire England UK
138 E2 **Market Drayton** Shropshire England UK
141 H3 **Market Rasen** Lincolnshire England UK
141 H3 **Market Weighton** East Riding of Yorkshire England UK
143 F2 **Markethill** Armagh Northern Ireland UK
199 H5 **Markham** *watercourse* Papua New Guinea
58 K1 **Markham, Mount** *mountain* Antarctica
125 K1 **Marki** Poland
120 L3 **Markitta** Sweden
142 D5 **Marklach** Dumfries and Galloway Scotland UK
82 I6 **Markle** Indiana USA
159 H3 **Markounda** Central African Republic
134 S6 **Markovo** Russian Federation
158 E2 **Markoye** Burkina Faso
182 E3 **Marks** Russian Federation
86 F3 **Marks** Mississippi USA
124 F2 **Marksuhl** Germany
127 J2 **Markt Bibart** Germany
130 C2 **Marktheidenfeld** Germany
124 F4 **Marktoberdorf** Germany
215 J7 **Markwell** Qld Australia
127 H1 **Marl** Germany
218 B3 **Marla** SA Australia
198 E5 **Marlasi** Indonesia
74 M6 **Marlboro** Alberta Canada
215 J7 **Marlborough** Qld Australia
124 B3 **Marle** France
86 C5 **Marlin** Texas USA
83 K7 **Marlinton** West Virginia USA
219 I7 **Marlo** Vic. Australia
139 G3 **Marlow** Buckinghamshire England UK
127 H2 **Marly** France
126 F1 **Marly** France
214 E6 **Marmadua** Qld Australia
126 E5 **Marmande** France
133 E5 **Marmara** Turkey
133 E5 **Marmara Adası** *island* Turkey
133 F5 **Marmara Denizi** *bay* Turkey
133 E6 **Marmara Gölü** *lake* Turkey
133 E5 **Marmaraereğlisi** Turkey
133 D6 **Marmarion** Greece
133 E6 **Marmaro** Greece
81 N3 **Marmarth** North Dakota USA
82 D8 **Marmaton** *watercourse* Kansas USA
122 I2 **Marmen** *lake* Sweden
216 G4 **Marmion, Lake** WA Australia
128 D4 **Marmolejo** Spain
83 M4 **Marmora** Ontario Canada
127 G3 **Marnay** France
120 I3 **Mårnes** Norway
132 D3 **Marneuli** Georgia
182 D5 **Marneuli** Georgia
124 F1 **Marnitz** Germany
181 H3 **Marniu** Arunachal Pradesh India
142 F3 **Marnoch** Aberdeenshire Scotland UK
218 F7 **Marnoo** Vic. Australia
159 H3 **Maro** Chad
163 I3 **Maroantsetra** Madagascar
220 F4 **Marokopa** New Zealand
186 D3 **Marol** Jammu and Kashmir India/Pakistan
179 M2 **Marol** Pakistan
139 I5 **Maromme** France
199 H4 **Maron Island** Papua New Guinea
163 F3 **Marondera** Zimbabwe
126 F4 **Maronne** *watercourse* France
215 K8 **Maroochydore** Qld Australia
212 F6 **Maroonah** WA Australia
216 D1 **Maroonah** WA Australia
198 A5 **Maros** Indonesia
163 I3 **Maroseranana** Madagascar
223 I4 **Marotiri, Îles** *islands* French Polynesia
130 E5 **Marotta** Italy
159 G2 **Maroua** Cameroon
163 H3 **Marovoay** Madagascar
163 I3 **Marovolo** Madagascar
214 D7 **Marqua** NT Australia
53 S9 **Marquesas Fracture Zone** *underwater feature* Pacific Ocean
87 J8 **Marquesas Keys** *island* Florida USA
82 H3 **Marquette** Michigan USA
86 C5 **Marquez** Texas USA
75 S7 **Marquis** Saskatchewan Canada
109 I3 **Marquis** St Lucia
109 I3 **Marquis, Cape** St Lucia
139 I4 **Marquise** France
223 I4 **Marquises, Îles** *islands* French Polynesia
100 E2 **Marquito** Venezuela
219 H4 **Marra** *watercourse* NSW Australia
159 I2 **Marra, Jebel** *range* Sudan
130 D4 **Marradi** Italy
216 E6 **Marradong** WA Australia
154 E2 **Marrakech** Morocco
77 V4 **Marralik** *watercourse* Quebec Canada
121 N3 **Marrasjärvi** Finland
121 N3 **Marrasjärvi** *lake* Finland
129 H4 **Marratxi** Spain
219 Q10 **Marrawah** Tas. Australia
218 D3 **Marree** SA Australia
142 E2 **Marrel** Highland Scotland UK
216 D1 **Marrilla** WA Australia
163 F3 **Marromeu** Mozambique
163 G2 **Marrupa** Mozambique
217 M3 **Marryat** *watercourse* SA Australia
83 R3 **Mars Hill** Maine USA
87 J3 **Mars Hill** North Carolina USA
157 G2 **Marsā al 'Alam** Egypt
155 J3 **Marsá al Burayqah** Libya
156 D1 **Marsā Maţrūh** Egypt
156 F3 **Marsā' Sha'b** Halaib Triangle
161 F3 **Marsabit** Kenya
131 E8 **Marsala** Italy
219 H5 **Marsden** NSW Australia
141 G3 **Marsden** West Yorkshire England UK
126 F5 **Marseillan** France
127 G5 **Marseille** France
141 F2 **Marsett** North Yorkshire England UK
218 F6 **Marsh, The** *marsh* Vic. Australia
87 M7 **Marsh Harbour** Bahamas
86 F6 **Marsh Island** *island* Louisiana USA
74 D2 **Marsh Lake** Yukon Territory Canada
141 G3 **Marsh Lane** Derbyshire England UK
214 C7 **Marshall** *watercourse* NT Australia
75 Q6 **Marshall** Saskatchewan Canada
158 B3 **Marshall** Liberia
86 E3 **Marshall** Arkansas USA
82 H7 **Marshall** Illinois USA
82 I5 **Marshall** Michigan USA
82 D4 **Marshall** Minnesota USA
82 E7 **Marshall** Missouri USA
86 D4 **Marshall** Texas USA
199 I6 **Marshall Bennett Islands** Papua New Guinea
223 I5 **Marshall Islands** *country* Pacific Ocean
76 L7 **Marshall Lake** Ontario Canada
82 E5 **Marshalltown** Iowa USA
123 O4 **Marshavitsy** Russian Federation
141 I3 **Marshchapel** Lincolnshire England UK
82 E8 **Marshfield** Missouri USA
82 F4 **Marshfield** Wisconsin USA
124 C3 **Marson** France
120 I4 **Marssjön** *lake* Sweden
122 I3 **Märsta** Sweden
122 F5 **Marstal** Denmark
122 F5 **Marstal Bugt** *bay* Denmark
139 F3 **Marston** Oxfordshire England UK
86 G2 **Marston** Missouri USA
86 C5 **Mart** Texas USA
131 D5 **Marta** *watercourse* Italy
194 C3 **Martaban, Gulf of** Myanmar
159 G3 **Martap** Cameroon
196 E5 **Martapura** Indonesia
159 G2 **Marte** Nigeria
132 E4 **Marten** Bulgaria
76 M7 **Marten Falls** Ontario Canada
132 B2 **Martfű** Hungary
86 B3 **Martha** Oklahoma USA
83 P6 **Marthas Vineyard** *island* Massachusetts USA
126 E4 **Marthon** France
90 D2 **Martí** Cuba
127 H3 **Martigny** Switzerland
127 G5 **Martigues** France
130 H2 **Martin** Slovakia
82 J8 **Martin** Kentucky USA
81 O5 **Martin** South Dakota USA
86 G2 **Martin** Tennessee USA
87 I4 **Martin Lake** Alabama USA
86 D4 **Martin Lake** Texas USA
58 Q2 **Martin Peninsula** Antarctica
132 A3 **Martinci** Serbia
91 I4 **Martinique** *French overseas territory* Caribbean
91 I4 **Martinique Passage** *strait* Caribbean
121 N4 **Martinniemi** Finland
221 B7 **Martins Bay** New Zealand
125 H3 **Martinsberg** Austria
83 M7 **Martinsburg** West Virginia USA
130 E5 **Martinsicuro** Italy
82 H7 **Martinsville** Indiana USA
87 L2 **Martinsville** Virginia USA
101 E5 **Martírio** Brazil
138 E2 **Martley** Worcestershire England UK
138 E4 **Martock** Somerset England UK
220 F5 **Marton** New Zealand
141 G2 **Marton** North Yorkshire England UK
138 D2 **Marton** Shropshire England UK
121 P5 **Martonvaara** Finland
128 E5 **Martos** Spain
72 H6 **Martre, Lac la** *lake* Northwest Territories Canada
121 P3 **Martti** Finland
182 G3 **Martuk** Kazakhstan
198 D5 **Maru** *island* Indonesia
182 G3 **Marudi** Malaysia
197 H2 **Marudu, Teluk** *bay* Malaysia
221 E6 **Maruia** *watercourse* New Zealand
221 E6 **Maruia Springs** New Zealand
219 I6 **Marulan** NSW Australia
123 J3 **Marum** Sweden
199 J5 **Marunga** Papua New Guinea
183 O3 **Marushka** Russian Federation
101 F4 **Marutani, Serra** *range* Brazil
178 G3 **Marv Dasht** Iran
122 E2 **Marvejols** France
216 F5 **Marvel Loch** WA Australia
86 F3 **Marvell** Arkansas USA
56 W1 **Marvin Spur** *underwater feature* Arctic Ocean
214 A2 **Mary** *watercourse* NT Australia
219 K1 **Mary** *watercourse* Qld Australia
182 I6 **Mary** Turkmenistan
213 J4 **Mary, Mount** NT Australia
212 C6 **Mary Anne Reef** WA Australia
214 E6 **Mary Kathleen** Qld Australia
214 B2 **Mary River Roadhouse** NT Australia
182 I6 **Mary Welaýaty** *admin. area* Turkmenistan
219 K1 **Maryborough** Qld Australia
162 D5 **Marydale** South Africa
214 B3 **Maryfield** NT Australia
214 B3 **Maryfield** *watercourse* NT Australia
75 U8 **Maryfield** Saskatchewan Canada
142 F4 **Marykirk** Aberdeenshire Scotland UK
85 L4 **Maryneal** Texas USA
142 E3 **Marypark** Moray Scotland UK
140 E2 **Maryport** Cumbria England UK
140 D2 **Maryport** Dumfries and Galloway Scotland UK
78 K6 **Mary's Harbour** Newfoundland and Labrador Canada
80 I7 **Marysvale** Utah USA
80 H2 **Marysville** British Columbia Canada
80 E7 **Marysville** California USA
81 Q7 **Marysville** Kansas USA
215 H5 **Maryvale** Qld Australia
219 K3 **Maryvale** Qld Australia
80 D6 **Maryville** Missouri USA
87 J3 **Maryville** Tennessee USA
100 B3 **Marzo, Cabo** *cape* Colombia
199 J4 **Masahet Island** Papua New Guinea
196 D2 **Masai** Malaysia
161 F4 **Masai Steppe** *plain* Tanzania
160 E4 **Masaka** Uganda
197 G5 **Masalembu Besar** *island* Indonesia
197 G5 **Masalembu Kecil** *island* Indonesia
198 B4 **Masamba** Indonesia
192 F4 **Masan** South Korea
161 F6 **Masasi** Tanzania
90 C5 **Masaya** Nicaragua
195 I4 **Masbate** *island* Philippines
155 G1 **Mascara** Algeria
54 J6 **Mascarene Basin** *underwater feature* Indian Ocean
54 I7 **Mascarene Plain** *underwater feature* Indian Ocean
54 K6 **Mascarene Plateau** *underwater feature* Indian Ocean
103 E6 **Mascote** Brazil
81 L2 **Masefield** Saskatchewan Canada
198 D6 **Masela** Indonesia
198 D6 **Masela** *island* Indonesia
120 K2 **Måselva** *watercourse* Norway
197 I4 **Masepe** *island* Indonesia
162 E5 **Maseru** Lesotho
161 F2 **Masha** Ethiopia
160 C5 **Mashala** Democratic Republic of Congo
162 F4 **Mashava** Zimbabwe
179 M2 **Masherbrum** *mountain* Pakistan
136 E2 **Mashevo** Ukraine
182 H7 **Mashhad** Iran
163 F3 **Mashonaland Central** *admin. area* Zimbabwe
163 F3 **Mashonaland East** *admin. area* Zimbabwe
162 E3 **Mashonaland West** *admin. area* Zimbabwe
193 J2 **Mashū-ko** *lake* Japan
160 B4 **Masi-Manimba** Democratic Republic of Congo
160 B4 **Masia-Mbio** Democratic Republic of Congo
198 E5 **Masian, Tanjung** *cape* Indonesia
161 E5 **Masimba** Tanzania
198 A4 **Masimbu** Indonesia
199 F5 **Masin** Indonesia
160 E3 **Masindi** Uganda
161 F4 **Masinga Reservoir** *lake* Kenya
195 H4 **Masinloc** Philippines
179 I6 **Maşīrah, Jazīrat** *island* Oman
160 D4 **Masisi** Democratic Republic of Congo
132 D2 **Masivul Ceahlău** *range* Romania
198 D4 **Masiwang** *watercourse* Indonesia
179 J2 **Masjed Negar** Afghanistan
178 G3 **Masjed Soleymān** Iran
143 C3 **Mask, Lough** *lake* Ireland
120 J4 **Maskaure** Sweden
120 J4 **Måskenåive** Sweden
132 E4 **Maslen Nos** *cape* Bulgaria
178 E4 **Maslīyah** Saudi Arabia
123 O2 **Maslovo** Russian Federation
121 R5 **Maslozero, Ozero** *lake* Russian Federation
163 J3 **Masoala, Tanjona** *cape* Madagascar
163 I4 **Masomeloka** Madagascar
86 B5 **Mason** Texas USA
216 F3 **Mason, Lake** WA Australia
221 B8 **Mason Bay** New Zealand
82 E5 **Mason City** Iowa USA
109 9 **Mason Hall** Trinidad and Tobago
74 D2 **Mason Landing** Yukon Territory Canada
197 J4 **Masoni** *island* Indonesia
83 L7 **Masontown** West Virginia USA
121 N1 **Måsøya** *island* Norway
164 3b **Maspalomas** Canary Islands
179 I5 **Masqaţ (Muscat)** Oman
187 D7 **Masqat** Maharashtra India
130 D4 **Massa** Italy

124 G5 **Massa Fiscaglia** Italy
83 P5 **Massachusetts Bay** Massachusetts USA
109 I5 **Massacre** Dominica
80 F6 **Massacre Lake** Nevada USA
155 J6 **Massaguet** Chad
155 J6 **Massakory** Chad
155 J6 **Massalassef** Chad
160 C4 **Massanga** Democratic Republic of Congo
159 G3 **Massangam** Cameroon
160 B5 **Massango** Angola
163 G2 **Massangulo** Mozambique
126 E5 **Massat** France
160 B5 **Massau** Angola
134 N6 **Massava** Russian Federation
157 F4 **Massawa** Eritrea
157 G4 **Massawa Channel** *strait* Eritrea
83 N4 **Massena** New York USA
159 H2 **Massenya** Chad
127 J3 **Masseria** Italy
74 E5 **Masset** British Columbia Canada
74 E6 **Masset Inlet** British Columbia Canada
126 E5 **Masseube** France
126 F4 **Massiac** France
123 M4 **Massiaru** Estonia
162 D2 **Massibi** Angola
126 F4 **Massif Central** *region* France
158 C2 **Massigui** Mali
154 E6 **Massina** Mali
163 F4 **Massingir** Mozambique
163 F4 **Massingir, Barragem de** *lake* Mozambique
81 L7 **Massive, Mount** Colorado USA
58 G2 **Masson Island** Antarctica
130 D5 **Massoncello, Monte** *mountain* Italy
124 B3 **Massy** France
221 F5 **Masterton** New Zealand
133 E6 **Masticho, Akra** *cape* Greece
131 C7 **Màstixi, Punta su** *cape* Sardinia Italy
122 G4 **Mästocka** Sweden
192 F4 **Masuda** Japan
120 M3 **Masugnsbyn** Sweden
159 G5 **Masuku (Franceville)** Gabon
187 D8 **Masur** Maharashtra India
196 D4 **Masurai, Bukit** *mountain* Indonesia
163 F4 **Masvingo** Zimbabwe
163 F4 **Masvingo** *admin. area* Zimbabwe
161 E4 **Maswa** Tanzania
198 E4 **Maswaar** *island* Indonesia
125 L2 **Masyevichy** Belarus
125 H1 **Maszewo** Poland
101 E3 **Mata, Serranía de** *range* Venezuela
108 B4 **Mata Amarilla** Argentina
103 E6 **Mata de São João** Brazil
101 F2 **Mata de Venado** Venezuela
101 F3 **Mata en Medio** Venezuela
162 E3 **Matabeleland North** *admin. area* Zimbabwe
162 E4 **Matabeleland South** *admin. area* Zimbabwe
223 9 **Matacaw Levu** *island* Fiji
83 K2 **Matachewan** Ontario Canada
85 I6 **Matachic** Mexico
191 H3 **Matad** Mongolia
160 A5 **Matadi** Democratic Republic of Congo
85 L3 **Matador** Texas USA
90 C4 **Matagalpa** Nicaragua
77 Q8 **Matagami** Quebec Canada
77 Q8 **Matagami, Lac** *lake* Quebec Canada
86 C6 **Matagorda Bay** Texas USA
86 C6 **Matagorda Island** Texas USA
86 C6 **Matagorda Peninsula** Texas USA
190 F5 **Mataigou** Ningxia Huizu Zizhiqu China
221 G5 **Mataikona** New Zealand
223 14 **Mataiva** *reef* French Polynesia
196 E3 **Matak** *island* Indonesia
218 G5 **Matakana** NSW Australia
220 G3 **Matakana Island** New Zealand
220 H3 **Matakaoa Point** New Zealand
221 E6 **Matakitaki** *watercourse* New Zealand
162 B2 **Matala** Angola
160 D4 **Matala** Democratic Republic of Congo
133 D8 **Matala** Greece
160 D4 **Matale** Democratic Republic of Congo
187 E10 **Matale** Sri Lanka
108 C3 **Matalinares, Punta** *cape* Argentina
154 D5 **Matam** Senegal
155 H6 **Matameye** Niger
83 N6 **Matamoras** Pennsylvania USA
88 E3 **Matamoros** Mexico
89 F3 **Matamoros** Mexico
197 I4 **Matana, Danau** *lake* Indonesia
195 I6 **Matanal Point** Philippines
161 F5 **Matandu** *watercourse* Tanzania
77 V8 **Matane** Quebec Canada
77 V8 **Matane** *watercourse* Quebec Canada
100 D3 **Matanegra** Colombia
90 D2 **Matanzas** Cuba
90 D2 **Matanzas** *admin. area* Cuba
106 D6 **Matanzilla, Pampa de la** *plain* Argentina
103 B8 **Matão** Brazil
105 I3 **Matão, Serra do** *range* Brazil
90 D5 **Matapalo, Cabo** *lake* Costa Rica
84 H6 **Matape** Mexico
83 R2 **Matapédia** *watercourse* Quebec Canada
83 R2 **Matapédia, Lac** *lake* Quebec Canada
101 G3 **Matappi** Suriname
106 D5 **Mataquito** *watercourse* Chile
121 P5 **Matara** Finland
187 E11 **Matara** Sri Lanka
133 B6 **Mataragka** Greece
197 H6 **Mataram** Indonesia
214 B3 **Mataranka** NT Australia
197 I4 **Matarape, Teluk** *bay* Indonesia
129 H3 **Mataró** Spain
132 C3 **Mătăsari** Romania
197 G5 **Matasiri** *island* Indonesia
121 P5 **Mätäsvaara** Finland
162 E6 **Matatiele** South Africa
221 C8 **Mataura** New Zealand
221 C7 **Mataura** *watercourse* New Zealand
223 12b **Mata'utu** Wallis and Futuna
100 E3 **Mataveni** Venezuela
220 2 **Matavera** Cook Islands New Zealand
109 5 **Mataveri** Isla de Pascua (Easter Island)
76 I5 **Matawak** Manitoba Canada
83 O3 **Matawin Reservoir** Quebec Canada
183 M4 **Matay** Kazakhstan
125 L2 **Matcze** Poland
100 D3 **Mate Palma** Colombia
105 F4 **Mateguá** Bolivia
88 E4 **Matehuala** Mexico
223 13a **Mateika** *island* Tuvalu
105 I5 **Mateira, Serra** *range* Brazil
103 A9 **Matelândia** Brazil
130 E5 **Matelica** Italy
109 9 **Matelot** Trinidad and Tobago
162 C3 **Matende** Angola
163 F3 **Matenga** Mozambique
90 C4 **Mateo** Honduras
131 G6 **Matera** Italy
132 A4 **Mateševo** Montenegro
155 H1 **Mateur** Tunisia
122 I1 **Matfors** Sweden
126 D4 **Matha** France
53 U6 **Mathematicians Seamounts** *underwater feature* Pacific Ocean
85 K1 **Matheson** Colorado USA
86 C6 **Mathis** Texas USA
214 A3 **Mathison** *watercourse* NT Australia
218 G6 **Mathoura** NSW Australia
133 A6 **Mathraki** *island* Greece
186 D5 **Mathura** Uttar Pradesh India
195 J6 **Mati** Philippines
161 F4 **Matia** *watercourse* Kenya
179 K4 **Matiari** Pakistan
102 D3 **Matias Olímpio** Brazil
89 G5 **Matías Romero** Mexico
163 H2 **Matibane** Mozambique
102 C3 **Matinha** Brazil
103 D8 **Matipó** Brazil
223 14a **Matiti** French Polynesia
121 Q6 **Matkasel'kya** Russian Federation
162 E4 **Matlabas** *watercourse* South Africa
139 F1 **Matlock** Derbyshire England UK
195 J4 **Matnog** Philippines
105 G4 **Mato Grosso** Brazil
105 H4 **Mato Grosso** *admin. area* Brazil
103 A6 **Mato Grosso, Planalto do** *region* Brazil
105 H5 **Mato Grosso do Sul** *admin. area* Brazil
105 I3 **Mato Verde** Brazil
103 D6 **Mato Verde** Brazil
163 F5 **Matola** Mozambique
77 U7 **Matonipi** *watercourse* Quebec Canada
77 U7 **Matonipi, Lac** *lake* Quebec Canada
161 G4 **Matooni, Raas** *cape* Somalia
128 B3 **Matosinhos** Portugal
188 E4 **Matou** Guangxi Zhuangzu Zizhiqu China
127 G3 **Matour** France
159 G5 **Matouti, Pointe** *cape* Gabon
179 I5 **Maṭraḥ** Oman
122 C2 **Matre** Norway
124 G4 **Matrei** Austria
158 B3 **Matru** Sierra Leone
120 I4 **Matsdal** Sweden
163 I4 **Matsiatra** *watercourse* Madagascar
189 H3 **Matsu Tao** *island* China
192 G4 **Matsue** Japan
193 H4 **Matsumoto** Japan
193 H4 **Matsusaka** Japan
192 G5 **Matsuyama** Japan
101 H3 **Matta** Suriname
77 N7 **Mattagami** *watercourse* Ontario Canada
106 F5 **Mattaldi** Argentina
87 M3 **Mattamuskeet, Lake** North Carolina USA
83 L3 **Mattawa** Ontario Canada
80 F3 **Mattawa** Washington USA
83 Q3 **Mattawamkeag Lake** Maine USA
217 O5 **Mattaweara Lagoon** SA Australia
130 B3 **Matten** Switzerland
127 H4 **Matterhorn** *mountain* Switzerland
91 F2 **Matthew Town** Bahamas
87 K3 **Matthews** North Carolina USA
221 F5 **Matthews, Mount** New Zealand
178 G5 **Maṭṭī, Sabkhat** United Arab Emirates
121 M2 **Mattiselva** *watercourse* Norway
120 H5 **Mattmar** Sweden
82 G7 **Mattoon** Illinois USA
124 G4 **Mattsee** *lake* Austria
197 F3 **Matu** Malaysia
197 F4 **Matua** Indonesia
135 AF9 **Matua, Ostrov** *island* Russian Federation
187 E10 **Matugama** Sri Lanka
223 9 **Matuku** *island* Fiji
162 C2 **Matumbo** Angola
181 G5 **Matupi** Myanmar
109 9 **Matura** Trinidad and Tobago
109 9 **Matura Bay** Trinidad and Tobago
101 F2 **Maturín** Venezuela
132 G1 **Matusov** Ukraine
197 J2 **Matutuang** *island* Indonesia
128 E2 **Matxitxako, Cabo** *cape* Spain
134 S6 **Matyl'ka** Russian Federation
186 F6 **Mau** Bihar India
186 E6 **Mau** Madhya Pradesh India
186 E6 **Mau Ranipur** Uttar Pradesh India
163 G2 **Maúa** Mozambique
86 C3 **Maud** Oklahoma USA
216 C1 **Maud, Point** WA Australia
58 A2 **Maud Rise** *underwater feature* Southern Ocean
218 G6 **Maude** NSW Australia
58 L1 **Maude, Cape** Antarctica
214 B3 **Maude Creek** NT Australia
105 G1 **Maués** Brazil
101 G6 **Maues Acu** *watercourse* Brazil
222 2 **Maug Islands** *islands* Northern Mariana Islands
140 D2 **Maughold Head** *cape* Isle of Man UK
84 inset **Maui** *island* Hawai'i USA
220 1 **Mauke** *island* Cook Islands New Zealand
121 N4 **Maula** Finland
106 D5 **Maule** *admin. area* Chile
106 C5 **Maule** *watercourse* Chile
106 D6 **Maule, Lago de** *lake* Chile
126 D3 **Maulévrier** France
108 B2 **Maullín** Chile
143 C3 **Maum** Ireland
82 I6 **Maumee** *watercourse* Indiana USA
86 E3 **Maumelle, Lake** Arkansas USA
198 B6 **Maumere** Indonesia
162 D3 **Maun** Botswana
130 F4 **Maun** *island* Croatia
84 inset **Mauna Kea** *volcano* Hawai'i USA
84 inset **Mauna Loa** *volcano* Hawai'i USA
84 inset **Maunaloa** Hawai'i USA
186 F6 **Maunath Bhanjan** Uttar Pradesh India
162 E4 **Maunatlala** Botswana
220 2 **Maungaroa** *volcano* Cook Islands New Zealand
181 G5 **Maungdaw (Sinchaigbyin)** Myanmar
194 C4 **Maungmagan Islands** Myanmar
72 G5 **Maunoir, Lac** *lake* Northwest Territories Canada
121 M2 **Maunu** Sweden
77 T7 **Maupertuis, Lac** *lake* Quebec Canada
223 14 **Maupihaa** *island* French Polynesia
80 E4 **Maupin** Oregon USA
122 F2 **Maura** Norway
125 K5 **Măureni** Romania
86 F5 **Maurepas, Lake** Louisiana USA
126 F4 **Mauriac** France
217 L4 **Maurice, Lake** SA Australia
154 D5 **Mauritania** *country* Africa
164 7b **Mauritius** *country* Indian Ocean
164 7 **Mauritius** *island* Mauritius
131 F6 **Mauro, Monte** *mountain* Italy
126 C2 **Mauron** France
126 F4 **Maurs** France
58 I2 **Maury Bay** Antarctica
57 E3 **Maury Channel** *underwater feature* Atlantic Ocean
125 G3 **Mauth** Germany
126 E5 **Mauvezin** France
126 D3 **Mauzé-sur-le-Mignon** France
163 G2 **Mavago** Mozambique
163 G4 **Mavanza** Mozambique
120 J3 **Mavas** Sweden
120 J3 **Mavasjaure** *lake* Sweden
162 C3 **Mavengue** Angola
162 D3 **Mavinga** Angola
213 G3 **Mavis Reef** WA Australia
132 D3 **Mavrodin** Romania
186 D6 **Mawana** Madhya Pradesh India
160 B5 **Mawanga** Democratic Republic of Congo
194 C5 **Mawdaung Pass** *mountain* Myanmar
220 H4 **Mawhai Point** New Zealand
181 H5 **Mawkme** Myanmar
Mawlaik *see* **Kalay** Myanmar
194 C3 **Mawlamyaing (Moulmein)** Myanmar
178 E4 **Mawqaq** Saudi Arabia
178 E7 **Mawr, Wādī** *watercourse* Yemen
58 E2 **Mawson (Australia)** *research station* Antarctica
58 L2 **Mawson Bank** *underwater feature* Ross Sea
58 E2 **Mawson Coast** Antarctica
58 E2 **Mawson Escarpment** *range* Antarctica
210 inset **Mawson Peak** Heard Island Australia
58 K2 **Mawson Peninsula** Antarctica
81 O3 **Max** North Dakota USA
161 H3 **Maxaas** Somalia
106 E4 **Maxán** Argentina
89 H4 **Maxcanú** Mexico
126 C3 **Maxent** France
74 J3 **Maxhamish Lake** British Columbia Canada
163 G4 **Maxixe** Mozambique
220 F4 **Maxwell** New Zealand
81 O6 **Maxwell** Nebraska USA
85 J2 **Maxwell** New Mexico USA
214 G6 **Maxwelton** Qld Australia
199 G5 **May** *watercourse* Papua New Guinea
58 L1 **May, Cape** Antarctica
142 F4 **May, Isle of** Scotland UK
215 H4 **May, Mount** Qld Australia
215 J7 **May Downs** Qld Australia
90 E3 **May Pen** Jamaica
216 E4 **Maya** WA Australia
196 F4 **Maya** *island* Indonesia
135 AC7 **Maya** *watercourse* Russian Federation
90 B3 **Maya Mountains** Belize
194 B4 **Mayabandar** Andaman and Nicobar Islands India
91 F2 **Mayaguana Island** Bahamas
91 F2 **Mayaguana Passage** Bahamas
91 H3 **Mayagüez** Puerto Rico
155 H6 **Mayahi** Niger
183 K7 **Mayakovskiy, Qullai** *mountain* Tajikistan
132 F2 **Mayaky** Ukraine
160 B5 **Mayala** Democratic Republic of Congo
198 D4 **Mayalibit, Teluk** *bay* Indonesia
192 F3 **Mayang-dong** *island* North Korea
188 E1 **Mayanhe** Gansu China
160 E3 **Mayania** *watercourse* Uganda
216 E6 **Mayanup** WA Australia
109 9 **Mayaro** Trinidad and Tobago
109 9 **Mayaro Bay** Trinidad and Tobago
142 D5 **Maybole** South Ayrshire Scotland UK
157 F5 **Maych'ew** Ethiopia
132 G1 **Maydanets'ke** Ukraine
182 J6 **Maydayobu** Uzbekistan
198 E4 **Mayege** Indonesia
124 D2 **Mayen** Germany
126 D2 **Mayenne** France
181 F2 **Mayer Kangri** *mountain* Xizang Zizhiqu China
126 E3 **Mayet** France
221 D6 **Mayfield** New Zealand
86 C2 **Mayfield** Kansas USA
86 G2 **Mayfield** Kentucky USA
84 G1 **Mayfield** Utah USA
85 J4 **Mayhill** New Mexico USA
183 L3 **Maykain** Kazakhstan
183 M4 **Maykamys** Kazakhstan
182 C5 **Maykop** Russian Federation
183 O3 **Mayma** Russian Federation
135 AC7 **Maymakan** *watercourse* Russian Federation
181 H4 **Maymyo** Myanmar
182 E2 **Mayna** Russian Federation
182 J6 **Maynamak** Uzbekistan
214 F7 **Mayne** *watercourse* Qld Australia
214 F7 **Maynes Peak** *mountain* Qld Australia
135 AK6 **Mayno-Amamkut** Russian Federation
135 AK6 **Mayno-Gytkino** Russian Federation
83 M4 **Maynooth** Ontario Canada
143 F3 **Maynooth** Ireland
108 B3 **Mayo** *watercourse* Argentina
72 F6 **Mayo** Yukon Territory Canada
143 C2 **Mayo** *admin. area* Ireland
109 9 **Mayo** Trinidad and Tobago
87 J5 **Mayo** Florida USA
108 B6 **Mayo, Cerro** *mountain* Chile
195 J6 **Mayo Bay** Philippines
159 G3 **Mayo Belwa** Nigeria
159 G3 **Mayo Darlé** Cameroon
159 G3 **Mayo Godi** *watercourse* Cameroon
159 H2 **Mayo-Kebbi Est** *admin. area* Chad
159 G3 **Mayo-Kebbi Ouest** *admin. area* Chad
105 E4 **Mayo Mayo** Bolivia
87 L2 **Mayo Reservoir** North Carolina USA
159 G5 **Mayoko** Congo
195 I4 **Mayon Volcano** Philippines
128 C5 **Mayor, Isla** *island* Spain
106 F6 **Mayor Buratovich** Argentina
220 G3 **Mayor Island (Tuhua)** New Zealand
105 F5 **Mayor Pablo Lagerenza** Paraguay
128 D2 **Mayorga** Spain
109 9 **Mayoro-Rio Claro** *admin. area* Trinidad and Tobago
164 6a **Mayotte** *French overseas department* Indian Ocean
195 I3 **Mayraira Point** Philippines
109 11 **Mayreau** St Vincent and the Grenadines
124 F4 **Mayrhofen** Austria
121 M5 **Mäyry** Finland
178 F3 **Maysān** *admin. area* Iraq
191 L2 **Mayskiy** Russian Federation
135 AB8 **Mayskiy, Khrebet** *range* Russian Federation
183 M3 **Mayskoye** Kazakhstan
75 R4 **Mayson Lake** Saskatchewan Canada
195 H5 **Maytiguid** *island* Philippines
197 J3 **Mayu** *island* Indonesia
187 E9 **Mayuram** Tamil Nadu India
81 Q3 **Mayville** North Dakota USA
142 inset **Maywick** Shetland Scotland UK
81 O6 **Maywood** Nebraska USA
135 AB6 **Mayya** Russian Federation
178 E6 **Mayzah** Saudi Arabia
162 E3 **Mazabuka** Zambia
102 B3 **Mazagão** Brazil
80 E2 **Mazama** British Columbia Canada
74 K8 **Mazama** Washington USA
126 F5 **Mazamet** France
88 E5 **Mazamitla** Mexico
179 H2 **Mazanābād** Iran
182 F7 **MazandarĀn** *admin. area* Iran
182 J7 **Mazār-e-Sharīf** Afghanistan
184 F5 **Mazar Tag** *mountain* Xinjiang Uygur Zizhiqu China
131 E8 **Mazara del Vallo** Italy
108 C4 **Mazarredo** Argentina
129 F5 **Mazarrón** Spain
101 F3 **Mazaruni** *watercourse* Guyana
88 C2 **Mazatán** Mexico
88 D4 **Mazatlán** Mexico
123 L4 **Mazeikiai** Lithuania
129 G2 **Mazères** France
130 F4 **Mazin** Croatia
83 M4 **Mazinaw Lake** Ontario Canada
123 L4 **Mazirbe** Latvia
84 G6 **Mazocahui** Mexico
160 D4 **Mazomeno** Democratic Republic of Congo
161 F5 **Mazomora** Tanzania
185 J4 **Mazong Shan** *mountain* Gansu China
163 F3 **Mazowe** *watercourse* Zimbabwe
125 K1 **Mazowieckie** *admin. area* Poland
156 D5 **Mazrub** Sudan
123 M4 **Mazsalaca** Latvia
162 E4 **Mazunga** Zimbabwe
136 D2 **Mazyr** Belarus
155 H2 **Mazzouna** Tunisia
159 G3 **Mba** Cameroon
163 F5 **Mbabane** Swaziland
164 8a **Mbachilé** Comoros
154 C6 **Mbacké** Senegal
159 H4 **Mbaïki** Central African Republic
159 G3 **Mbakaou** Cameroon
159 H4 **Mbako** Central African Republic
160 E5 **Mbala** Zambia
159 G4 **Mbalam** Cameroon
161 E3 **Mbale** Uganda
159 H3 **Mbali** Central African Republic
159 I3 **Mbali** *watercourse* Central African Republic
159 G4 **Mbalmayo** Cameroon
222 8a **Mbalo** Solomon Islands
159 G3 **Mbam** *watercourse* Cameroon
159 G5 **Mbama** Congo
161 E6 **Mbamba Bay** Tanzania
160 B4 **Mbandaka** Democratic Republic of Congo
159 G4 **Mbandjok** Cameroon
159 G4 **Mbandza** Congo
159 G4 **Mbang** Cameroon
159 G6 **M'banza Congo** Angola
160 A5 **Mbanza-Ngungu** Democratic Republic of Congo
154 C6 **Mbar** Senegal
160 E4 **Mbarara** Uganda
159 I3 **Mbari** *watercourse* Central African Republic
163 F2 **Mbati** Zambia
199 K5 **Mbava** *island* Solomon Islands
159 G3 **Mbé** Cameroon
159 H5 **Mbé** Congo
162 E3 **Mbembesi** Zimbabwe
161 F5 **Mbemkuru** *watercourse* Tanzania
164 8a **Mbéni** Comoros
159 G3 **Mbere** *watercourse* Cameroon
162 E4 **Mberengwa** Zimbabwe
158 B3 **Mbesi, Lake** Sierra Leone
163 F1 **Mbesuma** Zambia
161 E5 **Mbeya** Tanzania
161 E5 **Mbeya** *admin. area* Tanzania
159 H4 **Mbi** *watercourse* Central African Republic
159 G5 **Mbigou** Gabon
161 E6 **Mbinga** Tanzania
159 G4 **Mbini** *watercourse* Equatorial Guinea
159 G4 **Mbomo** Congo
159 I3 **Mbomou** *admin. area* Central African Republic
159 H5 **Mbon** Congo
160 D3 **Mboro** Democratic Republic of Congo
160 C2 **Mbotou** *watercourse* Central African Republic
159 G3 **Mboula** Cameroon
154 D6 **Mboun** Senegal
154 C6 **Mbour** Senegal
154 D5 **Mbout** Mauritania
159 H3 **Mbrés** Central African Republic
160 C5 **Mbuji-Mayi** Democratic Republic of Congo
160 C5 **Mbuji-Mayi** *watercourse* Democratic Republic of Congo
107 G4 **Mburucuyá** Argentina
223 9a **Mbutha** Fiji
161 F5 **Mchinga** Tanzania
163 F2 **Mchinji** Zambia
76 H4 **M'Clintock** Manitoba Canada
73 I4 **M'Clintock Channel** Nunavut Canada
72 G3 **M'Clure Strait** Northwest Territories Canada
162 E6 **Mdantsane** South Africa
128 D6 **M'diq** Morocco
129 I6 **M'Doukal** Algeria
194 E3 **Mê, Hon** *island* Vietnam
193 I2 **Me-akan-dake** *volcano* Japan
192 F5 **Me-shima** *island* Japan
86 C4 **Mead** Oklahoma USA
84 E2 **Mead, Lake** Nevada USA
72 D5 **Meade** *watercourse* Alaska USA
81 O8 **Meade** Kansas USA
128 B3 **Meadela** Portugal
142 D2 **Meadie, Loch** *lake* Scotland UK
216 D3 **Meadow** WA Australia
85 K4 **Meadow** Texas USA
80 I7 **Meadow** Utah USA
86 C5 **Meadowlakes** Texas USA
86 F5 **Meadville** Mississippi USA
83 K6 **Meadville** Pennsylvania USA
140 F2 **Meal Bank** Cumbria England UK
142 A2 **Mealasta** *island* Scotland UK
128 B3 **Mealhada** Portugal
78 I6 **Mealy Mountains** Newfoundland and Labrador Canada
219 I2 **Meandarra** Qld Australia
74 M3 **Meander River** Alberta Canada
102 C4 **Mearim** *watercourse* Brazil
120 J5 **Meåstrand** Sweden
143 F3 **Meath** *admin. area* Ireland
143 E3 **Meathas Troim** Ireland
198 E4 **Mebo, Gunung** *mountain* Indonesia
160 A5 **Mebridege** *watercourse* Angola
197 G6 **Mebulu, Tanjung** *cape* Indonesia
101 F3 **Mecalineta** Brazil
163 G3 **Mecanhelas** Mozambique
Mecca *see* **Makkah** Saudi Arabia
161 G2 **Mechāra** Ethiopia
127 G1 **Mechelen** Belgium
129 G6 **Mecheraa Asfa** Algeria
222 3 **Mecherchar** *island* Palau
155 F2 **Mecheria** Algeria
124 D2 **Mechernich** Germany
155 J6 **Mechimére** Chad
183 J4 **Mechkey-sor** *lake* Kazakhstan
216 E5 **Meckering** WA Australia
124 G1 **Mecklenburg-Vorpommern** *admin. area* Germany
122 F5 **Mecklenburger Bucht** *bay* Germany
163 G2 **Meconta** Mozambique
163 G2 **Mecuburi** *watercourse* Mozambique
163 H2 **Mecúfi** Mozambique
163 G2 **Mecula** Mozambique
213 H4 **Meda** WA Australia
213 H4 **Meda** *watercourse* WA Australia
128 C3 **Meda** Portugal
130 F4 **Medak** Croatia
187 E7 **Medak** Andhra Pradesh India
196 C3 **Medan** Indonesia
197 H6 **Medang** *island* Indonesia
100 D2 **Médanos, Istmo de** *peninsula* Venezuela
108 D4 **Medanosa, Punta** *cape* Argentina
75 V5 **Medard** Manitoba Canada
187 E10 **Medawachchiya** Sri Lanka
155 G1 **Médéa** Algeria
103 D7 **Medeiros Neto** Brazil
100 C3 **Medellín** Colombia
120 J5 **Medelpad** *region* Sweden
155 I2 **Medenine** Tunisia
154 C5 **Mederdra** Mauritania
133 F7 **Medet** Turkey
81 Q8 **Medford** Oklahoma USA
80 D5 **Medford** Oregon USA
82 F4 **Medford** Wisconsin USA
133 D5 **Médhousa** Greece
160 E2 **Medi** Sudan
106 E5 **Media Luna** Argentina
90 E2 **Media Luna** Cuba
128 F5 **Media Naranja, Punta de la** *cape* Spain
103 A9 **Medianeira** Brazil
129 G2 **Mediano, Embalse de** *lake* Spain
80 G3 **Medical Lake** Washington USA
130 D4 **Medicina** Italy
81 L6 **Medicine Bow** Wyoming USA
81 L6 **Medicine Bow Mountains** Wyoming USA
75 P7 **Medicine Hat** Alberta Canada
81 M2 **Medicine Lake** Montana USA
81 P8 **Medicine Lodge** Kansas USA
85 M3 **Medicine Park** Oklahoma USA
103 D7 **Medina** Brazil
195 J5 **Medina** Philippines
Medina *see* **Al Madīnah al Munawwarah** Saudi Arabia
83 L5 **Medina** New York USA
86 G3 **Medina** Tennessee USA
108 D2 **Medina, Ensenada de** *bay* Argentina
128 E2 **Medina de Pomar** Spain
128 D3 **Medina del Campo** Spain
154 D6 **Medina Gounas** Senegal
187 G6 **Medinipur** West Bengal India
106 D6 **Medio, Chihuido** *mountain* Argentina
88 D2 **Medio Camino** Mexico
100 C5 **Mediodía** Colombia
50 U6 **Mediterranean Ridge** *underwater feature* Mediterranean Sea
118 **Mediterranean Sea** Europe
129 H6 **Medjedel** Algeria
129 J5 **Medjez Sfa** Algeria
120 L4 **Medle** Sweden
135 U3 **Mednyy, Mys** *cape* Russian Federation
135 AI8 **Mednyy, Ostrov** *island* Russian Federation
82 F7 **Medora** Illinois USA
81 N3 **Medora** North Dakota USA
123 K5 **Medovoye** Russian Federation
129 G6 **Medrissa** Algeria
120 H5 **Medstugan** Sweden
125 I5 **Medumajdan** Croatia
132 B4 **Medveđa** Serbia
135 AH4 **Medvezh'i, Ostrov** *island* Russian Federation
134 T4 **Medvezhiy Yar** Russian Federation
193 H1 **Medvezh'ya, Gora** *mountain* Russian Federation
134 H6 **Medvezh'yegorsk** Russian Federation
139 H3 **Medway** *admin. area* England UK
132 C1 **Medyka** Ukraine
216 D3 **Meeberrie** WA Australia
216 D2 **Meedo** WA Australia
216 F3 **Meekatharra** WA Australia
81 L6 **Meeker** Colorado USA
143 D3 **Meelick** Galway Ireland
216 F4 **Meeline** WA Australia
79 J8 **Meelpaeg Lake** Newfoundland and Labrador Canada
143 D2 **Meenacross** Ireland
123 N3 **Meerapalu** Estonia
124 C2 **Meerhout** Belgium
219 H7 **Meerlieu** Vic. Australia
186 D5 **Meerut** Uttar Pradesh India
81 K4 **Meeteetse** Wyoming USA
138 C4 **Meeth** Devon England UK
161 F3 **Mēga** Ethiopia
161 F3 **Mega Escarpment** *range* Ethiopia
161 G2 **Megalo** Ethiopia
222 7 **Mégam** Vanuatu
133 B6 **Meganisi** *island* Greece
86 B4 **Megargel** Texas USA
187 G7 **Megasini** *mountain* Orissa India
181 G4 **Meghalaya** *admin. area* India
83 M2 **Mégiscane, Lac** *lake* Quebec Canada
178 B2 **Megisti** *island* Greece
123 Q2 **Megrega** Russian Federation
123 Q2 **Megrozero** Russian Federation
125 L5 **Mehadia** Romania
121 O1 **Mehamn** Norway
179 K4 **Mehar** Pakistan
212 E7 **Meharry, Mount** WA Australia
186 F5 **Mehdawal** Uttar Pradesh India
132 C3 **Mehedinți** *admin. area* Romania
122 E3 **Meheia** Norway
186 G6 **Meherpur** West Bengal India
123 N3 **Mehikoorma** Estonia
125 K4 **Méhkerék** Hungary
178 F2 **Mehrān** Iran
121 N4 **Mehtäkylä** Finland
179 L2 **Mehtar Lām** Afghanistan
106 C6 **Mehuín** Chile
189 G2 **Meicheng** Anhui China
159 G3 **Meidougou** Cameroon
138 D2 **Meifod** Powys Wales UK
143 F2 **Meigh** Newry and Mourne Northern Ireland UK
73 I2 **Meighen Island** Nunavut Canada
142 E4 **Meigle** Perth and Kinross Scotland UK
87 I5 **Meigs** Georgia USA
191 K4 **Meihekou** Jilin China
188 E3 **Meijiang** Guizhou China
189 G3 **Meijiang** Jiangxi China
181 H5 **Meiktila** Myanmar
120 L1 **Meiland** Norway
189 G3 **Meilin** Jiangxi China
128 C2 **Meira** Spain
127 I3 **Meiringen** Switzerland
189 G2 **Meishan** Anhui China
188 D2 **Meishan** Sichuan China
189 G2 **Meishan Shuiku** *lake* Anhui China
80 D6 **Meiss Lake** California USA
124 G2 **Meißen** Germany
188 D2 **Meixing** Sichuan China
189 G4 **Meizhou** Guangdong China
189 H3 **Meizhou Dao** *island* Fujian China
106 E4 **Mejicana** *mountain* Argentina
90 B4 **Mejicanos** El Salvador
108 D2 **Mejillón, Punta** *cape* Argentina
106 D2 **Mejillones** Chile
106 D2 **Mejillones, Bahía** *bay* Chile
223 15 **Mejit Island** Marshall Islands
159 E3 **Mejo** Nigeria
216 E3 **Meka** WA Australia
159 G4 **Mékambo** Gabon
157 F5 **Mekane Selam** Ethiopia
157 F5 **Mek'elē** Ethiopia
123 Q2 **Mekhbaza** Russian Federation
154 C5 **Mékhé** Senegal
179 L3 **Mekhtar** Pakistan
154 E2 **Meknès** Morocco
194 E5 **Mekong** *watercourse* Cambodia
188 C4 **Mekong** *watercourse* Yunnan China
194 E4 **Mekong** *watercourse* Laos
194 E3 **Mekong** *watercourse* Thailand
197 I5 **Mekongga, Teluk** *bay* Indonesia
121 Q5 **Mekrijärvi** *lake* Finland
160 C2 **Mela, Mount** Central African Republic
124 F4 **Melago** Italy
196 D3 **Melaka** Malaysia
196 D3 **Melaka** *admin. area* Malaysia
197 G2 **Melalap** Malaysia
219 R11 **Melaleuca, Mount** Tas. Australia
196 E4 **Melalo, Tanjung** *cape* Indonesia
52 M7 **Melanesian Basin** *underwater feature* Pacific Ocean
133 D6 **Melanios, Akra** *cape* Greece
133 B6 **Melátai** Greece
197 G4 **Melawi** *watercourse* Indonesia
80 G5 **Melba** Idaho USA
142 B2 **Melbost Borve** Na h-Eileanan Siar Scotland UK
218 G7 **Melbourne** Vic. Australia
139 F2 **Melbourne** Derbyshire England UK
86 F2 **Melbourne** Arkansas USA
87 K6 **Melbourne** Florida USA
139 E4 **Melbury Abbas** Dorset England UK
108 B3 **Melchor, Isla** *island* Chile
85 L7 **Melchor Múzquiz** Mexico
182 H4 **Meldikol** *lake* Kazakhstan
122 E5 **Meldorfer Bucht** *bay* Germany
159 I3 **Mélé** Central African Republic
156 C6 **Mélé** Central African Republic
76 G7 **Meleb** Manitoba Canada
222 3 **Melekeok** Palau
163 G3 **Melela** *watercourse* Mozambique
132 B3 **Melenci** Serbia
182 D2 **Melenki** Russian Federation
182 G3 **Meleuz** Russian Federation
77 T4 **Mélèzes, Rivière aux** *watercourse* Quebec Canada
159 H2 **Melfi** Chad
131 F6 **Melfi** Italy
120 H3 **Melfjorden** Norway
75 S6 **Melfort** Saskatchewan Canada
128 B2 **Melgaço** Portugal
128 D2 **Melgar de Fernamental** Spain
192 F2 **Melgunovka** *watercourse* Russian Federation
76 I1 **Meliadine Lake** Nunavut Canada
124 E5 **Melide** Switzerland
133 C5 **Meliki** Greece
128 E6 **Melilla** *autonomous Spanish city* Africa
132 C3 **Melinești** Romania
108 B3 **Melinka** Chile
197 H4 **Melintang, Danau** *lake* Indonesia
133 D8 **Melissa, Akra** *cape* Greece
136 E3 **Melitopol'** Ukraine
125 H3 **Melk** Austria
161 F3 **Melka Guba** Ethiopia
139 E3 **Melksham** Wiltshire England UK
130 D4 **Mella** *watercourse* Italy
121 N3 **Mellakoski** Finland
129 G6 **Mellakou** Algeria
156 C5 **Mellam** Sudan
122 G3 **Mellan Fryken** *bay* Sweden
120 H5 **Mellanfjärden** *bay* Sweden
120 K5 **Mellansel** Sweden
120 I5 **Mellansjö** Sweden
126 D3 **Melle** France
124 E1 **Melle** Germany
82 F3 **Mellen** Wisconsin USA
216 E4 **Mellenbye** WA Australia
120 M4 **Mellerstön** *island* Sweden
81 P4 **Mellette** South Dakota USA
131 F9 **Mellieħa** Malta
156 D5 **Mellit** Sudan
58 E2 **Mellor Glacier** *ice* Antarctica
138 E3 **Mells** Somerset England UK
122 I4 **Mellstaby** Sweden
124 E1 **Mellum** *island* Germany
141 F2 **Melmerby** Cumbria England UK
141 G2 **Melmerby** North Yorkshire England UK
125 H2 **Mělník** Czech Republic
123 O2 **Mel'nikovo** Russian Federation
123 O3 **Mel'nitsy** Russian Federation
107 H5 **Melo** Uruguay
163 G2 **Meloco** Mozambique
198 B6 **Melolo** Indonesia
136 G3 **Melovoye** Ukraine
120 H3 **Meløya** *island* Norway
72 D5 **Melozitna** *watercourse* Alaska USA
120 inset **Melrakkanes** *cape* Iceland
218 D5 **Melrose** SA Australia
216 G3 **Melrose** WA Australia
79 G10 **Melrose** Nova Scotia Canada
142 F5 **Melrose** Scottish Borders Scotland UK
81 R4 **Melrose** Minnesota USA
85 K3 **Melrose** New Mexico USA
81 L3 **Melstone** Montana USA
121 N3 **Meltaus** Finland
120 G5 **Meltingvatnet** *lake* Norway
218 D5 **Melton** SA Australia
218 G7 **Melton** Vic. Australia
87 I3 **Melton Hill Lake** Tennessee USA
139 G2 **Melton Mowbray** Leicester England UK
121 N3 **Meltosjärvi** Finland
163 G2 **Meluco** Mozambique
124 B3 **Melun** France
142 C3 **Melvaig** Highland Scotland UK
82 D7 **Melvern Lake** Kansas USA
142 E2 **Melvich** Highland Scotland UK
75 T7 **Melville** Saskatchewan Canada
86 F5 **Melville** Louisiana USA
215 H3 **Melville, Cape** Qld Australia
195 H6 **Melville, Cape** Philippines
78 I6 **Melville, Lake** Newfoundland and Labrador Canada
214 D2 **Melville Bay** NT Australia
72 G5 **Melville Hills** Northwest Territories Canada
214 A1 **Melville Island** NT Australia
72 H3 **Melville Island** Northwest Territories/Nunavut Canada
73 K5 **Melville Peninsula** Nunavut Canada
86 B5 **Melvin** Texas USA
143 D2 **Melvin, Lough** *lake* Ireland
124 E5 **Melzo** Italy
197 G4 **Memala** Indonesia
163 H2 **Memba** Mozambique
199 F4 **Memberamo** *watercourse* Indonesia
198 A6 **Memboro** Indonesia
128 C4 **Membrío** Spain
123 M4 **Mēmele** *watercourse* Latvia
124 F4 **Memmingen** Germany
196 F3 **Mempawah** Indonesia
82 E6 **Memphis** Missouri USA
86 F3 **Memphis** Tennessee USA
86 A3 **Memphis** Texas USA
83 O4 **Memphremagog, Lake** Quebec Canada
136 E2 **Mena** Ukraine
86 D3 **Mena** Arkansas USA
218 F4 **Mena Murtee** NSW Australia
215 H8 **Mena Park** Qld Australia
81 R3 **Menahga** Minnesota USA
140 D3 **Menai Bridge** Gwynedd Wales UK
155 G5 **Ménaka** Mali
198 C4 **Menanga** Indonesia
163 I4 **Menarandra** *watercourse* Madagascar
86 B5 **Menard** Texas USA
51 G14 **Menard Fracture Zone** *underwater feature* Pacific Ocean
128 D4 **Menasalbas** Spain
196 E4 **Mendanau** *island* Indonesia
196 E3 **Mendarik** *island* Indonesia
197 G4 **Mendawai** Indonesia
197 G4 **Mendawai** *watercourse* Indonesia
126 F4 **Mende** France
161 F2 **Mendebo** *plain* Ethiopia
56 S1 **Mendeleyev Abyssal Plain** *underwater feature* Arctic Ocean
56 S1 **Mendeleyev Ridge** *underwater feature* Arctic Ocean
127 H1 **Menden** Germany
86 G5 **Mendenhall** Mississippi USA
72 C7 **Mendenhall, Cape** Alaska USA
133 E6 **Menderes** Turkey
129 G6 **Mendes** Algeria
103 D8 **Mendes** Brazil
89 F3 **Méndez** Mexico
75 Q7 **Mendham** Saskatchewan Canada
161 F2 **Mendī** Ethiopia
138 E3 **Mendip Hills** England UK
216 G4 **Mendleyarri** WA Australia
85 I7 **Mendoceño** Mexico
80 C6 **Mendocino, Cape** California USA
80 D7 **Mendocino, Lake** California USA
53 R3 **Mendocino Fracture Zone** *underwater feature* Pacific Ocean
82 I5 **Mendon** Michigan USA
80 E8 **Mendota** California USA
82 G5 **Mendota, Lake** Wisconsin USA
106 D5 **Mendoza** Argentina
106 D5 **Mendoza** *admin. area* Argentina
104 C3 **Mendoza** Peru
133 E6 **Menemen** Turkey
126 F1 **Menen** Belgium
222 4 **Meneng Point** Nauru
133 E8 **Menetes** Greece
131 E8 **Menfi** Italy
159 G3 **Meng** *watercourse* Cameroon
188 F4 **Meng Jiang** *watercourse* Guangxi Zhuangzu Zizhiqu China
188 E3 **Meng Jiang** *watercourse* Guizhou China
191 I6 **Meng Shan** *range* Shandong China
197 G2 **Mengalum** *island* Malaysia
189 G1 **Mengcheng** Anhui China
124 E3 **Mengen** Germany
196 E5 **Menggala** Indonesia
197 G4 **Mengkatip** Indonesia
198 B4 **Mengkoka, Gunung** *mountain* Indonesia
188 D4 **Mengla** Yunnan China
188 C4 **Menglang** Yunnan China
188 C4 **Menglian** Yunnan China
188 D4 **Menglie** Yunnan China
188 C4 **Mengmao Zhen** Yunnan China
188 C4 **Mengmeng** Yunnan China
159 G4 **Mengong** Cameroon
188 F4 **Mengshan** Guangxi Zhuangzu Zizhiqu China
189 F3 **Mengshan** *mountain* Hunan China
188 C4 **Mengsuo** Yunnan China
191 I6 **Mengyin** Shandong China
189 F1 **Mengzhou** Henan China
77 V5 **Menihek** Newfoundland and Labrador Canada
77 V5 **Menihek Lakes** Newfoundland and Labrador Canada
218 F5 **Menindee** NSW Australia
218 F5 **Menindee Lake** NSW Australia
135 Z5 **Menkere** Russian Federation
81 Q5 **Menno** South Dakota USA
142 E5 **Mennock** Dumfries and Galloway Scotland UK
86 B2 **Meno** Oklahoma USA
133 C5 **Menoikion Oros** *range* Greece
82 H4 **Menominee** *watercourse* Michigan USA
162 C2 **Menongue** Angola
128 C5 **Menor, Isla** *island* Spain
129 I4 **Menorca (Minorca)** *island* Spain
155 F2 **Menouarar** Algeria
127 G4 **Mens** France
197 H3 **Mensalong** Indonesia
135 AD8 **Men'shikova, Ostrov** *island* Russian Federation
141 G3 **Menston** West Yorkshire England UK
196 D3 **Mentakab** Malaysia
197 H3 **Mentarang** *watercourse* Indonesia
196 C4 **Mentawai, Kepulauan** *islands* Indonesia
196 C4 **Mentawai, Selat** *strait* Indonesia
104 B4 **Mentiroso, Islas** *islands* Peru
196 E4 **Mentok** Indonesia
127 H5 **Menton** France
215 G6 **Mentone** Qld Australia
83 K6 **Mentor** Ohio USA
106 E6 **Menucos** Argentina
197 G2 **Menumbok** Malaysia
197 H3 **Menyapa, Gunung** *mountain* Indonesia
155 H1 **Menzel Bourguiba** Tunisia
131 D9 **Menzel Chaker** Tunisia
131 C8 **Menzel Jemil** Tunisia
155 I1 **Menzel Temime** Tunisia
216 G4 **Menzies** WA Australia
58 E2 **Menzies, Mount** Antarctica
124 E4 **Menziken** Switzerland
139 H3 **Meopham** Kent England UK
88 D2 **Meoqui** Mexico
160 A5 **Mepala** Angola
182 D5 **Mepists'karo, Mt** *mountain* Georgia
163 F2 **Meponda** Mozambique
124 D1 **Meppel** Netherlands
124 D1 **Meppen** Germany
129 F3 **Mequinenza, Embalse de** *lake* Spain
126 E3 **Mer** France
86 F4 **Mer Rouge** Louisiana USA
197 H3 **Merah** Indonesia
219 I4 **Merah North** NSW Australia
120 G5 **Meråker** Norway
217 M4 **Meramangye, Lake** SA Australia
82 F7 **Meramec** *watercourse* Missouri USA
124 F4 **Merano** Italy
79 K9 **Merasheen Island** Newfoundland and Labrador Canada
120 L3 **Merasjärvi** Sweden
130 C4 **Merate** Italy
162 D4 **Meratswe** *watercourse* Botswana
197 G4 **Meratus, Pegunungan** *range* Indonesia
196 D3 **Merbau** Indonesia
100 C5 **Merced** Ecuador
80 E8 **Merced** California USA

106 D4 **Mercedario, Cerro** *mountain* Argentina
107 G4 **Mercedes** Argentina
107 G5 **Mercedes** Argentina
107 G5 **Mercedes** Uruguay
220 F3 **Mercer** New Zealand
220 F3 **Mercury Bay** New Zealand
220 F3 **Mercury Islands (Iles d'Haussez)** New Zealand
73 M6 **Mercy, Cape** Nunavut Canada
126 C2 **Merdrignac** France
141 F3 **Mere** Cheshire England UK
139 E3 **Mere** Wiltshire England UK
222 7 **Méré Lava** *island* Vanuatu
218 G7 **Meredith** Vic. Australia
108 E5 **Meredith, Cape** Falkland Islands
85 L3 **Meredith, Lake** Texas USA
161 H3 **Mereeg** Somalia
136 F3 **Merefa** Ukraine
220 F3 **Meremere** New Zealand
220 F4 **Meremere** New Zealand
132 D3 **Mereniidesus** Romania
126 F2 **Méréville** France
182 F3 **Mergenevo** Kazakhstan
Mergui *see* **Myeik** Myanmar
159 G2 **Méri** Cameroon
130 B4 **Méribel** France
133 E5 **Meriç** Turkey
81 K1 **Merid** Saskatchewan Canada
89 H4 **Mérida** Mexico
128 C4 **Mérida** Spain
100 D2 **Mérida** Venezuela
100 D2 **Mérida** *admin. area* Venezuela
100 D2 **Mérida, Cordillera de** *range* Venezuela
139 F2 **Meriden** West Midlands England UK
83 O6 **Meriden** Connecticut USA
81 R5 **Meriden** Iowa USA
80 G5 **Meridian** Idaho USA
86 G4 **Meridian** Mississippi USA
85 C5 **Meridian** Texas USA
81 N7 **Meridith, Lake** Colorado USA
155 F2 **Meridja** Algeria
126 D4 **Mérignac** France
126 E5 **Mérigon** France
123 K2 **Merikarvia** Finland
125 L2 **Měřín** Czech Republic
215 J6 **Merinda** Qld Australia
120 F6 **Meringsdalen** Norway
215 H7 **Merino Downs** Qld Australia
198 E2 **Merir** *island* Palau
197 G3 **Merit** Malaysia
219 I1 **Merivale** Qld Australia
219 H1 **Merivale** *watercourse* Qld Australia
222 5 **Merizo** Guam
86 A4 **Merkel** Texas USA
123 M5 **Merkys** *watercourse* Lithuania
126 E1 **Merlimont-Plage** France
214 E4 **Mermaid Reef** WA Australia
213 K1 **Mermaid Shoal** *reef* NT Australia
81 P6 **Merna** Nebraska USA
155 H1 **Merouana** Algeria
156 E4 **Merowe** Sudan
215 F5 **Merredin** WA Australia
82 E8 **Merriam Woods** Missouri USA
218 G7 **Merriang** Vic. Australia
142 D5 **Merrick** *mountain* Scotland UK
82 G4 **Merrill** Wisconsin USA
82 F4 **Merrillan** Wisconsin USA
81 O5 **Merriman** Nebraska USA
218 D5 **Merriton** SA Australia
74 K7 **Merritt** British Columbia Canada
81 O5 **Merritt Reservoir** Nebraska USA
219 J5 **Merriwa** NSW Australia
218 G5 **Merriwagga** NSW Australia
218 G5 **Merrowie** *watercourse* NSW Australia
219 I4 **Merrygoen** NSW Australia
86 E5 **Merryville** Louisiana USA
219 I3 **Merrywinebone** NSW Australia
129 F6 **Mers el Hadjad** Algeria
157 G5 **Mersa Fatma** Eritrea
125 G3 **Mersch** Luxembourg
127 H2 **Merseburg** Germany
139 H3 **Mersea Island** England UK
124 F2 **Merseburg** Germany
141 F3 **Mersey** *watercourse* England UK
196 D3 **Mersing** Malaysia
197 G3 **Mersing, Bukit** *mountain* Malaysia
123 L4 **Mērsrags** *cape* Latvia
186 D5 **Merta City** Rajasthan India
138 D2 **Merthyr Cynog** Powys Wales UK
138 D3 **Merthyr Tydfil** Merthyr Tydfil Wales UK
138 D3 **Merthyr Tydfil** *admin. area* Wales UK
128 C5 **Mértola** Portugal
139 F1 **Merton** Norfolk England UK
155 H2 **Mertoutek** Algeria
218 E3 **Merty Merty** SA Australia
58 J2 **Mertz Glacier Tongue** *ice* Antarctica
85 L5 **Mertzon** Texas USA
124 B3 **Méru** France
161 F3 **Meru** Kenya
161 F4 **Meru, Mount** *volcano* Tanzania
197 H4 **Meruat, Tanjung** *cape* Indonesia
101 F3 **Merume Mountains** Guyana
197 H2 **Merutai** Malaysia
140 B4 **Mervyn** Ireland
88 F2 **Merweville** South Africa
80 D4 **Merwin, Lake** Washington USA
124 B3 **Méry** France
58 U2 **Merz Peninsula** Antarctica
135 E5 **Merzifon** Turkey
124 D3 **Merzig** Germany
196 D3 **Mesa** Indonesia
84 G4 **Mesa** Arizona USA
80 F3 **Mesa** Washington USA
85 I7 **Mesa de Coloradas** Mexico
85 H6 **Mesa Tres Rios** Mexico
82 E3 **Mesabi Range** Minnesota USA
77 P7 **Mésaconane, Pointe** Quebec Canada
131 G6 **Mesagne** Italy
196 E3 **Mesanak** *island* Indonesia
160 D4 **Mesaraba** Democratic Republic of Congo
88 E1 **Mescalero Ridge** *range* New Mexico USA
120 J4 **Meselefors** Sweden
222 6a **Meseong** *island* Federated States of Micronesia
128 D3 **Meseta** *region* Spain
160 C3 **Mesetas** Colombia
77 R7 **Mesgouez, Lac** *lake* Quebec Canada
85 I4 **Mesilla** New Mexico USA
131 B9 **Meskiana** Algeria
126 J5 **Mesnières-en-Bray** France
130 C3 **Mesocco** Switzerland
130 E4 **Mesola** Italy
133 B6 **Mesolongi** Greece
133 B6 **Mesolongiou, Limnothalassa** *bay* Greece
133 A6 **Mesongi** Greece
109 11a **Mesopotamia** St Vincent and the Grenadines
120 H3 **Mesøy** Norway
84 E2 **Mesquite** Nevada USA
86 C4 **Mesquite** Texas USA
84 E3 **Mesquite Lake** California USA
179 H2 **Meşr** Iran
155 G2 **Messaad** Algeria
163 G2 **Messalo** *watercourse* Mozambique
126 D5 **Messanges** France
120 L3 **Messaure** Sweden
120 G6 **Messelt** Norway
108 A4 **Messier, Canal** *strait* Chile
131 F7 **Messina** Italy
133 C7 **Messiniakos Kolpos** *bay* Greece
127 I3 **Meßkirch** Germany
134 Q5 **Messoyakha** *watercourse* Russian Federation
130 C2 **Meßstetten** Germany
133 C3 **Mesta** Bulgaria
133 C5 **Mesta** *watercourse* Bulgaria
124 F1 **Mestlin** Germany
130 G1 **Město Albrechtice** Czech Republic
125 I3 **Město Libavá** Czech Republic
133 D6 **Meston, Akra** *cape* Greece
130 E4 **Mestre** Italy
196 E4 **Mesuji** *watercourse* Indonesia
124 C4 **Mesvres** France
100 C4 **Meta** *admin. area* Colombia
91 G6 **Meta, Río** *watercourse* Colombia/Venezuela
77 U1 **Meta Incognita Peninsula** Nunavut Canada
79 K8 **Meta Pond** Newfoundland and Labrador Canada
132 C2 **Metaliferi, Munţii** *range* Romania
80 G2 **Metaline Falls** Washington USA
130 H5 **Metaljka** Montenegro
123 P3 **Metallostroy** Russian Federation
106 E3 **Metán** Argentina
197 G4 **Metangai** Indonesia
163 F2 **Metangula** Mozambique
132 A4 **Metanjac** Montenegro
163 G2 **Metarica** Mozambique
133 E5 **Metaxades** Greece
78 G6 **Metchin** *watercourse* Newfoundland and Labrador Canada
156 F5 **Metema** Ethiopia
54 F9 **Meteor Seamount** *underwater feature* Southern Ocean
133 B6 **Meteora** *monastery* Greece
89 F5 **Metepec** Mexico
199 I4 **Meteran** Papua New Guinea
124 B2 **Météren** France
90 E5 **Metetí** Panama
141 H3 **Metheringham** Lincolnshire England UK
142 F3 **Methlick** Aberdeenshire Scotland UK
221 D6 **Methven** New Zealand
142 E4 **Methven** Perth and Kinross Scotland UK
139 H2 **Methwold** Norfolk England UK
76 J8 **Metionga Lake** Ontario Canada
74 M3 **Metis** Alberta Canada
75 P6 **Metiskow** Alberta Canada
163 G2 **Metoro** Mozambique
196 E5 **Metro** Indonesia
121 P4 **Metsäkylä** Finland
123 M4 **Metsapoole** Estonia
104 C3 **Metsoquiari Alto** Peru
87 J4 **Metter** Georgia USA
216 F7 **Mettler** WA Australia
161 F2 **Metu** Ethiopia
197 G3 **Metulang** Indonesia
197 H3 **Metut** Indonesia
127 H2 **Metz** France
130 B2 **Metzervisse** France
126 C2 **Meu** *watercourse* France
196 C2 **Meulaboh** Indonesia
127 H2 **Meurthe** *watercourse* France
127 G1 **Meuse** *watercourse* Belgium
127 G2 **Meuse** *watercourse* France
138 C4 **Mevagissey** Cornwall England UK
188 D1 **Mewa** Sichuan China
141 G3 **Mexborough** South Yorkshire England UK
86 C5 **Mexia** Texas USA
102 B3 **Mexiana, Ilha** *island* Brazil
88 B1 **Mexicali** Mexico
88 D2 **Mexican Hat** Utah USA
84 F4 **Mexican Water** Arizona USA
88 C5 **Mexico** *country* North America
82 F7 **Mexico** Missouri USA
89 F5 **México** *admin. area* Mexico
90 B1 **Mexico, Gulf of** Caribbean
50 I7 **Mexico Basin** *underwater feature* Gulf of Mexico
México City *see* **Ciudad de México** Mexico
142 E2 **Mey** Highland Scotland UK
182 E6 **Meyāneh** Iran
179 K2 **Meydān Shahr** Afghanistan
124 G1 **Meyenburg** Germany
83 L7 **Meyersdale** Pennsylvania USA
127 G4 **Meylan** France
138 C2 **Meyllteyrn** Gwynedd Wales UK
179 J2 **Meymaneh** Afghanistan
178 G2 **Meymeh** Iran
135 AK6 **Meynypil'gyno** Russian Federation
159 G4 **Meyo Centre** Cameroon
81 L2 **Meyronne** Saskatchewan Canada
124 B5 **Meyrueis** France
89 F6 **Mezcalapa** *lake* Mexico
126 F5 **Mèze** France
134 J3 **Mezen'** Russian Federation
134 J5 **Mezen'** *watercourse* Russian Federation
126 G4 **Mézenc, Mount** *mountain* France
134 J5 **Mezenskaya Guba** *bay* Russian Federation
135 U4 **Mezenskiy** Russian Federation
134 L4 **Mezhdusharskiy, Ostrov** *island* Russian Federation
182 H2 **Mezhozernyy** Russian Federation
74 G4 **Meziadin Lake** British Columbia Canada
125 H4 **Mežica** Slovenia
126 G4 **Mézilhac** France
126 E4 **Mézin** France
132 B2 **Mezőcsát** Hungary
125 K4 **Mezőkeresztes** Hungary
125 K4 **Mezzano** Italy
130 E4 **Mezzogoro** Italy
161 E4 **Mfangano Island** Uganda
159 G4 **Mfou** Cameroon
123 P3 **Mga** Russian Federation
134 AD8 **Mgachi** Russian Federation
142 B5 **Mhàil, Rubh' a'** *cape* Scotland UK
187 D8 **Mhasvad** Maharashtra India
142 D3 **Mhòr, Loch** *lake* Scotland UK
187 D6 **Mhow** Madhya Pradesh India
181 G5 **Mi** *watercourse* Myanmar
182 G5 **Mi-shima** *island* Japan
194 F2 **Mia Sơn** Vietnam
142 B2 **Miabhaig** Na h-Eileanan Siar Scotland UK
125 L2 **Miączyn** Poland
89 F5 **Miahuatlán** Mexico
159 H3 **Miaméré** Central African Republic
84 G4 **Miami** Arizona USA
87 K8 **Miami** Florida USA
82 D8 **Miami** Oklahoma USA
86 A3 **Miami** Texas USA
87 K8 **Miami Beach** Florida USA
82 I7 **Miamisburg** Ohio USA
178 F3 **Mian Āb** Iran
179 L3 **Mian Channun** Pakistan
189 F1 **Mianchi** Henan China
178 F2 **Miāndoāb** Iran
182 E7 **Miandowab** Iran
197 I2 **Miangas** *island* Indonesia
195 J6 **Miangas (Indonesia)** *island* Indonesia
188 D3 **Mianning** Sichuan China
179 L2 **Mianwali** Pakistan
188 D2 **Mianyang** Sichuan China
188 D2 **Mianzhu** Sichuan China
188 H4 **Miaoli** Taiwan China
163 I3 **Miarinarivo** Madagascar
182 H2 **Miass** Russian Federation
122 I5 **Miastko** Poland
160 C5 **Mibalaie** Democratic Republic of Congo
132 D2 **Mica** Romania
106 D2 **Mica, Cerro de** *mountain* Chile
74 L6 **Mica Creek** British Columbia Canada
74 L6 **Mica Peak** British Columbia Canada
91 F2 **Micarro, Sierra de** *range* Cuba
163 G3 **Micaúne** Mozambique
87 J5 **Micosukee, Lake** Florida USA
199 H5 **Michael, Mount** Papua New Guinea
125 K3 **Michalovce** Slovakia
125 L1 **Michałowo** Poland
75 Q4 **Michel** Saskatchewan Canada
124 F2 **Michelau** Germany
127 I2 **Michelstadt** Germany
188 C3 **Micheng** Yunnan China
75 O7 **Michichi** Alberta Canada
82 H3 **Michigamme Reservoir** Michigan USA
70 **Michigan** *admin. area* USA
82 H4 **Michigan, Lake** Michigan USA
82 H6 **Michigan City** Indiana USA
78 I5 **Michinappi Lake** Newfoundland and Labrador Canada
108 B3 **Michinmahuida, Volcán** *volcano* Chile
82 I3 **Michipicoton** Ontario Canada
82 I3 **Michipicoton Bay** Ontario Canada
82 H3 **Michipicoton Island** Ontario Canada
88 E5 **Michoacán** *admin. area* Mexico
182 C3 **Michurinsk** Russian Federation
120 L5 **Mickelsörarna** *island* Finland
120 L4 **Mickelsträsk** Sweden
141 F2 **Mickle Fell** *mountain* England UK
141 G3 **Micklefield** West Yorkshire England UK
109 I3 **Micoud** St Lucia
199 I2 **Micronesia, Federated States of** *country* Oceania
50 N7 **Mid-Atlantic Ridge** *underwater feature* Atlantic Ocean
55 M5 **Mid-Indian Basin** *underwater feature* Indian Ocean
54 K5 **Mid-Indian Ridge** *underwater feature* Indian Ocean
52 M6 **Mid-Pacific Mountains** *underwater feature* Pacific Ocean
52 N6 **Mid-Pacific Seamount** *underwater feature* Pacific Ocean
142 inset **Mid Yell** Shetland Scotland UK
196 E3 **Midai** *island* Indonesia
81 N2 **Midale** Saskatchewan Canada
142 F1 **Midbea** Orkney Islands Scotland UK
124 B2 **Middelburg** Netherlands
162 D6 **Middelburg** South Africa
162 E5 **Middelburg** South Africa
124 C2 **Middelharnis** Netherlands
124 F1 **Middelkerke** Belgium
214 F4 **Middle** *watercourse* Qld Australia
80 E6 **Middle Alkali Lake** California USA
53 W6 **Middle America Trench** *underwater feature* Pacific Ocean
194 B4 **Middle Andaman** *island* Andaman and Nicobar Islands India
79 J8 **Middle Arm** Newfoundland and Labrador Canada
91 G2 **Middle Caicos** *island* Turks and Caicos Islands
80 E7 **Middle Fork Feather** *watercourse* California USA
75 S4 **Middle Foster Lake** Saskatchewan Canada
215 K6 **Middle Island** Qld Australia
216 H7 **Middle Island** WA Australia
109 I9 **Middle Island** St Kitts and Nevis
210 inset **Middle Islet** Ashmore Reef and Cartier Island Australia
75 S6 **Middle Lake** Saskatchewan Canada
214 G1 **Middle Peak** Qld Australia
139 F3 **Middle Winterslow** Wiltshire England UK
81 R2 **Middlebro** Manitoba Canada
211 inset **Middlegate** Norfolk Island Australia
221 D7 **Middlemarch** New Zealand
138 E4 **Middlemarsh** Dorset England UK
215 J7 **Middlemount** Qld Australia
141 G2 **Middlesbrough** Middlesbrough England UK
141 G2 **Middlesbrough** *admin. area* England UK
141 G2 **Middlesmoor** North Yorkshire England UK
214 F7 **Middleton** Qld Australia
79 F10 **Middleton** Nova Scotia Canada
141 F2 **Middleton** Cumbria England UK
141 G3 **Middleton** North Yorkshire England UK
139 F2 **Middleton** Warwickshire England UK
86 G3 **Middleton** Tennessee USA
82 G5 **Middleton** Wisconsin USA
139 F2 **Middleton Cheney** Northamptonshire England UK
84 A1 **Middletown** California USA
83 N6 **Middletown** New York USA
82 I7 **Middletown** Ohio USA
155 F2 **Midelt** Morocco
139 G4 **Midhurst** West Sussex England UK
125 F5 **Midi, Canal du** *watercourse* France
126 F4 **Midi-Pyrénées** *admin. area* France
126 E4 **Midland** WA Australia
83 L4 **Midland** Ontario Canada
82 I5 **Midland** Michigan USA
81 O4 **Midland** South Dakota USA
85 K5 **Midland** Texas USA
162 E3 **Midlands** *admin. area* Zimbabwe
142 E5 **Midlothian** *admin. area* Scotland UK
122 E6 **Midlum** Germany
80 H1 **Midnapore** Alberta Canada
163 I4 **Midongy Atsimo** Madagascar
126 D5 **Midou** *watercourse* France
126 D5 **Midouze** *watercourse* France
124 C1 **Midsland** Netherlands
122 D1 **Midsund** Norway
142 F4 **Midtown of Barras** Aberdeenshire Scotland UK
80 G4 **Midvale** Idaho USA
74 L8 **Midway** British Columbia Canada
87 K5 **Midway** Georgia USA
52 O5 **Midway Islands** *unincorporated US territory* Pacific Ocean
86 C3 **Midwest City** Oklahoma USA
136 G6 **Midyat** Turkey
159 G4 **Midyobo** Equatorial Guinea
132 C4 **Midzhur** *mountain* Serbia
125 K2 **Miechów** Poland
125 H1 **Miedwie, Jezioro** *lake* Poland
125 I2 **Międzyrzec Podlaski** Poland
121 M3 **Miekojärvi** *lake* Sweden
126 E5 **Miélan** France
125 K2 **Mielec** Poland
161 F5 **Miembwe** Tanzania
122 H4 **Mien** *lake* Sweden
219 R11 **Miena** Tas. Australia
178 C3 **Mizpe Ramon** Israel
218 G7 **Miepoll** Vic. Australia
89 F3 **Mier** Mexico
128 D2 **Mieres** Spain
182 D2 **Miesau** Germany
130 D3 **Miesbach** Germany
161 G2 **Mī'ēso** Ethiopia
125 I1 **Mieszków** Poland
125 H1 **Mieszkowice** Poland
122 O2 **Miettilä** Finland
127 K5 **Migliano** Italy
126 E3 **Migné** France
130 C5 **Mignole, Pointe di** *cape* Corsica France
161 E4 **Migori** Kenya
89 F5 **Miguel Alemán, Presa** *lake* Mexico
102 D4 **Miguel Alves** Brazil
88 E3 **Miguel Auza** Mexico
102 D5 **Miguel Calmon** Brazil
128 D4 **Miguel de la Madrid, Presa** *lake* Mexico
88 C3 **Miguel Hidalgo, Presa** *lake* Mexico
103 B8 **Miguelópolis** Brazil
132 B3 **Mihai Bravu** Romania
132 E3 **Mihajlovac** Serbia
133 G6 **Mihalıççık** Turkey
132 D2 **Mihesu de Câmpie** Romania
159 H3 **Mihi** *watercourse* Central African Republic
161 F6 **Mihumo Chini** Tanzania
123 N5 **Mikhalishki** Belarus
182 F5 **Mikhaylov Island** Antarctica
58 F2 **Mikhaylovka** Kazakhstan
183 M5 **Mikhaylovka** Kyrgyzstan
136 E2 **Mikhaylovka** Russian Federation
182 D3 **Mikhaylovka** Russian Federation
132 G3 **Mikhaylovskiy Pervaya** Ukraine
183 M3 **Mikhaylovskiy** Russian Federation
133 D5 **Miki** Greece
121 P4 **Mikitänjärvi** *lake* Finland
121 M4 **Mikkeli** Finland
120 K1 **Mikkelvik** Norway
75 N4 **Mikkwa** *watercourse* Alberta Canada
133 C3 **Mikosszéplak** Hungary
133 B5 **Mikra Prespa, Limni** *lake* Greece
133 C5 **Mikra Volvi** Greece
133 C6 **Mikrón Elevtherokhórion** Greece
123 P5 **Mikulino** Russian Federation
182 D1 **Mikulintsy** Ukraine
161 F5 **Mikumi** Tanzania
134 L6 **Mikun'** Russian Federation
193 H4 **Mikuni** Japan
193 H4 **Mikuni Sanmyaku** Japan
193 H5 **Mikura-jima** *island* Japan
218 E7 **Mil Lel** SA Australia
155 H1 **Mila** Algeria
219 Q10 **Milabena** Tas. Australia
82 E4 **Milaca** Minnesota USA
187 C10 **Miladhunmadulu Atoll** Maldives
102 E4 **Milagres** Brazil
100 C4 **Milán** Colombia
Milan *see* **Milano** Italy
87 J4 **Milan** Georgia USA
86 C2 **Milan** Kansas USA
81 R4 **Milan** Minnesota USA
85 I3 **Milan** New Mexico USA
160 B5 **Milando** Angola
124 E5 **Milano (Milan)** Italy
133 E7 **Milas** Turkey
131 F7 **Milazzo** Italy
131 F7 **Milazzo, Capo di** *cape* Italy
81 Q4 **Milbank** South Dakota USA
74 G6 **Milbanke Sound** British Columbia Canada
83 R4 **Milbridge** Maine USA
75 R7 **Milden** Saskatchewan Canada
218 F6 **Mildura** Vic. Australia
157 G5 **Milē** Ethiopia
109 12 **Mile and a Quarter** Barbados
157 G5 **Milē Wenz** *watercourse* Ethiopia
178 F2 **Mileh Sar** Iran
138 A2 **Milehouse** Ireland
125 L1 **Milejczyce** Poland
161 F6 **Milepa** Mozambique
219 J2 **Miles** Qld Australia
86 A5 **Miles** Texas USA
81 M3 **Miles City** Montana USA
182 D1 **Mileshino** Russian Federation
75 S8 **Milestone** Saskatchewan Canada
143 D4 **Milestone** Ireland
127 L2 **Milevsko** Czech Republic
143 E1 **Milford** Ireland
83 N7 **Milford** Delaware USA
81 Q6 **Milford** Nebraska USA
86 C4 **Milford** Texas USA
80 I7 **Milford** Utah USA
138 B3 **Milford Haven** Pembrokeshire Wales UK
81 Q7 **Milford Lake** Kansas USA
221 B7 **Milford Sound** New Zealand
221 B7 **Milford Sound** New Zealand
214 F5 **Milgarra** Qld Australia
216 F2 **Milgun** WA Australia
223 I5 **Mili Atoll** Marshall Islands
155 G1 **Miliana** Algeria
130 H4 **Miliči** Bosnia and Herzegovina
213 K1 **Milikapiti** NT Australia
213 K1 **Milingimbi** NT Australia
131 C6 **Milis** Sardinia Italy
130 H5 **Miljevina** Bosnia and Herzegovina
75 P8 **Milk** *watercourse* Alberta Canada
75 Q8 **Milk** *watercourse* Montana USA
156 E4 **Milk, Wādī El** *watercourse* Sudan
75 Q8 **Milk River** Alberta Canada
218 F5 **Milkengay, Lake** NSW Australia
80 D4 **Mill City** Oregon USA
139 I2 **Mill Green** Norfolk England UK
83 M6 **Mill Hall** Pennsylvania USA
58 T2 **Mill Inlet** *bay* Antarctica
58 G2 **Mill Island** Antarctica
73 L6 **Mill Island** Nunavut Canada
109 18 **Mill Reef** Antigua and Barbuda
215 I6 **Millaroo** Qld Australia
126 F5 **Millas** France
126 F4 **Millau** France
73 J9 **Mille Lacs, Lac des** *lake* Ontario Canada
82 E3 **Mille Lacs Lake** Minnesota USA
87 J4 **Milledgeville** Georgia USA
81 P4 **Miller** South Dakota USA
86 H2 **Millersville** Georgia USA
82 E4 **Miller** Nebraska USA
81 P4 **Miller** South Dakota USA
182 C4 **Millerovo** Russian Federation
214 E5 **Millers** *watercourse* Qld Australia
218 E3 **Millers** *watercourse* SA Australia
221 C7 **Millers Flat** New Zealand
82 I7 **Millersburg** Kentucky USA
83 K6 **Millersburg** Ohio USA
83 M6 **Millerstown** Pennsylvania USA
80 E6 **Millerton Lake** California USA
75 O6 **Millet** Alberta Canada
142 C5 **Millport** Scotland UK
126 F4 **Millevaches** France
143 F2 **Millford** Armagh Northern Ireland UK
142 C5 **Millhouse** Argyll and Bute Scotland UK
86 C5 **Milliean** Texas USA
140 E1 **Milliganton** Dumfries and Galloway Scotland UK
81 M6 **Milliken** Colorado USA
86 H2 **Millington** Tennessee USA
73 M9 **Millinocket** Maine USA
104 D6 **Milliri, Cerro** *mountain* Bolivia
143 G2 **Millisle** Ards Northern Ireland UK
219 J2 **Millmerran** Qld Australia
140 E2 **Millom** Cumbria England UK
86 G4 **Millport** Alabama USA
143 F4 **Millroad** Ireland
216 G3 **Millrose** WA Australia
86 G5 **Millry** Alabama USA
81 L5 **Mills** Wyoming USA
74 L2 **Mills Lake** Northwest Territories Canada
143 C4 **Millstreet** Ireland
141 F2 **Millthrop** Cumbria England UK
140 B4 **Milltown** Ireland
143 B4 **Milltown** Ireland
140 B2 **Milltown** Armagh Northern Ireland UK
143 G2 **Milltown** Larne Northern Ireland UK
140 B2 **Milltown** Newry and Mourne Northern Ireland UK
79 K9 **Milltown-Head of Bay d'Espoir** Newfoundland and Labrador Canada
143 C4 **Milltown Malbay** Ireland
214 F5 **Millungera** Qld Australia
86 E4 **Millwood Lake** Arkansas USA
86 E4 **Milly Milly** WA Australia
215 K7 **Milman** Qld Australia
128 D2 **Milmarcos** Spain
130 G5 **Milna** Croatia
142 E4 **Milnathort** Perth and Kinross Scotland UK
199 I6 **Milne Bay** Papua New Guinea
87 I4 **Milner** Georgia USA
78 E6 **Milner Lake** Newfoundland and Labrador Canada
81 Q1 **Milner Ridge** Manitoba Canada
85 K4 **Milnesand** New Mexico USA
141 F2 **Milnthorpe** Cumbria England UK
218 G1 **Milo** Qld Australia
75 O7 **Milo** Alberta Canada
83 R3 **Milo** Maine USA
158 C3 **Milo** *watercourse* Guinea
161 E5 **Milo** Tanzania
83 Q4 **Milo** Maine USA
132 B4 **Miločaj** Serbia
84 inset **Milolii** Hawai'i USA
133 D7 **Milos** Greece
133 D7 **Milos** *island* Greece
133 A5 **Milot** Albania
125 M1 **Milovidy** Belarus
125 J3 **Miłówka** Poland
218 G3 **Milparinka** NSW Australia
85 I8 **Milpas Viejas** Mexico
80 E8 **Milpitas** California USA
142 F5 **Milsington** Scottish Borders Scotland UK
79 F10 **Milton** Nova Scotia Canada
83 L5 **Milton** Ontario Canada
221 C8 **Milton** New Zealand
140 D2 **Milton** Dumfries and Galloway Scotland UK
142 D3 **Milton** Highland Scotland UK
142 D3 **Milton** Highland Scotland UK
142 E4 **Milton** Perth and Kinross Scotland UK
86 H5 **Milton** Florida USA
82 E6 **Milton** Iowa USA
83 O4 **Milton** Vermont USA
139 G2 **Milton Keynes** Milton Keynes England UK
139 G2 **Milton Keynes** *admin. area* England UK
82 D3 **Miltona, Lake** Minnesota USA
81 Q7 **Miltonvale** Kansas USA
189 G3 **Miluo** Hunan China
82 H5 **Milwaukee** Wisconsin USA
182 D3 **Milyakburra** NT Australia
183 L4 **Milybulak** Kazakhstan
199 J5 **Mimias, Cape** Papua New Guinea
217 M3 **Mimili** SA Australia
76 K7 **Miminiska Lake** Ontario Canada
126 D4 **Mimizan** France
126 D4 **Mimizan-Plage** France
159 G5 **Mimongo** Gabon
105 H6 **Mimoso** Brazil
103 D8 **Mimoso do Sul** Brazil
189 H3 **Min Jiang** *watercourse* Fujian China
188 D2 **Min Jiang** *watercourse* Sichuan China
188 F2 **Min'an** Hunan China
188 E3 **Min'gu** Guizhou China
88 E3 **Mina** Mexico
178 D5 **Miná** Saudi Arabia
77 W4 **Mina, Lac** *lake* Quebec Canada
90 D4 **Mina Columbus** Nicaragua
128 C5 **Mina de São Domingos** Portugal
106 D3 **Mina la Casualidad** Argentina
106 D6 **Mina La Escondida** Argentina
179 I4 **Mināb** Iran
76 F5 **Minago** *watercourse* Manitoba Canada
197 I3 **Minahasa, Semenanjung** *peninsula* Indonesia
123 P2 **Minala** Russian Federation
192 F5 **Minamata** Japan
216 G4 **Minara** WA Australia
133 F7 **Minare** Turkey
196 D3 **Minas** Indonesia
107 H5 **Minas** Uruguay
100 D4 **Minas, Cerros** *range* Colombia
100 B4 **Minas, Serranía de las** *range* Colombia
79 F10 **Minas Basin** Nova Scotia Canada
79 F10 **Minas Channel** Nova Scotia Canada
88 E3 **Minas de Barroterán** Mexico
107 H4 **Minas de Corrales** Uruguay
105 I5 **Minas Gerais** *admin. area* Brazil
103 D7 **Minas Novas** Brazil
89 G5 **Minatitlán** Mexico
88 D5 **Minatitlán** Mexico
181 H5 **Minbu** Myanmar
75 P6 **Minburn** Alberta Canada
181 G5 **Minbya** Myanmar
142 C2 **Minch, The** *strait* Scotland UK
88 E3 **Minchaca** Mexico
104 B1 **Minchana** Peru
216 F2 **Mindah Springs** WA Australia
195 J6 **Mindanao** *island* Philippines
181 G7 **Mindat** Myanmar
127 J2 **Mindel** *watercourse* Germany
127 J2 **Mindelheim** Germany
124 F3 **Mindelo** Cape Verde
164 4 **Minden** Ontario Canada
83 L4 **Minden** Nebraska USA
81 P6 **Mindibungu** WA Australia
213 I5 **Mindibungu** WA Australia
120 H4 **Mindlandet** *island* Norway
181 H5 **Mindon** Myanmar
218 F5 **Mindona, Lake** NSW Australia
195 I4 **Mindoro** *island* Philippines
192 F4 **Mine** *volcano* Japan
140 B4 **Mine Bridge** Ireland
143 E5 **Mine Head** *cape* Ireland
138 D3 **Minehead** Somerset England UK
103 A7 **Mineiros** Brazil
131 F8 **Mineo** Italy
86 B4 **Mineral Wells** Texas USA
130 D4 **Minerbe** Italy
105 F5 **Mineros** Bolivia
80 I7 **Minersville** Utah USA
184 E5 **Ming-tieh-kai Ho** *watercourse* Xinjiang Uygur Zizhiqu China
160 D6 **Minga** Democratic Republic of Congo
163 F2 **Minga** Zambia
182 E6 **Mingäçevir Su Anbari** *lake* Azerbaijan
159 I3 **Mingala** Central African Republic
79 F7 **Mingan** Quebec Canada
79 G7 **Mingan** *watercourse* Quebec Canada
218 E5 **Mingary** SA Australia
218 E4 **Mingary** *watercourse* SA Australia
183 K5 **Mingbuloq** Uzbekistan
215 I5 **Mingela** Qld Australia
216 D4 **Mingenew** WA Australia
214 E6 **Mingera** *watercourse* Qld Australia
189 F2 **Minggang** Anhui China
189 H2 **Mingguang** Anhui China
181 H4 **Mingin** Myanmar
220 G4 **Minginui** New Zealand
128 F4 **Minglanilla** Spain
191 K3 **Mingshui** Heilongjiang China
161 G6 **Minguri** Mozambique
189 F3 **Mingyue** Jilin China
190 G5 **Mingzhou** Shaanxi China
194 E3 **Minh Hóa** Vietnam
189 G3 **Minhe** Jiangxi China
181 H5 **Minhla** Myanmar
132 C4 **Minićevo** Serbia
187 C10 **Minicoy Island** Lakshadweep India
80 I5 **Minidoka** Idaho USA
216 H4 **Minigwal, Lake** WA Australia
123 K5 **Minija** *watercourse* Lithuania
216 C1 **Minilya** WA Australia
212 F3 **Minilya** *watercourse* WA Australia
216 D1 **Minilya Roadhouse** WA Australia
216 E1 **Mininer** WA Australia
158 C2 **Mininian** Côte d'Ivoire
75 U7 **Miniota** Manitoba Canada
78 H7 **Minipi** *watercourse* Newfoundland and Labrador Canada
78 H6 **Minipi Lake** Newfoundland and Labrador Canada
76 J7 **Miniss Lake** Ontario Canada
128 E3 **Ministra, Sierra** *range* Spain
108 C2 **Ministro Ramos Mexia** Argentina
104 D5 **Miñita** Chile
214 C3 **Miniyeri (Hodgson Downs)** NT Australia
Minjerriba *see* **North Stradbroke Island** Australia
188 D3 **Minjian** Sichuan China
198 E6 **Minjilang** NT Australia
214 B1 **Minjilang** NT Australia
74 M2 **Mink Lake** Northwest Territories Canada
190 D5 **Minle** Gansu China
159 F3 **Minna** Nigeria
58 L1 **Minna Bluff** Antarctica
193 J3 **Minna-jima** *island* Japan
81 Q7 **Minneapolis** Kansas USA
82 E4 **Minneapolis** Minnesota USA
81 O8 **Minneola** Kansas USA
82 E4 **Minnesota** *watercourse* Minnesota USA
82 D4 **Minnewaska, Lake** Minnesota USA
81 P2 **Minnewaukan** North Dakota USA
218 G1 **Minnie Downs** Qld Australia
219 K3 **Minnie Water** NSW Australia
76 J8 **Minnitaki Lake** Ontario Canada
128 B2 **Miño** *watercourse* Spain
82 F3 **Minong** Wisconsin USA
Minorca *see* **Menorca** Spain
81 O2 **Minot** North Dakota USA
156 D1 **Minqār al Majabirah** *mountain* Egypt
190 E5 **Minqin** Gansu China
178 E4 **Minsafa** Saudi Arabia
123 N6 **Minsk** Belarus
125 K1 **Mińsk Mazowiecki** Poland
136 C2 **Minskaya Voblasts'** *admin. area* Belarus
139 H3 **Minster** Kent England UK
159 G4 **Minta** Cameroon
217 M3 **Mintabie** SA Australia
184 E5 **Mintaka Pass** Xinjiang Uygur Zizhiqu China
179 M1 **Mintaka Pass** Pakistan
218 D5 **Mintaro** SA Australia
141 H3 **Minting** Lincolnshire England UK
142 F3 **Mintlaw** Aberdeenshire Scotland UK
81 O2 **Minto** Manitoba Canada
79 E9 **Minto** New Brunswick Canada
81 Q2 **Minto** North Dakota USA
77 R4 **Minto, Lac** *lake* Quebec Canada
58 L2 **Minto, Mount** *mountain* Antarctica
72 H4 **Minto Inlet** Northwest Territories Canada
159 G4 **Minton II** Cameroon
75 S8 **Minton** Saskatchewan Canada
183 P2 **Minusinsk** Russian Federation
159 G4 **Minvoul** Gabon
188 D1 **Minxian** Gansu China
82 I4 **Mio** Michigan USA
74 K6 **Miocene** British Columbia Canada
142 B4 **Miodar** Highland Scotland UK
127 G4 **Mions** France
126 D4 **Mios** France
132 D3 **Mioveni** Romania
218 D1 **Mipia, Lake** Qld Australia
178 D3 **Miqt** Jordan
185 H4 **Miquan** Xinjiang Uygur Zizhiqu China
79 J9 **Miquelon** St Pierre and Miquelon
79 J9 **Miquelon** *island* St Pierre and Miquelon
124 G5 **Mira** Italy
128 B3 **Mira** Portugal
128 B5 **Mira** *watercourse* Portugal
107 G2 **Mirabela** Paraguay
128 C4 **Mirabel** Spain
103 C7 **Mirabela** Brazil
103 C9 **Miracatu** Brazil
102 B5 **Miracema do Tocantins** Brazil
102 C4 **Mirador** Brazil
126 E4 **Miradoux** France
100 D4 **Miraflores** Colombia
100 C3 **Miraflores** Colombia
103 D8 **Miraí** Brazil
179 L3 **Miram Shah** Pakistan
89 F4 **Miramar** Mexico
89 F3 **Miramar** Mexico
104 D5 **Miramar** Peru
87 K8 **Miramar** Florida USA
127 G5 **Miramas** France
126 D4 **Mirambeau** France
79 F9 **Miramichi** New Brunswick Canada
79 F9 **Miramichi Bay** New Brunswick Canada
179 I4 **Mīrān Sū** Iran
108 C5 **Miranda** Argentina
105 G6 **Miranda** Brazil
105 G6 **Miranda** *watercourse* Brazil
100 B4 **Miranda** Colombia
101 E2 **Miranda** *admin. area* Venezuela
216 G3 **Miranda, Lake** WA Australia
106 D2 **Miranda, Sierra** *range* Chile
128 E2 **Miranda de Ebro** Spain
214 F4 **Miranda Downs** Qld Australia
124 F5 **Mirandola** Italy
103 B8 **Mirandópolis** Brazil
215 J6 **Mirani** Qld Australia
107 I2 **Mirante, Serra do** *range* Brazil
133 B5 **Miras** Albania
179 H6 **Mirbāţ** Oman
126 E3 **Mirebeau** France
127 H2 **Mirecourt** France
126 E5 **Mirepoix** France
132 C2 **Mireşu Mare** Romania
197 G2 **Miri** Malaysia
155 H6 **Miria** Niger
187 E8 **Mirialguda** Andhra Pradesh India
215 K8 **Miriam Vale** Qld Australia
107 H5 **Mirim, Lagoa** *lake* Brazil
198 E4 **Mirimiri** Indonesia
107 G4 **Miriñay** *watercourse* Argentina
105 F2 **Miriti** Brazil
100 D5 **Mirití-paraná** *watercourse* Colombia
214 E4 **Miriwinni** Qld Australia
179 J3 **Mīrjāveh** Iran
132 C4 **Mirkovo** Bulgaria
125 H5 **Mirna** Slovenia
58 G2 **Mirny (Russia)** *research station* Antarctica
135 X6 **Mirnyy** Russian Federation
125 M1 **Mironim** Belarus
130 F2 **Mirotice** Czech Republic
132 C4 **Mirovyane** Bulgaria
124 G1 **Mirow** Germany
179 L4 **Mirpur Khas** Pakistan
179 K5 **Mirpur Sakro** Pakistan
219 H6 **Mirrool** NSW Australia
161 H2 **Mirsale** Somalia
131 G7 **Mirto Crosia** Italy
133 C7 **Mirtoö Pelagos** *sea* Greece
162 F3 **Mirueo** Mozambique
181 G4 **Mirzaganj** Bangladesh
186 F6 **Mirzapur** Uttar Pradesh India
130 F5 **Misa** *watercourse* Italy
89 F5 **Misantla** Mexico
159 G2 **Misau** Nigeria
193 I3 **Misawa** Japan
195 G5 **Mischief Reef** Spratly Islands
125 L5 **Mischii** Romania
79 F9 **Miscou Island** New Brunswick Canada
218 F7 **Misery, Mount** Vic. Australia
194 B6 **Misha** Andaman and Nicobar Islands India
196 B1 **Misha** Tripura India
160 E5 **Mishamo** Tanzania
191 L3 **Mishan** Heilongjiang China
178 G3 **Mishān-e 'Olyā** Iran
193 H4 **Mishima** Japan
123 P5 **Mishutki** Belarus
121 O3 **Misijärvi** *lake* Finland
76 J6 **Misikeyask Lake** Ontario Canada
199 J6 **Misima Island** Papua New Guinea
84 F6 **Mision Santa Gertrudis** Mexico
107 G2 **Misión Yalve Sanga** Paraguay
107 H3 **Misiones** *admin. area* Argentina
107 G3 **Misiones** *admin. area* Paraguay
107 H3 **Misiones, Sierra de** *range* Argentina
130 H3 **Miske** Hungary
100 A1 **Miskitos, Cayos** *islands* Nicaragua
125 K4 **Miskolc** Hungary
125 H4 **Mislinja** Slovenia
104 D4 **Mismi, Nevado** *mountain* Peru
127 L4 **Mišnjak** Croatia
198 D4 **Misool** *island* Indonesia
82 F3 **Misquah Hills** *range* Minnesota USA
155 J2 **Misrātah** Libya
105 G2 **Missão** Brazil
158 C2 **Misseni** Mali
126 C3 **Missillac** France
77 N8 **Missinaibi** *watercourse* Ontario Canada
73 K9 **Missinaibi Lake** Ontario Canada
75 S5 **Missinipe** Saskatchewan Canada
81 O5 **Mission** South Dakota USA
86 B7 **Mission** Texas USA
84 D4 **Mission Bay** California USA
215 I4 **Mission Beach** Qld Australia
84 D4 **Mission Viejo** California USA
75 T6 **Missipuskiow** *watercourse* Saskatchewan Canada
154 D6 **Missira** Senegal
76 M6 **Missisa** *watercourse* Ontario Canada
76 M6 **Missisa Lake** Ontario Canada
77 P7 **Missisicabi** *watercourse* Quebec Canada
71 **Mississippi** *admin. area* USA
86 F3 **Mississippi** *watercourse* Arkansas USA
86 F5 **Mississippi** *watercourse* Louisiana USA
82 D3 **Mississippi** *watercourse* Minnesota USA
86 F5 **Mississippi** *watercourse* Mississippi USA
82 G8 **Mississippi** *watercourse* Missouri USA
86 G6 **Mississippi Delta** Louisiana USA
83 M4 **Mississippi Lake** Ontario Canada
86 G5 **Mississippi Sound** Mississippi USA
105 E2 **Missões** Brazil
80 I3 **Missoula** Montana USA
154 F2 **Missour** Morocco
71 **Missouri** *admin. area* USA
82 F7 **Missouri** *watercourse* Missouri USA
75 S8 **Missouri** *watercourse* Montana USA
82 D6 **Missouri** *watercourse* Nebraska USA
81 P5 **Missouri** *watercourse* South Dakota USA
86 D6 **Missouri City** Texas USA
81 R6 **Missouri Valley** Iowa USA
215 G7 **Mistake** *watercourse* Qld Australia
76 I1 **Mistake Bay** Nunavut Canada
213 J4 **Mistake Creek** NT Australia
79 G7 **Mistanipisipou** *watercourse* Quebec Canada
83 L2 **Mistaouac, Lac** *lake* Quebec Canada
77 S7 **Mistassibi** *watercourse* Quebec Canada
77 T7 **Mistassibi Nord-Est** *watercourse* Quebec Canada
77 S8 **Mistassini** *watercourse* Quebec Canada
77 S7 **Mistassini, Lac** *lake* Quebec Canada
77 X5 **Mistastin Lake** Newfoundland and Labrador Canada
75 T6 **Mistatim** Saskatchewan Canada
122 I4 **Misterhult** Sweden
90 D3 **Misteriosa Bank** *reef* Caribbean
138 E4 **Misterton** Somerset England UK
76 J4 **Mistikokan** *watercourse* Manitoba Canada
77 W5 **Mistinibi, Lac** *lake* Quebec Canada
77 U6 **Mistinic, Lac** *lake* Quebec Canada
106 F2 **Mistol Marcado** Argentina
131 F8 **Mistretta** Italy
133 C6 **Mistros** Greece
75 W4 **Mistuhekasookun** Manitoba Canada
75 K2 **Misty Lake** Manitoba Canada
160 C4 **Misumba** Democratic Republic of Congo
130 E3 **Misurina** Italy

120 I3 **Misvær** Norway
120 I3 **Misværfjorden** *bay* Norway
104 D4 **Mita** Peru
88 D4 **Mita, Punta de** *cape* Mexico
161 F6 **Mitande** Mozambique
156 F4 **Mitatib** Sudan
138 E3 **Mitcheldean** Gloucestershire England UK
219 H2 **Mitchell** Qld Australia
214 G3 **Mitchell** *watercourse* Qld Australia
138 B4 **Mitchell** Cornwall England UK
82 H7 **Mitchell** Indiana USA
81 N6 **Mitchell** Nebraska USA
80 E4 **Mitchell** Oregon USA
81 P5 **Mitchell** South Dakota USA
215 H4 **Mitchell, Lake** Qld Australia
87 J3 **Mitchell, Mount** North Carolina USA
87 H4 **Mitchell Lake** Alabama USA
213 K1 **Mitchell Point** NT Australia
214 C2 **Mitchell Range** NT Australia
140 A1 **Mitchells Town** Ireland
159 G4 **Mitémélé** *watercourse* Equatorial Guinea
108 A4 **Mitford, Cabo** *cape* Chile
179 L5 **Mithi** Pakistan
179 L4 **Mithrau** Pakistan
133 E6 **Mithymna** Greece
197 K3 **Miti** *island* Indonesia
218 G7 **Mitiamo** Vic. Australia
220 1 **Mitiaro** *island* Cook Islands New Zealand
134 K5 **Mitina** Russian Federation
193 I4 **Mito** Japan
104 C3 **Mitoc, Cerro** *mountain* Peru
161 F5 **Mitole** Tanzania
133 C5 **Mitrašinci** Macedonia
108 D6 **Mitre, Península** *peninsula* Argentina
221 B7 **Mitre Peak** *mountain* New Zealand
163 H2 **Mitsamiouli** Comoros
163 I2 **Mitsio, Nosy** *island* Madagascar
193 H4 **Mitsuke** Japan
219 H7 **Mitta Mitta** Vic. Australia
120 H5 **Mittådalen** Sweden
124 F1 **Mittellandkanal** *watercourse* Germany
127 J2 **Mittelneufnach** Germany
124 F4 **Mittenwald** Germany
124 G4 **Mittersill** Austria
127 K2 **Mitterteich** Germany
100 D4 **Mitú** Colombia
160 D5 **Mitumba, Chaîne des** *range* Democratic Republic of Congo
160 D4 **Mitumba, Monts** *range* Uganda
160 D5 **Mitwaba** Democratic Republic of Congo
159 G4 **Mitzic** Gabon
139 F2 **Mixbury** Oxfordshire England UK
90 B4 **Mixco** Guatemala
159 F2 **Miya** Nigeria
193 H4 **Miyake-jima** *island* Japan
193 I3 **Miyako** Japan
189 J4 **Miyako-jima** *island* Japan
189 J4 **Miyako Rettō** *island* Japan
182 G4 **Miyaly** Kazakhstan
192 F5 **Miyazaki** Japan
192 G4 **Miyoshi** Japan
191 H5 **Miyun** Beijing China
161 F2 **Mīzan Teferī** Ethiopia
155 I2 **Mizdah** Libya
143 G4 **Mizen Head** *cape* Ireland
190 G5 **Mizhi** Shaanxi China
132 C4 **Miziya** Bulgaria
181 G4 **Mizoram** *admin. area* India
105 E5 **Mizque** Bolivia
193 I3 **Mizusawa** Japan
120 K5 **Mjällom** Sweden
120 I3 **Mjelde** Norway
120 L5 **Mjölefjärden** *bay* Sweden
122 D2 **Mjølfell** Norway
120 K1 **Mjølvik** Norway
122 C2 **Mjømna** Norway
122 G4 **Mjörn** *lake* Sweden
122 F2 **Mjøsa** *lake* Norway
120 K5 **Mjösjöby** Sweden
120 H4 **Mjøsundvatnet** *lake* Norway
161 F5 **Mkokotoni** Tanzania
161 F5 **Mkondoa** *watercourse* Tanzania
161 F4 **Mkujani** Tanzania
161 E5 **Mkurusi** Tanzania
162 E2 **Mkushi** Zambia
125 H2 **Mladá Boleslav** Czech Republic
130 G4 **Mlaka** Croatia
160 E5 **Mlala Hills** *range* Tanzania
161 F5 **Mlandizi** Tanzania
125 K1 **Mława** Poland
125 I2 **Mleczno** Poland
161 F5 **Mligasi** *watercourse* Tanzania
164 8b **Mlima Benara** *mountain* Mayotte
130 G5 **Mljet** *island* Croatia
197 F5 **Mlonggo** Indonesia
125 J2 **Młynek** Poland
162 E4 **Mmashoro** Botswana
159 F3 **Mo** *watercourse* Cameroon
158 E3 **Mo** *watercourse* Ghana
122 G3 **Mo** Sweden
120 J5 **Mo** Sweden
158 E3 **Mo** *watercourse* Togo
120 I3 **Mo i Rana** Norway
91 F2 **Moa** Cuba
197 J6 **Moa** *island* Indonesia
81 K7 **Moab** Utah USA
223 9 **Moala** *island* Fiji
218 G7 **Moama** NSW Australia
221 D6 **Moana** New Zealand
143 E3 **Moate** Ireland
163 F3 **Moatize** Mozambique
220 F4 **Moawhango, Lake** New Zealand
160 D5 **Moba** Democratic Republic of Congo
193 I4 **Mobara** Japan
178 G3 **Mobārakeh** Iran
159 I4 **Mobaye** Central African Republic
82 E7 **Moberly** Missouri USA
74 K5 **Moberly Lake** British Columbia Canada
86 G5 **Mobile** Alabama USA
86 H5 **Mobile Bay** Alabama USA
86 H5 **Mobile Point** Alabama USA
218 F2 **Moble** Qld Australia
81 O4 **Mobridge** South Dakota USA
91 G3 **Moca** Dominican Republic
102 B3 **Mocajuba** Brazil
163 H3 **Moçambique** Mozambique
223 9 **Moce** *island* Fiji
106 C6 **Mocha, Isla** *island* Chile
105 E6 **Mochará, Cordillera de** *range* Bolivia
138 D2 **Mochdre** Powys Wales UK
125 J1 **Mochowo** Poland
162 E4 **Mochudi** Botswana
163 H2 **Mocìmboa da Praia** Mozambique
163 G2 **Mocìmboa do Rovuma** Mozambique
122 H4 **Möckeln** *lake* Sweden
218 F7 **Mockinya** Vic. Australia
124 G2 **Mockrehna** Germany
101 G4 **Moco-Moco Village** Guyana
100 B4 **Mocoa** Colombia
103 C8 **Mococa** Brazil
163 G4 **Mocoduene** Mozambique
85 I8 **Mocorito** Mexico
132 F2 **Mocra** Moldova
88 E4 **Moctezuma** Mexico
163 G3 **Mocuba** Mozambique
140 B4 **Mocurry Bridge** Ireland
127 H4 **Modane** France
186 C6 **Modasa** Gujarat India
127 G1 **Modave** Belgium
138 D4 **Modbury** Devon England UK
124 F5 **Modena** Italy
84 F2 **Modena** Utah USA
80 E8 **Modesto** California USA
131 F8 **Modica** Italy
162 E4 **Modimolle** South Africa
125 H2 **Modła** Poland
125 H1 **Modlęcin** Poland
125 L2 **Modliborzyce** Poland
198 E5 **Modowi** Indonesia
125 H4 **Modriach** Austria
130 H4 **Modriča** Bosnia and Herzegovina
125 H5 **Modruš** Croatia
218 H8 **Moe** Vic. Australia
163 G3 **Moebase** Mozambique
181 H4 **Moegaung** Myanmar
220 F3 **Moehau** *mountain* New Zealand
181 H4 **Moehnyin** Myanmar
197 K4 **Moeilijk** *island* Indonesia
160 B3 **Moekoe** *watercourse* Democratic Republic of Congo
122 E3 **Moel** *watercourse* Norway
140 D3 **Moelfre** Isle of Anglesey Wales UK
120 K2 **Moen** Norway
101 H3 **Moengo** Suriname
84 G2 **Moenkopi** Arizona USA
221 D7 **Moeraki Point** New Zealand
127 H1 **Moers** Germany
142 E5 **Moffat** Dumfries and Galloway Scotland UK
81 M8 **Moffat** Colorado USA
186 D4 **Moga** Punjab India
Mogadishu *see* **Muqdisho** Somalia
128 C3 **Mogadouro** Portugal
193 H3 **Mogami-gawa** *lake* Japan
164 3b **Mogán** Canary Islands
191 M2 **Mogdy** Russian Federation
102 F4 **Mogeiro** Brazil
125 I1 **Mogilno** Poland
130 E5 **Mogliano** Italy
135 Y8 **Mogocha** Russian Federation
191 I1 **Mogocha** Russian Federation
190 E3 **Mogod** Mongolia
181 H4 **Mogok** Myanmar
84 G3 **Mogollon Plateau** Arkansas USA
108 A4 **Mogotes, Cabo** *cape* Chile
135 AE4 **Mogotoyevo, Ozero** *lake* Russian Federation
219 I5 **Mogriguy** NSW Australia
159 H2 **Mogroum** Chad
216 E5 **Mogumber** WA Australia
74 J7 **Moha** British Columbia Canada
132 A3 **Mohács** Hungary
187 E7 **Mohala** Chhattisgarh India
162 E6 **Mohales Hoek** Lesotho
81 O2 **Mohall** North Dakota USA
155 G1 **Mohammadia** Algeria
154 E2 **Mohammedia** Morocco
84 F4 **Mohawk** Arizona USA
186 E6 **Mohdra** Madhya Pradesh India
191 J1 **Mohe** Heilongjiang China
135 Z8 **Mohe** Nei Mongol Zizhiqu China
164 8 **Mohéli (Mwali)** *island* Comoros
72 C6 **Mohican, Cape** Alaska USA
143 E3 **Mohill** Ireland
178 G4 **Mohkdān** Iran
121 Q5 **Möhkö** Finland
124 D4 **Möhlin** Switzerland
124 E2 **Möhnesee** *lake* Germany
57 G2 **Mohns Ridge** *underwater feature* Norwegian Sea
83 N6 **Mohnton** Pennsylvania USA
161 F5 **Mohoro** Tanzania
122 D3 **Moi** Norway
129 H3 **Moià** Spain
142 C4 **Moidart** *cape* Scotland UK
128 C3 **Moimenta da Beira** Portugal
219 R10 **Moina** Tas. Australia
142 C5 **Moineruadh** Argyll and Bute Scotland UK
132 E2 **Moinești** Romania
143 F2 **Moira** Armagh Northern Ireland UK
125 M4 **Moisei** Romania
77 V7 **Moisie** *watercourse* Quebec Canada
121 P4 **Moisiovaara** Finland
159 H3 **Moïssala** Chad
103 C7 **Moitinha** Brazil
123 J3 **Möja** *island* Sweden
85 K7 **Mojada, Sierra** *range* Mexico
84 C3 **Mojave** California USA
84 D3 **Mojave Desert** California USA
103 C8 **Moji Mirim** Brazil
188 D4 **Mojiang** Yunnan China
76 K7 **Mojikit Lake** Ontario Canada
125 G4 **Mojstrana** Slovenia
125 J3 **Mojtín** Slovakia
102 B3 **Moju** Brazil
102 B3 **Moju** *watercourse* Brazil
220 F4 **Mokau** New Zealand
220 F4 **Mokau** *watercourse* New Zealand
122 G2 **Møkeren** *lake* Norway
221 E5 **Mokihinui** *watercourse* New Zealand
222 6 **Mokil** *island* Federated States of Micronesia
120 H5 **Mokkavatnet** *lake* Norway
155 I1 **Moknine** Tunisia
181 H3 **Mokokchung** Nagaland India
159 G2 **Mokolo** Cameroon
160 C4 **Mokombe** *watercourse* Democratic Republic of Congo
162 E4 **Mokopane** South Africa
192 E4 **Mokp'o** South Korea
132 B4 **Mokra Gora** *range* Kosovo
132 B3 **Mokrin** Serbia
182 E3 **Mokrous** Russian Federation
121 N5 **Möksy** Finland
159 F3 **Mokwa** Nigeria
132 B3 **Mol** Serbia
181 H3 **Mol Len** *mountain* Nagaland India
75 S5 **Molanosa** Saskatchewan Canada
131 C6 **Molara, Isola** *island* Sardinia Italy
124 E5 **Molare** Italy
126 E5 **Molas** France
130 F4 **Molat** Croatia
130 F4 **Molat** *island* Croatia
198 B4 **Molawe** Indonesia
138 D1 **Mold** Flintshire Wales UK
183 M3 **Moldary** Kazakhstan
120 E5 **Molde** Norway
132 F2 **Moldova** *country* Europe
132 D2 **Moldova** *watercourse* Romania
125 K5 **Moldova Nouă** Romania
132 D3 **Moldoveanu, Vârful** *mountain* Romania
132 E2 **Moldovei, Câmpia** *region* Romania
132 C2 **Moldovenești** Romania
219 J3 **Mole** *watercourse* NSW Australia
158 D3 **Mole** *watercourse* Ghana
161 E5 **Mole** Tanzania
139 G3 **Mole** *watercourse* England UK
199 H4 **Mole Island** Papua New Guinea
126 B2 **Molène, Île de** *island* France
162 E4 **Molepolole** Botswana
139 G2 **Molesworth** Cambridgeshire England UK
123 M5 **Molėtai** Lithuania
131 G6 **Molfetta** Italy
198 B3 **Molibagu** Indonesia
106 D5 **Molina** Argentina
106 D5 **Molina** Chile
128 F3 **Molina de Aragón** Spain
129 F4 **Molinar, Embalse del** *lake* Spain
86 C2 **Moline** Kansas USA
105 E5 **Molinero** Bolivia
131 F8 **Molini, Capo** *cape* Italy
109 10a **Molinière Point** *cape* Grenada
84 E6 **Molino Lacy** Mexico
106 E3 **Molinos** Argentina
108 B2 **Molinos** Chile
128 D4 **Molinos de Matachel, Embalse de los** *lake* Spain
160 E5 **Moliro** Democratic Republic of Congo
131 F6 **Molise** *admin. area* Italy
121 N3 **Molkojärvi** *lake* Finland
124 G4 **Möll** *watercourse* Austria
138 D3 **Molland** Devon England UK
133 B5 **Mollas** Albania
122 G4 **Mölle** Sweden
105 E5 **Molle Punco** Bolivia
216 E5 **Mollerin Lake** WA Australia
129 G3 **Mollerussa** Spain
77 R5 **Mollet, Lacs** *lake* Quebec Canada
77 T5 **Molleville, Lac** *lake* Quebec Canada
57 G1 **Molloy Deep** *underwater feature* Greenland Sea
161 F4 **Molo** Kenya
163 G3 **Molocue** *watercourse* Mozambique
58 D2 **Molodezhnaya (Russia)** *research station* Antarctica
84 inset **Moloka'i** *island* Hawai'i USA
53 S5 **Molokai Fracture Zone** *underwater feature* Pacific Ocean
219 I5 **Molong** NSW Australia
105 G2 **Molongó** Brazil
162 D5 **Molopo** *watercourse* South Africa
133 C6 **Molos** Greece
159 H4 **Moloundou** Cameroon
132 F2 **Molovata** Moldova
124 C4 **Moloy** France
120 L5 **Molpe** Finland
76 G5 **Molson Lake** Manitoba Canada
198 D5 **Molu** *island* Indonesia
Molucca Sea *see* **Maluku, Laut** Indonesia
Moluccas *see* **Maluku** Indonesia
163 G3 **Molumbo** Mozambique
188 C2 **Moluo** Xizang Zizhiqu China
123 Q4 **Molvotitsy** Russian Federation
160 D6 **Molwe** Democratic Republic of Congo
221 C8 **Molyneaux Bay** New Zealand
160 C5 **Moma** Democratic Republic of Congo
163 G3 **Moma** Mozambique
135 AD5 **Moma** *watercourse* Russian Federation
199 F5 **Momats** *watercourse* Indonesia
218 F4 **Momba** NSW Australia
102 E4 **Mombaça** Brazil
130 E5 **Mombaroccio** Italy
161 F4 **Mombasa** Kenya
160 B4 **Momboyo** *watercourse* Democratic Republic of Congo
105 H5 **Mombuca, Serra da** *range* Brazil
199 F6 **Mombum** Indonesia
179 I3 **Mo'menābād, Kūh-e** *mountain* Iran
223 9a **Momi** Fiji
124 C2 **Momignies** Belgium
100 C2 **Mompós** Colombia
135 AE5 **Momskiy Khrebet** *range* Russian Federation
122 G5 **Møn** *island* Denmark
181 H3 **Mon** Nagaland India
194 C3 **Mon** *admin. area* Myanmar
109 13 **Mon Repos** St Lucia
219 H3 **Mona** Qld Australia
91 H3 **Mona, Isla** *island* Puerto Rico
90 D5 **Mona, Punta** *cape* Costa Rica
91 G3 **Mona Passage** *strait* Dominican Republic
80 J7 **Mona Reservoir** Utah USA
219 J5 **Mona Vale** NSW Australia
142 A3 **Monach Islands (Heisker Islands)** Scotland UK
127 H5 **Monaco** *country* Europe
127 H5 **Monaco** Monaco
142 D3 **Monadhliath Mountains** Scotland UK
120 M5 **Monafjärd** *bay* Finland
101 F2 **Monagas** *admin. area* Venezuela
143 F2 **Monaghan** Ireland
143 F2 **Monaghan** *admin. area* Ireland
218 F6 **Monak** NSW Australia
138 A2 **Monale** Ireland
142 C3 **Monar, Loch** *lake* Scotland UK
75 O8 **Monarch** Alberta Canada
74 I7 **Monarch Mountain** British Columbia Canada
105 F5 **Monas** Bolivia
74 L7 **Monashee Mountains** British Columbia Canada
131 G7 **Monasterace** Italy
155 I1 **Monastir** Tunisia
132 D1 **Monastyrys'ka** Ukraine
159 G4 **Monatélé** Cameroon
140 B4 **Monatore** Ireland
159 G3 **Monboré** Cameroon
125 H3 **Mönchdorf** Austria
121 R3 **Monchegorsk** Russian Federation
124 D2 **Mönchengladbach** Germany
128 B5 **Monchique** Portugal
75 R8 **Monchy** Saskatchewan Canada
88 E3 **Monclova** Mexico
126 D3 **Moncoutant** France
79 F9 **Moncton** New Brunswick Canada
107 H3 **Mondai** Brazil
81 Q6 **Mondamin** Iowa USA
128 E3 **Mondéjar** Spain
131 E7 **Mondello** Italy
155 J6 **Mondo** Chad
160 C4 **Mondombe** Democratic Republic of Congo
128 C2 **Mondoñedo** Spain
82 F4 **Mondovi** Wisconsin USA
216 H7 **Mondrain Island** WA Australia
161 F4 **Monduli** Tanzania
190 D2 **Mondy** Russian Federation
159 F3 **Mone** *watercourse* Cameroon
132 C2 **Moneasa** Romania
129 F3 **Monegrillo** Spain
129 F3 **Monegros, Los** *region* Spain
133 C7 **Monemvasia** Greece
193 I1 **Moneron, Ostrov** *island* Russian Federation
83 L6 **Monessen** Pennsylvania USA
128 C4 **Monesterio** Spain
127 G4 **Monestier-de-Clermont** France
143 E4 **Moneygall** Ireland
143 F2 **Moneymore** Cookstown Northern Ireland UK
130 C4 **Monferrato** *region* Italy
181 I5 **Mong Hsat** Myanmar
181 I5 **Mong Hsu** Myanmar
181 H5 **Mong Ne** Myanmar
181 I5 **Mong Ping** Myanmar
181 I4 **Mong Yai** Myanmar
181 I5 **Mong Yang** Myanmar
160 C3 **Monga** Democratic Republic of Congo
160 B3 **Mongala** *watercourse* Democratic Republic of Congo
160 E2 **Mongalla** Sudan
181 G3 **Mongar** Bhutan
219 I6 **Mongarlowe** NSW Australia
160 C4 **Mongemputu** Democratic Republic of Congo
131 E7 **Mongerbino, Capo** *cape* Italy
216 E4 **Mongers Lake** WA Australia
199 H5 **Mongi** *watercourse* Papua New Guinea
181 H5 **Mongkaing** Myanmar
156 B5 **Mongo** Chad
185 K3 **Mongolia** *country* Asia
190 D4 **Mongolian Plateau** Mongolia
159 G4 **Mongomo** Equatorial Guinea
213 I3 **Mongona, Mount** WA Australia
159 G2 **Mongonu** Nigeria
156 C5 **Mongororo** Chad
159 H4 **Mongoumba** Central African Republic
181 I5 **Mongpayak** Myanmar
162 D3 **Mongu** Zambia
162 C3 **Mongua** Angola
154 D5 **Mônguel** Mauritania
181 I5 **Mongyang** Myanmar
185 I3 **Monh Hajrhan** *mountain* Mongolia
124 F3 **Monheim** Germany
218 G5 **Monia Gap** NSW Australia
142 E5 **Moniaive** Dumfries and Galloway Scotland UK
75 P7 **Monitor** Alberta Canada
80 G7 **Monitor Range** Nevada USA
143 D3 **Monivea** Ireland
164 2 **Moniz, Porto** Madeira
90 C4 **Monjarás** Honduras
160 C4 **Monjuku** Democratic Republic of Congo
195 J6 **Monkayo** Philippines
163 F2 **Monkey Bay** Malawi
216 C2 **Monkey Mia** WA Australia
125 L1 **Mońki** Poland
218 E1 **Monkira** Qld Australia
138 C4 **Monkleigh** Devon England UK
160 C4 **Monkoto** Democratic Republic of Congo
138 D3 **Monksilver** Somerset England UK
138 E3 **Monmouth** Monmouthshire Wales UK
80 D4 **Monmouth** Oregon USA
74 J7 **Monmouth Mountain** British Columbia Canada
138 E3 **Monmouthshire** *admin. area* Wales UK
75 Q6 **Monnery** *watercourse* Saskatchewan Canada
121 Q5 **Mönni** Finland
222 8 **Mono** *island* Solomon Islands
158 E3 **Mono** *watercourse* Togo
90 D5 **Mono, Punta del** *cape* Nicaragua
84 C2 **Mono Lake** California USA
219 J2 **Monogorilby** Qld Australia
123 N2 **Monola** Finland
82 G5 **Monona** Wisconsin USA
131 G6 **Monopoli** Italy
132 D2 **Monor** Romania
109 9 **Monos** *island* Trinidad and Tobago
221 B7 **Monowai, Lake** New Zealand
194 B3 **Monoy** Myanmar
126 E4 **Monpazier** France
129 F3 **Monreal del Campo** Spain
87 J4 **Monroe** Georgia USA
86 E4 **Monroe** Louisiana USA
82 J6 **Monroe** Michigan USA
87 K3 **Monroe** North Carolina USA
82 G5 **Monroe** Wisconsin USA
82 H7 **Monroe Lake** Indiana USA
86 H5 **Monroeville** Alabama USA
158 B3 **Monrovia** Liberia
126 F1 **Mons** Belgium
122 G5 **Møns Klint** *cape* Denmark
128 C3 **Monsagro** Spain
103 E7 **Monsarás, Ponta de** *cape* Brazil
124 D2 **Monschau** Germany
102 D4 **Monsenhor Gil** Brazil
104 E6 **Monserrate** Bolivia
100 E3 **Monserrate** Colombia
158 C3 **Monsoro** *watercourse* Guinea
127 H4 **Mont, Col du** *pass* Italy
83 P3 **Mont-Apica** Quebec Canada
86 D6 **Mont Belvieu** Texas USA
127 H4 **Mont Cenis, Lac du** *lake* France
126 D5 **Mont-de-Marsan** France
83 N3 **Mont-Laurier** Quebec Canada
79 F8 **Mont-Louis** Quebec Canada
126 F5 **Mont-Louis** France
139 I5 **Mont-St-Aignan** France
101 H3 **Mont Valérien** French Guiana
127 H1 **Montabaur** Germany
199 I5 **Montagu Harbour** *bay* Papua New Guinea
80 D6 **Montague** California USA
82 H5 **Montague** Michigan USA
108 A4 **Montague, Isla** *island* Chile
72 E6 **Montague Island** Alaska USA
216 F3 **Montague Range** WA Australia
213 H3 **Montague Sound** WA Australia
126 D3 **Montaigu** France
129 F3 **Montalbán** Spain
128 E4 **Montalbo** Spain
155 J1 **Montalto** *mountain* Italy
127 H5 **Montalto Ligure** Italy
132 C4 **Montana** Bulgaria
132 C4 **Montana** *admin. area* Bulgaria
70 **Montana** *admin. area* USA
109 1c **Montaña** Netherlands Antilles
164 3d **Montaña Clara, Isla de** *island* Canary Islands
100 D3 **Montañas del Totumo** Colombia
103 D7 **Montanha** Brazil
128 B4 **Montargil, Barragem de** *lake* Portugal
126 E4 **Montauban** France
127 G3 **Montbard** France
126 F4 **Montbazens** France
127 H3 **Montbéliard** France
124 C5 **Montbrison** France
79 H7 **Montcevelles, Lac** *lake* Quebec Canada
126 G2 **Montcornet** France
126 E4 **Montcuq** France
126 F2 **Montdidier** France
106 F6 **Monte, Laguna del** *lake* Argentina
101 H5 **Monte Alegre** Brazil
103 B7 **Monte Alegre de Minas** Brazil
103 B8 **Monte Aprazível** Brazil
108 C5 **Monte Aymond** Argentina
103 D6 **Monte Azul** Brazil
212 C6 **Monte Bello Islands** WA Australia
104 C2 **Monte Belo** Brazil
127 H5 **Monte-Carlo** Monaco
103 C7 **Monte Carmelo** Brazil
162 E4 **Monte Christo** South Africa
106 E5 **Monte Comans** Argentina
219 J3 **Monte Cristo** Qld Australia
104 D2 **Monte Cristo** Brazil
124 G4 **Monte Croce Carnia, Passo di** *pass* Italy
108 C5 **Monte Dinero** Argentina
88 E4 **Monte Escobedo** Mexico
108 C5 **Monte León** Argentina
108 C5 **Monte León, Isla** *island* Argentina
106 D4 **Monte Patria** Chile
106 F3 **Monte Quemado** Argentina
131 C6 **Monte Rossu, Capo** *cape* Sardinia Italy
105 F3 **Monte Santo** Brazil
103 E5 **Monte Santo** Brazil
131 C6 **Monte Santu, Capo di** *cape* Sardinia Italy
81 L8 **Monte Vista** Colorado USA
219 I6 **Monteagle** NSW Australia
215 I7 **Monteagle** Qld Australia
105 F5 **Monteagudo** Bolivia
129 F4 **Montealegre del Castillo** Spain
126 E5 **Montech** France
100 A5 **Montecristi** Ecuador
131 D5 **Montecristo, Isola di** *island* Italy
130 E5 **Montefalco** Italy
90 E3 **Montego Bay** Jamaica
102 E4 **Monteiro** Brazil
214 A4 **Montejinni** NT Australia
127 G4 **Montélimar** France
128 B4 **Montemor-o-Nova** Portugal
89 F3 **Montemorelos** Mexico
126 D4 **Montendre** France
130 H5 **Montenegro** *country* Europe
163 G2 **Montepuez** Mozambique
163 G2 **Montepuez** *watercourse* Mozambique
80 E8 **Monterey** California USA
80 D8 **Monterey Bay** California USA
100 C2 **Montería** Colombia
105 F5 **Montero** Bolivia
100 C3 **Monterrey** Colombia
88 E3 **Monterrey** Mexico
102 C4 **Montes Altos** Brazil
103 D7 **Montes Claros** Brazil
106 F6 **Montes de Oca** Argentina
131 F6 **Montesarchio** Italy
128 D3 **Montesclaros** Spain
213 H3 **Montesquieu Islands** WA Australia
126 E5 **Montesquiou** France
130 D5 **Montevarchi** Italy
107 G5 **Montevideo** Uruguay
81 R4 **Montevideo** Minnesota USA
81 O8 **Montezuma** Kansas USA
129 H2 **Montgó, Cala** *cape* Spain
87 H4 **Montgomery** Alabama USA
213 H3 **Montgomery Island** WA Australia
127 H3 **Monthey** Switzerland
127 G2 **Monthois** France
131 C6 **Monti** Sardinia Italy
87 J5 **Monticello** Florida USA
87 J4 **Monticello** Georgia USA
82 F5 **Monticello** Iowa USA
87 I2 **Monticello** Kentucky USA
86 F5 **Monticello** Mississippi USA
81 K8 **Monticello** Utah USA
82 G5 **Monticello** Wisconsin USA
130 D4 **Montichiari** Italy
107 G4 **Montiel, Cuchilla de** *range* Argentina
126 E4 **Montignac** France
126 F2 **Montigny** France
83 M2 **Montigny, Lac de** *lake* Quebec Canada
128 B4 **Montijo** Portugal
128 C4 **Montijo** Spain
90 D6 **Montijo, Golfo de** *lake* Panama
128 D5 **Montilla** Spain
162 B2 **Montipa** Angola
105 I5 **Montividiu** Brazil
139 H5 **Montivilliers** France
126 F3 **Montluçon** France
126 F3 **Montmarault** France
75 T7 **Montmartre** Saskatchewan Canada
127 H4 **Montmélian** France
127 H5 **Montmeyan** France
126 E2 **Montmirail** France
126 E3 **Montmorillon** France
219 J1 **Monto** Qld Australia
121 O5 **Montola** Finland
128 F3 **Montón** Spain
128 D4 **Montoro, Embalse de** *lake* Spain
80 J5 **Montpelier** Idaho USA
81 P3 **Montpelier** North Dakota USA
83 O4 **Montpelier** Vermont USA
126 F5 **Montpellier** France
126 E4 **Montpon-Ménestérol** France
124 C4 **Montpont** France
82 J3 **Montreal** *watercourse* Ontario Canada
83 O4 **Montreal** Quebec Canada
75 S5 **Montréal** *watercourse* Saskatchewan Canada
124 C4 **Montréal** France
82 F3 **Montreal** Wisconsin USA
82 I3 **Montreal Island** Ontario Canada
126 E5 **Montréjeau** France
126 E3 **Montrésor** France
139 I4 **Montreuil** France
127 H3 **Montreux** Switzerland
127 G3 **Montrevel-en-Bresse** France
74 M8 **Montrose** British Columbia Canada
142 F4 **Montrose** Angus Scotland UK
86 F4 **Montrose** Arkansas USA
81 L7 **Montrose** Colorado USA
77 V8 **Monts, Pointe des** *cape* Quebec Canada
126 E3 **Monts-sur-Guesnes** France
126 F4 **Montsalvy** France
126 G3 **Montsauche** France
109 17 **Montserrat** *UK territory* Caribbean
109 17 **Montserrat** Montserrat
126 D2 **Montsûrs** France
80 F4 **Monument** Oregon USA
85 K4 **Monument** *watercourse* Texas USA
78 G1 **Monumental Island** Nunavut Canada
181 H4 **Monywa** Myanmar
124 E5 **Monza** Italy
162 E3 **Monze** Zambia
129 G3 **Monzón** Spain
130 D4 **Monzone** Italy
216 E6 **Moodiarrup** WA Australia
86 C5 **Moody** Texas USA
162 C5 **Mooifontein** Namibia
218 D3 **Moolawatana** SA Australia
83 L8 **Moomaw, Lake** West Virginia USA
218 E3 **Moomba** SA Australia
80 E6 **Moon Lake** California USA
214 E6 **Moonah** *watercourse* Qld Australia
218 E3 **Moonba, Lake** SA Australia
83 J2 **Moonbeam** Ontario Canada
219 J4 **Moonbi** NSW Australia
218 H8 **Moondarra** Vic. Australia
214 E6 **Moondarra, Lake** Qld Australia
219 J1 **Moonford** Qld Australia
215 I5 **Moongobulla** Qld Australia
218 H3 **Moongulla** NSW Australia
219 J2 **Moonie** Qld Australia
219 I2 **Moonie** *watercourse* Qld Australia
53 R5 **Moonless Mountains** *underwater feature* Pacific Ocean
218 C6 **Moonta** SA Australia
216 D4 **Moonyoonooka** WA Australia
143 D3 **Moor** Ireland
198 E4 **Moor, Kepulauan** *islands* Indonesia
216 D5 **Moora** WA Australia
218 E1 **Mooraberree** Qld Australia
218 F4 **Mooratchia Lake** NSW Australia
81 M4 **Moorcroft** Wyoming USA
122 D6 **Moordorf** Germany
219 K2 **Moore** Qld Australia
216 D5 **Moore** *watercourse* WA Australia
80 I5 **Moore** Idaho USA
81 K3 **Moore** Montana USA
86 C3 **Moore** Oklahoma USA
84 G1 **Moore** Utah USA
58 L2 **Moore, Cape** Antarctica
216 E4 **Moore, Lake** WA Australia
216 H2 **Moore, Mount** WA Australia
58 K1 **Moore Embayment** *bay* Antarctica
87 K7 **Moore Haven** Florida USA
219 K1 **Moore Park** Qld Australia
215 J4 **Moore Reefs** Coral Sea Islands Territory Australia
223 14a **Moorea** *island* French Polynesia
140 B2 **Moorefield** Armagh Northern Ireland UK
86 B2 **Mooreland** Oklahoma USA
78 H4 **Moores Harbour** Newfoundland and Labrador Canada
87 M7 **Moores Island** Bahamas
87 K3 **Mooresville** North Carolina USA
143 F2 **Moorfields** Ballymena Northern Ireland UK
81 Q3 **Moorhead** Minnesota USA
216 F5 **Moorine Rock** WA Australia
218 F5 **Moornanyah Lake** NSW Australia
218 G8 **Moorooduc** Vic. Australia
218 E6 **Moorook** SA Australia
214 C1 **Mooroongga Island** NT Australia
162 C6 **Moorreesburg** South Africa
77 O7 **Moose** *watercourse* Ontario Canada
76 G7 **Moose Island** Manitoba Canada
75 S7 **Moose Jaw** Saskatchewan Canada
75 S7 **Moose Jaw** *watercourse* Saskatchewan Canada
75 V6 **Moose Lake** Manitoba Canada
82 E3 **Moose Lake** Minnesota USA
77 O7 **Moose River** Ontario Canada
83 Q4 **Moosehead Lake** Maine USA
75 V7 **Moosehorn** Manitoba Canada
83 P4 **Moosilauke, Mount** New Hampshire USA
75 U7 **Moosomin** Saskatchewan Canada
77 O7 **Moosonee** Ontario Canada
163 G3 **Mopeia** Mozambique
162 D4 **Mopipi** Botswana
154 F6 **Mopti** Mali
154 F6 **Mopti** *admin. area* Mali
179 K3 **Moqor** Afghanistan
104 D5 **Moquegua** Peru
104 D5 **Moquegua** *admin. area* Peru
101 E2 **Moquetico** Venezuela
125 J4 **Mór** Hungary
159 G2 **Mora** Cameroon
128 B4 **Mora** Portugal
128 E4 **Mora** Spain
122 H2 **Mora** Sweden
82 E4 **Mora** Minnesota USA
106 D5 **Mora, Cerro** *mountain* Chile
129 F3 **Mora de Rubielos** Spain
132 A4 **Morača** *watercourse* Montenegro
105 H2 **Morada Bom Lugar** Brazil
186 E5 **Moradabad** Uttar Pradesh India
163 H3 **Morafenobe** Madagascar
218 G6 **Morago** NSW Australia
130 H5 **Morakovo** Montenegro
128 C3 **Moraleja** Spain
100 B4 **Morales** Colombia
100 C2 **Morales** Colombia
90 B4 **Morales** Guatemala
86 C6 **Morales** Texas USA
89 F4 **Morales, Laguna de** *lake* Mexico
163 I3 **Moramanga** Madagascar
86 B4 **Moran** Texas USA
101 F2 **Moranacas, Islas** *islands* Venezuela
215 J7 **Moranbah** Qld Australia
223 14 **Morane** *reef* French Polynesia
90 E3 **Morant Point** Jamaica
142 C4 **Morar** Highland Scotland UK
142 C4 **Morar, Loch** *lake* Scotland UK
127 H3 **Morat, Lac de** *lake* Switzerland
128 E3 **Morata de Tajuña** Spain
128 F4 **Moratalla** Spain
187 E10 **Moratuwa** Sri Lanka
125 H4 **Moravče** Slovenia
132 B3 **Moravița** Romania
132 C4 **Moravitsa** Bulgaria
125 J3 **Morávka** Czech Republic
125 I3 **Moravská Třebová** Czech Republic
125 J3 **Moravskoslezský Kraj** *admin. area* Czech Republic
216 E4 **Morawa** WA Australia
101 G2 **Morawhanna** Guyana
125 K2 **Morawica** Poland
125 J2 **Morawin** Poland
142 E3 **Moray** *admin. area* Scotland UK
215 I6 **Moray Downs** Qld Australia
142 E3 **Moray Firth** *bay* Scotland UK
214 A3 **Moray Range** NT Australia
124 D3 **Morbach** Germany
186 C6 **Morbi** Gujarat India
164 6b **Morbihan, Golfe du** *bay* French Southern and Antarctic Lands
126 D4 **Morcenx** France
100 D2 **Mórchipa** Venezuela
139 G2 **Morcott** Rutland England UK
218 F4 **Morden** NSW Australia
218 F4 **Morden** *watercourse* NSW Australia
218 G7 **Mordialloc** Vic. Australia
142 D2 **More, Loch** *lake* Scotland UK
122 D1 **Møre og Romsdal** *admin. area* Norway
81 N4 **Moreau** *watercourse* South Dakota USA
86 F5 **Moreauville** Louisiana USA
142 F5 **Morebattle** Scottish Borders Scotland UK
140 F2 **Morecambe** Lancashire England UK
140 E2 **Morecombe Bay** England UK
219 I3 **Moree** NSW Australia
126 E3 **Morée** France
142 C3 **Morefield** Highland Scotland UK
181 H4 **Moreh** Manipur India
139 I3 **Morehall** Kent England UK
199 G6 **Morehead** *watercourse* Papua New Guinea
86 G2 **Morehouse** Missouri USA
105 F3 **Moreira Cabral, Serra** *range* Brazil
81 M2 **Moreland** Saskatchewan Canada
88 E5 **Morelia** Mexico
215 G7 **Morella** Qld Australia
129 F3 **Morella** Spain
85 I7 **Morelos** Mexico
89 F5 **Morelos** *admin. area* Mexico
186 E5 **Morena** Madhya Pradesh India
128 D5 **Morena, Sierra** *range* Spain
106 D2 **Moreno, Bahía** *bay* Chile
108 D3 **Moreno, Isla** *island* Argentina
108 B5 **Moreno, Ventisquero** *glacier* Argentina
84 D4 **Moreno Valley** California USA
131 C6 **Mores** Sardinia Italy
140 E2 **Moresby** Cumbria England UK
74 E6 **Moresby Island** British Columbia Canada
124 C5 **Morestel** France
219 K2 **Moreton Bay** Qld Australia
219 K2 **Moreton Island (Gnoorganbin)** Qld Australia
138 D4 **Moretonhampstead** Devon England UK
127 H3 **Morez** France
138 C2 **Morfa** Pembrokeshire Wales UK
138 C3 **Morfa-Bach** Carmarthenshire Wales UK
138 C2 **Morfa Nefyn** Gwynedd Wales UK
218 D6 **Morgan** SA Australia
213 I3 **Morgan** *watercourse* WA Australia
86 F6 **Morgan City** Louisiana USA
80 E8 **Morgan Hill** California USA
183 P3 **Morgan Tajga** *mountain* Russian Federation
100 E3 **Morganito** Venezuela
82 H8 **Morgantown** Kentucky USA
83 L7 **Morgantown** West Virginia USA
128 B5 **Morgavel, Barragem de** *lake* Portugal
127 H3 **Morges** Switzerland
179 L2 **Morgh, Kowtal-e** *pass* Afghanistan
130 E4 **Morgo, Isola** *island* Italy
124 D3 **Morhange** France
79 G7 **Morhiban, Lac de** *lake* Quebec Canada
218 G8 **Moriac** Vic. Australia
85 I3 **Moriarty** New Mexico USA
158 C3 **Moribaya** Guinea
74 H5 **Morice Lake** British Columbia Canada
74 H5 **Moricetown** British Columbia Canada
179 L2 **Morich** Pakistan
101 F2 **Morichal** Venezuela
100 D4 **Morichal Viejo** Colombia
101 E2 **Morichalito** Venezuela
142 D3 **Morie, Loch** *lake* Scotland UK
199 G5 **Morigio Island** Papua New Guinea
159 F2 **Moriki** Nigeria
124 E2 **Moringen** Germany
123 P4 **Morino** Russian Federation
75 O6 **Morinville** Alberta Canada
193 I3 **Morioka** Japan
222 7 **Moriou** Vanuatu
101 F4 **Moriru** Brazil
219 J5 **Morisset** NSW Australia
142 D3 **Moriston** *watercourse* Scotland UK
121 M3 **Morjärv** Sweden
182 E2 **Morki** Russian Federation
135 X5 **Morkoka** *watercourse* Russian Federation
120 H6 **Mörkret** Sweden
126 C2 **Morlaix** France
74 E2 **Morley** *watercourse* Yukon Territory Canada
141 G2 **Morley** Durham England UK
141 G3 **Morley** West Yorkshire England UK
82 G8 **Morley** Missouri USA
74 E2 **Morley River** Yukon Territory Canada
84 G3 **Mormon Lake** Arizona USA
80 H5 **Mormon Reservoir** Idaho USA
109 16 **Morne-à-l'Eau** Guadeloupe
109 15 **Morne Raquette** Dominica
218 E1 **Morney** Qld Australia
214 F4 **Morning Inlet** *watercourse* Qld Australia
75 O6 **Morningside** Alberta Canada
214 E4 **Mornington Island** Qld Australia
179 K4 **Moro** Pakistan
195 I6 **Moro Gulf** Philippines
199 H5 **Morobe** Papua New Guinea
160 E3 **Morobo** Sudan
154 E2 **Morocco** *country* Africa
104 B3 **Morococha** Peru
143 D4 **Moroe** Ireland
161 F5 **Morogoro** Tanzania
161 F5 **Morogoro** *admin. area* Tanzania
162 D5 **Morokweng** South Africa
90 C4 **Morolica** Honduras
197 J5 **Moromaho** *island* Indonesia
163 H4 **Morombe** Madagascar
90 E2 **Morón** Cuba
100 D2 **Morón** Venezuela
190 D2 **Mörön** Mongolia
104 B1 **Morona** *watercourse* Peru
100 B5 **Morona-Santiago** *admin. area* Ecuador
163 H4 **Morondava** Madagascar
158 C3 **Morondo** Côte d'Ivoire
163 H2 **Moroni** Comoros
158 D3 **Moronou** Côte d'Ivoire
219 K3 **Mororo** NSW Australia
135 AG7 **Moroshechnoye** Russian Federation
197 K3 **Morotai** *island* Indonesia
197 K3 **Morotai, Selat** *strait* Indonesia
161 E3 **Moroto** Uganda
121 P2 **Morottaja** Finland
198 B4 **Morowali** Indonesia
182 D4 **Morozovsk** Russian Federation
124 D5 **Morozzo** Italy
141 G1 **Morpeth** Northumberland England UK
136 E6 **Morphou** Cyprus
103 B7 **Morrinhos** Brazil
220 F3 **Morrinsville** New Zealand
88 D2 **Morrión** Mexico
86 H4 **Morris** Alabama USA
82 G6 **Morris** Illinois USA
81 R4 **Morris** Minnesota USA
73 P2 **Morris Jesup, Kap** *cape* Greenland
57 E1 **Morris Jesup Rise** *underwater feature* Arctic Ocean
87 I3 **Morrison** Tennessee USA
84 F4 **Morristown** Arizona USA
87 J2 **Morristown** Tennessee USA
90 C5 **Morrito** Nicaragua
158 B3 **Morro** *watercourse* Sierra Leone
106 D3 **Morro, Punta** *cape* Chile
100 A5 **Morro, Punta del** *cape* Ecuador
103 B8 **Morro Agudo** Brazil
84 B3 **Morro Bay** California USA
164 3d **Morro del Jable** Canary Islands
103 D5 **Morro do Chapéu** Brazil
104 A2 **Mórrope** Peru
104 B2 **Morropón** Peru
102 C5 **Morros** Brazil
100 C2 **Morrosquillo, Golfo de** *bay* Colombia
163 G3 **Morrumbala** Mozambique
163 G4 **Morrumbene** Mozambique
122 H4 **Morrumsån** *watercourse* Sweden
122 E4 **Mors** *cape* Denmark
182 D2 **Morsansk** Russian Federation
58 I2 **Morse, Cape** Antarctica
131 C5 **Morsetta, Capo della** *cape* Corsica France
132 C1 **Morshyn** Ukraine
187 E7 **Morsi** Maharashtra India
121 S5 **Morskaya Masel'ga** Russian Federation
76 H8 **Morson** Ontario Canada
131 C9 **Morsott** Algeria
139 H2 **Morston** Norfolk England UK
126 D2 **Mortain** France
138 C3 **Morte Point** England UK
127 H3 **Morteau** France
138 C3 **Mortehoe** Devon England UK
127 I5 **Mortella, Punta** *cape* Corsica France
131 F7 **Mortelle** Italy

88 D3 **Mortero** Mexico
106 F4 **Morteros** Argentina
103 A6 **Mortes, Rio das** *watercourse* Brazil
122 I4 **Mörtfors** Sweden
90 E5 **Mortí** Panama
139 F3 **Mortimer** West Berkshire England UK
218 F8 **Mortlake** Vic. Australia
199 J2 **Mortlock Islands** Federated States of Micronesia
139 G2 **Morton** Lincolnshire England UK
82 G6 **Morton** Illinois USA
86 G4 **Morton** Mississippi USA
85 K4 **Morton** Texas USA
80 D3 **Morton** Washington USA
126 E2 **Mortrée** France
120 I5 **Mörtsjön** Sweden
120 I5 **Mörtsjön** *lake* Sweden
109 9 **Moruga** Trinidad and Tobago
218 H6 **Morundah** NSW Australia
219 J6 **Moruya** NSW Australia
218 H2 **Morven** Qld Australia
87 J5 **Morven** Georgia USA
138 E2 **Morville** Shropshire England UK
218 H8 **Morwell** Vic. Australia
123 P2 **Mor'ye** Russian Federation
123 O5 **Mosar** Belarus
120 I5 **Mosätt** Sweden
Moscow *see* **Moskva** Russian Federation
80 G3 **Moscow** Idaho USA
81 O8 **Moscow** Kansas USA
58 H2 **Moscow University Ice Shelf** Antarctica
140 F2 **Mosedale** Cumbria England UK
162 D5 **Moselebe** *watercourse* Botswana
127 H2 **Moselle** *watercourse* France
124 D2 **Moselle** *watercourse* Germany
79 G10 **Moser River** Nova Scotia Canada
80 F3 **Moses Lake** Washington USA
105 E5 **Mosetenes, Cordillera de** *range* Bolivia
105 F5 **Mosevi** Bolivia
134 K5 **Moseyevo** Russian Federation
221 D7 **Mosgiel** New Zealand
121 R3 **Mosha** Russian Federation
179 H2 **Moshajari** Iran
162 D5 **Moshaweng** *watercourse* South Africa
123 N3 **Moshchnyy, Ostrov** *island* Russian Federation
159 E3 **Moshi** *watercourse* Nigeria
161 F4 **Moshi** Tanzania
123 P5 **Moshkany** Belarus
199 J5 **Mosigo** Papua New Guinea
160 C3 **Mosite** Democratic Republic of Congo
120 H4 **Mosjøen** Norway
135 AD8 **Moskal'vo** Russian Federation
120 H3 **Mosken** *island* Norway
120 H2 **Moskenesøy** *island* Norway
120 K4 **Moskosel** Sweden
134 I7 **Moskovskaya Oblast'** *admin. area* Russian Federation
183 K6 **Moskva** Tajikistan
134 I7 **Moskva (Moscow)** Russian Federation
132 E2 **Moşna** Romania
140 B3 **Mosney Camp** Ireland
222 7 **Moso** *island* Vanuatu
124 F4 **Moso in Passiria** Italy
104 D4 **Mosoc Llacta** Peru
125 I4 **Mosoni-Duna** *watercourse* Hungary
85 K3 **Mosquero** New Mexico USA
129 F3 **Mosqueruela** Spain
89 I6 **Mosquitia** *region* Honduras
90 E5 **Mosquito, Punta** *cape* Panama
87 K6 **Mosquito Lagoon** Florida USA
72 F7 **Mosquito Lake** Alaska USA
90 D4 **Mosquitos, Costa de** *region* Nicaragua
90 D5 **Mosquitos, Golfo de los** *bay* Panama
122 F3 **Moss** Norway
219 J1 **Moss, Mount** Qld Australia
86 C4 **Moss Lake** Texas USA
219 J6 **Moss Vale** NSW Australia
123 K2 **Mossalafjärd** *bay* Finland
142 F3 **Mossat** Aberdeenshire Scotland UK
75 S8 **Mossbank** Saskatchewan Canada
221 C7 **Mossburn** New Zealand
162 D6 **Mossel Bay** South Africa
162 D6 **Mossel Bay** *bay* South Africa
159 G5 **Mossendjo** Congo
218 G5 **Mossgiel** NSW Australia
124 E3 **Mössingen** Germany
215 H4 **Mossman** Qld Australia
122 I2 **Mössön** Sweden
102 E4 **Mossoró** Brazil
75 T5 **Mossy** *watercourse* Saskatchewan Canada
80 D3 **Mossyrock** Washington USA
133 D5 **Most** Bulgaria
130 E3 **Most na Soči** Slovenia
155 G1 **Mostaganem** Algeria
130 G5 **Mostar** Bosnia and Herzegovina
107 I4 **Mostardas, Ponta de** *cape* Brazil
164 1a **Mosteiros** Azores
125 H2 **Mostek** Czech Republic
132 E3 **Mostiştea, Lacul** *lake* Romania
128 E3 **Móstoles** Spain
75 Q5 **Mostoos Hills** Saskatchewan Canada
183 N2 **Mostovoye** *lake* Russian Federation
132 G2 **Mostovoye** Ukraine
125 L2 **Mosty** Poland
197 H2 **Mostyn** Malaysia
140 E3 **Mostyn** Flintshire Wales UK
Mosul *see* **Al Mawşil** Iraq
122 E3 **Møsvatnet** *lake* Norway
156 F5 **Mot'a** Ethiopia
128 E4 **Mota del Cuervo** Spain
222 7 **Mota Lava** *island* Vanuatu
159 H4 **Motaba** *watercourse* Congo
90 B4 **Motagua** *watercourse* Guatemala
122 H3 **Motala** Sweden
139 E3 **Motcombe** Dorset England UK
160 B3 **Motenge-Boma** Democratic Republic of Congo
186 E6 **Moth** Uttar Pradesh India
142 E5 **Motherwell** North Lanarkshire Scotland UK
197 J3 **Moti** *island* Indonesia
186 F5 **Motihari** Bihar India
128 F4 **Motilla del Palancar** Spain
120 J4 **Mötingselberget** Sweden
220 G3 **Motiti Island** New Zealand
81 R3 **Motley** Minnesota USA
181 I4 **Motlong** Myanmar
101 F3 **Motó** Venezuela
162 D4 **Motokwe** Botswana
199 J6 **Motorina Island** Papua New Guinea
128 E5 **Motril** Spain
132 E1 **Motrunki** Ukraine
81 N3 **Mott** North Dakota USA
130 E4 **Motta di Livenza** Italy
131 G6 **Mottola** Italy
220 G3 **Motu** *watercourse* New Zealand
221 E5 **Motueka** New Zealand
221 E6 **Motunau Beach** New Zealand
181 H3 **Motuo** Xizang Zizhiqu China
104 B2 **Motupe** Peru
223 9 **Moturiki** *island* Fiji
220 2 **Motutapu** *island* Cook Islands New Zealand
220 F4 **Motutere** New Zealand
160 B3 **Mouali Gbangba** Congo
58 L2 **Moubray Bay** Antarctica
77 U6 **Mouchalagane** *watercourse* Quebec Canada
127 G3 **Mouchard** France
91 G2 **Mouchoir Bank** Turks and Caicos Islands
91 G2 **Mouchoir Passage** Turks and Caicos Islands
154 D5 **Moudjéria** Mauritania
127 H3 **Moudon** Switzerland
159 G5 **Mouenda** Gabon
123 L2 **Mouhijärvi** *lake* Finland
158 D2 **Mouhoun** *watercourse* Burkina Faso
158 D3 **Mouhoun (Black Volta)** *watercourse* Ghana
159 G5 **Mouila** Gabon
159 I3 **Mouka** Central African Republic
218 G6 **Moulamein** NSW Australia
128 C6 **Moulay-Bousselham** Morocco
109 13 **Moule a Chique, Cape** St Lucia
126 E3 **Mouliherne** France
126 F3 **Moulins** France
126 E3 **Moulismes** France
Moulmein *see* **Mawlamyaing** Myanmar
141 F3 **Moulton** Cheshire England UK
86 C6 **Moulton** Texas USA
58 P1 **Moulton, Mount** Antarctica
87 J5 **Moultrie** Georgia USA
87 K4 **Moultrie, Lake** South Carolina USA
181 G4 **Moulvibazar** Bangladesh
142 E4 **Moulzie** Angus Scotland UK
159 G5 **Mounana** Gabon
86 F4 **Mound Bayou** Mississippi USA
159 H3 **Moundou** Chad
82 G8 **Mounds** Illinois USA
86 C3 **Mounds** Oklahoma USA
159 G3 **Mounguel** Cameroon
121 M3 **Mounioälveri** *watercourse* Sweden
158 B3 **Mount, Cape** *cape* Liberia
218 G2 **Mount Alfred** Qld Australia
80 D4 **Mount Angel** Oregon USA
84 C6 **Mount Augusta** *volcano* Isla Guadeloupe Mexico
216 E2 **Mount Augustus** WA Australia
218 D6 **Mount Barker** SA Australia
216 E7 **Mount Barker** WA Australia
213 H4 **Mount Barnett** WA Australia
218 B3 **Mount Barry** SA Australia
211 inset **Mount Bates** Norfolk Island Australia
143 D3 **Mount Bellew Bridge** Ireland
221 F5 **Mount Bruce** New Zealand
218 H7 **Mount Buller Alpine Village** Vic. Australia
82 H7 **Mount Carmel** Illinois USA
80 F1 **Mount Cartier** British Columbia Canada
217 M2 **Mount Cavenagh** NT Australia
217 M5 **Mount Christie Siding** SA Australia
216 E2 **Mount Clere** WA Australia
215 I6 **Mount Coolon** Qld Australia
74 J7 **Mount Currie** British Columbia Canada
218 B2 **Mount Dare** SA Australia
214 B7 **Mount Denison** NT Australia
212 F6 **Mount Edgar** WA Australia
215 I6 **Mount Elsie** Qld Australia
54 J4 **Mount Error** *underwater feature* Indian Ocean
162 E6 **Mount Frere** South Africa
218 E7 **Mount Gambier** SA Australia
215 H4 **Mount Garnet** Qld Australia
82 J6 **Mount Gilead** Ohio USA
218 E4 **Mount Gipps** NSW Australia
214 E6 **Mount Guide** Qld Australia
140 A2 **Mount Hamilton** Strabane Northern Ireland UK
213 H4 **Mount Hart** WA Australia
218 G5 **Mount Hope** NSW Australia
215 I6 **Mount Hope** Qld Australia
218 B6 **Mount Hope** SA Australia
213 H4 **Mount House** WA Australia
86 E3 **Mount Ida** Arkansas USA
218 A2 **Mount Irwin** SA Australia
214 E6 **Mount Isa** Qld Australia
218 C5 **Mount Ive** SA Australia
83 L7 **Mount Jackson** Virginia USA
213 G4 **Mount Jowlaenga** WA Australia
87 H2 **Mount Juliet** Tennessee USA
216 E6 **Mount Kokeby** WA Australia
73 L9 **Mount-Laurier** Quebec Canada
214 A7 **Mount Liebig** NT Australia
216 F6 **Mount Madden** WA Australia
216 E4 **Mount Magnet** WA Australia
218 F5 **Mount Manara** NSW Australia
218 F2 **Mount Margaret** Qld Australia
216 H4 **Mount Margaret** WA Australia
219 H2 **Mount Maria** Qld Australia
215 H4 **Mount Molloy** Qld Australia
84 C2 **Mount Montgomery** Nevada USA
215 K7 **Mount Morgan** Qld Australia
79 I8 **Mount Moriah** Newfoundland and Labrador Canada
218 G1 **Mount Morris** Qld Australia
216 D3 **Mount Narryer** WA Australia
215 G5 **Mount Norman** Qld Australia
140 A3 **Mount Nugent** Ireland
86 G5 **Mount Olive** Mississippi USA
215 J6 **Mount Ossa** Qld Australia
79 L9 **Mount Pearl** Newfoundland and Labrador Canada
219 J1 **Mount Perry** Qld Australia
82 I5 **Mount Pleasant** Michigan USA
87 L4 **Mount Pleasant** South Carolina USA
86 H3 **Mount Pleasant** Tennessee USA
86 D4 **Mount Pleasant** Texas USA
80 J7 **Mount Pleasant** Utah USA
83 N6 **Mount Pocono** Pennsylvania USA
82 H5 **Mount Prospect** Illinois USA
214 C7 **Mount Riddock** NT Australia
216 D2 **Mount Sandiman** WA Australia
218 B2 **Mount Sarah** SA Australia
80 D6 **Mount Shasta** California USA
214 C7 **Mount Skinner** NT Australia
221 D6 **Mount Somers** New Zealand
212 D7 **Mount Stuart** WA Australia
215 H6 **Mount Sturgeon** Qld Australia
215 H5 **Mount Surprise** Qld Australia
215 G5 **Mount Turner** Qld Australia
83 M6 **Mount Union** Pennsylvania USA
216 F2 **Mount Vernon** WA Australia
86 H5 **Mount Vernon** Alabama USA
82 G7 **Mount Vernon** Illinois USA
82 I8 **Mount Vernon** Kentucky USA
83 J6 **Mount Vernon** Ohio USA
133 B6 **Mounta, Akra** *cape* Greece
100 A1 **Mountain** Colombia
81 Q2 **Mountain** North Dakota USA
76 D6 **Mountain Cabin** Saskatchewan Canada
87 J3 **Mountain City** Georgia USA
87 K2 **Mountain City** Tennessee USA
86 C5 **Mountain City** Texas USA
82 E8 **Mountain Grove** Missouri USA
86 E2 **Mountain Home** Arkansas USA
80 H5 **Mountain Home** Idaho USA
74 M6 **Mountain Park** Alberta Canada
86 B3 **Mountain Park** Oklahoma USA
101 G4 **Mountain Point** Guyana
214 B3 **Mountain Valley** NT Australia
75 O8 **Mountain View** Alberta Canada
84 inset **Mountain View** Hawai'i USA
82 F8 **Mountain View** Missouri USA
81 J6 **Mountain View** Wyoming USA
72 C6 **Mountain Village** Alaska USA
85 I3 **Mountainair** New Mexico USA
86 D3 **Mountainburg** Arkansas USA
142 E5 **Mountbenger** Scottish Borders Scotland UK
139 H4 **Mountfield** East Sussex England UK
143 E2 **Mountfield** Omagh Northern Ireland UK
143 E2 **Mountjoy** Omagh Northern Ireland UK
143 E3 **Mountmellick** Ireland
214 B1 **Mountnorris Bay** NT Australia
143 E4 **Mountrath** Ireland
138 B4 **Mount's Bay** England UK
219 I1 **Moura** Qld Australia
101 F5 **Moura** Brazil
128 C4 **Moura** Portugal
128 C4 **Mourão** Portugal
156 C4 **Mourdi, Dépression du** *pan* Chad
154 E6 **Mourdiah** Mali
126 D5 **Mourenx** France
215 I4 **Mourilyan** Qld Australia
133 D6 **Mourtzeflos, Akra** *cape* Greece
126 F1 **Mouscron** Belgium
199 H4 **Mouse Island** Papua New Guinea
159 H2 **Mousgougou** Chad
155 J6 **Moussoro** Chad
127 H5 **Moustiers-Sainte-Marie** France
194 B4 **Mouth of the Ayeyarwady (Irrawaddy)** *bay* Myanmar
127 H3 **Mouthe** France
179 K5 **Mouths of the Indus** *sea* Pakistan
127 H4 **Moûtiers** France
220 G3 **Moutohora Island** New Zealand
198 B3 **Moutong** Indonesia
164 8 **Moutsamoudou** Comoros
126 F2 **Mouy** France
159 G5 **Mouyondzi** Congo
155 J6 **Mouzarak** Chad
120 K2 **Movik** Norway
143 E1 **Moville** Donegal Ireland
81 Q5 **Moville** Iowa USA
101 G3 **Mowasi Mountains** Guyana
143 F2 **Mowhan** Armagh Northern Ireland UK
213 G5 **Mowla Bluff** WA Australia
162 D2 **Moxico** *admin. area* Angola
102 E5 **Moxotó** *watercourse* Brazil
143 F2 **Moy** Ireland
143 D2 **Moy** *watercourse* Ireland
143 F2 **Moy** Dungannon Northern Ireland UK
142 D4 **Moy** Highland Scotland UK
143 F2 **Moyad** Newry and Mourne Northern Ireland UK
161 F3 **Moyalē** Kenya
140 B1 **Moyarget** Moyle Northern Ireland UK
77 X5 **Moyen, Lac** *lake* Quebec Canada
159 H3 **Moyen-Chari** *admin. area* Chad
159 G5 **Moyen-Ogooué** *admin. area* Gabon
127 H2 **Moyenvic** France
135 V5 **Moyero** *watercourse* Russian Federation
75 N8 **Moyie** British Columbia Canada
75 M8 **Moyie Springs** Idaho USA
213 J3 **Moyle** *watercourse* NT Australia
143 F1 **Moyle** *admin. area* Northern Ireland UK
143 E2 **Moyle** Strabane Northern Ireland UK
138 C2 **Moylgrove** Pembrokeshire Wales UK
140 B3 **Moynalty** Ireland
143 D3 **Moyne** Ireland
197 H6 **Moyo** *island* Indonesia
104 B2 **Moyobamba** Peru
143 C3 **Moyour Bridge** Ireland
160 E4 **Moyowosi** *watercourse* Tanzania
155 J6 **Moyto** Chad
184 F5 **Moyu** Xinjiang Uygur Zizhiqu China
183 L4 **Moyynty** Kazakhstan
163 F3 **Mozambique** *country* Africa
163 H3 **Mozambique Channel** *strait* Mozambique/Madagascar
54 H9 **Mozambique Escarpment** *underwater feature* Indian Ocean
54 H8 **Mozambique Plateau** *underwater feature* Indian Ocean
103 B6 **Mozarlândia** Brazil
128 B3 **Mozelos** Portugal
124 E5 **Mozzanica** Italy
159 G5 **Mpama** *watercourse* Congo
160 E5 **Mpanda** Tanzania
162 E3 **Mpandamatenga** Botswana
159 G3 **Mpem** *watercourse* Cameroon
154 E6 **Mpessoba** Mali
163 F2 **Mpika** Zambia
159 H4 **Mpoko** *watercourse* Central African Republic
161 F5 **Mponde** *watercourse* Tanzania
163 F2 **Mponela** Malawi
162 E2 **Mpongwe** Zambia
160 E5 **Mporokoso** Zambia
158 D3 **Mpraeso** Ghana
160 E5 **Mpui** Tanzania
160 E5 **Mpulungu** Zambia
162 E5 **Mpumalanga** *admin. area* South Africa
159 I5 **Mpungu** Democratic Republic of Congo
161 F6 **Mpurukasese** Tanzania
162 E6 **Mqanduli** South Africa
130 G4 **Mrakovica** Bosnia and Herzegovina
125 J5 **Mramor** Bosnia and Herzegovina
130 H5 **Mratinje** Montenegro
181 G5 **Mrauk-U (Myohaung)** Myanmar
127 L4 **Mrkopalj** Croatia
125 K1 **Mroków** Poland
155 I1 **M'Saken** Tunisia
161 F5 **Msangasi** *watercourse* Tanzania
125 M1 **Mscibava** Belarus
125 G2 **Mšec** Czech Republic
125 H2 **Mšeno** Czech Republic
132 D1 **Mshanets** Ukraine
155 G1 **M'Sila** Algeria
123 Q3 **Mstinskiy Most** Russian Federation
125 K3 **Mszana Dolna** Poland
125 K2 **Mszczonów** Poland
161 F3 **Mtelo** *mountain* Kenya
161 F4 **Mtito Andei** Kenya
164 8b **Mtsamgamouji** Mayotte
182 D5 **Mtskheta** Georgia
163 F5 **Mtubatuba** South Africa
161 G6 **Mtwara** Tanzania
161 F6 **Mtwara** *admin. area* Tanzania
181 H4 **Mu-Se** Myanmar
223 10a **Mu'a** Tonga
163 G2 **Muaguide** Mozambique
163 F2 **Mualadzi** Mozambique
102 B3 **Muaná** Brazil
160 A5 **Muanda** Democratic Republic of Congo
194 E2 **Muang Et** Laos
194 D2 **Muang Hiam** Laos
194 D3 **Muang Hôngsa** Laos
194 D2 **Muang Houn** Laos
194 D2 **Muang Hup** Laos
194 D2 **Muang Khoa** Laos
194 E4 **Muang Khôngédôn** Laos
194 D2 **Muang La** Laos
194 E3 **Muang Mahaxai** Laos
194 D2 **Muang Meung** Laos
194 D2 **Muang Namo** Laos
194 D2 **Muang Ngoy** Laos
194 E3 **Muang Nong** Laos
194 D2 **Muang Ou Tai** Laos
194 D2 **Muang Paktha** Laos
194 D3 **Muang Phiang** Laos
194 E3 **Muang Phin** Laos
194 D2 **Muang Sing** Laos
194 E3 **Muang Songkhon** Laos
194 D3 **Muang Thadua** Laos
194 D2 **Muang Xon** Laos
194 D2 **Muangxay** Laos
163 F3 **Muanza** Mozambique
196 D3 **Muar** Malaysia
196 D3 **Muar** *watercourse* Malaysia
197 G2 **Muara** Brunei
197 H3 **Muara Pantai** *island* Indonesia
197 H3 **Muaraatap** Indonesia
196 D4 **Muarabeliti** Indonesia
197 G3 **Muarabemlelakidau** Indonesia
196 D4 **Muarabulian** Indonesia
196 D4 **Muarabungo** Indonesia
196 E5 **Muaradua** Indonesia
196 D4 **Muaraenim** Indonesia
197 G4 **Muarainu** Indonesia
197 H4 **Muarajawa** Indonesia
197 H4 **Muarakaman** Indonesia
196 D4 **Muaralabuh** Indonesia
196 D4 **Muaralakitan** Indonesia
197 H3 **Muaralasan** Indonesia
197 G4 **Muaralaung** Indonesia
197 H3 **Muaras Reef** Indonesia
196 D4 **Muarasabak** Indonesia
197 H3 **Muarasengajan** Indonesia
196 C4 **Muarasiberut** Indonesia
196 C4 **Muarasigep** Indonesia
196 C3 **Muarasipongi** Indonesia
196 D4 **Muaratebo** Indonesia
197 G4 **Muarateweh** Indonesia
197 H3 **Muarawahau** Indonesia
197 J4 **Muari** *island* Indonesia
179 K5 **Muāri, Rās** *cape* Pakistan
163 G3 **Muatua** Mozambique
160 E3 **Mubende** Uganda
159 G2 **Mubi** Nigeria
182 J6 **Muborak** Uzbekistan
198 E4 **Mubrani** Indonesia
196 E3 **Mubur** *island* Indonesia
160 B5 **Mucaba, Serra** *range* Angola
101 F4 **Mucajai** *watercourse* Brazil
101 F4 **Mucajaí, Serra do** *range* Brazil
163 F3 **Mucanha** *watercourse* Mozambique
212 F6 **Muccan** WA Australia
124 D2 **Much** Germany
138 E2 **Much Wenlock** Shropshire England UK
164 3b **Muchachos, Roque de los** *volcano* Canary Islands
104 E4 **Muchanes** Bolivia
104 E4 **Muchani, Serranía de** *range* Bolivia
216 D5 **Muchea** WA Australia
140 B4 **Muchwood Cross Roads** Ireland
142 B4 **Muck** *island* Scotland UK
218 E4 **Muck, Lake** NSW Australia
219 I2 **Muckadilla** Qld Australia
163 H2 **Mucojo** Mozambique
162 D2 **Muconda** Angola
162 B3 **Mucope** Angola
162 C3 **Mucope** *watercourse* Angola
163 G3 **Mucubela** Mozambique
105 E2 **Mucuim** *watercourse* Brazil
160 C6 **Mucumbo** *watercourse* Zambia
163 F3 **Mucumbura** Mozambique
100 D2 **Mucumpiz** Venezuela
162 C3 **Mucundi** Angola
163 G3 **Mucupia** Mozambique
101 F5 **Mucura** Brazil
103 E7 **Mucuri** Brazil
103 E7 **Mucuri** *watercourse* Brazil
103 D7 **Mucurici** Brazil
162 D2 **Mucussueje** Angola
80 I5 **Mud Lake** Idaho USA
82 B4 **Mud Lake Reservoir** South Dakota USA
74 J6 **Mud River** British Columbia Canada
196 D2 **Muda** *watercourse* Malaysia
142 D2 **Mudale** Highland Scotland UK
191 L4 **Mudanjiang** Heilongjiang China
130 C2 **Mudau** Germany
138 C3 **Muddiford** Devon England UK
81 N8 **Muddy Creek Reservoir** Colorado USA
187 D8 **Mudgal** Karnataka India
215 I8 **Mudge, Mount** Qld Australia
187 D7 **Mudhol** Andhra Pradesh India
187 D8 **Mudhol** Karnataka India
178 F7 **Mūdiyah** Yemen
75 R4 **Mudjatik** *watercourse* Saskatchewan Canada
187 D7 **Mudkhed** Maharashtra India
164 3b **Mudo, Punta del** *cape* Canary Islands
194 C3 **Mudon** Myanmar
133 E4 **Mŭdrets** Bulgaria
161 H2 **Mudug** *admin. area* Somalia
133 G5 **Mudurnu** Turkey
133 G5 **Mudurnu** *watercourse* Turkey
121 U5 **Mud'yuga** Russian Federation
163 G2 **Mueda** Mozambique
214 C7 **Mueller** *watercourse* NT Australia
213 I5 **Mueller Range** WA Australia
163 F2 **Muende** Mozambique
108 B4 **Muerte, Meseta de la** *plateau* Argentina
189 G3 **Mufu Shan** *mountain* Hunan China
162 E2 **Mufulira** Zambia
185 J6 **Mug Qu** *watercourse* Qinghai China
160 E5 **Mugewo** Tanzania
216 D3 **Muggon** WA Australia
136 D6 **Muğla** *admin. area* Turkey
156 D5 **Muhagiriya** Sudan
184 G6 **Muhala** Xinjiang Uygur Zizhiqu China
160 D5 **Muhala** Democratic Republic of Congo
179 L4 **Muhammad Ashraf** Pakistan
156 F3 **Muhammad Col** Sudan
161 E5 **Muhesi** *watercourse* Tanzania
127 K1 **Mühlberg** Germany
127 L2 **Mühldorf** Austria
58 A2 **Mühlig-Hofmann Mountains** Antarctica
130 F2 **Mühlviertel** *region* Austria
121 N5 **Muhola** Finland
121 O4 **Muhos** Finland
123 L3 **Muhu** *island* Estonia
161 F6 **Muhukuru** Tanzania
163 G2 **Muhula** Mozambique
160 D4 **Muhulu** Democratic Republic of Congo
161 F6 **Muhuwesi** *watercourse* Tanzania
194 E5 **Mui Ca Mau** *island* Vietnam
194 F5 **Mui Ca Na** *island* Vietnam
194 F5 **Mui Kê Ga** *island* Vietnam
194 E3 **Mui Ròn** *island* Vietnam
142 E4 **Muick, Loch** *lake* Scotland UK
163 G2 **Muidumbe** Mozambique
162 D2 **Muié** Angola
138 A2 **Muine Bheag** Ireland
142 E4 **Muir** Aberdeenshire Scotland UK
216 E7 **Muir, Lake** WA Australia
142 D4 **Muirhill** North Lanarkshire Scotland UK
142 D5 **Muirkirk** East Ayrshire Scotland UK
212 C6 **Muiron Islands** WA Australia
100 A4 **Muisne** Ecuador
163 G2 **Muite** Mozambique
121 P5 **Mujejärvi** Finland
194 C6 **Muk, Ko** *island* Thailand
197 G3 **Mukah** Malaysia
197 G3 **Mukah** *watercourse* Malaysia
160 C5 **Mukanga** Democratic Republic of Congo
194 E3 **Mukdahan** Thailand
141 F2 **Muker** North Yorkshire England UK
222 3 **Mukeru** Palau
76 M6 **Muketei** *watercourse* Ontario Canada
125 L1 **Mukhavets** Belarus
193 H1 **Mukhen** Russian Federation
80 D3 **Mukilteo** Washington USA
196 D4 **Mukomuko** Indonesia
182 J6 **Mukry** Turkmenistan
186 D4 **Muktsar** Punjab India
160 D5 **Mukunsa** Zambia
160 E5 **Mukupa Kaoma** Zambia
182 G4 **Mukur** Kazakhstan
76 G6 **Mukutawa** *watercourse* Manitoba Canada
187 C11 **Mulaku Atoll** Maldives
183 M4 **Mulaly** Kazakhstan
213 I6 **Mulan** WA Australia
191 K3 **Mulan** Heilongjiang China
163 G3 **Mulanje Mountains** Malawi
101 H5 **Mulato** Brazil
85 H6 **Mulatos** Mexico
109 15 **Mulâtre, Pointe** *cape* Dominica
86 D3 **Mulberry** Arkansas USA
72 D7 **Mulchatna** *watercourse* Alaska USA
106 C6 **Mulchén** Chile
133 D5 **Muldava** Bulgaria
124 G2 **Mulde** *watercourse* Germany
88 C3 **Mulegé** Mexico
185 I4 **Mulei** Xinjiang Uygur Zizhiqu China
197 I6 **Mules** *island* Indonesia
130 D3 **Mules** Italy
85 K3 **Muleshoe** Texas USA
163 G3 **Mulevala** Mozambique
218 H4 **Mulga** *watercourse* NSW Australia
219 J1 **Mulgildie** Qld Australia
216 E4 **Mulgine Hill** WA Australia
215 H4 **Mulgrave, Mount** Qld Australia
216 F2 **Mulgul** WA Australia
128 E5 **Mulhacén** *mountain* Spain
127 H3 **Mulhouse** France
199 F4 **Mulia** Indonesia
223 12c **Mulifanua** Samoa
191 L4 **Muling** Heilongjiang China
187 D9 **Mulki** Karnataka India
142 C4 **Mull** *island* Scotland UK
142 F1 **Mull Head** *cape* Scotland UK
143 F3 **Mullagh** Ireland
140 B3 **Mullagh** Ireland
143 B3 **Mullaghglass** Ireland
143 C2 **Mullaghnacross** Ireland
187 E10 **Mullaittivu** Sri Lanka
216 D5 **Mullaloo** WA Australia
143 E3 **Mullanalaghta** Ireland
143 D2 **Mullany's Cross** Ireland
81 O5 **Mullen** Nebraska USA
197 G3 **Müller, Pegunungan** *range* Indonesia
82 I4 **Mullet Lake** Michigan USA
216 D4 **Mullewa** WA Australia
124 D4 **Müllheim** Germany
214 E7 **Mulligan** *watercourse* Qld Australia
78 H5 **Mulligan** *watercourse* Newfoundland and Labrador Canada
86 B5 **Mullin** Texas USA
143 E3 **Mullingar** Ireland
87 L3 **Mullins** South Carolina USA
85 M2 **Mullinville** Kansas USA
182 F2 **Mullovka** Russian Federation
122 G4 **Mullsjö** Sweden
219 K3 **Mullumbimby** NSW Australia
123 L3 **Mullutu laht** *lake* Estonia
162 C3 **Mulondo** Angola
162 D3 **Mulongo Plain** *plain* Zambia
218 C3 **Muloorina** SA Australia
143 C3 **Mulrany** Mayo Ireland
122 G4 **Mulseryd** Sweden
187 E7 **Multai** Madhya Pradesh India
179 L3 **Multan** Pakistan
134 P6 **Multanovy** Russian Federation
121 N5 **Multia** Finland
100 B5 **Multitud** Ecuador
197 G2 **Mulu, Gunung** *mountain* Malaysia
160 D5 **Mulumbe, Monts** *range* Democratic Republic of Congo
218 F5 **Mulurulu Lake** NSW Australia
81 Q8 **Mulvane** Kansas USA
81 P1 **Mulvihill** Manitoba Canada
140 A2 **Mulvin** Strabane Northern Ireland UK
218 H6 **Mulwala** NSW Australia
214 F7 **Mulya** *watercourse* Qld Australia
134 N6 **Mulym'ya** Russian Federation
160 C3 **Muma** Democratic Republic of Congo
187 C7 **Mumbai** Maharashtra India
216 E6 **Mumballup** WA Australia
162 D2 **Mumbeji** Zambia
219 I5 **Mumbil** NSW Australia
214 E8 **Mumbleberry Lake** Qld Australia
138 D3 **Mumbles Head** *cape* Wales UK
162 B2 **Mumbondo** Angola
162 C2 **Mumbué** Angola
162 E2 **Mumbwa** Zambia
199 H5 **Mumeng** Papua New Guinea
161 E3 **Mumias** Kenya
Muminabad *see* **Leningrad** Tajikistan
101 G4 **Mumpututu, Serra** *range* Brazil
182 E4 **Mumra** Russian Federation
198 E5 **Mun** Indonesia
192 F4 **Mun-yeŏng** South Korea
197 I5 **Muna** *island* Indonesia
135 Z5 **Muna** *watercourse* Russian Federation
197 I5 **Muna, Selat** *strait* Indonesia
135 Y5 **Munakan** *watercourse* Russian Federation
197 G6 **Muncar** Indonesia
130 D2 **München (Munich)** Germany
74 I3 **Muncho Lake** British Columbia Canada
82 I6 **Muncie** Indiana USA
218 D1 **Muncoonie Lakes** Qld Australia
162 B3 **Munda** Angola
186 D5 **Munda** Rajasthan India
222 8 **Munda** Solomon Islands
135 AE5 **Mundar** Russian Federation
104 C3 **Mundaú** Brazil
139 I2 **Mundesley** Norfolk England UK
139 H2 **Mundford** Norfolk England UK
216 G1 **Mundiwindi** WA Australia
218 D3 **Mundowdna** SA Australia
186 B6 **Mundra** Gujarat India
217 K5 **Mundrabilla Motel** WA Australia
160 E2 **Mundri** Sudan
199 I5 **Mundua Island** Papua New Guinea
219 J1 **Mundubbera** Qld Australia
105 G2 **Mundurucus** Brazil
186 C5 **Mundwa** Rajasthan India
218 D4 **Mundy** *watercourse* SA Australia
128 E4 **Munera** Spain
219 H2 **Mungallala** Qld Australia
219 H2 **Mungallala** *watercourse* Qld Australia
215 H4 **Mungana** Qld Australia
186 E6 **Mungaoli** Madhya Pradesh India
163 F3 **Mungári** Mozambique
160 D3 **Mungbere** Democratic Republic of Congo
190 F3 **Mungenmort** Mongolia
186 G6 **Munger** Bihar India
214 F7 **Mungeroo Knobs** *mountain* Qld Australia
219 H5 **Mungery** NSW Australia
196 F3 **Mungguresak, Tanjung** *cape* Indonesia
126 C5 **Mungia** Spain
219 I3 **Mungindi** NSW Australia
162 C2 **Mungo** Angola
218 F5 **Mungo, Lake** *pan* NSW Australia
183 P3 **Mungun Tayga, Gora** *mountain* Russian Federation
191 G3 **Munhahaan** Mongolia
162 C2 **Munhango** Angola
185 I3 **Munhehairhan** Mongolia
223 9 **Munia** *island* Fiji
Munich *see* **München** Germany
81 P2 **Munich** North Dakota USA
100 D3 **Municipio de Arauquita** Venezuela
128 D3 **Muñico** Spain
129 F3 **Muniesa** Spain
82 H3 **Munising** Michigan USA
108 C5 **Munizaga** Chile
212 E7 **Munjina** WA Australia
75 W5 **Munk** Manitoba Canada
121 P2 **Munkelva** Norway
156 D2 **Munkhafaḍ al Qaṭṭārah** *pan* Egypt
190 D2 **Munku-Sardyk, Gora** *mountain* Russian Federation
183 R3 **Munku-Sasan, Gora** *mountain* Russian Federation
183 K3 **Munly** *mountain* Kazakhstan
124 F2 **Münnerstadt** Germany
221 6 **Munning, Point** Chatham Islands New Zealand
108 B5 **Muñoz Gamero, Península de** *península* Chile
219 S10 **Munro, Mount** Tas. Australia
76 F3 **Munroe Lake** Manitoba Canada
192 E4 **Munsan** South Korea
198 B5 **Munse** Indonesia
181 G4 **Munshiganj** Bangladesh
124 D3 **Munster** France
124 D2 **Münster** Germany
83 Q3 **Munsungan Lake** Maine USA
120 I4 **Munsvattnet** Sweden
216 F5 **Muntadgin** WA Australia
160 D5 **Mununga** Zambia
82 I3 **Munuscong Lake** Michigan USA
162 E3 **Munyati** *watercourse* Zimbabwe
121 M3 **Muodoslompolo** Sweden
121 P4 **Muojärvi** *lake* Finland
194 E2 **Mường Khương** Vietnam
194 D2 **Mường Tè** Vietnam
194 E3 **Mường Xén** Vietnam
121 M3 **Muonio** Finland
121 M3 **Muonionalusta** Sweden
120 L3 **Muorjevaara** Sweden
162 C3 **Mupa** Angola
163 G3 **Mupa** *watercourse* Mozambique
162 E3 **Mupfure** *watercourse* Zimbabwe
156 E4 **Muqaddam, Wādī** *watercourse* Sudan
178 F2 **Muqaq** Iraq
161 H3 **Muqdisho (Mogadishu)** Somalia
125 G4 **Mur** *watercourse* Austria
105 G1 **Mura** Brazil
130 G3 **Mura** *watercourse* Croatia
216 E6 **Muradup** WA Australia
196 B3 **Murai Reservoir** Singapore
193 H3 **Murakami** Japan
108 B4 **Murallón, Cerro** *mountain* Argentina
125 K3 **Muráň** Slovakia
134 K7 **Murashi** Russian Federation
123 M3 **Muraste** Estonia
126 F4 **Murat** France
136 G5 **Murat Nehri** *watercourse* Turkey
126 F5 **Murat-sur-Vèbre** France
133 E5 **Muratlı** Turkey
125 H4 **Murau** Austria
156 F3 **Murayr, Jazīrat** *island* Egypt
156 D1 **Muraysah, Ra's Al** *cape* Libya
124 E5 **Murazzano** Italy
187 C7 **Murbad** Maharashtra India
218 G7 **Murchison** Vic. Australia
216 D3 **Murchison** WA Australia
216 D3 **Murchison** *watercourse* WA Australia
221 E5 **Murchison** New Zealand
86 D4 **Murchison** Texas USA
78 G1 **Murchison, Cape** Nunavut Canada
58 L2 **Murchison, Mount** Antarctica
216 E3 **Murchison, Mount** WA Australia
76 K7 **Murchison Island** Ontario Canada
213 M6 **Murchison Range** NT Australia
129 F5 **Murcia** Spain
128 F5 **Murcia** *admin. area* Spain
128 F4 **Murcia** *region* Spain
74 K4 **Murdale** British Columbia Canada
81 O5 **Murdo** South Dakota USA
215 H3 **Murdoch Point** Qld Australia
79 F8 **Murdochville** Quebec Canada
133 E5 **Mürefte** Turkey
190 G3 **Muren** Mongolia
100 D5 **Mureru, Ilhas** *islands* Brazil
132 D2 **Mureş** *admin. area* Romania
132 D2 **Mureş** *watercourse* Romania
126 E5 **Muret** France
182 D5 **Muret** Georgia
132 F3 **Murfatlar** Romania
86 E3 **Murfreesboro** Arkansas USA
87 H3 **Murfreesboro** Tennessee USA
124 E3 **Murg** *watercourse* Germany
179 J2 **Murgap** *watercourse* Afghanistan
214 B1 **Murgenella** NT Australia
179 L3 **Murgha Kibzai** Pakistan
128 E2 **Murgia** Spain
219 J2 **Murgon** Qld Australia
220 2 **Muri** Cook Islands New Zealand
197 F5 **Muria, Gunung** *mountain* Indonesia
103 D8 **Muriaé** Brazil
126 A5 **Murias de Paredes** Spain
102 F5 **Murici** Brazil
162 D1 **Muriege** Angola
196 F3 **Murih** *island* Indonesia
199 J1 **Murilo** *island* Federated States of Micronesia
100 B3 **Murindó** Colombia
132 A4 **Murino** Montenegro
143 B4 **Muririgane** Ireland
120 L3 **Murjek** Sweden
134 H5 **Murmansk** Russian Federation
57 I2 **Murmansk Rise** *underwater feature* Barents Sea
134 H5 **Murmanskaya Oblast'** *admin. area* Russian Federation
121 R2 **Murmashi** Russian Federation
124 F4 **Murnau** Germany
218 D3 **Murnpeowie** SA Australia
129 F4 **Muro del Alcoy** Spain
163 I4 **Murodava** *watercourse* Madagascar
182 D2 **Murom** Russian Federation
193 I2 **Muroran** Japan
128 B2 **Muros** Spain
58 Q1 **Murphy, Mount** Antarctica
58 J2 **Murphy Bay** Antarctica
77 X3 **Murphy Head** Newfoundland and Labrador Canada
82 G8 **Murphysboro** Illinois USA
90 C4 **Murra** Nicaragua
142 E2 **Murra** Orkney Islands Scotland UK
218 H6 **Murrami** NSW Australia
218 G6 **Murray** *watercourse* NSW Australia
218 D6 **Murray** *watercourse* SA Australia
74 K5 **Murray** *watercourse* British Columbia Canada
86 G2 **Murray** Kentucky USA
86 C4 **Murray, Lake** Oklahoma USA
87 K3 **Murray, Lake** South Carolina USA
218 H7 **Murray, Mount** Vic. Australia
218 D6 **Murray Bridge** SA Australia
218 F6 **Murray Downs** NSW Australia
214 C6 **Murray Downs** NT Australia
53 R4 **Murray Fracture Zone** *underwater feature* Pacific Ocean
210 inset **Murray Hill** Christmas Island Australia
199 G6 **Murray Island** Australia
75 P8 **Murray Lake** Alberta Canada
199 G5 **Murray Range** Papua New Guinea
162 D6 **Murraysburg** South Africa
218 E6 **Murrayville** Vic. Australia
179 M2 **Murree** Pakistan
124 E3 **Murrhardt** Germany
218 H5 **Murrin Bridge** NSW Australia
143 C3 **Murrisk** Ireland
131 F8 **Murro di Porco, Capo** *cape* Italy
143 C3 **Murroogh** Ireland
219 I6 **Murrumbateman** NSW Australia
163 G3 **Murrupula** Mozambique
219 J4 **Murrurundi** NSW Australia
187 D7 **Murtajapur** Maharashtra India
127 H3 **Murten** Switzerland
130 F5 **Murter** Croatia
74 L6 **Murtle Lake** British Columbia Canada
218 F7 **Murtoa** Vic. Australia
121 P4 **Murtovaara** Finland
104 D3 **Muru** *watercourse* Brazil
90 C4 **Murubila** Nicaragua
197 G3 **Murud, Gunung** *mountain* Malaysia
135 V5 **Murukta** Russian Federation
197 G3 **Murung** *watercourse* Indonesia
220 G4 **Murupara** New Zealand
223 14 **Mururoa** *reef* French Polynesia
105 G1 **Murutinga** Brazil
86 D4 **Murvaul, Lake** Texas USA
186 E6 **Murwara** Madhya Pradesh India
219 K3 **Murwillumbah** NSW Australia
155 I3 **Murzūq** Libya
136 G5 **Muş** Turkey
136 G5 **Muş** *admin. area* Turkey
162 E3 **Musa** *watercourse* Zambia
123 L4 **Mūša** *watercourse* Lithuania
156 E2 **Mūsá, Jabal (Mount Sinai)** *mountain* Egypt
157 G5 **Mūsa Āli** *mountain* Eritrea
187 G6 **Musabani** Jharkhand India
160 C4 **Musadi** Democratic Republic of Congo
132 C4 **Musala** *mountain* Bulgaria
196 C3 **Musala** *island* Indonesia
158 B3 **Musala** Sierra Leone
192 F2 **Musan** North Korea
179 H4 **Musandam, Ra's** *cape* Oman
Muscat *see* **Masqaţ** Oman
82 F6 **Muscatine** Iowa USA
127 H1 **Müsch** Germany
199 G4 **Muschu Island** Papua New Guinea
86 H3 **Muscle Shoals** Alabama USA
76 H7 **Musclow Lake** Ontario Canada
83 Q5 **Muscongus Bay** Maine USA
160 E5 **Muse** Tanzania
160 D4 **Musenge** Democratic Republic of Congo
160 C5 **Musenge** Democratic Republic of Congo
79 L8 **Musgrave Harbour** Newfoundland and Labrador Canada
217 L3 **Musgrave Ranges** SA Australia
215 G3 **Musgrave Roadhouse** Qld Australia
160 C4 **Mushenge** Democratic Republic of Congo
160 B4 **Mushie** Democratic Republic of Congo
122 F5 **Musholm Bugt** *bay* Denmark
160 D6 **Mushoshi** Democratic Republic of Congo
196 E4 **Musi** *watercourse* Indonesia
104 C4 **Musia** Peru
52 P4 **Musicians Seamounts** *underwater feature* Pacific Ocean
178 E5 **Muşiddah** Saudi Arabia
162 F4 **Musina** South Africa
82 G2 **Muskeg Lake** Ontario Canada
74 L6 **Muskeg River** Alberta Canada
82 G5 **Muskego** Wisconsin USA
82 H5 **Muskegon** *watercourse* Michigan USA
86 D3 **Muskogee** Oklahoma USA
76 J6 **Muskrat Dam** Ontario Canada
76 J6 **Muskrat Dam Lake** Ontario Canada
74 J3 **Muskwa** *watercourse* British Columbia Canada
74 I4 **Muskwa Ranges** British Columbia Canada
75 V4 **Muskwesi** *watercourse* Manitoba Canada
156 F4 **Musmar** Sudan
123 M5 **Musninkai** Lithuania
162 E2 **Musofu** Zambia
161 E4 **Musoma** Tanzania
160 C5 **Musongoie** Democratic Republic of Congo
79 H7 **Musquaro, Lac** *lake* Quebec Canada
79 G10 **Musquodoboit Harbour** Nova Scotia Canada
199 I4 **Mussau Island** Papua New Guinea
142 E5 **Musselburgh** East Lothian Scotland UK
81 K3 **Musselshell** *watercourse* Montana USA
162 C2 **Mussende** Angola
126 E4 **Mussidan** France
162 D2 **Mussuma** Angola
162 D2 **Mussuma** *watercourse* Angola
124 C4 **Mussy-sur-Seine** France
123 N2 **Mustamaa** *island* Finland
86 C3 **Mustang** Oklahoma USA
120 L5 **Mustasaari** Finland
182 G3 **Mustayevo** Russian Federation
185 I3 **Muste** Mongolia
108 C2 **Musters** Argentina
108 C3 **Musters, Lago** *lake* Argentina
109 11 **Mustique** *island* St Vincent and the Grenadines

121 P2 Mustola Finland
76 M7 Muswabik Lake Ontario Canada
219 J5 Muswellbrook NSW Australia
125 K3 Muszyna Poland
136 E6 Mut Turkey
123 L2 Mutala Finland
220 4 Mutalau Niue New Zealand
162 E2 Mutanda Zambia
163 F3 Mutare Zimbabwe
100 B3 Mutatá Colombia
179 I5 Muṭayli' Oman
223 14b Mute, Motu island French Polynesia
178 F3 Muthanná, Al admin. area Iraq
142 E4 Muthill Perth and Kinross Scotland UK
199 G5 Muting Indonesia
163 F4 Mutirikwi, Lake Zimbabwe
100 B3 Mutis Colombia
198 C6 Mutis, Gunung mountain Indonesia
163 F3 Mutoko Zimbabwe
160 C5 Mutoto Democratic Republic of Congo
163 H2 Mutsamudu Comoros
160 C6 Mutshatsha Democratic Republic of Congo
193 I3 Mutsu Japan
193 I3 Mutsu-wan bay Japan
215 H7 Muttaburra Qld Australia
143 C4 Mutton Island Ireland
163 G2 Mutúali Mozambique
222 8 Mutuavi island Solomon Islands
103 E6 Mutuípe Brazil
103 D7 Mutum Brazil
105 H6 Mutum Brazil
100 D6 Mutum watercourse Brazil
105 E3 Mutumparaná Brazil
187 E10 Mutur Sri Lanka
198 E4 Muturi watercourse Indonesia
121 O2 Mutusjärvi lake Finland
121 N5 Muurame Finland
121 N5 Muurasjärvi Finland
121 N5 Muurasjärvi lake Finland
121 N5 Muuratjärvi lake Finland
121 N3 Muurola Finland
121 P5 Muuruvesi Finland
199 I6 Muwa Island Papua New Guinea
188 D3 Muxi Sichuan China
128 B2 Muxía Spain
162 B1 Muxima Angola
121 Q5 Muyezerskiy Russian Federation
160 E4 Muyinga Burundi
182 H5 Mŭynoq Uzbekistan
163 F2 Muyombe Zambia
105 E5 Muyu Khuchi Bolivia
159 F4 Muyuka Cameroon
179 M2 Muzaffarabad Pakistan
179 L3 Muzaffargarh Pakistan
186 D5 Muzaffarnagar Uttar Pradesh India
186 F5 Muzaffarpur Bihar India
184 G4 Muzat He watercourse Xinjiang Uygur Zizhiqu China
163 F3 Muze Mozambique
134 N5 Muzhi Russian Federation
100 C3 Muzo Colombia
88 E3 Múzquiz Mexico
184 F6 Muztag mountain Xinjiang Uygur Zizhiqu China
184 E5 Muztagata mountain Xinjiang Uygur Zizhiqu China
159 G4 Mvangan Cameroon
160 D2 Mvolo Sudan
159 G4 Mvoung watercourse Gabon
161 F5 Mvuha Tanzania
162 F3 Mvuma Zimbabwe
Mwali see Mohéli Comoros
161 F4 Mwanga Tanzania
160 D6 Mwangalala Democratic Republic of Congo
161 E5 Mwanisenga Tanzania
222 8 Mwaniwowo Solomon Islands
160 D5 Mwanza Democratic Republic of Congo
163 F3 Mwanza Malawi
161 E4 Mwanza Tanzania
161 E4 Mwanza admin. area Tanzania
160 C5 Mwanzangoma watercourse Democratic Republic of Congo
160 C4 Mweka Democratic Republic of Congo
161 F4 Mwele Tanzania
162 E2 Mwenda Zambia
160 C5 Mwene-Biji Democratic Republic of Congo
160 C5 Mwene-Ditu Democratic Republic of Congo
162 E2 Mwense Zambia
160 D5 Mweru, Lake Democratic Republic of Congo
160 D5 Mweru Wantipa, Lake Zambia
162 E3 Mwezi watercourse Zambia
160 C5 Mwilambwe Democratic Republic of Congo
161 F4 Mwingi Kenya
162 D2 Mwinilunga Zambia
194 E5 Mỹ Tho Vietnam
123 N5 Myadzye, Vozyeral lake Belarus
181 H5 Myaing Myanmar
123 O4 Myakishevo Russian Federation
135 AF6 Myakit Russian Federation
218 G6 Myall Vic. Australia
219 K5 Myall Lake NSW Australia
194 B3 Myanaung Myanmar
121 T4 Myandozero, Ozero lake Russian Federation
185 I3 Myangad Mongolia
190 E3 Myangan Ugalfat Uul mountain Mongolia
194 C2 Myanmar country Asia
121 Q3 Myantyuniyemi Russian Federation
194 B3 Myaungmya Myanmar
120 inset Mýdalsjökull mountain Iceland
181 G5 Myebon Myanmar
181 H5 Myede (Aunglan) Myanmar
194 C4 Myeik (Mergui) Myanmar
194 C5 Myeik Kyunzu island Myanmar
217 M2 Mygoora Lake NT Australia
181 H5 Myingyan Myanmar
194 C4 Myinmoletkat mountain Myanmar
181 H4 Myitkyina Myanmar
181 H5 Myittha Myanmar
130 G2 Myjava Slovakia
125 I3 Myjava watercourse Slovakia
122 E3 Mykle lake Norway
120 E5 Myklebost Norway
120 I3 Myklebostad Norway
136 E3 Mykolaïvs'ka Oblast' admin. area Ukraine
125 J3 Mykolajiw Ukraine
132 G2 Mykolayiv Ukraine
132 G2 Mykolayivka Ukraine
133 D7 Mykonos island Greece
132 D1 Mykulychyn Ukraine
121 N5 Myllymäki Finland
133 C7 Mylopotamos Greece
181 G4 Mymensingh Bangladesh
183 L4 Mynaral Kazakhstan
135 AB6 Myndagay Russian Federation
Myohuang see Mrauk-U Myanmar
218 G7 Myola Vic. Australia
218 D6 Mypolonga SA Australia
218 D6 Myponga SA Australia
122 E3 Myra Norway
120 I2 Myre Norway
120 G5 Myrhaug Norway
120 L4 Myrheden Sweden
133 D6 Myrina Greece
120 L5 Myrkky Finland
120 I2 Myrland Norway
120 G5 Myrmoen Norway
120 inset Mýrnatangi cape Iceland
132 G1 Myronivka Ukraine
213 H5 Myroodah WA Australia
143 C5 Myross Ireland
87 L4 Myrtle Beach South Carolina USA
80 D5 Myrtle Creek Oregon USA
80 C5 Myrtle Point Oregon USA
218 H7 Myrtleford Vic. Australia
133 D8 Myrtos Greece
120 I5 Myrviken Sweden
135 AL5 Mys Schmidta Russian Federation
121 R2 Mys Skorbeyevskiy Russian Federation
134 P4 Mys Taran Russian Federation
218 F7 Mysia Vic. Australia
125 H1 Myśliborskie, Jezioro lake Poland
187 D9 Mysore Karnataka India
135 AG5 Mysovaya Russian Federation
125 K1 Myszyniec Poland
182 D2 Myt Russian Federation
133 B6 Mytikas Greece
133 E6 Mytilini Greece
132 E1 Mytki Ukraine
130 H2 Mýtna Slovakia
81 J6 Myton Utah USA
120 inset Mývatn lake Iceland
161 F5 Mziha Tanzania
163 F2 Mzimba Malawi
163 F2 Mzuzu Malawi

N

142 B2 Na h-Eileanan Siar admin. area Scotland UK
194 E2 Na Hang Vietnam
142 B2 Na Hearadh island Scotland UK
194 D3 Na Klang Thailand
142 C3 na Sealga, Loch lake Scotland UK
142 C5 na Tràille, Rubha cape Scotland UK
194 E3 Na Wa Thailand
124 G3 Naab watercourse Germany
84 inset Nā'ālehu Hawai'i USA
160 D2 Na'am watercourse Sudan
155 F2 Naama Algeria
121 P4 Naamankajärvi lake Finland
123 L2 Naantali Finland
121 Q5 Naarva Finland
143 F3 Naas Ireland
214 B2 Nabarlek NT Australia
195 I5 Nabas Philippines
178 C2 Nabatîyé et Tahta Lebanon
122 I4 Nabbelund Sweden
216 G2 Nabberu, Lake WA Australia
182 F2 Naberezhnyye Chelny Russian Federation
72 E6 Nabesna Alaska USA
155 I1 Nabeul Tunisia
178 E7 Nabī Shu'ayb, Jabal an mountain Yemen
219 K5 Nabiac NSW Australia
161 E3 Nabilatuk Uganda
198 E4 Nabire Indonesia
79 G7 Nabisipi watercourse Quebec Canada
158 D2 Nabou Burkina Faso
223 9a Nabouwalu Fiji
141 G3 Naburn York England UK
161 E4 Nabuyongo Island Tanzania
163 H2 Nacala Mozambique
90 C4 Nacaome Honduras
163 G2 Nacaroa Mozambique
104 E3 Nacebe Bolivia
130 F2 Načeradec Czech Republic
85 N8 Nacha, Laguna La bay Mexico
182 E4 Nachalovo Russian Federation
78 D4 Nachicapau, Lac lake Quebec Canada
186 C5 Nachna Rajasthan India
194 B5 Nachuge Andaman and Nicobar Islands India
77 X3 Nachvak Fiord Newfoundland and Labrador Canada
84 B3 Nacimiento Reservoir California USA
218 D5 Nackara SA Australia
79 E10 Nackawic New Brunswick Canada
124 G1 Nackel Germany
88 C2 Naco Mexico
86 D5 Nacogdoches Texas USA
84 H5 Nacozari de Garcia Mexico
88 C2 Nacozari Viejo Mexico
139 I2 Nacton Suffolk England UK
223 9 Nacula island Fiji
143 D4 Nadanuller Beg Ireland
158 D2 Nadawali Ghana
120 E6 Naddvik Norway
223 9a Nadi Fiji
223 9a Nadi Bay Fiji
186 C6 Nadiad Gujarat India
155 F1 Nador Morocco
223 9a Naduri Fiji
125 M3 Nadvirna Ukraine
121 S5 Nadvoitsy Russian Federation
122 F2 Næren lake Norway
120 G4 Nærøy island Norway
141 H2 Nafferton East Riding of Yorkshire England UK
133 B6 Nafpaktos Greece
133 C7 Nafplio Greece
178 D4 Nafūd, An Saudi Arabia
181 G2 Nag Qu watercourse Xizang Zizhiqu China
195 I4 Naga Philippines
192 F5 Naga-shima island Japan
76 M8 Nagagami watercourse Ontario Canada
82 I2 Nagagami Lake Ontario Canada
193 H3 Nagai Japan
181 H3 Nagaland admin. area India
218 G7 Nagambie Vic. Australia
193 H4 Nagano Japan
193 H4 Nagaoka Japan
181 G3 Nagaon Assam India
187 E9 Nagappattinam Tamil Nadu India
186 E6 Nagar Madhya Pradesh India
154 D5 Nagara Mali
187 D10 Nagarcoil Tamil Nadu India
187 E8 Nagarjuna. Sagar lake Andhra Pradesh India
192 F5 Nagasaki Japan
120 J5 Nagasjön lake Sweden
192 F4 Nagato Japan
186 C5 Nagaur Rajasthan India
187 F7 Nagavali watercourse Andhra Pradesh India
186 D6 Nagda Madhya Pradesh India
85 I2 Nageezi New Mexico USA
120 J5 Naggen Sweden
161 E3 Nagichot Sudan
186 E5 Nagina Uttar Pradesh India
186 E5 Nagla Uttaranchal India
186 E5 Nagma Nepal
187 C7 Nagothana Maharashtra India
193 H4 Nagoya Japan
161 E3 Nagpotpot Sudan
187 E7 Nagpur Maharashtra India
187 E7 Nagri Chhattisgarh India
87 N3 Nags Head North Carolina USA
123 K2 Nagu Finland
91 G3 Nagua Dominican Republic
77 T2 Nagvaraaluk, Lac lake Quebec Canada
132 B1 Nagyhalász Hungary
130 H3 Nagykőrös Hungary
130 H2 Nagylóc Hungary
189 J3 Naha Japan
182 G7 Nahaldan Iran
74 J2 Nahanni Butte plain Northwest Territories Canada
74 J2 Nahanni Range Northwest Territories Canada
128 E3 Naharros Spain
179 I5 Nahdah Oman
124 D3 Nahe watercourse Germany
191 J3 Nahe Zhen Heilongjiang China
157 G1 Nahr al Furāt watercourse Syria
178 F3 Nahr Dijlah watercourse Iraq
104 C3 Nahuas Peru
108 B2 Nahuel Huapí, Lago lake Argentina
106 E5 Nahuel Mapá Argentina
108 C2 Nahuel Niyeu Argentina
87 K5 Nahunta Georgia USA
195 I4 Naic Philippines
88 D3 Naica Mexico
75 S6 Naicam Saskatchewan Canada
186 G6 Naihati West Bengal India
185 J6 Naij Gol He watercourse Qinghai China
198 B6 Naikliu Indonesia
138 E3 Nailsea North Somerset England UK
139 E3 Nailsworth Gloucestershire England UK
78 H4 Nain Newfoundland and Labrador Canada
179 H3 Nā'īn Iran
223 9a Naindi Fiji
186 E5 Nainital Uttaranchal India
187 E6 Nainpur Madhya Pradesh India
186 D6 Nainwa Rajasthan India
223 9 Nairai island Fiji
142 E3 Nairn Highland Scotland UK
216 E2 Nairn, Mount WA Australia
161 F4 Nairobi Kenya
161 F4 Nairobi Area admin. area Kenya
123 M3 Naissaar island Estonia
223 9 Naitaba island Fiji
161 F4 Naivasha Kenya
161 F4 Naivasha, Lake Kenya
178 G3 Najafābād Iran
128 E2 Nájera Spain
191 J3 Naji Nei Mongol Zizhiqu China
178 E6 Najrān Saudi Arabia
178 F6 Najrān admin. area Saudi Arabia
192 E4 Naju South Korea
192 F5 Nakadori-shima island Japan
158 D2 Nakambé watercourse Burkina Faso
192 G4 Nakano-shima island Japan
161 F6 Nakapanya Tanzania
192 F5 Nakatsu Japan
157 F4 Nakfa Eritrea
192 G2 Nakhodka Russian Federation
194 D4 Nakhon Pathom Thailand
194 E3 Nakhon Phanom Thailand
194 D4 Nakhon Ratchasima Thailand
194 D4 Nakhon Sawan Thailand
194 C5 Nakhon Si Thammarat Thailand
194 D5 Nakhon Srithammarat admin. area Thailand
194 D3 Nakhon Thai Thailand
74 E3 Nakina watercourse British Columbia Canada
76 L7 Nakina Ontario Canada
160 E4 Nakivali, Lake Uganda
72 D7 Naknek Alaska USA
161 E5 Nakonde Zambia
192 F6 Nakono-shima island Japan
132 B3 Nakovo Serbia
158 D2 Nakpanduri Ghana
122 F5 Nakskov Denmark
120 I5 Näkten lake Sweden
161 F4 Nakuru Kenya
74 M7 Nakusp British Columbia Canada
190 F3 Nalaih Mongolia
121 O5 Näläntöjärvi lake Finland
163 F4 Nalázi Mozambique
132 F3 Nalbant Romania
181 G3 Nalbari Assam India
182 D5 Nal'chik Russian Federation
120 I5 Nälden Sweden
187 D8 Naldurg Maharashtra India
187 E8 Nalgonda Andhra Pradesh India
121 P4 Näljänkä Finland
216 E5 Nalkain WA Australia
216 E3 Nallan WA Australia
133 G5 Nallıhan Turkey
77 S2 Nallusarqituq, Lac lake Quebec Canada
155 I2 Nālūt Libya
194 E2 Nam Định Vietnam
194 D3 Nam Ngum Reservoir Laos
163 G2 Namacala Mozambique
162 C3 Namacunde Angola
163 G3 Namacurra Mozambique
178 G2 Namak, Daryācheh-ye lake Iran
196 E4 Namang Indonesia
161 F4 Namanga Kenya
183 K5 Namangan Uzbekistan
183 K6 Namangan admin. area Uzbekistan
160 E5 Namanyere Tanzania
163 G2 Namapa Mozambique
162 C5 Namaqualand region South Africa
222 7 Namaram Vanuatu
198 E5 Namaripi, Tanjung cape Indonesia
199 G5 Namas Indonesia
198 E4 Namber Indonesia
161 F5 Nambiranji Tanzania
219 K2 Nambour Qld Australia
219 K4 Nambucca Heads NSW Australia
181 G2 Namco lake Xizang Zizhiqu China
120 H4 Namdalen region Norway
123 J3 Nämdö island Sweden
223 15 Namdrik Atoll Marshall Islands
223 9 Namenalala island Fiji
130 H2 Námestovo Slovakia
163 G3 Nametil Mozambique
75 U5 Namew Lake Saskatchewan Canada
181 H4 Namhsan Myanmar
163 G2 Namialo Mozambique
162 C4 Namib Desert Namibia
162 B3 Namibe Angola
162 B3 Namibe admin. area Angola
162 C4 Namibia country Africa
54 F7 Namibia Abyssal Plain underwater feature Atlantic Ocean
193 I4 Namie Japan
163 G3 Namiroe watercourse Mozambique
121 P2 Nammijärvi lake Finland
219 I4 Namoi watercourse NSW Australia
199 J2 Namoluk island Federated States of Micronesia
158 E3 Namon Togo
199 I1 Namonuito island Federated States of Micronesia
55 T4 Namonuito Atoll reef Caroline Islands
74 M4 Nampa Alberta Canada
80 G5 Nampa Idaho USA
154 E5 Nampala Mali
192 E3 Namp'o North Korea
196 D2 Nampong Pangkal Kalong Malaysia
163 G3 Nampula Mozambique
163 G2 Nampula admin. area Mozambique
198 C4 Namrole Indonesia
181 H3 Namsai Arunachal Pradesh India
181 H5 Namsang Myanmar
120 H4 Namsen watercourse Norway
120 G4 Namsos Norway
120 H4 Namsskogan Norway
120 H4 Namsvatn Norway
135 AA6 Namtsy Russian Federation
181 H4 Namtu Myanmar
74 H7 Namu British Columbia Canada
223 15 Namu Atoll Marshall Islands
223 9 Namuka-i-Lau island Fiji
163 G3 Namuli, Monte mountain Mozambique
163 G2 Namuno Mozambique
233 I2 Namur Belgium
233 I2 Namur admin. area Belgium
198 D5 Namwaan island Indonesia
162 E3 Namwala Zambia
192 E4 Namwŏn South Korea
135 AB5 Namy Russian Federation
195 G5 Namyit Island Spratly Islands
125 H2 Namysłów Poland
194 D3 Nan Thailand
194 D3 Nan admin. area Thailand
222 6b Nan Madol ruins Federated States of Micronesia
189 G3 Nan'an Jiangxi China
159 G3 Nana Cameroon
159 H3 Nana watercourse Central African Republic
159 H3 Nana watercourse Chad
159 H3 Nana Bakassa Central African Republic
160 C6 Nana Candundo Angola
219 K4 Nana Glen NSW Australia
159 H3 Nana-Grébizi, Préfecture de la admin. area Central African Republic
159 H3 Nana-Mambéré admin. area Central African Republic
193 I3 Nanae Japan
74 J8 Nanaimo British Columbia Canada
217 H6 Nanambinia WA Australia
219 I5 Nanami NSW Australia
219 J2 Nanango Qld Australia
193 H4 Nanao Japan
189 H4 Nan'ao Dao island Guangdong China
104 C1 Nanay watercourse Peru
188 E3 Nanbai Guizhou China
189 G3 Nanchang Jiangxi China
191 I5 Nanchangshan Shandong China
188 E2 Nanchong Sichuan China
196 B2 Nancowry island Andaman and Nicobar Islands India
194 B6 Nancowry island Andaman and Nicobar Islands India
126 D4 Nancras France
127 H2 Nancy France
221 B7 Nancy Sound New Zealand
186 E4 Nanda Devi mountain Uttaranchal India
186 E4 Nanda Kot mountain Uttaranchal India
188 E4 Nandan Guangxi Zhuangzu Zizhiqu China
90 C5 Nandayure Costa Rica
187 D7 Nanded Maharashtra India
163 F4 Nandi Zimbabwe
187 E8 Nandikotkur Andhra Pradesh India
188 F5 Nandu watercourse Hainan China
187 D7 Nandurbar Maharashtra India
187 E8 Nandyal Andhra Pradesh India
179 M2 Nanga Parbat mountain Pakistan
216 C3 Nanga Station WA Australia
197 G3 Nangah Bunut Indonesia
197 F4 Nangah Dedai Indonesia
197 G3 Nangah Embaloh Indonesia
197 F3 Nangah Kantuk Indonesia
197 G4 Nangah Kemangai Indonesia
197 F3 Nangah Ketungau Indonesia
197 F4 Nangah Pinoh Indonesia
197 G4 Nangah Serawai Indonesia
197 G3 Nangah Suruk Indonesia
197 G3 Nangah Tempuai Indonesia
195 I5 Nangalao island Philippines
161 F6 Nanganga Tanzania
179 L2 Nangarhār admin. area Afghanistan
197 F4 Nangataman Indonesia
197 F4 Nangatayap Indonesia
158 E3 Nangbéto, Retenue de lake Togo
126 F2 Nangis France
184 F6 Nanglong Kangri Xinjiang Uygur Zizhiqu China
192 E3 Nangnim-sanmaek North Korea
161 E3 Nangolet Sudan
191 H5 Nangong Hebei China
121 P2 Nangujärvi lake Finland
121 O2 Nanguvuono bay Finland
218 E7 Nangwarry SA Australia
191 H4 Nanhaoqian Hebei China
179 K3 Nānī Ghūnd Afghanistan
74 H6 Nanika Lake British Columbia Canada
178 G3 Nanizak Iran
189 I3 Nanji Shan range Zhejiang China
188 C3 Nanjian Yunnan China
188 E2 Nanjiang Sichuan China
189 F4 Nanjie Guangdong China
189 H2 Nanjing Jiangsu China
163 G1 Nanjirinji Tanzania
189 G2 Nankang Jiangxi China
192 G5 Nankoku Japan
162 C3 Nankova Angola
186 D4 Nankun mountain Jammu and Kashmir India/Pakistan
222 6b Nanlaud mountain Federated States of Micronesia
191 H6 Nanle Henan China
189 H2 Nanling Anhui China
188 F4 Nanliu Jiang watercourse Guangxi Zhuangzu Zizhiqu China
191 I6 Nanma Shandong China
181 F3 Nanmulinxue Xizang Zizhiqu China
188 E4 Nanning Guangxi Zhuangzu Zizhiqu China
216 D6 Nannup WA Australia
73 O6 Nanortalik Greenland
188 D4 Nanpan Jiang watercourse Yunnan China
186 E5 Nanpara Uttar Pradesh India
189 F4 Nanpeng Dao island Guangdong China
191 H5 Nanpi Hebei China
189 H3 Nanping Fujian China
188 D1 Nanping Sichuan China
189 H3 Nanpu Fujian China
189 I2 Nanqiao Shanghai China
189 H3 Nanri Dao island Fujian China
188 F4 Nansan Dao island Guangdong China
189 J3 Nansei-shoto (Ryukyu Islands, Japan) Japan
56 N1 Nansen Basin underwater feature Arctic Ocean
73 O2 Nansen Land region Greenland
73 J2 Nansen Sound bay Nunavut Canada
188 D4 Nansha Yunnan China
195 G5 Nanshan Island Spratly Islands
189 G4 Nanshui Shuiku lake Guangdong China
135 AD7 Nansikan, Ostrov island Russian Federation
161 E4 Nansio Tanzania
216 D4 Nanson WA Australia
77 R2 Nantais, Lac lake Quebec Canada
138 C2 Nantcwnlle Ceredigion Wales UK
126 D3 Nantes France
138 D1 Nantglyn Denbighshire Wales UK
196 D5 Nanti, Bukit mountain Indonesia
126 E3 Nantiat France
83 M6 Nanticoke Pennsylvania USA
75 O7 Nanton Alberta Canada
189 H2 Nantong Jiangsu China
189 H4 Nant'ou Taiwan China
58 U2 Nantucket Inlet bay Antarctica
83 Q6 Nantucket Island Massachusetts USA
83 P6 Nantucket Sound bay Massachusetts USA
163 G2 Nantulo Mozambique
138 E1 Nantwich Cheshire England UK
223 9 Nanuku Passage strait Fiji
223 9a Nanukuloa Fiji
222 1 Nanumanga island Tuvalu
222 1 Nanumea island Tuvalu
103 D7 Nanuque Brazil
198 C2 Nanusa, Kepulauan islands Indonesia
212 C7 Nanutarra Roadhouse WA Australia
188 D3 Nanxi Sichuan China
188 D4 Nanxi He watercourse Yunnan China
189 G3 Nanxiong Guangdong China
189 F2 Nanyang Henan China
189 G1 Nanyang Hu lake Shandong China
189 H2 Nanyi Hu lake Anhui China
193 I3 Nanyo Japan
161 F3 Nanyuki Kenya
181 H3 Nanyung Myanmar
189 H4 Nanzhao Fujian China
189 F1 Nanzhao Henan China
189 F2 Nanzhou Hunan China
129 G4 Nao, Cabo de la cape Spain
107 H4 Não Me Toque Brazil
77 T6 Naococane, Lac lake Quebec Canada
181 F4 Naogaon Bangladesh
197 G3 Naong, Bukit mountain Malaysia
186 D4 Naoshehra Jammu and Kashmir India/Pakistan
133 D7 Naousa Greece
188 F5 Naozhou Dao island Guangdong China
80 D7 Napa California USA
163 G2 Napaha Mozambique
72 H5 Napaktulik Lake Nunavut Canada
107 G6 Napaleofú Argentina
134 P4 Napalkovo Russian Federation
198 E4 Napanwainami Indonesia
186 C5 Napasar Rajasthan India
83 P6 Napeague Bay New York USA
82 G6 Naperville Illinois USA
79 J7 Napetipi watercourse Quebec Canada
181 I4 Naphan Myanmar
194 D3 Naphèng Laos
198 E4 Napido Indonesia
220 G4 Napier New Zealand
213 J4 Napier, Mount NT Australia
218 F7 Napier, Mount Vic. Australia
214 C1 Napier, Point NT Australia
213 I3 Napier Broome Bay WA Australia
213 H4 Napier Downs WA Australia
58 D2 Napier Mountains Antarctica
214 C2 Napier Peninsula NT Australia
75 U8 Napinka Manitoba Canada
Naples see Napoli Italy
87 K7 Naples Florida USA
81 K6 Naples Utah USA
188 E4 Napo Guangxi Zhuangzu Zizhiqu China
100 B5 Napo watercourse Ecuador
100 C5 Napo watercourse Peru
81 P3 Napoleon North Dakota USA
131 F6 Napoli (Naples) Italy
106 F6 Napostá Argentina
218 E2 Nappa Merrie Qld Australia
218 D1 Nappanerica, Lake Qld Australia
214 B7 Napperby NT Australia
218 D5 Napperby SA Australia
214 F2 Napranum Qld Australia
223 14 Napuka island French Polynesia
182 E7 Naqadeh Iran
100 D4 Naquén, Serranía range Colombia
123 J4 När Sweden
186 B6 Nara Gujarat India
154 E5 Nara Mali
85 K3 Nara Visa New Mexico USA
123 N5 Narach, Vozyera lake Belarus
218 E7 Naracoorte SA Australia
218 H5 Naradhan NSW Australia
191 H3 Naran Mongolia
185 I2 Naranbular Mongolia
100 B5 Naranjal Ecuador
100 B5 Naranjal Peru
90 C5 Naranjo Costa Rica
89 F4 Naranjos Mexico
194 D6 Narathiwat Thailand
194 D6 Narathiwat admin. area Thailand
181 G4 Narayanganj Bangladesh
187 E6 Narayanganj Madhya Pradesh India
219 J1 Narayen, Mount Qld Australia
132 D1 Narayev Ukraine
138 C3 Narbeth Pembrokeshire Wales UK
218 G7 Narbethong Vic. Australia
126 F5 Narbonne France
139 H2 Narborough Norfolk England UK
128 C2 Narcea watercourse Spain
194 B4 Narcondam Island Andaman and Nicobar Islands India
74 J6 Narcosli Creek British Columbia Canada
214 E5 Nardoo Qld Australia
199 I5 Narega Island Papua New Guinea
219 J6 Narellan NSW Australia
122 G2 Naren lake Sweden
50 L7 Nares Deep underwater feature Sargasso Sea
73 L3 Nares Strait Canada/Greenland
218 F2 Naretha Qld Australia
125 M1 Narew watercourse Belarus
125 L1 Narew Poland
125 L1 Narew watercourse Poland
125 L1 Narewka Poland
187 D8 Nargund Karnataka India
121 O5 Närhilä Finland
181 G4 Naria Bangladesh
100 B4 Nariño admin. area Colombia
84 G7 Narizon, Punta cape Mexico
186 D4 Narkanda Himachal Pradesh India
121 O3 Narkaus Finland
122 H3 Närke region Sweden
121 M3 Narken Sweden
187 D6 Narmada watercourse Madhya Pradesh India
186 D5 Narnaul Haryana India
216 F4 Narndee WA Australia
131 E5 Narni Italy
195 I5 Naro island Philippines
161 F4 Narok Kenya
128 B2 Narón Spain
219 J7 Narooma NSW Australia
182 D2 Narovchat Russian Federation
222 7 Narovorovo Vanuatu
120 L5 Närpes Finland
219 I4 Narrabri NSW Australia
142 C4 Narrachan Argyll and Bute Scotland UK
219 H3 Narran watercourse NSW Australia
219 H3 Narran Lake NSW Australia
218 H6 Narrandera NSW Australia
74 K5 Narraway watercourse British Columbia Canada
218 H5 Narriah Mountain NSW Australia
216 E7 Narrikup WA Australia
216 E6 Narrogin WA Australia
219 I5 Narromine NSW Australia
218 D6 Narrung SA Australia
218 F6 Narrung Vic. Australia
73 O6 Narsarsuaq Greenland
78 N1 Narsatsiaat Greenland
122 H2 Närsen lake Sweden
181 G4 Narsingdi Bangladesh
132 E3 Năruja Romania
125 K1 Naruszewo Poland
123 O3 Narva Estonia
121 M2 Närvä Sweden
123 N3 Narva Bay Estonia
120 J2 Narvik Norway
186 D5 Narwana Haryana India
214 B7 Narwietooma NT Australia
134 L5 Nar'yan-Mar Russian Federation
218 E3 Naryilco Qld Australia
183 O4 Narymskiy Khrebet range Kazakhstan
183 L5 Naryn Kyrgyzstan
183 L5 Naryn admin. area Kyrgyzstan
183 L5 Naryn watercourse Kyrgyzstan
159 F3 Nasarawa Nigeria
100 C5 Nasayá Colombia
120 I6 Näsberg Sweden
101 F4 Nascente Brazil
85 H2 Naschitti New Mexico USA
138 E3 Nash Newport Wales UK
86 B2 Nash Oklahoma USA
100 B5 Nashicta Ecuador
187 C7 Nashik Maharashtra India
81 L2 Nashua Montana USA
83 P5 Nashua New Hampshire USA
86 E4 Nashville Arkansas USA
82 G7 Nashville Illinois USA
81 P8 Nashville Kansas USA
86 Nashville Tennessee USA
158 D2 Nasia Ghana
158 D2 Nasia watercourse Ghana
130 H4 Našice Croatia
197 F3 Nasilat Indonesia
161 E2 Nasir Sudan
156 E3 Nāşir, Buḩayrat lake Egypt
186 D5 Nasirabad Rajasthan India
179 K4 Nasirabad Pakistan
179 J4 Nasirabad Pakistan
179 I3 Nask Iran
78 G5 Naskaupi watercourse Newfoundland and Labrador Canada
122 I3 Näsnaren lake Sweden
131 F7 Naso Italy
160 D6 Nasondoye Democratic Republic of Congo
223 9a Nasorolevu mountain Fiji
187 E7 Naspur Andhra Pradesh India
72 G7 Nass watercourse British Columbia Canada
121 M2 Naššа island Norway
159 F3 Nassarawa admin. area Nigeria
90 E1 Nassau Bahamas
83 O5 Nassau New York USA
222 1 Nassau Island Cook Islands New Zealand
87 K5 Nassau Sound Florida USA
83 N8 Nassawadox Virginia USA
124 F4 Nassereith Austria
158 D3 Nassian Côte d'Ivoire
73 N5 Nassuttooq bay Greenland
120 J4 Nästansjö Sweden
73 L7 Nastapoca watercourse Quebec Canada
73 L7 Nastapoka Islands Nunavut Canada
120 I5 Nästelsjön lake Sweden
123 M2 Nastola Finland
195 I4 Nasugbu Philippines
123 L3 Nasva Estonia
123 P4 Nasva Russian Federation
162 E4 Nata Botswana
162 E4 Nata watercourse Botswana
100 C4 Natagaima Colombia
102 F4 Natal Brazil
105 F2 Natal Brazil
80 H2 Natal British Columbia Canada
196 C3 Natal Indonesia
54 H8 Natal Basin underwater feature Indian Ocean
86 B6 Natalia Texas USA
78 G6 Natashquan watercourse Newfoundland and Labrador Canada
79 H7 Natashquan Quebec Canada
79 H7 Natashquan watercourse Quebec Canada
79 H7 Natashquan, Pointe de Quebec Canada
79 H7 Natashquan Est watercourse Quebec Canada
86 E5 Natchez Louisiana USA
86 F5 Natchez Mississippi USA
86 E5 Natchitoches Louisiana USA
127 H3 Naters Switzerland
223 9a Natewa Bay Fiji
194 B3 Nathaingchaung Myanmar
214 C3 Nathan watercourse NT Australia
214 C3 Nathan River NT Australia
129 H3 Nati, Punta cape Spain
158 E2 Natia-Boani Burkina Faso
74 I5 Nation watercourse British Columbia Canada
84 D4 National City California USA
101 H3 Nationale French Guiana
158 E2 Natitingou Benin
77 N1 Native Bay Nunavut Canada
105 E4 Natividad Bolivia
88 B3 Natividad, Isla island Mexico
103 C5 Natividade Brazil
181 H5 Natmauk Myanmar
181 H5 Natogyi Myanmar
85 M1 Natoma Kansas USA
85 H6 Nátora Mexico
181 F4 Natore Bangladesh
193 I3 Natori Japan
161 F4 Natron, Lake Tanzania
194 B3 Nattalin Myanmar
187 E9 Nattam Tamil Nadu India
120 L3 Nattavaara Sweden
121 N2 Nattvatnet lake Norway
77 T4 Natuak, Lac lake Quebec Canada
78 H5 Natuashish Newfoundland and Labrador Canada
196 E3 Natuna, Kepulauan islands Indonesia
196 F3 Natuna Besar island Indonesia
219 S10 Naturaliste, Cape Tas. Australia
216 D6 Naturaliste, Cape WA Australia
55 P8 Naturaliste Plateau underwater feature Indian Ocean
81 K7 Naturita Colorado USA
124 F4 Naturno Italy
162 C4 Nauchas Namibia
161 F7 Nauela Mozambique
107 I3 Naufragados, Ponta dos cape Brazil
213 K2 Nauiyu NT Australia
195 I4 Naujan, Lake Philippines
123 L4 Naujoji Akmenė Lithuania
186 C5 Naukh Rajasthan India
140 B3 Naul Ireland
162 B3 Naulila Angola
199 I4 Nauna Island Papua New Guinea
106 D6 Naunaucó, Sierra range Argentina
181 H3 Naung-Mon Myanmar
182 E5 Naurskaya Russian Federation
222 4 Nauru country Pacific Ocean
223 9a Nausori Fiji
120 K3 Nausta Sweden
120 K3 Naustajaure lake Sweden
120 K3 Nautijaur Sweden
123 K2 Nautiomaa island Finland
89 F4 Nautla Mexico
121 P2 Nautsi Russian Federation
122 C2 Nautsund Norway
179 L2 Nāv Afghanistan
160 D3 Nava watercourse Democratic Republic of Congo
88 E2 Nava Mexico
130 B4 Nava, Colle di pass Italy
128 D3 Nava de la Asunción Spain
126 F5 Navacelles, Cirque de point of interest France
128 D4 Navahermosa Spain
85 I2 Navajo Reservoir New Mexico USA
128 D3 Navalcán Spain
143 F3 Navan Ireland
123 O5 Navapolatsk Belarus
135 AK6 Navarin, Mys cape Russian Federation
108 C6 Navarino, Isla island Chile
120 J5 Navarn lake Sweden
128 F2 Navarra admin. area Spain
126 D5 Navarra region Spain
218 F7 Navarre Vic. Australia
126 C5 Navarrete Spain
86 C5 Navarro Mills Lake Texas USA
129 G3 Navàs Spain
128 C4 Navas del Madroño Spain
85 N5 Navasota watercourse Texas USA
91 F3 Navassa Island US territory Caribbean
78 M1 Navdlúnguaq bay Greenland
128 C3 Nave de Haver Portugal
142 D2 Naver watercourse Scotland UK
142 D2 Naver, Loch lake Scotland UK
106 E5 Navia Argentina
128 C2 Navia Spain
128 C2 Navia watercourse Spain
128 C2 Navia de Suarna Spain
106 D5 Navidad Chile
86 C6 Navidad watercourse Texas USA
91 G2 Navidad Bank underwater feature Atlantic Ocean
127 G3 Navilly France
103 A8 Naviraí Brazil
124 F4 Navis Austria
223 9 Naviti island Fiji
199 G6 Naviu Island Papua New Guinea
182 J6 Navoiy Uzbekistan
182 I5 Navoiy admin. area Uzbekistan
85 H7 Navojoa Mexico
88 D3 Navolato Mexico
122 H4 Nävragöl Sweden
158 D2 Navrongo Ghana
187 C7 Navsari Gujarat India
223 9a Navua Fiji
223 9a Navua watercourse Fiji
179 K2 Naw-e Tondakī Afghanistan
136 F7 Nawá Syria
179 L4 Nawa Kot Pakistan
181 F4 Nawabganj Bangladesh
179 K4 Nawabshah Pakistan
186 F6 Nawada Bihar India
186 D5 Nawalgarh Rajasthan India
179 L3 Nawan Kot Pakistan
187 C7 Nawapur Maharashtra India
181 H4 Nawngcho Myanmar
182 E6 Naxçhevan' Azerbaijan
133 D7 Naxos island Greece
187 F7 Nayagarh Orissa India
88 D4 Nayarit admin. area Mexico
223 9 Nayau island Fiji
179 K2 Naylowr Afghanistan
193 I2 Nayoro Japan
181 H5 Naypyidaw Myanmar
163 G2 Nayuchi Malawi
103 E6 Nazaré Brazil
128 B4 Nazaré Portugal
Nazareth see Nazerat Israel
85 K3 Nazareth Texas USA
54 K6 Nazareth Bank underwater feature Indian Ocean
222 7 Nazareth-Rantis Vanuatu
88 D3 Nazas Mexico
104 C4 Nazca Peru
53 Y9 Nazca Ridge underwater feature Pacific Ocean
189 K3 Naze Japan
139 I3 Naze, The cape England UK
178 C3 Nazerat (Nazareth) Israel
181 H3 Nazira Assam India
123 P3 Naziya Russian Federation
74 J6 Nazko British Columbia Canada
74 J6 Nazko watercourse British Columbia Canada
161 F2 Nazrēt Ethiopia
183 K2 Nazyvayevsk Russian Federation
154 D5 Nbâk Mauritania
160 D5 Nchelenge Zambia
162 D4 Ncojane Botswana
161 E4 Ndala Tanzania
162 B1 N'dalantando Angola
158 E3 Ndali Benin
159 I3 Ndanda Central African Republic
154 C5 Ndande Senegal
197 I6 Ndao island Indonesia
159 F3 Ndeji Nigeria
159 I3 Ndélé Central African Republic
159 G5 Ndendé Gabon
159 H3 Ndim Central African Republic
159 G5 Ndindi Gabon
154 C6 Ndioum Guènt Senegal
159 H2 N'Djamena Chad
159 I3 Ndji watercourse Central African Republic
159 G5 Ndjolé Gabon
159 F5 Ndogo, Lagune lake Gabon
159 G3 Ndok Cameroon

162 E2 **Ndola** Zambia
159 G3 **Ndop** Cameroon
158 D3 **Ndouci** Côte d'Ivoire
159 H3 **Ndoumbou** Central African Republic
133 A5 **Ndroq** Albania
222 7 **Ndui Ndui** Vanuatu
222 8a **Nduindui** Solomon Islands
161 F6 **Ndumbwe** Tanzania
160 D3 **Nduye** *watercourse* Democratic Republic of Congo
133 C6 **Nea Artaki** Greece
133 C5 **Nea Éfesos** Greece
133 C5 **Nea Kerdylia** Greece
133 C7 **Nea Kios** Greece
133 B6 **Nea Manolás** Greece
133 C5 **Nea Poteidaia** Greece
133 B6 **Nea Selévkia** Greece
219 H2 **Neabul** *watercourse* Qld Australia
143 F2 **Neagh, Lough** *lake* Northern Ireland UK
74 I8 **Neah Bay** Washington USA
77 Q2 **Neakongut, Baie** *bay* Quebec Canada
143 C3 **Neale** Ireland
217 K2 **Neale, Lake** NT Australia
218 B2 **Neales** *watercourse* SA Australia
132 E2 **Neanmț** *admin. area* Romania
133 C7 **Neapoli** Greece
135 AJ8 **Near Islands** Alaska USA
138 D3 **Neath** Neath Port Talbot Wales UK
138 D3 **Neath Port Talbot** *admin. area* Wales UK
158 D2 **Nebbou** Burkina Faso
198 B6 **Nebe** Indonesia
219 H3 **Nebine** *watercourse* Qld Australia
125 H5 **Nebljusi** Croatia
215 J6 **Nebo** Qld Australia
70 **Nebraska** *admin. area* USA
131 F8 **Nebrodi, Monti** *range* Italy
160 D3 **Nebulu** Democratic Republic of Congo
222 7 **Nécé** New Caledonia
82 F4 **Necedah** Wisconsin USA
74 I6 **Nechako** *watercourse* British Columbia Canada
86 D5 **Neches** *watercourse* Texas USA
100 C2 **Nechí** Colombia
91 F6 **Nechí** *watercourse* Colombia
125 G1 **Nechlin** Germany
129 J5 **Nechmeya** Algeria
124 E3 **Neckar** *watercourse* Germany
52 O6 **Necker Ridge** *underwater feature* Pacific Ocean
107 G6 **Necochea** Argentina
100 B2 **Necoclí** Colombia
160 A4 **Necuto** Angola
123 O5 **Nedal'** Belarus
120 H5 **Nedalshytta** Norway
132 D4 **Nedan** Bulgaria
120 J5 **Nedansjö** Sweden
86 E6 **Nederland** Texas USA
219 H4 **Nedgera** NSW Australia
123 M5 **Nedingis** *lake* Lithuania
77 S4 **Nedlouc** *watercourse* Quebec Canada
122 G3 **Nedre Fryken** *bay* Sweden
122 E2 **Nedre Hermdalsvatn** *lake* Norway
120 L3 **Nedre Kuouka** Sweden
122 H3 **Nedre Malingbosjön** *lake* Sweden
122 E3 **Nedre Tokke** *lake* Norway
124 D1 **Neede** Netherlands
214 A3 **Needham, Mount** NT Australia
139 I2 **Needham Market** Suffolk England UK
74 L8 **Needles** British Columbia Canada
84 E3 **Needles** California USA
139 F4 **Needles, The** *cape* England UK
85 K3 **Needmore** Texas USA
86 D6 **Needville** Texas USA
75 V8 **Neelin** Manitoba Canada
107 G3 **Ñeembucú** *admin. area* Paraguay
186 D6 **Neemuch** Madhya Pradesh India
75 V7 **Neepawa** Manitoba Canada
73 L4 **Neergaard Lake** Nunavut Canada
75 N5 **Neerlandia** Alberta Canada
124 F1 **Neetze** Germany
219 I3 **Neeworra** NSW Australia
157 F5 **Nefas Mewch'a** Ethiopia
155 H2 **Nefta** Tunisia
182 F6 **Neftçal** Azerbaijan
182 F3 **Neftegorsk** Russian Federation
182 G2 **Neftekamsk** Russian Federation
134 P6 **Nefteyugansk** Russian Federation
155 H1 **Nefza** Tunisia
160 B5 **Negage** Angola
154 E6 **Négala** Mali
197 G4 **Negara** Indonesia
197 G4 **Negara** *watercourse* Indonesia
161 F2 **Negëlē** Ethiopia
196 D3 **Negeri Sembilan** *admin. area* Malaysia
162 B2 **Negola** Angola
163 G2 **Negomane** Mozambique
187 E10 **Negombo** Sri Lanka
133 C5 **Negotino** Macedonia
85 J3 **Negra** New Mexico USA
108 C6 **Negra, Punta** *cape* Chile
106 D3 **Negra, Salar Punta** *lake* Chile
103 A7 **Negra, Serra** *range* Brazil
194 B4 **Negrais, Cape** Myanmar
130 D4 **Negrar** Italy
128 E5 **Negratín, Embalse de** *lake* Spain
128 B2 **Negreira** Spain
125 L4 **Negreni** Romania
213 J4 **Negri** *watercourse* NT Australia
155 H2 **Négrine** Algeria
106 E6 **Negro** *watercourse* Argentina
105 F4 **Negro** *watercourse* Bolivia
103 B9 **Negro** *watercourse* Brazil
107 G3 **Negro** *watercourse* Paraguay
107 H5 **Negro** *watercourse* Uruguay
85 N8 **Negro, Lago Mar** *bay* Mexico
106 E6 **Negro Muerto** Argentina
106 E6 **Negro Muerto, Laguna** *lake* Argentina
195 I5 **Negros** *island* Philippines
82 I2 **Negwazu Lake** Ontario Canada
132 E3 **Nehoiu** Romania
162 C3 **Nehone** Angola
185 L4 **Nei Mongol Zizhiqu** *admin. area* China
223 10 **Neiafu** Tonga
121 P2 **Neiden** Norway
75 R7 **Neidpath** Saskatchewan Canada
164 7a **Neiges, Piton des** *volcano* Réunion
188 E2 **Neijiang** Sichuan China
218 D4 **Neil, Mount** SA Australia
82 F4 **Neillsville** Wisconsin USA
219 I4 **Neilrex** NSW Australia
53 R10 **Neilson Reef** French Polynesia
142 D5 **Neilston** East Renfrewshire Scotland UK
125 H2 **Neiße** *watercourse* Poland
100 C4 **Neiva** Colombia
76 G3 **Nejanilini Lake** Manitoba Canada
161 F2 **Nejo** Ethiopia
161 F2 **Nek'emte** Ethiopia
76 D4 **Nekweaga Bay** Saskatchewan Canada
128 C3 **Nelas** Portugal
122 E3 **Nelaug** *lake* Norway
135 AF5 **Nelemnoye** Russian Federation
214 G6 **Nelia** Qld Australia
81 P5 **Neligh** Nebraska USA
135 AC7 **Nel'kan** Russian Federation
121 P2 **Nellim** Finland
187 E8 **Nellore** Andhra Pradesh India
106 F4 **Nelson** Argentina
218 E8 **Nelson** Vic. Australia
76 G5 **Nelson** *watercourse* Manitoba Canada
221 E5 **Nelson** New Zealand
141 F3 **Nelson** Lancashire England UK
84 E3 **Nelson** Nevada USA
199 I6 **Nelson, Cape** Papua New Guinea
108 A5 **Nelson, Estrecho** *strait* Chile
219 K5 **Nelson Bay** NSW Australia
74 I3 **Nelson Forks** British Columbia Canada
75 V5 **Nelson House** Manitoba Canada
81 L2 **Nelson Reservoir** Montana USA
163 F5 **Nelspruit** South Africa
199 J2 **Nema** *island* Federated States of Micronesia
182 F1 **Nema** Russian Federation
154 E5 **Néma** Mauritania
123 L5 **Neman** Russian Federation
82 J3 **Nemegos** Ontario Canada
82 J3 **Nemegosenda Lake** Ontario Canada
125 J4 **Németkér** Hungary
77 Q7 **Némiscau** Quebec Canada
77 Q7 **Némiscau** *watercourse* Quebec Canada
77 Q7 **Némiscau, Lac** *lake* Quebec Canada
124 B3 **Nemours** France
193 J2 **Nemuro** Japan
125 L2 **Nemyriv** Ukraine
191 K2 **Nen Jiang** *watercourse* Heilongjiang China
108 B2 **Nena, Punta** *cape* Chile
143 D4 **Nenagh** Ireland
72 E6 **Nenana** Alaska USA
222 8 **Nendö** *island* Solomon Islands
139 G2 **Nene** *watercourse* England UK
134 M5 **Nenetskiy Avtonomnyy Okrug** *admin. area* Russian Federation
223 14 **Nengo-Nengo** *island* French Polynesia
191 K2 **Nenjiang** Heilongjiang China
121 U4 **Nenoksa** Russian Federation
222 6a **Nenom, Mochun** *strait* Federated States of Micronesia
90 B4 **Nentón** Guatemala
133 C6 **Neo Monastiri** Greece
222 6a **Neoch** *reef* Federated States of Micronesia
82 D8 **Neodesha** Kansas USA
133 B6 **Néos Oropós** Greece
82 D8 **Neosho** *watercourse* Kansas USA
82 D8 **Neosho** Missouri USA
85 O2 **Neosho Falls** Kansas USA
85 O1 **Neosho Rapids** Kansas USA
135 W7 **Nepa** Russian Federation
135 W7 **Nepa** *watercourse* Russian Federation
218 D4 **Nepabunna** SA Australia
186 F5 **Nepal** *country* Asia
186 E5 **Nepalganj** Nepal
80 J7 **Nephi** Utah USA
73 M9 **Nepisiguit** *watercourse* New Brunswick Canada
160 D3 **Nepoko** *watercourse* Democratic Republic of Congo
87 K5 **Neptune Beach** Florida USA
218 B6 **Neptune Islands** SA Australia
58 U1 **Neptune Range** Antarctica
131 E5 **Nera** *watercourse* Italy
135 AE6 **Nera** *watercourse* Russian Federation
126 E4 **Nérac** France
219 K2 **Nerang** Qld Australia
191 H2 **Nerchinsk** Russian Federation
191 I2 **Nerchinskiy Khrebet** *range* Russian Federation
138 D1 **Nercwys** Flintshire Wales UK
122 H2 **Nerde Gärdsjö** Sweden
120 F5 **Nerdvika** Norway
126 D4 **Néré** France
123 M4 **Nereta** Latvia
130 H5 **Neretva** *watercourse* Bosnia and Herzegovina
78 N2 **Neria** Greenland
78 N2 **Neria** *bay* Greenland
162 D3 **Neriquinha** Angola
123 M5 **Neris** *watercourse* Lithuania
72 D7 **Nerka, Lake** Alaska USA
121 M5 **Nerkoonjärvi** *lake* Finland
120 E5 **Nerland** Norway
122 C1 **Nerlandsøy** *island* Norway
100 A6 **Ñermete, Punta** *cape* Peru
124 B4 **Nérondes** France
135 AG5 **Nerpich'ye, Ozero** *lake* Russian Federation
128 E4 **Nerpio** Spain
219 J6 **Nerriga** NSW Australia
132 F3 **Nerushay** Ukraine
128 C5 **Nerva** Spain
124 G5 **Nervesa** Italy
127 I4 **Nervi** Italy
135 Z7 **Neryungri** Russian Federation
124 C1 **Nes** Netherlands
134 J5 **Nes'** Russian Federation
122 E2 **Nesbyen** Norway
125 H2 **Neschwitz** Germany
132 E4 **Nesebŭr** Bulgaria
120 F5 **Neset** Norway
120 E5 **Nesjestranda** Norway
120 G5 **Nesjøen** *lake* Norway
76 L6 **Neskantaga** Ontario Canada
120 inset **Neskaupstaður** Iceland
72 B5 **Neskynpil'gyn, Laguna** Russian Federation
124 B3 **Nesle** France
120 H3 **Nesna** Norway
120 H3 **Nesøya** *island* Norway
142 D3 **Ness, Loch** *lake* Scotland UK
81 P7 **Ness City** Kansas USA
121 P1 **Nesseby** Norway
74 D3 **Nesselrode, Mount** British Columbia/Alaska Canada/USA
77 S8 **Nestaocano** *watercourse* Quebec Canada
126 E5 **Neste** *watercourse* France
123 L5 **Nesterov** Russian Federation
140 E3 **Neston** Cheshire England UK
139 E3 **Neston** Wiltshire England UK
133 D5 **Nestos** *watercourse* Greece
132 F2 **Nestoyita** Ukraine
122 D3 **Nesvatn** *lake* Norway
157 I5 **Nët** Yemen
178 C3 **Netanya** Israel
140 E1 **Nether Dalgliesh** Scottish Borders Scotland UK
218 E7 **Netherby** Vic. Australia
138 C3 **Nethercott** Devon England UK
124 **Netherlands** *country* Europe
91 G4 **Netherlands Antilles** *Dutch autonomous country* Caribbean
140 B4 **Nethertown** Ireland
142 E3 **Nethy Bridge** Highland Scotland UK
74 J2 **Netla** Northwest Territories Canada
131 G7 **Neto** *watercourse* Italy
130 F2 **Netolice** Czech Republic
127 I1 **Netphen** Germany
181 G4 **Netrakona** Bangladesh
125 H5 **Netretić** Croatia
82 E2 **Nett Lake** Minnesota USA
127 G2 **Nettancourt** France
73 L5 **Nettilling Lake** Nunavut Canada
218 F5 **Nettlegoe Lake** NSW Australia
139 H3 **Nettlestead** Kent England UK
86 G3 **Nettleton** Mississippi USA
131 C6 **Nettuno, Grotta di** Sardinia Italy
124 F3 **Neu-Ulm** Germany
127 L3 **Neuberg an der Mürz** Austria
125 H4 **Neubruck** Austria
127 H3 **Neuchâtel** Switzerland
124 D4 **Neuchâtel, Lac de** *lake* Switzerland
75 T7 **Neudorf** Saskatchewan Canada
124 E3 **Neuenstein** Germany
124 D3 **Neuf-Brisach** France
127 G2 **Neufchâteau** Belgium
124 C3 **Neufchâteau** France
139 I5 **Neufchâtel-en-Bray** France
125 H4 **Neuhaus** Austria
124 F2 **Neuhaus am Rennweg** Germany
127 I1 **Neuhof** Germany
124 C4 **Neuilly** France
130 G5 **Neum** Bosnia and Herzegovina
127 J2 **Neumarkt in der Oberpfalz** Germany
58 X2 **Neumayer (Germany)** *research station* Antarctica
122 E5 **Neumünster** Germany
194 D3 **Neun** *watercourse* Laos
125 I4 **Neunkirchen** Austria
134 Q4 **Neupokoyeva, Ostrov** *island* Russian Federation
125 H3 **Neupölla** Austria
106 D6 **Neuquén** Argentina
108 C2 **Neuquén** *admin. area* Argentina
106 D6 **Neuquén** *watercourse* Argentina
87 M3 **Neuse** *watercourse* North Carolina USA
124 D2 **Neuss** Germany
124 G1 **Neustrelitz** Germany
214 B6 **Neutral Junction** NT Australia
126 F4 **Neuvic d'Ussel** France
126 E3 **Neuville** France
126 E3 **Neuvy** France
122 E6 **Neuwerk** *island* Germany
70 **Nevada** *admin. area* USA
82 D8 **Nevada** Missouri USA
108 C3 **Nevada, Sierra** *range* Argentina
106 D3 **Nevada, Sierra** *mountain* Chile
128 E5 **Nevada, Sierra** *range* Spain
80 E7 **Nevada, Sierra** *range* California USA
80 E7 **Nevada City** California USA
106 D5 **Nevado, Cerro** *mountain* Argentina
123 N5 **Nevaišiu** *mountain* Lithuania
179 K3 **Nevay Deh** Afghanistan
123 L4 **Neveja** Latvia
125 H3 **Neveklov** Czech Republic
123 O4 **Nevel'** Russian Federation
125 M2 **Nevel'** Ukraine
135 AD9 **Nevel'sk** Russian Federation
193 I1 **Nevel'sk** Russian Federation
135 AD8 **Nevel'skogo, Proliv** *strait* Russian Federation
135 Z8 **Never** Russian Federation
191 J1 **Never** Russian Federation
121 M1 **Neverfjord** Norway
126 F3 **Nevers** France
219 H4 **Nevertire** NSW Australia
159 F4 **Neves** São Tomé and Príncipe
76 I2 **Nevill Bay** Nunavut Canada
75 R8 **Neville** Saskatchewan Canada
182 D5 **Nevinnomyssk** Russian Federation
109 19 **Nevis** *island* St Kitts and Nevis
81 R3 **Nevis** Minnesota USA
221 C7 **Nevis Crossing** New Zealand
109 19 **Nevis Peak** *volcano* St Kitts and Nevis
125 L3 **Nevitske** Ukraine
136 E5 **Nevşehir** Turkey
136 E5 **Nevşehir** *admin. area* Turkey
101 G4 **New** *watercourse* Guyana
142 E6 **New Abbey** Dumfries and Galloway Scotland UK
139 G3 **New Addington** Greater London England UK
74 G5 **New Aiyansh** British Columbia Canada
82 I7 **New Albany** Indiana USA
139 F3 **New Alresford** Hampshire England UK
218 D2 **New Alton Downs** SA Australia
101 G3 **New Amsterdam** Guyana
219 H3 **New Angledool** NSW Australia
215 G3 **New Bamboo** Qld Australia
83 P6 **New Bedford** Massachusetts USA
58 U2 **New Bedford Inlet** *bay* Antarctica
87 M3 **New Bern** North Carolina USA
141 G1 **New Bewick** Northumberland England UK
82 E7 **New Bloomfield** Missouri USA
86 D4 **New Boston** Texas USA
86 B6 **New Braunfels** Texas USA
143 E4 **New Bridge** Ireland
75 P7 **New Brigden** Alberta Canada
199 I5 **New Britain** *island* Papua New Guinea
83 O6 **New Britain** Connecticut USA
52 L8 **New Britain Trench** *underwater feature* Solomon Sea
87 I5 **New Brockton** Alabama USA
139 I2 **New Buckenham** Norfolk England UK
143 E2 **New Buildings** Londonderry Northern Ireland UK
222 7 **New Caledonia** *French territorial collectivity* Pacific Ocean
52 M10 **New Caledonia Basin** *underwater feature* Pacific Ocean
79 F8 **New Carlisle** Quebec Canada
81 L7 **New Castle** Colorado USA
82 I7 **New Castle** Kentucky USA
83 K6 **New Castle** Pennsylvania USA
140 E2 **New Cowper** Cumbria England UK
218 B1 **New Crown** NT Australia
142 D5 **New Cumnock** East Ayrshire Scotland UK
85 L4 **New Deal** Texas USA
142 F3 **New Deer** Aberdeenshire Scotland UK
186 D5 **New Delhi** Delhi India
74 M8 **New Denver** British Columbia Canada
141 G3 **New Edlington** South Yorkshire England UK
81 Q4 **New Effington** South Dakota USA
50 L6 **New England Seamounts** *underwater feature* Atlantic Ocean
82 F7 **New Florence** Missouri USA
126 D1 **New Forest** *region* England UK
222 8 **New Georgia** *island* Solomon Islands
199 K6 **New Georgia Group** *islands* Solomon Islands
222 8 **New Georgia Sound** *strait* Solomon Islands
82 G5 **New Glarus** Wisconsin USA
79 G10 **New Glasgow** Nova Scotia Canada
109 inset 9 **New Grant** Trinidad and Tobago
199 G5 **New Guinea** *island* Papua New Guinea
52 J8 **New Guinea Trench** *underwater feature* Pacific Ocean
156 F4 **New Halfa** Sudan
199 I4 **New Hanover** *island* Papua New Guinea
162 F5 **New Hanover** South Africa
80 I8 **New Harmony** Utah USA
83 O6 **New Haven** Connecticut USA
82 I6 **New Haven** Indiana USA
52 M9 **New Hebrides Bank** *underwater feature* Pacific Ocean
52 N10 **New Hebrides Trench** *underwater feature* Pacific Ocean
85 L4 **New Home** Texas USA
199 J4 **New Ireland** *island* Papua New Guinea
109 7 **New Island** Falkland Islands
83 L6 **New Kensington** Pennsylvania USA
90 E3 **New Kingston** Jamaica
215 H3 **New Laura** Qld Australia
81 O3 **New Leipzig** North Dakota USA
82 F5 **New Lisbon** Wisconsin USA
86 E5 **New Llano** Louisiana USA
83 O6 **New London** Connecticut USA
82 F6 **New London** Iowa USA
81 R4 **New London** Minnesota USA
82 F7 **New London** Missouri USA
82 G4 **New London** Wisconsin USA
142 D6 **New Luce** Dumfries and Galloway Scotland UK
86 G2 **New Madrid** Missouri USA
83 L7 **New Market** Virginia USA
80 G4 **New Meadows** Idaho USA
71 **New Mexico** *admin. area* USA
139 G3 **New Mill** Hertfordshire England UK
141 F3 **New Mills** Derbyshire England UK
138 D2 **New Mills** Powys Wales UK
139 F4 **New Milton** Hampshire England UK
216 E5 **New Norcia** WA Australia
86 F6 **New Orleans** Louisiana USA
142 F3 **New Pitsligo** Aberdeenshire Scotland UK
220 F4 **New Plymouth** New Zealand
87 J6 **New Port Richey** Florida USA
90 E1 **New Providence** *island* Bahamas
138 C2 **New Quay** Ceredigion Wales UK
138 D2 **New Radnor** Powys Wales UK
83 O6 **New Rochelle** New York USA
81 P3 **New Rockford** North Dakota USA
139 H4 **New Romney** Kent England UK
143 F4 **New Ross** Ireland
140 A3 **New Row** Ireland
81 O3 **New Salem** North Dakota USA
75 O6 **New Sarepta** Alberta Canada
142 E4 **New Scone** Perth and Kinross Scotland UK
218 G4 **New South Wales** *admin. area* Australia
216 F2 **New Springs** WA Australia
85 O1 **New Strawn** Kansas USA
72 D7 **New Stuyahok** Alaska USA
86 D5 **New Summerfield** Texas USA
143 E3 **New Town** Ireland
81 N3 **New Town** North Dakota USA
82 D4 **New Ulm** Minnesota USA
86 D5 **New Waverly** Texas USA
79 L8 **New-Wes-Valley** Newfoundland and Labrador Canada
79 K8 **New World Island** Newfoundland and Labrador Canada
139 F3 **New Yatt** Oxfordshire England UK
214 B1 **New Year Island** NT Australia
80 F6 **New Year Lake** Nevada USA
70 **New York** *admin. area* USA
83 N6 **New York** New York USA
220 E4 **New Zealand** *country* Oceania
52 M13 **New Zealand Plateau** *underwater feature* Southern Ocean
142 F1 **Newark** Orkney Islands Scotland UK
86 F3 **Newark** Arkansas USA
83 N7 **Newark** Delaware USA
83 N6 **Newark** New Jersey USA
83 J6 **Newark** Ohio USA
80 H7 **Newark Lake** Nevada USA
139 G1 **Newark-upon-Trent** Nottinghamshire England UK
82 I5 **Newaygo** Michigan USA
80 D4 **Newberg** Oregon USA
86 G2 **Newbern** Tennessee USA
87 J6 **Newberry** Florida USA
82 I3 **Newberry** Michigan USA
87 K3 **Newberry** South Carolina USA
84 D3 **Newberry Springs** California USA
141 G1 **Newbiggin-by-the-Sea** Northumberland England UK
87 J4 **Newborn** Georgia USA
138 C1 **Newborough** Isle of Anglesey Wales UK
75 O5 **Newbrook** Alberta Canada
142 F3 **Newburgh** Aberdeenshire Scotland UK
142 E4 **Newburgh** Fife Scotland UK
139 F3 **Newbury** West Berkshire England UK
83 P5 **Newburyport** Massachusetts USA
140 F2 **Newby Bridge** Cumbria England UK
219 J5 **Newcastle** NSW Australia
213 L4 **Newcastle** *watercourse* NT Australia
140 B4 **Newcastle** Ireland
143 F3 **Newcastle** Ireland
162 E5 **Newcastle** South Africa
109 19 **Newcastle** St Kitts and Nevis
143 G2 **Newcastle** Down Northern Ireland UK
86 C3 **Newcastle** Oklahoma USA
81 M5 **Newcastle** Wyoming USA
214 G1 **Newcastle Bay** Qld Australia
138 C2 **Newcastle Emlyn** Carmarthenshire Wales UK
138 E1 **Newcastle-under-Lyme** Staffordshire England UK
141 G1 **Newcastle upon Tyne** *admin. area* UK
141 G2 **Newcastle upon Tyne** Tyne and Wear England UK
214 B4 **Newcastle Waters** NT Australia
142 F5 **Newcastleton** Scottish Borders Scotland UK
85 H2 **Newcomb** New Mexico USA
81 O1 **Newdale** Manitoba Canada
216 F6 **Newdegate** WA Australia
139 G3 **Newdigate** Surrey England UK
81 N4 **Newell** South Dakota USA
217 J2 **Newell, Lake** WA Australia
75 P7 **Newell, Lake** Alberta Canada
77 V1 **Newell Sound** Nunavut Canada
86 F4 **Newellton** Louisiana USA
72 C7 **Newenham, Cape** Alaska USA
81 Q2 **Newfolden** Minnesota USA
83 P5 **Newfound Lake** New Hampshire USA
79 I8 **Newfoundland** *island* Newfoundland and Labrador Canada
78 G3 **Newfoundland and Labrador** *admin. area* Canada
50 N5 **Newfoundland Basin** *underwater feature* Atlantic Ocean
50 N6 **Newfoundland Rise** *underwater feature* Atlantic Ocean
75 N8 **Newgate** British Columbia Canada
214 A7 **Newhaven** NT Australia
139 H4 **Newhaven** East Sussex England UK
139 H4 **Newick** East Sussex England UK
85 J3 **Newkirk** New Mexico USA
81 Q8 **Newkirk** Oklahoma USA
218 B5 **Newland, Lake** SA Australia
215 I6 **Newlands** Qld Australia
216 F1 **Newman** WA Australia
82 H7 **Newman** Illinois USA
216 F1 **Newman, Mount** WA Australia
143 C4 **Newmarket** Ireland
139 H2 **Newmarket** Suffolk England UK
140 B2 **Newmills** Dungannon Northern Ireland UK
142 D3 **Newmills** Highland Scotland UK
87 I4 **Newnan** Georgia USA
139 G2 **Newnham** Hertfordshire England UK
138 A1 **Newpark** Ireland
91 G4 **Newport** Netherlands Antilles
141 H3 **Newport** East Riding of Yorkshire England UK
139 H2 **Newport** Essex England UK
139 F4 **Newport** Isle of Wight England UK
142 E2 **Newport** Highland Scotland UK
138 E3 **Newport** Newport Wales UK
138 E2 **Newport** Telford and Wrekin England UK
138 E3 **Newport** *admin. area* Wales UK
86 F3 **Newport** Arkansas USA
82 I7 **Newport** Kentucky USA
87 M3 **Newport** North Carolina USA
80 C4 **Newport** Oregon USA
83 M6 **Newport** Pennsylvania USA
83 P6 **Newport** Rhode Island USA
87 J3 **Newport** Tennessee USA
83 O4 **Newport** Vermont USA
83 M8 **Newport News** Virginia USA
139 G2 **Newport Pagnell** Milton Keynes England UK
138 B4 **Newquay** Cornwall England UK
143 F2 **Newry** Newry and Mourne Northern Ireland UK
143 F2 **Newry and Mourne** *admin. area* Northern Ireland UK
141 F3 **Newsholme** Lancashire England UK
218 G7 **Newstead** Vic. Australia
142 C5 **Newton** North Ayrshire Scotland UK
139 G2 **Newton** Northamptonshire England UK
142 F5 **Newton** Scottish Borders Scotland UK
82 G7 **Newton** Illinois USA
82 E6 **Newton** Iowa USA
81 Q7 **Newton** Kansas USA
83 P5 **Newton** Massachusetts USA
86 G4 **Newton** Mississippi USA
83 N6 **Newton** New Jersey USA
86 E5 **Newton** Texas USA
138 D4 **Newton Abbot** Devon England UK
219 K3 **Newton Boyd** NSW Australia
87 L3 **Newton Grove** North Carolina USA
142 F4 **Newton of Boysack** Angus Scotland UK
139 I2 **Newton St Faith** Norfolk England UK
142 D6 **Newton Stewart** Dumfries and Galloway Scotland UK
138 C3 **Newton Tracey** Devon England UK
142 F3 **Newtonhill** Aberdeenshire Scotland UK
143 C4 **Newtown** Ireland
143 E4 **Newtown** Ireland
140 F2 **Newtown** Cumbria England UK
139 F3 **Newtown** Hampshire England UK
138 E2 **Newtown** Herefordshire England UK
142 D3 **Newtown** Highland Scotland UK
138 D2 **Newtown** Powys Wales UK
143 E2 **Newtown Butler** Fermanagh Northern Ireland UK
142 F5 **Newtown St Boswells** Scottish Borders Scotland UK
140 B3 **Newtown Trim** Ireland
143 G2 **Newtownabbey** Newtownabbey Northern Ireland UK
143 G2 **Newtownabbey** *admin. area* Northern Ireland UK
143 G2 **Newtownards** Ards Northern Ireland UK
143 E2 **Newtownstewart** Strabane Northern Ireland UK
89 I2 **Newville** Alabama USA
77 V1 **Ney Harbour** Nunavut Canada
76 I5 **Ney Lake** Ontario Canada
182 D1 **Neya** Russian Federation
138 C3 **Neyland** Pembrokeshire Wales UK
179 H3 **Neyrīz** Iran
182 H7 **Neyshābūr** Iran
187 E9 **Neyveli** Tamil Nadu India
82 H2 **Nezah** Ontario Canada
89 F5 **Nezahualcóyotl** Mexico
89 G5 **Nezahualcóyotl, Presa** *lake* Mexico
123 O3 **Nezhadovo** Russian Federation
132 D1 **Nezvys'ko** Ukraine
194 E3 **Nga Sơn** Vietnam
197 F3 **Ngabang** Indonesia
159 H5 **Ngabé** Congo
198 E5 **Ngabordamlu, Tanjung** *cape* Indonesia
221 D5 **Ngakawau** New Zealand
159 G2 **Ngala** Nigeria
198 C3 **Ngalipaeng** Indonesia
197 I6 **Ngalu** Indonesia
198 B6 **Ngalu** Indonesia
159 H2 **Ngam** Chad
155 J6 **Ngama** Chad
162 D3 **Ngamaseri** *watercourse* Botswana
159 G4 **Ngambé** Cameroon
162 D4 **Ngami** *lake* Botswana
194 E2 **Ngân Sơn** Vietnam
154 C6 **Nganda** Senegal
216 G3 **Ngangganawili** WA Australia
180 E2 **Nganglaring Tsho** *lake* Xizang Zizhiqu China
180 D2 **Nganglong Kangri** *mountain* Xizang Zizhiqu China
160 D4 **Nganji** Democratic Republic of Congo
159 G3 **Ngaoundéré** Cameroon
196 E5 **Ngaras** Indonesia
222 3 **Ngardmau** Palau
220 F3 **Ngaruawahia** New Zealand
220 2 **Ngatangiia** Cook Islands New Zealand
222 6 **Ngatik** *island* Federated States of Micronesia
160 A3 **Ngato** Cameroon
197 F5 **Ngawi** Indonesia
221 F5 **Ngawi** New Zealand
194 C4 **Ngayanni Kyauk Taung** *mountain* Myanmar
159 G4 **Ngbala** Congo
222 3 **Ngcheangel** *island* Palau
222 3 **Ngercheluk** Palau
222 3 **Ngeriuns** *island* Palau
222 3 **Ngeruktabel** *island* Palau
223 9a **Nggamea** *island* Fiji
222 8 **Nggatokae** *island* Solomon Islands
222 8a **Nggela Pile** *island* Solomon Islands
222 8a **Nggela Sule** *island* Solomon Islands
198 C6 **Ngilmina** Indonesia
197 G6 **Ngliyep** Indonesia
194 E4 **Ngoc Linh** *mountain* Vietnam
198 C3 **Ngofakiaha** Indonesia
159 G4 **Ngoïla** Cameroon
159 H5 **Ngoko** Congo
159 H4 **Ngoko** *watercourse* Congo
162 D3 **Ngoma** Botswana
161 E5 **Ngomba** Tanzania
159 G4 **Ngomedzap** Cameroon
159 G3 **Ngong** Cameroon
161 E5 **Ngongo** Tanzania
185 K6 **Ngoring Hu** *lake* Qinghai China
160 B4 **Ngoso** Democratic Republic of Congo
159 H4 **Ngoto** Central African Republic
160 D2 **Ngouanga** *watercourse* Central African Republic
159 G4 **Ngoulemakong** Cameroon
159 G5 **Ngounié** *admin. area* Gabon
159 G5 **Ngounié** *watercourse* Gabon
155 J6 **Ngoura** Chad
155 J6 **Ngouri** Chad
155 I5 **Ngourti** Niger
159 G4 **Ngoyeboma** Congo
160 D4 **Ngozi** Burundi
161 E4 **Ngudu** Tanzania
159 G3 **Nguia Bouar** Central African Republic
155 I6 **Nguigmi** Niger
213 K1 **Nguiu** NT Australia
214 C3 **Ngukurr** NT Australia
198 F1 **Ngulu** *island* Federated States of Micronesia
222 7 **Nguna** *island* Vanuatu
163 F4 **Ngundu** Zimbabwe
220 F2 **Ngunguru Bay** New Zealand
197 I6 **Ngunju, Tanjung** *cape* Indonesia
197 G6 **Ngunut** Indonesia
159 G2 **Nguru** Nigeria
194 E2 **Nguyên Bình** Vietnam
162 E3 **Ngweze** *watercourse* Zambia
194 F4 **Nha Trang** Vietnam
162 D4 **Nhabe** *watercourse* Botswana
163 F3 **Nhacolo** Mozambique
163 F3 **Nhamatanda** Mozambique
101 G5 **Nhamundá** Brazil
101 G5 **Nhamundá** *watercourse* Brazil
162 C2 **N'harea** Angola
105 G5 **Nhecolândia** Brazil
162 B2 **Nhia** *watercourse* Angola
218 E7 **Nhill** Vic. Australia
162 D3 **Nhoma** Namibia
107 H4 **Nhu Pora** Brazil
214 D2 **Nhulunbuy** NT Australia
184 G5 **Ni-ya He** *watercourse* Xinjiang Uygur Zizhiqu China
191 J3 **Ni'erji** Nei Mongol Zizhiqu China
158 D3 **Niablé** Côte d'Ivoire
83 L5 **Niagara Falls** New York USA
83 L5 **Niagara Falls** *waterfall* New York USA
158 C2 **Niagassola** Guinea
197 G3 **Niah** Malaysia
218 E5 **Nialia Lake** NSW Australia
155 G6 **Niamey** Niger
154 E6 **Niamina** Mali
198 C2 **Niampak** Indonesia
190 E6 **Nianbo** Qinghai China
158 C2 **Niandan Koro** Guinea
158 C3 **Niandati** *watercourse* Guinea
219 J4 **Niangala** NSW Australia
161 F5 **Niangandu** Tanzania
160 D3 **Niangara** Democratic Republic of Congo
158 D2 **Niangoloko** Burkina Faso
86 E2 **Niangua** *watercourse* Missouri USA
158 B2 **Niantan** *watercourse* Guinea
189 G2 **Nianyushan Shuiku** *lake* Henan China
159 G5 **Niari** *admin. area* Congo
196 C3 **Nias** *island* Indonesia
163 G2 **Niassa** *admin. area* Mozambique
131 B6 **Nibaru, Punta de lu** *cape* Italy
76 K6 **Nibinamik** Ontario Canada
76 K6 **Nibinamik Lake** Ontario Canada
222 4 **Nibok** Nauru
123 K4 **Nīca** Latvia
90 C4 **Nicaragua** *country* Central America
90 C5 **Nicaragua, Lago de** *lake* Nicaragua
83 Q4 **Nicatous Lake** Maine USA
127 H5 **Nice** France
87 H5 **Niceville** Florida USA
135 AE4 **Nichalakh** Russian Federation
77 T6 **Nichicun, Lac** *lake* Quebec Canada
192 F5 **Nichinan** Japan
186 F5 **Nichlaul** Uttar Pradesh India
90 D2 **Nicholas Channel** Cuba
82 I8 **Nicholasville** Kentucky USA
87 J5 **Nicholls** Georgia USA
90 E1 **Nicholls Town** Bahamas
214 E4 **Nicholson** *watercourse* Qld Australia
213 J5 **Nicholson** WA Australia
213 J4 **Nicholson** *watercourse* WA Australia
82 J3 **Nicholson** Ontario Canada
219 I1 **Nicholson, Mount** Qld Australia
89 I4 **Nichupte, Laguna** *lake* Mexico
85 J5 **Nickel Creek Station** Texas USA
101 G3 **Nickerie** *admin. area* Suriname
81 P7 **Nickerson** Kansas USA
194 B6 **Nicobar Islands** Andaman and Nicobar Islands India
83 N2 **Nicobi Lake** Quebec Canada
89 H5 **Nicolás Bravo** Mexico
85 I6 **Nicolas Bravo** Mexico
131 F8 **Nicosia** Italy
136 E6 **Nicosia (Lefkosia)** Cyprus
131 F7 **Nicotera** Italy
90 C5 **Nicoya** Costa Rica
90 C5 **Nicoya, Golfo de** *lake* Costa Rica
90 C5 **Nicoya, Península de** *peninsula* Costa Rica
163 G3 **Nicuadala** Mozambique
79 J9 **Nid à l'Aigle, Cap du** *cape* St Pierre and Miquelon
123 K5 **Nida** Lithuania
125 K2 **Nida** *watercourse* Poland
141 G2 **Nidd** *watercourse* England UK
124 E2 **Nidda** Germany
124 E2 **Nidda** *watercourse* Germany
141 G2 **Nidderdale** *valley* England UK
122 E3 **Nidelva** *watercourse* Norway
195 H5 **Nido, El** Philippines
135 V6 **Nidym** *watercourse* Russian Federation
125 K1 **Nidzica** Poland
131 C7 **Niedda, Punta** *cape* Sardinia Italy
131 C6 **Nieddu, Capo** *cape* Sardinia Italy
125 H3 **Niederösterreich** *admin. area* Austria
124 E1 **Niedersachsen** *admin. area* Germany
181 E3 **Nielamu** Xizang Zizhiqu China
186 F5 **Nielamu** Nepal
159 H3 **Niem** Central African Republic
160 D5 **Niemba** Democratic Republic of Congo
125 I2 **Niemcza** Poland
121 P3 **Niemelä** Finland
121 Q5 **Niemijärvi** Finland
121 M3 **Niemis** Sweden
120 M3 **Niemisel** Sweden
121 N5 **Niemisvesi** *lake* Finland
154 D6 **Niéri Ko** *watercourse* Senegal
124 D2 **Niers** *watercourse* Germany
121 N3 **Niesi** Finland
125 H2 **Niesky** Germany
125 M1 **Niesłysz, Jezioro** *lake* Poland
125 J1 **Nieszawa** Poland
108 B3 **Nieto** Argentina
120 L3 **Nietsakjaure** *lake* Sweden
219 R10 **Nietta** Tas. Australia
101 H3 **Nieuw Amsterdam** Suriname
55 M8 **Nieuw Amsterdam Fracture Zone** *underwater feature* Indian Ocean
101 G3 **Nieuw Nickerie** Suriname
109 1b **Nieuwpoort** Netherlands Antilles
105 E4 **Nieve** Bolivia
88 E4 **Nieves** Mexico
164 3b **Nieves, Pico de las** *volcano* Canary Islands
198 D4 **Nif** Indonesia
136 E6 **Niğde** Turkey
136 E6 **Niğde** *admin. area* Turkey
159 F2 **Niger** *country* Africa
158 C2 **Niger** *watercourse* Guinea
154 E6 **Niger** *watercourse* Mali
155 G6 **Niger** *watercourse* Niger
159 F4 **Niger** *watercourse* Nigeria
54 E4 **Niger Fan** *underwater feature* Gulf of Guinea
159 F2 **Nigeria** *country* Africa
142 D3 **Nigg** Highland Scotland UK
142 D3 **Nigg Bay** Scotland UK
221 C7 **Nightcaps** New Zealand
83 K2 **Nighthawk Lake** Ontario Canada
164 5c **Nightingale Island** St Helena
108 B2 **Nihue, Punta** *cape* Chile
193 H4 **Nii-jima** *island* Japan
193 H4 **Niigata** Japan
192 G5 **Niihama** Japan
84 inset **Ni'ihau** *island* Hawai'i USA
193 I2 **Niikappu-gawa** *lake* Japan
192 G4 **Niimi** Japan
121 P5 **Niinivaara** Finland
121 O5 **Niinivesi** *bay* Finland
128 E5 **Níjar** Spain
132 A3 **Nijemci** Croatia
124 C1 **Nijkerk** Netherlands
124 C2 **Nijmegen** Netherlands
124 D1 **Nijverdal** Netherlands
133 C6 **Nikaia** Greece
220 2 **Nikao** Cook Islands New Zealand
134 H5 **Nikel'** Russian Federation
133 B5 **Niki** Greece
197 J6 **Nikinlki** Indonesia
76 J6 **Nikip Lake** Ontario Canada
133 C5 **Nikítas** Greece
182 D2 **Nikitino** Russian Federation
133 B5 **Nikodim** Macedonia
182 D5 **Nikolayevka** Russian Federation
182 E3 **Nikolayevsk** Russian Federation
135 AD8 **Nikolayevsk-na-Amure** Russian Federation
134 K7 **Nikol'sk** Russian Federation
182 E2 **Nikolsk** Russian Federation
160 E4 **Nikonga** *watercourse* Tanzania
136 E3 **Nikopol'** Ukraine
133 D7 **Nikouria** *island* Greece
130 H5 **Nikšić** Montenegro
222 1 **Nikumaroro** *island* Kiribati
222 1 **Nikunau** *island* Kiribati
156 E2 **Nīl, Nahr an (Nile)** *watercourse* Egypt
156 E4 **Nīl, Nahr an (Nile)** *watercourse* Sudan
198 D5 **Nila** *island* Indonesia
121 O5 **Nilakka** *lake* Finland
187 C11 **Nilandhoo Atoll** Maldives
Nile *see* **Nīl, Nahr an** Africa
219 R10 **Nile** Tas. Australia
156 E4 **Nile** *admin. area* Sudan
184 G4 **Nileke** Xinjiang Uygur Zizhiqu China
82 H6 **Niles** Michigan USA
120 L3 **Nilivaara** Sweden
218 D4 **Nilpena** SA Australia
218 B3 **Nilpinna** SA Australia
58 E2 **Nilsen Bay** Antarctica
186 D6 **Nimbahera** Rajasthan India
127 G5 **Nîmes** France
132 D2 **Nimigea de Sur** Romania
219 I7 **Nimmitabel** NSW Australia
74 H7 **Nimpkish Lake** British Columbia Canada
74 H7 **Nimpkish** *watercourse* British Columbia Canada
58 K1 **Nimrod Glacier** *ice* Antarctica
179 J3 **Nīmrūz** *admin. area* Afghanistan
123 N3 **Nina** Estonia
178 E2 **Nīnawá** *admin. area* Iraq
77 V4 **Ninawawe, Lac** *lake* Quebec Canada
162 D2 **Ninda** Angola
219 I3 **Nindigully** Qld Australia
187 C10 **Nine Degree Channel** *strait* Lakshadweep India
141 F2 **Ninebanks** Northumberland England UK
75 V8 **Ninette** Manitoba Canada
220 E2 **Ninety Mile Beach** New Zealand
55 M5 **Ninetyeast Ridge** *underwater feature* Indian Ocean
108 D3 **Ninfas, Punta** *cape* Argentina
188 D4 **Ning'er** Yunnan China
212 B7 **Ningaloo** WA Australia
191 L4 **Ning'an** Heilongjiang China
189 I2 **Ningbo** Zhejiang China
189 H3 **Ningde** Fujian China
189 I2 **Ninghai** Zhejiang China
191 I5 **Ninghe** Tianjin China
159 F2 **Ningi** Nigeria
191 H5 **Ningjin** Shandong China
189 G1 **Ningling** Henan China
188 E2 **Ningqiang** Shaanxi China
188 E1 **Ningshan** Shaanxi China
190 G5 **Ningwu** Shanxi China
188 E1 **Ningxia Huizu Zishiqu** *admin. area* China
191 H6 **Ningyang** Shandong China
194 E2 **Ninh Bình** Vietnam
194 F4 **Ninh Hòa** Vietnam
215 H3 **Ninian Bay** Qld Australia
199 H4 **Ninigo Group** *islands* Papua New Guinea
86 C3 **Ninnekah** Oklahoma USA
58 J2 **Ninnis Glacier Tongue** *ice* Antarctica
193 I3 **Ninohe** Japan
85 I5 **Niños Héroes de Chapultepec** Mexico
126 G1 **Ninove** Belgium
105 H6 **Nioaque** Brazil
81 P5 **Niobrara** *watercourse* Nebraska USA
73 R3 **Nioghalvfjerdsfjorden** *bay* Greenland
154 E6 **Niono** Mali
154 E5 **Nioro** Mali
154 C6 **Nioro du Rip** Senegal
126 D3 **Niort** France
199 G5 **Nipa** Papua New Guinea
187 D8 **Nipani** Karnataka India
91 F2 **Nipe, Bahia de** *bay* Cuba
163 G2 **Nipepe** Mozambique
187 D7 **Niphad** Maharashtra India
82 G2 **Nipigon, Lake** Ontario Canada
82 H2 **Nipigon Bay** Ontario Canada
75 Q5 **Nipin** *watercourse* Saskatchewan Canada
163 G3 **Nipiodi** Mozambique
79 F9 **Nipisiguit Bay** New Brunswick Canada
83 L3 **Nipissing, Lake** Ontario Canada
77 V7 **Nipissis, Lac** *lake* Quebec Canada
77 W7 **Nipisso, Lac** *lake* Quebec Canada
103 B6 **Niquelândia** Brazil

90 E2 **Niquero** Cuba
187 D8 **Nira** *watercourse* Maharashtra India
106 D6 **Ñire-Có** Argentina
108 B3 **Ñirehuao** Chile
187 E7 **Nirmal** Andhra Pradesh India
214 A7 **Nirrippi** NT Australia
123 N4 **Nirza** Latvia
132 B4 **Niš** Serbia
132 C4 **Nišava** *watercourse* Serbia
142 F5 **Nisbet House** Scottish Borders Scotland UK
131 F8 **Niscemi** Italy
132 C4 **Niševac** Serbia
192 G4 **Nishino-shima** *island* Japan
83 M3 **Nishkotea Lake** Quebec Canada
186 F5 **Nisi Khola** Nepal
102 F4 **Nísia Floresta** Brazil
121 O4 **Niskanselkä** *bay* Finland
76 K4 **Niskibi** *watercourse* Ontario Canada
121 M5 **Niskos** Finland
81 N4 **Nisland** South Dakota USA
122 G4 **Nissan** *watercourse* Sweden
199 J5 **Nissan Island** Papua New Guinea
122 E3 **Nisser** *lake* Norway
121 O5 **Nissilä** Finland
122 E4 **Nissum Bredning** *bay* Denmark
132 F2 **Nistru** *watercourse* Moldova
133 E7 **Nisyros** *island* Greece
212 F5 **Nita Downs** WA Australia
77 T6 **Nitchequon** Quebec Canada
107 K2 **Niterói** Brazil
142 D5 **Nith** *watercourse* Scotland UK
198 C6 **Nitibe** Timor-Leste (East Timor)
139 F4 **Niton** Isle of Wight England UK
75 N6 **Niton Junction** Alberta Canada
125 J3 **Nitra** Slovakia
125 J3 **Nitransky** *admin. area* Slovakia
124 B4 **Nitry** France
121 O2 **Nitsijärvi** *bay* Finland
223 12 **Niuafo'ou** *island* Tonga
223 12 **Niuatoputapu** *island* Tonga
220 inset **Niue** Pacific Ocean Nw Zealand territory
188 C3 **Niujing** Yunnan China
123 O2 **Niukkala** Finland
188 D3 **Niulan Jiang** *watercourse* Yunnan China
84 inset **Niuli'i** Hawai'i USA
222 1 **Niutao** *island* Tuvalu
189 I2 **Niutou Shan** *range* Zhejiang China
223 10a **Niutoua** Tonga
122 G5 **Nivå** Denmark
123 P2 **Niva** Russian Federation
121 N5 **Nivala** Finland
218 H1 **Nive** *watercourse* Qld Australia
126 D5 **Nive** *watercourse* France
127 G1 **Nivelles** Belgium
127 G1 **Nivelles** *admin. area* Belgium
126 F3 **Nivernais, Canal du** *watercourse* France
121 R3 **Nivskiy** Russian Federation
186 D5 **Niwai** Rajasthan India
186 E6 **Niwari** Madhya Pradesh India
82 E8 **Nixa** Missouri USA
181 I2 **Nixia** Sichuan China
86 C6 **Nixon** Texas USA
Niyazoba *see* **Nizovaya** Azerbaijan
189 I3 **Niyu Shan** *range* Zhejiang China
197 F3 **Niyut, Gunung** *mountain* Indonesia
181 G3 **Niz Hajo** Assam India
187 D7 **Nizam Sagar** *lake* Andhra Pradesh India
187 E7 **Nizamabad** Andhra Pradesh India
182 D2 **Nizhegorodskaya** *admin. area* Russian Federation
134 J7 **Nizhegorodskaya Oblast'** *admin. area* Russian Federation
121 T4 **Nizhmozero** Russian Federation
135 AH7 **Nizhne-Ozërnaya** Russian Federation
135 U8 **Nizhneudinsk** Russian Federation
183 R2 **Nizhneudinsk** Russian Federation
134 Q6 **Nizhnevartovsk** Russian Federation
121 Q4 **Nizhneye Kuyto, Ozero** *lake* Russian Federation
182 D4 **Nizhniy Chir** Russian Federation
182 C3 **Nizhniy Mamon** Russian Federation
134 J7 **Nizhniy Novgorod** Russian Federation
182 D2 **Nizhniy Novgorod** Russian Federation
134 M7 **Nizhniy Tagil** Russian Federation
182 H1 **Nizhniy Tagil** Russian Federation
134 L6 **Nizhniy Voch** Russian Federation
134 K7 **Nizhniy Yenangsk** Russian Federation
135 U7 **Nizhnyaya Poyma** Russian Federation
183 R2 **Nizhnyaya Poyma** Russian Federation
135 U6 **Nizhnyaya Tunguska** *watercourse* Russian Federation
182 H1 **Nizhnyaya Tura** Russian Federation
134 J5 **Nizhnyaya Zolotitsa** Russian Federation
123 N5 **Nizina Polatskaya** *region* Belarus
125 I2 **Nizina Śląska** *region* Poland
136 F6 **Nizip** Turkey
130 H2 **Nízke Tatry** *range* Slovakia
72 A6 **Nizkiy, Mys** *cape* Russian Federation
123 P5 **Nizkobor'ye** Belarus
182 E5 **Nizovaya** Azerbaijan
179 I5 **Nizwa'** Oman
120 K3 **Njavve** Sweden
Njazidja *see* **Grande Comore** Comoros
161 F5 **Njinjo** Tanzania
162 D3 **Njoko** *watercourse* Zambia
161 E5 **Njombe** Tanzania
161 E5 **Njombe** *watercourse* Tanzania
122 H4 **Njudung** *region* Sweden
120 J5 **Njurundabommen/Njurunda** Sweden
159 G4 **Nkam** *watercourse* Gabon
159 G5 **Nkayi** Congo
163 F2 **Nkhata Bay** Malawi
163 F2 **Nkhotakota** Malawi
159 G4 **Nkolabona** Gabon
159 F5 **Nkomi, Lagune** *lake* Gabon
160 E5 **Nkondwe** Tanzania
159 F4 **Nkongsamba** Cameroon
160 E5 **Nkundi** Tanzania
162 C3 **Nkurenkuru** Namibia
160 E3 **Nkusi** *watercourse* Uganda
158 E3 **Nkwanta** Ghana
158 C3 **Nlaklan** Liberia
181 H4 **Nmai** *watercourse* Myanmar
181 G4 **Noakhali** Bangladesh
218 D6 **Noarlunga** SA Australia
72 D5 **Noatak** *watercourse* Alaska USA
143 F3 **Nobber** Ireland
83 K4 **Nobel** Ontario Canada
192 F5 **Nobeoka** Japan
82 H6 **Noblesville** Indiana USA
105 G4 **Nobres** Brazil
218 F2 **Noccundra** Qld Australia
130 E5 **Nocera Umbra** Italy
88 E4 **Nochistlán** Mexico
131 G6 **Noci** Italy
218 F2 **Nockatunga** Qld Australia
218 G3 **Nocoleche** NSW Australia
86 C4 **Nocona** Texas USA
108 D4 **Nodales, Bahía de los** *bay* Argentina
82 D6 **Nodaway** *watercourse* Missouri USA
83 K3 **Noelville** Ontario Canada
122 H4 **Noen** *lake* Sweden
122 F5 **Noer** Germany
88 C2 **Nogales** Mexico
88 C2 **Nogales** Arizona USA
124 F5 **Nogara** Italy
134 T6 **Noginsk** Russian Federation
215 I8 **Nogoa** *watercourse* Qld Australia
107 G5 **Nogoyá** *watercourse* Argentina
125 J4 **Nógrad** *admin. area* Hungary
127 H2 **Nohfelden** Germany
192 E4 **Nohwa-do** *island* South Korea
83 M3 **Noire** *watercourse* Quebec Canada
126 C3 **Noirmoutier, Île de** *island* France
193 H4 **Nojiri-ko** *lake* Japan
179 J4 **Nok Kundi** Pakistan
222 8 **Noka** Solomon Islands
186 F6 **Nokha** Bihar India
186 C5 **Nokha** Rajasthan India
179 I4 **Nokhowch, Kūh-e** *mountain* Iran
135 Y7 **Nokhtuysk** Russian Federation
198 B4 **Nokilalaki, Gunung** *mountain* Indonesia
75 S7 **Nokomis** Saskatchewan Canada
155 I6 **Nokou** Chad
158 E3 **Nokoue, Lac** *lake* Benin
181 G4 **Nokrek Peak** *mountain* Meghalaya India
159 H4 **Nola** Central African Republic
131 F6 **Nola** Italy
215 G4 **Nolan** *watercourse* Qld Australia
124 C4 **Nolay** France
130 C4 **Noli, Capo di** *cape* Italy
87 H2 **Nolin Lake** Kentucky USA
182 F1 **Nolinsk** Russian Federation
199 G5 **Nomad** *watercourse* Papua New Guinea
215 G2 **Nomad Reef** Qld Australia
138 D4 **Nomansland** Devon England UK
77 O6 **Nomansland Point** Ontario Canada
218 G2 **Nombardie** Qld Australia
128 D3 **Nombela** Spain
108 C5 **Nombre, Cabo** *cape* Argentina
88 D4 **Nombre de Dios** Mexico
72 C6 **Nome** Alaska USA
127 H2 **Nomexy** France
190 F4 **Nomgon** Mongolia
133 C7 **Nómia** Greece
122 H4 **Nömmen** *lake* Sweden
223 10 **Nomuka** *island* Tonga
222 6 **Nomwin** *island* Federated States of Micronesia
75 Q2 **Nonacho Lake** Northwest Territories Canada
126 E2 **Nonancourt** France
130 D4 **Nonantola** Italy
72 D7 **Nondalton** Alaska USA
194 D3 **Nong Bua Lamphu** Thailand
191 M3 **Nong Jiang** *watercourse* Heilongjiang China
194 D3 **Nong Khai** Thailand
194 D4 **Nong Phai** Thailand
191 K4 **Nong'an** Jilin China
190 G5 **Nongchang** *mountain* Shaanxi China
122 H2 **Nöngen** *lake* Sweden
181 G4 **Nongkhlaw** Meghalaya India
163 F5 **Nongoma** South Africa
213 J5 **Nongra Lake** NT Australia
196 E3 **Nongsa** Indonesia
196 G5 **Nongsapura** Indonesia
181 G4 **Nongstoin** Meghalaya India
218 C5 **Nonning** SA Australia
158 B2 **Nono** *watercourse* Guinea
222 1 **Nonouti** *island* Kiribati
192 E4 **Nonsan** South Korea
76 H4 **Nonsuch** Manitoba Canada
109 18 **Nonsuch Bay** Antigua and Barbuda
194 D4 **Nonthaburi** Thailand
126 E4 **Nontron** France
72 D7 **Nonvianuk Lake** Alaska USA
127 I5 **Nonza** Corsica France
216 E3 **Nookawarra** WA Australia
218 C2 **Noolyeana, Lake** SA Australia
213 K2 **Noonamah** NT Australia
81 N2 **Noonan** North Dakota USA
216 F4 **Noondie, Lake** WA Australia
219 I2 **Noonga** Qld Australia
213 H5 **Noonkanbah** WA Australia
218 H3 **Noorama** *watercourse* Qld Australia
109 1a **Noord** Aruba
109 1a **Noordkaap** *cape* Aruba
91 G4 **Noordpunt** *cape* Netherlands Antilles
72 C5 **Noorvik** Alaska USA
219 K2 **Noosa Heads** Qld Australia
80 B2 **Nootka** British Columbia Canada
74 H8 **Nootka Island** British Columbia Canada
74 H8 **Nootka Sound** British Columbia Canada
218 F3 **Nooyeah Downs** Qld Australia
120 M5 **Nopankylä** Finland
122 I3 **Nora** Sweden
183 K6 **Norak** Tajikistan
74 H6 **Noralee** British Columbia Canada
100 C3 **Norcasia** Colombia
81 O7 **Norcatur** Kansas USA
159 G3 **Nord** *admin. area* Cameroon
77 R4 **Nord, Rivière du** *watercourse* Quebec Canada
160 D4 **Nord-Kivu** *admin. area* Democratic Republic of Congo
120 K1 **Nord-Kvaløy** *island* Norway
122 F2 **Nord-Mesna** *lake* Norway
122 E5 **Nord-Ostsee-Kanal** *watercourse* Germany
159 G3 **Nord-Ouest** *admin. area* Cameroon
126 F1 **Nord-Pas-de-Calais** *admin. area* France
120 L1 **Nord-Rekvik** Norway
120 H4 **Nord-Trøndelag** *admin. area* Norway
120 K4 **Nordanås** Sweden
120 J5 **Nordanede** Sweden
120 J5 **Nordankäl** Sweden
139 J4 **Nordausques** France
134 F3 **Nordaustlandet** *island* Norway
120 F5 **Nordbotn** Norway
121 M2 **Nordbotn** Norway
122 E5 **Nordby** Denmark
75 M6 **Nordegg** Alberta Canada
139 H2 **Nordelph** Norfolk England UK
124 D1 **Norden** Germany
141 F3 **Norden** Greater Manchester England UK
135 U3 **Nordenshel'da, Arkipelag** *islands* Russian Federation
58 L1 **Nordenskjöld Basin** *underwater feature* Ross Sea
124 D1 **Norderney** *island* Germany
122 F6 **Norderstedt** Germany
160 C5 **Nordeste** Angola
122 C2 **Nordfjordeid** Norway
127 J1 **Nordhausen** Germany
122 E4 **Nordjylland** *admin. area* Denmark
134 G4 **Nordkapp** *cape* Norway
134 G4 **Nordkinnhalvøya** *cape* Norway
120 K2 **Nordkjosbotn** Norway
121 O1 **Nordkynhalvøya** *peninsula* Norway
120 I3 **Nordland** *admin. area* Norway
120 H4 **Nordli** Norway
124 F3 **Nördlingen** Germany
120 K5 **Nordmaling** Sweden
122 D2 **Nordmannslågen** *lake* Norway
120 L2 **Nordmannvik** Norway
120 I2 **Nordmela** Norway
120 H6 **Nordomsjön** Sweden
124 D1 **Nordradde** *watercourse* Germany
120 I3 **Nordre-Bjøllåvatn** *lake* Norway
122 F2 **Nordre Osa** *watercourse* Norway
124 D2 **Nordrhein-Westfalen** *admin. area* Germany
120 G4 **Nordskjør** Norway
120 I3 **Nordskot** Norway
135 X4 **Nordvik** Russian Federation
120 F5 **Nordvika** Norway
120 H3 **Nordvikfjellet** *island* Norway
143 E4 **Nore** *watercourse* Ireland
122 E2 **Nore** Norway
143 E4 **Nore Bridge** Ireland
129 H2 **Norfeu, Cap de** *cape* Spain
139 H2 **Norfolk** *admin. area* England UK
81 Q5 **Norfolk** Nebraska USA
83 M8 **Norfolk** Virginia USA
219 Q10 **Norfolk, Mount** Tas. Australia
211 inset **Norfolk Island** *Australian territory* Pacific Ocean
52 M10 **Norfolk Ridge** *underwater feature* Pacific Ocean
86 E2 **Norfork Lake** Arkansas USA
124 D1 **Norg** Netherlands
75 V7 **Norgate** Manitoba Canada
75 R8 **Norge** Saskatchewan Canada
86 C7 **Norias** Texas USA
134 S5 **Noril'sk** Russian Federation
87 L2 **Norlina** North Carolina USA
82 G6 **Normal** Illinois USA
214 F5 **Norman** *watercourse* Qld Australia
86 C3 **Norman** Oklahoma USA
87 K3 **Norman, Lake** North Carolina USA
221 8 **Norman Inlet** Auckland Islands New Zealand
87 J5 **Norman Park** Georgia USA
72 G5 **Norman Wells** Northwest Territories Canada
215 H3 **Normanby** *watercourse* Qld Australia
Normandes, Îles *see* **Channel Islands** UK
126 E2 **Normandie (Normandy)** *region* France
Normandy *see* **Normandie** France
85 L6 **Normandy** Texas USA
86 C5 **Normangee** Texas USA
214 F4 **Normanton** Qld Australia
218 D6 **Normanville** SA Australia
83 L2 **Normetal** Quebec Canada
216 E7 **Nornalup** WA Australia
85 I7 **Norogachic** Mexico
164 6b **Noroît, Baie du** *bay* French Southern and Antarctic Lands
120 inset **Norðurfjörður** Iceland
120 inset **Norðurland Vestra** *admin. area* Iceland
86 E4 **Norphlet** Arkansas USA
75 T7 **Norquay** Saskatchewan Canada
106 D6 **Ñorquín** Argentina
108 B2 **Ñorquinco** Argentina
122 I2 **Norr-Bränningen** *lake* Sweden
122 F3 **Norr Bullaresjön** *lake* Sweden
122 H2 **Norr Hörken** *lake* Sweden
122 H2 **Norra Barken** *bay* Sweden
120 K3 **Norra Bergnäs** Sweden
120 J6 **Norra Dellen** *lake* Sweden
122 I3 **Norra Finnö** *island* Sweden
120 I4 **Norra Fjällnäs** Sweden
120 K4 **Norra Malånäs** Sweden
122 I4 **Norra Näsby** Sweden
120 I5 **Norra Skärvången** Sweden
120 I4 **Norra Storfjället** *island* Sweden
120 I4 **Norråker** Sweden
122 I2 **Norrala** Sweden
122 H3 **Norrälgen** *lake* Sweden
122 H4 **Norraryd** Sweden
120 J4 **Norrbäck** Sweden
120 J4 **Norrberg** Sweden
120 I5 **Norrböle** Sweden
120 L3 **Norrbotten** *admin. area* Sweden
120 K4 **Norrbyberg** Sweden
122 F5 **Nørre Alslev** Denmark
122 E4 **Nørre Lyngby** Denmark
122 E4 **Nørre Vorupør** Denmark
120 J5 **Norrfjärden** Sweden
123 K2 **Norrhavet** *bay* Finland
79 K8 **Norris Arm** Newfoundland and Labrador Canada
82 G8 **Norris City** Illinois USA
87 J2 **Norris Lake** Tennessee USA
79 J8 **Norris Point** Newfoundland and Labrador Canada
122 I3 **Norrköping** Sweden
122 I3 **Norrköpings Bukten** *bay* Sweden
120 L5 **Norrnäs** Finland
120 J5 **Norrstig** Sweden
123 J3 **Norrtälje** Sweden
122 H3 **Norsholm** Sweden
122 E3 **Norsjø** *lake* Norway
120 K4 **Norsjö** Sweden
73 R3 **Norske Øer** *island* Greenland
120 L1 **Norskehavet** *bay* Norway
222 7 **Norsup** Vanuatu
109 5 **Norte, Cabo** *cape* Isla de Pascua (Easter Island)
102 B2 **Norte, Canal do** *watercourse* Brazil
108 A3 **Norte, Punta** *cape* Chile
109 6a **Norte, Punta** *cape* Isla Róbinson Crusoe
105 G3 **Norte, Serra do** *range* Brazil
100 C2 **Norte de Santander** *admin. area* Colombia
107 G6 **Norte del Cabo San Antonio, Punta** *cape* Argentina
77 X4 **North** *watercourse* Newfoundland and Labrador Canada
58 L2 **North, Cape** Antarctica
79 H9 **North, Cape** Nova Scotia Canada
83 O5 **North Adams** Massachusetts USA
194 B4 **North Andaman** *island* Andaman and Nicobar Islands India
75 N1 **North Arm** Northwest Territories Canada
109 7 **North Arm** Falkland Islands
87 K4 **North Augusta** South Carolina USA
77 W3 **North Aulatsivik Island** Newfoundland and Labrador Canada
142 D5 **North Ayrshire** *admin. area* Scotland UK
195 H5 **North Balabac Strait** Philippines
216 E6 **North Bannister** WA Australia
75 Q6 **North Battleford** Saskatchewan Canada
77 U1 **North Bay** Nunavut Canada
83 L3 **North Bay** Ontario Canada
73 K7 **North Belcher Islands** Nunavut Canada
80 E2 **North Bend** British Columbia Canada
142 F4 **North Berwick** East Lothian Scotland UK
218 G4 **North Bourke** NSW Australia
82 D2 **North Branch** Ontario Canada
82 E4 **North Branch** Minnesota USA
194 B5 **North Brother Island** Andaman and Nicobar Islands India
91 G2 **North Caicos** *island* Turks and Caicos Islands
79 G9 **North Cape** Prince Edward Island Canada
221 11 **North Cape** Antipodes Islands New Zealand
221 9 **North Cape** Campbell Island New Zealand
109 8 **North Cape** South Georgia
220 E2 **North Cape (Otou)** New Zealand
76 J6 **North Caribou Lake** Ontario Canada
73 J8 **North Caribou Lake** Ontario Canada
71 **North Carolina** *admin. area* USA
141 H3 **North Cave** East Riding of Yorkshire England UK
142 C5 **North Channel** Northern Ireland/ Scotland UK
87 L4 **North Charleston** South Carolina USA
82 H5 **North Chicago** Illinois USA
191 H6 **North China Plain** Shandong China
141 H3 **North Cliffe** East Riding of Yorkshire England UK
213 G4 **North Cliffs** WA Australia
74 J8 **North Cowichan** British Columbia Canada
139 H2 **North Creake** Norfolk England UK
70 **North Dakota** *admin. area* USA
141 H3 **North Dalton** East Riding of Yorkshire England UK
216 D6 **North Dandalup** WA Australia
143 G2 **North Down** *admin. area* Northern Ireland UK
139 H3 **North Downs** *range* England UK
162 E4 **North-East** *admin. area* Botswana
221 7 **North East Island** Snares Islands New Zealand
214 D2 **North East Isles** NT Australia
141 H3 **North East Lincolnshire** *admin. area* England UK
210 inset **North East Point** Christmas Island Australia
222 1a **North East Point** Kiribati
161 G3 **North-Eastern** *admin. area* Kenya
220 F4 **North Egmont** New Zealand
91 F1 **North End Point** Bahamas
86 C2 **North Enid** Oklahoma USA
142 F4 **North Esk** *watercourse* Scotland UK
108 E5 **North Falkland Sound** Falkland Islands
52 N9 **North Fiji Basin** *underwater feature* Pacific Ocean
139 I3 **North Foreland** *cape* England UK
75 N8 **North Fork** *watercourse* British Columbia Canada
80 H2 **North Fork Flathead** *watercourse* Montana USA
85 M3 **North Fork Red** *watercourse* Oklahoma USA
77 O7 **North French** *watercourse* Ontario Canada
109 19 **North Friar's Bay** St Kitts and Nevis
213 L1 **North Goulburn Island** NT Australia
141 H2 **North Grimston** North Yorkshire England UK
219 K4 **North Haven** NSW Australia
211 inset **North Head** Lord Howe Island Australia
220 F3 **North Head** New Zealand
75 W2 **North Henik Lake** Nunavut Canada
161 F3 **North Horr** Kenya
141 H3 **North Hykeham** Lincolnshire England UK
214 D3 **North Island** NT Australia
216 C4 **North Island** WA Australia
220 E3 **North Island** New Zealand
164 9a **North Island** Seychelles
87 L4 **North Island** South Carolina USA
195 I5 **North Islet** Philippines
57 I2 **North Kanin Basin** *underwater feature* Barents Sea
210 inset **North Keeling Island** Cocos (Keeling) Islands Australia
141 H3 **North Kelsey** Lincolnshire England UK
142 D3 **North Kessock** Highland Scotland UK
141 H3 **North Killingholme** North Lincolnshire England UK
76 G3 **North Knife** *watercourse* Manitoba Canada
75 W3 **North Knife Lake** Manitoba Canada
73 J7 **North Knife Lake** Manitoba Canada
192 F3 **North Korea** *country* Asia
181 H3 **North Lakhimpur** Assam India
142 E5 **North Lanarkshire** *admin. area* Scotland UK
84 E2 **North Las Vegas** Nevada USA
141 H3 **North Lincolnshire** *admin. area* England UK
86 E3 **North Little Rock** Arkansas USA
139 F2 **North Littleton** Worcestershire England UK
81 P6 **North Loup** Nebraska USA
81 O5 **North Loup** *watercourse* Nebraska USA
82 D4 **North Mankato** Minnesota USA
139 G3 **North Marston** Buckinghamshire England UK
109 11 **North Mayreau Channel** *strait* St Vincent and the Grenadines
87 K8 **North Miami** Florida USA
138 D3 **North Molton** Devon England UK
76 E5 **North Moose Lake** Manitoba Canada
218 D4 **North Mulga** SA Australia
87 L4 **North Myrtle Beach** South Carolina USA
74 I1 **North Nahanni** *watercourse* Northwest Territories Canada
80 J6 **North Ogden** Utah USA
213 K2 **North Peron Island** NT Australia
138 D3 **North Petherton** Somerset England UK
81 O6 **North Platte** Nebraska USA
81 N6 **North Platte** *watercourse* Nebraska USA
219 Q10 **North Point** *cape* Tas. Australia
109 12 **North Point** *cape* Barbados
164 9b **North Point** *cape* Seychelles
164 5c **North Point** *cape* St Helena
57 **North Pole** Arctic
72 E6 **North Pole** Alaska USA
87 J7 **North Port** Florida USA
80 G4 **North Powder** Oregon USA
195 F3 **North Reef** Paracel Islands
194 B4 **North Reef Island** Andaman and Nicobar Islands India
75 X3 **North River** Manitoba Canada
141 F3 **North Rode** Cheshire England UK
142 F1 **North Ronaldsay** *island* Scotland UK
75 N6 **North Saskatchewan** *watercourse* Alberta Canada
75 R6 **North Saskatchewan** *watercourse* Saskatchewan Canada
139 J2 **North Sea** Northern Europe
75 U3 **North Seal** *watercourse* Manitoba Canada
194 B5 **North Sentinel Island** Andaman and Nicobar Islands India
142 C4 **North Shian** Argyll and Bute Scotland UK
220 F3 **North Shore** New Zealand
72 D5 **North Slope** *region* Alaska USA
141 I3 **North Somercotes** Lincolnshire England UK
138 E3 **North Somerset** *admin. area* England UK
143 C3 **North Sound** Ireland
142 F1 **North Sound, The** Scotland UK
76 I6 **North Spirit Lake** Ontario Canada
78 J5 **North Stag Islands** Newfoundland and Labrador Canada
141 F2 **North Stainmore** Cumbria England UK
219 J3 **North Star** NSW Australia
74 M4 **North Star** Alberta Canada
219 K2 **North Stradbroke Island (Minjerriba)** Qld Australia
220 E4 **North Taranaki Bight** New Zealand
142 F4 **North Tarbrax** Angus Scotland UK
72 G8 **North Thompson** *watercourse* British Columbia Canada
83 O4 **North Troy** Vermont USA
77 O6 **North Twin Island** Nunavut Canada
216 H7 **North Twin Peak Island** WA Australia
141 F1 **North Tyne** *watercourse* England UK
141 G1 **North Tyneside** *admin. area* England UK
North Uist *see* **Uibhist a Tuath** UK
74 J8 **North Vancouver** British Columbia Canada
75 O4 **North Wabasca Lake** Alberta Canada
162 D3 **North-West** *admin. area* Botswana
162 E5 **North West** *admin. area* South Africa
212 C6 **North West Cape** WA Australia
221 8 **North West Cape** Auckland Islands New Zealand
179 L2 **North-West Frontier** *admin. area* Pakistan
215 K7 **North West Island** Qld Australia
210 inset **North West Point** Christmas Island Australia
222 1a **North West Point** *cape* Kiribati
78 H6 **North West River** Newfoundland and Labrador Canada
162 E2 **North-Western** *admin. area* Zambia
141 H2 **North York Moors** *region* England UK
141 G2 **North Yorkshire** *admin. area* England UK
216 E5 **Northam** WA Australia
138 C3 **Northam** Devon England UK
216 D4 **Northampton** WA Australia
139 G2 **Northampton** Northamptonshire England UK
58 L2 **Northampton, Mount** *mountain* Antarctica
139 G2 **Northamptonshire** *admin. area* England UK
216 E7 **Northcliffe** WA Australia
58 G2 **Northcliffe Glacier** *ice* Antarctica
214 A4 **Northcote, Mount** NT Australia
138 C4 **Northcott** Cornwall England UK
195 G5 **Northeast Cay** *island* Spratly Islands
221 9 **Northeast Harbour** Campbell Island New Zealand
53 T7 **Northeast Pacific Basin** *underwater feature* Pacific Ocean
91 F2 **Northeast Point** Bahamas
90 E1 **Northeast Providence Channel** Bahamas
158 D3 **Northern** *admin. area* Ghana
163 F2 **Northern** *admin. area* Zambia
179 M2 **Northern Areas** *admin. area* Pakistan
160 D2 **Northern Bahr-el-Ghazal** *admin. area* Sudan
162 D5 **Northern Cape** *admin. area* South Africa
220 1 **Northern Cook Islands** Cook Islands New Zealand
156 D4 **Northern Darfur** *admin. area* Sudan
75 W4 **Northern Indian Lake** Manitoba Canada
140 B2 **Northern Ireland** *admin. area* UK
156 D4 **Northern Kordofan** *admin. area* Sudan
222 2 **Northern Mariana Islands** *US territory* Pacific Ocean
217 L2 **Northern Territory** *admin. area* Australia
82 E4 **Northfield** Minnesota USA
81 N2 **Northgate** North Dakota USA
82 I3 **Northland Station** Ontario Canada
138 C4 **Northlew** Devon England UK
81 R3 **Northome** Minnesota USA
86 H4 **Northport** Alabama USA
80 G2 **Northport** Washington USA
58 I2 **Norths Highland** *region* Antarctica
141 G1 **Northumberland** *admin. area* England UK
218 E8 **Northumberland, Cape** SA Australia
215 K6 **Northumberland Islands** Qld Australia
73 M9 **Northumberland Strait** Nova Scotia/ Prince Edward Island Canada
87 L3 **Northwest** North Carolina USA
50 N4 **Northwest Atlantic Mid-Ocean Canyon** *underwater feature* Atlantic Ocean
52 L4 **Northwest Pacific Basin** *underwater feature* Pacific Ocean
91 F2 **Northwest Point** Bahamas
87 M7 **Northwest Providence Channel** Bahamas
52 I9 **Northwest Shelf** *underwater feature* Indian Ocean
72 G6 **Northwest Territories** *admin. area* Canada
141 F3 **Northwich** Cheshire England UK
56 T1 **Northwind Abyssal Plain** *underwater feature* Arctic Ocean
56 T1 **Northwind Escarpment** *underwater feature* Arctic Ocean
56 T1 **Northwind Ridge** *underwater feature* Arctic Ocean
81 Q3 **Northwood** North Dakota USA
79 F10 **Norton** New Brunswick Canada
139 E3 **Norton** Gloucestershire England UK
139 H2 **Norton** Suffolk England UK
139 G4 **Norton** West Sussex England UK
81 P7 **Norton** Kansas USA
162 F3 **Norton** Zimbabwe
138 D3 **Norton Fitzwarren** Somerset England UK
138 E2 **Norton in Hales** Shropshire England UK
82 H5 **Norton Shores** Michigan USA
72 C6 **Norton Sound** Alaska USA
121 N3 **Norvajärvi** *lake* Finland
58 X2 **Norvegia, Cape** Antarctica
84 C4 **Norwalk** California USA
82 J6 **Norwalk** Ohio USA
120 F5 **Norway** *country* Europe
57 G2 **Norwegian Basin** *underwater feature* Norwegian Sea
73 J3 **Norwegian Bay** Nunavut Canada
73 R5 **Norwegian Sea** Iceland/Norway
141 H3 **Norwell** Nottinghamshire England UK
139 I2 **Norwich** Norfolk England UK
83 O6 **Norwich** Connecticut USA
142 inset **Norwick** Shetland Scotland UK
83 M4 **Norwood** Ontario Canada
81 K7 **Norwood** Colorado USA
82 E8 **Norwood** Missouri USA
193 H3 **Noshiro** Japan
142 F2 **Noss Head** *cape* Scotland UK
103 E5 **Nossa Senhora da Glória** Brazil
100 E4 **Nossa Senhora da Guia** Brazil
162 C4 **Nossob** *watercourse* Namibia
162 D5 **Nossop** *watercourse* Botswana
163 I4 **Nosy-varika** Madagascar
125 I4 **Noszlop** Hungary
125 I1 **Noteć** *watercourse* Poland
75 V5 **Notigi** Manitoba Canada
74 L4 **Notikewin** *watercourse* Alberta Canada
133 D7 **Notio Aigaio** *admin. area* Greece
131 F8 **Noto, Golfo di** *bay* Italy
193 J2 **Notoro-ko** *lake* Japan
121 Q2 **Notozero, Ozero** *lake* Russian Federation
73 M9 **Notre Dame, Monts** *range* Quebec Canada
79 K8 **Notre Dame Bay** Newfoundland and Labrador Canada
158 E3 **Notsé** Togo
138 D3 **Nottage** Bridgend Wales UK
77 P7 **Nottaway** *watercourse* Quebec Canada
87 I3 **Nottely Lake** Georgia USA
139 F2 **Nottingham** *admin. area* England UK
139 F2 **Nottingham** Nottingham England UK
77 Q1 **Nottingham Island** Nunavut Canada
141 G3 **Nottinghamshire** *admin. area* England UK
87 M2 **Nottoway** *watercourse* Virginia USA
154 C4 **Nouâdhibou** Mauritania
154 C5 **Nouakchott** Mauritania
154 C5 **Nouâmghâr** Mauritania
78 C5 **Noue, Lac de la** *lake* Quebec Canada
222 7 **Nouméa** New Caledonia
158 D2 **Nouna** Burkina Faso
159 G4 **Nouna** *watercourse* Gabon
121 P3 **Nousu** Finland
79 E8 **Nouvelle** Quebec Canada
222 7 **Nouvelle Calédonie** *island* New Caledonia
78 B1 **Nouvelle-France, Cap de** *cape* Quebec Canada
139 I4 **Nouvion** France
125 I4 **Nova** Hungary
105 F3 **Nova, Serra** *range* Brazil
104 D3 **Nova Amélia** Brazil
103 A8 **Nova Andradina** Brazil
125 J3 **Nová Baňa** Slovakia
160 A5 **Nova Caipemba** Angola
105 I4 **Nova Crixás** Brazil
102 F4 **Nova Cruz** Brazil
105 G5 **Nova Dourados** Brazil
163 F4 **Nova Golegã** Mozambique
130 E4 **Nova Gorica** Slovenia
103 D8 **Nova Iguaçu** Brazil
103 A8 **Nova Londrina** Brazil
163 F4 **Nova Mambone** Mozambique
105 G3 **Nova Monte Verde** Brazil
105 G4 **Nova Olímpia** Brazil
105 G1 **Nova Olinda** Brazil
105 G1 **Nova Olinda do Norte** Brazil
103 C7 **Nova Ponte, Represa** *lake* Brazil
107 I4 **Nova Prata** Brazil
125 I5 **Nova Rača** Croatia
102 D4 **Nova Russas** Brazil
73 M10 **Nova Scotia** *admin. area* Canada
103 E5 **Nova Soure** Brazil
132 E1 **Nova Ushytsya** Ukraine
132 A4 **Nova Varoš** Serbia
103 D7 **Nova Venécia** Brazil
125 M2 **Nova Verba** Ukraine
103 E7 **Nova Viçosa** Brazil
104 E1 **Nova Vida** Brazil
103 A6 **Nova Xavantina** Brazil
125 L5 **Novaci** Romania
125 J3 **Nováky** Slovakia
130 F4 **Novalja** Croatia
83 L4 **Novar** Ontario Canada
124 E5 **Novara** Italy
80 D7 **Novato** California USA
182 F4 **Novaya Kazanka** Kazakhstan
123 Q2 **Novaya Ladoga** Russian Federation
135 AE3 **Novaya Sibir', Ostrov** *island* Russian Federation
121 R2 **Novaya Titovka** Russian Federation
134 M4 **Novaya Zemlya** *island* Russian Federation
57 J2 **Novaya Zemlya Trough** *underwater feature* Karskoye More (Kara Sea)
132 E1 **Nove Selo** Ukraine
125 J4 **Nové Zámky** Slovakia
123 P4 **Novgorodskaya Oblast'** *admin. area* Russian Federation
125 K5 **Novi Bečej** Serbia
124 E5 **Novi Ligure** Italy
132 A3 **Novi Sad** Serbia
86 B5 **Novice** Texas USA
130 E4 **Novigrad** Croatia
193 I1 **Novikovo** Russian Federation
105 E5 **Novillero** Bolivia
100 B3 **Nóvita** Colombia
102 B2 **Novo, Lago** *lake* Brazil
105 E3 **Novo Apuá** Brazil
105 F2 **Novo Aripuanã** Brazil
103 D7 **Novo Cruzeiro** Brazil
105 I6 **Novo Horizonte** Brazil
125 H5 **Novo Mesto** Slovenia
132 B3 **Novo Miloševo** Serbia
105 H3 **Novo Mundo** Brazil
132 A3 **Novo Orahovo** Serbia
102 D4 **Novo Oriente** Brazil
100 E5 **Novo Paraíso** Brazil
133 C5 **Novo Selo** Macedonia
182 F3 **Novo-sergiyevskiy** Russian Federation
183 N2 **Novoaltaysk** Russian Federation
182 D3 **Novoanninskiy** Russian Federation
136 E3 **Novoaya Kakhovka** Ukraine
183 K6 **Novobod** Tajikistan
182 E2 **Novocheboksarsk** Russian Federation
182 C4 **Novocherkassk** Russian Federation
183 K3 **Novodolinka** Kazakhstan
134 J6 **Novodvinsk** Russian Federation
182 E5 **Novokayakent** Russian Federation
183 O2 **Novokuznetsk** Russian Federation
58 A2 **Novolazarevskaya (Russia)** *research station* Antarctica
123 O5 **Novolukoml'** Belarus
136 F1 **Novomoskovsk** Russian Federation
136 E3 **Novomoskovsk** Ukraine
132 G1 **Novomyrhorod** Ukraine
182 H3 **Novoorsk** Russian Federation
136 F3 **Novopskov** Ukraine
182 C5 **Novorossiysk** Russian Federation
183 K3 **Novorybinka** Kazakhstan
133 A5 **Novoselë** Albania
123 O5 **Novosëlki** Belarus
132 E1 **Novoselytsya** Ukraine
183 N2 **Novosibirsk** Russian Federation
183 M2 **Novosibirskaya Oblast'** *admin. area* Russian Federation
135 AE3 **Novosibirskiye Ostrova** *island* Russian Federation
136 F2 **Novosil'** Russian Federation
123 P4 **Novosokol'niki** Russian Federation
132 G2 **Novosvetlovka** Ukraine
182 H3 **Novotroitsk** Russian Federation
182 H3 **Novoural'sk** Russian Federation
182 E3 **Novouzensk** Russian Federation
132 G2 **Novovasil'yevka** Ukraine
125 M2 **Novovolyns'k** Ukraine
135 AA8 **Novovoskresenovka** Russian Federation
191 K2 **Novovoskresenovka** Russian Federation
132 C1 **Novoye Misto** Ukraine
183 M3 **Novoyego'ryevskoye** Russian Federation
134 L6 **Novozhilovskaya** Russian Federation
130 G4 **Novska** Croatia
125 I3 **Nový Jičín** Czech Republic
123 N5 **Novy Pahost** Belarus
135 W4 **Novyy** Russian Federation
134 L5 **Novyy Bor** Russian Federation
136 E3 **Novyy Buh** Ukraine
132 D1 **Novyy Rozdil** Ukraine
134 Q5 **Novyy Urengoy** Russian Federation
191 L2 **Novyy Urgal** Russian Federation
132 G2 **Novyye Bilyari** Ukraine
179 I2 **Now Bahār** Iran
179 J3 **Now Deh** Afghanistan
125 J2 **Nowa Brzeźnica** Poland
125 I2 **Nowa Ruda** Poland
125 L2 **Nowa Sarzyna** Poland
125 H2 **Nowa Sól** Poland
125 L1 **Nowa Wieś Ełcka** Poland
125 J1 **Nowe** Poland
219 J4 **Nowendoc** NSW Australia
125 K1 **Nowiny** Poland
76 E1 **Nowleye Lake** Nunavut Canada
125 K1 **Nowogród** Poland
219 J6 **Nowra** NSW Australia
125 L2 **Nowy Lubliniec** Poland
125 K3 **Nowy Sącz** Poland
125 J3 **Nowy Targ** Poland
76 F2 **Nowyak Lake** Nunavut Canada
80 H3 **Noxon Reservoir** Montana USA
86 G4 **Noxubee** *watercourse* Mississippi USA
159 G4 **Noya** *watercourse* Gabon
183 R3 **Noyan-khol'** *lake* Russian Federation
126 E3 **Noyant** France
126 G3 **Noyers** France
79 I7 **Noyrot, Lac** *lake* Quebec Canada
192 F5 **Nozaki-jima** *island* Japan
126 D3 **Nozay** France
127 H3 **Nozeroy** France
159 H5 **Nsa** Congo
160 B4 **Nsambi** Democratic Republic of Congo
159 G4 **Nsoc** Equatorial Guinea
162 E2 **Nsombo** Zambia
159 F3 **Nsukka** Nigeria
162 D2 **Ntambu** Zambia
160 B4 **Ntandembele** Democratic Republic of Congo
163 F2 **Ntcheu** Malawi
159 G4 **Ntem** *watercourse* Gabon
159 F4 **Ntoum** Gabon
160 E4 **Ntungamo** Uganda
162 E3 **Ntwetwe Pan** Botswana
188 C4 **Nu Jiang** *watercourse* Yunnan China
199 I6 **Nuakata Island** Papua New Guinea
198 C3 **Nuangan** Indonesia
187 F7 **Nuaparha** Orissa India
121 O4 **Nuasjärvi** *bay* Finland
156 E5 **Nuba Mountains** *range* Sudan
156 D4 **Nubian Desert** Sudan
156 E3 **Nubian Monuments** *point of interest* Egypt
106 D6 **Ñubile** *watercourse* Chile
198 F4 **Nuboai** Indonesia
74 H8 **Nuchatlitz Inlet** British Columbia Canada
86 B6 **Nueces** *watercourse* Texas USA
75 V3 **Nueltin Lake** Manitoba/Nunavut Canada
108 C6 **Nueva, Isla** *island* Chile
107 H3 **Nueva Alborada** Paraguay
89 F3 **Nueva Ciudad Guerrero** Mexico
104 D4 **Nueva Cruz** Peru
101 E2 **Nueva Esparta** *admin. area* Venezuela
107 G2 **Nueva Germania** Paraguay
90 D2 **Nueva Gerona** Cuba
100 C2 **Nueva Granada** Colombia
90 C5 **Nueva Guinea** Nicaragua
106 C6 **Nueva Imperial** Chile
107 G3 **Nueva Italia** Paraguay
100 B4 **Nueva Loja** Ecuador
108 B3 **Nueva Lubecka** Argentina
107 G5 **Nueva Palmira** Uruguay
106 F3 **Nueva Pompeya** Argentina
106 F6 **Nueva Roma** Argentina
88 E3 **Nueva Rosita** Mexico
106 C6 **Nueva Toltén** Chile
106 F5 **Nueve de Julio** Argentina
90 E2 **Nuevitas, Bahia de** *bay* Cuba
108 D3 **Nuevo, Golfo** *bay* Argentina
90 C4 **Nuevo Amanecer** Nicaragua
88 D2 **Nuevo Casas Grandes** Mexico
86 B7 **Nuevo Ciudad Guerrero** Mexico
100 C5 **Nuevo Horizonte** Peru
104 B4 **Nuevo Imperial** Peru
88 E5 **Nuevo Italia de Ruiz** Mexico
89 F3 **Nuevo Laredo** Mexico
89 F3 **Nuevo León** *admin. area* Mexico
105 E5 **Nuevo Mundo** Bolivia
104 C3 **Nuevo Mundo** Peru
89 F3 **Nuevo Padilla** Mexico
89 F4 **Nuevo Progreso** Mexico
85 K7 **Nuevo Reforma** Mexico
88 B2 **Nuevo Uruapan** Mexico
161 H2 **Nugaal** *admin. area* Somalia
216 E5 **Nugadong** WA Australia
221 C8 **Nugget Point** New Zealand
222 8a **Nughu Island** *island* Solomon Islands
122 G2 **Nuguren** *lake* Norway
199 J4 **Nuguria Islands** Papua New Guinea
186 D5 **Nuh** Haryana India
220 G4 **Nuhaka** New Zealand
223 13 **Nui** *island* Tuvalu
194 E2 **Nui Con Voi** Vietnam
72 D4 **Nuiqsut** Alaska USA
74 J5 **Nukko Lake** British Columbia Canada
223 14 **Nuku Hiva** *island* French Polynesia
223 10a **Nuku'alofa** Tonga
223 13 **Nukufetau** *island* Tuvalu
223 13 **Nukulaelae** *island* Tuvalu
220 3 **Nukunonu** *island* Tokelau New Zealand
220 3 **Nukunonu Village** Tokelau New Zealand
223 10a **Nukunuku** Tonga
52 L7 **Nukuoro Atoll** *reef* Micronesia
182 H5 **Nukus** Uzbekistan

223 14 **Nukutavake** *island* French Polynesia
223 14 **Nukutipipi** *island* French Polynesia
72 D6 **Nulato** Alaska USA
129 F4 **Nules** Spain
212 F6 **Nullagine** WA Australia
212 F6 **Nullagine** *watercourse* WA Australia
217 J5 **Nullarbor Plain** WA Australia
217 L5 **Nullarbor Roadhouse** SA Australia
219 J5 **Nullo Mountain** NSW Australia
77 Q3 **Nuluarniavik, Lac** *lake* Quebec Canada
191 I4 **Nulu'erhu Shan** *range* Liaoning China
198 E4 **Num** *island* Indonesia
159 G3 **Numan** Nigeria
160 D2 **Numatinna** *watercourse* Sudan
193 H4 **Numazu** Japan
196 E3 **Numbing** *island* Indonesia
214 C3 **Numbulwar** NT Australia
122 E2 **Numedal** *valley* Norway
219 I7 **Numeralla** NSW Australia
214 C7 **Numery** NT Australia
214 F5 **Numil Downs** Qld Australia
123 M2 **Numminen** Finland
78 H5 **Nunaksaluk Island** Newfoundland and Labrador Canada
75 X3 **Nunalla** Manitoba Canada
219 R10 **Nunamara** Tas. Australia
73 O7 **Nunap Isua (Kap Farvel)** *cape* Greenland
78 O2 **Nunarsuit** *island* Greenland
78 M1 **Nunasarnaq** *island* Greenland
77 Q4 **Nunavik** *region* Quebec Canada
72 I5 **Nunavut** *admin. area* Canada
100 C3 **Nunchía** Colombia
219 J4 **Nundle** NSW Australia
217 M5 **Nundroo** SA Australia
139 F2 **Nuneaton** Warwickshire England UK
216 F5 **Nungarin** WA Australia
219 I7 **Nungatta Mountain** NSW Australia
76 I7 **Nungesser Lake** Ontario Canada
163 G2 **Nungo** Mozambique
72 C6 **Nunivak Island** Alaska USA
121 N2 **Nunnanen** Finland
129 G4 **Nunó, Cap** *cape* Spain
104 D4 **Ñuñoa** Peru
143 G2 **Nuns Quarter** Ards Northern Ireland UK
218 F4 **Nuntherungie** NSW Australia
197 H2 **Nunukan** *island* Indonesia
188 E2 **Nuojiang** Sichuan China
121 Q5 **Nuorajärvi** *bay* Finland
121 O4 **Nuoritta** Finland
131 C6 **Nuoro** Sardinia Italy
121 O4 **Nuorunka** Finland
155 J4 **Nuqayy, Jabal** *range* Libya
178 E4 **Nuqrah** Saudi Arabia
125 L1 **Nur** Poland
183 L4 **Nura** Kazakhstan
178 F2 **Nūrābād** Iran
130 C4 **Nure** *watercourse* Italy
156 C5 **Nurei** Sudan
179 L2 **Nūrestān** *admin. area* Afghanistan
88 C2 **Nuri** Mexico
196 F4 **Nuri, Teluk** *bay* Indonesia
182 F2 **Nurlat** Russian Federation
182 E2 **Nurlaty** Russian Federation
120 M3 **Nurmasuanto** Sweden
121 P5 **Nurmes** Finland
121 Q5 **Nurmijärvi** Finland
121 M5 **Nurmo** Finland
124 F3 **Nürnberg** Germany
217 K4 **Nurrari Lakes** SA Australia
198 A5 **Nusa Tenggara Barat** *admin. area* Indonesia
198 B6 **Nusa Tenggara Timur** *admin. area* Indonesia
198 E5 **Nusawulan** Indonesia
136 G6 **Nusaybin** Turkey
198 D4 **Nusela, Kepulauan** *islands* Indonesia
132 D2 **Nuşeni** Romania
120 H2 **Nusfjord** Norway
179 K3 **Nushki** Pakistan
78 H4 **Nutak** Newfoundland and Labrador Canada
72 B5 **Nutauge, Laguna** *lagoon* Russian Federation
72 B5 **Nutepel'men** Russian Federation
179 K4 **Nuttal** Pakistan
214 C3 **Nutwood Downs** NT Australia
73 N4 **Nuugaatsiaap Tunua** *bay* Greenland
73 N6 **Nuuk** Greenland
121 O3 **Nuupas** Finland
223 14a **Nuupere, Pointe** *cape* French Polynesia
190 D4 **Nuur** *lake* Mongolia
73 N4 **Nuussuaq** *peninsula* Greenland
121 O4 **Nuutila** Finland
121 O2 **Nuvusskaidi** Finland
121 O2 **Nuvvus** Finland
186 F5 **Nuwakot** Nepal
162 C6 **Nuwerus** South Africa
216 E7 **Nuyts, Point** WA Australia
218 A5 **Nuyts Archipelago** SA Australia
159 G3 **Nwa** Cameroon
159 H3 **Nya** *watercourse* Chad
159 G4 **Nyabessan** Cameroon
216 F6 **Nyabing** WA Australia
161 F3 **Nyahururu** Kenya
181 G2 **Nyainqentanglha Shan** *range* Xizang Zizhiqu China
120 K5 **Nyåker** Sweden
134 N6 **Nyaksimvol'** Russian Federation
156 C5 **Nyala** Sudan
163 F3 **Nyamapanda** Zimbabwe
160 D2 **Nyamlell** Sudan
161 F6 **Nyamtumbo** Tanzania
134 J6 **Nyandomskiy Rayon** *range* Russian Federation
216 D1 **Nyang** WA Australia
181 F2 **Nyang Qu** *lake* Xizang Zizhiqu China
181 G3 **Nyang Qu** *watercourse* Xizang Zizhiqu China
159 G5 **Nyanga** *admin. area* Gabon
163 F3 **Nyanga** Zimbabwe
161 F5 **Nyangolo** Tanzania
160 E4 **Nyantakara** Tanzania
161 E4 **Nyanza** *admin. area* Kenya
160 D4 **Nyanza Lac** Burundi
130 H3 **Nyárlőrinc** Hungary
161 E6 **Nyasa, Lake** Africa
181 H5 **Nyaung-U** Myanmar
194 C3 **Nyaunglebin** Myanmar
122 F5 **Nyborg** Denmark
120 L5 **Nyby** Finland
121 N1 **Nyby** Norway
120 I5 **Nyby** Sweden
121 M3 **Nybyn** Sweden
159 G4 **Nyé** *watercourse* Gabon
73 N2 **Nyeboe Land** *region* Greenland
161 F4 **Nyeri** Kenya
135 AM6 **Nygchigen, Mys** *cape* Russian Federation
120 I4 **Nyhem** Sweden
160 E2 **Nyiel** Sudan
163 F2 **Nyika Plateau** *plain* Malawi
163 F2 **Nyimba** Zambia
214 C3 **Nyinpinti Point** NT Australia
125 L4 **Nyírbogát** Hungary
132 B2 **Nyíregyháza** Hungary
132 B1 **Nyírtura** Hungary
121 O5 **Nykälä** Finland
120 M5 **Nykarleby/Uusikaarlepy** Finland
122 F5 **Nykøbing** Denmark
122 I3 **Nyköping** Sweden
120 J5 **Nyland** Sweden
120 K5 **Nyliden** Sweden
218 H5 **Nymagee** NSW Australia
219 K3 **Nymboida** NSW Australia
125 H2 **Nymburk** Czech Republic
122 I3 **Nynäshamn** Sweden
219 H4 **Nyngan** NSW Australia
125 L1 **Nyoman** *watercourse* Belarus
159 G4 **Nyong** *watercourse* Cameroon
127 G4 **Nyons** France
218 G8 **Nyora** Vic. Australia
130 E2 **Nýrsko** Czech Republic
127 K2 **Nýrsko, Vodní nádrž** *lake* Czech Republic
121 P2 **Nyrud** Norway
125 I2 **Nysa** Poland
122 G3 **Nysäter** Sweden
122 G3 **Nysockensjön** *lake* Sweden
80 G5 **Nyssa** Oregon USA
122 F5 **Nysted** Denmark
120 F6 **Nystova** Norway
123 M2 **Nytkyn** *lake* Finland
121 Q4 **Nyuk, Ozero** *lake* Russian Federation
135 Z7 **Nyukzha** *watercourse* Russian Federation
160 D5 **Nyunzu** Democratic Republic of Congo
197 H3 **Nyurang** Indonesia
135 Y6 **Nyurba** Russian Federation
135 X6 **Nyuya** *watercourse* Russian Federation
121 M1 **Nyvoll** Norway
132 D1 **Nyzhniv** Ukraine
159 I3 **Nzako** Central African Republic
159 G5 **Nzambi** Congo
161 E4 **Nzega** Tanzania
158 C3 **Nzérékoré** Guinea
160 A5 **N'zeto** Angola
158 D3 **Nzi** *watercourse* Côte d'Ivoire
160 D6 **Nzilo, Lac** *lake* Democratic Republic of Congo
158 C3 **Nzo** *watercourse* Côte d'Ivoire
158 C3 **Nzoo** Guinea
160 E3 **Nzoro** *watercourse* Democratic Republic of Congo
Nzwani *see* **Angouan** Comoros

O

128 C2 **O Barco** Spain
128 B2 **O Castro** Spain
120 K4 **Ö Kikkejaure** *lake* Sweden
192 G5 **Ō-Shima** *island* Japan
86 D2 **O The Cherokees, Lake** Oklahoma USA
86 D4 **O' the Pines, Lake** Texas USA
142 B5 **Oa, Mull of** *cape* Scotland UK
81 P5 **Oacoma** South Dakota USA
139 F2 **Oadby** Leicester England UK
84 inset **O'ahu** *island* Hawai'i USA
81 L6 **Oak Creek** Colorado USA
86 A4 **Oak Creek Reservoir** Texas USA
86 H2 **Oak Grove** Kentucky USA
85 N4 **Oak Grove** Texas USA
86 F2 **Oak Grove Heights** Arkansas USA
80 D2 **Oak Harbor** Washington USA
87 K6 **Oak Hill** Florida USA
83 K8 **Oak Hill** West Virginia USA
215 H5 **Oak Hills** Qld Australia
87 L4 **Oak Island** North Carolina USA
75 U8 **Oak Lake** Manitoba Canada
82 H6 **Oak Lawn** Illinois USA
82 H6 **Oak Park** Illinois USA
81 P1 **Oak Point** Manitoba Canada
87 I3 **Oak Ridge** Tennessee USA
215 H6 **Oak Vale** Qld Australia
81 O1 **Oakburn** Manitoba Canada
86 E5 **Oakdale** Louisiana USA
81 Q5 **Oakdale** Nebraska USA
218 C4 **Oakden Hills** SA Australia
218 F6 **Oakdene** NSW Australia
138 E2 **Oakengates** Telford and Wrekin England UK
81 P3 **Oakes** North Dakota USA
80 G3 **Oakesdale** Washington USA
219 J2 **Oakey** Qld Australia
219 H3 **Oakey Park** Qld Australia
143 F3 **Oakfield** Ireland
218 F1 **Oakham** Qld Australia
139 G2 **Oakham** Rutland England UK
84 C2 **Oakhurst** California USA
76 F7 **Oakland** Manitoba Canada
80 D8 **Oakland** California USA
82 G7 **Oakland** Illinois USA
82 D6 **Oakland** Iowa USA
86 G3 **Oakland** Mississippi USA
86 C3 **Oakland** Oklahoma USA
80 D5 **Oakland** Oregon USA
218 H6 **Oaklands** NSW Australia
139 F3 **Oakley** Buckinghamshire England UK
80 I5 **Oakley** Idaho USA
81 O7 **Oakley** Kansas USA
86 H4 **Oakman** Alabama USA
212 F6 **Oakover** *watercourse* WA Australia
80 D5 **Oakridge** Oregon USA
219 R10 **Oaks** Tas. Australia
82 H7 **Oaktown** Indiana USA
220 F2 **Oakura** New Zealand
218 E5 **Oakvale** SA Australia
76 F8 **Oakville** Manitoba Canada
80 D3 **Oakville** Washington USA
85 O5 **Oakwood** Texas USA
215 J7 **Oaky Creek** Qld Australia
220 F2 **Oakura** New Zealand
221 D7 **Oamaru** New Zealand
220 E4 **Oaonui** New Zealand
84 F1 **Oasis** Utah USA
215 H5 **Oasis Roadhouse** Qld Australia
58 K2 **Oates Coast** Antarctica
219 R11 **Oatlands** Tas. Australia
89 F5 **Oaxaca** Mexico
89 F5 **Oaxaca** *admin. area* Mexico
183 N3 **Ob** *watercourse* Russian Federation
58 K2 **Ob' Bay** Antarctica
54 J10 **Ob' Tablemount** *underwater feature* Southern Ocean
82 I2 **Oba Lake** Ontario Canada
199 F5 **Obaa** Indonesia
82 I2 **Obakamiga Lake** Ontario Canada
83 M2 **Obalski Lake** Quebec Canada
193 G4 **Obama** Japan
159 F3 **Oban** Nigeria
142 C4 **Oban** Argyll and Bute Scotland UK
159 F3 **Oban Hills** *range* Nigeria
183 K6 **Obanbori Qayroqum** *lake* Tajikistan
83 N2 **Obatogamau** *watercourse* Quebec Canada
83 N2 **Obatogamau Lake** Quebec Canada
120 L5 **Obbola** Sweden
132 D2 **Obcina Feredeului** *region* Romania
74 M6 **Obed** Alberta Canada
123 M5 **Obeliai** Lithuania
130 C2 **Ober-Olm** Germany
130 D3 **Oberau** Germany
130 D2 **Oberbaar** Germany
130 C2 **Oberkirch** Germany
81 O7 **Oberlin** Kansas USA
86 E5 **Oberlin** Louisiana USA
127 H2 **Obernai** France
219 I5 **Oberon** NSW Australia
124 G3 **Oberösterreich** *admin. area* Austria
125 I4 **Oberpullendorf** Austria
124 F4 **Oberstaufen** Germany
124 F4 **Oberstdorf** Germany
124 G4 **Obertrumer See** *lake* Austria
125 I4 **Oberwart** Austria
197 J4 **Obi** *island* Indonesia
159 F3 **Obi** Nigeria
193 I2 **Obihiro** Japan
197 J4 **Obilatu** *island* Indonesia
127 K2 **Obing** Germany
192 G2 **Oblachnaya, Gora** *mountain* Russian Federation
182 D4 **Oblivskaya** Russian Federation
82 H7 **Oblong** Illinois USA
191 L3 **Obluchye** Russian Federation
136 F1 **Obninsk** Russian Federation
160 D2 **Obo** Central African Republic
157 G5 **Obock** Djibouti
132 F1 **Obodivka** Ukraine
160 D4 **Obokote** Democratic Republic of Congo
198 E4 **Obome** Indonesia
82 G2 **Obonga Lake** Ontario Canada
125 K3 **Oborín** Slovakia
132 D4 **Oborishte** Bulgaria
182 G6 **Oboy** Turkmenistan
136 F2 **Oboyan'** Russian Federation
186 F6 **Obra** Uttar Pradesh India
132 A3 **Obrež** Serbia
86 B4 **O'Brien** Texas USA
125 H5 **Obrov** Slovenia
130 H5 **Obrtići** Bosnia and Herzegovina
108 D6 **Observatorio, Isla** *island* Argentina
215 L4 **Observatory Cay** Coral Sea Islands Territory Australia
74 F5 **Observatory Inlet** British Columbia Canada
182 E2 **Obshaovka** Russian Federation
134 P5 **Obskaya Guba** *bay* Russian Federation
158 D3 **Obuasi** Ghana
159 F3 **Obudu** Nigeria
132 E4 **Obzor** Bulgaria
133 E5 **Ocakı** Turkey
87 J6 **Ocala** Florida USA
89 F4 **Ocampo** Mexico
88 E3 **Ocampo** Mexico
100 C2 **Ocaña** Colombia
128 E4 **Ocaña** Spain
102 E4 **Ocara** Brazil
100 B3 **Occidental, Cordillera** *range* Colombia
104 C4 **Occidental, Cordillera** *range* Peru
142 E2 **Occumster** Highland Scotland UK
83 N7 **Ocean City** New Jersey USA
74 H6 **Ocean Falls** British Columbia Canada
50 O6 **Oceanographer Fracture Zone** *underwater feature* Atlantic Ocean
84 D4 **Oceanside** California USA
222 5 **Oceanview** Guam
222 6a **Ocha** *island* Federated States of Micronesia
132 G2 **Ochakiv** Ukraine
193 H4 **Ochi-gata** *lake* Japan
142 D5 **Ochiltree** East Ayrshire Scotland UK
85 J6 **Ochoa** Texas USA
81 P1 **Ochre River** Manitoba Canada
142 E4 **Ochtertyre** Perth and Kinross Scotland UK
124 D1 **Ochtrup** Germany
87 J5 **Ocilla** Georgia USA
87 K6 **Ocklawaha Lake** Florida USA
142 B4 **Ockle** Highland Scotland UK
87 J5 **Ocmulgee** *watercourse* Georgia USA
132 E1 **Ocniţa** Moldova
104 C5 **Ocoña** *watercourse* Peru
87 J4 **Oconee** *watercourse* Georgia USA
219 I5 **O'Connell** NSW Australia
82 H4 **Oconto** Wisconsin USA
89 G6 **Ocós** Guatemala
89 G5 **Ocosingo** Mexico
90 C4 **Ocotal** Nicaragua
89 F5 **Ocotlán** Mexico
125 K4 **Öcsöd** Hungary
139 F5 **Octeville** France
214 C4 **October** *watercourse* NT Australia
214 C6 **Octy, Mount** NT Australia
90 D6 **Ocú** Panama
163 G2 **Ocua** Mozambique
100 E2 **Ocumare del Tuy** Venezuela
122 G4 **Od** Sweden
158 D3 **Oda** Ghana
192 G4 **Ōda** Japan
156 F3 **Oda, Jebel** *mountain* Sudan
199 F5 **Odammun** *watercourse* Indonesia
193 I3 **Ōdate** Japan
193 H4 **Odawara** Japan
76 H4 **O'Day** Manitoba Canada
122 D2 **Odda** Norway
75 V5 **Oddhill** Manitoba Canada
86 C7 **Odem** Texas USA
128 B5 **Odemira** Portugal
133 E6 **Ödemiş** Turkey
122 F5 **Odense** Denmark
122 F5 **Odense Fjord** *bay* Denmark
124 F2 **Oder** *watercourse* Germany
130 E4 **Oderzo** Italy
132 G2 **Odesa** Ukraine
136 D3/4 **Odes'ka Oblast'** *admin. area* Ukraine
75 T7 **Odessa** Saskatchewan Canada
81 Q4 **Odessa** Minnesota USA
82 E7 **Odessa** Missouri USA
85 K5 **Odessa** Texas USA
80 F3 **Odessa** Washington USA
183 K2 **Odesskoye** Russian Federation
126 C2 **Odet** *watercourse* France
128 C5 **Odiel** *watercourse* Spain
158 C3 **Odienné** Côte d'Ivoire
128 B4 **Odivelas, Barragem de** *lake* Portugal
58 U2 **Odom Inlet** *bay* Antarctica
126 D2 **Odon** *watercourse* France
85 L4 **O'Donnell** Texas USA
125 H1 **Odra** *watercourse* Poland
156 F4 **Odrus** *watercourse* Sudan
125 I3 **Odry** Czech Republic
139 F3 **Odstock** Wiltshire England UK
130 H4 **Odžaci** Serbia
130 H5 **Odžak** Montenegro
123 M4 **Odzes ezers** *lake* Latvia
163 F3 **Odzi** *watercourse* Zimbabwe
102 D4 **Oeiras** Brazil
102 B3 **Oeiras do Pará** Brazil
81 N5 **Oelrichs** South Dakota USA
127 K1 **Oelsnitz** Germany
82 F5 **Oelwein** Iowa USA
223 11 **Oeno Island** Pitcairn Islands
214 B2 **Oenpelli** NT Australia
192 E4 **Oeraro-do** *island* South Korea
124 F3 **Oettingen** Germany
127 J2 **Oettingen in Bayern** Germany
124 F4 **Oetz** Austria
124 F1 **Oetzen** Germany
78 B5 **Oeufs, Lac des** *lake* Quebec Canada
82 G7 **O'Fallon** Illinois USA
131 F6 **Ofanto** *watercourse* Italy
159 F3 **Ofe** *watercourse* Nigeria
131 E5 **Ofena** Italy
159 E3 **Offa** Nigeria
143 E3 **Offaly** *admin. area* Ireland
130 C1 **Offenbach am Main** Germany
81 P8 **Offerle** Kansas USA
106 D2 **Oficina Sara** Chile
133 E7 **Ofidoussa** *island* Greece
108 A4 **Ofqui, Istmo de** *peninsula* Chile
122 E3 **Ofte** Norway
223 12c **Ofu** *island* American Samoa
193 I3 **Ōfunato** Japan
197 G3 **Oga** *watercourse* Indonesia
193 H3 **Oga** Japan
161 H2 **Ogaden** *plain* Ethiopia
193 H4 **Ogaki** Japan
81 O6 **Ogallala** Nebraska USA
196 E4 **Ogan** *watercourse* Indonesia
193 I3 **Ogawara-ko** *lake* Japan
159 E3 **Ogbomosho** Nigeria
81 Q7 **Ogden** Kansas USA
80 J6 **Ogden** Utah USA
83 N4 **Ogdensburg** New York USA
122 E3 **Øgdern** *lake* Norway
223 9 **Ogea Driki** *island* Fiji
87 J4 **Ogeechee** *watercourse* Georgia USA
75 S8 **Ogema** Saskatchewan Canada
122 E3 **Ogge** *lake* Norway
130 C4 **Oggiono** Italy
193 H4 **Ogi** Japan
75 V7 **Ogilvie** Manitoba Canada
72 F5 **Ogilvie** *watercourse* Yukon Territory Canada
72 F6 **Ogilvie Mountains** Yukon Territory Canada
215 G2 **Ogilvie Reef** Qld Australia
108 C6 **Oglander, Bahía** *bay* Chile
131 B9 **Oglat Oulad Mahboub** Algeria
184 H6 **Oglung He** *watercourse* Xizang Zizhiqu China
215 J7 **Ogmore** Qld Australia
127 G3 **Ognon** *watercourse* France
198 B3 **Ogoamas, Gunung** *mountain* Indonesia
159 F3 **Ogoja** Nigeria
76 M7 **Ogoki** Ontario Canada
76 K7 **Ogoki** *watercourse* Ontario Canada
76 L7 **Ogoki Lake** Ontario Canada
76 K7 **Ogoki Reservoir** Ontario Canada
159 G5 **Ogooué** *watercourse* Congo
159 G5 **Ogooué** *watercourse* Gabon
159 G4 **Ogooué-Ivindo** *admin. area* Gabon
159 G5 **Ogooué-Lolo** *admin. area* Gabon
159 F5 **Ogooué-Maritime** *admin. area* Gabon
123 M4 **Ogre** Latvia
123 M4 **Ogres** *admin. area* Latvia
132 D3 **Ogrezeni** Romania
159 E3 **Ogun** *admin. area* Nigeria
159 E3 **Ogun** *watercourse* Nigeria
182 F6 **Ogurja Ada** *island* Turkmenistan
220 G4 **Ohaaki** New Zealand
221 B7 **Ohai** New Zealand
220 G4 **Ohakuri** New Zealand
155 H3 **Ohanet** Algeria
162 C3 **Ohangwena** *admin. area* Namibia
75 O6 **Ohaton** Alberta Canada
221 C7 **Ohau, Lake** New Zealand
127 G1 **Ohey** Belgium
106 D2 **O'Higgins** Chile
109 5 **O'Higgins, Cabo** *cape* Isla de Pascua (Easter Island)
108 B4 **O'Higgins, Cerro** *mountain* Chile
109 6a **O'Higgins, Punta** *cape* Isla Róbinson Crusoe
58 U2 **O'Higgins (Chile)** *research station* Antarctica
220 F4 **Ohingaiti** New Zealand
70 **Ohio** *admin. area* USA
82 G8 **Ohio** *watercourse* Illinois USA
82 H7 **Ohio** *watercourse* Indiana USA
82 J7 **Ohio** *watercourse* Kentucky USA
83 K7 **Ohio** *watercourse* Ohio USA
58 Q1 **Ohio Range** Antarctica
127 I1 **Ohm** *watercourse* Germany
120 I5 **Öhn** Sweden
223 10a **'Ohonua** Tonga
124 G2 **Ohře** *watercourse* Czech Republic
133 B5 **Ohrid** Macedonia
133 B5 **Ohrid, Lake** Macedonia
124 E3 **Öhringen** Germany
121 M3 **Ohtanajärvi** Sweden
121 M5 **Ohtola** Finland
220 F4 **Ohura** New Zealand
133 D7 **Oia** Greece
128 B3 **Oiã** Portugal
102 A2 **Oiapoque** *watercourse* Brazil
101 I4 **Oiapoque** French Guiana
101 H4 **Oiapoque** *watercourse* French Guiana
101 I3 **Oiapoque, Baía do** *bay* French Guiana
77 P6 **Oies, Baie des** *bay* Quebec Canada
83 P3 **Oies, Ile aux** *island* Quebec Canada
121 N4 **Oijärvi** Finland
193 I2 **Oikamanae-numa** *lake* Japan
121 O3 **Oikarainen** Finland
86 C2 **Oilton** Oklahoma USA
133 C6 **Oinoi** Greece
133 E6 **Oinoússai** Greece
126 F2 **Oise** *watercourse* France
139 I5 **Oisemont** France
91 J4 **Oistins** Barbados
192 F5 **Oita** Japan
133 C6 **Oiti** *mountain* Greece
121 M5 **Oivu** Finland
121 M5 **Öja** Finland
122 I3 **Öja** *island* Sweden
84 C3 **Ojai** California USA
121 N4 **Ojakylä** Finland
122 I2 **Öjaren** *lake* Sweden
120 I5 **Öjarssjön** *lake* Sweden
122 G2 **Öje** Sweden
120 L4 **Öjebyn** Sweden
106 E5 **Ojeda** Argentina
120 J5 **Öjen** *lake* Sweden
83 L4 **Ojibway Bay** Ontario Canada
88 D2 **Ojinaga** Mexico
120 I6 **Öjingen** *lake* Sweden
88 D2 **Ojito** Mexico
88 C2 **Ojo de Agua de Elías** Mexico
88 B3 **Ojo de Liebre, Laguna** *lake* Mexico
85 J6 **Ojo del Carrizo** Mexico
159 F3 **Oju** Nigeria
120 H6 **Öjvasseln** Sweden
199 G5 **Ok Tedi** *watercourse* Papua New Guinea
134 I8 **Oka** *watercourse* Russian Federation
162 C4 **Okahandja** Namibia
221 E6 **Okains Bay** New Zealand
78 H4 **Okak Islands** Newfoundland and Labrador Canada
162 C4 **Okakarara** Namibia
74 L8 **Okanagan Falls** British Columbia Canada
74 L7 **Okanagan Lake** British Columbia Canada
187 E10 **Okanda** Sri Lanka
159 G5 **Okandja** Gabon
159 G4 **Okano** *watercourse* Gabon
80 F1 **Okanogan** British Columbia Canada
80 F2 **Okanogan** Washington USA
197 H4 **Okaoka** Indonesia
179 M3 **Okara** Pakistan
86 C3 **Okarche** Oklahoma USA
221 D6 **Okarito** New Zealand
221 D6 **Okarito Lagoon** New Zealand
86 G4 **Okatibbee Lake** Mississippi USA
220 E4 **Okato** New Zealand
162 D3 **Okavango** *watercourse* Botswana
162 C3 **Okavango** *admin. area* Namibia
162 D3 **Okavango Delta** *swamp* Botswana
221 6 **Okawa Point** Chatham Islands New Zealand
192 G4 **Okayama** Japan
159 E3 **Oke-Iho** Nigeria
87 K7 **Okeechobee** Florida USA
87 K7 **Okeechobee, Lake** Florida USA
86 B2 **Okeene** Oklahoma USA
138 C4 **Okehampton** Devon England UK
86 C3 **Okemah** Oklahoma USA
159 F3 **Okene** Nigeria
124 F1 **Oker** *watercourse* Germany
135 AD8 **Okha** Russian Federation
186 G5 **Okhaldhunga** Nepal
135 AD7 **Okhotsk** Russian Federation
135 AF8 **Okhotsk, Sea of** Russian Federation
135 AC6 **Okhotskiy Perevoz** Russian Federation
121 Q4 **Okhtan"yarvi, Ozero** *lake* Russian Federation
136 E2 **Okhtyrka** Ukraine
123 Q4 **Okhvat** Russian Federation
220 F2 **Okiato** New Zealand
192 G4 **Oki-shotō** *island* Japan
189 J3 **Okinawa** Japan
189 J3 **Okinawa-shotō** *island* Japan
189 J3 **Okino-erabu** Japan
189 J3 **Okino-erabu-shima** *island* Japan
159 E3 **Okitipupa** Nigeria
71 **Oklahoma** *admin. area* USA
86 C3 **Oklahoma City** Oklahoma USA
130 G5 **Oklaj** Croatia
86 D3 **Okmulgee** Oklahoma USA
156 F3 **Ōkō, Wādī** *watercourse* Sudan
162 C4 **Okombahe** Namibia
125 L2 **Okopy Nowy** Poland
75 O7 **Okotoks** Alberta Canada
159 H5 **Okoyo** Congo
125 H3 **Okříšky** Czech Republic
125 K2 **Oksa** Poland
121 M3 **Oksajärvi** Sweden
121 N5 **Oksakoski** Finland
199 G5 **Oksapmin** Papua New Guinea
122 E5 **Oksby** Denmark
120 E5 **Oksenøya** *island* Norway
121 M1 **Øksfjord** Norway
121 M1 **Øksfjordjøkulen** *bay* Norway
134 L5 **Oksino** Russian Federation
120 G4 **Øksnes** Norway
120 I2 **Øksneshamn** Norway
222 2a **Okso Takpochao** *mountain* Northern Mariana Islands
134 I6 **Oksovskiy** Russian Federation
120 I3 **Okstindan** *mountain* Norway
86 D3 **Oktaha** Oklahoma USA
181 H5 **Oktwin** Myanmar
135 AA7 **Oktyabr'skiy** Russian Federation
182 G2 **Oktyabr'skiy** Russian Federation
135 U3 **Oktyabr'skoy Revolyutsii, Ostrov** *island* Russian Federation
193 H2 **Okushiri-tō** *volcano* Japan
158 E3 **Okuta** Nigeria
162 D4 **Okwa** *watercourse* Botswana
159 F3 **Okwa** *watercourse* Nigeria
120 inset **Olafsfjörður** Iceland
120 inset **Ólafsvík** Iceland
187 E9 **Olakkur** Tamil Nadu India
74 L8 **Olalla** British Columbia Canada
84 C2 **Olancha** California USA
90 C4 **Olanchito** Honduras
122 I4 **Öland** *island* Sweden
122 I4 **Ölands Norra Udde** *cape* Sweden
122 I4 **Ölands Sodra Udde** *cape* Sweden
121 Q3 **Olanga** Russian Federation
106 E2 **Olaroz Chico** Argentina
218 E5 **Olary** SA Australia
218 E5 **Olary** *watercourse* SA Australia
81 L7 **Olathe** Colorado USA
82 D7 **Olathe** Kansas USA
106 F6 **Olavarría** Argentina
100 B3 **Olave** Colombia
125 I2 **Oława** Poland
127 K1 **Olbernhau** Germany
131 C6 **Olbia** Sardinia Italy
132 B2 **Olcea** Romania
127 J2 **Olching** Germany
90 E2 **Old Bahama Channel** *strait* Cuba
219 K3 **Old Bonalbo** NSW Australia
213 H5 **Old Cherrabun** WA Australia
156 E4 **Old Dongola** Sudan
75 P3 **Old Fort** *watercourse* Alberta Canada
74 H5 **Old Fort** British Columbia Canada
87 J3 **Old Fort** North Carolina USA
75 N1 **Old Fort Providence** Northwest Territories Canada
75 N1 **Old Fort Rae** Northwest Territories Canada
72 D7 **Old Harbor** Alaska USA
143 D5 **Old Head of Kinsale** *cape* Ireland
87 H2 **Old Hickory Lake** Tennessee USA
140 F2 **Old Hutton** Cumbria England UK
213 I5 **Old Lamboo** WA Australia
139 H1 **Old Leake** Lincolnshire England UK
162 E2 **Old Mkushi** Zambia
79 L8 **Old Perlican** Newfoundland and Labrador Canada
143 E4 **Old Pike Bridge** Ireland
109 18 **Old Road** Antigua and Barbuda
109 19 **Old Road Town** St Kitts and Nevis
138 A2 **Old Ross** Ireland
138 A2 **Old Town** Ireland
141 F1 **Old Town** Northumberland England UK
83 Q4 **Old Town** Maine USA
81 M1 **Old Wives** Saskatchewan Canada
75 S7 **Old Wives Lake** Saskatchewan Canada
143 F3 **Oldbawn** Ireland
139 E2 **Oldbury** West Midlands England UK
138 E3 **Oldcastle** Monmouthshire Wales UK
120 F5 **Olden** Norway
124 E1 **Oldenburg** Germany
122 E5 **Oldenswort** Germany
120 L2 **Olderdalen** Norway
120 L1 **Olderfjord** Norway
120 E6 **Oldevatnet** *lake* Norway
143 F3 **Oldgrange** Ireland
141 F3 **Oldham** Greater Manchester England UK
143 C4 **Oldmill Bridge** Ireland
140 B3 **Oldtown** Ireland
140 A4 **Oldtown** Ireland
138 D3 **Oldways End** Devon England UK
83 L5 **Olean** New York USA
123 L5 **Olecko** Poland
130 C4 **Oleggio** Italy
128 C4 **Oleiros** Portugal
135 Z7 **Olekma** *watercourse* Russian Federation
135 Y8 **Olekminskiy Stanovik** *range* Russian Federation
132 H1 **Oleksandrivka** Ukraine
132 F2 **Oleksiyivka** Ukraine
127 G1 **Olen** Belgium
122 C3 **Ølen** Norway
121 R2 **Olenegorsk** Russian Federation
135 X5 **Olenëk** Russian Federation
135 Y5 **Olenëk** *watercourse* Russian Federation
135 Z4 **Olenekskiy Zaliv** *bay* Russian Federation
121 S3 **Olenitsa** Russian Federation
134 Q4 **Oleniy, Ostrov** *island* Russian Federation
183 L3 **Olenty** *watercourse* Kazakhstan
126 D4 **Oléron, Île d'** *island* France
125 I2 **Oleśnica** Poland
130 G2 **Olešnice** Czech Republic
125 J2 **Olesno** Poland
197 H6 **Olet Tongo** *mountain* Indonesia
126 F5 **Olette** France
124 D2 **Olfen** Germany
77 Q8 **Olga, Lac** *lake* Quebec Canada
Olga, Mount *see* **Kata Tjuta** Australia
57 H1 **Olga Basin** *underwater feature* Barents Sea
127 I4 **Olgiate Comasco** Italy
Ölgiy *see* **Ulgii** Mongolia
185 I3 **Ölgiy** Mongolia
128 C5 **Olhão** Portugal
121 N4 **Olhava** Finland
162 C4 **Olifants** *watercourse* Namibia
162 D5 **Olifantshoek** South Africa
102 F5 **Olinda** Brazil
103 E5 **Olindina** Brazil
195 I5 **Olingan** Philippines
122 H2 **Olingskog** Sweden
128 F2 **Olite** Spain
129 F4 **Oliva** Spain
214 G2 **Olive** *watercourse* Qld Australia
86 G3 **Olive Branch** Mississippi USA
103 C8 **Oliveira** Brazil
103 D6 **Oliveira dos Brejinhos** Brazil
102 E5 **Olivença** Brazil
128 C4 **Olivenza** Spain
74 L8 **Oliver** British Columbia Canada
75 T4 **Oliver Lake** Saskatchewan Canada
126 E3 **Olivet** France
81 R4 **Olivia** Minnesota USA
221 C7 **Olivine Range** New Zealand
105 I5 **Olívio Peres** Brazil
127 I3 **Olivone** Switzerland
132 D1 **Oliyiv** Ukraine
190 F5 **Oljoq** Nei Mongol Zizhiqu China
122 D2 **Øljuvatnet** *lake* Norway
132 B1 **Oľka** Slovakia
182 D3 **Olkhovka** Russian Federation
123 K2 **Olkiluoto** *island* Finland
86 E5 **Olla** Louisiana USA
142 inset **Ollaberry** Shetland Scotland UK
104 D6 **Ollagüe, Volcán** *volcano* Chile
129 F4 **Ollería** Spain
138 E2 **Ollerton** Shropshire England UK
121 O2 **Ollila** Finland
106 D4 **Ollita, Cordillera de** *range* Argentina
106 D4 **Ollitas** *mountain* Argentina
121 Q5 **Öllölä** Finland
130 B3 **Ollon** Switzerland
120 I5 **Ollsta** Sweden
127 H2 **Olm** Luxembourg
183 K6 **Olmaliq** Uzbekistan
128 D3 **Olmedo** Spain
161 F4 **Olmoti** *volcano* Tanzania
139 G2 **Olney** Milton Keynes England UK
86 B4 **Olney** Texas USA
79 H7 **Olomane** *watercourse* Quebec Canada
125 I3 **Olomouc** Czech Republic
125 I3 **Olomoucký Kraj** *admin. area* Czech Republic
123 Q2 **Olonets** Russian Federation
195 I4 **Olongapo** Philippines
197 G4 **Olongliko** Indonesia
126 D3 **Olonne-sur-Mer** France
129 H2 **Olonzac** France
126 D5 **Oloron-Sainte-Marie** France
223 12c **Olosega** *island* American Samoa
129 H2 **Olot** Spain
191 H2 **Olovyannaya** Russian Federation
135 AH5 **Oloyskiy Khrebet** *range* Russian Federation
124 D2 **Olpe** Germany
82 C7 **Olpe** Kansas USA
124 E2 **Olsberg** Germany
132 C1 **Olszanica** Poland
125 K2 **Olszany** Poland
125 K1 **Olsztyn** Poland
132 D3 **Olt** *admin. area* Romania
132 D3 **Olt** *watercourse* Romania
122 D3 **Oltedal** Norway
127 H3 **Olten** Switzerland
132 E3 **Olteniţa** Romania
132 E3 **Oltina, Lacul** *lake* Romania
85 K3 **Olton** Texas USA
136 G5 **Oltu** Turkey
189 H4 **Oluan Pi** *island* Taiwan China
128 E5 **Olula del Río** Spain
86 B3 **Olustee** Oklahoma USA
121 O4 **Olvasjärvi** Finland
128 D5 **Olvera** Spain
128 E4 **Olvera, Embalse de** *lake* Spain
133 E8 **Olymbos** Greece
80 D3 **Olympia** Washington USA
218 C4 **Olympic Dam** SA Australia
80 D3 **Olympic Mountains** Washington USA
133 C5 **Olympos** *mountain* Greece
136 E6 **Olympus, Mount** *mountain* Cyprus
135 AI6 **Olyutorskiy** Russian Federation
135 AJ7 **Olyutorskiy, Mys** *cape* Russian Federation
135 AJ6 **Olyutorskiy Poluostrov** *peninsula* Russian Federation
135 AI6 **Olyutorskiy Zaliv** *bay* Russian Federation
156 F5 **Om Hajēr** Eritrea
143 E2 **Omagh** *admin. area* Northern Ireland UK
143 E2 **Omagh** Omagh Northern Ireland UK
81 R6 **Omaha** Nebraska USA
162 C4 **Omaheke** *admin. area* Namibia
80 F2 **Omak Lake** Washington USA
191 N2 **Omal'skiy Khrebet** *range* Russian Federation
187 E9 **Omalur** Tamil Nadu India
179 H4 **Oman** *country* Middle East
179 I5 **Oman, Gulf of**
220 E2 **Omapere** New Zealand
220 E2 **Omapere, Lake** New Zealand
221 C7 **Omarama** New Zealand
77 P5 **Omarolluk Sound** Nunavut Canada
130 G4 **Omarska** Bosnia and Herzegovina
162 C4 **Omaruru** Namibia
104 B4 **Omas** Peru
162 C3 **Omatako** *watercourse* Namibia
162 C4 **Omatjete** Namibia
160 B2 **Ombella-M'poko** *admin. area* Central African Republic
139 E2 **Ombersley** Worcestershire England UK
122 C3 **Ombo** *island* Norway
196 C3 **Ombolata** Indonesia
159 F5 **Omboué** Gabon
156 E4 **Omdurman** Sudan
193 H4 **Ome** Japan
130 C4 **Omegna** Italy
219 H7 **Omeo** Vic. Australia
140 B2 **Omerbank** Ballymoney Northern Ireland UK
133 F5 **Ömerli Barajı** *lake* Turkey
90 C5 **Ometepe, Isla de** *island* Nicaragua
89 F5 **Ometepec** Mexico
143 B3 **Omey Island** Ireland
178 G3 **Omidīyeh** Iran
131 C5 **Omigna, Punta d'** *cape* Corsica France
123 K2 **Ominaisfjärden** *bay* Finland
74 I5 **Omineca** *watercourse* British Columbia Canada
74 H4 **Omineca Mountains** British Columbia Canada
130 G5 **Omiš** Croatia
130 F4 **Omišalj** Croatia
162 C4 **Omitara** Namibia
73 I4 **Ommanney Bay** Nunavut Canada
122 G4 **Ömmern** *lake* Sweden
190 E4 **Ömnögovi** *admin. area* Mongolia
161 F2 **Omo** *watercourse* Ethiopia
90 B4 **Omoa** Honduras
135 AB4 **Omoloy** *watercourse* Russian Federation
183 L2 **Omsk** Russian Federation
134 P7 **Omskaya Oblast'** *admin. area* Russian Federation
135 AG6 **Omsukchanskiy Khrebet** *range* Russian Federation
159 F3 **Omu-aran** Nigeria
159 F3 **Omuo** Nigeria
192 F5 **Omura** Japan
162 B3 **Omusati** *admin. area* Namibia
192 F5 **Omuta** Japan
128 E2 **Oña** Spain
84 H6 **Onabas** Mexico
86 D5 **Onalaska** Texas USA
82 F5 **Onalaska** Wisconsin USA
76 L8 **Onaman Lake** Ontario Canada
82 E3 **Onamia** Minnesota USA
198 A4 **Onang** Indonesia
159 G5 **Onangué, Lac** *lake* Gabon
83 K3 **Onaping-Levack** Ontario Canada
123 M2 **Onas landet** *island* Finland
73 L9 **Onatchiway, Lac** *lake* Quebec Canada
85 J3 **Onava** New Mexico USA
81 Q5 **Onawa** Iowa USA
106 F5 **Oncativo** Argentina
140 D2 **Onchan** Isle of Man UK
192 E3 **Onch'ŏn** North Korea
162 B3 **Oncócua** Angola
126 E3 **Oncques** France
129 F4 **Onda** Spain
162 C3 **Ondangwa** Namibia
129 G4 **Ondara** Spain
126 C5 **Ondarroa** Spain
103 C6 **Ondas** *watercourse* Brazil
125 K3 **Ondava** *watercourse* Slovakia
162 D6 **Onderstedorings** South Africa
162 C3 **Ondjiva** Angola
159 E3 **Ondo** Nigeria
159 F3 **Ondo** *admin. area* Nigeria
190 G3 **Öndörhaan** Mongolia
121 R5 **Ondozero** Russian Federation
121 R5 **Ondozero, Ozero** *lake* Russian Federation
223 14 **One, Motu** *island* French Polynesia
215 H3 **One and a Half Mile Opening** *reef* Qld Australia
213 G4 **One Arm Point** *cape* WA Australia
218 G6 **One Tree** NSW Australia
223 9 **Oneata** *island* Fiji
134 I6 **Onega** Russian Federation
134 I6 **Onega** *watercourse* Russian Federation
83 N5 **Oneida** New York USA
87 I2 **Oneida** Tennessee USA
83 N5 **Oneida Lake** New York USA
105 F3 **Oneide** Brazil
81 P5 **O'Neill** Nebraska USA
217 N2 **O'Neill Point** *mountain* NT Australia
135 AG9 **Onekotan, Ostrov** *island* Kuril Islands
105 F5 **Oñema** Bolivia
160 C4 **Onema Ututu** Democratic Republic of Congo
121 T4 **Onezhskaya Guba** *bay* Russian Federation
134 I6 **Onezhskiy Poluostrov** *peninsula* Russian Federation
134 I6 **Onezhskoye Ozero** *lake* Russian Federation
187 F7 **Ong** *watercourse* Orissa India
194 E5 **Ông Đốc** *watercourse* Vietnam
220 F4 **Ongarue** New Zealand
162 D6 **Ongers** *watercourse* South Africa
216 F6 **Ongerup** WA Australia
192 E4 **Ongjin** North Korea
187 E8 **Ongole** Andhra Pradesh India
191 H3 **Ongon** Mongolia
138 E2 **Onibury** Shropshire England UK
81 O4 **Onida** South Dakota USA
109 1c **Onima** Netherlands Antilles
198 D4 **Onin, Djazirah** *peninsula* Indonesia
77 T7 **Onistagane, Lac** *lake* Quebec Canada
159 F3 **Onitsha** Nigeria
121 P3 **Onkamo** Finland
121 P3 **Onkamojärvi** *lake* Finland
123 L2 **Onkijoki** Finland
121 O5 **Onkivesi** *bay* Finland
135 X5 **Onkuchakh** Russian Federation
223 9 **Ono** *island* Fiji
222 1 **Onotoa** *island* Kiribati
222 6 **Onoun** *island* Federated States of Micronesia
120 H3 **Onøya** Norway
128 B2 **Ons, Illa de** *island* Spain
122 F2 **Onsaker** Norway
162 C5 **Onseepkans** South Africa
212 C6 **Onslow** WA Australia
87 M3 **Onslow Bay** North Carolina USA
139 G3 **Onslow Village** Surrey England UK
193 H4 **Ontake-san** *mountain* Japan
73 J8 **Ontario** *admin. area* Canada
84 D3 **Ontario** California USA
80 G4 **Ontario** Oregon USA
83 M5 **Ontario, Lake** Canada/USA
129 F4 **Ontinyent** Spain
121 P4 **Ontojärvi** *lake* Finland
82 G3 **Ontonagon** Michigan USA
193 I2 **Ōnuma** *lake* Japan
101 H3 **Onverwacht** Suriname
59 K1 **Onyx** *watercourse* Antarctica
213 G4 **Oobagooma** WA Australia
218 D5 **Oodla Wirra** SA Australia

218 B2 Oodnadatta SA Australia
161 H2 Oodweyne Somalia
82 D8 Oolagahl Lake Oklahoma USA
217 L5 Ooldea SA Australia
217 L5 Ooldea Range SA Australia
214 A2 Oolloo NT Australia
214 A3 Oolloo Crossing NT Australia
74 F6 Oona River British Columbia Canada
214 C8 Ooraminna, Mount NT Australia
214 D6 Ooratippa NT Australia
82 H5 Oostburg Wisconsin USA
126 F1 Oostende Belgium
126 F1 Oostkamp Belgium
109 1b Oostpunt cape Netherlands Antilles
215 H4 Ootann Qld Australia
74 H6 Ootsa Lake British Columbia Canada
81 J6 Opal Wyoming USA
160 C4 Opala Democratic Republic of Congo
214 G7 Opalton Qld Australia
125 H3 Opařany Czech Republic
221 E5 Oparara New Zealand
83 L2 Opasatica Lake Quebec Canada
76 I6 Opasquia Lake Ontario Canada
82 J2 Opastika Ontario Canada
77 R7 Opataca, Lac lake Quebec Canada
77 Q7 Opataouaga, Lac lake Quebec Canada
127 L4 Opatija Croatia
125 I3 Opava Czech Republic
83 N2 Opawica Lake Quebec Canada
82 J2 Opazatika Lake Ontario Canada
87 I4 Opelika Alabama USA
86 E5 Opelousas Louisiana USA
83 N2 Opémisca Lake Quebec Canada
83 L4 Opeongo Lake Ontario Canada
124 E5 Opera Italy
124 C2 Opglabbeek Belgium
81 L2 Opheim Montana USA
196 C3 Ophir, Gunung volcano Indonesia
221 C7 Ophir New Zealand
127 K4 Opicina Italy
84 inset Opihikao Hawai'i USA
77 R6 Opinaca watercourse Quebec Canada
77 Q6 Opinaca, Réservoir Quebec Canada
77 N5 Opinnagau watercourse Ontario Canada
76 M6 Opinnagau Lake Ontario Canada
77 V6 Opiscotéo, Lac lake Quebec Canada
124 C1 Opmeer Netherlands
159 F4 Opobo Nigeria
123 O4 Opochka Russian Federation
77 V6 Opocopa Newfoundland and Labrador Canada
125 K2 Opoczno Poland
125 I2 Opole Poland
125 J2 Opolskie admin. area Poland
220 G4 Opotiki New Zealand
220 G4 Opoutama New Zealand
87 H5 Opp Alabama USA
120 F5 Oppdal Norway
122 E1 Oppdal Herad Norway
122 C2 Oppedal Norway
120 F5 Opphaug Norway
122 F2 Opphus Norway
131 G6 Oppido Lucano Italy
122 E2 Oppland admin. area Norway
120 F5 Oppsal Norway
75 U5 Optic Lake Manitoba Canada
85 L2 Optima Oklahoma USA
85 L2 Optima Lake Oklahoma USA
85 J3 Optimo New Mexico USA
221 D6 Opuha Lake New Zealand
220 E4 Opunake New Zealand
162 B3 Opuwo Namibia
130 G5 Opuzen Croatia
182 J6 Oqtosh Uzbekistan
132 B2 Oradea Romania
126 E4 Oradour-sur-Vayres France
132 B4 Orahovac Kosovo
130 G4 Orahovica Croatia
186 E6 Orai Uttar Pradesh India
121 O3 Orajärvi lake Finland
220 G4 Orakei Korako New Zealand
121 O3 Orakylä Finland
155 F1 Oran Algeria
100 C5 Orán Peru
181 G3 Orang Assam India
192 F3 Ŏrang North Korea
219 I5 Orange NSW Australia
127 G4 Orange France
162 C5 Orange watercourse Namibia
162 D5 Orange watercourse South Africa
84 D4 Orange California USA
86 E5 Orange Texas USA
101 I3 Orange, Cabo cape Brazil
51 T12 Orange Cone underwater feature Atlantic Ocean
84 C2 Orange Cove California USA
214 B8 Orange Creek NT Australia
86 C7 Orange Grove Texas USA
109 3 Orange Hill Isla de San Andrés
109 11a Orange Hill St Vincent and the Grenadines
87 J6 Orange Lake Florida USA
87 K5 Orange Park Florida USA
90 B3 Orange Walk Belize
87 K4 Orangeburg South Carolina USA
215 J1 Orangerie Bay Papua New Guinea
158 A2 Orango island Guinea-Bissau
158 A2 Orango-Zinho island Guinea-Bissau
131 C6 Orani Sardinia Italy
101 H4 Oranje Gebergte range Suriname
162 C5 Oranjemund Namibia
91 G4 Oranjestad Aruba
109 19 Oranjestad Netherlands Antilles
162 E4 Orapa Botswana
125 I5 Orašac Bosnia and Herzegovina
125 L5 Orăştioara de Sus Romania
120 M5 Oravainen Finland
120 K4 Öravan Sweden
132 B3 Oraviţa Romania
126 F5 Orb watercourse France
127 H3 Orbe Switzerland
126 E2 Orbec France
131 D5 Orbetello Italy
126 F5 Orbieu watercourse France
126 B5 Orbigo watercourse Spain
219 I7 Orbost Vic. Australia
122 I2 Örbyhus Sweden
58 V2 Orcadas (Argentina) research station Antarctica
128 E4 Orcera Spain
81 L7 Orchard City Colorado USA
126 E3 Orches France
219 K1 Orchid Beach Qld Australia
87 K7 Orchid Island Florida USA
124 B2 Orchies France
101 E2 Orchila, Isla island Venezuela
127 I5 Orchina, Punta d' cape Corsica France
127 H4 Orcières France
213 J3 Ord watercourse WA Australia
81 P6 Ord Nebraska USA
122 D3 Ørdalsvatn lake Norway
128 B2 Órdenes Spain
136 F5 Ordu Turkey
136 F5 Ordu admin. area Turkey
128 E2 Orduña Spain
81 N7 Ordway Colorado USA
159 E3 Ore Nigeria
122 D3 Øre lake Norway
139 H4 Ore East Sussex England UK
86 D4 Ore City Texas USA
120 K5 Örealven watercourse Sweden
122 H3 Örebro Sweden
122 H3 Örebro admin. area Sweden
123 P3 Oredezh Russian Federation
70 Oregon admin. area USA
82 G5 Oregon Illinois USA
82 J6 Oregon Ohio USA
80 D4 Oregon City Oregon USA
123 J2 Öregrund Sweden
123 J2 Öregrundsgrepen bay Sweden
136 F2 Orel Russian Federation
135 AD8 Orel', Ozero lake Russian Federation
100 B5 Orellana admin. area Ecuador
128 D4 Orellana, Embalse de lake Spain
128 D4 Orellana la Vieja Spain
80 J6 Orem Utah USA
122 H4 Ören lake Sweden
133 E7 Ören Turkey
182 G3 Orenburg Russian Federation
182 G3 Orenburgskaya Oblast' admin. area Russian Federation
107 G6 Orense Argentina
122 G3 Öresjö lake Sweden
122 H2 Oresjön lake Sweden
133 E5 Orestiada Greece
221 C7 Oreti watercourse New Zealand
220 F3 Orewa New Zealand
77 W6 Oreway Newfoundland and Labrador Canada
133 C5 Orfanou, Kolpos bay Greece
139 I2 Orford Suffolk England UK
139 I2 Orford Ness cape England UK
133 E7 Orfos, Akra cape Greece
219 I2 Organ, Mount Qld Australia
133 D5 Orgáni Greece
104 A2 Órganos Chico, Punta cape Peru
127 G3 Orgelet France
128 E5 Orgiva Spain
179 L3 Orgūn-e Kalān Afghanistan
133 F6 Orhaneli Turkey
133 F5 Orhangazi Turkey
133 E5 Orhaniye Turkey
133 F7 Orhanlı Turkey
132 F2 Orhei Moldova
190 E3 Orhon Mongolia
190 E3 Orhon admin. area Mongolia
190 E3 Orhon Gol watercourse Mongolia
190 E3 Orhontuul Mongolia
131 G6 Oria Italy
128 E2 Oria watercourse Spain
74 L8 Orient Washington USA
82 G2 Orient Bay Ontario Canada
87 M3 Oriental North Carolina USA
106 E2 Oriental, Cordillera range Bolivia
100 C3 Oriental, Cordillera range Colombia
104 D4 Oriental, Cordillera range Peru
106 F6 Oriente Argentina
105 E3 Oriente Brazil
105 F5 Oriente, Llanos del region Bolivia
218 E3 Orientos Qld Australia
128 F3 Orihuela del Tremedal Spain
133 A5 Orikum Albania
136 E3 Oril watercourse Ukraine
77 S6 Orillat, Lac lake Quebec Canada
83 L4 Orillia Ontario Canada
123 M2 Orimattila Finland
132 E1 Orinin Ukraine
100 E3 Orinoco watercourse Colombia/Venezuela
101 F2 Orinoco Delta Venezuela
199 G6 Oriomo Papua New Guinea
75 P8 Orion Alberta Canada
82 F6 Orion Illinois USA
81 Q3 Oriska North Dakota USA
83 N5 Oriskany New York USA
120 M5 Orismala Finland
187 F7 Orissa admin. area India
131 C7 Oristano Sardinia Italy
131 C7 Oristano, Golfo di bay Sardinia Italy
140 B3 Oristown Ireland
123 L2 Orisuo Finland
100 B4 Orito Colombia
123 M2 Orivesi Finland
121 P5 Orivesi bay Finland
101 H5 Oriximiná Brazil
89 F5 Orizaba Mexico
89 F4 Orizatlán Mexico
103 B7 Orizona Brazil
132 D4 Orizovo Bulgaria
120 F5 Orkanger Norway
122 H4 Örken lake Sweden
120 F5 Orkla watercourse Norway
162 E5 Orkney South Africa
142 E1 Orkney Islands Scotland UK
142 E1 Orkney Islands admin. area Scotland UK
85 K5 Orla Texas USA
80 D7 Orland California USA
82 H6 Orland Park Illinois USA
87 K6 Orlando Florida USA
132 D4 Orlea Romania
107 I4 Orleans Brazil
126 E3 Orléans France
83 O4 Orleans Vermont USA
126 F3 Orléans, Canal d' watercourse France
216 H6 Orleans Farms WA Australia
125 H3 Orlík, Vodní nádrž lake Czech Republic
182 E3 Orlov Gay Russian Federation
191 K2 Orlovka watercourse Russian Federation
132 F3 Orlovka Ukraine
136 F2 Orlovskaya Oblast' admin. area Russian Federation
125 M1 Orlya Belarus
133 G5 Ormanlı Turkey
130 B4 Ormea Italy
133 E5 Orménion Greece
133 C5 Ormília Greece
195 J5 Ormoc Philippines
220 G5 Ormondville New Zealand
120 J4 Ormsjön lake Sweden
140 F3 Ormskirk Lancashire England UK
127 H3 Ornans France
126 D2 Orne watercourse France
120 E6 Ornes Norway
120 H3 Ørnes Norway
131 F6 Orneta Italy
123 J3 Ornö island Sweden
120 K5 Örnsköldsvik Sweden
123 L3 Örö island Finland
84 G4 Oro Valley Arizona USA
100 D3 Orocué Colombia
158 D2 Orodara Burkina Faso
190 D4 Orog Nuur lake Mongolia
85 I4 Orogrande New Mexico USA
223 14a Orohena volcano French Polynesia
199 J2 Oroluk island Federated States of Micronesia
222 6 Oroluk reef Federated States of Micronesia
130 H4 Orom Serbia
104 B2 Oromina Peru
161 G2 Oromiya admin. area Ethiopia
79 E10 Oromocto New Brunswick Canada
79 E10 Oromocto Lake New Brunswick Canada
159 F4 Oron Nigeria
222 1 Orona island Kiribati
52 O8 Orona reef Phoenix Islands
79 D10 Orono Maine USA
142 B4 Oronsay island Scotland UK
104 D4 Oropesa Peru
195 I5 Oroquieta Philippines
102 E4 Orós Brazil
102 E4 Orós, Açude lake Brazil
131 C6 Orosei, Golfo di bay Sardinia Italy
128 B2 Oroso Spain
130 H3 Oroszlány Hungary
131 C6 Orotelli Sardinia Italy
135 AC4 Orotko, Ozero lake Russian Federation
132 C1 Orov Ukraine
80 E7 Oroville California USA
80 F2 Oroville Washington USA
80 E7 Oroville, Lake California USA
50 N4 Orphan Knoll underwater feature Atlantic Ocean
126 E2 Orphin France
139 H3 Orpington Greater London England UK
100 B3 Orpúa Colombia
191 J2 Orqohan Nei Mongol Zizhiqu China
122 H4 Orrefors Sweden
123 N2 Orrengrund island Finland
131 F6 Orria Italy
142 D3 Orrin Reservoir lake Scotland UK
120 H6 Orrmosjön lake Sweden
140 E2 Orroland Dumfries and Galloway Scotland UK
218 D5 Orroroo SA Australia
83 K4 Orrville Ontario Canada
122 H2 Orsa Sweden
120 K5 Örsbäck Sweden
122 I3 Örsbacken bay Sweden
123 P5 Orsha Belarus
127 H3 Orsières Switzerland
122 H4 Örsjö Sweden
122 I2 Orsjön bay Sweden
122 G2 Örsjön lake Sweden
182 H3 Orsk Russian Federation
123 J2 Örskär island Sweden
123 M3 Orslandet island Finland
132 C3 Orşova Romania
183 L4 Orta-bakanas watercourse Kazakhstan
133 G6 Ortaca Turkey
133 E7 Ortaköy Turkey
131 E5 Orte Italy
128 C2 Ortegal, Cabo cape Spain
120 H5 Orten lake Sweden
182 I7 Ortepa Afghanistan
126 D5 Orthez France
140 E2 Orthwaite Cumbria England UK
103 B9 Ortigueira Brazil
128 C2 Ortigueira Spain
84 G6 Ortíz Mexico
141 F2 Orton Cumbria England UK
139 G2 Orton Northamptonshire England UK
131 F5 Ortona Italy
81 Q4 Ortonville Minnesota USA
120 K4 Örträsk Sweden
120 K4 Örträskjön lake Sweden
124 F1 Örtze watercourse Germany
135 AA5 Orulgan, Khrebet range Russian Federation
182 E6 Orūmīyeh Iran
182 E6 Orūmīyeh, Daryācheh-ye (Lake Urmia) lake Iran
104 E5 Oruro Bolivia
104 E5 Oruro admin. area Bolivia
122 F3 Orust island Sweden
179 K3 Orūzgān admin. area Afghanistan
130 E5 Orvieto Italy
131 C6 Orvili, Punta cape Sardinia Italy
58 T1 Orville Coast Antarctica
133 C5 Orvilos range Greece
127 K5 Orvinio Italy
136 E2 Orzhitsa watercourse Ukraine
130 C4 Orzinuovi Italy
154 D3 Orzola Spain
120 G5 Os Norway
122 D2 Osa Norway
90 C5 Osa, Península de lake Costa Rica
75 T8 Osage Saskatchewan Canada
82 E5 Osage Iowa USA
82 E7 Osage watercourse Missouri USA
82 E7 Osage Beach Missouri USA
193 G4 Ōsaka Japan
81 R4 Osakis Minnesota USA
82 D4 Osakis, Lake Minnesota USA
127 I5 Osani Corsica France
132 B4 Osaonica Serbia
107 J2 Osasco Brazil
55 M6 Osborn Plateau underwater feature Indian Ocean
81 P7 Osborne Kansas USA
213 H3 Osborne Islands WA Australia
75 V5 Osborne Lake Manitoba Canada
125 J3 Oščadnica Slovakia
214 E5 Oscar, Mount Qld Australia
85 I6 Oscar Soto Maynez Mexico
82 E6 Osceola Iowa USA
142 B3 Ose Highland Scotland UK
132 A3 Osečina Serbia
123 P2 Osel'ki Russian Federation
120 G4 Osen Norway
122 F2 Osensjøen lake Norway
129 F3 Osera Spain
141 G3 Osgodby North Yorkshire England UK
183 K6 Osh Kyrgyzstan
183 K6 Osh admin. area Kyrgyzstan
162 C3 Oshakati Namibia
162 C3 Oshana admin. area Namibia
83 L5 Oshawa Ontario Canada
121 U6 Oshevenskiy Pogost Russian Federation
162 C3 Oshikango Namibia
162 C3 Oshikoto admin. area Namibia
162 C3 Oshikuku Namibia
162 C3 Oshivelo Namibia
81 N6 Oshkosh Nebraska USA
82 G4 Oshkosh Wisconsin USA
159 E3 Oshogbo Nigeria
178 G2 Oshtorān Kūh mountain Iran
160 B4 Oshwe Democratic Republic of Congo
132 D3 Osica de Sus Romania
125 J1 Osie Poland
125 J1 Osięciny Poland
125 J1 Osiek Poland
125 H1 Osiek, Jezioro lake Poland
130 H4 Osijek Croatia
132 D4 Osikovitsa Bulgaria
72 G7 Osilinka watercourse British Columbia Canada
130 E5 Osimo Italy
123 P5 Osinovka Belarus
132 B3 Osipaonica Serbia
162 C4 Osire Namibia
186 C5 Osiyan Rajasthan India
120 I5 Ösjön bay Sweden
82 E6 Oskaloosa Iowa USA
122 I4 Oskarshamn Sweden
Öskemen see Ust'-Kamenogorsk Kazakhstan
75 R6 Osler Saskatchewan Canada
122 F3 Oslo Norway
122 F2 Oslo admin. area Norway
199 G5 Oslobip Papua New Guinea
121 N3 Osma Finland
187 D7 Osmanabad Maharashtra India
136 F6 Osmaniye Turkey
136 F6 Osmaniye admin. area Turkey
121 O4 Osmankajärvi lake Finland
121 N4 Osmankijärvi lake Finland
123 O3 Os'mino Russian Federation
123 L3 Osmussaar island Estonia
81 P2 Osnabrock North Dakota USA
124 E1 Osnabrück Germany
76 J7 Osnaburgh House Ontario Canada
126 F2 Osny France
160 D4 Oso watercourse Democratic Republic of Congo
124 G4 Osoppo Italy
130 F4 Osor Croatia
108 B2 Osorno Chile
128 D2 Osorno Spain
108 B2 Osorno, Volcán volcano Chile
123 O6 Osovets Belarus
74 L8 Osoyoos British Columbia Canada
122 C2 Osøyri Norway
74 I4 Ospika watercourse British Columbia Canada
127 J4 Ospitaletto Italy
215 I2 Osprey Reef Coral Sea Islands Territory Australia
124 C2 Oss Netherlands
133 C5 Óssa Greece
125 K2 Ossa Poland
219 R10 Ossa, Mount Tas. Australia
128 E4 Ossa de Montiel Spain
126 E5 Osse watercourse France
159 F3 Osse watercourse Nigeria
141 G3 Ossett West Yorkshire England UK
125 G4 Ossiacher See lake Austria
82 F5 Ossian Iowa USA
77 W6 Ossokmanuan Reservoir Newfoundland and Labrador Canada
87 K5 Osssabaw Sound Georgia USA
130 F4 Oštarije Croatia
120 I5 Östavall Sweden
122 G2 Østby Norway
124 E1 Oste watercourse Germany
220 F3 Ostend New Zealand
124 F1 Osterburg Germany
122 F4 Østerby Denmark
122 G2 Österdalälven bay Sweden
120 G6 Østerdalen valley Norway
122 H3 Östergötland admin. area Sweden
122 E4 Østerild Denmark
122 H5 Østerlars Denmark
120 J4 Österноret Sweden
122 C2 Osterøya region Norway
120 I5 Östersund Sweden
122 F3 Østfold admin. area Norway
123 J2 Östhammar Sweden
120 J5 Östloning Sweden
122 G2 Östmark Sweden
120 L5 Ostnäs Sweden
120 L5 Östra Gloppet bay Finland
122 I3 Östra Hjälmaren bay Sweden
122 I3 Östra Husby Sweden
120 J4 Östra Mullejaure lake Sweden
122 G5 Östra Ringsjön lake Sweden
122 G3 Östra Silen lake Sweden
125 J3 Ostrava Czech Republic
125 I5 Oštrelj Bosnia and Herzegovina
125 J1 Ostróda Poland
136 F2 Ostrogozhsk Russian Federation
125 K1 Ostrołęka Poland
125 H2 Ostroměř Czech Republic
132 D4 Ostrov Bulgaria
132 E3 Ostrov Romania
123 O4 Ostrov Russian Federation
132 C4 Ostroveni Romania
123 O5 Ostrovno Belarus
135 AH7 Ostrovnoy Russian Federation
135 AG6 Ostrovnoy, Mys cape Russian Federation
182 D1 Ostrovskoye Russian Federation
125 K1 Ostrów Mazowiecka Poland
125 K2 Ostrowiec Świętokrzyski Poland
125 I2 Ostrzeszów Poland
131 G6 Ostuni Italy
127 H2 Ostwald France
125 L2 Osuchy Poland
76 L7 O'Sullivan Lake Ontario Canada
192 F5 Ōsumi-Shotō island Japan
159 E3 Osun admin. area Nigeria
128 D5 Osuna Spain
103 B8 Osvaldo Cruz Brazil
82 D8 Oswego Kansas USA
83 M5 Oswego New York USA
138 D2 Oswestry Shropshire England UK
125 J2 Oświęcim Poland
135 Z4 Ot-Siyen Russian Federation
107 I3 Otacílio Costa Brazil
77 N6 Otadaonanis watercourse Ontario Canada
221 D7 Otago Harbour New Zealand
221 D7 Otago Peninsula New Zealand
123 K2 Otajärvi lake Finland
221 F5 Otaki New Zealand
221 F5 Otaki Beach New Zealand
220 G4 Otane New Zealand
193 I2 Otaru Japan
221 C8 Otautau New Zealand
100 B4 Otavalo Ecuador
162 C3 Otavi Namibia
221 D7 Otekaieke New Zealand
78 D4 Otelnuk, Lac lake Quebec Canada
132 C3 Oţelu Roşu Romania
123 N3 Otepää Estonia
123 N3 Otepää kõrgustik range Estonia
121 O4 Oterma Finland
121 O4 Otermajärvi lake Finland
139 H3 Otford Kent England UK
185 K3 Otgon Mongolia
185 K3 Otgon Tenger Uul mountain Mongolia
80 F3 Othello Washington USA
75 R3 Otherside watercourse Saskatchewan Canada
133 C6 Othris mountain Greece
198 A4 Oti Indonesia
122 H3 Oti Sweden
221 D6 Otira watercourse New Zealand
81 N6 Otis Colorado USA
85 M1 Otis Kansas USA
78 C6 Otish, Monts range Quebec Canada
82 J5 Otisville Michigan USA
162 C3 Otjikondo Namibia
162 C4 Otjimbingwe Namibia
162 C4 Otjinene Namibia
162 C3 Otjitambi Namibia
162 C4 Otjiwarongo Namibia
162 C4 Otjosondu Namibia
162 C3 Otjozondjupa admin. area Namibia
141 G3 Otley West Yorkshire England UK
130 G2 Otnice Czech Republic
222 8 Otong Java island Solomon Islands
156 E5 Otoro, Jebel mountain Sudan
76 J7 Otoskwin watercourse Ontario Canada
75 T6 Otosquen Saskatchewan Canada
Otou see North Cape New Zealand
122 D3 Otra watercourse Norway
109 1 Otrabanda Netherlands Antilles
131 H6 Otranto Italy
131 H6 Otranto, Capo d' cape Italy
131 H6 Otranto, Strait of Italy
82 I4 Otsego Lake Michigan USA
158 E3 Otta Nigeria
120 F6 Otta watercourse Norway
120 F6 Ottavatn bay Norway
83 N4 Ottawa Ontario Canada
83 L3 Ottawa watercourse Ontario Canada
82 G6 Ottawa Illinois USA
82 D7 Ottawa Kansas USA
82 I6 Ottawa Ohio USA
82 H2 Otter Head cape Ontario Canada
77 O7 Otter Rapids Ontario Canada
81 R3 Otter Tail Lake Minnesota USA
138 D4 Otterford Somerset England UK
120 E5 Otterøya island Norway
138 D4 Otterton Devon England UK
122 F5 Otterup Denmark
138 D4 Ottery St Mary Devon England UK
127 G1 Ottignies Belgium
122 I2 Ottnaren lake Sweden
199 H5 Otto, Mount Papua New Guinea
73 K2 Otto Fiord Nunavut Canada
124 F4 Ottobeuren Germany
124 E5 Ottone Italy
120 K4 Ottonträsk Sweden
82 I6 Ottoville Ohio USA
120 H5 Ottsjön lake Sweden
82 E6 Ottumwa Iowa USA
82 E2 Otukamamoan Lake Ontario Canada
159 F3 Otukpa Nigeria
159 F3 Otukpo Nigeria
106 F3 Otumpa Argentina
104 B2 Otuzco Peru
108 A5 Otway, Bahía bay Chile
218 F8 Otway, Cape Vic. Australia
218 F8 Otway Range Vic. Australia
125 K1 Otwock Poland
124 F4 Ötztal valley Austria
194 D2 Ou watercourse Laos
194 D2 Ou Nua Laos
155 H6 Ouacha Niger
86 E4 Ouachita watercourse Arkansas USA
86 F5 Ouachita watercourse Louisiana USA
86 E3 Ouachita, Lake Arkansas USA
86 D3 Ouachita Mountains Oklahoma USA
222 7 Ouâco New Caledonia
154 C5 Ouâd Nâga Mauritania
159 I3 Ouadda Central African Republic
159 I2 Ouaddaï admin. area Chad
158 D2 Ouagadougou Burkina Faso
158 D2 Ouahigouya Burkina Faso
160 C2 Ouaka admin. area Central African Republic
160 C2 Ouaka watercourse Central African Republic
158 E3 Ouake Benin
154 E5 Oualâta Mauritania
154 D6 Oualia Mali
155 G6 Ouallam Niger
159 I3 Ouanda Djailé Central African Republic
159 H3 Ouandago Central African Republic
159 I4 Ouango Central African Republic
158 C3 Ouangolo-Dougou Côte d'Ivoire
126 F3 Ouanne, L' watercourse France
160 D2 Ouara watercourse Central African Republic
154 E6 Ouardé Mali
158 E2 Ouargaye Burkina Faso
155 H2 Ouargla Algeria
155 G5 Ouaritoufoulout Mali
154 E2 Ouarzazate Morocco
77 S8 Ouasiemsca watercourse Quebec Canada
155 G5 Ouatagouna Mali
126 F1 Oudenaarde Belgium
194 D2 Oudomxai admin. area Laos
126 D3 Oudon watercourse France
162 D6 Oudtshoorn South Africa
129 G6 Oued Lili Algeria
129 G6 Oued Taria Algeria
154 E2 Oued Zem Morocco
131 B8 Oued Zenati Algeria
222 7 Ouégoa New Caledonia
158 D3 Ouéllé Côte d'Ivoire
158 E3 Ouémé watercourse Benin
126 B2 Ouessant, Île d' island France
159 H4 Ouesso Congo
159 G3 Ouest admin. area Cameroon
164 6b Ouest, Île de l' island French Southern and Antarctic Lands
79 F8 Ouest, Pointe de l' cape Quebec Canada
154 E2 Ouezzane Morocco
127 G1 Ouffet Belgium
143 C3 Oughterard Ireland
159 H3 Ouham admin. area Central African Republic
159 H3 Ouham watercourse Central African Republic
159 H3 Ouham watercourse Chad
159 H3 Ouham-Pendé admin. area Central African Republic
155 F2 Oujda Morocco
129 G5 Oulad Bou Djemaa Algeria
121 N4 Oulainen Finland
121 P3 Oulankajoki watercourse Finland
143 F4 Oulart Ireland
158 E2 Oulé watercourse Burkina Faso
158 C3 Oulé watercourse Guinea
155 H2 Ouled Djellal Algeria
159 G3 Ouli Cameroon
159 I2 Oulou, Bahr watercourse Central African Republic
141 G2 Oulston North Yorkshire England UK
139 I2 Oulton Suffolk England UK
121 N4 Oulu Finland
121 O4 Oulujärvi bay Finland
121 N4 Oulujoki watercourse Finland
121 O4 Oulun admin. area Finland
124 D5 Oulx Italy
156 C4 Oum Chalouba Chad
131 B9 Oum el Bouaghi Algeria
159 H2 Oum-Hadjer Chad
129 I6 Oum Ladjoul Algeria
155 H3 Ounane, Djebel mountain Algeria
154 E2 Ounara Morocco
121 M2 Ounasjärvi lake Finland
121 N3 Ounasjoki watercourse Finland
121 N2 Ounastunturi island Finland
139 G2 Oundle Northamptonshire England UK
75 T8 Oungre Saskatchewan Canada
156 C4 Ounianga-Kebir Chad
159 H3 Ouogo Central African Republic
162 D4 Ouoxo watercourse Botswana
124 D3 Our watercourse Luxembourg
123 K2 Ouransaaristo island Finland
127 G2 Ource watercourse France
158 B2 Ouré-Kaba Guinea
102 C3 Ourém Brazil
128 B4 Ourém Portugal
128 C2 Ourense Spain
102 D4 Ouricuri Brazil
103 B8 Ourinhos Brazil
103 C5 Ouro watercourse Brazil
103 D8 Ouro Preto Brazil
105 F3 Ouro Preto do Oeste Brazil
105 G4 Ouro Verde Brazil
79 G8 Ours, Cap de l' cape Quebec Canada
124 C2 Ourthe watercourse Belgium
142 E2 Ousdale Highland Scotland UK
139 H2 Ousden Suffolk England UK
219 R11 Ouse Tas. Australia
141 G3 Ouse watercourse England UK
126 E5 Oust France
126 C3 Oust watercourse France
141 I3 Out Newton East Riding of Yorkshire England UK
121 O2 Outakoski Finland
79 D8 Outardes, Rivière aux watercourse Quebec Canada
79 D7 Outardes Quatre, Réservoir Quebec Canada
154 F2 Outat Oulad el Haj Morocco
57 F2 Outer Bailey underwater feature Atlantic Ocean
82 F3 Outer Island Wisconsin USA
219 S9 Outer Sister Island Tas. Australia
141 F2 Outhgill Cumbria England UK
162 C4 Outjo Namibia
121 P5 Outokumpu Finland
221 D7 Outram New Zealand
126 E1 Outreau France
139 H2 Outwell Cambridgeshire England UK
222 7 Ouvéa island New Caledonia
127 G4 Ouvèze watercourse France
139 H5 Ouville-la-Rivière France
218 F6 Ouyen Vic. Australia
124 E5 Ovada Italy
109 5 Ovahí, Caleta bay Isla de Pascua (Easter Island)
223 9 Ovalau island Fiji
159 G4 Ovan Gabon
122 H2 Ovanåker Sweden
128 B3 Ovar Portugal
199 K5 Ovau island Solomon Islands
132 B3 Ovča Serbia
100 C2 Ovejas Colombia
106 E5 Ovejas, Cerro de las mountain Argentina
219 K4 Oven Mountain NSW Australia
159 G4 Oveng Cameroon
218 H7 Ovens Vic. Australia
139 H2 Over Cambridgeshire England UK
142 E5 Over Dalgliesh Scottish Borders Scotland UK
139 F3 Over Kiddington Oxfordshire England UK
139 F3 Over Wallop Hampshire England UK
120 I5 Överammer Sweden
120 F5 Overås Norway
122 F3 Överby Sweden
75 T6 Overflowing watercourse Saskatchewan Canada
75 U6 Overflowing River Manitoba Canada
120 K2 Øvergard Norway
120 I5 Överhogdal Sweden
121 M3 Överkalix Sweden
120 L4 Överklinten Sweden
82 D7 Overland Park Kansas USA
216 D3 Overlander Roadhouse WA Australia
120 L5 Övermark Finland
121 M3 Övermorjärv Sweden
106 D5 Overo, Volcán volcano Argentina
120 K4 Överrödå Sweden
142 E6 Overton Dumfries and Galloway Scotland UK
139 F3 Overton Hampshire England UK
138 E2 Overton Wrexham Wales UK
86 D4 Overton Texas USA
121 M3 Övertorneå Sweden
120 I3 Överuman lake Sweden
132 F3 Ovidiu Romania
91 G3 Oviedo Dominican Republic
128 D2 Oviedo Spain
122 G1 Oviksfjällen range Sweden
123 K4 Oviši Latvia
190 E3 Övörhangay admin. area Mongolia
120 J5 Övra Sweden
120 I3 Övre Ältsvattnet lake Sweden
120 E6 Øvre Årdal Norway
120 I4 Övre Boksjön lake Sweden
120 H4 Øvre Fiplingvatnet lake Norway
122 G2 Övre Fryken lake Sweden
122 E2 Øvre Hein lake Norway
120 L2 Övre Soppero Sweden
120 L4 Övre Tväråsel Sweden
120 J5 Övsjöbyn Sweden
122 E5 Ovtrup Denmark
221 C8 Owaka New Zealand
159 H5 Owando Congo
193 H4 Owase Japan
82 D8 Owasso Oklahoma USA
82 E4 Owatonna Minnesota USA
218 D6 Owen SA Australia
216 G5 Owen, Lake WA Australia
221 E5 Owen, Mount New Zealand
54 J3 Owen Fracture Zone underwater feature Indian Ocean
194 C5 Owen Island Myanmar
221 E5 Owen River New Zealand
83 K4 Owen Sound Ontario Canada
199 H6 Owen Stanley Range Papua New Guinea
159 F3 Owena watercourse Nigeria
159 F4 Owendo Gabon
143 C2 Owenduff Ireland
80 F8 Owens watercourse California USA
84 C2 Owens Lake California USA
82 H8 Owensboro Kentucky USA
159 F3 Owerri Nigeria
143 D1 Owey Island Ireland
220 F4 Owhango New Zealand
109 11a Owia Bay St Vincent and the Grenadines
139 G3 Owlswick Buckinghamshire England UK
141 H3 Owmby Lincolnshire England UK
82 I5 Owosso Michigan USA
80 G5 Owyhee watercourse Oregon USA
80 G5 Owyhee, Lake Oregon USA
143 D2 Ox Mountains Ireland
104 C3 Oxapampa Peru
120 inset Öxarfjörður bay Iceland
75 T8 Oxbow Saskatchewan Canada
82 E2 Oxdrift Ontario Canada
133 B6 Oxeia island Greece
139 E3 Oxenton Gloucestershire England UK
221 E6 Oxford New Zealand
139 F3 Oxford Oxfordshire England UK
87 I4 Oxford Alabama USA
86 F2 Oxford Arkansas USA
81 Q8 Oxford Kansas USA
86 G3 Oxford Mississippi USA
83 N5 Oxford New York USA
87 L2 Oxford North Carolina USA
82 I7 Oxford Ohio USA
76 H5 Oxford Lake Manitoba Canada
139 F3 Oxfordshire admin. area England UK
122 G5 Oxie Sweden
89 H4 Oxkutzcab Mexico
218 H4 Oxley, Mount NSW Australia
214 B1 Oxley Island NT Australia
84 C3 Oxnard California USA
139 G3 Oxted Surrey England UK
139 F1 Oxton Nottinghamshire England UK
142 F5 Oxton Scottish Borders Scotland UK
133 D6 Oxylithos Greece
197 F3 Oya Malaysia
197 G3 Oya watercourse Malaysia
127 H4 Oyace Italy
104 D3 Oyague Peru
74 L7 Oyama British Columbia Canada
193 H4 Oyama Japan
120 F6 Øyangen lake Norway
101 H4 Oyapock watercourse French Guiana
122 D3 Øyarvatn lake Norway
183 N4 Oychilik Kazakhstan
120 F6 Øye Norway
159 G4 Oyem Gabon
75 P7 Oyen Alberta Canada
120 H4 Øyevatnet lake Norway
120 J2 Øyjorda Norway
142 D3 Oykel Bridge Highland Scotland UK
122 F3 Øymarksjøen lake Norway
159 H5 Oyo Congo
159 E3 Oyo admin. area Nigeria
104 B3 Oyón Peru
127 G3 Oyonnax France
183 L6 Oytal Kyrgyzstan
120 G5 Øyungen lake Norway
135 AF5 Oyusardakh Russian Federation
136 G5 Özalp Turkey
195 I5 Ozamiz Philippines
87 I5 Ozark Alabama USA
82 E8 Ozark Missouri USA
86 E3 Ozark Lake Arkansas USA
82 E8 Ozark Plateau Missouri USA
82 E7 Ozarks, Lake of the Missouri USA
125 K3 Ózd Hungary
132 F3 Ozerne Ukraine
135 AH7 Ozernoy, Zaliv bay Russian Federation
193 I1 Ozerskiy Russian Federation
80 C2 Ozette Lake Washington USA
76 K6 Ozhiski Lake Ontario Canada
135 AE5 Ozhogino Russian Federation
135 AE5 Ozhogino, Ozero lake Russian Federation
125 M3 Ozhydiv Ukraine
182 F3 Ozinki Russian Federation
85 L5 Ozona Texas USA
125 J2 Ozorków Poland
159 F3 Ozoro Nigeria
192 G5 Ozu Japan
182 D5 Ozurgeti Georgia

P

192 E3 P-aro Ho lake South Korea
158 D2 Pâ Burkina Faso
189 H4 Pa-Chao Tao island Taiwan China
194 C3 Pa Daet Thailand
180 D2 Pa-li Ho watercourse Xizang Zizhiqu China
188 C4 Pa-pien Ho watercourse Yunnan China
184 H4 Pa-yin-kou Ho watercourse Xinjiang Uygur Zizhiqu China
121 O2 Paaddos Finland
121 N5 Pääjärvi Finland
123 M2 Pääjärvi lake Finland
222 7 Paama island Vanuatu
73 O6 Paamiut Greenland
127 J2 Paar watercourse Germany
109 1a Paardenbaai bay Aruba
162 C6 Paarl South Africa
121 O2 Paatari lake Finland
121 O4 Paatinjärvi lake Finland
121 N4 Paavola Finland
142 A4 Pabaigh island Scotland UK
142 A3 Pabbay island Scotland UK
197 H5 Pabbiring, Kepulauan islands Indonesia
88 C3 Pabellones, Ensenada lake Mexico
125 J2 Pabianice Poland
104 D4 Pablo Amaya Bolivia
181 F4 Pabna Bangladesh
79 F8 Pabos Quebec Canada
79 F8 Pabos Mills Quebec Canada
123 M5 Pabradė Lithuania
104 D5 Pacae Peru
105 I1 Pacajá Brazil
101 I5 Pacajá watercourse Brazil
101 F3 Pacaraimã, Serra range Brazil
104 B2 Pacasmayo, Punta cape Peru
102 E3 Pacatuba Brazil
108 A5 Pacheco, Isla island Chile
133 D7 Pacheia island Greece
182 D2 Pachelma Russian Federation
85 I6 Pachera Mexico
131 F8 Pachino Italy
104 C4 Pachiri Peru
104 C3 Pachitea watercourse Peru
100 C3 Pacho Colombia
186 F5 Pachperwa Uttar Pradesh India
89 F4 Pachuca Mexico
82 F7 Pacific Missouri USA
58 O2 Pacific-Antarctic Ridge underwater feature Southern Ocean
80 E8 Pacific Grove California USA
52-53 Pacific Ocean
197 G5 Pacinan, Tanjung cape Indonesia
197 G5 Paciran Indonesia
197 F6 Pacitan Indonesia
218 E4 Packsaddle NSW Australia
100 D4 Pacoa Colombia
105 G5 Paçoca Brazil
104 D5 Pacocha Peru
90 E5 Pacora Panama
127 L2 Pacov Czech Republic
105 E2 Pacovalzinho Brazil
125 J1 Pacyna Poland
195 J6 Padada Philippines
179 K3 Padag Road Pakistan
197 I5 Padamarang island Indonesia
101 E4 Padamo, Rio watercourse Venezuela
186 C5 Padampur Rajasthan India
198 B5 Padang Indonesia
196 D4 Padang Indonesia
196 D3 Padang island Indonesia
196 D3 Padang Endau Malaysia
196 D4 Padangpanjang Indonesia
196 C3 Padangsidempuan Indonesia
196 F4 Padangtikar Indonesia
196 F4 Padangtikar island Indonesia
121 R5 Padany Russian Federation
197 G2 Padas watercourse Malaysia
101 F4 Padauari watercourse Brazil
122 E5 Padborg Denmark
187 C6 Paddhari Gujarat India

218 G5 **Paddington** NSW Australia
139 H3 **Paddock Wood** Kent England UK
75 S6 **Paddockwood** Saskatchewan Canada
197 I4 **Padeabesar** *island* Indonesia
125 K5 **Padej** Serbia
86 C3 **Paden** Oklahoma USA
124 E2 **Paderborn** Germany
132 C3 **Padeş** Romania
161 E3 **Padibe** Uganda
141 F3 **Padiham** Lancashire England UK
105 E5 **Padilla** Bolivia
132 B3 **Padina** Serbia
120 J3 **Padjelanta** *range* Sweden
76 G2 **Padlei** Nunavut Canada
121 S5 **Padmozero, Ozero** *lake* Russian Federation
124 F5 **Padova** Italy
187 C6 **Padra** Gujarat India
160 A5 **Padrão, Ponta** *cape* Angola
103 B6 **Padre Bernardo** Brazil
86 C7 **Padre Island** Texas USA
103 D7 **Padre Paraíso** Brazil
128 B2 **Padrón** Spain
186 C6 **Padru** Rajasthan India
131 C6 **Padru** Sardinia Italy
138 C4 **Padstow** Cornwall England UK
218 E7 **Padthaway** SA Australia
82 G8 **Paducah** Kentucky USA
86 A3 **Paducah** Texas USA
223 14a **Paea** French Polynesia
192 E4 **Paegnyŏng-do** *island* North Korea
191 K4 **Paektu San** *mountain* Jilin China
192 F2 **Paektu San** *mountain* North Korea
220 G3 **Paengaroa** New Zealand
220 F3 **Paeroa** New Zealand
163 F4 **Pafuri** South Africa
130 F4 **Pag** Croatia
105 H2 **Paga-Conta** Brazil
195 I6 **Pagadian** Philippines
196 D4 **Pagai Selatan** *island* Indonesia
196 D4 **Pagai Utara** *island* Indonesia
222 2 **Pagan** *island* Northern Mariana Islands
130 D5 **Paganico** Italy
196 D5 **Pagaralam** Indonesia
133 C6 **Pagasitikos Kolpos** *bay* Greece
197 G4 **Pagatan** Indonesia
194 C4 **Pagawyun** Myanmar
101 F3 **Pagé** Brazil
84 G2 **Page** Arizona USA
81 Q3 **Page** North Dakota USA
87 K3 **Pageland** South Carolina USA
196 E4 **Pagerdewa** Indonesia
109 8 **Paget, Mount** South Georgia
133 C6 **Pagkalos, Akra** *cape* Greece
130 B2 **Pagny** France
222 5 **Pago Bay** Guam
223 12 **Pago Pago** American Samoa
81 L8 **Pagosa Springs** Colorado USA
109 15 **Pagua Pointe** *cape* Dominica
82 I2 **Pagwachuan Lake** Ontario Canada
199 G5 **Pagwi** Papua New Guinea
84 inset **Pāhala** Hawai'i USA
186 D4 **Pahalgam** Jammu and Kashmir India/Pakistan
196 D2 **Pahang** *admin. area* Malaysia
196 D3 **Pahang** *watercourse* Malaysia
221 F5 **Pahaoa** New Zealand
90 D4 **Páhara, Laguna** *lake* Nicaragua
179 L3 **Paharpur** Pakistan
132 A2 **Páhi** Hungary
221 B8 **Pahia** New Zealand
221 B8 **Pahia Point** New Zealand
220 F5 **Pahiatua** New Zealand
121 O4 **Pahkakoski** Finland
121 O5 **Pahkamäki** Finland
84 inset **Pāhoa** Hawai'i USA
87 K7 **Pahokee** Florida USA
80 H8 **Pahranagat Range** Nevada USA
84 E2 **Pahrump** Nevada USA
80 G8 **Pahute Mesa** *range* Nevada USA
159 G3 **Pai** *watercourse* Nigeria
189 H4 **Pai-Sha Tao** *island* Taiwan China
105 G5 **Paiaguás** Brazil
142 A3 **Paible** Na h-Eileanan Siar Scotland UK
103 A8 **Paiçandu** Brazil
189 H3 **Paich'üan Liehtao (Taiwan)** *island* Taiwan China
100 C4 **Paicol** Colombia
123 M3 **Paide** Estonia
138 D4 **Paignton** Torbay England UK
123 M2 **Päijänne** *bay* Finland
159 F3 **Paiko** Nigeria
85 K8 **Paila** Mexico
194 D4 **Pailĭn** Cambodia
104 D4 **Pailipaya** Bolivia
104 E3 **Pailita** Bolivia
100 C2 **Pailitas** Colombia
105 F5 **Pailón** Bolivia
100 C3 **Paime** Colombia
126 C2 **Paimpol** France
196 D4 **Painan** Indonesia
83 K6 **Painesville** Ohio USA
123 L2 **Painio** *lake* Finland
77 P6 **Paint Hills Bay** Quebec Canada
75 W5 **Paint Lake** Manitoba Canada
86 B5 **Paint Rock** Texas USA
84 G3 **Painted Desert** Arkansas USA
82 J8 **Paintsville** Kentucky USA
100 C3 **Paipa** Colombia
142 B2 **Pairc** Na h-Eileanan Siar Scotland UK
222 7 **Païromé** New Caledonia
128 E2 **País Vasco** *admin. area* Spain
142 D5 **Paisley** Renfrewshire Scotland UK
80 E5 **Paisley** Oregon USA
121 O5 **Paisua** Finland
222 7 **Paita** New Caledonia
104 A2 **Paita** Peru
104 A2 **Paita, Bahía de** *bay* Peru
197 H2 **Paitan, Teluk** *bay* Malaysia
187 D7 **Paithan** Maharashtra India
121 M2 **Paittasjärvi** Sweden
120 K3 **Paittasjärvi** *lake* Sweden
105 F3 **Paixão, Serra da** *range* Brazil
121 M3 **Pajala** Sweden
100 A5 **Paján** Ecuador
106 D2 **Pajancha** Chile
164 3d **Pájara** Canary Islands
108 C4 **Pajarito, Puerto** *bay* Argentina
106 D4 **Pájaros, Islotes** *islands* Chile
161 E3 **Pajule** Uganda
121 O5 **Pajuskylä** Finland
123 N3 **Pajusti** Estonia
199 H4 **Pak Island** Papua New Guinea
194 C5 **Pak Nam Chumphon** Thailand
81 J2 **Pak-oghkee** Alberta Canada
194 D2 **Pak-Ou** Laos
194 D5 **Pak Phanang** Thailand
194 D6 **Pak Phayun** Thailand
125 I4 **Páka** Hungary
196 D2 **Paka** Malaysia
187 E9 **Pakala** Andhra Pradesh India
101 G3 **Pakaraima Mountains** Guyana
121 O5 **Pakarila** Finland
82 F2 **Pakashkan Lake** Ontario Canada
194 D3 **Pakbèng** Laos
194 C5 **Pakchan** *watercourse* Myanmar
89 H5 **Pakchén** Mexico
108 A4 **Pakenham, Cabo** *cape* Chile
121 Q4 **Pakhomova-Vara** Russian Federation
159 F2 **Paki** Nigeria
197 H6 **Pakijangan, Tanjung** *cape* Indonesia
222 6 **Pakin** *island* Federated States of Micronesia
123 K2 **Pakinainen** *island* Finland
179 J4 **Pakistan** *country* Asia
76 H5 **Pakitahokansik** Manitoba Canada
181 H5 **Pakokku** Myanmar
125 J1 **Pakość** Poland
75 P8 **Pakowki Lake** Alberta Canada
179 M3 **Pakpattan** Pakistan
130 G4 **Pakrac** Croatia
123 L5 **Pakruojis** Lithuania
132 A2 **Paks** Hungary
179 L2 **Paktīā** *admin. area* Afghanistan
179 K3 **Paktīkā** *admin. area* Afghanistan
186 G6 **Pakur** Jharkhand India
76 I7 **Pakwash Lake** Ontario Canada
76 D6 **Pakwaw Lake** Saskatchewan Canada
194 D3 **Pakxan** Laos
194 E4 **Pakxe** Laos
194 D2 **Pakxèng** Laos
159 G3 **Pala** Chad
196 E5 **Palabuhanratu, Teluk** *bay* Indonesia
91 F2 **Palacca Point** *cape* Bahamas
86 C6 **Palacios** Texas USA
187 E8 **Palacole** Andhra Pradesh India
129 H3 **Palafrugell** Spain
131 F8 **Palagonia** Italy
133 C8 **Palaiochora** Greece
133 B6 **Palaiochórion** Greece
133 B6 **Palairou, Ormos** *bay* Greece
187 D9 **Palakkad** Kerala India
162 D4 **Palamakoloi** Botswana
198 C4 **Palamea** Indonesia
129 H3 **Palamós** Spain
186 D4 **Palampur** Himachal Pradesh India
219 R9 **Palana** Tas. Australia
195 I3 **Palanan Bay** Philippines
132 G2 **Palanca** Moldova
187 E7 **Palandur** Maharashtra India
179 I3 **Palangān, Kūh-e** *mountain* Iran
197 G4 **Palangkaraya** Indonesia
187 D9 **Palani** Tamil Nadu India
186 C6 **Palanpur** Gujarat India
198 A5 **Palanro** Indonesia
162 E4 **Palapye** Botswana
82 G5 **Palatine** Illinois USA
135 AF6 **Palatka** Russian Federation
87 K6 **Palatka** Florida USA
131 C6 **Palau** Sardinia Italy
88 E3 **Palau** Mexico
198 E2 **Palau** *country* Oceania
52 J7 **Palau Trench** *underwater feature* Pacific Ocean
195 I3 **Palaui** *island* Philippines
196 E5 **Palausekopong, Tanjung** *cape* Indonesia
195 H5 **Palawan** *island* Philippines
52 H7 **Palawan Trough** *underwater feature* South China Sea
127 I5 **Palazzo, Punta** *cape* Corsica France
124 E5 **Palazzolo** Italy
105 E6 **Palca Grande** Bolivia
85 M1 **Palco** Kansas USA
125 K2 **Palczew** Poland
123 M3 **Paldiski** Estonia
138 D2 **Pale** Gwynedd Wales UK
198 B3 **Paleheh** Indonesia
196 E4 **Palembang** Indonesia
108 B3 **Palena** Chile
108 B3 **Palena, Lago** *lake* Argentina
128 D2 **Palencia** Spain
89 H5 **Palenque** Mexico
91 G3 **Palenque, Punta** *cape* Dominican Republic
186 E6 **Palera** Madhya Pradesh India
106 E3 **Palermo** Argentina
131 E7 **Palermo** Italy
104 D2 **Palestina** Brazil
106 D2 **Palestine** Chile
86 F3 **Palestine** Arkansas USA
86 D5 **Palestine** Texas USA
86 D4 **Palestine, Lake** Texas USA
101 H3 **Palétuviers, Pointe des** *cape* French Guiana
187 C7 **Palghar** Maharashtra India
107 I3 **Palhoça** Brazil
186 C6 **Pali** Rajasthan India
186 E6 **Pali** Uttar Pradesh India
197 G5 **Paliat** *island* Indonesia
130 H3 **Palić** Serbia
125 J4 **Palićko Jezero** *lake* Serbia
123 O5 **Palik** Belarus
222 6b **Palikir** Federated States of Micronesia
195 J6 **Palimbang** Philippines
131 F6 **Palinuro, Capo** *cape* Italy
133 C6 **Paliouri** Greece
133 C6 **Paliouri, Akra** *cape* Greece
133 B6 **Paliouria** Greece
81 K7 **Palisade** Colorado USA
127 G2 **Paliseul** Belgium
187 C7 **Palitana** Gujarat India
89 G5 **Palizada** Mexico
131 F8 **Palizzi** Italy
121 O4 **Paljakka** *mountain* Finland
187 E10 **Palk Bay** Sri Lanka
187 E10 **Palk Strait** India
123 M2 **Pälkänevesi** *lake* Finland
120 L3 **Pålkem** Sweden
186 F6 **Palkot** Jharkhand India
219 J3 **Pallamallawa** NSW Australia
215 I5 **Pallarenda** Qld Australia
143 E3 **Pallas** Ireland
143 D4 **Pallas Grean** Ireland
121 N2 **Pallasjärvi** *lake* Finland
182 E3 **Pallasovka** Russian Federation
104 E5 **Pallini** Bolivia
221 F5 **Palliser, Cape** New Zealand
221 F5 **Palliser Bay** New Zealand
186 D5 **Pallu** Rajasthan India
87 K6 **Palm Bay** Florida USA
109 1a **Palm Beach** *bay* Aruba
215 H4 **Palm Cove** Qld Australia
215 I5 **Palm Islands** Qld Australia
87 K7 **Palm Springs** Florida USA
103 C6 **Palma** *watercourse* Brazil
163 H2 **Palma** Mozambique
129 H4 **Palma** Spain
128 D5 **Palma del Río** Spain
104 E4 **Palma Seca** Bolivia
91 F2 **Palma Soriano** Cuba
107 H5 **Palmar, Punta del** *cape* Uruguay
102 F5 **Palmares** Brazil
107 I4 **Palmares do Sul** Brazil
103 B9 **Palmas** Brazil
103 B5 **Palmas** Brazil
158 C4 **Palmas, Cape** *cape* Liberia
90 D5 **Palmas Bellas** Panama
103 D6 **Palmas de Monte Alto** Brazil
84 C3 **Palmdale** California USA
103 B9 **Palmeira** Brazil
107 H3 **Palmeira das Missões** Brazil
102 D4 **Palmeirais** Brazil
105 G5 **Palmeiras** Brazil
103 C6 **Palmeiras** *watercourse* Brazil
103 B7 **Palmeiras de Goiás** Brazil
162 B1 **Palmeirinhas, Ponta das** *cape* Angola
217 M2 **Palmer** *watercourse* NT Australia
215 G4 **Palmer** *watercourse* Qld Australia
199 G5 **Palmer** *watercourse* Papua New Guinea
72 E6 **Palmer** Alaska USA
81 Q7 **Palmer** Kansas USA
81 P6 **Palmer** Nebraska USA
86 C4 **Palmer** Texas USA
58 T2 **Palmer (USA)** *research station* Antarctica
58 T2 **Palmer Archipelago** *islands* Antarctica
58 T2 **Palmer Land** *plain* Antarctica
215 H4 **Palmer River Roadhouse** Qld Australia
217 M2 **Palmer Valley** NT Australia
83 K5 **Palmerston** Ontario Canada
221 D7 **Palmerston** New Zealand
220 F5 **Palmerston North** New Zealand
220 1 **Palmerston** *island* Cook Islands New Zealand
215 J6 **Palmerston, Cape** Qld Australia
87 J7 **Palmetto** Florida USA
109 18 **Palmetto Point** Antigua and Barbuda
87 M8 **Palmetto Point** Bahamas
105 E4 **Palmira** Bolivia
100 B4 **Palmira** Colombia
109 10a **Palmiste Bay** Grenada
107 G5 **Palmitas** Uruguay
Palmyra *see* **Tadmur** Syria
82 H7 **Palmyra** Indiana USA
82 F7 **Palmyra** Missouri USA
52 P7 **Palmyra Atoll** *unincorporated US territory* Pacific Ocean
187 G7 **Palmyras Point** Orissa India
142 E6 **Palnackie** Dumfries and Galloway Scotland UK
101 F2 **Palo Blanco** Venezuela
86 B4 **Palo Pinto, Lake** Texas USA
106 F3 **Palo Santo** Argentina
109 inset 9 **Palo Seco** Trinidad and Tobago
84 E4 **Palo Verde** California USA
197 F3 **Paloh** Malaysia
120 L3 **Palohuornas** Sweden
121 M2 **Palojärvi** *lake* Finland
121 M2 **Palojoensuu** Finland
121 O5 **Palokangas** Finland
121 P5 **Palomäki** Finland
88 E3 **Palomas, Lago de** *lake* Mexico
198 B4 **Palopo** Indonesia
129 F5 **Palos, Cabo de** *cape* Spain
103 A9 **Palotina** Brazil
104 C4 **Palpa** Peru
218 E1 **Palparara** Qld Australia
122 E2 **Pålsbufjorden** *bay* Norway
120 L4 **Pålsträsk** Sweden
121 O4 **Paltamo** Finland
121 O4 **Paltaniemi** Finland
121 O4 **Paltaselkä** *bay* Finland
198 A4 **Palu** Indonesia
123 M5 **Paluknys** Lithuania
215 I5 **Paluma** Qld Australia
213 J3 **Palumpa** NT Australia
187 E9 **Palur** Tamil Nadu India
124 G4 **Paluzza** Italy
194 C4 **Palwa** Myanmar
186 D5 **Palwal** Haryana India
158 E2 **Pama** Burkina Faso
159 H4 **Pama** *watercourse* Central African Republic
218 F5 **Pamamaroo Lake** NSW Australia
197 I6 **Pamana, Pulau** *island* Indonesia
196 E5 **Pamanukan** Indonesia
164 8b **Pamanzi (Petite Terre)** *island* Mayotte
163 G4 **Pambarra** Mozambique
198 A3 **Pambero** Indonesia
75 R8 **Pambrun** Saskatchewan Canada
198 F4 **Pamdai** Indonesia
197 G5 **Pamekasan** Indonesia
196 E5 **Pameungpeuk** Indonesia
133 E6 **Pamfylla** Greece
125 I4 **Pamhagen** Austria
126 E5 **Pamiers** France
183 K6 **Pamir** *lake* Tajikistan
87 N3 **Pamlico Sound** North Carolina USA
83 P2 **Pamouscachiou, Lac** *lake* Quebec Canada
85 L3 **Pampa** Texas USA
104 C4 **Pampa Blanca** Peru
108 C3 **Pampa de Agnia** Argentina
106 F3 **Pampa de Infierno** Argentina
104 c2 **Pampa del Sacramento** *range* Peru
108 C3 **Pampa Pelada** *region* Argentina
104 C4 **Pampa Redonda** Peru
127 H4 **Pamparato** Italy
106 E5 **Pampas** *region* Argentina
104 C4 **Pampas** Peru
104 C4 **Pampas** *watercourse* Peru
104 D2 **Pampeiro** Brazil
126 F4 **Pampelonne** France
164 7b **Pamplemousses** Mauritius
83 L8 **Pamplin** Virginia USA
100 C3 **Pamplona** Colombia
128 F2 **Pamplona/Irunea** Spain
222 8 **Pamua** Solomon Islands
197 H4 **Pamukan, Teluk** *bay* Indonesia
133 G5 **Pamukova** Turkey
83 M8 **Pamunkey** *watercourse* Virginia USA
142 E2 **Pan** Orkney Islands Scotland UK
106 D3 **Pan de Azúcar** Chile
107 H5 **Pan de Azúcar** Uruguay
131 C7 **Pan di Zucchero, Scoglio** *island* Sardinia Italy
181 G2 **Pana** Xizang Zizhiqu China
159 G5 **Pana** Gabon
89 H4 **Panaba** Mexico
84 E2 **Panaca** Nevada USA
83 K3 **Panache, Lake** Ontario Canada
132 D2 **Panaci** Romania
186 E6 **Panagar** Madhya Pradesh India
196 E5 **Panaitan** *island* Indonesia
133 B6 **Panaitolikon** *range* Greece
187 C8 **Panaji** Goa India
90 D5 **Panama** *country* Central America
90 E5 **Panamá** Panama
100 B2 **Panamá, Bahía de** *bay* Panama
100 B3 **Panamá, Golfo de** *bay* Panama
53 X7 **Panama Basin** *underwater feature* Pacific Ocean
90 D5 **Panama Canal** Panama
87 I5 **Panama City** Florida USA
107 H4 **Panambi** Brazil
84 D2 **Panamint Range** California USA
199 J6 **Panapompom Island** Papua New Guinea
196 F3 **Panarik** Indonesia
199 J6 **Panatinane Island** Papua New Guinea
199 J6 **Panawina Island** Papua New Guinea
195 I5 **Panay** *island* Philippines
126 E4 **Panazol** France
80 H7 **Pancake Range** Nevada USA
132 B3 **Pančevo** Serbia
77 W6 **Panchia Lake** Newfoundland and Labrador Canada
189 I4 **Panchiao** Taiwan China
85 H5 **Pancho Villa** Mexico
132 B4 **Pančicev Vrh** *mountain* Serbia
197 G3 **Pancingapan, Bukit** *mountain* Indonesia
132 B2 **Pâncota** Romania
198 F4 **Pandaidori, Kepulauan** *islands* Indonesia
195 J4 **Pandan** Philippines
196 C4 **Pandan, Selat** *strait* Singapore
196 B4 **Pandan Reservoir** Singapore
197 G4 **Pandang** Indonesia
210 inset **Pandang, Pulo** *island* Cocos (Keeling) Islands Australia
214 G4 **Pandanus** *watercourse* Qld Australia
213 G4 **Pandanus Park** WA Australia
103 C6 **Pandeiros** *watercourse* Brazil
187 D8 **Pandharpur** Maharashtra India
187 E7 **Pandhurna** Madhya Pradesh India
218 D2 **Pandie Pandie** SA Australia
104 E3 **Pando** *admin. area* Bolivia
215 H1 **Pandora Entrance** *reef* Qld Australia
138 D2 **Pandy** Gwynedd Wales UK
138 E3 **Pandy** Monmouthshire Wales UK
123 M5 **Panevežio** *admin. area* Lithuania
123 M5 **Panevėžys** Lithuania
139 H3 **Panfield** Essex England UK
123 L3 **Panga** Estonia
223 10 **Pangai** Tonga
159 G5 **Pangala** Congo
161 F5 **Pangani** *watercourse* Tanzania
139 F3 **Pangbourne** West Berkshire England UK
218 H5 **Pange** *watercourse* NSW Australia
197 H4 **Pangean** Indonesia
222 8 **Panggoe** Solomon Islands
160 D4 **Pangi** Democratic Republic of Congo
197 G5 **Pangkah, Tanjung** *cape* Indonesia
197 F4 **Pangkalanbuun** Indonesia
196 C3 **Pangkalanlunang** Indonesia
196 E4 **Pangkalpinang** Indonesia
198 B4 **Pangkalsiang, Tanjung** *cape* Indonesia
73 M5 **Pangnirtung** Nunavut Canada
160 A5 **Pango Aluquem** Angola
104 C4 **Pangoa** Peru
159 I3 **Pangonda** Central African Republic
106 C6 **Panguipulli** Chile
80 I8 **Panguitch** Utah USA
196 C3 **Pangururan** Indonesia
195 I6 **Pangutaran** *island* Philippines
195 I6 **Pangutaran Group** *islands* Philippines
85 L3 **Panhandle** Texas USA
160 D5 **Pania-Mwanga** Democratic Republic of Congo
198 F4 **Paniai, Danau** *lake* Indonesia
133 D5 **Panichkovo** Bulgaria
222 7 **Panié, Mont** *mountain* New Caledonia
100 B5 **Panintsa** Peru
186 D5 **Panipat** Haryana India
104 D6 **Paniri, Cerro** *mountain* Chile
195 H5 **Panitan** Philippines
179 K2 **Panjāb** Afghanistan
183 J6 **Panjakent** Tajikistan
Panjang *see* **West Island** Australia
196 E5 **Panjang** Indonesia
197 H3 **Panjang** *island* Indonesia
196 D3 **Panjang, Selat** *strait* Indonesia
132 B3 **Panjevac** Serbia
179 J4 **Panjgur** Pakistan
191 J4 **Panjin** Liaoning China
179 L2 **Panjshir** *admin. area* Afghanistan
121 O5 **Panka** Finland
121 Q5 **Pankajärvi** *lake* Finland
121 Q5 **Pankakoski** Finland
130 G3 **Pankasz** Hungary
193 I2 **Panke-to** *lake* Japan
186 F6 **Panki** Jharkhand India
123 P5 **Pan'kovo** Russian Federation
159 F3 **Pankshin** Nigeria
188 D3 **Panlian** Sichuan China
186 E6 **Panna** Madhya Pradesh India
212 D6 **Pannawonica** WA Australia
179 L4 **Pano Aqil** Pakistan
103 B8 **Panorama** Brazil
82 D6 **Panorama Lake** Iowa USA
133 D8 **Panormos** Greece
187 E9 **Panruti** Tamil Nadu India
181 I4 **Pansam** Myanmar
191 K4 **Panshi** Jilin China
188 D3 **Panshui** Guizhou China
138 D2 **Pant-y-dwr** Powys Wales UK
129 G2 **Pantà d'Escales** *lake* Spain
197 H4 **Pantai** Indonesia
196 D2 **Pantai Remis** Malaysia
105 G5 **Pantanal** *region* Brazil
120 M5 **Päntäne** Finland
197 J6 **Pantar** *island* Indonesia
131 D8 **Pantelleria** Italy
131 D8 **Pantelleria, Isola di** *island* Italy
131 G6 **Pantenecianni, Punta** *cape* Italy
141 H3 **Panton** Lincolnshire England UK
120 M5 **Panttila** Finland
160 B4 **Panu** Democratic Republic of Congo
89 F4 **Pánuco** Mexico
187 C7 **Panvel** Maharashtra India
188 D3 **Panzhihua** Sichuan China
160 B5 **Panzi** Democratic Republic of Congo
90 B4 **Panzós** Guatemala
131 G7 **Paola** Italy
82 D7 **Paola** Kansas USA
81 L7 **Paonia Reservoir** Colorado USA
223 14a **Paopao** French Polynesia
159 H3 **Paoua** Central African Republic
125 I4 **Pápa** Hungary
84 inset **Pāpā** Hawai'i USA
131 F6 **Papa, Monte del** *mountain* Italy
142 F1 **Papa Westray** *island* Scotland UK
84 inset **Pāpa'aloa** Hawai'i USA
103 C7 **Papagaios** Brazil
101 F2 **Papagayos, Islas** *islands* Venezuela
84 inset **Pāpa'ikou** Hawai'i USA
220 F3 **Papakura** New Zealand
89 F5 **Papaloapan** *lake* Mexico
220 G3 **Papamoa Beach** New Zealand
88 E5 **Papanoa, Morro de** *cape* Mexico
89 F4 **Papantla de Olarte** Mexico
197 G2 **Papar** Malaysia
223 14a **Papara** French Polynesia
187 F7 **Paparhahandi** Orissa India
221 D6 **Paparoa Range** New Zealand
133 D7 **Papas, Akra** *cape* Greece
104 A2 **Papayal** Peru
223 14a **Papeete** French Polynesia
104 E5 **Papel Pampa** Bolivia
124 D1 **Papenburg** Germany
223 14a **Papenoo** French Polynesia
223 14a **Papeotai** French Polynesia
123 K4 **Papes ezers** *lake* Latvia
120 inset **Papey** *island* Iceland
136 E6 **Paphos** Cyprus
142 inset **Papil** Shetland Scotland UK
123 L4 **Papilė** Lithuania
81 Q6 **Papillion** Nebraska USA
123 M4 **Papilys** Lithuania
125 L3 **Papín** Slovakia
198 E5 **Papisoi, Tanjung** *cape* Indonesia
80 H8 **Papoose Lake** Nevada USA
106 D3 **Paposo** Chile
90 C4 **Paptalaya** Honduras
199 H6 **Papua, Gulf of** Papua New Guinea
199 H5 **Papua New Guinea** *country* Oceania
106 D5 **Papudo** Chile
217 K2 **Papulankutja (Blackstone)** WA Australia
194 C3 **Papun** Myanmar
214 A7 **Papunya** NT Australia
106 D2 **Paquica, Cabo** *cape* Chile
179 I4 **Par Kūh** Iran
87 K4 **Par Pond** South Carolina USA
105 H2 **Pará** *admin. area* Brazil
197 J3 **Para** *island* Indonesia
101 H3 **Para** *admin. area* Suriname
101 I5 **Pará, Ilha do** *island* Brazil
102 B3 **Pará, Rio do** *watercourse* Brazil
103 C7 **Pará de Minas** Brazil
124 E5 **Parabiago** Italy
216 E1 **Paraburdoo** WA Australia
101 G6 **Paracari** *watercourse* Brazil
104 B4 **Paracas, Península de** *peninsula* Peru
103 C7 **Paracatu** Brazil
103 C7 **Paracatu** *watercourse* Brazil
195 G3 **Paracel Islands** *disputed territory* Asia
218 D4 **Parachilna** SA Australia
179 L2 **Parachinar** Pakistan
81 K7 **Parachute** Colorado USA
102 E3 **Paracuru** Brazil
187 G7 **Paradip** Orissa India
83 M2 **Paradis** Quebec Canada
78 J6 **Paradise** *watercourse* Newfoundland and Labrador Canada
109 10a **Paradise** Grenada
101 G3 **Paradise** Guyana
80 E7 **Paradise** California USA
219 H8 **Paradise Beach** Vic. Australia
78 J6 **Paradise River** Newfoundland and Labrador Canada
75 P6 **Paradise Valley** Alberta Canada
198 A6 **Parado** Indonesia
102 C3 **Paragominas** Brazil
80 I8 **Paragonah** Utah USA
86 F2 **Paragould** Arkansas USA
105 F4 **Paragua** *watercourse* Bolivia
101 F3 **Paragua** *watercourse* Venezuela
103 E6 **Paraguaçu** *watercourse* Brazil
100 D2 **Paraguaná, Península de** *peninsula* Venezuela
107 G2 **Paraguay** *country* South America
105 G5 **Paraguay** *watercourse* Brazil
107 G2 **Paraguay** *watercourse* Paraguay
106 F6 **Paragüil** Argentina
101 F3 **Parai-tepuí** Venezuela
102 E4 **Paraíba** *admin. area* Brazil
102 D4 **Paraibano** Brazil
105 F3 **Paraibão** Brazil
101 H5 **Paraíso** Brazil
105 G2 **Paraíso** Brazil
103 A7 **Paraíso** Brazil
91 G3 **Paraíso** Dominican Republic
89 G5 **Paraíso** Mexico
102 B5 **Paraíso do Tocantins** Brazil
106 F6 **Paraje El Gavilán** Argentina
107 G2 **Paraje Tuyuyú** Paraguay
220 F3 **Parakai** New Zealand
120 L3 **Parakka** Sweden
158 E3 **Parakou** Benin
218 C4 **Parakylia Hill** SA Australia
187 F7 **Paralakhemundi** Orissa India
133 C7 **Paralia Tyrou** Greece
199 G6 **Parama Island** Papua New Guinea
101 H3 **Paramaribo** Suriname
102 D4 **Parambu** Brazil
103 D5 **Paramirim** *watercourse* Brazil
135 AG8 **Paramushir, Ostrov** *island* Kuril Islands
106 F4 **Paraná** Argentina
107 G3 **Paraná** *watercourse* Argentina
107 I3 **Paraná** *admin. area* Brazil
103 C6 **Paraná** *watercourse* Brazil
103 C6 **Paranã** Brazil
103 C6 **Paranã, Serra Geral do** *range* Brazil
101 G5 **Paraná Madeirinha** *watercourse* Brazil
100 E5 **Parana Mirim Pirajuanana** *watercourse* Brazil
103 B9 **Paranaguá** Brazil
103 B7 **Paranaíba** Brazil
103 B7 **Paranaíba** *watercourse* Brazil
103 B8 **Paranapanema** Brazil
103 B8 **Paranapanema** *watercourse* Brazil
107 I3 **Paranapiacaba, Serra** *range* Brazil
103 A8 **Paranavaí** Brazil
198 D4 **Parang** *island* Indonesia
195 I6 **Parang** Philippines
107 H2 **Paranhos** Brazil
187 E10 **Paranki Aru** *watercourse* Sri Lanka
223 14 **Paraoa** *island* French Polynesia
103 C7 **Paraopeba** *watercourse* Brazil
221 F5 **Paraparaumu** New Zealand
105 F5 **Parapeti** *watercourse* Bolivia
222 8 **Parara** *island* Solomon Islands
86 B7 **Paras** Mexico
186 F6 **Parasi** Chhattisgarh India
186 F6 **Parasi** Jharkhand India
133 E8 **Paraspori, Akra** *cape* Greece
104 C3 **Paratari** Brazil
103 C8 **Parati** Brazil
103 D6 **Paratinga** Brazil
218 D5 **Paratoo** SA Australia
102 B4 **Parauapebas** *watercourse* Brazil
102 A3 **Parauaquara, Serra** *mountain* Brazil
105 G2 **Parauari** *watercourse* Brazil
103 B7 **Paraúna** Brazil
181 F4 **Parbatipur** Bangladesh
187 D7 **Parbhani** Maharashtra India
125 J2 **Parcice** Poland
132 E1 **Parcova** Moldova
187 C7 **Pardi** Gujarat India
132 F3 **Pardina** Romania
107 G6 **Pardo** Argentina
105 E3 **Pardo** Bolivia
107 H2 **Pardo** *watercourse* Brazil
212 E6 **Pardoo Roadhouse** WA Australia
125 H2 **Pardubice** Czech Republic
125 I3 **Pardubický Kraj** *admin. area* Czech Republic
105 G4 **Parecis** Brazil
105 F4 **Parecis, Serra dos** *range* Brazil
164 3d **Pared, Puerto de la** *bay* Canary Islands
108 B4 **Pared Norte, Cerro** *mountain* Chile
108 B4 **Pared Sur, Cerro** *mountain* Chile
128 D2 **Paredes de Nava** Spain
106 D5 **Pareditas** Argentina
106 C5 **Paredones** Chile
102 E4 **Parelhas** Brazil
126 F4 **Pareloup, Lac de** *lake* France
222 6a **Parem** *island* Federated States of Micronesia
135 AH6 **Paren'** *watercourse* Russian Federation
220 E2 **Parengarenga Harbour** New Zealand
83 M2 **Parent, Lac** *lake* Quebec Canada
221 D7 **Pareora** New Zealand
198 A5 **Parepare** Indonesia
123 P4 **Parfino** Russian Federation
187 D8 **Pargi** Andhra Pradesh India
164 2 **Pargo, Ponta do** *cape* Madeira
100 E3 **Parguaza, Serranía de** *range* Venezuela
109 18 **Parham** Antigua and Barbuda
109 inset 9 **Paria, Gulf of** Trinidad and Tobago
101 F2 **Paria, Gulf of** Venezuela
101 F2 **Paria, Península de** *peninsula* Venezuela
196 D4 **Pariaman** Indonesia
101 E5 **Parica, Lago** *lake* Brazil
101 I4 **Paricás** Brazil
105 F2 **Paricatuba, Lago** *lake* Brazil
100 A2 **Parida, Isla** *island* Panama
106 D2 **Parihuana, Laguna** *lake* Bolivia
179 K4 **Pariko** Pakistan
101 E4 **Parima, Serra** *range* Venezuela
104 D5 **Parinacota, Nevado** *mountain* Chile
104 A2 **Pariñas, Punta** *cape* Peru
218 E6 **Paringa** SA Australia
221 C6 **Paringa** *watercourse* New Zealand
221 C6 **Paringa, Lake** New Zealand
132 C2 **Parîngul Mare, Vîrful** *mountain* Romania
101 G5 **Parintins** Brazil
103 C9 **Pariquera Açu** Brazil
83 K5 **Paris** Ontario Canada
126 F2 **Paris** France
222 1a **Paris** *ruins* Kiribati
80 J5 **Paris** Idaho USA
82 H7 **Paris** Illinois USA
86 G2 **Paris** Tennessee USA
86 D4 **Paris** Texas USA
214 F7 **Parisian** *watercourse* Qld Australia
82 I3 **Parisienne, Ile** *island* Ontario Canada
196 D2 **Parit Buntar** Malaysia
90 D5 **Parita** Panama
182 H2 **Parizh** Russian Federation
143 D2 **Park** Ireland
143 F4 **Park** Ireland
85 L1 **Park** Kansas USA
82 F4 **Park Falls** Wisconsin USA
82 F8 **Park Hills** Missouri USA
81 R3 **Park Rapids** Minnesota USA
81 Q2 **Park River** North Dakota USA
121 M3 **Parkajoki** Sweden
121 M3 **Parkalompolo** Sweden
132 G2 **Parkantsy** Ukraine
78 I6 **Parke Lake** Newfoundland and Labrador Canada
84 E3 **Parker** Arizona USA
81 M7 **Parker** Colorado USA
80 J5 **Parker** Idaho USA
81 Q5 **Parker** South Dakota USA
83 K7 **Parkersburg** West Virginia USA
219 I5 **Parkes** NSW Australia
139 I3 **Parkeston** Essex England UK
142 E5 **Parkgate** Dumfries and Galloway Scotland UK
83 K5 **Parkhill** Ontario Canada
215 K7 **Parkhurst** Qld Australia
120 K3 **Parkijaure** *bay* Sweden
121 N5 **Parkkila** Finland
121 N5 **Parkkima** Finland
75 O7 **Parkland** Alberta Canada
75 U8 **Parkman** Saskatchewan Canada
84 B2 **Parksdale** California USA
83 N8 **Parksley** Virginia USA
81 Q5 **Parkston** South Dakota USA
74 I8 **Parksville** British Columbia Canada
179 M2 **Parkutta** Pakistan
109 inset 9 **Parlatuvier** Trinidad and Tobago
187 D7 **Parli** Maharashtra India
187 C8 **Parli Vaijnath** Maharashtra India
84 C2 **Parlier** California USA
124 F5 **Parma** Italy
130 D4 **Parma** *watercourse* Italy
80 G5 **Parma** Idaho USA
86 G2 **Parma** Missouri USA
83 K6 **Parma** Ohio USA
102 D3 **Parnaíba** Brazil
102 C4 **Parnaíba** *watercourse* Brazil
51 O10 **Parnaíba Ridge** *underwater feature* Atlantic Ocean
102 C5 **Parnaibinha** *watercourse* Brazil
100 D4 **Parnaiuicava** Brazil
102 E5 **Parnamirim** Brazil
102 F4 **Parnamirim** Brazil
102 D4 **Parnarama** Brazil
133 C6 **Parnassos** *mountain* Greece
221 E6 **Parnassus** New Zealand
218 C6 **Parndana** SA Australia
130 H2 **Párnica** Slovakia
133 C7 **Parnon Oros** *range* Greece
123 M3 **Pärnu** Estonia
123 M3 **Pärnu** *watercourse* Estonia
123 M3 **Pärnu Laht** *bay* Estonia
123 M3 **Pärnumaa** *admin. area* Estonia
181 F3 **Paro Dzong** Bhutan
187 D7 **Parola** Maharashtra India
104 D6 **Paroma, Cerro** *mountain* Bolivia
218 F4 **Paroo** *watercourse* NSW Australia
133 D7 **Paros** *island* Greece
80 I8 **Parowan** Utah USA
127 H4 **Parpaillon** *range* France
106 D6 **Parral** Chile
219 J5 **Parramatta** NSW Australia
88 E3 **Parras** Mexico
128 D2 **Parres** Spain
138 E4 **Parrett** *watercourse* England UK
86 H4 **Parrish** Alabama USA
90 C5 **Parrita** Costa Rica
212 G7 **Parrngurr** WA Australia
79 F10 **Parrsboro** Nova Scotia Canada
72 G4 **Parry, Cape** Northwest Territories Canada
73 K5 **Parry Bay** Nunavut Canada
72 H4 **Parry Channel** Nunavut Canada
72 H3 **Parry Islands** Northwest Territories/Nunavut Canada
74 E5 **Parry Passage** British Columbia Canada
83 K4 **Parry Sound** Ontario Canada
124 F3 **Parsberg** Germany
123 K5 **Paršežeria ežeras** *lake* Lithuania
81 N3 **Parshall** North Dakota USA
123 P5 **Parshino** Belarus
74 J5 **Parsnip** *watercourse* British Columbia Canada
80 G1 **Parson** British Columbia Canada
139 H2 **Parson Drove** Cambridgeshire England UK
82 D8 **Parsons** Kansas USA
86 G3 **Parsons** Tennessee USA
83 L7 **Parsons** West Virginia USA
214 C2 **Parsons Range** NT Australia
121 O5 **Partala** Finland
131 E8 **Partanna** Italy
120 J3 **Pårtefjällen** *mountain* Sweden
126 D3 **Parthenay** France
133 C7 **Parthénion** Greece
82 J2 **Parthia** Ontario Canada
190 F3 **Partizan** Mongolia
125 J3 **Partizánske** Slovakia
141 I3 **Partney** Lincolnshire England UK
140 E2 **Parton** Cumbria England UK
142 D5 **Parton** Dumfries and Galloway Scotland UK
138 D3 **Partrishow** Powys Wales UK
143 C3 **Partry** Ireland
187 D7 **Partur** Maharashtra India
213 K1 **Paru** NT Australia
102 A3 **Paru** *watercourse* Brazil
101 E3 **Parú, Serranía** *range* Venezuela
101 G4 **Paru de Oeste** *watercourse* Brazil
179 J4 **Pārūd** Iran
101 F3 **Paruima Mission** Guyana
101 F3 **Parupá** Venezuela
222 8 **Paruru** Solomon Islands
132 G2 **Parutyne** Ukraine
179 K2 **Parvān** *admin. area* Afghanistan
179 K4 **Parwan** Pakistan
139 F1 **Parwich** Derbyshire England UK
125 J2 **Parzymiechy** Poland
179 J2 **Pasāband** Afghanistan
84 C3 **Pasadena** California USA
86 D6 **Pasadena** Texas USA
100 A5 **Pasado, Cabo** *cape* Ecuador
100 B5 **Pasaje** Ecuador
187 F6 **Pasan** Chhattisgarh India
198 A4 **Pasangkayu** Indonesia
181 H5 **Pasanglaw** Myanmar
196 D4 **Pasarbantal** Indonesia
196 D4 **Pasarseblat** Indonesia
196 D5 **Pasarseluma** Indonesia
198 B5 **Pasarwajo** Indonesia
121 O2 **Pasasjärvi** *lake* Finland
83 N2 **Pascagama** *watercourse* Quebec Canada
86 G5 **Pascagoula** Mississippi USA
90 C4 **Pascale** Honduras
104 C3 **Pasco** *admin. area* Peru
80 F3 **Pasco** Washington USA
103 E7 **Pascoal, Monte** *mountain* Brazil
214 E4 **Pascoe Inlet** Qld Australia
210 inset **Pascoe Passage** Ashmore Reef and Cartier Island Australia
196 E5 **Paseh** Indonesia
125 G1 **Pasewalk** Germany
76 C3 **Pasfield Lake** Saskatchewan Canada
123 Q2 **Pasha** Russian Federation
182 J6 **Pashxo'rt** Uzbekistan
123 O4 **Pasiene** Latvia
181 H3 **Pasighat** Arunachal Pradesh India
196 D3 **Pasir Gudang** Malaysia
196 D2 **Pasir Mas** Malaysia
196 C4 **Pasir Panjang** *admin. area* Singapore
196 E3 **Pasir Ris** *admin. area* Singapore
196 E3 **Pasir Ris Park** Singapore
196 D3 **Pasirpengarayan** Indonesia
179 J4 **Paskūh** Iran
217 H7 **Pasley Island** WA Australia
121 N3 **Pasmajärvi** Finland
121 N2 **Pasmajärvi** *lake* Finland
106 F6 **Pasman** Argentina
218 D4 **Pasmore** *watercourse* SA Australia
179 J4 **Pasni** Pakistan
198 D4 **Paso** Indonesia
100 D3 **Paso de Guajibo** Venezuela
100 D2 **Paso de las Dos Bocas** Venezuela
100 D3 **Paso de Los Bellacos** Venezuela
106 D6 **Paso de los Indios** Argentina
107 G5 **Paso de los Toros** Uruguay
107 G3 **Paso de Patria** Paraguay
88 E2 **Paso de San Antonio** Mexico
108 B4 **Paso del Águila** Argentina
100 E2 **Paso del Ganado** Venezuela
89 F5 **Paso del Macho** Mexico
100 D3 **Paso del Toro** Colombia
100 E2 **Paso El Caballo** Venezuela
101 F2 **Paso El Jabal** Venezuela
108 C4 **Paso Gobernador Gregores** Argentina
108 B3 **Paso Guenguel** Argentina
107 G2 **Paso Horqueta** Paraguay
108 B2 **Paso Limay** Argentina
108 E2 **Paso Mayor** Argentina
101 F2 **Paso Nuevo** Venezuela
108 B4 **Paso Rodolfo Roballos** Argentina
81 M1 **Pasqua** Saskatchewan Canada
72 I8 **Pasquia Hills** Saskatchewan Canada
140 A3 **Pass of Kilbride** Ireland
197 J6 **Passabe** Timor-Leste (East Timor)
143 F4 **Passage East** Ireland
212 C6 **Passage Islands** WA Australia
143 D5 **Passage West** Ireland
105 G2 **Passagem** Brazil
102 D4 **Passagem Franca** Brazil
101 F5 **Passarão, Ilhas** *islands* Brazil
124 G3 **Passau** Germany
127 H3 **Passavant** France
131 F8 **Passero, Capo** *cape* Italy
214 E4 **Passmore** *watercourse* Qld Australia
107 H4 **Passo Fundo** Brazil
107 H4 **Passo Real, Barragem** *lake* Brazil
103 C8 **Passos** Brazil
125 H1 **Passow** Germany
195 F3 **Passu Keah** *island* Paracel Islands
127 H4 **Passy** France
123 N5 **Pastavy** Belarus
100 B5 **Pastaza** *admin. area* Ecuador
100 B5 **Pastaza** *watercourse* Ecuador
100 B4 **Pasto** Colombia
105 F2 **Pasto Grande** Brazil
89 F6 **Pastoría, Laguna de** *lake* Mexico
105 E6 **Pastos** Bolivia
108 B3 **Pastos Blancos** Argentina
102 C4 **Pastos Bons** Brazil
85 J3 **Pastura** New Mexico USA
130 D4 **Pasubio, Monte** *mountain* Italy
197 G5 **Pasuruan** Indonesia
123 M4 **Pasvalys** Lithuania
123 L4 **Pašvitinys** Lithuania
132 A2 **Pásztó** Hungary
86 D4 **Pat Mayse Lake** Texas USA
104 D4 **Pata** Bolivia
159 I3 **Pata** Central African Republic
195 I6 **Pata** *island* Philippines
154 D6 **Pata** Senegal
104 C4 **Pata Corral** Peru
104 E5 **Patacamaya** Bolivia
106 D2 **Patache, Punta** *cape* Chile
108 B4 **Patagonia** *region* Argentina
84 G5 **Patagonia** Arizona USA
196 D5 **Patah, Gunung** *mountain* Indonesia
128 B4 **Pataias** Portugal
179 I3 **Patambar** Iran
78 C6 **Patamisk, Lac** *lake* Quebec Canada
187 E7 **Patan** Chhattisgarh India
186 C6 **Patan** Gujarat India
187 E6 **Patan** Madhya Pradesh India
186 F5 **Patan** Nepal
121 M5 **Patanan tekojärvi** *lake* Finland
159 F3 **Patani** Nigeria
79 E8 **Patapédia** *watercourse* Quebec Canada
104 C3 **Patarcocha, Cerro** *mountain* Peru
132 E3 **Pătârlagele** Romania
101 G3 **Pataro** *watercourse* Guyana
123 N3 **Pataste** Estonia
126 E2 **Patay** France
83 O6 **Patchogue** New York USA
138 E3 **Patchway** South Gloucestershire England UK
161 G4 **Paté** *island* Kenya
89 I2 **Pate Lake** Florida USA
Patea *see* **Doubtful Sound** New Zealand
159 F3 **Pategi** Nigeria
141 G2 **Pateley Bridge** North Yorkshire England UK
125 I1 **Paterek** Poland

130 E3 **Paternion** Austria
131 F6 **Paternopoli** Italy
80 F2 **Pateros** Washington USA
130 E2 **Patersdorf** Germany
218 H3 **Paterson** *watercourse* Qld Australia
75 V5 **Paterson** Manitoba Canada
83 N6 **Paterson** New Jersey USA
216 G2 **Paterson, Mount** WA Australia
221 C8 **Paterson Inlet** New Zealand
212 G6 **Paterson Range** WA Australia
187 F6 **Pathalgaon** Chhattisgarh India
186 D4 **Pathankot** Punjab India
187 D7 **Pathardi** Maharashtra India
186 E6 **Patharia** Madhya Pradesh India
194 B3 **Pathein (Bassein)** Myanmar
81 L5 **Pathfinder Reservoir** Wyoming USA
194 C5 **Pathiu** Thailand
194 D4 **Pathum Thani** Thailand
197 F5 **Pati** Indonesia
222 5 **Pati Point** Guam
186 D4 **Patiala** Punjab India
198 C4 **Patinti, Selat** *strait* Indonesia
133 E7 **Patmos** Greece
133 E7 **Patmos** *island* Greece
186 F6 **Patna** Bihar India
187 F7 **Patnagarh** Orissa India
136 G5 **Patnos** Turkey
103 A9 **Pato Branco** Brazil
187 D7 **Patoda** Maharashtra India
82 H7 **Patoka Lake** Indiana USA
121 N3 **Patokoski** Finland
135 Y7 **Patomskoye Nagor'ye** *region* Russian Federation
161 E3 **Patongo** Uganda
133 A5 **Patos** Albania
102 E4 **Patos** Brazil
107 I4 **Patos, Lagoa dos** *lake* Brazil
103 C7 **Patos de Minas** Brazil
106 E4 **Patquía** Argentina
133 B6 **Patra** Greece
100 D2 **Patrecitos** Venezuela
75 P7 **Patricia** Alberta Canada
85 K4 **Patricia** Texas USA
218 B4 **Patricia, Lake** SA Australia
108 A4 **Patricio Lynch, Isla** *island* Chile
141 H3 **Patrington** East Riding of Yorkshire England UK
58 S1 **Patriot Hills (Chile)** *research station* Antarctica
103 C7 **Patrocínio** Brazil
198 A5 **Pattalasang** Indonesia
194 D6 **Pattani** Thailand
194 D6 **Pattani** *admin. area* Thailand
140 F2 **Patterdale** Cumbria England UK
80 E8 **Patterson** California USA
87 J5 **Patterson** Georgia USA
222 7 **Patteson Passage** *strait* Vanuatu
186 F6 **Patti** Uttar Pradesh India
131 F7 **Patti** Italy
131 F7 **Patti, Golfo di** *bay* Italy
187 D8 **Pattikonda** Andhra Pradesh India
221 6 **Pattisson, Cape** Chatham Islands New Zealand
53 U4 **Patton Escarpment** *underwater feature* Pacific Ocean
53 R2 **Patton Seamount** *underwater feature* Pacific Ocean
187 E9 **Pattukkottai** Tamil Nadu India
72 G7 **Pattullo, Mount** British Columbia Canada
102 E4 **Patu** Brazil
75 R5 **Patuanak** Saskatchewan Canada
100 B5 **Patuca** Ecuador
89 I6 **Patuca** *watercourse* Honduras
90 C4 **Patuca, Punta** *cape* Honduras
187 D7 **Patur** Maharashtra India
83 M7 **Patuxent** *watercourse* Maryland USA
58 T1 **Patuxent Range** Antarctica
88 E5 **Pátzcuaro, Lago de** *lake* Mexico
126 D5 **Pau** France
103 E6 **Pau Brasil** Brazil
105 G5 **Pau Prêto** Brazil
220 F3 **Pauanui** New Zealand
101 H3 **Paubasoe** Suriname
132 C2 **Păuca** Romania
104 D4 **Paucartambo** Peru
126 D4 **Pauillac** France
104 E2 **Pauini** Brazil
104 D2 **Pauini** *watercourse* Brazil
181 H5 **Pauk** Myanmar
181 H5 **Paukhaung** Myanmar
181 G5 **Pauktaw** Myanmar
138 B4 **Paul** Cornwall England UK
78 H4 **Paul Island** Newfoundland and Labrador Canada
216 E7 **Paul Valley** WA Australia
72 G5 **Paulatuk** Northwest Territories Canada
84 F3 **Paulden** Arizona USA
102 F4 **Paulista** Brazil
102 E5 **Paulo Afonso** Brazil
163 F5 **Paulpietersburg** South Africa
83 M8 **Pauls Crossroads** Virginia USA
194 C3 **Paung** Myanmar
181 H4 **Paungbyin** Myanmar
194 B3 **Paungde** Myanmar
187 E7 **Pauni** Maharashtra India
186 E4 **Pauri** Uttaranchal India
124 G1 **Pausin** Germany
120 J4 **Pauträsk** Sweden
120 J4 **Pauträsket** *lake* Sweden
84 inset **Pa'uwela** Hawai'i USA
223 13a **Pava** *island* Tuvalu
121 P2 **Pavdejarvi** *lake* Finland
178 F2 **Pāveh** Iran
139 G2 **Pavenham** Bedfordshire England UK
124 E5 **Pavia** Italy
74 K7 **Pavilion** British Columbia Canada
139 H5 **Pavilly** France
125 M2 **Pavitstsye** Belarus
132 F1 **Pavlivka** Ukraine
183 L3 **Pavlodar** Kazakhstan
183 M3 **Pavlodarskaya oblast'** *admin. area* Kazakhstan
72 C7 **Pavlof Volcano** Alaska USA
183 L2 **Pavlogradka** Russian Federation
136 E3 **Pavlohrad** Ukraine
183 K3 **Pavlovka** Kazakhstan
182 G2 **Pavlovka** Russian Federation
123 J5 **Pavlovo** Russian Federation
182 D2 **Pavlovo** Russian Federation
87 J5 **Pavo** Georgia USA
123 M5 **Pavoverė** Lithuania
222 8 **Pavuvu** *island* Solomon Islands
123 O3 **Pavy** Russian Federation
77 R3 **Pavy, Lac** *lake* Quebec Canada
160 D3 **Pawa** Democratic Republic of Congo
196 B5 **Pawai, Pulau** *island* Singapore
197 F4 **Pawan** *watercourse* Indonesia
82 C8 **Pawhuska** Oklahoma USA
75 U5 **Pawistik** Manitoba Canada
125 K1 **Pawłowo** Poland
81 O7 **Pawnee** *watercourse* Kansas USA
81 Q8 **Pawnee** Oklahoma USA
86 C6 **Pawnee** Texas USA
81 Q6 **Pawnee City** Nebraska USA
81 P7 **Pawnee Rock** Kansas USA
83 P6 **Pawtucket** Rhode Island USA
194 C4 **Pawut** Myanmar
85 N1 **Paxico** Kansas USA
133 B6 **Paxoi** Greece
133 B6 **Paxoi** *island* Greece
87 H5 **Paxton** Florida USA
82 G6 **Paxton** Illinois USA
134 N5 **Pay-Khoy, Khrebet** *range* Russian Federation
198 C3 **Payahe** Indonesia
196 D4 **Payakumbuh** Indonesia
100 B4 **Payán** Colombia
182 J6 **Payariq** Uzbekistan
127 H3 **Payerne** Switzerland
80 G4 **Payette** Idaho USA
77 U3 **Payne, Baie** *bay* Quebec Canada
73 L7 **Payne, Lac** *lake* Quebec Canada
219 Q11 **Payne Bay** Tas. Australia
216 E4 **Paynes Find** WA Australia
81 R4 **Paynesville** Minnesota USA
197 G3 **Payong, Tanjong** *cape* Malaysia
126 D3 **Pays de la Loire** *admin. area* France
107 G5 **Paysandú** Uruguay
107 G5 **Paysandú** *admin. area* Uruguay
84 G3 **Payson** Arizona USA
75 U5 **Payuk** Manitoba Canada
106 D6 **Payún, Cerro** *volcano* Argentina
187 D9 **Payyannur** Kerala India
88 C3 **Paz, Bahía de la** *bay* Mexico
106 D1 **Paza, Cerro de** *mountain* Chile
103 E5 **Paza, Ponta** *cape* Brazil
136 G5 **Pazar** Turkey
132 D4 **Pazardzhik** *admin. area* Bulgaria
133 F6 **Pazarlar** Turkey
130 E4 **Pazin** Croatia
125 J3 **Pcim** Poland
223 10a **Pea** Tonga
103 A8 **Peabiru** Brazil
81 Q7 **Peabody** Kansas USA
72 H7 **Peace** *watercourse* Alberta Canada
72 G7 **Peace** *watercourse* British Columbia Canada
87 J7 **Peace** *watercourse* Florida USA
75 O3 **Peace Point** Alberta Canada
74 M4 **Peace River** Alberta Canada
139 G4 **Peacehaven** East Sussex England UK
84 F3 **Peach Springs** Arizona USA
74 L8 **Peachland** British Columbia Canada
87 I4 **Peachtree City** Georgia USA
164 5a **Peak, The** *mountain* Ascension
216 G6 **Peak Charles** WA Australia
215 I7 **Peak Vale** Qld Australia
218 B3 **Peake** SA Australia
218 B3 **Peake** *watercourse* SA Australia
195 H5 **Peaked Point** Philippines
121 O2 **Peäldujävri** *lake* Finland
84 D3 **Pearblossom** California USA
213 J3 **Pearce Point** NT Australia
128 C2 **Peares, Embalse dos** *lake* Spain
86 F4 **Pearl** Mississippi USA
89 H2 **Pearl** *watercourse* Mississippi USA
52 O5 **Pearl and Hermes Atoll** *reef* USA
84 inset **Pearl Harbor** Hawai'i USA
86 D6 **Pearland** Texas USA
86 B6 **Pearsall** Texas USA
87 J5 **Pearson** Georgia USA
218 B5 **Pearson Isles** SA Australia
195 G5 **Pearson Reef** Spratly Islands
73 I3 **Peary Channel** Nunavut Canada
73 O2 **Peary Land** *region* Greenland
86 B3 **Pease** *watercourse* Texas USA
212 E6 **Peawah** *watercourse* WA Australia
76 M5 **Peawanuck** Ontario Canada
163 G3 **Pebane** Mozambique
109 7 **Pebble Island** Falkland Islands
197 F5 **Pecangakan** Indonesia
103 D7 **Peçanha** Brazil
132 F3 **Peceneaga** Romania
77 P6 **Pêche, Rivière la** *watercourse* Quebec Canada
132 E3 **Pechea** Romania
121 Q2 **Pechenga** Russian Federation
132 D1 **Pechenizhyn** Ukraine
134 M5 **Pechora** Russian Federation
134 M6 **Pechora** *watercourse* Russian Federation
134 M5 **Pechorskaya Guba** *bay* Russian Federation
134 M5 **Pechorskoye More** *sea* Russian Federation
123 N4 **Pechory** Russian Federation
132 B2 **Pecica** Romania
132 B3 **Peciu Nou** Romania
158 A2 **Pecixe, Ilha de** *island* Guinea-Bissau
131 C7 **Pecora, Capo** *cape* Sardinia Italy
131 D5 **Pecoraro, Punta del** *cape* Italy
85 J3 **Pecos** New Mexico USA
85 J3 **Pecos** *watercourse* New Mexico USA
85 K5 **Pecos** Texas USA
85 K5 **Pecos** *watercourse* Texas USA
124 B2 **Pecq** Belgium
125 J4 **Pécs** Hungary
90 D6 **Pedasí** Panama
219 R11 **Pedder, Lake** Tas. Australia
162 E6 **Peddie** South Africa
91 G3 **Pedernales** Dominican Republic
86 B5 **Pedernales** *watercourse* Texas USA
106 D3 **Pedernales, Salar de** *pan* Chile
122 H5 **Pedersker** Denmark
121 M5 **Pedersöre** Finland
198 C3 **Pediwang** Indonesia
102 E5 **Pedra** Brazil
103 D7 **Pedra Azul** Brazil
131 C6 **Pedra Bianca, Punta** *cape* Sardinia Italy
102 E4 **Pedra Branca** Brazil
105 F3 **Pedra Branca** Brazil
101 I4 **Pedra Branca do Amapari** Brazil
154 B5 **Pedra Lume** Cape Verde
105 F4 **Pedras Negras** Brazil
103 C8 **Pedregulho** Brazil
101 I5 **Pedreira** Brazil
102 B5 **Pedro Afonso** Brazil
53 Y6 **Pedro Bank** *underwater feature* Caribbean Sea
100 A5 **Pedro Carbo** Ecuador
88 E3 **Pedro Carrizales** Mexico
102 D4 **Pedro II** Brazil
107 H2 **Pedro Juan Cabellero** Paraguay
106 F6 **Pedro Luro** Argentina
128 E5 **Pedro-Martínez** Spain
102 F4 **Pedro Velho** Brazil
129 F3 **Pedrola** Spain
87 L3 **Pee Dee** *watercourse* South Carolina USA
218 E6 **Peebinga** SA Australia
142 E5 **Peebles** Scottish Borders Scotland UK
218 B1 **Peebles, Mount** NT Australia
212 C6 **Peedamulla** WA Australia
74 K4 **Peejay** British Columbia Canada
72 F5 **Peel** *watercourse* Yukon Territory Canada
140 D2 **Peel** Isle of Man UK
221 D6 **Peel Forest** New Zealand
73 J4 **Peel Sound** Nunavut Canada
125 G1 **Peene** *watercourse* Germany
127 G1 **Peer** Belgium
218 C2 **Peera Peera Poolanna Lake** SA Australia
216 D7 **Peerabeelup** WA Australia
75 S8 **Peerless** Montana USA
75 N6 **Peers** Alberta Canada
218 F4 **Peery Lake** NSW Australia
81 N6 **Peetz** Colorado USA
133 B5 **Péfkos** Greece
128 E5 **Pegalajar** Spain
219 P9 **Pegarah** Tas. Australia
221 B8 **Pegasus, Port** New Zealand
221 E6 **Pegasus Bay** New Zealand
130 D2 **Pegnitz** Germany
128 B4 **Pego do Altar, Barragem do** *lake* Portugal
Pegu *see* **Bago** Myanmar
198 E3 **Pegun** *island* Indonesia
139 I3 **Pegwell Bay** England UK
158 E2 **Péhonko** Benin
106 F5 **Pehuajó** Argentina
189 G1 **Peicheng** Jiangsu China
142 B3 **Peinchorran** Highland Scotland UK
108 B5 **Peineta, Cerro** *mountain* Argentina
130 D3 **Peio** Italy
133 C7 **Peiraias** Greece
124 F4 **Peiting** Germany
103 B6 **Peixe** *watercourse* Brazil
107 J2 **Peixoto, Represa** *lake* Brazil
196 E3 **Pejantan** *island* Indonesia
197 F5 **Pekalongan** Indonesia
196 D3 **Pekan** Malaysia
196 D3 **Pekanbaru** Indonesia
121 P4 **Pekankylä** Finland
121 M3 **Pekanpäa** Finland
77 V6 **Pékans** *watercourse* Quebec Canada
221 E6 **Peketa** New Zealand
82 G6 **Pekin** Illinois USA
Peking *see* **Beijing** China
121 O3 **Pekkala** Finland
135 AJ5 **Pekul'ney, Khrebet** *range* Russian Federation
108 B3 **Pelados, Cerros** *mountain* Argentina
131 E9 **Pelagie, Isole** *island* Italy
133 B5 **Pelagonija** *region* Macedonia
196 D3 **Pelalawan** Indonesia
196 F4 **Pelapis** *island* Indonesia
179 K4 **Pelar** Pakistan
197 H3 **Pelawanbesar** Indonesia
100 C2 **Pelaya** Colombia
104 D4 **Pelechuco** Bolivia
109 I4 **Pelée, Montagne** *volcano* Martinique
222 3 **Peleliu** *island* Palau
197 I4 **Peleng** *island* Indonesia
198 B4 **Peleng, Selat** *strait* Indonesia
198 B4 **Peleng, Teluk** *bay* Indonesia
160 C4 **Pelenge** Democratic Republic of Congo
86 H4 **Pelham** Alabama USA
87 I5 **Pelham** Georgia USA
125 H3 **Pelhřimov** Czech Republic
78 B3 **Pélican, Lac du** *lake* Quebec Canada
109 I8 **Pelican Bay** Antigua and Barbuda
75 O5 **Pelican Lake** Alberta Canada
82 E2 **Pelican Lake** Minnesota USA
75 O5 **Pelican Mountains** Alberta Canada
75 T5 **Pelican Narrows** Saskatchewan Canada
81 Q3 **Pelican Rapids** Minnesota USA
214 D3 **Pelican Spit** NT Australia
100 B5 **Pelileo** Ecuador
88 D2 **Pelillo** Mexico
133 B5 **Pelister** *mountain* Macedonia
87 H4 **Pell City** Alabama USA
133 C5 **Pélla** Greece
162 C5 **Pella** South Africa
108 D2 **Pellegrini, Lago** *lake* Argentina
199 G4 **Pelleluhu Islands** Papua New Guinea
130 E4 **Pellestrina, Isola di** *island* Italy
130 B4 **Pellice** *watercourse* Italy
214 C8 **Pellinore, Mount** NT Australia
121 N3 **Pello** Finland
122 E5 **Pellworm** *island* Germany
72 F6 **Pelly** *watercourse* Yukon Territory Canada
73 J5 **Pelly Bay** Nunavut Canada
74 F1 **Pelly Lakes** Yukon Territory Canada
74 E2 **Pelly Mountains** Yukon Territory Canada
197 H5 **Pelokang** *island* Indonesia
133 C7 **Peloponnisos** *admin. area* Greece
218 G4 **Pelora Lake** NSW Australia
131 F7 **Peloro, Capo** *cape* Italy
221 E5 **Pelorus** *watercourse* New Zealand
221 E5 **Pelorus Sound** New Zealand
107 H4 **Pelotas** Brazil
216 C4 **Pelsaert Group** *islands* WA Australia
216 C4 **Pelsaert Island** WA Australia
121 N2 **Peltovuoma** Finland
83 Q4 **Pemadumcook Lake** Maine USA
181 G3 **Pemagatsel** Bhutan
198 B4 **Pemali, Tanjung** *cape* Indonesia
196 F3 **Pemangkat** Indonesia
196 C3 **Pematangsiantar** Indonesia
163 H2 **Pemba** Mozambique
161 F5 **Pemba Island** *island* Tanzania
161 F4 **Pemba North** *admin. area* Tanzania
161 F5 **Pemba South** *admin. area* Tanzania
216 E7 **Pemberton** WA Australia
80 D1 **Pemberton Meadows** British Columbia Canada
75 M6 **Pembina** *watercourse* Alberta Canada
81 Q2 **Pembina** North Dakota USA
82 H4 **Pembine** Wisconsin USA
199 F5 **Pembre** Indonesia
138 C3 **Pembrey** Carmarthenshire Wales UK
138 E2 **Pembridge** Herefordshire England UK
83 M4 **Pembroke** Ontario Canada
109 inset 9 **Pembroke** Trinidad and Tobago
138 C3 **Pembroke** Pembrokeshire Wales UK
87 K4 **Pembroke** Georgia USA
86 H2 **Pembroke** Kentucky USA
77 O1 **Pembroke, Cape** Nunavut Canada
87 K7 **Pembroke Pines** Florida USA
138 C3 **Pembrokeshire** *admin. area* Wales UK
219 K4 **Pembrooke** NSW Australia
197 G4 **Pembuanghulu** Indonesia
139 H3 **Pembury** Kent England UK
127 K2 **Pemfling** Germany
197 F4 **Pemuar** Indonesia
187 C7 **Pen** Maharashtra India
181 G5 **Pen** *watercourse* Myanmar
138 C1 **Pen-y-groes** Gwynedd Wales UK
138 D1 **Pen-y-stryt** Denbighshire Wales UK
85 I6 **Peña Blanca** Mexico
100 B4 **Peña Colorada** Colombia
128 E2 **Peñacerrada** Spain
128 D3 **Peñafiel** Spain
109 inset 9 **Penal** Trinidad and Tobago
109 inset 9 **Penal-Débé** *admin. area* Trinidad and Tobago
128 E3 **Peñalara, Pico** *mountain* Spain
102 C3 **Penalva** Brazil
198 E5 **Penambulai** *island* Indonesia
103 B8 **Penápolis** Brazil
128 D3 **Peñaranda de Bracamonte** Spain
218 F6 **Penarie** NSW Australia
128 E4 **Peñarroya, Embalse de** *lake* Spain
138 D3 **Penarth** Vale of Glamorgan Wales UK
108 C5 **Peñas, Cabo** *cape* Argentina
128 D2 **Peñas, Cabo de** *cape* Spain
108 A4 **Penas, Golfo de** *bay* Chile
101 F2 **Peñas, Punta** *cape* Venezuela
83 M6 **Penbrook** Pennsylvania USA
138 C2 **Penbryn** Ceredigion Wales UK
138 C2 **Pencarreg** Carmarthenshire Wales UK
80 G2 **Pend Oreille, Lake** Idaho USA
159 H3 **Pendé** *watercourse* Central African Republic
158 B3 **Pendembu** Sierra Leone
102 E4 **Pendências** Brazil
212 G4 **Pender Bay** WA Australia
138 C3 **Pendine** Carmarthenshire Wales UK
80 F4 **Pendleton** Oregon USA
196 D4 **Pendopo** Indonesia
187 E6 **Pendra** Chhattisgarh India
160 D4 **Pene-Mende** Democratic Republic of Congo
196 F4 **Penebangan** *island* Indonesia
189 H4 **P'eng-Hu Tao** *island* Taiwan China
187 E7 **Penganga** *watercourse* Maharashtra India
162 F4 **Penge** South Africa
196 F3 **Pengiki** *island* Indonesia
191 I5 **Penglai** Shandong China
107 I3 **Penha** Brazil
126 B2 **Penhir, Pointe de** *cape* France
128 B4 **Peniche** Portugal
142 E5 **Penicuik** Midlothian Scotland UK
197 G6 **Penida** *island* Indonesia
127 K1 **Penig** Germany
129 G3 **Peñíscola** Spain
131 F8 **Penisola Magnisi** *cape* Italy
141 G3 **Penistone** South Yorkshire England UK
89 G5 **Peñitas, Presa** *lake* Mexico
102 C5 **Penitente, Serra do** *range* Brazil
125 H1 **Penkun** Germany
138 C2 **Penllech** Gwynedd Wales UK
138 D1 **Penmachno** Conwy Wales UK
138 D2 **Penmaenpool** Gwynedd Wales UK
126 B3 **Penmarch** France
126 B3 **Penmarch, Pointe de** *cape* France
140 D3 **Penmon** Isle of Anglesey Wales UK
187 E9 **Pennadam** Tamil Nadu India
138 D2 **Pennal** Gwynedd Wales UK
75 Q7 **Pennant** Saskatchewan Canada
138 C2 **Pennant** Ceredigion Wales UK
138 D2 **Pennant** Powys Wales UK
138 D2 **Pennant-Melangell** Powys Wales UK
138 C3 **Pennard** Swansea Wales UK
127 K5 **Penne** Italy
131 G6 **Penne, Punta** *cape* Italy
214 F2 **Pennefather** *watercourse* Qld Australia
58 M2 **Pennel Bank** *underwater feature* Ross Sea
58 L2 **Pennell Coast** Antarctica
218 C6 **Penneshaw** SA Australia
87 K6 **Penney Farms** Florida USA
141 F2 **Pennines** *range* England UK
83 K7 **Pennsboro** West Virginia USA
70 **Pennsylvania** *admin. area* USA
74 K6 **Penny** British Columbia Canada
58 K1 **Penny Point** Antarctica
76 I4 **Pennycutaway** *watercourse* Manitoba Canada
83 Q4 **Penobscot** *watercourse* Maine USA
83 Q4 **Penobscot Bay** Maine USA
218 E7 **Penola** SA Australia
88 D3 **Peñón Blanco** Mexico
129 G4 **Peñón de Ifach** *cape* Spain
217 M5 **Penong** SA Australia
90 D5 **Penonomé** Panama
138 C2 **Penrhos** Gwynedd Wales UK
138 D3 **Penrhos** Powys Wales UK
220 1 **Penrhyn (Tongareva)** *island* Cook Islands New Zealand
53 Q8 **Penrhyn Atoll** *reef* Cook Islands New Zealand
53 Q8 **Penrhyn Basin** *underwater feature* Pacific Ocean
219 J5 **Penrith** NSW Australia
140 F2 **Penrith** Cumbria England UK
215 J6 **Penrith Island** Qld Australia
138 B4 **Penryn** Cornwall England UK
86 H5 **Pensacola** Florida USA
86 H5 **Pensacola Bay** Florida USA
58 U1 **Pensacola Mountains** Antarctica
105 H4 **Pensão Sêca** Brazil
218 F7 **Penshurst** Vic. Australia
186 D4 **Pensi La** *pass* Jammu and Kashmir India/Pakistan
197 H2 **Pensiangan** Malaysia
78 K6 **Pensons Arm** Newfoundland and Labrador Canada
133 B5 **Pentalofos** Greece
222 7 **Pentecost** *island* Vanuatu
77 V7 **Pentecôte** *watercourse* Quebec Canada
74 L8 **Penticton** British Columbia Canada
215 H6 **Pentland** Qld Australia
142 E2 **Pentland Firth** *bay* Scotland UK
142 E5 **Pentland Hills** *range* Scotland UK
142 F2 **Pentland Skerries** *islands* Scotland UK
140 D3 **Pentraeth** Isle of Anglesey Wales UK
138 D2 **Pentre** Powys Wales UK
138 D3 **Pentre-bâch** Powys Wales UK
138 C3 **Pentre Galar** Pembrokeshire Wales UK
138 C3 **Pentre-Morgan** Carmarthenshire Wales UK
138 D1 **Pentrefoelas** Conwy Wales UK
82 H5 **Pentwater** Michigan USA
123 M3 **Penu** Estonia
196 E4 **Penuba** Indonesia
196 E4 **Penuguan** Indonesia
196 D2 **Penunjuk, Tanjung** *cape* Malaysia
138 C2 **Penuwch** Ceredigion Wales UK
85 K5 **Penwell** Texas USA
138 D2 **Peny-bryn** Gwynedd Wales UK
138 D2 **Penybont** Powys Wales UK
138 D2 **Penybontfawr** Powys Wales UK
75 R2 **Penylan Lake** Northwest Territories Canada
140 D3 **Penysarn** Isle of Anglesey Wales UK
198 C5 **Penyu, Kepulauan** *islands* Indonesia
196 F5 **Penyu, Tulek** *bay* Indonesia
182 E2 **Penza** Russian Federation
81 M1 **Penzance** Saskatchewan Canada
138 B4 **Penzance** Cornwall England UK
124 F4 **Penzberg** Germany
182 D3 **Penzenskaya Oblast'** *admin. area* Russian Federation
135 AI6 **Penzhina** *watercourse* Russian Federation
135 AH6 **Penzhinskaya Guba** *bay* Russian Federation
135 AI6 **Penzhinskiy Khrebet** *range* Russian Federation
124 G1 **Penzlin** Germany
84 F4 **Peoria** Arizona USA
82 G6 **Peoria** Illinois USA
85 K4 **Pep** New Mexico USA
133 B5 **Pepellash** Albania
77 S7 **Pépeshquasati** *watercourse* Quebec Canada
58 J2 **Pépin, Cape** Antarctica
107 H3 **Pepiri Guaçú** *watercourse* Argentina
133 E5 **Peplos** Greece
213 K3 **Peppimenarti** NT Australia
100 C3 **Peque** Colombia
88 B3 **Pequeña, Punta** *cape* Mexico
103 D6 **Pequeno, Verde** *watercourse* Brazil
82 D3 **Pequot Lakes** Minnesota USA
130 G3 **Pér** Hungary
121 O3 **Perä-Posio** Finland
196 D2 **Perak** *admin. area* Malaysia
123 K1 **Perälä** Finland
128 D4 **Peraleda del Zaucejo** Spain
129 F3 **Perales del Alfambra** Spain
106 F6 **Peralta** Argentina
128 F2 **Peralta** Spain
133 D8 **Perama** Greece
161 F6 **Peramiho** Tanzania
121 P4 **Peranka** Finland
121 N5 **Peränne** *lake* Finland
121 M5 **Peräseinäjoki** Finland
196 C3 **Perbaungan** Indonesia
79 F8 **Percé** Quebec Canada
126 E2 **Perche, Collines du** *range* France
130 G2 **Perchtoldsdorf** Austria
142 F3 **Percie** Aberdeenshire Scotland UK
213 H6 **Percival Lakes** WA Australia
82 G7 **Percy** Illinois USA
215 K6 **Percy Isles** Qld Australia
102 C5 **Perdida** *watercourse* Brazil
107 G2 **Perdido, Serra do** *range* Brazil
86 H5 **Perdido Bay** Alabama USA
107 J2 **Perdões** Brazil
132 C1 **Perechyn** Ukraine
100 C3 **Pereira** Colombia
103 B8 **Pereira Barreto** Brazil
182 D3 **Perelazovskiy** Russian Federation
182 F3 **Perelyub** Russian Federation
58 H2 **Peremennyy, Cape** Antarctica
132 F1 **Peremoga** Ukraine
187 C9 **Peremul Par** *island* Lakshadweep India
104 C3 **Perené** Peru
216 E4 **Perenjori** WA Australia
132 F2 **Peresecina** Moldova
125 M2 **Perespa** Ukraine
132 D3 **Peretu** Romania
183 L6 **Pereval Akbaytal** *pass* Tajikistan
184 F4 **Pereval Bedel'** *pass* Xinjiang Uygur Zizhiqu China
183 M5 **Pereval Bedel'** *pass* Kyrgyzstan
183 L6 **Pereval Chyyyrchyk Asnuusu** *pass* Kyrgyzstan
184 E5 **Pereval Karaart** *pass* Xinjiang Uygur Zizhiqu China
183 L6 **Pereval Karaart** *pass* Tajikistan
182 E5 **Pereval Khalakhurkats** *pass* Russian Federation
184 E5 **Pereval Kipchak** *pass* Xinjiang Uygur Zizhiqu China
183 L6 **Pereval Kipchak** *pass* Kyrgyzstan
182 D5 **Pereval Klukhorskiy** *pass* Russian Federation
182 D5 **Pereval Sharivtsek** *pass* Russian Federation
183 L6 **Pereval Taldyk** *pass* Kyrgyzstan
184 E5 **Pereval Turugart** *pass* Xinjiang Uygur Zizhiqu China
183 L6 **Pereval Turugart** *pass* Kyrgyzstan
183 L6 **Pereval Urum-Bash** *pass* Kyrgyzstan
182 D2 **Perevoz** Russian Federation
132 F1 **Pereyma** Ukraine
125 H3 **Perg** Austria
106 F5 **Pergamino** Argentina
127 K5 **Pergola** Italy
81 R3 **Perham** Minnesota USA
196 D2 **Perhentian Besar, Pulao** *island* Malaysia
121 N5 **Perho** Finland
121 M5 **Perhonjoki** *watercourse* Finland
83 P2 **Péribonka** *watercourse* Quebec Canada
79 C7 **Péribonka, Lac** *lake* Quebec Canada
106 E3 **Perico** Argentina
90 D2 **Perico** Cuba
84 G4 **Peridot** Arizona USA
126 D2 **Périers** France
126 E4 **Périgueux** France
100 C2 **Perija, Sierra de** *range* Venezuela
124 E5 **Perino** Italy
105 F3 **Periquitos** Brazil
132 D3 **Periş** Romania
132 E3 **Perişoru** Romania
133 D6 **Peristera** *island* Greece
133 C6 **Peristerio** Greece
108 B4 **Perito Moreno** Argentina
133 B6 **Perivolion** Greece
196 E4 **Perkat, Tanjung** *cape* Indonesia
125 M1 **Perkavičy** Belarus
86 C3 **Perkins** Oklahoma USA
100 B2 **Perlas, Archipíelago de las** *islands* Panama
90 D4 **Perlas, Laguna de** *lake* Nicaragua
90 D4 **Perlas, Punta de** *cape* Nicaragua
124 F1 **Perleberg** Germany
81 Q3 **Perley** Minnesota USA
132 B3 **Perlez** Serbia
196 D2 **Perlis** *admin. area* Malaysia
134 M7 **Perm'** Russian Federation
182 G1 **Perm'** Russian Federation
133 B5 **Përmet** Albania
134 M7 **Permskiy Kray** *admin. area* Russian Federation
130 F4 **Permuda** Croatia
127 L4 **Permuda** *island* Croatia
123 N2 **Pernaja** Finland
102 E5 **Pernambuco** *admin. area* Brazil
51 P10 **Pernambuco Plain** *underwater feature* Atlantic Ocean
51 O10 **Pernambuco Seamounts** *underwater feature* Atlantic Ocean
130 F4 **Pernat** Croatia
218 C4 **Pernatty Lagoon** SA Australia
132 C4 **Pernik** *admin. area* Bulgaria
125 H4 **Pernitz** Austria
121 O3 **Pernu** Finland
216 C2 **Peron North, Cape** WA Australia
216 C2 **Peron Peninsula** WA Australia
89 F5 **Perote** Mexico
193 I2 **Perouse Strait, La** Russian Federation
126 F5 **Perpignan** France
197 H3 **Perpuk, Tanjung** *cape* Indonesia
106 C6 **Perquenco** Chile
138 B4 **Perranporth** Cornwall England UK
76 I7 **Perrault Lake** Ontario Canada
218 F1 **Perrier, Mount** Qld Australia
216 G4 **Perrinvale Outcamp** WA Australia
84 D4 **Perris** California USA
85 J3 **Perro, Laguna de** *lake* New Mexico USA
126 C2 **Perros-Guirec** France
124 D4 **Perroy** Switzerland
212 E7 **Perry** *watercourse* WA Australia
87 J5 **Perry** Florida USA
87 J4 **Perry** Georgia USA
82 F7 **Perry** Missouri USA
86 C2 **Perry** Oklahoma USA
58 I2 **Perry Bay** Antarctica
82 J6 **Perrysburg** Ohio USA
86 A2 **Perryton** Texas USA
86 E3 **Perryville** Arkansas USA
82 G8 **Perryville** Missouri USA
122 H2 **Persbo** Sweden
221 9 **Perseverance Harbour** Campbell Island New Zealand
105 F4 **Perseverancia** Bolivia
105 E3 **Perseverancia** Bolivia
83 M3 **Pershing Lake** Quebec Canada
139 E2 **Pershore** Worcestershire England UK
Persian Gulf, The *see* **Gulf, The** Middle East
122 I4 **Persnäs** Sweden
216 D5 **Perth** WA Australia
83 M4 **Perth** Ontario Canada
142 E4 **Perth** Perth and Kinross Scotland UK
142 D4 **Perth and Kinross** *admin. area* Scotland UK
55 O7 **Perth Basin** *underwater feature* Indian Ocean
219 I5 **Perthville** NSW Australia
121 U4 **Pertominsk** Russian Federation
127 G5 **Pertuis** France
106 E6 **Perú** Argentina
104 C3 **Peru** *country* South America
82 H6 **Peru** Indiana USA
53 X9 **Peru Basin** *underwater feature* Pacific Ocean
53 Y10 **Peru-Chile Trench** *underwater feature* Pacific Ocean
132 A4 **Perućac** Serbia
130 E5 **Perugia** Italy
103 C9 **Peruíbe** Brazil
121 N3 **Perunkajärvi** Finland
126 F1 **Péruwelz** Belgium
183 K3 **Pervomayka** Kazakhstan
182 D2 **Pervomaysk** Russian Federation
132 G1 **Pervomays'k** Ukraine
183 N3 **Pervomayskiy** Kazakhstan
182 H6 **Pervomayskiy** Turkmenistan
197 F4 **Pesaguan** Indonesia
197 F4 **Pesaguan** *watercourse* Indonesia
130 E5 **Pesaro** Italy
102 B2 **Pescada, Ponta da** *cape* Brazil
84 A2 **Pescadero** California USA
104 C5 **Pescadores, Punta** *cape* Peru
109 inset 9 **Pescadores, Punta** *cape* Venezuela
131 F5 **Pescara** Italy
132 F1 **Peschana** Ukraine
121 S5 **Peschanoye** Russian Federation
193 J2 **Peschanoye, Ozero** *lake* Russian Federation
182 F5 **Peschanyy, Mys** *cape* Kazakhstan
135 Y4 **Peschanyy, Ostrov** *island* Russian Federation
131 G6 **Peschici** Italy
131 E5 **Pescina** Italy
90 D6 **Pesé** Panama
179 L2 **Peshawar** Pakistan
133 B5 **Peshkopi** Albania
120 L3 **Peske** Sweden
124 C4 **Pesmes** France
84 G6 **Pesqueira** Mexico
126 D4 **Pessac** France
124 G1 **Pessin** Germany
125 J4 **Pest** *admin. area* Hungary
135 AG6 **Pëstraya Dresva** Russian Federation
58 N1 **Pestrud Bank** *underwater feature* Ross Sea
88 E5 **Petacalco, Bahía** *bay* Mexico
121 P5 **Petäiskylä** Finland
121 O2 **Petäjäsaaret** *island* Finland
121 N5 **Petäjävesi** Finland
86 G5 **Petal** Mississippi USA
133 D7 **Petalida, Akra** *cape* Greece
196 D3 **Petaling Jaya** Malaysia
133 D7 **Petalioi** *island* Greece
80 D7 **Petaluma** California USA
127 G2 **Pétange** Luxembourg
197 H4 **Petangis** Indonesia
90 B4 **Petapa** Guatemala
100 E2 **Petare** Venezuela
88 E5 **Petatlán** Mexico
88 E5 **Petatlán, Morro de** *cape* Mexico
163 F2 **Petauke** Zambia
83 M4 **Petawawa** Ontario Canada
82 G4 **Petenwell Lake** Wisconsin USA
58 R2 **Peter I Island** *Norwegian dependency* Antarctica
76 I1 **Peter Lake** Nunavut Canada
75 Q4 **Peter Pond Lake** Saskatchewan Canada
82 J2 **Peterbell** Ontario Canada
218 F8 **Peterborough** Vic. Australia
83 L4 **Peterborough** Ontario Canada
139 G2 **Peterborough** Peterborough England UK
139 G2 **Peterborough** *admin. area* England UK
83 P5 **Peterborough** New Hampshire USA
142 C3 **Peterburn** Highland Scotland UK
138 E2 **Peterchurch** Herefordshire England UK
142 F3 **Peterculter** Aberdeen Scotland UK
142 G3 **Peterhead** Aberdeen Scotland UK
141 G2 **Peterlee** Durham England UK
214 B8 **Petermann** *watercourse* NT Australia
73 Q4 **Petermann Bjerg** *mountain* Greenland
73 M2 **Petermann Gletscher** *ice* Greenland
217 K2 **Petermann Ranges** NT Australia
106 D5 **Peteroa, Volcán** *volcano* Chile
78 C3 **Peters, Lac** *lake* Quebec Canada
138 C4 **Peters Marland** Devon England UK
78 E1 **Peters Point** Nunavut Canada
127 I1 **Petersberg** Germany
74 E4 **Petersburg** Alaska USA
81 P6 **Petersburg** Nebraska USA
81 Q3 **Petersburg** North Dakota USA
85 L4 **Petersburg** Texas USA
83 M8 **Petersburg** Virginia USA
83 L7 **Petersburg** West Virginia USA
58 H2 **Petersen Bank** *underwater feature* Southern Ocean
139 G3 **Petersfield** Hampshire England UK
83 K8 **Peterstown** West Virginia USA
140 B3 **Petersville** Ireland
132 B1 **Pétervására** Hungary
79 K8 **Peterview** Newfoundland and Labrador Canada
215 H4 **Petford** Qld Australia
123 O4 **Peti** Russian Federation
109 I6 **Petit-Bourg** Guadeloupe
109 I6 **Petit-Canal** Guadeloupe
109 I6 **Petit Cul-de-Sac Marin** *bay* Guadeloupe
77 S4 **Petit Lac des Loups Marins** *lake* Quebec Canada
77 W6 **Petit Lac Joseph** *lake* Newfoundland and Labrador Canada
77 V7 **Petit Lac Manicouagan** *lake* Quebec Canada
79 I7 **Petit Mécatina** *watercourse* Quebec Canada
79 I7 **Petit Mécatina, Île du** *island* Quebec Canada
109 I3 **Petit Piton** *volcano* St Lucia
129 G5 **Petit Port** Algeria
83 P3 **Petit-Rivière** Quebec Canada
79 F9 **Petit-Rocher** New Brunswick Canada
109 inset 9 **Petit Valley** Trinidad and Tobago
79 F10 **Petitcodiac** New Brunswick Canada
83 O2 **Petite Lièvre** *watercourse* Quebec Canada
164 7b **Petite Rivière Noire, Piton de la** *volcano* Mauritius
91 I4 **Petite Rivière Salée** Martinique
109 I5 **Petite Savane Point** *cape* Dominica
Petite Terre *see* **Pamanzi** Mayotte
109 I6 **Petite Terre, Îles de la** *islands* Guadeloupe
74 L3 **Petitot** *watercourse* Alberta Canada
74 J2 **Petitot** *watercourse* Northwest Territories Canada
77 V5 **Petitsikapau Lake** Newfoundland and Labrador Canada
121 O3 **Petkula** Finland
89 H4 **Peto** Mexico
82 I4 **Petoskey** Michigan USA
76 I6 **Petownikip Lake** Ontario Canada
192 F2 **Petra Velikogo, Zaliv** *island* Russian Federation
58 P1 **Petras, Mount** *mountain* Antarctica
123 O2 **Petraselkä** *bay* Finland
221 6 **Petre Bay** Chatham Islands New Zealand
129 F4 **Petrer** Spain
132 D3 **Petreşti** Romania
125 L5 **Petrila** Romania
130 G4 **Petrinja** Croatia
125 L4 **Petriş** Romania
132 G2 **Petrivka** Ukraine
106 D4 **Petro, Cerro de** *mountain* Chile
123 O3 **Petrodvorets** Russian Federation
128 F4 **Pétrola, Laguna Salada de** *lake* Spain
86 B3 **Petrolia** Texas USA
102 D5 **Petrolina** Brazil
103 B7 **Petrolina de Goiás** Brazil
183 L2 **Petropavlovka** Russian Federation
Petropavlovsk *see* **Petropavlovskiy** Kazakhstan
135 AG8 **Petropavlovsk-Kamchatskiy** Russian Federation
182 J2 **Petropavlovskiy** Kazakhstan
103 D8 **Petrópolis** Brazil
50 P5 **Petrov Fracture Zone** *underwater feature* Atlantic Ocean
121 P5 **Petrovaara** Finland
132 B3 **Petrovac** Serbia
125 J5 **Petrovci** Croatia
182 E3 **Petrovsk** Russian Federation
190 F2 **Petrovsk-zabaykalskiy** Russian Federation
136 F3 **Petrovs'ke** Ukraine
121 S5 **Petrovskiy Yam** Russian Federation
182 G2 **Petrovskoye** Russian Federation
182 C3 **Petrovskoye** Russian Federation
123 R2 **Petrozavodsk** Russian Federation
121 O2 **Petsikko** Finland
143 E2 **Pettigo** Fermanagh Northern Ireland UK
219 I6 **Pettitts** NSW Australia
183 J2 **Petukhovo** Russian Federation
139 G4 **Petworth** West Sussex England UK
125 G3 **Peuerbach** Austria
196 C2 **Peuetsagu, Gunung** *volcano* Indonesia
77 P6 **Peuplier, Rivière du** *watercourse* Quebec Canada
121 O3 **Peurasuvanto** Finland
120 J3 **Peuraure** Sweden
120 J3 **Peuraure** *lake* Sweden
196 C2 **Peureula** Indonesia
135 AJ5 **Pevek** Russian Federation
139 H4 **Pevensey Bay** East Sussex England UK
139 F3 **Pewsey** Wiltshire England UK
122 D6 **Pewsum** Germany
126 D5 **Peyrehorade** France
124 B5 **Peyreleau** France
126 E4 **Peyrissac** France
85 J1 **Peyton** Colorado USA
126 F5 **Pézenas** France
179 L3 **Pezu** Pakistan
127 J3 **Pfaff, Wilder** *mountain* Austria
86 C5 **Pflugerville** Texas USA
124 E3 **Pforzheim** Germany
124 E4 **Pfullendorf** Germany
124 F4 **Pfunds** Austria
124 E3 **Pfungstadt** Germany
194 D4 **Phai Sali** Thailand
163 F4 **Phalaborwa** South Africa
186 C5 **Phalodi** Rajasthan India
127 H2 **Phalsbourg** France
187 D8 **Phaltan** Maharashtra India
194 F5 **Phan Rí Cửa** Vietnam
194 F5 **Phan Thiết** Vietnam
194 C5 **Phangnga** Thailand
194 C5 **Phangnga** *admin. area* Thailand
186 G5 **Phaplu** Nepal
194 B3 **Phapon (Pyapon)** Myanmar
86 B7 **Pharr** Texas USA
194 E2 **Phát Diệm** Vietnam
194 D6 **PhattHalung** *admin. area* Thailand
194 C3 **Phayao** Thailand
194 D3 **Phayao** *admin. area* Thailand
194 D4 **Phayuta Khiri** Thailand
181 H4 **Phek** Nagaland India
214 C3 **Phelp** *watercourse* NT Australia
76 D3 **Phelps Lake** Saskatchewan Canada
87 M3 **Phelps Lake** North Carolina USA
87 I4 **Phenix City** Alabama USA
194 D3 **Phetchabun** Thailand
194 C4 **Phetchaburi** Thailand
194 E4 **Phiafai** Laos
194 D3 **Phichit** Thailand
194 D3 **Phichit** *admin. area* Thailand
86 G4 **Philadelphia** Mississippi USA
83 N7 **Philadelphia** Pennsylvania USA
156 E3 **Philae** *ruin* Egypt
138 C4 **Philham** Devon England UK
81 O4 **Philip** South Dakota USA
211 inset **Philip Island** Norfolk Island Australia
72 E5 **Philip Smith Mountains** Alaska USA
127 G1 **Philippeville** Belgium
83 K7 **Philippi** West Virginia USA
214 E8 **Philippi, Lake** Qld Australia
52 I6 **Philippine Basin** *underwater feature* Philippine Sea
195 J3 **Philippine Sea** Philippines
52 I6 **Philippine Trench** *underwater feature* Philippine Sea
195 J4 **Philippines** *country* Oceania
109 20 **Philipsburg** Netherlands Antilles
80 I3 **Philipsburg** Montana USA
140 B3 **Philipstown** Ireland
186 D4 **Phillaur** Punjab India
218 G8 **Phillip, Port** *bay* Vic. Australia
214 C5 **Phillip Creek** NT Australia
218 G8 **Phillip Island** Vic. Australia
86 C3 **Phillips** Oklahoma USA
82 F4 **Phillips** Wisconsin USA
73 K2 **Phillips Inlet** Nunavut Canada
213 I4 **Phillips Range** WA Australia
81 P7 **Phillipsburg** Kansas USA
83 N6 **Phillipsburg** Pennsylvania USA
218 B3 **Phillipson, Lake** SA Australia
83 O5 **Philmont** New York USA
80 D4 **Philomath** Oregon USA
75 P5 **Philomena** Alberta Canada
87 K2 **Philpott Lake** Virginia USA
219 H7 **Phipps, Mount** Vic. Australia

194 D3 **Phitsanulok** Thailand
Phnom Penh *see* **Phnum Pénh** Cambodia
194 E5 **Phnum Pénh (Phnom Penh)** Cambodia
88 B1 **Phoenix** Arizona USA
222 1 **Phoenix Islands** Kiribati
194 D4 **Phon** Thailand
194 D2 **Phong Thô** Vietnam
194 D2 **Phongsali** Laos
194 D2 **Phongsali** *admin. area* Laos
194 D3 **Phonhong** Laos
194 D3 **Phonsavan** Laos
219 P9 **Phoques Bay** Tas. Australia
142 E3 **Phorp** Moray Scotland UK
194 E4 **Phouphieng Bolovens** Laos
194 C5 **Phra Thong, Ko** *island* Thailand
194 D3 **Phrae** Thailand
194 E3 **Phú Bài** Vietnam
194 D3 **Phu Khieo** Thailand
194 D3 **Phu Kra Dung** Thailand
194 E3 **Phú Lộc** Vietnam
194 E2 **Phủ Lý** Vietnam
194 D5 **Phu Quoc, Đao** *island* Vietnam
194 E2 **Phù Yên** Vietnam
162 D4 **Phuduhudu** Botswana
194 C6 **Phuket** Thailand
194 C5 **Phuket** *admin. area* Thailand
194 C6 **Phuket, Ko** *island* Thailand
187 F7 **Phulabani** Orissa India
194 E4 **Phumĭ Kâmpóng Trâlach** Cambodia
194 E4 **Phumĭ Mlu Prey** Cambodia
194 D4 **Phumĭ Sâmraông** Cambodia
162 E5 **Phuthaditjhaba** South Africa
194 D4 **Phutthaisong** Thailand
181 G5 **Pi** *watercourse* Myanmar
103 E5 **Piaçabuçu** Brazil
124 E5 **Piacenza** Italy
79 C7 **Piacouadie, Lac** *lake* Quebec Canada
124 F5 **Piadena** Italy
77 P5 **Piagochioui** *watercourse* Quebec Canada
220 F3 **Piako** *watercourse* New Zealand
219 I3 **Pian** *watercourse* NSW Australia
102 E4 **Piancó** Brazil
130 D5 **Pianella** Italy
190 G5 **Pianguan** Shanxi China
124 F5 **Pianoro** Italy
131 F5 **Pianosa, Isola** *island* Italy
222 6a **Pianu, Mochun** *strait* Federated States of Micronesia
75 Q8 **Piapot** Saskatchewan Canada
125 H1 **Piasek** Poland
132 E2 **Piatra Neamţ** Romania
102 D4 **Piauí** *admin. area* Brazil
102 D4/5 **Piauí** *watercourse* Brazil
130 E3 **Piave** *watercourse* Italy
131 F8 **Piazza Armerina** Italy
161 E2 **Pibor** *watercourse* Sudan
161 E2 **Pibor Post** Sudan
82 H2 **Pic** *watercourse* Ontario Canada
105 F5 **Picacho, Serranía El** *range* Bolivia
100 B4 **Picacho Bujío** *mountain* Colombia
106 F2 **Picada Catorce de Mayo** Paraguay
130 F4 **Pićan** Croatia
126 F2 **Picardie** *admin. area* France
126 F2 **Picardie** *region* France
86 G5 **Picayune** Mississippi USA
104 D5 **Pichalo, Punta** *cape* Chile
86 D2 **Picher** Oklahoma USA
186 E6 **Pichhor** Madhya Pradesh India
106 E6 **Pichi Mahuida** Argentina
104 D4 **Pichigua** Peru
100 B3 **Pichimá** Colombia
100 B5 **Pichincha, Volcán** *volcano* Ecuador
104 D5 **Pichu Pichu, Nevado de** *mountain* Peru
89 G5 **Pichucalco** Mexico
81 O3 **Pick City** North Dakota USA
141 G3 **Pickburn** South Yorkshire England UK
86 G4 **Pickens** Mississippi USA
86 G4 **Pickensville** Alabama USA
82 F2 **Pickerel Lake** Ontario Canada
141 H2 **Pickering** North Yorkshire England UK
141 H2 **Pickering, Vale of** *valley* England UK
82 I3 **Pickford** Michigan USA
141 G2 **Pickhill** North Yorkshire England UK
76 J7 **Pickle Lake** Ontario Canada
141 F3 **Pickmere** Cheshire England UK
81 Q6 **Pickrell** Nebraska USA
81 P5 **Pickstown** South Dakota USA
86 G3 **Pickwick Lake** Mississippi USA
164 1 **Pico** *island* Azores
131 E6 **Pico** Italy
100 A5 **Pico, Punta** *cape* Peru
108 C3 **Pico de Salamanca** Argentina
164 1b **Pico Negro, Punta** *cape* Azores
104 D4 **Pico Tres, Nevado** *mountain* Peru
102 D4 **Picos** Brazil
104 B2 **Picota** Peru
219 J6 **Picton** NSW Australia
219 R11 **Picton, Mount** Tas. Australia
79 G10 **Pictou** Nova Scotia Canada
79 G10 **Pictou Island** Nova Scotia Canada
75 O8 **Picture Butte** Alberta Canada
102 E4 **Picuí** Brazil
106 D6 **Picún Leufú** Argentina
182 C5 **Picunda** Georgia
179 J4 **Pidarak** Pakistan
164 8a **Pidjani** Comoros
218 C4 **Pidleeomina, Lake** SA Australia
132 H1 **Pidlisne** Ukraine
187 E10 **Pidurutalagala** *mountain* Sri Lanka
100 B3 **Pié de Pató** Colombia
85 H3 **Pie Town** New Mexico USA
125 K1 **Piecki** Poland
164 1b **Piedade** Azores
100 C3 **Piedecuesta** Colombia
Piedmont *see* **Piemonte** Italy
82 F8 **Piedmont** Missouri USA
86 C3 **Piedmont** Oklahoma USA
108 B3 **Piedra Blanca** Chile
108 C4 **Piedra Clavada** Argentina
108 B2 **Piedra del Águila** Argentina
106 F6 **Piedra Echada** Argentina
128 D4 **Piedrabuena** Spain
128 C2 **Piedrafita** Spain
100 C4 **Piedras** Colombia
107 G5 **Piedras, Punta** *cape* Argentina
104 D3 **Piedras, Rio de Las** *watercourse* Peru
88 E2 **Piedras Negras** Mexico
121 N4 **Piehinki** Finland
121 O5 **Pieksämäki** Finland
123 N1 **Pieksänjärvi** *lake* Finland
128 E2 **Pielagas** Spain
121 O5 **Pielavesi** Finland
121 O5 **Pielavesi** *lake* Finland
121 P5 **Pielinen** *bay* Finland
219 Q10 **Pieman, Lake** Tas. Australia
130 B4 **Piemonte** *admin. area* Italy
125 M3 **Pieniaki** Ukraine
125 H2 **Pieńsk** Poland
130 D5 **Pienza** Italy
142 C4 **Pier** Highland Scotland UK
125 J1 **Pieranie** Poland
80 H3 **Pierce** Idaho USA
76 I5 **Pierce Lake** Ontario Canada
107 G6 **Pieres** Argentina
81 O4 **Pierre** South Dakota USA
126 E4 **Pierre-Buffière** France
83 K2 **Pierre Lake** Ontario Canada
139 I5 **Pierrepont** France
109 inset 9 **Pierreville** Trinidad and Tobago
75 U8 **Pierson** Manitoba Canada
87 K6 **Pierson** Florida USA
120 K3 **Piertinjaure** Sweden
82 D4 **Pierz** Minnesota USA
125 K2 **Pierzchnica** Poland
120 J3 **Pieskehaure** *lake* Sweden
125 H1 **Pieski** Poland
125 I3 **Piešťany** Slovakia
162 F5 **Piet Retief** South Africa
162 F5 **Pietermaritzburg** South Africa
131 F6 **Pietracatella** Italy
124 D5 **Pietraporzio** Italy
127 J5 **Pietrasanta** Italy
131 F6 **Pietre Nere, Punta** *cape* Italy
132 C3 **Pietroasa** Romania
132 D4 **Pietroşani** Romania
132 D2 **Pietrosul** *mountain* Romania
125 H2 **Pietrzyków** Poland
130 E3 **Pieve di Cadore** Italy
127 K4 **Pieve di Soligo** Italy
164 5c **Pig Beach** St Helena
82 G2 **Pigeon** *watercourse* Ontario Canada
109 16 **Pigeon** Guadeloupe
82 J5 **Pigeon** Michigan USA
221 E6 **Pigeon Bay** New Zealand
75 O6 **Pigeon Lake** Alberta Canada
130 B5 **Pigna** Italy
131 F6 **Pignola** Italy
220 F3 **Piha** New Zealand
121 O5 **Pihkainmäki** Finland
121 O4 **Pihkala** Finland
123 O2 **Pihlajavesi** *lake* Finland
121 N5 **Pihtipudas** Finland
121 N4 **Piippola** Finland
121 P4 **Piispajärvi** *lake* Finland
89 G6 **Pijijiapan** Mexico
76 H7 **Pikangikum Lake** Ontario Canada
219 J3 **Pikedale** Qld Australia
123 L4 **Pikeliai** Lithuania
222 6 **Pikelot** *island* Federated States of Micronesia
81 M7 **Pikes Peak** Colorado USA
82 J7 **Piketon** Ohio USA
83 J8 **Pikeville** Kentucky USA
87 I3 **Pikeville** Tennessee USA
195 J6 **Pikit** Philippines
159 H4 **Pikounda** Congo
75 W5 **Pikwitonei** Manitoba Canada
124 G5 **Pila** Italy
125 I1 **Piła** Poland
107 G3 **Pilagá** *watercourse* Argentina
108 C2 **Pilahué** Argentina
186 D5 **Pilani** Rajasthan India
102 D5 **Pilão Arcado** *watercourse* Brazil
106 F4 **Pilar** Argentina
107 G3 **Pilar** Paraguay
195 I4 **Pilar** Philippines
108 A5 **Pilar, Cabo** *cape* Chile
103 C8 **Pilar do Sul** Brazil
195 I6 **Pilas** *island* Philippines
128 C5 **Pilas** Spain
126 D4 **Pilat, Dune du** *dunes* France
125 I2 **Piława** Poland
213 D7 **Pilbara** *region* NT Australia
212 E6 **Pilbara** WA Australia
108 B2 **Pilcaniyeu** Argentina
125 H2 **Pilchowicie, Jezioro** *lake* Poland
105 F6 **Pilcomayo** *watercourse* Bolivia
106 F2 **Pilcomayo** *watercourse* Paraguay
125 I1 **Pile, Jezioro** *lake* Poland
162 F4 **Pilgrims Rest** South Africa
141 H3 **Pilham** Lincolnshire England UK
106 E2 **Pili, Cerro** *mountain* Chile
186 E5 **Pilibhit** Uttar Pradesh India
125 J2 **Pilica** *watercourse* Poland
101 G4 **Pilinawa** Guyana
130 H3 **Pilis** Hungary
100 B3 **Piliza** Colombia
219 S11 **Pillar, Cape** Tas. Australia
100 B5 **Píllaro** Ecuador
138 C4 **Pillaton** Cornwall England UK
138 D2 **Pilleth** Powys Wales UK
219 I4 **Pilliga** NSW Australia
140 F3 **Pilling** Lancashire England UK
80 D7 **Pillsbury, Lake** California USA
123 P6 **Pil'nya** Belarus
106 D6 **Pilolil** Argentina
128 D2 **Piloña** Spain
75 V8 **Pilot Mound** Manitoba Canada
80 F4 **Pilot Rock** Oregon USA
138 E4 **Pilsdon** Dorset England UK
Pilsen *see* **Plzeň** Czech Republic
140 A4 **Piltown** Ireland
120 K4 **Pilträsk** Sweden
135 AD8 **Pil'tun, Zaliv** *bay* Russian Federation
132 B2 **Pilu** Romania
134 P6 **Pim** Russian Federation
84 H4 **Pima** Arizona USA
84 G6 **Pimas** Mexico
105 F3 **Pimenta Bueno** Brazil
102 D4 **Pimenteiras** Brazil
105 F4 **Pimenteiras do Oeste** Bolivia
104 B2 **Pimentel** Peru
187 C7 **Pimpri Chinchwad** Maharashtra India
125 M1 **Pina** *watercourse* Belarus
129 F3 **Pina** Spain
88 B2 **Pinacate, Sierra del** *mountain* Mexico
186 E5 **Pinahat** Uttar Pradesh India
84 H4 **Pinaleno Mountains** Arkansas USA
100 C4 **Piñalito** Colombia
195 I4 **Pinamalayan** Philippines
196 C2 **Pinang** *admin. area* Malaysia
196 D2 **Pinang** *island* Malaysia
197 H2 **Pinangah** Malaysia
196 D4 **Pinangteluk** Indonesia
129 H4 **Pinar, Cap des** *cape* Spain
90 D2 **Pinar del Río** Cuba
90 D2 **Pinar del Rio** *admin. area* Cuba
100 B5 **Piñas** Ecuador
195 I4 **Pinatubo, Mount** *volcano* Philippines
76 H7 **Pinawa** Manitoba Canada
139 G2 **Pinchbeck** Lincolnshire England UK
80 I2 **Pincher** Alberta Canada
75 O8 **Pincher Creek** Alberta Canada
100 B5 **Pincho** Ecuador
105 G4 **Pindaiuval** Brazil
105 G5 **Pindaival** Brazil
216 D4 **Pindar** WA Australia
102 C4 **Pindaré** *watercourse* Brazil
102 C3 **Pindaré Mirim** Brazil
181 H5 **Pindaya** Myanmar
103 D5 **Pindobaçu** Brazil
133 B6 **Pindos Oros** *range* Greece
105 G2 **Pindoval** Brazil
186 C6 **Pindwara** Rajasthan India
74 J5 **Pine** *watercourse* British Columbia Canada
75 U7 **Pine** *watercourse* Manitoba Canada
84 G3 **Pine** Arizona USA
83 N7 **Pine Beach** New Jersey USA
75 T5 **Pine Bluff** Saskatchewan Canada
86 F3 **Pine Bluff** Arkansas USA
81 M6 **Pine Bluffs** Wyoming USA
219 I4 **Pine Clump** NSW Australia
214 A2 **Pine Creek** NT Australia
86 D3 **Pine Creek Lake** Oklahoma USA
76 G7 **Pine Dock** Manitoba Canada
80 F8 **Pine Flat Reservoir** California USA
214 B7 **Pine Gap** NT Australia
219 I4 **Pine Grove** NSW Australia
214 B7 **Pine Hill** NT Australia
86 H5 **Pine Hill** Alabama USA
86 C5 **Pine Island** Texas USA
58 R2 **Pine Island Bay** Antarctica
58 R1 **Pine Island Glacier** *ice* Antarctica
87 J7 **Pine Island Sound** Florida USA
215 K6 **Pine Peak Island** Qld Australia
218 E5 **Pine Point** NSW Australia
75 N2 **Pine Point** Northwest Territories Canada
81 N5 **Pine Ridge** Nebraska USA
75 U7 **Pine River** Manitoba Canada
75 R5 **Pine River** Saskatchewan Canada
74 J5 **Pine Valley** British Columbia Canada
129 H3 **Pineda** Spain
84 G3 **Pinedale** Arizona USA
81 K5 **Pinedale** Wyoming USA
134 K6 **Pinega** *watercourse* Russian Federation
80 G3 **Pinehurst** Idaho USA
86 E5 **Pinehurst** Texas USA
76 K6 **Pineimuta** *watercourse* Ontario Canada
133 B6 **Pineios** *watercourse* Greece
86 E5 **Pineland** Texas USA
87 J7 **Pinellas Park** Florida USA
87 K4 **Pineridge** South Carolina USA
124 D5 **Pinerolo** Italy
131 F5 **Pineto** Italy
84 H3 **Pinetop-Lakeside** Arizona USA
87 J4 **Pineview** Georgia USA
86 E5 **Pineville** Louisiana USA
82 D8 **Pineville** Missouri USA
83 K8 **Pineville** West Virginia USA
82 D2 **Pinewood** Minnesota USA
76 H8 **Piney** Manitoba Canada
127 G2 **Piney** France
87 J6 **Piney Point** Florida USA
212 E6 **Pinga** *watercourse* WA Australia
190 E6 **Ping'an** Qinghai China
216 F6 **Pingaring** WA Australia
188 E3 **Pingba** Guizhou China
189 G3 **Pingchuan** Fujian China
191 H5 **Pingding** Shanxi China
189 F1 **Pingdingshan** Henan China
189 G3 **Pingdu** Jiangxi China
191 I6 **Pingdu** Shandong China
222 6 **Pingelap** *island* Federated States of Micronesia
216 E6 **Pingelly** WA Australia
191 I5 **Pinggu** Beijing China
188 E3 **Pinghu** Guizhou China
189 I2 **Pinghu** Zhejiang China
188 F4 **Pingle** Guangxi Zhuangzu Zizhiqu China
188 F2 **Pingli** Shaanxi China
190 F6 **Pingliang** Gansu China
190 F5 **Pingluo** Ningxia Huizu Zishiqu China
188 E4 **Pingma** Guangxi Zhuangzu Zizhiqu China
188 F4 **Pingnan** Guangxi Zhuangzu Zizhiqu China
164 6 **Pingouins, Île des** *island* French Southern and Antarctic Lands
191 I5 **Pingquan** Hebei China
216 F6 **Pingrup** WA Australia
191 H5 **Pingshan** Hebei China
188 D3 **Pingshan** Yunnan China
191 H5 **Pingshu** Hebei China
189 H3 **Pingtan** Fujian China
189 H4 **P'ingtung** Taiwan China
78 G3 **Pinguksoak, Mount** Newfoundland and Labrador Canada
188 E3 **Pingxi** Guizhou China
190 F6 **Pingxiang** Gansu China
188 E4 **Pingxiang** Guangxi Zhuangzu Zizhiqu China
189 G3 **Pingxiang** Jiangxi China
190 G5 **Pingyao** Shanxi China
191 I6 **Pingyi** Shandong China
191 H5 **Pingyuan** Shandong China
188 C4 **Pingyuan** Yunnan China
188 E3 **Pingzhaio** Guizhou China
103 B9 **Pinhão** Brazil
102 C3 **Pinheiro** Brazil
107 H4 **Pinheiro Machado** Brazil
105 H1 **Pinhel** Brazil
128 C3 **Pinhel** Portugal
196 C3 **Pini** *island* Indonesia
199 J5 **Pinipel Island** Papua New Guinea
216 D6 **Pinjarra** WA Australia
87 M3 **Pink Hill** North Carolina USA
74 J4 **Pink Mountain** British Columbia Canada
125 I4 **Pinka** *watercourse* Austria
125 I4 **Pinkafeld** Austria
213 J3 **Pinkerton Range** NT Australia
219 J3 **Pinkett** NSW Australia
218 F2 **Pinkilla** Qld Australia
181 H4 **Pinlebu** Myanmar
140 D1 **Pinminnoch** South Ayrshire Scotland UK
142 D5 **Pinmore** South Ayrshire Scotland UK
218 E6 **Pinnaroo** SA Australia
133 D5 **Pinnes, Akra** *cape* Greece
127 I5 **Pino** Corsica France
106 D6 **Pino Hachado** Argentina
128 C3 **Pinofranqueado** Spain
197 F4 **Pinoh** *watercourse* Indonesia
88 D3 **Pinole** Mexico
80 D8 **Pinole** California USA
128 E5 **Pinos Puente** Spain
129 F4 **Pinoso** Spain
89 F5 **Pinotepa Nacional** Mexico
222 7 **Pins, Île des** *island* New Caledonia
136 C2 **Pinsk** Belarus
84 H3 **Pinta** Arizona USA
109 4 **Pinta, Canal de** *strait* Archipiélago de Colon (Galapagos Islands)
109 4 **Pinta, Isla** *island* Archipiélago de Colón (Galapagos Islands)
105 I4 **Pintado** *watercourse* Brazil
121 O4 **Pintamo** Finland
197 H2 **Pintasan** Malaysia
216 D4 **Pintharuka** WA Australia
105 E5 **Pinto** Bolivia
108 B4 **Pinturas** *watercourse* Argentina
79 J7 **Pinware** Newfoundland and Labrador Canada
142 D5 **Pinwherry** South Ayrshire Scotland UK
128 C3 **Pinzio** Portugal
109 4 **Pinzón, Isla** *island* Archipiélago de Colon (Galapagos Islands)
195 I4 **Pio Duran** Philippines
102 D4 **Pio IX** Brazil
102 C3 **Pio XII** Brazil
84 E2 **Pioche** Nevada USA
160 D5 **Piodi** Democratic Republic of Congo
130 D5 **Piombino** Italy
53 S4 **Pioneer Fracture Zone** *underwater feature* Pacific Ocean
80 I4 **Pioneer Mountains** Montana USA
134 S3 **Pioner, Ostrov** *island* Russian Federation
220 F4 **Piopio** New Zealand
131 F6 **Pioppi** Italy
101 F5 **Piorini, Lago** *lake* Brazil
124 D5 **Piossasco** Italy
130 E4 **Piove di Sacco** Italy
106 E4 **Pipanaco, Salar de** *lake* Argentina
139 F2 **Pipe Ridware** Staffordshire England UK
133 D6 **Piperi** *island* Greece
76 J6 **Pipestone** *watercourse* Ontario Canada
81 Q5 **Pipestone** Minnesota USA
82 E2 **Pipestone Lake** Ontario Canada
159 I3 **Pipi** *watercourse* Central African Republic
132 E2 **Pipirig** Romania
79 C8 **Pipmuacan, Réservoir** *lake* Quebec Canada
212 E6 **Pippingarra** WA Australia
75 S5 **Piprell Lake** Saskatchewan Canada
187 D6 **Pipri** Madhya Pradesh India
187 D7 **Pipri** Maharashtra India
126 D3 **Pipriac** France
75 V5 **Pipun** Manitoba Canada
133 A5 **Piqeras** Albania
103 C8 **Piquete** Brazil
104 C4 **Piquipata** Peru
105 F6 **Piquirenda** Paraguay
103 A9 **Piquiri** *watercourse* Brazil
183 J7 **Pir Nakhchīr** Afghanistan
186 D4 **Pir Panjal Range** Jammu and Kashmir India/Pakistan
179 I3 **Pīr Shūrān** *mountain* Iran
103 B7 **Piracanjuba** Brazil
103 C8 **Piracicaba** Brazil
102 D3 **Piracuruca** Brazil
103 B9 **Piraí do Sul** Brazil
100 E4 **Piraiuara** Brazil
103 B8 **Piraju** Brazil
103 B8 **Pirajuí** Brazil
108 B4 **Pirámide, Cerro** *mountain* Chile
124 G5 **Piran** Slovenia
107 G3 **Pirané** Argentina
101 H5 **Piranga, Serra da** *range* Brazil
105 H2 **Piranhaquara** Brazil
101 E5 **Piranhas** Brazil
103 B7 **Piranhas** Brazil
102 C3 **Pirapemas** Brazil
103 B8 **Pirapó** *watercourse* Brazil
103 C7 **Pirapora** Brazil
103 B8 **Pirapozinho** Brazil
105 E2 **Pirapucu** Brazil
91 F2 **Pirates Well** Bahamas
105 H6 **Piratini** Brazil
102 B2 **Piratuba, Lago** *lake* Brazil
101 G5 **Piratucu** *watercourse* Brazil
77 T7 **Piraube, Lac** *lake* Quebec Canada
108 C3 **Piré Mahuida, Sierra** *range* Argentina
108 B2 **Pirehueico** Chile
103 B6 **Pirenópolis** Brazil
103 B7 **Pires do Rio** Brazil
104 D4 **Pirhua, Cerro** *mountain* Peru
102 C3 **Piriá** *watercourse* Brazil
107 G3 **Piribebuy** Paraguay
199 F5 **Pirimapun** Indonesia
133 C5 **Pirin** *range* Bulgaria
102 D4 **Piripiri** Brazil
105 G5 **Pirizeiro** Brazil
213 K1 **Pirlangimpi** NT Australia
127 H2 **Pirmasens** Germany
125 G2 **Pirna** Germany
142 C5 **Pirnmill** North Ayrshire Scotland UK
109 16 **Pirogue** Guadeloupe
220 F3 **Pirongia** New Zealand
220 F3 **Pirongia** *volcano* New Zealand
132 C4 **Pirot** Serbia
126 D2 **Pirou** France
84 H5 **Pirtleville** Arizona USA
139 G3 **Pirton** Hertfordshire England UK
198 D4 **Piru** Indonesia
197 K4 **Piru, Teluk** *bay* Indonesia
130 D5 **Pisa** Italy
221 C7 **Pisa Range** New Zealand
198 D4 **Pisang** *island* Indonesia
198 D4 **Pisang, Kepulauan** *islands* Indonesia
104 B4 **Pisco** Peru
132 C2 **Pişcolt** Romania
125 H3 **Písek** Czech Republic
188 D3 **Pisha** Sichuan China
184 F5 **Pishan** Xinjiang Uygur Zizhiqu China
132 F1 **Pishchanka** Ukraine
197 I5 **Pising** Indonesia
84 B3 **Pismo Beach** California USA
158 B3 **Piso, Lake** *lake* Liberia
105 F4 **Piso Firme** Bolivia
104 C2 **Pisqui** *watercourse* Peru
106 D3 **Pissis, Cerro** *mountain* Argentina
126 D4 **Pissos** France
121 P4 **Pista** *watercourse* Finland
127 J5 **Pistoia** Italy
76 I1 **Pistol Bay** Nunavut Canada
133 A5 **Pistull** Albania
138 C2 **Pistyll** Gwynedd Wales UK
128 D3 **Pisuerga** *watercourse* Spain
125 K1 **Pisz** Poland
125 L2 **Piszczac** Poland
80 E6 **Pit** *watercourse* California USA
77 W6 **Pitaga** Newfoundland and Labrador Canada
100 C4 **Pital** Colombia
90 C5 **Pital** Costa Rica
100 B4 **Pitalito** Colombia
103 B9 **Pitanga** Brazil
103 C7 **Pitangui** Brazil
105 F4 **Pitari, Lagoa** *lake* Brazil
218 F6 **Pitarpunga Lake** NSW Australia
223 11 **Pitcairn Island** Pacific Ocean
223 11 **Pitcairn Islands** *UK overseas territory* Pacific Ocean
138 E2 **Pitchford** Shropshire England UK
120 L4 **Piteå** Sweden
120 L4 **Piteälven** *watercourse* Sweden
182 D2 **Pitelino** Russian Federation
182 E3 **Piterka** Russian Federation
132 D3 **Piteşti** Romania
216 E5 **Pithara** WA Australia
124 B3 **Pithiviers** France
223 14b **Piti Aau, Motu** *island* French Polynesia
102 F4 **Pitimbu** Brazil
88 B2 **Pitiquito** Mexico
123 K2 **Pitkäluoto** Finland
123 P2 **Pitkyaranta** Russian Federation
121 P2 **Pitkyayarvi** Russian Federation
142 E4 **Pitlochry** Perth and Kinross Scotland UK
142 F3 **Pitmedden** Aberdeenshire Scotland UK
159 G3 **Pitoa** Cameroon
188 D2 **Pitong** Sichuan China
109 13 **Pitons, Anse des** *bay* St Lucia
142 F4 **Pitscottie** Fife Scotland UK
139 G2 **Pitsford Reservoir** England UK
74 G6 **Pitt Island** British Columbia Canada
221 6 **Pitt Island (Rangiauria)** Chatham Islands New Zealand
74 J8 **Pitt Lake** British Columbia Canada
221 6 **Pitt Strait** Chatham Islands New Zealand
142 D3 **Pittentrail** Highland Scotland UK
142 F4 **Pittenweem** Fife Scotland UK
82 D8 **Pittsburg** Kansas USA
86 D4 **Pittsburg** Texas USA
83 L6 **Pittsburgh** Pennsylvania USA
82 F7 **Pittsfield** Illinois USA
79 D10 **Pittsfield** Maine USA
83 O5 **Pittsfield** Massachusetts USA
219 J2 **Pittsworth** Qld Australia
161 F5 **Pitu** *watercourse* Tanzania
76 M7 **Pitukupi Lake** Ontario Canada
214 E7 **Pituri** *watercourse* Qld Australia
124 F4 **Pitztal** *valley* Austria
103 C8 **Piuí** Brazil
199 J5 **Piul Island** Papua New Guinea
103 D8 **Piúma** Brazil
104 A2 **Piura** Peru
104 A2 **Piura** *admin. area* Peru
104 A2 **Piura** *watercourse* Peru
80 I7 **Piute Reservoir** Utah USA
105 G4 **Piúva** Brazil
77 N7 **Pivabiska** *watercourse* Ontario Canada
132 F1 **Pivdennyy Buh** *watercourse* Ukraine
125 H5 **Pivka** Slovenia
130 H4 **Pivnice** Serbia
130 H5 **Pivško Jezero** *lake* Montenegro
89 H5 **Pixoyal** Mexico
128 D5 **Pizarra** Spain
100 B3 **Pizarro** Colombia
159 F3 **Pizhi** Nigeria
182 E1 **Pizhma** Russian Federation
189 H1 **Pizhou** Jiangsu China
131 G7 **Pizzo** Italy
131 F5 **Pizzo, Punta di** *cape* Italy
127 K5 **Pizzuto, Monte** *mountain* Italy
120 K4 **Pjesker** *lake* Sweden
124 G1 **Plaaz** Germany
105 H1 **Placas** Brazil
79 L9 **Placentia** Newfoundland and Labrador Canada
79 K9 **Placentia Bay** Newfoundland and Labrador Canada
85 H1 **Placerville** Colorado USA
132 D4 **Plachkovtsi** Bulgaria
104 E3 **Plácido de Castro** Bolivia
142 C5 **Pladda** *island* Scotland UK
82 F5 **Plain** Wisconsin USA
86 E4 **Plain Dealing** Louisiana USA
82 H7 **Plainfield** Indiana USA
82 G4 **Plainfield** Wisconsin USA
87 I4 **Plains** Georgia USA
81 O8 **Plains** Kansas USA
85 K4 **Plains** Texas USA
81 Q5 **Plainview** Nebraska USA
85 L3 **Plainview** Texas USA
81 P7 **Plainville** Kansas USA
124 A3 **Plaisir** France
196 E4 **Plaju** Indonesia
133 D5 **Plaka** Greece
133 D5 **Plaka, Akra** *cape* Greece
75 O5 **Plamondon** Alberta Canada
197 H6 **Plampang** Indonesia
85 J7 **Plan de Ayala** Mexico
129 I2 **Plan-de-Cuques** France
130 E2 **Planá** Czech Republic
91 F2 **Plana Cays** *islands* Bahamas
100 C4 **Planadas** Colombia
103 C6 **Planaltina** Brazil
101 H5 **Planalto Maracanaquará** *region* Brazil
132 B3 **Plandište** Serbia
215 J8 **Planet** *watercourse* Qld Australia
100 C2 **Planeta Rica** Colombia
124 G3 **Plánice** Czech Republic
108 D2 **Planicie de los Vientos** *region* Argentina
86 C4 **Plano** Texas USA
133 B7 **Plános** Greece
124 F4 **Plansee** *lake* Austria
87 J6 **Plant City** Florida USA
87 K7 **Plantation** Florida USA
128 C3 **Plasencia** Spain
125 H5 **Plaški** Croatia
133 B5 **Plasnica** Macedonia
79 E9 **Plaster Rock** New Brunswick Canada
130 E2 **Plasy** Czech Republic
100 A5 **Plata, Isla de La** *island* Ecuador
108 B3 **Plata, Lago La** *lake* Argentina
106 D3 **Plata, Punta** *cape* Chile
107 G5 **Plata, Rio de la** *watercourse* Argentina
104 C3 **Platanal** Peru
131 E8 **Platani** *watercourse* Italy
133 B6 **Plataria** Greece
159 F3 **Plateau** *admin. area* Nigeria
184 G6 **Plateau of Tibet** Xizang Zizhiqu China
159 H5 **Plateaux** *admin. area* Congo
134 F2 **Platen, Kap** *cape* Norway
88 E4 **Plateros** Mexico
125 L1 **Platerów** Poland
129 H3 **Platja d'Aro** Spain
75 Q7 **Plato** Saskatchewan Canada
100 C2 **Plato** Colombia
81 L8 **Platoro Reservoir** Colorado USA
81 O6 **Platte** *watercourse* Nebraska USA
81 P5 **Platte** South Dakota USA
164 9 **Platte Island** Seychelles
81 M6 **Platteville** Colorado USA
82 F5 **Platteville** Wisconsin USA
124 G3 **Plattling** Germany
83 O4 **Plattsburgh** New York USA
124 G1 **Plau am See** Germany
124 G2 **Plauen** Germany
124 G1 **Plauer See** *lake* Germany
132 A4 **Plav** Montenegro
125 K3 **Plavnica** Slovakia
130 F4 **Plavnik** *island* Croatia
134 R4 **Plavnikovye, Ostrova** *island* Russian Federation
136 F2 **Plavsk** Russian Federation
194 F4 **Plây Ku** Vietnam
164 3d **Playa Blanca** Canary Islands
88 E5 **Playa Corrida de San Juan, Punta** *cape* Mexico
100 E4 **Playa de Candela** Venezuela
164 3a **Playa de la Americas** Canary Islands
164 3b **Playa de Mogán** Canary Islands
89 I4 **Playa del Carmen** Mexico
164 3b **Playa del Ingles** Canary Islands
101 E2 **Playa e Riedra, Embalse** *lake* Venezuela
100 C5 **Playa Paiche** *region* Peru
108 B2 **Playa Pilolcura** Chile
101 G2 **Playa Point** *cape* Guyana
164 3b **Playa Puerto Rico** Canary Islands
88 B2 **Playa Unión** Mexico
100 A5 **Playas** Ecuador
85 H5 **Playas Lake** New Mexico USA
219 H1 **Playfair, Mount** *peak* Qld Australia
214 D5 **Playford** *watercourse* NT Australia
139 I2 **Playford** Suffolk England UK
75 V6 **Playgreen Lake** Manitoba Canada
81 O2 **Plaza** North Dakota USA
84 F4 **Pleasant, Lake** Arizona USA
213 K2 **Pleasant, Mount** NT Australia
74 C3 **Pleasant Camp** Alaska USA
87 I3 **Pleasant Hill** Tennessee USA
221 D7 **Pleasant Point** New Zealand
89 F1 **Pleasant Valley** Texas USA
75 S6 **Pleasantdale** Saskatchewan Canada
82 D7 **Pleasanton** Kansas USA
86 B6 **Pleasanton** Texas USA
76 N7 **Pledger Lake** Ontario Canada
124 F3 **Pleinfeld** Germany
124 G2 **Pleiße** *watercourse* Germany
132 C3 **Pleniţa** Romania
214 C7 **Plenty** *watercourse* NT Australia
81 M2 **Plentywood** Montana USA
134 J6 **Plesetsk** Russian Federation
126 C2 **Pleslin** France
125 M5 **Pleşoiu** Romania
125 I2 **Pleszew** Poland
77 T7 **Plétipi, Lac** *lake* Quebec Canada
126 E3 **Pleumartin** France
132 D4 **Pleven** Bulgaria
81 M3 **Plevna** Montana USA
218 F2 **Plevna Downs** Qld Australia
123 L4 **Plieņciems** Latvia
197 G3 **Plieran** *watercourse* Malaysia
123 K5 **Plikiai** Lithuania
123 L4 **Plinkšių ežeras** *lake* Lithuania
123 O5 **Plisa** Belarus
130 H5 **Pljevlja** Montenegro
125 J1 **Płock** Poland
132 B4 **Pločnik** Serbia
126 C3 **Ploemeur** France
126 C2 **Ploeuc** France
132 E3 **Ploieşti** Romania
133 E6 **Plomari** Greece
126 F4 **Plomb du Cantal** *mountain* France
127 H3 **Plombières-les-Bains** France
219 K4 **Plomer Point** NSW Australia
125 H1 **Płoń, Jezioro** *lake* Poland
126 B3 **Plonéour-Lanvern** France
125 K1 **Płońsk** Poland
132 E1 **Plop** Moldova
132 F2 **Plopi** Moldova
132 C2 **Plopiş** Romania
132 C3 **Plopşoru** Romania
123 P4 **Ploskosh'** Russian Federation
126 C2 **Plouaret** France
126 C3 **Plouay** France
126 C2 **Plougasnou** France
126 B2 **Plougastel-Daoulas** France
126 C2 **Plouha** France
126 C3 **Plouharnel** France
133 D4 **Plovdiv** Bulgaria
133 D5 **Plovdiv** *admin. area* Bulgaria
82 G4 **Plover** Wisconsin USA
138 E2 **Plowden** Shropshire England UK
126 B3 **Plozévet** France
139 H3 **Pluckley** Kent England UK
76 G8 **Plum Coulee** Manitoba Canada
81 P1 **Plumas** Manitoba Canada
143 E2 **Plumbridge** Strabane Northern Ireland UK
86 E3 **Plumerville** Arkansas USA
125 I3 **Plumlov** Czech Republic
80 G3 **Plummer** Idaho USA
81 Q3 **Plummer** Minnesota USA
217 I4 **Plumridge Lakes** WA Australia
162 E4 **Plumtree** Zimbabwe
139 G2 **Plungar** Leicester England UK
123 L5 **Pluszkiejmy** Poland
88 C2 **Plutarco Elias Calles, Presa** *lake* Mexico
91 I3 **Plymouth** Montserrat
109 inset 9 **Plymouth** Trinidad and Tobago
138 C4 **Plymouth** *admin. area* England UK
138 C4 **Plymouth** Plymouth England UK
82 H6 **Plymouth** Indiana USA
82 E4 **Plymouth** Minnesota USA
80 I6 **Plymouth** Utah USA
138 D4 **Plymtree** Devon England UK
123 O3 **Plyussa** Russian Federation
124 G3 **Plzeň (Pilsen)** Czech Republic
124 G3 **Plzeňský Kraj** *admin. area* Czech Republic
214 B7 **Pmara Jutunta** NT Australia
125 I1 **Pniewy** Poland
158 D2 **Pô** Burkina Faso
130 D4 **Po** *watercourse* Italy
130 E4 **Po, Delta del** Italy
197 F3 **Po, Tanjong** *cape* Malaysia
181 E3 **Po Ho** *watercourse* Xizang Zizhiqu China
103 D8 **Poá** Brazil
88 E3 **Poanas** Mexico
219 R10 **Poatina** Tas. Australia
184 F4 **Pobeda Peak** *mountain* Xinjiang Uygur Zizhiqu China
130 E2 **Poběžovice** Czech Republic
125 I1 **Pobiedziska** Poland
122 I5 **Pobrzeże Koszalińskie** *region* Poland
86 F2 **Pocahontas** Arkansas USA
102 C4 **Poção de Pedras** Brazil
86 C3 **Pocasset** Oklahoma USA
80 I5 **Pocatello** Idaho USA
192 F3 **Poch'ŏn** North Korea
78 H5 **Pocket Knife Lake** Newfoundland and Labrador Canada
125 G3 **Pocking** Germany
141 H3 **Pocklington** East Riding of Yorkshire England UK
103 E5 **Poço Verde** Brazil
103 D6 **Poções** Brazil
83 N7 **Pocomoke City** Maryland USA
104 D5 **Poconchile** Chile
105 G5 **Poconé** Brazil
103 C8 **Poços de Caldas** Brazil
90 D5 **Pocrí** Panama
132 B2 **Pocsaj** Hungary
133 C5 **Podareš** Macedonia
123 O4 **Podberez'ye** Russian Federation
130 G4 **Podbrđe** Bosnia and Herzegovina
130 G4 **Podbrdo** Bosnia and Herzegovina
125 H4 **Podčetrtek** Slovenia
123 P4 **Poddor'ye** Russian Federation
183 M5 **Podeba Peak** *mountain* Kyrgyzstan
125 H1 **Podelzig** Germany
130 H5 **Podgorica** Montenegro
134 R7 **Podgornoye** Russian Federation
183 N1 **Podgornoye** Russian Federation
135 AE9 **Podgornyy** Kuril Islands
193 K2 **Podgornyy** Russian Federation
132 C1 **Podhorod'** Slovakia
130 G5 **Podhum** Bosnia and Herzegovina
187 E8 **Podile** Andhra Pradesh India
132 D2 **Podişul Transilvaniei (Transylvanian Basin)** *region* Romania
130 G2 **Podivín** Czech Republic
125 K2 **Podkarpackie** *admin. area* Poland
133 D5 **Podkova** Bulgaria
125 L1 **Podlaskie** *admin. area* Poland
132 E2 **Podoleni** Romania
136 F1 **Podol'sk** Russian Federation
154 D5 **Podor** Senegal
132 D1 **Podorozhnoye** Ukraine
123 O4 **Podsevy** Russian Federation
104 A2 **Poechos, Reservorio** *lake* Peru
163 G4 **Poelela, Lagoa** *lake* Mozambique
132 C2 **Poeni** Romania
218 C1 **Poeppel, Lake** NT Australia
162 C5 **Pofadder** South Africa
136 E2 **Pogar** Russian Federation
127 J5 **Poggi Alti** *mountain* Italy
130 D5 **Poggibonsi** Italy
130 E5 **Poggiodomo** Italy
125 H3 **Pöggstall** Austria
135 AD8 **Pogibi** Russian Federation
132 B4 **Pogled** *mountain* Serbia
133 B5 **Pogradec** Albania
198 B4 **Poh** Indonesia
192 F4 **P'ohang** South Korea
220 F5 **Pohangina** New Zealand
121 O4 **Pohjanmaa** *region* Finland
121 O3 **Pohjaslahti** Finland
121 P4 **Pohjavaara** Finland
123 N1 **Pohjois-Virmas** *lake* Finland
222 6 **Pohnpei** *admin. area* Federated States of Micronesia
222 6 **Pohnpei** *island* Federated States of Micronesia
125 K3 **Pohorelá** Slovakia
132 F1 **Pohrebyshche** Ukraine
186 D6 **Pohri** Madhya Pradesh India
132 D3 **Poiana Mărului** Romania
160 C4 **Poie** Democratic Republic of Congo
132 D2 **Poienile de Sub Munte** Romania
198 C3 **Poigar** Indonesia
101 H4 **Poimró** Brazil
58 H2 **Poinsett, Cape** Antarctica
82 C4 **Poinsett, Lake** South Dakota USA
86 D4 **Point** Texas USA
80 D7 **Point Arena** California USA
86 F6 **Point au Fer Island** Louisiana USA
218 B1 **Point Eremophila** *mountain* NT Australia
109 inset 9 **Point Fortin** Trinidad and Tobago
109 inset 9 **Point Fortin** *admin. area* Trinidad and Tobago
72 C5 **Point Hope** Alaska USA
72 H5 **Point Lake** Northwest Territories Canada
79 K9 **Point Lance** Newfoundland and Labrador Canada
72 C5 **Point Lay** Alaska USA
219 K4 **Point Lookout** *mountain* NSW Australia
219 K2 **Point Lookout** Qld Australia
83 N6 **Point Pleasant** New Jersey USA
83 J7 **Point Pleasant** West Virginia USA
217 H3 **Point Robert** WA Australia
217 H4 **Point Salvation** WA Australia
126 F4 **Point Sublime** France
79 E8 **Pointe-à-la-Croix** Quebec Canada
109 15 **Pointe-à-Peine** *cape* Dominica
109 inset 9 **Pointe-à-Pierre** Trinidad and Tobago
109 16 **Pointe-à-Pitre** Guadeloupe
83 K4 **Pointe au Baril Station** Ontario Canada
79 D8 **Pointe-Lebel** Quebec Canada
109 15 **Pointe Michel** Dominica
159 G5 **Pointe-Noire** Congo
109 16 **Pointe-Noire** Guadeloupe
139 G2 **Pointon** Lincolnshire England UK
84 inset **Poipu** Hawai'i USA
124 D5 **Poirino** Italy
212 E5 **Poissonnier Point** WA Australia
77 W6 **Poissons** *watercourse* Newfoundland and Labrador Canada
124 C3 **Poissons** France
124 B3 **Poissy** France
126 E3 **Poitiers** France
126 E3 **Poitou** *region* France
126 D4 **Poitou-Charentes** *admin. area* France
164 9 **Poivre Islands** Seychelles
139 I5 **Poix-de-Picardie** France
124 C3 **Poix-Terron** France
125 I1 **Pojezierze Pomorskie** *region* Poland
85 I3 **Pojoaque** New Mexico USA
186 C5 **Pokaran** Rajasthan India
220 F3 **Pokeno** New Zealand
186 F5 **Pokhara** Nepal
121 N2 **Pokka** Finland
160 D3 **Poko** Democratic Republic of Congo
183 K5 **Pokrovka** Kyrgyzstan
132 G2 **Pokrovka** Ukraine
132 G2 **Pokrovs'ke** Ukraine
182 C4 **Pokrovskoye** Russian Federation
125 H5 **Pokupsko** Croatia
179 K2 **Pol-e 'Alam** Afghanistan
178 F2 **Pol-e Dokhtar** Iran
179 K2 **Pol-e-Khomrī** Afghanistan
123 P4 **Pola** Russian Federation
128 D2 **Pola de Laviana** Spain
128 D2 **Pola de Lena** Spain
128 C2 **Pola de Somiedo** Spain
130 G5 **Polače** Croatia
125 J1 **Poland** *country* Europe
222 1a **Poland** Kiribati
125 K2 **Połaniec** Poland
104 D6 **Polapi, Cerro** *mountain* Chile
58 V1 **Polar Plateau** Antarctica
123 O5 **Polatsk** Belarus
142 D5 **Polbae** Dumfries and Galloway Scotland UK
142 C2 **Polbain** Highland Scotland UK
120 L3 **Polcirkeln** Sweden
106 D6 **Polcura** Chile
122 I5 **Pólczno** Poland
218 B5 **Polda** SA Australia
121 U5 **Pole** Russian Federation
56 O1 **Pole Abyssal Plain** *underwater feature* Arctic Ocean
198 D4 **Polee** *island* Indonesia
139 H4 **Polegate** East Sussex England UK
77 Q3 **Polemond** *watercourse* Quebec Canada
123 K5 **Polessk** Russian Federation
198 A4 **Polewali** Indonesia
125 K4 **Polgár** Hungary
214 B8 **Polhill, Mount** NT Australia
159 G3 **Poli** Cameroon
133 B5 **Poliçan** Albania
131 F7 **Policastro, Golfo di** *bay* Italy
215 I6 **Police** *watercourse* Qld Australia
125 H1 **Police** Poland
125 I3 **Polička** Czech Republic
131 G6 **Policoro** Italy
127 G3 **Poligny** France
133 C5 **Polikarpion** Greece
195 I4 **Polillo** *island* Philippines
195 I4 **Polillo Islands** Philippines
131 G7 **Polistena** Italy
130 H5 **Polje** Bosnia and Herzegovina
130 G5 **Polje** Croatia
125 I2 **Polkowice** Poland
87 K3 **Polkton** North Carolina USA
142 D2 **Polla** Highland Scotland UK
187 D9 **Pollachi** Tamil Nadu India
124 E2 **Polle** Germany
122 C3 **Pollestad** Norway
75 P7 **Pollockville** Alberta Canada
143 E4 **Pollrone** Ireland
140 B4 **Pollshane** Ireland
221 C7 **Pollux, Mount** New Zealand
121 P1 **Polmak** Norway
121 O2 **Polmakuatnet** *lake* Finland
125 I1 **Polne** Poland
82 G6 **Polo** Illinois USA
136 F3 **Pologi** Ukraine

218 F4 **Poloko Lake** NSW Australia
162 E4 **Polokwane** South Africa
195 J6 **Polomolok** Philippines
123 O4 **Polonoye** Russian Federation
123 O5 **Polota** Belarus
135 AC5 **Polousnyy, Kryazh** *range* Russian Federation
125 L5 **Polovragi** Romania
138 C4 **Polperro** Cornwall England UK
138 C4 **Polruan** Cornwall England UK
80 H3 **Polson** Montana USA
130 H2 **Poltár** Slovakia
136 E3 **Poltava** Ukraine
136 E3 **Poltavs'ka Oblast'** *admin. area* Ukraine
183 K2 **Poludino** Kazakhstan
187 E9 **Polur** Tamil Nadu India
123 N3 **Põlva** Estonia
85 I3 **Polvadera** New Mexico USA
123 N3 **Põlvamaa** *admin. area* Estonia
121 P5 **Polvela** Finland
121 P5 **Polvijärvi** Finland
133 D7 **Polyaigos** *island* Greece
182 C5 **Polyana** Russian Federation
132 C1 **Polyana** Ukraine
121 R2 **Polyarnyy** Russian Federation
134 N5 **Polyarnyy Ural** *range* Russian Federation
121 R3 **Polyarnyye Zori** Russian Federation
133 C5 **Polygyros** Greece
198 E4 **Pom** Indonesia
104 B3 **Pomabamba** Peru
130 D5 **Pomarance** Italy
123 L2 **Pomarkku** Finland
130 H3 **Pomáz** Hungary
102 E4 **Pombal** Brazil
128 B4 **Pombal** Portugal
133 D8 **Pómbia** Greece
101 G3 **Pomeroon Point** *cape* Guyana
101 G3 **Pomeroon-Supenaam** *admin. area* Guyana
140 B2 **Pomeroy** Cookstown Northern Ireland UK
80 G3 **Pomeroy** Washington USA
131 E6 **Pomezia** Italy
162 D5 **Pomfret** South Africa
132 G1 **Pomichna** Ukraine
82 E8 **Pomme de Terre Lake** Missouri USA
122 H5 **Pommersche Bucht** *bay* Germany
121 O3 **Pomokaira** *island* Finland
84 D3 **Pomona** California USA
82 D7 **Pomona Lake** Kansas USA
132 E4 **Pomoriysko Ezero** *lake* Bulgaria
125 I1 **Pomorskie** *admin. area* Poland
87 K7 **Pompano Beach** Florida USA
103 C7 **Pompeéu** Brazil
105 G2 **Pompeu** Brazil
89 H4 **Pomuch** Mexico
76 I5 **Ponask Lake** Ontario Canada
81 Q8 **Ponca City** Oklahoma USA
91 H3 **Ponce** Puerto Rico
87 K8 **Ponce De Leon Bay** Florida USA
81 L7 **Poncha Springs** Colorado USA
77 Q7 **Poncheville, Lac** *lake* Quebec Canada
213 H3 **Pond, Cape** WA Australia
81 Q8 **Pond Creek** Oklahoma USA
73 L4 **Pond Inlet** Nunavut Canada
100 C2 **Ponedera** Colombia
130 C5 **Ponente, Riviera di** *coast* Italy
222 7 **Ponérihouen** New Caledonia
128 C2 **Ponferrada** Spain
194 D3 **Pong** Thailand
159 F4 **Pongara, Pointe** *cape* Gabon
220 G5 **Pongaroa** New Zealand
192 F4 **Ponghwa** South Korea
160 D2 **Pongo** *watercourse* Sudan
163 F5 **Pongola** South Africa
158 D2 **Poni** *watercourse* Burkina Faso
125 I2 **Poniec** Poland
198 B4 **Ponindilisa, Tanjung** *cape* Indonesia
123 P5 **Ponizov'ye** Russian Federation
187 D9 **Ponnani** Kerala India
198 E5 **Pono** Indonesia
75 O6 **Ponoka** Alberta Canada
197 F5 **Ponorogo** Indonesia
195 I5 **Ponot** Philippines
134 J5 **Ponoy** Russian Federation
134 I5 **Ponoy** *watercourse* Russian Federation
198 B4 **Ponrang** Indonesia
77 U5 **Pons** *watercourse* Quebec Canada
126 D4 **Pons** France
127 G1 **Pont-à-Celles** Belgium
127 H2 **Pont-à-Mousson** France
138 C3 **Pont Antwn** Carmarthenshire Wales UK
127 G3 **Pont-d'Ain** France
126 F4 **Pont-de-Salars** France
129 G2 **Pont de Suert** Spain
126 B3 **Pont-l'Abbé** France
138 D2 **Pont-Robert** Powys Wales UK
127 G4 **Pont-St-Esprit** France
105 G3 **Ponta da Divisão** Brazil
164 1b **Ponta da Ilha** *cape* Azores
164 1b **Ponta da Terra** *cape* Azores
164 1a **Ponta Delgade** Azores
164 1b **Ponta do Arrife** *cape* Azores
164 1b **Ponta do Pico** *volcano* Azores
164 2 **Ponta do Sol** Madeira
103 B9 **Ponta Grossa** Brazil
105 H6 **Ponta Porã** Brazil
126 D5 **Pontacq** France
103 B8 **Pontal** Brazil
102 D5 **Pontal** *watercourse* Brazil
103 B9 **Pontal do Paraná** Brazil
103 B7 **Pontalina** Brazil
138 D3 **Pontardawe** Neath Port Talbot Wales UK
138 C3 **Pontardulais** Carmarthenshire Wales UK
127 H3 **Pontarlier** France
126 F4 **Pontaumur** France
77 Q7 **Pontax** *watercourse* Quebec Canada
86 F5 **Pontchartrain, Lake** Louisiana USA
126 C3 **Pontchâteau** France
103 A7 **Ponte Branca** Brazil
105 G4 **Ponte de Pedra** Brazil
128 B4 **Ponte de Sor** Portugal
131 C5 **Ponte-Leccia** Corsica France
103 D8 **Ponte Nova** Brazil
128 B2 **Ponteareas** Spain
124 G4 **Pontebba** Italy
141 G3 **Pontefract** West Yorkshire England UK
105 H5 **Ponteira** Brazil
75 R8 **Ponteix** Saskatchewan Canada
141 G1 **Ponteland** Northumberland England UK
138 D2 **Ponterwyd** Ceredigion Wales UK
105 G4 **Pontes e Lacerda** Brazil
138 E2 **Pontesbury** Shropshire England UK
128 B2 **Pontevedra** Spain
82 G6 **Pontiac** Illinois USA
196 F4 **Pontianak** Indonesia
124 B4 **Pontigny** France
126 D2 **Pontmain** France
103 D5 **Ponto Novo** Brazil
216 H5 **Ponton** *watercourse* WA Australia
75 V5 **Ponton** Manitoba Canada
126 D5 **Pontonx-sur-l'Adour** France
143 C3 **Pontoon** Mayo Ireland
130 C4 **Pontremoli** Italy
127 I3 **Pontresina** Switzerland
138 D2 **Pontrhydfendigaid** Ceredigion Wales UK
138 E3 **Pontrilas** Herefordshire England UK
138 D3 **Pontsticill** Powys Wales UK
138 D3 **Pontypridd** Rhondda Cynon Taff Wales UK
220 F3 **Ponui Island** New Zealand
131 E6 **Ponza, Isola di** *island* Italy
131 E6 **Ponziane, Isole** *island* Italy
218 B5 **Poochera** SA Australia
159 G5 **Pool** *admin. area* Congo
138 D2 **Pool Quay** Powys Wales UK
139 F4 **Poole** *admin. area* England UK
139 F4 **Poole** Poole England UK
218 E3 **Poole, Mount** NSW Australia
139 F4 **Poole Bay** England UK
142 C3 **Poolewe** Highland Scotland UK
218 C2 **Poolowanna, Lake** SA Australia
218 F5 **Pooncarie** NSW Australia
217 K3 **Poondinna, Mount** SA Australia
218 F4 **Poopelloe Lake** NSW Australia
104 E5 **Poopó** Bolivia
104 E5 **Poopó, Lago** *lake* Bolivia
220 F2 **Poor Knights Islands** New Zealand
123 N3 **Pööra** Estonia
75 U2 **Poorfish Lake** Nunavut Canada
181 H5 **Popa, Mount** *mountain* Myanmar
123 K4 **Pope** Latvia
132 C2 **Popești** Romania
139 F3 **Popham** Hampshire England UK
218 E5 **Popiltah Lake** NSW Australia
76 G6 **Poplar** *watercourse* Manitoba Canada
81 M2 **Poplar** Montana USA
81 M2 **Poplar** *watercourse* Montana USA
82 F3 **Poplar** Wisconsin USA
82 F8 **Poplar Bluff** Missouri USA
80 G1 **Poplar Creek** British Columbia Canada
76 H6 **Poplar Hill** Ontario Canada
86 G5 **Poplarville** Mississippi USA
197 F6 **Popoh** Indonesia
131 E5 **Popoli** Italy
222 8a **Popomanaseu, Mount** Solomon Islands
130 H5 **Popov Do** Montenegro
123 O4 **Popovka** Russian Federation
100 B4 **Popoyán** Colombia
125 K3 **Poprad** Slovakia
90 B3 **Poptún** Guatemala
220 G5 **Porangahau** New Zealand
103 B6 **Porangatu** Brazil
125 M1 **Porazava** Belarus
187 B7 **Porbandar** Gujarat India
74 F6 **Porcher Island** British Columbia Canada
124 G5 **Porcia** Italy
103 D8 **Porciúncula** Brazil
103 C6 **Porcos** *watercourse* Brazil
132 C2 **Porcsalma** Hungary
128 D5 **Porcuna** Spain
72 E5 **Porcupine** *watercourse* Alaska USA
78 J6 **Porcupine, Cape** Newfoundland and Labrador Canada
50 Q5 **Porcupine Abyssal Plain** *underwater feature* Atlantic Ocean
50 Q4 **Porcupine Bank** *underwater feature* Atlantic Ocean
75 T6 **Porcupine Plain** Saskatchewan Canada
126 C2 **Pordic** France
127 J3 **Pordoi, Passo** *pass* Italy
100 D3 **Pore** Colombia
130 E4 **Poreč** Croatia
103 B8 **Porecatu** Brazil
123 P4 **Porech'ye** Russian Federation
108 D2 **Pórfido, Punta** *cape* Argentina
158 E2 **Porga** Benin
123 K2 **Pori** Finland
142 D3 **Porin** Highland Scotland UK
221 F5 **Porirua** New Zealand
120 K3 **Porjus** Sweden
123 O4 **Porkhov** Russian Federation
123 M3 **Porkkala** *peninsula* Finland
123 M3 **Porkkalafjärden** *bay* Finland
101 F2 **Porlamar** Venezuela
138 D3 **Porlock** Somerset England UK
128 D2 **Porma** *watercourse* Spain
126 B5 **Porma, Embalse de** *lake* Spain
132 D1 **Pormortsy** Ukraine
214 F3 **Pormpuraaw** Qld Australia
126 C3 **Pornic** France
120 L2 **Porojärvi** *lake* Finland
121 P5 **Porokylä** Finland
135 AD9 **Poronaysk** Russian Federation
197 G5 **Porong** Indonesia
194 E4 **Porông** *watercourse* Cambodia
133 C7 **Poros** Greece
121 R5 **Porosozero** Russian Federation
125 K4 **Poroszló** Hungary
121 Q2 **Porovaara** Russian Federation
132 E4 **Poroy** Bulgaria
130 F4 **Porozina** Croatia
58 I2 **Porpoise Bay** Antarctica
221 C8 **Porpoise Bay** New Zealand
127 H3 **Porrentruy** Switzerland
143 C3 **Porridgetown** Ireland
121 O1 **Porsangen** *bay* Norway
121 N1 **Porsangerhalvøya** *peninsula* Norway
196 C3 **Porsea** Indonesia
120 L3 **Porsi** Sweden
133 G6 **Porsuk** *watercourse* Turkey
133 G6 **Porsuk Barajı** *lake* Turkey
160 E3 **Port** Democratic Republic of Congo
143 D2 **Port** Ireland
121 O2 **Port** Norway
74 I8 **Port Alberni** British Columbia Canada
220 F3 **Port Albert** New Zealand
74 D4 **Port Alexander** Alaska USA
162 E6 **Port Alfred** South Africa
74 H7 **Port Alice** British Columbia Canada
86 F5 **Port Allen** Louisiana USA
80 D2 **Port Angeles** Washington USA
142 C4 **Port Appin** Argyll and Bute Scotland UK
219 R11 **Port Arthur** Tas. Australia
86 E6 **Port Arthur** Texas USA
142 B5 **Port Askaig** Argyll and Bute Scotland UK
79 I8 **Port au Port Bay** Newfoundland and Labrador Canada
79 I8 **Port au Port Peninsula** Newfoundland and Labrador Canada
91 F3 **Port-au-Prince** Haiti
218 C5 **Port Augusta** SA Australia
82 J4 **Port Austin** Michigan USA
164 6b **Port-aux-Français** French Southern and Antarctic Lands
129 H2 **Port-Barcarès** France
86 F5 **Port Barre** Louisiana USA
194 B5 **Port Blair** Andaman and Nicobar Islands India
79 K8 **Port Blandford** Newfoundland and Labrador Canada
218 C5 **Port Broughton** SA Australia
218 F8 **Port Campbell** Vic. Australia
77 V7 **Port-Cartier** Quebec Canada
220 F3 **Port Charles** New Zealand
142 B5 **Port Charlotte** Argyll and Bute Scotland UK
74 E6 **Port Clements** British Columbia Canada
221 B8 **Port Craig** New Zealand
79 F8 **Port-Daniel, Baie de** Quebec Canada
196 D3 **Port Dickson** Malaysia
215 H4 **Port Douglas** Qld Australia
74 F5 **Port Edward** British Columbia Canada
162 F6 **Port Edward** South Africa
162 E6 **Port Elizabeth** South Africa
109 11 **Port Elizabeth** St Vincent and the Grenadines
142 B5 **Port Ellen** Argyll and Bute Scotland UK
140 D2 **Port Erin** Isle of Man UK
74 G5 **Port Essington** British Columbia Canada
138 C3 **Port-Eynon** Swansea Wales UK
218 F8 **Port Fairy** Vic. Australia
220 F3 **Port Fitzroy** New Zealand
159 F5 **Port-Gentil** Gabon
86 F5 **Port Gibson** Mississippi USA
159 F4 **Port Harcourt** Nigeria
74 H7 **Port Hardy** British Columbia Canada
221 E5 **Port Hardy** New Zealand
79 H10 **Port Hawkesbury** Nova Scotia Canada
212 E6 **Port Hedland** WA Australia
83 O4 **Port Henry** New York USA
83 L5 **Port Hope** Ontario Canada
78 J6 **Port Hope Simpson** Newfoundland and Labrador Canada
109 7 **Port Howard** Falkland Islands
83 J5 **Port Huron** Michigan USA
86 C7 **Port Isabel** Texas USA
126 C3 **Port-Joinville** France
219 J6 **Port Kembla** NSW Australia
218 B5 **Port Kenny** SA Australia
126 F5 **Port-la-Nouvelle** France
195 I6 **Port Languyan** Philippines
86 C6 **Port Lavaca** Texas USA
83 N5 **Port Leyden** New York USA
218 B6 **Port Lincoln** SA Australia
142 D6 **Port Logan** Dumfries and Galloway Scotland UK
83 L4 **Port Loring** Ontario Canada
109 16 **Port-Louis** Guadeloupe
164 7b **Port Louis** Mauritius
218 E8 **Port MacDonnell** SA Australia
74 H7 **Port McNeill** British Columbia Canada
219 K4 **Port Macquarie** NSW Australia
90 E3 **Port Maria** Jamaica
74 J8 **Port Mellon** British Columbia Canada
79 F8 **Port-Menier** Quebec Canada
72 C7 **Port Moller** Alaska USA
142 B4 **Port Mor** Highland Scotland UK
199 H6 **Port Moresby** Papua New Guinea
79 F11 **Port Mouton Island** Nova Scotia Canada
142 B3 **Port na Long** Highland Scotland UK
142 B2 **Port nan Giuran** Na h-Eileanan Siar Scotland UK
142 A3 **Port nan Long** Na h-Eileanan Siar Scotland UK
218 C6 **Port Neill** SA Australia
91 F2 **Port Nelson** Bahamas
76 I4 **Port Nelson** Manitoba Canada
80 B1 **Port Neville** British Columbia Canada
142 B2 **Port Nis** Na h-Eileanan Siar Scotland UK
162 C5 **Port Nolloth** South Africa
109 inset 9 **Port of Spain** Trinidad and Tobago
109 inset 9 **Port of Spain** *admin. area* Trinidad and Tobago
220 G3 **Port Ohope** New Zealand
87 K6 **Port Orange** Florida USA
80 C5 **Port Orford** Oregon USA
83 L4 **Port Perry** Ontario Canada
218 D5 **Port Pirie** SA Australia
138 C4 **Port Quin** Cornwall England UK
74 I8 **Port Renfrew** British Columbia Canada
218 C6 **Port Rickaby** SA Australia
214 C3 **Port Roper** NT Australia
83 K5 **Port Rowan** Ontario Canada
87 K4 **Port Royal** South Carolina USA
87 K4 **Port Royal Sound** South Carolina USA
Port Said *see* **Būr Sa'īd** Egypt
87 I6 **Port Saint Joe** Florida USA
127 G5 **Port-St-Louis-du-Rhône** France
87 K7 **Port Saint Lucie** Florida USA
140 D2 **Port St Mary** Isle of Man UK
82 J5 **Port Sanilac** Michigan USA
79 J7 **Port Saunders** Newfoundland and Labrador Canada
162 F6 **Port Shepstone** South Africa
212 F5 **Port Smith** WA Australia
219 R10 **Port Sorell** Tas. Australia
109 7 **Port Stephens** Falkland Islands
156 F4 **Port Sudan** Sudan
138 D3 **Port Talbot** Neath Port Talbot Wales UK
126 F5 **Port-Vendres** France
222 7 **Port-Vila** Vanuatu
121 R2 **Port-Vladimir** Russian Federation
220 F3 **Port Waikato** New Zealand
218 D6 **Port Wakefield** SA Australia
82 H5 **Port Washington** Wisconsin USA
142 D6 **Port William** Dumfries and Galloway Scotland UK
82 F3 **Port Wing** Wisconsin USA
164 4a **Porta Gouveia** Cape Verde
142 C5 **Portachoillan** Argyll and Bute Scotland UK
105 F5 **Portachuelo** Bolivia
100 B4 **Portachuelo, Cordillera** *range* Colombia
143 F2 **Portadown** Armagh Northern Ireland UK
82 I5 **Portage** Michigan USA
80 I6 **Portage** Utah USA
76 F8 **Portage La Prairie** Manitoba Canada
83 Q3 **Portage Lake** Maine USA
140 A1 **Portahack** Donegal Ireland
81 N2 **Portal** North Dakota USA
128 C4 **Portalegre** Portugal
128 C4 **Portalegre** *admin. area* Portugal
85 K3 **Portales** New Mexico USA
128 C2 **Portas, Embalse das** *lake* Spain
142 C5 **Portavadie** Argyll and Bute Scotland UK
143 G2 **Portavogie** Ards Northern Ireland UK
126 D2 **Portbail** France
83 L7 **Porte Crayon, Mount** West Virginia USA
101 G5 **Porteira** Brazil
102 B3 **Portel** Brazil
128 C4 **Portel** Portugal
86 D3 **Porter** Oklahoma USA
75 R4 **Porter Lake** Saskatchewan Canada
74 F3 **Porter Landing** British Columbia Canada
109 11a **Porter Point** *cape* St Vincent and the Grenadines
84 C2 **Porterville** California USA
138 B3 **Portfield Gate** Pembrokeshire Wales UK
142 E2 **Portgower** Highland Scotland UK
138 D3 **Porth** Rhondda Cynon Taff Wales UK
138 B4 **Porthleven** Cornwall England UK
138 C4 **Portholland** Cornwall England UK
138 B4 **Porthoustock** Cornwall England UK
138 C3 **Porthyrhyd** Carmarthenshire Wales UK
131 C6 **Porticcio** Corsica France
128 D3 **Portillo** Spain
128 B5 **Portimão** Portugal
121 O3 **Portimo** Finland
129 G4 **Portinatx** Spain
138 E3 **Portishead** North Somerset England UK
142 F3 **Portknockie** Moray Scotland UK
218 E8 **Portland** Vic. Australia
86 F4 **Portland** Arkansas USA
83 P5 **Portland** Maine USA
80 D4 **Portland** Oregon USA
86 C7 **Portland** Texas USA
218 E8 **Portland Bay** Vic. Australia
79 J7 **Portland Creek Pond** Newfoundland and Labrador Canada
138 E4 **Portland Harbour** England UK
74 F5 **Portland Inlet** British Columbia Canada
220 G4 **Portland Island** New Zealand
90 E3 **Portland Point** Jamaica
215 G2 **Portland Roads** Qld Australia
143 E3 **Portlaoise** Ireland
143 E4 **Portlaw** Ireland
142 F3 **Portlethen** Aberdeenshire Scotland UK
90 E3 **Portmore** Jamaica
79 D8 **Portneuf-sur-Mer** Quebec Canada
135 V4 **Portnyagino, Ozero** *lake* Russian Federation
102 D3 **Porto** Brazil
131 C5 **Porto** Corsica France
128 B3 **Porto** Portugal
128 B3 **Porto** *admin. area* Portugal
102 A4 **Porto Alegre** Brazil
107 I4 **Porto Alegre** Brazil
103 A8 **Porto Alegre** Brazil
105 F4 **Pôrto Amarante** Brazil
162 B2 **Porto Amboim** Angola
100 E5 **Pôrto Antunes** Brazil
101 I4 **Pôrto Arari** Brazil
130 D5 **Porto Azzurro** Italy
103 A8 **Pôrto Barra do Ivinheima** Brazil
107 I3 **Porto Belo** Brazil
105 F3 **Pôrto Bicentenário** Brazil
105 H3 **Pôrto Cajueiro** Brazil
105 H5 **Pôrto Cedro** Brazil
105 H2 **Pôrto da Lontra** Brazil
105 F4 **Pôrto da Telha** Brazil
103 A6 **Pôrto de Meinacos** Brazil
102 A3 **Pôrto de Moz** Brazil
105 H4 **Pôrto do Angico** Brazil
105 F4 **Pôrto do Massacás** Brazil
105 G2 **Pôrto do Palhal** Brazil
105 G5 **Pôrto do Sará** Brazil
105 G3 **Pôrto dos Gaúchos** Brazil
105 H4 **Pôrto dos Meinacos** Brazil
131 E8 **Porto Empedocle** Italy
105 G4 **Pôrto Esperança** Brazil
105 G4 **Porto Esperidião** Brazil
103 C8 **Pôrto Feliz** Brazil
102 C4 **Pôrto Franco** Brazil
101 H5 **Pôrto Franco** Brazil
105 H4 **Pôrto Fundação** Brazil
105 H2 **Pôrto Fundo** Brazil
101 I4 **Pôrto Grande** Brazil
133 C7 **Pórto Káyio** Greece
105 G5 **Pôrto Manduri** Brazil
105 G6 **Porto Murtinho** Brazil
103 B5 **Porto Nacional** Brazil
158 E3 **Porto-Novo** Benin
164 4 **Porto Novo** Cape Verde
101 H4 **Pôrto Poet** Brazil
107 H2 **Porto Primavera, Represa** *lake* Brazil
130 E5 **Porto Recanati** Italy
130 E5 **Porto San Giorgio** Italy
127 K5 **Porto Sant'Elpidio** Italy
164 2 **Porto Santo, Ilha de** *island* Madeira
105 I3 **Pôrto São Domingos** Brazil
105 G5 **Pôrto São José Velho** Brazil
103 E7 **Pôrto Seguro** Brazil
105 G4 **Pôrto Tenente Marques** Brazil
131 C6 **Porto Torres** Sardinia Italy
103 B9 **Pôrto União** Brazil
105 F3 **Pôrto Velho** Brazil
104 C3 **Pôrto Walter** Brazil
90 E5 **Portobelo** Panama
120 L5 **Pörtom** Finland
105 F5 **Porton** Bolivia
100 A5 **Portoviejo** Ecuador
142 C6 **Portpatrick** Dumfries and Galloway Scotland UK
143 F3 **Portraine** Ireland
138 B4 **Portreath** Cornwall England UK
142 B3 **Portree** Highland Scotland UK
143 F1 **Portrush** Coleraine Northern Ireland UK
143 E1 **Portsalon** Ireland
139 F4 **Portsmouth** Hampshire England UK
83 P5 **Portsmouth** New Hampshire USA
82 J7 **Portsmouth** Ohio USA
83 M8 **Portsmouth** Virginia USA
83 P5 **Portsmouth Harbor** New Hampshire USA
142 F3 **Portsoy** Aberdeenshire Scotland UK
143 F1 **Portstewart** Coleraine Northern Ireland UK
121 O2 **Porttipahdan tekojärvi** *lake* Finland
128 C4 **Portugal** *country* Europe
100 D2 **Portuguesa** *admin. area* Venezuela
104 C4 **Portuguesa, Nevado** *mountain* Peru
143 D3 **Portumna** Ireland
143 C2 **Porturlin** Ireland
83 L5 **Portville** New York USA
140 D2 **Portyerrock** Dumfries and Galloway Scotland UK
108 B5 **Porvenir** Chile
123 M2 **Porvoo/Borgå** Finland
121 R3 **Por'ya Guba** Russian Federation
128 D4 **Porzuna** Spain
128 D2 **Posada** Spain
107 H3 **Posadas** Argentina
108 B4 **Posadas, Lago** *lake* Argentina
58 F2 **Posadowsky Bay** Antarctica
127 J3 **Poschiavo** Switzerland
104 C4 **Posco** Peru
108 C5 **Posesión, Bahía** *bay* Argentina
121 P3 **Posio** Finland
121 P3 **Posionjärvi** *lake* Finland
198 B4 **Poso** Indonesia
197 I4 **Poso** *watercourse* Indonesia
198 B4 **Poso, Teluk** *bay* Indonesia
192 E4 **Posŏng** South Korea
183 N3 **Pospelikha** Russian Federation
103 C6 **Posse** Brazil
159 H3 **Possel** Central African Republic
164 6 **Possession, Île de la** *island* French Southern and Antarctic Lands
109 8 **Possession Bay** South Georgia
86 B4 **Possum Kingdom Lake** Texas USA
85 L4 **Post** Texas USA
80 G3 **Post Falls** Idaho USA
214 C8 **Post Hill** NT Australia
131 E5 **Posta** Italy
131 F6 **Posta Piana** Italy
155 G4 **Poste Weygand (Balise 250)** Algeria
124 G5 **Postioma** Italy
162 D5 **Postmasburg** South Africa
105 H3 **Pôsto Alto Manissaua** Brazil
105 H2 **Pôsto Cocraimoro** Brazil
105 H2 **Pôsto Curua** Brazil
105 F4 **Pôsto Fiscal Rolim de Moura** Brazil
105 H4 **Pôsto Indígena Batovi** Brazil
130 G5 **Posušje** Bosnia and Herzegovina
198 B6 **Pota** Indonesia
82 J3 **Potagannissing Bay** Michigan USA
215 G3 **Potallah** *watercourse* Qld Australia
88 C3 **Potam** Mexico
101 G3 **Potaro-Siparuni** *admin. area* Guyana
162 E5 **Potchefstroom** South Africa
132 D3 **Potcoava** Romania
86 B6 **Poteet** Texas USA
182 E3 **Potemkino** Russian Federation
131 F6 **Potenza** Italy
130 E5 **Potenza** *watercourse* Italy
130 E5 **Potenza Picena** Italy
221 B8 **Poteriteri, Lake** New Zealand
128 D2 **Potes** Spain
86 B6 **Poth** Texas USA
102 D4 **Poti** *watercourse* Brazil
182 D5 **Poti** Georgia
130 G5 **Potirna** Croatia
159 G2 **Potiskum** Nigeria
120 L2 **Potka** Norway
80 G3 **Potlatch** Idaho USA
222 7 **Potnarvin** Vanuatu
130 G5 **Potoci** Bosnia and Herzegovina
132 F1 **Potoki** Ukraine
82 H6 **Potomac** Illinois USA
83 M7 **Potomac** *watercourse* Virginia USA
83 M7 **Potomac** *watercourse* West Virginia USA
132 A1 **Pôtor** Slovakia
158 B3 **Potoru** Sierra Leone
105 E5 **Potosí** Bolivia
106 E2 **Potosí** *admin. area* Bolivia
90 C5 **Potosí** Nicaragua
82 F8 **Potosi** Missouri USA
82 F5 **Potosi** Wisconsin USA
105 G5 **Potrerito de la Noria** Bolivia
105 F5 **Potrero** Bolivia
100 C4 **Potrero** Colombia
83 N2 **Potrincourt Lake** Quebec Canada
124 G1 **Potsdam** Germany
187 F7 **Pottangi** Orissa India
82 D7 **Pottawatomie** *watercourse* Kansas USA
81 N6 **Potter** Nebraska USA
77 W1 **Potter Island** Nunavut Canada
139 E3 **Potterne** Wiltshire England UK
139 G3 **Potters Bar** Hertfordshire England UK
142 F3 **Potterton** Aberdeenshire Scotland UK
143 E4 **Pottlerath** Ireland
78 J5 **Pottles Bay** Newfoundland and Labrador Canada
139 G2 **Potton** Bedfordshire England UK
86 E3 **Pottsville** Arkansas USA
83 M6 **Pottsville** Pennsylvania USA
187 E10 **Pottuvil** Sri Lanka
81 Q8 **Potwin** Kansas USA
126 D3 **Pouancé** France
74 K5 **Pouce Coupe** British Columbia Canada
164 7b **Poudre d'Or** Mauritius
83 O6 **Poughkeepsie** New York USA
124 B4 **Pouilly** France
83 L2 **Poularies** Quebec Canada
143 C5 **Poulgorm Bridge** Ireland
83 P2 **Poulin-de-Courval, Lac** *lake* Quebec Canada
221 D6 **Poulter** *watercourse* New Zealand
139 F3 **Poulton** Gloucestershire England UK
140 F3 **Poulton-le-Fylde** Lancashire England UK
222 7 **Poum** New Caledonia
133 D6 **Pounta, Akra** *cape* Greece
133 C6 **Pourion** Greece
106 F6 **Pourtalé** Argentina
105 G3 **Pouso Alegre** Brazil
103 C8 **Pouso Alegre** Brazil
121 P4 **Poussu** Finland
194 D4 **Poŭthisăt** Cambodia
158 D2 **Pouy-Tenga** Burkina Faso
126 D3 **Pouzauges** France
129 I1 **Pouzilhac** France
121 S5 **Povenets** Russian Federation
220 G4 **Poverty Bay** New Zealand
132 A3 **Povlen, Mali** *mountain* Serbia
128 B3 **Póvoa de Varzim** Portugal
182 D3 **Povorino** Russian Federation
192 G2 **Povorotnyy, Mys** *island* Russian Federation
83 L3 **Powassan** Ontario Canada
84 D4 **Poway** California USA
81 L4 **Powder** *watercourse* Wyoming USA
218 G1 **Powell** *watercourse* Qld Australia
82 J6 **Powell** Ohio USA
81 K4 **Powell** Wyoming USA
84 G2 **Powell, Lake** Utah USA
214 C7 **Powell, Mount** NT Australia
74 I7 **Powell Lake** British Columbia Canada
216 G6 **Powell Point** WA Australia
90 E1 **Powell Point** Bahamas
74 I8 **Powell River** British Columbia Canada
87 J2 **Powell River** Tennessee USA
143 D5 **Power Head** *cape* Ireland
81 N2 **Powers Lake** North Dakota USA
76 G7 **Powerview** Manitoba Canada
83 M8 **Powhatan** Virginia USA
139 E2 **Powick** Worcestershire England UK
125 I1 **Powidz** Poland
215 H6 **Powlathanga, Lake** Qld Australia
138 D2 **Powys** *admin. area* Wales UK
105 H4 **Poxoréo** Brazil
222 7 **Poya** New Caledonia
196 A3 **Poyan Reservoir** Singapore
189 G3 **Poyang** Jiangxi China
189 G2 **Poyang Hu** *lake* Jiangxi China
191 K2 **Poyarkovo** Russian Federation
82 G4 **Poygan, Lake** Wisconsin USA
143 F2 **Poyntz Pass** Armagh Northern Ireland UK
128 B2 **Poyo** Spain
133 F6 **Poyrazdamları** Turkey
121 N2 **Pöyrisjärvi** *lake* Finland
123 N2 **Pöyry** Finland
123 L2 **Pöytyä** Finland
89 F4 **Poza Rica** Mexico
130 G4 **Požega** Croatia
123 K5 **Pozezdrze** Poland
136 E2 **Pozhnya** *watercourse* Ukraine
125 I1 **Poznań** Poland
125 I4 **Poznanovec** Croatia
128 E5 **Pozo Alcón** Spain
106 F2 **Pozo Anta** Paraguay
101 F3 **Pozo Azul** Venezuela
105 F4 **Pozo Blanco** Bolivia
107 G2 **Pozo Colorado** Paraguay
105 G5 **Pozo de Buey** Paraguay
106 E3 **Pozo Hondo** Argentina
128 D4 **Pozoblanco** Spain
128 F4 **Pozohondo** Spain
108 D2 **Pozos, Punta** *cape* Argentina
104 C3 **Pozuzo** Peru
131 F8 **Pozzallo** Italy
131 F8 **Pozzillo, Lago di** *lake* Italy
131 C6 **Pozzo di Borgo, Punta di** *mountain* Corsica France
131 F6 **Pozzuoli** Italy
130 D5 **Pozzuolo** Italy
158 D3 **Pra** *watercourse* Ghana
196 E4 **Prabumulih** Indonesia
128 B4 **Pracana, Barragem de** *lake* Portugal
130 F2 **Prachatice** Czech Republic
128 C2 **Prada, Embalse de** *lake* Spain
125 I2 **Praděd** *mountain* Czech Republic
126 F4 **Pradelles** France
100 B4 **Pradera** Colombia
126 F5 **Prades** France
103 E7 **Prado** Brazil
100 C4 **Prado** Colombia
Prague *see* **Praha** Czech Republic
125 H2 **Praha** *admin. area* Czech Republic
125 H2 **Praha (Prague)** Czech Republic
126 D3 **Prahecq** France
132 D3 **Prahova** *admin. area* Romania
125 L5 **Prahovo** Serbia
164 4a **Praia** Cape Verde
164 1b **Praia da Vitória** Azores
163 F5 **Praia do Bilene** Mozambique
164 1b **Praia do Norte** Azores
101 F5 **Praia do Vinte e Oito** Brazil
103 C9 **Praia Grande** Brazil
132 D2 **Praid** Romania
164 1b **Prainha** Azores
102 A3 **Prainha** Brazil
101 I5 **Prainha** Brazil
215 H6 **Prairie** Qld Australia
218 G2 **Prairie** Qld Australia
215 H6 **Prairie** *watercourse* Qld Australia
80 F4 **Prairie City** Oregon USA
85 L3 **Prairie Dog Town Fork of the Red** *watercourse* Texas USA
82 F5 **Prairie du Chien** Wisconsin USA
215 H7 **Prairie Peak** Qld Australia
81 P7 **Prairie View** Kansas USA
194 D4 **Prakhon Chai** Thailand
194 C4 **Pran Buri** Thailand
123 M3 **Prangli** *island* Estonia
90 D4 **Pranza** Nicaragua
196 C3 **Prapat** Indonesia
164 9a **Praslin** *island* Seychelles
109 13 **Praslin** St Lucia
108 A4 **Prat, Isla** *island* Chile
103 B7 **Prata** Brazil
103 B7 **Prata** *watercourse* Brazil
186 D6 **Pratapgarh** Rajasthan India
186 E6 **Pratapgarh** Uttar Pradesh India
189 G5 **Pratas Island** China
130 D5 **Prato** Italy
126 F5 **Prats-de-Mollo-la-Preste** France
81 P8 **Pratt** Kansas USA
56 U3 **Pratt Seamount** *underwater feature* Pacific Ocean
87 H4 **Prattville** Alabama USA
127 G3 **Prauthoy** France
128 C2 **Pravia** Spain
125 I2 **Prawików** Poland
88 D2 **Praxédis Guerrero** Mexico
197 H6 **Praya** Indonesia
123 O5 **Prazaroki** Belarus
194 E4 **Preah** *watercourse* Cambodia
125 I5 **Predavac** Croatia
125 G4 **Predlitz** Austria
124 G4 **Predoi** Italy
130 H5 **Predolje** Bosnia and Herzegovina
130 F4 **Predošćica** Croatia
140 F3 **Preesall** Lancashire England UK
122 F5 **Preetz** Germany
77 N1 **Prefontaine, Cape** Nunavut Canada
123 K5 **Pregolya** *watercourse* Russian Federation
130 F3 **Pregrada** Croatia
123 N4 **Preiļi** Latvia
123 N4 **Preiļu** *admin. area* Latvia
83 L2 **Preissac, Lac** *lake* Quebec Canada
130 F1 **Přelouč** Czech Republic
130 E4 **Premantura** Croatia
126 F3 **Prémery** France
74 F4 **Premier** British Columbia Canada
86 B7 **Premont** Texas USA
125 J3 **Prenčov** Slovakia
132 F2 **Prenistrului, Dealurile** *range* Moldova
216 H3 **Prenti Downs** WA Australia
82 F4 **Prentice** Wisconsin USA
214 C5 **Prentice Lake** NT Australia
86 G5 **Prentiss** Mississippi USA
135 AI8 **Preobrazhenskoye** Russian Federation
194 B4 **Preparis Island** Andaman and Nicobar Islands India
194 B4 **Preparis North Channel** Andaman and Nicobar Islands India
194 B4 **Preparis South Channel** Andaman and Nicobar Islands India
130 G2 **Přerov** Czech Republic
122 G5 **Prerow** Germany
131 G6 **Presciutto, Punta** *cape* Italy
84 F3 **Prescott** Arizona USA
86 E4 **Prescott** Arkansas USA
80 F3 **Prescott** Washington USA
213 H6 **Prescott Lakes** WA Australia
84 F3 **Prescott Valley** Arizona USA
221 B8 **Preservation Inlet** New Zealand
81 O5 **Presho** South Dakota USA
106 F3 **Presidencia Roque Sáenz Peña** Argentina
53 R10 **President Thiers Seamount** *underwater feature* Pacific Ocean
103 B8 **Presidente Bernardes** Brazil
102 C4 **Presidente Dutra** Brazil
103 A8 **Presidente Epitácio** Brazil
107 G2 **Presidente Hayes** *admin. area* Paraguay
105 F3 **Presidente Médici** Brazil
103 A6 **Presidente Murtinho** Brazil
103 B8 **Presidente Prudente** Brazil
103 B8 **Presidente Venceslau** Brazil
88 D4 **Presidio** *watercourse* Mexico
85 J6 **Presidio** Texas USA
125 K3 **Prešov** Slovakia
125 K3 **Prešovský** *admin. area* Slovakia
133 D5 **Prespa** *mountain* Bulgaria
133 B5 **Prespa, Lake** Macedonia
83 Q3 **Presque Isle** Maine USA
109 14 **Presqu'île la Caravelle** Martinique
76 J8 **Press Lake** Ontario Canada
126 E3 **Pressac** France
127 J2 **Pressath** Germany
140 E3 **Prestatyn** Denbighshire Wales UK
120 I2 **Presteid** Norway
138 D2 **Presteign** Powys Wales UK
138 E2 **Presthope** Shropshire England UK
140 F3 **Preston** Lancashire England UK
142 F5 **Preston** Scottish Borders Scotland UK
80 J5 **Preston** Idaho USA
85 M2 **Preston** Kansas USA
82 E5 **Preston** Minnesota USA
212 D6 **Preston, Cape** WA Australia
216 D6 **Preston, Lake** WA Australia
216 D6 **Preston Beach** WA Australia
139 F2 **Preston on Stour** Warwickshire England UK
142 F5 **Prestonpans** East Lothian Scotland UK
82 J8 **Prestonsburg** Kentucky USA
58 N1 **Prestrud Inlet** *bay* Antarctica
142 D5 **Prestwick** South Ayrshire Scotland UK
103 C7 **Preto** *watercourse* Brazil
101 G5 **Preto da Eva** *watercourse* Brazil
105 F2 **Preto do Igapo-acu** *watercourse* Brazil
162 E5 **Pretoria (Tshwane)** South Africa
126 F3 **Préveranges** France
81 N6 **Prewitt Reservoir** Colorado USA
194 E5 **Prey Vêng** Cambodia
130 F4 **Prezid** Croatia
130 F4 **Prezid** Slovenia
191 I2 **Priargunsk** Russian Federation
72 C7 **Pribilof Islands** Alaska USA
130 H4 **Priboj** Bosnia and Herzegovina
132 A4 **Priboj** Serbia
125 L2 **Priborovo** Belarus
218 C6 **Price** SA Australia
81 J7 **Price** Utah USA
81 J7 **Price** *watercourse* Utah USA
194 B4 **Price, Cape** Andaman and Nicobar Islands India
218 D5 **Price Hill** SA Australia
86 H3 **Priceville** Alabama USA
86 G5 **Prichard** Alabama USA
109 10a **Prickly Bay** Grenada
109 10a **Prickly Point** *cape* Grenada
139 H2 **Prickwillow** Cambridgeshire England UK
138 E3 **Priddy** Somerset England UK
132 B4 **Pridvorica** Serbia
128 E3 **Priego** Spain
123 L4 **Priekule** Latvia
123 K5 **Priekulė** Lithuania
124 G4 **Prien** Germany
123 L5 **Prienai** Lithuania
162 D5 **Prieska** South Africa
142 C3 **Priest Island** Scotland UK
80 G2 **Priest Lake** Idaho USA
80 F3 **Priest Rapids Lake** Washington USA
125 J3 **Prievidza** Slovakia
130 F4 **Prijeboj** Croatia
132 A4 **Prijepolje** Serbia
132 B4 **Prijevor** Serbia
158 D3 **Prikro** Côte d'Ivoire
133 B5 **Prilep** Macedonia
123 P4 **Priluki** Russian Federation
129 G4 **Prima, Punta** *cape* Spain
130 E2 **Přimda** Czech Republic
108 D2 **Primera Angostura** Argentina
106 F4 **Primero** *watercourse* Argentina
85 L7 **Primero de Mayo** Mexico
88 A1 **Primo Tapia** Mexico
123 O2 **Primorsk** Russian Federation
136 E4 **Primorskiy** Ukraine
190 F2 **Primorskiy Khrebet** *range* Russian Federation
135 AB10 **Primorskiy Kray** *admin. area* Russian Federation
123 K5 **Primor'ye** Russian Federation
75 Q5 **Primrose Lake** Saskatchewan Canada
75 Q6 **Prince** Saskatchewan Canada
75 S6 **Prince Albert** Saskatchewan Canada
162 D6 **Prince Albert** South Africa
58 K1 **Prince Albert Mountains** Antarctica
72 H4 **Prince Albert Peninsula** Northwest Territories Canada
72 H4 **Prince Albert Sound** Northwest Territories Canada
72 G4 **Prince Alfred, Cape** Northwest Territories Canada
73 L5 **Prince Charles Island** Nunavut Canada
58 E2 **Prince Charles Mountains** Antarctica
78 C2 **Prince-de-Galles, Cap du** *cape* Quebec Canada
54 H9 **Prince Edward Fracture Zone** *underwater feature* Southern Ocean
79 G9 **Prince Edward Island** *admin. area* Canada
74 J6 **Prince George** British Columbia Canada
73 I3 **Prince Gustaf Adolf Sea** Nunavut Canada
58 C2 **Prince Harald Coast** Antarctica
72 C5 **Prince of Wales, Cape** Alaska USA
76 H3 **Prince of Wales Fort** Manitoba Canada
214 G1 **Prince of Wales Island** Qld Australia
73 J4 **Prince of Wales Island** Nunavut Canada
74 E5 **Prince of Wales Island** Alaska USA
72 H4 **Prince of Wales Strait** Northwest Territories Canada
58 C2 **Prince Olav Coast** Antarctica
72 H3 **Prince Patrick Island** Northwest Territories Canada
213 H3 **Prince Regent** *watercourse* WA Australia
73 J4 **Prince Regent Inlet** Nunavut Canada
74 F5 **Prince Rupert** British Columbia Canada
109 15 **Prince Rupert Bay** Dominica
72 E6 **Prince William Sound** Alaska USA
139 G3 **Princes Risborough** Buckinghamshire England UK
109 inset 9 **Princes Town** Trinidad and Tobago
109 inset 9 **Princes Town** *admin. area* Trinidad and Tobago
102 E4 **Princesa Isabel** Brazil
83 N7 **Princess Anne** Maryland USA
58 A2 **Princess Astrid Coast** Antarctica
215 H3 **Princess Charlotte Bay** Qld Australia
58 F2 **Princess Elizabeth Land** *plain* Antarctica
58 X2 **Princess Martha Coast** Antarctica
58 B2 **Princess Ragnhild Coast** Antarctica
74 G6 **Princess Royal Island** British Columbia Canada
74 K8 **Princeton** British Columbia Canada
82 G6 **Princeton** Illinois USA
82 H8 **Princeton** Kentucky USA
82 E6 **Princeton** Missouri USA
218 F8 **Princetown** Vic. Australia
138 D4 **Princetown** Devon England UK
84 inset **Princeville** Hawai'i USA
159 F4 **Príncipe** *island* São Tomé and Príncipe
74 F6 **Principe Channel** British Columbia Canada
80 E4 **Prineville** Oregon USA
80 E4 **Prineville Reservoir** Oregon USA
81 N5 **Pringle** South Dakota USA
196 E5 **Pringsewu** Indonesia
90 D4 **Prinzapolka** Nicaragua
211 inset **Prion Lake** Macquarie Island Australia
128 B2 **Prior, Cabo** *cape* Spain
139 F2 **Priors Marston** Warwickshire England UK
123 O2 **Priozersk** Russian Federation
134 N6 **Pripolyarnyy Ural** *range* Russian Federation
121 Q2 **Prirechnyy** Russian Federation

132 E4 **Priseltsi** Bulgaria
136 F2 **Pristen** Russian Federation
132 B4 **Priština** Kosovo
81 N8 **Pritchett** Colorado USA
186 E6 **Prithvipur** Madhya Pradesh India
77 V1 **Pritzler Harbour** Nunavut Canada
127 G4 **Privas** France
78 E4 **Privert, Lac** *lake* Quebec Canada
132 D1 **Privetnoye** Ukraine
182 D1 **Privolzhsk** Russian Federation
182 E3 **Privolzhskiy** Russian Federation
182 E3 **Privolzhskoye** Russian Federation
132 B4 **Prizren** Kosovo
131 E8 **Prizzi** Italy
130 G4 **Prnjavor** Bosnia and Herzegovina
132 A3 **Prnjavor** Serbia
142 B5 **Proaig** Argyll and Bute Scotland UK
197 G5 **Probolinggo** Indonesia
138 C4 **Probus** Cornwall England UK
74 M8 **Procter** British Columbia Canada
86 B4 **Proctor Lake** Texas USA
187 E8 **Proddatur** Andhra Pradesh India
77 Q2 **Profond, Pointe du** *cape* Quebec Canada
100 C5 **Progreso** Ecuador
89 H4 **Progreso** Mexico
85 I5 **Progreso** Mexico
88 B1 **Progreso** Mexico
123 K5 **Prokhladnoye** Russian Federation
182 D5 **Prokhladnyy** Russian Federation
135 AC7 **Prokof'yeva, Ostrov** *island* Russian Federation
133 C6 **Prokopion** Greece
183 O2 **Prokopyevsk** Russian Federation
132 B4 **Prokuplje** Serbia
123 P3 **Proletariy** Russian Federation
Prome *see* **Pyay** Myanmar
105 H5 **Promissão** Brazil
103 B8 **Promissão** Brazil
107 I2 **Promissão, Represa** *lake* Brazil
104 B3 **Promontorio Salinas** *cape* Peru
123 P6 **Pronya** *watercourse* Belarus
74 I4 **Prophet** *watercourse* British Columbia Canada
74 J3 **Prophet River** British Columbia Canada
103 E5 **Propriá** Brazil
122 G5 **Prorer Wiek** *bay* Germany
215 J6 **Proserpine, Lake** Qld Australia
125 J2 **Prosna** *watercourse* Poland
214 G5 **Prospect** Qld Australia
109 12 **Prospect** Barbados
87 K3 **Prosperity** South Carolina USA
164 5b **Prosperous Bay** St Helena
125 I2 **Prószków** Poland
81 P8 **Protection** Kansas USA
133 D5 **Proti** Greece
130 F2 **Protivín** Czech Republic
134 O6 **Protochnyye** Russian Federation
127 H5 **Provence-Alpes-Côte d'Azur** *admin. area* France
83 P6 **Providence** Rhode Island USA
82 H8 **Providence** Kentucky USA
80 J6 **Providence** Utah USA
164 9 **Providence Island** Seychelles
100 C3 **Providencia** Colombia
88 C2 **Providencia** Mexico
109 2 **Providencia, Isla de (Colombia)** *island* Colombia
105 F3 **Providência, Serra da** *range* Brazil
91 F2 **Providenciales Island** Turks and Caicos Islands
160 D3 **Province Orientale** *admin. area* Democratic Republic of Congo
126 F2 **Provins** France
80 J6 **Provo** Utah USA
75 P6 **Provost** Alberta Canada
158 D3 **Pru** *watercourse* Ghana
103 B9 **Prudentópolis** Brazil
141 G2 **Prudhoe** Northumberland England UK
124 D2 **Prüm** Germany
124 D2 **Prüm** *watercourse* Germany
131 C5 **Prunelli-di-Fiumorbo** Corsica France
218 F6 **Prungle** NSW Australia
130 H2 **Pruské** Slovakia
125 J1 **Pruszcz** Poland
125 K1 **Pruszków** Poland
132 E2 **Prut** *watercourse* Moldova
132 E1 **Prut** *watercourse* Romania
132 D1 **Prut** *watercourse* Ukraine
123 N5 **Prūto ežeras** *lake* Belarus
123 Q2 **Pryazha** Russian Federation
58 F2 **Prydz Bay** Antarctica
136 E2 **Pryluky** Ukraine
125 K1 **Przasnysz** Poland
125 I1 **Przechlewo** Poland
125 I2 **Przeczów** Poland
125 J2 **Przedbórz** Poland
125 H2 **Przemków** Poland
125 L3 **Przemyśl** Poland
125 L2 **Przeworsk** Poland
125 K2 **Przysucha** Poland
125 K2 **Przytyk** Poland
122 J5 **Przywidz** Poland
133 D6 **Psara** Greece
133 D6 **Psara** *island* Greece
133 C6 **Psaromita, Akra** *cape* Greece
133 D6 **Psathoura** *island* Greece
182 C5 **Psebay** Russian Federation
133 D8 **Pseira** *island* Greece
136 E2 **Psel** *watercourse* Russian Federation
133 E7 **Pserimos** *island* Greece
182 C5 **Pshada** Russian Federation
133 D8 **Psiloritis** *mountain* Greece
123 O4 **Pskov** Russian Federation
123 N3 **Pskov, Lake** *lake* Russian Federation
123 O4 **Pskovskaya Oblast'** *admin. area* Russian Federation
136 E2 **Ps'ol** *watercourse* Ukraine
130 E1 **Pšov** Czech Republic
125 H1 **Pszczew** Poland
125 J3 **Pszczyna** Poland
77 T4 **Ptarmigan** *watercourse* Quebec Canada
133 C6 **Pteleos** Greece
125 H4 **Ptuj** Slovenia
188 D4 **Pu-la Ho** *watercourse* Yunnan China
199 G4 **Pua** *watercourse* Papua New Guinea
197 I4 **Puah** *island* Indonesia
84 inset **Puakō** Hawai'i USA
106 F6 **Puan** Argentina
223 12c **Pu'apu'a** Samoa
181 G2 **Pubao** Xizang Zizhiqu China
104 E6 **Puca Apacheta** Bolivia
104 C1 **Pucacuro** Peru
104 C3 **Pucallpa** Peru
104 D5 **Pucapacheta, Cerro** *mountain* Peru
104 E5 **Pucara** Bolivia
125 L2 **Puchaczów** Poland
188 F1 **Pucheng** Shaanxi China
182 D2 **Puchezh** Russian Federation
192 E4 **Puch'ŏn** South Korea
195 I5 **Pucio Point** Philippines
123 J5 **Pucka, Zatoka** *bay* Poland
121 O4 **Pudasjärvi** Finland
188 E3 **Puding** Guizhou China
134 Q7 **Pudino** Russian Federation
180 E2 **Pudog Zangbo** *watercourse* Xizang Zizhiqu China
121 T6 **Pudozh** Russian Federation
188 D3 **Pudu He** *watercourse* Yunnan China
187 E9 **Puducherry** Puducherry India
220 2 **Pue** Cook Islands New Zealand
89 F5 **Puebla** Mexico
89 F5 **Puebla** *admin. area* Mexico
128 D5 **Puebla, Embalse de la** *lake* Spain
128 D4 **Puebla de Alcocer** Spain
128 E3 **Puebla de Beleña** Spain
128 C2 **Puebla de Brollón** Spain
128 D4 **Puebla de Don Rodrigo** Spain
128 D2 **Puebla de Lillo** Spain
128 C4 **Puebla de Obando** Spain
81 M7 **Pueblo** Colorado USA
128 E5 **Pueblo de Don Fadrique** Spain
100 C4 **Pueblo de Indios** Colombia
104 B3 **Pueblo Libre** Peru
106 F6 **Pueblo Nuevo** Argentina
100 C2 **Pueblo Nuevo** Colombia
104 B2 **Pueblo Nuevo** Peru
90 B4 **Pueblo Nuevo Tiquisate** Guatemala
109 2 **Pueblo Viejo** Isla de Providencia
90 D5 **Pueblo Viejo** Panama
100 D3 **Pueblo Viejo** Venezuela
89 F4 **Pueblo Viejo, Laguna de** *lake* Mexico
88 C3 **Pueblo Yaqui** Mexico
106 E6 **Puelches** Argentina
106 E6 **Puelén** Argentina
128 D5 **Puente-Genil** Spain
128 D4 **Puente Nuevo, Embalse de** *lake* Spain
126 C5 **Puente Viesgo** Spain
128 F5 **Puentes, Embalse de** *lake* Spain
128 C2 **Puentes de Garcia Rodríguez** Spain
85 I3 **Puerco** *watercourse* New Mexico USA
88 C2 **Puerta Cajón** Mexico
106 F2 **Puerta de Díaz** Argentina
84 E5 **Puertecitos** Mexico
100 C5 **Puerto** Peru
108 B3 **Puerto Aguirre** Chile
108 B3 **Puerto Aisén** Chile
105 F4 **Puerto Alegre** Bolivia
100 D5 **Puerto Alfonso** Colombia
90 D5 **Puerto Armuelles** Panama
101 F3 **Puerto Arturo** Venezuela
100 B4 **Puerto Asís** Colombia
100 E3 **Puerto Ayacucho** Venezuela
109 4 **Puerto Ayora** Archipiélago de Colón (Galapagos Islands)
107 G2 **Puerto Bahía Negra** Paraguay
109 4 **Puerto Baquerizo Moreno** Archipiélago de Colón (Galapagos Islands)
90 B4 **Puerto Barrios** Guatemala
100 C5 **Puerto Benjamín García** Colombia
100 C3 **Puerto Berrío** Colombia
85 H5 **Puerto Blanca** Mexico
85 I7 **Puerto Blanco** Mexico
100 C3 **Puerto Boyacá** Colombia
104 C3 **Puerto Breu** Peru
90 D4 **Puerto Cabezas** Nicaragua
108 B3 **Puerto Cahacabuco** Chile
100 D5 **Puerto Caimán** Colombia
88 C3 **Puerto Cancún** Mexico
84 E6 **Puerto Canoas** Mexico
100 D5 **Puerto Carlos** Colombia
91 H6 **Puerto Carreño** Colombia
90 C3 **Puerto Castilla** Honduras
100 C2 **Puerto Catatumbo** Venezuela
104 B2 **Puerto Chicama** *bay* Peru
108 B3 **Puerto Cisnes** Chile
108 C5 **Puerto Coig** Argentina
100 D4 **Puerto Colombia** Colombia
100 C2 **Puerto Colombia** Colombia
100 E4 **Puerto Colombia** Venezuela
100 C4 **Puerto Concordia** Colombia
90 C4 **Puerto Cortés** Honduras
100 C4 **Puerto Cuba** Colombia
108 B5 **Puerto Curtze** Chile
164 3a **Puerto de la Cruz** Canary Islands
154 C3 **Puerto de la Estaca** Spain
164 3 **Puerto de Rosario** Canary Islands
104 E4 **Puerto de Tumupasa** Bolivia
164 3d **Puerto del Rosario** Canary Islands
108 D4 **Puerto Deseado** Argentina
104 B2 **Puerto Díaz** Peru
90 B4 **Puerto El Triunfo** El Salvador
100 B2 **Puerto Escondido** Colombia
88 C3 **Puerto Escondido** Mexico
90 D5 **Puerto Escondido** Panama
108 D6 **Puerto Español** Argentina
104 D3 **Puerto Estirón de Marcos** Peru
104 D3 **Puerto Fortaleza** Peru
100 B5 **Puerto Francisco de Orellanas** Ecuador
104 C2 **Puerto Franco** Peru
100 C3 **Puerto Gaitán** Colombia
100 C5 **Puerto Grau** Peru
108 B4 **Puerto Guadal** Chile
104 D5 **Puerto Guaqui** Bolivia
104 D4 **Puerto Heath** Bolivia
100 C4 **Puerto Huitoto** Colombia
100 B5 **Puerto Ila** Ecuador
108 B4 **Puerto Ingeniero Ibáñez** Chile
109 6a **Puerto Inglés** *bay* Isla Róbinson Crusoe
106 F2 **Puerto Irigoyen** Argentina
104 D4 **Puerto Leguía** Peru
100 C5 **Puerto Leguízamo** Colombia
90 D4 **Puerto Lempira** Honduras
105 F4 **Puerto Leytón** Bolivia
89 B2 **Puerto Libertad** Mexico
100 D3 **Puerto Limón** Colombia
90 D5 **Puerto Limón** Costa Rica
108 D2 **Puerto Lobos** Argentina
84 F5 **Puerto Lobos** Mexico
128 F5 **Puerto Lumbreras** Spain
89 G6 **Puerto Madero** Mexico
108 D3 **Puerto Madryn** Argentina
104 C3 **Puerto Mairo** Peru
104 D4 **Puerto Maldonado** Peru
105 E4 **Puerto Márquez** Bolivia
100 C4 **Puerto Mercedes** Colombia
100 E3 **Puerto Miranda** Venezuela
108 B2 **Puerto Montt** Chile
100 D5 **Puerto Nariño** Colombia
108 B5 **Puerto Natales** Chile
105 E5 **Puerto Nuevo** Bolivia
100 D4 **Puerto Nuevo** Colombia
90 E2 **Puerto Padre** Cuba
88 D2 **Puerto Palomas** Mexico
104 B1 **Puerto Pardo** Peru
104 C2 **Puerto Parinari** Peru
105 F4 **Puerto Pastos** Bolivia
100 D4 **Puerto Peñalito** Colombia
88 B2 **Puerto Peñasco** Mexico
104 B3 **Puerto Perdido** *bay* Peru
108 D3 **Puerto Pirámides** Argentina
104 B3 **Puerto Pisana** Peru
105 F6 **Puerto Potosí** Bolivia
195 H5 **Puerto Princesa** Philippines
100 C4 **Puerto Príncipe** Colombia
108 C5 **Puerto Progreso** Chile
108 B3 **Puerto Puyuguapi** Chile
108 B3 **Puerto Quellón** Chile
105 G5 **Puerto Quijarro** Bolivia
108 C6 **Puerto Remolino** Argentina
100 C5 **Puerto Reyes** Colombia
91 H3 **Puerto Rico** *unincorporated US territory* Caribbean
100 C4 **Puerto Rico** Colombia
50 L8 **Puerto Rico Trench** *underwater feature* Atlantic Ocean
100 D3 **Puerto Rondón** Colombia
107 G3 **Puerto Rosario** Paraguay
104 E3 **Puerto Ruiz** Bolivia
108 D2 **Puerto San Antonio Este** Argentina
90 B4 **Puerto San José** Guatemala
104 B3 **Puerto Santa** Peru
108 C5 **Puerto Santa Cruz** Argentina
100 C5 **Puerto Santander** Colombia
91 F5 **Puerto Santander** Colombia
100 C2 **Puerto Santander** Venezuela
88 A2 **Puerto Santo Tomás** Mexico
105 F6 **Puerto Sucre** Bolivia
104 C2 **Puerto Supay** Peru
104 B3 **Puerto Supe** Peru
104 D4 **Puerto Tahuantinsuyo** Peru
108 B4 **Puerto Tranquilo** Chile
100 C3 **Puerto Triunfo** Colombia
100 C5 **Puerto Triunfo** Peru
88 D4 **Puerto Vallarta** Mexico
109 4 **Puerto Velasco Ibarra** Archipiélago de Colón (Galapagos Islands)
100 C5 **Puerto Victoria** Colombia
105 F4 **Puerto Viejo** Bolivia
106 D3 **Puerto Viejo** Chile
109 4 **Puerto Villamil** Archipiélago de Colón (Galapagos Islands)
108 C3 **Puerto Visser** Argentina
100 C3 **Puerto Wilches** Colombia
108 B5 **Puerto Yartou** Chile
100 C4 **Puerto Yavilla** Colombia
108 B5 **Puerto Zenteno** Chile
128 D4 **Puertollano** Spain
107 G2 **Puesto Alambique** Paraguay
100 C5 **Puesto Arturo** Peru
106 F2 **Puesto Bullain** Paraguay
106 F2 **Puesto Curupayty** Paraguay
106 F2 **Puesto Dorado** Paraguay
107 G2 **Puesto González** Paraguay
106 F2 **Puesto Jabalí** Paraguay
104 D4 **Puesto Moscoso** Bolivia
106 F2 **Puesto Pavón** Paraguay
107 G2 **Puesto Santa Rosa** Paraguay
223 14a **Pueu** French Polynesia
88 D4 **Puga** Mexico
182 E3 **Pugachev** Russian Federation
186 C5 **Pugal** Rajasthan India
188 D3 **Puge** Sichuan China
127 H5 **Puget-sur-Argens** France
131 G6 **Puglia** *admin. area* Italy
109 5 **Puhi** *volcano* Isla de Pascua (Easter Island)
121 O4 **Puhos** Finland
125 L5 **Pui** Romania
160 D2 **Puig** Sudan
129 G3 **Puig-reig** Spain
126 F1 **Puisieux** France
132 F3 **Puiu, Lacul** *lake* Romania
158 B3 **Pujehun** Sierra Leone
210 inset **Puji, Tanjong** *cape* Cocos (Keeling) Islands Australia
100 B5 **Pujilí** Ecuador
104 D5 **Pujocucho** Peru
192 E3 **Pujon** North Korea
192 E3 **Pujon-ho** *lake* North Korea
221 D7 **Pukaki** *watercourse* New Zealand
221 D6 **Pukaki, Lake** New Zealand
222 1 **Pukapuka** *island* Cook Islands New Zealand
223 14 **Pukapuka** *island* French Polynesia
121 Q4 **Pukari** Finland
223 14 **Pukarua** *island* French Polynesia
217 M3 **Pukatja** SA Australia
122 H4 **Pukavik** Sweden
122 H4 **Pukaviksbukten** *bay* Sweden
192 F3 **Pukch'ŏng** North Korea
132 A4 **Pukë** Albania
220 F3 **Pukekohe** New Zealand
221 E6 **Puketeraki Range** New Zealand
221 C8 **Puketi** New Zealand
220 G5 **Puketoi Range** New Zealand
130 E4 **Pula** Croatia
130 G3 **Pula** Hungary
131 C7 **Pula** Sardinia Italy
131 C7 **Pula, Capo di** *cape* Sardinia Italy
133 A5 **Pulaj** Albania
180 D2 **Pulan** Xizang Zizhiqu China
191 J5 **Pulandian** Liaoning China
197 G4 **Pulangpisau** Indonesia
199 I2 **Pulap** *island* Federated States of Micronesia
197 I5 **Pulasi** *island* Indonesia
83 M5 **Pulaski** New York USA
83 K8 **Pulaski** Virginia USA
199 F5 **Pulau** *watercourse* Indonesia
196 C4 **Pulautelo** Indonesia
125 K2 **Puławy** Poland
125 L2 **Pulemets** Ukraine
127 K3 **Pulfero** Italy
138 E1 **Pulford** Cheshire England UK
187 E7 **Pulgaon** Maharashtra India
138 E4 **Pulham** Dorset England UK
124 D2 **Pulheim** Germany
187 E9 **Pulicat Lake** Andhra Pradesh India
198 C3 **Pulisan, Tanjung** *cape* Indonesia
121 N2 **Pulju** Finland
121 O5 **Pulkonkoski** Finland
80 G3 **Pullman** Washington USA
124 D4 **Pully** Switzerland
198 D2 **Pulo Anna** *island* Palau
194 C5 **Pulo Buda** Myanmar
195 I3 **Pulog, Mount** *mountain* Philippines
121 R2 **Pulozero** Russian Federation
121 S5 **Pulozero, Ozero** *lake* Russian Federation
75 U7 **Pulp River** Manitoba Canada
128 F5 **Pulpí** Spain
88 C3 **Púlpito, Punta** *cape* Mexico
125 G2 **Pulsnitz** *watercourse* Germany
120 L2 **Pulsujärvi** Sweden
222 6 **Pulusuk** *island* Federated States of Micronesia
199 I2 **Puluwat** *island* Federated States of Micronesia
186 D4 **Pulwama** Jammu and Kashmir India/Pakistan
161 E4 **Puma** Tanzania
104 C4 **Pumacahuanca** Peru
104 C4 **Pumasillo, Cerro** *mountain* Peru
188 E4 **Pumiao** Guangxi Zhuangzu Zizhiqu China
105 E5 **Puna** Bolivia
100 A5 **Puná, Isla** *island* Ecuador
223 14a **Punaauia** French Polynesia
221 D6 **Punakaiki** New Zealand
181 F3 **Punakha** Bhutan
187 D10 **Punalur** Kerala India
186 C5 **Punasar** Rajasthan India
130 F4 **Punat** Croatia
105 E5 **Punata** Bolivia
186 D4 **Punch** Jammu and Kashmir India/Pakistan
163 F4 **Punda Maria** South Africa
187 C7 **Pune** Maharashtra India
123 M2 **Punelia** *lake* Finland
196 D3 **Punggol** *admin. area* Singapore
192 F3 **P'ungsan** North Korea
160 D4 **Punia** Democratic Republic of Congo
105 E5 **Punilla** Bolivia
106 D4 **Punilla, Cordillera de la** *range* Chile
186 D4 **Punjab** *admin. area* India
179 L3 **Punjab** *admin. area* Pakistan
123 O2 **Punkaharju** Finland
179 M2 **Punmah Glacier** Pakistan
213 G7 **Punmu** WA Australia
75 S7 **Punnichy** Saskatchewan Canada
104 D4 **Puno** Peru
104 D5 **Puno** *admin. area* Peru
84 F7 **Punta Abreojos** Mexico
106 F6 **Punta Alta** Argentina
108 B5 **Punta Arenas** Chile
100 D2 **Punta Cardón** Venezuela
104 C5 **Punta Colorada** Peru
88 C3 **Punta Coyote** Mexico
106 D4 **Punta de Diaz** Chile
106 D5 **Punta del Agua** Argentina
164 3a **Punta del Hidalgo** Canary Islands
108 B5 **Punta del Monte** Argentina
108 D3 **Punta Delgada** Argentina
90 B3 **Punta Gorda** Belize
87 J7 **Punta Gorda** Florida USA
90 C4 **Punta Piedra** Honduras
88 B3 **Punta Prieta** Mexico
131 F8 **Punta Secca** Italy
128 C5 **Punta Umbría** Spain
164 3b **Puntagorda** Canary Islands
90 C5 **Puntarenas** Costa Rica
159 F4 **Puntas, Cabo dos** *cape* Equatorial Guinea
88 B2 **Puntas Coloradas** Mexico
218 D3 **Puntawolona, Lake** SA Australia
104 C2 **Puntilla** Peru
100 A5 **Puntilla, La** *cape* Ecuador
100 D2 **Punto Fijo** Venezuela
83 L6 **Punxsutawney** Pennsylvania USA
121 O4 **Puokio** Finland
121 O4 **Puolanka** Finland
120 L3 **Puoltikasvaara** Sweden
121 M3 **Puostijärvi** *lake* Sweden
120 L3 **Puottaure** Sweden
105 E5 **Pupayoj** Bolivia
130 G5 **Pupnat** Croatia
220 E5 **Puponga** New Zealand
104 E2 **Pupunha** Brazil
104 C4 **Puquio** Peru
134 Q5 **Pur** *watercourse* Russian Federation
134 S4 **Pura** *watercourse* Russian Federation
186 E5 **Puranpur** Uttar Pradesh India
106 C6 **Puraquina** Chile
199 H5 **Purari** *watercourse* Papua New Guinea
86 C3 **Purcell** Oklahoma USA
74 M7 **Purcell Mountains** British Columbia Canada
82 E8 **Purdy** Missouri USA
199 H4 **Purdy Islands** Papua New Guinea
123 M3 **Purekkari Neem** *cape* Estonia
106 C6 **Purén** Chile
220 F4 **Pureora** New Zealand
220 F4 **Pureora** *volcano* New Zealand
219 K2 **Purga** Qld Australia
85 K2 **Purgatoire** *watercourse* Colorado USA
187 E7 **Puri** Chhattisgarh India
187 F7 **Puri** Orissa India
194 B4 **Purian Point** Myanmar
100 C4 **Purificación** Colombia
88 D5 **Purificación** Mexico
89 F3 **Purificación** *watercourse* Mexico
134 S4 **Purinskoye, Ozero** *lake* Russian Federation
120 K3 **Purkijaur** *lake* Sweden
187 D7 **Purna** Maharashtra India
100 C5 **Purna Susa** Colombia
121 T4 **Purnema** Russian Federation
186 G6 **Purnia** Bihar India
218 F8 **Purnim** Vic. Australia
120 L3 **Purnu** Sweden
121 P4 **Purnuvaara** Finland
75 P8 **Purple Springs** Alberta Canada
108 B2 **Purranque** Chile
100 D1 **Purruruhu** Colombia
138 E3 **Purton** Gloucestershire England UK
139 F3 **Purton** Wiltshire England UK
139 F3 **Purton Stoke** Wiltshire England UK
77 S2 **Purtuniq** Quebec Canada
105 F4 **Purubi** Bolivia
197 G4 **Purukcahu** Indonesia
186 G6 **Puruliya** West Bengal India
100 B4 **Purún, Punta de** *cape* Colombia
104 E3 **Purus** *watercourse* Brazil
199 G6 **Purutu Island** Papua New Guinea
123 O2 **Puruvesi** *bay* Finland
86 G5 **Purvis** Mississippi USA
197 F5 **Purwodadi** Indonesia
196 F5 **Purwokerto** Indonesia
197 G5 **Purworejo** Indonesia
139 G2 **Pury End** Northamptonshire England UK
192 F2 **Puryŏng** North Korea
197 F3 **Pusa** Malaysia
187 D7 **Pusad** Maharashtra India
192 F4 **Pusan (Busan)** South Korea
197 F3 **Pusat Damai** Indonesia
83 Q4 **Pushaw Lake** Maine USA
135 AG8 **Pushchino** Russian Federation
186 D5 **Pushkar** Rajasthan India
121 T4 **Pushlakhta** Russian Federation
83 M2 **Puskitamika Lake** Quebec Canada
125 K2 **Pustków** Poland
132 C1 **Pustomyty** Ukraine
135 AH6 **Pustoretsk** Russian Federation
123 O4 **Pustoška** Russian Federation
121 S5 **Pustoye, Ozero** *lake* Russian Federation
125 K4 **Pusztaföldvár** Hungary
198 C6 **Putain** Indonesia
197 H2 **Putalan** Malaysia
181 H3 **Putao (Fort Hertz)** Myanmar
220 F4 **Putaruru** New Zealand
220 G4 **Putauaki** *volcano* New Zealand
189 H3 **Putian** Fujian China
104 D4 **Putina** Peru
197 F4 **Puting, Tanjung** *cape* Indonesia
123 P6 **Put'ki** Belarus
121 O3 **Putkivaara** Finland
89 F5 **Putla de Guerrero** Mexico
124 G1 **Putlitz** Germany
132 B1 **Putnok** Hungary
199 J5 **Puto** Papua New Guinea
189 I2 **Puto Shan** *range* Zhejiang China
135 U5 **Putorana, Plato** *region* Russian Federation
123 K2 **Putsaari** *island* Finland
127 H2 **Puttelange** France
219 J5 **Putty** NSW Australia
100 C4 **Putumayo** *admin. area* Colombia
100 C5 **Putumayo** *watercourse* Colombia
100 C5 **Putumayo** *watercourse* Peru
197 G3 **Putusibau** Indonesia
132 D2 **Putyla** Ukraine
84 inset **Pu'uanahulu** Hawai'i USA
121 P5 **Puukari** Finland
121 M4 **Puukkofjärden** *bay* Sweden
121 N4 **Puukkokumpu** Finland
123 N2 **Puula** *lake* Finland
123 O2 **Puumala** Finland
84 inset **Pu'uwai** Hawai'i USA
77 Q2 **Puvirnituq** *bay* Quebec Canada
77 Q2 **Puvirnituq** *watercourse* Quebec Canada
77 Q3 **Puvirnituq, Baie de** Quebec Canada
77 Q2 **Puvirnituq, Lac de** *lake* Quebec Canada
82 F8 **Puxico** Missouri USA
102 F4 **Puxinanã** Brazil
126 F4 **Puy-Guillaume** France
80 D3 **Puyallup** Washington USA
191 H5 **Puyang** Hebei China
191 H6 **Puyang** Henan China
189 H2 **Puyang** Zhejiang China
108 B2 **Puyehue** Chile
126 F5 **Puylaurens** France
100 B5 **Puyo** Ecuador
192 E4 **Puyŏ** South Korea
221 B8 **Puysegur Point** New Zealand
108 B3 **Puyuguapi, Canal** *strait* Chile
123 L4 **Puzes ezers** *lake* Latvia
129 F4 **Puzol** Spain
161 F5 **Pwani** *admin. area* Tanzania
138 B3 **Pwllcrochan** Pembrokeshire Wales UK
138 C2 **Pwllheli** Gwynedd Wales UK
135 AF7 **P'yagina, Poluostrov** *peninsula* Russian Federation
134 Q6 **Pyakupur** *watercourse* Russian Federation
121 U3 **Pyalitsa** Russian Federation
121 S5 **Pyal'ma** Russian Federation
123 Q1 **Pyal'vozero** Russian Federation
121 Q3 **Pyaozero, Ozero** *lake* Russian Federation
121 Q4 **Pyaozerskiy** Russian Federation
Pyapon *see* **Phapon** Myanmar
134 T4 **Pyasina** *watercourse* Russian Federation
134 S5 **Pyasino, Ozero** *lake* Russian Federation
134 R4 **Pyasinskiy Zaliv** *bay* Russian Federation
181 H5 **Pyawbwe** Myanmar
194 B3 **Pyay (Prome)** Myanmar
123 N2 **Pyhäjärvi** *bay* Finland
121 P5 **Pyhäjärvi** *lake* Finland
121 N4 **Pyhäjoki** Finland
121 N4 **Pyhäjoki** *watercourse* Finland
123 N2 **Pyhältö** Finland
121 N4 **Pyhänkoski** Finland
121 O4 **Pyhäntä** Finland
123 K2 **Pyhäranta** Finland
121 N5 **Pyhäsalmi** Finland
121 P5 **Pyhäselkä** Finland
121 P5 **Pyhäselkä** *bay* Finland
123 L2 **Pyhöjärvi** *lake* Finland
181 H4 **Pyin-U-Lwin** Myanmar
181 H5 **Pyinmana** Myanmar
138 D3 **Pyle** Bridgend Wales UK
121 N5 **Pylkönmäki** Finland
133 B7 **Pylos** Greece
123 K2 **Pyntäinen** Finland
192 E3 **Pyŏktong** North Korea
192 E4 **P'yongil-do** *island* South Korea
192 E3 **P'yŏngsan** North Korea
192 E4 **P'yŏngt'aek** South Korea
192 E3 **P'yŏngyang** North Korea
85 K5 **Pyote** Texas USA
212 D6 **Pyramid** WA Australia
216 G6 **Pyramid Lake** WA Australia
80 F6 **Pyramid Lake** Nevada USA
125 M2 **Pyratyn** Ukraine
129 G2 **Pyrenees** *range* France/Spain
133 D6 **Pyrgi** Greece
133 B5 **Pyrgoi** Greece
133 D8 **Pyrgos** Greece
125 H1 **Pyrzyce** Poland
134 K7 **Pyshchug** Russian Federation
123 N4 **Pytalovo** Russian Federation
194 C3 **Pyu** Myanmar
186 F5 **Pyuthan** Nepal
138 C4 **Pyworthy** Devon England UK
123 M1 **Pyyrinlahti** Finland

Q

178 C3 **Qā'al Jafr** *watercourse* Jordan
73 M3 **Qaanaaq** Greenland
178 F3 **Qādisīyah, Al** *admin. area* Iraq
179 I2 **Qā'en** Iran
78 O2 **Qaersuarssuk** *island* Greenland
178 F3 **Qafās** Iraq
178 G5 **Qaffāy, Al** *island* United Arab Emirates
191 J3 **Qagan Nuur** *lake* Jilin China
191 H4 **Qagan Nuur** *lake* Nei Mongol Zizhiqu China
185 K6 **Qaidam He** *watercourse* Qinghai China
156 E5 **Qala'en Nahl** Sudan
179 K2 **Qalagai** Afghanistan
179 K3 **Qalāt** Afghanistan
178 E6 **Qal'at Bīshah** Saudi Arabia
179 K2 **Qal'eh-ye Khān** Afghanistan
179 J2 **Qal'eh-ye Now** Afghanistan
77 R3 **Qalluviartuuq, Lac** *lake* Quebec Canada
183 K2 **Qalybek Koli** *lake* Kazakhstan
73 J6 **Qamanirjuaq Lake** Nunavut Canada
182 J6 **Qamashi** Uzbekistan
156 B1 **Qamīnis** Libya
157 H5 **Qandala** Somalia
182 E7 **Qanqanlu** Iran
178 F3 **Qāpī** Iran
73 O6 **Qaqortoq** Greenland
78 M1 **Qaqqarsuaq** *mountain* Greenland
179 K2 **Qarah Bāgh** Afghanistan
182 H4 **Qarakol** *lake* Kazakhstan
183 M3 **Qarasor Koli** *lake* Kazakhstan
156 D1 **Qārat al Mashrūkah** *mountain* Egypt
161 H2 **Qardho** Somalia
178 G2 **Qareh Chāy** *watercourse* Iran
182 H3 **Qarghaly Bogeni** *lake* Kazakhstan
185 H5 **Qarqan He** *watercourse* Xinjiang Uygur Zizhiqu China
182 J6 **Qarqīn** Afghanistan
182 J6 **Qarshi** Uzbekistan
182 J6 **Qashqadaryo** *admin. area* Uzbekistan
73 N5 **Qasigiannguit** Greenland
178 E4 **Qaşīm, Al** *admin. area* Saudi Arabia
190 G5 **Qasq** Nei Mongol Zizhiqu China
155 J2 **Qaşr Aḩmad** Libya
156 D2 **Qaşr al Farāfirah** Egypt
156 C1 **Qaşr al Qarn** *point of interest* Libya
156 C1 **Qaşr ash Shaqqah** *point of interest* Libya
155 J2 **Qaşr Bū Hādī** Libya
156 E3 **Qaşr Ibrīm** *point of interest* Egypt
78 O2 **Qassimiut** Greenland
78 N1 **Qassit** *bay* Greenland
178 E7 **Qa'ţabab** Yemen
178 G5 **Qatar** *country* Middle East
136 F6 **Qattinah, Buhayrat** *lake* Syria
182 F7 **Qazvīn** Iran
223 9 **Qele Levu** *island* Fiji
78 N1 **Qeqertarsuaq** Greenland
73 N5 **Qeqertarsuaq (Disko)** *island* Greenland
78 M1 **Qeqertarsuatsiaat** Greenland
73 N4 **Qeqertarsuatsiaq** *island* Greenland
73 N5 **Qeqertarsuup Tunua** *bay* Greenland
179 H4 **Qeshm** Iran
179 H4 **Qeshm, Jazīreh-ye** *island* Iran
189 G1 **Qi Xian** Henan China
190 D6 **Qiabuqia** Qinghai China
188 E1 **Qian He** *watercourse* Shaanxi China
191 J5 **Qian Shan** *range* Liaoning China
188 E1 **Qian Xian** Shaanxi China
191 I5 **Qian'an** Hebei China
191 J4 **Qian'an** Jilin China
191 J3 **Qianguozhen** Jilin China
188 E2 **Qianjiang** Chongqing China
189 F2 **Qianjiang** Hubei China
188 F3 **Qianling** Hunan China
188 E3 **Qianxi** Guizhou China
188 E1 **Qianyang** Shaanxi China
190 G6 **Qiaoshan** Shaanxi China
190 E6 **Qiaotou** Qinghai China
188 D3 **Qiaowa** Sichuan China
188 E2 **Qiaozhuang** Sichuan China
182 E7 **Qīdar** Iran
184 H5 **Qiemo** Xinjiang Uygur Zizhiqu China
156 E2 **Qifţ** Egypt
191 K2 **Qike** Heilongjiang China
73 M5 **Qikiqtarjuaq** Nunavut Canada
77 V3 **Qikirtajuaq Island** Nunavut Canada
179 J4 **Qila Safed** Pakistan
77 Q3 **Qilalugalik, Lac** *lake* Quebec Canada
191 I4 **Qilaotu Shan** *range* Hebei China
185 K5 **Qilian Shan** *range* Gansu China
185 J5 **Qilian Shan** *range* Qinghai China
73 M3 **Qimusseriarsuaq** *bay* Greenland
188 E1 **Qin Ling** *range* Jiangsu China
156 E2 **Qinā** Egypt
156 E2 **Qinā, Wādī** *watercourse* Egypt
188 E1 **Qin'an** Gansu China
189 G3 **Qincheng** Jiangxi China
188 F2 **Qing Jiang** *watercourse* Hubei China
191 K3 **Qing'an** Heilongjiang China
190 F6 **Qingcheng** Gansu China
191 I6 **Qingdao** Shandong China
191 H6 **Qingfeng** Henan China
191 K3 **Qinggang** Heilongjiang China
181 H2 **Qinghai** *admin. area* China
190 D6 **Qinghai Hu** *lake* Qinghai China
185 K6 **Qinghai Nanshan** *range* Qinghai China
185 I3 **Qinghe** Xinjiang Uygur Zizhiqu China
189 H1 **Qingkou** Jiangsu China
188 E3 **Qinglong** Guizhou China
191 I5 **Qinglong** Hebei China
189 I2 **Qingpu** Shanghai China
189 G2 **Qingquan** Hubei China
191 K3 **Qingshan** Heilongjiang China
190 G5 **Qingshuihe** Nei Mongol Zizhiqu China
190 F5 **Qingtongxia** Ningxia Huizu Zishiqu China
190 E6 **Qingyuan** Gansu China
189 G4 **Qingyuan** Guangdong China
191 J4 **Qingyuan** Liaoning China
191 H5 **Qingzhou** Hebei China
191 I6 **Qingzhou** Shandong China
191 I5 **Qinhuangdao** Hebei China
189 G3 **Qinjiang** Jiangxi China
190 G6 **Qinshui** Shanxi China
191 G6 **Qinxian** Shanxi China
188 E4 **Qinzhou** Guangxi Zhuangzu Zizhiqu China
188 E4 **Qinzhou Wan** *bay* Guangxi Zhuangzu Zizhiqu China
188 F5 **Qionghai** Hainan China
181 G3 **Qiongjie** Xizang Zizhiqu China
188 D2 **Qionglai** Sichuan China
188 F5 **Qiongshan** Hainan China
188 D2 **Qiongxi** Sichuan China
188 F5 **Qiongzhou Haixia (Hainan Strait)** Hainan China
191 J3 **Qiqihar** Heilongjiang China
78 D3 **Qirniraujaq, Pointe** *cape* Quebec Canada
185 I4 **Qitai** Xinjiang Uygur Zizhiqu China
191 L3 **Qitaihe** Heilongjiang China
189 H2 **Qiupu** *watercourse* Anhui China
191 I5 **Qixia** Shandong China
189 H3 **Qixing Liedao** *island* Fujian China
183 K3 **Qiyakty Koli** *lake* Kazakhstan
178 G2 **Qom** Iran
178 G2 **Qom Rūd** *watercourse* Iran
Qomolangmo Feng *see* **Everest, Mount** China/Nepal
184 G6 **Qong Muztag** *mountain* Xinjiang Uygur Zizhiqu China
182 H4 **Qopasor Koli** *lake* Kazakhstan
183 K6 **Qo'qon** Uzbekistan
182 I6 **Qorako'l** Uzbekistan
182 H5 **Qoraqalpog'iston** *admin. area* Uzbekistan
178 F2 **Qorveh** Iran
179 K2 **Qosh Tirdawān** Afghanistan
182 J6 **Qo'shrabot** Uzbekistan
179 H3 **Qoţrom** Iran
183 J6 **Qo'ytosh** Uzbekistan
219 I7 **Quaama** NSW Australia
107 I4 **Quadros, Lagoa dos** *lake* Brazil
215 J7 **Quail Island** Qld Australia
216 E6 **Quairading** WA Australia
74 I8 **Qualicum Beach** British Columbia Canada
218 F6 **Quambatook** Vic. Australia
219 H4 **Quambone** NSW Australia
214 F6 **Quamby** Qld Australia
194 E2 **Quan Đao Cô Tô** *island* Vietnam
194 E5 **Quan Đao Nam Du** *island* Vietnam
194 E2 **Quan Đao Trà Bán** *island* Vietnam
194 E2 **Quan Hóa** Vietnam
86 B3 **Quanah** Texas USA
213 H5 **Quanbun Butte** *mountain* WA Australia
218 E5 **Quandong** NSW Australia
109 15 **Quanery, Anse** *bay* Dominica
194 E2 **Quảng Uyên** Vietnam
189 G3 **Quanjiang** Jiangxi China
189 H4 **Quanzhou** Fujian China
188 F3 **Quanzhou** Guangxi Zhuangzu Zizhiqu China
75 S7 **Qu'Appelle** *watercourse* Saskatchewan Canada
77 U2 **Quaqtaq** Quebec Canada
107 G4 **Quaraí** *watercourse* Brazil
159 F3 **Quarar** *watercourse* Nigeria
142 inset **Quarff** Shetland Scotland UK
128 B5 **Quarteira** Portugal
130 E5 **Quarto** Italy
76 H1 **Quartzite Lake** Nunavut Canada
84 E4 **Quartzsite** Arizona USA
138 E2 **Quatford** Shropshire England UK
100 E5 **Quati Parana** *watercourse* Brazil
109 11 **Quatre, Île à** *island* St Vincent and the Grenadines
164 7b **Quatre Bornes** Mauritius
107 I3 **Quatro Barras** Brazil
164 1b **Quatro Ribeiras** Azores
74 G7 **Quatsino Sound** British Columbia Canada
138 E2 **Quatt** Shropshire England UK
182 H6 **Qūchān** Iran
183 L3 **Qudaykol** *lake* Kazakhstan
194 E3 **Quế Phong** Vietnam
219 I6 **Queanbeyan** NSW Australia
83 P3 **Québec** Quebec Canada
73 L8 **Québec** *admin. area* Canada
105 H6 **Quebra Côco** Brazil
107 G4 **Quebracho** Uruguay
106 E3 **Quebracho Coto** Argentina
90 D5 **Quebrada Canoa** Panama
101 F2 **Quebrada Honda** Venezuela
100 C3 **Quebradona, Embalse** *lake* Colombia
108 A2 **Quedal, Cabo** *cape* Chile
58 L1 **Queen Alexandra Range** Antarctica
74 I7 **Queen Bess, Mount** British Columbia Canada
74 E6 **Queen Charlotte** British Columbia Canada
109 7 **Queen Charlotte Bay** Falkland Islands
74 E6 **Queen Charlotte Islands** British Columbia Canada
74 G7 **Queen Charlotte Sound** British Columbia Canada
74 H7 **Queen Charlotte Strait** British Columbia Canada
82 E6 **Queen City** Missouri USA
86 D4 **Queen City** Texas USA
84 G4 **Queen Creek** Arizona USA
72 H2 **Queen Elizabeth Islands** Nunavut Canada
58 K1 **Queen Elizabeth Mountains** Antarctica
58 C2 **Queen Fabiola Mountains** Antarctica
58 G2 **Queen Mary Coast** Antarctica
164 5c **Queen Mary's Peak** *volcano* St Helena
109 8 **Queen Maud Bay** South Georgia
73 I5 **Queen Maud Gulf** Nunavut Canada
58 B2 **Queen Maud Land** *plain* Antarctica
58 L1 **Queen Maud Mountains** Antarctica
213 J3 **Queens Channel** NT Australia
73 J3 **Queens Channel** Nunavut Canada
162 E3 **Queen's Mine** Zimbabwe
141 G3 **Queensbury** West Yorkshire England UK
218 G2 **Queensland** *admin. area* Australia
55 T6 **Queensland Plateau** *underwater feature* Coral Sea
75 O7 **Queenstown** Alberta Canada
221 C7 **Queenstown** New Zealand
196 C4 **Queenstown** *admin. area* Singapore
162 E6 **Queenstown** South Africa
189 I3 **Queerao** *island* Zhejiang China
106 E6 **Quehué** Argentina
108 B3 **Queilén** Chile
102 B3 **Queimada, Ilha** *island* Brazil
103 E5 **Queimadas** Brazil
105 H6 **Queiroz** Brazil
160 B5 **Quela** Angola
126 D3 **Quèlaines** France
163 G3 **Quelimane** Mozambique
104 C4 **Quellocochа** Peru
160 A5 **Quelo** Angola
128 B4 **Queluz** Portugal
105 G1 **Quem Diria** Brazil
162 D2 **Quembo** *watercourse* Angola
106 F6 **Quemú-Quemú** Argentina
139 I4 **Quend-Plage-les-Pins** France
139 F3 **Quenington** Gloucestershire England UK
90 C5 **Quepos** Costa Rica
106 F6 **Quequén Salado** *watercourse* Argentina
104 E5 **Querarani** Bolivia
104 A2 **Querecotillo** Peru
105 H4 **Querência** Brazil
103 A8 **Querência do Norte** Brazil
88 E4 **Querétaro** Mexico
89 F4 **Querétaro** *admin. area* Mexico
88 C2 **Querobabi** Mexico
90 C5 **Quesada** Costa Rica
74 J6 **Quesnel** British Columbia Canada
74 J6 **Quesnel** *watercourse* British Columbia Canada
74 K6 **Quesnel Lake** British Columbia Canada
91 F2 **Quest, Pointe** *cape* Haiti
85 J2 **Questa** New Mexico USA
82 F2 **Quetico** Ontario Canada
108 C2 **Quetrequile** Argentina
179 K3 **Quetta** Pakistan
90 B4 **Quetzaltenango** Guatemala
162 B2 **Queve** *watercourse* Angola
100 B5 **Quevedo** Ecuador
83 M2 **Quévillon, Lac** *lake* Quebec Canada
126 D4 **Queyrac** France
195 H5 **Quezon** Philippines
195 I4 **Quezon City** Philippines
191 H6 **Qufu** Shandong China
142 E2 **Quholm** Orkney Islands Scotland UK
162 B2 **Quibala** Angola
100 B3 **Quibdó** Colombia
81 S2 **Quibell** Ontario Canada
126 C3 **Quiberon** France
126 C3 **Quiberon, Baie de** *bay* France
160 B5 **Quibocolo** Angola
100 D2 **Quíbor** Venezuela
104 C4 **Quichuaña** Peru
74 H5 **Quick** British Columbia Canada
160 B5 **Quiculungo** Angola
139 H2 **Quidenham** Norfolk England UK
108 B2 **Quidico** Chile
74 E2 **Quiet Lake** Yukon Territory Canada
75 P4 **Quigley** Alberta Canada
162 B3 **Quihita** Angola
108 C2 **Quila Mahuida, Altiplanicie del** *region* Argentina
106 D6 **Quilachanquil** Argentina
90 C4 **Quilalí** Nicaragua
108 A3 **Quilán, Cabo** *cape* Chile
108 A3 **Quilán, Isla** *island* Chile
104 D4 **Quilca, Nevado** *mountain* Peru
162 B2 **Quilenda** Angola
162 B2 **Quilengues** Angola
106 D6 **Quili Malal** Argentina
75 S7 **Quill Lakes** Saskatchewan Canada
126 F5 **Quillan** France
106 D5 **Quillota** Chile
104 B4 **Quilmaná** Peru
107 G5 **Quilmes** Argentina
218 G2 **Quilpie** Qld Australia
106 D5 **Quilpué** Chile
160 B5 **Quimbele** Angola
104 E5 **Quime** Bolivia
106 F3 **Quimilí** Argentina
126 B3 **Quimper** France
126 C3 **Quimperlé** France
143 D4 **Quin** Ireland
195 I4 **Quinalasag** *island* Philippines
80 D3 **Quinault** *watercourse* Washington USA
104 D4 **Quince Mil** Peru
100 C3 **Quinchía** Colombia
87 I5 **Quincy** Florida USA

83 P5 **Quincy** Massachusetts USA
82 F7 **Quincy** Missouri USA
80 F3 **Quincy** Washington USA
106 E5 **Quines** Argentina
163 H3 **Quinga** Mozambique
127 G3 **Quingey** France
72 C7 **Quinhagak** Alaska USA
101 E3 **Quinigua, Serranía** *range* Venezuela
106 F6 **Quiñihual** Argentina
195 I5 **Quiniluban** *island* Philippines
100 B4 **Quininde** *watercourse* Ecuador
86 C4 **Quinlan** Texas USA
80 F6 **Quinn** *watercourse* Nevada USA
80 H7 **Quinn Canyon Range** Nevada USA
216 D5 **Quinns Rocks** WA Australia
89 H5 **Quintana Roo** *admin. area* Mexico
128 E4 **Quintanar de la Orden** Spain
128 E3 **Quintanar de la Sierra** Spain
106 E5 **Quinto** *watercourse* Argentina
129 F3 **Quinto** Spain
83 L3 **Quinze, Lac des** *lake* Quebec Canada
163 H2 **Quionga** Mozambique
102 E5 **Quipapá** Brazil
106 C6 **Quirhue** Chile
85 H7 **Quiriego** Mexico
162 C2 **Quirima** Angola
101 F5 **Quirimiri, Lago** *lake* Brazil
219 J4 **Quirindi** NSW Australia
103 B7 **Quirinópolis** Brazil
106 F5 **Quiroga** Argentina
88 E5 **Quiroga** Mexico
128 C2 **Quiroga** Spain
100 D2 **Quisiro** Venezuela
126 G5 **Quissac** France
162 C2 **Quissongo** Angola
90 D4 **Quita Sueño Bank** *reef* Colombia
162 C2 **Quitapa** Angola
85 L3 **Quitaque** Texas USA
163 H2 **Quiterajo** Mozambique
106 F3 **Quitilipi** Argentina
87 J5 **Quitman** Georgia USA
86 G4 **Quitman** Mississippi USA
86 D4 **Quitman** Texas USA
100 B5 **Quito** Ecuador
84 F5 **Quitovac** Mexico
106 C6 **Quitratúe** Chile
102 E4 **Quixadá** Brazil
105 F3 **Quixadá** Brazil
102 E4 **Quixeramobim** Brazil
102 E4 **Quixeré** Brazil
188 E2 **Qujiang** Sichuan China
188 D3 **Qujing** Yunnan China
185 J6 **Qumar He** *watercourse* Qinghai China
216 C2 **Quobba** WA Australia
216 C2 **Quobba, Point** WA Australia
73 J6 **Quoich** *watercourse* Nunavut Canada
142 C3 **Quoich, Loch** *lake* Scotland UK
216 C2 **Quoin Head** WA Australia
213 J3 **Quoin Island** NT Australia
82 F2 **Quorn** Ontario Canada
178 C2 **Quornet es Sausda** *mountain* Lebanon
183 J6 **Qŭrghonteppa** Tajikistan
77 V3 **Qurlutuq** *watercourse* Quebec Canada
179 I5 **Quryāt** Oman
156 E2 **Quş** Egypt
188 D2 **Qushan** Sichuan China
181 G3 **Qushui** Xizang Zizhiqu China
181 G3 **Qusong** Xizang Zizhiqu China
183 L3 **Qutau** *mountain* Kazakhstan
178 E2 **Quwasi** Iraq
190 F6 **Quwu Shan** *range* Gansu China
181 F3 **Quxia** Xizang Zizhiqu China
194 E3 **Quỳ Châu** Vietnam
194 F4 **Quy Nhơn** Vietnam
188 F3 **Quyang** Hunan China
194 D2 **Quỳnh Nhai** Vietnam
191 H6 **Quzhou** Hebei China
189 H3 **Quzhou** Zhejiang China
183 J3 **Qypshaq Koli** *lake* Kazakhstan
183 L2 **Qyzylqaq Koli** *lake* Kazakhstan

R

87 I4 **R. L. Harris Reservoir** Alabama USA
194 C5 **Ra, Ko** *island* Thailand
125 H4 **Raab** *watercourse* Austria
121 N4 **Raahe** Finland
121 P5 **Rääkkylä** Finland
197 G5 **Raas** *island* Indonesia
142 C3 **Raasay** *island* Scotland UK
121 N2 **Raattama** Finland
125 H5 **Rab** Croatia
125 I4 **Rába** *watercourse* Hungary
159 F2 **Rabah** Nigeria
156 E5 **Rabak** Sudan
198 E5 **Rabal** Indonesia
126 E5 **Rabastens** France
131 F9 **Rabat** Malta
154 E2 **Rabat** Morocco
213 J6 **Rabbit Flat Roadhouse** NT Australia
75 T3 **Rabbit Lake Mine** Saskatchewan Canada
74 L2 **Rabbitskin** *watercourse* Northwest Territories Canada
125 I3 **Rábca** *watercourse* Austria
120 J4 **Råberg** Sweden
223 9a **Rabi** *island* Fiji
109 4 **Rábida, Isla** *island* Archipiélago de Colon (Galapagos Islands)
178 D5 **Rābigh** Saudi Arabia
181 G5 **Rabnabad Islands** Bangladesh
164 1a **Rabo de Peixe** Azores
89 F3 **Rabón, Laguna El** *lake* Mexico
132 C3 **Rabrovo** Bulgaria
132 A3 **Rača** Bosnia and Herzegovina
132 D3 **Răcari** Romania
91 F2 **Raccoon Cay** *island* Bahamas
130 F3 **Rače** Slovenia
79 L9 **Race, Cape** Newfoundland and Labrador Canada
194 E5 **Rạch Giá** Vietnam
194 C6 **Racha Noi, Ko** *island* Thailand
194 C6 **Racha Yai, Ko** *island* Thailand
89 F3 **Rachal** Texas USA
82 H5 **Racine** Wisconsin USA
82 J2 **Racine Lake** Ontario Canada
74 I3 **Racing** *watercourse* British Columbia Canada
125 M5 **Racoviţa** Romania
123 L6 **Raczki** Poland
100 B2 **Rada, Punta de la** *cape* Colombia
108 C3 **Rada Tilly** Argentina
132 B4 **Radan** *region* Serbia
122 G2 **Rådasjön** *lake* Sweden
124 G3 **Radbuza** *watercourse* Czech Republic
82 I8 **Radcliff** Kentucky USA
141 F3 **Radcliffe** Greater Manchester England UK
122 F3 **Råde** Norway
127 K1 **Radebeul** Germany
83 K8 **Radford** Virginia USA
186 C6 **Radhanpur** Gujarat India
101 F4 **Radiador** Brazil
127 J4 **Radici, Foce delle** *pass* Italy
77 Q6 **Radisson** Quebec Canada
75 M7 **Radium Hot Springs** British Columbia Canada
109 inset 9 **Radix, Point** Trinidad and Tobago
58 R1 **Radlinski, Mount** *mountain* Antarctica
125 H4 **Radlje ob Dravi** Slovenia
120 L3 **Rådnejaure** *lake* Sweden
132 D4 **Radnevo** Bulgaria
125 K2 **Radom** Poland
132 C4 **Radomir** Bulgaria
125 J2 **Radomsko** Poland
125 K2 **Radoszyce** Poland
133 E5 **Radovets** Bulgaria
132 C4 **Radovnica** Serbia
122 C2 **Radøy** *island* Norway
138 E3 **Radstock** Bath and North East Somerset England UK
217 N6 **Radstock, Cape** SA Australia
132 F2 **Rădulenii Vechi** Moldova
75 S8 **Radville** Saskatchewan Canada
125 L3 **Radymno** Poland
186 E5 **Rae Bareli** Uttar Pradesh India
75 M1 **Rae-Edzo** Northwest Territories Canada
73 K5 **Rae Isthmus** Nunavut Canada
87 L3 **Raeford** North Carolina USA
124 D2 **Raeren** Belgium
221 C7 **Raes Junction** New Zealand
216 G4 **Raeside, Lake** WA Australia
220 F4 **Raetihi** New Zealand
106 F4 **Rafaela** Argentina
159 I4 **Rafaii** Central African Republic
131 E8 **Raffadali** Italy
142 C2 **Raffin** Highland Scotland UK
162 F3 **Raffingora** Zimbabwe
178 E3 **Rafḩā** Saudi Arabia
131 D8 **Rafrāf** Tunisia
179 H3 **Rafsanjān** Iran
121 M1 **Rafsbotn** Norway
75 U5 **Rafter** Manitoba Canada
127 I3 **Rafz** Switzerland
160 D2 **Raga** Sudan
160 D2 **Raga** *watercourse* Sudan
123 M4 **Ragana** Latvia
195 J6 **Ragang, Mount** *mountain* Philippines
195 I4 **Ragay Gulf** Philippines
91 F2 **Ragged Island** Bahamas
109 12 **Ragged Point** *cape* Barbados
143 D2 **Raghly** Ireland
186 C5 **Raghu Nathpura** Rajasthan India
215 K7 **Raglan** Qld Australia
220 F3 **Raglan** New Zealand
138 E3 **Raglan** Monmouthshire Wales UK
220 F3 **Raglan Harbour** New Zealand
221 E5 **Raglan Range** New Zealand
122 G3 **Råglanda** Sweden
120 J4 **Rågoliden** Sweden
100 C3 **Ragonvalia** Colombia
124 G1 **Ragösen** Germany
77 U8 **Ragueneau** Quebec Canada
120 J5 **Ragunda** Sweden
131 F8 **Ragusa** Italy
123 M5 **Raguva** Lithuania
156 E5 **Rahad** *watercourse* Sudan
159 I2 **Rahad El Berdi** Sudan
156 C5 **Rahad el Berdi** Sudan
121 O2 **Rahajärvi** *lake* Finland
159 F2 **Rahama** Nigeria
143 E3 **Raheen** Ireland
157 G5 **Raheita** Eritrea
179 L4 **Rahimyar Khan** Pakistan
140 A3 **Rahincuill** Ireland
121 M4 **Rahja** Finland
143 G2 **Raholp** Down Northern Ireland UK
129 G6 **Rahouia** Algeria
106 D6 **Rahue** *mountain* Chile
106 D6 **Rahué** Argentina
187 D7 **Rahuri** Maharashtra India
221 E5 **Rai Valley** New Zealand
131 E5 **Raiano** Italy
196 E3 **Raibu** *island* Indonesia
187 D8 **Raichur** Karnataka India
186 F6 **Raidih** Jharkhand India
186 G6 **Raiganj** West Bengal India
187 F7 **Raigarh** Chhattisgarh India
187 F7 **Raighar** Orissa India
197 I6 **Raijua** *island* Indonesia
80 H7 **Railroad Valley** Nevada USA
78 D6 **Raimbault, Lac** *lake* Quebec Canada
124 F3 **Rain** Germany
219 K1 **Rainbow Beach** Qld Australia
74 L3 **Rainbow Lake** Alberta Canada
80 D3 **Rainier** Washington USA
198 C2 **Rainis** Indonesia
141 F3 **Rainow** Cheshire England UK
82 E2 **Rainy Lake** Ontario Canada
73 J9 **Rainy River** Ontario Canada
123 K1 **Raippaluoto (Vallgrund)** *island* Finland
187 E7 **Raipur** Chhattisgarh India
186 D5 **Raipur** Rajasthan India
223 15a **Rairik** Marshall Islands
121 O3 **Räisälä** Finland
186 D6 **Raisen** Madhya Pradesh India
121 O4 **Raiskio** Finland
142 E4 **Raith** Perth and Kinross Scotland UK
223 14 **Raivavae** *island* French Polynesia
187 E7 **Raj Nandgaon** Chhattisgarh India
197 G5 **Raja** *island* Indonesia
196 C3 **Raja, Ujung** *cape* Indonesia
198 D4 **Raja Ampat, Kepulauan** *islands* Indonesia
196 E5 **Rajabasa, Gunung** *volcano* Indonesia
187 E8 **Rajahmundry** Andhra Pradesh India
121 O3 **Rajala** Finland
187 F7 **Rajam** Andhra Pradesh India
123 M2 **Rajamäki** Finland
197 F3 **Rajang** Malaysia
197 G3 **Rajang** *watercourse* Malaysia
179 L3 **Rajanpur** Pakistan
187 E8 **Rajapur** Andhra Pradesh India
186 C5 **Rajasthan** *admin. area* India
120 I4 **Rajastrand/Söfors** Sweden
186 D4 **Rajauri** Jammu and Kashmir India/Pakistan
186 G5 **Rajbiraj** Nepal
186 D6 **Rajgarh** Madhya Pradesh India
186 D5 **Rajgarh** Rajasthan India
196 E4 **Rajik** Indonesia
192 F2 **Rajin** North Korea
132 B4 **Rajince** Serbia
125 I3 **Rajka** Hungary
187 C6 **Rajkot** Gujarat India
187 G7 **Rajnagar** Orissa India
187 C7 **Rajpipla** Gujarat India
187 D7 **Rajpur** Madhya Pradesh India
186 C6 **Rajsamand** Rajasthan India
181 F4 **Rajshahi** Bangladesh
181 F4 **Rajshahi** *admin. area* Bangladesh
187 C7 **Rajula** Gujarat India
222 1 **Rakahanga** *island* Cook Islands New Zealand
160 E4 **Rakai** Uganda
221 D6 **Rakaia** *watercourse* New Zealand
221 E6 **Rakaia Huts** New Zealand
132 B1 **Rakamaz** Hungary
179 M2 **Rakaposhi** *mountain* Pakistan
180 D2 **Rakas Lake** Xizang Zizhiqu China
123 N6 **Rakaw** Belarus
139 G3 **Rake** West Sussex England UK
125 H5 **Rakek** Slovenia
194 B3 **Rakhine** *admin. area* Myanmar
181 H5 **Rakhine Yoma** Myanmar
132 D1 **Rakhiv** Ukraine
123 P2 **Rakh'ya** Russian Federation
223 9a **Rakiraki** Fiji
196 F5 **Rakit** *island* Indonesia
136 E2 **Rakitnoye** Russian Federation
130 H4 **Rakitovica** Croatia
123 N3 **Rakke** Estonia
161 H2 **Rako** Somalia
162 D4 **Rakops** Botswana
125 J3 **Raková** Slovakia
125 K2 **Raków** Poland
121 M3 **Räktjärv** *lake* Sweden
182 F5 **Rakushechnyy, Mys** *cape* Kazakhstan
120 G5 **Råkvåg** Norway
123 N3 **Rakvere** Estonia
122 H4 **Ralången** *lake* Sweden
86 G4 **Raleigh** Mississippi USA
87 L3 **Raleigh** North Carolina USA
87 M3 **Raleigh Bay** North Carolina USA
80 I2 **Raley** Alberta Canada
125 L3 **Ralivka** Ukraine
78 E3 **Ralleau, Lac** *lake* Quebec Canada
164 6b **Rallier du Baty, Péninsule** *peninsula* French Southern and Antarctic Lands
85 L4 **Ralls** Texas USA
219 H6 **Ralvona** NSW Australia
132 B3 **Ram** Serbia
90 C4 **Rama** Nicaragua
105 F3 **Rama-Rama** Brazil
187 F8 **Ramachandrapuram** Andhra Pradesh India
105 G5 **Ramada del Pato** Bolivia
104 E5 **Ramadilla** Bolivia
106 D2 **Ramaditas** Chile
187 E7 **Ramagundam** Andhra Pradesh India
81 M7 **Ramah** Colorado USA
186 D5 **Raman** Punjab India
187 D9 **Ramanagaram** Karnataka India
187 E10 **Ramanathapuram** Tamil Nadu India
187 C8 **Ramas, Cape** Goa India
142 B3 **Ramasaig** Highland Scotland UK
162 E5 **Ramatlabama** South Africa
120 H2 **Ramberg** Norway
127 H2 **Rambervillers** France
187 F7 **Rambha** Orissa India
126 E2 **Rambouillet** France
215 L1 **Rambuso** Papua New Guinea
199 H4 **Rambutyo Island** Papua New Guinea
187 D8 **Ramdurg** Karnataka India
138 C4 **Rame** Cornwall England UK
138 C4 **Rame Head** *cape* England UK
79 J9 **Ramea** Newfoundland and Labrador Canada
79 J9 **Ramea Islands** Newfoundland and Labrador Canada
186 G5 **Ramechhap** Nepal
187 E10 **Rameswaram** Tamil Nadu India
187 F6 **Ramgarh** Chhattisgarh India
186 F6 **Ramgarh** Jharkhand India
187 C8 **Ramgarh** Maharashtra India
186 D5 **Ramgarh** Rajasthan India
178 G3 **Rāmhormoz** Iran
214 C2 **Ramingining** NT Australia
108 A5 **Ramírez, Isla** *island* Chile
161 G2 **Ramis** *watercourse* Ethiopia
186 F6 **Ramkola** Chhattisgarh India
156 C3 **Ramlat Rabyānah** *desert* Libya
178 C3 **Ramm, Jabal** *mountain* Jordan
122 E4 **Ramme** Denmark
186 E5 **Ramnagar** Uttar Pradesh India
132 D3 **Râmnicu Vâlcea** Romania
136 F2 **Ramon** Russian Federation
85 J3 **Ramon** New Mexico USA
82 D8 **Ramona** Oklahoma USA
81 Q4 **Ramona** South Dakota USA
88 E3 **Ramos Arizpe** Mexico
107 G6 **Ramos Otero** Argentina
127 J3 **Ramosch** Switzerland
140 E2 **Rampside** Cumbria England UK
187 E7 **Rampur** Andhra Pradesh India
186 D4 **Rampur** Himachal Pradesh India
186 E6 **Rampur** Madhya Pradesh India
187 F7 **Rampur** Orissa India
186 C6 **Rampur** Rajasthan India
186 E5 **Rampur** Uttar Pradesh India
181 G5 **Ramree** Myanmar
181 G5 **Ramree Island** Myanmar
214 C2 **Ramsay, Mount** NT Australia
122 H3 **Ramsberg** Sweden
141 F3 **Ramsbottom** Greater Manchester England UK
120 J5 **Ramsele** Sweden
140 D2 **Ramsey** Isle of Man UK
139 G2 **Ramsey** Cambridgeshire England UK
138 B3 **Ramsey Island** Wales UK
139 G2 **Ramsey St Marys** Cambridgeshire England UK
181 G3 **Ramsing** *mountain* Xizang Zizhiqu China
120 I5 **Ramsjö** Sweden
120 J2 **Ramsund** Norway
187 F7 **Ramtek** Chhattisgarh India
199 H5 **Ramu** *watercourse* Papua New Guinea
120 J5 **Ramvik** Sweden
159 G2 **Ran** Nigeria
120 I3 **Rana** *watercourse* Norway
186 D6 **Rana Pratap Sagar** *lake* Madhya Pradesh India
198 B6 **Ranaka, Gunung** *volcano* Indonesia
186 D6 **Ranapur** Madhya Pradesh India
197 H2 **Ranau** Malaysia
196 D5 **Ranau, Danau** *lake* Indonesia
106 D5 **Rancagua** Chile
126 F5 **Rance** *watercourse* France
105 I6 **Rancharia** Brazil
74 F2 **Rancheria** Yukon Territory Canada
85 I5 **Rancheria** Mexico
85 I7 **Rancheria Valerio** Mexico
81 L4 **Ranchester** Wyoming USA
186 F6 **Ranchi** Jharkhand India
88 D3 **Rancho Benton** Mexico
88 D3 **Rancho de Agujas** Mexico
88 D2 **Rancho de las Lilas** Mexico
88 E3 **Rancho El Altos** Mexico
88 E2 **Rancho El Milagro** Mexico
88 A2 **Rancho El Salado** Mexico
88 A2 **Rancho Grande** Mexico
88 E3 **Rancho Guadalupe** Mexico
88 B2 **Rancho Guadalupe** Mexico
88 C2 **Rancho La Junta** Mexico
88 C2 **Rancho La Noria** Mexico
88 D3 **Rancho La Puerta** Mexico
88 E2 **Rancho Los Cabezones** Mexico
84 D4 **Rancho Mirage** California USA
88 C2 **Rancho Monumento** Mexico
88 B2 **Rancho Pozo Hielo Estrella** Mexico
88 E3 **Rancho San Francisco** Mexico
88 D2 **Rancho San Francisco** Mexico
88 E3 **Rancho Santa Fe** Mexico
105 H6 **Rancho São Francisco** Brazil
89 F3 **Rancho Sol de Mayo** Mexico
105 E5 **Rancho Tarueca** Bolivia
90 D2 **Rancho Veloz** Cuba
88 E4 **Rancho Verde** Mexico
100 D2 **Ranchogrande** Colombia
108 B2 **Ranco, Lago** *lake* Chile
218 H6 **Rand** NSW Australia
157 G5 **Randa** Djibouti
86 B7 **Randado** Texas USA
82 D3 **Randall** Minnesota USA
126 F3 **Randan** France
120 H5 **Rånddalen** Sweden
122 F4 **Randers** Denmark
120 K3 **Randijaur** Sweden
120 K3 **Randijaure** *bay* Sweden
127 H3 **Randogne** Switzerland
81 Q5 **Randolph** Nebraska USA
83 L5 **Randolph** New York USA
79 L8 **Random Island** Newfoundland and Labrador Canada
198 F4 **Randowaya** Indonesia
120 F6 **Randsverk** Norway
120 M4 **Råneå** Sweden
120 L3 **Råneälven** *watercourse* Sweden
120 G4 **Ranemsletta** Norway
126 D2 **Rânes** France
75 P6 **Ranfurly** Alberta Canada
221 D7 **Ranfurly** New Zealand
181 G4 **Rangamati** Bangladesh
181 G3 **Rangapara** Assam India
220 F4 **Rangataua** New Zealand
221 6 **Rangatira Island** Chatham Islands New Zealand
220 E2 **Rangaunu Harbour** New Zealand
83 P4 **Rangeley** Maine USA
81 K6 **Rangely** Colorado USA
86 B4 **Ranger** Texas USA
82 J3 **Ranger Lake** Ontario Canada
181 G3 **Rangia** Assam India
Rangiauria *see* **Pitt Island** New Zealand
221 E6 **Rangiora** New Zealand
220 E2 **Rangiputa** New Zealand
223 14 **Rangiroa** *island* French Polynesia
220 G4 **Rangitaiki** New Zealand
220 G4 **Rangitaiki** *watercourse* New Zealand
221 D7 **Rangitata** New Zealand
221 D6 **Rangitata** *watercourse* New Zealand
220 G4 **Rangitikei** *watercourse* New Zealand
221 F5 **Rangitoto Islands** New Zealand
196 E5 **Rangkasbitung** Indonesia
188 C2 **Rangke** Sichuan China
181 H3 **Rangku** Arunachal Pradesh India
192 E3 **Rangnim** North Korea
181 F4 **Rangpur** Bangladesh
196 D3 **Rangsang** *island* Indonesia
186 C6 **Rani** Rajasthan India
187 D8 **Ranibennur** Karnataka India
186 G6 **Raniganj** West Bengal India
186 F6 **Ranijula Peak** *mountain* Chhattisgarh India
186 C6 **Raniwara** Rajasthan India
178 E2 **Rāniyah** Iraq
214 D5 **Ranken** *watercourse* NT Australia
122 G3 **Ränken** *lake* Sweden
85 L5 **Rankin** Texas USA
76 I1 **Rankin Inlet** Nunavut Canada
218 H5 **Rankins Springs** NSW Australia
186 B6 **Rann of Kachchh** Gujarat India
123 N3 **Ranna** Estonia
215 K8 **Rannes** Qld Australia
142 D4 **Rannoch Moor** *region* Scotland UK
122 G3 **Rannsjön** *lake* Sweden
123 N3 **Rannu** Estonia
159 F2 **Rano** Nigeria
163 I4 **Ranohira** Madagascar
77 O7 **Ranoke** Ontario Canada
187 C6 **Ranoli** Gujarat India
121 M4 **Rånön** *island* Sweden
222 8 **Ranonnga** *island* Solomon Islands
194 D6 **Ranot** Thailand
163 I4 **Ranotsara Avatatra** Madagascar
120 I4 **Ransarn** *lake* Sweden
198 E4 **Ransiki** Indonesia
122 G2 **Ransjön** *lake* Sweden
81 P7 **Ransom** Kansas USA
122 I3 **Ransta** Sweden
121 M3 **Rantajärvi** Sweden
121 P5 **Rantasalmi** Finland
197 G4 **Rantau** Indonesia
196 D3 **Rantau** *island* Indonesia
196 D3 **Rantaukampar** Indonesia
197 G4 **Rantaupanjang** Indonesia
196 C3 **Rantauprapat** Indonesia
197 G4 **Rantaupulut** Indonesia
198 B4 **Rantemario, Gunung** *mountain* Indonesia
82 G6 **Rantoul** Illinois USA
121 N4 **Rantsila** Finland
121 O4 **Ranua** Finland
222 7 **Ranwas** Vanuatu
191 M3 **Raohe** Heilongjiang China
127 H2 **Raon-l'Étape** France
130 D4 **Raossi** Italy
220 5 **Raoul Island** Kermadec Islands New Zealand
191 J4 **Raoyang He** *watercourse* China
223 14 **Rapa** *island* French Polynesia
123 L5 **Rapa** Poland
186 C6 **Rapar** Gujarat India
106 D5 **Rapel** *watercourse* Chile
108 A4 **Ráper, Cabo** *cape* Chile
73 M5 **Raper, Cape** Nunavut Canada
143 E2 **Raphoe** Ireland
81 O1 **Rapid City** Manitoba Canada
81 N4 **Rapid City** South Dakota USA
75 Q5 **Rapid View** Saskatchewan Canada
123 M3 **Rapla** Estonia
123 M3 **Raplamaa** *admin. area* Estonia
123 N2 **Rapojärvi** *lake* Finland
102 C4 **Raposa** Brazil
197 H4 **Rappang** Indonesia
120 J3 **Rappen** *lake* Sweden
183 K6 **Rāqh** Afghanistan
83 N5 **Raquette Lake** New York USA
163 G3 **Raraga** *watercourse* Mozambique
214 D1 **Raragala Island** NT Australia
223 14 **Raroia** *island* French Polynesia
127 H3 **Raron** Switzerland
220 1 **Rarotonga** *island* Cook Islands New Zealand
178 F7 **Ra's al Kalb** Yemen
179 H4 **Ra's al Khaymah** United Arab Emirates
131 C9 **Râs el Aïoun** Algeria
155 F2 **Râs el Ma** Algeria
154 F5 **Râs el Mâ** Mali
156 E2 **Ra's Ghārib** Egypt
127 L4 **Raša** Croatia
195 H5 **Rasa** *island* Philippines
108 D2 **Rasa, Punta** *cape* Argentina
108 D4 **Rasa Chica, Isla** *island* Argentina
121 O5 **Räsälä** Finland
164 3a **Rasca, Punta de la** *cape* Canary Islands
124 G2 **Raschau** Germany
132 F2 **Raşcov** Moldova
123 L5 **Raseiniai** Lithuania
190 E3 **Rashaant** Mongolia
190 E2 **Rashaant** Mongolia
156 E5 **Rashad** Sudan
143 F2 **Rasharkin** Ballymoney Northern Ireland UK
156 E1 **Rashīd** Egypt
178 F3 **Rashnūdī** Iran
182 F6 **Rasht** Iran
132 D3 **Răşinari** Romania
130 G3 **Rasinja** Croatia
123 O1 **Rasivaara** Finland
141 G2 **Raskelf** North Yorkshire England UK
73 J5 **Rasmussen Basin** Nunavut Canada
132 D3 **Râşnov** Romania
164 4 **Raso** *island* Cape Verde
217 I4 **Rason, Lake** WA Australia
132 E3 **Rasova** Romania
132 C4 **Rasovo** Bulgaria
186 F6 **Rasra** Uttar Pradesh India
135 AF9 **Rasshua, Ostrov** *island* Kuril Islands
193 L1 **Rasshua, Ostrov** *lake* Russian Federation
182 D3 **Rasskazovo** Russian Federation
135 AF5 **Rassokha** *watercourse* Russian Federation
124 E3 **Rastatt** Germany
120 L2 **Råsto** *island* Sweden
120 L2 **Råstojaure** *lake* Sweden
132 C4 **Rastu** Romania
122 H3 **Råsvalen** *lake* Sweden
199 H4 **Rat Island** Papua New Guinea
135 AK8 **Rat Island** Alaska USA
75 V4 **Rat Lake** Manitoba Canada
75 O2 **Rat River** Northwest Territories Canada
220 F4 **Rata** New Zealand
142 C3 **Ratagan** Highland Scotland UK
196 E5 **Ratai, Gunung** *mountain* Indonesia
120 L5 **Ratan** Sweden
120 I5 **Rätan** Sweden
186 D5 **Ratangarh** Rajasthan India
187 F6 **Ratanpur** Chhattisgarh India
186 C6 **Ratanpur** Gujarat India
186 E6 **Rath** Uttar Pradesh India
143 D4 **Ráth Luirc** Ireland
143 F3 **Rathangan** Ireland
140 B4 **Rathanna** Ireland
82 E6 **Rathbun Lake** Iowa USA
138 A1 **Rathconnellwood** Ireland
143 F3 **Rathcoole** Ireland
140 B3 **Rathcor** Ireland
143 F3 **Rathcore** Ireland
143 D4 **Rathcormack** Ireland
219 K3 **Rathdowney** Qld Australia
143 F4 **Rathdrum** Ireland
181 G5 **Rathedaung** Myanmar
140 B3 **Rathfeigh** Ireland
143 F2 **Rathfriland** Newry and Mourne Northern Ireland UK
143 D4 **Rathkeale** Ireland
143 F1 **Rathlin Island** Northern Ireland UK
141 F2 **Rathmell** North Yorkshire England UK
143 E1 **Rathmelton** Ireland
143 C4 **Rathmore** Ireland
143 E1 **Rathmullan** Ireland
143 F4 **Rathnageeragh** Ireland
143 F4 **Rathnew** Ireland
143 C4 **Rathomin Bridge** Ireland
140 A3 **Rathowen** Ireland
143 F3 **Rathtroane** Ireland
143 F4 **Rathvilly** Ireland
186 D6 **Ratlam** Madhya Pradesh India
138 E2 **Ratlinghope** Shropshire England UK
187 C8 **Ratnagiri** Maharashtra India
187 E10 **Ratnapura** Sri Lanka
125 M2 **Ratne** Ukraine
123 M6 **Ratnyčia** Lithuania
143 F3 **Ratoath** Ireland
85 J2 **Raton** New Mexico USA
134 R6 **Ratta** Russian Federation
142 E2 **Rattar** Highland Scotland UK
121 N3 **Rattosjärvi** *lake* Finland
142 E4 **Rattray** Perth and Kinross Scotland UK
142 G3 **Rattray Head** *cape* Scotland UK
120 L5 **Ratu** Sweden
123 N2 **Ratula** Finland
74 E4 **Ratz, Mount** British Columbia/Alaska Canada/USA
124 F1 **Ratzeburger See** *lake* Germany
197 K3 **Rau** *island* Indonesia
125 L5 **Râu-de-Mori** Romania
132 D3 **Râu Sadului** Romania
196 D3 **Raub** Malaysia
107 G6 **Rauch** Argentina
135 AI5 **Rauchua** *watercourse* Russian Federation
108 B3 **Rauco** Chile
121 O3 **Raudanjoki** Finland
121 O5 **Raudanvesi** *lake* Finland
121 N5 **Raudaskylä** Finland
77 W5 **Raude, Lac** *lake* Quebec Canada
120 F5 **Raudsand** Norway
120 I3 **Raudvatnet** *lake* Norway
120 inset **Raufarhöfn** Iceland
121 N3 **Rauhala** Finland
104 B3 **Raujunte, Nevado** *mountain* Peru
120 I4 **Raukasjön** *lake* Sweden
123 K2 **Rauma** Finland
123 M4 **Rauna** Latvia
139 G2 **Raunds** Northamptonshire England UK
220 F4 **Raurimu** New Zealand
187 F6 **Raurkela** Orissa India
220 F4 **Raurimu** New Zealand
193 J2 **Rausu-dake** *volcano* Japan
132 F2 **Raut** *watercourse* Moldova
121 O5 **Rautalampi** Finland
120 K3 **Rautas** Sweden
120 K2 **Rautasjärvi** *lake* Sweden
121 P5 **Rautavaara** Finland
123 L2 **Rautavesi** *bay* Finland
123 M2 **Rautavesi** *lake* Finland
121 N4 **Rautio** Finland
123 O2 **Rautjärvi** Finland
120 I3 **Rauvatn** Norway
130 F5 **Rava** *island* Croatia
125 L2 **Rava-Rus'ka** Ukraine
131 E8 **Ravanusa** Italy
179 H3 **Rāvar** Iran
183 K6 **Ravat** Kyrgyzstan
83 O5 **Ravena** New York USA
86 F2 **Ravenden** Arkansas USA
140 E2 **Ravenglass** Cumbria England UK
139 I2 **Raveningham** Norfolk England UK
124 G5 **Ravenna** Italy
82 J8 **Ravenna** Kentucky USA
81 P6 **Ravenna** Nebraska USA
86 C4 **Ravenna** Texas USA
124 E4 **Ravensburg** Germany
141 H2 **Ravenscar** North Yorkshire England UK
75 Q8 **Ravenscrag** Saskatchewan Canada
215 H4 **Ravenshoe** Qld Australia
138 E1 **Ravensmoor** Cheshire England UK
216 G6 **Ravensthorpe** WA Australia
141 F2 **Ravenstonedale** Cumbria England UK
215 I6 **Ravenswood** Qld Australia
179 M3 **Ravi** *watercourse* Pakistan
86 C3 **Ravia** Oklahoma USA
126 F5 **Raviège, Lac de la** *lake* France
73 Q5 **Ravn, Kap** *cape* Greenland
125 H4 **Ravne** Slovenia
130 H4 **Ravno Selo** Serbia
120 K5 **Rävsön** Sweden
120 J3 **Råvvejaure** *lake* Sweden
141 H2 **Raw** North Yorkshire England UK
125 K2 **Rawa Mazowiecka** Poland
222 1 **Rawaki** *island* Kiribati
179 M2 **Rawalpindi** Pakistan
178 E2 **Rawandoz** Iraq
196 D4 **Rawas** *watercourse* Indonesia
186 D6 **Rawatbhata** Rajasthan India
186 D5 **Rawatsar** Rajasthan India
75 U5 **Rawebb** Manitoba Canada
220 E2 **Rawene** New Zealand
220 F2 **Rawhiti** New Zealand
194 C6 **Rawi, Ko** *island* Thailand
125 I2 **Rawicz** Poland
217 I5 **Rawlinna** WA Australia
81 L6 **Rawlins** Wyoming USA
217 J2 **Rawlinson, Mount** WA Australia
108 D3 **Rawson** Argentina
58 N1 **Rawson Mountains** Antarctica
143 E1 **Ray** Ireland
81 N2 **Ray** North Dakota USA
79 I9 **Ray, Cape** Newfoundland and Labrador Canada
87 J5 **Ray City** Georgia USA
75 W2 **Ray Lake** Nunavut Canada
86 C4 **Ray Roberts Lake** Texas USA
197 G4 **Raya, Bukit** *mountain* Indonesia
187 E8 **Rayachoti** Andhra Pradesh India
187 D8 **Rayadurg** Andhra Pradesh India
187 F7 **Rayagada** Orissa India
191 L2 **Raychikhinsk** Russian Federation
135 AF9 **Raykoke, Ostrov** *island* Russian Federation
133 D5 **Raykovo** Bulgaria
141 F1 **Raylees** Northumberland England UK
75 O8 **Raymond** Alberta Canada
80 D3 **Raymond** Washington USA
86 C7 **Raymondville** Texas USA
82 D7 **Raymore** Missouri USA
221 8 **Raynal, Mount** Auckland Islands New Zealand
58 D2 **Rayner Glacier** Antarctica
89 G5 **Rayón** Mexico
89 F4 **Rayón** Mexico
194 D4 **Rayong** Thailand
121 M5 **Räyrinki** Finland
83 M6 **Raystown Lake** Pennsylvania USA
82 D7 **Raytown** Missouri USA
86 F4 **Rayville** Louisiana USA
179 L3 **Razani** Pakistan
178 E3 **Razāzah, Buḩayrat ar** *lake* Iraq
132 E2 **Războieni** Romania
130 G4 **Razboj** Bosnia and Herzegovina
182 D6 **Razdan** Armenia
179 I3 **Razeh** Iran
178 G2 **Rāzeqan** Iran
132 E4 **Razgrad** Bulgaria
132 E4 **Razgrad** *admin. area* Bulgaria
132 F3 **Razim, Lacul** *lake* Romania
123 N4 **Rāznas** *lake* Latvia
126 D3 **Ré, Île de** *island* France
139 H2 **Reach** Cambridgeshire England UK
80 C1 **Read Island** British Columbia Canada
139 G3 **Reading** Berkshire England UK
139 G3 **Reading** *admin. area* England UK
83 N6 **Reading** Pennsylvania USA
141 F2 **Reagill** Cumbria England UK
103 E5 **Real** *watercourse* Brazil
128 B3 **Real** Portugal
103 A9 **Realeza** Brazil
106 E5 **Realicó** Argentina
88 C2 **Realito** Mexico
126 F5 **Réalmont** France
223 14 **Reao** *island* French Polynesia
142 E2 **Reay** Highland Scotland UK
131 C8 **Rebaa Oulad Yahia** Tunisia
124 B3 **Rebais** France
120 K1 **Rebbenesøy** *island* Norway
216 H5 **Rebecca, Lake** WA Australia
88 C2 **Rebeico** Mexico
198 E5 **Rebi** Indonesia
121 Q5 **Reboly** Russian Federation
128 C3 **Rebordelo** Portugal
128 B2 **Rebordelo** Spain
183 N2 **Rebrikha** Russian Federation
133 B5 **Reç** Albania
108 A5 **Recalada, Isla** *island* Chile
130 E5 **Recanati** Italy
128 E3 **Recas** Spain
127 G3 **Recey-sur-Ource** France
129 G6 **Rechaïga** Algeria
123 P4 **Rechane** Russian Federation
216 H7 **Recherche, Archipelago of the** WA Australia
132 E4 **Rechitsa** Bulgaria
132 D1 **Rechka** Ukraine
136 D2 **Rechytsa** Belarus
125 H5 **Rečica** Croatia
102 F5 **Recife** Brazil
162 E6 **Recife, Cape** South Africa
124 D2 **Recklinghausen** Germany
130 D4 **Recoaro Terme** Italy
195 I6 **Recodo** Philippines
107 G4 **Reconquista** Argentina
58 W1 **Recovery Glacier** Antarctica
105 F2 **Recreio** Brazil
103 D8 **Recreio** Brazil
100 C5 **Recreo** Peru
86 F2 **Rector** Arkansas USA
139 I3 **Reculver** Kent England UK
125 H1 **Recz** Poland
125 J2 **Ręczno** Poland
215 G4 **Red** *watercourse* Qld Australia
Red *see* **Yuan** China
86 E4 **Red** *watercourse* Louisiana USA
81 Q3 **Red** *watercourse* Minnesota USA
82 C3 **Red** *watercourse* North Dakota USA
79 J7 **Red Bay** Newfoundland and Labrador Canada
216 C2 **Red Bluff** *cape* WA Australia
80 D6 **Red Bluff** California USA
85 K5 **Red Bluff Reservoir** Texas USA
82 G7 **Red Bud** Illinois USA
81 L7 **Red Cliff** Colorado USA
218 F6 **Red Cliffs** Vic. Australia
76 I5 **Red Cross Lake** Manitoba Canada
75 O6 **Red Deer** Alberta Canada
75 N7 **Red Deer** *watercourse* Alberta Canada
75 T6 **Red Deer** *watercourse* Saskatchewan Canada
74 K5 **Red Deer Creek** British Columbia Canada
75 U6 **Red Deer Lake** Manitoba Canada
75 N4 **Red Earth Creek** Alberta Canada
140 A3 **Red Gate** Ireland
212 D6 **Red Hill** WA Australia
86 B2 **Red Hills** *range* Kansas USA
79 J8 **Red Indian Lake** Newfoundland and Labrador Canada
79 K9 **Red Island** Newfoundland and Labrador Canada
218 C4 **Red Lake** SA Australia
76 I7 **Red Lake** Ontario Canada
84 E3 **Red Lake** Arizona USA
82 C3 **Red Lake** *watercourse* Minnesota USA
81 K6 **Red Lake** Wyoming USA
81 Q3 **Red Lake Falls** Minnesota USA
81 K4 **Red Lodge** Montana USA
Red River *see* **Hong, Song** China
85 J2 **Red River** New Mexico USA
219 K3 **Red Rock** NSW Australia
82 G2 **Red Rock** Ontario Canada
81 Q8 **Red Rock** Oklahoma USA
178 D5/6 **Red Sea** Middle East
156 F4 **Red Sea** *admin. area* Sudan
83 K7 **Red Spruce Knob** *mountain* West Virginia USA
76 I5 **Red Sucker Lake** Manitoba Canada
75 O6 **Red Willow** Alberta Canada
78 H5 **Red Wine** *watercourse* Newfoundland and Labrador Canada
82 E4 **Red Wing** Minnesota USA
122 F2 **Redalen** Norway
196 D2 **Redang** *island* Malaysia
218 F7 **Redbank** Vic. Australia
75 R6 **Redberry Lake** Saskatchewan Canada
141 H3 **Redbourne** North Lincolnshire England UK
142 D3 **Redburn** Highland Scotland UK
141 F2 **Redburn** Northumberland England UK
219 I2 **Redcap, Mount** Qld Australia
141 G2 **Redcar** Redcar and Cleveland England UK
141 H2 **Redcar and Cleveland** *admin. area* England UK
80 D6 **Redding** California USA
139 F2 **Redditch** Worcestershire England UK
125 I4 **Réde** Hungary
102 E4 **Redenção** Brazil
102 B4 **Redenção** Brazil
155 H2 **Redeyef** Tunisia
81 P4 **Redfield** South Dakota USA
77 V6 **Redfir Lake** Newfoundland and Labrador Canada
138 A1 **Redford** Ireland
85 J6 **Redford** Texas USA
109 inset 9 **Redhead** Trinidad and Tobago
218 D5 **Redhill** SA Australia
143 D3 **Redhill** Ireland
139 G3 **Redhill** Surrey England UK
84 D3 **Redlands** California USA
139 F4 **Redlynch** Wiltshire England UK
80 E4 **Redmond** Oregon USA
80 D3 **Redmond** Washington USA
124 F3 **Rednitz** *watercourse* Germany
126 C3 **Redon** France
91 I3 **Redonda** *island* Antigua and Barbuda
109 inset 9 **Redonda, Isla** *island* Venezuela
109 5 **Redonda, Punta** *cape* Isla de Pascua (Easter Island)
128 B2 **Redondela** Spain
128 C4 **Redondo** Portugal
106 E2 **Redondo, Cerro** *mountain* Chile
77 V5 **Redore** Newfoundland and Labrador Canada
142 C3 **Redpoint** Highland Scotland UK
85 H4 **Redrock** New Mexico USA
138 B4 **Redruth** Cornwall England UK
199 H6 **Redscar Bay** Papua New Guinea
74 J6 **Redstone** British Columbia Canada
72 G6 **Redstone** *watercourse* Northwest Territories Canada
85 H1 **Redvale** Colorado USA
75 O6 **Redwater** Alberta Canada
86 D4 **Redwater** Texas USA
142 E4 **Redwells** Fife Scotland UK
81 R4 **Redwood Falls** Minnesota USA
143 E3 **Ree, Lough** *lake* Ireland
82 I5 **Reed City** Michigan USA
75 U5 **Reed Lake** Manitoba Canada
81 N3 **Reeder** North Dakota USA
139 I2 **Reedham** Norfolk England UK
84 C2 **Reedley** California USA
141 H3 **Reedness** East Riding of Yorkshire England UK
80 C5 **Reedsport** Oregon USA
215 I8 **Reedy** *watercourse* Qld Australia
58 P1 **Reedy Glacier** Antarctica
215 H5 **Reedy Springs** Qld Australia
218 C6 **Reef Point** SA Australia
219 H6 **Reefton** NSW Australia
86 G2 **Reelfoot Lake** Tennessee USA
143 B5 **Reenard Cross** Ireland
124 D2 **Rees** Germany
221 C7 **Rees** *watercourse* New Zealand
108 E5 **Rees Harbour** Falkland Islands
80 G6 **Reese** *watercourse* Nevada USA
141 G2 **Reeth** North Yorkshire England UK
140 A4 **Reevanagh** Ireland
86 H4 **Reform** Alabama USA
89 H5 **Reforma** Mexico
210 inset **Refuge, Port** Cocos (Keeling) Islands Australia
108 B3 **Refugio, Isla** *island* Chile
125 H1 **Rega** *watercourse* Poland
128 D6 **Regaïa** Morocco
124 G3 **Regen** *watercourse* Germany
102 D4 **Regeneração** Brazil
124 G3 **Regensburg** Germany
124 G3 **Regenstauf** Germany
81 N3 **Regent** North Dakota USA
103 B8 **Regente Feijó** Brazil
155 G3 **Reggane** Algeria
130 D5 **Reggello** Italy
131 F7 **Reggio di Calabria** Italy
124 F5 **Reggio nell'Emilia** Italy
132 D2 **Reghin** Romania
102 B1 **Regina** Brazil
75 S7 **Regina** Saskatchewan Canada
75 S7 **Regina Beach** Saskatchewan Canada
106 D5 **Región Metropolitana** *admin. area* Chile
131 G7 **Regione Calabria** *region* Italy
103 C9 **Registro** Brazil
103 B6 **Registro do Araguaia** Brazil
122 H3 **Regna** Sweden
212 D6 **Regnard Bay** WA Australia
183 J6 **Regor** Tajikistan
142 E3 **Regoul** Highland Scotland UK
121 Q4 **Regozero** Russian Federation
130 E1 **Rehau** Germany
186 E6 **Rehli** Madhya Pradesh India
162 C4 **Rehoboth** Namibia
83 N7 **Rehoboth Bay** Delaware USA
83 N7 **Rehoboth Beach** Delaware USA
199 I5 **Reibeck Bay** Papua New Guinea
77 X3 **Reichel Head** Newfoundland and Labrador Canada
127 H2 **Reichshoffen** France
217 K5 **Reid** WA Australia
213 K4 **Reid, Mount** NT Australia
215 I5 **Reid River** Qld Australia
142 C3 **Reidh, Rubha** *cape* Scotland UK
219 I6 **Reids Flat** NSW Australia
87 J4 **Reidsville** Georgia USA
87 L2 **Reidsville** North Carolina USA
142 C2 **Reiff** Highland Scotland UK
139 G3 **Reigate** Surrey England UK
129 I2 **Reillanne** France
124 C3 **Reims** France
108 A5 **Reina Adelaida, Archipiélago de la** *islands* Chile
75 T5 **Reindeer** *watercourse* Saskatchewan Canada
75 W6 **Reindeer Island** Manitoba Canada

76 D4 **Reindeer Lake** Manitoba/Saskatchewan Canada
120 H3 **Reine** Norway
220 E2 **Reinga, Cape** New Zealand
124 E3 **Reinheim** Germany
120 J3 **Reinoksvatnet** *lake* Norway
128 D2 **Reinosa** Spain
120 K2 **Reinøy** *island* Norway
121 N1 **Reinøya** *island* Norway
122 F2 **Reinsvatnet** *lake* Norway
120 E5 **Reinsvik** Norway
120 L2 **Reisaelva** *watercourse* Norway
124 G3 **Reisbach** Germany
121 N5 **Reisjärvi** Finland
142 E2 **Reiss** Highland Scotland UK
120 G5 **Reitan** Norway
162 E5 **Reitz** South Africa
122 H3 **Rejmyre** Sweden
Rekohua *see* **Chatham Island** New Zealand
122 C2 **Reksteren** *island* Norway
120 J3 **Rekvatnet** *lake* Norway
123 L5 **Rėkyvos ežeras** *lake* Lithuania
143 C5 **Releagh** Ireland
81 P5 **Reliance** South Dakota USA
155 G1 **Relizane** Algeria
130 H3 **Rém** Hungary
155 I2 **Remada** Tunisia
104 C3 **Remanso** Brazil
214 E6 **Remarkable, Mount** Qld Australia
218 D5 **Remarkable, Mount** SA Australia
221 C7 **Remarkables, The** *range* New Zealand
104 D2 **Remate de Males** Brazil
197 F5 **Rembang** Indonesia
197 F5 **Rembang, Teluk** *bay* Indonesia
120 I4 **Remdalen** Sweden
88 D3 **Remedios, Los** *watercourse* Mexico
90 B4 **Remedios, Punta** *cape* El Salvador
128 B2 **Remedios, Punta dos** *cape* Spain
124 D1 **Remels** Germany
132 D2 **Remetea** Romania
125 I4 **Remetinec** Croatia
83 J2 **Remi Lake** Ontario Canada
164 9 **Remire Island** Seychelles
101 H3 **Remire-Montjoly** French Guiana
127 H2 **Remiremont** France
120 J5 **Remmarbäcken** Sweden
104 C4 **Remolino** Peru
127 G5 **Remoulins** France
196 E3 **Rempang** *island* Indonesia
124 D2 **Remscheid** Germany
82 D5 **Remsen** Iowa USA
83 N5 **Remsen** New York USA
101 H4 **Remune** Brazil
124 C5 **Rémuzat** France
122 F2 **Rena** Norway
120 G5 **Rena** *watercourse* Norway
126 D3 **Renac** France
58 T2 **Renaud Island** Antarctica
130 E4 **Renče** Slovenia
185 K2 **Renchinlhumbe** Mongolia
82 G7 **Rend Lake** Illinois USA
123 L4 **Renda** Latvia
188 D3 **Rende** Yunnan China
131 G7 **Rende** Italy
222 8 **Rendova** *island* Solomon Islands
79 D7 **René-Levasseur, Île** *island* Quebec Canada
124 B2 **Renesse** Netherlands
142 D5 **Renfrewshire** *admin. area* Scotland UK
120 H3 **Renga** *island* Norway
187 F7 **Rengali Reservoir** Orissa India
196 E5 **Rengasdengklok** Indonesia
196 D4 **Rengat** Indonesia
189 G3 **Renhua** Guangdong China
188 E3 **Renhuai** Guizhou China
132 F3 **Reni** Ukraine
108 B3 **Reñihué** Chile
142 B3 **Renish Point** Scotland UK
77 O7 **Renison** Ontario Canada
218 E6 **Renmark** SA Australia
120 F5 **Rennebu** Norway
222 8 **Rennell** *island* Solomon Islands
108 B5 **Rennell, Islas** *islands* Chile
222 8 **Rennell and Bellona** *admin. area* Solomon Islands
74 E6 **Rennell Sound** British Columbia Canada
214 B5 **Renner Springs** NT Australia
126 D2 **Rennes** France
122 C3 **Rennesøy** *island* Norway
58 K2 **Rennick Bay** Antarctica
58 K2 **Rennick Glacier** Antarctica
58 L2 **Rennick Trough** *underwater feature* Southern Ocean
75 S2 **Rennie Lake** Northwest Territories Canada
141 G1 **Rennington** Northumberland England UK
74 M5 **Reno** Alberta Canada
130 D4 **Reno** *watercourse* Italy
80 F7 **Reno** Nevada USA
86 C4 **Reno** Texas USA
83 M6 **Renovo** Pennsylvania USA
191 H5 **Renqiu** Hebei China
120 K2 **Rensjön** Sweden
120 L4 **Renström** Sweden
133 B6 **Rentina** Greece
80 D3 **Renton** Washington USA
186 F6 **Renukut** Uttar Pradesh India
198 B6 **Reo** Indonesia
158 D2 **Réo** Burkina Faso
104 C3 **Repartición** Peru
104 D5 **Repartición** Peru
105 F3 **Repartimento** Brazil
182 I6 **Repetek** Turkmenistan
120 L5 **Replot** Finland
120 L5 **Replotfjärden** *island* Finland
121 N2 **Repokaira** *island* Finland
220 G4 **Reporoa** New Zealand
82 E8 **Republic** Missouri USA
80 F2 **Republic** Washington USA
105 F4 **República** Brazil
81 Q7 **Republican** *watercourse* Kansas USA
73 K5 **Repulse Bay** Nunavut Canada
104 C2 **Requena** Peru
129 F4 **Requena** Spain
101 E3 **Requena** Venezuela
126 F4 **Réquista** France
122 F5 **Rerik** Germany
143 C5 **Rerrin** Ireland
87 I3 **Resaca** Georgia USA
130 D4 **Resana** Italy
218 E6 **Rescue, Mount** SA Australia
108 A4 **Rescue, Punta** *cape* Chile
53 BB6 **Researcher Ridge** *underwater feature* Atlantic Ocean
103 C8 **Resende** Brazil
103 B9 **Reserva** Brazil
104 D3 **Reserva Extrema** Brazil
108 C5 **Reserva Fiscal** Chile
75 T6 **Reserve** Saskatchewan Canada
85 H4 **Reserve** New Mexico USA
182 F7 **Reshteh-ye Kūhhā-ye Alborz** *range* Iran
107 G3 **Resistencia** Argentina
132 B3 **Reşiţa** Romania
132 A4 **Resnik** Montenegro
73 J4 **Resolute** Nunavut Canada
78 F5 **Résolution, Lac** *lake* Quebec Canada
78 F2 **Resolution Island** Nunavut Canada
221 B7 **Resolution Island** New Zealand
105 H5 **Resolvido** Brazil
142 C4 **Resourie** Highland Scotland UK
103 D7 **Resplendor** Brazil
182 C5 **Respublika Adygeya** *admin. area* Russian Federation
182 G2 **Respublika Bashkortostan** *admin. area* Russian Federation
135 X8 **Respublika Buryatiya** *admin. area* Russian Federation
182 E5 **Respublika Dagestan** *admin. area* Russian Federation
134 H6 **Respublika Kareliya** *admin. area* Russian Federation
134 L6 **Respublika Komi** *admin. area* Russian Federation
182 E2 **Respublika Mariy El** *admin. area* Russian Federation
182 D2 **Respublika Mordoviya** *admin. area* Russian Federation
135 AA6 **Respublika Sakha** *admin. area* Russian Federation
182 D5 **Respublika Severnaya Osetiya** *admin. area* Russian Federation
182 F2 **Respublika Tatarstan** *admin. area* Russian Federation
79 E9 **Restigouche** *watercourse* New Brunswick/Quebec Canada
81 O2 **Reston** Manitoba Canada
142 F5 **Reston** Scottish Borders Scotland UK
90 B4 **Retalhuleu** Guatemala
220 F4 **Retaruke** New Zealand
126 D4 **Rétaud** France
141 H3 **Retford** Nottinghamshire England UK
124 C3 **Rethel** France
133 D8 **Rethymno** Greece
124 C2 **Retie** Belgium
126 D3 **Retiers** France
100 D5 **Retiro** Brazil
105 G5 **Retiro** Brazil
105 G5 **Retiro Carrapatinho** Brazil
105 H5 **Retiro Central** Brazil
105 H5 **Retiro do Buriti** Brazil
105 G5 **Retiro do Presidente** Brazil
105 H6 **Retiro Monte Belo** Brazil
218 F1 **Retreat** Qld Australia
125 H3 **Retz** Austria
124 G1 **Reuden** Germany
126 F3 **Reuilly** France
164 7a **Réunion** *French overseas department* Indian Ocean
164 7 **Réunion** *island* Indian Ocean
129 G3 **Reus** Spain
196 C3 **Reusam** *island* Indonesia
124 C2 **Reusel** Netherlands
127 I3 **Reuss** *watercourse* Switzerland
124 E3 **Reutlingen** Germany
127 J3 **Reutte** Austria
121 S3 **Revda** Russian Federation
126 F5 **Revel** France
58 T2 **Revelle Inlet** *bay* Antarctica
74 L7 **Revelstoke** British Columbia Canada
74 L7 **Revelstoke, Lake** British Columbia Canada
163 G2 **Révia** Mozambique
88 C5 **Revillagigedo, Islas** *islands* Mexico
74 F5 **Revillagigedo Channel** Alaska USA
74 F5 **Revillagigedo Island** Alaska USA
124 C3 **Revin** France
127 K1 **Řevničov** Czech Republic
124 F4 **Revò** Italy
121 N4 **Revonlahti** Finland
121 N1 **Revsbotn** *bay* Norway
120 J2 **Revsnes** Norway
122 I4 **Revsudden** Sweden
120 I5 **Revsund** Sweden
120 I5 **Revsundssjön** *bay* Sweden
163 F3 **Revubue** *watercourse* Mozambique
130 I2 **Revúca** Slovakia
186 E6 **Rewa** Madhya Pradesh India
75 Q6 **Reward** Saskatchewan Canada
186 D5 **Rewari** Haryana India
58 S2 **Rex, Mount** *mountain* Antarctica
80 J5 **Rexburg** Idaho USA
81 O7 **Rexford** Kansas USA
80 H2 **Rexford** Montana USA
100 B2 **Rey, Isla del** *island* Panama
85 K7 **Rey, Lago del** *lake* Mexico
88 E3 **Rey, Laguna del** *watercourse* Mexico
120 inset **Reyðarfjörður** *bay* Iceland
104 E4 **Reyes** Bolivia
104 E3 **Reyes** Bolivia
80 D7 **Reyes, Point** California USA
104 B4 **Reyes, Punta** *cape* Peru
120 inset **Reykholt** Iceland
120 inset **Reykjahlíð** Iceland
57 E2 **Reykjanes Ridge** *underwater feature* Atlantic Ocean
120 inset **Reykjanestá** *cape* Iceland
120 inset **Reykjavík** Iceland
213 K2 **Reynolds** *watercourse* NT Australia
81 R2 **Reynolds** Manitoba Canada
87 I4 **Reynolds** Georgia USA
82 H6 **Reynolds** Indiana USA
81 Q3 **Reynolds** North Dakota USA
89 F3 **Reynosa** Mexico
138 C4 **Rezare** Cornwall England UK
123 N4 **Rēzekne** Latvia
123 N4 **Rēzeknes** *admin. area* Latvia
181 H2 **Rezhaka** Xizang Zizhiqu China
132 F2 **Rezina** Moldova
133 F5 **Rezovo** Bulgaria
130 D4 **Rezzato** Italy
130 B4 **Rezzo** Italy
81 N3 **Rhame** North Dakota USA
138 D2 **Rhandir-mwyn** Carmarthenshire Wales UK
138 D2 **Rhayader** Powys Wales UK
124 D2 **Rhede** Germany
127 H2 **Rhein** *watercourse* France
124 D3 **Rheinau** Germany
124 D1 **Rheine** Germany
124 D3 **Rheinland-Pfalz** *admin. area* Germany
138 D1 **Rhewl** Denbighshire Wales UK
83 O6 **Rhinebeck** New York USA
82 G4 **Rhinelander** Wisconsin USA
124 G1 **Rhinkanal** *watercourse* Germany
160 E3 **Rhino Camp** Uganda
124 G1 **Rhinow** Germany
138 C2 **Rhiw** Gwynedd Wales UK
130 C4 **Rho** Italy
Rhodes *see* **Rodos** Greece
133 D5 **Rhodope Mountains** *range* Bulgaria
86 C4 **Rhome** Texas USA
138 D3 **Rhondda** Rhondda Cynon Taff Wales UK
138 D3 **Rhondda Cynon Taff** *admin. area* Wales UK
127 G4 **Rhône** *watercourse* France
108 A3 **Rhone, Puerto** *bay* Chile
127 G4 **Rhône-Alpes** *admin. area* France
138 D3 **Rhoose** Vale of Glamorgan Wales UK
138 C3 **Rhos** Carmarthenshire Wales UK
140 E3 **Rhôs-on-Sea** Conwy Wales UK
138 C2 **Rhós-y-llan** Gwynedd Wales UK
138 D2 **Rhosgoch** Powys Wales UK
138 D1 **Rhosllanerchrugog** Wrexham Wales UK
140 D3 **Rhosneigir** Isle of Anglesey Wales UK
138 C3 **Rhossili** Swansea Wales UK
155 H1 **Rhoufi** Algeria
142 D4 **Rhu** Argyll and Bute Scotland UK
140 E3 **Rhuallt** Denbighshire Wales UK
142 C5 **Rhubodach** Argyll and Bute Scotland UK
140 E3 **Rhuddlan** Denbighshire Wales UK
138 C2 **Rhydcymmerau** Carmarthenshire Wales UK
138 C2 **Rhydlios** Gwynedd Wales UK
140 E3 **Rhyl** Denbighshire Wales UK
138 D3 **Rhymney** Caerphilly Wales UK
142 F3 **Rhynie** Aberdeenshire Scotland UK
159 F4 **Riaba** Equatorial Guinea
102 C4 **Riachão** Brazil
103 C5 **Riachão das Neves** Brazil
103 E5 **Riachão do Jacuípe** Brazil
103 D6 **Riacho de Santana** Brazil
108 E2 **Riachos, Islas de los** *islands* Argentina
103 B6 **Rialma** Brazil
129 G3 **Rialp, Pantà de** *lake* Spain
219 J4 **Riamukka** NSW Australia
181 G3 **Riang** Arunachal Pradesh India
128 B2 **Rianjo** Spain
127 G5 **Rians** France
186 D4 **Riasi** Jammu and Kashmir India/Pakistan
120 G5 **Riasten** *lake* Norway
196 D3 **Riau** *admin. area* Indonesia
124 D4 **Riaz** Switzerland
129 G3 **Riba-roja, Pantà de** *lake* Spain
128 C2 **Ribadeo** Spain
128 D2 **Ribadesella** Spain
129 G2 **Ribagorça** *region* Spain
132 D4 **Ribaritsa** Bulgaria
103 A8 **Ribas do Rio Pardo** Brazil
128 B4 **Ribatejo** *region* Portugal
163 G2 **Ribáuè** Mozambique
141 F2 **Ribble** *watercourse* England UK
141 F2 **Ribblesdale** *valley* England UK
215 H3 **Ribbon Reef** Qld Australia
141 F3 **Ribchester** Lancashire England UK
122 E5 **Ribe** Denmark
103 B9 **Ribeira** *watercourse* Brazil
128 B3 **Ribeira** Portugal
164 2 **Ribeira Brava** Madeira
164 4a **Ribeira da Barca** Cape Verde
103 E5 **Ribeira do Pombal** Brazil
164 1a **Ribeira Grande** Azores
164 4a **Ribeira Prata** Cape Verde
102 F5 **Ribeirão** Brazil
105 E3 **Ribeirão** Brazil
103 B9 **Ribeirão Branco** Brazil
103 B6 **Ribeirão Cascalheira** Brazil
105 I3 **Ribeirão Crisostomo** *watercourse* Brazil
103 C8 **Ribeirão Preto** Brazil
131 E8 **Ribera** Italy
128 B2 **Ribera** Spain
128 C4 **Ribera del Fresno** Spain
126 E4 **Ribérac** France
105 E3 **Riberalta** Bolivia
130 H4 **Ribnica** Bosnia and Herzegovina
125 H5 **Ribnica** Slovenia
132 F2 **Rîbniţa** Moldova
130 D5 **Ribolla** Italy
75 P6 **Ribstone** Alberta Canada
193 I2 **Ribun tō** *island* Japan
212 D6 **Rica, Mount** WA Australia
100 B4 **Ricaurte** Ecuador
131 F6 **Riccia** Italy
84 E3 **Rice** California USA
86 C4 **Rice** Texas USA
83 L4 **Rice Lake** Ontario Canada
82 F4 **Rice Lake** Wisconsin USA
108 B5 **Rice Trevor, Islas** *islands* Chile
87 K5 **Riceboro** Georgia USA
75 P5 **Rich Lake** Alberta Canada
82 E2 **Richan** Ontario Canada
75 R6 **Richard** Saskatchewan Canada
87 J3 **Richard B. Russell Lake** Georgia USA
163 F5 **Richards Bay** South Africa
75 R3 **Richards Lake** Saskatchewan Canada
75 P3 **Richardson** *watercourse* Alberta Canada
75 P3 **Richardson Lake** Alberta Canada
72 F5 **Richardson Mountains** Northwest Territories/Yukon Territory Canada
221 C7 **Richardson Mountains** New Zealand
81 N3 **Richardton** North Dakota USA
79 J7 **Riche, Point** Newfoundland and Labrador Canada
126 E3 **Richelieu** France
82 C2 **Richer** Manitoba Canada
81 M3 **Richey** Montana USA
80 H5 **Richfield** Idaho USA
80 I7 **Richfield** Utah USA
143 F2 **Richill** Armagh Northern Ireland UK
87 I4 **Richland** Georgia USA
82 I5 **Richland** Michigan USA
80 G4 **Richland** Oregon USA
86 C5 **Richland** Texas USA
80 F3 **Richland** Washington USA
87 J3 **Richland Balsam** *mountain* North Carolina USA
82 F5 **Richland Center** Wisconsin USA
86 B5 **Richland Springs** Texas USA
83 K8 **Richlands** Virginia USA
219 J5 **Richmond** NSW Australia
215 G6 **Richmond** Qld Australia
219 R11 **Richmond** Tas. Australia
74 J8 **Richmond** British Columbia Canada
83 O4 **Richmond** Quebec Canada
162 D6 **Richmond** South Africa
109 11a **Richmond** St Vincent and the Grenadines
80 D8 **Richmond** California USA
82 I7 **Richmond** Indiana USA
82 I8 **Richmond** Kentucky USA
86 F4 **Richmond** Louisiana USA
83 M8 **Richmond** Virginia USA
221 E5 **Richmond Range** New Zealand
83 N5 **Richmondville** New York USA
75 Q7 **Richmound** Saskatchewan Canada
143 E3 **Richmount Hill** Ireland
86 E4 **Richwood** Louisiana USA
83 K7 **Richwood** West Virginia USA
139 G3 **Rickmansworth** Hertfordshire England UK
81 K8 **Rico** Colorado USA
128 D3 **Ricobayo, Embalse de** *lake* Spain
178 E7 **Ridā'** Yemen
58 E2 **Riddell Nunataks** *range* Antarctica
130 B3 **Riddes** Switzerland
80 D5 **Riddle** Oregon USA
123 L4 **Rideļi** Latvia
76 M7 **Ridge** *watercourse* Ontario Canada
84 D3 **Ridgecrest** California USA
75 S6 **Ridgedale** Saskatchewan Canada
86 F4 **Ridgeland** Mississippi USA
87 K4 **Ridgeland** South Carolina USA
215 K7 **Ridgelands** Qld Australia
83 K5 **Ridgetown** Ontario Canada
87 L2 **Ridgeway** Virginia USA
82 G5 **Ridgeway** Wisconsin USA
81 L7 **Ridgway** Colorado USA
132 A3 **Riđica** Serbia
139 G2 **Ridlington** Rutland England UK
141 F1 **Ridsdale** Northumberland England UK
120 J3 **Riebnes** *lake* Sweden
100 D3 **Riecito** *watercourse* Venezuela
124 G3 **Ried** Austria
127 I2 **Riedern** Germany
124 E3 **Riedlingen** Germany
126 B5 **Riego de la Vega** Spain
120 G5 **Rien** *lake* Norway
127 K1 **Riesa** Germany
131 F8 **Riesi** Italy
162 D6 **Rietbron** South Africa
162 D5 **Rietfontein** South Africa
131 E5 **Rieti** Italy
126 E5 **Rieumes** France
129 H1 **Rieupeyroux** France
141 G2 **Rievaulx** North Yorkshire England UK
127 H5 **Riez** France
189 G3 **Rifeng** Jiangxi China
80 D3 **Riffe Lake** Washington USA
81 L7 **Rifle** Colorado USA
161 F3 **Rift Valley** *admin. area* Kenya
155 I6 **Rig-Rig** Chad
123 M4 **Rīga** Latvia
123 L4 **Riga, Gulf of** Estonia/Latvia
123 M4 **Rīgas** *admin. area* Latvia
80 J5 **Rigby** Idaho USA
142 B3 **Rigg** Highland Scotland UK
80 G4 **Riggins** Idaho USA
142 E5 **Righead** Dumfries and Galloway Scotland UK
78 I5 **Rigolet** Newfoundland and Labrador Canada
142 E5 **Rigside** South Lanarkshire Scotland UK
123 L3 **Riguldi** Estonia
123 M2 **Riihimäki** Finland
121 O3 **Riipijärvi** *lake* Finland
58 W2 **Riiser-Larsen Basin** *underwater feature* Southern Ocean
58 W2 **Riiser-Larsen Ice Shelf** Antarctica
58 C2 **Riiser-Larsen Peninsula** Antarctica
58 B2 **Riiser-Larsen Sea** Antarctica
123 M3 **Riisipere** Estonia
123 K2 **Riispyy** Finland
121 P4 **Riitakylä** Finland
159 F2 **Rijau** Nigeria
130 F4 **Rijeka** Croatia
181 F3 **Rikaze** Xizang Zizhiqu China
121 P5 **Rikkavesi** *lake* Finland
181 H3 **Rikor** Arunachal Pradesh India
193 I3 **Rikuzentakata** Japan
132 C4 **Rila** *range* Bulgaria
126 E3 **Rillé** France
159 F2 **Rima** *watercourse* Nigeria
178 E4 **Rimah, Wādī ar** *watercourse* Saudi Arabia
223 14 **Rimatara** *island* French Polynesia
196 E4 **Rimau** *island* Indonesia
125 J3 **Rimavská Baňa** Slovakia
75 N6 **Rimbey** Alberta Canada
130 E4 **Rimini** Italy
186 D3 **Rimo Glacier** Jammu and Kashmir India/Pakistan
79 D8 **Rimouski** Quebec Canada
79 D8 **Rimouski** *watercourse* Quebec Canada
80 E3 **Rimrock Lake** Washington USA
142 D2 **Rimsdale, Loch** *lake* Scotland UK
197 H6 **Rinca** *island* Indonesia
108 C5 **Rincón** Argentina
88 E4 **Rincón de Romos** Mexico
128 F2 **Rincón de Soto** Spain
107 G5 **Rincón del Bonete, Lago artificial de** *lake* Uruguay
109 7 **Rincon Grande Settlement** Falkland Islands
120 F5 **Rindal** Norway
133 D7 **Rineia** *island* Greece
140 B4 **Ring** Ireland
219 R10 **Ringarooma Bay** Tas. Australia
122 I3 **Ringarum** Sweden
186 D5 **Ringas** Rajasthan India
143 G2 **Ringboy** Ards Northern Ireland UK
122 F5 **Ringe** Denmark
120 G6 **Ringebu** Norway
122 D2 **Ringedalsvatnet** *lake* Norway
142 D6 **Ringford** Dumfries and Galloway Scotland UK
86 E4 **Ringgold** Louisiana USA
122 D5 **Ringkøbing Fjord** *lake* Denmark
139 I2 **Ringland** Norfolk England UK
86 C3 **Ringling** Oklahoma USA
122 G2 **Ringnäs** Sweden
140 B3 **Ringsend** Ireland
143 F1 **Ringsend** Coleraine Northern Ireland UK
122 I3 **Ringsön** *island* Sweden
139 G2 **Ringstead** Northamptonshire England UK
122 F5 **Ringsted** Denmark
218 G7 **Ringwood** Vic. Australia
139 F4 **Ringwood** Hampshire England UK
139 I3 **Ringwould** Kent England UK
123 O2 **Rinkilä** Finland
142 C6 **Rinns of Galloway** *peninsula* Scotland UK
124 E1 **Rinteln** Germany
104 D5 **Río Blanco** Bolivia
90 C4 **Río Blanco** Nicaragua
85 I1 **Rio Blanco** Colorado USA
101 F2 **Río Bonito** Venezuela
108 B5 **Río Bote** Argentina
104 E3 **Rio Branco** Brazil
105 G4 **Rio Branco** Brazil
89 F3 **Río Bravo** Mexico
86 B7 **Rio Bravo** Texas USA
105 H6 **Rio Brilhante** Brazil
103 D8 **Rio Casca** Brazil
90 E2 **Río Cauto** Cuba
108 B2 **Río Chico** Argentina
108 C4 **Río Chico** Argentina
108 B3 **Río Cisnes** Chile
103 C8 **Rio Claro** Brazil
106 C6 **Río Claro** Chile
109 inset 9 **Rio Claro** Trinidad and Tobago
108 E2 **Rio Colorado, Delta del** *region* Argentina
106 E5 **Río Cuarto** Argentina
103 D8 **Rio das Ostras** Brazil
163 G4 **Rio das Pedras** Mozambique
103 D8 **Rio de Janeiro** Brazil
107 K2 **Rio de Janeiro** *admin. area* Brazil
90 D6 **Río de Jesús** Panama
89 G5 **Río de Teapa** Mexico
80 C6 **Rio Dell** California USA
107 I3 **Rio do Sul** Brazil
90 C4 **Río Esteban** Honduras
108 C5 **Río Gallegos** Argentina
108 C5 **Río Grande** Argentina
104 E6 **Río Grande** Bolivia
107 H5 **Rio Grande** Brazil
106 D2 **Río Grande** Chile
88 E4 **Río Grande** Mexico
106 E3 **Río Grande, Salar de** *pan* Argentina
86 B7 **Rio Grande City** Texas USA
102 E4 **Rio Grande do Norte** *admin. area* Brazil
107 H4 **Rio Grande do Sul** *admin. area* Brazil
81 L8 **Rio Grande Reservoir** Colorado USA
51 O13 **Rio Grande Rise** *underwater feature* Atlantic Ocean
108 B4 **Río Guenguel, Pampa del** *region* Argentina
86 C7 **Rio Hondo** Texas USA
106 E3 **Río Hondo, Embalse** *lake* Argentina
89 H4 **Rio Lagartos** Mexico
128 B4 **Rio Maior** Portugal
105 H4 **Rio Manso, Represa do** *lake* Brazil
130 D5 **Rio Marina** Italy
108 B3 **Río Mayo** Argentina
106 F3 **Río Muerto** Argentina
88 C3 **Río Muerto** Mexico
104 E5 **Río Mulatos** Bolivia
103 B9 **Rio Negrinho** Brazil
108 C2 **Río Negro** *admin. area* Argentina
103 B9 **Rio Negro** Brazil
107 G5 **Río Negro** *admin. area* Uruguay
105 H4 **Rio Novo** Brazil
107 H4 **Rio Pardo** Brazil
103 D6 **Rio Pardo de Minas** Brazil
108 B3 **Río Pico** Argentina
103 D8 **Rio Pomba** Brazil
103 C7 **Rio Preto, Serra do** *range* Brazil
85 I3 **Rio Rancho** New Mexico USA
103 E5 **Rio Real** Brazil
106 E5 **Río Tercero** Argentina
102 F4 **Rio Tinto** Brazil
105 I5 **Rio Verde** Brazil
105 H5 **Rio Verde de Mato Grosso** Brazil
100 C2 **Río Viejo** Colombia
86 C4 **Rio Vista** Texas USA
100 B5 **Riobamba** Ecuador
129 F3 **Riodeva** Spain
100 C2 **Ríohacha** Colombia
104 B2 **Rioja** Peru
105 I5 **Riolândia** Brazil
126 F4 **Riom** France
126 F4 **Riom-ès-Montagnes** France
100 C3 **Rionegro** Colombia
131 F6 **Rionero in Vulture** Italy
182 D5 **Rioni** *watercourse* Georgia
126 G3 **Riorges** France
100 C3 **Riosucio** Colombia
100 B3 **Riosucio** Colombia
127 G4 **Riotord** France
75 R3 **Riou Lake** Saskatchewan Canada
104 E3 **Riozinho** Brazil
102 A4 **Riozinho** *watercourse* Brazil
130 F4 **Ripač** Bosnia and Herzegovina
130 D5 **Ripalti, Punta dei** *cape* Italy
139 F1 **Ripley** Derbyshire England UK
141 G2 **Ripley** North Yorkshire England UK
86 G3 **Ripley** Mississippi USA
82 J7 **Ripley** Ohio USA
86 C2 **Ripley** Oklahoma USA
86 G3 **Ripley** Tennessee USA
129 H2 **Ripoll** Spain
141 G2 **Ripon** North Yorkshire England UK
104 C4 **Riquillacasa, Cerro** *mountain* Peru
126 F2 **Ris-Orangis** France
130 H5 **Risan** Montenegro
160 D4 **Risasa** Democratic Republic of Congo
120 I4 **Risbäck** Sweden
120 I6 **Risbrunn** Sweden
138 E2 **Risbury** Herefordshire England UK
139 H2 **Risby** Suffolk England UK
138 D3 **Risca** Caerphilly Wales UK
100 A2 **Risco** Panama
120 F5 **Rise** Norway
141 H3 **Rise** East Riding of Yorkshire England UK
141 H3 **Riseholme** Lincolnshire England UK
139 G2 **Riseley** Bedfordshire England UK
186 E4 **Rishikesh** Uttaranchal India
193 I2 **Rishiri-tō** *island* Japan
193 I2 **Rishiri-zan** *volcano* Japan
86 B4 **Rising Star** Texas USA
74 J7 **Riske Creek** British Columbia Canada
142 E5 **Riskinhope** Scottish Borders Scotland UK
126 E2 **Risle** *watercourse* France
120 K4 **Risliden** Sweden
86 E4 **Rison** Arkansas USA
122 E3 **Risør** Norway
120 I2 **Risøyhamn** Norway
124 E3 **Riß** *watercourse* Germany
120 I4 **Rissjön** *lake* Sweden
120 I5 **Rissna** Sweden
123 M3 **Risti** Estonia
121 Q2 **Ristikent** Russian Federation
121 P3 **Ristilä** Finland
121 N5 **Ristinselkä** *bay* Finland
132 B4 **Ristovac** Serbia
120 L3 **Risträsk** Sweden
122 G3 **Risveden** *region* Sweden
102 F4 **Rita** Brazil
85 K3 **Rita Blanca** *watercourse* Texas USA
215 I5 **Rita Island** Qld Australia
194 B4 **Ritchie's Archipelago** Andaman and Nicobar Islands India
222 5 **Ritidian Point** Guam
162 C3 **Rito** Angola
58 X2 **Ritscher Upland** *plain* Antarctica
180 D2 **Ritu** Xizang Zizhiqu China
80 F3 **Ritzville** Washington USA
199 J6 **Riu, Mount** Papua New Guinea
123 N2 **Riutanselkä** *bay* Finland
121 O2 **Riutula** Finland
127 J4 **Riva** Italy
106 F3 **Rivadavia** Argentina
106 D5 **Rivadavia** Argentina
124 E5 **Rivanazzano** Italy
139 F3 **Rivar** Wiltshire England UK
90 C5 **Rivas** Nicaragua
127 G4 **Rive-de-Gier** France
158 C3 **River Cess** Liberia
87 H5 **River Falls** Alabama USA
219 K1 **River Heads** Qld Australia
79 F10 **River Hebert** Nova Scotia Canada
84 B1 **River Reservoir** California USA
215 H6 **River View** Qld Australia
106 F6 **Rivera** Argentina
107 H4 **Rivera** Uruguay
107 H4 **Rivera** *admin. area* Uruguay
80 E8 **Riverbank** California USA
140 B4 **Riverchapel** Ireland
87 I4 **Riverdale** Georgia USA
75 R7 **Riverhurst** Saskatchewan Canada
216 G4 **Riverina** WA Australia
108 A3 **Rivero, Isla** *island* Chile
75 U7 **Rivers** Manitoba Canada
159 F4 **Rivers** *admin. area* Nigeria
216 H5 **Rivers, Lake** WA Australia
75 S8 **Rivers, Lake of the** Saskatchewan Canada
74 H7 **Rivers Inlet** British Columbia Canada
143 F3 **Riversdale** Dublin Ireland
221 G5 **Riversdale Beach** New Zealand
84 D4 **Riverside** California USA
80 F2 **Riverside** Washington USA
81 M6 **Riverside Reservoir** Colorado USA
214 E5 **Riversleigh** Qld Australia
80 J6 **Riverton** Utah USA
81 K5 **Riverton** Wyoming USA
127 G4 **Rives** France
86 C7 **Riviera** Texas USA
87 K7 **Riviera Beach** Florida USA
83 O3 **Rivière-à-Pierre** Quebec Canada
83 O2 **Rivière-au-Doré** Quebec Canada
79 F7 **Rivière-au-Tonnerre** Quebec Canada
164 7b **Rivière de Rempart** Mauritius
164 7b **Rivière des Anguilles** Mauritius
79 D9 **Rivière-du-Loup** Quebec Canada
79 C9 **Rivière Ouelle** Quebec Canada
77 V8 **Rivière-Pentecôte** Quebec Canada
79 F7 **Rivière-St-Jean** Quebec Canada
109 14 **Rivière-Salée** Martinique
132 G1 **Rivne** Ukraine
136 C2 **Rivne** Ukraine
136 C2 **Rivnens'ka Oblast'** *admin. area* Ukraine
140 A2 **Rivory** Ireland
162 D3 **Rivungo** Angola
192 F3 **Riwon** North Korea
178 E5 **Riyāḍ, Ar** *admin. area* Saudi Arabia
Riyadh *see* **Ar Riyāḍ** Saudi Arabia
179 G2 **Rizāb-e Mayām** Iran
136 G5 **Rize** Turkey
136 G5 **Rize** *admin. area* Turkey
191 I6 **Rizhao** Shandong China
131 G7 **Rizzuto, Capo** *cape* Italy
122 D3 **Rjuven** *region* Norway
154 C5 **Rkîz** Mauritania
128 E3 **Roa** Spain
109 5 **Roa, Punta** *cape* Isla de Pascua (Easter Island)
140 A3 **Roachtown** Ireland
109 21 **Road Town** British Virgin Islands
120 E5 **Roald** Norway
120 J5 **Röan** Sweden
81 K7 **Roan Plateau** Colorado USA
126 G3 **Roanne** France
89 I1 **Roanoke** Georgia USA
87 M2 **Roanoke** *watercourse* North Carolina USA
83 L8 **Roanoke** Virginia USA
87 M2 **Roanoke Rapids** North Carolina USA
88 E1 **Roaring Springs** Texas USA
143 C5 **Roaringwater Bay** Ireland
132 D3 **Roata de Jos** Romania
90 C3 **Roatán** Honduras
90 C3 **Roatán, Isla de** *island* Honduras
179 H2 **Robāṭ-e Khān** Iran
179 I2 **Robāṭ-e Mūreshq** Iran
179 I2 **Robāṭ-e Samangān** Iran
74 M6 **Robb** Alberta Canada
87 L3 **Robbins** North Carolina USA
219 Q10 **Robbins Island** Tas. Australia
218 D7 **Robe** SA Australia
212 C6 **Robe** *watercourse* WA Australia
161 F2 **Robē** Ethiopia
124 F5 **Robecco** Italy
58 J2 **Robert, Cape** Antarctica
58 D2 **Robert Glacier** Antarctica
85 L5 **Robert Lee** Texas USA
86 D3 **Robert S. Kerr Reservoir** Oklahoma USA
87 J4 **Roberta** Georgia USA
142 F5 **Roberton** Scottish Borders Scotland UK
78 C2 **Roberts, Lac** *lake* Quebec Canada
58 K2 **Roberts Butte** *plain* Antarctica
162 C6 **Robertson** South Africa
79 I7 **Robertson, Lac** *lake* Quebec Canada
58 L2 **Robertson Bay** Antarctica
77 P5 **Robertson Bay** Nunavut Canada
58 U2 **Robertson Island** Antarctica
216 G1 **Robertson Range** WA Australia
158 B3 **Robertsport** Liberia
218 D5 **Robertstown** SA Australia
140 A4 **Robertstown** Ireland
73 L9 **Roberval** Quebec Canada
73 N2 **Robeson Channel** Canada/Greenland
123 N5 **Robežnieki** Latvia
142 B2 **Robhanais, Rubha** *cape* Scotland UK
141 H2 **Robin Hood's Bay** North Yorkshire England UK
214 D4 **Robinson** *watercourse* NT Australia
86 C5 **Robinson** Texas USA
109 6a **Róbinson Crusoe, Isla** *island* Juan Fernández Archipiélago
214 D4 **Robinson River** NT Australia
79 I8 **Robinsons** *watercourse* Newfoundland and Labrador Canada
218 F6 **Robinvale** Vic. Australia
75 U7 **Roblin** Manitoba Canada
105 G5 **Roboré** Bolivia
128 E3 **Robregordo** Spain
75 Q8 **Robsart** Saskatchewan Canada
74 L6 **Robson, Mount** British Columbia Canada
86 A4 **Roby** Texas USA
130 F4 **Roč** Croatia
128 B4 **Roca, Cabo da** *cape* Portugal
108 C6 **Roca Nassau** *island* Chile
89 G5 **Roca Partida, Punta** *cape* Mexico
131 H6 **Roca Vecchia** Italy
88 B3 **Rocas Alijos** *island* Mexico
131 G6 **Rocca Imperiale** Italy
131 F6 **Roccadaspide** Italy
131 F8 **Roccalumera** Italy
131 E6 **Roccamonfina** Italy
130 D5 **Roccastrada** Italy
131 G7 **Roccella Ionica** Italy
106 F6 **Rocha** Argentina
107 H5 **Rocha** Uruguay
107 H5 **Rocha** *admin. area* Uruguay
128 B5 **Rocha, Barragem do Monte da** *lake* Portugal
141 F3 **Rochdale** Greater Manchester England UK
128 C5 **Roche, Cabo** *cape* Spain
127 G4 **Roche-la-Molière** France
88 D3 **Rochéachic** Mexico
83 M2 **Rochebaucourt** Quebec Canada
126 E4 **Rochechouart** France
127 G1 **Rochefort** Belgium
126 D4 **Rochefort** France
77 S3 **Rochefort, Lac** *lake* Quebec Canada
87 J5 **Rochelle** Georgia USA
75 O2 **Rocher River** Northwest Territories Canada
109 17 **Roche's Bluff** *cape* Montserrat
126 D3 **Rocheservière** France
218 G7 **Rochester** Vic. Australia
139 H3 **Rochester** Medway England UK
141 F1 **Rochester** Northumberland England UK
82 E4 **Rochester** Minnesota USA
83 P5 **Rochester** New Hampshire USA
83 M5 **Rochester** New York USA
86 B4 **Rochester** Texas USA
82 J5 **Rochester Hills** Michigan USA
140 A4 **Rochestown** Ireland
139 H3 **Rochford** Essex England UK
82 C5 **Rock** *watercourse* Minnesota USA
221 C7 **Rock and Pillar Range** New Zealand
74 I7 **Rock Bay** British Columbia Canada
80 F2 **Rock Creek** British Columbia Canada
83 M7 **Rock Hall** Maryland USA
82 G2 **Rock Harbor** Michigan USA
87 K3 **Rock Hill** South Carolina USA
86 D3 **Rock Island** Oklahoma USA
80 E3 **Rock Island** Washington USA
81 P2 **Rock Lake** North Dakota USA
80 G3 **Rock Lake** Washington USA
143 F1 **Rock Port** Moyle Northern Ireland UK
81 M6 **Rock River** Wyoming USA
90 E1 **Rock Sound** Bahamas
84 F3 **Rock Springs** Arizona USA
81 K6 **Rock Springs** Wyoming USA
81 Q5 **Rock Valley** Iowa USA
58 J2 **Rock X** *island* Antarctica
50 Q4 **Rockall Bank** *underwater feature* Atlantic Ocean
50 Q4 **Rockall Rise** *underwater feature* Atlantic Ocean
80 D4 **Rockaway Beach** Oregon USA
142 E6 **Rockcliffe** Dumfries and Galloway Scotland UK
86 C5 **Rockdale** Texas USA
58 P1 **Rockefeller Plateau** *plain* Antarctica
127 H2 **Rockenhausen** Germany
142 E3 **Rockfield** Highland Scotland UK
82 G5 **Rockford** Illinois USA
82 E5 **Rockford** Iowa USA
82 I6 **Rockford** Ohio USA
81 M2 **Rockglen** Saskatchewan Canada
215 K7 **Rockhampton** Qld Australia
214 C5 **Rockhampton Downs** NT Australia
216 D6 **Rockingham** WA Australia
215 I5 **Rockingham Bay** Qld Australia
82 B2 **Rocklake** North Dakota USA
79 D10 **Rockland** Maine USA
218 F7 **Rocklands Reservoir** Vic. Australia
212 D7 **Rocklea** WA Australia
87 K6 **Rockledge** Florida USA
83 M3 **Rockliffe** Ontario Canada
80 E7 **Rocklin** California USA
109 inset 9 **Rockly Bay** Trinidad and Tobago
87 I4 **Rockmart** Georgia USA
83 N4 **Rockport** Ontario Canada
82 H8 **Rockport** Indiana USA
82 J4 **Rockport** Michigan USA
86 C6 **Rockport** Texas USA
85 L5 **Rocksprings** Texas USA
101 G3 **Rockstone** Guyana
85 J1 **Rockvale** Colorado USA
140 A4 **Rockview** Ireland
82 H7 **Rockville** Indiana USA
84 F2 **Rockville** Utah USA
214 F5 **Rocky** *watercourse* Qld Australia
86 B3 **Rocky** Oklahoma USA
81 N7 **Rocky Ford** Colorado USA
216 E7 **Rocky Gully** WA Australia
87 M3 **Rocky Mount** North Carolina USA
75 N6 **Rocky Mountain House** Alberta Canada
74 H3 **Rocky Mountains** Alberta/British Columbia Canada
85 J2 **Rocky Mountains** Colorado USA
80 I3 **Rocky Mountains** Montana USA
81 K6 **Rocky Mountains** Wyoming USA
213 K1 **Rocky Point** NT Australia
80 D2 **Rocky Point** British Columbia Canada
211 inset **Rocky Point** Norfolk Island Australia
218 C6 **Rocky River** SA Australia
124 C3 **Rocroi** France
124 F2 **Rodach** *watercourse* Germany
124 D3 **Rodalben** Germany
122 F5 **Rødby** Denmark
140 B4 **Roddenagh** Ireland
79 J7 **Roddickton** Newfoundland and Labrador Canada
122 E5 **Rødding** Denmark
122 E5 **Rødekro** Denmark
129 F2 **Rodellar** Spain
122 E5 **Rodenäs** Germany
122 F3 **Rødenessjøen** *lake* Norway
106 D4 **Rodeo** Argentina
88 D3 **Rodeo** Mexico
85 H5 **Rodeo** New Mexico USA
216 E3 **Roderick** *watercourse* WA Australia
76 H7 **Roderick Lake** Ontario Canada
124 D4 **Rodersdorf** Switzerland
104 E6 **Rodespampa** Bolivia
127 K1 **Rodewisch** Germany
126 F4 **Rodez** France
123 J3 **Rödhamnsfjärden** *bay* Finland
133 C5 **Rodholívos** Greece
124 G3 **Roding** Germany
139 H3 **Roding** *watercourse* England UK
218 B1 **Rodinga, Mount** NT Australia
183 M3 **Rodino** Russian Federation
134 M5 **Rodionovo** Russian Federation
139 E3 **Rodmarton** Gloucestershire England UK
125 M4 **Rodna** Romania
220 F3 **Rodney, Cape** New Zealand
109 13 **Rodney Bay** St Lucia
182 H3 **Rodnikovka** Kazakhstan
133 A5 **Rodonit, Gjiri i** *bay* Albania
133 F7 **Rodos (Rhodes)** Greece
133 F7 **Rodos (Rhodes)** *island* Greece
120 H3 **Rødøy** Norway
120 L1 **Rødøy** *island* Norway
120 H3 **Rodøya** *island* Norway
120 H4 **Rødøya** *island* Norway
164 7 **Rodrigues, Île** *island* Mauritius
54 K6 **Rodrigues Ridge** *underwater feature* Indian Ocean
120 G4 **Rødseidet** Norway
122 E2 **Rødungen** *lake* Norway
122 G5 **Rødvig** Denmark
143 F1 **Roe** *watercourse* Northern Ireland UK
216 H5 **Roe, Lake** WA Australia
217 J6 **Roe Plains** WA Australia
212 D6 **Roebourne** WA Australia
212 G5 **Roebuck Bay** WA Australia
212 G4 **Roebuck Plains** WA Australia
212 G4 **Roebuck Roadhouse** WA Australia
162 E4 **Roedtan** South Africa
124 C/D2 **Roer** *watercourse* Netherlands
73 K6 **Roes Welcome Sound** Nunavut Canada
126 F1 **Roeselare** Belgium
130. G5 **Rogač** Croatia
104 E4 **Rogagua, Laguna** *lake* Bolivia
105 E4 **Rogaguado, Laguna** *lake* Bolivia
122 D3 **Rogaland** *admin. area* Norway
142 D2 **Rogart** Highland Scotland UK
125 H4 **Rogaška Slatina** Slovenia
125 I4 **Rogašovci** Slovenia
139 G3 **Rogate** West Sussex England UK
130 H5 **Rogatica** Bosnia and Herzegovina
124 F1 **Rogätz** Germany
122 G2 **Røgden** *lake* Sweden
120 H5 **Rogen** *lake* Sweden
83 L3 **Roger, Lac** *lake* Quebec Canada
74 M7 **Rogers** British Columbia Canada
86 C5 **Rogers** Texas USA
82 J4 **Rogers City** Michigan USA
84 D3 **Rogers Lake** California USA
79 F9 **Rogersville** New Brunswick Canada
77 P5 **Roggan** *watercourse* Quebec Canada
77 Q5 **Roggan, Lac** *lake* Quebec Canada
109 5 **Roggeveen, Cabo** *cape* Isla de Pascua (Easter Island)
53 W10 **Roggeveen Basin** *underwater feature* Pacific Ocean
120 I3 **Rognan** Norway
130 F5 **Rogoznica** Croatia

122 H2 **Rogsjön** *lake* Sweden
80 C5 **Rogue** *watercourse* California USA
223 15a **Roguron** *island* Marshall Islands
126 C2 **Rohan** France
80 D7 **Rohnert Park** California USA
124 D4 **Rohr** Switzerland
127 H2 **Rohrbach-lès-Bitche** France
179 K4 **Rohri Canal** *watercourse* Pakistan
186 D4 **Rohru** Himachal Pradesh India
186 D5 **Rohtak** Haryana India
194 D3 **Roi-Et** Thailand
129 F5 **Roig, Cabo** *cape* Spain
123 M2 **Roine** *bay* Finland
181 H3 **Roing** Arunachal Pradesh India
121 P2 **Roiro** *island* Finland
126 F2 **Roisel** France
123 L4 **Roja** Latvia
108 B3 **Rojas, Isla** *island* Chile
89 F4 **Rojo, Cabo** *cape* Mexico
91 H3 **Rojo, Cabo** *cape* Puerto Rico
196 D3 **Rokan** *watercourse* Indonesia
214 G2 **Rokeby** Qld Australia
123 M5 **Rokiškis** Lithuania
120 F5 **Røkkem** Norway
120 I3 **Røkland** Norway
120 L4 **Roknäs** Sweden
132 G1 **Rokytne** Ukraine
76 G8 **Roland** Manitoba Canada
164 6b **Roland, Île du** *island* French Southern and Antarctic Lands
122 E4 **Rold** Denmark
122 D3 **Røldalsvatnet** *lake* Norway
100 B3 **Roldanillo** Colombia
81 P2 **Rolette** North Dakota USA
120 J2 **Rolla** *island* Norway
81 O8 **Rolla** Kansas USA
82 F8 **Rolla** Missouri USA
81 P2 **Rolla** North Dakota USA
215 J8 **Rolleston** Qld Australia
221 D6 **Rolleston Range** New Zealand
83 L3 **Rollet** Quebec Canada
82 I8 **Rolling Fork** *watercourse* Kentucky USA
86 F4 **Rolling Fork** Mississippi USA
120 H3 **Rolvåg** Norway
121 M1 **Rolvsøya** *island* Norway
219 I2 **Roma** Qld Australia
197 J5 **Roma** *island* Indonesia
131 E6 **Roma (Rome)** Italy
87 L4 **Romain, Cape** South Carolina USA
79 G7 **Romaine** *watercourse* Quebec Canada
141 F2 **Romaldkirk** Durham England UK
132 C4 **Roman** Bulgaria
124 C5 **Romanche** *watercourse* France
51 P10 **Romanche Fracture Zone** *underwater feature* Atlantic Ocean
51 P10 **Romanche Gap** *underwater feature* Atlantic Ocean
78 E4 **Romanet, Lac** *lake* Quebec Canada
132 D3 **Romania** *country* Europe
130 H5 **Romanija** Bosnia and Herzegovina
87 K8 **Romano, Cape** Florida USA
90 E2 **Romano, Cayo** *island* Cuba
135 X8 **Romanovka** Russian Federation
191 G1 **Romanovka** Russian Federation
182 D3 **Romanovka** Russian Federation
123 K5 **Romanovo** Russian Federation
127 G4 **Romans-sur-Isère** France
72 C6 **Romanzof, Cape** Alaska USA
127 H2 **Rombas** France
199 F4 **Rombebai, Danau** *lake* Indonesia
195 I4 **Romblon** *island* Philippines
Rome *see* **Roma** Italy
87 I3 **Rome** Georgia USA
83 N5 **Rome** New York USA
120 L4 **Romelsön** *island* Sweden
81 M8 **Romeo** Colorado USA
122 F2 **Romerike** *region* Norway
139 H3 **Romford** Greater London England UK
154 E2 **Rommani** Morocco
83 L7 **Romney** West Virginia USA
136 E2 **Romny** Ukraine
122 E5 **Rømø** *island* Denmark
196 D3 **Rompin** *watercourse* Malaysia
121 P5 **Romppala** Finland
124 E2 **Romrod** Germany
139 F4 **Romsey** Hampshire England UK
122 F3 **Rømsjøen** *lake* Norway
132 D2 **Romuli** Romania
187 D8 **Ron** Karnataka India
194 C5 **Ron Phibun** Thailand
142 C1 **Rona** *island* Scotland UK
125 M4 **Rona de Sus** Romania
80 H3 **Ronan** Montana USA
120 I4 **Rönäs** Sweden
142 A3 **Ronay** *island* Scotland UK
90 E4 **Roncador, Cay** *island* Colombia
105 I4 **Roncador, Serra do** *range* Brazil
83 K8 **Ronceverte** West Virginia USA
128 D5 **Ronda** Spain
105 F4 **Ronda das Salinas** Brazil
105 G4 **Ronda do Sul** Brazil
120 F6 **Rondane** *range* Norway
122 F4 **Rønde** Denmark
109 15 **Ronde, Pointe** *cape* Dominica
91 I4 **Ronde Island** Grenada
105 F3 **Rondônia** *admin. area* Brazil
105 H5 **Rondonópolis** Brazil
122 C2 **Rong** Norway
188 F3 **Rong Jiang** *watercourse* Guangxi Zhuangzu Zizhiqu China
194 D3 **Rong Kwang** Thailand
189 H2 **Rongcheng** Anhui China
188 F4 **Rongcheng** Guangxi Zhuangzu Zizhiqu China
191 H5 **Rongcheng** Hebei China
189 F2 **Rongcheng** Hubei China
191 J5 **Rongcheng** Shandong China
223 15 **Rongelap Atoll** *reef* Marshall Islands
120 H4 **Røngen** *bay* Norway
223 15 **Rongerik Atoll** *reef* Marshall Islands
189 G3 **Rongjiang** Jiangxi China
189 G2 **Rongjiawan** Hunan China
188 F3 **Rongshui** Guangxi Zhuangzu Zizhiqu China
223 14a **Roniu** *volcano* French Polynesia
121 P5 **Rönkönvaara** Finland
122 F4 **Rönnäng** Sweden
120 J4 **Rönnäs** Sweden
122 H5 **Rønne** Denmark
58 T2 **Ronne Entrance** *strait* Antarctica
58 U1 **Ronne Ice Shelf** Antarctica
122 H4 **Ronneby** Sweden
120 L4 **Rönnskär** *island* Sweden
216 C2 **Ronsard, Cape** WA Australia
126 F1 **Ronse** Belgium
105 H4 **Ronuro** *watercourse* Brazil
198 E4 **Rooin** *island* Indonesia
164 5c **Rookery Point** *cape* St Helena
141 H3 **Roos** East Riding of Yorkshire England UK
105 F3 **Roosevelt** *watercourse* Brazil
86 B3 **Roosevelt** Oklahoma USA
81 K6 **Roosevelt** Utah USA
74 I3 **Roosevelt, Mount** British Columbia Canada
58 M1 **Roosevelt Island** Antarctica
121 N5 **Roosinpohja** Finland
143 E1 **Roosky** Ireland
123 M3 **Roosna-Alliku** Estonia
143 D5 **Rooves Beg** Ireland
120 I4 **Ropen** *lake* Sweden
214 B3 **Roper** *watercourse* NT Australia
87 M3 **Roper** North Carolina USA
214 C3 **Roper Bar** NT Australia
214 C3 **Roper Valley** NT Australia
85 K4 **Ropesville** Texas USA
120 L2 **Ropi** *mountain* Finland
125 J3 **Ropice** Czech Republic
123 O3 **Ropsha** Russian Federation
127 H4 **Roquebillière** France
129 H2 **Roquebrun** France
129 H2 **Roquecourbe** France
129 F1 **Roquefort** France
120 G5 **Røra** Norway
142 E2 **Rora Head** *cape* Scotland UK
101 F4 **Roraima** *admin. area* Brazil
101 F3 **Roraima, Monte** *mountain* Venezuela
101 F4 **Rorainópolis** Brazil
122 E3 **Rore** *bay* Norway
186 D5 **Rori** Haryana India
122 F4 **Rörö** Sweden
120 G5 **Røros** Norway
120 I3 **Rørstad** Norway
120 G4 **Rørvik** Norway
132 G1 **Ros'** *watercourse* Ukraine
91 F2 **Rosa, Lake** Bahamas
88 C3 **Rosa, Punta** *cape* Mexico
216 D6 **Rosa Brook** WA Australia
100 B4 **Rosa Zárate** Ecuador
128 B3 **Rosal** Spain
128 C5 **Rosal de la Frontera** Spain
88 D2 **Rosales** Mexico
80 G3 **Rosalia** Washington USA
109 5 **Rosalia, Punta** *cape* Isla de Pascua (Easter Island)
109 15 **Rosalie** Dominica
90 D3 **Rosalind Bank** *underwater feature* Caribbean
84 C3 **Rosamond Lake** California USA
120 I5 **Rosången** *lake* Sweden
127 G4 **Rosans** France
142 E3 **Rosarie** Moray Scotland UK
106 F5 **Rosario** Argentina
105 E4 **Rosario** Bolivia
104 E6 **Rosario** Bolivia
85 H7 **Rosario** Mexico
100 C2 **Rosario** Venezuela
90 D2 **Rosario, Cayo del** *island* Cuba
90 C3 **Rosario Bank** *underwater feature* Caribbean
106 E3 **Rosario de la Frontera** Argentina
106 E3 **Rosario de Lerma** Argentina
104 C4 **Rosario de Yauca** Peru
107 G5 **Rosario del Tala** Argentina
107 H4 **Rosário do Sul** Brazil
105 G4 **Rosário Oeste** Brazil
88 A1 **Rosarito** Mexico
143 F4 **Rosbercon** Ireland
81 P4 **Roscoe** South Dakota USA
85 L4 **Roscoe** Texas USA
126 C2 **Roscoff** France
143 D3 **Roscommon** Ireland
143 D3 **Roscommon** *admin. area* Ireland
140 A4 **Rosconnell Bridge** Ireland
143 E4 **Roscrea** Ireland
214 C3 **Rose** *watercourse* NT Australia
131 H5 **Rose** Montenegro
52 P9 **Rose Atoll** *reef* American Samoa
164 7b **Rose Belle** Mauritius
74 F6 **Rose Harbour** British Columbia Canada
87 L3 **Rose Hill** North Carolina USA
74 H5 **Rose Lake** British Columbia Canada
74 F5 **Rose Point** British Columbia Canada
91 I4 **Roseau** Dominica
81 R2 **Roseau** Minnesota USA
218 D1 **Roseberth** Qld Australia
219 Q10 **Rosebery** Tas. Australia
75 O7 **Rosebud** Alberta Canada
75 O7 **Rosebud** *watercourse* Alberta Canada
86 C5 **Rosebud** Texas USA
80 D5 **Roseburg** Oregon USA
75 O7 **Rosedale** Alberta Canada
141 H2 **Rosedale Abbey** North Yorkshire England UK
156 E5 **Roseires Reservoir** *lake* Sudan
86 F5 **Roseland** Louisiana USA
139 H4 **Roselands** East Sussex England UK
212 D6 **Rosemary Island** WA Australia
82 C2 **Rosenfeld** Manitoba Canada
130 E3 **Rosenheim** Germany
86 E5 **Rosepine** Louisiana USA
129 H2 **Roses** Spain
129 H2 **Roses, Golfo de** *bay* Spain
130 E5 **Roseto degli Abruzzi** Italy
143 F3 **Rosetown** Ireland
80 E7 **Roseville** California USA
82 F6 **Roseville** Illinois USA
219 K2 **Rosewood** Qld Australia
162 C5 **Rosh Pinah** Namibia
182 C2 **Roshal** Russian Federation
132 F2 **Roshcha** Ukraine
123 O2 **Roshchino** Russian Federation
142 C4 **Roshven** Highland Scotland UK
130 D5 **Rosia** Italy
125 M5 **Roşia** Romania
125 I3 **Rosice** Czech Republic
214 C3 **Rosie** *watercourse* NT Australia
132 B2 **Roşiori** Romania
143 C3 **Roskeeda** Ireland
143 D2 **Roskeeragh Point** Ireland
122 G5 **Roskilde** Denmark
133 A5 **Roskovec** Albania
136 E2 **Roslavl'** Russian Federation
122 E4 **Roslev** Denmark
121 R2 **Roslyakova** Russian Federation
219 I6 **Roslyn** NSW Australia
80 E3 **Roslyn** Washington USA
82 H2 **Roslyn Lake** Ontario Canada
128 C4 **Rosmaninhal** Portugal
133 B5 **Rosoman** Macedonia
132 F1 **Rososha** Ukraine
126 C3 **Rosporden** France
76 G8 **Ross** Manitoba Canada
143 C4 **Ross** Ireland
143 F3 **Ross** Ireland
221 D6 **Ross** New Zealand
140 D2 **Ross** Dumfries and Galloway Scotland UK
86 C5 **Ross** Texas USA
164 6b **Ross, Mont** *volcano* French Southern and Antarctic Lands
211 inset **Ross, Point** Norfolk Island Australia
58 M1 **Ross Bank** *underwater feature* Ross Sea
77 V6 **Ross Bay Junction** Newfoundland and Labrador Canada
143 E4 **Ross Bridge** Ireland
143 C5 **Ross Carbery** Ireland
210 inset **Ross Hill** Christmas Island Australia
58 M1 **Ross Ice Shelf** Antarctica
58 L1 **Ross Island** Antarctica
75 V5 **Ross Island** Manitoba Canada
80 E2 **Ross Lake** Washington USA
86 G4 **Ross R. Barnett Reservoir** Mississippi USA
214 C7 **Ross River** NT Australia
215 I5 **Ross River Dam** Qld Australia
58 M1 **Ross Sea** Antarctica
143 D2 **Rossan Point** Ireland
131 G7 **Rossano** Italy
219 R10 **Rossarden** Tas. Australia
143 D2 **Rossbeg** Ireland
75 U7 **Rossburn** Manitoba Canada
83 L4 **Rosseau Lake** Ontario Canada
199 J6 **Rossel Island** Papua New Guinea
215 G4 **Rosser** *watercourse* Qld Australia
140 A2 **Rossgeir** Ireland
140 C2 **Rossglass** Down Northern Ireland UK
79 F10 **Rossignol, Lake** Nova Scotia Canada
143 D2 **Rossinver** Ireland
122 G4 **Rossjön** *lake* Sweden
122 D3 **Rosskreppfjorden** *lake* Norway
74 M8 **Rossland** British Columbia Canada
143 F4 **Rosslare Harbour** Ireland
143 F4 **Rosslare Point** Ireland
140 A2 **Rosslea** Fermanagh Northern Ireland UK
143 D2 **Rossnowlagh** Ireland
154 C5 **Rosso** Mauritania
131 C5 **Rosso, Capo** *cape* Corsica France
131 E9 **Rosso, Monte** *mountain* Italy
120 J5 **Rossön** Sweden
136 F2 **Rossosh'** Russian Federation
120 H4 **Røssvatnet** *lake* Norway
215 H3 **Rossville** Qld Australia
75 W6 **Rossville** Manitoba Canada
120 F5 **Rossvoll** Norway
120 H3 **Røst** Norway
120 H3 **Røst** *island* Norway
57 G2 **Røst Bank** *underwater feature* Norwegian Sea
120 K2 **Rosta** Norway
120 K2 **Rostavatn** *lake* Norway
75 R6 **Rosthern** Saskatchewan Canada
122 G5 **Rostock** Germany
120 L2 **Rostonsölkä** *range* Sweden
182 C4 **Rostov-na-Donu** Russian Federation
182 C4 **Rostovskaya** *admin. area* Russian Federation
120 I4 **Röströmssjön** *lake* Sweden
120 H5 **Røstvollen** Norway
132 F3 **Roşu, Lacul** *lake* Romania
120 I3 **Røsvik** Norway
120 L4 **Rosvik** Sweden
87 I3 **Roswell** Georgia USA
85 J4 **Roswell** New Mexico USA
222 2 **Rota** *island* Northern Mariana Islands
198 B6 **Rote, Selat** *strait* Indonesia
124 E1 **Rotenburg an der Wümme** Germany
124 F3 **Roth** Germany
139 H4 **Rother** *watercourse* England UK
58 T2 **Rothera (United Kingdom)** *research station* Antarctica
141 G3 **Rotherham** South Yorkshire England UK
139 G3 **Rotherwick** Hampshire England UK
142 E3 **Rothes** Moray Scotland UK
79 F10 **Rothesay** New Brunswick Canada
142 C5 **Rothesay** Argyll and Bute Scotland UK
58 T2 **Rothschild Island** Antarctica
139 G2 **Rothwell** Northamptonshire England UK
198 B6 **Roti** Indonesia
213 G1 **Roti, Pulau** *island* Indonesia
121 O5 **Rotimo** *lake* Finland
218 G5 **Roto** NSW Australia
220 F4 **Rotoaira, Lake** New Zealand
220 G4 **Rotoiti** New Zealand
220 G4 **Rotoiti, Lake** New Zealand
220 F4 **Rotorangi, Lake** New Zealand
221 E5 **Rotoroa, Lake** New Zealand
220 G4 **Rotorua** New Zealand
220 G4 **Rotorua, Lake** New Zealand
220 F3 **Rotowaro** New Zealand
124 G3 **Rott** *watercourse* Germany
142 E4 **Rottal** Angus Scotland UK
218 E4 **Rotten Swamp** SA Australia
124 G3 **Rottenburg** Germany
124 C2 **Rotterdam** Netherlands
124 E3 **Röttingen** Germany
122 H4 **Rottnen** *lake* Sweden
216 D5 **Rottnest Island** WA Australia
124 E3 **Rottweil** Germany
106 F6 **Rotura del Colorado** *watercourse* Argentina
120 I5 **Rötviken** Sweden
129 J5 **Rouached** Algeria
126 F1 **Roubaix** France
123 L3 **Rõude** Estonia
126 E2 **Rouen** France
127 H3 **Rouffach** France
126 D3 **Rougé** France
77 S6 **Rouget, Lac** *lake* Quebec Canada
221 C7 **Rough Ridge** *range* New Zealand
82 H8 **Rough River Lake** Kentucky USA
129 G5 **Rouina** Algeria
75 S7 **Rouleau** Saskatchewan Canada
219 J3 **Round Hill** NSW Australia
83 M4 **Round Lake** Ontario Canada
83 O5 **Round Lake** New York USA
219 K4 **Round Mountain** NSW Australia
84 D1 **Round Mountain** Nevada USA
86 B5 **Round Mountain** Texas USA
79 J8 **Round Pond** *lake* Newfoundland and Labrador Canada
86 C5 **Round Rock** Texas USA
78 C6 **Roundeyed, Lac** *lake* Quebec Canada
81 K3 **Roundup** Montana USA
142 E1 **Rousay** *island* Scotland UK
143 E2 **Rousky** Omagh Northern Ireland UK
126 F5 **Roussillon** *region* France
78 B2 **Rouxel, Lac** *lake* Quebec Canada
124 B4 **Rouy** France
73 L9 **Rouyn-Noranda** Quebec Canada
190 F6 **Rouyuan** Gansu China
121 O3 **Rovala** Finland
121 N3 **Rovaniemi** Finland
120 F5 **Rovatnet** *lake* Norway
125 M1 **Rovbitsk** Belarus
136 F3 **Rovenki** Russian Federation
136 F3 **Roven'ky** Ukraine
124 F5 **Roverbella** Italy
133 C6 **Roviaî** Greece
194 E4 **Rôviĕng Tbong** Cambodia
124 F5 **Rovigo** Italy
130 E4 **Rovinj** Croatia
121 N2 **Rovisuvanto** Finland
121 Q5 **Rovkul'skoye, Ozero** *lake* Russian Federation
182 E3 **Rovnoye** Russian Federation
222 7 **Rowa Islands** *islands* Vanuatu
76 I8 **Rowan Lake** Ontario Canada
139 E3 **Rowde** Wiltshire England UK
219 R10 **Rowella** Tas. Australia
140 E3 **Rowen** Conwy Wales UK
219 I3 **Rowena** NSW Australia
73 L5 **Rowley Island** Nunavut Canada
212 E4 **Rowley Shoals** *reef* WA Australia
138 E3 **Rowlstone** Herefordshire England UK
158 A2 **Roxa** *island* Guinea-Bissau
195 I5 **Roxas** Philippines
195 I4 **Roxas** Philippines
195 H5 **Roxas** Philippines
87 L2 **Roxboro** North Carolina USA
109 inset 9 **Roxborough** Trinidad and Tobago
214 E7 **Roxborough Downs** Qld Australia
221 C7 **Roxburgh** New Zealand
218 C4 **Roxby Downs** SA Australia
122 H3 **Roxen** *lake* Sweden
86 F5 **Roxie** Mississippi USA
128 C5 **Roxo, Barragem do** *lake* Portugal
139 G2 **Roxton** Bedfordshire England UK
86 D4 **Roxton** Texas USA
80 C1 **Roy** British Columbia Canada
85 J3 **Roy** New Mexico USA
80 I6 **Roy** Utah USA
109 7 **Roy Cove** Falkland Islands
212 E7 **Roy Hill** WA Australia
81 R5 **Royal** Iowa USA
219 J5 **Royal, Mount** NSW Australia
109 8 **Royal Bay** South Georgia
82 H6 **Royal Center** Indiana USA
195 G6 **Royal Charlotte Reef** Spratly Islands
80 F3 **Royal City** Washington USA
139 F2 **Royal Leamington Spa** Warwickshire England UK
58 K1 **Royal Society Range** Antarctica
139 H3 **Royal Tunbridge Wells** Kent England UK
82 G3 **Royale, Isle** *island* Michigan USA
126 D4 **Royan** France
127 G4 **Roybon** France
126 E4 **Royère** France
120 H4 **Røyrvik** Norway
120 F6 **Røysheim** Norway
139 G2 **Royston** Hertfordshire England UK
141 G3 **Royston** South Yorkshire England UK
87 J3 **Royston** Georgia USA
77 S5 **Roz, Lac** *lake* Quebec Canada
132 B4 **Rožaje** Montenegro
125 M1 **Różanka** Belarus
128 C2 **Rozas, Embalse de las** *lake* Spain
132 G2 **Rozdil'na** Ukraine
85 M1 **Rozel** Kansas USA
182 F2 **Rozhdestveno** Russian Federation
132 F1 **Rozhnyatovka** Ukraine
125 M2 **Rozhyshche** Ukraine
78 D2 **Rozière, Baie de** *bay* Quebec Canada
125 K1 **Rozogi** Poland
132 A4 **Rrapë** Albania
133 A5 **Rrapëza-Rshat** Albania
182 D3 **Rtishchevo** Russian Federation
125 L5 **Rtkovo** Serbia
189 G2 **Ru'ning** Henan China
138 D2 **Ruabon** Wrexham Wales UK
162 B3 **Ruacana** Namibia
220 G4 **Ruahine Range** New Zealand
220 F2 **Ruakaka** New Zealand
220 G4 **Ruakituri** *watercourse* New Zealand
138 B5 **Ruan Minor** Cornwall England UK
220 F4 **Ruapehu, Mount** *volcano* New Zealand
221 C8 **Ruapuke Island** New Zealand
163 F2 **Ruarwe** Malawi
220 H3 **Ruatoria** New Zealand
161 F5 **Ruawa** Tanzania
220 F3 **Ruawai** New Zealand
178 G6 **Rub' Al Khālī, Ar** Saudi Arabia
130 D4 **Rubano** Italy
120 K2 **Rubben** *island* Norway
161 F5 **Rubeho** Tanzania
160 D3 **Rubi** *watercourse* Democratic Republic of Congo
103 B6 **Rubiataba** Brazil
124 F5 **Rubiera** Italy
183 N3 **Rubtsovsk** Russian Federation
72 D6 **Ruby** Alaska USA
75 T6 **Ruby Beach** Saskatchewan Canada
80 H6 **Ruby Lake** Nevada USA
80 H6 **Ruby Mountains** Nevada USA
213 I5 **Ruby Plains** WA Australia
215 I7 **Rubyvale** Qld Australia
123 K4 **Rucava** Latvia
189 G4 **Rucheng** Guangdong China
189 G3 **Rucheng** Hunan China
123 O3 **Ruch'i** Russian Federation
121 V3 **Ruch'i** Russian Federation
88 D4 **Rucias** Mexico
83 L7 **Ruckersville** Virginia USA
139 H3 **Ruckinge** Kent England UK
182 G6 **Rūd-e Atrak** *watercourse* Iran
178 G3 **Rūd-e Beshar** *watercourse* Iran
179 I2 **Rūd-e Kāl Shūr** *watercourse* Iran
178 F3 **Rūd-e Kārūn** *watercourse* Iran
179 H3 **Rūd-e Kor** *watercourse* Iran
178 G4 **Rūd-e Mand** *watercourse* Iran
178 G4 **Rūd-e Shur** *watercourse* Iran
179 I2 **Rūd Jām** *watercourse* Iran
127 K4 **Ruda** Italy
218 C5 **Rudall** SA Australia
212 G7 **Rudall** *watercourse* WA Australia
123 M5 **Rudamina** Lithuania
179 I4 **Rūdān** Iran
132 B4 **Rudare** Serbia
123 O3 **Ruddilovo** Russian Federation
75 U5 **Ruddock** Manitoba Canada
125 H5 **Rude** Croatia
122 F5 **Rude** Denmark
132 F1 **Rude Selo** Ukraine
123 M5 **Rūdiškės** Lithuania
178 G3 **Rūdkhāneh-ye Helleh** *watercourse* Iran
182 E6 **Rudkhaneh-ye Qotur** *lake* Iran
132 C1 **Rudky** Ukraine
125 I2 **Rudna** Poland
123 M5 **Rudnia** Lithuania
132 B4 **Rudnica** Serbia
125 K2 **Rudnik** Poland
125 J2 **Rudniki** Poland
125 L2 **Rudno** Poland
123 O3 **Rudno** Russian Federation
123 O6 **Rudnya** Belarus
123 P5 **Rudnya** Belarus
123 Q4 **Rudnya** Russian Federation
182 D3 **Rudnya** Russian Federation
125 M2 **Rudnya** Ukraine
182 I3 **Rudnyy** Kazakhstan
86 C7 **Rudolph** Texas USA
182 F6 **Rūdsar** Iran
126 E1 **Rue** France
130 B3 **Rue** Switzerland
128 D3 **Rueda** Spain
81 L7 **Ruedi Reservoir** Colorado USA
156 E5 **Rufa'a** Sudan
127 J5 **Rufeno, Monte** *mountain* Italy
126 E3 **Ruffec** France
124 C5 **Ruffieux** France
161 F5 **Rufiil** *watercourse* Tanzania
106 F5 **Rufino** Argentina
162 E3 **Rufunsa** Zambia
80 E4 **Rufus** Oregon USA
138 D2 **Rug** Denbighshire Wales UK
189 H2 **Rugao** Jiangsu China
139 F2 **Rugby** Warwickshire England UK
81 P2 **Rugby** North Dakota USA
139 F2 **Rugeley** Staffordshire England UK
122 G5 **Rügen** *island* Germany
138 E3 **Rugeway** South Gloucestershire England UK
126 E2 **Rugles** France
121 R4 **Rugozero** Russian Federation
160 D5 **Rugurfu** *watercourse* Tanzania
161 F5 **Ruhangino** Tanzania
124 F1 **Rühen** Germany
160 D4 **Ruhengeri** Rwanda
125 G2 **Ruhland** Germany
123 L4 **Ruhnu** Estonia
123 L4 **Ruhnu** *island* Estonia
124 D2 **Ruhr** *watercourse* Germany
161 F5 **Ruhudji** *watercourse* Tanzania
189 H3 **Rui'an** Zhejiang China
188 F1 **Ruicheng** Shanxi China
85 J6 **Ruidosa** Texas USA
85 J4 **Ruidoso** New Mexico USA
85 J4 **Ruidoso Downs** New Mexico USA
121 N3 **Ruikka** Finland
126 F4 **Ruines** France
77 U4 **Ruisseau-Highfall** *watercourse* Quebec Canada
164 2 **Ruivo, Pico** *volcano* Madeira
88 D4 **Ruiz** Mexico
88 D2 **Ruiz Cortines** Mexico
132 C4 **Rujen** *mountain* Macedonia
123 M4 **Rūjiena** Latvia
179 H4 **Rūk** Iran
121 P5 **Rukavesi** *bay* Finland
123 O4 **Rukovo** Russian Federation
198 C5 **Rukua** Indonesia
160 E5 **Rukwa** *admin. area* Tanzania
161 E5 **Rukwa, Lake** *lake* Tanzania
120 I6 **Rulbo** Sweden
86 B4 **Rule** Texas USA
219 K1 **Rules Beach** Qld Australia
86 F4 **Ruleville** Mississippi USA
197 J7 **Rulhieres, Cape** Australia
188 F3 **Rulin** Hunan China
188 C2 **Rulong** Sichuan China
123 N5 **Rum** Belarus
125 I4 **Rum** Hungary
142 B3 **Rum** *island* Scotland UK
91 F2 **Rum Cay** *island* Bahamas
213 K2 **Rum Jungle** NT Australia
159 F2 **Ruma** Nigeria
132 A3 **Ruma** Serbia
178 F4 **Rumāḥ** Saudi Arabia
160 D2 **Rumbek** Sudan
198 E4 **Rumberpon** *island* Indonesia
128 E4 **Rumblar, Embalse del** *lake* Spain
138 C4 **Rumford** Cornwall England UK
121 P5 **Rummukkala** Finland
121 P5 **Rumo** Finland
193 I2 **Rumoi** Japan
160 D4 **Rumonge** Burundi
163 F2 **Rumphi** Malawi
179 J4 **Rumra** Pakistan
215 H4 **Rumula** Qld Australia
161 F3 **Rumuruti** Kenya
198 D5 **Run** *island* Indonesia
143 C5 **Runalunn** Ireland
221 D6 **Runanga** New Zealand
220 G3 **Runaway, Cape** New Zealand
90 E3 **Runaway Bay** Jamaica
132 C3 **Runcu** Romania
122 C1 **Runde** *island* Norway
163 F4 **Runde** *watercourse* Zimbabwe
120 K2 **Rundhaug** Norway
162 C3 **Rundu** Namibia
197 J5 **Runduma** *island* Indonesia
120 K5 **Rundvik** Sweden
161 E5 **Rungwa** Tanzania
160 E5 **Rungwa** Tanzania
161 E5 **Rungwa** *watercourse* Tanzania
161 E5 **Rungwe** *mountain* Tanzania
132 B4 **Runica** Macedonia
123 J3 **Runmarö** *island* Sweden
122 H2 **Runn** *lake* Sweden
214 D4 **Running** *watercourse* NT Australia
85 K3 **Running Water** *watercourse* Texas USA
122 I4 **Runnö** *island* Sweden
219 H3 **Runnymede** Qld Australia
222 6 **Ruo** *island* Federated States of Micronesia
121 N3 **Ruokojärvi** Finland
121 O3 **Ruopsa** Finland
185 H5 **Ruoqiang** Xinjiang Uygur Zizhiqu China
121 O5 **Ruotaanmäki** Finland
123 M2 **Ruotsalainen** *lake* Finland
123 L1 **Ruovesi** *bay* Finland
127 L4 **Rupa** Croatia
181 G3 **Rupa** Arunachal Pradesh India
108 B2 **Rupanco, Lago** *lake* Chile
163 F2 **Rupashe** *watercourse* Malawi
196 D3 **Rupat** *island* Indonesia
132 D2 **Rupea** Romania
214 G6 **Rupert** *watercourse* Qld Australia
77 P7 **Rupert** *watercourse* Quebec Canada
80 I5 **Rupert** Idaho USA
77 P7 **Rupert, Baie de** *bay* Quebec Canada
58 O1 **Rupert Coast** Antarctica
161 F5 **Rupia** Tanzania
161 F6 **Ruponda** Tanzania
124 G1 **Ruppiner See** *lake* Germany
187 G7 **Rupsa** Orissa India
132 D4 **Ruptsi** Bulgaria
101 G4 **Rupununi** *watercourse* Guyana
124 D2 **Rur** *watercourse* Germany
223 14 **Rurutu** *island* French Polynesia
163 F3 **Rusape** Zimbabwe
132 D4 **Ruse** Bulgaria
143 F3 **Rush** Ireland
81 P7 **Rush Center** Kansas USA
139 F3 **Rushall** Wiltshire England UK
191 J6 **Rushan** Shandong China
139 G2 **Rushden** Northamptonshire England UK
82 F5 **Rushford** Minnesota USA
163 F3 **Rushinga** Zimbabwe
181 H3 **Rushon** Arunachal Pradesh India
139 G2 **Rushton** Northamptonshire England UK
139 E1 **Rushton Spencer** Staffordshire England UK
75 S7 **Rushville** Saskatchewan Canada
82 F6 **Rushville** Illinois USA
82 I7 **Rushville** Indiana USA
218 G7 **Rushworth** Vic. Australia
86 D5 **Rusk** Texas USA
120 J5 **Ruske** Sweden
123 P2 **Ruskeala** Russian Federation
120 K4 **Ruskele** Sweden
122 H4 **Rusken** *lake* Sweden
121 P5 **Ruskila** Finland
123 K5 **Rusnė** Lithuania
123 L3 **Russarö** *island* Finland
142 C3 **Russel** Highland Scotland UK
75 U7 **Russell** Manitoba Canada
81 P7 **Russell** Kansas USA
81 R4 **Russell** Minnesota USA
73 J4 **Russell Island** Nunavut Canada
75 U4 **Russell Lake** Manitoba Canada
75 S4 **Russell Lake** Saskatchewan Canada
82 I8 **Russell Springs** Kentucky USA
86 H3 **Russellville** Alabama USA
86 E3 **Russellville** Arkansas USA
86 H2 **Russellville** Kentucky USA
121 M1 **Russeluft** Norway
120 L2 **Russelv** Norway
120 I5 **Russfjärden** *bay* Sweden
80 D7 **Russian** *watercourse* California USA
193 I1 **Russian Federation** *country* Russian Federation
183 L2 **Russkaya Polyana** Russian Federation
135 U3 **Russkiy, Ostrov** *island* Russian Federation
135 AE4 **Russkoye Ust'ye** Russian Federation
215 G8 **Russleigh** Qld Australia
125 I4 **Rust** Austria
179 K4 **Rustam Khan Shahr** Pakistan
179 I5 **Rustāq** Oman
162 E5 **Rustenburg** South Africa
86 E4 **Ruston** Louisiana USA
125 H2 **Ruszów** Poland
123 L2 **Rutajärvi** *lake* Finland
160 D4 **Rutana** Burundi
128 D5 **Rute** Spain
162 F4 **Rutenga** Zimbabwe
127 I1 **Rüthen** Germany
83 L3 **Rutherglen** Ontario Canada
142 E2 **Ruthers of Howe** Highland Scotland UK
124 E4 **Rüthi** Switzerland
213 I2 **Ruthieres, Cape** WA Australia
138 D1 **Ruthin** Denbighshire Wales UK
81 Q4 **Ruthton** Minnesota USA
142 E6 **Ruthwell** Dumfries and Galloway Scotland UK
125 L1 **Rutki** Poland
139 G2 **Rutland** *admin. area* England UK
81 Q3 **Rutland** North Dakota USA
83 O5 **Rutland** Vermont USA
194 B5 **Rutland Island** Andaman and Nicobar Islands India
214 F3 **Rutland Plains** Qld Australia
139 G2 **Rutland Water** *lake* England UK
130 B4 **Rutor, Testa del** *mountain* Italy
121 N4 **Ruukki** Finland
121 Q5 **Ruunaa** Finland
121 Q5 **Ruunaanjärvi** *lake* Finland
123 N4 **Ruusmäe** Estonia
121 P3 **Ruuvaoja** Finland
161 F6 **Ruvuma** *watercourse* Mozambique
161 F6 **Ruvuma** *admin. area* Tanzania
178 D3 **Ruwayshid, Wādī** *watercourse* Jordan
103 D6 **Ruy Barbosa** Brazil
182 J3 **Ruzayevka** Kazakhstan
182 D2 **Ruzayevka** Russian Federation
125 M1 **Ruzhany** Belarus
189 F1 **Ruzhou Zhen** Henan China
132 F1 **Ruzhyn** Ukraine
130 G5 **Ružić** Croatia
123 N4 **Ružina** Latvia
132 A2 **Ruzsa** Hungary
160 E4 **Rwanda** *country* Africa
160 E3 **Rwenzori** *range* Uganda
160 E4 **Rweru, Lake** *lake* Rwanda
122 E4 **Ry** Denmark
123 O2 **Ryabovo** Russian Federation
132 E4 **Ryakhovo** Bulgaria
86 C3 **Ryan** Oklahoma USA
85 J5 **Ryan** Texas USA
142 D6 **Ryan, Loch** *bay* Scotland UK
218 G4 **Ryandale** NSW Australia
123 O5 **Ryasna** Belarus
182 C2 **Ryazan'** Russian Federation
182 C2 **Ryazanskaya Oblast'** *admin. area* Russian Federation
134 H5 **Rybachiy, Poluostrov** *peninsula* Russian Federation
183 N4 **Rybach'ye** Kazakhstan
183 L5 **Rybach'ye** Kyrgyzstan
132 H2 **Rybal'che** Ukraine
183 L4 **Rybalka Tas-aral** Kazakhstan
125 J2 **Rybnik** Poland
125 J1 **Rybno** Poland
125 K1 **Rybno** Poland
123 J6 **Rychliki** Poland
125 I2 **Rychnov nad Kněžnou** Czech Republic
125 J1 **Rychwał** Poland
123 N5 **Rychy, Vozyera** *lake* Belarus
74 L5 **Rycroft** Alberta Canada
58 S2 **Rydberg Peninsula** Antarctica
139 F4 **Ryde** Isle of Wight England UK
218 G8 **Rye** Vic. Australia
139 H4 **Rye** East Sussex England UK
139 H4 **Rye Bay** England UK
139 H4 **Rye Harbour** East Sussex England UK
80 F6 **Rye Patch Reservoir** Nevada USA
140 A3 **Ryefield** Ireland
139 E3 **Ryeford** Gloucestershire England UK
81 K3 **Ryegate** Montana USA
141 H3 **Ryehill** East Riding of Yorkshire England UK
139 G2 **Ryhall** Rutland England UK
125 K2 **Ryki** Poland
75 O6 **Ryley** Alberta Canada
136 E2 **Ryl'sk** Russian Federation
219 I5 **Rylstone** NSW Australia
125 I3 **Rýmařov** Czech Republic
138 E4 **Ryme Intrinseca** Dorset England UK
122 H4 **Rymmen** *lake* Sweden
122 H2 **Rymnäsbodarna** Sweden
121 T2 **Rynda** Russian Federation
123 N2 **Ryökäsvesi** *lake* Finland
192 E3 **Ryong-yŏn** North Korea
193 H3 **Ryōtsu** Japan
125 J1 **Rypin** Poland
125 I1 **Rytel** Poland
141 G3 **Ryther** North Yorkshire England UK
121 O4 **Rytinki** Finland
121 O5 **Rytky** Finland
139 F2 **Ryton on Dunsmore** Warwickshire England UK
132 B1 **Rytro** Poland
122 H5 **Rytterknægten** *mountain* Denmark
Ryukyu Islands *see* **Nansei Shotō** Japan
52 I5 **Ryukyu Trench** *underwater feature* Pacific Ocean
123 P2 **Ryuttyu** Russian Federation
125 L2 **Rzeszów** Poland
125 H1 **Rzewnowo** Poland
125 J2 **Rzgón** Poland

S

124 C1 **'s-Gravenhage (The Hague)** Netherlands
124 C2 **'s-Hertogenbosch** Netherlands
194 D3 **Sa** Thailand
194 E5 **Sa Déc** Vietnam
129 H4 **Sa Dragonera** *island* Spain
194 F4 **Sa Huỳnh** Vietnam
194 D4 **Sa Kaeo** Thailand
194 D2 **Sa Pa** Vietnam
159 G4 **Saa** Cameroon
222 8 **Sa'a** Solomon Islands
123 M2 **Sääksjärvi** Finland
123 L2 **Sääksjärvi** *lake* Finland
122 G5 **Saal** Germany
124 F2 **Saale** *watercourse* Germany
127 H2 **Saales** France
126 E2 **Saâne** *watercourse* France
130 B3 **Saanen** Switzerland
74 J8 **Saanich** British Columbia Canada
124 D3 **Saarbrücken** Germany
123 L4 **Sääre** Estonia
123 M3 **Sääre** Estonia
123 L3 **Saaremaa** *admin. area* Estonia
123 L3 **Saaremaa** *island* Estonia
121 N3 **Saarenkylä** Finland
121 O3 **Saari-Kämä** Finland
121 O4 **Saariharju** Finland
121 N5 **Saarijärvi** Finland
123 M1 **Saarijärvi** *lake* Finland
121 M3 **Saaripudas** Finland
121 O2 **Saariselka** *island* Finland
121 O2 **Saariselkä** Finland
124 D3 **Saarland** *admin. area* Germany
78 O2 **Saarloq** Greenland
127 H2 **Saarlouis** Germany
142 C3 **Saasaig** Highland Scotland UK
127 H2 **Saasenheim** France
121 O3 **Sääskilahti** Finland
105 I2 **Saba** Brazil
109 20 **Saba** *island* Netherlands Antilles
130 H4 **Šabac** Serbia
129 H3 **Sabadell** Spain
193 H4 **Sabae** Japan
197 H2 **Sabah** *admin. area* Malaysia
196 D3 **Sabak** Malaysia
197 H5 **Sabalana** *island* Indonesia
197 H5 **Sabalana, Kepulauan** *archipelago* Indonesia
100 C5 **Sabana** Colombia
100 D4 **Sabana** Colombia
101 H3 **Sabana** Suriname
90 D2 **Sabana, Archipiélago de** *islands* Cuba
100 C3 **Sabana de Torres** Colombia
91 G3 **Sabana Yegua** Dominican Republic
100 C3 **Sabanalarga** Colombia
89 H5 **Sabancuy** Mexico
90 B3 **Sabancuy, Bancos de** *reef* Mexico
101 F3 **Sabaneta** Venezuela
101 F2 **Sabaneta, Punta** *cape* Venezuela
199 F5 **Sabang** Indonesia
196 B2 **Sabang** Indonesia
90 E5 **Sabanitas** Panama
158 E3 **Sabari** Ghana
187 E7 **Sabari** *watercourse* Chhattisgarh India
197 H5 **Sabaru** *island* Indonesia
198 B4 **Sabbang** Indonesia
155 I3 **Sabhā** Libya
163 F4 **Sabi** *watercourse* Zimbabwe
156 F4 **Sabidana, Jebel** *mountain* Sudan
163 F5 **Sabie** Mozambique
162 F5 **Sabie** South Africa
123 L4 **Sabile** Latvia
82 J7 **Sabina** Ohio USA
86 B6 **Sabinal** Texas USA
90 E2 **Sabinal, Cayo** *island* Cuba
129 F2 **Sabiñánigo** Spain
88 E3 **Sabinas** Mexico
88 E3 **Sabinas** *watercourse* Mexico
88 E3 **Sabinas Hidalgo** Mexico
86 E5 **Sabine** *watercourse* Louisiana USA
86 D4 **Sabine** *watercourse* Texas USA
77 S3 **Sabine, Lac** *lake* Quebec Canada
218 B4 **Sabine, Mount** SA Australia
86 E6 **Sabine Lake** Louisiana USA
125 K3 **Sabinov** Slovakia
77 U5 **Sable** *watercourse* Quebec Canada
79 F11 **Sable, Cape** Nova Scotia Canada
87 K8 **Sable, Cape** Florida USA
79 I11 **Sable Island** Nova Scotia Canada
126 D3 **Sablé-sur-Sarthe** France
83 P2 **Sables, Rivière aux** *watercourse* Quebec Canada
127 G5 **Sablon, Pointe du** *cape* France
128 C3 **Sabor** *watercourse* Portugal
83 M3 **Sabourin, Lac** *lake* Quebec Canada
198 E4 **Sabra, Tanjung** *cape* Indonesia
155 I2 **Sabrātah** Libya
126 D4 **Sabres** France
58 H2 **Sabrina Coast** Antarctica
195 I2 **Sabtang** *island* Philippines
182 F6 **Sabu Chal** Iran
198 D4 **Sabuda** *island* Indonesia
128 C3 **Sabugal** Portugal
82 F5 **Sabula** Iowa USA
198 B4 **Sabulu** Indonesia
196 C4 **Sabulubek** Indonesia
197 G5 **Sabunten** *island* Indonesia
178 E6 **Şabyā** Saudi Arabia
182 H7 **Sabzevār** Iran
179 I4 **Sabzvārān** Iran
80 F3 **Sacajawea, Lake** Washington USA
100 C3 **Sácama** Colombia
108 C3 **Sacanana** Argentina
159 H6 **Sacandica** Angola
90 B4 **Sacapulas** Guatemala
131 E6 **Sacco** *watercourse* Italy
128 E3 **Sacedón** Spain
100 C4 **Sachene** Colombia
76 J5 **Sachigo** *watercourse* Ontario Canada
76 I6 **Sachigo Lake** Ontario Canada
192 F4 **Sach'on** South Korea
72 G4 **Sachs Harbour** Northwest Territories Canada
127 K1 **Sachsen** *admin. area* Germany
124 F2 **Sachsen-Anhalt** *admin. area* Germany
125 H1 **Sachsendorf** Germany
179 K3 **Sachu** Pakistan
130 E4 **Sacile** Italy
79 F10 **Sackville** New Brunswick Canada
81 L2 **Saco** Montana USA
103 C7 **Sacramento** Brazil
80 E7 **Sacramento** California USA
80 E7 **Sacramento** *watercourse* California USA
85 J4 **Sacramento Mountains** New Mexico USA
128 E5 **Sacratif, Cabo** *cape* Spain
100 B5 **Sacraurcu** *mountain* Ecuador
131 F6 **Sacro, Monte** *mountain* Italy
132 C2 **Săcueni** Romania
105 G4 **Sacuriuina** *watercourse* Brazil
164 8b **Sada** Mayotte
162 E6 **Sada** South Africa
129 F2 **Sádaba** Spain
136 F6 **Şadad** Syria
178 E7 **Şa'dah** Yemen
197 H4 **Sadang** *watercourse* Indonesia
194 D6 **Sadao** Thailand
197 F4 **Sadau** Indonesia
182 F7 **Sadd-e Sefid Rud, Daryacheh-ye** *lake* Iran
179 L2 **Sadda** Pakistan
120 K3 **Saddajaure** *bay* Sweden
142 C5 **Saddell** Argyll and Bute Scotland UK
139 F2 **Saddington** Leicester England UK
74 L5 **Saddle Hills** Alberta Canada
194 B4 **Saddle Peak** *mountain* Andaman and Nicobar Islands India
218 D6 **Saddleworth** SA Australia
100 B4 **Sade** Ecuador
140 F2 **Sadgill** Cumbria England UK
179 H6 **Şadḥ** Oman
161 F2 **Sadi** Ethiopia
154 D6 **Sadiola** Mali
181 H3 **Sadiya** Assam India
86 C4 **Sadler** Texas USA
109 19 **Sadlers** St Kitts and Nevis
128 B4 **Sado** *watercourse* Portugal

193 H4 **Sadoga-shima** *island* Japan
197 F3 **Sadong** *watercourse* Malaysia
132 F2 **Sadova** Moldova
132 C4 **Sadova** Romania
132 G2 **Sadova** Ukraine
182 D4 **Sadovoye** Russian Federation
187 D7 **Sadri** Madhya Pradesh India
125 H2 **Sadská** Czech Republic
120 J3 **Sädvajaure** *lake* Sweden
120 J3 **Sädvaluspen** Sweden
199 H4 **Sae Islands** Papua New Guinea
120 E5 **Sæbø** Norway
122 F4 **Sæby** Denmark
128 D2 **Saelices del Rio** Spain
124 D1 **Saerbeck** Germany
120 G4 **Sætervika** Norway
158 D2 **Safané** Burkina Faso
178 E5 **Şaffāqah** Saudi Arabia
122 G3 **Säffle** Sweden
84 H4 **Safford** Arizona USA
139 H2 **Saffron Walden** Essex England UK
154 E2 **Safi** Morocco
178 E7 **Safi** Yemen
136 E1 **Safonovo** Russian Federation
135 AK6 **Safonovo** Russian Federation
192 F5 **Saga** Japan
181 H5 **Sagaing** Myanmar
181 H4 **Sagaing** *admin. area* Myanmar
82 J2 **Saganash Lake** Ontario Canada
125 H2 **Sagar** Germany
187 D8 **Sagar** Karnataka India
186 E6 **Sagar** Madhya Pradesh India
187 G7 **Sagar Island** West Bengal India
Sagarmatha *see* **Everest, Mount** China/Nepal
135 AA4 **Sagastyyr** Russian Federation
72 E5 **Sagavanirktok** *watercourse* Alaska USA
195 I5 **Sagay** Philippines
120 K2 **Sagelvvatnet** *lake* Norway
120 J3 **Saggat** *bay* Sweden
123 J2 **Saggöfjärden** *bay* Finland
82 J5 **Saginaw** Michigan USA
82 J4 **Saginaw Bay** Michigan USA
182 G4 **Sagiz** Kazakhstan
182 G4 **Sagiz** *watercourse* Kazakhstan
78 G3 **Saglek Bay** Newfoundland and Labrador Canada
197 I4 **Sago** *island* Indonesia
105 F3 **Sagrada Paixão, Serra da** *range* Brazil
128 B5 **Sagres** Portugal
128 B5 **Sagres, Ponta de** *cape* Portugal
178 E6 **Sagrit** Saudi Arabia
90 D2 **Sagua la Grande** Cuba
81 L7 **Saguache** Colorado USA
85 I7 **Saguarachi** Mexico
79 C8 **Saguenay** *watercourse* Quebec Canada
125 J3 **Ságújfalu** Hungary
129 F4 **Sagunto** Spain
125 J4 **Ságvár** Hungary
186 D6 **Sagwara** Rajasthan India
182 F5 **Sagyndyk, Mys** *cape* Kazakhstan
100 C2 **Sahagún** Colombia
128 D2 **Sahagún** Spain
179 H5 **Şaḩam** Oman
139 H2 **Saham Hills** Norfolk England UK
186 E5 **Sahanpur** Uttar Pradesh India
154 E4 **Sahara** *desert* North Africa
186 D5 **Saharanpur** Uttar Pradesh India
178 G5 **Sahbā', Wādī as** *watercourse* Saudi Arabia
133 E5 **Şahin** Turkey
179 M3 **Sahiwal** Pakistan
178 F2 **Sahneh** Iran
121 N5 **Sahrajärvi** Finland
74 J3 **Sahtaneh** *watercourse* British Columbia Canada
88 C2 **Sahuarachic** Mexico
88 C2 **Sahuaripa** Mexico
84 G5 **Sahuarita** Arizona USA
88 B2 **Sahuaro** Mexico
181 H2 **Sahuteng** Qinghai China
101 H4 **Saï** French Guiana
194 D6 **Sai Buri** Thailand
199 G6 **Saibai Island** Australia
155 G2 **Saïda** Algeria
178 C2 **Saïda (Sidon)** Lebanon
182 E7 **Sā'īdābād** Iran
155 F1 **Saïdia** Morocco
181 F4 **Saidpur** Bangladesh
Saigon *see* **Hồ Chí Minh** Vietnam
181 G4 **Saiha** Mizoram India
190 E3 **Saihan** Mongolia
190 E3 **Saihan-ovoo** Mongolia
191 G4 **Saihan Tal** Nei Mongol Zizhiqu China
190 G4 **Saihandulaan** Mongolia
121 P3 **Saija** Finland
192 F5 **Saiki** Japan
188 C2 **Sailaitang** Qinghai China
127 G4 **Saillans** France
198 D4 **Sailolof** Indonesia
123 O2 **Saimaa** *lake* Finland
121 P5 **Säimen** Finland
88 E4 **Saín Alto** Mexico
77 S5 **Saindon, Lacs** *lakes* Quebec Canada
142 F5 **St Abb's Head** *cape* Scotland UK
126 F5 **St-Affrique** France
138 B4 **St Agnes** Cornwall England UK
138 A5 **St Agnes** *island* England UK
127 G4 **St-Agrève** France
126 E3 **St-Aignan** France
219 J5 **St Albans** NSW Australia
139 G3 **St Albans** Hertfordshire England UK
139 E4 **St Alban's Head** *cape* England UK
75 O6 **St Albert** Alberta Canada
83 O3 **St-Alexis-des-Monts** Quebec Canada
124 B5 **Saint-Amans-la-Lozère** France
129 H2 **Saint-Amans-Soult** France
76 F7 **St Ambroise** Manitoba Canada
126 G4 **St-Ambroix** France
127 H2 **Saint-Amé** France
127 G3 **St-Amour** France
79 D9 **St-André** Quebec Canada
126 E3 **Saint-André** France
164 7a **Saint-André** Réunion
101 G3 **Saint Andrew Point** *cape* Guyana
87 K5 **Saint Andrew Sound** Georgia USA
79 E10 **St Andrews** New Brunswick Canada
142 F4 **St Andrews** Fife Scotland UK
142 F4 **St Andrews Bay** Scotland UK
139 E5 **St Anne** Alderney Channel Islands UK
73 M9 **Saint-Anne-des-Monts** Quebec Canada
140 E1 **St Ann's** Dumfries and Galloway Scotland UK
79 H9 **St Anns Bay** Nova Scotia Canada
82 E5 **Saint Ansgar** Iowa USA
79 K7 **St Anthony** Newfoundland and Labrador Canada
80 J5 **Saint Anthony** Idaho USA
79 F9 **Saint-Antoine** New Brunswick Canada
126 E4 **Saint-Antonin** France
218 F7 **St Arnaud** Vic. Australia
221 E6 **St Arnaud Range** New Zealand
140 E3 **St Asaph** Denbighshire Wales UK
213 K1 **St Asaph Bay** NT Australia
79 I7 **St-Augustin** Quebec Canada
87 K6 **Saint Augustine** Florida USA
87 K6 **Saint Augustine Beach** Florida USA
79 I7 **St-Augustine Nord-Ouest** *watercourse* Quebec Canada
138 C4 **St Austell** Cornwall England UK
138 C4 **St Austell Bay** England UK
126 F4 **Saint-Bard** France
91 I3 **St Barthélemy** *French overseas collectivity* Caribbean
109 19 **St Barthélemy** *island* St Barthélemy
221 C7 **St Bathans Range** New Zealand
126 E5 **St-Béat** France
140 E2 **St Bees Head** *cape* England UK
124 B4 **Saint Benin** France
164 7a **Saint-Benoît** Réunion
127 G2 **Saint-Blin** France
138 E3 **St Briavels** Gloucestershire England UK
79 K9 **St Bride's** Newfoundland and Labrador Canada
138 B3 **St Bride's Bay** Wales UK
126 C2 **St-Brieuc** France
126 C2 **St-Brieuc, Baie de** *bay* France
75 S6 **St Brieux** Saskatchewan Canada
83 L5 **St Catharines-Niagara** Ontario Canada
86 G5 **Saint Catherine, Lake** Louisiana USA
109 10a **St Catherine, Mount** *volcano* Grenada
83 inset **St Catherine Point** Bermuda
139 F4 **St Catherine's Point** England UK
87 K5 **Saint Catherines Sound** Georgia USA
126 E4 **St-Céré** France
127 H3 **Saint-Cergue** Switzerland
126 F4 **St-Cernin** France
127 G5 **St-Chamas** France
127 G4 **St-Chamond** France
82 F7 **Saint Charles** Missouri USA
126 F4 **St-Chély-d'Apcher** France
219 J5 **St Clair** NSW Australia
219 R11 **St Clair, Lake** Tas. Australia
83 J5 **St Clair, Lake** Ontario Canada
84 G4 **Saint Clair, Lake** Arizona USA
127 G3 **St-Claude** France
109 16 **Saint-Claude** Guadeloupe
138 C3 **Saint Clears** Wales UK
126 D3 **Saint-Clément-des-Baleines** France
82 D4 **Saint Cloud** Minnesota USA
142 G3 **St Combs** Aberdeenshire Scotland UK
216 C2 **St Cricq, Cape** WA Australia
127 G4 **St Cristol, Plateau de** *region* France
79 E10 **St Croix** *watercourse* Canada/USA
109 21 **St Croix** *island* US Virgin Islands
82 E4 **Saint Croix Falls** Wisconsin USA
126 F5 **Saint-Cyprien-Plage** France
83 N2 **Saint-Cyr** *watercourse* Quebec Canada
79 C8 **Saint-David-de-Falardeau** Quebec Canada
109 10a **St David's** Grenada
138 B3 **St David's** Pembrokeshire Wales UK
138 B3 **St David's Head** *cape* Wales UK
83 inset **St David's Island** Bermuda
126 F2 **St-Denis** France
164 7a **Saint-Denis** Réunion
126 D3 **Saint-Denis-d'Oléron** France
126 D2 **Saint-Denis-le-Gast** France
138 E3 **St Devereux** Herefordshire England UK
127 H2 **St-Dié** France
124 C3 **St-Dizier** France
138 C2 **St Dogmells** Pembrokeshire Wales UK
81 Q6 **Saint Edward** Nebraska USA
124 C5 **St-Égrève** France
72 E7 **St Elias, Cape** Alaska USA
72 E6 **St Elias, Mount** Alaska USA
74 A2 **St Elias Mountains** British Columbia/Yukon Territory/Alaska Canada/USA
82 G7 **Saint Elmo** Illinois USA
126 F3 **St-Éloy-les-Mines** France
126 D4 **Saint-Émilion** France
138 B4 **St Erth** Cornwall England UK
127 G4 **St-Étienne** France
127 G4 **Saint-Étienne-les-Orgues** France
91 I3 **St Eustatius** *island* Netherlands Antilles
79 D8 **St-Fabien** Quebec Canada
126 D3 **Saint-Félix** France
142 G3 **St Fergus** Aberdeenshire Scotland UK
127 H4 **Saint-Firmin** France
127 I5 **St-Florent** Corsica France
126 F2 **St-Florentin** France
126 F4 **St-Flour** France
126 E3 **Saint-Flovier** France
78 C3 **St-Fond** *watercourse* Quebec Canada
83 Q3 **St Francis** *watercourse* Canada/USA
81 O7 **Saint Francis** Kansas USA
79 L9 **St Francis, Cape** Newfoundland and Labrador Canada
162 D6 **St Francis, Cape** South Africa
83 P4 **St Francis, Lake** Quebec Canada
86 F5 **Saint Francisville** Louisiana USA
109 16 **Saint-François** Guadeloupe
79 C8 **Saint-Fulgence** Quebec Canada
127 I3 **St Gallen** Switzerland
126 E5 **St-Gaudens** France
126 E3 **St-Gaultier** France
83 P2 **St-Gédéon** Quebec Canada
124 B5 **St-Geniez-d'Olt** France
219 I3 **St George** Qld Australia
83 inset **St George** Bermuda
87 K4 **Saint George** South Carolina USA
84 F2 **Saint George** Utah USA
199 J5 **Saint George, Cape** Papua New Guinea
80 C6 **St George, Point** California USA
213 H3 **St George Basin** WA Australia
72 C7 **St George Island** Alaska USA
87 I6 **Saint George Sound** Florida USA
83 P3 **St-Georges** Quebec Canada
91 I4 **St George's** Grenada
79 I8 **St George's Bay** Newfoundland and Labrador Canada
79 H10 **St George's Bay** Nova Scotia Canada
194 B6 **St George's Channel** Andaman and Nicobar Islands India
143 G4 **St George's Channel** *strait* Ireland/UK
199 J5 **Saint George's Channel** *strait* Papua New Guinea
75 Q5 **St George's Hill** Saskatchewan Canada
83 inset **St George's Island** Bermuda
78 B2 **St-Germain, Lac** *lake* Quebec Canada
139 F5 **Saint-Germain-des-Vaux** France
138 C4 **St Germans** Cornwall England UK
126 F1 **Saint-Ghislain** Belgium
126 C3 **St-Gildas, Pointe de** *cape* France
126 E5 **St-Girons** France
126 D5 **Saint-Girons-en-Marensin** France
138 C3 **St Govan's Head** *cape* Wales UK
83 O3 **St-Grégoire** Quebec Canada
138 D2 **Saint Harmon** Powys Wales UK
164 5b **St Helena** *British overseas territory* Atlantic Ocean
164 5b **St Helena** *island* Atlantic Ocean
162 C6 **St Helena Bay** *bay* South Africa
87 K4 **Saint Helena Sound** South Carolina USA
219 S10 **St Helens** Tas. Australia
140 F3 **St Helens** *admin. area* England UK
80 D4 **Saint Helens** Oregon USA
219 S10 **St Helens Point** Tas. Australia
126 C2 **St Helier** Jersey Channel Islands UK
83 P3 **St-Henri-de-Lévis** Quebec Canada
81 Q3 **Saint Hilaire** Minnesota USA
126 F3 **Saint-Hilaire-près Pionsat** France
124 B4 **Saint-Honoré** France
73 L9 **Saint-Hyacinthe** Quebec Canada
82 I4 **Saint Ignace** Michigan USA
80 H3 **Saint Ignatius** Montana USA
138 C3 **St Ishmael** Carmarthenshire Wales UK
139 G2 **St Ives** Cambridgeshire England UK
138 B4 **St Ives** Cornwall England UK
138 B4 **St Ives Bay** England UK
81 Q2 **Saint James** Manitoba Canada
126 D2 **St-James** France
82 F8 **Saint James** Missouri USA
74 F7 **St James, Cape** British Columbia Canada
221 E6 **St James Range** New Zealand
73 L9 **St-Jean, Lac** *lake* Quebec Canada
126 C3 **St-Jean-de-Monts** France
91 F3 **Saint-Jean du Sud** Haiti
126 D5 **St-Jean-Pied-de-Port** France
79 C9 **St-Jean-Port-Joli** Quebec Canada
83 O4 **St-Jean-sur-Richelieu** Quebec Canada
83 N4 **St-Jérôme** Quebec Canada
86 C4 **Saint Jo** Texas USA
80 H3 **St Joe** *watercourse* Idaho USA
79 E10 **St John** New Brunswick Canada
79 E9 **St John** *watercourse* Canada/USA
158 C3 **St John** *watercourse* Liberia
109 21 **St John** *island* US Virgin Islands
81 P8 **Saint John** Kansas USA
79 K8 **St John, Cape** Newfoundland and Labrador Canada
79 J7 **St John Bay** Newfoundland and Labrador Canada
79 E10 **St John Harbour** New Brunswick Canada
79 J7 **St John Island** Newfoundland and Labrador Canada
109 18 **Saint John's** Antigua and Barbuda
79 L9 **St John's** Newfoundland and Labrador Canada
85 H3 **Saint Johns** Arizona USA
82 I5 **Saint Johns** Michigan USA
91 I3 **Saint John's Flat** Netherlands Antilles
109 18 **Saint John's Harbour** *bay* Antigua and Barbuda
143 D2 **St John's Point** Ireland
143 G2 **St John's Point** Northern Ireland UK
109 17 **St John's Village** Montserrat
109 14 **Saint-Joseph** Martinique
222 7 **Saint Joseph** New Caledonia
164 7a **Saint-Joseph** Réunion
109 inset 9 **Saint Joseph** Trinidad and Tobago
82 D7 **Saint Joseph** Missouri USA
76 J7 **St Joseph, Lake** Ontario Canada
87 I6 **Saint Joseph Bay** Florida USA
164 9 **Saint Joseph Island** Seychelles
86 C7 **St Joseph Island** Texas USA
87 J6 **Saint Joseph Sound** Florida USA
83 P3 **St-Josephe-de-Beauce** Quebec Canada
143 C4 **Saint Joseph's** Ireland
126 F4 **Saint-Julien-aux-Bois** France
126 E4 **St-Junien** France
138 B4 **St Just** Cornwall England UK
126 D5 **Saint-Justin** France
138 B4 **St Keverne** Cornwall England UK
109 19 **St Kitts** *island* St Kitts and Nevis
91 I3 **St Kitts and Nevis** *country* Caribbean
213 I3 **St Lambert, Cape** WA Australia
126 E5 **St-Lary-Soulan** France
81 Q1 **Saint-Laurent** Manitoba Canada
129 H2 **St-Laurent-de-Cerdans** France
129 H2 **St-Laurent-de-la-Salanque** France
101 H3 **Saint-Laurent-du-Maroni** French Guiana
139 H5 **Saint-Laurent-en-Caux** France
215 J7 **St Lawrence** Qld Australia
109 12 **St Lawrence** Barbados
79 K9 **St Lawrence** Newfoundland and Labrador Canada
79 D8 **St Lawrence** *watercourse* Canada/USA
139 H3 **St Lawrence** Essex England UK
81 P4 **Saint Lawrence** South Dakota USA
79 H9 **St Lawrence, Cape** Nova Scotia Canada
79 G8 **St Lawrence, Gulf of** Canada
72 B6 **St Lawrence Island** Alaska USA
81 O1 **Saint Lazare** Manitoba Canada
80 G1 **Saint Leon** British Columbia Canada
126 E4 **St-Léonard-de-Noblat** France
164 7a **Saint-Leu** Réunion
138 B4 **St Levan** Cornwall England UK
78 K6 **St Lewis** Newfoundland and Labrador Canada
78 J6 **St Lewis** *watercourse* Newfoundland and Labrador Canada
78 K6 **St Lewis Sound** Newfoundland and Labrador Canada
126 E5 **Saint-Lizier** France
126 D2 **St-Lô** France
75 S6 **St Louis** Saskatchewan Canada
109 16 **Saint-Louis** Guadeloupe
164 7a **Saint-Louis** Réunion
154 C5 **St-Louis** Senegal
82 I5 **Saint Louis** Michigan USA
82 F7 **Saint Louis** Missouri USA
79 F9 **Saint-Louis-de-Kent** New Brunswick Canada
127 H3 **St-Loup-sur-Semouse** France
109 13 **St Lucia** *country* Caribbean
163 F5 **St Lucia** South Africa
163 F5 **St Lucia, Lake** *lake* South Africa
91 I4 **St Lucia Channel** St Lucia
79 K7 **St Lunaire-Griquet** Newfoundland and Labrador Canada
126 D3 **St-Maixent-l'École** France
126 C2 **St-Malo, Golfe de** *bay* France
126 G5 **Saint-Mamert-du-Gard** France
91 F3 **Saint-Marc** Haiti
91 F3 **St-Marc, Canal de** *strait* Haiti
101 H4 **St Marcel, Mont** *mountain* French Guiana
75 R8 **St Marie** Montana USA
80 G3 **St Maries** Idaho USA
109 10a **St Mark Bay** Grenada
143 F3 **Saint Marnocks** Ireland
109 20 **St Martin** *French overseas collectivity* Caribbean
109 20 **St Martin** *island* Caribbean
109 14 **St-Martin, Cap** *cape* Martinique
76 F7 **St Martin, Lake** Manitoba Canada
126 D3 **St-Martin-de-Ré** France
138 A5 **St Martin's** *island* England UK
181 G5 **St Martin's Island** Myanmar
129 G2 **St-Martory** France
75 O8 **St Mary** *watercourse* Alberta Canada
75 M8 **St Mary** *watercourse* British Columbia Canada
75 O8 **St Mary** Montana USA
79 E10 **St Mary, Cape** Nova Scotia Canada
199 H6 **Saint Mary, Mount** Papua New Guinea
218 D4 **St Mary Peak** SA Australia
80 I2 **St Mary Reservoir** Alberta Canada
219 S10 **St Marys** Tas. Australia
142 F2 **St Mary's** Orkney Islands Scotland UK
109 inset 9 **Saint Marys** Trinidad and Tobago
138 A5 **St Mary's** *island* England UK
87 K5 **Saint Marys** Georgia USA
83 L6 **Saint Marys** Pennsylvania USA
79 K9 **St Mary's, Cape** Newfoundland and Labrador Canada
79 L9 **St Mary's Bay** Newfoundland and Labrador Canada
221 D7 **St Marys Range** New Zealand
126 B2 **St-Mathieu, Pointe de** *cape* France
72 B6 **St Matthew Island** Alaska USA
199 I4 **Saint Matthias Group** *islands* Papua New Guinea
126 F2 **St-Maur-des-Fossés** France
138 B4 **St Mawes** Cornwall England UK
127 G5 **St-Maximin-la-Ste-Baume** France
126 D4 **St-Médard-en-Jalles** France
215 I5 **St Michael, Mount** Qld Australia
125 G4 **St Michael im Lungau** Austria
138 E2 **St Michaels** Worcestershire England UK
126 B2 **St-Michel, Réservoir de** *lake* France
127 H4 **St-Michel-de-Maurienne** France
73 L9 **Saint-Michel-des-Saints** Quebec Canada
127 G2 **St-Mihiel** France
142 F4 **St Monans** Fife Scotland UK
130 C3 **St Moritz** Switzerland
139 G2 **St Neots** Cambridgeshire England UK
138 B3 **St Nicholas** Pembrokeshire Wales UK
139 I5 **Saint-Nicolas-d'Aliermont** France
127 L3 **St Nikolai** Austria
124 B2 **St-Omer** France
83 Q3 **St-Pacôme** Quebec Canada
126 D5 **St-Palais** France
79 D9 **St-Pamphile** Quebec Canada
79 D9 **St-Pascal** Quebec Canada
83 M3 **St-Patrice, Lac** *lake* Quebec Canada
109 17 **Saint Patrick's** Montserrat
75 P6 **St Paul** Alberta Canada
79 J7 **St Paul** *watercourse* Quebec Canada
101 H3 **Saint-Paul** French Guiana
158 B3 **St Paul** *watercourse* Liberia
164 7a **Saint-Paul** Réunion
72 B7 **St Paul** Alaska USA
135 AM7 **St Paul** *island* Alaska USA
82 D8 **Saint Paul** Kansas USA
82 E4 **Saint Paul** Minnesota USA
81 P6 **Saint Paul** Nebraska USA
87 J2 **Saint Paul** Virginia USA
158 E3 **St Paul, Cape** Ghana
164 6 **Saint-Paul, Île** *island* French Southern and Antarctic Lands
79 H9 **St Paul Island** Nova Scotia Canada
72 B7 **St Paul Island** Alaska USA
126 G4 **Saint-Paul-le-Jeune** France
109 19 **Saint Paul's** Saint Kitts and Nevis
87 L3 **Saint Pauls** North Carolina USA
79 J8 **St Paul's Inlet** Newfoundland and Labrador Canada
223 11a **St Paul's Point** *cape* Pitcairn Islands
217 M6 **St Peter Island** SA Australia
122 E5 **St Peter-Ording** Germany
126 C2 **St Peter Port** Guernsey Channel Islands UK
79 G9 **St Peters** Prince Edward Island Canada
82 F7 **Saint Peters** Missouri USA
St Petersburg *see* **Sankt-Peterburg** Russian Federation
87 J7 **Saint Petersburg** Florida USA
164 7a **Saint-Philippe** Réunion
101 H4 **Saint Pierre** French Guiana
109 14 **Saint-Pierre** Martinique
164 7a **Saint-Pierre** Réunion
79 J9 **St-Pierre** St Pierre and Miquelon
79 J9 **St-Pierre, Île** *island* St Pierre and Miquelon
83 O3 **St-Pierre, Lac** *lake* Quebec Canada
79 F8 **St-Pierre, Pointe** *cape* Quebec Canada
79 J9 **St Pierre and Miquelon** *French overseas territorial collectivity* North America
126 D4 **St-Pierre-d'Oléron** France
139 F5 **Saint-Pierre-Église** France
164 9 **Saint Pierre Island** Seychelles
76 G8 **St-Pierre-Jolys** Manitoba Canada
126 F3 **St-Pierre-le-Moûtier** France
138 C4 **St Pinnock** Cornwall England UK
83 L3 **St Placide** Quebec Canada
126 C2 **St-Pol-de-Léon** France
125 H3 **St Pölten** Austria
129 H2 **St-Pons-de-Thomières** France
126 F3 **St-Pourçain-sur-Sioule** France
79 E9 **St-Quentin** New Brunswick Canada
126 F2 **St-Quentin** France
127 G4 **Saint-Rambert-d'Albon** France
83 P3 **St-Raphaël** Quebec Canada
129 J2 **St-Raphaël** France
83 P3 **St-Raymond** Quebec Canada
126 D2 **St-Rémy** France
126 F3 **Saint-Révérien** France
139 I4 **Saint-Riquier** France
139 I5 **St-Saëns** France
126 F3 **Saint-Satur** France
126 E3 **Saint-Savin** France
126 F5 **Saint-Sernin-sur-Rance** France
126 D5 **St-Sever** France
79 D9 **St-Siméon** Quebec Canada
87 K5 **Saint Simons Sound** Georgia USA
83 O2 **St-Stanislas** Quebec Canada
83 R4 **St Stephen** Maine USA
87 L4 **Saint Stephen** South Carolina USA
126 E5 **St-Sulpice** France
126 D4 **St-Symphorien** France
83 K5 **St Thomas** Ontario Canada
109 21 **St Thomas** *island* US Virgin Islands
83 O3 **St-Tite** Quebec Canada
83 P3 **St-Tite-des-Caps** Quebec Canada
127 H5 **St-Tropez** France
127 H5 **St-Tropez, Cap de** *cape* France
127 G1 **St-Truiden** Belgium
127 G4 **St-Vallier** France
126 D3 **Saint-Varent** France
125 H4 **St Veit an der Glan** Austria
124 D5 **St-Vincent** Italy
109 11 **St Vincent** *island* St Vincent and the Grenadines
81 Q2 **Saint Vincent** Minnesota USA
218 D6 **St Vincent, Gulf** SA Australia
91 I4 **St Vincent and the Grenadines** *country* Caribbean
91 I4 **St Vincent Passage** St Vincent and the Grenadines
87 I6 **Saint Vincent Sound** Florida USA
75 Q6 **St Walburg** Saskatchewan Canada
138 E3 **St Weonards** Herefordshire England UK
126 E4 **Saint-Yrieix-la-Perche** France
79 C9 **St-Zacharie** Quebec Canada
81 Q2 **Sainte Anne** Manitoba Canada
101 H3 **Sainte-Anne** French Guiana
109 16 **Sainte-Anne** Guadeloupe
109 14 **Sainte-Anne** Martinique
75 N6 **Ste Anne, Lac** *lake* Alberta Canada
77 V8 **Sainte-Anne-des-Monts** Quebec Canada
83 O4 **Ste-Anne-des-Plaines** Quebec Canada
83 N3 **Ste-Anne-du-Lac** Quebec Canada
164 9b **Sainte Anne Island** Seychelles
159 F5 **Ste-Catherine, Pointe** *cape* Gabon
126 E1 **Sainte-Cécile-Plage** France
83 P3 **Ste-Claire** Quebec Canada
127 H3 **Sainte-Croix** Switzerland
127 H5 **Ste-Croix, Lac de** *lake* France
126 E4 **Ste-Foy-la-Grande** France
82 F8 **Sainte Genevieve** Missouri USA
79 D9 **Ste-Hélène** Quebec Canada
126 D3 **Ste-Hermine** France
83 P3 **Ste-Justine** Quebec Canada
83 Q2 **Ste-Luce** Quebec Canada
109 14 **Sainte-Luce** Martinique
83 O3 **Ste-Madeleine** Quebec Canada
109 16 **Sainte-Marguerite** Guadeloupe
109 16 **Sainte-Marie** Guadeloupe
109 14 **Sainte-Marie** Martinique
127 H2 **Sainte-Marie-aux-Mines** France
131 D8 **Sainte Marie du Zit** Tunisia
127 H5 **Sainte-Maxime** France
109 17 **Sainte-Rose** Montserrat
164 7a **Sainte-Rose** Réunion
75 V7 **Sainte-Rose-du-Lac** Manitoba Canada
164 7a **Sainte-Suzanne** Réunion
83 O3 **Ste-Thècle** Quebec Canada
126 D4 **Saintes** France
126 G5 **Stes Maries, Golfe des** *bay* France
127 G5 **Stes-Maries-de-la-Mer** France
143 G2 **Saintfield** Down Northern Ireland UK
190 F3 **Saintsagaan** Mongolia
106 D6 **Sainuco** Argentina
126 E2 **Sainville** France
186 E4 **Saipal** *mountain* Nepal
222 2 **Saipan** Northern Mariana Islands
222 2 **Saipan** *island* Northern Mariana Islands
222 3 **Saipan** Palau
181 G4 **Sairang** Mizoram India
106 E2 **Sairecábur, Cerro** *mountain* Chile
129 H2 **Saissac** France
193 H4 **Saitama** Japan
192 F5 **Saito** Japan
181 G4 **Saitual** Mizoram India
121 M2 **Saivomuotka** Sweden
190 F4 **Saiwusu** Nei Mongol Zizhiqu China
104 D5 **Sajama, Nevado** *mountain* Bolivia
181 F3 **Sajia** Xizang Zizhiqu China
132 B3 **Šajkaš** Serbia
125 K3 **Sajó** *watercourse* Hungary
105 E5 **Sajpuco** Bolivia
162 D6 **Sak** *watercourse* South Africa
123 N3 **Saka** Estonia
161 F2 **Saka** Ethiopia
123 K4 **Saka** Latvia
120 L3 **Sakajärvi** Sweden
178 D3 **Sakākā** Saudi Arabia
197 H5 **Sakala** *island* Indonesia
77 Q6 **Sakami** Quebec Canada
77 R6 **Sakami** *watercourse* Quebec Canada
77 Q6 **Sakami, Lac** *lake* Quebec Canada
160 D6 **Sakania** Democratic Republic of Congo
220 3 **Sakaofo** *island* Tokelau New Zealand
133 E5 **Sakar** *range* Bulgaria
199 H5 **Sakar Island** Papua New Guinea
163 H4 **Sakaraha** Madagascar
133 G5 **Sakarya** *admin. area* Turkey
133 G5 **Sakarya (Adapazırı)** Turkey
193 H3 **Sakata** Japan
83 J3 **Sakatawi Lake** Ontario Canada
192 E3 **Sakchu** North Korea
183 M2 **Sakhalin** *lake* Russian Federation
135 AD8 **Sakhalin, Ostrov** *island* Russian Federation
135 AD8 **Sakhalinskaya Oblast'** *admin. area* Russian Federation
135 AD8 **Sakhalinskiy Zaliv** *bay* Russian Federation
Saki *see* **Sheki** Azerbaijan
123 L5 **Šakiai** Lithuania
196 C5 **Sakijang Bendera, Pulau** *island* Singapore
196 D5 **Sakijang Pelepah, Pulau** *island* Singapore
179 K3 **Sakīr Gharūna** *mountain* Pakistan
199 G6 **Sakiramke** Indonesia
189 I4 **Sakishima-shotō** *island* Japan
121 P3 **Säkkilänvaara** Finland
123 L3 **Sakla** Estonia
194 E3 **Sakon Nakhon** Thailand
182 I4 **Saksaulskiy** Kazakhstan
193 H4 **Saku** Japan
192 F5 **Sakura-jima** *volcano* Japan
76 J6 **Sakwaso Lake** Ontario Canada
123 L2 **Säkylä** Finland
164 4 **Sal** *island* Cape Verde
91 H5 **Sal, Cayo de** *island* Venezuela
90 C4 **Sal, Punta** *cape* Honduras
90 D2 **Sal Cay** *island* Bahamas
100 A5 **Sal Chico, Punta** *cape* Peru
164 4 **Sal Rei** Cape Verde
53 W10 **Sala y Gómez Ridge** *underwater feature* Pacific Ocean
197 I4 **Salabangka, Kepulauan** *islands* Indonesia
123 M4 **Salacgrīva** Latvia
106 D3 **Salada, Bahía** *bay* Chile
108 C3 **Salada, Gran Laguna** *lake* Argentina
84 E4 **Salada, Laguna** *lake* Mexico
107 G5 **Saladillo** Argentina
106 F5 **Saladillo** *watercourse* Argentina
106 F4 **Salado** *watercourse* Argentina
106 D3 **Salado** *watercourse* Chile
107 G4 **Salado, Lago** *lake* Argentina
106 D3 **Salado, Nevado Ojos del** *mountain* Argentina
158 D3 **Salaga** Ghana
88 B1 **Salaga, Laguna** *lake* Mexico
178 E2 **Şalaḩ Ad Dīn** *admin. area* Iraq
121 O5 **Salahmi** Finland
223 12c **Sala'ilua** Samoa
132 C2 **Sălaj** *admin. area* Romania
162 D4 **Salajwe** Botswana
155 J6 **Salal** Chad
156 F3 **Salâla** Sudan
179 H6 **Şalālah** Oman
106 D4 **Salamanca** Chile
88 E4 **Salamanca** Mexico
128 D3 **Salamanca** Spain
83 L5 **Salamanca** New York USA
108 C3 **Salamanca, Pampa de** *region* Argentina
163 F5 **Salamanga** Mozambique
159 I2 **Salamat** *admin. area* Chad
159 H3 **Salamat, Bahr** *watercourse* Chad
199 H5 **Salamaua** Papua New Guinea
223 12c **Salamumu** Samoa
190 G5 **Salaqi** Nei Mongol Zizhiqu China
106 E3 **Salar de Pocitos** Argentina
179 I3 **Sālārābād** Iran
128 C2 **Salas** Spain
128 E2 **Salas de los Infantes** Spain
129 H2 **Salasc** France
197 F5 **Salatiga** Indonesia
194 E4 **Salavan** Laos
104 B3 **Salaverry** Peru
198 D4 **Salawati** *island* Indonesia
187 B6 **Salaya** Gujarat India
106 F6 **Salazar** Argentina
164 7a **Salazie** Réunion
126 F3 **Salbris** France
104 C4 **Salcantay, Nevado** *mountain* Peru
88 C2 **Salcedo** Mexico
132 C3 **Salcia** Romania
138 D4 **Salcombe** Devon England UK
133 F7 **Salda Gölü** *lake* Turkey
128 D2 **Saldaña** Spain
162 C6 **Saldanha** South Africa
123 L4 **Saldus** Latvia
123 L4 **Saldus** *admin. area* Latvia
141 F3 **Sale** Greater Manchester England UK
197 H6 **Saleh, Teluk** *bay* Indonesia
223 12c **Sale'imoa** Samoa
134 O5 **Salekhard** Russian Federation
223 12c **Salelologa** Samoa
187 E9 **Salem** Tamil Nadu India
109 17 **Salem** Montserrat
138 C3 **Salem** Carmarthenshire Wales UK
86 F2 **Salem** Arkansas USA
82 G8 **Salem** Kentucky USA
82 F8 **Salem** Missouri USA
83 K6 **Salem** Ohio USA
80 D4 **Salem** Oregon USA
81 Q5 **Salem** South Dakota USA
83 K8 **Salem** Virginia USA
122 H4 **Salen** *bay* Sweden
131 F6 **Salerno** Italy
131 F6 **Salerno, Golfo di** *bay* Italy
105 I3 **Sales** Brazil
121 O5 **Sälevä** *lake* Finland
141 F3 **Salford** Greater Manchester England UK
103 E5 **Salgado** Brazil
121 M2 **Salgganjávri** *lake* Norway
125 J3 **Salgótarján** Hungary
102 E5 **Salgueiro** Brazil
190 F2 **Salhit** Mongolia
106 E4 **Sali** *watercourse* Argentina
130 F5 **Sali** Croatia
143 C3 **Saliahoona** Ireland
197 J3 **Salibabu** *island* Indonesia
109 inset 9 **Salibea** Trinidad and Tobago
81 M7 **Salida** Colorado USA
126 D5 **Salies-de-Béarn** France
136 C2 **Salihorsk** Belarus
77 Q4 **Salikuit Islands** Nunavut Canada
163 F2 **Salima** Malawi
197 H3 **Salimbatu** Indonesia
128 C2 **Salime, Embalse de** *lake* Spain
181 H5 **Salin** Myanmar
81 Q7 **Salina** Kansas USA
80 J7 **Salina** Utah USA
89 G5 **Salina Cruz** Mexico
106 D5 **Salina Llancanelo** *lake* Argentina
91 F2 **Salina Point** Bahamas
103 D7 **Salinas** Brazil
100 A5 **Salinas** Ecuador
88 E4 **Salinas** Mexico
80 E8 **Salinas** California USA
84 B2 **Salinas** *watercourse* California USA
104 B3 **Salinas, Bahía** *bay* Peru
129 F4 **Salinas, Laguna de** *lake* Spain
106 E4 **Salinas, Pampas de las** *lake* Argentina
91 G3 **Salinas, Punta** *cape* Dominican Republic
100 A5 **Salinas, Punta** *cape* Ecuador
109 6a **Salinas, Punta** *cape* Isla Róbinson Crusoe
105 G4 **Salinas, Serra das** *range* Brazil
104 B4 **Salinas de Otuma** Peru
106 E4 **Salinas Grandes** *lake* Argentina
142 E4 **Saline** Fife Scotland UK
86 E3 **Saline** *watercourse* Arkansas USA
81 P7 **Saline** *watercourse* Kansas USA
109 inset 9 **Saline Bay** Trinidad and Tobago
86 E5 **Saline Lake** Louisiana USA
104 A2 **Salinera Colán** Peru
129 H4 **Salines, Cap de Ses** *cape* Spain
91 I5 **Salines, Point** Grenada
181 H5 **Salingyi** Myanmar
124 C4 **Salins** France
218 D6 **Salisbury** SA Australia
109 15 **Salisbury** Dominica
139 F3 **Salisbury** Wiltshire England UK
83 N7 **Salisbury** Maryland USA
217 H7 **Salisbury Island** WA Australia
77 Q1 **Salisbury Island** Nunavut Canada
222 5 **Salisbury Junction** Guam
139 F3 **Salisbury Plain** England UK
80 H2 **Salish Mountains** Montana USA
132 D2 **Săliştea de Sus** Romania
88 E3 **Salitillo** Mexico
104 A2 **Salitral** Peru
103 D5 **Salitre** *watercourse* Brazil
106 D3 **Salitrosa** *watercourse* Chile
81 Q5 **Salix** Iowa USA
122 H4 **Saljen** *lake* Sweden
132 F1 **Sal'kovo** Ukraine
121 P3 **Salla** Finland
104 D4 **Sallalli** Peru
127 H4 **Sallanches** France
122 E4 **Salling** *cape* Denmark
140 B3 **Sallins** Ireland
120 J3 **Sallohaure** *lake* Sweden
77 R1 **Salluit** Quebec Canada
156 D1 **Sallūm, Khalīj as** *bay* Egypt/Libya
143 D5 **Sally Port** Ireland
186 F5 **Sallyana** Nepal
123 P2 **Salmi** Russian Federation
121 P3 **Salmivaara** Finland
74 M8 **Salmo** British Columbia Canada
79 F9 **Salmon** *watercourse* New Brunswick Canada
80 I4 **Salmon** Idaho USA
80 H4 **Salmon** *watercourse* Idaho USA
74 L7 **Salmon Arm** British Columbia Canada
216 G6 **Salmon Gums** WA Australia
80 H4 **Salmon River Mountains** Idaho USA
213 I4 **Salmond** *watercourse* WA Australia
121 S3 **Sal'nitsa** Russian Federation
160 B3 **Salo** Central African Republic
123 L2 **Salo** Finland
128 F4 **Salobral, Laguna del** *lake* Spain
123 M4 **Saločiai** Lithuania
100 D3 **Saloma** Colombia
109 14 **Salomon, Cap** *cape* Martinique
126 G2 **Salon** France
186 E5 **Salon** Uttar Pradesh India
127 G5 **Salon-de-Provence** France
160 C4 **Salonga** *watercourse* Democratic Republic of Congo
133 D5 **Salonikos, Akra** *cape* Greece
74 F3 **Saloon** British Columbia Canada
128 C4 **Salorino** Spain
125 I4 **Šalovci** Slovenia
123 N2 **Salpausselkä** *range* Finland
105 F2 **Salsa, Igarape Cabeceira do** *watercourse* Brazil
106 E4 **Salsacate** Argentina
129 G3 **Salsadella** Spain
120 G4 **Salsbruket** Norway
126 F5 **Salses-le-Château** France
75 O3 **Salt** *watercourse* Alberta Canada
139 E2 **Salt** Staffordshire England UK
84 G4 **Salt** *watercourse* Arkansas USA
82 F7 **Salt** *watercourse* Missouri USA
218 D7 **Salt Creek** SA Australia
85 J5 **Salt Flat** Texas USA
85 M2 **Salt Fork Arkansas** *watercourse* Kansas USA
85 L3 **Salt Fork Red** *watercourse* Texas USA
218 F4 **Salt Lake** NSW Australia
80 J6 **Salt Lake City** Utah USA
80 I7 **Salt Marsh Lake** Utah USA
75 O2 **Salt River** Northwest Territories Canada
80 E7 **Salt Springs Reservoir** California USA
84 C1 **Salt Wells** Nevada USA
106 E3 **Salta** Argentina
106 E3 **Salta** *admin. area* Argentina
138 C4 **Saltash** Cornwall England UK
75 T7 **Saltcoats** Saskatchewan Canada
142 D5 **Saltcoats** North Ayrshire Scotland UK
120 I3 **Saltdalen** *valley* Norway
120 I3 **Saltdalselva** *watercourse* Norway
120 I3 **Saltdalsfjorden** *bay* Norway
143 F4 **Saltee Islands** Ireland
141 I3 **Saltfleetby St Clement** Lincolnshire England UK
122 G5 **Saltholm** *island* Denmark
133 G6 **Saltık** Turkey
88 E3 **Saltillo** Mexico
86 G3 **Saltillo** Mississippi USA
142 E2 **Saltness** Orkney Islands Scotland UK
106 F5 **Salto** Argentina
103 C8 **Salto** Brazil
107 G4 **Salto** Uruguay
107 G4 **Salto** *admin. area* Uruguay
89 G5 **Salto de Agua** Mexico
107 H3 **Salto del Guairá** Paraguay
107 G4 **Salto Grande, Embalse de** *lake* Argentina
103 A9 **Salto Osório, Represa** *lake* Brazil
120 K3 **Saltoluokta** Sweden
141 H2 **Salton** North Yorkshire England UK
84 E4 **Salton Sea** California USA
105 E5 **Saltos** Bolivia
221 D6 **Saltwater Lagoon** New Zealand
182 C2 **Saltyki** Russian Federation
87 K4 **Saluda** South Carolina USA
197 I4 **Salue Timpaus, Selat** *strait* Indonesia
197 I4 **Saluebesar** *island* Indonesia
195 I5 **Salug** Philippines
186 D6 **Salumbar** Rajasthan India
187 F7 **Salur** Andhra Pradesh India
124 D5 **Saluzzo** Italy
108 A5 **Salvación, Bahía** *bay* Chile
216 G2 **Salvado, Mount** WA Australia
106 E4 **Salvador** Argentina
104 D4 **Salvador** Bolivia
103 E6 **Salvador** Brazil
86 F6 **Salvador, Lake** Louisiana USA
109 7 **Salvador, Port** Falkland Islands
91 G3 **Salvaleón de Higüey** Dominican Republic
88 E4 **Salvatierra** Mexico
126 C5 **Salvatierra** Spain
219 H1 **Salvator, Mount** Qld Australia
128 B2 **Salvora, Illa de** *island* Spain
138 E4 **Salway Ash** Dorset England UK
Salween *see* **Khong, Mae Nam** Myanmar
109 inset 9 **Salybia** Trinidad and Tobago
124 F2 **Salza** *watercourse* Germany
124 G4 **Salzach** *watercourse* Austria
124 G4 **Salzburg** Austria
124 G4 **Salzburg** *admin. area* Austria
124 F1 **Salzgitter** Germany
124 F1 **Salzwedel** Germany
186 C5 **Sam** Rajasthan India
86 D5 **Sam Rayburn Reservoir** Texas USA
194 E3 **Sầm Sơn** Vietnam
199 G4 **Sama Atoll** *reef* Papua New Guinea
85 I7 **Samachic** Mexico
179 I5 **Şamad** Oman
126 D5 **Samadet** France
196 E4 **Samak, Tanjung** *cape* Indonesia
178 E6 **Samakh** Saudi Arabia
196 F3 **Samalantan** Indonesia
195 I6 **Samales Group** *islands* Philippines
135 AN8 **Samalga Pass** *strait* Alaska USA
156 E2 **Samālūţ** Egypt
91 G3 **Samaná, Cabo** *cape* Dominican Republic
91 F2 **Samana Cay** *island* Bahamas
104 B3 **Samanco, Bahía** *lake* Peru
183 J7 **SamangĀn** *admin. area* Afghanistan
133 F5 **Samanlı Dağları** *range* Turkey
77 S8 **Samaqua** *watercourse* Quebec Canada
195 J5 **Samar Sea** Philippines
90 C5 **Sámara** Costa Rica
182 F2 **Samara** Russian Federation
199 I6 **Samarai** Papua New Guinea
218 H7 **Samaria, Mount** Vic. Australia
197 H4 **Samarinda** Indonesia
182 J6 **Samarqand** Uzbekistan
182 J6 **Samarqand** *admin. area* Uzbekistan
178 E2 **Sāmarrā'** Iraq
182 F3 **Samarskaya Oblast'** *admin. area* Russian Federation
183 N3 **Samarskoye** Kazakhstan
125 M2 **Samary** Ukraine
186 F6 **Samastipur** Bihar India
104 E3 **Samaúma** Brazil
160 C3 **Samba** Democratic Republic of Congo
160 D4 **Samba** Democratic Republic of Congo
197 G4 **Samba** *watercourse* Indonesia
160 B5 **Samba Caju** Angola
197 H3 **Sambaliung Pergunungan** *range* Indonesia
187 F7 **Sambalpur** Orissa India
163 H3 **Sambao** *watercourse* Madagascar
198 B5 **Sambapolulu, Gunung** *mountain* Indonesia
197 F4 **Sambar, Tanjung** *cape* Indonesia
196 F3 **Sambas** Indonesia
163 J2 **Sambava** Madagascar
186 E5 **Sambhal** Uttar Pradesh India
186 D5 **Sambhar Salt Lake** Rajasthan India
197 H3 **Sambit** *island* Indonesia
102 D4 **Sambito** *watercourse* Brazil
162 C2 **Sambo** Angola
197 H4 **Samboja** Indonesia
106 F5 **Samborombon** *watercourse* Argentina
107 G5 **Samborombón, Bahía** *bay* Argentina
139 F2 **Sambourne** Warwickshire England UK
192 F4 **Samch'ŏk** South Korea
181 G3 **Samdrup Jongkhar** Bhutan
161 F4 **Same** Tanzania
124 A2 **Samer** France
162 E2 **Samfya** Zambia
157 I5 **Samhah** *island* Yemen
197 I3 **Samia, Tanjung** *cape* Indonesia
192 F3 **Samjiyŏn** North Korea
121 M5 **Sammatti** Finland
155 I3 **Samnū** Libya
223 12c **Samoa** *unincorporated US territory* Pacific Ocean

52 P9 **Samoa Basin** *underwater feature* Pacific Ocean
124 D4 **Samoëns** France
130 G2 **Šamorín** Slovakia
133 E7 **Samos** Greece
133 E7 **Samos** *island* Greece
128 C2 **Samos** Spain
196 C3 **Samosir** *island* Indonesia
133 D5 **Samothraki** *island* Greece
132 D4 **Samovodene** Bulgaria
182 D3 **Samoylovka** Russian Federation
158 D3 **Sampa** Ghana
106 E5 **Sampacho** Argentina
197 G5 **Sampang** Indonesia
138 D4 **Sampford Arundel** Somerset England UK
138 D4 **Sampford Courtenay** Devon England UK
138 D4 **Sampford Peverell** Devon England UK
197 G4 **Sampit** Indonesia
197 G4 **Sampit** *watercourse* Indonesia
197 G4 **Sampit, Teluk** *strait* Indonesia
198 B5 **Sampolawa** Indonesia
76 I6 **Sampson Lake** Ontario Canada
100 C2 **Sampués** Colombia
199 J5 **Sampun** Papua New Guinea
160 D5 **Sampwe** Democratic Republic of Congo
157 F5 **Samrē** Ethiopia
120 G5 **Samsjøen** *lake* Norway
122 G4 **Sämsjön** *lake* Sweden
122 F5 **Samsø** *island* Denmark
87 H5 **Samson** Alabama USA
192 E3 **Samsu** North Korea
136 F5 **Samsun** Turkey
136 F5 **Samsun** *admin. area* Turkey
181 F3 **Samtse** Bhutan
214 C5 **Samuel, Mount** NT Australia
181 G4 **Samurou** Manipur India
194 D4 **Samut Prakan** Thailand
194 E4 **San** *watercourse* Cambodia
154 F6 **San** Mali
125 L3 **San** *watercourse* Poland
128 B2 **San Adrián, Cabo de** *cape* Spain
100 B4 **San Agustín** Colombia
84 E6 **San Agustin** Mexico
195 J6 **San Agustin, Cape** Philippines
85 I4 **San Agustin, Plains of** New Mexico USA
100 C3 **San Alberto** Colombia
107 H3 **San Alberto** Paraguay
85 I4 **San Andreas Mountains** New Mexico USA
105 E4 **San Andrés** Bolivia
100 A1 **San Andrés** Colombia
109 3 **San Andrés** Isla de San Andrés
109 3 **San Andrés, Isla de** *island* Colombia
89 F4 **San Andres, Laguna de** *lake* Mexico
126 B5 **San Andrés del Rabanedo** Spain
85 L5 **San Angelo** Texas USA
100 C2 **San Antero** Colombia
104 D4 **San Antón** Peru
106 D3 **San Antonia** Chile
89 H5 **San Antonio** Belize
105 E5 **San Antonio** Bolivia
106 D5 **San Antonio** Chile
100 C5 **San Antonio** Colombia
104 C1 **San Antonio** Peru
195 I4 **San Antonio** Philippines
84 B2 **San Antonio** *watercourse* California USA
87 J6 **San Antonio** Florida USA
85 I4 **San Antonio** New Mexico USA
86 B6 **San Antonio** Texas USA
85 N6 **San Antonio** *watercourse* Texas USA
100 E4 **San Antonio** Venezuela
90 C2 **San Antonio, Cabo de** *cape* Cuba
129 G4 **San Antonio, Cabo de** *cape* Spain
100 A5 **San Antonio, Isla** *island* Ecuador
108 D2 **San Antonio, Puerto** *bay* Argentina
129 G4 **San Antonio Abad** Spain
195 H5 **San Antonio Bay** Philippines
86 C6 **San Antonio Bay** Texas USA
88 D2 **San Antonio de Bravo** Mexico
104 C4 **San Antonio de Cusicancha** Peru
85 L8 **San Antonio de las Alazanas** Mexico
106 E3 **San Antonio de los Cobres** Argentina
104 E5 **San Antonio de Nor Kala** Bolivia
105 E4 **San Antonio de Rivera** Bolivia
108 D2 **San Antonio Oeste** Argentina
84 B3 **San Antonio Reservoir** California USA
106 E4 **San Augustin de Valle Fértil** Argentina
86 D5 **San Augustine** Texas USA
105 E4 **San Bartolo** Bolivia
108 D6 **San Bartolomé, Cabo** *cape* Argentina
128 C5 **San Bartolomé de la Torre** Spain
130 E5 **San Benedetto del Tronto** Italy
88 C5 **San Benedicto, Isla** *island* Mexico
90 B3 **San Benito** Guatemala
86 C7 **San Benito** Texas USA
88 B2 **San Benito, Islas** *islands* Mexico
84 D3 **San Bernardino** California USA
84 D3 **San Bernardino Mountains** California USA
106 D5 **San Bernardo** Chile
88 C3 **San Bernardo** Mexico
106 E4 **San Blas** Argentina
88 D4 **San Blas** Mexico
90 E5 **San Blas, Archipiélago de** *islands* Panama
90 E5 **San Blas, Cordillera de** *range* Panama
90 E5 **San Blas, Punta** *cape* Panama
104 E4 **San Borja** Bolivia
105 G5 **San Borja** Bolivia
84 F7 **San Bruno** Mexico
88 C3 **San Buenaventura** Mexico
88 E3 **San Buenaventura** Mexico
106 D5 **San Carlos** Argentina
105 F5 **San Carlos** Bolivia
106 D6 **San Carlos** Chile
109 7 **San Carlos** Falkland Islands
86 B8 **San Carlos** Mexico
90 C5 **San Carlos** Nicaragua
107 G2 **San Carlos** Paraguay
107 G2 **San Carlos** *watercourse* Paraguay
195 I5 **San Carlos** Philippines
100 D2 **San Carlos** Venezuela
106 F6 **San Carlos de Bolívai** Argentina
100 C4 **San Carlos de Guaroa** Colombia
100 D2 **San Carlos del Zulia** Venezuela
84 G4 **San Carlos Reservoir** Arizona USA
131 E8 **San Cataldo** Italy
84 D4 **San Clemente** California USA
128 E5 **San Clemente, Embalse de** *lake* Spain
107 G6 **San Clemente del Tuyú** Argentina
88 A1 **San Clemente Island** California USA
222 8 **San Cristobal** *island* Solomon Islands
106 F4 **San Cristóbal** Argentina
106 D2 **San Cristóbal** Chile
90 D2 **San Cristóbal** Cuba
107 H3 **San Cristóbal** Paraguay
100 C3 **San Cristóbal** Venezuela
109 4 **San Cristóbal, Isla** *islands* Archipiélago de Colón (Galapagos Islands)
154 C3 **San Cristóbal de la Laguna** Spain
89 G5 **San Cristóbal de las Casas** Mexico
105 F5 **San Diablo, Serranía** *range* Bolivia
100 C2 **San Diego** Colombia
88 A1 **San Diego** California USA
86 B7 **San Diego** Texas USA
108 D6 **San Diego, Cabo** *cape* Argentina
84 D4 **San Diego Bay** California USA
88 D3 **San Diego de Alcalo** Mexico
88 E4 **San Diego de la Unión** Mexico
88 C2 **San Dionisio** Mexico
127 K4 **San Donà di Piave** Italy
88 D2 **San Elizario** Texas USA
90 C4 **San Esteban** Honduras
85 K6 **San Esteban** Mexico
108 A4 **San Estéban, Golfo** *bay* Chile
88 B2 **San Esteban, Isla** *island* Mexico
131 E6 **San Felice Circeo** Italy
106 D5 **San Felipe** Chile
100 E4 **San Felipe** Colombia
88 E4 **San Felipe** Mexico
88 B2 **San Felipe** Mexico
100 D2 **San Felipe** Venezuela
108 C5 **San Felipe, Bahía** *bay* Chile
89 J4 **San Felipe, Cayos de** *island* Cuba
89 H5 **San Felipe, Laguna** *lake* Mexico
85 I7 **San Felipe de Jesus** Mexico
91 G3 **San Felipe de Puerto Plata** Dominican Republic
90 D5 **San Félix** Panama
107 G5 **San Félix** Uruguay
85 J7 **San Fermin** Mexico
107 G5 **San Fernando** Argentina
106 D5 **San Fernando** Chile
89 F3 **San Fernando** Mexico
195 I4 **San Fernando** Philippines
109 inset 9 **San Fernando** Trinidad and Tobago
109 inset 9 **San Fernando** *admin. area* Trinidad and Tobago
84 C3 **San Fernando** California USA
100 E3 **San Fernando de Apure** Venezuela
106 E4 **San Fernando del Valle de Catamarca** Argentina
100 C5 **San Fernendo** Peru
109 inset 9 **San Francique** Trinidad and Tobago
106 F4 **San Francisco** Argentina
105 F5 **San Francisco** Bolivia
100 D5 **San Francisco** Colombia
90 C5 **San Francisco** Costa Rica
90 B4 **San Francisco** El Salvador
85 H5 **San Francisco** Mexico
90 D5 **San Francisco** Panama
195 J5 **San Francisco** Philippines
80 D8 **San Francisco** California USA
85 H4 **San Francisco** *watercourse* New Mexico USA
100 A4 **San Francisco, Cabo de** *cape* Ecuador
84 A2 **San Francisco Bay** California USA
85 J8 **San Francisco de Asis** Mexico
89 I6 **San Francisco de Coray** Honduras
91 G3 **San Francisco de Macorís** Dominican Republic
108 C4 **San Francisco de Paula, Cabo** *cape* Argentina
88 E4 **San Francisco del Rincón** Mexico
129 G4 **San Francisco Javier** Spain
100 B3 **San Francisco Solano, Punta** *cape* Colombia
84 F6 **San Francisquito** Mexico
100 B4 **San Gabriel** Ecuador
89 F5 **San Gabriel Casa Blanca** Mexico
84 D3 **San Gabriel Mountains** California USA
106 F6 **San Germán** Argentina
100 C3 **San Gil** Colombia
124 G5 **San Giorgio di Nogaro** Italy
108 D3 **San Gregorio, Bahía** *bay* Argentina
85 K6 **San Guillermo** Mexico
88 B3 **San Hipólito, Punta** *cape* Mexico
90 B3 **San Ignacio** Belize
105 F4 **San Ignacio** Bolivia
88 D4 **San Ignacio** Mexico
104 B2 **San Ignacio** Peru
88 B3 **San Ignacio, Laguna** *lake* Mexico
100 B4 **San Ignacio, Punta** *cape* Colombia
105 E4 **San Ignacio de Moxo** Bolivia
105 F5 **San Ignacio de Velasco** Bolivia
88 E2 **San Ildefonso** Mexico
195 I4 **San Ildefonso, Cape** Philippines
195 I3 **San Ildefonso Peninsula** *cape* Philippines
90 D5 **San Isidro** Costa Rica
84 F7 **San Isidro** Mexico
85 I5 **San Isidro** Mexico
86 B7 **San Isidro** Texas USA
107 H3 **San Isidro de Curuguaty** Paraguay
100 C2 **San Jacinto** Colombia
195 I4 **San Jacinto** Philippines
84 D4 **San Jacinto** California USA
107 G4 **San Jaime** Argentina
129 F5 **San Javier** Spain
89 G5 **San Jerónimo Ixtepec** Mexico
105 F4 **San Joaguin** *watercourse* Bolivia
105 E4 **San Joaquín** Bolivia
107 G3 **San Joaquín** Paraguay
80 E8 **San Joaquin** California USA
80 E8 **San Joaquin** *watercourse* California USA
85 K3 **San Jon** New Mexico USA
106 F4 **San Jorge** Argentina
100 C4 **San Jorge** Colombia
222 8 **San Jorge** *island* Solomon Islands
108 C4 **San Jorge, Golfo** *bay* Argentina
195 I4 **San Jose** Philippines
195 J6 **San Jose** Philippines
80 E8 **San Jose** California USA
82 G6 **San Jose** Illinois USA
107 G6 **San José** Argentina
104 E4 **San José** Bolivia
105 F2 **San José** Brazil
106 C6 **San José** Chile
100 B4 **San José** Colombia
90 C5 **San José** Costa Rica
90 B3 **San José** Guatemala
90 C4 **San José** Honduras
89 F4 **San José** Mexico
84 G7 **San José** Mexico
129 G4 **San José** Spain
107 G5 **San José** *admin. area* Uruguay
108 D3 **San José, Cabo** *cape* Argentina
108 D3 **San José, Golfo** *bay* Argentina
88 C3 **San José, Isla** *island* Mexico
90 E5 **San José, Isla** *island* Panama
88 C3 **San José de Bácum** Mexico
84 G6 **San José de Baviácora** Mexico
90 C4 **San José de Bocay** Nicaragua
195 I5 **San Jose de Buenavista** Philippines
101 E3 **San José de Camani** Venezuela
88 B3 **San José de Castro** Mexico
107 G4 **San José de Feliciano** Argentina
101 E2 **San José de Guanipa** Venezuela
106 D4 **San José de Jáchal** Argentina
85 I6 **San José de la Ermita** Mexico
84 E6 **San José de las Palomas** Mexico
107 G5 **San José de Mayo** Uruguay
100 E2 **San José de Tiznados** Venezuela
88 E3 **San José del Aguaje** Mexico
106 F3 **San José del Boquerón** Argentina
105 E4 **San José del Carrito** Bolivia
100 C4 **San José del Guaviare** Colombia
90 C4 **San José del Potrero** Honduras
85 N6 **San Jose Island** Texas USA
106 D4 **San Juan** Argentina
106 D4 **San Juan** *admin. area* Argentina
104 E4 **San Juan** Bolivia
164 3a **San Juan** Canary Islands
108 B5 **San Juan** Chile
89 F3 **San Juan** *watercourse* Mexico
100 C5 **San Juan** Peru
91 H3 **San Juan** Puerto Rico
109 inset 9 **San Juan** Trinidad and Tobago
85 H2 **San Juan** *watercourse* Utah USA
108 D6 **San Juan, Cabo** *cape* Argentina
159 F4 **San Juan, Cabo** *cape* Equatorial Guinea
100 C4 **San Juan, Llanos de** *region* Colombia
90 E2 **San Juan, Loma** *region* Cuba
90 B4 **San Juan, Punta** *lake* El Salvador
109 5 **San Juan, Punta** *cape* Isla de Pascua (Easter Island)
109 2 **San Juan, Punta** *cape* Isla de Providencia
109 6a **San Juan Bautista** Isla Róbinson Crusoe
107 G3 **San Juan Bautista** Paraguay
104 C4 **San Juan Bautista** Peru
88 D4 **San Juan de Abajo** Mexico
100 C4 **San Juan de Arama** Colombia
100 D2 **San Juan de Colón** Venezuela
100 C2 **San Juan de Guía, Cabo de** *cape* Colombia
100 B4 **San Juan de La Costa** Colombia
164 3a **San Juan de la Rambla** Canary Islands
100 D2 **San Juan de los Cayos** Venezuela
100 E2 **San Juan de los Morros** Venezuela
100 B2 **San Juan de Urabá** Colombia
100 C2 **San Juan del Cesar** Colombia
90 D5 **San Juan del Norte** Nicaragua
90 D5 **San Juan del Norte, Bahía de** *bay* Nicaragua
89 E4 **San Juan del Río** Mexico
90 C5 **San Juan del Sur** Nicaragua
104 D4 **San Juan Grande** Peru
80 D2 **San Juan Islands** Washington USA
109 inset 9 **San Juan-Laventille** *admin. area* Trinidad and Tobago
85 I2 **San Juan Mountains** Colorado USA
85 I7 **San Juan Nepomuceno** Mexico
89 H4 **San Juan Ote** Mexico
90 B4 **San Juan Sacatepéquez** Guatemala
84 F7 **San Juanico** Mexico
84 F7 **San Juanico, Laguna** Mexico
88 B3 **San Juanico, Punta** *cape* Mexico
85 I7 **San Juanito** Mexico
88 D4 **San Juanito, Isla** *island* Mexico
108 C4 **San Julián** Argentina
108 C4 **San Julián, Bahía** *bay* Argentina
108 C4 **San Julián, Gran Bajo de** *region* Argentina
106 F4 **San Justo** Argentina
107 G2 **San Lázaro** Paraguay
88 B3 **San Lázaro, Cabo** *cape* Mexico
86 C5 **San Leanna** Texas USA
130 E5 **San Leo** Italy
128 E3 **San Leonardo de Yagüe** Spain
100 B4 **San Lorenz de Esmeraldas** Ecuador
107 G4 **San Lorenzo** Argentina
105 E4 **San Lorenzo** Bolivia
100 C4 **San Lorenzo** Colombia
90 C4 **San Lorenzo** Honduras
85 I6 **San Lorenzo** Mexico
104 D4 **San Lorenzo** Peru
100 A5 **San Lorenzo, Cabo** *cape* Ecuador
88 B2 **San Lorenzo, Isla** *island* Mexico
108 C4 **San Lorenzo, Monte** *mountain* Argentina
105 F5 **San Lorenzo, Serranía** *range* Bolivia
128 E4 **San Lorenzo de la Parrilla** Spain
131 C7 **San Lotemzo, Capo** *cape* Sardinia Italy
88 C4 **San Lucas** Mexico
85 J6 **San Lucas** Mexico
84 B2 **San Lucas** California USA
100 C3 **San Lucas, Serranía de** *range* Colombia
106 E5 **San Luis** Argentina
106 E5 **San Luis** *admin. area* Argentina
91 F2 **San Luis** Cuba
90 B3 **San Luis** Guatemala
90 C4 **San Luis** Honduras
109 3 **San Luis** Isla de San Andrés
88 B2 **San Luis** Mexico
104 C4 **San Luis** Peru
81 M8 **San Luis** Colorado USA
88 B2 **San Luís, Isla** *island* Mexico
105 F4 **San Luis, Laguna** *lake* Bolivia
100 D2 **San Luis, Sierra de** *range* Venezuela
89 F5 **San Luis Acatlán** Mexico
88 E4 **San Luis de la Paz** Mexico
85 J8 **San Luis del Cordero** Mexico
84 B3 **San Luis Obispo** California USA
88 E4 **San Luis Potosí** Mexico
88 E4 **San Luis Potosí** *admin. area* Mexico
80 E8 **San Luis Reservoir** California USA
84 D4 **San Luis Rey** *watercourse* California USA
88 B1 **San Luis Río Colorado** Mexico
88 B2 **San Luisito** Mexico
107 G6 **San Manuel** Argentina
85 I4 **San Marcial** New Mexico USA
88 C3 **San Marcial, Punta** *cape* Mexico
131 E8 **San Marco, Capo** *cape* Italy
104 E4 **San Marcos** Bolivia
105 E6 **San Marcos** Bolivia
100 C2 **San Marcos** Colombia
89 F5 **San Marcos** Mexico
104 B2 **San Marcos** Peru
84 D4 **San Marcos** California USA
86 C6 **San Marcos** Texas USA
88 C3 **San Marcos, Isla** *island* Mexico
130 E5 **San Marino** San Marino
106 D5 **San Martín** Argentina
105 F4 **San Martin** *watercourse* Bolivia
108 C5 **San Martín** Chile
100 C4 **San Martín** Colombia
104 B2 **San Martín** *admin. area* Peru
89 G5 **San Martin, Volcán** *volcano* Mexico
58 T2 **San Martín (Argentina)** *research station* Antarctica
108 B2 **San Martín de los Andes** Argentina
195 I3 **San Mateo** Philippines
85 I3 **San Mateo** New Mexico USA
100 B4 **San Mateo, Bahía** *bay* Ecuador
100 C2 **San Mateo, Serranía de** *range* Colombia
89 G5 **San Mateo del Mar** Mexico
90 B4 **San Mateo Ixtatán** Guatemala
85 I4 **San Mateo Mountains** New Mexico USA
105 G5 **San Matías** Brazil
108 D2 **San Matías, Golfo** *bay* Argentina
127 H4 **San Mauro Torinese** Italy
127 K4 **San Michele al Tagliamento** Italy
106 E6 **San Miguel** Argentina
105 F5 **San Miguel** Bolivia
105 F4 **San Miguel** *watercourse* Bolivia
100 B4 **San Miguel** Colombia
100 B5 **San Miguel** Ecuador
100 B4 **San Miguel** *watercourse* Ecuador
88 C2 **San Miguel** Mexico
90 E5 **San Miguel** Panama
107 G3 **San Miguel** Paraguay
104 C4 **San Miguel** Peru
90 E5 **San Miguel, Golfo de** *bay* Panama
195 I4 **San Miguel Bay** Philippines
104 B3 **San Miguel de Cauri** Peru
88 C2 **San Miguel de Horcasitas** *watercourse* Mexico
106 E3 **San Miguel de Tucumán** Argentina
104 E4 **San Miguel del Bala** Bolivia
107 G5 **San Miguel del Monte** Argentina
84 B3 **San Miguel Island** California USA
195 H6 **San Miguel Islands** Philippines
88 D3 **San Miguel Papasquiaro** Mexico
89 G5 **San Miguel Quetzaltepec** Mexico
104 D3 **San Miguelito** Bolivia
90 C5 **San Miguelito** Nicaragua
90 E5 **San Miguelito** Panama
90 B4 **San Miquel** El Salvador
90 D2 **San Nicolás** Cuba
90 C4 **San Nicolás** Honduras
101 E2 **San Nicolás** Venezuela
104 C4 **San Nicolás, Bahía** *bay* Peru
106 F5 **San Nicolás de los Arroyos** Argentina
88 E3 **San Nicolás de los Garzas** Mexico
164 3b **San Nicolás de Tolentino** Canary Islands
84 C4 **San Nicolas Island** California USA
85 I8 **San Nicolas Sitio de Arriba** Mexico
100 C2 **San Onofre** Colombia
108 C6 **San Pablo** Argentina
108 B2 **San Pablo** Chile
100 C2 **San Pablo** Colombia
195 I4 **San Pablo** Philippines
88 B3 **San Pablo, Punta** *cape* Mexico
85 I7 **San Pablo Balleza** Mexico
107 G3 **San Pablo de Ycuámandyyú** Paraguay
131 F8 **San Paolo** Italy
88 D5 **San Patricio** Mexico
107 G5 **San Pedro** Argentina
90 C3 **San Pedro** Belize
105 E6 **San Pedro** Bolivia
88 C3 **San Pedro** Mexico
85 H5 **San Pedro** *watercourse* Mexico
107 G3 **San Pedro** *admin. area* Paraguay
104 D3 **San Pedro** Peru
84 G4 **San Pedro** *watercourse* Arkansas USA
158 C4 **San Pédro** Côte d'Ivoire
108 A2 **San Pedro, Bahía** *bay* Chile
106 E2 **San Pedro, Nevado de** *mountain* Argentina
90 D5 **San Pedro, Punta** *lake* Costa Rica
85 H5 **San Pedro, Rio de** *watercourse* Mexico
84 C4 **San Pedro Channel** California USA
84 H6 **San Pedro de la Cueva** Mexico
85 K8 **San Pedro de las Colonias** Mexico
91 G3 **San Pedro de Macorís** Dominican Republic
128 D3 **San Pedro de Rozados** Spain
100 B2 **San Pedro de Urabá** Colombia
107 G3 **San Pedro de Ycuamandiyú** Paraguay
85 J8 **San Pedro del Gallo** Mexico
107 G3 **San Pedro del Paraná** Paraguay
126 C5 **San Pedro Manrique** Spain
84 E5 **San Pedro Martir** Mexico
89 F6 **San Pedro Pochutla** Mexico
90 B4 **San Pedro Sula** Honduras
86 C7 **San Perlita** Texas USA
130 D5 **San Piero in Bagno** Italy
127 I4 **San Pietro Vara** Italy
88 B2 **San Quintín** Mexico
88 A2 **San Quintín, Cabo** *cape* Mexico
106 D5 **San Rafael** Argentina
104 D4 **San Rafael** Peru
80 D8 **San Rafael** California USA
81 J7 **San Rafael** *watercourse* Utah USA
84 C3 **San Rafael Mountains** California USA
105 F4 **San Ramón** Bolivia
90 C5 **San Ramón** Costa Rica
104 C3 **San Ramón** Peru
130 B5 **San Remo** Italy
89 H5 **San Román** Mexico
100 D1 **San Román, Cabo** *cape* Venezuela
222 2a **San Roque** Northern Mariana Islands
84 E7 **San Roque, Punta** *cape* Mexico
86 B5 **San Saba** Texas USA
107 G4 **San Salvador** Argentina
91 F1 **San Salvador** *island* Bahamas
90 B4 **San Salvador** El Salvador
109 4 **San Salvador, Isla** *island* Archipiélago de Colón (Galapagos Islands)
106 E3 **San Salvador de Jujuy** Argentina
131 F5 **San Salvo** Italy
108 C5 **San Sebastián** Argentina
108 C5 **San Sebastián, Cabo** *cape* Argentina
164 3a **San Sebastián de la Gomera** Canary Islands
89 F5 **San Sebastián Zinacatepec** Mexico
131 F6 **San Severo** Italy
84 B3 **San Simeon** California USA
85 H4 **San Simon** Arizona USA
105 F4 **San Simón** Bolivia
106 D5 **San Vicente** Chile
108 D6 **San Vicente, Cabo** *cape* Argentina
128 C4 **San Vicente de Alcántara** Spain
100 C3 **San Vicente de Chucurí** Colombia
100 C4 **San Vicente del Caguán** Colombia
130 D5 **San Vincenzo** Italy
128 C3 **San Vitero** Spain
90 D5 **San Vito** Costa Rica
131 G6 **San Vito, Capo** *cape* Italy
131 E7 **San Vito lo Capo** Italy
100 D4 **San Yanaro** Colombia
89 F3 **San Ygnacio** Mexico
86 B7 **San Ygnacio** Texas USA
85 I3 **San Ysidro** New Mexico USA
88 B3 **San Zacharías** Mexico
178 E7 **Şan'ā'** *admin. area* Yemen
178 E7 **Şan'ā' (Sanaa)** Yemen
161 H1 **Sanaag** *admin. area* Somalia
158 D2 **Sanaba** Burkina Faso
58 X2 **SANAE IV (South Africa)** *research station* Antarctica
142 B5 **Sanaigmore** Argyll and Bute Scotland UK
72 C8 **Sanak Island** Alaska USA
88 D3 **Sanalona, Presa** *lake* Mexico
178 E5 **Sanām** Saudi Arabia
197 J4 **Sanana** *island* Indonesia
186 C6 **Sanand** Gujarat India
178 F2 **Sanandaj** Iran
154 E6 **Sanando** Mali
132 B3 **Sânandrei** Romania
107 I3 **Sananduva** Brazil
159 G4 **Sananga** *watercourse* Cameroon
158 C2 **Sanankoroba** Mali
100 D2 **Sanare Abajo** Venezuela
199 I6 **Sanaroa Island** Papua New Guinea
222 6a **Sanat** *island* Federated States of Micronesia
187 D6 **Sanawad** Madhya Pradesh India
81 P3 **Sanborn** North Dakota USA
126 F3 **Sancerre** France
128 D3 **Sanchidrián** Spain
186 C6 **Sanchore** Rajasthan India
195 J5 **Sanco Point** Philippines
197 J1 **Sanco Point** *cape* Philippines
126 F3 **Sancoins** France
128 C5 **Sancti Petri, Isla** *island* Spain
90 E2 **Sancti Spíritus** Cuba
90 E2 **Sancti Spiritus** *admin. area* Cuba
128 C3 **Sancti-Spíritus** Spain
141 H3 **Sancton** East Riding of Yorkshire England UK
81 K1 **Sanctuary** Saskatchewan Canada
126 F4 **Sancy, Puy de** *mountain* France
75 P5 **Sand** *watercourse* Alberta Canada
122 F2 **Sand** Norway
199 G4 **Sand** *watercourse* Papua New Guinea
162 E4 **Sand** *watercourse* South Africa
120 L4 **Sand** Sweden
215 J6 **Sand Bay** Qld Australia
187 C9 **Sand Cay** *island* Lakshadweep India
164 9 **Sand Cay** *island* Seychelles
81 O6 **Sand Hills** Nebraska USA
72 C6 **Sand Islands** Alaska USA
76 H7 **Sand Lake** Ontario Canada
72 C7 **Sand Point** Alaska USA
86 C2 **Sand Springs** Oklahoma USA
193 G4 **Sanda** Japan
142 C5 **Sanda Island** Scotland UK
179 K4 **Sandadkot** Pakistan
197 F4 **Sandai** Indonesia
142 C3 **Sandaig** Highland Scotland UK
197 H2 **Sandakan** Malaysia
197 H2 **Sandakan, Teluk** *bay* Malaysia
123 R1 **Sandal, Ozero** *lake* Russian Federation
178 E6 **Şandalīyah** Saudi Arabia
131 C7 **Sandalo, Capo** *cape* Sardinia Italy
194 E4 **Sândăn** Cambodia
162 D2 **Sandando** Angola
142 F1 **Sanday Sound** Scotland UK
138 E1 **Sandbach** Cheshire England UK
120 L2 **Sandbukt** Norway
122 F3 **Sande** Norway
122 C3 **Sandeid** Norway
211 inset **Sandell Bay** Macquarie Island Australia
122 F2 **Sander** Norway
58 D2 **Sandercock Nunataks** *mountain* Antarctica
85 K5 **Sanderson** Texas USA
87 J4 **Sandersville** Georgia USA
86 G5 **Sandersville** Mississippi USA
120 I2 **Sandes** Norway
212 F5 **Sandfire Roadhouse** WA Australia
141 F2 **Sandford** Cumbria England UK
58 I2 **Sandford Glacier** Antarctica
142 F1 **Sandgarth** Orkney Islands Scotland UK
120 inset **Sandgerði** Iceland
142 D6 **Sandhead** Dumfries and Galloway Scotland UK
120 I3 **Sandhornøya** *island* Norway
139 G3 **Sandhurst** Bracknell Forest England UK
136 F6 **Şandī** Syria
159 I4 **Sandiki** *watercourse* Central African Republic
133 G6 **Sandıklı** Turkey
186 E5 **Sandila** Uttar Pradesh India
196 D4 **Sanding** *island* Indonesia
125 H3 **Sandl** Austria
120 J5 **Sandnäset** Sweden
122 C3 **Sandnes** Norway
120 I2 **Sandnes** Norway
142 inset **Sandness** Shetland Scotland UK
120 H3 **Sandnessjøen** Norway
160 C5 **Sandoa** Democratic Republic of Congo
105 I4 **Sandolândia** Brazil
125 K2 **Sandomierz** Poland
139 E2 **Sandon** Staffordshire England UK
121 M4 **Sandön** *island* Sweden
100 B4 **Sandoná** Colombia
132 B2 **Sándorfalva** Hungary
214 C6 **Sandover** *watercourse* NT Australia
198 E4 **Sandow** Indonesia
139 F4 **Sandown** Isle of Wight England UK
120 K1 **Sandoy** *island* Faroe Islands
80 G2 **Sandpoint** Idaho USA
142 F1 **Sandquoy** Orkney Islands Scotland UK
142 A4 **Sandray** *island* Scotland UK
76 G7 **Sandridge** Manitoba Canada
122 D3 **Sandsavatnet** *lake* Norway
216 F3 **Sandstone** WA Australia
82 E3 **Sandstone** Minnesota USA
120 J2 **Sandstrand** Norway
187 F7 **Sandur** *watercourse* Chhattisgarh India
82 J5 **Sandusky** Michigan USA
82 J6 **Sandusky** Ohio USA
120 F6 **Sandvatnet** *lake* Norway
162 C6 **Sandveld** *plain* South Africa
120 K2 **Sandvik** Norway
122 I4 **Sandvik** Sweden
122 F3 **Sandvika** Norway
122 I2 **Sandviken** Sweden
141 F4 **Sandwell** *admin. area* England UK
139 I3 **Sandwich** Kent England UK
78 J6 **Sandwich Bay** Newfoundland and Labrador Canada
142 inset **Sandwick** Shetland Scotland UK
214 D4 **Sandy** *watercourse* NT Australia
214 E5 **Sandy** *watercourse* Qld Australia
139 G2 **Sandy** Bedfordshire England UK
211 inset **Sandy Bay** Macquarie Island Australia
75 T5 **Sandy Bay** Saskatchewan Canada
90 C3 **Sandy Bay** Honduras
219 K1 **Sandy Cape** Qld Australia
219 Q10 **Sandy Cape** Tas. Australia
83 M5 **Sandy Creek** New York USA
219 J3 **Sandy Flat** NSW Australia
214 D3 **Sandy Hill** NT Australia
78 K6 **Sandy Hook** Newfoundland and Labrador Canada
82 J7 **Sandy Hook** Kentucky USA
78 K6 **Sandy Islands** Newfoundland and Labrador Canada
75 O5 **Sandy Lake** Alberta Canada
79 J8 **Sandy Lake** Newfoundland and Labrador Canada
76 I6 **Sandy Lake** Ontario Canada
75 R4 **Sandy Lake** Saskatchewan Canada
75 T5 **Sandy Narrows** Saskatchewan Canada
218 H8 **Sandy Point** Vic. Australia
212 G4 **Sandy Point** *cape* WA Australia
164 5c **Sandy Point** *cape* St Helena
143 F3 **Sandyford** Ireland
182 I6 **Sandyklygum** *lake* Turkmenistan
128 E2 **Sanfelices** Spain
120 H5 **Sånfjället** *mountain* Sweden
216 E3 **Sanford** *watercourse* WA Australia
76 G8 **Sanford** Manitoba Canada
85 J2 **Sanford** Colorado USA
87 L3 **Sanford** North Carolina USA
85 L3 **Sanford** Texas USA
192 F4 **Sang-do** *island* South Korea
162 C2 **Sanga** Angola
154 F6 **Sanga** Mali
120 J5 **Sånga** Sweden
187 D7 **Sangamner** Maharashtra India
179 K3 **Sangan** Pakistan
218 H6 **Sangar** NSW Australia
135 AA6 **Sangar** Russian Federation
158 B2 **Sangarédi** Guinea
186 D5 **Sangaria** Rajasthan India
133 C7 **Sángas** Greece
159 G3 **Sangbé** Cameroon
195 I6 **Sangboy Islands** Philippines
160 D5 **Sange** Democratic Republic of Congo
179 K2 **Sange Shāndeh** Afghanistan
197 H6 **Sangeang** *island* Indonesia
132 D2 **Sângeorz-Băi** Romania
84 C2 **Sanger** California USA
86 C4 **Sanger** Texas USA
197 H6 **Sanggar, Teluk** *bay* Indonesia
197 F3 **Sanggau** Indonesia
196 F3 **Sanggauledo** Indonesia
197 J3 **Sanggeluhang** *island* Indonesia
159 H4 **Sangha** *admin. area* Congo
159 H4 **Sangha** *watercourse* Congo
159 H4 **Sangha-Mbaéré** *admin. area* Central African Republic
197 J3 **Sangihe, Kepulauan** *islands* Indonesia
121 O4 **Sanginkylä** Finland
197 J3 **Sangir** *island* Indonesia
185 K2 **Sangiyn Dalay Nuur** *lake* Mongolia
192 F4 **Sangju** South Korea
197 G5 **Sangkapura** Indonesia
197 H3 **Sangkulirang** Indonesia
197 H3 **Sangkulirang, Teluk** *bay* Indonesia
187 D8 **Sangli** Maharashtra India
186 D6 **Sangod** Rajasthan India
187 D8 **Sangola** Maharashtra India
100 B5 **Sangolquí** Ecuador
198 D3 **Sangowo** Indonesia
85 J2 **Sangre de Cristo Range** Colorado/New Mexico USA
109 inset 9 **Sangre Grande** Trinidad and Tobago
109 inset 9 **Sangre Grande** *admin. area* Trinidad and Tobago
101 G2 **Sangretal Bay** Guyana
181 G3 **Sangri** Xizang Zizhiqu China
131 F5 **Sangro** *watercourse* Italy
120 J4 **Sängsjön** *lake* Sweden
192 E4 **Sangtae-do** *island* South Korea
75 N6 **Sangudo** Alberta Canada
105 G3 **Sangue, Rio do** *watercourse* Brazil
126 D4 **Sanguinet** France
108 C4 **Sanguineto, Bahía** *bay* Argentina
158 B2 **Sangulana** Guinea
163 F4 **Sangutane** *watercourse* Mozambique
183 K6 **Sangvor** Tajikistan
191 H5 **Sangyuan** Hebei China
158 C2 **Sanhala** Côte d'Ivoire
188 E3 **Sanhe** Guizhou China
156 E2 **Sanhûr** Egypt
133 C5 **Sani** Greece
87 J7 **Sanibel** Florida USA
87 J7 **Sanibel Island** Florida USA
101 H3 **Saniki** Suriname
77 P4 **Sanikiluaq** Nunavut Canada
104 E5 **Sanipaya** Bolivia
125 L4 **Sanislău** Romania
122 G5 **Sanitz** Germany
188 F3 **Sanjiang** Guizhou China
190 D6 **Sanjiaocheng** Qinghai China
194 C3 **Sankamphaeng** Thailand
158 B3 **Sankanbiaiwa** *mountain* Guinea
158 C2 **Sankarani** *watercourse* Guinea
130 F3 **Sankt Aegyd am Neuwalde** Austria
127 K2 **Sankt Florian** Austria
124 E4 **Sankt Gallen** Switzerland
124 E3 **Sankt Georgen** Germany
127 H1 **Sankt Goar** Germany
122 H5 **Sankt Olof** Sweden
123 P3 **Sankt-Peterburg (St Petersburg)** Russian Federation
160 C4 **Sankuru** *watercourse* Democratic Republic of Congo
136 F6 **Şanlıurfa** Turkey
136 F6 **Şanlıurfa** *admin. area* Turkey
131 C7 **Sanluri** Sardinia Italy
189 I3 **Sanmen Wan** *bay* Zhejiang China
189 F1 **Sanmenxia** Henan China
189 H3 **Sanming** Fujian China
142 B4 **Sanna** Highland Scotland UK
78 N2 **Sannerut** *island* Greenland
135 AC4 **Sannikova, Proliv** *strait* Russian Federation
142 C5 **Sannox** North Ayrshire Scotland UK
125 L3 **Sanok** Poland
154 E5 **Sanpaka** Mali
194 C3 **Sanpatong** Thailand
142 E5 **Sanquhar** Dumfries and Galloway Scotland UK
109 inset 9 **Sans Souci** Trinidad and Tobago
158 B2 **Sansale** Guinea
154 E6 **Sansanding** Mali
189 F4 **Sanshui** Guangdong China
130 G4 **Sanski Most** Bosnia and Herzegovina
158 C2 **Sanso** Mali
220 F5 **Sanson** New Zealand
190 E3 **Sant** Mongolia
190 F2 **Sant** Mongolia
130 C4 **Sant' Anna, Punta** *cape* Italy
129 G3 **Sant Carles de la Ràpita** Spain
129 G3 **Sant Jordi, Golfo de** *bay* Spain
129 G3 **Sant Mateu** Spain
100 B4 **Santa Ana** Colombia
100 A5 **Santa Ana** Ecuador
90 B4 **Santa Ana** El Salvador
90 B3 **Santa Ana** Guatemala
90 C4 **Santa Ana** Honduras
85 I8 **Santa Ana** Mexico
104 C4 **Santa Ana** Peru
222 8 **Santa Ana** *island* Solomon Islands
84 D4 **Santa Ana** California USA
85 I3 **Santa Ana Pueblo** New Mexico USA
86 B5 **Santa Anna** Texas USA
105 G4 **Santa Bárbara** Brazil
100 C3 **Santa Bárbara** Colombia
90 B4 **Santa Bárbara** Guatemala
90 B4 **Santa Bárbara** Honduras
88 D3 **Santa Bárbara** Mexico
129 G3 **Santa Bárbara** Spain
84 C3 **Santa Barbara** California USA
164 1b **Santa Bárbara, Serra de** *volcano* Azores
107 H2 **Santa Bárbara, Serra de** *range* Brazil
84 B3 **Santa Barbara Channel** California USA
128 C5 **Santa Bárbara de Casa** Spain
91 G3 **Santa Bárbara de Samaná** Dominican Republic
84 C4 **Santa Barbara Island** California USA
103 C8 **Santa Branca** Brazil
106 D3 **Santa Catalina** Chile
88 A1 **Santa Catalina, Gulf of** California USA
109 2 **Santa Catalina, Isla de** *island* Isla de Providencia
84 C4 **Santa Catalina Island** California USA
107 I3 **Santa Catarina** *admin. area* Brazil
85 L8 **Santa Catarina** Mexico
105 H6 **Santa Catarina, Serra** *range* Brazil
109 1b **Santa Caterina** Netherlands Antilles
107 I3 **Santa Cecília** Brazil
131 H6 **Santa Cesarea Terme** Italy
100 D5 **Santa Clara** Colombia
90 E2 **Santa Clara** Cuba
88 E3 **Santa Clara** Mexico
88 D2 **Santa Clara** *watercourse* Mexico
104 B2 **Santa Clara** Peru
85 H4 **Santa Clara** New Mexico USA
84 F2 **Santa Clara** Utah USA
128 B5 **Santa Clara, Barragem de** *lake* Portugal
109 6 **Santa Clara, Isla** *island* Juan Fernández Archipiélago
84 C3 **Santa Clarita** California USA
129 H3 **Santa Coloma de Gramanet** Spain
131 F8 **Santa Croce, Capo** *cape* Italy
109 4 **Santa Cruz** Archipiélago de Colón (Galapagos Islands)
108 C4 **Santa Cruz** *admin. area* Argentina
108 B5 **Santa Cruz** *watercourse* Argentina
109 1a **Santa Cruz** Aruba
105 F5 **Santa Cruz** Bolivia
106 F2 **Santa Cruz** *admin. area* Bolivia
105 G5 **Santa Cruz** Brazil
164 4a **Santa Cruz** Cape Verde
106 D5 **Santa Cruz** Chile
90 C5 **Santa Cruz** Costa Rica
164 2 **Santa Cruz** Madeira
89 H5 **Santa Cruz** Mexico
84 G5 **Santa Cruz** Mexico
195 I4 **Santa Cruz** Philippines
195 H4 **Santa Cruz** Philippines
80 D8 **Santa Cruz** California USA
109 4 **Santa Cruz, Isla** *island* Archipiélago de Colón (Galapagos Islands)
88 C3 **Santa Cruz, Isla** *island* Mexico
108 C5 **Santa Cruz, Puerto** *bay* Argentina
103 E7 **Santa Cruz Cabrália** Brazil
128 E2 **Santa Cruz de Bezana** Spain
91 G3 **Santa Cruz de El Seibo** Dominican Republic
164 1b **Santa Cruz de Graciosa** Azores
164 3b **Santa Cruz de la Palma** Canary Islands
164 3a **Santa Cruz de Tenerife** Canary Islands
90 D2 **Santa Cruz del Norte** Cuba
102 E4 **Santa Cruz do Capibaribe** Brazil
103 B8 **Santa Cruz do Rio Pardo** Brazil
107 H4 **Santa Cruz do Sul** Brazil
84 C4 **Santa Cruz Island** California USA
89 F5 **Santa Cruz Xoxocotlán** Mexico
85 J8 **Santa Domingo** Mexico
128 E3 **Santa Domingo de Silos** Spain
104 E4 **Santa Elena** Bolivia
100 A5 **Santa Elena** Ecuador
100 A5 **Santa Elena** *admin. area* Ecuador
89 H4 **Santa Elena** Mexico
100 C5 **Santa Elena** Peru
100 A5 **Santa Elena, Bahía de** *bay* Ecuador
90 C5 **Santa Elena, Cabo** *cape* Costa Rica
105 H5 **Santa Elvira** Brazil
128 D4 **Santa Eufemia** Spain
131 F7 **Santa Eufemia, Golfo di** *bay* Italy
129 F3 **Santa Eulalia** Spain
129 G4 **Santa Eulalia del Río** Spain
106 F4 **Santa Fe** Argentina
106 F4 **Santa Fe** *admin. area* Argentina
195 I4 **Santa Fe** Philippines
85 J3 **Santa Fe** New Mexico USA
90 E5 **Santa Fé** Panama
109 4 **Santa Fé, Isla** *island* Archipiélago de Colon (Galapagos Islands)
103 B8 **Santa Fé do Sul** Brazil
87 J6 **Santa Fe Lake** Florida USA
100 B3 **Santa Genoveva de Docorodó** Colombia
105 H5 **Santa Helena** Brazil
103 B7 **Santa Helena de Goiás** Brazil
88 E3 **Santa Inés** Mexico
100 D2 **Santa Inés** Venezuela
102 C3 **Santa Inês** Brazil
108 B5 **Santa Inés, Isla** *island* Chile
106 E6 **Santa Isabel** Argentina
105 G5 **Santa Isabel** Brazil
109 2 **Santa Isabel** Isla de Providencia
88 B2 **Santa Isabel** Mexico
222 8 **Santa Isabel** *island* Solomon Islands
101 E4 **Santa Isabel** Venezuela
88 B2 **Santa Isabel, Sierra** *range* Mexico
101 E5 **Santa Isabel do Rio Negro** Brazil
107 G4 **Santa Lucia** *watercourse* Argentina
100 C5 **Santa Lucía** Colombia
100 C2 **Santa Lucía** Colombia
100 A5 **Santa Lucía** Ecuador
104 D4 **Santa Lucía** Peru
108 A5 **Santa Lucía, Cabo** *cape* Chile
84 B2 **Santa Lucia Range** California USA
105 H5 **Santa Luisa, Sierra de** *range* Brazil
102 C4 **Santa Luzia** Brazil
164 4 **Santa Luzia** *island* Cape Verde
128 B3 **Santa Luzia, Barragem de** *lake* Portugal
105 F3 **Santa Luzia d'Oeste** Brazil
106 F4 **Santa Margarita** Argentina
84 B3 **Santa Margarita** California USA
88 B3 **Santa Margarita, Isla** *island* Mexico
164 1 **Santa Maria** *island* Azores
105 F4 **Santa María** Bolivia
107 H4 **Santa Maria** Brazil
164 4 **Santa Maria** Cape Verde
88 D2 **Santa Maria** *watercourse* Mexico
109 1b **Santa Maria** Netherlands Antilles
107 G3 **Santa María** Paraguay
195 I3 **Santa Maria** Philippines
84 B3 **Santa Maria** California USA
222 7 **Santa Maria** *island* Vanuatu
162 B2 **Santa Maria, Cabo de** *cape* Angola
163 F5 **Santa Maria, Cabo de** *cape* Mozambique
128 C5 **Santa Maria, Cabo de** *cape* Portugal
91 F2 **Santa Maria, Cape** Bahamas
90 E2 **Santa Maria, Cayo** *island* Cuba
109 4 **Santa María, Isla** *island* Archipiélago de Colón (Galapagos Islands)
106 C6 **Santa María, Isla** *island* Chile
89 F5 **Santa María Asunción Tlaxiaco** Mexico
102 E5 **Santa Maria da Boa Vista** Brazil
103 C6 **Santa Maria da Vitória** Brazil
101 E2 **Santa María de Ipire** Venezuela
88 E3 **Santa María de Mohovano** Mexico
126 B5 **Santa María del Páramo** Spain
88 E4 **Santa María del Río** Mexico
131 F6 **Santa Maria di Castellabate** Italy
102 C3 **Santa Maria do Pará** Brazil
103 D7 **Santa Maria do Suaçuí** Brazil
128 D3 **Santa María la Real de Nieva** Spain
89 F6 **Santa María Xadani** Mexico
131 F7 **Santa Marina Salina** Italy
100 C2 **Santa Marta** Colombia
84 F7 **Santa Marta** Mexico
128 C4 **Santa Marta** Spain
100 C2 **Santa Marta, Cienaga Grande de** *lake* Colombia

100 C2 **Santa Marta, Sierra Nevada de** *range* Colombia
128 D3 **Santa Marta de Tormes** Spain
84 C4 **Santa Monica Bay** California USA
128 D3 **Santa Olalla** Spain
84 C3 **Santa Paula** California USA
102 D4 **Santa Quitéria** Brazil
102 D3 **Santa Quitéria do Maranhão** Brazil
104 C3 **Santa Rita** Brazil
100 D4 **Santa Rita** Colombia
88 C4 **Santa Rita** Mexico
101 F3 **Santa Rita** Venezuela
101 G5 **Santa Rita, Ilha** *island* Brazil
103 A8 **Santa Rita do Pardo** Brazil
106 E6 **Santa Rosa** Argentina
105 F6 **Santa Rosa** Bolivia
105 F3 **Santa Rosa** Brazil
107 H3 **Santa Rosa** Brazil
108 B2 **Santa Rosa** Chile
109 1b **Santa Rosa** Netherlands Antilles
107 G3 **Santa Rosa** Paraguay
104 B2 **Santa Rosa** Peru
84 F4 **Santa Rosa** Arizona USA
80 D7 **Santa Rosa** California USA
85 J3 **Santa Rosa** New Mexico USA
86 C7 **Santa Rosa** Texas USA
100 E3 **Santa Rosa** Venezuela
90 C3 **Santa Rosa, Punta** *cape* Mexico
100 E4 **Santa Rosa de Amanadona** Venezuela
90 B4 **Santa Rosa de Copán** Honduras
104 C3 **Santa Rosa de Dinamarca** Peru
100 C3 **Santa Rosa de Osos** Colombia
105 F5 **Santa Rosa del Sara** Bolivia
100 C3 **Santa Rosa del Sur** Colombia
84 B4 **Santa Rosa Island** California USA
100 C5 **Santa Rosa Menaje** Colombia
84 D4 **Santa Rosa Mountains** California USA
80 G6 **Santa Rosa Range** Nevada USA
86 H5 **Santa Rosa Sound** Florida USA
88 B3 **Santa Rosalía** Mexico
101 E3 **Santa Rosalía** Venezuela
84 E6 **Santa Rosaliita** Mexico
106 F3 **Santa Sylvina** Argentina
128 B3 **Santa Tecla** *region* Portugal
105 G5 **Santa Teresa** Bolivia
103 B6 **Santa Teresa** *watercourse* Brazil
86 B8 **Santa Teresa** Mexico
100 E2 **Santa Teresa** Venezuela
100 B6 **Santa Teresita** Ecuador
84 F7 **Santa Tomas** Mexico
105 E6 **Santa Victoria, Sierra** *range* Argentina
103 B7 **Santa Vitória** Brazil
107 H5 **Santa Vitória do Palmar** Brazil
84 C3 **Santa Ynez** *watercourse* California USA
128 D5 **Santaella** Spain
131 D5 **Sant'Agostino, Punta** *cape* Italy
188 E2 **Santai** Sichuan China
103 E5 **Santaluz** Brazil
197 H4 **Santan** Indonesia
197 H4 **Santan, Tanjung** *cape* Indonesia
102 B3 **Santana** Brazil
164 2 **Santana** Madeira
107 H4 **Santana, Coxilha de** *range* Brazil
107 H4 **Santana da Boa Vista** Brazil
102 D3 **Santana do Acaraú** Brazil
102 B5 **Santana do Araguaia** Brazil
107 H4 **Santana do Livramento** Brazil
102 E4 **Santana do Matos** Brazil
100 C3 **Santander** *admin. area* Colombia
128 E2 **Santander** Spain
89 F3 **Santander Jiménez** Mexico
127 I4 **Sant'Angelo Lodigiano** Italy
131 C7 **Sant'Antioco** Sardinia Italy
127 I5 **Sant'Appiano, Monte** *mountain* Corsica France
80 J7 **Santaquin** Utah USA
101 H5 **Santarém** Brazil
128 B4 **Santarém** Portugal
128 B4 **Santarém** *admin. area* Portugal
90 E2 **Santaren Channel** Bahamas
84 D4 **Santee** California USA
87 J3 **Santeetlah Lake** North Carolina USA
130 E4 **Sant'Erasmo, Isola** *island* Italy
130 C4 **Sant'Erasmo, Punta** *cape* Italy
107 H4 **Santiago** Brazil
164 4 **Santiago** *island* Cape Verde
106 D5 **Santiago** Chile
100 B4 **Santiago** *watercourse* Ecuador
88 E3 **Santiago** Mexico
90 D5 **Santiago** Panama
107 G3 **Santiago** Paraguay
195 I3 **Santiago** Philippines
108 A5 **Santiago, Cabo** *cape* Chile
88 D4 **Santiago, Grande de** *watercourse* Mexico
159 F4 **Santiago, Punta** *cape* Equatorial Guinea
105 G5 **Santiago, Serranía de** *range* Bolivia
104 B3 **Santiago de Chuco** Peru
128 B2 **Santiago de Compostela** Spain
91 F2 **Santiago de Cuba** Cuba
90 E3 **Santiago de Cuba** *admin. area* Cuba
89 F4 **Santiago de la Peña** Mexico
91 G3 **Santiago de los Caballeros** Dominican Republic
104 D4 **Santiago de Pacaguaras** Bolivia
106 E3 **Santiago del Estero** Argentina
106 F3 **Santiago del Estero** *admin. area* Argentina
164 3a **Santiago del Teide** Canary Islands
105 F5 **Santiago del Torno** Bolivia
88 D4 **Santiago Ixcuintla** Mexico
89 F5 **Santiago Miahuatlán** Mexico
85 K6 **Santiago Mountains** Texas USA
88 D3 **Santiago Papasquiaro** Mexico
76 N1 **Santianna Point** Nunavut Canada
189 I3 **Santiao Chiao** *island* Taiwan China
128 C3 **Santibáñez el Bajo** Spain
198 B3 **Santigi** Indonesia
197 I3 **Santigi, Tanjung** *cape* Indonesia
185 J3 **Santmargants** Mongolia
164 2 **Santo, Porto** Madeira
128 C4 **Santo Aleixo** Portugal
103 E6 **Santo Amaro** Brazil
107 I3 **Santo Amaro da Imperatriz** Brazil
103 B8 **Santo Anastácio** Brazil
103 C8 **Santo André** Brazil
128 B4 **Santo André** Portugal
107 H4 **Santo Ângelo** Brazil
102 F5 **Santo Antão** Brazil
164 4 **Santo Antão** *island* Cape Verde
159 F4 **Santo António** São Tomé and Príncipe
102 F4 **Santo Antônio** Brazil
105 I5 **Santo Antônio da Barra** Brazil
102 A3 **Santo Antônio da Cachoeira** Brazil
105 I3 **Santo Antônio da Solta** Brazil
103 E6 **Santo Antônio de Jesus** Brazil
100 E5 **Santo Antônio do Içá** Brazil
105 G4 **Santo Antônio do Leverger** Brazil
107 J2 **Santo Antônio do Monte** Brazil
103 A9 **Santo Antônio do Sudoeste** Brazil
102 B3 **Santo Antônio do Tauá** Brazil
105 E4 **Santo Domingo** Bolivia
91 G3 **Santo Domingo** Dominican Republic
100 B4 **Santo Domingo** Ecuador
85 L6 **Santo Domingo** Mexico
88 E4 **Santo Domingo** Mexico
89 H5 **Santo Domingo** *watercourse* Mexico
100 B5 **Santo Domingo de los Colorados** Ecuador
89 G5 **Santo Domingo Tehuantepec** Mexico
103 E6 **Santo Estêvão** Brazil
131 F8 **Santo Pietro** Italy
124 G5 **Santo Stino di Livenza** Italy
128 B3 **Santo Tirso** Portugal
105 G5 **Santo Tomás** Bolivia
84 D5 **Santo Tomás** Mexico
90 C4 **Santo Tomás** Nicaragua
104 C4 **Santo Tomas** Peru
107 G4 **Santo Tomé** Argentina
108 B3 **Santo Victoria** Chile
129 F3 **Santolea, Embalse de** *lake* Spain
139 H2 **Santon Downham** Norfolk England UK
128 E2 **Santoña** Spain
131 E6 **Sant'Onofrio** Italy
218 E3 **Santos** Qld Australia
107 J2 **Santos** Brazil
51 N12 **Santos Plateau** *underwater feature* Atlantic Ocean
188 F5 **Sanya** Hainan China
188 E1 **Sanyuan** Shaanxi China
160 B5 **Sanza Pombo** Angola
189 G4 **Sanzao Dao** *island* Guangdong China
105 G5 **São Benedito** Brazil
102 D3 **São Benedito do Rio Preto** Brazil
102 C3 **São Bento** Brazil
102 E4 **São Bento** Brazil
105 E2 **São Bernado** Brazil
102 D3 **São Bernardo** Brazil
107 H4 **São Borja** Brazil
104 D3 **São Brás** Brazil
103 C8 **São Carlos** Brazil
103 C6 **São Desidério** Brazil
103 A8 **São Domingos** Brazil
105 F3 **São Domingos** *watercourse* Brazil
164 4a **São Domingos** Cape Verde
128 B5 **São Domingos** Portugal
102 C4 **São Domingos do Maranhão** Brazil
101 F5 **São Felipe** Brazil
103 D6 **São Felipe** Brazil
128 B3 **São Félix da Marinha** Portugal
103 B5 **São Felix do Araguaia** Brazil
102 B4 **São Félix do Xingu** Brazil
103 D8 **São Fidélis** Brazil
164 4 **São Filipe** Cape Verde
103 C6 **São Francisco** Brazil
103 D6 **São Francisco** *watercourse* Brazil
107 I3 **São Francisco, Ilha de** *island* Brazil
107 H4 **São Francisco de Assis** Brazil
107 I4 **São Francisco de Paula** Brazil
107 H4 **São Gabriel** Brazil
100 E5 **São Gabriel da Cachoeira** Brazil
102 B4 **São Geraldo do Araguaia** Brazil
105 H5 **São Gonçalo** Brazil
102 F4 **São Gonçalo do Amarante** Brazil
103 C7 **São Gotardo** Brazil
101 F4 **São Gregório** Brazil
105 H5 **São Jerônimo, Serra de** *range* Brazil
105 G5 **São João** Brazil
102 C3 **São João, Ilhas de** *island* Brazil
105 F3 **São João, Serra de** *range* Brazil
103 D8 **São João da Barra** Brazil
103 C8 **São João da Boa Vista** Brazil
103 C6 **São João da Ponte** Brazil
102 C3 **São João de Pirabas** Brazil
105 I5 **São João do Aporé** Brazil
102 B4 **São João do Araguaia** Brazil
103 D6 **São João do Paraíso** Brazil
102 D5 **São João do Piauí** Brazil
159 F4 **São João dos Angolares** São Tomé and Príncipe
102 D4 **São João dos Patos** Brazil
103 D7 **São João Evangelista** Brazil
103 D8 **São João Nepomuceno** Brazil
107 I4 **São Joaquim** Brazil
164 1 **São Jorge** *island* Azores
164 2 **São Jorge, Ponta de** *cape* Madeira
104 D2 **São José** Brazil
104 E3 **São José** Brazil
105 H6 **São José** Brazil
102 E5 **São José da Tapera** Brazil
105 F2 **São José de Cuxo** Brazil
102 C3 **São José de Ribamar** Brazil
102 E4 **São José do Belmonte** Brazil
103 A6 **São José do Couto** Brazil
102 E4 **São José do Egito** Brazil
105 G5 **São José do Piquiri** Brazil
103 B8 **São José do Rio Preto** Brazil
103 C8 **São José dos Campos** Brazil
103 B9 **São José dos Pinhais** Brazil
104 C2 **São Leopoldo** Brazil
104 C3 **São Lorentino** Brazil
105 H5 **São Lourenço** Brazil
103 C8 **São Lourenço** Brazil
164 2 **São Lourenço, Ponta de** *cape* Madeira
103 B7 **São Lourenço, Serra** *range* Brazil
107 I4 **São Lourenço do Sul** Brazil
103 A9 **São Lourenço d'Oeste** Brazil
102 C3 **São Luís** Brazil
105 G2 **São Luís** Brazil
105 H5 **São Luís** Brazil
103 B7 **São Luís de Montes Belos** Brazil
102 F5 **São Luís do Quitunde** Brazil
101 F4 **São Luiz** Brazil
107 H4 **São Luiz Gonzaga** Brazil
107 I4 **São Marcos** Brazil
103 C7 **São Marcos** *watercourse* Brazil
164 1b **São Mateus** Azores
103 E7 **São Mateus** Brazil
102 C4 **São Mateus do Maranhão** Brazil
103 B9 **São Mateus do Sul** Brazil
164 1 **São Miguel** *island* Azores
101 I4 **São Miguel** Brazil
102 F4 **São Miguel** Brazil
103 B6 **São Miguel do Araguaia** Brazil
102 C3 **São Miguel do Guamá** Brazil
103 A9 **São Miguel do Iguaçu** Brazil
164 4 **São Nicolau** *island* Cape Verde
103 C8 **São Paulo** Brazil
107 I2 **São Paulo** *admin. area* Brazil
100 D5 **São Paulo de Olivença** Brazil
103 C8 **São Pedro** Brazil
102 E5 **São Pedro** *watercourse* Brazil
128 B4 **São Pedro da Cadeira** Portugal
107 H4 **São Pedro do Sul** Brazil
102 C4 **São Raimundo das Mangabeiras** Brazil
102 D5 **São Raimundo Nonato** Brazil
164 1b **São Roque do Pico** Azores
164 1b **São Sebastião** Azores
105 F3 **São Sebastião** Brazil
103 C8 **São Sebastião, Ilha de** *island* Brazil
163 G4 **São Sebastião, Ponta** *cape* Mozambique
103 C8 **São Sebastião do Paraíso** Brazil
107 H4 **São Sepé** Brazil
103 C8 **São Simão** Brazil
103 B7 **São Simão, Barragem de** *lake* Brazil
128 B5 **São Teotónio** Portugal
159 F4 **São Tomé** São Tomé and Príncipe
159 F5 **São Tomé** *island* São Tomé and Príncipe
103 D8 **São Tomé, Cabo de** *cape* Brazil
159 F4 **São Tomé and Príncipe** *country* Africa
164 4 **São Vicente** *island* Cape Verde
164 2 **São Vicente** Madeira
128 B5 **São Vicente, Cabo de** *cape* Portugal
105 G4 **São Vicente, Serra de** *range* Brazil
91 G3 **Saona, Isla** *island* Dominican Republic
124 C4 **Saône** *watercourse* France
187 E7 **Saoner** Maharashtra India
77 P7 **Saouayane, Pointe** *cape* Quebec Canada
103 C5 **Sapão** *watercourse* Brazil
198 D4 **Saparua** Indonesia
100 E5 **Sapateiro, Lago** *lake* Brazil
197 H6 **Sape, Selak** *strait* Indonesia
159 F3 **Sapele** Nigeria
87 K5 **Sapelo Sound** Georgia USA
88 D3 **Sapién** Mexico
133 B7 **Sapientza** *island* Greece
90 E6 **Sapo, Serranía del** *range* Panama
104 B2 **Saposoa** Peru
215 I7 **Sapphire** Qld Australia
123 K2 **Säppi** *island* Finland
193 I2 **Sapporo** Japan
131 F6 **Sapri** Italy
192 E4 **Sapsi-do** *island* South Korea
121 P4 **Sapsoperä** Finland
195 J6 **Sapu** Philippines
197 G5 **Sapudi** *island* Indonesia
86 C3 **Sapulpa** Oklahoma USA
197 G5 **Sapulu** Indonesia
197 H2 **Sapulut** Malaysia
179 I2 **Sāq** Iran
78 O2 **Saqqamiut** Greenland
182 E7 **Saqqez** Iran
104 C2 **Saquena** Peru
179 J3 **Sar Banāder** Afghanistan
182 J7 **Sar-e Pol** Afghanistan
179 K2 **Sar-E Pol** *admin. area* Afghanistan
108 C5 **Sara** Argentina
158 D2 **Sara** Burkina Faso
104 C4 **Sara Sara, Nevado** *mountain* Peru
194 D4 **Saraburi** Thailand
194 D4 **Saraburi** *admin. area* Thailand
131 E7 **Saraceno, Punta del** *cape* Italy
218 B2 **Sarah, Mount** SA Australia
182 I7 **Sarahs** Turkmenistan
182 D2 **Sarai** Russian Federation
123 K4 **Saraiäi** Latvia
187 F7 **Saraipali** Chhattisgarh India
121 O4 **Säräisniemi** Finland
105 I4 **Saraiva** Brazil
133 B4 **Saraj** Macedonia
121 O4 **Sarajärvi** Finland
130 H5 **Sarajevo** Bosnia and Herzegovina
133 C6 **Sarakiniko, Akra** *cape* Greece
133 D6 **Sarakino** *island* Greece
182 G3 **Saraktash** Russian Federation
86 G5 **Saraland** Alabama USA
123 O3 **Saralog** Russian Federation
181 H4 **Saramati** *mountain* Myanmar
126 E3 **Saran** France
183 K3 **Saran'** Kazakhstan
197 F4 **Saran, Gunung** *mountain* Indonesia
132 B2 **Sáránd** Hungary
195 J6 **Sarangani** Philippines
195 J6 **Sarangani** *island* Philippines
195 J6 **Sarangani Bay** Philippines
195 J6 **Sarangani Islands** Philippines
182 E2 **Saransk** Russian Federation
182 G2 **Sarapul** Russian Federation
135 AC9 **Sarapul'skoye** Russian Federation
191 M3 **Sarapul'skoye** Russian Federation
87 J7 **Sarasota** Florida USA
87 J7 **Sarasota Bay** Florida USA
186 E4 **Saraswati** *watercourse* Uttaranchal India
81 L6 **Saratoga** Wyoming USA
83 O5 **Saratoga Lake** New York USA
197 F3 **Saratok** Malaysia
182 E3 **Saratov** Russian Federation
182 E3 **Saratovskaya Oblast'** *admin. area* Russian Federation
179 J4 **Sarāvān** Iran
197 G3 **Sarawak** *admin. area* Malaysia
136 H5 **Saray** Turkey
154 D6 **Saraya** Senegal
133 F7 **Sarayköy** Turkey
133 E5 **Saraylar** Turkey
125 I1 **Sarbia** Poland
132 A2 **Sárbogárd** Hungary
142 E2 **Sarclet** Highland Scotland UK
82 D8 **Sarcoxie** Missouri USA
183 K7 **Sard Āb** *pass* Afghanistan
179 K3 **Sardāgh** Afghanistan
128 B5 **Sardão, Cabo** *cape* Portugal
186 D5 **Sardarshahr** Rajasthan India
131 C6 **Sardegna** *admin. area* Italy
161 F3 **Sardendida Plain** *plain* Kenya
90 C5 **Sardinal** Costa Rica
Sardinia *see* **Sardegna**
87 K4 **Sardis** Georgia USA
86 G3 **Sardis** Mississippi USA
86 G3 **Sardis Lake** Mississippi USA
120 J3 **Sarektjåkkå** *mountain* Sweden
197 G4 **Sarempaka, Gunung** *mountain* Indonesia
86 E4 **Sarepta** Louisiana USA
127 I3 **Sargans** Switzerland
50 L7 **Sargasso Sea** Atlantic Ocean
104 B1 **Sargento Puño** Peru
85 I1 **Sargents** Colorado USA
179 L3 **Sargodha** Pakistan
183 L4 **Sargumei** Kazakhstan
159 H3 **Sarh** Chad
158 C3 **Sarhala** Côte d'Ivoire
182 G7 **Sārī** Iran
133 E8 **Saría** Greece
133 E8 **Sariá** *island* Greece
123 N5 **Sariai** Lithuania
199 I6 **Sariba Island** Papua New Guinea
198 E4 **Saribi, Tanjung** *cape* Indonesia
84 G5 **Saric** Mexico
222 2 **Sarigan** *island* Northern Mariana Islands
197 F3 **Sarikel** Malaysia
133 E7 **Sarıkemer** Turkey
133 E5 **Sarıköy** Turkey
133 F7 **Sarılar** Turkey
196 B2 **Sarimbun Reservoir** Singapore
215 J6 **Sarina** Qld Australia
215 J6 **Sarina Beach** Qld Australia
129 F3 **Sariñena** Spain
161 G3 **Sarinleey** Somalia
156 C2 **Sarīr Kalanshiyū Ar Ramlī Al Kabīr** *desert* Libya
192 E3 **Sariwŏn** North Korea
133 G5 **Sarıyar Barajı** *lake* Turkey
126 C2 **Sark** *island* Channel Islands UK
120 J3 **Sårkåjaure** *lake* Norway
183 M4 **Sarkand** Kazakhstan
186 C5 **Sarkari Tala** Rajasthan India
121 M3 **Särkijärvi** Finland
121 N2 **Särkijärvi** *lake* Finland
133 G6 **Şarkîkaraağaç** Turkey
123 O2 **Särkisalmi** Finland
133 E6 **Sarköy** Turkey
82 B2 **Sarles** North Dakota USA
199 F4 **Sarmi** Indonesia
108 C3 **Sarmiento** Argentina
108 B5 **Sarmiento, Lago** *lake* Chile
108 B6 **Sarmiento, Monte** *mountain* Chile
132 C3 **Sarmizegetusa** Romania
138 D2 **Sarn** Powys Wales UK
120 H6 **Särna** Sweden
130 E5 **Sarnano** Italy
186 F6 **Sarnath** Uttar Pradesh India
138 C2 **Sarnau** Ceredigion Wales UK
127 I3 **Sarnen** Switzerland
187 E6 **Sarni** Madhya Pradesh India
83 J5 **Sarnia** Ontario Canada
125 G1 **Sarnow** Germany
198 B4 **Saroako** Indonesia
196 D4 **Sarolangun** Indonesia
193 J2 **Saroma-ko** *lake* Japan
199 G6 **Sarore** Indonesia
133 E5 **Saros Körfezi** *bay* Turkey
134 O5 **Saroto** Russian Federation
182 D2 **Sarova** Russian Federation
178 F2 **Sarpol-e Z̧ahāb** Iran
122 F3 **Sarpsborg** Norway
126 C5 **Sarracín** Spain
124 D3 **Sarralbe** France
127 H2 **Sarre-Union** France
127 H2 **Sarrebourg** France
127 H2 **Sarreguemines** France
154 E6 **Sarro** Mali
131 C7 **Sarròch** Sardinia Italy
185 I3 **Sarsai** Mongolia
142 D2 **Sarsgrum** Highland Scotland UK
140 A4 **Sart Cross Roads** Kilkenny Ireland
131 C6 **Sartène** Corsica France
126 D3 **Sarthe** *watercourse* France
133 C5 **Sarti** Greece
127 I4 **Sartirana Lomellina** Italy
123 M5 **Sartų Ežeras** *lake* Lithuania
134 N6 **Sartyn'ya** Russian Federation
133 E6 **Saruhanlı** Turkey
121 M5 **Sarvikas** Finland
121 P5 **Sarvikumpu** Finland
120 H5 **Särvsjö** Sweden
186 D5 **Sarwar** Rajasthan India
123 N5 **Sar"ya** Belarus
182 H4 **Sarybasat** Kazakhstan
136 E4 **Sarych, Mys** *cape* Ukraine
182 H5 **Sarygamysh Köli** *lake* Turkmenistan
183 L3 **Sarykiyak** Kazakhstan
Sarykomey *see* **Sargumei** Kazakhstan
182 I3 **Sarykopa** *lake* Kazakhstan
182 I3 **Saryqopa Koli** *lake* Kazakhstan
183 L4 **Saryshagan** Kazakhstan
183 K4 **Sarysu** *watercourse* Kazakhstan
182 F3 **Saryumir** Kazakhstan
182 I7 **Saryýazy Suwhowdany** *lake* Turkmenistan
126 C3 **Sarzeau** France
107 J2 **Sarzedo** Brazil
183 M3 **Sarzhal** Kazakhstan
133 C4 **Sasa** Macedonia
161 G2 **Sasabeneh** Ethiopia
76 H7 **Sasaginnigak Lake** Manitoba Canada
196 C3 **Sasak** Indonesia
222 8 **Sasamungga** Solomon Islands
197 H6 **Sasar, Tanjung** *cape* Indonesia
186 F6 **Sasaram** Bihar India
105 E5 **Sasasama** Bolivia
132 D2 **Saschiz** Romania
132 C3 **Săsciori** Romania
132 E2 **Sascut** Romania
125 J4 **Sásd** Hungary
192 F5 **Sasebo** Japan
72 I8 **Saskatchewan** *admin. area* Canada
75 S6 **Saskatchewan** *watercourse* Saskatchewan Canada
75 R6 **Saskatoon** Saskatchewan Canada
135 X4 **Saskylakh** Russian Federation
182 D2 **Sasovo** Russian Federation
158 C4 **Sass Town** Liberia
219 R10 **Sassafras** Tas. Australia
121 N3 **Sassali** Finland
121 O3 **Sassalinjärvi** *lake* Finland
158 C4 **Sassandra** Côte d'Ivoire
158 C3 **Sassandra** *watercourse* Côte d'Ivoire
131 C6 **Sassari** Sardinia Italy
124 E5 **Sassello** Italy
199 G6 **Sassie Island** Australia
130 D4 **Sasso Marconi** Italy
130 E5 **Sassoferrato** Italy
183 M4 **Sasyqköl** *lake* Kazakhstan
154 D6 **Satadougou** Mali
186 E6 **Satai** Madhya Pradesh India
187 D7 **Satana** Maharashtra India
132 E1 **Sataniv** Ukraine
81 O8 **Satanta** Kansas USA
128 C3 **Satão** Portugal
187 D8 **Satara** Maharashtra India
135 AB5 **Satara** Russian Federation
222 6 **Satawal** *island* Federated States of Micronesia
160 C3 **Satéma** Democratic Republic of Congo
197 H5 **Satengar** *island* Indonesia
120 K3 **Satihaure** *lake* Sweden
104 C3 **Satipo** Peru
158 D2 **Satiri** Burkina Faso
100 C3 **Sativanorte** Colombia
182 H2 **Satka** Russian Federation
181 F4 **Satkhira** Bangladesh
186 E6 **Satna** Madhya Pradesh India
132 B1 **Sátoraljaújhely** Hungary
133 C5 **Satovcha** Bulgaria
122 F6 **Satow** Germany
222 6 **Satowan** *island* Federated States of Micronesia
183 J4 **Satpayev** Kazakhstan
187 D7 **Satpura Range** Madhya Pradesh India
86 G5 **Satsuma** Alabama USA
192 F6 **Satsunan-shotō** *island* Japan
194 D4 **Sattahip** Thailand
121 M3 **Sattajärvi** Sweden
120 L3 **Satter** Sweden
138 D4 **Satterleigh** Devon England UK
186 D3 **Satti** Jammu and Kashmir India/Pakistan
132 C2 **Satu Mare** Romania
132 C2 **Satu Mare** *admin. area* Romania
197 G4 **Satui** Indonesia
194 D4 **Satuk** Thailand
194 C6 **Satun** *admin. area* Thailand
101 F3 **Sauata** Brazil
197 G5 **Saubi** *island* Indonesia
88 B1 **Sauceda Mountains** Arizona USA
88 D2 **Saucillo** Mexico
122 D3 **Sauda** Norway
120 inset **Sauðárkrókur** Iceland
178 F5 **Saudi Arabia** *country* Middle East
105 G4 **Saueruina** *watercourse* Brazil
82 H5 **Saugatuck** Michigan USA
142 F5 **Saughtree** Scottish Borders Scotland UK
126 F4 **Saugues** France
101 G5 **Sauiá** Brazil
126 D4 **Saujon** France
82 D4 **Sauk Rapids** Minnesota USA
121 P5 **Saukko** Finland
123 L2 **Saukkola** Finland
121 N3 **Saukkoriipi** Finland
198 E4 **Saukorem** Indonesia
143 G2 **Saul** Down Northern Ireland UK
101 H4 **Saül** French Guiana
122 E3 **Sauland** Norway
126 E3 **Sauldre** *watercourse* France
127 I2 **Saulgau** Germany
124 C4 **Saulieu** France
127 G4 **Sault** France
126 D5 **Sault-de-Navailles** France
82 I3 **Sault Ste Marie** Ontario Canada
124 D4 **Saulx** France
127 H3 **Saulxures** France
183 J2 **Saumalkol (Volodarskoye)** Kazakhstan
126 D3 **Saumur** France
121 P5 **Saunajärvi** *lake* Finland
121 O3 **Saunavaara** Finland
58 N1 **Saunders Coast** Antarctica
109 7 **Saunders Island** Falkland Islands
138 C3 **Saundersfoot** Pembrokeshire Wales UK
183 O4 **Saur, Khrebet** *range* Kazakhstan
120 inset **Saurbær** Iceland
199 I5 **Sauren** Papua New Guinea
162 D1 **Saurimo** Angola
90 C4 **Sausa** Honduras
198 E4 **Sausapor** Indonesia
162 C2 **Sautar** Angola
91 I4 **Sauteurs** Grenada
120 L3 **Sautusjärvi** *lake* Sweden
77 S6 **Sauvolles, Lac** *lake* Quebec Canada
126 F4 **Sauxillanges** France
106 F2 **Sauzal** Paraguay
126 E3 **Sauzé-Vaussais** France
130 H4 **Sava** *watercourse* Bosnia and Herzegovina
130 G4 **Sava** *watercourse* Croatia
131 G6 **Sava** Italy
223 12 **Savai'i** *island* Samoa
120 G5 **Savalen** *lake* Norway
158 E3 **Savalou** Benin
77 T7 **Savane** *watercourse* Quebec Canada
163 G3 **Savane** Mozambique
109 1a **Savaneta** Aruba
86 D3 **Savanna** Oklahoma USA
87 K4 **Savannah** Georgia USA
87 J3 **Savannah** *watercourse* South Carolina USA
90 C3 **Savannah Bight** Honduras
194 E3 **Savannakhet** Laos
82 F2 **Savanne** Ontario Canada
76 J7 **Savant Lake** Ontario Canada
120 L5 **Sävar** Sweden
133 E6 **Savaştepe** Turkey
162 C3 **Savate** Angola
126 E5 **Save** *watercourse* France
163 F3 **Save** *watercourse* Zimbabwe
158 E3 **Savé** Benin
178 G2 **Sāveh** Iran
122 G4 **Säven** *lake* Sweden
126 D3 **Savenay** France
126 E5 **Saverdun** France
127 H2 **Saverne** France
121 O5 **Säviä** Finland
127 H3 **Savièse** Switzerland
124 F5 **Savigno** Italy
121 P5 **Savijärvi** Finland
121 P5 **Savikylä** Finland
127 H4 **Savines-le-Lac** France
182 E3 **Savinka** Russian Federation
136 F3 **Savintsy** Ukraine
121 O4 **Saviselkä** Finland
130 H5 **Šavnik** Montenegro
222 8 **Savo** *island* Solomon Islands
76 M8 **Savoff** Ontario Canada
74 K7 **Savona** British Columbia Canada
124 E5 **Savona** Italy
109 1b **Savonet** Netherlands Antilles
123 O2 **Savonlinna** Finland
121 P5 **Savonranta** Finland
72 B6 **Savoonga** Alaska USA
212 F7 **Savory** *watercourse* WA Australia
198 B6 **Savu** Indonesia
198 B6 **Savu** *island* Indonesia
198 B6 **Savu, Kepulauan** *islands* Indonesia
Savu Sea *see* **Sawu, Laut** Indonesia
130 E4 **Savudrija** Croatia
121 P3 **Savukoski** Finland
223 9a **Savusavu Bay** Fiji
162 D3 **Savuti** Botswana
181 H5 **Saw** Myanmar
136 G6 **Şawāb, Wādī aş** Syria
198 D4 **Sawai, Teluk** *bay* Indonesia
186 D6 **Sawai Madhopur** Rajasthan India
197 G4 **Sawan** Indonesia
194 C3 **Sawankhalok** Thailand
81 L7 **Sawatch Range** Colorado USA
75 U4 **Sawbill** Manitoba Canada
77 V6 **Sawbill** Newfoundland and Labrador Canada
179 H6 **Sawdā', As** *island* Oman
178 E6 **Sawdā, Jabal** *mountain* Saudi Arabia
156 E2 **Sawhāj** Egypt
194 B5 **Sawi Bay** Andaman and Nicobar Islands India
158 D3 **Sawla** Ghana
139 F2 **Sawley** Derbyshire England UK
179 H6 **Şawqirah** Oman
139 H2 **Sawston** Cambridgeshire England UK
181 I3 **Sawt-Law** Myanmar
219 K4 **Sawtell** NSW Australia
80 H5 **Sawtooth Range** Idaho USA
80 E2 **Sawtooth Ridge** Washington USA
212 F1 **Sawu** Indonesia
197 I6 **Sawu, Laut (Savu Sea)** Indonesia
81 P8 **Sawyer** Kansas USA
81 O2 **Sawyer** North Dakota USA
129 F4 **Sax** Spain
101 G3 **Saxakalli** Guyana
123 J3 **Saxarfjorden** *bay* Sweden
214 F5 **Saxby** *watercourse* Qld Australia
139 I2 **Saxham Street** Suffolk England UK
141 H3 **Saxilby** Lincolnshire England UK
139 I2 **Saxmundham** Suffolk England UK
127 H2 **Saxon-Sion** France
154 F6 **Say** Mali
155 G6 **Say** Niger
182 G5 **Say-utes** Kazakhstan
54 K6 **Saya de Malha Bank** *underwater feature* Indian Ocean
198 D3 **Sayafi** *island* Indonesia
183 M4 **Sayak** Kazakhstan
187 C7 **Sayan** Gujarat India
183 P3 **Sayano-Shushenskoye Vodokhranilishche** *lake* Russian Federation
183 P3 **Sayanskiy Khrebet** *range* Russian Federation
182 I6 **Saýat** Turkmenistan
90 B3 **Sayaxché** Guatemala
182 E4 **Saykhin** Kazakhstan
157 G5 **Saylac** Somalia
82 E6 **Saylorville Lake** Iowa USA
121 N5 **Säynätsalo** Finland
184 G4 **Sayram Hu** *lake* Xinjiang Uygur Zizhiqu China
86 B3 **Sayre** Oklahoma USA
88 E5 **Sayula** Mexico
89 G5 **Sayula de Alemán** Mexico
178 F7 **Say'ūn** Yemen
74 I7 **Sayward** British Columbia Canada
135 AC5 **Sayylyk** Russian Federation
125 H3 **Sázava** Czech Republic
125 H3 **Sázava** *watercourse* Czech Republic
179 M2 **Sazin** Pakistan
155 F3 **Sbaa** Algeria
155 H1 **Sbeitla** Tunisia
216 G6 **Scaddan** WA Australia
126 C2 **Scaër** France
140 E2 **Scafell Pike** *mountain* England UK
141 H3 **Scalby** East Riding of Yorkshire England UK
131 F7 **Scalea** Italy
131 F7 **Scalea, Capo** *cape* Italy
140 F2 **Scalehouses** Cumbria England UK
140 E2 **Scales** Cumbria England UK
142 inset **Scalloway** Shetland Scotland UK
142 C3 **Scalpay** *island* Scotland UK
141 H3 **Scamblesby** Lincolnshire England UK
72 C6 **Scammon Bay** Alaska USA
142 C4 **Scamodale** Highland Scotland UK
141 H2 **Scampston** North Yorkshire England UK
75 O7 **Scandia** Alberta Canada
160 B5 **Scandica** Angola
131 C5 **Scandola, Pointe** *cape* Corsica France
130 D5 **Scansano** Italy
142 E2 **Scapa Flow** *bay* Scotland UK
80 D4 **Scappoose** Oregon USA
142 F1 **Scar** Orkney Islands Scotland UK
142 C4 **Scarba** *island* Scotland UK
109 inset 9 **Scarborough** Trinidad and Tobago
141 H2 **Scarborough** North Yorkshire England UK
195 H4 **Scarborough Shoal** *island* Philippines
143 B5 **Scariff Island** Ireland
142 B4 **Scarinish** Highland Scotland UK
142 A2 **Scarp** *island* Scotland UK
126 F1 **Scarpe** *watercourse* France
143 D4 **Scarriff** Ireland
141 H3 **Scartho** North East Lincolnshire England UK
143 F2 **Scarva** Armagh Northern Ireland UK
79 I9 **Scatarie Island** Nova Scotia Canada
142 D3 **Scatraig** Highland Scotland UK
223 9 **Scatterbreak Channel** *strait* Fiji
141 H3 **Scawby** North Lincolnshire England UK
215 J6 **Scawfell Island** Qld Australia
218 B5 **Sceale Bay** SA Australia
75 Q7 **Sceptre** Saskatchewan Canada
124 F1 **Schaalsee** *lake* Germany
127 I3 **Schaffhausen** Switzerland
124 C1 **Schagen** Netherlands
124 G3 **Schardenberg** Austria
124 G3 **Schärding** Austria
122 E6 **Scharhörn** *island* Germany
127 I3 **Schattdorf** Switzerland
82 G5 **Schaumburg** Illinois USA
124 E3 **Schefflenz** Germany
125 H3 **Scheibbs** Austria
132 C3 **Schela** Romania
80 H7 **Schell Creek Range** Nevada USA
124 C2 **Schelle** Belgium
83 O5 **Schenectady** New York USA
82 H6 **Schererville** Indiana USA
86 B6 **Schertz** Texas USA
124 E4 **Schesaplana** *mountain* Austria/Switzerland
127 J2 **Scheßlitz** Germany
142 D4 **Schiehallion** *mountain* Scotland UK
127 I3 **Schiers** Switzerland
124 F1 **Schilde** *watercourse* Germany
127 H2 **Schiltigheim** France
124 D3 **Schirmeck** France
131 F8 **Schisò, Capo** *cape* Italy
125 G4 **Schladming** Austria
127 K3 **Schleching** Germany
122 E5 **Schlei** *bay* Germany
127 H1 **Schleiden** Germany
199 I4 **Schleinitz Range** Papua New Guinea
124 F2 **Schleiz** Germany
122 E5 **Schleswig-Holstein** *admin. area* Germany
124 F2 **Schleusingen** Germany
124 E2 **Schlitz** Germany
109 14 **Schœlcher** Martinique
85 M1 **Schoenchen** Kansas USA
133 D7 **Schoinoussa** *island* Greece
83 L4 **Schomberg** Ontario Canada
124 G3 **Schomberg** Germany
125 G1 **Schöneiche Berlin** Germany
124 G3 **Schönsee** Germany
83 Q4 **Schoodic Lake** Maine USA
124 C1 **Schoorl** Netherlands
124 E3 **Schorndorf** Germany
109 1b **Schottegat** *bay* Netherlands Antilles
219 S11 **Schouten Island** Tas. Australia
199 H5 **Schrader Range** Papua New Guinea
127 I2 **Schramberg** Germany
125 H3 **Schrems** Austria
83 O5 **Schroon Lake** New York USA
124 E4 **Schruns** Austria
75 P7 **Schuler** Alberta Canada
143 C5 **Schull** Ireland
86 D3 **Schulter** Oklahoma USA
84 C1 **Schurz** Nevada USA
81 Q6 **Schuyler** Nebraska USA
124 F3 **Schwabach** Germany
124 E3 **Schwäbisch Hall** Germany
124 E2 **Schwalm** *watercourse* Germany
127 I3 **Schwanden** Switzerland
197 G4 **Schwaner, Pegunungan** *range* Indonesia
122 E5 **Schwansen** *peninsula* Germany
58 D2 **Schwartz Range** Antarctica
124 F2 **Schwarza** *watercourse* Germany
124 G2 **Schwarze Elster** *watercourse* Germany
127 J3 **Schwaz** Austria
125 H1 **Schwedt** Germany
124 D3 **Schweich** Germany
124 F2 **Schweinfurt** Germany
127 I3 **Schwyz** Switzerland
131 E8 **Sciacca** Italy
142 D2 **Sciberscross** Highland Scotland UK
131 F8 **Scicli** Italy
126 E2 **Scie** *watercourse* France
82 I8 **Science Hill** Kentucky USA
131 F7 **Scilla** Italy
82 J7 **Scioto** *watercourse* Ohio USA
84 F1 **Scipio** Utah USA
80 I7 **Scipio Lake** Utah USA
131 C6 **Scirocco, Punta di** *cape* Sardinia Italy
75 U7 **Sclater** Manitoba Canada
138 C3 **Scleddau** Pembrokeshire Wales UK
81 M2 **Scobey** Montana USA
80 J7 **Scofield Reservoir** Utah USA
131 C6 **Scoglietti, Punta** *cape* Sardinia Italy
140 B2 **Scolboa** Antrim Northern Ireland UK
139 I2 **Scole** Norfolk England UK
131 C6 **Scomunica, Punta della** *mountain* Sardinia Italy
219 J5 **Scone** NSW Australia
142 B3 **Sconser** Highland Scotland UK
86 G4 **Scooba** Mississippi USA
131 C5 **Scopa, Punta alla** *cape* Corsica France
124 E5 **Scopello** Italy
73 Q4 **Scoresby Land** *plain* Greenland
126 C2 **Scorff** *watercourse* France
141 G2 **Scotch Corner** North Yorkshire England UK
143 F2 **Scotch Street** Armagh Northern Ireland UK
143 E2 **Scotch Town** Omagh Northern Ireland UK
141 H3 **Scothern** Lincolnshire England UK
83 L4 **Scotia** Ontario Canada
81 P6 **Scotia** Nebraska USA
83 O5 **Scotia** New York USA
58 U3 **Scotia Sea** Antarctica
142 **Scotland** *admin. area* UK
86 B4 **Scotland** Texas USA
75 Q8 **Scotsguard** Saskatchewan Canada
219 I1 **Scott** *watercourse* Qld Australia
75 Q6 **Scott** Saskatchewan Canada
86 E5 **Scott** Louisiana USA
74 G7 **Scott, Cape** British Columbia Canada
215 J6 **Scott, Mount** Qld Australia
58 L1 **Scott Base (New Zealand)** *research station* Antarctica
81 O7 **Scott City** Kansas USA
58 K1 **Scott Coast** Antarctica
58 G2 **Scott Glacier** Antarctica
73 L4 **Scott Inlet** Nunavut Canada
74 G7 **Scott Islands** British Columbia Canada
75 R3 **Scott Lake** Saskatchewan Canada
58 D2 **Scott Mountains** Antarctica
55 Q6 **Scott Plateau** *underwater feature* Indian Ocean
212 F3 **Scott Reef** WA Australia
141 H3 **Scotter** Lincolnshire England UK
142 F5 **Scottish Borders** *admin. area* Scotland UK
141 G2 **Scotton** North Yorkshire England UK
219 K4 **Scotts Head** NSW Australia
109 15 **Scotts Head** *cape* Dominica
215 J7 **Scotts Peak** Qld Australia
80 D8 **Scotts Valley** California USA
81 N6 **Scottsbluff** Nebraska USA
87 H3 **Scottsboro** Alabama USA
82 I7 **Scottsburg** Indiana USA
219 R10 **Scottsdale** Tas. Australia
84 G4 **Scottsdale** Arizona USA
83 L8 **Scottsville** Virginia USA
82 H5 **Scottville** Michigan USA
142 C2 **Scourie** Highland Scotland UK
142 inset **Scousburgh** Shetland Scotland UK
143 E3 **Scrabby** Cavan Ireland
142 E2 **Scrabster** Highland Scotland UK
82 D5 **Scranton** Iowa USA
81 N3 **Scranton** North Dakota USA
83 N6 **Scranton** Pennsylvania USA
139 I2 **Scratby** Norfolk England UK
87 K5 **Screven** Georgia USA
199 G4 **Screw** *watercourse* Papua New Guinea
139 F2 **Scropton** Derbyshire England UK
218 D5 **Scrub, Mount** SA Australia
109 20 **Scrub Island** Anguilla
218 B5 **Scrubby Peak** SA Australia
83 L4 **Scugog, Lake** Ontario Canada
141 H3 **Scunthorpe** North Lincolnshire England UK
127 J3 **Scuol** Switzerland
142 A3 **Scurrival Point** Scotland UK
132 D3 **Scurtu Mare** Romania
132 A4 **Scutari, Lake** Albania
132 E3 **Scutelnici** Romania
82 F2 **Sea Gull Lake** Minnesota USA
83 N7 **Sea Isle City** New Jersey USA
109 7 **Sea Lion Islands** Falkland Islands
139 I2 **Sea Palling** Norfolk England UK
143 D5 **Sea View** Ireland
103 D6 **Seabra** Brazil
216 F5 **Seabrook, Lake** WA Australia
87 K4 **Seabrook Island** South Carolina USA
143 E2 **Seacor** Ireland
86 C6 **Seadrift** Texas USA
139 H4 **Seaford** East Sussex England UK
215 J6 **Seaforth** Qld Australia
86 C4 **Seagoville** Texas USA
141 G2 **Seaham** Durham England UK
77 W6 **Seahorse** Newfoundland and Labrador Canada
76 H3 **Seal** *watercourse* Manitoba Canada
58 X2 **Seal Bay** Antarctica
164 5c **Seal Bay** St Helena
79 J8 **Seal Cove** Newfoundland and Labrador Canada
78 H5 **Seal Lake** Newfoundland and Labrador Canada
86 C6 **Sealy** Texas USA
142 D5 **Seamill** North Ayrshire Scotland UK
84 E3 **Searchlight** Nevada USA
82 I3 **Searchmont** Ontario Canada
86 F3 **Searcy** Arkansas USA
84 D3 **Searles** California USA
84 D3 **Searles Lake** California USA
79 D10 **Searsport** Maine USA
140 E2 **Seascale** Cumbria England UK
80 E8 **Seaside** California USA
80 D4 **Seaside** Oregon USA
140 E2 **Seathwaite** Cumbria England UK
138 D4 **Seaton** Devon England UK
139 G2 **Seaton** Rutland England UK
141 G1 **Seaton Delaval** Northumberland England UK
58 D2 **Seaton Glacier** Antarctica
141 H3 **Seaton Ross** East Riding of Yorkshire England UK
109 18 **Seatons** Antigua and Barbuda
80 D3 **Seattle** Washington USA
141 G2 **Seave Green** North Yorkshire England UK
139 F4 **Seaview** Isle of Wight England UK
219 K4 **Seaview, Mount** NSW Australia
221 E6 **Seaward Kaikoura Range** New Zealand
198 B6 **Seba** Indonesia
83 P5 **Sebago Lake** Maine USA
197 H4 **Sebakung** Indonesia
197 G4 **Sebamban** Indonesia
197 G4 **Sebangan, Teluk** *bay* Indonesia
196 E3 **Sebangka** *island* Indonesia
196 C5 **Sebarok, Pulau** *island* Singapore
78 H6 **Sebaskachu** *watercourse* Newfoundland and Labrador Canada
106 F4 **Sebastián Elcano** Argentina
88 B2 **Sebastián Vizcaíno, Bahía** *bay* Mexico
83 Q4 **Sebasticook Lake** Maine USA
Sebastopol *see* **Sevastopol'** Ukraine
197 F4 **Sebayan, Bukit** *mountain* Indonesia
156 F4 **Sebderat** Eritrea
155 F2 **Sebdou** Algeria
83 Q4 **Sebec Lake** Maine USA
154 E6 **Sébékoro** Mali
133 G5 **Seben** Turkey
125 L5 **Sebeş** Romania
125 K4 **Sebes-Körös** *watercourse* Hungary
196 E5 **Sebesi** *island* Indonesia

132 C2 **Sebiş** Romania
196 D4 **Seblat, Gunung** *mountain* Indonesia
83 Q4 **Seboeis Lake** Maine USA
83 Q4 **Seboomook Lake** Maine USA
82 H8 **Sebree** Kentucky USA
87 K7 **Sebring** Florida USA
195 J6 **Sebu** Philippines
197 G3 **Sebuah** Malaysia
101 F3 **Sebucán** Venezuela
197 H4 **Sebuku** *island* Indonesia
197 H2 **Sebuku** *watercourse* Indonesia
197 H3 **Sebuku, Teluk** *bay* Indonesia
197 F3 **Sebuyau** Malaysia
198 E4 **Sebyar** *watercourse* Indonesia
108 B4 **Seca, Laguna** *lake* Argentina
88 D2 **Sección Alsacia** Mexico
108 C5 **Sección Gap** Argentina
108 B3 **Sección Tapera** Chile
125 J2 **Secemin** Poland
127 G2 **Séchault** France
77 U6 **Séchelles, Lac** *lake* Quebec Canada
74 J8 **Sechelt** British Columbia Canada
104 A2 **Sechura** Peru
104 A2 **Sechura, Ensenada de** *bay* Peru
126 F1 **Seclin** France
84 G3 **Second Mesa** Arizona USA
126 D3 **Secondigny** France
164 4 **Secos, Ilhéus** *islands* Cape Verde
221 B7 **Secretary Island** New Zealand
187 E8 **Secunderabad** Andhra Pradesh India
132 B2 **Secusigiu** Romania
123 M4 **Seda** Latvia
82 E7 **Sedalia** Missouri USA
218 D6 **Sedan** SA Australia
127 G2 **Sedan** France
82 C8 **Sedan** Kansas USA
85 K2 **Sedan** New Mexico USA
214 F6 **Sedan Dip** Qld Australia
141 F2 **Sedbergh** Cumbria England UK
143 D4 **Sedboro** Tipperary Ireland
221 F5 **Seddon** New Zealand
127 G4 **Séderon** France
215 I7 **Sedgeford** Qld Australia
81 Q8 **Sedgwick** Kansas USA
154 C6 **Sédhiou** Senegal
124 G4 **Sedico** Italy
75 S7 **Sedley** Saskatchewan Canada
84 G3 **Sedona** Arizona USA
155 H1 **Sédrata** Algeria
80 D2 **Sedro-Woolley** Washington USA
197 H3 **Sedulang** Indonesia
123 L5 **Šeduva** Lithuania
126 D2 **Sée** *watercourse* France
75 N7 **Seebe** Alberta Canada
76 I6 **Seeber Lake** Ontario Canada
124 G4 **Seeboden** Austria
127 I3 **Seedorf** Switzerland
127 J3 **Seefeld in Tirol** Austria
124 F1 **Seehausen** Germany
58 R1 **Seelig, Mount** *mountain* Antarctica
217 I5 **Seemore Downs** WA Australia
126 E2 **Sées** France
124 F2 **Seesen** Germany
133 E6 **Seferihisar** Turkey
154 E6 **Séféto** Mali
179 G4 **Sefīdār, Kūh-e** *mountain* Iran
132 B3 **Sefkerin** Serbia
162 E4 **Sefophe** Botswana
154 F2 **Sefrou** Morocco
140 F3 **Sefton** *admin. area* England UK
221 E6 **Sefton** New Zealand
221 D6 **Sefton, Mount** New Zealand
161 G2 **Segag** Ethiopia
154 D6 **Ségala** Mali
120 G6 **Segalstad** Norway
197 H2 **Segama** *watercourse* Malaysia
196 D3 **Segamat** Malaysia
125 L5 **Segarcea** Romania
159 E2 **Ségbana** Benin
198 E4 **Sege** Indonesia
198 A5 **Segeri** Indonesia
134 H6 **Segezha** Russian Federation
129 I6 **Seggana** Algeria
222 8 **Seghe** Solomon Islands
129 H5 **Seghouane** Algeria
120 L1 **Seglvik** Norway
131 E6 **Segni** Italy
181 G2 **Segong** Xizang Zizhiqu China
129 F4 **Segorbe** Spain
154 E6 **Ségou** Mali
154 E6 **Ségou** *admin. area* Mali
100 C3 **Segovia** Colombia
121 R5 **Segozerskoye, Ozero** *lake* Russian Federation
129 G3 **Segre** *watercourse* Spain
126 E2 **Ségrie** France
135 AM8 **Seguam Island** Alaska USA
155 I4 **Séguédiné** Niger
158 C3 **Séguéla** Côte d'Ivoire
158 D2 **Séguénéga** Burkina Faso
86 C6 **Seguin** Texas USA
88 B3 **Segunda Etapa** Mexico
106 F4 **Segundo** *watercourse* Argentina
128 F4 **Segura** *watercourse* Spain
128 E5 **Segura, Sierra de** *range* Spain
107 G6 **Segurola** Argentina
162 D4 **Sehithwa** Botswana
124 E1 **Sehnde** Germany
197 J4 **Seho** *island* Indonesia
186 D6 **Sehore** Madhya Pradesh India
199 I6 **Sehulea** Papua New Guinea
179 K4 **Sehwan** Pakistan
128 C3 **Seia** Portugal
129 J6 **Seïar** Algeria
81 N7 **Seibert** Colorado USA
126 D3 **Seiche** *watercourse* France
120 G4 **Seierstad** Norway
77 U6 **Seignelay** *watercourse* Quebec Canada
126 D5 **Seignosse** France
181 H5 **Seikpyu** Myanmar
121 M1 **Seiland** *island* Norway
121 M1 **Seilandsjøkelen** *bay* Norway
126 E4 **Seilhac** France
127 H2 **Seille** *watercourse* France
122 C2 **Seim** Norway
132 F3 **Seimeni** Romania
126 B2 **Sein, Île de** *island* France
121 M5 **Seinäjärvi** *lake* Finland
121 M5 **Seinäjoki** Finland
121 M5 **Seinäjoki** *watercourse* Finland
126 E2 **Seine** *watercourse* France
126 D2 **Seine, Baie de la** *bay* France
50 Q6 **Seine Abyssal Plain** *underwater feature* Atlantic Ocean
50 Q6 **Seine Seamount** *underwater feature* Atlantic Ocean
132 C2 **Seini** Romania
121 O3 **Seipäjärvi** Finland
197 G4 **Seipinang** Indonesia
123 L5 **Seirijis** *lake* Lithuania
139 E2 **Seisdon** Staffordshire England UK
214 G1 **Seisia** Qld Australia
197 H4 **Sejaka** Indonesia
196 F3 **Sejangkung** Indonesia
122 F5 **Sejerby** Denmark
122 F5 **Sejerø** *island* Denmark
122 F5 **Sejerø Bugt** *bay* Denmark
104 E4 **Sejeruma, Serranía** *range* Bolivia
123 L5 **Sejny** Poland
194 D3 **Seka** Thailand
197 F3 **Sekadau** Indonesia
197 H3 **Sekatak, Teluk** *bay* Indonesia
196 D4 **Sekayu** Indonesia
188 C2 **Seke** Sichuan China
133 F7 **Seki** *watercourse* Turkey
189 I3 **Sekibi-sho** *island* Japan
121 L2 **Sekkemo** Norway
181 G4 **Sekmai Bazar** Manipur India
162 D4 **Sekoma** Botswana
158 D4 **Sekondi** Ghana
157 F5 **Sek'ot'a** Ethiopia
196 D3 **Sekudai** Malaysia
196 F3 **Sekura** Indonesia
120 G5 **Sela** Norway
80 E3 **Selah** Washington USA
196 F3 **Selakau** Indonesia
197 F3 **Selalang** Malaysia
196 D3 **Selangor** *admin. area* Malaysia
199 I4 **Selapiu Island** Papua New Guinea
131 C7 **Selargius** Sardinia Italy
197 G5 **Selatan, Tanjung** *cape* Indonesia
196 D4 **Selatpanjang** Indonesia
72 C5 **Selawik** Alaska USA
197 I5 **Selayar** *island* Indonesia
197 I5 **Selayar, Selat** *strait* Indonesia
124 G2 **Selb** Germany
122 C2 **Selbjørn** *island* Norway
120 G5 **Selbustrand** Norway
141 G3 **Selby** North Yorkshire England UK
81 O4 **Selby** South Dakota USA
83 N7 **Selbyville** Delaware USA
132 A4 **Selcë** Albania
133 E7 **Selçuk** Turkey
81 O7 **Selden** Kansas USA
72 D7 **Seldovia** Alaska USA
198 D4 **Sele** Indonesia
131 F6 **Sele** *watercourse* Italy
162 E4 **Selebi Phikwe** Botswana
161 F5 **Selegu** *mountain* Tanzania
135 AB8 **Selemdzhinsk** Russian Federation
191 L2 **Selemdzhinsk** Russian Federation
191 M1 **Selemdzhinskiy Khrebet** *range* Russian Federation
133 F6 **Selendi** Turkey
160 B4 **Selenge** Democratic Republic of Congo
190 E2 **Selenge** Mongolia
190 F2 **Selenge** *admin. area* Mongolia
190 E2 **Selenge Moron** *watercourse* Mongolia
133 A5 **Selenicë** Albania
135 AD5 **Selennyakh** *watercourse* Russian Federation
127 H2 **Sélestat** France
120 L4 **Selet** Sweden
123 O2 **Seleznëvo** Russian Federation
123 P5 **Selezni** Russian Federation
120 inset **Selfoss** Iceland
81 O3 **Selfridge** North Dakota USA
154 D5 **Sélibabi** Mauritania
84 F3 **Seligman** Arizona USA
82 E8 **Seligman** Missouri USA
123 O4 **Selikhnovo** Russian Federation
159 I4 **Sélim** Central African Republic
156 D3 **Selima** *spring* Sudan
135 AB7 **Selingde** Russian Federation
158 C2 **Sélingué, Lac de** *lake* Mali
154 D6 **Selinnkegni** Mali
133 C4 **Selishte** Bulgaria
123 M3 **Seliste** Estonia
132 C4 **Selište** Serbia
196 E4 **Seliu** *island* Indonesia
122 C1 **Selje** Norway
122 D3 **Seljestad** Norway
122 E3 **Seljordsvatnet** *lake* Norway
121 P3 **Selkälä** Finland
76 G7 **Selkirk** Manitoba Canada
74 L7 **Selkirk Mountains** British Columbia/Idaho Canada/USA
138 E3 **Sellack** Herefordshire England UK
219 S10 **Sellars Lagoon** Tas. Australia
91 F3 **Selle, Massif de la** *range* Haiti
126 E3 **Selles** France
127 G3 **Sellières** France
139 I3 **Sellindge** Kent England UK
84 G5 **Sells** Arizona USA
83 K3 **Sellwood** Ontario Canada
135 AC4 **Sellyakhskaya Guba** *bay* Russian Federation
125 I5 **Sellye** Hungary
86 H4 **Selma** Alabama USA
84 C2 **Selma** California USA
87 L3 **Selma** North Carolina USA
86 G3 **Selmer** Tennessee USA
130 G3 **Selnica** Croatia
125 I4 **Selo** Slovenia
126 E3 **Selommes** France
197 H6 **Selong** Indonesia
127 G3 **Selongey** France
139 G4 **Selsey** West Sussex England UK
139 G4 **Selsey Bill** *cape* England UK
120 J5 **Seltjäm/Seltjärn** Sweden
198 D5 **Selu** *island* Indonesia
196 E2 **Seluan** *island* Indonesia
126 D2 **Sélune** *watercourse* France
127 J3 **Selva** Italy
120 F5 **Selva** Norway
105 E3 **Selvas** *region* Brazil
101 E3 **Selvas** *region* Venezuela
80 H3 **Selway** *watercourse* Idaho USA
214 F6 **Selwyn** Qld Australia
75 S2 **Selwyn Lake** Northwest Territories Canada
72 I7 **Selwyn Lake** Saskatchewan Canada
74 F1 **Selwyn Mountains** Northwest Territories/Yukon Territory Canada
222 7 **Selwyn Strait** Vanuatu
132 D2 **Selyatyn** Ukraine
125 H4 **Selzthal** Austria
163 F3 **Semacueza** Mozambique
198 E4 **Semai** *island* Indonesia
196 C5 **Semakau, Pulau** *island* Singapore
196 E5 **Semangka, Teluk** *bay* Indonesia
75 S7 **Semans** Saskatchewan Canada
197 F5 **Semarang** Indonesia
197 H4 **Semaras** Indonesia
186 F6 **Semaria** Chhattisgarh India
197 F3 **Sematan** Malaysia
197 I6 **Semau** *island* Indonesia
197 H4 **Semayang, Danau** *lake* Indonesia
160 E4 **Sembabule** Uganda
197 H3 **Sembakung** *watercourse* Indonesia
196 C2 **Sembawang** *admin. area* Singapore
159 G4 **Sembé** Congo
136 H6 **Semdinli** *mountain* Turkey
125 J5 **Semeljci** Croatia
182 D2 **Semenov** Russian Federation
121 T6 **Semënovo** Russian Federation
196 D3 **Semenyih** Malaysia
139 H2 **Semer** Suffolk England UK
197 G6 **Semeru, Gunung** *volcano* Indonesia
133 E5 **Semetli** Turkey
125 H5 **Semič** Slovenia
135 AJ8 **Semichi Islands** Alaska USA
72 D7 **Semidi Islands** Alaska USA
197 G4 **Semilat** Indonesia
136 F2 **Semiluki** Russian Federation
81 L5 **Seminoe Reservoir** Wyoming USA
85 K4 **Seminole** Texas USA
87 I5 **Seminole, Lake** Georgia USA
183 M3 **Semipalatinsk** Kazakhstan
195 I4 **Semirara** *island* Philippines
178 G3 **Semiron** Iran
197 F3 **Semitau** Indonesia
183 L3 **Semizbugy** Kazakhstan
139 E3 **Semley** Wiltshire England UK
76 H5 **Semmens Lake** Manitoba Canada
179 I2 **Semnān** Iran
182 G7 **Semnān** *admin. area* Iran
197 H2 **Sempang Mangayau, Tanjong** *cape* Malaysia
197 H2 **Semporna** Malaysia
197 G6 **Sempu** *island* Indonesia
127 G3 **Semur-en-Auxios** France
194 E4 **Sên** *watercourse* Cambodia
104 D3 **Sena Madureira** Brazil
103 B7 **Senador Canedo** Brazil
104 E3 **Senador Guiomard** Brazil
102 B3 **Senador José Porfírio** Brazil
102 E4 **Senador Pompeu** Brazil
157 F5 **Sen'afe** Eritrea
197 H2 **Senaja** Malaysia
196 B6 **Senang, Pulau** *island* Singapore
162 D3 **Senanga** Zambia
197 F3 **Senaning** Indonesia
129 I2 **Sénas** France
193 I3 **Sendai** Japan
124 D2 **Senden** Germany
187 D7 **Sendhwa** Madhya Pradesh India
196 D3 **Senebui, Tanjung** *cape* Indonesia
125 I3 **Senec** Slovakia
81 Q7 **Seneca** Kansas USA
82 D8 **Seneca** Missouri USA
80 F4 **Seneca** Oregon USA
83 M5 **Seneca Lake** New York USA
127 G1 **Seneffe** Belgium
154 D6 **Senegal** *country* Africa
154 D5 **Sénégal** *lake* Mauritania
131 C6 **Senetosa, Capu di** *cape* Corsica France
82 I3 **Seney** Michigan USA
160 E5 **Senga Hill** Zambia
197 H3 **Sengata** Indonesia
161 E4 **Sengerema** Tanzania
199 G4 **Senggi** Indonesia
182 E2 **Sengiley** Russian Federation
182 F5 **Sengirli, Mys** *cape* Kazakhstan
196 D3 **Sengkang** *admin. area* Singapore
108 C3 **Senguer** *watercourse* Argentina
162 E3 **Sengwa** *watercourse* Zimbabwe
125 I3 **Senica** Slovakia
106 D6 **Senillosa** Argentina
133 G6 **Senirkent** Turkey
131 G6 **Senise** Italy
130 F4 **Senj** Croatia
120 J2 **Senja** *island* Norway
132 B4 **Senje** Serbia
189 I3 **Senkaku-shotō** *disputed territory* South China Sea
158 C3 **Senko** Guinea
75 Q6 **Senlac** Saskatchewan Canada
162 D5 **Senlac** South Africa
126 F2 **Senlis** France
194 E4 **Senmonorom** Cambodia
156 E5 **Sennar** Sudan
156 E5 **Sennar** *admin. area* Sudan
121 S6 **Sennaya Guba** Russian Federation
138 B4 **Sennen** Cornwall England UK
132 D4 **Sennik** Bulgaria
123 O5 **Senno** Belarus
132 F4 **Senokos** Bulgaria
127 H2 **Senones** France
89 H5 **Señor** Mexico
183 O3 **Senrinskiy Khrebet** *range* Russian Federation
124 B3 **Sens** France
90 B4 **Sensuntepeque** El Salvador
183 N3 **Sentas** Kazakhstan
125 H4 **Šentilj** Slovenia
84 F4 **Sentinel** Arizona USA
86 B3 **Sentinel** Oklahoma USA
217 M3 **Sentinel Hill** SA Australia
74 J5 **Sentinel Peak** British Columbia Canada
58 S1 **Sentinel Range** Antarctica
196 D5 **Sentosa** *island* Singapore
76 I2 **Sentry Island** Nunavut Canada
199 G4 **Senu** *watercourse* Papua New Guinea
159 F4 **Senye** Equatorial Guinea
197 H3 **Senyiur** Indonesia
192 F4 **Seongju** South Korea
187 E6 **Seoni** Madhya Pradesh India
187 E6 **Seoni Chhapara** Madhya Pradesh India
187 D6 **Seoni Malwa** Madhya Pradesh India
Seoul *see* **Sŏul** South Korea
197 H5 **Sepanjang** *island* Indonesia
85 H4 **Separ** New Mexico USA
221 E5 **Separation Point** New Zealand
197 H3 **Sepasu** Indonesia
105 E3 **Sepatini** *watercourse* Brazil
197 F3 **Sepauk** Indonesia
126 F3 **Sépeaux** France
222 8 **Sepi** *island* Solomon Islands
199 G5 **Sepik** *watercourse* Papua New Guinea
192 E3 **Sep'o** North Korea
123 K5 **Sępopol** Poland
181 G3 **Seppa** Arunachal Pradesh India
77 V7 **Sept-Îles** Quebec Canada
91 G3 **Septentrional, Cordillera** *range* Dominican Republic
162 D3 **Sepupa** Botswana
196 E5 **Seputih** *watercourse* Indonesia
87 I3 **Sequatchie** *watercourse* Tennessee USA
128 D3 **Sequillo** *watercourse* Spain
198 D5 **Sera** *island* Indonesia
182 D3 **Serafimovich** Russian Federation
85 J3 **Serafina** New Mexico USA
127 G1 **Seraing** Belgium
198 D4 **Seram** *island* Indonesia
197 K4 **Seram, Laut (Ceram Sea)** Indonesia
198 F4 **Serami** Indonesia
196 E5 **Serang** Indonesia
196 D3 **Serangoon** *admin. area* Singapore
196 E3 **Serangoon Harbour** Singapore
196 F3 **Serasan** *island* Indonesia
196 F3 **Serasan, Selat** *strait* Indonesia
130 D5 **Seravezza** Italy
196 F3 **Seraya** *island* Indonesia
132 B3 **Serbia** *country* Europe
132 E1 **Serbinovtsy** Ukraine
132 G2 **Serbka** Ukraine
181 G4 **Serchhip** Mizoram India
157 G5 **Serdo** Ethiopia
182 D3 **Serdobsk** Russian Federation
72 B5 **Serdtse-Kamen', Mys** *cape* Russian Federation
193 J2 **Serebryanoye, Ozero** *lake* Russian Federation
182 D1 **Sereda** Russian Federation
132 C1 **Seredne** Ukraine
126 F3 **Serein** *watercourse* France
154 C6 **Serekunda** Gambia
196 D3 **Seremban** Malaysia
128 D4 **Serena, Embalse de la** *lake* Spain
128 D4 **Serena, La** *region* Spain
161 E4 **Serengeti Plain** *plain* Tanzania
162 F2 **Serenje** Zambia
126 C3 **Sérent** France
105 E6 **Sereré** Bolivia
132 D1 **Seret** *watercourse* Ukraine
133 D7 **Serfopoula** *island* Greece
182 E2 **Sergach** Russian Federation
191 H3 **Sergelen** Mongolia
121 T5 **Sergievo** Russian Federation
134 O6 **Serginskiy** Russian Federation
103 E5 **Sergipe** *admin. area* Brazil
132 G2 **Sergiyivka** Ukraine
121 T3 **Sergozero, Ozero** *lake* Russian Federation
197 G2 **Seria** Brunei
197 F3 **Serian** Malaysia
196 E5 **Seribu, Kepulauan** *islands* Indonesia
196 C3 **Seribudolok** Indonesia
133 D7 **Serifos** *island* Greece
78 D5 **Sérigny** *watercourse* Quebec Canada
78 D5 **Sérigny, Lac** *lake* Quebec Canada
159 I2 **Seringa** *watercourse* Central African Republic
102 B4 **Seringa, Serra da** *range* Brazil
104 D3 **Seringal Sacado** Brazil
212 G2 **Seringapatam Reef** WA Australia
133 F7 **Serinhisar** Turkey
199 G6 **Serki** Papua New Guinea
124 B3 **Sermaises** France
198 D6 **Sermata** *island* Indonesia
198 D6 **Sermata, Kepulauan** *islands* Indonesia
73 M3 **Sermersuaq (Humboldt Gletscher)** *glacier* Greenland
78 N2 **Sermersuut** *island* Greenland
78 N2 **Sermilik** *bay* Greenland
128 C3 **Sernancelhe** Portugal
182 F2 **Sernovodsk** Russian Federation
182 F2 **Sernur** Russian Federation
125 K1 **Serock** Poland
109 1a **Seroe Colorado** Aruba
128 E5 **Serón** Spain
162 D3 **Seronga** Botswana
129 G3 **Seròs** Spain
134 N7 **Serov** Russian Federation
162 E4 **Serowe** Botswana
128 C5 **Serpa** Portugal
101 G5 **Serpa, Ilha de** *island* Brazil
83 P2 **Serpent** *watercourse* Quebec Canada
154 E6 **Serpent, Vallée du** *valley* Mali
217 K4 **Serpentine Lakes** SA Australia
109 inset 9 **Serpent's Mouth** *strait* Trinidad and Tobago
136 F1 **Serpukhov** Russian Federation
103 D8 **Serra** Brazil
103 B6 **Serra da Mesa, Represa** *lake* Brazil
131 E8 **Serradifalco** Italy
131 C7 **Serramanna** Sardinia Italy
103 C8 **Serrana** Brazil
90 D4 **Serrana Bank** *reef* Colombia
90 E4 **Serranilla Bank** *underwater feature* Caribbean Sea
164 1b **Serrata** Azores
126 F2 **Serre** *watercourse* France
127 G4 **Serres** France
133 C5 **Serres** Greece
106 E4 **Serrezuela** Argentina
103 E5 **Serrinha** Brazil
105 H6 **Serrito** Brazil
103 D7 **Serro** Brazil
131 G7 **Sersale** Italy
128 B4 **Sertã** Portugal
102 E5 **Sertânia** Brazil
103 B8 **Sertanópolis** Brazil
196 E5 **Sertung** *island* Indonesia
198 D5 **Serua** *island* Indonesia
196 C2 **Seruai** Indonesia
196 F4 **Serutu** *island* Indonesia
197 G4 **Seruyan** *watercourse* Indonesia
123 N5 **Servach** *watercourse* Belarus
190 D4 **Serven Uul** *mountain* Mongolia
218 E7 **Serviceton** Vic. Australia
130 E5 **Servigliano** Italy
198 C6 **Serwaru** Indonesia
72 B5 **Serykh Gusey, Ostrova** *island* Russian Federation
197 H3 **Sesayap** Indonesia
197 H3 **Sesayap** *watercourse* Indonesia
160 D3 **Sese** Democratic Republic of Congo
76 J7 **Seseganaga Lake** Ontario Canada
128 E3 **Seseña** Spain
162 B3 **Sesfontein** Namibia
162 D3 **Sesheke** Zambia
128 B4 **Sesimbra** Portugal
121 M4 **Seskarö** Sweden
140 A2 **Seskinore** Omagh Northern Ireland UK
90 B4 **Sesori** El Salvador
162 D2 **Sessa** Angola
120 J2 **Sessaya** *island* Norway
124 F2 **Seßlach** Germany
130 E3 **Sesto** Italy
124 E5 **Sesto Calende** Italy
123 L5 **Šeštokai** Lithuania
127 I4 **Sestri Levante** Italy
124 D5 **Sestriere** Italy
123 O2 **Sestroretsk** Russian Federation
127 J3 **Sesvenna, Piz** *mountain* Italy/Switzerland
192 F5 **Setaka** Japan
126 F5 **Sète** France
103 C7 **Sete Lagoas** Brazil
120 K2 **Setermoen** Norway
164 1a **Setes Cicades, Caldeira das** *lake* Azores
122 D3 **Setesdal** *valley* Norway
155 H1 **Sétif** Algeria
139 F4 **Setley** Hampshire England UK
74 J7 **Seton Portage** British Columbia Canada
120 I3 **Setså** Norway
154 E2 **Settat** Morocco
159 F5 **Setté Cama** Gabon
135 AC6 **Sette-Daban, Khrebet** *range* Russian Federation
122 F3 **Setten** *lake* Norway
75 V5 **Setting Lake** Manitoba Canada
141 F2 **Settle** North Yorkshire England UK
210 inset **Settlement** Christmas Island Australia
158 E3 **Setto** Benin
126 G3 **Settons, Lac des** *lake* France
128 B4 **Setúbal** Portugal
128 B4 **Setúbal** *admin. area* Portugal
126 D4 **Seudre** *watercourse* France
126 D4 **Seugne** *watercourse* France
124 C3 **Seuil-d'Argonne** France
120 J3 **Seukojaure** *lake* Sweden
76 I7 **Seul, Lac** *lake* Ontario Canada
196 B2 **Seulimeum** Indonesia
124 C4 **Seurre** France
182 E6 **Sevana Lich** *lake* Armenia
132 E4 **Sevar** Bulgaria
154 F6 **Sévaré** Mali
133 A5 **Sevaster** Albania
136 E4 **Sevastopol'** Ukraine
123 O2 **Sevast'yanovo** Russian Federation
127 I3 **Sevelen** Switzerland
140 A4 **Seven** Ireland
86 F4 **Seven Devils Lake** Arkansas USA
78 G3 **Seven Islands Bay** Newfoundland and Labrador Canada
138 D3 **Seven Sisters** Neath Port Talbot Wales UK
86 B6 **Seven Sisters** Texas USA
81 Q1 **Seven Sisters Falls** Manitoba Canada
218 D5 **Sevenhill** SA Australia
139 H3 **Sevenoaks** Kent England UK
75 P8 **Sevenpersons** Alberta Canada
215 K8 **Seventeen Seventy** Qld Australia
135 AI6 **Sever** Russian Federation
126 F4 **Sévérac-le-Château** France
103 B8 **Severínia** Brazil
107 H4 **Severino Ribeiro** Brazil
76 I6 **Severn** *watercourse* Ontario Canada
221 E6 **Severn** *mountain* New Zealand
162 D5 **Severn** South Africa
138 E2 **Severn** *watercourse* England/Wales UK
76 J6 **Severn Lake** Ontario Canada
134 S5 **Severnaya** *watercourse* Russian Federation
134 N6 **Severnaya Sos'va** *watercourse* Russian Federation
135 W3 **Severnaya Zemlya** *island* Russian Federation
135 X7 **Severo-Baykal'-skoye Nagor'ye** *region* Russian Federation
183 O3 **Severo-Chuyskiy Khr** *mountain* Russian Federation
183 K2 **Severo-Kazakhstanskaya Oblast'** *admin. area* Kazakhstan
135 U4 **Severo-Sibirskaya Nizmennost'** *region* Russian Federation
134 I6 **Severodvinsk** Russian Federation
134 H5 **Severomorsk** Russian Federation
86 C2 **Severy** Kansas USA
121 P2 **Sevettijärvi** Finland
84 F1 **Sevier** *watercourse* Utah USA
84 F1 **Sevier Bridge Reservoir** Utah USA
84 F1 **Sevier Desert** Utah USA
84 F1 **Sevier Lake** Utah USA
128 D5 **Sevilla** Spain
159 G4 **Sevilla de Niefang** Equatorial Guinea
132 D4 **Sevlievo** Bulgaria
130 F3 **Sevnica** Slovenia
124 B3 **Sevran** France
190 E4 **Sevrei** Mongolia
158 B3 **Sewa** *watercourse* Sierra Leone
74 E6 **Sewall** British Columbia Canada
87 K7 **Sewall's Point** Florida USA
72 E6 **Seward** Alaska USA
81 Q6 **Seward** Nebraska USA
72 C5 **Seward Peninsula** Alaska USA
199 G6 **Sewerimabu** Papua New Guinea
74 L5 **Sexsmith** Alberta Canada
85 J7 **Sextin** Mexico
134 P4 **Sëyakha** Russian Federation
134 O4 **Sëyakha** *watercourse* Russian Federation
89 H5 **Seyaplaya** Mexico
90 B3 **Seybaplaya** Mexico
164 9 **Seychelles** *country* Indian Ocean
164 9b **Seychellois, Morne** *mountain* Seychelles
182 I6 **Seýdi** Turkmenistan
120 inset **Seyðisfjörður** Iceland
133 G6 **Seyitgazi** Turkey
133 F6 **Seyitömer** Turkey
136 F2 **Seym** *watercourse* Russian Federation
82 I7 **Seymour** Indiana USA
86 B4 **Seymour** Texas USA
109 4 **Seymour, Isla** *islands* Archipiélago de Colon (Galapagos Islands)
76 G7 **Seymourville** Manitoba Canada
127 H4 **Seyne** France
127 H4 **Seynod** France
133 E6 **Seyrek** Turkey
127 G4 **Seyssel** France
179 K3 **Seyyed Būs** Afghanistan
130 E4 **Sežana** Slovenia
124 B3 **Sézanne** France
133 D8 **Sfakion** Greece
132 F3 **Sfântu Gheorghe** Romania
132 D3 **Sfântu Gheorghe** Romania
155 I2 **Sfax** Tunisia
131 C7 **Sferracavallo, Capo** *cape* Sardinia Italy
133 C8 **Sfinárion** Greece
142 A4 **Sgallairidh** Na h-Eileanan Siar Scotland UK
189 G3 **Sha Xi** *lake* Fujian China
189 H3 **Sha Xi** *watercourse* Fujian China
188 E1 **Shaanxi** *admin. area* China
82 G6 **Shabbona** Illinois USA
161 H3 **Shabeellaha Dhexe** *admin. area* Somalia
161 G3 **Shabeellaha Hoose** *admin. area* Somalia
161 H3 **Shabeelle, Webi** *watercourse* Somalia
182 C4 **Shabel'sk** Russian Federation
132 F4 **Shabla** Bulgaria
132 F4 **Shabla** *cape* Bulgaria
77 V6 **Shabo** Newfoundland and Labrador Canada
78 E6 **Shabogamo Lake** Newfoundland and Labrador Canada
76 K7 **Shabuskwia Lake** Ontario Canada
184 F5 **Shache** Xinjiang Uygur Zizhiqu China
189 H3 **Shacheng** Fujian China
189 H3 **Shacheng Gang** *lake* Fujian China
216 E5 **Shackleton** WA Australia
75 Q7 **Shackleton** Saskatchewan Canada
58 K1 **Shackleton Coast** Antarctica
58 G2 **Shackleton Ice Shelf** Antarctica
58 L1 **Shackleton Inlet** *bay* Antarctica
58 W1 **Shackleton Range** Antarctica
178 F3 **Shādegān** Iran
81 N4 **Shadehill Reservoir** South Dakota USA
182 I2 **Shadrinsk** Russian Federation
156 E2 **Shadwan Island** Egypt
80 D5 **Shady Cove** Oregon USA
215 I8 **Shady Downs** Qld Australia
86 D3 **Shady Point** Oklahoma USA
82 H6 **Shafer, Lake** Indiana USA
58 K2 **Shafer Peak** *mountain* Antarctica
84 C3 **Shafter** California USA
85 J6 **Shafter** Texas USA
139 E3 **Shaftesbury** Dorset England UK
210 inset **Shag Island** Heard Island Australia
221 D7 **Shag Point** New Zealand
76 L5 **Shagamu** *watercourse* Ontario Canada
76 L5 **Shagamu Lake** Ontario Canada
183 Q3 **Shagonar** Russian Federation
196 D3 **Shah Alam** Malaysia
179 K2 **Shāh Fūladī** *mountain* Afghanistan
187 E8 **Shahabad** Andhra Pradesh India
187 D8 **Shahabad** Karnataka India
186 E5 **Shahabad** Uttar Pradesh India
179 J4 **Shāhābād** Iran
179 H4 **Shahābī** Iran
187 D7 **Shahada** Maharashtra India
132 G3 **Shahany, Ozero** *lake* Ukraine
179 K4 **Shahdadpur** Pakistan
186 E6 **Shahdol** Madhya Pradesh India
191 H6 **Shahe** Hebei China
186 E6 **Shahgarh** Madhya Pradesh India
178 G4 **Shahīd** Iran
186 E5 **Shahjahanpur** Uttar Pradesh India
187 C6 **Shahpur** Gujarat India
187 D8 **Shahpur** Karnataka India
179 K4 **Shahpur** Pakistan
179 K4 **Shahpur Chakar** Pakistan
186 D6 **Shahpura** Rajasthan India
179 H3 **Shahr-e Bābak** Iran
178 G3 **Shahr-e Kord** Iran
178 G3 **Shahrezā** Iran
183 J6 **Shahriston** Tajikistan
178 E3 **Sha'īb Ḩisb** *watercourse* Iraq
179 K3 **Shaighalu** Pakistan
179 K4 **Shaikh Salar** Pakistan
100 B5 **Shaimi, Cordillera de** *range* Peru
186 D6 **Shajapur** Madhya Pradesh India
162 D3 **Shakawe** Botswana
76 K8 **Shakespeare Island** Ontario Canada
179 H5 **Shakhbūt** Oman
157 G5 **Shakhs, Ras** *cape* Eritrea
183 K3 **Shakhtinsk** Kazakhstan
182 C4 **Shakhty** Russian Federation
159 E3 **Shaki** Nigeria
72 C6 **Shaktoolik** Alaska USA
161 F2 **Shala, Lake** Ethiopia
183 M3 **Shalakterek** *lake* Kazakhstan
139 F3 **Shalbourne** Wiltshire England UK
183 M3 **Shalday** Kazakhstan
139 H3 **Shalford** Essex England UK
185 J6 **Shaliu He** *watercourse* Qinghai China
190 D5 **Shaliuhe** Qinghai China
182 F3 **Shalkar** *lake* Kazakhstan
182 H4 **Shalkar (Shalqar)** Kazakhstan
182 I3 **Shalkar-karashatau** *lake* Kazakhstan
87 L4 **Shallotte** North Carolina USA
58 E2 **Shallow Bay** Antarctica
218 E1 **Shallow Lake** Qld Australia
85 L4 **Shallowater** Texas USA
Shalqar *see* **Shalkar** Kazakhstan
188 C2 **Shalulie Shan** *range* Sichuan China
181 H3 **Shaluni** *mountain* Xizang Zizhiqu China
161 E5 **Shama** *watercourse* Tanzania
190 F2 **Shamaat** Mongolia
76 I5 **Shamattawa** Manitoba Canada
76 M5 **Shamattawa** *watercourse* Ontario Canada
160 E2 **Shambe** Sudan
161 F2 **Shambu** Ethiopia
83 M6 **Shamokin** Pennsylvania USA
123 Q2 **Shamoksha** Russian Federation
75 R7 **Shamrock** Saskatchewan Canada
86 A3 **Shamrock** Texas USA
179 I5 **Shams, Jabol** *mountain* Oman
163 F3 **Shamva** Zimbabwe
181 H5 **Shan** *admin. area* Myanmar
181 H5 **Shan Plateau** Myanmar
190 F5 **Shanba** Nei Mongol Zizhiqu China
189 H4 **Shancheng** Fujian China
140 B2 **Shanco** Monaghan Ireland
190 E5 **Shandan** Gansu China
189 H1 **Shandong** *admin. area* China
179 L2 **Shandur Pass** Pakistan
162 E3 **Shangani** *watercourse* Zimbabwe
188 E3 **Shangchao** Guangxi Zhuangzu Zizhiqu China
189 G2 **Shangcheng** Henan China
189 F4 **Shangchuan Dao** *island* Guangdong China
190 E6 **Shangchuankou** Qinghai China
191 H4 **Shangdu** Nei Mongol Zizhiqu China
189 I2 **Shanghai** *admin. area* China
189 I2 **Shanghai** Shanghai China
188 C3 **Shangpa** Yunnan China
189 H2 **Shangpai** Anhui China
189 G1 **Shangqiu** Henan China
189 H3 **Shangrao** Jiangxi China
100 C3 **Shangri-Lá** Colombia
184 F5 **Shangyou Shuiku** *lake* Xinjiang Uygur Zizhiqu China
191 K3 **Shangzhi** Heilongjiang China
188 F1 **Shangzhou** Shaanxi China
190 F6 **Shanhe** Gansu China
179 K4 **Shank** Pakistan
186 G5 **Shankarpur** Bihar India
140 B3 **Shankill** Ireland
139 F4 **Shanklin** Isle of Wight England UK
140 B3 **Shanlis Cross Roads** Ireland
216 E7 **Shannon** WA Australia
143 D4 **Shannon** Ireland
143 D4 **Shannon** *watercourse* Ireland
86 G3 **Shannon** Mississippi USA
218 E3 **Shannon, Mount** NSW Australia
143 C4 **Shannon, Mouth of the** *bay* Ireland
76 E3 **Shannon Lake** Manitoba Canada
73 R3 **Shannon Øer** *island* Greenland
185 I4 **Shanshan** Xinjiang Uygur Zizhiqu China
135 AC7 **Shantarskiye Ostrova** *island* Russian Federation
186 G6 **Shantipur** West Bengal India
189 G4 **Shantou** Guangdong China
221 D6 **Shantytown** New Zealand
104 B2 **Shanusi** Peru
189 G4 **Shanwei** Guangdong China
189 F1 **Shanxi** *admin. area* China
188 F1 **Shanyang** Shaanxi China
191 G5 **Shanyin** Shanxi China
189 G4 **Shaoguan** Guangdong China
189 H3 **Shaowu** Fujian China
189 H2 **Shaoxing** Zhejiang China
140 F2 **Shap** Cumbria England UK
100 C5 **Shapajal** Peru
160 C4 **Shapembe** Democratic Republic of Congo
188 D2 **Shaping** Sichuan China
142 F1 **Shapinsay** *island* Scotland UK
78 H5 **Shapio Lake** Newfoundland and Labrador Canada
123 P3 **Shapki** Russian Federation
178 F4 **Shaqrā'** Saudi Arabia
156 D5 **Sharafa** Sudan
179 J4 **Sharak** Pakistan
179 K2 **Sharan** Afghanistan
179 K3 **Sharan Jogizai** Pakistan
179 H6 **Sharbithāt, Ra's** *cape* Oman
183 J5 **Shardara Bogeni** *lake* Uzbekistan
182 H7 **Shāreh** Iran
185 J3 **Sharga** Mongolia
190 D4 **Sharga Morit Uul** *mountain* Mongolia
193 J2 **Sharidake** *volcano* Japan
190 F2 **Sharingol** Mongolia
215 I3 **Shark Reef** Coral Sea Islands Territory Australia
156 E2 **Sharm ash Shaykh** Egypt
86 B2 **Sharon** Kansas USA
81 Q3 **Sharon** North Dakota USA
83 K6 **Sharon** Pennsylvania USA
81 O7 **Sharon Springs** Kansas USA
82 I7 **Sharonville** Ohio USA
216 G6 **Sharpe, Lake** WA Australia
81 P4 **Sharpe, Lake** South Dakota USA
76 I5 **Sharpe Lake** Manitoba Canada
76 H7 **Sharpstone Lake** Ontario Canada
179 M3 **Sharqpur** Pakistan
134 K7 **Shar'ya** Russian Federation
182 E1 **Shar'ya** Russian Federation
162 E4 **Shashe** Botswana
162 E4 **Shashe** *watercourse* Zimbabwe
80 D6 **Shasta, Mount** *volcano* California USA
80 D6 **Shasta Lake** California USA
216 G6 **Shaster, Lake** WA Australia
132 E1 **Shatava** Ukraine
86 B2 **Shattuck** Oklahoma USA
218 E6 **Shaugh, Mount** SA Australia
138 C4 **Shaugh Prior** Devon England UK
75 Q8 **Shaunavon** Saskatchewan Canada
81 L7 **Shavano, Mount** Colorado USA
80 F8 **Shaver Lake** California USA
121 Q5 **Shaverki** Russian Federation
212 E6 **Shaw** *watercourse* WA Australia
86 F4 **Shaw** Mississippi USA
215 J6 **Shaw Island** Qld Australia
82 G4 **Shawano** Wisconsin USA
82 G4 **Shawano Lake** Wisconsin USA
138 E2 **Shawbury** Shropshire England UK
73 L9 **Shawinigan** Quebec Canada
86 C3 **Shawnee** Oklahoma USA
74 J8 **Shawnigan Lake** British Columbia Canada
184 G4 **Shaya** Xinjiang Uygur Zizhiqu China
178 C4 **Shaybārā** *island* Saudi Arabia
156 E5 **Shaykh Jok** Sudan
183 K6 **Shazud** Tajikistan
125 M1 **Shchara** *watercourse* Belarus
136 F2 **Shchëkino** Russian Federation
134 L5 **Shchel' yayur** Russian Federation
183 M3 **Shcherbakty** Kazakhstan
183 O3 **Shebalino** Russian Federation
82 F2 **Shebandowan** Ontario Canada
138 C4 **Shebbear** Devon England UK
136 F2 **Shebekino** Russian Federation
182 J7 **Sheberghān** Afghanistan
82 H5 **Sheboygan** Wisconsin USA
82 H5 **Sheboygan Falls** Wisconsin USA
193 I1 **Shebunino** Russian Federation
79 F9 **Shediac** New Brunswick Canada
79 F9 **Shediac Bay** New Brunswick Canada
143 E3 **Sheelin, Lough** *lake* Ireland
74 H7 **Sheemahant** *watercourse* British Columbia Canada
80 G6 **Sheep Creek Reservoir** Nevada USA
162 F5 **Sheepmoor** South Africa
143 C5 **Sheep's Head** *cape* Ireland
138 C4 **Sheepwash** Devon England UK
139 H3 **Sheerness** Kent England UK
79 G10 **Sheet Harbour** Nova Scotia Canada
141 G3 **Sheffield** South Yorkshire England UK
85 L5 **Sheffield** Texas USA
79 J8 **Sheffield Lake** Newfoundland and Labrador Canada
139 F3 **Shefford Woodlands** West Berkshire England UK
187 E7 **Shegaon** Maharashtra India
187 D7 **Shegaon** Maharashtra India
134 R7 **Shegarka** *watercourse* Russian Federation
161 G2 **Shēh Husēn** Ethiopia
75 T7 **Sheho** Saskatchewan Canada
142 C2 **Sheigra** Highland Scotland UK
156 F5 **Shek Husen** Ethiopia
82 I2 **Shekak** *watercourse* Ontario Canada
183 K5 **Sheker** Kyrgyzstan
179 M3 **Shekhupura** Pakistan
182 E5 **Sheki** Azerbaijan
183 N2 **Shelabolikha** Russian Federation
135 AJ4 **Shelagskiy, Mys** *cape* Russian Federation
82 E7 **Shelbina** Missouri USA
79 F11 **Shelburne** Nova Scotia Canada
215 G1 **Shelburne Bay** Qld Australia
82 H5 **Shelby** Michigan USA
86 F4 **Shelby** Mississippi USA
80 J2 **Shelby** Montana USA
87 K3 **Shelby** North Carolina USA
82 I7 **Shelbyville** Indiana USA
82 E7 **Shelbyville** Missouri USA
87 H3 **Shelbyville** Tennessee USA
82 G7 **Shelbyville, Lake** Illinois USA
138 D4 **Sheldon** Devon England UK
81 R5 **Sheldon** Iowa USA
82 D8 **Sheldon** Missouri USA
81 Q3 **Sheldon** North Dakota USA
135 V8 **Shelekhov** Russian Federation
190 E2 **Shelekhov** Russian Federation
135 AG7 **Shelikhova, Zaliv** *bay* Russian Federation
72 D7 **Shelikof Strait** Alaska USA
75 R6 **Shell Lake** Saskatchewan Canada
75 R6 **Shellbrook** Saskatchewan Canada
74 J6 **Shelley** British Columbia Canada
80 I5 **Shelley** Idaho USA
219 J6 **Shellharbour** NSW Australia
87 I5 **Shellman** Georgia USA
81 Q3 **Shelly** Minnesota USA
74 M7 **Shelter Bay** British Columbia Canada
83 O6 **Shelton** Connecticut USA
80 D3 **Shelton** Washington USA
181 G3 **Shemgang** Bhutan
183 N3 **Shemonaikha** Kazakhstan
191 H6 **Shen Xian** Shandong China
214 B4 **Shenandoah** NT Australia
190 G5 **Shenchi** Shanxi China
156 E4 **Shendi** Sudan
181 H2 **Shengda** Xizang Zizhiqu China
158 B3 **Shenge** Sierra Leone
133 B5 **Shëngjergj** Albania
133 A5 **Shëngjin** Albania
185 H4 **Shengli Daban** *pass* Xinjiang Uygur Zizhiqu China
188 C3 **Shengping** Yunnan China
134 J6 **Shenkursk** Russian Federation
158 C3 **Shenkwehn** *watercourse* Liberia
190 G5 **Shenmu** Shaanxi China
188 F4 **Shentang Shan** *mountain* Guangxi Zhuangzu Zizhiqu China
191 J4 **Shenyang** Liaoning China
191 H5 **Shenze** Hebei China
181 F2 **Shenzha** Xizang Zizhiqu China
189 G4 **Shenzhen** Guangdong China
186 C6 **Sheoganj** Rajasthan India
186 D6 **Sheopur** Madhya Pradesh India
58 O2 **Shepard Island** Antarctica
82 I5 **Shepherd** Michigan USA
86 D5 **Shepherd** Texas USA
218 G7 **Shepparton** Vic. Australia
139 H3 **Sheppey, Isle of** England UK
138 E3 **Shepton Mallet** Somerset England UK
182 E7 **Shera** Iran
73 K4 **Sherard, Cape** Nunavut Canada
141 G2 **Sheraton** Durham England UK
138 E4 **Sherborne** Dorset England UK
158 B3 **Sherbro Island** Sierra Leone
73 L9 **Sherbrooke** Quebec Canada
83 N5 **Sherburne** New York USA
143 F3 **Shercock** Ireland
156 E4 **Shereiq** Sudan
86 E3 **Sheridan** Arkansas USA
84 B1 **Sheridan** California USA
80 I4 **Sheridan** Montana USA
81 L4 **Sheridan** Wyoming USA

73 M2 Sheridan, Cape Nunavut Canada
218 B5 Sheringa SA Australia
139 I2 Sheringham Norfolk England UK
143 C5 Sherkin Island Ireland
186 E5 Sherkot Uttar Pradesh India
212 D6 Sherlock watercourse WA Australia
82 G7 Sherman Illinois USA
83 L5 Sherman New York USA
86 C4 Sherman Texas USA
73 J5 Sherman Basin Nunavut Canada
58 R2 Sherman Island Antarctica
81 P6 Sherman Reservoir Nebraska USA
83 Q4 Sherman Station Maine USA
142 D3 Sherramore Highland Scotland UK
75 U5 Sherridon Manitoba Canada
143 F2 Sherrigrim Dungannon Northern Ireland UK
86 E3 Sherwood Arkansas USA
82 I6 Sherwood Ohio USA
75 O6 Sherwood Park Alberta Canada
82 J4 Sheshegwaning Ontario Canada
143 C2 Sheskin Ireland
74 F3 Sheslay British Columbia Canada
133 A5 Shetaj Albania
104 C2 Shetebo Peru
82 D4 Shetek, Lake Minnesota USA
142 inset Shetland admin. area Scotland UK
142 inset Shetland Islands Scotland UK
182 F5 Shetpe Kazakhstan
Shevchenko see Aktau Kazakhstan
182 H4 Shevchenko, Zaliv lake Kazakhstan
132 F3 Shevchenkove Ukraine
81 R3 Shevlin Minnesota USA
135 Y6 Sheya Russian Federation
81 P3 Sheyenne North Dakota USA
82 B3 Sheyenne watercourse North Dakota USA
182 E7 Sheykhlar Iran
123 P4 Sheykino Russian Federation
142 B3 Shiant Islands Scotland UK
135 AG9 Shiashkotan, Ostrov island Kuril Islands
178 F7 Shibām Yemen
190 G6 Shibao Shaanxi China
179 K2 Shibar, Kowtal-e pass Afghanistan
193 H4 Shibata Japan
135 AA8 Shibazhan Heilongjiang China
76 K6 Shibogama Lake Ontario Canada
193 I2 Shibunotsunai-to lake Japan
189 H3 Shicheng Fujian China
191 J5 Shicheng Dao island Liaoning China
191 J6 Shidao Shandong China
183 L3 Shiderty watercourse Kazakhstan
142 C4 Shiel, Loch lake Scotland UK
142 C3 Shiel Bridge Highland Scotland UK
214 D2 Shield, Cape NT Australia
142 C3 Shieldaig Highland Scotland UK
188 D3 Shifang Sichuan China
138 E2 Shifnal Shropshire England UK
178 G6 Shiḥan, Wādī watercourse Yemen
184 H4 Shihezi Xinjiang Uygur Zizhiqu China
161 H2 Shiikh Somalia
133 A5 Shijak Albania
189 G4 Shijiao Guangdong China
191 H5 Shijiazhuang Hebei China
189 H2 Shijiu Hu lake Jiangsu China
76 J8 Shikag Lake Ontario Canada
193 I2 Shikaribetsu-ko lake Japan
179 K4 Shikarpur Pakistan
162 D3 Shikela watercourse Zambia
193 H4 Shikine-jima island Japan
186 E5 Shikohabad Uttar Pradesh India
192 G5 Shikoku island Japan
192 G5 Shikoku-sanchi Japan
189 G4 Shikongkong mountain Guangdong China
Shikotan, Ostrov see Shikotan-tō Kuril Islands
193 J2 Shikotan-tō (Ostrov Shikotan) island Kuril Islands
193 I2 Shikotsu-ko lake Japan
182 H3 Shil'da Russian Federation
141 G2 Shildon Durham England UK
179 I5 Shileh Iran
186 G5 Shiliguri West Bengal India
181 F3 Shiliguri admin. area West Bengal India
188 F5 Shiliu Hainan China
191 H2 Shilka watercourse Russian Federation
186 E4 Shilla mountain Himachal Pradesh India
142 A3 Shillay island Scotland UK
143 F4 Shillelagh Ireland
158 B3 Shilling, Cape cape Sierra Leone
83 K2 Shillington Ontario Canada
181 G4 Shillong Meghalaya India
182 E3 Shil'naya Balka Kazakhstan
81 P2 Shilo Manitoba Canada
190 G6 Shilou Shanxi China
135 C2 Shilovo Russian Federation
185 K3 Shiluustei Mongolia
135 AA8 Shimanovsk Russian Federation
188 C3 Shimen Yunnan China
186 D4 Shimla Himachal Pradesh India
192 F5 Shimo Koshiko-jima island Japan
193 H4 Shimoda Japan
187 D9 Shimoga Karnataka India
192 F5 Shimonoseki Japan
123 P3 Shimsk Russian Federation
142 D2 Shin, Loch lake Scotland UK
190 D3 Shina-under Mongolia
179 H5 Shināş Oman
178 E2 Shindir Iraq
190 D3 Shinejinst Mongolia
86 C6 Shiner Texas USA
160 C4 Shinga Democratic Republic of Congo
139 I2 Shingle Street Suffolk England UK
82 H3 Shingleton Michigan USA
183 M4 Shingozha Kazakhstan
193 G5 Shingu Japan
179 K3 Shinkay Afghanistan
193 F2 Shintuya Peru
192 E3 Shinwŏn North Korea
161 E4 Shinyanga Tanzania
161 E4 Shinyanga admin. area Tanzania
193 I3 Shiogama Japan
193 G5 Shiono-misaki island Japan
83 N7 Ship Bottom New Jersey USA
79 G10 Ship Harbour East Nova Scotia Canada
189 G2 Shipai Anhui China
188 D4 Shiping Yunnan China
78 G5 Shipiskan Lake Newfoundland and Labrador Canada
79 F9 Shippegan New Brunswick Canada
83 M6 Shippensburg Pennsylvania USA
83 L6 Shippenville Pennsylvania USA
85 H2 Shiprock New Mexico USA
77 T8 Shipshaw watercourse Quebec Canada
139 F2 Shipston on Stour Warwickshire England UK
138 E2 Shipton Shropshire England UK
135 AH8 Shipunskiy, Mys cape Russian Federation
188 E3 Shiqian Guizhou China
189 G4 Shiqiao Guangdong China
188 E1 Shiquan Shaanxi China
180 D2 Shiquan He watercourse Xizang Zizhiqu China
180 D2 Shiquanhe Xizang Zizhiqu China
183 J6 Shir Khan Afghanistan
183 P2 Shira lake Russian Federation
193 I3 Shiragami-dake volcano Japan
193 H4 Shirane-san mountain Japan
193 I2 Shiraoi Japan
58 N1 Shirase Bank underwater feature Ross Sea
58 N1 Shirase Coast Antarctica
58 C2 Shirase Glacier Antarctica
178 G3 Shīrāz Iran
187 D7 Shirdi Maharashtra India
163 F3 Shire watercourse Malawi
141 G3 Shirebrook Derbyshire England UK
139 F1 Shirland Derbyshire England UK
139 F2 Shirley West Midlands England UK
109 I8 Shirley, Cape Antigua and Barbuda
132 C4 Shiroki Dol Bulgaria
132 G2 Shirokolanovka Ukraine
135 AC4 Shirokostan, Poluostrov peninsula Russian Federation
187 D7 Shirpur Maharashtra India
56 R3 Shirshov Ridge underwater feature Bering Sea
182 H6 Shīrvān Iran
72 C8 Shishaldin Volcano Alaska USA
189 H4 Shishi Fujian China
72 C5 Shishmaref Alaska USA
189 F2 Shishou Hubei China
140 C1 Shiskine North Ayrshire Scotland UK
100 B5 Shitihuaca Ecuador
190 F3 Shivee Gov Mongolia
82 I7 Shively Kentucky USA
186 D6 Shivpuri Madhya Pradesh India
187 C6 Shivrajpur Gujarat India
163 F2 Shiwa Ngandu Zambia
190 G5 Shiwan Shaanxi China
188 F2 Shiyan Hubei China
182 I3 Shiyli lake Kazakhstan
189 H1 Shizilu Shandong China
190 F5 Shizuishan Ningxia Huizu Zizhiqu China
193 I2 Shizunai Japan
193 H4 Shizuoka Japan
125 L3 Shklo Ukraine
182 D3 Shklovo Russian Federation
123 P5 Shklow Belarus
132 A4 Shkodër Albania
133 B5 Shkumbin watercourse Albania
132 F1 Shlyakhova Ukraine
134 S2 Shmidta, Ostrov island Russian Federation
135 AD8 Shmidta, Poluostrov peninsula Russian Federation
123 O5 Sho, Vozyera lake Belarus
75 U7 Shoal Lake Manitoba Canada
76 H8 Shoal Lake Ontario Canada
76 G7 Shoal Lakes Manitoba Canada
219 J6 Shoalhaven Heads NSW Australia
192 G4 Shobara Japan
192 G4 Shodo-shima island Japan
83 N6 Shoemakersville Pennsylvania USA
182 I6 Shofirkon Uzbekistan
134 P4 Shokal'skogo, Ostrov island Russian Federation
183 L3 Sholakkor lake Kazakhstan
121 R4 Shomba Russian Federation
121 R4 Shombozero, Ozero lake Russian Federation
182 H4 Shomishkol' Kazakhstan
51 S14 Shona Ridge underwater feature Atlantic Ocean
181 G3 Shongar Dzong Bhutan
82 D3 Shooks Minnesota USA
138 C4 Shop Cornwall England UK
183 L3 Shoptykol' Kazakhstan
179 K4 Shoran Pakistan
77 N1 Shoran Bay Nunavut Canada
182 E6 Shorbachy Azerbaijan
183 J6 Sho'rchi Uzbekistan
80 D3 Shoreline Washington USA
183 K5 Shorobe Botswana
212 D2 Short, Lake SA Australia
216 F6 Short, Mount WA Australia
183 K3 Shortandy Kazakhstan
222 8 Shortland island Solomon Islands
183 J4 Shoshkakol lake Kazakhstan
84 D3 Shoshone California USA
80 H5 Shoshone Idaho USA
81 J4 Shoshone Lake Wyoming USA
80 G6 Shoshone Mountains Nevada USA
162 E4 Shoshong Botswana
81 K5 Shoshoni Wyoming USA
136 E2 Shostka Ukraine
221 C7 Shotover watercourse New Zealand
139 F2 Shotteswell Warwickshire England UK
191 I6 Shouguang Shandong China
191 H5 Shouyang Shanxi China
84 G3 Show Low Arizona USA
156 F5 Showak Sudan
134 J5 Shoyna Russian Federation
132 G1 Shpola Ukraine
132 F1 Shpykiv Ukraine
138 E2 Shrawardine Shropshire England UK
86 E4 Shreveport Louisiana USA
139 F2 Shrewley Warwickshire England UK
138 E2 Shrewsbury Shropshire England UK
187 C7 Shrivardhan Maharashtra India
143 C4 Shrone Ireland
139 H2 Shropham Norfolk England UK
138 E2 Shropshire admin. area England UK
138 F2 Shrubhill Galway Ireland
183 L5 Shu Kazakhstan
191 K3 Shuangcheng Heilongjiang China
190 G5 Shuanghuyu Shaanxi China
188 F3 Shuangjiang Hunan China
191 J4 Shuangliao Jilin China
191 K4 Shuangyang Jilin China
191 L3 Shuangyashan Heilongjiang China
189 G2 Shuangzhong Jiangxi China
156 C1 Shu'bah, Wādī ash watercourse Libya
183 J4 Shubar-tengiz lake Kazakhstan
182 G3 Shubarkuduk Kazakhstan
189 G2 Shucheng Anhui China
189 H1 Shucheng Jiangsu China
185 E5 Shufu Xinjiang Uygur Zizhiqu China
184 F4 Shuiding Xinjiang Uygur Zizhiqu China
189 G2 Shuihu Anhui China
188 E1 Shuiluocheng Gansu China
189 G4 Shuizhai Guangdong China
191 K4 Shulan Jilin China
184 E5 Shule Xinjiang Uygur Zizhiqu China
185 K5 Shule He watercourse Gansu China
183 J5 Shūlgerah Afghanistan
190 G5 Shulinzhao Nei Mongol Zizhiqu China
82 F5 Shullsburg Wisconsin USA
123 P3 Shum Russian Federation
72 C8 Shumagin Islands Alaska USA
162 E3 Shumba Zimbabwe
132 E4 Shumen admin. area Bulgaria
182 I1 Shumikha Russian Federation
135 AG8 Shumshu, Ostrov island Kuril Islands
189 G4 Shunde Guangdong China
121 S5 Shun'ga Russian Federation
182 C1 Shunga Russian Federation
189 F3 Shunling Hunan China
189 F3 Shunyi Beijing China
121 Q4 Shuopolakshа, Ozero lake Russian Federation
86 G4 Shuqualak Mississippi USA
182 F6 Shuraabad Azerbaijan
179 H2 Shūrab Iran
182 H6 Shurak Iran
183 L3 Shureksor Koli lake Kazakhstan
182 J6 Shurguzar Uzbekistan
178 G3 Shūrjestān Iran
162 E3 Shurugwi Zimbabwe
182 I6 Shurxuk Uzbekistan
178 F3 Shūsh Iran
178 F3 Shūshtar Iran
74 L7 Shuswap Lake British Columbia Canada
215 J6 Shute Harbour Qld Australia
121 S6 Shuya Russian Federation
182 D2 Shuya Russian Federation
72 D7 Shuyak Island Alaska USA
121 S4 Shuyeretskoye Russian Federation
123 O4 Shvanibakhovo Russian Federation
181 H4 Shwebo Myanmar
194 B3 Shwedaung Myanmar
181 H4 Shwego Myanmar
194 C3 Shwegyin Myanmar
181 H4 Shweli watercourse Myanmar
181 H4 Shweudaung mountain Myanmar
183 L3 Shybyndy Koli lake Kazakhstan
183 L3 Shyganak lake Kazakhstan
183 K5 Shymkent (Chimkent) Kazakhstan
194 D3 Si Racha Thailand
194 E4 Si Sa Ket Thailand
198 E5 Sia Indonesia
142 B2 Siabost Na h-Eileanan Siar Scotland UK
196 C3 Siabu Indonesia
179 M2 Siachen Glacier Pakistan
142 B2 Siadar Uarach Na h-Eileanan Siar Scotland UK
179 J2 Siāhkākī Afghanistan
196 D3 Siak watercourse Indonesia
179 M3 Sialkot Pakistan
179 H5 Siallum Papua New Guinea
101 E3 Siamacu, Sabana region Venezuela
196 E3 Siantan island Indonesia
101 E4 Siapa watercourse Venezuela
195 J5 Siargao island Philippines
195 I6 Siasi Philippines
195 I6 Siasi island Philippines
195 I5 Siaton Philippines
198 C3 Siau island Indonesia
123 L5 Šiauliai Lithuania
123 L5 Šiaulių admin. area Lithuania
90 E2 Sibanicú Cuba
100 C3 Sibaté Colombia
182 H3 Sibay Russian Federation
163 F5 Sibaya, Lake lake South Africa
75 P7 Sibbald Alberta Canada
130 F5 Šibenik Croatia
100 C4 Sibenia Colombia
Siberia see Sibir' Russian Federation
56 Q1 Siberia Abyssal Plain underwater feature Arctic Ocean
196 C4 Siberut island Indonesia
196 C4 Siberut, Selat strait Indonesia
199 G6 Sibidiri Papua New Guinea
196 B3 Sibigo Indonesia
135 W/X5 Sibir' (Siberia) region Russian Federation
134 Q4 Sibiryakova, Ostrov island Russian Federation
159 G5 Sibiti Congo
132 D3 Sibiu Romania
132 D3 Sibiu admin. area Romania
139 H3 Sible Hedingham Essex England UK
81 R5 Sibley Iowa USA
86 E4 Sibley Louisiana USA
100 E5 Sibó Brazil
196 C3 Siboliga Indonesia
196 C3 Siborongborong Indonesia
181 H3 Sibsagar Assam India
139 H1 Sibsey Lincolnshire England UK
197 F3 Sibu Malaysia
195 F6 Sibuco Philippines
195 I6 Sibuguey Bay Philippines
159 H3 Sibut Central African Republic
197 G2 Sibuti Malaysia
195 H6 Sibutu island Philippines
195 H6 Sibutu Passage strait Philippines
195 I4 Sibuyan island Philippines
195 I4 Sibuyan Sea Philippines
84 G5 Sibyl Arizona USA
132 C2 Sic Romania
74 L7 Sicamous British Columbia Canada
195 I3 Sicapoo, Mount mountain Philippines
218 D4 Siccus watercourse SA Australia
104 C5 Sicera Peru
132 C4 Sićevo Serbia
188 E4 Sicheng Guangxi Zhuangzu Zizhiqu China
132 B3 Sichevița Romania
181 J2 Sichuan admin. area China
125 G7 Sicié, Cap cape France
131 E8 Sicilia admin. area Italy
131 F8 Sicilia island Italy
131 E8 Sicilian Channel Mediterranean Sea
139 H2 Sicklesmere Suffolk England UK
90 C4 Sicsayeri Honduras
132 D2 Siculeni Romania
132 A3 Šid Serbia
75 S1 Sid Lake Northwest Territories Canada
197 F3 Sidas Indonesia
138 D4 Sidbury Devon England UK
143 F3 Siddan Ireland
186 C6 Siddhapur Gujarat India
140 E2 Siddick Cumbria England UK
141 F3 Siddington Cheshire England UK
187 E7 Siddipet Andhra Pradesh India
137 G7 Side Turkey
138 C3 Sideby Finland
199 I6 Sideia Island Papua New Guinea
120 K5 Sidensjö Sweden
131 G7 Siderno Italy
133 E8 Sideros, Akra cape Greece
138 D4 Sidford Devon England UK
186 E5 Sidhauli Uttar Pradesh India
186 E6 Sidhi Madhya Pradesh India
129 G6 Sidi Algeria
155 G1 Sidi Aïssa Algeria
155 G1 Sidi Ali Algeria
129 F6 Sidi Ali Boussidi Algeria
156 D1 Sidi Barrâni Egypt
129 F6 Sidi Bel Abbes Algeria
129 G6 Sidi Bou Bekeur Algeria
155 H2 Sidi Bou Zid Tunisia
131 C8 Sidi Ferjani Tunisia
153 D1 Sidi Ifni Morocco
154 E2 Sidi Kacem Morocco
155 G2 Sidi Khaled Algeria
129 H6 Sidi Ladjel Algeria
154 E2 Sidi Slimane Morocco
154 E2 Sidi Smaïl Morocco
136 C3 Sidikalang Indonesia
139 H4 Sidlesham West Sussex England UK
58 P1 Sidley, Mount mountain Antarctica
138 D4 Sidmouth Devon England UK
215 G2 Sidmouth, Cape Qld Australia
74 J8 Sidney British Columbia Canada
81 P2 Sidney Manitoba Canada
82 D6 Sidney Iowa USA
81 M3 Sidney Montana USA
81 N6 Sidney Nebraska USA
82 I6 Sidney Ohio USA
87 J3 Sidney Lanier, Lake Georgia USA
158 C2 Sido Mali
198 B3 Sidoan Indonesia
197 G5 Sidoarjo Indonesia
181 H5 Sidoktaya Myanmar
Sidon see Saïda Lebanon
86 F4 Sidon Mississippi USA
123 L5 Sidory Poland
108 I6 Sidrolândia Brazil
120 I3 Sidsjö Sweden
120 K4 Siebnesjaure lake Sweden
125 L1 Siedlce Poland
124 D2 Sieg watercourse Germany
124 D2 Siegen Germany
120 J3 Sieldutjåkkå watercourse Sweden
199 I4 Siemens, Cape Papua New Guinea
125 K2 Siemiatycze Poland
194 E4 Siĕmpang Cambodia
194 D4 Siĕmréab Cambodia
188 E4 Si'en Guangxi Zhuangzu Zizhiqu China
130 D5 Siena Italy
125 L2 Sieniawa Poland
125 J2 Sieniеca Różana Poland
125 K2 Sienno Poland
125 J2 Sieradz Poland
124 D4 Sierentz France
128 D2 Siero Spain
125 J1 Sierpc Poland
108 D2 Sierra, Punta cape Argentina
108 E2 Sierra Chata Argentina
108 C3 Sierra Colorada Argentina
106 D5 Sierra Gorda Chile
108 D2 Sierra Grande Argentina
158 B3 Sierra Leone country Africa
50 Q9 Sierra Leone Basin underwater feature Atlantic Ocean
50 P9 Sierra Leone Rise underwater feature Atlantic Ocean
84 C3 Sierra Madre Mountains California USA
85 K7 Sierra Mojada Mexico
108 C3 Sierra Nevada Argentina
108 C3 Sierra Pailemán Argentina
88 E4 Sierra Vieja Mexico
84 G5 Sierra Vista Arizona USA
83 N3 Siesta, Lac de la lake Quebec Canada
104 B2 Siete de Junio Peru
132 D2 Șieu-Odorhei Romania
121 N5 Sievi Finland
160 G5 Sifeni Ethiopia
137 D7 Sifnos island Greece
155 F1 Sig Algeria
136 H4 Sig Russian Federation
133 E6 Sığacık Körfezi bay Turkey
223 9a Sigatoka Fiji
120 I2 Sigerfjord Norway
138 D4 Sigford Devon England UK
73 N4 Sigguup Nunaa region Greenland
196 B2 Sigli Indonesia
120 inset Siglufjörður Iceland
120 D5 Signa Italy
139 F3 Signet Oxfordshire England UK
125 F4 Signy-l'Abbaye France
196 C4 Sigoisooinan Indonesia
82 E6 Sigourney Iowa USA
133 D6 Sigri Greece
130 B3 Sigriswil Switzerland
128 E3 Sigüenza Spain
158 C2 Siguiri Guinea
123 M4 Sigulda Latvia
80 J7 Sigurd Utah USA
196 C3 Sihabuhabu, Gunung mountain Indonesia
136 G5 Sıhanköy Turkey
Sihanoukville see Kâmpóng Saôm Cambodia
187 C7 Sihor Gujarat India
186 E6 Sihor Madhya Pradesh India
189 F4 Sihui Guangdong China
121 N4 Siikajoki Finland
121 N4 Siikajoki watercourse Finland
123 N1 Siilinjärvi Finland
136 G6 Siirt Turkey
136 G6 Siirt admin. area Turkey
222 6a Siis island Federated States of Micronesia
189 I2 Sijiao Shan range Zhejiang China
178 E2 Sijin Iraq
196 D4 Sijunjung Indonesia
222 8 Sikaiana island Solomon Islands
196 D4 Sikakap Indonesia
74 J4 Sikanni Chief British Columbia Canada
186 D5 Sikar Rajasthan India
179 L2 Sikārām Sar mountain Afghanistan
158 C2 Sikasso Mali
158 C2 Sikasso admin. area Mali
133 C6 Sikea Greece
120 L4 Sikeå Sweden
198 B5 Sikeli Indonesia
82 G8 Sikeston Missouri USA
120 L4 Sikfors Sweden
194 D4 Sikhiu Thailand
193 H1 Sikhote-Alin Russian Federation
135 AC9 Sikhote Alin range Russian Federation
101 H4 Sikini French Guiana
133 D7 Sikinos island Greece
120 E6 Sikkelbreen glacier Norway
186 G5 Sikkim admin. area India
125 J5 Siklós Hungary
198 C3 Siko island Indonesia
162 D3 Sikongo Zambia
120 J4 Siksele Sweden
120 J4 Siksjö Sweden
120 J4 Siksjö/Siksjöhöjden Sweden
135 Z5 Siktyakh Russian Federation
197 H2 Sikuati Malaysia
128 C2 Sil watercourse Spain
122 I5 Šilalė Lithuania
130 D3 Silandro Italy
86 G5 Silas Alabama USA
123 L5 Šilavotas Lithuania
194 B5 Silawaih Agam mountain Indonesia
195 I5 Silay Philippines
127 L4 Silba Croatia
181 G4 Silchar Assam India
76 H4 Silcox Manitoba Canada
133 F5 Şile Turkey
140 E2 Silecroft Cumbria England UK
133 D5 Silen Bulgaria
124 E4 Silenen Switzerland
215 H5 Silent Hill Qld Australia
87 L3 Siler City North Carolina USA
187 E8 Sileru watercourse Andhra Pradesh India
155 G4 Silet Algeria
183 K3 Sileti Bŏgeni lake Kazakhstan
183 L2 Siletitengiz Koli lake Kazakhstan
80 D4 Siletz Oregon USA
186 E5 Silgarhi Nepal
181 G3 Silghat Assam India
164 9a Silhouette island Seychelles
138 C2 Silian Ceredigion Wales UK
155 H1 Siliana Tunisia
136 E6 Silifke Turkey
134 J5 Siligir watercourse Russian Federation
161 G1 Silil watercourse Somalia
223 12c Silisili, Mount volcano Samoa
132 D3 Silistea Romania
132 E3 Silistra admin. area Bulgaria
133 F5 Silivri Turkey
122 H2 Siljan lake Sweden
122 F2 Siljuberget Norway
129 F4 Silla Spain
123 N3 Sillamäe Estonia
121 M5 Sillanpää Finland
130 D4 Sillara, Monte mountain Italy
122 G2 Sillerö Sweden
158 D2 Silli Burkina Faso
187 D7 Sillod Maharashtra India
126 C2 Sillon de Talbert peninsula France
140 E2 Silloth Cumbria England UK
120 J5 Sillre Sweden
122 I2 Sillvik Sweden
142 F3 Sillyearn Moray Scotland UK
196 E1 Silo Silo Papua New Guinea
86 D2 Siloam Springs Arkansas USA
136 G6 Silopi Turkey
120 J2 Silsand Norway
86 D5 Silsbee Texas USA
76 H5 Silsby Lake Manitoba Canada
81 L7 Silt Colorado USA
80 C5 Siltcoos Lake Oregon USA
75 S7 Silton Saskatchewan Canada
197 F3 Siluas Indonesia
159 F3 Siluko Nigeria
159 F3 Siluko watercourse Nigeria
122 G5 Silvåkra Sweden
136 G5 Silvan Turkey
105 G5 Silvânia Brazil
103 B7 Silvânia Brazil
187 C7 Silvassa Dadra and Nagar Haveli India
75 V7 Silver Bay Manitoba Canada
82 E3 Silver Bay Minnesota USA
85 H4 Silver City New Mexico USA
81 M7 Silver Cliff Colorado USA
74 L7 Silver Creek British Columbia Canada
81 Q6 Silver Creek Nebraska USA
83 L5 Silver Creek New York USA
82 G2 Silver Islet Ontario Canada
82 I6 Silver Lake Indiana USA
82 E7 Silver Lake Missouri USA
80 E5 Silver Lake Oregon USA
80 D3 Silver Lake Washington USA
82 G2 Silver Mountain Ontario Canada
84 D2 Silver Peak Range Nevada USA
84 C1 Silver Springs Nevada USA
139 F2 Silverstone Northamptonshire England UK
74 K8 Silvertip Mountain British Columbia Canada
218 E4 Silverton NSW Australia
74 M8 Silverton British Columbia Canada
138 D4 Silverton Devon England UK
81 L8 Silverton Colorado USA
85 I3 Silverton Texas USA
75 U7 Silverwood Manitoba Canada
128 B4 Silves Portugal
130 F5 Silvi Italy
138 E2 Silvington Shropshire England UK
77 Q5 Silvy, Lac lake Quebec Canada
135 AD4 Sil'yeyaki Russian Federation
133 C5 Simantra Greece
188 C4 Simao Yunnan China
105 E5 Simão Dias Brazil
195 I4 Simara island Philippines
73 L9 Simard, Lac lake Quebec Canada
133 F6 Simav watercourse Turkey
106 C6 Simba, Volcán volcano Chile
127 K2 Simbach am Inn Germany
122 C2 Simbăta Romania
199 J4 Simberi Island Papua New Guinea
159 I2 Simbi, Ouadi watercourse Chad
222 8 Simbo island Solomon Islands
83 K5 Simcoe Ontario Canada
83 L4 Simcoe, Lake Ontario Canada
187 F6 Simdega Jharkhand India
196 E3 Simei admin. area Singapore
135 W6 Simenga Russian Federation
132 C3 Simeria Romania
131 F8 Simeto watercourse Italy
196 C3 Simeulue island Indonesia
84 C3 Simi Valley California USA
186 E5 Simikot Nepal
194 C5 Similan, Ko island Thailand
74 K8 Similkameen watercourse British Columbia Canada
159 I3 Simindou Central African Republic
100 C3 Simiti Colombia
133 C5 Simitli Bulgaria
161 E4 Simiyu watercourse Tanzania
81 M7 Simla Colorado USA
127 H2 Simmern Germany
86 F5 Simmesport Louisiana USA
75 Q8 Simmie Saskatchewan Canada
123 L5 Simnas Lithuania
121 N4 Simo Finland
102 D4 Simões Brazil
121 O3 Simojärvi lake Finland
121 N4 Simojoki watercourse Finland
101 H3 Simon French Guiana
74 L5 Simonette watercourse Alberta Canada
75 U5 Simonhouse Manitoba Canada
138 D3 Simonsbath Somerset England UK
122 I3 Simonstorp Sweden
196 E4 Simpang Indonesia
196 D2 Simpang Empat Malaysia
196 D3 Simpang Renggam Malaysia
123 O2 Simpelejärvi lake Finland
102 D4 Simplício Mendes Brazil
75 S7 Simpson Saskatchewan Canada
75 P8 Simpson Montana USA
218 C1 Simpson Desert NT Australia
75 O2 Simpson Islands Northwest Territories Canada
80 G7 Simpson Park Mountains Nevada USA
73 K5 Simpson Peninsula Nunavut Canada
87 J3 Simpsonville South Carolina USA
78 F6 Sims Lake Newfoundland and Labrador Canada
80 E4 Simtustus, Lake Oregon USA
196 C4 Simuk island Indonesia
123 N3 Simuna Estonia
197 F3 Simunjan Malaysia
195 H6 Simunul island Philippines
135 AF9 Simushir, Ostrov island Kuril Islands
193 L1 Simushir, Ostrov lake Russian Federation
195 G5 Sin Cowe Island Spratly Islands
108 B5 Sin Nombre, Península peninsula Chile
104 D4 Sina Peru
161 H2 Sina Dhaqa Somalia
196 C3 Sinabang Indonesia
196 C3 Sinabung volcano Indonesia
156 E2 Sinai peninsula Egypt
Sinai, Mount see Mūsa, Jabal Egypt
132 D3 Sinaia Romania
88 D3 Sinaloa admin. area Mexico
88 D3 Sinaloa watercourse Mexico
88 C3 Sinaloa de Leyva Mexico
179 J2 Sinay Afghanistan
162 E3 Sinazongwe Zambia
181 H5 Sinbaungwe Myanmar
100 C2 Sincé Colombia
100 C2 Sincelejo Colombia
Sinchaigbyin see Maungdaw Myanmar
214 F3 Sinclair watercourse Qld Australia
75 U8 Sinclair Manitoba Canada
81 L6 Sinclair Wyoming USA
87 J4 Sinclair, Lake Georgia USA
101 G3 Sinclair Landing Guyana
132 C2 Sîncraiu Romania
186 D6 Sind watercourse Madhya Pradesh India
163 F2 Sinda Zambia
196 E5 Sindangbarang Indonesia
198 B6 Sindeh, Teluk bay Indonesia
130 C2 Sindelfingen Germany
187 D8 Sindgi Karnataka India
179 K4 Sindh admin. area Pakistan
187 D8 Sindhnur Karnataka India
156 C4 Sindī, Wādī watercourse Sudan
131 C6 Sindia Sardinia Italy
133 F6 Sındırgı Turkey
158 E2 Sinende Benin
83 N7 Sinepuxent Bay Maryland USA
128 B5 Sines Portugal
128 B5 Sines, Cabo de cape Portugal
121 N3 Sinettä Finland
121 O5 Sinettäjärvi lake Finland
199 I5 Sinewit, Mount Papua New Guinea
158 C3 Sinfra Côte d'Ivoire
156 E5 Singa Sudan
186 E5 Singahi Bhiraura Uttar Pradesh India
196 D3 Singapore country Asia
196 D3 Singapore Singapore
196 C3 Singapore Island Singapore
196 E3 Singapore Strait Singapore
197 G6 Singaraja Indonesia
223 12a Singavé Wallis and Futuna
223 12a Singavé, Mont mountain Wallis and Futuna
194 D4 Singburi admin. area Thailand
130 C3 Singen Germany
132 E3 Singeru Romania
161 E4 Singida Tanzania
161 E5 Singida admin. area Tanzania
198 B5 Singkang Indonesia
196 D4 Singkarak Indonesia
196 F3 Singkawang Indonesia
196 E4 Singkep island Indonesia
196 C3 Singkil Indonesia
196 C3 Singkuang Indonesia
214 E5 Single watercourse Qld Australia
122 F3 Singlefjorden bay Norway
219 J5 Singleton NSW Australia
216 E4 Singleton, Mount WA Australia
123 J2 Singö island Sweden
120 J5 Singsjön lake Sweden
120 I5 Singsjön/Slättön Sweden
194 B6 Sinh Ho Vietnam
192 E3 Sinhŭng North Korea
182 H3 Siniy Shikhan Russian Federation
130 G5 Sinj Croatia
192 E4 Sinji-do island South Korea
156 E5 Sinkat Sudan
192 E3 Sinmi-do island North Korea
124 E2 Sinn watercourse Germany
101 H3 Sinnamary French Guiana
101 H3 Sinnamary, Fleuve watercourse French Guiana
132 F3 Sinoie, Lacul lake Romania
136 E5 Sinop Turkey
136 E5 Sinop admin. area Turkey
159 E3 Sinou Nigeria
192 F3 Sinp'o North Korea
130 C3 Sins Switzerland
132 D2 Sinsimion Romania
135 AA6 Sinsk Russian Federation
124 C2 Sint-Amands Belgium
109 1b Sint Christoffelberg mountain Netherlands Antilles
109 20 Sint Eustatius island Netherlands Antilles
109 20 Sint Maarten Netherlands territory Caribbean
109 20 Sint Maarten island Netherlands Antilles
109 1a Sint Nicolaas Aruba
197 F3 Sintang Indonesia
86 C6 Sinton Texas USA
100 C2 Sinu watercourse Colombia
191 J5 Sinŭiju Liaoning China
161 H2 Sinujiif Somalia
196 E5 Sinumbra Indonesia
124 E3 Sinzheim Germany
127 H1 Sinzig Germany
125 J4 Sió watercourse Hungary
195 I6 Siocon Philippines
125 J4 Siófok Hungary
127 H3 Sion Switzerland
143 E2 Sion Mills Strabane Northern Ireland UK
78 M1 Sioraq plain Greenland
126 F4 Sioule watercourse France
81 Q5 Sioux Center Iowa USA
81 Q5 Sioux City Iowa USA
81 Q5 Sioux Falls South Dakota USA
76 J7 Sioux Lookout Ontario Canada
82 D5 Sioux Rapids Iowa USA
104 C4 Sipaci Peru
197 H2 Sipadan, Pulau island Malaysia
101 H4 Sipaliwini admin. area Suriname
195 I5 Sipang, Tanjong cape Malaysia
109 9 Siparia Trinidad and Tobago
109 9 Siparia admin. area Trinidad and Tobago
104 E5 Sipe Sipe Bolivia
100 B3 Sipí Colombia
191 J4 Siping Jilin China
197 G2 Sipitang Malaysia
75 W5 Sipiwesk Manitoba Canada
75 W5 Sipiwesk Lake Manitoba Canada
58 P2 Siple, Mount mountain Antarctica
58 N1 Siple Coast Antarctica
58 P2 Siple Island Antarctica
195 I4 Sipocot Philippines
121 N4 Sipola Finland
130 G4 Šipovo Bosnia and Herzegovina
86 H4 Sipsey watercourse Alabama USA
196 C4 Sipura island Indonesia
196 C4 Sipura, Selat strait Indonesia
157 I5 Şiqirah Yemen
195 I5 Siquijor island Philippines
90 D5 Siquirres Costa Rica
74 K6 Sir Alexander, Mount British Columbia Canada
178 G5 Şīr Banī Yās island United Arab Emirates
179 H4 Şīr Bū Nu'āyr (UAE) island United Arab Emirates
214 D3 Sir Edward Pellew Group islands NT Australia
213 I2 Sir Graham Moore Islands WA Australia
218 B6 Sir Isaac, Point SA Australia
194 C5 Sir J. Malcolm Island Myanmar
74 H1 Sir James MacBrien, Mount Northwest Territories Canada
218 C6 Sir Joseph Banks Group islands SA Australia
74 M7 Sir Sandford, Mount British Columbia Canada
74 L6 Sir Wilfrid Laurier, Mount British Columbia Canada
187 D9 Sira Karnataka India
122 D3 Sira Norway
122 D3 Sira watercourse Norway
131 F8 Siracusa (Syracuse) Italy
181 F4 Sirajganj Bangladesh
129 G6 Sirat Algeria
158 E2 Sirba watercourse Burkina Faso
158 F5 Sircajahuira Peru
179 I3 Sirch Iran
122 D3 Sirdalsvatn lake Norway
74 M8 Sirdar British Columbia Canada
183 J6 Sirdaryo Uzbekistan
183 J6 Sirdaryo admin. area Uzbekistan
161 F2 Sirē Ethiopia
199 H5 Sirebi watercourse Papua New Guinea
82 E4 Siren Wisconsin USA
132 D1 Siret watercourse Ukraine
186 G5 Sirha Nepal
215 L1 Siri, Cape Papua New Guinea
132 B2 Şiria Romania
132 A3 Sirig Serbia
197 F3 Sirik, Tanjong cape Malaysia
196 E3 Siriwo watercourse Indonesia
179 H3 Sirjān Iran
121 N3 Sirkka Finland
121 N3 Sirkkakoski Finland
121 O1 Sirma Norway
186 D6 Sirmaur Madhya Pradesh India
186 E6 Sirmour Madhya Pradesh India
132 D3 Sirna Romania
136 G6 Şırnak Turkey
136 G6 Şırnak admin. area Turkey
186 C6 Sirohi Rajasthan India
196 C3 Sirombu Indonesia
161 E3 Sironko Uganda
187 E7 Sirpur Andhra Pradesh India
179 H4 Sirri, Jazireh-ye island Iran
186 D5 Sirsa Haryana India
187 E7 Sirsa Maharashtra India
186 F6 Sirsa Uttar Pradesh India
186 F6 Sirsi Chhattisgarh India
187 D8 Sirsi Karnataka India
186 D6 Sirsi Madhya Pradesh India
187 E7 Sirsilla Andhra Pradesh India
160 E3 Sirsiri Sudan
187 D7 Sirur Maharashtra India
123 M5 Širvėnos ežeras lake Lithuania
123 M5 Širvintos Lithuania
127 K4 Sisak Croatia
127 K4 Šišan Croatia
128 E4 Sisante Spain
191 I6 Sishui Shandong China
182 E6 Sisiani Lernmants pass Azerbaijan
73 N5 Sisimiut Greenland
75 U5 Sisipuk Lake Manitoba Canada
82 G3 Siskiwit Bay Michigan USA
120 I3 Sisovatnet lake Norway
84 B3 Sisquoc watercourse California USA
124 D4 Sissach Switzerland
121 M5 Sissala Finland
199 G4 Sissano Papua New Guinea
81 Q4 Sisseton South Dakota USA
79 E9 Sisson Branch Reservoir New Brunswick Canada
124 B3 Sissonne France
179 J3 Sīstān Daryācheh-ye watercourse Afghanistan
179 I4 Sīstān Va Balūchestān admin. area Iran
126 F4 Sisteron France
214 E7 Sisters, The mountain Qld Australia
219 Q10 Sisters Beach Tas. Australia
194 B5 Sisters Islands Andaman and Nicobar Islands India
120 F5 Sistranda Norway
132 E3 Sita Buzăului Romania
186 D6 Sitamau Madhya Pradesh India
163 I3 Sitampiky Madagascar
188 E3 Sitang Guizhou China
188 E3 Sitang Guizhou China
186 E6 Sitapur Madhya Pradesh India
186 E5 Sitapur Uttar Pradesh India
120 J3 Sitasjaure lake Sweden
133 C5 Sithonia peninsula Greece
105 F5 Sítio Castanhal Brazil
101 F4 Sítio do Pino Brazil
104 E5 Sítio Novo Brazil
105 F3 Sítio Paraná Brazil
72 F7 Sitka Alaska USA
132 B4 Sitnica watercourse Kosovo
120 K3 Sitojaure lake Sweden
156 D2 Sitrah Egypt
124 C1 Sittard Netherlands
139 H3 Sittingbourne Kent England UK
156 F5 Sittona Eritrea
181 G5 Sittwe (Akyab) Myanmar
197 F3 Situbondo Indonesia
198 B5 Siumpu island Indonesia
223 12c Siumu Samoa
198 B4 Siuna Indonesia
90 C4 Siuna Nicaragua
123 M2 Siuntio Finland
123 L4 Šiupyliai Lithuania
186 G6 Siuri West Bengal India
121 O4 Siuruanjoki watercourse Finland
132 F3 Siutghiol, Lacul lake Romania
132 A3 Sivac Serbia
187 D10 Sivakasi Tamil Nadu India
135 AA8 Sivaki Russian Federation
121 P5 Sivakka Finland
136 F5 Sivas Turkey
136 F5 Sivas admin. area Turkey
133 F6 Sivaslı Turkey
154 D5 Sivé Mauritania
123 P3 Siverskiy Russian Federation
156 D2 Siwah Egypt
156 D2 Siwah, Wāḥāt lake Egypt
186 F5 Siwan Bihar India
186 C6 Siwana Rajasthan India
127 G5 Six-Fours-les-Plages France
109 I2 Six Men's Bay Barbados
90 D5 Sixaola Costa Rica
141 H3 Sixhills Lincolnshire England UK
189 H1 Sixian Anhui China
143 E2 Sixmilecross Omagh Northern Ireland UK
124 D4 Sixt France
156 F3 Siyāl, Jazā'ir island Sudan
188 E4 Siyang Guangxi Zhuangzu Zizhiqu China
162 D3 Siyowe watercourse Zambia
126 B2 Sizun France
122 F5 Sjælland island Denmark
122 F5 Sjaunjaape island Sweden
122 E3 Sjåvatnet lake Norway
120 I3 Sjisjka Sweden
122 E2 Sjoa watercourse Norway
120 G4 Sjøåsen Norway
122 G5 Sjöbo Sweden

120 E5 **Sjøholt** Norway
122 E4 **Sjørup** Denmark
120 J2 **Sjøvegan** Norway
120 I4 **Sjulsåsen** Sweden
120 F6 **Skåbu** Norway
136 E3 **Skadovs'k** Ukraine
120 H5 **Skækervatnet** *lake* Norway
73 R3 **Skærfjorden** *bay* Greenland
120 inset **Skagafjörður** *bay* Iceland
120 inset **Skagaströnd** Iceland
120 inset **Skagatá** *cape* Iceland
120 G4 **Skage** Norway
122 F4 **Skagen** Denmark
122 H3 **Skagern** *lake* Sweden
134 C7 **Skagerrak** *strait* Norway
122 I4 **Skäggenäs** *island* Sweden
80 E2 **Skagit** *watercourse* Washington USA
72 F7 **Skagway** Alaska USA
121 N1 **Skáiddajávri** *lake* Norway
121 N1 **Skáidi** Norway
142 D2 **Skail** Highland Scotland UK
133 C7 **Skála** Greece
133 E7 **Skála** Greece
125 J2 **Skała** Poland
133 D6 **Skala Eresou** Greece
133 D5 **Skala Marion** Greece
120 I5 **Skålan** Sweden
122 G4 **Skälderviken** *bay* Sweden
130 G2 **Skalica** Slovakia
132 E4 **Skalitsa** Bulgaria
121 Q1 **Skallelv** Norway
120 J5 **Skallsjön** *lake* Sweden
120 I4 **Skalmodal** Sweden
133 D5 **Skaloti** Greece
120 H5 **Skalsvattnet** *lake* Sweden
122 G4 **Skåne** *admin. area* Sweden
120 J4 **Skansholm** Sweden
133 D6 **Skantzoura** *island* Greece
122 G3 **Skåpafors** Sweden
122 I3 **Skåra** Sweden
120 J2 **Skarberget** Norway
130 F4 **Škarda** *island* Croatia
120 K4 **Skarda** Sweden
214 G1 **Skardon** *watercourse* Qld Australia
179 M2 **Skardu** Pakistan
122 E4 **Skarp-Salling** Denmark
120 F5 **Skarsøy** *island* Norway
120 F6 **Skarstind** *mountain* Norway
120 J4 **Skarvsjön** *lake* Sweden
125 K2 **Skaryszew** Poland
122 G2 **Skasen** *lake* Norway
127 K2 **Skašov** Czech Republic
122 H2 **Skattungen** *lake* Sweden
123 L5 **Skaudvilė** Lithuania
122 E4 **Skave** Denmark
122 G3 **Skaven** Sweden
142 inset **Skaw** Shetland Scotland UK
125 J3 **Skawina** Poland
154 C4 **Skaymat** Western Sahara
74 F6 **Skedans** British Columbia Canada
123 J3 **Skedviken** *lake* Sweden
122 H3 **Skedvisjön** *lake* Sweden
74 G5 **Skeena** *watercourse* British Columbia Canada
74 G4 **Skeena Mountains** British Columbia Canada
120 inset **Skeggjastaðir** Iceland
141 I3 **Skegness** Lincolnshire England UK
120 G4 **Skei** Norway
132 B3 **Skela** Serbia
132 A4 **Skelani** Bosnia and Herzegovina
101 G3 **Skeldon** Suriname
162 B3 **Skeleton Coast** *region* Namibia
216 F5 **Skeleton Rock** *mountain* WA Australia
120 L4 **Skellefteå** Sweden
120 K4 **Skellefteälven** *watercourse* Sweden
120 L4 **Skelleftebukten** *bay* Sweden
120 L4 **Skelleftehamn** Sweden
143 B5 **Skelligs Rocks** Ireland
85 L3 **Skellytown** Texas USA
142 D5 **Skelmorlie** North Ayrshire Scotland UK
74 E6 **Skelu Bay** British Columbia Canada
142 F1 **Skelwick** Orkney Islands Scotland UK
130 G4 **Skender Vakuf** Bosnia and Herzegovina
138 E3 **Skenfrith** Monmouthshire Wales UK
133 C5 **Skepastón** Greece
120 J5 **Skeppshamn** Sweden
142 C5 **Skeroblingarry** Argyll and Bute Scotland UK
143 F3 **Skerries** Ireland
143 F2 **Skerries** Armagh Northern Ireland UK
125 L3 **Skhidni Karpaty** *range* Ukraine
155 I2 **Skhira** Tunisia
122 F3 **Ski** Norway
133 C6 **Skiathos** *island* Greece
82 D8 **Skiatook** Oklahoma USA
120 L2 **Skibotn** Norway
125 M1 **Skidal'** Belarus
140 E2 **Skiddan** *mountain* England UK
74 F6 **Skidegate Inlet** British Columbia Canada
86 C6 **Skidmore** Texas USA
122 E3 **Skien** Norway
125 L2 **Skierbieszów** Poland
120 K3 **Skierfajaure** *bay* Sweden
125 K2 **Skierniewice** Poland
155 H1 **Skikda** Algeria
122 H4 **Skillingaryd** Sweden
133 B7 **Skinari, Akra** *cape* Greece
140 E2 **Skinburness** Cumbria England UK
74 F6 **Skincuttle Inlet** British Columbia Canada
120 inset **Skinnastaður** Iceland
186 D4 **Skio** Jammu and Kashmir India/Pakistan
141 F3 **Skipton** North Yorkshire England UK
139 G2 **Skirbeck** Lincolnshire England UK
142 E2 **Skirza** Highland Scotland UK
120 K2 **Skitenelv** Norway
122 E4 **Skive** Denmark
120 G5 **Skjækra** *watercourse* Norway
122 G2 **Skjærberget** Norway
120 F6 **Skjåk** Norway
120 inset **Skjálfandafljót** *watercourse* Iceland
120 inset **Skjálfandi** *bay* Iceland
120 H4 **Skjåvika** Norway
120 H4 **Skjelbreid** Norway
120 G5 **Skjelstad** Norway
122 E5 **Skjern** Denmark
120 I3 **Skjerstad** Norway
120 L1 **Skjervøy** Norway
120 L1 **Skjervøy** *island* Norway
120 K2 **Skjold** Norway
120 E6 **Skjolden** Norway
120 J2 **Skjombotn** Norway
121 O3 **Skjutövn-Omr** *island* Finland
135 Z4 **Sklad** Russian Federation
183 K6 **Skobeleva, Pik** *mountain* Kyrgyzstan
120 J2 **Skodbergvatnet** *lake* Norway
120 E5 **Skodje** Norway
130 F3 **Škofja Loka** Slovenia
121 N2 **Skoganvarre** Norway
121 P2 **Skogerøya** *island* Norway
121 P2 **Skogfoss** Norway
122 G3 **Skoghall** Sweden
120 G5 **Skogn** Norway
120 K1 **Skogsfjord** Norway
138 B3 **Skokholm Island** Wales UK
82 H5 **Skokie** Illinois USA
132 C1 **Skole** Ukraine
121 M4 **Skomakarfjärden** *bay* Sweden
138 B3 **Skomer Island** Wales UK
132 F1 **Skomoroshki** Ukraine
120 I3 **Skonseng** Norway
75 N8 **Skookumchuck** British Columbia Canada
133 C6 **Skopelos** Greece
133 C6 **Skopelos** *island* Greece
133 B4 **Skopje** Macedonia
125 I2 **Skorogoszcz** Poland
122 C2 **Skorpa** Norway
122 C2 **Skorpa** *island* Norway
120 J5 **Skorped** Sweden
122 E4 **Skørping** Denmark
122 E3 **Skottevik** Norway
133 C6 **Skourta** Greece
122 G3 **Skövde** Sweden
191 J1 **Skovorodino** Russian Federation
83 Q4 **Skowhegan** Maine USA
75 V7 **Skownan** Manitoba Canada
133 C5 **Skra** Greece
130 F4 **Skrad** Croatia
120 L3 **Skröven** Sweden
163 F4 **Skukuza** South Africa
120 E5 **Skuløya** *island* Norway
120 K2 **Skulsfjord** Norway
125 J1 **Skulsk** Poland
123 M4 **Skulte** Latvia
82 F6 **Skunk** *watercourse* Iowa USA
123 K4 **Skuodas** Lithuania
121 N1 **Skuotanjar'ga** *peninsula* Norway
120 inset **Skútustaðir** Iceland
120 I2 **Skutvika** Norway
132 F1 **Skvyra** Ukraine
133 C5 **Skydra** Greece
142 B3 **Skye** *island* Scotland UK
80 E3 **Skykomish** Washington USA
133 D6 **Skyros** Greece
133 D6 **Skyros** *island* Greece
58 S1 **Skytrain Ice Rise** Antarctica
123 N5 **Slabodka** Belarus
143 F4 **Slade** Ireland
140 B3 **Slade** Ireland
120 K4 **Slagnäs** Sweden
141 F3 **Slaidburn** Lancashire England UK
122 H3 **Slaka** Sweden
196 F5 **Slamet, Gunung** *volcano* Indonesia
125 K3 **Slaná** *watercourse* Slovakia
143 F3 **Slane** Ireland
125 K3 **Slanec** Slovakia
132 E4 **Slannik** *range* Bulgaria
130 G5 **Slano** Croatia
123 O3 **Slantsy** Russian Federation
125 H2 **Slaný** Czech Republic
86 A2 **Slapout** Oklahoma USA
120 J3 **Slappejaure** *lake* Sweden
120 K4 **Släppträsket** *lake* Sweden
139 F2 **Slapton** Northamptonshire England UK
125 J2 **Śląskie** *admin. area* Poland
82 H2 **Slate Islands** Ontario Canada
130 G4 **Slatina** Bosnia and Herzegovina
130 G4 **Slatina** Croatia
130 G2 **Slatinice** Czech Republic
132 C3 **Slătioara** Romania
85 L4 **Slaton** Texas USA
86 F5 **Slaughter** Louisiana USA
86 C3 **Slaughterville** Oklahoma USA
72 H7 **Slave** *watercourse* Alberta/Northwest Territories Canada
158 E3 **Slave Coast** *coast* Africa
75 N5 **Slave Lake** Alberta Canada
183 M3 **Slavgorod** Russian Federation
193 K2 **Slavnoye, Ozero** *lake* Russian Federation
125 H3 **Slavonice** Czech Republic
130 H4 **Slavonski Brod** Croatia
81 R5 **Slayton** Minnesota USA
143 B4 **Slea Head** *cape* Ireland
139 G2 **Sleaford** Lincolnshire England UK
218 B6 **Sleaford Bay** SA Australia
142 C3 **Sleat, Sound of** *bay* Scotland UK
75 R5 **Sled Lake** Saskatchewan Canada
86 F3 **Sledge** Mississippi USA
73 L7 **Sleeper Islands** Nunavut Canada
141 H2 **Sleights** North Yorkshire England UK
197 F5 **Sleman** Indonesia
120 K4 **Sleng** *lake* Sweden
58 W1 **Slessor Glacier** Antarctica
122 C3 **Sletta** *bay* Norway
122 F4 **Sletterhage** *cape* Denmark
86 G5 **Slidell** Louisiana USA
122 E2 **Slidrefjord** *bay* Norway
120 I3 **Slierogaise** *mountain* Sweden
140 B2 **Slieve** Ireland
143 E1 **Slievebane** Ireland
143 E4 **Slieveroe** Ireland
142 B3 **Sligachan** Highland Scotland UK
143 D2 **Sligo** Ireland
143 D2 **Sligo** *admin. area* Ireland
143 D2 **Sligo Bay** Ireland
90 D4 **Slilmasía** Nicaragua
129 H6 **Slim** Algeria
138 E3 **Slimbridge** Gloucestershire England UK
130 D3 **Slingia** Italy
142 F3 **Slioch** Aberdeenshire Scotland UK
220 F3 **Slipper Island** New Zealand
120 G5 **Slipra** Norway
123 J4 **Slite** Sweden
132 E4 **Sliven** Bulgaria
130 F4 **Slivnica** Croatia
132 C4 **Slivnitsa** Bulgaria
125 J1 **Śliwice** Poland
123 N5 **Sloboda** Belarus
123 P5 **Sloboda** Russian Federation
132 E3 **Slobozia Bradului** Romania
80 G2 **Slocan Lake** British Columbia Canada
124 D1 **Slochteren** Netherlands
74 E3 **Sloko** *watercourse* British Columbia Canada
125 K2 **Słomniki** Poland
221 C8 **Slope Point** New Zealand
139 G3 **Slough** *admin. area* England UK
139 G3 **Slough** Slough England UK
125 K5 **Slovac** Serbia
122 C2 **Sløvåg** Norway
125 J3 **Slovakia** *country* Europe
125 M1 **Slovatyche** Belarus
125 H5 **Slovenia** *country* Europe
132 D1 **Slovita** Ukraine
134 S3 **Slozhnyy, Ostrov** *island* Russian Federation
125 H1 **Słubice** Poland
136 C2 **Sluch** *watercourse* Ukraine
124 B2 **Sluis** Netherlands
125 H5 **Slunj** Croatia
122 I5 **Słupsk** Poland
143 B3 **Slyne Head** *cape* Ireland
190 E2 **Slyudyanka** Russian Federation
86 E4 **Smackover** Arkansas USA
122 H4 **Smaland** *region* Sweden
120 G5 **Småland** Norway
122 F5 **Smålandsfarvandet** *bay* Denmark
139 I2 **Smallburgh** Norfolk England UK
138 E4 **Smallridge** Devon England UK
78 F6 **Smallwood Reservoir** Newfoundland and Labrador Canada
123 N5 **Smalvas ežeras** *lake* Lithuania
130 F3 **Šmartno** Slovenia
121 M4 **Småskären** *island* Sweden
75 S6 **Smeaton** Saskatchewan Canada
123 O3 **Smerdi** Russian Federation
142 E2 **Smerral** Highland Scotland UK
83 L6 **Smethport** Pennsylvania USA
125 H2 **Smidary** Czech Republic
191 M3 **Smidovich** Russian Federation
125 M2 **Smidyn** Ukraine
132 G1 **Smila** Ukraine
75 Q7 **Smiley** Saskatchewan Canada
86 C6 **Smiley** Texas USA
133 D5 **Smilyan** Bulgaria
132 D4 **Smîrdioasa** Romania
127 L1 **Smiřice** Czech Republic
132 E4 **Smirnenski** Bulgaria
135 AD9 **Smirnykh** Russian Federation
75 N5 **Smith** Alberta Canada
74 H3 **Smith** *watercourse* British Columbia Canada
83 K4 **Smith, Cape** Ontario Canada
72 G5 **Smith Arm** Northwest Territories Canada
73 L3 **Smith Bay** Nunavut Canada
72 D4 **Smith Bay** Alaska USA
81 P7 **Smith Center** Kansas USA
58 Q1 **Smith Glacier** Antarctica
58 T2 **Smith Island** Antarctica
73 L6 **Smith Island** Nunavut Canada
87 M4 **Smith Island** North Carolina USA
87 L2 **Smith Mountain Lake** Virginia USA
74 H3 **Smith River** British Columbia Canada
73 L3 **Smith Sound** Canada/Greenland
74 H5 **Smithers** British Columbia Canada
87 L3 **Smithfield** North Carolina USA
83 L7 **Smithfield** Pennsylvania USA
83 M4 **Smiths Falls** Ontario Canada
82 H8 **Smiths Grove** Kentucky USA
210 inset **Smithson Bight** *bay* Christmas Island Australia
219 Q10 **Smithton** Tas. Australia
82 E7 **Smithton** Missouri USA
87 I5 **Smithville** Georgia USA
86 G3 **Smithville** Mississippi USA
86 C5 **Smithville** Texas USA
79 H9 **Smokey, Cape** Nova Scotia Canada
130 G5 **Smokvica** Croatia
72 H8 **Smoky** *watercourse* Alberta Canada
218 A5 **Smoky Bay** SA Australia
218 A5 **Smoky Bay** SA Australia
76 D6 **Smoky Burn** Saskatchewan Canada
77 N7 **Smoky Falls** Ontario Canada
81 O7 **Smoky Hill** *watercourse* Kansas USA
81 P7 **Smoky Hills** Kansas USA
120 F5 **Smøla** *island* Norway
182 F3 **Smolenka** Russian Federation
136 E1 **Smolensk** Russian Federation
134 H7 **Smolenskaya Oblast'** *admin. area* Russian Federation
132 G1 **Smolino** Ukraine
123 P6 **Smolitsa** Belarus
133 D5 **Smolyan** *admin. area* Bulgaria
132 C4 **Smolyanovtsi** Bulgaria
123 P5 **Smolyany** Belarus
73 K9 **Smooth Rock Falls** Ontario Canada
76 K7 **Smoothrock Lake** Ontario Canada
75 R5 **Smoothstone** *watercourse* Saskatchewan Canada
75 R5 **Smoothstone Lake** Saskatchewan Canada
125 M2 **Smorzhiv** Ukraine
132 E1 **Smotrych** Ukraine
122 G5 **Smygehamn** Sweden
58 S2 **Smyley Island** Antarctica
109 7 **Smylie Channel** Falkland Islands
87 H3 **Smyrna** Tennessee USA
140 D2 **Snaefell** *mountain* Isle of Man UK
120 inset **Snæfellsjökull** *mountain* Iceland
132 E3 **Snagov, Lacul** *lake* Romania
139 H2 **Snailwell** Cambridgeshire England UK
141 G3 **Snaith** East Riding of Yorkshire England UK
213 J4 **Snake** *watercourse* NT Australia
80 G3 **Snake** *watercourse* Idaho USA
80 F3 **Snake** *watercourse* Washington USA
213 K1 **Snake Bay** NT Australia
80 H7 **Snake Range** Nevada USA
74 J3 **Snake River** British Columbia Canada
80 I5 **Snake River Plain** Idaho USA
141 G2 **Snape** North Yorkshire England UK
139 I2 **Snape** Suffolk England UK
123 L2 **Snappertuna** Finland
121 M5 **Snåre** Finland
221 B9 **Snares, The** *islands* New Zealand
74 L6 **Snaring** *watercourse* Alberta Canada
120 H4 **Snåsa** Norway
120 H4 **Snåsvatnet** *bay* Norway
138 D2 **Snead** Powys Wales UK
87 H3 **Snead** Alabama USA
124 C1 **Sneek** Netherlands
143 C5 **Sneem** Ireland
78 H5 **Snegamook Lake** Newfoundland and Labrador Canada
77 W5 **Snelgrove Lake** Newfoundland and Labrador Canada
220 F3 **Snells Beach** New Zealand
139 H2 **Snettisham** Norfolk England UK
132 C1 **Snina** Slovakia
74 M5 **Snipe Lake** Alberta Canada
132 E1 **Snitkov** Ukraine
142 B3 **Snizort, Loch** *bay* Scotland UK
120 F5 **Snøhetta** *mountain* Norway
136 E2 **Snopot'** Russian Federation
120 F5 **Snota** *mountain* Norway
120 H3 **Snøtinden** *mountain* Norway
219 R10 **Snow Hill** Tas. Australia
83 N7 **Snow Hill** Maryland USA
58 U2 **Snow Hill Island** Antarctica
75 U5 **Snow Lake** Manitoba Canada
80 H6 **Snow Water Lake** Nevada USA
72 I6 **Snowbird Lake** Northwest Territories Canada
138 C1 **Snowdon** *mountain* Wales UK
75 Q1 **Snowdrift** *watercourse* Northwest Territories Canada
84 G3 **Snowflake** Arizona USA
218 D5 **Snowtown** SA Australia
80 I6 **Snowville** Utah USA
219 I7 **Snowy** *watercourse* NSW Australia
219 I7 **Snowy Mountains** NSW Australia
91 F2 **Snug Corner** Bahamas
194 E4 **Snuŏl** Cambodia
86 B3 **Snyder** Oklahoma USA
85 L4 **Snyder** Texas USA
83 L7 **Snyder Knob** *mountain* West Virginia USA
192 E4 **So-do** *island* South Korea
198 D4 **Soabuwe** Indonesia
100 C3 **Soacha** Colombia
121 M2 **Soadnojávri** *lake* Norway
163 I3 **Soalala** Madagascar
179 L2 **Soan** *watercourse* Pakistan
192 E4 **Soan-do** *island* South Korea
123 P1 **Soanlahti** Russian Federation
80 F3 **Soap Lake** Washington USA
199 G5 **Soari** *watercourse* Papua New Guinea
163 H4 **Soaserana** Madagascar
198 C3 **Soasiu** Indonesia
100 C3 **Soatá** Colombia
142 B3 **Soay** *island* Scotland UK
162 C2 **Soba Matias** Angola
192 E4 **Sobaek-sanmaek** South Korea
105 E4 **Soberante** Bolivia
120 I2 **Søberg** Norway
199 G4 **Sobger** *watercourse* Indonesia
125 K2 **Sobienie-Jeziory** Poland
182 C2 **Sobinka** Russian Federation
135 AG8 **Sobolevo** Russian Federation
125 K2 **Sobolew** Poland
125 K2 **Sobótka** Poland
102 D5 **Sobradinho, Represa de** *lake* Brazil
102 D3 **Sobral** Brazil
128 E2 **Sobrón, Embalse de** *lake* Spain
194 E5 **Sóc Trăng** Vietnam
182 C5 **Sochi** Russian Federation
192 E4 **Söch'ŏn** South Korea
223 14 **Societé, Îles de la** *island* French Polynesia
87 L3 **Society Hill** South Carolina USA
141 G2 **Sockburn** Darlington England UK
132 B2 **Socodor** Romania
125 K5 **Socol** Romania
106 D3 **Socompa** Chile
106 D3 **Socompa, Volcán** *volcano* Chile
103 C8 **Socorro** Brazil
100 C3 **Socorro** Colombia
85 K7 **Socorro** Mexico
195 J5 **Socorro** Philippines
85 I3 **Socorro** New Mexico USA
85 I5 **Socorro** Texas USA
88 C5 **Socorro, Isla** *island* Mexico
100 C3 **Socotá** Colombia
Socotra *see* **Suquṭrā** Yemen
128 F4 **Socovos** Spain
74 J6 **Soda Creek** British Columbia Canada
84 C3 **Soda Lake** California USA
80 J5 **Soda Springs** Idaho USA
121 O3 **Sodankylä** Finland
87 I3 **Soddy-Daisy** Tennessee USA
122 I4 **Söderåkra** Sweden
122 H3 **Söderälgen** *lake* Sweden
123 L3 **Söderby** Estonia
123 J2 **Söderfjärden** *bay* Finland
122 I2 **Söderhamn** Sweden
122 I3 **Södermanland** *admin. area* Sweden
122 I3 **Södertälje** Sweden
120 L5 **Söderudden** Finland
156 D5 **Sodiri** Sudan
161 F2 **Sodo** Ethiopia
122 H2 **Södra Barken** *bay* Sweden
123 K1 **Södra Björkön** *island* Finland
122 F3 **Södra Bullaresjön** *lake* Sweden
122 I2 **Södra Dellen** *lake* Sweden
122 I3 **Södra Enby** Sweden
122 I3 **Södra Finnö** *island* Sweden
120 J4 **Södra Insjö** Sweden
122 F3 **Södra Kornsjön** *lake* Sweden
123 J2 **Södra Kvarken** *bay* Sweden
120 I4 **Södra Storfjället** *island* Sweden
120 J4 **Södra Tresund** Sweden
120 L5 **Södra Vallgrund** Finland
125 H5 **Sodražica** Slovenia
197 J6 **Soë** Indonesia
163 G3 **Sofala** *admin. area* Mozambique
Sofia *see* **Sofiya** Bulgaria
163 I3 **Sofia** *watercourse* Madagascar
132 F2 **Sofia** Moldova
133 C7 **Sofiko** Greece
132 C4 **Sofiya** *admin. area* Bulgaria
132 C4 **Sofiya (Sofia)** Bulgaria
132 G1 **Sofiyevka** Ukraine
132 G1 **Sofiyivka** Ukraine
135 AC8 **Sofiysk** Russian Federation
135 AB8 **Sofiysk** Russian Federation
120 J2 **Søfjord** Norway
121 Q4 **Sofporog** Russian Federation
133 E7 **Sofrana** *island* Greece
181 G2 **Sog Qu** *watercourse* Xizang Zizhiqu China
100 C3 **Sogamoso** Colombia
100 C3 **Sogamoso** *watercourse* Colombia
199 H5 **Sogeram** *watercourse* Papua New Guinea
183 J6 **Soghd** *admin. area* Tajikistan
122 D2 **Sogn og Fjordane** *admin. area* Norway
120 E6 **Sogndalsfjøra** Norway
122 C2 **Sognefjorden** *bay* Norway
122 C2 **Sognesjøen** *bay* Norway
161 F3 **Sogo Hills** *plain* Kenya
195 J5 **Sogod** Philippines
195 J5 **Sogod Bay** Philippines
133 E6 **Soğucak** Turkey
133 F7 **Söğüt** Turkey
133 G5 **Söğüt** Turkey
192 E5 **Sŏgwip'o** South Korea
Sohag *see* **Sawhāj** Egypt
139 H2 **Soham** Cambridgeshire England UK
132 E3 **Sohatu** Romania
192 E4 **Soheugsan-do** *island* South Korea
190 F2 **Sohor, Gora** *mountain* Russian Federation
192 E3 **Sohung** North Korea
126 G1 **Soignies** Belgium
132 C3 **Şoimuş** Romania
121 N5 **Soini** Finland
121 P5 **Soisalo** *island* Finland
126 F2 **Soissons** France
186 C6 **Sojat** Rajasthan India
125 I4 **Söjtör** Hungary
162 E4 **Sojwe** Botswana
192 F3 **Sokch'o** South Korea
160 C5 **Sokele** Democratic Republic of Congo
182 C5 **Sokhumi** Georgia
125 M2 **Sokil** Ukraine
121 M5 **Soklot** Finland
122 E2 **Sokna** Norway
132 B4 **Sokobanja** Serbia
158 E3 **Sokodé** Togo
193 I1 **Sokol** Russian Federation
130 H5 **Sokolac** Bosnia and Herzegovina
125 L1 **Sokolany** Poland
154 E6 **Sokolo** Mali
125 L1 **Sokołów Podlaski** Poland
125 L3 **Sokolya** Ukraine
154 C6 **Sokone** Senegal
121 P2 **Sokosti** *mountain* Finland
159 F2 **Sokoto** Nigeria
159 F2 **Sokoto** *admin. area* Nigeria
159 F2 **Sokoto** *watercourse* Nigeria
125 K3 **Sol'** Slovakia
182 G3 **Sol-iletsk** Russian Federation
160 D5 **Sola** Democratic Republic of Congo
195 I3 **Solana** Philippines
84 D4 **Solana Beach** California USA
221 B8 **Solander Islands** New Zealand
102 F4 **Solânea** Brazil
107 G6 **Solanet** Argentina
100 C4 **Solano** Colombia
85 J3 **Solano** New Mexico USA
108 C3 **Solano, Bahía** *bay* Argentina
187 D8 **Solapur** Maharashtra India
124 E5 **Solaro** Italy
198 C3 **Solat, Gunung** *mountain* Indonesia
125 H4 **Solčava** Slovenia
127 I5 **Solche, Pointe de** *cape* Corsica France
100 B5 **Soldado Luna** Peru
135 AI6 **Soldatovo** Russian Federation
127 J3 **Sölden** Austria
82 D5 **Soldier** *watercourse* Iowa USA
72 D6 **Soldotna** Alaska USA
125 K2 **Solec nad Wisłą** Poland
106 F4 **Soledad** Argentina
100 C2 **Soledad** Colombia
84 B2 **Soledad** California USA
101 E3 **Soledad** Venezuela
88 E3 **Soledad de Abajo** Mexico
88 E4 **Soledad Díez Gutiérrez** Mexico
107 H4 **Soledade** Brazil
182 D4 **Solenoye** Russian Federation
122 F2 **Sølensjøen** *lake* Norway
139 F4 **Solent, The** *strait* England UK
131 C6 **Solenzara** Corsica France
158 D2 **Solenzo** Burkina Faso
120 L5 **Solf** Finland
122 H4 **Solgen** *lake* Sweden
130 D4 **Soliera** Italy
139 F2 **Solihull** West Midlands England UK
134 M7 **Solikamsk** Russian Federation
131 D8 **Soliman** Tunisia
124 D2 **Solingen** Germany
162 C4 **Solitaire** Namibia
214 B7 **Solitaire, Mount** NT Australia
122 G3 **Söljeflagen** *bay* Sweden
130 E4 **Solkan** Slovenia
120 J5 **Sollefteå** Sweden
122 I3 **Sollentuna** Sweden
129 H4 **Sóller** Spain
122 C2 **Sollsvika** Norway
197 F5 **Solo** *watercourse* Indonesia
121 O2 **Solojärvi** *lake* Finland
196 D4 **Solok** Indonesia
81 Q7 **Solomon** Kansas USA
199 K5 **Solomon Islands** *country* Oceania
199 I5 **Solomon Sea** Papua New Guinea
83 Q4 **Solon** Maine USA
83 K6 **Solon** Ohio USA
82 F3 **Solon Springs** Wisconsin USA
182 J4 **Solonchak Arys** *lake* Kazakhstan
182 H6 **Solonchakovyye Vpadiny Unguz** *lake* Turkmenistan
183 N3 **Soloneshnoye** Russian Federation
198 B6 **Solor** *island* Indonesia
198 B6 **Solor, Kepulauan** *islands* Indonesia
223 12c **Solosolo** Samoa
127 H3 **Solothurn** Switzerland
132 C2 **Solotvyno** Ukraine
121 S4 **Solovetskiy** Russian Federation
121 S4 **Solovetskiye Ostrova** *island* Russian Federation
136 E1 **Solov'yëvo** Russian Federation
191 J1 **Solov'yevsk** Russian Federation
133 F5 **Sölöz** Turkey
120 G4 **Solsem** Norway
129 G3 **Solsona** Spain
132 A2 **Solt** Hungary
124 E1 **Soltau** Germany
183 O3 **Solton** Russian Federation
123 P3 **Sol'tsy** Russian Federation
133 B5 **Solunska Glava** *mountain* Macedonia
84 B3 **Solvang** California USA
122 H4 **Sölvesborg** Sweden
120 E6 **Solvorn** Norway
142 E6 **Solway Firth** *bay* Scotland UK
162 E2 **Solwezi** Zambia
186 C6 **Som** Rajasthan India
193 I4 **Soma** Japan
126 F1 **Somain** France
54 J5 **Somali Basin** *underwater feature* Indian Ocean
161 I1 **Somali Peninsula** *peninsula* Somalia
161 H2 **Somalia** *country* Africa
161 F5 **Somanga** Tanzania
179 I2 **Sombā** Iran
127 G3 **Sombernon** France
130 H4 **Sombor** Serbia
88 E4 **Sombrerete** Mexico
109 20 **Sombrero** *island* Anguilla
196 B2 **Sombrero Channel** *strait* India
194 B6 **Sombrero Channel** Andaman and Nicobar Islands India
106 F2 **Sombrero Negro** Argentina
107 I4 **Sombrio** Brazil
107 I4 **Sombrio, Lagoa do** *lake* Brazil
124 C2 **Someren** Netherlands
123 L2 **Somerniemi** Finland
83 N7 **Somers Point** New Jersey USA
83 inset **Somerset** Bermuda
138 E3 **Somerset** *admin. area* England UK
85 I1 **Somerset** Colorado USA
82 I8 **Somerset** Kentucky USA
83 J7 **Somerset** Ohio USA
86 B6 **Somerset** Texas USA
162 E6 **Somerset East** South Africa
83 inset **Somerset Island** Bermuda
73 J4 **Somerset Island** Nunavut Canada
162 C6 **Somerset West** South Africa
219 J4 **Somerton** NSW Australia
139 F3 **Somerton** Oxfordshire England UK
138 E3 **Somerton** Somerset England UK
84 E4 **Somerton** Arizona USA
83 N6 **Somerville** New Jersey USA
86 G3 **Somerville** Tennessee USA
86 C5 **Somerville** Texas USA
85 N5 **Somerville Lake** Texas USA
132 C2 **Someş** *watercourse* Romania
132 C2 **Someşu Cald** *watercourse* Romania
132 C2 **Someşu Mic** *watercourse* Romania
120 K2 **Sommarøy** Norway
120 J2 **Sommarøy** *island* Norway
126 E1 **Somme** *watercourse* France
126 E1 **Somme, Baie de la** *bay* France
122 H4 **Sommen** *lake* Sweden
126 G5 **Sommières** France
126 E3 **Sommières-du-Clain** France
120 H4 **Sømna** *island* Norway
125 I4 **Somogy** *admin. area* Hungary
223 9a **Somosomo** Fiji
90 C4 **Somotillo** Nicaragua
90 C4 **Somoto** Nicaragua
187 F7 **Sompeta** Andhra Pradesh India
125 J1 **Sompolno** Poland
139 G4 **Sompting** West Sussex England UK
108 C2 **Somuncurá, Meseta de** *plateau* Argentina
186 F6 **Son** *watercourse* Madhya Pradesh India
194 D2 **Sơn La** Vietnam
129 H4 **Son Servera** Spain
124 F5 **Sona** Italy
90 D5 **Soná** Panama
135 AC8 **Sonakh** Russian Federation
183 K3 **Sonaly** Kazakhstan
183 K3 **Sonaly** Kazakhstan
186 E6 **Sonar** *watercourse* Madhya Pradesh India
181 H3 **Sonari** Assam India
192 F2 **Sŏnbong** North Korea
192 E3 **Sonch'ŏn** North Korea
128 E2 **Soncillo** Spain
124 F4 **Sondalo** Italy
121 R5 **Sondaly** Russian Federation
122 E5 **Sønderho** Denmark
122 E4 **Søndervig** Denmark
78 N2 **Søndre Storø** *island* Greenland
Søndre Strømfjord *see* **Kangerlussuaq** Greenland
187 F7 **Sonepur** Orissa India
122 E2 **Soneren** *lake* Norway
159 G4 **Song** Gabon
197 G3 **Song** Malaysia
194 F4 **Sông Cầu** Vietnam
194 E2 **Song Da (Black)** *watercourse* Vietnam
194 E2 **Song Hông (Red)** *watercourse* Vietnam
188 D4 **Song Ko** *watercourse* Yunnan China
183 L5 **Song-Köl** *lake* Kyrgyzstan
191 I5 **Song Ling** *range* Liaoning China
194 D2 **Sông Mã** Vietnam
189 F1 **Song Xian** Henan China
158 E3 **Songaw Lagoon** *bay* Ghana
188 F2 **Songbai** Hubei China
161 F6 **Songea** Tanzania
122 D3 **Songevatnet** *lake* Norway
192 E3 **Sŏnggan** North Korea
199 G4 **Songgato** *watercourse* Indonesia
191 L3 **Songhua Jiang** *watercourse* Heilongjiang China
192 E3 **Songhwa** North Korea
185 J3 **Songino** Mongolia
187 D7 **Songir** Maharashtra India
194 D6 **Songkhla** Thailand
194 D3 **Songkhram** *watercourse* Thailand
194 D6 **Songkla** *admin. area* Thailand
188 C3 **Songmai** Sichuan China
192 E4 **Söngnam** South Korea
192 E3 **Songnim** North Korea
161 F5 **Songo Songo** *island* Tanzania
188 D2 **Songpan** Sichuan China
188 E3 **Songshan** Guizhou China
188 F3 **Songtao** Guizhou China
161 E5 **Songwe** *watercourse* Tanzania
192 E3 **Sŏngwŏn** North Korea
188 D3 **Songyang** Yunnan China
191 J3 **Songyuan** Jilin China
189 H3 **Songyuan** Zhejiang China
189 F2 **Songzi** Hubei China
186 F6 **Sonhat** Chhattisgarh India
186 D5 **Sonipat** Haryana India
104 E6 **Soniquera** Bolivia
121 N3 **Sonka** Finland
121 O5 **Sonkajärvi** Finland
121 O5 **Sonkari** *lake* Finland
179 K4 **Sonmiani** Pakistan
127 J1 **Sonneberg** Germany
75 R6 **Sonningdale** Saskatchewan Canada
102 C5 **Sono** *watercourse* Brazil
88 C2 **Sonora** *admin. area* Mexico
88 C2 **Sonora** *watercourse* Mexico
80 E8 **Sonora** California USA
85 L5 **Sonora** Texas USA
88 B2 **Sonoyta** Mexico
178 F2 **Sonqor** Iran
128 E4 **Sonseca** Spain
100 C3 **Sonsón** Colombia
122 E2 **Sønstevatn** *lake* Norway
127 I1 **Sontra** Germany
161 H2 **Sool** *admin. area* Somalia
107 G4 **Sopas** *watercourse* Uruguay
78 D1 **Soper** *watercourse* Nunavut Canada
87 J4 **Soperton** Georgia USA
213 I5 **Sophie Downs** WA Australia
198 D3 **Sopi, Tanjung** *cape* Indonesia
132 F1 **Sopin** Ukraine
133 B5 **Sopište** Macedonia
160 D2 **Sopo** *watercourse* Sudan
193 K2 **Sopochnoye, Ozero** *lake* Russian Federation
133 B5 **Sopot** Albania
123 J5 **Sopot** Poland
132 B3 **Şopotu Nou** Romania
121 O3 **Soppela** Finland
125 I4 **Sopron** Hungary
186 D3 **Sopur** Jammu and Kashmir India/Pakistan
198 C3 **Soputan, Gunung** *volcano* Indonesia
222 6a **Sopweru, Mochun** *strait* Federated States of Micronesia
120 H3 **Sør-Arnøy** Norway
122 H2 **Sör Hörken** *lake* Sweden
182 G4 **Sor Kaydak** *lake* Kazakhstan
182 G4 **Sor Mertvyy Kultuk** *lake* Kazakhstan
122 F2 **Sør-Mesna** *lake* Norway
58 B2 **Sør Rondane Mountains** Antarctica
120 G5 **Sør-Trøndelag** *admin. area* Norway
120 L1 **Sør Tverrfjord** Norway
121 P2 **Sør Varanger Herad** Norway
131 E6 **Sora** Italy
187 F7 **Sorada** Orissa India
120 J5 **Söråker** Sweden
120 H3 **Sørarnøy** *island* Norway
104 D4 **Sorata** Bolivia
104 C4 **Soraya** Peru
128 E5 **Sorbas** Spain
124 F5 **Sorbolo** Italy
121 M4 **Sörbrändofjärden** *bay* Sweden
120 J5 **Sörbygden** Sweden
135 AB6 **Sordoginskiy Khrebet** *range* Russian Federation
83 O3 **Sorel** Quebec Canada
73 L9 **Sorel-Tracy** Quebec Canada
219 R11 **Sorell** Tas. Australia
219 Q11 **Sorell, Cape** Tas. Australia
219 R11 **Sorell, Lake** Tas. Australia
124 E5 **Soresina** Italy
199 K5 **Sorezaru Point** Solomon Islands
122 I3 **Sörfjärden** *bay* Sweden
120 I3 **Sørfjordmoen** Norway
122 I1 **Sörfors** Sweden
129 I1 **Sorgues** France
129 H2 **Sorgues** *watercourse* France
128 E3 **Soria** Spain
107 G5 **Soriano** *admin. area* Uruguay
196 C3 **Sorikmarapi** *volcano* Indonesia
104 B2 **Soritor** Peru
134 D3 **Sørkappøya** *cape* Norway
183 L3 **Sorkopa** *lake* Kazakhstan
120 H3 **Sørland** Norway
120 F5 **Sørleka** *island* Norway
120 H4 **Sørli** Norway
120 J2 **Sørli** Norway
142 D5 **Sorn** East Ayrshire Scotland UK
122 F5 **Sorø** Denmark
187 G7 **Soro** Orissa India
109 1c **Sorobon** Netherlands Antilles
132 F1 **Soroca** Moldova
103 C8 **Sorocaba** Brazil
182 G3 **Sorochinsk** Russian Federation
123 O4 **Sorokino** Russian Federation
199 G1 **Sorol** *island* Federated States of Micronesia
159 G3 **Sorombéo** Cameroon
198 D4 **Sorong** Indonesia
102 B4 **Sororó** *watercourse* Brazil
161 E3 **Soroti** Uganda
121 M1 **Sørøya** *island* Norway
128 B4 **Sorraia** *watercourse* Portugal
86 F5 **Sorrento** Louisiana USA
120 J2 **Sørrollnes** Norway
120 K2 **Sørruisa** Norway
123 N1 **Sorsavesi** *lake* Finland
120 J4 **Sorsele** Sweden
122 G2 **Sörsjön** Sweden
131 C6 **Sorso** Sardinia Italy
195 J4 **Sorsogon** Philippines
129 G2 **Sort** Spain
123 P2 **Sortavala** Russian Federation
120 I2 **Sortland** Norway
120 G5 **Sørungen** *lake* Norway
120 H3 **Sorvær** Norway
120 H3 **Sørvågen** Norway
120 H5 **Sörvattnet** Sweden
120 J2 **Sørvik** Norway
120 G5 **Sørvika** Norway
120 I5 **Sörviken** Sweden
129 G1 **Sos** France
129 F2 **Sos del Rey Católico** Spain
192 E4 **Sŏsan** South Korea
77 Q7 **Soscumica, Lac** *lake* Quebec Canada
123 O3 **Sosedno** Russian Federation
125 H5 **Sošice** Croatia
136 E2 **Soskovo** Russian Federation
135 W6 **Sosna** Russian Federation
136 F2 **Sosna** *watercourse* Russian Federation
106 D5 **Sosneado** *mountain* Argentina
125 I1 **Sośnica** Poland
125 M3 **Sosniv** Ukraine
134 L6 **Sosnogorsk** Russian Federation
121 S4 **Sosnovets** Russian Federation
183 M3 **Sosnovka** Kazakhstan
183 L5 **Sosnovka** Kyrgyzstan
121 V3 **Sosnovka** Russian Federation
182 D2 **Sosnovka** Russian Federation
123 O4 **Sosnovo** Russian Federation
123 O3 **Sosnovo** Russian Federation
123 P2 **Sosnovo** Russian Federation
121 R4 **Sosnovyy** Russian Federation
123 O3 **Sosnovyy Bor** Russian Federation
134 R6 **Sosnovyy Bor** Russian Federation
125 J2 **Sosnowiec** Poland
121 N4 **Soso** Finland
127 H5 **Sospel** France
159 H4 **Sosso** Central African Republic
125 H4 **Šoštanj** Slovenia
91 G3 **Sosúa** Dominican Republic
164 4 **Sotavento, Ilhas do** *island* Cape Verde
122 F3 **Sotefjorden** *bay* Sweden
108 C2 **Sotera, Laguna** *lake* Argentina
105 E3 **Soterio** *watercourse* Brazil
121 P4 **Sotkamo** Finland
106 E4 **Soto** Argentina
109 1b **Soto** Netherlands Antilles
89 F4 **Soto La Marina** Mexico
89 F4 **Soto La Marina** *watercourse* Mexico
129 F2 **Sotonera, Embalse de** *lake* Spain
158 E3 **Sotouboua** Togo
128 D2 **Sotresgudo** Spain
122 H3 **Sottern** *lake* Sweden
89 H4 **Sotuta** Mexico
159 G4 **Souanké** Congo
158 C3 **Soubré** Côte d'Ivoire
109 13 **Soucis** St Lucia
221 E5 **Soucis, Cape** New Zealand
214 D6 **Soudan** NT Australia
82 E3 **Soudan** Minnesota USA
159 F4 **Souellaba, Pointe** *cape* Cameroon
126 F3 **Souesmes** France
127 H2 **Soufflenheim** France
133 E5 **Soufli** Greece
109 16 **Soufrière** *volcano* Guadeloupe
109 17 **Soufrière** *volcano* Montserrat
109 13 **Soufrière** St Lucia
109 11a **Soufrière** *volcano* St Vincent and the Grenadines
155 G1 **Sougueur** Algeria
126 E4 **Souillac** France
127 G2 **Souilly** France
155 H1 **Souk Ahras** Algeria
128 D6 **Souk-el-Arba-des-Beni-Hassan** Morocco
131 C8 **Souk-el Khemis** Tunisia
155 G6 **Soukoukoutane** Niger
192 E4 **Sŏul (Seoul)** South Korea
126 D4 **Soulac-sur-Mer** France
141 F2 **Soulby** Cumbria England UK
130 B3 **Soultz** France
127 G1 **Soumagne** Belgium
129 F2 **Soumoulou** France
138 E1 **Sound** Cheshire England UK
138 C4 **Sound, The** *bay* England UK
194 B4 **Sound Island** Andaman and Nicobar Islands India
75 P7 **Sounding Creek** Alberta Canada
154 C6 **Soungrougrou** *watercourse* Senegal
178 C2 **Soûr (Tyre)** Lebanon
155 G1 **Sour el Ghozlane** Algeria
126 D2 **Sourdeval** France
102 B3 **Soure** Brazil
128 B3 **Soure** Portugal
75 U8 **Souris** Manitoba Canada
75 U8 **Souris** *watercourse* Manitoba Canada
75 T8 **Souris** *watercourse* Saskatchewan Canada
79 G9 **Souris** Prince Edward Island Canada
81 O2 **Souris** *watercourse* North Dakota USA
133 C6 **Sourpi** Greece
102 E4 **Sousa** Brazil
128 C4 **Sousel** Portugal
155 I1 **Sousse** Tunisia
126 D5 **Soustons** France
126 D5 **Soustons, Étang de** *lake* France
159 E2 **Souta** *watercourse* Benin
162 D6 **South Africa** *country* Africa
214 B2 **South Alligator** NT Australia
214 B2 **South Alligator** *watercourse* NT Australia
58 T3 **South America** *continent*
194 B5 **South Andaman** *island* Andaman and Nicobar Islands India
78 H4 **South Aulatsivik Island** Newfoundland and Labrador Canada
218 B3 **South Australia** *admin. area* Australia
55 R8 **South Australian Basin** *seabed*
142 D5 **South Ayrshire** *admin. area* Scotland UK
140 D1 **South Balloch** South Ayrshire Scotland UK
76 I7 **South Bay** Ontario Canada
83 J4 **South Baymouth** Ontario Canada
82 H6 **South Bend** Indiana USA
80 D3 **South Bend** Washington USA
74 H6 **South Bentinck** British Columbia Canada
215 J7 **South Blackwater** Qld Australia
87 L2 **South Boston** Virginia USA
138 D4 **South Brent** Devon England UK
79 J8 **South Brook** Newfoundland and Labrador Canada
194 B5 **South Brother Island** Andaman and Nicobar Islands India
219 R11 **South Bruny Island** Tas. Australia
216 F5 **South Burracoppin** WA Australia
221 B8 **South Cape (Whiore)** New Zealand
71 **South Carolina** *admin. area* USA
141 H3 **South Cave** East Riding of Yorkshire England UK
139 F3 **South Cerney** Gloucestershire England UK
83 K7 **South Charleston** West Virginia USA

141 G1 **South Charlton** Northumberland England UK
195 G4 **South China Sea**
195 G4 **South China Sea** Asia
82 D8 **South Coffeyville** Oklahoma USA
70 **South Dakota** *admin. area* USA
87 K6 **South Daytona** Florida USA
142 B2 **South Dell** Na h-Eileanan Siar Scotland UK
215 K4 **South Diamond Island** Coral Sea Islands Territory Australia
139 G4 **South Downs** *range* England UK
162 E4 **South-East** *admin. area* Botswana
219 R11 **South East Cape** Tas. Australia
218 H8 **South East Point** Vic. Australia
222 1a **South East Point** Kiribati
213 I6 **South Esk Tablelands** WA Australia
52 N10 **South Fiji Basin** *underwater feature* Pacific Ocean
52 O10 **South Fiji Ridge** *underwater feature* Pacific Ocean
139 I3 **South Foreland** *cape* England UK
81 L8 **South Fork** Colorado USA
81 N7 **South Fork Republican** *watercourse* Colorado USA
80 D6 **South Fork Trinity** *watercourse* California USA
109 19 **South Friar's Bay** Saint Kitts and Nevis
58 H1 **South Geomagnetic Pole** Antarctica
109 8 **South Georgia** *island* South Georgia
42 **South Georgia and the South Sandwich Islands** *UK territory* Southern Ocean
51 N15 **South Georgia Ridge** *underwater feature* Scotia Sea
138 E3 **South Gloucestershire** *admin. area* England UK
213 L1 **South Goulburn Island** NT Australia
219 K3 **South Grafton** NSW Australia
142 B3 **South Harris** *island* Scotland UK
139 G4 **South Harting** West Sussex England UK
81 Q8 **South Haven** Kansas USA
82 H5 **South Haven** Michigan USA
211 inset **South Head** Lord Howe Island Australia
220 F3 **South Head** New Zealand
212 E6 **South Hedland** WA Australia
73 J6 **South Henik Lake** Nunavut Canada
87 L2 **South Hill** Virginia USA
52 K5 **South Honshu Ridge** *underwater feature* Pacific Ocean
161 F3 **South Horr** Kenya
58 H3 **South Indian Basin** *underwater feature* Southern Ocean
215 K6 **South Island** Qld Australia
221 C6 **South Island** New Zealand
210 inset **South Island (Atas)** Cocos (Keeling) Islands Australia
195 H5 **South Islet** Philippines
109 7 **South Jason** *island* Falkland Islands
210 inset **South Keeling Islands** Cocos (Keeling) Islands Australia
75 W3 **South Knife** *watercourse* Manitoba Canada
75 W3 **South Knife Lake** Manitoba Canada
75 W3 **South Knife Lake** Manitoba Canada
192 F4 **South Korea** *country* Asia
139 G1 **South Kyme** Lincolnshire England UK
80 F7 **South Lake Tahoe** California USA
142 E5 **South Lanarkshire** *admin. area* Scotland UK
139 I2 **South Lopham** Norfolk England UK
81 P6 **South Loup** *watercourse* Nebraska USA
58 J1 **South Magnetic Pole** Antarctica
139 H4 **South Malling** East Sussex England UK
87 K8 **South Miami** Florida USA
138 D3 **South Molton** Devon England UK
73 J8 **South Moose Lake** Manitoba Canada
83 M7 **South Mountains** Pennsylvania USA
74 H2 **South Nahanni** *watercourse* Northwest Territories Canada
90 E3 **South Negril Point** *cape* Jamaica
52 M10 **South New Hebrides Trench** *underwater feature* Pacific Ocean
141 H3 **South Newbald** East Riding of Yorkshire England UK
58 U2 **South Orkney Islands** *UK territory* Antarctica
86 C7 **South Padre Island** Texas USA
222 1a **South Passage** *strait* Kiribati
138 E4 **South Petherton** Somerset England UK
85 L3 **South Plains** Texas USA
214 D3 **South Point** NT Australia
91 F2 **South Point** Bahamas
109 12 **South Point** *cape* Barbados
210 inset **South Point** Christmas Island Australia
86 G6 **South Point** Louisiana USA
58 F1 **South Pole** Antarctica
83 P5 **South Portland** Maine USA
139 H2 **South Raynham** Norfolk England UK
141 I3 **South Reston** Lincolnshire England UK
83 L4 **South River** Ontario Canada
142 F2 **South Ronaldsay** *island* Scotland UK
58 V2 **South Sandwich Fracture Zone** *underwater feature* Atlantic Ocean
75 P7 **South Saskatchewan** *watercourse* Alberta/Saskatchewan Canada
75 W3 **South Seal** *watercourse* Manitoba Canada
58 U2 **South Shetland Islands** Antarctica
51 L16 **South Shetland Trough** *underwater feature* Southern Ocean
81 Q5 **South Sioux City** Nebraska USA
80 E4 **South Sister** *volcano* Oregon USA
52 M9 **South Solomon Trench** *underwater feature* Pacific Ocean
141 I3 **South Somercotes** Lincolnshire England UK
73 L5 **South Spicer Island** Nunavut Canada
139 G2 **South Stoke** Lincolnshire England UK
219 K2 **South Stradbroke Island** Qld Australia
220 F4 **South Taranaki Bight** *bay* New Zealand
55 S9 **South Tasman Rise** *underwater feature* Southern Ocean
216 E5 **South Trayning** WA Australia
84 G4 **South Tucson** Arizona USA
77 P6 **South Twin Island** Nunavut Canada
141 G2 **South Tyneside** *admin. area* England UK
75 O5 **South Wabasca Lake** Alberta Canada
215 H3 **South Warden Reef** Qld Australia
214 E4 **South Wellesley Islands** Qld Australia
210 inset **South West Bay** Heard Island Australia
221 B8 **South West Cape** New Zealand
215 K4 **South West Cay** *island* Coral Sea Islands Territory Australia
214 D3 **South West Island** NT Australia
222 1a **South West Point** Kiribati
211 inset **South West Point** Macquarie Island Australia
164 5b **South West Point** *cape* St Helena
86 G6 **South West Point** Louisiana USA
219 K4 **South West Rocks** NSW Australia
85 M4 **South Wichita** *watercourse* Texas USA
78 K6 **South Wolf Island** Newfoundland and Labrador Canada
139 H3 **South Woodham Ferrers** Essex England UK
139 H2 **South Wootton** Norfolk England UK
139 F2 **Southam** Warwickshire England UK
83 K4 **Southampton** Ontario Canada
139 F4 **Southampton** *admin. area* England UK
139 F4 **Southampton** Southampton England UK
83 O6 **Southampton** New York USA
76 L1 **Southampton Island** Nunavut Canada
86 G3 **Southaven** Mississippi USA
139 H3 **Southborough** Kent England UK
221 E6 **Southbridge** New Zealand
221 9 **Southeast Harbour** Campbell Island New Zealand
55 M9 **Southeast Indian Ridge** *seabed*
53 W12 **Southeast Pacific Basin** *underwater feature* Pacific Ocean
91 F2 **Southeast Point** Bahamas
218 E7 **Southend** SA Australia
142 C5 **Southend** Argyll and Bute Scotland UK
139 H3 **Southend** *admin. area* England UK
139 H3 **Southend-on-Sea** Southend England UK
75 T4 **Southend Reindeer** Saskatchewan Canada
162 D4 **Southern** *admin. area* Botswana
163 G2 **Southern** *admin. area* Malawi
162 E3 **Southern** *admin. area* Zambia
221 D6 **Southern Alps (Ka Tiritiri O Te Moana)** *range* New Zealand
87 M8 **Southern Bight** *bay* Bahamas
216 E5 **Southern Brook** WA Australia
220 1 **Southern Cook Islands** Cook Islands New Zealand
216 F5 **Southern Cross** WA Australia
156 D5 **Southern Darfur** *admin. area* Sudan
79 L9 **Southern Harbour** Newfoundland and Labrador Canada
216 H6 **Southern Hills** WA Australia
75 V4 **Southern Indian Lake** Manitoba Canada
156 E5 **Southern Kordofan** *admin. area* Sudan
162 D3 **Southern Lueti** *watercourse* Zambia
58 F3 **Southern Ocean**
87 L3 **Southern Pines** North Carolina USA
87 N2 **Southern Shores** North Carolina USA
138 D3 **Southerndown** Vale of Glamorgan Wales UK
139 H2 **Southery** Norfolk England UK
75 S7 **Southey** Saskatchewan Canada
90 E3 **Southfield** Jamaica
82 J5 **Southfield** Michigan USA
74 I7 **Southgate** *watercourse* British Columbia Canada
139 H3 **Southminster** Essex England UK
139 I2 **Southolt** Suffolk England UK
219 R11 **Southport** Tas. Australia
140 E3 **Southport** Merseyside England UK
87 M4 **Southport** North Carolina USA
141 H3 **Southrey** Lincolnshire England UK
87 H4 **Southside** Alabama USA
142 F2 **Southtown** Orkney Islands Scotland UK
138 E4 **Southwell** Dorset England UK
139 G1 **Southwell** Nottinghamshire England UK
195 G5 **Southwest Cay** *island* Spratly Islands
54 J8 **Southwest Indian Ridge** *seabed*
53 S12 **Southwest Pacific Basin** *underwater feature* Pacific Ocean
139 I2 **Southwold** Suffolk England UK
120 L3 **Soutojärvi** *lake* Sweden
132 D2 **Sovata** Romania
123 K5 **Sovetsk** Russian Federation
134 K7 **Sovetsk** Russian Federation
135 AD9 **Sovetskaya Gavan'** Russian Federation
123 O2 **Sovetskiy** Russian Federation
134 R5 **Sovetskoye, Ozero** *lake* Russian Federation
120 E5 **Søvik** Norway
120 E5 **Sövik** Norway
130 G5 **Sovra** Croatia
162 E4 **Sowa** Botswana
162 E4 **Sowa Pan** *pan* Botswana
76 J8 **Sowden Lake** Ontario Canada
140 F2 **Sowerby Row** Cumbria England UK
162 E5 **Soweto** South Africa
183 K6 **So'x** Tajikistan
192 E4 **Soyang-ho** *lake* South Korea
160 A5 **Soyo** Angola
132 E4 **Sozopol** Bulgaria
124 C2 **Spa** Belgium
109 1a **Spaans Lagoen** *bay* Aruba
109 1b **Spaanse Water** *bay* Netherlands Antilles
58 T2 **Spaatz Island** Antarctica
135 AE7 **Spafar'yeva, Ostrov** *island* Russian Federation
128 E4 **Spain** *country* Europe
218 D5 **Spalding** SA Australia
75 S6 **Spalding** Saskatchewan Canada
139 G2 **Spalding** Lincolnshire England UK
139 G2 **Spaldwick** Cambridgeshire England UK
125 G3 **Spálené Poříčí** Czech Republic
123 M4 **Spalviškiai** Lithuania
139 G2 **Spanby** Lincolnshire England UK
127 I1 **Spangenberg** Germany
80 G3 **Spangle** Washington USA
81 M8 **Spanish Peaks** Colorado USA
109 18 **Spanish Point** Antigua and Barbuda
109 21 **Spanish Town** British Virgin Islands
90 E3 **Spanish Town** Jamaica
140 E2 **Spark Bridge** Cumbria England UK
87 J5 **Sparks** Georgia USA
82 G6 **Sparland** Illinois USA
101 H3 **Sparouine, Montagnes de la** *range* Suriname
Sparta *see* **Sparti** Greece
87 K2 **Sparta** North Carolina USA
87 I3 **Sparta** Tennessee USA
82 F5 **Sparta** Wisconsin USA
87 K3 **Spartanburg** South Carolina USA
133 C7 **Sparti (Sparta)** Greece
131 G8 **Spartivento, Capo** *cape* Italy
141 F2 **Spartylea** Northumberland England UK
75 N8 **Sparwood** British Columbia Canada
192 G2 **Spassk-Dal'niy** Russian Federation
121 R5 **Spasskaya Guba** Russian Federation
123 P3 **Spasskaya Polist'** Russian Federation
183 J3 **Spasskoye** Kazakhstan
133 C7 **Spathi, Akra** *cape* Greece
78 K6 **Spear Harbour** Newfoundland and Labrador Canada
75 R4 **Spear Lake** Saskatchewan Canada
140 A3 **Spear Vale** Cavan Ireland
81 N4 **Spearfish** South Dakota USA
212 E7 **Spearhole** *watercourse* WA Australia
85 L2 **Spearman** Texas USA
81 P8 **Spearville** Kansas USA
109 7 **Speedwell Island** Falkland Islands
141 H2 **Speeton** North Yorkshire England UK
125 H4 **Speikkogel** *mountain* Austria
161 E4 **Speke Gulf** *bay* Tanzania
82 H7 **Spencer** Indiana USA
82 D5 **Spencer** Iowa USA
81 P5 **Spencer** Nebraska USA
87 K3 **Spencer** North Carolina USA
72 C5 **Spencer, Point** Alaska USA
218 C6 **Spencer Gulf** SA Australia
77 P6 **Spencer Island** Nunavut Canada
74 K7 **Spences Bridge** British Columbia Canada
141 G2 **Spennymoor** Durham England UK
122 E2 **Sperillen** *lake* Norway
82 C2 **Sperling** Manitoba Canada
131 C7 **Sperone, Capo** *cape* Sardinia Italy
140 A2 **Sperrin** Strabane Northern Ireland UK
86 D2 **Sperry** Oklahoma USA
133 C7 **Spetses** *island* Greece
142 D3 **Spey** *watercourse* Scotland UK
142 E3 **Spey Bay** Moray Scotland UK
142 E3 **Spey Bay** Scotland UK
124 E3 **Speyer** Germany
109 9 **Speyside** Trinidad and Tobago
125 L2 **Spiczyn** Poland
83 K4 **Spider Bay** Ontario Canada
58 I2 **Spieden, Cape** Antarctica
124 D1 **Spiekeroog** *island* Germany
127 H3 **Spiez** Switzerland
120 L3 **Spikberg** Sweden
120 L1 **Spildra** *island* Norway
124 G4 **Spilimbergo** Italy
75 M7 **Spillimacheen** British Columbia Canada
141 I3 **Spilsby** Lincolnshire England UK
218 C6 **Spilsby Island** SA Australia
179 K3 **Spin Buldak** Afghanistan
127 G2 **Spincourt** France
130 C4 **Spinetta** Italy
213 J3 **Spirit Hill Station** NT Australia
80 G3 **Spirit Lake** Idaho USA
82 D5 **Spirit Lake** Iowa USA
82 D5 **Spirit Lake** Iowa USA
74 L5 **Spirit River** Alberta Canada
125 K3 **Spišská Stará Ves** Slovakia
125 K3 **Spišské Vlachy** Slovakia
210 inset **Spit Bay** Heard Island Australia
212 E6 **Spit Point** WA Australia
210 inset **Spit Point** Heard Island Australia
134 E3 **Spitsbergen** *island* Norway
57 H1 **Spitsbergen Bank** *underwater feature* Barents Sea
57 F1 **Spitsbergen Fracture Zone** *underwater feature* Greenland Sea
123 N3 **Spitsino** Russian Federation
124 G4 **Spittal** Austria
140 D2 **Spittal** Dumfries and Galloway Scotland UK
138 C3 **Spittal** Pembrokeshire Wales UK
127 K3 **Spittal an der Drau** Austria
142 E4 **Spittal of Glenshee** Perth and Kinross Scotland UK
123 M2 **Spjutsund** Finland
86 D5 **Splendora** Texas USA
130 G5 **Split** Croatia
77 P4 **Split Island** Nunavut Canada
75 W4 **Split Lake** Manitoba Canada
75 W4 **Split Lake** Manitoba Canada
219 J4 **Split Rock Reservoir** NSW Australia
80 G3 **Spokane** Washington USA
130 E5 **Spoleto** Italy
82 F6 **Spoon** *watercourse* Illinois USA
82 F4 **Spooner** Wisconsin USA
133 E7 **Sporades (Dodecanese)** *island* Greece
125 M1 **Sporawskaye, Vozyera** *lake* Belarus
120 I5 **Sporrsjön** *bay* Sweden
78 K6 **Spotted Island** Newfoundland and Labrador Canada
80 G3 **Sprague** Washington USA
195 F5 **Spratly Island** Spratly Islands
195 G5 **Spratly Islands** *disputed territory* South China Sea
80 F4 **Spray** Oregon USA
125 G1 **Spree** *watercourse* Germany
122 F5 **Sprenge** Germany
141 H3 **Spridlington** Lincolnshire England UK
214 F7 **Spring** *watercourse* Qld Australia
75 O8 **Spring Coulee** Alberta Canada
82 F5 **Spring Green** Wisconsin USA
82 F5 **Spring Grove** Minnesota USA
87 L3 **Spring Lake** North Carolina USA
84 E2 **Spring Mountains** Nevada USA
219 I3 **Spring Plains** NSW Australia
75 Q3 **Spring Point** Saskatchewan Canada
109 7 **Spring Point** Falkland Islands
82 E5 **Spring Valley** Minnesota USA
162 C5 **Springbok** South Africa
82 I7 **Springboro** Ohio USA
84 F2 **Springdale** Utah USA
80 G2 **Springdale** Washington USA
85 J2 **Springer** New Mexico USA
86 C3 **Springer** Oklahoma USA
85 H3 **Springerville** Arizona USA
221 D6 **Springfield** New Zealand
81 N8 **Springfield** Colorado USA
87 K4 **Springfield** Georgia USA
82 G7 **Springfield** Illinois USA
82 I8 **Springfield** Kentucky USA
83 O5 **Springfield** Massachusetts USA
81 R4 **Springfield** Minnesota USA
82 E8 **Springfield** Missouri USA
82 J7 **Springfield** Ohio USA
80 D4 **Springfield** Oregon USA
86 H2 **Springfield** Tennessee USA
82 G7 **Springfield, Lake** Illinois USA
162 E6 **Springfontein** South Africa
79 F10 **Springhill** Nova Scotia Canada
74 J7 **Springhouse** British Columbia Canada
85 K3 **Springlake** Texas USA
221 E6 **Springs Junction** New Zealand
215 J8 **Springsure** Qld Australia
86 C4 **Springtown** Texas USA
214 F7 **Springvale** Qld Australia
213 I4 **Springvale Hill** WA Australia
81 P5 **Springview** Nebraska USA
83 L5 **Springville** New York USA
80 J6 **Springville** Utah USA
75 Q7 **Springwater** Saskatchewan Canada
122 E2 **Sprogen** *lake* Norway
120 G4 **Sprova** Norway
75 R6 **Spruce** *watercourse* Saskatchewan Canada
83 L7 **Spruce Knob** *mountain* West Virginia USA
87 J3 **Spruce Pine** North Carolina USA
84 F1 **Spry** Utah USA
131 G7 **Spulico, Capo** *cape* Italy
85 L4 **Spur** Texas USA
82 C2 **Spurgrave** Manitoba Canada
141 I3 **Spurn Head** *cape* England UK
72 D6 **Spurr, Mount** Alaska USA
221 E6 **Spy Glass Point** New Zealand
81 O1 **Spy Hill** Saskatchewan Canada
125 K1 **Spychowo** Poland
83 Q3 **Squa Pan Lake** Maine USA
74 J8 **Squamish** British Columbia Canada
74 J7 **Squamish** *watercourse* British Columbia Canada
217 I3 **Square Hill** WA Australia
83 Q3 **Square Lake** Maine USA
80 F1 **Squilax** British Columbia Canada
131 G7 **Squillace** Italy
131 G7 **Squillace, Golfo di** *bay* Italy
217 J3 **Squires, Mount** WA Australia
76 N7 **Squirrel** *watercourse* Ontario Canada
197 F5 **Sragen** Indonesia
143 C2 **Srah** Ireland
143 E4 **Srahbaun** Ireland
143 D5 **Sraleigh** Ireland
197 F5 **Srandakan** Indonesia
143 E1 **Srath** Ireland
132 B4 **Srbica** Kosovo
194 D5 **Srê Âmbĕl** Cambodia
130 H4 **Srebrenik** Bosnia and Herzegovina
132 E4 **Sredets** Bulgaria
135 AG7 **Sredinnyy, Khrebet** *range* Russian Federation
132 D4 **Sredna Gora** *range* Bulgaria
135 W6 **Sredne-Sibirskoye Ploskogor'ye** *range* Russian Federation
135 AF9 **Srednego, Ostrov** *island* Kuril Islands
193 L1 **Srednego, Ostrov** *lake* Russian Federation
135 AF5 **Srednekolymsk** Russian Federation
121 Q4 **Sredneye Kuyto, Ozero** *lake* Russian Federation
191 L2 **Sredniy Urgal** Russian Federation
135 AF7 **Sredniy** Russian Federation
135 AB8 **Sredniy Urgal** Russian Federation
132 B3 **Srednjevo** Serbia
132 D4 **Srednogorie** Bulgaria
135 AH6 **Srednyaya Itkana** Russian Federation
179 K3 **Sreh Chānhānd Tānah** Afghanistan
125 I1 **Śrem** Poland
194 D4 **Srêng** *watercourse* Cambodia
191 I2 **Sretensk** Russian Federation
187 E10 **Sri Jayewardenepura Kotte** Sri Lanka
187 E10 **Sri Lanka** *country* Asia
187 E9 **Sriharikota Island** Andhra Pradesh India
186 G6 **Srinagar** Bihar India
186 D3 **Srinagar** Jammu and Kashmir India/Pakistan
186 G6 **Srirampur** Jharkhand India
183 O3 **Srostki** Russian Federation
132 B3 **Srpska Crnja** Serbia
120 H5 **Staa/Sta** Sweden
214 F4 **Staaten** *watercourse* Qld Australia
120 F5 **Stabben** *island* Norway
122 E4 **Staby** Denmark
142 D2 **Stack, Loch** *lake* Scotland UK
142 D1 **Stack Skerry** *island* Scotland UK
138 C3 **Stackpole** Pembrokeshire Wales UK
124 B2 **Staden** Belgium
122 C1 **Stadhavet** *bay* Norway
122 C1 **Stadlandet** *island* Norway
125 L1 **Stadniki** Poland
124 E2 **Stadtallendorf** Germany
127 J2 **Stadtbergen** Germany
124 F2 **Stadtilm** Germany
124 D2 **Stadtkyll** Germany
130 C3 **Stäfa** Switzerland
142 B3 **Staffin** Highland Scotland UK
139 E2 **Stafford** Staffordshire England UK
81 P8 **Stafford** Kansas USA
141 G3 **Staffordshire** *admin. area* England UK
140 B2 **Staffordstown** Antrim Northern Ireland UK
131 E8 **Stagnone, Punta dello** *cape* Italy
120 G6 **Stai** Norway
123 M4 **Staicele** Latvia
141 G3 **Stainburn** North Yorkshire England UK
141 G2 **Staindrop** Durham England UK
139 G3 **Staines** Surrey England UK
108 B5 **Staines, Península** *peninsula* Chile
141 F2 **Stainforth** North Yorkshire England UK
141 G2 **Stainton** North Yorkshire England UK
141 H2 **Staintondale** North Yorkshire England UK
142 D6 **Stairhaven** Dumfries and Galloway Scotland UK
125 L3 **Stakčín** Slovakia
123 M5 **Stakliškės** Lithuania
132 B4 **Stalać** Serbia
138 E4 **Stalbridge** Dorset England UK
127 H3 **Stalden** Switzerland
131 G7 **Stalettì, Punta di** *cape* Italy
139 I2 **Stalham** Norfolk England UK
Stalingrad *see* **Volgograd** Russian Federation
141 F2 **Stalling Busk** North Yorkshire England UK
120 L2 **Stalojaure** *lake* Sweden
120 I4 **Stalon** Sweden
125 L2 **Stalowa Wola** Poland
123 N5 **Stalti** Latvia
81 M1 **Stalwart** Saskatchewan Canada
215 G6 **Stamford** Qld Australia
139 G2 **Stamford** Lincolnshire England UK
83 O6 **Stamford** Connecticut USA
86 B4 **Stamford** Texas USA
86 B4 **Stamford, Lake** Texas USA
141 H3 **Stamford Bridge** North Yorkshire England UK
80 E7 **Stampede Reservoir** California USA
162 C4 **Stampriet** Namibia
120 I3 **Stamstik** Norway
120 H2 **Stamsund** Norway
82 D6 **Stanberry** Missouri USA
139 F4 **Stanbridge** Dorset England UK
58 W1 **Stancomb-Wills Glacier** Antarctica
75 O8 **Stand Off** Alberta Canada
75 O7 **Standard** Alberta Canada
162 E5 **Standerton** South Africa
141 F3 **Standish** Greater Manchester England UK
187 D9 **Stanely** *lake* Tamil Nadu India
139 H2 **Stanfield** Norfolk England UK
80 F4 **Stanfield** Oregon USA
139 G2 **Stanford** Bedfordshire England UK
82 I8 **Stanford** Kentucky USA
81 J3 **Stanford** Montana USA
84 C2 **Stanford, Mount** California USA
139 F3 **Stanford in the Vale** Oxfordshire England UK
122 F2 **Stange** Norway
58 S2 **Stange Sound** *strait* Antarctica
163 F5 **Stanger** South Africa
139 H2 **Stanhoe** Norfolk England UK
141 F2 **Stanhope** Durham England UK
139 G2 **Stanion** Northamptonshire England UK
130 F5 **Stankovci** Croatia
219 Q10 **Stanley** Tas. Australia
74 K6 **Stanley** British Columbia Canada
79 E9 **Stanley** New Brunswick Canada
109 7 **Stanley** Falkland Islands
141 G2 **Stanley** Durham England UK
142 E4 **Stanley** Perth and Kinross Scotland UK
80 H4 **Stanley** Idaho USA
81 N2 **Stanley** North Dakota USA
218 H7 **Stanley, Mount** Vic. Australia
75 S5 **Stanley Mission** Saskatchewan Canada
219 R9 **Stanley Point** Tas. Australia
162 E4 **Stanmore** Zimbabwe
219 J3 **Stannum** NSW Australia
135 Y7 **Stanovoye Nagor'ye** *region* Russian Federation
127 I3 **Stans** Switzerland
218 C6 **Stansbury** SA Australia
213 J6 **Stansmore Range** WA Australia
139 H3 **Stansted Mountfitchet** Essex England UK
219 J3 **Stanthorpe** Qld Australia
139 F2 **Stanton** Gloucestershire England UK
139 H2 **Stanton** Suffolk England UK
82 J8 **Stanton** Kentucky USA
86 G3 **Stanton** Tennessee USA
85 L4 **Stanton** Texas USA
138 E2 **Stanton Long** Shropshire England UK
139 F2 **Stanton on the Wolds** Nottinghamshire England UK
139 F2 **Stanton under Bardon** Leicester England UK
219 J6 **Stanwell Park** NSW Australia
140 F2 **Stanwix** Cumbria England UK
124 F4 **Stanzach** Austria
132 A3 **Stapar** Serbia
124 D1 **Staphorst** Netherlands
139 H3 **Staplehurst** Kent England UK
81 R3 **Staples** Minnesota USA
140 B3 **Staplestown** Ireland
138 E2 **Stapleton** Herefordshire England UK
81 O6 **Stapleton** Nebraska USA
125 K2 **Stąporków** Poland
121 N1 **Stappane** *island* Norway
87 L3 **Star** North Carolina USA
86 F4 **Star City** Arkansas USA
133 C5 **Star Dojran** Macedonia
125 L1 **Stara Kamionka** Poland
132 D4 **Stara Planina** *range* Bulgaria
125 L3 **Stara Sil'** Ukraine
132 E1 **Stara Synyava** Ukraine
125 I3 **Stará Turá** Slovakia
132 E1 **Stara Ushytsya** Ukraine
125 M2 **Stara Vyzhivka** Ukraine
125 K1 **Stara Wieś** Poland
132 D4 **Stara Zagora** Bulgaria
132 D4 **Stara Zagora** *admin. area* Bulgaria
125 K2 **Starachowice** Poland
121 Q2 **Staraya** Russian Federation
123 O5 **Staraya Byelitsa** Belarus
123 P3 **Staraya Russa** Russian Federation
123 P4 **Staraya Toropa** Russian Federation
76 G8 **Starbuck** Manitoba Canada
81 R4 **Starbuck** Minnesota USA
80 F3 **Starbuck** Washington USA
222 1 **Starbuck Island** Kiribati
138 D4 **Starcross** Devon England UK
125 I2 **Staré Město** Czech Republic
86 D2 **Stark** Kansas USA
81 M8 **Starkville** Colorado USA
86 G4 **Starkville** Mississippi USA
81 P2 **Starkweather** North Dakota USA
124 F4 **Starnberger See** *lake* Germany
133 B5 **Staro Gradsko** Macedonia
132 E4 **Staro Oryakhovo** Bulgaria
130 H5 **Staro Slano** Bosnia and Herzegovina
183 N3 **Staroaleyskoye** Russian Federation
136 F3 **Starobelsk** Ukraine
136 E2 **Starodub** Russian Federation
132 E1 **Starokostyantyniv** Ukraine
134 K7 **Starovercheskaya** Russian Federation
123 O3 **Staroye Gorkolovo** Russian Federation
182 C2 **Staroyur'yevo** Russian Federation
140 D1 **Starr** East Ayrshire Scotland UK
135 AE6 **Starry Eschan** Russian Federation
138 D4 **Start Bay** England UK
138 D4 **Start Point** England UK
133 D5 **Startsevo** Bulgaria
81 J6 **Starvation Reservoir** Utah USA
125 L2 **Stary Dzików** Poland
125 K3 **Stary Sącz** Poland
132 D1 **Staryy Oleksynets'** Ukraine
136 F2 **Staryy Oskol** Russian Federation
132 E1 **Staryy Ostropil'** Ukraine
132 C1 **Staryy Sambir** Ukraine
83 M6 **State College** Pennsylvania USA
86 G5 **State Line** Mississippi USA
87 K4 **Statesboro** Georgia USA
87 K3 **Statesville** North Carolina USA
138 E3 **Stathe** Somerset England UK
214 F3 **Station** *watercourse* Qld Australia
213 K4 **Station Hill** NT Australia
156 E4 **Station No. 10** Sudan
156 E3 **Station No. 5** Sudan
156 E3 **Station No. 6** Sudan
131 G6 **Statte** Italy
122 C3 **Stavanger** Norway
132 A3 **Stave** Serbia
74 J8 **Stave Lake** British Columbia Canada
221 D6 **Staveley** New Zealand
140 F2 **Staveley** Cumbria England UK
141 G3 **Staveley** Derbyshire England UK
141 G2 **Staveley** North Yorkshire England UK
127 G1 **Stavelot** Belgium
75 O7 **Stavely** Alberta Canada
122 F3 **Stavern** Norway
132 D4 **Stavertsi** Bulgaria
132 G2 **Stavki** Ukraine
125 M2 **Stavky** Ukraine
124 C1 **Stavoren** Netherlands
182 D4 **Stavropol'** Russian Federation
182 D4 **Stavropol'skiy Kray** *admin. area* Russian Federation
133 D8 **Stavros, Akra** *cape* Greece
133 B5 **Stavroskiádion** Greece
132 F2 **Stavrove** Ukraine
123 J3 **Stavsnäs** Sweden
132 G1 **Stavyshche** Ukraine
215 G6 **Stawell** *watercourse* Qld Australia
218 F7 **Stawell** Vic. Australia
125 L1 **Stawiski** Poland
125 J2 **Stawiszyn** Poland
138 D2 **Staylittle** Powys Wales UK
83 K4 **Stayner** Ontario Canada
80 D4 **Stayton** Oregon USA
74 J3 **Steamboat** British Columbia Canada
81 L6 **Steamboat Springs** Colorado USA
141 G2 **Stean** North Yorkshire England UK
138 D3 **Steart** Somerset England UK
72 C6 **Stebbins** Alaska USA
132 D1 **Stebni** Ukraine
132 C1 **Stebnik** Ukraine
141 G3 **Steel Bank** South Yorkshire England UK
87 H4 **Steele** Alabama USA
81 P3 **Steele** North Dakota USA
58 U2 **Steele Island** Antarctica
82 F8 **Steelville** Missouri USA
127 G1 **Steenbergen** Netherlands
80 F5 **Steens Mountains** Oregon USA
73 N3 **Steenstrup Gletscher** *glacier* Greenland
216 C3 **Steep Point** WA Australia
75 V7 **Steep Rock** Manitoba Canada
82 F2 **Steep Rock Lake** Ontario Canada
139 G2 **Steeple Gidding** Cambridgeshire England UK
109 7 **Steeple Jason** *island* Falkland Islands
82 F2 **Steeprock Lake** Ontario Canada
58 M1 **Steershead Crevasses** *valley* Antarctica
132 F2 **Ştefan Vodă** Moldova
58 E2 **Stefansson Bay** Antarctica
73 I4 **Stefansson Island** Nunavut Canada
108 C3 **Steffen, Cerro** *mountain* Argentina
132 C2 **Ştei** Romania
125 H4 **Steiermark** *admin. area* Austria
120 I3 **Steigen** Norway
124 F3 **Stein** Germany
142 B3 **Stein** Highland Scotland UK
125 G4 **Stein an der Enns** Austria
127 J3 **Steinach** Austria
124 E2 **Steinau** Germany
76 G8 **Steinbach** Manitoba Canada
105 H4 **Steinen** *watercourse* Brazil
124 D1 **Steinfurter Aa** *watercourse* Germany
124 F4 **Steingaden** Germany
162 C4 **Steinhausen** Namibia
124 E1 **Steinhuder Meer** *lake* Germany
120 G4 **Steinkjer** Norway
162 C5 **Steinkopf** South Africa
120 E5 **Steinshamn** Norway
121 P2 **Steinskjærnes** Norway
122 C2 **Steinslandsvatnet** *lake* Norway
132 F3 **Stejaru** Romania
126 G1 **Stekene** Belgium
183 M2 **Steklyannoye** *lake* Russian Federation
162 D5 **Stella** South Africa
124 F1 **Stelle** Germany
122 I4 **Stenåsa** Sweden
124 C3 **Stenay** France
120 K2 **Stenbacken** Sweden
124 F1 **Stendal** Germany
123 L4 **Stende** Latvia
122 H4 **Stengårdshultasjön** *lake* Sweden
218 C6 **Stenhouse Bay** SA Australia
132 B3 **Stenjevac** Serbia
122 J4 **Stenkumla** Sweden
142 inset **Stenness** Shetland Scotland UK
133 E8 **Steno Karpathou** *bay* Greece
133 C7 **Stenon** Greece
122 H4 **Stensjön** *lake* Sweden
120 K3 **Stenträsk** Sweden
142 B2 **Steòrnabhagh** Na h-Eileanan Siar Scotland UK
132 E1 **Stepanki** Ukraine
123 O4 **Stepankino** Russian Federation
130 H5 **Stepen** Bosnia and Herzegovina
130 E2 **Stephansposching** Germany
81 Q2 **Stephen** Minnesota USA
86 E4 **Stephens** Arkansas USA
109 7 **Stephens, Port** *bay* Falkland Islands
221 F5 **Stephens Island** New Zealand
76 H4 **Stephens Lake** Manitoba Canada
74 D3 **Stephens Passage** Alaska USA
82 H4 **Stephenson** Michigan USA
58 T2 **Stephenson, Mount** *mountain* Antarctica
86 B4 **Stephenville** Texas USA
79 I8 **Stephenville Crossing** Newfoundland and Labrador Canada
182 D5 **Stepnoye** Russian Federation
183 N3 **Stepnoye** *lake* Russian Federation
183 K3 **Stepnyak** Kazakhstan
133 C6 **Sterea Ellada** *admin. area* Greece
162 D6 **Sterling** South Africa
81 N6 **Sterling** Colorado USA
82 G6 **Sterling** Illinois USA
81 P7 **Sterling** Kansas USA
82 I4 **Sterling** Michigan USA
80 J7 **Sterling** Utah USA
85 L5 **Sterling City** Texas USA
82 J5 **Sterling Heights** Michigan USA
182 G2 **Sterlitamak** Russian Federation
133 C7 **Sterna** Greece
122 E2 **Sternbusjøen** *lake* Norway
121 T6 **Steshëvskaya** Russian Federation
139 H2 **Stetchworth** Cambridgeshire England UK
127 L1 **Štětí** Czech Republic
199 I5 **Stettin Bay** Papua New Guinea
125 H1 **Stettiner Haff (Zalew Szczeciński)** *bay* Poland
75 O6 **Stettler** Alberta Canada
83 K6 **Steubenville** Ohio USA
139 G3 **Stevenage** Hertfordshire England UK
82 G4 **Stevens Point** Wisconsin USA
218 B2 **Stevenson** *watercourse* SA Australia
87 I3 **Stevenson** Alabama USA
76 H6 **Stevenson Lake** Manitoba Canada
142 D5 **Stevenston** North Ayrshire Scotland UK
82 H5 **Stevensville** Michigan USA
80 H3 **Stevensville** Montana USA
122 G5 **Stevns Klint** *cape* Denmark
215 G3 **Stewart** *watercourse* Qld Australia
74 G5 **Stewart** British Columbia Canada
214 C1 **Stewart, Cape** NT Australia
75 S6 **Stewart Creek** Saskatchewan Canada
221 C8 **Stewart Island** New Zealand
73 K5 **Stewart Lake** Nunavut Canada
82 F6 **Stewart Lake** Illinois USA
75 R7 **Stewart Valley** Saskatchewan Canada
142 D5 **Stewarton** East Ayrshire Scotland UK
82 E5 **Stewartville** Minnesota USA
79 G10 **Stewiacke** Nova Scotia Canada
139 G4 **Steyning** West Sussex England UK
162 E6 **Steynsburg** South Africa
125 H3 **Steyr** Austria
125 H4 **Steyr** *watercourse* Austria
125 H2 **Stěžery** Czech Republic
125 K2 **Stężyca** Poland
127 I4 **Stezzano** Italy
139 H2 **Stibbard** Norfolk England UK
138 C4 **Sticker** Cornwall England UK
141 I3 **Stickford** Lincolnshire England UK
139 H1 **Stickney** Lincolnshire England UK
81 P5 **Stickney** South Dakota USA
124 C1 **Stiens** Netherlands
139 H2 **Stiffkey** Norfolk England UK
120 H3 **Stigen** *island* Norway
124 F5 **Stiglia** Italy
131 G6 **Stigliano** Italy
74 F4 **Stikine** British Columbia Canada
74 F4 **Stikine** *watercourse* British Columbia Canada
74 F3 **Stikine Plateau** British Columbia Canada
85 L5 **Stiles** Texas USA
86 C5 **Stillhouse Hollow Lake** Texas USA
86 C2 **Stillwater** Oklahoma USA
80 F7 **Stillwater Range** Nevada USA
83 N5 **Stillwater Reservoir** New York USA
131 G7 **Stilo** Italy
131 G7 **Stilo, Punta** *cape* Italy
139 G2 **Stilton** Cambridgeshire England UK
85 L3 **Stinnett** Texas USA
133 C5 **Štip** Macedonia
214 B6 **Stirling** NT Australia
213 J4 **Stirling** *watercourse* NT Australia
214 F4 **Stirling** Qld Australia
218 D6 **Stirling** SA Australia
75 O8 **Stirling** Alberta Canada
83 M4 **Stirling** Ontario Canada
142 D4 **Stirling** *admin. area* Scotland UK
142 E4 **Stirling** Stirling Scotland UK
218 C5 **Stirling North** SA Australia
216 E7 **Stirling Range** WA Australia
80 H3 **Stites** Idaho USA
132 B1 **Štítnik** Slovakia
141 H3 **Stixwould** Lincolnshire England UK
121 M1 **Stjernøya** *island* Norway
120 G5 **Stjørdalselva** *watercourse* Norway
120 G5 **Stjordalshalsen** Norway
122 G2 **Støa** Norway
125 I1 **Stobno** Poland
130 G5 **Stobreć** Croatia
120 J6 **Stocka** Sweden
139 F3 **Stockbridge** Hampshire England UK
86 C6 **Stockdale** Texas USA
75 T7 **Stockholm** Saskatchewan Canada
122 J3 **Stockholm** Sweden
81 Q4 **Stockholm** South Dakota USA
219 H6 **Stockinbingal** NSW Australia
138 D4 **Stockland** Devon England UK
214 E7 **Stockport** Qld Australia
141 F3 **Stockport** Greater Manchester England UK
51 O11 **Stocks Seamount** *underwater feature* Atlantic Ocean
120 L5 **Stöcksjö** Sweden
80 E8 **Stockton** California USA
82 F5 **Stockton** Illinois USA
81 P7 **Stockton** Kansas USA
82 E8 **Stockton** Missouri USA
219 J5 **Stockton Bight** *bay* NSW Australia
86 E2 **Stockton Lake** Missouri USA
141 G2 **Stockton-on-Tees** *admin. area* England UK
141 G2 **Stockton-on-Tees** Stockton-on-Tees England UK
138 E2 **Stockton on Teme** Worcestershire England UK
88 E2 **Stockton Plateau** Texas USA
125 K1 **Stoczek** Poland
125 K2 **Stoczek Łukowski** Poland
125 G3 **Stod** Czech Republic
120 J5 **Stöde** Sweden
120 J5 **Stödesjön** *lake* Sweden
194 E4 **Stŏeng Trêng** Cambodia
142 C2 **Stoer** Highland Scotland UK
142 C2 **Stoer, Point of** *cape* Scotland UK
193 J2 **Stokap, Gora** *volcano* Russian Federation
139 G2 **Stoke Albany** Northamptonshire England UK
139 H2 **Stoke By Clare** Suffolk England UK
138 E2 **Stoke Heath** Shropshire England UK
139 I2 **Stoke Holy Cross** Norfolk England UK
138 E2 **Stoke Lacy** Herefordshire England UK
139 E1 **Stoke-on-Trent** *admin. area* England UK
139 E1 **Stoke-on-Trent** Stoke-on-Trent England UK
139 E3 **Stoke Orchard** Gloucestershire England UK
138 E2 **Stoke Prior** Herefordshire England UK
139 E2 **Stoke Prior** Worcestershire England UK
108 B6 **Stokes, Bahía** *bay* Chile
221 F5 **Stokes, Mount** New Zealand
219 P10 **Stokes Point** Tas. Australia
213 K3 **Stokes Range** NT Australia
138 E2 **Stokesay** Shropshire England UK
139 I2 **Stokesby** Norfolk England UK
141 G2 **Stokesley** North Yorkshire England UK
120 F4 **Stokkøya** *island* Norway
120 G4 **Stokksund** Norway
120 I2 **Stokmarknes** Norway
130 G5 **Stolac** Bosnia and Herzegovina
183 N3 **Stolbourkha** Kazakhstan
135 AC4 **Stolbovoy, Ostrov** *island* Russian Federation
138 D3 **Stolford** Somerset England UK
136 C2 **Stolin** Belarus
122 C3 **Stolmen** *island* Norway
132 E2 **Stolniceni-Prăjescu** Romania
132 D3 **Stolnici** Romania
125 J1 **Stolno** Poland
122 D2 **Stolsheimen** *island* Norway
101 G3 **Stondansie Projekt** *lake* Suriname
138 E3 **Stone** Gloucestershire England UK
139 H3 **Stone** Kent England UK
139 E2 **Stone** Staffordshire England UK
138 E3 **Stone Allerton** Somerset England UK
142 F4 **Stone of Morphie** Aberdeenshire Scotland UK
140 A4 **Stoneen** Ireland
141 H2 **Stonegrave** North Yorkshire England UK
83 P3 **Stoneham** Quebec Canada
141 F1 **Stonehaugh** Northumberland England UK
142 F4 **Stonehaven** Aberdeenshire Scotland UK
215 G8 **Stonehenge** Qld Australia
74 J6 **Stoner** British Columbia Canada
139 F3 **Stonesfield** Oxfordshire England UK
86 E4 **Stonewall** Louisiana USA
86 G4 **Stonewall** Mississippi USA
86 C3 **Stonewall** Oklahoma USA
138 E3 **Stoney Stratton** Somerset England UK
139 F2 **Stoneygate** Leicester England UK
120 J2 **Stonglandseidet** Norway
78 K6 **Stony Island** Newfoundland and Labrador Canada
76 G7 **Stony Mountain** Manitoba Canada
75 S3 **Stony Rapids** Saskatchewan Canada
142 inset **Stonybreck** Shetland Scotland UK
143 F2 **Stonyford** Lisburn Northern Ireland UK
164 5c **Stonyhill Point** *cape* St Helena
77 N7 **Stooping** *watercourse* Ontario Canada
120 I4 **Stor-Björkvattnet** *bay* Sweden
120 I4 **Stor-Byvattnet** *lake* Sweden
120 J4 **Stor Dainan** *lake* Sweden
120 K5 **Stor Degersjön** *lake* Sweden
120 J5 **Stor-Finnsjön** *lake* Sweden
120 I4 **Stor Laison** *lake* Sweden
120 J5 **Stor-Laxsjön** *lake* Sweden
120 K3 **Stor-Mattaure** *lake* Sweden
120 H5 **Stor-Stensjön** *lake* Sweden
120 L4 **Stor-Teuger** *lake* Sweden
120 I5 **Stor-Valsjön** *lake* Sweden
122 H3 **Storå** Sweden
122 I3 **Stora Ålö** *island* Sweden
122 I4 **Stora Alvaret** *region* Sweden
120 J4 **Stora Arasjön** *lake* Sweden
122 I4 **Stora Askö** *island* Sweden
122 G3 **Stora Bör** *lake* Sweden
122 G4 **Stora Färgen** *lake* Sweden
120 I5 **Stora Foskvattnet** *lake* Sweden
122 G3 **Stora Gla** *lake* Sweden

120 J5 **Stora Grundsjön** *lake* Sweden
122 G3 **Stora Hästefjorden** *lake* Sweden
122 I4 **Stora Karlsö** *island* Sweden
120 K4 **Stora Kvammarn** *lake* Sweden
122 F3 **Stora Le** *lake* Sweden
120 K3 **Stora Lulevatten** *bay* Sweden
122 H3 **Stora Rängen** *lake* Sweden
120 K3 **Stora Sjöfallet** *waterfall* Sweden
120 J4 **Stora Skyrsjön** *lake* Sweden
120 J5 **Stora Tågsjön** *lake* Sweden
120 K5 **Stora Tällvattnet** *lake* Sweden
122 I3 **Stora Värtan** *bay* Sweden
120 I3 **Storåga** *watercourse* Norway
120 F5 **Storås** Norway
120 K4 **Storavan** *bay* Sweden
121 M5 **Storbacka** Finland
120 H6 **Storbäcken** Sweden
120 K4 **Storberg** Sweden
122 C3 **Stord** *island* Norway
120 L1 **Stordalen** Norway
120 G5 **Stordalsfjorden** *bay* Norway
130 F3 **Štore** Slovenia
122 C2 **Store Kalsøy** *island* Norway
73 R3 **Store Koldewey** *island* Greenland
120 G5 **Store Korssjøen** *lake* Norway
121 M1 **Store Kvalfjord** Norway
122 G5 **Store Lyngby** Denmark
120 H4 **Store Majavatnet** *lake* Norway
120 I3 **Store Malvatnet** *lake* Norway
120 I2 **Store Molla** *island* Norway
120 H4 **Store Namsvatnet** *lake* Norway
121 P2 **Store Sametti** *lake* Norway
122 C2 **Store Sotra** *island* Norway
121 N1 **Store Tamsøya** *island* Norway
122 D3 **Store Urevatnet** *lake* Norway
120 I3 **Storeakersvatnet** *lake* Norway
120 G5 **Støren** Norway
122 I2 **Storfjärden** *bay* Sweden
120 K2 **Storfjord** Norway
122 E2 **Storfjorden** *lake* Norway
122 H3 **Storfors** Sweden
120 I3 **Storforshei** Norway
120 F5 **Storfosna** *island* Norway
120 I4 **Storfulvurn** *lake* Sweden
120 I3 **Storglomvatnet** *lake* Norway
122 H2 **Storhamrasjön** *lake* Sweden
120 I5 **Storhögen** Sweden
120 I3 **Storjord** Norway
120 I3 **Storjorda** Norway
120 I4 **Storjorm** *bay* Sweden
120 J4 **Storjuktan** *lake* Sweden
122 I2 **Storjungfrun** *island* Sweden
120 L4 **Storkågeträsk** *lake* Sweden
72 I4 **Storkerson Peninsula** Nunavut Canada
123 K2 **Storklyndan** *island* Finland
123 K2 **Storlandet** *island* Finland
120 H5 **Storlien** Sweden
219 R11 **Storm Bay** Tas. Australia
82 D5 **Storm Lake** Iowa USA
76 I8 **Stormy Lake** Ontario Canada
120 F5 **Storodden** Norway
121 M4 **Storöhamn** Sweden
120 K5 **Storön** *island* Sweden
120 H3 **Storøya** *island* Norway
123 M2 **Storpellinge** *island* Finland
139 G4 **Storrington** West Sussex England UK
121 M1 **Storsandes** Norway
120 H5 **Störsätern** Sweden
120 H5 **Storsjö** Sweden
122 F2 **Storsjøen** *lake* Norway
120 I5 **Storsjön** *bay* Sweden
120 J6 **Storsjön** *lake* Sweden
120 I4 **Storsjouten** *lake* Sweden
120 L2 **Storslett** Norway
120 K2 **Storsteinnes** Norway
120 L4 **Storsund** Sweden
75 U8 **Storthoaks** Saskatchewan Canada
120 J4 **Storuman** Sweden
120 J4 **Storuman** *lake* Sweden
120 I4 **Storväktaren** *lake* Sweden
120 H4 **Storvatnet** *lake* Norway
120 J4 **Storvindeln** *lake* Sweden
124 F2 **Stößen** Germany
120 H3 **Støtvær** *island* Norway
75 T8 **Stoughton** Saskatchewan Canada
82 G5 **Stoughton** Wisconsin USA
142 C4 **Stoul** Highland Scotland UK
139 I3 **Stour** *watercourse* England UK
76 H6 **Stout Lake** Ontario Canada
142 F1 **Stove** Orkney Islands Scotland UK
141 H3 **Stow** Lincolnshire England UK
142 F5 **Stow** Scottish Borders Scotland UK
83 K6 **Stow** Ohio USA
138 D2 **Stowe** Shropshire England UK
139 H2 **Stowmarket** Suffolk England UK
125 M2 **Stoyaniv** Ukraine
132 E4 **Stozher** Bulgaria
124 G5 **Stra** Italy
124 G2 **Straach** Germany
143 E2 **Strabane** *admin. area* Northern Ireland UK
143 E2 **Strabane** Strabane Northern Ireland UK
132 E3 **Strachina, Lacul** *lake* Romania
142 C4 **Strachur** Argyll and Bute Scotland UK
132 C4 **Stradalovo** Bulgaria
143 E3 **Stradbally** Ireland
124 E5 **Stradella** Italy
82 E8 **Strafford** Missouri USA
219 Q11 **Strahan** Tas. Australia
143 F1 **Straid** Moyle Northern Ireland UK
143 G2 **Straid** Newtownabbey Northern Ireland UK
122 H4 **Stråken** *lake* Sweden
125 G3 **Strakonice** Czech Republic
132 E4 **Straldzha** Bulgaria
140 A2 **Stralongford** Omagh Northern Ireland UK
122 G5 **Stralsund** Germany
143 E3 **Stramillian** Ireland
139 F2 **Stramshall** Staffordshire England UK
143 E2 **Stranagalwilly** Strabane Northern Ireland UK
125 H3 **Strančice** Czech Republic
120 E5 **Stranda** Norway
122 E2 **Strandafjord** *bay* Norway
122 D2 **Strandavatnet** *lake* Norway
122 F4 **Strandby** Denmark
143 G2 **Strangford Lough** *bay* Northern Ireland UK
214 B3 **Strangways** *watercourse* NT Australia
214 B7 **Strangways, Mount** NT Australia
218 C3 **Strangways Springs** SA Australia
143 E2 **Stranorlar** Ireland
142 C6 **Stranraer** Dumfries and Galloway Scotland UK
132 E3 **Străoane** Romania
127 H2 **Strasbourg** France
81 M1 **Strasbourg Station** Saskatchewan Canada
125 G1 **Strasburg** Germany
81 O3 **Strasburg** North Dakota USA
124 F2 **Straßberg** Germany
83 K5 **Stratford** Ontario Canada
220 F4 **Stratford** New Zealand
86 C3 **Stratford** Oklahoma USA
85 K2 **Stratford** Texas USA
82 F4 **Stratford** Wisconsin USA
139 F3 **Stratford Tony** Wiltshire England UK
139 F2 **Stratford-upon-Avon** Warwickshire England UK
142 E2 **Strath** Highland Scotland UK
218 D6 **Strathalbyn** SA Australia
142 D5 **Strathaven** South Lanarkshire Scotland UK
218 G7 **Strathbogie Ranges** Vic. Australia
77 T1 **Strathcona Islands** Nunavut Canada
214 F6 **Strathfield** Qld Australia
214 G7 **Strathfillan** Qld Australia
214 G3 **Strathgordon** Qld Australia
142 C3 **Strathkanaird** Highland Scotland UK
214 G4 **Strathmore** Qld Australia
75 O7 **Strathmore** Alberta Canada
142 D2 **Strathmore** *watercourse* Scotland UK
142 D2 **Strathnavar** *valley* Scotland UK
83 K5 **Strathroy** Ontario Canada
142 D2 **Strathy Point** Scotland UK
133 C5 **Stratoni** Greece
138 C4 **Stratton** Cornwall England UK
138 E4 **Stratton** Dorset England UK
81 N7 **Stratton** Colorado USA
81 O6 **Stratton** Nebraska USA
120 F5 **Straum** Norway
122 E3 **Straume** Norway
120 I2 **Straume** Norway
120 I3 **Straumen** Norway
125 G1 **Strausberg** Germany
81 J6 **Strawberry Reservoir** Utah USA
86 B4 **Strawn** Texas USA
125 G3 **Strážný** Czech Republic
218 B5 **Streaky Bay** SA Australia
218 B5 **Streaky Bay** SA Australia
143 E3 **Streamstown** Ireland
76 M6 **Streatfield Lake** Ontario Canada
218 F7 **Streatham** Vic. Australia
139 F3 **Streatley** West Berkshire England UK
82 G6 **Streator** Illinois USA
125 H3 **Středočeský Kraj** *admin. area* Czech Republic
143 E3 **Street** Ireland
141 H2 **Street** North Yorkshire England UK
138 E3 **Street** Somerset England UK
81 P3 **Streeter** North Dakota USA
125 L5 **Strehaia** Romania
127 K1 **Strehla** Germany
125 L3 **Strelki** Ukraine
212 E6 **Strelley** *watercourse* WA Australia
121 U3 **Strel'na** Russian Federation
123 O4 **Stremutka** Russian Federation
138 D4 **Strete** Devon England UK
138 E2 **Stretford** Herefordshire England UK
139 E2 **Stretton** Staffordshire England UK
214 C2 **Stretton, Mount** NT Australia
73 S6 **Streymoy** *island* Faroe Islands
124 G3 **Stříbro** Czech Republic
142 F3 **Strichen** Aberdeenshire Scotland UK
83 K2 **Strickland** Ontario Canada
199 G5 **Strickland** *watercourse* Papua New Guinea
124 C2 **Strijen** Netherlands
133 C5 **Strimonas** *watercourse* Greece
120 G5 **Strindfjorden** *bay* Norway
120 I3 **Strindvatnet** *lake* Norway
86 C3 **Stringtown** Oklahoma USA
120 K4 **Strittjomvare** Sweden
130 G5 **Striževo** Bosnia and Herzegovina
132 F1 **Strizhavka** Ukraine
182 F1 **Strizhi** Russian Federation
108 B4 **Strobel, Laguna** *lake* Argentina
108 D2 **Stroeder** Argentina
120 K4 **Ström** Sweden
142 E2 **Stroma, Island of** Scotland UK
120 J4 **Strömåker** Sweden
122 I2 **Strömaren** *lake* Sweden
120 J6 **Strömbacka** Sweden
131 F7 **Stromboli, Isola** *island* Italy
142 C3 **Stromeferry** Highland Scotland UK
120 J4 **Strömnäs** Sweden
142 E2 **Stromness** Orkney Islands Scotland UK
109 8 **Stromness Bay** South Georgia
120 J6 **Strömsbruk** Sweden
81 Q6 **Stromsburg** Nebraska USA
120 K2 **Strømsmo** Norway
120 I3 **Strømsnes** Norway
122 F3 **Strömstad** Sweden
120 I5 **Strömsund** Sweden
142 D4 **Stronachlachar** Stirling Scotland UK
142 D2 **Stronechrubie** Highland Scotland UK
142 D4 **Stronenaba** Highland Scotland UK
86 E4 **Strong** Arkansas USA
199 H5 **Strong, Mount** Papua New Guinea
81 Q7 **Strong City** Kansas USA
142 F1 **Stronsay** *island* Scotland UK
142 C4 **Strontian** Highland Scotland UK
140 B1 **Stroove** Ireland
125 K3 **Stropkov** Slovakia
125 H3 **Stropnice** *watercourse* Czech Republic
124 D5 **Stroppo** Italy
219 J5 **Stroud** NSW Australia
139 E3 **Stroud** Gloucestershire England UK
75 R6 **Struan** Saskatchewan Canada
122 E4 **Struer** Denmark
162 D6 **Struisbaai** South Africa
143 E2 **Strule** *watercourse* Northern Ireland UK
130 D2 **Strullendorf** Germany
133 C5 **Struma** *watercourse* Bulgaria
138 B2 **Strumble Head** *cape* Wales UK
132 F3 **Strumok** Ukraine
133 C5 **Strumyani** Bulgaria
83 K6 **Struthers** Ohio USA
77 P6 **Strutton Islands** Nunavut Canada
132 D4 **Stryama** Bulgaria
162 D5 **Strydenburg** South Africa
75 N8 **Stryker** Montana USA
122 E2 **Strykken** *lake* Norway
125 J2 **Stryków** Poland
125 I1 **Strykowo** Poland
120 K4 **Stryksele** Sweden
120 E6 **Stryn** Norway
122 D2 **Strynsvatnet** *lake* Norway
125 J3 **Stryszawa** Poland
132 G2 **Stryukovo** Ukraine
132 C1 **Stryy** Ukraine
132 C1 **Stryy** *watercourse* Ukraine
125 I1 **Strzałkowo** Poland
218 E3 **Strzelecki** *watercourse* SA Australia
218 E3 **Strzelecki Desert** SA Australia
125 J1 **Strzelno** Poland
125 K1 **Strzyże** Poland
125 K3 **Strzyżów** Poland
215 I5 **Stuart** Qld Australia
87 K7 **Stuart** Florida USA
82 D6 **Stuart** Iowa USA
81 P5 **Stuart** Nebraska USA
86 C3 **Stuart** Oklahoma USA
87 K2 **Stuart** Virginia USA
74 I5 **Stuart Lake** British Columbia Canada
221 B7 **Stuart Mountains** New Zealand
218 B3 **Stuart Range** SA Australia
214 B8 **Stuart Well** NT Australia
76 G8 **Stuartburn** Manitoba Canada
139 F4 **Stubbington** Hampshire England UK
109 11a **Stubbs** St Vincent and the Grenadines
136 C2 **Stubia** *watercourse* Ukraine
132 C3 **Štubik** Serbia
132 C4 **Studena** Bulgaria
136 E2 **Studenets** Russian Federation
139 F4 **Studland** Dorset England UK
122 I3 **Studsvik** Sweden
124 G1 **Stuer** Germany
122 H1 **Stugun** Sweden
120 G5 **Stugusjøen** *lake* Norway
124 E1 **Stuhr** Germany
76 I5 **Stull Lake** Ontario Canada
132 D2 **Stulpicani** Romania
82 B3 **Stump Lake** North Dakota USA
121 M2 **Stuorajávri** *mountain* Norway
121 P2 **Stuorát Golmmesjávri** *lake* Finland
121 O1 **Stuorra Sopmir** *lake* Norway
130 H4 **Stupari** Bosnia and Herzegovina
141 H3 **Sturgate** Lincolnshire England UK
58 L2 **Sturge Island** Antarctica
82 E7 **Sturgeon** Missouri USA
75 W6 **Sturgeon Bay** Manitoba Canada
82 I4 **Sturgeon Bay** Michigan USA
82 H4 **Sturgeon Bay** Wisconsin USA
74 M5 **Sturgeon Heights** Alberta Canada
74 M5 **Sturgeon Lake** Alberta Canada
76 J5 **Sturgeon Lake** Ontario Canada
75 T7 **Sturgis** Saskatchewan Canada
82 H8 **Sturgis** Kentucky USA
82 I6 **Sturgis** Michigan USA
81 N4 **Sturgis** South Dakota USA
123 L4 **Stūri** Latvia
122 H4 **Sturkö** Sweden
139 H2 **Sturmer** Essex England UK
139 E4 **Sturminster Newton** Dorset England UK
132 A2 **Štúrovo** Slovakia
131 C6 **Sturraggia, Capo sa** *cape* Sardinia Italy
213 J5 **Sturt** *watercourse* NT Australia
218 E3 **Sturt, Mount** NSW Australia
218 C6 **Sturt Bay** SA Australia
213 J5 **Sturt Creek** WA Australia
216 G4 **Sturt Meadows** WA Australia
218 D2 **Sturt Stony Desert** SA Australia
218 E5 **Sturt Vale** SA Australia
162 E6 **Stutterheim** South Africa
124 E3 **Stuttgart** Germany
86 F3 **Stuttgart** Arkansas USA
120 inset **Stykkishólmur** Iceland
125 M2 **Styr** *watercourse* Ukraine
197 G3 **Suai** Malaysia
198 C6 **Suai** Timor-Leste (East Timor)
100 C3 **Suaita** Colombia
156 F4 **Suakin** Sudan
157 F4 **Suakin Archipelago** *islands* Sudan
192 E3 **Suan** North Korea
160 C5 **Suana** Democratic Republic of Congo
88 C2 **Suaqui Grande** Mexico
100 B4 **Suárez** Colombia
199 I6 **Suau** Papua New Guinea
158 D4 **Sub-Comoé** *admin. area* Côte d'Ivoire
196 E5 **Subang** Indonesia
181 G3 **Subankhata** Assam India
161 E2 **Sūbāt** *watercourse* Sudan
196 F3 **Subi Besar** *island* Indonesia
81 O8 **Sublette** Kansas USA
80 D4 **Sublimity** Oregon USA
132 A2 **Subotica** Serbia
139 I2 **Subourne** Suffolk England UK
161 F4 **Subugo** *mountain* Kenya
143 D4 **Subulter** Ireland
75 Q7 **Success** Saskatchewan Canada
84 C2 **Success, Lake** California USA
126 D3 **Sucé** France
132 E2 **Suceava** Romania
132 D2 **Suceava** *admin. area* Romania
130 G4 **Sučevići** Croatia
123 J5 **Suchacz** Poland
125 H1 **Suchań** Poland
89 G6 **Suchiate** Mexico
125 L1 **Suchowola** Poland
132 D2 **Suciu de Sus** Romania
143 D3 **Suck** *watercourse* Ireland
138 E2 **Suckley** Worcestershire England UK
199 H6 **Suckling, Cape** Papua New Guinea
199 I6 **Suckling, Mount** Papua New Guinea
105 E5 **Sucre** Bolivia
100 B4 **Sucre** Colombia
100 C2 **Sucre** Colombia
100 C2 **Sucre** *admin. area* Colombia
100 A5 **Sucre** Ecuador
101 F2 **Sucre** *admin. area* Venezuela
109 3 **Sucre, Cayo** *island* Isla de San Andrés
100 B5 **Sucúa** Ecuador
101 F4 **Sucuba** Brazil
100 B5 **Sucumbíos** *admin. area* Ecuador
105 G2 **Sucunduri** *watercourse* Brazil
105 H5 **Sucuriu** *watercourse* Brazil
100 C5 **Sucusari** Peru
159 G4 **Sud** *admin. area* Cameroon
79 G8 **Sud, Pointe du** *cape* Quebec Canada
164 9b **Sud, Pointe du** *cape* Seychelles
160 D4 **Sud-Kivu** *admin. area* Democratic Republic of Congo
159 F3 **Sud-Ouest** *admin. area* Cameroon
79 G8 **Sud-Ouest, Pointe du** *cape* Quebec Canada
136 E4 **Sudak** Ukraine
156 D5 **Sudan** *country* Africa
85 K3 **Sudan** Texas USA
83 K3 **Sudbury** Ontario Canada
139 H2 **Sudbury** Suffolk England UK
125 M2 **Sudche** Ukraine
84 B3 **Sudden** California USA
120 K4 **Suddesjaur** Sweden
124 F1 **Sude** *watercourse* Germany
122 E5 **Süderoogsand** *island* Germany
125 H2 **Sudety** *region* Poland
179 H5 **Sudi** Oman
182 D1 **Sudislavi** Russian Federation
199 G7 **Sudley** QLD Australia
182 C2 **Sudogda** Russian Federation
120 L3 **Sudok** Sweden
196 B5 **Sudong, Pulau** *island* Singapore
156 E2 **Sudr** Egypt
182 E5 **Sudur** Azerbaijan
120 inset **Suðurland** *admin. area* Iceland
120 inset **Suðurnes** *admin. area* Iceland
73 S6 **Suðuroy** *island* Faroe Islands
160 D2 **Sue** *watercourse* Sudan
Suez *see* **As Suways** Egypt
Suez, Gulf of *see* **Suways, Khalīj as** Egypt
156 E1 **Suez Canal** *watercourse* Egypt
199 H4 **Suf Island** Papua New Guinea
75 P7 **Suffield** Alberta Canada
139 I2 **Suffolk** *admin. area* England UK
87 M2 **Suffolk** Virginia USA
81 N7 **Sugar City** Colorado USA
86 D6 **Sugar Land** Texas USA
164 5b **Sugar Loaf Point** *cape* St Helena
219 K5 **Sugarloaf Point** NSW Australia
186 F5 **Sugauli** Bihar India
195 J5 **Sugbuhan Point** Philippines
219 I7 **Suggan Buggan** Vic. Australia
75 T5 **Suggi Lake** Saskatchewan Canada
196 D3 **Sugi** Indonesia
138 E2 **Sugnall** Staffordshire England UK
181 G4 **Sugnu** Manipur India
195 H6 **Sugut** *watercourse* Malaysia
195 H6 **Sugut, Tanjong** *cape* Malaysia
161 F3 **Suguta** *watercourse* Kenya
185 J5 **Suhai Hu** *lake* Qinghai China
132 D4 **Suhaia** Romania
132 D4 **Suhaia, Lacul** *lake* Romania
179 H5 **Şuḩār** Oman
190 F2 **Sühbaatar** Mongolia
191 H3 **Sühbaatar** *admin. area* Mongolia
187 C9 **Suheli Par** *island* Lakshadweep India
127 J1 **Suhl** Germany
130 G4 **Suhopolje** Croatia
189 F4 **Sui Jiang** *watercourse* Guangdong China
189 H4 **Sui'an** Fujian China
105 H3 **Suiá-Missu** *watercourse* Brazil
130 G5 **Šuica** Bosnia and Herzegovina
189 G3 **Suicheng** Fujian China
188 F4 **Suicheng** Guangdong China
191 L4 **Suifenhe** Heilongjiang China
191 K3 **Suihua** Heilongjiang China
121 M2 **Suijavaara** Sweden
191 K3 **Suileng** Heilongjiang China
188 E2 **Suining** Sichuan China
121 P3 **Suininki** *lake* Finland
192 E3 **Suip-ch'on** *watercourse* South Korea
127 G2 **Suippe** *watercourse* France
143 E4 **Suir** *watercourse* Ireland
84 A1 **Suisun** California USA
189 G1 **Suixi** Anhui China
191 I5 **Suizhong** Liaoning China
189 G2 **Suizhou** Hubei China
105 F4 **Sujalito** Bolivia
186 D5 **Sujangarh** Rajasthan India
179 K5 **Sujawal** Pakistan
191 I5 **Suji** Hebei China
196 E5 **Sukabumi** Indonesia
196 E5 **Sukadana** Indonesia
197 F4 **Sukadana, Teluk** *bay* Indonesia
197 F4 **Sukaraja** Indonesia
197 F4 **Sukaramai** Indonesia
197 H2 **Sukau** Malaysia
192 E3 **Sukch'ŏn** North Korea
186 D6 **Suket** Rajasthan India
121 O5 **Sukeva** Finland
135 Y5 **Sukhana** Russian Federation
123 P6 **Sukhari** Belarus
125 M1 **Sukhinichi** Belarus
136 E1 **Sukhinichi** Russian Federation
134 J7 **Sukhona** *watercourse* Russian Federation
194 C3 **Sukhothai** Thailand
194 C3 **Sukhothai** *admin. area* Thailand
199 G6 **Suki** Papua New Guinea
156 E5 **Suki** Sudan
121 R5 **Sukkozero** Russian Federation
179 K4 **Sukkur** Pakistan
194 C6 **Sukon, Ko** *island* Thailand
193 H1 **Sukpay** *watercourse* Russian Federation
162 C4 **Sukses** Namibia
135 AF6 **Suksukan** Russian Federation
192 G5 **Sukumo** Japan
198 B6 **Sukun** *island* Indonesia
120 H5 **Sul** Norway
122 C2 **Sula** *island* Norway
134 L5 **Sula** *watercourse* Russian Federation
198 C4 **Sula, Kepulauan** *islands* Indonesia
121 Q5 **Sula, Ozero** *lake* Russian Federation
142 B1 **Sula Sgeir** *island* Scotland UK
179 L3 **Sulaiman Range** Pakistan
182 E5 **Sulak** Russian Federation
120 G5 **Sulåmoen** Norway
197 H6 **Sulat** *island* Indonesia
195 J5 **Sulat** Philippines
198 B4 **Sulawesi (Celebes)** *island* Indonesia
198 A4 **Sulawesi Barat** *admin. area* Indonesia
198 A4 **Sulawesi Selatan** *admin. area* Indonesia
198 B4 **Sulawesi Tengah** *admin. area* Indonesia
198 B5 **Sulawesi Tenggara** *admin. area* Indonesia
198 C3 **Sulawesi Utara** *admin. area* Indonesia
178 D5 **Sulaym** Saudi Arabia
178 F2 **Sulaymānīyah, As** *admin. area* Iraq
178 F5 **Sulayyimah** Saudi Arabia
178 F4 **Şulbūkh** Saudi Arabia
122 D3 **Suldal** Norway
122 D3 **Suldalsvatnet** *lake* Norway
142 D1 **Sule Skerry** *island* Scotland UK
125 H1 **Sulęcin** Poland
159 F3 **Suleja** Nigeria
125 J2 **Sulejów** Poland
197 H3 **Suleman, Teluk** *bay* Indonesia
120 F5 **Sulfjorden** *bay* Norway
125 M1 **Sulichevo** Belarus
132 F3 **Sulina** Romania
124 E1 **Sulingen** Germany
120 J3 **Sulitjelma** *mountain* Norway
123 M2 **Sulkava** Finland
123 O2 **Sulkava** Finland
121 O5 **Sulkavanjärvi** Finland
121 M5 **Sulkavankylä** Finland
104 A2 **Sullana** Peru
143 C5 **Sullane** *watercourse* Ireland
133 F6 **Süller** Turkey
82 G7 **Sullivan** Illinois USA
214 A4 **Sullivan, Mount** NT Australia
74 H7 **Sullivan Bay** British Columbia Canada
75 O7 **Sullivan Lake** Alberta Canada
138 D3 **Sully** Vale of Glamorgan Wales UK
82 E6 **Sully** Iowa USA
125 I2 **Sulmierzyce** Poland
133 E5 **Süloğlu** Turkey
86 E5 **Sulphur** Louisiana USA
86 C3 **Sulphur** Oklahoma USA
86 D4 **Sulphur Springs** Texas USA
84 F1 **Sulphurdale** Utah USA
82 J3 **Sultan** Ontario Canada
156 C1 **Sultan** Libya
80 E3 **Sultan** Washington USA
186 F5 **Sultanpur** Uttar Pradesh India
134 K6 **Sul'tsa** Russian Federation
160 C4 **Sulu** Democratic Republic of Congo
195 I6 **Sulu Archipelago** Philippines
52 I7 **Sulu Basin** *underwater feature* Sulu Sea
195 H6 **Sulu Sea** Philippines
195 J5 **Suluan** *island* Philippines
183 K6 **Sülüktü** Kyrgyzstan
156 C1 **Sulūq** Libya
187 E9 **Suluru** Andhra Pradesh India
183 L6 **Suluu-Istik** *watercourse* Tajikistan
120 H5 **Sulviken** Sweden
182 E3 **Sulyayevka** Russian Federation
58 N1 **Sulzberger Bay** Antarctica
124 F3 **Sulzemoos** Germany
132 B3 **Šumadiji** Serbia
197 H4 **Sumaianyar** Indonesia
161 G2 **Sumalē** *admin. area* Ethiopia
103 C8 **Sumaré** Brazil
134 S6 **Sumarokovo** Russian Federation
199 G4 **Sumasuma Island** Papua New Guinea
196 D4 **Sumatera (Sumatra)** *island* Indonesia
196 D4 **Sumatera Barat** *admin. area* Indonesia
196 D4 **Sumatera Selatan** *admin. area* Indonesia
196 C3 **Sumatera Utara** *admin. area* Indonesia
Sumatra *see* **Sumatera** Indonesia
124 G3 **Šumava** *range* Czech Republic
197 H6 **Sumba** *island* Indonesia
160 B3 **Sumba, Île** *island* Democratic Republic of Congo
197 H6 **Sumba, Selat** *strait* Indonesia
182 G6 **Sumbar** *watercourse* Turkmenistan
197 H6 **Sumbawa** *island* Indonesia
197 H6 **Sumbawabesar** Indonesia
160 E5 **Sumbawanga** Tanzania
162 B2 **Sumbe** Angola
196 F5 **Sumber** Indonesia
191 I3 **Sumber** Mongolia
190 F3 **Sumber** Mongolia
196 D4 **Sumbing, Gunung** *volcano* Indonesia
160 E5 **Sumbu** Zambia
158 B3 **Sumbuya** Sierra Leone
102 E4 **Sumé** Brazil
125 I4 **Sümeg** Hungary
197 G5 **Sumenep** Indonesia
182 F6 **Sumgait** Azerbaijan
123 N1 **Sumiainen** Finland
178 E4 **Sumlah** Saudi Arabia
121 N5 **Summasjärvi** *lake* Finland
216 D3 **Summer Hill** WA Australia
142 C2 **Summer Isles** Scotland UK
80 E5 **Summer Lake** Oregon USA
215 I7 **Summerdell** Qld Australia
162 C4 **Summerdown** Namibia
85 K3 **Summerfield** Texas USA
143 F3 **Summerhill** Ireland
74 L8 **Summerland** British Columbia Canada
79 G9 **Summerside** Prince Edward Island Canada
87 K4 **Summerton** South Carolina USA
140 A3 **Summerville** Ireland
86 F5 **Summit** Mississippi USA
86 D3 **Summit** Oklahoma USA
81 Q4 **Summit** South Dakota USA
74 I3 **Summit Lake** British Columbia Canada
221 E6 **Sumner, Lake** New Zealand
85 J3 **Sumner, Lake** New Mexico USA
74 E4 **Sumner Strait** Alaska USA
198 A5 **Sumpangbinangae** Indonesia
181 H3 **Sumrabum** Myanmar
86 G5 **Sumrall** Mississippi USA
121 P4 **Sumsa** Finland
136 E2 **Sum'ska Oblast'** *admin. area* Ukraine
121 S4 **Sumskiy Posad** Russian Federation
87 K4 **Sumter** South Carolina USA
186 D3 **Sumur** Jammu and Kashmir India/Pakistan
136 E2 **Sumy** Ukraine
162 E5 **Sun City** South Africa
80 H5 **Sun Valley** Idaho USA
187 F7 **Sunabeda** Orissa India
193 I2 **Sunagawa** Japan
186 D6 **Sunaj** Madhya Pradesh India
186 D4 **Sunam** Punjab India
181 G4 **Sunamgonj** Bangladesh
83 O5 **Sunapee Lake** New Hampshire USA
159 G3 **Sunati** *watercourse* Nigeria
87 I2 **Sunbright** Tennessee USA
81 R4 **Sunburg** Minnesota USA
80 J2 **Sunburst** Montana USA
218 G7 **Sunbury** Vic. Australia
139 G3 **Sunbury** Surrey England UK
106 F4 **Sunchales** Argentina
106 F3 **Suncho Corral** Argentina
192 E4 **Sunch'ŏn** South Korea
123 K2 **Sund** Finland
120 I3 **Sund** Norway
122 F3 **Sund** Sweden
196 E5 **Sunda, Selat** *strait* Indonesia
55 O4 **Sunda Shelf** *seabed*
120 F5 **Sundan** Norway
81 M4 **Sundance** Wyoming USA
186 D4 **Sundar Nagar** Himachal Pradesh India
122 F5 **Sundby** Denmark
121 M5 **Sundby** Finland
141 G2 **Sunderland** *admin. area* England UK
141 G2 **Sunderland** Tyne and Wear England UK
124 E2 **Sundern** Germany
120 H5 **Sundet** Sweden
120 K4 **Sundö** Sweden
120 M4 **Sundom** Sweden
85 K4 **Sundown** Texas USA
75 N7 **Sundre** Alberta Canada
122 J4 **Sundre** Sweden
83 L4 **Sundridge** Ontario Canada
120 J5 **Sundsvall** Sweden
120 K5 **Sundsvallsbukten** *bay* Sweden
120 G4 **Sundsvoll** Norway
82 I5 **Sunfield** Michigan USA
84 G4 **Sunflower** Arizona USA
86 F4 **Sunflower** Mississippi USA
197 F3 **Sungai Ayak** Indonesia
196 D2 **Sungai Petani** Malaysia
196 D3 **Sungaiapit** Indonesia
196 D3 **Sungaiguntung** Indonesia
196 F4 **Sungaikakap** Indonesia
196 E4 **Sungailiat** Indonesia
196 D4 **Sungaipenuh** Indonesia
196 F3 **Sungaipinyuh** Indonesia
196 F3 **Sungairaya** Indonesia
196 E4 **Sungalpadang** Indonesia
196 C3 **Sunggal** Indonesia
198 A5 **Sungguminasa** Indonesia
163 F3 **Sungo** Mozambique
196 E4 **Sungsang** Indonesia
136 E5 **Sungurlu** Turkey
131 C6 **Suni** Sardinia Italy
85 I5 **Sunland Park** New Mexico USA
120 G4 **Sunnan** Norway
122 H2 **Sunnansjö** Sweden
120 F5 **Sunndalen** *valley* Norway
120 F5 **Sunndalsøra** Norway
120 I5 **Sunne** Sweden
122 G3 **Sunnemo** Sweden
75 P7 **Sunnynook** Alberta Canada
84 E1 **Sunnyside** Nevada USA
81 J7 **Sunnyside** Utah USA
80 E3 **Sunnyside** Washington USA
80 D8 **Sunnyvale** California USA
85 L2 **Sunray** Texas USA
87 K7 **Sunrise** Florida USA
105 G5 **Sunsas, Serranía** *range* Bolivia
86 E5 **Sunset** Louisiana USA
86 C4 **Sunset** Texas USA
87 L4 **Sunset Beach** North Carolina USA
218 E6 **Sunset Country** *region* Vic. Australia
135 AD6 **Suntar Khayata, Khrebet** *range* Russian Federation
123 M4 **Suntaži** Latvia
179 J4 **Suntsar** Pakistan
161 F2 **Suntu** Ethiopia
192 E4 **Sunwi-do** *island* North Korea
191 K2 **Sunwu** Heilongjiang China
158 D3 **Sunyani** Ghana
121 N5 **Suolahti** Finland
135 X4 **Suolama** *watercourse* Russian Federation
121 P4 **Suolijärvi** Finland
121 O4 **Suolijärvi** *lake* Finland
121 P2 **Suolisjärvi** *lake* Finland
121 O2 **Suolisvuono** *bay* Finland
121 O1 **Suolojav'ri** *lake* Norway
123 N2 **Suomijärvi** *bay* Finland
121 P4 **Suomussalmi** Finland
190 E6 **Suonaihai** Qinghai China
190 E6 **Suonan** Gansu China
121 O5 **Suonenjoki** Finland
194 E5 **Suong** Cambodia
123 N2 **Suontee** *lake* Finland
121 O5 **Suontienselkä** *lake* Finland
120 K3 **Suorva** Sweden
121 N2 **Šuosjav'ri** Norway
121 N5 **Suotuperä** Finland
123 Q1 **Suoyarvi** Russian Federation
123 Q1 **Suoyarvi, Ozero** *lake* Russian Federation
104 B3 **Supe** Peru
84 G4 **Superior** Arizona USA
80 H3 **Superior** Montana USA
81 P6 **Superior** Nebraska USA
82 E3 **Superior** Wisconsin USA
89 G5 **Superior, Laguna** *lake* Mexico
82 H3 **Superior, Lake** Canada/USA
194 D4 **Suphan Buri** Thailand
194 C4 **Suphanburi** *admin. area* Thailand
131 E6 **Supino** Italy
198 E4 **Supiori** *island* Indonesia
213 J5 **Supplejack Downs** NT Australia
58 U1 **Support Force Glacier** Antarctica
192 E3 **Supung** North Korea
125 L4 **Supuru de Jos** Romania
178 E6 **Sūq al 'Ajamah** Saudi Arabia
156 D5 **Şuq'at Al Jamal** Sudan
189 H1 **Suqian** Jiangsu China
157 I5 **Suquṭrá (Socotra)** *islands* Yemen
179 I5 **Şūr** Oman
109 5 **Sur, Cabo** *cape* Isla de Pascua (Easter Island)
84 A2 **Sur, Point** California USA
109 3 **Sur, Punta** *cape* Isla de San Andrés
182 E2 **Sura** Russian Federation
182 E2 **Sura** *watercourse* Russian Federation
179 K4 **Surab** Pakistan
197 G5 **Surabaya** Indonesia
122 I3 **Surahammar** Sweden
132 E3 **Suraia** Romania
197 F5 **Surakarta** Indonesia
198 A4 **Suramana** Indonesia
130 H2 **Šurany** Slovakia
219 I2 **Surat** Qld Australia
187 C7 **Surat** Gujarat India
221 C8 **Surat Bay** New Zealand
194 C5 **Surat Thani** Thailand
194 C5 **Surat Thani** *admin. area* Thailand
186 C5 **Suratgarh** Rajasthan India
136 E2 **Surazh** Russian Federation
215 I7 **Surbiton** Qld Australia
131 H6 **Surbo** Italy
186 C6 **Surendranagar** Gujarat India
83 N7 **Surf City** New Jersey USA
87 M3 **Surf City** North Carolina USA
219 K2 **Surfers Paradise** Qld Australia
139 G2 **Surfleet** Lincolnshire England UK
187 C7 **Surgana** Maharashtra India
126 D3 **Surgères** France
134 P6 **Surgut** Russian Federation
134 S6 **Surgutikha** Russian Federation
179 H3 **Sūrīān** Iran
187 E8 **Suriapet** Andhra Pradesh India
195 J5 **Surigao** Philippines
195 J5 **Surigao Strait** Philippines
194 D4 **Surin** Thailand
194 D4 **Surin** *admin. area* Thailand
101 H3 **Suriname** *country* South America
100 D3 **Suripa** *watercourse* Venezuela
186 E5 **Surkhet** Nepal
121 P2 **Surnujärvi** *lake* Finland
121 P2 **Surnuvuono** *bay* Finland
104 D5 **Suropa** Bolivia
182 D4 **Surovikino** Russian Federation
105 E3 **Surprêsa** Brazil
214 F4 **Surprise** *watercourse* Qld Australia
74 E3 **Surprise** British Columbia Canada
84 F4 **Surprise** Arizona USA
83 N2 **Surprise, Lac** *lake* Quebec Canada
214 A6 **Surprise, Lake** NT Australia
219 J4 **Surprise, Mount** NSW Australia
219 I1 **Surprise Mountain** Qld Australia
81 M2 **Surprise Valley** Saskatchewan Canada
74 J8 **Surrey** British Columbia Canada
139 G3 **Surrey** *admin. area* England UK
75 U8 **Surrey** North Dakota USA
182 E2 **Surskoye** Russian Federation
155 J2 **Surt** Libya
155 J2 **Surt, Khalīj** *bay* Libya
120 inset **Surtsey** *island* Iceland
100 E5 **Surubim** Brazil
101 F4 **Surucucus, Serra dos** *range* Brazil
193 H4 **Suruga-wan** *bay* Japan
196 D4 **Surulangun** Indonesia
101 G4 **Surumatra** Guyana
85 I8 **Surutato** Mexico
182 J6 **Surxondaryo** *admin. area* Uzbekistan
100 C3 **Susa** Colombia
124 D5 **Susa** Italy
130 G5 **Sušac** *island* Croatia
130 F4 **Susak** *island* Croatia
192 G5 **Susaki** Japan
123 P3 **Susanino** Russian Federation
131 H5 **Šušanj** Montenegro
80 E6 **Susanville** California USA
124 G3 **Sušice** Czech Republic
120 I4 **Susna** *watercourse* Norway
186 D6 **Susner** Madhya Pradesh India
189 G2 **Susong** Anhui China
100 A4 **Suspiro, Punta** *cape* Ecuador
129 H3 **Susqueda, Pantà de** *lake* Spain
106 E2 **Susques** Argentina
79 F10 **Sussex** New Brunswick Canada
219 J6 **Sussex Inlet** NSW Australia
163 F3 **Sussundenga** Mozambique
74 H4 **Sustut** *watercourse* British Columbia Canada
161 F4 **Susua** *mountain* Kenya
222 8 **Susubona** Solomon Islands
197 H2 **Susul** Malaysia
222 2a **Susupe** Northern Mariana Islands
133 F6 **Susurluk** Turkey
125 J1 **Susz** Poland
183 P3 **Sut-khol', Ozero** *lake* Russian Federation
185 J3 **Sutay Uul** *mountain* Mongolia
138 C4 **Sutcombe** Devon England UK
133 G7 **Sütçüler** Turkey
162 D6 **Sutherland** South Africa
81 O6 **Sutherland** Nebraska USA
221 B7 **Sutherland Sound** New Zealand
80 D5 **Sutherlin** Oregon USA
186 D4 **Sutlej** *watercourse* Punjab India
123 O4 **Sutoki** Russian Federation
80 E7 **Sutter Creek** California USA
139 G2 **Sutterton** Lincolnshire England UK
76 M1 **Sutton** *watercourse* Nunavut Canada
83 L4 **Sutton** Ontario Canada
76 M5 **Sutton** *watercourse* Ontario Canada
140 B3 **Sutton** Ireland
139 G3 **Sutton** Greater London England UK
139 I2 **Sutton** Norfolk England UK
141 H3 **Sutton** Nottinghamshire England UK
138 E2 **Sutton** Staffordshire England UK
139 I2 **Sutton** Suffolk England UK
81 Q6 **Sutton** Nebraska USA
139 G2 **Sutton Bassett** Northamptonshire England UK
139 H2 **Sutton Bridge** Lincolnshire England UK
139 F2 **Sutton Coldfield** West Midlands England UK
215 H6 **Sutton Downs** Qld Australia
139 F1 **Sutton in Ashfield** Nottinghamshire England UK
76 M5 **Sutton Lake** Ontario Canada
141 I3 **Sutton on Sea** Lincolnshire England UK
141 H3 **Sutton-on-Trent** Nottinghamshire England UK
139 H2 **Sutton St Edmund** Lincolnshire England UK
139 E3 **Sutton Veny** Wiltshire England UK
139 F3 **Sutton Wick** Oxfordshire England UK
215 I6 **Suttor** *watercourse* Qld Australia
154 D6 **Sutukoba** Gambia
135 AB5 **Sutun'ya** Russian Federation
72 D7 **Sutwik Island** Alaska USA
222 8 **Su'u** Solomon Islands
160 E2 **Suud** *swamp* Sudan
123 L3 **Suur Katel** *bay* Estonia
123 N4 **Suur Munamägi** *mountain* Estonia
121 Q5 **Suuri Onkamojärvi** *lake* Finland
121 P5 **Suurijärvi** *lake* Finland
223 9a **Suva** Fiji
133 B5 **Suva Gora** *range* Macedonia
132 B4 **Suva Reka** Kosovo
121 O3 **Suvanto** Finland
121 P5 **Suvasvesi** *bay* Finland
131 G7 **Suvero, Capo** *cape* Italy
132 H2 **Suvorovka** Ukraine
197 G4 **Suwakong** Indonesia
123 L5 **Suwałki** Poland
87 J5/6 **Suwannee** *watercourse* Georgia/Florida USA
192 F6 **Suwanose-jima** *island* Japan
220 1 **Suwarrow Atoll** *reef* Cook Islands New Zealand
156 E2 **Suways, Khalīj as (Gulf of Suez)** *bay* Egypt
192 E4 **Suwŏn** South Korea
189 G1 **Suyahu Shuiku** *lake* Henan China
183 N3 **Suykbulak** Kazakhstan
182 F5 **Suz, Mys** *cape* Kazakhstan
193 H4 **Suzaka** Japan
103 C8 **Suzano** Brazil
182 C2 **Suzdal** Russian Federation
189 G1 **Suzhou** Anhui China
189 H2 **Suzhou** Jiangsu China
193 H4 **Suzuka** Japan
127 J4 **Suzzara** Italy
122 H2 **Svabensverk** Sweden
121 O1 **Svæholtklubben** *cape* Norway
121 O1 **Sværholthalvøya** *peninsula* Norway
134 D3 **Svalbard** *island* Norway
134 D3 **Svalbard** *Norway territory* Norway
132 C1 **Svalyava** Ukraine
120 J4 **Svanabyn** Sweden
120 L3 **Svanisträsket** *lake* Sweden
120 K3 **Svannäs** Sweden
122 C2 **Svanøy** Norway
122 C2 **Svanøy** *island* Norway
121 Q2 **Svanvik** Norway
120 L3 **Svappavaara** Sweden
120 inset **Svartá** *watercourse* Iceland
122 H3 **Svartå** Sweden
122 D3 **Svartevatn** *lake* Norway
120 I3 **Svartisen** *island* Norway
123 J3 **Svartlöga** *island* Sweden
123 J3 **Svartlögafjärden** *bay* Sweden
122 I2 **Svartnäs** Sweden
123 J3 **Svartsö** *island* Sweden
121 M3 **Svartträsk** Sweden
120 J4 **Svärtträsk/Gunnarsberg** Sweden
125 M2 **Svaryn'** Belarus
136 F3 **Svatove** Ukraine
194 D4 **Svay Chék** Cambodia
182 E1 **Svecha** Russian Federation
123 M5 **Svėdasai** Lithuania
120 K5 **Svedje** Sweden
120 I5 **Sveg** Sweden
120 I5 **Svegsjön** *lake* Sweden
122 C3 **Sveio** Norway
123 K5 **Švėkšna** Lithuania
122 F5 **Svendborg** Denmark
120 H4 **Svenningdal** Norway
120 K2 **Svensby** Norway
120 L4 **Svensbyfjärden** *bay* Sweden
134 G3 **Svenskøya** *island* Norway
120 I5 **Svenstavik** Sweden
123 M5 **Šventoji** *watercourse* Lithuania
136 F3 **Sverdlovs'k** Ukraine
134 N7 **Sverdlovskaya Oblast'** *admin. area* Russian Federation
73 J3 **Sverdrup Channel** Nunavut Canada
134 Q4 **Sverdrupa, Ostrov** *island* Russian Federation
182 D4 **Svetlograd** Russian Federation
182 H3 **Svetlyy** Russian Federation
182 D4 **Svetlyy Yar** Russian Federation
123 O2 **Svetogorsk** Russian Federation
125 K3 **Svidník** Slovakia
124 G3 **Švihov** Czech Republic
123 L3 **Sviibi** Estonia
130 G5 **Svilaja** *region* Croatia
133 E5 **Svilengrad** Bulgaria
122 H4 **Svinhult** Sweden
132 C3 **Svinița** Romania
123 N5 **Svir, Vozyera** *lake* Belarus
123 Q2 **Sviritsa** Russian Federation
123 N5 **Svirkos** Lithuania
123 Q2 **Svir'stroy** Russian Federation
132 D4 **Svishtov** Bulgaria
125 M1 **Svislach** Belarus
125 K3 **Svit** Slovakia
125 I3 **Svitava** *watercourse* Czech Republic
130 G2 **Svitavy** Czech Republic
132 D4 **Svoboda** Bulgaria
191 K2 **Svobodnyy** Russian Federation
132 C4 **Svođe** Serbia
125 J4 **Svodín** Slovakia
130 G4 **Svodna** Bosnia and Herzegovina
132 C4 **Svoge** Bulgaria
130 H4 **Svojat** Bosnia and Herzegovina
120 I2 **Svolvær** Norway
130 G2 **Svratka** Czech Republic
132 C4 **Svrljig** Serbia
123 N5 **Svyantsyanskiya Hrady** *region* Belarus
57 K1 **Svyataya Anna Fan** *underwater feature* Arctic Ocean
57 K1 **Svyataya Anna Trough** *underwater feature* Arctic Ocean
125 N1 **Svyatitsa** Belarus
134 J5 **Svyatoy Nos, Mys** *cape* Russian Federation
123 Q2 **Svyatozero** Russian Federation
123 N5 **Svylionys** Lithuania
139 F2 **Swadlincote** Derbyshire England UK
139 H2 **Swaffham** Norfolk England UK
215 L6 **Swain Reefs** Qld Australia

222 1 **Swains Island** American Samoa
162 C4 **Swakop** *watercourse* Namibia
162 B4 **Swakopmund** Namibia
141 F2 **Swale** *watercourse* England UK
164 5c **Swales Fell** *volcano* St Helena
141 H3 **Swallow** Lincolnshire England UK
195 G6 **Swallow Reef** Spratly Islands
77 U5 **Swampy Bay** *watercourse* Quebec Canada
77 N6 **Swan** *watercourse* Ontario Canada
218 F6 **Swan Hill** Vic. Australia
75 N5 **Swan Hills** Alberta Canada
90 D3 **Swan Islands** Honduras
74 G5 **Swan Lake** British Columbia Canada
81 P2 **Swan Lake** Manitoba Canada
75 U6 **Swan Lake** Manitoba Canada
76 J5 **Swan Lake** Ontario Canada
82 D4 **Swan Lake** Minnesota USA
80 I3 **Swan Lake** Montana USA
75 T6 **Swan Plain** Saskatchewan Canada
218 D6 **Swan Reach** SA Australia
75 U6 **Swan River** Manitoba Canada
82 E3 **Swan River** Minnesota USA
219 J3 **Swan Vale** NSW Australia
215 G8 **Swan Vale** Qld Australia
80 J5 **Swan Valley** Idaho USA
160 D6 **Swana-Mume** Democratic Republic of Congo
139 F4 **Swanage** Dorset England UK
139 H3 **Swanley** Kent England UK
218 H7 **Swanpool** Vic. Australia
219 J5 **Swansea** NSW Australia
219 S11 **Swansea** Tas. Australia
138 D3 **Swansea** Swansea Wales UK
138 D3 **Swansea** *admin. area* Wales UK
87 K4 **Swansea** South Carolina USA
138 D3 **Swansea Bay** Wales UK
81 O6 **Swanson Reservoir** Nebraska USA
83 O4 **Swanton** Vermont USA
141 G1 **Swarland** Northumberland England UK
179 L2 **Swat** *watercourse* Pakistan
163 F5 **Swaziland** *country* Africa
120 J4 **Sweden** *country* Europe
214 E4 **Sweers Island** Qld Australia
80 D4 **Sweet Home** Oregon USA
82 E7 **Sweet Springs** Missouri USA
138 C4 **Sweetshouse** Cornwall England UK
86 A4 **Sweetwater** Texas USA
81 K5 **Sweetwater** *watercourse* Wyoming USA
125 I2 **Świdnica** Poland
125 L2 **Świdnik** Poland
125 J1 **Świecie** Poland
125 J1 **Świekatowo** Poland
125 J2 **Święta Anna** Poland
125 K2 **Świętokrzyskie** *admin. area* Poland
75 R7 **Swift Current** Saskatchewan Canada
80 D3 **Swift Reservoir** Washington USA
74 F2 **Swift River** Yukon Territory Canada
124 C1 **Swifterbant** Netherlands
139 F3 **Swindon** *admin. area* England UK
139 E3 **Swindon** Gloucestershire England UK
139 F3 **Swindon** Swindon England UK
139 G2 **Swineshead** Lincolnshire England UK
143 D3 **Swinford** Ireland
140 B4 **Swinn** Ireland
142 F5 **Swinton** Scottish Borders Scotland UK
124 **Switzerland** *country* Europe
142 B4 **Swordle** Highland Scotland UK
143 F3 **Swords** Ireland
134 P5 **Syaday-Kharvuta** Russian Federation
135 AD5 **Syagannakh** Russian Federation
135 Z5 **Syalakh** Russian Federation
121 R6 **Syamozero, Ozero** *lake* Russian Federation
123 Q2 **Syas'stroy** Russian Federation
182 E1 **Syava** Russian Federation
143 B4 **Sybil Point** Ireland
125 I2 **Syców** Poland
123 K2 **Sydänmaa** Finland
122 E5 **Syddanmark** *admin. area* Denmark
219 J5 **Sydney** NSW Australia
80 D2 **Sydney** British Columbia Canada
79 H9 **Sydney** Nova Scotia Canada
211 inset **Sydney Bay** Norfolk Island Australia
80 B2 **Sydney Inlet** British Columbia Canada
214 E4 **Sydney Island** Qld Australia
76 H7 **Sydney Lake** Ontario Canada
79 H9 **Sydney Mines** Nova Scotia Canada
139 G1 **Syerston** Nottinghamshire England UK
136 F3 **Syeverodonets'k** Ukraine
133 C7 **Sykea** Greece
81 P3 **Sykeston** North Dakota USA
134 L6 **Syktyvkar** Russian Federation
87 H4 **Sylacauga** Alabama USA
120 H5 **Sylarna** *mountain* Norway
138 C3 **Sylen** Carmarthenshire Wales UK
181 G4 **Sylhet** Bangladesh
181 G4 **Sylhet** *admin. area* Bangladesh
122 E5 **Sylt** *island* Germany
120 E5 **Sylte** Norway
87 J3 **Sylva** North Carolina USA
76 G7 **Sylvan** Manitoba Canada
81 P7 **Sylvan Grove** Kansas USA
75 N6 **Sylvan Lake** Alberta Canada
75 N6 **Sylvan Lake** Alberta Canada
216 G1 **Sylvania** WA Australia
75 S6 **Sylvania** Saskatchewan Canada
87 K4 **Sylvania** Georgia USA
82 J6 **Sylvania** Ohio USA
214 E7 **Sylvester** *watercourse* Qld Australia
214 C5 **Sylvester, Lake** NT Australia
85 M2 **Sylvia** Kansas USA
74 I3 **Sylvia, Mount** British Columbia Canada
142 inset **Symbister** Shetland Scotland UK
133 E7 **Symi** Greece
133 E7 **Symi** *island* Greece
142 D5 **Symington** South Ayrshire Scotland UK
122 E2 **Syndin** *lake* Norway
122 E3 **Syndle** *lake* Norway
138 C2 **Synod Inn** Ceredigion Wales UK
132 G1 **Synyukha** *watercourse* Ukraine
58 C2 **Syowa (Japan)** *research station* Antarctica
Syracuse *see* **Siracusa** Italy
81 O8 **Syracuse** Kansas USA
81 Q6 **Syracuse** Nebraska USA
83 M5 **Syracuse** New York USA
182 I4 **Syradarya** *watercourse* Kazakhstan
182 I4 **Syrdarya** *watercourse* Kazakhstan
121 N5 **Syri** Finland
136 F6 **Syria** *country*
136 F6 **Syria** *country* Middle East
133 E7 **Syrna** *island* Greece
133 D7 **Syros** *island* Greece
122 I4 **Syrsan** *lake* Sweden
122 D2 **Sysenvatnet** *lake* Norway
121 O5 **Sysmä** *lake* Finland
122 G2 **Sysslebäck** Sweden
183 Q3 **Systyg-Kem** Russian Federation
121 M2 **Syväjärvi** Finland
121 O5 **Syvänsi** *lake* Finland
121 P5 **Syväri** *lake* Finland
121 O2 **Syysjärvi** *lake* Finland
182 E2 **Syzran** Russian Federation
125 L4 **Szabolcs-Szatmar-Bereg** *admin. area* Hungary
125 J2 **Szadek** Poland
199 G5 **Szaga Lake** Papua New Guinea
125 J5 **Szajk** Hungary
125 J5 **Szalánta** Hungary
132 B1 **Szalonna** Hungary
125 L4 **Szamos** *watercourse* Hungary
130 H3 **Szank** Hungary
125 I4 **Szany** Hungary
132 B2 **Szarvas** Hungary
125 H1 **Szczecin** Poland
Szczeciński, Zalew *see* **Stettiner Haff** Poland
125 J2 **Szczekociny** Poland
123 N5 **Szczerby** Belarus
125 L1 **Szczuczyn** Poland
123 K5 **Szczurkowo** Russian Federation
125 K1 **Szczytno** Poland
125 J2 **Szczyty** Poland
132 A1 **Szécsény** Hungary
132 B2 **Szeged** Hungary
125 K4 **Szeghalom** Hungary
132 B1 **Székely** Hungary
132 A2 **Székesfehérvár** Hungary
132 A2 **Szekszárd** Hungary
122 J5 **Szemud** Poland
132 B1 **Szendrő** Hungary
130 H3 **Szentendre** Hungary
132 B2 **Szentes** Hungary
125 I4 **Szentőrinc** Hungary
125 I4 **Szigetvár** Hungary
125 H2 **Szklarska Poręba** Poland
132 B2 **Szolnok** Hungary
130 G3 **Szombathely** Hungary
125 J4 **Szorosad** Hungary
125 L1 **Sztabin** Poland
125 I1 **Szubin** Poland
125 K2 **Szydłów** Poland
125 K2 **Szydłowiec** Poland
125 J2 **Szynkielów** Poland

T

189 H4 **Ta Hsu** *island* Taiwan China
194 E5 **Ta Khmau** Cambodia
184 G5 **Ta-li-mu Ho (Tarim He)** *watercourse* Xinjiang Uygur Zizhiqu China
75 N8 **Ta Ta Creek** British Columbia Canada
142 C3 **Taagan** Highland Scotland UK
195 I4 **Taal, Lake** *lake* Philippines
198 E5 **Taam** *island* Indonesia
104 D5 **Taapacá, Cerro** *mountain* Chile
121 N3 **Taapajärvi** Finland
216 E6 **Taarblin Lake** WA Australia
125 J4 **Tab** Hungary
156 D5 **Tabago Hills** Sudan
85 J6 **Tabaloapa** Mexico
104 B2 **Tabalosos** Peru
197 G6 **Tabanan** Indonesia
197 H3 **Tabang** Indonesia
199 I4 **Tabar Islands** Papua New Guinea
155 H1 **Tabarka** Tunisia
179 H2 **Ţabas** Iran
88 E4 **Tabasco** Mexico
89 G5 **Tabasco** *admin. area* Mexico
156 E5 **Tabat** Sudan
104 D2 **Tabatinga** Brazil
107 I2 **Tabatinga** Brazil
219 K3 **Tabbimoble** NSW Australia
218 G6 **Tabbita** NSW Australia
155 F3 **Tabelbala** Algeria
155 H2 **Taberdga** Algeria
198 E5 **Taberfane** Indonesia
122 H4 **Taberg** Sweden
140 B4 **Taberlomina** Ireland
109 19 **Tabernacle** Saint Kitts and Nevis
128 E5 **Tabernas** Spain
81 J6 **Tabiona** Utah USA
196 D4 **Tabir** *watercourse* Indonesia
102 E4 **Tabira** Brazil
222 1 **Tabiteuea** *island* Kiribati
100 E2 **Tablantico** Venezuela
108 A3 **Tablaruca, Punta** *cape* Chile
195 I4 **Tablas** *island* Philippines
106 D4 **Tablas, Cabo** *cape* Chile
195 I4 **Tablas Strait** Philippines
129 H5 **Tablat** Algeria
79 H8 **Table, Cap de la** *cape* Quebec Canada
164 7a **Table, Pointe de la** *cape* Réunion
78 J6 **Table Bay** Newfoundland and Labrador Canada
199 I6 **Table Bay** Papua New Guinea
220 H4 **Table Cape** New Zealand
79 K6 **Table Head** Newfoundland and Labrador Canada
194 B4 **Table Island** Andaman and Nicobar Islands India
82 E8 **Table Rock Lake** Missouri USA
213 I4 **Tableland** WA Australia
215 I7 **Tabletop, Mount** Qld Australia
128 C2 **Taboada** Spain
125 H3 **Tábor** Czech Republic
135 AE4 **Tabor** Russian Federation
81 Q5 **Tabor** South Dakota USA
87 L3 **Tabor City** North Carolina USA
161 E5 **Tabora** Tanzania
161 E5 **Tabora** *admin. area* Tanzania
134 N7 **Tabory** Russian Federation
158 C4 **Tabou** Côte d'Ivoire
219 H5 **Tabratong** NSW Australia
182 E6 **Tabrīz** Iran
222 1 **Tabuaeran** *island* Kiribati
199 G5 **Tabubil** Papua New Guinea
128 F3 **Tabuenca** Spain
195 I3 **Tabuk** Philippines
178 C4 **Tabūk** Saudi Arabia
178 D4 **Tabūk** *admin. area* Saudi Arabia
219 K3 **Tabulam** NSW Australia
198 B4 **Tabulan** Indonesia
196 C3 **Tabuyung** Indonesia
222 7 **Tabwémasana, Mount** *volcano* Vanuatu
122 J3 **Täby** Sweden
101 H4 **Tacalé** Brazil
88 E5 **Tacámbaro de Codallos** Mexico
89 G6 **Tacaná, Volcán** *volcano* Mexico
184 G3 **Tacheng** Xinjiang Uygur Zizhiqu China
181 I5 **Tachileik** Myanmar
100 D3 **Táchira** *admin. area* Venezuela
130 E2 **Tachov** Czech Republic
198 B5 **Tacipi** Indonesia
105 F2 **Taciua, Lago** *lake* Brazil
195 J5 **Tacloban** Philippines
104 D5 **Tacna** Peru
104 D5 **Tacna** *admin. area* Peru
106 F3 **Taco Pozo** Argentina
80 D3 **Tacoma** Washington USA
163 G3 **Tacuane** Mozambique
105 G5 **Tacuara** Bolivia
104 E4 **Tacuaral, Serranía de** *range* Bolivia
107 G3 **Tacuaras** Paraguay
107 H4 **Tacuarembó** Uruguay
107 H5 **Tacuarembó** *admin. area* Uruguay
107 H5 **Tacuarí** *watercourse* Uruguay
107 G2 **Tacuatí** Paraguay
85 H6 **Tacupeto** Mexico
195 J6 **Tacurong** Philippines
101 F4 **Tacutu** *watercourse* Brazil
141 G3 **Tadcaster** North Yorkshire England UK
157 G5 **Tadjourah** Djibouti
157 G5 **Tadjourah, Golfe de** *bay* Djibouti
155 G2 **Tadjrouna** Algeria
139 F3 **Tadley** Hampshire England UK
75 T7 **Tadmore** Saskatchewan Canada
136 F6 **Tadmur (Palmyra)** Syria
100 B3 **Tadó** Colombia
76 F3 **Tadoule Lake** Manitoba Canada
79 D8 **Tadoussac** Quebec Canada
192 E4 **Taeajŏn** South Korea
192 E4 **Taean** South Korea
192 F3 **Taebaek sanmaek** South Korea
192 E4 **Taebu-do** *island* South Korea
192 E3 **T'aech'ŏn** North Korea
192 E4 **Taech'ong-do** *island* North Korea
192 E3 **Taedong-gang** *watercourse* North Korea
192 F4 **Taegu** South Korea
192 E3 **Taegwan** North Korea
192 E3 **Taehung** North Korea
192 E3 **Taehwa-do** *island* North Korea
192 E4 **Taenanji-do** *island* South Korea
192 F4 **T'aepaek** South Korea
192 E4 **Taeyonp'yong-do** *island* South Korea
223 12 **Tafahi** *island* Tonga
128 F2 **Tafalla** Spain
129 J6 **Tafassour** Algeria
198 E5 **Tafermaar** Indonesia
138 D3 **Taff** *watercourse* Wales UK
106 E3 **Tafi Viejo** Argentina
120 E5 **Tafjord** Norway
154 E3 **Tafraoute** Morocco
178 G2 **Tafresh** Iran
80 F1 **Taft** British Columbia Canada
179 H3 **Taft** Iran
84 C3 **Taft** California USA
86 C7 **Taft** Texas USA
120 L5 **Täftefjärden** *bay* Sweden
194 B6 **Tafwap** Andaman and Nicobar Islands India
223 12c **Taga** Samoa
132 D2 **Ţaga** Romania
179 J4 **Tagas** Pakistan
195 I5 **Tagbilaran** Philippines
180 E2 **Tagchagpu Ri** *mountain* Xizang Zizhiqu China
155 F2 **Taghit** Algeria
143 F4 **Taghmon** Ireland
74 D2 **Tagish** Yukon Territory Canada
74 D3 **Tagish Lake** British Columbia Canada
130 E3 **Tagliamento** *watercourse* Italy
130 E4 **Tagliamento, Punta** *cape* Italy
195 I5 **Tagolo Point** Philippines
182 H5 **Tagta** Turkmenistan
182 I7 **Tagtabazar** Turkmenistan
103 C6 **Taguatinga** Brazil
199 J6 **Tagula** Papua New Guinea
199 J6 **Tagula Island** Papua New Guinea
195 J6 **Tagum** Philippines
Tagus *see* **Tejo** Portugal
74 L7 **Tahaetkun Mountain** British Columbia Canada
196 D2 **Tahan, Gunung** *mountain* Malaysia
155 H4 **Tahat, Mont** *mountain* Algeria
191 J2 **Tahe** Heilongjiang China
223 14 **Tahiti** *island* French Polynesia
223 14a **Tahiti Iti** French Polynesia
223 14a **Tahiti Nui** French Polynesia
80 C5 **Tahkenitch Lake** Oregon USA
123 L3 **Tahkuna Nina** *cape* Estonia
86 D3 **Tahlequah** Oklahoma USA
74 F3 **Tahltan** British Columbia Canada
80 E7 **Tahoe, Lake** California USA
72 I4 **Tahoe Lake** Nunavut Canada
85 L4 **Tahoka** Texas USA
155 H6 **Tahoua** Niger
74 H8 **Tahsis** British Columbia Canada
156 E2 **Ţahţā** Egypt
133 F6 **Tahtaköprü** Turkey
74 H6 **Tahtsa Lake** British Columbia Canada
104 D3 **Tahuamanu** *watercourse* Bolivia
223 14 **Tahuata** *island* French Polynesia
198 C3 **Tahulandang** *island* Indonesia
198 C3 **Tahuna** Indonesia
158 C3 **Taï** Liberia
194 D3 **Tai** Thailand
189 H2 **Tai Hu** *lake* Jiangsu China
Tai Shan *see* **Yuhuang Ding** China
191 I6 **Tai Shan** *range* Shandong China
191 I6 **Tai'an** Shandong China
188 E1 **Taibai Shan** *mountain* Shaanxi China
191 J5 **Taibao D** *mountain* Shandong China
189 H4 **T'aichung** Taiwan China
221 D7 **Taieri** *watercourse* New Zealand
221 D8 **Taieri Mouth** New Zealand
188 E3 **Taigong** Guizhou China
191 H5 **Taihang Shan** *range* Hebei China
191 H6 **Taihang Shan** *range* Shanxi China
220 F4 **Taihape** New Zealand
189 G1 **Taihe** Anhui China
189 F4 **Taihe** Guangdong China
188 E2 **Taihe** Sichuan China
189 G2 **Taihu** Anhui China
191 J3 **Taikang** Heilongjiang China
194 B3 **Taikkyi** Myanmar
191 J3 **Tailai** Heilongjiang China
196 C4 **Taileleo** Indonesia
218 D6 **Tailem Bend** SA Australia
135 U6 **Taimba** Russian Federation
121 N5 **Taimoniemi** Finland
158 D3 **Tain** *watercourse* Ghana
142 D3 **Tain** Highland Scotland UK
189 H4 **T'ainan** Taiwan China
133 C7 **Tainaro, Akra** *cape* Greece
104 C4 **Taino** Peru
103 D6 **Taiobeiras** Brazil
199 J5 **Taiof Island** Papua New Guinea
198 B4 **Taipa** Indonesia
121 N4 **Taipale** Finland
121 N3 **Taipale** Finland
121 O4 **Taipaleenharju** Finland
189 H4 **T'aipao** Taiwan China
189 I3 **T'aipei** Taiwan China
189 G4 **Taiping** Guangdong China
188 E4 **Taiping** Guangxi Zhuangzu Zizhiqu China
188 E4 **Taiping** Guangxi Zhuangzu Zizhiqu China
196 D2 **Taiping** Malaysia
221 D6 **Taipo** *watercourse* New Zealand
102 F4 **Taipu** Brazil
191 H6 **Taiqian** Henan China
192 F6 **Taira-shima** *island* Japan
140 D1 **Tairlaw** South Ayrshire Scotland UK
220 F3 **Tairua** New Zealand
196 D4 **Tais** Indonesia
189 F4 **Taishan** Guangdong China
185 J3 **Taishir** Mongolia
196 D4 **Taitaitanopo** *island* Indonesia
108 A4 **Taitao, Península de** *peninsula* Chile
221 E6 **Taitapu** New Zealand
104 E2 **Taititu** Brazil
189 I4 **T'aitung** Taiwan China
189 I4 **Taitung Shan** *range* Taiwan China
121 P4 **Taivalkoski** Finland
189 I4 **Taiwan** *admin. area* China
189 H4 **Taiwan** *island* Taiwan China
189 H4 **Taiwan Strait** Taiwan China
189 H2 **Taixing** Jiangsu China
88 E5 **Taixtan** Mexico
156 E5 **Taiyara** Sudan
183 K2 **Taiynsha (Krasnoarmeysk)** Kazakhstan
191 G5 **Taiyuan** Shanxi China
190 G6 **Taiyue Shan** *range* Shanxi China
189 H2 **Taizhou** Jiangsu China
189 I3 **Taizhou** Zhejiang China
178 E7 **Ta'izz** Yemen
182 H6 **Taj Ed Din** Iran
108 A3 **Tajamar, Punta** *cape* Chile
155 I4 **Tajarḩī** Libya
128 E3 **Tajera, Embalse de la** *lake* Spain
104 E4 **Tajibo** Bolivia
183 K6 **Tajikistan** *country*
193 H4 **Tajimi** Japan
85 I6 **Tajirachic** Mexico
128 E3 **Tajo** *watercourse* Spain
105 E6 **Tajsara, Cordillera de** *range* Bolivia
128 E3 **Tajuña** *watercourse* Spain
194 C3 **Tak** Thailand
194 C3 **Tak** *admin. area* Thailand
223 15 **Taka Atoll** Marshall Islands
182 E7 **Takāb** Iran
189 J3 **Takabanare-jima** *island* Japan
161 G3 **Takabba** Kenya
58 Q1 **Takahe, Mount** *mountain* Antarctica
193 I3 **Takahoko-numa** *lake* Japan
221 E5 **Takaka** New Zealand
198 A5 **Takalar** Indonesia
101 G3 **Takama** Guyana
164 9b **Takamaka** Seychelles
192 G4 **Takamatsu** Japan
192 F5 **Takanabe** Japan
193 H4 **Takaoka** Japan
220 G5 **Takapau** New Zealand
189 K2 **Takara-jima** *island* Japan
223 14 **Takaroa** *island* French Polynesia
162 D4 **Takatshwane** Botswana
220 F3 **Takatu Point** New Zealand
192 F5 **Take-shima** *island* Japan
196 C2 **Takengon** Indonesia
122 H3 **Tåkern** *lake* Sweden
182 F7 **Takestān** Iran
194 E5 **Takêv** Cambodia
183 K7 **TakhĀr** *admin. area* Afghanistan
129 G6 **Takhemaret** Algeria
74 D2 **Takhini** Yukon Territory Canada
74 C2 **Takhini** *watercourse* Yukon Territory Canada
179 J3 **Takht** Afghanistan
179 L3 **Takht-i-Sulaiman** *mountain* Pakistan
182 D4 **Takhta** Russian Federation
155 H6 **Takiéta** Niger
75 U5 **Takipy** Manitoba Canada
197 G4 **Takisung** Indonesia
221 B7 **Takitimu Mountains** New Zealand
193 I3 **Takizawa** Japan
193 J2 **Takkobu-numa** *lake* Japan
74 H5 **Takla Lake** British Columbia Canada
74 I5 **Takla Landing** British Columbia Canada
184 G5 **Taklamakan Desert** Xinjiang Uygur Zizhiqu China
Taklamakan Shamo *see* **Taklamakan Desert** China
158 D4 **Takoradi** Ghana
158 E3 **Takpamba** Togo
74 E3 **Taku** British Columbia Canada
74 E3 **Taku** *watercourse* British Columbia Canada
194 C5 **Takua Pa** Thailand
159 F3 **Takum** Nigeria
160 B4 **Takundi** Democratic Republic of Congo
220 1 **Takutea** *island* Cook Islands New Zealand
120 K2 **Takvatnet** *lake* Norway
77 S7 **Takwa** *watercourse* Quebec Canada
186 D6 **Tal** Madhya Pradesh India
179 L2 **Tal** Pakistan
138 C2 **Tal-gareg** Ceredigion Wales UK
185 I3 **Tal Nuur** *lake* Mongolia
219 J5 **Tal Tal Mountain** NSW Australia
140 E3 **Tal-y-Cafn** Conwy Wales UK
138 D2 **Tal-y-llyn** Gwynedd Wales UK
138 C1 **Tal-y-sarn** Gwynedd Wales UK
107 H5 **Tala** Uruguay
123 O5 **Talachyn** Belarus
140 E3 **Talacre** Flintshire Wales UK
223 10a **Talafo'ou** Tonga
108 C3 **Talagapa** Argentina
187 C7 **Talaja** Gujarat India
86 D2 **Talala** Oklahoma USA
90 D5 **Talamanca, Cordillera de** *range* Costa Rica
196 F5 **Talang** Indonesia
196 D4 **Talang, Gunung** *volcano* Indonesia
90 C4 **Talanga** Honduras
196 E4 **Talangbatu** Indonesia
196 E4 **Talangbetutu** Indonesia
127 G3 **Talant** France
179 L2 **Talao Kandao** *pass* Pakistan
104 A2 **Talara** Peru
104 A2 **Talara, Bahía de** *bay* Peru
183 K5 **Talas** Kyrgyzstan
183 K5 **Talas** *admin. area* Kyrgyzstan
183 K5 **Talas** *watercourse* Kyrgyzstan
199 I5 **Talasea** Papua New Guinea
187 C7 **Talasri** Maharashtra India
198 C2 **Talaud, Kepulauan** *islands* Indonesia
128 F4 **Talave, Embalse de** *lake* Spain
128 D4 **Talavera de la Reina** Spain
212 F7 **Talawana** WA Australia
214 F5 **Talawanta** Qld Australia
199 I5 **Talawe, Mount** *volcano* Papua New Guinea
186 E6 **Talbehat** Uttar Pradesh India
219 I6 **Talbingo** NSW Australia
218 F7 **Talbot** Vic. Australia
213 I2 **Talbot, Cape** WA Australia
217 J3 **Talbot, Mount** WA Australia
213 I5 **Talbot, Mount** WA Australia
73 L3 **Talbot Inlet** Nunavut Canada
76 F5 **Talbot Lake** Manitoba Canada
87 I4 **Talbotton** Georgia USA
106 D5 **Talca** Chile
106 C6 **Talcahuano** Chile
86 D4 **Talco** Texas USA
183 M5 **Taldy-su** Kyrgyzstan
183 M5 **Taldykorgan** Kazakhstan
183 K3 **Taldysay** Kazakhstan
132 D3 **Talea** Romania
126 D4 **Talence** France
138 D2 **Talerddig** Powys Wales UK
183 M5 **Talgar** Kazakhstan
138 D3 **Talgarth** Powys Wales UK
156 F4 **Talguharai** Sudan
123 M3 **Tali** Estonia
160 E2 **Tali Post** Sudan
198 C4 **Taliabu** *island* Indonesia
124 D5 **Taliard** France
195 J5 **Talibon** Philippines
86 D3 **Talihina** Oklahoma USA
187 D8 **Talikota** Karnataka India
101 H4 **Talimã** Brazil
195 I5 **Talisay** Philippines
197 H3 **Talisayan** Indonesia
142 B3 **Talisker** Highland Scotland UK
197 H6 **Taliwang** Indonesia
72 D6 **Talkeetna** Alaska USA
178 E2 **Tall 'Afar** Iraq
179 J3 **Tall Kala** Afghanistan
217 M5 **Tallacootra, Lake** SA Australia
142 C3 **Talladale** Highland Scotland UK
87 H4 **Talladega** Alabama USA
87 I5 **Tallahassee** Florida USA
142 D5 **Tallaminnoch** South Ayrshire Scotland UK
140 B3 **Tallanstown** Ireland
87 I4 **Tallapoosa** Georgia USA
127 H4 **Tallard** France
218 H5 **Tallebung, Mount** NSW Australia
216 D4 **Tallering Peak** WA Australia
138 D3 **Talley** Carmarthenshire Wales UK
74 H6 **Tallheo** British Columbia Canada
218 H5 **Tallimba** NSW Australia
123 M3 **Tallinn** Estonia
121 Q4 **Talloreka** Russian Federation
143 D4 **Tallow** Ireland
86 F4 **Tallulah** Louisiana USA
121 O5 **Talluskylä** Finland
81 N2 **Talmage** Saskatchewan Canada
126 D4 **Talmont** France
134 S5 **Talnakh** Russian Federation
136 D3 **Tal'ne** Ukraine
160 E1 **Talodi** Sudan
222 5 **Talofofo** Guam
86 B2 **Taloga** Oklahoma USA
135 AE7 **Talon** Russian Federation
183 K7 **Tāloqān** Afghanistan
58 K2 **Talos Dome** *mountain* Antarctica
182 C3 **Talovaya** Russian Federation
73 J5 **Taloyoak** Nunavut Canada
109 9 **Talparo** Trinidad and Tobago
191 I3 **Talping Ling** *mountain* Nei Mongol Zizhiqu China
87 I5 **Talquin, Lake** Florida USA
138 C2 **Talsarn** Ceredigion Wales UK
138 C2 **Talsarnau** Gwynedd Wales UK
123 L4 **Talsi** Latvia
123 L4 **Talsu** *admin. area* Latvia
106 D3 **Taltal** Chile
75 O2 **Taltson** *watercourse* Northwest Territories Canada
196 D3 **Talu** Indonesia
198 B3 **Taludaa** Indonesia
198 D4 **Taluti, Teluk** *bay* Indonesia
121 M1 **Talvik** Norway
219 I3 **Talwood** Qld Australia
140 D3 **Talwrn** Isle of Anglesey Wales UK
138 D3 **Talybont** Powys Wales UK
194 F4 **Tam Kỳ** Vietnam
128 D2 **Tama** Spain
82 E6 **Tama** Iowa USA
197 G3 **Tama Abu, Banjaran** *range* Malaysia
216 C3 **Tamala** WA Australia
182 D3 **Tamala** Russian Federation
158 D3 **Tamale** Ghana
197 F4 **Tamalung** Indonesia
128 C3 **Tamames** Spain
197 G5 **Taman** Indonesia
222 1 **Tamana** *island* Kiribati
154 E2 **Tamanar** Morocco
102 F5 **Tamandaré** Brazil
105 I5 **Tamandaré** Brazil
107 G6 **Tamangueyú** Argentina
155 I3 **Tamanhint** Libya
154 E6 **Tamani** Mali
192 G4 **Tamano** Japan
155 H4 **Tamanrasset** Algeria
138 C4 **Tamar** *watercourse* England UK
109 7 **Tamar Harbour** *bay* Falkland Islands
100 C3 **Tamara** Colombia
87 K7 **Tamarac** Florida USA
164 7b **Tamarin** Mauritius
132 E4 **Tamarino** Bulgaria
129 G3 **Tamarite de Litera** Spain
106 D2 **Tamarugel, Pampa de** *region* Chile
125 L2 **Tamashowka** Belarus
125 J4 **Tamási** Hungary
89 F3 **Tamaulipas** *admin. area* Mexico
88 E5 **Tamazula de Gordiano** Mexico
154 D6 **Tambacounda** Senegal
197 I5 **Tambalongang** *island* Indonesia
197 F4 **Tambanmunjul** Indonesia
158 E2 **Tambao** Burkina Faso
219 I4 **Tambar Springs** NSW Australia
103 C8 **Tambaú** Brazil
198 B5 **Tambea** Indonesia
196 E3 **Tambelan, Kepulauan** *islands* Indonesia
196 E3 **Tambelan Besar** *island* Indonesia
216 E7 **Tambellup** WA Australia
197 G5 **Tamberu** Indonesia
104 E6 **Tambillo** Bolivia
104 B2 **Tambillo** Peru
104 C5 **Tambillo** Peru
106 D4 **Tambillos, Nevados de los** *range* Chile
197 H2 **Tambisan** Malaysia
218 H1 **Tambo** Qld Australia
219 H7 **Tambo** *watercourse* Vic. Australia
104 C4 **Tambo** Peru
104 D5 **Tambo** *watercourse* Peru
158 C3 **Tambo, Lac de** *lake* Côte d'Ivoire
104 B3 **Tambo del Sol** Peru
104 A2 **Tambo Grande** Peru
100 D5 **Tambo Yaguas** Peru
100 D5 **Tambo Yanayacu** Peru
163 H3 **Tambohorano** Madagascar
198 B4 **Tamboli** Indonesia
104 D4 **Tambopata** Peru
104 D4 **Tambopata** *watercourse* Peru
162 B3 **Tambor** Angola
197 H6 **Tambora, Gunung** *volcano* Indonesia
102 D4 **Tamboril** Brazil
219 K2 **Tamborine** Qld Australia
182 D3 **Tambov** Russian Federation
182 D3 **Tambovskaya Oblast'** *admin. area* Russian Federation
128 B2 **Tambre** *watercourse* Spain
197 H3 **Tambu, Teluk** *bay* Indonesia
197 H2 **Tambulanan, Bukit** *mountain* Malaysia
160 D2 **Tambura** Sudan
197 H2 **Tambuyukon, Gunung** *mountain* Malaysia
154 D5 **Tâmchekket** Mauritania
183 L5 **Tamchy** Kyrgyzstan
182 H3 **Tamdy** Kazakhstan
100 D3 **Tame** Colombia
85 I8 **Tameapa** Mexico
128 C3 **Tâmega** *watercourse* Portugal/Spain
108 B4 **Tamel Aike** Argentina
133 D7 **Tamelos, Akra** *cape* Greece
141 F3 **Tameside** *admin. area* England UK
155 H5 **Tamgak, Adrar** *mountain* Niger
183 J4 **Tamgaly** *lake* Kazakhstan
158 B2 **Tamgué, Massif du** *mountain* Guinea
89 F4 **Tamiahua** Mexico
89 F4 **Tamiahua, Laguna de** *lake* Mexico
196 C2 **Tamiang** *watercourse* Indonesia
196 C2 **Tamiang, Ujung** *cape* Indonesia
187 E9 **Tamil Nadu** *admin. area* India
178 E2 **Ta'mīm, At** *admin. area* Iraq
197 G4 **Taminglayang** Indonesia
132 B3 **Tamiš** *watercourse* Serbia
121 U4 **Tamitsa** Russian Federation
143 F2 **Tamlaght** Magherafelt Northern Ireland UK
129 J5 **Tamlouka** Algeria
123 N2 **Tammijärvi** *lake* Finland
123 N2 **Tammio** *island* Finland
122 I2 **Tämnaren** *lake* Sweden
132 C3 **Tamnič** Serbia
155 G6 **Tamou** Niger
87 J7 **Tampa** Florida USA
85 N1 **Tampa** Kansas USA
87 J7 **Tampa Bay** Florida USA
196 E5 **Tampang** Indonesia
123 L2 **Tampere** Finland
88 B2 **Tampico** Mexico
89 F4 **Tampico** Mexico
196 D3 **Tampin** Malaysia
196 E3 **Tampines** *admin. area* Singapore
198 B5 **Tampo** Indonesia
125 G4 **Tamsweg** Austria
181 H4 **Tamu** Myanmar
222 5 **Tamuning** Guam
219 J4 **Tamworth** NSW Australia
139 F2 **Tamworth** Staffordshire England UK
192 E4 **Tamyang** South Korea
183 L4 **Tan** Kazakhstan
155 H3 **Tan Emellel** Algeria
189 F4 **Tan Jiang** *watercourse* Guangdong China
194 E3 **Tân Kỳ** Vietnam
154 D3 **Tan-Tan** Morocco
161 G4 **Tana** *watercourse* Kenya
121 P1 **Tana Bru** Norway
156 F5 **T'ana Häyk'** *lake* Ethiopia
193 G5 **Tanabe** Japan
103 B8 **Tanabi** Brazil
132 E2 **Tanacu** Romania
121 P1 **Tanafjorden** *bay* Norway
135 AL8 **Tanaga Island** Alaska USA
196 F5 **Tanah, Tanjung** *cape* Indonesia
196 D2 **Tanah Merah** Malaysia
196 C4 **Tanahbala** *island* Indonesia
197 H4 **Tanahgrogot** Indonesia
197 I5 **Tanahjampea** *island* Indonesia
197 H3 **Tanahkuning** Indonesia
196 C4 **Tanahmasa** *island* Indonesia
196 D3 **Tanahputih** Indonesia
181 H3 **Tanaing** Myanmar
197 H5 **Tanakeke** *island* Indonesia
186 E5 **Tanakpur** Uttaranchal India
134 Q4 **Tanama** *watercourse* Russian Federation
214 A5 **Tanami Desert** NT Australia
72 D5 **Tanana** Alaska USA
72 E6 **Tanana** *watercourse* Alaska USA
163 H4 **Tanandava** Madagascar
121 P1 **Tananes** Norway
195 I4 **Tanauan** Philippines
139 H5 **Tancarville** France
189 H1 **Tancheng** Shandong China
192 F3 **Tanch'ŏn** North Korea
158 D3 **Tanda** Côte d'Ivoire
187 D6 **Tanda** Madhya Pradesh India
186 F5 **Tanda** Uttar Pradesh India
132 C3 **Tanda** Serbia
154 F5 **Tanda, Lac** *lake* Mali
195 J5 **Tandag** Philippines
218 G7 **Tandarra** Vic. Australia
197 H2 **Tandek** Malaysia
155 F5 **Tanderiouel** *watercourse* Mali
107 G6 **Tandil** Argentina
107 G6 **Tandil, Sierra del** *range* Argentina
159 H3 **Tandjilé** *admin. area* Chad
122 G2 **Tandö** Sweden
179 K4 **Tando Adam** Pakistan
179 K4 **Tando Allahyar** Pakistan
179 K5 **Tando Bago** Pakistan
218 F5 **Tandou, Lake** NSW Australia
143 F2 **Tandragee** Armagh Northern Ireland UK
195 I6 **Tandubatu** *island* Philippines
218 F5 **Tandure Lake** NSW Australia
192 F5 **Tanega-shima** *island* Japan
120 G5 **Tanem** Norway
198 B5 **Tanete** Indonesia
198 C4 **Taneti** *island* Indonesia
143 E3 **Tang** Ireland
189 H3 **Tang Yu** *island* Fujian China
161 F5 **Tanga** Tanzania
161 F5 **Tanga** *admin. area* Tanzania
199 J4 **Tanga Islands** Papua New Guinea
216 F2 **Tangadee** WA Australia
187 E10 **Tangalla** Sri Lanka
160 D5 **Tanganyika, Lake** Tanzania
102 F4 **Tangará** Brazil
120 H5 **Tångböle** Sweden
189 F3 **Tangdukou** Hunan China
58 D2 **Tange Promontory** *peninsula* Antarctica
122 F2 **Tangen** Norway
154 E1 **Tanger (Tangier)** Morocco
196 E5 **Tangerang** Indonesia
181 G2 **Tanggula (Dangla) Shan** *range* Xizang Zizhiqu China
181 G2 **Tanggula Shan** *mountain* Xizang Zizhiqu China
181 G2 **Tanggula Shankou** *pass* Xizang Zizhiqu China
191 I5 **Tanghai** Hebei China
189 F2 **Tanghe** Henan China
179 L2 **Tangi** Pakistan
Tangier *see* **Tanger** Morocco
220 F5 **Tangimoana** New Zealand
86 F5 **Tangipahoa** Louisiana USA
198 B4 **Tangkelemboke, Gunung** *mountain* Indonesia
196 E5 **Tangkittebak, Gunung** *mountain* Indonesia
181 G3 **Tangla** Assam India
187 E7 **Tangla** Maharashtra India
181 F2 **Tanglha Range** Xizang Zizhiqu China
220 E2 **Tangowahine** New Zealand
215 H6 **Tangorin** Qld Australia
196 B2 **Tangse** Indonesia
191 I5 **Tangshan** Hebei China
186 E3 **Tangtse** Jammu and Kashmir India/Pakistan
100 B4 **Tangua** Colombia
158 E2 **Tanguiéta** Benin
189 G4 **Tangxi Shuiku** *lake* Guangdong China
181 I4 **Tangyan** Myanmar
191 H6 **Tangyin** Henan China
191 L3 **Tangyuan** Heilongjiang China
103 D6 **Tanhaçu** Brazil
121 O3 **Tanhua** Finland
123 O2 **Tani** Finland
181 H2 **Taniantaweng Shan** *range* Xizang Zizhiqu China
198 D6 **Tanimbar, Kepulauan** *islands* Indonesia
101 E3 **Tanimiña** Venezuela
122 H2 **Täningen** *lake* Sweden
194 C4 **Tanintharyi** *admin. area* Myanmar
198 E4 **Tanisapata** Indonesia
198 D4 **Taniwel** Indonesia
219 I7 **Tanja** NSW Australia
196 D3 **Tanjong Karang** Malaysia
196 D3 **Tanjong Malim** Malaysia
197 G4 **Tanjung** Indonesia
196 D4 **Tanjungagung** Indonesia
197 H4 **Tanjungaru** Indonesia
196 D3 **Tanjungbalai** Indonesia
198 C4 **Tanjungbaliha** Indonesia
196 D3 **Tanjungbatu** Indonesia
197 H3 **Tanjungbuayabuaya** *island* Indonesia
196 E4 **Tanjungpandan** Indonesia
196 E3 **Tanjungpinang** Indonesia
196 C3 **Tanjungpura** Indonesia
196 E4 **Tanjungraja** Indonesia
197 H3 **Tanjungredeb** Indonesia
196 F4 **Tanjungsaleh** *island* Indonesia
196 F4 **Tanjungsatai** Indonesia
197 H3 **Tanjungselor** Indonesia
197 F4 **Tanjungwaringin** Indonesia
121 O2 **Tankapirtti** Finland
140 B4 **Tankardstown** Carlow Ireland
158 D3 **Tankuw** *watercourse* Ghana
189 H2 **Tanmu Shan** *range* Zhejiang China
124 F2 **Tann** Germany
130 E2 **Tann** Germany
222 7 **Tanna** *island* Vanuatu
120 H5 **Tännäs** Sweden
120 H5 **Tänndalen** Sweden
124 F2 **Tanne** Germany
74 L8 **Tanner, Mount** British Columbia Canada
121 N4 **Tannila** Finland
82 F2 **Tannin** Ontario Canada
183 P3 **Tannu-Ola, Khrebet** *range* Russian Federation
178 G4 **Tannūrah, Ra's** *cape* Saudi Arabia
158 D3 **Tano** *watercourse* Ghana
186 C5 **Tanot** Rajasthan India
155 H6 **Tânout** Niger
154 E2 **Tanout Ou Filal, Tizi** *pass* Morocco
187 C7 **Tansa** *watercourse* Maharashtra India
186 F5 **Tansen** Nepal
219 K2 **Tansey** Qld Australia
156 E1 **Ţanţā** Egypt
181 H5 **Tantabin** Myanmar
218 E7 **Tantanoola** SA Australia
127 H2 **Tantonville** France
189 I2 **Tantou Shan** *range* Zhejiang China
74 F6 **Tanu** British Columbia Canada
161 F4 **Tanu** *watercourse* Kenya
187 E8 **Tanuku** Andhra Pradesh India
214 C4 **Tanumbirini** NT Australia
122 F3 **Tanumshede** Sweden
218 D6 **Tanunda** SA Australia
138 D2 **Tanygrisiau** Gwynedd Wales UK
135 AK5 **Tanyurer** *watercourse* Russian Federation
161 E5 **Tanzania** *country* Africa
74 F3 **Tanzilla** *watercourse* British Columbia Canada
190 E6 **Tao He** *watercourse* Gansu China
188 D1 **Tao He** *watercourse* Jiangsu China
189 I2 **Taohua Dao** *island* Zhejiang China
189 F3 **Taohuajiang** Hunan China
191 J3 **Taonan** Jilin China
223 15 **Taongi Atoll** *island* Marshall Islands
131 F8 **Taormina** Italy
85 J2 **Taos** New Mexico USA
154 F4 **Taoudenni** Mali
129 G5 **Taougrite** Algeria
155 F2 **Taourirt** Morocco
190 E6 **Taoyang** Gansu China
189 I4 **T'aoyüan** Taiwan China
189 H2 **Taozhou** Anhui China
89 G6 **Tapachula** Mexico
105 F5 **Tapado** Bolivia
196 D2 **Tapah** Malaysia
105 G2 **Tapajós** *watercourse* Brazil
196 C3 **Tapaktuan** Indonesia
107 F6 **Tapalqué** Argentina
196 D4 **Tapan** Indonesia
101 H4 **Tapanahoni** *lake* Suriname
221 C7 **Tapanui** New Zealand
196 C3 **Tapanuli, Teluk** *bay* Indonesia
101 H5 **Tapará, Ilha Grande do** *island* Brazil
101 H5 **Tapará, Serra do** *range* Brazil
198 C4 **Tapat** *island* Indonesia
105 E2 **Tapauá** *watercourse* Brazil
103 A8 **Tapejara** Brazil
107 H4 **Tapejara** Brazil
105 G5 **Tapenema** Bolivia
101 F5 **Tapera** Brazil
102 E4 **Taperoá** Brazil
103 E6 **Taperoá** Brazil
158 C3 **Tapeta** Liberia
194 D3 **Taphan Hin** Thailand
187 D7 **Tapi** *watercourse* Madhya Pradesh India
187 D7 **Tapi** *watercourse* Maharashtra India
108 B5 **Tapi Aike** Argentina
195 I6 **Tapiantana Group** *islands* Philippines
197 F4 **Tapinbini** Indonesia
199 H6 **Tapini** Papua New Guinea
121 O3 **Tapionniemi** Finland
103 D5 **Tapiramutá** Brazil
103 B5 **Tapirapé** *watercourse* Brazil
101 E4 **Tapirapecó, Sierra** *range* Venezuela
105 G4 **Tapirapuã** Brazil
105 G4 **Tapirapuã, Serra do** *range* Brazil
186 G5 **Taplejung** Nepal
158 E2 **Tapoa** *watercourse* Burkina Faso
130 G3 **Tapolca** Hungary
198 A4 **Tappalang** Indonesia
80 F1 **Tappen** British Columbia Canada
81 P3 **Tappen** North Dakota USA
193 H3 **Tappi-numa** *lake* Japan
220 F3 **Tapu** New Zealand
221 E5 **Tapuae-o-Uenuku** *mountain* New Zealand
220 H3 **Tapuaeroa** *watercourse* New Zealand
195 I6 **Tapul** *island* Philippines
195 I6 **Tapul Group** *islands* Philippines
196 C3 **Tapulonanjing** *mountain* Indonesia
179 H6 **Ţāqah** Oman
105 H5 **Taquari** Brazil
107 I4 **Taquari** Brazil
105 H5 **Taquari, Serra do** *range* Brazil
103 B8 **Taquaritinga** Brazil
103 B8 **Taquarituba** Brazil
108 C3 **Taquetrén, Laguna** *lake* Argentina
130 E4 **Tar** Croatia
132 A2 **Tar** Hungary
87 M3 **Tar** *watercourse* North Carolina USA
219 J2 **Tara** Qld Australia
132 A4 **Tara** *watercourse* Montenegro
159 G3 **Taraba** *admin. area* Nigeria
159 G3 **Taraba** *watercourse* Nigeria
155 I2 **Tārabulus (Tripoli)** Libya
132 F3 **Taraclia** Moldova

155 I3 Tarāghin Libya
100 D4 Taraira Brazil
164 3d Tarajalejo Canary Islands
197 H3 Tarakan Indonesia
197 H3 Tarakan island Indonesia
133 G5 Taraklı Turkey
189 I4 Tarama-jima island Japan
198 C6 Taramana Indonesia
186 D6 Tarana Madhya Pradesh India
186 D5 Taranagar Rajasthan India
220 F4 Taranaki admin. area New Zealand
220 F4 Taranaki (Egmont), Mount volcano New Zealand
128 E3 Tarancón Spain
142 A3 Taransay island Scotland UK
142 A3 Taransay, Sound of bay Scotland UK
131 G6 Taranto Italy
131 G7 Taranto, Golfo di bay Italy
221 D7 Taranui New Zealand
104 D5 Tarapacá admin. area Chile
222 8 Tarapaina Solomon Islands
100 B5 Tarapoa Ecuador
104 B2 Tarapoto Peru
179 H5 Ţaraq United Arab Emirates
127 G4 Tarare France
107 G5 Tarariras Uruguay
127 G5 Tarascon France
126 E5 Tarascon-sur-Ariège France
132 G1 Tarashcha Ukraine
132 G1 Tarasovka Ukraine
134 K5 Tarasovo Russian Federation
155 H3 Tarat Algeria
105 E5 Tarata Bolivia
222 1b Taratai Kiribati
222 1b Taratai island Kiribati
104 D3 Tarauacá Brazil
104 D2 Tarauacá watercourse Brazil
223 14a Taravao French Polynesia
222 1 Tarawa island Kiribati
199 G4 Tarawai Island Papua New Guinea
220 G4 Tarawera New Zealand
220 G4 Tarawera, Lake New Zealand
220 G4 Tarawera, Mount volcano New Zealand
183 K5 Taraz (Zhambyl) Kazakhstan
128 F3 Tarazona Spain
128 F4 Tarazona de la Mancha Spain
184 F3 Tarbagatai Shan range Xinjiang Uygur Zizhiqu China
183 N4 Tarbagatai Shan range Kazakhstan
183 N4 Tarbagatavy, Khrebet range Kazakhstan
183 N4 Tarbagatay Kazakhstan
142 E3 Tarbat Ness cape Scotland UK
143 C4 Tarbert Ireland
126 E5 Tarbes France
142 C2 Tarbet Highland Scotland UK
142 D5 Tarbolton South Ayrshire Scotland UK
87 M3 Tarboro North Carolina USA
215 G8 Tarcombe Qld Australia
218 B4 Tarcoola SA Australia
219 H6 Tarcutta NSW Australia
126 D5 Tardets-Sorholus France
126 E4 Tardoire watercourse France
216 D4 Tardun WA Australia
219 K4 Taree NSW Australia
121 M3 Tärendö Sweden
178 E6 Ţarfā, Ra's at cape Saudi Arabia
156 E2 Ţarfā, Wādī Aţ watercourse Egypt
154 D3 Tarfaya Morocco
142 F4 Tarfside Angus Scotland UK
128 D6 Targa Morocco
125 K1 Targowo Poland
132 E3 Târgu Bujor Romania
132 C3 Târgu Jiu Romania
132 D2 Târgu-Mureş Romania
132 E2 Târgu Secuiesc Romania
154 F2 Targuist Morocco
155 I2 Tarhūnah Libya
190 E2 Tarialan Mongolia
100 D4 Tariana Brazil
190 D3 Tariat Mongolia
179 H5 Ţarīf United Arab Emirates
128 D5 Tarifa Spain
128 D6 Tarifa, Punta de cape Spain
195 I3 Tarigtig Point Philippines
105 E6 Tarija Bolivia
106 E2 Tarija admin. area Bolivia
129 H6 Tarik Ibn Ziad Algeria
198 F4 Tariku watercourse Indonesia
219 I2 Tarilla Qld Australia
178 G7 Tarīm Yemen
Tarim He see Ta-li-mu Ho China
184 H4 Tarim He watercourse Xinjiang Uygur Zizhiqu China
88 E4 Tarimoro Mexico
179 K3 Tarīn Kowt Afghanistan
199 F4 Taritatu watercourse Indonesia
121 N5 Tarjannevesi bay Finland
134 Q6 Tarko-Sale Russian Federation
158 D3 Tarkwa Ghana
195 I4 Tarlac Philippines
218 D6 Tarlee SA Australia
140 F3 Tarleton Lancashire England UK
125 M4 Târlişua Romania
214 D7 Tarlton Downs NT Australia
104 C3 Tarma Peru
143 C4 Tarmon Ireland
126 E5 Tarn watercourse France
120 I4 Tärnaby Sweden
179 K3 Tarnak Rūd watercourse Afghanistan
120 I4 Tärnasjön lake Sweden
120 E5 Tårnes Norway
121 Q2 Tårnet Norway
122 H4 Tärnö island Sweden
125 K2 Tarnobrzeg Poland
130 H3 Tárnok Hungary
126 D5 Tarnos France
125 K3 Tarnov Slovakia
125 K5 Târnova Romania
125 K2 Tarnów Poland
125 I1 Tarnówka Poland
130 C4 Taro watercourse Italy
179 H4 Ţārom Iran
219 K2 Tarome Qld Australia
181 G3 Tarong Xizang Zizhiqu China
219 I1 Taroom Qld Australia
122 E5 Tarp Germany
132 C1 Tarpa Hungary
87 J6 Tarpon Springs Florida USA
100 C5 Tarqui Peru
131 D5 Tarquinia Italy
214 C5 Tarrabool Lake NT Australia
120 J3 Tarradalen valley Sweden
164 4a Tarrafal Cape Verde
129 G3 Tarragona Spain
120 K3 Tårrajaur Sweden
139 E4 Tarrant Gunville Dorset England UK
221 C7 Tarras New Zealand
129 G3 Tàrrega Spain
142 E3 Tarrel Highland Scotland UK
122 F4 Tårs Denmark
155 J4 Tarso Emissi mountain Chad
136 E6 Tarsus Turkey
106 F2 Tartagal Argentina
130 D4 Tartaro, Fiume watercourse Italy
101 I4 Tartarugal Grande Brazil
126 D5 Tartas France
123 N3 Tartu Estonia
219 I2 Tartulla watercourse Qld Australia
123 N3 Tartumaa admin. area Estonia
136 E6 Tartus Syria
220 G4 Taruarau watercourse New Zealand
103 B8 Tarumã Brazil
182 E5 Tarumovka Russian Federation
194 C6 Tarutao, Ko island Thailand
196 C3 Tarutung Indonesia
132 F2 Tarutyne Ukraine
120 F5 Tarva island Norway
121 O5 Tarvaala Finland
120 F5 Tarvahavet bay Norway
123 L2 Tarvainen Finland
135 AD6 Tas-Kystabyt, Khrebet range Russian Federation
135 AB4 Tas-Tumus Russian Federation
85 H7 Tasajeras Mexico
155 I3 Tasāwah Libya
182 J5 Tasbuget Kazakhstan
88 D2 Táscate Mexico
83 L2 Taschereau Quebec Canada
74 J7 Taseko Lakes British Columbia Canada
183 K5 Tash-Kömür Kyrgyzstan
184 E5 Tashiku'ergan Xinjiang Uygur Zizhiqu China
179 H3 Tashk, Daryācheh-ye lake Iran
Tashkent see Toshkent Uzbekistan
123 K4 Tāši Latvia
77 T3 Tasialujjuaq, Lac lake Quebec Canada
77 R3 Tasiat, Lac lake Quebec Canada
196 F5 Tasikmalaya Indonesia
77 U3 Tasiujaq Quebec Canada
77 X4 Tasiuyak Tasialua Lake Newfoundland and Labrador Canada
120 I4 Tåsjö Sweden
120 I4 Tåsjön lake Sweden
183 M4 Taskesken Kazakhstan
183 R3 Taskyl-Sajtyg, Gora mountain Russian Federation
221 E5 Tasman admin. area New Zealand
221 E5 Tasman Bay New Zealand
52 K13 Tasman Fracture Zone underwater feature Tasman Sea
219 R11 Tasman Head Tas. Australia
221 E5 Tasman Mountains New Zealand
219 R11 Tasman Peninsula Tas. Australia
52 L11 Tasman Plain underwater feature Tasman Sea
211 P8 Tasman Sea Oceania
219 Q10 Tasmania admin. area Tas. Australia
132 A2 Tass Hungary
155 H5 Tassara Niger
77 S3 Tassialouc, Lac lake Quebec Canada
73 P5 Tassiilaq Greenland
158 E2 Tassiné watercourse Benin
77 Q7 Tast, Lac du lake Quebec Canada
183 N4 Tastau, Gora mountain Kazakhstan
74 E6 Tasu Sound British Columbia Canada
222 8 Tasure Solomon Islands
130 H3 Tát Hungary
154 E3 Tata Morocco
198 C6 Tata Mailau, Gunung mountain Timor-Leste (East Timor)
125 J4 Tatabánya Hungary
132 A2 Tataháza Hungary
223 14 Tatakoto island French Polynesia
79 G10 Tatamagouche Nova Scotia Canada
222 8 Tatamba Solomon Islands
155 I2 Tataouine Tunisia
130 F4 Tatar Varoš Croatia
132 E1 Tătărăşeni, Lacul lake Romania
132 F3 Tatarbunary Ukraine
133 G6 Tatarlı Turkey
123 P5 Tatarsk Russian Federation
183 L2 Tatarsk Russian Federation
135 AD9 Tatarskiy Proliv strait Russian Federation
132 E3 Tătarul, Lacul lake Romania
197 G3 Tatau Malaysia
199 J4 Tatau Island Papua New Guinea
190 F2 Tataurovo Russian Federation
198 E4 Tatawa Indonesia
215 H4 Tate watercourse Qld Australia
108 A5 Tate, Cabo cape Chile
219 I7 Tate, Mount NSW Australia
193 H4 Tateyama Japan
193 H4 Tateyama volcano Japan
74 M2 Tathlina Lake Northwest Territories Canada
178 E6 Tathlīth Saudi Arabia
178 E6 Tathlīth, Wādī watercourse Saudi Arabia
219 I7 Tathra NSW Australia
105 F6 Tatí Bolivia
75 W2 Tatinnai Lake Nunavut Canada
182 E3 Tatishchevo Russian Federation
181 H5 Tatkon Myanmar
74 I7 Tatla Lake British Columbia Canada
74 I7 Tatlayoko Lake British Columbia Canada
76 J4 Tatnam, Cape Manitoba Canada
74 G4 Tatogga British Columbia Canada
132 A1 Tatry, Nízke range Slovakia
74 C3 Tatshenshini watercourse British Columbia Canada
182 D4 Tatsinskiy Russian Federation
103 C8 Tatuí Brazil
85 K4 Tatum New Mexico USA
86 D4 Tatum Texas USA
218 G7 Tatura Vic. Australia
136 G5 Tatvan Turkey
138 E4 Tatworth Somerset England UK
223 12 Tau island American Samoa
102 D4 Tauá Brazil
220 F4 Taumarunui New Zealand
222 6a Tauanap, Mochun strait Federated States of Micronesia
103 C8 Taubaté Brazil
124 E3 Tauber watercourse Germany
127 J2 Tauberzell Germany
182 F5 Tauchik Kazakhstan
127 H3 Täuffelen Switzerland
160 E2 Taufikia Sudan
220 G4 Tauhara volcano New Zealand
220 G5 Taumatawhakatangihangakoauauotamateapokai-whenuakitanatahu mountain New Zealand
162 D5 Taung South Africa
181 H5 Taungdwingyi Myanmar
181 H5 Taunggyi Myanmar
194 C3 Taunggyi Tanen watercourse Thailand
194 C4 Taungnyo Range Myanmar
181 H5 Taungup Myanmar
179 L3 Taunsa Pakistan
138 D3 Taunton Somerset England UK
83 P6 Taunton Massachusetts USA
220 G4 Taupo New Zealand
220 F4 Taupo, Lake New Zealand
220 E2 Taupo Bay New Zealand
52 L11 Taupo Tablemount underwater feature Tasman Sea
123 L5 Tauragė Lithuania
123 L5 Tauragės admin. area Lithuania
100 C3 Tauramena Colombia
220 G3 Tauranga New Zealand
199 H5 Tauri watercourse Papua New Guinea
131 G7 Taurianova Italy
131 H7 Taurisano Italy
123 M4 Taurkalne Latvia
220 E2 Tauroa Point New Zealand
123 L4 Tausalo ežeras lake Lithuania
223 14a Tautiri French Polynesia
121 N4 Tauvo Finland
133 E6 Tavaklı Turkey
76 I1 Tavani Nunavut Canada
127 H3 Tavannes Switzerland
128 B3 Tavarede Portugal
102 E4 Tavares Brazil
121 Q3 Tavayarvi, Ozero lake Russian Federation
134 O7 Tavda Russian Federation
182 J1 Tavda Russian Federation
134 N7 Tavda watercourse Russian Federation
139 I2 Taverham Norfolk England UK
161 F4 Taveta Kenya
223 9 Taveuni island Fiji
128 C5 Tavira Portugal
128 C5 Tavira, Ilha de cape Portugal
138 C4 Tavistock Devon England UK
183 M3 Tavolzhan Kazakhstan
Tavoy see Dawei Myanmar
133 F6 Tavşanlı Turkey
223 9a Tavua Fiji
138 D4 Taw watercourse England UK
187 E6 Tawa lake Madhya Pradesh India
197 H2 Tawai, Bukit mountain Malaysia
223 9a Tawake Fiji
86 C4 Tawakoni, Lake Texas USA
214 C4 Tawallah Range NT Australia
181 G3 Tawang Arunachal Pradesh India
82 J4 Tawas City Michigan USA
75 O5 Tawatinaw Alberta Canada
75 O5 Tawatinaw watercourse Alberta Canada
197 H2 Tawau Malaysia
197 H2 Tawau, Teluk bay Malaysia
156 D5 Taweisha Sudan
195 I6 Tawi Tawi island Philippines
156 C5 Tawila Sudan
120 I5 Täxan Sweden
89 F5 Taxco Mexico
142 E4 Tay watercourse Scotland UK
216 G6 Tay, Lake WA Australia
142 D4 Tay, Loch lake Scotland UK
194 E5 Tây Ninh Vietnam
195 I4 Tayabas Bay Philippines
197 F4 Tayan Indonesia
219 J5 Tayan Peak NSW Australia
198 E5 Tayandu Indonesia
198 E5 Tayandu island Indonesia
198 D5 Tayandu, Kepulauan islands Indonesia
179 I2 Tāybād Iran
121 R2 Taybola Russian Federation
161 G3 Tayeeglow Somalia
133 E5 Tayfur Turkey
183 O2 Tayga Russian Federation
135 AH6 Taygonos, Mys cape Russian Federation
135 AH6 Taygonos, Poluostrov peninsula Russian Federation
214 C6 Taylor watercourse NT Australia
84 G3 Taylor Arizona USA
86 E4 Taylor Arkansas USA
82 J5 Taylor Michigan USA
81 P6 Taylor Nebraska USA
86 C5 Taylor Texas USA
86 G5 Taylorsville Mississippi USA
87 K3 Taylorsville North Carolina USA
80 J6 Taylorsville Utah USA
82 G7 Taylorville Illinois USA
178 D4 Taymā' Saudi Arabia
135 U6 Taymura watercourse Russian Federation
134 T5 Taymyr Russian Federation
135 V4 Taymyr, Ozero lake Russian Federation
135 V3 Taymyr, Poluostrov peninsula Russian Federation
139 F3 Taynton Oxfordshire England UK
142 C4 Taynuilt Argyll and Bute Scotland UK
88 D3 Tayoltita Mexico
142 B5 Tayovullin Argyll and Bute Scotland UK
142 F4 Tayport Fife Scotland UK
135 U7 Tayshet Russian Federation
195 H5 Taytay Philippines
195 H5 Taytay Bay Philippines
197 F5 Tayu Indonesia
101 F3 Tayucay Venezuela
134 R5 Taz watercourse Russian Federation
154 F2 Taza Morocco
193 I3 Tazawa-ko lake Japan
75 Q2 Tazin watercourse Northwest Territories Canada
75 Q3 Tazin Lake Saskatchewan Canada
156 C2 Tāzirbū Libya
134 P5 Tazovskaya Guba bay Russian Federation
134 Q5 Tazovskiy Russian Federation
155 H4 Tazrouk Algeria
154 E2 Tazzarine Morocco
182 D5 Tbilisi Georgia
158 E3 Tchamba Togo
158 E3 Tchaourou Benin
74 I5 Tchentlo Lake British Columbia Canada
158 E3 Tchetti Benin
159 G5 Tchibanga Gabon
155 H5 Tchighozérine Niger
155 H5 Tchin-Tabaradene Niger
159 G3 Tcholliré Cameroon
86 F4 Tchula Mississippi USA
123 J5 Tczew Poland
221 B7 Te Anau New Zealand
221 B7 Te Anau, Lake New Zealand
220 H3 Te Araroa New Zealand
220 G4 Te Aute New Zealand
220 F4 Te Awamutu New Zealand
220 G4 Te Awanga New Zealand
220 E2 Te Hapua New Zealand
220 G4 Te Haroto New Zealand
220 F3 Te Henga (Bethells Beach) New Zealand
220 G3 Te Kaha New Zealand
220 E2 Te Kao New Zealand
220 G4 Te Karaka New Zealand
220 E3 Te Kopuru New Zealand
220 F4 Te Kuiti New Zealand
220 2 Te Manga volcano Cook Islands New Zealand
220 E2 Te Paki New Zealand
221 D6 Te Pirita New Zealand
220 G3 Te Puke New Zealand
220 G4 Te Teko New Zealand
221 B8 Te Waewae Bay New Zealand
Te Waihora see Ellesmere, Lake New Zealand
220 G4 Te Whaiti New Zealand
101 E5 Tea watercourse Brazil
81 Q5 Tea South Dakota USA
89 H4 Teabo Mexico
88 D4 Teacapán Mexico
85 K4 Teague New Mexico USA
86 C5 Teague Texas USA
216 G2 Teague, Lake WA Australia
223 14a Teahupoo French Polynesia
109 7 Teal Inlet Falkland Islands
141 H3 Tealby Lincolnshire England UK
222 1b Teaoraereke Kiribati
89 G5 Teapa Mexico
214 C6 Teatree watercourse NT Australia
223 14a Teavaro French Polynesia
199 F4 Teba Indonesia
128 D5 Teba Spain
155 G6 Tébarat Niger
196 F3 Tebas Indonesia
141 F2 Tebay Cumbria England UK
197 F3 Tebedu Malaysia
155 H1 Tébessa Algeria
196 C3 Tebingtinggi Indonesia
196 D4 Tebingtinggi Indonesia
106 D2 Tebinquiche, Laguna lake Chile
196 D4 Tebo watercourse Indonesia
155 H1 Tébourba Tunisia
155 H1 Téboursouk Tunisia
88 E5 Tecalitlán Mexico
88 A1 Tecate Mexico
126 F5 Tech watercourse France
158 D3 Techiman Ghana
108 B3 Tecka Argentina
89 F5 Tecoanapa Mexico
89 H4 Tecoh Mexico
84 E4 Tecolote Mexico
88 D4 Tecolotlán Mexico
88 E5 Tecomán Mexico
89 F5 Tecomate, Laguna lake Mexico
85 H6 Tecoriname Mexico
88 C2 Tecoripa Mexico
88 E5 Tecpán de Galeana Mexico
89 G5 Tecpatán Mexico
88 D4 Tecuala Mexico
81 Q6 Tecumseh Nebraska USA
161 G3 Ted Somalia
215 H5 Teddy Mountain Qld Australia
107 G6 Tedín Uriburu Argentina
182 H6 Tedzhenskiy Oazis watercourse Turkmenistan
90 D4 Tee Kamp Nicaragua
85 H2 Teec Nos Pos Arizona USA
183 P3 Teeli Russian Federation
121 P4 Teeriranta Finland
141 F2 Tees watercourse England UK
141 G2 Tees Bay England UK
141 F2 Teesdale valley England UK
185 J3 Teetsenuul Mongolia
223 13a Tefala island Tuvalu
101 E5 Tefé Brazil
105 E2 Tefé watercourse Brazil
101 E5 Tefé, Lago lake Brazil
133 F7 Tefenni Turkey
139 E3 Teffont Magna Wiltshire England UK
196 F5 Tegal Indonesia
124 D2 Tegelen Netherlands
120 J5 Tegelträsket lake Sweden
159 F2 Tegina Nigeria
182 I3 Tegissor Koli lake Kazakhstan
132 B2 Téglás Hungary
138 C3 Tegryn Pembrokeshire Wales UK
222 7 Tégua island Vanuatu
108 B2 Tegualda Chile
90 C4 Tegucigalpa Honduras
155 H5 Teguidda-n-Tessoumt Niger
164 3d Teguise Canary Islands
84 C3 Tehachapi California USA
80 D6 Tehama California USA
73 J5 Tehek Lake Nunavut Canada
158 D3 Téhini Côte d'Ivoire
123 M2 Tehinselkä bay Finland
83 K4 Tehkummah Ontario Canada
178 G2 Tehrān Iran
182 F7 Tehrān admin. area Iran
186 E4 Tehri Uttaranchal India
89 F5 Tehuacán Mexico
88 C2 Tehuachi Mexico
89 G6 Tehuantepec, Golfo de bay Mexico
89 G5 Tehuantepec, Istmo de region Mexico
53 W6 Tehuantepec Ridge underwater feature Pacific Ocean
108 C4 Tehuelches Argentina
164 3a Teide, Pico de volcano Canary Islands
138 D4 Teignmouth Devon England UK
218 E4 Teilta NSW Australia
123 L2 Teisko Finland
156 E4 Teiti Sudan
102 E4 Teixeira Brazil
128 C3 Teixoso Portugal
85 K8 Tejaban de la Rosita Mexico
197 G6 Tejakula Indonesia
182 H6 Tejen Turkmenistan
164 3a Tejina Canary Islands
128 C4 Tejo (Tagus) watercourse Portugal
88 E5 Tejupan, Punta cape Mexico
81 Q6 Tekamah Nebraska USA
221 D7 Tekapo watercourse New Zealand
221 D6 Tekapo, Lake New Zealand
89 H4 Tekax de Álvaro Obregón Mexico
183 J5 Teke Kazakhstan
183 K2 Teke Koli lake Kazakhstan
182 H4 Tekeli Kazakhstan
184 F4 Tekes He watercourse Xinjiang Uygur Zizhiqu China
184 G4 Tekesi Xinjiang Uygur Zizhiqu China
125 L5 Tekija Serbia
184 F6 Tekiliktag mountain Xinjiang Uygur Zizhiqu China
136 C5 Tekirdağ admin. area Turkey
187 F7 Tekkali Andhra Pradesh India
196 F3 Tekong, Pulau island Singapore
196 F3 Tekong Kechil, Pulau island Singapore
198 B4 Teku Indonesia
178 C3 Tel Aviv-Yafo Israel
160 D6 Tela Democratic Republic of Congo
90 C4 Tela Honduras
182 E5 T'elavi Georgia
125 H3 Telč Czech Republic
132 D2 Telciu Romania
164 3b Telde Canary Islands
160 C3 Tele watercourse Democratic Republic of Congo
196 C3 Tele Indonesia
197 G4 Telegapulang Indonesia
86 B5 Telegraph Texas USA
219 K4 Telegraph Point NSW Australia
120 K3 Telejaur Sweden
223 13a Telele island Tuvalu
103 B9 Telêmaco Borba Brazil
122 E3 Telemark admin. area Norway
197 H3 Telen watercourse Indonesia
133 E7 Telendos island Greece
132 D3 Teleorman admin. area Romania
155 H4 Telertheba, Djebel mountain Algeria
105 H4 Teles Pires watercourse Brazil
109 10a Telescope Point cape Grenada
183 O3 Teletskoye, Ozero lake Russian Federation
212 G6 Telfer WA Australia
76 H8 Telford Manitoba Canada
138 E2 Telford Telford and Wrekin England UK
83 N6 Telford Pennsylvania USA
138 E2 Telford and Wrekin admin. area England UK
124 F4 Telfs Austria
124 D2 Telgte Germany
90 C4 Telica Nicaragua
158 B2 Télimélé Guinea
132 D4 Telish Bulgaria
125 K3 Telkibánya Hungary
74 H5 Telkwa British Columbia Canada
72 C5 Teller Alaska USA
219 I3 Telleraga NSW Australia
108 C4 Tellier Argentina
124 C2 Tellin Belgium
100 C4 Tello Colombia
185 K3 Telmen Mongolia
185 K3 Telmen Nuur lake Mongolia
196 C4 Telok Blangah admin. area Singapore
108 C3 Telsen Argentina
123 L5 Telšiai Lithuania
123 L5 Telšiai admin. area Lithuania
197 F4 Telukbatang Indonesia
196 D4 Telukbayur Indonesia
196 C3 Telukdalam Indonesia
196 D4 Telukkuantan Indonesia
197 F4 Telukmelano Indonesia
196 E5 Teluknaga Indonesia
196 C3 Teluknibung Indonesia
196 F4 Telukpakedai Indonesia
187 E10 Telulla Sri Lanka
158 D3 Tema Ghana
222 1b Temaiku island Kiribati
196 F3 Temaju island Indonesia
106 D4 Temas de Socos Chile
88 D4 Temascal Mexico
223 14 Tematangi island French Polynesia
135 U5 Tembenchi watercourse Russian Federation
196 D4 Tembesi watercourse Indonesia
196 D4 Tembilahan Indonesia
162 E5 Tembisa South Africa
160 B5 Tembo Aluma Angola
163 F2 Tembwe Zambia
138 E2 Teme watercourse England UK
84 D4 Temecula California USA
194 D6 Temengor, Tasik lake Malaysia
155 F5 Téméra Mali
196 D3 Temerloh Malaysia
196 E3 Temiang island Indonesia
196 D2 Temiang, Bukit mountain Malaysia
198 D4 Teminabuan Indonesia
183 K3 Temirtau Kazakhstan
77 T7 Témiscamie watercourse Quebec Canada
83 L3 Témiscaming Quebec Canada
83 L3 Témiscamingue, Lac lake Quebec Canada
79 D9 Témiscouata, Lac lake Quebec Canada
121 N4 Temmes Finland
182 D2 Temnikov Russian Federation
219 H6 Temora NSW Australia
88 C2 Temósachic Mexico
222 8 Temotu admin. area Solomon Islands
89 H4 Temozón Mexico
84 G4 Tempe Arizona USA
100 C5 Tempestad Peru
196 D4 Tempino Indonesia
131 C6 Tempio Pausania Sardinia Italy
86 C5 Temple Texas USA
138 C2 Temple Bar Ceredigion Wales UK
215 G2 Temple Bay Qld Australia
139 I3 Temple Ewell Kent England UK
89 J2 Temple Terrace Florida USA
143 E4 Templemore Ireland
140 A1 Templemoyle Ireland
214 E6 Templeton watercourse Qld Australia
143 E4 Templetuohy Ireland
143 E2 Tempo Fermanagh Northern Ireland UK
89 F4 Tempoal watercourse Mexico
89 F4 Tempoal de Sánchez Mexico
127 G1 Temse Belgium
106 C6 Temuco Chile
221 D7 Temuka New Zealand
188 D3 Temuli Sichuan China
182 H3 Temyasovo Russian Federation
122 D6 Ten Boer Netherlands
194 A5 Ten Degree Channel Andaman and Nicobar Islands India
214 E7 Ten Mile Hills Qld Australia
216 G2 Ten Mile Lake WA Australia
79 K8 Ten Mile Pond Newfoundland and Labrador Canada
81 L4 Ten Sleep Wyoming USA
87 K8 Ten Thousand Islands Florida USA
100 B5 Tena Ecuador
89 H4 Tenabó Mexico
123 L2 Tenala Finland
127 G4 Tenay France
138 E2 Tenbury Wells Worcestershire England UK
138 C3 Tenby Pembrokeshire Wales UK
126 G4 Tence France
157 G5 Tendaho Ethiopia
127 H4 Tende France
127 H4 Tende, Colle di pass France
156 E5 Tendelti Sudan
155 F2 Tendrara Morocco
164 3 Tenerife island Canary Islands
155 G1 Ténès Algeria
197 J3 Tenga Indonesia
197 H5 Tengah, Kepulauan islands Indonesia
188 F4 Tengcheng Guangxi Zhuangzu Zizhiqu China
188 C3 Tengchong Yunnan China
182 F5 Tenge Kazakhstan
198 D5 Tenggara, Kepulauan islands Indonesia
197 H4 Tenggarong Indonesia
190 E5 Tengger Shamo Nei Mongol Zizhiqu China
194 D6 Tenggol island Malaysia
197 H2 Tenghilan Malaysia
183 L3 Tengiz lake Kazakhstan
189 H1 Tengzhou Shandong China
218 F1 Tenham Qld Australia
100 B5 Teniente López Peru
106 F2 Teniente Ochoa Paraguay
106 F6 Teniente Origone Argentina
104 B2 Teniente Pinglo Peru
80 D3 Tenino Washington USA
187 D10 Tenkasi Tamil Nadu India
160 D6 Tenke Democratic Republic of Congo
72 B5 Tenkergynpil'gyn, Laguna lake Russian Federation
86 D3 Tenkiller Ferry Lake Oklahoma USA
158 D2 Tenkodogo Burkina Faso
80 C5 Tenmile Lake Oregon USA
130 E5 Tenna watercourse Italy
131 E8 Tenna, Punta cape Italy
122 G2 Tennänget Sweden
214 C5 Tennant Creek NT Australia
71 Tennessee admin. area USA
86 G2 Tennessee watercourse Kentucky/Tennessee USA
127 G1 Tenneville Belgium
120 J2 Tennevoll Norway
87 J4 Tennille Georgia USA
121 P3 Tenniöjoki watercourse Finland
106 D5 Teno Chile
164 3a Teno, Punta de cape Canary Islands
197 G2 Tenom Malaysia
89 H5 Tenosique de Pino Suárez Mexico
80 G3 Tensed Idaho USA
81 R3 Tenstrike Minnesota USA
182 H4 Tenteksor lake Kazakhstan
182 I3 Tenteksor Koli lake Kazakhstan
198 B4 Tentena Indonesia
139 H3 Tenterden Kent England UK
219 K3 Tenterfield NSW Australia
198 B3 Tentolomatinan, Gunung mountain Indonesia
128 B2 Teo Spain
88 E4 Teocaltiche Mexico
103 A8 Teodoro Sampaio Brazil
103 D7 Teófilo Otoni Brazil
195 I6 Teomabal island Philippines
186 E6 Teonthar Madhya Pradesh India
89 G5 Teopisca Mexico
133 B5 Teovo Macedonia
158 D3 Tepa Ghana
198 D5 Tepa Indonesia
220 4 Tepa Point Niue New Zealand
88 E5 Tepalcatepec Mexico
121 N2 Tepasto Finland
88 D3 Tepehuanes Mexico
163 G2 Tepere Mozambique
89 F4 Tepetzintla Mexico
197 H3 Tepianlangsat Indonesia
88 D4 Tepic Mexico
104 C2 Tepiche watercourse Peru
124 G3 Teplá Czech Republic
125 G2 Teplice Czech Republic
134 L6 Teplogorka Russian Federation
88 B2 Tepoca, Punta cape Mexico
85 I7 Teporéchi Mexico
223 14 Tepoto island French Polynesia
121 N3 Tepsa Finland
223 13a Tepuka island Tuvalu
87 K7 Tequesta Florida USA
88 E4 Tequila Mexico
129 H2 Ter watercourse Spain
124 D1 Ter Apel Netherlands
155 G6 Téra Niger
128 C2 Tera watercourse Spain
222 1 Teraina island Kiribati
160 E2 Terakeka Sudan
184 E6 Teram Kangri Peak mountain Asia
130 E5 Teramo Italy
123 K4 Tērande Latvia
218 F8 Terang Vic. Australia
108 B3 Terao Chile
125 L2 Teratyn Poland
198 D5 Terbang Selatan island Indonesia
198 D5 Terbang Utara island Indonesia
196 E5 Terbanggi-besar Indonesia
164 1b Terceira island Azores
101 H4 Terceiro Acampamento Brazil
106 F5 Tercero watercourse Argentina
183 R3 Tere-khol' lake Russian Federation
132 C1 Tereblya Ukraine
125 L5 Teregova Romania
182 D5 Terek watercourse Russian Federation
183 J4 Terekty Kazakhstan
183 O4 Terekty Kazakhstan
182 E2 Teren'ga Russian Federation
196 D2 Terengganu admin. area Malaysia
105 H6 Terenos Brazil
196 F4 Terentang Indonesia
124 F4 Terento Italy
132 E1 Tereshpol' Ukraine
102 D4 Teresina Brazil
100 D4 Teresita Colombia
103 D8 Teresópolis Brazil
194 B5 Teressa island Andaman and Nicobar Islands India
132 C1 Teresva Ukraine
128 C5 Terges, Ribeira de watercourse Portugal
178 E7 Terifa Yemen
121 M5 Terjärv Finland
130 D3 Terlano Italy
76 I1 Term Point Nunavut Canada
136 F5 Terme Turkey
219 J6 Termeil NSW Australia
218 D4 Termination Hill SA Australia
131 E8 Termini Imerese Italy
89 H5 Términos, Laguna de lake Mexico
155 I5 Termit-Kaoboul Niger
183 J6 Termiz Uzbekistan
198 C3 Ternate Indonesia
77 U6 Ternay, Lac lake Quebec Canada
127 L3 Ternberg Austria
193 H2 Terney Russian Federation
131 E5 Terni Italy
130 G3 Ternitz Austria
132 F1 Ternivka Ukraine
136 C3 Ternopil's'ka Oblast' admin. area Ukraine
132 G1 Ternovka Ukraine
136 E2 Terny Ukraine
218 D5 Terowie SA Australia
135 AE9 Terpeniya, Mys cape Russian Federation
135 AD9 Terpeniya, Zaliv bay Russian Federation
107 H2 Terra Boa Brazil
162 D5 Terra Firma South Africa
103 D6 Terra Nova Brazil
58 L1 Terra Nova Bay Antarctica
103 A8 Terra Rica Brazil
103 B8 Terra Roxa Brazil
101 G5 Terra Santa Brazil
74 G5 Terrace British Columbia Canada
131 E6 Terracina Italy
129 G2 Terradets, Pantà de lake Spain
120 H4 Terråk Norway
86 C4 Terral Oklahoma USA
218 G3 Terramia NSW Australia
129 H3 Terrassa Spain
126 E5 Terraube France
109 16 Terre-de-Bas Guadeloupe
109 16 Terre-de-Bas island Guadeloupe
109 16 Terre-de-Haut Guadeloupe
109 16 Terre-de-Haut island Guadeloupe
82 H7 Terre Haute Indiana USA
89 H2 Terrebonne Bay Louisiana USA
86 C4 Terrell Texas USA
108 E5 Terrible, Cape Falkland Islands
108 B5 Terromontos, Pampa de region Chile
86 F4 Terry Mississippi USA
81 M3 Terry Montana USA
219 J3 Terry Hie Hie NSW Australia
143 D3 Terryglass Ireland
124 C1 Terschelling island Netherlands
131 C7 Tertenia Sardinia Italy
122 E5 Tertius island Germany
100 C4 Teruel Colombia
129 F3 Teruel Spain
132 E4 Tervel Bulgaria
121 O5 Tervo Finland
121 N3 Tervola Finland
123 P2 Tervu Russian Federation
218 F5 Teryaweynya Lake NSW Australia
125 H4 Terz Austria
185 J2 Tes Mongolia
185 J2 Tes Mongolia
85 N1 Tescott Kansas USA
158 D3 Teselima Ghana
156 F4 Teseney Eritrea
72 D4 Teshekpuk Lake Alaska USA
190 E2 Teshig Mongolia
88 C3 Tesia Mexico
74 E2 Teslin Yukon Territory Canada
74 D2 Teslin watercourse Yukon Territory Canada
74 E3 Teslin Lake British Columbia Canada
132 D3 Teslui Romania
103 A7 Tesouro Brazil
123 P3 Tësovo-Netyl'skiy Russian Federation
123 P3 Tesovskiy Russian Federation
155 G4 Tessalit Mali
155 H6 Tessaoua Niger
122 E2 Tesse lake Norway
124 E4 Tesserete Switzerland
163 F4 Tessolo Mozambique
139 F3 Test watercourse England UK
155 H1 Testour Tunisia
126 F5 Têt watercourse France
74 I6 Tetachuck Lake British Columbia Canada
106 D2 Tetas, Punta cape Chile
139 E3 Tetbury Gloucestershire England UK
138 E2 Tetchill Shropshire England UK
163 F3 Tete Mozambique
163 F3 Tete admin. area Mozambique
222 8 Tetepare island Solomon Islands
79 D7 Tétépisca, Lac lake Quebec Canada
124 D3 Téterchen France
124 G1 Teterow Germany
141 H3 Tetford Lincolnshire England UK
89 H4 Tetiz Mexico
141 H3 Tetney Lincolnshire England UK
80 I3 Teton watercourse Montana USA
81 J5 Teton Range Wyoming USA
154 E1 Tétouan Morocco
121 U3 Tetrino Russian Federation
124 E4 Tettnang Germany
182 E2 Tetyushi Russian Federation
106 F3 Teuco watercourse Argentina
131 C7 Teulada Sardinia Italy
129 G4 Teulada Spain
76 G7 Teulon Manitoba Canada
198 D5 Teun island Indonesia
196 B2 Teunom watercourse Indonesia
121 M3 Teurajärvi Sweden
107 I4 Teutônia Brazil
216 G4 Teutonic WA Australia
120 L5 Teuva Finland
223 14b Tevairoa island French Polynesia
131 E5 Tevere watercourse Italy
139 H2 Teversham Cambridgeshire England UK
142 F5 Teviot watercourse Scotland UK
142 F5 Teviothead Scottish Borders Scotland UK
122 I2 Tevsjön bay Sweden
197 G4 Tewah Indonesia
197 G4 Teweh watercourse Indonesia
142 F4 Tewel Aberdeenshire Scotland UK
139 E3 Tewkesbury Gloucestershire England UK
142 B5 Texa island Scotland UK
86 C6 Texana, Lake Texas USA
89 G1 Texarkana Arkansas USA
86 D4 Texarkana Texas USA
71 Texas admin. area USA
86 D6 Texas City Texas USA
124 C1 Texel island Netherlands
85 L2 Texhoma Oklahoma USA
85 K3 Texico New Mexico USA
85 K2 Texline Texas USA
86 C3 Texoma, Lake Oklahoma USA
162 E5 Teyateyaneng Lesotho
127 K5 Tezio, Monte mountain Italy
89 F5 Teziutlán Mexico
181 G3 Tezpur Assam India
181 H3 Tezu Arunachal Pradesh India
194 D2 Tha watercourse Laos
73 J6 Tha-anne watercourse Nunavut Canada
194 D3 Tha Bo Thailand
162 E5 Thaba Putsoa mountain Lesotho
194 B3 Thabaung Myanmar
162 E4 Thabazimbi South Africa
214 E4 Thabugan Point Qld Australia
86 C4 Thackerville Oklahoma USA
194 D2 Thafa Laos
194 E2 Thái Bình Vietnam
194 E3 Thái Hòa Vietnam
194 E2 Thái Nguyên Vietnam
194 D3 Thailand country
194 D5 Thailand, Gulf of Thailand
187 D7 Thair Maharashtra India
181 F3 Thakurgaon Bangladesh
179 L2 Thal Pakistan
155 H1 Thala Tunisia
76 G7 Thalberg Manitoba Canada
124 F2 Thale Germany
194 D6 Thale Luang lake Thailand
127 K1 Thalheim Germany
80 E2 Thalia British Columbia Canada
219 I3 Thallon Qld Australia
162 E4 Thamaga Botswana
182 I3 Thaman-akkol lake Kazakhstan
179 H6 Thamarīt Oman
223 9a Thambia island Fiji
139 G3 Thame Buckinghamshire England UK
220 F3 Thames New Zealand
139 F3 Thames watercourse England UK
220 F3 Thames, Firth of bay New Zealand
194 C5 Than Kyun Myanmar
194 D2 Than Uyên Vietnam
194 C4 Thanbyuzayat Myanmar
181 H5 Thandaung Myanmar
194 B3 Thandwe Myanmar
186 D5 Thanesar Haryana India
194 E3 Thanh Chương Vietnam
194 E3 Thanh Hóa Vietnam
187 E9 Thanjavur Tamil Nadu India
194 C3 Thanlwin (Salween) watercourse Myanmar
194 C3 Thanlyin Myanmar
127 H3 Thann France
179 K4 Thano Ahmad Khan Pakistan
76 G2 Thaolintoa Lake Nunavut Canada
194 C5 Thap Sakae Thailand
186 C5 Thar Desert Rajasthan India
186 C6 Thara Gujarat India
186 C6 Tharad Gujarat India
161 F4 Tharaka Kenya
218 F3 Thargomindah Qld Australia
178 E2 Tharthār, Buḩayrat ath lake Iraq
178 E2 Tharthār, Wādī ath watercourse Iraq
133 D5 Thasos Greece
133 D5 Thasos island Greece
194 E2 Thất Khê Vietnam
194 E3 That Phanom Thailand
139 F3 Thatcham West Berkshire England UK
84 H4 Thatcher Arizona USA
194 C3 Thaton Myanmar
179 K5 Thatta Pakistan
139 H3 Thaxted Essex England UK
86 G3 Thaxton Mississippi USA
194 C4 Thayawthadangyi Kyun Myanmar
82 D8 Thayer Kansas USA
86 F2 Thayer Missouri USA

181 H5 **Thayet** Myanmar
81 J5 **Thayne** Wyoming USA
181 H5 **Thazi** Myanmar
219 I1 **The Battery** Qld Australia
218 F2 **The Blue Hills** Qld Australia
109 20 **The Bottom** Netherlands Antilles
199 J6 **The Calvados Chain** *islands* Papua New Guinea
140 B4 **The Cedars** Ireland
218 D6 **The Coorong** *watercourse* SA Australia
142 D3 **The Craigs** Highland Scotland UK
109 12 **The Crane** Barbados
140 A3 **The Downs** Ireland
140 B1 **The Drones** Ballymoney Northern Ireland UK
214 D1 **The English Companys Islands** NT Australia
219 J5 **The Entrance** NSW Australia
139 H2 **The Fens** England UK
143 F3 **The Five Roads** Ireland
219 J2 **The Gums** Qld Australia
The Hague *see* **Den Haag/'s-Gravenhage** Netherlands
86 C5 **The Hills** Texas USA
221 D7 **The Hunters Hills** *range* New Zealand
211 inset **The Lagoon** Lord Howe Island Australia
143 F4 **The Little Crosses** Ireland
215 H5 **The Lynd** Qld Australia
218 F6 **The Marsh** *swamp* Vic. Australia
142 C2 **The Minch** *strait* Scotland UK
214 E6 **The Monument** Qld Australia
109 19 **The Narrows** *strait* Saint Kitts and Nevis
142 F1 **The North Sound** Scotland UK
75 U6 **The Pas** Manitoba Canada
164 5a **The Peak** *mountain* Ascension
143 E3 **The Pigeons** Ireland
221 C7 **The Remarkables** *range* New Zealand
219 H6 **The Rock** NSW Australia
143 D4 **The Rodney** Ireland
196 E6 **The Settlement** Christmas Island Australia
109 21 **The Settlement** British Virgin Islands
140 B2 **The Sheddings** Ballymena Northern Ireland UK
214 E7 **The Sisters** *mountain* Qld Australia
143 F2 **The Six Towns** Magherafelt Northern Ireland UK
221 B9 **The Snares** *islands* New Zealand
218 B3 **The Twins** SA Australia
75 T5 **The Two Rivers** Saskatchewan Canada
109 20 **The Valley** Anguilla
86 C3 **The Village** Oklahoma USA
126 E1 **The Weald** *region* England UK
82 I3 **Theano Point** Ontario Canada
84 F4 **Theba** Arizona USA
213 I3 **Theda** WA Australia
81 O6 **Thedford** Nebraska USA
131 C9 **Thelepte** Tunisia
72 I6 **Thelon** *watercourse* Northwest Territories Canada
127 J1 **Themar** Germany
78 D6 **Thémines** *watercourse* Quebec Canada
126 D3 **Thénezay** France
155 G1 **Thenia** Algeria
155 G1 **Theniet El Had** Algeria
126 E4 **Thenon** France
214 A6 **Theo, Mount** NT Australia
77 Q7 **Théodat, Lac** *lake* Quebec Canada
219 J1 **Theodore** Qld Australia
75 T7 **Theodore** Saskatchewan Canada
88 C1 **Theodore Roosevelt Lake** Arizona USA
126 F3 **Théols** *watercourse* France
126 F2 **Thérain** *watercourse* France
215 I7 **Theresa, Lake** Qld Australia
164 9b **Thérèse, Île** *island* Seychelles
133 C5 **Thermaïkos Kolpos** *bay* Greece
126 D5 **Thermes-d'Armagnac** France
58 W1 **Theron Mountains** Antarctica
72 G4 **Thesiger Bay** Northwest Territories Canada
133 B6 **Thessalia** *admin. area* Greece
133 C5 **Thessaloniki** Greece
139 H2 **Thetford** Norfolk England UK
83 P3 **Thetford Mines** Quebec Canada
127 H4 **Théus** France
127 G1 **Theux** Belgium
212 C6 **Thevenard Island** WA Australia
73 L7 **Thévenet, Lac** *lake* Quebec Canada
124 B3 **Thiais** France
76 H4 **Thibaudeau** Manitoba Canada
86 F6 **Thibodaux** Louisiana USA
82 D2 **Thief Lake** Minnesota USA
81 Q2 **Thief River Falls** Minnesota USA
58 R1 **Thiel Mountains** Antarctica
124 F5 **Thiene** Italy
126 F4 **Thiers** France
77 R3 **Thiersant, Lac** *lake* Quebec Canada
154 C6 **Thiès** Senegal
161 F4 **Thika** Kenya
187 C10 **Thiladhunmathi Atoll** Maldives
154 D5 **Thilogne** Senegal
181 F3 **Thimphu** Bhutan
120 inset **Þingeyri** Iceland
120 inset **Þingvallavatn** *lake* Iceland
194 D3 **Thinkèo** Laos
157 G5 **Thio** Eritrea
222 7 **Thio** New Caledonia
133 D7 **Thira** *island* Greece
133 D7 **Thirasia** *island* Greece
219 J6 **Thirroul** NSW Australia
141 G2 **Thirsk** North Yorkshire England UK
216 G6 **Thirsty, Mount** WA Australia
216 D5 **Thirsty Point** WA Australia
187 D10 **Thiruvananthapuram** Kerala India
187 E9 **Thiruvarur** Tamil Nadu India
120 inset **Þistilfjörður** *bay* Iceland
218 C6 **Thistle Island** SA Australia
133 C6 **Thisvi** Greece
195 G5 **Thitu Island** Spratly Islands
194 E4 **Thiu Kaho Phanom Dong Rak** Thailand
133 C6 **Thívai** Greece
126 E4 **Thiviers** France
120 inset **Þjórsá** *watercourse* Iceland
76 E3 **Thlewiaza** *watercourse* Manitoba Canada
194 D5 **Thô Chu, Đao** *island* Vietnam
75 Q2 **Thoa** *watercourse* Northwest Territories Canada
194 C3 **Thoen** Thailand
194 D3 **Thoeng** Thailand
162 F4 **Thohoyandou** South Africa
104 E5 **Thola Palca** Bolivia
124 C2 **Tholen** Netherlands
133 B7 **Tholón** Greece
212 D8 **Thomas** *watercourse* WA Australia
86 B3 **Thomas** Oklahoma USA
218 C2 **Thomas, Lake** SA Australia
138 C3 **Thomas Chapel** Pembrokeshire Wales UK
82 E7 **Thomas Hill Reservoir** Missouri USA
73 J2 **Thomas Hubbard, Cape** Nunavut Canada
143 D3 **Thomas Street** Roscommon Ireland
87 I4 **Thomaston** Georgia USA
86 H5 **Thomasville** Alabama USA
87 J5 **Thomasville** Georgia USA
127 H1 **Thommen** Belgium
91 G3 **Thomonde** Haiti
75 W5 **Thompson** Manitoba Canada
81 Q3 **Thompson** North Dakota USA
80 H3 **Thompson Falls** Montana USA
74 H7 **Thompson Sound** British Columbia Canada
84 H1 **Thompson Springs** Utah USA
82 G8 **Thompsonville** Illinois USA
72 H4 **Thomsen** *watercourse* Northwest Territories Canada
142 E3 **Thomshill** Moray Scotland UK
215 G8 **Thomson** *watercourse* Qld Australia
87 J4 **Thomson** Georgia USA
221 C7 **Thomson Mountains** New Zealand
221 B7 **Thomson Sound** New Zealand
130 B4 **Thônes** France
124 D4 **Thônex** Switzerland
127 H3 **Thonon-les-Bains** France
85 H3 **Thoreau** New Mexico USA
120 inset **Þórisvatn** *lake* Iceland
120 inset **Þorlákshöfn** Iceland
141 G2 **Thormanby** North Yorkshire England UK
141 G2 **Thornaby on Tees** Stockton-on-Tees England UK
138 E3 **Thornbury** South Gloucestershire England UK
86 C5 **Thorndale** Texas USA
139 I2 **Thorndon** Suffolk England UK
141 H3 **Thorne** South Yorkshire England UK
74 E5 **Thorne Bay** Alaska USA
139 G2 **Thorney** Peterborough England UK
140 B2 **Thornford** Ireland
138 E4 **Thornford** Dorset England UK
141 G3 **Thornhill** Derbyshire England UK
142 E5 **Thornhill** Dumfries and Galloway Scotland UK
142 D4 **Thornhill** Stirling Scotland UK
140 A4 **Thornpack** Ireland
140 E2 **Thornthwaite** Cumbria England UK
138 A1 **Thornton** Ireland
140 E3 **Thornton** Lancashire England UK
86 E4 **Thornton** Arkansas USA
84 B1 **Thornton** California USA
139 G1 **Thornton le Fen** Lincolnshire England UK
141 H3 **Thornton le Moor** Lincolnshire England UK
214 E5 **Thorntonia** Qld Australia
88 E2 **Thorntonville** Texas USA
215 G6 **Thornville** *watercourse* Qld Australia
139 F1 **Thorpe** Derbyshire England UK
139 I2 **Thorpeness** Suffolk England UK
120 inset **Þórshöfn** Iceland
122 E4 **Thorsminde** Denmark
138 D4 **Thorverton** Devon England UK
126 D3 **Thouars** France
181 H4 **Thoubal** Manipur India
126 D3 **Thouet** *watercourse* France
212 E6 **Thouin, Cape** WA Australia
126 F2 **Thourotte** France
84 C3 **Thousand Oaks** California USA
139 G2 **Thrapston** Northamptonshire England UK
80 J4 **Three Forks** Montana USA
188 F2 **Three Gorges Dam** Hubei China
188 E2 **Three Gorges Reservoir** Chongqing China
75 O7 **Three Hills** Alberta Canada
219 Q10 **Three Hummock Island** Tas. Australia
52 N11 **Three Kings Basin** *underwater feature* Pacific Ocean
220 E2 **Three Kings Islands** New Zealand
84 G4 **Three Points** Arizona USA
158 D4 **Three Points, Cape** *cape* Ghana
216 F2 **Three Rivers** WA Australia
85 I4 **Three Rivers** New Mexico USA
86 B6 **Three Rivers** Texas USA
214 C5 **Three Ways Roadhouse** NT Australia
138 A2 **Three Wells** Ireland
139 G2 **Threekingham** Lincolnshire England UK
141 F2 **Thringarth** Durham England UK
141 G2 **Thrintoft** North Yorkshire England UK
187 D9 **Thrissur** Kerala India
86 B4 **Throckmorton** Texas USA
141 G1 **Thropton** Northumberland England UK
212 F7 **Throssel Range** WA Australia
217 I3 **Throssell, Lake** WA Australia
74 M8 **Thrums** British Columbia Canada
139 F3 **Thruxton** Hampshire England UK
194 F4 **Thu Bon** *watercourse* Vietnam
161 F4 **Thua** *watercourse* Kenya
194 D2 **Thuận Châu** Vietnam
214 F2 **Thud Point** Qld Australia
126 G4 **Thueyts** France
127 G1 **Thuin** Belgium
218 G6 **Thule** NSW Australia
75 O3 **Thultue Lake** Alberta Canada
127 H3 **Thun** Switzerland
73 K9 **Thunder Bay** Ontario Canada
82 G2 **Thunder Bay** Ontario Canada
82 J4 **Thunder Bay** Michigan USA
75 R7 **Thunder Creek** Saskatchewan Canada
86 C3 **Thunderbird, Lake** Oklahoma USA
80 F8 **Thunderbolt Peak** California USA
194 C5 **Thung Song** Thailand
194 E3 **Thường Xuân** Vietnam
141 G3 **Thurcroft** South Yorkshire England UK
124 A1 **Thurgarton** Norfolk England UK
124 F2 **Thüringen** *admin. area* Germany
124 F2 **Thüringer Wald** *region* Germany
215 I5 **Thuringowa** Qld Australia
139 G2 **Thurlby** Lincolnshire England UK
143 E4 **Thurles** Ireland
218 F3 **Thurloo Downs** NSW Australia
124 F2 **Thurnau** Germany
139 H3 **Thurnham** Kent England UK
139 G2 **Thurning** Northamptonshire England UK
139 H3 **Thurrock** *admin. area* England UK
214 G1 **Thursday Island** Qld Australia
83 N4 **Thurso** Ontario Canada
142 E2 **Thurso** Highland Scotland UK
142 E2 **Thurso** *watercourse* Scotland UK
58 R2 **Thurston Island** Antarctica
127 I3 **Thusis** Switzerland
74 H4 **Thutade Lake** British Columbia Canada
139 I2 **Thuxton** Norfolk England UK
141 F2 **Thwaite** North Yorkshire England UK
58 Q2 **Thwaites Glacier Tongue** *ice* Antarctica
141 H2 **Thwing** East Riding of Yorkshire England UK
122 E4 **Thy** *cape* Denmark
122 E4 **Thyborøn** Denmark
218 F2 **Thylungra** Qld Australia
133 E7 **Thymaina** *island* Greece
213 K3 **Thymanan, Mount** NT Australia
155 G5 **Ti-n-Azabo** Mali
214 B7 **Ti-Tree** NT Australia
189 G2 **Tiancheng** Hubei China
188 E2 **Tianchi** Sichuan China
188 D3 **Tiandiba** Sichuan China
102 D3 **Tianguá** Brazil
191 I5 **Tianjin** *admin. area* China
191 I5 **Tianjin** Tianjin China
158 D2 **Tiankoura** Burkina Faso
188 E4 **Tianlin** Guangxi Zhuangzu Zizhiqu China
189 H3 **Tianma** Zhejiang China
189 G2 **Tianmen** Hubei China
191 I4 **Tianshan** Nei Mongol Zizhiqu China
188 E1 **Tianshui** Gansu China
189 I2 **Tiantai** Zhejiang China
189 G2 **Tiantang** Anhui China
191 I4 **Tianyi** Nei Mongol Zizhiqu China
191 H5 **Tianzhen** Shanxi China
155 G1 **Tiaret** Algeria
164 3d **Tias** Canary Islands
223 12c **Ti'avea** Samoa
100 C3 **Tibacuy** Colombia
103 B9 **Tibagi** Brazil
103 B8 **Tibagi** *watercourse* Brazil
100 C3 **Tibaná** Colombia
132 E2 **Ţibana** Romania
159 G3 **Tibati** Cameroon
138 E3 **Tibberton** Gloucestershire England UK
158 C3 **Tibé, Pic de** *mountain* Guinea
155 G3 **Tiberghamine** Algeria
155 J4 **Tibesti** *desert* Libya
Tibet *see* **Xizang Zizhiqu** China
186 F5 **Tibrikot** Nepal
122 H3 **Tibro** Sweden
100 C2 **Tibú** Colombia
100 B3 **Tibuga, Ensenada** *bay* Colombia
91 F3 **Tiburon** Haiti
90 E5 **Tiburón, Cabo** *cape* Colombia
88 B2 **Tiburón, Isla** *island* Mexico
132 E4 **Ticha** Bulgaria
219 I5 **Tichborne** NSW Australia
83 M4 **Tichborne** Ontario Canada
77 S7 **Tichégami** *watercourse* Quebec Canada
81 L1 **Tichfield** Saskatchewan Canada
154 E5 **Tichît** Mauritania
154 D4 **Tichla** Western Sahara
127 I3 **Ticino** *watercourse* Switzerland
218 F3 **Tickalara** Qld Australia
138 E2 **Ticklerton** Shropshire England UK
141 H3 **Tickton** East Riding of Yorkshire England UK
89 H4 **Ticul** Mexico
104 C3 **Ticumpina** Peru
218 H8 **Tidal River** Vic. Australia
139 F3 **Tidcombe** Wiltshire England UK
83 R3 **Tide Head** New Brunswick Canada
138 E3 **Tidenham** Gloucestershire England UK
122 H4 **Tidersrum** Sweden
154 D5 **Tidjikja** Mauritania
79 G10 **Tidnish** Nova Scotia Canada
198 C3 **Tidore** *island* Indonesia
143 C4 **Tiduff** Ireland
139 F3 **Tidworth** Wiltshire England UK
158 C3 **Tiébissou** Côte d'Ivoire
191 J4 **Tiefa** Liaoning China
124 G3 **Tiefenbach** Germany
124 C2 **Tiel** Netherlands
154 C6 **Tiel** Senegal
191 K3 **Tieli** Heilongjiang China
191 J4 **Tieling** Liaoning China
194 E5 **Tien Giang (Mekong)** *watercourse* Vietnam
194 E2 **Tiền Hải** Vietnam
184 F4 **Tien Shan** *range* Xinjiang Uygur Zizhiqu China
158 C3 **Tieningboue** Côte d'Ivoire
121 Q5 **Tiensuu** Finland
126 D3 **Tiercé** France
215 J7 **Tieri** Qld Australia
122 I2 **Tierp** Sweden
85 I2 **Tierra Amarilla** New Mexico USA
128 C4 **Tierra Barros** *region* Spain
89 F5 **Tierra Colorada** Mexico
108 C6 **Tierra del Fuego** *admin. area* Argentina
100 B2 **Tierralta** Colombia
88 E4 **Tierranueva** Mexico
128 D4 **Tiétar** *watercourse* Spain
103 B8 **Tietê** *watercourse* Brazil
214 D7 **Tietkens, Mount** NT Australia
218 A2 **Tieyon** SA Australia
126 D3 **Tiffauges** France
82 J6 **Tiffin** Ohio USA
87 J5 **Tifton** Georgia USA
198 C4 **Tifu** Indonesia
128 E6 **Tifziouine** Morocco
197 G2 **Tiga** *island* Malaysia
222 7 **Tiga, Île** *island* New Caledonia
159 F2 **Tiga Reservoir** *lake* Nigeria
164 3b **Tigalete** Canary Islands
195 I4 **Tigaon** Philippines
196 D4 **Tigapuluh, Pegunungan** *range* Indonesia
182 F5 **Tigen** Kazakhstan
74 M8 **Tiger** Washington USA
215 H5 **Tiger Hill** Qld Australia
132 F2 **Tigheciului, Dealurile** *range* Moldova
132 F2 **Tighina** Moldova
198 F5 **Tigi, Danau** *lake* Indonesia
135 AG7 **Tigil'** *watercourse* Russian Federation
183 N3 **Tigiretskiy Khrebet** *range* Russian Federation
159 G3 **Tignère** Cameroon
124 D5 **Tignes** France
79 F9 **Tignish** Prince Edward Island Canada
222 8 **Tigoa** Solomon Islands
156 F5 **Tigray** *admin. area* Ethiopia
104 B2 **Tigre** Peru
104 C2 **Tigre** *watercourse* Peru
104 D4 **Tigre, Serranía del** *range* Bolivia
Tigris River *see* **Dijlah, Nahr** Syria
154 C5 **Tiguent** Mauritania
155 G5 **Tiguezefene** Niger
156 E2 **Tīh, Jabal at** *desert* Egypt
121 O5 **Tihilä** Finland
89 F4 **Tihuatlán** Mexico
186 D5 **Tijara** Rajasthan India
106 C6 **Tijeral** Chile
85 I3 **Tijeras** New Mexico USA
155 I2 **Tijī** Libya
88 A1 **Tijuana** Mexico
107 I3 **Tijucas, Baía de** *bay* Brazil
103 B7 **Tijuco** *watercourse* Brazil
90 B3 **Tikal** Guatemala
186 E6 **Tikamgarh** Madhya Pradesh India
72 D6 **Tikchik Lake** Alaska USA
159 H3 **Tikem** Chad
182 C4 **Tikhoretsk** Russian Federation
123 Q3 **Tikhvin** Russian Federation
53 S9 **Tiki Basin** *underwater feature* Pacific Ocean
90 D4 **Tikiraya** Honduras
129 I5 **Tikjda** Algeria
121 N5 **Tikkakoski** Finland
78 G4 **Tikkoatokak Bay** Newfoundland and Labrador Canada
220 G4 **Tikokino** New Zealand
222 1 **Tikopia** *island* Solomon Islands
187 F7 **Tikra** *watercourse* Orissa India
178 E2 **Tikrīt** Iraq
121 R4 **Tiksha** Russian Federation
121 Q3 **Tiksheozero, Ozero** *lake* Russian Federation
Tikus *see* **Direction Island** Cocos (Keeling) Islands Australia
218 F5 **Til Til** NSW Australia
89 G5 **Tila** Mexico
198 B3 **Tilamuta** Indonesia
186 F6 **Tilaya** *lake* Jharkhand India
219 J7 **Tilba Tilba** NSW Australia
124 C2 **Tilburg** Netherlands
83 J5 **Tilbury** Ontario Canada
139 H3 **Tilbury** Thurrock England UK
106 E2 **Tilcara** Argentina
82 G7 **Tilden** Illinois USA
81 Q5 **Tilden** Nebraska USA
86 B6 **Tilden** Texas USA
155 G5 **Tilemsès** Niger
155 G6 **Tillabéri** Niger
155 G6 **Tillabéri** *admin. area* Niger
80 C4 **Tillamook Bay** Oregon USA
80 C4 **Tillamook Head** *cape* Oregon USA
196 B1 **Tillanchang Dwip** *island* Andaman and Nicobar Islands India
194 B5 **Tillanchong** *island* Andaman and Nicobar Islands India
127 G3 **Tille** *watercourse* France
75 P7 **Tilley** Alberta Canada
155 G5 **Tillia** Niger
126 E3 **Tilly** France
77 R6 **Tilly, Lac** *lake* Quebec Canada
142 F3 **Tillyfar** Aberdeenshire Scotland UK
142 F3 **Tillyfourie** Aberdeenshire Scotland UK
214 B7 **Tilmouth Well** NT Australia
133 E7 **Tilos** *island* Greece
133 E7 **Tilos, Akra** *cape* Greece
218 G4 **Tilpa** NSW Australia
139 F3 **Tilshead** Wiltshire England UK
138 E2 **Tilstock** Shropshire England UK
138 E1 **Tilston** Cheshire England UK
123 N4 **Tilža** Latvia
122 E4 **Tim** Denmark
136 F2 **Tim** Russian Federation
83 L3 **Timagami** Ontario Canada
83 L3 **Timagami, Lake** Ontario Canada
132 F1 **Timanovka** Ukraine
134 L6 **Timanskiy Kryazh** *region* Russian Federation
164 1b **Timão, Pico** *volcano* Azores
221 D7 **Timaru** New Zealand
130 E3 **Timau** Italy
86 F6 **Timbalier Bay** Louisiana USA
154 E5 **Timbedgha** Mauritania
75 S5 **Timber Bay** Saskatchewan Canada
213 K3 **Timber Creek** NT Australia
81 O4 **Timber Lake** South Dakota USA
85 L3 **Timbercreek Canyon** Texas USA
100 B4 **Timbiquí, Bahía de** *bay* Colombia
102 D4 **Timbiras** Brazil
100 B4 **Timbiré** Ecuador
132 E3 **Timboeşti** Romania
Timbuktu *see* **Tombouctou** Mali
198 A2 **Timbun Mata** *island* Malaysia
155 H1 **Timgad** Algeria
155 H5 **Timia** Niger
100 C5 **Timicurillo** Peru
155 G3 **Timimoun** Algeria
135 AF5 **Timir-Atakh-Tas** Russian Federation
132 B3 **Timiş** *admin. area* Romania
132 B3 **Timiş** *watercourse* Romania
83 L3 **Timiskaming Station** Quebec Canada
132 B3 **Timişoara** Romania
134 N6 **Timkapaul'** Russian Federation
73 K9 **Timmins** Ontario Canada
87 L3 **Timmonsville** South Carolina USA
132 C3 **Tîmna** Romania
132 C4 **Timok** *watercourse* Serbia
143 F4 **Timolin** Ireland
102 D4 **Timon** Brazil
131 C6 **Timone, Punta** *cape* Sardinia Italy
197 J6 **Timor** *island* Timor-Leste (East Timor)
198 C6 **Timor-Leste (East Timor)** *country* Asia
198 C6 **Timor Sea** Indonesia/Australia
52 I8 **Timor Trough** *underwater feature* Timor Sea
103 D7 **Timóteo** Brazil
155 F3 **Timoudi** Algeria
197 G4 **Timpah** Indonesia
85 K2 **Timpas** Colorado USA
86 D5 **Timpson** Texas USA
135 AA7 **Timpton** *watercourse* Russian Federation
120 J5 **Timrå** Sweden
87 H3 **Tims Ford Lake** Tennessee USA
142 A2 **Timsgearraidh** Na h-Eileanan Siar Scotland UK
182 J3 **Timtuir Koli** *lake* Kazakhstan
156 C1 **Tin, Ra's at** *cape* Libya
221 B8 **Tin Range** New Zealand
195 J6 **Tinaca Point** Philippines
195 I4 **Tinaga** *island* Philippines
143 F4 **Tinahely** Ireland
164 3d **Tinajo** Canary Islands
222 8 **Tinakula** *volcano* Solomon Islands
198 A4 **Tinambung** Indonesia
100 D2 **Tinaquillo** Venezuela
215 H4 **Tinaroo, Lake** Qld Australia
132 B2 **Tinca** Romania
214 B3 **Tindal** NT Australia
158 E2 **Tindangou** Burkina Faso
164 3d **Tindaya** Canary Islands
154 E3 **Tindouf** Algeria
156 C5 **Tiné** Sudan
127 H4 **Tinée** *watercourse* France
128 C2 **Tineo** Spain
154 E2 **Tinerhir** Morocco
154 E3 **Tinfouchy** Algeria
196 E3 **Tinggi** *island* Malaysia
219 J3 **Tingha** NSW Australia
158 B3 **Tingi Mountains** *range* Guinea
104 C3 **Tingo María** Peru
158 C2 **Tingréla** Côte d'Ivoire
122 H4 **Tingsryd** Sweden
106 D5 **Tinguiririca, Volcán** *volcano* Chile
120 F5 **Tingvoll** Norway
142 E1 **Tingwall** Orkney Islands Scotland UK
199 I4 **Tingwon Group** *islands* Papua New Guinea
199 I4 **Tingwon Island** Papua New Guinea
189 G3 **Tingzhou** Fujian China
194 E3 **Tĩnh Gia** Vietnam
194 E2 **Tĩnh Túc** Vietnam
103 E6 **Tinharé, Ilha de** *island* Brazil
222 2 **Tinian** *island* Northern Mariana Islands
77 R3 **Tininnirusiq, Lac** *lake* Quebec Canada
220 G4 **Tiniroto** New Zealand
197 G3 **Tinjar** *watercourse* Malaysia
196 E5 **Tinjil** *island* Indonesia
143 F3 **Tinkerslane** Ireland
158 C2 **Tinkisso** *watercourse* Guinea
122 E3 **Tinnoset** Norway
122 E3 **Tinnsjo** *lake* Norway
143 D3 **Tinny Park** Ireland
106 E4 **Tinogasta** Argentina
198 B3 **Tinombo** Indonesia
133 D7 **Tinos** Greece
133 D7 **Tinos** *island* Greece
129 F5 **Tiñoso, Cabo** *cape* Spain
199 J5 **Tinputz** Papua New Guinea
126 F2 **Tinqueux** France
181 H3 **Tinsukia** Assam India
138 C4 **Tintagel** Cornwall England UK
154 D5 **Tîntâne** Mauritania
197 H3 **Tintang** Indonesia
155 G4 **Tintejert, Adrar** *mountain* Algeria
138 E3 **Tintern Parva** Monmouthshire Wales UK
106 F3 **Tintina** Argentina
218 E6 **Tintinara** SA Australia
128 C5 **Tinto** *watercourse* Spain
221 G5 **Tinui** New Zealand
81 N2 **Tioga** North Dakota USA
100 B5 **Tioloma** *mountain* Ecuador
199 F4 **Tiom** Indonesia
196 E3 **Tioman** *island* Malaysia
106 D2 **Tiomonte** Chile
83 L6 **Tionesta** Pennsylvania USA
198 D5 **Tioor** *island* Indonesia
154 E6 **Tioribougou** Mali
155 F6 **Tiou** Burkina Faso
155 G1 **Tipasa** Algeria
121 P4 **Tipasoja** Finland
90 C4 **Tipitapa** Nicaragua
143 D4 **Tipperary** Ireland
143 D4 **Tipperary** *admin. area* Ireland
142 F4 **Tipperty** Aberdeenshire Scotland UK
84 C2 **Tipton** California USA
82 H6 **Tipton** Indiana USA
81 P7 **Tipton** Kansas USA
86 B3 **Tipton** Oklahoma USA
86 G2 **Tiptonville** Tennessee USA
139 H3 **Tiptree** Essex England UK
187 D9 **Tiptur** Karnataka India
101 G4 **Tipuru Village** Brazil
88 E5 **Tiquicheo** Mexico
100 D4 **Tiquie** *watercourse* Brazil
100 C2 **Tiquisio** Colombia
105 F3 **Tira-Cerveja** Brazil
102 C3 **Tiracambu, Serra do** *range* Brazil
107 J2 **Tiradentes** Brazil
Tirana *see* **Tiranë** Albania
133 A5 **Tiranë (Tirana)** Albania
124 F4 **Tirano** Italy
181 H3 **Tirap** Arunachal Pradesh India
218 C2 **Tirari Desert** SA Australia
132 F2 **Tiraspol** Moldova
221 G5 **Tiraumea** New Zealand
133 E6 **Tire** Turkey
215 H6 **Tiree** Qld Australia
142 B4 **Tiree** *island* Scotland UK
179 L2 **Tirich Mir** *mountain* Pakistan
186 E4 **Tirido** Jammu and Kashmir India/Pakistan
100 E4 **Tiriquín** Venezuela
139 E3 **Tirley** Gloucestershire England UK
218 F4 **Tirlta** NSW Australia
124 G4 **Tirol** *admin. area* Austria
132 B3 **Tirol** Romania
159 I3 **Tiroungoulou** Central African Republic
214 E4 **Tirranna Roadhouse** Qld Australia
127 K2 **Tirschenreuth** Germany
187 G7 **Tirtol** Orissa India
108 B2 **Tirúa, Cabo** *cape* Chile
187 E9 **Tiruchchirappalli** Tamil Nadu India
187 D10 **Tirumangalam** Tamil Nadu India
187 D10 **Tirunelveli** Tamil Nadu India
187 E9 **Tirupati** Andhra Pradesh India
187 D9 **Tiruppur** Tamil Nadu India
187 D9 **Tirur** Kerala India
187 E9 **Tirutturaippundi** Tamil Nadu India
187 D10 **Tiruvalla** Kerala India
187 E9 **Tiruvannamalai** Tamil Nadu India
187 E9 **Tiruvottiyur** Tamil Nadu India
132 B4 **Tisa** *watercourse* Serbia
139 E3 **Tisbury** Wiltshire England UK
75 S6 **Tisdale** Saskatchewan Canada
123 O4 **Tishino** Russian Federation
130 F1 **Tišice** Czech Republic
122 G2 **Tisjön** *lake* Sweden
155 H4 **Tiska, Mont** *mountain* Algeria
122 E2 **Tisleifjorden** *lake* Norway
132 C3 **Tismana** Romania
120 K2 **Tisnes** Norway
130 H2 **Tisovec** Slovakia
155 G1 **Tissemsilt** Algeria
181 F3 **Tista** *watercourse* West Bengal India
121 M4 **Tistersöfjärden** *bay* Sweden
120 H4 **Tisvatnet** *lake* Norway
132 B3 **Tisza** *watercourse* Serbia
125 L3 **Tisza** *watercourse* Ukraine
125 K4 **Tiszabura** Hungary
125 K3 **Tiszadob** Hungary
125 K4 **Tiszakécske** Hungary
125 K3 **Tiszalök** Hungary
132 B2 **Tiszaörs** Hungary
132 B2 **Tiszasas** Hungary
155 H4 **Tit** Algeria
181 H3 **Titabar** Assam India
58 I1 **Titan Dome** *mountain* Antarctica
158 D2 **Titao** Burkina Faso
139 F4 **Titchfield** Hampshire England UK
132 B3 **Titel** Serbia
132 D3 **Titeşti** Romania
104 D4 **Titicaca, Lago** *lake* Peru
220 2 **Titikaveka** Cook Islands New Zealand
187 F7 **Tititea (Mount Aspiring)** New Zealand
187 F7 **Titlagarh** Orissa India
138 E2 **Titley** Herefordshire England UK
133 B5 **Titov Vrv** *mountain* Macedonia
120 F5 **Titran** Norway
82 I5 **Tittabawassee** *watercourse* Michigan USA
127 J2 **Titting** Germany
160 D3 **Titule** Democratic Republic of Congo
179 I3 **Titūn** Iran
87 K6 **Titusville** Florida USA
83 L6 **Titusville** Pennsylvania USA
142 B2 **Tiumpan Head** *cape* Scotland UK
196 E4 **Tiung, Tanjung** *island* Indonesia
161 F4 **Tiva** *watercourse* Kenya
154 C6 **Tivaouane** Senegal
131 H5 **Tivat** Montenegro
122 H3 **Tived** Sweden
138 E1 **Tiverton** Cheshire England UK
138 D4 **Tiverton** Devon England UK
109 10a **Tivoli** Grenada
131 E6 **Tivoli** Italy
160 C1 **Tiwal** *watercourse* Sudan
195 I4 **Tiwi** Philippines
198 B5 **Tiworo, Selat** *strait* Indonesia
139 E2 **Tixall** Staffordshire England UK
198 E5 **Tiyo, Pegunungan** *range* Indonesia
179 H4 **Tizaj** Iran
88 E4 **Tizapán el Alto** Mexico
155 G1 **Tizi Ouzou** Algeria
89 H4 **Tizimín** Mexico
184 F5 **Tiznap He** *watercourse* Xinjiang Uygur Zizhiqu China
154 E3 **Tiznit** Morocco
101 G3 **Tjakkatjakka Ston** Suriname
120 K3 **Tjaktjajaure** *lake* Sweden
120 J3 **Tjålmejaure** *lake* Sweden
120 K3 **Tjåmotis** Sweden
120 K3 **Tjåmotisjaure** *bay* Sweden
120 J5 **Tjärn** Sweden
120 K3 **Tjäura** Sweden
120 J3 **Tjeggelvas** *bay* Sweden
120 J2 **Tjeldøya** *island* Norway
120 E5 **Tjelle** Norway
130 H5 **Tjentište** Bosnia and Herzegovina
124 C1 **Tjeukemeer** *lake* Netherlands
120 J3 **Tjidtjak** *range* Sweden
123 J3 **Tjockö** *island* Sweden
122 F3 **Tjörn** *island* Sweden
122 G5 **Tjörnarp** Sweden
120 H4 **Tjøtta** Norway
217 I3 **Tjukayirla Roadhouse** WA Australia
120 J4 **Tjulträsk** Sweden
122 H4 **Tjurken** *lake* Sweden
122 F4 **Tjuvkil** Sweden
123 N2 **Tjuvö** Finland
181 G4 **Tlabung** Mizoram India
88 E3 **Tlahualilo de Zaragoza** Mexico
88 E4 **Tlajomulco de Zúñiga** Mexico
88 E5 **Tlalchapa** Mexico
89 F5 **Tlalnepantla** Mexico
89 F5 **Tlanalapan** Mexico
89 F4 **Tlanchinol** Mexico
89 F5 **Tlapa de Comonfort** Mexico
88 E4 **Tlaquepaque** Mexico
88 E4 **Tlatenango de Sánchez Román** Mexico
89 F5 **Tlaxcala** Mexico
89 F5 **Tlaxcala** *admin. area* Mexico
155 F2 **Tlemcen** Algeria
129 J6 **Tletz** Algeria
129 J6 **Tlidjen** Algeria
125 J3 **Tlmače** Slovakia
125 K1 **Tłuszcz** Poland
155 J3 **Tmassah** Libya
193 H4 **To-shima** *island* Japan
196 D3 **Toa Payoh** *admin. area* Singapore
142 inset **Toab** Shetland Scotland UK
74 H3 **Toad** *watercourse* British Columbia Canada
74 I3 **Toad River** British Columbia Canada
163 I3 **Toamasina** Madagascar
163 I3 **Toamasina** *admin. area* Madagascar
181 H2 **Toba** Xizang Zizhiqu China
193 H4 **Toba** Japan
179 K4 **Toba** Pakistan
196 C3 **Toba, Danau** *lake* Indonesia
87 K2 **Tobaccoville** North Carolina USA
109 9 **Tobago** *admin. area* Trinidad and Tobago
109 9 **Tobago** *island* Trinidad and Tobago
198 D4 **Tobalai** *island* Indonesia
128 F4 **Tobarra** Spain
192 G5 **Tobe** Japan
101 F2 **Tobe Jube, Bahía** *bay* Venezuela
101 F2 **Tobejuba, Punta** *cape* Venezuela
140 B3 **Tober** Ireland
143 D2 **Tobercurry** Ireland
143 D3 **Toberdan** Ireland
214 D7 **Tobermorey** NT Australia
142 B4 **Tobermory** Highland Scotland UK
142 C4 **Toberonochy** Argyll and Bute Scotland UK
140 B4 **Toberpatrick** Ireland
198 D3 **Tobi** *island* Palau
81 Q6 **Tobias** Nebraska USA
103 E5 **Tobias Barreto** Brazil
213 H6 **Tobin Lake** WA Australia
75 T6 **Tobin Lake** Saskatchewan Canada
75 T6 **Tobin Lake** Saskatchewan Canada
196 E4 **Toboali** Indonesia
158 B3 **Tobokani Point** *cape* Liberia
182 I3 **Tobol** *watercourse* Kazakhstan
182 I2 **Tobol** *watercourse* Russian Federation
183 J1 **Tobol'sk** Russian Federation
158 E2 **Tobré** Benin
134 L5 **Tobseda** Russian Federation
142 B2 **Tobson** Na h-Eileanan Siar Scotland UK
122 G3 **Tobyn** Sweden
104 B3 **Tocache Nuevo** Peru
104 E4 **Tocahuara** Bolivia
100 C3 **Tocaima** Colombia
102 C4 **Tocantinópolis** Brazil
102 B5 **Tocantins** *admin. area* Brazil
102 B5 **Tocantins** *watercourse* Brazil
87 J3 **Toccoa** Georgia USA
130 C3 **Toce** *watercourse* Italy
132 F2 **Tochylove** Ukraine
138 E3 **Tockington** South Gloucestershire England UK
122 F3 **Töcksfors** Sweden
109 9 **Toco** Trinidad and Tobago
90 C4 **Tocoa** Honduras
101 F4 **Tocobiren, Serra** *range* Brazil
106 D2 **Toconce** Chile
106 D2 **Tocopilla** Chile
106 E2 **Tocorpuri, Cerros de** *mountain* Chile
218 G6 **Tocumwal** NSW Australia
100 D2 **Tocuyo, Rio** *watercourse* Venezuela
122 E1 **Todalen** Norway
120 F5 **Todalsfjellet** *island* Norway
214 C7 **Todd** *watercourse* NT Australia
139 F3 **Toddington** Gloucestershire England UK
198 C4 **Todeli** Indonesia
139 F2 **Todenham** Gloucestershire England UK
140 F2 **Todhills** Cumbria England UK
142 D4 **Todholes** Stirling Scotland UK
132 E2 **Todireşti** Romania
218 B2 **Todmorden** SA Australia
141 F3 **Todmorden** West Yorkshire England UK
103 E6 **Todos os Santos, Bahia de** *bay* Brazil
105 E3 **Todos Santos** Bolivia
88 C4 **Todos Santos** Mexico
183 Q3 **Todzha** *lake* Russian Federation
143 C5 **Toe Head** *cape* Ireland
142 A3 **Toe Head** *cape* Scotland UK
75 O6 **Tofield** Alberta Canada
80 C2 **Tofino** British Columbia Canada
139 G2 **Toft** Cambridgeshire England UK
142 inset **Toft** Shetland Scotland UK
122 H2 **Toftan** *lake* Sweden
122 H2 **Toftbyn** Sweden
82 F3 **Tofte** Minnesota USA
122 H3 **Toften** *lake* Sweden
122 E5 **Tofterup** Denmark
122 E5 **Toftlund** Denmark
223 10 **Tofua** *island* Tonga
161 G2 **Tog Wajaale** Ethiopia
222 7 **Toga** *island* Vanuatu
161 H2 **Togdheer** *admin. area* Somalia
161 H1 **Togga Miriye** *watercourse* Somalia
219 I6 **Togganoggera** NSW Australia
140 B3 **Togher** Ireland
72 C7 **Togiak** Alaska USA
198 B4 **Togian** *island* Indonesia
198 B4 **Togian, Kepulauan** *islands* Indonesia
130 E2 **Töging** Germany
156 F4 **Tognuf** Eritrea
158 E3 **Togo** *country* Africa
199 G6 **Togo** Papua New Guinea
158 C3 **Togobala** Guinea
185 H5 **Tograsay He** *watercourse* Xinjiang Uygur Zizhiqu China
183 N2 **Toguchin** Russian Federation
Toguz *see* **Togyz** Kazakhstan
182 H4 **Togyz** Kazakhstan
186 D5 **Tohana** Haryana India
223 14a **Tohiea** *volcano* French Polynesia
136 H5 **Tohil** Turkey
121 Q5 **Tohmajärvi** Finland
123 P1 **Tohmajärvi** *lake* Finland
121 N5 **Toholampi** Finland
87 K6 **Tohopekaliga Lake** Florida USA
123 M3 **Tohvri** Estonia
220 4 **Toi** Niue New Zealand
123 L2 **Toijala** Finland
198 B4 **Toili** Indonesia
130 C4 **Toirano** Italy
121 M5 **Toisvesi** *lake* Finland
121 O5 **Toivakka** Finland
121 O5 **Toivala** Finland
84 D1 **Toiyabe Range** Nevada USA
133 B5 **Tojaci** Macedonia
198 B4 **Tojo** Indonesia
104 D4 **Tojuyo** Peru
104 C4 **Tojyanca** Peru
72 E6 **Tok** Alaska USA
101 G4 **Toka Village** Guyana
220 F4 **Tokaanu** New Zealand
193 I2 **Tokachi-dake** *volcano* Japan
193 H4 **Tokamachi** Japan
156 F4 **Tokar** Sudan
182 D3 **Tokarevka** Russian Federation
130 H2 **Tokarnia** Poland
189 J3 **Tokashiki-shima** *island* Japan
136 F5 **Tokat** Turkey
136 F5 **Tokat** *admin. area* Turkey
192 E3 **Tŏkch'ŏn** North Korea
220 3 **Tokelau** *NZ territory* Pacific Ocean
125 K3 **Toki** Poland
136 E3 **Tokmak** Ukraine
183 L5 **Tokmok** Kazakhstan
132 A2 **Tokod** Hungary
220 F5 **Tokomaru** New Zealand
220 H4 **Tokomaru Bay** New Zealand
220 F4 **Tokoroa** New Zealand
158 C3 **Tokounou** Guinea
121 Q5 **Tokrajärvi** Finland
121 U5 **Toksha-Kuznetsova** Russian Federation
72 C6 **Toksook Bay** Alaska USA
123 P2 **Toksovo** Russian Federation
183 N4 **Tokty** Kazakhstan
223 10 **Toku Island** Tonga
133 F6 **Tokul** Turkey
189 J3 **Tokuno-jima** *mountain* Japan
192 G4 **Tokushima** Japan
193 H4 **Tōkyō** Japan
222 6a **Tol** *island* Federated States of Micronesia
220 H4 **Tolaga Bay** New Zealand
163 I5 **Tôlanaro** Madagascar
86 C4 **Tolar** Texas USA
106 E3 **Tolar, Cerro** *mountain* Argentina
142 B2 **Tolastaidh** Na h-Eileanan Siar Scotland UK
185 I3 **Tolbo** Mongolia
185 I3 **Tolbo Nuur** *lake* Mongolia
58 T1 **Tolchin, Mount** *mountain* Antarctica
103 A9 **Toledo** Brazil
106 D3 **Toledo** Chile
128 D4 **Toledo** Spain
82 G7 **Toledo** Illinois USA
82 J6 **Toledo** Ohio USA
80 D4 **Toledo** Oregon USA
128 E4 **Toledo, Montes de** *range* Spain
86 E5 **Toledo Bend Reservoir** Louisiana USA
195 I5 **Toledo City** Philippines
127 K5 **Tolentino** Italy
129 I6 **Tolga** Algeria
120 G5 **Tolga** Norway
163 H4 **Toliara** Madagascar
163 H4 **Toliara** *admin. area* Madagascar
198 B3 **Tolitoli, Teluk** *bay* Indonesia
122 G4 **Tolken** *lake* Sweden
123 J5 **Tolkmicko** Poland
123 K5 **Tolko** Poland
141 G3 **Toll Bar** South Yorkshire England UK
142 G3 **Toll of Birness** Aberdeenshire Scotland UK
139 E4 **Tollard Royal** Wiltshire England UK
124 G1 **Tollense** *watercourse* Germany
141 G2 **Tollerton** North Yorkshire England UK
142 B3 **Tolmachan** Na h-Eileanan Siar Scotland UK
123 O3 **Tolmachevo** Russian Federation
132 A2 **Tolna** Hungary
125 J4 **Tolna** *admin. area* Hungary
81 P3 **Tolna** North Dakota USA
198 B4 **Tolo, Teluk** *bay* Indonesia
199 H5 **Tolokiwa Island** Papua New Guinea
121 N3 **Tolonen** Finland
198 D3 **Tolonuu** *island* Indonesia
128 E2 **Tolosa** Spain
121 Q5 **Tolosenmäki** Finland
139 E4 **Tolpuddle** Dorset England UK
192 E4 **Tolsan-do** *island* South Korea
191 J5 **Tolshan Dao** *island* Liaoning China
142 B2 **Tolsta Head** *cape* Scotland UK
135 AG7 **Tolstoy, Mys** *cape* Russian Federation
100 C2 **Tolú** Colombia
89 F5 **Toluca** Mexico
121 P3 **Tolva** Finland
142 E3 **Tolvah** Highland Scotland UK
121 Q3 **Tolvand, Ozero** *lake* Russian Federation
121 S5 **Tolvuya** Russian Federation
182 F2 **Tol'yatti** Russian Federation
183 O2 **Tom** *watercourse* Russian Federation
220 E2 **Tom Bowling Bay** New Zealand
212 D7 **Tom Price** WA Australia
212 D7 **Tom Price, Mount** WA Australia
72 E6 **Tom White, Mount** Alaska USA
158 D2 **Toma** Burkina Faso
75 N6 **Tomahawk** Alberta Canada
82 G4 **Tomahawk** Wisconsin USA
132 F2 **Tomai** Moldova
193 I2 **Tomakomai** Japan
80 D7 **Tomales Bay** California USA
197 G2 **Tomani** Malaysia
223 9 **Tomanivi** *mountain* Fiji
128 B4 **Tomar** Portugal
193 I1 **Tomari** Russian Federation
104 E5 **Tomás Barrón** Bolivia
107 G4 **Tomás Gomensoro** Uruguay
132 F1 **Tomashpil'** Ukraine
125 L2 **Tomaszów Lubelski** Poland
125 K2 **Tomaszów Mazowiecki** Poland
142 E3 **Tomatin** Highland Scotland UK
88 D5 **Tomatlán** Mexico
105 G4 **Tombador, Serra do** *range* Brazil
86 D5 **Tomball** Texas USA
222 8 **Tombe** Solomon Islands
127 J5 **Tombe, Punta le** *cape* Italy
86 G4 **Tombigbee** *watercourse* Alabama USA

86 G3 **Tombigbee** *watercourse* Mississippi USA
160 A5 **Tomboco** Angola
154 F5 **Tombouctou (Timbuktu)** Mali
84 G5 **Tombstone** Arizona USA
162 B3 **Tombua** Angola
142 E4 **Tomchulan** Perth and Kinross Scotland UK
142 E3 **Tomdow** Moray Scotland UK
193 I3 **Tome** Japan
163 F4 **Tome** Mozambique
102 B3 **Tomé Açu** Brazil
198 B5 **Tomea** *island* Indonesia
130 G4 **Tomina** Bosnia and Herzegovina
158 B2 **Tominé** *watercourse* Guinea
219 I5 **Tomingley** NSW Australia
198 B4 **Tomini, Teluk** *bay* Indonesia
154 F6 **Tominian** Mali
128 B3 **Tomiño** Spain
142 E3 **Tomintoul** Moray Scotland UK
217 K3 **Tomkinson Ranges** SA Australia
120 H3 **Tomma** *island* Norway
142 F3 **Tomnaven** Moray Scotland UK
100 D3 **Tomo** *watercourse* Colombia
85 I6 **Tomochic** Mexico
160 B3 **Tomori** Central African Republic
133 B5 **Tomorit, Maja e** *mountain* Albania
222 1 **Tömotu Noi** *island* Solomon Islands
135 W7 **Tompa** Russian Federation
198 B4 **Tompira** Indonesia
75 Q7 **Tompkins** Saskatchewan Canada
198 A4 **Tompo** Indonesia
84 C2 **Toms Place** California USA
213 K4 **Toms Rock** *mountain* NT Australia
183 N2 **Tomsk** Russian Federation
134 R7 **Tomskaya Oblast'** *admin. area* Russian Federation
138 C2 **Ton-fanau** Gwynedd Wales UK
129 H3 **Tona** Spain
88 D3 **Tónachic** Mexico
89 G5 **Tonalá** Mexico
100 E5 **Tonantins** Brazil
131 C6 **Tonara** Sardinia Italy
80 F2 **Tonasket** Washington USA
83 L5 **Tonawanda** New York USA
100 B4 **Tonchigüe** Ecuador
128 B3 **Tondela** Portugal
154 D6 **Tondidji** Mali
138 D3 **Tondu** Bridgend Wales UK
140 B1 **Tonduff** Moyle Northern Ireland UK
216 E7 **Tone** *watercourse* WA Australia
138 E3 **Tone** *watercourse* England UK
58 Q1 **Toney Mountain** *mountain* Antarctica
199 H4 **Tong Island** Papua New Guinea
223 10 **Tonga** *country* Oceania
160 E2 **Tonga** Sudan
52 O9 **Tonga Trench** *underwater feature* Pacific Ocean
163 F5 **Tongaat** South Africa
223 10a **Tongamama'o** Tonga
220 F4 **Tongaporutu** New Zealand
Tongareva *see* **Penrhyn** Cook Islands New Zealand
222 7 **Tongariki** *island* Vanuatu
220 F4 **Tongariro, Mount** *volcano* New Zealand
223 10a **Tongatapu** *island* Tonga
223 10 **Tongatapu Group** *islands* Tonga
189 G2 **Tongbai** Henan China
189 G2 **Tongcheng** Anhui China
Tongchuan *see* **Santai** China
188 F1 **Tongchuan** Shaanxi China
192 E4 **Tongduch'ŏn** South Korea
127 G1 **Tongeren** Belgium
189 G4 **Tonggu Zhang** *mountain* Guangdong China
192 F4 **Tonghae** South Korea
189 G3 **Tonghai** Jiangxi China
191 K3 **Tonghe** Heilongjiang China
191 K4 **Tonghua** Jilin China
191 L3 **Tongjiang** Heilongjiang China
192 E3 **Tongjoson-man** *bay* North Korea
Tongking, Gulf of *see* **Tonkin, Gulf of** China/Vietnam
188 E4 **Tongle** Guangxi Zhuangzu Zizhiqu China
191 J4 **Tongliao** Nei Mongol Zizhiqu China
189 H2 **Tongling** Anhui China
189 H2 **Tonglu** Zhejiang China
218 F4 **Tongo** NSW Australia
222 7 **Tongoa** *island* Vanuatu
108 A3 **Tongoi, Bahía** *bay* Chile
158 D2 **Tongomayél** Burkina Faso
106 D4 **Tongoy** Chile
195 I6 **Tongquil** *island* Philippines
188 F3 **Tongren** Guizhou China
188 F5 **TongShi** Hainan China
185 J6 **Tongtian He** *lake* Qinghai China
185 J6 **Tongtian He** *watercourse* Qinghai China
181 H2 **Tongtian He** *watercourse* Sichuan China
142 D2 **Tongue** Highland Scotland UK
81 L4 **Tongue** *watercourse* Montana USA
158 B2 **Tongué** Guinea
142 D2 **Tongue Bay** Scotland UK
90 E1 **Tongue of the Ocean** *strait* Bahamas
81 L4 **Tongue River Reservoir** Montana USA
190 F6 **Tongxin** Ningxia Huizu Zizhiqu China
189 G1 **Tongxu** Henan China
192 F4 **T'ongyŏng** South Korea
191 J4 **Tongyu** Jilin China
191 H5 **Tongzhou** Beijing China
189 I2 **Tongzhou** Jiangsu China
188 D3 **Tongzilin** Sichuan China
185 J3 **Tonhul** Mongolia
100 E4 **Tonina** Venezuela
160 D2 **Tonj** Sudan
186 D5 **Tonk** Rajasthan India
81 Q8 **Tonkawa** Oklahoma USA
81 N1 **Tonkin** Saskatchewan Canada
194 F2 **Tonkin, Gulf of** Vietnam
214 G7 **Tonkoro** Qld Australia
194 E4 **Tônlé Sap** *lake* Cambodia
126 D4 **Tonnay-Boutonne** France
126 D4 **Tonnay-Charente** France
126 E4 **Tonneins** France
82 G2 **Tonnere, Pointe au** *cape* Ontario Canada
126 F3 **Tonnerre** France
120 H3 **Tonnes** Norway
193 I3 **Tōno** Japan
222 6a **Tonoas** *island* Federated States of Micronesia
106 F2 **Tonono** Argentina
84 F4 **Tonopah** Arizona USA
84 D1 **Tonopah** Nevada USA
90 D6 **Tonosí** Panama
162 E4 **Tonota** Botswana
122 F3 **Tønsberg** Norway
215 I5 **Toobanna** Qld Australia
219 I3 **Toobeah** Qld Australia
158 C3 **Toobli** Liberia
218 G7 **Tooborac** Vic. Australia
216 E5 **Toodyay** WA Australia
219 K2 **Toogoolawah** Qld Australia
214 F7 **Toolebuc** Qld Australia
218 F6 **Tooleybuc** NSW Australia
218 B5 **Tooligie** SA Australia
217 I6 **Toolinna Cove** WA Australia
218 E7 **Toolondo** Vic. Australia
219 I4 **Tooloon** NSW Australia
143 D3 **Toomard** Ireland
218 G3 **Toomaroo, Lake** Qld Australia
143 C3 **Toombeola** Ireland
140 B2 **Toome** Antrim Northern Ireland UK
218 G2 **Toompine** Qld Australia
87 J4 **Toomsboro** Georgia USA
143 D4 **Toomyvara** Tipperary Ireland
219 I5 **Toongi** NSW Australia
223 14b **Toopua, Motu** *island* French Polynesia
143 B5 **Toor** Ireland
140 B1 **Toor** Ballymoney Northern Ireland UK
143 C4 **Toorboney** Ireland
143 C3 **Tooreen** Ireland
143 C3 **Tooreengarve** Ireland
219 J2 **Toowoomba** Qld Australia
214 A4 **Top Springs** NT Australia
132 F3 **Topalu** Romania
84 F1 **Topaz Slough** *lake* Utah USA
183 N3 **Topchikha** Russian Federation
141 G2 **Topcliffe** North Yorkshire England UK
82 D7 **Topeka** Kansas USA
183 O2 **Topki** Russian Federation
74 H5 **Topley** British Columbia Canada
132 C4 **Topli Do** Serbia
132 D2 **Toplița** Romania
164 1b **Topo** Azores
84 E3 **Topock** Arizona USA
104 D5 **Topohoco** Bolivia
132 B3 **Topola** Serbia
130 H2 **Topol'čany** Slovakia
132 E4 **Topolchane** Bulgaria
135 AC6 **Topolinyy** Russian Federation
88 C3 **Topolobampo** Mexico
132 B3 **Topolovățu Mare** Romania
133 E4 **Topolovgrad** Bulgaria
133 D5 **Topolovo** Bulgaria
132 D3 **Toporu** Romania
121 Q4 **Topozero** Russian Federation
121 R4 **Topozero, Ozero** *lake* Russian Federation
83 R4 **Topsfield** Maine USA
138 D4 **Tor Bay** England UK
131 G7 **Torano Castello** Italy
101 H3 **Torarica Meer** *lake* Suriname
120 M3 **Torasjärvi** Sweden
142 B4 **Torastan** Highland Scotland UK
104 D5 **Torata** Peru
142 E3 **Torbain** Moray Scotland UK
133 E6 **Torbalı** Turkey
219 K1 **Torbanlea** Qld Australia
179 I2 **Torbat-e Ḩeydarīyeh** Iran
179 I2 **Torbat-e Jām** Iran
138 D4 **Torbay** *admin. area* England UK
138 D4 **Torbryan** Devon England UK
75 T6 **Torch** *watercourse* Saskatchewan Canada
125 M2 **Torchyn** Ukraine
139 I5 **Torcy-le-Grand** France
132 B3 **Torda** Serbia
128 D3 **Tordesillas** Spain
125 J5 **Tordinci** Croatia
121 M4 **Töre** Sweden
142 D3 **Tore** Highland Scotland UK
129 H2 **Torelló** Spain
198 B4 **Toreo** Indonesia
138 D3 **Torfaen** *admin. area* Wales UK
122 D2 **Torfinnsvatnet** *lake* Norway
124 G2 **Torgau** Germany
185 K2 **Torgon Nuur** *lake* Mongolia
122 H4 **Torhamn** Sweden
122 I4 **Torhamns Udde** *cape* Sweden
189 J3 **Tori-shima** *island* Japan
100 B4 **Toribío** Colombia
128 E3 **Torija** Spain
215 K7 **Torilla Peninsula** Qld Australia
124 D5 **Torino** Italy
105 H5 **Toriparu** Brazil
161 E3 **Torit** Sudan
102 E5 **Toritama** Brazil
103 A7 **Torixoreu** Brazil
123 N3 **Torma** Estonia
121 Q5 **Törmälä** Finland
121 O2 **Törmänen** Finland
121 N4 **Törmäperä** Finland
121 N3 **Törmäsjärvi** *lake* Finland
213 G4 **Torment, Point** WA Australia
128 D3 **Tormes** *watercourse* Spain
122 H4 **Törn** *lake* Sweden
80 H2 **Tornado Mountain** British Columbia Canada
125 K3 **Tornaľa** Slovakia
128 D3 **Tornavacas** Spain
142 F3 **Tornaveen** Aberdeenshire Scotland UK
120 L3 **Torneälven** *watercourse* Sweden
120 K2 **Torneträsk** *bay* Sweden
78 F3 **Torngat Mountains** Newfoundland and Labrador/Quebec Canada
121 N4 **Tornio** Finland
132 A3 **Tornjoš** Serbia
106 F6 **Tornquist** Argentina
100 B3 **Toro** Colombia
128 D3 **Toro** Spain
122 I3 **Torö** *island* Sweden
160 E3 **Toro** Uganda
106 D4 **Toro, Cerro del** *mountain* Argentina
100 D3 **Toro Pintado** Venezuela
155 G6 **Torodi** Niger
135 AC8 **Torom** Russian Federation
108 C3 **Torongeñeu, Sierra de** *range* Argentina
83 L5 **Toronto** Ontario Canada
86 D2 **Toronto** Kansas USA
86 D2 **Toronto Lake** Kansas USA
125 I4 **Torony** Hungary
123 P4 **Toropets** Russian Federation
161 E3 **Tororo** Uganda
104 C4 **Tororume** Peru
136 E6 **Toros Daglan** Turkey
105 E5 **Torotoro** Bolivia
122 G4 **Torpa** Sweden
122 I3 **Torpfjön** *bay* Sweden
142 F3 **Torphins** Aberdeenshire Scotland UK
138 C4 **Torpoint** Cornwall England UK
120 J5 **Torpshammar** Sweden
107 H4 **Torquato Severo** Brazil
218 G8 **Torquay** Vic. Australia
75 T8 **Torquay** Saskatchewan Canada
138 D4 **Torquay** Torbay England UK
142 B3 **Torran** Highland Scotland UK
84 C4 **Torrance** California USA
85 J3 **Torrance** New Mexico USA
128 B4 **Torrão** Portugal
128 D4 **Torre de Abraham, Embalse de la** *lake* Spain
128 D5 **Torre del Águila, Embalse de la** *lake* Spain
124 D5 **Torre Pellice** Italy
128 D4 **Torrecampo** Spain
128 E2 **Torrecilla en Cameros** Spain
105 E5 **Torrecillas** Bolivia
128 E5 **Torredonjimeno** Spain
128 C4 **Torrejón el Rubio** Spain
128 E3 **Torrelaguna** Spain
130 D5 **Torrenieri** Italy
218 C4 **Torrens, Lake** SA Australia
215 H6 **Torrens Creek** Qld Australia
88 E3 **Torreón** Mexico
128 C4 **Torreorgaz** Spain
107 I4 **Torres** Brazil
128 D2 **Torres, Cabo** *cape* Spain
222 7 **Torres Islands** *island* Vanuatu
128 B4 **Torres Novas** Portugal
199 G6 **Torres Strait** Australia
128 B4 **Torres Vedras** Portugal
80 J7 **Torrey** Utah USA
120 I5 **Torrflonäs** Sweden
199 G4 **Torricelli Mountains** *range* Papua New Guinea
138 C4 **Torridge** *watercourse* England UK
142 C3 **Torridon** Highland Scotland UK
128 D4 **Torrijos** Spain
142 B3 **Torrin** Highland Scotland UK
122 H1 **Torringen** *lake* Sweden
75 O7 **Torrington** Alberta Canada
81 M5 **Torrington** Wyoming USA
120 L3 **Torrivaara** Sweden
120 H5 **Torrön** *bay* Sweden
122 H3 **Torrvarpen** *lake* Sweden
123 O2 **Torsa** *lake* Finland
120 H5 **Torsborg** Sweden
73 S6 **Tórshavn** Faroe Islands
120 J2 **Torsken** Norway
120 M5 **Torsön** *island* Finland
120 K1 **Torsvåg** Norway
120 E5 **Torsvatnet** *lake* Norway
132 A2 **Törtel** Hungary
84 G4 **Tortilla Flat** Arizona USA
183 L3 **Tortkuduk** Kazakhstan
109 21 **Tortola** *island* British Virgin Islands
121 M3 **Tortola** Finland
101 F2 **Tortola, Isla** *island* Venezuela
128 D3 **Tórtoles de Esgueva** Spain
131 C7 **Tortolì** Sardinia Italy
124 E5 **Tortona** Italy
129 G3 **Tortosa** Spain
129 G3 **Tortosa, Cap de** *cape* Spain
91 F2 **Tortue, Île de la** *island* Haiti
101 H3 **Tortue, Monts** *range* French Guiana
109 4 **Tortuga, Isla** *island* Archipiélago de Colón (Galapagos Islands)
84 G7 **Tortuga, Isla** *island* Mexico
101 E2 **Tortuga, Isla La** *island* Venezuela
100 B4 **Tortugas, Golfo** *bay* Colombia
198 D4 **Torubi** *island* Indonesia
198 B4 **Torue** Indonesia
132 C1 **Torun'** Ukraine
125 J1 **Toruń** Poland
122 G4 **Torup** Sweden
140 E2 **Torver** Cumbria England UK
120 E5 **Torvik** Norway
120 E5 **Torvikbukt** Norway
121 O3 **Torvinen** Finland
215 G4 **Torwood** Qld Australia
143 D1 **Tory Island** Ireland
100 A5 **Tosagua** Ecuador
192 E3 **T'osan** North Korea
120 H4 **Tosbotn** Norway
162 D5 **Tosca** South Africa
88 C3 **Tosca, Punta** *cape* Mexico
142 C3 **Toscaig** Highland Scotland UK
130 D5 **Toscana** *admin. area* Italy
131 D5 **Toscano, Arcipelago** *islands* Italy
120 H4 **Tosenfjorden** *bay* Norway
183 J6 **Toshkent** *admin. area* Uzbekistan
183 K5 **Toshkent (Tashkent)** Uzbekistan
123 P3 **Tosno** Russian Federation
185 J5 **Toson Hu** *lake* Qinghai China
120 H5 **Tossåsen** Sweden
122 G3 **Tösse** Sweden
143 F2 **Tossy** Ireland
106 F4 **Tostado** Argentina
219 I7 **Tostaree** Vic. Australia
139 H2 **Tostock** Suffolk England UK
135 X4 **Tostuya** Russian Federation
132 B2 **Tószeg** Hungary
100 C3 **Tota, Laguna de** *lake* Colombia
122 D3 **Totak** *lake* Norway
187 E10 **Totapola** *mountain* Sri Lanka
221 E5 **Totaranui** New Zealand
142 D2 **Totegan** Highland Scotland UK
162 D4 **Toteng** Botswana
139 I5 **Tôtes** France
222 6a **Totiw** *island* Federated States of Micronesia
132 B2 **Tótkomlós** Hungary
139 F4 **Totland** Isle of Wight England UK
138 D4 **Totnes** Devon England UK
101 G3 **Totness** Suriname
76 K6 **Totogan Lake** Ontario Canada
90 B4 **Totonicapán** Guatemala
104 D5 **Totora** Bolivia
106 E4 **Totoralejos** Argentina
100 B4 **Totoró** Colombia
158 C3 **Totota** Liberia
223 9 **Totoya** *island* Fiji
182 F3 **Totskoye** Russian Federation
120 G4 **Tøttdal** Norway
219 H5 **Tottenham** NSW Australia
139 G3 **Tottenham** Greater London England UK
218 F7 **Tottington** Vic. Australia
139 H2 **Tottington** Norfolk England UK
139 F4 **Totton** Hampshire England UK
192 G4 **Tottori** Japan
154 D4 **Touajil** Mauritania
158 C3 **Touba** Côte d'Ivoire
154 C6 **Touba** Senegal
154 D6 **Toubéré Bafal** Senegal
154 E2 **Toubkal, Jbel** *mountain* Morocco
159 H3 **Touboro** Cameroon
126 F3 **Toucy** France
129 J6 **Touffana** Algeria
158 D2 **Tougan** Burkina Faso
158 D2 **Tougouri** Burkina Faso
222 7 **Touho** New Caledonia
154 D5 **Touil** Mauritania
155 G2 **Touil, Oued** *watercourse* Algeria
154 E6 **Toukoto** Mali
158 E2 **Toukountouna** Benin
127 G2 **Toul** France
158 C3 **Toulépleu** Côte d'Ivoire
189 H4 **Touliu** Taiwan China
79 E7 **Toulnustouc** *watercourse* Quebec Canada
127 G5 **Toulon** France
124 C4 **Toulon-sur-Arroux** France
126 E5 **Toulouse** France
155 I4 **Toummo** Libya
158 C3 **Toumodi** Côte d'Ivoire
181 H5 **Toungoo** Myanmar
126 E2 **Touques** *watercourse* France
158 C3 **Toura, Monts** *range* Côte d'Ivoire
128 B2 **Toural** Spain
155 J6 **Tourba** Chad
126 F1 **Tourcoing** France
128 B2 **Touriñán, Cabo** *cape* Spain
139 F5 **Tourlaville** France
126 F1 **Tournai** Belgium
124 B3 **Tournan** France
126 E5 **Tournay** France
127 G4 **Tournon-sur-Rhône** France
124 C4 **Tournus** France
102 F4 **Touros** Brazil
159 G3 **Touroua** Cameroon
126 E2 **Tourouvre** France
126 E3 **Tours** France
129 I2 **Tourves** France
126 E2 **Toury** France
129 F4 **Tous, Embalse de** *lake* Spain
155 J4 **Toussidе, Pic** *mountain* Chad
211 inset **Toutcher, Cape** Macquarie Island Australia
75 V7 **Toutes Aides** Manitoba Canada
162 D6 **Touwsrivier** South Africa
124 G2 **Toužim** Czech Republic
190 F3 **Tov** *admin. area* Mongolia
122 E3 **Tovdalselv** *watercourse* Norway
108 D3 **Tovita, Isla** *island* Argentina
132 D1 **Tovste** Ukraine
141 G2 **Tow Law** Durham England UK
193 I3 **Towada-ko** *lake* Japan
219 K4 **Towallum** NSW Australia
198 B5 **Towari** Indonesia
139 G2 **Towcester** Northamptonshire England UK
74 I6 **Towdystan** British Columbia Canada
140 A4 **Tower Bridge** Ireland
218 F8 **Tower Hill** Vic. Australia
215 H6 **Towerhill** *watercourse* Qld Australia
85 K1 **Towner** Colorado USA
81 O2 **Towner** North Dakota USA
214 C3 **Towns** *watercourse* NT Australia
80 J3 **Townsend** Montana USA
216 F3 **Townsend, Mount** WA Australia
76 H1 **Townsend Lake** Nunavut Canada
108 B6 **Townshend, Punta** *cape* Chile
215 I5 **Townsville** Qld Australia
198 B4 **Towori, Teluk** *bay* Indonesia
179 K3 **Towrzi** Afghanistan
138 C2 **Towyn** Ceredigion Wales UK
193 I2 **Tōya-ko** *lake* Japan
88 C3 **Toyachic** Mexico
85 K5 **Toyah** Texas USA
193 H4 **Toyama** Japan
125 M2 **Toykut** Ukraine
193 H4 **Toyokawa** Japan
192 G4 **Toyooka** Japan
121 M5 **Töysä** Finland
184 G6 **Toze Kangri** *mountain* Xizang Zizhiqu China
155 H2 **Tozeur** Tunisia
178 E2 **Tozkhurmato** Iraq
182 D5 **Tqvarch'eli** Georgia
194 E2 **Trà Lĩnh** Vietnam
194 E5 **Trà Vinh** Vietnam
128 C3 **Trabazos** Spain
178 C2 **Trâblous (Tripoli)** Lebanon
123 M5 **Traby** Belarus
136 F5 **Trabzon** Turkey
136 F5 **Trabzon** *admin. area* Turkey
79 F9 **Tracadie-Sheila** New Brunswick Canada
104 D2 **Tracoá** Brazil
81 R4 **Tracy** Minnesota USA
124 E5 **Tradate** Italy
57 G2 **Traena Bank** *underwater feature* Norwegian Sea
120 H3 **Trænfjorden** *bay* Norway
82 E5 **Traer** Iowa USA
131 C6 **Traessu, Monte** *mountain* Sardinia Italy
79 G10 **Trafalgar** Nova Scotia Canada
128 C5 **Trafalgar, Cabo de** *cape* Spain
213 H3 **Trafalgar, Mount** WA Australia
141 F3 **Trafford** *admin. area* England UK
87 K7 **Trafford, Lake** Florida USA
108 B2 **Traful, Lago** *lake* Argentina
128 F3 **Tragacete** Spain
132 E2 **Traian** Romania
108 B3 **Traiguén** Chile
74 M8 **Trail** British Columbia Canada
73 Q4 **Traill Øer** *island* Greenland
213 I4 **Traine** *watercourse* WA Australia
102 E5 **Traipu** Brazil
100 D5 **Traira, Serranía de** *range* Colombia
102 E3 **Trairi** Brazil
123 M5 **Trakai** Lithuania
123 M5 **Trakai** *region* Lithuania
133 C7 **Trakhiá** Greece
143 C4 **Tralee** Ireland
143 C4 **Tralee Bay** Ireland
194 E2 **Trạm Tấu** Vietnam
143 E4 **Tramore** Ireland
143 E4 **Tramore Bay** Ireland
131 F6 **Tramutola** Italy
122 H3 **Tranås** Sweden
106 E3 **Trancas** Argentina
88 E4 **Trancoso** Mexico
194 C6 **Trang** Thailand
194 C6 **Trang** *admin. area* Thailand
198 E5 **Trangan** *island* Indonesia
219 H5 **Trangie** NSW Australia
131 G6 **Trani** Italy
163 I4 **Tranomaro** Madagascar
120 I2 **Tranøy** Norway
107 H4 **Tranqueras** Uruguay
126 D2 **Trans** France
58 K1 **Transantarctic Mountains** Antarctica
132 D2 **Transilvaniei, Câmpia** *region* Romania
122 G2 **Transtrand** Sweden
132 D3 **Transylvanian Alps** *range* Romania
Transylvanian Basin *see* **Podişul Transilvaniei** Romania
142 E2 **Trantlemore** Highland Scotland UK
106 E6 **Trapalcó** Argentina
106 D6 **Trapatrapa** Chile
100 E3 **Trapichote** Venezuela
80 E1 **Trapp Lake** British Columbia Canada
127 J1 **Trappstadt** Germany
218 H8 **Traralgon** Vic. Australia
104 D2 **Traru** Brazil
128 C3 **Trás-os-Montes** *region* Portugal
181 G3 **Trashigang** Bhutan
130 E5 **Trasimeno, Lago** *lake* Italy
120 L5 **Träskvik** Finland
86 E3 **Traskwood** Arkansas USA
194 D5 **Trat** *admin. area* Thailand
106 D6 **Tratayén** Argentina
125 H3 **Traun** Austria
127 K3 **Traunsee** *lake* Austria
127 K3 **Traunstein** Germany
127 J4 **Travagliato** Italy
131 G6 **Trave, Punta del** *cape* Italy
218 F5 **Travellers Lake** NSW Australia
84 C2 **Traver** California USA
82 I4 **Traverse City** Michigan USA
78 H6 **Traverspine** *watercourse* Newfoundland and Labrador Canada
89 F2 **Travis, Lake** Texas USA
130 G4 **Travnik** Bosnia and Herzegovina
124 E5 **Travo** Italy
138 C2 **Trawsfynydd, Llyn** *lake* Wales UK
178 D3 **Ţraybil** Iraq
216 E5 **Trayning** WA Australia
130 H4 **Trbuk** Bosnia and Herzegovina
138 C2 **Tre-groes** Ceredigion Wales UK
138 D2 **Tre-Taliesin** Ceredigion Wales UK
138 C3 **Tre-Vaughan** Carmarthenshire Wales UK
214 B7 **Treachery, Mount** NT Australia
140 A2 **Treantagh** Ireland
142 B3 **Treaslane** Highland Scotland UK
199 J5 **Treasury Islands** Solomon Islands
124 G1 **Trebbin** Germany
122 G5 **Trebel** *watercourse* Germany
125 H3 **Třebíč** Czech Republic
127 L4 **Trebnje** Slovenia
130 F2 **Třeboň** Czech Republic
138 D3 **Treborough** Somerset England UK
138 D3 **Trecastle** Powys Wales UK
138 D3 **Tredegar** Blaenau Gwent Wales UK
195 G3 **Tree Island** Paracel Islands
138 B4 **Treen** Cornwall England UK
122 E5 **Treene** *watercourse* Germany
138 D2 **Trefeglwys** Powys Wales UK
124 F2 **Treffurt** Germany
138 B3 **Trefgarn Owen** Pembrokeshire Wales UK
138 C2 **Trefilan** Ceredigion Wales UK
140 E3 **Trefnant** Denbighshire Wales UK
138 D1 **Trefriw** Conwy Wales UK
138 D2 **Tregaron** Ceredigion Wales UK
138 C4 **Tregoney** Cornwall England UK
215 K4 **Tregrosse Reefs** Coral Sea Islands Territory Australia
126 C2 **Tréguier** France
138 D2 **Tregynon** Powys Wales UK
75 V8 **Treherne** Manitoba Canada
190 F1 **Trehgolowi Gorez** *mountain* Russian Federation
142 D4 **Treig, Loch** *lake* Scotland UK
126 E4 **Treignac** France
107 H5 **Treinta y Tres** Uruguay
107 H5 **Treinta y Tres** *admin. area* Uruguay
120 I5 **Trekilen** Sweden
127 H4 **Tréla Tête, Aiguilles de** *mountain* France
108 D3 **Trelew** Argentina
138 E3 **Trelleck** Monmouthshire Wales UK
138 D2 **Trelystan** Powys Wales UK
125 I4 **Trema** Croatia
138 C2 **Tremadog** Gwynedd Wales UK
138 C2 **Tremadog Bay** Wales UK
138 C4 **Tremail** Cornwall England UK
75 V7 **Tremaine** Manitoba Canada
138 C4 **Trematon** Cornwall England UK
74 I5 **Trembleur Lake** British Columbia Canada
103 D6 **Tremedal** Brazil
85 J3 **Trementina** New Mexico USA
131 F5 **Tremiti, Isole** *islands* Italy
80 I6 **Tremonton** Utah USA
129 G2 **Tremp** Spain
138 B4 **Trenance** Cornwall England UK
125 J3 **Trenčiansky** *admin. area* Slovakia
130 H2 **Trenčín** Slovakia
122 E4 **Trend** Denmark
130 G4 **Trenkovo** Croatia
106 F5 **Trenque Lauquen** Argentina
138 E4 **Trent** Dorset England UK
139 F2 **Trent** *watercourse* England UK
81 Q5 **Trent** South Dakota USA
86 A4 **Trent** Texas USA
139 E2 **Trent Vale** Stoke-on-Trent England UK
87 M3 **Trent Woods** North Carolina USA
130 D3 **Trentino-Alto Adige** *admin. area* Italy
124 F4 **Trento** Italy
87 J6 **Trenton** Florida USA
87 I3 **Trenton** Georgia USA
82 E6 **Trenton** Missouri USA
83 N6 **Trenton** New Jersey USA
86 G3 **Trenton** Tennessee USA
86 C4 **Trenton** Texas USA
79 L9 **Trepassey** Newfoundland and Labrador Canada
79 L9 **Trepassey Bay** Newfoundland and Labrador Canada
106 F6 **Tres Arroyos** Argentina
105 G4 **Três Barras** Brazil
103 B9 **Três Barras** Brazil
105 F2 **Tres Casas, Lago** *lake* Brazil
108 C4 **Tres Cerros** Argentina
103 C8 **Três Corações** Brazil
104 D5 **Tres Cruces** Bolivia
106 D4 **Tres Cruces** Chile
107 H3 **Três de Maio** Brazil
128 E6 **Tres Forcas, Cap** *cape* Morocco
106 F3 **Tres Isletas** Argentina
103 B8 **Três Lagoas** Brazil
108 B4 **Tres Lagos** Argentina
103 C7 **Três Marias, Represa de** *lake* Brazil
108 A4 **Tres Montes, Cabo** *cape* Chile
108 A4 **Tres Montes, Península** *peninsula* Chile
88 E5 **Tres Palos** Mexico
89 F5 **Tres Palos, Laguna** *lake* Mexico
107 H3 **Três Passos** Brazil
89 G6 **Tres Picos** Mexico
106 F6 **Tres Picos, Cerro** *mountain* Argentina
85 J2 **Tres Piedras** New Mexico USA
108 B1 **Tres Pinos** Chile
84 E5 **Tres Pozos** Mexico
108 D4 **Tres Puntas, Cabo** *cape* Argentina
90 B3 **Tres Puntas, Cabo de** *cape* Guatemala
103 D8 **Três Rios** Brazil
138 A5 **Tresco** *island* England UK
120 E5 **Tresfiord** Norway
142 B4 **Treshnish** Highland Scotland UK
131 F6 **Tresino, Punta** *cape* Italy
133 B5 **Treska** *watercourse* Macedonia
123 N4 **Treski** Estonia
128 E2 **Trespaderne** Spain
142 E4 **Tressait** Perth and Kinross Scotland UK
126 E3 **Tresson** France
125 H3 **Třešť** Czech Republic
141 H3 **Treswell** Nottinghamshire England UK
120 L2 **Tretta** Norway
120 G6 **Tretten** Norway
83 N2 **Trève, Lac La** *lake* Quebec Canada
108 B3 **Trevelín** Argentina
126 F4 **Tréves** France
127 K5 **Trevi** Italy
138 B3 **Trevine** Pembrokeshire Wales UK
124 G5 **Treviso** Italy
128 C3 **Trevões** Portugal
138 C2 **Trevor** Gwynedd Wales UK
138 B4 **Trevose Head** *cape* England UK
214 G8 **Trewalla** Qld Australia
219 I5 **Trewilga** NSW Australia
138 C4 **Trewithian** Cornwall England UK
138 B4 **Trewolla** Cornwall England UK
138 C4 **Trewornan** Cornwall England UK
130 B3 **Treyvaux** Switzerland
124 E5 **Trezzo** Italy
132 C4 **Trgovište** Serbia
133 E7 **Tria Nisia** *island* Greece
219 R11 **Triabunna** Tas. Australia
126 D3 **Triaize** France
219 K4 **Trial Bay** NSW Australia
78 K6 **Triangle** Newfoundland and Labrador Canada
181 H3 **Triangle, The** *region* Myanmar
133 F7 **Trianta** Greece
75 T8 **Tribune** Saskatchewan Canada
81 O7 **Tribune** Kansas USA
106 E6 **Trica Có** Argentina
106 D6 **Tricao Malal** Argentina
124 G4 **Tricesimo** Italy
218 G5 **Trida** NSW Australia
126 E5 **Trie-sur-Baïse** France
125 H4 **Trieben** Austria
124 D3 **Trier** Germany
125 G5 **Trieste** Italy
126 C2 **Trieux** *watercourse* France
132 E2 **Trifeşti** Romania
133 B6 **Trikala** Greece
123 M4 **Trikāta** Latvia
136 E6 **Trikomo** Cyprus
199 F5 **Trikora, Puncak** *mountain* Indonesia
130 G5 **Trilj** Croatia
140 A2 **Trillick** Omagh Northern Ireland UK
128 E3 **Trillo** Spain
143 F3 **Trim** Ireland
139 I2 **Trimingham** Norfolk England UK
139 I3 **Trimley St Mary** Suffolk England UK
127 I3 **Trimmis** Switzerland
100 A5 **Trinchera, Punta** *cape* Ecuador
187 E10 **Trincomalee** Sri Lanka
102 D4 **Trindade** Brazil
103 B7 **Trindade** Brazil
51 **Trindade, Ilha da** *Brazilian territory* Atlantic Ocean
139 G3 **Tring** Hertfordshire England UK
218 F1 **Trinidad** Qld Australia
105 E4 **Trinidad** Bolivia
100 D3 **Trinidad** Colombia
90 E2 **Trinidad** Cuba
90 B4 **Trinidad** Honduras
109 9 **Trinidad** *island* Trinidad and Tobago
107 G5 **Trinidad** Uruguay
80 C6 **Trinidad** California USA
81 M8 **Trinidad** Colorado USA
108 A4 **Trinidad, Golfo** *bay* Chile
108 E2 **Trinidad, Isla** *island* Argentina
91 I5 **Trinidad and Tobago** *country* Caribbean
131 E8 **Trinità, Lago della** *lake* Italy
131 G6 **Trinitapoli** Italy
101 H3 **Trinité, Montagnes de la** *range* French Guiana
79 L8 **Trinity** Newfoundland and Labrador Canada
80 D6 **Trinity** *watercourse* California USA
87 L3 **Trinity** North Carolina USA
86 D5 **Trinity** Texas USA
86 C5 **Trinity** *watercourse* Texas USA
215 H4 **Trinity Bay** Qld Australia
73 N9 **Trinity Bay** Newfoundland and Labrador Canada
72 D7 **Trinity Islands** Alaska USA
194 B5 **Trinkat** *island* Andaman and Nicobar Islands India
156 F4 **Trinkitat** Sudan
124 E5 **Trino** Italy
131 F6 **Triolo** *watercourse* Italy
87 I3 **Trion** Georgia USA
131 G7 **Trionto, Capo** *cape* Italy
196 C2 **Tripa** *watercourse* Indonesia
133 C7 **Tripoli** Greece
Tripoli *see* **Tārabulus** Libya
130 E5 **Triponzo** Italy
133 B7 **Tripotama** Greece
127 J1 **Triptis** Germany
181 G4 **Tripura** *admin. area* India
79 I7 **Triquet, Lac** *lake* Quebec Canada
124 F4 **Trisanna** *watercourse* Austria
122 E5 **Trischen** *island* Germany
164 5c **Tristan da Cunha** *island* St Helena
158 A2 **Tristao, Îles** *island* Guinea-Bissau
164 2 **Tristão, Ponta do** *cape* Madeira
143 C2 **Tristia** Ireland
132 D2 **Tritenii de Jos** Romania
79 K8 **Triton** Newfoundland and Labrador Canada
198 E4 **Triton, Teluk** *bay* Indonesia
195 F4 **Triton Island** Paracel Islands
105 E3 **Triunfo** Bolivia
105 F3 **Triunfo** Brazil
89 H5 **Triunfo** Mexico
131 F6 **Trivento** Italy
130 G4 **Trn** Bosnia and Herzegovina
125 I3 **Trnava** Slovakia
125 I3 **Trnavský** *admin. area* Slovakia
132 C3 **Trnjane** Serbia
130 H5 **Trnovo** Bosnia and Herzegovina
199 I6 **Trobriand Islands** Papua New Guinea
75 O7 **Trochu** Alberta Canada
77 P6 **Trodely Island** Nunavut Canada
138 C2 **Troedyraur** Ceredigion Wales UK
125 H4 **Trofaiach** Austria
130 B4 **Trofarello** Italy
120 H4 **Trofors** Norway
130 G5 **Trogir** Croatia
132 D4 **Troianul** Romania
77 R7 **Troilus, Lac** *lake* Quebec Canada
164 7a **Trois-Bassins** Réunion
79 D8 **Trois-Pistoles** Quebec Canada
109 15 **Trois Pitons, Morne** *volcano* Dominica
83 O3 **Trois-Rivières** Quebec Canada
109 16 **Trois-Rivières** Guadeloupe
127 H1 **Troisvierges** Luxembourg
182 I2 **Troitsk** Russian Federation
183 N3 **Troitskoye** Russian Federation
182 D4 **Troitskoye** Russian Federation
89 I6 **Trojas** Honduras
120 G5 **Trolla** Norway
121 O1 **Trollbukta** Norway
122 G3 **Trollhättan** Sweden
120 E5 **Trolltindan** *mountain* Norway
101 G5 **Trombetas** *watercourse* Brazil
164 6a **Tromelin, Île** French Southern and Antarctic Lands
108 D1 **Tromen, Volcán** *volcano* Argentina
122 E3 **Trømoya** *island* Norway
122 G5 **Tromper Wiek** *bay* Germany
162 E6 **Trompsburg** South Africa
120 K2 **Troms** *admin. area* Norway
120 K2 **Tromsø** Norway
120 K2 **Tromvik** Norway
142 inset **Trondavoe** Shetland Scotland UK
120 G5 **Trondheim** Norway
120 G5 **Trondheimsfjorden** *bay* Norway
120 H4 **Trones** Norway
120 I3 **Trones** Norway
181 G3 **Trongsa** Bhutan
130 E5 **Tronto** *watercourse* Italy
126 E3 **Trôo** France
142 D5 **Troon** South Ayrshire Scotland UK
124 C2 **Trooz** Belgium
103 C6 **Tropeiros, Serra dos** *range* Brazil
80 I8 **Tropic** Utah USA
88 C3 **Troquero** Mexico
134 M5 **Trosh** Russian Federation
75 S8 **Trossachs** Saskatchewan Canada
136 E2 **Trostyanets'** Ukraine
132 E2 **Trotuş** *watercourse* Romania
91 F3 **Trou du Nord** Haiti
109 13 **Trou Gras Point** *cape* St Lucia
109 11a **Troumaka** St Vincent and the Grenadines
86 D4 **Troup** Texas USA
142 F3 **Troup Head** *cape* Scotland UK
75 N4 **Trout** *watercourse* Alberta Canada
84 F1 **Trout Creek** Utah USA
74 K2 **Trout Lake** Northwest Territories Canada
74 K2 **Trout Lake** Northwest Territories Canada
76 I7 **Trout Lake** Ontario Canada
79 I8 **Trout River** Newfoundland and Labrador Canada
140 F2 **Troutbeck** Cumbria England UK
80 D4 **Troutdale** Oregon USA
139 E3 **Trowbridge** Wiltshire England UK
139 I2 **Trowse Newton** Norfolk England UK
Troy *see* **Truva** Turkey
87 I5 **Troy** Alabama USA
82 J5 **Troy** Michigan USA
80 H2 **Troy** Montana USA
82 I6 **Troy** Ohio USA
83 M6 **Troy** Pennsylvania USA
86 G2 **Troy** Tennessee USA
86 C5 **Troy** Texas USA
132 D4 **Troyan** Bulgaria
126 G2 **Troyes** France
132 G2 **Troyits'ke** Ukraine
130 G5 **Trpanj** Croatia
132 B4 **Trpezi** Montenegro
130 H5 **Trsa** Montenegro
125 J3 **Trstená** Slovakia
132 B4 **Trstenik** Serbia
214 D1 **Truant Island** NT Australia
75 S8 **Truax** Saskatchewan Canada
127 H3 **Trub** Switzerland
128 C2 **Truchas** Spain
80 E7 **Truckee** California USA
182 E4 **Trudfront** Russian Federation
127 G3 **Trugny** France
100 B3 **Trujillo** Colombia
90 C4 **Trujillo** Honduras
104 B3 **Trujillo** Peru
128 D4 **Trujillo** Spain
100 D2 **Trujillo** Venezuela
100 D2 **Trujillo** *admin. area* Venezuela
132 C1 **Trukhanov** Ukraine
138 D4 **Trull** Somerset England UK
196 C3 **Trumon** Indonesia
139 H2 **Trumpington** Cambridgeshire England UK
126 E2 **Trun** France
127 I3 **Trun** Switzerland
132 C4 **Trŭn** Bulgaria
139 I2 **Trunch** Norfolk England UK
219 H5 **Trundle** NSW Australia
194 E2 **Trùng Khánh** Vietnam
194 E5 **Trúng Lón, Hòn** *island* Vietnam
215 I5 **Trunk Reef** Qld Australia
219 I5 **Trunkey Creek** NSW Australia
218 D6 **Truro** SA Australia
79 G10 **Truro** Nova Scotia Canada
138 B4 **Truro** Cornwall England UK
197 H2 **Trus Madi, Gunung** *mountain* Malaysia
197 G2 **Trusan** Malaysia
197 G2 **Trusan** *watercourse* Malaysia
139 F2 **Trusley** Derbyshire England UK
87 H4 **Trussville** Alabama USA
132 D4 **Trŭstenik** Bulgaria
122 F4 **Trustrup** Denmark
74 J4 **Trutch** British Columbia Canada
85 I4 **Truth or Consequences** New Mexico USA
133 E6 **Truva (Troy)** *site* Turkey
126 F4 **Truyère** *watercourse* France
133 B6 **Trygon** Greece
87 J3 **Tryon** North Carolina USA
220 F3 **Tryphena** New Zealand
133 D6 **Trypiti, Akra** *cape* Greece
122 G2 **Trysil** Norway
122 F2 **Trysilelva** *watercourse* Norway
125 I1 **Trzcianka** Poland
125 L1 **Trzcianne** Poland
125 H1 **Trzciel** Poland
125 H1 **Trzcińsko Zdrój** Poland
125 H2 **Trzebień** Poland
125 H1 **Trzebież** Poland
125 I2 **Trzebnica** Poland
125 I1 **Trzemeszno** Poland
125 H4 **Tržič** Slovenia
185 J3 **Tsagaan Nuur** *lake* Mongolia
191 H3 **Tsagaan Ovoo** Mongolia
190 D2 **Tsagaan Uul** *mountain* Mongolia
190 F3 **Tsagaandelger** Mongolia
190 F2 **Tsagaannuul** Mongolia
185 I2 **Tsagaannuur** Mongolia
182 E4 **Tsagan-Nur** Russian Federation
185 J3 **Tsaganhairhan** Mongolia
120 J3 **Tsäkkok** *island* Sweden
87 J6 **Tsala Apopka Lake** Florida USA
159 G5 **Tsama** Congo
133 B6 **Tsamantas** Greece
190 E2 **Tsaraan-uure** Mongolia
185 J3 **Tsaraanchuluut** Mongolia
185 J2 **Tsaraanhairhan** Mongolia
185 K2 **Tsaraannuur** Mongolia
163 I3 **Tsaramandroso** Madagascar
163 I3 **Tsarantanana** Madagascar
186 D4 **Tsarap Lingti Chu** *watercourse* Jammu and Kashmir India/Pakistan
163 I2 **Tsaratanama, Massif du** *range* Madagascar
132 E4 **Tsarev Brod** Bulgaria
132 E4 **Tsarevo** Bulgaria
185 I3 **Tsast Uul** *mountain* Mongolia
182 D4 **Tsatsa** Russian Federation
162 D4 **Tsau** Botswana
74 I4 **Tsay Keh Dene** British Columbia Canada
81 O3 **Tschida, Lake** North Dakota USA
185 J3 **Tseel** Mongolia
190 F3 **Tseel** Mongolia
183 O2 **Tselinnoye** Russian Federation
185 I3 **Tsengel** Mongolia
190 D2 **Tsengel** Mongolia
190 E3 **Tsenher** Mongolia
185 I3 **Tsetseg** Mongolia
185 J3 **Tsetseg Nuur** *lake* Mongolia
162 D4 **Tsetseng** Botswana
190 D2 **Tsetserleg** Mongolia
190 E3 **Tsetserleg** Mongolia
190 E3 **Tsetserleg** Mongolia
158 E3 **Tsévié** Togo
162 D5 **Tshabong** Botswana
160 C5 **Tshala** Democratic Republic of Congo
160 A4 **Tshela** Democratic Republic of Congo
160 C4 **Tshenge-Oshwe** Democratic Republic of Congo
160 C5 **Tshibala** Democratic Republic of Congo
160 C5 **Tshibuka** Democratic Republic of Congo
160 C5 **Tshibwika** Democratic Republic of Congo
160 C5 **Tshikapa** Democratic Republic of Congo
160 C5 **Tshilenge** Democratic Republic of Congo
162 F4 **Tshipise** South Africa
160 C5 **Tshisenge** Democratic Republic of Congo

160 C5 **Tshitanzu** Democratic Republic of Congo
186 E4 **Tsho Moriri** *lake* Jammu and Kashmir India/Pakistan
160 D5 **Tshofa** Democratic Republic of Congo
162 E3 **Tsholotsho** Zimbabwe
162 D4 **Tshootsha** Botswana
160 C4 **Tshupa** *watercourse* Democratic Republic of Congo
Tshwane *see* **Pretoria** South Africa
182 D4 **Tsimlyansk** Russian Federation
182 D4 **Tsimlyanskoye Vodokhranilishche** *lake* Russian Federation
162 D5 **Tsineng** South Africa
163 I3 **Tsinjoarivo** Madagascar
162 C3 **Tsintsabis** Namibia
163 I5 **Tsiombe** Madagascar
135 X8 **Tsipa** *watercourse* Russian Federation
135 AC7 **Tsipanda** Russian Federation
135 X8 **Tsipikan** Russian Federation
163 I3 **Tsiribihina** *watercourse* Madagascar
163 I3 **Tsiroanomandidy** Madagascar
163 I4 **Tsitondroina** Madagascar
74 I6 **Tsitsutl Peak** British Columbia Canada
182 D5 **Ts'khinvali** Georgia
162 D3 **Tsodilo Hills** *range* Botswana
162 E6 **Tsolo** South Africa
162 E6 **Tsomo** South Africa
185 J3 **Tsort** Mongolia
193 H4 **Tsu** Japan
182 E4 **Tsubu** Russian Federation
193 I3 **Tsugarū-kaikyō** *strait* Japan
162 C3 **Tsumeb** Namibia
162 D3 **Tsumkwe** Namibia
193 H4 **Tsuru** Japan
193 I2 **Tsuru-numa** *lake* Japan
193 H4 **Tsuruga** Japan
192 G5 **Tsurugi-san** *volcano* Japan
193 H3 **Tsuruoka** Japan
192 F4 **Tsushima** *island* Japan
192 G4 **Tsuyama** Japan
162 D4 **Tswaane** Botswana
121 R2 **Tsypnavolok** Russian Federation
128 C3 **Tua** *watercourse* Portugal
196 E5 **Tua, Tanjung** *cape* Indonesia
220 F3 **Tuakau** New Zealand
143 D3 **Tuam** Ireland
221 E5 **Tuamarina** New Zealand
219 K1 **Tuan** Qld Australia
194 D2 **Tuấn Giáo** Vietnam
196 C3 **Tuangku** *island* Indonesia
104 D4 **Tuanuni** Bolivia
182 C5 **Tuapse** Russian Federation
197 H2 **Tuaran** Malaysia
196 A4 **Tuas** *admin. area* Singapore
223 12c **Tuasivi** Samoa
197 G5 **Tuban** Indonesia
197 G3 **Tubau** Malaysia
195 H5 **Tubbataha Reefs** Philippines
143 D4 **Tubber** Ireland
143 E4 **Tubbrid** Ireland
160 C5 **Tubeya-Dita** Democratic Republic of Congo
195 I6 **Tubigan** *island* Philippines
128 E2 **Tubilla del Agua** Spain
126 G1 **Tubize** Belgium
158 B3 **Tubmanburg** Liberia
223 9 **Tubou** Fiji
156 C1 **Tubruq** Libya
223 14 **Tubuaï** *island* French Polynesia
223 14 **Tubuaï, Îles** *islands* French Polynesia
90 E5 **Tubualá** Panama
88 C2 **Tubutama** Mexico
100 D4 **Tucana** Brazil
103 E5 **Tucano** Brazil
108 B1 **Tucapel, Punta** *cape* Chile
105 G5 **Tucavaca** *watercourse* Bolivia
130 G5 **Tučepi** Croatia
126 F5 **Tuchan** France
88 D3 **Tucheachi** Mexico
74 G2 **Tuchitua** Yukon Territory Canada
74 I3 **Tuchodi** *watercourse* British Columbia Canada
125 I1 **Tuchola** Poland
125 K3 **Tuchów** Poland
216 F3 **Tuckanarra** WA Australia
84 G4 **Tucson** Arizona USA
108 B4 **Tucu Tucu** Argentina
102 B3 **Tucumã** Brazil
106 E3 **Tucumán** *admin. area* Argentina
85 K3 **Tucumcari** New Mexico USA
104 B2 **Túcume** Peru
101 F2 **Tucupita** Venezuela
102 B3 **Tucuruí** Brazil
102 B4 **Tucuruí, Represa de** *lake* Brazil
128 F2 **Tudela** Spain
216 E7 **Tudor** WA Australia
78 F5 **Tudor, Lac** *lake* Quebec Canada
123 P5 **Tudorovo** Belarus
123 N3 **Tudulinna** Estonia
159 F2 **Tudun Wada** Nigeria
128 C3 **Tuela** *watercourse* Portugal
181 H3 **Tuensang** Nagaland India
102 B3 **Tueré** *watercourse* Brazil
136 F5 **Tufanbeyli** Turkey
181 F3 **Tufanganj** West Bengal India
132 E3 **Tufeşti** Romania
126 E2 **Tuffé** France
53 R3 **Tufts Plain** *underwater feature* Pacific Ocean
139 G2 **Tugby** Leicester England UK
138 E2 **Tugford** Shropshire England UK
185 J3 **Tugreg** Mongolia
197 H3 **Tuguan Maputi** *island* Indonesia
195 I3 **Tuguegarao** Philippines
191 H5 **Tuguiwula** Nei Mongol Zizhiqu China
135 AC8 **Tugur** Russian Federation
Tuhua *see* **Mayor Island** New Zealand
133 B5 **Tuin** Macedonia
101 E5 **Tuina** Brazil
164 3d **Tuineje** Canary Islands
181 G4 **Tuivaw** *watercourse* Mizoram India
123 M4 **Tūja** Latvia
104 E5 **Tujuria** Bolivia
182 H2 **Tukan** Russian Federation
198 C5 **Tukangbesi, Kepulauan** *islands* Indonesia
77 P4 **Tukarak Island** Nunavut Canada
132 C1 **Tukhol'ka** Ukraine
220 G4 **Tukituki** *watercourse* New Zealand
156 C1 **Tūkrah** Libya
72 F5 **Tuktoyaktuk** Northwest Territories Canada
123 L4 **Tukuma** *admin. area* Latvia
123 L4 **Tukums** Latvia
135 AA8 **Tukuringra, Khrebet** *range* Russian Federation
182 E5 **Tukuy-Mekteb** Russian Federation
223 12c **Tula** American Samoa
89 F4 **Tula** Mexico
136 F1 **Tula** Russian Federation
58 D2 **Tula Mountains** Antarctica
222 8 **Tulagi** Solomon Islands
185 I6 **Tulagt Ar Gol** *watercourse* Qinghai China
185 K5 **Tulai He** *watercourse* Gansu China
185 K5 **Tulai Nanshan** *range* Gansu China
80 E2 **Tulameen** British Columbia Canada
89 F4 **Tulancingo** Mexico
196 E5 **Tulangbawang** *watercourse* Indonesia
132 B4 **Tulare** Serbia
84 C2 **Tulare** California USA
81 P4 **Tulare** South Dakota USA
84 C3 **Tulare Lake Bed** California USA
85 I4 **Tularosa** New Mexico USA
88 D1 **Tularosa Valley** New Mexico USA
187 F7 **Tulasi** *mountain* Chhattisgarh India
178 D2 **Ţulayḩah** Iraq
100 B4 **Tulcan** Ecuador
132 F3 **Tulcea** Romania
132 F3 **Tulcea** *admin. area* Romania
142 E4 **Tulchan Lodge** Angus Scotland UK
132 F1 **Tul'chyn** Ukraine
89 F5 **Tulcingo del Valle** Mexico
104 D5 **Tulduni** Chile
80 E6 **Tule Lake Sump** California USA
80 E6 **Tulelake** California USA
76 F1 **Tulemalu Lake** Nunavut Canada
86 C6 **Tuleta** Texas USA
127 G4 **Tulette** France
162 E4 **Tuli** *watercourse* Zimbabwe
85 L3 **Tulia** Texas USA
72 G6 **Tulita** Northwest Territories Canada
218 B6 **Tulka** SA Australia
143 D3 **Tulla** Ireland
142 D4 **Tulla, Loch** *lake* Scotland UK
143 E1 **Tullagh** Ireland
140 B3 **Tullaghanoge** Ireland
87 H3 **Tullahoma** Tennessee USA
143 C5 **Tullakeel** Ireland
218 G6 **Tullakool** NSW Australia
219 H5 **Tullamore** NSW Australia
143 E3 **Tullamore** Ireland
126 E4 **Tulle** France
120 K2 **Tulleng** Norway
120 I5 **Tulleråsen** Sweden
218 H5 **Tullibigeal** NSW Australia
142 C4 **Tullich** Argyll and Bute Scotland UK
142 E3 **Tullich** Highland Scotland UK
143 C4 **Tullig** Ireland
130 G2 **Tulln** Austria
84 B2 **Tulloch Reservoir** California USA
143 F4 **Tullow** Ireland
215 H4 **Tully** Qld Australia
215 H4 **Tully** *watercourse* Qld Australia
83 M5 **Tully** New York USA
215 I5 **Tully Heads** Qld Australia
143 F3 **Tullyallen** Ireland
140 B3 **Tullygowan** Ireland
143 D4 **Tullylease** Ireland
140 C2 **Tullymurry** Down Northern Ireland UK
140 B4 **Tullytusk** Ireland
143 C3 **Tullywee Bridge** Ireland
214 G7 **Tulmer** Qld Australia
132 E3 **Tulnici** Romania
106 D2 **Túlor** Chile
121 Q5 **Tulos** Russian Federation
121 Q5 **Tulos, Ozero** *lake* Russian Federation
134 M6 **Tulpan** Russian Federation
121 P3 **Tulppio** Finland
86 D2 **Tulsa** Oklahoma USA
74 E3 **Tulsequah** British Columbia Canada
186 F5 **Tulsipur** Nepal
134 I8 **Tul'skaya Oblast'** *admin. area* Russian Federation
101 F4 **Tulu-Tuloi, Serra** *range* Brazil
100 B3 **Tuluá** Colombia
185 I4 **Tulufan** Xinjiang Uygur Zizhiqu China
89 I4 **Tulum** Mexico
135 V8 **Tulun** Russian Federation
199 J5 **Tulun Islands** Papua New Guinea
197 F6 **Tulungagung** Indonesia
195 H5 **Tuluran** *island* Philippines
182 C2 **Tuma** Russian Federation
199 I6 **Tuma Island** Papua New Guinea
100 B4 **Tumaco** Colombia
100 B4 **Tumaco, Bahía de** *bay* Colombia
121 S2 **Tumannyy** Russian Federation
135 AC4 **Tumat** Russian Federation
160 C4 **Tumba** Democratic Republic of Congo
122 I3 **Tumba** Sweden
160 B4 **Tumba, Lac** *lake* Democratic Republic of Congo
197 G4 **Tumbangmiri** Indonesia
197 G4 **Tumbangsamba** Indonesia
197 G4 **Tumbangsenamang** Indonesia
197 F4 **Tumbangtiti** Indonesia
106 E2 **Tumbaya** Argentina
104 A1 **Tumbes** Peru
100 A5 **Tumbes** *admin. area* Peru
74 K5 **Tumbler Ridge** British Columbia Canada
219 H6 **Tumblong** NSW Australia
218 C6 **Tumby Bay** SA Australia
191 L4 **Tumen** Jilin China
191 G3 **Tumentsogt** Mongolia
190 D2 **Tumerbular** Mongolia
198 A2 **Tumindao** *island* Philippines
75 U7 **Tummel** Manitoba Canada
142 D4 **Tummel Bridge** Perth and Kinross Scotland UK
196 D2 **Tumpat** Malaysia
198 B4 **Tumpu, Gunung** *mountain* Indonesia
187 E7 **Tumsar** Maharashtra India
158 D2 **Tumu** Ghana
Tumuc-Humac Mountains *see* **Tumucumaque, Serra** Brazil
101 H4 **Tumucumaque, Serra (Tumuc-Humac)** *range* Brazil
187 F7 **Tumudibandh** Orissa India
158 D3 **Tuna** Ghana
91 H3 **Tuna, Punta** *cape* Puerto Rico
100 D4 **Tunahí, Sierra** *range* Colombia
100 C4 **Tunaima, Laguna** *lake* Colombia
105 E6 **Tunal** Bolivia
185 K2 **Tunamal Nuur** *lake* Mongolia
109 9 **Tunapuna** Trinidad and Tobago
109 9 **Tunapuna-Piarco** *admin. area* Trinidad and Tobago
106 F6 **Tunas, Sierra del las** *range* Argentina
156 D2 **Tunaydah** Egypt
136 F5 **Tunceli** Turkey
136 F5 **Tunceli** *admin. area* Turkey
188 F5 **Tunchang** Hainan China
161 E5 **Tunduma** Tanzania
161 F6 **Tunduru** Tanzania
132 D4 **Tundzha** *watercourse* Bulgaria
190 D2 **Tunel** Mongolia
159 F3 **Tunga** Nigeria
191 I1 **Tungir** *watercourse* Russian Federation
197 H2 **Tungku** Malaysia
120 inset **Tungnaá** *watercourse* Iceland
74 G2 **Tungsten** Northwest Territories Canada
121 R4 **Tunguda** Russian Federation
120 inset **Tungufljót** *watercourse* Iceland
135 AA6 **Tunguskhaya** Russian Federation
134 T6 **Tunguskoye Plato** *region* Russian Federation
198 E5 **Tunguwatu** Indonesia
190 F3 **Tunhel** Mongolia
86 F3 **Tunica** Mississippi USA
155 I1 **Tunis** Tunisia
131 D8 **Tunis, Golfe de** *bay* Tunisia
155 H2 **Tunisia** *country* Africa
100 C3 **Tunja** Colombia
212 E7 **Tunnel** *watercourse* WA Australia
87 I3 **Tunnel Hill** Georgia USA
122 E2 **Tunnhovdfjorden** *bay* Norway
123 O2 **Tunnila** Finland
120 H4 **Tunnsjøen** *lake* Norway
120 I5 **Tunnvågen** Sweden
122 F5 **Tunø** *island* Denmark
122 D2 **Tunsbergdalsvatnet** *lake* Norway
141 G2 **Tunstall** North Yorkshire England UK
102 C4 **Tuntum** Brazil
78 H4 **Tunungayualok Island** Newfoundland and Labrador Canada
77 Q3 **Tunusualuk, Lac** *lake* Quebec Canada
106 D5 **Tunuyán** Argentina
106 E5 **Tunuyán** *watercourse* Argentina
181 G4 **Tunzang** Myanmar
189 H1 **Tuo He** *watercourse* Anhui China
188 D4 **Tuodian** Yunnan China
180 D2 **Tuoding** Xizang Zizhiqu China
191 I5 **Tuoji Dao** *island* Shandong China
188 F3 **Tuojiang** Hunan China
189 F3 **Tuojiang** Hunan China
190 G5 **Tuoketuo** Nei Mongol Zizhiqu China
185 H4 **Tuokexun** Xinjiang Uygur Zizhiqu China
184 G3 **Tuoli** Xinjiang Uygur Zizhiqu China
120 L3 **Tuolpukka** Sweden
121 N4 **Tuomioja** Finland
188 E4 **Tuoniang Jiang** *watercourse* Guangxi Zhuangzu Zizhiqu China
184 H3 **Tuoputiereke** Xinjiang Uygur Zizhiqu China
185 I6 **Tuotuo He** *watercourse* Qinghai China
143 D5 **Tuough Bridge** Ireland
103 B8 **Tupã** Brazil
223 14 **Tupai** *island* French Polynesia
105 F2 **Tupana** *watercourse* Brazil
101 F4 **Tupari** Brazil
86 C3 **Tupelo** Oklahoma USA
103 B8 **Tupi Paulista** Brazil
191 I1 **Tupik** Russian Federation
105 G1 **Tupinambarama, Ilha** *island* Brazil
123 O3 **Tupisyno** Russian Federation
105 E6 **Tupiza** Bolivia
74 K5 **Tupper** British Columbia Canada
83 N4 **Tupper Lake** New York USA
182 I6 **Tuprakkala** Turkmenistan
191 J3 **Tuquan** Nei Mongol Zizhiqu China
132 A2 **Tura** Hungary
181 G4 **Tura** Meghalaya India
135 V6 **Tura** Russian Federation
182 J1 **Tura** *watercourse* Russian Federation
178 E5 **Turabah** Saudi Arabia
178 E5 **Turabah, Wādī** *watercourse* Saudi Arabia
104 C4 **Turajaja** Peru
135 Z4 **Turakh** Russian Federation
220 F5 **Turakina** New Zealand
221 F5 **Turakirae Head** New Zealand
132 A3 **Turalići** Bosnia and Herzegovina
199 G5 **Turama** *watercourse* Papua New Guinea
135 AB8 **Turana, Khrebet** *range* Russian Federation
220 F4 **Turangi** New Zealand
132 A1 **Turany** Slovakia
179 I6 **Tur'at Maşirah** *sea* Oman
125 J2 **Turawskie, Jezioro** *lake* Poland
123 M3 **Turba** Estonia
100 C2 **Turbaco** Colombia
179 J4 **Turbat** Pakistan
87 L4 **Turbeville** South Carolina USA
125 K2 **Turbia** Poland
142 C4 **Turbiskill** Argyll and Bute Scotland UK
100 B2 **Turbo** Colombia
132 C3 **Turceni** Romania
121 U5 **Turchasovo** Russian Federation
104 D5 **Turco** Bolivia
132 F3 **Turcoaia** Romania
104 E4 **Turcocala** Bolivia
143 E1 **Ture** Ireland
212 D7 **Turee** *watercourse* WA Australia
216 F1 **Turee Creek** WA Australia
128 D3 **Turégano** Spain
223 14 **Tureia** *island* French Polynesia
125 J1 **Turek** Poland
123 M2 **Turenki** Finland
142 F3 **Turfgate** Aberdeenshire Scotland UK
182 I3 **Turgay** Kazakhstan
183 K3 **Turgay** Kazakhstan
182 I4 **Turgay** *watercourse* Kazakhstan
185 I2 **Turgen** Mongolia
185 I2 **Turgen Uul** *mountain* Mongolia
83 L2 **Turgeon** *watercourse* Quebec Canada
83 L2 **Turgeon, Lac** *lake* Quebec Canada
132 E4 **Tŭrgovishte** Bulgaria
136 F5 **Turhal** Turkey
131 G6 **Turi** Italy
123 M3 **Türi** Estonia
129 F4 **Turia** *watercourse* Spain
102 C3 **Turiaçu** Brazil
102 C3 **Turiaçu** *watercourse* Brazil
102 C3 **Turiaçu, Baía de** *bay* Brazil
161 F5 **Turiani** Tanzania
125 K5 **Turija** Serbia
219 I5 **Turill** NSW Australia
101 F2 **Turimiquire, Serrania de** *range* Venezuela
75 O8 **Turin** Alberta Canada
182 I1 **Turinsk** Russian Federation
125 M2 **Turiys'k** Ukraine
130 G5 **Turjaci** Croatia
125 H5 **Turjak** Slovenia
132 C1 **Turka** Ukraine
161 F3 **Turkana, Lake** *lake* Kenya
133 E7 **Türkbükü** Turkey
139 F3 **Turkdean** Gloucestershire England UK
133 E5 **Türkeli Adası** *island* Turkey
183 J5 **Turkestan** Kazakhstan
132 B2 **Túrkeve** Hungary
136 E5 **Turkey** *country* Asia
218 F4 **Turkey** *watercourse* NSW Australia
85 L3 **Turkey** Texas USA
215 K8 **Turkey Beach** Qld Australia
Turkey Creek *see* **Warmun** Australia
219 J2 **Turkey Mountain** Qld Australia
182 D3 **Turki** Russian Federation
182 I6 **Türkmenabat** Turkmenistan
182 F6 **Türkmenbaşy** Turkmenistan
182 F6 **Türkmenbaşy Aýlagy** *bay* Turkmenistan
182 H6 **Turkmenistan** *country*
91 G2 **Turks and Caicos Islands** *British overseas territory* Caribbean
91 G2 **Turks Islands** Turks and Caicos Islands
91 G2 **Turks Islands Passage** *channel* Turks and Caicos Islands
123 L2 **Turku/Åbo** Finland
80 E8 **Turlock** California USA
103 D7 **Turmalina** Brazil
125 K3 **Turňa nad Bodvou** Slovakia
220 G5 **Turnagain, Cape** New Zealand
199 G6 **Turnagain Island** Australia
138 E2 **Turnastone** Herefordshire England UK
78 I5 **Turnavik Islands** Newfoundland and Labrador Canada
75 U6 **Turnberry** Manitoba Canada
142 D5 **Turnberry** South Ayrshire Scotland UK
90 C3 **Turneffe Islands** Belize
212 E6 **Turner** *watercourse* WA Australia
75 Q8 **Turner** Montana USA
75 N7 **Turner Valley** Alberta Canada
140 B4 **Turner's** Ireland
158 B3 **Turners Peninsula** *peninsula* Sierra Leone
139 E4 **Turners Puddle** Dorset England UK
125 H4 **Türnitz** Austria
75 Q4 **Turnor Lake** Saskatchewan Canada
125 H2 **Turnov** Czech Republic
81 P8 **Turon** Kansas USA
125 K1 **Turośl** Poland
219 J7 **Tuross Head** NSW Australia
125 I1 **Turowo** Poland
Turpan *see* **Tulufan** China
85 I1 **Turquoise Lake** Colorado USA
125 G4 **Turrach** Austria
219 I4 **Turrawan** NSW Australia
86 F3 **Turrell** Arkansas USA
142 D4 **Turret Bridge** Highland Scotland UK
90 D5 **Turrialba** Costa Rica
142 F3 **Turriff** Aberdeenshire Scotland UK
178 F2 **Tursāq** Iraq
182 H5 **Türtkŭl** Uzbekistan
82 F3 **Turtle Flambeau** *lake* Wisconsin USA
214 G1 **Turtle Head Island** Qld Australia
197 H2 **Turtle Islands** Philippines
75 Q6 **Turtle Lake** Saskatchewan Canada
82 E4 **Turtle Lake** Wisconsin USA
213 J3 **Turtle Point** NT Australia
75 Q6 **Turtleford** Saskatchewan Canada
134 R5 **Turukhan** *watercourse* Russian Federation
134 S5 **Turukhansk** Russian Federation
133 G7 **Turunçova** Turkey
182 G4 **Turush** Kazakhstan
103 B7 **Turvo** *watercourse* Brazil
125 M2 **Tur'ya** Ukraine
132 A1 **Turzovka** Slovakia
132 C2 **Tusa** Romania
106 E2 **Tusaquilla** Argentina
86 H4 **Tuscaloosa** Alabama USA
86 H4 **Tuscaloosa, Lake** Alabama USA
131 D5 **Tuscania** Italy
83 M6 **Tuscarora Mountains** Pennsylvania USA
82 G7 **Tuscola** Illinois USA
86 B4 **Tuscola** Texas USA
87 J2 **Tusculum** Tennessee USA
86 H3 **Tuscumbia** Alabama USA
127 I5 **Tuselli, Punta alli** *cape* Corsica France
120 G5 **Tuset** Norway
140 E1 **Tushielaw** Scottish Borders Scotland UK
190 F2 **Tushig** Mongolia
123 L5 **Tushino** Russian Federation
86 C3 **Tushka** Oklahoma USA
123 N2 **Tuskas** Finland
87 I4 **Tuskegee** Alabama USA
120 J2 **Tussøya** *island* Norway
120 I4 **Tustervatnet** *lake* Norway
120 E5 **Tustna** *island* Norway
125 K2 **Tuszów Narodowy** Poland
179 J2 **Tuta** Afghanistan
179 J2 **Tūtachī** Afghanistan
220 G4 **Tutaekuri** *watercourse* New Zealand
223 13a **Tutaga** *island* Tuvalu
139 F2 **Tutbury** Staffordshire England UK
187 E10 **Tuticorin** Tamil Nadu India
220 G4 **Tutira** New Zealand
197 G2 **Tutoh** *watercourse* Malaysia
102 D3 **Tutóia** Brazil
134 T5 **Tutonchana** *watercourse* Russian Federation
135 T5 **Tutonchana, Vozvyshennost'** *range* Russian Federation
197 G2 **Tutong** Brunei
132 E2 **Tutova** Romania
74 D3 **Tutshi Lake** British Columbia Canada
86 C3 **Tuttle** Oklahoma USA
82 C7 **Tuttle Creek Lake** Kansas USA
120 J3 **Tutturjaure** *lake* Sweden
78 O2 **Tuttutooq** *island* Greenland
85 I6 **Tutuaca** Mexico
198 C6 **Tutuala** Timor-Leste (East Timor)
223 12 **Tutuila** *island* American Samoa
220 F2 **Tutukaka** New Zealand
162 E4 **Tutume** Botswana
222 8a **Tutumu** Solomon Islands
104 D5 **Tutupaca, Volcán** *volcano* Peru
86 F3 **Tutwiler** Mississippi USA
123 L3 **Tuudi** Estonia
121 N3 **Tuuliharju** Finland
121 Q5 **Tuupovaara** Finland
123 O1 **Tuusjärvi** Finland
123 O2 **Tuusjärvi** *lake* Finland
121 P5 **Tuusniemi** Finland
109 5 **Tuutapu** *volcano* Isla de Pascua (Easter Island)
222 13 **Tuvalu** *country* Oceania
58 S2 **Tuve, Mount** *mountain* Antarctica
190 G3 **Tuvshinshiree** Mongolia
190 E3 **Tuvshruuleh** Mongolia
223 9 **Tuvuca** *island* Fiji
82 C2 **Tuxedo** Manitoba Canada
81 M1 **Tuxford** Saskatchewan Canada
141 H3 **Tuxford** Nottinghamshire England UK
89 G5 **Tuxtla Gutiérrez** Mexico
194 E4 **Tuỳ Đức** Vietnam
194 F4 **Tuy Hòa** Vietnam
74 F3 **Tuya Lake** British Columbia Canada
136 E5 **Tuz Gölü** *lake* Turkey
133 E7 **Tuzburgazı** Turkey
182 E1 **Tuzha** Russian Federation
131 H5 **Tuzi** Montenegro
130 H4 **Tuzla** Bosnia and Herzegovina
133 E5 **Tuzla** Turkey
133 G6 **Tuzlukçu** Turkey
132 C1 **Tuzsér** Hungary
122 G4 **Tvååker** Sweden
120 K4 **Tvärålund** Sweden
120 J4 **Tväråträsk** Sweden
122 E3 **Tvedestrand** Norway
134 I7 **Tver'** Russian Federation
120 K2 **Tverrfjellet** *island* Norway
134 H7 **Tverskaya Oblast'** *admin. area* Russian Federation
122 F4 **Tversted** Denmark
130 H2 **Tvrdošín** Slovakia
125 I2 **Twardogóra** Poland
142 E1 **Twatt** Orkney Islands Scotland UK
162 C5 **Twee Rivier** Namibia
83 M4 **Tweed** Ontario Canada
140 E1 **Tweed** *watercourse* Scotland UK
142 E5 **Tweedsmuir** Scottish Borders Scotland UK
214 E7 **Twelve Mile Mountain** Qld Australia
139 G2 **Twenty** Lincolnshire England UK
84 D3 **Twentynine Palms** California USA
217 J6 **Twilight Cove** *bay* WA Australia
79 K8 **Twillingate** Newfoundland and Labrador Canada
80 I4 **Twin Bridges** Montana USA
88 E2 **Twin Buttes Reservoir** Texas USA
87 J4 **Twin City** Georgia USA
80 H5 **Twin Falls** Idaho USA
79 K8 **Twin Lakes** Newfoundland and Labrador Canada
85 I1 **Twin Lakes Reservoir** Colorado USA
216 D3 **Twin Peaks** WA Australia
218 E5 **Twin Wells** NSW Australia
162 E2 **Twingi** Zambia
80 E2 **Twisp** Washington USA
124 D1 **Twist** Germany
124 E2 **Twiste** Germany
84 B3 **Twitchell Reservoir** California USA
164 5a **Two Boats Village** Ascension
81 N8 **Two Buttes Reservoir** Colorado USA
75 M5 **Two Creeks** Alberta Canada
109 18 **Two Feet Bay** Antigua and Barbuda
84 G3 **Two Guns** Arizona USA
82 F3 **Two Harbors** Minnesota USA
214 E7 **Two Hills** Qld Australia
75 P6 **Two Hills** Alberta Canada
76 J6 **Two River Lake** Ontario Canada
82 H4 **Two Rivers** Wisconsin USA
88 D1 **Two Rivers Reservoir** New Mexico USA
221 D6 **Two Thumb Range** New Zealand
219 I7 **Twofold Bay** NSW Australia
125 J2 **Tworóg** Poland
139 F3 **Twyford** Hampshire England UK
139 G2 **Twyford** Leicester England UK
139 E2 **Twyning** Gloucestershire England UK
138 D3 **Twynllanan** Carmarthenshire Wales UK
138 D2 **Ty-nant** Gwynedd Wales UK
87 J5 **Ty Ty** Georgia USA
132 C1 **Tyachiv** Ukraine
219 K3 **Tyagarah** NSW Australia
138 E2 **Tyberton** Herefordshire England UK
125 J2 **Tychy** Poland
74 D4 **Tyee** Alaska USA
218 H8 **Tyers** Vic. Australia
74 G2 **Tyers** *watercourse* Yukon Territory Canada
122 H2 **Tyfors** Sweden
135 AA8 **Tygda** Russian Federation
122 E2 **Tyin** *lake* Norway
125 K3 **Tylawa** Poland
120 G5 **Tyldal** Norway
81 Q4 **Tyler** Minnesota USA
86 D4 **Tyler** Texas USA
86 F5 **Tylertown** Mississippi USA
132 G2 **Tylihul's'kyy Lyman** *lake* Ukraine
135 AB8 **Tyl'skiy Khrebet** *range* Russian Federation
134 R6 **Tym** *watercourse* Russian Federation
122 H5 **Tymień** Poland
72 A6 **Tymna, Laguna** Russian Federation
140 B2 **Tynan** Armagh Northern Ireland UK
135 Z7 **Tynda** Russian Federation
81 Q1 **Tyndall** Manitoba Canada
81 Q5 **Tyndall** South Dakota USA
120 J5 **Tynderö** Sweden
142 D4 **Tyndrum** Stirling Scotland UK
141 G2 **Tyne** *watercourse* England UK
79 G9 **Tyne Valley** Prince Edward Island Canada
122 G2 **Tyngsjö** Sweden
121 N4 **Tynkä** Finland
132 G1 **Tynovka** Ukraine
120 G5 **Tynset** Norway
121 N4 **Typpö** Finland
121 N3 **Typpyrä** Finland
121 P4 **Tyräjärvi** *lake* Finland
121 P4 **Tyrävaara** Finland
125 L3 **Tyrawa Wołoska** Poland
Tyre *see* **Soûr** Lebanon
122 F2 **Tyrifjorden** *bay* Norway
219 K4 **Tyringham** NSW Australia
191 L2 **Tyrma** Russian Federation
191 L2 **Tyrma** *watercourse* Russian Federation
121 N4 **Tyrnävä** Finland
86 A2 **Tyrone** Oklahoma USA
83 L6 **Tyrone** Pennsylvania USA
86 F3 **Tyronza** Arkansas USA
75 V5 **Tyrrell** Manitoba Canada
218 F6 **Tyrrell, Lake** Vic. Australia
127 J5 **Tyrrhenian Sea** Italy
135 AC6 **Tyry** *watercourse* Russian Federation
132 C/D1 **Tysa** *watercourse* Ukraine
122 C3 **Tysnesøy** *island* Norway
122 C2 **Tysse** Norway
122 I3 **Tystberga** Sweden
139 E3 **Tytherton Lucas** Wiltshire England UK
123 L5 **Tytuvėnai** Lithuania
182 F5 **Tyub-Karagan, Mys** *cape* Kazakhstan
183 K2 **Tyukalinsk** Russian Federation
135 Y6 **Tyukyan** *watercourse* Russian Federation
182 F4 **Tyulen'i Ostrova** *island* Kazakhstan
182 G3 **Tyul'gan** Russian Federation
182 J1 **Tyumen'** Russian Federation
134 O7 **Tyumenskaya Oblast'** *admin. area* Russian Federation
135 AB6 **Tyungyulyu** Russian Federation
183 Q3 **Tyva** *admin. area* Russian Federation
138 D2 **Tywi** *watercourse* Wales UK
138 C2 **Tywyn** Gwynedd Wales UK
100 B5 **Tzungüi** Ecuador

U

192 E5 **U-do** *island* South Korea
223 14 **Ua Huka** *island* French Polynesia
223 14 **Ua Pu** *island* French Polynesia
101 F3 **Uacauyén** Venezuela
UAE *see* **United Arab Emirates**
90 E5 **Ualá** Panama
101 F3 **Uaray, Sierra de** *range* Venezuela
101 E5 **Uarini** Brazil
212 C7 **Uaroo** WA Australia
101 E3 **Uasadi, Cerros** *range* Venezuela
101 G5 **Uatumã** *watercourse* Brazil
102 E5 **Uauá** Brazil
101 F3 **Uaua, Cerro** *mountain* Venezuela
100 E4 **Uaupés** *watercourse* Brazil
132 B3 **Ub** Serbia
103 D8 **Ubá** Brazil
159 G2 **Uba** Nigeria
199 I5 **Ubai** Papua New Guinea
186 D6 **Ubaidullaganj** Madhya Pradesh India
103 E6 **Ubaitaba** Brazil
102 D3 **Ubajara** Brazil
160 B3 **Ubangi** *watercourse* Central African Republic
159 H4 **Ubangi** *watercourse* Congo
100 C3 **Ubaque** Colombia
103 E6 **Ubatã** Brazil
100 C3 **Ubaté** Colombia
103 C8 **Ubatuba** Brazil
179 L4 **Ubauro** Pakistan
127 H4 **Ubaye** *watercourse* France
178 E3 **Ubayyiḑ, Wādī al** Iraq
192 F5 **Ube** Japan
128 E4 **Úbeda** Spain
103 C7 **Uberaba** Brazil
103 B7 **Uberlândia** Brazil
198 F5 **Ubia, Gunung** *mountain* Indonesia
196 E3 **Ubin, Pulau** *island* Singapore
183 M2 **Ubinskoye** *lake* Russian Federation
132 C1 **Ubľa** Slovakia
108 C3 **Ubledo, Laguna** *lake* Argentina
130 G5 **Ubli** Croatia
130 H5 **Ubli** Montenegro
194 E4 **Ubon Ratchathani** Thailand
128 D5 **Ubrique** Spain
197 G6 **Ubud** Indonesia
160 D4 **Ubundu** Democratic Republic of Congo
90 C4 **Ucacabatla** Honduras
182 I6 **Üçajy** Turkmenistan
104 C3 **Ucayali** *admin. area* Peru
104 C3 **Ucayali** *watercourse* Peru
128 E3 **Uceda** Spain
135 U6 **Uchami** Russian Federation
135 T6 **Uchami** *watercourse* Russian Federation
183 M4 **Ucharal** Kazakhstan
214 C4 **Ucharonidge** NT Australia
104 B3 **Uchiza** Peru
183 K5 **Uchqurghon** Uzbekistan
135 AB7 **Uchur** *watercourse* Russian Federation
139 H4 **Uckfield** East Sussex England UK
80 C2 **Ucluelet** British Columbia Canada
133 E6 **Üçpınar** Turkey
131 F7 **Ucria** Italy
89 H5 **Ucum** Mexico
135 AB8 **Uda** *watercourse* Russian Federation
182 E4 **Udachnoye** Russian Federation
135 X5 **Udachnyy** Russian Federation
186 C6 **Udaipur** Rajasthan India
186 E6 **Udaipura** Madhya Pradesh India
178 E4 **Ūḑākh** Saudi Arabia
187 E10 **Udangudi** Tamil Nadu India
187 E8 **Udayagiri** Andhra Pradesh India
130 F4 **Udbina** Croatia
122 F5 **Udby** Denmark
122 F4 **Udbyhøj** Denmark
122 F3 **Uddevalla** Sweden
122 G3 **Uddheden** Sweden
142 E5 **Uddington** South Lanarkshire Scotland UK
120 J4 **Uddjaure** *bay* Sweden
124 C2 **Uden** Netherlands
187 D7 **Udgir** Maharashtra India
186 D4 **Udhampur** Jammu and Kashmir India/Pakistan
124 G4 **Udine** Italy
58 P3 **Udintsev Fracture Zone** *underwater feature* Southern Ocean
134 L7 **Udmurtskaya Respublika** *admin. area* Russian Federation
135 Y7 **Udokan, Khrebet** *range* Russian Federation
194 D3 **Udon Thani** Thailand
222 6a **Udot** *island* Federated States of Micronesia
120 K3 **Udtja** Sweden
187 D9 **Udupi** Karnataka India
135 AD8 **Udyl', Ozero** *lake* Russian Federation
135 Y4 **Udzha** Russian Federation
197 I4 **Uëbonti** Indonesia
125 H1 **Uecker** *watercourse* Germany
193 H4 **Ueda** Japan
198 B4 **Uekuli** Indonesia
160 D3 **Uele** *watercourse* Democratic Republic of Congo
135 Y4 **Uele** *watercourse* Russian Federation
72 C5 **Uelen** Russian Federation
135 AL5 **Uel'kal** Russian Federation
124 F1 **Uelzen** Germany
185 I3 **Uench** Mongolia
160 D3 **Uere** *watercourse* Democratic Republic of Congo
124 E1 **Uetersen** Germany
124 F1 **Uetze** Germany
182 G2 **Ufa** Russian Federation
138 D4 **Uffculme** Devon England UK
138 E2 **Uffington** Shropshire England UK
139 I2 **Ufford** Suffolk England UK
162 B4 **Ugab** *watercourse* Namibia
123 L4 **Ugāle** Latvia
160 E5 **Ugalla** *watercourse* Tanzania
160 E3 **Uganda** *country* Africa
132 B4 **Ugao** Serbia
131 H7 **Ugento** Italy
182 D5 **Ugheltekhili Nakra** *pass* Georgia
128 E5 **Ugíjar** Spain
127 H4 **Ugine** France
78 G3 **Ugjuktok Fiord** Newfoundland and Labrador Canada
178 E4 **'Uglah** Saudi Arabia
135 AD9 **Uglegorsk** Russian Federation
130 F4 **Ugljan** Croatia
183 M3 **Uglovskoye** Russian Federation
72 A6 **Ugol'naya, Bukhta** *bay* Russian Federation
132 B3 **Ugrinovci** Serbia
135 Y5 **Ugumun** Russian Federation
132 D4 **Ugŭrchin** Bulgaria
133 F6 **Uğurluca** Turkey
132 C1 **Uh** *watercourse* Slovakia
125 I3 **Uherské Hradiště** Czech Republic
130 G2 **Uherský Brod** Czech Republic
124 G3 **Úhlava** *watercourse* Czech Republic
125 L2 **Uhniv** Ukraine
127 H4 **Uia Bessanese** *mountain* France
142 A3 **Uibhist a Tuath (North Uist)** *island* Scotland UK
123 L4 **Ūibzde** Latvia
142 B3 **Uig** Highland Scotland UK
160 B5 **Uíge** Angola
160 B5 **Uíge** *admin. area* Angola
223 10 **'Uiha Island** Tonga
192 E3 **Ŭiju** North Korea
182 G3 **Uil** Kazakhstan
182 G3 **Uil** *watercourse* Kazakhstan
121 Q5 **Uimaharju** Finland
84 F2 **Uinkaret Plateau** Arkansas USA
81 J6 **Uinta Mountains** Utah USA
102 E4 **Uiraúna** Brazil
162 B4 **Uis Mine** Namibia
142 B4 **Uisken** Highland Scotland UK
162 E6 **Uitenhage** South Africa
124 D1 **Uithuizen** Netherlands
124 E4 **Uitikon** Switzerland
78 G3 **Uivak, Cape** Newfoundland and Labrador Canada
223 15 **Ujae Atoll** Marshall Islands
222 15 **Ujelang Atoll** Marshall Islands
125 K4 **Újfehértó** Hungary
193 G4 **Uji** Japan
198 E5 **Ujir** *island* Indonesia
186 D6 **Ujjain** Madhya Pradesh India
132 B2 **Újkígyós** Hungary
197 G3 **Ujohbilang** Indonesia
125 I1 **Ujście** Poland
UK *see* **United Kingdom**
135 AH7 **Uka** Russian Federation
187 C7 **Ukai Sagar** *lake* Gujarat India
78 H5 **Ukasiksalik Island** Newfoundland and Labrador Canada
159 F2 **Ukata** Nigeria
189 K3 **Uke-shima** *island* Japan
135 AJ6 **Ukelayat** Russian Federation
134 L6 **Ukhta** Russian Federation
222 8 **Uki** *island* Solomon Islands
80 D7 **Ukiah** California USA
80 F4 **Ukiah** Oregon USA
161 E5 **Ukimbo** Tanzania
121 P2 **Ukonselkä** *lake* Finland
132 G1 **Ukraine** *country* Europe
134 K6 **Uktym** Russian Federation
162 B2 **Uku** Angola
192 F5 **Uku-shima** *island* Japan
161 E3 **Ukutat** *watercourse* Uganda
123 O5 **Ula** *watercourse* Belarus
133 F7 **Ula** Turkey
190 E4 **Ulaan Nuur** *lake* Mongolia
190 F3 **Ulaanbaatar (Ulan Bator)** Mongolia
185 I2 **Ulaangom** Mongolia
185 I2 **Ulaanhus** Mongolia
185 K2 **Ulaanuul** Mongolia
135 AB5 **Ulaga** Russian Federation
135 AC6 **Ulakhan-Bom, Khrebet** *range* Russian Federation
135 AE6 **Ulakhan-Chistay, Khrebet** *range* Russian Federation
219 I5 **Ulan** NSW Australia
190 F5 **Ulan** Nei Mongol Zizhiqu China
Ulan Bator *see* **Ulaanbaatar** Mongolia
190 F5 **Ulan Buh Shamo** Nei Mongol Zizhiqu China
135 W8 **Ulan-Burgasy, Khrebet** *range* Russian Federation
182 D4 **Ulan-Erge** Russian Federation
190 G4 **Ulan Hua** Nei Mongol Zizhiqu China
182 E4 **Ulan-Khol** Russian Federation
190 F5 **Ulan Suhai** *lake* Nei Mongol Zizhiqu China
190 F2 **Ulan-Ude** Russian Federation
190 G4 **Ulan-ull** Mongolia
191 J3 **Ulanhot** Nei Mongol Zizhiqu China
125 L2 **Ulanów** Poland
222 8 **Ulawa** *island* Solomon Islands
199 I5 **Ulawun, Mount** *volcano* Papua New Guinea
135 AD6 **Ul'beya** *watercourse* Russian Federation
104 D3 **Ulbio** Brazil
142 E2 **Ulbster** Highland Scotland UK
141 H3 **Ulceby Skitter** North Lincolnshire England UK
192 F4 **Ulchin** South Korea
131 H6 **Ulcinj** Montenegro
122 G5 **Ule näbbe** *cape* Sweden
191 G2 **Ulety** Russian Federation
133 A5 **Ulëz** Albania
124 D2 **Ulft** Netherlands
185 I2 **Ulgii** Mongolia
Uliastai *see* **Uliastay** Mongolia
185 J3 **Uliastay** Mongolia
125 L3 **Ulič** Slovakia
222 3 **Ulimang** Palau
160 D4 **Ulindi** *watercourse* Democratic Republic of Congo
222 6 **Ulithi** *island* Federated States of Micronesia
125 K5 **Uljma** Serbia
121 N4 **Uljuan tekojärvi** *lake* Finland
74 I6 **Ulkatcho** British Columbia Canada
183 K2 **Ulken Qaraoy Koli** *lake* Kazakhstan
121 N4 **Ulkokrunni** *island* Finland
128 B2 **Ulla** *watercourse* Spain
219 J6 **Ulladulla** NSW Australia
142 C3 **Ullapool** Highland Scotland UK
122 G4 **Ullared** Sweden
120 L3 **Ullatti** Sweden
121 M5 **Ullava** Finland
121 N5 **Ullavanjärvi** *lake* Finland
216 E1 **Ullawarra** WA Australia
120 K4 **Ullbergsträsk** Sweden
130 H3 **Üllés** Hungary
128 E2 **Ullibarri, Embalse de** *lake* Spain
142 B3 **Ullinish** Highland Scotland UK
108 B5 **Ulloa, Península** *peninsula* Chile
120 K2 **Ullsfjorden** *bay* Norway
140 F2 **Ullswater** *lake* England UK
124 E3 **Ulm** Germany
123 K4 **Ulmale** Latvia
219 K3 **Ulmarra** NSW Australia
125 L4 **Ulmeni** Romania
132 F2 **Ulmu** Moldova
122 E2 **Ulnes** Norway
130 H5 **Ulog** Bosnia and Herzegovina
219 K4 **Ulong** NSW Australia
218 D2 **Uloowaranie, Lake** SA Australia
135 AF4 **Ulovo** Russian Federation
120 L2 **Uløya** *island* Norway
192 F4 **Ulreuno-do** *island* South Korea
125 G3 **Ulrichsberg** Austria
120 I5 **Ulriksfors** Sweden
141 H3 **Ulrome** East Riding of Yorkshire England UK
122 E2 **Ulsåk** Norway
192 F4 **Ulsan** South Korea
124 F2 **Ulster** *watercourse* Germany
120 I2 **Ulsvåg** Norway
120 K3 **Ultevis** *mountain* Sweden
218 F6 **Ultima** Vic. Australia
104 C2 **Ultraoriental, Cordillera** *range* Peru
198 C3 **Ulu** Indonesia
135 AA6 **Ulu** Russian Federation
196 D3 **Ulu Tiram** Malaysia
89 I6 **Ulua** *watercourse* Honduras
133 F5 **Ulubat Gölü** *lake* Turkey
133 F6 **Ulubey** Turkey
133 G6 **Uluborlu** Turkey
133 F5 **Uludağ** *mountain* Turkey
163 F5 **Ulundi** South Africa
185 H3 **Ulungur Hu** *lake* Xinjiang Uygur Zizhiqu China
217 L2 **Uluru (Ayers Rock)** *mountain* NT Australia
142 C4 **Uluvalt** Highland Scotland UK
220 4 **Uluvehi Landing** Niue New Zealand
142 B4 **Ulva** *island* Scotland UK
140 E2 **Ulverston** Cumbria England UK
219 R10 **Ulverstone** Tas. Australia
122 H3 **Ulvettern** *bay* Sweden
123 N3 **Ulvi** Estonia
123 K2 **Ulvila** Finland
120 K5 **Ulvön** *island* Sweden
135 AD7 **Ul'ya** *watercourse* Russian Federation
132 G1 **Ul'yanovka** Ukraine
182 E2 **Ul'yanovsk** Russian Federation
182 E2 **Ul'yanovskaya Oblast'** *admin. area* Russian Federation
81 O8 **Ulysses** Kansas USA
190 E3 **Ulziit** Mongolia
190 E3 **Ulziit** Mongolia
190 D3 **Ulziit** Mongolia
190 F4 **Ulziit** Mongolia
190 G3 **Ulziit** Mongolia
160 D3 **Uma** Democratic Republic of Congo
130 E4 **Umag** Croatia
159 F3 **Umaisha** Nigeria
222 6a **Uman** *island* Federated States of Micronesia
89 H4 **Umán** Mexico

132 L1 **Uman'** Ukraine
106 D4 **Umango, Cerro** *mountain* Argentina
198 E5 **Umari** Indonesia
102 E4 **Umarizal** Brazil
187 F7 **Umarkot** Orissa India
179 L4 **Umarkot** Pakistan
218 D2 **Umaroona Lake** SA Australia
222 5 **Umatac** Guam
87 K6 **Umatilla** Florida USA
80 F4 **Umatilla** Oregon USA
121 S3 **Umba** Russian Federation
214 D2 **Umbakumba** NT Australia
217 M2 **Umbeara** NT Australia
160 C2 **Umbelasha** *watercourse* Sudan
198 B4 **Umbele** *island* Indonesia
130 E5 **Umbertide** Italy
218 E4 **Umberumberka, Mount** NSW Australia
199 H5 **Umboi** *island* Papua New Guinea
121 S3 **Umbozero, Ozero** *lake* Russian Federation
127 J3 **Umbrail, Piz** *mountain* Italy/Switzerland
130 E5 **Umbria** *admin. area* Italy
199 I4 **Umbukul** Papua New Guinea
218 C3 **Umbum** *watercourse* SA Australia
162 E3 **Ume** *watercourse* Zimbabwe
120 L5 **Umeå** Sweden
120 K4 **Umeälven** *watercourse* Sweden
82 D1 **Umfreville Lake** Ontario Canada
78 G4 **Umiakovik Lake** Newfoundland and Labrador Canada
73 O6 **Umiiviip Kangertiva** *bay* Greenland
84 inset **'Umikoa** Hawai'i USA
77 Q4 **Umiujaq** Quebec Canada
163 F5 **Umlazi** South Africa
178 D5 **Umm al Birak** Saudi Arabia
179 H4 **Umm al Qaywayn** United Arab Emirates
178 D5 **Umm 'Amâyin** Saudi Arabia
156 C1 **Umm ar Rizam** Libya
179 H5 **Umm as Samim** Oman
178 G4 **Umm ash Shubrum** Qatar
156 D5 **Umm Badr** Sudan
156 D5 **Umm Bel** Sudan
156 E5 **Umm Dam** Sudan
156 D5 **Umm Dhibbān** Sudan
155 J3 **Umm Farud** Libya
156 D5 **Umm Keddada** Sudan
178 D4 **Umm Lajj** Saudi Arabia
156 D5 **Umm Marahik** Sudan
178 F3 **Umm Qaşr** Iraq
156 D5 **Umm Qawzayn** Sudan
178 E6 **Umm Rahţā'** Saudi Arabia
156 E5 **Umm Ruwaba** Sudan
156 D1 **Umm Sa'ad** Libya
159 I1 **Umm Saggat, Wadi** *watercourse* Sudan
156 E5 **Umm Saiyala** Sudan
178 G4 **Umm Şalāl Muḥammad** Qatar
178 D5 **Umm Samā'** Saudi Arabia
156 D5 **Umm Shugeira** Sudan
156 D5 **Umm Sidrah** Saudi Arabia
122 G5 **Ummanz** *island* Germany
72 C8 **Umnak Island** Alaska USA
120 J4 **Umnassjön** *lake* Sweden
190 G3 **Umnegelder** Mongolia
135 U5 **Umnym, Khrebet** *range* Russian Federation
163 G2 **Umpuhua** Mozambique
133 G6 **Umraniye** Turkey
187 E7 **Umred** Maharashtra India
187 E7 **Umri** Andhra Pradesh India
198 E4 **Umsini, Gunung** *mountain* Indonesia
162 E6 **Umtata** South Africa
159 F3 **Umuahia** Nigeria
103 A8 **Umuarama** Brazil
162 E6 **Umzimkulu** South Africa
162 E4 **Umzingwani** *watercourse* Zimbabwe
162 F6 **Umzinto** South Africa
130 G4 **Una** *watercourse* Bosnia and Herzegovina
103 E6 **Una** Brazil
187 C7 **Una** Gujarat India
186 D4 **Una** Himachal Pradesh India
121 U4 **Una** Russian Federation
87 J4 **Unadilla** Georgia USA
103 C7 **Unaí** Brazil
72 C6 **Unalakleet** Alaska USA
72 C8 **Unalaska** Alaska USA
72 C8 **Unalaska Island** Alaska USA
162 G3 **Unango** Mozambique
222 6 **Unanu** *island* Federated States of Micronesia
106 E6 **Unanué** Argentina
102 E4 **Unare** *watercourse* Venezuela
101 E2 **Unare, Laguna de** *lake* Venezuela
121 N3 **Unari** Finland
121 N3 **Unari** *lake* Finland
198 D4 **Unauna** *island* Indonesia
129 F2 **Uncastillo** Spain
85 I1 **Uncompahgre** *watercourse* Colorado USA
81 L7 **Uncompahgre Peak** Colorado USA
81 K7 **Uncompahgre Plateau** Colorado USA
122 H3 **Unden** *lake* Sweden
122 H3 **Undenäs** Sweden
190 D3 **Under-ulaan** Mongolia
218 E6 **Underbool** Vic. Australia
185 J2 **Underhangai** Mongolia
120 H5 **Undersåker** Sweden
190 F3 **Undershil** Mongolia
190 F3 **Undershireet** Mongolia
81 O3 **Underwood** North Dakota USA
214 E5 **Undilla** Qld Australia
192 F2 **Undok** North Korea
198 B6 **Undu, Tanjung** *cape* Indonesia
198 D4 **Undur** Indonesia
123 K3 **Undva Nina** *cape* Estonia
101 E5 **Uneiuxi** *watercourse* Brazil
121 T5 **Unezhma** Russian Federation
197 F5 **Ungaran** Indonesia
218 H5 **Ungarie** NSW Australia
218 C6 **Ungarra** SA Australia
78 B3 **Ungava, Péninsule d'** *peninsula* Quebec Canada
78 D3 **Ungava Bay** Quebec Canada
132 E2 **Ungheni** Moldova
132 D3 **Ungheni** Romania
132 D3 **Ungra** Romania
100 B2 **Unguia** Colombia
123 M4 **Ungura ezers** *lake* Latvia
132 E2 **Ungureni-Hora** Romania
162 G4 **Ungwana Bay** Kenya
214 D3 **Ungwariba Point** NT Australia
186 D6 **Unhel** Madhya Pradesh India
130 F1 **Unhošť** Czech Republic
102 D4 **União** Brazil
102 D4 **União da Vitória** Brazil
105 I9 **União de Minas** Brazil
105 H3 **União do Sul** Brazil
87 J2 **Unicoi** Tennessee USA
130 G2 **Uničov** Czech Republic
125 J2 **Uniejów** Poland
130 F4 **Unije** Croatia
130 F4 **Unije** *island* Croatia
222 6a **Unikar, Mochun** *strait* Federated States of Micronesia
72 C8 **Unimak Island** Alaska USA
101 F5 **Unini** *watercourse* Brazil
106 E5 **Unión** Argentina
109 10a **Union** Grenada
107 G3 **Unión** Paraguay
82 F7 **Union** Missouri USA
81 R6 **Union** Nebraska USA
80 G4 **Union** Oregon USA
87 K3 **Union** South Carolina USA
83 K8 **Union** West Virginia USA
195 G5 **Union Atoll** Spratly Islands
87 I4 **Union City** Georgia USA
83 L6 **Union City** Pennsylvania USA
86 G2 **Union City** Tennessee USA
88 D5 **Unión de Tula** Mexico
80 E3 **Union Gap** Washington USA
89 G5 **Unión Hidalgo** Mexico
109 10 **Union Island** Grenada
91 I4 **Union Island** St Vincent and the Grenadines
87 J4 **Union Point** Georgia USA
87 I4 **Union Springs** Alabama USA
84 B1 **Union Valley Reservoir** California USA
162 D6 **Uniondale** South Africa
86 H4 **Uniontown** Alabama USA
86 D2 **Uniontown** Kansas USA
83 L7 **Uniontown** Pennsylvania USA
80 G3 **Uniontown** Washington USA
82 J5 **Unionville** Michigan USA
82 E6 **Unionville** Missouri USA
179 H5 **United Arab Emirates** *country* Middle East
137 F4 **United Kingdom (UK)** *country* Europe
70 **United States of America (USA)** *country* North America
73 K2 **United States Range** Nunavut Canada
75 Q6 **Unity** Saskatchewan Canada
160 D2 **Unity** *admin. area* Sudan
162 B4 **Unjab** *watercourse* Namibia
186 C6 **Unjha** Gujarat India
120 H4 **Unkervatnet** *lake* Norway
186 E5 **Unnao** Uttar Pradesh India
122 G4 **Unnaryd** Sweden
122 G4 **Unnen** *lake* Sweden
122 H2 **Unntorp** Sweden
121 P5 **Unnukka** *bay* Finland
192 E3 **Unsan** North Korea
192 E3 **Ŭnsan** North Korea
120 M5 **Untamala** Finland
186 F6 **Untari** Jharkhand India
124 G4 **Untertilliach** Austria
122 G1 **Unterueckersee** *lake* Germany
74 F4 **Unuk** *watercourse* British Columbia Canada
136 F5 **Ünye** Turkey
182 D1 **Unzha** Russian Federation
134 J7 **Unzha** *watercourse* Russian Federation
131 D5 **Uomo, Capo d'** *cape* Italy
101 F3 **Uonán** Venezuela
194 E2 **Uông Bi** Vietnam
189 I3 **Uotsuri-shima** *island* Japan
90 C5 **Upala** Costa Rica
102 E4 **Upanema** Brazil
101 F2 **Upata** Venezuela
139 F3 **Upavon** Wiltshire England UK
160 D3 **Upemba, Lac** *lake* Democratic Republic of Congo
123 L4 **Upenieki** Latvia
73 N4 **Upernavik** Greenland
81 O2 **Upham** North Dakota USA
195 J6 **Upi** Philippines
130 J2 **Úpice** Czech Republic
162 D5 **Upington** South Africa
123 M2 **Upinniemi** Finland
138 E3 **Upleadon** Gloucestershire England UK
187 C7 **Upleta** Gujarat India
138 E4 **Uplyme** Devon England UK
123 N4 **Upmala** Latvia
120 J3 **Upmas** *lake* Sweden
121 Q3 **Upoloksha** Russian Federation
222 1 **Upolu** *island* Samoa
84 inset **'Upolu Point** Hawai'i USA
80 G1 **Upper Arrow Lake** British Columbia Canada
220 G4 **Upper Atiamuri** New Zealand
86 H3 **Upper Bear Creek Reservoir** Alabama USA
139 G2 **Upper Benefield** Northamptonshire England UK
142 F4 **Upper Birnie** Aberdeenshire Scotland UK
139 G2 **Upper Borth** Ceredigion Wales UK
142 E2 **Upper Camster** Highland Scotland UK
138 D2 **Upper Chapel** Powys Wales UK
83 N4 **Upper Chateaugay Lake** New York USA
139 F1 **Upper Denton** Cumbria England UK
75 S4 **Upper Foster Lake** Saskatchewan Canada
76 I7 **Upper Goose Lake** Ontario Canada
141 H2 **Upper Helmsley** North Yorkshire England UK
142 E5 **Upper Howecleuch** South Lanarkshire Scotland UK
139 F1 **Upper Hulme** Staffordshire England UK
79 E9 **Upper Kent** New Brunswick Canada
80 E5 **Upper Klamath Lake** Oregon USA
74 D2 **Upper Laberge** Yukon Territory Canada
84 A1 **Upper Lake** California USA
74 G2 **Upper Liard** Yukon Territory Canada
140 A2 **Upper Lough Erne** *lake* Northern Ireland UK
82 E2 **Upper Manitou Lake** Ontario Canada
109 9 **Upper Manzanilla** Trinidad and Tobago
221 E5 **Upper Moutere** New Zealand
79 G10 **Upper Musquodoboit** Nova Scotia Canada
161 E2 **Upper Nile** *admin. area* Sudan
196 C3 **Upper Peirce Reservoir** Singapore
82 G4 **Upper Red Lake** Minnesota USA
83 N4 **Upper Saranac Lake** New York USA
196 C3 **Upper Seletar Reservoir** Singapore
139 F3 **Upper Slaughter** Gloucestershire England UK
219 J2 **Upper Spring Creek** Qld Australia
215 H5 **Upper Stone** Qld Australia
139 F4 **Upper Street** Hampshire England UK
221 E5 **Upper Takaka** New Zealand
101 G4 **Upper Takutu-Upper Essequibo** *admin. area* Guyana
76 J6 **Upper Windigo Lake** Ontario Canada
122 G3 **Upphärad** Sweden
139 G2 **Uppingham** Rutland England UK
122 I3 **Uppsala** Sweden
122 I2 **Uppsala** *admin. area* Sweden
82 F2 **Upsala** Ontario Canada
141 G2 **Upsall** North Yorkshire England UK
79 E9 **Upsalquitch** *watercourse* New Brunswick Canada
87 N2 **Upshur Bay** Virginia USA
215 I5 **Upstart, Cape** Qld Australia
143 D5 **Upton** Ireland
138 C4 **Upton** Cornwall England UK
139 E4 **Upton** Dorset England UK
139 F4 **Upton** Hampshire England UK
139 G2 **Upton** Norfolk England UK
141 H3 **Upton** Nottinghamshire England UK
139 D3 **Upton** Somerset England UK
83 J8 **Upton** Kentucky USA
81 M4 **Upton** Wyoming USA
138 E3 **Upton Bishop** Herefordshire England UK
138 D4 **Upton Pyne** Devon England UK
139 E3 **Upton St Leonards** Gloucestershire England UK
139 E3 **Upton Scudamore** Wiltshire England UK
139 H2 **Upwell** Cambridgeshire England UK
139 G2 **Upwood** Cambridgeshire England UK
123 L5 **Upyna** Lithuania
121 R2 **Ura-Guba** Russian Federation
130 C5 **Urabá, Golfo de** *bay* Colombia
125 H1 **Urad** Poland
101 F3 **Uraday** Venezuela
123 M2 **Urajärvi** *lake* Finland
182 F4 **Ural** *watercourse* Kazakhstan
182 H3 **Ural** *watercourse* Russian Federation
219 J4 **Uralla** NSW Australia
135 AA8 **Uralovka** Russian Federation
182 F3 **Ural'sk** Kazakhstan
182 H2 **Ural'skiy Khrebet** *range* Russian Federation
160 E5 **Urambo** Tanzania
187 D8 **Uran Islampur** Maharashtra India
218 G6 **Urana** NSW Australia
218 H6 **Urana, Lake** NSW Australia
214 E6 **Urandangi** Qld Australia
86 E5 **Urania** Louisiana USA
75 Q3 **Uranium City** Saskatchewan Canada
214 C3 **Urapunga** NT Australia
101 F4 **Uraricaa** *watercourse* Brazil
101 F4 **Uraricoera** *watercourse* Brazil
131 C7 **Uras** Sardinia Italy
187 D8 **Uravakonda** Andhra Pradesh India
182 E2 **Urazovka** Russian Federation
82 G6 **Urbana** Illinois USA
82 J6 **Urbana** Ohio USA
127 K5 **Urbania** Italy
102 D3 **Urbano Santos** Brazil
130 E5 **Urbino** Italy
131 C5 **Urbino, Étang d'** *lake* Corsica France
125 I3 **Určice** Czech Republic
104 D4 **Urcos** Peru
182 E4 **Urda** Kazakhstan
100 B5 **Urdaneta** Ecuador
195 I4 **Urdaneta** Philippines
126 D5 **Urdos** France
183 N4 **Urdzhar** Kazakhstan
141 G2 **Ure** *watercourse* England UK
198 E4 **Urema** *watercourse* Indonesia
134 K7 **Uren'** Russian Federation
220 F4 **Urenui** New Zealand
222 7 **Uréparapara** *island* Vanuatu
88 C2 **Ures** Mexico
185 J3 **Urgamal** Mongolia
182 H5 **Urganch** Uzbekistan
133 E6 **Urganlı** Turkey
190 G4 **Urgen** Mongolia
142 B3 **Urgha** Na h-Eileanan Siar Scotland UK
136 E5 **Ürgüp** Turkey
157 F5 **Uri Wenz** *watercourse* Ethiopia
100 C4 **Uribe** Colombia
108 A5 **Uribe, Canal** *strait* Chile
100 C2 **Uribia** Colombia
125 L5 **Uricani** Romania
82 E7 **Urich** Missouri USA
190 E3 **Uringuur** Mongolia
104 C4 **Urinpay** Peru
85 I7 **Urique** Mexico
218 F3 **Urisino** NSW Australia
104 C3 **Urituyacu** *watercourse* Peru
132 D2 **Uriu** Romania
124 C1 **Urk** Netherlands
135 E5 **Urkarakh** Russian Federation
109 I8 **Urlings** Antigua and Barbuda
Urmia, Lake *see* **Orūmīyeh, Daryācheh-ye** Iran
159 F3 **Uromi** Nigeria
121 S5 **Urosozero** Russian Federation
183 K6 **Ŭroteppa** Tajikistan
182 D5 **Urozhaynoye** Russian Federation
141 G2 **Urra** North Yorkshire England UK
100 B3 **Urrao** Colombia
108 E2 **Urre Lauquen, Laguna** *lake* Argentina
107 F4 **Urrúnaga, Embalse de** *lake* Spain
89 F5 **Ursulo Galván** Mexico
120 L4 **Ursviken** Sweden
125 J1 **Urszulewo** Poland
182 H3 **Urtazym** Russian Federation
103 B6 **Uruaçu** Brazil
192 F5 **Uruana** Brazil
84 D5 **Uruapan** Mexico
105 F2 **Urupiara, Lago** *lake* Brazil
105 H1 **Uruará** Brazil
104 C4 **Urubamba** *watercourse* Peru
105 F4 **Urubichá** Bolivia
101 G5 **Urubu** *watercourse* Brazil
101 G5 **Urucará** Brazil
136 E2 **Urucje** Russian Federation
105 F2 **Urucu** *watercourse* Brazil
103 E6 **Uruçuca** Brazil
102 C4 **Uruçuí** Brazil
102 C5 **Uruçuí, Serra do** *range* Brazil
102 C4 **Uruçuí Preto** *watercourse* Brazil
103 C6 **Urucuia** *watercourse* Brazil
101 H5 **Urucuricaia, Ilha** *island* Brazil
101 G5 **Urucurituba** Brazil
107 G4 **Uruguaiana** Brazil
107 G5 **Uruguay** *watercourse* Argentina
107 G5 **Uruguay** *country* South America
105 E6 **Uruguayito** Bolivia
222 6 **Urukthapel** *island* Palau
100 D2 **Urumaco** Venezuela
182 D5 **Urup** Russian Federation
135 AF9 **Urup, Ostrov** *island* Kuril Islands
103 B8 **Urupês** Brazil
135 Z8 **Urusha** Russian Federation
160 E5 **Uruwira** Tanzania
104 C4 **Urusyaccasa** Peru
124 B3 **Ury** France
183 O3 **Uryl** Kazakhstan
134 K7 **Urzhum** Russian Federation
109 21 **US Virgin Islands** *unincorporated US territory* Caribbean
192 F5 **Usa** Japan
USA *see* **United States of America** North America
134 M5 **Usa** *watercourse* Russian Federation
136 D5 **Uşak** *admin. area* Turkey
136 D5 **Uşak** Turkey
103 O6 **Usakino** Belarus
162 C4 **Usakos** Namibia
58 K2 **Usarp Mountains** Antarctica
178 E4 **'Usaylah** Saudi Arabia
109 7 **Usborne, Mount** Falkland Islands
132 B4 **Ušće** Serbia
122 H6 **Usedom** *island* Germany
216 C3 **Useless Loop** WA Australia
161 E4 **Usengi** Kenya
123 O5 **Ushachy** Belarus
134 Q2 **Ushakova, Ostrov** *island* Russian Federation
135 AL4 **Ushakovskoye** Russian Federation
121 U4 **Ushan** Iran
75 T6 **Usherville** Saskatchewan Canada
135 AK5 **Ushkan'iy, Gory** *range* Russian Federation
183 Q3 **Ushpe-khol'** *lake* Russian Federation
183 L3 **Ushtagan** Kazakhstan
183 M4 **Ushtobe** Kazakhstan
108 C6 **Ushuaia** Argentina
135 AH5 **Ushurakchan, Khrebet** *range* Russian Federation
123 L4 **Usi** Latvia
104 C3 **Usina Taparabo** Brazil
124 E2 **Usingen** Germany
199 H5 **Usino** Papua New Guinea
76 L5 **Usisko** *watercourse* Ontario Canada
74 H5 **Usk** British Columbia Canada
138 E3 **Usk** Monmouthshire Wales UK
138 D3 **Usk** *watercourse* Wales UK
138 D3 **Usk Reservoir** *lake* Wales UK
122 C3 **Uskedalen** Norway
122 H3 **Usken** *lake* Sweden
182 C3 **Usman'** Russian Federation
123 P5 **Usmyn'** Russian Federation
135 V8 **Usol'ye-Sibirskoye** Russian Federation
193 I3 **Usoriyama-ko** *lake* Japan
123 D5 **Uspallata** Argentina
183 M3 **Uspenka** Kazakhstan
183 K4 **Uspenskiy** Kazakhstan
182 D5 **Uspenskiy** Russian Federation
126 F4 **Ussel** France
192 G2 **Ussuri** *watercourse* Russian Federation
192 F2 **Ussuriysk** Russian Federation
135 AJ5 **Ust'-Belaya** Russian Federation
135 W6 **Ust'-Chayka Zimor'ye** Russian Federation
134 L6 **Ust'-Chërnaya** Russian Federation
135 V7 **Ust' Ilimsk** Russian Federation
135 V7 **Ust'-Ilimskiy Vodokhranilishche** *lake* Russian Federation
134 P7 **Ust' Ishim** Russian Federation
135 AH7 **Ust'-Kamchatsk** Russian Federation
183 N3 **Ust'-Kamenogorsk (Öskemen)** Kazakhstan
135 Y8 **Ust'-Karenga** Russian Federation
191 I2 **Ust'-Karsk** Russian Federation
135 AG7 **Ust'-Khayryuzovo** Russian Federation
135 W7 **Ust' Kut** Russian Federation
182 C4 **Ust'-Labinsk** Russian Federation
134 M5 **Ust' Lyzha** Russian Federation
134 L6 **Ust' Nem** Russian Federation
135 AD6 **Ust' Nera** Russian Federation
135 AB8 **Ust' Niman** Russian Federation
135 AB5 **Ust'-Olenëk** Russian Federation
135 AE6 **Ust' Omchug** Russian Federation
190 E1 **Ust'-Ordynskiy** Russian Federation
135 V8 **Ust'-Ordynskiy Buryatskiy AO** *admin. area* Russian Federation
134 S7 **Ust'-Ozernoye** Russian Federation
134 T7 **Ust'-Pit** Russian Federation
134 R5 **Ust'-Port** Russian Federation
135 AB6 **Ust'-Tatta** Russian Federation
136 M6 **Ust' Un'ya** Russian Federation
134 M5 **Ust' Usa** Russian Federation
135 AG7 **Ust'-Voyampolka** Russian Federation
135 AC4 **Ust' Yansk** Russian Federation
134 O5 **Ust'-Yuribey** Russian Federation
125 G2 **Ústecký Kraj** *admin. area* Czech Republic
130 C3 **Uster** Switzerland
122 E3 **Ustevatn** *lake* Norway
125 H2 **Ústí nad Labem** Czech Republic
132 F2 **Ustia** Moldova
130 H5 **Ustibar** Bosnia and Herzegovina
131 E7 **Ustica, Isola di** *island* Italy
125 I5 **Ustka** Poland
183 N3 **Ustokamenogorskoye Vodokhranilishche** *lake* Kazakhstan
133 E4 **Ustrem** Bulgaria
125 L3 **Ustrzyki Dolne** Poland
125 L3 **Ustrzyki Górne** Poland
90 E5 **Ustupo** Panama
125 M2 **Ustyluh** Ukraine
132 H2 **Ustynivka** Ukraine
198 B6 **Usu** *island* Indonesia
90 B4 **Usulután** El Salvador
123 O5 **Usvyach'ye, Vozyera** *lake* Belarus
123 O4 **Usvyach'ye, Vozyera** *lake* Russian Federation
123 P5 **Usvyaty** Russian Federation
198 F5 **Uta** Indonesia
198 F5 **Uta** *watercourse* Indonesia
70 **Utah** *admin. area* USA
218 G4 **Utah Lake** NSW Australia
80 J6 **Utah Lake** Utah USA
121 O4 **Utajärvi** Finland
197 H6 **Utan** Indonesia
121 J5 **Utanede** Sweden
104 C3 **Utcuyacu** Peru
81 R5 **Ute** Iowa USA
129 F3 **Utebo** Spain
162 D3 **Utembo** *watercourse* Angola
123 M5 **Utena** Lithuania
123 M5 **Utenos** *admin. area* Lithuania
135 AJ5 **Utesiki** Russian Federation
161 F5 **Utete** Tanzania
194 C4 **Uthai Thani** *admin. area* Thailand
120 F5 **Uthaug** Norway
105 G4 **Utiariti** Brazil
81 O7 **Utica** Kansas USA
86 F4 **Utica** Mississippi USA
83 N5 **Utica** New York USA
83 J6 **Utica** Ohio USA
129 F4 **Utiel** Spain
220 F4 **Utiku** New Zealand
72 H7 **Utikuma Lake** Alberta Canada
183 P2 **Utinoye** *watercourse* Russian Federation
223 I5 **Utirik Atoll** Marshall Islands
90 C4 **Utla-Almuk** Honduras
122 H4 **Utlängan** *island* Sweden
122 D2 **Utne** Norway
192 F5 **Uto** Japan
123 J3 **Utö** *island* Sweden
138 D4 **Uton** Devon England UK
214 C7 **Utopia** NT Australia
123 P3 **Utorgosh** Russian Federation
129 D4 **Utracán, Valle de** *valley* Argentina
186 F5 **Utraula** Uttar Pradesh India
124 C1 **Utrecht** Netherlands
100 B3 **Utría, Ensenada de** *bay* Colombia
121 O2 **Utsjoki** Finland
120 H3 **Utskarpen** Norway
58 E2 **Utstikkar Bay** Antarctica
182 E4 **Utta** Russian Federation
186 E5 **Uttar Pradesh** *admin. area* India
194 D3 **Uttaradit** Thailand
194 D3 **Uttaradit** *admin. area* Thailand
186 E4 **Uttarakhand** *admin. area* India
186 E4 **Uttarkashi** Uttaranchal India
124 G4 **Uttendorf** Austria
83 L4 **Utterson** Ontario Canada
120 K4 **Utterträsk** Sweden
139 F2 **Uttoxeter** Staffordshire England UK
135 AB5 **Uttyakh** Russian Federation
222 1 **Utupua** *island* Solomon Islands
104 E6 **Uturunco, Cerro** *mountain* Bolivia
120 G4 **Utvorda** Norway
191 G3 **Uulbayan** New Mongolia
73 N4 **Uummannaq** Greenland
73 N4 **Uummannaq Fjord** Greenland
121 N5 **Uurainen** Finland
121 O5 **Uurainen** *lake* Finland
185 I2 **Üüreg Nuur** *lake* Mongolia
123 M3 **Uuri** Estonia
120 M5 **Uuro** Finland
123 K2 **Uusikaupunki** Finland
162 B3 **Uutapi** Namibia
121 P4 **Uva** Finland
132 A4 **Uvac** Serbia
87 J4 **Uvalda** Georgia USA
86 B6 **Uvalde** Texas USA
182 D3 **Uvarovo** Russian Federation
222 1 **Uvea** *island* Wallis and Futuna
133 E6 **Uvecik** Turkey
121 F6 **Uveral** Venezuela
160 E5 **Uvinza** Tanzania
185 I2 **Uvs** *admin. area* Mongolia
185 I2 **Uvs Nuur** *lake* Mongolia
160 C4 **Uvungo** Democratic Republic of Congo
192 G5 **Uwajima** Japan
199 F5 **Uwebu** Indonesia
156 D3 **Uweinat, Jebel** *mountain* Sudan
196 E3 **Uwi** *island* Indonesia
199 G5 **Uwimmerah** *watercourse* Indonesia
83 L4 **Uxbridge** Ontario Canada
139 G3 **Uxbridge** Greater London England UK
135 AD5 **Uyandi** Russian Federation
190 E3 **Uyanga** Mongolia
134 T7 **Uyar** Russian Federation
142 inset **Uyeasound** Shetland Scotland UK
134 R3 **Uyedineniya, Ostrov** *island* Russian Federation
159 F3 **Uyo** Nigeria
160 E4 **Uyowa** Tanzania
181 H4 **Uyu** *watercourse* Myanmar
104 E6 **Uyuni** Bolivia
104 E6 **Uyuni, Salar de** *pan* Bolivia
182 H5 **Uzbekistan** *country*
182 G6 **Uzboy** *watercourse* Turkmenistan
108 C3 **Uzcudun** Argentina
125 K5 **Uzdin** Serbia
125 K1 **Uzdowo** Poland
126 E4 **Uzerche** France
127 G4 **Uzès** France
136 D2 **Uzh** *watercourse* Ukraine
132 D1 **Uzhhorod** Ukraine
132 C1 **Uzhok** Ukraine
132 B5 **Užice** Serbia
182 D3 **Uzlovaya** Russian Federation
125 L2 **Uzlovoye** Russian Federation
132 A3 **Uzovnica** Serbia
133 E6 **Uzun Ada** *island* Turkey
133 F5 **Uzunköprü** Turkey
123 L5 **Užventis** Lithuania
130 C3 **Uzwil** Switzerland

V

88 C1 **V-Cross-T Lake** New Mexico USA
159 I3 **Va** *watercourse* Central African Republic
121 N5 **Vaajakoski** Finland
121 O4 **Vaala** Finland
121 O4 **Vaalajärvi** Finland
123 O3 **Vaalajärvi** *lake* Finland
123 N2 **Vaalimaa** Finland
124 D2 **Vaals** Netherlands
121 O5 **Vaaraperä** Sweden
123 N2 **Vaaraslahti** Finland
126 E3 **Vaas** France
120 L5 **Vaasa** Finland
120 M5 **Vaasa** *admin. area* Finland
123 M1 **Vaasanjärvi** Finland
125 J4 **Vác** Hungary
107 H4 **Vacaria** Brazil
108 B4 **Vacas, Sierra de las** *range* Argentina
80 E7 **Vacaville** California USA
126 E4 **Vacha** Russian Federation
121 R5 **Vache, Île-à-** *island* Haiti
78 B2 **Vachon** *watercourse* Quebec Canada
187 C7 **Vada** Maharashtra India
122 H3 **Vaddö** *island* Sweden
80 D3 **Vader** Washington USA
123 F3 **Vaderöfjorden** *bay* Sweden
182 E2 **Vadfoss** Norway
182 D2 **Vadinsk** Russian Federation
85 J2 **Vadito** New Mexico USA
187 C6 **Vadodara** Gujarat India
123 M5 **Vadokliai** Lithuania
121 P1 **Vadsø** Norway
124 H3 **Vadstena** Sweden
124 E4 **Vaduz** Liechtenstein
122 C2 **Værlandet** *island* Norway
120 H3 **Værøy** *island* Norway
122 C3 **Våg** Norway
122 C3 **Våga** Norway
134 J6 **Vaga** *watercourse* Russian Federation
120 F6 **Vågåmo** Norway
73 S6 **Vágar** *island* Faroe Islands
120 F6 **Vågåvatn** *bay* Norway
120 C6 **Våge** Norway
121 P2 **Vagge** Norway
122 I3 **Väggö** *island* Sweden
222 8 **Vaghena** *island* Solomon Islands
128 B3 **Vagos** Portugal
122 C2 **Vagsøy** *island* Norway
123 N4 **Vagula Järv** *lake* Estonia
130 G2 **Váh** *watercourse* Slovakia
121 N5 **Vahanka** Finland
123 M2 **Vaheri** Finland
223 14 **Vahitahi** *island* French Polynesia
178 G2 **Vahnabad** Iran
58 V1 **Vahsel Bay** Antarctica
122 L2 **Vahto** Finland
86 G4 **Vaiden** Mississippi USA
126 D2 **Vaiges** France
109 5 **Vaihu** Isla de Pascua (Easter Island)
187 D7 **Vaijapur** Maharashtra India
123 L3 **Väike-Pakri** *island* Estonia
120 K3 **Vaikijaur** Sweden
120 K3 **Vaikijaur** *lake* Sweden
81 L7 **Vail** Colorado USA
199 H5 **Vailala** *watercourse* Papua New Guinea
126 F2 **Vailly** France
126 F3 **Vailly-sur-Sauldre** France
120 J3 **Vaimok** *lake* Sweden
123 N4 **Vainava** Latvia
223 10a **Vaini** Tonga
187 D7 **Vairag** Maharashtra India
127 G4 **Vaison-la-Romaine** France
223 14b **Vaitape** French Polynesia
223 14a **Vaitumaa** French Polynesia
223 13 **Vaitupu** *island* Tuvalu
223 12b **Vaitupu** Wallis and Futuna
120 K3 **Vajmat** Sweden
132 A3 **Vajska** Serbia
125 I4 **Vajszló** Hungary
159 I3 **Vakaga** *admin. area* Central African Republic
122 H2 **Vakern** Sweden
183 K6 **Vakhsh** *watercourse* Tajikistan
120 K3 **Vakkotavarekåtan** Sweden
132 A2 **Vál** Hungary
83 N3 **Val-David** Quebec Canada
127 G2 **Val-de-Meuse** France
130 B4 **Val-d'Isère** France
73 L9 **Val-d'Or** Quebec Canada
83 M2 **Val-Laflamme** Quebec Canada
75 R8 **Val Marie** Saskatchewan Canada
124 C4 **Val-Suzon** France
133 C5 **Valandovo** Macedonia
120 L2 **Valanhamn** Norway
125 J3 **Valaská Belá** Slovakia
133 D6 **Valaxa** *island* Greece
125 M5 **Vâlcea** *admin. area* Romania
108 C2 **Valcheta** Argentina
83 O4 **Valcourt** Quebec Canada
127 H3 **Valdahon** France
128 D4 **Valdecañas, Embalse de** *lake* Spain
128 E5 **Valdeinfierno, Embalse de** *lake* Spain
128 E4 **Valdepeñas** Spain
128 D3 **Valderaduey** *watercourse* Spain
128 D2 **Valderas** Spain
131 E7 **Valderice** Italy
120 E5 **Valderøya** Norway
129 G3 **Valderrobres** Spain
108 D3 **Valdés, Caleta** *bay* Argentina
108 D3 **Valdés, Península** *peninsula* Argentina
100 B4 **Valdez** Ecuador
72 E6 **Valdez** Alaska USA
108 B2 **Valdivia** Chile
58 E2 **Valdivia Abyssal Plain** *underwater feature* Southern Ocean
130 D4 **Valdobbiadene** Italy
87 J5 **Valdosta** Georgia USA
120 I5 **Våle** Sweden
80 G5 **Vale** Oregon USA
128 C4 **Vale da Amoreira** Portugal
128 C3 **Vale de Espinho** Portugal
105 H4 **Vale dos Sonhos** Brazil
138 D4 **Vale of Glamorgan** *admin. area* Wales UK
132 E3 **Valea Argovei** Romania
125 L4 **Valea Ierii** Romania
125 L4 **Valea lui Mihai** Romania
132 D2 **Valea Lungă** Romania
132 D3 **Valea Mare-Pravăț** Romania
132 E3 **Valea Mărului** Romania
74 L6 **Valemount** British Columbia Canada
103 E6 **Valença** Brazil
128 B3 **Valença** Portugal
102 D4 **Valença do Piauí** Brazil
126 E4 **Valence** France
126 E5 **Valence-sur-Baïse** France
100 B2 **Valencia** Colombia
195 J6 **Valencia** Philippines
129 F4 **Valencia** Spain
109 8 **Valencia** Trinidad and Tobago
100 D2 **Valencia** Venezuela
129 F4 **Valencia, Golfo de** *bay* Spain
129 D4 **Valencia de Don Juan** Spain
128 D4 **Valencia de las Torres** Spain
143 B5 **Valencia Island** Ireland
129 F4 **Valenciana** *admin. area* Spain
128 D4 **Valencid del Mombuey** Spain
126 F1 **Valenciennes** France
127 J5 **Valentano** Italy
103 E5 **Valente** Brazil
127 H3 **Valentigney** France
102 D4 **Valentim, Serra do** *range* Brazil
88 D2 **Valentín Gómez Farías** Mexico
85 I3 **Valentine** Arizona USA
81 O5 **Valentine** Nebraska USA
85 J5 **Valentine** Texas USA
124 E5 **Valenza** Italy
100 D2 **Valera** Venezuela
105 H5 **Valério** Brazil
122 D2 **Valevatnet** *lake* Norway
123 M4 **Valgamaa** *admin. area* Estonia
123 N3 **Valgma** Estonia
80 I2 **Valier** Montana USA
131 C6 **Valinco, Golfe de** *bay* Corsica France
132 D3 **Vălişoara** Romania
121 O4 **Välitalo** Finland
132 A3 **Valjevo** Serbia
123 N4 **Valka** Latvia
123 M4 **Valkas** *admin. area* Latvia
123 M5 **Valkininkai** Lithuania
136 E3 **Valky** Ukraine
58 C1 **Valkyrie Dome** *mountain* Antarctica
123 J4 **Vall** Sweden
129 F3 **Vall d'Alba** Spain
129 F4 **Vall d'Uixó** Spain
219 K4 **Valla Beach** NSW Australia
128 D3 **Valladolid** Spain
132 C2 **Vállaj** Hungary
78 D6 **Vallard, Lac** *lake* Quebec Canada
131 F6 **Vallata** Italy
120 H5 **Vallbo** Sweden
122 D1 **Valldal** Norway
106 D4 **Valle Cura, Río de** *watercourse* Argentina
130 B4 **Valle d'Aosta** *admin. area* Italy
106 E6 **Valle Daza** Argentina
106 E6 **Valle de La Pascua** Venezuela
88 D3 **Valle de Olivos** Mexico
88 B3 **Valle de Vizcaíno** Mexico
100 B4 **Valle del Cauca** *admin. area* Colombia
100 B4 **Valle del Guamuez** Colombia
89 F3 **Valle Hermoso** Mexico
90 C4 **Valle Kuikuinita** Nicaragua
84 E5 **Valle La Trinidad** Mexico
90 C4 **Vallecillo** Honduras
85 M7 **Vallecillo** Mexico
106 E4 **Vallecito** Argentina
85 I2 **Vallecito Reservoir** Colorado USA
100 C2 **Valledupar** Colombia
105 E5 **Vallegrande** Bolivia
80 D7 **Vallejo** California USA
131 E8 **Vallelunga Pratameno** Italy
106 J5 **Vallen** Sweden
106 D4 **Vallenar** Chile
120 I4 **Vallenäs** Sweden
126 D3 **Vallet** France
131 F9 **Valletta** Malta
143 C2 **Valley** Ireland
140 D3 **Valley** Isle of Anglesey Wales UK
87 I4 **Valley** Alabama USA
81 Q6 **Valley** Nebraska USA
81 Q8 **Valley Center** Kansas USA
81 Q3 **Valley City** North Dakota USA
83 K3 **Valley East** Ontario Canada
82 D7 **Valley Falls** Kansas USA
195 I3 **Valley Head** *cape* Philippines
86 C5 **Valley Mills** Texas USA
84 B1 **Valley Springs** California USA
86 C4 **Valley View** Texas USA
74 M5 **Valleyview** Alberta Canada
Vallgrund *see* **Raippaluoto** Finland
86 D4 **Valliant** Oklahoma USA
80 G2 **Vallican** British Columbia Canada
122 G5 **Vällinge** Sweden
120 J4 **Vallnäs** Sweden
122 I4 **Vållö** *island* Sweden
127 H3 **Vallorbe** Switzerland
129 G3 **Valls** Spain
120 H5 **Valmåsen** Sweden
123 M4 **Valmiera** Latvia
123 M4 **Valmieras** *admin. area* Latvia
139 H5 **Valmont** France
120 G4 **Valøya** Norway
123 N5 **Valozhyn** Belarus
103 B8 **Valparaíso** Brazil
106 D5 **Valparaíso** Chile
106 D5 **Valparaíso** *admin. area* Chile
100 C4 **Valparaíso** Colombia
88 E4 **Valparaíso** Mexico
82 H6 **Valparaiso** Indiana USA
128 C3 **Valparaiso, Embalse de** *lake* Spain
126 B5 **Valporquero, Cuevas de** Spain
130 H4 **Valpovo** Croatia
126 F5 **Valras-Plage** France
198 F6 **Vals, Tanjung** *cape* Indonesia
187 C7 **Valsad** Gujarat India
120 I4 **Valsjöbyn** Sweden
120 I4 **Valsjön** *bay* Sweden
120 L5 **Valsörarna** *island* Finland
162 D5 **Valspan** South Africa
122 G3 **Valstad** Sweden
121 P5 **Valtimo** Finland
136 F2 **Valuyki** Russian Federation
128 E4 **Valverde de Júcar** Spain
128 C3 **Valverde del Fresno** Spain
132 D2 **Vama** Romania
132 D3 **Vama Buzăului** Romania
130 G1 **Vamberk** Czech Republic
123 L2 **Vammala** Finland
133 D8 **Vamos** Greece
133 E6 **Vamvakas, Akra** *cape* Greece
136 G5 **Van** Turkey
136 G5 **Van** *admin. area* Turkey
138 D2 **Van** Powys Wales UK
86 D4 **Van** Texas USA
83 O3 **Van Bruyssel** Quebec Canada
86 D3 **Van Buren** Arkansas USA
83 R3 **Van Buren** Maine USA
82 F8 **Van Buren** Missouri USA
194 F4 **Văn Canh** Vietnam
198 F4 **Van Daalen** *watercourse* Indonesia
213 K1 **Van Diemen, Cape** NT Australia
214 A1 **Van Diemen Gulf** NT Australia
136 G5 **Van Gölü (Lake Van)** *lake* Turkey
85 J5 **Van Horn** Texas USA
215 G4 **Van Lee** Qld Australia
194 F4 **Van Ninh** Vietnam
194 F4 **Van Phong, Vinh** *bay* Vietnam
198 F4 **Van Rees, Pegunungan** *range* Indonesia
162 D5 **Van Zylsrus** South Africa
182 D6 **Vanadzor** Armenia
123 M2 **Vanajavesi** *lake* Finland
80 C2 **Vananda** British Columbia Canada
77 R2 **Vanasse, Lac** *lake* Quebec Canada
223 14 **Vanavana** *island* French Polynesia
83 R4 **Vanceboro** Maine USA
87 M3 **Vanceboro** North Carolina USA
82 J7 **Vanceburg** Kentucky USA
74 J8 **Vancouver** British Columbia Canada
80 D4 **Vancouver** Washington USA
216 F7 **Vancouver, Cape** WA Australia
80 C2 **Vancouver Island** British Columbia Canada
59 K1 **Vanda, Lake** Antarctica
82 F7 **Vandalia** Missouri USA
123 N4 **Vandāni** Latvia
74 I5 **Vanderhoof** British Columbia Canada
162 D5 **Vanderkloof** South Africa
214 D3 **Vanderlin, Cape** NT Australia
214 D3 **Vanderlin Island** NT Australia
122 G3 **Vanderydvattnet** *lake* Sweden
127 H2 **Vandoeuvre-lès-Nancy** France
83 O3 **Vandry** Quebec Canada
120 H3 **Vandved** *island* Norway
122 G3 **Vänern** *bay* Sweden
122 E2 **Vang** Norway
58 T2 **Vang, Mount** *mountain* Antarctica
163 I4 **Vangaindrano** Madagascar
123 M4 **Vangaži** Latvia
139 H3 **Vange** Essex England UK
120 J5 **Vängel** Sweden
120 G5 **Vangshylla** Norway
122 D2 **Vangsvatnet** *lake* Norway
120 J2 **Vangsvik** Norway
75 R8 **Vanguard** Saskatchewan Canada
222 8 **Vangunu** *island* Solomon Islands
123 M2 **Vanhanselkä** *bay* Finland
187 C7 **Vani** Maharashtra India
120 K4 **Vänjaurbäck** Sweden
132 C3 **Vânjule Mare** Romania
135 AL5 **Vankarem** Russian Federation
72 B5 **Vankarem, Laguna** *lagoon* Russian Federation
123 L2 **Vankavesi** *bay* Finland
120 K1 **Vanna** *island* Norway
120 K1 **Vannareid** Norway
120 K5 **Vännäs** Sweden
120 K5 **Vännäsby** Sweden
126 F2 **Vanne** *watercourse* France
126 C3 **Vannes** France
78 E5 **Vannes, Lac** *lake* Quebec Canada
120 L4 **Vånören** *island* Sweden
162 C6 **Vanrhynsdorp** South Africa
214 F4 **Vanrook** Qld Australia
214 F4 **Vanrook** *watercourse* Qld Australia
213 I3 **Vansittart Bay** WA Australia
219 S10 **Vansittart Island** Tas. Australia
73 K5 **Vansittart Island** Nunavut Canada
122 H3 **Vänstern** *lake* Sweden
123 M2 **Vantaa** Finland
81 L2 **Vantage** Saskatchewan Canada
123 N2 **Vanttausjärvi** *lake* Finland
121 O3 **Vanttauskoski** Finland
223 9 **Vanua Balavu** *island* Fiji
222 7 **Vanua Lava** *island* Vanuatu
223 9 **Vanua Levu** *island* Fiji
223 9 **Vanua Vatu** *island* Fiji
222 7 **Vanuatu** *country* Oceania
194 D3 **Vanviang** Laos
222 7 **Vao** New Caledonia
128 C2 **Vao, Embalse de** *lake* Spain
125 I2 **Vápenná** Czech Republic
132 F1 **Vapnyarka** Ukraine
127 H4 **Var** *watercourse* France
164 1a **Vara, Pico da** *mountain* Azores
104 C2 **Varadero** Peru
124 D5 **Varaita** *watercourse* Italy
121 N3 **Varajärvi** Finland
123 N4 **Varakļāni** Latvia
122 G2 **Varaldsjøen** *lake* Sweden
122 D2 **Varaldsøy** *region* Norway
158 D3 **Varalé** Côte d'Ivoire
178 G2 **Varāmīn** Iran
186 F6 **Varanasi** Uttar Pradesh India
121 P1 **Varangerbotn** Norway
121 Q2 **Varangerfjorden** *bay* Norway
121 P1 **Varangerhalvøya** *peninsula* Norway
131 F6 **Varano, Lago di** *lake* Italy
130 C4 **Varazze** Italy
122 G4 **Varberg** Sweden
133 B6 **Varda** Greece
179 K2 **Vardak** *admin. area* Afghanistan
187 E8 **Vardannapet** Andhra Pradesh India
133 B5 **Vardar** *watercourse* Macedonia
122 E5 **Varde** Denmark

182 E6 **Vardenis** Armenia
132 D4 **Vardim** Bulgaria
127 I5 **Vardiola, Cap** *cape* Corsica France
123 M3 **Vardja** Estonia
121 Q1 **Vardø** Norway
124 E1 **Varel** Germany
158 A2 **Varela** Guinea-Bissau
127 H3 **Varen** Switzerland
139 H5 **Varengeville-sur-Mer** France
124 B4 **Varennes** France
124 E5 **Varese** Italy
132 C2 **Vârfurile** Romania
122 G3 **Vårgårda** Sweden
106 D5 **Vargas** Argentina
100 E2 **Vargas** *admin. area* Venezuela
102 E5 **Vargem** *watercourse* Brazil
132 D2 **Vârghiş** Romania
103 C8 **Varginha** Brazil
120 L4 **Vargön** *island* Sweden
122 C3 **Varhaug** Norway
133 D7 **Vari** Greece
125 K4 **Variaş** Romania
125 J3 **Varín** Slovakia
122 H3 **Väringen** *lake* Sweden
133 B5 **Váris** Greece
123 N3 **Varja** Estonia
120 I4 **Värjaren** *lake* Sweden
120 K3 **Varjisträsk** Sweden
102 D4 **Varjota** Brazil
121 O5 **Varkaus** Finland
123 J3 **Värmdolandet** *island* Sweden
122 G3 **Varmeln** *lake* Sweden
122 G3 **Värmland** *admin. area* Sweden
122 G3 **Värmlandsnäs** *peninsula* Sweden
132 E4 **Varna** Bulgaria
132 E4 **Varna** *admin. area* Bulgaria
122 H4 **Värnamo** Sweden
122 G2 **Värnäs** Sweden
121 P1 **Varnesodden** *cape* Norway
123 L5 **Varniai** Lithuania
125 H2 **Varnsdorf** Czech Republic
123 N5 **Varnyany** Belarus
121 P3 **Värriö** Finland
104 E3 **Varsovia** Bolivia
138 D3 **Varteg** Torfaen Wales UK
121 P4 **Vartius** Finland
136 G5 **Varto** Turkey
120 L4 **Varuträsket** *lake* Sweden
123 K4 **Värve** Latvia
134 Q6 **Var'yegan** Russian Federation
107 H3 **Várzea** *watercourse* Brazil
103 C7 **Várzea da Palma** Brazil
105 G4 **Várzea Grande** Brazil
103 C6 **Varzelândia** Brazil
130 C4 **Varzi** Italy
134 I5 **Varzino** Russian Federation
183 J6 **Varzob** Tajikistan
121 T3 **Varzuga** Russian Federation
124 B4 **Varzy** France
125 I4 **Vas** *admin. area* Hungary
120 I5 **Vås** Sweden
223 13a **Vasafua** *island* Tuvalu
121 P3 **Vasaraperä** Finland
125 L3 **Vásárosnamény** Hungary
123 N3 **Vasavere** Estonia
128 E2 **Vasca, Costa** *region* Spain
125 L4 **Vaşcău** Romania
139 I5 **Vascoeuil** France
109 8 **Vashel, Cape** South Georgia
132 D1 **Vashkivtsi** Ukraine
134 O6 **Vashnël** Russian Federation
214 A1 **Vashon Head** NT Australia
178 F2 **Vasiān** Iran
125 J5 **Vašica** Serbia
121 O2 **Vasikkaselkä** *bay* Finland
133 D5 **Vasil Kolarov, Yazovir** *reservoir* Bulgaria
127 I5 **Vasina, Pointe de la** *cape* Corsica France
222 1a **Vaskess Bay** Kiribati
123 J4 **Väskinde** Sweden
123 L2 **Vaskio** Finland
121 M5 **Vaskivesi** *bay* Finland
123 N3 **Vasknarva** Estonia
121 O2 **Vaskojoki** *watercourse* Finland
132 E2 **Vaslui** Romania
132 E2 **Vaslui** *admin. area* Romania
83 M2 **Vassan** Quebec Canada
81 R2 **Vassar** Manitoba Canada
82 J5 **Vassar** Michigan USA
120 H6 **Vassbo** Sweden
216 D6 **Vasse** WA Australia
122 H2 **Vässinjärvi** *lake* Sweden
122 I3 **Vassunda** Sweden
120 I4 **Västansjö** Sweden
123 M3 **Vastemõisa** Estonia
120 J3 **Vastenjaure** *lake* Sweden
122 I3 **Västerås** Sweden
122 I3 **Västeråsfjärden** *bay* Sweden
120 J4 **Västerbotten** *admin. area* Sweden
122 G2 **Västerdalälven** *watercourse* Sweden
120 J3 **Västerfjäll** Sweden
122 J4 **Västergarn** Sweden
120 J5 **Västernorrland** *admin. area* Sweden
122 G4 **Vastersjön** *lake* Sweden
122 I4 **Västervik** Sweden
121 N5 **Vastinki** Finland
121 P5 **Västinniemi** Finland
122 I3 **Västmanland** *admin. area* Sweden
131 F5 **Vasto** Italy
122 G4 **Västra Fegen** *lake* Sweden
120 I4 **Västra Fiskåvattnet** *lake* Sweden
122 G3 **Västra Götaland** *admin. area* Sweden
120 K4 **Västra Kikkejaure** *lake* Sweden
122 G3 **Västra Örten** *lake* Sweden
122 G5 **Västra Ringsjön** *lake* Sweden
122 G3 **Västra Silen** *lake* Sweden
120 I4 **Västra Tåsjö** Sweden
120 L5 **Västra Yttermark** Finland
122 I4 **Västrum** Sweden
123 N4 **Vastseliina** Estonia
123 N3 **Vasula** Estonia
121 M5 **Vasunmäki** Finland
125 I4 **Vasvár** Hungary
136 D2 **Vasyl'kiv** Ukraine
134 Q7 **Vasyugan** *watercourse* Russian Federation
126 E3 **Vatan** France
123 Q1 **Vatchelskoye, Ozero** *lake* Russian Federation
142 B3 **Vaternish Point** Scotland UK
133 C7 **Vathí** Greece
133 E7 **Vathy** Greece
131 E6 **Vatican City** *country* Europe
131 F7 **Vaticano, Capo** *cape* Italy
73 R6 **Vatnajökull** *ice* Iceland
122 D3 **Vatndalsvatnet** *lake* Norway
120 inset **Vatneyri** Iceland
120 inset **Vatnsdalsá** *watercourse* Iceland
123 J3 **Vätö** *island* Sweden
223 9 **Vatoa** *island* Fiji
163 I3 **Vatomandry** Madagascar
186 C6 **Vatrak** *watercourse* Gujarat India
142 B3 **Vatten** Highland Scotland UK
122 H3 **Vättern** *bay* Sweden
223 9 **Vatu Vara** *island* Fiji
223 9a **Vatukoula** Fiji
223 9a **Vatulele** *island* Fiji
132 G1 **Vatutine** Ukraine
135 AJ6 **Vatyna** Russian Federation
124 C3 **Vaubecourt** France
127 G2 **Vaucouleurs** France
85 J3 **Vaughn** New Mexico USA
78 C5 **Vaulezar, Lac** *lake* Quebec Canada
100 D4 **Vaupés** *admin. area* Colombia
100 D4 **Vaupés (Uaupés)** *watercourse* Brazil/Colombia
126 G5 **Vauvert** France
139 F5 **Vauville** France
127 G2 **Vaux-sur-Sûre** Belgium
186 C6 **Vav** Gujarat India
122 E2 **Vavatn** *lake* Norway
223 10 **Vava'u Group** *islands* Tonga
223 10 **Vava'u Island** Tonga
74 L7 **Vavenby** British Columbia Canada
125 M1 **Vawkavysk** Belarus
75 Q6 **Vawn** Saskatchewan Canada
122 I2 **Växbo** Sweden
123 J3 **Vaxholm** Sweden
122 H4 **Växjö** Sweden
121 Q2 **Vaydaguba** Russian Federation
134 M4 **Vaygach** Russian Federation
134 N4 **Vaygach, Ostrov** *island* Russian Federation
121 O2 **Väylä** Finland
121 M3 **Väylänpää** Sweden
121 O4 **Väyrylä** Finland
133 E5 **Vaysal** Turkey
103 C7 **Vazante** Brazil
130 H2 **Važec** Slovakia
124 C5 **Veauche** France
81 Q4 **Veblen** South Dakota USA
120 L4 **Vebomark** Sweden
124 D1 **Vecht** *watercourse* Germany
124 E1 **Vechta** Germany
164 3b **Vecindario** Canary Islands
128 D3 **Vecinos** Spain
123 N4 **Veclaicene** Latvia
125 J4 **Vecsés** Hungary
123 N4 **Vecumi** Latvia
120 J5 **Veda** Sweden
187 E9 **Vedaranniyam** Tamil Nadu India
122 G4 **Veddige** Sweden
132 D3 **Vedea** *watercourse* Romania
120 I4 **Vedjeön** Sweden
123 Q2 **Vedlozero** Russian Federation
130 G4 **Vedro Polje** Croatia
142 inset **Veensgarth** Shetland Scotland UK
123 L3 **Veere** Estonia
124 B2 **Veere** Netherlands
120 H4 **Vefsna** *watercourse* Norway
120 G4 **Vega** *island* Norway
85 K3 **Vega** Texas USA
128 C2 **Vega de Espinareda** Spain
128 E4 **Vega del Jabalón, Embalse de la** *lake* Spain
58 U2 **Vega Island** Antarctica
104 A2 **Vega Moro** Peru
85 I1 **Vega Reservoir** Colorado USA
101 E2 **Vega Vieja** Venezuela
100 C3 **Vegachí** Colombia
128 C2 **Vegadeo** Spain
123 L4 **Vegeriai** Lithuania
122 E4 **Vegger** Denmark
131 G6 **Veglie** Italy
75 O6 **Vegreville** Alberta Canada
123 M2 **Vehkajärvi** *lake* Finland
121 P5 **Vehmersalmi** Finland
107 G3 **Veinticinco de Diciembre** Paraguay
106 E6 **Veinticinco de Mayo** Argentina
123 L5 **Veisiejai** *lake* Lithuania
120 E6 **Veitastrondvatnet** *lake* Norway
122 E5 **Vejle** Denmark
123 K2 **Vekara** *island* Finland
100 C1 **Vela, Cabo de la** *cape* Colombia
164 1b **Velas** Azores
90 C5 **Velas, Cabo** *cape* Costa Rica
106 E4 **Velasco, Sierra de** *range* Argentina
132 B1 **Vel'aty** Slovakia
107 H5 **Velázquez** Uruguay
162 C6 **Velddrif** South Africa
124 D2 **Velen** Germany
125 J4 **Velencei-tó** *lake* Hungary
133 B5 **Veles** Macedonia
130 F2 **Velešín** Czech Republic
100 C3 **Vélez** Colombia
128 D5 **Vélez-Málaga** Spain
128 E5 **Vélez-Rubio** Spain
103 C7 **Velhas** *watercourse* Brazil
101 G5 **Velho Mocambo de Santana** Brazil
182 E5 **Velichayevskoye** Russian Federation
130 G4 **Velika** Croatia
125 M2 **Velika Hlusha** Ukraine
130 F4 **Velika Kladuša** Bosnia and Herzegovina
132 B3 **Velika Plana** Serbia
135 AJ6 **Velikaya** *watercourse* Russian Federation
121 S5 **Velikaya Guba** Russian Federation
125 H5 **Velike Lašče** Slovenia
132 B3 **Veliki Crljeni** Serbia
130 G5 **Veliki Drvenik** *island* Croatia
125 K5 **Veliki Gaj** Serbia
132 C4 **Veliki Izvor** Serbia
132 B4 **Veliki Kupci** Serbia
132 C1 **Velikiy Lyuben'** Ukraine
123 P3 **Velikiy Novgorod** Russian Federation
134 K6 **Velikiy Ustyug** Russian Federation
123 P4 **Velikiye-Luki** Russian Federation
125 K5 **Veliko Laole** Serbia
125 K5 **Veliko Selo** Serbia
136 C4 **Veliko Tŭrnovo** Bulgaria
130 H4 **Velimirovac** Croatia
138 C2 **Velindre-farchog** Pembrokeshire Wales UK
154 D6 **Vélingara** Senegal
127 K5 **Velino, Monte** *mountain* Italy
123 P5 **Velizh** Russian Federation
125 I3 **Velká Bíteš** Czech Republic
125 J3 **Veľká Fatra** *range* Slovakia
124 G3 **Velká Hleďsebe** Czech Republic
125 K3 **Veľká Ida** Slovakia
132 A1 **Veľká Udiča** Slovakia
125 J3 **Velké Karlovice** Czech Republic
125 I2 **Velké Poříčí** Czech Republic
134 D3 **Velkomstpynten** *cape* Norway
130 H2 **Veľký Krtíš** Slovakia
125 I4 **Veľký Meder** Slovakia
222 8 **Vella Lavella** *island* Solomon Islands
131 E6 **Velletri** Italy
124 E2 **Vellmar** Germany
187 E9 **Vellore** Tamil Nadu India
124 C1 **Velsen** Netherlands
134 J6 **Vel'sk** Russian Federation
134 K5 **Vel't** Russian Federation
122 G2 **Velta** Norway
81 O2 **Velva** North Dakota USA
127 L1 **Velvary** Czech Republic
133 C5 **Velvendos** Greece
132 C1 **Velyatyn** Ukraine
132 F2 **Velyka Mykhaylivka** Ukraine
125 L3 **Velyki Luchky** Ukraine
132 F2 **Velykoploske** Ukraine
132 C1 **Velykyy Bereznyy** Ukraine
50 N8 **Vema Fracture Zone** *underwater feature* Atlantic Ocean
54 F8 **Vema Seamount** *underwater feature* Atlantic Ocean
54 K6 **Vema Trench** *underwater feature* Indian Ocean
122 E4 **Vemb** Denmark
120 H5 **Vemdalen** Sweden
122 G5 **Ven** *island* Sweden
122 H4 **Vena** Sweden
127 I5 **Venaco** Corsica France
100 C3 **Venadillo** Colombia
90 D5 **Venado, Isla del** *island* Nicaragua
106 F5 **Venado Tuerto** Argentina
131 F6 **Venafro** Italy
81 N6 **Venango** Nebraska USA
124 D5 **Venaria** Italy
127 H4 **Venasca** Italy
127 H5 **Vence** France
128 E3 **Vencías, Embalse de las** *lake* Spain
123 K5 **Venckai** Lithuania
128 B4 **Vendas Novas** Portugal
126 D4 **Vendays-Montalivet** France
126 D3 **Vendée** *region* France
122 I2 **Vendelsjön** *lake* Sweden
127 G2 **Vendeuvre-sur-Barse** France
109 10a **Vendôme** Grenada
100 D4 **Venecia** Colombia
121 O4 **Veneheitto** Finland
121 N3 **Venejärvi** Finland
121 M5 **Veneskoski** Finland
80 D4 **Veneta** Oregon USA
72 E5 **Venetie** Alaska USA
121 N5 **Venetjoen tekojärvi** *lake* Finland
130 D4 **Veneto** *admin. area* Italy
121 N5 **Venetpalo** Finland
136 F1 **Venëv** Russian Federation
130 E4 **Venezia, Golfo di** *bay* Italy
130 E4 **Venezia (Venice)** Italy
91 H6 **Venezuela** *country* South America
100 D2 **Venezuela, Golfo de** *bay* Venezuela
50 L8 **Venezuelan Basin** *underwater feature* Caribbean Sea
121 O4 **Vengasaho** Finland
120 K2 **Vengsøya** *island* Norway
187 C8 **Vengurla** Maharashtra India
72 D7 **Veniaminof Volcano** Alaska USA
Venice *see* **Venezia** Italy
87 J7 **Venice** Florida USA
127 G4 **Vénissieux** France
122 G2 **Venjan** Sweden
122 G2 **Venjanssjön** *lake* Sweden
187 E9 **Venkatagiri** Andhra Pradesh India
75 U7 **Venlaw** Manitoba Canada
138 D4 **Venn Ottery** Devon England UK
217 O7 **Vennachar Point** SA Australia
122 D3 **Vennesla** Norway
131 F6 **Venosa** Italy
120 I3 **Venset** Norway
124 F4 **Vent** Austria
123 K4 **Venta** *watercourse* Latvia
123 L4 **Venta** Lithuania
123 L5 **Venta** *watercourse* Lithuania
108 D6 **Ventana, Punta** *cape* Argentina
128 D5 **Ventas de Zafarraya** Spain
104 D5 **Ventilla** Bolivia
90 D5 **Ventisqueros, Cerro** *mountain* Costa Rica
139 F4 **Ventnor** Isle of Wight England UK
131 E6 **Ventotene, Isola** *island* Italy
123 K4 **Ventspils** Latvia
123 K4 **Ventspils** *admin. area* Latvia
100 E3 **Ventuari** *watercourse* Venezuela
86 C4 **Venus** Texas USA
218 B5 **Venus Bay** SA Australia
218 G8 **Venus Bay** Vic. Australia
88 E3 **Venustiano Carranza** Mexico
88 E3 **Venustiano Carranza, Presa** *lake* Mexico
127 K3 **Venzone** Italy
123 M5 **Vepriai** Lithuania
121 P5 **Vepsä** Finland
121 P5 **Vepsänjärvi** *lake* Finland
106 F4 **Vera** Argentina
128 F5 **Vera** Spain
108 D3 **Vera, Bahía** *bay* Argentina
103 D6 **Vera Cruz** Brazil
89 F5 **Veracruz** Mexico
89 F5 **Veracruz** *admin. area* Mexico
100 D4 **Veradal** Colombia
120 H5 **Veravatnet** *lake* Sweden
125 M2 **Verba** Ukraine
127 H3 **Verbier** Switzerland
124 E5 **Vercelli** Italy
109 19 **Verchild's Mountain** *volcano* St Kitts and Nevis
120 H5 **Verdal** *island* Norway
120 G5 **Verdalsøra** Norway
105 I4 **Verde** Brazil
103 A7 **Verde** *watercourse* Brazil
107 G2 **Verde** *watercourse* Paraguay
84 G3 **Verde** *watercourse* Arkansas USA
128 C2 **Verde, Costa** *region* Spain
108 E2 **Verde, Península** *peninsula* Argentina
104 C4 **Verdecocha, Cerro** *mountain* Peru
86 B3 **Verden** Oklahoma USA
86 C2 **Verdigris** *watercourse* Kansas USA
85 O2 **Verdigris** *watercourse* Oklahoma USA
103 B7 **Verdinho, Serra do** *range* Brazil
127 H5 **Verdon** *watercourse* France
127 G2 **Verdun** France
75 T7 **Veregin** Saskatchewan Canada
123 O5 **Veremeyevo** Belarus
132 C3 **Verendin** Romania
158 B2 **Verga, Cap** *cape* Guinea
107 H5 **Vergara** Uruguay
127 J4 **Vergato** Italy
214 G7 **Vergemont, Mount** Qld Australia
83 O4 **Vergennes** Vermont USA
123 N3 **Vergi** Estonia
128 C3 **Verín** Spain
123 N3 **Veriora** Estonia
135 AG8 **Verkhne Kolpakora Urochishche** Russian Federation
135 X7 **Verkhneangarskiy Khrebet** *range* Russian Federation
121 Q2 **Verkhnetulomskiy** Russian Federation
121 Q4 **Verkhneye Kuyto, Ozero** *lake* Russian Federation
121 S5 **Verkhneye Volozero, Ozero** *lake* Russian Federation
182 E4 **Verkhniy Baskunchak** Russian Federation
182 D5 **Verkhniy Chegem** Russian Federation
121 S3 **Verkhniy Vyalozërskiy** Russian Federation
182 E3 **Verkhniy Yeruslan** Russian Federation
135 AA7 **Verkhnyaya Amga** Russian Federation
132 D1 **Verkhnyaya Lipitsa** Ukraine
134 J6 **Verkhnyaya Toyma** Russian Federation
132 D1 **Verkhovyna** Ukraine
135 AB5 **Verkhoyanskiy Khrebet** *range* Russian Federation
183 N3 **Verkhuba** Kazakhstan
125 M2 **Verkhy** Ukraine
124 E2 **Verl** Germany
81 K1 **Verlo** Saskatchewan Canada
120 F5 **Verma** Norway
126 F2 **Vermand** France
102 C4 **Vermelho** *watercourse* Brazil
126 F3 **Vermenton** France
125 K5 **Vermeş** Romania
130 D3 **Vermiglio** Italy
75 P6 **Vermilion** *watercourse* Alberta Canada
86 F6 **Vermilion Bay** Louisiana USA
82 E3 **Vermilion Lake** Minnesota USA
82 E3 **Vermilion Range** *range* Minnesota USA
81 S2 **Vermillion** Ontario Canada
81 Q5 **Vermillion** South Dakota USA
82 C5 **Vermillion** *watercourse* South Dakota USA
133 B5 **Vermio** *range* Greece
109 11a **Vermont** St Vincent and the Grenadines
70 **Vermont** *admin. area* USA
132 A4 **Vermosh** Albania
136 E2 **Vern** *watercourse* Ukraine
58 T2 **Vernadsky (Ukraine)** *research station* Antarctica
81 K6 **Vernal** Utah USA
127 H3 **Vernayaz** Switzerland
83 K3 **Verner** Ontario Canada
124 D4 **Vernier** Switzerland
74 L7 **Vernon** British Columbia Canada
126 E2 **Vernon** France
87 I5 **Vernon** Florida USA
86 B3 **Vernon** Texas USA
80 I6 **Vernon** Utah USA
77 R3 **Vernon, Lac** *lake* Quebec Canada
216 F2 **Vernon, Mount** WA Australia
86 E5 **Vernon Lake** Louisiana USA
109 16 **Vernou** Guadeloupe
130 B2 **Verny** France
87 K7 **Vero Beach** Florida USA
133 C5 **Veroia** Greece
127 H4 **Verolengo** Italy
131 E6 **Veroli** Italy
124 F5 **Verona** Italy
81 P3 **Verona** North Dakota USA
86 F6 **Verret, Lake** Louisiana USA
126 F2 **Versailles** France
82 I7 **Versailles** Indiana USA
82 I7 **Versailles** Kentucky USA
127 H3 **Versoix** France
127 H3 **Versoix** Switzerland
154 C6 **Vert, Cap** *cape* Senegal
104 D2 **Vertentes** Brazil
90 E2 **Vertientes** Cuba
106 E2 **Vertientes Sulfhídricas** Bolivia
126 D3 **Vertou** France
126 G2 **Vertus** France
122 G4 **Verum** Sweden
127 G1 **Verviers** Belgium
75 S8 **Verwood** Saskatchewan Canada
139 F4 **Verwood** Dorset England UK
133 C5 **Véryi** Greece
121 N5 **Vesanka** Finland
121 O5 **Vesanto** Finland
125 I4 **Vése** Hungary
182 D4 **Veselovskoye Vodokhranilishche** *lake* Russian Federation
123 J5 **Vesëloye** Russian Federation
123 M2 **Vesijako** *lake* Finland
123 M2 **Vesijärvi** *lake* Finland
123 L3 **Veskijärv** *lake* Estonia
121 O2 **Veskoniemi** Finland
126 F2 **Vesle** *watercourse* France
123 P2 **Vesnino** Russian Federation
127 H3 **Vesoul** France
103 D7 **Vespasiano** Brazil
124 E5 **Vespolate** Italy
122 G4 **Vessigebro** Sweden
122 D3 **Vest-Agder** *admin. area* Norway
122 D3 **Vestbygd** Norway
134 D5 **Vesterålen** *island* Norway
78 N2 **Vesterland** *island* Greenland
120 inset **Vestfirðir** *admin. area* Iceland
120 I3 **Vestfjorden** *bay* Norway
122 E3 **Vestfjorden** *lake* Norway
122 F3 **Vestfold** *admin. area* Norway
58 F2 **Vestfold Hills** *range* Antarctica
120 inset **Vestmannaeyjar** Iceland
73 Q6 **Vestmannaeyjar** *island* Iceland
120 E5 **Vestnes** Norway
124 F5 **Vestone** Italy
122 C3 **Vestre Bokn** *island* Norway
121 P1 **Vestre Jakobselv** Norway
58 X2 **Veststraumen Glacier** *ice* Antarctica
120 inset **Vesturland** *admin. area* Iceland
120 G5 **Vestvik** Norway
125 I4 **Veszprém** Hungary
125 I4 **Veszprém** *admin. area* Hungary
132 B2 **Vésztő** Hungary
223 9 **Vetavuaa** *island* Fiji
121 M5 **Veteli** Finland
133 B5 **Vetersko** Macedonia
182 E1 **Vetluga** Russian Federation
132 E4 **Vetovo** Bulgaria
132 D4 **Vetren** Bulgaria
133 C4 **Vetren** Macedonia
132 E4 **Vetrino** Bulgaria
125 H2 **Vetschau** Germany
121 O2 **Vetsijärvi** *lake* Finland
121 O2 **Vetsikko** Finland
120 L3 **Vettasjärvi** Sweden
120 L3 **Vettasjärvi** *lake* Sweden
139 H5 **Veules-les-Roses** France
139 H5 **Veulettes-sur-Mer** France
126 F1 **Veurne** Belgium
120 E5 **Vevang** Norway
222 8 **Veve, Mount** *volcano* Solomon Islands
161 E2 **Veveno** *watercourse* Sudan
127 H3 **Vevey** Switzerland
124 D4 **Vex** Switzerland
120 M5 **Vexala** Finland
123 O3 **Veymarn** Russian Federation
127 G4 **Veynes** France
126 F3 **Vézelay** France
126 E4 **Vézère** *watercourse* France
121 T4 **Vezhmozero, Ozero** *lake* Russian Federation
136 E5 **Vezirköprü** Turkey
120 J5 **Vi** Sweden
126 E2 **Viabon** France
105 E6 **Viacha** Bolivia
124 F5 **Viadana** Italy
199 H4 **Viai Island** Papua New Guinea
107 I4 **Viamão** Brazil
106 F5 **Viamonte** Argentina
108 C6 **Viamonte** Argentina
86 D3 **Vian** Oklahoma USA
102 C3 **Viana** Brazil
128 E2 **Viana** Spain
128 C4 **Viana do Alentejo** Portugal
128 B3 **Viana do Castelo** *admin. area* Portugal
127 H2 **Vianden** Luxembourg
194 D3 **Viangchan (Vientiane)** Laos
103 B7 **Vianópolis** Brazil
121 N4 **Viantie** Finland
128 D5 **Viar** *watercourse* Spain
130 D5 **Viareggio** Italy
123 K2 **Viasvesi** *bay* Finland
126 F4 **Viaur** *watercourse* France
131 G7 **Vibo Valentia** Italy
86 B7 **Viboras** Texas USA
122 E4 **Viborg** Denmark
126 E2 **Vibraye** France
82 F8 **Viburnum** Missouri USA
129 H3 **Vic** Spain
126 E5 **Vic-en-Bigorre** France
126 E5 **Vic-Fezensac** France
126 F4 **Vic-sur-Cère** France
88 C3 **Vicam** Mexico
128 E5 **Vícar** Spain
104 A2 **Vice** Peru
102 F4 **Vicência** Brazil
88 E4 **Vicente Guerrero** Mexico
88 B2 **Vicente Guerrero** Mexico
84 E4 **Vicente Guerrero** Mexico
86 B9 **Vicente Guerrero, Presa** *lake* Mexico
124 F5 **Vicenza** Italy
100 D3 **Vichada** *admin. area* Colombia
100 D3 **Vichada** *watercourse* Colombia
107 H4 **Vichadero** Uruguay
126 F3 **Vichy** France
86 B2 **Vici** Oklahoma USA
86 A5 **Vick** Texas USA
84 F4 **Vicksburg** Arizona USA
86 F4 **Vicksburg** Mississippi USA
101 F4 **Viçosa** Brazil
103 D8 **Viçosa** Brazil
102 B2 **Vicosa, Ilha** *island* Brazil
102 D3 **Viçosa do Ceará** Brazil
132 D2 **Vicovu de Jos** Romania
132 D2 **Vicovu de Sus** Romania
75 U7 **Victor** Manitoba Canada
82 E6 **Victor** Iowa USA
83 M5 **Victor** New York USA
58 C2 **Victor, Mount** *mountain* Antarctica
218 D5 **Victor, Mount** SA Australia
58 J2 **Victor Bay** Antarctica
218 D6 **Victor Harbor** SA Australia
106 F5 **Victoria** Argentina
218 G7 **Victoria** *admin. area* Australia
214 A4 **Victoria** *watercourse* NT Australia
105 G5 **Victoria** Bolivia
74 J8 **Victoria** British Columbia Canada
79 L9 **Victoria** Newfoundland and Labrador Canada
79 G9 **Victoria** Prince Edward Island Canada
106 C6 **Victoria** Chile
131 F8 **Victoria** Malta
164 9 **Victoria** Seychelles
81 P7 **Victoria** Kansas USA
86 C6 **Victoria** Texas USA
108 B3 **Victoria, Isla** *island* Chile
218 E5 **Victoria, Lake** NSW Australia
161 E4 **Victoria, Lake** *lake* Uganda
219 R10 **Victoria, Mount** Tas. Australia
181 G5 **Victoria, Mount** Myanmar
199 H6 **Victoria, Mount** Papua New Guinea
73 L3 **Victoria and Albert Mountains** Nunavut Canada
76 G7 **Victoria Beach** Manitoba Canada
73 O2 **Victoria Fjord** Greenland
72 H4 **Victoria Island** Northwest Territories/Nunavut Canada
218 F5 **Victoria Lake** NSW Australia
79 J8 **Victoria Lake** Newfoundland and Labrador Canada
58 K1 **Victoria Land** *plain* Antarctica
160 E3 **Victoria Nile** *watercourse* Uganda
219 K2 **Victoria Point** Qld Australia
221 E6 **Victoria Range** New Zealand
214 A4 **Victoria River Downs** NT Australia
214 A3 **Victoria River Roadhouse** NT Australia
83 L4 **Victoria Road** Ontario Canada
162 D6 **Victoria West** South Africa
195 I5 **Victorias** Philippines
73 L9 **Victoriaville** Quebec Canada
106 E6 **Victorica** Argentina
84 D3 **Victorville** California USA
217 M2 **Victory Downs** NT Australia
76 H1 **Victory Lake** Nunavut Canada
106 D4 **Vicuña** Chile
106 E5 **Vicuna Mackenna** Argentina
101 I5 **Vida Nova** Brazil
84 E3 **Vidal** California USA
84 E3 **Vidal Junction** California USA
123 L4 **Vidāle** Latvia
87 J4 **Vidalia** Georgia USA
86 F5 **Vidalia** Louisiana USA
125 L1 **Vidamlya** Belarus
127 H5 **Vidauban** France
86 C6 **Vidaurri** Texas USA
122 E4 **Videbæk** Denmark
120 inset **Víðidalsá** *watercourse* Iceland
128 C4 **Vidigueira** Portugal
132 C4 **Vidin** *admin. area* Bulgaria
123 J3 **Vidinge** *island* Sweden
128 C2 **Vidio, Cabo** *cape* Spain
186 D6 **Vidisha** Madhya Pradesh India
123 Q2 **Vidlitsa** Russian Federation
86 D5 **Vidor** Texas USA
122 G4 **Vidöstern** *lake* Sweden
130 G4 **Vidovci** Croatia
130 H4 **Vidovice** Bosnia and Herzegovina
132 D3 **Vidraru, Lacul** *lake* Romania
129 H3 **Vidrieres** Spain
120 L4 **Vidsel** Sweden
126 D3 **Vie** *watercourse* France
108 D2 **Viedma** Argentina
108 B4 **Viedma, Lago** *lake* Argentina
108 B4 **Viedma, Ventisquero** *glacier* Argentina
109 15 **Vieille Case** Dominica
128 B4 **Vieira de Leiria** Portugal
126 C5 **Vieja** *region* Spain
85 J5 **Vieja, Sierra** *range* Texas USA
121 P5 **Vieki** Finland
121 P5 **Viekinjärvi** *lake* Finland
129 G2 **Vielha** Spain
127 G1 **Vielsalm** Belgium
124 F2 **Vienenburg** Germany
Vienna *see* **Wien** Austria
82 G8 **Vienna** Illinois USA
83 M7 **Vienna** Virginia USA
83 K7 **Vienna** West Virginia USA
127 G4 **Vienne** France
126 E3 **Vienne** *watercourse* France
Vientiane *see* **Viangchan** Laos
91 H3 **Vieques** Puerto Rico
91 H3 **Vieques** *island* Puerto Rico
121 O5 **Vieremä** Finland
126 F3 **Vierzon** France
88 E3 **Viesca** Mexico
123 M4 **Viesīte** Latvia
131 G6 **Vieste** Italy
194 E2 **Việt Trì** Vietnam
120 K3 **Vietas** Sweden
194 E3 **Vietnam** *country*
109 16 **Vieux-Bourg** Guadeloupe
109 16 **Vieux-Fort** Guadeloupe
101 F1 **Vieux Fort** St Lucia
109 16 **Vieux-Fort, Pointe du** *cape* Guadeloupe
101 H3 **Vieux Grand-Santi** French Guiana
109 16 **Vieux-Habitants** Guadeloupe
127 G4 **Vif** France
88 E3 **Viga, Cerro de la** *mountain* Mexico
195 I3 **Vigan** Philippines
124 E5 **Vigevano** Italy
120 I5 **Vigge** Sweden
102 B3 **Vigia** Brazil
128 C4 **Vigia, Barragem da** *lake* Portugal
100 B3 **Vigía del Fuerte** Colombia
127 K5 **Vignanello** Italy
124 F5 **Vignola** Italy
131 F5 **Vignola, Punta** *cape* Italy
131 C6 **Vignola Mare l'Agnata** Sardinia Italy
128 B2 **Vigo** Spain
139 E2 **Vigo** Worcestershire England UK
122 C1 **Vigra** *island* Norway
130 B2 **Vigy** France
121 N4 **Vihanti** Finland
179 L3 **Vihari** Pakistan
126 D3 **Vihiers** France
179 L3 **Vihowa** Pakistan
123 O1 **Vihtari** Finland
123 M2 **Vihti** Finland
123 M2 **Vihtijärvi** Finland
123 L2 **Viiala** Finland
121 M3 **Viikusjärvi** Sweden
121 P5 **Viinijärvi** *lake* Finland
132 E2 **Viişoara** Romania
121 P5 **Viitaniemi** Finland
121 N5 **Viitasaari** Finland
123 N3 **Viitna** Estonia
186 D6 **Vijainagar** Rajasthan India
187 E8 **Vijayawada** Andhra Pradesh India
100 B4 **Vijes** Colombia
120 inset **Vík** Iceland
120 H3 **Vik** Norway
121 O3 **Vikajärvi** Finland
186 D4 **Vikasnagar** Uttaranchal India
120 E5 **Vike** Norway
198 C6 **Vikeke** Timor-Leste (East Timor)
120 H4 **Viken** Sweden
122 H3 **Vikern** *lake* Sweden
133 C5 **Vikhren** *mountain* Bulgaria
75 P6 **Viking** Alberta Canada
120 G4 **Vikna** *island* Norway
132 D1 **Vikno** Ukraine
122 D2 **Vikøyri** Norway
120 K2 **Vikran** Norway
122 C2 **Viksdalsvatnet** *lake* Norway
120 J5 **Viksjö** Sweden
122 I2 **Viksjön** *lake* Sweden
120 F5 **Vikum** Norway
105 G4 **Vila Bela da Santíssima Trindade** Brazil
100 D5 **Vila Bittencourt** Colombia
104 D2 **Vila Calmon** Brazil
105 F1 **Vila Camará** Brazil
164 4 **Vila da Ribeira Brava** Cape Verde
106 F4 **Vila de María** Argentina
102 F4 **Vila do Conde** Brazil
164 4 **Vila do Maio** Cape Verde
128 C3 **Vila Flor** Portugal
128 B4 **Vila Franca de Xira** Portugal
164 1a **Vila Franca do Campo** Azores
105 G2 **Vila Nova** Brazil
164 4 **Vila Nova Sintra** Cape Verde
105 H4 **Vila Paredão** Brazil
101 F4 **Vila Pereira** Brazil
128 B3 **Vila Praia de Âncora** Portugal
128 C3 **Vila Real** Portugal
128 C3 **Vila Real** *admin. area* Portugal
128 C5 **Vila Real de Santo António** Portugal
105 I3 **Vila Rica** Brazil
101 F4 **Vila Tepequém** Brazil
101 I4 **Vila Velha** Brazil
103 D8 **Vila Velha** Brazil
128 C4 **Vila Viçosa** Portugal
104 C3 **Vilacamba, Cordillera** *range* Peru
164 3a **Vilaflor** Canary Islands
129 G3 **Vilafranca del Penedès** Spain
126 C3 **Vilaine** *watercourse* France
163 H3 **Vilanandro, Tanjona** *cape* Madagascar
163 G4 **Vilankulos** Mozambique
129 G3 **Vilanova i la Geltrú** Spain
104 D5 **Vilaque** Bolivia
128 B3 **Vilar do Paraíso** Portugal
81 N8 **Vilas** Colorado USA
120 I3 **Vilasund** Sweden
106 C6 **Vilcún** Chile
122 E4 **Vildbjerg** Denmark
128 C3 **Vilela** Portugal
120 J4 **Vilhelmina** Sweden
105 F4 **Vilhena** Brazil
133 C6 **Vilia** Greece
135 AG6 **Viliga-Kushka** Russian Federation
123 N5 **Viliya** *watercourse* Belarus
123 M3 **Viljandi** Estonia
123 M3 **Viljandimaa** *admin. area* Estonia
162 E5 **Viljoenskroon** South Africa
121 P5 **Viljolahti** Finland
123 L5 **Vilkaviškis** Lithuania
123 M4 **Viļķene** Latvia
123 L5 **Vilkija** Lithuania
134 Q4 **Vil'kitskogo, Ostrov** *island* Russian Federation
135 V3 **Vil'kitskogo, Proliv** *strait* Russian Federation
88 D2 **Villa Ahumada** Mexico
106 F3 **Villa Ángela** Argentina
100 D2 **Villa Bruzual** Venezuela
90 B4 **Villa Canales** Guatemala
106 E4 **Villa Carlos Paz** Argentina
108 B4 **Villa Cerro Castillo** Chile
90 D2 **Villa Clara** *admin. area* Cuba
89 G5 **Villa Corzo** Mexico
104 B3 **Villa Culebras** Peru
88 E5 **Villa de Álvarez** Mexico
88 E4 **Villa de Cos** Mexico
100 E2 **Villa de Cura** Venezuela
85 L8 **Villa de Garcia** Mexico
107 G5 **Villa del Carmen** Uruguay
128 D3 **Villa del Prado** Spain
128 D5 **Villa del Río** Spain
100 C3 **Villa del Rosario** Colombia
106 E4 **Villa Dolores** Argentina
107 G3 **Villa Florida** Paraguay
88 E4 **Villa Guerrero** Mexico
88 D4 **Villa Hidalgo** Mexico
106 E5 **Villa Huidobro** Argentina
105 F6 **Villa Ingavi** Bolivia
88 C3 **Villa Insurgentes** Mexico
84 F6 **Villa Jesus Maria** Mexico
88 C3 **Villa Juárez** Mexico
106 D4 **Villa Krause** Argentina
108 B3 **Villa Mañihuales** Chile
106 F5 **Villa María** Argentina
108 B2 **Villa Mascardi** Argentina
85 J7 **Villa Matamoros** Mexico
106 E5 **Villa Mercedes** Argentina
90 B4 **Villa Nueva** Guatemala
101 F2 **Villa Nueva** Venezuela
107 G4 **Villa Ocampo** Argentina
88 D3 **Villa Ocampo** Mexico
106 F4 **Villa Ojo de Agua** Argentina
107 G3 **Villa Oliva** Paraguay
88 D3 **Villa Orestes Pereyra** Mexico
100 B4 **Villa Rica** Colombia
104 C3 **Villa Rica** Peru
106 E4 **Villa San Martin** Argentina
130 E3 **Villa Santina** Italy
107 H5 **Villa Sara** Uruguay
106 D4 **Villa Unión** Argentina
88 D4 **Villa Unión** Mexico
88 E2 **Villa Unión** Mexico
106 E5 **Villa Valeria** Argentina
105 F5 **Villa Yapacaní** Bolivia
128 E2 **Villabona** Spain
128 D3 **Villabrágima** Spain
128 D3 **Villacastín** Spain
125 G4 **Villach** Austria
131 C7 **Villacidro** Sardinia Italy
128 D2 **Villada** Spain
128 D2 **Villadiego** Spain
130 C3 **Villadossola** Italy
131 E8 **Villafrati** Italy
128 E3 **Villafruela** Spain
100 B4 **Villagarzón** Colombia
109 6a **Villagra, Bahia** *bay* Isla Róbinson Crusoe
107 G4 **Villaguay** Argentina
89 G5 **Villahermosa** Mexico
128 E4 **Villahermosa** Spain
126 D2 **Villaines-la-Juhel** France
121 P5 **Villala** Finland
128 C2 **Villalba** Spain
128 E3 **Villalba de la Sierra** Spain
107 G3 **Villalbin** Paraguay
85 L7 **Villaldama** Mexico
128 D2 **Villalón de Campos** Spain
106 F6 **Villalonga** Argentina
131 C7 **Villamar** Sardinia Italy
128 D5 **Villamartín** Spain
105 F6 **Villamontes** Bolivia
128 E2 **Villano, Cabo** *cape* Spain
100 D3 **Villanueva** Colombia
88 E4 **Villanueva** Mexico
128 D4 **Villanueva de Córdoba** Spain
128 D4 **Villanueva de la Serena** Spain
128 C4 **Villanueva del Fresno** Spain
125 J5 **Villány** Hungary
128 E4 **Villapalacios** Spain
131 C7 **Villaputzu** Sardinia Italy
128 C3 **Villar de Peralonso** Spain
128 C4 **Villar del Rey** Spain
128 C4 **Villar del Rey, Embalse de** *lake* Spain
127 G4 **Villard-de-Lans** France
106 F6 **Villarino Viejo** Argentina
131 F8 **Villarosa** Italy
128 D2 **Villarramiel** Spain
106 C6 **Villarrica** Chile
107 G3 **Villarrica** Paraguay
106 C6 **Villarrica, Lago** *lake* Chile
108 C2 **Villarrica, Volcán** *volcano* Chile
128 E4 **Villarrobledo** Spain
124 C5 **Villars-les-Dombes** France
129 J2 **Villars-sur-Var** France
128 D3 **Villatoro** Spain
100 C3 **Villavicencio** Colombia
126 B5 **Villaviciosa** Spain
100 C4 **Villavieja** Colombia
106 E2 **Villazón** Argentina
124 D3 **Villé** France
126 F4 **Villefort** France
126 E5 **Villefranche-de-Lauragais** France
126 F4 **Villefranche-de-Panat** France
126 F4 **Villefranche-de-Rouergue** France
127 G4 **Villefranche-sur-Saône** France
108 D3 **Villegas, Valle** *valley* Argentina
127 H3 **Villeneuve** Switzerland
126 D5 **Villeneuve-de-Marsan** France
126 F3 **Villeneuve-sur-Allier** France
126 E4 **Villeneuve-sur-Lot** France
126 F5 **Villepinte** France
126 E4 **Villeréal** France
83 P3 **Villeroy** Quebec Canada
124 C2 **Villers-la-Ville** Belgium
127 H3 **Villersexel** France
126 E4 **Villesèque** France
100 C3 **Villeta** Colombia
127 G4 **Villeurbanne** France
162 E5 **Villiers** South Africa
123 J3 **Villinge** *island* Sweden
128 D2 **Villodrigo** Spain
124 G5 **Villorba** Italy
123 M5 **Vilniaus** *admin. area* Lithuania
123 M5 **Vilnius** Lithuania
104 E5 **Viloco** Bolivia
123 M1 **Vilppula** Finland
127 J3 **Vils** Austria
124 F3 **Vils** *watercourse* Germany
132 G1 **Vil'shanka** Ukraine
132 G1 **Vil'shanka** *watercourse* Ukraine
124 G3 **Vilshofen** Germany
130 H5 **Vilusi** Montenegro
104 D4 **Viluyo** Peru
127 G1 **Vilvoorde** Belgium
182 E6 **Vilyashchay** *watercourse* Azerbaijan
123 N5 **Vilyeyskaye, Vozyera** *lake* Belarus
135 Y6 **Vilyuy** *watercourse* Russian Federation
135 Z6 **Vilyuysk** Russian Federation
135 X5 **Vilyuyskoye Plato** *region* Russian Federation
135 X6 **Vilyuyskoye Vodokhranilishche** *lake* Russian Federation
128 B2 **Vimianzo** Spain
128 C4 **Vimieiro** Portugal
128 C3 **Vimioso** Portugal
122 H4 **Vimmerby** Sweden
121 M5 **Vimpeli** Finland
125 G3 **Vimperk** Czech Republic
159 H3 **Vina** *watercourse* Cameroon
106 D5 **Viña del Mar** Chile
106 D5 **Viña Sausiño** Chile
129 G3 **Vinaròs** Spain
124 C5 **Vinay** France
122 G4 **Vinberg** Sweden
78 B5 **Vincelotte, Lac** *lake* Quebec Canada
82 H7 **Vincennes** Indiana USA
58 H2 **Vincennes Bay** Antarctica
211 inset **Vincent Point** Norfolk Island Australia
100 B5 **Vinces** Ecuador
106 D4 **Vinchina** Argentina
127 J5 **Vinci** Italy
120 J3 **Vindelälven** *watercourse* Sweden
120 K4 **Vindelgransele** Sweden
120 K4 **Vindeln** Sweden
187 D6 **Vindhya Range** Madhya Pradesh India
123 J3 **Vindö** *island* Sweden
122 I3 **Vindommen** *lake* Sweden
83 N7 **Vineland** New Jersey USA
126 E3 **Vineuil** France
132 B2 **Vinga** Romania
120 G5 **Vingelen** Norway
194 E3 **Vinh** Vietnam
194 E5 **Vĩnh Châu** Vietnam
194 E3 **Vĩnh Lộc** Vietnam
194 E5 **Vĩnh Long** Vietnam
194 E2 **Vinh Thuc, Đao** *island* Vietnam
194 E2 **Vĩnh Tuy** Vietnam
128 C3 **Vinhais** Portugal
125 H5 **Vinica** Slovenia
58 S1 **Vinison Mastif** *mountain* Antarctica
82 D8 **Vinita** Oklahoma USA
122 D2 **Vinje** Norway
120 I3 **Vinknes** Norway
130 H4 **Vinkovci** Croatia
125 K3 **Vinné** Slovakia
136 D3 **Vinnyts'ka Oblast'** *admin. area* Ukraine
136 D3 **Vinnytsya** Ukraine

122 I4 **Vinö** *island* Sweden
132 D4 **Vinogradets** Bulgaria
120 F5 **Vinsternes** Norway
120 F6 **Vinstra** Norway
120 F6 **Vinstra** *watercourse* Norway
74 K7 **Vinsulla** British Columbia Canada
132 E3 **Vintileasca** Romania
122 I2 **Vintjärn** Sweden
104 E5 **Vinto** Bolivia
82 E5 **Vinton** Iowa USA
86 E5 **Vinton** Louisiana USA
85 I5 **Vinton** Texas USA
83 L8 **Vinton** Virginia USA
132 C3 **Vinţu de Jos** Romania
128 E3 **Vinuesa** Spain
187 E8 **Vinukonda** Andhra Pradesh India
82 F6 **Viola** Illinois USA
86 C2 **Viola** Kansas USA
58 U2 **Violante Inlet** *bay* Antarctica
218 G7 **Violet Town** Vic. Australia
162 C5 **Vioolsdrif** South Africa
130 E4 **Vipava** *watercourse* Slovenia
130 D3 **Vipiteno** Italy
130 F4 **Vir** Croatia
130 F4 **Vir** *island* Croatia
125 H4 **Vir** Slovenia
195 J4 **Virac** Philippines
186 C6 **Viramgam** Gujarat India
134 I6 **Virandozero** Russian Federation
187 C7 **Virar** Maharashtra India
179 L5 **Virawah** Pakistan
121 Q5 **Virda** Russian Federation
75 U8 **Virden** Manitoba Canada
85 H4 **Virden** New Mexico USA
126 D2 **Vire** *watercourse* France
122 H4 **Viren** *lake* Sweden
123 N4 **Vireši** Latvia
108 C5 **Vírgenes, Cabo** *cape* Argentina
84 E2 **Virgin** *watercourse* Nevada USA
84 F2 **Virgin** Utah USA
91 H3 **Virgin Gorda** *island* Virgin Islands
Virgin Islands (UK) *see* **British** Virgin Islands
91 H3 **Virgin Islands (USA)** *US territory* Caribbean
84 F2 **Virgin Mountains** Arkansas USA
143 E3 **Virginia** Ireland
162 E5 **Virginia** South Africa
71 **Virginia** *admin. area* USA
82 F7 **Virginia** Illinois USA
82 E3 **Virginia** Minnesota USA
83 N8 **Virginia Beach** Virginia USA
223 9a **Viria** Fiji
120 J3 **Virihaure** *lake* Sweden
130 G3 **Virje** Croatia
121 O4 **Virkkunen** Finland
121 O5 **Virmaanpää** Finland
121 O5 **Virmas** *lake* Finland
121 O5 **Virmasvesi** *bay* Finland
123 N2 **Virolahden Kirkonkylä** Finland
130 G4 **Virovitica** Croatia
131 H5 **Virpazar** Montenegro
121 M5 **Virrat** Finland
104 B2 **Virrey Nuevo** Peru
122 H4 **Virserum** Sweden
121 P2 **Virtaniemi** Finland
121 O5 **Virtasalmi** Finland
127 G2 **Virton** Belgium
132 C3 **Vîrtopu** Romania
104 B3 **Virú** Peru
130 G5 **Vis** Croatia
130 G5 **Vis** *island* Croatia
162 D6 **Vis** *watercourse* South Africa
84 C2 **Visalia** California USA
187 C7 **Visavadar** Gujarat India
195 I5 **Visayan Islands** Philippines
195 I5 **Visayan Sea** Philippines
124 E1 **Visbek** Germany
122 F4 **Visborg** Denmark
122 J4 **Visby** Sweden
72 H4 **Viscount Melville Sound** *strait* Northwest Territories/Nunavut Canada
127 G1 **Visé** Belgium
132 A4 **Višegrad** Bosnia and Herzegovina
127 K3 **Visentin, Col** *mountain* Italy
102 C3 **Viseu** Brazil
128 C3 **Viseu** Portugal
128 C3 **Viseu** *admin. area* Portugal
187 F8 **Vishakhapatnam** Andhra Pradesh India
132 F3 **Vishnëvoye** Ukraine
123 N5 **Vishnewskaye, Vozyera** *lake* Belarus
120 K4 **Viskasjön** *lake* Sweden
186 C6 **Visnagar** Gujarat India
127 L4 **Višnja Gora** Slovenia
125 H2 **Višňova** Czech Republic
127 H3 **Visp** Switzerland
120 J4 **Vispsjön** *lake* Sweden
133 B6 **Vissani** Greece
187 E8 **Vissannapeta** Andhra Pradesh India
122 H4 **Vissjön** *lake* Sweden
130 E5 **Visso** Italy
84 D4 **Vista** California USA
101 E5 **Vista Alegre** Brazil
105 G5 **Vista Alegre** Brazil
100 C4 **Vista Hermosa** Colombia
122 G3 **Visten** *lake* Sweden
120 L4 **Vistheden** Sweden
133 D5 **Vistonias, Ormos** *bay* Greece
133 D5 **Vistonida, Limni** *lake* Greece
123 L5 **Vištytis** Lithuania
123 L5 **Vištytis** *lake* Russian Federation
132 D4 **Vit** *watercourse* Bulgaria
187 D8 **Vita** Maharashtra India
179 L3 **Vitakri** Pakistan
120 L4 **Vitberget** Sweden
123 O5 **Vitebsk/Vitsyebskaya Voblasts'** *admin. area* Belarus
100 C3 **Viterbo** Colombia
131 E5 **Viterbo** Italy
133 B5 **Vithkuq** Albania
223 9 **Viti Levu** *island* Fiji
223 9a **Viti Levu Bay** Fiji
199 H5 **Vitiaz Strait** Papua New Guinea
105 E6 **Vitichi** Bolivia
128 C3 **Vitigudino** Spain
135 X7 **Vitim** Russian Federation
135 Y8 **Vitim** *watercourse* Russian Federation
191 G1 **Vitimskoye Ploskogor'ye** Russian Federation
135 X8 **Vitimskoye Ploskogor'ye** *region* Russian Federation
130 G5 **Vitina** Bosnia and Herzegovina
133 C7 **Vitina** Greece
133 B5 **Vitolište** Macedonia
104 C5 **Vitor** *watercourse* Peru
103 D8 **Vitória** Brazil
103 D6 **Vitória da Conquista** Brazil
128 E2 **Vitoria-Gasteiz** Spain
51 O12 **Vitória Seamount** *underwater feature* Atlantic Ocean
104 D3 **Vitória Velha** Brazil
102 C4 **Vitorino Freire** Brazil
126 D2 **Vitré** France
127 G5 **Vitrolles** France
123 P5 **Vitsyebsk** Belarus
120 L3 **Vittangi** Sweden
120 L2 **Vittangivaara** *lake* Sweden
127 G3 **Vitteaux** France
127 G2 **Vittel** France
120 L4 **Vittjärv** Sweden
131 F8 **Vittoria** Italy
124 G5 **Vittorio Veneto** Italy
121 M3 **Vitvattnet** Sweden
52 N9 **Vityaz Trench** *underwater feature* Pacific Ocean
129 F4 **Viver** Spain
128 C2 **Vivero** Spain
130 C4 **Viverone, Lago di** *lake* Italy
135 U5 **Vivi** *watercourse* Russian Federation
76 G8 **Vivian** Manitoba Canada
86 E4 **Vivian** Louisiana USA
199 I6 **Vivigani** Papua New Guinea
218 C6 **Vivonne Bay** SA Australia
107 G6 **Vivoratá** Argentina
223 9 **Viwa** *island* Fiji
104 D4 **Vizcachane** Peru
104 E6 **Vizcachilla** Bolivia
88 B3 **Vizcaíno, Sierra** *range* Mexico
128 E2 **Vizcaya, Golfo de** *bay* Spain
133 E5 **Vize** Turkey
134 Q3 **Vize, Ostrov** *island* Russian Federation
187 F7 **Vizianagaram** Andhra Pradesh India
78 B3 **Vizien** *watercourse* Quebec Canada
125 G5 **Vižinada** Croatia
121 Q3 **Viziyarvi, Ozero** *lake* Russian Federation
133 A5 **Vjosë** *watercourse* Albania
132 E3 **Vlădeni** Romania
132 F3 **Vlădeşti** Romania
132 C4 **Vladičin Han** Serbia
182 D5 **Vladikavkaz** Russian Federation
134 J7 **Vladimir** Russian Federation
182 C2 **Vladimirskaya** *admin. area* Russian Federation
192 F2 **Vladivostok** Russian Federation
133 B7 **Vlakhópoulon** Greece
212 C6 **Vlaming Head** WA Australia
132 B4 **Vlase** Serbia
130 H4 **Vlasenica** Bosnia and Herzegovina
125 H3 **Vlašim** Czech Republic
132 C4 **Vlasinsko Jezero** *lake* Serbia
183 P2 **Vlas'yevo** *lake* Russian Federation
124 C1 **Vlieland** *island* Netherlands
124 B2 **Vlissingen** Netherlands
133 C6 **Vlochos** Greece
133 A5 **Vlorë** Albania
133 A5 **Vlorës, Gjiri i** *bay* Albania
124 E1 **Vlotho** Germany
125 G3 **Vltava** *watercourse* Czech Republic
182 I6 **Vobkent** Uzbekistan
133 E4 **Voden** Bulgaria
132 G1 **Vodjanoye** Ukraine
121 T5 **Vodla** Russian Federation
125 H3 **Vodňany** Czech Republic
127 K4 **Vodnjan** Croatia
124 D2 **Voerde** Germany
124 E5 **Voghera** Italy
120 F5 **Vognill** Norway
127 K2 **Vohenstrauß** Germany
163 I4 **Vohilava** Madagascar
163 I5 **Vohimena, Tanjon'i** *cape* Madagascar
161 F4 **Voi** Kenya
161 F4 **Voi** *watercourse* Kenya
125 M5 **Voiceşti** Romania
127 G2 **Void-Vacon** France
123 M3 **Võidu** Estonia
132 C3 **Voineasa** Romania
127 G2 **Voire** *watercourse* France
127 G4 **Voiron** France
125 H4 **Voitsberg** Austria
123 M3 **Võivaku** Estonia
122 E5 **Vojens** Denmark
120 J4 **Vojmsjön** *lake* Sweden
130 F4 **Vojnić** Croatia
125 H4 **Vojnik** Slovenia
199 H4 **Vokeo Island** Papua New Guinea
121 Q4 **Voknavolok** Russian Federation
104 E6 **Volcán, Cerro** *volcano* Argentina
108 F1 **Volcán, Sierra del** *range* Argentina
84 inset **Volcano** Hawai'i USA
183 M3 **Volchikha** Russian Federation
120 E5 **Volda** Norway
134 I7 **Volga** *watercourse* Russian Federation
81 Q4 **Volga** South Dakota USA
182 D4 **Volgodonsk** Russian Federation
182 D4 **Volgograd** Russian Federation
182 D3 **Volgogradskaya** *admin. area* Russian Federation
133 B7 **Volimai** Greece
132 F2 **Volintiri** Moldova
130 G5 **Voljevac** Bosnia and Herzegovina
125 H4 **Völkermarkt** Austria
123 Q3 **Volkhov** Russian Federation
123 Q3 **Volkov** *watercourse* Russian Federation
123 O6 **Volma** Belarus
136 E3 **Vol'n'ansk** Ukraine
136 F3 **Volnovakha** Ukraine
135 T4 **Volochanka** Russian Federation
132 E1 **Volochys'k** Ukraine
134 K5 **Volokovaya** Russian Federation
121 R5 **Voloma** Russian Federation
133 C6 **Volos** Greece
123 O3 **Voloshovo** Russian Federation
123 O5 **Volosovo** Belarus
123 P4 **Volot** Russian Federation
125 L3 **Volovets'** Ukraine
123 P2 **Voloyarvi** Russian Federation
121 S5 **Volozero, Ozero** *lake* Russian Federation
182 E3 **Vo'lsk** Russian Federation
158 E3 **Volta** *watercourse* Ghana
158 D3 **Volta, Lake** *lake* Ghana
213 H3 **Voltaire, Cape** WA Australia
130 D5 **Volterra** Italy
127 I4 **Voltri** Italy
121 M5 **Voltti** Finland
131 F6 **Volturno** *watercourse* Italy
108 E1 **Voluntad** Argentina
133 C5 **Volvi, Limni** *lake* Greece
136 C2 **Volyns'ka Oblast'** *admin. area* Ukraine
182 E2 **Volzhsk** Russian Federation
182 D4 **Volzhskiy** Russian Federation
122 G5 **Vombsjön** *lake* Sweden
223 9a **Vomo** *island* Fiji
216 H3 **Von Treuer Tableland** WA Australia
132 D4 **Voneshta Voda** Bulgaria
87 I3 **Vonore** Tennessee USA
123 N3 **Võõpsu** Estonia
120 inset **Vopnafjörður** Iceland
120 inset **Vopnafjörður** *bay* Iceland
123 M5 **Voranava** Belarus
124 E4 **Vorarlberg** *admin. area* Austria
133 B5 **Voras** *range* Macedonia
133 D6 **Voreio Aigaio** *admin. area* Greece
121 S5 **Vorenzha** Russian Federation
57 G2 **Voring Plateau** *underwater feature* Norwegian Sea
181 G3 **Vorjing** *mountain* Xizang Zizhiqu China
181 H3 **Vorjing** *mountain* Arunachal Pradesh India
134 N5 **Vorkuta** Russian Federation
123 L3 **Vormsi** *island* Estonia
182 C3 **Vorob'yevka** Russian Federation
108 F2 **Vorohué, Punta** *cape* Argentina
136 F2 **Voronezh** Russian Federation
136 F2 **Voronezh** *watercourse* Russian Federation
182 C3 **Voronezhskaya Oblast'** *admin. area* Russian Federation
57 L1 **Voronin Trough** *underwater feature* Arctic Ocean
135 U3 **Voronina, Ostrov** *island* Russian Federation
57 F1 **Voronov Plateau** *underwater feature* Arctic Ocean
123 O3 **Voronovo** Russian Federation
132 G1 **Voronoye** Ukraine
132 H2 **Vorontsovka** Ukraine
135 AE5 **Vorontsovo** Russian Federation
123 P5 **Vorony** Belarus
125 M3 **Voronyaky** *region* Ukraine
182 E2 **Vorotynets** Russian Federation
58 B2 **Vorposten Peak** *mountain* Antarctica
120 L2 **Vorterøy** *island* Norway
123 N3 **Võrtsjärv** *lake* Estonia
123 N4 **Võru** Estonia
183 K6 **Vorukh** Tajikistan
123 N4 **Võrumaa** *admin. area* Estonia
127 H2 **Vosges** *range* France
123 L5 **Vosiliškis** Lithuania
133 B5 **Voskopojë** Albania
132 H2 **Voskresens'ke** Ukraine
182 E2 **Voskresenskoye** Russian Federation
182 G2 **Voskresenskoye** Russian Federation
121 R2 **Vosmus** Russian Federation
132 H2 **Vossiyatskoye** Ukraine
134 I5 **Vostochnaya Litsa** Russian Federation
183 N4 **Vostochno-Kazakstanskaya Oblast'** *admin. area* Kazakhstan
135 AH4 **Vostochno-Sibirskoye More** *sea* Russian Federation
135 U8 **Vostochnyy Sayan** *range* Russian Federation
59 G1 **Vostok, Lake** Antarctica
58 H1 **Vostok (Russia)** *research station* Antarctica
222 1 **Vostok Island** Kiribati
123 M3 **Võsu** Estonia
222 7 **Vot Tandé** *island* Vanuatu
125 H3 **Votice** Czech Republic
182 G1 **Votkinsk** Russian Federation
222 7 **Votlo** Vanuatu
133 B6 **Votonosion** Greece
124 C3 **Voué** France
128 C3 **Vouga** *watercourse* Portugal
127 G3 **Vougeot** France
133 C8 **Voukolies** Greece
126 D3 **Vouvant** France
133 C8 **Vouxa, Akrotirio** *cape* Greece
127 G2 **Vouziers** France
126 E2 **Voves** France
160 D2 **Vovondo** *watercourse* Central African Republic
121 Q4 **Voynitsa** Russian Federation
222 8 **Voza** Solomon Islands
132 G2 **Voznesens'k** Ukraine
183 K3 **Voznesenka** Kazakhstan
183 K2 **Vozvyshenka** Kazakhstan
122 E4 **Vrå** Denmark
122 G4 **Vrå** Sweden
132 C4 **Vrachesh** Bulgaria
132 G2 **Vradiyivka** Ukraine
132 E3 **Vrancea** *admin. area* Romania
135 AL4 **Vrangelya, Ostrov** *island* Russian Federation
131 H5 **Vranj** Montenegro
132 B4 **Vranje** Serbia
133 A5 **Vrap** Albania
132 C3 **Vrata** Romania
132 B4 **Vratnica** Macedonia
132 C4 **Vratsa** *admin. area* Bulgaria
130 G4 **Vrbanja** Bosnia and Herzegovina
125 J5 **Vrbanja** Croatia
130 G4 **Vrbas** *watercourse* Bosnia and Herzegovina
132 A3 **Vrbas** Serbia
125 I5 **Vrbaška** Bosnia and Herzegovina
130 G4 **Vrbovljani** Croatia
130 F4 **Vrbovsko** Croatia
125 H2 **Vrchlabí** Czech Republic
125 K5 **Vrčin** Serbia
125 H3 **Vrdy** Czech Republic
162 C6 **Vredenburg** South Africa
162 C6 **Vredendal** South Africa
101 G3 **Vreed en Hoop** Guyana
130 F5 **Vrgada** *island* Croatia
130 G5 **Vrgorac** Croatia
125 I5 **Vrhopolje** Bosnia and Herzegovina
125 H5 **Vrhovine** Croatia
214 G1 **Vrilya Point** Qld Australia
133 B7 **Vrísai** Greece
122 G3 **Vristulven** *lake* Sweden
133 B6 **Vromonas** *island* Greece
139 I4 **Vron** France
133 B5 **Vronterón** Greece
133 B6 **Vrosina** Greece
132 B3 **Vršac** Serbia
130 E4 **Vrsar** Croatia
130 F4 **Vrsi** Croatia
123 O3 **Vruda** Russian Federation
130 F5 **Vrulje** Croatia
133 B5 **Vrutok** Macedonia
162 D5 **Vryburg** South Africa
162 F5 **Vryheid** South Africa
125 I3 **Vsetín** Czech Republic
72 C8 **Vsevidof, Mount** Alaska USA
123 P3 **Vsevolozhsk** Russian Federation
194 E2 **Vụ Bản** Vietnam
223 9 **Vuagava** *island* Fiji
160 D3 **Vube** Democratic Republic of Congo
132 D4 **Vŭbel** Bulgaria
124 C2 **Vught** Netherlands
125 H4 **Vuhred** Slovenia
125 J5 **Vuka** Croatia
132 C4 **Vukan** Bulgaria
130 H4 **Vukovar** Croatia
162 E5 **Vukuzakhe** South Africa
195 G3 **Vuladdore Reef** Paracel Islands
75 O7 **Vulcan** Alberta Canada
131 F7 **Vulcano, Isola** *island* Italy
132 E4 **Vŭlchidol** Bulgaria
125 M5 **Vultureşti** Romania
132 E3 **Vulturu de Jos** Romania
194 E5 **Vũng Tàu** Vietnam
223 9a **Vunindawa** Fiji
223 9 **Vunisei** Fiji
120 J3 **Vuoggatjålmjaure** *lake* Sweden
121 O2 **Vuogojavri** *lake* Finland
123 N2 **Vuohijärvi** *lake* Finland
121 O3 **Vuojärvi** Finland
120 K3 **Vuojat** Sweden
121 P4 **Vuokatti** Finland
121 P4 **Vuokkijärvi** *lake* Finland
121 P5 **Vuokko** Finland
120 K3 **Vuolep Kaitumjaure** *lake* Sweden
121 O4 **Vuolijoki** Finland
120 L3 **Vuollerim** Sweden
120 K3 **Vuolvojaure** *bay* Sweden
121 M3 **Vuomajärvi** Sweden
121 N2 **Vuontisjärvi** Finland
121 P2 **Vuopioniemi** Finland
121 P3 **Vuori-Yarvi, Ozero** *lake* Russian Federation
121 N5 **Vuorilahti** Finland
121 P4 **Vuosanganjärvi** *lake* Finland
123 M1 **Vuosjärvi** *lake* Finland
121 P3 **Vuosnayarvi, Ozero** *lake* Russian Federation
121 O3 **Vuostimo** Finland
123 O1 **Vuotjärvi** *lake* Finland
121 O2 **Vuotso** Finland
120 L3 **Vuottas** Sweden
121 O4 **Vuottolahti** Finland
121 P3 **Vuotunki** Finland
125 M5 **Vurpăr** Romania
123 N5 **Vustsye** Belarus
132 E2 **Vutcani** Romania
132 F2 **Vvedenka** Ukraine
121 S3 **Vyalozero, Ozero** *lake* Russian Federation
187 C7 **Vyara** Gujarat India
121 Q5 **Vyartsilya** Russian Federation
134 L7 **Vyatka** *watercourse* Russian Federation
136 E1 **Vyaz'ma** Russian Federation
182 E4 **Vyazovka** Russian Federation
182 D3 **Vyazovka** Russian Federation
123 N5 **Vyazyn'** Belarus
123 O2 **Vyborg** Russian Federation
134 K6 **Vychegda** *watercourse* Russian Federation
123 O5 **Vydritsa** Belarus
123 O5 **Vyesnitsk** Belarus
121 S5 **Vygozero, Ozero** *lake* Russian Federation
132 C1 **Vyhorlat** *mountain* Slovakia
123 P5 **Vykhodtsy** Belarus
182 D2 **Vyksa** Russian Federation
132 F3 **Vylkove** Ukraine
125 L3 **Vylok** Ukraine
134 L6 **Vym'** *watercourse* Russian Federation
134 Q6 **Vyngapur** Russian Federation
132 D1 **Vynnyky** Ukraine
123 O3 **Vyra** Russian Federation
123 P3 **Vyritsa** Russian Federation
138 D2 **Vyrnwy, Lake** Wales UK
182 C4 **Vyselki** Russian Federation
132 C1 **Vyshkove** Ukraine
123 O3 **Vyskatka** Russian Federation
123 P4 **Vyskod'** Russian Federation
130 G2 **Vyškov** Czech Republic
125 H3 **Vysočina Kraj** *admin. area* Czech Republic
125 L1 **Vysokaye** Belarus
135 AE3 **Vysokiy, Mys** *cape* Russian Federation
135 AI6 **Vyvenka** *watercourse* Russian Federation
132 D1 **Vyzhnytsya** Ukraine
193 I1 **Vzmor'ye** Russian Federation

W

87 K2 **W. Kerr Scott Reservoir** North Carolina USA
158 D2 **Wa** Ghana
161 G3 **Waajid** Somalia
76 H6 **Waasagomach** Manitoba Canada
160 E2 **Waat** Sudan
199 G5 **Waawoi** *watercourse* Papua New Guinea
76 L7 **Wababimiga Lake** Ontario Canada
76 K7 **Wabakimi Lake** Ontario Canada
75 N6 **Wabamun Lake** Alberta Canada
72 H7 **Wabasca** *watercourse* Alberta Canada
82 I6 **Wabash** Indiana USA
82 H7 **Wabash** *watercourse* Indiana USA
76 L7 **Wabassi** *watercourse* Ontario Canada
140 E2 **Waberthwaite** Cumbria England UK
156 E3 **Wabi, Wādī** *watercourse* Sudan
161 G2 **Wabi Gestro** *watercourse* Ethiopia
161 G2 **Wabi Shēbelē** *watercourse* Ethiopia
76 I8 **Wabigoon Lake** Ontario Canada
76 M7 **Wabimeig Lake** Ontario Canada
199 J6 **Waboma Island** Papua New Guinea
75 V5 **Wabowden** Manitoba Canada
125 J1 **Wąbrzeźno** Poland
189 G2 **Wabu-hu** *lake* Anhui China
199 G6 **Wabuda Island** Papua New Guinea
76 M5 **Wabuk Point** Ontario Canada
77 V6 **Wabush** Newfoundland and Labrador Canada
84 C1 **Wabuska** Nevada USA
87 L3 **Waccamaw, Lake** North Carolina USA
89 J2 **Waccasassa Bay** Florida USA
161 F3 **Wach'īlē** Ethiopia
124 E2 **Wächtersbach** Germany
77 W7 **Waco** Quebec Canada
86 C5 **Waco** Texas USA
86 C5 **Waco Lake** Texas USA
81 P7 **Waconda Lake** Kansas USA
179 K4 **Wad** Pakistan
156 D5 **Wad Banda** Sudan
156 D5 **Wad Hassib** Sudan
156 E5 **Wad Medani** Sudan
156 E4 **Wad Rawa** Sudan
155 J3 **Waddān** Libya
124 C1 **Waddeneilanden** *region* Netherlands
216 F5 **Wadderin** WA Australia
218 G6 **Waddi** NSW Australia
216 E5 **Waddington** WA Australia
83 N3 **Waddington** Quebec Canada
83 N4 **Waddington** New York USA
74 I7 **Waddington, Mount** British Columbia Canada
78 F5 **Wade Lake** Newfoundland and Labrador Canada
138 E4 **Wadeford** Somerset England UK
75 T7 **Wadena** Saskatchewan Canada
81 R3 **Wadena** Minnesota USA
124 D3 **Wadern** Germany
124 E2 **Wadersloh** Germany
87 K3 **Wadesboro** North Carolina USA
213 J3 **Wadeye** NT Australia
187 D7 **Wadgaon** Maharashtra India
79 L8 **Wadham Islands** Newfoundland and Labrador Canada
159 I2 **Wadi Fira** *admin. area* Chad
156 E3 **Wādī Halfa** Sudan
159 I2 **Wadibra** *watercourse* Sudan
75 S5 **Wadin Bay** Saskatchewan Canada
87 I4 **Wadley** Alabama USA
87 J4 **Wadley** Georgia USA
125 J3 **Wadowice** Poland
83 K6 **Wadsworth** Ohio USA
187 D7 **Wadwani** Maharashtra India
86 C6 **Waelder** Texas USA
58 P1 **Waesche, Mount** *mountain* Antarctica
191 J5 **Wafangdian** Liaoning China
198 C4 **Waflia** Indonesia
142 E2 **Wag** Highland Scotland UK
199 G4 **Wagasu** *watercourse* Papua New Guinea
124 E1 **Wagenfeld** Germany
101 G3 **Wageningen** Suriname
108 A4 **Wager, Isla** *island* Chile
73 K5 **Wager Bay** Nunavut Canada
219 H6 **Wagga Wagga** NSW Australia
218 G7 **Waggarandall** Vic. Australia
216 E6 **Wagin** WA Australia
81 P5 **Wagner** South Dakota USA
85 J3 **Wagon Mound** New Mexico USA
86 D3 **Wagoner** Oklahoma USA
125 H1 **Wągrowiec** Poland
84 F1 **Wah Wah Mountains** Utah USA
158 D2 **Wahabu** Ghana
198 D4 **Wahai** Indonesia
158 E3 **Wahala** Togo
78 C6 **Wahemen, Lac** *lake* Quebec Canada
84 inset **Wahiawā** Hawai'i USA
158 C2 **Wahiré** Côte d'Ivoire
81 Q6 **Wahoo** Nebraska USA
81 Q3 **Wahpeton** North Dakota USA
156 C2 **Wāḥūt Jalū** Libya
84 inset **Waiakoa** Hawai'i USA
220 H3 **Waiapu** *watercourse* New Zealand
221 C7 **Waiatoto** *watercourse* New Zealand
221 E6 **Waiau** New Zealand
221 E6 **Waiau** *watercourse* New Zealand
125 H3 **Waidhofen** Austria
198 B6 **Waienga-one** *bay* Indonesia
198 D4 **Waigama** Indonesia
217 K3 **Waigen Lakes** WA Australia
198 D4 **Waigeo** *island* Indonesia
220 F3 **Waiheke Island** New Zealand
220 F3 **Waihi** New Zealand
220 F3 **Waihi Beach** New Zealand
221 D6 **Waiho** *watercourse* New Zealand
221 E5 **Waihopai** *watercourse* New Zealand
198 A6 **Waikabubak** Indonesia
221 C7 **Waikaia** New Zealand
221 C7 **Waikaka** New Zealand
221 F5 **Waikanae** New Zealand
220 F3 **Waikare, Lake** New Zealand
220 G4 **Waikaremoana, Lake** New Zealand
220 F4 **Waikato** *admin. area* New Zealand
220 F3 **Waikato** *watercourse* New Zealand
221 C8 **Waikawa** New Zealand
198 A6 **Waikelo** Indonesia
218 D6 **Waikerie** SA Australia
84 inset **Waiki'i** Hawai'i USA
220 G4 **Waikite Valley** New Zealand
221 D7 **Waikouaiti** New Zealand
221 E6 **Waikuku Beach** New Zealand
84 inset **Wailua** Hawai'i USA
220 G4 **Waimana** *watercourse* New Zealand
220 G4 **Waimarama** New Zealand
221 D7 **Waimate** New Zealand
198 A6 **Waimanguar** Indonesia
84 inset **Waimea** Hawai'i USA
222 8 **Wainaworasi** Solomon Islands
141 I3 **Wainfleet All Saints** Lincolnshire England UK
198 B6 **Waingapu** Indonesia
101 G3 **Waini** *watercourse* Guyana
101 G2 **Waini Point** *cape* Guyana
221 F5 **Wainuioru** New Zealand
72 C4 **Wainwright** Alaska USA
220 F4 **Waiouru** New Zealand
198 F4 **Waipa** Indonesia
84 inset **Waipahu** Hawai'i USA
221 C8 **Waipapa Point** New Zealand
221 E6 **Waipara** New Zealand
75 N7 **Waiparous** Alberta Canada
220 G4 **Waipawa** New Zealand
220 G4 **Waipawa** *watercourse* New Zealand
220 H4 **Waipiro Bay** New Zealand
220 E2 **Waipoua Settlement** New Zealand
220 F2 **Waipu** New Zealand
220 G4 **Waipukurau** New Zealand
220 G4 **Wairakei** New Zealand
221 E5 **Wairau** *watercourse* New Zealand
160 E3 **Wairingo** *watercourse* Uganda
220 G4 **Wairoa** New Zealand
220 G4 **Wairoa** *watercourse* New Zealand
198 B6 **Wairunu** Indonesia
221 D6 **Waitaha** *watercourse* New Zealand
220 G4 **Waitahanui** New Zealand
221 C7 **Waitahuna** New Zealand
220 F3 **Waitakere** New Zealand
221 D7 **Waitaki** *watercourse* New Zealand
220 F2 **Waitangi** New Zealand
220 F4 **Waitara** New Zealand
220 F4 **Waitara** *watercourse* New Zealand
220 F5 **Waitarere** New Zealand
214 C7 **Waite** *watercourse* NT Australia
58 Q2 **Waite, Cape** Antarctica
211 inset **Waite, Mount** Macquarie Island Australia
220 E2 **Waitiki Landing** New Zealand
220 F3 **Waitoa** New Zealand
220 F3 **Waiuku** New Zealand
220 F4 **Waitomo Caves** New Zealand
220 F4 **Waitotara** New Zealand
220 F4 **Waitotara** *watercourse* New Zealand
80 F3 **Waitsburg** Washington USA
199 I6 **Waiwa** Papua New Guinea
220 F3 **Waiwera** New Zealand
193 H4 **Wajima** Japan
161 G3 **Wajir** Kenya
160 C3 **Waka** Democratic Republic of Congo
161 F2 **Waka** Ethiopia
198 B6 **Waka** Indonesia
198 C4 **Waka, Tanjung** *cape* Indonesia
101 G4 **Wakadanawa** Brazil
221 E5 **Wakamarama Range** New Zealand
193 G4 **Wakasa-wan** *bay* Japan
221 C7 **Wakatipu, Lake** New Zealand
75 S6 **Wakaw** Saskatchewan Canada
223 9 **Wakaya** *island* Fiji
199 F4 **Wakde** *island* Indonesia
87 L3 **Wake Forest** North Carolina USA
52 M6 **Wake Island** *unincorporated US territory* Pacific Ocean
81 P7 **WaKeeney** Kansas USA
221 E5 **Wakefield** New Zealand
141 G3 **Wakefield** West Yorkshire England UK
82 G3 **Wakefield** Michigan USA
83 M8 **Wakefield** Virginia USA
78 B2 **Wakeham, Baie** *bay* Quebec Canada
194 B3 **Wakema** Myanmar
139 G2 **Wakerley** Northamptonshire England UK
85 N2 **Wakita** Oklahoma USA
193 I2 **Wakkanai** Japan
199 I5 **Wako** Papua New Guinea
218 G6 **Wakool** NSW Australia
75 V8 **Wakopa** Manitoba Canada
162 C2 **Waku Kungo** Angola
78 E5 **Wakuach, Lac** *lake* Quebec Canada
83 K1 **Wakwayowkastic** *watercourse* Ontario Canada
160 D2 **Wal Athiang** Sudan
198 B5 **Walanae** *watercourse* Indonesia
125 I2 **Wałbrzych** Poland
219 J4 **Walcha** NSW Australia
124 F4 **Walchensee** *lake* Germany
139 I2 **Walcott** Norfolk England UK
80 I5 **Walcott, Lake** Idaho USA
213 H4 **Walcott Inlet** WA Australia
127 G1 **Walcourt** Belgium
125 I1 **Wałcz** Poland
130 C3 **Wald** Switzerland
161 F3 **Walde** *watercourse* Ethiopia
75 R7 **Waldeck** Saskatchewan Canada
127 I1 **Waldeck** Germany
81 L6 **Walden** Colorado USA
81 L6 **Walden Reservoir** Colorado USA
124 D3 **Waldkirch** Germany
124 E4 **Waldkirch** Switzerland
124 G3 **Waldkraiburg** Germany
87 J6 **Waldo** Florida USA
80 D5 **Waldo Lake** Oregon USA
80 C4 **Waldport** Oregon USA
86 D3 **Waldron** Arkansas USA
58 H2 **Waldron, Cape** Antarctica
125 H3 **Waldviertel** *region* Austria
198 B4 **Walea, Selat** *strait* Indonesia
198 B4 **Waleakodi** *island* Indonesia
216 E5 **Walebing** WA Australia
138 D2 **Wales** *admin. area* UK
84 G1 **Wales** Utah USA
78 C2 **Wales Island** Nunavut Canada
141 H3 **Walesby** Nottinghamshire England UK
158 D2 **Walewale** Ghana
82 F6 **Walford** Iowa USA
219 I4 **Walgett** NSW Australia
58 Q1 **Walgreen Coast** Antarctica
81 Q2 **Walhalla** North Dakota USA
214 C4 **Walhallow** NT Australia
160 D4 **Walikale** Democratic Republic of Congo
198 E5 **Walir** *island* Indonesia
199 G4 **Walis Island** Papua New Guinea
218 G6 **Waljeers, Lake** NSW Australia
215 H4 **Walkamin** Qld Australia
216 D4 **Walkaway** WA Australia
141 F3 **Walkden** Greater Manchester England UK
214 F4 **Walker** *watercourse* Qld Australia
82 I5 **Walker** Michigan USA
81 R3 **Walker** Minnesota USA
215 H3 **Walker Bay** Qld Australia
87 L7 **Walker Cay** Bahamas
109 7 **Walker Creek** Falkland Islands
218 D6 **Walker Flat** SA Australia
76 G5 **Walker Lake** Manitoba Canada
84 C1 **Walker Lake** Nevada USA
58 R2 **Walker Mountains** Antarctica
83 K4 **Walkerton** Ontario Canada
81 N5 **Wall** South Dakota USA
212 D7 **Wall, Mount** WA Australia
218 H6 **Walla Walla** NSW Australia
80 F3 **Walla Walla** Washington USA
219 J4 **Wallabadah** NSW Australia
216 C4 **Wallabi Group** *islands* WA Australia
219 K5 **Wallabi Point** NSW Australia
214 F3 **Wallaby Island** Qld Australia
81 O6 **Wallace** Nebraska USA
87 M3 **Wallace** North Carolina USA
75 N5 **Wallace Mountain** Alberta Canada
83 J5 **Wallaceburg** Ontario Canada
221 C8 **Wallacetown** New Zealand
219 H3 **Wallam** *watercourse* Qld Australia
216 E5 **Wallambin, Lake** WA Australia
219 H2 **Wallan** *watercourse* Qld Australia
219 J3 **Wallangarra** NSW Australia
218 C5 **Wallaroo** SA Australia
140 E3 **Wallasey** Merseyside England UK
127 I2 **Walldürn** Germany
162 C6 **Wallekraal** South Africa
219 I6 **Wallendbeen** NSW Australia
83 N6 **Wallenpaupack, Lake** Pennsylvania USA
86 D5 **Waller** Texas USA
219 J5 **Wallerawang** NSW Australia
124 G3 **Wallersdorf** Germany
124 G4 **Wallersee** *lake* Austria
127 J3 **Wallgau** Germany
109 11a **Wallilabou** St Vincent and the Grenadines
216 G4 **Walling Rock** WA Australia
139 F3 **Wallingford** Oxfordshire England UK
223 12 **Wallis, Îles** *island* Wallis and Futuna
223 12 **Wallis and Futuna** *French overseas territory* Pacific Ocean
80 G4 **Wallowa Lake** Oregon USA
142 inset **Walls** Shetland Scotland UK
122 E5 **Wallsbüll** Germany
219 I2 **Wallumbilla** Qld Australia
219 I5 **Walmer** NSW Australia
140 E2 **Walney, Isle of** England UK
82 D6 **Walnut** Iowa USA
86 G3 **Walnut** Mississippi USA
87 K2 **Walnut Cove** North Carolina USA
87 M3 **Walnut Creek** North Carolina USA
86 F2 **Walnut Ridge** Arkansas USA
86 C4 **Walnut Springs** Texas USA
218 F6 **Walpeup** Vic. Australia
216 E7 **Walpole** WA Australia
81 O2 **Walpole** Saskatchewan Canada
77 P6 **Walrus, Pointe** *lake* Quebec Canada
77 N1 **Walrus Island** Nunavut Canada
141 G4 **Walsall** *admin. area* England UK
139 F2 **Walsall** West Midlands England UK
81 M8 **Walsenburg** Colorado USA
215 H4 **Walsh** *watercourse* Qld Australia
81 J2 **Walsh** Alberta Canada
81 N8 **Walsh** Colorado USA
139 H2 **Walsham le Willows** Suffolk England UK
124 E1 **Walsrode** Germany
87 I5 **Walter F. George Reservoir** Georgia USA
87 K4 **Walterboro** South Carolina USA
86 B3 **Walters** Oklahoma USA
54 I8 **Walters Shoal** *underwater feature* Indian Ocean
81 Q5 **Walthill** Nebraska USA
87 K5 **Walthourville** Georgia USA
138 D2 **Walton** Powys Wales UK
85 N1 **Walton** Kansas USA
138 C3 **Walton East** Pembrokeshire Wales UK
162 B4 **Walvis Bay** Namibia
54 E7 **Walvis Ridge** *underwater feature* Atlantic Ocean
141 F1 **Walwick** Northumberland England UK
138 B3 **Walwyn's Castle** Pembrokeshire Wales UK
160 E3 **Wamala, Lake** Uganda
158 D3 **Wamanfo** Ghana
198 E5 **Wamar** *island* Indonesia
160 D3 **Wamba** Democratic Republic of Congo
160 B5 **Wamba** *watercourse* Democratic Republic of Congo
159 F3 **Wamba** Nigeria
199 F5 **Wamena** Indonesia
180 E2 **Wamo Zangbo** *watercourse* Xizang Zizhiqu China
218 F5 **Wampo** NSW Australia
76 H8 **Wampum** Manitoba Canada
90 C4 **Wampusirpi** Honduras
81 L6 **Wamsutter** Wyoming USA
198 C4 **Wamulan** Indonesia
219 K2 **Wamuran** Qld Australia
181 I5 **Wan Singpyin** Myanmar
179 L3 **Wana** Pakistan
218 G3 **Wanaaring** NSW Australia
221 C7 **Wanaka** New Zealand
221 C7 **Wanaka, Lake** New Zealand
109 1c **Wanapa** Netherlands Antilles
83 K3 **Wanapitei Lake** Ontario Canada
218 E6 **Wanbi** SA Australia
90 C4 **Wanblán** Nicaragua
221 D7 **Wanbrow, Cape** New Zealand
156 F5 **Wancha** Ethiopia
198 B5 **Wanci** Indonesia
198 F4 **Wandai** Indonesia
101 G3 **Wandaik Village** Guyana
216 E3 **Wandarrie** WA Australia
73 R2 **Wandel Sea** Greenland
216 E6 **Wandering** WA Australia
75 O5 **Wandering River** Alberta Canada
188 C4 **Wanding** Yunnan China
218 E7 **Wando Bridge** Vic. Australia
219 I2 **Wandoan** Qld Australia
199 H5 **Wandokai** Papua New Guinea
218 G7 **Wandong** Vic. Australia
139 G3 **Wandsworth** Greater London England UK
86 C3 **Wanette** Oklahoma USA
124 F2 **Wanfried** Germany
194 D3 **Wang Saphung** Thailand
160 D3 **Wanga** Democratic Republic of Congo
218 G3 **Wangamana** NSW Australia
218 G6 **Wanganella** NSW Australia
220 F4 **Wanganui** New Zealand
221 D6 **Wanganui** *watercourse* New Zealand
216 G3 **Wangarrai** WA Australia
158 D3 **Wangasi-turu** Ghana
191 I6 **Wangcon** Shandong China
181 F3 **Wangdi Phodrang** Bhutan
191 H5 **Wangdu** Hebei China
198 B6 **Wanggamet, Gunung** *mountain* Indonesia
198 E4 **Wanggar** *watercourse* Indonesia
198 B5 **Wangiwangi** *island* Indonesia
189 G2 **Wangjiang** Anhui China
191 K3 **Wangkui** Heilongjiang China
82 J3 **Wangoon Lake** Ontario Canada
191 L4 **Wangqing** Jilin China
189 H1 **Wangying** Jiangsu China
187 E7 **Wani** Maharashtra India
90 C4 **Waní** Nicaragua
160 D3 **Wanie Rukula** Democratic Republic of Congo
218 B6 **Wanilla** SA Australia
222 8 **Wanione** Solomon Islands
186 C6 **Wankaner** Gujarat India
161 G3 **Wanlaweyn** Somalia
75 U5 **Wanless** Manitoba Canada
139 F2 **Wanlip** Leicester England UK
217 K4 **Wanna Lakes** WA Australia
216 E5 **Wannamal** WA Australia
216 D5 **Wanneroo** WA Australia
216 E1 **Wannery** *watercourse* WA Australia
188 F5 **Wanning** Hainan China
218 F7 **Wannon** Vic. Australia
139 G2 **Wansford** Peterborough England UK
188 F3 **Wanshan** Guizhou China
220 G5 **Wanstead** New Zealand
139 F3 **Wantage** Oxfordshire England UK
83 K3 **Wanup** Ontario Canada
214 D2 **Wanyanmera Point** NT Australia
188 E2 **Wanyuan** Sichuan China
127 G1 **Wanze** Belgium
189 H2 **Wanzhi** Anhui China
188 E2 **Wanzhou** Chongqing China
124 F1 **Wanzleben** Germany
82 I6 **Wapakoneta** Ohio USA
76 J5 **Wapaseese** *watercourse* Ontario Canada
75 S5 **Wapawekka Lake** Saskatchewan Canada
75 V4 **Wapawsik** Manitoba Canada
76 K6 **Wapekeka** Ontario Canada
75 U7 **Wapella** Saskatchewan Canada
82 F6 **Wapello** Iowa USA
212 C6 **Wapet Camp** WA Australia
76 J7 **Wapikaimaski Lake** Ontario Canada
76 I5 **Wapikani** *watercourse* Manitoba Canada
76 L6 **Wapikopa Lake** Ontario Canada
74 L5 **Wapiti** *watercourse* Alberta Canada
138 E3 **Wapley** South Gloucestershire England UK
198 F4 **Wapoga** *watercourse* Indonesia
198 C4 **Wapotih** Indonesia
86 F2 **Wappapello, Lake** Missouri USA
199 G5 **Wapumba Island** Papua New Guinea
79 I7 **Wapustagamau, Lac** *lake* Quebec Canada
188 D1 **Waqên** Sichuan China
125 L3 **Wara** Poland
158 B3 **Wara Wara Mountains** *range* Sierra Leone
160 D2 **Warab** Sudan
160 D2 **Warab** *admin. area* Sudan
198 D4 **Warakaraket** *island* Indonesia
217 K2 **Warakurna Roadhouse** WA Australia
212 D6 **Warambie** WA Australia
161 G2 **Warandab** Ethiopia
187 E8 **Warangal** Andhra Pradesh India
219 Q10 **Waratah** Tas. Australia
218 H8 **Waratah Bay** Vic. Australia
139 G2 **Warboys** Cambridgeshire England UK
214 G8 **Warbreccan** Qld Australia
75 N6 **Warburg** Alberta Canada
218 G6 **Warburn** NSW Australia
218 D2 **Warburton** *watercourse* SA Australia
217 J3 **Warburton** WA Australia
124 D2 **Warche** *watercourse* Belgium
124 C3 **Warcq** France
218 H1 **Ward** *watercourse* Qld Australia
221 F5 **Ward** New Zealand
86 F3 **Ward** Arkansas USA
58 T2 **Ward, Mount** *mountain* Antarctica
74 F5 **Ward Cove** Alaska USA
199 I6 **Ward Hunt Strait** Papua New Guinea
218 C6 **Wardang Island** SA Australia
219 K3 **Wardell** NSW Australia
162 E5 **Warden** South Africa
80 F3 **Warden** Washington USA
75 P7 **Wardlow** Alberta Canada
198 E4 **Wardo** Indonesia
85 K2 **Ware** Texas USA
139 E4 **Wareham** Dorset England UK
198 F4 **Waren** Indonesia
214 F7 **Warenda** Qld Australia
139 G2 **Waresley** Cambridgeshire England UK
215 K7 **Warginburra Peninsula** Qld Australia
199 I6 **Wari Island** Papua New Guinea
219 J3 **Warialda** NSW Australia
198 E5 **Warilau** *island* Indonesia
122 F6 **Warin** Germany
141 F1 **Wark** Northumberland England UK
219 I2 **Warkon** Qld Australia
220 F3 **Warkworth** New Zealand
141 G2 **Warlaby** North Yorkshire England UK
84 D1 **Warm Springs** Nevada USA
80 F5 **Warm Springs Reservoir** Oregon USA
198 E4 **Warmandi** Indonesia
123 K5 **Warmia** *region* Poland
139 G2 **Warmington** Northamptonshire England UK

125 K1 **Warminsko-Mazurskie** *admin. area* Poland
124 E1 **Warmsen** Germany
213 J4 **Warmun (Turkey Creek)** WA Australia
216 F4 **Warne** *watercourse* WA Australia
122 G5 **Warnemünde** Germany
75 O8 **Warner** Alberta Canada
86 D3 **Warner** Oklahoma USA
81 P4 **Warner** South Dakota USA
216 D7 **Warner Glen** WA Australia
80 E6 **Warner Mountains** California USA
87 J4 **Warner Robins** Georgia USA
105 F5 **Warnes** Bolivia
218 C6 **Warooka** SA Australia
216 D6 **Waroona** WA Australia
198 F4 **Waropen, Teluk** *bay* Indonesia
199 G5 **Waropko** Indonesia
76 F6 **Warpath** *watercourse* Manitoba Canada
219 J2 **Warra** Qld Australia
214 F8 **Warra** *watercourse* Qld Australia
214 F7 **Warra Hill** Qld Australia
218 H6 **Warragoon** NSW Australia
218 D3 **Warrakalanna, Lake** SA Australia
218 E5 **Warrakoo** NSW Australia
214 C3 **Warrakunta Point** NT Australia
218 B5 **Warramboo** SA Australia
218 D2 **Warrandirinna Lake** SA Australia
212 F6 **Warrawagine** WA Australia
218 E5 **Warrawenia Lake** NSW Australia
218 G2/3 **Warrego** *watercourse* NSW/Qld Australia
214 B5 **Warrego Mine** NT Australia
218 G1 **Warrego Range** Qld Australia
219 H4 **Warren** NSW Australia
83 K3 **Warren** Ontario Canada
143 F1 **Warren** Moyle Northern Ireland UK
86 E4 **Warren** Arkansas USA
82 I6 **Warren** Indiana USA
82 J5 **Warren** Michigan USA
81 Q2 **Warren** Minnesota USA
82 K6 **Warren** Ohio USA
83 L6 **Warren** Pennsylvania USA
214 F5 **Warren Vale** Qld Australia
140 B2 **Warrenpoint** Newry and Mourne Northern Ireland UK
82 G7 **Warrensburg** Illinois USA
82 E7 **Warrensburg** Missouri USA
87 J4 **Warrenton** Georgia USA
80 D3 **Warrenton** Oregon USA
83 M7 **Warrenton** Virginia USA
159 F3 **Warri** Nigeria
219 H4 **Warrigal** NSW Australia
218 B3 **Warriner** *watercourse* SA Australia
221 D7 **Warrington** New Zealand
141 F3 **Warrington** *admin. area* England UK
218 F8 **Warrnambool** Vic. Australia
81 R2 **Warroad** Minnesota USA
216 C1 **Warroora** WA Australia
219 I4 **Warrumbungle Range** NSW Australia
214 B1 **Warruwi** NT Australia
183 K7 **Warsaj** Afghanistan
Warsaw *see* **Warszawa** Poland
82 F6 **Warsaw** Illinois USA
82 I6 **Warsaw** Indiana USA
82 E7 **Warsaw** Missouri USA
83 L5 **Warsaw** New York USA
87 L3 **Warsaw** North Carolina USA
83 J6 **Warsaw** Ohio USA
83 M8 **Warsaw** Virginia USA
139 F1 **Warslow** Staffordshire England UK
75 O5 **Warspite** Alberta Canada
125 K1 **Warszawa (Warsaw)** Poland
125 J2 **Warta** Poland
125 H1 **Warta** *watercourse* Poland
141 H3 **Warter** East Riding of Yorkshire England UK
75 Q7 **Wartime** Saskatchewan Canada
140 F2 **Warton** Lancashire England UK
187 E7 **Warud** Maharashtra India
90 C4 **Warunta** Honduras
199 G4 **Waruta** *watercourse* Indonesia
219 K3 **Warwick** Qld Australia
86 C3 **Warwick** Oklahoma USA
83 P6 **Warwick** Rhode Island USA
139 F2 **Warwickshire** *admin. area* England UK
75 N8 **Wasa** British Columbia Canada
214 G1 **Wasaga** Qld Australia
83 L4 **Wasaga Beach** Ontario Canada
81 P1 **Wasagaming** Manitoba Canada
159 F2 **Wasagu** Nigeria
222 7 **Wasaka** Vanuatu
84 G1 **Wasatch Range** Utah USA
84 C3 **Wasco** California USA
80 E4 **Wasco** Oregon USA
159 F3 **Wase** *watercourse* Nigeria
75 Q6 **Waseca** Saskatchewan Canada
82 E4 **Waseca** Minnesota USA
217 I3 **Wash** *watercourse* WA Australia
139 H2 **Wash, The** *bay* England UK
81 O3 **Washburn** North Dakota USA
82 F3 **Washburn** Wisconsin USA
141 G2 **Washfold** North Yorkshire England UK
138 D4 **Washford Pyne** Devon England UK
187 D7 **Washim** Maharashtra India
139 G4 **Washington** West Sussex England UK
70 **Washington** *admin. area* USA
83 M7 **Washington** District of Columbia USA
87 J4 **Washington** Georgia USA
82 G6 **Washington** Illinois USA
82 H7 **Washington** Indiana USA
82 F6 **Washington** Iowa USA
81 Q7 **Washington** Kansas USA
86 E5 **Washington** Louisiana USA
82 F7 **Washington** Missouri USA
87 M3 **Washington** North Carolina USA
83 K6 **Washington** Pennsylvania USA
84 F2 **Washington** Utah USA
58 L2 **Washington, Cape** Antarctica
86 F4 **Washington, Lake** Mississippi USA
83 P4 **Washington, Mount** New Hampshire USA
82 H4 **Washington Island** Wisconsin USA
73 M2 **Washington Land** *region* Greenland
86 A3 **Washita** *watercourse* Texas USA
80 F7 **Washoe Lake** Nevada USA
76 G7 **Washow Bay** Manitoba Canada
80 F3 **Washtucna** Washington USA
72 E6 **Wasilla** Alaska USA
158 E3 **Wasimi** Nigeria
198 E5 **Wasir** *island* Indonesia
198 C5 **Wasiri** Indonesia
178 F3 **Wāsiţ** *admin. area* Iraq
76 G4 **Waskaiowaka Lake** Manitoba Canada
75 R6 **Waskesiu Lake** Saskatchewan Canada
90 C4 **Waslala** Nicaragua
125 I2 **Wąsosz** Poland
90 D4 **Waspam** Nicaragua
139 F2 **Wasperton** Warwickshire England UK
90 C4 **Waspuk** Nicaragua
141 G2 **Wass** North Yorkshire England UK
154 D6 **Wassadou** Senegal
87 K5 **Wassaw Sound** *strait* Georgia USA
158 B2 **Wassou** Guinea
127 G2 **Wassy** France
140 E2 **Wast Water** *lake* England UK
199 H5 **Wasu** Papua New Guinea
199 G6 **Wasua** Papua New Guinea
84 C1 **Wasuk Range** Nevada USA
77 R8 **Waswanipi** Quebec Canada
77 Q8 **Waswanipi, Lac** *lake* Quebec Canada
83 K2 **Watabeag Lake** Ontario Canada
79 I7 **Watagheistic, Île** *island* Quebec Canada
198 B5 **Watampone** Indonesia
101 G3 **Watamung Mountains** Guyana
87 J2 **Watauga Lake** Tennessee USA
138 D3 **Watchet** Somerset England UK
78 G3 **Watchman Island** Newfoundland and Labrador Canada
82 F2 **Watcomb** Ontario Canada
90 E2 **Water Cays** *islands* Bahamas
75 N7 **Water Valley** Alberta Canada
85 L5 **Water Valley** Texas USA
142 E5 **Waterbeck** Dumfries and Galloway Scotland UK
162 C4 **Waterberg** Namibia
83 O6 **Waterbury** Connecticut USA
83 O4 **Waterbury** Vermont USA
76 C3 **Waterbury Lake** Saskatchewan Canada
87 K3 **Wateree Lake** South Carolina USA
139 F1 **Waterfall** Staffordshire England UK
211 inset **Waterfall Lake** Macquarie Island Australia
143 E4 **Waterford** Ireland
143 E4 **Waterford** *admin. area* Ireland
75 S3 **Waterfound** *watercourse* Saskatchewan Canada
143 D4 **Watergrasshill** Ireland
140 E1 **Waterhead** Dumfries and Galloway Scotland UK
76 F6 **Waterhen Lake** Manitoba Canada
75 Q5 **Waterhen Lake** Saskatchewan Canada
75 Q5 **Waterhen Lake** Saskatchewan Canada
127 G1 **Waterloo** Belgium
158 B3 **Waterloo** Sierra Leone
109 9 **Waterloo** Trinidad and Tobago
142 C3 **Waterloo** Highland Scotland UK
82 F7 **Waterloo** Illinois USA
82 E5 **Waterloo** Iowa USA
218 F5 **Waterloo Lake** NSW Australia
75 Q3 **Waterloo Lake** Saskatchewan Canada
139 F4 **Waterlooville** Hampshire England UK
142 E3 **Waterside** Aberdeenshire Scotland UK
82 G3 **Watersmeet** Michigan USA
80 I2 **Waterton Park** Alberta Canada
81 Q4 **Watertown** South Dakota USA
82 G5 **Watertown** Wisconsin USA
143 B5 **Waterville** Ireland
83 Q4 **Waterville** Maine USA
82 E4 **Waterville** Minnesota USA
83 N5 **Waterville** New York USA
80 E3 **Waterville** Washington USA
82 H5 **Watervliet** Michigan USA
83 O5 **Watervliet** New York USA
139 G3 **Watford** Hertfordshire England UK
81 N3 **Watford City** North Dakota USA
76 D4 **Wathaman** *watercourse* Saskatchewan Canada
82 D7 **Wathena** Kansas USA
216 E5 **Watheroo** WA Australia
74 M5 **Watino** Alberta Canada
83 M5 **Watkins Glen** New York USA
139 F3 **Watlington** Oxfordshire England UK
198 D5 **Watmuri** Indonesia
86 B3 **Watonga** Oklahoma USA
75 S7 **Watrous** Saskatchewan Canada
85 J3 **Watrous** New Mexico USA
160 D3 **Watsa** Democratic Republic of Congo
82 H6 **Watseka** Illinois USA
160 C4 **Watsi** Democratic Republic of Congo
160 C4 **Watsi Kengo** Democratic Republic of Congo
214 F2 **Watson** *watercourse* Qld Australia
217 L5 **Watson** SA Australia
75 S6 **Watson** Saskatchewan Canada
58 O1 **Watson Escarpment** *range* Antarctica
74 G2 **Watson Lake** Yukon Territory Canada
80 E8 **Watsonville** California USA
58 J2 **Watt Bay** Antarctica
139 J4 **Watten** France
142 E2 **Watten, Loch** *lake* Scotland UK
130 D3 **Wattens** Austria
76 F2 **Watterson Lake** Nunavut Canada
219 I5 **Wattle Flat** NSW Australia
139 H2 **Watton** Norfolk England UK
87 I3 **Watts Bar Lake** Tennessee USA
198 D5 **Watubela, Kepulauan** *islands* Indonesia
198 B6 **Watumanuk, Tanjung** *cape* Indonesia
198 B4 **Watuwila, Bukit** *mountain* Indonesia
198 E4 **Wau** Indonesia
160 D2 **Wau** Sudan
160 D2 **Wau** *watercourse* Sudan
82 C4 **Waubay Lake** South Dakota USA
81 R3 **Waubun** Minnesota USA
214 C6 **Wauchope** NT Australia
87 K7 **Wauchula** Florida USA
81 R2 **Waugh** Manitoba Canada
212 F6 **Waukarlycarly, Lake** WA Australia
82 H5 **Waukegan** Illinois USA
82 G5 **Waukesha** Wisconsin USA
86 C2 **Waukomis** Oklahoma USA
82 F5 **Waukon** Iowa USA
81 O6 **Wauneta** Nebraska USA
82 G5 **Waupun** Wisconsin USA
86 C3 **Waurika** Oklahoma USA
86 B3 **Waurika Lake** Oklahoma USA
82 G4 **Wausau** Wisconsin USA
82 H4 **Wausaukee** Wisconsin USA
139 I2 **Waveney** *watercourse* England UK
220 F4 **Waverley** New Zealand
82 E5 **Waverly** Iowa USA
82 E7 **Waverly** Missouri USA
81 Q6 **Waverly** Nebraska USA
83 M6 **Waverly** Pennsylvania USA
86 H2 **Waverly** Tennessee USA
87 I4 **Waverly Hall** Georgia USA
127 G1 **Wavre** Belgium
194 C3 **Waw** Myanmar
82 I3 **Wawa** Ontario Canada
159 E3 **Wawa** Nigeria
77 Q5 **Wawa, Lac** *lake* Quebec Canada
76 K6 **Wawakapewin** Ontario Canada
75 V8 **Wawanesa** Manitoba Canada
82 F2 **Wawang Lake** Ontario Canada
90 C4 **Wawina** Honduras
198 B4 **Wawo** Indonesia
75 T8 **Wawota** Saskatchewan Canada
86 C4 **Waxahachie** Texas USA
87 K3 **Waxhaw** North Carolina USA
127 H1 **Waxweiler** Germany
216 G3 **Way, Lake** WA Australia
223 9 **Waya** *island* Fiji
198 D3 **Wayag** *island* Indonesia
90 C4 **Wayawás** Nicaragua
87 J5 **Waycross** Georgia USA
198 C4 **Wayhaya** Indonesia
198 C4 **Waykilo** Indonesia
82 I5 **Wayland** Michigan USA
83 M5 **Wayland** New York USA
90 C4 **Waylaska** Nicaragua
86 C3 **Wayne** Oklahoma USA
87 K4 **Waynesboro** Georgia USA
86 H3 **Waynesboro** Tennessee USA
83 L7 **Waynesboro** Virginia USA
82 E8 **Waynesville** Missouri USA
87 J3 **Waynesville** North Carolina USA
81 P8 **Waynoka** Oklahoma USA
159 G2 **Waza** Cameroon
186 F6 **Wazirganj** Bihar India
76 J6 **Weagamow Lake** Ontario Canada
126 E1 **Weald, The** *region* England UK
141 F2 **Wear** *watercourse* England UK
141 F2 **Wear Head** Durham England UK
214 D4 **Wearyan** *watercourse* NT Australia
158 B3 **Weasua** Liberia
86 B3 **Weatherford** Oklahoma USA
82 E8 **Weaubleau** Missouri USA
76 G6 **Weaver Lake** Manitoba Canada
141 F3 **Weaverham** Cheshire England UK
75 Q7 **Webb** Saskatchewan Canada
87 I5 **Webb** Alabama USA
86 F4 **Webb** Mississippi USA
213 J7 **Webb, Mount** WA Australia
215 H6 **Webb Lake** Qld Australia
83 K3 **Webbwood** Ontario Canada
52 J8 **Weber Basin** *underwater feature* Banda Sea
85 K3 **Weber City** New Mexico USA
124 F1 **Weberin** Germany
81 Q4 **Webster** South Dakota USA
82 E5 **Webster City** Iowa USA
81 P7 **Webster Reservoir** Kansas USA
125 K2 **Węchadłow** Poland
198 C3 **Weda** Indonesia
198 D3 **Weda, Teluk** *bay* Indonesia
58 V2 **Weddell Abyssal Plain** *underwater feature* Weddell Sea
109 7 **Weddell Island** Falkland Islands
58 V2 **Weddell Sea** Southern Ocean
218 F7 **Wedderburn** Vic. Australia
221 D7 **Wedderburn** New Zealand
124 E1 **Wedel** Germany
219 R11 **Wedge, Mount** Tas. Australia
213 H3 **Wedge Hill** WA Australia
218 C6 **Wedge Island** SA Australia
216 D5 **Wedge Island** WA Australia
138 E3 **Wedmore** Somerset England UK
139 E2 **Wednesbury** West Midlands England UK
87 I4 **Wedowee** Alabama USA
198 E5 **Weduar, Tanjung** *cape* Indonesia
219 I6 **Wee Jasper** NSW Australia
219 I4 **Wee Waa** NSW Australia
80 D6 **Weed** California USA
198 D4 **Weeim** *island* Indonesia
141 H3 **Weel** East Riding of Yorkshire England UK
216 G1 **Weelarrana** WA Australia
216 E4 **Weelhamby Lake** WA Australia
219 I3 **Weemelah** NSW Australia
127 G1 **Weert** Netherlands
127 I3 **Weesen** Switzerland
219 I4 **Weetaliba** NSW Australia
218 H5 **Weethalle** NSW Australia
139 F2 **Weethley** Warwickshire England UK
139 H2 **Weeting** Norfolk England UK
74 G6 **Weewanie** British Columbia Canada
215 H7 **Weewondilla** Qld Australia
222 6 **Weey** *island* Federated States of Micronesia
124 F2 **Wegeleben** Germany
196 B2 **Weh, Pulau** *island* Indonesia
156 F5 **Wehni** Ethiopia
124 D4 **Wehr** Germany
188 E1 **Wei He** *watercourse* Jiangsu China
191 I4 **Weichang** Hebei China
125 H1 **Weichensdorf** Germany
125 H4 **Weichselboden** Austria
189 G2 **Weidoushan Shuiku** *lake* Hubei China
191 I6 **Weifang** Shandong China
191 J5 **Weihai** Shandong China
189 G1 **Weihui** Henan China
124 E3 **Weil** Germany
124 E2 **Weil** *watercourse* Germany
124 E2 **Weilburg** Germany
219 H3 **Weilmoringle** NSW Australia
124 F2 **Weimar** Germany
86 C6 **Weimar** Texas USA
188 F1 **Weinan** Shaanxi China
86 F3 **Weiner** Arkansas USA
86 B4 **Weinert** Texas USA
124 E3 **Weinheim** Germany
214 F2 **Weipa** Qld Australia
80 H3 **Weippe** Idaho USA
188 E1 **Weiqu** Shaanxi China
86 G4 **Weir** Mississippi USA
85 N5 **Weir** Texas USA
87 K6 **Weir, Lake** Florida USA
76 H4 **Weir River** Manitoba Canada
216 F5 **Weira** WA Australia
83 K6 **Weirton** Ohio USA
80 G4 **Weiser** Idaho USA
188 C3 **Weishan** Yunnan China
189 H1 **Weishan Hu** *lake* Shandong China
189 G1 **Weishi** Henan China
87 I3 **Weiss Lake** Alabama USA
124 G2 **Weiße Elster** *watercourse* Germany
124 G4 **Weißensee** *lake* Austria
124 F2 **Weißer Main** *watercourse* Germany
189 H2 **Weitang** Zhejiang China
125 H3 **Weitra** Austria
75 R4 **Weitzel Lake** Saskatchewan Canada
190 E6 **Weiyuan** Qinghai China
188 C4 **Weiyuan** Yunnan China
125 H4 **Weiz** Austria
188 F4 **Weizhou Dao** *island* Guangxi Zhuangzu Zizhiqu China
221 E6 **Weka Pass** New Zealand
221 E5 **Wekakura Point** New Zealand
75 V5 **Wekusko** Manitoba Canada
75 V5 **Wekusko Lake** Manitoba Canada
218 B2 **Welbourn Hill** SA Australia
141 H2 **Welburn** North Yorkshire England UK
82 D8 **Welch** Oklahoma USA
83 K8 **Welch** West Virginia USA
138 C4 **Welcombe** Devon England UK
216 E3 **Weld Range** WA Australia
157 F5 **Weldiya** Ethiopia
122 I6 **Wełdkowo** Poland
86 C3 **Weleetka** Oklahoma USA
139 F2 **Welford** Northamptonshire England UK
218 F1 **Welford, Mount** Qld Australia
53 R2 **Welker Seamount** *underwater feature* Pacific Ocean
161 F2 **Welk'īt'ē** Ethiopia
162 E5 **Welkom** South Africa
141 G2 **Well** North Yorkshire England UK
155 G6 **Wèlla Sofon Gari** Niger
139 G2 **Welland** *watercourse* England UK
214 E4 **Wellesley Islands** Qld Australia
139 G1 **Wellingore** Lincolnshire England UK
219 I5 **Wellington** NSW Australia
218 D6 **Wellington** SA Australia
80 C2 **Wellington** British Columbia Canada
83 M5 **Wellington** Ontario Canada
221 F5 **Wellington** New Zealand
221 F5 **Wellington** *admin. area* New Zealand
138 D4 **Wellington** Somerset England UK
81 M6 **Wellington** Colorado USA
81 Q8 **Wellington** Kansas USA
84 C1 **Wellington** Nevada USA
86 A3 **Wellington** Texas USA
81 J7 **Wellington** Utah USA
108 A4 **Wellington, Archipiélago** *islands* Chile
108 A4 **Wellington, Isla** *island* Chile
219 H8 **Wellington, Lake** Vic. Australia
219 R11 **Wellington, Mount** Tas. Australia
221 F5 **Wellington Harbour** New Zealand
143 F4 **Wellingtonbridge** Ireland
85 K4 **Wellman** Texas USA
138 E3 **Wells** Somerset England UK
80 H6 **Wells** Nevada USA
83 N5 **Wells** New York USA
86 D5 **Wells** Texas USA
216 H3 **Wells, Lake** WA Australia
213 I4 **Wells, Mount** WA Australia
76 E4 **Wells Lake** Manitoba Canada
83 M6 **Wellsboro** Pennsylvania USA
139 F2 **Wellsborough** Leicester England UK
220 F3 **Wellsford** New Zealand
216 F7 **Wellstead** WA Australia
82 I4 **Wellston** Michigan USA
83 J7 **Wellston** Ohio USA
86 C3 **Wellston** Oklahoma USA
82 D7 **Wellsville** Kansas USA
83 M5 **Wellsville** New York USA
83 K6 **Wellsville** Ohio USA
80 J6 **Wellsville** Utah USA
84 E4 **Wellton** Arizona USA
213 K2 **Welltree** NT Australia
139 H2 **Welney** Norfolk England UK
84 inset **Welokā** Hawai'i USA
125 H3 **Wels** Austria
86 E5 **Welsh** Louisiana USA
138 B3 **Welsh Hook** Pembrokeshire Wales UK
138 D2 **Welshpool** Powys Wales UK
140 E2 **Welton** Cumbria England UK
141 H3 **Welton le Wold** Lincolnshire England UK
161 H2 **Welwel** Ethiopia
139 G3 **Welwyn Garden City** Hertfordshire England UK
124 E3 **Welzheim** Germany
160 C4 **Wema** Democratic Republic of Congo
161 E4 **Wembere** *watercourse* Tanzania
74 L5 **Wembley** Alberta Canada
139 G3 **Wembley** Greater London England UK
161 G2 **Wemell** *watercourse* Ethiopia
77 P6 **Wemindji** Quebec Canada
189 G1 **Wen Xian** Henan China
191 H5 **Wen'an** Hebei China
80 E3 **Wenatchee** Washington USA
80 E3 **Wenatchee Mountains** Washington USA
181 F2 **Wenbu** Xizang Zizhiqu China
103 B8 **Wenceslau Braz** Brazil
188 E2 **Wenchang** Sichuan China
188 F5 **Wencheng** Hainan China
158 E2 **Wenchiki** Ghana
80 H5 **Wendell** Idaho USA
191 J5 **Wendeng** Shandong China
198 E4 **Wendesi** Indonesia
158 B2 **Wéndou Mbôrou** Guinea
139 G3 **Wendover** Buckinghamshire England UK
80 H6 **Wendover** Utah USA
138 B4 **Wendron** Cornwall England UK
82 J3 **Wenebegon Lake** Ontario Canada
188 D2 **Wenehuan** Sichuan China
189 G3 **Wenfeng** Jiangxi China
219 J2 **Wengenville** Qld Australia
139 I2 **Wenhaston** Suffolk England UK
188 D3 **Wenjiang** Sichuan China
188 D4 **Wenlan** Yunnan China
189 I3 **Wenling** Zhejiang China
214 G2 **Wenlock** *watercourse* Qld Australia
222 6 **Weno** Federated States of Micronesia
222 6a **Weno** *island* Federated States of Micronesia
188 D3 **Wenping** Yunnan China
188 E2 **Wenquan** Chongqing China
189 G2 **Wenquan** Hubei China
184 G4 **Wenquan** Xinjiang Uygur Zizhiqu China
141 F2 **Wensleydale** *valley* England UK
184 F4 **Wensu** Xinjiang Uygur Zizhiqu China
139 H2 **Wensum** *watercourse* England UK
141 G3 **Wentbridge** West Yorkshire England UK
138 E2 **Wentnor** Shropshire England UK
218 E6 **Wentworth** NSW Australia
81 Q5 **Wentworth** South Dakota USA
75 N3 **Wentzel Lake** Alberta Canada
189 F1 **Wenxi** Shanxi China
188 D2 **Wenxian** Gansu China
189 F3 **Wenxing** Hunan China
157 F5 **Wenz** *spring* Ethiopia
189 H3 **Wenzhou** Zhejiang China
138 E2 **Weobley** Herefordshire England UK
162 E5 **Wepener** South Africa
160 D2 **Wer Ping** Sudan
125 G1 **Werbellinsee** *lake* Germany
124 G2 **Werbig** Germany
162 D5 **Werda** Botswana
127 K1 **Werdau** Germany
124 G1 **Werder** Germany
161 H2 **Werdēr** Ethiopia
124 D2 **Werdohl** Germany
124 G4 **Werfen** Austria
198 E4 **Weri** Indonesia
124 D1 **Werlte** Germany
127 K1 **Wermsdorf** Germany
124 E3 **Wern** *watercourse* Germany
215 G6 **Werna** *watercourse* Qld Australia
214 E5 **Wernadinga** Qld Australia
130 E2 **Wernberg-Köblitz** Germany
219 I6 **Werong, Mount** NSW Australia
219 J6 **Werri Beach** NSW Australia
218 G7 **Werribee** Vic. Australia
219 J4 **Werris Creek** NSW Australia
127 I2 **Wertheim** Germany
101 F3 **Werushima Range** Guyana
126 F1 **Wervik** Belgium
198 D6 **Werwaru** Indonesia
124 D2 **Wesel** Germany
124 E1 **Weser** *watercourse* Germany
109 15 **Wesley** Dominica
83 R4 **Wesley** Maine USA
125 K2 **Wesoła** Poland
125 K1 **Wesołowo** Poland
214 D1 **Wessel, Cape** NT Australia
214 D1 **Wessel Islands** NT Australia
81 P4 **Wessington Springs** South Dakota USA
86 F5 **Wesson** Mississippi USA
86 C5 **West** Texas USA
139 H2 **West Acre** Norfolk England UK
214 B2 **West Alligator** *watercourse* NT Australia
82 G5 **West Allis** Wisconsin USA
58 Q1 **West Antarctica** *region* Antarctica
213 I3 **West Arm** *watercourse* WA Australia
213 J4 **West Baines** *watercourse* NT Australia
178 C3 **West Bank** *disputed territory* Middle East
139 H2 **West Barsham** Norfolk England UK
78 J5 **West Bay** Newfoundland and Labrador Canada
86 G6 **West Bay** Louisiana USA
82 G5 **West Bend** Wisconsin USA
181 F4 **West Bengal** *admin. area* India
140 C1 **West Bennan** North Ayrshire Scotland UK
139 H3 **West Bergholt** Essex England UK
139 F3 **West Berkshire** *admin. area* England UK
139 H2 **West Bilney** Norfolk England UK
86 H4 **West Blocton** Alabama USA
139 F2 **West Bromwich** West Midlands England UK
91 F2 **West Caicos** *island* Turks and Caicos Islands
218 C6 **West Cape** SA Australia
221 B7 **West Cape** New Zealand
52 J7 **West Caroline Basin** *underwater feature* Pacific Ocean
141 G1 **West Chevington** Northumberland England UK
221 D6 **West Coast** *admin. area* New Zealand
196 C4 **West Coast Park** Singapore
87 K4 **West Columbia** South Carolina USA
139 G4 **West Dean** West Sussex England UK
139 H2 **West Dereham** Norfolk England UK
82 E6 **West Des Moines** Iowa USA
215 K4 **West Diamond Islet** Coral Sea Islands Territory Australia
142 F4 **West Drums** Angus Scotland UK
142 D4 **West Dunbartonshire** *admin. area* Scotland UK
87 L7 **West End** Bahamas
87 L7 **West End Point** Bahamas
81 Q3 **West Fargo** North Dakota USA
199 H1 **West Fayu** *island* Federated States of Micronesia
86 D3 **West Fork** Arkansas USA
79 E10 **West Grand Lake** Maine USA
139 F3 **West Grimstead** Wiltshire England UK
216 G7 **West Group** *islands* WA Australia
139 F2 **West Haddon** Northamptonshire England UK
141 H3 **West Halton** North Lincolnshire England UK
83 O6 **West Haven** Connecticut USA
81 R2 **West Hawk Lake** Manitoba Canada
86 F3 **West Helena** Arkansas USA
142 B4 **West Hynish** Highland Scotland UK
58 F2 **West Ice Shelf** Antarctica
139 F3 **West Ilsley** West Berkshire England UK
91 H3 **West Indies** *islands* Caribbean
214 D3 **West Island** NT Australia
210 inset **West Island** Cocos and Keeling Islands
194 B4 **West Island** Andaman and Nicobar Islands India
210 inset **West Island (Panjang)** Cocos (Keeling) Islands Australia
210 inset **West Islet** Ashmore Reef and Cartier Island Australia
80 J6 **West Jordan** Utah USA
140 E3 **West Kirby** Merseyside England UK
82 H6 **West Lafayette** Indiana USA
86 C5 **West Lake Hills** Texas USA
139 F3 **West Lavington** Wiltshire England UK
82 J8 **West Liberty** Kentucky USA
142 E5 **West Linton** Scottish Borders Scotland UK
138 C4 **West Looe** Cornwall England UK
83 K5 **West Lorne** Ontario Canada
142 E5 **West Lothian** *admin. area* Scotland UK
139 E4 **West Lulworth** Dorset England UK
162 D2 **West Lunga** *watercourse* Zambia
52 J6 **West Mariana Basin** *underwater feature* Atlantic Ocean
86 F3 **West Memphis** Arkansas USA
139 H3 **West Mersea** Essex England UK
78 H5 **West Micmac Lake** Newfoundland and Labrador Canada
139 H2 **West Newton** Norfolk England UK
162 E4 **West Nicholson** Zimbabwe
82 D5 **West Okoboji Lake** Iowa USA
87 K7 **West Palm Beach** Florida USA
82 F8 **West Plains** Missouri USA
79 H11 **West Point** Nova Scotia Canada
86 G4 **West Point** Mississippi USA
81 Q6 **West Point** Nebraska USA
83 M8 **West Point** Virginia USA
87 I4 **West Point Lake** Georgia USA
75 M5 **West Prairie** *watercourse* Alberta Canada
138 C4 **West Putford** Devon England UK
74 I6 **West Road** *watercourse* British Columbia Canada
139 H2 **West Roe** Suffolk England UK
139 H2 **West Rudham** Norfolk England UK
141 F2 **West Stonesdale** North Yorkshire England UK
139 G4 **West Sussex** *admin. area* England UK
141 G2 **West Tanfield** North Yorkshire England UK
124 C1 **West-Terschelling** Netherlands
143 D1 **West Town** Ireland
82 F5 **West Union** Iowa USA
83 K7 **West Union** West Virginia USA
80 J6 **West Valley City** Utah USA
70 **West Virginia** *admin. area* USA
80 H6 **West Wendover** Nevada USA
219 H5 **West Wyalong** NSW Australia
81 J4 **West Yellowstone** Montana USA
195 G5 **West York Island** Spratly Islands
218 B5 **Westall, Point** SA Australia
74 L8 **Westbank** British Columbia Canada
82 F4 **Westboro** Wisconsin USA
83 P5 **Westbrook** Maine USA
85 L4 **Westbrook** Texas USA
138 E2 **Westbury** Shropshire England UK
81 M2 **Westby** Montana USA
142 E5 **Wester Deans** Scottish Borders Scotland UK
141 H2 **Westerdale** North Yorkshire England UK
122 E5 **Westerland** Germany
214 B4 **Western** *watercourse* NT Australia
161 E3 **Western** *admin. area* Kenya
222 8 **Western** *admin. area* Solomon Islands
162 D2 **Western** *admin. area* Zambia
216 G4 **Western Australia** *admin. area* Australia
160 D2 **Western Bahr-el-Ghazal** *admin. area* Sudan
162 D6 **Western Cape** *admin. area* South Africa
221 7 **Western Chain** *islands* Snares Islands New Zealand
159 I2 **Western Darfur** *admin. area* Sudan
210 inset **Western Entrance** *port* Cocos (Keeling) Islands Australia
160 D2 **Western Equatoria** *admin. area* Sudan
199 H4 **Western Island** Papua New Guinea
83 K4 **Western Islands** *islands* Ontario Canada
156 D5 **Western Kordofan** *admin. area* Sudan
154 D4 **Western Sahara** *disputed territory* Africa
79 F10 **Western Shore** Nova Scotia Canada
124 D2 **Westerwald** *region* Germany
142 inset **Westerwick** Shetland Scotland UK
139 H4 **Westfield** East Sussex England UK
83 L5 **Westfield** New York USA
82 G5 **Westfield** Wisconsin USA
142 F3 **Westhill** Aberdeenshire Scotland UK
80 D2 **Westholme** British Columbia Canada
81 O2 **Westhope** North Dakota USA
215 G7 **Westland** Qld Australia
218 G3 **Westlea** Qld Australia
139 I2 **Westleton** Suffolk England UK
75 O5 **Westlock** Alberta Canada
219 I2 **Westmar** Qld Australia
143 E3 **Westmeath** *admin. area* Ireland
218 F7 **Westmere** Vic. Australia
83 M7 **Westminster** Maryland USA
214 E4 **Westmoreland** Qld Australia
87 H2 **Westmoreland** Tennessee USA
84 E4 **Westmorland** California USA
197 G2 **Weston** Malaysia
221 D7 **Weston** New Zealand
139 G4 **Weston** Hampshire England UK
141 H3 **Weston** Nottinghamshire England UK
138 E2 **Weston** Shropshire England UK
80 F4 **Weston** Oregon USA
83 K7 **Weston** West Virginia USA
82 G4 **Weston** Wisconsin USA
77 P6 **Weston Island** Nunavut Canada
139 F2 **Weston Subedge** Gloucestershire England UK
138 E3 **Weston-super-Mare** North Somerset England UK
139 F2 **Weston Underwood** Derbyshire England UK
138 E3 **Westonzoyland** Somerset England UK
85 O1 **Westphalia** Kansas USA
109 7 **Westpoint Island** Falkland Islands
143 C3 **Westport** Ireland
221 D5 **Westport** New Zealand
81 P4 **Westport** South Dakota USA
80 C3 **Westport** Washington USA
109 1b **Westpunt** *cape* Netherlands Antilles
75 U6 **Westray** Manitoba Canada
142 E1 **Westray Firth** *bay* Scotland UK
142 F5 **Westruther** Scottish Borders Scotland UK
86 D3 **Westville** Oklahoma USA
140 E2 **Westward** Cumbria England UK
138 C3 **Westward** Devon England UK
86 F6 **Westwego** Louisiana USA
74 L7 **Westwold** British Columbia Canada
215 K7 **Westwood** Qld Australia
221 B7 **Wet Jacket Arm** *bay* New Zealand
77 P5 **Wetalltok Bay** Nunavut Canada
198 D5 **Wetan** *island* Indonesia
198 C5 **Wetar** *island* Indonesia
198 C6 **Wetar, Selat** *strait* Indonesia
75 O6 **Wetaskiwin** Alberta Canada
161 F5 **Wete** Tanzania
83 M2 **Wetetnagami Lake** Quebec Canada
140 F2 **Wetheral** Cumbria England UK
141 G3 **Wetherby** West Yorkshire England UK
76 G5 **Wetikoweskwattam** Manitoba Canada
181 H4 **Wetlet** Myanmar
125 L3 **Wetlina** Poland
85 J1 **Wetmore** Colorado USA
124 D2 **Wetter** Germany
139 F1 **Wetton** Staffordshire England UK
86 C3 **Wetumka** Oklahoma USA
87 H4 **Wetumpka** Alabama USA
141 H2 **Wetwang** East Riding of Yorkshire England UK
86 C3 **Wewoka** Oklahoma USA
143 F4 **Wexford** Ireland
143 F4 **Wexford** *admin. area* Ireland
143 F4 **Wexford Harbour** Ireland
139 G3 **Wey** *watercourse* England UK
82 G4 **Weyauwega** Wisconsin USA
124 E1 **Weyhe** Germany
79 F10 **Weymouth** Nova Scotia Canada
138 E4 **Weymouth** Dorset England UK
215 G2 **Weymouth, Cape** Qld Australia
90 E1 **Weymyss Bight** Bahamas
220 G3 **Whakaari-White Island** *volcano* New Zealand
220 G3 **Whakatane** New Zealand
220 G4 **Whakatane** *watercourse* New Zealand
219 I3 **Whalan** *watercourse* NSW Australia
194 C5 **Whale Bay** Myanmar
141 G3 **Whaley Bridge** Derbyshire England UK
220 F2 **Whananaki** New Zealand
220 F5 **Whangaehu** New Zealand
220 F4 **Whangaehu** *watercourse* New Zealand
220 F3 **Whangamata** New Zealand
220 F4 **Whanganui** *watercourse* New Zealand
220 E5 **Whanganui Inlet** New Zealand
220 F3 **Whangaparaoa** New Zealand
220 E2 **Whangape** New Zealand
220 F3 **Whangape, Lake** New Zealand
220 E2 **Whangape Harbour** New Zealand
220 F3 **Whangapoua Harbour** New Zealand
220 F2 **Whangarei** New Zealand
220 F2 **Whangarei Harbour** New Zealand
220 E2 **Whangaroa** New Zealand
220 F2 **Whangaruru** New Zealand
220 F2 **Whangaruru Harbour** New Zealand
77 Q5 **Whapmagoostui** Quebec Canada
221 G5 **Whareama** New Zealand
141 F2 **Wharfe** *watercourse* England UK
141 G2 **Wharfedale** *valley* England UK
86 C6 **Wharton** Texas USA
58 K1 **Wharton, Mount** Antarctica
55 O6 **Wharton Basin** *underwater feature* Indian Ocean
221 D6 **Whataroa** *watercourse* New Zealand
142 D6 **Whauphill** Dumfries and Galloway Scotland UK
218 G5 **Whealbah** NSW Australia
82 F6 **Wheatland** Iowa USA
81 M5 **Wheatland** Wyoming USA
81 M6 **Wheatland Reservoir** Wyoming USA
81 Q4 **Wheaton** Minnesota USA
82 D8 **Wheaton** Missouri USA
139 E2 **Wheaton Aston** Staffordshire England UK
138 D3 **Wheddon Cross** Somerset England UK
78 E4 **Wheeler** *watercourse* Quebec Canada
80 D4 **Wheeler** Oregon USA
86 A3 **Wheeler** Texas USA
86 H3 **Wheeler Lake** Alabama USA
84 C3 **Wheeler Ridge** California USA
83 K6 **Wheeling** West Virginia USA
216 E3 **Whela** *watercourse* WA Australia
214 E7 **Whelan, Mount** Qld Australia
139 F3 **Whelford** Gloucestershire England UK
141 G2 **Whenby** North Yorkshire England UK
Whenua Hou *see* **Codfish Island** New Zealand
139 F2 **Whetstone** Leicester England UK
84 G5 **Whetstone** Arizona USA
141 G2 **Whickham** Tyne and Wear England UK
218 B6 **Whidbey, Point** SA Australia
218 B6 **Whidbey Isles** SA Australia
138 D4 **Whiddon Down** Devon England UK
143 C5 **Whiddy Island** *island* Ireland
212 D6 **Whim Creek** WA Australia
217 L3 **Whinham, Mount** SA Australia
142 G3 **Whinnyfold** Aberdeenshire Scotland UK
Whiore *see* **South Cape** New Zealand
139 G3 **Whipsnade** Bedfordshire England UK
100 B4 **Whiskey** Colombia
76 E3 **Whiskey Jack Lake** Manitoba Canada
80 I2 **Whisky Gap** Alberta Canada
214 C6 **Whistleduck** *watercourse* NT Australia
74 J7 **Whistler** British Columbia Canada
219 P9 **Whistler Point** Tas. Australia
139 F1 **Whiston** Staffordshire England UK
87 M2 **Whitakers** North Carolina USA
140 E2 **Whitbeck** Cumbria England UK
79 L9 **Whitbourne** Newfoundland and Labrador Canada
138 E2 **Whitbourne** Herefordshire England UK
141 H2 **Whitby** North Yorkshire England UK
139 F3 **Whitchurch** Hampshire England UK
138 E3 **Whitchurch** Herefordshire England UK
138 E2 **Whitchurch** Shropshire England UK
83 L5 **Whitchurch-Stouffville** Ontario Canada
138 E4 **Whitcombe** Dorset England UK
86 F3 **White** *watercourse* Arkansas USA
81 K6 **White** *watercourse* Colorado USA
82 H7 **White** *watercourse* Indiana USA
84 E2 **White** *watercourse* Nevada USA
81 N5 **White** *watercourse* South Dakota USA
138 D4 **White Ball** Somerset England UK
79 J8 **White Bay** Newfoundland and Labrador Canada
78 I6 **White Bear** *watercourse* Newfoundland and Labrador Canada
75 Q7 **White Bear** Saskatchewan Canada
78 H4 **White Bear Island** Newfoundland and Labrador Canada
78 I5 **White Bear Lake** Newfoundland and Labrador Canada
80 G4 **White Bird** Idaho USA
84 G2 **White Canyon** Utah USA
86 F5 **White Castle** Louisiana USA
81 M1 **White City** Saskatchewan Canada
85 N1 **White City** Kansas USA
215 J7 **White Cliff** Qld Australia
218 F4 **White Cliffs** NSW Australia
216 H4 **White Cliffs** WA Australia
85 L3 **White Deer** Texas USA
216 G5 **White Flag Lake** WA Australia
75 S6 **White Fox** Saskatchewan Canada
86 E3 **White Hall** Arkansas USA
78 G3 **White Handkerchief, Cape** Newfoundland and Labrador Canada
79 H9 **White Hill** Nova Scotia Canada
58 D2 **White Island** Antarctica
73 K5 **White Island** Nunavut Canada
216 G2 **White Lake** WA Australia
83 M4 **White Lake** Ontario Canada
82 I2 **White Lake** Ontario Canada
86 E6 **White Lake** Louisiana USA
81 P5 **White Lake** South Dakota USA
81 P5 **White Lake** South Dakota USA
72 C6 **White Mountain** Alaska USA
84 C2 **White Mountain** California USA
215 H6 **White Mountains** Qld Australia
White Nile *see* **Abiad, Bahr el** Sudan
156 E5 **White Nile** *admin. area* Sudan
86 E4 **White Oak Lake** Arkansas USA
82 F2 **White Otter Lake** Ontario Canada
87 J2 **White Pine** Tennessee USA
84 E1 **White Pine Range** Nevada USA
82 H8 **White Plains** Kentucky USA
83 O6 **White Plains** New York USA
82 I2 **White River** Ontario Canada
81 O5 **White River** South Dakota USA
84 E1 **White River Valley** Nevada USA
74 J8 **White Rock** British Columbia Canada
80 E4 **White Salmon** Washington USA
White Sea *see* **Beloye More** Russian Federation
86 C4 **White Settlement** Texas USA
85 H4 **White Signal** New Mexico USA
87 J5 **White Springs** Florida USA
78 C1 **White Strait** Nunavut Canada
81 J3 **White Sulphur Springs** Montana USA
158 D2 **White Volta** *watercourse* Ghana
138 A2 **Whitechurch** Ireland
221 D6 **Whitecliffs** New Zealand
75 N5 **Whitecourt** Alberta Canada
76 H7 **Whitedog** Ontario Canada
82 E3 **Whiteface** *watercourse* Minnesota USA
85 K4 **Whiteface** Texas USA
82 E3 **Whiteface Reservoir** Minnesota USA
140 A1 **Whitefield** Ireland
80 H2 **Whitefish** Montana USA
83 J3 **Whitefish Bay** Ontario Canada
82 I3 **Whitefish Bay** Michigan USA
76 I5 **Whitefish Lake** Manitoba Canada
85 L3 **Whiteflat** Texas USA
219 R11 **Whitefoord** Tas. Australia
138 C3 **Whiteford Point** Wales UK
143 D4 **Whitegate** Ireland
143 E4 **Whitehall** Ireland
142 F1 **Whitehall** Orkney Islands Scotland UK
80 I4 **Whitehall** Montana USA
82 J7 **Whitehall** Ohio USA
83 K7 **Whitehall** West Virginia USA
82 F4 **Whitehall** Wisconsin USA
140 E2 **Whitehaven** Cumbria England UK
142 F3 **Whitehills** Aberdeenshire Scotland UK
74 D2 **Whitehorse** Yukon Territory Canada
76 H8 **Whitemouth** Manitoba Canada
82 D2 **Whitemouth** *watercourse* Manitoba Canada
82 D2 **Whitemouth Lake** Manitoba Canada
74 L4 **Whitemud** *watercourse* Alberta Canada
142 D2 **Whiten Head** *cape* Scotland UK
139 F3 **Whiteparish** Wiltshire England UK
85 J4 **Whites City** New Mexico USA
143 F3 **Whites Town** Ireland
74 H6 **Whitesail Lake** British Columbia Canada
75 N3 **Whitesand** *watercourse* Alberta Canada
75 T7 **Whitesand** *watercourse* Saskatchewan Canada
86 C4 **Whitesboro** Texas USA

87 I4 **Whitesburg** Georgia USA
140 B2 **Whitesides Corner** Ballymena Northern Ireland UK
138 D4 **Whitestaunton** Somerset England UK
142 C5 **Whitestone** Argyll and Bute Scotland UK
76 J7 **Whitestone Lake** Ontario Canada
82 H8 **Whitesville** Kentucky USA
83 K8 **Whitesville** West Virginia USA
75 S8 **Whitetail** Montana USA
87 L3 **Whiteville** North Carolina USA
86 G3 **Whiteville** Tennessee USA
82 G5 **Whitewater** Wisconsin USA
90 D1 **Whitewater Bay** Florida USA
76 K7 **Whitewater Lake** Ontario Canada
141 F3 **Whitewell** Lancashire England UK
75 T7 **Whitewood** Saskatchewan Canada
86 C4 **Whitewright** Texas USA
141 F2 **Whitfield** Northumberland England UK
75 U6 **Whithorn** Manitoba Canada
142 D6 **Whithorn** Dumfries and Galloway Scotland UK
74 E3 **Whiting** *watercourse* Alaska USA
83 R4 **Whiting** Maine USA
142 C5 **Whiting Bay** North Ayrshire Scotland UK
139 H2 **Whitington** Norfolk England UK
75 R6 **Whitkow** Saskatchewan Canada
81 J2 **Whitla** Alberta Canada
138 C3 **Whitland** Carmarthenshire Wales UK
87 K3 **Whitmire** South Carolina USA
58 Q1 **Whitmore Mountains** Antarctica
83 L4 **Whitney** Ontario Canada
138 D2 **Whitney** Herefordshire England UK
86 C5 **Whitney, Lake** Texas USA
84 C2 **Whitney, Mount** California USA
83 N5 **Whitney Point** New York USA
142 F5 **Whitnmuir** Scottish Borders Scotland UK
140 E2 **Whitrigg** Cumbria England UK
138 C4 **Whitsand Bay** England UK
138 E3 **Whitson** Newport Wales UK
139 I3 **Whitstable** Kent England UK
215 J6 **Whitsunday Group** *islands* Qld Australia
215 J6 **Whitsunday Island** Qld Australia
141 G1 **Whittingham** Northumberland England UK
138 D2 **Whittington** Shropshire England UK
139 G2 **Whittlesey** Cambridgeshire England UK
139 H2 **Whittlesford** Cambridgeshire England UK
138 D2 **Whitton** Powys Wales UK
214 F8 **Whitulania** *watercourse* Qld Australia
141 G3 **Whitwell** Derbyshire England UK
76 C2 **Wholdaia Lake** Northwest Territories Canada
218 C5 **Whyalla** SA Australia
218 C5 **Whyalla, Mount** SA Australia
79 H10 **Whycocomagh** Nova Scotia Canada
192 E4 **Wi-do** *island* South Korea
216 F5 **Wialki** WA Australia
101 G3 **Wiapri** Guyana
142 A3 **Wiay** *island* Scotland UK
81 M3 **Wibaux** Montana USA
139 F2 **Wibtoft** Warwickshire England UK
157 F5 **Wich'alē** Ethiopia
81 Q8 **Wichita** Kansas USA
125 K2 **Wichta** Poland
142 E2 **Wick** Highland Scotland UK
138 D3 **Wick** Vale of Glamorgan Wales UK
139 G2 **Wicken** Northamptonshire England UK
84 F4 **Wickenburg** Arizona USA
216 E6 **Wickepin** WA Australia
86 D3 **Wickes** Arkansas USA
85 K5 **Wickett** Texas USA
139 H3 **Wickford** Essex England UK
213 K4 **Wickham** *watercourse* NT Australia
212 D6 **Wickham** WA Australia
139 F4 **Wickham** Hampshire England UK
219 P9 **Wickham, Cape** Tas. Australia
108 E5 **Wickham Heights** *range* Falkland Islands
139 I2 **Wickham Market** Suffolk England UK
139 H2 **Wickhambrook** Suffolk England UK
80 E5 **Wickiup Reservoir** Oregon USA
82 G8 **Wickliffe** Kentucky USA
143 F4 **Wicklow** Ireland
143 F4 **Wicklow** *admin. area* Ireland
143 G4 **Wicklow Head** *cape* Ireland
143 F3 **Wicklow Mountains** Ireland
139 I2 **Wickmere** Norfolk England UK
125 J2 **Widawa** Poland
199 J5 **Wide Bay** Papua New Guinea
138 D4 **Widecombe in the Moor** Devon England UK
58 B2 **Widerøe, Mount** Antarctica
75 N5 **Widewater** Alberta Canada
218 H3 **Widgeegoara** *watercourse* Qld Australia
216 G5 **Widgiemooltha** WA Australia
218 H6 **Widgiewa** NSW Australia
198 D4 **Widi, Kepulauan** *islands* Indonesia
140 F3 **Widnes** Merseyside England UK
140 C2 **Widows Row** Newry and Mourne Northern Ireland UK
138 D4 **Widworthy** Devon England UK
125 I1 **Więcbork** Poland
124 D2 **Wied** *watercourse* Germany
77 P4 **Wiegand Island** Nunavut Canada
124 D2 **Wiehl** Germany
122 G5 **Wiek** Germany
125 I1 **Wiele** Poland
125 I1 **Wieleń** Poland
125 I1/2 **Wieleńskie, Jezioro** *lake* Poland
125 I1 **Wielichowo** Poland
125 I1 **Wielimie, Jezioro** *lake* Poland
125 H1 **Wielkie, Jezioro** *lake* Poland
125 I1 **Wielkopolskie** *admin. area* Poland
124 B2 **Wielsbeke** Belgium
125 J2 **Wieluń** Poland
125 I3 **Wien** *admin. area* Austria
130 G2 **Wien (Vienna)** Austria
125 I3 **Wiener Neudorf** Austria
125 L2 **Wieprz** *watercourse* Poland
122 I5 **Wieprza** *watercourse* Poland
125 K2 **Wierzchosławice** Poland
125 I1 **Wierzchowo, Jezioro** *lake* Poland
127 I1 **Wiesbaden** Germany
124 E1 **Wietze** Germany
141 F3 **Wigan** Greater Manchester England UK
86 G5 **Wiggins** Mississippi USA
139 F3 **Wigginton** Oxfordshire England UK
141 F2 **Wigglesworth** North Yorkshire England UK
139 F4 **Wight, Isle of** England UK
138 E2 **Wigmore** Herefordshire England UK
214 D1 **Wigram Island** NT Australia
141 H3 **Wigsley** Nottinghamshire England UK
140 E2 **Wigton** Cumbria England UK
142 D6 **Wigtown** Dumfries and Galloway Scotland UK
140 D2 **Wigtown Bay** Scotland UK
75 N8 **Wigwam** *watercourse* British Columbia Canada
85 J1 **Wigwam** Colorado USA
76 K6 **Wigwascence Lake** Ontario Canada
125 I2 **Wijewo** Poland
157 F5 **Wik'ro** Ethiopia
130 C3 **Wila** Switzerland
218 E4 **Wilangee** NSW Australia
81 Q6 **Wilber** Nebraska USA
83 L4 **Wilberforce** Ontario Canada
221 D6 **Wilberforce** *watercourse* New Zealand
214 D1 **Wilberforce, Cape** NT Australia
80 F3 **Wilbur** Washington USA
139 H2 **Wilburton** Cambridgeshire England UK
86 D3 **Wilburton** Oklahoma USA
139 H2 **Wilby** Norfolk England UK
218 F4 **Wilcannia** NSW Australia
138 E3 **Wilcrick** Newport Wales UK
214 F6 **Wild** *watercourse* Qld Australia
58 K2 **Wild, Cape** Antarctica
81 K3 **Wild Horse Lake** Montana USA
80 H6 **Wild Horse Reservoir** Nevada USA
125 H4 **Wildalpen** Austria
124 G1 **Wildberg** Germany
75 W5 **Wilde** Manitoba Canada
199 F5 **Wildeman** *watercourse* Indonesia
80 G5 **Wilder** Idaho USA
83 M7 **Wilderness** Virginia USA
212 F8 **Wilderness, Lake** WA Australia
212 G4 **Wilderness Camp** WA Australia
74 M6 **Wildhay** *watercourse* Alberta Canada
214 B2 **Wildman** *watercourse* NT Australia
81 N2 **Wildrose** North Dakota USA
216 D3 **Wileri** WA Australia
139 F2 **Wilford** Nottingham England UK
199 H5 **Wilhelm, Mount** Papua New Guinea
58 G2 **Wilhelm II Coast** Antarctica
58 F2 **Wilhelm II Land** *plain* Antarctica
101 G4 **Wilhelmina Gebergte** *range* Suriname
124 E4 **Wilhelmsdorf** Germany
122 E6 **Wilhelmshaven** Germany
83 N6 **Wilkes-Barre** Pennsylvania USA
58 H2 **Wilkes Land** *plain* Antarctica
87 K2 **Wilkesboro** North Carolina USA
142 E3 **Wilkhaven** Highland Scotland UK
215 I7 **Wilkin, Mount** Qld Australia
58 T2 **Wilkins Coast** Antarctica
58 T2 **Wilkins Sound** *strait* Antarctica
83 L6 **Wilkinsburg** Pennsylvania USA
217 M4 **Wilkinson Lakes** SA Australia
87 J5 **Willacoochee** Georgia USA
218 G3 **Willacora** Qld Australia
218 E7 **Willalooka** SA Australia
80 D4 **Willamina** Oregon USA
218 G5 **Willandra** *watercourse* NSW Australia
80 C3 **Willapa Bay** Washington USA
82 E8 **Willard** Missouri USA
85 I3 **Willard** New Mexico USA
80 I6 **Willard** Utah USA
219 J1 **Willawa** Qld Australia
219 K4 **Willawarrin** NSW Australia
218 H6 **Willbriggie** NSW Australia
84 H4 **Willcox** Arizona USA
88 C1 **Willcox Playa** *pan* Arizona USA
91 G4 **Willemstad** Netherlands Antilles
141 H2 **Willerby** North Yorkshire England UK
138 D2 **Willersley** Herefordshire England UK
139 H3 **Willesborough Lees** Kent England UK
75 Q3 **William** *watercourse* Saskatchewan Canada
218 C3 **William, Lake** SA Australia
218 F7 **William, Mount** Vic. Australia
221 C8 **William, Port** New Zealand
86 H4 **William "Bill" Dannelly Reservoir** Alabama USA
218 C3 **William Creek** SA Australia
217 I2 **William Lambert, Mount** WA Australia
78 F2 **William-Smith, Cap** *cape* Quebec Canada
181 G4 **Williamnagar** Meghalaya India
214 F6 **Williams** *watercourse* Qld Australia
216 E6 **Williams** WA Australia
84 F3 **Williams** Arizona USA
80 D7 **Williams** California USA
81 R2 **Williams** Minnesota USA
58 L2 **Williams, Cape** Antarctica
214 A4 **Williams, Mount** NT Australia
58 E2 **Williams, Point** Antarctica
81 L7 **Williams Fork Reservoir** Colorado USA
90 E1 **Williams Island** Bahamas
74 J6 **Williams Lake** British Columbia Canada
76 J7 **Williams Lake** Ontario Canada
55 M10 **Williams Seamount** *underwater f eature* Southern Ocean
82 E6 **Williamsburg** Iowa USA
85 O1 **Williamsburg** Kansas USA
87 I2 **Williamsburg** Kentucky USA
85 I4 **Williamsburg** New Mexico USA
83 M8 **Williamsburg** Virginia USA
87 J2 **Williamson** West Virginia USA
84 C2 **Williamson, Mount** California USA
58 H2 **Williamson Glacier** *ice* Antarctica
83 M7 **Williamsport** Maryland USA
83 M6 **Williamsport** Pennsylvania USA
87 M3 **Williamston** North Carolina USA
82 I7 **Williamstown** Kentucky USA
127 H1 **Willich** Germany
212 G4 **Willie Creek** WA Australia
214 B5 **Willieray, Mount** NT Australia
109 18 **Willikies** Antigua and Barbuda
75 O6 **Willingdon** Alberta Canada
139 H4 **Willingdon** East Sussex England UK
75 M7 **Willingdon, Mount** Alberta Canada
127 I1 **Willingen** Germany
141 H3 **Willingham by Stowe** Lincolnshire England UK
141 G2 **Willington** Durham England UK
109 8 **Willis Islands** South Georgia
215 K4 **Willis Islets** Coral Sea Islands Territory Australia
162 D6 **Williston** South Africa
87 J6 **Williston** Florida USA
81 N2 **Williston** North Dakota USA
87 K4 **Williston** South Carolina USA
72 G7 **Williston Lake** British Columbia Canada
138 D3 **Williton** Somerset England UK
80 D7 **Willits** California USA
75 T8 **Willmar** Saskatchewan Canada
81 R4 **Willmar** Minnesota USA
218 D5 **Willochra** SA Australia
218 D4 **Willochra** *watercourse* SA Australia
218 D6 **Willoughby, Cape** SA Australia
109 18 **Willoughby Bay** Antigua and Barbuda
74 K6 **Willow** *watercourse* British Columbia Canada
72 E6 **Willow** Alaska USA
86 B3 **Willow** Oklahoma USA
81 M2 **Willow Bunch** Saskatchewan Canada
81 M2 **Willow Bunch Lake** Saskatchewan Canada
81 O2 **Willow City** North Dakota USA
75 O7 **Willow Creek** Alberta Canada
80 G6 **Willow Creek Reservoir** Nevada USA
74 L1 **Willow Lake** Northwest Territories Canada
81 Q4 **Willow Lake** South Dakota USA
82 G4 **Willow Reservoir** Wisconsin USA
82 F8 **Willow Springs** Missouri USA
219 J4 **Willow Tree** NSW Australia
81 N1 **Willowbrook** Saskatchewan Canada
74 J1 **Willowlake** *watercourse* Northwest Territories Canada
162 D6 **Willowmore** South Africa
214 B6 **Willowra** NT Australia
80 D7 **Willows** California USA
162 E6 **Willowvale** South Africa
214 E6 **Wills** *watercourse* Qld Australia
213 J6 **Wills, Lake** WA Australia
86 D4 **Wills Point** Texas USA
218 D6 **Willunga** SA Australia
139 F2 **Wilmcote** Warwickshire England UK
83 N7 **Wilmington** Delaware USA
87 M3 **Wilmington** North Carolina USA
82 J7 **Wilmington** Ohio USA
82 I8 **Wilmore** Kentucky USA
86 F4 **Wilmot** Arkansas USA
81 Q4 **Wilmot** South Dakota USA
141 F3 **Wilmslow** Cheshire England UK
139 F2 **Wilnecote** Staffordshire England UK
218 D4 **Wilpena** *watercourse* SA Australia
218 F2 **Wilson** *watercourse* Qld Australia
213 I4 **Wilson** *watercourse* WA Australia
76 I1 **Wilson** *watercourse* Nunavut Canada
86 F3 **Wilson** Arkansas USA
86 F5 **Wilson** Louisiana USA
87 M3 **Wilson** North Carolina USA
86 C3 **Wilson** Oklahoma USA
85 L4 **Wilson** Texas USA
108 B6 **Wilson, Cabo** *cape* Chile
73 K5 **Wilson, Cape** Nunavut Canada
80 F3 **Wilson Creek** Washington USA
58 K2 **Wilson Hills** *range* Antarctica
216 E7 **Wilson Inlet** WA Australia
85 M1 **Wilson Lake** Kansas USA
81 O6 **Wilsonville** Nebraska USA
80 D4 **Wilsonville** Oregon USA
124 E1 **Wilstedt** Germany
122 E6 **Wilster** Germany
124 D1 **Wilsum** Germany
125 H2 **Wilthen** Germany
219 J6 **Wilton** NSW Australia
214 C2 **Wilton** *watercourse* NT Australia
138 E3 **Wilton** Herefordshire England UK
138 D3 **Wilton** Somerset England UK
139 F3 **Wilton** Wiltshire England UK
83 P4 **Wilton** Maine USA
81 O3 **Wilton** North Dakota USA
139 F3 **Wiltshire** *admin. area* England UK
127 G2 **Wiltz** Luxembourg
216 G3 **Wiluna** WA Australia
76 F5 **Wimapedi** *watercourse* Manitoba Canada
81 P3 **Wimbledon** North Dakota USA
139 H2 **Wimblington** Cambridgeshire England UK
75 O7 **Wimborne** Alberta Canada
139 F4 **Wimborne St Giles** Dorset England UK
139 I4 **Wimereux** France
87 I6 **Wimico, Lake** Florida USA
127 H2 **Wimmenau** France
124 D4 **Wimmis** Switzerland
90 C4 **Wina** Nicaragua
74 M5 **Winagami Lake** Alberta Canada
82 H6 **Winamac** Indiana USA
218 G2 **Winbin** *watercourse* Qld Australia
138 E3 **Wincanton** Somerset England UK
139 H4 **Winchelsea** East Sussex England UK
214 D2 **Winchelsea Island** NT Australia
83 N4 **Winchester** Ontario Canada
221 D7 **Winchester** New Zealand
139 F3 **Winchester** Hampshire England UK
80 G3 **Winchester** Idaho USA
82 I8 **Winchester** Kentucky USA
82 J7 **Winchester** Ohio USA
83 L7 **Winchester** Virginia USA
72 F5 **Wind** *watercourse* Yukon Territory Canada
81 K5 **Wind** *watercourse* Wyoming USA
81 K5 **Wind River Range** Wyoming USA
218 C4 **Windabout, Lake** SA Australia
83 L6 **Windber** Pennsylvania USA
75 N7 **Windermere** British Columbia Canada
140 E2 **Windermere** *lake* England UK
162 C4 **Windhoek** Namibia
216 H3 **Windidda** WA Australia
76 J6 **Windigo** *watercourse* Ontario Canada
83 O2 **Windigo** *watercourse* Quebec Canada
76 J6 **Windigo Lake** Ontario Canada
216 F4 **Windimurra** WA Australia
81 Q7 **Windom** Kansas USA
81 R5 **Windom** Minnesota USA
86 D4 **Windom** Texas USA
218 F1 **Windorah** Qld Australia
58 G2 **Winds, Bay of** Antarctica
219 J5 **Windsor** NSW Australia
216 F4 **Windsor** WA Australia
79 F10 **Windsor** Nova Scotia Canada
82 J5 **Windsor** Ontario Canada
83 O4 **Windsor** Quebec Canada
139 G3 **Windsor** Windsor and Maidenhead England UK
80 D7 **Windsor** California USA
87 M3 **Windsor** North Carolina USA
87 M2 **Windsor** Virginia USA
139 G3 **Windsor and Maidenhead** *admin. area* England UK
162 D5 **Windsorton** South Africa
75 T7 **Windthorst** Saskatchewan Canada
86 B4 **Windthorst** Texas USA
218 F2 **Windulla** *watercourse* Qld Australia
221 11 **Windward Islands** Antipodes Islands New Zealand
91 F2 **Windward Passage** *marina channel* Caribbean
221 D6 **Windwhistle** New Zealand
216 E7 **Windy Harbour** WA Australia
143 F3 **Windy Harbour** Ireland
76 E2 **Windy Lake** Nunavut Canada
76 F8 **Windygates** Manitoba Canada
82 B2 **Windygates** North Dakota USA
181 H4 **Wine-maw** Myanmar
75 P5 **Winefred Lake** Alberta Canada
101 G3 **Wineperu** Guyana
75 N6 **Winfield** Alberta Canada
86 H4 **Winfield** Alabama USA
81 Q8 **Winfield** Kansas USA
87 I2 **Winfield** Tennessee USA
86 D4 **Winfield** Texas USA
83 K7 **Winfield** West Virginia USA
138 D2 **Winforton** Herefordshire England UK
81 O3 **Wing** North Dakota USA
213 K3 **Wingate Mountains** NT Australia
141 G1 **Wingates** Northumberland England UK
Wingellina *see* **Irrunytju** Australia
219 J4 **Wingen** NSW Australia
81 R3 **Winger** Minnesota USA
219 K4 **Wingham** NSW Australia
83 K5 **Wingham** Ontario Canada
198 C6 **Wini** Indonesia
81 K3 **Winifred** Montana USA
213 G7 **Winifred, Lake** WA Australia
76 L5 **Winisk** *watercourse* Ontario Canada
76 L6 **Winisk Lake** Ontario Canada
85 K5 **Wink** Texas USA
84 G4 **Winkelman** Arizona USA
124 G3 **Winklarn** Germany
214 D5 **Winkle** *watercourse* NT Australia
76 G8 **Winkler** Manitoba Canada
124 G4 **Winklern** Austria
74 M8 **Winlaw** British Columbia Canada
80 D3 **Winlock** Washington USA
218 E3 **Winnathee** NSW Australia
82 G5 **Winnebago, Lake** Wisconsin USA
214 A5 **Winnecke** *watercourse* NT Australia
214 D7 **Winnecke, Mount** NT Australia
80 G6 **Winnemucca** Nevada USA
80 F6 **Winnemucca Lake** Nevada USA
81 P5 **Winner** South Dakota USA
81 K3 **Winnett** Montana USA
86 E5 **Winnfield** Louisiana USA
82 D3 **Winnibigoshish, Lake** Minnesota USA
216 D1 **Winning** WA Australia
76 G8 **Winnipeg** Manitoba Canada
76 G7 **Winnipeg** *watercourse* Manitoba Canada
73 J8 **Winnipeg, Lake** Manitoba Canada
76 G7 **Winnipeg Beach** Manitoba Canada
75 V7 **Winnipegosis** Manitoba Canada
73 J8 **Winnipegosis, Lake** Manitoba Canada
83 P5 **Winnipesaukee, Lake** New Hampshire USA
86 F4 **Winnsboro** Louisiana USA
78 G6 **Winokapau Lake** Newfoundland and Labrador Canada
84 G3 **Winona** Arizona USA
81 O7 **Winona** Kansas USA
82 F4 **Winona** Minnesota USA
86 G4 **Winona** Mississippi USA
82 F8 **Winona** Missouri USA
86 D4 **Winona** Texas USA
124 D1 **Winschoten** Netherlands
124 E1 **Winsen** Germany
141 F3 **Winsford** Cheshire England UK
138 D3 **Winsford** Somerset England UK
140 F2 **Winskill** Cumbria England UK
139 G3 **Winslow** Buckinghamshire England UK
84 G3 **Winslow** Arizona USA
81 Q6 **Winslow** Nebraska USA
139 F3 **Winson** Gloucestershire England UK
139 F1 **Winster** Derbyshire England UK
87 K2 **Winston-Salem** North Carolina USA
122 D6 **Winsum** Netherlands
87 K6 **Winter Garden** Florida USA
87 K6 **Winter Park** Florida USA
124 E2 **Winterberg** Germany
139 E4 **Winterborne Kingston** Dorset England UK
138 E4 **Winterborne Steepleton** Dorset England UK
139 F3 **Winterbourne Bassett** Wiltshire England UK
139 F3 **Winterbourne Dauntsey** Wiltshire England UK
79 D10 **Winterport** Maine USA
86 B5 **Winters** Texas USA
82 D6 **Winterset** Iowa USA
127 I3 **Winterthur** Switzerland
79 L9 **Winterton** Newfoundland and Labrador Canada
139 I2 **Winterton-on-Sea** Norfolk England UK
87 M3 **Winterville** North Carolina USA
141 I3 **Winthorpe** Lincolnshire England UK
79 D10 **Winthrop** Maine USA
82 D4 **Winthrop** Minnesota USA
80 E2 **Winthrop** Washington USA
215 G7 **Winton** Qld Australia
221 C8 **Winton** New Zealand
87 M2 **Winton** North Carolina USA
139 G2 **Winwick** Cambridgeshire England UK
141 F3 **Winwick** Warrington England UK
124 F2 **Wipper** *watercourse* Germany
196 E4 **Wiralaga** Indonesia
198 E4 **Wiriagar** *watercourse* Indonesia
139 F1 **Wirksworth** Derbyshire England UK
198 D5 **Wirmaf** Indonesia
218 D5 **Wirrabara** SA Australia
140 E3 **Wirral** *admin. area* England UK
218 B3 **Wirrida, Lake** SA Australia
219 H3 **Wirriwa** NSW Australia
218 B5 **Wirrulla** SA Australia
222 6a **Wisas** *island* Federated States of Micronesia
139 H2 **Wisbech** Cambridgeshire England UK
79 D10 **Wiscasset** Maine USA
70 **Wisconsin** *admin. area* USA
82 F5 **Wisconsin** *watercourse* Wisconsin USA
82 G5 **Wisconsin Dells** Wisconsin USA
58 P1 **Wisconsin Range** Antarctica
82 G4 **Wisconsin Rapids** Wisconsin USA
87 J2 **Wise** Virginia USA
75 R7 **Wiseton** Saskatchewan Canada
75 T7 **Wishart** Saskatchewan Canada
142 E5 **Wishaw** North Lanarkshire Scotland UK
81 P3 **Wishek** North Dakota USA
161 H2 **Wisil Dabarow** Somalia
125 K2 **Wisła** *watercourse* Poland
125 K3 **Wisłoka** *watercourse* Poland
122 F6 **Wismar** Germany
86 F5 **Wisner** Louisiana USA
81 Q6 **Wisner** Nebraska USA
139 I4 **Wissant** France
127 H2 **Wissembourg** France
139 H2 **Wissey** *watercourse* England UK
138 E2 **Wistanstow** Shropshire England UK
74 H6 **Wistaria** British Columbia Canada
86 D3 **Wister** Oklahoma USA
86 D3 **Wister Lake** Oklahoma USA
139 G2 **Wistow** Cambridgeshire England UK
141 G3 **Wistow** North Yorkshire England UK
162 E5 **Witbank** South Africa
162 C5 **Witbooisvlei** Namibia
75 R6 **Witchekan Lake** Saskatchewan Canada
218 D4 **Witchelina** SA Australia
139 G1 **Witham** *watercourse* England UK
139 H3 **Witham** Essex England UK
141 H3 **Withcall** Lincolnshire England UK
139 G2 **Withcote** Leicester England UK
82 F4 **Withee** Wisconsin USA
141 I3 **Withernsea** East Riding of Yorkshire England UK
139 H2 **Withersfield** Suffolk England UK
140 F2 **Witherslack** Cumbria England UK
139 F3 **Withington** Gloucestershire England UK
138 E2 **Withington** Herefordshire England UK
141 F3 **Withnell** Lancashire England UK
138 D3 **Withypool** Somerset England UK
79 L9 **Witless Bay** Newfoundland and Labrador Canada
139 G3 **Witley** Surrey England UK
139 F3 **Witney** Oxfordshire England UK
125 J1 **Witonia** Poland
82 G7 **Witt** Illinois USA
212 E7 **Wittenoom** WA Australia
125 H2 **Wittichenau** Germany
124 F1 **Wittingen** Germany
124 D3 **Wittlich** Germany
84 F4 **Wittmann** Arizona USA
122 G5 **Wittow** *island* Germany
124 G1 **Wittstock** Germany
199 I5 **Witu Islands** Papua New Guinea
162 C4 **Witvlei** Namibia
138 D3 **Wiveliscombe** Somerset England UK
76 H4 **Wivenhoe** Manitoba Canada
139 H3 **Wivenhoe** Essex England UK
219 K2 **Wivenhoe, Lake** Qld Australia
90 C4 **Wiwilí** Nicaragua
139 H2 **Wixoe** Essex England UK
86 C5 **Wixon Valley** Texas USA
101 H3 **W.J. van Blommestein Meer** *lake* Suriname
125 K1 **Wkra** *watercourse* Poland
122 J5 **Władysławowo** Poland
125 J1 **Włocławek** Poland
125 J2 **Włoszczowa** Poland
124 F1 **Wöbbelin** Germany
139 G3 **Woburn** Bedfordshire England UK
218 H7 **Wodonga** Vic. Australia
124 C1 **Woerden** Netherlands
130 B2 **Woerth** France
58 A2 **Wohlthat Mountains** Antarctica
139 I4 **Woincourt** France
199 H6 **Woitape** Papua New Guinea
125 K3 **Wojaszówka** Poland
125 J1 **Wójcin** Poland
198 E5 **Wokam** *island* Indonesia
181 H3 **Wokha** Nagaland India
74 L5 **Woking** Alberta Canada
139 G3 **Woking** Surrey England UK
214 G6 **Wokingham** *watercourse* Qld Australia
139 G3 **Wokingham** *admin. area* England UK
125 L2 **Wola Obszańska** Poland
125 J2 **Wolbrom** Poland
82 I6 **Wolcottville** Indiana USA
141 H3 **Wold Newton** North East Lincolnshire England UK
125 G1 **Woldegk** Germany
199 G2 **Woleai** *island* Federated States of Micronesia
52 K7 **Woleai Atoll** *reef* Caroline Islands
159 G4 **Woleu-Ntem** *admin. area* Gabon
75 P5 **Wolf** *watercourse* Alberta Canada
74 E2 **Wolf** *watercourse* Yukon Territory Canada
82 D7 **Wolf** *watercourse* Kansas USA
82 G4 **Wolf** *watercourse* Wisconsin USA
109 4 **Wolf, Isla** *island* Archipiélago de Colón (Galapagos Islands)
109 4 **Wolf, Volcán** *volcano* Archipiélago de Colón (Galapagos Islands)
74 F2 **Wolf Lake** Yukon Territory Canada
81 L4 **Wolf Mountains** Montana USA
81 M2 **Wolf Point** Montana USA
213 I5 **Wolfe** *watercourse* WA Australia
124 G2 **Wolfen** Germany
127 I3 **Wolfenschiessen** Switzerland
139 H2 **Wolferton** Norfolk England UK
85 L4 **Wolfforth** Texas USA
124 G4 **Wolfgangsee** *lake* Austria
138 C3 **Wolf's Castle** Pembrokeshire Wales UK
125 H4 **Wolfsberg** Austria
124 F1 **Wolfsburg** Germany
125 G3 **Wolfsegg am Hausruck** Austria
127 H3 **Wolfwil** Switzerland
127 I3 **Wolhusen** Switzerland
125 H1 **Wolin** Poland
219 I5 **Wollar** NSW Australia
108 C6 **Wollaston, Isla** *island* Chile
75 T3 **Wollaston Lake** Saskatchewan Canada
75 T3 **Wollaston Lake** Saskatchewan Canada
72 H5 **Wollaston Peninsula** Northwest Territories/Nunavut Canada
214 D4 **Wollogorang** NT Australia
219 J5 **Wollombi** NSW Australia
219 K4 **Wollomombi** NSW Australia
219 J6 **Wollongong** NSW Australia
158 B3 **Wologizi Mountains** Liberia
125 L3 **Wołosate** Ukraine
125 I2 **Wołów** Poland
75 T7 **Wolseley** Saskatchewan Canada
81 P4 **Wolsey** South Dakota USA
141 G2 **Wolsingham** Durham England UK
73 L6 **Wolstenholme, Cap** *cape* Quebec Canada
124 D1 **Wolvega** Netherlands
139 F3 **Wolvercote** Oxfordshire England UK
141 F4 **Wolverhampton** *admin. area* England UK
139 E2 **Wolverhampton** West Midlands England UK
75 M4 **Wolverine** *watercourse* Alberta Canada
214 G2 **Wolverton** Qld Australia
139 G2 **Wolverton** Milton Keynes England UK
219 I1 **Womblebank** Qld Australia
141 H2 **Wombleton** North Yorkshire England UK
141 G3 **Wombwell** South Yorkshire England UK
179 K2 **Wonay, Kowtal-e** *pass* Afghanistan
198 E4 **Wondiwoi, Pegunungan** *mountain* Indonesia
215 H4 **Wonga** Qld Australia
218 G4 **Wongalara Lake** NSW Australia
214 G6 **Wongan** Qld Australia
216 E5 **Wongan Hills** WA Australia
219 I5 **Wongarbon** NSW Australia
216 G3 **Wongawol** WA Australia
214 E7 **Wongitta, Lake** Qld Australia
219 I2 **Wongle** Qld Australia
192 E4 **Wŏnju** South Korea
218 D4 **Wonoka** SA Australia
197 F5 **Wonosari** Indonesia
197 F5 **Wonosobo** Indonesia
198 C6 **Wonreli** Indonesia
192 E3 **Wŏnsan** North Korea
218 G8 **Wonthaggi** Vic. Australia
218 H8 **Wonwron** Vic. Australia
213 I4 **Wood** *watercourse* WA Australia
75 R8 **Wood** *watercourse* Saskatchewan Canada
58 L2 **Wood Bay** Antarctica
139 I2 **Wood Dalling** Norfolk England UK
213 H4 **Wood Islands** WA Australia
79 G10 **Wood Islands** Prince Edward Island Canada
75 R8 **Wood Mountain** Saskatchewan Canada
81 P6 **Wood River** Nebraska USA
139 G2 **Wood Walton** Cambridgeshire England UK
198 F7 **Woodah, Isle** NT Australia
216 E6 **Woodanilling** WA Australia
214 E5 **Woodbine** *watercourse* Qld Australia
87 K5 **Woodbine** Georgia USA
81 Q7 **Woodbine** Kansas USA
210 inset **Woodbine Bank** Ashmore Reef and Cartier Island Australia
221 E5 **Woodbourne** New Zealand
219 K3 **Woodburn** NSW Australia
80 D4 **Woodburn** Oregon USA
87 I4 **Woodbury** Georgia USA
83 N7 **Woodbury** New Jersey USA
87 H3 **Woodbury** Tennessee USA
74 G5 **Woodcock** British Columbia Canada
139 F3 **Woodcott** Hampshire England UK
219 K3 **Woodenbong** NSW Australia
140 B4 **Woodenbridge** Ireland
218 G7 **Woodend** Vic. Australia
142 E5 **Woodfoot** Dumfries and Galloway Scotland UK
214 B7 **Woodforde** *watercourse* NT Australia
84 C1 **Woodfords** California USA
140 B3 **Woodfort** Ireland
219 K1 **Woodgate** Qld Australia
141 H3 **Woodhall Spa** Lincolnshire England UK
214 E6 **Woodhouse, Mount** Qld Australia
212 F6 **Woodie Woodie Mine** WA Australia
84 C2 **Woodlake** California USA
79 E10 **Woodland** Maine USA
87 M2 **Woodland** North Carolina USA
80 D4 **Woodland** Washington USA
81 M7 **Woodland Park** Colorado USA
76 G7 **Woodlands** Manitoba Canada
196 C2 **Woodlands** *admin. area* Singapore
199 J6 **Woodlark Island** Papua New Guinea
76 G8 **Woodridge** Manitoba Canada
139 H2 **Woodrising** Norfolk England UK
214 D6 **Woodroffe** *watercourse* NT Australia
217 L3 **Woodroffe, Mount** SA Australia
87 J3 **Woodruff** South Carolina USA
214 B4 **Woods, Lake** NT Australia
73 J9 **Woods, Lake of the** Canada/USA
78 F5 **Woods Lake** Newfoundland and Labrador Canada
215 H4 **Woods Peak** Qld Australia
218 D7 **Woods Well** SA Australia
86 C6 **Woodsboro** Texas USA
83 K7 **Woodsfield** Ohio USA
84 G1 **Woodside** Utah USA
86 B4 **Woodson** Texas USA
219 I5 **Woodstock** NSW Australia
214 G5 **Woodstock** Qld Australia
212 E6 **Woodstock** WA Australia
79 E9 **Woodstock** New Brunswick Canada
83 K5 **Woodstock** Ontario Canada
139 F3 **Woodstock** Oxfordshire England UK
82 G5 **Woodstock** Illinois USA
140 A4 **Woodstown** Ireland
219 H2 **Woodvale** Qld Australia
218 G7 **Woodvale** Vic. Australia
220 F5 **Woodville** New Zealand
87 H3 **Woodville** Alabama USA
86 F5 **Woodville** Mississippi USA
86 D5 **Woodville** Texas USA
86 B2 **Woodward** Oklahoma USA
86 E5 **Woodworth** Louisiana USA
195 G3 **Woody Island** Paracel Islands
75 T5 **Woody Lake** Saskatchewan Canada
138 E2 **Woofferton** Herefordshire England UK
139 E4 **Wool** Dorset England UK
138 C3 **Woolacombe** Devon England UK
213 K2 **Woolaning** NT Australia
138 E3 **Woolaston** Gloucestershire England UK
214 C2 **Woolen** *watercourse* NT Australia
219 K4 **Woolgoolga** NSW Australia
138 E2 **Woolhope** Herefordshire England UK
219 K3 **Wooli** NSW Australia
213 K2 **Woolianna** NT Australia
216 G5 **Woolibar** WA Australia
139 E4 **Woolland** Dorset England UK
58 R1 **Woollard, Mount** *mountain* Antarctica
77 S7 **Woollett, Lac** *lake* Quebec Canada
219 J4 **Woolooma** NSW Australia
138 E2 **Woolstaston** Shropshire England UK
216 G6 **Woolyeenyer Hill** WA Australia
219 H6 **Woomargama** NSW Australia
83 P5 **Woonsocket** Rhode Island USA
138 E2 **Woonton** Herefordshire England UK
141 G1 **Wooperton** Northumberland England UK
218 E7 **Woorak** Vic. Australia
216 D2 **Wooramel** *watercourse* WA Australia
216 D2 **Wooramel Roadhouse** WA Australia
218 H8 **Woorarra** Vic. Australia
218 F7 **Woorndoo** Vic. Australia
83 K6 **Wooster** Ohio USA
139 G2 **Wooton** Northamptonshire England UK
219 K5 **Wootton** NSW Australia
139 F3 **Wootton Bassett** Wiltshire England UK
139 F2 **Wootton Wawen** Warwickshire England UK
161 G1 **Woqooyi Galbeed** *admin. area* Somalia
127 H3 **Worben** Switzerland
214 F2 **Worbody Point** Qld Australia
162 C6 **Worcester** South Africa
139 E2 **Worcester** Worcestershire England UK
83 P5 **Worcester** Massachusetts USA
139 E2 **Worcestershire** *admin. area* England UK
138 E2 **Worfield** Shropshire England UK
124 G4 **Wörgl** Austria
198 E5 **Workai** *island* Indonesia
140 E2 **Workington** Cumbria England UK
141 G3 **Worksop** Nottinghamshire England UK
124 C1 **Workum** Netherlands
141 I3 **Worlaby** Lincolnshire England UK
81 L5 **Worland** Wyoming USA
138 E1 **Worleston** Cheshire England UK
139 H2 **Worlington** Suffolk England UK
126 F1 **Wormhout** France
124 E3 **Worms** Germany
138 C3 **Worms Head** *cape* Wales UK
127 L2 **Wörnharts** Austria
139 I4 **Wornicourt** France
124 F3 **Wörnitz** *watercourse* Germany
130 C2 **Wörrstadt** Germany
139 I2 **Worstead** Norfolk England UK
139 I3 **Worth** Kent England UK
127 I2 **Wörth** Germany
85 N5 **Wortham** Texas USA
125 H4 **Wörther See** *lake* Austria
109 12 **Worthing** Barbados
139 G4 **Worthing** West Sussex England UK
81 R5 **Worthington** Minnesota USA
82 J6 **Worthington** Ohio USA
198 C4 **Wosi** Indonesia
198 D5 **Wotap** *island* Indonesia
223 15 **Wotje Atoll** Marshall Islands
138 C4 **Wotter** Devon England UK
198 B4 **Wotu** Indonesia
215 K7 **Wowan** Qld Australia
197 I5 **Wowoni** *island* Indonesia
197 I5 **Wowoni, Selat** *strait* Indonesia
196 C2 **Woyla** *watercourse* Indonesia
218 F4 **Woytchugga, Lake** NSW Australia
125 J2 **Woźniki** Poland
141 H3 **Wragby** Lincolnshire England UK
56 Q1 **Wrangel Abyssal Plain** *underwater feature* Arctic Ocean
74 E4 **Wrangell** Alaska USA
74 E4 **Wrangell Island** Alaska USA
72 E6 **Wrangell Mountains** Alaska USA
139 H1 **Wrangle** Lincolnshire England UK
142 C2 **Wrath, Cape** Scotland UK
141 H3 **Wrawby** North Lincolnshire England UK
138 E3 **Wraxall** Somerset England UK
81 N6 **Wray** Colorado USA
215 M7 **Wreck Reefs** Coral Sea Islands Territory Australia
222 1a **Wrecks, Bay of** Kiribati
141 H2 **Wrelton** North Yorkshire England UK
138 E1 **Wrenbury** Cheshire England UK
139 I2 **Wreningham** Norfolk England UK
87 J4 **Wrens** Georgia USA
75 O8 **Wrentham** Alberta Canada
138 E1 **Wrexham** *admin. area* Wales UK
138 E1 **Wrexham** Wrexham Wales UK
221 C8 **Wreys Bush** New Zealand
81 M5 **Wright** Wyoming USA
58 U2 **Wright Inlet** *bay* Antarctica
58 Q2 **Wright Island** Antarctica
86 D4 **Wright Patman Lake** Texas USA
83 K5 **Wright Point** Ontario Canada
59 K1 **Wright Valley** Antarctica
86 E3 **Wrightsville** Arkansas USA
87 J4 **Wrightsville** Georgia USA
72 G6 **Wrigley** Northwest Territories Canada
58 P2 **Wrigley Gulf** *bay* Antarctica
125 I2 **Wrocław** Poland
125 I2 **Wroniniec** Poland
215 G4 **Wrotham Park** Qld Australia
139 F3 **Wroughton** Swindon England UK
139 F4 **Wroxall** Isle of Wight England UK
81 O1 **Wroxton** Saskatchewan Canada
125 H1 **Września** Poland
125 I2 **Wschowa** Poland
188 E2 **Wu Jiang** *watercourse* Chongqing China
184 H3 **Wu-mu-ha-ko Yen-tse** *lake* Xinjiang Uygur Zizhiqu China
188 F2 **Wu Shan** *range* Hubei China
189 H4 **Wu'an** Fujian China
216 E5 **Wubin** WA Australia
191 K4 **Wuchang** Heilongjiang China
189 G2 **Wuchang Hu** *lake* Anhui China
189 H2 **Wucheng** Anhui China
191 H5 **Wucheng** Shandong China
189 H4 **Wuchiu Yü (Taiwan)** *island* Taiwan China
188 F4 **Wuchuan** Guangdong China
191 K3 **Wudalianchi** Heilongjiang China
191 I4 **Wudan** Nei Mongol Zizhiqu China
159 F2 **Wudil** Nigeria
218 B5 **Wudinna** SA Australia
218 B5 **Wudinna, Mount** SA Australia
188 D1 **Wudu** Gansu China
188 F2 **Wufeng** Hubei China
188 D3 **Wufeng** Yunnan China
189 G1 **Wugang** Henan China
188 F3 **Wugang** Hunan China
189 G3 **Wugong Shan** *mountain* Jiangxi China
190 F5 **Wuhai** Nei Mongol Zizhiqu China
189 G2 **Wuhan** Hubei China
189 H1 **Wuhe** Anhui China
189 H2 **Wuhu** Anhui China
191 H5 **Wuji** Hebei China
189 H2 **Wujiang** Jiangsu China
159 F3 **Wukari** Nigeria
188 D4 **Wuliang Shan** *range* Yunnan China
198 D5 **Wuliaru** *island* Indonesia
188 F3 **Wuling Shan** *range* Hunan China
191 H3 **Wuliyasitai** Nei Mongol Zizhiqu China
198 D5 **Wulmasa** Indonesia
185 H4 **Wulumuqi** Xinjiang Uygur Zizhiqu China
198 D5 **Wulur** Indonesia
159 G3 **Wum** Cameroon
189 G3 **Wumei Shan** *mountain* Jiangxi China
188 E4 **Wuming** Guangxi Zhuangzu Zizhiqu China
124 E1 **Wümme** *watercourse* Germany
160 E2 **Wunagak** Sudan
181 H5 **Wundwin** Myanmar
218 E6 **Wunkar** SA Australia
127 I1 **Wünnenberg** Germany
76 K6 **Wunnummin Lake** Ontario Canada
76 K6 **Wunnummin Lake** Ontario Canada
124 E1 **Wunstorf** Germany
181 H4 **Wuntho** Myanmar
124 D2 **Wupper** *watercourse* Germany
162 C6 **Wuppertal** South Africa
190 F6 **Wuqi** Shaanxi China
184 E5 **Wuqia** Xinjiang Uygur Zizhiqu China
189 G1 **Wuquan** Henan China
216 E4 **Wurarga** WA Australia
159 F2 **Wurno** Nigeria
83 N6 **Wurtsboro** New York USA
219 J1 **Wuruma, Lake** Qld Australia
127 J1 **Wurzbach** Germany
130 C2 **Würzburg** Germany
127 K1 **Wurzen** Germany
188 D1 **Wushan** Gansu China
184 F4 **Wushi** Xinjiang Uygur Zizhiqu China
222 7 **Wusi** Vanuatu
54 D8 **Wüst Seamount** *underwater feature* Atlantic Ocean
124 G1 **Wusterwitz** Germany
184 G4 **Wusu** Xinjiang Uygur Zizhiqu China
191 H5 **Wutai Shan** *range* Shanxi China
219 J2 **Wutul** Qld Australia
199 G4 **Wuvulu Island** Papua New Guinea
190 E5 **Wuwei** Gansu China
188 F2 **Wuxi** Chongqing China
189 H2 **Wuxi** Jiangsu China
188 F2 **Wuxia** Chongqing China
191 G6 **Wuxiang** Shanxi China
188 F4 **Wuxuan** Guangxi Zhuangzu Zizhiqu China
189 G2 **Wuxue** Hubei China
188 E3 **Wuyang** Guizhou China
191 H5 **Wuyi** Hebei China
189 G3 **Wuyi Shan** *range* Fujian China
189 H3 **Wuyishan** Fujian China
190 F4 **Wuyuan** Nei Mongol Zizhiqu China
189 G2 **Wuyue Shuiku** *lake* Henan China
189 H3 **Wuyun** Zhejiang China
190 F5 **Wuzhong** Ningxia Huizu Zizhiqu China
189 F4 **Wuzhou** Guangxi Zhuangzu Zizhiqu China
189 F4 **Wuzhu Zhou** *island* Guangdong China
214 G4 **Wyaaba** *watercourse* Qld Australia
216 E5 **Wyalkatchem** WA Australia
219 K3 **Wyan** NSW Australia
51 T13 **Wyandot Seamount** *underwater feature* Atlantic Ocean
218 G2 **Wyandra** Qld Australia
218 G3 **Wyara, Lake** Qld Australia
139 G2 **Wyberton** Lincolnshire England UK
138 E1 **Wybunbury** Cheshire England UK
218 F7 **Wycheproof** Vic. Australia
139 F2 **Wychnor** Staffordshire England UK

214 C6 **Wycliffe Well** NT Australia
216 E4 **Wydgee** WA Australia
138 E3 **Wye** *watercourse* England/Wales UK
219 J5 **Wyee** NSW Australia
138 E4 **Wyke Regis** Dorset England UK
219 R11 **Wylds Craig** *mountain* Tas. Australia
217 H6 **Wylie Scarp** WA Australia
212 D7 **Wyloo** WA Australia
139 F3 **Wylye** Wiltshire England UK
75 R7 **Wymark** Saskatchewan Canada
81 Q6 **Wymore** Nebraska USA
219 I7 **Wyndham** NSW Australia
213 J3 **Wyndham** WA Australia
221 C8 **Wyndham** New Zealand
108 B5 **Wyndham, Monte** *mountain* Chile
143 D4 **Wyndham's Bridge** Ireland
81 Q3 **Wyndmere** North Dakota USA
74 M8 **Wynndel** British Columbia Canada
86 F3 **Wynne** Arkansas USA
86 C3 **Wynnewood** Oklahoma USA
72 H4 **Wynniatt Bay** Northwest Territories Canada
82 C8 **Wynona** Oklahoma USA
75 S7 **Wynyard** Saskatchewan Canada
217 L4 **Wyola Lake** SA Australia
70 **Wyoming** *admin. area* USA
82 F5 **Wyoming** Iowa USA
82 I5 **Wyoming** Michigan USA
81 J5 **Wyoming Range** Wyoming USA
219 J5 **Wyong** NSW Australia
139 E2 **Wyre Piddle** Worcestershire England UK
214 G6 **Wyreema** Qld Australia
139 F2 **Wysall** Nottinghamshire England UK
125 K2 **Wyśmierzyce** Poland
125 L2 **Wysokie** Poland
125 L1 **Wysokie Mazowieckie** Poland
125 J2 **Wyszanów** Poland
125 K1 **Wyszków** Poland
125 K1 **Wyszogród** Poland
87 K2 **Wytheville** Virginia USA
218 G7 **Wyuna** Vic. Australia
57 F2 **Wyville-Thomson Ridge** *underwater feature* Atlantic Ocean

X

162 C1 **Xá-Muteba** Angola
157 I5 **Xaafuun** Somalia
161 I1 **Xaafuun, Raas** *cape* Somalia
181 F3 **Xab Qu** *watercourse* Xizang Zizhiqu China
162 D4 **Xade** Botswana
163 F5 **Xai-Xai** Mozambique
194 D3 **Xainabouli** *admin. area* Laos
161 H2 **Xalin** Somalia
194 E3 **Xam Tai** Laos
102 B4 **Xambioá** Brazil
194 E2 **Xamnua** Laos
162 D4 **Xanagas** Botswana
194 D3 **Xanakham** Laos
180 D2 **Xang Qu** *watercourse* Xizang Zizhiqu China
162 B3 **Xangongo** Angola
124 D2 **Xanten** Germany
133 D5 **Xanthi** Greece
104 D3 **Xapuri** Brazil
161 H3 **Xarardheere** Somalia
129 G4 **Xarraca, Punta** *cape* Spain
190 D2 **Xatgal** Mongolia
129 F4 **Xátiva** Spain
162 D4 **Xau, Lake** *lake* Botswana
107 I2 **Xavantes, Represa de** *lake* Brazil
103 B5 **Xavantes, Serra dos** *range* Brazil
180 E2 **Xaxa Zangbo** *watercourse* Xizang Zizhiqu China
194 D3 **Xayabouli** Laos
194 D2 **Xeng** *watercourse* Laos
82 J7 **Xenia** Ohio USA
101 F4 **Xeriuini** *watercourse* Brazil
128 C2 **Xermade** Spain
188 E2 **Xi He** *watercourse* Sichuan China
189 F4 **Xi Jiang** *watercourse* Guangdong China
189 G2 **Xi Xian** Henan China
189 F1 **Xia Xian** Shanxi China
189 H1 **Xia Zhen** Shandong China
191 I5 **Xiabancheng** Hebei China
188 D2 **Xia'er** Sichuan China
191 H6 **Xiajin** Shandong China
189 H4 **Xiamen** Fujian China
189 H4 **Xiamen** Fujian China
188 E1 **Xi'an** Shaanxi China
189 F3 **Xiang Jiang** *lake* Hunan China
189 F3 **Xiang Jiang** *watercourse* Hunan China
189 G1 **Xiangcheng** Henan China
188 C3 **Xiangcheng** Yunnan China
181 H2 **Xiangda** Qinghai China
189 F2 **Xiangfan** Hubei China
190 G6 **Xiangfen** Shanxi China
188 F2 **Xiangfeng** Hubei China
189 H2 **Xianghe** Anhui China
189 G3 **Xiangjiang** Jiangxi China
194 D3 **Xiangkhoang** Laos
194 D3 **Xiangkhoang Plateau** Laos
188 E2 **Xiangkou** Chongqing China
190 G6 **Xiangning** Shanxi China
180 D2 **Xiangquan He** *watercourse* Xizang Zizhiqu China
188 C4 **Xiangshan** Yunnan China
189 H1 **Xiangshui** Jiangsu China
189 F3 **Xiangtan** Hunan China
191 H6 **Xiangyuan** Shanxi China
189 H3 **Xianju** Zhejiang China
189 G2 **Xianjuemiao Shuiku** *lake* Hubei China
189 G2 **Xianning** Hubei China
188 D2 **Xianshui** Sichuan China
188 C2 **Xianshui He** *watercourse* Sichuan China
189 G2 **Xiantao** Hubei China
189 H3 **Xianxia Ling** *range* Fujian China
188 E1 **Xianyang** Shaanxi China
191 K3 **Xiao Hinggan Ling** *range* Heilongjiang China
188 D3 **Xiao Jiang** *watercourse* Yunnan China
189 H3 **Xiao Xi** *lake* Zhejiang China
191 J5 **Xiaochangshan Dao** *island* Liaoning China
189 G2 **Xiaogan** Hubei China
189 G3 **Xiaogang** Jiangxi China
188 F4 **Xiaojiang** Guangxi Zhuangzu Zizhiqu China
188 F4 **Xiaojiang Shuiku** *lake* Guangxi Zhuangzu Zizhiqu China
189 F3 **Xiaopu** Hunan China
191 J4 **Xiaoshi** Liaoning China
189 H4 **Xiaoxi** Fujian China
189 F2 **Xiaoxita** Hubei China
190 G5 **Xiaoyi** Shanxi China
188 C2 **Xiaqiong** Sichuan China
188 E2 **Xiasi** Sichuan China
181 F3 **Xiasima** Xizang Zizhiqu China
189 G3 **Xiayang** Hunan China
189 G1 **Xiayi** Henan China
188 D3 **Xichang** Sichuan China
191 H5 **Xicheng** Hebei China
189 F1 **Xichuan** Henan China
181 F3 **Xiege'er** Xizang Zizhiqu China
188 F5 **Xieyang Dao** *island* Guangxi Zhuangzu Zizhiqu China
189 G1 **Xifei He** *watercourse* Anhui China
190 F6 **Xifeng** Gansu China
191 J4 **Xifeng** Liaoning China
190 F5 **Xigang** Ningxia Huizu Zizhiqu China
188 E1 **Xihan Shui** *watercourse* Jiangsu China
188 D3 **Xihe Shuiku** *lake* Yunnan China
188 E1 **Xihe Xian** Gansu China
189 G1 **Xihua** Henan China
190 F6 **Xihuachi** Gansu China
189 G2 **Xilang Hu** *lake* Hubei China
191 I4 **Xiliao** *lake* Nei Mongol Zizhiqu China
185 K6 **Xiligou** Qinghai China
191 H4 **Xilinhaote** Nei Mongol Zizhiqu China
191 J1 **Xilinji** Heilongjiang China
89 F4 **Xilitla** Mexico
190 F5 **Xin** Nei Mongol Zizhiqu China
189 G3 **Xin Jiang** *watercourse* Jiangxi China
189 H2 **Xin'an** Anhui China
189 F1 **Xin'an** Henan China
188 E3 **Xin'an** Guizhou China
189 H2 **Xinanjiang Shuiku** *lake* Zhejiang China
191 H4 **Xinbaolage** Nei Mongol Zizhiqu China
191 K4 **Xinbin** Liaoning China
189 H2 **Xinchang** Zhejiang China
189 H3 **Xincheng** Fujian China
189 F4 **Xincheng** Guangdong China
188 E4 **Xincheng** Guangxi Zhuangzu Zizhiqu China
188 D3 **Xincheng** Sichuan China
188 D2 **Xindu** Sichuan China
188 C2 **Xindu** Sichuan China
189 G4 **Xinfeng Jiang** *lake* Guangdong China
190 G5 **Xing Xian** Shanxi China
191 I5 **Xingcheng** Hebei China
191 I5 **Xingcheng** Liaoning China
162 C1 **Xinge** Angola
191 H5 **Xinghe** Nei Mongol Zizhiqu China
189 H2 **Xinghua** Jiangsu China
189 H3 **Xinghua Wan** *bay* Fujian China
185 H4 **Xinjiang Uygur Zizhiqu** *admin. area* China
191 I5 **Xinglong** Hebei China
189 G4 **Xingning** Guangdong China
188 E3 **Xingren** Guizhou China
188 E3 **Xingshan** Guizhou China
191 H5 **Xingtai** Hebei China
102 A4 **Xingu** *watercourse* Brazil
189 G1 **Xingyang** Henan China
188 D3 **Xingyi** Guizhou China
191 H4 **Xinhaote** Nei Mongol Zizhiqu China
184 G4 **Xinhe** Xinjiang Uygur Zizhiqu China
189 G4 **Xinhua** Guangdong China
188 D3 **Xinhua** Sichuan China
188 E4 **Xinhua** Yunnan China
188 F3 **Xinhuang** Hunan China
189 F4 **Xinhui** Guangdong China
191 I4 **Xinhui** Nei Mongol Zizhiqu China
190 E6 **Xining** Qinghai China
191 H5 **Xinji** Hebei China
189 G2 **Xinji** Henan China
188 D2 **Xinjin** Sichuan China
188 E4 **Xinjing** Guangxi Zhuangzu Zizhiqu China
191 I4 **Xinkai He** *watercourse* Nei Mongol Zizhiqu China
191 H5 **Xinle** Hebei China
188 F2 **Xinling** Hubei China
188 D2 **Xinmian** Sichuan China
191 J4 **Xinmin** Liaoning China
190 F6 **Xinning** Gansu China
188 E4 **Xinning** Guangxi Zhuangzu Zizhiqu China
188 E2 **Xinning** Sichuan China
189 G2 **Xinshi** Hubei China
188 D3 **Xinshiba** Sichuan China
191 I6 **Xintai** Shandong China
189 G1 **Xinxiang** Henan China
189 G2 **Xinyang** Henan China
189 F2 **Xinye** Henan China
188 F4 **Xinyi** Guangdong China
189 H1 **Xinyi** Jiangsu China
189 G3 **Xinyu** Jiangxi China
185 K5 **Xinyuan** Qinghai China
184 G4 **Xinyuan** Xinjiang Uygur Zizhiqu China
190 F5 **Xinzhao Shan** *mountain* Nei Mongol Zizhiqu China
188 E4 **Xinzhou** Guangxi Zhuangzu Zizhiqu China
189 G2 **Xinzhou** Hubei China
191 G5 **Xinzhou** Shanxi China
189 H4 **Xiongdi Yu** *island* Fujian China
189 H3 **Xiongshi** Jiangxi China
191 H5 **Xiongzhou** Hebei China
191 H5 **Xiping** Shanxi China
189 H3 **Xiping** Zhejiang China
103 D5 **Xique Xique** Brazil
104 D2 **Xirua** *watercourse* Brazil
188 D4 **Xisa** Yunnan China
190 F5 **Xishanzui** Nei Mongol Zizhiqu China
158 B2 **Xitole** Guinea-Bissau
189 G2 **Xiu Shui** *watercourse* Jiangxi China
189 G3 **Xiugu** Jiangxi China
188 D4 **Xiushan** Yunnan China
189 I2 **Xiushan Dao** *island* Zhejiang China
191 J5 **Xiuyan** Liaoning China
190 G5 **Xiuyan** Shaanxi China
180 E3 **Xixabangma Feng** *mountain* Xizang Zizhiqu China
189 F1 **Xixia** Henan China
190 G6 **Xixian** Shanxi China
190 G6 **Xixian** *mountain* Shanxi China
188 E2 **Xixiang** Shaanxi China
189 H3 **Xiyang Dao** *island* Fujian China
188 E4 **Xiyang Jiang** *watercourse* Yunnan China
181 F2 **Xizang Zizhiqu** *admin. area* China
89 H5 **Xkanhá** Mexico
182 H5 **Xo'jayli** Uzbekistan
182 H5 **Xorazm** *admin. area* Uzbekistan
89 H5 **Xpujil** Mexico
189 H2 **Xuancheng** Anhui China
191 H5 **Xuanhua** Hebei China
188 D3 **Xuanwei** Yunnan China
189 G1 **Xuchang** Henan China
189 H2 **Xucheng** Jiangsu China
161 G3 **Xuddur** Somalia
161 H2 **Xudun** Somalia
188 C3 **Xue Shan** *range* Yunnan China
190 G5 **Xuejiawan** Nei Mongol Zizhiqu China
190 E6 **Xueshan** *mountain* Gansu China
189 G3 **Xujiang** Jiangxi China
191 K2 **Xun He** *watercourse* Heilongjiang China
181 G2 **Xung Qu** *watercourse* Xizang Zizhiqu China
191 H6 **Xunxian** Henan China
188 F2 **Xunyang** Shaanxi China
188 E1 **Xunyi** Shaanxi China
188 F5 **Xuwen** Guangdong China
188 E3 **Xuyong** Sichuan China
189 H1 **Xuzhou** Jiangsu China
133 D5 **Xylagani** Greece

Y

188 D2 **Ya'an** Sichuan China
198 C4 **Yaba** Indonesia
159 F4 **Yabassi** Cameroon
158 C3 **Yabayo** Côte d'Ivoire
107 G3 **Yabebyry** Paraguay
161 F3 **Yabēlo** Ethiopia
105 F4 **Yabeta** Bolivia
132 D4 **Yablanitsa** Bulgaria
132 E4 **Yablanovo** Bulgaria
135 AI5 **Yablon** *watercourse* Russian Federation
191 G2 **Yablon Ovyy Khrebet** *range* Russian Federation
123 P2 **Yablonovka** Russian Federation
135 X8 **Yablonovyy Khrebet** *range* Russian Federation
132 D1 **Yabluniv** Ukraine
132 D1 **Yablun'ka** Ukraine
159 E2 **Yabo** Nigeria
190 E5 **Yabrai Shan** *range* Nei Mongol Zizhiqu China
100 C5 **Yabuyanos** Peru
223 9 **Yacata** *island* Fiji
188 F5 **Yacha** Hainan China
80 C4 **Yachats** Oregon USA
188 E3 **Yachi He** *lake* Guizhou China
80 D4 **Yacolt** Washington USA
100 E3 **Yacuaray** Venezuela
106 F2 **Yacuiba** Argentina
105 E4 **Yacuma** *watercourse* Bolivia
107 G3 **Yacyretá Apipé, Embalse** *lake* Paraguay
182 H6 **Yadak** Iran
187 D8 **Yadgir** Karnataka India
187 D8 **Yadiki** Andhra Pradesh India
182 E2 **Yadrin** Russian Federation
189 I4 **Yaeyama Rettō** *island* Japan
155 I2 **Yafran** Libya
223 9 **Yagasa** *island* Fiji
133 F6 **Yağcılar** Turkey
58 T3 **Yaghan Basin** *underwater feature* Southern Ocean
121 Q5 **Yaglyayarvi** Russian Federation
182 G6 **Yagman** Turkmenistan
159 H2 **Yagoua** Cameroon
90 E2 **Yaguajay** Cuba
107 H4 **Yaguari** *watercourse* Uruguay
100 D5 **Yaguas** Peru
84 H6 **Yagui** *watercourse* Mexico
160 C3 **Yahila** Democratic Republic of Congo
160 C4 **Yahisuli** Democratic Republic of Congo
75 M8 **Yahk** British Columbia Canada
88 E4 **Yahualica** Mexico
160 C3 **Yahuma** Democratic Republic of Congo
194 C4 **Yai (Ye)** Myanmar
193 H4 **Yaita** Japan
164 3d **Yaiza** Canary Islands
193 H4 **Yaizu** Japan
89 G5 **Yajalón** Mexico
216 G3 **Yakabindie** WA Australia
199 G4 **Yakamul** Papua New Guinea
72 A5 **Yakan, Mys** *cape* Russian Federation
218 F3 **Yakara** Qld Australia
191 I2 **Yakeshi** Nei Mongol Zizhiqu China
80 E3 **Yakima** Washington USA
132 C4 **Yakimovo** Bulgaria
160 C3 **Yakiri** Democratic Republic of Congo
182 J6 **Yakkabog'** Uzbekistan
179 J4 **Yakmach** Pakistan
158 D2 **Yako** Burkina Faso
160 C3 **Yakoma** Democratic Republic of Congo
160 C3 **Yakonga** Democratic Republic of Congo
192 F5 **Yaku-shima** *island* Japan
193 I2 **Yakumo** Japan
74 B3 **Yakutat** Alaska USA
74 A3 **Yakutat Bay** Alaska USA
135 AA6 **Yakutsk** Russian Federation
181 G2 **Yala** Xizang Zizhiqu China
158 D2 **Yala** Ghana
187 E10 **Yala** Sri Lanka
194 D6 **Yala** Thailand
194 D6 **Yala** *admin. area* Thailand
158 C3 **Yalakoro** Guinea
217 L5 **Yalata** SA Australia
217 L5 **Yalata Roadhouse** SA Australia
217 L5 **Yalata Swamp** SA Australia
215 J6 **Yalboroo** Qld Australia
74 K8 **Yale** British Columbia Canada
82 J5 **Yale** Michigan USA
80 D4 **Yale Lake** Washington USA
216 E3 **Yalgar** *watercourse* WA Australia
158 D2 **Yalgo** Burkina Faso
216 E4 **Yalgoo** WA Australia
160 C4 **Yali** Democratic Republic of Congo
160 C3 **Yalibongo** Democratic Republic of Congo
159 I3 **Yalinga** Central African Republic
89 H4 **Yalkubul, Punta** *cape* Mexico
216 D3 **Yallalong** WA Australia
219 J3 **Yallaroi** NSW Australia
215 H8 **Yalleroi** Qld Australia
158 D2 **Yallo** Burkina Faso
218 G5 **Yallock** NSW Australia
159 H3 **Yaloké** Central African Republic
188 D3 **Yalong Jiang** *watercourse* Sichuan China
133 F5 **Yalova** *admin. area* Turkey
136 D4 **Yalpugh, Ozero** *lake* Ukraine
136 E4 **Yalta** Ukraine
132 E1 **Yaltushkiv** Ukraine
191 K4 **Yalu** *watercourse* Jilin China
160 C3 **Yalufi** Democratic Republic of Congo
182 J2 **Yalutorovsk** Russian Federation
160 C4 **Yaluwe** Democratic Republic of Congo
133 G6 **Yalvaç** Turkey
135 AC8 **Yam-Alin', Khrebet** *range* Russian Federation
109 5 **Yama, Punta** *cape* Isla de Pascua (Easter Island)
83 O3 **Yamachiche** Quebec Canada
192 F4 **Yamaguchi** Japan
134 O4 **Yamal, Poluostrov** *peninsula* Russian Federation
134 P5 **Yamalo-Nenetskiy Avtonomnyy Okrug** *admin. area* Russian Federation
190 G2 **Yamarovka** Russian Federation
91 G3 **Yamasá** Dominican Republic
219 K3 **Yamba** NSW Australia
219 P9 **Yambacoona** Tas. Australia
214 B7 **Yambah** NT Australia
158 B2 **Yambering** Guinea
100 D4 **Yambí, Mesa de** *region* Colombia
160 D3 **Yambio** Sudan
219 I5 **Yambira Mountain** NSW Australia
161 F2 **Yambo** Ethiopia
132 E4 **Yambol** Bulgaria
132 E4 **Yambol** *admin. area* Bulgaria
104 B2 **Yambrasbamba** Peru
134 R4 **Yambuto, Ozero** *lake* Russian Federation
104 B3 **Yamcay, Cerro** *mountain* Peru
198 D5 **Yamdena** *island* Indonesia
181 H5 **Yamethin** Myanmar
195 I2 **Y'Ami** *island* Philippines
199 F5 **Yamin, Puncak** *mountain* Indonesia
218 E2 **Yamma Yamma (MacKillop), Lake** Qld Australia
158 C3 **Yamoussoukro** Côte d'Ivoire
81 L6 **Yampa** Colorado USA
81 K6 **Yampa** *watercourse* Colorado USA
132 F1 **Yampil'** Ukraine
198 D4 **Yamtu, Tanjung** *cape* Indonesia
186 D4 **Yamunanagar** Haryana India
187 E10 **Yan Oya** *watercourse* Sri Lanka
191 I5 **Yan Shan** *range* Hebei China
132 C4 **Yana** Bulgaria
135 AB5 **Yana** *watercourse* Russian Federation
158 B3 **Yana** Sierra Leone
199 I6 **Yanaba Island** Papua New Guinea
104 B3 **Yanacancha** Peru
104 B3 **Yanahuanca** Peru
187 F8 **Yanam** Puducherry India
104 D4 **Yanama** Peru
190 G6 **Yan'an** Shaanxi China
104 D4 **Yanaoca** Peru
182 G2 **Yanaul** Russian Federation
100 C5 **Yanayacu** Peru
178 D5 **Yanbu' al Baḩr** Saudi Arabia
218 F4 **Yancannia** NSW Australia
218 F4 **Yancannia** *watercourse* NSW Australia
87 L2 **Yanceyville** North Carolina USA
189 H1 **Yancheng** Jiangsu China
188 D2 **Yancheng** Sichuan China
188 D2 **Yancheng** Sichuan China
216 D5 **Yanchep** WA Australia
190 F5 **Yanchi** Ningxia Huizu Zizhiqu China
190 G6 **Yanchuan** Shaanxi China
218 H6 **Yanco** NSW Australia
218 G4 **Yanda** *watercourse* NSW Australia
158 E3 **Yanda** Togo
216 G3 **Yandal** WA Australia
218 E3 **Yandama** *watercourse* NSW Australia
188 D2 **Yandao** Sichuan China
222 7 **Yandé, Île** *island* New Caledonia
212 E6 **Yandeyarra** WA Australia
216 D3 **Yandi** WA Australia
219 K2 **Yandina** Qld Australia
223 9a **Yandua** *island* Fiji
158 C2 **Yanfolila** Mali
188 D4 **Yang-Tsung Hai** *lake* Yunnan China
159 I3 **Yangalia** Central African Republic
160 C3 **Yangambi** Democratic Republic of Congo
189 F4 **Yangcheng** Guangdong China
188 E3 **Yangchuan** Guizhou China
189 F4 **Yangchun** Guangdong China
223 9 **Yangganga** *island* Fiji
191 H5 **Yanggao** Shanxi China
190 F5 **Yanghe** Ningxia Huizu Zizhiqu China
183 K5 **Yangiqŭrghon** Uzbekistan
183 K5 **Yangiyŭl** Uzbekistan
189 F4 **Yangjiang** Guangdong China
189 G4 **Yangming** Guangdong China
194 C3 **Yangon** *admin. area* Myanmar
194 C3 **Yangon (Rangoon)** Myanmar
121 T5 **Yangory** Russian Federation
121 R5 **Yangozero, Ozero** *lake* Russian Federation
191 H5 **Yangqu Shan** *mountain* Shanxi China
191 H5 **Yangquan** Shanxi China
188 F4 **Yangshuo** Guangxi Zhuangzu Zizhiqu China
Yangtze *see* **Jinsha** China
188 E1 **Yanguan** Gansu China
128 E2 **Yanguas** Spain
191 I5 **Yangxin** Shandong China
192 F3 **Yangyang** South Korea
189 H2 **Yangzhou** Jiangsu China
188 E1 **Yangzhou** Shaanxi China
104 D4 **Yani** Bolivia
218 B5 **Yaninee, Lake** SA Australia
121 S5 **Yanishpole** Russian Federation
121 Q6 **Yanis"yarvi, Ozero** *lake* Russian Federation
191 L4 **Yanji** Jilin China
188 D3 **Yanjing** Sichuan China
188 D3 **Yanjing** Yunnan China
135 Y7 **Yankan, Khrebet** *range* Russian Federation
158 D3 **Yankoman** Ghana
188 E2 **Yankou** Sichuan China
81 Q5 **Yankton** South Dakota USA
216 D1 **Yannarie** *watercourse* WA Australia
135 AD4 **Yano-Indigirskaya Nizmennost'** *region* Russian Federation
135 AC6 **Yano-Oymyakonskoye Nagor'ye** *region* Russian Federation
132 C1 **Yanoshi** Ukraine
134 R5 **Yanov-Stan** Russian Federation
185 H4 **Yanqi** Xinjiang Uygur Zizhiqu China
191 H5 **Yanqing** Beijing China
191 K3 **Yanshou** Heilongjiang China
135 AB5 **Yanskiy** Russian Federation
135 AB4 **Yanskiy Zaliv** *bay* Russian Federation
218 G3 **Yantabulla** NSW Australia
191 J5 **Yantai** Shandong China
218 F3 **Yantara Lake** NSW Australia
123 J5 **Yantarnyy** Russian Federation
132 D4 **Yantra** *watercourse* Bulgaria
100 B5 **Yantzaza** Ecuador
223 9a **Yanutua** *island* Fiji
139 F3 **Yanworth** Gloucestershire England UK
190 G6 **Yanzhang** Shaanxi China
191 H6 **Yanzhou** Shandong China
193 G4 **Yao** Japan
188 E1 **Yao Xian** Shaanxi China
194 C6 **Yao Yai, Ko** *island* Thailand
189 H2 **Yaodu** Anhui China
160 A3 **Yaoundé** Cameroon
222 6 **Yap** *admin. area* Federated States of Micronesia
222 6 **Yap** *island* Federated States of Micronesia
52 J7 **Yap Trench** *underwater feature* Pacific Ocean
105 E5 **Yapacani** *watercourse* Bolivia
104 A2 **Yapato, Punta** *cape* Peru
198 F4 **Yapen** *island* Indonesia
198 E4 **Yapen, Selat** *strait* Indonesia
107 G4 **Yapeyú** Argentina
214 F5 **Yappar** *watercourse* Qld Australia
199 G5 **Yapsiei** Papua New Guinea
223 9 **Yaqeta** *island* Fiji
88 C2 **Yaqui** *watercourse* Mexico
90 E2 **Yara** Cuba
100 D2 **Yaracuy** *admin. area* Venezuela
182 H6 **Yaradzhi** Turkmenistan
218 G1 **Yaraka** Qld Australia
133 F7 **Yaraş** Turkey
133 F6 **Yarbasan** Turkey
138 D4 **Yarcombe** Devon England UK
218 B5 **Yardea** SA Australia
136 D6 **Yardımcı Burnu** *cape* Turkey
139 I2 **Yare** *watercourse* England UK
105 G5 **Yaré** Bolivia
222 4 **Yaren** Nauru
100 C4 **Yari** *watercourse* Colombia
194 D6 **Yaring** Thailand
214 E6 **Yaringa** *watercourse* Qld Australia
216 D2 **Yaringa** WA Australia
100 D2 **Yaritagua** Venezuela
184 E5 **Yarkant He** *watercourse* Xinjiang Uygur Zizhiqu China
217 L5 **Yarle Lakes** SA Australia
216 D6 **Yarloop** WA Australia
181 F3 **Yarlung Zangbo Jiang** *watercourse* Xizang Zizhiqu China
141 G2 **Yarm** Stockton-on-Tees England UK
132 E1 **Yarmolyntsi** Ukraine
79 E11 **Yarmouth** Nova Scotia Canada
139 F4 **Yarmouth** Isle of Wight England UK
182 E1 **Yarnsk** Russian Federation
125 M2 **Yaroslavichi** Ukraine
182 C1 **Yaroslavl'** Russian Federation
182 C1 **Yaroslavskaya Oblast'** *admin. area* Russian Federation
216 D4 **Yarra Yarra Lakes** WA Australia
215 H4 **Yarrabah** Qld Australia
216 F3 **Yarrabubba** WA Australia
215 G3 **Yarraden** Qld Australia
219 I4 **Yarragrin** NSW Australia
212 C6 **Yarraloola** WA Australia
219 J2 **Yarraman** Qld Australia
219 H4 **Yarrawin** NSW Australia
218 G7 **Yarrawonga** Vic. Australia
212 F6 **Yarrie** WA Australia
134 P5 **Yarro-To** Russian Federation
219 J3 **Yarrowford** NSW Australia
142 F5 **Yarrowford** Scottish Borders Scotland UK
214 E4 **Yarrum** Qld Australia
218 F6 **Yarto** Vic. Australia
136 E1 **Yartsevo** Russian Federation
100 C3 **Yarumal** Colombia
185 J3 **Yaruu** Mongolia
106 D2 **Yarvicoya, Cerro** *mountain* Chile
132 E1 **Yaryshev** Ukraine
160 C4 **Yasa** Democratic Republic of Congo
135 AF5 **Yasachnaya** *watercourse* Russian Federation
178 G5 **Yāsāt, Al** *island* United Arab Emirates
159 F2 **Yashi** Nigeria
184 G6 **Yashil Tsho** *lake* Xizang Zizhiqu China
182 E4 **Yashkul'** Russian Federation
194 E4 **Yasothon** Thailand
219 I6 **Yass** NSW Australia
219 I6 **Yass** *watercourse* NSW Australia
158 E2 **Yassine** *watercourse* Benin
123 P4 **Yasski** Russian Federation
183 L6 **Yassy** *watercourse* Kyrgyzstan
178 G3 **Yāsūj** Iran
125 M1 **Yasyel'da** *watercourse* Belarus
105 E3 **Yata** *watercourse* Bolivia
155 G6 **Yatakala** Niger
138 E3 **Yate** South Gloucestershire England UK
222 7 **Yaté** New Caledonia
75 M3 **Yates** *watercourse* Alberta Canada
76 G1 **Yathkyed Lake** Nunavut Canada
160 C3 **Yatolema** Democratic Republic of Congo
181 H5 **Yatsauk** Myanmar
193 H4 **Yatsuga-take** *volcano* Japan
192 F5 **Yatsushiro** Japan
138 E3 **Yatton** North Somerset England UK
91 H3 **Yauco** Puerto Rico
104 B3 **Yauya** Peru
187 D7 **Yaval** Maharashtra India
183 K6 **Yavan** Tajikistan
100 D4 **Yavaraté** Brazil
88 C3 **Yávaros** Mexico
187 E7 **Yavatmal** Maharashtra India
90 E5 **Yaviza** Panama
125 L3 **Yavoriv** Ukraine
132 C1 **Yavory** Ukraine
184 G5 **Yawatongguz He** *watercourse* Xinjiang Uygur Zizhiqu China
158 B3 **Yawri Bay** *bay* Sierra Leone
139 G2 **Yaxley** Cambridgeshire England UK
160 C4 **Yayama** Democratic Republic of Congo
133 E6 **Yaylaköy** Turkey
179 H3 **Yazd** Iran
179 H3 **Yazd** *admin. area* Iran
133 E7 **Yazıköy** Turkey
86 F4 **Yazoo City** Mississippi USA
125 H4 **Ybbs** *watercourse* Austria
107 G2 **Yby Yaú** Paraguay
107 G3 **Ybycuí** Paraguay
122 F5 **Yderby** Denmark
122 E5 **Yding Skovhøj** *mountain* Denmark
122 H4 **Ydrefors** Sweden
Ye *see* **Yai** Myanmar
181 G5 **Ye Kyun** Myanmar
181 H4 **Ye-u** Myanmar
83 N7 **Yeadon** Pennsylvania USA
216 E6 **Yealering** WA Australia
138 D4 **Yealmpton** Devon England UK
191 I4 **Yebaishou** Liaoning China
155 J4 **Yebbi Bou** Chad
156 B3 **Yebbi Bou** Chad
129 F2 **Yebra de Basa** Spain
129 F4 **Yecla** Spain
88 C2 **Yécora** Mexico
181 H5 **Yedashe** Myanmar
161 F2 **YeDedub Bihēroch Bihēresboch na Hizboch** *admin. area* Ethiopia
141 H2 **Yedingham** North Yorkshire England UK
161 G3 **Yeed** Somalia
198 D4 **Yef Lio** Indonesia
183 L3 **Yegindybulak** Kazakhstan
160 E3 **Yei** Sudan
160 E3 **Yei** *watercourse* Sudan
158 D3 **Yeji** Ghana
160 C3 **Yekana** Democratic Republic of Congo
182 H2 **Yekaterinburg** Russian Federation
193 J2 **Yekateriny, Proliv** *lake* Russian Federation
183 M4 **Yekiasha** Kazakhstan
160 C3 **Yekokora** *watercourse* Democratic Republic of Congo
74 I5 **Yekooche** British Columbia Canada
182 D3 **Yelan'** Russian Federation
132 G2 **Yelanets'** Ukraine
219 J3 **Yelarbon** Qld Australia
182 D2 **Yelatma** Russian Federation
187 D8 **Yelbarga** Karnataka India
108 B3 **Yelcho, Lago** *lake* Chile
133 F6 **Yeleğen** Turkey
136 F2 **Yelets** Russian Federation
154 D5 **Yelimané** Mali
135 AD8 **Yelizavety, Mys** *cape* Russian Federation
135 AG8 **Yelizovo** Russian Federation
182 F2 **Yelkhovka** Russian Federation
187 D8 **Yellapur** Karnataka India
140 B3 **Yellow Furze** Ireland
75 S8 **Yellow Grass** Saskatchewan Canada
82 E4 **Yellow Lake** Minnesota USA
218 H5 **Yellow Mountain** NSW Australia
189 I1 **Yellow Sea (Huang Hai)**
216 F5 **Yellowdine** WA Australia
140 B4 **Yellowford** Ireland
75 N1 **Yellowknife** Northwest Territories Canada
81 J4 **Yellowstone** *watercourse* Montana USA
81 J4 **Yellowstone Lake** Wyoming USA
86 E2 **Yellville** Arkansas USA
80 D3 **Yelm** Washington USA
134 S6 **Yeloguy** *watercourse* Russian Federation
183 N4 **Yel'tay** Kazakhstan
190 G6 **Yan'an** Shaanxi China
214 E6 **Yelvertoft** Qld Australia
138 C4 **Yelverton** Devon England UK
73 K2 **Yelverton Bay** Nunavut Canada
159 F3 **Yelwa** Nigeria
185 J5 **Yema He** *watercourse* Gansu China
185 J5 **Yema Nanshan** *range* Gansu China
87 K4 **Yemassee** South Carolina USA
178 F7 **Yemen** *country*
123 O5 **Yemenets** Russian Federation
159 G4 **Yen** Cameroon
194 E2 **Yên Bái** Vietnam
194 E2 **Yên Châu** Vietnam
194 E2 **Yên Viên** Vietnam
121 Q3 **Yëna** Russian Federation
159 F4 **Yenagoa** Nigeria
136 F3 **Yenakiyevo** Ukraine
181 H5 **Yenangyaun** Myanmar
198 E4 **Yende** Indonesia
158 D3 **Yendi** Ghana
159 G5 **Yénéganou** Congo
160 C4 **Yenge** *watercourse* Democratic Republic of Congo
158 B3 **Yengema** Sierra Leone
184 E5 **Yengisar** Xinjiang Uygur Zizhiqu China
219 J5 **Yengo, Mount** NSW Australia
188 C3 **Yengsheng** Yunnan China
133 E6 **Yenice** Turkey
133 F6 **Yenicekent** Turkey
133 E6 **Yenifoça** Turkey
133 E7 **Yenihisar** Turkey
133 F6 **Yeniköy** Turkey
133 G7 **Yenimahalle** Turkey
133 F6 **Yenişehir** Turkey
133 F5 **Yenişehir** Turkey
134 T7 **Yenisey** *watercourse* Russian Federation
134 T7 **Yeniseysk** Russian Federation
134 T7 **Yeniseyskiy Kryazh** *range* Russian Federation
134 R4 **Yeniseyskiy Zaliv** *bay* Russian Federation
127 G4 **Yenne** France
121 T2 **Yenozero, Ozero** *lake* Russian Federation
138 E4 **Yeo** *watercourse* England UK
217 I3 **Yeo Lake** WA Australia
192 E4 **Yeongheung-do** *island* South Korea
219 I5 **Yeoval** NSW Australia
138 E4 **Yeovil** Somerset England UK
88 C2 **Yepachic** Mexico
134 P5 **Yepoko** Russian Federation
215 K7 **Yeppoon** Qld Australia
182 H6 **Yerbent** Turkmenistan
182 D6 **Yerevan** Armenia
183 L3 **Yereymentau** Kazakhstan
80 F7 **Yerington** Nevada USA
134 Q6 **Yerkalnadeypur** *watercourse* Russian Federation
132 G1 **Yerky** Ukraine
133 E5 **Yerlisu** Turkey
57 G1 **Yermak Plateau** *underwater feature* Arctic Ocean
58 K2 **Yermak Point** Antarctica
134 L5 **Yermitsa** Russian Federation
85 J7 **Yermo** Mexico
135 Z8 **Yerofey Pavlovich** Russian Federation
135 AI5 **Yeropol** Russian Federation
126 F2 **Yerres** *watercourse* France
182 E3 **Yershov** Russian Federation
134 K6 **Yërtom** Russian Federation
104 B3 **Yerupajá, Nevado** *mountain* Peru
178 C3 **Yerushaylim/Al Quds (Jerusalem)** *disputed territory* Middle East
139 H5 **Yerville** France
138 D4 **Yes Tor** *mountain* England UK
129 F2 **Yesa, Embalse de** *lake* Spain
181 H5 **Yesagyo** Myanmar
183 M5 **Yesik** Kazakhstan
182 J3 **Yesil'** Kazakhstan
182 D5 **Yessentuki** Russian Federation
135 V5 **Yessey** Russian Federation
135 V5 **Yessey, Ozero** *lake* Russian Federation
141 G1 **Yetlington** Northumberland England UK
126 C3 **Yeu, Île d'** *island* France
123 P5 **Yevdokimovichi** Belarus
136 E4 **Yevpatoriya** Ukraine
135 AB9 **Yevreyskaya** *admin. area* Russian Federation
191 L3 **Yevreyskaya Avtonomnaya Oblast'** *admin. area* Russian Federation
158 E3 **Yewa** *watercourse* Nigeria
182 C4 **Yeysk** Russian Federation
188 F2 **Yezhou** Hubei China
188 F2 **Yezhou** Hubei China
107 H3 **Ygatimí** Paraguay
126 D5 **Ygos-Saint-Saturnin** France
135 Y6 **Ygyatta** *watercourse* Russian Federation
107 H3 **Yhú** Paraguay
191 K3 **Yi'an** Heilongjiang China
188 D3 **Yibin** Sichuan China
189 F2 **Yichang** Hubei China
189 F2 **Yicheng** Hubei China
190 G6 **Yicheng** Shanxi China
189 F1 **Yichuan** Henan China
191 K3 **Yichun** Heilongjiang China
189 G3 **Yichun** Jiangxi China
189 F2 **Yidu** Hubei China
133 G5 **Yığılca** Turkey
222 5 **Yigo** Guam
189 H3 **Yijiang** Jiangxi China
190 G6 **Yijun** Shaanxi China
191 L3 **Yilan** Heilongjiang China
136 F5 **Yıldız Dağı** *mountain* Turkey
188 D3 **Yili He** *watercourse* Yunnan China
216 E6 **Yilliminning** WA Australia
188 D4 **Yilong Hu** *lake* Yunnan China
189 F1 **Yima** Henan China
199 G4 **Yimi** *watercourse* Papua New Guinea
133 C6 **Yimnón** Greece
190 G4 **Yin Shan** *range* Nei Mongol Zizhiqu China
190 F5 **Yinchuan** Ningxia Huizu Zizhiqu China
216 H5 **Yindana, Lake** WA Australia
216 H5 **Yindarlgooda, Lake** WA Australia
216 H5 **Yindi** WA Australia
181 H2 **Yinduo** Xizang Zizhiqu China
191 H5 **Ying Xian** Shanxi China
189 G2 **Yingcheng** Hubei China
189 G4 **Yingde** Guangdong China
188 F5 **Yinggen** Hainan China
191 J5 **Yingkou** Liaoning China
189 G2 **Yingshang** Anhui China
189 H3 **Yingtan** Jiangxi China
159 G4 **Yingui** Cameroon
189 G2 **Yining** Jiangxi China
184 G4 **Yining** Xinjiang Uygur Zizhiqu China
181 H4 **Yinmabin** Myanmar
216 E2 **Yinnetharra** WA Australia
181 H2 **Yi'ong Zangbo** *watercourse* Xizang Zizhiqu China
161 F2 **Yirga Alem** Ethiopia
161 F2 **Yirga Ch'efē** Ethiopia
160 E2 **Yirol** Sudan
214 D2 **Yirrkala** NT Australia
188 D4 **Yisa** Yunnan China
189 H1 **Yishan** Jiangsu China
191 I6 **Yishui** Shandong China
196 D2 **Yishun** *admin. area* Singapore
190 E5 **Yitiaoshan** Gansu China
191 K4 **Yitong** Jilin China
185 J4 **Yiwu** Xinjiang Uygur Zizhiqu China
188 D4 **Yiwu** Yunnan China
189 H2 **Yiwu** Zhejiang China
189 F1 **Yiyang** Henan China
189 F3 **Yiyang** Hunan China
189 F3 **Yizhang** Hunan China
189 H2 **Yizheng** Jiangsu China
188 E4 **Yizhou** Guangxi Zhuangzu Zizhiqu China
191 H5 **Yizhou** Hebei China
191 J4 **Yizhou** Liaoning China
123 L2 **Yläne** Finland
121 N4 **Yli-Ii** Finland
121 P3 **Yli-Kitka** *lake* Finland
121 N5 **Yli-Lesti** Finland
121 M2 **Yli-Muonio** Finland
121 P3 **Yli-Suolijärvi** *lake* Finland
121 M5 **Ylihärmä** Finland
121 N4 **Ylikärppä** Finland
121 O4 **Ylikiiminki** Finland
121 M3 **Ylinenjärvi** Finland
121 N3 **Ylipää** Finland
120 M5 **Ylistaro** Finland
121 M3 **Ylitornio** Finland
121 N4 **Ylivieska** Finland
121 M5 **Yliviirre** Finland
120 H4 **Ylvingen** Norway
120 H4 **Ylvingen** *island* Norway
73 Q3 **Ymer Nunatak** *mountain* Greenland
73 Q4 **Ymer Øer** *island* Greenland
74 M8 **Ymir** British Columbia Canada
122 G3 **Ymsen** *lake* Sweden
122 H3 **Yngen** *lake* Sweden
183 K4 **Yntaly** Kazakhstan
138 D3 **Ynysddu** Caerphilly Wales UK
86 C6 **Yoakum** Texas USA
159 G2 **Yobe** *admin. area* Nigeria
193 I2 **Yobetsu-dake** *volcano* Japan
157 G5 **Yoboki** Djibouti
105 E5 **Yocalla** Bolivia
138 E2 **Yockleton** Shropshire England UK
85 J1 **Yoder** Colorado USA
81 M6 **Yoder** Wyoming USA
199 F5 **Yodom** Indonesia
199 F5 **Yofor** Indonesia
197 F5 **Yogyakarta** Indonesia
197 F6 **Yogyakarta** *admin. area* Indonesia
192 E4 **Yŏju** South Korea
159 H4 **Yokadouma** Cameroon
141 H3 **Yokefleet** East Riding of Yorkshire England UK
216 H6 **Yokinup Bay** WA Australia
159 G3 **Yoko** Cameroon
189 J3 **Yokoate-shima** *island* Japan
193 H4 **Yokohama** Japan
193 I3 **Yokote** Japan
186 D4 **Yol** Himachal Pradesh India
159 G3 **Yola** Nigeria
160 C4 **Yolombo** Democratic Republic of Congo
182 I6 **Yolöten** Turkmenistan
100 C4 **Yomaira** Colombia
159 G5 **Yombi** Gabon
158 C3 **Yomou** Guinea
181 G3 **Yomtam** Arunachal Pradesh India
199 F5 **Yomuka** Indonesia
126 D3 **Yon** *watercourse* France
222 5 **Yona** Guam
192 G4 **Yonago** Japan
189 I4 **Yonaguni Jima** *island* Japan
192 E4 **Yonan** North Korea
80 D5 **Yoncalla** Oregon USA
189 H3 **Yong'an** Fujian China
188 E2 **Yongchang** Chongqing China
190 E5 **Yongchang** Gansu China
190 E6 **Yongdeng** Gansu China
188 D3 **Yongding** Yunnan China
192 F4 **Yŏngdŏk** South Korea
189 F3 **Yongfeng** Hunan China
188 F4 **Yongfu** Guangxi Zhuangzu Zizhiqu China
192 E4 **Yŏnggwang** South Korea
190 G6 **Yonghe** Shanxi China
192 E3 **Yŏnghŭng** North Korea
188 F1 **Yongji** Shanxi China
188 E3 **Yongjing** Guizhou China
192 F4 **Yŏngju** South Korea
188 F1 **Yongle** Shaanxi China
189 G3 **Yongning** Jiangxi China
188 E1 **Yongqing** Gansu China
191 H5 **Yongqing** Hebei China
192 F4 **Yŏngwol** South Korea
188 E3 **Yongxi** Guizhou China
189 G3 **Yongxing** Hunan China
188 E3 **Yongyang** Guizhou China
189 F3 **Yongzhou** Hunan China
158 B3 **Yonibana** Sierra Leone
83 O6 **Yonkers** New York USA
126 F2 **Yonne** *watercourse* France
154 D5 **Yonoféré** Senegal
192 F3 **Yŏnsa** North Korea
218 H6 **Yoogali** NSW Australia
100 C3 **Yopal** Colombia
216 E5 **York** WA Australia
141 G3 **York** *admin. area* England UK
141 G3 **York** York England UK
86 G4 **York** Alabama USA
81 Q6 **York** Nebraska USA
83 M7 **York** Pennsylvania USA
87 K3 **York** South Carolina USA
87 M2 **York** *watercourse* Virginia USA
214 G1 **York, Cape** Qld Australia
108 A5 **York, Isla Duque de** *island* Chile
213 H3 **York, Mount** WA Australia
76 I4 **York Factory** Manitoba Canada
75 W4 **York Landing** Manitoba Canada
213 H3 **York Sound** WA Australia
83 M6 **York Springs** Pennsylvania USA
218 C6 **Yorke Peninsula** SA Australia
218 C6 **Yorketown** SA Australia
219 K3 **Yorklea** NSW Australia
216 E5 **Yorkrakine** WA Australia
141 H2 **Yorkshire Wolds** *region* England UK

75 T7 Yorkton Saskatchewan Canada
86 C6 Yorktown Texas USA
216 E6 Yornaning WA Australia
216 E7 Yornup WA Australia
90 C4 Yoro Honduras
189 J3 Yoro-shima island Japan
193 H4 Yoroi-gata lake Japan
189 J3 Yoron-jima island Japan
158 D2 Yorosso Mali
138 E2 Yorton Shropshire England UK
160 C3 Yoseki Democratic Republic of Congo
84 C2 Yosemite Village California USA
182 E2 Yoshkar-Ola Russian Federation
192 E5 Yoso-do island South Korea
192 E4 Yosu South Korea
100 B4 Yotoco Colombia
100 C2 Yotójohoin Colombia
188 E4 You Jiang watercourse Guangxi Zhuangzu Zizhiqu China
188 F3 You Shui watercourse Hunan China
189 H3 You Xi watercourse Fujian China
189 G3 You Xian Hunan China
216 F4 Youangarra WA Australia
129 F6 Youb Algeria
188 C4 Youdian Yunnan China
188 D1 Youganning Qinghai China
143 E5 Youghal Ireland
143 E5 Youghal Bay Ireland
158 B2 Youkounkoun Guinea
141 G3 Youlgreave Derbyshire England UK
216 E5 Youndegin WA Australia
219 I6 Young NSW Australia
75 S7 Young Saskatchewan Canada
107 G5 Young Uruguay
221 6 Young, Cape Chatham Islands New Zealand
87 J3 Young Harris Georgia USA
58 K2 Young Island Antarctica
220 G4 Young Nicks Head cape New Zealand
218 G3 Youngerina NSW Australia
218 C4 Younghusband, Lake SA Australia
83 K6 Youngstown Ohio USA
83 L6 Youngsville Pennsylvania USA
83 L6 Youngwood Pennsylvania USA
154 F5 Youvarou Mali
77 Q2 Youville, Monts D' mountains Quebec Canada
189 H3 Youxi Fujian China
191 L3 Youyi Heilongjiang China
123 N2 Yövesi bay Finland
218 G2 Yowah Qld Australia
218 G2 Yowah watercourse Qld Australia
219 I7 Yowrie NSW Australia
139 F2 Yoxall Staffordshire England UK
139 I2 Yoxford Suffolk England UK
219 H2 Yoyo Park Qld Australia
136 E5 Yozgat Turkey
136 E5 Yozgat admin. area Turkey
123 L2 Ypäjä Finland
107 G2 Ypané watercourse Paraguay
139 H5 Yport France
121 N4 Yppäri Finland
82 J5 Ypsilanti Michigan USA
121 P4 Ypykkä Finland
107 G6 Yráizoz Argentina
80 D6 Yreka California USA
199 I4 Ysabel Channel strait Papua New Guinea
138 D1 Ysbyty Ifan Conwy Wales UK
126 G4 Yssingeaux France
122 G5 Ystad Sweden
138 D3 Ystalyfera Powys Wales UK
138 D2 Ystrad Ffin Carmarthenshire Wales UK
138 D3 Ystradfellte Powys Wales UK
183 M5 Ysyk-Köl admin. area Kyrgyzstan
183 M5 Ysyk-Köl lake Kyrgyzstan
142 F3 Ythan watercourse Scotland UK
122 D2 Ytre Frønningan Norway
121 O1 Ytre Korsnes Norway
122 E3 Ytre Ramse Norway
120 inset Ytri-Rangá watercourse Iceland
120 I5 Ytterån Sweden
120 I5 Ytterhogdal Sweden
121 M5 Ytterjeppo Finland
122 G2 Yttermalung Sweden
120 K5 Yttre Lemelsjön lake Sweden
135 AB6 Ytyk-Kyuyel' Russian Federation
198 D4 Yu island Indonesia
189 H4 Yu Shan mountain Taiwan China
189 H4 Yu-Weng Tao island Taiwan China
191 H5 Yu Xian Shanxi China
188 F3 Yuan Jiang watercourse Hunan China
188 D4 Yuan Jiang watercourse Yunnan China
189 G3 Yuan Shui watercourse Jiangxi China
188 F3 Yuanbao Shan mountain Guangxi Zhuangzu Zizhiqu China
188 E1 Yuanjiazhuang Shaanxi China
191 J2 Yuanlin Nei Mongol Zizhiqu China
188 F3 Yuanling Hunan China
188 D3 Yuanma Yunnan China
191 G5 Yuanping Shanxi China
185 J5 Yuanquan Gansu China
189 G4 Yuanshan Guangdong China
199 H5 Yuat watercourse Papua New Guinea
80 E7 Yuba City California USA
161 F2 Yubdo Ethiopia
84 D3 Yucaipa California USA
100 C4 Yucalito Colombia
89 H4 Yucatán admin. area Mexico
90 B3 Yucatán, Península de region Mexico
53 X5 Yucatan Basin underwater feature Caribbean Sea
90 C2 Yucatán Channel Mexico
84 E3 Yucca Arizona USA
84 D3 Yucca Valley California USA
191 H6 Yucheng Shandong China
191 J2 Yudi Shan mountain Nei Mongol Zizhiqu China
182 G6 Yūdkā Iran
135 AC6 Yudoma-Krestovskaya Russian Federation
188 D3 Yuecheng Sichuan China
185 J6 Yuegaitan Qinghai China
191 L3 Yuelai Heilongjiang China
214 B7 Yuelamu NT Australia
214 A7 Yuendumu NT Australia
184 E5 Yuepuhu Xinjiang Uygur Zizhiqu China
189 G2 Yueyang Hunan China
188 E2 Yueyang Sichuan China
135 AC7 Yugorenok Russian Federation
134 N5 Yugorskiy Poluostrov peninsula Russian Federation
134 J6 Yugra watercourse Russian Federation
189 H2 Yuhang Zhejiang China
188 C3 Yuhu Yunnan China
189 I3 Yuhuan Zhejiang China
189 I3 Yuhuan Dao island Zhejiang China
191 I6 Yuhuang Ding (Tai Shan) mountain Shandong China
216 E3 Yuin WA Australia
188 D2 Yujin Sichuan China
135 AG5 Yukagirskoye Ploskogor'ye region Russian Federation
133 F6 Yukari Mezit Turkey
133 E6 Yukarıbey Turkey
182 F2 Yukhmachi Russian Federation
136 E1 Yukhnov Russian Federation
123 P4 Yukhovo Russian Federation
160 B4 Yuki Democratic Republic of Congo
123 P2 Yukki Russian Federation
72 E6 Yukon watercourse Yukon Territory Canada
72 D6 Yukon watercourse Alaska USA
72 C6 Yukon River Delta Alaska USA
72 E6 Yukon Territory admin. area Canada
136 H6 Yüksekova Turkey
192 F5 Yukuhashi Japan
182 H3 Yuldybayevo Russian Federation
212 E6 Yule watercourse WA Australia
58 L2 Yule Bay Antarctica
219 I2 Yuleba Qld Australia
184 H4 Yuli Xinjiang Uygur Zizhiqu China
188 F4 Yulin Guangxi Zhuangzu Zizhiqu China
190 G5 Yulin Shaanxi China
108 B3 Yulton, Lago lake Chile
121 R4 Yuma Russian Federation
84 E4 Yuma Arizona USA
81 N6 Yuma Colorado USA
182 G3 Yumaguzino Russian Federation
105 F6 Yumao, Cerros de range Bolivia
160 B4 Yumbi Democratic Republic of Congo
100 B4 Yumbo Colombia
185 K5 Yumen Gansu China
188 F2 Yun Xian Hubei China
216 D4 Yuna WA Australia
135 AM8 Yunaska Island Alaska USA
188 F1 Yuncheng Shanxi China
133 C4 Yundola Bulgaria
188 D3 Yunfu Sichuan China
215 H4 Yungaburra Qld Australia
188 C3 Yunhe Yunnan China
189 H3 Yunhe Zhejiang China
189 H4 Yunling Fujian China
189 G2 Yunmeng Hubei China
188 D4 Yunnan admin. area China
218 D5 Yunta SA Australia
191 H4 Yunwu Shan mountain Beijing China
188 F2 Yunxi Hubei China
188 E2 Yunxi Sichuan China
188 E2 Yunyang Chongqing China
217 M3 Yunyarinyi (Kenmore Park) SA Australia
106 C6 Yupehue Chile
188 E3 Yuping Guizhou China
188 D4 Yuping Yunnan China
105 F6 Yuquirendita Bolivia
104 D5 Yura Peru
123 M5 Yuratsishki Belarus
133 F6 Yüreğil Turkey
183 N2 Yurga Russian Federation
134 Q4 Yuribey Russian Federation
134 P5 Yuribey watercourse Russian Federation
104 B2 Yurimaguas Peru
135 U7 Yurokhta Russian Federation
134 K5 Yuroma Russian Federation
134 O7 Yurovsk Russian Federation
104 E5 Yuruma Bolivia
184 F6 Yurungkax He watercourse Xinjiang Uygur Zizhiqu China
90 C4 Yuscarán Honduras
121 Q4 Yushkozero Russian Federation
191 K4 Yushu Jilin China
182 J7 Yūsof Mīrzā'ī Afghanistan
182 E4 Yusta Russian Federation
189 F3 Yutan Hunan China
81 Q6 Yutan Nebraska USA
191 I5 Yutian Hebei China
189 H3 Yutou Dao island Fujian China
107 G3 Yuty Paraguay
124 D3 Yutz France
188 E3 Yuxi Guizhou China
188 D4 Yuxi Yunnan China
189 I2 Yuyao Zhejiang China
100 B4 Yuyero Colombia
193 I3 Yuzawa Japan
182 D2 Yuzha Russian Federation
132 G2 Yuzhne Ukraine
193 I1 Yuzhno-Kamyshovyy Khrebet range Russian Federation
183 J5 Yuzhno-Kazakhstanskaya Oblast' admin. area Kazakhstan
135 X7 Yuzhno-Muyskiy Khrebet range Russian Federation
135 AD9 Yuzhno Sakhalinsk Russian Federation
183 N2 Yuzhnyy Russian Federation
135 AG7 Yuzhnyy, Mys cape Russian Federation
183 O3 Yuzhnyy Altay, Khrebet range Kazakhstan
190 E6 Yuzhong Gansu China
191 H5 Yuzhou Hebei China
189 G1 Yuzhou Henan China
127 H3 Yverdon Switzerland
139 H5 Yvetot France
124 C2 Yvoir Belgium
181 H5 Ywangan Myanmar
122 I4 Yxern lake Sweden
123 J3 Yxlan island Sweden
182 H5 Ýylanly Turkmenistan
126 F3 Yzeure France

Z

181 H2 Za Qu watercourse Qinghai China
190 E3 Zaamar Mongolia
190 E3 Zaamar Uul mountain Mongolia
124 C1 Zaanstad Netherlands
128 D6 Zaaroura Morocco
132 B3 Žabalj Serbia
132 B3 Žabari Serbia
178 E7 Zabīd Yemen
130 H5 Žabljak Montenegro
130 G4 Žabno Croatia
125 K2 Żabno Poland
179 K3 Zābol admin. area Afghanistan
179 J3 Zābol Iran
125 M2 Zabolottsy Ukraine
123 O5 Zabor'ye Belarus
123 P5 Zabor'ye Russian Federation
132 B2 Zăbrani Romania
158 D2 Zabre Burkina Faso
130 G2 Zábřeh Czech Republic
130 G5 Zabrišće Bosnia and Herzegovina
125 J2 Zabrze Poland
125 K3 Zabrzeż Poland
125 H4 Zabukovica Slovenia
182 F4 Zaburunye Kazakhstan
90 B4 Zacapa Guatemala
88 E5 Zacapú Mexico
88 E4 Zacatecas Mexico
88 E4 Zacatecas admin. area Mexico
133 B7 Zacharo Greece
86 F5 Zachary Louisiana USA
123 O5 Zachist'ye Belarus
125 H1 Zachodniopomorskie admin. area Poland
124 G1 Zachow Germany
125 H2 Žacléř Czech Republic
89 F4 Zacualtipán Mexico
194 C5 Zadetkale Kyun Myanmar
194 C5 Zadetkyi Kyun Myanmar
82 J2 Zadi Lake Ontario Canada
125 J2 Zadzim Poland
156 E2 Za'farānah Egypt
186 D4 Zafarwal Punjab India
132 E3 Zafirovo Bulgaria
128 C4 Zafra Spain
127 K3 Žaga Slovenia
199 G6 Zagai Island Qld Australia
131 E6 Zagarolo Italy
155 I1 Zaghouan Tunisia
133 C5 Zagkliveri Greece
132 E3 Zagon Romania
133 C6 Zagorá Greece
154 E2 Zagora Morocco
125 H4 Zagorci Slovenia
130 F4 Zagreb Croatia
188 D2 Zagu'nao Sichuan China
181 F2 Zagungngomar mountain Xizang Zizhiqu China
125 K4 Zagyva watercourse Hungary
179 I3 Zāhedān Iran
187 D8 Zahirabad Andhra Pradesh India
178 C2 Zahlé Lebanon
124 G2 Zahna Germany
123 N4 Zaiceva Latvia
132 F2 Zaim Moldova
108 B2 Zaina Yegua Argentina
128 E6 Zaïo Morocco
160 A5 Zaire admin. area Angola
136 B3 Zakarpats'ka Oblast' admin. area Ukraine
182 E5 Zakataly Azerbaijan
136 F1 Zakharovo Russian Federation
136 B2 Zakhidnyy Buh watercourse Ukraine
178 E1 Zakho Iraq
121 T2 Zakhrebetnoye Russian Federation
159 F3 Zaki Biam Nigeria
125 L2 Zaklików Poland
125 J3 Zakopane Poland
125 K1 Zakroczym Poland
125 L2 Zakrzówek Poland
132 E1 Zakupne Ukraine
133 B7 Zakynthos island Greece
125 I4 Zala admin. area Hungary
125 I4 Zala watercourse Hungary
125 I4 Zalaegerszeg Hungary
125 I4 Zalakomár Hungary
130 G3 Zalalövő Hungary
128 C5 Zalamea la Real Spain
159 G2 Zalanga Nigeria
191 J3 Zalantun Nei Mongol Zizhiqu China
135 V8 Zalari Russian Federation
183 S2 Zalari Russian Federation
132 C2 Zalau Romania
125 H4 Žalec Slovenia
132 B1 Zalesie Poland
125 J1 Zalewo Poland
178 E5 Ẓalim Saudi Arabia
156 C5 Zalingei Sudan
123 K5 Zalivino Russian Federation
132 H2 Zaliznyy Port Ukraine
132 D1 Zaliztsi Ukraine
126 C5 Zalla Spain
123 L5 Žaltytis lake Lithuania
123 P4 Zaluch'ye Russian Federation
194 B3 Zalun Myanmar
132 C2 Zam Romania
155 G6 Zama Niger
74 L3 Zama Lake Alberta Canada
104 C4 Zamaca Peru
189 J3 Zamami-jima island Japan
186 F6 Zamania Uttar Pradesh India
163 G3 Zambeze watercourse Mozambique
160 C6 Zambezi watercourse Angola
160 C6 Zambezi Zambia
162 D2 Zambezi watercourse Zambia
162 E3 Zambezi Escarpment range Zambia
163 G3 Zambezia admin. area Mozambique
162 E2 Zambia country Africa
195 I6 Zamboanga Philippines
125 L1 Zambrów Poland
163 F3 Zambué Mozambique
125 H2 Zamek Czocha lake Poland
159 F2 Zamfara admin. area Nigeria
159 F2 Zamfara watercourse Nigeria
100 B6 Zamora Ecuador
89 I6 Zamora Honduras
100 B5 Zamora watercourse Peru
128 D3 Zamora Spain
100 B6 Zamora-Chinchipe admin. area Ecuador
88 E5 Zamora de Hidalgo Mexico
125 L2 Zamość Poland
178 D5 Zamrat 'Aqabah Saudi Arabia
100 D2 Zamuro, Punta cape Venezuela
101 F3 Zamuro, Sierra del range Venezuela
104 B2 Zaña Peru
159 G5 Zanaga Congo
128 E4 Záncara watercourse Spain
83 J7 Zanesville Ohio USA
105 G5 Zanetti Brazil
158 C2 Zangasso Mali
159 I4 Zangba Central African Republic
159 F2 Zango Nigeria
184 H6 Zangser Kangri mountain Xizang Zizhiqu China
191 H5 Zanhuang Hebei China
182 E7 Zanjān Iran
182 E7 Zanjān admin. area Iran
108 D2 Zanjón de Oyuela Argentina
186 D4 Zanskar watercourse Jammu and Kashmir India/Pakistan
123 L4 Zante Latvia
217 H5 Zanthus WA Australia
158 C2 Zantié Bougou Mali
134 K6 Zanul'ye Russian Federation
161 F5 Zanzibar Tanzania
161 F5 Zanzibar Island island Tanzania
161 F5 Zanzibar North admin. area Tanzania
161 F5 Zanzibar South and Central admin. area Tanzania
161 F5 Zanzibar West admin. area Tanzania
193 I3 Zaō-zan volcano Japan
159 H3 Zaorosongou Central African Republic
189 F3 Zaoshi Hunan China
123 Q2 Zaostrov'ye Russian Federation
189 F2 Zaoyang Hubei China
183 Q2 Zaozernyy Russian Federation
189 H1 Zaozhuang Shandong China
81 O3 Zap North Dakota USA
132 B4 Zapadna Morava watercourse Serbia
123 Q4 Zapadnaya Dvina Russian Federation
182 C4 Zapadno Kapitalnaya Russian Federation
182 F3 Zapadno-Kazakhstanskaya Oblast' admin. area Kazakhstan
135 AD9 Zapadno Sakhalinskiye Gory range Russian Federation
134 Q6 Zapadno-Sibirskaya Ravnina mountain Russian Federation
72 A4 Zapadnyy, Mys Russian Federation
121 S2 Zapadnyy Kil'din Russian Federation
183 P3 Zapadnyy Sayan range Russian Federation
106 D6 Zapala Argentina
106 E2 Zapaleri, Cerro mountain Chile
86 B7 Zapata Texas USA
108 B5 Zapata, Cerro mountain Chile
90 D2 Zapata, Península de peninsula Cuba
100 C3 Zapatoca Colombia
100 C2 Zapatosa, Cienaga de lake Colombia
85 J7 Zapién Mexico
104 D5 Zapiga Chile
51 N14 Zapiola Ridge underwater feature Atlantic Ocean
51 P13 Zapiola Seamount underwater feature Atlantic Ocean
123 O3 Zapol'ye Russian Federation
88 E4 Zapopan Mexico
136 E3 Zaporizhzhya Ukraine
136 E3 Zaporiz'ka Oblast' admin. area Ukraine
123 P2 Zaporozhskoye Russian Federation
131 F6 Zapponeta Italy
125 M1 Zaprudy Belarus
Zaqatala see Zakataly Azerbaijan
190 D3 Zar Mongolia
100 D3 Zaracure Colombia
182 I5 Zarafshon Uzbekistan
100 C3 Zaragoza Colombia
88 D2 Zaragoza Mexico
129 F3 Zaragoza Spain
133 D6 Zárakes Greece
179 H3 Zarand Iran
179 J3 Zaranj Afghanistan
123 N5 Zarasai Lithuania
107 G5 Zárate Argentina
100 C2 Zarate, Cienaga de watercourse Colombia
128 E2 Zarautz Spain
136 F1 Zaraysk Russian Federation
101 E2 Zaraza Venezuela
121 Q3 Zarechensk Russian Federation
125 M1 Zarechka Belarus
123 O5 Zarech'ye Belarus
74 E4 Zarembo Island Alaska USA
179 K3 Zarghūn Shahr Afghanistan
159 F2 Zaria Nigeria
125 K2 Żarnów Poland
125 J2 Żarnowiec Poland
122 I5 Żarnowieckie, Jezioro lake Poland
123 P5 Zaruby Belarus
132 F1 Zarudintsy Ukraine
100 B5 Zaruma Ecuador
104 A1 Zarumilla Peru
125 H2 Żary Poland
135 AC3 Zarya, Proliv strait Russian Federation
182 H4 Zarya Oktyabrya Kazakhstan
164 3d Zarza, Pico de la mountain Canary Islands
155 H3 Zarzaïtine Algeria
100 B3 Zarzal Colombia
155 I2 Zarzis Tunisia
128 B2 Zas Spain
121 Q3 Zasheek Russian Federation
123 N5 Zaslawkaye Vodaskhovishcha lake Belarus
125 H3 Zásmuky Czech Republic
132 D1 Zastavna Ukraine
162 E6 Zastron South Africa
125 G2 Žatec Czech Republic
125 J3 Zator Poland
132 F2 Zatyshshya Ukraine
123 M4 Zaube Latvia
132 A4 Zaumsko Serbia
125 L3 Zavadka Ukraine
58 F2 Zavadovskiy Island Antarctica
133 B5 Zavalinë Albania
86 D5 Zavalla Texas USA
132 D1 Zavalov Ukraine
178 G2 Zavāreh Iran
178 G2 Zavāreh Iran
185 J3 Zavhan Mongolia
185 J3 Zavhanmandal Mongolia
125 M2 Zavidov Ukraine
125 N1 Zavine Belarus
191 L2 Zavitinsk Russian Federation
132 A3 Zavlaka Serbia
183 N2 Zavodskoy Russian Federation
130 G3 Zavrč Slovenia
135 AF7 Zav'yalova, Ostrov island Russian Federation
125 J2 Zawadzkie Poland
125 J2 Zawiercie Poland
155 J3 Zawilah Libya
155 K2 Zāwiyat Masūs Libya
125 J3 Zawoja Poland
125 I2 Zawonia Poland
125 I3 Zaya watercourse Austria
178 G3 Zāyandeh Rūd watercourse Iran
123 P5 Zaykovo Belarus
183 N4 Zaysan Kazakhstan
183 N4 Zaysan, Ozero lake Kazakhstan
90 E2 Zaza, Presa lake Cuba
100 D2 Zazárida Venezuela
132 D1 Zbarazh Ukraine
125 H1 Zbąszynek Poland
125 I1 Zbąszyńskie, Jezioro lake Poland
132 A4 Zboriste mountain Serbia
132 D1 Zboriv Ukraine
125 K3 Zborowice Poland
125 L1 Zbucz Poland
124 G2 Žďár Czech Republic
125 H3 Žďar nad Sázavou Czech Republic
130 G4 Zdenci Croatia
130 F1 Zdiby Czech Republic
125 H5 Zdihovo Croatia
125 H1 Zdroisko Poland
125 J1 Zduny Poland
125 J2 Zdzieszowice Poland
138 D4 Zeal Monachorum Devon England UK
75 R7 Zealandia Saskatchewan Canada
222 2 Zealandia Bank island Northern Mariana Islands
139 E3 Zeals Wiltshire England UK
80 B2 Zeballos British Columbia Canada
131 F8 Żebbuġ Malta
87 I4 Zebulon Georgia USA
130 F4 Zeča island Croatia
125 H1 Zechin Germany
219 Q10 Zeehan Tas. Australia
216 G6 Zeehan WA Australia
124 B2 Zeeland admin. area Netherlands
162 E5 Zeerust South Africa
158 E3 Zegbeli Ghana
125 K3 Żegocina Poland
81 M1 Zehner Saskatchewan Canada
214 B7 Zeil, Mount NT Australia
123 M4 Žeimelis Lithuania
123 L5 Žeimiai Lithuania
125 G2 Zeisholz Germany
127 K1 Zeitz Germany
123 O2 Zelënaya Roshcha Russian Federation
121 R3 Zelenoborskiy Russian Federation
123 K5 Zelenogradsk Russian Federation
132 E1 Zelënyye Kurilovtsy Ukraine
124 G3 Železná Ruda Czech Republic
125 H4 Železniki Slovenia
136 E2 Zeleznogorsk Russian Federation
155 G2 Zelfana Algeria
124 D1 Zelhem Netherlands
133 B5 Želino Macedonia
133 C6 Zelio Greece
125 H3 Želivka, Vodní nádrž lake Czech Republic
124 D2 Zell Germany
124 D4 Zell Switzerland
130 E3 Zell am See Austria
130 D3 Zell am Ziller Austria
124 E4 Zellersee bay Germany
125 J2 Zelów Poland
125 H4 Zeltweg Austria
123 M5 Želva Lithuania
132 C4 Zemen Bulgaria
132 E2 Zemeş Romania
182 D2 Zemetchino Russian Federation
160 D2 Zémio Central African Republic
134 M3 Zemlya Frantsa-Iosifa island Russian Federation
155 G1 Zemmora Algeria
86 B2 Zenda Kansas USA
179 I4 Zendeh, Kūh-e mountain Iran
179 J2 Zendeh Jān Afghanistan
189 G4 Zeng Jiang watercourse Guangdong China
189 G4 Zengcheng Guangdong China
130 G4 Zenica Bosnia and Herzegovina
55 O7 Zenith Plateau underwater feature Indian Ocean
129 H6 Zenzach Algeria
130 H4 Žepče Bosnia and Herzegovina
87 J6 Zephyrhills Florida USA
184 F5 Zepu Xinjiang Uygur Zizhiqu China
124 G2 Zerbst Germany
185 I3 Zereg Mongolia
183 K3 Zerenda Kazakhstan
155 H2 Zeribet el Oued Algeria
132 B2 Zerind Romania
183 N3 Zerkalnoye lake Russian Federation
127 J3 Zernez Switzerland
182 C4 Zernograd Russian Federation
133 B5 Zerqan Albania
100 C3 Zetaquira Colombia
132 D2 Zetea Romania
124 D1 Zetel Germany
193 H1 Zeva watercourse Russian Federation
124 E1 Zeven Germany
130 D4 Zevio Italy
191 K1 Zeya Russian Federation
191 K1 Zeya Dam Russian Federation
135 AA8 Zeyskoye Vodokhranilishche lake Russian Federation
128 C3 Zêzere watercourse Portugal
178 C2 Zgharta Lebanon
125 J2 Zgierz Poland
125 K1 Zgniłocha Poland
125 M1 Zhabinka Belarus
182 I3 Zhailma Kazakhstan
182 I3 Zhaksy-alakol' lake Kazakhstan
182 I4 Zhaksy-kylysh lake Kazakhstan
183 L3 Zhalauly Koli lake Kazakhstan
183 K3 Zhaltyr Kazakhstan
183 M3 Zhaltyr Kazakhstan
182 G4 Zhamansor Kazakhstan
183 K3 Zhamantuz lake Kazakhstan
Zhambyl see Taraz Kazakhstan
183 K4 Zhambyl Kazakhstan
183 K5 Zhambylskaya oblast' admin. area Kazakhstan
181 H3 Zhamu Xizang Zizhiqu China
183 N3 Zhanaozen Kazakhstan
182 I4 Zhanay Kazakhstan
182 F4 Zhanbay Kazakhstan
191 H4 Zhangbei Hebei China
189 H3 Zhangcheng Fujian China
188 C4 Zhangfeng Yunnan China
188 D2 Zhanggu Sichuan China
191 K4 Zhangguangcai Ling range Heilongjiang China
188 E1 Zhangjiachuan Gansu China
188 F2 Zhangjiajie Hunan China
191 H5 Zhangjiakou Hebei China
189 F3 Zhangjiang Hunan China
190 F5 Zhangjiapan Shaanxi China
189 H3 Zhangping Fujian China
189 G3 Zhangshu Jiangxi China
191 J4 Zhangwu Liaoning China
190 D5 Zhangye Gansu China
189 H4 Zhangzhou Fujian China
191 J5 Zhangzi Dao island Liaoning China
188 F4 Zhanjiang Guangdong China
135 AG3 Zhannetty, Ostrov island Russian Federation
182 G4 Zhanterek Kazakhstan
183 K3 Zhanybekshalkar lake Kazakhstan
188 D2 Zhao Zhen Sichuan China
191 K3 Zhaodong Heilongjiang China
189 G3 Zhaojne Jiangxi China
188 F4 Zhaoping Guangxi Zhuangzu Zizhiqu China
189 F4 Zhaoqing Guangdong China
188 E1 Zhaoren Shaanxi China
184 G4 Zhaosu Xinjiang Uygur Zizhiqu China
188 D3 Zhaotong Yunnan China
191 K3 Zhaoyuan Heilongjiang China
191 I5 Zhaoyuan Shandong China
191 K3 Zhaozhou Heilongjiang China
123 N5 Zhardzyazhzha Belarus
182 G4 Zharkamys Kazakhstan
182 I3 Zharman Koli lake Kazakhstan
136 D3 Zhashkiv Ukraine
188 F1 Zhashui Shaanxi China
181 G3 Zhatang Xizang Zizhiqu China
188 E3 Zhaxi Yunnan China
183 K4 Zhayrem Kazakhstan
189 G1 Zhecheng Henan China
188 C4 Zhedao Yunnan China
189 H3 Zhejiang admin. area China
182 J3 Zhekekol lake Kazakhstan
134 O3 Zhelaniya, Mys cape Russian Federation
183 L2 Zhelezinka Kazakhstan
134 L6 Zheleznodorozhnyy Russian Federation
189 G2 Zhelin Shuiku lake Jiangxi China
188 E4 Zhelou Guizhou China
188 F3 Zhenbao Ding mountain Guangxi Zhuangzu Zizhiqu China
191 H5 Zhengkou Hebei China
189 G1 Zhengzhou Henan China
191 J3 Zhenlai Jilin China
188 E3 Zhenning Guizhou China
188 F2 Zhenping Shaanxi China
190 G6 Zhenw-udong Shaanxi China
189 G2 Zhenyang Henan China
190 F6 Zhenyuan Gansu China
182 H3 Zhety-kol" lake Russian Federation
182 J4 Zhezdi Bogeni lake Kazakhstan
183 J4 Zhezkazgan Kazakhstan
123 O3 Zhglino Russian Federation
189 H2 Zhicheng Zhejiang China
135 W8 Zhigalovo Russian Federation
188 F3 Zhijiang Hunan China
188 E3 Zhijin Guizhou China
132 C4 Zhilentsi Bulgaria
135 X4 Zhillinda Russian Federation
189 F4 Zhilong Guangdong China
100 B5 Zhimbrue Ecuador
188 D1 Zhiqingsongduo Qinghai China
182 I3 Zhitikara Kazakhstan
123 O2 Zhitkovo Russian Federation
182 E4 Zhitkur Russian Federation
189 G4 Zhiwan Dao island Guangdong China
136 D2 Zhlobin Belarus
179 L3 Zhob Pakistan
76 G8 Zhoda Manitoba Canada
123 O5 Zhodzina Belarus
135 AF3 Zhokhova, Ostrov island Russian Federation
190 G5 Zhong-yang Shanxi China
188 D3 Zhong'an Yunnan China
188 E3 Zhongcheng Sichuan China
188 D3 Zhongcheng Yunnan China
188 E3 Zhongduo Chongqing China
188 E3 Zhonghe Chongqing China
189 G4 Zhongshan Guangdong China
189 F4 Zhongshan Guangxi Zhuangzu Zizhiqu China
58 F2 Zhongshan (China) research station Antarctica
188 D3 Zhongshu Yunnan China
188 D4 Zhongshu Yunnan China
188 E1 Zhongtai Gansu China
190 F5 Zhongwei Ningxia Huizu Zizhiqu China
188 D3 Zhongxin Yunnan China
189 H1 Zhongxing Jiangsu China
189 G4 Zhongyang Liedao island Guangdong China
125 M2 Zhorany Ukraine
132 F1 Zhornishche Ukraine
123 O5 Zhortay Belarus
183 K3 Zhosaly lake Kazakhstan
188 E2 Zhou He watercourse Sichuan China
181 H2 Zhoujun Qinghai China
189 G1 Zhoukou Henan China
188 E2 Zhoukou Sichuan China
188 D1 Zhouqu Gansu China
189 I2 Zhoushan Dao island Zhejiang China
132 H1 Zhovnino Ukraine
125 M3 Zhovtantsi Ukraine
132 D1 Zhovten' Ukraine
132 F3 Zhovtyy Yar Ukraine
191 J5 Zhuanghe Liaoning China
189 I3 Zhuangyuan'ao island Zhejiang China
191 I6 Zhucheng Shandong China
189 G4 Zhuhai Guangdong China
189 H2 Zhuji Zhejiang China
189 I2 Zhujia Jian island Zhejiang China
136 F1 Zhukovskiy Russian Federation
189 G2 Zhumadian Henan China
188 D1 Zhuogenima Gansu China
191 H5 Zhuolu Hebei China
191 H5 Zhuozhou Hebei China
190 F5 Zhuozi Shan mountain Nei Mongol Zizhiqu China
191 G5 Zhuozishan Nei Mongol Zizhiqu China
183 K3 Zhuravlevka Kazakhstan
188 F2 Zhushan Hubei China
188 F2 Zhushan Hubei China
188 F2 Zhuxi Hubei China
189 G3 Zhuzhou Hunan China
125 M2 Zhyryche Ukraine
136 D2 Zhytomyr Ukraine
136 D2 Zhytomyrs'ka Oblast' admin. area Ukraine
189 F3 Zi Shui lake Hunan China
158 C3 Zia Town Liberia
158 C3 Ziama mountain Guinea
125 J3 Žiar nad Hronom Slovakia
191 I6 Zibo Shandong China
128 C4 Zibreira Portugal
125 H4 Žice Slovenia
189 G4 Zicheng Guangdong China
132 E4 Zidarovo Bulgaria
179 K4 Zidi Pakistan
123 L4 Židikai Lithuania
101 H4 Zidok French Guiana
132 E3 Ziduri Romania
125 I2 Ziębice Poland
123 K5 Zięby Poland
125 H2 Zielona Góra Poland
125 J1 Zieluń Poland
124 B2 Zierikzee Netherlands
124 G1 Ziesar Germany
123 M5 Žiežmariai Lithuania
156 E1 Ziftá Egypt
194 B3 Zigon Myanmar
188 D2 Zigong Sichuan China
154 C6 Ziguinchor Senegal
124 G2 Žihle Czech Republic
190 D6 Ziketan Qinghai China
179 I4 Zīkūkī Iran
136 E5 Zile Turkey
123 N4 Zīle Latvia
125 J3 Žilina Slovakia
181 F2 Ziling Tsho lake Xizang Zizhiqu China
125 J3 Žilinsky admin. area Slovakia
155 J3 Zillah Libya
80 E3 Zillah Washington USA
123 O4 Zilupe Latvia
135 V8 Zima Russian Federation
89 F4 Zimapán Mexico
89 F5 Zimatlán de Álvarez Mexico
162 E3 Zimbabwe country Africa
125 L4 Zimbor Romania
179 K2 Zin Afghanistan
159 G2 Zina Cameroon
88 E5 Zinapécuaro Mexico
155 H6 Zinder Niger
155 H6 Zinder admin. area Niger
161 F5 Zinga Mulika Tanzania
124 B2 Zingem Belgium
122 G5 Zingst island Germany
100 E6 Zinho watercourse Brazil
158 D2 Ziniaré Burkina Faso
178 F7 Zinjibār Yemen
136 E2 Zin'kiv Ukraine
132 E1 Zin'kov Ukraine
154 E6 Zinzana Mali
109 19 Zion St Kitts and Nevis
158 E3 Zion watercourse Togo
76 J7 Zionz Lake Ontario Canada
88 E5 Zirándaro Mexico
186 D6 Zirapur Madhya Pradesh India
123 K4 Ziras Latvia
131 C8 Zirba Tunisia
125 I4 Zirc Hungary
130 F3 Žiri Slovenia
130 F5 Žirje Croatia
130 F5 Žirje island Croatia
179 H5 Zirkūh (UAE) island United Arab Emirates
124 F4 Zirl Austria
123 M5 Žirnajų ežeras lake Lithuania
127 J2 Zirndorf Germany
181 G3 Ziro Arunachal Pradesh India
125 I3 Zistersdorf Austria
132 B3 Žitište Serbia
102 C4 Zitiua watercourse Brazil
132 B4 Žitkovac Serbia
132 B4 Žitni Potok Serbia
188 E2 Zitong Chongqing China
127 L1 Zittau Germany
130 H4 Živinice Bosnia and Herzegovina
161 F2 Ziway Ethiopia
161 F2 Ziway, Lake Ethiopia
190 F6 Ziwu Ling mountain Gansu China
189 G3 Zixing Hunan China
191 H5 Ziya He watercourse Hebei China
189 H2 Ziyang Jiangxi China
188 E2 Ziyang Shaanxi China
188 D2 Ziyang Sichuan China
127 I3 Zizers Switzerland
132 D4 Zlataritsa Bulgaria
125 J3 Zlaté Moravce Slovakia
132 A4 Zlatibor Serbia
132 A4 Zlatibor range Serbia
132 C2 Zlatna Romania
130 G3 Zlatná na Ostrove Slovakia
182 H2 Zlatoust Russian Federation
135 AB8 Zlatoustovsk Russian Federation
123 K4 Zlēkas Latvia
125 I3 Zlín Czech Republic
125 I3 Zlínský Kraj admin. area Czech Republic
155 I2 Zlīṭan Libya
130 F2 Zliv Czech Republic
125 H2 Złotoryja Poland
130 H4 Zmajevac Croatia
183 N3 Zmeinogorsk Russian Federation
136 F3 Zmiyiv Ukraine
125 L2 Znamenka Belarus
183 M3 Znamenka Kazakhstan
125 I3 Znojmo Czech Republic
124 C1 Zoetermeer Netherlands
124 E5 Zogno Italy
161 F5 Zoissa Tanzania
186 D3 Zoji La pass Jammu and Kashmir India/Pakistan
87 K7 Zolfo Springs Florida USA
132 D1 Zolochiv Ukraine
135 AA8 Zolotaya Gora Russian Federation
132 H1 Zolotonosha Ukraine
132 D1 Zolotyy Potik Ukraine
125 L2 Żołynia Poland
132 A2 Zomba Hungary
163 G3 Zomba Malawi
183 J6 Zomin Uzbekistan
180 E3 Zongga Xizang Zizhiqu China
160 D3 Zongia Democratic Republic of Congo
160 B3 Zongo Democratic Republic of Congo
136 D5 Zonguldak Turkey
136 D5 Zonguldak admin. area Turkey
131 C6 Zonza Corsica France
128 D4 Zorita Spain
104 A1 Zorritos Peru
125 M2 Zosin Poland
155 J4 Zouar Chad
191 H6 Zoucheng Shandong China
154 D4 Zouérat Mauritania
132 F1 Zozov Ukraine
190 E3 Zrdenemandan Mongolia
132 B3 Zrenjanin Serbia
129 J6 Zribet Ahmed Algeria
133 C5 Zrnovci Macedonia
132 A2 Zsámbék Hungary
124 G2 Zschortau Germany
183 K7 Zu Afghanistan
100 E2 Zuata watercourse Venezuela
125 J3 Zuberec Slovakia
132 B4 Zubin Potok Kosovo
136 F2 Zubkovo Russian Federation
182 D2 Zubova Polyana Russian Federation
182 F2 Zubovka Russian Federation
123 P5 Zubovo Belarus
125 L2 Zubowice Poland
132 B4 Žuč Serbia
130 D3 Zuckerhütl mountain Austria
128 E2 Zudaire Spain
129 F3 Zuera Spain
128 C5 Zufre Spain
128 C5 Zufre, Embalse de lake Spain
127 I3 Zug Switzerland
182 D5 Zugdidi Georgia
159 F2 Zugu Nigeria
188 E1 Zuitou Shaanxi China
128 D4 Zújar watercourse Spain
125 L2 Żuków Poland
100 D2 Zulia admin. area Venezuela
124 D2 Zülpich Germany
126 F1 Zulte Belgium
126 C5 Zumaia Spain
58 T1 Zumberge Coast Antarctica
124 C2 Zundert Netherlands
181 H4 Zunheboto Nagaland India
191 I5 Zunhua Hebei China
85 H3 Zuni Mountains New Mexico USA
85 H3 Zuni Pueblo New Mexico USA
188 E3 Zunyi Guizhou China
191 H5 Zuoquan Shanxi China
191 G5 Zuoyun Shanxi China
130 H4 Županja Croatia
156 C3 Zurgh, Jabal mountain Libya
127 I3 Zürich Switzerland
125 J1 Żuromin Poland
100 A4 Zurones, Punta cape Ecuador
159 F2 Zuru Nigeria
130 D2 Zusam watercourse Germany
193 H4 Zushi Japan
124 F1 Züsow Germany
130 F5 Žut island Croatia
127 L4 Žuta Lokva Croatia
190 G4 Zuunebayan Mongolia
190 E3 Zuunebayan-ylaan Mongolia
185 J2 Zuunegov Mongolia
185 J2 Zuunehangai Mongolia
190 F3 Zuunmod Mongolia
123 L5 Žuvintas lake Lithuania
155 I2 Zuwārah Libya
182 F1 Zuyevka Russian Federation
216 C3 Zuytdorp Cliffs WA Australia
216 C3 Zuytdorp Point WA Australia
123 O3 Zvad Russian Federation
132 C4 Zverino Bulgaria
123 M5 Žverno ežeras lake Lithuania
133 E4 Zvezdets Bulgaria
123 M4 Zvirgzde Latvia
162 F4 Zvishavane Zimbabwe
125 J3 Zvolen Slovakia
130 H4 Zvornik Bosnia and Herzegovina
158 C3 Zwedru Liberia
127 H3 Zweisimmen Switzerland
125 H3 Zwettl Austria
127 K1 Zwickau Germany
124 G2 Zwickauer Mulde watercourse Germany
125 L2 Zwierzyniec Poland
124 G3 Zwiesel Germany
124 D1 Zwolle Netherlands
86 E5 Zwolle Louisiana USA
124 G2 Zwönitz Germany
125 K1 Żyrardów Poland
135 AF5 Zyryanka Russian Federation
183 N3 Zyryanovsk Kazakhstan
125 L2 Żyrzyn Poland
125 J3 Żywiec Poland

PUBLISHER
Gordon Cheers

ASSOCIATE PUBLISHER
Janet Parker

ART DIRECTOR
Stan Lamond

DESIGNERS
Peta Zoubakin, Robert Taylor

Cover Design
Stan Lamond

CONTRIBUTORS
Donald J. Berg, John Cook, Roman Cybriwsky, David Hamper, Quintin Wight, Willow Wight

EDITORS
Loretta Barnard, Helen Cooney, Kate Etherington, James Inglis, Heather Jackson, Jan Watson

CARTOGRAPHIC CONSULTANTS
Damien Demaj, John Frith

CARTOGRAPHERS
Munmun Adhikari, Will Adnams, Stewart Adrain, Imran Ahmad, Galen Barnett, Sushmita Bhaduri, Clare Brown, Sam Brown, Terry Bush, Vaclav Cerny, Indrajit Chakraborty, Ruth Coombs, Lawrence Crissman, Martin Darlison, Subhodip Ghosh Dastidar, Alison Davies, Linda Dawes, Damien Demaj, Adam Derringer, Liz Donnelly, Peeyush Dubey, Mark Eldridge, Alison Ewington, Mark Fairbairn, Kim Farrington, Heather Francisco, John Frith, Matt Goodchild, Erin Greb, Casey Greene, Alan Grimwade, Matthew Hampton, Paul Hyatt, Robin Hyatt, Jaibhagwan, Ravi Kant, Kevin Klein, Sanjay Kumar, Don Larsen, Scott Lockheed, Craig MacAlpine, Rob McCaleb, Laura McCormick, David McCutcheon, David Maltby, Ed Merritt, Greg Moore, Kate Morrill, Wayne Murphy, David Murray, Jatin Nankana, Lynn Neal, Joe Nunn, Alan Palfreyman, Nitin Pande, Amritanjan Pandey, Jerome Parkin, Alok Pathak, Jacob Patrylick, Max Peatman, Tim Rideout, Beth Robertson, Riju Roy, Kelly Sandefer, Julie Sheridan, Prem Singh, Alan Smith, Roger Smith, George Stoll, Matthew Townsend, Gail Townsley, Hans Van der Maarel, Clare Varney, Martin von Wyss, Allison Walls, Marcella Warner, Jonathan Wyss, Amelia Zander

PRODUCTION
Simone Coupland, Bernard Roberts

First published in 2009 in Canada by Reader's Digest Association (Canada) ULC
P O Box 11763 Stn Centre Ville
Montreal, QC
H3C 6W5,
Canada
Website: www.rd.ca

Produced by Millennium House Pty Ltd
52 Bolwarra Road, Elanora Heights
NSW, 2101, Australia
Ph: (612) 9970 6850
Fax: (612) 9913 3500
Email: info@millenniumhouse.com.au
Website: www.millenniumhouse.com.au

ISBN: 978-1-55475-019-1

Printed in China by Sing Cheong Printing Co Ltd
Color Separation by Pica Digital Pte Ltd, Singapore

AUTHORS
Millennium House would be happy to receive submissions from authors. Please send brief submissions to: editor@millenniumhouse.com.au

PHOTOGRAPHERS AND ILLUSTRATORS
Millennium House would be happy to receive submissions from photographers or illustrators. Please send submissions to: editor@millenniumhouse.com.au

PICTURE CREDITS

All images © Millennium House unless otherwise noted.

6 (top) © Corbis Australia; 6 (left) © Corbis Australia; 7 (top) © Corbis Australia; 10 (left) © Corbis Australia; 10 (right) © Corbis Australia; 11 © Corbis Australia; 12–13 NASA images by Reto Stöckli, based on data from NASA and NOAA/Earth Observatory; 23 (top) NASA Visible Earth Image courtesy the SeaWiFS Project, NASA/Goddard Space Flight Center, and ORBIMAGE; 26 (top) US Navy/U.S. Marine Corps photo by Pfc. Jeremiah Handeland; 26 (bottom) ISS Astronaut Photography/Image Science & Analysis Group, Johnson Space Center; 27 NASA Earth Observatory/Image by Kerri Rose, based on data copyrighted by Space Imaging; 28 (top) NASA Earth Observatory/Image Science & Analysis Laboratory, Johnson Space Center; 64 (bottom left) NASA Earth Observatory/NASA/GSFC/MITI/ERSDAC/JAROS, and U.S./Japan ASTER Science Team; 116 (bottom) NASA Earth Observatory/Image by Robert Simmon, NASA's Earth Observatory, based on data copyright Space Imaging; 168 (bottom left) NASA Earth Observatory/NASA images courtesy of the NASA/GSFC/MITI/ERSDAC/JAROS, and U.S./Japan ASTER Science Team.

Pages 2–3: A young girl from northern Mozambique wears a traditional face mask known as musiro. This natural paste—extracted from tree branches—is worn by the women of northern Mozambique for protection from the sun and is also applied as part of the beauty regime.

KEY TO MAP PAGES

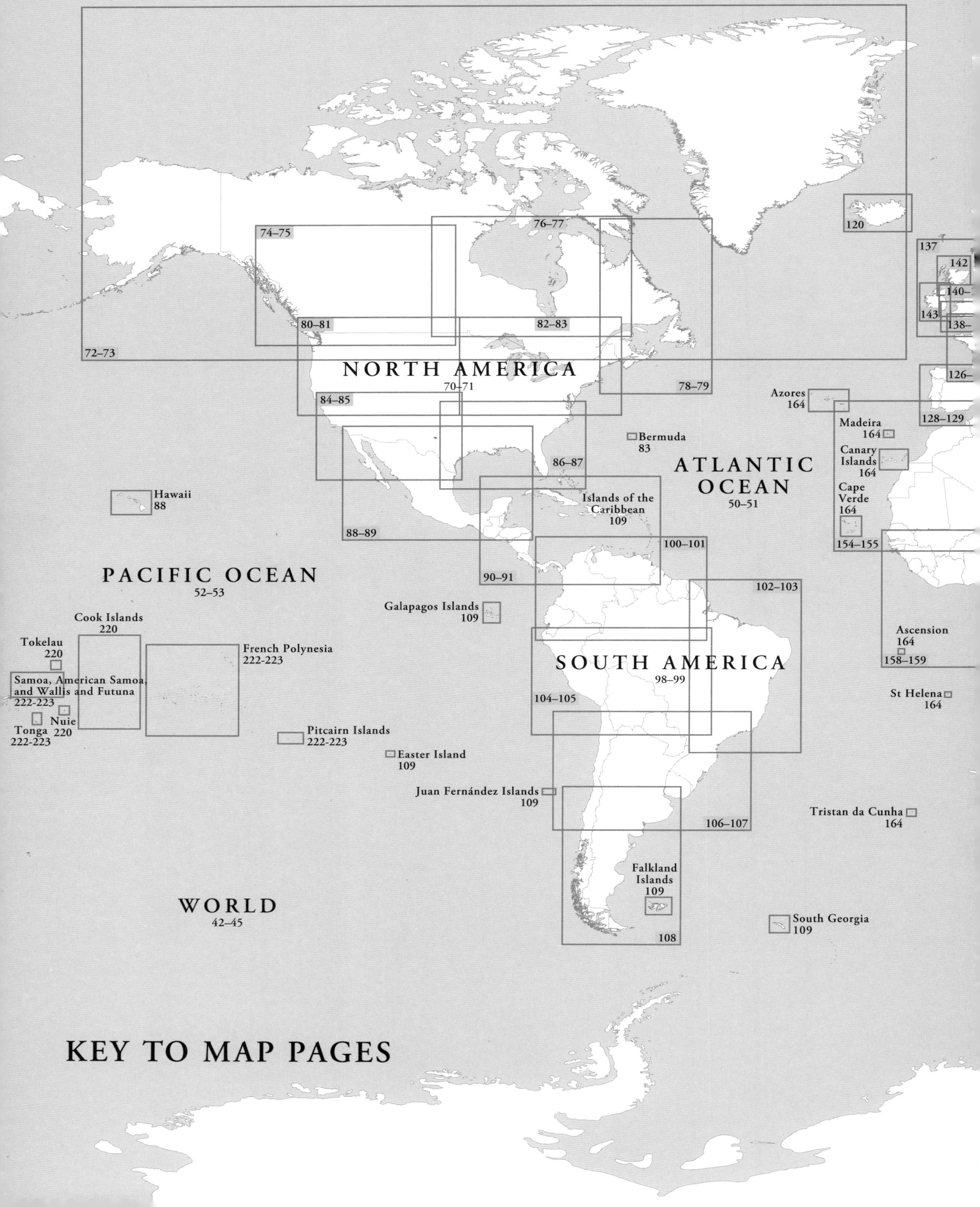

72–73
74–75
76–77
78–79
80–81
82–83
84–85
86–87
88–89
90–91
NORTH AMERICA
70–71
120
137
142
140–
143
138–
126–
128–129
Azores
164
Madeira
164
Canary Islands
164
Cape Verde
164
154–155
Bermuda
83
ATLANTIC OCEAN
50–51
Islands of the Caribbean
109
100–101
102–103
Hawaii
88
PACIFIC OCEAN
52–53
Galapagos Islands
109
Ascension
164
158–159
Cook Islands
220
Tokelau
220
French Polynesia
222-223
SOUTH AMERICA
98–99
Samoa, American Samoa, and Wallis and Futuna
222-223
104–105
St Helena
164
Nuie
220
Tonga
222-223
Pitcairn Islands
222-223
Easter Island
109
Juan Fernández Islands
109
106–107
Tristan da Cunha
164
Falkland Islands
109
South Georgia
109
108
WORLD
42–45